T0397597

# THE OXFORD GUIDE TO THE MALAYO-POLYNESIAN LANGUAGES OF SOUTHEAST ASIA

# OXFORD GUIDES TO THE WORLD'S LANGUAGES



PUBLISHED

**The Oxford Guide to Australian Languages**
*Edited by* Claire Bowern

**The Oxford Guide to the Bantu Languages**
*Edited by* Ellen Hurst, Nancy Kula, Lutz Marten, and Jochen Zeller

**The Oxford Guide to the Malayo-Polynesian Languages of Southeast Asia**
*Edited by* Alexander Adelaar and Antoinette Schapper

**The Oxford Guide to the Romance Languages**
*Edited by* Adam Ledgeway and Martin Maiden

**The Oxford Guide to the Transeurasian Languages**
*Edited by* Martine Robbeets and Alexander Savelyev

**The Oxford Guide to the Uralic Languages**
*Edited by* Marianne Bakró-Nagy, Johanna Laakso, and Elena Skribnik

IN PREPARATION

**The Oxford Guide to the Afroasiatic Languages**
*Edited by* Sabrina Bendjaballah and Chris Reintges

**The Oxford Guide to the Atlantic Languages of West Africa**
*Edited by* Friederike Lüpke

**The Oxford Guide to the Languages of the Central Andes**
*Edited by* Matthias Urban

**The Oxford Guide to the Papuan Languages**
*Edited by* Nicholas Evans and Sebastian Fedden

**The Oxford Guide to the Slavonic Languages**
*Edited by* Jan Fellerer and Neil Bermel

**The Oxford Guide to the Tibeto-Burman Languages**
*Edited by* Kristine Hildebrandt, Yankee Modi, David Peterson, and Hiroyuki Suzuki

THE OXFORD GUIDE TO THE

# Malayo-Polynesian Languages of Southeast Asia

EDITED BY

Alexander Adelaar and Antoinette Schapper

OXFORD
UNIVERSITY PRESS

Great Clarendon Street, Oxford, OX2 6DP,
United Kingdom

Oxford University Press is a department of the University of Oxford. It furthers the University's objective of excellence in research, scholarship, and education by publishing worldwide. Oxford is a registered trade mark of Oxford University Press in the UK and in certain other countries



Published in the United States of America by Oxford University Press
198 Madison Avenue, New York, NY 10016, United States of America

British Library Cataloguing in Publication Data
Data available

Library of Congress Control Number: 2022944578

ISBN 9780198807353

DOI: 10.1093/oso/9780198807353.001.0001

Printed and bound by
CPI Group (UK) Ltd, Croydon, CR0 4YY



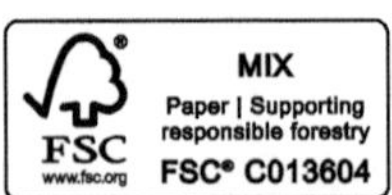

# Short contents

# Detailed contents

# Series preface

We know that the close study of individual language families and linguistic areas is vital both to the synchronic and diachronic study of language and to cognitive science more widely. Comparative investigations of this type stimulate exciting synergies between different subdisciplines of linguistics, such as language change, contact linguistics, sociolinguistics, linguistic typology, textual philology, and microvariation in grammar, sound, and meaning within and across languages. Besides reflecting and encouraging the links between these subdomains, the fundamental goal of the series is to publish high-quality, substantial reference works which represent a set of theoretically informed and systematic guides to what is known about the world's languages.

Each *Guide* focuses on a particular language family, subfamily, or areal grouping, and is edited by leading authorities, who bring together contributions from the best international scholars in the field. The *Guides* aim to show the more general theoretical significance of the languages' history, linguistic and sociolinguistic characteristics, and overall to provide an indispensable reference tool both to specialist scholars and students and to professional linguists. The approach adopted in all the *Guides* is systematic and comparative, informed by the latest research and theoretical and methodological perspectives, and, where appropriate, the authors draw on relevant work in such fields as anthropology, archaeology, and cognitive science.

Adam Ledgeway and Martin Maiden
*University of Cambridge and University of Oxford*

# Acknowledgements

The editors have a number of debts to acknowledge.

Over ten long years, the production of this volume has involved a great effort by editors, authors, and others. Work on this volume began in 2014 and, despite impediments such as a global pandemic, it has proceeded steadily. Special thanks go to Nikolaus Himmelmann, Malcolm Ross, and Laurence A. Reid, each of whom provided useful advice and suggestions at different stages in the planning and execution of this volume. Angela Terrill assisted with the preparation of the manuscript for Oxford University Press, while Vicki Sunter and Deborah Maloney at the press oversaw the production of the volume. Many thanks to Owen Edwards, who produced the maps for the volume with great efficiency.

The editors would like to take this opportunity to commemorate Robert "Bob" Blust and William "Billy" McConvell, both of whom died while this volume was in production. We are very grateful for the chapters that they contributed to this volume. Bob's legacy within Austronesian linguistics is enormous, while Billy's will never be realised, for he was taken from us long before his time. We dedicate this volume to their memory.

Alexander Adelaar gratefully acknowledges the support of the European Regional Development Fund Project "Sinophone Borderlands – Interaction at the Edges" (CZ.02.1.01/0.0/0.0/16_019/0000791) that he received in the final editorial stages of this volume. He also gratefully acknowledges the hospitality and infrastructural support he received as a Principal Fellow at the Asia Institute of the University of Melbourne and as a Visiting Scholar at the Department of Linguistics (Fachbereich für Sprachwissenschaft), University of Cologne.

Antoinette Schapper would like to acknowledge that research grants from several research organizations supported her editorial and research work for this volume. They are: the Netherlands Organisation for Scientific Research VENI project "The evolution of the lexicon: Explorations in lexical stability, semantic shift and borrowing in a Papuan language family", the Volkswagen Stiftung DoBeS project "Aru languages documentation", the Australian Research Council project "Waves of words" (ARC, DP180100893), and the OUTOFPAPUA project funded by the European Research Council (grant agreement no. 848532).

# Abbreviations and conventions

## ABBREVIATIONS

| | |
|---|---|
| 1 | first person |
| 2 | second person |
| 3 | third person |
| A | Actor/Agent-like argument |
| a.o. | among others |
| AA | Austro-Asiatic |
| AB | absolute lexical alternation |
| ABIL | abilitative (can, able to) |
| ABL | ablative |
| ABS | absolutive |
| ABSTR | abstract |
| ACC | accusative |
| ACCIDENT | accidental |
| ACD | Austronesian Comparative Dictionary |
| ACHIEV | achievement |
| ACROSS.RIVER | direction across river |
| ACT | active |
| ADDR | addressee |
| ADJ | adjective |
| ADPOS | adposition |
| ADV | adverb/adverbializer |
| ADVS | adversative |
| AF | actor focus |
| AFF | affirmative |
| AGR | agreement |
| AGT | agent(ive) |
| AL | alienable |
| ALL | allative |
| ALONG.COAST | direction along coast |
| AN | Austronesian |
| AND | andative |
| ANIM | animate |
| ANTIP | antipassive |
| APPL | applicative |
| APRX | approximative |
| ART | article |
| ASP | aspectual marker |
| ASSOC | associative |
| AT | actor topic |
| ATT | attenuative |
| ATTR | attributive |
| AUX | auxiliary |
| AV | actor/active voice |
| AWAY.FROM.RIVER | direction away from river |
| BCE | before current era |
| BEG | begun aspect |
| BEN | benefactive |
| BP | Before Present |
| BPhyl | Bayesian phylogenetics |
| BSS | Bali-Sasak-Sumbawa |
| C | consonant |
| CAUS | causative |
| CC | consonant cluster |
| CE | Current Era |
| CEB | Central-East Barito |
| CEL | Celebic |
| CEMP | Central Eastern Malayo-Polynesian |
| CIRC | circumfix |
| CIRCV | circumstantial voice |
| CIS | cislocative |
| CL | clitic |
| CLF | classifier |
| CLZN | Central Luzon |
| CMP | Central Malayo-Polynesian |
| CNT | counting prefix |
| CO | "co-"/ sharing relation |
| COLL | collective |
| COM | comitative |
| COMP | complementizer |
| COMPAR | comparative |
| COMPL | completive |
| CompM | Comparative Method |
| COMS | commiserative |
| CONJ | conjunction |
| CONSEC | consecutive |
| CONT | continuative |
| CONTR | contrastive |
| COP | copula |
| CORE | core (case/argument) |
| COS | change of state |

| | |
|---|---|
| CSP | Central and Southern Philippines |
| CV | conveyance voice |
| DAT | dative |
| DEF | definite |
| DEIC | deictic |
| DEM | demonstrative |
| DEP | dependent |
| DER | derivational |
| DET | determiner |
| DETRANS | detransitivizer |
| DEX | indexer |
| DIM | diminutive |
| DIR | directional |
| DISC | discourse marker |
| DIST | distal |
| DISTR | distributive |
| DNA | deoxyribonucleic acid |
| DO | double object construction |
| DO | dynamic verb stem former |
| DOWN | down (vertically) |
| DOWNCOAST | direction downcoast |
| DOWNHILL | direction downhill |
| DOWNRIVER | direction downriver |
| DU | dual |
| DUR | durative |
| DV | dative voice |
| DYN | dynamic |
| EF | East Formosan languages |
| EGIDS | Expanded Graded Intergeneration Disruption Scale |
| EMO | emotional involvement |
| EMP | Eastern Malayo-Polynesian |
| EMPH | emphatic |
| EP | end point |
| EPIS | epistemic |
| EQ | equative |
| ERG | ergative |
| ESS | essive |
| EV | experiencer voice |
| EVID | evidential |
| EXCL | exclusive |
| EXCLAM | exclamative |
| EXHR | exhortative |
| EXIST | existential |
| F | feminine |
| FACT | factitive |
| FAM | familiar |
| FILL | filler |
| FIN | final |
| FOC | focus |
| FUT | future |
| G | goal/recipient of a three-place verb |
| G1, G2, ... | first generation, second generation, ... |
| GCPH | Greater Central Philippines |
| GEN | genitive |
| GENR | generic |
| GER | gerund |
| GIV | given |
| GNB | Greater North Borneo |
| GRT | greeting |
| GWB | Greater West Bomberai |
| HAB | habitual |
| HES | hesitation |
| HIGH | higher elevation |
| HNS | Homorganic Nasal Substitution |
| HON | honorific |
| HORT | hortative |
| HR | high register |
| HSY | hearsay |
| HUM | human |
| HYP | hypothetical |
| IAM | iamitive |
| ID | identifying |
| IDEO | ideophone |
| ILL | illocutionary force marker |
| IMM | immediate |
| IMP | imperative |
| INAN | inanimate |
| INCEP | inceptive |
| INCH | inchoative |
| INCL | inclusive |
| IND | indicative |
| INDEF | indefinite |
| INF | infinitive |
| INFR | inferential |
| INFRM | informal |
| INS | inserted nasal sound |
| INSTR | instrument |
| INTNS | intensive/intensifier |
| INTERJ | interjection |
| INTR | intransitive |
| INV | inverse voice |
| INVS | invisible |
| IP | intonational phrase |
| IPA | International Phonetic Alphabet |
| IPF | imperfect |

| | |
|---|---|
| IPFV | imperfective |
| IRR | irrealis |
| ISEA | Insular Southeast Asia/Island Southeast Asia |
| ITER | iterative |
| IV | instrumental voice |
| k.o. | kind of |
| kya | thousand years ago |
| L1, L2, ... | first language, second language, ... |
| LAND | direction landward |
| LCM | locative case marker |
| LEVEL | level elevation |
| LIG | ligature |
| LNK | linker |
| LOC | locative |
| LOW | lower elevation |
| LR | low register |
| LV | locative voice |
| M | male/masculine |
| MCORD | Meso-Cordilleran |
| MD | middle semantics |
| MED | medial |
| MIA | Middle-Indo-Aryan |
| MID | middle voice |
| MIRA | mirative |
| MOD | mood marker |
| MODER | moderate degree |
| MP | Malayo-Polynesian |
| MPSEA | Malayo-Polynesian languages of Southeast Asia |
| MSEA | Mainland Southeast Asia |
| mtDNA | mitochondrial DNA (maternally inherited) |
| MULT | multiple subjects |
| MUT | mutation |
| *N-* | nasal prefix |
| N | nasal or noun (in context) |
| NAO | non-actor-oriented |
| NB | North Borneo |
| NC | nasal + consonant |
| NCONTR | non-contrastive |
| NCORD | Northern Cordilleran |
| NEB | Northeast Barito |
| NEC | necessity |
| NEG | negative/negator |
| NEGEXIST | negative existential |
| NEUT | neutral |
| NFIN | nonfinite |
| NHUM | non-human |
| NIA | New-Indo-Aryan |
| NLZN | Northern Luzon |
| NMLG | Northern Malagasy |
| NMLS | non-Malayic languages of Sumatra |
| NMLZ | nominalizer/nominalization |
| NMP | Nuclear-Malayo-Polynesian |
| NOM | nominative |
| NONFIN | non-final |
| NP | Noun Phrase |
| NPAT | nonpatient |
| NPERS | non-personal article/marker |
| NPIV | non-pivot |
| NPST | non-past |
| NSG | non-singular |
| NSUBJ | non-subject core argument |
| NUM | numeral |
| NVOL | non-volitional |
| NWB | Northwest Barito |
| O | object-like argument of transitive verb |
| o.a. | one another |
| OB | oblique lexical alternation |
| OBJ | object |
| OBL | oblique |
| OM | Official Malagasy |
| OPN | open space |
| ORD | ordinal |
| OT | object topic |
| OV | object(ive) voice |
| P | patient-like argument of transitive verb |
| p.c. | personal communication |
| PAN | Proto-Austronesian |
| PAR | paragogic |
| PART | particle |
| PARTV | partitive |
| PASS | passive |
| PAT | patient(ive) |
| PBSS | Proto-Bali-Sasak-Sumbawa |
| PC | Proto-Chamic |
| PCEL | Proto-Celebic |
| PECM | Proto-Eastern Central Maluku |
| PCR | Polymerase Chain Reaction |
| PCS | Proto-Central Sarawak |
| PDVS | Phonation Driven Vowel Shift |
| PECEL | Proto-Eastern Celebic |
| PEF | Proto-East Formosan |
| PEJ | pejorative |
| PERS | personal article/marker |

| | |
|---|---|
| PFV | perfective |
| PGCPH | Proto-Greater Central Philippines |
| PGNB | Proto-Greater North Borneo |
| PGWB | Proto-Greater West Bomberai |
| PH | Philippine |
| PhP | phonological phrase |
| PIV | pivot |
| PKW | Proto-Kaili-Wolio |
| PL | plural |
| PLD | Proto-Land Dayak |
| PLURACT | pluractional |
| PM | Proto-Malayic |
| PMJ | Proto-Malayo-Javanic |
| PMLG | Proto-Malagasy |
| PMM | Proto-Moken-Moklen |
| PMP | Proto-Malayo-Polynesian |
| PNB | Proto-North Borneo |
| PNLZN | Proto-Northern Luzon |
| PNMP | Proto-Nuclear-Malayo-Polynesian |
| PNS | Proto-North Sarawak |
| PO | prepositional object construction |
| POL | polite |
| POS | positive |
| POSS | possessive |
| POT | potentive |
| PP | prepositional phrase |
| PPH | Proto-Philippines |
| PRCS | precise space |
| PRED | predicate/predicative |
| PREP | preposition |
| PRETEND | pretendative |
| PRF | perfect |
| PRO | pronoun |
| PROG | progressive |
| PROH | prohibitive |
| PROS | prospective |
| PROX | proximal/proximate |
| PRS | present |
| PSB | Proto-Sama Bajaw |
| PSEB | Proto-Southeast Barito |
| PSHWNG | Proto-South Halmahera-West New Guinea |
| PSM | possessum |
| PSR | possessor |
| PSS | Proto-Sasak-Sumbawa |
| PSSul | Proto-South Sulawesi |
| PST | past |
| PSUM | Proto-Sumatran |
| PTAP | Proto-Timor-Alor-Pantar |
| PTCP | participle |
| PUNC | punctual |
| PURP | purposive |
| PV | patient voice |
| PWIN | Proto-Western Indonesian |
| PWMP | Proto-Western Malayo-Polynesian |
| Q | question marker |
| QF | quantifier float |
| QUAL | qualifier |
| QUANT | quantifier |
| QUT | quotative |
| RASH | Raja Ampat–South Halmahera |
| RC | relative clause |
| RCT | recent |
| REAL | realis |
| RECOG | recognitional deictic |
| RECP | reciprocal |
| REDUP | reduplication |
| REF | referent status |
| REFL | reflexive |
| REL | relativizer/relative clause marker |
| RES | resultative |
| ROOT | root modality |
| RPRT | reportative |
| RS | reported speech |
| RV | reason voice |
| S | single argument of intransitive clause |
| s.t. | something |
| S1, S2, ... | speaker 1, speaker 2, ... |
| $S_A$ | single argument of active intransitive clause |
| SB | Sama-Bajaw |
| SBJ | subject |
| SBJV | subjunctive |
| SEA | Southeast Asia |
| SEA | direction seaward |
| SEB | Southeast Barito |
| SEP | separator |
| SEQ | sequential |
| SF | stem former |
| SG | singular |
| SHWNG | South Halmahera–West New Guinea |
| SI | S-infix |
| SIL | Summer Institute of Linguistics |
| SIM | similitive |
| SIMT | simultaneous |
| SOC | social/sociative |

| | |
|---|---|
| SPEC | specifier |
| SS | South Sulawesi |
| STAT | stative |
| $S_U$ | single argument of non-active intransitive clause |
| SUM | Sumatran |
| SUPER | superlative |
| SV | subject voice |
| SVC | serial verb construction |
| SW | switch |
| SWB | Southwest Barito |
| T | theme of a three-place verb |
| TAG | sentence tag |
| TAM | tense-aspect-mood |
| TAP | Timor-Alor-Pantar |
| TH | thematic vowel |
| TNS | Teun-Nila-Serua |
| TOP | topic |
| TOWARD.RIVER | toward the river |
| TR | transitive |
| TRANS | translocative |
| TRI | trial |
| TV | theme voice |
| U | undergoer |
| UP | direction up vertically |
| UPCOAST | direction upcoast |
| UPHILL | direction uphill |
| UPRIVER | direction upriver |
| UV | undergoer voice |
| V | verb or vowel (in context) |
| VBLZ | verbalizer/verbalization |
| VEN | venitive |
| VER | veridical |
| VERB | verbal marker |
| VI | intransitive verb |
| VIS | visible |
| VOC | vocative |
| VP | verb phrase |
| vs. | versus |
| VT | transitive verb |
| VV | vowel sequence |
| WH | content question word/interrogative proform |
| WIN | Western Indonesian |
| WMP | Western Malayo-Polynesian |

Note that in some cases, an abbreviation may occur in both small caps and uppercase forms. Where it is in small caps, it is a gloss for a particular form (be it a morpheme or a lexeme). Where it appears in uppercase, it refers to a construction or a word class.

## CONVENTIONS

| | |
|---|---|
| - | morpheme boundary |
| ~ | boundary between reduplicant and its base |
| ~ | (if preceded and followed by a space) indicating variant forms of a single item |
| = | clitic boundary |
| # | word boundary |
| ˈ... | primary stress |
| ˌ... | secondary stress |
| <...> | infix, infixation |
| *... | (followed by a sound/word in non-italicised script:) indicates reconstructed sound or etymon |
| *... | (followed by a sound, word, phrase or clause, in italics:) indicates ungrammaticality |
| [...] | square brackets used for phonetic representation |
| /.../ | slashes used for phonemic representation, underlying morphemes, etc. |
| ← | comes from, derives from (synchronically) |
| → | becomes (synchronically) |
| < | came from, derived from (diachronically) |
| > | became (diachronically) |
| ø | zero realization (of a phoneme or morpheme) |

# The contributors

Alexander Adelaar *Sinophon Project, Palacký University and Asia Institute, University of Melbourne*
Karl Anderbeck *SIL International and Institut Alam dan Tamadun Melayu, Universiti Kebangsaan*
I Wayan Arka *Australian National University and Universitas Udayana*
Laura Arnold *University of Edinburgh*
Leif Asplund *Stockholm University*
Peter Bellwood *Australian National University*
Juliette Blevins *City University of New York*
† Robert A. Blust *University of Hawai'i at Mānoa*
Nicolas Brucato *CNRS and Université Paul Sabatier, Toulouse*
Marc Brunelle *University of Ottawa*
Murray Cox *Massey University and Te Pūnaha Matatini (New Zealand Centre of Research Excellence for Complex Systems)*
Mark Donohue *The Living Tongues Institute for Endangered Languages*
Michael C. Ewing *Asia Institute, University of Melbourne*
Emily Gasser *Swarthmore College*
David Gil *Max Planck Institute for Evolutionary Anthropology, Leipzig*
Simon J. Greenhill *Max Planck Institute for Evolutionary Anthropology, Leipzig*
Charles Grimes *Unit Bahasa dan Budaya, Kupang and Australian National University*
John T. Hajek *Asia Institute, University of Melbourne*
William C. Hall *SIL, Philippines*
Nikolaus P. Himmelmann *Universität zu Köln*
Gary Holton *University of Hawai'i at Mānoa*
Tom Hoogervorst *Royal Netherlands Institute of Southeast Asian and Caribbean Studies (KITLV)*
Penelope Howe *Independent scholar*
Hsiao-chun Hung *Australian National University*
Joshua Jensen *EMU International*
David Kamholz *The Long Now Foundation*
Daniel Kaufman *Queens College, City University of New York, and ELA*
Yukinori Kimoto *University of Hyogo*
Paul Kroeger *Dallas International University*
Hsiu-chuan Liao *National Tsing Hua University*
Jason Lobel *University of Hawai'i at Mānoa*
Veronika Mattes *Karl-Franzens-Universität, Graz*
† William McConvell *Western Sydney University*
Bradley McDonnell *University of Hawai'i at Mānoa*
Tim McKinnon *Quantitative Scientific Solutions*
David Mead *Sulawesi Language Alliance*
Francesca Moro *Università degli Studi dell'Insubria*
Naonori Nagaya *University of Tokyo*
Leah Pappas *University of Hawai'i at Mānoa*
Lawrence Reid *University of Hawai'i at Mānoa*
François-Xavier Ricaut *CNRS and Université Paul Sabatier, Toulouse*
Sonja Riesberg *Laboratoire et Civilisations à Tradition Orale, CNRS*
Malcolm C. Ross *Australian National University*
Antoinette Schapper *Laboratoire et Civilisations à Tradition Orale, CNRS, and Vrije Universiteit Amsterdam*
Thomas Schwaiger *Karl-Franzens-Universität, Graz*
Asako Shiohara *Tokyo University of Foreign Studies*
Paul Sidwell *Language Intelligence*
Peter Slomanson *Tampere University*
Alexander D. Smith *National University of Singapore*
Christina L. Truong *University of Hawai'i at Mānoa*
René van den Berg *SIL International*
Johan van der Auwera *University of Antwerp*
Daniel van Olmen *Lancaster University*
Jozina Vander Klok *Humboldt Universität, Berlin*
Ljuba Veselinova *Stockholm University*
Frens Vossen *University of Antwerp*
Jiang Wu *Leiden University*
Erik Zobel *Independent scholar*
R. David Zorc *Language Research Center and Dunwoody Press (retired)*

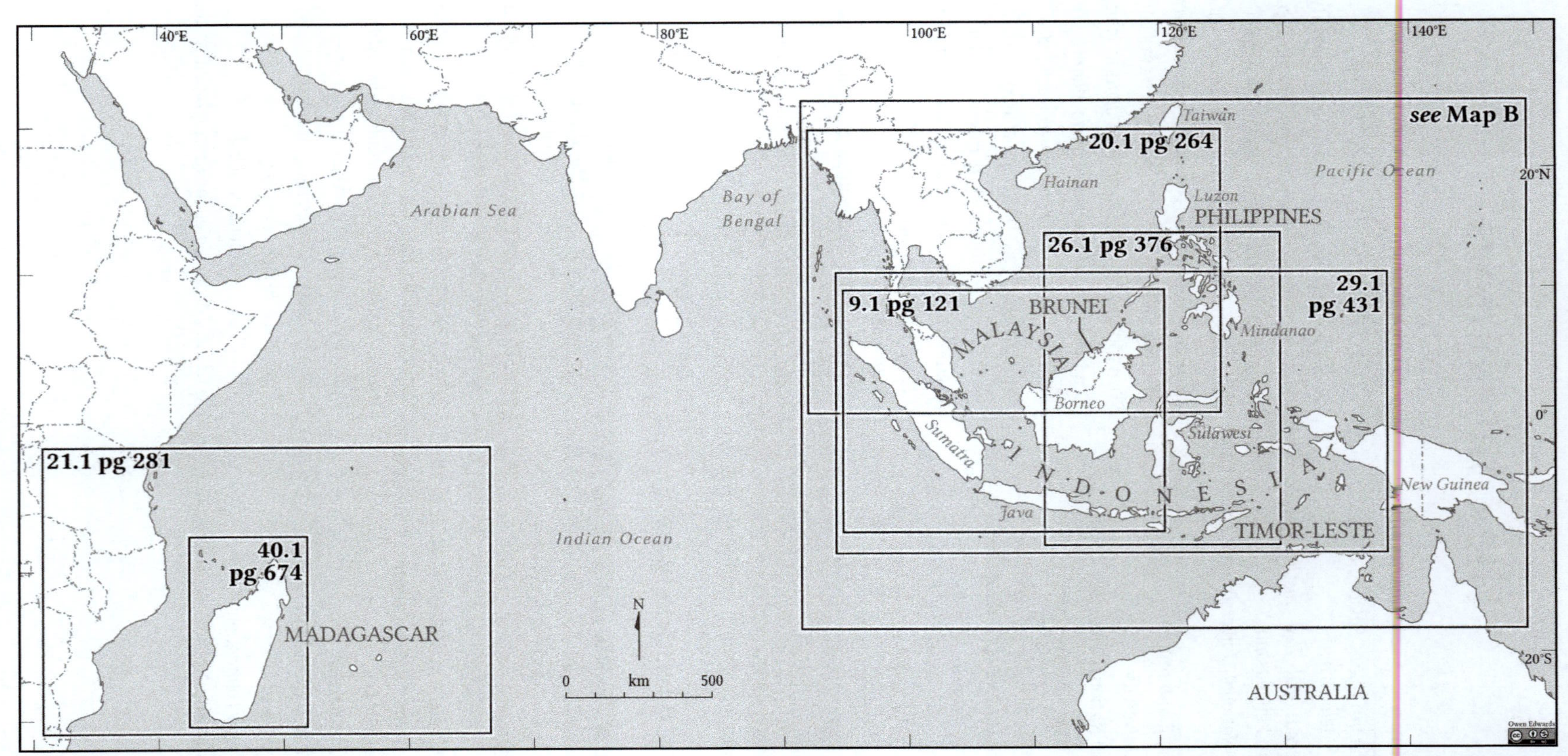


**Map A.** Guide to the language maps in this volume.

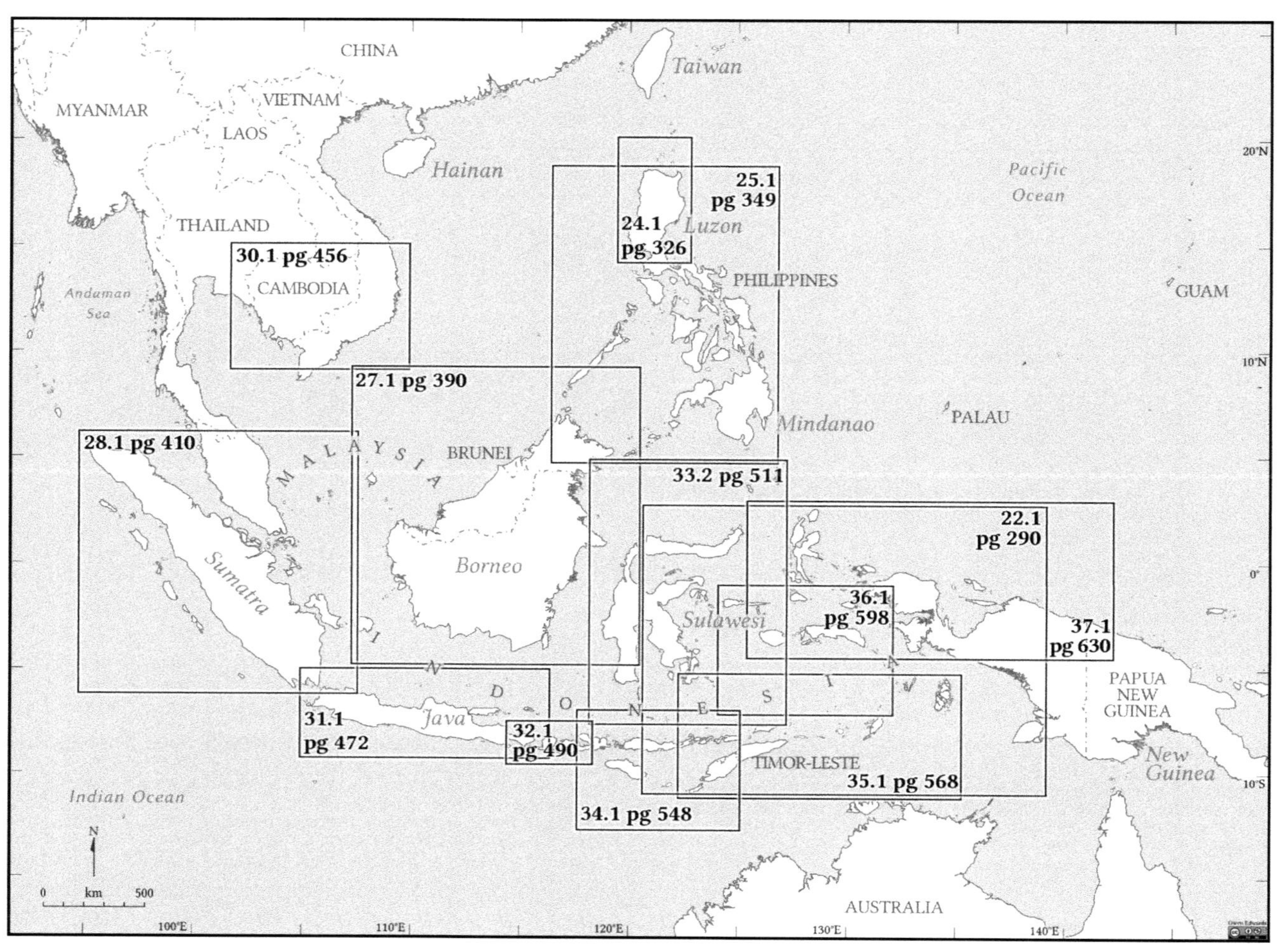


**Map B.** Guide to the language maps in this volume.

CHAPTER 1

# Introduction

ALEXANDER ADELAAR AND ANTOINETTE SCHAPPER

## 1.1 Scope of the volume

This volume is a comprehensive reference work on the Malayo-Polynesian languages of Southeast Asia. The Malayo-Polynesian languages constitute a primary branch of the Austronesian language family. The Austronesian languages of Taiwan (Formosa) form the other primary branches of the family, and fall outside the scope of this volume. Also not covered are those Malayo-Polynesian languages belonging to the Oceanic subgroup, spoken (for the most part) in the Pacific. These two exclusions leave close to 800 Austronesian languages, scattered across the modern nation states of the Philippines, China, Vietnam, Cambodia, Burma, Thailand, Malaysia, Indonesia, Brunei Darussalam, and Timor-Leste (East Timor), within the purview of the book. Also included are Yami on Taiwan's outlying Orchid Island, together with three more distant Malayo-Polynesian outliers which have their closest relatives in Southeast Asia: Palauan and Chamorro, spoken in Micronesia; and Malagasy, spoken in Madagascar and on Mayotte in the Comoros. Maps 1 and 1.1 situate the languages covered in the volume within the distribution of the Austronesian family as a whole.

The Southeast Asian triangle that encompasses the Malayo-Polynesian languages covered in this volume constitutes a cohesive object of study. After the initial settlement of speakers of Proto-Malayo-Polynesian (PMP) in the northern Philippines around 4000 years ago, speakers of Malayo-Polynesian languages dispersed in all directions across Island South Asia. Deep and continuous ethno-linguistic contacts and interactions between different groups speaking Austronesian languages, as well as with speakers of non-Austronesian languages (including Austroasiatic and Papuan languages), have resulted over millennia in large swathes of the area sharing many broad typological characteristics. The region also forms an integrated macro-area from the point of view of cultural and historical influences in more recent times. Large parts of the Southeast Asian triangle have experienced the same or similar waves of cultural and religious change. The effects of Indianization from about the third century, Islamization from the thirteenth century, as well as subjugation to western European colonial powers from the sixteenth century onwards are shared over much of the region under study in this volume. The presence of Malay and Javanese loanwords across the whole of Island Southeast Asia, into Mainland Southeast Asia and out into Madagascar further demonstrates the interconnectedness of the region in terms of indigenous networks.

## 1.2 Aims and rationale for the volume

The large size and wide geographical distribution of the Austronesian language family mean that it is always difficult to study as a whole. Our aim in this volume is to represent a wide range of scholarly viewpoints on Austronesian languages, as well as to achieve high levels of detail in description and accuracy in generalization. All too often, we feel, Austronesian languages have been excessively homogenized, and the diversity of ideas on their history underrepresented, in the broader scholarly world of linguistics. By limiting the scope of our volume to the Malayo-Polynesian languages of Southeast Asia (henceforth, MPSEA), we could ensure that our aims of granularity and diversity were met.

As mentioned in the preceding section, the Formosan and Oceanic languages are excluded from the volume. The twenty or so Formosan languages are not Malayo-Polynesian, but constitute several independent first-order branches of Austronesian. The issues involving them are somewhat different from those affecting MPSEA languages, be it in terms of their structures, their prehistory, or the foreign influences on them. They are the topic of a separate, dedicated volume that has recently appeared (Li, Zeitoun, and De Busser 2023). The Oceanic subgroup has some 450 languages. Dealing with a group of this size in addition to the close to 800 MPSEA languages would have made in-depth treatments of subgroups and of typological variation impossible within a single volume. The Oceanic languages also have a distinctly separate history from the MPSEA languages. Speakers of Proto-Oceanic settled in the area of the Bismarck Islands around 3500 years ago. Since that time, Oceanic languages have developed almost entirely

Alexander Adelaar and Antoinette Schapper, *Introduction.* In: *The Oxford Guide to the Malayo-Polynesian Languages of Southeast Asia.* Edited by: Alexander Adelaar and Antoinette Schapper, Oxford University Press. © Alexander Adelaar and Antoinette Schapper (2024). DOI: 10.1093/oso/9780198807353.003.0001

in isolation from MPSEA languages and can be regarded as a distinct object of study, although many interrelated issues exist (for instance, the role of Papuan contact). The handbook edited by Lynch, Ross and Crowley (2002) provides an excellent overview of the Oceanic subgroup.

There is a thriving descriptive linguistic tradition for MPSEA languages, and although there are many gaps, the languages of most parts of the region are represented by numerous grammars of varying lengths. Given the substantial and ongoing investment by linguists in creating grammatical materials for the region, we opted not to include sketch grammars in this volume. Besides the impossibility of capturing the diversity of the many MPSEA languages in a dozen or so sketches, several volumes consisting mostly of sketches already exist for these languages—notably, Tryon (1995a), and Adelaar and Himmelmann (2005). Instead, this volume includes synthesising chapters written by specialist linguists that give in-depth historical and typological overviews of MPSEA languages, discuss key issues, and identify questions for future research.

The present volume builds on a great many existing works, but two form particularly important points of departure. The first is Himmelmann's seminal article (2005a) "The Austronesian languages of Asia and Madagascar: Typological characteristics". This provided many insights into the typological divisions among Austronesian languages, and is, rightly, still highly cited by Austronesianists. However, it is ultimately restricted in the observations it is able to make due to its limited sampling of the large number of languages and the broad range of phenomena it covers. The second is perhaps the most significant handbook in the area of Austronesian linguistics. Appearing a little over a decade ago, Robert Blust's (2009c) *The Austronesian languages* is an influential work based on the knowledge accumulated by its author in forty years of scholarship. It presents a single vision, covering all aspects of Austronesian linguistics, but selectively illustrated. While slightly smaller in scope, the present volume builds on Blust's (2009c) significant legacy, but approaches the subject matter differently. Most notably, we take a diversity perspective and aim to cover all linguistic regions of the MPSEA area in detail, incorporating the many different viewpoints on their history and typology.

## 1.3 Organization of the volume

The chapters in this volume are organised into four broad themes. Part I deals with historical linguistics, including excursions into human genetics, archaeology, and cultural history. Part II treats contact and sociolinguistics, including contact languages, diasporas, language contact, multilingualism, language standardization, and language endangerment. Part III and Part IV of the volume are dedicated to describing the diverse typologies of MPSEA languages. Up to now these languages have been subject to little in-depth typologization. Existing attempts at typological characterizations are either too coarse-grained or too localized to provide a true picture of Malayo-Polynesian typological diversity in Southeast Asia. Part III provides detailed typological overviews of coherent groupings of MPSEA languages. Part IV overviews the distribution of variation in important typological domains for the languages across the whole MPSEA area. Each of the four sections is outlined below.

### 1.3.1 Part I. Historical linguistics

From a comparative historical perspective, the Austronesian language family and its Malayo-Polynesian branch are among the best-studied language groups in the world. Yet essential information, in particular around critical debates, about Malayo-Polynesian comparative historical linguistics has never been available in an accessible, single-volume format. The present book is designed to fill this gap by providing a systematic, detailed overview of the languages in question, organized both by region and linguistic classification.

The two opening chapters deal with high-level issues in the historical study of MPSEA languages. Chapter 2 situates the Malayo-Polynesian languages within the wider Austronesian language family and overviews the reconstructed features of their parent, Proto-Malayo-Polynesian. Chapter 3 considers methodological issues in the classification and subgrouping of Malayo-Polynesian languages. It compares applications of the traditional Comparative Method and newer Bayesian phylogenetics in Austronesian historical linguistics, arguing that they present complementary rather than competing approaches. Together they can be used to elucidate contentious points in the Malayo-Polynesian tree.

The following three chapters take a broader view of Malayo-Polynesian language history, beyond linguistics as such. Chapter 4 offers a view into the world of the speakers of Proto-Malayo-Polynesian, their culture (houses, village structure), subsistence (agriculture, maritime technology), and social organization (marriage, kinship relations). Chapter 5 is concerned with human genetics. Whilst acknowledging that Austronesian languages originated in Taiwan, it points out that the flow of DNA from Taiwan was not very pronounced, suggesting a much greater role for language shift among pre-existing populations, particularly in the Philippines, in the dispersal of Austronesian languages. Chapter 6 discusses the archaeological evidence for the spread of speakers of Austronesian languages from Taiwan into the Philippines and then across the Southeast Asian region and beyond. It offers a somewhat different view of Malayo-Polynesian prehistory from that presented in Chapter 5, taking the stance that it was primarily the migration of Malayo-Polynesian speaking agriculturists that drove the dispersal of the Austronesian languages beyond Taiwan.

The remaining nine chapters are primarily concerned with the subgrouping and reconstruction of MPSEA languages. Chapters 7 to 14 are regionally focused. They provide state-of-the-art, critical evaluations of the differing classifications that are currently proposed, offering detailed accounts of the various subgroups, both at high and low cladistic levels. It will become apparent to the reader that many proposed subgroups in the MPSEA domain between Proto-Malayo-Polynesian and Proto-Oceanic are still hotly debated. Similarly, the reader will observe in these chapters that there is still a great reliance on phonological and lexical comparison as the basis for classification of MPSEA languages. In the Austronesian linguistic tradition, comparatively little attention has been paid to morphosyntax, although grammatical change is discussed in several chapters of this volume.

By bringing together these chapters on Malayo-Polynesian historical linguistics, we have sought to create an account which is more comprehensive, multifaceted, and detailed than any comparable study to date.

### 1.3.2 Part II. Sociolinguistics and Language Contact

The topics addressed in this section concern language ecology, multilingualism, language standardization, language contact, contact languages, and diaspora languages. They are united by the fact that they deal with language change, especially through contact, and therefore build on the historical linguistic studies of the previous section.

Three chapters focus on current plurilingual contact. Chapter 15 is concerned with language ecology, drawing together issues surrounding the language endangerment crisis affecting MPSEA languages and describing patterns of language vitality in insular Southeast Asian countries and Madagascar. It sets out the ideologies, government and education policies, attitudes, action programmes, and other forces that give rise to varying degrees of indigenous language vitality, including rapid language shift and language loss. Chapter 16 illustrates multilingualism in action by means of code-switching. Rather than being "messy" and standing in the way of the neat description of a target language, code-switching is shown to exhibit structural linguistic patterns in its own right, and to be indicative of the sociolinguistic circumstances that give rise to them. Chapter 17 deals with language policy and the politics of language. In insular Southeast Asian nations, the elevation of one regional language to the status of national language has often reinforced the marginalization of other languages. This chapter brings together a series of case studies highlighting both official language development, and its impact on minority languages, in diverse parts of the region.

Chapters 18 and 19 deal with contact languages. These are languages that unambiguously result from contact, having source languages that are still spoken and a clearly identifiable history of contact and convergence. Chapter 18 details some salient features of contact languages from different parts of Southeast Asia and elsewhere. It also clarifies various terminological definitions, and reports on current debates in this area, such as the issue of whether there is a causal association between collective adult second language acquisition and morphosyntactic simplification. Chapter 19 deals more specifically with heritage languages—that is, immigrant minority languages spoken in diaspora contexts. This chapter shows how heritage languages diverge systematically from the language as spoken by speakers in the source location, principally as a result of collective bilingualism and crosslinguistic influences on second generation migrants.

Chapters 20 to 23 look at the diverse influences exerted on MPSEA languages by unrelated languages belonging to different groups. Chapter 20 shows that many languages in the western part of the MPSEA area have varying amounts of lexical borrowing from, and phonological convergence with, languages of Mainland Southeast Asia. Chapter 21 is a short history of the contact that has occurred between several MPSEA languages and languages of coastal East Africa. In particular it focuses on the various influences from Austronesian and Bantu languages that can be seen to have shaped the phonology, verbal morphosyntax, and deictic system of Malagasy, refuting the idea that Malagasy reflects PMP morphosyntax in a near-unchanged form. Chapter 22 looks at contact with so-called Papuan languages in the eastern part of the MPSEA area. It argues that while the effects of shifts from Papuan languages are widely recognised in the morphosyntax of eastern MPSEA languages, scholars have been too quick to dismiss the idea of Papuan lexical influence. Finally, Chapter 23 gives a brief account of the many and important influences exerted down the ages on MPSEA languages by languages originally spoken far outside Southeast Asia in India, China, the Middle East, and Europe.

### 1.3.3 Part III. Areal overviews

Part III gives typological overviews of pragmatic groupings of MPSEA languages, presented over seventeen chapters. In traditional typology based on broad classifications of linguistic phenomena, complex and often subtle typological differences, particularly between related languages, are easily lost. The prevalence of genealogically balanced sampling, coupled with the wide adoption of highly cladistic representations of the Austronesian family tree, has led many global studies to include only one or two MPSEA languages. Consequently, the group is undersampled and its heterogeneity underestimated in much of the current literature. As with many language families, however, closer scrutiny reveals significant variation in the distributional and constructional details of individual features across MPSEA languages. In the context of the ongoing pivot toward multivariate approaches to typological classification alongside the use of genealogically dense samples, the MPSEA languages offer fertile ground for future study. In particular, there is still much scope for the typological study of historically related form–function pairs and their attested developments in MPSEA languages. Chapters in this part of the volume give many insights into the subtle variations that exist between genealogical and areal groupings of MPSEA languages.

Chapters 24 to 40 are written by authors with specialist knowledge of the languages covered, each bringing out the most important and characteristic features of the languages under discussion, both in relation to each other and within the wider MPSEA context. Most chapters in this section survey a large number of languages, on average between forty and ninety, found in a contiguous area. A few deal with smaller groupings of closely related and/or geographically clustered languages: Chapter 30 on Chamic languages; Chapter 32 on lects of the Bali-Sasak-Sumbawa cluster; Chapter 28 on the non-Malayic languages of Sumatra and the Barrier Islands; and Chapter 31 on the languages of Java. Languages which belong to a single subgroup but are widely dispersed geographically are discussed in Chapter 26 on the Sama-Bajaw languages, and in Chapter 29 on the Malayic languages of Borneo, Sumatra, the Malay Peninsula, and eastern Indonesia. There are also three chapters on individual geographical outliers among the MPSEA languages: Chamorro (Chapter 38); Palauan (Chapter 39); and Malagasy (Chapter 40).

Taken together, the chapters in this section offer a rich picture of the structure of MPSEA languages and its variations. They also set out the major lacunae in our documentary knowledge of MPSEA languages, thereby providing clear directions for future efforts in language documentation and description.

### 1.3.4 Part IV. Featural overviews

This part presents twelve chapters overviewing key domains of typological variation across MPSEA languages.

Different levels of phonological structure are dealt with in Chapters 41, 42, and 43, each highlighting regional norms and deviations from them. Chapter 41 examines the segmental inventories of the MPSEA languages and investigates what forces shaped their consonant and vowel inventories. Chapter 42 surveys suprasegmental systems and proposes a new typology of stress in MPSEA languages based on four prototypes featuring different associations between phrase-marking edge tone combinations and the segmental string. Chapter 43 discusses a range of phonotactic properties of MPSEA languages that are crosslinguistically unusual, highlighting notable patterns of nasal–plosive resolution and the variation in widely found constraints on root shapes.

Four chapters deal with characteristics that are of particular typological interest within the Austronesian family. Chapter 44 looks at the morphological profiles of MPSEA languages. Its approach is quantitative, comparing the morphological characteristics of MPSEA languages with those of other groups, both Austronesian and unrelated. It highlights the fact that in global perspective, many MPSEA languages show an unusually low degree of morphological elaboration. Reduplication, treated in depth in Chapter 45, is a uniquely important feature of morphology in MPSEA languages, as it is in all Austronesian languages. Chapter 47 presents a detailed treatment of the voice systems of MPSEA languages. This chapter is of particular significance because the typologically unusual nature of voice in Austronesian languages, and the distinct terminology used within the Austronesianist tradition to describe it, have often proved inaccessible to non-specialists. Chapter 51 deals with phasal polarity, a domain that has traditionally been little studied, but is central in aspect marking, with phasal polarity markers typically occurring with high frequency in MPSEA languages.

Contact is invoked in severable chapters as a likely cause of variation in types across the MPSEA area. This is a particularly important argument in Chapter 46, which charts word order patterns across the MPSEA languages to show clines running north to south and west to east. Shifts away from conservative Austronesian word order patterns are argued to result from contact with speakers of non-Austronesian languages that were present in Southeast Asia at the time of the Austronesian expansion. Chapter 50, on negation types, also attributes some major variables in MPSEA languages to contact. At the same time, the authors emphasize that the MPSEA negation patterns fit squarely within well-known typologies of negation: standard and prohibitive negators tend to be different and usually occur early in a negated clause, while negative indefinites are typically based on an existential strategy.

Several chapters present challenges to existing ideas about the distribution of types. Chapter 48 surveys the structural characteristics of basic and marked adnominal

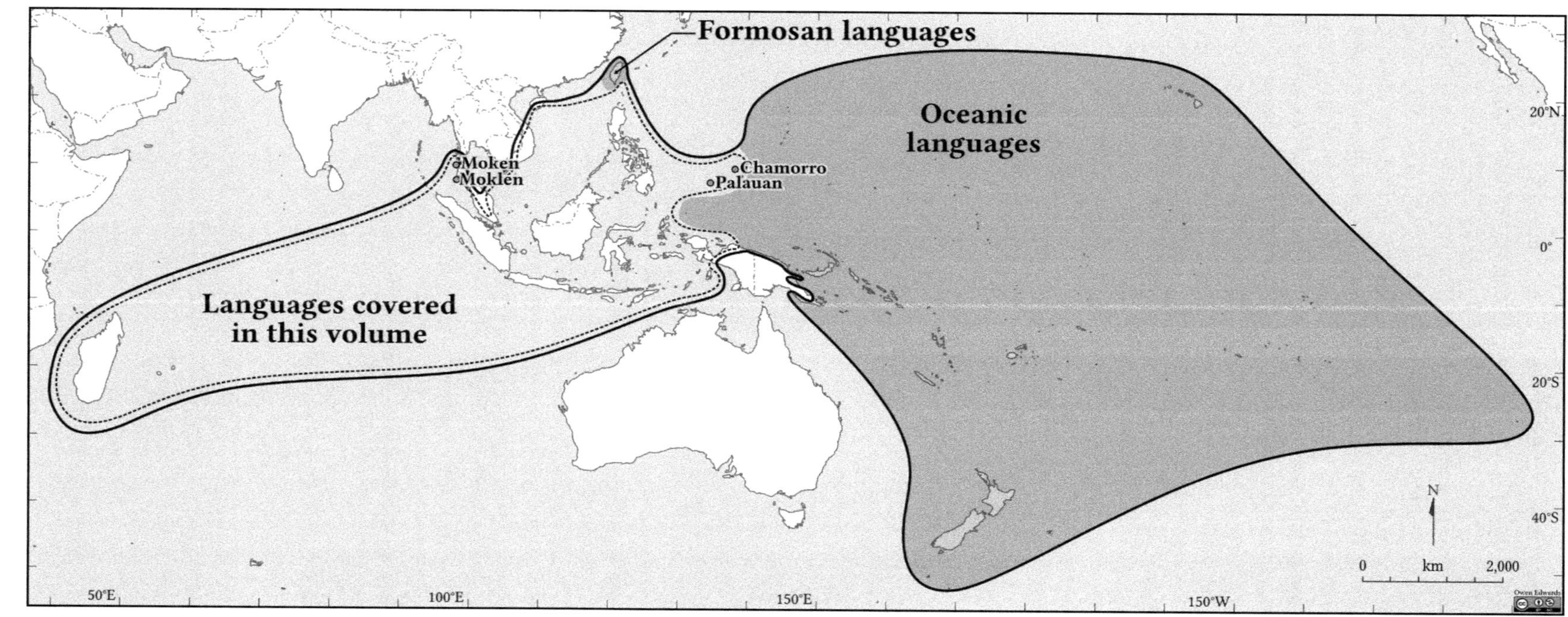


**Map 1.1.** The position of the Malayo-Polynesian languages of Southeast Asia within the Austronesian language family.

possessive constructions and shows that reversals in the order of possessor and possessum are found in marked constructions throughout the area. What is more, this chapter points out how differential possessive marking, often inaccurately conflated with '(in)alienability', is not limited to languages of eastern MPSEA, but is also found in Borneo, and to a lesser extent in Luzon and Sulawesi. Chapter 49 discusses systems of spatial orientation in MPSEA languages and contests the long-standing assumption that within this group the seaward–landward orientation is the fundamental axis of orientation. In reality, the MPSEA languages employing seaward–landward systems are less numerous than those using riverine, coastal, and cardinal systems.

Finally, Chapter 52 considers free pronouns. These tend to be stable in form and meaning throughout the MPSEA language group. However, there is much local variation in subsidiary and associated features such as politeness, number (dual, trial, and quadral), gender, animacy, and pronominal use of other lexical categories. These are not representative of the entire MPSEA region.

# PART I
# Historical Linguistics

CHAPTER 2

# Proto-Malayo-Polynesian

## *Its place within the Austronesian language family, reconstruction, and daughters*

ALEXANDER D. SMITH

## 2.1 Introduction

The Austronesian (AN) language family has several first-order subgroups. Most are located in Taiwan (the so-called *Formosan* languages) and only one, Malayo-Polynesian (MP), is located outside Taiwan. MP is by far the largest Austronesian subgroup, and all AN languages that are spoken outside of Taiwan belong to the MP subgroup. The northernmost MP languages are the Batanic languages, spoken on the small islands between mainland Taiwan and northern Luzon, Philippines. From here the languages fan out and are spoken throughout the Philippines, Malaysia, Indonesia, Madagascar, mostly coastal areas of New Guinea, Solomon Islands, Vanuatu, New Caledonia, Fiji, and the inhabited Polynesian and Micronesian islands. This chapter focuses on the historical development and interrelatedness of the MP languages of Asia and Madagascar as well as two languages spoken in Micronesia: Chamorro and Palauan. The chapter also discusses the reconstruction of Proto-Malayo-Polynesian (PMP), the hypothetical common ancestor language from which all MP languages descend.

Several topics will be discussed in this chapter, regarding both PMP as a language and the internal subgrouping of MP. To begin, the chapter includes a discussion of the putative properties of PMP itself in §2.2, including aspects of its phonology (§2.2.1) and morphosyntax (§2.2.2). Comparative evidence gives us a clear understanding of what PMP was like as a spoken language, although areas of disagreement exist among specialists. §2.3 discusses such topics as canonical word-shape, phonotactics, stress, voice morphology, word-order, pivot (or subject) selection (see also Kroeger and Riesberg, this volume, §47.3.3), and voice's effect on extraction in WH-movement and relative clause gapping. The chapter continues with an overview of evidence supporting a Malayo-Polynesian subgroup and its position within Austronesian (§2.3). There is a large collection of phonological, lexical, and morphosyntactic evidence which supports the existence of a MP subgroup, and MP itself enjoys widespread acceptance among Austronesian specialists. The chapter will also, however, quickly review some competing proposals that do not recognize the traditional MP subgroup, for the sake of completeness (§2.3.6). Finally, the chapter will conclude with a discussion on the internal subgrouping of MP in §2.4. Recent proposals argue that MP has little internal structure (that is, it has multiple primary branches), although a model with only two primary divisions has dominated theories of MP subgrouping for decades. These two opposing viewpoints are dubbed 'binary-MP' and 'diverse-MP' models for MP internal subgrouping, and the discussion in §2.4 favours the diverse-MP model over the binary-MP model.

## 2.2 Proto-Malayo-Polynesian

The discussion begins with PMP as a language, focusing on its phonology and morphosyntax. PMP had mostly disyllabic lexemes, no complex onsets or codas, and a phonological inventory of four vowels and up to twenty-one consonants. Regarding morphosyntax, it displayed a high degree of synthesis, especially on the verb, was verb-initial, and had a complex voice system that selected arguments for extraction. These observations are supported by robust comparative evidence and examples from modern Austronesian languages will be used to provide examples of the types of constructions that probably follow directly from PMP. The phonology is discussed first.

### 2.2.1 Proto-Malayo-Polynesian phonology

PMP had a smaller phonemic inventory than Proto-Austronesian (PAN) due to the several mergers that took

Alexander D. Smith, *Proto-Malayo-Polynesian*. In: *The Oxford Guide to the Malayo-Polynesian Languages of Southeast Asia.* Edited by: Alexander Adelaar and Antoinette Schapper, Oxford University Press. © Alexander D. Smith (2024). DOI: 10.1093/oso/9780198807353.003.0002

place between PAN and PMP (§2.3). There is some disagreement regarding a few of the reconstructed phonemes, and Tables 2.1 and 2.2 show what might be considered the least controversial (with appropriate qualifications, of course). This section begins with the consonants, then moves on to the vowels.

#### 2.2.1.1 *Consonants and word-shape*

Due to longstanding traditions in the field the PMP (and PAN) graphemes *j, *z, *R, *r, and *D do not correspond clearly with their reconstructed phonetic forms. Regarding *j, Blust (1999a, 2013a) has stated that *j was a palatalized velar stop, written phonetically as [gʲ]. PMP *z was the post-alveolar affricate [ʤ] and *c was [ʧ], the voiceless counterpart to *z, but is reconstructed without evidence from multiple primary branches, casting some doubt on its validity (see Ross 1992). The phonemes *t and *d were distinguished not only by voice, but also by place of articulation. *t was produced with a dental articulation, as it still is in many languages, and *d, along with *s, *n, and *l, was produced with an alveolar articulation (see Blevins, this volume, §41.2.3). Dempwolff (1934–1938) reconstructs a single retroflex *D, although both Dahl (1976) and Zorc (1987) argue that there was no general distinction between *d and *D. Blust (2013a: 575), however, argues that the retroflex is supported, although with minimal attestation and strict phonotactic limitations; it was only found in word-final position. All words that began with a vowel likely contained a glottal stop onset, which is retained in many Philippine languages where prefixes on otherwise vowel-initial words reveal a glottal stop. It is not clear, however, that glottal stop formed any meaningful contrasts with other consonants.

Finally, another important orthographic convention is the use of a capital *R for what was probably an alveolar trill, while *r is used for an alveolar flap. In languages where *R remains rhotic, it is mostly an alveolar trill. Languages where reflexes of *R surface as velar (like Malay and Land Dayak varieties in West Borneo) probably reflect a historically convergent change where *R, [r], moved back, becoming g, ɣ, ʀ, or another velar/uvular consonant, as it is more common for an alveolar trill to shift to a velar or uvular articulation than it is for a velar or uvular to shift to a trilled r. These changes parallel familiar changes in Europe, where Italic and Germanic languages show velar and uvular pronunciations of *r* in a contact zone that overlaps with modern France and Germany. PMP *R is therefore reconstructed as alveolar, (but see Adelaar 2005a, who postulates that *R was velar). (See Table 2.1.)

Although the phonological inventory of PMP was simpler when compared to PAN with respect to phonemic inventory, word-shape was more complex. A close examination of the *Austronesian Comparative Dictionary* (*ACD*; Blust and Trussel 2020) reveals a consonant cluster restriction in PAN vocabulary; clusters were common in reduplicated monosyllabic roots (words like *bəjbəj 'to tie by winding'), but in regular two-syllable roots, word-internal clusters are exceptionally rare, and where they are reconstructed it is done so without Formosan evidence, which suggests that they were, in fact, not present in PAN. This had changed in PMP, which had many root-internal consonant clusters other than those formed by reduplication of monosyllables. There was thus a complexification of canonical shape, from PAN CVCV(C) to PMP CV(C)CV(C).

#### 2.2.1.2 *Vowels*

The vowels are less controversial than the consonants, and there is widespread agreement that PMP had four vowels, depicted in Table 2.2. There were also four diphthongs restricted to word-final position, *-ay, *-aw, *-uy, and *-iw.

**Table 2.1** Proto-Malayo-Polynesian consonants

| | Labial | Dental | Alveolar | Palatal | Retroflex | Palatalized-velar | Velar | Uvular | Glottal |
|---|---|---|---|---|---|---|---|---|---|
| Plosive | *p/*b | *t | /*d | | /(*D) | /*j | *k/*g | *q | (*ʔ) |
| Affricate | | | | (*c)/ *z | | | | | |
| Fricative | | | *s | | | | | | *h |
| Nasal | *m | | *n | *ñ | | | *ŋ | | |
| Lateral | | | *l | | | | | | |
| Flap | | | *r | | | | | | |
| Trill | | | *R | | | | | | |

**Table 2.2** Proto-Malayo-Polynesian vowels

| | Front | Central | Back |
|---|---|---|---|
| High | *i | | *u |
| Mid | | *ə | |
| Low | | *a | |

The vowels *i, *u, and *a had no distributional restrictions in either PAN or PMP. Schwa, on the other hand, was subject to several unique restrictions. First, schwa could appear in closed final syllables but not open final ones (Blust 2000a: 88; Smith 2018b). Second, at the PAN level, schwa was underrepresented in word-initial position in two-syllable roots (only the numerals *əsa and *ənəm contained word-initial schwa), but this changed in PMP which contains numerous examples of word-initial schwa. In three-syllable roots, however, schwa was still banned from occurring in initial position. Third, although schwa was utilized in the patient voice suffix *-ən, it was not used in any prefixing or infixing morphology. In fact, *-ən is the sole morpheme (excluding roots) where schwa was used. Finally, in many modern western Austronesian languages schwa cannot bear stress in open penultimate syllables, a prosodic system which Smith (2018b) reconstructs all the way to PAN.

#### 2.2.1.3 *Stress*

The status of stress in PAN and PMP is fraught with disagreement. Much of the literature on stress is concerned with the reconstructability of a contrastive (phonemic) stress system to either PMP or PAN. For example, Pejros (1994); Ross (1992); Wolff (1991); and Zorc (1978) have argued for reconstructing contrastive stress all the way to PAN. The proposals vary in quality, but they all have in common a reliance on Philippine data (Philippine languages maintain a unique concentration of contrastive stress systems in Austronesian). Ross (1992) specifically tried to show systematic correspondences between Philippine stress and Rukai, a language of Taiwan, but Blust (1997a) showed a lack of consistency in the correspondence sets, and contrastive stress has never been definitively reconstructed to either PMP or PAN.

Although the status of phonemic stress remains an issue of debate, there are other important observations about PMP stress that can be made, and these observations all deal with schwa, its distributional restrictions, and its ability to bear stress. As pointed out earlier, schwa was subject to unique restrictions not found on the other vowels. In many modern AN languages, schwa is not stressed in penultimate syllables and is furthermore extra-short throughout AN. Smith (2018b) has argued specifically that schwa, at both the PAN and PMP level, was unstressed in penultimate position and caused stress shift to the final syllable (but see Ross 1992 who argued that schwa *could* bear stress in the penultimate syllable).

The main issue with reconstructing a stressable schwa in open penultimate syllables to PMP is that the linguistic evidence overwhelmingly supports reconstructing a schwa that could not bear stress in this position. For example, Zorc (1972) demonstrated that where schwa appeared in an open penultimate syllable, it caused stress to shift to the final syllable in several Philippine languages, a process that he reconstructs to Proto-Philippines. Adelaar (1981) reports a similar pattern in Karo Batak and Dairi-Pakpak where penultimate stress shifts to the final syllable if the penultimate vowel is schwa, and Blust (2000a: 90–2) posits a similar pattern for pre-Chamorro.

In Formosan languages there is a mixture of systems. For instance, the Budai dialect of Rukai has contrastive stress while Amis has word-final stress. However, there are also examples of Formosan languages with a stress system similar to that found in western MP languages. Thao, for example, has penultimate stress except where a historical PAN schwa appeared in the penultimate syllable, in which case stress is final (Blust 2013a: 255). The same pattern also applies to Paiwan (Chen 2004: 36–9). It is difficult to look at this evidence and not conclude that PMP stress could not fall on schwa in open penultimate syllables and that this system was inherited from PAN.

Schwa may therefore be reconstructed to the major proto-languages as unstressable where it appeared in penultimate position. In Proto-Oceanic schwa had shifted to *o and stress appeared on the penultimate mora (Lynch 2000), so schwa-related phenomena are restricted to the western languages. Even in Philippine languages where stress is contrastive, reflexes of penultimate schwa do not typically receive stress. This suggests that even if contrastive stress were reconstructed to the proto-language, it would not involve penultimate schwa which never appeared stressed. One may reconstruct, for example, PMP *ˈmata 'eye', *ˈbulu 'body hair', and *ˈpitu 'seven' with penultimate stress but *dəˈpah 'a fathom', *təˈlu 'three', and *bəˈsuR 'full; satiated' with final stress.

#### 2.2.1.4 *Summary*

Taken together a clear picture of the phonology of PMP can be reconstructed. Because more than ninety percent of the lexicon of PAN was disyllabic (Chrétien 1965), a canonical shape of CV(C)CV(C) can be reconstructed to PAN. One can further state that if the penultimate syllable was schwa, that stress was final: Cə'CV(C). There were no words of the shape *CVCə or *əCVCVC, and schwa was also absent from infixing or prefixing morphology. It is unclear what the stress pattern was in reduplicated monosyllables like *bəjbəj 'to tie by winding'. It is also unclear how Philippine stress became contrastive. There is a connection between word-final stress and the presence of schwa in reconstructed vocabulary as pointed out by Zorc (1972), but this does not explain all cases of word-final stress and work remains to be done both on the Philippine subgroup, the interrelatedness of Philippine languages, and the ultimate origin of Philippine stress systems.

## 2.2.2 Verbal morphology and voice

PMP was morphologically complex especially on verbs which were marked with several inflectional and derivational morphemes. PMP had a Philippine-type four-voice system (also called Multiple Undergoer Voice) that closely resembled the PAN system reconstructed in Adelaar 2005a; Chen 2017; and Wolff 1973. (Table 2.3 incorporates proposals from both Chen and Adelaar.) Much of the PMP verbal morphology was inherited from PAN, but the language was also innovative with regards to morphology, which forms part of the evidence in favour of MP as a subgroup (see §3 for the subgrouping evidence). The main difference between PMP and PAN with regard to voice morphology is the addition of the homorganic nasal substitution prefix *maŋ- 'actor voice' which was used alongside *<um>, possibly as a marker of transitive AV, whereas PMP *<um> was used mostly, but not exclusively, as an intransitive AV infix. Finally, verbal morphology operated in tandem with a series of particles that appeared before nominal arguments and indicated their relationship to the verb, their grammatical category as pivot, their semantic category, and other information such as number and whether the noun was common. These case markers are discussed more after the verbal morphology.

### 2.2.2.1 *Verbal morphology*

In Table 2.3 both PAN and PMP verbal voice morphology is indicated using labels from Chen (2017: 21). AV is actor voice, PV is patient voice, LV is locative voice, and IV is instrumental voice (sometimes called circumstantial voice). Voice selection determines pivot, discussed more in the following.

The syntax of this voice system has received much attention, due in no small part to the fact that voice was not a transitivity or valency altering process like it is in languages with more familiar passives; typical AV, PV, LV, and circumstantial constructions were all transitive. In fact, PV was the preferred transitive voice, as it still is in many Austronesian languages. This type of valency non-alternating voice system is dubbed "symmetrical voice", and it is largely an Austronesian phenomenon (Himmelmann 2005a).

PMP voice was responsible for selecting which argument was privileged for extraction in, for example, WH-movement and relative clause formation. The term 'extraction', as it is used here, means the movement of a typically post-verbal argument into pre-verbal position. In a two-argument sentence with an agent and patient, the actor voice (AV) allowed for agent extraction and patient voice (PV) allowed for patient extraction. Examples from Toba Batak demonstrate the voicing requirement for extraction (from Erlewine 2018) reflected in a modern language:

**Table 2.3** PAN and PMP voice morphology (Adelaar 2005a; Chen 2017)

| **Indicative** | | | AV | PV | LV | IV |
|---|---|---|---|---|---|---|
| | Neutral | PAN | *<um> | *-ən | *-an | *Si- |
| | | PMP | *<um><br>*maŋ- | *-ən | *-an | *i- |
| | Perfective | PAN | *<umin> | *<in> | *<in> -an | *Si- <in> |
| | | PMP | *<umin> | *<in> | *<in> -an | *i- <in> |
| **Optative/Hortative** | | PAN | *-a | *-aw | *-ay | -anay |
| | | PMP | *-a | *-aw | *-ay | (anay) |
| **Imperative/Negative** | | PAN | Ø | *-u | *-i | *-an |
| | | PMP | Ø | *-a | *-i | *-an |

Toba Batak

(1) a. *ise* *mang-allang* *babi* ___
who AV-eat pork

b. **ise* *di-allang* ___ *babi*
who PV-eat pork
'who ate pork?' (Erlewine 2018: 665)

c. **aha* *man-uhor* ___ *si* *Poltak*
what AV-buy PERS Poltak

d. *aha* *di-tuhor* *si* *Poltak* ___
what PV-buy PERS Poltak
'what did Poltak buy?' (Erlewine 2018: 665)

In (1a) and (1b) *ise* 'who' (the agent) can be fronted to preverbal position only in AV while in c and d, *aha* 'what' (the patient) may only be fronted in PV. The same restriction was noted in relativization in Toba Batak (Keenan and Comrie 1977) and in other Austronesian languages (see Kroeger and Riesberg, this volume, §47.2.2). In Lun Bawang as spoken at Long Semadoh, for example, Mortensen (2018, personal communication) demonstrates that agents are extractable only in AV, patients only in PV, and instruments only in IV. In the following examples one can see that the instrument *inih anət* 'this rope' can be fronted in relative clauses only in example (2c), which utilizes IV. Examples (2a) and (2b), which utilize AV and PV respectively, are ungrammatical when instrument extraction is attempted from the relative sentence.

Lun Bawang (Long Semadoh dialect)

(2) a. **inih* *anət* *luk* *pian=kuh* *iko*
this rope REL want=1SG.GEN 2SG.PIV
*ŋabət* *kərubau*
tie.AV buffalo

b. **inih* *anət* *luk* *pian=kuh* *bət-in=muh*
this rope REL want=1SG.GEN tie-PV=2SG.PIV
*kərubau*
buffalo

c. *inih* *anət* *luk* *pian=kuh* *pi-ŋabət=muh*
this rope REL want=1SG.GEN IV-tie=2SG.PIV
*kərubau*
buffalo
'This is the rope that I want you to use to tie up a buffalo.' (Mortensen 2018)

The requirement that voice match the role of the WH-word was only strictly required with WH fronting. In many languages, including Toba Batak (Erlewine 2018) and Cebuano Bisaya, to name only two, non-pivot WH-words are grammatical as long as they remain *in situ*.

Extraction restrictions, while ubiquitous as examples of Austronesian syntax, are more loosely applied in relativization. Typically, Austronesian voice is described as also restricting relativization to only pivot arguments, similar to the requirement that WH extraction only targets pivots. Bondoc (2018) has shown, however, that at least Tagalog and Cebuano Bisaya allow for the relativization of non-pivot arguments (but still do not allow relativization of obliques). It is understood that relativization, at the PMP level, was strictly pivot-only, just like WH-movement, but that pivot-only relativization restrictions have been loosened in some daughter languages.

To summarize, PMP had a series of affixes that carried voice, aspectual, and modal information. This section focused on voice, and how voice indicated pivot selection. Pivots are the arguments which are available for extraction in WH-movement, relativization, and focus. Beyond this, voice selection also indicated the pivot's special status even without extraction. In Tagalog, for example, *ang*-marked pivots are interpreted as definite, and non-pivots as nonspecific (see Rackowski 2002). Although Tagalog *ang-* does not follow directly from PMP, the reconstructed language did have a series of nominal case markers that indicated which argument was pivot and thus had a special relationship with the verb. They are discussed in more detail in the following section.

#### 2.2.2.2 *Case markers*

Blust (2015a), Reid (2006a), Ross (2006), and others have reconstructed a series of case marking particles that directly marked nouns as pivot (nominative) and non-pivot (genitive, oblique, and locative). The forms of the case markers in each reconstruction differ from one another, but they typically share the same functions. "Nominative" case markers, to use Blust's terminology, appear on whichever argument is selected by the verb as pivot; the agent in AV, the patient in PV, the subject in intransitive clauses, and so forth. Agents appeared in the genitive case in non-actor voice sentences and were cliticized to the VP as an enclitic if they were pronominal or were otherwise marked with the genitive case marker. Locative case markers appeared on locative arguments (if the locative is not also pivot), and the oblique case markers appeared on other non-core arguments.

Case markers fit into a paradigm of a consonant onset that corresponded with case, and a vowel, which corresponded with other properties of the argument (singular, plural, common noun). To summarize, an *s- onset indicated that the following argument was pivot, *n- that the following argument was genitive, *k- that the following argument was oblique, and *d- that the following argument was locative. The onsets combined with a vowel nucleus, either *-i for a singular noun, *-a for a plural noun, or *-u for a common noun regardless of plurality. Schwa was naturally excluded. A singular, non-common agent in AV would therefore have been immediately preceded by the *si case marker, a plural non-pivot agent would have been preceded by *na, a common noun oblique by *ku, and so forth. The case marking system that Blust reconstructs for PMP is shown below in Table 2.4.

**Table 2.4** PMP case markers (Blust 2015a)

| PMP | Pivot | Non-Pivot | | |
|---|---|---|---|---|
| | NOM | GEN | OBL | LOC |
| Singular | *si | *ni | *ki | *di |
| Plural | *sa | *na | *ka | *da |
| Common | - | *nu | *ku | *du |

The case markers are retained in many languages that reflect the PMP multiple-undergoer voice system, but are also found in languages that have reduced the old voice system. In Cebuano Bisaya, for example, the case marker *ni has fused with the pronoun *aku, producing the pronominal *naku?* for the non-pivot patient. Similarly, *si fused with pronominal pivots, creating Cebuano Bisaya *siya* for the third person singular pivot agent (from *si ia). The locative marker is quickly recognizable in the Malay locative *di*, as in, *di mana* 'where' or *di sini* 'here'. The use of *k- initial case markers as oblique markers is found throughout both the Philippines and Taiwan (see Blust 2015a for a full list of evidence).

2.2.2.3 *Summary*

PMP, as the evidence above suggests, had complex verbal morphosyntax that selected an argument as pivot, that is, it was able to move to preverbal position in various syntactic contexts. Nouns themselves were also marked with pre-nominal case markers. PMP sentences with two arguments could thus occur as in example (3). In this example, a two-argument sentence may appear in either AV or PV, with the voice-determined-pivot either *in situ* or fronted to pre-verbal position. In (4), a three argument sentence may select from several possible pivots. Case markers are labelled NOM, GEN, OBL, and LCM (locative case marker, to distinguish it from LOC, the locative argument).

(3) a.      [AV-VERB NOM-AGT OBL-PAT]
AGT [AV-VERB ___ OBL-PAT]

b.      [VERB-PV=AGT.GEN NOM-PAT]
PAT [VERB-PV=AGT.GEN ___]

(4) a.      [AV-VERB NOM-AGT GEN-PAT LCM-LOC]
AGT [AV-VERB ___ GEN-PAT LCM-LOC]

b.      [VERB-PV=AGT.GEN NOM-PAT LCM-LOC]
PAT [VERB-PV=AGT.GEN ___ LCM-LOC]

c.      [VERB-PV=AGT.GEN NOM-LOC OBL-PAT]
LOC [VERB-LV=AGT.GEN ___ OBL-PAT]

## 2.3 Malayo-Polynesian within Austronesian

Early scholarship on Austronesian languages tended to have a bias for Malayo-Polynesian data and therefore did not recognize a primary division between Formosan languages and MP. Dempwolff's reconstruction of *Uraustronesisch* [Proto-Austronesian] (Dempwolff 1934–1938), for example, contained only MP data, and therefore does not represent a true 'Proto-Austronesian' reconstruction. As Formosan evidence became more widely available, however, it became increasingly clear that the Formosan languages contained distinctions not found in the languages outside Taiwan and that MP is a separate linguistically defined subgroup. Evidence for MP includes a large and growing set of exclusively shared phonological, lexical, and morphosyntactic innovations. These innovations are explained in more detail below and reflect a strong consensus among those working in MP. Although there are examples of subgrouping hypotheses that dismantle MP, mentioned in brief below, the subgroup is not controversial and there is no serious argument against its validity.

### 2.3.1 Phonological evidence for Malayo-Polynesian

The phonological innovations defining MP are numerous, and of varying quality. Blust (2001a) likens the gathering of MP evidence to building a wall, one stone at a time; no single stone (or sound change) can be singled out as defining the entire subgroup, but together the evidence for MP is compelling. Some of the longest-standing evidence is presented below, with a few examples to distinguish MP from the Formosan languages. These are: i) the merger of PAN *C and *t as PMP *t; ii) the merger of PAN *N and *n as PMP *n; and iii) the shift of PAN *S to PMP *h (Dahl 1976, Mills 1975a).[1]

Table 2.5, below, shows the merger of PAN *t and *C using reflexes of PAN *qaCay 'liver' and *pitu 'seven'. In the two Formosan languages, Puyuma and Paiwan, *C and *t have distinct reflexes, but in all MP languages, including the four in Table 2.5, *C and *t have identical reflexes:

**Table 2.5** Merger of PAN *t and *C as PMP *t

| PAN | | *qaCay 'liver' | *pitu 'seven' |
|---|---|---|---|
| *Formosan* | Puyuma | *haṭay* | *pitu* |
| | Paiwan | *qatsay* | *pitʃu* |
| PMP | | *qatay | *pitu |
| *Malayo-Polynesian* | Tagalog | *atáy* | *pitó* |
| | Malagasy | *àti* | *fitu* |
| | Palauan (*t > ð) | *ʔað* | *wið* |
| | Hawaiian (*t > *k*) | *ake* | *hiku* |

The same pattern is observable in reflexes of *N and *n in Table 2.6. The Formosan languages retain a distinction between *N and *n but all MP languages reflect *N and *n as a single phoneme.

**Table 2.6** Merger of PAN *n and *N as PMP *n

| PAN | | *aNak 'offspring' | *danaw 'lake' |
|---|---|---|---|
| *Formosan* | Puyuma | *alak* | *danaw* |
| | Paiwan | *alʸak* | *dʒanaw* |
| PMP | | *anak | *danaw |
| *Malayo-Polynesian* | Tagalog | *anák* | *dánaw* |
| | Malagasy | *ànaka* | *rànu* ('water') |
| | Malay | *anak* | *danaw* |
| | Termanu | *ana* | *dano* |

Table 2.7 shows the typical reflexes of PAN *S [s] which shifted to *h in PMP. This is a common sound change, and does not provide compelling evidence on its own, but is nevertheless part of the large list of changes that define MP. It is difficult to find robust evidence for this change outside of the Philippines (since most languages have further deleted *h), but beyond reflexes of *duSa (in Table 2.7), reflexes of PAN *Sapuy 'fire' in a few MP languages also show this change: Bunun (*Formosan*) *sapuð* but Itbayaten *hapoy* and Western Bukidnon Manobo *hapuy*.

[1] PAN *C was an alveolar affricate [ts] and *N was probably a lateral, distinct from *l, as it is reflected as a lateral in several Formosan languages, although its exact phonetic properties are not agreed upon. *S was an alveolar fricative [s], which is distinct from the palatalized *s [ʃ], although PAN *S merged with *h as PMP *h and *s [ʃ] shifted to *s [s], a change that is not represented in the orthography.

**Table 2.7** Shift of PAN *S to PMP *h

| PAN | | *duSa 'two' |
|---|---|---|
| *Formosan* | Kavalan | *zusa* |
| | Squliq Atayal | *rusa* |
| | Amis | *tosa* |
| PMP | | *duha |
| *Malayo-Polynesian* | Itbayaten | *doha* |
| | Cebuano | *duhá* |
| | Hiligaynon | *duhá* |
| | Masbatenyo | *duhá* |

*S also underwent irregular changes in PMP which provide additional evidence for the subgroup. These are: (i) the irregular deletion of *S in some words where it should have shifted to *h; and (ii) the irregular metathesis of PAN *CVCVS to PMP *CVhVC (Tsuchida 1976). Examples of the first change are found in MP reflexes of PAN *Səpat 'four', which irregularly became PMP *əpat. Two well-known examples of the latter change are printed in Table 2.8 below, where PAN *bukəS 'hair' became PMP *buhək and *tapəS 'to winnow' became *tahəp. An additional example of *S being irregularly deleted (not indicated on the table) is the locative voice prefix *Si-, which is reflected with Atayal *si-*, Bunun *is-* (with metathesis), and Paiwan *si-*, but with *i-* in MP without exception.

**Table 2.8** Irregular metathesis and deletion of *S in PMP

| PAN | | *bukəS 'head hair' | *tapəS 'to winnow' | *Səpat 'four' |
|---|---|---|---|---|
| *Formosan* | Pazeh | - | *tapəs* | *səpat* |
| | Kavalan | *bukəs* | *tapəs* | *ʔu-spat* |
| | Saisiyat | *bokəsh* | - | - |
| | Thao | *fukish* | *tapish* | - |
| PMP | | *buhək | *tahəp | *əpat |
| *Malayo-Polynesian* | Itbayaten | *vohok* | *tahəp* | *apat* |
| | Cebuano | *buhúk* | *tahup* | *upát* |
| | Tetun | *buuk* | - | *faat* |

The phonological evidence for MP is typically interpreted as providing strong support for MP as a subgroup. The combined mergers of *t and *C as PMP *t and *N and *n as PMP *n, as well as narrowly conditioned and irregular changes like the metathesis of *CVS to MP *hVC and irregular deletion of *S in words like PMP *əpat 'four' and *i- 'circumstantial voice prefix' (PAN *Səpat and *Si) are compelling. It is also worth noting that Blust (2001a) points out a narrowly conditioned sound change whereby PAN *R became PMP *l in the environment _Vj. The only two examples that are given are *baRuj 'dove' > PMP *baluj and PAN *baRija 'batten of the loom' > PMP *balija. The evidence is slight and the change quite narrowly conditioned. The change is therefore not as compelling as other evidence, but nevertheless adds to the already robust list of evidence. In addition to the phonological evidence the subgroup is also defined by morphosyntactic innovations, strengthening the MP hypothesis. Some of this evidence is shown in Table 2.9.

### 2.3.2 Homorganic nasal substitution as a PMP innovation

An important morphological innovation that separates MP from Formosan subgroups is homorganic nasal substitution (Henceforth HNS), a morphophonological process that was associated with two PMP prefixes, *paŋ- 'instrumental nominalizer' and *maŋ- 'actor voice'. *paŋ- and *maŋ- form a p/m pairing, a feature found throughout Austronesian that Blust (2013a: 372) describes as referring "to the presence of pairs of prefixes which differ only in that one has p- and the other m-". Ross (1995a) and later Smith (2017b) both list HNS as a MP-defining innovation, although it has also been implied as evidence for *Western* Malayo-Polynesian (see §2.4 for more on why WMP is probably not a valid subgroup).

HNS is a process whereby the final nasal of *paŋ- or *maŋ- (sometimes written *paN- and *maN-) assimilated to the place of, and came to replace, the initial consonant of the root. Examples from Malay, where *maŋ- is reflected as *məŋ-* (written *meng-*) display HNS if the root-initial consonant is voiceless: *panas* 'hot' > *memanaskan* /məŋ-panas-kan/ 'to heat'; *tulis* 'letter' > *menulis* /məŋ-tulis/ 'to write'; *sakit* 'sick' > *menyakiti* /məŋ-sakit-i/ 'to hurt s.o.'. Examples with reflexes of *paŋ- are also prevalent in Malay, for example, *sakit* > *penyakit* /pəŋ-sakit/ 'disease; illness.' In some languages, HNS in the actor voice was reduced to only the nasal element, for example, Kenyah *tali* 'rope' > *nali* /ŋ-tali/ 'to make rope' or *pana* 'hot' > *mana* /ŋ-pana/ 'to heat; to cook'. HNS is a widespread morphophonological process, found in the Philippines, most AN languages of Malaysia and Indonesia, Chamorro, and Palauan, and there are even examples of HNS in fossilized forms in Oceanic (Smith 2017b). There are not, however, any examples of HNS in Taiwan, suggesting that the process was innovated in PMP, inherited in most daughter languages, and survives throughout western Austronesian languages.

### 2.3.3 *maR-

A second set of prefixes, PMP *paR- and *maR-, are also reconstructable to PMP and may constitute another set of morphological innovations (Adelaar 2005a: 6). PMP *paR- was associated with numerals and, depending on the root, could mean 'do *x* number of times' or '1/*x*' as in Malay *pərdua* 'half' or *sapertiga* 'one third'. Comparative evidence suggests that *maR- is indeed a PMP innovation, but that *paR- can be reconstructed to PAN, meaning that its presence in MP is a retention not an innovation. The evidence that *paR- is reconstructable to PAN is from Tamalakaw Puyuma *paR-x-(ən)* 'do *x* times', which forces us to reconstruct *paR- to PAN.

PMP *maR-, however, does not have Formosan evidence and may therefore be included in the list of PMP morphological innovations. It is notable, however, that MP languages utilize reflexes of *maR- in the same way as *paR- with numerals; reflexes of *maR- are attached to numbers to denote division where *maR-*x* is translated as 'divide into *x*'. Some examples include: Itbayaten *mi-roha* 'again, repeat, restore, do again'; Bikol *mag-duwá* 'to double; to divide into two parts'; Malagasy *mi-roa* 'to divide into two'; Toba Batak *mar-dua* 'divide into two, to halve'; and others. From a historical perspective, PAN *paR- may have become PMP *maR- through the process of pseudo-nasal substitution where, through a family-wide dispreference for non-identical sequential labial onsets (Chrétien 1965), the infix *<um> triggered deletion of the preceding syllable if it began with *p-. This gives the following history: PAN *paR- > pre PMP *p<um>aR- > PMP *maR-. If this case is true, then *paŋ-, *maŋ-, and *maR- form MP evidence, but *paR- does not.

### 2.3.4 The second person politeness shift

MP is also defined by the shift of PAN *-mu 'second person plural genitive' to PMP *-mu 'second person singular genitive' (Blust 1977a). The motivation for such a change is a cross-cultural aversion for directly addressing peers, which resulted in a similar shift from Early Modern English *you* 'second person plural accusative' to Present Day English *you* 'second person singular/plural'. In Austronesian, this change targeted the genitive short form, but not the full pronoun, *kamu 'second person plural', which remained plural. Although one might argue that a motivated politeness shift may have occurred as multiple parallel innovations, the evidence that this change occurred in PMP and was inherited by its daughter languages is found throughout MP with no known exceptions, with the *ACD* providing dozens of examples of the politeness shift in MP and no examples of *-mu reflected as a dedicated plural.

### 2.3.5 Other morphological evidence

Although they have not been explicitly mentioned in the literature as evidence for MP, there are a few additional observations of MP morphology that should be mentioned. Several affixes are only attested in MP languages and include the following: the prefix *ha- 'adjective of measure', with evidence from Ifugao *a-*, Bikol *ha-*, Cebuano *ha-*, Kadazan Dusun *a-*, Malagasy *a-*, Javanese *a-*, Makasar *a-*, Arosi *a-*, and others; the suffix *-i 'local transitive', with evidence from Malay *-i*, Toba Batak *-i*, Wolio *-i*, Fijian *-i*, and others; the prefix *ta- 'spontaneous or involuntary action', with evidence from Tagalog *ta-*, Iban *tə-*, Fijian *ta-*, and others; and the use of *sa- 'one' with *ŋa-, a ligature which connects numerals, in the numerals *sa-ŋa-puluq 'ten' and *sa-ŋa-Ratus 'one hundred'. Note that *sa-puluq is attested in Formosan languages, but it is never used in conjunction with *ŋa-. These examples cannot be reconstructed to PAN and may form additional morphological evidence for MP.

All of this evidence, as summarized in Table 2.9, points to a clear division between MP languages and the languages of Taiwan. Although there are competing hypotheses on the position of MP, the consensus is that there was a discreet PMP language that is coordinate with the several AN primary branches in Taiwan. Some of the competing proposals are discussed briefly below.

**Table 2.9** MP-defining innovations

| PMP innovations from PAN | | | PMP new innovations (No PAN reconstruction) |
|---|---|---|---|
| PAN | | PMP | PMP |
| *t, *C | > | *t | *maŋ- 'actor voice (transitive)' |
| *n, *N | > | *n | *paŋ- 'instrumental nominalizer' |
| *S | > | *h, Ø (irregular) | *maR- 'do *x* times' |
| *CVS# | > | *hVC# (irregular) | *ha- 'adjective of measure' |
| *RVj | > | *lVj | *-i 'local transitive' |
| *=mu (2PL) | > | *=mu (2S) | *ta- 'spontaneous or involuntary action' |

### 2.3.6 Proposals against MP

There have been multiple proposals over the decades which directly or indirectly dismantle Malayo-Polynesian in favour of a different family tree, or which nest MP within a Formosan group, although none of these proposals enjoy wide acceptance. The discussion begins with Dyen's various proposals on Austronesian subgrouping, before highlighting a parallel proposal from Wolff.

Dyen was known for positing dramatically different lexicostatistic and "homomeric" classifications of Austronesian languages. His lexicostatistical classification of Austronesian, for example, posits forty separate primary branches, with the majority in Melanesia and no separation of MP and Formosan (Dyen 1962, 1965a). The shortcomings of lexicostatistical methods have already been thoroughly dealt with (Blust 2000b) and need not be discussed further, except to point out that the results are not widely accepted. Dyen (1995) later proposes a Homomeric classification, which again differs from most other subgrouping hypotheses. Homomery uses a collection of cognate sets with the same distribution over a set of languages as the basis for subgrouping proposals (Dyen 1995: 463). The method explicitly does not differentiate between retentions and innovations. The resulting proposal groups Philippine and Indonesian languages together with Formosan in a group named 'Hesperonesian' and is based on a set of supposed shared cognates which may or may not be innovations. If anything, the homomeric classifications might demonstrate contact between Taiwan and the Philippines, but because of the conflation of retentions and innovations, the proposal itself does not have a solid grounding.

Wolff (1995) made a similar proposal, based on observations of lexical similarities between languages of the Philippines and Taiwan. He groups Formosan and Philippine together and hypothesizes "dialectical variation in the protolanguage" and "a period of common development between the Philippines and Taiwan after the eastern languages split off." (Wolff 1995: 573). Wolff's and Dyen's proposals stem from the observation that Formosan and Philippine languages share many typological features. Both groups are composed of mostly verb-initial languages, reflect complex morphological systems, and are widely known for having Philippine-type voice systems. All of these similarities, however, appear to be retentions from PAN and therefore should have no impact on subgrouping arguments. Philippine languages reflect the totality of sound changes already described which define MP. This basic observation has more weight than the large amount of lexical, morphological, and syntactic similarity between Formosan and Philippine languages that has been adduced.

### 2.3.7 Amis, East Formosan, and Malayo-Polynesian

Another recurring hypothesis that has appeared in various publications over the past several decades posits an exclusive genetic relationship between Malayo-Polynesian languages and the East Formosan (EF) languages of Taiwan, including Amis, Kavalan, and Siraya. Earlier contact between the Amis and MP speakers to the south has been noted, for example, by Ross (1995a: 102 footnote 26) who suggested that the name Amis reflects PAN *qamis 'north' and stated that ". . .it is possible that they [the Amis] were given this name by the Malayo-Polynesian speakers of the islands to the south, who remembered the Amis as their stay-at-home relatives. However, there is currently no linguistic support for this." Ross's point does not posit a genetic relationship, however. It was rather Reid (1982) who earlier proposed a distinct "Amis-Extra Formosan" (Extra Formosan includes MP) subgroup which represented a primary branch of Austronesian, with Amis and Extra-Formosan equidistant daughter languages. This view also appears in Starosta 1995.

Reid's earlier proposal states that Amis-Extra Formosan is defined by a merger of *C and *t as *t, and *N and *n as *n. These changes, of course, define MP, but if they are shared with Amis, it would require one to take Amis-Extra Formosan seriously. Blust (1999a: 54) goes into detail why these sound changes cannot be used to link Amis and MP, but the most serious objection is that Amis is an East Formosan language and Proto-East Formosan kept *n and *N distinct (although it did merge *n with *j. See Li 2004 and below). MP thus does not form an exclusive subgroup with Amis alone, but others have pointed to the larger East Formosan subgroup as a possible sister to MP.

Although the theory of an Amis-Extra Formosan or an East Formosan-Malayo-Polynesian connection has persisted for some time, there is reason to doubt a special genetic connection between the subgroups. As already mentioned, Li (2004) makes clear in his comparison of Basay, Kavalan, Amis, and Siraya, that PAN *N and *n remained distinct in Proto-East Formosan, although it had merged in PMP. Li also demonstrates that Proto-East Formosan had merged *j and *n as PEF *n, but PMP kept *j distinct. Thus, the only common sound change between EF and MP is the merger of *t and *C, but this change alone does not provide convincing evidence. In MP it is the totality of changes plus the special significance of irregular deletions (e.g. *S > Ø in some lexemes), irregular metathesis (e.g. *bukəS > *buhək), and morphosyntactic innovations that define the subgroup, not simply the *t/*C merger. To demonstrate the point, one need only observe that East Formosan languages do not provide the only examples of a parallel *t/*C merger in Taiwan. MP also shares the merger of *t and *C with Bunun, but of course no special relationship has been proposed between these two. With this in mind, *C > *t is a sound change that has occurred in demonstrably parallel innovations both within and without Taiwan, and further, this is the most likely explanation for its presence in both EF and MP.

## 2.4 The internal subgrouping of Malayo-Polynesian

Competing hypotheses on the internal classification of MP can be divided into two opposing models, binary-MP models which posit nested binary splits from MP to subgroups therein, and diverse-MP models which favour a rake-like family tree with limited internal structure and multiple primary branches. Both hypotheses are well represented in the literature, but there has been a recent movement away from a binary-MP model towards a diverse-MP model. The most recent proposal, and that which is endorsed in this chapter, is from Smith (2017b) who posits nine primary branches. Smith's model is discussed first, in the context of other diverse-MP models, and after that will look at some of the competing models including the oft-cited binary-MP model from Blust (1977a, 1982, 1983/1984, 1993a, 1995a) which splits MP into two primary subgroups, Western Malayo-Polynesian and Central-Eastern Malayo-Polynesian, and Zobel's (2002) model which splits MP into a 'Nuclear' Malayo-Polynesian group and a second catch-all group consisting of non-nuclear MP languages.

### 2.4.1 Diverse-MP models

The 'diverse-MP' models, which posit multiple primary branches rather than only two, have been argued for in various contexts for the last two to three decades and have slowly grown in popularity. A family tree with multiple primary branches is advantageous because it follows naturally from a history whereby speakers of PMP came to occupy island Southeast Asia in a single, rapid population expansion. These types of movements, as noted in Nichols (1997); Ross (1988); and elsewhere, tend to produce rake-like family trees with many primary branches or linkages with no well-defined subgroups. The connection between population movement and family tree shape means that diverse-MP models can provide a linguistic complement to the archaeological record in Island Southeast Asia, discussed in more detail later on in this section.

Earlier studies laid the groundwork for a diverse-MP subgrouping, for example, Adelaar (2005a) and Ross (1995a, 2005) both expressed reservations about the binary split of MP into Western and Central-Eastern subgroups, and attempted to established an inventory of less controversial microgroups as a starting point. Adelaar posits twenty-three microgroups within MP and Ross posits twenty-four, although they leave the question about how these microgroups fit together within MP open for further research. More recently, Smith (2017b) proposed a model which does away with a binary split from PMP in favour of a rake-like structure with several primary branches. Smith's proposal dismantles WMP and groups the twenty-three to twenty-four microgroups from Adelaar and Ross into nine primary branches. Elaborating on an earlier attempt by Blust (2010b), it accepts several large internal subgroups including Western Indonesian, South Sulawesi, and Celebic (CEL). More details on these subgroups are discussed after Figure 2.1, which shows the current subgrouping hypothesis.

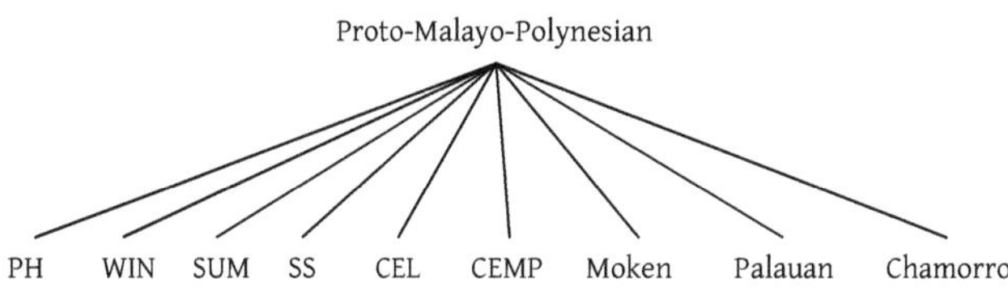


**Figure 2.1** Current hypothesis of Malayo-Polynesian internal subgrouping (Smith 2017b).

The evidence for this subgrouping is based both on original observations and a collection of earlier work. Western Indonesian is lexically defined with evidence compiled first by Blust (2010b) and later expanded upon by Smith (2017a). Three phonological changes: i) the merger of PMP *d and *j [g$^j$] as PWIN *d; ii) the place-assimilation of heterorganic nasal-plosive clusters to homorganic; and iii) the full assimilation of non-nasal heterorganic clusters also define WIN (see Smith, this volume, §8.3.4). The Sumatran subgroup (SUM) is based on Nothofer (1986) who first proposed a relationship between Enggano, the other Sumatran Barrier-Island languages, and Batak varieties. Smith (2017b) added Nasal to the group and pointed to the merger of PMP *j and *g as PSUM *g as evidence. South Sulawesi (SS) and Celebic are based on Mills (1975a) and Mead (2003a) respectively. Palauan, Chamorro, and Moken (discussed in more detail below) are considered isolates within Malayo-Polynesian because of their geographical isolation, lack of any shared phonological innovations, and the presence of innovations found in each language not present in any other MP language or subgroup. CEMP remains unchanged, but the subgroup has been criticized for lack of evidence (see §2.4.5 for more on CEMP). Smith (2017b) keeps a Philippine node but remains agnostic as to the status of the subgroup.

## 2.4.2 Isolates within MP

The diverse-MP model of Smith (2017b) allows for several primary branches of MP with only one surviving language (or dialect group, as is the case with Moken). Isolates within a family arise when a group of speakers is isolated from the wider community early in the history of a language family and remain isolated until their language is sufficiently differentiated. They can also arise when most languages in a subgroup are lost, leaving behind only one member which then becomes the sole representative of the group. Several hypotheses have proposed isolates within MP, including Chamorro, Moken/Moklen, Enggano, Nasal, and Palauan (Anderbeck and Aprilani 2013; Blust 2000a, 2009b; Edwards 2015; Larish 1999, 2005; Reid 2002b; Smith 2017b). In Smith 2017b, Enggano and Nasal are grouped within the Sumatran subgroup, but Chamorro, Moken/Moklen, and Palauan remain as isolates. Some scholars group Chamorro with Philippine languages on the basis of its verbal system (Topping 1973), within Formosan (for similar reasons, Starosta and Pagotto 1985; Starosta 1995), or within Nuclear Malayo-Polynesian (Zobel 2002). Blust (2000a) and Smith (2017b), however, both consider Chamorro an isolate within Malayo-Polynesian, with Smith giving it the status of primary branch. Palauan has been the topic of fewer classificatory hypotheses but is considered by Smith (2017b) to be an isolate, equidistant from Chamorro within Malayo-Polynesian.

Moken and Moklen have also had a history of sparse linguistic attention, but Larish (1999, 2005) and Bay (1995) provide valuable resources. Larish (1999, repeated in 2005) argues for a Moken-Moklen-Aceh-Chamic-Malayic subgroup. Blust (2010b), following Larish, places Moken within Greater North Borneo (GNB), a classification which suggests that Moken speakers initially migrated from the same region as Malay speakers and that their historical phonological diversion is the result of recent, rapid sound change. It is not impossible that a language could change so completely so quickly. Parallel cases of dramatic phonological changes abound in Borneo, for example (see Blust 2001b;

Smith 2017a). However, the evidence used to include Moken within GNB was a single semantic shift, PMP *tuzuq 'to point' to Proto-Greater North Borneo *tuzuq 'seven' but Blust himself points out that the supposed reflexes of *tuzuq have phonological irregularities in Moken, casting doubt on their validity as evidence. Smith (2017b) classifies Moken as an isolate within MP, forming one of three single-language primary branches along with Chamorro and Palauan. The reason for its classification as a primary branch is the change of PMP *j to Moken *y*, found nowhere else in western Austronesian languages, along with its overall aberrant nature and geographical distance from any possible sister.

### 2.4.3 CMP and CEMP

The status of Central-Eastern Malayo-Polynesian, as well as Central Malayo-Polynesian, is not challenged by Smith (2017b), but the evidence for these subgroups has been called into question elsewhere. Much of the debate centres around Central Malayo-Polynesian, and this discussion therefore begins with CMP.

CMP includes, according to Blust (1993a: 242), languages that "stretch from Bimanese, on the island of Sumbawa, eastward through the Lesser Sunda chain of Indonesia as far as the Aru Islands, and then northwest into the central Moluccas, inclusive of the Sula Archipelago." Although often referred to as a subgroup, CMP is not supported by strong innovations found throughout member languages, but rather by a list of overlapping innovations that unify CMP languages through a chain of sound changes. The distribution of sound changes in CMP thus more closely resembles that of an innovation defined linkage as per Ross (1988) rather than a traditional subgroup. After Blust, Donohue and Grimes (2008) point to the lack of subgroup-wide attestation of sound changes as a reason to dismantle CMP. Although both points of view acknowledge the incomplete attestation of sound changes in CMP languages, they reach rather different conclusions. Donohue and Grimes suggest that CMP contains multiple primary branches of MP itself, and that some languages of southern Sulawesi may subgroup with CMP languages rather than with Celebic, while Blust (in both 1993a and as a response to Donohue and Grimes, Blust 2009a) contends that the distribution of evidence supports CMP as a linkage, if not a traditional subgroup.

The evidence for CEMP, however, is more robust than CMP, but still not as strong as, say, MP. Blust (1993a) lists only a handful of regular phonological innovations which define CEMP, including the merger of PMP *c and *s as PCEMP *s, a change that has little subgrouping value considering its almost universal attestation in Island Southeast Asia. A second sound change is the deletion of $C_1$ in word-internal consonant clusters in reduplicated monosyllables, *$CVC_1C_2VC$ > $CVC_2VC$, except for where $C_1$ was a nasal and $C_2$ an obstruent, in which case $C_1$ assimilated to the place of $C_2$ (PMP *bukbuk > PCEMP *bubuk 'wood weevil', but PMP *dəmdəm > PCEMP *dəndəm 'dark'). CEMP languages are not alone in treating medial consonants this way, but it does appear that the change is found in all CEMP languages, which suggests that it was inherited.

These innovations combine with a list of irregular changes that shifted *ə to either CEMP *o or *e, which results in a six-vowel system, expanded from PMP's four-vowel system. In addition to this, some lexical innovations appear to be shared by all CEMP languages, including important innovations such as *kandoRa 'cuscus' and *mansaR/mansəR 'bandicoot', words that were likely innovated when Austronesian speakers crossed the Wallace line into the Pacific floral and faunal zones (although this evidence has been challenged, see Schapper 2011b.) Although some of the CEMP evidence is stronger than others, the regular and irregular phonological innovations, along with a list of exclusively shared lexical replacement innovations, give CEMP a more solid footing than CMP. CMP itself is not a traditional subgroup, but a network of closely related languages in an innovation-defined linkage. Such linkage is to be expected, considering how rapidly Austronesian speakers spread into the Lesser Sunda islands.

### 2.4.4 The Island Southeast Asian archaeological record and Austronesian expansion

As mentioned earlier, a diverse-MP subgrouping with multiple primary branches fits better into the archaeological history of Island Southeast Asia than a binary model. In Island Southeast Asia the arrival of Austronesian speakers is typically associated with the arrival of the Neolithic 'Austronesian cultural package', defined as follows. The Neolithic culture of Austronesian speaking people is thought to have descended from a coastal Neolithic culture known as the Dapenkeng culture which existed in Taiwan around 1,000 years before the Austronesian expansion into ISEA (Chang 1995). This early culture had pottery, sea resource technology, stone tools, domesticated rice and foxtail millet, and domesticated animals, all of which are also reconstructed to Proto-Austronesian vocabulary, providing strong evidence for an agriculturalist society. The Austronesian cultural package, descended from the Dapenkeng culture, spread out of Taiwan into the northern Philippines around 4500 Before Present (BP), before spreading further into Borneo, Java, Sumatra, Sulawesi, Timor, Halmahera, the Marianas, and Palau between 4000 and 3500BP (Bellwood 2007; Kirch

2002 and citations therein; Ward et al. 1998). The islands of Southeast Asia, including Borneo, Sulawesi Sumatra, Java, and Timur, have archaeological sites with Neolithic culture dating back to around 4000BP (Bellwood 2007; Flenley 1988; Glover 1976, 1977a, b; Stuijts 1993). The archaeological evidence thus paints a certain picture; the totality of Island Southeast Asia was settled by bearers of the Austronesian cultural package at around the same time. The Austronesian expansion into the area was therefore rapid and eventually lead to the settlement of areas further to the east and the establishment of the Lapita Culture in the Bismarck Archipelago soon thereafter (Kirch 2002, citations therein).

There is an expectational relationship between the manner of population expansion and the resulting impact on linguistic relations. To summarize, when a group expands quickly into a large geographical area, one expects many languages directly descended from a single protolanguage; that is, a rake-like tree structure. The reason for this is simple. If, for example, Island Southeast Asia was settled by Austronesian speaking people in a single migration out of the northern Philippines (ultimately from Taiwan), it follows that they spoke the same language or closely related dialects of PMP at the time of initial expansion. In a vacuum, each new settlement would eventually evolve into its own language, related closely to the languages around it but forming no cohesive genetic structure (François [2014], for example, hypothesizes that all linguistic units form in this way, that linkages are the rule, and that tree-like structure arise artificially as languages expand, contract, and die). In reality, languages expand at the expense of others. Although it is reasonable to assume that PMP spread over such a great area in such a short amount of time that the language of each settlement would ultimately be directly descended from PMP, the social context of linguistic interaction, common development, linguistic expansion, and extinction, mean that a limited number of primary branches will remain in any subgrouping. This remains an area of debate, but whichever specific internal subgrouping gains wide acceptance, it will likely be quite different from the previous, binary-branching model, and will instead have limited internal structure with a rake-like family tree such as that proposed in Smith 2017b.

### 2.4.5 Previous subgrouping proposals

More traditional models of MP internal subgrouping typically fall into the Binary-MP category, that is, a MP node that splits into two subgroups. Perhaps the most well-known and oft-cited example of a binary-MP model is the Western Malayo-Polynesian model (Blust 1977a, 1982, 1983/1984, 1993a, 1995a). In this proposal, Malayo-Polynesian splits into two groups: Western and Central-Eastern Malayo-Polynesian. Western Malayo-Polynesian (WMP) is a 'catch-all' subgroup that includes all languages not delegated to Central-Eastern Malayo-Polynesian (CEMP) and includes the languages of the Philippines, most of Western Indonesia, Malaysia, Mainland Southeast Asia, Malagasy, Palauan, and Chamorro. This model is often cited in more general literature including, for example, in Tryon (1995b); Blust (2013a); Bellwood (2007); and others.

The modern Western Malayo-Polynesian subgroup first appeared in Blust 1977a, as part of a wider argument on higher-order Austronesian subgrouping. In this early study WMP appeared in a tree representation of Malayo-Polynesian but was not discussed further nor defended with linguistic evidence. Blust's proposal at this point was a tripartite internal subgrouping with WMP, Central Malayo-Polynesian (CMP) and Eastern Malayo-Polynesian (EMP) as equidistant members of MP. The binary model appeared later, with CMP and EMP combined into Central-Eastern Malayo-Polynesian (CEMP) (Blust 1982, 1983/1984, 1993a, 2009a).

No true defence of WMP as a subgroup has ever been attempted, and any evidence for WMP is usually referred to as a side note. The most consistently referenced evidence has been Homorganic Nasal Substitution. Blust (1999a: 633), for example, pointed out that homorganic nasal substitution is restricted to "most languages of the Philippines and western Indonesia. . . and in Palauan and Chamorro. . ." and similar statements pop up in other publications (Blust 2000a, b, 2013a). Along with these references to HNS, however, Blust has also pointed out the deficiencies in the WMP model (see, e.g. Blust 1984/1985: 56, 2013a: 741, 2014a: 313). Blust (2000a); Ross (1995a); and Smith (2017b) all point out that HNS appears as fossilized morphology in some Oceanic languages, which forces its reconstruction as a morphophonological process to PMP. This in turn favours the interpretation that HNS in WMP languages is a retention and thus has no subgrouping value. At the moment, therefore, WMP is supported by no linguistic evidence.

Scholars working in MP internal subgrouping have long been aware of the shortcomings of the WMP model, as noted by Ross (2005: 4–7) who states that "The literature often refers to a discrete 'Proto-Western Malayo-Polynesian', but there is no evidence. . . that such a language ever existed". Edwards (2015); Anderbeck and Aprilani (2013); and Smith (2017b) have all proposed recent dissolvements of WMP, and support for WMP as a subgroup, despite regular citation, is almost non-existent.

Besides Blust's WMP model, Zobel (2002) has proposed an MP subgroup with two main divisions. One division consists of the languages of the Philippines, Borneo (excluding Malayic), and languages of Northern Sulawesi (presumably the Philippine languages of Sulawesi). This first division is a catch-all group, and does not necessarily represent a single subgroup on its own. The other, labelled 'Nuclear Malayo-Polynesian' (NMP), contains Chamorro, Palauan, Malayic, and all other languages of western Indonesian (including languages of Sumatra, Java, Bali, Lombok, Sumbawa, Sulawesi) and CEMP. NMP, unlike the first division, is a proper subgroup for which Zobel lists a set of exclusive innovations. The proposal itself relies entirely on morphological evidence, summarized below:

1. NMP languages have a set of preverbal person-agreeing affixes on the verb that are derived from the PMP possessive set.
2. They have differential uses of *maŋ- and *‹um›, with *maŋ- being used in antipassive and *<um> in active sentences.
3. They use the affix combinations *maŋ- -i, and *‹um› -i, which was absent in PMP.

Because there are no phonological innovations that define Nuclear Malayo-Polynesian (NMP), the morphological evidence stands alone in defining the subgroup. Zobel's divisions also challenge many lower-level subgrouping proposals from earlier studies. Malayic, for example, is placed within NMP while the other languages of Borneo are placed outside NMP, a proposal that differs significantly from other proposals from Adelaar (1992a) and Blust (2005c) who proposed that Malayic languages originate from Borneo and subgroup with what Blust (2010b) later called "Greater North Borneo" (see also Smith 2017a, and Smith, this volume, §8.2, §8.3.1). This subgroup contains Malay, Iban, and closely related languages of Borneo as well as many languages formally excluded from Zobel's NMP, Land Dayak, Central Sarawak, Kayanic, and North Borneo (itself containing North Sarawak, Southwest Sabah, and Northeast Sabah).

Zobel's proposal also implies a revised history of the dispersal of people into Island Southeast Asia. According to the NMP proposal, NMP languages originated from the island of Sulawesi, and spread into islands further to the west, including Sumatra, Java, and Borneo (although in Borneo, only Malayic and Tamanic are NMP). This implies one of two possible scenarios regarding Austronesian languages in the area: i) The non-NMP languages of Borneo are what remain after the spread of NMP languages into western Indonesia; or ii), Western Indonesia was initially settled by people who first sailed through Sulawesi. The second scenario is difficult to defend, as archaeological evidence shows that Island Southeast Asia was settled more-or-less simultaneously by bearers of the Austronesian 'cultural package'. If PNMP was a distinct language spoken in Sulawesi, it follows that it would have developed for some time as a unit before dispersing into its current location. This brings us back to the advantages of a rake-like family tree; the rake-like tree of Smith (2017b) better complements the archaeological record, since a rake-like structure is itself indicative of rapid population movements.

## 2.5 Conclusion

Malayo-Polynesian is the largest subgroup in the Austronesian family with a well-established history of comparative study. Because of this long history of scholarship, a consensus has developed in support of both the validity of MP as a first-order Austronesian subgroup as well as the linguistic properties of Proto-Malayo-Polynesian, the hypothetical ancestor language from which all MP languages are said to descend. Regarding the properties of PMP itself, this chapter showed that PMP was phonologically similar to PAN; it had a canonical two-syllable word with a four-vowel system and typically penultimate stress with stress shift to the final syllable occurring under certain conditions. PMP was not identical to PAN, however, and had undergone simultaneous reduction in the phoneme inventory due to consonant mergers and canonical-shape complexification through the innovation of non-reduplicated roots with internal homorganic nasal+stop clusters. The chapter also discussed PMP morphosyntax, which was complex, and largely inherited from PAN. PMP was a verb-initial Philippine-type language with associated verbal morphosyntax and the 'Multiple-undergoer' Philippine-type voice system. It also likely maintained a system of extraction restrictions, which meant that only arguments whose thematic roles were marked through voice selection could undergo processes such as WH-extraction and relative clause gapping. PMP also innovated morphology not found in the *Formosan* languages, including homorganic nasal substitution as an active morphophonological process in *maŋ- and *paŋ- and may have further innovated a prefix of the shape *maR- through pseudo nasal substitution.

The chapter also discussed the internal subgrouping of MP, which has less of a consensus. MP was historically split into two subgroups under the long-standing Western Malayo-Polynesian model, but some researchers have begun to question the assertion that PMP split into two primary branches and instead are proposing internal subgrouping models with numerous primary branches of MP. These new models, earlier dubbed the 'diverse-MP' models, better reconcile the linguistic interrelatedness of MP languages with the archaeological record regarding the spread of Austronesian Neolithic culture into Island Southeast Asia. The diverse-MP models fit well with a historical migration model whereby speakers of PMP came to occupy vast areas of Island Southeast Asia as part of a single large-scale movement of people, with subsequent diversification of PMP into its daughter languages happening thereafter. There remains much work to be done in MP comparative linguistics, particularly in areas dealing with first-order subgroups and the interrelatedness of MP languages utilizing a diverse-MP model. This is a promising area for further research and it will be interesting to see how these issues are resolved as more work is done in this area.

CHAPTER 3

# Methods in Malayo-Polynesian comparative-historical linguistics

MALCOLM ROSS AND SIMON J. GREENHILL

## 3.1 Introduction

This chapter is about methods used to work out relationships among Malayo-Polynesian (MP) languages — or languages in any language family.

The principal method in use today, and indeed throughout the history of MP comparative-historical studies, is the classical comparative method (CompM) of linguistics—'of linguistics' because the term 'comparative method' is sometimes also used for methods in other disciplines (e.g. anthropology) and 'classical' because the method is central to most systematic work in comparative-historical linguistics since its formulation by the Neogrammarians, a group of Danish and German scholars active from the 1860s. A nascent version of the method underlies Schleicher's (1861) comparative grammar of the Indo-European languages, which includes the first 'family tree' (phylogeny) of a language family. Two decades later, Brugmann's (1884) evaluation of the shared innovations on which relationships among Indo-European languages were based deals with issues that still occupy historical linguists today.

A recent newcomer to the suite of methods in comparative-historical linguistics is Bayesian phylogenetics (BPhyl), which uses modified versions of software devised by evolutionary biologists to work out relationships among species on the basis of their DNA. The earliest linguistic publication using BPhyl is Gray and Atkinson's (2003) analysis of the early history of Indo-European. This provoked considerable controversy among historical linguists and led to beliefs among some that BPhyl was lexicostatistics in a new guise or was being advanced as a replacement for the comparative method. Neither claim is true (Greenhill and Gray 2009, 2012). The CompM and BPhyl are complementary, as we explain below (§3.4).

Although MP's internal relationships are the subject of Chapter 2 (Smith, this volume), we cannot discuss the application of methods to MP without alluding to the higher-order phylogeny of Austronesian on which most Austronesianist historical linguists agree. This is shown in Figure 3.1. It shows that MP includes all Austronesian languages spoken outside Taiwan (alias Formosa). Such a grouping was first proposed by Dahl (1973) and fleshed out by Mills (1975a) and Blust (1977a), who each independently named it 'Malayo-Polynesian' (Blust 2013a: 748). Blust (1977a) also provided an internal subgrouping of MP, which, along with the introduction of CEMP in Blust (1983/1984), gives us the skeleton of the phylogeny in Figure 3.1. The Formosan and western Malayo-Polynesian languages appear there as grey blocks. The blocks indicate that they are **not** subgroups, but simply collections of languages which probably include more than one subgroup. Each protolanguage shown in Figure 3.1, other than Proto-Austronesian (whose prehistory is little known), underwent a set of shared innovations relative to the node 'above' it (to its left in Figure 3.1). These innovations are inherited by the daughters of the protolanguage and are evidence that the latter form a subgroup. Proto-Central-EMP is shown with a dashed vertical line. This says that it was a language that broke up into a dialect network. The horizontal dashed line indicates that the central Malayo-Polynesian languages emerged from a part of that dialect network. The little fan at the right-hand end of the line symbolizes the fact that the central Malayo-Polynesian languages are a linkage, that is, a collection of languages whose relationship is attested by overlapping innovations but which is not defined by innovations that all its member languages share.

The matters referred to in the previous paragraph are discussed in detail in Chapter 10 of Blust (2013a). Blust's volume, with 816 pages of text, is by far the most detailed reference on the Austronesian languages, and especially on their history and the history of the field, and we owe a great deal to it.

Figure 3.1 includes the Oceanic subgroup, which lies outside the purview of this volume, but is a large and well-defined subgroup of MP languages that we cannot completely ignore.

The remainder of this chapter is organized as follows: §3.2 describes the CompM and something of its applications to

Malcolm Ross and Simon J. Greenhill, *Methods in Malayo-Polynesian comparative-historical linguistics.* In: *The Oxford Guide to the Malayo-Polynesian Languages of Southeast Asia.* Edited by: Alexander Adelaar and Antoinette Schapper, Oxford University Press.  DOI: 10.1093/oso/9780198807353.003.0003

MP languages; §3.3 briefly surveys the history of the CompM and other methods in MP studies. It may seem strange to place history between sections on the CompM and BPhyl, but so much depends on the central concept of the CompM, namely the shared innovations, that this order was adopted in order to avoid numerous forward references. §3.4 describes some challenges in the application of the CompM and BPhyl to MP comparative-historical studies, and offers some conclusions and looks to the future.

## 3.2 The classical comparative method and Malayo-Polynesian

### 3.2.1 Describing the comparative method

Figure 3.1 represents the results of applying the CompM to Austronesian and MP languages over much of the history of Austronesian scholarship (see §3.3.1). As indicated in our explanation of Figure 3.1 above, the essence of the CompM lies in the description and reconstruction of innovations exclusively shared by a group of languages. It is inferred that these innovations occurred in a language that was the group's parent. This language thus becomes a node in a proposed phylogeny, and the languages are said to form a subgroup, as described in most textbooks of historical linguistics (see, e.g., Bynon 1977: 63–70; Campbell 2013: 174–84; Crowley and Bowern 2010: 110–15; Trask 2015: 169–74).

Since any innovation is by definition relative to some earlier condition in which the innovation has not yet happened, working out shared innovations depends (necessarily) on knowing something of the prior history of a group of languages, and this entails figuring out that prior history. Again, this is textbook stuff. The following brief instructions for the CompM are adapted from Ross and Durie (1996: 6–7).

(1) a. Collect putative cognate sets—lexical items and morphological paradigms—for languages of the family.
  b. Work out regular sound correspondences from these cognate sets.
  c. Reconstruct the protolanguage of the family:
    i. reconstruct the protophonology from the sound correspondences, using knowledge of frequently occurring directions of sound change (see, for example, Blevins 2004a).
    ii. reconstruct protomorphemes (morphological paradigms and lexical items) from the cognate sets collected in (a), using the reconstructed protophonology.
  d. Establish innovations (phonological, lexical, semantic, morphological) shared by groups of languages within the family relative to the reconstructed protolanguage.
  e. Tabulate the innovations established in (d) to arrive at an internal classification of the family, a 'family tree' or phylogeny.
  f. Construct an etymological dictionary, tracing borrowings, semantic change, and so forth, of the lexicon of the family (or of member languages of the family).

Witness to the fact that these steps have been carried out for much of MP is Blust and Trussel's (2020) immense and highly informative online comparative dictionary of Austronesian (see also Blust and Trussel 2013). Each reconstructed lexical item is supported by a cognate set and often a discussion note. The dictionary's one lacuna is that it does not show the sound correspondences on which the reconstructions are based, but there is no doubt that they *are* based mainly on regular sound correspondences. The one exception to this generalization is that inserted nasals in western MP languages and contrasts between plain and prenasalized stops in CMP (see, for example, Mills 1991) languages seem to be ignored. This huge work reflects Blust's application of the CompM to MP, which is also responsible for many of the insights in Blust (2013a: 737–49), where known MP subgroups are listed with discussion of the innovations that define them and references to more detailed accounts (many of them Blust's own).

Two book-length applications of the CompM to subgroups within western MP deserve mention. Adelaar (1992a) and Thurgood (1999) analyse and describe the history of, respectively, the Malayic languages and the Chamic languages.

### 3.2.2 Challenges in applying the comparative method

#### 3.2.2.1 *Effects of language contact*

The CompM as encapsulated by the steps in (1a–f) is not without its challenges. These can be roughly divided into two sets: (i) those caused by seemingly recalcitrant data; and (ii) analyst biases in the selection of shared innovations by which to define subgroups.

Recalcitrant data are all due, one way or another, to contact among speakers. If contact is between speakers of closely related dialects or languages (isolects), then an innovation may spread beyond the boundary of the innovating isolect. This process slows down only when the isolects become different enough for regular communication across their boundaries to be difficult. If there are a number of such innovations which have spread in different directions, perhaps at different times, the outcome is a linkage, a collection of overlapping innovations/isoglosses which defy subgrouping (Ross 1988: 8). Most work on linkages in MP languages has concerned parts of the Oceanic subgroup. The isolects of

Fiji are descended from a linkage which had broken into two at one point, then reintegrated, then broken again at a somewhat different point (Geraghty 1983; Ross 1997). François (2011) gives a detailed study of a small linkage in northern Vanuatu. Such detailed work on the languages to which this volume is devoted has yet to take place, but it is clear than the CMP grouping as described by Blust (1993a, 2013a: 739) is a linkage, and so is what Blust (2013a: 60–1) calls the Bisayan complex in the Philippines, described by Zorc (1977).

In instances such as those in the previous paragraph, the data are 'recalcitrant' only in the sense that they do not conform to the expectations of linguists who want bundles of coterminous innovations that allow them to draw trees. The phenomenon of non-coterminous innovations is well enough known in western European linguistics from, for example, the Rhenish Fan.

Contact also occurs, of course, between languages that are distantly related or unrelated. The fact that varieties of Malay have functioned as a lingua franca in parts of Indonesia for at least 1,200 years, and perhaps longer, has led to numerous lexical borrowings into other MP languages from Malay. Some of these are impossible to recognize because the relevant sound correspondences in Malay and the borrowing language are the same, making it impossible to determine whether the word is inherited or borrowed, and impeding the subgrouping of some languages of western Indonesia (Smith 2017b).

Ongoing bilingualism and language shift bring other challenges. The outcomes of these two phenomena are sometimes confused. In the case of ongoing bilingualism, particularly in small scale speech communities with no shared convention motivating linguistic conservatism, one language is reshaped semantically and morphosyntactically on the model of the other, a phenomenon that Ross (2007) calls 'metatypy'. Semantic reshaping results from word-for-word translation, such that the two languages come to use words of equivalent meaning with identical semantic range. The typological divide between the MP languages of western and eastern Indonesia is probably due to contact with (and early bilingualism in) typologically quite different non-Austronesian languages (Donohue 2007).

Language shift is sometimes said to have a similar effect, that is, speakers of a non-Austronesian language have shifted to an Austronesian one and brought their morphosyntax with them. It is more likely, though, that what they bring to their new language is their phonology ('a foreign accent'). Even this is probable only when shift is sudden and incomplete **and** the resulting aberrant isolect survives. But this must be a rare occurrence. More typically, shift is spread over several generations. A circumstance arises where children learn not only their community's heritage language but also a second language spoken by a neighbouring community or as a lingua franca. Over a number of generations two consequences are possible. One is that their heritage language undergoes metatypy on the model of the second language. Alternatively the heritage language is gradually lost and shift to the second language becomes complete. Since children learn languages well, the second language will not display contact phenomena other than the import of culturally specific lexicon from the heritage language (Ross 2014). This is illustrated by Reid's (1994a) study of the lexicon of languages of Philippine Negritos. The latter are apparently descended from groups living in the Philippines before the arrival of MP speakers, and came to participate in symbiotic relationships with the latter, shifting to their MP languages over generations but retaining in their isolect items of specialist lexicon from their now forgotten heritage languages.

It could be objected that contact with un- or distantly related languages has no place in a discussion of the CompM as the CompM does not deal directly with contact. This is true, but every CompM practitioner encounters the effects of contact sooner or later, at least in the form of cognate sets that do not conform to regular sound correspondences because the cognate words have been borrowed. To ignore these is to ignore evidence about the history of the languages under study.

#### 3.2.2.2 *Conditions on the reconstruction of exclusively shared innovations*

This takes us to the second set of challenges in the application of the CompM. A shared innovation needs to satisfy two conditions in order to be attributed to the exclusively shared common ancestor of a subgroup's languages. These are (a) that it has not been borrowed across language boundaries. and (b) that it has not occurred independently in the different members of the subgroup. We refer to these as the 'no borrowing' and 'no independent innovation' conditions. Shared innovations may be lexical, syntactic, phonological, or morphological. Of these, lexicon often fails the no borrowing condition, disastrously so in western Indonesia, as noted above. Syntax is borrowed less frequently, but syntactic borrowing occurs when contact leads to metatypy. Because children learn the phonemic system and the inflectional morphology of their heritage isolect early on, and both resist subsequent change, phonological changes and innovations in bound morphology largely satisfy the 'no borrowing' condition (Ringe et al. 2002). Sound change, however, famously fails the 'no independent innovation' condition because most sound changes are natural phonetic changes that recur in different places and at different times (Nakhleh et al. 2005). It seems to follow that only rare sound changes should be attributed to the exclusively shared common ancestor of a subgroup's languages. This appears to leave only changes in bound morphology satisfying both conditions.

The survey in the previous paragraph seems to bring us to a dead end, but there is a way out. In order to support the reconstruction of an exclusively shared protolanguage one can often identify collections of shared innovations that do not co-occur naturally. Thus Proto-Malayo-Polynesian (PMP) itself is supported by three phonological mergers: Proto-Austronesian (PAN) *C and *t > PMP *t; PAN *N and *n > PMP *n; and PAN *S and *h > PMP *h. The last of these has lexical exceptions (Blust 2013a: 747–8). The PAN sequence *consonant + *vowel + word-final *S often becomes PMP *h + *vowel + *consonant, as in PAN *CaqiS 'to sew' vs. PMP *tahiq. The 'politeness shift' in pronouns identified by Blust (1977a) entailed a complex set of morphological innovations in PMP (Ross 2006). In the case of PMP, careful work over decades has paid off. Blust (2001a) uses the metaphor of building a wall one stone at a time to describe the gradual discovery of innovations supporting MP.

Of the four areas of innovation, only the lexicon is not a closed set. It thus provides more data points to work with, and, although exceptions like western Indonesia do occur, one can usually spot borrowed items because their source is readily recognized or because the cognate set contains exceptions to regular sound correspondences. Some MP subgroups have been postulated on the basis of lexicon alone. One is EMP (Blust 1978). Another is the Philippines (Zorc 1986; Blust 2019b).

Satisfying the 'no borrowing' and 'no independent innovation' conditions obviously forces CompM practitioners to make choices, as they must estimate the probability that a given innovation satisfies the two conditions—an estimate that is usually intuitive rather than objective. A danger around choice is the temptation to choose innovations that fit one's hypothesis, the more so if one has a commitment to trees rather than to linkages. We return to this issue in §3.4.

## 3.3 History of methods used in Malayo-Polynesian comparative-historical linguistics

The CompM has been paramount in the history of Austronesian historical studies. Lexicostatistics and homomerics popped up in the middle of this history, then more or less disappeared again. In recent decades BPhyl has appeared, complementing the CompM.

### 3.3.1 The comparative method

Blust (2013a: 519–60) provides a magisterial historical survey of applications of the CompM to MP languages, and most of this short section is drawn from it.

The CompM as we have outlined it in (1) did not come to fruition in MP studies until Otto Dempwolff's first CompM publication on MP in 1920. However, it was preceded by a long, gradual build-up. Van der Tuuk (1865) gives three sound correspondences between a few west Indonesian and Philippine languages. In his 1884 Leiden dissertation, Brandes expanded these to include fifteen other languages, including Siraya of Taiwan, which he labelled 'Formosan'. Kern expanded the comparative phonology of MP languages to include Oceanic languages, presenting many widely distributed cognate sets. He worked first on Fijian (Kern 1886), then on Anejom (south Vanuatu) (Kern 1906b), showing that the latter is an MP language. Brandstetter had a capacity to read and process every description and every grammar of an MP language he could lay hands on. He published "a number of well-organised, clearly written and neatly interlocking essays and monographs" and thereby "produced a systematic overview of the then-current comparative knowledge of the languages of island Southeast Asia. . ." (Blust 2013a: 531).

Blust comments that up to this point no systematic phonological MP reconstruction had been attempted. This came when Dempwolff (1920) showed, contrary to a prevailing belief, that what are now called Oceanic languages were appropriate subjects for systematic comparative work. This was followed by further papers in 1925 and 1927. In the latter, Dempwolff recognized Proto-Oceanic (*Urmelanesisch*) and set out the phonological mergers that define it. This prepared the way for the three-volume *Vergleichende Lautlehre der austronesischen Sprachen* (Comparative phonology of the Austronesian languages, 1934, 1937, 1938), which in many respects forms the basis of present-day MP historical linguistics, fulfilling all the requirements of the CompM (§3.2.2.1), listing innovations that define the Oceanic subgroup along with evidence for them and providing a collection of PMP reconstructions.

Although Dempwolff used the term 'Austronesian' in his title, the work includes no Formosan data and is therefore a reconstruction of PMP. Dempwolff was followed by Dyen, who replaced Dempwolff's PMP orthography with one that was easier to type, and which remains the basis of PMP orthography today. In Dyen (1965b) he showed that Proto-Austronesian can only be reconstructed adequately if Formosan languages (i.e. indigenous languages of Taiwan) are included in the analysis. Dyen was followed in turn by Blust and Trussel (2020), whose prodigious output and online dictionary have made an enormous contribution to the comparative-historical study of MP that includes the phylogeny shown in Figure 3.1 and the *magnum opus* (Blust 2013a) on which this section is based.

### 3.3.2 Lexicostatistics and homomeric lexical classification

Although there have been numerous lexicostatistical forays into relationships among smallish groups of MP languages, only one has sought to embrace the entire Austronesian family, published as Dyen (1965a). For each pair of languages in the group under study, the lexicostatistician calculates the percentage of items, typically in a version of the 200-word Swadesh list, that are cognate, where 'cognate' in practice often means just 'similar in form', rather than 'descended from the same ancestral word'. The percentages are then used to construct a tree. Dyen thus sought to disambiguate the relationships among a sample of 245 languages, drawn from 371 wordlists. His finding was that the greatest lexical heterogeneity was found in Melanesia (i.e. in and around New Guinea) and used the principle of greatest diversity (Dyen 1956) to declare it to be the Austronesian homeland. Only much later in his life did he instead publicly accept that Taiwan was the probable homeland. With hindsight it is clear that two factors contributed to Dyen's mistake. One is that the diversity of Melanesian lexica is attributable to bilingualism in Papuan languages (§3.2.2.1), about which far more is known today than in 1965. The other is the major methodological flaw of lexicostatistics: its failure to distinguish a pair of cognates that are the result of innovation from a pair that reflects retention. Distinguishing innovation from retention is crucial to subgrouping, and its failure to do so leaves lexicostatisticians open to major errors.

Dyen was also responsible for 'homomeric lexical classification'. A homomery is a collection of cognate sets that are coterminous, that is, they occur in the same set of languages. In one respect, this echoes the CompM, which looks for coterminous shared innovations. But, like lexicostatistics, the method offers no way of distinguishing between innovations and retentions. Just one (rather arcane) paper on the method was published (Dyen 1990). It was mentioned again in Dyen (1995), after which it disappeared from view.

### 3.3.3 Bayesian phylogenetics

Bayesian phylogenetics (BPhyl) is sometimes confused with lexicostatistics. This is wrong. BPhyl is in two respects more closely allied with the CompM. First, BPhyl seeks to model the exclusively shared innovations languages have in common, not how many words on a list they share. Thus the CompM and BPhyl are mutually reinforcing. Second, applying the CompM, in order to identify cognates in wordlists, is a precondition for the successful application of BPhyl.

Bayesian phylogenetic methods are a class of computational tools designed in evolutionary biology for inferring evolutionary histories of species. Recently, these have been applied to a range of linguistic questions. This application might seem unusual at first glance. However, just as the classification and subgrouping of languages is vital to historical linguistics, the grouping of species is vital to evolutionary biology. This similarity of purpose has led to a long history of "curious parallels" (Atkinson and Gray 2005) between the two disciplines. Many of the same ideas can be found in both disciplines, for example, linguists since the neogrammarians have stressed the importance of identifying historically related groups using shared innovations rather than shared retentions. Biologists do the same (Hennig 1966).

In fact, biologists invented 'numerical taxonomic' methods that were almost identical to lexicostatistics (Sokal and Sneath 1963), but just as in linguistics, it became apparent that these approaches were seriously flawed, chiefly because they did not distinguish innovations from retentions or allow rates of change to vary (see Greenhill and Gray 2009). However, biologists worked to overcome these issues, leading to the development of a range of 'phylogenetic' methods, the most powerful of which are Bayesian phylogenetic methods (for more complete overviews of BPhyl see Greenhill and Gray 2009, 2012). These phylogenetic methods directly build the retention/innovation distinction into the mathematical modelling underlying these tools, and have constructed many methods for allowing rates of change to vary across lineages and over time.

The application of phylogenetic methods to the linguistic data complements the comparative method. Indeed most applications have, to date, taken the cognate sets as identified by the comparative method as input. The case in point here, the application of BPhyl to the Austronesian Basic Vocabulary Database (Greenhill et al. 2008), is an example of the complementarity between BPhyl and the CompM. Of the CompM instructions listed in (1), steps (a), (b), (c), and (f) were carried out by specialists in the various parts of the Austronesian family who used known sound correspondences and lexical reconstructions in order to organize the lexical items in the database into cognate sets — these became the first components of the analysis, the *data*.

After the data, the next key component of a BPhyl analysis is a *model* of cognate change. This model specifies in a probabilistic manner how cognates change over time along a lineage. The simplest model would allow a lineage, at each point in time to gain or lose a cognate set (mimicking the process of innovation or loss respectively). In this model, any given cognate set could be gained or lost from a lineage at the same rate. However, this is not very realistic and a more complicated model would allow cognates to be gained and lost at different rates, perhaps building in an assumption that cognates are born rarely (in a parent language) but can be lost often (from the daughter languages). A commonly used model in phylolinguistics is the *covarion* which allows cognates to be gained and lost at different rates, so that each cognate can switch between a 'fast' and 'slow' rate, mimicking bursts of change over time (Penny et al. 2001).

The final key component of a BPhyl analysis is the *likelihood*. The likelihood is a numerical value that is proportional to the fit of the data onto a tree given the model. This likelihood is calculated by estimating the most probable fit of each single cognate to the tree using the model and multiplying together these probabilities to give a single score. Trees that fit the data well, according to the model, will have better likelihoods than those that explain the data the worst. This likelihood approach directly infers where each cognate set is innovated and where it is retained. Furthermore, the likelihood approach allows us to test between different models: the likelihood of each model is proportional to its fit to the data, so the model with the highest likelihood is the 'best-fitting model'.

How do we find the best trees with the data and model using the likelihood? Bayesian phylogenetic approaches generally work like this:

(2) a. Start with a randomly generated tree and calculate the likelihood.
  b. Randomly choose a *parameter* to change (e.g. move a branch on the tree, or change the rate of cognate change, or alter the overall rate of change).
  c. Calculate the likelihood of the new tree and parameter combination.
  d. Occasionally store the tree and parameters (i.e. we store the tree and parameters every 1,000th or 10,000th generation so that the trees we store are statistically independent of each other).
  e. If the likelihood is better, keep the new tree and parameters.
    If the likelihood is worse, reject the new tree and parameters.
  f. Repeat steps b–e millions of times.

This is a common approach to solving computational problems called a Markov Chain Monte Carlo algorithm ('MCMC', Gilks et al. 1996). Here, the analysis initially starts with random guesses at the tree and parameters and successively 'tweaks' the tree or parameters in step (b) and then keeps improvements in step (e). After running the analysis for a long time, the estimates of the tree and parameters should have converged to good estimates—where the data are explained well under the model and the tree. We then throw away the initial random guesses (called 'burn-in') and are left with a sample of thousands of trees and parameters called the *posterior probability distribution* (or *posterior* for short).

The outcome of a Bayesian MCMC analysis is therefore not just a single tree, but a collection of many trees. This *posterior* has the advantage over single tree approaches in that it provides a way to handle conflicting signals caused by non-tree-like processes such as borrowing or areal diffusion (Greenhill et al. 2009)—if there is appreciable signal for these conflicting groupings then they should be present in the posterior. Therefore, the proportion of trees in the posterior containing a given group is a natural measure of its support in the data, for example, a group that is present in 100% of the trees in the posterior is strongly supported by all the data, while a group that is present in only 75% of the trees is only moderately supported while anything less than 50% is weak. Further, at the end of §3.2.2.2 we noted that a CompM practitioner's choice of innovations is often intuitive and that there exists a temptation to 'cherry-pick' one's innovations to fit one's hypothesis. These dangers are avoided by BPhyl given that all the data are equally weighted. Steps (d) and (e) under (1) above are thus removed from the potential dangers of linguist intuition and performed objectively and statistically.

The BPhyl analyses of Austronesian languages (Gray et al. 2009; Greenhill et al. 2010) show that, first, the Formosan languages in Taiwan form several first-order branches of Austronesian as demonstrated by Blust (1999a), and this is followed by a very strongly supported MP node (p=1.00). Within MP there are some well-supported groups. Second, the Philippines languages are strongly grouped together (p=1.00) and indicate some well supported microgroups within the Philippines (Blust 1991b), for example: Bashiic (p=1.00); Cordilleran (p=1.00); Central Luzon (p=0.97); Palawanic (p=0.70); Central Philippines (p=1.00); Manobo (p=1.00); and Subanun (p=1.00). Two expected microgroups are located with their regional neighbours in Sulawesi, rather than with their Philippine sisters: Sangiric and Minahasan. Blust (1991b) provides evidence that Gorontalo-Mongondowic languages group with Central Philippines to create the Greater Central Philippines subgroup. However, the phylogeny strongly places (p=1.00) these languages at the base of the entire Philippines group. Gorontalo-Mongondowic has undergone substantial sound change and this placement may represent difficulties in identifying cognate terms. This is not a fault of BPhyl. It is because BPhyl relies for its input on linguists coding cognate sets accurately, a task that at times verges on the impossible.

Third, the phylogenies show strong to moderate support for most of the expected western MP subgroups: Celebic (p=0.99, Sneddon 1993; Mead 2003a); Greater South

Sulawesi (p=1.00, Adelaar 1994b); North Sarawak (p=0.90, Blust 1974a). Other groups are less well attested, however, including North Borneo (p=0.64, Blust 1998b); Malayic (p=0.78, Adelaar 1992a); Chamic (p=0.72, Thurgood 1999); and Barito (p=0.56, Hudson 1967). Hudson himself doubted the Barito grouping, writing, "the lexicostatistical evidence does not warrant putting West Barito into an immediate taxonomic group East Barito and Barito-Mahakam" (1978: 22). The trees do not link the Sama-Bajaw languages to Barito to form Greater Barito (Blust 1991b), but place them with the Philippines languages—presumably reflecting the high levels of contact-induced change between these groups (Blust 1991b). Nor do they indicate support for the Barrier Islands/North Sumatra subgroup (Nothofer 1986). Such mismatches between BPhyl and the CompM are exceptions. Because BPhyl and the CompM usually generate similar results, and the input data have been coded by practitioners of the CompM, there is a strong motivation for the latter to carefully review their codings.

## 3.4 Challenges and conclusions

MP has already served as a proving ground for BPhyl (Gray et al. 2009; Greenhill et al. 2010) and for cooperation between practitioners of the CompM and of BPhyl. There is room, however, for an even closer integration of the two approaches in the challenge to figure out the histories of MP languages. Contrary to the belief of some of our colleagues, the two approaches are complementary, as they are founded on the same conceptual framework: drawing trees in which a node is defined by the innovations that its children share. Neither can successfully displace the other. The linguist applies their knowledge of (i) the languages under study and (ii) the kinds of language change that are common or possible or impossible. This knowledge is vital, but leaves room for less than complete objectivity. The phylogeneticist, on the other hand, uses BPhyl to generate hypotheses that are objective and statistically based. The challenge is then to resolve the mismatches when the CompM and BPhyl give different results like those noted above.

The linguist wants to know which data have led to BPhyl's posterior tree. At present this demand is difficult for the phylogeneticist to accede to. This is because the posterior tree sums up a large number of different trees, each embodying different decisions, and an effective means of summarizing and outputting the data that have fed these decisions is yet to be formulated—but is not impossible.

The phylogeneticist, meanwhile, wonders if the cognate recognitions are so inadequate that BPhyl has failed ('garbage in, garbage out'). Figuring out the discrepancies can be difficult, as the authors have learned from work with the Austronesian Basic Vocabulary Database, yet the overall agreements between the CompM and BPhyl are certainly good enough for the mismatches to be worth pursuing.

An important mismatch concerns the MP languages of eastern Indonesia. Figure 3.1 presents the conventional picture given by the CompM. Central-EMP is a branch of MP,

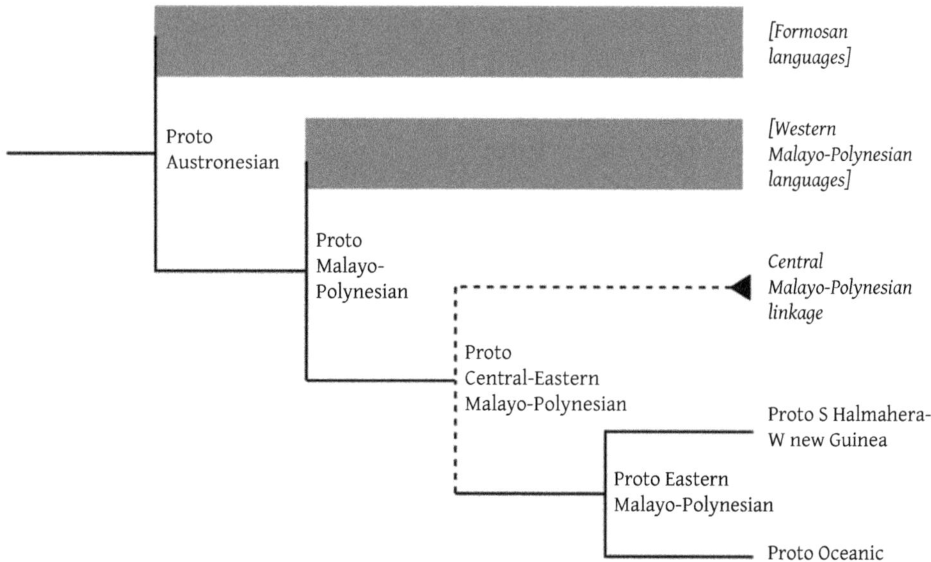


**Figure 3.1** Higher-order phylogeny of Austronesian. The grey blocks indicate that these collections of languages are not subgroups, and probably include more that one subgroup.

and divides into a CMP linkage and an EMP branch. The BPhyl tree published by Gray et al. (2009) contradicts this picture. Central-EMP is much less directly descended from PMP and forms a branch with the groups that occupy Sulawesi and nearby islands. Central-EMP itself is divided into a branch containing three groups (an extended Bima-Sumba, West and Central Flores, and East Flores-Lembata) and a branch that divides in turn into two isolates and four further branches—one of them EMP.

These are important mismatches, doubly interesting because they have been the subject of controversy among linguists. There are at least three threads here. Blust (2008) finds no evidence for a long accepted group that includes Bima and Sumba, but he groups the latter with Hawu (Savu). The BPhyl tree confirms the Sumba-Hawu link but also includes Bima as a first-order offshoot of the extended Bima-Sumba group. This mismatch matters because it concerns the western boundary of CEMP. A second thread concerns CEMP, established by Blust (1982) on the basis of terms for marsupials. This evidence was challenged by Schapper (2011b) but the subgroup was reasserted by Blust (2012). The third thread relates to CMP, which made its appearance in Blust's (1977a) tree but was defined by shared innovations only by Blust (1993a), who noted that the pattern of innovations was that of a linkage, not a proper subgroup. Blust (1993a) also offered more evidence for CEMP. Donohue and Grimes (2008) challenged the integrity of both CEMP and CMP, suggesting that the latter did not even form a linkage. They claimed that a number of the innovations reported by Blust are also reflected in certain western MP languages.

We do not want to take a side in these controversies, but we do want to take them seriously. Blust's work is thoroughly grounded in the CompM, yet the BPhyl tree gives different results from his in several instances. Are there problems with Blust's data or with the data that served as input for the BPhyl tree? Were the input data poorly coded? And which data led specifically to the BPhyl results? Resolutions to these conflicts require more and better descriptions of the languages included under 'CMP' and further comparative work. They also require checking and polishing of the input to BPhyl (is a modified 200-word Swadesh list sufficient input?) and the capacity to spit out innovations that underlie the consensus tree.

The question of whether one can talk of a CMP linkage is a challenge for both the CompM and BPhyl (§3.2.2.1), because both methods assume a tree with distinct nodes as their outcome. BPhyl performs better than the CompM in this respect, because each node in the posterior—the 'consensus' tree—is marked with a percentage showing what proportion of the trees sampled it was found in. The BPhyl tree has no CMP node. Its Central-Eastern node was found in 80% of sampled trees. Of the nodes that parent languages conventionally assigned to CMP, the Bima-Sumba-Flores-Lembata branch occurred in all (!) sampled trees, whilst the second (huge) branch was found in 82%.

The absence of a CMP node suggests that the western most part of CEMP is in places untreelike, that is, it forms a linkage. One way of conceptualizing this dimension of a phylogeny is as a gradient of treelikeness—from totally treelike (where every node is present in the posterior, as described in §3.3.3) to totally *un*treelike yet still displaying relatedness. The Central Maluku-Aru and Yamdena-North Bomberai groups, found respectively in only 54% and 56% of sampled trees, are untreelike in this way—almost half the trees found do not include these groups. This challenges us to determine the point below which a percentage is historically meaningful.

Treelikeness can be quantified in a number of ways, but two commonly used methods are the δ-score (Holland et al. 2002) and Q-residual (Gray et al. 2010). These two measures quantify how much each language is involved in conflicting distributions of innovations (i.e. are all the cognates that are present in this language consistent with one tree topology, or do some cognates indicate an alternative set of relationships?). These methods work by breaking the dataset up into 'quartets' of all possible groupings of four languages, and then inferring the branch lengths of each possible grouping in that quartet. If the branch lengths pattern such that they support a single tree topology, then the score is zero. If there is a conflicting distribution of innovations, then the score will range up to 1.0. The difference between the measures, mathematically, is that the δ-score normalizes the score using a normalization constant, while the Q-residual is a simpler metric (see Gray et al. 2010 for more details).

In practice, the δ-score seems to track conflict better (such as might be found in a linkage or dialect chain situation), while the Q-residual seems to track noise in the data better (such as might be found if the data were problematic or cognate codings were not done carefully; Greenhill, in prep). We can calculate these two scores for the Malayo-Polynesian languages from the Gray et al. (2009) data using the software package *phylogemetric* (v1.0.0, Greenhill 2016) and visualize them in Figure 3.2. On average, the median δ score is 0.375 (standard deviation = 0.0279) while the median Q-residual is 0.0014 (s.d. = 0.00028). The dark grey lines on Figure 3.2 show these median scores. We can see that the CMP languages tend to have notably higher δ and Q-residual scores, suggesting that the difficulty resolving the subgroupings here is due to a mixture of linkage-like processes as well as substantially noisy data. Other subgroups show different patterns. Greater Barito, for example,

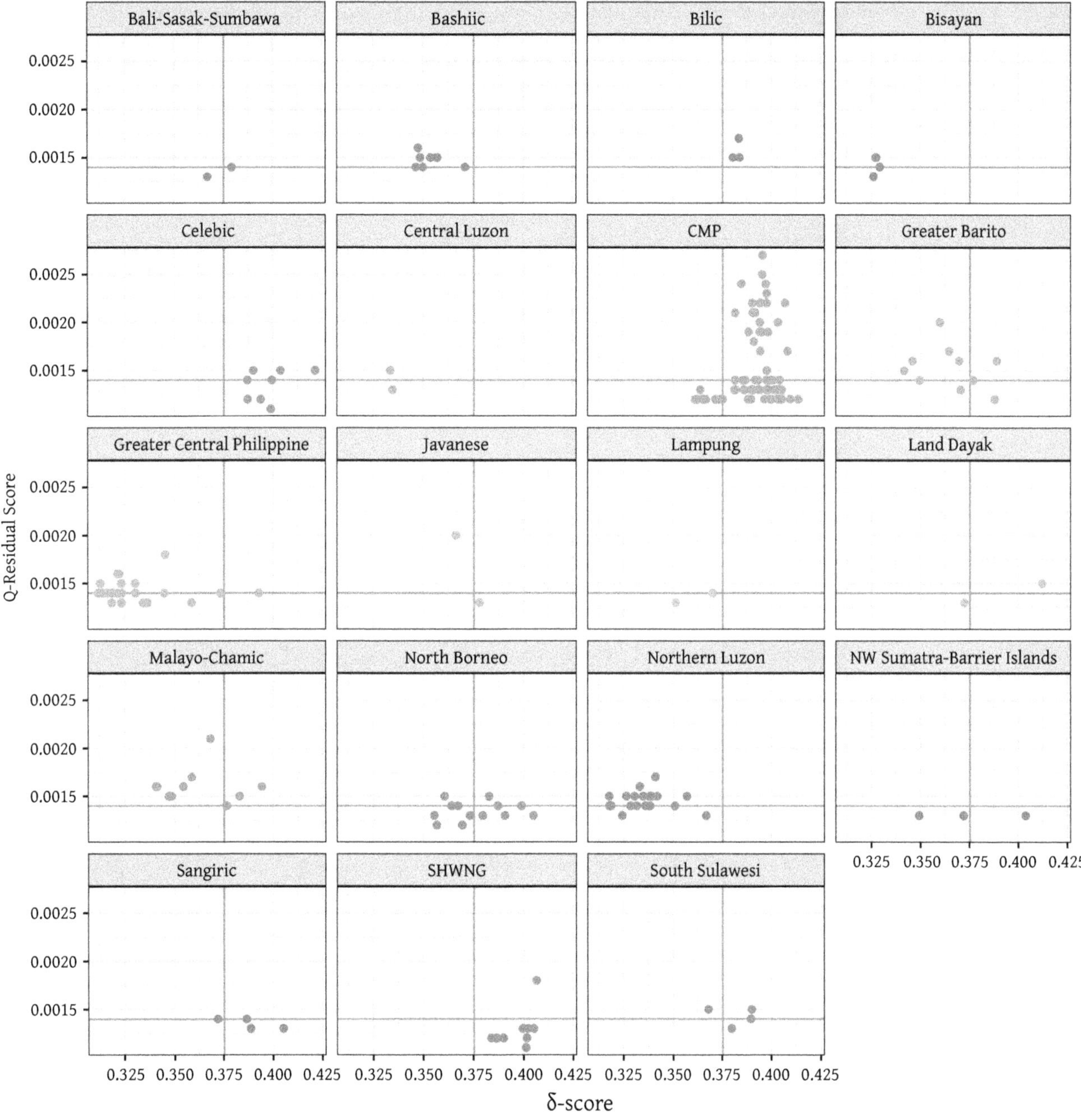


**Figure 3.2** Scatterplot showing the δ and Q-residual scores for different Malayo-Polynesian language groups. The dark gray lines show the median values of each score, languages above the horizontal line show higher amounts of noise, while the languages to the right of the vertical line show more conflicting signal.

has some languages with high Q-residuals, but only moderate δ scores suggesting a noisy but not conflicted history. In contrast, Celebic has high δ scores but low Q-residuals suggesting a conflicted history with little noise. Yet another pattern is seen in the Greater Central Philippines group, which has both little conflict and little noise, consistent with the hypothesis by Blust (1991b) that it is a relatively recent expansion. A noticeable outlier within Malayo-Chamic is the Melayu-Brunei dialect of Malay, with high levels of noise, while within the Javanese group, the Old Javanese variety also has high levels of noise but an average level of conflict.

Clarifying and formalizing the treelikeness continuum in this way has potential to build a bridge or two between comparative-historical linguistics and contact linguistics, subfields that at times seem barely to overlap. In the process we will perhaps discover that there are different untreelike configurations that can be formally defined.

Applying the CompM is painstakingly slow work, but there are now computer applications to perform steps (a), (b) and (c) of (1) above (List et al. 2017). Work with these is only just beginning, and it remains to be seen whether they replicate human application of the CompM closely enough to save time and labour.

# CHAPTER 4

# Linguistic approaches to Austronesian culture history

ROBERT BLUST

## 4.1 Introduction

This chapter addresses linguistic contributions to the culture history of the Austronesian-speaking peoples of Southeast Asia and Madagascar. Given the potential scope of this subject, and limitations on length, most topics will be treated briefly, referring the reader to earlier publications for further details. The most in-depth treatment will be on kinship, marriage and social organization, since with rare exceptions (e.g. Benveniste 1973[1969]), these have received far less attention than material culture.

Linguistic evidence for human prehistory is based on the reconstruction of vocabulary, which in turn derives from application of the comparative method, a set of procedures for inferring aspects of prehistoric languages from the traces left in their attested descendants. Although it was first developed over 200 years ago by such pioneers as Jacob Grimm and Rasmus Rask (Pedersen 1931: 30–43), the comparative method has fared better than most ideas of that vintage. Indeed, along with Darwin's theory of evolution by means of natural selection, it is regarded by many as one of the major intellectual achievements of the nineteenth century. Landmark tests of its validity are found in Verner (1967[1875]); Saussure (1879); and Bloomfield (1925), and discussions of its continuing value are found in many other works, of which only Baldi (1990), Durie and Ross (1996), and any recent textbook, such as Campbell (2020) need be cited here.

Most treatments of the comparative method are concerned with how to infer the shapes of words. However, since inferences about culture history depend equally on the *meaning* of reconstructed words, the reader is referred to Benveniste (1973[1969]), and Blust (1987, 2010a) for discussion and illustration of the principles of semantic reconstruction. Previous broad surveys of the linguistic evidence for Austronesian (AN) culture history are found in Blust (1976, 1995b, 1996a), and more narrowly-focused studies in Blust (1980a, b, 1981a, b, 1986/1987, 1987, 1991a, 1992b, 1993b, 1996b, 1999b, 2005a, b, 2010c, 2013b, 2017c, 2018a), as well as comments on the interrelationship of historical linguistics and archaeology in Blust (1976, 2017a, b).

The topics addressed in this brief compass are: house, village, and community (§4.2); agriculture (§4.3); maritime technology (§4.4); and kinship, marriage, and social organization (§4.5). Because it requires the resources of more than one academic discipline to fully understand, most attention will be paid to the last of these.

## 4.2 House, village, and community

Despite occasional statements to the contrary (Murdock 1964; Bulbeck 2008), it is clear that most AN speakers have been sedentary agriculturalists throughout their linguistically reconstructable history, with only rare reversions to a foraging lifestyle, nearly all of which have occurred in insular Southeast Asia south of Taiwan (Kreemer 1912; Hildebrand 1982; Hemley 2003; Blust 2015b). Major linguistic reconstructions supporting this inference for the area in question are shown in Table 4.1. Supporting evidence for all linguistic reconstructions in this chapter may be found in Blust and Trussel (2020), and will be cited here only where it is necessary to clarify semantic distinctions.

This set of terms may not be exhaustive, but it is sufficiently complete to remove any doubt that PMP speakers, like PAN speakers before them, lived in villages that contained several types of structures, including family dwellings (*Rumaq), a public building that probably served primarily as a meeting house (*balay), separate bachelor's quarters (*kamaliR), and granaries (*lepaw). In addition, as will be shown in greater detail below, they recognized a broad distinction between inhabited territory (*banua), and wilderness (*halas).

The distinction between PMP *banua and *natad merits a brief comment. The *banua, as will be explained below, described all land recognized by the community as providing its material and spiritual support. This would necessarily

Robert Blust, *Linguistic approaches to Austronesian culture history*. In: *The Oxford Guide to the Malayo-Polynesian Languages of Southeast Asia*. Edited by: Alexander Adelaar and Antoinette Schapper, Oxford University Press. © Robert Blust (2024). DOI: 10.1093/oso/9780198807353.003.0004

**Table 4.1** Linguistic reconstructions relating to house and village in the Malayo-Polynesian languages of insular Southeast Asia

| PMP | English |
|---|---|
| *ataŋ | crossbeam |
| *balay | meeting house |
| *banua | inhabited territory (opp. to wilderness) |
| *bara | support beams in a house |
| *baRat | crossbeam |
| *bilik | room in a house |
| *bubuŋ(-an) | ridgepole |
| *dalikan | trivet for cooking pot |
| *dapuR | hearth |
| *diŋdiŋ | wall of a house |
| *hadiRi | housepost |
| *haRezan | notched log ladder |
| *hili | village |
| *kamaliR | bachelor's house |
| *kasaw | rafter |
| *kataman | door, doorway |
| *kulub | log or bamboo ridgepole cover (PWMP) |
| *lepaw | granary |
| *lipuq | village |
| *natad | cleared area around house/in village |
| *pager | fence |
| *papan | plank |
| *paRa | storage rack above hearth |
| *qatep | roof, thatch |
| *Rumaq | house, family dwelling |
| *saleR | floor of a house |
| *surambi(q) | extension to a house (PWMP) |

have encompassed forested land, including groves of fruit trees. Reflexes of *natad, however, refer specifically to cleared ground within a village, an area that would be safe from the dangers of noxious insects and poisonous reptiles, because any cover that might conceal them had been removed. Representative forms appear in Table 4.2.

**Table 4.2** Reflexes of PMP *natad in representative languages of insular Southeast Asia

| PMP | *natad | cleared around around house/in village |
|---|---|---|
| WMP | | |
| Bikol | *nátad* | the front yard of a house |
| | *ka-nátad* | a neighbour |
| Cebuano | *nátad* | yard of house; sphere of work or activity |
| Kadazan Dusun | *natad* | courtyard, house compound |
| Tombonuwo | *natad* | yard |
| Lun Dayeh | *natad* | a resting place made along a jungle trek |
| Kelabit | *natad* | open ground near longhouse where children like to play spinning tops |
| Rejang | *nateut* | the village square, open space in the centre of the village |
| Old Javanese | *natar* | yard (in front or around building, house, temple, etc.) |
| CEMP | | |
| Rembong | *natar* | village; yard around a house |
| Kambera | *nataru* | front yard of a house; village square |
| Yamdena | *natar* | dance and gathering place, village square |
| Kei | *natat* | yard, bald part |

My last comment on this section of the PMP vocabulary will concern the construction of the house. Unlike the typical brush shelters of foragers, the AN house, as far back as linguistic evidence is found (PAN *Rumaq), was clearly made of heavy timbers that had to be obtained by the felling of appropriate trees, and the adzing of the logs until they were suitable for the various purposes to which they were put.

It is clear that the first step in constructing a traditional AN house was to erect the foundation posts (*hadiRi). These were uprights that had to be secured by sinking them into postholes and insuring that they remained stable. Various horizontal crossbeams were then laid across the houseposts. Two of these are represented by the PMP terms *ataŋ and *baRat. For the former term, Hanunoo in the central Philippines has *átaŋ* 'one of the underlying crosspieces used in constructing the flooring of a house', Maranao in the southern Philippines has *antaŋ-an* 'framework (as of a house); base line', Kelabit in northern Sarawak has *ataŋ* 'crossbeam in house construction', and Kédang in the Lesser Sunda islands of eastern Indonesia has *ataŋ* 'house beam'. For the second term, Ngaju Dayak in southeast Borneo has *bahat* 'crossbeam', Dairi-Pakpak in northern Sumatra has *barat* 'athwart or across (as a barrier)', Tae' in central Sulawesi has *baraʔ* 'two long beams of the house', Makasar has *barat-aŋ* 'bamboo outrigger connectors', and Termanu in the Lesser Sundas has *ba* 'lie crosswise, as a log across the road'. These glosses are insufficient for clarifying the distinction between PMP *ataŋ and *baRat. One term presumably referred to beams that ran parallel to the ridgepole and supported the crossbeams on which the floor (probably of split bamboo) was placed. Clearly distinct from these were the rafters (*kasaw), which supported the ridged roof structure, and so were placed at an angle between the support beams for the floor and the ridgepole. Finally, it is apparent from the details of this description that the floor of the PMP house, which has been preserved most faithfully in insular Southeast Asia, was raised off the ground, and the house was thus entered by means of a notched log ladder (*haRezan).

While 'house' and 'village' refer to physical structures, the idea of community is more abstract.

What do we mean when we speak of a 'human community'? Clearly it is a collection of people, but for it to be a community it must be a collection of people sharing common values and attitudes toward the natural and social world that supports them. These values and attitudes can differ dramatically across cultures. We need only think of the European attitude toward the new lands they encountered in the Americas as against that of the native peoples they replaced by war, disease, or forced removal. To the new arrivals, land was a commodity, something to be bought and sold like anything in a marketplace. If it could not be bought, it was taken by force or deceit. To the native people the land was something given by the Creator for the use of his children, who were obligated to use it wisely and pass it on unharmed to those who came after them; it was in some ways an extension of the divine being who had made it, and for this reason it was sacred. We see this theme repeated again and again in the tragic history of the native peoples of North America who were repeatedly pressed into ever smaller tracts and asked to sell what little connection they still had to the sacred places they loved. No one expressed the total disconnect between the European and native American perspectives on this matter more poignantly than the Squamish leader Chief Seattle in his famous 1854 reply to President Franklin Pierce—a stunningly simple and beautiful oration that begins:

> *The Great Chief in Washington sends word that he wishes to buy our land.*
>
> *The Great Chief also sends us words of friendship and good will. This is kind of him, since we know he has little need of our friendship in return.*
>
> *But we will consider your offer, for we know that if we do not sell, the white man may come with guns and take our land.*
>
> *How can you buy or sell the sky, the warmth of the land? This idea is strange to us.*
>
> *If we do not own the freshness of the air and the sparkle of the water how can you buy them?*
>
> *Every part of this earth is sacred to my people. Every shining pine needle, every sandy shore, every mist in the dark woods, every clearing and humming insect is holy in the memory and experience of my people. The sap which courses through the trees carries the memories of the red man.*
>
> *The white man's dead forget the country of their birth when they go to walk among the stars. Our dead never forget this beautiful earth, for it is the mother of the red man. We are part of the earth and it is part of us.*

It is not merely that native Americans and immigrant Americans saw their relationship to the land in very different ways—each found the other's perspective *incomprehensible*. Could this insight help us understand the nature of community in early AN society?

It is at first unclear how we should proceed to find evidence of the native-speaker attitude toward community. If we look at terms for 'village', for example, we can reconstruct PAN *asaŋ, and the unrelated PMP *lipuq (Blust and Trussel 2020). But this gains us nothing, for we have simply found the equivalents in some AN languages of an English semantic category. What we need instead is to discover a native semantic category in AN languages which may differ from the categories encoded in English words in much the same way that the native American attitude toward the land differed from that of the European invaders who displaced them.

This raises issues of lexicography that can be illustrated with the term *banua from Table 4.3. As noted in Blust (1987), the difference between an extended word list (which is what many 'dictionaries' are), and a genuine dictionary, is that the latter tries to capture the native semantic categories rather than merely representing them partially through the categories of the compiler's language, a distinction that Saussure (1959[1915]) labelled 'signification' (= translation equivalent) vs. 'value' (= full meaning). One of the 'house' words that is explored in Blust (1987)

**Table 4.3** Reflexes of PMP *banua

| 'Territory supporting the life of a community' | | | |
|---|---|---|---|
| **WMP** | Itbayaten | *vanua* | landing place, port |
| | Pangasinan | *banwá* | sun |
| | Kapampangan | *banwá* | year, sky, heaven |
| | Hiligaynon | *banwá* | town, community; a compactly settled area usually larger than a village but smaller than a city |
| | Subanon | *meg-banua* | to live, dwell |
| | Embaloh[a] | *banua* | country, land, commoner |
| | Malay | *benua* | large expanse of land; empire; continent; mainland in contrast to island; to the old Malays even a large island like Java was a *benua* |
| | Toba Batak | *banua* | land, district, region |
| | | *banua ginjaŋ* | upper world, heaven |
| | | *banua toŋa on* | middle world, Earth |
| | | *banua toru* | underworld, world of the dead |
| | Mentawai | *manua* | sky, heaven |
| | Tondano | *wanua* | village |
| | Pamona | *banua* | house |
| | | *wanua* | den of an animal |
| | Palauan | *bəlúu* | country, village, place |
| **CMP** | Selaru | *hnu(a)* | village |
| | Yamdena | *pnue* | village |
| **SHWNG** | Buli | *pnu* | village |
| | Ansus | *wanu* | village; house |
| **OC** | Emira | *anua* | house |
| | Duke of York | *wanua* | land, country |
| | Motu | *hanua* | village, town |
| | Pokau | *vanua* | land |
| | Molima | *vanua* | house |
| | Mono-Alu | *fanua* | fellow clansman |
| | Bugotu | *vanua* | land, island |
| | Longgu | *vanua* | people |
| | Fijian | *vanua* | land, region, place; used in a number of weather expressions |
| | Samoan | *fanua* | land, field; afterbirth, placenta |
| | Hawaiian | *honua* | land, earth |

[a] Maloh is also used in the scientific literature. However, it is an Iban exonym. The people designated with it are also called Embaloh; they refer to themselves and their language as Ambalo or Tamambalo.

is *banua, and its glosses in the modern languages vary considerably, as shown by the following selective sample (WMP = Western Malayo-Polynesian, CMP = Central Malayo-Polynesian, SHWNG = South Halmahera–West New Guinea, OC = Oceanic):

Selecting only glosses that occur in both primary branches of Malayo-Polynesian, namely WMP vs. the rest, we find that the following meanings can be attributed to PMP:

1. village (Tondano, Palauan, Selaru, Buli, Motu, etc.)
2. house (Pamona, Ansus, Emira, Molima)
3. land (Embaloh, Toba Batak, Duke of York, Bugotu, Fijian, Hawaiian, etc.)
4. place (Palauan, Fijian)

As already seen, there is a straightforward PMP term for 'village' (*lipuq), and as noted in Blust (1987), there are better-supported PMP terms for 'house' (*Rumaq) and 'land' (*taneq), leaving us with the rather vague notion of 'place', which is unsatisfactory. The meaning of PMP *banua apparently included the notions 'village', 'house', and 'land', to which we might add 'people' by matching Embaloh *banua* 'commoner' with Mono-Alu *fanua* 'fellow clansman', or Longgu *vanua* 'people'. But this is little more than a string of English equivalents, not a coherent conceptual unity. What we have done so far, in the terms of Saussure (1959[1915]: 114), is find various *significations* of PMP *banua, but not its semantic *value*. As stated in an earlier publication "signification defines meaning through a reference point that is outside the system of a language, while value defines meaning through systemic coherence" (Blust 1987: 88).

Fortunately, not all lexicographers fall back on one-word English translations of native concepts; a few try to *explain* a native concept for which there is no single English word, and in the present case we see this in two widely separated languages, the WMP language Iban, a close relative of Malay spoken in southwest Borneo, and 'Āre'āre, an Oceanic language spoken in the southeast Solomons. For the first of these languages Richards (1981: 215) gives Iban *menoa/menua* 'area of land held and used by distinct community, esp. longhouse, including house, farms, gardens, fruit groves, cemetery, water and all forest within half a day's journey. Use of the *m.* is only gained and maintained by much effort and danger, and by proper rites to secure and preserve a ritual harmony of all within it and the unseen forces involved.' Following this description Richards adds the English glosses 'home', 'abode', 'place', 'district', 'country', 'region'. For the second language Geerts (1970) gives 'Āre'āre *hanua* 'land, as opposed to *āsi* sea; district, place, country, island', but then adds: 'the territory, area, where a person lives, where his possessions are, such as food, bamboo, trees, pigs, water and graves, is called his *hanua*'.

The detailed agreement of these glosses in distantly related languages cannot be accidental. Both specifically mention an inhabited territory which includes the necessities of life: food, water, and the graves of the ancestors, whose blessings are needed for the prosperity of their descendants. In short, PMP *banua was a tract of inhabited land (as opposed to virgin forest) which provided the life support of the community, both material and spiritual. The likelihood that this gloss is correct is strikingly confirmed by the otherwise mysterious semantic reflex 'afterbirth, placenta', which is attesed in three Polynesian languages, Tongan (*fonua*), Samoan (*fanua*), and Rennellese (*henua*). What could be a more perfect parallel for the total life support of the community than the organ that provides the total life support of the unborn foetus?

We are lucky in this case to have two glosses that were produced by lexicographers who strove to capture the full sense of the native concept, rather than simply presenting a collection of semantic fragments that happen to coincide with single words of English. But this is an accident we cannot expect to be repeated whenever needed, and it is anyone's guess how many valid glosses that provide important insights into culture history have been concealed under the cover of inadequate lexicography which, once illuminated, might open up an understanding of a worldview very different from our own.[1]

## 4.3 Agriculture

From the earliest period to which linguistic data provides insight, AN speakers had grain agriculture in addition to horticulture and the gathering of wild plants. The term 'agriculture' ('field cultivation') will be used here in its broadest possible sense to indicate the cultivation of grain crops, some tree crops, tubers, and such special categories as sugarcane. Table 4.4 presents the core PMP reconstructions that relate to this aspect of culture.

With regard to tree crops it is not always easy to determine whether a particular type of tree was cultivated for its fruit, or whether it was sufficiently plentiful in the wild to allow harvesting without cultivation. For this reason, I have excluded such widespread plants as *bulu-an 'rambutan', *duRi-an 'durian', *niuR 'coconut', *paŋedan 'pandanus' (fruits eaten in some areas), and *pahuq and *wai

[1] Pawley (2005) has addressed the semantics of POC *panua (< PMP *banua), and reached similar conclusions, differing only in whether he sees the semantic diversity of the reflexes as a product of semantic fragmentation, or as a continuation of a collection of related meanings that were already discrete in the protolanguage.

**Table 4.4** Linguistic reconstructions relating to agriculture in the Malayo-Polynesian languages of insular Southeast Asia

| PMP | English |
|---|---|
| *ampaw | empty husk (of rice, etc.) |
| *bataR | broomcorn millet |
| *beRas | husked rice |
| *beteŋ | foxtail millet |
| *binehiq | seed rice |
| *buRaw | drive animals from the fields |
| *eRik/*irik | thresh grains by trampling |
| *hemay | cooked rice |
| *kuluR | breadfruit |
| *laqia | ginger |
| *lepaw | granary |
| *lesuŋ | mortar |
| *niRu | winnowing basket |
| *pajay | rice plant, rice in the field |
| *paspas | thresh grains by beating |
| *punti | banana |
| *qahelu | pestle |
| *qani | to harvest |
| *qapa | empty husk |
| *qeta | rice husk |
| *qubi | yam |
| *qumah | swidden |
| *ququs | to chew on sugarcane |
| *Rambia | sago |
| *sukun | breadfruit sp. |
| *tahep | to winnow grains |
| *tales | taro |
| *tebuh | sugarcane |
| *teRep | tree with fruit similar to breadfruit (PWMP) |
| *zaRami | rice stubble |

'mango'. However, both the banana and breadfruit appear to have been widely cultivated, as were root crops such as yams (*qubi) and taro (*tales).

The material of Table 4.4 shows that AN speakers in insular Southeast Asia continued the tradition of rice and millet cultivation that their ancestral communities had established more than a millennium earlier in Taiwan. With regard to the relative importance of these two cereal crops there can be no question that rice was the dominant member of the pair, as in the great majority of cultures in the Philippines and western Indonesia–Malaysia it is the *sine qua non* of each daily meal. Only in eastern Indonesia and some marginal areas of western Indonesia–Malaysia, as the Melanau coastal zone of Sarawak, does it yield its position to sago as the pre-eminent starch.

Some of the terms in Table 4.4, such as *lesuŋ 'mortar' and *qahelu 'pestle' apply indifferently to any grain crop (or, less commonly, to other types of plants), but are overwhelmingly associated in the ethnographic record with the pounding of rice grains to loosen the husk, which is then threshed and winnowed off to transform *pajay into *beRas, which remains in storage until it is cooked. Terms such as *zaRami could, in principle, apply to the stalks of grain crops left in the field after the harvest, whether this crop was rice or millet, but in the great majority of languages in which a reflex of this term is found the sources specify that it is the stubble of the rice plant.

The last thing I will comment on is sugarcane. This appears to have been cultivated from an early time, and is a plant that was carried by AN speakers into the Pacific as far as Hawai'i, far from the region in which it was first domesticated.

## 4.4 Maritime technology

Given the largely insular environment in which they live, there is little question that AN speakers have had a strong maritime orientation throughout their history. In some areas this was lost, as certain groups moved inland over time, and lost their ancestral connection with the sea, as with the Bontok, Kankanaey, Ifugao and other peoples of the mountainous interior of northern Luzon, the Manobo and other groups of interior Mindanao, the Kayan, Kenyah, Kelabit and other groups of central Borneo, the interior populations of Madagascar, the Batak peoples of northern Sumatra, or various Toraja groups of central Sulawesi. In other areas, as the islands reaching from approximately Bali to Timor, the settlers remained in physical contact with the sea, but came to associate the forces of life and growth with the mountainous interior of the islands on which they live, and the sea with all things dangerous and negative (Covarrubias 1937). However, in the great majority of AN-speaking communities, across a vast swath of islands in both Southeast Asia and the Pacific, contact with the sea remained a basic part of their lives, and to live in this environment required skill both with the construction of seaworthy watercraft, and with the methods of navigation over distances that in the Pacific often brought one out of sight of land. Table 4.5 shows the major PMP reconstructions connected with maritime technology in insular Southeast Asia and Madagascar.

**Table 4.5** PMP and lower-order terms for maritime technology in insular Southeast Asia

| PMP | English |
|---|---|
| *(pa)-aluja | to paddle a canoe |
| *beRsay | canoe paddle |
| *duluŋ | prow of a canoe |
| *katiR | small outrigger canoe |
| *labuq | to drop anchor, moor a boat |
| *laŋen | rollers for beaching a canoe |
| *layaR | sail of a canoe |
| *limas | canoe bailer; to bail out a canoe |
| *lujan | load a canoe with cargo |
| PWMP | |
| *lunas | keel of a boat |
| *qabaŋ | canoe (probably used on rivers) |
| *qulin | rudder; to steer a boat |
| *Rakit | raft (of bamboo) |
| *saRman | outrigger float |
| *sauq | anchor; to moor |
| *seŋkar | thwart or ribs of a boat |
| *(m)-udi | stern of a boat |
| PCEMP | |
| *waŋka | seagoing canoe |

The terms in Table 4.5 show that the AN-speaking peoples of insular Southeast Asia reached this area by means of the outrigger canoe, a sailing craft that in this part of the AN world is equipped with outriggers on each side to provide greater stability, but less manoeuvrability and speed than is true of the single-outrigger canoes of the Pacific (Doran 1981: 78, 79).

In general, terminology relating to sailing and navigation is richer in the Pacific, where the land masses are smaller and the distances between them greater than in insular Southeast Asia (Pawley and Pawley 1994). Within the Philippines and Indonesia–Malaysia, most sailing was done between closely spaced islands, so that one was rarely out of sight of land for more than a day. More important for sailing in insular Southeast Asia than in the Pacific were the seasonal winds connected with the monsoon rains. The Buginese and Makassarese traders who collected sea cucumbers (also called tripang, or bêche-de-mer) for the Chinese market, and Bird of Paradise plumes for the European market, traditionally sailed east to the Aru islands with the west monsoon (*habaRat), and back to south Sulawesi some months later with the east monsoon (*timuR), a pattern of voyaging that was observed firsthand as a passenger by the renowned English naturalist Alfred Russel Wallace during fourteen years of collecting natural history specimens for the British Museum in the middle of the nineteenth century (Wallace 1962[1869]). Other voyages connected with the tripang, or bêche-de-mer market took the 'Macassans' to Arnhem Land in northern Australia, where AN loanwords connected with sailing entered some of the local Australian languages (Walker and Zorc 1981; Macknight 2011).

Malay speakers were among the most active sailors in Island Southeast Asia, a consequence of their role as traders for goods from the Malay archipelago which were traded out to India and beyond through the Strait of Malacca, and to China through the southern Philippines. As a result of centuries of voyaging widely between the Asian mainland and New Guinea, local Malay dialects grew up wherever stable trading colonies became established. Thus, while the Malayic homeland was almost certainly southwest Borneo, with secondary migrations to southern Sumatra and the Malay peninsula (Adelaar 1992a; Collins and Sariyan 2006) at least a dozen geographically displaced Malay dialects that derive from earlier trading colonies are found from Jakarta in the west to the Bird's Head peninsula of New Guinea in the east (Adelaar 2005b: 203).

Partly as a consequence of the wide trade contacts of Malay sailors, beginning as early as the seventh century with the Indianized state of Sriwijaya in southern Sumatra, likely trading partners in the Barito river basin of southeast Borneo were drawn out into long exploratory voyages of their own, leading to the settlement of Madagascar (Dahl 1951, 1991; Adelaar 1989), and to the development of commercially motivated houseboat nomadism by groups known variously as Sama and Bajaw in both the Philippines and various parts of Indonesia (Blust 2005a, 2007c). In both of these groups the eight-point Malay sailing compass was adopted, providing direct linguistic evidence that the movement of these non-Malayic peoples from the same region of southeast Borneo was prompted by close trading contacts with Malays, who were already accomplished navigators (Blust 2007c: 103).

## 4.5 Kinship, marriage, and social organization

The PMP kinship terminology, drawn from the Austronesian Comparative Dictionary (Blust and Trussel 2020), is shown in Table 4.6. Standard kinship abbreviations are used except where generalization is needed for a more concise representation in tabular format (e.g. 'GP' rather than FF, FM, MF, MM); +1, -1, etc. mark generations above and below EGO).

**Table 4.6** PMP consanguineal kinship terms

| Generation: | +2: | +1 | EGO |
|---|---|---|---|
| | *(t)-empu GP (recip.) | *(t)-ina M/MZ | *kaka e//Sb |
| | *bubu GP (add.) | *(t)-ama F/FB | *huaji y//Sb |
| | *aki GF | *baba F | *ñaRa B (w.s.) |
| | *baqi GM | *mama FB | *betaw Z (m.s.) |
| | *ma-tuqah MB? | | |
| | *aya FZ | | |
| **Generation:** | **-2** | **-1** | |
| | *(t)-empu GC (recip.) | *anak C | |
| | *kempu GC | *kam-anak-an BC/ZC | (PWMP) |
| | *bubu GC (add.) | | |

Details needing explanation for generations +2 and -2 include the following: i) *empu was a reciprocal term for grandparents and their grandchildren; it apparently was an address term when used alone, and was converted to a term of reference when prefixed with *t-; ii) *bubu appears to have been an affectionate term for the same reciprocal relationship; iii) although *empu did not distinguish gender, gender-specific grandparental terms *aki 'GF' and *baqi 'GM' were also used, but were not extended to grandchildren; and iv) *kempu applied only to the -2 generation, and did not distinguish gender. Grandparental terms probably also meant 'ancestor', although a distinct, but sparsely attested word *anduŋ appears to have referred to ancestors in general.[2]

Details needing explanation for generations +1 and -1 include the following: i) terms for parents and their same sex siblings were identical, although a separate term can also be reconstructed for 'FB', but not for 'MZ'; ii) *baba apparently was a childish name for 'father', part of the globally distributed set of 'mama/papa' terms that has arisen independently in languages around the world (Jakobson 1960); and iii) *ma-tuqah is challenging. Milke (1958) reconstructed *matuqa 'mother's brother' for Proto-Oceanic, but reflexes of this word in most languages of insular Southeast Asia mean 'parent-in-law'; if the two are related this suggests (without clearly demonstrating) that PMP *ma-tuqah meant 'MB/WF', which would imply a system of matrilateral cross-cousin marriage. The fact that *aya probably meant 'FZ', with reflexes having this meaning in several Oceanic languages, but meaning either 'father' or 'mother' in Southeast Asia, also implies that PMP had a distinct term for 'MB', further strengthening the case for the tentative gloss given here to PMP *ma-tuqah. For consanguineal terms the first descending generation holds little interest, as the only kin terms reconstructed to date mean 'child' and 'nephew/niece', which is morphologically derived from 'child'.

As will be seen, interest in the consanguineal terminology for PMP centres on Ego's generation. In his foundational, but now superseded reconstruction, Dempwolff (1934–1938), whose study for methodological reasons was limited to eleven languages, (none from eastern Indonesia), recognized only three sibling terms. In current orthography these were: *betaw 'sibling of the opposite sex'; *aji 'relative (mostly younger)', which is a 'doublet' of the same term *huaji 'relative (mostly of the opposite sex)'; and *kaka 'older sibling'. It can be seen at once that Dempwolff's glosses for these terms show no systemic coherence, and it is now clear that his reconstruction of sibling terms was seriously flawed.

The set of PMP affinal kinship terms (Table 4.7) is considerably smaller than the set of reconstructed consanguineal terms, and is more problematic, as only *qasawa has a gloss that can be completely trusted. Reflexes of *ma-tuqah have already been discussed in relation to Table 4.6—there are tantalizing indications that it meant both 'MB' and 'WF', although in most languages of western Indonesia it refers to the more general category 'parent-in-law'. Complicating the interpretation of kinship meanings in connection with this term is that its basic sense is 'aged, mature', leaving open the possibility that some kinship senses in the modern languages are historically secondary.

[2] Observations that are irrelevant to the structure of the system, but are part of the reconstructed terminology include the unexplained vowel variation in *empu, *ampu, *impu, and *umpu 'GP/GC (recip.)'.

**Table 4.7** PMP affinal kinship terms

| AFFINAL TERMS | | |
|---|---|---|
| Generation: | +1 | EGO |
| | *ma-tuqah WF? | *qasawa 'spouse' |
| | *bayaw BIL (m.s.) | |
| | *hipaR BW/ZH/WB/WZ/HB/HZ | |
| | *idas 'affine of Ego's generation' | |

Reflexes of PMP *hipaR are widespread, and invariably refer to a brother-in-law or sister-in-law, although the precise set of affines included is difficult to determine, either because of vagueness in the glosses given by sources, or because of conflict when the glosses are explicit, as where *ipag* in Isnag of northern Luzon is glossed 'BW (m.s.), ZH (w.s.), WZ, HB', but *ifar* in Fordata of eastern Indonesia is glossed 'ZH (m.s.), BW (w.s.)'. In the first case the set of siblings-in-law are the spouses of one's parallel siblings, or the parallel siblings of one's spouse, while in the second case the set is the spouses of one's cross-siblings, and these are only two among a number of differently constituted affines of Ego's generation that are associated with this term. To further complicate matters, PMP *hipaR 'opposite side, as of a river' may ultimately be the same form, with a symbolic value in kinship that is yet to be elucidated (Adelaar 1988: 72).

Much the same is true of PMP *idas, which clearly designated an affinal category of Ego's generation that must have differed from that of *hipaR. To cite an example or two to illustrate the problem of semantic reconstruction with this term, in Timugon Murut of Sabah *ilas* is glossed 'HBW', but not 'WZH', while in Mentawai of the Barrier islands west of Sumatra *ira* is given as 'brother-in-law, sister-in-law, woman speaking', hence WHB/WHZ/WZH/WBW.

Reflexes of *bayaw (PWMP) refer overwhelmingly to a male affine of Ego's generation, although the specification that this is for a male speaker is not supported by all witnesses. Finally, the search for PMP affinal terms for the -1 generation has so far yielded no clear results, and PMP *tuRaŋ apparently was an umbrella term for 'kinsman, relative'.

Without a more in-depth analysis little can be concluded about PMP descent or marriage from the kinship terminology presented above. So far as the data reveals, sibling terms also referred to cousins, meaning that PMP social structure was 'Hawaiian' in type. However, it is clear that if matrilateral cross-cousin marriage was preferred, the terms for MBD and FZS could not have been identical to those for siblings. This problem has long eluded linguistic reconstruction, probably because the terms for cross-cousins had other, broader meanings that are better attested in the linguistic record. Several of the terminologies from eastern Indonesia suggest that the MBD was designated by a reflex of PMP *b<in>ahi 'female, woman' and the FZS by a reflex of PMP *laki or *ma-Ruqanay 'male, man', but support for this inference remains elusive, and is complicated by reflexes of the same term meaning 'sister' or 'wife' in closely related languages, as Manggarai *wina* 'MBD, wife', Sika *whine* 'Z (m.s.)' < PMP *b<in>ahi 'female, woman'.

The use of linguistic evidence to infer the history of the marriage system in PMP society was first attempted in Blust (1980a), and taken up in greater detail in Blust (1993b). In both papers it was concluded that PMP society was based on unilineal descent and a system of asymmetric exchange (i.e. preferential matrilateral cross-cousin marriage) that is revealed by the history of sibling terms. At the heart of the argument is a widespread pattern of change called 'the cross-sibling substitution drifts' (CSSDs). Oral presentations to groups of both linguists and social anthropologists on several occasions has convinced me that few listeners in either audience understood the logic of the argument, and for this reason the presentation is laid out here in carefully controlled steps.

### 4.5.1 PMP siblings: Two terms or four?

Inferences about descent or marriage in prehistoric language communities have traditionally relied heavily on cousin terminology. However, since at least Murdock (1968), it has been recognized on the basis of extensive crosscultural sampling that the structure of sibling terminologies may, in many cases, provide more reliable information on this topic. For this reason it is critical that we begin with an explicit justification of the reconstructed sibling terms that appear in Table 4.6.

STEP 1. As noted elsewhere (e.g. Blust 1993b), PMP reconstructions require evidence from at least two primary branches of the MP group, i.e. WMP and CEMP. Although it need not concern us here, WMP may itself contain more than one MP branch (Smith 2017b and Smith, this volume, §2.4.1).

STEP 2. Dempwolff (1934–1938) recognized only three early Malayo-Polynesian sibling terms, with glosses that show no systemic coherence, and most later writers have recognized only two: *kaka 'older sibling'; *huaji 'younger sibling'. This leads to step 3.

**Table 4.8** Comparative evidence for PMP *kaka, *huaji, *ñaRa, and *betaw

| A) Parallel siblings | | | | | |
|---|---|---|---|---|---|
| PMP | | *kaka | 'e//Sb' | *huaji | 'y//Sb' |
| WMP: | Toba Batak | *haha* | 'e//Sb' | *aŋgi* | 'y//Sb' |
| | Ngaju Dayak | *kaka* | 'e//Sb (ref.)' | *andi* | 'y//Sb (ref.)' |
| CMP: | Manggarai | (*kaʔe*) | 'e//Sb' | *ase* | 'y//Sb' |
| | Termanu | *kaʔa* | 'e//Sb' | *fadi* | 'y//Sb' |
| | Soboyo | *kaka* | 'eSb' | (*uliʔ*) | 'ySb' |

| B) Cross siblings | | | | | |
|---|---|---|---|---|---|
| PMP | | *ñaRa | 'B (w.s.)' | *betaw | 'Z (m.s.)' |
| WMP: | Toba Batak | --- | | *i-boto* | 'xSb' |
| | Ngaju Dayak | *ñahɛ* | 'B (w.s.)' | *betaw* | 'Z (m.s.)' |
| CMP: | Manggarai | *nara* | 'B (w.s.)' | *weta* | 'Z (m.s.)' |
| | Termanu | *na* | 'B (w.s.)' | *feto* | 'Z (m.s.)' |
| | Soboyo | *naha* | 'B (w.s.)' | *foto* | 'Z (m.s.)' |

STEP 3. Leaving Dempwolff's limited sample (eleven languages), it quickly becomes apparent that many languages of eastern Indonesia have four sibling terms distinguished by relative sex (male speaker/female speaker) and by relative age (older/younger). More important, these terms are generally cognate with one another and with equivalent terms in some WMP languages, allowing all four to be reconstructed to PMP, as shown in Table 4.8.[3]

Although reflexes of the cross-sibling terms are rare in WMP languages, they agree in meaning with similar forms in CEMP languages, and except for Manggarai *kaʔe* and Soboyo *uliʔ*, show regular sound correspondences. Since this is not likely to be due to chance or borrowing, there is little alternative but to assign them to PMP, a decision that is further supported by Berawan (northern Sarawak) *betaw* 'sister' and Simalungun *botow* 'xSb'.

Accepting Ngaju Dayak *ñahɛ* 'B (w.s.)' as native raises another question: why would reflexes of *ñaRa be rarer than reflexes of *betaw in WMP languages? It is non-controversial that most fieldworkers, both in anthropology and in linguistics, are (or were in the past) male, as were the informants from whom they collected primary data. A relative sex parameter in the sibling terminology is commonplace in CEMP languages, but rare in WMP. The first question that a male fieldworker collecting data for a WMP language is likely to ask is 'what are the words for "brother" and "sister"?'. Since relative age in sibling terms is almost universal in AN languages, the informant probably would respond with terms for elder and younger parallel siblings, and 'sister', which might easily be recorded as 'elder brother/younger brother' and 'sister'. If it were then asked whether the elder/younger distinction also applies to sisters the answer from a male speaker could well be 'no', since it doesn't apply for him.

What term, if any, would be lost in such an incomplete data-collection process? Almost certainly, it would be the term for 'brother (woman speaking)', since the male fieldworker may not bother to ask the same questions of a female informant. The phenomenon of male dominance in data collection is thus sufficient by itself to account for the likelihood that if any sibling term in a relative sex terminology is overlooked, it will be 'brother (woman speaking)', as seen in Dempwolff's incongruous three-term system, which reflects in some ways the limitations of his sources. The conclusion reached so far, then, is that PMP had four sibling terms distinguished both by relative sex and relative age.

STEP 4. As noted in Blust (1980a, 1993b), Murdock (1968) drew on a sample of 800 societies in showing that the presence of a relative sex parameter in sibling terms is strongly

[3] Ngaju Dayak data is from the Katingan dialect (cf. Blust 1993b: 50, fn. 14); forms in parentheses are non-cognate.

associated with lineal descent. As in any statistical distribution, it is possible that PMP was an exception to the probability calculus linking relative sex in sibling terms with lineal descent, but given the reported statistics it is more likely that it conformed to this correlation. Tentatively, then, we can assume that PMP society operated on the basis of lineal principles rather than bilateral kindreds.

## 4.5.2. PMP siblings: Four terms or six?

If this were all there was to the history of sibling terms in AN languages the matter would be settled: we reconstruct four PMP sibling terms, conclude that descent probably was unilineal, and our job is done.

What makes the AN case more interesting, both for Austronesian specialists and for general kinship theorists, is that the story does not end here. Rather, in addition to *ñaRa and *betaw, there is a second set of cross-sibling terms spanning the major divide between WMP and CEMP languages much like the primary set of cross-sibling terms. However, this second set differs from the first in an important feature, namely that while *ñaRa and *betaw have only kinship meanings, the second set of cross-sibling terms is homophonous with the words for 'male' and 'female', or a reflex of PMP *anak 'child, offspring', plus 'male/female'. In other words, they look like 'male/female' or 'male child/female child'. Extensive documentation of this second set of cross-sibling terms is given in Blust (1993b). A representative sample is given in Table 4.9 (F = morpheme glossed 'female', M = morpheme glossed 'male'; note that PMP *bahi = 'female', and PMP *laki and *(ma)-Ruqanay both = 'male', with an unknown difference of meaning).

Perhaps the first question to ask is why a language would have two sets of sibling terms with the same meaning, and if it did, why this would be true for cross-siblings, but not parallel siblings. It is noteworthy that no attested language uses members of both sets interchangeably, suggesting that they never co-existed in a single language as alternative cross-sibling terms, although 'mixed' terminologies occur, as with Sika *whine* (Set 2), and *nara* (Set 1).

In addition, the morphological difference between *ñaRa and *betaw vs. Malagasy *ana bavy/ana dahi*, or Kambera *ana wini/ana mini*, recalls the observation of Sapir (1916: 434ff) that words which are analysable into smaller meaningful parts are more likely to be recent additions to a language than words with no internal morphological structure. In the present case we should qualify this as specifying historically secondary addition to the kinship terminology rather than recent addition to the language. As a first clue, then, this

**Table 4.9** Evidence for a second set of cross-sibling terms in WMP and CEMP languages

| *(anak) bahi 'Z (m.s.)' | *(anak) laki/*ma-Ruanay 'B (w.s.)' |
|---|---|
| WMP: | WMP: |
| Bontok *ka-babai-an* (*ka-F-an*) | Bontok *ka-lalaki-an* (*ka-M-an*) |
| Bugkalot *be:kur* (F) | Bugkalot *laki* (M) |
| Maranao *bebai* (F) | Maranao *laki* (M) |
| Malagasy *ana bavy* (*anak + F) | Malagasy *ana dahi* (*anak + M) |
| Middle Malay *kelaway* (F) | Middle Malay *moanay* (M) |
| Tae' *anak dara* (*anak + virgin) | Tae' *anak muane* (*anak + M) |
| CEMP: | CEMP: |
| Sika *whine* (F) | Sika (*nara*) |
| Adonara Lamaholot *bine* (F) | Adonara Lamaholot (*naa*) |
| Kambera *ana wini* (*anak + F) | Kambera *ana mini* (*anak + M) |
| Hawu *na weni* (*anak + F) | Hawu *na mone* (*anak + M) |

observation suggests that while PMP *ñaRa, *betaw designated cross-siblings, the second set of cross-sibling terms originally had some other meaning that was more readily derivable from its parts. But if so, what other meaning? And why would the terms in Table 4.9 replace terms that already distinguished cross-siblings? Again, to facilitate comprehension I will break the discussion into discrete steps.

STEP 5. As just noted, the first thing to keep in mind is that the terms in Table 4.9 probably were replacements for PMP *ñaRa and *betaw. The second thing to keep in mind is that it is much harder to achieve a unique reconstruction for this second set of terms, which differ in whether or not they include *anak, and in the morpheme for 'male' (or, less commonly, 'female'). We might first ask, then, what would motivate replacing monomorphemic terms for 'B (w.s.)', and 'Z (m.s.)' with the general terms 'male', and 'female'. Gender terms (M/F) are often used for 'husband/wife' in AN languages, replacing the gender-neutral PMP *qasawa 'spouse', but it would be decidedly odd for this usage to be extended to cross-siblings, where any suggestion of marriage would violate the most basic incest taboos.

STEP 6. This leads us to consider the possibility that the use of 'male/female' as replacement terms for *ñaRa/betaw is historical shorthand for *anak + male/female. In other words, if we assume that the reconstructed terms in Table 4.9 contained *anak, as their reflexes still do in some WMP and CEMP languages, it is simpler to derive the modern forms without this morpheme by loss than to derive those with it by addition of an element that should have been unnecessary if the terms 'male/female' already distinguished cross-siblings by gender.

But this leads us into another apparent *cul-de-sac*: words with the structure *anak +male/female are identical to terms for 'son/daughter' in most AN languages, and there is no more reason to believe that original cross-sibling terms would be replaced by words for 'son' and 'daughter' than that they would be replaced by words for 'husband' and 'wife'. Since neither option makes structural sense something is clearly escaping us here, and this is perhaps the most difficult part of the argument for non-linguists to follow. Does the reflex of *anak in Malagasy *ana bavy/ana dahi*, or Kambera *ana wini/ana mini* really mean 'child'? Or, even more obscurely, do the terms for 'male/female' represent the sex of the cross-sibling, or a broader social category?

STEP 7. As noted in Blust (1993b), there is evidence from differences in possessive patterns of both WMP and CMP languages that *anak, in the cross-sibling terms, cannot be glossed 'child'. For Tae', van der Veen (1940: 17ff) cites *anak muane-na* 'her brother', but *anak-na muane* 'his/her son', showing divergent possessive patterns for terms that are structurally identical in their basic forms. What greatly enhances the importance of this observation is that Fischer (1957: 5, n), citing Onvlee, reports a parallel pattern in Kambera, where *ana mini-ŋgu* means 'my brother (w.s.)', but *ana-ŋgu mini* is 'my son' (of either a man or a woman). Given its possessive form, a construction such as Tae' *anak-na muane* must therefore be analysed as 'his/her child (who is male)', while *anak muane-na* must be analysed as 'her *anak muane*', and likewise for Kambera. In Table 4.9, then, reflexes of PMP *anak *cannot* mean 'child'. So, what could they mean in these terms for cross-siblings?

STEP 8. Blust and Trussel (2020) gloss PMP *anak both as 'child', and as 'dependent or component part of something larger'. Examples include: *anak i banua 'fellow villager, fellow community member'; *anak i lima 'little finger'; *anak i mata 'pupil of the eye'; *anak i panaq 'arrow'; and *anak i sumpit 'blowpipe dart'. With regard to living languages, Wilkinson (1959: 27) lists Malay *anak* 'child; young (of animal); one (of a party, set or series); important component part; smaller of two'. Most to the point, the anthropologist Masri Singarimbun (1975: 113) notes that although Karo Batak *anak* means 'child', it is "often used in expressions to indicate 'the people of' (e.g. *anak gunung*, upstream or highland people; *anak jahejahe*, downstream or lowland people)," and he therefore recommends that Karo Batak *anak beru* (anak + 'female') 'wife-takers' be glossed as 'the people of the woman', 'the woman's people' or 'one's daughter's (or sister's) family'.

STEP 9. The recognition that *anak in the historically secondary cross-sibling terms probably meant something like 'kin group' or 'collection of related people' rather than 'child' takes us an important step forward. But what could 'male group' or 'female group' mean in terms used by cross-siblings to refer to one another? At this point it is useful to recall that, based entirely on cultural evidence without reference to language, F.A.E. van Wouden (1935) posited an original system of 'circulating connubium' among the great majority of AN-speaking societies in eastern Indonesia. By this he meant a system of asymmetric exchange with a minimum of four descent groups, in which A was wife-giver to B, B to C, C to D, and D to A. In this system every descent group is both wife-giver and wife-taker, but never to the same group. Ideally in such a system a man should marry his classificatory mother's brother's daughter, since this cements the exchange relationship between lineages established by marriages in previous generations. Could this type of marriage system help to make sense of the data in Table 4.9? We already know that *anak did not mean 'child' in the replacement terms for cross-siblings. What, then, do 'male/female' mean in terms glossed as 'male group/female group'?

STEP 10. It might initially be assumed that a sister would call her brother 'member of the male group' because he is male, and vice-versa. However, a consideration of asymmetric exchange systems does not support this interpretation. Lévi-Strauss (1969[1949]) posited an 'axis of generalized exchange' reaching from Siberia through mainland and insular Southeast Asia to aboriginal Australia, a claim that essentially extended the kind of marriage/alliance system van Wouden (1968[1935]) had posited for eastern Indonesia to a much wider geographical region. Taking this up, Needham (1962) pointed out that such marriage-based political arrangements are 'total systems' in the sense that they manifest a dualistic cosmological scheme for ordering the cultural world on both social and material levels. He illustrates this with the system of symbolic classification used by the Tibeto-Burman-speaking Purum of Burma. Needham's table includes twenty-nine pairs of opposed terms used by this group, but we can get by with the eight shown in Table 4.10.

STEP 11. The first thing to note about this table is that it is typical of societies based on asymmetric exchange ('circulating connubium'), regardless of their linguistic affiliations.

**Table 4.10** Scheme of Purum symbolic classification (after Needham 1962: 96)

| Left | Right |
|---|---|
| Affines | Kin |
| Wife-takers | Wife-givers |
| Inferior | Superior |
| Female | Male |
| Earth | Sky |
| Bad death | Good death |
| Profane | Sacred |

Going back to Step 8 recall that the Karo Batak anthropologist Masri Singarimbun described the term *anak beru* (anak + female) as 'the people of the woman', 'the woman's people', or 'one's daughter's (or sister's) family', and that these are also the wife-takers in relation to one's own lineage. This is not an isolated occurrence of the equation *anak + female = wife-takers, *anak + male = wife-givers, as seen in Table 4.11, where the same equation is repeated in Toba Batak of Sumatra, and in a number of the languages of eastern Indonesia.

**Table 4.11** Reflexes of PMP *anak + m/f meaning 'wife-givers/wife-takers'

| WMP | wife-takers | wife-givers |
|---|---|---|
| Karo Batak | *anak beru* (*anak + F) | (*kalimbubu*) |
| Toba Batak | *anak boru* (*anak + F) | (*hula hula*) |
| CMP | | |
| Manggarai | *anak wina* (< *anak + F) | *anak rona* (< *anak + M) |
| Atoni | *an feto* (< *anak + F) | *an mone* (< *anak + M) |
| Tetun | *feto sawa* (F + girdle) | *uma mane* (house + M) |
| Huaulu | *haha pina* 'veranda +F' | *haha mana* 'veranda +M' |

Why would semantically equivalent terms for affinal alliance groups and cross-siblings exist in related languages? Briefly, there are four logical possibilities:

(1) chance
(2) transfer from PMP cross-sibling terms to affinal alliance groups
(3) transfer from PMP affinal alliance terms to cross-siblings
(4) transfer from terms that had some other still undefined meaning to *both* affinal alliance groups and cross-siblings.

Alternative (1) is clearly unconvincing. Alternative (2) is equally unconvincing, since there is no evidence that Type 2 cross-sibling terms co-existed with *ñaRa and *betaw in PMP, nor any clear reason why a language would need two morphologically unrelated sets of kin terms in the same meanings. Alternative (4) is speculative, leaving (3) as the only plausible choice, and one that was adopted by Valeri (1980: 185) for the Huaulu of Seram in discussing *hahamana* and *hahapina*, terms which designate wife-giving and wife-taking groups in a system of asymmetric exchange: "Literally, 'hahamana' means 'male veranda'; 'hahapina' 'female veranda'. 'Veranda' here is a synecdoche for 'house' (*luma*): it symbolizes the social group associated with the luma in its relationship to another group, since the veranda is the part of the house reserved for social encounters .. . Not surprisingly, 'hahamana' is also glossed 'male child' and 'hahapina' 'female child'. It is evident that in native conceptualisation the wife-giving/wife-taking relationship is subsumed under more fundamental relationships: children of the brother/children of the sister, brother/sister, and finally, male/female."

STEP 12. Although Valeri's glosses 'male child' and 'female child' probably should be altered to 'member of the male group/female group', as noted above, his analysis of the Huaulu terminology provides a model for what almost certainly has happened in many descendants of PMP: over time a pressure developed for a woman to call her brother 'male group/wife-giver' because her son was expected to marry his daughter, making him wife-giver to her son. In the same way, a man began to call his sister 'female group/wife-taker' not because of *her* role, but because of that of her son. From the standpoint of the individual the key relationship in this system of social organization appears to have been between mother's brother and sister's son, but from the standpoint of lineage affiliation it was between siblings of opposite sex, since it was their relationship which was the foundation for the social order in the next generation.

This may seem contradictory at first, since it follows that the wife-givers are then 'the man's people', or the 'male group', even though they provide women in the exchange relation. It follows further that the terms 'male/female' do not refer to the sex of the husband and wife, but to the sex of the siblings who pledge their children in this relationship: since a man gives his daughter to his sister's son, he belongs to the 'male' (= 'superior', 'wife-giving') group, while his sister's son is a member of the 'female' (= 'inferior', 'wife-taking') group. The terms 'male/female' in the historically secondary cross-sibling terms thus refer to the labels in the dualistic classification system illustrated in Table 4.10, not to the sexes of the siblings themselves.

STEP 13. The only thing left to explain is the concept of drift, first proposed by the linguist Edward Sapir in 1921 in order to account for parallel changes in languages that had separated from a common ancestor, but then evolved along similar lines as a result of the continued operation of inherited structural pressures. Sapir's examples need not concern us here beyond noting that irregular plurals that were innovated in English *mouse*: *mice* and High German *Maus*: *Mäuse* arose through historically independent changes from an ancestral form *mus-i, rather than through a single change in an immediate common ancestor. In much the same way terms for wife-giving and wife-taking groups in a system of asymmetric alliance (Table 4.11) replaced reflexes of PMP *ñaRa and *betaw in some languages, either wholly or in part, while other languages retained the original cross-sibling terms unchanged. In short, the CSSD are important both because they imply a PMP system of asymmetric exchange, and because they are the first known example of a linguistic drift powered not by structural pressures in language, but rather by structural pressures in the sociocultural system.

## 4.6 Conclusions

Linguistic reconstruction has given us a picture of the lifeways of a population that began to migrate into island Southeast Asia from Taiwan about 4,000 years ago. We cannot expect it to be a complete picture, but it provides some insights that are not available from the archaeological record taken alone (cf. Blust 1976). Ultimately, a more complete picture of Austronesian culture history may be possible with greater interdisciplinary collaboration.

Historical linguists and archaeologists have had a fruitful dialogue about the human past in this part of the world for roughly the past four decades, but the very different nature of the raw material in these two disciplines means that the kinds of inferences reached will be largely complementary. For future progress in understanding issues such as the history of kinship and social organization, where more than one academic discipline can contribute to answering the same questions, it would be desirable to see more collaboration between historical linguists and social/cultural anthropologists.

CHAPTER 5

# Human genetic approaches to Malayo-Polynesian prehistory

FRANÇOIS-XAVIER RICAUT, NICOLAS BRUCATO, AND MURRAY P. COX

## 5.1 Introduction[1]

The biology of human groups across Island Southeast Asia (ISEA*) and New Guinea was first studied using blood group information in the 1920s (Bais and Verhoef 1924; Heydon and Murphy 1924). Molecular anthropology had been founded as a discipline only five years before (Hirszfeld and Hirszfeld 1919). Along with the first major works of modern social anthropology published in the 1910s and 1920s (e.g. Malinowski 1922), molecular anthropology similarly benefitted from the stimulating environment of Southeast Asia and the Pacific.

A hundred years later, research on the genetic diversity of this region has advanced tremendously, but with the same broad intent: to reconstruct regional prehistory by investigating the inherited genetic characters of its modern peoples. The earliest research focussed on blood proteins, particularly the ABO blood group*, and offered little insight into prehistory beyond the consistent, if somewhat blurry, distinction between Southeast Asian and Papuan peoples (Mourant et al. 1976; Cavalli-Sforza et al. 1994).

Molecular anthropology advanced quickly in the late 1980s and early 1990s, with new molecular techniques like the Polymerase Chain Reaction (PCR) allowing the first direct observation of changes in DNA* molecules. Molecular studies rapidly switched to the maternally inherited mitochondrial DNA (mtDNA*) and paternally inherited Y chromosome*, providing the first estimates of the timing and movements of human groups. Subsequent automation and miniaturization now enable the analysis of whole genome* sequences—the entire DNA of an individual—at community, regional, and global scales. These 'genomic' studies have come to dominate molecular anthropology and are revealing the biological history of Southeast Asia with ever greater precision. It is therefore now particularly timely to integrate this biological knowledge with the burgeoning information emerging from linguistic studies.

[1] Technical terms are explained in a glossary at the end of the chapter. The terms that appear in the glossary are followed by an asterisk when they are first used in the text.

## 5.2 Genetic diversity before the Austronesian era

The current scientific consensus is that modern humans arose in Africa around 300,000 years ago (300kya*) (Hublin et al. 2017), before dispersing around 70kya to settle throughout the world. Increasing genetic and archaeological evidence suggests the possibility of multiple dispersals out of Africa by early modern humans, which has caused debate among scholars, with some arguing that this may simply result from bias in data analysis (Pagani et al. 2016; Bae et al. 2017; O'Connell et al. 2018). Regardless, dating of early archaeological sites indicates that these first travellers probably arrived in, and spread across, Island Southeast Asia within just a few thousand years (O'Connell et al. 2018), creating, in the process, an ancient genetic layer that is still easily observable in the region today.

### 5.2.1 Island Southeast Asia hosts multiple major genetic ancestries

A key overarching feature of Island Southeast Asia is the distribution of two major genetic ancestries, Papuan and Asian. Distribution frequencies vary considerably between islands, and a west–east cline in the proportion of the two ancestries is clearly observable (Abdulla et al. 2009; Xu et al. 2012; Hudjashov et al. 2017). The Papuan component can be traced back to the first anatomically modern humans who arrived in Sunda (the ancient Asian land mass that extended eastward to Borneo and Bali) and Sahul (the land mass to the east comprising modern New Guinea, Australia, and Tasmania). Papuan ancestry reaches its highest

François-Xavier Ricaut, Nicolas Brucato, and Murray P. Cox, *Human genetic approaches to Malayo-Polynesian prehistory*. In: *The Oxford Guide to the Malayo-Polynesian Languages of Southeast Asia*. Edited by: Alexander Adelaar and Antoinette Schapper, Oxford University Press. © François-Xavier Ricaut, Nicolas Brucato, and Murray P. Cox (2024).
DOI: 10.1093/oso/9780198807353.003.0005

frequency today in eastern Indonesia, New Guinea, and Australia, but is essentially absent west of the Wallace line. This absence reflects the fact that the islands of Wallacea, the vast archipelago between Sunda and Sahul, were always separated by deep water straits from Sunda and Sahul, thus forming a barrier against migrating fauna and flora, and often slowing down human migration, with the notable exception of modern humans who settled >50kya in Sahul, and possibly some archaic hominins (Clarkson et al. 2017; Jacobs et al. 2019). This geography, mediated by Wallace's bio-geographical line, shaped human genetic diversity in the region until much later climatic changes, such as rising sea levels, and drove human responses in the Holocene*, such as the development of new maritime technologies.

The second main genetic component was thought to result from the much later Neolithic* expansion of Austronesian-speaking farmers (6–4kya) from Mainland Asia and/or Taiwan into Island Southeast Asia and the Pacific (Gray et al. 2009; Ko et al. 2014; Bellwood 2017). However, this two-layer settlement model—an initial spread in the late Pleistocene* and a subsequent mid-Holocene 'out-of-Taiwan' expansion (Bellwood 1997)—is often the lens through which the prehistory of this region is interpreted. Thus genetic variation is often categorized either as autochthonous, meaning the first 'Papuan' settlement of the region, or a later Asian input usually interpreted as 'Austronesian' (Friedlaender et al. 2008; Kayser et al. 2008).

### 5.2.2 Regional settlement was complex

This simple model has been challenged, and today a much more complex picture has emerged, broadly supporting an Austronesian population origin in Taiwan and the Philippines, but without large scale population replacement related to its dispersal across all areas of Island Southeast Asia. Instead, the regional genetic landscape was also shaped by rising sea levels at the end of the last glacial maximum (18–7kya), which is proposed to have been an important driver of human mobility across the region during the late Pleistocene (Solheim et al. 2006; Karafet et al. 2010; Soares et al. 2011, 2016).

New analyses of uniparental markers on the mtDNA and Y chromosomes, coupled with autosomal* marker sets, and whole genome sequences, suggest several settlement phases for Island Southeast Asia and New Guinea (see Figure 5.1).

#### 5.2.2.1 *After the Out of Africa expansion*

The arrival of the first settlers in Island Southeast Asia >50kya (Westaway et al. 2017) left a genetic signal that

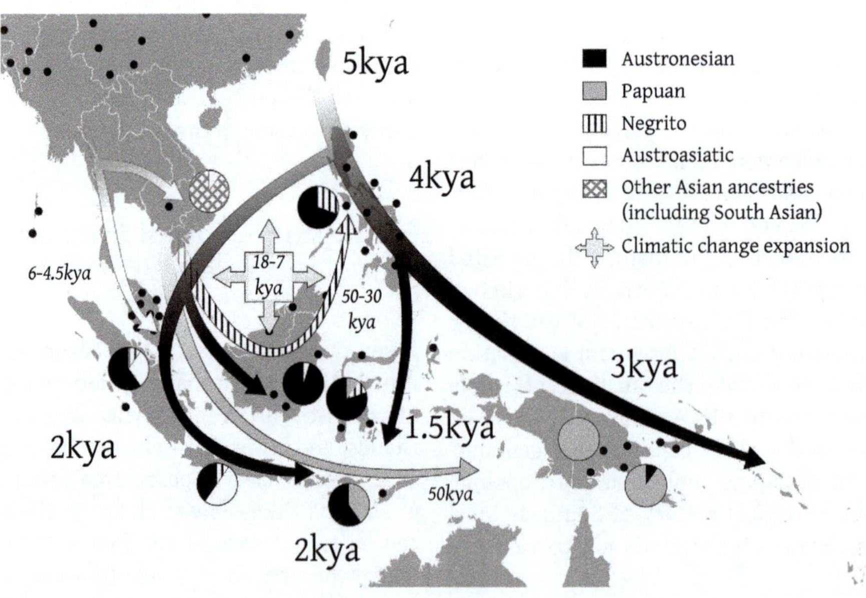


**Figure 5.1** Approximate genetic mixture proportions between the Austronesian genetic component and other genetic components for populations across Island Southeast Asia.

is still visible in modern populations from the Andaman Islands, Negritos* in the Philippines and Malaysia, New Guineans and Indigenous Australians (Mallick et al. 2016; Brzozowska et al. 2019). These first settlers were phenotypically Australo-Papuan and were once distributed much more widely across Island Southeast Asia than today (Howells 1976), as attested by the 'deep skull' from Niah Cave in Borneo (Krigbaum and Datan 2005). These first settlers met and interbred with the archaic hominins they encountered en route. Consequently, the genomes of modern Island Southeast Asian populations contain high proportions of archaic ancestry in their genomes: from Neanderthals in western Eurasia (typically 2–4%; Sankararaman et al. 2014), admixture with Denisovans in Southeast Asia (2–6% in Negritos from the Philippines, New Guineans and Indigenous Australians, and <1% in South and East Asian groups; Reich et al. 2011; Jacobs et al. 2019), and likely with two unknown hominin groups (<1% in Island Southeast Asian populations), possibly even including some *Homo erectus* lineages present in Island Southeast Asia (e.g. *Homo floresiensis)* (Teixeira and Cooper 2019). The biological advantages of archaic hominin genes are attested in some Asian populations: examples include the gene variant that allows modern Tibetans to survive the high altitudes of the Himalayas, which derives from Denisovans (Huerta-Sánchez et al. 2014), and archaic variants of genes allowing immunity and dietary adaptations in the eastern groups of Island Southeast Asia (Jacobs et al. 2019). The human genome is thus a mosaic formed from repeated mixing events with other human-like species.

The first modern human settlers into Island Southeast Asia also introduced genetic lineages still present to the region today, representing 30% of the modern Y chromosome lineages. These lineages are mostly in the basal C and K haplogroups*, and their downstream branching lineages M and S, as well as mitochondrial DNA lineages (P, Q, S, O, M21, M73, M47, N21, R14, and further unresolved M* and R* clades), which today have a spotty distribution across both Mainland and Island Southeast Asia west of the Wallace line (Karafet et al. 2010; Tumonggor et al. 2013; Soares et al. 2016). Interestingly, in contrast to mtDNA, many early male lineages remain at appreciable frequencies in Island Southeast Asia, reflecting either later expansions during the Pleistocene (broadly from 30 to 12kya) that occurred well after the initial settlement period (Karafet et al. 2010;Tumonggor et al. 2013), and/or a higher resilience of certain male lineages.

#### 5.2.2.2 *Climate change during the last glacial maximum and the postglacial period*

These events led to a rise in sea levels (18–7kya) stimulating the dispersal of Sunda populations. Almost half of all available land was lost, and more than 25,000 islands appeared, driving the emergence of more maritime-orientated cultures in Island Southeast Asia (Solheim et al. 2006). These dispersals within the southeast of Sunda (today Mainland Southeast Asia, Sumatra, Java, and Borneo) and from there across all of Mainland and Island Southeast Asia included 40 to 50% of all mtDNA and Y chromosome lineages observed in the region today (Soares et al. 2016). For example, during this period, some lineages moved from Mainland Asia southward to Island Southeast Asia (mtDNA haplogroups B5b1, N9a, and R9b; and Y haplogroups O2a1, O3, and O1a) (Brandão et al. 2016; Soares et al. 2016) in agreement with the spread of Hoabinhian* culture from Mainland Southeast Asia into Sumatra (Bellwood 2017), and likely reflecting multiple population movements of hunter-gatherers. Ancient DNA now also supports the idea of Asian ancestry in western Island Southeast Asia during the late Pleistocene (Lipson et al. 2018; McColl et al. 2018). The expansion of the ancestor haplogroup (B4a1a) of the so-called 'Polynesian motif'* (popularly named for its high frequency among Polynesians) followed the same route. Its spread began sometime in the last 20–10kya from Mainland Southeast Asia and reached Near Oceania including the Bismarck Archipelago 10–8kya, where the 'Polynesian motif' was well established by the mid-Holocene (around 6kya) (Soares et al. 2008, 2011), before it expanded eastward into the Pacific, and westward into East Indonesia and later Madagascar. Other data support gene flow from Island Southeast Asia toward the Philippines and Taiwan, as evidenced by autosomal genome-wide data (Abdulla et al. 2009) and mtDNA lineages (haplogroup E; Soares et al. 2008) within the last 8,000 years, but possibly predating the Neolithic. The exact time frames for these contacts are still open to debate, but the presence of a Mainland Southeast Asian genetic substrate in Island Southeast Asia, pre-dating the Austronesian dispersal, is now well attested and dated to the late Pleistocene or very early Holocene (Karafet et al. 2010; Jinam et al. 2012; Vallée et al. 2016).

#### 5.2.2.3 *An initial mid-Holocene (~6-4.5kya) small scale migration from Mainland Southeast Asia*

This event was probably related to Neolithic movements, and involved paddle-impressed ceramics and was possibly accompanied by Austroasiatic languages (Spriggs 2012). The migration had a genetic impact (5 to 30%) on much of western Island Southeast Asia, mainly on the Malay Peninsula, western Indonesia, and Borneo, with decreasing impact towards eastern Indonesia, a minor impact in the Philippines and was absent in Taiwan (Soares et al. 2016). For example, mtDNA haplogroups B5a1 and F1a1a, appear to have originated in Mainland Southeast Asia, and are rare or absent in both Taiwan and the Philippines. There is, however, limited archaeological and linguistic evidence for this contact in western Indonesia (Bellwood 2017). The presence of a Mainland Southeast Asian genetic substrate in Indonesia has been confirmed by ancient DNA studies (Lipson et al. 2018; McColl et al. 2018), as well as modern maternal (e.g. B5a1 and F1a1a) and paternal (e.g. O-M95) lineages and autosomal data (Karafet et al. 2010; Jinam et al. 2012; Lipson et al. 2014; Soares et al. 2016; Mörseburg et al. 2016; Hudjashov et al. 2017).

#### 5.2.2.4 *A second mid-Holocene Neolithic wave*

This wave archaeologically marked by red-slipped pottery in the initial phase, encompasses the proposed 'out-of-Taiwan' migration (Bellwood and Dizon 2008) from mainland China into Taiwan (8–6kya) and from Taiwan into the Philippines and Island Southeast Asia (from ~5kya), ultimately reaching farther west into the Pacific (2.5–1kya) and east across the Indian Ocean (1kya) (Brandão et al. 2016; Brucato et al. 2017; Hudjashov et al. 2017). These dispersals are discussed in the sections below.

Possible migration paths for the different genetic components into and through Island Southeast Asia since the arrival of the first modern humans >50 kya are shown. Five main ancestries can be identified. Two are related to indigenous population arrivals in Island Southeast Asia (>50 kya): Papuans ('Melanesians') (grey) in eastern Island Southeast Asia; and Negritos (dashed) in western Island Southeast Asia. Two are related to mid-Holocene dispersals of Asian populations: Mainland Southeast Asian or Austroasiatic speakers (white); and aboriginal Taiwanese/Philippines or Austronesian speakers (black). Other Asian ancestries are also shown (squares). (Modified from Lipson et al. 2014 and Hudjashov et al. 2017.)

## 5.3 Genetic signals of the Austronesian expansion

Malayo-Polynesian languages are found today across Island Southeast Asia (the Indonesian archipelago and Philippines), coastal areas of Mainland Southeast Asia, and the eastern African island of Madagascar. With nearly 400 million speakers worldwide, it is the most important Austronesian language subgroup. Linguistic, archaeological, and genetic evidence all point to Taiwan as the most likely origin of expanding Austronesian speakers, whose outward dispersal began 4.5–4kya (Bellwood et al. 1995; Gray et al. 2009; Ko et al. 2014). The Austronesian expansion spread rapidly across Island Southeast Asia, reaching the Philippines by 4–3.5kya and Borneo and Sulawesi by 3.5–3kya. Appearing in western Melanesia by 3.5–2.5kya, the settlement of the remote and previously uninhabited islands of the Pacific Ocean quickly followed (Bellwood 2017). Ultimately, the Austronesian expansion spread westward across the Indian Ocean to Madagascar and the Comoros a little before 1kya (Brucato et al. 2017). Simulation modelling suggests that Austronesian individuals with Asian genetic ancestry spread at a rate of ~4km/year (Vallée et al. 2016) in agreement with previous estimates from archaeology (3km/year; Bellwood et al. 1995), and language phylogenies (6.5km/year; Gray et al. 2009).

### 5.3.1 The transition to Neolithic lifestyles was complex

Although this broad-brush history is now well established and supported, multiple lines of evidence suggest that the Neolithic transition in Island Southeast Asia was more complex than a simple movement of genes, languages, and technology solely out of Taiwan. Debate has traditionally revolved around whether the Austronesian dispersal was primarily a movement of people, accompanied by admixture with local populations, or was instead driven by transfers of language, culture, and technology. Recent studies analysing genome-scale data and previous complementary uniparental marker studies, from hundreds of populations, have revealed several key points about these aspects of the Austronesian expansion.

The Neolithic dispersal from Taiwan significantly impacted the Philippines, accounting for 30–40% of current genetic diversity and all Philippine languages now being Austronesian languages, but it had a much lower, sometimes negligible, impact on the rest of Island Southeast Asia. Interestingly, this out-of-Taiwan genetic input into the Philippines is present in their paternal, maternal, and autosomal DNA, for most Filipino ethnolinguistic groups including the Negrito* groups. However, there are no clear patterns of sex-biased admixture, although more analysis still needs to be done (Abdulla et al. 2009; Delfin et al. 2011, 2014). Nonetheless, there is geographic structuring, in the Cordilleran-related (Austronesian) and Mainland Southeast Asian-based contributions to the ancestry of Negritos and non-Negrito Filipinos. The general pattern is that the northern ethnic groups have a higher proportion of Cordilleran-related ancestry (Austronesian), while the southern ethnic groups have a higher proportion of Mainland Southeast Asian-based ancestry. In the south, the coastal populations have a higher proportion of Cordilleran-related ancestry in contrast to the inland groups (Delfin et al. 2011, 2014; Maximilian Larena, p.c., 11 November 2019).

Filipino groups also appear to be genetically very heterogeneous based on their Y chromosome and mtDNA diversity, which could result from population isolation, genetic drift, and anthropological processes, such as the practices of patrilocality and matrilocality. Genetic relationships between Negrito and non-Negrito groups reveal some affinities based on autosomal DNA, but differences based on Y chromosome and mtDNA are best explained by isolation between these groups and limited recent admixture (Abdulla et al. 2009; Delfin et al. 2011). Some Negrito groups (e.g. the Mamanwa, Aeta, and Agta) harbour genetic traces from the initial settlement of the region, and genetic links with descendants from this initial colonization in Melanesia, Australia, and possibly South Asia (Y lineage C-M9 with Australia and Melanesia, mtDNA haplogroup P with Melanesia, and haplogroup N11b with South Asia) (Delfin et al. 2014), and post-colonization links from the Late Pleistocene (18–10kya) with South Asia (mtDNA haplogroup M52). Filipino groups have closer genetic affinity with populations in Southeast Asia and Taiwan and more ancient links with South Asia, Melanesia, and Australia.

Some maternal lineages (e.g. mtDNA haplogroups M7c3, D5, F1a, Y2a, B4b1) and paternal lineages (e.g. Y chromosome haplogroups O1a) have been identified as out-of-Taiwan markers (Karafet et al. 2010; Soares et al. 2016), and have a similar (20% or higher) frequency in Taiwan and the Philippines than in other Austronesian-speaking populations, a pattern also visible in the autosomal data (Mörseburg et al. 2016). The Austronesian genetic component in Taiwan/Philippines decreases by at least a third in the mtDNA, Y chromosome, and autosomal DNA of other Island Southeast Asian populations (Soares et al. 2016; Mörseburg et al. 2016), and no strong sex-biased admixture is observed in relation to the Austronesian expansion (i.e. there is no significant divergence in the male and female contribution across Island Southeast Asia). This may reflect low scale migration with a strong linguistic impact, with language shift playing the major role.

However, populations from the Philippines also made genetic contributions in early phases of the Austronesian expansion (Mörseburg et al. 2016; Hudjashov et al. 2017). Each admixed eastern Indonesian population today includes both a Philippine and western Indonesian-like source, likely representing Holocene movements of Asian farming groups (both Austronesian and Mainland Southeast Asian Neolithic), as well as contributions from populations representing local indigenous ancestry (genetically close to the Papuan genetic signature). One reason for the lack of clear Taiwanese sources may be because the aboriginal populations of Taiwan were heavily affected by post-Austronesian movements from mainland East Asia, and thus no longer represented the ancestral Austronesian gene pool, which may lie today in the Philippines, where groups such as the Kankanaey harbour genetic links to Taiwanese aboriginals and the highest genetic component generally associated with the Austronesian expansion (Mörseburg et al. 2016). This pattern might also be explained by the dominance of language and culture transfers during the early phases of the Neolithic expansion from Taiwan into the Philippines, followed by people with predominantly Philippine ancestry driving later demic diffusion into the Indonesian archipelago.

### 5.3.2 The Austronesian expansion was an extended process

Whereas the wave of Austronesian speakers from the Taiwan/Philippines region left a common genetic trace across the whole of eastern Indonesia, but was relatively small compared to the Philippines (Soares et al. 2016), the details and dates of this contact vary considerably not only between islands, such as Flores and Alor, but also within individual islands, such as the populations of Rampasasa and Bama on Flores. Genetic admixture times in eastern Indonesia between Papuan-like and western Indonesian/Philippines-like sources lie within a narrow timeframe of ~2kya, but suggest that it took migrants at least 500 years to travel from the islands around the Wallace line to the easternmost parts of eastern Indonesia and New Guinea. Dates for Austronesian genetic contact in eastern Indonesia are still approximately a millennium younger than the earliest Neolithic archaeological evidence from the region. This could reflect: i) either several waves of people leaving Taiwan or the Philippines, spanning multiple generations, which would bias date estimates later than the first arrival of the Neolithic archaeological assemblage (Sedghifar et al. 2015); or ii) there may have been a substantial time lag between the spread of culture and technological traditions, and the beginning of extensive genetic contacts between incoming farming groups and native inhabitants in Island Southeast Asia (Lansing et al. 2007), as has been observed in other regions with incoming Neolithic groups (Europe and Near Oceania) (Lipson et al. 2018; Malmström et al. 2015).

Interestingly, recent studies have identified at least three broad genomic classes that dominate the gene pool of Island Southeast Asian individuals: Papuan ancestry (dating from the initial settlement period >50kya); mainland Asian ancestry (from the late Pleistocene 30–10kya); and mid-Holocene Neolithic ancestries from Island (Taiwan/Philippines) and Mainland Southeast Asia (Lipson et al. 2014; Karafet et al. 2010; Jinam et al. 2012; Soares et al. 2016; Hudjashov et al. 2017). Analyses of isolated populations from Borneo, such as the Ma'anyan, have also identified a new genetic component (Kusuma et al. 2016a). This newly discovered ancestry occurs at low levels in many populations across Island Southeast Asia and retains ancient links to Austronesian diversity. This may reflect a complex picture of Austronesian ancestry and possible genetic signatures of the diffusion of two different Austronesian groups from Taiwan (possibly related to cultural groups linked to cord-marked and red-slipped pottery materials) (Spriggs 2007). This needs to be investigated further.

### 5.3.3 The Austronesian expansion into the Indian and Pacific Oceans was associated with the Polynesian motif

The most famous Austronesian genetic signal is perhaps the mtDNA lineage called the 'Polynesian motif' (B4a1a1a) and related forms, as a marker for tracing the late-Holocene expansion of Austronesian-speaking populations into the Pacific and the Indian Oceans (see also §5.2.2.2). The current view is that the Polynesian motif arose about 6kya, perhaps in the Bismarck Archipelago east of New Guinea, from where it dispersed more widely as part of later population movements (Soares et al. 2011). The Polynesian motif is largely restricted to the east of the Wallace line, from eastern Indonesia (up to 7.4% in Timor) to the Pacific islands (where it approaches fixation* in some populations), with only sporadic occurrences further west (e.g. in Bali and Borneo) (Cox et al. 2012; Tumonggor et al. 2013; Kusuma et al. 2015). Curiously, a variant of the Polynesian motif called the 'Malagasy motif' (B4a1a1b; Razafindrazaka et al. 2010) is a key genetic marker of the westward Austronesian expansion into the Indian Ocean. It is exceptionally common in Malagasy populations (13–50%; Razafindrazaka et al. 2010; Cox et al. 2012; Pierron et al. 2017), is likely to be present in the Comoros (Msaidie et al. 2011; Mazières et al. 2018), and has been detected in individuals from East Africa and the Arabian Peninsula (Brucato et al. 2019).

Single locus (mtDNA and Y chromosome) and genome-wide genetic data support the view that the spread of Neolithic red-slipped pottery and Austronesian languages in Island Southeast Asia was accompanied by seafarers dispersing from the vicinity of Taiwan. Beyond the Philippines, however, the primary mechanism for their spread was probably more often acculturation, at least in later periods of the Austronesian spread. Current analyses support a scenario in which language shifts played the major role, rather than large-scale population replacement (see §5.4; Donohue and Denham 2010). Subsequently, different, but interrelated processes, acted in the east and west. The Austronesian migration took several centuries to spread across the eastern part of the archipelago, where genetic admixture* postdates the archaeological signal. In contrast, western Indonesia has a more complicated admixture history shaped by interactions with mainland Asian and Austronesian newcomers, which for some populations occurred more than once.

### 5.3.4 Social behaviours and demographic drivers

As should now be evident, genetics is providing an increasingly detailed picture of population movements from mainland Asia, through Island Southeast Asia, and out into the Pacific during the farming revolution. Equally, however, critical aspects of this process remain poorly understood. A key example is how social behaviours interacted with demographic drivers to create the patterns of genetic diversity observed across Island Southeast Asia today.

Some analyses based on mtDNA, Y chromosome, and autosomal data do not support highly divergent Austronesian genetic contributions into Island Southeast Asia from male and female sources (Soares et al. 2016). However, a growing body of data (Cox et al. 2010; Hage & Marck 2003) shows that Asian DNA variants appear more frequently on female sex-linked parts of the genome. Recent computer modelling to quantify human movements across Island Southeast Asia with a focus on Asian-Papuan genetic ancestry (Vallée et al. 2016) was performed using genetic variation in 2,299 individuals from eighty-four populations across Island Southeast Asia, spanning Taiwan in the north, Sumatra in the west, and New Guinea in the east (Cox et al. 2010; Karafet et al. 2010; Tumonggor et al. 2014; Wilder et al. 2011; Tumonggor et al. 2013). The results suggest that observed genetic patterns are best explained by elevated birth rates as one driver behind the expansion of individuals with Asian ancestry, when marriage was more strongly favoured between Asian women and Papuan men, or alternately, that the children of such marriages had a social or biological advantage. The cause of this bias is unknown, but it is nonetheless a strikingly important, if poorly understood, feature of Island Southeast Asian prehistory.

However, while acknowledging that migration and fecundity had an important role in population expansion and admixture, some of these approaches may not always differentiate among the different Asian ancestries present in Island Southeast Asia since late Pleistocene. Clarifying sex-biased admixture for the different genetic ancestries is a matter of ongoing inquiry.

## 5.4 Links between gene–language associations at large and small scales

Many studies have noted strong associations between genes and languages at a global scale (Cavalli-Sforza et al. 1988; Nettle 2007), but ultimately, all of these large gene–language patterns must arise from processes that occur at the level of communities. Diamond and Bellwood (2003) proposed that the linked spread of prehistoric farmers and their languages caused many of these correlations. In its simplest form, their model proposes that genetic and linguistic variation co-evolves as the genes and languages of farmers replace those of the hunter-gatherers they encounter.

Of course, discrepancies between genetic and linguistic patterns can easily arise in many different ways (Chen et al. 1995), including genetic admixture without language change or language replacement (Posth et al. 2018). These and related processes occur whenever migrating farmers meet resident hunter-gatherers, including the expansion of Austronesian speakers into regions long occupied by indigenous populations, particularly in eastern Indonesia and New Guinea. However, gene–language studies typically sample at geographic scales that are too coarse to analyse these contact zones.

### 5.4.1 Language and genetics correlate even over small geographical distances

Lansing et al. (2007) undertook perhaps the only small-scale gene–language study in Island Southeast Asia, focusing on the eastern Indonesian island of Sumba. Sumba is a useful case study system because it is remote and remains culturally conservative. Contact between villages is limited and population sizes are low. Because of this history, a large number of languages are spoken on the island relative to its small size (220 x 75km).

Analysing 200-word Swadesh lists using traditional comparative linguistic approaches to identify cognates, this study found that, on average, ~35% of the Swadesh lexicon descends directly from Proto-Austronesian (PAn). The island's languages cluster into five subgroups, with comparative linguistic analysis strongly supporting an origin of Sumbanese languages from a single ancestral Austronesian language, Proto-Sumba. 352 men from eight villages were genotyped for seventy-one Y chromosome markers, and seventeen Y chromosome haplogroups were identified. A statistically significant correlation was found between linguistic and genetic distances ($r = 0.36$, $P = 0.023$), the first time such a pattern had been identified over such a small geographical area. To verify that this association emerged within the time frame of the Austronesian expansion, Lansing et al. (2007) estimated the divergence time of the two most geographically distant communities, Rindi and Kodi, using an isolation-with-migration coalescent simulation model. The upper limit of the 95% confidence interval was 4,875 years, consistent with the Austronesian expansion.

### 5.4.2 Language and genetic change are co-dominant

Focusing just on the Austronesian genetic components of the Sumba study, a positive correlation was found between the percentages of Austronesian-associated haplogroup O and retained PAN cognates in the eight villages ($r = 0.627$, $P = 0.047$). The most likely explanation is that intermarriage between expanding farmers and existing local residents led to progressively lower frequencies of Austronesian-associated haplogroup O Y chromosomes and PAN cognates at increasing distances from the founding island source population. Rather than elite dominance, where a few individuals can impose their language on a resident population, the retention of PAN lexicon is instead governed simply by the proportion of men present in the population with Austronesian paternal ancestry.

Similar small-scale gene–language associations have since been identified on Timor (Lansing et al. 2017), suggesting that they may be a general feature of eastern Indonesia. These patterns imply that social interactions between expanding farmers and resident hunter-gatherers may largely explain community-level language evolution during the Neolithic expansion. While more commonly viewed from a mile-high regional lens, the Austronesian expansion ultimately played out at the village level. Whether the co-evolution processes described here can explain gene–language patterns observed at continental scales remains an open question, as these studies on Sumba and

Timor are the most detailed investigations undertaken so far. It is likely, however, that similar processes occurred across other Austronesian/non-Austronesian contact zones, such as in New Guinea, and during later periods, Madagascar.

## 5.5 Later Austronesian movements within and beyond Island Southeast Asia

From around 6kya, the development of long distance seafaring technologies placed Island Southeast Asia at the centre of new maritime corridors that crossed vast swaths of two oceans: the Indian Ocean to the west, and the Pacific Ocean to the east (Beaujard 2012; Fuller et al. 2011; Lawler 2014). These contacts have contributed to the genetic diversity of Island Southeast Asian populations by: (i) driving the exchange of goods, ideas, cultures, and people around the Indo-Pacific region; and (ii) stimulating the emergence of sea-oriented peoples who acted as regional links between populations with different genomic backgrounds.

### 5.5.1 Historical trading networks influenced Asian gene flow within Island Southeast Asia and beyond

Genetic admixture patterns of around 200 populations from Island Southeast Asia and the Indian Ocean rim were reconstructed from genomic data, and reveal a close association between bouts of human migration and trade volumes during the last 2,000 years (Brucato et al. 2017). Temporal oscillations in trading activity match: (i) phases of contraction and expansion in migration and population admixture; (ii) major expansions following the expansion of the Silk Roads in the fifth century AD; (iii) the rise of maritime routes in the eleventh century CE; and (iv) a drastic restructuring of the trade network following the arrival of Europeans in the sixteenth century AD. The economic fluxes of the Indian Ocean trade network therefore directly shaped genetic exchange, the most striking example being Asian gene flow to Madagascar and the Comoros at the end of the first millennium AD (see §5.5.4) (Brucato et al. 2016, 2017). This represents the only major Asian gene flow identified on the western rim of the Indian Ocean, while minor and recent (nineteenth century AD) Asian contributions have been detected in East Africa and South Arabia, suggesting that Asian gene flow across the Indian Ocean was part of a lengthy process (Brucato et al. 2019). Other genetic admixture events among populations were detected during this period (second to sixteenth centuries AD) but only took place within Island Southeast Asia itself.

### 5.5.2 South Asia influenced Island Southeast Asia during the historic period

One of the main genetic influences in Island Southeast Asia during the historic period came from western Eurasia—India and later the Near East—from the first century BC to the sixteenth century AD (Lawler 2014). This influence, in the form of cultural and trading networks, became widespread in Island Southeast Asia, where Hindu Malay Empires, such as Śrīvijaya and Majapahit, reigned over large parts of the region. Genomic analysis of Island Southeast Asian populations (>3,000 individuals) show that the Indian subcontinent is the main modern genetic contributor to the Island Southeast Asian gene pool, and its genetic signature is also found in Mainland Southeast Asia (Malay and Burmese). In Island Southeast Asia, it impacted over 40% of populations. These events are genetically dated as starting around 400BC (Mörseburg et al. 2016), and potentially as early as 2000BC (Pugach et al. 2013), with a midpoint during the period of the Hindu kingdoms in Indonesia (seventh to sixteenth century AD) (Kusuma et al. 2016b). Frequency distributions of western Eurasian genetic variants show a sex biased admixture pattern, with western Eurasian paternal lineages (e.g. R1a1a, R2a) found more commonly (4.5%) than western Eurasian maternal lineages (1.5%), probably due to a male bias in trading activities. The highest frequency of western Eurasian Y chromosome lineages is observed in Sulawesi (Bajau, 26%), Java (15%), and Bali (11%), and for western Eurasian mtDNA in Gayo (13%), Pantar (10%), and Java (8%). Further, the origins of these paternal lineages are more diverse than the corresponding maternal lineages, predominantly tracing back to Southwest and South Asia, and the Indian subcontinent, respectively. Indianized kingdoms in Island Southeast Asia likely played a major role in dispersing western Eurasian lineages because these kingdoms geographically overlap with the current distribution of individuals carrying western Eurasian genetic markers (Karafet et al. 2010; Pugach et al. 2013; Kusuma et al. 2016b; Mörseburg et al. 2016).

### 5.5.3 Sea nomads are a modern proxy for early Austronesian expansions

Within this broader regional context, several human groups in Island Southeast Asia have long maintained a sea-oriented way of life, often based on fishing (maritime hunter-gatherers) and facilitators of interregional trade. These groups are perhaps the best modern proxy to understand the earlier dispersal of Austronesian groups across Island Southeast Asia. The well-known examples of sea nomads are the Urak Lawoi'—a Malay-speaking population based around the islands of southern Thailand, the Moken—an Austronesian-speaking group located in peninsular Burma and southern Thailand, and the Bajau—another Austronesian speaking group. The latter is the biggest of the three with over one million people scattered along the coast of Sabah in Malaysia, the southern Philippines and Indonesia (Sopher 1977; Nuraini 2008). Before European sailors began venturing into Southeast Asia, the Bajau were involved in long distance maritime trading networks, reaching Singapore in the west, and as far as New Guinea and northern Australia to the east (Nuraini 2008). Genomic analysis of several Bajau communities from Sulawesi, and south and north Borneo, has depicted a complex genetic history involving creolization and multiple admixture events starting in the fourth century AD. For instance, the Bajau from Sulawesi resulted from an admixture between ancestral Bugis (90%) and a Papuan group (10%) (Kusuma et al. 2017). The Bajau communities appeared to be a genetically distinct group with genetic influences from western and eastern Indonesia, and even beyond (South Asian and Papuan), but with a single ultimately shared population origin converging on southern Sulawesi. However, linguistic and genetic evidence points to quite different locations for the Bajau origin: in southern Sulawesi for the gene pool, and in southeast Borneo for the languages. This may result from the expanding influence of the Malay Kingdom of Śrīvijaya from the seventh century AD onward, which modified population structures and interactions in southeast Borneo and triggered population movements, such as the likely migration of Banjarese people to Madagascar (Kusuma et al. 2016a; Brucato et al. 2016).

The complexity of the Bajau genomic profile provides a striking reflection of their history, mediated by both migratory and local admixture events. All Bajau communities share a common culture and genetic heritage, but experienced sex biased gene flow from populations surrounding them (in general, men from other groups married women from within the Bajau population). A similar pattern is also observed in other sea nomad populations in Southeast Asia, such as the Moken (Dancause et al. 2009). This genetic structure is in part due to a process of maritime creolization (Nagatsu 2013), whereby populations exhibit closer genetic connections with neighbouring groups than distant Bajau populations.

Finally, some Bajau groups from southeast Borneo are among the few populations west of the Wallace line to carry a genetic input also found in the Malagasy (Pierron et al. 2017), but which likely traces its ancestry to New Guinea or eastern Indonesia (e.g. Y chromosome haplogroup M1a and mtDNA haplogroups Q1 and B4a1a1) (Kusuma et al. 2015, 2017). This suggests that, while still unresolved, the Bajau may have played a role in the Indonesian settlement of Madagascar (Kusuma et al. 2015, 2017).

### 5.5.4 Crossing the Indian Ocean to Madagascar

At the dawn of the second millennium AD, the existing Indian Ocean maritime network was expanding and intensifying, connecting the Austronesian world to major new territories, including Madagascar and the Comoros (Beaujard 2005). Located 500km east of continental Africa and 6,000km from Southeast Asia, the current inhabitants of these islands are the direct descendants of one of the most remarkable migrations in human history, still wrapped up in mystery as it is not attested by any written source and archaeological studies remain elusive.

#### 5.5.4.1 *Austronesians left a genetic legacy in East Africa*

A human presence on Madagascar seems to have occurred more than 3kya, at least transiently, but no connection to Southeast Asia can be made at that stage (Hansford et al. 2018). The earliest presence of permanent settlements on Madagascar and the Comoros is indicated by archaeological analyses of ancient crop remains dated around the end of the first millennium, which reveal that Asian species, such as rice, dominated agricultural subsistence from the early stages of settlement on these islands (Crowther et al. 2016). On the African continent and nearby coastal islands, Asian crops are only identified in minor proportions, suggesting that Southeast Asian cultures were only limited to these two insular territories and not more widely spread.

Currently, inhabitants of Madagascar speak Malagasy, which is a West Malayo-Polynesian language in the Austronesian language family. It is related to languages spoken in the Southeast Barito region of Borneo, such as the one spoken by the Ma'anyan. The Ma'anyan are an indigenous ethnic group representing approximately 70,000 individuals today, cultivating dry rice on shifting fields, but also gathering forest products. They do not exhibit any particular mastery of seafaring technologies or navigational knowledge, raising questions about how a closely related language travelled across the vast Indian Ocean and came to be spoken in Madagascar (Kusuma et al. 2016a). Moreover, the genetic composition of the Ma'anyan tends to weakly coincide with the genetic patrimony of Malagasy and Comorian populations.

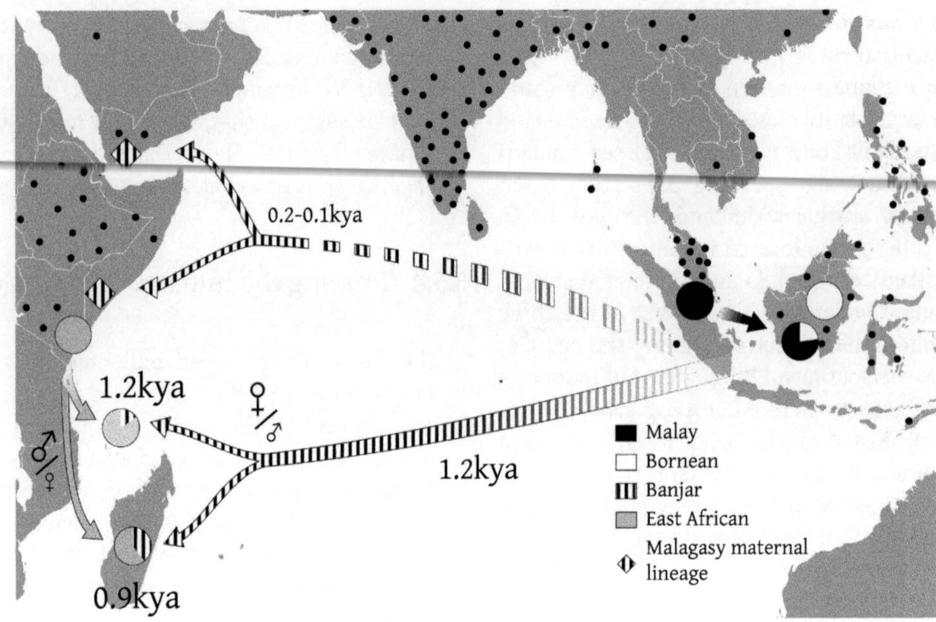


**Figure 5.2** Model scenario to explain Asian genetic ancestry in the offshore African Islands of Madagascar and the Comoros.

*Notes*: Black dots highlight other populations included in the high density genomic data set. Sex-biased gene flow is represented by male and female symbols. The arrows show migration events, with indicative routes, and dates are inferred from genetic admixture and coalescence analyses. (Modified from Brucato et al. 2016, 2018 and Cox et al. 2012.)

The Austronesian genetic inheritance accounts for 10% of the Comorian genome and 35% of the Malagasy genome, the rest coming from East African Bantu groups (Brucato et al. 2018; Pierron et al. 2014) (see Figure 5.2). Considerable variation is present in Madagascar since the Austronesian component can reach up to 74% in groups located in the central highlands, such as the Merina, but it is nonetheless homogenous in its characteristics, meaning that all individuals share the same Austronesian component (Pierron et al. 2017). This suggests that the Austronesian genetic inheritance in all these islands came from one unique source and spread rapidly across the territory. A clear example is represented by the discovery of the mtDNA haplotype named the 'Malagasy motif' (B4a1a1b) (Razafindrazaka et al. 2010). It branches off from the phylogenetic lineage of the Polynesian motif, as previously mentioned, and represents up to 21% of all Malagasy maternal lineages. Despite being present in such high proportions across the island, very few different haplotypes have been detected, strongly indicating a rapid expansion from a common origin (Pierron et al. 2017). The Malagasy motif is accompanied by other Austronesian maternal lineages accounting for up to 50% of the total Malagasy maternal background. Based on this mtDNA diversity, simulations favour a scenario in which Madagascar was settled approximately 1,200 years ago, a date which corresponds to linguistic evidence showing that migrations were post-seventh century AD (Adelaar 1989). The number of migrants was very small, including possibly as few as thirty women (Cox et al. 2012). This fairly low estimated number supports the possibility that the settlement of Madagascar was not part of a large-scale planned settlement from Indonesia, but rather a small and perhaps even unique transoceanic crossing.

### 5.5.4.2 *Migration from southeast Borneo was rapid*

It might be thought that Madagascar and the Comoros archipelago represent a large and diverse region from an ecological and cultural perspective, but whole genome analysis shows that both populations share the same Austronesian genetic background (Brucato et al. 2018). This information was insufficient to determine whether the Austronesian genome arrived first on one of the two islands, but it did reveal that the admixture process with the African genome occurred first in the Comoros (see Figure 5.2). The earliest detected admixture event in Madagascar occurred during the late eleventh century AD in groups located on the easternmost coast of the island (Pierron et al. 2017). This postdates the earliest date of admixture in the Comoros, which is estimated to have occurred in the eighth century AD for the Anjouan community, an eastern island in the archipelago. These dates coincide broadly with the time frame of Austronesian settlement in each region as inferred from linguistic (Adelaar 1989) and archaeological data (Crowther et al. 2016). For example, analyses of ancient crop remains suggest older dates for Asian crops in the Comoros (eighth–eleventh centuries AD) compared to Madagascar (eleventh–thirteenth centuries AD) (Crowther et al. 2016). More archaeological and genetic data from the north of Madagascar, where Austronesians are thought to have first settled on the island, are currently lacking to ground this conclusion, but it is remarkable that genetic and archaeological analyses broadly converge chronologically by pointing to the Comoros as the earliest presence of Austronesians in the East Africa region.

Outside these two territories, the Austronesian legacy is almost absent. The Malagasy motif is only found in three of 14,461 individuals from around the Indian Ocean rim, in three Somalian and south Yemeni individuals whose whole genomes suggest that their maternal inheritance comes from a recent secondary contact with Malagasy or Indonesians (Brucato et al. 2019) (see Figure 5.2). The absence of the Malagasy motif in coastal populations coincides with the fact that no Austronesian gene flow to the western rim of the Indian Ocean was inferred when analysing whole genomes from 187 coastal populations (Brucato et al. 2017). Coastal stops during the migration may still have occurred, but did not leave detectable genetic traces in modern populations. Simulations based on detailed oceanographic, wind, and climatic data have determined that, depending on seasonal weather, a direct route from northern Indonesia to the Comoros and Madagascar, as well as in the reverse direction, is feasible (Fitzpatrick and Callaghan 2008). This coincides with linguistic evidence on Malagasy language showing no evidence of multiple migration layers (Adelaar 2009a, 2009b, 2016a; Simon 2006). For example, Sanskrit words in Malagasy are more likely to have first been borrowed into Malay before being passed on to Malagasy, rather than through direct contacts with Indian costal groups during the migration (Adelaar 1989). These multiple lines of evidence indicate that the route of migration to Madagascar and the Comoros was rapid and direct.

#### 5.5.4.3 *Who were the first Malagasy?*

The phylogenetically closest maternal lineages to the Malagasy motif—the Polynesian motif—are more frequently found in remote Oceania, far from the expected location in Borneo based on linguistic data. Linguistically, the closest language to Malagasy is the Ma'anyan, spoken by a southeast Bornean group (Dahl 1951). But when studied genetically, this population has a composition that does not fully correspond to the Austronesian legacy found in Malagasy and the Comoros (Kusuma et al. 2016a). This disjunction between genetic and linguistic data points towards a more complex settlement scenario.

Relative to the genetic diversity of thirty-five Island Southeast Asian populations, the Austronesian component of the genomes of Malagasy and Comorian groups is closely related to the Banjarese, another southeast Bornean population (Brucato et al. 2016). Currently the Banjarese speak a Malay dialect, but genetically they are the descendants of an admixture event between Malay and Ma'anyan individuals (see Figure 5.2). The Banjarese are thus a population with composite ethnic ancestry that emerged from the long-standing presence of Malays in Borneo, creating an admixed community with local Austronesian-speaking groups speaking languages closely related to Ma'anyan. Established on the islands of Sumatra and Java, Hindu Malay Kingdoms such as Śrīvijaya (sixth–thirteenth centuries AD) (Beaujard 2012) traded with far-distant regions, notably with East African populations. They extended their influence across all of the Southeast Asian islands, including in Borneo where they established several trading posts, such as one in the city of Banjarmasin in southeast Borneo (Beaujard 2012; Ras 1968). As related in the only Banjarese historical records available, the *Hikayat Banjar* ('Tale of Banjar') (Ras 1968), the main city of the Banjarese population was a major trading post in the former Malay Empire. This probably favoured interactions with inland groups in Borneo, such as peoples linguistically very closely related to the current Ma'anyan (Adelaar 2009b), but also with other populations such as the Bajau sea nomads (Beaujard 2012; Kusuma et al. 2015). Since the Banjarese originated from an admixture of Malays and groups whose language(s) were very closely related to Ma'anyan and other Southeast Barito languages at a time preceding the supposed date of migration to Madagascar and the Comoros (i.e. around 1,000 years ago), the ancestors of the Banjarese presumably still spoke a Southeast Barito language that was close to what can be reconstructed for Proto-Malagasy (Adelaar 2017). This scenario reconciles both the linguistic and genetic data, strengthening a scenario that places the Banjarese as the main Austronesian parental populations of the Malagasy and the Comorians.

The settlement of Madagascar occurred relatively recently, and the complexity of its settlement can therefore be reconstructed with some precision. Such reconstruction is naturally more challenging for older settlement processes. However, it is perhaps reasonable to assume that the spread of Austronesian speaking populations across Island Southeast Asia during the Neolithic proceeded in similarly complex ways. While Austronesian history is often presented in a simple form, in all likelihood it was an equally complex and multifaceted process.

## 5.6 Conclusions

Both linguistics and genetics take variation seen in the present and use it to extrapolate into the past. Due to this shared conceptual framework, each field has considerable potential to inform the other. Linguistic evidence, including the distribution and affinities of languages, can provide information that clarifies the reasons why certain patterns of genetic diversity emerged. Similarly, genetic evidence can inform and constrain hypotheses about past interactions between groups of language speakers. Fine-scale study of the co-evolution of linguistic and genetic diversity can lead to new insight into how communities of speakers engage and interact. Beyond the similarities, there are instances where genetic and linguistic evidence disagree. These are almost certainly exciting areas where population density, environment constraints, and social structures have interacted in non-standard or understudied ways. The extraordinary linguistic and genetic diversity of Island Southeast Asia presents a nearly unparalleled opportunity to investigate these questions. Many of the models that can be developed for Island Southeast Asia would be of considerable use to other regions and other language families, perhaps notably the farming expansions linked to the spread of Austroasiatic and the Trans-New Guinea languages, but equally many other systems around the world.

## 5.7 Glossary

**ABO blood group:** the ABO blood group system was discovered in 1901 by Karl Landsteiner, the first evidence that blood group variation exists in humans. A and B are antigens (proteins) on the surface of red blood cells. This defines four groups of individuals: those carrying the A antigen allele only, the B antigen allele only, both alleles (AB), or neither (O). Blood groups are inherited from both parents, like autosomal DNA, and due to variation in blood groups around world populations, they were the first genetic marker to be used to reconstruct human history.

**Allele:** one of potentially many alternative forms of a segment of DNA (such as a gene) at the same location on the chromosome. Alleles are distinguished by one or more mutations. The proportion of a given allele usually varies between different populations and its modern geographic distribution can inform on its place of origin and subsequent human movements.

**Autosomal DNA:** autosomal DNA is contained in the twenty-two pairs of chromosomes (autosomes) that are not involved in determining a person's sex (the X and Y chromosomes; mitochondrial DNA is also not considered autosomal). Autosomal DNA recombines each generation, and is inherited equally from both parents.

**DNA:** the informational macromolecule that encodes genetic information.

**Fixation:** the process by which one allele increases in a population until all other alleles go extinct and only that single allele remains.

**Genetic admixture:** the formation of a hybrid population (or individual) through the mixing of two genetically distinguishable populations (or parents). Admixture is determined statistically by the presence of different genetic ancestries in a population or individual. Caution is needed with interpretation, as it can be difficult to connect a given genetic ancestry with any specific historical event.

**Genetic drift:** the random change of allele frequencies in a population over time. Genetic drift has a particularly big effect on human groups with small population sizes.

**Genome:** the total content of genetic information in an organism, including the mitochondrial DNA, the X and Y sex chromosomes, and the autosomes.

**Haplogroup:** a group of closely related mtDNA or Y chromosome sequences that share a recent common ancestor, called the most recent common ancestor (MRCA). Mutations that accumulate along the DNA sequences allow relationships within and between mtDNA and Y chromosome lineages to be represented as a tree-like structure called a phylogenetic tree. Haplogroups often, but not always, have a geographically restricted distribution. Haplogroups are usually identified by a letter of the alphabet, in the order of their discovery, and refinements consist of additional number and letter combinations.

**Hoabinhian:** a term used to define the hunter-gatherer tradition (i.e. subsistence economy and lithic technology) of a population mostly located in Mainland Southeast Asia from around 44kya until the development of agriculture in the region around 5kya.

**Holocene:** the epoch following the Pleistocene, starting from 11.7kya and continuing to the present.

**Island Southeast Asia (ISEA):** a maritime region including Indonesia, Brunei, the East Malaysia region of Malaysia, Singapore, East Timor, the Philippines, and Taiwan.

**Kya:** thousand years ago.

**Mainland Southeast Asia (MSEA):** the region including the modern countries of Myanmar, Thailand, Peninsular Malaysia, Laos, Cambodia, and Vietnam, bordered by the Indian Ocean to the west and the Pacific Ocean to the east.

**Mitochondrial DNA (mtDNA):** mtDNA is a small circular piece of DNA contained in mitochondria (energy producing organelles), which occurs in thousands of copies per cell. Mitochondria and their DNA are maternally inherited, and all mtDNA types identified in living people thus far can be traced back to common matrilineal ancestor that lived approximatively 200kya in Africa. Currently ~5,400 major mtDNA types (haplogroups) have been identified (https://www.phylotree.org).

**Molecular clock:** the finding that mutations occur at a sufficiently regular rate to allow divergence between two sequences to be accurately related to the time those sequences split from a common ancestor. In other words, the divergence time between two sequences can be measured by the number of mutations accumulated between molecular sequences. A sophisticated body of statistical models, which have been extensively validated, are now available to apply this dating (Cox 2019).

**Negrito:** individuals who possess a pygmy phenotype (dark-skinned, small stature) and live in Southeast Asia and Oceania.

**Neolithic:** the period starting from the development of agriculture—around 12kya in the Near East—until the development of metal tools. The Neolithic period began at different times in different places around the world. In Island Southeast Asia, its start is usually associated with the arrival of the Austronesian cultural complex around 5kya.

**Pleistocene:** the geological epoch between ~2.5 million years ago and 11.7kya. The end of the Pleistocene corresponds with the end of the last glacial period.

**Polynesian motif:** a mitochondrial DNA sequence with a specific set of mutations that is found at its highest frequencies in Polynesian populations, but which originated in Island Southeast Asia. A closely related lineage is found in Madagascar.

**Y chromosome:** the male-specific sex chromosome, which is passed solely along the patrilineal line, from father to son. The portion of the Y chromosome that does not recombine with the X chromosome is used to define haplogroups and to study human genetic history. The patrilineal ancestor of all Y chromosome lineages found in people today is estimated to have lived ~240kya in Africa. Currently more than 420 major Y chromosome types (haplogroups) have been identified (https://www.phylotree.org/Y).

CHAPTER 6

# Archaeological correlations for the dispersal of the Malayo-Polynesian languages of Southeast Asia, western Micronesia, and Madagascar

Hsiao-chun Hung and Peter Bellwood

## 6.1 Introduction

Today, Austronesian (AN) languages are spoken by almost 400 million people in Southeast Asia (SEA), the Pacific Islands, and Madagascar. AN was the most widespread language family in the world prior to the sixteenth century, and the dispersal of its major Malayo-Polynesian (MP) subgroup, which encompasses all AN-speaking regions outside Taiwan, from Madagascar to Easter Island, represents one of the most fascinating episodes of migration in the history of mankind. This chapter discusses the prehistory behind the MP languages of Southeast Asia, western Micronesia, and Madagascar, from the perspective of the archaeological record.

In order to understand the history of MP dispersal, it is necessary to compare historical perspectives from at least four independent disciplines: comparative linguistics, archaeology, genetics, and human skeletal anthropology. Only the last two deal directly with the biology of human migration. However, comparative linguistics can theoretically provide powerful support to a biological scenario if the assumption is made that the initial spread of a major language family such as AN occurred with a spread of its speakers.

In this chapter, the authors make this assumption, rather than spread by language shift alone, without population movement. This is partly because of corroborating genetic and biological evidence for an AN population migration, despite the obvious reality of admixture with pre-existing non-AN populations, especially in the islands that lie close to New Guinea (see Ricaut, Brucato, and Cox, chapter 5, this volume).

In this regard, we acknowledge that frequent adoption of MP languages by former Papuan (or non-AN) speakers might have occurred in the eastern regions of Island SEA (Donohue and Denham 2010), leading to considerable quantities of contact-induced change. However, these adoptions caused the MP language expansion process to terminate rather than to continue further. Language shift can only spread a language or language family if the people who have undertaken the shift then migrate onwards. MP languages were never established permanently in Australia or along the New Guinea coastline south of the Bird's Head in precolonial times, and this suggests that their speakers admixed with non-AN populations in the Moluccas and Lesser Sundas, and remained thereafter in place. In genetic terms, this eastern Indonesian admixture between MP and Papuan populations commenced between 3,000 and 2,000 years ago, as we discuss below.

In the remainder of this chapter, it will be assumed that the AN languages spread hand in hand from Taiwan into Island SEA with migrations of their early speakers, who carried a material and economic culture that can be recognized in the record of archaeology. This scientific discipline provides information on chronology, material culture, subsistence economy, and other lifestyle factors, and it also recovers crucial skeletal remains. But archaeology, like comparative linguistics, does not present primary evidence for genetic migration.

## 6.2 Archaeological models of Austronesian dispersal

Credible explanations for Austronesian dispersal based on linguistic and biological observations go back into the late eighteenth century, for instance with the English navigator James Cook and his scientific colleague Johann Reinhold

Hsiao-chun Hung and Peter Bellwood, *Archaeological correlations for the dispersal of the Malayo-Polynesian languages of Southeast Asia, western Micronesia, and Madagascar*. In: *The Oxford Guide to the Malayo-Polynesian Languages of Southeast Asia*. Edited by: Alexander Adelaar and Antoinette Schapper, Oxford University Press. © Hsiao-chun Hung and Peter Bellwood (2024). DOI: 10.1093/oso/9780198807353.003.0006

Forster (Thomas et al. 1996). During the early twentieth century, Austrian ethnologist Robert Heine-Geldern (1932: 574) brought in archaeological evidence for the first time, using especially stone adzes and megaliths, to propose a route for Austronesian migration from China via the Malay Peninsula into Island SEA. Today, this route has been superseded by the strong evidence for an archaeological, linguistic, and genetic movement via Taiwan and the Philippines rather than the Malay Peninsula, an idea foreshadowed by Forster in 1778.

This chapter focuses on the Out of Taiwan hypothesis for Austronesian origins and dispersals, but first we will comment on other relevant models. We have already commented on the suggestion that language shift was the major driver of AN expansion (Donohue and Denham 2010), and find it unconvincing as an explanation on a sufficiently broad scale. We also find unconvincing the idea that MP-speaking migrants spread initially with a hunting-gathering or maritime-collecting economy, without food production from domesticated plants and animals (as suggested by Szabó and O'Connor 2004; Bulbeck 2008; O'Connor 2015).

Given that virtually all AN speakers were competent food producers when they entered the record of written history and anthropology, it makes sense that they were also food producers before their expansion commenced, as suggested by many linguistic reconstructions, and by the rapidly increasing archaeological record that we review below. Otherwise, one has to postulate multiple transitions from hunting and gathering to agriculture, and also to explain how Austronesian-speakers come to have such a large vocabulary of cognate terms related to food production with domesticated plants and animals. Borrowing alone could not create the observed patterns in language and material culture.

In the recent past, there have been other archaeological hypotheses that have negated or downplayed the role of Taiwan as the source region for the AN language family. One of these was the Nusantao hypothesis of archaeologist Wilhelm G. Solheim II (1984–1985, 2006), paralleled by William Meacham's (1984–1985, 1995) view that Island SEA supported a largely independent emergence and evolution of Neolithic societies, separate from any major intrusion or expansion from southern China or Taiwan. Solheim believed that ancestral ANs (*Nusantao*) developed a language to facilitate trade networks over a vast and diverse geographic space, extending from the coast of Vietnam to the Bismarck Archipelago, and northwards into coastal southern China (Solheim 2006: 90). Both Solheim and Meacham regarded the AN settlement of Taiwan as coming from the south.

The Nusantao model is no longer supported by the archaeological record. Solheim stressed the stylistic links between Sa Huynh pottery in Vietnam and Kalanay pottery in the Philippines as diagnostic evidence for his ancient Nusantao seafaring network. However, these pottery assemblages are Iron Age in date, post-dating 2,500 years ago (e.g. Reinecke et al. 2002; Yamagata 2012; Hung et al. 2013), and linked with a trade in nephrite ornaments sourced to Taiwan (e.g. Hung et al. 2007). They are too young to bear any relevance for understanding initial MP expansion (see §6.10, Mainland Southeast Asia).

Another hypothesis, the multiple routes model, suggests that ancient Austronesians may have reached the Philippines directly from the Asian mainland with no connections at all with Taiwan, which was reached independently and thereafter isolated (Tsang 1992, 2012). This model has also been proposed recently by geneticists based on comparisons of DNA in living Philippine populations (Larena et al. 2021), but it cannot account for observations based in archaeology or linguistics. Such opinions will require ancient DNA for support, and none is yet available from the initial phases of Austronesian dispersal in Taiwan or Island SEA.

Contrary to the viewpoints just described, numerous Neolithic and Iron Age links have been revealed during the past two decades between Taiwan and the northern Philippines (see §6.5, From Taiwan to the Philippines). Taiwan has an older chronology in Island SEA by at least a millennium for many aspects of Neolithic material culture, including pottery manufacture. Furthermore, Taiwan was never completely isolated in the way that the multiple routes model suggests.

There is another hypothesis that modifies the significance of Taiwan in the creation of living Island SEA populations, even if it does not attempt to remove it altogether. In this proposal, Neolithic settlers from Mainland SEA (sometimes claimed as early speakers of Austroasiatic languages, as suggested by Anderson 2005; Blench 2010c; Chia 2016; Simanjuntak et al. 2016; Simanjuntak 2017), arrived with cord-marked pottery in western Island SEA before Malayo-Polynesians, especially in Sumatra, Java, and Borneo. A separate movement then brought red-slipped pottery with MP linguistic expansion from Taiwan through the Philippines and into the central and eastern islands of Indonesia, as suggested by the Out of Taiwan hypothesis.

These postulated western and eastern dispersals, if really separate from each other, could represent the respective movements of Neolithic populations from Taiwan and from Mainland SEA into Island SEA. We return to these issues in the following sections on Borneo and

Sumatra, where this bipartite hypothesis has been most strongly applied. However, available archaeological evidence for the early Neolithic movement from Mainland SEA into Borneo remains rather small, except perhaps for northern Sumatra, and the issue is complicated by the possibility of a common pre-Austronesian and pre-Austroasiatic linguistic substratum that might once have existed across the exposed bed of the South China Sea during late glacial times, prior to 10,000 years ago (Adelaar 1995b).

## 6.3 The Out of Taiwan hypothesis for AN dispersal

We now describe the Out of Taiwan hypothesis, which uses the background Farming/Language Dispersal hypothesis of archaeologist Colin Renfrew (Bellwood and Renfrew 2002) to explain one of the major motives for AN dispersal, this being food production. The hypothesis suggests a movement of ancestral AN-speaking peoples into Taiwan from southern China at around 5,000 years ago, prior to the linguistic break-up of Proto-Austronesian, arriving as food producers with a portable domesticated repertoire of rice, millets, pigs, and dogs, together with pottery, weaving technology, and polished stone tools. From Taiwan, they began to move south by boat into the Philippines, about 4,200 years ago.

The Out of Taiwan hypothesis nowadays receives strong support not only from archaeology and linguistics, but also from ancient human genetics (e.g. Ko et al. 2014; Skoglund et al. 2016; McColl et al. 2018; Yang et al. 2020; Tätte et al. 2021; Chambers and Edinur 2021), and the archaeobotany of paper mulberry and rice (e.g. Chang et al. 2015; Deng et al. 2020). The new human genetic/genomic evidence is discussed by Ricaut, Brucato, and Cox (this volume, §5.2.2, §5.3.1–2).

In addition, there is more to the Out of Taiwan hypothesis from a biological perspective than just the human genetics. An important skeletal transition, from an indigenous Australo-Papuan craniofacial morphology to an immigrant Asian Neolithic one, has also been identified in many regions of East and Southeast Asia, including southern China, Japan, Taiwan, Thailand, Vietnam, Malaysia, and Indonesia (Matsumura et al. 2018, 2019). On a broad scale, this transition can be correlated with the spread of Neolithic assemblages associated with supine burials (extended on their backs, facing upwards) with grave goods, replacing earlier Pre-Neolithic flexed (with legs bent) burials without goods. The transition was a direct reflection of the initial migrations of many different agricultural populations across eastern Asia, presumably speaking ancestral languages in the Austronesian, Austroasiatic, Sino-Tibetan, and Kra-Dai language families (e.g. Bellwood 2005; Zhang and Hung 2010; Higham 2014).

During the past two decades, more discoveries with reliable archaeological dating have become available from Island SEA. This new weight of evidence allows a more informed appraisal of the several hypotheses discussed above. We now review this evidence on a geographical and chronological basis, commencing with the role of Taiwan.

## 6.4 Taiwan, Island Southeast Asia, and the western half of the MP distribution

Within the AN language family, the MP-SEA languages consist of a number of regional subgroups within the major (and Extra-Taiwan) Malayo-Polynesian subgroup (Smith 2017b; Blust 2019a). To the east, they abut Papuan languages in New Guinea, and in adjacent islands such as Halmahera, Timor, Alor, and Pantar. To the west, they abut Austroasiatic languages in Peninsular Malaysia and Vietnam. There is a strong likelihood that both of these non-AN language groups were associated with food producing populations before the MP expansion, which might explain why that expansion was limited in extent on the Southeast Asian mainland and in New Guinea.

Exactly what linguistic situation existed in Island SEA before the MP expansion began is unclear, since all previous languages apart from Papuan ones, in and close to New Guinea, are extinct, apart from survivals through substrate phenomena. The archaeological record does not support a widespread occurrence of pre-MP food production in these islands, a circumstance that could explain the MP success in replacing non-AN languages in the Philippines and throughout most of Indonesia. Hunter-gatherer populations would not have provided demographic resistance to MP settlement on the scale that would be expected from other demographically competitive populations of farmers.

Before moving into the archaeology of Island SEA, it is necessary first to reiterate the significance of Taiwan as the linguistic homeland for Proto-AN, even though this island is not discussed in detail in this article. Robert Blust (e.g. 1984/1985, 1995b, 2019a) has long argued for a geographical expansion of AN languages beginning in Taiwan, following on from earlier observations by Chang et al. (1964) and Dahl (1973). Taiwan still retains today the majority of the primary AN subgroups.

About 5000–4800BP, a major change occurred in Taiwan with the arrival of Neolithic cultures from the southern mainland of China. Prior to this, the island was inhabited by small hunter-gatherer populations who appear to have existed as a very thin population occupying caves and coastal open sites. By 4800BP, a Neolithic culture of southern Chinese origin was well established around the Taiwan coast. It is especially well known from sites buried very deeply beneath the southwestern coastal plain close to the modern city of Tainan. The Nanguanli and Nanguanlidong sites here are particularly important because of their remains of rice and both foxtail and broomcorn millet cultivation, decorated pottery, domesticated dogs, stone bark-cloth beaters, spindle whorls for spinning fibres, polished stone axes and spear points, and marine shell knives and body ornaments (Tsang 2005; Tsang et al. 2017).

None of these categories had antecedents in the older Palaeolithic cultures of the island—they were brought in from outside Taiwan and all have antecedents in southern China. However, a specific female clone of the paper mulberry tree that was used for bark-cloth production across the AN world has recently been revealed by chloroplast genetic research as indigenous to Taiwan (Chang et al. 2015).

It is assumed that these Neolithic settlers crossed Taiwan Strait from the south-coastal mainland of China, possibly by paddling or sailing rafts or dugout canoes, probably as yet without outriggers according to linguistic observations (Pawley and Pawley 1994; and see Blust, this volume, §4.4). They occupied Taiwan for about 800–600 years before moving further, and during this time they developed a series of cultural expressions marked by the use of pottery that was often decorated with a surface coat of red-ochre paint (red-slipped pottery).

By 4200–4000BP, some Austronesians were ready to move on from Taiwan. It was at this time, presumably, that some people carried away from that island the linguistic innovations that marked the birth of the MP subgroup. Somehow, they were able to circumvent the northward-flowing Kuroshio Current in their seacraft, in order to reach the northern Philippines. This is where our reconstruction starts (Figure 6.1).

## 6.5 From Taiwan to the Philippines

### 6.5.1 The Batanes Islands

Between the southern tip of Taiwan and the northern coast of Luzon, the Luzon Strait is about 350 kilometres wide. It contains seventeen islands in the Batanes and Babuyan groups, together with the island of Lanyu (Botel Tobago) with its Yami (Tao) language, of recent Batanes origin, situated close to the Taiwan mainland. Until recently, it was thought by some that the northwards-flowing Kuroshio Current would have made southward movement across the Luzon Strait extremely difficult (Solheim 1984–1985: 81, and see debate by Bellwood 1984–1985), in accordance with the Nusantao theory that the AN languages must have originated somewhere south of Taiwan. This opinion has not stood the test of time, and recent archaeology in the Batanes Islands confirms an arrival of Neolithic settlers from Taiwan at about 4200BP. Because the Batanes, Babuyans, and the northern Luzon coast provide a chain of island intervisibility, Neolithic settlers also reached northern Luzon at about the same time.

The beginning of the Neolithic pottery sequence in the Batanes is represented by an assemblage from Reranum Cave on Itbayat Island (Bellwood and Dizon 2013). This incorporated a small quantity of fine cord-marked pottery of a type unknown in other Batanes sites, and clearly derived from the Early to Middle Neolithic pottery sequence in Taiwan (c. 4500–4000BP). This Reranum cord-marked pottery is identical, for instance, to pottery of this date range unearthed from the Kending sites at the southern tip of Taiwan. Most of the pottery from Reranum, however, is red-slipped or plain but not cord-marked, and more closely related to red-slipped pottery in eastern Taiwan, especially from the south-eastern coastal Neolithic site of Chaolaiqiao, and several contemporary sites (c. 4200BP, Hung 2005, 2008). Zhenhua Deng et al. (2018) report rice phytoliths in high quantities from Chaolaiqiao.

By 3200BP, larger Batanes artifact assemblages are known from sites at Sunget on Batan Island, Savidug on Sabtang Island, and Anaro on Itbayat Island. They include plain, red-slipped and circle-stamped pottery with ring-feet and handles, biconical terracotta spindle whorls, adzes made of Taiwan volcanic rock and jade (nephrite, from the Fengtian source near Hualian, eastern Taiwan), Taiwan slate points, and Taiwan-style double-notched pebble fishing net sinkers.

Taiwan and the Batanes were undoubtedly in frequent contact throughout prehistory, the Kuroshio Current notwithstanding. We see this not only in pottery styles, but also through a presence of Taiwan stone tools and jade ornaments in Batanes, the latter including a specific form of *lingling-o* earring with three circumferential projections (Figure 6.2). At Anaro, blanks of imported Fengtian jade were worked on-site into *lingling-o* and other ornaments using a Taiwan technology of stone knives for grooving and snapping (nephrite is too hard for flaking) (Hung and Iizuka 2013), and possibly also tubular bamboo drills that could have been used in combination with sand abrasive and water. Given the wide Late Neolithic to Iron Age distribution of *lingling-o* earrings of Fengtian jade in the Philippines, northern Borneo, central and southern Thailand, and southern Vietnam, it is apparent that contacts involving Taiwan and the MP-SEA world continued for at least 2,000 years after Neolithic settlement in Batanes commenced (Hung et al. 2007).

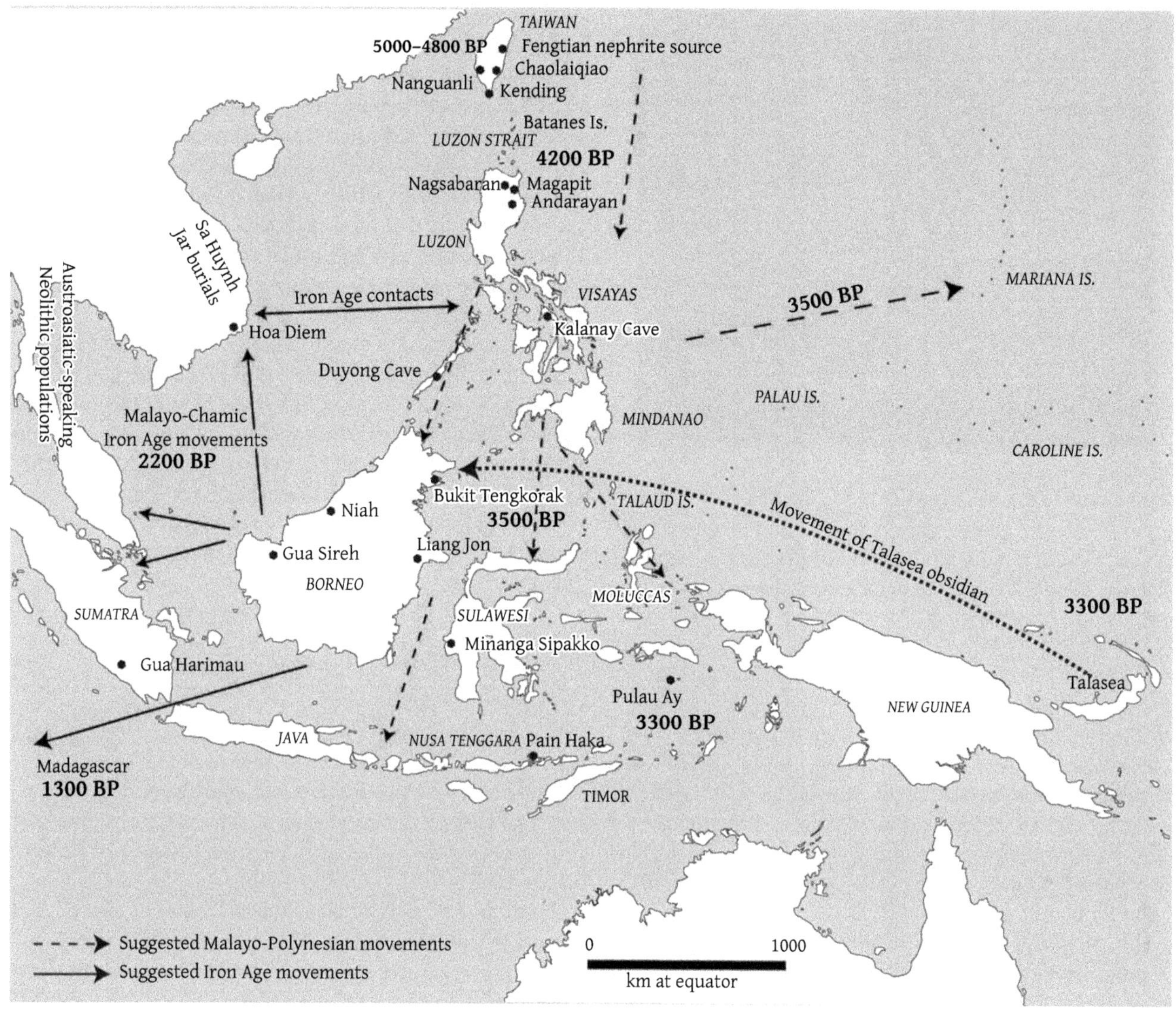


**Figure 6.1** Sites mentioned in the text, with schematic migration directions of MP-speakers during the Neolithic and Iron Age.

## 6.5.2 Luzon

The broad Cagayan Valley of northern Luzon contains the densest concentration of prehistoric sites in the Philippines. Many that lie close to the river itself are formed from large mounds of discarded food shell (shell middens), of a local species that lives in the lower estuarine part of the valley. Many of these shell middens overlie deeper and older layers of alluvial silt that also contain artefacts. The cultural sequence in the Cagayan Valley extends from Palaeolithic, mostly found in limestone caves in the nearby Peñablanca Massif, through Neolithic, into Iron Age, the last two phases found beneath and within the shell middens. The oldest Neolithic sites in the Cagayan Valley that can convincingly be equated with an arrival of speakers of (Proto)-MP languages date between 4200 and 4000BP.

For instance, the Gaerlan shell midden near the town of Lal-lo, on the east bank of the Cagayan River, has plain and red-slipped pottery that dates to c. 4100–4000BP, according to three radiocarbon dates, overlying a Palaeolithic layer beneath the midden (Garong 2002; Ogawa 2005: 11, 30). A nearby site at Nagsabaran has a shell midden with mainly Iron Age pottery that overlies a deep alluvial deposit with red-slipped Neolithic pottery, here with the important

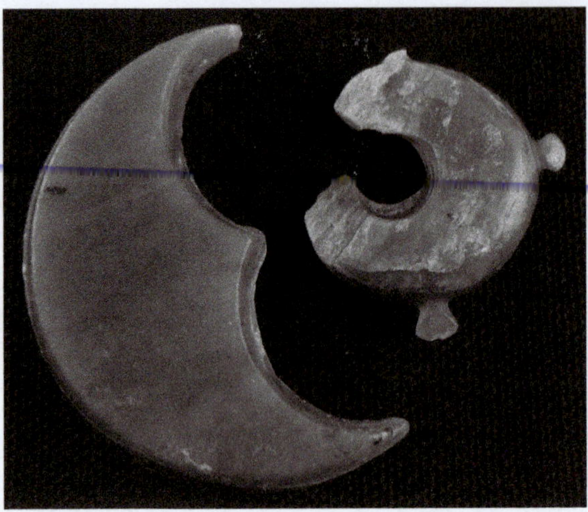

**Figure 6.2** Left: drilled green Fengtian (eastern Taiwan) nephrite blank from Savidug, discarded during the manufacture of circular ornaments. Right: Fengtian green nephrite *lingling-o* ear ornament, c.3 cm maximum diameter, found at Savidug Dune Site, Sabtang Island, Batanes, c.2500 BP.

addition of comb-stamped (with lines of punctate or dentate impressions) and circle-stamped motifs infilled with white lime. This was found in association with bones of domestic pigs of probable Taiwan origin, a fragment of a Taiwan nephrite bracelet, stone adzes, and baked clay spindle whorls (Hung 2008; Piper et al. 2009; Amano et al. 2013) (Figure 6.3).

The chronology for the Neolithic layer at Nagsabaran ranges between 4200/4000 and 2600BP (Hung 2008, 2016; Hung et al. 2011). A very dense charcoal layer exists at the base of the site, presumably representing vegetation clearance by its first settlers (Carson and Hung 2018). Ancient DNA study of a Nagsabaran human skeleton indicates that the inhabitants were most closely related to recent Formosans (represented by the Amis population of southeastern Taiwan) and other Filipinos (McColl et al. 2018).

In broader perspective, it is important to note that the Nagsabaran type of red-slipped and stamped pottery, often called punctate-stamped or dentate-stamped pottery by archaeologists, is an extremely important marker of MP migration through the Philippines and onwards to regions such as northern Sulawesi, the Mariana Islands, and Island Melanesia. In the last region, such dentate-stamped pottery belongs to the Lapita culture, which was antecedent to later Polynesian cultures in the central and eastern Pacific (e.g. Summerhayes 2007; Carson 2018).

Many other shell midden sites in the Cagayan Valley have a sequence similar to that from Nagsabaran, for instance at Catugan (Tanaka 1998), Irigayen (De la Torre 2000), and Magapit (Aoyagi et al. 1993). The Magapit shell midden is an amalgam of five seemingly separate smaller middens, distributed for 800 metres along the top and side of a limestone hill on the east bank of the Cagayan River. Most of the Magapit pottery is plain or red-slipped, dated between c. 3500 and 2800BP (Aoyagi et al. 1993), and it contains large amounts of the punctate- and circle-stamped red-slipped pottery that characterized Nagsabaran.

Beside animal domestication, these early Neolithic migrants into the Cagayan Valley had a knowledge of rice farming. Rice grains and banana phytoliths radiocarbon dated to 3200–3000BP have been found in the Neolithic layers in Nagsabaran and Magapit (Carson and Hung 2018). Eighty kilometres south of Nagsabaran, the riverine interfluve site of Andarayan has produced a direct radiocarbon date of 4000–3400BP for a rice husk inclusion in pottery (Snow et al. 1986).

### 6.5.3 The Visayas and Palawan

The Batungan Cave sites on Masbate Island in the Visayas (Solheim 1968) have a pottery sequence similar to that in the Cagayan Valley, with Neolithic red-slipped and stamped pottery like that from Nagsabaran and Magapit, also like that found in the oldest sites in the Mariana Islands in western Micronesia.

Palawan has rich archaeological remains but limited chronological information. During the 1960s, archaeologist Robert Fox excavated a flexed burial in Duyong Cave, western Palawan, that was provided with polished stone and *Tridacna* shell adzes, shell lime-containers (presumably used in betel chewing), and shell ornaments. Fox related the burial to an indirect uncalibrated radiocarbon date of 4630BP±250 (Fox 1970: 17), although this rather ancient date remains unverified in other sites. The flexed Duyong Cave posture is typical of pre-Neolithic burials across Southeast Asia, and it is possible that this person was an indigenous hunter-gatherer who came into contact with MP-speaking immigrants with a Neolithic material culture.

To summarize the Philippine situation from the perspective of MP dispersal, it is apparent that Neolithic settlers arrived from Taiwan via Batanes at about 4200BP. Because the Philippine archipelago is unique in Island SEA in having so many small islands around protected inland seas, it is likely that Neolithic settlement proceeded quickly from Luzon to Mindanao. The oldest pottery found so far in the

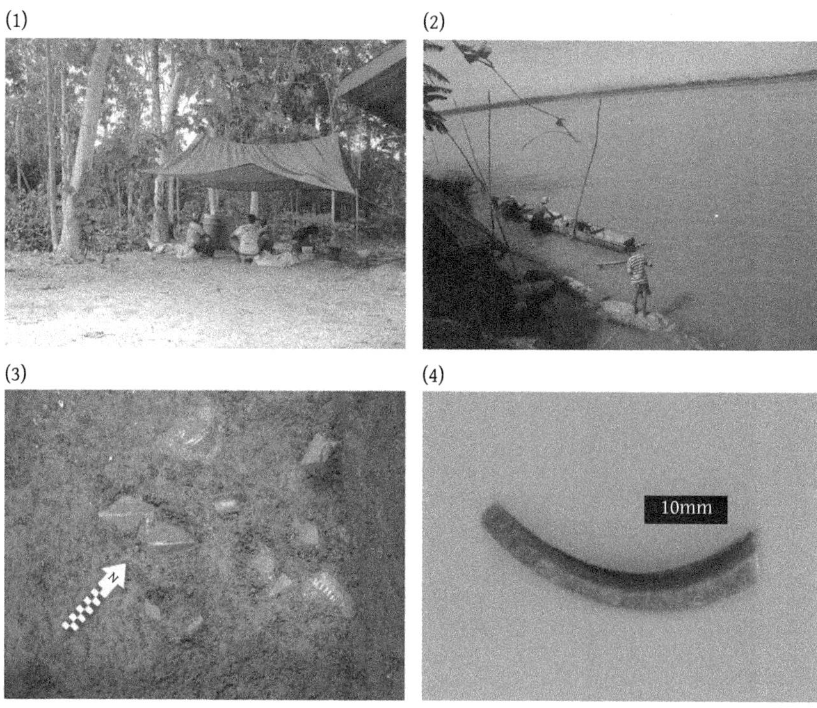


**Figure 6.3** (1) Archaeological excavation at Nagsabaran, Lal-lo, Cagayan Province, northern Luzon; (2) the Cagayan River near Nagsabaran; (3) potsherds and a deer mandible exposed during excavations at Nagsabaran; (4) bracelet fragment of Taiwan (Fengtian) jade from a Neolithic context at Nagsabaran.

Philippines is plain or red-slipped, with a small proportion of Taiwan Middle Neolithic style cord-marked pottery in Batanes. By 3500BP, the tradition of stamped decoration with lime-infilling had apparently spread southwards to at least the Visayas, and eastwards across more than 2,000 kilometres of open ocean to reach the Mariana Islands. By 3300BP it had also spread into the Bismarck Archipelago to the east of New Guinea, to establish the Lapita culture that spread through Island Melanesia and western Polynesia (e.g. Summerhayes 2007; Kirch 2017).

## 6.6 Western Micronesia

Although the Mariana and Palau Islands of western Micronesia are geographically outside Island SEA, their languages are non-Oceanic Malayo-Polynesian in the terminology of Robert Blust, hence they do not belong to the major Oceanic subgroup of MP languages (see Smith, this volume, §2.4.1, and Zobel, this volume, §38.1, §38.7, and §39.1, §39.8). Therefore, they are discussed in this chapter as direct extensions of the Island SEA Neolithic record.

### 6.6.1 The Mariana Islands

The Mariana and Palau Islands were the first regions reached by MP-speaking populations that did not have prior human settlement. The earliest Marianas Neolithic assemblage includes well-made red-slipped pottery with dentate-stamped and lime-infilled designs, plus other artefacts such as stone adzes, shell beads, and shell fish-hooks (e.g. Spoehr 1957; Butler 1994, 1995; Craib 1993, 1999; Carson 2008, 2014, 2016; Carson and Hung 2012, 2017). Most of the early decorated pottery is of a type best represented at the Achugao site in Saipan (Butler 1994, 1995) and the House of Taga in Tinian (Spoehr 1957; Pellett and Spoehr 1961; Carson and Hung 2012; Carson 2018).

The homeland for the first Marianas settlers, the ancestors of the Chamorro, must have been in a region where the diagnostic decorated pottery was produced prior to 3500BP. This date (Carson and Kurashina 2012; Carson 2020) is slightly older than the emergence of dentate-stamped Lapita pottery in Melanesia and Polynesia (Summerhayes 2007, 2010). The closest parallels of the earliest Marianas pottery, with supporting chronology, occur in the northern

**Figure 6.4** Red-slipped pottery with dentate-stamped and lime-infilled designs excavated from the House of Taga on Tinian, Mariana Islands (1,2), compared with similar sherds from Nagsabaran (3,4) and Magapit (5) in the Cagayan Valley, Northern Luzon.

and central Philippines (Hung et al. 2011; Carson et al. 2013) (Figure 6.4).

In addition to the archaeological record, ancient pollen and sediment studies in the Mariana Islands have identified the existence of an anthropogenic impact horizon involving forest clearance, mostly dating to around 3500BP, with some suggestions for an even older date back to 4200BP (Athens and Ward 2005). In lake-bed and swamp profiles in Guam, Tinian, and Saipan, this impact horizon is revealed by a sudden influx of charcoal, coincident with increased sedimentation, reductions in native plant taxa, and the appearances of second-growth vegetation and introduced species. Among the last, pollen of *Areca catechu* (the 'betel nut', possibly of Philippine origin) offers a special insight into the presence of a culturally important stimulant.

The Marianas case is especially important, as this is potentially the oldest recorded seaborne migration by humans to extend across more than 2,000 kilometres of continuous ocean (e.g. Spoehr 1957; Craib 1999; Blust 2000a, 2019a; Hung et al. 2011; Carson 2014). Although suggestions exist, based on analysis of winds and currents, for movement to the Marianas via other islands to the south, such as Palau, the Moluccas, or even New Guinea (Fitzpatrick and Callaghan 2013), the archaeologically attested Philippines-Marianas connection is the most consistent with findings in linguistics and ancient genetics (Pugach et al. 2021).

The indigenous Chamorro language of the Marianas was derived from an early MP source in the northern or central Philippines according to Robert Blust (2000a, 2019a), and in order to get there the ancestral Chamorros might have taken a route similar to that used in a recent simulation exercise, in which a dugout canoe was paddled from Taiwan across the track of the Kuroshio Current to emerge downstream, on its eastern side, in the Ryukyu Archipelago (Normile 2019; Servick 2019). A similar movement would have been possible from the central Philippines during the summer season of periodic westerly winds, and by paddling or sailing, the crew could eventually have reached currents in the western Pacific that bear towards the northern Marianas, as did the Spanish more than 3,000 years later (Figure 6.1).

### 6.6.2 The Palau Islands

The earliest attested human presence in the Palau Islands dates to around 3300–3000BP, likely from a central or eastern Indonesian origin. Early sites are represented by Chelechol ra Orrak (Fitzpatrick 2003; Nelson and Fitzpatrick 2006; Fitzpatrick and Nelson 2011), the Ulong Island site (Clark et al. 2006), and Ngatpang (Liston 2009). The material culture in early Palauan sites includes plain pottery and stone adzes. The red-slipped, stamped and lime infilled pottery found in the Philippines and Marianas has not so far been found in this group of islands.

So far, the oldest burials in Palau come from Chelechol ra Orrak Cave (c. 3000 to 2000BP), located on Orrak Island. At least thirty-one fragmentary skeletons were discovered here, although the only grave goods were three pearl shell (*Pinctada margaritifera*) scraper/grater tools, traditionally regarded as women's money (Fitzpatrick 2003; Fitzpatrick and Nelson 2011). Stable isotope analysis of diet on the bones from Chelechol ra Orrak suggests that early Palauans were heavily dependent on marine foods (Stone et al. 2019). Reddish-black stains on the front teeth, a marker of areca nut ('betel') chewing, were identified on all analysed dentitions found at this site, and *Areca catechu* pollen has been identified from the same time range in Palau, as in the Marianas (Athens and Ward 2001: 170).

Interestingly, this practice of betel nut chewing was widely spread in Southeast Asia and western Micronesia before 3000BP. As mentioned above, several shell lime containers were found at Duyong Cave in Palawan, and the individual buried here also had betel-stained teeth (Fox 1970). Lime, calcium hydroxide, together with a leaf of *Piper methysticum*, is one of the three ingredients of betel nut chewing, the third being the areca nut itself. Shell lime containers (Ray 1981: 235–6; Carucci and Mitchell 1990; Carson 2008) and teeth with betel staining have been reported from several archaeological sites such as Apurguan in Guam (Douglas et al. 1997), Alaguan in Rota (Hocart and Fankhauser 1996), Song Keplek in East Java (Noerwidi et al. 2020), and Gua Harimau in Sumatra (Noerwidi et al. 2016).

## 6.7 Borneo

Across the Sulawesi and Sulu Seas from the Philippines, the island of Borneo also has an archaeological record that can be related to the arrival, possibly around 3500BP, of MP-speaking populations with Neolithic material culture derived from Taiwan and the Philippines. This is especially the case in Sabah, where Neolithic assemblages have been found in many caves. One of the most important is the rock-shelter and open site of Bukit Tengkorak, on the rim of an extinct volcano near Semporna, which has red-slipped pottery dated to c. 3300–3000BP (Bellwood and Koon 1989; Chia 2008, 2016; Bellwood 2017). Two adult male skeletons directly dated to 3,000 years ago, found in a nearby site called Bukit Kamiri, have dental affinities with existing Island Southeast Asian and Chinese Neolithic populations (Eng 2009).

Bukit Tengkorak has been intensively studied for several decades (Bellwood 1989; Chia 2003, 2008), and while it does have some decorated pottery, it appears to lack the specific kind of dentate- and circle-stamped pottery that is typical of the sites dated to 3500–3300BP in the Philippines and Marianas. This may be because the layers with decorated pottery in Bukit Tengkorak are younger than this migration horizon. Nevertheless, the site has also produced shell tools and ornaments, stone adzes, and agate microblade drills (for working shell). Small chips of volcanic glass (obsidian) were imported from two different Melanesian sources used in Lapita times, these being the Admiralty Islands north of New Guinea and the Kutao/Bao source on the Talasea Peninsula of northern New Britain (identified in Figure 6.1; Bellwood 1989). An additional sourcing study on a green mica ornament from Bukit Tengkorak suggests a Mindoro Island source in the central Philippines (Hung and Iizuka 2017). These far-flung contacts are quite remarkable, and hint at the ability of early speakers of MP languages to maintain contacts over extremely wide areas.

In Indonesian Kalimantan, several Neolithic cave sites located close to the Mangkalihat Peninsula of Kalimantan Timur (East Kalimantan), such as Liang Jon, have red-slipped pottery dated to c. 2900BP (Chazine and Ferrié 2008; Plutniak et al. 2014) that is similar to that from Bukit Tengkorak, Magapit, and Nagsabaran. These occurrences support a continuing spread of early MP speakers down the eastern side of Borneo.

For a long time, scholars have suggested that the archaeological record of western Borneo differs from that on the eastern side of the island, especially in its emphasis on paddle-impressed pottery, including cord-marked, rather than on the red-slipped and punctate/dentate-stamped pottery that characterized movement through the Philippines (e.g. Chia 2016). Such paddle-impressed pottery has been reported from the Niah Caves (e.g. Harrisson 1957; Barker et al. 2011), from Lubang Angin in Gunung Mulu National Park, and from the Neolithic occupation cave of Gua Sireh in western Sarawak (Datan and Bellwood 1991; Datan 1993).

However, the exact date of this paddle-impressed pottery has never been clear. Although the Neolithic layers in the Niah Caves date between 3500 and 2400BP (Lloyd-Smith 2012, 2013; Lindsay Lloyd-Smith, p.c. 2020), Franca Cole has observed that the oldest pottery ("the early earthenware phase", c. 2800 to 2200BP) at Niah is red-slipped (see the red pigment in Cole 2012: 188, Fig. 7.5r) rather than paddle-impressed, and that cord-marked pottery appeared only later, during the Metal Age from c. 1300BP onwards (Cole 2012: 224).

A single rice grain dated directly by C14 to older than 4000BP, embedded in a sherd from Gua Sireh and once thought to mark an early arrival of rice farmers in Borneo, is now thought to be of natural origin within the potting clay (Barron et al. 2020), hence not relevant for discussing dates for pottery manufacture (Barron et al. 2020; and see also Cochrane et al. 2021, where this date is linked erroneously to pottery manufacture). The overall western Borneo ceramic sequence thus remains very uncertain, and suggestions, discussed above, that favour a Mainland Southeast Asian Neolithic substratum in western Borneo connected with an early spread of cord-marked pottery from Vietnam or Thailand (see §6.2) remain unverified. Cord-marked pottery was common in Taiwan from 5000–4800BP until about 3500BP, and it predated 4000BP in Torongan Cave in the Batanes, so the Taiwan-Philippine region could also serve as a possible source.

Borneo is an extremely large island, with a rugged interior that can be difficult to penetrate away from major rivers. Unlike the Philippines, it is very likely that this island witnessed rather different Neolithic cultures on its western and eastern coasts, with little movement across the island. Recent excavations in caves and open sites in central Borneo, near the headwaters of the Kapuas River which rises on the west coast, have revealed an arrival of impressed pottery-using peoples at about 3,000 years ago (Kusmartono et al. 2017). Presumably, these were western Borneo MP speakers who travelled up the rivers in Sarawak and West Kalimantan, particularly the Kapuas itself. They would have found the deep interior of Borneo virtually uninhabited at this time, although a small number of stone tools do indicate an occasional human presence going back well into the Palaeolithic.

## 6.8 Eastern Indonesia

### 6.8.1 Sulawesi

In the Talaud Islands between Mindanao and Sulawesi, a small amount of red-slipped Neolithic pottery has been reported from the rock-shelter of Leang Tuwo Mane'e on Karakelang Island (Bellwood 1976), with a possible commencement date of about 3500BP (Tanudirjo 2001: 160; Bellwood 2019: 88).

In Sulawesi itself, similar red-slipped pottery has been reported from several open sites, including Paso in northern Sulawesi (Bellwood 1976), and Minanga Sipakko and Kamassi in West Sulawesi (e.g. Simanjuntak et al. 2008; Anggraeni et al. 2014; Hakim 2014). The last two sites, located close together near the township of Kalumpang, provide the most significant sequence of Neolithic material culture and subsistence economy in all of Indonesia.

Minanga Sipakko and Kamassi have been studied intensively since the 1950s (Van Stein Callenfels 1951; Van Heekeren 1972). Kamassi is a hill-flank site in which much material has been redeposited from a higher hilltop level that is now eroded away. Minanga Sipakko is pristine in its preservation within an abandoned and well-preserved alluvial terrace of the Karama River. In terms of context, when this site was first occupied about 3,500 years ago, Neolithic populations were spreading from the Philippines around the coastline of Sulawesi, where coastlines and river mouths had recently been drowned by the postglacial sea level rise. The many Neolithic sites that must have been established in such situations have since been buried under tens of metres of sediment, and are for all practical purposes invisible to archaeologists who lack massive bulldozers, or immense luck. Most Neolithic assemblages in Indonesia come from remote limestone caves, and such sites are unlikely to contain coherent evidence for any subsistence activity beyond hunting and gathering.

Minanga Sipakko comes as a kind of saviour for this difficult situation (Figure 6.5, no. 1 and no. 2). It lies one hundred kilometres inland in the incised valley of the fast-flowing Karama River, and it has been sealed under a manageable one or two metres of protective Karama alluvium on a terrace above the river. The site, like Kamassi, has produced an assemblage of red-slipped pottery that has remarkable parallels in the Neolithic Philippines and eastern Taiwan, especially the above-mentioned site of Chaolaiqiao. The radiocarbon chronology for the initial phase of occupation at Minanga Sipakko, based on many samples from stratified occupation layers, is between 3500 and 3300BP (Deng et al. 2020). Besides pottery, other Neolithic artefacts from the two Kalumpang sites include stone adzes, stone bark-cloth beaters, ground slate projectile points, a green nepheline bead (visually similar to green jade), and a penannular ear ornament (Figure 6.5, no. 3).

The most important contribution from these two sites, particularly Minanga Sipakko, is towards an understanding of the subsistence economy. Bones of domesticated pigs (*Sus scrofa*) occurred in both sites, together with those of the native wild boar *Sus celebensis*. These two species can be differentiated from their teeth (Piper et al. 2009). Domesticated pigs were thus brought by the first Neolithic settlers to Sulawesi, as to the Cagayan Valley (above) and the northern Moluccas (below). It is likely that dogs arrived too, but evidence for their presence outside Neolithic Taiwan is not as strong as that for domesticated pigs.

Perhaps most importantly, a recent analysis of phytoliths (microscopic silica bodies found in plants) from all the layers at Minanga Sipakko has revealed that rice (*Oryza sativa*), with the diagnostic phytolith morphology of domesticated varieties (Figure 6.5, no. 4), was grown in the vicinity of the site. Phytoliths from discarded husks also indicate that the harvests were de-husked and processed into food on the site (Deng et al. 2020). These rice phytoliths were in direct association with the red-slipped pottery, and they provide what is so far the most convincing direct evidence for rice farming in Indonesia, as early as 3500BP. They reflect a remarkable instance of survival in a protected river terrace, a situation that might be difficult to replicate in future research in a landscape of severe tropical soil erosion and deposition.

Red-slipped pottery with dentate stamping, circle impression, and red painting, possibly pre-dating 3000BP, has also been reported from the Mansiri site in North Sulawesi. The pottery decoration is similar to that in middle Lapita assemblages in the southwest Pacific, and the excavators suggest that, it might represent a backflow of ideas and people from east to west (Azis et al. 2018), like the Talasea obsidian at Bukit Tengkorak in Sabah.

### 6.8.2 The Moluccas

The early Neolithic in the Moluccas is best represented by the Uattamdi rock shelter on Kayoa Island, near Halmahera

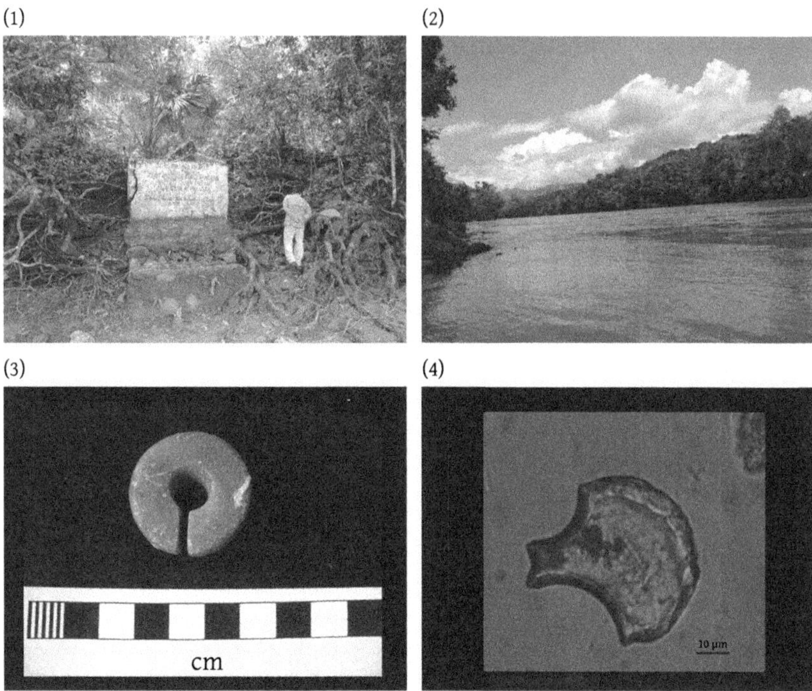


**Figure 6.5** (1) The riverside setting of the Minanga Sipakko site, Karama Valley; (2) the Karama River near Minanga Sipakko; (3) a steatite ear pendant from Kamassi; (4) rice bulliform phytolith from Minanga Sipakko with convex-edge indentations characteristic of domesticated *Oryza sativa*.

(Bellwood 2019), and the Pulau Ay open site in the Banda Islands (Lape et al. 2018). Both contain red-slipped pottery dating from about 3300BP, and both have bones of domestic pigs and possibly dogs. Pulau Ay has also yielded starch grains of *Dioscorea spp.* (yams), *Metroxylon sagu* (sago), and *Myristica fragrans* (nutmeg).

The overall archaeological record of the Halmahera region (Bellwood 2019) suggests that Uattamdi represented a Neolithic enclave, with its red-slipped pottery, inserted into a region that was otherwise at that time without pottery manufacture. All other excavated sites in the northern Moluccas lacked pottery until after 2500BP, by which time the older red-slipped tradition had lost its original coherence and was replaced by regional styles of a later date, mainly from the Metal Age. This suggests that pottery manufacture spread into other communities in Morotai and Halmahera from an MP source. Because these two islands contain most indigenous Papuan-speaking populations today, this supports the view expressed previously that the MP dispersal ceased in this southeastern part of Indonesia as a result of admixture with the indigenous population.

This view is also supported by analysis of ancient human DNA samples from Uattamdi and the Morotai Island site of Tanjung Pinang, dating to about 2,500–1,500 years ago. These indicate that there was considerable genetic admixture by this time between Asian-related and indigenous western Pacific populations. Molecular clock analysis suggests that this admixture commenced in eastern Indonesia soon after 3000BP. Presumably, it reflected interbreeding between immigrant Malayo-Polynesians and indigenous Papuan-speaking groups. The individuals analysed have between 64 and 70% Asian-related ancestry calculated from their whole genomes, the rest coming from Papuan ancestry (Oliveira et al. 2020).

Another conclusion from the North Moluccan archaeological project conducted during the 1990s is that this region was not directly involved in any hypothetical spread of MP-speaking populations along the northern coastline of New Guinea into Oceania. The dentate- and circle-stamped pottery style that typifies the Lapita culture in Island Melanesia, and its contemporaries in northern Sulawesi, the Marianas, and Philippines, does not occur in relevant contexts in either the Moluccas or New Guinea, except for late Lapita sites in south eastern Papua New Guinea. These represent back-movements from the Bismarcks. The migration that led to the establishment of the Lapita culture in the Bismarck archipelago at about 3300BP appears to have travelled from Island SEA by sea, entirely to the north of New Guinea and perhaps via the Admiralty Islands.

### 6.8.3 The Lesser Sunda Islands (Nusa Tenggara)

The Lesser Sunda Islands have very few well-dated Neolithic assemblages because most archaeological research has concentrated on caves in limestone regions unsuitable for food production. However, it was noted many years ago by Ian Glover (1977a: 46) that "The first pottery in Timor, in particular a thin, hard-fired ware, often burnished and sometimes with a red slip, is rather close to the earliest pottery found by Bellwood in the Talaud Islands".

Recent excavations by Sue O'Connor (2015) have recovered Neolithic pottery from more cave sites in Timor-Leste, with red-slipped sherds as a minor component. There is otherwise very little dated Neolithic pottery from the Lesser Sundas. However, the Neolithic site of Pain Haka in eastern Flores is particularly important for its burial evidence, which includes fifty-five individuals inhumed in earth graves as well as in large pottery jars (Galipaud et al. 2016), the last being a tradition of burial first attested in Taiwan at about 4200BP. The Pain Haka burials date to 3000BP and are associated with Neolithic artefacts. The most significant observation about them is that a number had skeletal elements missing, including skulls.

Evidence for skull removal is found at roughly the same time at Nagsabaran in the Cagayan Valley (Hung 2008), at Liang Jon in East Kalimantan (Chazine and Ferrié 2008), at Ritidian on Guam, Marianas (Carson 2017), and in the Lapita burial ground at Teouma on Efate Island in Vanuatu (Bedford et al. 2006). This seems to be beyond coincidence, and may reflect inherited behaviour connected with a veneration of ancestors through activities connected with skull removal and later reburial. One Lapita burial at Teouma had three skulls placed on its chest, behaviour more likely related to veneration than head-hunting (Bellwood and Hiscock 2018: Fig. 9.30).

## 6.9 The western Indo-Malaysian archipelago

Relatively little is known about the spread of Neolithic assemblages through Java and Sumatra. In southern Sumatra, Pondok Selabe (Silabe) cave 1 contained three cultural layers, including pre-Neolithic (4500 to 3100BP), Neolithic (2700BP), and Metal Age (after 2700BP). The Neolithic layer is stated to have cord-marked pottery (Forestier et al. 2006) as does Loyang Mendale cave in Aceh, northern Sumatra (Wiradnyana and Setiawan 2011).

**Figure 6.6** (1) excavations in Gua Harimau; (2) extended Metal Age burials (numbers 23 and 24) in the upper layer; (3) a flexed burial (number 79) of Australo-Papuan craniofacial affinity from the Pre-Neolithic phase in the lower layer.

The most important Neolithic site in western Indonesia is undoubtedly the cave of Gua Harimau in southern Sumatra, where more than eighty-four human burials (with many still unexcavated) range from pre-Neolithic (5700 to 4400BP), through late Neolithic (2700 to 2400BP), to Metal Age (2400 to 1700BP) in date (Simanjuntak 2016; Matsumura et al. 2018) (Figure 6.6). A few cord-marked sherds similar to those from Pondok Selabe, and some red-slipped sherds, have also been found in this site (Ansyori 2016), but the details are not yet fully published.

Craniofacial morphometric analysis has revealed that the Metal Age individuals from Gua Harimau exhibit close affinities with AN-speaking populations in Taiwan and Island SEA, whereas the older pre-Neolithic population had affinities with both ancient and recent Indigenous populations in Australia and New Guinea (Matsumura et al. 2018, 2019). No Neolithic burials have yet been analysed from this site. A possible genetic connection with Mainland SEA is also reflected in a recent ancient DNA study of two individuals unearthed from Loyang Ujung Cave (near Loyang Mendale) in northern Sumatra, dated to about 2,000 years ago (hence Metal Age). They reveal an admixed genomic ancestry signature between those of modern Austroasiatic-speaking peoples in Mainland SEA, and Austronesian-speaking Amis in Taiwan (McColl et al. 2018). Admixture at this relatively recent date, however, is not unexpected.

## 6.10 Mainland Southeast Asia

Neolithic cultures were widely established across the mainland of Southeast Asia and down into the Malay Peninsula by 4500BP. They reveal few connections in pottery styles and other artefacts with Neolithic cultures in Island SEA, apart from the possible connections associated with impressed and cord-marked pottery discussed above for Sumatra and Borneo. The migrations of the Chams, Malays, and Moken appear, at present, to have been Metal Age in date and to have originated, according to linguistic observations on Malay and Chamic, in western Borneo (Blust 1994, 2010b).

In support, the archaeological record reveals intensive contact between Island and Mainland SEA between 2500 and 1500BP (Figure 6.1), especially through trade and exchange involving metals, glass beads, Taiwan nephrite ornaments, and similarities in pottery decoration. Wilhelm Solheim II (1957) noted long ago that there were marked similarities between pottery found by the early twentieth century Guthe

Expedition in caves in the central Philippines, and that associated with the Sa Huynh tradition of Iron Age jar burial along the central coast of Vietnam. He coined the concept of the 'Sa Huynh-Kalanay Interaction Sphere', as discussed above in connection with his Nusantao hypothesis. There can be little doubt that this was in some way associated with the contemporary movement of Chamic speakers to Vietnam, even if an archaeological link with the Philippines appears to conflict with the well-established linguistic link between Chamic and the Malayic languages of western Borneo origin.

The Sa Huynh-Kalanay Iron Age Interaction Sphere has attracted a great deal of interest from archaeologists in recent years. The most relevant sites are located in central and south-central Vietnam, Peninsular Thailand, the Philippines, and western Borneo (e.g. Solheim 1964, 2006; Fox 1970; Loofs-Wissowa 1982; Yamagata 2012; Hung et al. 2013; Favereau and Bellina 2016). Sites in these regions share similar styles of decorated pottery, jar burial practice, and especially personal jewellery (jade earrings, glass beads, carnelian beads). The jade items, in particular, include penannular *lingling-o* and double animal-headed ear pendants made of Fengtian nephrite from eastern Taiwan (e.g. Hung et al. 2007; Hung and Iizuka 2017), as discussed above in connection with the Batanes Islands.

It has also been shown that some Iron Age pottery found in Ko Din Cave on Samui Island, Gulf of Thailand, is identical in form and decoration to vessels from Kalanay Cave on Masbate Island, central Philippines (Solheim 1964, 2006), and also to pottery in the Hoa Diem Iron Age jar burial site in Cam Rang Bay, southern Vietnam (Yamagata 2012) (Figure 6.7). These are quite remarkable long-distance and convincing connections. Likely dates for both Malayic and Chamic migration to the mainland of Southeast Asia seem to relate to such materials, and fall between 1800 and 1500BP.

## 6.11 Madagascar

Madagascar lies 6,000 kilometres west of Island SEA, and in terms of linguistic and genetic evidence it was probably settled by a population under Srivijayan (South Sumatra) political control, but of southern Borneo linguistic origin. Suggested dates fall between 1600 and 1500BP (Dahl 1951) or between 1400 and 1300BP (Adelaar 2009b; Kusuma et al.

**Figure 6.7** Pottery vessels of identical form and decoration from Kalanay Cave, Masbate, Visayas (1–2); and from Hoa Diem, Khanh Hoa Province, southern Vietnam (3–4). (Courtesy: National Museum of the Philippines and Khanh Hoa Museum.)

2015). As noted by Dahl and Adelaar, the Malagasy language contains Sanskrit loans mediated through Malay or Javanese. In terms of exact origin, archaeological evidence as currently known neither confirms nor denies a likelihood for Borneo, and no archaeologists have yet claimed that any specific pottery assemblage in Madagascar resembles that from any specific location in Indonesia.

There is currently disagreement as to when Madagascar was first settled by humans (e.g. Dewar et al. 2013; Anderson et al. 2018; Hansford et al 2018; Mitchell 2019). This does not directly affect discussion about the date of arrival of the Malagasy, but there is an important contextual issue involved if humans were there beforehand, as opposed to being entirely absent. For example, the Ambohiposa and Lakaton'i Anja sites in northern Madagascar are claimed to show early forager occupation with a stone tool technology dating back to at least 4000BP (Dewar et al. 2013). Two evaluations of the distributions of radiocarbon dates from Madagascar also suggest a human presence by at least 2000BP (Douglass et al. 2019; Godfrey et al. 2019). The arrival of a herding and farming economy on the island is currently dated between 1300 and 1100BP (Godfrey et al. 2019), thus supporting the linguistic inferences that pertain to early Malagasy settlement.

Archaeobotanical data show that the Indonesian settlers brought Asian crops to Madagascar. Plant assemblages dating 1300 through 1000BP contain both *indica* and *japonica* rice, and South Asian mung beans (Crowther et al. 2016). The introduction of Southeast Asian crops such as bananas, taro, greater yam, and sugar cane into tropical Africa in the period from 2000 to 1900BP, or before (Beaujard 2017; Power et al. 2019), might also have impacted on early Malagasy food production, perhaps with the arrival of Bantu-speaking farmers.

## 6.12 Conclusion

In this chapter, we have examined the footprints left by the first speakers of MP-SEA languages in Island SEA and western Micronesia. The Neolithic archaeological signature, that matches the pattern of language dispersal, appeared about 5000–4800BP in Taiwan and spread into the northern Philippines after a one-millennium pause between 4200 and 4000BP. About 3500BP, people emerged from the Philippines to cross more than 2,000 kilometres of open sea to the Marianas Islands in western Micronesia. Others moved southwards between 3500 and 3300BP into Borneo, Sulawesi, and the Moluccas. Further movements into Java, Sumatra (Figure 6.8), and Melanesia were underway by 3000–2700BP, although MP movements to Vietnam, Peninsular Malaysia, and Madagascar were later in time, focused on the Metal Age (2500 to 1300BP).

Many possibilities have been suggested about the ultimate causes of AN expansion. These include the spread of rice agriculture and resultant population growth (Bellwood 1985: 223, 2005, 2017; Carson and Hung 2018), demands for valued marine and tropical forest products (Chang and Goodenough 1996: 51), a search for new trade contacts (Thiel 1984–1985: 127), an effective maritime technology (Anderson 2005: 39–40), a founder ideology that would encourage veneration of those who led successful colonising expeditions (Bellwood 1996), adverse environmental impacts (Anderson 2005: 40; Bellwood 2005: 135; Carson and Hung 2018), and more. In our view, all probably worked hand in hand, to varying degrees in different situations.

One final comment is necessary on the concept of a driving force behind the AN migration as a whole, including from China to Taiwan. An availability of boats goes without question. But it is important to reiterate that virtually all AN-speaking populations at European contact were farmers, with a highly transportable economy based on domesticated crops and animals. They could not possibly have become farmers through independent trajectories of adoption or invention across the AN-speaking world after the migration had occurred. They must, according to Occam's Razor, have been farmers before it began. This point was made at the beginning of this chapter, and increasing archaeological evidence is in support.

**Figure 6.8** Austronesian rice farmers in northern Sumatra.

This need not mean all early MP migrants were specialized rice farmers. They certainly never took rice farming into Oceania, at least not beyond the Marianas. Besides maritime resources, crops indigenous to Island SEA and Melanesia, such as yams, aroids (taro), bananas, breadfruit and coconuts (and perhaps also chickens, indigenous to Mainland SEA) also played major roles in MP subsistence. However, archaeological and genetic records make it clear that the pigs and dogs, rice and millets, and the paper mulberry tree for bark-cloth were present in Taiwan right at the start of the MP expansion process, not adopted later as it progressed through Island SEA.

The MP economy adapted as it travelled, from large and resource-rich continental islands to resource-poor oceanic ones, and from an original baseline with cereal production in southern China towards one based more and more on fruits and tubers, especially in non-seasonal equatorial climates unsuited to annual rice. Without food production from domesticated plants and animals that could be transported between islands there could have been no Malayo-Polynesian migration as we know it today.

## Acknowledgements

We thank Robert Blust, Sander Adelaar, and Antoinette Schapper for valuable comments on linguistic aspects of this chapter.

CHAPTER 7

# Historical linguistics of the Philippines

R. David Zorc, Jason W. Lobel, and William Hall

## 7.1 Introduction

The Philippines, a nation of over 7,000 islands, is located just south of Taiwan, northeast of Borneo, and due north of the Indonesian island of Sulawesi. Its 179 living, indigenous languages mostly belong to the Philippine subfamily (cf. Blust 2019b),[1] and 171 of the 190 members of the Philippine subfamily are spoken within its borders.

Philippine languages were among the first languages in Asia to be the subject of western linguistic study. The first documentation of a Philippine language took place in 1522 when Pigafetta (1525: 51v–53r) elicited an inconsistently transcribed list of Old Cebuano (some of which, however, is actually Malay). Less than a century later, the documentation and description of several major Philippine languages began with the work of a number of Spanish friar-linguists in the first decades of the Spanish occupation of the Philippines. These works provide not only invaluable data on archaic features and vocabulary items, which can aid in lexical and grammatical reconstruction, but also important clues about the migration history of certain languages. In some cases (e.g. Old Bikol and Old Ilonggo/Hiligaynon), this four-century-old data reveals ancient languages which are different enough to be considered separate from their modern counterparts.

The contact languages that have contributed the most to Philippine lexicons over the past millennium are Malay (primarily pre-1600), Spanish (from the 1500s to 1800s), and English (starting with the arrival of the Thomasites in 1901, but especially in the modern era with widespread access to English-language television, music, and social media). Borrowings from Arabic, largely borrowed via Malay, are most common in the languages of Islamized populations in the southern Philippines and their neighbours, as well as in northern Sulawesi. Finally, several Chinese languages (Hokkien, Minan, Southern Min) have left their mark on Philippine lexicons in the areas of commerce and cuisine.

This survey will provide an overview of the Philippine microgroups (§7.2), some phonological developments relevant to Proto-Philippines and its various daughter languages (§7.3), and subgrouping issues and controversies (§7.4). It should be noted that the subgroups, languages, and axes mentioned through this chapter have been established based on not only phonological innovations but also significant replacement innovations for well-established PAN or PMP reconstructions: for example, the 8,139 cognate sets in Blust and Trussel's (2020) *Austronesian Comparative Dictionary* include over 720 high-level etymologies that each contain two or more pages of invaluable comparative evidence.

## 7.2 The Philippine languages

Following Blust (1991b, 2019b); Charles (1974); Reid (1989); Robinson and Lobel (2013); Lobel (2010, 2013a); and Zorc (1977, 2019), the languages of the Philippine subfamily can be assigned to the following thirteen primary branches, listed roughly from north to south:

1. Batanic/Bashiic
2. Northern Luzon ('Cordilleran')
3. Central Luzon
4. Umiray Dumaget
5. Manide-Alabat
6. North Mangyan
7. Greater Central Philippines (and Palawanic)
8. Kalamianic
9. Inati
10. Southwestern Mindanao
11. Southeastern Mindanao
12. Sangiric
13. Minahasan

[1] The seven Sama-Bajaw languages (see Kaufman, this volume, chapter 26) spoken in the Philippines are not included in this number as they belong to the Greater Barito subgroup (Blust 2007c). Note that our count of Philippine languages differs from the Ethnologue (Eberhard et al. 2019) in (i) the inclusion of seven languages (Bulalakawnon, Northern Samarenyo, Samā IGaCOS, Tawlet Subanen/Kalibugan, Tigwa Manobo, Klata, and Tasaday) not listed therein, and (ii) the exclusion of several others which are either unattested, not genetically Philippine, or simply dialects of another listed language.

R. David Zorc, Jason W. Lobel, and William Hall, *Historical linguistics of the Philippines.* In: *The Oxford Guide to the Malayo-Polynesian Languages of Southeast Asia.* Edited by: Alexander Adelaar and Antoinette Schapper, Oxford University Press. © R. David Zorc, Jason W. Lobel, and William Hall (2024). DOI: 10.1093/oso/9780198807353.003.0007

### 7.2.1 Batanic/Bashiic

The northernmost subgroup in the Philippines is Batanic (or 'Bashiic'), consisting of Itbayaten, Ivatan, and Ibatan/Babuyan spoken on the Batanes Islands off the northern tip of Luzon, plus the Yami language of Orchid Island within the national borders of Taiwan. The internal and external relationships of these languages have been studied by Scheerer (1908) and Conant (1908); Dempwolff (1926); Tsuchida, Yamada, and Moriguchi (1987); Yang (2002); Ross (2005); Gallego (2014); and Blust (2017d, 2019b). Included among the numerous lexical innovations defining this subgroup are *batah 'say, tell', *bubun 'bury', *bulək 'belly', *dalmət 'heavy', *hilak 'white', *kadam 'rat', *muhdan 'nose', *makpahad 'bitter', and *taur 'heart'.

### 7.2.2 Northern Luzon

Formerly known as 'Cordilleran', the Northern Luzon subgroup consists of seven branches: Ilokano, Cagayan Valley, Northeastern Luzon, Central Cordilleran, Southern Cordilleran, Alta, and Arta, each of which is dealt with in the following subsections. Lawrence Reid (1979, 1989, 1991, 2006b) and Ronald Himes (1997, 1998, 2005) are the primary scholars who have addressed either the entire subgroup or various branches thereof.

#### 7.2.2.1 *Ilokano*

Spoken by nearly ten per cent of the Philippine population, Ilokano is now the major trade language in most of northern Luzon, a position once held by Ibanag, which may explain the widespread /g/ reflexes of *R in Ilokano where /r/ would be expected in native Ilokano forms (cf. Tharp 1974). Its two-way history of borrowing makes it difficult to identify Ilokano lexical innovations, although some candidates include *dúrek* 'earwax', *isú* 'he/she (3SG.NOM)', *kaladkad* 'climb', *lapáyag* 'ear', and *punpun* 'bury'. There are two main dialects of Ilokano: a northern dialect reflecting earlier *ə as /e/ and having the form *saán* /saʔán/ for 'no', and a southern dialect in which *ə is preserved as /ə/ and the word for 'no' is *haán* /haʔán/.

#### 7.2.2.2 *Cagayan Valley*

The Cagayan Valley subgroup includes Adasen, the three Atta languages (Atta Faire, Atta Pamplona, and Atta Pudtol), Central Cagayan Agta, Gaddang, Ga'dang, Ibanag, Itawis, Isnag, Malaweg, and Yogad. It was formerly proposed that the Cagayan Valley and Northeastern Luzon subgroups formed a 'Northern Cordilleran' node within Northern Luzon (or 'Cordilleran'), but Robinson and Lobel (2013) found no evidence to support such a grouping after a more thorough survey of the Northeastern Luzon languages. Cagayan Valley innovations include *agə́l 'liver', *agída 'they (3PL.NOM)', *aŋ(ə)tiŋ 'afraid', *dákəs 'bad', *dapíŋ 'dirty', *əbíŋ 'child', *po:ray 'angry, brave', *saŋáw (temporal: now, recent past, a little later), *təkaw 'borrow', *to:lay 'person', *ubo:bug 'speak', and *ŭgaŋ 'sweat'.

#### 7.2.2.3 *Northeastern Luzon*

This subgroup includes five Aboriginal (or 'Negrito'[2]) Filipino languages—Dupaningan Agta, Pahanan Agta, Dinapigue Agta, Casiguran Agta,[3] and Nagtipunan Agta, all spoken on or near the Pacific coast of northeastern Luzon by groups self-identifying as 'Agta'—plus the Paranan language of the ethnic-Austronesian inhabitants of Palanan town. Robinson and Lobel's (2013) is the only historical-comparative study of these languages, although Headland (1975) published an earlier study based on lexicostatistics and mutual intelligibility. Innovations within this group include *ləbbút 'boil (water)', *ladúʔ 'fever', *putát 'full', *madəggáʔ 'heavy', *démət 'arrive', *sánig 'hear, listen', *tóglad 'push', and *bakál 'stab'.

#### 7.2.2.4 *Central Cordilleran*

This large group of languages includes Balangao, Isinay, Luba, Manabo, Northern Kankanaey, Southern Kankanaey, and various languages known by the names 'Itneg' (Binongan, Inlaod, Maeng, Masadiit, Moyadan, and Banao), 'Kalinga' (Butbut, Limos, Lubuagan, Mabaka Valley, Majukayang, Southern, and Tanudan); 'Bontok' (Northern, Southern, Central, Eastern, and Southwestern) and 'Ifugao' (Amganad, Batad, Mayoyao, and Tuwali).[4] Innovations defining the Central Cordilleran subgroup include *ʔákaw 'steal' (with unexplained loss of the *t- of earlier *takaw), *ʔalməŋ 'laugh', *baʔúd 'tie, tether', *bagáŋ 'neck' (semantic shift from PAN *baRqaŋ 'molar'), *tágu 'person, human' (with insertion of -g- into PAN *Cau), *tubu 'leaf' (semantic specialization of PMP *tubuq 'grow, sprout'), *tuŋʔal 'bone'

[2] The second author, as well as Mirante (2014) and Louward Zubiri (p.c., 5/27/2020) have observed that many Aboriginal Filipinos disapprove of the term 'Negrito', which will therefore be avoided in this chapter.

[3] Usually referred to as 'Casiguran Dumagat' in the literature, following its primary scholar Thomas Headland, this and other groups speaking NE Luzon languages actually refer to themselves as 'Agta', while *dumagat* is a generic Tagalog term referring to any of the Aboriginal Filipino groups near the Pacific coast of northern and central Luzon, including the Umiray Dumaget, the Alta, and the Agta, and other Aboriginal Filipinos on Alabat Island.

[4] Bayninan Ifugao and Kiangan Ifugao, both included in Reid (1971) are actually dialects of Kallahan/Kalanguya and Tuwali Ifugao, respectively.

(a metathesis of PWMP *tuqəlaŋ), *tupə́k 'mouth', *waŋwaŋ 'river', and *wasít 'throw'.

#### 7.2.2.5 *Southern Cordilleran*

The Southern Cordilleran subgroup, for which Himes (1998) is the primary historical-comparative work, includes Bugkalot (also known as Ilongot), Pangasinan, I-wak, Ibaloi, Kalanguya, Keley-i Kallahan, and Karao. Zorc (1979) has studied the historical development of contrastive accent in Pangasinan. Innovations defining this group include *ʔəgə́s 'intestines', *ʔaləgə́y 'stand', *baklaŋ 'body', *ballə́g 'big', *dálin 'earth, soil', *ʔəsə́l 'speak', *sakə́y 'one', *táwən 'sky', and *səlí 'foot'.

#### 7.2.2.6 *Alta*

This subgroup consists of Northern Alta and Southern Alta (Reid 1991; Garcia-Laguia 2018; Abreu 2018), spoken by Aboriginal Filipino populations living both along the eastern coast of north-central Luzon between the towns of Baler and Dingalan in Aurora Province, and upriver from those areas. Proposed innovations include *bitlay 'carry on shoulder', *dakəl 'flood', *ibut 'lost', *iʔə 'this', *lanis 'sweet', *lutit 'mud', *mudoŋ 'mountain', and *pənaŋ 'hot (of weather)'.

#### 7.2.2.7 *Arta*

This near-extinct language spoken by a small Aboriginal Filipino population living near Maddela, Quirino Province, was discovered by Reid (1989), who identified almost 150 unique forms (e.g. *binguèt* /biŋuət/ 'night', *bukágan* /buka:gan/ 'woman', and *bunbun* 'house') and noted that its rate of retention of PMP lexicon was among the lowest figures 26.9%) known for any Philippine language, with Arta preserving reflexes of only fifty-one out of 189 PMP reconstructions. Arta currently has around a dozen first- and second-language speakers, and Kimoto (2017a, b) is the primary scholar on this language.

### 7.2.3 Central Luzon (and Remontado)

The Central Luzon subgroup consists of two branches, one of which is Kapampangan, and the other the Sambalic or Sambali-Ayta group, which includes Botolan Sambal, 'Tina' Sambal,[5] Bolinao, Ayta Mag-antsi, Ayta Mag-indi, Ayta Abellen, Ayta Ambala, and Ayta Bataan. The primary study of this subgroup is Himes (2012). Kapampangan and Sambalic share a number of innovations, including *ʔəmíʔ 'urine', *gurut 'back', *uŋut 'coconut (generic)' (< PPH *huŋut 'coconut shell cup'), *taklaʔ 'excrement, to defecate' (also found in Remontado and Iraya), and *tələk 'deaf' (borrowed into Pangasinan). Innovations unique to the Sambalic group include *anag 'termite' (cf. PAN *aNay), *bəkraw 'throat', *dalúnut 'smooth', *dayi 'still, yet', *dəbləm 'dark', *duday 'urine', *kudpal 'thick', *láləʔ 'deep', *maʔín 'have, there is', and *rayʔəp 'cold'.

Special mention should be made of the moribund Remontado language (also referred to in the literature by Hatang-Kayi, or the unfortunate misnomer 'Sinauna' or 'Sinauna Tagalog' meaning 'Archaic/Aboriginal Tagalog') spoken by some 300 adult Remontados in the highlands of Tanay and General Nakar towns east of Manila (Lobel and Surbano 2019). Following Santos (1975), most scholars, including Blust (1991b) and Himes (2012) have included Hatang-Kayi in the Central Luzon group, but Lobel and Surbano (2019) question this based on the limited size of earlier data sets, much of which was ambiguous as to whether it was borrowed or inherited.

### 7.2.4 Umiray Dumaget

The Umiray Dumaget language—which has at least a northern/coastal and southern/inland dialect,[6] and possibly a third dialect on Polillo Island—is spoken over a considerable part of central-eastern Luzon, now primarily in inland and highland parts of the elaborate river networks of the area, but as late as the 1970s and 1980s, also along a stretch of the coastline of northeastern Luzon from near Baler in the north to near General Nakar in the south (MacLeod 1972). Other than a New Testament translation and various literacy materials developed by Tom and Pat Macleod of SIL-Philippines during their work among the Dumaget from the 1950s to the 1980s, little has appeared on this highly unique language whose numerous innovations include *sagú* 'blood', *órat* 'water', and *tapúk* 'rain' (Lobel, Andrada, et al. n.d.). Himes (2002) suggests assigning Umiray Dumaget to the Greater Central Philippine subgroup, but Lobel (2013a) rejects this, arguing that Himes's analysis suffered from a lack of distinction between retentions, innovations, and borrowings. Instead, based on a much larger body of evidence

[5] 'Tina' is placed in quotation marks because at least some speakers consider it offensive, and the Ethnologue no longer includes it as the primary name of the language. However, the removal of this identifier leaves only 'Sambal', which becomes ambiguous as to which of the two Sambali languages is being referred to.

[6] In the southern dialect area, some Dumaget self-identify as *Bulus*, a term neither used nor recognized as an ethnic identifier by speakers from other areas, who only self-identify as *Dumaget* /dumagét/ (cognate with Tagalog *dumágat* /dumágat/). Finally, despite its misapplication in the literature, no Dumaget self-identify as 'Agta' (which simply means 'person, human being' in their language), nor are they referred to as such by Tagalogs.

including complete sets of functors, Lobel places Umiray Dumaget as a primary branch of the Philippine subfamily, not closely related to any of the other Philippine languages.

### 7.2.5 Manide-Alabat

The small Manide-Alabat subgroup consists of two languages spoken by Aboriginal Filipino populations in south-central Luzon: Inagta Alabat and Manide. Both languages were virtually unknown prior to work by Lobel over the past two decades, with Lobel (2010, 2013a) and Lobel et al. (2020) representing the only published linguistic analysis of these languages. These two closely related languages do not have any other close relatives, although related languages may once have been spoken by other aboriginal groups in Quezon Province who now speak only Tagalog as their native language, such as the 'Katabagan' of Catanauan and the so-called 'Ayta' of Tayabas town. Noteworthy features of these two languages include not only their large amounts of unique vocabulary, but also their vowel shifts which affect /a/ and /u/ after voiced stops and glides: Low Vowel Fronting (a shift shared with other Aboriginal Filipino languages along the Pacific coast of Luzon, cf. Lobel n.d. a) and Low Vowel Backing in both languages, and Back Vowel Fronting in Manide. Proto-Manide-Alabat innovations include *seŋul 'sit', *panagbey 'swim', *pálaʔ 'die, kill', *katlub 'tongue', *seweŋ 'ear', *gemes 'rain', *peleŋut 'mosquito', *ma-lemʔat 'white', *suʔeŋ 'thorn', *hiʔnew 'wind (n.)', *beʔdis 'faeces', and over 200 others (Lobel n.d. b).

### 7.2.6 North Mangyan

The North Mangyan subgroup consists of the Alangan, Iraya, and Tadyawan languages spoken in the northern half of Mindoro Island. Major works include Zorc (1974b) and Barbian (1977), both of which also cover the South Mangyan languages. Forms that appear to be unique to this group include *apu 'there is, exists, have', *dulaŋ 'knee', *nakay 'what?', *Rataŋ 'hold', and the unexplained addition of -y in *duway 'two' from PAN *duSa.

### 7.2.7 Greater Central Philippines

The Greater Central Philippine (GCPH) subgroup, first proposed by Blust (1991b), combines seven Philippine subgroups (Central Philippines, Manobo, Subanen, Danaw, South Mangyan, Mongondow-Gorontalo, and Palawanic) on the basis of both shared lexical innovations and the *R > /g/ shift. Of the ninety-four innovations that Blust presented to establish this group, it is clear from Blust and Trussel (2020) that twenty-eight are retentions from PAN, PMP, PWMP, or PPH. The sixty-six that remain include *ʔəbúh 'cough', *darág 'yellow', *haldək 'fear', *pispis 'bird', and *púnuʔ 'leader, chief' (a semantic shift and metathesis of PMP *puqun 'base of a tree; cause; source, origin'). Zorc, however, questions the inclusion of the Palawanic languages in this subgroup (cf. §7.2.7.7), given the small number of GCPH innovations reflected by them vis-à-vis other GCPH languages. Likewise, Lobel (2013a, 2016b) has raised the possibility that Molbog, the southernmost language included in the Palawanic subgroup, may instead be more closely related to the Bonggi language of Sabah, Malaysia (cf. §7.4.4), a language which Blust (2010b) argues is most closely related to the Ida'anic languages of Sabah.

#### 7.2.7.1 *Central Philippines*

The approximately fifty members of this group, which consists of Tagalog, Mamanwa, and the various Bikol, Bisayan, and Mansakan languages, are spoken natively from southern Luzon to Sulu and southeastern Mindanao, and are spoken as a first language by over 60% of the Philippine population, primarily Tagalog (28%), the national language; Cebuano (13.1%); Hiligaynon (Ilonggo) (7.5%), Bikol (6%),[7] and Waray (3.4%).

##### 7.2.7.1.1 Tagalog

Chosen as the National Language or 'Wikang Pambansa' in 1937, Tagalog is the most widely studied Philippine language. Besides having been the donor of countless borrowings in dozens of proximate languages, Tagalog in premodern times was also the recipient of numerous loanwords, primarily from Malay, including forms ultimately from Arabic and Sanskrit (Wolff 1976); Kapampangan (whose territory was at certain times the centre of trade and power in the Philippines); and Chinese (Chan-Yap 1980). Due to its reciprocal borrowing relationships, as well as to its solitude (along with Kasiguranin) in its branch of the Central Philippine subgroup, it is exceedingly difficult to identify lexicon unique to Tagalog, but candidates include *búti* 'good, well', *dumí* 'dirt, dirtiness', *saán* /saʔán/ 'where?', *sagót* 'answer', *tagál* 'long (of time)', *tandâ* /tandáʔ/ 'old (person)', *tanóng* /tanúŋ/ 'ask', *upô* /ʔupúʔ/ 'sit', and *úsok* 'smoke'. Dialects outside of Manila often include historically important features such as the retention of post-consonantal glottal

[7] It is unclear whether this number includes all Bikol languages or only Central Bikol; and whether the three Bisayan languages in the Bikol Region—Masbatenyo, Northern Sorsoganon, and Southern Sorsoganon—may have also been inadvertently included.

stops (e.g. *gab-í* /gabʔí/ 'night', *big-át* /bigʔát/ 'heaviness, weight', and *ngay-on* /ŋayʔún/ 'today, now', vs. *gabí, bigát,* and *ngayón* in Manila Tagalog); and stress differences (e.g. *bitúin* /bitúʔin/ 'star' and *díyan* 'there, near addressee' vs. *bituín* /bituʔín/ ~ *bitwín* /bitwín/ 'star' and *diyán* ~ *dyan* in Manila Tagalog, respectively).

#### 7.2.7.1.2 Bisayan

The primary study of the approximately forty languages belonging to the Bisayan subgroup (some of which are spoken at the southeastern corner of Luzon, in northeastern Mindanao, and in the Sulu archipelago) is Zorc (1977), in which thirty-six Bisayan speech varieties were compared on the basis of functor analysis, shared innovations, and lexicostatistics. Innovations defining the entire Bisayan subgroup include *dakúʔ 'big', *damgu 'dream', *gəgma 'love', *hibadú 'know how to do, know (facts)', *lúʔuy 'pity', *-naʔ 'root of 2nd-position deictics', and *siŋgit 'shout'. Zorc's five-way division of the Bisayan languages—Central, Western, Southern, Cebuano, and Asi—has been adopted by all subsequent authors writing about these languages, with the sole exception of Gallman (1997), whose proposed Northeastern Mindanao group, containing Cebuano, South Bisayan, Mansakan, and Mamanwa, has not been accepted by other authors, and is best explained as the result of an East Mindanao axis (cf. §7.4.2).

The Western Bisayan subgroup consists of not only 'standard' Kalibonhon Aklanon and the 'standard' Kinaray-a around San Jose de Buenavista in Antique, but also a number of minor languages including Bulalakawnon, Inonhan, Ratagnon, Malaynon, Buruanganon, Nabasnon, Pandananon, Libertadnon, Jamindanganon-Mambusaonon, Panayanon Binukidnon (sometimes referred to as 'Sulod'), and numerous 'non-standard' dialects of Kinaray-a in the provinces of Iloilo, Capiz, and Antique. Innovations defining this subgroup include *ayán 'go', *-gi (root of 1st-person deictic), *haŋgəd 'big, many', *hilə́ŋ 'drunk', *hiŋgaʔ 'lie down', *kasalpan 'west', *libáyən 'sibling', *ráhaʔ 'cook', *tána 'he/she, him/her (NOM)', and *sánda 'they, them (NOM)'.

The Central Bisayan subgroup consists of the major languages Hiligaynon, Waray-Waray, and Masbatenyo, as well as numerous minor languages including Romblomanon, Northern Sorsoganon, Southern Sorsoganon-Northwestern Samarenyo, Northern Samarenyo, Bantayanon, Utudnon, Kinabalian, Porohanon and possibly also the Northern Binukidnon and Southern Binukidnon languages of Negros Island whose position has yet to be determined. Innovations defining this subgroup include *irúy 'mother', *kadáʔ 'go there (near addressee)', *kánam 'play', *píraw 'sleepy', and *sumat 'say, converse'.

The Cebuano branch of the Bisayan subgroup consists of a single language, Cebuano, represented by numerous dialects throughout the central Visayan Islands. Dialects in the southern third of Cebu Island, the eastern coast of Bohol Island, the southwestern coast of Leyte Island, and the eastern coast of Negros Island retain more conservative phonological and grammatical features than the Cebuano spoken in Cebu City and northern Cebu Island, and throughout Mindanao as an immigrant or second language. As with Tagalog, finding unique forms for Cebuano is difficult due to its extended and complex history of both contributing and borrowing lexicon through contact with various Bisayan, Mansakan, and Manobo languages, but candidates include *daghan* 'many', *hagbung* /hagbuŋ/ 'fall', *húnung* /húnuŋ/ 'stop', *kámu* 'cook', *kubut* 'hold', and the genitive common noun case marker *ug*.

The Southern Bisayan subgroup consists of Surigaonon, Butuanon, Tandaganon/Tagon-on (called 'Naturalis' in Zorc 1977, after the term speakers used with Zorc to distinguish their language from the Cebuano of nearby towns) and Tausug. Innovations include *bugáʔ 'afraid', *hiram 'mosquito' (borrowed into Kamayo, Ata Manobo, and Dibabawon), *kawáʔ 'get, take' (a reshaping of PPH *kúhaʔ), *kunsələm 'tomorrow', *pisak 'mud', and *yupúʔ 'short'.

The Asi subgroup consists of a single language, Asi (also known as Bantoanon), which is spoken in five towns, each with its own distinct dialect: Banton, Corcuera (on Simara Island), Concepcion (on the island known variously as Sibale, Concepcion, and Maestro de Campo), and Odiongan and Calatrava towns on Tablas Island. The Asi language is distinguished phonologically by a triad of shifts: PPH *d > /r/, *y > /d/, and *l > /y/, for example, *gador* 'emphatic marker' < PGCPH *gayəd. The five dialects share a number of innovations including *ásì* /ásiʔ/ 'why?' (from which the language gets its name), *bagúntor* 'mountain', *guyáh* 'laugh', *hidáit* /hidáʔit/ 'love' (other Bisayan *gəgma), *insulíp* 'tomorrow', *kag* 'nominative common noun case marker' (most Central Philippine *ang* ~ *an*), *kumán* 'earlier (in the same day)', and *nak* 'linker' (other Philippine *nga or *na). A number of other forms hint at external contacts that speakers of this language may have had over the past millenium, sharing *bilá-bilá* 'butterfly' with Romblomanon; *dútà* /dútaʔ/ 'earth' with Cebuano *yútà* /yútaʔ/; *maádo* /maʔádu/ 'good, well' with Cebuano and Central Bisayan *maáyo* /maʔáyu/ 'good'; *rampog* 'raincloud' with Central Bisayan *dampəg; and *taybu* 'dust' with Rinconada Bikol and Libon Bikol *talbu*.

#### 7.2.7.1.3 Bikol

The Bikol subgroup consists of eight languages native only to the Bikol Region in southeastern Luzon. The primary study of these languages is McFarland (1974), while Lobel

(2004, 2005, 2013a) has done a considerable amount of additional work. The subgroups within the Bikol node are Northern Bikol (McFarland's 'Coastal Dialects'), consisting of a single language often called 'Central Bikol' or 'Naga Bikol', spoken in various dialects primarily along the northern coast of the Bikol Region from Daet through Naga, Partido, and Legaspi to the northern coast of Sorsogon, plus in the southern half of Catanduanes Island; Southern Bikol (McFarland's 'Inland Dialects'), consisting of the Rinconada Bikol ('Iriga'),[8] Buhi-non ('Buhi Bikol'), Libon Bikol ('Libon'), West Albay Bikol ('Oas'), and Miraya Bikol ('Daraga') languages; Northern Catanduanes Bikol ('Pandan') consisting of a single language spoken throughout the northern half of Catanduanes Island; and Inagta Bikol, a language spoken by the Agta of Mt. Isarog and Mt. Iriga/Asog in Camarines Sur province (Lobel n.d.c). Not included in the Bikol subgroup are the three Bisayan languages that are native to the Bikol Region, Northern Sorsoganon ('Sorsogon'), Southern Sorsoganon ('Gubat'), and Masbatenyo ('Masbate'), the first two of which are most often simply called 'Bikol' by their speakers in spite of actually belonging to the Central Bisayan subgroup (Zorc 1977). Innovations defining the Bikol subgroup include *bayúŋ 'bird', *ʔəsád ~ *sarúʔ 'one', *gədaʔan 'die, kill', *həlay 'long (time)', *payú 'head', *rahay 'good', and *sadáy 'small'.

#### 7.2.7.1.4 Mansakan

The Mansakan subgroup consists of nine languages split between three branches: Kamayo (with a northern and southern dialect) in the Northern branch; Mansaka, Davawenyo, Samā IGaCOS[9] and the various dialects of Mandaya[10] in the Central branch; and Kāgan, Kalagan[11] and Tagakaulo in the Southern branch. Zorc (1977) was the first scholar to propose a Mansakan subgroup, which Gallman (1979) later referred to as a 'South-East Mindanao' node within what he would later (1997) propose as an East Mindanao subgroup (a grouping which no other scholars have accepted). Proto-Mansakan innovations include *atulun 'fire', *daʔig 'many', *hambuŋ 'afternoon', *hikəl 'laugh', *kamayu 'to you (2PL.OBL)', *kisələm 'tomorrow', *kulkulhun 'fingernail', *lumun 'sibling', *tiyayuʔ 'cry, weep', and *yaʔan '3SG.NOM'.

[8] The remaining alternate names in parentheses in these two paragraphs are those used by McFarland (1974).

[9] This little-known language, spoken on the Island Garden City of Samal ('IGaCOS') near Davao City and sometimes referred to as 'Samal', should not be confused with the only distantly related Sama languages.

[10] Not including the group identifying as Mandaya in Monkayo town, who in fact speak Dibabawon, not Mandaya.

[11] While *Kāgan* /kaagan/ is simply the native pronunciation of *Kalagan*, the latter is usually used in the Davao region to refer to the Islamic ethnolinguistic group, while the former is used to refer to the non-Muslim group.

#### 7.2.7.1.5 Mamanwa

The Mamanwa language is spoken by an Aboriginal Filipino population of the same name native to the northeastern Mindanao provinces of Surigao del Norte, Surigao del Sur, and Agusan del Norte, with small but long-established migrant communities on the eastern Visayan islands of Samar, Leyte, and Biliran. In spite of the fact that the vast majority of its lexicon appears to be borrowed from neighbours such as Kamayo, Surigaonon, Agusan Manobo, and Cebuano, Mamanwa retains a number of functors which point to a non-Central Philippine origin. Most of our knowledge about this language is the product of the decades that missionary sisters Helen Miller and Jeanne Miller spent working among the Mamanwa (Miller 1964, 1973; Miller and Miller 1969, 1976, 1991), with only Lobel (e.g. 2013a) having done additional work on this group in the decades since. Unique Mamanwa forms include *kamahan* 'monkey' and *nao* /naʔo/ 'I, my (1SG.GEN)', and a handful of borrowings hint at past interactions with Mansakan (e.g. *atmuʔ 'full, replete', *kamayu '2PL.OBL', *kulkulhun 'fingernail', *lumun 'sibling'); South Bisayan (e.g. *dəkag 'itch', *laʔas 'old, of person', *ləpəs 'rope', *taʔəd 'many'); and Manobo (e.g. *bubuŋ 'mountain', *buhiʔ 'full, sated', *ʔimpis 'egg').

### 7.2.7.2 *Manobo*

The Manobo subgroup consists of at least nineteen languages spoken throughout central and eastern Mindanao. Elkins (1974, 1984) has addressed the entire group in great detail, while Zorc (1974a) and Harmon (1977) have addressed the position of Kagayanen (a geographically distant member of the Northern Manobo subgroup) and Burton (1996) presents a study of borrowing relationships between various Manobo and Mansakan languages. Following Elkins plus Lobel's subsequent work on the entire group (including languages for which data was unavailable to Elkins), the nineteen Manobo languages can be classified into five branches: Northern, including Talaandig-Higaonon, Kinamiging, Banwaon, and Kagayanen; Southern, including Tagabawa, Sarangani Manobo, Cotabato Manobo, and Tasaday; Core-Western, including Obo Manobo, Ilianen Manobo, Western Bukidnon Manobo, and Pulangiyen Manobo; Core-Central, including Ata Manobo, Matig Salug Manobo, and Tigwa Manobo; and Core-Eastern, including Agusan Manobo, Rajah Kabungsuwan Manobo, Umajamnon, and Dibabawon. Among the hundreds of Proto-Manobo lexical innovations reconstructed by Elkins (1974, 1984) are *ʔahaʔ 'see', *ʔaram 'choose', *bakəsan 'snake', *din '3SG.GEN', *rimusəng 'sweat', *gətək 'belly', *laŋəsa 'blood' (although Southern Manobo has *dipanug), *lipədəŋ 'sleep', *pinənuʔu 'sit', and *tabak 'answer'.

#### 7.2.7.3 *Subanen*

The Subanen subgroup consists of seven languages spoken in the Zamboanga Peninsula in western Mindanao: Northern Subanen, Southern Subanen, Eastern Subanen, Central Subanen, Western Subanon, Western Kolibugan, and Salug-Godod Subanen (including Tawlet/Kalibugan). The primary division in this subgroup is between a Western branch which contains Western Subanon and Western Kolibugan, and the Nuclear branch which contains the other five. Early work on these languages includes Christie (1909) and Finley and Churchill (1913), while more recent work has been done by Hall (1987); Daguman (2004); Lobel and Hall (2010); Lobel (2013a); and Estioca (2020). This subgroup is defined by several phonological innovations and over seventy lexical innovations (Lobel 2013a), including *dupiʔ 'rain', *gəbək 'run', *gəŋay 'gills', *ləgdəŋ 'straight', *m[a]-ikaʔ 'small', *tapuk 'lungs', and *tərawan 'spear'.

#### 7.2.7.4 *Danaw*

The Danaw (or 'Danao') subgroup includes Maranao, the various dialects of the Maguindanaon and Iranun languages in central and western Mindanao, and the Eastern Sabah and Western Sabah dialects of Iranun in Sabah, Malaysia. While the late Howard McKaughan contributed substantially to our knowledge of these languages (1958, 1959, 1962, 2002a, b, c; McKaughan and Macaraya 1967, 1996), very little comparative work has been done on this subgroup other than a handful of articles (Allison 1979; Fleischman 1981; and Lobel and Riwarung 2009, 2011).[12] Innovations defining the group are both lexical (e.g. *mayaw 'hot', *agag 'dry in sun', *idtug 'throw') and phonological, including complex rules reducing earlier consonant clusters to the eleven clusters permissible in Proto-Danaw.

#### 7.2.7.5 *South Mangyan*

The South Mangyan subgroup consists of the Hanunoo, Buhid, Eastern Tawbuwid, Western Tawbuwid, and Bangon languages spoken in central and southern Mindoro Island. Zorc (1974b) has treated the internal subgrouping of the Mangyan languages in general, while Pennoyer (1980) addressed the relationship between Buhid and the Tawbuwid languages.[13] Very few lexical innovations have been identified for this subgroup so far (e.g. *labuŋ 'leaf', *siraŋ-siraŋ 'daily'), while a handful of forms are shared exclusively with Bisayan (e.g. *badás 'sand') or Bikol (e.g. *túkaw 'sit'), likely due to contact with these two groups at some point in the past.

#### 7.2.7.6 *Mongondow-Gorontalo*

One of three Philippine subgroups located outside of the geographical Philippines, along with Sangiric (§7.2.12) and Minahasan (§7.2.13), the Mongondow-Gorontalo subgroup consists of nine languages spoken in central northern Sulawesi, Indonesia: Mongondow, Lolak, Bintauna, Kaidipang, Bolango, Suwawa, Buol, Gorontalo, and the now-extinct Ponosakan. Recent work on these languages includes that of James Sneddon and late Indonesian scholar H. T. Usup (Usup 1984, 1986; Sneddon and Usup 1986; Sneddon 1991; Lobel 2011, 2015, 2016a; and Lobel and Paputungan 2017).[14] Following Charles (1974), Blust (1991b) groups the Mongondow-Gorontalo languages in the Greater Central Philippine subgroup. The 140 Proto-Mongondow-Gorontalo lexical innovations identified by Lobel (n.d. d) include *boyod 'rat', *buloy 'spouse', *gogoyon 'hungry', *mo-lanit 'sharp (of edge)', *lituʔ 'sit', *liyoŋ 'forget', *oŋkag 'river', *porok 'smoke (n.)', and *utas 'sibling'.

#### 7.2.7.7 *Palawanic*

The Palawanic subgroup is generally defined as consisting of Batak, Aborlan Tagbanwa, Molbog, and various languages spoken by groups identifying as Palawan ~ Pala-wan,[15] including Brooke's Point Palawan, Central Palawan, Southwest Palawan, and the closely related languages of the Panimusan (long-Islamized coastal groups who do not identify as 'Palawan' but whose language is nevertheless largely identical to that of the non-Muslim Palawan people). Thiessen (1981) is the only study of the entire subgroup. Scebold (2003) later introduced the Central Tagbanwa language, for which data was not previously available. Blust (1991b) argues that these languages form one of seven nodes of the Greater Central Philippine macrogroup, but Zorc questions

[12] Many authors have asserted that there was a difference in endonyms between the Iranun of Mindanao and the Iranun of Sabah. In fact, both groups refer to themselves exclusively as 'Iranun' (sometimes spelled 'Iranon'), while names such as 'Ilanun' and 'Illanun' are exclusively exonyms used in Malay, Maguindanaon, and English.

[13] Barbian (1977) contains an invaluable expanded wordlist, but the subgrouping analysis contained therein is highly problematic, based on shared features and ignoring innovations and important differences between the languages. Likewise, Barbian treats Ratagnon as a Mangyan language, when it clearly belongs to the Western Bisayan group.

[14] Lobel is currently working on a dictionary and grammar of the now-extinct Ponosakan and the moribund Lolak.

[15] The latter reflecting the conservative reflex /palaʔwan/ found in the Palawan dialects that preserve /ʔC/ clusters.

this since, in spite of sharing the *R > *g shift, the number of PGCPH lexical innovations found in the Palawanic languages is minimal, a fact that could also indicate that Proto-Palawanic was the earliest to split from Proto-GCPH. The Palawanic languages share a number of lexical innovations including *bakal 'throw', *bəgit 'bird', *gərəŋ 'back', *rayak 'pull', and *tabuk 'smoke'. The Northern and Southern branches of Palawanic are distinguished by forms such as *kəʔdəŋ 'dog' in the former corresponding to *idəŋ in the latter, both replacing PAN *asu. The Southern branch is further distinguished by innovations such as *dələk 'rain', *kəsit 'laugh', and *tipusəd 'sibling'.

### 7.2.8 Kalamianic

The Kalamianic subgroup consists of the Agutaynen, Calamian Tagbanwa, and Karamianen languages, all located on islands between northern Palawan, southern Mindoro, and western Panay. Himes (2007) is the primary historical-comparative work on these languages, which are distinguished by the phonological shifts of PMP/PPH *R > *l and *q > *k. Lexical innovations defining the Kalamianic subgroup include *aliŋət 'near', *aniŋ 'say', *ələd 'fear', *gəʔəd 'bolo', *guʔuy 'call', *kandas 'liver', *kulit 'white', *tan- '3rd-person pronominal formative', and *yawaʔ 'you (2SG.NOM)'.

### 7.2.9 Inati and the Ata of Negros

While the existence of the Ete/'Ati'[16] people of Panay Island had been known since the Spanish occupation of the Philippines, it wasn't until Pennoyer (1986–1987) that any data from, or description of, their language surfaced, and little Inati data has appeared in the literature outside of that included by Pennoyer and in Lobel (2013a). The language appears to form a primary branch of the Philippine subfamily (Blust 1991b: 80), with Blust noting that "[u]niquely among languages in the Philippines, it has merged *R and *d in at least final position (intervocalically pre-Inati *d became /r/, and subsequently pre-Inati *R became /d/)", for example, *kadat* 'bite', *kiturud* 'sleep', *paridus* 'bathe'. There are also a large number of unique forms and features in the functor subsets, but the vast majority of its lexicon has been borrowed from neighbouring Bisayan languages on Panay, primarily Kinaray-a and Aklanon, but also Hiligaynon (Ilonggo). Unique lexical items include *sapiw* 'house', *awuy* 'yes', *nalang* 'no', *umê* 'arrive', *dugúk* 'go', *ngadin* 'don't know', *pegek* 'chicken', *betleng* 'put', *da-it* 'rain', *miyá* 'what?', *ki-ara* 'where?', *mesned* 'far', *himpun* 'fire', and *gine* 'also'.

It should be noted that the Ete/'Ati' of Panay, Guimaras, and Boracay islands are distinct from the Ata people of Negros Island (who in turn should not be confused with the linguistically and ethnically distinct Ata Manobo of central Mindanao, who are closely related to the neighbouring Tigwa and Matigsalug Manobo). The Ata of Negros Island are descendants of a once widespread population encountered by the Spanish in the sixteenth century (Rahman and Maceda 1955; Scott 1984, 1992), thus compelling them to name the island 'Negros' (from the Spanish plural for 'black', or, in this context, 'Black person'). The most important linguistic distinction is that while the Ati and the Ata have distinct ethnic identities, only the Ati retain a complete language distinct from those of their neighbours, whereas Lobel, in multiple visits to Ata communities throughout the island, has found only three Ata who can remember even fragments of an Inata language distinct from the neighbouring Binukidnon languages native to the mountains of Negros Island. Unique Inata forms where these few individuals were in linguistic agreement during these separately collected elicitations include *din-ay* 'there (far from speaker and addressee)', *kan-ay* 'go there', *dihna* 'here', *bangut* 'man', *tairan* 'woman', *kukuyuban* 'house', and *tukub* 'eat' (Lobel n.d. e).

[16] Note that *Ete* /ete/ (likely underlying *ata, as /a/ raises to [ɛ] ~ [æ] in the Inete language) and *Inete* /inete/ are the endonyms for the group and its language, respectively, while *Ati* and *Inati* are the Bisayan corruptions thereof.

### 7.2.10 Southwestern Mindanao

The Southwest Mindanao subgroup consists of Tboli (sometimes called 'Tagabili'), Koronadal Blaan, Sarangani Blaan, and the more distantly related Teduray (also called 'Tiruray'). Innovations defining the Southwest Mindanao subgroup include *bakuŋ 'deaf', *butəŋ 'night', *dawin 'loincloth' (vs. PMP *bahaR), *deʔe 'many', *kodog 'boil (water)', *isaq 'break open, hatch' (vs. PAN *pəcəq), *kuwah 'oar, paddle', *lakay 'tail feather of rooster' (vs. PMP *lawi), and *Rasan 'skinny'. The Tboli-Blaan node is defined by innovations such as *boŋ 'big', *fayah 'tomorrow', *kahuŋ 'swim' (vs. PAN *Nanguy), *kahiʔ 'salt' (vs. PAN *qasiN), and *litəʔ 'blood' (cf. PAN *Nitəq 'sap').

### 7.2.11 Southeastern Mindanao

This group consists of the various dialects of the Klata language (also known as Bagobo Klata, Giangan, or Diangan), spoken in Magpet town in Cotabato province, and in the Baguio, Calinan, Marilog, and Tugbog districts of Davao City. This moribund language was only recently discovered to be distinct from all other southern Philippine languages (cf. Evans 2017 and Zorc 2019). It is no longer generally being passed on to children, largely due to intermarriage with Cebuanos and other local groups. A few of its unique vocabulary items include the plural marker *bɛ* (vs. Proto-Southern-Philippines *maŋa), *benne'* /benneʔ/ 'cry, weep' (vs. PAN *Caŋis), *byoo* /byoʔo/ 'year' (vs. PMP *taqun, PPH *dagʔun), *klammag* 'star' (vs. PAN *bituqən), *kulung* 'back' (vs. PAN *likud), *lammi* 'new' (vs. PAN *baqəRuh), *ongob* /oŋob/ 'fingernail' (vs. PMP *kukuh), and *paya* 'big' (vs. PAN *Raya, PMP *laba, PPH *dakəl).

### 7.2.12 Sangiric

Separated from one another by the maritime border between the Philippines and Indonesia, the five Sangiric languages have been recognized as a primary branch of the Philippine subgroup since Sneddon (1984), the primary work on this subgroup. Three of these languages (Sangir/Sangihe, Talaud, and Sangil) are spoken on a series of small islands between southeastern Mindanao and northeastern Sulawesi, while the other two (Ratahan/Pasan and Bantik) were traditionally spoken in the Minahasa subprovince on the mainland of northeastern Sulawesi. Like the vast majority of languages native to northeastern Sulawesi, the Sangiric languages within the national borders of Indonesia are all moribund and highly endangered, seldom spoken, and not being learned by anyone younger than the 'grandparent generation', as the entire population has switched to Manado Malay. Innovations identified by Sneddon (1984) include *akeʔ 'water', *babəlaw 'afternoon', *busak 'banana', *iaʔ 'I (1SG.NOM)', *payaŋ 'thigh', *pepe 'urine', *siŋaʔ 'know a person', *tanak 'live, dwell', *təbay 'old (of object)', *təmbuʔ 'head', *tipu 'smoke', *timbonan 'head', *t[io]ŋkaRia 'ear', *tətuR 'hot coals, embers', and *tolay 'tail'. Note that the Sangiric and Minahasan groups, bordering on one another in some areas, share a handful of innovations, including *dou ~ *r$_2$eʔo 'thirst', *paluka 'shoulder', *həŋisəʔ ~ *rəngis 'burn', *dirihəʔ ~ *ririh 'yellow', *tagas 'low tide, ebb', *təkəl 'sleep', *tumpa 'descend, alight', *tunay 'thorn', and *utak 'hair' (< PMP *utək 'brain').

### 7.2.13 Minahasan

The Minahasan languages are spoken exclusively on the mainland of northeastern Sulawesi, in what was formerly the subprovince or 'regency' of Minahasa (now broken up into several smaller regencies). Sneddon (1978) assigned these five languages—Tontemboan, Tonsawang, Tonsea, Tondano, and Tombulu—to the Philippine subfamily, a position also adopted by Blust (1991b). Similar to the Sangiric languages, all of the Minahasan languages except Tonsawang are moribund, with even elderly Minahasans now speaking Manado Malay much more frequently than their ancestral languages, which virtually no children are currently learning. Proto-Minahasan innovations identified by Sneddon (1978) include *baŋkoʔ 'big', *bər$_2$ən 'eye', *bisa 'which?, where?', *datə 'cold', *ələp 'drink', *əŋah 'cough', *biaʔi 'here', *kəʔkəʔ 'laugh', *pəntuʔ 'bitter', *tələb 'fly (away)', and *tiəy 'pig'.

## 7.3 Phonological developments

Much has been written on both the synchronic phonologies of Philippine languages, and on various aspects of the historical phonology of the Philippine subfamily or various branches thereof, starting with such noteworthy early works as Conant (1911, 1912, 1916) and Dempwolff (1925). This section will therefore present only a very brief overview of Philippine phonology and phonological developments.

### 7.3.1 Consonants

Proto-Philippines can be reconstructed with a phonological system consisting of twenty consonants and four vowels (Blust p.c., 9/28/2020). Synchronically, the vast majority of Philippine languages have either three- or four-vowel systems, and most commonly a sixteen-member consonant inventory, as illustrated in Table 7.1.

The following relatively rare consonants are also known to occur in some languages:

a) /β/ (*-b-) in Central Cagayan Agta and some Manobo and Sangiric languages
b) /f/ (< *p) in Koronadal Blaan, Sarangani Blaan, Teduray, Tawbuwid, and Bangon
c) voiced velar approximant /ɰ/ (< *l) in Buhi-non Bikol and Aklanon (written <e> in the latter)
d) interdental approximant /ð̞/ (< *l and sometimes *r) in Southern Catanduanes Bikol, Kagayanen, the Cajidiocan dialect of Romblomanon, and some Mandaya dialects
e) retroflex tap [ɽ] (< *l preceding /i/ or /e/ if not following another /i/ or /e/), in Mongondow, Lolak, and certain other Mongondow-Gorontalo languages
f) retroflex lateral approximant [ɭ] (< *l adjacent to any combination of the vowels /a o u/ whether word-initial, word-final, or intervocalic) in Mongondow, Lolak, and certain other Mongondow-Gorontalo languages (Lobel and Paputungan 2017)

**Table 7.1** The phoneme system of Proto-Philippines (Blust p.c., 9/28/2020) and the most common Philippine phoneme system

**THE PHONEME SYSTEM OF PROTO-PHILIPPINES**

| CONSONANTS | | | | | VOWELS | |
|---|---|---|---|---|---|---|
| *p | *t | | *k | *q | *ʔ | *i | *u |
| *b | *d | *j | *g | | | *ə |
| | *s | | | | *h | *a |
| *m | *n | *ñ | *ŋ | | | |
| | *l | | | | | |
| | *r | | | *R | | |
| *w | *y | | | | | |

**THE MOST COMMON PHILIPPINE PHONEME SYSTEM**

| CONSONANTS | | | | VOWELS | |
|---|---|---|---|---|---|
| p | t | k | ʔ | i | u |
| b | d | g | | (ə/ɨ/o) | |
| | s | | h | a | |
| m | n | ŋ | | | |
| | l | | | | |
| | r | | | | |
| w | y | | | | |

g) a series of heavy voiceless obstruents /p' t' k' s'/ in Maranao (< Proto-Danaw *bp, *dt, *gk, and *ds, respectively) (Lobel and Riwarung 2009, 2011)
h) a series of aspirated voiceless obstruents /$p^h$ $t^h$ $k^h$ $s^h$/ in Southern Subanen (< Proto-Subanen *kp, *kt, *gk, and *ks, respectively) (Lobel and Hall 2010).

The glottal fricative /h/ is found in many Philippine languages, sometimes as a continuation of PMP *h (< PAN *S), other times as a reflex of other PMP/PPH phonemes such as *s, *r, or *R, and, in some languages, only in forms borrowed from Spanish, Malay, or English. PMP *h itself is continued as /h/ in Itbayaten, Manide, Inagta Alabat, most Central Philippine languages (including Tagalog, Mamanwa, and at least some members of the Bikol, Bisayan, and Mansakan subgroups), and several mostly northern Manobo languages (Talaandig-Higaonon (Binukid), Kinamiging, Banwaon, and Umajamnon).[17] Other sources of /h/ in Philippine languages include:

a) *s > /h/ in Amganad Ifugao, Ayta Abellen, Ayta Ambala, Ayta Bataan, Ayta Mag-antsi, Balangao, Batad Ifugao, Bayninan Ifugao, Botolan Sambal, Kalanguya, Keley-i Kallahan, Koronadal Blaan, Sarangani Blaan, and Tboli; and sporadically in all of the Northeastern Luzon languages except Casiguran Agta
b) *r > /h/ in Pahanan Agta, Casiguran Agta, Nagtipunan Agta, Dinapigue Agta and the southern dialect of Dupaningan Agta
c) *l > /h/ in Ivatan, and sporadically in Tagalog and some dialects of Bantayanon
d) *R, *g > /h/ in Ponosakan, Suwawa, and Gorontalo (plus *b > /h/ in some environments in Gorontalo)
e) *R > /h/ in Minahasan, and in a handful of etyma in Mamanwa
f) *k > /h/ in Southern Subanen and Buhid
g) *p, *q > /h/ in Tboli
h) *b, *d, *j, *R, *r > /h/ in Central Cagayan Agta.

The occurrence of word-final /h/ is limited to Itbayaten, Ayta Abellen, Tina Sambal, Mamanwa, Aklanon, Surigaonon (primarily in dialects in Surigao del Sur), Bantayanon (at least in rural dialects), Northern Samarenyo, and Eastern Samar Waray.[18] Thus PAN *CiŋaS, PMP *tiŋah 'food stuck in teeth' > Itbayaten *tiñah*, Aklanon, Mamanwa *tiŋáh*. Likewise,

[17] A number of other languages such as Casiguran Agta have /h/ < *h in borrowings but not in inherited forms.

[18] There are differences in the retention of word-final /h/ between reduplicated monosyllables (e.g. *muhmuh 'rice crumbs') and words of other forms (e.g. *təbuh 'sugarcane'), with some languages such as Bantayanon, Surigaonon, and some dialects of Waray-Waray preserving word-final *h in the former but not the latter.

other than in words of the shape CVhCVh in the aforementioned languages, few others preserve /h/ as a reflex of PMP *h in non-word-final coda position, such as Inata *dihna* 'here', Northern Binukidnon *dihni* 'here', Manide, Inagta Alabat *beh-en* /behʔen/ 'sneeze'. Finally, an underlying word-final /h/ is posited on orthographically vowel-final words in certain other languages like Tagalog and Cebuano, but it is only pronounced when inflected, for example, *natiŋahán* 'happened to have food stuck in one's teeth' (although this morphophonemic /h/ is far more regular in Tagalog than in Cebuano).

### 7.3.2 Vowels

Proto-Philippines had a four-vowel system (*a *i *u *ə), and most of its daughter languages have three or four phonemic vowels. Languages that have three-vowel systems have merged PPH *ə with either *a, *i, or *u. Those that have four-vowel systems are split between those that continue *ə as a tense high central vowel /ɨ/, a lax mid central vowel /ə/, a mid back vowel /o/ (phonetically [ɔ] in some languages), and a mid front vowel /e/. Languages with more than four vowels include:

a) Casiguran Agta, described in Headland and Headland (1974) as having an eight-vowel system consisting of /a e ɛ i o ɔ u ɨ/
b) The Oas dialect of Miraya Bikol, which has monophthongized sequences of *au (> /o/), *ai (> /e/), and *aə (> /ɯ/) while maintaining a distinct reflex of *ə, producing a seven-vowel system consisting of /a e i o u ɨ ɯ/
c) A number of Mongondow-Gorontalo languages, in which a non-etymological /e/ appears alongside an /o/ reflex of *ə, yielding a five-vowel system consisting of /a e i o u/.

Furthermore, educated and/or urban speakers of many other Philippine languages have acquired a non-native distinction between /e/ and /i/, and /o/ and /u/, even though these two vowels (/e/ and /o/) are not otherwise contrastive in the native lexicon of their languages. However, Spanish and English loanwords are adapted to the native phonology for most speakers of Philippine languages, even major languages like Tagalog, Cebuano, Ilokano, and Hiligaynon (Ilonggo).

Finally, the Maranao language of central Mindanao is unique in having developed a system of voice register (Lobel and Riwarung 2009, 2011) reminiscent of that found in certain Mon-Khmer languages, in which earlier consonant clusters have developed into the unitary heavy consonants mentioned earlier in this section, which have a raising and tensing effect on the following vowel. Although acoustic analysis is still lacking, it is clear that what initially appear to be eight distinct vowels in Maranao are instead two complementary sets of four vowel allophones, with each set occurring after a separate set of consonants.

## 7.4 Issues and controversies

By far the largest controversy in the historical linguistics literature on Philippine and Philippine-type languages has been the question of whether or not there is sufficient evidence to posit a 'Proto-Philippines', that is, whether the languages of the Philippines (minus the Sama-Bajaw languages) plus Yami in Taiwan and the Sangiric, Minahasan, and Mongondow-Gorontalo languages of Sulawesi in Indonesia, are more closely related to one another than to any other languages. One of the major issues that have been resolved (see Zorc and Almarines 2022) is the appearance of innovations that cross-cut genetic boundaries established by the comparative method which are *axis relationships*, geographic and sociolinguistic unities among languages based on subsequent trade and cultural ties. These will be discussed in the following sections.

### 7.4.1 Proto-Philippines

As Blust (2019b) notes, the existence of a Philippine subfamily was largely assumed for much of the twentieth century, and rarely debated until Reid (1982) argued against it in a now-retracted paper (Reid 2020) based primarily on the presence or absence of what he claimed was an "intrusive nasal" (in spite of providing neither a list of such forms nor thorough evidence to support his claim). In response, Zorc (1986) presented ninety-eight lexical Proto-Philippine innovations that had not previously appeared in the literature. Little more appeared on the issue for almost two decades until Ross (2005) revisited the issue in his reanalysis of the position of the Batanic languages, pointing out the lack of evidence for a Proto-Philippines beyond what he characterized as a relatively small number of lexical items which he believed could have been borrowed through contact. However, while working on his Austronesian Comparative Dictionary (Blust and Trussel 2020), Blust has identified hundreds of lexical items unique to the Philippine languages, ultimately publishing a comprehensive treatise (Blust 2019b) defending the existence of a Proto-Philippines based on over a thousand lexical innovations and the merger of proto-phonemes *z and *d (as opposed to the retention of both *ñ and *n). Since the appearance of Blust (2019b), reaction papers appeared in the 2020 issue of *Oceanic Linguistics* can be summarized as follows:

(1) Zorc (2020), generally supportive of Blust's arguments, proposes that the complex accent patterns exclusive to the Philippines (cf. Smith, chapter 2, this volume) and the reconstruction of an initial PPH *y- may provide additional supporting evidence for a Proto-Philippines, identifying nine minimal pairs for accent reconstructed for PPH within Blust's article. Zorc also deals with the lack of true vowel sequences and the need to reconstruct glottal stop in all positions (initial, intervocalic, preconsonantal, post-consonantal, and word-final) both in most microgroups and for PPH itself. He proposes that forms shared exclusively between Bashiic and Ilokano were most probably the product of a Bashiic-Ilokano Axis, and disputes the value of Casiguran Agta as any more than a 'witness' language due to evidence of heavy borrowing from Tagalog and/or Kasiguranin.

(2) Liao (2020) and Reid (2020) are more critical, with Liao pointing out that none of Blust's proposed PPH innovations are retained in all of its daughter branches, and argues that "[i]ssues with. . . negative evidence cannot be eased simply by drastically increasing the number of lexical innovations. . . not established through. . . bottom-up reconstruction". Similar to Zorc (2020), Reid notes problems with Blust's reconstruction of *q instead of *ʔ in certain cases, including thirty-nine etyma with no Tboli or Kalamianic evidence; six etyma where either Tboli or Kalamianic justify *q; and three etyma where Agutaynen has irregular reflexes. Reid also revisits prenasalization (-NC- clusters), unknown in Formosan languages except in reduplicated monosyllables (Dahl 1976: 128), and difficult to reconstruct for PPH except as the product of syncope of words infixed with *<um> or *<in>.

It remains to be seen what further discussion will surface on this issue. Combined with the merger of *d and *z and the apparent innovation of phonemic accent, the sheer number of lexical innovations presented by Blust (2019b) would seem to complicate any arguments that they are simply the result of borrowing. However, it is likely that the lack of grammatical innovations (understandable in light of the relative conservativity of the Philippine languages as a whole) will motivate at least some authors to continue to question the validity of this grouping.

### 7.4.2 The complicating factors of axis relationships

In writing his dissertation in 1972–1973, Zorc was confronted with a number of innovations that were spread across various otherwise well-established subgroups, for example, the replacement of PAN *bəli 'to buy' (retained in Tagalog, Tausug, Mansaka, and Bilic) by *bakál in Aklanon *bakáe* /bakáu̯/, Asi, Romblomanon *bakáy*, Bulalakawnon, Kinaray-a, Caluyanen, Hiligaynon, Masbatenyo, Hanunoo, and all Bikol languages *bakál*. As this form *bakál cuts across four separate discrete subgroups (West Bisayan, Central Bisayan, Bikol, and South Mangyan), Zorc posited forms with this distribution as evidence of a North Bisayan 'Axis'.[19] It is clear from evidence in Reid (1971) and Zorc (ongoing) that analogous replacements have occurred throughout the Philippines: Waray, Cebuano, Surigaonon, Mamanwa, Kamayo, Kagayanen, and several Mansakan dialects have *palít* (from PPH *palít 'exchange' [ACD], possibly related to Dempwolff's *palit 'return gift'), suggesting an Eastern Mindanao Axis; Kalamianic and Palawanic have *alaŋ, supporting a Palawan–Kalamian Axis; Northern Philippine languages have either *gátaŋ or *láku?, suggesting a northern Luzon Axis; South Cordilleran has *tuŋgal, which is unique to that subgroup; and the Danao languages, Dibabawon and Western Bukidnon Manobo share *pamasa* 'buy' (possibly from Persian *bāzār* 'market' via Malay *pasar* + *paN-). Each of these replacements represents 'leakage' (in the terminology of Blust 2019b for loans across genetic boundaries) from one well-established subgroup into other neighbouring languages where significant trade or social networks once existed. These post-split innovations give the false impression of a genetic subgrouping, whereas what they actually indicate is a significant sociolinguistic replacement phenomenon.

Thus far, Zorc has uncovered evidence for the following eight axis relationships (note that some languages such as Ilokano, Tagalog, and Hanunoo are included in two or more such axes):

[19] Zorc coined the term 'axis' in 1972, since which similar phenomena have been described as 'network' by Milroy and Milroy (1985), and as 'linkage' by Pawley and Ross (1995) and Ross (1988). Note that this phenomenon could also be accounted for by the German terms 'Sprachbund' and 'Sprechbund'.

1) **Bashiic–Ilokano axis** [Ilokano and the Batanic/Bashiic languages]
*dúyuR 'coconut-shell receptacle for food or water': Ilokano *dúyog*, Yami, Itbayaten, Ibatan *royoy*, Ivatan *duyuy*.
*kəláʔat 'sudden, abrupt': Ilokano *kelláʔat*, Itbayaten *akxat*.
*laŋlaŋ 'eat together as a group': Ilokano *ag-la-laŋláŋ* 'to eat together', Itbayaten *xaŋxaŋ* 'eating in a group (at least two)', Ibatan *haŋhaŋ* 'two people eat together'.
*Rábat 'flotsam': Ilokano *gábat* 'flotsam, debris, stray, straggler, loot', Isamorong Ivatan *yavat* 'driftwood'.
*RaRáŋ 'large marine mollusk (Turbo marmoratus)': Ilokano *raráŋ* 'kind of large, elongated mollusk with a pointed shell; mother-of-pearl', Itbayaten *yayaŋ* 'seashell with a shutter or lid: Turbo marmoratus (larger of the two Turbo varieties)', Ivatan *yayaŋ* 'turbo shell', Ibatan *yayaŋ* 'kind of large sea snail'.

2) **Northern Luzon axis** [Ilokano, Cagayan Valley, and Central Cordilleran]
*layús 'flood': Ilokano, Gaddang, Manabo, Luba, Itneg and Isinai.
*lukməg 'fat': Ilokano, Luba, Bontok, and Isnag.
*sabáli 'other, different': Isnag, Ilokano, Manabo, Itneg, and Balangao.
*salʔit 'lightning': Isnag, Ilokano, Itneg, and Kalinga.
*suʔpit 'narrow': Isnag, Malaweg, Kalinga, and Manabo.

3) **Central Luzon axis** [Central and South Cordilleran]
*bətík 'run': Amganad Ifugao, Kiangan Ifugao, Ibaloi, Kallahan, and Pangasinan.
*bútəŋ 'drunk': Isinai, Kiangan Ifugao, Northern and Southern Kankanaey, Inibaloi.
*dagə́m 'wind': Isinai, Northern and Southern Kankanaey, Ibaloi, Kalanguya, and Pangasinan.
*imuk 'mosquito': Isinai, Ibaloi, and Kalanguya.
*taláw 'star': Balangao, Bontok, Luba, Kankanay, Ibaloi, Kalanguya.

4) **Southern Luzon axis** [Tagalog, Sambalic, Kapampangan, Remontado, Pangasinan, Casiguran Agta, Bikol, and Hanunoo]
*alikabúk 'dust': Tagalog, Kapampangan, Botolan Sambal, Ayta Mag-Indi, Bulalakawnon, and Casiguran Agta.
*buláti 'earthworm': Tagalog, Kapampangan, Botolan Sambal, Remontado, and Masbatenyo.
*damúlag 'carabao': Kapampangan, Sambalic, Northern Bikol, and Southern Bikol.
*páwəs 'sweat': Kapampangan *páwas*, Tagalog *páwis* (borrowed by Remontado and Casiguran Agta).
*tiʔris 'urine': Northern Bikol, Tadyawan, and Pangasinan; Hanunoo 'millipede secretion'.

5) **North Bisayan axis** [West Bisayan, Central Bisayan, Asi, Bikol, and Hanunoo]
*bahə́l 'big': Aklanon, Kinaray-a, Looknon, Bulalakawnon, Datagnon, Kuyonon, and Romblomanon.
*bəʔə́l 'take': Aklanon, Kinaray-a, Bulalakawnon, Datagnon, Kuyonon, Asi, Romblomanon, and Hanunoo.
*hambal 'say, speak': Aklanon, Kinaray-a, Bulalakawnon, Caluyanen, Asi, Hiligaynon, Romblomanon, Masbatenyo, and Kagayanen.
*indu 'your (2PL.OBL)': Caluyanen, Kuyonon, Northern Bikol, Romblomanon, and Asi.
*isará 'one': Aklanon, Kinaray-a, Pandananon, Bulalakawnon, Caluyanen, Kuyonon, Hanunoo, and Kagayanen.
*taʔú 'give': Aklanon, Kinaray-a, Pandananon, Bulalakawnon, Caluyanen, Romblomanon, Asi, Northern Bikol, and Rinconada Bikol.

6) **Palawan–Kalamian axis** [Kalamianic and Palawanic]
*alaŋ 'buy': Calamian Tagbanwa, Aborlan Tagbanwa, Batak (note also Palawan *ələn*).
*bəlag 'not so' [NEG]: Agutaynen, Karamianen, Palawan, and Molbog; Aborlan Tagbanwa 'different'.
*kumba 'lungs': Calamian Tagbanwa, Karamianen, Central Tagbanwa, and Aborlan Tagbanwa.
*luwak 'plant, dibble (v.)': Calamian Tagbanwa, Agutayen, Karamianen, Batak, Aborlan Tagbanwa, and Palawan.
*tagək 'blood': Calamian Tagbanwa, Karamianen, Batak, and Central Tagbanwa.

7) **Palawan–Mindoro axis** [North and South Mangyan, Kalamianic, and Palawanic]
*[h]abuat 'long': Kalamianic, Palawanic, North Mangyan, and South Mangyan.
*aŋbəʔ 'rat': Aborlan Tagbanwa, Batak, Hanunoo, Buhid, and West Bisayan.
*bílug 'body': Northern Palawanic, North Mangyan, and South Mangyan.

*hampaŋ 'say, speak': Batak, Aborlan Tagbanwa, Palawan, and Hanunoo (cf. PBIS *hampaŋ 'play').
*kawa 'you (2SG.NOM)': Kalamianic *yawaʔ (< *i-kawa), Central Tagbanwa and Tadyawan *kawa*.

8) **Eastern Mindanao axis** [South Bisayan, Mansakan, Mamanwa, Manobo, Danaw, and Subanen]
*allaŋ 'slave': Mansakan, Dibabawon, and Sarangani Manobo.
*baʔal 'make': Western Bukidnon Manobo, Subanen, Maranao, and Maguindanaon.
*dayaw 'good': South Bisayan, Mansakan, Mamanwa, Ata Manobo, and Dibabawon.
*sidan 'they (3PL.NOM)' (with addition of final nasal to PMP *sida): Mamanwa, Kamayo, Mansakan, and Subanen.

### 7.4.3 Relationship of Bashiic/Batanic, Central Luzon, and North Mangyan

In his treatment of the Mangyan languages of Mindoro, Zorc (1977: 34) pointed out the division between the North Mangyan (Iraya, Alangan, and Tadyawan) and South Mangyan (Hanunoo, Buhid, Western and Eastern Tawbuwid, and Bangon) languages, and suggested the possibility of a 'North Extension' containing not only the North Mangyan languages but also Batanic/Bashiic and Central Luzon (i.e. Kapampangan and the Sambali-Ayta languages). This 'North Extension' was based on the merger of PAN *R with *y, not generally found elsewhere among Philippine languages, as well as a handful of putative lexical innovations, including *dagul 'big', *udi 'left (side)', and *dimlaʔ 'cold'. Neither McFarland (1980) nor Blust (1991b, 2019b) accept the inclusion of Batanic/Bashiic in this grouping, but far more research and documentation is still needed for all of these languages. Note that the presence of forms reflecting *R as /y/ instead of /g/ or /l/ in members of the South Mangyan, Palawanic, and Kalamianic subgroups may turn out to be evidence that an ancient member of Zorc's North Extension may have once been a prestige language in the area: for example, Calamian Tagbanwa, Karamianen, some Batak *ikuy* 'tail' (< *ikuR); Agutaynen *ki-yuy* /kiʔyuy/ 'egg' (< *qitəluR); Agutaynen *niyuy* 'coconut' (< *niyuR); Batak, Aborlan Tagbanwa *punyangan* 'parent-in-law' (< *tuRaŋ); and Kalamianic *waiʔ 'water' (< *wahiR).

### 7.4.4 The position of Molbog and Bonggi

The languages of the Philippine province of Palawan have been demonstrated by a number of authors (e.g. Zorc 1977; Thiessen 1981; Blust 1991b, 2010b; Himes 2007) to be split between a Kalamianic group and a Palawanic group, both belonging to the Philippine subfamily. Likewise, the majority of the languages of Sabah (as well as a handful of others spoken in Sarawak, Brunei, and the Indonesian province of Kalimantan Utara) are known to belong to two subgroups, Southwest Sabah and Ida'anic/Northeast Sabah (Blust 1998b, 2010b; Lobel 2013a), neither of which immediately subgroups with the languages of the Philippines (Blust 1998b) in spite of their Philippine-type features. However, one controversy remains with regard to these two groups: the position of Molbog and Bonggi. Molbog is spoken primarily on the Philippine island of Balabac off the southern tip of Palawan, neighbouring minor islands, and a handful of communities near the southern tip of Palawan plus two perhaps century-old communities on Banggi Island off the northwestern tip of Sabah. Bonggi, on the other hand, is spoken on the aforementioned Malaysian island of Banggi plus Balambangan Island to its immediate west. Thiessen (1981) treats both languages as members of the Palawanic group, while Blust (2010b) argues that Bonggi subgroups with the Ida'anic languages (Ida'an, Begak, Sungai Seguliud, Subpan, and the elusive Buludupi) in a 'Northeast Sabah' subgroup within his Greater North Borneo grouping. Lobel (2013a), on the other hand, notes striking similarities (but admittedly not shared innovations) suggesting a closer connection between Molbog and Bonggi in a Molbog-Bonggi subgroup whose external relationships have yet to be determined. While Blust's data linking Bonggi to the Ida'anic languages appear to be quite strong, the similarities Lobel notes between Molbog and Bonggi still warrant further investigation: The Palawan-Sabah area is clearly at the border of Philippine and non-Philippine languages, but what remains to be understood is whether Molbog and Bonggi were once two closely related languages that came under mutually exclusive influences, one (Molbog) from languages to its north, the other (Bonggi) from the languages to its south. If not, then the similarities shared by these two languages, one each from the Philippine and Greater North Borneo macrogroups, are the result of a contact-induced convergence whose further investigation may shed light on the undocumented social history of this little-studied border zone.

### 7.4.5 The position of the languages of Sabah

Much less a 'controversy' among scholars of Philippine and Philippine-type languages than simply an 'issue' warranting mention is the position of the languages of Sabah in light of their Philippine-type grammatical characteristics. In very few places outside of the geographical Philippines and northern Borneo is the Philippine-type focus and case-marking system retained, with large pockets in Taiwan and northern Sulawesi (the latter belonging to the Philippine subfamily), and a small number of more distant holdouts in Madagascar (Malagasy), Java (Old Javanese), and Sumatra (Batak). However, as Blust (1998b, 2010b, 2013a) points out, evidence from the Formosan languages in Taiwan clearly and uncontroversially indicates that the 'Philippine-type' structure is in fact a retention from Proto-Austronesian (or, at the very least, a protolanguage forming a primary branch thereof), and the lack of shared phonological and lexical innovations indicates that none of the languages originally native to Borneo belong to the Philippine subfamily. This was not immediately apparent in the early years of Austronesian scholarship, prior to the emergence of larger amounts of data on Malagasy and the Formosan languages of Taiwan. Today, however, no 'controversy' remains in this regard, and subsequent authors (e.g. Lobel 2013a, 2016b; Smith 2017a) have accepted Blust's separation of the languages of northern Borneo from the Philippine subfamily.

### 7.4.6 Migration and historical levelling

Blust (1991b, 2005a) calls attention to the relatively low level of diversity found among modern Philippine languages in comparison to their presumed length of time in the Philippines after the departure of speakers of Proto-Malayo-Polynesian from what is now the country of Taiwan. To explain this, Blust proposes two periods of language levelling: the first in which speakers of Proto-Philippines expanded throughout the Philippines at the expense of speakers of other Malayo-Polynesian subgroups that were presumably present in the area at that time; and a second, during which speakers of Proto-Greater Central Philippines expanded throughout not only the central and southern Philippines but also northern Sulawesi, levelling non-GCPH languages that had previously been spoken in those areas.

A number of other levelling episodes could also be added to Blust's list. Inete/Inati, the language of the aboriginal Ete/Ati of Panay, appears to be a primary branch of the Philippine subfamily (Pennoyer 1986–1987; Blust 1991b, 2019b), and was present in its current location prior to the expansion of speakers of Bisayan languages into the western Visayan Islands. On neighbouring Negros Island, the various Bukidnon peoples are clearly remnants of earlier Bisayan-speaking populations who fled into the mountains to maintain their freedom during the Spanish occupation (George Largado p.c., 2006) and became minoritized by the massive influx of Cebuanos and Ilonggos in the mid-nineteenth century (Scott 1984, 1992). In Luzon, many parts of the Pacific coast of central Luzon were inhabited almost exclusively by the Umiray Dumaget when Canadian missionaries Thomas and Pat Macleod arrived in the area in the 1960s (as evidenced by numerous reports and thousands of photographs archived by SIL-Philippines); half a century later, virtually no Dumaget communities can be found along the coast, with Tagalogs having now taken over the land that the Dumagets' ancestors had lived on since time immemorial (Lubita Andrada p.c.; Salvador Cruz p.c.). What has happened with the Dumagets over the past fifty years has occurred many times over the past 500 years or so, as many native populations, now largely confined to upland areas in Luzon, Palawan, and Mindanao, report that their ancestors once moved freely between coastal and interior areas prior to the arrival of the groups now living along the coast, who, based on linguistic evidence, are clearly much more recent arrivals.

In other cases, however, remnants of levelled populations still exist even in coastal areas: for example, early Spanish documents make no mention of Cebuano speakers on Leyte Island, and appear to suggest a somewhat wider distribution of Waray-Waray on that island. Today's Baybayanon (Rubino 2005b) and Kinabalian languages (Lobel 2013a) appear to represent remnants of Warayan dialects that existed prior to the expansion of Cebuano along the western and southern coasts of Leyte Island. In northeastern Luzon, the still-coastal Agta have yet to be fully displaced from their ancestral waters, although the expansion of Tagalogs from the south and Ilokanos from the north are slowly minoritizing both them and the natives of the town centre of Casiguran (note that the Kasiguranin language spoken by the latter largely developed from a mix of Tagalog and Casiguran Agta).

### 7.4.7 Aboriginal Filipinos

In addition to the 'ethnic Austronesian' population, an estimated 15,000 Aboriginal Filipinos[20] are also native to the Philippines, and the population of Filipinos with at least one aboriginal grandparent may be as large as 100,000. Most of these populations live on the fringes of modern Philippine society, and a number of authors have written about the violence, discrimination, and other abuse that these populations regularly suffer (see discussion in Lobel 2013a). Thomas Headland, Lawrence Reid, and Jason Lobel are among the most widely published scholars on the languages of aboriginal Filipinos, several of which form primary

[20] This number could be as high as 75,000, if we include the 10,000 Iraya Mangyans and 50,000 Ata, Tigwa, and Matigsalug Manobos of Mindanao, large portions of whose populations clearly have 'Negrito'-like physical characteristics.

branches of the Philippine macrogroup (e.g. Inati, Umiray Dumaget, Manide, and Inagta Alabat) and preserve highly conservative features lost in all other Philippine languages. Headland and Blood (2002) and Lobel (2013a: 55–102) give a more extended overview of Aboriginal Filipino populations and their languages.

## 7.5 Conclusion

Although an impressive amount of historical-comparative work has been done on Philippine languages over the past century, much work remains, and is even more urgent due to the rate at which the numbers of fully fluent native speakers of many of these languages have been diminishing over the past several decades. For various reasons—including intermarriage, the rise of the internet and social media, and the expansion of electricity and mobile phone networks into rural areas —tens of millions of Philippine youth are no longer growing up competent in their parents' language(s). It is therefore imperative that as much documentation as possible be completed before these languages disappear, especially since an unfortunately large number of Philippine languages still lack even basic documentation, such as a sketch grammar, dictionary, or text collection, let alone a reference grammar (see Ewing and Kimoto, chapter 15, this volume).

In planning future fieldwork, scholars should strive to go far beyond the relatively short wordlists of the past (e.g. the Swadesh 100- and 200-item lists, and the SIL 372-item list) and collect not only longer wordlists (e.g. those developed by Zorc and Lobel, each with well over 1,500 items) and extensive sentence lists, but also recordings of spontaneous speech. In particular, collections of texts, ideally accompanied by audio recordings, allow researchers to collect invaluable information about such topics as local history, customs and traditions, flora and fauna, recipes, biographies of important people, and origin myths. Similarly, historical-comparative work must move beyond simply reconstructing lexical items, and pay more attention to the reconstruction of morphology, grammar, and discourse. A considerable amount of morphology marking verbs, nouns, pronouns, deictics, numerals, and modifiers remains to be reconstructed, and grammatical paradigms particular to each language need to be mapped alongside those reconstructed for Proto-Philippines. Additional research is also needed on Philippine accent patterns, which may prove to be a highly significant innovation unique to the Philippine subfamily (Zorc 2020; Smith, chapter 2, this volume), absent from both Formosan languages and non-Philippine Malayo-Polynesian languages.

Finally, additional research will also hopefully allow us to determine the genetic position of certain languages like Umiray Dumaget, Inati, Manide, Inagta Alabat, Remontado, Molbog, and Bonggi. If it turns out that some or all of these languages are, in fact, primary branches of the Philippine subfamily, then this will also help revise our understanding of Proto-Philippines and even possibly of higher-level nodes in the Austronesian family tree.

The authors are well aware of and apologize to several Filipino scholars who have published on the topic of this paper such as Cecilio Lopez, Ernesto Constantino, Teodoro Llamzon, and Consulo Paz. Constraints of space have not allowed their contributions to be acknowledged.

## Acknowledgements

We wish to express our heartfelt gratitude to all of our native speaker friends and consultants who provided the data on the languages covered herein. We are likewise grateful for the invaluable feedback from Robert Blust, Lawrence Reid, and Hsiu-chuan Liao, as well as from the late John Lynch, to whose memory this chapter is dedicated.

# CHAPTER 8

# Historical linguistics of Borneo

Alexander D. Smith

## 8.1 Introduction

Borneo, in the centre of Island Southeast Asia, is an area of considerable linguistic diversity. There are over one hundred languages spoken throughout Borneo, although precise numbers are difficult to determine. The languages of Borneo have played an important role in the field of Austronesian comparative linguistics, due in no small part to the island's central location, which led Adelaar (1995b) to refer to the island as a "cross-roads for comparative Austronesian linguistics". With this in mind, this chapter will focus on the historical and comparative study of these languages; how they are related to one another and the linguistic properties of the protolanguage(s) from which they descend. Two Austronesian subgroups in Borneo—Tamanic and Malayic—will be excluded from the present discussion, however. Tamanic will be excluded because of its close genetic relationship with the South Sulawesi subgroup (*see* Mead, this volume, §12.3.10) and Malayic because of Malay's wide geographic spread throughout Island and Mainland Southeast Asia (*see* Anderbeck, this volume, §9.1 + fn.2).

This chapter thus focuses on the remaining Austronesian languages of Borneo and their subgroupings. It takes a bottom-up approach to Bornean historical linguistics, dealing first with lower-to-mid-level subgroups that enjoy consensus support before discussing competing hypotheses on higher-level subgrouping. It also discusses the lexical evidence for linguistic subgroups in Borneo, focusing on innovated faunal terms which act as critical evidence for an ancestor language from which all modern languages of Borneo descend. Finally, it looks at how historical linguistics and subgrouping can be used to better understand the recent history of population movement among the people of Borneo.

The chapter will also reference Borneo's current political divisions, so a brief review is provided before moving on to the linguistic analysis. Borneo is divided between three nations: Malaysia, Indonesia, and Brunei. The Malaysian portion of Borneo is located mostly in the north and west (the Malaysian states of Sabah in the north and Sarawak in the west). The Indonesian portion is the largest, and occupies eastern, southern, and western Borneo (North, East, South, Central, and West Kalimantan). Brunei is located entirely on Borneo, roughly in between the Malaysian states of Sarawak and Sabah. Some subgroups have a distribution that roughly aligns with political divisions, for example, the languages of Sabah consist of two linguistically defined subgroups that are largely found in the state of Sabah, and the Barito languages make up the dominant indigenous language group in Central and South Kalimantan. Other language groups do not conform to modern political boundaries.

## 8.2 Languages and subgroups

According to Blust (2010b) and Smith (2017a) there are two main subgroups on Borneo—Greater North Borneo and Barito-Basap—each with numerous internal divisions. Details on these first-order subgroups can be found in §8.3. This section rather focuses on the mid-to-lower level subgroups. The major linguistic divisions within Greater North Borneo are: North Borneo (the languages of Sabah plus Dayic, Kenyah, Berawan-Lower Baram, and Bintulu); Land Dayak; Kayanic (Kayan, Ngorek, Merap, Segai-Modang); Central Sarawak (Melanau, Kajang, Punan, Müller-Schwaner); and Malayic (Malay, Iban, Kanayatn [Kendayan] and other so-called 'Malayic Dayak' languages). Basap-Barito contains the under-described Basap language of eastern Kalimantan and the more robustly described Barito languages of south-central Borneo (including Malagasy), and Sama-Bajaw. These major subgroups are discussed below, starting with Sabahan languages in the north and working south to Barito before concluding with remarks on higher-order subgrouping and a family tree.

### 8.2.1 Sabahan languages

Sabahan languages are unlike most other languages of Borneo in that they generally retain the PMP 'Philippine-type' or 'multiple undergoer' voice system, including robust verbal morphology that indicates voice, mood, aspect,

Alexander D. Smith, *Historical linguistics of Borneo*. In: *The Oxford Guide to the Malayo-Polynesian Languages of Southeast Asia*. Edited by: Alexander Adelaar and Antoinette Schapper, Oxford University Press. © Alexander D. Smith (2024). DOI: 10.1093/oso/9780198807353.003.0008

a verb-initial word order, and other hallmarks of Philippine systems. In this respect, they are superficially more similar to the languages of the Philippines or Taiwan than they are to the more southern languages of Borneo. Regarding their linguistic position, there are several hypotheses on the historical relations of Sabahan languages. An older hypothesis groups Sabahan languages with Philippine languages, separate from the other languages of Borneo (see Dyen 1965a or Prentice 1971). This hypothesis appeals to the typological similarity of Sabahan and Philippine languages, although the similarities in question are now considered retentions from PMP and therefore not suitable for subgrouping. Hudson (1978: 20–1) also notes the similarities between Sabahan and Philippine languages and lists 'Idahan' (which included all languages considered Southwest and Northeast Sabah) under his 'Exo-Bornean' classification. He notes that Ida'anic shares several features with both Philippine and Bornean languages, but refers to Sabahan languages as 'Philippinic', suggesting a genetic relationship.

The current view is that the languages of Sabah group with the other languages of Borneo (Blust 1998b, 2010b; Lobel 2013b; Smith 1984), a view that has not yet been challenged by scholars currently working in Borneo. There are two 'Sabahan' groups, Southwest and Northeast Sabah and a third group, Lun Dayeh, with significant attestation in southern Sabah but which subgroups more closely with languages in Sarawak. 'Sabahan' is not necessarily a linguistic classification, and although Blust (1998b) does mention the possibility of a Sabahan subgroup that includes only Southwest and Northeast Sabah, it has not been defended on linguistic grounds.

Southwest Sabah is the largest subgroup in Sabah and has been proposed under various names by Smith (1984); Blust (1998b, 2010b); and Lobel (2013b). The term 'Southwest Sabah' itself is from Blust (1998b), who chose the name because the area of highest genetic diversity is in the southwest area of Sabah. Evidence for the subgroup is limited but contains lexical innovations that were recently organized by Smith (2017a). Southwest Sabah is divided into two large subgroups, Greater Dusunic and Greater Murutic, following Lobel (2013b). Internally, Greater Dusunic contains the Sabah Dusun languages, Sabah Bisaya, Lotud, and Paitanic languages while Greater Murutic contains Papar, Tatana', Murutic, and Tidung.

Northeast Sabah was proposed in Blust (2010b). It contains the Ida'anic languages of northeastern Sabah (Ida'an dialects, Sungai Seguluid, Begak) together with Bonggi, a language spoken on Bonggi island just off the northern coast of Sabah. Ida'anic and Bonggi are geographically separated from one another by a relatively homogenous section of Southwest Sabahan languages. Under the current hypothesis Northeast Sabahan languages must have been geographically contiguous at some point in their history and stretched along the entire eastern coast of Sabah. In the more recent past, however, Southwest Sabah expanded eastward and severed the line of Northeast Sabahan languages effectively 'stranding' Bonggi from the Ida'anic languages. The evidence for such a subgroup is lexical: there are roughly nineteen innovations proposed in Blust (2010b) that define the subgroup.

Lobel (2013b, 2016b) provides a counter proposal to Northeast Sabah, arguing that Bonggi subgroups most closely with Molbog, a Philippine language spoken on a nearby island. Lobel's argument for grouping Molbog and Bonggi together rests on comparisons of 'functors', functional words including pronouns, that he claims are more resistant to borrowing and change and therefore provide higher quality evidence for subgrouping than other lexical categories. The following three viewpoints summarize contemporary hypotheses on Bonggi and Molbog: i) Bonggi and Molbog form a subgroup within the Greater Central Philippine group; ii) Bonggi and Molbog form a subgroup within Northeast Sabah; and iii) Bonggi and Molbog do not form a subgroup, and belong to separate subgroups: Bonggi with Northeast Sabah and Molbog with Greater Central Philippines. Lobel (2013b, 2016b) supports i and ii as two possible interpretations of his subgrouping while Blust (2010b) and Smith (2017a) support iii.

### 8.2.2 North Sarawak

North Sarawak (NS) languages are situated mostly along the Baram River and its upper reaches, but Lun Dayeh, part of the Dayic subgroup of North Sarawak, is represented by dialects in Sabah just north of the border with present day Sarawak. It is divided into four main subgroups: Dayic (also dubbed Kelabit-Lun Dayeh [Hudson 1978]); Kenyah; Berawan-Lower Baram (Berawan Dialects, Kiput, Narum, Miri); and Bintulu, a single language spoken in and around Bintulu town south of the Baram river. The four North Sarawak subgroups are mostly uncontroversial, although the boundaries of the Kenyah subgroup have been the subject of debate. Blust (2010b) and Smith (2015a, b), for example, include Sebop, Penan, and all groups that identify as Kenyah, (excluding Murik) in the Kenyah subgroup, whereas Soriente (2003) places both Sebop and Penan in a separate Sebop-Penan group and also lists several languages considered by Blust and Smith as Kenyah within her Kayan subgroup (Lebo' Vo', Uma Pawe, Lebo' Kulit). This chapter follows the subgrouping of Blust and Smith. Regarding evidence for North Sarawak, the defining feature of this subgroup is found in reflexes of PMP voiced stops *b, *d, *j, *z, and *g which developed into phonetically complex or historically unexpected stops where they appear immediately following a penultimate schwa. Blust (1974a) reconstructed these as PNS 'voiced aspirates', *bʰ, *dʰ (from PMP *d and *j), *jʰ (from PMP *z), and *gʰ (Blust 2010b). In the Bario dialect of Kelabit, these stops are retained as voiced aspirates, but surface as implosive stops, voiced stops, voiceless stops, and fricatives in various other North Sarawak languages. Table 8.1 gives examples of all of the voiced stop reflexes after schwa in numerous North Sarawak languages. Notice the diversity in reflexes of the voiced stops, which is argued to follow from the phonetically complex terminally devoiced stops of PNS (Table 8.1).

**Table 8.1** Reflexes of PNS terminally devoiced stops

| | 'sugarcane' | 'woman' | 'ladder' | 'lie down' |
|---|---|---|---|---|
| PNS | *təbʰu | *dədʰuR | *Rəjʰan | *pəgʰəl |
| Lebo' Vo' | *təɓu* | *ləɗo* | *fan* | *pəɠən* |
| Lepo' Tau | *təpu* | *ləto* | *can* | *pəkən* |
| Bintulu | *təɓəw* | *ɣəɗu* | *kəfan* | *məɠən* 'sleep' |
| Lun Dayeh | *təfuh* | *dəsur* | *əsan* | - |
| Bario Kelabit | *təbpuh* | *dədtur* | *ədtan* | *pəgkəl* 'put to sleep' |
| Miri | *təfuh* | - | *asɛn* | *makil* |
| Kiput | *təsəw* | - | *asin* | *məkən* |
| Long Terawan Berawan | *təppuh* | *dicu* | *acin* | - |

These reflexes of voiced obstruents after a penultimate schwa, which follow from terminally devoiced obstruents in PNS, constitute the only piece of phonological evidence yet proposed for North Sarawak. Although this is a high-quality sound change, similar reflexes are found in Northeast Sabah languages. In §8.3, the same terminal devoicing phenomenon will be shown to form evidence for a North Borneo subgroup. This calls into question the strength of using these reflexes as NS evidence, because they may be retentions rather than innovations. What this means for the validity of NS remains to be worked out.

### 8.2.3 Central Sarawak

The Central Sarawak (CS) classification is a recent proposal from Smith (2017a) and therefore is less widely accepted but it is comprised of several smaller, well-established subgroups: Melanau (Chou 2002; Rensch 2012); Kajang (Smith 2017a); Punan; and Müller-Schwaner (Smith 2017a; Sellato and Soriente 2015). Melanau, Kajang, and Punan are located along the Rejang river in Sarawak, Malaysia, although Punan speakers are also found throughout Borneo in small groups, sometimes practising a nomadic hunter-gatherer lifestyle, and Müller-Schwaner is found in the upper reaches of the Kapuas and Mahakam rivers in Kalimantan, Indonesia. Melanau and Kajang have been grouped together in a Melanau-Kajang subgroup (see Simons and Fennig 2018) but the similarities that are shared between these two groups appear to also be shared with Punan and Müller-Schwaner, so it is better to group all four in a single subgroup, Central Sarawak. The linguistic evidence for Central Sarawak contains lexical innovations and irregular sound changes, the most important of which is an irregular development in reflexes of the PMP word *takaw 'to steal', described in more detail below.

Like most languages of Borneo, Melanau, Kajang, Punan, and Müller-Schwaner maintained PMP *a in penultimate syllables. However, they did change this *a to *i* in specifically conditioned cases. Reflexes of PMP *takaw 'to steal' should thus reflect *a as *a* in all these subgroups, but it appears that an irregular change took place which changed PMP *a to PCS *i in this word. Examples are organized below in example set (1) below:

(1) **Melanau:**
Mukah Melanau *tikaw/mənikaw*, Dalat Melanau *mənikaw*, Kanowit *nikaw*, Sarikei Melanau *mənikaw.*
**Kajang:**
Sekapan *məñikaw*, Kejaman *ñikaw*, Lahanan *ñikaw.*
**Punan:**
Punan Bah *mañikuow*, Punan Lisum *ñiko*, Punan Tubu *ñikow*, Punan Aput *ñikow*, Beketan *ñikow*, Ukit *ñiko*, Buket *ñiko*.
**Müller-Schwaner:**
Kereho *ñiku*, Hovongan *ñiko*, Seputan *ñiku*, Aoheng *ñiku*.

Most of the words were recorded with homorganic nasal substitution, and Kajang, Punan, and Müller-Schwaner show an additional irregular palatalization of the nasal. What is clear, however, is that all languages reflect PCS *tikaw/mənikaw, where *a from PMP *takaw/manakaw became *i in the penultimate syllable with no clear motivation, and where no other reflexes of PAN or PMP words show a parallel irregular change. Because of the lack of motivation, but subgroup-wide attestation, the simplest explanation is that *a became *i once in this word and was inherited in the daughter languages. This is, in turn, evidence for a Central Sarawak subgroup because an irregular and unmotivated change is unlikely to occur in multiple unrelated innovations. Other evidence for the subgroup includes a longer list of additional lexical replacement innovations that can be found in Smith (2017a).

### 8.2.4 Land Dayak

The largest work to date on Land Dayak 'Proto-Land Dayak' (PLD) is Rensch et. al (2012), in addition to Smith (2017a, 2019a), who discusses Land Dayak internal subgrouping and the phonological shape of Proto-Land Dayak. Rensch et al. and Smith agree that Land Dayak forms a discrete subgroup located along the mid Kapuas river in West Kalimantan, Indonesia and southern Sarawak, Malaysia. Phonological evidence for Land Dayak includes a merger of *R and *l as PLD *r except where *R was between two low vowels, in which case it merged with *y in addition to some exclusive lexical replacement innovations (Smith 2019a: 113–14). The Land Dayak languages have received special attention because of apparent similarities between Land Dayak and Aslian (Mon-Khmer) languages in the words 'to die' (PLD *kəbəs) and 'to bathe' (PLD *mamuh), pointed out by Adelaar (1995b: 90). It's difficult to reach a confident conclusion with only these two words, but these similarities could point to past contact between Land Dayak and Aslian, a situation that would have arisen through the robust trade networks that existed in the South China Sea. Additional work on Land Dayak, some older, some newer, includes Buck (1933); Chong (2008); and Reijffert (1956) in addition to the studies mentioned earlier. Also, Sommerlot (2020) provides a look at the comparative syntax of Land Dayak and surrounding languages in West Kalimantan.

### 8.2.5 Kayanic

Kayanic languages are spoken throughout the upriver areas of Sarawak and Kalimantan and can be divided into two types: the better-studied Kayan and Murik-Merap (or Ngorek) groups, and the lesser-studied but phonologically innovative Segai-Modang group. Published works on Kayanic tend to focus on the Kayan languages (Blust 1977b, 2002a; Clayre and Cubit 1974; Effendy et al. 2006; Metcalf 1974; Rousseau 1974; Southwell 1990; among many others) and Murik-Merap (Blust 1974b; Soriente 2003; Smith 2017c) but the Segai-Modang languages have also received some recent attention (Astar et al 2002; Guerreiro 1996; Revel-Macdonald 1982; Smith 2019b; Wati et al 2002). There is little disagreement concerning the composition of Kayanic (Kayan, Murik-Merap, and Segai-Modang), but some issues should be addressed. Hudson (1978) also placed the Müller-Schwaner languages in the Kayanic branch of his Kayan-Kenyah group, where Penihing and Seputan (both Müller-Schwaner) are listed under Long Paka' Kayan-Penyabung, itself listed under Kayanic. Although Ethnologue uses Hudson's classification, most scholars working in the area today do not subgroup Müller-Schwaner languages with Kayan. Sellato and Soriente (2015: 350), for example, separate Müller-Schwaner languages from Kayan, claiming instead that Müller-Schwaner languages are "rooted in an old Western Borneo linguistic substratum". Smith (2017a) places Müller-Schwaner in Central Sarawak.

The linguistic evidence for Kayan, Murik-Merap, and Segai-Modang as individual subgroups is strong, but the evidence linking these three groups together into Kayanic is less robust and relies on lexical innovations and irregular sound changes. For example, the first segment in the well-supported PMP word *bibiR 'lips' irregularly changed to *s in Kayanic languages, giving Proto-Kayanic *sibih (*-R regularly became *-h in Proto-Kayanic)[1] from *bibiR. The Kayanic evidence for *sibih is given in example (2) below:

(2) **Kayan-Murik:**
Murik *ebeh* (*s- regularly deleted), Long Naah *siveh*, Data Dian *sifeh*, Bahau *sifeh*, Balui Liko *hiveh*, Busang *hiveh*.
**Segai-Modang:**
Long Gelat *səwaẖ*, Modang *səwayh*, Kelai *suwɛh*, Wahau *sweh*.

PMP *bibiR has a well-established etymology, and there doesn't seem to be any potential borrowing source, both because 'lip' is a stable word, unlikely to be borrowed in the first place, and also because Kayanic languages are the only languages in Borneo (or anywhere in the Austronesian world for that matter) where this irregular change is attested. There are additionally no languages where *b- regularly became *s- which might act as a source. The most likely explanation, then, is that *bibiR changed to *sibih only once and was inherited from a common ancestor by modern Kayanic languages. Additional evidence can be found in Smith 2017a.

### 8.2.6 Barito-Basap

Barito-Basap is, like Central Sarawak, a recent proposal from Smith (2017a, 2018a), although its largest member, Barito, has been the subject of multiple studies. It combines the

[1] A possible etymology for this form is that *isi-n bibiR 'flesh of the lips', a form that is sometimes used to describe the lips, fused together, creating Proto-Kayanic *sibih. It's difficult to test this hypothesis, though, and either way, the resulting form *sibih is unique to Kayanic languages.

Greater Barito subgroup (Barito combined with Sama-Bajaw (SB)) with the underdocumented Basap language spoken in small numbers by groups living in eastern Kalimantan. Barito famously includes Malagasy, which includes the many dialects spoken on the island of Madagascar whose speakers left the Barito river Basin roughly 1,300 years ago (Adelaar 1989) and the various Barito languages of the Barito river basin in Central Kalimantan including various Ngaju languages spoken further upriver and in western Central Kalimantan. Hudson (1967, 1978) provides early works on the internal subgrouping of what he called the Barito "family" and Durasid (1980/1981) provides a reconstruction of Proto-Barito. Hudson recognized several subgroups within Barito, namely: Northwest Barito (NWB); Southwest Barito (SWB); Southeast Barito (SEB, which includes Malagasy); Central-East Barito (CEB); Northeast Barito (NEB); and Barito-Mahakam, which is comprised of Tunjung and closely related dialects.

More recently, Smith (2018a) has proposed a linkage relationship between Barito languages (see Ross 1988 for more on linkages). In a linkage, sound changes are spread throughout member languages in such a way that no single sound change is found in all member languages and there is no non-arbitrary way to divide the languages into internal subgroups. For example, if four languages A, B, C, D, form a linkage, we may find shared innovations between A, B, and C, and another set of innovations shared between B, C, and D, but no shared innovations between A and D. This is precisely the situation found in Barito, where several sound changes are found in a chain-like distribution as indicated in Table 8.2, modified from Smith (2018a).

The Barito Linkage hypothesis assumes several past proposals. First, it includes Malagasy as a Southeast Barito language, closely related to Ma'anyan, Samihim, and Dusun Witu (Dahl 1951, 1977; Adelaar 1989, 1995a). In fact, Smith's proposal retains all of the smaller internal subgroups, but simply reanalyses their mutual relationships. Second, the Sama-Bajaw languages are included in the linkage (as demonstrated in Blust 2007c). They are spoken in the Sulu Archipelago area of the Philippines, in small coastal settlements in northern and eastern Borneo, around the coast of Sulawesi, scattered throughout the Island between Borneo and Madura. The Barito languages, Malagasy, and Sama-Bajaw then form a larger group with Basap. Basap is still poorly documented but the presence of lexical innovations that are exclusively shared between Barito and Basap suggests that they were at one point part of a large dialect network that stretched along the eastern coast of Borneo (Smith 2018a).

**Table 8.2** Distribution of sound change in Barito

| | *R > h | *ə > e | *z > d | *-r > y | *b > w | *-d > r | *-l > -r |
|---|---|---|---|---|---|---|---|
| NWB | + | | | | | | |
| SWB | + | + | | | | + | |
| Yakan (S-B) | + | + | + | | | | |
| SEB | | + | + | + | | | |
| CEB | | + | + | + | + | | |
| NEB | | | + | + | + | + | + |
| Tunjung | + | | | | + | + | + |

To review, the languages of Borneo can be split into several subgroups. This section gave an overview of most of these subgroups, including Southwest Sabah, Northeast Sabah, North Sarawak, Central Sarawak, Kayanic, Land Dayak, and Barito-Basap. At this mid-to-lower level, there is not much controversy over the makeup of each subgroup, but there has been historically less of a consensus regarding how these subgroups are organized into larger higher-order subgroups. This topic is discussed in the following section, §8.3.

## 8.3 Higher-order subgrouping in Borneo

In this chapter, 'higher-order' subgrouping refers to the grouping of already established subgroups into larger genetic units. Higher-order subgrouping naturally involves the comparison of all languages of Borneo, although because of the size of the island and a general lack of linguistic data, relatively few studies have attempted to address island-wide subgrouping. The most recent study dealing with the entirety of Borneo is from Smith (2017a, b), which informs much of the present chapter, although other hypotheses are discussed as well. Smith claims that all indigenous languages of Borneo (excluding Tamanic) are descended from a single common ancestor, earlier dubbed *Proto-Western Indonesian* (PWIN) by Blust (2010b). Western Indonesian may be a primary branch of Proto-Malayo-Polynesian, although both the validity of WIN and its precise location within MP is still a matter of debate. Two primary groups of WIN are found on Borneo, Greater North Borneo, and Basap-Barito. Other studies that predate Blust (2010b) and Smith (2017a) did not propose a single discrete protolanguage for Borneo. The most notable of these earlier publications are Ray's (1913) *The Languages of Borneo*, Hudson's (1978) manuscript *Linguistic relations among Bornean peoples with special reference to Sarawak: An interim report*, and Adelaar's (1995b) overview of the subgrouping situation in Borneo, with a focus on Malayic, Malagasy, Tamanic, and Land Dayak.

This section provides an overview of the various proposals on Bornean higher-level subgrouping, beginning with earlier proposals, especially those from Hudson (1978) which continues to have an impact on Bornean linguistics. Afterward, the current proposal from Smith (2017a, b) is discussed, starting with the North Borneo proposal, before moving 'up the tree' to the Greater North Borneo, and finally, Western Indonesian proposals. The proposal from Smith (2017a, b) is shown in Figure 8.1 below. Note that branch number three is not a single subgroup, but rather a collection of languages that are classified under Western Indonesian, but whose exact position has not been worked out.

WESTERN INDONESIAN

1. Greater North Borneo
    a. North Borneo
        Northeast Sabah
        Southwest Sabah
        North Sarawak
    b. Central Sarawak
    c. Kayanic
    d. Land Dayak
    e. Malayic
2. Barito-Basap
    a. Barito (including Malagasy and Sama-Bajaw)
    b. Basap
3. *Languages outside Borneo excluding CMP and languages of Sulawesi*

**Figure 8.1** Western Indonesian and its member subgroups.

## 8.3.1 Past proposals on higher-order subgrouping

Hudson (1978) was a landmark study in its scope, since it dealt with the linguistic relations of Borneo in a truly island-wide manner. He proposes two main groups: Exo-Bornean (those languages which he argued originate from outside the island); and Endo-Bornean (those which originate from within Borneo). His Exo-Bornean groups include Sabahan, Malayic, and Tamanic languages. Endo-Bornean groups are East Barito, West Barito, Barito-Mahakam, Land Dayak, Apo Duat (Dayic), Rejang-Baram, and Kayan-Kenyah. The major difference between Hudson and the Blust-Smith proposal is that Hudson did not propose a single ancestor from which all languages of Borneo descend. There are also differences regarding the composition of member groups as well as on the intermediate levels of subgrouping, that is, how different subgroups are paired together below the first-order Exo-/Endo-Bornean distinction.

Regarding the intermediate level subgroups from Hudson, his proposed Rejang-Baram and Kayan-Kenyah subgroups differ in sometimes substantial ways from Smith (2017a). Rejang-Baram and its internal divisions, Baram-Tinjar, Rejang-Bintulu, Lower Rejang, and Rejang-Sajau, for example, are still regularly repeated in the linguistic literature although they have been superseded by subgrouping hypotheses which utilize more complete datasets. In fact, Hudson (1978: 25) states that the Rejang-Baram subgroup as a whole is "quite provisional", and correctly predicted that it would be drastically changed with future research. Hudson never presents evidence to justify the larger Rejang-Bintulu group, and rather focuses his discussion on the four divisions within. Of the four internal divisions, two are no longer valid: Rejang-Bintulu and Rejang-Sajau. Rejang-Bintulu originally linked Bintulu and Kajang languages in a single subgroup. Other proposals, however, have placed Kajang either with Melanau languages in a single Melanau-Kajang subgroup or with the larger Central Sarawak subgroup (Smith 2017a). Bintulu, on the other hand, appears to subgroup with North Sarawak, not Melanau, since it has implosive reflexes of voiced stops after penultimate schwa, a key diagnostic not found in Melanau languages (Blust 1974a). Rejang-Sajau contains several of the Punan dialects not listed in the Rejang-Bintulu group, along with Merap and Sajau. Smith (2017a, c) demonstrated that Merap shares certain sound changes with Ngorek (which implies that Merap is a Kayanic language), and later showed that Sajau is likely another dialect of Punan, distinct from Basap and thus should be within the Punan subgroup (Smith 2018a).

The Kayan-Kenyah proposal is not only found in Hudson's work, but is also defended by Soriente (Soriente 2003, 2008) and challenged by Smith (2015a). Soriente (2003) contains a thorough analysis along with supporting linguistic data for Kayan-Kenyah, including a list of claimed shared phonological innovations. It is not necessary to reanalyse these works here, but Smith (2015a) argues that the proposed Kayan-Kenyah shared phonological innovations are either of low quality (common and found in other subgroups) or do not withstand close scrutiny (some sound changes have been erroneously assigned) and therefore does not endorse the view that Kenyah and Kayanic form an exclusive subgroup.

The final critique of Hudson (1978) involves the classification of Barito languages, which appear listed as three separate groups: East Barito; West Barito; and Barito-Mahakam. As already discussed, Barito languages form a linkage relationship with one another (Smith 2018a), and although Hudson had earlier grouped Barito together as a family (Hudson 1967), the classification in his later work appears to list them as three separate entities (Hudson 1978). The Greater North Borneo hypothesis and the larger Western Indonesian hypothesis, both discussed in more detail in the remainder of this section, both assume a Barito subgroup (whether a traditional subgroup or a linkage). No proposal has suggested an immediate subgrouping relationship between Barito and another subgroup in Borneo. In this respect, both older and newer subgrouping hypotheses (including the Western Indonesian hypothesis, discussed in §8.3.4) agree that Barito languages are uniquely distinct among Bornean languages.

### 8.3.2 North Borneo

The chapter now turns to issues in higher-order subgrouping based on proposals from Blust (2010b) and later Smith (2017a). First is a discussion of North Borneo (NB), followed by its immediate ancestor Greater North Borneo, and finally, Western Indonesian, the hypothetical ancestral language to all languages of Borneo. Regarding North Borneo, the subgroup includes both major Sabahan subgroups: Southwest Sabah and Northeast Sabah, together with North Sarawak. NB was first proposed in Blust 1998b, and elaborated upon in Blust 2010b. The subgroup is defined mostly by the effects that gemination in the onsets of final syllables, which became PNB terminally devoiced geminate stops. There are also a few apparent lexical innovations that were identified by Smith (2017a) that are discussed briefly in this section.

Regarding the gemination of consonants, PMP *ə was extra short, and wherever it appeared in the penultimate syllable it caused the automatic gemination of the onset of the final syllable: *CəCVC > *CəC:VC. Automatic gemination of stops after schwa is found in many Austronesian languages and is not unique to Borneo but is nevertheless responsible for important sound changes. North Borneo is the only known Austronesian subgroup where these geminates developed terminal devoicing in historically voiced obstruents, that is, where the long consonant starts voiced but ends voiceless (Blust 2010b writes them as voiced aspirates, *b$^h$ [b͡p$^h$], *d$^h$ [d͡t$^h$], *j$^h$ [d͡ʧ$^h$], and *g$^h$ [g͡k$^h$]). The motivation for this sound change is simple: after voiced stops lengthened in PNB, the inherent difficulty in maintaining airflow over the vocal folds while simultaneously stopping airflow in the mouth caused the stops to lose voicing before the completion of articulation. Two out of three primary branches—North Sarawak and Northeast Sabah—reflect terminal devoicing in the following examples where *b from Proto-Malayo-Polynesian *təbu 'sugarcane' first underwent lengthening, *təbbu, and finally terminal devoicing, *təb$^h$u, where *b$^h$ was a single phonological segment. The terminal devoicing is retained in Begak (Northeast Sabah) *təbpu*, and Bario Kelabit (North Sarawak) *təbpuh*.

The question of whether terminal devoicing arose in separate parallel developments in Northeast Sabah and North Sarawak, or if it is a retention from these two groups most recent common ancestor Proto-North Borneo, is still a matter of debate. An argument for the latter position is strengthened by the observation that terminally devoiced stops of this kind are exceptionally rare. Decades ago, Ladefoged (1971) claimed that no such sounds existed but later acknowledged terminally devoiced stops in at least two languages, including Kelabit (Ladefoged and Maddieson 1996; see Blust 2018b for more on this contentious issue). From a historical point of view, the rarity of these consonants suggests that a single change, where voiced geminate obstruents underwent terminal devoicing in Proto-North Borneo, is more economical as it posits fewer rare sound changes than the alternative. However, as noted earlier in §8.2.2, if terminal devoicing of obstruents is in fact an inheritance from PNB, it removes the only piece of phonological evidence in support of North Sarawak.

Finally, the lexical evidence for North Borneo is slight, but includes an innovation that closed a semantic gap in words for various pigs. Austronesian languages tend to distinguish two types of pig: wild and domestic. At the PMP level, two words are reconstructed for the cover-term 'pig': *bəRək 'wild pig'; and *babuy 'pig'. The latter reconstruction was a general term that was used for any type of pig, domestic or wild. There was not, however, a word that referred strictly to the domesticated pig, and this is where PNB appears to have made an innovation. The term *bakas can be reconstructed to PNB with evidence from Bintulu *bakas*, Kelabit *baka*, Kiput *baka*, Kadazan Dusun *bakas*, Murut *bakas*, and Ida'anic *bakas*. All languages, except Ida'anic, retain the strict meaning 'domestic pig'. In Ida'anic, the word has generalized to mean any pig, domestic or wild.

### 8.3.3 Greater North Borneo

North Borneo combines with the remaining non-Barito subgroups, Kayanic, Central Sarawak, Land Dayak, and Malayic, to form Greater North Borneo (GNB), the largest and most diverse higher-order subgroup under Western Indonesian. GNB is defined by lexical innovations and has no strong phonological evidence. As shown in Figure 8.1, it comprises five lower subgroups, namely North Borneo, Land Dayak,

Kayanic, Central Sarawak, and Malayic. The list of lexical innovations which define Greater North Borneo is quite large, but the most important lexical evidence comes from reflexes of PMP *pitu, which are found throughout Island Southeast Asia but are conspicuously absent in the proposed Greater North Borneo group. Instead, GNB languages reflect a lexical replacement. To summarize, GNB languages reflect PMP *tuzuq 'to point' as 'seven' (Malay *tujuh* for example), which then replaced PMP *pitu (Blust 2010b). Barito languages maintain *pitu (Ma'anyan, Dusun Witu *pitu*) although some Barito languages have borrowed *tujuh* from a Greater North Bornean source. There is not enough space to enumerate every piece of lexical evidence for GNB, but Smith (2017a) lists thirty-one additional lexical innovations, including both new lexemes as well as those from Blust (2010b). Since GNB, as a subgroup, hinges on purely lexical evidence, its status remains somewhat precarious, although no attempts have yet been made to challenge the proposal.

### 8.3.4 The Western Indonesian proposal

According to Blust (2010b) and later Smith (2017a), Greater North Borneo and Barito-Basap combine to form the putative Western Indonesian subgroup. Originally, Western Indonesian included all the languages of Borneo, plus all Austronesian languages to the west excluding the languages of Sulawesi and languages of the Central-Eastern Malayo-Polynesian group. This original proposal therefore included the non-Malayic languages of Sumatra (Batak and Sumatran Barrier Island languages). Smith (2017b: 443), however, restricts Western Indonesian to only the "indigenous languages of Borneo, plus some of the Austronesian languages of Sumatra (excluding Batak, Barrier Islands languages, and Nasal), Javanese, Madurese, Balinese, Sasak, and Sumbawa." This chapter adopts the more restrictive subgrouping of Smith.

Like GNB, Western Indonesian is primarily a lexically defined subgroup. Smith (2017a) provides thirty-five innovations, including nine that are either lexical replacement innovations or synonymic innovations (innovations that create a synonym, but do not replace the inherited word), and twenty-seven that are either innovated/new concepts or involve words without known etymologies. Some of the evidence is quite widespread, including the replacement of PMP *qaRta 'outsider; alien person' with PWIN *qulun. Many of the innovated concepts have to do with the plant and animal life found on Borneo, a situation that arose through Borneo's geographical position. The entire island of Borneo lies on the Sunda shelf, the southern extension of the Asian continental shelf which contains mainland Southeast Asia, Taiwan, the greater Sunda Islands including Sumatra and Java, Borneo, and the South China Sea but excludes most of the Philippines. During the last glacial maximum, the islands on the Sunda Shelf were part of Mainland Southeast Asia. As a result of this recent history, the islands themselves have similar flora and fauna with Mainland Southeast Asia including megafauna like elephants, rhinoceroses, large cats, and deer, and smaller terrestrial mammals such as the pangolin, and birds such as the hornbills, and myna, which are absent from islands located off the Sunda shelf, including most Philippine islands, that were never part of the mainland.

The boundary between islands within the Mainland Southeast Asian flora and fauna zone and islands outside of the zone is referred to as the Wallace line, named after Alfred Russel Wallace, English naturalist and evolutionary biologist. Because land masses on opposing sides of the Wallace line have easily observable differences in plant and animal life, it can serve an important role in linguistic subgrouping, particularly where a single group travels across the Wallace line and gives original names to new plants and animals. Blust (1982) demonstrated the importance of the Wallace line in Southeast Asia with respect to Austronesian marsupial naming conventions further east, but it may also be applied to the historical population movements of Austronesian speaking people from Taiwan through the Philippines into Borneo. When Austronesian speaking people migrated south into the northern Philippines, they entered an area without the familiar animals found in Taiwan, including the clouded leopard (PAN *lukəNaw) and the barking deer (PAN *sakəC), both of which are reconstructable to PAN using exclusively Formosan evidence. The vocabulary associated with these animals was thus lost, and when Austronesian speaking people re-entered the Mainland Southeast Asian zone upon their arrival in Borneo, new names were invented for these animals. Following Blust's logic, if a single name for a newly (re)discovered animal is found with regular sound correspondences throughout the island it implies that the animal was named once by a group ancestral to speakers of languages that reflect the new term. If multiple names for the same animal are found throughout the island, it implies that it was named multiple times by separate groups and thus does not form a subgrouping argument. Importantly, if a single name is recorded for a newly (re)discovered animal but with irregular sound correspondences, it implies that the name was borrowed between groups, and it also does not form any type of subgrouping evidence. In Borneo, the first scenario is by far the most common. There are multiple animal names specifically associated with the Mainland Southeast Asian zone that are found concentrated in Western Indonesian languages. These words have regular sound correspondences, suggesting inheritance from a common ancestor (i.e. PWIN). Some of the major lexical innovations regarding flora and fauna are reviewed here.

Borneo has eight species of primate: five monkeys; two apes; and the western tarsier. Several of these animals have names that may be reconstructed to PWIN with robust attestation throughout the island. In alphabetical order of reconstruction these are: *bəduk/*bəRuk 'pig-tailed macaque'; *buRis 'silver-leaf monkey'; *kəlabit 'gibbon'; *kəlasi 'red-leaf monkey'; *kəraq 'long-tailed macaque'; *kəRiw 'orangutan'; and *ukəd 'western tarsier'. The proboscis monkey is also found throughout the island but a protoword cannot yet be reconstructed. Beyond the primates, Borneo is home to multiple species of large mammals and languages have broad agreement on the reconstructed terms for many of the native mammals, including *kuliR 'clouded leopard', *biRuaŋ 'Malayan Sun Bear', *təməduR 'Sumatran Rhinoceros', and *təlaqus 'barking deer'. Other animals whose names and subsequent reconstructions are important for subgrouping in Borneo are *butbut 'coucal' (a species of bird), *kubuŋ 'flying fox', *dəŋən 'river otter', and *ma-tuRun 'binturong'. All this evidence, considering regular sound correspondences throughout Borneo, suggests that a single group of Austronesian-speaking people entered the island and were responsible for naming these new creatures.

Lexical evidence for subgrouping, no matter its robustness or quality, will always be criticized from the view that borrowing may better explain similarities between apparent lexical innovations. Borrowing will always be a special issue for lexical evidence, for the simple reason that sound changes are rarely borrowed, but individual words may be easily borrowed. It is not, however, a detriment to the comparative method that borrowing occurs. Borrowings can often be straightforwardly identified by comparative analysis. The cases where borrowings may be difficult to identify are where borrowings occurred in the early history of a group of languages, before sufficient differentiation has taken place between the phonologies of the languages involved. In these cases of early borrowing, borrowed vocabulary will often appear phonologically native. This is where the present hypothesis, that lexical innovations associated with the naming of new animals define a linguistic subgroup, faces its most serious challenge. It may be fruitful to improve upon or challenge the Western Indonesian hypothesis by identifying cases where the proposed lexical innovations are found outside of WIN.

WIN is not, however, only defined by lexical evidence, and although the reconstructed phonology of PWIN is only slightly removed from PMP it is still possible to identify sound changes which define the subgroup. As already mentioned, the original Western Indonesian hypothesis from Blust included the non-Malayic languages of Sumatra (Batak and Sumatran Barrier Island languages). However, Smith (2017b) points out that the WIN innovations found in Batak may be the product of borrowing. Additionally, all known WIN languages exhibit a merger of PMP *d and *j [gʲ] as PWIN *d, but Batak, Barrier Island, and Nasal do not reflect this merger. Instead, these languages merged PMP *j and *g as *g*. Smith argues that the merger of *j and *g in these languages excludes them from WIN, and instead proposed that they form a Sumatran subgroup. Another WIN sound change is the simplification of PMP heterorganic clusters in PWIN. There are two ways that clusters simplified, Nasal-plosive clusters became homorganic (*diŋdiŋ 'wall' became PWIN *dindiŋ, for example), and non-nasal clusters fully assimilated (PMP *baqbaq 'mouth' became PWIN *babbaq). Again, Sumatran languages do not reflect these changes (*diŋdiŋ > Toba Batak *diŋdiŋ* and *baqbaq > Simular *baʔba*). These sound changes, (i) merger of *j and *d, (ii) place assimilation of heterorganic nasal-plosive clusters, and (iii) full assimilation of non-nasal heterorganic clusters, are not unique to Western Indonesian, but their totality across the subgroup suggests that they are reconstructable to PWIN, providing some level of phonological differentiation between this protolanguage and PMP.

Finally, regarding the division of WIN into GNB and Basap-Barito, the proposal hinges on the presence of lexical evidence grouping all GNB languages together to the exclusion of Barito, already discussed. As for the possibility that Barito languages form a closer subgrouping relationship with other languages within WIN, not much has been proposed other than the recognition that groups like the Sama-Bajaw and Malagasy be included *within* Barito. One may speculate that Barito forms a closer relationship with non-Bornean WIN languages, but so far, no such proposal has been made, and it is questionable whether any special subgrouping relationship will be found between Barito and other WIN subgroups.

To review, Bornean higher-order subgrouping has enjoyed a recent renewal of interest in comparative Austronesian linguistics. Older proposals have been updated with a new model that posits a single ancestor, WIN, from which all Bornean languages descend. The WIN languages of Borneo are themselves split into two groups, Greater North Borneo and Barito-Basap. As it stands, however, the current state of Bornean comparative linguistics may change as an increasing amount of linguistic work is being done on the island. Many of the subgroups discussed so far have only lexical innovations as evidence, which many scholars view as less substantial than phonological or morphological evidence. There is also the issue of data availability, particularly in southwestern Borneo, where much comparative work remains to be done and the Western Indonesian hypothesis may very well undergo alterations as more research is conducted in Borneo.

## 8.4 Morphosyntax

Based on our current understanding of PMP morphosyntax, there appears to be little separating PWIN from PMP in this area. Evidence from Sabahan and Dayic languages, as well as Malagasy, indicate that PWIN maintained much of the PMP morphosyntax. It is also difficult at this time to reconstruct the morphology of PWIN, considering the overall lack of consensus on even the existence of the subgroup. We can, however, highlight some of the major morphosyntactic properties of WIN which provide evidence that PWIN had a conservative, Philippine-type voice system and associated morphosyntax. For more on the morphosyntax of Bornean languages, Kroeger and Smith (chapter 27, this volume) provide a typology overview, and Kroeger and Riesberg (chapter 47, this volume) examine voice and transitivity 'Western Malayo-Polynesian', which includes Borneo.

### 8.4.1 Homorganic nasal substitution

Proto-Malayo-Polynesian innovated homorganic nasal substitution as a morphophonological process whereby a prefix (*maŋ- or *paŋ-) assimilated to and replaced the first consonant of the root (Ross 1995a; Smith 2017b). Both *maŋ- and *paŋ- are retained in Borneo, but where *paŋ- is retained mostly unchanged, *maŋ- has undergone significant phonological reduction in a number of languages.

In many modern languages, *maŋ- has been reduced to only the nasal segment *ŋ-*, resulting in synchronic obstruent–nasal alternations. For example, Lebo' Vo' has the noun *tapan* 'winnowing basket' but the verb *napan* 'to winnow' which consists of a reduced reflex of *maŋ- and the root, *ŋ-tapan*. Other languages display variation in *maŋ- prefix reduction. In Punan Bah, for example, *tovoa̰ŋ* 'felling trees' is verbalized as *mənovoa̰ŋ*, but *kayuow* 'headhunting' as either *məŋañuow* 'to headhunt' with the full prefix or as *ŋañuow* with the reduced prefix and no meaning change.[2]

Reduction of prefixes to only the homorganic segment affects only reflexes of *maŋ-, never *paŋ-. If reduction were simply a phonological phenomenon, it is unexpected that there are no languages that retain *maŋ- without deleting /ma/, while reducing *paŋ- to only the homorganic nasal. Languages like Punan Bah, which alternate freely between *məŋ-* and *ŋ-*, also never alternate between *pəŋ-* and *ŋ-*, nor are there any languages that alternate only between full and reduced reflexes of *paŋ- but never *maŋ-. There must be other factors at play which affect reduction. Examples from genetically diverse languages in Borneo show how reduction targets *maŋ- (Table 8.3):

**Table 8.3** Reflexes of *maŋ- and *paŋ- in Bornean languages

| PMP | *maŋ- | *paŋ- |
|---|---|---|
| Kelabit | *ŋ-* 'transitive verb' | *pəŋ-* 'instrumental nominalizer' |
| Lebo' Vo' | *ŋ-* 'transitive verb' | *pəŋ-* nominalizer |
| Ngaju | *ŋ-* 'verb' | *pəŋ-* nominalizer |
| Ngorek | *ŋ-* 'verb' | *pəŋ-* nominalizer |

There are two scenarios which might explain *maŋ's propensity for simplification. The first one is the result of frequency. Reflexes of *maŋ- are better attested cross-linguistically and in texts. Second, *maŋ- may be analysed as internally complex, consisting of a *ma- prefix with a homorganic nasal *ŋ- (*ma-ŋ-). Sommerlot 2021, for example, has argued for this analysis as a result of morphological reanalysis. An internal division based on a comparison of the initial /pa/ segment in *paŋ-, and, say, *pa- 'causative' is less plausible, which may motivate the loss of *ma- but not *pa-. An alternative explanation for this is phonological. Under such an analysis the two nasal elements of the prefix assimilate, resulting in an apparent deletion of the initial *ma-, whereas *paŋ- resists assimilation because the non-nasal initial consonant and the nasal are not sufficiently similar to trigger assimilation.

### 8.4.2 Voice morphology

Voice in Austronesian has attracted special attention, especially regarding Philippine-type or 'multiple-undergoer' voice, whereby languages utilize multiple, transitive voices to select which participant may be moved in situations such as relative clause gapping or WH-fronting. In Proto-Austronesian, verbal morphology agreed with the privileged participant; the infix <um> 'Actor Voice' indicated that the agent was the privileged participant, *-ən did so for the patient, *-an for the locative, and *Si- for the instrumental and benefactive. The PAN system of verbal morphology was inherited into PMP and further into WIN.

Borneo is a transition zone between Philippine-type languages in Sabah and Indonesian-type languages in central and southern Borneo. Historically, however, the loss of

[2] This example also shows onset-driven nasal spreading, which triggers the alternation between *y* and *ñ* in examples with a nasal prefix. See Kroeger and Smith (this volume, §27.2.4) for more on this phenomenon.

Philippine-type verbal morphology in a diverse range of Bornean languages must be the result of parallel innovation. Outside of Sabah, where much of the old verbal morphology is retained, bits and pieces of Philippine-type voice are found, suggesting that the full PMP Philippine-type voice system was retained in the immediate common ancestor to all Bornean languages. Clayre (1996) provides a thorough overview of voice in Borneo, and the reader is encouraged to read this earlier work for a fuller understanding or Boutin (1988) for a focused look at the conservative morphology of Sabahan languages. A short overview is also given in the space below. In Table 8.4, verbal morphology is compared between Kimaragang (a language of Sabah; Kroeger 2005a, 2010, 2017), Malagasy (on the island of Madagascar, but nevertheless closely related to Barito languages), and Lun Bawang (a language of central Borneo; Mortensen 2018). Philippine-type verbal morphology is retained in each language to varying degrees.

**Table 8.4** Voice morphology in three Western Indonesian languages

| | PAN | PMP | Kimarangan | Malagasy | Lun Bawang |
|---|---|---|---|---|---|
| AV | *-um- | *-um- | | *-om-* | *m-, -əm-, -u-* |
| | | *maŋ- | *moŋ-* | *man-/mi-* | *ŋ-* |
| PV | *-ən | *-ən | *-on* | *-ina* | *-ən, -in* |
| LV | *-an | *-an | *-an* | *-ana* | - |
| IV | *Si- | *i- | *i-* | *a-* | *piŋ-* (< *i-paŋ-) |

Kimarangan maintains the four distinct voices from PMP, along with regular reflexes of the associated verbal morphology (*maŋ- > *moŋ-*, *-ən > *-on*, *-an > *-an*, and *i- > *i-*). Malagasy keeps the actor voice prefix *maŋ-, the patient voice and locative voice suffixes, has reduced the PMP IV prefix *i- to *a- via prepenultimate vowel reduction, and keeps *-um- in a restricted set of verbs. Lun Bawang maintains reflexes of *-um- with allophonic variants, has reduced *maŋ- to the nasal component, and has fused the IV prefix *i- with *paŋ- 'instrumental nominalizer' giving Lun Bawang *piŋ-* which is rare but does appear in elicited instrumental voice constructions. The original locative voice suffix, *-an, was lost. Without a doubt, most of the morphosyntactically conservative languages are in the north, but the retention of verbal voice morphology in Malagasy, originally from southern Borneo, suggests that the other languages of Borneo lost voice morphology after the languages began to diversify. Malagasy left Borneo before voice simplification took hold, giving a rare glimpse into the early linguistic landscape of southern Borneo. This also means that the elimination of voice morphology does not serve as a useful subgrouping tool, since it was apparently a change that spread across subgrouping boundaries rather than a change that was inherited from a common ancestor.

Bornean languages that have reduced the verbal voice morphology can give insights into how this system changed over time. Kelabit, for example, is a close sister language to Lun Bawang but does not have an active Philippine-type voice system. Instead, Kelabit reflexes of verbal voice morphology have been reanalysed as strictly nominal. Kelabit *-an*, a reflex of *-an 'locative voice' is a locative nominalizer, forming nouns indicating the location of an action: *gatum* 'act of joining together' > *gətum-an* 'a joint' and *gəta* 'act of crossing' > *gəta-an* 'bridge over a river crossing'. Kelabit *-ən* reflects PMP *-ən 'patient voice' and is used as a patient nominalizer: *irup* 'drinking' > *rup-ən* 'thing to be drank, a drink', *pasiw* 'act of selling' > *pəsiw-ən* 'item for sale, merchandise', and *patur* 'explanation' > *pətur-ən* 'something to be explained earnestly or in detail'.

It is possible that these affixes had a nominalizing function even in PAN, and that their shift in function, from a voice function to a nominalizing function, is a narrowing of their historical function rather than a shift. Starosta et al. (1981), for example, proposed that the original function of the morphemes was nominalization, with the voice function arising after, but Beguš (2016) presents a compromise position and reconstructs both a nominalizing and voice function to PAN. If the nominalizing function coexisted with the voice function in PMP, then the nominalizing function of these affixes only became their primary function as the voice system was reduced.

Another interesting change that occurred in several languages of Borneo involves the perfective infix *<in>, which is reflected in many languages south of Sabah as the default PV marker, a situation that arose through an interaction of allomorphy and voice reduction. In PMP, perfective aspect constructions in the patient voice utilized *<in> 'perfective', but had a zero allomorph for the patient suffix *-ən. After *-ən was eliminated from the morphology in many languages, reflexes of *<in> became the only indicator of patient voice. In a language like Kanowit, for example, reflexes of *-ən 'patient voice' have no verbal function and therefore are not involved in the formation of patient voice sentences. Kanowit *<ən>*, from PMP *<in> 'perfective' acts as the only indicator of patient voice:

Kanowit

(3) a. *gitin* 'to pinch'
*bukut* 'to punch'
*tapəl* 'to slap'

b. *ŋitin* /ŋ-gitin/ 'pinch AV'
*mukut* /ŋ-bukut/ 'punch AV'
*napəl* /ŋ-tapəl/ 'slap AV'

c. *gənitin* /g<ən>itin/ 'pinch PV'
*bənukut* /b<ən>ukut/ 'punch PV'
*tənapəl* /t<ən>apəl/ 'slap PV'

The use of *<in> to indicate passive or patient voice is widespread and not limited to Borneo. In some languages, like Mukah Melanau (Blust 1988a), the patient voice is both marked by a reflex of *<in> and inherently past tense, a situation that follows from the historical function of *<in> as a perfective marker. Since it is possible to reconstruct *-ən as the patient voice marker for PWIN with data from Sabahan languages and Malagasy, *<in> could not have been the primary indicator of PV at that higher level, and where *<in> is the main indicator of PV, it must be the result of more recent parallel innovation.

There are several languages that, like Kanowit, reduced the Multiple Undergoer Voice system to a two-voice active–passive system, but unlike Kanowit, deleted the inherited PV morphology and indicate passive with innovated morphology. Clayre (1996) points out some of these languages, which use an innovated periphrastic passive marked by the function word *an*, or a phonetically similar variant, in passive constructions. Clayre analyses *an* as following from the verb 'to make', and documents the word in Sa'ban, Murik, and Kayan. Additional research shows that the form is even more widespread, as data from Smith (2017a) shows *an* in Busang, Gaai, Kelai, Lebo' Vo', and, perhaps through contact, in Lahanan, a Kajang language in the Central Sarawak group. Sommerlot (2020) finds structurally similar periphrastic passives in Land Dayak, but with a formally distinct function word marking the passive. Example (8), which demonstrates a passive in Ribun, is from Sommerlot (2020). In Busang and Lahanan (examples (4) and (5) respectively), *an* parallels the examples from Clayre (1996), that is, *an* appears immediately before the demoted agent, but Gaai and Lebo' Vo' (examples (6) and (7) respectively) use *an* (or a phonetically similar variant) in a previously unreported position, as a pre-verbal particle that appears immediately before a sentence-medial verb, with the agent, if it appears at all, at the end.

Busang

(4) *anak ana an hinan naʔ moʔ*
child that PASS mother 3SG.GEN breastfeed
'The child is being breastfed by its mother.'
(Smith, field notes)

Lahanan

(5) *anak inan m-itiʔ an tinan nah*
child that VERB-breast PASS mother 3SG.GEN
'That child is being breastfed by its mother.'
(Smith, field notes)

Gaai

(6) a. *koy en bal oʔ*
1SG PASS hit 3SG
'I was hit by him.'

b. *guhŋan cəwʔ en əwk*
rice that PASS wrap
'The rice is wrapped.' (Smith, field notes)

Lebo' Vo'

(7) *ləpah aan nutoŋ sapay ɓəlaɓaw ray kuʔən*
already PASS burn shirt rat DM by
*sinaw laʔiŋ*
Sinaw Laing
'The rat shirts were already burned by Sinaw Laing.'
(Smith, field notes)

Ribun

(8) *Buah han leq oko m-iyo*
fruit that UV 1SG.I AV[3]-cut
'The fruit is cut by me.' (Sommerlot 2020)

The structural differences between languages, and the spread of *an* across subgrouping boundaries suggests that *an* as a passive is the product of drift, possibly triggered through contact in central Borneo, frustrating efforts to use this innovation as evidence for linguistic subgroups. The use of a formally distinct passive marker in structurally similar constructions in Land Dayak suggests further drift, motivated by the loss of inherited verbal morphology. A more thorough discussion of these and other voice patterns in Borneo can be found in Kroeger and Smith (this volume, §27.3.1.1).

Languages of Borneo south of Sabah therefore show the same tendency for voice reduction and passive-voice innovation, although strategies for voice reduction do not clearly coincide with subgrouping boundaries. It was shown that there are two typical historical paths that languages of Borneo have taken in response to voice reduction with special reference to the passive or patient voice: (i) re-analysis of existing voice morphology into an active–passive system; and (ii) complete loss of verbal morphology with innovated forms used to mark the new passive. Finally, the question of how these morphosyntactic changes may inform our

[3] Sommerlot notes that passive voice in Land Dayak often retains active morphology on the verb, possibly tied to tense/aspect.

understanding of the linguistic history and interrelatedness of Bornean languages remains open. There are clear typological patterns: Philippine-type multiple undergoer languages with complex verbal morphology are common in the north and Malagasy, while reduced systems are found throughout the remainder of the island. Malayic languages, in particular, appear to have a unique morphosyntax (Kroeger and Riesberg, this volume, §47.5.1), and the languages of central Borneo have varying degrees of morphological reduction and syntactic innovation. The study of comparative morphosyntax in Borneo is therefore an area where additional research may provide interesting new perspectives on the island's linguistic history.

## 8.5 Linguistic insights on recent migrations in Borneo

It has long been recognized that linguistic subgrouping can inform hypotheses of historical population movement, centres of dispersal, and homelands (Diebold 1960; Dyen 1956; Nichols 1997). In short, the centre for dispersal is usually the area of highest first-order genetic diversity. For Austronesian that is Taiwan, home to the highest concentration of AN primary branches (Blust 1999a; Ross 2009; and others). The same principle can be applied in Borneo, where new hypotheses on linguistic subgrouping allow for additional study of the historical movements of indigenous people and the pinpointing of areas of high first-order linguistic diversity. Thanks to a large catalogue of oral histories gathered in anthropological studies, the linguistic and anthropological evidence together provide a clear understanding of the recent internal migration history of Borneo, with special reference to central Sarawak. There are several major events that I will discuss: (i) the migration of Kenyah into the Apo Kayan central highlands, resulting in Kayan movement out from the central highlands; (ii) the northward expansion of the Iban into central and northern Sarawak; and finally, (iii) how these migration events may be viewed as triggering the Punan to abandon permanent settlements and take up a nomadic hunter-gatherer lifestyle.

The historical migrations of the people of Borneo are best understood with relation to major river systems. Map 8.1 gives the locations of the major Bornean rivers. The rivers are described in clockwise order starting in the north. The Kinabatangan is the northernmost river in the map and the only large river in Sabah. The Sesayap, Kayan, and Berau rivers follow directly south of the Kinabatangan, in Indonesian Borneo. This area is mixed with Kayan and Kenyah speaking villages, but was historically majority Kayan. The Mahakam river, in central-east Borneo, is today home to Kenyah and Kayanic languages, as well as Müller-Schwaner in the headwaters. The Barito (a large river that is part of the Barito river basin, itself home to several large rivers in close proximity) is home to most Barito languages. The Kapuas is the westernmost major river and was historically home to Malayic and Land Dayak speaking communities. The Rejang is across the international border from the Kapuas and is the homeland of the Central Sarawak subgroup. Finally, the Baram River is located in northern Sarawak, and is home to most of the North Sarawak languages.

### 8.5.1 The Kenyah homeland

As stated above, the North Sarawak group has four primary branches: Bintulu, Berawan-Lower Baram, Kenyah, and Dayic. The last three of these are located on the Baram river, an indication that the Baram is the likely North Sarawak homeland. As far as the Kenyah languages are concerned, they are divided into a Highland and Lowland group, both found along the Baram. Although Highland Kenyah languages have come to occupy much of East and North Kalimantan, Lowland languages remain restricted to Sarawak, supporting the hypothesis that Proto-Kenyah was also spoken along the Baram River.

### 8.5.2 The Kayan homeland

The Apo Kayan, a highland area in central Borneo includes headwaters of part of the Mahakam, Kayan, and Bahau rivers, is home to Kayan and other groups that speak Kayanic languages, Bahau, Murik, Merap, and possibly Segai-Modang (Guerreiro 1996: 205–6; Smith 2017a). The area is the ancestral home of the Kayan but is today dominated by speakers of relatively homogenous Highland Kenyah languages (Metcalf 1974; Sellato 1980, 1986; Nyipa 1956). If the Kenyah homeland is the Baram River, this implies that their presence in the Apo Kayan is the result of migration. The movement of Kenyah speakers into the Apo Kayan set off a chain reaction, as Kayan speakers were forced out of the highlands and migrated to areas further down river. Kayan speakers today occupy the middle courses of all major river systems whose headwaters are accessible from the Apo Kayan. This includes Baram River Kayan, Rejang River Kayan, Mendalam

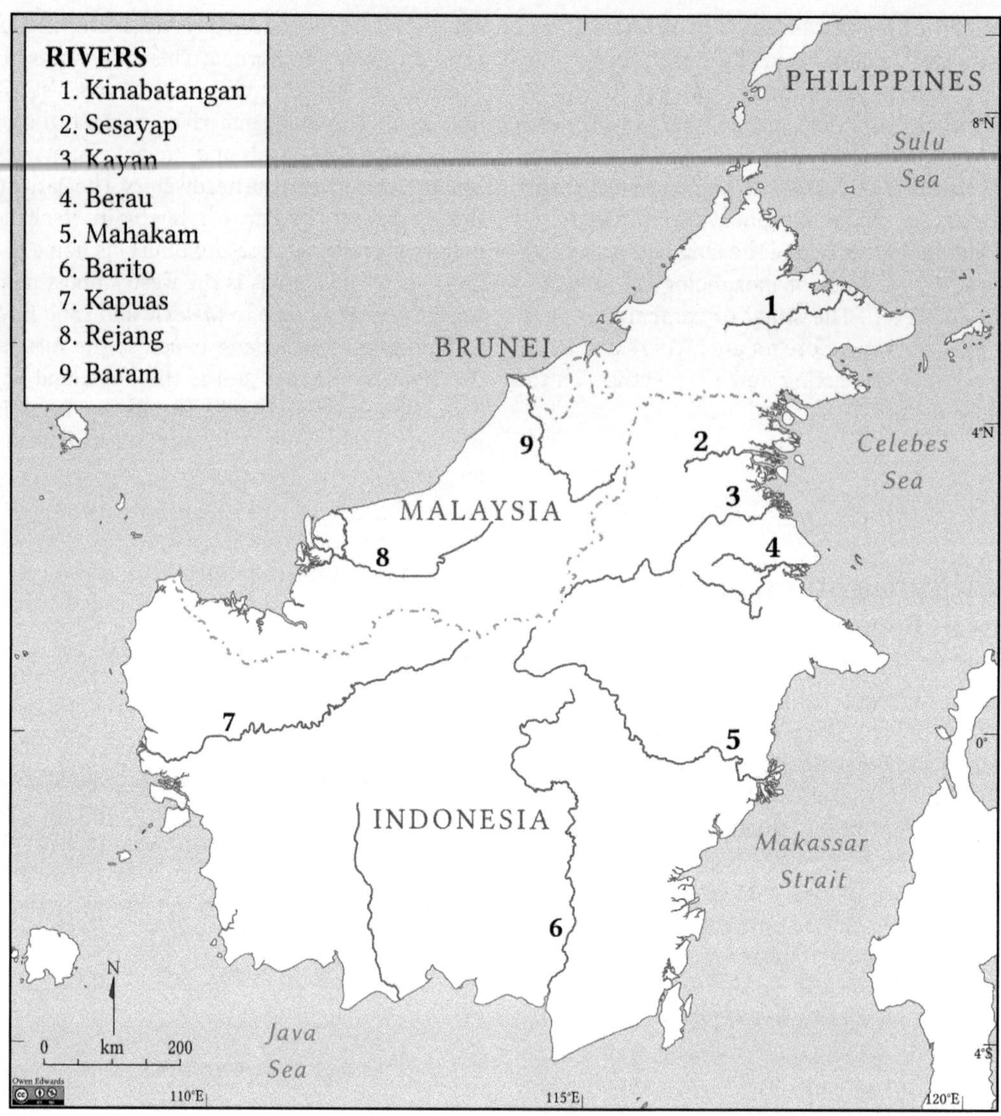


**Map 8.1** The rivers of Borneo.

(Kapuas River) Kayan, and Kayan speakers along the Mahakam river. Linguistically, the languages spoken in these various Kayan strongholds are relatively homogenous, with observable dialectical variation but widespread mutual intelligibility. Again, this implies a recent migration.

### 8.5.3 The Iban homeland

Iban are one of the more dominant groups in Sarawak, although the Iban originate from modern Kapuas Hulu regency in West Kalimantan, Indonesia. At some point towards the end of the 1700s and beginning of the 1800s, Iban settlers began migrating over the mountainous watershed boundaries that separate modern West Kalimantan from Sarawak (Sutlive 1978: 20; Sandin 1994). The Rejang river, home to the ancestor groups to modern Central Sarawak languages, is not far north of this border. We can discern from this that the position of the Iban, as the dominant linguistic group in the Rejang river area, arose through the demise and assimilation of other groups with longer histories in Sarawak. There is documentation of at least one such group, the Sru Dayak, for whom a single non-Iban 170-item wordlist exists (Bailey 1968), but who were quickly assimilated by the Iban.

### 8.5.4 Punan dispersal and the breakup of Central Sarawak

Central Sarawak is divided into at least three primary subgroups, Melanau, Kajang, and Punan-Müller-Schwaner. All three are located on the Rejang river or in its watershed. It would follow from this that the Rejang is the Central Sarawak homeland, as it is the area of highest linguistic diversity. Central Sarawak languages that are found in other parts of the island are therefore considered more recent migrations.

Two major outside groups migrated into lands that traditionally belonged to speakers of Central Sarawak. First, there was the migration of Kayan-speaking people into the upper Rejang from the Apo Kayan highlands in the centre of the island, which were driven by Kenyah expansion into the Apo Kayan. Second, Iban-speaking people migrated from the border region with West Kalimantan into the lower and middle stretches of the Rejang, overrunning the native populations and causing at least one documented linguistic extinction event.

Although these migrations have had a significant impact on the linguistic situation along the Rejang, the river is still home to several smaller language groups, namely the Melanau, Kajang, and Punan. These languages belong to the Central Sarawak subgroup (Smith 2017a) and their geographical locations are described in more detail in Map 8.2. Melanau languages are located at the mouths of the Balingian, Mukah, Dalat, and Rejang rivers, as well as further upriver in the towns of Kanowit and Kapit. Kajang languages are located in the Belaga area, although some have been relocated when the Balui river was flooded after the construction of the Bakun dam. There are only a few small villages of Kajang speakers, and their numbers cannot be more than a few thousand. Punan languages along the Rejang are concentrated between Kapit and Belaga, including Punan Bah, but most Punan dialects are spoken elsewhere on the island by small, widely dispersed groups. Most of the map corresponds to areas where Iban and Kayan speakers far out-number speakers of Central Sarawak languages. The Rejang itself, and the large Baleh tributary, are majority Iban, and the Balui and Murum are now occupied mainly by Kayanic-speaking people.

The question of the origins of hunter-gathering groups in Borneo is closely related to both the linguistic realities of the languages they speak, and our knowledge of a tumultuous recent past where at least two simultaneous intrusions into the Central Sarawak homeland displaced native groups. It has been argued multiple times that there were bands of hunter-gatherers present in Borneo at Austronesian arrival, and that modern Punan groups are their descendants (see Brosius 1988; Sellato 1988 for reactions to contrary claims; or Sellato and Soriente 2015 regarding the "ancient Pin nomads"). It is argued elsewhere, however, that modern hunter-gatherers are descended from settled groups who abandoned agriculture and took to the forests in the recent past (see Blust 2015b; Hoffman 1986; Smith 2015b).

The issue remains controversial, but there is evidence that the Punan are not descended from ancient hunter-gatherers but are instead the descendants of settled groups who were driven from their homeland by invading forces.

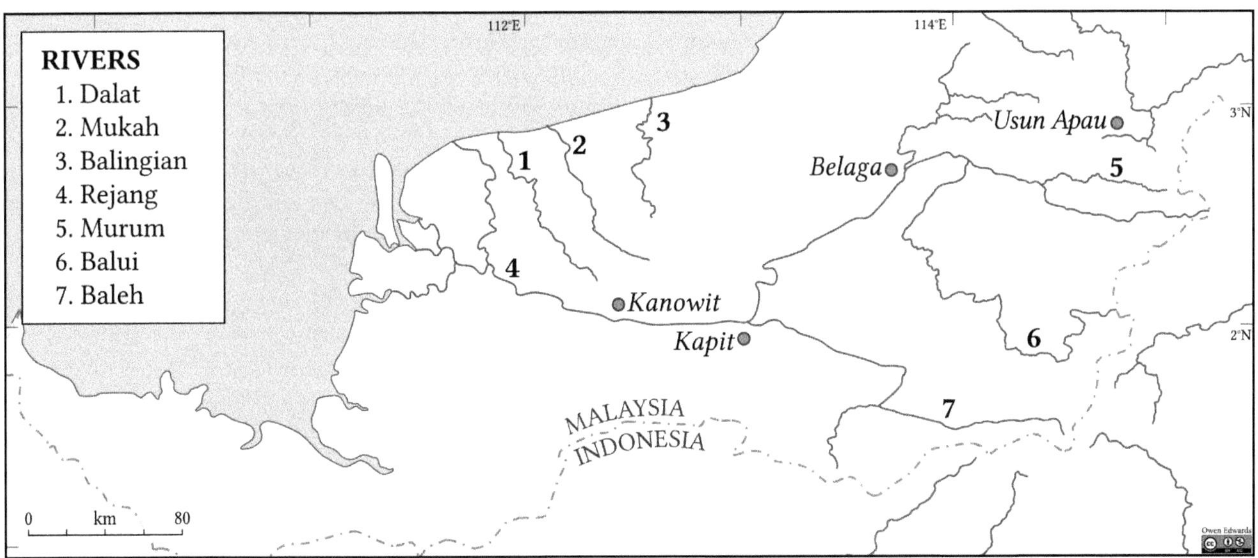


**Map 8.2** The Rejang river and its tributaries.

That evidence is, the Iban and Kayanic expansions, our knowledge of at least one formerly agricultural Punan group that was assimilated into the Iban, linguistic evidence suggesting that Punan languages form a discrete subgroup, itself part of the larger Central Sarawak group, the observation that Punan languages are mutually intelligible, and linguistic and oral history that suggests that the Punan originate from the Rejang river (Smith 2017a; Sellato 1994: 21–48, 2001: 33; Kaboy 1974; Sandin 1980). This evidence does not support the 'original hunter-gathers' hypothesis. Rather, it is clear that when Kayan and Iban speakers took over the Rejang river, the original inhabitants either contracted into small isolated groups (Melanau and Kajang, for example), were absorbed into the expanding group (as happened to the Sru), or fled. Speakers of Punan languages who are found in far-flung corners of the island are, under this view, descendants of those who fled during invasion by outside groups. The indigenous people of Borneo (and speakers of Austronesian languages more generally) have a long history of migration and expansion, and a hypothesis whereby the Punan were forced into nomadism, as the result of warfare and territorial expansion, fits well into the known history of the Rejang river.

## 8.6 Conclusion

The subgrouping hypotheses and discussion of migrations discussed throughout this chapter rely heavily on recent proposals (Smith 2017a; Blust 2010b). The main hypothesis is that the languages of Borneo are descended from a single common ancestor, Proto-Western Indonesian, and that PWIN itself descends directly from PMP. As a language, PWIN was similar to PMP. It was verb-initial, had a Philippine-type system of verbal morphology and voice selection that probably differed little from that reconstructed to PMP. Phonologically, it differed from PMP in the merger of *j and *d as *d, and assimilation of heterorganic stops to homorganic (*diŋdiŋ > *dindiŋ 'wall', for example), but otherwise had undergone no notable phonological changes. What defines the subgroup is rather a set of lexical innovations closely tied to the Mainland Southeast Asian fauna that Austronesian speaking people encountered when they crossed the Wallace line and moved into Borneo from the Philippines. This evidence is considered strong enough for subgrouping because of the regularity of sound correspondences in diagnostic lexemes across all Bornean languages.

The internal subgrouping of the languages of Borneo has also received several revisions as a result of recent work. This includes a proposed Central Sarawak subgroup that is historically based along the Rejang river and includes the Melanau, Kajang, Punan, and Müller-Schwaner subgroups. The nature of the interrelatedness of Barito languages, which includes Malagasy and Sama-Bajaw, has also undergone recent revisionary proposals, including the proposed inclusion of Basap within Barito and the re-analysis of Barito as an innovation-defined linkage rather than a traditional subgroup. Much of this progress is because research is on the rise concerning the languages of East and North Kalimantan, an area that has traditionally been left out in favour of Sarawak.

Finally, the chapter discussed the relationship between linguistic subgrouping and the study of historical population movements. Special attention was given to the area along the Rejang river, which has been the centre of two important migration events that led to dramatic changes in the geographical distribution of languages in Borneo. Both linguistic and anthropological evidence support the hypothesis that the Rejang river is the historical home of Central Sarawak languages, including the Punan group which is currently thinly spread throughout the island. Contrary to hypotheses that the Punan descend directly from groups of hunter-gatherers that have lived on the island for centuries, the linguistic evidence suggests that the groups who historically lived along the Rejang river were forced out by the northward expansion of Iban out of West Kalimantan. This is coupled with the downriver movement of Kayanic-speaking people which was triggered in turn by their expulsion from the Apo Kayan highlands by Kenyah speakers.

CHAPTER 9

# Historical linguistics of the Malayic subgroup

Karl Anderbeck

## 9.1 Introduction

Malay is one of the best known Austronesian languages, and for good reason. Malayic languages stretch from the Netherlands and Sri Lanka in the west, finding their geographical centre in Sumatra, Peninsular Malaysia, and Borneo, and to Ambon and Papua (western New Guinea) in the east. In modern times four countries, Indonesia, Malaysia, Singapore, and Brunei, have designated varieties of Malay as national languages. Standard Malay was equally well known in previous centuries, used by Dutch and British colonial governments, and this usage was due to an even earlier prominence of Malay in the maritime trade of Island Southeast Asia. Standard Malay has played an equally oversized role in Austronesian comparative scholarship, with scholars such as Brandstetter (1911, 1915) and Dempwolff (1934, 1937, 1938) heavily utilizing Standard Malay sources in their reconstructions (see Blust 1980c: 1–5 for a review).

The label 'Malay'/'Melayu' represents a diverse set of linguistic practices; this was apparent to the earliest European observers, and even earlier to Southeast Asians themselves (as seen in the discussion of 'good language' in the *Malay Annals/Sejarah Melayu*). Adelaar and Prentice (1996: 674) roughly divided these speech varieties (or lects) into three 'sociolect' categories: (i) Court Malay (the ancestor of Standard Malay/Indonesian); (ii) vehicular Malay (the contact varieties spoken in various ports of Indonesia, Malaysia, and elsewhere); and (iii) 'inherited' or 'vernacular' Malay, lects spoken in Sumatra, the Malay Peninsula, and Borneo in (one presumes) an unbroken line from Proto-Malayic.[1] Adelaar and Prentice use the term 'pidgin Malay derived', but I will use 'vehicular Malay' following Paauw (2008). As pointed out in Hoogervorst (2011: 73), Adelaar and Prentice basically follow a distinction first made by Abdullah Hassan (1969) between "bazaar Malay, literary Malay and colloquial Malay (Bahasa Melayu Lisan)". It should be noted, as Adelaar and Prentice admit, that these categories are by no means watertight or all explanatory.[2]

It took until the twentieth century for linguists to perceive that other lects, not represented as 'Malay', were also closely related to Malay (Wilkinson 1922; picked up again in Hudson 1970). Today it is recognized that lects such as Urak Lawoi' in Thailand, Jakun and Temuan in Peninsular Malaysia, Lom, Sekak, Kubu, and Lubu in Sumatra, Kendayan, Menterap, and Iban in Borneo, and Bacan in Maluku should be classified as 'Malayic', or members of a single family with Malay. As a result of this realization, Collins (2001: 388) coined the socially oriented term 'canonical Malay' as a way of referring to "those Malayic variants spoken by Muslims", allowing that other Malayic varieties may not be recognized as 'Malay' while still being closely related linguistically.

Accounting for the inherent difficulty of counting languages, on the basis of the mutual intelligibility criterion proposed by Hockett (1960: 321–30) and Voegelin and Voegelin (1977: 4), Anderbeck (2018: 283–6) estimated that fifty-four Malayic languages (or dialect clusters) are spoken in total, the largest number spoken in Borneo and Sumatra respectively.[3]

The most significant attempt to provide a definition for a Malayic subgroup and reconstruct its protolanguage was the 1992 revision of Adelaar's (1985) PhD dissertation (Adelaar 1992a). This chapter will therefore summarize Adelaar's conclusions while providing updates and highlighting points of differences with other scholars. For his reconstruction, Adelaar primarily used source materials from

[1] Whether the various vehicular lects should be considered creoles is briefly treated later in this chapter and in Slomanson, this volume, §18.2.1.

[2] For example, this chapter argues that linguistic assimilation to Malay is occurring to this day in the heartland of 'inherited Malay', and Malay in the main centres of diffusion was spoken by an extremely diverse set of humanity and has been so since the days of Malacca in the fourteenth century (Wheatley 1961: 312–13) and even Srivijaya and Jambi in the seventh century (Edwards McKinnon 1985).

[3] Anderbeck's count includes two standard languages, sixteen (inherited) canonical Malay languages, twenty-three (inherited) Malayic-but-not-canonical-Malay languages, and thirteen vehicular Malay languages. Of the thirty-nine clusters of mutually intelligible inherited dialects (Malay and non-Malay), twenty are spoken on Borneo, while the nineteen remaining languages/clusters are split between Sumatra (13), the Malay Peninsula (6), and Maluku (Bacan).

Karl Anderbeck, *Historical linguistics of the Malayic subgroup*. In: *The Oxford Guide to the Malayo-Polynesian Languages of Southeast Asia*. Edited by: Alexander Adelaar and Antoinette Schapper, Oxford University Press. © Karl Anderbeck (2024). DOI: 10.1093/oso/9780198807353.003.0009

the following six lects: Standard Malay, Minangkabau (central west Sumatra), Serawai (southwest Sumatra), Jakarta Malay/Betawi (Java), Banjar Hulu (southeast Borneo), and Iban (northwest Borneo). Malayic documentation naturally has increased substantially since Adelaar's original work in the early 1980s, so this chapter will bring in evidence from other lects not included earlier.[4]

The goal of this chapter is to present a clear definition of the Malayic language family, discuss reconstructions of Proto-Malayic (henceforth PM), including its phonology, morphology, and lexicon, and review attempts to both situate Malayic within the larger Malayo-Polynesian language family and subgroup and determine the PM homeland. The chapter shifts into documenting the lateral influence of Malay on other languages, then concludes with a summary of aspects of Malayic cultural history and a review of current scholarship and remaining problems and controversies in Malayic historical linguistics.

## 9.2 Malayic phonology

The phoneme system and phonotactic constraints reconstructed by Adelaar have provoked little controversy and are largely accepted.[5] See Table 9.1 and Table 9.2 for a summary of the reconstructed vowel and consonant phoneme systems.

**Table 9.1** PM vowel and diphthong phoneme system

| | Front | | Back |
|---|---|---|---|
| High | *i | | *u |
| Mid | | *ə | |
| Low | | *a | |
| Diphthongs | *-ay | | *-aw |

Source: Adelaar (1992a)

I will not attempt to provide evidence for each phoneme (cf. Adelaar 1992a: 32–101), but will focus on a few issues which particularly would benefit from further comment.

First of all, I compare PM phonemes to those of its best-reconstructed ancestor language, Proto-Malayo-Polynesian (PMP). The PM normal vowel system is quite similar to the reconstructed PMP system (*i, *u, *e, *a) except that *e merged with *a prior to final *h. Diphthongs underwent more substantial changes. Two PMP diphthongs split: *-ay to PM *-ay and *i; and PMP *-aw to PM *-aw and *-u, while *-uy and *-iw merged to PM *i.[6] The PMP semivowel *w was also lost in initial position.

PMP consonants also evince significant stability through to PM. PMP occlusives (stops and affricates) remain unchanged with the following exceptions. First, PMP voiced stops devoice word-finally. PMP *d, *j merge to PM *d, -t, and, at least as a symbol, PMP *z changes to PM *j, while PMP *d is retained as PM *d and weakens finally to *-r. Slightly more controversially, PMP *R and *r were considered to have merged into PM *r (*ɣ). PMP post-uvular consonants *q weakened to PM *h, and PMP *h > Ø with some exceptions discussed in Adelaar (1992a: 198).

The relative stability of PMP segments masks additional ferment in PM phonotactics. Major phonotactic changes, besides the final devoicing and other changes already mentioned, mostly are of a simplifying or reducing nature. Medial heterorganic consonant clusters with nasals are made homorganic, like PMP *demdem > PM *dəndəm, and other consonant clusters are reduced to the second component, for example, PMP *bejbej > PM *bəbət. Similarly, many words of more than two syllables were reduced to disyllables via a few processes (processes that continue to current times in many lects).

The resulting PM word structure tended heavily towards disyllabic lexemes with a *CV(N)CVC structure, where C is optional. Hence forms like *təluɣ 'egg' < PMP *qatelur, *hantu 'ghost' < PMP *qanitu, and *buah 'fruit'.

While many phenomena in daughter lects show some inconsistencies, Malayic phonology contains relatively few difficulties compared to most other language families in the region (for Chamic cf. Thurgood 1999 and Brunelle and Jensen, this volume, §30.2; and Rensch et al. 2012 for Proto-Bidayuhic), and Adelaar's reconstruction of its phonology is widely accepted. Three areas of difficulty can be highlighted here: antepenultimate vowel quality, ultimate schwa, and final glottal stop.

Antepenultimate vowel reconstructions. Given the tendency towards disyllabicity in Malayic, most Malayic lects neutralize (to ə) if they do not entirely elide antepenultimate vowels, for example, *səmaŋat* 'spirit (of a living being)' < *sumaŋət. Evidence, therefore, for a bottom-up reconstruction of antepenultimate vowels is in short supply.

[4] Malay(ic) bibliographies are Voorhoeve (1955) for Sumatra and Cense and Uhlenbeck (1958) for Borneo. Later ones are Teeuw (1961) and Collins (1990, 1995a, b, 1996). Most recently, the study of languages in Borneo has been served by a new bibliography (Blust and Smith 2014).

[5] With apologies to specialists in the field, this and subsequent sections contain numerous generalizations which would require, did space permit, careful rehearsal of caveats and counterexamples for complete accuracy.

[6] Adelaar mentions two other PMP diphthongs, *-ey and *-ew, but these have both been abandoned by scholars (cf. Blust 2013a: 590–1 for a review).

**Table 9.2** PM consonant phoneme system

| | | Labial | Dental | Alveolar | Palatal | Velar | Glottal |
|---|---|---|---|---|---|---|---|
| Stops/affricates | voiceless | *p | *t | | *c | *k | *ʔ |
| | voiced | *b | | *d | *j | *g | |
| Nasals | | *m | | *n | *ɲ | *ŋ | |
| Fricatives | | | | *s | | | *h |
| Liquids | | | | *l | | *ɣ | |
| Semivowels | | *w | | | *y | | |

*Source*: Adelaar (1992a)

In some cases, like the example here (PMP *sumaŋed), a PMP reconstruction is available for reference, but this is exceptional. Adelaar (1992a: 50–1) relied on two lects which, apparently, do not neutralize to schwa for his reconstructions, Banjar Hulu and Minangkabau. Sometimes these two—geographically distant—lects agree on their realization of antepenultimate vowels, in which case the reconstruction is straightforward. The difficulty lies when they conflict with each other and/or with the PMP reconstruction. To compound the shakiness of the reconstructions, both Banjar Hulu and Minangkabau (at least, the dialect used by Adelaar) do not have schwa at all in their phonological systems, which leads to the possibility that either or both lects innovated *a*, *i*, or *u* in that environment from an earlier *ə.

A difficulty which involves a much higher proportion of reconstructions is the issue of whether **ə* in ultimate closed syllables (corresponding to PMP **e*) can be reconstructed for Proto-Malayic, since almost all Malayic lects reflect PMP **e* as *a* in the ultima. Discussed at length in Adelaar (1992a: 33–9), Adelaar's evidence for reconstructing ultimate *ə (primarily, close correspondence with PMP reflexes) is not insubstantial and cannot easily be dismissed; however, significant questions arise. First, while documentation of Malayic lects has increased substantially since the time of Adelaar's reconstruction, no known Malayic-speaking area with any significant distance to Java still retains final closed *ə. (Anderbeck 2019a).[7] Javanese, Sundanese, and Balinese all retain the ultimate *e/*a distinction, and the few Malayic lects that seem to reflect PMP *e as *ə*, Jakarta Malay, Balinese Malay, and Palembang Malay, have had significant and documented contact with Javanese, Sundanese, and/or Balinese. All other documented Malayic lects have merged these two segments, including relic lects such as Haji of South Sumatra (Anderbeck 2007a), Urak Lawoi' of the islands off Thailand's west coast (Hogan 1988; Steinhauer 2008), Central Kalimantan Dayak Malayic (Wood 2000), and Bacan of Maluku (Collins 1986a). While this is primarily an argument from dialect distribution, its force should not be minimized. Barring a very early subgroup composed of all Malayic lects in Sumatra, the Malay Peninsula, and Borneo except the subset mentioned above, what are the odds that every single lect besides the three mentioned above merged two phonemes in the final syllable? Second, the seventh-century (1340BP) 'Old Malay' inscriptions, transliterated and translated by Çoedès, do not show an ultimate *a*: *ə* distinction (Blust 1988b: 13). To maintain the claim of a Proto-Malayic with ultimate schwa, the ancestor of Jakarta Malay must have split from this 'Old Malay' at an earlier point. If we consider 950BP as the approximate settlement date of Jakarta (Blust 1988b: 8),[8] we must ask ourselves where these speakers were located prior to moving to Jakarta.

A third difficulty in reconstructing PM phonemes is found in Adelaar (1992a: 63–9, 71–2), namely the reconstruction of *ʔ, reconstructed only in word-final position. In his argument, Adelaar very tentatively[9] draws a line between glottal stops occurring at the end of various words in Iban, and Proto-Austronesian/Proto-Hesperonesian *S, *H, or *ʔ, or PMP *h or *ʔ, for example, Iban *bukaʔ* 'open' < PMP *bukaʔ, Iban *baruʔ* 'hibiscus' < Proto-Austronesian (PAN) *ba:RuH. This view of glottal stop as retention was quickly disputed by Nothofer (1994a), who argued that Iban's glottal stop was

[7] Evidence from Tioman Malay, mentioned in Adelaar (1992a: 38–9) as an example of retained non-merger, actually exhibits what Mckinnon (2012) labelled "phonation driven vowel shift".

[8] It is unclear whether the AD1000 [950BP] date in Blust (1988b: 8) is more than speculation.

[9] As explained in Adelaar (2004b), the reconstruction arose not because the evidence in favour of final *ʔ was strong, but rather because counter-evidence was deemed insufficient.

not only an innovation but an areal feature. (Perhaps contradictorily, Nothofer also argued for glottal stop as a feature by which Malayic could be subgrouped; see below.) The discussion has continued beyond these two publications (e.g. Thurgood (1999: 308), who basically agrees with Nothofer that glottal stop is from contact), but suffice it to say the status of glottal stop as a valid feature of Proto-Malayic is not well accepted.

The discussion now turns from problems with the reconstruction to modern-day reflexes. The hundreds of different Malayic lects spoken today exhibit a vast profusion of phonological innovations from PM, and numerous publications have described them from the perspective of single lects (e.g. Steinhauer's (2008) study of Thailand's Urak Lawoi') or on a broader scale (cf. Collins' (1983b) dialectology of Malaysia's Ulu Terengganu, Grijns' (1991) variationist monograph on Jakarta Malay, or Asmah Haji Omar's (2008) overview of Peninsular Malay). In summarizing them, it is helpful to observe the three sociolectal categories introduced earlier. First, 'Court Malay', represented by Standard Malay. In many ways, Standard Malay is the most phonologically conservative of Malayic lects, which makes sense given its significant dependence on 'frozen' written forms. Bypassing the controversial issues mentioned above, one of the few significant Standard Malay phonological innovations is the lowering of PM high vowels **i* and **u* in certain lexemes but not in others, for example, Standard Malay *nene/k* < *niniʔ 'grandparent, ancestor', *oraŋ* 'person' < *uraŋ, and *pohon* 'tree' < *puhun. Explanations for this split likely involve more than one mechanism and require separate consideration of penultimate (likely phonemic) vs. ultimate (likely non-phonemic) environments.

Significant consonant innovations include the non-phonemic debuccalization of final *k in Standard Malay, for example, *beloʔ* 'turn' < *biluk, change from *ɣ as back fricative to apical flap in Standard Indonesian, and the loss of initial *h in approximately a third of reconstructed words, including a majority of cases where *h is followed by *a, for example, *atap* 'roof' < *hatəp, *abu* 'ash' < *habu.

Moving now to inherited Malayic and vehicular Malay lects, the single greatest generalization which can be made about phonological innovations is that final VC tends to be the least stable. In contact varieties of Malay, for example, simple loss of final stops is common; one sees forms such as *dapa* 'get' from earlier *dapat*, and *lia* 'see' < *lihat. As one of the most extreme examples in inherited Malayic, many Minangkabau (west and central Sumatran) lects underwent an ordered set of changes affecting nearly all final closed environments (*-VC), and usually culminating in vowel change and debuccalization of the consonant (Adelaar 1995c: 436–7; Anderbeck 2008: 50–3). Hence *iduyʔ* 'live' < *hidup, *isoʔ* 'suck' < *hisap, *takuyʔ* 'afraid' < *takut, and *bareh* 'uncooked rice' < *bəras. In terms of geographical distribution within inherited Malayic, this mutation of final syllables is most common among the canonical Malay lects of Sumatra and the Malay Peninsula. Three other innovations common in this same subset of lects are the sporadic lowering of high vowels (discussed above), the loss of *h, and the mutation of final *-a. With PM *h, the most common environment in which *h is lost is in initial position, such as *idup* 'live' < **hidup*. This innovation is ubiquitous in parts of Sumatra and the Malay Peninsula. Loss of medial *h (e.g. *liat* 'see' < *lihat) is less common but still much more common than loss of final *h, which is generally restricted to Trade Malays and port areas (Paauw 2007; Anderbeck 2008: 40, 80; McDowell and Anderbeck 2020: 57–61).

A well-known innovation involving final open syllables is the mutation of final *a, for example, Jambi Malay *mato* 'eye' < *mata. In Sumatra, it is rare for final open *a not to change to another vowel, whether *o* or *e* or even *u* in Duano. In Borneo and the Malay Peninsula final *a mutation is not universal but still common.

A likely Javanese-linked innovation is the simplification of final *-aw and *-ay sequences, usually to *-o* and *-e* (Nothofer 1975: 84–94, 1996: 76). While not all similarly appearing cases may be attributable to Javanese influence, this innovation is frequently seen in areas of known Javanese historical influence where Javanese loanwords are also seen in greater number, such as Palembang and Jambi (city) in Sumatra, Jakarta and Balinese Malay, and vehicular Malays.

Three mutations as common in Bornean Malayic as elsewhere are variable plosion of final nasals (e.g. *ujatn*, *ujant* < *hujan 'rain'), variable nasalization of final plosives (e.g. *aɲutn*, *aɲunt*, < *haɲut 'drift'), and weakening or disappearance of medial voiced stops in nasal–stop clusters (*anʲiŋ*, *aɲiŋ*, *eɲekŋ* < *anjiŋ* 'dog'). These innovations can be treated as a set because they often co-occur. As these also occur in non-Malayic languages, they seem to be an areal phenomenon. Much more could be, and has been, said about them (for example, see Blust 1997b; Seidlitz 2005a; Anderbeck 2008; Durvasula 2009).

An innovation very common in Borneo and in vehicular Malay varieties, less so elsewhere in inherited Malayic, is the mutation of *ə in penultimate syllables. For example, different dialects of Minangkabau variously reflect *ənəm 'six' as *ənam*, *anam*, or *onam*. In Borneo, Malayic lects retaining *ə are in the minority, mostly in coastal canonical Malay and Ibanic (Iban-related) lects. Other reflexes include *a* (where the segment merges with *a), *o* (commonest in western Borneo), and *e*. In eastern Indonesian vehicular Malay lects, *ə has disappeared entirely and merged with *a.

Finally, *ɣ exhibits a profusion of different reflexes. These reflexes add support to the contention of the original segment as a (voiced) back (velar/uvular) fricative (Collins 1986a: 181, 1987: 42; Adelaar 1992a: 86) rather than an apical flap. One of the most common reflexes of *ɣ is apical flap, occurring in close to half of inherited Malayic dialects, including most Dayak Malayic lects in western Borneo. However, evidence that the directionality of change was *ɣ > *r* and not, say, *r > ɣ, is found, for example, in Central Kalimantan Dayak Malayic. In one subset, surrounded by other *r*-ful lects, *ɣ is consistently reflected as *y* and Ø. This is a natural sound change from a back fricative, but not from a velar flap or trill. In much more limited form, writers such as Nothofer (1997a: 10) have noted the same change in certain lexemes only, the most frequent being *bəsay* 'big' < *bəsaɣ, in otherwise *r*-ful (or ɣ-ful) lects. This single change can be seen sprinkled throughout other subsets of western Bornean Malayic.

In lects that generally do not innovate to an apical flap, *ɣ is volatile in different ways, whether because of devoicing, palatalizing, eliding (fully or partially), or even a change into *ʔ*. Occasionally, mutation of *ɣ is accompanied by a change in the preceding vowel. One of the most complex of these changes is the merger of *-ar, *-ir, and *-ur words to *o(ɰ)* in the Upper Musi dialect cluster, in a process which likely involved four independent steps (lenition of the fricative and secondary lip rounding leading to vocalic manifestations and often complete disappearance of the fricative; McDowell and Anderbeck 2020: 67–8).

## 9.3 Malayic morphology

This section is able to present only the barest sketch of reconstructed PM morphology, points of similarity and difference with PMP, and patterns of reflexes in Malayic languages. The subject received fifty pages in Adelaar (1992a), which was itself both preceded and followed by scores of publications of both synchronic and diachronic nature. To give a sense of the subject matter's complexity, Adelaar's treatment covered 'only' the most common affixes to nouns and verbs. After a summary table (Table 9.3), this section begins with verbal affixes.

Adelaar (1984) reconstructed PM *pAr- (continuing PAN *paR-) and *(mb)Ar- (PAN *maR-). The former was evidently used to form transitive verbs and the latter to form intransitive verbs (among other things). The two exist in paradigmatic relationship. Hence Iban *bejalay* 'walk' and *pejalay* 'move (object)'.

In the same article he reconstructs the "location-oriented transitivizing suffix" *-i (no pre-Malayic affix provided), for example, Standard Malay *air* 'water' and *airi* 'water (object)'.

**Table 9.3** PM reconstructed affixes treated in this section

| Verbal affixes | Other affixes |
|---|---|
| *pAr- | *kA- -an(1) |
| *(mb)Ar- | *kA- -an(2) |
| *-i | *pAN- (-an) |
| *akAn (preposition) | *pAr- (-an) |
| *tAr- | *b(a) |
| *mAN(1)- | *ŋ |
| *mAN(2)- | |
| *-aʔ | |
| *maka- | |
| *-an(1) | |
| *-an(2) | |
| *-An | |

Building on Ras (1970) and Collins (1981; reprinted in 1986a), Adelaar (1984: 410) reconstructed the preposition *akAn. While not a suffix, it became attached to the verbs it followed in many PM daughter lects as a transitivizing suffix. Its earlier form can be seen in Bacan *lapas* 'free (adj.)' and *lapas akaŋ* 'to free, to let loose (object)', and in Banjar (Banjarese Malay) and Brunei Malay in similar situations. In Classical Malay, *-kan* and *akan* are still in variation.

Another verbal prefix is *tAr- which was neutral to the active/passive opposition, and "which conveyed the notion of unintentionality and potentiality" (Adelaar 1992a: 155). In Standard Malay, for example, the prefix can be attached to *buka* 'open' to create *terbuka* 'open(ed); opened (by mistake)'.

The focus-marking prefixes *mAN(1)- and intransitive verb marker *mAN(2)-, were both reconstructed (Adelaar 1992a: 159–61), also subjunctive marker *-aʔ, which Adelaar (1992a: 164) considers to be a continuation of PAN subjunctive suffix *-a as reconstructed by Wolff (1973: 90). Also reconstructed was the (rare) transitive marker *maka-.

Much has been written about the possible origins of Standard Malay passive prefix *di-*. The debate and various positions to that time were summarized in Adelaar (2005d), where he primarily responds to a paper by van den Berg (2004b) (which traces *di-* through Old Malay *ni-* to Proto-Austronesian *-in-). Adelaar instead concludes the origins of *di* were not as an affix but as a preposition.[10] The same article discusses (p.132) the PM (and PAN) reciprocal prefix *si-.

[10] The debate has continued since that article, including in Adelaar (2009c).

Three likely related suffixes were reconstructed (Adelaar 1992a: 173): *-an(1); *-an(2); and *-An. *-an(1) could denote reciprocality or collectivity, among other things. *-an(2) and *-An formed nouns of different types. Two circumfixes were reconstructed (Adelaar 1992a: 178): *kA- -an(1) and *kA- -an(2). *kA- -an(1) formed non-volitional verbs usually with an adversative meaning, and *kA- -an(2) formed nouns from adjectives and stative intransitive verbs.

Nominal prefixes and circumfixes reconstructed include PM *pAN-, *pAr-, *pAN- -an, and *pAr- -an (Adelaar 1992a: 192–3).

Adelaar (2004a) was concerned with two 'lost' (fossilized) PM morphemes: *b(a) 'someone who functions like [kinship term]', and the enclitic ligature *ŋ "apparently used between quantifiers and following nouns, and after pronouns introducing relative clauses", which is a continuation of the PMP morpheme of the same shape. The former can be seen in Standard Malay words *bətina* 'female', derived from PM *b(a)- + *tina* 'mother; wife' and *budak* 'child, domestic' < *b(a)- + *uda 'young' + *-ʔ. The latter may be illustrated with the common Standard Malay relativizer yaŋ, which < *ia '3rd person singular' + *ŋ, and baraŋ 'thing, object, article' < PMP *baRa 'marker of incertitude' +*ŋ. An example of a more lexical nature is PM *buruŋ, likely derived from PMP *buRaw 'drive off, chase away' plus the ligature.

One generalization that can be made is that many modern Malayic languages have lost most or all of their suffixes, for example, Iban, northern Peninsular Malay lects, and vehicular Malay lects. This fits with a broader trend which can be observed, that non-standard Malayic lects tend to be substantially more isolating than the morphologically more conservative Standard Malay (Gil 2009b: 4).[11]

## 9.4 Malayic lexicon

With Malay's dominance in Southeast Asian linguistics comes corresponding high-quality lexicographic resources. The temptation in a discussion of lexicon, given available materials, is to heavily weight Standard Indonesian/Malay, because lexicographic resources thin quickly for non-standard Malayic lects. This section will attempt to resist that temptation and give space to other subsets of Malayic.

At the outset it can be noted that Standard Malay has been the recipient of significant linguistic influence. Some of the major influences on Malay, whether Standard or other, have been Indian languages, especially Sanskrit, also Javanese, Arabic, and, more recently, Portuguese, Dutch, and English (see Jones 2007 and Hoogervorst, this volume, chapter 23).

Despite the historical bias due to the dominance of Standard Malay in comparative linguistics, and its numerous borrowings from donor languages, it still seems that, at the level of basic vocabulary, Standard Malay is more lexically conservative and more closely reflects earlier protolanguages. In a study involving a revised version of the Swadesh 200 wordlist, Blust (1988b: 14) concluded, "Of the 216 languages sampled to date Standard Malay shows the highest percentage of retained Proto-Malayo-Polynesian basic vocabulary of any Austronesian language,[12] retaining 58% of its basic vocabulary." The next closest Malayic lect sampled was Iban, at 54.3%. In general, Malayic lects contained the highest PMP retention percentages in comparison with other Austronesian languages. Of the Malayic basic vocabulary which was not retained, innovation patterns are not easy to detect, but two things stand out (Adelaar 1992a: 200–4): body parts (of humans and animals) underwent a high proportion of replacement, and many verbs required the reconstruction of two synonyms, one a PMP reflex and the other an innovated form.

Blust (1988b: 14) noted that "Adelaar's reconstructions show a close correspondence with Standard Malay forms"; the question is, is the correspondence too close? It would seem so. In another lexical study, Anderbeck (2018: 220–4) applied a clustering algorithm to a lexicostatistic comparison of most documented Malayic lects of Sumatra, the Malay Peninsula, Borneo, and Java/Bali. When the program was instructed to produce two clusters, in one cluster were all the lects of Sumatra, the Malay Peninsula, Java/Bali, Ambonese Malay, Standard Malay, and most of the coastal Bornean canonical Malay lects (Pontianak, Sambas, Sarawak, Brunei, and Berau). The second cluster was composed of all Interior Kalimantan lects (including Iban and Kendayan) plus Banjar (southern Borneo). A Proto-Malayic wordlist was included in the study, and fell solidly into the first 'canonical Malay' cluster. This is unsurprising in that this first cluster contains four of Adelaar's six main source lects for his reconstruction. This (and other clustering work reported in Anderbeck 2018) demonstrates that interior/western Bornean Malayic indeed contains a high level of lexical diversity (see discussion on homeland in §9.6.1). Table 9.4 contains some of the most widespread lexemes if interior Bornean vocabulary were to be given increased weight in Proto-Malayic reconstructions, organized roughly in decreasing order of strength of representation.

[11] Banjar and Kendayan are exceptions to this rule.

[12] Of course, one can argue this from the opposite direction, that Standard Malay has unduly influenced reconstructions of protolanguages. This is likely also true but diminishes over time as scholarship in other Austronesian languages increases.

**Table 9.4** Possible PM reconstructions from interior western Borneo

| PM reconstruction | Earlier reconstructions (Blust and Trussel 2020) |
|---|---|
| *kəbat 'tie' | PWMP (Western PMP) *$kabat_1$ 'wrap, bundle up' |
| *tapuk 'hide (verb)' | PWMP *$tapuk_3$ 'hide oneself' |
| *bujur 'straight' | PWMP *-zur 'thrust out; extend' |
| *ɣaŋkay 'dry' | PWMP *Raŋkay 'dry' |
| *cəlap 'cold' | |
| *suman 'cook' | |
| *kəlit 'steal' | |
| *ɣiŋkaŋ 'thin, skinny' | |

Modern-day Malayic lects tend to consistently retain PM nouns and adjectives,[13] while verbs show much greater tendency towards replacement, semantic drift, and even irregular sound changes than do nouns or adjectives. Some of the innovated verbs exhibit merely semantic drift, for example, *tikəm 'stab', which shows up in lists variously as 'stab', 'throw', 'discard', and 'spear', while other verbs seem to have simply appeared from nowhere, such as *kətap~kətup* 'bite'.

Among the larger groups of dialects, Ibanic-related and Kendayan-related lects are lexically quite distinct from other lects. The latter set shares a fair bit of vocabulary with Land Dayak/Bidayuhic lects, for example, *tareɲeŋ* 'ear', *ɲocok* 'drink', and *ka* 'at, in'. But two of the most lexically aberrant smaller lects are Haji of South Sumatra and Duano in the Riau Islands (Anderbeck 2018: 221–5). Haji (exonym: Aji) is an archaic lect on the linguistic border between Lampung- and Malayic-speaking areas, with approximately a third of its basic vocabulary borrowed from Lampung (Anderbeck 2007a). Duano (the people also known as Orang Kuala or Desin Dola') is more complex. As briefly treated by Anderbeck (2012: 272–4) and in more depth below, while it is possible that Duano has gone through sound changes of unprecedented (for Malayic) thoroughness and oddness, it is more likely the case that Duano is originally non-Malayic but has significantly assimilated to Malayic. Either way, the result is that only 63% of its vocabulary can be traced back to PM (the average in the study was 79%). A few examples of aberrant Duano vocabulary are: *saŋu* (< *saŋa) 'river'; *ia* 'water'; *desin* 'person'; *dolaʔ* 'sea'; *ayo* 'we (excl.)'; and *asaŋ* 'mouth'. Even more striking is the retention in Duano of reflexes of PMP *beRŋi 'night', *lipen 'tooth', and *laŋuy 'swim', as these are attested nowhere else in Malayic. As discussed below, I regard these as part of Duano's Austronesian-but-not-Malayic substratum.

[13] As is the case cross-linguistically (Tadmor, Haspelmath, and Taylor 2010).

Over the many past centuries, Malay has been the most influential and prolific donor language for dozens of Southeast Asian languages. What may not be immediately apparent, however, is that the recipient languages have also included other Malayic lects. Blust (2005c: 85–7) develops an argument based on the presence of Indian and Arabic loans in the many interior Malayic lects of Borneo which have never been Indianized directly, an argument which points toward an intermediary lect like Malay. This is the same line of argumentation fruitfully pursued by Collins in a number of research programs and publications (Collins 1983b, 1987, 2004 among many others), tracing the course of rivers and finding the spread of linguistic innovations, whether morphosyntactic, phonological, or lexical.

## 9.5 Malayic definition and subgrouping

### 9.5.1 External relationships

Malayic lects are clearly closely related below the Malayo-Polynesian level, but how, and which lects can be properly considered 'Malayic'? The discussion was kick-started with Dyen's (1965a) lexicostatistical classification of Austronesian, where he posited (among many other things) a 'Malayic Hesion', dividing into a 'Malayan subfamily' consisting of lects like Malay, Minangkabau, and Kerinci in one branch, and then Madurese and Acehnese in two separate branches. This Malayic Hesion was said to be part of a larger 'Javo-Sumatra Hesion' (also including Lampung, Sundanese, and Javanese) from which one of his students, Bernd Nothofer, reconstructed 'Proto-Malayo-Javanic' (1975). In response, Blust (1981c) argued that languages such as Sundanese and Cham were more closely related to Malay than Nothofer's languages, and suggested a new subgroup, also labelled 'Malayic' but with different constituent members. Specifically, this 'Malayic subgroup' was divided into four groups: (i) the languages identified by Dyen and Nothofer as members of the 'Malayan subfamily'; (ii) northwest Bornean lects Kendayan ('Salako') and Iban; (iii) Sundanese (Java), Embaloh (interior Borneo), and Rejang (Sumatra), and Bidayuhic languages; and (iv) Acehnese, Cham, and Jarai, which are still considered more closely related to each other than to other languages (see Brunelle, this volume, §11.2–4).

As noted in the introduction, Adelaar's reconstruction substantially narrowed the scope of the term 'Malayic', restricting it to the first two of Blust's groups (Malayan and Iban-Salako).[14] Since the time of this landmark publication, Adelaar's definition of 'Malayic' has been widely accepted, and no significant challenges have been mounted to the validity of the Malayic subgroup.[15]

A look at Adelaar's defining criteria for Malayic (2005c: 360) provides more specificity to the discussion, and allows for newly documented lects to be tested against them.

1. PMP *j > *d*
2. PMP *z > *j*
3. PMP *w- > Ø
4. PMP *R (and *r) > *r* (here ɣ)
5. PMP *q > *h*
6. PMP *h > Ø (except between vowels, or if the following vowel is a schwa)
7. PMP *-iw > *-i*
8. PMP *-uy > *-i*
9. split of *-ay to -ay and *-i*
10. split of *-aw to *aw* and *u*
11. cluster reduction
12. nasal became homorganic to following stop
13. final voiced stops became devoiced
14. homorganic nasal accretion between initial schwa and following stop
15. vowel metathesis in PMP *qudip 'to live' (Blust 1981c)

Duano provides an interesting test case for the Malayic definition. Given the fifteen criteria above, should Duano be considered Malayic? For the sake of space, I will only consider a few criteria, namely reflexes of PMP *q (#5), PMP *z (#2), PMP *-uy (#8), and PMP *-ay (#9). And while attested Duano lects display many words matching the Malayic pattern, I will here highlight a few of the numerous words which do not.[16]

First, PMP *q, which came to Proto-Malayic as *h, is reflected in Duano in a way that is basically unknown in Malayic, as *k* and later derivatives. See Table 9.5.

**Table 9.5** Reflexes of PMP *q in Duano

| PMP | Duano | Proto-Malayic |
|---|---|---|
| *qulu 'head' | *kulu* | *hulu(ʔ) |
| *qijuhuŋ 'nose' | *kəloŋo* | *hiduŋ |
| *taqu 'know' | *taɣu* | *tahu(ʔ) |
| *qatay 'liver' | *ɣati* | *hati |
| *bunuq 'kill' | *bunaʔ* | *bunuh |
| *buaq 'fruit' | *buaʔ* | *buah |

Note that Duano *k* is often spirantized to fricative; cf. Duano *ɣoyu* 'wood' < PMP **kahiw*.

Moving on, in Malayic, PMP *-uy merged with *-i (criterion 8), but Duano *məloŋoy* 'swim' < PMP *laŋuy. PMP *z became PM **j*, but Duano *duaʔ* 'far' < PMP *zauq (with vowel metathesis). Finally, PMP *-ay often > PM **i*, including PM *[h]ui 'rattan' (Adelaar 1992b: 390) < PMP *quay, but Duano *χai* (Kähler 1946).

It is clear that the phonological reflexes in the above words fall outside the definition of Malayic. Additionally, it is shown above that Duano has retained PMP lexical items deemed to have been replaced in PM. These two streams of evidence allow us to conclude that Duano contains both significant Malayic and non-Malayic elements. The question that arises is which subset is likely to be older. Given that Duano is currently geographically surrounded by Malayic lects, it is a much likelier scenario that Duano was originally a Western Malayo-Polynesian language which has significantly but only partially assimilated to Malayic.

I now return to the topic of subgrouping. There has been a considerable amount of scholarly back-and-forth with earlier subgrouping proposals above the Malayic level. These have included Western Malayo-Polynesian (Blust 1977a, 1978), Malayo-Javanic (Nothofer 1975), Hesperonesian/Western Hesperonesian (Mahdi 1988), and Malayo-Sumbawan (Adelaar 2005c). As Smith (this volume, §2.4.5) points out, these proposals have enjoyed various measures of popularity and acceptance for a time, but without producing lasting scholarly consensus. The one exception is that groups one, two, and four in Blust (1981c) are generally accepted to be closely related, and thus a 'Malayo-Chamic subgroup' (Blust 1981c, 1994) consisting of languages in these groups seems fairly well-attested.

Most recently, Blust proposed a 'Greater North Bornean' subgroup, "that incorporates Malayo-Chamic, Moken, Rejang, Sundanese, and all other languages of Borneo except the Barito family" (Blust 2010b: 44). (It also excludes the Tamanic subgroup which belongs to the Greater South Sulawesi group, see Adelaar 1994b and Mead, this volume, §12.3.10). Additionally, Blust suggested that Greater North Borneo "forms part of a more encompassing 'Western

[14] Adelaar did not imply an affiliation between Iban and Salako, nor has any such affiliation been later defended.

[15] An exception is Ross' (2004) preliminary exploration which wondered, on the basis of morphological evidence, whether Old Malay should be excluded from Adelaar's Malayic; see also Adelaar's (2008) response and the summary later in this chapter. It has also been suggested that Duano may not be genetically Malayic (Benjamin 2009; Anderbeck 2012 and below in this chapter), but in any case Duano was not part of the original definition of Malayic.

[16] Duano data are mainly taken from Seidlitz (2005b) with some additions from Kähler (1946).

Indonesian' subgroup that includes all Austronesian languages of mainland Southeast Asia, Madagascar, and the Greater Sunda Islands, but not the languages of Sulawesi" (same). Smith (2017a) spent considerable effort in adducing additional (mostly lexical) evidence for Greater North Bornean and Western Indonesian subgroups. Time will tell whether the newest proposals fare better than the ones they followed.

### 9.5.2 The internal structure of Malayic

The Malayic dialect network has been the site of numerous waves of cultural influence, migrations, cultural assimilation, and other factors which make subgrouping difficult. This section attempts to provide a glimpse into this confusing and confused dialect network. Much ink has been spilled in the attempt to demonstrate comparative subgroups below the level of Malayic, involving some of the best-known figures of current Austronesian scholarship. Even properly summarizing the various arguments would take multiple pages. At the risk of minimizing important work, I will here just attempt a thumbnail sketch.

The initial proposals by Dyen, Nothofer, and Blust have already been mentioned. Adelaar (1985) followed Blust (his PhD thesis adviser) in assuming a separate branch for Iban(ic), but was criticized by Nothofer (1988) for not presenting clear criteria for either of the two branches (Ibanic and the remainder). Nothofer's article was the first serious attempt to put forth evidence for an Ibanic branch (mostly of a phonological and lexical nature) and remains necessary reading in Malayic studies. However, Adelaar, in his revised dissertation (1992a) and a follow-up article (1993) took a more agnostic stance, holding that Nothofer's purported evidence was inconsistent and inconclusive.

Ross (2004) joined the classification debate but focused on morphosyntactic evidence. He proposed, based on this evidence, that Kendayan ('Kanayatn' in his publication) was a separate primary branch of Malayic, and that all other Malayic lects could be traced to 'Proto-Nuclear Malayic'. The primary evidence for this division was Kendayan aspect marking, and the application of the prefix *di-*, allegedly different from all other Malayic varieties. Also, as noted above, he judged Old Malay as not fitting within Adelaar's (1992a) definition of 'Malayic', as it had not yet acquired the Undergoer marker *di-*, and still reflects the PMP prefix **maR-* instead of *ber-* which is more common in contemporary Malayic lects. While Adelaar (2008) acknowledged that a separate branch for Kendayan was "not implausible in itself", he also judged Ross's evidence as unconvincing. In relation to Kendayan, he produced evidence that Undergoer voice is also not usually expressed with *di-* in other, non-Kendayan Malayic lects (namely on the Malay peninsula), thereby eliminating the argument for a primary branch for Kendayan. In the case of Old Malay, he argued that *di-* as Undergoer marker should not be reconstructed for Proto-Malayic, given its absence in various Malayic varieties. This took away Ross' argument for excluding Old Malay in the Malayic language group.

Meanwhile, linguistic fieldwork in the Malayic sphere, particularly in western Borneo, increased the knowledge of more peripheral Malayic lects. The numerous publications resulting from this fieldwork have brought out more and more evidence of close connections between this lower order group or that, evidence bearing both synchronic and diachronic interest. Just two examples will be offered here, both directly pertaining to western Borneo. The first is Nothofer's research on Bangka Island (1994a, 1995, 1997b), which lies between Sumatra and Kalimantan. In these publications, Nothofer laid out an impressive array of evidence connecting lects as distant as Iban, Sarawak Malay, Salako (Kendayan), Ketapang Dayak Malayic, and Bangka Malay. This evidence included irregular phonological innovations such as final glottal stop from *-r or *-h, and culminated in Nothofer's (1997a) proposal of a 'Western Bornean Malayic' subgroup.

The second example, perhaps even more bottom-up than the previous example, is the research conducted in Ketapang by Collins, Nothofer, Dedy Asfar, and Sujarni Alloy (multiple publications). This research not only yielded innovations differentiating a number of different Ketapang lects from each other but suggested an ordering of these innovations which could be used to establish historical relationships. The problem is that subgrouping proposals arising from these studies have typically been low-level, based on one or two innovations, and inconsistent with other proposals (Adelaar 2004b: 14–18).

The subgrouping arguments above explicitly or implicitly seek to establish (or refute) the existence of subgroups based on exclusively shared innovations, whether lexical, phonological, or grammatical. Preferably the positive argument provides not just one but several exclusively shared innovations with the same lectal distribution. The mental model involved in this paradigm is called the 'family-tree model' (Campbell 2013: 165). In its simplest form, the family-tree model posits the existence of a homogeneous speech community from which a subsection splits and migrates elsewhere. These migrations, staged over time, occur before and after various innovations appear within the ancestral language. Thus tracking the distribution of the innovations gives insight into migrations and possibly homeland, and allows for the identification of subgroups.

The biggest problem with the tree model and its assumptions is that it is far from proven that these assumptions are truly the norm.[17] If speakers gradually spread out without breaking contact with each other, the (simple) tree model is incapable of accurately representing the resulting situation. In such a case, a non-homogeneous Malayic *dialect linkage* (Ross 1988: 8) would be more appropriate to represent that reality. It may be that making a convincing subgrouping argument for Malayic under the assumptions of the tree model is simply impossible (compare Adelaar 1992a: IV).[18]

The latest foray into Malayic subgrouping struggles with these same historical/linguistic circumstances. Smith (2017a) is an ambitious and impressive historical-comparative dissertation which includes in its scope all the languages of Borneo. With such breadth, any particular language family can receive only so much attention, Malayic included. In the latter case, an additional handicap in Smith's treatment is that much of Malayic is spoken outside of Borneo and is therefore not covered in the dissertation, thus a complete subgrouping proposal could not be given. Smith further limits himself to sound changes, and sound changes of high quality, which he defines as "those which are unlikely to be the product of chance, diffusion, or convergence" (p. 188). In other words, morphosyntax and lexicosemantics remain to be included in his subgrouping proposal.

After examining a number of possibilities within his own (rather extensive and phonetically detailed) data, Smith finds three sound changes which are conducive to a subgrouping. One (deletion of **l*) affects (only) a subset of Kendayan. Another (sporadic addition of glottal stop) is the singular high-quality sound change Smith finds to define Ibanic. Hearkening back to Nothofer's work, Smith's third sound change is PMP "*-R > *-ʔ in Iban and 'Malayic Dayak' (better, Dayak Malayic) (p. 188), for example, *ikur 'tail' > *ekoʔ*, *butir 'grain' > *butiʔ*.

Smith's Malayic subgrouping proposals, as they currently stand, do not allow for a convincing subgrouping of Malayic. First, each of Smith's three subgroups are based on a single innovation. Second, as an artefact of the Borneo-only scope of the dissertation, the first two innovations are low-level and do not help us place, for example, Ibanic within the overall Malayic subgroup. Third, Smith's highest-level subgroup, West Bornean Malayic, relies on a sound change (PMP *-R > *-ʔ) for which the evidence presented in Anderbeck (2018: 187–91, 2019b) more likely points to diffusion rather than inheritance. In brief, this innovation typically appears in more innovative lects. However, it does not in closely related but conservative/relic lects. For instance, it occurs on the Sumatran coast but fades as one moves inland, and in most Ibanic lects but not in those at Ibanic's northern and southern peripheries (Sebuyau, Remun, Sekujam). The same pattern repeats itself elsewhere.

At a minimum, even if a successful subgrouping proposal for Malayic will never be made, allowing for the difficulties inherent in such an enterprise, it seems safe to say that all major scholars involved in Malayic historical linguistics (Adelaar included) would agree that Proto-Malayic as reconstructed by Adelaar (1992a), based as it was on the best documentation of the time, unduly favours Sumatran and Peninsular Malay at the expense of Bornean Malayic.

## 9.6 Culture history

In the imaginations of some, the term 'Malay' conjures up scenes of peasant farmers toiling in wet rice fields under a steaming tropical sun. For others, the same term may evoke images of able seamen offloading bundles of spices in far-flung ports. Both images have some basis in reality, which is, of course, significantly more complex. Today, speakers of Malayic lects exist in (rapidly diminishing) hunter-gatherer societies, as nomadic sea-gatherers, as slash-and-burn agriculturists, as both wet-rice and dry-rice cultivators, as tradesmen, plus as a whole range of more 'modern' occupations. The wide range of ecological niches occupied by Malayic speakers, in so many regions, begs the question of how Malayic lects spread to such a large area, what evidence there is of migrations, and from where the earliest speakers migrated. I begin with the last question.

### 9.6.1 The homeland of Proto-Malayic

Where did Malayic first originate? Where did speech communities first use, as their vernacular, something that we would (later) identify as Proto-Malayic? Map 9.1 is a graphic of the current geographical distribution of vernacular Malayic.

If we work backward from the historical attestation of Malay in the Straits polities of Malacca and Riau-Johor, we arrive at Srivijaya and Jambi of southeastern Sumatra, where both the term *Melayu* (or *Malayu*) was first attested (Andaya 2008: 19) and the earliest Old Malay inscription was found (Çoedès 1930). It is this geographical connection, plus the clear pattern of maritime distribution of Malay, that led some to posit the area connected with the Srivijaya and

[17] See François (2014) for a good discussion of this, also the short explanation in Smith (this volume, §2.4.4).

[18] However, see Jacques and List (2018) for an argument against this agnosticism.

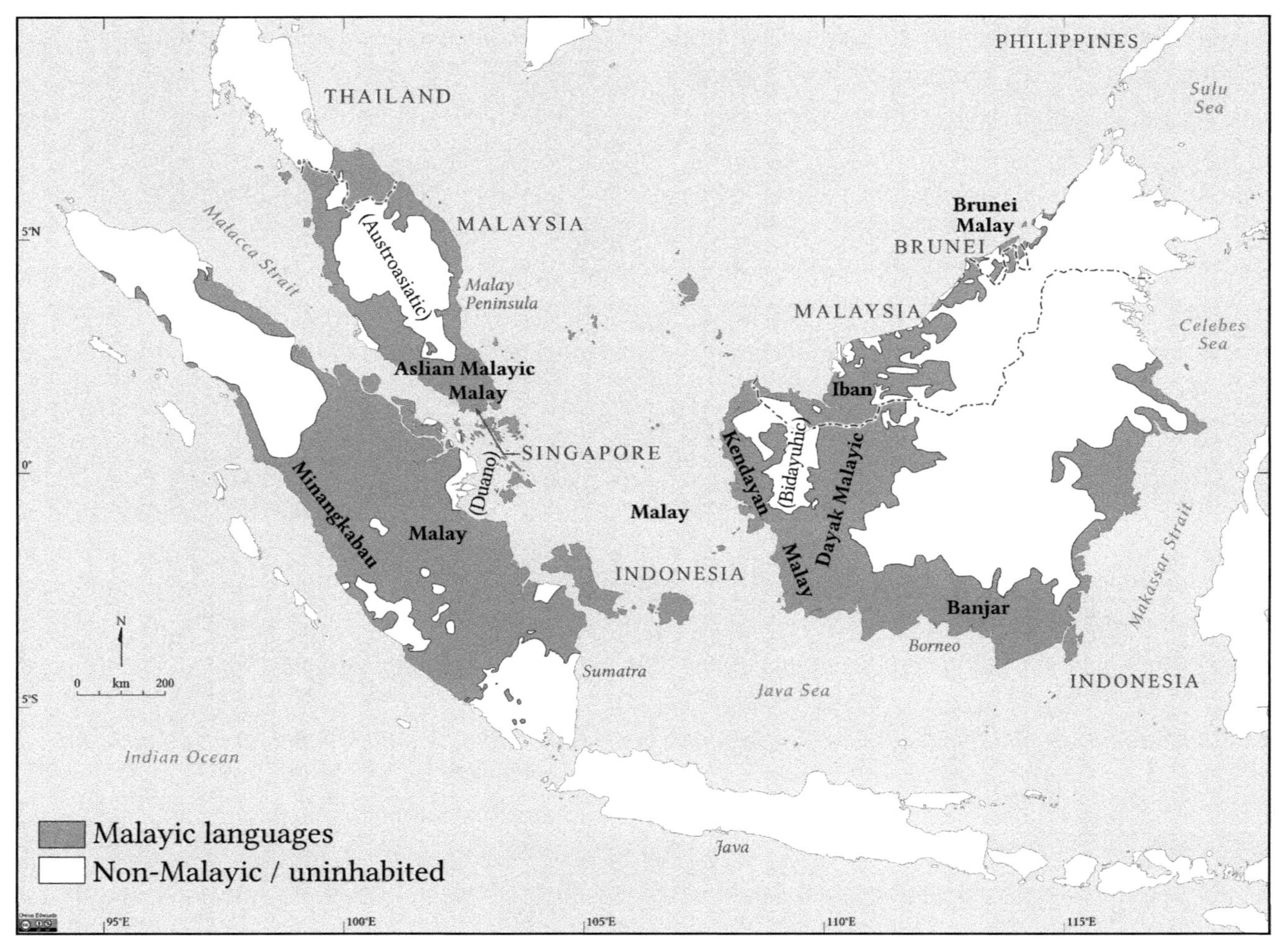


**Map 9.1** Current distribution of vernacular Malayic.

*Source*: Adapted from a 2021 map by SIL International®. Language data from Alloy et al 2008 (West Kalimantan) and SIL International® (elsewhere).

Jambi empires as the homeland of Malay (as discussed in Adelaar 2004b: 3).

However, once other languages were included in a broadened *Malayic* family, the question of a Malayic homeland needed to be newly addressed. Scholarly attention over the past thirty years has been most strongly focused on (usually western) Borneo as the homeland of Malayic (Blust 1984/1985; Adelaar 2004b; Collins 2006) perhaps beginning 2,000 years ago (Blust 1988b; Adelaar 2004b). While the arguments for a homeland are too complex to cover here, one of the key criteria is the 'centre of gravity' concept (Sapir 1916). Which area contains the greatest genetic diversity? Given that the largest number of subgrouping proposals (whether generally accepted or not) involves lects in western Borneo, and given the significant genetic divergence of Kendayan and Iban, this area seems a strong contender for Malayic homeland.

Without a successful subgrouping proposal for Malayic, one could posit that a region containing archaisms or comparatively rare retentions may at least give hints about the homeland, as these often indicate relatively great time depths in a particular location. Deciding what qualifies as a 'rare archaism' is an exercise fraught with opportunities for cherry-picking, however. To explore this topic in the context of Malayic, I provide five examples of possible phonological archaisms, and five lexical, all taken from common wordlist items so as to limit the sample (examples taken from Anderbeck and Cooper 2017).

The five potential phonological archaisms/retentions are: pre-Malayic antepenultimate vowels *a, *i, and *u; non-lowered penultimate high vowels *i and *u; and initial and medial *h in selected words. Of these three, the first has the circularity problems mentioned above, and the second is found in each of the three main inherited Malayic areas. The third (*h) may be more promising.

Reflexes of PMP *q regularly became PM *h, but have an interesting distribution among inherited Malayic lects. Standard Malay is phonologically one of the most conservative lects as regards reflexes of PM *h, yet even in certain Standard Malay words *h has been lost, such as (in Indonesian) *baru* 'new' < PM *bAharu, *atap* 'roof' < *hatəp, *berak* 'defecate' < *ba-hiraʔ, *alu* 'pestle' < *halu, and *asap* 'smoke' < (I argue) PM *hasəp. Similar words are found in Standard Malay with loss of *h in medial position: tua 'old' < *tuha and *tiaŋ* 'post' < *tihaŋ, and *tau* 'know' < *tahu and *tai* 'excrement' < *tahi (pronunciation; written forms retain *h*). To simplify, I here discuss the two lexemes which most rarely retain *h, 'smoke' and 'roof'.[19] The Malayic lects (usually, subsets) which retain *h in both words are split between Sumatra and Borneo: in Sumatra, Lubu, Kubu, Kaur, and Haji retain *h. All are either socially or geographically peripheral to Sumatran Malayic. On Borneo, Brunei Malay in the northeast, and Pesaguan and Delang (Dayak Malayic) in the southwest retain *h. Pesaguan and Delang are certainly not as geographically or socially central as, say, Bornean Canonical Malay, but are not as peripheral as the conservative Sumatran lects above, while Brunei Malay is not peripheral at all.[20]

The next two irregular sound changes are PM *dilah 'tongue' (PMP *dilaq), which in most lects metathesized to *lidah*, and PM *lihər 'neck' (PMP *liqeR), which in most lects innovated to *lihir (usually obtaining lowered vowels in the end, such as Standard Malay *leher*). In its unmetathesized state, *dilah* can be found in western Borneo alone, namely in most Kendayan and Ibanic lects, plus also in scattered Dayak Malayic lects in Central Kalimantan and far upstream regions of the Kapuas river basin. Retention of *lihər (with the final vowel always reflected as *a*) has a very different distribution, found almost exclusively in southern Sumatra (including Bangka island). Outside this area, *lihər only appears twice in the corpus, once in Central Kalimantan and once in West Kalimantan, and in both of these cases it is unclear whether to view the final vowel as a reflex of an intermediate *a or simply as vowel lowering due to the presence of final *ɣ.

Shifting the discussion to lexical retentions, I focus here on retentions in basic vocabulary from PMP which have largely been replaced in Malayic lects. The five selected retentions are the rarest in my corpus; one is so rare that a PM reflex was not reconstructed in Adelaar (1992a). The commonest is PM *sida 'they' < PMP *si-iDa (Blust 1977a: 11), which is usually replaced with *mereka* or other words, but is retained in large swaths of western Bornean Malayic. Next in terms of frequency is PM *təlu 'three', which has usually been replaced with the Indic *tiga*. Reflexes of *təlu are retained in western Borneo in Kendayan lects and often in Central Kalimantan. They are also found further east, in Banjar Hulu, Berau Malay (East Kalimantan), and Bacan (Maluku), although some of these eastern varieties may have borrowed *təlu* from Javanese. Less frequent yet are reflexes of PM *kunit 'curcuma, yellow' (PMP *kunij 'curcuma') which, with the meaning 'yellow', has been replaced with *kuniŋ* in nearly all Malayic lects. Reflexes of *kunit meaning 'yellow' can still be found scattered in Kendayan, Ibanic, and Bangka Malay lects, and in Bacan. Highly rare are reflexes of PM *sira 'salt' (PMP *qasiRa), found only (in my corpus)

[19] Adelaar (1992a) noted that *h was likeliest to elide when preceding *a, as is the case for these two examples.

[20] Upstream Banjar, a very cosmopolitan southeast Bornean variety, also strongly retains **h*. While it does not seem to have a reflex of PMP *qasep 'smoke', observe *hatap* 'roof'.

in Brunei and Bacan.[21] Finally, we find one retention from PMP unreconstructed in PM due to its rarity, namely PMP *baReq 'swell', usually replaced by *bəŋkak but still found in Kendayan, one witness in Ketapang Dayak Malayic (also western Borneo), and Berau Malay.[22]

What may we infer from these facts? Dialectologists refer to areas with archaic features as 'relic areas' (Andersen 1988). Relic areas have at least two features: they display relatively great time depth; and they have not undergone as much of the levelling which so often occurs when different speech communities are in contact. Because of the second feature, relic areas are often found in peripheral, relatively isolated locations, such as Icelandic, or the Norwegian spoken by immigrants in the United States. Hence not only can retentions not be used for subgrouping, but because of the likelihood of levelling elsewhere their relative time depth must be cautiously interpreted. Nevertheless, the strong preponderance of Borneo in the rare phonological and lexical innovations discussed here lends additional weight to questions of homeland.

If the proposed Greater North Borneo (GNB) subgroup continues to gain scholarly favour, the idea of (western) Borneo as the homeland of Malayic receives a significant boost. The majority of the higher-order GNB subgroups are found in western–northern Borneo (from southwest to northeast: Malayic (Malayo-Chamic), Land Dayak, Central Sarawak, Kayanic, North Borneo), while the others are scattered further west, between western Thailand (Moken), southwestern Sumatra (Rejang), and western Java (Sundanese). Malayo-Chamic itself is spoken in Vietnam-Cambodia, the Malay Peninsula, Sumatra, Borneo, and elsewhere. The centre of linguistic diversity for GNB would thus seem to be squarely in Borneo, suggesting from parsimony if nothing else that Malayo-Chamic also originated on Borneo.

Likely from western Borneo, then, Malayic lects diffused (whether through migration or contact) to Sumatra, the Malay Peninsula, and the islands in the Strait of Malacca. In the Malay Peninsula Malayic speakers likely encountered or were drawn from Austroasiatic speakers, but the mostly coastal settlement patterns there may indicate shorter time depth (Kruspe 2004: 17–18). Time depths for Sumatra seem relatively longer, as Malay is spoken from east to west coasts including the Barisan mountain range, in a fairly long north–south swath. Thus Malayic on Sumatra likely represents a levelling of previously greater linguistic diversity, and many of the current linguistic neighbours of Malay on Sumatra, Batak in the north, Barrier Island languages to the west, Rejang, Nasal, and Lampung to the south, are likely holdouts against this Malayic intrusion (Smith 2017b).

Evidence has accumulated over time for this assimilation. The case of Duano has already been discussed above. A second example is the southern segment of the Malay Peninsula. The Malay Peninsula is home to a large variety of Austroasiatic (Aslian) languages which probably predate the arrival of Austronesian languages (Benjamin 1976: 83). However, the further south one travels in the Malay Peninsula, the likelier it is that non-Malay/tribal groups will speak a variety of Malay instead of an Aslian language. Hajek (1996: 4–5) is representative of a number of linguists in stating:

> Linguistic assimilation of aboriginal populations to some form of Malay has of course been underway for centuries everywhere on the peninsula, but is most pervasive and complete in the southern half. The diffusion of Malay amongst the southern Asli appears to have spread inland and partly along the coast from Johor northward into Melaka, Negeri Sembilan, and Selangor, and also along the coast into Pahang.

Blagden (1906) contains a massive vocabulary of various aboriginal languages spoken in the Malay Peninsula. Given the cultural pressures strongest in the south, it is not surprising that the two languages (Kenaboi and Rasa) understood as extinct and represented now only by lists in that volume were both spoken in the southern part of the peninsula. That the linguistic change is "assimilation" (Hajek's term) and not simple replacement by Malay of earlier languages can be shown through the case of Jakun, spoken today in Pahang and Johor. Jakun is currently classified in the Ethnologue as Malayic, and in most respects seems no less Malayic than any other Malayic lect. Wordlists taken in the early 2000s (Seidlitz 2005a) show high lexical similarity with, for example, Johor Malay. Nevertheless, some Aslian words are evident in the fourteen Jakun wordlists, particularly in the pronoun system[23] but in other vocabulary as well. Blagden also includes 'Jakun' lists in the same geographical region, but these lists are over 50% Aslian (Austroasiatic) vocabulary, seemingly Semelai. If the geographical placement of Blagden's lists is to be believed, either Semelai territory has shrunk over the past century, or the speech of the southernmost Semelai communities has been mostly assimilated to Malay.

A third and final example is of the Sekak (Sekah/Loncong/Sawang/Laut) sea people of Belitung Island. Two sources were published exactly a century apart, the first a Dutch-language article with two folk tales in

[21] Adelaar (1992a: 141) notes that Pigafetta's 16th century wordlist contains *sira* 'salt'. Given the seeming Brunei and North Moluccan provenance of Pigafetta's Malay data (Collins and Novotny 1991), this fits the modern-day distribution of *sira* quite well.

[22] See §9.5.1 for examples of PMP retentions in Duano, which are in contrast deemed to be a non-Malayic substratum.

[23] For example, *ayih* 'you (singular)' and *hiʔ* 'you (plural)'. Timothy Phillips (p.c. 2018) considers pronoun systems the most stable indicator among Aslian languages of language progeny.

the 'Sekah' language (Riedel 1881), and the second a brief linguistic book by the Indonesian government (Napsin et al. 1981). The 1881 stories include otherwise unknown vocabulary items like *bəŋkur* 'breast', *ayau* 'person', *mənam* 'female', *umar* 'blood', *marus* 'white', *dudut* 'tail', *tuyu* 'rice', and *di rapak* 'where'. An analysis comparing the vocabulary of the two publications (Anderbeck and Tadmor, nd) demonstrates distinct continuity between the two witnesses, both in lexicon and in sound changes. However, it is noteworthy that many of these otherwise unknown words had seemingly disappeared a century later in the government study. Whether beginning with an Austroasiatic substratum like Jakun, Austronesian-not-Malay like Duano, or an unknown substratum like Kenaboi (Benjamin and Bradley 1983) and Sekak,[24] assimilation to Malay is far beyond mere hypothesis and means that the current Malay-speaking area was formerly host to a substantially greater level of linguistic diversity.

As foreshadowed above, it may be possible for scholars to differentiate between the homeland of *Malayic* as a language family, and the place of origin of *Malay/Melayu* as an identity (Adelaar 1988: 74; Blust 1988b; Tadmor 2002, 2006). It is not possible to make a categorical linguistic distinction between Malay and non-Malay-but-Malayic (this would be equivalent to a subgrouping argument), yet see the above discussion about 'canonical Malay' and the early attestations of Malay in southeastern Sumatra. Here we begin to see Malay as an identity or *representation* (Calvet 2006). This linguistic representation became attached to the somewhat amorphous and geographically shifting polity which for centuries controlled or had significant influence over the brisk India–China mercantile traffic through the Straits of Malacca. Beginning in Srivijaya (modern Palembang) and Jambi in the seventh century (1500BP) or earlier, then shifting to Malacca by the fifteenth century (600BP), then to Riau-Johor after Malacca's capture by the Portuguese, this mercantile traffic spread (probably multiple varieties of) Malay and a Malay identity throughout the areas bordering the Strait but even further to ports as far as Batavia (Jakarta), Makassar, Brunei, Kupang, Ambon, and Manila. With the religious conversion of key leaders, the Malay identity became closely related to Islam and spread also via education, culture, and kinship networks. Hence today Malay identity is part of a loose cultural 'package' encompassing language, religion, socioeconomic patterns (including fishing and wet rice farming), diet, and dress, but even this identity is paired with more localized identities such as 'Johor' or 'Sambas'. Meanwhile, millions of speakers of other Malayic lects hold to identities such as 'Dayak' (interior, non-Muslim), 'Orang Laut' (semi-nomadic people of the sea), 'Ambonese', 'Papuan', and many more.

If we shift our attention to the ports where vehicular Malay spread, we also find complex social and linguistic histories, differing with each port in question. B.D. Grimes (1991) is a linguistically aware history of one port, namely that of Ambon, Maluku. The picture she paints is of a busy, multilingual port from the sixteenth century (500BP) at the latest, where the language of commerce eventually became dominant not only in the commercial sphere but also among a large and growing population of residents. Today, Ambonese Malay bears elements common to many vehicular Malays, evidence of a fairly robust trading language (Adelaar and Prentice 1996; Paauw 2008) throughout the region, but with its own peculiarities due to its unique history.

A debate between linguists in the area is whether these vehicular Malays, in particular those of eastern Indonesia, should be considered creoles or languages that have evolved regularly from Austronesian. Collins (1980a) argued against what he considered careless applications of the term *creole* in the case of languages such as Ambonese Malay, and he and several other linguists argue that we should consider vehicular Malay lects as legitimately 'Malay' as other lects closer to the homeland. B.D. Grimes (1991) is representative of the creole position, arguing that Ambonese Malay is a "nativised pidgin/creole". This author's contention is that both positions are applications of particular (differing) mental models of the same linguistic situation (although likely with different extrapolations into the historical past). Models are not reality; they just describe aspects of reality through a certain lens, and as such explain certain things and obscure others. A (post-)creole model helps explain certain aspects of Ambonese Malay's linguistic structure and sociohistorical functioning, while a genetic linguistics model explains other aspects and highlights Ambonese Malay's relationship to the broader world of Malayic.

## 9.7 Conclusion

This whirlwind tour of Malayic has left many places and topics unexplored, others touched on with unsatisfying brevity, and lingered in other, rather odd and out of the way, locales. The diversity of the descendants of Proto-Malayic and related scholarship is such that a full treatment would require several dedicated volumes, but this chapter has attempted to illustrate some of the diversity of Malayic in terms of geography, culture, phonology, morphology, and lexicon. Along the way, weak points of the reconstruction of the protolanguage were discussed. It then placed Malayic languages in the context of Malayo-Polynesian, defining and testing

[24] The seeming (but unproven) Austronesian substratum of Sekah seems to evince no connection with Duano's substratum.

the definition of 'Malayic' with the case of Duano, and discussed the thorny issue of Malayic subgrouping, concluding that we are still without an acceptable subgrouping proposal. From there, old and new evidence for the homeland of Proto-Malayic was brought forth, and the chapter concludes with a discussion of language contact in the Malayic world. As other scholarly works have done, the final section argues for a long history of contact, assimilation, and replacement which made the Malayic (especially Malay) world ever larger, yet still diverse in new ways.

CHAPTER 10

# Historical linguistics of the languages of Sumatra, Java, the Lesser Sunda Islands, and Moken-Moklen

ALEXANDER ADELAAR

## 10.1 Introduction

This chapter is about the linguistic history of the languages of Sumatra, Java, the Lesser Sunda Islands and Moken-Moklen. It gives an overview of the various subgrouping hypotheses that have been proposed for the languages in this southwestern MPSEA fringe area, and it discusses the principles on which these hypotheses have been built. It does not include the Malayic languages, which are traditionally spoken on the southern coasts of the South China Sea and are treated in Anderbeck (this volume, chapter 9). It also does not include Acehnese, which is spoken in North Sumatra and is closely related to the Chamic languages in Vietnam and Cambodia. It will be discussed in Brunelle (this volume, chapter 11). The languages will be discussed in a basically West–East order, and, as far as possible, in the context of larger genetic configurations to which they may belong.

Historical research on these languages has concentrated on phonology and lexicon, except for Edwards (2015) which also deals with grammatical developments in Enggano.

The chapter is mostly concerned with subgrouping proposals that have been made over the last four decades. Several smaller language configurations and isolates are discussed. They are detailed here for the sake of clarity.

Moken-Moklen is a group of closely related languages (including Moken and Moklen) which are spoken in the Mergui Archipelago (on the border between southwest Myanmar and northwest Thailand). Their position within the Malayo-Polynesian subgroup remains uncertain (see Smith, this volume, §2.4.2; for contact history, see Sidwell, this volume, §20.5).

Non-Malayic languages of Sumatra include the Barrier Island languages, which supposedly form a subgroup, although the membership of two of them (Enggano, and to a less extent Mentawai) is problematic; the Batak languages, a close-knit and transparent subgroup in northern Sumatra; and the Lampungic languages, a dialect chain in southern Sumatra. They also include Gayo, Nasal, and Rejang, three Sumatran languages resisting subgrouping (see also Truong and McDonnell, this volume, chapter 28, including Map 28.1).

Non-Malayic languages of Java are Javanese, Sundanese, Madurese (see also Vander Klok, this volume, chapter 31, including Map 31.1). Together with Malay they were treated as a genetic subgroup by Nothofer (1975). However, they are no longer considered to be closely related.

Bali-Sasak-Sumbawa (or BSS) is a coherent subgroup of languages spoken in respectively Bali, Lombok, and West Sumbawa (see Shiohara and Arka, this volume, chapter 32, including Map 32.1).

The following sections in this chapter deal in more detail with the genetic affiliations of the above languages. §10.2 explains the major subgroups and subgrouping devices that are currently used. §10.3 discusses Moken-Moklen; §10.4, the Barrier Island languages, Batak languages, and Enggano; and §10.5, Gayo, Rejang, Nasal, and Lampungic (i.e. languages of Sumatra other than Malayic and Batak ones and Acehnese); §10.6, the languages of Java; and §10.7, the languages of Bali, Lombok, and West Sumbawa. §10.8 is an appraisal of the use of *tuzuq 'seven' and of PMP *j as subgrouping evidence. Concluding remarks follow in §10.9.

## 10.2 Major subgroups and subgrouping devices

Robert Blust (2010b) and Alexander Smith (2017b) are currently the main protagonists in the classification of the languages in question. For a better understanding of the complicated issues that currently play a role in this classification, it is necessary from the outset to take notice of

Alexander Adelaar, *Historical linguistics of the languages of Sumatra, Java, the Lesser Sunda Islands, and Moken-Moklen*. In: *The Oxford Guide to the Malayo-Polynesian Languages of Southeast Asia*. Edited by: Alexander Adelaar and Antoinette Schapper, Oxford University Press. © Alexander Adelaar (2024). DOI: 10.1093/oso/9780198807353.003.0010

the subgroups that they propose and the diagnostic devices that they have been using.

All languages investigated in this chapter belong to Blust's Western Indonesian (henceforth WIN) subgroup. It is based on lexical evidence, including botanical and zoological terms. This evidence was initially rather limited but it has recently been augmented with more lexical evidence by Smith (2017b). Blust classifies a large part of the WIN languages into a further (smaller) group called the 'Greater North Borneo' subgroup (henceforth GNB), which includes the languages of most of Borneo as well as the Malayic languages, the Chamic languages, the Moken-Moklen languages, Sundanese, and Rejang. Blust's main diagnostic device for establishing the GNB subgroup is that the languages in it have replaced *pitu, the original Austronesian numeral for 'seven', with *tuzuq, a word which originally meant 'to point with the index'. In contrast, other languages in the WIN group still have a reflex of *pitu for 'seven' (and by and large also kept the original meaning of *tuzuq).

Smith (2017b) rejects the WIN subgroup as defined by Blust and splits it into three primary Malayo-Polynesian subgroups, to wit Moken-Moklen, Sumatran, and WIN 'proper' (the latter maintaining GNB as a subdivision within it). Smith's main criterion for this further split is that the member languages in the resulting three subgroups each have their own reflex of PMP *-j-. Many Sumatran languages reflect it as *g* (or at least, as a consonant that has developed from an intermediate *-g-), Moken-Moklen languages reflect it as *y*, and other WIN languages reflect it as *d* (or *r*, which is a development thereof).

Other classifications that have been proposed in the last two decades are Zobel (2002) and Adelaar (2005c). Zobel (2002) distinguishes a Nuclear Malayo-Polynesian subgroup which encompasses Indonesian languages on the southwestern fringes of MPSEA, languages of central and southern Sulawesi, Chamorro and Palauan, and the CEMP languages. His classification is based on morphosyntactic evidence (see the discussion in Smith, this volume, §2.4.5). Based on phonological and lexical evidence, Adelaar's (2005c) 'Malayo-Sumbawan' subgroup excludes Javanese and puts BSS on a par with Malayic and Aceh-Chamic in one division, and Sundanese and Madurese in two other ones (see further §10.8).

## 10.3 Moken and Moklen

The westernmost languages, Moken-Moklen, have a rather unique phonological history.[1] Larish (1999) presents a subgrouping hypothesis in which Proto-Moken-Moklen is closely related to Malayo-Chamic. His Moken-Moklen–Aceh-Chamic-Malayic subgroup consists of two branches, Moken-Moklen and Aceh-Chamic-Malayic. Thurgood (1999: 58) opposes such a relationship, pointing out the unusual Moken-Moklen change from *q to *k* and the different ways final high vowels became diphthongized (PMP *-i > Proto-Malayic *-i, Proto-Chamic *-ɛy; PMP *-u > Proto-Malayic *-u, Proto-Chamic *-ɔw); whereas in Moken-Moklen both vowels have merged to *-oi*. Moken-Moklen furthermore merged PMP *R and *l whereas Malayic and Chamic reflect these as respectively *r* and *l*. (See comparative wordlist in Table 10.1.)

Blust (2010b) includes Moken-Moklen in the GNB group because they have a reflex of *tuzuq for 'seven'. Smith (2017b) contests this, considering the pair an isolate within the Malayo-Polynesian language group. He refers to Blust's own observation that *tuzuq reflexes meaning 'seven' are also found in some languages which cannot belong to GNB (such as Makasar). He also points out that Moken-Moklen as well as some of the GNB languages in Borneo itself show irregularities in their reflexes of *tuzuq. Furthermore, in contrast to many GNB languages, Moken-Moklen languages do not merge PMP *j and *d, but distinguish them as respectively *y* and *d* (compare PMP *qudip 'alive' > *kodip* and *daqan 'branch' > *dakan* vs. *qijuŋ > *yoŋ* and *qajəŋ 'charcoal' > *kayaŋ*). This is a reason for him to exclude these languages from GNB, instead affording them a separate branch status within Malayo-Polynesian.

## 10.4 Barrier Island languages, Batak languages, and Enggano

The Barrier Island languages along Sumatra's west coast are Simeulue, Sigulai (also called Sikule, Sikhule), Nias, Mentawai, and Enggano. They are often assumed to form a genetic subgroup (see Nothofer 1986), although the inclusion of Enggano is very uncertain as this language differs dramatically from other MPSEA languages. The major Batak languages are the Southern Batak ones Toba Batak, Angkola, Mandailing, and Simalungun, and the Northern Batak ones, Karo Batak, Dairi-Pakpak, and Alas. Gayo is sometimes assumed to be closely related to the Batak languages, but the relationship has never been demonstrated and is unlikely (see §10.5.1).[2] At a higher (more distant) level, the Barrier Island and Batak languages are also considered to form a genetic group on account of the large amount of lexical in-

[1] See Larish (1999, 2005) for information about differences between these closely related languages.

[2] McDonnell and Truong (this volume, §28.1, fn.2) already pointed to the lack of evidence for an inclusion of Gayo in the Barrier Island–Batak subgroup.

**Table 10.1** Comparative wordlist of PMP, Malayic, Chamic, and Moken

| PMP | Malayic | Chamic | Moken |
|---|---|---|---|
| *quzan 'rain' | *hujan | *huja:n | *kojan* |
| *qudip 'to live; alive' | *hidup | *hudip | *kodip* |
| *tanəq 'earth, soil' | *tanah | *tanah | *tanak* 'land; country' |
| *batu 'stone' | *batu | *batɔw | *batoi* (/bato:e:/bätoi) |
| *waRi 'day; sun' | *hari | *hurɛy | *aloi* |
| *Ratus 'hundred' | *ratus | *ratus | *lato* |
| *lima 'five' | *lima | *lima | *lèma* |
| *tuzuq 'to point with the index finger' | *tujuh 'seven' | *tujuh 'seven' | *luju:k* and *duyu:k* 'seven' |

novations that they exclusively share and on the assumption that they both reflect PMP *j as *g* or, in some cases, as a consonant which must have been *g at an earlier stage (Nothofer 1986). In Simeulue, Sigulai, and Nias, PMP *j became *x*; in Mentawai, *g*; and in Enggano, *h*.

## 10.4.1 Barrier Island languages and Enggano

The comparative wordlist in Table 10.2 brings out the phonological differences between the assumed members of the Barrier Island subgroup. In Edwards' (2015: 83–4) classification, Simeulue, Sigulai, and Nias form the core of this subgroup, whereas Mentawai is a less integrated member, and Enggano is no member at all as it has a totally different phonological history from the other languages (Edwards 2015), even if it shares with Mentawai a development from *w to b. (This is different from Nothofer's classification (1986: 105), in which Sigulai, Nias, and Mentawai are grouped closely together whereas Simeulue is somewhat more remote, and an even more remote Enggano is still provisionally included).

Edwards (2015) investigates the phonological, lexical, and morphosyntactic history of Enggano. He provides a comprehensive body of evidence to show that it is a member of the Austronesian language family, rejecting the position of earlier scholars (Capell 1982; Blench 2014) who disputed this. His main arguments are that in spite of the unusual sound changes that Enggano has undergone since PMP (such as *w > *b*; *t > *k*; *s > *k*; *m > *b*; *n > *d*; *ŋ, j > *h*), these changes are often very regular; furthermore, Enggano also appears to have retained a large part of PMP verb morphology and pronouns. Compare the following genitive suffixes: *-ʔVu* '1SG.GEN' (*=(ŋ)ku); *-bu* '2SG.GEN' (< *=mu); *-dia* '3SG.GEN' (< *n-ia); *-dai* '1PL.EXCL.GEN' (< *n-ami); *-ka* '1DU.INCL.GEN' (< *=ta); *kaʔa* '1PL.INCL.GEN' (< *=ta + plural extender); *-d(i)u* '2PL.GEN' (< *=miu); *-da* '3PL.GEN' (< *=da).

Edwards is doubtful about a common history between Enggano and other Barrier Island languages. The following three phonological changes seem to suggest such a history:

(1) PMP *j > Enggano *h*, Simeulue, Sigulai, Nias *x* (<-> Mentawai *g*, ɣ; Proto-Batak *g[3]);
PMP *k > Enggano *ʔ*, Sigulai, Nias *ʔ*, *Ø*, Simeulue *k*, *ʔ*, *Ø* (<-> Mentawai *k*, *ʔ*; Proto-Batak *k);
PMP *w > Enggano *b*, Mentawai *b* (<-> Sigulai, Nias, Simeulue *w*, *Ø*; Proto-Batak *w, sØ)

Edwards does not consider these changes a basis for including Enggano in a Barrier Island–Batak subgroup. In this language, not only PMP *j but also PMP *ŋ became *h*. Edwards (2015: 64) assumes that at an earlier point in Enggano phonological history *ŋ had first become *g, which is in line with the fact that, in this language, PMP *m and *n also became denasalized, (becoming *b and *d respectively, although they maintain nasal allophones).[4] This *g subsequently became *ɣ, which then merged with PMP *j to *x before it took its final shape *h*. Edwards does not think that *ŋ could eventually have led to Simeulue, Sigulai, and Nias

[3] Edwards provides Toba Batak cognates but these Proto-Batak phonemes (based on Adelaar 1981) are uncontroversial and phonologically more illustrative.

[4] Incidentally, Enggano has a palatal nasal phoneme, but the status of palatal nasals is very uncertain in the phonological history of both Enggano (Edwards 2015: 62) and Malayo-Polynesian.

**Table 10.2** Comparative wordlist of PMP, the Barrier Island languages, and Proto-Batak[a]

| PMP | Simeulue | Sigulai | Nias | Mentawai | Enggano | Toba Batak |
|---|---|---|---|---|---|---|
| *anak 'offspring' | *anaʔ* | *ono* | *ono* | — | *e-ara* | *anak* |
| *baqbaq 'mouth' | *baba, baʔba* | *bafa* | *bawa* | — | *e-papa* 'cheek' | *baba* |
| *bəli 'to buy' | *bəli* | *bıli* | *bõli=õli*[b] | — | *e-odi* 'price' | *boli* 'bride price' |
| *buluŋ 'medicinal herbs' | *boluŋ* | *bulu* | *bulu* | *buluk* | *e-pudu* 'leaf' | *buluŋ* 'leaf' |
| *bunuq 'to kill' | *bunu, funu* | *bunu* | *bunu* | *munu* | *pudu* | *bunu* |
| *dəŋəR 'to hear' | — | ? | *roŋo* | ? | *ki-dohoi* 'listen' | — |
| *duha 'two' | *dua, rua* | *dua* | *dua, rua* | *dua, rua* | *ʔa-dua, ʔa-rua* | *dua* |
| *ikuR 'tail' | *iuʔ* | *xixio* | ? | ? | *e-iʔo* | *ihur* |
| *kaka 'older sibling' | *kakaʔ* | *kakaʔ* | *aʔa* | — | *ʔaʔa* | *haha* |
| *kita 1PL. INCL. | *ita* | *ʔita* | *(yaʔ)ita* | *sita*, (North) *ita* | *ʔika* (1du.incl.) | *hita* |
| *latəŋ 'stinging nettle' | *lalateŋ* | *lato* | *lato* | *lalatek* | — | — |
| *lima 'five' | *lima, limo* | ? | *lima* | *lima* | *ʔadiba* | *lima* |
| *mata 'eye' | *mata* | *mata* | — | *mata* | *e-baka* | *mata* |
| *ŋajan 'name' | *kahan, kaxan* | ? | ? | *ŋagan, gagan* | — | — |
| *pajay 'rice in field' | *axae, ahae* | *faxe* | *faxe* | — | — | (P-Batak *pagey) |
| *pija 'how much/many' | *ixa* | *iga, ida* | — | *piga* | (?) *ʔa/piaha* | *piga* |
| *pusəj 'navel; centre' | — | ? | *fusõ* | *pusou* | *e-puko* | *pusok* |
| *qajəŋ 'charcoal' | *axəŋ* | *axo* | *axo* | ? | *agoŋ* | |
| *qijuŋ 'nose' | *ixuŋ* | *nixu* | *ixu* | — | *e-ihu* | *iguŋ* |
| *quluh 'head' | *ulu* | — | — | — | *e-(ʔ)udu* | *ulu* |
| *Rumaq 'house' | *luma* | — | *omo* | *uma* | *e-uba* | *(ruma)* |
| *Rusuk 'chest; rib' | *lusuʔ* | *rosuʔ* | *osu* | *ʔusuʔ* | *e-uku* | *rusuk* |
| *taliŋa 'ear' | — | — | *taliŋa* | *taliŋa* | *e-kadiha* | — |
| *taqi 'excrement' | *tai* | *tai* | *tai* | *tanai* | *e-kai* | *te* |
| *təlu 'three' | *təlu, təlo* | *tölu* | *tõlu* | *telu* | *ʔakoru, ʔakodu* | *tolu* |
| *si-ia 3SG. | *ia, ie* | ? | *i, yaʔia* | *ʔiya, siya* | *kia* | — |
| *si(ŋ)jəm 'ant' | *sirəm* | *iröm* | *sixõ* | *sigep* | *e-kiho* [e-kiço] | — |
| *Sua(ŋ)ji 'y. sibling' | *axi, ahi* | *axi* | *axi* | *bagi* | *ãhãi* | *aŋgi* |
| *[w]walu 'eight' | *olo* | *olu* | *walu* | *balu* | — | *alu* |
| *siwa 'nine' | *siwa* | *siwa* | *siwa* | *siba* | — | *sia* |
| *wanan 'right-side' | *enawan* | — | *e-daba* (with metathesis of *d/b*) | — | | |
| *wahiR 'water' | *oiʔ, oil* | ? | *we* | *oi/nan* | *e-bee* | *aek* 'juice' |

[a] The information in this list is taken from Nothofer (1986: 100–2); Edwards (2015); Kähler (1963: xxi–xxii); Blust and Trussel (2020).
[b] Some of the original vowels were adjusted according to current spelling conventions.

*x* or to Mentawai *g* or ɣ (or Proto-Batak *g). He therefore finds it doubtful that the *j reflexes in all these languages went through a partly common history: a joint development from *j to *x is not obvious because the change is natural enough to have happened independently in these languages, whether *j was a velar stop (Wolff 1988: 131–2), a velar fricative (Ross 1992: 36), or a palatalized voiced velar stop (Blust 2013a: 554). And even if this presumed joint development would be taken as evidence for including Enggano in the Barrier Island group, it would clash with the inclusion of Batak and Mentawai in the same group because a change from *x to (Batak) *g* or (Mentawai) ɣ is phonetically unusual (Edwards 2015: 83).

According to Edwards (2015: 64) the developments of PMP *j and *ŋ in Enggano are staged as follows:

(2) Stage 1: PMP *ŋ > *g
PMP *j > *j
Stage 2: *g, *j > *ɣ
Stage 3: *ɣ > Enggano *h* ~ *ç*

As to the other sound changes, the one from *k to *ʔ* or *Ø* is phonologically too general to have diagnostic value, and while *w > *b* is more meaningful, it should also be rejected as subgrouping evidence because it is found in only two Barrier Island languages (Enggano and Mentawai). The change is moreover not entirely unique and could be due to areal contact as it also occurs in Rejang and Lampung in Sumatra (Edwards 2015: 84; see also §10.5.3 for Rejang and §10.5.4 for Lampung).

After a careful evaluation of the phonological, morphological, and lexical evidence (including evidence from allegedly shared phonological irregularities), Edwards decides against subgrouping Enggano with the Barrier Island languages, and to give the language an independent isolate status within Malayo-Polynesian. He is even doubtful that the other Barrier Island languages form a subgroup: Simeulue, Sigulai, and Nias may together qualify as one, but Mentawai would not integrate well in it (Edwards 2015: 94).

The pathway taken from PMP *j to its current reflexes in Barrier Island and Batak languages also became an important detail in Smith's (2017b) classification, as the history of *j would be the cornerstone, two years later, of his distinction between a West Indonesian and a Sumatran subgroup. He does include Enggano in the Barrier Island subgroup, arguing that PMP *j first merged with *g to *g; later on it also merged with *ŋ to *g. The latter in turn evolved into ɣ, before it finally became modern Enggano *h*. In other Barrier Island–Batak languages, *j first merged with *g to *g in Batak languages or to ɣ and *g* in Mentawai, and it ended up as *x* in Nias, Sigulai, and Simeulue. Like Edwards, Smith brings the Enggano change from (PMP *ŋ, *j >) *ŋ > to *g > *h* in line with the fact that, in this language, all PMP final nasals became denasalized. In this scenario, the stage between PMP *j and Enggano *h* was not *ŋ, which would have been phonologically implausible, but *g, which solves that problem.

The developments of PMP *j in Barrier Island and Batak languages can be staged as follows:

(3) Stage 1: PMP *j > Proto-Barrier Island–Batak *g
Stage 2: Proto-Barrier Island–Batak *g merges with *ŋ > *g
Stage 3: *g > *ɣ > Enggano *h*
*g > Proto-Batak *g > Simalungun Batak *g*, Northern Batak *g*, *-ŋ*, Southern Batak *g*, *-k*
*g > Mentawai *g*, ɣ
*g > *ɣ > Nias, Sigulai, and Simeulue *x*

In this way, Smith tries to demonstrate that Enggano and all Barrier Island and Batak languages went through a common stage in which PMP *j became *g, and to provide critical evidence for their inclusion in the Barrier Island–Batak subgroup. Smith's argument is a forceful one, but it remains a question whether the evidence of this one phonological development weighs up against the impressive body of evidence adduced by Edwards (2015) from several levels of linguistics and even from other disciplines.

## 10.4.2 Batak languages

Compared with the Barrier Island languages, the Batak languages form a transparent and close-knit subgroup, and the phonological reconstruction of Proto-Batak is a straightforward affair (Adelaar 1981). Of its members, Toba Batak, Mandailing, Angkola, and Simalungun constitute a Southern branch, and Karo Batak, Dairi-Pakpak, and Alas, a Northern branch (see Figure 10.1).

Phonological features that are typical for the various Batak languages are as follows:

(4) PMP *ə > Northern Batak *ə*, Southern Batak *o*
PMP *-aw > Simalungun *-ow*, other Batak *-o*
PMP *-ay > Simalungun *-ey*, other Batak *-e*
PMP *-uy > Simalungun *-uy*, other Batak *-e*, *-i*

PMP *w-, *-w- > Northern Batak *u-*, *Ø-*, *-w-*, Southern Batak Ø
PMP *q > Northern Batak *h, Simalungun Batak Ø, *-h*, other Southern Batak Ø
PMP non-final *k > Northern Batak *k*, Southern Batak *h*
PMP *-j- > all Batak languages *-g-*
PMP *-j > Northern Batak *ŋ*, Simalungun *g*, other Southern Batak *k*
PMP no stress Northern Batak lacks stress, Southern Batak has distinctive stress

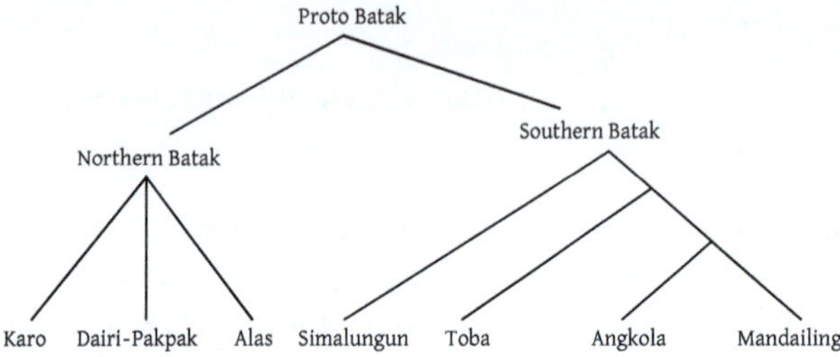


**Figure 10.1** Genealogical tree of Batak languages.

Simalungun Batak shares linguistic features with both Northern and Southern Batak, and due to its seemingly intermediate position, Voorhoeve (1955) gave it the status of a third division within the Batak group. However, Adelaar (1981) classifies it as an early split-off within Southern Batak because it shares important innovative phonological developments with the Southern Batak varieties such as the changes from Proto-Batak/PMP *k- and *-k- to *h*, from Proto-Batak/PMP *ə to *o*, and from Proto-Batak/PMP *c to *s*, as well as the development of distinctive stress. In contrast, commonalities between Simalungun and Northern Batak are often the result of borrowing or are retentions from Proto-Batak (e.g. the maintenance of *-h (< PMP *q)). Also significant is that Simalungun maintained Proto-Batak final voiced stops, which is relatively more in alignment with the corresponding Southern Batak final voiceless stops than with the corresponding Northern Batak final nasals. Examples:

(5) Proto-Batak *kalak 'human being' > Simalungun, other Southern Batak *halak*, Northern Batak *kalak*;
Proto-Batak *aku 'I, me' > Simalungun, other Southern Batak *ahu*, Northern Batak *aku*;
Proto-Batak *kərbow 'buffalo' > Southern Batak *horbo*, Simalungun *horbow*, Northern Batak *kərbo*;
Proto-Batak *pərəh 'to squeeze out' > Southern Batak *poro*, Simalungun *poroh*, Northern Batak *pərəh*;
Proto-Batak *pucuk 'sprout, young leaf' > Simalungun, other Southern Batak *pusuk*, Northern Batak *pucuk*;
Proto-Batak *abab 'ashes' > Southern Batak *abap*, Simalungun *abab*, Northern Batak *abam*;
Proto-Batak *dələg 'mountain' > Southern Batak *dolok*, Simalungun *dolog*, Northern Batak *dələŋ*;
Proto-Batak *sərəd 'sting' > Southern Batak *sorot* 'to sting', Simalungun *sorod* '(a) sting', Northern Batak *sərən*

Stress is distinctive, as seen, for example, in Southern Batak *bàgas* 'house' vs. *bagàs* 'deep'; and in Simalungun *bàyu* 'to braid, plait' vs. *bayù* 'new'; *tòbu* 'sugarcane' vs. *tobù* 'sweet'.

N.B. Before moving on to the next section, it is worth mentioning some alternative viewpoints on the classification of the Barrier Island and Batak languages. Several scholars have referred to possible links between the Barrier Island–Batak languages and languages in Sulawesi, the Philippines, and even as far as Oceania.

Willms (1955) investigated lexical borrowing into Mentawai. Along with loanwords from other Barrier Island languages (Nias and Simeulue), he also listed ninety-seven supposedly from Sulawesi languages. Nothofer (1986: 88) refers to unpublished work by Kähler, in which the latter points to a Philippine–Sulawesi substratum in Barrier Island languages and is particularly struck by the occurrence of shared vocabulary. Nothofer (1994b) argues that Sumatra, the Barrier Islands, the Batak region, and parts of Sulawesi and the Philippines initially formed a Paleo-Hesperonesian (early Malayo-Polynesian) language area, which was largely supplanted by Hesperonesian (later Malayo-Polynesian) languages later on. He considers the vocabulary shared specifically by languages in the said Barrier Islands, Batak region, and parts of Sulawesi and the Philippines as part of a substratum.

According to Capell (1982: 5, 6, 15), Enggano is not an Austronesian language but one that has a structure "sui generis" (p.5). He nevertheless still classifies it together with other Barrier Island languages in his "Oceanic-type" languages (p.15). Mahdi (1988) proposes a primarily eastern and western split within the Austronesian family tree. He classifies Enggano together with Makuva (a language of Timor Leste called Lovaia in Mahdi 1988) in a Paleo-Hesperonesian subdivision of Eastern Austronesian, and Nias and Mentawai together with Philippine languages, Sulawesi languages, and

Palauan in Western Austronesian. One of his devices for distinguishing certain subgroups is the term for human being that their members share: Enggano and Makuva are both in a 'hartanic' group because their term for human being derives from *qaRta. By the same token, Malay and the languages of Java are in an 'Urangic' subgroup as they have reflexes of *uRaŋ as default terms for 'human being'.

## 10.5 The other Sumatran languages: Gayo, Nasal, Rejang, and Lampung(ic)

These languages are treated separately in sections 10.5.1–4.

### 10.5.1 Gayo

In comparison to other languages associated with the Barrier Island–Batak group, Gayo has been rather neglected. The old language atlases from Esser (1938) and Salzner (1960) classify it in a Sumatran group which is basically geographically defined. On the basis of lexicostatistics, Dyen (1965a) classified it in a separate 'Hesperonesian' division including Balinese, Sasak, 'Dayak', and the Javo-Sumatran languages but excluding the Batak ones. However, Soravia (1984) is in favour of a close genetic link between Gayo and Batak. In his grammatical sketch of Alas (Soravia 2007), he also gives lexicostatistical evidence to support a Batak-Gayo subgroup. In particular, his percentages for Karo (48%) and Alas (55%) are very high. Nothofer (1986: 87) notes that Lafeber (1922) mentioned a Batak-Gayo group. Nothofer also adds Gayo material to his comparative lists, but he does not actually discuss its classification (Nothofer 1986: 107). Blust (2013a: 78) remarked that "Acehnese, Gayo and the Batak languages represent three quite distinct subgroups". Smith (2017b), whose phonologically defined Sumatra group is rather different from that of Esser (1938) and Salzner (1960, does not mention Gayo.[5]

Taking the evolution of PMP *j as indicative, it appears that in five cases Gayo has lost *j whereas in four[6] other cases it agrees with various Batak languages in reflecting *ŋg*, final *k* or final *ŋ*. Compare the following nine cognate sets[7]:

(6)

| PMP | Gayo | Toba Batak | Karo Batak |
|---|---|---|---|
| *pija 'how much/many' | *piyən, piən* | *piga* | *piga* |
| *qijuŋ 'nose' | *iuŋ* | *iguŋ* | *iguŋ* |
| *qaləjaw 'day' | *lô* | — | — |
| *qapəjuh 'gall, bile' | *pau* | *pogu* | *pegu* |
| *bajas 'inside' (Dempwolff 1938) | *was* | *bagàs* | *bagas* |
| *[hu]aji 'younger sibling' | *eŋ$^{g}$i* | *aŋgi* | *agi* |
| *pusəj 'navel' | *pusok* (Blust and Trussel 2020) | *pusok* | *pusuŋ* |
| *kuñij 'curcuma' | *kuniŋ* | *hunik* | *kuniŋ* |
| (PWMP *ubaj 'medicine' [Adelaar 2005c: 371]) | *uak*[8] | *obok* 'antidote' | — |

The Ø reflex in *pi(y)ən*,[9] *iuŋ*, *lô*, *pau*, and *was* does not agree with reflexes of *j in other Sumatran languages. Theoretically, it could be analysed as the ultimate reduction of an original *g (i.e. *g > *h > Ø), in which case it is still somehow included in the Barrier Island–Batak subgroup, or even as the ultimate reduction of an intermediate *y, which would suggest a genetic affiliation with Moken and Moklen, all things being equal. (However, in the latter case not all things are equal, as many other phonological changes in Moken and Moklen are rather idiosyncratic).

In other cases, Gayo forms agree with Batak ones. However, the agreement is not with a single Batak variety but with two varieties that differ from one another, reducing the evidential value for a close genetic relationship between Gayo and Batak. In *eŋ$^{g}$i* (exhibiting a 'barred nasal')[10] and *pusok*, Gayo has the reflexes *g* and *-k* (< *g), which it shares with Southern Batak languages such as Toba Batak. In *kuniŋ*, however, it has a final *ŋ*, which is in agreement with Northern Batak languages such as Karo Batak. While there is much lexical evidence shared between Gayo and Batak, suggesting on first sight a common history between the two, some of the shared lexicon is due to borrowing from Batak into Gayo. For instance, Gayo *bətih* 'to know' phonologically agrees with Karo Batak *mətəh* (< *bətəh*) and Toba Batak *um-*

[5] Nor does Edwards, but his focus is by definition limited to the classification of Enggano (Edwards 2015: 82).

[6] *ubaj is based on evidence from Sundanese (*ubar*), Balinese (*ubad*), and Malay (*obat*). Toba Batak *obok* may be related provided that *u and *a in *ubaj underwent vowel harmony; however, this is a speculation, as such harmony is not usual in Toba Batak.

[7] Gayo also has *araŋ* 'live coal' which reflects PMP *qajəŋ (same meaning; Eades 2005). It must be a loanword from Malay, as the latter also has *araŋ* 'live coal'.

[8] I am grateful to Erik Zobel for drawing my attention to this Gayo reflex of *ubaj.

[9] The *y* in *piyən* is the orthographic expression of a non-phonemic glide.

[10] That is, an original homorganic nasal + voiced stop in which the velic closure is minimal (or even absent) and nasality is prevented from spreading to the following vowel (see further Truong and McDonnell, this volume, §28.2.1.1, fn. 5).

*boto* (same meaning): while it looks like an exclusively shared innovation, it must be a Batak loanword as Gayo regularly lost initial and medial *b in inherited vocabulary; compare *atu* 'stone' (< *batu), *oros* 'uncooked rice' (< *bəRas), *inih* 'seedling' (< *binəhiq), *ulan* 'moon' (< *bulan), *uak* 'medicine' (< *ubaj).[11]

In summary, it has become clear that in Gayo the inherited reflex of PMP *-j- is Ø and not *-g-, and that part of the lexicon that Gayo shares with Batak languages is demonstrably borrowed from the latter into the former. As it stands, there is no conclusive evidence for a close relationship between Gayo and the Batak languages.

### 10.5.2 Nasal

Anderbeck and Aprilani (2013) try to determine the classificatory position of Nasal. There is precious little lexical material for this language, but from what is available, it is apparent that much of Nasal's lexicon is borrowed from the neighbouring Malayic and Lampungic languages.

There are some similarities between Nasal and Lampung varieties (Lampungic) which are not shared with Malayic. The most prominent of these is the debuccalization of final stops, for example, Nasal *hasuʔ* 'smoke' (< Proto-Western-Malayo-Polynesian *qasəp), *lawuʔ* 'sea' (< PMP *lahud 'towards the sea'), *uwoʔ* 'head hair' (< PMP *buhək).

However, Anderbeck and Aprilani point out that other commonalities, such as the presence of a final diphthong *-uy and the distinction between *a and *ə in final closed syllables, carry little weight as they are retentions from PMP, or they are too widespread in western MPSEA languages to be significant, as with the change from *q to *h*. They also point out some important distinctions between Nasal and Lampungic. Among these are the maintenance of *-ay, which became *-i* in Lampungic (e.g. Nasal *hənay*, Lampungic *həni* 'sand'), and the different reflexes of PMP non-initial *R in Nasal (l) and Lampungic (y or Ø), for example, *qasira 'salt'> Nasal *sila*, Lampungic *sia; *qatəluR 'egg' > Nasal *hatəlul* and Lampungic *hatəluy. (Moreover, Nasal and Lampungic have very different histories in terms of lexical borrowing.)

The authors conclude that Nasal is not part of the Lampungic group. They then investigate if the two are closely related and possibly derive from an exclusively shared ancestral language, but this proposition also runs into trouble because the only possible phonological support for this, debuccalization, can be shown to be a post-Proto-Lampungic development that also affected many loanwords. It must have spread from Lampungic into Nasal.

They also compare Nasal to Rejang, which equally shows the change from *R to *l*. However, in spite of the highly emblematic value of this change, it did not happen under exactly the same conditions in both languages, yielding some otherwise regular sets in which Nasal has an l corresponding to Rejang *r*. The fact that Nasal does not significantly agree with other Sumatran languages in its historical developments led the authors to conclude tentatively that it was an isolate and a branch in itself within the Malayo-Polynesian language group (Anderbeck and Aprilani 2013: 12). For the sake of completeness, Nasal evidence for PMP *j is not helpful either for a classification as it remains inconclusive. Possible reflexes are *x*, *h*, *d*, or *-ʔ*: compare PMP *pija 'how much/many' > *pixo*; *pajay 'rice in field' > *pahay*; *qapəjuh 'gall, bile' > *əmpədu*; *[hu]aji 'younger sibling' > *adıʔ*; *pusəj 'navel' > *pusuʔ*; and *quləj 'maggot' > *uluʔ* 'caterpillar'.

Smith (2017b: 454) also tries to find out if Nasal can be classified with other languages in or around Sumatra but he too is unable to find the necessary diagnostic evidence. He deems it unlikely that it is a member of the GNB subgroup because it has *pitu* for 'seven'. Culling from the limited data eight words that qualify at first sight as evidence for an inclusion in his WIN subgroup, he shows that half of them are clearly borrowed from (most likely) Malay, whereas the remaining ones are also suspected of being borrowed. He considers *hulon* 'person, human being', as evidence for the inclusion of Nasal into the WIN subgroup, provided that it is not a Malay loan.[12] However, he concedes that a single word is not sufficient evidence for this inclusion.

It is obviously still early days for a classification of Nasal, considering the limited resources that are available and the current lack of historical research at all linguistic levels involving this language.

### 10.5.3 Rejang

According to Voorhoeve (1955), Rejang is closely related to Malay. However, Blust (1984) estimates that the similarities

[11] Then again, a case like *uluŋ* 'leaf' is ambiguous: on the one hand, it is a local innovation shared with Batak languages (which have *buluŋ* 'leaf'); on the other, it has lost initial *b, which tends to happen in inherited languages rather than in loanwords. (The diagnostic value of *b- > Ø needs further investigation).

[12] *qulun 'outsider' is one of the lexical innovations that Smith (2017b) adduces in support of the WIN group. He reasons that if Nasal *hulon* is a regular reflex of WIN *qulun, this language should be classified as WIN, but if Nasal has borrowed Malay *(h)ulun* 'slave', its classification remains undecided. However, borrowing from Malay is unlikely as a semantic change from 'slave' or 'servant' to 'person' would be odd.

between the two languages are often the result of borrowing from Malay into Rejang. In a phonological history of the latter, he analyses the rather remarkable sound changes it has undergone. They include PMP *w > b, *R > l, ʔ, or Ø, *-k and *-q > ʔ, the development of so-called barred nasals (see fn.11), and various complicated and staged vocalic changes leading to a large number of diphthongs and even triphthongs. Compare the following examples (taken from Blust 1984):

(7)

| PMP | Rejang |
|---|---|
| *wahiR 'water' | *bioa* |
| *wari 'day' | *bilay* |
| *ñawa 'breathe' | *ñabəy* |
| *baqəRu 'new' | *bələw* |
| *daRaq 'blood' | *daleaʔ* |
| *qasiRa 'salt' | *siləy* |
| *qapəju 'gall (bladder)' | *pəgəw* |
| *tuRun 'to descend' | *tuʔun* |
| *qapuR 'lime' | *opoa* |
| *danaw 'lake' | *danuəw* (*danoa*) |
| *buRuk 'rotten' | *buʔuʔ* |
| *ipən 'tooth' | *epen* |
| *uləj 'maggot' | *olok* |

Blust makes typological comparisons with other Austronesian languages having undergone complicated vocalic changes such as Trukese and Kerinci. In Blust (2010b: 69–70) he classifies Rejang in GNB because of *tujuaʔ* 'seven'. In a similar vain, while Smith (2017b: 452) does not focus on the classification of Rejang, he also concludes that it must be a GNB language because it has "an apparently native reflex of *tuzuq 'seven'". In a footnote he makes a further observation that although this language is quite different from other Sumatran languages, its retention of -q (< *-q) instead of instead of showing -h makes it difficult to "brush aside" *tujuaʔ* as a loanword.

In other words, its final syllable with diphthongized vowel and glottal stop should be a guarantee that it is not borrowed. But in fact, these features do not give that guarantee as they are also found in loanwords. Compare loanwords like *Atjiaʔ*[13] 'Aceh', *Uleaʔ Talo*, a Rejang adaptation the Arabic *Allah Taʕāla* 'God The Elevated', *Mekeaʔ* 'Mecca' (Malay *Məkah*), *sugiaʔ* 'wealthy' (< Javanese *sugih*), *pluaʔ* 'a work gang' (most likely < Dutch *ploeg* [plux] 'team (of workers); soccer team') (Jaspan 1984). Apparently, the final *h* of their source words became *-ʔ* in Rejang. As a result, the phonemic structure of the resulting loanwords can no longer be distinguished from that of native lexicon. Rejang *tujuaʔ* must be borrowed, especially in light of the fact that it co-occurs with *dlapeun* 'eight' (< *dua-alap-an, 'eight') and *smbileun* 'nine' (< *(ə)sa-ambil-an 'nine'). The latter numerals are even more suspected of borrowing as they bear traces of a suffix *-an, whereas Rejang has no suffixes. Compare Malay *dəlapan* 'eight' and *səmbilan* 'nine' (see further §10.8).

The phenomenon of remodelling loanwords such that they cannot be distinguished from inherited vocabulary, even if there is no structural motivation for it, has been noticed in the history of various other languages. Aikio (2006) calls it "etymological nativization of loanwords" in his discussion of similar cases in the adoption of Finnish loanwords into Saami and of Spanish loanwords into Basque (among others). Nash (1997) and Evans (1998) use the term "correspondence mimicry" for manifestations of it in Australian languages.

Smith (2017b: 455) also claims that Rejang merged PMP *d and *j (presumably to *d*), but this is inaccurate in two respects. First, whereas in the Rawas dialect, final *j does merge with *d and *t into *-t* (McGinn 2003), in the Lebong dialect it is kept distinct, becoming -k instead (Jaspan 1984), as demonstrated below:

(8)

| PMP | Rawas | Lebong |
|---|---|---|
| *laləj 'mosquito' | *dalət* | *daleuk* |
| *pusəj 'navel' | *pusət* | *posok* |
| *quləj 'maggot' | *ulət* 'caterpillar' | *olok* 'caterpillar' |
| *lahud 'seaward' | *laut* 'sea' | *laweut* 'sea' |
| *tukəd 'prop' | *tokot* 'stick' | *tokot* 'stick' |
| *kabut 'fog' | *kabut* | *kabuet* |
| *həpat 'four' | *pat* | *pat* |

Second, in both the Rawas and other dialects (including Lebong), intervocalic *j became g (in two instances) or Ø (in three instances); *d remains d in this position:

(9)

| PMP | Rawas | Lebong |
|---|---|---|
| *ŋajan 'name' | *gén* | *gän* |
| *qapəju 'gall, bile' | *pəgəw* | *pəgaw* |
| *pajay 'rice-plant' | *pai* | *pai* |
| *qajəŋ 'charcoal' | *aʔaŋ* | *aʔaŋ* |
| *qijuŋ 'nose' | *yuŋ* | ? |
| *qudaŋ 'shrimp' | *udaŋ* | *udaŋ* |
| *tiduR 'to sleep' | *tidua* | *tidua* |
| *qudip 'to live; alive' | *idup* | *idup* |

It appears that in Rejang, PMP *j did not merge with PMP *d except in final position, and only in the Rawas dialect. In the Lebong dialect *j and *d have been kept distinct all along in all positions. Smith's arguments for considering Rejang a

[13] The 'tj' in this word is a feature of colonial spelling. It is written as 'c' in modern Indonesian spelling.

member of the WIN group and excluding it from his Sumatran group are not critical enough and part of them can be falsified.

Note incidentally the partial analogy with *j reflexes in Gayo, which has four instances of Ø, and three instances of *-g-/-k*.

For the sake of completeness, subgrouping attempts by McGinn are mentioned here. McGinn (1999) is an attempt to link up Rejang with Malay and Mukah Melanau (Sarawak) on the basis of morphological comparisons. McGinn (2003) uses phonological arguments to subgroup Rejang with the Bukar Sadong dialects, a division of the Land Dayak group (see Smith, this volume, §8.2.4). See Adelaar (2007a) for a critical review.

## 10.5.4 Lampung(ic)

There are three main Lampung dialects, Lampung Api (or Pesisir), Komering, and Lampung Nyo (or Abung). Anderbeck (2007b) made a thorough phonological and lexical reconstruction of Proto-Lampung using lexical evidence from twenty-three subdialects. He offers a list of fifteen "defining characteristics of Lampungic" (Anderbeck 2007b: 7). Some of these are not unusual among western MPSEA languages and are therefore not so relevant for subgrouping. However, other ones are shared with Sundanese and are possible evidence for a direct relationship between both languages. The most diagnostic change among these is the one from PMP *R to Proto-Lampungic *y; examples:

(10) PMP *wahiR 'water' > Sundanese *cai*, Proto-Lampungic *wai;
PMP *buRuk 'rotten' > Sundanese *buyuk*, Proto-Lampungic *buyuʔ;
PMP *təRas 'hard' > Sundanese *tias*, Proto-Lampungic *tias;
PMP *bəRas 'unhusked rice' > Sundanese *beas*, Proto-Lampungic *bias;
PMP *qulaR 'snake' > Sundanese *oray*, Proto-Lampungic *ulay;
PMP *baRəq 'swollen' > Proto-Lampungic *bayəh, Sundanese *bayah* (*a* in last syllable unexplained)

Compare also: Malay *kura-kura*, Javanese *kura*, Balinese *kəkua*, Toba Batak *hura-hura*, Sundanese *kuya*, Proto-Lampungic *kuya 'tortoise'.

However, there are also cases in which either Lampungic or Sundanese lack the expected y:

(11) PMP *bəRat 'heavy' > Proto-Lampungic *biat, Sundanese *birat*

Anderbeck also mentions PMP *-iw to Proto-Lampungic and Sundanese *-(y)u as a shared innovation, but this change occurs only in two instances. One of these (PMP *kahiw 'wood' > *kayu*) is not significant because the resulting form also emerges in many other languages in the area. The other (PMP *baRiw 'beginning to spoil' > Lampungic dialects *bayu* 'spoiled') does have a (Baduy) Sundanese counterpart *wayuq* 'fermented drink' but Nothofer (1975: 215) tends to analyse it as a Javanese loanword.

Finally, Anderbeck points out that the Sunda-Lampung subgroup is further strengthened by the circumstance that the Sundanese and Lampung speaking areas are adjacent, and by the existence of the following two cognates which are shared among Lampungic, Sundanese, and Javanese and were adduced by Nothofer (1985: 297): Proto-Malayo-Javanic (PMJ) *pa-waRi 'dry in the sun' > Sundanese *poe*, Javanese *pé*, Lampung *paway*; PMJ *pitək 'gadfly' > Sundanese *pitik*, Javanese *pitaq*, Lampung *pitoq*. But this lexical evidence is neither sufficient, nor is it critical considering the presence of Javanese reflexes. Furthermore, cognates of *pa-waRi are also found in Sulawesi languages.[14]

Another feature, debuccalization of final (voiceless) occlusives, is typical of Lampungic varieties, but Anderbeck shows that it is not diagnostic for reconstruction and subgrouping purposes because one of the twenty-three Lampungic subdialects, Paku, escaped this form of levelling. Examples of debuccalization are shown in (12) (Anderbeck 2007b: 14):

(12) Proto-Lampungic *pahit 'bitter' > Komering (Paku) *pahit*, Komering (Kayu Agung Asli) *pahiʔ*, Nyo (Kota Bumi) *pahiʔ*
Proto-Lampungic *hasəp 'smoke' > Komering (Paku) *hasop*, Komering (Kayu Agung Asli) *hasoʔ*, Nyo (Kota Bumi) *asəʔ*
Proto-Lampungic *sərəp 'needle' > Komering (Paku) *sawop*, Komering (Kayu Agung Asli)*soʁoʔ*, Nyo (Kota Bumi) *səʁəʔ*
Proto-Lampungic *huət 'husk of rice' > Komering (Paku) *huət*, Komering (Kayu Agung Asli) *huoʔ*, Nyo (Kota Bumi) *uəʔ*

While tempting, the evidence for a Sunda-Lampung subgroup remains insufficient.

Note incidentally that if a Sunda-Lampung subgroup were to be established, it would put another strain on the use of a reflex of *tuzuq for 'seven' as subgrouping evidence, as Sundanese has *tujuh*, whereas Lampung varieties maintained a reflex of *pitu.

[14] Erik Zobel (p.c.) points to the Sulawesi cognates Tialo *puagi*, Pendau *puai* (Himmelmann 2001), and Proto-Bungku-Tolaki *puai (Mead 1998).

## 10.6 The languages of Java

Many historical linguistic observations had been made about the languages of Java in the nineteenth and early twentieth centuries, and Dempwolff (1934, 1937, 1938) made systematic use of Javanese material in his reconstruction of PMP. However, it was not until 1965 that these languages became the subject of a more detailed classification, when Dyen (1965a) included them in a lexicostatistical study which had the entire Austronesian language family in its scope. He grouped Javanese together with Sundanese, Malay, and Madurese. (Some other languages which he closely affiliated with specifically Malay were Minangkabau, Kerinci, Lampung, and Acehnese). Dyen's Javo-Sumatran became the basis of an important thesis, published ten years later, by Nothofer, who used Javanese, Sundanese, Malay, and Madurese for a reconstruction of the phonology and lexicon of PMJ (Nothofer 1975: 1). It appeared at a time when very little systematic research had been conducted on the history of the languages concerned, and lexicostatistics was still considered as a scientific basis for subgrouping. Nothofer followed Dyen's method of reconstructing additional protophonemes whenever a sound correspondence left exceptions (rather than 'resigning' to the likelihood that these exceptions—or at least, some of them—are the result of borrowing or other irregular factors). These additional protophonemes were indicated with capital letters and/or given a number (*$R_1$, *$R_2$, *$R_3$, etc.). The advantage of this diversification of protophonemes was that irregular sound correspondences were made explicit and given their own symbol.[15] A number of Nothofer's PMJ phonemes were problematic. Some consonant series were based on Javanese and Madurese retroflexes and on Madurese and Old Javanese aspirated voiced stops, which in all likelihood are attributable to South Asian influence (although their development in Madurese is more complex than in other Malayo-Javanic languages). PMJ *q (a glottal stop) was reconstructed on the basis of a non-phonemic Sundanese glottal stop, which occurs by default before initial vowels, between like vowels, and after final vowels, and which corresponds to Ø in Malay, Javanese, and East Madurese, and *-h* in West Madurese (Nothofer 1975: 179). Finally, PMJ geminate consonants were reconstructed based on Madurese, in which they have become contrastive. (Malay and Javanese also have geminated consonants, but in these languages they are not phonemic). Compare the word pairs in Table 10.3.

Blust (1981c) made some critical observations. For one thing, Malayo-Javanic included languages which did not belong in the group (e.g. Javanese, which even by lexicostatistical standards is not as close to other Malayo-Javanic languages as the latter are to one another). At the same time, it failed to include languages that do belong. Blust (1981c:

[15] A somewhat less fortunate consequence of reconstructing protophonemes in this way is that the more protophonemes are added, the less realistic the resulting phoneme system tends to become.

**Table 10.3** Comparative wordlist of PMP, PMJ, Sundanese, Javanese, Malay, and Madurese.

| PMP | PMJ | Sundanese | Javanese | Malay | Madurese |
|---|---|---|---|---|---|
| *qatəp 'roof' | *qatəp | *hatɨp* | *atəp* | *(h)atap* | *ataq* |
| *bəsiq 'iron' | *Bəssiq | *bɨsiq* | *wəsi* (loanword?) | *bəsi* | *bəssè(h)* |
| *habuq 'ashes' | *haBuq | *hawuq* 'furnace' | *awu* | *(h)abu* | *abu(h)* (loanword?) |
| — | *biruq 'blue' | *biruq* | *biru* (loanword?) | *biru* | *bhiru(h)* 'green' |
| *bənər 'true; honest' | *bənnər | *bɨnɨr* | *bənər* | *bənar* | *bhənnar* |
| *baRaq$_1$ 'lung' | *baR$_1$ah | *bayah* | — | — | *bháyá* |
| *paRih 'ray-fish' | *paR$_2$iq | *pariq* | *pé* | *pari* | *parè(h)* |
| *Rusuk 'rib' | *R$_3$usuk 'rib' | *qusuk* 'rafter' | *usóq* 'rafter' | *rusuk* 'rib' | *ròsòq* 'rib' |
| *ləbət 'dense' | *ləbbət 'full with fruit' | *lɨbɨt* | — | *ləbat* | *ləbbháq* 'full with fruit' |
| *wada 'to exist' | *waDaq | — | *ora* 'not' | *ada* | *báḍá(h)* |
| — | *wuyah 'salt' | *quyah* | (Old Javanese *wuyah*) | — | *buyá* |

459) singled out Iban: this language also maintains the distinction between *b and *w when occurring between *a's, whereas Nothofer (1975: 81) considered the distinction lost in PMJ since PMP *b and *w had merged to *w* in Malay, Javanese, and Sundanese, and to *h* in Madurese. Compare the following cognate sets (Blust 1981c: 459):

(13) PMP *tabaR 'tasteless, unsalted, unsweetened' > Iban *tabar* (same meaning), Malay, Sundanese *tawar*, Javanese *tawa* 'tasteless, powerless, sweet', Madurese *tabar* 'uncooked';
PMP *laban 'opposed, against' > Iban *laban* (same meaning), Malay, Javanese, Sundanese *lawan*, Madurese *laban* 'opponent';
PMP *ñawa 'soul, breath' > Iban *ñawa* 'life, existence', Malay, Javanese, Sundanese *ñawa*, Madurese *ñaba* 'soul, spirit';
PMP *awaŋ 'atmosphere' > Iban *awan* (final *n* unexplained) 'air', Malay, Javanese, Sundanese *awaŋ-awaŋ*, Madurese *abaŋ-abaŋ* 'airspace'

Furthermore, the distorting effects of lexical borrowing from Javanese and Malay into other languages were not sufficiently recognized. Nor was it sufficiently recognized that a high rate of shared vocabulary between two members in a wider language group is not significant for their subgrouping if the shared vocabulary items are retentions. Blust suggested that a high retention rate of core vocabulary may be the reason why Malay and Madurese have so much basic vocabulary in common.

Blust also argued for the use of qualitatively based lexical innovations, especially numerals. In Malay and Sundanese, PMP *pitu 'seven' was replaced by *tujuh* and its cognates, PMP *wwalu 'eight' by Malay *dəlapan* and Sundanese *dalapan* (< *dua + *alap-an), and PMP *siwa 'nine' by Malay *səmbilan*, Sundanese *sambilan* (< *(ə)sa + *ambilan); in Javanese and Madurese, *siwa was replaced by *saŋa* 'nine'. He proposed an alternative classification of languages relative to their genetic distance to Malay, which is now outdated. It was based on the *tuzuq device discussed above and on the vowel metathesis in PMP *qudip 'to live; alive' which had taken place in Malayic languages (compare Proto-Malayic *hidup). Four degrees of relatedness were distinguished. In the first degree were Malay, Minangkabau, Kerinci, and 'Middle-Malay' (Besemah and Seraway in Southeast Sumatra); in the second degree, Salako and Iban (Malayic languages in western Borneo); in the third degree, Sundanese, Embaloh ('Maloh', in Borneo), and Rejang (Sumatra); and in the fourth degree, Acehnese (Sumatra) and Cham and Jarai (both in Vietnam and Cambodia).

In his evaluation of the position of Madurese, Blust should also have highlighted that in this language PMP *j had become *l* (as seen, for instance, in *èlòŋ* 'nose' < *PMP *qijuŋ).[16] This sound change has not gone unnoticed in the literature but nor has it been given due recognition in the wider context of subgrouping evidence. As evidence it is relatively much stronger than an elevated lexicostatistical percentage in need of further scrutiny, and it gives extra weight to Blust's arguments against unqualified use of the latter.

In his reply to Blust, Nothofer (1985) accepted the latter's objections in general outline and refined some of the subgrouping conclusions he had drawn in Nothofer (1975). But he also justifiably opposed Blust's assertion that until relatively recently Sundanese and Malay had never been in close contact, and he rejected his arguments based on numerals. He still maintained the Malayo-Javanic subgroup, while acknowledging that Javanese is more distantly related to the other members. He adduced new lexical support for the subgroup, which now also included Lampung and Iban. As discussed above, he also provided some evidence for a close relationship between Sundanese and Lampung.

Notwithstanding the critical observations outlined above, Nothofer (1975) still stands out as a systematic and well-documented work based on methodological principles that were common at the time of its appearance.

As mentioned in §10.2, in Adelaar's (2005c) Malayo-Sumbawan, Javanese is excluded; it puts Malayic, Chamic (+ Acehnese), and the BSS languages on a par in one primary branch, and Sundanese and Madurese in two others. This subgroup is rejected by Blust (2010b), who includes Sundanese and Malayic in GNB, (see §10.8 for an evaluation of these alternatives).

In conclusion, the languages of Java clearly do not show the same close kinship to one another as do the Batak, Lampungic, or BSS languages. The phonological features and lexicon they have in common are also the result of a very long history of contact. This contact has been both global (e.g. from the Indian subcontinent) and local. It has also strongly affected BSS languages. Locally, Malay and Javanese have, for a very long time, been hegemonic languages and major sources of influence, both on other Austronesian languages (in Java, but also elsewhere in MPSEA) as on one another. Other factors such as a high common retention rate of basic vocabulary (between Malay and Madurese) as suggested by Blust may also play a distorting role in earlier subgrouping attempts.

The current default assumption is that the languages of Java simply do not form a genetic subgroup, something that becomes even more likely if their common history and similarities due to contact are taken into account. In terms of genetic distance, it has become clear that Javanese is further removed from Malay, Sundanese, and Madurese than the latter are from one another, and Malay (possibly also Sundanese) is more significantly related to various languages outside Java than it is to languages within. Further research based on more than phonology and lexicon alone is needed to bring more clarity in the issue.

[16] Other instances are *alè?* 'younger sibling' (< *(hu)aji); *pəlləs* 'smarting like when hit with thin rattan' (< *hapəjəs 'smarting, stinging pain'); *bálá* 'to announce, say' (< *bajaq 'to tell, inform; ask, inquire').

## 10.7 Balinese-Sasak-Sumbawa

BSS was outlined for the first time in 1938 in Esser's linguistic atlas. The latter had previously classified Balinese with Javanese and Madurese, in line with the prevailing viewpoints at the time and instigated by the fact that Balinese had much of its lexicon in common with Javanese. However, this common lexicon was much more a feature of high register Balinese than of low Balinese, which in every respect is more original than High Balinese and is more akin to Sasak and Sumbawa. Esser's (1938) subgrouping was taken over in the linguistic atlases of Salzner (1960) and Wurm and Hattori (1981–1983). Note that it was basically impressionistic: it was not based on systematic linguistic research but rather on philological insight in Balinese and Javanese. However, it was confirmed by lexicostatistical research conducted by Dyen (1982: 32), whose 'Balic' covers the same languages. As to the external classification of BSS, as indicated previously, Adelaar (2005c) groups it together with Malayic and Chamic (and Acehnese) in a Malayo-Sumbawan macrogroup. Blust (2010b) includes these language groups in his WIN subgroup, disagreeing with the close affiliation between them as implied in Adelaar (2005c) (see §10.8).

Mbete's PhD thesis (1990) divides the BSS languages into a Balinese and a Sasak-Sumbawa branch and he uses these languages for a reconstruction of the phonology and basic lexicon of PBSS. Basing himself on the Bali Dataran dialect of Balinese, the Ngeto-ngeté dialect of Sasak, and the Sumbawa Besar dialect of Sumbawa, he applies the comparative method and uses an approach which is strictly from bottom up.

His evidence for a BSS subgroup consists of forty-one exclusively shared lexical innovations vis-à-vis PMP[17] and a handful of formal innovations involving metathesis (Mbete 1990: 74–6). He also provides shared lexicostatistical percentages for Balinese, Sasak, Sumbawa, Javanese, Bima, and Manggarai, showing that the first three languages score significantly higher in shared vocabulary with one another than they do with the latter three (Mbete 1990: 66).

As Mbete's approach is from the bottom upwards, he does not use sound changes from PMP to BSS languages to test his subgroup, although he discusses these changes in a later chapter on "Reflexes of P[roto] A[ustronesia]n phonemes in [Proto-Bali-Sasak-Sumbawa]". Most PBSS sound correspondences are not particularly impressive as they are either PMP retentions or tend to be similar to ones that happened in Malayic and other languages in the region (such as the loss of *w-, and the change from *j to *d* and *-t*). Somewhat more diagnostic are individual irregular sound changes such as the loss of last syllable shown in *kənawan*, the denasalization shown in *tajəp*, the vowel raising in *taek*, or the reduplication in *ka~kən, as shown in (14).

(14) PMP *wada 'exist' > PBSS *adaq > Balinese *adə*, PSS (Proto-Sasak Sumbawa) *adaq > Sasak, Sumbawa *adaq*
PMP *waRi 'sun; day' > PBSS *ari > Balinese *ai*
PMP *qijuŋ 'nose' > PBSS *iduŋ > Balinese, Sasak *iduŋ*, *iruŋ*, Sumbawa *iduŋ*
PMP *(ŋ)ajan 'name' > PBSS *adan > Balinese *adan*, PSS *aran > Sasak, Sumbawa *aran*
PMP *tumid 'heel' > PBSS *tumed > Sasak *tumet* 'heel', Balinese *tumed* 'push with the foot'
PMP *ka-wanan 'right side' > PBSS *kənawan > Balinese *kənawan*, Sasak *kawan*, Sumbawa *kanan*
(?PMP) *pəniŋ 'dizzy' > PBSS *pinəŋ > Balinese *peneŋ*, PSS *pinəŋ
PMP *nahik 'to climb, go up' > PBSS *taek > Sasak *taek*, Sumbawa (*ən-*)*tek*
PMP *tazim, *tazəm 'sharp point; to whet' > PBSS *tajəp 'sharp'> Balinese, Sasak *tajep*, Sumbawa *tajam* (< Malay?)
PMP *kaʔən 'food' > PBSS *ka~kən > Sasak *kakən*, Sumbawa *kakan*

Mbete's Sasak-Sumbawa microgroup is based on phonological, lexical, and lexicostatistical evidence. His main phonological evidence for distinguishing a Balinese branch vs. a Sasak-Sumbawa one is as follows:

Phonological changes:

(15) PBSS *-a > Balinese *-ə* (not in all dialects)
PBSS voiced final occlusives > PSS devoicing of final occlusives
PBSS *-d- > PSS *-d-, *-r-;
PBSS *r, *R > PSS *r;
PBSS *R > Balinese Ø-, -Ø-, *-h*;
PBSS *-q > Balinese *-h*, PSS *-q*
PBSS *-w- > Balinese Ø, PSS *-w-*
PBSS *əRV > Balinese VV
PBSS heterorganic nasal + stop clusters become homorganic
PBSS heterorganic clusters of unlike stops are reduced to their last stop

[17] Mbete uses Proto-Austronesian (PAN) as a reference point, but for reasons of phonological transparency and given the topic of the current volume, PMP is used instead.

Examples:

(16) PBSS *səRəb 'to glance, spy, lurk' > Balinese *səəb*, PSS *sərəp*
PBSS *uRad 'vein, nerve' > Balinese *uad*, PSS *urat > Sasak, Sumbawa *urat*
PBSS *əmpug 'split, peeled' > Balinese *əmpug*, PSS *əmpuk
PBSS *bəgaq 'just, only, enough' > Balinese *bəgah*, PSS *bəgaq
PBSS *adan 'name' > Balinese *adan*, PSS *aran
PBSS *siwa 'nine' > Balinese *siə*, PSS *siwaʔ > Sasak, Sumbawa *siwaʔ* (with irregular ʔ accretion)
PBSS *ada > Balinese *adə*, PSS *adaʔ > Sasak *araʔ*, Sumbawa *adaʔ* (with irregular -ʔ accretion)
PBSS *Ratus 'hundred' > Balinese *-atus*, PSS *ratus > Sasak *ratus*, Sumbawa *ratis*[18]
PBSS *pəRut 'to shrink' > Balinese *puut*, PSS *pərut
PBSS *bəRas 'rice (uncooked)' > Balinese *baas*, PSS *bəras
PBSS *kaRuŋ 'male (of animals)' > Balinese *kauŋ*, PSS *karuŋ
PBSS *akaR 'root' > Balinese *akah*, PSS *akar
PBSS *diŋdiŋ 'wall' > Balinese *diŋdiŋ*, PSS *dindiŋ
PBSS *tabtab 'to knock hard' > Balinese *tabtab*, PSS *tatap > Sasak, Sumbawa *tatap*

Mbete's lexical evidence consists of thirty-one lexical innovations (Mbete 1990: 79–80).

Finally, Mbete gives the following lexicostatistical percentages for basic vocabulary shared among Balinese, Sasak, and Sumbawa: Sasak-Balinese 51%; Sumbawa-Balinese 49%; Sasak-Sumbawa 64%. They show a significant gap between Balinese on the one hand and Sasak and Sumbawa on the other.

As indicated before, Adelaar's (2005c) Malayo-Sumbawan subgroup places Malayic, Chamic, and the BSS languages on a par in one primary branch, and Sundanese and Madurese in two other ones. It is rejected by Blust (2010b) on various grounds. One concerns the evidential force of Adelaar's sound changes. While conceding that there are many phonological developments shared between the Malayic, Chamic, and BSS languages, Blust considers most of these insignificant because they are also frequently observed in languages outside the group (e.g. PMP *q > *h*, *R, *r > *r*, *h > Ø). Another ground is the applicability of some changes: some phonological developments are not properly shared. They do not yield a representative protoform at the Malayic-Chamic-BSS level because they do not occur in all languages that are diagnostic for such a subgroup (as with reflexes of *-ay, *-uy, *-iw), or, if they do occur, they differ to the extent that they must have followed independent pathways (as with PMP *w-). Moreover, Blust considers the fact that BSS languages lack a reflex of *tuzuq meaning 'seven' as crucial evidence for rejecting their inclusion in the same subgroup as Malayic and Chamic.

Blust's assessment is coherent, except for the undue value he attaches to Chamic *tuzuq reflexes, which are likely to be borrowed from Malay (see §10.8).

[18] In Sumbawa, last syllable *u often changes to i, as in (PMP) *niuR 'cocospalm; coconut' > *ñir*; *tahun 'agricultural cycle; year' > *tin*; *Ratus 'hundred' > *ratis*; *tuhəd 'knee' (> *əntut) > *əntit* (Mbete 1990: 108–9).

## 10.8 The use of *tuzuq 'seven' and PMP *j as subgrouping evidence: an appraisal

These reflexes deserve extra focus as their use is a recurrent theme in the subgrouping proposals in this chapter. While, in general, both are useful diagnostic devices for subgrouping, it has also become increasingly clear that their value is not absolute with regard to the languages under discussion.

Concerning reflexes of *tuzuq 'seven', Blust already conceded that Makasar *tuju* (in Sulawesi) must be borrowed from Malay. However, borrowing must also be at the origin of Rejang *tujuaq* and of *tuzuq reflexes in Chamic languages, Sundanese, Moken-Moklen, and Simeulue.

The following are indications that this, in fact, must be the case.

- In Rejang, *tujuaq* 'seven' occurs along with reflexes of *dua-alap-an, 'eight' and *(ə)sa-ambil-an 'nine', which are clearly borrowed from Malay. This increases the likelihood that *tujuaq* is also borrowed. Furthermore, whereas its phonological appearance suggests that it is inherited, parallel phonological developments in other loanwords in Rejang show that this is not necessarily the case (§10.5.3).
- The situation in Chamic is comparable to that in Rejang. There is no direct evidence that *tuzuq reflexes are borrowed but the fact that they co-occur with reflexes of *dua-alap-an, 'eight' and *(ə)sa-ambil-an 'nine' (and in the Chamic case, also reflexes of *(ə)sa-alap-an 'nine'), makes it likely that they are. Like Rejang, Chamic languages lack reflexes of the roots *alap and *ambil, and they also lack reflexes of the suffix *-an. (In fact, both Rejang and Chamic languages lack suffixes). Moreover, in Chamic, reflexes of *dua + *alapan, *(e)sa + *alapan, and *(e)sa + ambil-an have very unstable meanings. This is abundantly demonstrated in Thurgood (1999: 38–9), where it is shown, among others, that in Ede (also Rhade or Rade) and Jarai, reflexes for 'nine' and 'eight' were reversed, and in some other cases, *dua + *alapan, *(e)sa

+ *alapan, and *(e)sa + ambil-an compete in denoting the same numerical values.[19] On the other hand, in standard and literary forms of Malay, the morphemic structure and semantics of these compound numerals are transparent.

- Gayo has inherited numerals but systematically uses Malay numerals alongside them (Eades 2005: 86). In Simeulue, inherited *ito/itu* and *tujuh* (< Malay) exist side by side (Blust 2010b: 69). Both languages clearly demonstrate the dominant (and ongoing) influence of Malay on the lexicons of languages in the western fringes of the MPSEA region, including on their numeral systems.

Malayic and Chamic are obviously closely related, and it may be that this relationship excludes other Malayo-Polynesian languages, as proposed by Blust (2010b) and Thurgood (1999). However, the absence of *tuzuq reflexes for 'seven' in BSS languages is not *by itself* a sufficiently robust argument for denying them a coordinate position in a subgroup with Malayic and Chamic. Nor is the presence of these reflexes in Chamic languages critical evidence for a close relationship between Chamic and Malayic, as it is likely that they were borrowed from Malay.

Sundanese *tujuh* could also be borrowed from Malay (although here the evidence is less compelling as Sundanese could theoretically also have acquired its terms for 'seven', 'eight', and 'nine' independently). Along with *tujuh* it has also *dalapan* 'eight' (< *dua *alap-an 'two taken away') and *salapan* 'nine' (< *(ə)a *alap-an 'one taken away'). Note furthermore Old Javanese *ḍolapan* 'eight', which occurs sporadically alongside *wwalu* and is clearly borrowed from Malay.

So it is important to keep in mind that reflexes of *tuzuq 'seven' are not necessarily inherited, even if they show inherited phonology. There are several ways in which languages could have acquired them other than through membership in the GNB subgroup. They could be borrowed (in which case their phonological shape may or may not give them away); they could be calque translations; or they could be the result of independent parallel developments.

The limited use of *j reflexes as evidence for subgrouping has also become obvious. Here again, the device is not without value, but it is clearly co-dependent on other evidence. Moreover, the evidence of *j is complicated by the fact that languages often do not have a uniform reflex: for instance, Gayo has Ø and g; Rejang has *-g-*, *-Ø-*, *-k*, and *-t*; Nasal has *x*, *h*, *d*, and *-ʔ*; Madurese has *l* and *-ʔ*.[20] Furthermore, closely related languages may still have different reflexes of *j, as in South Sulawesi languages, where Bugis and Tamanic have *s*, and Makasar has *r* (< *d). These South Sulawesi *j reflexes may be relatively recent. Mills (1975a) tried to reconcile them by reconstructing Proto-South Sulawesi *z, but this is unsatisfactory: a change from *z to *s* can be accounted for, but one from *z to *d/r* is odd.

Neither Smith's WIN subgroup nor his Sumatran subgroup are clearly defined by a uniform reflex of *j. About the merger of *j and *d in WIN languages, Smith (2017b: 455–6) writes that "there are no languages that unambiguously belong to Western Indonesian (either Greater North Borneo, or Barito) that do not reflect this merger, and it can likely be reconstructed to the immediate ancestor of these languages." It is not immediately clear if he is including WIN languages in Sumatra and Java in his statement, but in the same context he does mention Rejang as another WIN language in which the merger occurred. However, the merger occurred only to a very limited extent (§10.5.3). Furthermore, if his statement was meant to include all WIN languages, it ignores Madurese, which reflects PMP *j as *l* and *-ʔ*. In Sumatran languages, another concern is the hitherto missed *j > Ø reflex which is predominant in Gayo and is also seen in part of the Rejang cognates.

Finally, in both the case of GNB and of WIN, the inclusion of outlier languages such as Moken-Moklen in the GNB group (only based on sharing a *tuzuq reflex for 'seven', as done by Blust), and Rejang in the WIN group as defined by Smith (only based on a merger of *j and *d to *d/-t*, which moreover is questionable) is unsatisfactory because it is based on insufficient evidence. Including them seems to do no more than rescue the subgroups involved, which would otherwise lack a critical exclusive innovation to define them.

To summarize, evidence based on *tuzuq or on the shape of a *j reflex is insufficient by itself. Moreover, if not given absolute diagnostic value, various pieces of other and possibly more promising subgrouping evidence may fall into place. For instance, there would no longer be a compelling reason to include Moken-Moklen with the GNB languages. Without further evidence, that inclusion is rather a stretch, given the idiosyncratic phonological history of Moken-Moklen and its eccentric position in relation to Borneo.

[19] Thurgood (1999) himself is convinced that the Chamic forms for 'seven', 'eight', and 'nine' are evidence for subgrouping Chamic with Malayic (p.38), pointing out that some of the confusion regarding *(əsa)-alapan and *dua-alapan also exists in Minangkabau and Kerinci. However, this merely shows that the latter languages must have borrowed these numerals from the same literary Malay acrolect as the Chamic languages did.

[20] Note that in Madurese, PMP final *l remained *-l*, in contrast to *-j > *-ʔ*. It shows that, in this language, final *j did not first change to *l before ending as *-ʔ*, and that *j and *l only merged in intermediate position.

## 10.9 Concluding remarks

The classification of the languages focused on in this chapter remains largely unsolved. Three subgroups are uncontroversial, namely Batak, Lampungic, and BSS. Subgrouping Lampungic and Sundanese at a higher cladistic node seems promising but needs further investigation. As to the Barrier Island languages, Simeulue, Sigulai, and Nias form a cohesive subgroup, but further inclusions involving Enggano or Mentawai, remain problematic. The classifications of Enggano, Mentawai, Nasal, Gayo, Rejang, Moken-Moklen, and the languages of Java remain uncertain and need further investigation. A close relationship between Batak and Gayo remains undecided.

While the evidence of an innovative numeral like *tuzuq or a complex phonological reconstruction like PMP *j may be strong in itself, it still needs to be assessed in context. More generally, in the languages under investigation, subgrouping devices that have absolute diagnostic value are unlikely to be found.

At the risk of stating the obvious, the only promising approach to a classification of the languages in this chapter is to systematically conduct research from the bottom upwards while investigating data at all linguistic levels (including morphosyntax and semantic taxonomies). The results of this research should also be brought into a wider perspective involving contact history and recent research in other disciplines, including archaeology, human genetics, anthropology, and ethnobotany.

## Acknowledgements

I am indebted to Bradley McDonnell, Laurie Reid, Antoinette Schapper, and Erik Zobel, for their valuable feedback on earlier drafts of this chapter.

CHAPTER 11

# Historical linguistics of the Chamic languages

MARC BRUNELLE

## 11.1 Introduction

The lexical and phonological similarities between Chamic languages and between Chamic and other Malayo-Polynesian languages of Southeast Asia are so striking that they have probably always been obvious to native speakers. However, they were only noted in academic work in the late nineteenth century. The first scholarly mention of the Austronesian affiliation of Chamic seems attributable to Étienne-François Aymonier (1889: 6), who believed that Austronesian and Mon-Khmer[1] were related and that Chamic was a transitional group between these two families. As for the genetic relation between Chamic languages, it was first noted, albeit briefly, in Aymonier and Cabaton (1906: vii).

In this short chapter, I will review evidence about the specific position of the Chamic family within Malayo-Polynesian and about its internal subgrouping. I will address three main questions: the relation of Chamic to Malayic and other Malayo-Polynesian languages of Southeast Asia (§11.2); the relation of Chamic to Acehnese (§11.3); and subgrouping within Chamic itself (§11.4). Note that reconstructed Proto-Malayo-Polynesian (PMP) and Proto-Chamic (PC) forms are taken from Thurgood (1999), unless specified otherwise.

## 11.2 Chamic, Malayic, and Malayo-Polynesian

A special difficulty when discussing the genetic affiliation of Chamic is that its closest relatives are Malayo-Polynesian languages of Southeast Asia whose subgrouping is still being worked out (Adelaar 2005a; Blust 2010b; Smith 2017b). For this reason, a good starting point for a discussion of the position of Chamic in Malayo-Polynesian is its long-noticed relationship with Malayic. To my knowledge, Robert Blust was the first linguist to establish that Chamic and Malayic are closely connected based on systematic phonological and lexical innovations rather than impressionistic similarities (Blust 1981c, 1994). The phonological innovations identified by Blust are a shift from PMP *q to *h, a merger between PMP *R and *r without merger with other protophonemes, the loss of PMP *w in initial position, and the introduction of an *h in the form *mata hari 'sun'. As for innovated lexical items, they include *gigi 'tooth' and *besi 'iron', and the numerals *tuzuq 'seven', *dua lapan 'eight', and *salipan/*sambilan 'nine' (see Adelaar 2005c: 384 for evidence that Chamic 'eight' and 'nine' may be Malay loans). Although all these innovations are found sporadically in other languages of the region, Blust judged that their co-occurrence in Chamic and Malayic was sufficient to establish the existence of a Malayo-Chamic group.

Based on fourteen phonological innovations complemented with lexical evidence, Adelaar (2005c) proposed that Malayic and Chamic are part of a Malayo-Sumbawan group comprising several languages of Western Indonesia and the Malaysian Peninsula. Within Malayo-Sumbawan, however, Adelaar deemed that the lexical and phonological evidence as to whether Malayic is closer to Chamic or to a Balinese-Sasak-Sumbawa subgroup was equivocal. More recently, Blust (2010b), followed by Smith (2017b), has proposed to include a Malayo-Chamic subgroup in a Greater-North-Borneo (GNB) group that would also comprise Moken, Rejang, Sundanese, and all the languages of Borneo except the Barito languages. According to this scenario, Malayo-Chamic would have been spoken in the Kapuas river basin, in Borneo, before its speakers sailed to Sumatra and Mainland Southeast Asia. Although the Greater-North-Borneo and the Malayo-Sumbawan hypotheses are not compatible in terms of linguistic reconstruction, they are both consistent with an early migration from Borneo.

Similarities between Malayic and Chamic, and Moken-Moklen have also been invoked to posit a Moken-Moklen-Aceh-Chamic-Malayic group, that would have split into

[1] As the existence of a Mon-Khmer subgroup within Austroasiatic has recently been questioned, I will use the term "Austroasiatic" in this chapter, even when previous authors used "Mon-Khmer". The move away from the latter label and its historical implications can also be seen in Sidwell, this volume, chapter 20.

Marc Brunelle, *Historical linguistics of the Chamic languages.* In: *The Oxford Guide to the Malayo-Polynesian Languages of Southeast Asia.* Edited by: Alexander Adelaar and Antoinette Schapper, Oxford University Press. © Marc Brunelle (2024). DOI: 10.1093/oso/9780198807353.003.0011

Moken-Moklen, on the one hand, and Aceh-Chamic-Malayic, on the other (Larish 1999). Although Malayo-Chamic and Moken-Moklen share innovations, most seem to be found in other languages of the area, and many appear to be common typological changes (Blust 1994). While Blust (2010b) treats Moken as a non-Malayo-Chamic branch of GNB, Smith (2017b) radically sets it apart as a different branch of Malayo-Polynesian.

To sum up, it seems fairly uncontroversial that Chamic and Malayic are closely related, but in the absence of an established classification of the other Malayo-Polynesian languages of Southeast Asia, it remains an open question whether they form an exclusive subgroup within a larger branch of Malayo-Polynesian or are part of a group that includes other members.

## 11.3 Chamic and Acehnese

It has long been recognized that Chamic languages share similarities with Acehnese, despite the distance and geographical obstacles that separate them (Niemann 1891). While there is a general consensus that the languages are close relatives (Blagden 1929; Blust 1994; I. V. Collins 1975; J. T. Collins 1991; Cowan 1991; Durie 1985; Niemann 1891; Shorto 1975; Sidwell 2005; Thurgood 1999), there remains minor disagreement about their exact relationship. The traditional view is that Acehnese is a sister to Chamic in an Aceh-Chamic group, as in (1a) (Blust 1994; Brunelle 2019; Durie 1990; Shorto 1975; Sidwell 2006), but Thurgood (1999) proposed that Acehnese is a Chamic language on a par with other Chamic subgroups, as in (1b).

(1) a.

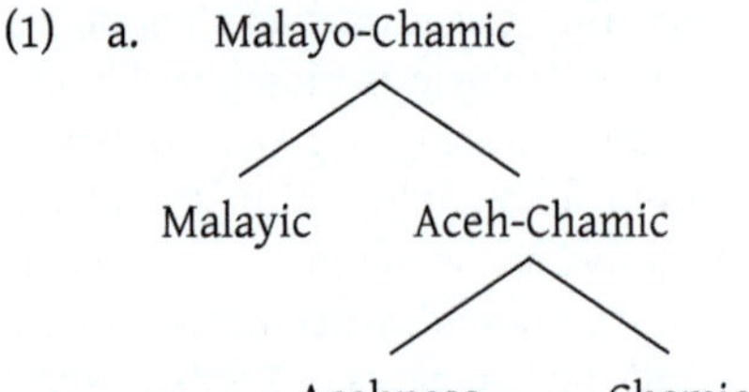


b.

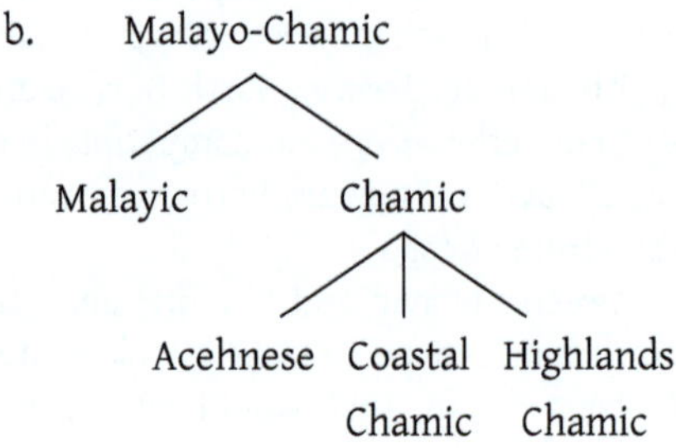


The evidence that Acehnese and Chamic are closer to each other than to languages of the Malayic branch mainly comes from three phonological innovations (weaker evidence is argued against in Sidwell 2005). The first one is the lengthening of PMP short *a before most final consonants, but not before *q (Shorto 1975; Sidwell 2006; Thurgood 1999). Long *a: was then diphthongized in Acehnese. This is illustrated in (2).

(2)

| Proto-Malayo-Polynesian (PMP) | Proto-Chamic (PC) | Acehnese |
|---|---|---|
| *palaj 'palm of hand' | *pala:t | [paluɯət] |
| *epat 'four' | *pa:t | [puɯət] |
| *bulan 'moon' | *bula:n | [buluɯən] |
| *qudaŋ 'shrimp' | *huda:ŋ | [uduɯəŋ] |
| *daraq 'blood' | *darah | [darah] |
| *panaq 'shoot an arrow' | *panah | [panah] |

Sidwell (2006) claimed that this phonological innovation is not only shared by Chamic and Acehnese, but also by Malayic varieties and by Moken-Moklen. However, he provided no Malayic evidence, and a close inspection of the Moken-Moklen correspondences given in Larish (1999) shows that in that subgroup, the lengthening of PMP *a occurred before all consonants, including PMP *q. This would suggest that, despite similarities, Moken-Moklen underwent the lengthening independently from Chamic and Acehnese.

The second phonological innovation shared by Chamic and Acehnese is the diphthongization of PMP final *i and *u (Blust 1994; Sidwell 2006; Shorto 1975; Thurgood 1999). Final high vowels are only found in forms in which they were originally followed by PMP *R, a coda that dropped at a later stage. This is shown in (3).

(3)

| Proto-Malayo-Polynesian (PMP) | | Proto-Chamic (PC) | Acehnese |
|---|---|---|---|
| *tali | 'rope' | *talɛj | [talɔə] |
| *beli | 'buy' | *blɛj | [blɔə] |
| *balu | 'widowed' | *balɔw | [balɛə] |
| *ikuR | 'tail' | *ʔiku | [iku] |
| *niuR | 'coconut' | *laʔu | [u] |

High vowel diphthongization is also attested in Moken-Moklen (Larish 1999), but in these languages, PMP *-R was changed to /-n/ rather than deleted, which would again suggest that they are outside Aceh-Chamic.

The last phonological innovation, in (4), is only shared by Acehnese and Chamic. It is the loss of the vowel of PMP penultimate syllables between a stop and *l, *r, and *h, yielding the clusters *Cr, *Cl, *Ch (Blust 1994: note 7; Sidwell 2006; Thurgood 1999).

(4)

| Proto-Malayo-Polynesian (PMP) | Proto-Chamic (PC) | Acehnese |
|---|---|---|
| *puluq 'ten' | *pluh | [siploh] |
| *beli 'buy' | *blɛj | [bloə] |
| *buRuk 'spoiled; rotten' | *bruʔ | [broʔ] |
| *taqu 'to know' | *thɔw | [thɛə] |

A more systematic comparison of these Aceh-Chamic phonological innovations with evidence from Malayic varieties is needed, but at this stage, there seem to be strong grounds for considering that Acehnese and Chamic do indeed form a subgroup. However, the innovations above are not sufficient to decide if Acehnese is a sister to Chamic within Aceh-Chamic (1a) or a member of the Chamic subgroup (1b).

While most scholars settled for the first option, Cowan (1991) and Thurgood (1999) opted for the second, based on a combination of linguistic evidence and historical conjecture. The linguistic evidence is that Chamic and Acehnese share Austroasiatic loanwords that can either be reconstructed to PC, like *krɔŋ 'river', *cim 'bird', and *kaːŋ 'jaw', or are shared by Acehnese and some Chamic languages, without being reconstructable to PC (marked with $^{X}$), such as $^{X}$cagəu 'Malaysian bear' and $^{X}$kəmuan 'nephew; sister's son' (Blust 1994; Durie 1990; Shorto 1975; Thurgood 1999). These two layers of loans suggest that some Austroasiatic words were borrowed at a stage were Aceh-Chamic was a unified language, while others were borrowed relatively late after the break-up of Chamic into distinct varieties. This would be consistent with the view that Acehnese and Chamic shared a long common history and parted recently. Cowan and Thurgood then took the bold step to associate this late separation of Acehnese from Chamic with the fall of the Cham capitals of Indrapura and Vijaya to the Vietnamese in 982 and 1471 (Cowan 1991; Thurgood 1999, 2007). Thurgood also hypothesized that most Austroasiatic loanwords in Acehnese come from the Katuic branch, that is nowadays spoken near the former site of Indrapura (Thurgood 1999, 2007).

I have already argued in detail that there is little to no historical evidence for a significant migration of Acehnese speakers from central Vietnam in 982 or 1471 (Brunelle 2019). I will here focus on the linguistic evidence. As pointed out by Thurgood (1999), a first important observation is that Acehnese does not seem to share Austroasiatic loanwords with a specific Chamic language or subgroup. (In fact, Durie (1985) noted that it does not share any Austroasiatic phonological innovations with a specific Chamic language or subgroup). This suggests that contact with Austroasiatic occurred very early, before the break-up of Aceh-Chamic. The number of Austroasiatic loanwords shared by Acehnese and Chamic also seems relatively small: a close inspection of Thurgood's (1999) lexicon by Sidwell (2005), following Dyen (2001), reveals that only twenty-eight words of Austroasiatic origin are shared by Acehnese and Chamic but not by neighbouring Austronesian languages, to which we could add twelve words of unknown origins. More importantly, there are suggestive distributional asymmetries in Thurgood's reconstructed Proto-Chamic lexicon: while 71.2% of Austronesian vocabulary has reflexes in both Acehnese and Chamic, it is the case for only 9.4% of Austroasiatic words and 8.9% of words of unknown origins (Sidwell 2006). This is evidence that many (if not most) loans of Austroasiatic and unknown origins were borrowed independently in Acehnese and Chamic.

From what language were these words borrowed then? Sidwell (2006) concluded that the large majority of them (200/277) have a Bahnaric cognate, but that many also have close cognates in other Austroasiatic branches. Moreover, those that do not have Austroasiatic cognates outside Bahnaric could be Chamic words borrowed into Bahnaric rather than the opposite. As for a possible Katuic origin of Austroasiatic loans in Aceh-Chamic, Sidwell (2006) conducted an inspection of sixty-three reconstructed Proto-Chamic etyma of Austroasiatic origin that have Katuic cognates in Thurgood (1999) and found that only six of them were closer to Katuic than to Bahnaric, and that a single one only had a Katuic cognate. There is therefore hardly any evidence that Acehnese was ever in close contact with Katuic, which invalidates the scenario according to which it would have been spoken close to Indrapura before a migration to Aceh. Various hypotheses are compatible with the presence of Austroasiatic loans in both Acehnese and Chamic, but the absence of any indication that they were borrowed after Chamic broke up into different dialects/languages would suggest that they were adopted early on, before the split of Aceh-Chamic. We should also consider the distinct possibility that most Austroasiatic loanwords were borrowed independently by Acehnese and Chamic, which would rule them out as evidence for subgrouping. In fact, it has even been proposed that the lexicon shared by Austroasiatic and Chamic might have been borrowed from a non-Austroasiatic extinct language typologically similar to Austroasiatic (Sidwell 2006). The evidence thus weighs in favour of the conservative tree in (1a), where Acehnese is a sister to Chamic rather than a Chamic language.

This opens the question of where the split between Acehnese and Chamic happened. If evidence for an Austroasiatic presence in insular Southeast Asia before the arrival of Malayo-Polynesian speakers is to be taken seriously (Blench 2010c), it could have occurred before the ancestors of Aceh-Chamic speakers left Borneo (Adelaar 1995b). Other possible scenarios include contact between Aceh-Chamic and Austroasiatic in various areas of Mainland Southeast Asia (including present-day central Vietnam) before Acehnese and Chamic split (Blust 1994; Durie 1985; Sidwell 2005, 2006), and even a migration from Aceh to central Vietnam (Dyen 2001).

## 11.4 Chamic subgrouping and reconstruction

Three reconstructions of Proto-Chamic have been proposed so far. Lee (1966) based his on Eastern Cham, Jarai, and Ede transcriptions, and on original materials collected on Northern Raglai. Ten years later, Burnham (1976) revisited Lee's reconstruction, making minor amendments and adding Haroi data. More recently, Thurgood (1999) used data from all Chamic languages for which comprehensive vocabularies were at his disposal (Jarai, Ede, Haroi, Tsat, Northern Raglai, Chru, Eastern Cham, and Western Cham). Since then, additional evidence has become available for other dialects of Raglai (Cát Gia and different varieties of Southern Raglai), for Eastern Jarai, and for Bih, a variety closely related to Ede (Jensen 2014; Lee 1998; V. H. Nguyễn 2003, 2007; T. M. T. Nguyễn 2013a, b; Tạ 2009). A map illustrating the geographical distribution of Chamic languages is available in Brunelle and Jensen (chapter 30, Map 30.1).

Before discussing subgrouping, the use of the terms 'Cham' and 'Chamic' in previous sources needs to be clarified. They have sometimes been used interchangeably and several proposed subgroups of Chamic languages have names that contain 'Cham', even if they do not include Cham dialects proper. These include Burnham's Highland Cham and Lowland Cham, and Thurgood's Northern Cham (the term 'Hainan Cham' has also been used by Benedict and Thurgood to designate Tsat). I will not rename these subgroups, but will restrict my own use of the term 'Cham' to the language that is spoken in the provinces of Ninh Thuận and Bình Thuận, in south-central Vietnam, and that has spread to the Vietnamese Mekong delta and Cambodia since the seventeenth century. It includes two main dialects: Eastern Cham (south-central Vietnam); and Western Cham (Cambodia and Mekong delta).

The first subgrouping of Chamic languages was put forward by Lee (1966) and was largely based on lexicostatistic comparisons. Lee was well aware that this was a limitation, and presented his classification as "tentative statements" (Lee 1966: 8). He proposed to group all languages except Jarai and Ede into a southern group, split between Northern Raglai and all other Chamic languages. Despite shared lexical evidence and phonological innovations, he remained non-committed as to the grouping of Jarai and Ede as a single Northern Chamic branch or as separate sisters of Southern Chamic. In his MA thesis, Burnham (1976) developed and amended Lee's subgrouping, and proposed the tree in (5) based on both phonological and lexicostatistic evidence. Burnham backed up Lee's proposed split between Northern Chamic (Ede and Jarai) and Southern Chamic (Northern Raglai and Eastern Cham) with a number of phonological innovations and renamed the two groups Highland Cham and Lowland Cham, respectively. The phonological innovations invoked by Burnham included a much lower rate of debuccalization of coda stops in Highland than in Lowland Cham, the debuccalization of PC *s as [-ʲh] in Highland Cham but as [-h] in Lowland Cham, and the preservation of the PC contrast between -r and -l in Highland Cham but their neutralization in Lowland Cham. However, Burnham's main modification to Lee's subgrouping was to propose that Haroi constitutes a third branch within Chamic as it is ambivalent with respect to these phonological innovations.

Thurgood (1999) radically departs from the subgroupings in Lee (1966) and Burnham (1976) and proposes the tree classification in (6). Leaving aside his treatment of Acehnese, which was discussed in the previous section, he divides Chamic languages into two groups, Highlands Chamic and Coastal Chamic, a split that is claimed to have developed "after the Vietnamese began moving south" without much explanation (Thurgood, 1999: 43). Thurgood's Coastal Chamic includes Cham dialects and Haroi, while Highlands Chamic is split into two groups: Jarai and Ede, on the one hand, and a group that includes Chru, Northern Raglai, and Tsat, on the other. This latter unnamed group is in turn divided into Chru and Northern Cham, which contains Northern Raglai and Tsat.

(5)

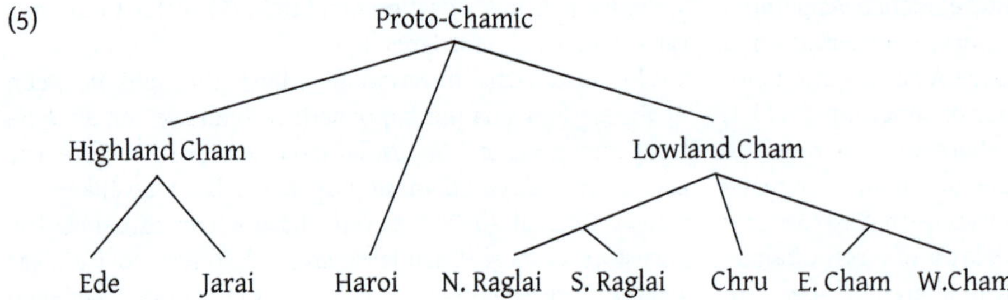

(6)

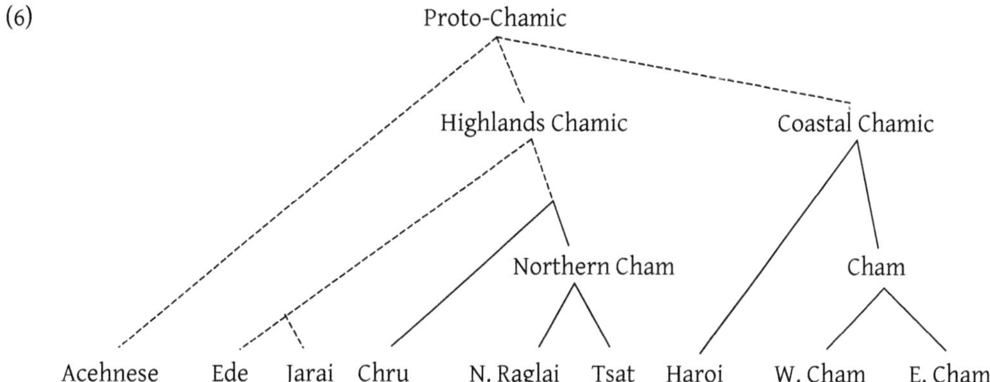


The important discrepancies between Thurgood's subgrouping, on the one hand, and Lee and Burnham's, on the other, are partly attributable to the sources to which they had access, but also stem from Thurgood's parallel use of linguistic reconstruction and historical conjecture. In addition, two important factors, recognized in Thurgood (1999), make the classification of Chamic languages especially challenging. The first one is that Chamic languages probably formed at some point in the past one or more dialect chains within which linguistic innovations diffused as waves (also 'linkages' or 'dialect continua'), rather than a patchwork of isolated communities regularly splitting off from each other. In fact, dialect continua spanning different Chamic languages appear to have survived to this day. There is evidence for a dialect continuum including Chru, Raglai, and possibly even Eastern Cham in Lâm Đồng, Bình Thuận, Ninh Thuận, and Khánh Hòa provinces in south-central Vietnam. Chru speakers living in the district of Đơn Dương, in the province of Lâm Đồng, are in frequent contact with Southern Raglai speakers from the district of Ma Nới, in the province of Ninh Thuận, about 35km to the southeast. I have witnessed interactions between speakers of these two communities in which all interlocutors used their (very similar) native varieties without the slightest misunderstanding. A similar mutual intelligibility holds between Southern Raglai speakers from Ma Nới and Northern Raglai speakers from the district of Bác Ái, in the province of Ninh Thuận, 50km to the northeast. The Northern Raglai in Bác Ái are in turn adamant that they have no difficulty communicating with Northern Raglai speakers from the province of Khánh Hòa (although I have not seen this first hand). This suggests that there is no clear linguistic break between these Chru and Raglai dialects, but rather gradual change as one travels from village to village. Perhaps more surprising is the level of intelligibility between the Eastern Cham varieties spoken in Ninh Thuận province, and Chru and Raglai dialects. Eastern Cham peddlers regularly travel to Chru and Raglai communities to sell used clothes and traditional medicine, and participants in the resulting commercial transactions normally all use their native languages. Although this is all based on anecdotal observations, the high level of intelligibility between Chamic varieties spoken in south-central Vietnam suggests that they may form a dialect continuum, even if there is no evidence of lexical diffusion.

The second special problem faced by Chamic diachronic linguistics is the intensity of contact between Chamic and Austroasiatic. Various contact scenarios have been proposed, ranging from large-scale language shifts to a low, but constant, rate of intermarriage (Brunelle 2020; Thurgood 2000), but the impact of Austroasiatic on the lexicon and structures of Chamic languages is undeniable. This poses special problems: not only is it often difficult to sort out contact-induced and regular internal change, but similar innovations in different Chamic varieties may have developed independently because of contact with separate, yet similar Austroasiatic languages. For instance, the formation of register in distant Chamic languages could be attributed to contact with different registral Austroasiatic languages. The issue is even more pronounced with lexical evidence, as Austroasiatic loans may have been borrowed independently from closely related languages by different Chamic varieties.

In the following pages, I will critically review Thurgood's subgrouping in (6). For each branch, the validity of his interpretation of the data will be confirmed or questioned. New evidence not yet available to him in 1999 will also be brought forward. For clarity's sake, I will start with lower groupings in (6) and will gradually work my way up.

Within Highlands Chamic, Jarai and Ede seem to form a well-established subgroup. As noted by Lee (1966), they share a number of lexical innovations (including a unique reversal of 'eight' and 'nine'), and as pointed out by Burnham (1976) and by Thurgood (1999), are more conservative than all other Chamic varieties in that they do not debuccalize their coda stops, and debuccalize PC *-s into /-ʲh/. (Note that Thurgood (1999: 46) attributes these shared features to retention and contact). More generally, Ede and Jarai are mutually intelligible in northern Đắk Lắk province, where they are in close contact; speakers of the two languages report understanding each other without explicit instruction.

Evidence regarding the Northern Chamic subgroup, which includes Northern Raglai and Tsat (a Chamic language spoken in Hainan) is more controversial. Thurgood (1999) proposes to group these two languages based on linguistic and historical evidence. As I have already argued against Thurgood's historical scenario and raised doubt about the northern origin of Tsat and Raglai elsewhere (Brunelle 2019), I will concentrate on the linguistic evidence. The two innovations put forward to group Northern Raglai and Tsat are the loss of PC *-s after long *a: and nasal preplosion.

In all Chamic languages, *-s and *-h have merged to /-h/ in most contexts, as can be seen in the first four words in (7). In Northern Raglai, the /-h/ is preserved, while in Tsat, it has been regularly transphonologized into a high tone /$^{55}$/. Moreover, as can be seen in the last four examples of (7), Northern Raglai and Tsat share an exception: after PC long *a:, they both lost the *-h. In Tsat, *-a in final syllables then regularly developed a low tone /$^{11}$/ or a high tone /$^{33}$/ depending on the voicing of the initial, as all other open syllables.

(7)

| Proto-Chamic (PC) | Northern Raglai | Tsat |
|---|---|---|
| *lipih 'thin (material)' | [lupih] | [pi$^{55}$] |
| *panah 'to shoot; bow' | [panãh] | [na$^{55}$] |
| *tikus 'rat' | [tukuh] | [(na$^{11}$) ku$^{55}$] |
| *deras 'fast; short time' | [drah] | [sia$^{55}$] |
| *ʔata:s 'far; above; long' | [ata] | [ta$^{33}$] |
| *kapa:s 'cotton' | [kappa] | [pa$^{33}$] |
| *kaka:s 'fish scales' | [kaka] | [ka$^{33}$] |
| *bra:s 'husked rice' | [bra] | [phia$^{11}$] |

The presence of this common exception appears to constitute solid evidence for subgrouping. However, there are also contexts, exemplified in (8), where Tsat has lost PC final *-h, but not Northern Raglai.

(8)

| Proto-Chamic (PC) | Northern Raglai | Tsat |
|---|---|---|
| *ratus 'hundred' | [ratuh] | [tu$^{33}$] |
| *ɓuh NEGATION | [ɓuh] | [pu$^{33}$] |
| *radɛh 'vehicle' (post-PC) | [radeh] | [the$^{11}$] |
| *asɛh 'horse' (post-PC) | [aseh] | [se$^{33}$] |

The second relevant innovation is nasal preplosion. In Northern Raglai, PC final nasals are typically denasalized, whereas Tsat has post-glottalized nasals, as shown in (9). Thurgood treats these changes as a shared innovation, assuming an intermediate stage with nasal preplosion (PC *-m, -n, -ŋ > *-pm, -tn, -kŋ).

(9)

| Proto-Chamic (PC) | Northern Raglai | Tsat |
|---|---|---|
| *dalam 'inside' | [dalap] | [lanʔ$^{42}$] |
| *dua-lapan 'eight' | [lapat] | [pa:nʔ$^{42}$] |
| *haŋ 'hot; spicy' | [hak] | [ha:ŋʔ$^{42}$] |

Interestingly, there is one context in which preplosion seems to have failed in both languages: syllables with nasal onsets, as in PC *ʔaŋin 'wind', Northern Raglai /aŋĩn/, Tsat /ŋin$^{33}$/. The presence of a shared innovation and of common exception to this innovation would normally be strong evidence for subgrouping. However, a closer look at the data reveals that Tsat nasal post-glottalization seems limited to certain short vowels (PC *a, *ɔ), but applies in all vocalic contexts in Northern Raglai (Brunelle 2019). Furthermore, preplosion and its failure after nasal onsets are common in languages of the area and could thus be treated as areal features: within Chamic, several Raglai dialects whose data were not available to Thurgood (1999) exhibit preplosion, denasalization, and sometimes even a post-glottalization identical to that of Tsat (Brunelle and Jensen, this volume §30.2.5; Lee 1998; Nguyễn 2003); nasal preplosion is even found as far as in the Western Jarai dialect of Cambodia (Brunelle and Jensen, this volume, §30.2.5). Outside Chamic, nasal preplosion is commonly attested in other Austronesian and Aslian languages (Adelaar 1995b; Blust 2013a: §4.3.1.4).

That the two innovations invoked to group Northern Raglai and Tsat do not perfectly match, and that the second is attested in many related languages (and, of course, unrelated ones), suggests that a close re-examination of the Northern Chamic subgroup is needed. Thurgood's arguments are not necessarily wrong, but the inclusion of more exhaustive Raglai dialectal data could lead to a significant reorganization of his Northern Chamic subgroup. In any case, the unnamed node that groups Chru and Northern Chamic in (6) is more questionable. In Thurgood (1999: 44), it is justified by "shared similarities among the nasal vowels" and by a "simple note in Grimes (1988: 615), which states without further comment that Southern Roglai [Raglai] is closely related to Chru and Northern Roglai". Unfortunately, regular correspondences between the nasal vowels of Chru and

Northern Raglai are not established in Thurgood's chapter on 'Nasals and Nasalization'. The fact that Proto-Chamic nasal vowels are preserved in these two varieties is suggestive, but as contrastive nasal vowels also exist in Western Jarai (Brunelle and Jensen, this volume, §3.2.3), this may be a retention rather than an innovation. As for the similarity between Chru and Raglai dialects, it has already been mentioned in the discussion of dialect continua, but it does not entail that other Chamic varieties do not resemble Chru and Raglai.

Turning to Thurgood's Coastal Chamic, there is no reason to question the fact that Eastern Cham and Western Cham form a close subgroup. Mutual intelligibility between all Eastern and Western Cham dialects is strong, even if it can be hindered by the presence of Vietnamese loanwords in varieties spoken in Vietnam and of Khmer loanwords in varieties spoken in Cambodia. All Eastern and Western Cham dialects share unique innovations like register systems largely based on pitch (Brunelle 2009a, 2012; Brunelle and Jensen, this volume, §30.2.4) and the raising of PC *a to /ɨ/ after nasals. What is less solidly established is the grouping of Haroi and the two Cham dialects (Eastern Cham and Western Cham) as Coastal Chamic. Thurgood claims that Haroi is closer to Western Cham than to Eastern Cham because vowel quality plays a significant role in their register systems and because PC *ə corresponds to /ɨ/ in the reflexes of the words *bəŋ 'to eat' and *dəŋ 'to stand' in Haroi and the Western Cham dialect of Kompong Thom (other Western Cham dialects retain /ə/ in these words). Lack of sufficient data about Kompong Thom Cham in Headley (1991) makes it difficult to assess if the correspondence between reflexes of PC *ə is regular. However, it is clear that the register systems of Haroi and Cham are too different to be treated as a shared innovation: not only are the patterns of diphthongization they condition distinct, but the development of Haroi register was accompanied by an aspiration of onset stops that is unattested in Kompong Thom and other Cham dialects (Brunelle 2005b, 2006; Lee 1977; Mundhenk and Goschnick 1977).

The last subgrouping that needs to be discussed in (6) is the split between Highlands and Coastal Chamic. Thurgood (1999) establishes it based on three features of Coastal languages: a greater monosyllabicity, the preservation of a contrast between implosives and voiced stops, and the presence of register. Monosyllabization does not hold scrutiny as a criterion for separating Coastal and Highlands Chamic. Out of the languages of Thurgood's Coastal branch, Colloquial Eastern Cham did become largely monosyllabic (Brunelle 2009b), but there is no evidence that there is more than sporadic monosyllabization in Western Cham and in Haroi. On the opposite, monosyllabization is attested in his Highlands Chamic: Tsat is fully monosyllabic (Thurgood et al. 2014), and there is evidence for monosyllabization in several Raglai dialects (Tạ 2009).

As for the other two criteria, they actually boil down to a single one as the devoicing of voiced stops, which is the primary motivation for registrogenesis, is also what leads to the loss of the contrast between implosives and voiced stops. It turns out that devoicing and registrogenesis do not neatly divide Thurgood's Highlands and Coastal Chamic. Eastern Cham, Western Cham, and Haroi are clearly register languages, but register and obstruent devoicing are also found in Chru and Raglai dialects (Brunelle et al. 2020; Brunelle et al. 2022; Lee 1998; Tạ 2009), and seem to have been an important mechanism in Tsat tonogenesis (Maddieson and Pang 1993). Jarai also shows signs of devoicing and register formation (Jensen 2014).

To summarize this section, most of the Chamic subgroups previously proposed in the literature are in need of a reassessment with more emphasis on exclusively shared innovations. There are currently no strong arguments for the two-way split between Highlands Chamic and Coastal Chamic proposed by Thurgood (1999), or for lumping together Haroi and Cham dialects as an exclusive subgroup. The Northern Cham group is supported by more (though not entirely) regular correspondences, but may need to be reassessed in light of Raglai dialectal evidence that was not available to Thurgood in 1999. As for the group including Chru, Northern Raglai, and Tsat, it is not currently supported by regular innovations, but should nonetheless be taken seriously as Chru and Raglai dialects do appear to form a tight dialect continuum. In the end, the only groups that do not seem controversial are those formed by Eastern and Western Cham dialects and by Jarai and Ede. The latter corresponds to Lee's Northern Chamic and to Burnham's Highland Cham.

## 11.5 Conclusion

In this chapter, I have proposed a critical assessment of previous proposals on the genetic relationship between Chamic and other Malayo-Polynesian languages and between Chamic languages. Based on a review of the literature about the relationship between Chamic and other Malayo-Polynesian languages in §11.2, I suggested that Malayic and Chamic are closely related, even if their exact relation with other Malayo-Polynesian languages of Southeast Asia remains to be worked out. In §11.3, I reviewed the evidence about the exact relationship between Acehnese and Chamic and concluded that Acehnese is probably a sister to Chamic within an Aceh-Chamic group rather than a branch of Chamic. In §11.4, I went over previous phylogenetic classifications of the Chamic family and showed that the evidence for most previously proposed Chamic subgroups is weaker than appears as few of them are supported by uncontroversial phonological and lexical innovations.

CHAPTER 12

# Sulawesi historical linguistics

DAVID MEAD

## 12.1 Introduction

The island of Sulawesi in Indonesia is home to more than one hundred indigenous languages (see van den Berg and Mead, this volume, §33.1).[1] It is uncontroversial that all of these languages belong to the large Austronesian language family. However, ideas about how they are related to one another in a genetic classification—that is to say, how they are best parcelled into subgroups based on criteria that indicate a period of shared historical development—has been a process of discovery. This process in fact took place in two distinct phases.

The first phase, which occurred during the late Dutch colonial period, can be regarded as an inventorying of about sixty languages, many of them newly documented,[2] and developing a reasoned basis for classifying them into more than a dozen subgroups. This phase came to a close with the advent of World War II.

A second phase commenced decades later. With improved data on a full range of languages, new researchers were able to revisit the old subgroupings. Some subgroups were combined, another was split, while a handful of languages were transferred from one subgroup to another. From this process emerged what can be regarded as the ten established subgroups of today: Sangiric, Minahasan, Gorontalo-Mongondow, Tomini-Tolitoli, Kaili-Pamona, Saluan-Banggai, Bungku-Tolaki, Muna-Buton, Wotu-Wolio, and South Sulawesi (see Map 33.1 in van den Berg and Mead, this volume, chapter 33).

I have adopted these two phases as an organizing principle for this chapter. §12.2 discusses the picture of subgrouping of Sulawesi languages that emerged during the Dutch colonial period, principally through the work of Nicolaus Adriani and Hendrik van der Veen. §12.3 discusses the changes that later researchers made to these subgroups, and their reasons for making these changes. A final section discusses the search for higher level relationships between the established subgroups and externally to languages outside of Sulawesi. By providing an overview of the subgroups and the arguments supporting each, I hope the reader will quickly gain an appreciation of the major issues that historical-comparative linguists have faced over the years working with Sulawesi languages.

## 12.2 Historical-comparative work during the Dutch colonial period

The modern era of Sulawesi historical-comparative linguistics begins with the Dutch linguist Nicolaus Adriani. Arriving in Indonesia in 1894, within a year he had joined Alb. C. Kruyt in Poso, Central Sulawesi. Together they made several trips through ungoverned territories to ascertain the borders of the Pamona (or, as then known, Bare'e) language area, opportunities which they used to collect information on surrounding languages. Through these personal forays, communication with missionary colleagues and civil administrators, and accessing archival material[3] and the available literature, Adriani amassed an unprecedented amount of material on the languages of Sulawesi.

The results of Adriani's investigations into language relationships were published as the first part of the third volume of *De Bare'e-sprekende Toradja's van Midden-Celebes* (Adriani and Kruyt 1914). Across 350 pages, he lays out his view of language relationships over almost the whole of the island of Sulawesi. The omission of the 'Philippine' languages of northern Sulawesi (Bolaang-Mongondow and the Sangiric and Minahasan languages) was not due to unfamiliarity.[4]

[1] Three indigenous languages belong to language groups centered outside of Sulawesi and are not considered in this study: Manado Malay; Makassar Indonesian; and Indonesian Bajau.

[2] Only Bugis, Makasar, and languages of northern Sulawesi had a strong research tradition predating the twentieth century; see Noorduyn (1991a) regarding what was known about Sulawesi languages prior to 1900.

[3] Specifically the manuscripts collection of the Bataviaasch Genootschap van Kunsten en Wetenschappen, including hand-written word lists, and materials assembled by the late Dr J. G. F. Riedel.

[4] Prior to his arrival in Indonesia Adriani had published a grammar and text collection of Sangir (Adriani 1893, 1894), and later spent two years in Minahasa assisting the elderly Johannes Schwarz with a Tontemboan text collection and dictionary (Schwarz 1907, 1908).

David Mead, *Sulawesi historical linguistics*. In: *The Oxford Guide to the Malayo-Polynesian Languages of Southeast Asia*. Edited by: Alexander Adelaar and Antoinette Schapper, Oxford University Press. © David Mead (2024). DOI: 10.1093/oso/9780198807353.003.0012

Rather, Adriani felt these languages had been adequately covered elsewhere.[5]

Despite its attempted coverage, Adriani had only a coarse awareness of the languages of western and southeastern Sulawesi. Three years after Adriani's death, van der Veen (1929) provided a needed revision regarding the language situation in western Sulawesi. In fact van der Veen's article was an acknowledged update, seeking to replicate for Toraja Sa'dan what Adriani had done, on a larger scale, for Pamona. His groupings and map thus were designed to integrate with and supplement those published earlier by Adriani. Details regarding the complicated language situation in southeastern Sulawesi, particularly on Muna and Buton islands, however, emerged only decades later (see §12.3.7).

After his death, Adriani's mantle passed largely to his one-time understudy, Samuel J. Esser. Thirty-five years Adriani's junior, Esser was on track to produce deeper studies of languages across a broad swath of central Sulawesi. Publications during his lifetime included treatises on Mori (Esser 1927, 1933), Kaili (Esser 1934), and Kulawi (Adriani and Esser 1939), and a cross-linguistic study of preverbal person markers (Esser 1929). A picture of Esser's wide-ranging interests, which also ran to language relationships, emerges from his reports published posthumously by Noorduyn (1963). As discussed below, not a few of the subgrouping changes made by later researchers were presaged in Esser's writings. However, Esser's promising career was cut short by his death during World War II, and far too many of his unpublished language materials were never recovered.[6]

Two strengths characterize Adriani's research.[7] First, he operated on the conviction that every language had a contribution to make to science, thus even the smallest language was worthy of attention. Second, he adopted a scientific approach to language classification based on 'phonetic laws', that is to say, patterns of regular sound correspondences between languages. The following excerpt is typical of his discussions.

> Normally *j* became *s* [in Lalaki] just as in Bungku and Mori, e.g. *ase* (chin), Bare'e [Pamona] *aje*; *mosa'a* (bad), Bare'e *maja'a*; *mosodo* (poke at), Bare'e *monjolo*; *usa* (rain), Bare'e *uja*; *kasu* (tree), Bare'e *kaju*; *sala* (path), Bare'e *jaya*; *oposu* (gall), Bare'e *apoju*; *oseu* (needle), Bare'e *ijau*, Malay *jarum*. . . . Also not a single example of *nj* is found, nor of *ny*. Malay *ny* is represented by *n*, e.g. *hanuno* (his one), Malay *anunya*; *mo'ana* (plait), Malay *anyam*.
>
> (Adriani and Kruyt 1914: 220–1, my translation)

Languages that exhibited similar patterns of sound correspondences could be considered related. Sometimes he also looked at pronouns, genitive constructions, and verb and noun morphology. What strikes the modern comparativist, however, is his nearly complete lack of reconstructed forms.[8] Furthermore while one can deduce, from his sound correspondences, a set of (conditioned or unconditioned, ordered or unordered) sound changes that must have operated historically to produce present-day forms—one might infer for example: "original Indonesian *ñ* merged everywhere with *n* in Lalaki, Mori, and Bungku"—Adriani seldom stated these changes explicitly. He also rarely expressed language relationships using tree diagrams or other hierarchical structure. Rather it seems his interest was in drawing rings around related languages, and in practice he often emphasized the fuzzy, transitional nature of the boundaries where language groups bordered each other.

Combining Adriani's and van der Veen's results, by 1930 the following picture had emerged of language groups across the island of Sulawesi. Adriani considered the first three groups to be Philippine languages, a topic I return to in §12.4.1.

1. **Sangiric group** (including Bantik and Ratahan spoken on the mainland)
2. **Minahasan group**
3. Bolaang-Mongondow (including Lolak and Ponosakan)
4. Gorontalic group
5. Tominic group
6. West Torajan group (Kaili, Kulawi, Lindu, Uma)
7. East Torajan group (Pamona, Bada, Behoa, Napu, Rampi)
8. **Loinan group** (including Banggai)
9. **Bungku-Mori group**
10. Muna-Buton group
11. Makasar-Bugis group (including Wotu)
12. Sadang group
13. Mandar group
14. Luwu-Masenrempulu group
15. Pitu Ulunna Salu group

[5] For language maps, Adriani directed his readers to the *Taalkaart van de Minahasa* (Brandes 1894), and, for the Sangiric and Talaud languages, the *Taalkaart van Celebes* (Holle 1894). In 1925 he published an overview of the Minahasan languages including a review of the linguistic literature up to that time.

[6] A list of Esser's unpublished language materials, collated by W. Kern, can be found in van Ronkel (1947: 165–8).

[7] A third hallmark was his abiding interest in etymology. His notes on word lists and vernacular language texts often digressed to mention this or that connection between words in different languages.

[8] In Adriani's defense lack of reconstructed forms was broadly characteristic of the infant field of comparative Austronesian studies at that time (Blust 1980c: 2), although Adriani's Swiss contemporary, Renward Brandstetter, was making progress in that direction (e.g. Brandstetter 1906b, 1911).

The four groups that appear in bold (1, 2, 8, and 9) have stood the test of time. In fact each has been the subject of a modern historical-comparative study that has established the genetic validity of the group, its internal subgrouping, and the chain of historical sound changes that lead to present-day forms (respectively Sneddon 1984, 1978; Mead 2003b, 1998). The other groups have had to be amended, and therein lies a tale. Their stories are told below.

## 12.3 Historical-comparative work in the post-independence era

Following Adriani, historical-comparative research on the island of Sulawesi took a half-century hiatus. When it resumed, the new practitioners were able to benefit from advances in the field of Austronesian comparative linguistics that had been pioneered by the likes of Otto Dempwolff, Isidore Dyen, and Robert Blust.

The new era also benefitted from a renewed interest, fuelled in part by survey teams sent out by the Summer Institute of Linguistics, to identify every last language and dialect spoken across the island of Sulawesi. This push included: surveys of Central Sulawesi (Barr and Barr 1979); South Sulawesi (Grimes and Grimes 1987 and several follow-up surveys);[9] a survey of North Sulawesi (Merrifield and Salea 1996); and a survey of the Bungku-Tolaki languages of southeastern Sulawesi (Mead 1999). If Adriani knew of some sixty languages, today that number stands at over one hundred.

In general, Sulawesi historical-comparative work has proceeded in an amicable manner. Most revisions to Adriani's classifications have been regarded as necessary updates based on closer inspection of improved data. Areas of ongoing debate are noted below.

I begin by reviewing studies of the four uncontroversial subgroups, highlighting some of their principal conclusions, before moving on to other cases where changes have been made to Adriani and van der Veen's subgroups.

### 12.3.1 The Sangiric subgroup

Sangiric, the northernmost of Sulawesi's subgroups, comprises five languages. Bantik and Ratahan are spoken on the mainland of northern Sulawesi, Sangir (Sangíhe) and Talaud are spoken in archipelagos to the north of mainland Sulawesi, while Sangil is spoken in the southern Philippines.

[9] Follow-up surveys can be found in the two volumes edited by Timothy Friberg (1987, 1991); see also the summary by Friberg and Laskowske (1989).

Sneddon (1984) places Sangir, Sangil, and Talaud in a northern group, particularly as all three languages exhibit metathesis of *t* and *s* (e.g. Proto-Malayo-Polynesian (PMP) *Ratus 'hundred' > Sangir *hasuʔ*, Sangil *rasuʔ*, Talaud *z̥asutta*). On somewhat slimmer evidence he placed Bantik and Ratahan in a southern group (Sneddon 1984: 54–7).

A number of changes characterize the Sangiric languages as a whole. A partial list includes: lowering of PMP *i and *u preceding final *q; replacement of *ə in final syllables by another vowel (but sometimes retention of *ə when preceded by a laryngeal); vowel dissimilation of *-$V_1$q$V_1$- to *-$V_1$qə-; vowel dissimilation of *-a$C_1$a$C_2$ > *-a$C_1$e$C_2$ provided $C_2$ was alveolar or dental; nasal assimilation or consonant cluster reduction in repeated monosyllables, often with shift of the penultimate vowel to schwa; loss of PMP *q and *h; and shift of final *a to *e in certain pronominal forms. Selected examples are given in Table 12.1; see Sneddon (1984: 5ff.) for further discussion and examples.

**Table 12.1** Reflexes of selected PMP etyma in Proto-Sangiric

| PMP | Proto-Sangiric | |
|---|---|---|
| *qatəp | *qatup | 'roof' |
| *hikət | *ikit | 'tie' |
| *uliq | *ule | 'return' |
| *bunuq | *buno | 'kill' |
| *puqun | *puən | 'trunk' |
| *Raqan | *Raən | 'light (in weight)' |
| *habaRat | *baRet | 'west wind' |
| *zalan | *dalen | 'road' |
| *bunbun | *bumbun | 'heap' |
| *diŋdiŋ | *dəndiŋ | 'wall' |
| *bulbul | *bəbul | 'pluck' |
| *kiskis | *kəkis | 'scrape' |

In addition to his discussion of sound changes, Sneddon's study includes more than fifty pages of Proto-Sangiric lexical reconstructions.

### 12.3.2 The Minahasan subgroup

The Minahasan subgroup comprises five languages spoken on the mainland near the tip of Sulawesi's northern peninsula. The three northernmost languages, Tonsea, Tondano, and Tombulu, are closely related, followed by Tontemboan, and finally Tonsawang, lexically and morphologically the most divergent of the Minahasan languages. Sneddon's 1978 investigation of historical sound change in the Minahasan languages supports this classification.[10]

When looking for outside witnesses for Proto-Minahasan reconstructions, Sneddon often resorted to Zorc's *Proto-Philippine Finder List* (1971a) as a matter of convenience, while taking a neutral position on whether the Minahasan languages were Philippine languages in a genetic sense (Sneddon 1978: 11, 15). Sneddon characterized his own work as a detailed comparative analysis of a small set of closely related languages, determining its internal relationships and reconstructing the parent language's sound system and lexicon.

Later Sneddon (1989: 5) highlighted two innovations which he felt made a strong case for establishing Minahasan as a valid genetic group: (a) the metathesis of initial PMP *R with a following vowel, e.g. *Ramut > *ahmut 'root' (note: PMP *R shifted to *h in Proto-Minahasan); and (b) a somewhat complicated pattern whereby schwa either harmonized with a neighbouring vowel or shifted to a mid-front vowel under influence of a contiguous laryngeal (*h, *ʔ). Examples of harmonization (always next to a *medial* laryngeal) are *tuqəD > *tuʔud 'stump' and *bəRas > *bahas 'husked rice'; examples of shift to a mid-front vowel are *saləR > *saleh 'floor', *ləməq > *ləmeʔ 'weak', and *kəRət 'cut; reap' > *kehet 'tap sugar palm'. Also significant in my opinion is the split of PMP *j, which merged with *d finally and following schwa but was retained elsewhere (for which Sneddon writes $*r_2$) (Sneddon 1989: 98); examples include PMP *luluj > *lulud 'shin', *səjəm > *sədəm 'ant', *qapəju > *apədu 'gall; bile', *ŋajan > $*ŋar_2an$ 'name', *ijuŋ > $*n\text{-}ir_2uŋ$ 'nose', and *kuja > $*kur_2a$ 'how'. Changes of a more mundane nature which distinguish Proto-Minahasan from Proto-Malayo-Polynesian, however, were left unaddressed.

### 12.3.3 The Saluan-Banggai subgroup

One of the principal results of Mead's (2003b) investigation of the Saluan-Banggai subgroup (i.e. Adriani's Loinan group) is that Banggai should be included within it—despite its low percentage of shared lexicon, and intimations that it was a language isolate or belonged with Moluccan languages. His study outlines twelve sound changes shared by all languages and a further eleven changes which occurred in one or more languages. Balantak and Banggai both exhibit lowering of *u > o preceding final *q and reflect PMP *R as respectively *r* and *l*. They compose an eastern subgroup against the western languages, Saluan, Andio, Bobongko, and Batui, where *R > *Ø-Ø-y. Mead's paper lacks Proto-Saluan-Banggai reconstructions and failed to address certain vowel changes (vowel harmonization) in Balantak.

### 12.3.4 The Bungku-Tolaki subgroup

The fifteen languages of the Bungku-Tolaki subgroup (i.e. Adriani's Bungku-Mori group) are spoken across mainland southeastern Sulawesi, some of its offshore islands, and into neighbouring areas of Central Sulawesi. Based on sound changes and other innovations, Mead (1998: 117ff.) divides these languages into eastern and western branches. Surprisingly this division crosscuts the Mori area: Mori Bawah is more closely related to Bungku, Wawonii, Kulisusu, and Moronene than it is to its presumed sister languages, Mori Atas and Padoe, which group instead with Tolaki. Another unexpected result: while all present-day Bungku-Tolaki languages are vocalic, there is internal evidence for reconstructing reflexes of nearly all PMP word-final consonants (Mead 1996, 1998: 71ff.). Final consonant loss must be an areal feature. Besides the fate of final consonants, Mead identifies more than fifteen other sound changes which distinguish Proto-Bungku-Tolaki from its Proto-Malayo-Polynesian ancestor (Mead 1998: 20ff.), and appends a list of Proto-Bungku-Tolaki reconstructions.

Four of the more interesting changes which characterize all Bungku-Tolaki languages and are reconstructed for the protolanguage are (a) split of PMP *s into *s and *h without discernible conditioning environment (e.g. *siku > *hiku 'elbow', *siwa > *sio 'nine', *isi > *ihi 'flesh', *ŋisi > *ŋisi 'tooth'); (b) subsequent unconditioned shift of PMP *z to *s (e.g. *zalan > *salaɴ 'road', *qazay > *ase 'chin'); (c) shift of PMP *w to *h word initially but lost word medially (e.g. *walu > *halu 'eight', *sawah > *saa 'python'); and (d) loss of initial PMP *R with vowel fronting (e.g. *Ratus > *etu° 'hundred', *Rusuk > *ihuQ 'rib', *Rəkən > *ekoɴ 'base for cookpot'). The first two changes (among others) link the Bungku-Tolaki and Muna-Buton languages, while the second two changes are unique to Bungku-Tolaki (but see further §12.3.7).

[10] This classification differs only slightly from one given by Adriani (1925), who had posited a closer relationship between Tontemboan and Tonsawang.

### 12.3.5 Gorontalo and Mongondow

Gorontalo and Mongondow are two of the major languages of northern Sulawesi. Adriani classified these languages separately, placing only Mongondow within his Philippines group. However Charles noted "striking similarity in the vocabularies and (to a point) in the phonological histories of Mongondow and Gorontalo" (Charles 1974: 487). When discussing historical sound change in Gorontalo, Noorduyn (1982) considered it a given that Gorontalo and Mongondow were closely related.

Historical-comparative work on the Gorontalo-Mongondow languages was carried out by the Indonesian linguist Hunggu Tadjuddin Usup in a series of articles (Usup 1981a, b, 1984) that culminated in his 1986 doctoral thesis. As summarized in Sneddon and Usup (1986: 410), sound changes that characterize the Gorontalo-Mongondow languages as a whole are the shift of PMP *ə > *o (e.g. *qatəp > *qatop 'roof', *ənəm > *onom 'six'); consonant cluster simplification, including nasal assimilation (e.g. *bulbul > *bubul 'body hair', *kiskis > *kikis 'scrape', *kəmkəm > *koŋkom 'handful'); and the shift of PMP *a > *ə > *o in repeated monosyllables (e.g. *tadtad > *totad 'chop up'). Sneddon (1989: 86) adds ten potential lexical innovations unique to Gorontalo-Mongondow.

Following in the steps of Adriani and Kruyt (1914: 192), Usup promoted a further subclassification of Gorontalic languages into an eastern group comprising Kaidipang, Bolango, Atinggola, Suwawa, and Bintauna, and a western group comprising Gorontalo and Buol.[11] However, a closer investigation (Sneddon and Usup 1986) revealed that most sound changes must have diffused across the Gorontalic area, and therefore cannot be used for subgrouping in a genetic inheritance model. In addition, Lolak, at one time known as 'Old Mongondow' (Wilken and Schwarz 1868: 189), was treated by Usup as a Mongondowic language. However Sneddon (1991) argues that Lolak is better considered a Gorontalic language that has borrowed heavily from Mongondow.

Significant works beyond those mentioned above include Lobel's reconstruction of Gorontalo-Mongondow pronominal forms, and his presentation of Ponosakan phonology from a historical perspective (Lobel 2011, 2015).

### 12.3.6 Wotu and the Wotu-Wolio languages

The small Wotu language is spoken at the head of the Gulf of Bone. Throughout most of the twentieth century, researchers were misled by Wotu's geographic location, and debated whether it was more closely related to Pamona or to Bugis. Adriani (1898: 150) noted that Wotu shared some points of similarity with Bugis, and others with Pamona, without coming to a firm conclusion, but he later classified it with Bugis (Adriani and Kruyt 1914: 353). Esser (1938) included Wotu with Pamona in his 'Toraja' group, but later reversed himself (Esser 1961: 385). Salzner (1960) classified Wotu as a South Sulawesi language. Mills (1975a: 604–12) favoured a connection with Pamona, with apparent South Sulawesi features via later influence from Bugis. Sneddon (1983: note 9) simply cited the opinion that data did not allow Wotu to be classified.[12] Only after the lexicostatistical study by Grimes and Grimes (1987: 62) was it recognized that Wotu's closest affinities lay instead with Wolio and other languages of the (as then known) Muna-Buton group.

Sirk concurred with this classification, but felt the Muna-Buton group could not be maintained as it was conceived at the time: "What seems much more likely is that Wotu, Laiyolo and Wolio, possibly with some unknown dialects of Buton, etc., constitute a separate group which does not embrace Muna" (Sirk 1988: 11). This was confirmed by Donohue (2004a). Comparing the reflexes of PMP *b, *ə, *j, *q, *R, *z, *w, *-uy, and *-iq in nine languages, he concluded that five—Wotu, Wolio, Kamaru, Laiyolo, and Kalao—should be removed from Muna-Buton and placed in their own group, which he termed the Wotu-Wolio languages. This move was necessary and has not been disputed since.

No definitive internal classification of the Wotu-Wolio languages exists. However it is generally assumed that Wolio and Kamaru (both spoken on Buton Island) share a closer relationship to each other than they do to any of the other languages, and likewise for Kalao, Laiyolo, and Barang-Barang (spoken on or near the southern tip of Selayar Island, together sometimes referred to as the Kalao subgroup).

### 12.3.7 Internal subgrouping of the Muna-Buton languages

As for the remaining Muna-Buton languages, notably it took linguists a number of years to gain an appreciation of their diversity. Adriani knew of only four languages: Muna, Tukang Besi (his 'Wandji'), Bonerate, and Cia-Cia (his 'Binongko'), the latter two of which he left unclassified (Adriani and Kruyt 1914: 242, 265–72, 353–4). Esser (1938) reported the same four languages. Anceaux (1978) recognized two additional languages, Pancana and Lasalimu,[13] while van den Berg (1991a) added Liabuku, Kioko, Kambowa, Busoa, and Kaimbulawa. Donohue (2000) brought to light the significant split between northern and southern Tukang Besi and

[11] For locations of these languages, see the maps in Sneddon and Usup (1986: 408) and Sneddon (1991: 300).

[12] On the position of Wotu, see also Noorduyn (1991a: 134) and Donohue (2004a: 25).

[13] Supporting data published posthumously (Anceaux 2016).

(1)

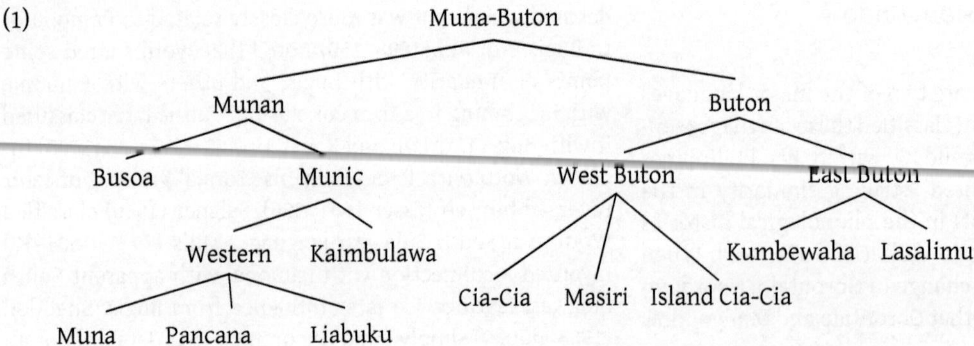


the relationship of both to Bonerate, and later was the first (Donohue 2004a) to report on the Kumbewaha language. Finally Mead (2017) argues for elevating Kaisabu from (previously underdescribed) Cia-Cia dialect to separate language. Against this background, it is unsurprising that a comprehensive historical-comparative study of the Muna-Buton languages has yet to be undertaken.

The only internal classification of the Muna-Buton languages to date is one advanced by Donohue (2004a: 33), shown in example (1). But it lacks supporting evidence, and several languages were omitted, including Tukang Besi, Bonerate, Kioko, Kambowa, and Kaisabu.[14]

Van den Berg (2003) addressed the position of the Tukang Besi languages (including Bonerate). He concluded that they share nine sound changes with other Muna-Buton languages, but are distinguished by their reflexes of PMP *R (*h* in Tukang Besi, but *y with subsequent vowel colouring and loss in other Muna-Buton languages), *j (lost via *y in both groups, but only the other Muna-Buton languages exhibit vowel colouring), and *-uy (Tukang Besi *-u*, other Muna-Buton languages *-i*). See Table 12.2.

Accordingly van den Berg proposed that the first split was between the Tukang Besi languages and the rest of Muna-Buton (a group which he calls Nuclear Muna-Buton).

Within Nuclear Muna-Buton, I am confident about Donohue's Butonic branch. Languages in this group (Kaisabu, Cia-Cia, Kumbewaha, and Lasalimu) are united by the split of *q into *k (preceding *i and *u) and *h (elsewhere), with the subsequent loss of *h in Lasalimu. Van den Berg (1991c: 311–12) noted this sound change in Cia-Cia, but it can be demonstrated for the other languages as well. See Table 12.3.

The existence of a Munan branch along Donohue's lines requires additional study before it can be established. Van den Berg is to be commended for his pioneering work (1991a, b, 2001, 2003), and his list of "sporadic sound changes within the Muna-Buton group" (van den Berg 2003: 96–7) could even be viewed as a roadmap to future work. However, as of this writing, there are no published sources of data for Kaimbulawa or Liabuku, and only minimal data for Pancana. These gaps will have to be filled before the story of sound change and subgrouping within Muna-Buton can be fully elucidated.

[14] He apparently would also elevate Masiri and Island Cia-Cia (Adriani's 'Binongko') to language status.

**Table 12.2** Reflexes of PMP *R, *j, and *-uy in Tukang Besi and other Muna-Buton languages

| PMP | *daRaq 'blood' | *ŋajan 'name' | *qulej 'worm' | *babuy 'pig' |
|---|---|---|---|---|
| Proto-Muna-Buton | *raRa | *ŋaya | *quloy 'snake' | *wawuy |
| Tukang Besi | *raha* | *ngaa* | *ulo* | *wawu* |
| Cia-Cia | *rea* | *ngea* | *kule* | *wawi* |
| Muna | *rea* | *nea* | *ghule* | *wewi* |

**Table 12.3** Reflexes of PMP *q in Butonic languages

| PMP | *quhun 'mushroom' | *taqi 'excrement' | *qabu 'ashes' | *paqa 'thigh' |
|---|---|---|---|---|
| Kaisabu | *kuu* | *taki* | *habu* | *paha* |
| Cia-Cia | *kuʔu* | *taki* | *habu* | *paha* |
| Kumbewaha | *kuʔu* | *taki* | *habu* | *paha* |
| Lasalimu | *kuʔu* | *taki* | *awu* | *paa* |

As stated above, van den Berg adduced nine shared sound changes as evidence for linking the Tukang Besi languages with the remaining Muna-Buton languages. However most of these changes are shared with the Bungku-Tolaki languages. When one asks, on what basis is Tukang Besi linked with Muna-Buton, vis-à-vis Bungku-Tolaki, the evidence from sound change amounts to: (a) loss of final consonants (presumed for the Tukang Besi and Muna-Buton ancestor, but known to be an areal feature in Bungku-Tolaki); and (b) loss of PMP *w initially, vs. shift to *h in Proto-Bungku-Tolaki (Mead 2003a: 123–4). In fact evidence advanced for the last change in Tukang Besi consists to date of only two forms of the numeral eight, cf. Tukang Besi, Muna *oalu*, Tolaki *hoalu* (free form) (< PMP *wawalu), and Tukang Besi, Muna *alu*, Tolaki *halu* (form used in numeral compounds) (< PMP *walu). This is thin evidence indeed. Beyond this, a distinction between realis vs. irrealis nominative markers is present in Tukang Besi and all Muna-Buton languages (van den Berg 2003: 98ff.; van den Berg and Mead, this volume, §33.6.4), but is absent in Bungku-Tolaki languages. Demonstrating that this distinction can be reconstructed for the parent language and is not just an areal feature would strengthen the case for including Tukang Besi with Muna-Buton.

### 12.3.8 Ledo and the Wotu-Wolio languages

In a 1939 report, Esser referred to "similarities that had earlier been identified between Wotu and Ledo (the principle dialect of Kaili)" (Esser, cited in Noorduyn 1963: 358–9, my translation)—but mentioned no specifics beyond their negative terms (respectively *laedo* and *ledo*). Given their geographical separation—Wotu at the head of the Gulf of Bone, and Ledo centred around Palu Bay on the Makassar Strait—a connection between these languages would indeed be curious.

Recently more examples were adduced by van den Berg (2008: 101–4), and the issue is fully addressed in Zobel (2020). Similarities include the reflex of penultimate *ə as /a/ in Wotu-Wolio languages and Ledo, where other Kaili-Pamona languages (including other Kaili dialects) have /o/; the reflex of PMP *z as /d/, where other Kaili-Pamona languages have /ʤ/;[15] and the retention of initial *b where other Kaili-Pamona languages shifted to /w/. The forms in Table 12.4 are exemplary; Pamona is used in this data set to represent other Kaili-Pamona languages.

Looking primarily at vowel correspondences, van den Berg (2008: 103–4) thought that similarities between Ledo

[15] But independently also /d/ in Kulawi, Lindu, and Sedoa, and often Uma (Martens 1997).

**Table 12.4** Reflexes of PMP *ə, *z, and *b in Wotu, Wolio, and Ledo vs. other Kaili dialects and Pamona

| PMP | *təŋaq 'middle' | *kəna 'strike' | *təlu 'three' | PCel *qəli 'buy' |
|---|---|---|---|---|
| Wotu, Wolio | *tanga* | *kana* | *talu* | *ali* |
| Ledo | *tanga* | *kana* | *talu* | *ali* |
| other Kaili dialects | *tongo* | *kono* | *tolu* | *oli* |
| Pamona | *tongo* | *kono* | *togo/tou* | *oli* |
| **PMP** | *zəlay 'Job's tears' | *zilaq 'tongue' | *quzan 'rain' | *qazay 'chin' |
| Wotu, Wolio | *dale* | *dila* | *uda* | *ade* |
| Ledo | *dale* | *dila* | *uda* | *ade* |
| other Kaili dialects | *jole* | *jila* | *uja* | *aje* |
| Pamona | *jole* | *jila* | *uja* | *aje* |
| **PMP** | *bulan 'moon' | *bibiR 'lips' | *babuy 'pig' | *bulu 'feather' |
| Wotu, Wolio | *bula* | *biwi* | *bawu* | *bulu* |
| Ledo | *bula* | *biwi* | *bawu* | *bulu* |
| other Kaili dialects | *wula* | *wiwi* | *wawu* | *wulu* |
| Pamona | *wula* | *wiwi* | *wawu* | *wulu* |

and the Wotu-Wolio languages could be explained by influence, at an early stage, from South Sulawesi languages. Zobel (2020: 318–19) proposed that Ledo be joined to the Wotu-Wolio subgroup, suggesting that Ledo has characteristics of a mixed language: a predominant Wotu-Wolio substratum in vocabulary, but grammar matching surrounding languages.

Without seeking to diminish Zobel's conclusions, it may nonetheless be premature to move Ledo into the Wotu-Wolio subgroup. First there is the theoretical question of how mixed languages are to be classified—to wit, is Ledo primarily a Kaili language that has been relexified, or a Wotu-Wolio language that has been regrammaticalized? Second, the opposition between 'Ledo Kaili' and 'other Kaili varieties' is more complex than indicated by Table 12.4. For example both Ledo and Doi use *biwi* 'lips' (other Kaili varieties: *wiwi*); in addition to Ledo *uda* 'rain' one also encounters *uda* in the Doi, Edo, Ado, Tado, and Tara varieties of Kaili (elsewhere *uja*) (Evans 1991). It would be instructive—if someone were to undertake a dialect geography study[16]—to determine where isogloss boundaries fall among the sixteen or so known varieties of Kaili. In fact there may not be an easy dividing line between which dialects follow along with Ledo and which do not.[17]

Earlier Esser had proposed to account for the similarities between Wotu, Wolio, and Ledo by emigration to Buton Island and Palu, as recounted in Wotu folktales (Esser 1961: 384; Noorduyn 1963: 359). Seeing as how today the core Wotu-Wolio languages are dispersed along the margins of Bone Bay, present locations must have been attained by a seaward expansion. Possibly this dispersal occurred in the thirteenth century when, according to the archaeological record, Wotu emerged as an early important political centre on the Gulf of Bone (Bulbeck 2000).[18] Zobel (2020: 14) also adduces evidence for a Wotu-Wolio substratum in Mamuju, further confirming the presence of (Proto) Wotu-Wolio speakers along the Makassar Strait.

## 12.3.9 Limola as a Badaic language

Limola—widely known by its Bugis exonym Lemolang—is spoken in the Baebunta area at the confluence of the Baebunta and Rongkong rivers in northeastern South Sulawesi. Limola presents a case similar to Wotu described above: a language geographically separated from its next of kin, influenced by surrounding languages, and initially presenting a puzzle as to its classification.

Limola data was first reported by van der Veen, who saw in it resemblances to Rampi (van der Veen 1929: 93–6). Esser collected data on Limola during visits in 1935 and 1939, but came to a different conclusion: "I have not been able to establish anything more concerning a close link of Rampi' with the Limola language of Waiboenta . . . Limola links up much more closely with Bada'" (Esser, cited in Noorduyn 1963: 355, my translation).

In the wake of World War II and the loss of his Limola texts and notes, Esser's hypothesis was mostly forgotten, and linguists in the new era started over on its classification. Sirk suggested that Limola was possibly an "aboriginal non-South Sulawesi language" (1981: 34). Grimes and Grimes (1987: 53–4) classified Limola as a South Sulawesi isolate on lexicostatistical evidence, while Yamaguchi (2003) argued Limola was likely a Bungku-Tolaki language. Martens (1997) accumulated preliminary evidence—in terms of exclusively shared vocabulary—that suggested Limola related closely to the Badaic languages. Following an in-depth study, Zobel affirmed that both "the phonological history and the basic lexical stock of Limola point at a relation to the Badaic languages" (Zobel 2017b); see Table 12.5.[19] Today the Badaic heritage of Limola can no longer be doubted.

**Table 12.5** Lexical items (both retentions and innovations) with identical or near-identical forms in Limola and Bada

| Limola | Bada | |
|---|---|---|
| *vutu-na* | *wutuʔ* | 'elder sibling' |
| *ovase* | *waheʔ* | 'blood' |
| *ile* | *ile* | 'snake' |
| *ikodo* | *kodo* | 'I' |
| *tave* | *taweʔ* | 'leaf' |
| *otampo* | *tampoʔ* | 'earth' |
| *ivoi* | *iwoiʔ* | 'below' |
| *mearo* | *mearo* | 'wake up' |
| *meluu* | *meluʔu* | 'swim' |
| *ilalu* | *ilalu* | 'inside' |
| *opuru* | *puru* | 'bile' |
| *-insa* | *-isa* | 'know' |

Archaeological evidence indicates that the Baebunta area has been continuously inhabited for the past two thousand years (Bulbeck and Caldwell 2000: 65), so it is possible that Limola is indeed a 'relic' language that predates the arrival of speakers of South Sulawesi languages in this part of the island. Based on certain toponyms, Esser felt that Limola must at one time have been spoken more widely (Noorduyn 1963: 352).

## 12.3.10 Revisions to the notion of a South Sulawesi group

Two questions have arisen concerning the South Sulawesi language group: what languages should be included in it, and how are those languages related to each other?

[16] Evans (1991) is a step in this direction. For an overview of Kaili dialects, see Mead (2014).

[17] At any rate it certainly does *not* fall along the lines of how Kaili Ledo is currently defined in the Ethnologue (encompassing Ledo, Tado, Doi, Ija, Taa, Ado, Edo, Rai, Tara, Ta'a, and Kori).

[18] A thirteenth-century expansion also accords with the founding of the Wolio kingdom on Buton Island by Wa Kaa Kaa, traditionally dated to 1311CE.

[19] Data in Table 12.5 has been reproduced directly from Zobel (2017b).

On his language map of the Netherlands East Indies, Esser (1938) introduced—without comment—the notion of a South Celebes group as a combination of van der Veen's Makasar-Bugis, Sadang, Mandar, Luwu-Masenrempulu, and Pitu Ulunna Salu groups. He also included Seko, a language[20] of which van der Veen had been aware, but did not include in any of his groupings. Mills (1975a) accepted this grouping when he set out to reconstruct their common ancestor, Proto-South Sulawesi.[21]

Recently two more groups have been added to South Sulawesi. Adelaar (1994b) has convincingly demonstrated that the Embaloh and Taman languages of central Borneo (with Kalis sometimes recognized as a third language, together the 'Tamanic languages') are, despite their geographic location, genetically South Sulawesi languages closely related to Bugis. Two changes which unite Bugis and Tamanic against the rest of South Sulawesi are the reflex of PMP *j as *s*, and the irregular loss of initial *p in certain lexemes (Adelaar 1994b: 34). Compare Table 12.6.

**Table 12.6** PMP *j > *s* and sporadic loss of initial *p in Bugis and Tamanic

| PMP | *qaləjaw 'sun' | *pajay 'field rice' | *punti 'banana' | *pusuq 'heart' |
|---|---|---|---|---|
| Bugis | *əsso* | *ase* | *utti* | *uso* |
| Tamanic | *aso* | *ase* | *unti* | *usoʔ* |

Second, both Zobel (2017b) and McConvell (unpublished b) remove the Badaic languages (including Limola, see §12.3.9) from Kaili-Pamona and place them in South Sulawesi closely related to Seko. According to Zobel, the changes which unite Seko and Badaic as opposed to the rest of South Sulawesi are merger of PMP *z, *d, and *j as *d-r-ʔ*, and loss of *R in all positions, but only after colouring a preceding *a in the final syllable (PMP *-aR > *-eR > *-e). In addition, schwa in final syllables is regularly reflected as *i* unless affected by a following *p, *m, or *q. However, a few exceptional cases argue that the shift of *ə to *i* occurred after the breakup of Proto-Seko-Badaic.

With the inclusion of Tamanic and Badaic, it is clear that some of Mills' notions about sound change need to be amended.

All South Sulawesi languages exhibit the lowering of PMP *i and *u to PSSul *e and *o preceding final *q. Mills postulated the subsequent loss of *q in all positions as a feature of Proto-South Sulawesi, but in fact PMP *q is reflected as *Ø-ʔ-ʔ* in Bada and Behoa (Martens 1997), as *Ø-Ø-ʔ* in Tamanic (Adelaar 1994b: 5), and as *Ø-Ø-V:* (lengthened final vowel) in Seko (Laskowske 2007). A reflex of PMP *q must be reconstructed for the protolanguage.

All South Sulawesi languages exhibit a reduction in the number of consonant contrasts allowed word finally (Mills 1975b: 212), for example, Makasar *-n*, *-ŋ*, *-ʔ*, *-r*, *-l*, *-s*, Toraja Sa'dan *-n*, *-ŋ*, *-k*, *-ʔ*, Bugis *-ŋ*, *-ʔ*, Bada *-ʔ*. However given the relatively complete set of final consonants found in Tamanic, final consonant loss must be regarded as an areal feature and cannot be used for subgrouping as Mills supposed (1975a: 491).

Taking a broad view of subgroups within South Sulawesi, we can distinguish: (a) in the far north the Seko-Badaic languages; (b) in the south (and in central Borneo) the Bugis-Tamanic languages; (c) further south of Bugis, the Makasaric languages (Makasar, Bentong, Konjo, and Selayar) occupying the southwestern corner of the peninsula and Selayar Island; and (d) between Bugis and Seko-Badaic, a large group, the Northern South Sulawesi languages, that encompasses all the remaining languages.[22] How these groups are related to one another in a genetic classification, however, is at present a matter of debate, with two authors presenting different views.

McConvell's (unpublished b) view is summarized in (2).[23] He argues that Bugis-Tamanic and Makasaric share an immediate common node. He includes Seko-Badaic within his Northern South Sulawesi group, as Mills (1975a: 443) did earlier for Seko.

Zobel (2017b) on the other hand elevates Seko-Badaic to a position coordinate to the other South Sulawesi languages. His view is represented in (3).

The difference between the two amounts to this: McConvell sees affinities between Seko-Badaic and certain languages of the Northern South Sulawesi group, and ascribes those similarities to (closer or more distant degrees of) genetic relationship; Zobel, on the other hand, sees ripples of influence that radiated southward from Seko-Badaic, affecting the Northern South Sulawesi languages over a span of time. Some of the earliest ripples affected Proto-Northern

[20] In actuality a complex of four languages: Seko Padang, Seko Tengah, Panasuan, and Budong-Budong (Laskowske 2007). As noted in Friberg and Laskowske (1989: 8), Talondo' may be a fifth Seko language closely related to Panasuan—Van der Veen (1929: 62–3) in fact had previously identified Talondo' as a Seko-speaking village—but this possibility has yet to be properly investigated.

[21] For a systematic listing of South Sulawesi innovations, Sirk (1989) is a better guide than Mills (1975a, b).

[22] With the possible exception of Mandar, per Mills (1975a), although now it is usually included.

[23] From McConvell (unpublished b). In order to focus on the larger picture, this diagram omits many details regarding his subgroups within Northern South Sulawesi.

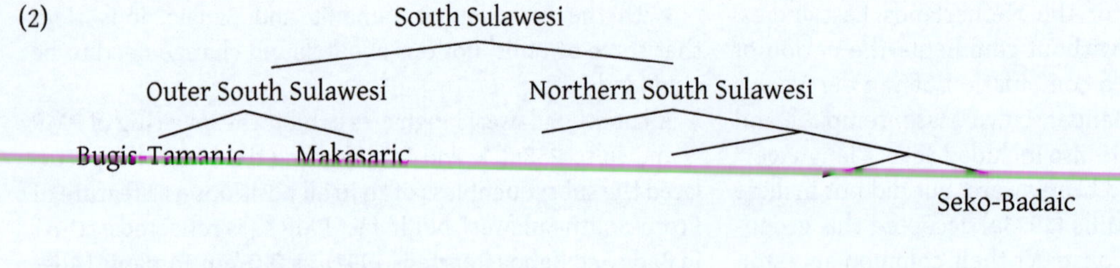


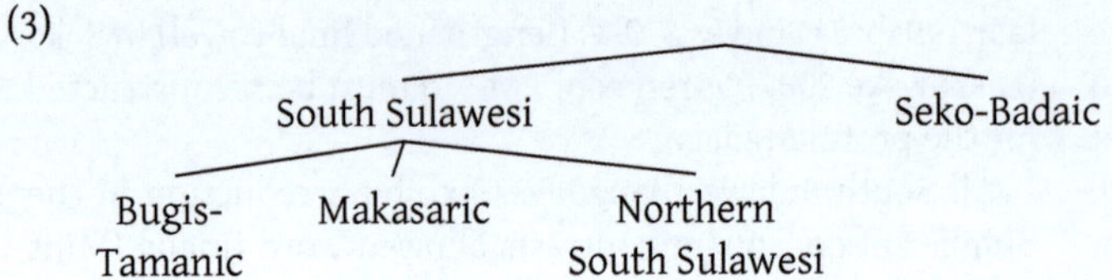


South Sulawesi itself. Unravelling which similarities are the result of genetic inheritance reflecting a period of common development, and which are due to horizontal transmission through contact, will go a long way toward sorting out a classification of the South Sulawesi languages.

## 12.4 The search for higher level connections

From time to time, linguists who have investigated Sulawesi languages from a historical-comparative perspective have turned their attention to the 'big picture': how are the established subgroups related to one another at higher levels? An early proposal by Adriani saw a stream of migration that split near Gorontalo, whereby central, eastern, and southeastern Sulawesi were populated; see Figure 12.1.

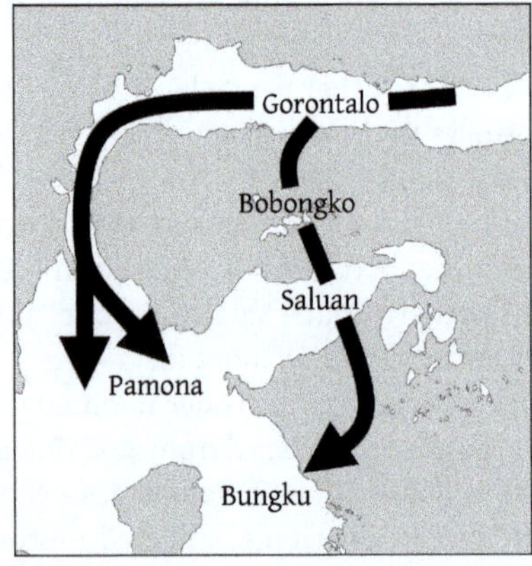


**Figure 12.1** Migration of Austronesian peoples into Sulawesi, per Nicolaus Adriani

In Adriani's own words:

> By its relationship with Bobongko (on the Togian Islands) and Gorontalo, the Loinan language points to a southward migration of the inhabitants of the north half of the northern peninsula, which divided near present-day Gorontalo: the Loinan [Saluan] branch proceeded via the Togian islands to the further shore east of Tanjung Api, spreading thence to the east (Balantak) and to the south (Bungku), while another branch proceeded to the west and then to the south, and then south of the equator a further branch separated back in an easterly direction. So, one may consider that Bare'e [Pamona], as the most eastern extension of this last-named side flow, was arrested up against Loinan.
>
> (Adriani and Kruyt 1914: 89, my translation)

The following subsections discuss recent investigations, including some studies that went looking for higher level relationships but came up empty. Adriani was on to something, but, as emerges below, his hypothesis can be accepted only in part.

### 12.4.1 The Philippine languages of northern Sulawesi

The Sangiric, Minahasan, and Gorontalo-Mongondow subgroups of northern Sulawesi have long been considered Philippine languages.[24] This classification was based on several points of similarity, particularly their rich systems of

[24] The claim that northern Sulawesi and Philippine languages group together goes back at least to Adriani (1893: 1–2), who identified Sangir, Talaud, Bantik, Ratahan, Ponosakan, and Mongondow as Philippine languages, but curiously (and without comment) placed the five Minahasan languages in a 'sub-Philippine' group that stood closer to the other languages of Sulawesi.

verb morphology. Brandstetter (1906a) compared northern Sulawesi languages favourably with Philippine languages in terms of vocabulary, morphology, and retention of final consonants; he also noted *R reflected as /g/ (but conveniently restricted his attention to Mongondow and Ponosakan, as in fact *R had shifted to *h in all his other northern Sulawesi languages). Adriani (1925) mentioned again the rich morphology, also articles, retention of final consonants, and the general lack of palatal consonants in northern Sulawesi and Philippine languages.

At one point Sneddon (1984: 11–12) had proposed that the Sangiric and Minahasan groups shared a close relationship, but five years later reversed himself. Examining the evidence closely, he found no solid basis for linking the Sangiric, Minahasan, or Gorontalo-Mongondow languages closely with each other or in fact with any other language group of Sulawesi. He concluded that "the search for close affinities [of the three North Sulawesi subgroups] must be directed northward, to the languages of the Philippines" (Sneddon 1989: 103).

In 1991, Blust identified the Gorontalo-Mongondow languages as belonging to his newly proposed Greater Central Philippines group (1991b). In a word, the Gorontalo-Mongondow languages are relatively recent arrivals in Sulawesi (circa 500BC) and share closer affiliations with Tagalog, Cebuano, and other Greater Central Philippine languages than they do with any language group on Sulawesi.

There are also grounds for including the Minahasan and Sangiric languages in a broader Philippines group. As confirmed by Sneddon (1989: 97ff.), PMP *d and *z merged in Proto-Sangiric and probably also merged in Proto-Minahasan—although he noted a handful of exceptions where it appears that intervocalic *d shifted to Proto-Minahasan *r prior to *z merging with remaining instances of *d.[25] The merger of PMP *d and *z is characteristic of other Philippine languages and was attributed by Charles (1974: 480) to their common ancestor, Proto-Philippines. Normally a single change of this general nature—which has also occurred elsewhere in the Austronesian language family—would be considered of low diagnostic value for defining a subgroup. However it has been supplemented with a large body of proposed Proto-Philippines lexical innovations beginning with Zorc (1986) and expanded by Blust (2005a, 2019b) to more than one thousand reconstructions. Whether this evidence will be sufficient to win over past detractors (e.g. Reid 1982; Ross 2005; Smith 2017b) remains an open question. See the lengthier discussion in Zorc, Lobel, and Hall, this volume, §7.4.1.

[25] I reviewed Sneddon's Proto-Minahasan reconstructions (Sneddon 1978: 120ff.) and found more instances of intervocalic PMP *d merging with reflexes of PMP *j and *r (seven) than of it merging with *z (three). Still, the small number of examples makes it difficult to extrapolate that Proto-Minahasan retained a distinction that had been lost in Proto-Philippines. Relevant examples are in Mead (nd b).

### 12.4.2 South Sulawesi

Starting from his work in South Sulawesi, Mills investigated but could find no basis for grouping South Sulawesi languages with the Kaili-Pamona, Bungku-Tolaki, or Muna-Buton groups, which he collectively referred to as the 'Toraja' languages (Mills 1975a: 517–19, 1981: 60). Sirk reached the same conclusion. While Sirk (1981) identified several 'old' lexical items which South Sulawesi languages shared with their neighbours, particularly Kaili-Pamona languages, and structural similarities which they shared with languages of southeastern Sulawesi, he concluded that such similarities merely pointed to a long period of contact.

Ross, however, has suggested that South Sulawesi may not be as distinct from their neighbours to the north as is often supposed, at least typologically. He partially reconstructs a 'Proto-Sulawesi' system of verb morphology, from which South Sulawesi systems could also be derived (Ross 2002a: 462–4). McConvell (unpublished a) reviews the relatively weak phonological evidence for linking the languages of central and southeastern Sulawesi with South Sulawesi languages (e.g. loss of *h*, monophthongization of *-aw and *-ay, nasal assimilation), and adds to it around fifty lexical innovations in support of a group which he calls Central-Southern Sulawesi. Whether a supergroup encompassing all the 'non-Philippine' languages of Sulawesi comes to be accepted remains to be seen.

### 12.4.3 Celebic and the outliers: Rampi, Totoli, and Boano

Mills' notion of a 'Toraja' group embracing the languages across a broad swath of central and southeastern Sulawesi, however, has persisted. Renaming it the Celebic supergroup, van den Berg (1996a: 94) sketched out a reasoned basis for grouping together the Kaili-Pamona, Bungku-Tolaki, and Muna-Buton (including Wotu-Wolio) languages. Mead (2003a) adduced additional evidence allowing the Tominic and Saluan-Banggai languages also to be placed within this group. Internally he posited an Eastern Celebic group comprising Saluan-Banggai, Bungku-Tolaki, and Muna-Buton. More recently Zobel (2020) has proved a close relationship between the Kaili-Pamona and Wotu-Wolio groups (at the same time transferring Ledo from the former to the latter; see §12.3.8), and in a companion paper (Zobel 2017a) argues for placing the Tominic languages alongside Saluan-Banggai in the Eastern Celebic group. Taken together, the picture

(4)

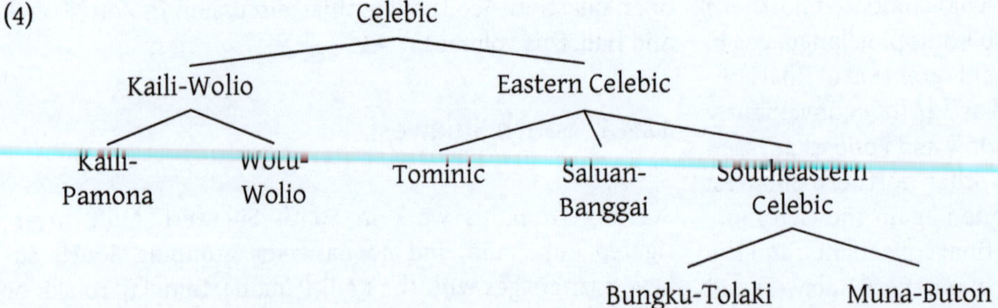


of subgrouping within Celebic that has emerged is given in example (4).[26]

The phonological innovations which distinguish Celebic languages as a whole are shift of PMP *j to *y; consonant cluster reduction; monophthongization of PMP *-ay and *-aw as *e and *o; and shift of PMP *d > *r (Mead 2003b).

As argued by Zobel (2017a, 2020), the two branches below Celebic are distinguished primarily by certain vowel changes. All Kaili-Wolio languages exhibit the merger of *ə and *a in final syllables and the subsequent colouring of this vowel by final *-s and *-R (prior to final consonant loss). Eastern Celebic languages exhibit the shift of *ə to *o in final syllables; the shift of *a to *ə in the antepenultimate syllable; the lowering of *-iq > *eq;[27] and the assimilation of *-au to *oo. Examples are given in Table 12.7.

All present-day Celebic languages have five-vowel systems (*i*, *e*, *a*, *o*, *u*), but have lost inherited schwa in various ways—for example (and at risk of over-simplification) shift to *a* (Ledo and Wotu-Wolio), harmonization with a following vowel (Tominic and Balantak), and shift to *o* (other languages).

In a work of this scope, it would be impossible to trace consonant reflexes in every daughter language. Notably, however, Balantak and all Southeastern Celebic languages exhibit the shift of PMP *z to *s (whereas its usual reflex in other Celebic languages is /ʤ/ or /d/). PMP *q is widely reflected as glottal stop or zero except in Nuclear Muna-Buton, where its reflexes include /ɣ/, /k/, and /h/. Strikingly, outside of Tominic and Saluan-Banggai nearly all Celebic languages have lost final consonants, but this must be regarded as an areal feature (Sneddon 1993; Mead 1996).

If the innovations defining Celebic are accepted as definitive, then three languages must be excluded from Celebic which traditionally have been given a place within it: Rampi, Totoli, and Boano.

[26] With the inclusion of the Tominic languages, spoken in the northwest, the label 'Eastern Celebic' is awkward, but a more suitable cover term has yet to be proposed.

[27] But not the parallel lowering of *-uq > *oq.

**Table 12.7** Reflexes of selected PMP etyma in Proto-Celebic, Proto-Kaili-Wolio, and Proto-Eastern Celebic

| PMP | PCel | PKW | PECel | |
|---|---|---|---|---|
| *səjəm | *səyəm | *səya | *səyom | 'ant' |
| *qatəp | *qatəp | *ataʔ | *qatop | 'roof' |
| *zalan | *zalan | *jala | *zalan | 'road' |
| *təŋəs | *təŋəs | *təŋe | *təŋos | 'wrap' |
| *panas | *panas | *pane | *panas | 'hot' |
| *dəŋəR | *rəŋəR | *rəŋå | *rəŋoR | 'hear' |
| *bəsaR | *bəsaR | *bəså | *bəsaR | 'big' |
| *qaləjaw | *qaləyo | *əyo | *qələyo | 'sun' |
| *bali-an | *balian | *balia | *bəlian | 'shaman' |
| *putiq | *putiq | *putiʔ | *puteq | 'white' |
| *uliq | *uliq | *-uliʔ | *-uleq | 'return' |
| *tau | *tau | *tau | *too | 'person' |
| *dahun | *raun | *rau | *roon | 'leaf' |

### 12.4.3.1 *Rampi*

The Rampi homeland is an isolated highland valley near the border between South and Central Sulawesi, located south of Bada, east of Seko, north of Limola and Luwu', and west of Pamona. Adriani included Rampi with the Badaic languages (his East Torajan Mountain group), but noted its somewhat separate position (Adriani and Kruyt 1914: 133–42, 351). Kruyt (1938) moved these languages to his West Toraja group, at the same time elevating Rampi to its own position, as Martens (1997) also did for Rampi within his Southern Kaili-Pamona group.

Recently the position of Rampi has been reinvestigated by Zobel (2017b) and McConvell (unpublished a), and both concur that Rampi belongs neither with Celebic nor with South Sulawesi. On the one hand, Rampi reflects PMP *j between vowels as *r*, and word finally as glottal stop. This shift unites it with Seko-Badaic, but excludes it from Celebic (where *j > *y and further to zero contiguous to a front vowel); see Table 12.8.

**Table 12.8** Reflexes of PMP *j in Rampi vs. Proto-Celebic

| PMP | *qapəju 'gall; bile' | *t-uaji 'younger sibling' | *laləj 'fly' | *quləj 'caterpillar' |
|---|---|---|---|---|
| Rampi | *poru* | *tuari* | *olaliʔ* | *iliʔ* |
| PCel | *qapəyu | *tuai | *laloy | *uloy |

On the other hand Rampi reflects PMP *-uq and *-iq as *uʔ* and *iʔ*, without exhibiting the vowel lowering that broadly characterizes South Sulawesi languages including Seko and Badaic; see Table 12.9.

**Table 12.9** Reflexes of PMP *-uq and *-iq in Rampi vs. Proto-South Sulawesi

| PMP | *tubuq 'live' | *puluq 'ten' | *putiq 'white' | *uliq 'return' |
|---|---|---|---|---|
| Rampi | *tuwuʔ* | *puluʔ* | *puhiʔ* | *hɨliʔ* |
| PSSul | *tuwoq | *puloq | *puteq | *uleq |

Zobel concludes, "Much more data is needed for a final assessment of the position of Rampi. At the current stage it is clear that it contains at least two strata, one clearly related to Seko-Badaic, the other derived from Proto-Kaili-Wotu-Wolio; and probably also an archaic layer that is only distantly related to its neighbours (Seko-Badaic, South Sulawesi, Celebic)" (Zobel 2017b). Amazingly, even today there is no published description of Rampi phonology (that could for example verify the number of vowel contrasts),[28] and only minimal resources on its word stock.[29]

### 12.4.3.2 *Totoli and Boano*

Totoli and Boano are two closely related languages found at the crook of the neck of northern Sulawesi, where Celebic languages abut the Gorontalo-Mongondow languages. Adriani and Kruyt (1914) included Totoli and Boano in their Tominic group. Recognizing their divergent nature, Himmelmann placed these two languages in a northern subgroup ('Totolic') vs. the remaining ('Tominic') languages, further noting "it remains to be established that all these languages together in fact form a genetic group" (Himmelmann 2001: 20). However Totoli and Boano reflect *-a(h)u- as *au*, and *-iq as *i* and *iʔ* respectively (Zobel 2017a: 2; McConvell unpublished a). These retentions exclude them from Eastern Celebic. See Table 12.10; Tomini is used in this data set to represent other Tominic languages.

**Table 12.10** Reflexes of PMP *-a(h)u- and *-iq in Totoli and Boano vs. Tominic

| PMP | *i-kau 'you' (sg.) | *tau 'person' | *putiq 'white' | *piliq 'choose' |
|---|---|---|---|---|
| Totoli | *kau* | *tau* | *puti* | *pili* |
| Boano | *cau* | *tau* | *putiʔ* | *piliʔ* |
| Tomini | *iʔoo* | *too* | *memeas* | *pile* |

Furthermore Totoli and Boano exhibit the merger of PMP *j and *d as *l*,[30] which would exclude them from Celebic altogether (Zobel 2017a: 2; McConvell unpublished a); see Table 12.11.

**Table 12.11** Reflexes of PMP *j in Totoli and Boano

| PMP | *ŋajan 'name' | *pijan 'when' | *pusəj 'navel' | *bukij 'mountain' |
|---|---|---|---|---|
| Totoli | *ngalan* | *pilan* | *pisol* | *bukil* |
| Boano | *langan* | *pilan* | *pusol* | *bukil* |

On the other hand, Totoli shares a grammatical peculiarity with Bobongko and Saluan, namely that the applicative suffix *-i* alternates with *-an*; examples and details lie beyond the scope of this chapter, but see the summary shown in Table 12.12.[31]

Unless this applicative alternation can be shown to be a retention from a higher level, perhaps Totoli and Boano do not fall so far from Celebic after all.

[28] Adriani reports six vowels (Adriani and Kruyt 1914: 133), while Martens (1997) reports seven with the distinct possibility of dialectal variation.

[29] These are limited to a few word lists (Barr and Barr 1979: 99–101; Wumbu et al. 1986: 109–22; Grimes and Grimes 1987: 98ff; Martens 1997) and whatever lexical material that can be gleaned from the description of Rampi in Adriani and Kruyt (1914: 133–42) and the Rampi texts compiled by Woensdregt (1929).

[30] Presumably through an *r stage; cf. also Totoli, Boano *lui* 'thorn' (< PMP *duRi); Totoli *laa*, Boano *laʔa* 'blood' (< PMP *daRaq); Boano *ulang* 'shrimp' (< PMP *qudaŋ); Totoli, Boano *takol* 'climb' (< PMP *takəd).

[31] See Totoli examples in Himmelmann and Riesberg (2013: 420, and the summary in Table 9). For Bobongko see Mead (2001a: 77–8, nd a). That the same pattern is found in Saluan is from my personal field notes.

**Table 12.12** Contexts in which the applicative suffix *-i* alternates with *-an* in Totoli, Bobongko, and Saluan

| | Realis | Nonrealis |
|---|---|---|
| Actor Voice | *-i* | *-i* |
| Undergoer Voice | *-an* | *-i* |

## 12.5 Conclusions

For over a century, historical-comparative linguists have been refining our notions of how the languages of Sulawesi are related to one another. Collectively this effort has resulted in the identification of ten lower-level groupings. From roughly north to south these are the Sangiric, Minahasan, Gorontalo-Mongondow, Tomini-Tolitoli, Kaili-Pamona, Saluan-Banggai, Bungku-Tolaki, Muna-Buton, Wotu-Wolio, and South Sulawesi subgroups. Six subgroups, cutting a swath from northwest to southeast across the island of Sulawesi, have been shown to be related to each other in a Celebic supergroup (§12.4.3), while the Gorontalo-Mongondow languages have been shown to be related to other Central Philippine languages such as Tagalog and Cebuano (§12.4.1). Still open to debate are whether the South Sulawesi languages link with Celebic (§12.3.2), or the Minahasan and Sangiric languages to a Philippines group (§12.3.1).

At the same time that we have improved our understanding of subgroups and the evidence, particularly from sound change, that supports these groupings, the position of three languages has become less clear. Rampi, spoken in an isolated upland valley near the border between South and Central Sulawesi, appears not to group with either the Celebic or South Sulawesi languages (§12.4.3.1). Unfortunately, even today, materials on Rampi phonology, word stock, and grammar remain on the thin side. Totoli and Boano are two closely related languages spoken in the border area between Celebic and Gorontalo-Mongondow languages; however, they appear not to group with the Tominic languages (where they were traditionally placed) nor even within Celebic (§12.4.3.2).

It should also be noted that while some things have come to light about sound change in the Tominic and Wotu-Wolio languages, there is ample room for small-scale yet detailed comparative analyses that would reconstruct their parent languages and establish internal relationships. The data for a comparative study of Tominic has been available now for two decades (Himmelmann 2001).

While several studies have approached one or another Muna-Buton language from a historical-comparative perspective, a clear understanding of internal relationships within this group has yet to emerge (§12.3.7). Once the requisite data has been procured, this should be a fascinating study. At the same time a minor question should be answered concerning the Tukang Besi languages. Presently considered to be a first order branch within Muna-Buton, the possibility exists they should be elevated to a separate branch within Southeastern Celebic.

For some time it has been known that Mills' (1975a: 490ff.) internal classification of South Sulawesi languages has needed to be reworked. Within South Sulawesi, the Makasaric, Bugis-Tamanic, and Seko-Badaic groupings seem well established, with remaining languages falling into a generally recognized Northern South Sulawesi group. But how these groups relate to each other, or even how the Northern South Sulawesi group is internally structured, remains an open question (§12.3.10).

Beyond these issues, we can of course continue to look for higher-level connections between the South Sulawesi, Celebic, Minahasan, or Sangiric languages that would group them with each other or with subgroups outside of Sulawesi *below* the level of Proto-Malayo-Polynesian. (As noted above, this question has been answered for the Gorontalo-Mongondow languages.) On this search, however, we may have gone as far as investigations of historical sound change can take us. Higher-level relationships will have to be established on other considerations, such as lexical or grammatical innovations.

CHAPTER 13

# Historical linguistics of the Central Malayo-Polynesian languages

ERIK ZOBEL

## 13.1 Introduction

This chapter is about the MPSEA languages of the Lesser Sunda Islands (excluding Balinese, Sasak, Sumbawa), the Moluccas (excluding Halmahera), and a few MP languages spoken along the coast of the Bomberai Peninsula at the western coast of New Guinea. These languages were united in a 'Central Malayo-Polynesian' (CMP) subgroup by Blust (1977a, 1993a), as will be described in §4 below. Central Malayo-Polynesian as a genetic grouping—either as subgroup or as linkage—remains controversial until present. Some scholars dismiss CMP entirely as a subgroup or linkage, and only accept it as an umbrella term for the MP languages (excluding the SHWNG subgroup, cf. Kamholz, this volume, Chapter 14) in a typological and contact area which is referred to as 'East Nusantara' (Klamer, Reesink, and van Staden 2008) or 'Linguistic Wallacea' (Schapper 2015a). This chapter gives an overview of the various proposed CMP subgroups, and evaluates the validity of CMP as a genetically cohesive group. The label CMP will be used in a neutral way, and is not committed to the validity of this grouping as a genealogical unit.

Based on earlier work by Jonker (1918) and others, Esser (1938) assigned the Austronesian languages of the Lesser Sunda Islands, the Moluccas, and western New Guinea to four subgroups: Bima-Sumba, Ambon-Timor, Sula-Bacan, and South Halmahera–West New Guinea, the first three of which correspond to CMP. The border separating Bima-Sumba and Ambon-Timor lies on the island of Flores, between the Lio and Sika speech areas.

The first predecessor of CMP as a single coherent group is found in Dyen's (1965a) lexicostatistical classification of the Austronesian languages. Here, Dyen placed the languages of the Lesser Sunda islands east of Sumbawa (represented by 'Sumba', Hawu, Sika, 'Solor'), southwest Maluku (Leti, Kisar), southeast Maluku–New Guinea (Sekar, Kei, 'Kuiwai'), and the central Maluku ('Ambon', Paulohi, Buru) into a Moluccan linkage. Dyen's overall results were heavily criticized since they failed to reproduce obvious subgroups which were already established based on quantitative evidence (most notably the Oceanic subgroup). His 'Moluccan linkage', however, largely coincides with CMP as later proposed by Blust (1977a, 1983/1984).

In the following discussion, §13.2 presents a list of the smallest uncontroversial units of CMP; §13.3 then discusses some of the major subgrouping proposals that classify the low-level subgroups of §13.2 into larger subgroups. Blust's CMP hypothesis itself is presented in §13.4, together with a critical discussion. §13.5 closes with an outlook for further research in the classification of the CMP languages.

## 13.2 Low-level subgroups within Central Malayo-Polynesian

The following list of low-level subgroups represents the minimal consensus that can be extracted from the major extant subgrouping proposals. Some of the divisions presented here may appear over-atomistic, but they are the result of interlocking classification schemes. The low-level subgroups are presented in four geographical areas, organised in a counter-clockwise direction around the Banda Sea.

| Geographical area | Microgroups |
|---|---|
| 1. Bima-Sumba-Flores | 1. Bima<br>2. Sumba-Hawu<br>3. Western-Central Flores<br>4. Flores-Lembata |
| 2. Timor–southwest Maluku | 1. Rote-Meto<br>2. Helong<br>3. Central Timor<br>4. Tetun-Habun<br>5. Idate-Lakalei<br>6. Kawaimina |

*continued*

Erik Zobel, *Historical linguistics of the Central Malayo-Polynesian languages*. In: *The Oxford Guide to the Malayo-Polynesian Languages of Southeast Asia*. Edited by: Alexander Adelaar and Antoinette Schapper, Oxford University Press. © Erik Zobel (2024). DOI: 10.1093/oso/9780198807353.003.0013

| Geographical area | Microgroups |
|---|---|
| | 7. Makuva |
| | 8. Wetar-Galolen |
| | 9. Kisar Luangic |
| | 10. East Damar |
| | 11. Teun-Nila-Serua (TNS) |
| | 12. Babar |
| 3. Southeast Maluku–New Guinea | 1. Selaru |
| | 2. Tanimbar-Kei |
| | 3. Teor-Kur |
| | 4. North Bomberai |
| | 5. Kowiai |
| | 6. Aru |
| 4. Central Maluku | 1. Banda-Geser |
| | 2. East Seram |
| | 3. Nunusaku |
| | 4. Buru |
| | 5. Sula-Taliabu |

I will restrict myself to a very short characterization of each subgroup, concentrating on unusual sound changes, or sound changes which are generally considered diagnostic for low-level subgrouping. These are for instance reflexes of PMP *d, *z, *j, *R in most CMP areas (these will be discussed in 5.3), and the fate of *p in the languages of the Timor–southwest Maluku area.

## 13.2.1 The Bima-Sumba-Flores area

### 13.2.1.1 *Bima*

Spoken in the eastern part of Sumbawa Island, Bima is the westernmost language included within CMP by Blust. Jonker (1896) stated that Bima is most closely related to the languages of Sumba, and less closely to Hawu; Blust (2008), however, does not find evidence to corroborate this claim, and treats Bima as an isolate branch of CMP.

As a characteristic areal feature of CMP, Bima shows loss of antepenultimate syllables in words such as *liro* < *qaləjaw 'day'; *dolu* < *qatəluR 'egg'. An unusual sound change is the unconditioned split of PMP *t to *t* or *d*. The coronals *d and *z merged to *r* (with a few cases of *d*), while *j split into *r* and *l*.

### 13.2.1.2 *Sumba-Hawu*

The Sumba-Hawu languages include the languages of Sumba (e.g. Kambera, Weyewa), Hawu, and Dhao. This subgroup is based on lexical evidence presented by Blust (2008).

Hawu and Dhao are notable for the retention of *z as a distinct palatal implosive *f*, as in *fara* 'road' < *zalan.

### 13.2.1.3 *Western-Central Flores*

This subgroup consists of two branches, Western Flores and Central Flores. Lexical and phonological evidence for Western-Central Flores is presented by Fernandez (1990, 1996) and Schmidt (2014). The Western Flores languages comprise Komodo, Manggarai, and a number of smaller languages spoken directly to the east of Manggarai (e.g. Rembong). The Central Flores branch includes, for example, Ende, Lio, Ngadha; the most divergent member is Palu'e.

In almost all Western-Central Flores languages, the coronals *d/*z/*j have merged, with reflexes ranging from *s* (Manggarai), *z* (Rembong, Ngadha), to *r* (Komodo, Ende). The only exception is Lio, which has a distinct reflex of *z/*j as lamino-palatal *dʒ*, next to *r* from *d (Elias 2018). PMP *R retained a distinct reflex, but often merges with *d in individual languages (e.g. Lio).

### 13.2.1.4 *Flores-Lembata*

Flores-Lembata comprises Sika, Kedang, and the Lamaholot lects. Fricke (2019) divides the latter into three branches, Western, Central, and Eastern Lamaholot. The status of the Lamaholot varieties as dialects of a single language or multiple individual languages is disputed, but Lamaholot is uncontroversial as a classificatory unit that excludes Sika and Kedang.

Sika is the westernmost MP language that displays three typical areal features of CMP languages: (a) preposed possessors; (b) phonetic merger of personal subject prefixes with the verb stem, resulting in initial consonant variations such as *tani* ~ *dani* 'cry'; and (c) metathesis of high vowels into following syllables across morpheme boundaries. While the former two are regular features of Sika's synchronic structure, the latter only has a fossilized reflex with the verb *ʔa* 'eat' (e.g. *goa* < *mkua < *mu-kan 'you (sg.) eat', *gea* < *mkia < *mi-kan 'you (pl.) eat').

The PMP coronals *d/*z/*j all merge to Proto-Flores-Lembata *d, while PMP *R retains a different reflex.

## 13.2.2 The Timor–southwest Maluku area

This section is based on Mills (1991), Taber (1993), Hull (1998), van Engelenhoven (2009, 2010a), and Edwards (2018a). Since these proposals show significant differences in many important details, I have chosen to present the low-level subgroups of this area in a very fine-grained way.[1]

#### 13.2.2.1 *Rote-Meto*

This group is discussed in detail by Edwards (2018a, b). Geographically, it is divided into the Rote lects spoken on Roti, and the Uab Meto lects spoken in western Timor. The Rote cluster can be divided into two branches, West Rote and East Rote, each of which shares features with the Meto cluster which are not found in the other branch. Edwards explains this with an initial split of Rote-Meto into Meto + West Rote as one branch and East Rote as another branch, and subsequent diffusion of East Rote features into Meto.

The PMP coronals *d/*z/*j show a complex distribution of reflexes in Proto-Rote-Meto as reconstructed by Edwards: *d and *z always have distinct reflexes: PMP *z became *ɗ in all positions, while PMP *d became *d initially and *r medially. PMP medial *j has split into two reflexes: either it merged with PMP *z to *ɗ, or it became *d (thus displaying the same reflexes as *initial* *d). PMP *p weakened to *h, while *R became zero.

#### 13.2.2.2 *Helong*

Helong is spoken in the area around Kupang in western Timor. Although it is located between Rote and Uab Meto, it is clearly distinct from Rote-Meto (Edwards 2018c).

As in Flores-Lembata, the PMP coronals *d/*z/*j merged; *R underwent a split into *l* and zero. Unusual features in the areal context are the retention of the velar nasal *ŋ, and the devoicing of *w to *f* or *p*, depending on dialect.

#### 13.2.2.3 *Central Timor*

The Central Timor subgroup was proposed by Edwards (2019), and comprises Kemak, Tokodede, Mambae, and Welaun. Their most distinctive feature is that *ŋ became a stop (Kemak, Tokodede, Mambae: *g*; Welaun: *k*).

The PMP coronals *d, *z, *j remained distinct: *z shifted to *s* (although there are few instances where it became *d* or *r*), *j to *l*, and *d to *r* (e.g. Kemak *usa* < *quzan 'rain', *pila* < *pija 'how many', *rae* < *daRəq 'earth'). *R was lost in Kemak, Tokodede and Welaun, but was partially retained as *r* in Mambae (e.g. *lara* < *daRaq 'blood').

Welaun takes a special position among the Central Timor languages. In Welaun, *p became *h* (unlike the other Central Timor languages, where it became *p* or *f*), and *ə became *o* (as in Tetun-Habun, whereas most other languages in the Timor–southwest Maluku area have *e*), for example, *loka* < *dəŋəR 'hear' (cf. Kemak *rega*).

#### 13.2.2.4 *Tetun-Habun*

Hull (1998) proposed the Tetun-Habun group, although he notes that their shared history might be the result of Tetun influence on Habun. Since this grouping has not been contested, it is tentatively adopted here.

A characteristic feature of Tetun-Habun is the reflex of *ə as *o*, against near-universal *e* in all other languages of the Timor–southwest Maluku area.[2] In Tetun, the coronals *d and *j merged into *r*, while *z became *d*; *p is mostly retained as *h*, while *R became zero in all positions (Hull 1998, 2000).

#### 13.2.2.5 *Idate-Lakalei*

Hull (1998) proposed a low-order group comprising Idate and Lakalei (called 'Idalaka' by Hull), and this is tentatively adopted here. He further included Idate-Lakalei in his 'Timoric B' group next to Kemak, Tokodede, and Mambae. However, Edwards (2019) does not include Idate and Lakalei in his Central Timor subgroup.

A quick inspection of the Idate data in Hull (1998) indeed shows little agreement with Kemak, Tokodede, and Mambae. On the other hand, it has some features in common with the Wetar and Kisar-Luangic languages, such as loss of *p; non-zero reflexes of *R as *r* (only sporadically so in Central Timor); and *n* for *ŋ (which became *k* in Central Timor), which is shared with almost all other languages of the Timor area.

#### 13.2.2.6 *Kawaimina*

The Kawaimina (also called 'Eastern Timor') subgroup comprises Kairui, Waima'a, Midiki, and Naueti. The most notable feature of this subgroup is the occurrence of ejectives, aspirated stops, voiceless and glottalized sonorants, which have emerged through fusion of initial consonant clusters, for example, Waima'a *l̥ai* 'quick' < *pa-laRiw; *wˀai* 'dry in the sun' < *ka-waRi; *tʰaku* 'afraid' < *ka-takut (Schapper 2020a: 400–2).

Apart from these very unusual innovative initial segments, Kawaimina languages show full agreement with Tetun in their reflexes of *d/*z/*j/*R and *p.

[1] Two sets of subgroups are actually 'unnecessarily' detailed, because, as will be seen in §13.3.2., they are never assigned to different higher-order groups in any extant proposal: 1. Rote-Meto, Tetun-Habun, Kawaimina and 2. Kisar-Luangic, East Damar, TNS. I have nevertheless refrained from putting them into two 'macro' low-level subgroups (which could be called 'Nuclear Timor' and 'Nuclear southwest Maluku'), because this would create spurious units that no scholar has actually proposed.

[2] Reflexes other than *e* are only found in Welaun (*ə > *o*), and in West Damar (*ə > *a*).

#### 13.2.2.7 *Makuva*

Makuva was spoken on the eastern tip of Timor. It is one of the few CMP languages and the only language in the Timor–southwest Maluku area which has retained PMP *z as a palatal; *d remained unchanged in initial position, while in other positions, it merged with *j and *R to *r*. Initial *p became *h*, whereas in other positions, it became zero (van Engelenhoven 2009).

#### 13.2.2.8 *Wetar-Galolen*

The Wetar-Galolen subgroup comprises Wetar, a dialect cluster; Galolen with two dialects, one spoken on Wetar island, and one on the northern coast of Timor right across Wetar; it most probably also includes Hresuk and Dadu'a.

Based on the material in Taber (1993), Wetar and Galolen share the shift of *z to *s*, but they went opposite ways with regards to *j and *R: in Wetar, *R merged with *d as *r*, while *j became zero (probably via an intermediate *y, e.g. *nean* < *nayan 'name' < *ŋajan); in Galolen, *j merged with *d as *r*, whereas *R became zero. Hresuk appears to have retained PMP *ŋ as a velar nasal, which makes it the only language to do so in the Timor–southwest Maluku area next to Helong (§2.2.2). All other languages in the area have shifted *ŋ to *n* or a velar stop.

#### 13.2.2.9 *Kisar-Luangic*

This subgroup comprises Roma, Kisar, and the Luangic languages Leti, Luang, and Wetan. It was first proposed as a subgroup by Mills (1991) and van Engelenhoven (1995), although Jonker (1932) had already observed that Leti is most closely related to the other Luangic languages, and a little more distantly to Kisar and Roma.

The most characteristic diachronic feature of Kisar-Luangic is the reflex of PMP *z as a voiceless stop, which merges with *t (the latter became *t* in Luangic and Roma, and shifted further to *k* in Kisar). The other voiced coronals, *d and *j, merged with *R to *r*. Like in all other low-level subgroups of the southwest Maluku islands, *p became zero, and *ŋ merged with *n.

#### 13.2.2.10 *East Damar*

East Damar is spoken on Damar Island next to West Damar (which belongs to the Babar subgroup). It is among the least documented languages in the southwest Maluku area.

A characteristic sound change of East Damar is the merger of *d/*j/*R to *r* (Taber 1993). It is the only southwest Maluku language in which *z has not become a voiceless obstruent, but is reflected as *l* and *r*.

#### 13.2.2.11 *Teun-Nila-Serua (TNS)*

The Teun-Nila-Serua languages, conventionally abbreviated as TNS, were originally spoken on three islands in the Banda Sea, before their speakers were relocated to Seram in the late twentieth century.

Based on Taber (1993) and van Engelenhoven (2010a), characteristic sound changes are the merger of *z and *s to *s* (shared with the Central Timor and Wetar-Galolen languages), and the merger of *d, *j, and *R to *r* in Nila and Serua. In Teun, however, *j and *R were lost.

#### 13.2.2.12 *Babar*

The Babar languages are spoken on the Babar Islands and in the western part of Damar. They were recognized as a subgroup by Taber (1993) based on lexicostatistical evidence, and further supported by phonological evidence by van Engelenhoven (2010a).

All Babar languages share the following sound changes (based on Taber 1993 and van Engelenhoven 2010a): *s became a stop (*d* in the North Babar languages, *t* in the South Babar languages; thus merging with *nd/*nt), and *z became *h* or Ø. As in Teun, both *R and *j became Ø, while *d remained distinct as *r*.

The Babar languages can be divided in two main branches, North Babar (which includes West Damar) and South Babar. Each underwent quite drastic further sound changes. In the South Babar languages, *t became *k* (in some languages also *x*, *ʔ*), and *a was raised to *e*, *o*, or *u* (e.g. Southeast Babar *mox* < *mata 'eye'). In the North Babar languages, final high vowels changed to voiceless obstruents (*i > *s*, *u > *k*, *x*, *ʔ*; e.g. Daweloor *adk* < *asu 'dog', *waws* < *babi < *babuy 'pig').

### 13.2.3 The southeast Maluku–New Guinea area

#### 13.2.3.1 *Selaru*

Selaru (together with the virtually undescribed Seluwasan) is spoken in the southernmost part of the Tanimbar Islands. It is quite distinct from other languages in the area.

The phonological history of Selaru has not yet been systematically studied, except for a preliminary discussion by Mills (1991). It shows only little agreement with its closest neighbours, viz. the Tanimbar-Kei languages, but some common points with Kisar-Luangic, such as the merger of *d, *j, *R to *r*, and the complete loss of *p. PMP *z remained distinct and became *s*.

#### 13.2.3.2 *Tanimbar-Kei*

This subgroup comprises Yamdena, Fordata, and Kei and was established by Mills (1991). The most conservative of the three is Yamdena, while Fordata and Kei are more innovative, and display features only shared among these two.

In Yamdena, *z became *d*, while *j and *R merged with *r as *r*. In initial position, *d merged with *z, but medially, *d became *r*.[3]

#### 13.2.3.3 *Teor-Kur*

Teor-Kur is spoken in the Banda Sea at the border area between the south Maluku and central Maluku areas. It is one of the least documented CMP languages. The only published lexical material is found in Wallace (1962[1869]).

According to Collins (1982a), Teor-Kur has merged *d/*j/*l to *l*, and *z/*R to *r*.

#### 13.2.3.4 *North Bomberai*

The North Bomberai languages Arguni, Sekar, Onin, and Uruangnirin are spoken at the northern and western coast of the Bomberai peninsula in West Papua. Blust (1993a) presented lexical evidence for a link between the North Bomberai languages and Tanimbar-Kei, being most closely related to Yamdena.

#### 13.2.3.5 *Kowiai*

Like the North Bomberai languages (§13.2.3.4), Kowiai is spoken at the coast of West Papua. Not much language data is available (Tismeer 1913 and a wordlist by Roland Walker in Greenhill, Blust, and Gray 2008), but it is sufficient to link Kowiai to the CMP languages, especially to the easternmost languages in the central Maluku area (see §13.2.4).

Kowiai further shows close links - especially lexically - to Irarutu, a hitherto unclassified Central-Eastern Malayo-Polynesian language spoken in the northern part of the Bomberai peninsula (Schapper and Zobel, forthcoming). Some of the lexcial innovations shared by Kowiai and Irarutu are also found in the Banda-Geser languages.

Based on the available data, the following sound changes are noted: *d/*z/*R/*l have merged to *r*, while *j became *s*. The labials *b and *p merged as *f*, while *y became *l*.

#### 13.2.3.6 *Aru*

The fourteen Aru languages are the easternmost subgroup among the CMP languages. They are generally accepted as a coherent subgroup. Lexically, the Aru languages are quite aberrant, as can be seen from their low scores in lexicostatistical studies (e.g. Hughes 1987; Taber 1993). Proto-Aru is reconstructed by Nivens (nd b), and Blust (2014b) gave a detailed outline of the phonological history of one of the Aru languages, viz. Dobel.

In Proto-Aru, *j and *R merged to *R, while *d and *z became *r and *y, respectively. PMP *p is reflected as *ɸ, while *b became *p. Fortition of *b to *p is a very rare sound change among CMP languages, which is elsewhere only found in a small number of Nunusaku languages (Collins 1983a).[4] Most CMP languages have a fricative reflex (*v*, *β*, *f*, *h*) for *b.

### 13.2.4 The central Maluku area

#### 13.2.4.1 *Banda-Geser*

The Banda-Geser languages comprise Banda and the 'Seran-Laut' languages. Banda was originally spoken on the Banda Islands south of Seram. It is now only spoken by two small communities on Kei Besar, which are descendants of survivors of the Banda massacre in the seventeenth century (Collins and Kaartinen 1998). The Seran-Laut languages (Geser, Bati, Watubela) are spoken on the eastern part of Seram and the adjacent Seran-Laut islands.

Collins (1986b) bases this low-level subgroup on one sound change, the merger of *d/*z/*R to *r* (which shifted further to *l* in Watubela). Otherwise, the two branches of this group have little in common: PMP *j merged with *l to *l* in Banda, whereas the Seran-Laut languages display merger of *j and *s to *s*.

A remarkable feature is the retention of PMP *q as *k* in Watubela in all positions (*katlu* 'egg' < *qatəluR, *lalak* 'blood' < *daRaq).

#### 13.2.4.2 *East Seram*

Also proposed by Collins (1986b), the East Seram subgroup comprises Bobot, Masiwang, and the Seti languages.

A characteristic sound change is the merger of PMP *d/*z/*j/*l to *l*, while *R remained distinct from these sounds. The shift of *ŋ to *k* is unusual in the area, only matched by a parallel change in Central Timor (cf. §13.2.2.3).

#### 13.2.4.3 *Nunusaku*

The Nunusaku languages are spoken in western and central Seram, on Ambon, and on adjacent smaller islands. Proposed by Collins (1986b), this large group (consisting of twenty-six languages) corresponds to the 'Sub-Ambon' and 'Sub-Seram' groups posited by Stresemann (1927). The position of a small group of languages in the border area of Nunusaku and East Seram (e.g. Nuaulu, Manusela) is unclear; classified as Nunusaku in Collins (1983a) based on qualitative

[3] Mills has *d > *d*, but the medial reflex *r* is visible in *morip* < *maqudip 'alive', *sire* < *sida 'they'.

[4] In SHWNG languages, the shift *b > *p* is quite common (Kamholz 2014).

evidence, they are assigned to two separate micro-groups in the lexicostatistical SIL surveys (Taguchi 1989; Loski and Loski 1989).

Characteristic sound shifts are the mergers of PMP *z/*d to Proto-Nunusaku *d and of *l/*R/*j to *l.

#### 13.2.4.4 *Buru*

The island of Buru is home to a cluster of closely related dialects. One language which was spoken on Buru but is now extinct was Hukumina. Its exact position in relation to Buru cannot be established due to scarcity of data.

Unlike in most other CMP languages, *d, *z, *j, and *R did not merge in Buru (Collins 1981).

#### 13.2.4.5 *Sula-Taliabu*

Sula-Taliabu comprises the languages of the Sula Islands: Mangole, Sanana, Kadai, Taliabu. Blust (1981d) discusses the phonological history of the Soboyo dialect of Taliabu. Bloyd (2020) presents a bottom-up reconstruction of Proto-Sula, the common ancestor of Mangole and Sanana.

As in Buru, *d, *z, *j, and *R did not merge in Sula-Taliabu (Collins 1981).

## 13.3 Proposals for mid-level subgroups

All low-level subgroups listed in the preceding section are classified by Blust as CMP. Before discussing the evidence for CMP as a whole, in this section I want to present the mid-level subgroups that have been proposed for the languages of the CMP area.

As can be seen from Tables 13.1 to 13.3, there is considerable disagreement in many details, which is partly due to the methodologies employed. For instance, the classifications by Mills (1991), Collins (1981, 1983a, 1986b, and Edwards (2018a) are based phonological evidence, whereas, for example, Chlenov (1980), Hughes (1987), and Taber (1993) employ lexicostatistical scores. Further, most of these studies only cover a restricted geographic area, and thus fail to recognize possible connections with languages outside of that range (e.g. Fernandez 1990; Taber 1993).

### 13.3.1 Proposals for the Bima-Sumba-Flores area

In the Bima-Sumba-Flores area, the major point of disagreement is the position of Bima and the Flores-Lembata languages, whereas a closer link between the Sumba-Hawu and Western-Central Flores languages is generally accepted (Table 13.1).

Esser (1938, following Jonker 1918) placed a major subgroup border between Western-Central Flores and Flores-Lembata languages, putting the former together with Bima and Sumba-Hawu in a 'Bima-Sumba' group and assigning the latter to an 'Ambon-Timor group' which also includes almost all low-level subgroups listed in §13.2.2 to 13.2.4.

Blust (2008) excluded Bima from Esser's Bima-Sumba, but found "limited support" for a closer relation between the remaining languages, viz. Sumba-Hawu and Western-Central Flores.

Fernandez (1990) reconstructs a common protolanguage (Proto-Flores) for Western-Central Flores and Flores-Lembata, but since he does not compare the languages of Flores with external languages, 'Proto-Flores' may well represent a higher ancenstral language from which other languages besides Western-Central Flores and Flores-Lembata could have descended.

Hull (1998), without citing evidence, groups all languages of the Bima-Sumba-Flores area in a 'Florinic' group. Fricke (2019) proposes the same subgroup under the name 'Bima-Lembata', based on a single phonological innovation, viz. the irregular split of PMP *b to Proto-Bima-Lembata *b and *w. Fricke's proposal can be viewed as tentative at best and needs to be corroborated by more solid evidence.

### 13.3.2 Proposals for the Timor–southwest Maluku and southeast Maluku–New Guinea areas

The subgrouping proposals for the Timor–southwest Maluku and southeast Maluku–New Guinea areas will be discussed here together, since there is some overlap

**Table 13.1** Proposals for the Bima-Sumba-Flores area

| | Esser (1938) | Blust (2008) | Fernandez (1990) | Hull (1998) | Fricke (2019) |
|---|---|---|---|---|---|
| Bima | Bima-Sumba | Bima | not discussed | Florinic | Bima-Lembata |
| Sumba-Hawu | | Sumba-Hawu + WC Flores | | | |
| WC Flores | | | Flores | | |
| Flores-Lembata | Ambon-Timor (cf. Tables 2+3) | not discussed | | | |

**Table 13.2** Proposals for the Timor–south Maluku area

<table>
<tr><th></th><th>Esser (1938)</th><th>Chlenov (1980)</th><th>Hughes (1987)</th><th>Mills (1991)</th><th>Taber (1993)</th><th>Hull (1998)</th><th>Edwards (2018a)</th></tr>
<tr><td>Central Timor</td><td rowspan="16">Ambon-Timor (cf. Tables 1+3)</td><td rowspan="8">not discussed</td><td rowspan="12">not discussed</td><td>not discussed</td><td rowspan="7">Timor (no details)</td><td>Timoric B</td><td>Central Timor</td></tr>
<tr><td>Helong</td><td rowspan="4">Timor</td><td rowspan="3">Timoric A</td><td>Helong</td></tr>
<tr><td>Rote-Meto</td><td rowspan="10">Timor-Wetar-Babar</td></tr>
<tr><td>Tetun-Habu</td></tr>
<tr><td>Idate-Lakalei</td><td>Timoric B</td></tr>
<tr><td>Kawaimina</td><td rowspan="2">not discussed</td><td>Timoric A</td></tr>
<tr><td>Makuva</td><td>Arafuric</td></tr>
<tr><td>Wetar-Galoli</td><td>Timor</td><td rowspan="4">Timor > SW Maluku</td><td>Timoric A</td></tr>
<tr><td>Kisar-Luangic</td><td rowspan="5">Moluccan > southwest</td><td rowspan="6">southeast Maluku</td><td rowspan="3"></td></tr>
<tr><td>East Damar</td></tr>
<tr><td>TNS</td></tr>
<tr><td>Babar</td><td>Babar</td><td rowspan="3">Arafuric</td></tr>
<tr><td>Selaru</td><td>Selaru</td><td>not discussed</td><td rowspan="4">not discussed</td></tr>
<tr><td>Tanimbar-Kei[a]</td><td>Moluccan > Yamdena</td><td rowspan="2">Tanimbar-Kei</td><td>Tanimbar-Kei</td></tr>
<tr><td>Teor-Kur</td><td>Moluccan > Kei-Kur</td><td rowspan="2">not discussed</td><td>not discussed</td><td rowspan="2">not discussed</td></tr>
<tr><td>Aru</td><td>Aru</td><td>Aru</td><td>Aru</td></tr>
</table>

[a] Blust (1993a) includes North Bomberai in Tanimbar-Kei.

between these two areas in the extant subgrouping schemes. The major proposals are summarized in Table 13.2.

In Esser's classification, all languages of the two areas were assigned to the 'Ambon-Timor' group (Esser 1938). All later classifications recognize three main 'centres of gravity': one group focusing around the languages of Timor, another one comprising the languages of the Kei and Tanimbar islands, and the Aru languages as a clearly distinct unit recognized by all scholars. Major disagreement is about the position of Selaru and the languages of southwest Maluku.

Based on lexicostatistical methods, Chlenov (1980) posited a 'Moluccan' subgroup, with three branches in the southern Maluku area: (a) southwestern Moluccan (corresponding to Kisar-Luangic, East Damar, TNS, Babar, Selaru); (b) Yamdena; and (c) 'Kei-Kur' (comprising Tanimbar-Kei minus Yandena, and Teor-Kur). Three more branches of 'Moluccan' are located in the central Maluku area (cf. §13.2.4). The languages of Timor are not covered in Chlenov's subgrouping. Hughes (1987) agrees in his classification of the languages of southeast Maluku with Chlenov in grouping Teor-Kur together with Fordata-Kei, which he links in turn to Yamdena.

Like Chlenov, Mills (1991) also groups the languages of southwest Maluku with their neighbours further east, based on a detailed discussion of phonological evidence. He groups Kisar-Luangic and Teun-Nila-Serua together under label 'Barat Daya' (='southwest [Maluku]'), with Selaru as their closest relative (thus agreeing with Chlenov). Barat Daya-Selaru in turn is placed together with Tanimbar-Kei into a 'southeast Maluku' subgroup. The languages of Timor (represented in Mills' discussion by Rote, Meto, Tetun, and Galolen) form a distinct group. Hull (1998) made a similiar division between the languages of Timor and the languages of southern Maluku. He assigned the languages of Timor (including Wetar-Galolen, but excluding Makuva) to two groups, viz. 'Timoric A' or 'Fabronic' (Helong, Rote-Meto, Tetun-Habun, Kawaimina, Wetar-Galolen) and 'Timoric B' or 'Ramelaic' (Central Timor and Idate-Lakalei). The 'Arafuric' languages comprise Makuva and the languages of southern Maluku (excluding Aru).

Taber (1993) presented a lexicostatisical study of the languages of southwest Maluku. It was the first systematic and comprehensive attempt to classify these languages and remains the only published source for many of them until present. Taber posits three subgroups in the area: (i) the southwest Maluku group (Wetar-Galolen, Kisar-Luangic, East Damar, Teun-Nila-Serua); (ii) the Babar group; and (iii) West Damar as group level isolate. The southwest Maluku group is provisionally assigned to a higher-order Timor group. West Damar and the Babar languages, however, are excluded from this Timor group.

In a series of papers, van Engelenhoven (1995, 2003, 2009, 2010a) discussed the classification of the languages of southwest Maluku and their relation to the languages of Timor. He presented conclusive evidence for the inclusion of West Damar with the Babar languages, and proposed a closer link between Kisar-Luangic, Makuva, and the Kawaimina languages. The position of the southwest Maluku languages among the languages of Timor is confirmed by Edwards (2018a). Unlike van Engelenhoven, however, he excludes Helong and Central Timor from the bulk of the Timor languages; he unifies the latter together with the languages of southwest Maluku in a 'Timor-Wetar-Babar' group. Edwards leaves open the question of a closer relation between Helong, Central Timor, and Timor-Wetar-Babar on a higher level, as well as of a possible link with languages external to the area.

The position of Selaru still remains uncertain. A link with the southwest Maluku languages, as proposed by Chlenov and Mills, appears not unlikely and merits to be further investigated,[5] especially with regards to the proposals by Taber, van Engelenhoven, and Edwards, who group the languages of southwest Maluku as nested within a larger Timor group.

The Aru languages are generally considered a group of their own by all scholars who cover them (Chlevov 1980; Collins 1982a; Hughes 1987; Taber 1993), without any specific links to other low-order subgroups.

### 13.3.3 Proposals for the central Maluku area

Unlike the first three areas, the central Maluku area has not received much attention from historical linguists in the last thirty years. The most relevant proposals are illustrated in Table 13.3.

A pioneering study of the languages of Buru, Ambon, and Seram was undertaken by Stresemann (1927), which represents one of the earliest systematic applications of the comparative method to Austronesian languages. In this study, Stresemann derived the Buru and Nunusaku languages from a 'Proto-Ambon' ('*Ur-Ambon*') parent language. Sula-Taliabu, East Seram, and Banda-Geser are explicitly excluded from this subgroup.

[5] Selaru shows more lexical agreement with languages to the west than with the Tanimbar-Kei group, its immediate neighbours, for example, *nem* 'to fly' (Leti *nema*; but Yamdena *turim*), *ktahi* 'leaf' (Leti *tavi*; but Yamdena *done*).

**Table 13.3** Proposals for the central Maluku area

<table>
<tr><th></th><th>Stresemann (1927)</th><th>Esser (1938)</th><th>Chlenov (1980)</th><th>Collins (1983a, 1986b)</th></tr>
<tr><td rowspan="2">Sula-Taliabu</td><td rowspan="2">not discussed</td><td rowspan="2">Sula-Bacan</td><td>Moluccan > Sula</td><td rowspan="4">Central Maluku > Western</td></tr>
<tr><td>Moluccan > Soboyo</td></tr>
<tr><td>Buru</td><td rowspan="2">Ambon</td><td rowspan="4">Ambon-Timor (cf. Tables 1+2)</td><td rowspan="4">Moluccan > Central</td></tr>
<tr><td>Nunusaku</td></tr>
<tr><td>East Seram</td><td rowspan="2">not discussed</td><td rowspan="2">Central Maluku > Eastern</td></tr>
<tr><td>Banda-Geser</td></tr>
</table>

In Esser's language map (Esser 1938), all Central Maluku languages except for Sula-Taliabu are assigned to the 'Ambon-Timur' macrogroup. Sula-Taliabu is grouped in a 'Sula-Bacan' subgroup, together with Bacan, a language now known to be a Malayic language that has been strongly influenced by neighbouring languages.

Based on a lexicostatistical count, Chlenov (1980) included all languages of this area in his 'Moluccan' subgroup (see §13.3.2), assigning Sula and Taliabu ('Soboyo') to individual sub-branches, and uniting the remaining ones in the 'Central Moluccan' sub-branch.

Collins (1981, 1983a, 1986b) posited a 'Central Maluku' subgroup with two branches, Western Central Maluku (Sula-Taliabu, Buru) and Eastern Central Maluku (Nunusaku, East Seram, Banda-Geser). Characteristic sound shifts are the mergers PMP *mb/*mp > Proto-Central Maluku *mb, PMP *md/*nt > Proto-Central Maluku *nd, and further the merger of *z and *d in Proto-Eastern Central Maluku.

After Collins, no comparative studies about the Central Maluku languages have been undertaken (except for lexicostatistical SIL surveys), so the validity of this subgroup still awaits further evaluation. The diagnostic value of the mergers of the NC-clusters *mb/*mp > *mb and *nd/*nt > *nd is minimal, since it is shared by many other CMP low-order subgroups. Other mergers proposed by Collins such as *d/*D > *d, *z/*Z > *Z, *-ay/*-əy > *-ay involve phonemic contrasts which are now generally considered spurious. The point for each of the sub-branches appears stronger, but clearly needs to be corroborated by more qualitative evidence beyond phonological arguments.

One language which has not been discussed before in the context of the Central Maluku languages is Kowiai. Located on the western coast of New Guinea (thus in the southeast Maluku–New Guinea area), it shares several features with the Eastern Central Maluku languages (e.g. *tif* 'fly' < Proto-(Eastern) Central Maluku *tibu), especially the Seran-Laut languages. Sound changes shared with the latter are: merger of *d/*z/*R to *r*; merger of *j and *s to *s*; the shift of *ə to *o* in the penultimate and to *a* in in the final syllable.

## 13.4 Central Malayo-Polynesian as a subgroup or linkage

Blust mentioned the Central Malayo-Polynesian group for the first time in 1977 (Blust 1977a). In Blust (1983/1984) he presented evidence for a Central-Eastern Malayo-Polynesian (CEMP) branch that comprises the CMP and Eastern Malayo-Polynesian (EMP) languages. At that stage, CMP was defined as the residual group of CEMP languages not included in EMP.

More evidence for CEMP was brought forward in Blust (1993a), where he also laid out concrete arguments for CMP as a 'linkage' as defined by Ross (1988) (for a definition, see Smith, this volume, §8.2.6). The concept of a linkage was seen as more apt for a description of CMP than that of a coherent subgroup, since none of the proposed innovations characterizing CMP is found in all of its member languages.

### 13.4.1 Blust's proposed innovations

Blust presented the following innovations as evidence for the CMP linkage:

1. Loss of the antepenultimate syllable in trisyllables beginning in *V- and *hV-, and also in *qV- for languages which have a zero reflex of *q.
2. Glide truncation in final diphthongs: *-ay > -a, *-aw > -a, *-uy > -u.
3. 'Post-nasal voicing' of voiceless stops: *mp > *mb*, *nt > *nd*, *ŋk > *ŋg*. This often also affects secondary NC-clusters which have arisen through reduction of the

stative prefix *ma-, or the person marking prefixes *mu-, *na- etc. For example, many languages have a reflex of PMP *maputiq 'white' that went through the intermediate stages *mputiq > *mbutiq.

4. Lexical innovations.

Donohue and Grimes (2008) raised several points of critique, which were addressed in Blust (2009a). The following subsections discuss these innovations based on Blust's arguments and the ensuing critical observations made by Donohue and Grimes.

#### 13.4.1.1 *Apheresis of *V-, *hV-, and *qV-*

The loss of antepenultimate syllables of the shape *(h)V- is a recurrent change in CMP languages but it is clearly not restricted to these, as was observed by Donohue and Grimes (2008) and acknowledged by Blust (2009a). This sound change is brought about by a strong drift towards a 'trochaic' word type, that is, disyllabic words with penultimate stress. The same drift is also seen in the loss of vowels in antepenultimate syllables, which also underlies the change discussed in §13.4.3 below.

Apheresis remained a productive process even after the loss of syllables of the shape *(h)V-, and also operated on syllables of the same shape which developed as a result of regular loss of an initial consonant, most commonly *q (e.g. Manggarai *telo*, Geser *tolu* < PMP *qatəluR).[6]

Clearly, Donohue and Grimes are correct with their critique that apheresis is an areal phenomenon which is not even restricted to the CMP area, and thus cannot serve as evidence for a CMP subgroup or linkage.

#### 13.4.1.2 *Glide truncation*

The term glide truncation was coined by Blust (1993a) for the reduction of PMP final diphthongs in which the final glide is simply dropped, thus leading to the merger of *-ay, *-aw, and *-a into *-a*, and *-uy and *-u into *-u* (which in turn can undergo further sound changes). This contrasts with monophthongization, which is a more common type of simplification of diphthongs, as in *-ay > *-e*, *-aw > *-o*, *-uy > *-i*. Monophthongization is very common outside the CMP area, but is also widespread among CMP languages (for instance, in the languages of Timor).

The distribution of glide truncation leaves a coherent picture mostly in the eastern part of the CMP area (Eastern Central Maluku + Tanimbar-Kei), while its occurrence in the area from southwest Maluku to Bima is more sporadic. Blust tried to explain this distribution by diffusion within the linkage model, but this explanation fails because chaining is often disrupted, as was correctly observed by Donohue and Grimes (2008). In fact, glide truncation and monophthongization of the same final diphthong sometimes even occurs within a single low-level subgroup, as, for example, in Kisar-Luangic, where only Roma shows glide truncation of *-ay to *-a*, whereas Kisar and Luang have monophthongization to *-i*; or TNS, with Teun and Nila having *-a* for *-ay, against Serua which has *-i*.

Therefore, the distribution of glide truncation must (at least partially) be the result of parallel changes. In the case of the Eastern Central Maluku languages, glide truncation—as the name implies—is only one aspect of the general loss of final consonants (e.g. in Hitu, the truncation of *matay 'dead' to *mata* is matched by *anak > *ana* 'child').

In other cases, for example with Kisar-Luangic and TNS in southwest Maluku, this explanation does not work, since final consonants were systematically retained here. Instead, we might posit that *-ay first became *-e in Proto-Kisar-Luangic and Proto-TNS, as in the languages of Timor. Subsequently, *-e merged with either *-i (Kisar, Luang, Serua) or *-a (Roma, Teun, Nila).[7] That means, what appears to be glide truncation in Roma and Teun is actually the result of a two-step sound change. The trigger of the second step must have been the general trend towards reducing the number of vowel phonemes in the unstressed final syllable: *a and *ə generally merge to *a in all southwest Maluku languages, while *i and *u merge to *i in the eastern southwest Maluku area (Wetan, South Babar).

Since glide truncation is not distributed over a contiguous area and has emerged independently as the result of two different sound change mechanisms, it cannot serve as a defining feature for CMP even in the weaker form of a linkage. The occurrence of glide truncation which is almost exclusively confined to CMP languages must therefore be explained by some shared areal typological trigger. As a common denominator between the loss of final consonants (as in Eastern Central Maluku) and the reduction of phonemical vowel contrast in the final syllable, one may posit the unstressed position to be the main trigger. Glide truncation is thus linked to the trochaic root model that also triggered the apheresis described in the preceding section.

#### 13.4.1.3 *Postnasal voicing*

The methodologically weakest part in the exchange between Blust and Donohue and Grimes concerns 'postnasal voicing'.

[6] Loss of *qV- is however not observed in Watubela, which is exceptional among CMP languages in having preserved *q as *k*: Watubela *katlu* < *qatəluR 'egg'.

[7] This is confirmed by the fact that final *-əq has the same reflexes as *-ay in these languages (e.g. *mbasəq > Leti *pasi*, Roma *paha* 'wash clothes', Jonker 1932). In non-final syllables, the reflex of *ə always is *e*, so *e as a common reflex of *-əq (following the loss of *q) and *-ay is very plausible.

Blust (1993a, 2009a) primarily describes this as a voicing process in the second segment in clusters of the type *mp, etc, which affects both primary (i.e. original) clusters, but also secondary clusters which have emerged through syncope of an unstressed vowel. Donohue and Grimes (2008) interpret 'postnasal voicing' literally and try to dismiss Blust's evidence by citing counterexamples where for example *mp has become *p* in CMP languages such as Helong and Imroing. However, both parties miss the main point: as already shown by Collins (1981) and Mills (1991) for smaller units of CMP,[8] postnasal voicing is just one aspect of the *mergers* of PMP *mp/*mb, *nt/*nd, *ŋk/*ŋg (called NC-clusters in the following discussion) into the prenasalized stops *ᵐb, *ⁿd, *ᵑg. Subsequent sound changes do often lead to systematic devoicing of *ᵐb, *ⁿd, *ᵑg to p, t, k (e.g. in the Babar languages), but this does not disprove postnasal voicing as a recurrent feature in almost all CMP languages, if correctly understood.

Nevertheless, the merger of NC-clusters is not a defining feature for CMP: it is lacking in the westernmost part of the area (e.g. in Manggarai), but it is found ouside of CMP (with primary NC-clusters), for example, in Proto-Oceanic (*mb/*mp > *b; *ŋg/*ŋk > *g), in some SHWNG languages, and some languages on Sulawesi (e.g. Tolaki).

More significant is the emergence of *secondary* NC-clusters, which then undergo the same sound changes as primary NC-clusters. Secondary NC-clusters arise through loss of an antepenulte vowel which is preceded by a word-initial nasal. Very common in CMP languages is the reduction of PMP *maputiq 'white' and *mapanas 'hot' to respectively *ᵐbuti and *ᵐbanas (Blust 2009a).

Secondary NC-clusters which have emerged through syncope of the vowel in the pronominal prefixes *mu-, *na-, *mi- are found in the Flores-Lembata and Eastern Central Maluku languages, resulting in inflectional verb paradigms with initial consonant mutations. These alternations are illustrated in Table 13.4 with examples from Sika (Flores-Lembata, Fricke 2013) and Asilulu (Eastern Central Maluku, Blust 1993a).

We can assume that both languages went through an intermediate stage with vowel syncope in all prefixes (*k-panaw, *m-panaw etc.); such a stage is represented in other CMP languages (e.g. Uab Meto). At the next stage, initial obstruents (*k/*t/*d) were simply dropped, while clusters of nasal + obstruent underwent assimilation to existing prenasalized stops.

Since there is no other evidence that would support an especially close relation between Flores-Lembata and Eastern Central Maluku, the loss of initial obstruents in CC-clusters and the emergence of secondary NC-clusters must be an independent parallel development—in spite of the highly distinctive outcome. Its occurrence in the CMP area is triggered by three areal features: reduction of antepenultimate vowels to zero, reduction/loss of consonant clusters, and the development of phonemic prenasalized stops.

**Table 13.4** Initial consonant mutations in Sika and Asilulu

| | Sika 'walk' | Asilulu 'weep' |
|---|---|---|
| 1SG | *ku-panaw > *pano > ***pano*** | *ku-taŋis > *tani > ***tani*** |
| 2SG | *mu-panaw > *ᵐbano > ***bano*** | *mu-taŋis > *ⁿdani > ***rani*** |
| 3SG | *na-panaw > *ᵐbano > ***bano*** | *na-taŋis > *ⁿdani > ***rani*** |
| 1PL.INCL | *ta-panaw > *pano > ***pano*** | *ta-taŋis > *tani > ***tani*** |
| 1PL.EXCL | *ma-panaw > *ᵐbano > ***bano*** | *ka-taŋis > *tani > ***tani*** |
| 2PL | *mi-panaw > *ᵐbano > ***bano*** | *mi-taŋis > *ⁿdani > ***rani*** |
| 3PL | *da-panaw > *pano > ***pano*** | *da-taŋis > *tani > ***tani*** |

#### 13.4.1.4 *Lexical innovations*

Blust listed twenty-eight lexical innovations which are unevenly distributed over the CMP area, but are proposed to be restricted to the CMP languages only (Blust 1993a: 267ff.). This list has not yet been systematically scrutinized, but some items have apparent cognates in non-CMP languages and thus cannot serve as evidence for CMP. The following ones have cognates in Sulawesi languages: *letay 'bridge' (cf. Makasar *lete* 'bridge'); *lemba 'carry on a stick' (cf. Makasar *lémbaraʔ*, Bugis *lempa:*); *gae 'hang' (Tukang Besi *nggae*); and *uta 'chaff' (Pamona *ota*, Proto-Bungku-Tolaki *ota). Two further items were later reassigned by Blust to Proto-Malayo-Polynesian. (*ketu 'pluck off'; *ta 'not'), while *tetu 'peck' appears to stem from a variant *tə(k)tuk of PMP *tuktuk.[9]

The remaining twenty-one Proto-CMP reconstructions have a very patchy distribution and give little evidence of

[8] Nivens (nd b) also posits these mergers for Proto-Aru: PMP *mp/*mb > Proto-Aru *b, *nt/*nd > *d.

[9] Note that *tetu is based on Ngadha, Paulohi *tetu*; both languages have lost final *k.

chaining that would be indicative of a linkage. Only five of these have reflexes in Bima, Sumba-Hawu, or Western-Central Flores; lexical evidence alone in fact actually lends stronger support for a less inclusive subgroup that matches Esser's 'Ambon-Timor'.

### 13.4.2 Assessment

Based on the preceding discussion of Blust's proposed innovations for the CMP linkage, we can summarize that at the current state of research, the concept of CMP as a genealogical unit (either as subgroup or linkage) remains unproven. Although many common features superficially point to a common origin of the CMP languages, all of these are most likely the result of parallel development due to areal convergence.

## 13.5 Topics for further research

As has become visible from §§13.3 and 13.4, comparative research in the CMP area is still in a developing state, both in terms of scope and depth. Systematic comparative studies that incorporate evidence from phonology, lexicon, and morphology are highly needed to fully unravel the linguistic history of the CMP languages. This also applies to the wider question of the Central-Eastern Malayo-Polynesian subgroup (CEMP), which is not addressed here. Argument against Blust's evidence for CEMP, as brought forward by Donohue and Grimes (2008) and Schapper (2011b), also weaken the case for CMP.

### 13.5.1 Influence from non-AN languages

An important question that still needs to be properly addressed is the potential influence from non-AN languages on CMP languages. Such an influence has been repeatedly claimed, for example, by Capell (1976) who attributed the structural erosion from the inherited MPSEA model observed in the languages of the western Wallacea (Flores and Hawu) to a non-AN substratum. However, he essentially did so by virtue of their divergent nature alone, without taking into account internal mechanisms of change, and without material evidence of such a non-AN substratum. In his time, such conjectures remained speculative due to the restricted knowledge of and lack of research about both AN and non-AN languages in the area.

The situation has considerably changed since then, especially in the last twenty years. For many languages (both AN and non-AN), detailed descriptive studies have become available, and studies about shared typological characteristics and lexical diffusion across language families in and around Wallacea have shed new light on the internal ramifications in the area (Klamer 2002b; Donohue 2004b; Donohue and Denham 2009; Schapper 2015a). These studies also indicate that the exchange between AN and non-AN languages was bidirectional. See Schapper, this volume, §22.4–5, for more discussion and illustration.

A notable step forward in the search for concrete traces of non-AN influence are Edwards' pioneering efforts to extract internal evidence for potentially non-AN lexical strata in the Rote-Meto languages of the western Timor area (Edwards 2018b).

### 13.5.2 Wider perspectives within MPSEA

Next to the internal comparison between CMP and CEMP languages, and the influence of non-AN languages on MPSEA in Wallacea, wider connections to western MPSEA must also be considered. Donohue and Grimes (2008) have shown that some of the innovations proposed for CMP and CEMP are also found in western MP languages, yet the implications from this observation remain undiscussed: did these innovations occur independently, or can they serve as diagnostic innovations for alternative higher-order subgroups comprising subsets of CEMP (or of CMP alone) together with MPSEA languages in western Indonesia?

For example, one recurrent feature of CMP languages is the person-marking of verbs by means of subject prefixes which are derived from PMP genitive pronouns. Table 13.5 gives examples from a few representative languages.[10]

In some CMP languages, these subject prefixes are missing, for example, in the Western-Central Flores group, Hawu, Kemak, or Buru. In the case of Hawu, we can postulate that this must be a result of a relatively late loss, since in closely related Dhao, subject prefixes are still found, albeit to a very restricted number of verbs. Elsewhere, intermediate stages with reduced sets are found in the languages of Timor (Schapper 2020a). Compare also the subject prefixes which left a residual trace as initial consonant mutations in Sika and Eastern Central Maluku languages (as discussed in §13.4.1.3).

Functionally, these subject prefixes are generally employed for the subject argument of transitive verbs and intransitive verbs. A number of CMP languages (e.g. Uab Meto (Edwards 2020)), use these prefixes with *nominative alignment*, but in others (e.g. Selaru (Coward 2005)), subject prefixes are used in an agreement system with *semantic*

[10] The data are from Klamer (1998), Balukh (2020), Edwards (2020), van Engelenhoven (2004), Drabbe (1926b), Kakerissa et al. (1986), Blust (1993a).

**Table 13.5** Subject prefixes in CMP languages

| | Kambera | Dhao | Meto | Leti | Yamdena | Geser | Asilulu |
|---|---|---|---|---|---|---|---|
| 1SG | *ku-* | *ku-* | *ʔu-* | *u-* | *ku-* | *Ø* | *Ø* |
| 2SG | *mu-* | *mu-* | *mu-* | *mu-* | *mu-* | *N-* | *N-* |
| 3SG | *na-* | *na-* | *na-* | *na-* | *na-* | *na-* | *N-* |
| 1PL.INCL | *ta-* | *ta-* | *ta-* | *ta-* | *ta-* | *ta-* | *Ø* |
| 1PL.EXCL | *ma-* | *ŋa-* | *mi-* | *ma-* | *ma-* | *a-* | *Ø* |
| 2PL | *mi-* | *mi-* | *mi-* | *mi-* | *mi-* | *N-* | *N-* |
| 3PL | *da-* | *ra-* | *na-* | *ra-* | *ra-* | *ra-* | *Ø* |

*alignment*, which is an important areal feature of Wallacea (Schapper 2015a).

As mentioned by Blust (1993a) and critically discussed by Donohue and Grimes (2008), these subject prefixes also appear in EMP and certain western MPSEA, as exemplified in Table 13.6 (see also van den Berg and Mead, this volume, §33.5.4 for further examples).[11]

**Table 13.6** Subject prefixes in EMP and western MPSEA

| | EMP | | western MPSEA | | | |
|---|---|---|---|---|---|---|
| | Buli | Yapese | Kulawi | Simeulue | Chamorro | Old Javanese |
| 1SG | *k-* | *gu-* | *ku-* | *u-* | *hu-* | *k-* |
| 2SG | *m-* | *mu-* | *mu-* | *mu-* | *un-* | *m-* |
| 3SG | *n-* | *i-* | *na-* | *ni-* | *(ha-)* | *n-* |
| 1PL.INCL | *t-* | *da-* | *ta-* | *ta-* | *ta-* | *t-* |
| 1PL.EXCL | *k-* | *gu-* | *ki-* | *mai-* | *in-* | *kam-* |
| 2PL | *f-* | *mu-* | *mi-* | *mi-* | *en-* | ? |
| 3PL | *d-* | *ra-* | *ra-* | *da-* | *ha-* | *r-* |

In western MPSEA, these subject prefixes are either fully restricted to occur with transitive verbs only (as in Kulawi or Simeulue [formerly Simalur]), or are employed with *split-ergative alignment*, that is, they are generally used with transitive verbs, but also with intransitive verbs. Where split-ergative alignment occurs, it is based on tense/aspect/mood, or syntactic environment.

Both Donohue and Grimes (2008) and Blust (2009a) consider these subject prefixes to be the result of multiple independent innovations, which may also explain the functional difference between the CMP and western MPSEA languages. For the latter, Wolff (1996) proposed a two-step scenario that describes how the subject prefixes were innovated, and this is cited by Donohue and Grimes and Blust as a possible scenario for the CMP languages too. However, they fail to explain why the scenario proposed by Wolff—which only explains the emergence of subject prefixes for transitive verbs—resulted in nominative or semantic alignment in CMP low-level subgroups.

Given the wide distribution of subject prefixes in CMP languages, it appears more likely that subject prefixes already had been innovated in the ancestral language (or ancestral languages) before they entered into Wallacea.[12] After the entry into Wallacea and contact with pre-existing non-AN languages, the use of subject prefixes was remodelled in accordance with the areal feature of semantic alignment. The non-AN and mutually unrelated North Halmahera and Timor-Alor-Pantar languages in the area widely display semantic alignment, so it is likely that this already was an areal feature at the time of the arrival of AN speakers, and subsequently diffused into the CMP languages to various degrees (Donohue 2004b).

### 13.5.3 Phonological convergence

One remarkable fact in the phonological histories of the CMP languages is that they have quite similar synchronic sound systems. They usually have five vowel systems, and certain consonants are usually lacking, especially palatal consonants, and dorsal continuants such as [ŋ] and [ɣ ~ ʁ]). However, it is clear that rather different pathways must have been followed from PMP to the individual daughter languages.

This is most clearly visible with reflexes of the PMP coronals *d, *z, *j, and the dorsal fricative or trill *R. Among these, *z, *j (for which a palatal realization can be assumed), and *R are incompatible with the areal phonological model. Mostly, these have shifted to *d*, *r*, *l* (*z often also becomes *s*), but the involved mergers display almost all possible permutations even among languages spoken over a relatively small area (such as Timor Island, or the islands of Central Maluku), as can been seen in Tables 13.7 and 13.8. This is in contrast with the western and northern parts of MPSEA,

[11] The data are from Maan (1951), Jensen (1977), Adriani and Esser (1939), Damsté (1916), Zobel (this volume, chapter 38), and Kern (1906a).

[12] It is even possible that subject pronouns emerged as a single innovation in a protolanguage ancestral to CMP (or even CEMP) and the abovementioned western MPSEA, as was argued by Zobel (2002).

**Table 13.7** Reflexes of *R and the coronals *d/*z/*j in selected CMP (proto)languages[a]

| PMP | *z | *d | *j | *R |
|---|---|---|---|---|
| Bima | ɗ/r | ɗ/r | r/l | ø |
| Hawu | ɗ$^{y}$ | ɗ/r | ɗ/r | ø |
| Proto-Central Flores | *j | *d | *j | *r |
| Proto-Flores-Lembata | *d | *d | *d | *r |
| Proto-Rote-Meto | *ɗ | *d/*-r- | *ɗ/*d | ø |
| Mambae | s | r | l | ø/r |
| Tetun | d | r | r | ø |
| Galolen | s | r | r | ø |
| Wetar | s | r | ø | r |
| Makuva | j | d-/-r- | r | r |
| Proto-Kisar-Luangic | *t | *r | *r | *r |
| Teun | s | r | ø | ø |
| Selaru | s | r | r | r |
| Yamdena | d | d-/-r- | r | r |
| Teor-Kur | r | l | l | r |
| Proto-Aru | *y | *r | *R | *R |
| Geser | r | r | s | r |
| Bobot | l | l | l | w |
| Proto-Nunusaku | *d | *d | *l | *l |
| Buru | ø | r | l/ ø | h |
| Sula | y | l | l/ ø | ø |

[a] For a detailed list of the reflexes of various PMP sounds in the languages of the Timor–southwest Maluku area, see Edwards (2018b: 87).

where patterns of mergers for *d/*z/*j (and to a lesser degree, *R) are much more stable over larger areas (Table 13.8, see also Adelaar, this volume, chapter 10).

This can be interpreted in two ways. Either we are dealing here with the result of early diversification shortly after the breakup of PMP (= the 'rapid expansion'-model), in which case Donohue and Grimes' model of many first-order branches of MP in the CMP area would be the most fitting (Donohue and Grimes 2008: 116). Or the current situation was brought about through the relatively late entry of a phonologically conservative ancestor (or ancestors) into an area with a pre-existing areal phonological model, arriving via various separate entry points. This would have resulted

**Table 13.8** Patterns of mergers of *z, *d, *j, *R in CMP[a]

| CMP | |
|---|---|
| Merger type | Languages/Protolanguages |
| none | Proto-Rote-Meto, Mambae, Buru, Sula |
| *z/*d | Bima |
| *d/*j | Hawu, Tetun, Galolen, (Makuva, Yamdena)[b] |
| *z/*j | Proto-Central Flores |
| *d/*R | Wetar |
| *j/*R | Teun, Proto-Aru, (Makuva, Yamdena) |
| *z/*R and *d/ *j | Teor-Kur |
| *z/*d and *j/*R | Proto-Nunusaku |
| *z/*d/*j | Proto-Flores-Lembata, Bobot |
| *d/*j/*R | Proto-Kisar-Luangic, Selaru |
| *z/*d/*R | Geser |
| **other MP** | |
| Merger type | Languages/Protolanguages |
| none | Madurese, Moken, Rejang, Proto-Celebic, Chamorro, Proto-SHWNG[c] |
| *z/*d | Proto-Philippines, Proto-South Sulawesi,[d] Barrier Islands-Batak[e] |
| *d/*j | Proto-Great North Borneo, Lampung, Javanese, Proto-Bali-Sasak-Sumbawa |
| *z/*j | Oceanic (excluding Admirality Islands) |
| *z/*d and *j/*R | Palauan |

[a] This is only about mergers of *z/*d/*j/*R among each other. It does not exclude that one or more of these have merged with other protophonemes.

[b] Since *j never appears in initial position, the Makuva and Yamdena data can be either interpreted as merger of *j with *d, or as merger of *j with *R.

[c] Most SHWNG languages display a merger of *d and *z (Kamholz 2014).

[d] Most South Sulawesi languages and many Philippine languages further merge *z/*d with *j.

[e] The Barrier Islands-Batak languages are a proposed subgroup that comprises Simeulue, Sigulai, Nias, Mentawai, Enggano, Gayo, and the Batak languages. The validity of this subgroup is disputed (see Adelaar, this volume, §10.4.1–2, §10.5.1, and McDonnell and Truong, this volume, § 28.1 fn.2), and no reconstruction of Proto-Barrier Islands-Batak has yet been made. They are listed here together since all of them show merger of *d and *z, while *j and *R each are treated differently.

in multiple parallel paths for the adaptation of the conservative ancestral language to the dominant typological model in Wallacea.

Clearly, phonological evidence alone does not suffice to decide which of these two scenarios better reflects the prehistorical migrations that brought the CMP languages into this part of Insular Southeast Asia. Only wider comparative studies that also discuss lexicon and morphology, and furthermore also take non-CMP languages into consideration, will enable us to get a clearer picture here.

## 13.6 Conclusion

As we have seen in §13.4.2, there is insufficient evidence for CMP as a subgroup that is defined by commonly shared innovations, or as a linkage that displays actual chaining of shared innovations. The character and distribution of the proposed innovations rather points to convergence and parallel development, most likely triggered by contact with non-AN languages. Some common features may go back to a higher-level ancestor, while innovations with a limited distribution might serve as a starting point for positing locally more confined mid-level subgroups. We cannot fully exclude that further studies might uncover compelling evidence in support of the original CMP proposal, but at the current state of research, the label CMP serves at best as a catch-all term for CEMP languages not belonging to EMP—and CEMP itself is still a disputed classificatory unit.

This has a precedent in the concept of Western Malayo-Polynesian. The idea of WMP as a subgroup has been abandoned (Smith 2017b), but nevertheless it has been useful as a cover term for non-CEMP Malayo-Polynesian languages, as long as the actual divisions in western NP area are not yet fully established. With our increasing knowledge about these divisions (see Smith, this volume, §2.4.1), however, the need for a cover term is diminishing. In the same way, a better understanding of the linguistic history of the Lesser Sunda Islands and Maluku will likely lead to the same fate for the concept of CMP.

## Acknowledgements

I am indebted to Antoinette Schapper and Sander Adelaar for their comments and suggestions, and to Rick Nivens for sharing with me his data and insights about the Aru languages.

CHAPTER 14

# Historical linguistics of the South Halmahera–West New Guinea subgroup

DAVID KAMHOLZ

## 14.1 Introduction

South Halmahera–West New Guinea (SHWNG) is a subgroup of Austronesian containing thirty-eight languages spoken on the southern portion of the island of Halmahera, in the Raja Ampat islands, in Cenderawasih Bay, and near the mouth of the Mamberamo River. (See Gasser, Arnold, and Kamholz, this volume, Map 37.1, for a map of their locations.) SHWNG is a sister to the much larger and more well-studied Oceanic subgroup. Together, these two subgroups make up Eastern Malayo-Polynesian.

The time depth of Proto-South Halmahera–West New Guinea (henceforth PSHWNG) is as great as 3,500 years (Kamholz 2014: 16). The most likely homeland for PSHWNG, based on number of primary branches, is southern Cenderawasih Bay (Kamholz 2014: 142). SHWNG languages preserve only a small core of inherited Austronesian vocabulary and morphology; a given language typically has no more than 100 words retained from Proto-Malayo-Polynesian.

This chapter covers the innovations that define the SHWNG subgroup (§14.2), the boundaries of the subgroup (§14.3), an internal subgrouping within SHWNG (§14.4), other phonological developments (§14.5), and a PSHWNG reconstruction (§14.6).

## 14.2 Defining PSHWNG

Adriani and Kruyt (1914: 3:302–5) were the first to propose the subgroup that later became known as SHWNG. Blust (1978) was the first to propose exclusively shared innovations supporting the SHWNG subgroup. Blust's innovations have been evaluated and modified by Ross (1995a), and again by Kamholz (2014). The following eleven recurrent sound changes and two irregular/sporadic changes are the principal evidence that has been used to define PSHWNG:[1]

1. PMP *q > Ø
2. PMP *h > Ø
3. PMP *g > Ø
4. PMP *t > *s /_*i
5. PMP *s, *j > *s
6. PMP *n, *ñ > *n
7. PMP *d > *l
8. PMP *z > *l
9. PMP *k > Ø
10. PMP *ə > *o in penultimate syllables
11. PMP *a, *ə > *a in final syllables
12. Lexically-specific vowel syncope
13. Irregular *ə > *e in PMP *pəñu 'the green turtle'

Together these changes form a distinctive profile that convincingly demonstrates the unity of the subgroup. But exactly how good is the evidence for the changes? The small number of Austronesian reflexes and unevenness of available documentation can make this hard to determine. In my view, despite some messiness, the case for PSHWNG is quite strong. The changes, though not all exceptionless, are recurrent across SHWNG languages. Independent innovation or borrowing cannot easily account for this pattern. The most plausible explanation is that SHWNG languages descend from a common ancestor in which these changes were complete or (in some cases that are discussed below) partially complete.

The remainder of this section summarizes the strength of evidence for these thirteen changes and how probative each one is for supporting PSHWNG. Exceptions are given special

[1] Changes are given from Proto-Malayo-Polynesian (PMP), since there has been little reconstruction at the level of Proto-Central Eastern Malayo-Polynesian (PCEMP) and Proto-Eastern Malayo-Polynesian (PEMP) and they are not thought to have undergone many changes.

David Kamholz, *Historical linguistics of the South Halmahera–West New Guinea subgroup*. In: *The Oxford Guide to the Malayo-Polynesian Languages of Southeast Asia*. Edited by: Alexander Adelaar and Antoinette Schapper, Oxford University Press. © David Kamholz (2024). DOI: 10.1093/oso/9780198807353.003.0014

attention, as they provide additional insight into the nature of the changes. For much more detail and supporting forms, see Kamholz (2014).

Changes 1–6 are well supported, with no significant complications. Other than Change 5 (PMP *s, *j > *s), none are particularly unusual, either from a cross-linguistic or Austronesian perspective.

Change 7 (PMP *d > *l) is well supported, with some lexical exceptions. The typical outcome is *l* in South Halmahera and Raja Ampat languages and *r* in Cenderawasih Bay and Mamberamo languages, as in PCEMP *dua 'two' > Sawai *-lu*, Yerisiam *rúu-hí*. The exceptions are as follows: Raja Ampat languages reflect *d* in PMP *dəŋəR 'hear' (e.g. Ma'ya *'do$^{12}$n*) and *r* in PMP *ma-diŋdiŋ 'cold' (e.g. Ma'ya *mari'rin* in several dialects), instead of expected *l*; the Cenderawasih Bay languages Umar and Yaur reflect *d* in PCEMP **dua* 'two' (compare Umar *e-dih* and Yaur *ré-dú-hè*), instead of expected *r*; and the Umar words *drin* and *tot* (< **tod* with final devoicing) also show *d* in PMP *ma-diŋdiŋ 'cold' and PCEMP **todan* 'sit', respectively. However, the otherwise pervasive regularity of the change suggests that the change PMP *d > *l is indeed diagnostic for subgrouping.

Change 8 (PMP *z > *l) is based on only a few attested reflexes, but is attested across the SHWNG region. Examples include PMP *zalan 'road' > Taba *lolan*, Ma'ya (Salawati dialect) *'lili$^{3}$n*, Moor *ràrin-a*; PMP *kazupay 'rat' > Sawai *luf*, Biga *kaluf*, Ambai *karu*. In Umar, Yaur, and Yerisiam apparently PMP *z > Ø, but there are only four total reflexes of protoforms across the three languages, so it is hard to know if this is really an exception to the sound change or may have some other explanation. The examples are PMP *haRəzan 'notched log ladder' > Yaur *ròn* (with loss of initial **ha*) and PMP *zalan 'road' > Umar *jar*; Yerisiam *jáàrà* (where apparently *za > *a > *ya > *ja); and PMP *ma-tazim/ma-tazəm 'sharp' > Umar *mtan*.

Change 9 (PMP *k > Ø) is attested in some form across all of SHWNG, but there is substantial irregularity. Cases of *k surviving as *k* are found across the region, particularly in South Halmahera languages (first noted by Blust 1978: 204) and Moor, and sporadically elsewhere. Examples of loss include PCEMP *kayu 'wood' > Taba *ai*, Ma'ya *'ai(o)*, Umar *ae*, Waropen *ai*; PMP *manuk 'bird' > Sawai *manɛ*, Ambel *mani*, Biak *man*, Waropen *mani*. Examples of retention include PCEMP *kayu 'wood' > Gebe *kay*, Moor *kaʔúat-a*; PMP *manuk 'bird' > Gane *manik*, Taba *manik* 'chicken'; PMP *kutu 'louse' > Moor (Hirom dialect) *kúʔ-a*, Warembori *ki-ro*. Available evidence weighs against the change PMP *k > Ø being complete in PSHWNG, but it is also not plausibly a coincidence that it is widespread within the subgroup. Most likely a precursor was present in PSHWNG.

Changes 10 (PMP *ə > *o in penultimate syllables) and 11 (PMP *a, *ə > *a in final syllables) are best treated together. They are generally well attested outside of Raja Ampat languages, for example: PMP *ənəm 'six' > Buli *wonam*, Ambai *wonan*; PMP *təlu 'three' > Taba *-tol*, Waropen *or-o*, Wamesa *toru*, Yerisiam *kóorí-hé*; PMP *tanəm 'to plant' > Gebe *ƒatanam*, Moor *ʔanam-î*, Serui-Laut *tanam*. In Raja Ampat, *ə takes on the quality of the preceding or following syllable nucleus in such cases when (i) the word was not monosyllabic at the time of the change and (ii) the other nucleus was not *ə. Examples include PMP *qitəluR 'egg' > Biga *tolo*, PMP *mañak 'fat, grease' > Ma'ya (Salawati dialect) *ma'na$^{3}$*; PCEMP *qenəp 'lie down to sleep' > Ma'ya (Salawati dialect) *-e'ne$^{3}$f*. In other contexts, most Raja Ampat languages show *ə > *o, a clear trace of change 11: PMP *Rəbək 'to fly' > Ma'ya (Salawati dialect) *-'opo$^{3}$*; PMP *ma-pənuq 'full' > Matbat *fo$^{3}$n*. Ambel and As appear to reflect *a* in penultimate syllables, as in PMP *qitəluR 'egg' > Ambel *tálo*, As *talo*; PMP *ənəm 'six' > Ambel *wanóm*, As *wanom*.[2] In the context of the overall evidence for SHWNG, the most plausible explanation for the Raja Ampat data is that changes 10 and 11 occurred in PSHWNG and later vowel changes in Raja Ampat languages obscured the result.

Change 12 (lexically specific vowel syncope) is characterized by vowel loss in the penultimate syllable, sometimes followed by cluster reduction; schematically, $C_1VC_2V > C_1C_2V$ ($> C_2V$). Syncope is attested in all SHWNG languages except Moor. It occurs only in a subset of protowords, which heavily overlap across languages. Typical examples are PMP *mañak 'fat; grease' > Buli *mna*, Matbat *mna$^{12}$*, Yaur *mnáa-rè*; PMP *banua 'village' > Ma'ya *'pnu$^{3}$*, Matbat *nu$^{3}$*, Biak *mənu*, Yerisiam *nú*. The lack of perfect uniformity across words affected and lack of attestation in Moor suggest that syncope was not complete in PSHWNG. However, some precursor must have been present, or variation between syncopated and unsyncopated forms; otherwise, the result would have been much more lexically variable than what we observe. The recurrent evidence for this idiosyncratic change across SHWNG could not easily have arisen independently or through borrowing, so it is best explained as a result of common inheritance from PSHWNG.

Change 13 (irregular *ə > *e in PMP *pəñu 'the green turtle') is attested across the SHWNG region. The only exception is Umar *ono*, which shows the expected outcome from

[2] Initial *w-* is attested in reflexes of PMP *ənəm 'six' in a number of widely separated CEMP languages (Blust and Trussel 2020). It is most likely a PCEMP innovation and thus unrelated to the outcome of *ə in this word. The fact that the second vowel is *o* in Ambel and As suggests a previous stage where both vowels harmonized as *o*, after which the first vowel changed: *wənəm > *wonam/*wonəm > *wonom > *wanom*.

change 10 (perhaps reflecting variation in PSHWNG). While this change only affects a single word, it is distinctive and sets SHWNG languages apart.

## 14.3 Boundaries

The westernmost SHWNG language is Taba, spoken on the island of Makian near Halmahera.

Blust (1993a) determined that five Austronesian languages of the Bomberai peninsula—Onin, Sekar, Uruangnirin, Arguni, and Kowiai—do not belong to SHWNG. Data was not available for Bedoanas and Erokwanas, but given their location along the north coast of the peninsula (quite far from known SHWNG languages), they are also unlikely to be SHWNG.

Blust (1993a) and Kamholz (2014) concluded that there is no positive or negative evidence for including Irarutu and closely related Kuri in SHWNG.

The easternmost SHWNG languages are Warembori and Yoke. All Austronesian languages further east are Oceanic, the geographically closest of which are the Sarmi coast languages (Grace 1971).

## 14.4 Internal subgrouping and innovations

Prior to Kamholz (2014), there was no SHWNG-wide subgrouping proposal on the basis of shared innovations. The most significant earlier works were Anceaux's (1961) lexicostatistical classification of Cenderawasih Bay languages, Blust's (1978) subgrouping of South Halmahera languages, Silzer's (1983) proposal of a Western Yapen group, and Remijsen's (2001a) proposal of a Raja Ampat–South Halmahera group (henceforth 'RASH').

Kamholz (2014) evaluated all SHWNG languages for which data was available and proposed an internal subgrouping based on shared phonological and morphological innovations. This section contains a modestly updated version based on newer data. The subgrouping is shown in Table 14.1.[3]

Morphological innovations only take into consideration verbal subject marking and inalienable possessive marking. Forms are considered innovations if they have no clear earlier Austronesian source (using reconstructions from Proto-Malayo-Polynesian, Proto-Central-Eastern Malayo-Polynesian, and Proto-Eastern Malayo-Polynesian), or if they are specific enough for this not to matter. The term *cross-paradigmatic innovation* is used for a set of morphological innovations that reshape a whole paradigm or subparadigm in a way that is clearly evident.

**Table 14.1** SHWNG internal subgrouping

- Tandia
- Moor
- Waropen
- Warembori
- Yoke
- **Proto-Nuclear Cenderawasih Bay**
  - **Proto-Biakic**–Biak, Roon, Dusner, Meoswar
  - **Proto-Yapen**
    - **Proto-Western Yapen**–Wamesa, Wooi, Ansus, Marau, Ambai
      - **Proto-Central Yapen**–Pom, Munggui, Papuma, Serui-Laut, Busami
    - **Proto-Eastern Yapen**–Kurudu, Wabo
  - **Proto-Southwest Cenderawasih Bay**
    - Umar
    - **Proto-Yaur-Yerisiam**–Yaur, Yerisiam
- **Proto-Raja Ampat–South Halmahera**
  - Ambel
  - Biga
  - Batta
  - Salawati
  - As
  - **Proto-Ma'ya-Matbat**–Ma'ya, Matbat
  - **Proto-South Halmahera**
    - Gebe
    - **Proto-Central-Eastern South Halmahera**–Buli, Maba, Patani, Sawai
    - **Proto-Southern South Halmahera**–Gane, Taba

[3] The changes are as follows: Proto-Ambel-Biga has been abandoned because after surveying Biga in 2015, I found that the innovation on which the subgroup was based did not in fact exist. New data has improved support for Proto-Eastern Yapen and Proto-Ma'ya-Matbat. Proto-Cenderawasih Bay has been renamed Proto-Nuclear Cenderawasih Bay to avoid confusion with the geographic region.

Most SHWNG languages fall under the two top-level subgroups, Nuclear Cenderawasih Bay and RASH. Impressionistically, there is more diversity within the Nuclear Cenderawasih Bay subgroup than within the RASH subgroup. Five languages (Tandia, Moor, Waropen, Warembori, and Yoke) do not belong to either subgroup and are considered primary branches.

Better documentation and comparative work may be able to reveal additional subgroups and 'unflatten' some primary-branch languages at the level of PSHWNG and, particularly, at the level of Proto-Raja Ampat–South Halmahera.

Proto-Nuclear Cenderawasih Bay is defined by three morphological innovations in subject marking: the 2SG subject infix *‹u›, the 3SG subject infix *‹i›, and the 3SG vocalic conjugation subject prefix *dy- (see Gasser, Arnold, and Kamholz, this volume, §37.2.6 for examples of infixation and §37.3.3.1 for examples of subject and object marking). The *dy- prefix is likely the historical source of the *‹i› infix (Gasser 2015).

Proto-Biakic is defined by three innovations: PMP *u, *i, *ə > *e* ~ *ə* in final closed syllables of polysyllabic words (examples: PMP *qapuR 'lime; calcium' > Biak *afər*, Dusner *aper*; PMP *qasin 'saltiness' > Biak *masən* 'salt', Dusner *masen* 'salt'; PCEMP *qenəp 'lie down' > Biak *enəf*, Dusner *enep*); a cross-paradigmatic innovation in subject marking; and a cross-paradigmatic innovation in inalienable possessive marking. Additional morphosyntactic innovations are likely discernible, for example alienable possessive marking with the form *ve* (see Gasser, Arnold, and Kamholz, this volume, §37.3.6 on possession), but these have not been systematically investigated.

Proto-Yapen is defined by the innovation of the 2SG vocalic conjugation subject prefix *bu- (as in Ambai *bu-*, Kurudu *b-*). Although this is only a single innovation, it is quite distinctive: inherited 2SG forms did not have *b*, so the most plausible explanation is that the innovation occurred only once, in the common ancestor of Yapen languages.

Proto-Western Yapen is defined by several innovations in inalienable possessive marking (3SG *-mpai*, 3SG *-na/-ni*, plural *-mi/-mu*) and the innovation of the plural vocalic conjugation linking consonant *-t-. An example of the latter is the Ambai 2PL vocalic conjugation subject prefix *met-* (compare with its absence in Kurudu *my-*). Other innovations can likely be posited; Silzer (1983: 232) notes several shared by Wamesa and Ambai.

Proto-Central Yapen is defined by the change of the 2SG vocalic conjugation subject prefix (inherited Proto-Western Yapen) from *bu- to *w-. Although a relatively minor change, it is more parsimonious to suppose that the change happened once rather than several times independently.

Proto-Eastern Yapen is defined by four morphological innovations: the change of the Proto-Yapen 2SG vocalic conjugation subject prefix *bu- to *b-, the 1SG vocalic conjugation prefix *ay-, the 1SG inalienable prefix *a-, and the 3SG inalienable suffix *-wai. Other innovations are likely to exist, but existing documentation is not sufficient to identify them.[4]

Proto-Southwest Cenderawasih Bay is defined by two phonological innovations: PMP *z > Ø (see §14.2 for examples) and irregular *u > *i* in PMP *punti 'banana' (Umar *idi*, Yaur *ìdí-e*, Yerisiam *píití*). Neither is very secure, so the validity of the subgroup should be considered tentative.

Proto-Yaur-Yerisiam is defined by a single innovation: PMP *ŋ > Ø. Examples include PMP *laŋit 'sky' > Yerisiam ***ráakátè***; PMP *taŋis 'to cry' > Yaur *ʔàáh-rè*, Yerisiam ***káhé***. Although this innovation is rather distinctive—loss of a nasal in all positions is unusual—arguably no single phonological innovation is sufficient to firmly establish a subgroup, and this subgroup should be considered tentative.[5]

Proto-Raja Ampat–South Halmahera is defined by two innovations: PMP *R > Ø, and the 1SG/2SG subject infix *‹y› (see §26.2.6 for more on infixation). Examples of PMP *R > Ø include PMP *Rumaq 'house' > Gane *um*, Sawai *um*, Biga *um*, Ma'ya *'u³m*; PMP *wahiR 'fresh water' > Sawai *wɔɛ*, Taba *woya*, Gebe *wa*, Ambel *we*, Biga *wey*, Ma'ya (Salawati) *'waya³*.

Proto-Ma'ya-Matbat is defined by two innovations: a shared tonal system (Arnold 2018b) and the 1PL.INCL inalienable suffix *-n. Additionally, the epenthetic final *o* found on words with Fall or Low Fall tone (as in Ma'ya *'be(o)*, Magey Matbat *be²¹(o)* 'give') may be a shared innovation.

Proto-South Halmahera is defined by two innovations: the 2PL subject prefix *f- and the 1PL.INCL inalienable possessive suffix *-d.

Proto-Central-Eastern South Halmahera is defined by a cross-paradigmatic innovation in inalienable possessive marking. There are likely other innovations in phonology, morphosyntax, and lexicon, but these have not yet been identified.

Proto-Southern South Halmahera is defined by the loss of inalienable possessive marking. There is also a variety of lexical items unique to this group (Blust 1978: 199), for example: Taba *battól*, Gane *batól* 'star'; Taba *-wom*, Gane *wom* 'to come'; Taba *kakle*, Gane *kiklé* 'hair'; Taba *gamós*, Gane *gamós* 'dry'. There are likely other innovations in phonology and morphosyntax, but these have not yet been identified.

[4] The innovations in inalienable possession only came to light from survey data I collected on Kurudu and Wabo in 2015.

[5] Since parallel sound changes are widely attested, it is much better to have multiple shared changes that support a subgroup. See Kamholz (2014: 5) for a discussion of the relative value of different kinds of changes for subgrouping.

## 14.5 Other phonological developments

There are several noteworthy and individual-language sound changes and tendencies across the SHWNG region that do not line up with subgroups.

Most languages underwent PMP *p > *f*; the exceptions are Dusner and Yerisiam. Typical examples include PEMP *pat 'four' > Buli *fat*, Taba *-hot*, Ambel *fat*, Maˈya *fa*[12]*t*, Biak *fiak*, Dusner *pati*, Wamesa *at*; PCEMP *marip 'laugh' > Buli *a-mlif*, Taba *-(ha)mlih*, Biga *mlif*, Biak *mbrif*, Wamesa *mari*; PMP *punti 'banana' > Moor *hút-a*, Umar *idi*, Yaur *ìdí-e*, Yerisiam *píítí* (with *f* > *h* in Taba and Moor, and *f* > *h* > Ø in Wamesa, Umar, and Yaur).

Several languages underwent PMP *b > *p*. This outcome is regular in South Halmahera languages. It is sporadic in Raja Ampat languages other than Matbat (where it does not occur): some reflexes have *p*, while others have *b*. Typical examples include PMP *bunuq 'kill' > Buli *pun*, Taba *-pun*, Gebe *-pun*, Biga *bun*, Maˈya *bun*; PMP *Rəbək 'to fly' > Buli *opa*, Taba *-opa*, Gebe *-opo*, Biga *-ubu*, Maˈya (Salawati) *-ˈopo*[3]; PMP *batu 'stone' > Buli *pāt*, Gebe *ka-pat*, Biga *kapat*, Maˈya *ka-ˈpa*[12]*t*; PMP *bəRay 'give' > Maˈya *ˈbe(o)*.

Several languages underwent PMP *b > *β*. The change occurred regularly in Dusner, Moor, and Yaur, and sporadically in Ambai, Ansus, Serui-Laut, Wamesa, Kurudu, Waropen, Umar, and Yerisiam. All of these languages except Dusner and Moor show further changes from *β* > *w* (> Ø), in most cases also sporadically. Examples include PMP *baRa 'arm' > Dusner *vra*, Moor *veréa*, Yaur *vra-*, Ambai *wara*, Ansus *warau*, Serui-Laut *wara*, Wamesa *vara*, Waropen *va(ha)-*; PMP *baqəRu 'new' > Ambai *waworu*, Ansus *waworu*, Serui-Laut *vavoru*, Wamesa *vavoru*, Kurudu *vivoru*, Waropen *voa~boa*; PMP *buaq 'fruit' > Moor *vó*, Ambai *bon*, Serui-Laut *bo*, Wamesa *buo*, Waropen *vo*, Yerisiam *ú*.[6]

Several languages underwent PMP *t > *k*: Biak, Roon, Yaur, Yerisiam, Moor, Waropen, and Warembori. In Moor (with exceptions) and Yaur, there was a further change of *k* > *ʔ*, after which in Yaur *ʔ* > Ø except word-initially on verbs.[7] Examples include PMP **batu* 'stone' > Yerisiam *áakú*, Moor *váʔ-a*; PEMP *pat 'four' > Biak *fiak*, Yerisiam *áakà*, Yaur *r-ía-hè*, Moor *áʔ-ó*, Waropen *ako*; PMP *tunu 'roast food over a fire' > Biak *kun*, Yaur *ʔún-dè*, Yerisiam *kúun-á*, Moor *ʔun-î*, Warembori *kuni*; PMP *kutu 'louse' > Biak *uk*, Moor (Hirom) *kúʔ-a*, Yaur *óò-jé*, Yerisiam *úukú*. These *t > *k* change are mostly consistent with Blust's (2004a) observation that *t > *k* typically occurs in languages that have lost **k*. However, Moor and Warembori both retain *k as *k* in some words, so a structural explanation may not be possible for these languages.

[6] The letter *v* represents [β].

[7] Yaur does not have phonemic word-initial glottal stops on other parts of speech.

Many languages underwent PMP *a > *ya* word-initially. The change followed PMP *q > Ø. It occurred in all RASH languages and sporadically in Cenderawasih Bay languages, with subsequent *y* > *l* in some Raja Ampat languages and *y* > *j* in some Cenderawasih Bay languages. Examples include PCEMP *api 'fire' > Buli *yap*, Gebe *yap*, As *yap*, Ambel *lap*, Maˈya *ˈla*[12]*p*, Yerisiam *jáai*; PMP *qasu 'smoke' > Sawai *mɛ**yas***, Taba ***yas**o*, As *kap**yas***, Maˈya *ˈla*[12]*s*.

PMP *u > *i* in final syllables is found sporadically across SHWNG. Examples include PMP *manuk 'bird' > Buli *mani*, Taba *manik* 'chicken', Gebe *mani*, Ambel *mani*, Maˈya (Salawati) *ˈmini*[12], Waropen *mani*; PMP *susu 'female breast' > Ambai *ui*, Yaur *húhì-e*; PMP *təlu 'three' > Dusner *tori*, Yerisiam *kóorí-hé*.

Final vowel loss (in words that did not undergo syncope) is found regularly in RASH languages, Biak, and Dusner, and sporadically elsewhere. It followed the loss of PMP *q, and in RASH languages it preceded the loss of PMP *R and *k. Examples include PMP *bunuq 'kill' > Buli *pun*, Taba *-pun*, Gebe *-pun*, Ambel *bun*, Matbat *bu*[3]*n*, Maˈya *ˈbu*[3]*n*, Biak *mun*, Dusner *mun*, Ambai *mun*, Wamesa *mun*, Yoke *mu*; PMP *lima 'five' > Buli *lim*, Taba *-lim*, Gebe *pi-lim*, Ambel *lim*, Matbat *li*[3]*m*, Maˈya *ˈli*[3]*m*, Biak *rim*, Dusner ***rim**bi*, Ambai *rin*, Serui-Laut *ri*, Moor *rím-ó*, Warembori ***rin**ti*, Yoke ***rim**si*.

Umar underwent syncope to a much greater extent than other languages. Typical examples are PMP *kuRita 'octopus' > *kte*; PMP *manuk 'bird' > *mna*; PMP *tunu 'to roast' > *tnu*.

Yerisiam, Ambel, and Maˈya have tonal innovations conditioned by vowel height. In Yerisiam, word-final *a* caused a change from high to low tone (Kamholz 2014: 106), as in PMP *daRaq 'blood > Yerisiam *rárà*, and PMP *bab‹in›ahi 'woman' > Yerisiam *îinà*. In the Metnyo dialect of Ambel, non-high vowels caused Proto-Ambel toneless syllables to receive high tone (Arnold 2020), as in *sa 'ascend' > Metnyo *sá* and **fon* 'full' > Metnyo *hón*. In Maˈya, non-high vowels caused Proto-Maˈya-Matbat high-tone syllables to receive rising tone (Arnold 2018b), as in *yap$^{H}$ 'fire' > *ˈla*[12]*p* and *nen$^{H}$ 'mother' > *ˈne*[12]*n*. These three changes were apparently all independent. Tonal developments triggered by vowel height are rare cross-linguistically, and it is noteworthy that it has happened three times in SHWNG. For a theoretical overview of this phenomenon, see Arnold (2020).

## 14.6 PSHWNG reconstruction

The principal inherited morphology that is available for potential PSHWNG reconstruction is subject marking and inalienable possessive paradigms. Van den Berg (2009) and Kamholz (2015) have attempted to reconstruct aspects of

**Table 14.2** Selected 1PL.EXCL vocalic conjugation subject forms across SHWNG

| | |
|---|---|
| Moor | *n-* |
| Tandia | *ami-* |
| Warembori | *am-* |
| Waropen | *angg-* |
| **Nuclear Cenderawasih Bay** | |
| **Southern Cenderawasih Bay** | |
| Umar | *em-* |
| **Yaur-Yerisiam** | |
| Yaur | *om-* |
| Yerisiam | *ne=m-* |
| **Biakic** | |
| Biak | *nkw-* |
| Dusner | *nd-* |
| **Yapen** | |
| **Western Yapen** | |
| Wamesa | *amat-* |
| **Eastern Yapen** | |
| Kurudu | *nm-* |
| **RASH** | |
| Ambel | *am-* |
| As | *am-* |
| Biga | *m-* |
| Fiawat | *l-* |
| **South Halmahera** | |
| Gebe | *k-* |
| **Central-Eastern South Halmahera** | |
| Patani | *k-* |
| Sawai | *k-* |
| **Southern South Halmahera** | |
| Gane | *am-* |
| Taba | *a=* |
| **Ma'ya-Matbat** | |
| Ma'ya (Kawe) | *w-* |
| Ma'ya (Salawati) | *m-, ma-* |
| Matbat | *n-* |

(Kamholz 2014 and fieldnotes)

these paradigms, but my current view is that evidence is too ambiguous at present to do so convincingly. Independent pronouns evidently have developed repeatedly over the history of SHWNG languages into bound forms in these paradigms. The starting point for these developments was highly similar, since most independent pronouns are inherited Austronesian forms. One cannot straightforwardly know if particular bound forms (often only one or two segments long) represent shared or independent innovations, or if a language used to have a particular bound form and later replaced it with another reduced pronoun form.

To better illustrate the issue, consider the 1PL.EXCL vocalic conjugation subject forms in Table 14.2. Most of the forms are consistent with an origin from the PMP 1PL.EXCL pronoun **kami*; the only languages where this is particularly implausible are Biak, Dusner, Fiawat, and Ma'ya (Kawe). However, the attestation of *ami-* in Tandia and *k-* in South Halmahera effectively prevent us from reconstructing anything for PSHWNG other than the full form *kami. Alternatives are theoretically possible but difficult to substantiate. For example, since Tandia is the only language that reflects the final vowel of *kami, we could posit a PSHWNG subject marker *kam- that coexisted with the independent pronoun *kami, and that Tandia's inherited *kam- was later replaced by a newly reduced *kami > *ami-*. We could even go further and posit PSHWNG *am-, which would then require assuming that Gebe and Proto-Central Eastern South Halmahera independently replaced their inherited forms with a newly reduced *kami > *k-*. But in order to convincingly propose complex scenarios of this sort, we would need more convincing supporting data. It is simpler to assume that PSHWNG simply had the unreduced *kami and that it persisted in that form at least into the primary branches of SHWNG, after which different bound forms arose independently.

This confound does not arise with bound forms that are not derived from Austronesian pronouns, such as the South Halmahera 2PL subject prefix *f-*, or with thoroughgoing cross-paradigmatic innovations. Most morphological innovations used above to define subgroups are of this kind. However, many paradigm elements do not contain such innovations, making it difficult to convincingly reconstruct whole paradigms even for many subgroups, let alone at the PSHWNG level.

Another way that one could, in principle, avoid the confound of inherited Austronesian pronouns is to find distinctive cross-paradigmatic innovations, but available evidence does not allow us to reconstruct any such innovations back to PSHWNG. It may seem plausible that one could reconstruct infixal subject marking of some kind, since it is attested in all but five SHWNG languages. However, the specific infixing innovations of Proto-Raja Ampat–South Halmahera and Proto-Nuclear Cenderawasih Bay are clearly different and not plausibly shared. Infixal subject marking is an areal tendency that goes beyond SHWNG—for example,

**Table 14.3** PSHWNG lexical reconstructions

| PSHWNG | *Reflexes* |
|---|---|
| *aka 'bite' | Matbat *n-a*$^{21}$*t*, Umar *wat*, Yerisiam *áaká*, Moor ***aʔì*** |
| *alai, *salai 'dig' | Gane *ólai*, Gebe *-alai*, Ambai *arai*, Wamesa *sarai*, Umar *hrae* |
| *am, *em 'see' | Taba *-am*, Gane *am*, Gebe *-em*, Ma'ya *'w-e*$^{12}$*m*, Biga *em*, Biak *mam*, Dusner *man* |
| *as 'swim' | Buli *yas*, Patani *yɔs*, Gebe *-yas*, Biga *as*, As *as*, Matbat *la*$^{3}$*s*, Ma'ya (Misool) *'w-a*$^{12}$*s*, Biak *ās*, Wamesa as, Umar ***ejah***, Moor ***áta***, Warembori ***ate*** |
| *asan 'sun; day' | Ma'ya (Misool) *'lyasa*$^{12}$*n*, Matbat *la*$^{121}$, Ambai *aha* |
| *ata 'to smoke (food)' | Umar *ta*, Yerisiam *ákáai*, Moor *aʔà* |
| *ba 'big' | Taba ***ba****kan*, Biak *ba*, Ambai *baba*, Wamesa *baba*, Yaur *né-****bá****túe*, Waropen *ba* |
| *bi 'live; be alive' | Biga *bi*, Ma'ya (Salawati) *wa'bi*$^{12}$, Serui-Laut *been* |
| *bisik 'sick' | Buli *bisik*, Biak *bis* |
| *bus 'white' | Ambel *ambu*, Biga *babus*, Matbat *bu*$^{3}$, Ma'ya *'bu*$^{3}$*s*, Ambai *bua*, Wamesa *vusa* |
| *dum 'drink' | Buli *dom*, Gebe *-dom*, Ma'ya (Kawe, Wauyai) *dum*, Yaur *rùm-né* |
| *el 'mountain' | Gebe *el*, Ambel *il*, Biga *il*, Matbat *he*$^{3}$*l*, Ma'ya *'ye*$^{3}$*l*, Moor *éra*, Yerisiam ***éer****ídìa* |
| *iap 'k.o. brown fish' | Buli *iaf*, Waropen *ia* |
| *katem 'one' | Ambel *kitem*, Biga *katem*, As *tem*, Matbat *te*$^{3}$*m*, Ma'ya *ka'te*$^{12}$*m*, Umar *kotem* |
| *lali 'dirty' | As *lali*, Ambai ***rari****ka*, Wamesa ***rari****ai*, Yerisiam *ó****rárí****íjárà* |
| *lan 'song' | Matbat *la*$^{3}$*n*, Wamesa *ran(u)* |
| *le 'land(ward)' | Ma'ya *'le*$^{3}$, Dusner *re*, Ambai *rei*, Wamesa *rei*, Moor *ré*, Waropen *re* |
| *ma-lom 'wet' | Sawai *n-mɛlom*, Ma'ya *ma'lo*$^{12}$*m*, Umar *brom*, Yaur *né-****márò*** |
| *ma-sun 'heavy' | Biga *masun*, As *mason*, Waropen *mahuna* |
| *tuat 'buy' | Gane *tua*, Umar *tuat* |
| *una 'know' | Taba *-unak*, Gane *unak*, Gebe *una*, Ambel *tun*, Biga *uno*, As *nun*, Ma'ya *'w-un(o)*, Umar *nune* |
| *utin 'hundred' | Sawai *witɛn-čɔ*, Taba *utin*, Wamesa *utin* 'twenty', Umar *utinho kotem* 'one hundred', Yaur *útín rèebé* 'one hundred' |

it is also found in Arguni and several languages of Aru and the Tanimbar islands—so it is likely not a coincidence that both subgroups developed infixation, but no system can be reconstructed.

Despite these challenges, better documentation and more careful analysis may make it possible to reconstruct more individual paradigm elements and morphosyntactic constructions at the level of PSHWNG.

Little work has been done on PSHWNG lexical reconstruction. Blust and Trussel (2020) list only two forms (*bisik 'sick' and *iap 'kind of brown fish'), but much more can be done. The appendix to Kamholz (2014) contains many SHWNG cognate sets without a known Austronesian etymology (also available in Kamholz nd). Table 14.3 contains some new-PSHWNG reconstructions using this data. I have reconstructed forms to PSHWNG only if they are attested in at least two primary branches of SHWNG and do not show clear evidence of borrowing. As richer lexical data becomes available, the prospects for reconstructing the PSHWNG lexicon should only improve.

# PART II

# Sociolinguistics and Language Contact

CHAPTER 15

# Vitality, maintenance, and documentation among the Malayo-Polynesian languages of Southeast Asia

MICHAEL C. EWING AND YUKINORI KIMOTO

## 15.1 Introduction

Shifting multilingualisms, economic development, and changing social and political circumstances are associated with decline in the vitality of many Malayo-Polynesian (and other) languages of Southeast Asia. Specifics differ between the countries of the region, yet these complex language ecologies can all lead to what Tupas (2015) calls the "inequalities of multilingualism" that often involve devaluing of some, usually indigenous, languages and valorization of other regional, national, or international languages.

Awareness of language endangerment and concomitant threats to linguistic diversity and the human rights of speech communities became acute in the late twentieth century, with a number of documenting projects and maintenance activities being undertaken over the past two decades. Adelaar (2010a) provides an overview of language documentation in the Austronesian world up to 2010. Among the major international bodies who actively support or operate projects working in this area are: the Endangered Languages Documentation Programme (ELDP) based at the Berlin-Brandenburg Academy of Sciences and Humanities; the Volkswagen Foundation; UNESCO; the Dynamic Language Infrastructure – Documenting Endangered Languages (DLI-DEL) programme of the National Endowment for the Humanities and National Science Foundation; and SIL International. Many regionally based initiatives also play a role in supporting the documentation, including: the Komisyon sa Wikang Filipino (Commission on the Filipino Language); the Indonesian Badan Pengembangan dan Pembinaan Bahasa (Language Development and Advancement Agency, formerly known as the Pusat Bahasa 'Language Centre'); and the Malaysian Dewan Bahasa dan Pustaka (Institute of Language and Literature).

Multiple interrelated factors are involved when communities shift from using one language to another (Himmelmann 2010a; Abtahian and Cohn 2018). This chapter provides an overview of the language ecologies of six key jurisdictions where Malayo-Polynesian languages of Southeast Asia are found: the Philippines, Malaysia, Brunei, Indonesia, East Timor (Timor Leste), and Madagascar. It explores different forces that give rise to varying degrees of indigenous language vitality and highlights some representative language maintenance activities being undertaken by community members, government and non-government organizations, and researchers.

## 15.2 Philippines

The Philippines is home to rich linguistic and cultural diversity. The country is broadly divided into three island groups: Luzon, Visayas, and Mindanao, from north to south. *Ethnologue* (Eberhard, Simons, and Fennig 2020) lists 186 languages as spoken in the country, of which 175 are indigenous, and nine are non-indigenous including those by used relatively recent immigrant populations (e.g. Basque, Spanish, Mandarin Chinese, and Sindhi).[1] Filipinos are mostly multilingual: as well as their mother tongue, most speak Filipino, the national language, and English, an official language. Speakers of smaller languages may also use another language of wider regional communication, such as Cebuano in the Visayan area and Ilokano in northern Luzon, and may also learn other languages after marriage or relocation. Filipino, formerly called Pilipino, was developed primarily

[1] It should be noted that the count adopted by *Ethnologue* is not a list of mutually unintelligible 'languages', but also includes different varieties or dialects. It would be practically impossible to assess the mutual intelligibility for each pair of any combination of the 186 languages. It is also difficult to distinguish languages from dialects/varieties due to oft-attested language dialect continua, a well-known case in Bikol and Visayan areas (Zorc 1977; Mintz and Britanico 1985). Similar issues obtain for *Ethnologue* data reported for the other countries discussed below.

Michael C. Ewing and Yukinori Kimoto, *Vitality, maintenance, and documentation among the Malayo-Polynesian languages of Southeast Asia*. In: *The Oxford Guide to the Malayo-Polynesian Languages of Southeast Asia*. Edited by: Alexander Adelaar and Antoinette Schapper, Oxford University Press. © Michael C. Ewing and Yukinori Kimoto (2024).
DOI: 10.1093/oso/9780198807353.003.0015

based on, hence almost identical with, Tagalog. English, as well as Filipino, is an official language in the country, first introduced in the American colonial period as the medium of instruction. Today, most Filipinos can use English in spite of longstanding anti-colonial reactions. The following description surveys Austronesian languages spoken in the country that are in danger of extinction.

In terms of the numbers of speakers, there is a skewed distribution of indigenous languages in the Philippines, just as with the distribution of the world's languages. According to Eberhard et al. (2020), two languages, Tagalog and Cebuano are learned as the first language by just over 50% of the total population in the Philippines. Languages with between one and ten million speakers include seven indigenous languages—Ilokano, Hiligaynon, Waray-Waray, Central Bikol, Kapampangan, Pangasinan, Maguindanaon—and one non-indigenous language—Nin Nan Chinese. These ten languages together account for more than 83% of the total L1 speakers. The remaining languages amount to 174, but are spoken by only about 17% of the population. In particular, the Philippine archipelago is home to various Negrito groups, who must have been present there for tens of thousands of years and are physically distinct from the Austronesian migrants who first entered the area around 4000BP (see Reid 2013 and the references therein). Since the arrival of Austronesian speakers, all Negrito groups shifted to speaking a variety of Austronesian languages. In the contemporary period, many speakers of Negrito languages are shifting to more politically and economically powerful languages such as Tagalog, Ilokano, Kapampangan, and Cebuano. Many of the other smaller languages are also gradually losing speakers as they shift to major or neighbouring languages.

### 15.2.1 Endangered languages in the Philippines

Eberhard et al. (2020) assess the vitality of each language using the Expanded Graded Intergenerational Disruption Scale (EGIDS),[2] and the following description focuses on some of the most severely endangered languages measured as 7 (Shifting), 8a (Moribund), 8b (Nearly extinct), and 9 (Dormant) by EGIDS. Note that Sorsogon Ayta [8b Nearly Extinct] listed in Eberhard et al. (2020) does not have any reliable information regarding the existence of the language.

Batak [7 Shifting] is a Negrito language[3] spoken in Puerto Princesa in central Palawan island. Tajolosa (2010: 55–6) identifies three Batak communities: Kalakuasan, Riyandakan, and Pangapin. The ethnolinguistic population is reported as 416 in the 2010 census (Tajolosa 2010: 49). The speakers are multilingual with Kuyonon, Tagbanwa, and Tagalog, and lexical and grammatical mixture with these languages was attested.[4] Butuanon [7 Shifting] is a language spoken in Butuan city, Agusan de Norte province in Mindanao island. This is one of the few languages for which detailed sociolinguistic study was conducted (Kobari 2009). 71,500 speakers of Butuanon are reported in Eberhard et al. (2020), but Kobari (2009) illustrates that, in spite of a strong ethnic identity as Butuanon, their linguistic competence both in lexicon and grammar is significantly declining in younger generations, influenced by Cebuano, the dominant language in the region.

Arta [8a Moribund] is a Negrito language spoken by nine native speakers and around forty L2 speakers in Nagtipunan, Quirino province, and Dinalungan and Casiguran, Aurora province. There is no distinctive speech community exclusively composed of Arta speakers, and all of them live in Casiguran Agta community in Nagtipunan and Casiguran. All the children shifted to Casiguran Agta as their L1, and acquire Ilokano and Tagalog as L2. Remontado [8a Moribund] is spoken by approximately 325 people in rural communities located in a border area between Rizal and Quezon provinces, east of Manila. The majority of the community members are intermarried with Tagalogs, Ilokanos, Alkanons, and Umiray Dumagets. Currently only the half of the members can speak the language, and most of these speakers are over the age of fifty (Lobel and Surbano 2019). Inagta Alabat [8a Moribund] is one of the two Negrito languages distributed in eastern Quezon province, southeast of Manila, together with Manide [6b Threatened]. Inagta Alabat currently spoken in Lopez town is a critically endangered language, with the number of attested speakers fewer than ten in Alabat island and four in Lopez (Lobel, Alpay, R. Barreno, and E. Barreno 2020). This moribund status of the language involves intermarriage with Negrito and non-Negrito neighbours in Alabat island and the massive influx of Manide people from Carmines Norte into Lopez town (Lobel et al. 2020: 2). In Mountain province in northern Luzon, there are a number of dialects/languages that form the Bontok macrolanguage group, including Central, Eastern, Southern, Northern, and Southwestern Bontok. Eberhard et al. (2020) list the latter two languages—Northern Bontok in Sadanga and Southwestern Bontok in Bontoc—as 8a Moribund. However, according to Reid (p.c.), all macro-Bontok varieties are severely endangered, and in daily conversation, these local languages are mixed with, or completely replaced with,

[2] See Quakenbush and Simons (2015) for a history and explanation of EGIDS and its application to Austronesian languages.

[3] A 'Negrito' language here simply means an Austronesian language spoken by a Negrito population, with no implication for linguistic classification. In fact, there is no major subgroup that is exclusively composed of Negrito languages.

[4] Tajolosa (2010: 64–8), however, claims that the mixture does not show language attrition.

Ilokano and Tagalog/Filipino. He thus estimates that all of the varieties of macro-Bontok will be eventually lost (see Reid 2009d for the change in the culture and social structure of Bontok communities and their impacts on language).

Central Tagbanwa [8b Nearly extinct] is a non-Negrito language spoken in Roxas, San Vicente, Taytay municipalities located in north Palawan island. A detailed sociolinguistic survey was conducted by Robert A. Scebold, who states that "there were probably less than 300 adults who competently spoke Tagbanwa in 1992, one third of whom have probably passed away since then" (Scebold 2003: 23). Their language use is shifting into Kuyonon [5 Developing], and Tagalog. Katubung Agta, Isarog Agta, or Inagta Partido [8b Nearly Extinct], and Mt. Iriga Agta or Rinconada Inagta [6b Threatened] are two Negrito languages in Camarines Sur province in the Bikol Region of southern Luzon. Eberhard et al. (2020) count five or six speakers for Isarog Agta and 1,500 for Mt. Iriga Agta. Isarog Agta does not constitute a speech community, and Lobel (2013a: 68) reports that he found more Mt. Iriga Agta speakers than Isarog Agta in the community, with no known speakers under the age of sixty.

Two languages are measured as 9 (Dormant). One is Eskayan, a constructed language based on Cebuano, English, and Spanish. It was allegedly created by an ancestral individual referred to as Pinay (Kelly 2015). No L1 users exist and it is only used by approximately 550 in five villages of southeast Bohol. The other is Ratagnon, a language spoken in the extreme south tip of Mindoro Occidental province, including Ilin islands. The language is genetically close to Kuyonon (Zorc 1977). Eberhard et al. (2020) state that the last known speaker may have survived into the 2010s.

There are even more languages that show signs of endangerment. First, there are twenty-six languages that are judged as 6b (Threatened), including Northern Alta, Southern Alta, Ati, Ibatan, and Isinay. For example, Isinay [6b Threatened], a language spoken in Nueva Vizcaya, Luzon, is used in some areas (Dupax del Sur and Bambang), but there are no young people speaking Isinay, shifting to Ilokano or Tagalog/Filipino even at home, and one area (Aritao) has only a few individuals speaking the language (Lawrence A. Reid, p.c.). In other cases, languages not judged as endangered in EGIDS are gradually losing speaker numbers or domains of language use, so there is no guarantee that these 'safe' languages will be stable. Headland (2010) maintains that Casiguran Agta [5 Developed], although not assessed as endangered in EGIDS, is undergoing radical change in language use. The growing rate of intermarriage with Tagalog or Ilokano people is accelerating the use of such major languages at home. Pangasinan [3 Wider communication], one of the major languages as stated above, is losing domains of language use, and the speakers are now aware of its endangered status, primarily due to the massive influx of Ilokano immigrants, and subsequent change in language use (Anderson and Anderson 2007).

There are several general characteristics identified across many endangered languages in the Philippines. First, since the Philippines is a highly multilingual country, there is a multi-layered contrast between the majority and minority groups at different levels. In the case of the previously mentioned Arta, speakers assimilate to the relative majority of Casiguran Agta at the community level, who in turn are a minority to Ilokano people at the wider regional level, who again have a smaller population than Tagalog at the countrywide level. Due to this multi-layered multilingualism, language attrition or shift may occur at different minority–majority contrasts. For example, Headland (2010) warns that Casiguran Agta is definitely endangered, shifting into Tagalog. Viewed from the perspective of Arta, however, it is the Casiguran Agta language which is driving Arta into extinction, since the Casiguran Agta language is now commonly used in the Arta-Agta communities.

Another feature is that self-confidence in language proficiency normally does not follow actual proficiency of a given endangered language (Headland 2003; Tajolosa 2010; Kobari 2009). It is generally the case in the Philippines that the users of endangered languages show a positive attitude towards the languages as a locus of ethnicity or as an important identity marker, and self-assessment for language proficiency or language use gains a high score. However, Kobari (2009) reveals that, in Butuanon, objective tests for language proficiency result in low scores, with extensive mixture with Cebuano. He proposes "the economy of distinction" principle, whereby salient structural features can be reduced as long as the language works as an ethnic distinction marker. Headland (2003) also maintains that Casiguran Agta is endangered not because it is not being spoken, but because it has been radically transformed into a creolized variant without being noticed by the users, a process that can be seen in other parts of the Austronesian speaking world as well. Here we can identify the discrepancy between the actual language proficiency and 'language ideology', that is, language user's beliefs about language constructed based on their limited knowledge or perception of language (Silverstein 1979, 1985).

### 15.2.2 Major factors responsible for language endangerment

The most common scenario whereby the language of a small population becomes endangered involves a massive influx of in-migration into the territory. This immigration scenario is observed in Ibatan (Gallego 2020), Arta (Kimoto 2017a), Casiguran Agta (Headland 1986, 2003, 2010), Central Tagbanwa (Scebold 2003), Manide (Lobel 2013a), and Butuanon (Kobari 2009). Immigration normally does not negatively affect the vitality of the languages if the immigrants are a relatively smaller population and do not intrude into the existent communities. However, if the communities have undergone a massive influx of outsiders, and the population of the newcomers has outnumbered the old communities, then a critical point will be reached in which balanced symbiosis collapses, and the majority's language begins to threaten the smaller languages. For example, Quirino province of northern Luzon witnessed the immigration of diverse ethnic groups from Cordillera such as Bontok, Ifugao, and Kalinga, and from the north such as Gaddang, Yogad, and Ibanag, but their languages did not become the language for wider communication. The real impact on the endangerment of Arta is the Ilokano group. They far outnumbered the other tribal populations, and Ilokano came to be used as a regional lingua franca.

Language endangerment may often be accelerated by increasing exogamy, and also involve discrimination and exclusion from majorities. If newly arrived and original residents build tighter social relationships with increased intermarriage between the majority and minority groups, then language attrition becomes more serious. Headland's longitudinal survey on marriage patterns among the Casiguran Agta reveals a rapid growth of exogamy with Tagalog speakers, accompanied by significant increase in the use of Tagalog at home. By the same token, the immigration of Kuyonon speakers into the Central Tagbanwa area has increased intermarriage between these groups. Central Tagbanwa speakers have become a minority and are shifting to Kuyonon. Discrimination also discourages the use of their mother tongue. It is often observed that the majority may hold derogatory attitudes towards neighbouring minorities. Several fieldworkers have reported that majority groups look down on minorities and joke about them and their languages. García-Laguía (2018) mentions that Northern Alta speakers have experienced being laughed at, and thus hesitated to speak their language in public. Such derogatory attitudes by the majority are pervasive, but seem to be particularly directed with racial overtones towards Negrito peoples. Additionally, the massive influx of newcomers in the territories may result in a 'push chain', that is, driving away the original inhabitants to more remote areas. If a small population group becomes involved in a push chain, it may have a devastating impact on language vitality. The Arta originally lived in Aglipay, Quirino province of northern Luzon, but were driven away from the area after an increased number of immigrants began cultivating the land that once was the Arta's hunting area. The Arta people then became scattered among different Casiguran Agta communities in Quirino and Aurora provinces, and their language became moribund.

Modernization and sociocultural changes have also had significant impacts on indigenous languages, as is also observed outside the Philippines. In the educational context, use of Tagalog/Filipino as the language of instruction has shaped the way young people interact with each other. Also, as lamented by Reid (2009d), many of the traditional rituals and social practices have been lost in the community in Bontok. "The working group system (*obfo*) has disintegrated. Girls' dormitories (*pangis*) that once played a key role in the establishment of working groups have disappeared" (Reid 2009d: 19). The spread of the internet and mobile devices is also completely changing the way people interact with friends and family. Research conducted in 2015 on Maranao-speaking people shows that on Facebook, English is by far the dominant language for communication (Latip-Yusoph 2016).[5] She suspects the lack of orthography in the local language may be relevant to the result. But it may also be due to the fact that Facebook and similar technologies are strongly associated with Western 'cool' culture. This result suggests that indigenous languages are being replaced by more powerful languages in such new domains even when communicating with family and close friends.

### 15.2.3 Recent documentation projects

A large body of linguistic and sociolinguistic documentation has been conducted in the Philippines long before language endangerment became at worldwide issue (e.g. Vanoverbergh 1937, 1954; Reid 1971; Zorc 1977; Quakenbush 1989). Here, a sample of current or ongoing documentation projects are focused on. Alexandro García-Laguía has been documenting Northern Alta, a Negrito language spoken by fewer than 300 people in Aurora, the Eastern side of Luzon island. His doctoral dissertation dealt with grammar and texts of the language (García-Laguía 2018) and all the 175 sessions are deposited in ELAR (Endangered Language Archive). Maria Kristina Gellego is conducting a sociolinguistic documentation project on Ibatan, spoken in the

[5] This is also illustrated among author Kimoto's Facebook friends whose native language is Casiguran Agta. Although their communication is largely limited within speech community members, they tend to use simple English, Tagalog, and Ilokano.

island of Babuyan Claro, Cagayan, Philippines. Funded by ELDP, the documentation project focuses on the sociolinguistic dynamics of the language and the contact-induced change affected by Ilokano. Jason Lobel has been devoting himself to the documentation and description of a number of Negrito languages. His dissertation includes a large amount of first-hand sociolinguistic information and grammatical description of Philippine Negrito and non-Negrito languages (which he renames 'Black Filipino'). His publications include Maranao phonology (Lobel and Riwarung 2011), Remontado phonology and morphology (Lobel and Surbano 2019), Inagta Alabat phonology and grammar (Lobel, Alpay, R. Barreno, and E. Barreno 2020), to list a few. Laura Robinson archived data and has several publications about Dupaningan Agta, a Negrito language. She published a reference grammar based on her own dissertation, archived eighty sessions (elicitation sessions, wordlists, stories, and songs) in PARADISEC in Australia (Robinson 2006), and also published on ethical and technical issues in language documentation (Honeyman and Robinson 2007; Robinson 2010). Yukinori Kimoto, has been working on Arta. In an ELDP-funded project, he deposited a collection of audio and video recordings in ELAR (Kimoto 2017c). His publications include educational material based on an Arta text, a reference grammar (Kimoto 2017a), and audio-synchronized narrative texts with morphological and syntactic glossing (Kimoto 2019). Finally, Lawrence A. Reid is currently collaborating on and supervising a community-based dictionary of the Isinay language (Reid and Salvador-Amores 2016).

## 15.3 Malaysia

Malaysia is an ethnically diverse country whose population consists of approximately 55% Malays, 25% people of Chinese ancestry (speaking a number of Chinese languages), 13% other indigenous groups, and 7% of Indian ancestry (mostly Tamil speaking) (Coluzzi 2017a). *Ethnologue* (Eberhard et al. 2020) currently lists 133 living languages spoken in Malaysia. Of these, twenty-one are non-indigenous and nine are varieties of Malay, meaning that 103 of these languages are spoken by the 13% of the population that is non-Malay indigenous. These indigenous minority languages include Austronesian languages and also Austroasiatic languages spoken by older inhabitants of the region, called Orang Asli ('original people'). Standard Malay is the official national language, while there are several varieties of vernacular Malay spoken in different parts of the country. English is also very widely used, functioning as a de facto second language, which is often preferred for interethnic communication (Coluzzi 2017a).

The regions that now make up Malaysia came under expanding British hegemony through the eighteenth to twentieth centuries. During this period, large numbers of Chinese and Indian labourers were brought into the region to work in mining and agriculture, leading to the rather unusual current ethnic mix (Coluzzi 2017b). Prior to independence in 1957, both Malay and English were official languages; after independence, Malay became the sole official language, while English retained official status for a ten-year transitional period (Asmah Haji Omar 1982). Despite decades of language planning, Malay has not yet been able to reach the goal of being a fully realized, unifying national language, that both Malays and non-Malays can identify with (Coluzzi 2017b). Historically, strong ethnic identification vis-à-vis the Muslim Malays, and the existence of English as an alternative lingua franca, have helped many communities retain their ethnic languages. Yet, as outlined below, the prominence of Malay, particularly in education, means that, in the twenty-first century, several indigenous languages are now becoming threatened.

Of the Austronesian languages spoken in Malaysia, Malay, in its standard and vernacular varieties, is quite strong due to its position as national language and language of the largest ethnic group. A number of Malay varieties dominate the languages spoken on the Malay peninsula, where indigenous minority languages include the Austroasiatic languages of the Semang and Senoi Orang Asli. These Aslian languages are generally still vigorous (Coluzzi 2017a), but are outside the purview of this chapter. The Austronesian minority languages of Malaysia are found in the states of Sarawak and Sabah in the north of Borneo, where they coexist with varieties of Malay (and non-indigenous minority languages). While some of these Austronesian minority languages are considered vigorous or stronger, the vast majority are considered threatened or more seriously endangered (Eberhard et al. 2020). Iban is one of the stronger languages, having a plurality of speakers in the state of Sarawak which is about 29% ethnically Iban, compared to 26% Chinese and 22% Malay (Ting and Ling 2013). Iban has a certain level of prestige and is even used by some non-Iban speakers for social and business purposes. It is also heard on the Malaysian public broadcaster and appears in special columns in the newspapers. Iban is not used as a medium of instruction, but is taught as a subject in some schools (Ting and Ling 2013).

Even among the more vigorous minority languages, there are signs that younger speakers are using their ethnic languages less frequently than older speakers. Additionally, all minority languages in Malaysia are showing signs of change, including Malay loanwords and Malay morphosyntactic and phonological features, and all "are experiencing different degrees of language shift, which may be faster or slower depending on various factors, like the size of the community, whether it is concentrated or dispersed, whether it has a written form and/or it is taught at school, if it is at least partially supported by some media, and so on" (Coluzzi 2017a: 217).

Anonby (2020) outlines this process in detail for Sebuyau, a variety of Iban spoken in Sarawak. Sebuyau speakers recognize ongoing language shift, with younger speakers describing the language of elders as 'purer', while the older speakers pejoratively refer to younger people's speech as 'New Sebuyau', due to mixing with Malay. Despite these changes, Sebuyau remains quite vigorous in its home territory, where people maintain stable diglossia, using Sebuyau among themselves and using Malay when speaking to others. In contrast, Sebuyau speakers residing in urban areas, with greater diversity and more intense interethnic interactions, are much more likely to shift to Malay as their dominant language. Coluzzi (2017a) presents Bidayuh as another vigorous language of Sarawak,[6] attributing its strength to factors such as high levels of endogamy among those living in the traditional Bidayuh area; continuing to be the majority ethnic group in their region, retaining close-knit social networks, traditional values, and positive attitudes toward their language, while at the same time accepting ideologies of modernity through education and mass media (in Malay and English), and conversion to Christianity which differentiates them from the majority Malays and helps maintain their separate identity. Complementing this pattern, we find that in the case of greater interethnic interaction, language shift is occurring more quickly. In exogamous marriages, the family language is often a variety of Malay, rather than either ethnic language of the parents. Those who migrate to urban areas, and in particular those who attend university, tend to lose their heritage language. Coluzzi (2020) suggests that with 42% of Malaysians attending university, this trend in language loss does not bode well for the overall vitality of minority languages in Malaysia.

In Sabah state, the vitality of the main indigenous language, Kadazan-Dusun, varies by location. In some areas it is quite strong, even being used for educational purposes, but in other regions is appears to be threatened (Ting and Tham 2014). Sabah Malay is the lingua franca of Sabah state, often learned by children before starting school, where they then learn Standard Malay (Smith and Smith 2017). Local groups have been working with SIL International and UNESCO, to develop their heritage languages, for example an Iranun trilingual picture book (Iranun, Malay, and English), and playschools for Iranun, Tobilung, Kimaragan, Serudung Murut, Rungus, and West Coast Bajau children. These programmes involve adult family members and other older community members engaging with the children.

In Sarawak, the Sarawak variety of Malay, Iban, and English, are all used as lingua francas. About a quarter of the Sarawak population is of Chinese ancestry, speaking various Chinese languages and using Mandarin as an in-group lingua franca. It is the presence of standard Malay within the education system that plays an important role in language maintenance and shift. Sebuyau speakers have claimed that their language was stronger during the time of English medium education (Anonby 2020). They feel that the change to Malay medium education from the 1970s helped precipitate the influence of Malay on their own language and the gradual shift that has been reported among younger members of the community. As a response to this pressure from Malay, the Bidayuh, Iban, and Kelabit communities have initiated mother tongue based multilingual education beginning at preschool, with the intention that children will learn Malay and English once they are in school but are still in need of support language documentation and materials development (McLellan 2014).

Anonby (2020) points out that Malaysian government policy encourages, at least indirectly, the social and economic segregation of different ethnic groups, a practice that may, in turn, help some groups maintain their language. Part of this has to do with religious differences, where Malay identity is strongly linked to Islam, and many of the minority groups are either Christian or still maintain indigenous religious practices. This association of language with religious and ethnic identity is one incentive for Christian groups to maintain their ethnic languages to distinguish themselves from Muslim Malays. Nonetheless, Ting and Ling (2013) report increasing use of Malay among youth. In a survey they conducted of Sarawak teenagers (13–17 years old), these young speakers reported often using Malay rather than ethnic languages in school friendships and on social media. This move to Malay was not as strong among speakers of Iban, Penan, Kelabit, Sa'ban, and Murut,[7] who reported that they use their heritage language more often than Malay. Sercombe (2020) has also reported that the Penan of Sarawak do not codeswitch as frequently as the Penan of Brunei. Young speakers of Bidayuh, Kenyah, and Kayan report using Malay and their ethnic language equally and Ting and Ling (2013) consider these languages still quite vigorous. Young speakers of Bisaya, Kiput, Berawan, and Melanau, however, report far more extensive use of Malay, indicating these languages are more vulnerable. This is particularly the case for Melanau, about half of whom are in fact Muslim and

[6] Note however, that *Ethnologue* (Eberhard et al. 2020) lists four varieties of Bidayuh [sdo, sne, bth, trx] and categorizes them all as threatened.

[7] Ting and Ling (2013) do not differentiate between varieties of Murut, of which Eberhard et al. (2020) list ten.

so take on attributes associated with Islam in Malaysia, including use of Malay. Yet, in all cases—vigorous as well as more threatened languages—Ting and Ling (2103) predict that increasing multilingualism, a lack of stable diglossia, and pressure from the role of standard Malay as the national language will be detrimental to maintenance of ethnic languages.

## 15.4 Brunei

Brunei Darussalam, a small kingdom on the north coast of Borneo, is home to ten indigenous languages: Malay, Kedayan, Tutong, Belait, Dusun, Bisaya, Murut, Iban, Penan, and Mukah (Coluzzi 2011). Large populations of the latter three languages also reside in Malaysia. The Brunei government considers these to be dialects of Malay, despite being classified on linguistic grounds as separate languages (McLellan 2014). Brunei Malay is the language of the majority and politically dominant ethnic group, who make up about 65% of the population. The other nine indigenous languages are spoken by about a quarter of the population. About ten per cent of the population are of Chinese ancestry, with the older generations speaking a variety of Chinese languages and the younger shifting to Mandarin. Brunei Malay is the default lingua franca of the country, while Standard Malay is mainly used in government offices and to facilitate communication with Malaysia and Indonesia. English serves as a de facto additional national language (Coluzzi 2011).

Malay remains vigorous and, since at least the mid-twentieth century, increased pressure to use Malay has caused a shift away from the other indigenous languages in a process that includes both Islamicization and Malayicization, or 'Bruneization' (Noor Azam 2005), in what Noor Azam and Siti Ajeerah (2016) have claimed is voluntary acquiescence on the part of the ethnic groups themselves. The result is that all the indigenous languages other than Malay are considered vulnerable, with Belait the most critically endangered, followed by Tutong, Dusun, and Penan. Dusun, for example, has been shown to be undergoing rapid shift. In a test of active and passive knowledge of the language, Noor Azam and Siti Ajeerah (2016) found that respondents over ninety years of age recorded 90% accuracy, while those between fifteen and thirty years of age recorded 37% receptive accuracy and only 11% active accuracy. Some other languages, particularly Iban, appear to remain somewhat stronger (Coluzzi 2011), but Noor Azam and Siti Ajeerah (2016) stress that across the country younger speakers are shifting to what they call pan-Brunei Malay. The Penan population in Brunei is relatively small and their language shows many innovations from both Malay and Iban. Sercombe (1996, 2020) describes the Eastern Penan of Brunei as having a complex composite identity. They identify with neighbours such as the Iban and also with the wider non-Malay community through use of a regionally inflected variety of Malay. A number of Penan have also converted to Islam and have thereby adopted aspects of Brunei Malay identity, while continuing to consider themselves Penan.

There is no space for indigenous languages as the medium of instruction in education. English has long been the main language of higher education, and is now increasingly important as the language of instruction in secondary and primary schools, while all classes not taught in English are taught in Standard Malay (Coluzzi 2011). At the same time, the University of Brunei Darussalam now teaches Iban, Tutong, and Dusun as subjects within a recently initiated Borneo Languages programme. This initiative has helped to raise the status of indigenous languages and promote positive attitudes towards them among the wider population, but it is yet to be seen whether this initiative will improve language vitality.

## 15.5 Indonesia

Indonesia has great language diversity (second only to Papua New Guinea), with estimates of 350 (Cribb 2000) to 710 (Eberhard et al. 2020) languages spoken (with the caveat mentioned above that *Ethnologue* makes finer grained distinctions between varieties than many others do). More than two thirds of indigenous Indonesian languages are Austronesian, with the remainder categorized as Papuan, although a much larger proportion of the population is Austronesian speaking, as most Papuan languages have relatively small speaker populations. Indonesia is home to the largest Austronesian language by first-language speaker population: Javanese (68.2 million). Other large languages with over a million speakers include Indonesian (42.8 M as a first language), Sundanese (32.4 M), Malay (4.9 M), Minangkabau (4.2 M), Bugis (3.9 M), Acehnese (3.5 M), Balinese (3.3 M), and Sasak (3.2 M). However, the majority of indigenous languages have speaker populations in the thousands (or fewer). The larger languages are predominately found in the western part of the archipelago and as one moves east there are increasing numbers of languages with smaller speaker populations. About 50% of the languages of Indonesia are spoken in the regions of Maluku and Papua, which have about 5% of the population (Collins 2019) and there is a much higher incidence of language endangerment in eastern Indonesia compared with western Indonesia (Florey 2005b). Anderbeck (2015) estimates that less than half (46%) the languages of Indonesia remain vital, being used in a wide variety of domains, in a stable diglossic relationship with Indonesian and with clear transmission to the next generation. Approximately one quarter are vulnerable, with domains of use declining and younger speakers shifting to primarily using Indonesian or some other language of wider communication. Well over one quarter of Indonesian languages are dying and may be lost in one or two generations.

### 15.5.1 Historic and contemporary causes of language endangerment

The contemporary linguistic ecology of Indonesia has been shaped by a complex history of migration, trade, and shifting political power, which has seen waves of influence from outside the region. This has included the rise of Indianized Hindu-Buddhist states and the concomitant influence of Sanskrit on languages of the region, followed by the introduction of Islam and with it the Arabic language. As the Netherlands established itself as the dominant colonial power in the region, Dutch developed a stronger influence than the previously important colonial language of Portuguese. The languages of Chinese migrants have also influenced local languages. The current globalized dominance of English as an international lingua franca is also strongly felt in Indonesia. Two key and closely related developments from this history that impact directly on language maintenance today are the consolidation of political power across the entire archipelago and the establishment of a variety of Malay, renamed Indonesian, as the national language (Adelaar 2000). The ascendence of Indonesian has been considered a 'miracle' of language planning (Fishman 1978; for a more nuanced discussion see Errington 1998b), yet during the early decades of Indonesian independence the local languages of the archipelago for the most part continued to thrive. More recently the dominance of Indonesian has contributed to the shift away from, and in many cases the endangerment of, local indigenous languages. The authoritarian Suharto regime, in power from the mid-1960s until 1998, oversaw an exponential increase in the use of Indonesian, propelled by the expansion of education and mass communication throughout the archipelago. During this time local languages had little official support. While bi- or multilingualism with Indonesian as a second language remained the norm in the early decades after Indonesian independence, increasing numbers of children are now growing up as first-language speakers of Indonesian, with only a cursory knowledge of their heritage language. While command of Indonesian is crucial for economic success in contemporary Indonesia, as Arka (2013) points out, speaking only Indonesian at the expense of the local language does not, in itself, guarantee a good job and can in fact cause social dislocation. As part of the post-Suharto democratization process, much government power has been decentralized under a policy of regional autonomy. There is now a renewed interest in the maintenance and revitalization of local languages, although much work remains.

Within Indonesia's rich lingua-scape, the government idealizes a stable diglossia, with the national language intended for public interactions and regional languages for personal contexts, while international languages are appropriate for dealings external to the country. This neat division has been recently reimagined in the emotionally laden government formulation that citizens should "'love' their local languages, 'use' their one shared national language, Indonesian, and 'study' foreign languages" (Zentz 2015a: 52). Yet the roles played by these differing scales of language are more complex than this. International languages and Indonesian are being used in an expanding range of domains, with a corresponding reduction in use of local languages, resulting in fewer opportunities for the natural acquisition of local language and culture (Arka 2015). When there is a break in intergenerational transmission of language, as observed by Jukes (2010) for Ratahan (Toratán) of Sulawesi, language acquisition takes on an obscure quality and speakers may feel learning needs external motivation and can no longer be done 'naturally' at home. Thus the focus of acquiring local languages shifts to school contexts, where they become associated with formality and evaluation, adding to discomfort and stress.

Local languages can differ in their scaled relation to each other and to languages of wider communication, as we also saw for the Philippines. For example, Bali is dominated by Balinese speakers and the vitality of their language benefits from government recognition of traditional social institutions and the relative prosperity of the province. As Arka notes, "traditional leadership tied to the traditional social structure for the whole ethnic group is important for the survival of the culture and language of the ethnic group against external pressures or influences" (2007: 80). On the other hand, a minority ethnolinguistic group in an administrative region dominated by another group may be doubly disadvantaged. Arka (2007) discusses the Rongga of Flores for whom poor economic conditions and the dismantling of local institutions by the Indonesian government decrease local autonomy and contribute to language attrition, spurred by pressure from the locally dominant Manggarai, as well as from Malay and Indonesian. In contrast to both these scenarios, Maluku province is home to several indigenous languages, none of which is dominant (Florey and Ewing 2010). While the rhetoric of support for local languages has been strong, it is difficult to implement large-scale revitalization programmes due to diversity of languages. Additionally, the prominent role of Ambonese Malay, the local lingua franca, augmented by the growing importance of Indonesian, encourages a shift away from small local languages (Musgrave and Ewing 2006). Similarly, speakers of Minahasan languages in northern Sulawesi are shifting to Manado Malay (Brickell 2018). In both cases, people often express a stronger sense of identity in terms the broader region rather than their local ethnolinguistic group (Brickell 2018; Florey and Ewing 2010). Yet another language situation is exemplified by Lampung province, where the Lampung-speaking people are now the minority in their homeland, due to large-scale transmigration in the twentieth century, primarily from Java and Bali, and this ethnic diversity has encouraged the use of Indonesian. However, Putra (2018) reports a trend in which many young people in Lampung are embracing a regional identity, which includes learning the Lampung language, even when their ethnic ancestry is from other parts of the country.

Social change is often accompanied by language shift and two areas of change that have strongly affected local languages in Indonesia include education and demographics.

During the period after Indonesian independence, local languages were often used in the first three years of primary education, to be replaced by Indonesian from grade four onwards, but today Indonesian is the language of instruction from the outset of schooling. It has been reported that as a result, parents across the country often shift to speaking Indonesian with their children to prepare them for school, whereas in the past they would have spoken their own local language, leaving Indonesian for later formal study. Now it is the local languages that are forced into formal study (if studied at all). *Muatan lokal* 'local content' is a space of a few hours a week in the curriculum for content not specified in the national curriculum and this is sometimes used for teaching local languages, but there are numerous obstacles, predominately involving resources (lack of teachers and materials) and competition for other topics that might be taught (*muatan lokal* is often used for other cultural instruction or for additional English lessons). The option of having a local language as the language of instruction is simply not a possibility given the way the role of the national language is constructed (Tollefson 2013; Zentz 2015a).

Movements of people have long been associated with language shift. For example, in the sixteenth century, a trade centre was established on Ambon island in Maluku by the newly arrived Europeans and this precipitated the loss of indigenous local languages and a shift to Ambonese Malay in nearby communities, followed by a similar shift in villages that later converted to Christianity. At the time, villages that converted to Islam and were thus less directly associated with colonial intrusion, were more likely to retain their local languages (Collins 2019). In contemporary Indonesia, with dramatically increased movement and interaction between people of different backgrounds, Muslim villages in Maluku have also started the shift towards Ambonese Malay as their predominant language (Musgrave and Ewing 2006). In a similar vein, accelerated social change and population movements across contemporary Indonesia are contributing to a rapid increase in language endangerment. This shift is primarily driven by intensified interaction between people from heterogeneous ethnolinguistic backgrounds, which drives greater use of languages of wider communication, whether Indonesian or regional lingua francas. With this comes a reduction in opportunities to use local indigenous languages and, eventually, the end of transfer to younger generations. Arka (2015) notes this is especially the case in urban areas, while in rural areas, local languages may still be used more frequently in a wider range of domains. However, Pepinsky, Abtahian, and Cohn (2020) have shown convincingly that this is due not so much to urbanization per se, but to the strong effect that ethnic diversity has on the shift to speaking Indonesian. That is, regions that are ethnically homogeneous, whether rural or urban, are much more likely to maintain the local language, whereas regions that are ethnically diverse, whether rural or urban, have a much higher probability of shifting to Indonesian, with that probability being even higher in urban areas. Furthermore, when people return from urban to rural areas, they often bring with them more prestigious, cosmopolitan ways of interacting which can effect language use in the home villages (Anderbeck 2015: 20). Use of contemporary media—including television and other mass media, mobile phones, and social networking—also exposes people to language geared toward mixed communities and promotes use of Indonesian (and English).

Despite the exponential growth in the use of Indonesian, often at the expense of the local language, there remains what Abtahian and Cohn call an "ideology of multilingualism" (2018: 110), projected by the nation motto *bhinneka tunggal ika* 'unity in diversity', with the result that people often assume local languages have greater vitality than they do. For example, in the early 2000s, older speakers of Rutah (Amahai) in Maluku reported stronger language vitality than was objectively the case (Margaret Florey, p.c.), and speakers of threatened Wamesa in West Papua are not concerned that children are not acquiring the language, despite feeling proud of the language, and they assume it will continue to be used in the future (Gasser 2017a). Similarly, Javanese speakers have reported to author Ewing that it is not a problem if children speak Indonesian as a first language because it is assumed they will pick up Javanese later, something that often does not happen. It has regularly been observed that communities only become aware of language shift once it is very far along. Arka (2013) found that raising awareness around language displacement in minority communities is difficult and that elders, in various minority communities he has worked with, only became aware of the threat of language endangerment when they were asked to reflect on language use in the old days compared to today.

### 15.5.2 Recent documentation and maintenance activities

Recent documentation work on Austronesian languages of Indonesia includes, for example, research on various Malay and Malayic varieties of Sumatra, including work by Yanti (2010) on Jambi Malay, Ernanda (2017) on Kerinci, and an overview of Southern Sumatran Malay lects by McDowell and Anderbeck (2020). McDonnell (2016b) has documented Besemah and has recently started a project on Nasal (see also Anderbeck and Aprilani 2013). Also in the Sumatra region, Leukon has been documented by Lubis (2019). Brickell (2016b) has documented Tonsawang of the Minahasa district in North Sulawesi. Soriente (2020) has conducted extensive documentation of Kenyah, Kayan, and other languages of Borneo. In West Papua, Arnold (2018a) has worked on Ambel. For a review of other documentation work in Eastern Indonesia, see Sawaki and Arka (2018).

In addition to research projects, capacity building within local communities is crucial, in order to help maintain or reinvigorate local languages and provide sustainable support for a range of language vitality activities. Jukes, Shiohara, and Yanti (2017) report on a recent series of workshops held in different locations across Indonesia in collaboration between Indonesian and international researchers, which aimed to increase awareness and skills around language documentation among Indonesian academics and students. Arka (2007) suggests that strengthening traditional social structures and working with a range of stakeholders is also crucial in language maintenance programmes. Many dynamic language maintenance projects target both elders, who are knowledge bearers, and youth, who carry this knowledge into the future (Arka 2013). Putra (2018) highlights this in his work on youth language activists. These activists have been working with elders to produce Lampung language YouTube videos and encourage school students to use Lampung on social media. Such multimodal, cross-generational initiatives have been useful in shifting the nature of the local language ecology. Contemporary technologies help "youth learn, use and advocate for their Indigenous languages, offering hope for supporting language vitality in the future" (Putra 2018: 7). Putra (2018) also points out that such work takes advantage of opportunities afforded by urbanization, modernization, and globalization, conditions which are often seen as detrimental to the maintenance of indigenous languages. Collins (2019) also notes that electronic communications can expand opportunities to use local heritage languages even as urbanization strengthens the role of the national language.

## 15.6 East Timor

As of 2003, most indigenous languages of East Timor (Timor Leste) were relatively vigorous. At that time, only the Austronesian languages Makuva (also called Maku'a or Lóvaia) was considered in serious trouble (Hajek, Himmelmann, and Bowden 2003), while Idate, Waima'a, and Naueti were considered potentially under threat due to population displacement (Hajek 2002). Today, according to *Ethnologue* (Eberhard et al. 2020), Makuva is considered nearly extinct while Naueti is in fact considered vigorous. Idate and Waima'a, along with Habun, Kairui-Midiki, and Lakalei, are considered threatened. The other nine Austronesian languages of East Timor (as well as the Papuan languages of the country) are classified as vigorous or stronger.

As we have seen elsewhere, changes in language vitality can be closely linked to government policies, demographic movements and social change. Three clear historical stages in East Timor include colonization by the Portuguese up to 1975, the occupation and annexation by Indonesia from 1975 to 1999, and the subsequent East Timorese independence which continues to the present. East Timorese society has long been characterized as a stable multilingual society, a situation which has helped local languages remain vigorous, and the introduction of Portuguese during the colonial period added to the linguistic ecology without destabilizing multilingual practice (Hajek 2002). During this time, Portuguese was the language of education, the church, and military, and East Timorese elites were co-opted into the colonial project through an official policy of 'assimilation', which included the adoption of Portuguese (Taylor-Leech 2008).

The occupation of East Timor by Indonesia after the Portuguese withdrawal in 1975 caused great social disruption, which had a negative effect on the vitality of local languages. As well as population displacement, the death of hundreds of thousands of East Timorese and the arrival of tens of thousands of migrants from different parts of Indonesia, a rapid programme of Indonesianization was also introduced. This included the introduction of Indonesian as the language of instruction at all levels of education and its use in government and media. Conversion to Catholicism, which began under the Portuguese, accelerated under Indonesian occupation (Taylor-Leech 2008). While Portuguese had been the language of the Church during the colonial period, under Indonesian occupation Tetun (also called Tetum)—a local Austronesian language, with a history as a regional lingua franca—rather than Indonesian, became the language of Church activities (Cabral and Martin-Jones 2018). This promoted the wider use of Tetun as a lingua franca and acted as a counterweight to Indonesianization. While Portuguese was banned by the Indonesian government, it played a key role in the guerrilla fight for independence, and thus lost its association with European colonialism to became a symbol of resistance (Cabral and Martin-Jones 2018; da Costa Cabral 2019). With support for Indonesian by the Indonesian government and for Tetun by the Catholic church, local languages were neglected (Hajek 2002).

Layers of social identity which existed prior to independence have only grown more complex, with the result that the role of languages in independent East Timor has been "hotly contested" (Taylor-Leech 2008). Portuguese and Tetun have been established as co-official languages, a status that was agreed to after lengthy debate and consensus building (Cabral and Martin-Jones 2018). Indonesian and English remain important exogenous working languages. Da Costa Cabral (2019: 46) points out that the colonial and occupying powers promoted a 'monolingual order' and that with the independence of East Timor, this monolingual order ended. In addition to the co-official languages, the constitution recognizes the ethnolocal languages as 'national languages', to be valued and developed by the state, and while people generally continue to use their local languages for non-official purposes related to their more traditional identities, in the early years of independence they did not receive official or practical support (Taylor-Leech 2013). Today, multilingualism is generally viewed positively but most of the discourse is around multilingualism with Tetun, Portuguese, and English, without regard to local languages (da Costa Cabral 2019). This sets up what Taylor-Leech (2008) describes as a combination of both established and ad hoc power relationships, which has produced the kinds of unequal multilingualisms outlined by Tupas (2015) and has led to the increased vulnerability of several indigenous languages mentioned above.

A case in point is Makuva, which has become nearly extinct due to a number of factors as discussed in Hajek et al. (2003). These include that it has always had a fairly small speaker population, which had long been dominated by the much larger population of speakers of the more prestigious Papuan language, Fataluku. The region of eastern East Timor where Makuva speakers lived has had a long history of migrations and the language was already in decline from the early twentieth century. Major population displacement during World War II saw the end of intergenerational transfer of the language. In the early twenty-first century, descendants of Makuva speakers have shifted fully to Fatuluku, both in terms of language use and ethnic identity. Van Engelenhoven (2010b: 179) suggests that use of Makuva nonetheless continues in attenuated form, elevated through 'language concealment' to the status of ritual language among these (now) Fatuluku speakers.

Greater support for other local languages now seems to be possible, due to changes in education policy in the past decade. Previously, in the first years of transition to independence, Indonesian was still the predominant language of education while Portuguese was being (re)introduced. By 2004, Tetun was given a place with Portuguese, but their respective roles were not always clear and the goal appeared to be assimilation to Portuguese rather than a balanced bilingualism (Cabral and Martin-Jones 2018; Taylor-Leech 2013). In 2008 the Ministry of Education initiated a debate on the role of mother tongues in education. New guidelines were released in 2011, which suggested the use of students' mother tongue as language of instruction in preschool and for introducing literacy in Grade 1, then moving to bilingual education in the mother tongue, and Tetun during Grades 2 and 3. This would be followed by bilingual education in Tetun and Portuguese from Grade 4, with the mother tongue becoming a subject of instruction. This process has only been introduced as pilot programmes in three districts, which include the Austronesian languages Baikeno and Galolen and the Papuan language Fataluku. This has set up an ideological conflict. On the one hand, there are those who take the nationalist view that use of local languages in education would devalue Tetun and Portuguese and lead to national disunity. On the other hand, there are those who take the educationist perspective that use of mother tongues in early education promotes better educational outcomes. They add that in the long term this will further strengthen the nation and the use of the co-official languages, since those who do not already speak Portuguese or Tetun will be given access to these languages via mother tongue based education. Supporters of this programme see it as promoting equality and social inclusion, while detractors claim it confuses students (Taylor-Leech 2013, 2019). The mother tongue approach also raises the issue that speaker populations do not line up with districts and schools so that there will always be student populations who speak multiple mother tongues and decisions about which local language to privilege in education will disadvantage some students (Cabral and Martin-Jones 2018; Taylor-Leech 2013). This potentially creates localized language hierarchies and exacerbates inequalities of multilingualism. While these programmes have been introduced from the central government, they have also generated a fair amount of local interest. Cabral and Martin-Jones (2018) stress the importance of even more extensive cooperation with local stakeholders, such as parents, teachers, and community groups, to ensure linguistic communities have a strong voice in their preferred outcomes. At the same time, Portuguese and English immersion programmes in private schools further "reinforce elitism and exacerbate educational inequalities" (Taylor-Leech 2019: 310), which could further alienate students from local languages. In any case, teachers are an important part of the process as they "engag[e] in small, local acts of linguistic citizenship" and "interpret and appropriate language-in-education policies in ways that are fine-tuned to local social and linguistic conditions" (Cabral and Martin-Jones 2018: 121).

## 15.7 Madagascar

Malagasy, spoken on the eastern African island of Madagascar, can be characterized as a macrolanguage, including several closely related varieties which often diverge enough that they are not properly thought of as dialects. *Ethnologue* (Eberhard et al. 2020) includes eleven varieties of Malagasy within this classification, although Kikusawa (2012) suggests this may under-represent the actual diversity of Malagasy sublanguages (see also Hoogervorst, this volume, §17.2.1). The Merina variety of Central Malagasy is the basis of the standardized, national language. All other varieties of Malagasy are classified as vigorous by *Ethnologue*. Dahl (2011) points out that Madagascar is unusual among African nations in having a single dominant (macro)language, rather than being a highly multilingual nation. We can point out that Madagascar is similarly unusual compared to the highly multilingual Austronesian-dominant countries of Southeast Asia discussed in this chapter, yet possible threats to language vitality may still be seen.

The Merina kingdom began to consolidate power in Madagascar in the early nineteenth century, at the same time British missionaries arrived and produced a bible translation in the Merina variety of Malagasy (Bouwer 2005). With the establishment of Christianity as the state religion in the 1860s, the influence of the Merina language was bolstered by government and church. The language ecology of Madagascar changed dramatically when the French annexed the island in 1896 and imposed the same assimilationist policy used across their colonies, which prioritized the use of French and supressed indigenous cultures (Spolsky 2018), thus "alienating the population from its own cultural roots" (Dahl 2011: 52). But even with the promotion of French throughout the country, Merina Malagasy continued to have a stronger national role than other varieties because many in the educated indigenous workforce of the French colonial administration were from the dominant Merina speaking area of the capital, Antananarivo. In the early twentieth century, the French government shifted to a bilingual education policy with mother tongue varieties of Malagasy in the lower grades and French in higher grades, but by the 1930s, French was made the sole official language with Malagasy treated as a foreign language in schools (Bouwer 2005). Language policy continued to shift after Madagascar's independence in 1960. French and Malagasy were made official languages; nonetheless, French continued to play an important role in public life and education. After a socialist takeover of government in the 1970s, Malagasy was raised to the status of national language, and a programme of *malgachisation* 'Malagasization' saw a shift to Malagasy as the language of education. There was dissatisfaction with this policy because French remained an important language of administration and was perceived as key to upward mobility (Verdier 2013), and in the 1990s there was a return to French as the language of instruction. Educational reforms introduced in 2008 saw a return to Malagasy as the language of instruction, with both French and English taught as subjects and a transition to French as language of instruction in higher grades. This oscillation between French and Malagasy has been described as driven by immediate political imperatives, rather than long-term planning (Bouwer 2005), and has had a deleterious effect on educational outcomes (Dahl 2011). There also continues to be a stigma attached to Malagasy, being considered poorly adapted to the modern world compared to French (Verdier 2013).

While a linguistic analytical approach highlights the differences between the sublanguages of Malagasy (see Howe, this volume, §40.1), language ideology within Madagascar often stresses linguistic unity for political purposes and only recognizes minor regional variations, despite difficulties of intelligibility between the standard and some regional varieties (Bouwer 2005). This has implications for documentation and support of the different varieties of Malagasy, as most research focuses on the dominant Merina variety. Kikusawa (2012) suggests that the ongoing promotion of the standard variety and ideological erasure of localized Malagasy sublanguages may have a levelling effect as standard features replace local features. Such a levelling process could have implications for the long term vitality of regional varieties. There have been hardly any language maintenance projects or research on language endangerment in Madagascar, despite the clear need for such work.

## 15.8 Concluding observations

Himmelmann (2010a) points out that simply cataloguing levels of language vitality does not give us insights into the mechanisms by which rapid language shift occurs. Rather, we need to think in terms of scenarios of language vitality because different communities will experience diverse social, economic, and political scenarios leading to language shift. In this chapter we have laid out broad national trends found across six countries in Southeast Asia with major populations who speak Malayo-Polynesian languages, as well as several representative examples of different language vitality scenarios in specific communities. A number of key recurring themes have emerged.

While language shift does often occur in communities "for reasons of political or economic expedience, without necessarily being pressured to do so" (McLellan 2014: 16), it is still important to question why shift is perceived as politically or economically expedient, and whether inequalities of access, power, and agency render such choices less than equitable. Coluzzi (2017a), discussing language vitality in Malaysia, points out that language maintenance need not be about enforcing a traditional lifestyle, but rather working to ensure people have local infrastructure and opportunities which allow authentic choice, as well as countering narratives and circumstances that conspire against local languages and encourage language shift.

May points out that "language loss is not only, perhaps not even primarily, a linguistic issue - it has much more to do with power, prejudice, (unequal) competition and, in many cases, overt discrimination and subordination" (2012: 4). Inequalities exemplified in this chapter arise as each society continues to evolve language ideologies, policies, and actions affected by their colonial pasts, current national ambitions, and localized aspirations of communities and individuals, in the context of a complex globalizing world. These complex sociopolitical and historical contexts often give rise the multi-layered multilingualisms illustrated several times above. A local language may be dominated by a national language, but at the same time dominate other, smaller local languages and pressures to shift may come from a variety of sources and move in a variety of competing directions. Education policy clearly plays a crucial role in language vitality throughout the region, setting expectations around the status and relationship between national, local and international languages. For example, the Philippines and East Timorese governments have initiated vigorous debates around the role of mother tongues in schools, while, in other countries, such issues are often not discussed at the national level and communities who speak (mostly smaller) local languages are generally unsupported and left to their own devices. Such government policies will in turn affect parents' attitudes and actions regarding transmission of heritage languages to the younger generation.

In discussing endangered minority languages of Borneo, McLellan (2014) presents a number of maintenance and revitalization strategies including documentation, mother tongue based bilingual education, as well as language study in higher education, development of new media resources, and improving the prestige of the language. These include top-down and bottom-up strategies and McLellan (2014) points out that crucially these must be deployed together with long term goals in mind—there is no simple quick fix. It is also clear from the cases discussed above that multiple stakeholders are involved, including communities, governments, non-government organizations, and academics. Successful maintenance of heritage languages comes from working together on multiple fronts. It is about building capacity for documenting, learning, and passing on language, and also crucially for building opportunities within communities that allow languages and cultures to be nurtured and adapted in order to thrive into the future.

CHAPTER 16

# Multilingualism

David Gil

## 16.1 Introduction

We tend to think of languages as discrete and reified entities, but this is an idealization. Out there in the real world, different languages, as well as different varieties of the same language, meet and combine to form complex linguistic ecologies. Indeed, the default situation is one in which speakers, and the communities which they constitute, enjoy mastery of more than just a single language variety, a state of affairs that is typically referred to as *multilingualism*.

Multilingualism comes in a number of distinct guises, often associated with different and more specific terms. *Bilingualism* refers to a situation where exactly two languages are involved. *Diglossia* is often used to describe a situation in which 'low' and 'high' registers of the same language constitute the two idealized end-points of a continuum. In this chapter, the term multilingualism is used to cover both of the above cases, as well as others in which a single speaker, or, more commonly, a community of speakers, enjoys mastery of two or more distinct languages and/or varieties of the same language.

This chapter presents an overview of multilingualism as manifest in MPSEA languages, the Malayo-Polynesian languages of Southeast Asia (as defined in the introduction to this volume). Attention is limited to contemporary multilingualism, even though multilingualism was undoubtedly present also in past times, as far back as we are able to reconstruct. Multilingualism may be classified in accordance with a variety of cross-cutting criteria; in this chapter, the focus is on the identities of the dialects and languages involved, and the sociolinguistic relationships that obtain among them. §16.2 introduces a classificatory schema characterizing the relationships among the dialects or languages in a multilingual situation. §§16.3, 16.4, and 16.5 then survey multilingualism within individual MPSEA languages, across MPSEA languages, and between MPSEA and non-Austronesian languages respectively. §16.6 offers some brief concluding remarks. The main goal of this chapter is to provide a sense of the pervasiveness of multilingualism, and the diversity of its forms and associated contexts, throughout the MPSEA-speaking region.

In this chapter, multilingualism in action is illustrated by means of *code-switching*, a naturalistically occurring phenomenon in which two or more distinct varieties or languages alternate within the same text, utterance, or even word. For some, code-switching represents the 'mess' that needs to be cleared away in order to arrive at a pure and unadulterated description of a pristine target language; however, in many cases, code-switching may be revealing of structural linguistic patterns and also the sociolinguistic circumstances that give rise to these patterns. The naturalistic examples presented in this chapter are taken from a combination of oral and written sources.[1]

## 16.2 Asymmetric multilingualism: The exotericity scale

Cases of multilingualism may be classified in accordance with the relationship that obtains among the participating dialects and languages. While, in some instances, the relevant dialects and languages stand in a symmetric relationship to one another, more commonly, the relationship between them is asymmetric.

Asymmetric multilingualism may be characterized in terms of the distinction between two modes of communication, *esoteric* and *exoteric*. Accordingly, dialects and languages may also be characterized as esoteric or exoteric to the extent that they are typically used for esoteric or exoteric communication. In particular, dialects and languages

[1] In the examples cited in this chapter, the dialect or language associated with each morpheme is indicated by a letter code directly above it. For oral utterances, the source of each utterance is indicated beneath it in brackets: those labelled DG are from the author's own unpublished corpus, while those labelled JFS are from the open-access Max Planck Institute Jakarta Field Station corpus (Gil, Tadmor, Bowden, and Taylor 2015), where, for each such utterance, its unique numerical ID code is indicated. In the case of written utterances, the first line presents the utterance italicized precisely as it was written, complete with emoticons, expressive orthographic idiosyncrasies as well as spelling mistakes; following that, it is represented one more time in a normalized orthography. All other data cited in this chapter, unless otherwise attributed, is from the author's own fieldwork.

David Gil, *Multilingualism*. In: *The Oxford Guide to the Malayo-Polynesian Languages of Southeast Asia*. Edited by: Alexander Adelaar and Antoinette Schapper, Oxford University Press.
 DOI: 10.1093/oso/9780198807353.003.0016

may be positioned on a set of interrelated scales together constituting the *scale of exotericity*, as indicated in (1):

| (1) | *The scale of exotericity:* | *esoteric* | — | *exoteric* |
|---|---|---|---|---|
| (a) | *modality:* | oral | — | written |
| (b) | *area:* | small | — | large |
| (c) | *polity:* | regional | — | national |
| (d) | *status:* | unofficial | — | official |
| (e) | *population:* | small | — | large |
| (f) | *societal complexity:* | low | — | high |
| (g) | *contextuality:* | private | — | public |
| (h) | *community identity:* | intra-group | — | inter-group |
| (i) | *power:* | low | — | high |
| (j) | *prestige:* | low | — | high |

While the ten scales shown in (1) above are logically independent of one another, they are related through a complex network of causal relationships, and therefore tend to cluster empirically. This provides the motivation for viewing them as realizations of a single more abstract scale, that of exotericity, on which particular dialects and languages are positioned.[2]

Asymmetric multilingualism involves dialects or languages falling on different points of the exotericity scale. To see this, consider the case of multilingualism on the island of Roon, in the Cenderawasih Bay region of Western New Guinea. The local language, Roon, belonging to the South Halmahera–West New Guinea subgroup of Malayo-Polynesian, ticks all the esoteric boxes: (a) it is almost exclusively used orally; (b) it is spoken on just one small island; (c) it is associated with a specific region within a larger country; (d) it has no official status; (e) its population of speakers is very small, between 1000 and 2000; (f) it is spoken by a relatively egalitarian group of low societal complexity; (g) it is typically used in private contexts; (h) it is used almost exclusively amongst ethnic Roon people speaking to each other; (i) it bestows little or no power on its speakers within the larger society; and (j) it is not associated with any kind of prestige within the larger society.

However, on the island of Roon, many people are competent also in the national language, Standard Indonesian, which lies right at the other, exoteric, end of the scale: (a) it is primarily written; (b) it is spoken over a large area spanning some 5,000 kilometres; (c) it is used across an entire country; (d) it is the official language of the country; (e) it is used to varying degrees by a very large population numbering well over 200 million; (f) it is spoken across populations of high societal complexity; (g) it is used almost exclusively in the public domain; (h) it is commonly used for inter-group communication across ethnic and other categories; (i) it confers power on its speakers; and (j) its use is judged to be prestigious. Thus, since Roon and Standard Indonesian occupy opposite poles of the exotericity scale, bilingualism involving Roon and Standard Indonesian presents an extreme case of asymmetric bilingualism.

While the asymmetry of Roon–Standard Indonesian multilingualism is quite typical throughout the MPSEA-speaking region and beyond, the reality is often considerably more complex. Still on the island of Roon, a third language is present, one that is used much more commonly than Standard Indonesian, namely the local colloquial variety of Indonesian, commonly referred to as Papuan Malay. In terms of the exotericity scale in (1), Papuan Malay falls somewhere in the middle. With respect to three of the scales it is esoteric: (a) it is primarily used orally; (c) it is associated with a specific region within a larger country; and (d) it has no official status. However, with regard to the remaining seven scales it is mid-range: (b) it is spoken over a moderately large area; (e) it is used by a comparatively large population of over one million; (f) it is spoken across populations of moderate to high societal complexity; (g) it is used in both private and public domains; (h) it is spoken by diverse ethnic groups albeit associated with a larger Papuan identity; (i) it confers a moderate amount of power on its speakers; and (j) its use is judged to be more prestigious than Roon though less than Standard Indonesian. In conjunction, then, Roon, Papuan Malay, and Standard Indonesian are strung out on the scale of exotericity, from maximally esoteric through mid-range to maximally exoteric, resulting in a situation of asymmetric trilingualism.

## 16.3 Multilingualism within individual languages

Although there is no principled and clear-cut distinction between what constitutes varieties of a single language as opposed to several different languages, it is still useful, for expository purposes, to distinguish between multilingualism within individual languages and multilingualism across different languages. For example, in the case discussed in the previous section, use of Papuan Malay and Standard Indonesian constitutes a case of multilingualism within a single language, Malay/Indonesian, while use of Roon alongside either Papuan Malay or Standard Indonesian presents an instance of multilingualism across different languages.

Multilingualism within individual languages occurs when a community of speakers enjoys mastery over two or more dialects, registers, or other varieties that are sufficiently close to each other to be considered representative of one

[2] The distinction between esoteric and exoteric communication was introduced by Thurston (1987) and further developed by Wray and Grace (2007) and others. As defined in (1) above, the exotericity scale also gives expression to the distinction between 'low' and 'high' language varieties, following Ferguson (1959) and others.

and the same language. Typically, in such cases, the similarities between the language varieties make it easier for multilingualism to be maintained.

Multilingualism within individual languages may be either symmetric or asymmetric, in accordance with the exotericity scale in (1) above. Symmetric multilingualism, in which the participating language varieties occupy similar positions on the exotericity scale, is most readily exemplified by the commonplace state of affairs involving two neighbouring locations, each with its own distinct dialect of the same language. Such cases abound throughout the MPSEA-speaking area and of course elsewhere. An example is provided by two closely related dialects of Malay spoken in Riau province in east-central Sumatra in Indonesia, Siak Malay, and Insular Riau Malay. Near the geographical boundary between the two dialects, speakers are familiar with both dialects, and may mix freely between the two, as illustrated in the following example of code-switching in the narration of a folktale:

(2) Siak Malay (SM)/Insular Riau Malay (IRM)

| = | SM | SM | = | = |
|---|---|---|---|---|
| *A,* | *"nangko* | *nangko* | *lah",* | *a,* |
| DEIC | jackfruit | jackfruit | FOC | DEIC |

| =:= | IRM | IRM | = | SM |
|---|---|---|---|---|
| *"ini* | *berape* | *nangke* | *satu* | *nangko?"* |
| DEM:DEM.PROX | how.much | jackfruit | one | jackfruit |

'"Okay, jackfruit then", he said, "so how much is it for one jackfruit?"' (DG)

One of the most emblematic features distinguishing these two dialects, as well as many other dialects of Malay/Indonesian, is the form of word-final historical *-a*; while in Siak Malay it is *-o*, in Insular Riau Malay it is *-e* (pronounced [ə]). In the above example, the same word, for 'jackfruit', occurs three times as *nangko* but also once as *nangke*; an additional instance of word-final *-e* occurs also in *berape* 'how much'. Since the two dialects are very similar, many forms (marked with the '=' symbol) are common to both dialects; however, in cases that they are not, the narrator appears to switch freely between Siak Malay and Insular Riau Malay forms, with no obvious regularities governing the alternation.

In asymmetric multilingualism, the language varieties involved occupy significantly different positions on the exotericity scale in (1). Depending on their position on the scale, such varieties may be characterized as *basilectal*, *mesolectal*, or *acrolectal*. Often, the conditioning factor is geography: the higher dialect will be more urban, the lower dialect more rural. An example of such diglossia is provided by Minangkabau, spoken in western Sumatra in Indonesia. In Minangkabau, the dialect of highest prestige is that associated with the provincial capital Padang; it accordingly functions as a kind of lingua franca available to speakers of various other dialects of Minangkabau. The following example illustrates code-switching between Padang Minangkabau and a more peripheral dialect, Tapus Minangkabau, spoken in and around the eponymous small town:

(3) Tapus Minangkabau (TM)/Padang Minangkabau (PM)

| = | = | TM | TM | =:= | = |
|---|---|---|---|---|---|
| *La* | *berang* | *gu* | *ko* | *inyo* | *tadi* |
| PFV | angry | 1SG | ALL | PERS:3 | PST.PROX |

| TM | PM | =:=:=:TM |
|---|---|---|
| *du,* | *bareh* | *disesera'ã* |
| DEM.DIST | uncooked.rice | PAT:DISTR~scatter:ASSOC |

'I was angry at him earlier, the rice was all over the place'
(JFS 160529191730674816895322)

Most of the conversation in which this utterance occurs is in the Tapus dialect; however, every now and then forms from Padang Minangkabau are interspersed—in the above example *bareh* 'uncooked rice' instead of the Tapus form *boreh*.

A major subtype of such diglossia involves national languages, where colloquial varieties of the language coexist alongside an official standardized version. This is readily observable throughout the MPSEA-speaking area, including: Tagalog (also known as Pilipino or Filipino) in the Philippines; Malay in Malaysia, Singapore, and Brunei; Indonesian in Indonesia; Tetun Dili (also known as Tetum) in Timor-Leste; and Malagasy in Madagascar. Typically, colloquial and standard varieties constitute a lectal cline, with speakers moving up and down the scale according to context. However, there are significant differences with respect to how this plays out in the various countries of the MPSEA area.

The situation in Indonesia is possibly the most complex of all, combining features shared with other MPSEA-speaking countries with features that are perhaps unique to Indonesia; for a variety of perspectives see Wolff and Poedjosoedarmo (1982); Adelaar and Prentice (1996); Collins (1998); Errington (1998a); Sneddon (2003a); Gil (2009c, 2020a); and others. A substantially simplified schematic representation of Malay/Indonesian multiglossia in Indonesia is provided in Figure 16.1 below.

In Figure 16.1, further left is more esoteric, further right more exoteric. To the left are a set of Malay dialects, spoken primarily by ethnic Malays in Sumatra and Borneo, some of which formed the basis for the standardization of the national language, which later became known as Indonesian.[3] At right is Standard Indonesian. In the big box in

[3] The use of language names for varieties of Malay/Indonesian spoken in Sumatra and Borneo is a common source of confusion. In general, for any

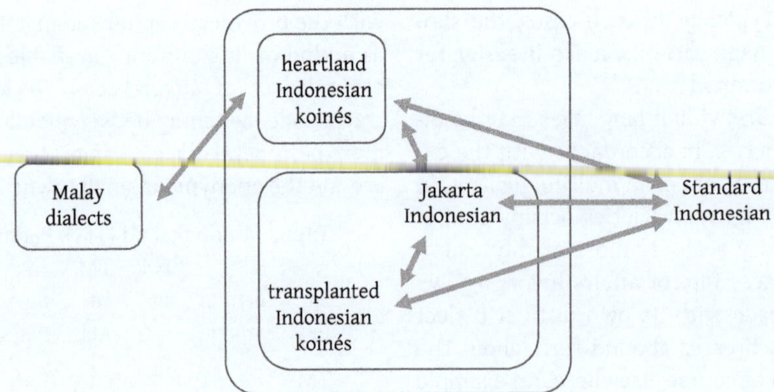


**Figure 16.1** Multiglossia in the Malay/Indonesian of Indonesia.

the middle are a set of koiné varieties of colloquial Indonesian, belonging to two distinct subtypes, depending on the identity of the local languages. While heartland koinés are spoken in regions where the local language is a variety of Malay, transplanted koinés are spoken in regions where the local language is one of the over 700 other languages of Indonesia. Among the latter subtype, the koiné of the capital city, Jakarta Indonesian, occupies a privileged position. In Figure 16.1, distinct varieties of Malay and Indonesian are connected by arrows, representing commonly occurring cases of diglossia.

One of the most widespread forms of diglossia in Malay/Indonesian is that between between colloquial and standard varieties of Indonesian, represented by the three arrows to the right.[4] One such case is that between Papuan Malay and Standard Indonesian, mentioned in the previous section. Another such case is illustrated in (4) below, involving code-switching between Kupang Malay, a transplanted Indonesian koiné spoken in the eponymous city near the western tip of Timor, and Standard Indonesian:[5]

Kupang Malay (KM)/Standard Indonesian (SI)

(4)

| =:= | = | = | =:= | KM |
|---|---|---|---|---|
| *ini* | *tahun* | *lalu* | *ini* | *dong* |
| DEM:DEM.PROX | year | pass | DEM:DEM.PROX | 3PL |

| KM | =:SI | =:= | = |
|---|---|---|---|
| *pi* | *bersihkan* | *ini* | *pasar* |
| go | clean:EP | DEM:DEM.PROX | market |

'Last year they went and cleaned up the marketplace'
(JFS 150971343531163912090908)

Example (4) is from a conversational text, largely in Kupang Malay, though many of the forms are actually shared by Kupang Malay and Standard Indonesian. However, one form, the causative suffix *-kan* in *bersihkan*, is unambiguously from Standard Indonesian; the equivalent colloquial Kupang Malay construction would have been periphrastic, *kasi bersi*, with *kasi* 'give'. The choice of the standard construction *bersihkan* is perhaps motivated by the subject matter, a market cleanup, which is typically organized by the neighbourhood functionaries, who might assert their authority by using a more formal linguistic register. Indeed, politicians' speeches, in Indonesia and elsewhere, often start out very officially, gradually becoming more folksy, before switching back to the standard language for a formal conclusion. Similar instances of diglossia between colloquial varieties and the national language are readily observed in other MPSEA-speaking countries, though in many cases, the colloquial varieties of the national languages remain underdescribed.

When colloquial and standard languages come together in a single utterance, two alternative analyses are available. The first, presupposed in the above discussion, posits code-switching between distinct basilectal and acrolectal registers. However, in other cases, similar utterances might be said to instantiate a single intermediate register, or *mesolect*.

given location, there is a clear distinction, in both linguistic form and sociolinguistic patterns of usage, between Malay and Indonesian; for example, in Riau province, Riau Malay and Riau Indonesian constitute distinct language varieties. However, there is no sharp boundary between Malay dialects and other related languages belonging to the Malayic language group, such as Minangkabau, Bangkinang, Kerinci, and so forth. Accordingly, in several regions, language varieties may be referred to inconsistently, either as dialects of Malay or as separate languages, in which latter case their names typically involve a toponym providing a geographical designation of where they are spoken.

[4] The middle one of these three arrows, that connecting Jakarta Indonesian and Standard Indonesian, represents the diglossia that forms the subject of Sneddon's (2003a) important study. However, as suggested by Figure 16.1, this is just one of a wide range of diglossic situations that are characteristic of the complex Malay/Indonesian linguistic landscape.

[5] In eastern Indonesia—unlike in Sumatra and Borneo, cf. Footnote 3—the terms Malay and Indonesian are used interchangeably to refer to transplanted koinés such as Kupang Malay/Indonesian, Papuan Malay/Indonesian, and so forth. The choice of the term Malay in this chapter echoes the expressed preferences of a majority of the speakers, and also the increasingly common usage of scholars (see also Slomanson, this volume, §18.4).

Consider the following example from Jakarta Indonesian, the largest and most important variety of colloquial Indonesian, represented separately in Figure 16.1.

(5) Jakarta Indonesian (JI)/Standard Indonesian (SI)

| =:= | = | =:JI | = | = | JI |
|---|---|---|---|---|---|
| *Rajanya* | *kamu* | *pindahin* | *dulu,* | *kalo* | *nggak* |
| king:ASSOC | 2 | move:EP | before | TOP | NEG |

| SI:= | = | SI |
|---|---|---|
| *kumakan,* | *mati* | *kau* |
| 1SG:eat | die | 2SG |

'Move your king first, if you don't I'll capture it, you'll be dead'
(JFS 482105110241030403)

In the above example, involving an adult playing chess with a young child, two Standard Indonesian forms stand out, in what is otherwise a quintessentially informal context. One is the second person singular pronoun *kau*, which occurs here as part of a conventionalized collocation *mati kau*, probably originating in cartoons and other similar television programmes, many of which are in the standard language—a clear case of code-switching. But it is the second form that is of interest to us here, namely, the proclitic first person singular pronoun *ku-*, occurring in the so-called *second passive* construction (Chung 1976). In general, the second passive construction is present in Standard Indonesian but absent from the most basilectal Jakarta Indonesian; however, it is also commonly observed in a colloquial speech style often associated with more educated people—see Cole, Hermon, and Tjung (2006) for discussion of the second passive in this register. Conversely, there are a number of features of basilectal Jakarta Indonesian which are also present in this speech style, while absent from the standard language; two such features occurring in example (5) above are the end-point (causative/applicative) suffix *-in* and the negative marker *nggak*. Thus, a mirror image pattern is effected, in which the second passive percolates downwards while the forms *-in* and *nggak* percolate upwards, resulting in an overlapping zone, occupied by example (5)—a zone which may accordingly be characterized as mesolectal. This state of affairs is represented schematically in Figure 16.2 below, zooming in on the arrow connecting Jakarta Indonesian and Standard Indonesian in Figure 16.1.

While it sometimes difficult or even impossible to adjudicate between alternative code-switching and mesolectal analyses, in other cases, various arguments can be invoked in support of one or another of the two. In order for code-switching to be possible, speakers must enjoy mastery of both of the relevant codes. In cases such as the above, while all speakers are fluent in the basilect, only a subset of them are capable of communicating in the acrolect. Thus, to the extent that speakers unfamiliar with the acrolect make use of a feature such as the second passive, this feature would accordingly be attributed to a distinct mesolectal register.

A second argument pertains to features which, unlike those represented in Figure 16.2, are uniquely mesolectal, while absent from both basilectal and acrolectal registers; the presence of such features provides direct support for an third and autonomous mesolectal register. An example of a uniquely mesolectal feature in the cline between Jakarta Indonesian and Standard Indonesian is provided by the use of the associative marker *-nya* in attributive possessive constructions: whereas in basilectal and acrolectal registers, attributive possession is expressed though bare juxtaposition (e.g. *buku Ali* (book Ali) 'Ali's book'), in the mesolect, the marker *-nya* is often employed, resulting in a head-marking strategy (e.g. *bukunya Ali* (book:ASSOC Ali)). This state of affairs is represented in Figure 16.3.

Further examples of uniquely mesolectal features are found in other Indonesian koinés. An example of such a feature in the cline between Riau Indonesian and Standard Indonesian involves the form of the end-point suffix: whereas in basilectal and acrolectal registers, it is *-kan* (recall the Standard Indonesian *-kan* in example (4) above), in a more trendy, urban mesolect, the form *-in* (cf. the Jakarta Indonesian *-in* in example (5) above) may be used in its place. Yet another uniquely mesolectal feature pertains to the location of word stress. For the most part, in colloquial varieties of Malay/Indonesian, stress is final in the west, including Peninsular Malaysia, Sumatra, Borneo, and West Nusa Tenggara, but mostly penultimate in the east, including Sulawesi, Maluku, East Nusa Tenggara, and Papua.[6] However, in Standard Indonesian, stress is said to be largely penultimate. Accordingly, in the west, a cline is in evidence between basilectal final stress and acrolectal penultimate. However, in the east, the situation is more complicated: whereas in basilectal and acrolectal registers, stress is mostly penultimate, there also exists a distinct mesolectal register with final stress—this register is associated in part with migrants from the west, but in part also with contexts of a more formal nature, though not to the extent that they would license the use of Standard Indonesian. Examples such as these underscore the importance of mesolects within the linguistic landscape of Malay/Indonesian, thereby highlighting the

[6] For eastern varieties, the qualification *mostly* penultimate is necessary because, for most such varieties, there are various classes of words that buck the predominant pattern and take final stress. It should also be noted that in at least some of these varieties, the domain of stress may be phrasal rather than lexical (see Gil 2006 for Riau Indonesian, Lai, Tynan, and Park 2010 for Kupang Malay, and Kaufman and Himmelmann (this volume, §42.4.1–42.4.3) more generally for languages of the region). However, even in those cases where the domain is phrasal, stress remains a property of individual words; thus, in eastern varieties, the location (penultimate or final) of stress is dependent on the identity of the word, even though it may be manifest only when the word occurs in phrase-final position.

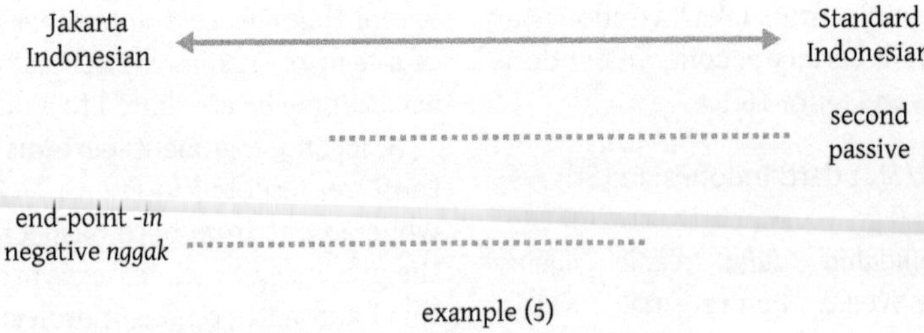


**Figure 16.2** The lectal cline between Jakarta Indonesian and Standard Indonesian.

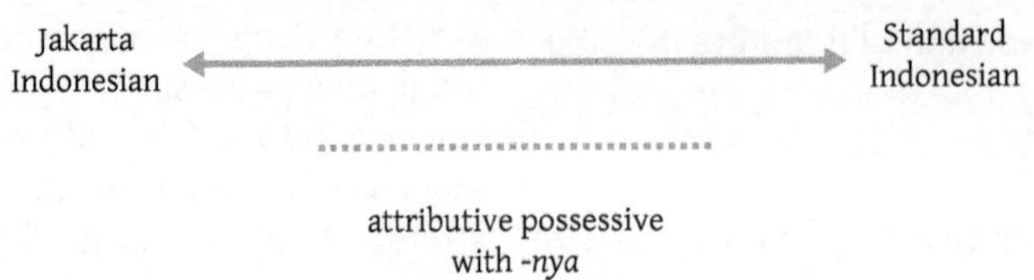


**Figure 16.3** A uniquely mesolectal feature.

complexity of diglossic situations in Malay/Indonesian. Similar mesolectal features are likely to be present also in other major MPSEA languages.

In general, national languages such as Indonesian, Malay, Tagalog, Tetun Dili, Malagasy, Palauan, and Chamorro are based on local languages originally associated with a specific ethnicity. However, even when the language becomes a national language, it may continue to function also as a regional language, maintaining its ethnic identification; such a situation results in a whole new range of diglossic situations, which differ substantially from one country to another.

In Indonesia, the national language Indonesian is derived from Malay, spoken by several million people mostly on the islands of Sumatra and Borneo. In terms of people's attitudes, Malay is considered to be as distinct from Indonesian as is any other language, such as Mentawai, Javanese, or Roon; however, from a linguistic point of view, it is clear that many varieties of Malay are sufficiently similar to Indonesian to merit characterization as dialects of a single language, as represented in Figure 16.1 above.

Thus, in a typical location in a Malay-speaking area of Sumatra or Borneo, ethnic Malay speakers are typically, at the very least, triglossic, enjoying mastery of a local dialect of Malay, a local heartland koiné variety of Indonesian, and Standard Indonesian. While each of these three language varieties tends to be used in a different set of contexts, speakers often choose to engage in code-switching. Example (6) illustrates code-switching in Riau province between the Siak dialect of Malay (cf. example (2) above) and the local heartland koiné Riau Indonesian:

Siak Malay (SM)/Riau Indonesian (RI)

| (6) | RI | SM | SM |
|---|---|---|---|
| | *"Nama* | *adek* | *siapo"* |
| | name | younger.sibling | who |

'"What's your name?", he asked him' (DG)

And example (7) illustrates code-switching amongst Siak Malay, Riau Indonesian, and also Standard Indonesian:

Siak Malay (SM)/Riau Indonesian (RI)/Standard Indonesian (SI)

| (7) | = | = | SM/RI | SI:= | SM |
|---|---|---|---|---|---|
| | *Datang* | *lah,* | *udah* | *membusuk* | *muko* |
| | arrive | FOC | PRF | AGT:rotten | face |

| SM/RI:RI/SI | = |
|---|---|
| *mamaknya* | *kan* |
| mother:ASSOC | Q |

'When he arrived, his mother's face was already decomposed' (DG)

For the most part, the heartland Indonesian koinés are less sociolinguistically distinctive than either their neighbouring Malay varieties or their transplanted koiné counterparts in other parts of Indonesia; speakers typically don't have special names for them, and linguists have not, for the most part, afforded them the attention that they deserve. This raises the question to what extent such heartland Indonesian koinés constitute conventionalized linguistic varieties, as opposed to, say, ad hoc mixtures of Standard Indonesian and the local varieties of Malay. For Riau Indonesian, at least, there is plenty of evidence to support its existence as an autonomous linguistic variety, making reference to linguistic features present in Riau Indonesian but absent from both local Malay and Standard Indonesian; such features include the lack of a phonemic schwa, the end-point suffix *-in* (discussed above for Jakarta Indonesian), the negative marker *ndak*, the form *kasi* 'give', and colexification of 'green' and 'blue' (Gil 2009c). Presumably, similar arguments can be adduced for most or all of the other heartland Indonesian koinés.

Outside of western Indonesia, however, there is no clear analogue in the MPSEA-speaking world to the triglossia constituted by local Malay dialects, heartland Indonesian koinés, and Standard Indonesian; this is because there is no clear parallel to the distinction, within western Indonesia, between Malay and Indonesian language varieties. In Malaysia, the expression *bahasa Malaysia* 'Malaysian language' is sometimes offered as a 'national' alternative to the more ethnically-loaded *bahasa Melayu* 'Malay language'; however, this distinction is entirely terminological, and does not correspond to any linguistic reality. Similarly, in the Philippines, the terms *Pilipino* or *Filipino* are proposed as alternatives to *Tagalog*, in order to bolster the national status of the language in a multiethnic archipelago; however, apart from a token and rather artificial addition of a handful of words from other Philippine languages, there is little linguistic reality to the distinction between Pilipino/Filipino and Tagalog, despite attempts to engineer such differences. As with Malay/Indonesian, a distinction may be drawn between heartland dialects of Tagalog, such as, for example, that of Batangas (Pancorbo 1989), and transplanted varieties, such as that of Davao (Rubrico 2012); these latter transplanted varieties are then sometimes argued to provide more appropriate referents for terms such as *Pilipino* or *Filipino*. However in heartland Tagalog-speaking locations such as Batangas, there is, so far, to the best of my knowledge at least, no reported evidence for a third intermediate mesolectal variety inbetween, say, Batangas Tagalog and Standard Tagalog—a variety that would be analogous to Riau Indonesian, in-between Riau Malay and Standard Indonesian.

A potential analogue to the triglossia involving local Malay dialects, heartland Indonesian koinés, and Standard Indonesian might perhaps be found in Timor Leste, where a regional ethnically-associated language, Tetun Terik, constitutes the basis for the standard language, Tetun Dili. For the parallel with western Indonesia to be complete, there would have to exist a conventionalized variety of Tetun Dili spoken alongside Tetun Terik in the Tetun Terik region that is distinct both from standard Tetun Dili and from the Tetun Dili spoken in other parts of Timor Leste; such a variety would thus be analogous to heartland Indonesian koinés such as Riau Indonesian. Some form of Tetun Dili is indeed spoken in Tetun Terik regions (Antoinette Schapper p.c.), and anecdotal evidence suggests that it may perhaps meet the condition of being a distinct and conventionalized regional variety of Tetun Dili (Catharina Williams-van Klinken p.c.); however, a clearer picture of the linguistic landscape of that particular region must await future investigation.

In Figure 16.1, the large box in the middle encloses a variety of Indonesian koinés spoken throughout the archipelago. In principle each koiné is associated with its own particular region; however, since some regions are more influential than others, their associated koinés also assume greater importance, and may end up spreading into other regions, where they coexist alongside the local Indonesian koinés, typically functioning as a more mesolectal variety, often associated with trendy youth culture. Such varieties may accordingly be referred to as *transregional* Indonesian koinés.

An example of such a transregional koiné is provided by Kupang Malay. In its function as a primary koiné variety, Kupang Malay is restricted to the city of Kupang and its outskirts; in surrounding regions, the local Indonesian koinés are already quite different. However, in some of these surrounding regions, including the remainder of West Timor and parts of the island of Flores, Kupang Malay is also present as a mesolectal alternative to the local Indonesian koinés, where it is most clearly evidenced in certain emblematic features such as the pronouns and negators. For example, in Atambua in West Timor, the first person singular pronoun is *saya* ~ *sa* in the local koiné, contrasting with either *saya* or *aku* in Standard Indonesian; however, in certain contexts, people may also make use of the Kupang Malay *beta* ~ *be*. The presence of Kupang Malay in places such as Atambua thus results in a triglossic situation involving the local Indonesian koiné, Kupang Malay, and Standard Indonesian.

The most well-known transregional Indonesian koiné, however, is Jakarta Indonesian, which functions as a mesolectal lingua franca throughout Indonesia and even beyond. Its ubiquity is such that it is sometimes referred to simply as *Colloquial Indonesian*, though given the large number of other distinct varieties of colloquial Indonesian that are spoken throughout the archipelago, this terminology is inappropriate and potentially misleading. Outside of Jakarta, Jakarta Indonesian is commonly encountered in movies, advertising, and social media, where it is often used, even in intraethnic communication, to signal what might be characterized as a trendy, outwards-oriented world view. It is also the register of choice for colloquial communication between people from different parts of Indonesia.

An illustration of the latter function of Jakarta Indonesian is provided by the following short written dialogue from Facebook Messenger, in which speakers separated by two time zones, having become acquainted mere moments earlier, are negotiating a cooperative video gaming session:

Riau Indonesian (RI)/Papuan Malay (PM)/Jakarta Indonesian (JI)

(8) RC *ayo kita mabar*
YB *Malas ko nubbb*
RC *siapa yg nuubb*
YB *Koo too* 😂😂😂😂
RC *ayo buktikan*
RC *saya udh pro player*
YB *Ohh besok saja kalo sekarang ngak ada paket data gue*

| | | | |
|---|---|---|---|
| RC | RI/JI | RI/JI | = |
| | *Ayo* | *kita* | *mabar* |
| | EXHR | 1PL | play.together |

'Come on, let's play co-op'

| | | | |
|---|---|---|---|
| YB | = | PM | = |
| | *Malas* | *ko* | *nub* |
| | not.feel.like | 2SG | newbie |

'Naah, you're a newbie'

| | | | |
|---|---|---|---|
| RC | = | = | = |
| | *Siapa* | *yang* | *nub* |
| | who | REL | newbie |

'Who's a newbie'

| | | |
|---|---|---|
| YB | PM | PM |
| | *Ko* | *to* |
| | 2SG | Q |

'You are, aren't you'

| | | |
|---|---|---|
| RC | RI/JI | =:RI |
| | *Ayo* | *buktikan* |
| | EXHR | prove:EP |

'Come on, let's prove it'

| | | | |
|---|---|---|---|
| RC | = | RI/RJ | = |
| | *Saya* | *udah* | *pro player* |
| | 1SG | PRF | pro player |

'I'm already a pro player'

| | | | | | | |
|---|---|---|---|---|---|---|
| YB | = | = | PM | = | = | RI/JI |
| | *Oh* | *besok* | *saja* | *kalo* | *sekarang* | *nggak* |
| | oh | tomorrow | only | TOP | now | NEG |

| | | | |
|---|---|---|---|
| = | = | = | Jl |
| *ada* | *paket* | *data* | *gue* |
| exist | package | data | 1SG |

'Oh, tomorrow then, right now I don't have a data package'

In (8) above, the interlocutors are RC, an ethnic Malay from Riau, whose dominant languages are Siak Malay and Riau Indonesian, and YB, an ethnic Mee from Papua, whose dominant language is Papuan Malay. The interlocutors are not familiar with each others' dialects of Malay/Indonesian, but what makes them able to communicate easily in the above text are two factors: first, the obvious similarities between the two dialects, and secondly, the familiarity of both interlocutors with Jakarta Indonesian, which functions as a bridge between the interlocutors' home dialects. Thus, for example, YB is familiar with the words *ayo* and *nggak* used by RC because, although absent from Papuan Malay, they are present not only in Riau but also in Jakarta Indonesian; similarly RC is familiar with the word *gue* used by YB because, although absent from both Riau Indonesian and Papuan Malay, it is an emblematic feature of Jakarta Indonesian, which YB is using not just for communicative efficacy but also in order to signal his worldliness and desirability as a gaming partner. In example (8), then, both interlocutors are making use of their multiglossic competence in Jakarta Indonesian; accordingly, the dialogue as a whole provides an instance of three-way code-switching involving Riau Indonesian, Papuan Malay, and Jakarta Indonesian. In summary, then, in most of Indonesia outside of the capital city, Jakarta Indonesian facilitates a situation of triglossia involving the local Indonesian koiné, Jakarta Indonesian, and Standard Indonesian.

Outside of Indonesia, a similar if somewhat less salient role as a transregional koiné is perhaps displayed in Malaysia by Kuala Lumpur Malay, though its local provenance from the capital city is not usually acknowledged, and the variety in question is more commonly referred to simply as *Colloquial Malay*. Thus, in some parts of Malaysia, a similar triglossia is in evidence, involving a local variety of Malay, Kuala Lumpur Malay, and Standard Malay. Following is a Facebook comment exhibiting code-switching between Sabah Malay, Kuala Lumpur Malay, and Standard Malay:

Sabah Malay (SbM)/Kuala Lumpur Malay (KLM)/Standard Malay (StM)

(9) *saman jrr itu urg supaya mereka dapat ape yg patut*

| | | | | |
|---|---|---|---|---|
| = | KLM | =:= | SbM | StM |
| *Saman* | *je* | *itu* | *urang* | *supaya* |
| penalty | NEG.FOC | DEM:DEM.DIST | person | so.that |

| | | | | |
|---|---|---|---|---|
| StM | = | KLM | = | = |
| *mereka* | *dapat* | *ape* | *yang* | *patut* |
| 3PL | get | what | REL | deserve |

'Penalize those people so that they get what they deserve'

As noted in the discussion of (2) above, one of the most emblematic features of Malay/Indonesian is the realization of word-final historical *-a*: while in Sabah Malay and in Standard Malay it is *-a*, in Kuala Lumpur Malay it is a schwa, which, in social media, is typically written either as *-e* or as *-er* (the latter mimicking a non-rhotic English spelling). In example (9) above, the presence of the Kuala Lumpur

Malay final schwa is signalled in the original spelling in two places, illustrating both orthographic practices: first *ape*, and secondly *jrr*, a stylistic variant on the more common *jer*.

Elsewhere, a potentially similar case of triglossia emerges from Rubrico's (2012) description of Tagalog in Davao, and in particular, her distinction between two local varieties, *FVD*, the Filipino Variety of Davao, and *FMM*, "the Tagalog-English code switch of Metro Manila which has pervaded the area" (p.14). To the extent that the latter is a stabilized variety into which the English-origin expressions are incorporated as loans, then it might perhaps be viewed as an example of a transregional koiné, functioning as a mesolect sandwiched inbetween local Davao and standard varieties of Tagalog.[7] Whether other such cases exist of triglossia involving a transregional colloquial variety of the national language in a mesolectal role must remain open to future investigation.

The various kinds of multilingualism discussed in this section may be compounded, resulting in multiglossic situations of ever-increasing complexity. For example, a villager belonging to the Orang Asli community on Padang island in Riau province in Sumatra (not to be confused with the better-known Orang Asli of Malaysia) might easily be familiar with, and make occasional use of, up to six different varieties of Malay/Indonesian, illustrated here with respect to their different pronunciations of the word *apa* 'what': Orang Asli Malay—[apaʔ]; Siak Malay—[apo]; Insular Riau Malay—[apə]; Riau Indonesian—[apa]; Jakarta Indonesian—[apa] ~ [ape]; and Standard Indonesian—[apa].

## 16.4 Multilingualism across MPSEA languages

Multilingualism across languages occurs when a community of speakers enjoys mastery over two or more languages that are sufficiently different from each other to preclude mutual intelligibility based on shared linguistic features.

As was the case for language-internal multilingualism in the preceding section, it is useful to distinguish between symmetric cases, in which the languages involved are of roughly equal status to one another, and asymmetric cases, in which the languages involved differ substantially in terms of the various factors subsumed under the exotericity scale in (1).

[7] Alternatively, if, as described by Rubrico, both FVD and FMM are systems defined by productive code-switching, the former between Tagalog and Cebuano, the latter between Tagalog and English, then a mixture of FVD and FMM would appear to constitute a rather curious case of seemingly recursive code-switching between code-switchings, in which the languages underpinning the code-switching are Cebuano, Tagalog, and English.

Symmetric multilingualism may occur in urban areas, where migrants from different regions, each with their own language, live side by side, and speak each others' languages to varying degrees of fluency. Some examples of this might include Javanese, Madurese, and others in the Indonesian city of Surabaya, and Zambaleño, Ilokano, and others in the Philippine city of Olongapo. Symmetric multilingualism may also occur in rural areas, near the geographical boundaries between different languages. Thus, on the island of Yapen in the Cenderawasih Bay in northwest New Guinea, speakers of Wooi over sixty years old "also speak Biak, Pom, Ansus and Wandamen [all South Halmahera–West New Guinea languages] with different degrees of fluency" (Sawaki 2016: 14). Other examples include Minangkabau and Mandailing on the island of Sumatra in Indonesia, Tausug and Bajau in the Sulu archipelago in the Philippines as well as parts of Sabah in Malaysia, and Bih and Ede (also Rhade or Rade) in the highlands of Dak Lak province in Vietnam (Nguyễn 2013b). An illustration of symmetric multilingualism from the western tip of the island of Java, involving Sundanese and the Banten dialect of Javanese is provided in (10) below:

Sundanese (S)/Banten Javanese (BJ)

| (10) | S | S | BJ | = | = | BJ |
|---|---|---|---|---|---|---|
| | *Kumaha* | *kumaha* | *iye* | *kan.* | *Ih* | *wis?* |
| | how | how | yes | Q | EXCLAM | PRF |

'What about it, is it already over?'
(JFS 839179182340230310)

Turning to asymmetric multilingualism, the most extreme case is that involving language endangerment and incipient death. For example, as of 2019, the last two elderly speakers of Tandia, spoken on the Gulf of Wondama in West Papua, had already forgotten much of their language, which, in their daily life, has been replaced by the neighbouring language Wamesa. In other cases, language endangerment and death is not absolute, but only relative to a particular location. In the same region, Roon is still relatively robust and in common use by children on the eponymous island; however, people from Roon living in the small nearby town of Wasior are typically less fluent in Roon than they are in Wamesa. Similar scenarios can be observed throughout the MPSEA-speaking area.

While some languages fall by the wayside, others accumulate additional power and prestige, and are used beyond the ethnic group with which they were originally associated, thereby assuming the role of trade languages or lingua francas; in such cases, they enter into diglossic situations alongside the local languages. Some examples of lingua francas include Biak, spoken (until recently) throughout much of coastal northwest New Guinea; Minangkabau, commonly used across a large swathe of central Sumatra; Cebuano, spoken in large parts of the Visayas and Mindanao; and Ilokano, used in much of northern Luzon. Example (11) is a passage from a narrative text in Dupaningan Agta incorporating a substantial number of forms from the regionally dominant Ilokano:

Dupaningan Agta (D)/Ilokano (I)

(11) I-I I I
*ma-gapu* *ta* *masansansan*
ACCIDENT-reason because frequently

D D D I=D D D
*konna* *hito* *a* *napintas=la* *ito* *a*
like OBL.it LNK good=just it LNK

I-I=D
*ma-apit=mi*
ACCIDENT-harvest=1PL.EXCL.GEN

I-I-I-I=D=D=I=D
*i-law-lawa-an=mi=bi=ngarud=dan*
TV-REDUP~wide-LV=1PL.EXCL.GEN=also=then=already

D-D
*nag-sikaw*
COMPL.AV-swidden
'Because our harvests were frequently good like that, so we enlarged our swidden farms' (Robinson (2008: 325)

In the text from which this example is taken, code-switching is rampant, taking place not only between words but also word-internally.[8]

One of the most important types of asymmetric multilingualism is that involving bilingualism between a local language and the national language—either in its standardized version, or, perhaps more commonly, in one of its colloquial forms. Given the existence of over 700 languages in Indonesia, and over 100 in both Malaysia and the Philippines, the national language provides a means for its population to communicate with each other across ethnic boundaries, as well as a tool for the state to exert its centralizing control. However, once such bilingualism is established, it takes on a life of its own, with the national language assuming a variety of additional functions, some widespread, others more specific to the circumstances of particular speech communities. In doing so, it inevitably enters into competition with the local languages, leading to a continually diminishing repertoire of functions for the local languages, a process that may eventually lead to language endangerment and death.

Typically, people tend to use the regional language for more intimate matters, and the national language for affairs associated with the public domain. For example, in Jakarta, speakers of the appropriate ethnicity might prefer Sundanese or Javanese for discussing family affairs, but Indonesian for talking about business or politics. Sometimes the distinction between esoteric and exoteric domains can be quite subtle. Padang, the provincial capital of West Sumatra province in Indonesia, is renowned for its local cuisine served in a distinctive style; however, an increasing number of restaurants offer generic Indonesian and even international food. When summoning a waiter, the choice of address term typically depends on the category of the restaurant. While in smaller and more modest Padang-style restaurants, the waiter will usually be called using the Padang Minangkabau address term *uda* 'elder brother', in a general Indonesian restaurant, he will typically be summoned with the equivalent Indonesian language term *mas* 'elder brother'—even though, in both cases, the waiter is likely to be an ethnic Minangkabau. In cases such as these, the choice of code marks the nature of the interaction: local language for intimate esoteric contexts, national language for more public exoteric situations.

A specific semantic domain in which code-switching commonly undergoes conventionalization is that of animals and the edible dishes that are made from them. In Minangkabau, the general word for 'fish' is *lauak*; however, the names of cooked dishes involving fish typically make use of the Indonesian word *ikan*, for example *ikan gulai* 'curried fish', or *ikan salai* 'smoked fish'. The systematicity of such collocations suggests that in Minangkabau *ikan* may be in the process of developing into a loanword with a meaning something along the lines of 'cooked fish'. A similar pattern is evident for other animal words, and in other local languages of Indonesia such as Javanese—and of course, a parallel development in known to have taken place in Middle English, resulting in contemporary pairs such as *cow/beef* and *pig/pork*, where the current English word for the foodstuff comes from the Old French word for the animal.

Another semantic domain in which code-switching between local and national languages is in the process of becoming conventionalized is that of numerals. In Indonesia, in certain specific contexts such as time-telling and prices, speakers conversing in a local language will typically use an Indonesian language numeral rather than one from the local language. Example (12), from the Muarasiberut

[8] Examples such as the above resemble other possible cases of word-internal code-switching described by Redouane (2005); Petersen (2009); and others, thereby providing further apparent counterexamples to the claim that code-switching cannot occur word internally—see Budzhak-Jones (1998). Further instances of word-internal code-switching can be observed also in (14), (18), and (20).

dialect of Mentawai, off the west coast of Sumatra, illustrating a time-telling context, contains two occurrences of the Indonesian numeral *empat*:

Muarasiberut Mentawai (M)/West Sumatra Indonesian (I)

(12)

| M | M | I | = | I | I |
|---|---|---|---|---|---|
| *tubut* | *sobi* | *sekitar* | *jam* | *empat* | *lah* |
| very | yesterday | around | hour | four | FOC |

| I | I | M | M | M |
|---|---|---|---|---|
| *jam* | *empat* | *ne* | *tet* | *nek* |
| hour | four | DEM.PROX | PART | DEM.PROX |

| M | M | = | M | I |
|---|---|---|---|---|
| *sokut* | *ka* | *anu* | *ka* | *dekat* |
| banyan | OBL | whatchamacallit | OBL | near |

M:M
*gettekku*
taro:POSS1SG
'Yesterday around four o'clock under the banyan tree, whatchamacallit, near my taro field'. (JFS 626832083141201108)

Similar patterns of code-switching occur throughout Indonesia, in languages as diverse as Minangkabau, Javanese, Bima, and Roon. Elsewhere, code-switching of numerals in contexts such as these occurs also in Malaysia, where speakers of local languages such as Tausug are likely to use the Standard Malay numerals, as well as in Timor Leste, where speakers of local languages such as Baikeno may use numerals from the erstwhile national language Indonesian. Similar patterns of code-switching involving numerals in MPSEA and various non-Austronesian languages are discussed in §16.5 below.

A rather special role is assumed by the Indonesian national language in some parts of Java. The Javanese language is renowned for its intricate system of speech levels, in which, in some regions, up to five different levels are available, depending on the specifics of the relationship between the interlocutors. Needless to say, such a system is difficult to master, and a minefield to navigate successfully: choose the wrong form for a word such as 'say' (*kandha*, *sanjang*, *criyos*, *matur*, or *ngendika* in Central Javanese—see Conners 2020), and offence can be caused. Accordingly, many Javanese make a conscious decision to avoid the inevitable pitfalls by stepping outside the system and using Indonesian instead of Javanese.

In many other cases, however, it is harder to pinpoint a specific reason for the use of the national language. In the following example, from a narrative text in Roon, the occurrence of a single word from Papuan Malay, *setiap* 'every', would seem to reflect the speaker's inability—either temporary or permanent—to come up with the appropriate construction in Roon:

Roon (R)/Papuan Malay (PM)

(13)

| PM | R:R | R | R:R |
|---|---|---|---|
| *Setiap* | *kofarar* | *i* | *kobado* |
| every | 1PL.INCL:run | 3.SG.ANIM | 1PL.INCL:carry |

| = | R | R:R | R:R |
|---|---|---|---|
| *e* | *pom* | *nawa* | *riso* |
| Q | bag | 3PL.INAN:DEM.DIST | 3SG.INAN:accompany |

R:R:R
*kobadori*
1PL.ANIM:carry:3SG.INAN
'Every time we go to the gardens, we carry those bags.' (DG)

Examples such as the above highlight how code-switching may eventually lead to replacement and change, either of entire languages or of subsystems thereof. In the Padang dialect of Minangkabau, it is common for the voice prefixes to be replaced by the corresponding and very similar prefixes in the local Indonesian koiné:

Padang Minangkabau (PM)/West Sumatran Indonesian (I)

(14)

| = | I:PM | PM |
|---|---|---|
| *Sebab,* | *bepetatah-petitiah* | *ko* |
| reason | NPAT-proverb | DEM.PROX |

| I:PM:PM | PM | PM | =:PM |
|---|---|---|---|
| *mempalamak* | *kato* | *untuak* | *didanga* |
| AGT:CAUS:nice | word | for | PAT:hear |

'Because speaking in proverbs makes words nice to hear' (JFS 999382095047111207)

In the above example, the Minangkabau prefixes *ba-* and *mam-* are replaced by their Indonesian counterparts *be-* and *mem-*; as suggested in Fadlul et al (2013), this apparent pattern of code-switching may perhaps be in the process of becoming conventionalized as an instance of loan morphology.

A common venue for code-switching between regional and national languages is provided by social media. In some cases, different interlocutors prefer different codes, as in the following Facebook comments on a posted photograph, by members of the migrant Tausug community in Kota Kinabalu, Malaysia, involving code-switching between Tausug and Sabah Malay:

Sabah Malay (SbM)/Tausug (T)

(15)
RKH *nag onu he abang ha hawlian yan??*😂😂
SRH *Baruu aku perasann*😆
ZJ *Nag karate hi Remy ha tykud*😂😂😂😂
SRH *ZJ baru aku perasan c remy d belakang*

RKH T:T T T T T
*Nagunu hi Abang ha hawlihan*
AT.REAL:what PERS.TOP Abang OBL rear

T
*yan?*
there
'What's the kid at the back doing?'

SRH SbM SbM SbM
*Baru aku perasan*
new 1SG notice
'I just noticed'

ZJ T:T T T T T
*Nagkarate hi Remy ha taykud*
AT.REAL:karate PERS.TOP Remy OBL rear
'It's Remy doing karate at the back'

SRH SbM SbM SbM SbM SbM SbM
*ZJ Baru aku perasan si Remy*
ZJ new 1SG notice PERS Remy

SbM SbM
*di belakang*
LOC rear
'ZJ I just noticed Remy at the back'

In other cases, a single interlocutor mixes the regional and national languages for no clearly discernible reason, as in the following Facebook comment from the Philippines:

Ilokano (I)/Tagalog (T)

(16) *bagong buhay ka ah? Sabayan kan to nu malpas detoy nga seagames*

T:T T = = T:T
*bagong buhay ka ah? Sabayan*
new:LNK life 2SG.TOP Q together:OBJ.FOC

=:I I I I I
*kan tu nu malpas daytoy*
2SG.ABS:PUNCT FUT PART finished DEM.PROX

I =
*nga seagames*
LNK SEA Games
'Having a new life? Will do it with you after the SEA Games'

In cases such as the above, code-switching is probably most appropriately analysed as a marker of style, with the national language Tagalog signifying greater worldliness than the regional language Ilokano.

In a few cases, the national languages of the MPSEA-speaking region spread beyond their associated political boundaries, resulting in yet additional instances of multilingualism. In Kota Kinabalu, Malaysia, a variety of Tagalog is sometimes used, alongside local languages such as Tausug and Bajau, by the Philippine migrant community. Conversely, in parts of Zamboanga, in the Philippines, a form of Sabah Malay is sometimes used as a trade language. Perhaps the most significant use of a national language extraterritorially is that of Indonesian in Timor Leste, which was part of Indonesia until it achieved independence in 2002. Unlike most parts of eastern Indonesia, there is no distinctive colloquial Indonesian koiné associated with Timor Leste; nevertheless, a version of Indonesian bearing a somewhat closer resemblance to Standard Indonesian is in widespread use in many parts of Timor Leste, and is still being acquired by children born in the post-independence era. Indeed, in eastern parts of Timor Leste, Indonesian is, or at least was until recently, in more widespread use than the national language Tetun Dili (Antoinette Schapper pc). The following Facebook example, from a speaker in Dili, commenting on a photoshopped image of the football star Cristiano Ronaldo with breasts and a low-slung red dress, following the loss of his team, Real Madrid, to Borussia Dortmund, illustrates code-switching between Indonesian and Tetun Dili:

Tetun Dili (TD)/Indonesian (I)

(17) *Ita,,,sai at ona,,,,,,,,beralih profesi setelah menelan kekalahan dari Borrusia Dortmud,,,,Liman ain mamar hotu,,,,*

TD TD TD TD I:I
*Ita sai aat ona beralih*
1PL.INCL go.out bad already NON.PAT:switch

I I:I I:I
*profesi setelah menelan*
profession one:PFV AGT:swallow

I:I:I I =
*kekalahan dari Borussia Dortmund*
ABSTR:lose:CIRC from Borussia Dortmund

TD TD TD TD
*Liman ain mamar hotu*
hand foot soft all
'You've broken down, just switch your profession after losing to Borussia Dortmund, you've gone weak'

The various kinds of multilingualism discussed in this section may combine to yield linguistic landscapes involving multilingualism of increasing degrees of complexity. The following passage, from the same text as (11) above, illustrates three-way multilingualism between the local language Dupaningan Agta, the dominant regional language Ilokano, and the national language Tagalog:

Dupaningan Agta (D)/Ilokano (I)/Tagalog (T)

(18) I I T=D=D D
*Ta ti balak=mi=n ayenan*
because the plan=1PL.EXCL.GEN=already now

| I=D | D | I=D | D |
|---|---|---|---|
| *mapan=kami* | *ha* | *abagatan=aye* | *a* |
| AT.go=1PL.EXCL.NOM | OBL | south=this | LNK |

D-D
*mag-lati*
AT-rattan
'Our plan now is that we will go to the south to collect rattan' (Robinson 2008: 334)

Moreover, multilingualism across languages also combines with multilingualism within languages, of the kinds considered in the preceding section. For example, the Orang Asli speaker with the six varieties of Malay/Indonesian mentioned at the end of the preceding section, when heading to the nearest market town Sungai Apit, is likely to converse also in the languages of the major migrant communities of the region, primarily Minangkabau and Bangkinang, and possibly also Javanese.

## 16.5 Multilingualism across MPSEA and non-Austronesian languages

MPSEA languages are in contact not only with each other but also with other non-MPSEA languages, which are almost exclusively non-Austronesian.[9] Resulting is a wide variety of cases of symmetric and asymmetric multilingualism involving combinations of MPSEA and non-Austronesian languages.

One family of cases involves multilingualism among regional languages, MPSEA and non-Austronesian. One example of this is bilingualism on the island of Makian in the North Maluku province of Indonesia, between Taba of the South Halmahera–West New Guinea branch of Austronesian and non-Austronesian West Makian, belonging to the North Halmahera family (Bowden 2001: 23). Other examples include bilingualism in Timor Leste between Malayo-Polynesian Mambae and the Timor-Alor-Pantar language Bunaq (Schapper 2010a: 12), and in Vietnam between Chamic Bih and the Bahnaric language Mnong (Nguyễn 2013b). A far-flung example from across the Indian Ocean, on the French-governed island of Mayotte, is that of bilingualism between Kibushi (Bushi) a dialect of Malagasy, and Shimaore, a variety of the Bantu language Comoran. Finally, a recently extinct case is that reconstructed for the Manokwari region of the New Guinea Bird's Head between Biak and a hypothetical language closely related to the otherwise isolate language Hatam, resulting in the mixed language Mansim (Reesink 2002a).

A second category of cases is that of bilingualism between varieties of two national languages, one MPSEA and one non-Austronesian, in or near border regions, where on one side the MPSEA language is the national one, while on the other side the non-Austronesian one is. In the Malay peninsula and to its north, varieties of Malay are spoken in Thailand and even Myanmar, while varieties of Thai are spoken across the border in Malaysia. In central New Guinea, on both sides of the political boundary, Standard Indonesian and Papuan Malay are in contact with Tok Pisin in the north and with English in the south—the latter two being official languages of Papua New Guinea.

A third group of cases is formed by multilingualism between an MPSEA national language and one or more non-Austronesian regional languages; in all such cases, the national language is in fact Malay/Indonesian. In Malaysia, most speakers of Aslian languages, a branch of the Austroasiatic family, are fluent also in one or more varieties of Malay. Similarly, in eastern parts of Indonesia, most speakers of non-Austronesian languages, belonging to numerous different and unrelated families, are also fluent in one or more varieties of Malay/Indonesian. The following Facebook conversation provides an example of code-switching between Papuan Malay and four different languages of the large Trans-New-Guinea family: Yali and Dani of the Dani subgroup, Ngalum of the Asmat-Awyu-Ok subgroup, and Mek of the Mek subgroup:

Papuan Malay (PM)/Yali (Y)/Dani (D)/Ngalum (Ng)/Mek (Mk)

(19)
| | |
|---|---|
| OKN | *Mantap nare...* |
| YS | *Telep..yepmum..nare wa* |
| OKN | *YS nare.posisi?* |
| YS | *Nabyal Holandia nare* |
| OKN | *Iya kwn ...sy msh di kota injil.* |
| UB | *Aiiii kk YS Ninti laha ari uuu wisssss yeheiiiii* 😂 |
| YS | *Ae Ae syg..* <br> *Hualliken..* <br> *Itu sdh* 😉 |
| UB | *YS wi wa uuuu yikheee htmt kk pribadi* |
| YS | *Urtius Balingga huall* |

OKN
| PM | Y |
|---|---|
| *Mantap* | *nare* |
| cool | 1SG.GEN:brother |

'Cool bro'

[9] Exceptions to the non-Austronesian nature of the non-MPSEA languages are found in the Northern Mariana Islands, Guam, Palau, and parts of northern New Guinea, where MPSEA languages are in contact with Austronesian languages of the Oceanic group.

YS Ng Mk Y
*Telep yepmum nare*
greetings greetings 1SG.GEN:brother

Y/D
*wa*
greetings
'Greetings bro'

OKN = Y PM
*YS nare posisi*
YS 1SG.GEN:brother location
'YS, where are you now?'

YS = = Y
*Nabyal Holandia nare*
Nabyal Holandia 1SG.GEN:brother
'Nabyal, in Holandia bro'

OKN PM PM PM PM PM PM
*Iya kawan saya masih di kota*
yes friend 1SG still LOC city

PM
*injil*
gospel
'Yeah friend, I'm still in the city of the gospel'

UB = PM = Y
*Ai kaka YS nindi*
EXCLAM elder.sibling YS liver

Y Y D/Y Y Y
*laha ari u wis yehei*
go:3SG.IMM.PST DEM say EXCLAM EXCLAM
'Wow, bro, I'm really surprised'

YS D/Y D/Y PM
*Ae ae sayang*
EXCLAM EXCLAM compassion

D:D PM:PM PM
*hualiaken itu suda*
testicle:penis:ERG DEM:DEM.DIST PRF
'Hey, friend, respect, bro, yeah'

UB = D/Y D/Y D/Y D:D:D
*YS wi wa u ikhe*
YS GRT GRT say say:FACT:3SG.SBJ

PM PM PM
*hormat kaka pribadi*
respect elder.sibling private
'YS, Thanks, respect to you too'

YS = = D
*Urtius Balingga hual*
Urtius Balingga testicle
'Urtius Balingga, respect'

A fourth and mirror-image category of cases involves multilingualism between one or more local MPSEA languages and a national non-Austronesian language. Within these, a further distinction pertains to the identity of the national non-Austronesian languages: Asian or European. The former case, of Asian national languages, is instantiated by the local MPSEA languages spoken across Mainland Southeast Asia: Moken in Myanmar, Moken and Moklen in Thailand, various Chamic languages in Cambodia and Vietnam, and Hainan Cham in the People's Republic of China—in all of these cases, the local MPSEA languages are spoken alongside versions of the respective national languages. Following is an example of code-switching between Hainan Cham and the local Sanya dialect of Mandarin:

Hainan Cham (HC)/Sanya Mandarin (SM)

(20) HC:HC SM:HC HC:SM
*ʔa$^{21}$t$^{h}$aj$^{21}$ k$^{h}$iaŋʔ$^{33}$ɓu$^{55}$ ʔa$^{21}$ko$^{33}$*
CLF:younger.brother see:see CLF:older.brother

HC:SM HC SM HC:HC
*ʔa$^{21}$sa:w$^{21}$ za:jʔ$^{33}$, tsa:w$^{33}$ɗajʔ$^{43}$ naw$^{33}$za: ŋʔ$^{33}$*
CLF:wife come receive 3:PL

HC HC HC HC
*le$^{55}$ nok$^{24}$ le$^{55}$ t$^{h}$a$^{21}$*
kill chicken kill duck
'Younger brother saw his older brother and sister-in-law come. To receive them, he killed a chicken and a duck.'
(Thurgood, Thurgood, and Fengxiang 2014)

The latter case is that of a European national language spoken alongside local MPSEA languages—a legacy of colonialism. Examples of this are observable on the French island of Mayotte, where French is used alongside Kibushi, the local dialect of Malagasy; in Timor Leste, where the national language Portuguese is spoken alongside regional MPSEA languages such as Mambae, Kemak, and Baikeno; and in eastern Malaysia and the Philippines, where the official language English is spoken alongside a wide variety of local MPSEA languages. Following is a Facebook example of code-switching between English and Kapampangan, spoken on the island of Luzon in the Philippines:

Kapampangan (K)/English (E)

(21) *Damputan deng bage bage king bitis ban e duduku. Perhaps the most nostalgic scenes of my childhood growing up in Magalang...*

K:K K:K K~K K
*Damputan déng bagé-bágé king*
pick.up:OT.FUT DEM.MED:LNK DISTR~thing OBL.SG

K K K
*bitis bán é*
foot so.that NEG

<K>K E E E E
*dúrukû. Perhaps the most nostalgic*
<AT.PRS>bow.down

E E E E
*scenes of my childhood*

E E E E
*growing up in Magalang*
'Picking up things with your feet so that you don't have to bow down anymore. Perhaps the most nostalgic scenes of my childhood growing up in Magalang.'

In several countries of the MPSEA-speaking region, the role of national language is shared, in one way or another, by a European language and a local MPSEA language, resulting in yet another class of cases of bilingualism. In the Philippines, English is an official language alongside Tagalog, and is in widespread use amongst more educated people. An example of code-switching between English and a regional Philippine language was given in (21) above; following is a similar Facebook example of code-switching between English and the other national language, Tagalog:

Tagalog (T)/English (E)
(22) *Cow Label! I still ask family to bring that for me every time they come visit. Pero bawal daw ipasok dito.*

😂😂😂😂

= E E E E E E E
*Cow Label! I still ask family to bring that*

E E E E E E E
*for me every time they come visit*

T T T T:T T
*Pero bawal daw ipasok dito*
but forbid RS OT:enter here
'Cow Label! I still ask the family to bring that for me every time they come to visit. But they say it's not allowed to bring it in.'

Such code-switching is so common that it even has its own name, *Taglish*. Whereas educated people are generally quite fluent in a local variety of English, people with lesser education know much less English; however, their own language is still replete with loanwords from English, attesting to the far-reaching effect that contact with English has had on Tagalog.

A rather similar situation is present also in Malaysia, reflected in a speech style sometimes referred to as *Manglish*, combining elements of Malay and English. Here too, educated people often find it difficult to complete a sentence in one of the languages without code-switching into the other, to the extent that people of lower socioeconomic status, fluent only in Malay, sometimes experience difficulties in communicating across the social divide. The following example is from a Kuala Lumpur university student's classroom oral literature review:

Kuala Lumpur Malay (KLM)/Standard Malay (SM)/English (E)
(23) KLM/SM KLM/SM E SM KLM/SM
*Dia banyak explain pada orang*
3 much OBL person

KLM/SM KLM E
*lain punya studies*
other POSS
'He explains other people's studies a lot' (DG)

In Singapore there are four official languages: English, Malay, Mandarin, and Tamil. English is the first among equals, and is the major language of administration; however, Malay is the designated 'national' language, and is used for ceremonial purposes, such as the national anthem. In everyday life, Singaporean English, and its more basilectal variant known as Singlish, are predominant; however, for interethnic communication, Bazaar Malay is often used alongside Singlish.

Out in the Pacific, in Palau, English and Palauan share the role of official languages; in Guam, English and Chamorro are official; while in the Northern Mariana Islands, English and Chamorro are official languages beside Carolinian, belonging to the Oceanic branch of the Malayo-Polynesian language family.

In addition to English, two other European languages function as national languages alongside indigenous MPSEA national languages. In Madagascar, French and Malagasy are the two national languages, resulting in widespread bilingualism, as exemplified in the following instance of code-switching in an email (discussing the organization of the International Conference on Austronesian Linguistics 14ICAL in Antananarivo in 2018):

Malagasy (M)/French (F)
(24) *Marina ny voalazan'ny Vice-Président. Na izany aza, indraindray tsy ary ho tonga hisoratra anarana anio daholo ny olona, fa aleo tonga dia tandremana ny efa voatsimpona: produits laitiers, gluten, épices (poivre, piment, moutarde, carry ?...), pas de sucre pour les diabétiques.*

M M M:M M F
*Marina ny voalazan' ny Vice-Président*
true DET PASS:say DET Vice-President

M M M M M M
*Na izany aza, indraindray tsy ary*
or that even sometimes NEG and

M M M:M M M
*ho tonga hisoratra anarana anio*
FUT come FUT:register name today

M M M M M M
*daholo ny olona, fa aleo tonga*
all DET people COMPL better come

M M M M M:M
*dia tandremana ny efa voatsimpona*
TOP cared.for DET already PASS:collect

F:F F:F:F F F:F
*produits laitiers, gluten, épices*
product:PL milk:ADJ:PLM gluten spice:PL

F F F F F
*(poivre, piment, moutarde, curry) pas*
pepper chili mustard curry NEG

F F F F F:F
*de sucre pour les diabétiques*
POSS sugar for DEF.PL diabetic:PL
'What the Vice-President says is true. However, given that everyone will not come to register today, it is best to keep those already collected: dairy products, gluten, spices (pepper, chili, mustard, curry), no sugar for diabetics.'

And in Timor Leste, Portuguese and Tetun Dili are both official languages, as illustrated in the following parallel text in a Facebook comment:

Tetun Dili (T)/Portuguese (P)
(25) *Rahun kmnek tinan foun 2020 nian ba família no belun sira hotu. Boas entradas em 2020 para todos os familiares e amigos.*

T T T T = T
*Rahun kmanek tinan foun 2020 nian*
celebration wonderful year new POSS

T T T T T T
*ba familia no belun sira hotu*
OBL family and friend 3PL all

P P P = P
*Boas entradas em 2020 para*
good:PLF wish:PLF in 2020 for

P P P P P
*todos os familiares e amigos*
all: PLM DEF.PLM relative:PLM and friend:PLM
'Best wishes for the new year 2020 to all relatives and friends'

In both Madagascar and Timor Leste, as in the Philippines and Malaysia previously, multilingualism involving the national language of European provenance is much more common amongst people of higher socioeconomic status.

Of the predominantly MPSEA-speaking countries, Indonesia and Brunei are the only two in which an MPSEA language is the sole national language. However, whereas in Indonesia, the erstwhile colonial language Dutch is virtually absent from the contemporary linguistic landscape, in Brunei, English still plays a major role in administration, education, and everyday life.

It is worth noting that the English, French, and Portuguese of MPSEA-speaking countries is often quite different from the more familiar varieties of these languages spoken in Europe. Indeed, the region also plays host to a handful of European-lexifier creole languages, including Chavacano in the Philippines, Papiá Kristang in Malaysia, and the recently extinct Batavia Creole in Indonesia—all of which have contributed further to the multilingualism of their respective speech communities.

Yet another family of cases of multilingualism involving MPSEA plus non-Austronesian languages involves speech communities representing the products of relatively recent migration over the course of the last few centuries. These fall into two categories. The first is that of MPSEA speakers migrating to other parts of the world, as represented by Surinamese Javanese, assorted varieties of Malay such as Sri Lankan Malay, the Malay dialects of the Cocos and Christmas Islands of Australia, Melayu Sini in the Netherlands, and, more generally, any number of migrant communities speaking MPSEA languages in Europe, the Persian Gulf, Oceania, and the Americas; some of these cases are discussed in more detail in Moro and Slomanson (chapter 19, this volume). The second mirror-image category is that of speakers of non-Austronesian languages migrating into the MPSEA-speaking region.

Foremost amongst these are the overseas Chinese, present in large numbers throughout Mainland and Island Southeast Asia. Most commonly, Chinese people speak the local languages in addition to their own ones, though in some cases, they have fashioned their own varieties of the local languages; for example in Sumatra and the Malay peninsula, they speak distinctive dialects of Malay/Indonesian. Interestingly, in such cases, non-Chinese people often use the Chinese dialect of Malay/Indonesian when speaking to Chinese people, thereby adding yet another level of complexity to their own multiglossic Malay/Indonesian repertoires. For example, in Riau province in Sumatra, non-Chinese people might use features such as the second-person singular pronoun *lu* or the prenominal attributive possessive construction with *punya* when speaking to Chinese people, but not amongst themselves. On the other hand, non-Chinese people in these same regions tend not to speak Chinese, though there are exceptions. Following is an example of Malay–Chinese code-switching taken from a conversation amongst a group of ethnic Teochew speakers in Pontianak, West Kalimantan, Indonesia:[10]

Pontianak Malay (P)/Teochew (T)/Hakka (H)

| (26) | P | H | T | P | P | P | P |
|---|---|---|---|---|---|---|---|
| | *bukan...* | *coni* | *ho* | *kalo* | *warna* | *rambut* | *kan* |
| | NEG | why | yes | TOP | colour | hair | Q |

| P | P | P:P:P:P | H | T |
|---|---|---|---|---|
| *pasti* | *di* | *siniqnya* | *can* | *hoq* |
| sure | LOC | LOC:DEM:DEM.PROX:ASSOC | real | very |

| H | T/H | P |
|---|---|---|
| *chut* | *sék,* | *kan* |
| go.out | colour | Q |

'No, how come when you dye your hair, the colour will be always be more visible here, right?'
(JFS 15102211182676144151314)

Second to the Chinese, the next largest migrant population in MPSEA-speaking countries is of South Asian provenance; the greatest concentration of these is in Malaysia and Singapore, though they can also be found in other countries. Among these, the largest group is of Tamil speakers—as noted above, Tamil is one of the official languages of Singapore. However, a wide variety of other South Asian languages, both Dravidian and Indo-Aryan, continue to be spoken by the respective communities throughout the region; to cite just one example, in Semporna, in eastern Sabah, Malaysia, one may even encounter Pashto being spoken alongside the more widespread Tausug, Bajau, and Sabah Malay.

A further category of multilingualism involving MPSEA languages and non-Austronesian languages from outside the region is formed by global languages, of which there are two notable cases. The first is that of Arabic, the holy language of Islam. Although few people in MPSEA-speaking countries are able to converse in Arabic, a significant number of Muslims can read from the Koran and participate in Arabic-language prayers. The multi-layered presence of Arabic in the local MPSEA languages is illustrated in the following Facebook posting from Padang, in Indonesia:

Indonesian (I)/Arabic (A)

(27) *Silaturahmi...Alhamdulillah...Selamat Ulang Tahun Audrey sayang semoga sehat selalu ...jadi cucu sholehah..barokallahu fii umriik...Aamiin..*

| A(>I) | A>I | (A>)I | I |
|---|---|---|---|
| *Silaturahmi* | *Alhamdulillah* | *Selamat* | *Ulang* |
| fraternity | praise.be.to.God | greetings | repeat |

| I | I | I | I | (A>)I |
|---|---|---|---|---|
| *Tahun* | *Audrey* | *sayang* | *semoga* | *sehat* |
| year | Audrey | compassion | one:may | healthy |

| I:I | I | I | A(>I) |
|---|---|---|---|
| *selalu* | *jadi* | *cucu* | *sholehah* |
| one:pass | become | grandchild | pious.F |

| A(>I) | A(>I) | A(>I) | (A>)I |
|---|---|---|---|
| *barokallahu* | *fi* | *umrik* | *Amin* |
| God's.blessing | in | your.age | amen |

'Fraternity, praise be to God, happy birthday dear Audrey, may you be healthy, and always be a pious grand-daughter, God's blessings in your life, amen'

In the above example, *silaturahmi*, *sholehah*, and *barokallahu fi umrik*, marked A(>I), are Arabic expressions that are partly integrated into Indonesian but are still less likely to be known by a non-religious person with no knowledge of Arabic; their presence in the above text might perhaps be considered to constitute an instance of code-switching.[11] Somewhat more integrated into Indonesian is the expression *Alhamdulillah*, marked A>I, which is commonly used also by non-religious Muslims, and less commonly also by non-Muslims when talking to Muslims.[12] Exhibiting yet a further degree of integration into Indonesian are the words *selamat*, *sehat*, and *amin*, marked (A>)I, which are fully-fledged loanwords; while the former two are devoid of any religious connotations, the latter, although clearly bearing a religious meaning, is not specific to Islam, being used also by Christians.

A curious use of Arabic as a marker of social identity can be observed amongst the male-to-female transgender community of Manokwari in West Papua. In Papuan Malay, as in many other languages of the region, oaths are a commonly occurring linguistic feature; however their form and provenance splits down ethnic and religious lines. While the indigenous Papuans, who are predominantly Christian, use Christian-based exclamations such as *yerus* 'Jerusalem' and *dara yesnat* 'blood of Jesus of Nazareth', the migrant population, who are largely Muslim, employ Arabic-based

[10] In addition to the code-switching between Pontianak Malay and Chinese, the Chinese forms themselves appear to originate in two distinct Sinitic languages, Teochew and Hakka, as indicated in (26). It is not clear whether this constitutes an instance of code-switching between Teochew and Hakka, or, alternatively, is representative of a single newly emergent shared code resulting from dialect levelling within Chinese.

[11] Nevertheless, in (27), these expressions are glossed as they are understood in Indonesian, and not in accordance with the original Arabic.

[12] In this respect, Indonesia is more liberal than neighbouring Malaysia, where the use of Islamic expressions such as greetings and oaths by non-Muslims is strictly forbidden.

exclamations, such as *alhamdulillah* 'praise be to God' (above) and *astagafirullah* 'I seek forgiveness from God'. In most cases, this division is strictly maintained. However, the transgender community, who are ethnically mixed between Christian Papuans and Muslim migrants, uniformly use the Muslim oaths, which, in the case of the Papuans in the community, constitutes an exceptional instance of Christian Papuans using Arabic-based oaths. The explanation for this, presumably, is that the transgender community of Manokwari models itself culturally on the mainstream Indonesian transgender community, which, like the country as a whole, is predominantly Muslim. Thus, paradoxically, the use of Arabic in this particular case becomes a marker of exotericity and modernity.

The second global language present in the linguistic landscape of MPSEA-speaking languages is of course English. Whereas in the Philippines, Malaysia, and Singapore, English is ubiquitous in its role as a national language, it is in countries such as Madagascar, Timor Leste, and Indonesia, where it has no official status and its presence is, in general, much less noticeable, that its function as a world language can be observed more directly. In Indonesia, where most people speak little or no English, the English language still crops up in a variety of places. For some, it is a marker of social status; in some upper-class families, parents may speak to their children in English. For others, it may perhaps represent an attempt by speakers to distance themselves from a dominant Indonesian culture and mark themselves as citizens of the world. And then, especially in social media, English is simply cool. The following Facebook comment illustrates code-switching between English and Biak:

Biak (B)/English (E)

(28) *Kwain ma buk oras beja fe Rwoer monda be mansar suine suwose fawawi na nabore........you're not gonna waste yout time..*

<B>B B B:B B
*Kwain ma buk oras*
<2SG>sit hither 2SG:give time

B:B:B B <B> B
*bedya fe rwowr monda*
2SG.POSS:3SG:SPEC down <2SG>hear only

B B:B B:B:B
*be mansar suine*
2SG.POSS male:old 3DU:SPEC:DEM.PROX

B:B B~B B B:B
*suwose fawawi na nabore*
3DU:talk know~NMLZ 3PL.INAN 3PL.INAN:much

E E E E E E E
*you're not going to waste your time*

'Come, sit, give your time, and listen to your elders talking, they are full of knowledge, you're not going to waste your time'

Several of the categories of multilingualism between MPSEA and non-Austronesian languages considered in this section find prominent expression in the specific semantic domain of numerals—already discussed in §16.3 above, cf. example (12). Here, too, such code-switching typically involves specific contexts such as time-telling and prices. Grammatical descriptions of many Philippine languages, including both regional languages and the national language Tagalog, will often provide three different sets of numerals, one in the indigenous language, one in English, and one in the erstwhile national language Spanish. In such cases, while the English numerals may, for some speakers, be analysable in terms of code-switching, the Spanish numerals would seem to be fully-fledged loans—given that most Pilipinos speak little or no Spanish. Similarly, in Timor Leste, speakers of the national language Tetun Dili, make use of three different sets of numerals—indigenous, Indonesian, and Portuguese (van Klinken and Hajek 2018). In example (29), a Tetun Dili numeral *walu* co-occurs alongside a Portuguese numeral *dozi i meia*:

Tetun Dili (T)/Portuguese (P)

(29) T T T T T P
*Ami tama tuku walu sai dozi*
1PL.EXCL enter o'clock eight exit twelve

P P
*i meia*
and half

'We start school at 8 o'clock and finish at 12.30'
(van Klinken and Hajek 2018: 65)

While the occurrence of Tetun Dili and Portuguese numerals side by side might point towards a code-switching analysis, the non-standard spelling of the Portuguese *dozi i meia* suggests that the form in question might be in the process of being integrated into Tetun Dili. In all of these cases, the language associated with the numerals would appear to be higher on the scale of exotericity represented in (1). This is true both for cases of national vs. regional MPSEA languages as discussed in §16.3, and for cases of non-Austronesian colonial vs. MPSEA languages as illustrated here.

A somewhat different instantiation of the same principle is offered by a set of currency terms in Jakarta Indonesian, consisting of forms such as *go cap* 'fifty (thousand Rupiah)', *pek go* 'hundred and fifty (thousand Rupiah)', and others. Originally from Hokkien Chinese, these terms have been fully integrated into Jakarta Indonesian, where in contemporary speech they are understood as referring exclusively to currency units of thousands of Rupiah. Although Hokkien is the language of an ethnic minority within Indonesia, when the terms first entered Indonesian they were associated with Chinese trading and commerce, which, from the perspective of the indigenous Malay/Indonesian population, might perhaps have represented modernity and worldliness, that is to say, higher on the scale of exotericity in (1).

Going back in time, similar patterns of asymmetric bilingualism have given rise to many instances of numeral borrowings, ranging from the Malay/Indonesian *juta* 'million' borrowed from Sanskrit (Gonda 1973: 383), to the higher numerals in the Bahnaric language Chrau borrowed from Cham (Grant 2007: 120)—the latter providing an instance of numeral borrowing in the opposite direction, from MPSEA to non-Austronesian languages.

The final case of multilingualism between MPSEA and non-Austronesian languages considered in this chapter is that between MPSEA languages and the various sign languages of the region. For the most part, oral-manual multilingualism is limited, on the one hand, to oral-language literacy amongst the deaf community, and on the other hand, to a very limited number of hearing people who have acquired sign language fluency, most commonly either as family members of deaf signers, or as workers in the deaf community, for example as interpreters. However, a special case of oral-manual multilingualism is provided by village sign languages, sign languages used in small and usually rural communities, where, for various reasons, there is a larger-than-usual incidence of deafness, as a result of which the hearing people in the community are also proficient in the local sign language. A well-documented case is that of Bengkala village in Bali, Indonesia (Marsaja 2008; de Vos 2012). Of a population of close to 3,000 people, over 2% are deaf, and communicate in the local sign language Kata Kolok; however, well over half of the hearing population are also fluent in the sign language. As described by de Vos (2012: 27) "Kata Kolok is the default language when one of the communication partners is deaf. Hearing signers also use Kata Kolok when they need to communicate over large distances—e.g. across the river—or when working in the fields using nois[y] farming equipment."

## 16.6 Conclusion

As illustrated in this chapter, multilingualism—within MPSEA languages, across MPSEA languages, and between MPSEA and non-Austronesian languages—is the norm for the region, as indeed are the corresponding forms of multilingualism in many other parts of the world. A speaker from near Manokwari in West Papua with whom I am familiar grew up bilingual in Papuan Malay and his native non-Austronesian language Meyah, but early on also acquired proficiency in two other Malay/Indonesian varieties, Jakarta Indonesian and Standard Indonesian; in addition he picked up Javanese from the *transmigrasi* (migrant) community that shared his village, as well as two other non-Austronesian languages, Sougb and Hatam, from people in the surrounding villages. Plus also a smattering of Biak and English. Although his linguistic proficiency is above average even for that particular region, it is by no means exceptional.

The ubiquity of multilingualism throughout the MPSEA region bears a number of important consequences for linguistic studies both within the region and beyond. Diachronically, language contact due to multilingualism plays a major role in historical processes such as, for example, the simplification undergone by Malayo-Polynesian languages as they originally spread south from the Philippines into the Indonesian archipelago (Donohue and Denham 2020; Gil 2020a), and, more recently, the development of trade varieties of Malay/Indonesian (Adelaar and Prentice 1996; Paauw 2008) and of creoles, the latter comprising both MPSEA-lexifier creoles such as Baba Malay (Ansaldo and Matthews 1999) and non-Austronesian-lexifier creoles such as Chavacano (Steinkrüger 2008a). Synchronically, multilingualism and pervasive code-switching presents the fieldworker with a methodological challenge, often calling for a sometimes rather arbitrary decision as to whether a particular form or construction should be attributed to the dialect or language being described, or perhaps to some other dialect or language with which it is in contact. Such difficulties may point towards alternative approaches to linguistic description and analysis in which the basic unit of study is not the language as a whole but rather the linguistic ecologies of individuals and their associated speech communities (Enfield 2003).

## Acknowledgements

I am grateful to the Department of Linguistics at the Max Planck Institute for Evolutionary Anthropology and its director Bernard Comrie for the extensive and long-term support that made possible the research represented in this chapter, and to the staff of the MPIEVA Jakarta Field Station for their years and years of labour, some small fruits of which are represented here. I would also like to thank Julibeletu Alabes, Rudy Chandra, Thomas Conners, Hilário de Sousa, Shirley Dita, Sajed Ingilan, Santi Kurniati, Manbero Oridek Mnusefer, Mike Pangilinan, Ileana Paul, Sonja Riesberg, Sven Siegmund, and Demianus Wasage for assistance with some of the data cited in this chapter.

CHAPTER 17

# Language policy and the politics of language

Tom Hoogervorst

## 17.1 Introduction

This chapter deals with issues surrounding language policy and the politics of language for a selection of MPSEA languages. I briefly describe their histories, literary traditions, and the influence of language engineers in colonial and postcolonial times. Across the region, early nationalists saw themselves confronted with great ethnolinguistic diversity within colonially inherited borders. In several instances, the choice to elevate one out of many regional languages as the national language reinforced processes of marginalization. Modern language institutes from Madagascar to East Timor face the task of standardizing 'their' national language, developing it, and bringing it up to par with world languages in terms of school curricula, literary productions, and specialized vocabulary. At the same time, these institutes are responsible for the protection of regional languages, with fluctuating degrees of success. In addition to top-down language policies, media and popular culture have assumed equally important roles in shaping today's linguistic landscapes.

This is not the first overview of the policies and politics of MPSEA languages. Steinhauer (2005) provides a comparison between different nation states. This chapter, by contrast, juxtaposes a selection of specific case studies that illustrate common developments across MPSEA languages. In two sections, it first highlights official (or national) languages and then regional (or minority) languages. The official languages examined here are Malagasy, Malay and Indonesian, Tagalog, and Tetun, while Cham, Javanese, Kapampangan, and—again—Malay are the regional languages considered.

## 17.2 National languages

### 17.2.1 Malagasy

Malagasy is one of the official languages of the Republic of Madagascar, the other one being French. Two Malagasy varieties, Kibushi and Kiantalaotse, are spoken in parts of the French-governed island of Mayotte, where they have no official status. Malagasy is a Southeast Barito language originating from Borneo's southeastern coast. The historical development of this language is described by Adelaar (this volume, chapter 21) and the contemporary linguistic features by Howe (this volume, chapter 40). In view of its size, Madagascar displays a remarkably homogenous linguistic landscape. Although Malagasy exhibits a number of dialects, their structural similarity and the mutual intelligibility between most of them conventionally qualify Malagasy as a single language, although there is some disagreement on this issue (Kikusawa 2012). Apart from the French, sizeable ethnolinguistic minorities include Arabs, Chinese, Indians, and Comorians, whose languages have no official status.

The Malagasy language has historically been written in an Arabic-derived script, preceding its romanized orthography. The former is known as *Sorabe*, of which seventeenth and eighteenth-century manuscripts in an archaic form of coastal Southeast Malagasy have survived. It is not precisely known how widespread this script was on the island. For some time, Sorabe literacy was monopolized by scribes from the Antemoro community. It was also briefly adopted by the upland courts, prior to their move towards romanization. The activities of French missionaries notwithstanding, widespread literacy in the Roman alphabet only began in 1818 with the arrival of the London Missionary Society. Romanized Malagasy played an important role in the expansive bureaucracy developed under King Radama I (1793–1828) in collaboration with British missionaries.

Despite the existence of Sorabe writing, the roots of Malagasy standardization—based on the Merina dialect of the island's central highlands—can be traced to this period of precolonial contact with Europeans. The Welsh linguist David Jones (1796–1841) proved a key collaborator in the court-initiated development of a Malagasy romanization, Bible translation, industrialized printing, literacy projects, and educational development from the 1820s (Jackson 2013: 24–36). In the waning days of slavery, a Malagasy-literate diaspora emerged in Cape Town, Mauritius, and elsewhere in the Indian Ocean. Their epistolary traditions provide some insightful examples of early written Malagasy (Larson 2009).

Tom Hoogervorst, *Language policy and the politics of language.* In: *The Oxford Guide to the Malayo-Polynesian Languages of Southeast Asia.* Edited by: Alexander Adelaar and Antoinette Schapper, Oxford University Press. © Tom Hoogervorst (2024). DOI: 10.1093/oso/9780198807353.003.0017

Through a centralized government and printing press, a unified, literary form of Merina Malagasy developed into the island's prestige language, a status it has kept to date. This so-called Standard Malagasy (*Malagasy ofisialy*) continues to be associated with the ethnic Merina elites and other groups in proximity to state power (Jackson 2013). Under French colonialism (1895–1960), the role of Malagasy as a language of bureaucracy, education, and literacy was diminished in favour of French, although the Merina variety was still favoured over the other dialects. Non-Merina varieties, such as Sakalava, received some attention from missionaries (Rosnes 2019), yet never developed a comparable literary tradition. Unofficial forms of Malagasy played a role in anticolonial mobilization before 1960 and in socialist activism preceding the May 1972 revolution (Jackson 2013: 41–3, 48–50).

The Malagasy Academy (*Académie Malgache* or *Akademia Malagasy*) is an important institution for scholarship on the Malagasy language. Founded in 1902 in the spirit of the Académie Française, this learned society was dedicated to the study of Malagasy history, linguistics, literature, archaeology, and ethnography (Poisson and Barbier 1952). Next to academic publications, which include a number of dialect dictionaries, the institute is also involved in setting up norms of correct Malagasy (Verdier 2013: 97). As is the case with many institutes established as part of the colonial project, the Académie Malgache has attempted to reinvent itself over the past decades. It now aims to develop Malagasy scholarship through frequent public events and conferences. In addition to its original preoccupations with language and culture, the institute has expanded its focus to health and sustainable development.

In 1972, a policy of Malgachization was implemented under Gabriel Ramanantsoa (1906–1979), Madagascar's second president. Its primary aim was to make the nation's French-dominated institutions more Malagasy (Turcotte 1981). To the chagrin of people from the coastal peripheries, this effectively meant a substitution of French by the Merina dialect, even though many politicians had origins outside the central highlands. Both co-existed as official languages, something that has lasted until the present day. Malagasy varieties associated with coastal groups, urban lower classes, descendants of enslaved Africans, and other marginalized groups have a history of being ridiculed in the printed media (Jackson 2013: 166–86). At present, non-Merina varieties of Malagasy are at risk of losing their specific features (Kikusawa 2012). Today's multimedia landscape has afforded a bigger platform for these non-hegemonic varieties. A number of hip hop artists, for instance, produce music in the Sakalava dialect of the island's west coast (Boyer-Rossel 2014).

The official Malagasy orthography continues to be based on the early nineteenth-century compromise between King Radama I and the British and French missionaries he collaborated with. Unlike many other European-style orthographies, it has from the outset rejected the graphs <c>, <q>, and <x>. The letters <u> and <w> are also absent in the official spelling. In written representations of spoken language, such as online chatting, an ad hoc colloquial spelling is used (Verdier 2013). Speakers of Kibushi and Kiantalaotse prefer an orthography closer to that of Comorian languages.

### 17.2.2 Malay and Indonesian

Malay is a national language in Indonesia, Malaysia, Singapore, and Brunei Darussalam, and a minority language in Thailand, Sri Lanka, and other countries (see §17.3.4). It belongs to the Malayo-Chamic family and exhibits considerable dialectal diversity (Anderbeck, this volume, §9.5.2, §9.6.2). Historically spoken on both sides of the Straits of Malacca, Malay has long been in contact with other languages and has adopted and transmitted several loanwords (Hoogervorst, this volume, §23.1, §23.2.2). With an epigraphic record dating back to the seventh century CE, it also has one of the oldest written traditions among Austronesian languages, second only to that of Cham (see §17.3.1). The earliest Malay inscriptions are written in an Indic-derived script closely related to those of Cham, Javanese, Tagalog, Kapampangan, etc. From the fourteenth century onwards, the Arabic-derived *Jawi* script gradually became the dominant way of writing Malay. Encouraged by missionaries and colonial authorities, Malay was increasingly written in various romanizations in the second half of the nineteenth century, although many ethnic Malays preferred to use Jawi into the twentieth century.

Like other Austronesian languages with a literary tradition, the gap between written and spoken Malay is considerable. Historically, prestigious registers, typically written in Jawi, featured in classical literature, diplomatic letters, legal codes, and at the courts of Borneo, Sumatra, and the Malay Peninsula. On the lower end of the multiglossic spectrum is a wide range of Malay vernaculars (Gil, this volume, chapter 16). The varieties spoken by ethnic Malays are popularly considered to be more 'pure' than those of eastern Indonesia and—historically—of Batavia (now Jakarta). Systematic attempts to standardize this regionally diverse language started under European colonialism. In this regard, missionaries played a pioneering role, albeit not an extremely effective one. Internal debates on the preferable type of Malay for a Bible translation—either in an idiom that was understandable to a broad readership or one that met the approval of both indigenous and European elites—raged on for centuries. An English-based romanization entered usage among the missionaries of British Malaya (now West Malaysia and Singapore), whereas a Dutch-based romanization prevailed in the Netherlands Indies (now Indonesia).

The first attempt to standardize romanized Malay came in 1901 from the Dutch linguist Charles Adriaan van Ophuijsen (1854–1917) and formed the basis of the modern Indonesian orthography. Similar efforts emerged in British Malaya and British North Borneo, leading in 1904 to the 'Romanized Malay Spelling' developed by Richard James Wilkinson (1867–1941) and subsequently adjusted by Zainal Abidin bin Ahmad or Za'aba (1895–1973). As a result of colonial and postcolonial language politics, Indonesia and Malaysia display slightly different standardizations, while Singapore and Brunei primarily follow the Malaysian model. In Indonesia, the adoption of Malay as the national language has been an unequivocal decision. The language did not suffer from the association with a single ethnicity, as it was widely adopted by people from non-Malay backgrounds. In addition, it had a thriving print culture. The Japanese occupation, with its ban on the use of European languages, greatly increased the domains in which 'Indonesian' (*Bahasa Indonesia*) could establish itself. The Agency for the Development and Promotion of Language (*Badan Pengembangan dan Pembinaan Bahasa*) is responsible for the description, documentation, and standardization of Indonesian and the preservation of regional languages.

A different situation unfolded in Malaysia, where Malay is associated with the country's (relatively small) ethnic Malay majority. Somewhat controversially, Malay has been elevated as the nation's single national language at the cost of minority languages and English (Leow 2016). Akin to the coinage of Indonesian, the resultant standardization was termed 'Malaysian' (*Bahasa Malaysia*), although it was temporarily reverted to 'Malay' (*Bahasa Melayu*) from 1986 to 2007 (Wong and Edwards 2007). In addition, English, Mandarin, and—to some extent—Tamil constitute languages of education. Established in 1956, Malaysia's Institute of Language and Literature (*Dewan Bahasa dan Pustaka*) is the governmental body responsible for the standardization and development of the Malay language and the publication of books and other resources on this topic. Housed since 1957 in Kuala Lumpur and later also in various regional offices, the institute's website contains various online materials and services to assist people in using its authorized type of Malay.

Singapore distinguishes between 'official languages' (English, Malay, Mandarin, and Tamil) and the 'national language' (Malay). The latter can be heard in military drills, the national anthem, and other ceremonial functions, whereas English functions as the de facto working language. While Malay continues to be a vibrant mother tongue among Singapore's Malay community, the city's specific variety of Bazaar Malay—historically used as an inter-ethnic means of oral communication—is currently restricted to the older generations. In Brunei Darussalam, Malay likewise functions as the national language (*Bahasa Kebangsaan*). As in Malaysia, the Malays constitute the largest ethnic group, in addition to Chinese, Indian, and indigenous (Austronesian-speaking) communities. A multiglossic situation exists between standard Malay and a continuum of colloquial dialects known as Brunei Malay. The usage of standard Malay is relatively limited and restricted to official settings and national media, whereas Brunei Malay widely functions as a lingua franca and vehicle of popular culture. In addition, Brunei has its own courtly register. The Brunei Institute of Language and Literature (*Dewan Bahasa dan Pustaka Brunei*), established in 1960, governs the nation's language policy, which includes the publication of a number of journals and a dictionary of Brunei Malay.

Indonesian and Malaysian language engineers established closer contacts from the 1970s, although differences between the two Malay standardizations persist in the realm of neologisms and the influence of spoken language. One of the greatest collaborative successes in this regard is the adoption in 1972 of a uniform orthography, known in Malaysia as the New Romanized Spelling (*Ejaan Rumi Baharu*) and in Indonesia as the Enhanced Spelling (*Ejaan Yang Disempurnakan*). This orthographic reform led to the homogenization of much but not all Malay vocabulary. From 1985, language planners from Brunei joined their ranks, collaboratively establishing the Language Council of Brunei-Indonesia-Malaysia (*Majlis Bahasa Brunei-Indonesia-Malaysia*), in which Singapore has the status of observer. This organization holds recurrent seminars and other activities and issues its own publications.

Standardization has also taken place in the realm of Jawi writing. In earlier times, the inability of this script to indicate minute phonological differences—especially in the realm of vowels—arguably contributed to its success, as it eroded regional variation between the dialects of Sumatra, Borneo, and the Malay Peninsula (in which vowel distinction played an important role). While the Malay World has known various spelling traditions (Vikør 1988) and Jawi newspapers may have played some role in reducing orthographic diversity during colonial times, the standardization of this script only began in postcolonial times. In 1986, Malaysia's Institute of Language and Literature introduced the Guidelines of the Enhanced Jawi Spelling (*Pedoman Ejaan Jawi yang Disempurnakan*), detailing the prescribed usage of diacritics, word boundaries, and vowels. Its standardization is an ongoing process, in which Jawi keyboards and other digital tools are of growing significance (Dungcik 2015). As a script associated with the heritage of ethnic Malays, Jawi has a symbolic status in Brunei, Singapore, most Malaysian states, and a number of Indonesian provinces. At present, education in Jawi—in addition to romanized Malay—is offered in Malaysia, Singapore, Brunei, southern Thailand (see §17.3.4), and in many regions of Sumatra in Indonesia (Rizki 2020).

### 17.2.3 Filipino

Filipino is the co-official language of the Republic of the Philippines alongside English. It is a standardized form of Tagalog, a Central Philippine language originating from the Manila Bay area and the central and southern parts of Luzon. Like a number of other Philippine languages, it was initially written in an Indic-derived syllabary known as *Baybayin*. The first romanization of Tagalog was introduced under Spanish colonialism. Like the romanizations of other Philippine languages, it was largely based on the Spanish orthography. A Catholic literature in Tagalog took shape in the late sixteenth century (Rafael 1988), whereas a mechanized printing industry emerged during the American colonial period (1898–1946). At the same time, the implementation of English as a medium of education suppressed Spanish as well as the indigenous languages (Smolicz 1986: 99–100).

The choice of Tagalog as the official language of the Philippines was never without controversy. The notion of a monolingual state was complicated by the presence of several other major languages, such as Bikol, Cebuano, Hiligaynon, Ilokano, Kapampangan (see §17.3.3), Pangasinan, and Waray-Waray, which played important roles in their respective regions of origin. These languages were often erroneously called 'dialects' during the American period (Gonzalez 1999: 135), as remains the case today in non-linguist circles. The First Philippine Republic (1899–1901) had to partly rely on Spanish to facilitate communication between its diverse politicians, many of whom had limited knowledge of Tagalog. In the same way, their successors were often stuck with English for that purpose. While Tagalog has long been common in and around the colonial capital, widespread proficiency in especially the southern parts of the archipelago only became a reality in the second half of the twentieth century.

As a literary language of the nation's political and economic centre, Tagalog nevertheless managed to hold on to its privileged position despite the challenges. The authoritative Institute of National Language (*Surian ng Wikang Pambansa*) officially instituted it as the national language (*Wikang Pambansa*) in 1937, even though at the time it had fewer speakers than Cebuano. The compilation of an official orthography, grammar, and dictionary soon followed. Like elsewhere in Southeast Asia, Tagalog received a boost during the Japanese occupation, when competing European languages were outlawed. It remained an official language after the Philippine independence in 1946 and was renamed *Pilipino* in 1959, displaying a similar de-ethnicized philosophy as 'Indonesian' and 'Malaysian' (see §17.2.2).

Supported by centralized media and education, Pilipino spread rapidly across the archipelago, although it encountered fierce hostility in some regions, in particular Cebu and the parts of Mindanao where Bisayan languages are spoken. Under the constitution of 1973, Pilipino retained its status of official language alongside English. Its name change, which was further amended to *Filipino* in 1987, was clearly an attempt to dissociate the national language from the Tagalog ethnicity and, at least in theory, have it incorporate elements from other large languages. So far, however, Filipino has remained closer to Tagalog than many non-Tagalogs would have hoped. In that sense, it came to fulfil a similar role to Merina in Madagascar (see §17.2.1): a language associated with proximity to the centralized government. In terms of prestige and upward mobility it continues to compete with English, the language of the former colonizer.

After several name changes (Gonzalez 1999: 135–6), the institute governing language policy became known in 1992 as the Commission on the Filipino Language (*Komisyon sa Wikang Filipino*). This national language institute produced a standardized orthography and a map and atlas of Philippine languages. It is responsible for Filipino language development and the protection of regional languages. Initially, regional languages were shunned from education out of fear that they would undermine nationalism and promote regionalism (Smolicz 1986). The Philippine authorities have shown themselves considerably more open-minded to multilingualism in recent times. From 2009, several educational institutes have adopted the UNESCO strategy of mother tongue based multilingual education (MTB-MLE), using the first language of the students in a classroom setting, while still maintaining Filipino and English in the curriculum (Cruz and Mahboob 2018). The future will tell whether this policy can take away the sense of marginalization experienced by ethnolinguistic minorities.

In an attempt to 'indigenize' the Spanish-based orthography of Tagalog, the so-called *Abakada* alphabet was adopted for the national language in 1940. It meant a validation of proposals first formulated in the late nineteenth century—including by the Filipino nationalist José Rizal (1861–1896)—to do away with the Spanish letters <c>, <ll>, <ñ>, and <qu>. In 2013, the Commission on the Filipino Language institutionalized its latest orthographic reform: the National Orthography (*Ortograpiyang Pambansa*). Unlike the earlier *Abakada* alphabet, with its reduced set of letters, the new spelling was supposed to be applicable to all Philippine languages. For this reason, the number of graphs was increased. Next to the default letters of the Latin alphabet, the <ñ>, <ng>, and schwa <ë> have been added. As yet, the orthography is less optimally equipped to mark the glottal stop, long vowels, and word stress, revealing its Tagalog-specific origins.

### 17.2.4 Tetun Dili

Tetun (written in the official Portuguese influenced orthography as *Tetum*) is an official language of the Democratic Republic of Timor-Leste (East Timor), alongside Portuguese. It is an interethnic contact language, sometimes referred to in the literature as Tetun Dili—and earlier as Tetun Prasa (*Tétum-Praça*). The language developed in colonial times in and around the capital Dili as a lingua franca based on more conservative rural dialects known as Tetun Terik, but with many Portuguese elements (see Slomanson, this volume, §18.7).

Parts of Timor were under Portuguese control from the sixteenth century. As the colony's high-prestige language, Portuguese was used—albeit mostly in the capital—for administrative purposes and has deeply influenced Tetun Dili. However, fluent speakers remained a small minority (Hajek 2000). Especially from the 1950s, Portuguese was the language of governance and education, confining Tetun and other local languages to the oral domain and forbidding them at schools. The Portuguese-influenced Tetun of the colony's urbanites stood in contrast with the variety used in the Catholic Church, which was more influenced by Tetun Terik (Williams-van Klinken et al. 2002: 3–4). Most early writings in Tetun were ecclesiastical in nature. Similar to Malay in Indonesia (see §17.2.2), Tetun Dili was relatively egalitarian and not explicitly linked to one specific ethnic group, granting it the favour of the country's early nationalists (van Engelenhoven 2006).

National independence, however, proved to be a short-lived reality. In 1976, East Timor was violently incorporated by the neighbouring Republic of Indonesia. For more than two decades, Indonesian became the official language, ousting Portuguese and ignoring Tetun and other local languages. Tetun and Portuguese played mutually complementary roles in the underground anti-Indonesian resistance movement and also in the East Timorese diaspora. From the 1980s, Tetun was also elevated across the island to the liturgical language of Catholicism, especially after the Indonesian government had diminished the role of Portuguese (Hajek 2000; Taylor-Leech 2009). Even today, a large part of the non-journalistic media and literature in Tetun is produced within the clerical realm.

East Timor achieved its independence in 2002, following a UN-led transitional administration in 1999. The National Institute of Linguistics (*Instituto Nacional de Linguistica* or *Institutu Nasionál Linguístika nian*) was established in 2001 during the interim government, with Tetun and Portuguese functioning as the co-official languages. As part of the National University of East Timor (*Universidade Nasionál Timór Lorosa'e*) in Dili, its tasks are those expected of a language institute: to develop the national language, expand its vocabulary, standardize its orthography, and disseminate materials to achieve these aims. Standard Tetun (*Tetun Ofisiál*) is largely modelled after Tetun Dili. The national language institute is also responsible for the protection of local languages. As with Tagalog and Merina Malagasy, the official status of Tetun is broadly accepted albeit not universally adopted. In the Fataluku- and Makasae-speaking eastern parts of the island, for example, Portuguese and subsequently Indonesian have been historically preferred to communicate with other ethnolinguistic communities, yet this has now almost completely shifted to Tetun.

A major challenge for language engineers has been to cast off the stigma of Tetun as a chiefly oral language. Already under the Indonesian occupation, the Fretilin literacy committee favoured orthographic conventions that would do justice to the phonology of Tetun rather than Portuguese, such as <k> instead of <qu> and <aun> instead of <ão>. In addition, the International Academic Committee for the Development of East Timorese Languages (IACDETL), formerly based in Sydney, proposed <ll> and <ñ> to replace respectively <lh> and <nh>. In this *ortografia padronizada* (standardized spelling), the apostrophe <'> was used to represent the glottal stop, even though this phoneme is absent in Tetun Dili. Doing so ensured that the orthography would not be rejected by speakers of Tetun Terik (van Engelenhoven 2006: 117; Ross 2017: 43–4). Recently, the Dili Institute of Technology set up a phonemic orthography for use in its Tetun language courses that casts off many of the irregularities of the official orthography, but it has not yet gained wide currency (Ross 2017: 44–5).

The success of Tetun as a national language has been impressive in view of its negligence under two different occupying forces. It has made great strides in achieving widespread literacy among the younger generations. Tetun proficiency, which was already high in early independence times, has increased through education, newspapers, and other media (Taylor-Leech 2009). The national radio and television broadcaster *Rádio Televisão Timor Leste-Emprensa Publika* in particular hosts numerous programmes in Tetun, many of which can be accessed through their website. Education has since 2002 taken place in Tetun and Portuguese, while Indonesian (and Indonesian-language textbooks) continued to be used unofficially until at least 2010. In addition, recent pilots in mother tongue based multilingual education have been undertaken with Baikeno (an Uab Meto lect), Fataluku, and Galolen (Taylor-Leech 2013; Cabral and Martin-Jones 2018).

## 17.3 Regional languages

### 17.3.1 Cham

Turning now to the regional languages, this section will first call attention to Cham, a minority language in Vietnam and Cambodia belonging to the Malayo-Chamic family (Brunelle and Jensen, this volume, chapter 30; Brunelle, this volume, §11.2). With an epigraphical record that has conventionally (though not conclusively) been dated to the fifth century CE, it has the oldest known written tradition of any Austronesian language. The original homeland of the Cham people covers much of the Vietnamese coastline. In the wake of the southward territorial expansion of the Việt, particularly from the late fifteenth century, many Chams were pushed to the highlands. Their westward migration into Cambodia has been an additional result of these changing power dynamics.

Cham epigraphy has received ample scholarly attention, particularly by philologists trained in France, which has lasted from colonial times until the present day. In addition, modern Cham exhibits a prestigious literary form. This register enjoys a high status within the community itself, both among Muslims and Hindus. In everyday life, two distinct colloquial varieties can be distinguished: Eastern Cham and Western Cham. The former has its basis in the Vietnamese provinces of Ninh Thuận and Bình Thuận. The latter is primarily found in small settlements in Cambodia, the Vietnamese provinces of Tây Ninh and An Giang, and Ho Chi Minh City. In addition to the literary-colloquial distinction, bilingualism with Khmer (in Cambodia) and Vietnamese (in Vietnam) is widespread.

Throughout its written history, Cham has used a number of closely related Indic scripts, which were never historically standardized and display internal variation. A continuum of slightly different alphabets collectively known as *Akhar Thrah* (pronounced as *Akhar Srak* in Western Cham) existed from the seventeenth century and has attracted the attention of European scholars from the late nineteenth century (Aymonier 1889). The use of Indic scripts has a stronger tradition in Vietnam than in Cambodia. In Cambodia, an Arabic-derived script known as *Jawi* (see §17.2.2) has risen in popularity from the nineteenth century, partly substituting Akhar Thrah (Bruckmayr 2019). In Vietnam, Akhar Thrah is currently in use among the Eastern Cham and Jawi among the Western Cham. In addition, Vietnam's Cham Bani community uses another localized Arabic-derived script known as *Akhar Bani*. Most Cham speakers have traditionally been unsympathetic towards romanization, although French and Vietnamese linguists have proposed a number of different systems and the internet has changed the orthographic preferences of the younger generations. Starting with the Cham–Vietnamese–French dictionary of Moussay (1971), several Cham dictionaries feature a romanization using Vietnamese diacritics (Bùi 1997). This spelling is not directly understandable to Chams from Cambodia.

Various communal efforts to study and protect Cham varieties have emerged. Some of the most renowned Cham scholars from Vietnam were trained at the Po Klong High School (*Trường Trung học Pô-Klong*), an ethnic-minority school that operated in the late 1960s and early 1970s and used Vietnamese and Cham. Publications issued in the Republic of Vietnam (1955–1975), chiefly by the Cham Cultural Centre (*Centre Culturel Cham*), tend to focus on literary Cham. Under the Socialist Republic of Vietnam (1976–present), the study of Cham and other minority languages received a degree of support from the Ministry of Education. A number of journals and publication series devoted themselves to the Cham language and culture, whereas the Committee for Drafting School Textbooks in Cham (*Ban Biên soạn Sách chữ Chăm*) was commissioned to standardize the language and script for its use in school curricula. The provinces Ninh Thuận and Bình Thuận have seen the development of local-language curricula (for Eastern Cham). In Cambodia, political and scholarly efforts have so far not precipitated the emergence of a widely adopted standardization.

Education in Eastern Cham has suffered a number of setbacks. Besides financial hardship, attempts in Ninh Thuận and Bình Thuận to cast the heterogenous traditions of written Cham into an educational mould have stumbled upon considerable controversy. Efforts to reform written Cham—which, like English, exhibits an archaic spelling—and bring it closer to the spoken language were fiercely criticized by traditionalists inside and outside Vietnam. Their concerns were not without basis. Not only did the new system yield disappointing results in improving Cham literacy, it also orthographically alienated the community from their rich classical literature (Brunelle 2008). Despite ongoing efforts to improve literacy in Akhar Thrah, the majority of Cham people rely on Vietnamese in writing. In Cambodia, Khmer has become the chief vehicle of literacy.

At the same time, the position of the Jawi script is gaining some ground among the Western Cham communities of Tây Ninh and An Giang. From the late 1990s, the Vietnamese Ministry of Education has allowed this script to be taught in public schooling (Bruckmayr 2019: 358). Closer collaborations between Cham Muslims and Malaysian

Muslims have started to bear their fruits. A Malay-Cham dictionary in Jawi, published in 2012 by the National University of Malaysia (*Universiti Kebangsaan Malaysia*) and compiled by two Cambodian and two Vietnamese Chams, can be seen as an authoritative standard work in this regard (Bruckmayr 2019: 334).

With its previously disconnected speech communities in Cambodia and Vietnam, and—more recently—in Malaysia and the USA, the Cham language has managed to find its way into new forms of media. The Vietnamese website Champaka.info, containing various pieces on language and culture, ran from 2006 to 2015. The Champa Youth Society (*Hội Thanh Niên Champa*), also based in Vietnam, is currently active on the social media. Pop artists singing in Cham have found YouTube to be a useful infrastructure to reach larger audiences. One of the best known networks at present is *Bangsa Cham Media*, which is run from Seattle. Active on Facebook, YouTube, and Instagram, this community provides information on language, culture, Islam, and relevant news. It uses the Jawi script. Even though TrueType fonts have been developed for the Indic Cham scripts, ad hoc romanization has become widespread across the social media.

### 17.3.2 Javanese

Javanese is the largest Austronesian language in terms of mother tongue speakers. Originating from the Indonesian island Java, it boasts a rich literary tradition going back to the ninth century. Throughout its long history, Javanese developed into a regional high-prestige language, influencing a number of Austronesian languages in its vicinity. The courtly form of Javanese, developed in early-colonial times in the Mataram principalities of Central Java—an area known as the *Kejawen*—is known for its sophisticated language registers (Vander Klok, this volume, §31.2). Javanese is also the first Austronesian language to develop a newspaper industry, dating from 1855. The Javanese press was patronized by the local gentry (*priyayi*) and remained vibrant into the twentieth century.

Like Cham, Javanese was first written down in a variety of related Indic scripts. These differed across time and place, and no top-down efforts at standardization are in evidence in precolonial times. An Arabic-derived script (*Pegon*), comparable to the Jawi script used for Malay and Cham, coexisted with the Indic scripts from at least early-colonial times and is still used in some Islamic institutions. The Javanese printing industry relied on a Central Javanese Indic script popularly known as *Hanacaraka*. In the common perception, the courtly cities of Yogyakarta and Solo (Surakarta) counted as the centres of Javanese culture, language, and literature, as remains the case today. The literary register from this part of Java has long received the greatest scholarly interest and continues to be seen as the norm. Javanese has been romanized in different ways, of which a Dutch-based orthography and an Indological tradition were both in use in colonial times.

Due to its sophisticated system of honorific registers and its association with a specific ethnicity—albeit Indonesia's largest—there have been no serious attempts to implement Javanese as Indonesia's official language, a capacity for which Malay proved much better equipped (see §17.2.2). Although Indonesia's Javanese majority left a clear imprint on the development of standard Indonesian, a greater influence went in the opposite direction. To bridge interdialectal differences or avoid linguistically encoded hierarchies, speakers of Javanese now increasingly adopt Indonesian when they cannot place each other. With standard Indonesian being institutionalized for administrative and educational purposes, Javanese has gradually been pushed into the domestic and cultural realm. High levels of literacy in the Javanese script remain exceptional outside Java's cultural elites. A number of Javanese magazines, all in romanized script, continue to suffice the needs of the Javanese literary scene.

Indonesia's attitudes towards regional languages changed considerably in the wake of the Reformation Period in 1998. Under the previous, centralized government, the use of Javanese—including in the media—was chiefly restricted to the cultural sphere, while Indonesian was used for non-folkloristic topics. With the new decentralization policy, Indonesian provinces could assert a greater influence on the creation of local school curricula (*muatan lokal*) and local-language media. In 2003, Surabaya was the first to host the local news in the city's specific dialect of Javanese. This dialect, which is quite distinct from the Central Javanese standard, was also widely used in political campaigning, commercial advertisements, graffiti, T-shirts, and even street signs (Hoogervorst 2009).

Other Javanese dialects—such as Osing, Cirebonan, and Banyumasan—soon followed suit. While most Javanese publications had historically been produced in the Central Javanese standard, various books have recently appeared in local varieties. Nevertheless, most schools stick to teaching materials in standard Javanese, chiefly because no dialect materials are available as yet. It remains to be seen how long this will last, especially because port cities such as Surabaya and Semarang have more inhabitants than Yogyakarta and Solo combined. That being said, the colonial-era institutionalization of the Kejawen as the cradle of Javanese culture continues to resonate strongly today. Most speakers find the Central Javanese dialects more refined than those of the coastal areas (*Pasisir*), making the former more suitable for literature and education.

At present, the Javanese script is no longer commonly used in handwriting, even though basic knowledge of *Hanacaraka* is included in school curricula. As a result, access to Javanese manuscripts is decreasing even in educated circles, with public signs often abounding in misspellings, especially outside Yogyakarta and Solo. The community has almost universally adopted the Latin alphabet, in a romanization resembling that of Indonesian. In analogy with Indic and Arabic-derived Javanese scripts, some writers distinguish between the so-called 'retroflex' <dh> and <th> and the dental equivalents <d> and <t>, as well as the high-mid front unrounded vowel <é> and the schwa <e>. These distinctions are especially maintained in dictionaries and literary texts. They are prescribed by the Yogyakarta Language Centre (*Balai Bahasa Yogyakarta*), a local branch of Indonesia's *Badan Pengembangan dan Pembinaan Bahasa* (Balai Bahasa Yogyakarta 2006). In online communication, however, they are not always deemed necessary. A slightly different standardization is in use among the Javanese community in Suriname, who—in accordance with other Surinamese languages—use <ty> for the voiceless palatal stop where Indonesian Javanese uses <c>.

Despite a strong lexical and grammatical influence from Indonesian, the Javanese language is not in serious danger. Its speakers do not suffer from hostility between different regional groups, at least not to the same extent as the Malagasy speech community (see §17.2.1). It has also not recently had to negotiate and implement a standardization, like Tetun and Cham, with all the associated difficulties. Ideas of 'correct' Javanese are widely accepted and go back to colonial times, and even within dialects, there are clear notions of good and bad usage. In this regard, the news broadcasts of JTV Surabaya often draw criticism for their perceived inauthenticity. Nevertheless, the Javanese language abounds in all its variety across the social media landscape. It also has a thriving grassroots publishing industry far outsizing that of colonial times.

### 17.3.3 Kapampangan

Kapampangan is a Central Luzon language spoken in Pampanga and the border areas of the surrounding provinces, such as southern Tarlac. At present, the Kapampangan form the sixth-largest ethnolinguistic group in the Philippines, after Tagalog, Cebuano, Ilokano, Hiligaynon, and Waray-Waray. The language was historically written in an Indic-derived syllabary, which is currently known under the names *Kulitan* or *Sulat Kapampangan*. In colonial times, Kapampangan was among the languages intensively studied by Spanish friar-linguists, who published grammatical and lexicographic works on the language. Kapampangan Bible translations, songs, poetry, theatre genres, and other literature flourished in colonial times (Manlapaz 1981; Icban-Castro 1981), using a Spanish-based romanization. From 1907, under the American occupation, various Kapampangan newspapers and other periodicals entered circulation (Manlapaz 1981: 6).

The role of Kapampangans in Philippine history has been one of considerable complexity. The Pampanga province has long facilitated insurgences against foreign invaders, including Spaniards, Japanese, and Americans. At the same time, Kapampangan people supplied elite mercenaries to the Spanish and even Dutch colonial armies. Doing so granted the community certain privileges under the Spanish occupation. Kapampangans were widely represented in political and intellectual circles in colonial times, as remains the case today. Like nationalists from other ethnolinguistic groups, most Kapampangan politicians learned Tagalog, fuelled by pan-Philippine loyalty and in preparation for a fruitful participation in the independent nation state.

As had been the case with regional languages elsewhere in the Philippines, the official status of Tagalog—in its standardized incarnation of Filipino—and English ousted Kapampangan from the realms of schools, government buildings, and economic centres, while it remained in use in the domestic sphere and in the Roman Catholic and Methodist Church (Pangilinan 2009). The imposition of Filipino in the Kapampangan heartlands did not encounter the same levels of resistance as it did in the Bisayan-speaking areas, which are considerably further removed from Manila.

Various efforts have been dedicated to the preservation of the Kapampangan language and culture. The chief institution in this regard is the *Akademyang Kapampangan* (AKKAP). Founded in 1937 for the promotion of literature in an indigenized romanization of the language, this centre has been revived in the late 1980s (Dizon 2000: 3). Due to the efforts of the poet José Gallardo (1918–1986), the Akademya has directed its attention to the protection of the Kapampangan language (Pangilinan 2006). In 2001, the Juan D. Nepomuceno Center for Kapampangan Studies was founded at the Holy Angel University in Angeles. This centre of research and education houses a library and a museum. It has produced a number of dictionaries and other books on the Kapampangan language.

In contrast with Javanese (see §17.3.2), the Kapampangan community lacks sufficient markets to develop a viable publishing industry. Although poetry and other cultural manifestations have generated popular interest, the production of newspapers—akin to those of colonial times—is hampered by financial restraints. Historically, other problems included a lack of accessible materials and lukewarm attitudes from within the community (Manlapaz 1981: 1). Finally, Kapampangan literacy suffers from a persistent dispute regarding the preferred orthography, not unlike the predicament of Eastern Cham (§17.3.1). The town of Bacolor (Bakulud) is the cradle of a respected literary tradition written in the Spanish orthography. A competing tradition developed in the port city of Guagua (Wawa), inspired by José Rizal's proposal to indigenize Philippine languages and do away with such colonial relicts as the Spanish graphs <c>, <ll>, <ñ>, and <qu>. None of these orthographies, nor any of the alternative proposals that followed them, is currently accepted by the entire community (Pangilinan 2006).

Due mostly to the aforementioned financial difficulties, an important part of Kapampangan language activism takes place online. In 1995, the so-called K-List was established to promote Kapampangan advocacy. These efforts gave rise to the *Batiáuan Foundation*, established in 1997, which aims to preserve, promote, and popularize the Kapampangan language. Also spearheading were the Yahoo Group *Academia ning Amanung Sisuan International* and the online forums *Electronic Kabalen* and *Pampanga Online*. As regards the regional media, the news bulletin *News Patrol Kapampangan* has previously issued broadcasts in Kapampangan, but—reminiscent of the Surabayan Javanese news bulletin (see §17.3.2)—their idiom was perceived to be inauthentic and ungrammatical (Pangilinan 2006). Although printed journals in Kapampangan are not at present economically viable, some of the English-language newspapers and journals printed in Pampanga sporadically feature pieces in Kapampangan.

### 17.3.4 Malay

While standardized Malay serves as the national language of Indonesia, Malaysia, Singapore, and Brunei, other Malay varieties constitute regional languages. As mentioned previously, Malay is remarkably heterogenous. It has long been acquired by speakers of neighbouring languages, but also Chinese, Arabs, and Europeans. These contact varieties are often designated as Bazaar Malay or Low Malay. Despite their low status in the eyes of language engineers and other elites, such varieties gained a certain degree of prominence in colonial times as vehicles of administration, missionary zeal, interethnic communication, and the industrialized press. Local-born Chinese communities—and, in Java, the urban middle classes more broadly—played a crucial role in the production and promotion of romanized Malay newspapers and popular books. They did so in their own distinct forms of Malay, which co-existed and competed with more prestigious varieties.

In Indonesia, the success of standardized Malay has not brought an end to pre-existing dialectal diversity. Rather, a situation of multiglossia came into being, in which speakers of regional Malay varieties can switch between their basilect, formal Indonesian, and colloquial Indonesian as used in the media (Gil, this volume, chapter 16). In the wake of Indonesia's decentralization policies of 1998 (§17.3.2), an unprecedented role has been afforded to regional languages such as Javanese and local Malay varieties. On a provincial scale, varieties such as Manado Malay and Papuan Malay are frequently employed alongside standard Indonesian in an attempt to authorize localness (Goebel et al. 2017). The use of regional Malay dialects is also extremely prevalent in popular culture, including in music, short stories in local newspapers (otherwise in standard Indonesian), and online media. While such efforts undoubtedly take place at the cost of even smaller minority languages, they have strengthened the position of Malay varieties with a strong regional usage. A number of Malayic languages (closely related to Malay), such as Banjar and Minangkabau, have likewise managed to grow despite the hegemony of standard Malay. The same can be said about Iban in Sarawak (Malaysia).

In Malaysia, Singapore, and Brunei, a distinction can be made between formal (standard) Malay, Bazaar Malay spoken by ethnic Chinese and Indians, and vernacular Malay spoken by ethnic Malays. The latter differs vastly across regions, as does its status. In Brunei, it can be found in wide range of domains (see §17.2.2). In Malaysia, like in Indonesia, the public use of local dialects is common in areas with a strong regional identity. The popular My Clean Kelantan Campaign (*Kempen Kelantanku Bersih*) of 2018, for example, made extensive use of the Kelantan dialect to stimulate local involvement. In Sabah, the local discourse particle *bah*—which is also found in other languages from the region and has a wide range of functions (Hoogervorst 2011)—features prominently in government communications and commercial advertisements. Meanwhile, Malaysia's 'default' form of colloquial Malay, as heard in popular media, is that of the southern Malay Peninsula, just as Indonesia's equivalent is that of Jakarta.

The Malayic varieties of Thailand can be divided into four major groups: Pattani Malay, Nonthaburi Malay, Satun Malay, and Urak Lawoi'. In addition, some speakers have knowledge of (Malaysian) standard Malay. Historically, the Thai government pursued a monolingual policy, marginalizing its Malay varieties to the point of severe endangerment (Tadmor 2004). While Thai remains firmly established as the national language, a new language policy in 2010 has granted some room for regional languages in local media and education. The Pattani Malay community, which has previously endured violent conflicts between separatists and the Thai government, has profited the most from these developments. Their specific dialect is now increasingly heard in news broadcasts, television programmes, and popular music. While its usage was historically restricted to religious education, in recent years a system of bilingual education has been introduced (Huebner 2019). Next to the traditional Jawi script, a Thai-based script is also in use for this variety.

Among the Malays of Sri Lanka (Slomanson, this volume, §18.9, Moro and Slomanson, this volume, §19.2), discussions have centred on whether the speech community should adopt a more standardized type of Malay—as prescribed by Malaysian language engineers—or legitimize and develop their own heritage variety, which has converged phonologically, grammatically, and lexically with Tamil and Sinhala (Rassool 2014). A romanization that takes into account the specific phonological character of Sri Lankan Malay exists, but has not been universally accepted. Incidentally, this system exhibits the orthographic conventions of <dh> and <th> for dental stops and <d> and <t> for their retroflex counterparts, which is the reverse of what we see in Javanese (see §17.3.2). Sri Lankan Malay is also sporadically written in the Sinhalese and Tamil script. In the case of Cocos Malay (Slomanson, this volume, chapter 18; Moro and Slomanson, this volume, §19.3), English-medium education and closer contacts with the broader Malay-speaking community may weaken the position of the low-prestige basilect over time, yet at present it is viable (Welsh 2015).

Other Malay-speaking communities have not developed meaningful language policies. In East Timor, a localized variety of Indonesian is still widely understood, but lacks official and communal recognition. The Kawthaung district of Myanmar is home to some small settlements of people with Malay ancestry, known locally as Pashu, who speak an as yet poorly described Malay variety alongside Burmese. Since Malay is regarded as a foreign language by the Myanmar government, neither this local dialect nor standard Malay have any place in the national language policy. Some Muslim Chams of Vietnam and Cambodia, supported by the Malaysian government and religious institutions, have adopted a broader pan-Malay identity. As a result, it is not uncommon to find speakers of Malaysian Malay in these communities. The Moluccan community in the Netherlands (see Moro and Slomanson, this volume, §19.6) have developed customized educational material for Melayu Sini (their distinct Malay variety) as part of the Dutch policy of mother tongue instruction (*onderwijs in eigen taal*) from 1985 to 2004 (Pattiiha 2000). They use neither the colonial nor the most recent Indonesian spelling, but an intermediate form common from 1947 to 1972.

## 17.4 Concluding remarks

The histories, politics, and policies of MPSEA languages reflect a number of shared developments. Several national languages can be traced back to the lingua franca of the colonial capital, which was itself typically a pre-colonial centre of trade, political power, and cultural prestige. With the exception of Tetun, many of the prominent languages possessed Indic-derived and/or Arabic-derived writing traditions. Western colonialism often consolidated pre-existing tensions between the centre and the periphery, which persist until the present day. This was effectuated through control over linguistic knowledge production, efforts at standardization, and the introduction of printed media. The Japanese occupation from 1941 to 1945 paved the way for Malay, Tagalog, and other national languages to establish themselves in an unprecedented range of domains.

While most national languages in the region are either associated with the former colonizers or the nation's largest ethnic group, we see some exceptions, such as Malay in Indonesia and Tagalog in the Philippines. In general, languages that lack honorific registers and other hierarchical features were preferred as national languages. This worked to the favour of Malay at the expense of Javanese, and of Tetun at the expense of other indigenous languages of East Timor. Name changes were common as additional means to dissociate national languages from specific ethnicities, yielding Indonesian, Malaysian, and Filipino. Promises by language engineers to substantially enrich such national languages by incorporating influences from regional languages have generally not come to fruition, at least not in the official realm.

In colonial times, indigenous languages were subordinated to Dutch, English, French, Portuguese, or Spanish. The selection, typically in late-colonial times, of one of the regional languages as the national language gave rise to new processes of exclusion. Despite efforts to promote national languages as transethnic in character, some are perceived by ethnolinguistic minorities to behave just like colonial languages. A number of speech communities have managed to achieve relative stability, Javanese being a good example, whereas many others face endangerment. Their vitality depends on a variety of factors. The existence of strong and entertaining local-language media has proven to be conducive, notwithstanding complaints about their artificiality. Exclusivist gate-keepers presiding over 'correct' usage tend to be detrimental to the vitality of regional languages. In some cases, such as Cham, connections between the homeland and the diaspora have led to new infrastructures of language maintenance.

The last decades saw a number of positive strides for some of the larger regional languages. Their classroom usage—commonly penalized in colonial and early independence times—now increasingly receives government support, with a growing number of education ministries experimenting with bilingual education. This has strengthened multilingual practices in the Philippines, East Timor, Thailand, and elsewhere, creating a situation in which regional languages, national languages, and the languages of erstwhile colonial powers coexist and complement each other. With the notable exception of Dutch, European languages continue to ensure upward mobility and grant their speakers access to broader networks. Meanwhile, small yet dedicated groups of enthusiasts—often operating online and in collaboration with diasporas worldwide—continue to struggle for the protection of regional languages and the revival of indigenous scripts. Their success is dependent on the support of national governments, international organizations, and especially the respective speech communities.

## Acknowledgements

I am indebted to Alexander Adelaar, Marc Brunelle, John Hajek, Mike Pangilinan, Lawrence Reid, Antoinette Schapper, David Zorc, and Penelope Howe for their valuable and gratefully received comments on different parts of this chapter.

CHAPTER 18

# Malayo-Polynesian contact languages in Southeast Asia and the creole controversy

PETER SLOMANSON

## 18.1 Introduction

This chapter will provide a concise summary of the controversy surrounding how and when to categorize a number of Malayo-Polynesian languages as contact varieties, as well as brief descriptions of selected varieties. In some cases, in which most vocabulary is drawn from colonial languages, the required categorization will be obvious. In others, the necessary language categories are less clear. The issue is complicated by the extent of historical language contact and the range of language types that have resulted from pre-colonial and colonial language contact scenarios in a range of local and national settings. In this chapter, the term 'creole' will refer to language varieties with a pidgin predecessor, although this definition is not uncontroversial in the language contact literature. The creole vs. mixed language status of the most divergent Malayo-Polynesian contact languages, in which the signs of language contact due to bilingualism are immediately apparent, is difficult to determine due to different interpretations of the terms. The more general umbrella term 'contact language' is not a precise one either, and its meaning is rendered still less precise by the fact that all languages have experienced some degree of contact with other languages, due to periods of varying degrees of bilingualism. The varieties to be discussed here are those that unambiguously resulted from contact, generally because the history of contact and convergence are recent and therefore clearly identifiable as such, and the grammatical source languages are still spoken, often by native speakers of the contact variety. If we could look back far enough, we would likely find that certain so-called historical languages (those not ordinarily classified as contact languages), were also contact languages. In this chapter, I will refer to informal spoken varieties, whatever their status, as colloquial Malay, which will be equivalent to the common term 'low' (Dutch *laag*) in traditional non-technical western accounts. Contact varieties will be referred to as such, regardless of whether or not the non-Malay influence was predominantly local (Austronesian or Papuan) or non-Austronesian (i.e. Hokkien or Tamil). The colloquial vs. formal or literary linguistic contrast in the Malay world is almost two millennia old, strongly associated with Indianized elite court culture prior to Islamization, as well as its successor cultures following Islamization. The chapter concerns the colloquial varieties and the role of language contact in their development.

## 18.2 Which contact language types?

### 18.2.1 Pidgins, pidgin-derived varieties, and creoles

A history of language contact, in the sense of collective second language acquisition by a population of adults, may explain grammatical complexity contrasts between related language varieties, when there is less complexity (by whatever definition) in the putative contact variety or varieties. According to one approach, this scenario necessarily indicates a history of contact and this type of explanation is necessarily valid. This approach surfaces implicitly in Adelaar and Prentice (1996), who describe Malay contact varieties in general as Pidgin-Malay Derived (PMD). Adelaar (2005b) includes the criterion of voice morphology in this characterization. While western Indonesian, Formosan, and Philippine languages typically feature a symmetrical voice system, the putative contact varieties do not. They do not distinguish voice except in an imitative form, where the use of *di-* may have recently been introduced, and are not reflective of the contact variety's inherited voice morphology, which uses a free-standing auxiliary rather than an affix. There is a striking lack of consensus on the view that the contact varieties are necessarily creoles, in part because the criterion of relative lack of bound morphology describes the grammatical systems of colloquial Malay varieties generally, and also because some derivational and functional morphology

Peter Slomanson, *Malayo-Polynesian contact languages in Southeast Asia and the creole controversy.* In: *The Oxford Guide to the Malayo-Polynesian Languages of Southeast Asia.* Edited by: Alexander Adelaar and Antoinette Schapper, Oxford University Press. © Peter Slomanson (2024). DOI: 10.1093/oso/9780198807353.003.0018

is typically retained. This holds even for the diasporic varieties, spoken outside the boundaries of states in which a variety of Malay has official status. Adelaar himself (2005b: 216) refers, for example, to several verbal affixes in Cocos Malay. These are present in other contact varieties as well, including *bə(r)-* as an intransitive verb marker, *baku-* as a marker of reciprocality or repetitive and diffuse action, *tə(r)-* to form intransitive verbs denoting lack of control, *kə-. . .-an* to form intransitive verbs denoting lack of control and adversativity, *di-* to mark agentless passives, and *-kan* to indicate the contextual or implied presence of a recipient.

One way of distinguishing between the positions taken on the matter of identifying vernacular and contact language types, including a hypothetical creole type, would be to contrast those characterizations focusing on linguistic features (exemplified by Adelaar and Prentice), with those focusing on historical breaks in intergenerational transmission (henceforth BIT), although both are technically criteria for establishing prior pidginization. The first approach, as well as the term PMD itself, are discussed and opposed in Paauw (2008: 15), without much elaboration, but citing an ostensible lack of diachronic evidence for the existence of a range of PMD varieties with Malayo-Polynesian substrata. So for Paauw, heavily Chinese and Tamil-influenced varieties, for example, would be unproblematic if the respective roles of their non-Malayo-Polynesian substrate languages were well documented. Gil (2009c) adopts a similar position with respect to Riau Indonesian, a vernacular contact variety with no external (sociohistorical) evidence of BIT, and therefore lacking justification for categorization as a creole or for having been one. A compromising counterargument would be that, as Gil acknowledges, the speakers of Riau Indonesian come from a range of ethnolinguistic backgrounds, the language they are speaking is a variety of informal Indonesian, and morphosyntactically reduced adult L2 varieties can converge, leading to grammatical changes in the usage of L1 speakers. The fact that Riau Indonesian does not now have a reduced lexical inventory, and the lack of an identifiable BIT in the present period, does not actually rule out a pidgin past. Such a history could make it an expanded pidgin, or a creole, or else simply another category of contact variety to which not all contact linguists would apply either of the preceding labels. Gil treats the reduced functional marking and other pidgin-like features of Riau Indonesian as areal. This should not preclude the possibility that areal influences in addition to the multilingual ecology and historical acquisition context contributed to the current language's grammatical profile, although Gil (2009c) places the relevant contact scenario in a much earlier period.

McWhorter (2008a) is the strongest version of the claim that there is *necessarily* (even in the absence of diachronic evidence) a causal association of collective adult second language acquisition with (especially) morphosyntactic simplification, in which all spoken varieties of Malay are nativized pidgins, including those not conventionally regarded as contact varieties. McWhorter's claim was challenged in Gil (2020a). For McWhorter, vehicular Malay varieties are not just contact languages, but historical creoles in a narrow sense. From a creolist perspective, grammatical processes leading to simplification may have played out iteratively, over the history of the Malay language, rather than at a single stage, as in the Bickertonian view, in which creolization is punctual (Bickerton 1981). This would then resemble the scenario familiar from certain Indo-European language groups, such as the continental Scandinavian languages, whose inflectional morphology simplified through periods of extensive bilingualism in Low German, but without undergoing pidginization or creolization.

The uncontroversial definition of the term 'creole' until the 1970s (Hall 1969) was a grammatically radical contact language that arises when an unexpanded pidgin acquires its first cohort of native speakers. It has been disputed, however, that creolization *requires* a pidgin stage and it has been frequently and vigorously disputed that creoles constitute a linguistically identifiable class of languages. The claim that they do constitute a distinctive class of languages is a large part of what motivated the growth of creolistics as a subfield of linguistics, however this was based on the observation that the Atlantic creoles, all of which have had European lexical sources, have morphosyntactic and phonological properties in common across lexical source languages.

Particularly disputed, most notably by Mufwene (2002) and de Graff (2003) is the older claim that creoles, as an ostensible distinctive class of languages, are identifiable, not just by the types of sociolinguistic configuration or ecology in which they are created, but in their structural simplicity, in comparison with other ('historical') languages that evolved without the BIT of a lexifier. In that debate, McWhorter and de Graff represent the strongest opposing claims, for and against distinctive simplicity, respectively. Of the two authors, only McWhorter has raised the issue directly with respect to western Malayo-Polynesian languages, including Malay.

The definition of contact languages as language varieties that were structurally simplified as a result of collective adult second language acquisition is weakened when we observe indisputably radical contact languages that have developed various types of functional and morphosyntactic complexity that are not present in their lexical source languages. The absence of a historical BIT is one explanation for this objection. However that absence is frequently impossible to verify with any certainty, so it cannot rise above the status of a useful proposal. Several languages of this complexified type have been loosely categorized as 'mixed' (having a traditional lexicon, but largely borrowed or replicated grammar). On the matter of which specific (particularly Malay-based) languages can genuinely be referred to as creoles, the lack of agreement extends beyond the debate between McWhorter and Gil. Wolff (1997) reserves that status for varieties whose speakers descend from L1 speakers of non-Austronesian languages such as Hokkien and Hakka, specifically with reference to varieties of Malay and Javanese, involving frequent code-switching between the two, as spoken by ethnic Chinese (Peranakan) people on Java.

The most extensive comparative work specifically focusing on the eastern contact varieties of Malay is Paauw (2008). He adopts the more conservative position that the loss or absence of inflection may or may not indicate a history of intermittent contact with speakers of other languages, but it is no indication of a history of pidginization and creolization when viewed from the position that a pidgin stage is required in order to yield a variety that could be characterized as a creole. All of the ostensible contact varieties, other than those mostly spoken by people of non-Austronesian-speaking ancestry, are, and have been, based on informal spoken Malay. The contact varieties are not so clearly differentiated from informal spoken Malay varieties (including various urban varieties in Indonesian and Malaysia) that those varieties can be identified as creoles based on linguistic features alone. On the Gil–McWhorter debate, Paauw (2008) writes that

> McWhorter (2008a) has attempted to demonstrate that *all* Low Malay varieties are creolized, and gives a number of arguments, with reference to Riau Indonesian, a colloquial Indonesian variety spoken in Sumatra by speakers of an "inherited" variety of Malay, as described by Gil (1994, 2000, 2001). McWhorter's points have been addressed by Gil (2008), based on whose argumentation it seems unlikely that Low Malay is itself the result of creolization, as there is no evidence for large-scale language contact in the Malay homeland unless it happened over 2,000 years ago, in the original migrations of Malay speakers from the Malay homeland in Borneo.

McWhorter's characterization is also problematic in the following sense. Even if we cannot identify evidence for large-scale pidginization, Malay was certainly used as an interethnic communication vehicle for hundreds of years preceding European colonization. That this function of Malay over time led to profound changes in its spoken varieties is in keeping with observed tendencies in other parts of the world. This scenario does not require pidginization and creolization, though it does require adult second language acquisition and collective bilingualism. Gil (2020a) argued that Minangkabau, a historical non-contact Malayic variety, and Siak Malay, a historical (i.e. 'non-contact') Malay variety, are just as morphologically simple as Riau Indonesian. His claim is not that the processes McWhorter proposed as contributing factors were irrelevant to the simplicity of the Malay contact varieties, but that ultimately creolization in any sense of the term was not required. Instead, minimal inflectional morphology, minimal categorial (part of speech) distinctions, and simpler associational semantics are all areal features in overlapping linguistic areas. The area with minimal inflectional morphology, for example, is geographically extensive. Each linguistic area is characterized by different areal properties, the aforementioned three of which happen to be found in varieties such as Riau Indonesian, which is located at the areal intersection between typological isoglosses. The effect of this is to assert that regarding a colloquial Malay variety as necessarily a former creole because it has *little* inflectional morphology is unmotivated, and not based on available diachronic evidence.

According to Adelaar (2018: 579)

> Gil's argument that grammatical simplification can also be triggered from within a language is essentially correct. Discussants in the debate about the sociolinguistic origins of Malay varieties tend to use arguments based only on general linguistic typology and sociolinguistics. However, historical linguistic evidence clearly shows that Malayic grammars underwent considerable simplification due to two sound changes, namely the merger of schwa and */a/ in final syllables to ɑ and the neutralization of vowels to schwa in antepenultimate syllables (Adelaar 1992)[1]. These changes together brought about the merger and loss of many affixes in the history of Malayic varieties. They also caused the erosion of the original Austronesian verbal morphosyntax, reducing its morphological four-voice system to one only opposing agent and patient voice.

## 18.2.2 Mixed languages

The term mixed [language] has been used by contact linguists to refer to a type of contact language that cannot be characterized as a creole, pidgin, or former pidgin. It is a type of language resulting from the blending of two languages spoken by bilinguals which may become nativized as a community language, after which the initial communal bilingualism may be lost in subsequent

[1] Appearing as Adelaar (1992a) in the references for the present volume.

generations of speakers. The two Dutch lexicon languages and one Spanish lexicon language described in this chapter (Pecok, Javindo, and Chabacano, respectively), as well as Sri Lankan Malay, and possibly Nonthaburi Malay in Thailand are candidates for this classification. The extent to which languages could be categorized as mixed is less clear for Malayo-Polynesian language varieties not spoken outside of a Malayo-Polynesian-speaking territory, or for Malayo-Polynesian language varieties not spoken in a Malayo-Polynesian-speaking territory by people of other linguistic ancestries.

The fact that persistent language contact as such has been a feature of large numbers of communities throughout the Malayo-Polynesian-speaking world throughout its history has yielded many contact varieties whose grammatical properties are unambiguously a product of collective second language acquisition and bilingualism. The intergroup communicative functions of Malay contributed to the creation of such contact vernaculars, and the resulting extent of variation across varieties and within speech communities remains underdocumented. The relative lack of texts reflecting earlier developmental stages is partly a result of the deeply ingrained diglossia which has long been a prominent feature of Malay linguistic culture. This means that the spoken language is largely absent from texts which might otherwise have served as evidence of changes in the grammar of the language. This dynamic was further strengthened in the modern period by the standardizing linguistic policies of the independent states of Indonesia, Malaysia, Singapore, and Brunei.

In his treatment of mixed languages, Bakker (2000) distinguishes between intertwined languages and converted languages. Intertwined languages, as with mixed languages generally, combine lexical material from one donor language, and morphosyntactic properties of another. The functional markers, including phonologically bound morphology, continue to be expressed using the actual forms inherited from the grammatical source language. Intertwined languages may, in practice, be indistinguishable from intrasentential code-switching, but the code-switching is conventionalized and becomes a part of the new mixed language's grammar. This aligns well with the characterization in Wolff (1997) of the ingroup language of the Peranakan Chinese community in Java. Intertwined languages appear to be relatively rare among the languages of the world.

Converted languages, by contrast, use morphological material from one language to express the morphosyntax and functional contrasts of the other language. This means that in practice, all of the lexical items and functional markers, with the exception of later open-class borrowings, are taken from the lexical source language. The contact language's grammar converges on the morphosyntax of the grammatical donor language, though without ever completely replicating the donor language's morphosyntactic system.

One of the clearest cases of a converted language, increasingly well described since the early years of the current millennium, and for the first time by a linguist in Adelaar (1991), is Sri Lankan Malay. This is the only living converted Malayo-Polynesian language.[2]

Among the varieties that have been characterized as pidgin-derived, some are in fact still pidgins, in the sense that their influence from non-Malayic (and non-Austronesian) languages is apparent, and in the sense that the language is primarily spoken as an auxiliary language by native speakers of other languages (for example, Singapore Indian Malay). Several of the grammatical properties characterizing pidgins and potentially pidgin-derived contact varieties are discussed in Adelaar and Prentice (1996); Adelaar (2005b); and Paauw (2008). The feature categories include plural pronouns based on *orang* ('person'). The selection of (i.e. first, second, and/or third) person forms varies from variety to variety. A second common feature is the use of possessor–possessed constructions conjoined by a linker derived from the word *punya*, where formal varieties have the construction possessed–possessor, with no linker. In Sri Lankan Malay, for example, 'my friend's house' is as in (1), whereas in formal varieties, this is expressed as in (2). That is, with the possessor on the right.

Sri Lankan Malay

| (1) | *go pe* | *tumman* | *pe* | *ruma* |
|---|---|---|---|---|
| | 1SG POSS | friend | POSS | house |

'my friend's house'

Standard Malay/Indonesian

| (2) | *rumah* | *teman* | *saya/aku* |
|---|---|---|---|
| | house | friend | 1SG |

'my friend's house'

Additional features are the pre-verbal expression of progressive aspect with the existential marker *ada*, and the use of periphrastic causatives with *kasi* ('give') and *bikin* ('make'). (In Sri Lankan Malay, the final vowel in *ada* is weakened or deleted. The form has come to mark present tense, with post-verbal auxiliaries used to express progressive aspect). The periphrastic causatives alternate in some varieties with the use of morphological causatives, involving the suffix *-kan* in Cocos and Baba Malay, and *-king* in Sri Lankan Malay. Iamdanush and Pittayaporn (2014) discuss three periphrastic constructions in Pattani Malay, a variety

[2] There are converted Oceanic languages spoken in Papuan New Guinea, such as Takia, whose convergence on the grammar of Waskia is described in Ross (2001).

spoken by approximately one million speakers in southern Thailand. In those constructions, the function and etymology is analogous with constructions in other contact Malay varieties, however the three are semantically differentiated from each other, in that their use is constrained by features such as animacy and agentivity. These include the *waʔ* ('do') construction, in which *waʔ* also has the unreduced form *buwaʔ*, cognate with *buat* ('make'). In (3) and (4), the constraints on the use of this form are that the causer must be animate, and the causation must be non-agentive or involuntary. The authors conclude that the functional semantics of the periphrastic causatives in Pattani Malay are closer to their Thai counterparts than to periphrastic causatives in other Malay varieties.

(3) *adɔ s-ɔɣɛ waʔ pasu ɟatoh*
have INDEF-man CAUS vase fall
'Someone caused the vase to fall.' (Doomkum 1984: 137)

(4) *sah waʔ kitɔ ɣusiŋ*
Sah CAUS 1SG sad
'Sah made me sad.' (Doomkum 1984: 137)

Note that this type of construction can be thought of as consisting of two clauses. In (3), the vase is found in the subject position of a complement clause which is controlled from the higher clause. If the word order were such that the causative verb were inseparable, yielding the order 'CAUS fall vase', then there would be just one subject, and it would be more plausible to treat the causativizer as a functional modifier of the verb *ɟatoh*.

The following sections consist of brief descriptions of selected individual contact languages.

## 18.3 Singapore Bazaar Malay

Singapore Bazaar Malay, a highly variable expanded pidgin, is indisputably a contact language, and the non-Austronesian languages that have historically influenced its grammar are still actively spoken by many of the most active users of the pidgin. The subvarieties described are strongly associated with older ethnic Chinese, which is due to the demography of the country, although the pidgin is used to communicate with ethnic Malays, Tamils, and others. It is a local subvariety of the Bazaar Malay pidgin historically used generally, and previously more extensively, as an intergroup language in the Straits, including the Malaysian peninsula, as well as in other parts of the archipelago. It is a non-nativized pidgin, and in that sense distinguished from nativized but pidgin-derived varieties, such as Baba Malay.

Bao and Aye (2010) highlight the significance of Chinese substrate-derived topic prominence, in which the sentential topic appears at the left periphery of the sentence, variably as a left dislocation structure co-indexed with a pronominal element within the clause, and variably as a simple topicalization co-indexed with a gap. Following other authors, the earliest of whom is Chao (1968), this is referred to as English-style topic structure, since the analogous construction is sayable in English, as contrasted with Chinese-style topic structure, in which the topic does not involve a lexical copy of a (null or overt) constituent in the main body of the sentence. The following (5) and (6) are examples of the aforementioned types of English-style topic structure.

Singapore Bazaar Malay Left Dislocation
(5) [*Anjing*]$_{TOP}$ [*dia gigit sama dia punya tangan*]$_S$
dog 3SG bite with 3SG POSS hand
'The dog, it bit his hand.' (Bao and Aye 2010: 156)

Singapore Bazaar Malay Topicalization
(6) [*Apa sayur dia cakap*]$_{TOP}$ [*saya tahu e*]$_S$
what vegetable 3SG speak 1SG know
'What vegetables he mentions, I know.'
(Bao and Aye 2010: 156)

The variety has been documented *inter alia* in the sketch description in Aye (2013). That description and others make reference to the SVO basic order of the language. We should however also note the existence of a related subvariety spoken by people of Indian descent, Singapore Indian Malay, in which the dominant major constituent order is SOV, as it is in Sri Lankan Malay, with both languages spoken by many Tamil–Malay bilinguals. Singapore Indian Malay is extensively described in Muthiah (2007). According to Muthiah, the SOV basic order has been lost in younger speakers, although it is unclear to what extent this extends variably to other surface orders that can be regarded as implicationally related to that basic order. As an expanded pidgin, there are not many morphological contrasts with other colloquial Malay varieties. Muthiah enumerates a number of contrasts with the more familiar Chinese varieties of Singapore Bazaar Malay, all of which follow from the historical and partly synchronic SOV status of the Indian variety. These include the fact that a lexical verb can occur before its causativizer, the fact that compounds can be head-final, that noun phrases are strictly head-final with no post-nominal modifiers, that the VP is head final and clauses are left-branching. Imperatives also display OV ordering. Other features contrast with Indian-influenced varieties spoken elsewhere. For example, whereas in the absence of a morphological passive in Sri Lankan Malay, the periphrastic passive with *kena* has been generalized and lost its adversative meaning, the Indian variety of Singapore Bazaar Malay has no passivization strategy. The position of nominal quantifiers such as *suma* ('all') is variable, occurring both pre- and post-nominally within noun phrases. Unlike Sri Lankan Malay, Singapore Bazaar Malay does not have postpositions, however both languages have prenominal relative clauses. According to Muthiah, the bracketed relative clause in the SVO example in (7) has *buku* as its head, and the possession marker *pinga* (from *punya*) as a modifier of the head. In a Sri Lankan Malay translation of this sentence, the verbs would be tense-marked, but there would be no overt marker of relativization.

Singapore Indian Malay
(7) *Dia baca* [[ *saya bili pinga* ] *buku* ].
3SG read 1SG buy POSS book
'He is reading the book that I bought.'
(Muthiah 2007: 109)

## 18.4 Eastern Malay contact varieties

The eastern Malay contact varieties have a range of lexical and structural properties in common, which justifies characterizing them as forming a distinctive subgroup. There is a fair amount of literature on individual varieties, including van Minde (1997) on Ambonese Malay, Stoel (2005) on Manado Malay, and Kluge (2014) on Papuan Malay. There has been relatively little literature comparing them systematically, a gap that will hopefully be closed in the future. Paauw (2008) is a descriptive PhD dissertation in which the author compares seven Malay contact varieties spoken in eastern Indonesia, contact varieties previously identified as such in Adelaar and Prentice (1996). Paauw distinguishes those varieties from Baba Malay, Singapore Bazaar Malay, Java Malay, and other arguably creolized varieties associated primarily with ethnic Chinese communities, particularly on the Malay peninsula and throughout the island of Java. The seven varieties include Manado Malay on Sulawesi, Larantuka Malay on Flores, Kupang Malay on Timor, Ambon Malay, Banda Malay in the Banda islands, North Moluccan Malay, and Papuan Malay. The labels foster the illusion that those varieties are necessarily highly differentiated, and that they are internally unitary. Papuan Malay, for example, is spoken differently on different coasts and different nearby islands, with the variety associated with the north Papuan coast closest to North Moluccan Malay. Although all of these are contact languages with large numbers of L1 and L2 speakers in historically multilingual areas, calling them creoles in the canonical sense of the term presupposes a sociohistorical context in which a more functionally elaborated grammatical system was lost as the result of acquisition by adults who created a pidgin. This historical account, as referred to previously, remains controversial. Varieties of Malay with relatively little bound morphology have been spoken throughout the archipelago for centuries. Therefore the acquisition by adults of an already morphologically reduced variety in the context of trade and migration cannot be characterized as pidginization, but simply as acquisition, subject to adstratal influence from other languages. While these varieties are, in that sense, not pidgins or creoles, they are also not mixed languages. They are contact languages by virtue of the historical effects of bilingualism in local non-Malayic languages.[3]

One grammatical system, in which we find cross-dialectal parallels in syntax and significant variation in form, is negation (see Table 18.1). One of the features that sets the eastern contact Malay varieties (with the exception of Manado Malay) apart from most other contact varieties is the presence of *tarada* or the reduced form *tara* (from *tidak ada*). In

[3] According to Adelaar and Prentice (1996), pidginization did not take place in eastern Indonesia, but much earlier in the Strait of Malacca, with a substantial Chinese role, in the thirteenth century.

**Table 18.1** Negators in selected eastern Malay contact varieties (adapted from Paauw 2008)

| | Primary neg | Alternate negs | Contrastive neg | Prohibitive neg | Neg aspect |
|---|---|---|---|---|---|
| Manado Malay | *nyanda* | *nim-* | *bukang* | *jang(ang)* | *bolong* |
| North Moluccan Malay | *tarada* | | *bukang* | *jang* | *bolong* |
| Ambonese Malay | *seng* | *tar, tra, sondor* | *bukang* | *jang(ang)* | *balong* |
| Kupang Malay | *son(de)* | *tar-* | *bukan* | *jang* | *balong* |
| Larantuka Malay | *te* | *ne, tərada* | *bukang* | *janga* | *bəlong* |
| Papuan Malay | *t(a)ra(da)* | *tida* | *buka(n)* | *jangang* | *balom* |

spite of their status as closed class functional items, some of the negators are borrowed from colonial languages. In Ambonese Malay, for example, the primary negator *seng* is from Portuguese *sem* 'without' and the alternate negator *sondor* is from Dutch *zonder* 'without'. These items are used in non-finite contexts in the source languages, in participial and infinitival clauses (cf. English 'without eating rice'). Malay does not feature clauses in which a verb can be analysed as non-finite, consequently these forms have been reanalysed as straightforward negators of verbal and adjectival predicates, functionally analogous with *tidak* in formal Malay/Indonesian. *Bukan(g)*, as in formal Malay/Indonesian, negates all constituents contrastively ('*not* x, but y'), as well as nominal predicates. *Jang* and its variants is the prohibitive negative or negative imperative marker, and *bolong* (formal Malay/Indonesian *belum*) can be translated as 'not yet'.

Kluge (2014: 178) provides a reduplicated example of the prohibitive negator or negative imperative marker in Papuan Malay (8), explaining that *jangang* in this context denotes intensity. We should additionally note however that the semantics of this sentence clearly demonstrate a negative irrealis/subjunctive meaning associated with the same etymon in other Malay varieties.[4] It was glossed as a reduplicated negative imperative marker, however the predicate *hujang* ('rain') has no overt or implied agent. This favours a negative irrealis/subjunctive interpretation over a negative imperative one.

Papuan Malay

(8) *...tapi jangang~jangang hujang di tenga*
but NEG.IMP~REDUP rain at middle
*jalang*
street
'[I want to go to (my) gardens,] but **let's hope** it **won't** rain in the middle of the way.'

A similar example from Ambonese Malay is found in van Minde (1997: 117). For the sentence in (9), *jang* was glossed in that monograph as 'don't' (i.e. negative imperative), however the house is not a plausible addressee, and *jang* would more adequately be translated as 'if only were not...'. The idiomatic English translation ought to have been 'if only this were not a house of kings', in which the verb is not past but irrealis (subjunctive).

Ambonese Malay

(9) *Ini jang kong raja~raja pung ruma!*
this don't EXCLAM king~REDUP POSS house
'If only this is not a house of kings!'

[4] This will be discussed further in the section on Sri Lankan Malay, a variety in which this form is not, however, reduplicated.

## 18.5 Pecok and Javindo

There are two intertwined languages associated with the island of Java in Indonesia, Pecok (van Rheeden 1995) and Javindo (de Gruiter 1994), both of which are now moribund or extinct, but which were described within historical memory. Moseley (2007) claims that Pecok still has first- and second-language speakers. Note that there was also a (lexically) Portuguese-based contact variety spoken on Java, Tugu, that was an important language of intergroup communication between local Indonesians and the Dutch in the early colonial period. This was heavily influenced by Malay, but also by other Asian Portuguese contact varieties. Detailed description and representative texts are found in Maurer (2011). Portuguese-based contact varieties have long been spoken in regions where they are in contact with Malay. Another example is Papia Kristang, a severely endangered language spoken in Singapore and Malaysia (Baxter 2013).

In Pecok, most closed class functional morphology comes either from Dutch or Malay, however, its pronouns are drawn from Dutch exclusively. The syntax of the language is Malay-derived and in various respects, it does not align with the syntax of Dutch. Particularly striking is the complete absence of the Dutch verb-second constraint requiring the main verb or auxiliary to appear in second position, so that there is no subject/main verb or auxiliary inversion in main clauses as there is obligatorily in Dutch, as in (10) and (11).

Pecok

(10) *Op een dah ik ontmoet Si Bentiet bij de*
on a day 1SG meet Si Bentiet at the
*Pasar Gambir.*
market Gambir
'One day I met Si Bentiet at the Gambir market.'
(van Rheeden 1995: 108)[5]

Dutch

(11) *Op een dag ontmoette ik Si Bentiet bij de*
on a day meet.PST 1SG Si Bentiet at the
*Gambir-markt.*
Gambir market
'One day I met Si Bentiet at the Gambir market.'

Another clear case in which Pecok (12) contrasts syntactically with Dutch (13) but parallels Malay (14), is seen in the fact that interrogative constituents frequently remain *in situ*

[5] I have modified the examples from van Rheeden (1995) in certain cases for format and lexical precision. For example, *jangkerik* had been translated as 'grasshopper', rather than as 'cricket'.

and are not obligatorily fronted in conventional (non-echo) questions.

Pecok
(12) *Jij gaan naar waar?*
2SG go to where
'Where are you going?'

Dutch
(13) *Waar ga je naar toe?*
where go 2SG towards
'Where are you going?'

Malay
(14) *Lu pergi ke mana?*
2SG go to where
'Where are you going?'

Negation mostly follows lexical verbs in Pecok, as it does in Dutch main clauses (van Rheeden 1995: 117), so the predominant linear order does not replicate that of Malay.

Pecok
(15) *Djangkriek hij laat niet los.*
cricket 3SG let NEG loose
'The cricket did not release it.'

Malay
(16) *Jangkerik tidak lepaskan.*
cricket NEG release
'The cricket did not release it.'

Dutch
(17) *De krekel liet niet los.*
DET cricket let NEG loose
'The cricket did not release it.'

Negated imperatives in Pecok (18) correspond with the linear order found in Malay (19), whereas the Dutch order is variable. The Pecok example in (18) uses the infinitival form of the verb, which is an optional strategy for Dutch imperatives. The Pecok order appears to follow from the ability of Dutch to extrapose objects in such imperatives. That extraposition gives us an infinitival verb phrase with verb–object order, although object–verb order is actually the less marked option in Dutch infinitival imperatives. At the same time, object–verb order does not occur in other sentence types in Pecok either, so the verb–object order in (18) is not surprising.

Pecok
(18) *Niet meer ferbeteren Nederlandse taal.*
NEG longer correct Dutch language
'Do not correct my Dutch anymore.'
(van Rheeden 1995: 118)

Malay
(19) *Jangan betulkan bahasa Belanda aku lagi.*
NEG.IMP correct language Dutch 1SG more
'Do not correct my Dutch anymore.'

Dutch
(20) *Niet meer verbeteren mijn Nederlands.*
NEG longer correct 1SG.POSS Dutch
'Do not correct my Dutch.'

Sentences containing negated nominal predicates are comparable in their respective linear orders in the three languages, however the construction in Pecok, as in Malay, lacks a copula. At the same time, whereas the Malay construction requires a constituent negator (22), and the usual Dutch construction requires a negative quantifier (23), the Pecok construction makes use of the general negation element *niet* from Dutch (21), and no determiner.

Pecok
(21) *Ik niet chon.*
1SG NEG dog
'I am not a dog.'

Malay
(22) *Aku bukan anjing.*
1SG NEG dog
'I am not a dog.'

Dutch
(23) *Ik ben geen hond.*
1SG am NEG.QUANT dog
'I am not a dog.' (lit. I am no dog.)

The term Javindo originates with de Gruiter (1994), who spoke the language while growing up in the Javanese city of Semarang. De Gruiter treats the grammar of Javindo as coterminous with the grammar of Javanese. This may be true to a great extent, if Javindo were indeed a language organized the way Anglo-Romani is, essentially a variety of English with Romani lexical items. The claim falls through, however, when we see that negation in Javindo (24) differs in its distribution from negation in Javanese (25).

Javindo
(24) *Ik koop niet beras.*
1SG buy NEG rice
'I do not buy rice.'

Javanese
(25) *Aku ora tuku beras.*
1SG NEG buy rice
'I do not buy rice.'

Dutch

(26) *Ik* *koop* *geen* *rijst.*
1SG buy NEG.QUANT rice
'I do not buy rice.'

Dutch

(27) *Rijst* *koop* *ik* *niet.*
rice buy 1SG NEG
'Rice I do not buy.'

Negation never precedes a finite verb in declarative main clauses in Dutch as it does in Javanese. This is reflected in the Javindo example, which follows the Dutch order, as is the case with Pecok. As is characteristic of mixed languages generally, the fact that a property of the grammar of Dutch was in some sense a model for its counterpart in the grammar of Javindo does not necessarily yield a straightforward morphosyntactic parallel between the languages. While the negation element *niet* 'not' appears post-verbally in Dutch (as opposed to Javanese and Pecok), that distribution is not found in subordinate clauses, whereas there is no such constraint differentiating between clause types in Javindo or Pecok. The negation element need not be adjacent to the verb in Dutch, as we can see from the subject–verb inversion example in (27), whereas the two elements are consistently adjacent in Javindo (24). In Dutch, the separability of verb and negation is clear with subject–verb inversion, whereas in Javindo, which does not have such inversion, the verb and its negator are adjacent, and never separable (de Gruiter 1994: 154).

De Vries (1997) attributes the Austronesianness of both Pecok and Javindo to a strong tendency to promote non-agents ("non-actor-oriented sentences"), which accounts for the alternating presence of Dutch-derived *wor* (from the Dutch passive auxiliary *worden* and the Malay/Javanese passive prefix *di-*, used with non-agent topics.[6] The morphology of Javindo is a subset of the morphology of Javanese, just as the Tamil-derived aspectual morphology of Sri Lankan Malay is a subset of the aspectual morphology of Tamil. There is a clear contrast in the contexts in which these languages came into existence however. Most Sri Lankan Malay speakers, if not all, were native speakers who acquired Tamil as an L2, whereas Pecok and Javindo developed among native speakers of Malay and Javanese speaking an L2 variety of Dutch. In both scenarios, grammatical systems are porous and in that sense 'mixed'. With respect to the passive construction, Javindo makes use of Javanese person-marked passives, at least in first person (28).

[6] According to van Rheeden (1995: 121–2), tokens of the Dutch-derived Pecok construction with *wor* as the passive marker, probably supported by the (adversative) passive auxiliary *kena*, from vernacular Malay, were much less frequent than *di-*.

Javindo

(28) *Jij* *taq-helpe-ni.*
2SG 1SG.NAO-help-TR
'You are helped by me.' (de Vries 1997: 354)

Note that the meaning of Javanese *taq-* is hortative, so a more idiomatic translation would be 'let me help you' (K.A. Adelaar, p.c.). According to de Vries (1997: 356), *taq-* was also used (though perhaps infrequently) in Pecok, as a result of contact with Javanese in Batavia. The example in (29), containing only Dutch morphemes and demonstrating the use of *wor*, could be from either Javindo or Pecok.

Javindo/Pecok

(29) *Als* *wij* *Indo,* *wij* *wor* *ge-haat* *door* *iedereen.*
as 1PL Indo 1PL NAO PTCP-hate by everyone
'As for Indos, we are hated by everyone.'
(de Vries 1997: 357)

Pecok

(30) *Kleren* *njang* *di-wassen* *door* *die* *frou,* *bruin.*
clothes REL NAO-wash by DET woman brown
'Clothes that are washed by that woman are brown.'
(de Vries 1997: 356)

## 18.6 Chabacano

Chabacano is spoken in a handful of communities in the Philippines, in all but one of which the language is clearly endangered. In the community centred around the city of Zamboanga City, the variety referred to as Zamboangueño (and Chavacano) is widely spoken natively by all generations among approximately half of the population of about 600,000 inhabitants, and by more as a second language. It is also spoken by a majority of the inhabitants of the island of Basilan. Two endangered Chabacano varieties spoken near Manila are Ternate Chabacano and Cavite Chabacano. These varieties are spoken in the towns after which they are named. Together they have approximately seven thousand speakers (Sippola 2013).

In Zamboanga City, the language is extensively used in local media, including print media (*Voz de Mindanao*) as well as internet news videos (*TV Patrol Chavacano*). This area is found in a part of Mindanao that is close to Sabah, Malaysian Borneo. It is also spoken in Kampung Air, near Semporna, due to migration from Mindanao. The language is a canonical creole in the sense that it evolved from a pidginized

Spanish variety, as used by speakers of Hiligaynon, Cebuano, and other Malayo-Polynesian languages, as well as speakers of Hokkien, and to some extent both Mexican Spanish and Nahuatl. Albalá (2003) discusses the extensive lexical impact of Nahuatl:

> Among the American languages that gave words to the languages of the Philippines, Náhuatl stands out. It was the "general language" (*lengua general*) of Mexico from where many of the expeditions towards the Pacific departed, and from where the Philippine galleon set sail. I have studied the Indoamericanisms present in sixteen Malayo-Polynesian languages from the Pacific area comprised of the archipelagos of the Philippines, the Mariana Islands, the Caroline Islands, and the Palau Islands. Of the 111 Indoamerican etymologies I have found, fifty-five, just under half, are Nahua words, and this would seem to indicate that this language was not unknown to the sailors and passengers on the Acapulco galleon. The Spanish that reached the Pacific territory was especially influenced by the Mexican languages, particularly Náhuatl. Once more, the linguistic facts reflect the historical reality that Mexico was the major centre of activity and Manila was a dependent territory of the Mexican viceroys until Mexico's independence in 1820.

As a Philippine language, albeit for the most part lexically Romance, Chabacano verbs precede their subjects. Plural number is marked by the pre-nominal clitic *manga*, and definite direct object status is marked by the preposition *kon* (etymologically 'with'). The use of *kon* as a direct object marker is a parallel with the direct object marker *kun* found in descriptions of Tugu (Batavian Portuguese) and Malayo-Portuguese in general. This is discussed with respect to those varieties (and their potential influence on Cape Dutch/Afrikaans) in den Besten (2000). There is no animacy requirement for this marker.

The fact that the unmarked declarative word order in Chabacano varieties is VSO aligns with the canonical word order of the indigenous coterritorial languages. The pronominal paradigm is etymologically mixed, with items drawn from Spanish and from Malayo-Polynesian languages. An example of the latter is the first person plural pronouns in Chavacano that are of Hiligaynon origin, preserving the contrast between inclusive and exclusive (Steinkrüger 2013). The subject forms are *kitá* (inclusive) and *kamé* (exclusive), and their respective object counterparts are *kanáton* and *kanámon*.

Chavacano

| (31) | *Ya-komprá* | *ya* | *le* | *éste* | *líbro.* |
|---|---|---|---|---|---|
| | PFV-buy | already | 3SG | this | book |

'S/he already bought this book.'
(Steinkrüger 2013: 159)

For detailed discussion of the genesis of Chavacano, see Parkvall and Jacobs (2018).

## 18.7 Tetun Dili

Vehicular Malay was historically present in Timor Leste (the eastern part of Timor island and an independent republic) until the mid-nineteenth century (Hajek 2000, citing Fox 1997), but its diffusion was effectively resisted by the Portuguese. Of the indigenous Austronesian and Papuan languages on the island of Timor, the Austronesian language Tetun assumed the role of local lingua franca and eventually became the dominant language in Dili, although it is not indigenous to Dili. This resembles, in some respects, the relationship that developed historically between Betawi (Jakarta Malay), as the Malay variety spoken in Batavia, and its Sundanese-speaking hinterland in western Java. As Tetun assumed this role, it also changed, so that now there are at least two major varieties of Tetun, the traditional rural varieties collectively known as Tetun-Terik, and a contact variety, Tetun Dili, spoken natively in Dili by people of various ethnolinguistic family backgrounds, and as a second language in non-Tetun-speaking areas elsewhere in the country, including the politically East Timorese island of Atauro.

Tetun Dili is not a creole in the canonical sense, but more like a mixed language, in that the lexicon remains predominantly Tetun. Though it draws heavily on Portuguese (and on Malay) lexically, it is not a Portuguese contact variety in the sense that Pecok and Javindo are Dutch contact varieties, but rather a Tetun contact variety. There is no diachronic evidence, in the form of actual attestations, for an actual pidgin stage. The relationship of Tetun Dili to Tetun Terik then seems to parallel the relationship of vehicular Malay to formal Malay, except that formal Malay was little used as a spoken register for centuries, until it was made the linguistic vehicle for Indonesian and Malaysian nationalism. The parallel is found in the recent social history, including the relative youth and extent of morphological reduction in the contact variety of Tetun associated with Dili. In both Jakarta and Dili, a vernacular with historical origins in another area became the general vernacular in a national capital, taking on new societal functions. The Portuguese colonizers appear to have favoured (the contact variety of) Tetun in the way the Dutch colonial population in Batavia once favoured (Asian contact) Portuguese (Groeneboer 1993) and latterly Malay, contributing to the association of contact Malay with Batavia, and contact Tetun with Dili. Williams-van Klinken and Hajek (2020, 2020) contains an analysis of two different classes of construction, both involving the nominal derivational suffix *-dor* from Portuguese. In the first construction, new lexical items are derived with *-dor*, a productive agentive suffix for humans (e.g. *moderadór* for 'chairperson') and for instruments (e.g. *agrafadór* for 'stapler'). The second *-dor* (often spelled *door*) is only associated with human agents with respect to "a habitual activity, which is usually negatively valued". The root can be a transitive verb, an intransitive verb, or an adjective. The lexical (as opposed to phrasal) status of the second type of construction is less obvious, since it can contain a transitive verb and its object, involving incorporation of the object in a VO sequence, to which the suffix is able to attach, i.e. *lori-lia-door* for 'rumour-monger' from carry-word-AGENT.

Tetun Dili
(32) *Heis, o para kesar door!*
EXCLAM 2SG SO tell.on AGT
'Hey, you're such a telltale!'
(Williams-van Klinken and Hajek 2020: 381)

For detailed discussion of the mixed status of Tetun Dili, see also Williams-van Klinken and Hajek (2018, 2019).

## 18.8 Nonthaburi Malay

Nonthaburi Malay is spoken in central Thailand, in a number of villages in the vicinity of Bangkok. Unlike Pattani Malay, still extensively spoken in an area near northern Malaysia, Malay in central Thailand is obsolescent. Not only does it have no official status locally, but the fact that it is not stably associated with any sociolinguistic domains means that its continued transmission and use have little to stabilize or perpetuate them (Tadmor 2014). This remains the variety of Malay that has been most strongly influenced by contact with Thai. This is not the only diasporic settlement originating in southern Thailand and northern Malaysia. There is also a small and similarly endangered linguistic community in the Kawthaung district in southern Myanmar, speaking a variety related to Kedah Malay.

Tadmor (1995), which focuses on the nature and effects of intensive Thai-(Pattani) Malay language contact in central Thailand, distinguishes between relexification and restructuralization, both of which he treats as being subject to some degree of speaker control. With respect to the extensive restructuring that has taken place in Nonthaburi Malay, morphological devices found in conservative varieties of Malay were replaced with periphrastic means of conveying the same contrasts, constituting interference from Thai. While Pattani Malay, the source variety for Nonthaburi Malay, has limited productive affixation, Nonthaburi Malay does not have functional (as opposed to derivational) affixation inherited from an earlier stage in its history. Tadmor concedes that the morphological reduction that he finds in the variety is not necessarily an effect of interference from Thai, but may constitute a logical continuation of processes already found in Pattani Malay when that variety was brought to central Thailand. He also states that it may be attributable to the changes that obsolescent languages have been found to be subject to elsewhere. However, Nonthaburi Malay does contain a number of productive derivational prefixes that are modelled on analogous prefixes found in Thai, so it would be inaccurate to claim that the overall morphological effect of language contact has been subtractive.

Certainly the fact that Thai and Nonthaburi Malay have this system of prefixes means that these are not straightforwardly isolating languages. Some of the prefixes establish the syntactic categories of their respective hosts and some are nominal classifiers that establish the semantic class to which their respective hosts belong. In Table 18.2, taken from Tadmor (1995: 232), we see some of the prefixes in question, separated from their hosts by spaces in the phonetic representations of Nonthaburi Malay and Thai lexical items. Tadmor states that "the loss of affixation is closely related to the development of pseudo-prefixes: the function of the first was taken over by the second." These derivational markers are bound as genuine prefixes. Characterizing them as pseudo-prefixes because of their lexical meaning does not actually establish a clear contrast with the

**Table 18.2** Noun derivation in Nonthaburi Malay and Thai

| English | Nonthaburi Malay | Thai | Gloss | Standard Malay | Pattani Malay |
|---|---|---|---|---|---|
| eater | *ʔɔɣiŋ̃ makiŋ̃* | *kʰon kin* | person+eat | *pemakan* | *m:akɔ* |
| player | *ʔɔɣiŋ̃ maᵉŋ* | *kʰon lên* | person+play | *pemain* | *m:aⁱŋ* |
| food | *hɔʔ makiŋ̃* | *kʰɔ̌:ŋ kin* | thing+eat | *makanan* | *makɛnɛ* |
| game | *hɔʔ maᵉŋ* | *kʰɔ̌:ŋ lên* | thing+play | *mainan* | *maⁱŋnɛ* |

standard Malay morphology in the table, which is derivational. The relevant affixes in Nonthaburi Malay are similarly derivational in function, whatever their etymologies. This follows from the author's claim that the function of the Malay morphology was taken over by the 'new' morphology in Nonthaburi Malay. This is not to criticize Tadmor's characterization of these prefixes in Nonthaburi Malay as lexical (they are), but simply to point out that they can be analysed as derivational when used as prefixes. The first morpheme in the Nonthaburi Malay translations of eater and player in Table 18.2 are based (etymologically) on Malay *orang*, a lexical item which also figures in bound pronominal morphology in other contact Malay varieties, for example *derang* in Sri Lankan Malay, meaning 'they', a contraction of *dia-orang* or *de-orang*. The following examples (33) and (34) from Tadmor (1995) demonstrate how clearly some aspects of word order have changed in Nonthaburi Malay under contact conditions.

Nonthaburi Malay
(33) *cɔ:n kin mây dây*
John eat NEG can
'John cannot eat.' (Tadmor 1995: 244)

Nonthaburi Malay
(34) *amɔ gi tɔʔ leh*
1SG go NEG can
'I cannot go.' (Tadmor 1995: 245)

The corresponding order in most Malay varieties is 'subject NEG MODAL verb'. The order in which negation intervenes between a preceding lexical verb and a following coverb (not necessarily a modal) is characteristic of both Thai and Nonthaburi Malay.

## 18.9 Sri Lankan Malay

One of the expected features of overseas heritage languages (see also Moro and Slomanson, this volume, chapter 19) is a tendency to converge on the grammar of the dominant language or other languages of the host society over time, with maintenance of the heritage language as a distinct code for ingroup functions. In the case of Sri Lankan Malay, this process has come close to its logical endpoint. There are only a small number of grammatical retentions attributable to other Malay varieties, including the (pre-verbal) ordering of functional markers, including tense, modality, and negation, relative to the simple forms of lexical verbs. Auxiliary verbs, for example in the perfect construction, are inflected separately (Slomanson 2008). Nevertheless, aside from the fact that most functional modifiers of verbs appear in pre-verbal position, there is some variation in the status of complementizers, not all of which appear clause-finally. The quotative complementizer *kata* does appear clause-finally, as is expected in a canonical SOV language.

Sri Lankan Malay
(35) *Go ince ka e-minta ambe sigaret*
1SG 3SG from PST-ask PRG cigarette
*ja-minung kata.*
NEG.INF-smoke QUT
'I was asking him not to smoke cigarettes.'

In the southeastern variety, and possibly elsewhere, the progressive aspect marker *ambe* (Slomanson 2011: 393–6) is a post-verbal clitic, and anomalously, the tense complementizer *kapan* ('when') precedes and cliticizes to the verb, wherever it appears, in complementary distribution with tense markers.

Sri Lankan Malay
(36) *Musba-mama iskul atu kapan-(*si-)kutumun...*
Musba-uncle school DET when-(*PST-)see
'When Uncle Musba saw a school. . .'

The aspect marker *ambe* may be derived from Malay *sambil* ('while'), with the /s/-aphaeresis in closed class words that is characteristic of Jakartanese. The aphaeresis may have occurred in Sri Lanka, on the model of Jakartanese forms, such as the iamitive marker *(s)udah*. Aspectual *ambe* is a further reduced form of *ambil*, which can lead to descriptive confusion, because the verb *ambil* ('take') has also been reduced to *ambe*, as it has been in other Malay varieties (for example Manadonese), rendering that form homophonous with the complementizer. In Kupang Malay, the form has been further reduced to *ame* (Paauw 2008: 158). There is no evidence that the process of variably deleting final /l/ for *ambil* and for *(s)ambil* (the complementizer) began simultaneously. The verb *ambil/ambe* occurs in serial verb constructions in which its meaning is not aspectual. Not all of the language's syntactic properties can necessarily be attributed to contact influence from other Sri Lankan languages exclusively. What appears to be due to areal convergence may simply be vestigial. For example, the presence of (obligatorily) prenominal demonstrative determiners in Sri Lankan Malay is a property also found in Southeast Asian contact varieties, including Baba Malay, Manado Malay, and variably in Cocos Malay (Adelaar 2005b: 214–15). In other respects, Sri Lankan Malay has adapted to the complementation patterns of the larger ambient languages on the island, as well as to their discourse-pragmatic conventions, for example in the chaining of conjunctive participles as adjuncts, in order to convey temporal sequence (Slomanson 2016).

Sri Lankan Malay

(37) *Iskuul* *na* *a(bbi)s-pi,* *Miflal* *attu=nyanyi*
school P ASP.NFIN-go Miflal IND=song
*su-tulis,* *mulbar* *abbis-belajar.*
PST-write Tamil ASP.NFIN-learn
'Having gone to school, Miflal wrote a song, having learned Tamil.'

Malay

(38) *Apa* *yang* *guru* *baca?*
what REL teacher read
'What are you reading?'

Sri Lankan Malay

(39) *Lorang(*=yang)* *buk=yang* *si-baca.*
2SG.POL(*=ACC) book=ACC PST-read
'You read the book.'

Whereas other contact Malay varieties are able to chain related event clauses in a sequence without requiring overt marking of subordination, Sri Lankan Malay requires the conjunctive participle strategy ubiquitous in the Sri Lankan and southern South Asian linguistic areas for marking individual events in a temporal sequence. In that strategy, the most recent event is consistently tense-marked and is therefore finite (37), whereas each related subsequent event is marked as a participle. At the same time, the new information status of a temporally subordinate predicate marked in this way can be highlighted by displacement to the right edge of the sentence (as with *mulbar a(bbi)s-belajar* in (37)), however its morphology continues to mark non-primary status in the event sequence.

Sri Lankan Malay features cliticized case morphology, including accusative case morphology, using Malay items to mark contrasts modelled on their equivalents in the [other] languages in the Sri Lankan sprachbund. At the same time, other Malay contact varieties also feature object marking. *Pa*, for example, can mark animate direct objects in Manado Malay (Watuseke and Watuseke-Politton 1981). It is therefore not justifiable to treat this as necessarily a development driven solely by convergence on the structural and functional conventions of the Sri Lankan linguistic area. For many speakers, accusative case markers are obligatory in definite patient noun phrases, regardless of animacy, as in Tamil. In dialect areas, including highland areas in which there has been greater influence from Sinhala, they may not be obligatory. As with all contact vernaculars for which there is only minimal evidence from earlier developmental stages, linguistically plausible hypothesis formation is an important means of reconstructing the contact vernacular's grammatical development. According to one proposal (Slomanson 2006), the accusative case marker was introduced as a generalization of a reanalysed accusative-marked interrogative phrase, *apa yang*, in which the interrogative cleft becomes an accusative-marked object (38). The reanalysed status of *yang* was generalized to include accusative case-marking of non-interrogative noun phrases (39). In the process, Sri Lankan Malay *yang* became ungrammatical with interrogative subjects, and ungrammatical with subjects generally.

Sri Lankan Malay has developed an infinitive, marked by *me-* and *-nang* respectively at opposite ends of the verb. Slomanson (2018b) demonstrates that this infinitive has significant parallels with the development of *to*-infinitives in the Old English period, a process that was argued for by Los (2005). In the view of Los, what look like ordinary dative constructions were actually finite clauses that, in their persistent irrealis interpretation, progressively replaced subjunctives. The Sri Lankan Malay construction features both of these properties.

Malay

(40) *Dia suka* [ *makan* *nasi* ].
3SG like eat rice
'S/he likes to eat rice.'

Sri Lankan Malay

(41) *Dia* [*nasi* *me-makang-nang* ] *a-suka.*
3SG rice INF-eat-to PRS-like
'S/he likes to eat rice.'

What appears to be the 'same' form as the pre-verbal *me-* in other varieties of Malay (which is an allomorph of meN-), is more plausibly a phonologically reduced variant of *mau* (already reduced to *mo* in eastern Indonesian contact varieties). The clitic *na(ng)* that post-nominally marks dative/allative status is post-verbal in the Sri Lankan Malay infinitive. In addition to developing an infinitive through the reanalysis of existing forms, Sri Lankan Malay has also developed a marker of negated infinitives, which is in complementary distribution with *me-*. This negation element, *jang*, from Malay *jang(an)*, marks negative non-finite verbs generally, including negative participles. The Sri Lankan form may be based on the non-imperative irrealis/subjunctive meaning of *jang(an)* in Malay (Slomanson 2021). Irrealis (and purposive) meanings are common in Sri Lankan Malay infinitives, both positive and negative. Although the Sri Lankan Malay infinitive is characterized, not just by pre-verbal *me*, but by post-verbal *na(ng)*, there is some variation in whether or not *na(ng)* is expressed. With respect to the etymological source, this form is a preposition in varieties of Javanese, a language spoken natively by a high status and numerous subgroup among the community's founder population. See for example Krauße 2017: 39, containing the following (42):

Javanese

(42) *Budhal langsóng arèk-'é* ***nang*** *saf ngarep*
depart directly child-DEF **ADPOS** row front
*dhéwé, Mèg.*
SUPER Meg
'She will immediately go to the front row, Meg.'

In nominal contexts, Sri Lankan Malay *na*(*ng*) functions as a dative/allative marker. The use of *jang*(*an*) in irrealis contexts in Malay varieties maps directly to the Sri Lankan Malay infinitive. This is exemplified with verbs that can take *jang*(*an*) + verb as their complement (43). In Sri Lankan Malay, subject control is common in infinitival complementation, as in (44), in which Miflal wants Miflal (i.e. himself) not to smoke cigarettes. Miflal, the overt subject of the main clause with *kemauan* ('want') is coreferential with the understood subject in the infinitival clause. The Malay lexical source varieties did not have infinitives, however features of certain embedded clauses in those varieties, including the modal character of affirmative *mau*/*mo* and the subjunctive character of negative *jang*(*an*), are conducive to the reanalysis that took place in the development of new complementation patterns in the Malay contact language in Sri Lanka.

Malay

(43) *Aku harap mereka jangan mengulang cerita itu.*
1SG hope 3PL NEG repeat story DET
'I hope they don't repeat that story.'

Sri Lankan Malay

(44) *Miflal-nang sigaret-pada jang-minung nang*
Miflal-DAT cigarettes-PL NEG.INF-smoke INF
*kemauan.*
want
'Miflal wants not to smoke cigarettes.'

## 18.10 Conclusion

The goal of this chapter has been to introduce the reader to the study of MPSEA contact languages, providing brief descriptions of noteworthy properties of selected languages. Part of this presentation necessitated discussion of the persistent controversy surrounding which MPSEA languages to classify as contact varieties, and how to subclassify individual varieties as pidgins, pidgin-derived varieties, creoles or former creoles, and mixed languages. With respect to these classifications, the last word has not been said. At the same time, as a subdiscipline, research into MPSEA contact languages is relatively young. Further descriptive research on individual languages is needed, and in some cases even the most basic descriptive work needs to be done. Also needed will be comparative work along the lines of Paauw (2008), but including more contact languages and more contact language types. This should present interested field linguists, historical linguists, and theoreticians with intriguing opportunities and challenges. Their results can be expected to cast light on pervasive as well as local patterns of change. A promising feature of this research will be the potential benefit derived from developments in partly overlapping research areas, including research on heritage languages, pidgins, creoles, mixed languages, and areal linguistics. The latter includes historically informed areal linguistics, involving the reconstruction of morphosyntactic and other effects of collective adult second language acquisition and areal convergence.

We can also benefit from insights from work in typology, as well as in formal grammatical investigation, in which we investigate the extent to which the grammatical outcomes in MPSEA contact languages were predictable based on processes that have been observed in the development of contact languages in other language families. Comparison with unrelated contact languages and distant language areas may benefit from corpora containing attestations of earlier stages in those other [non-Malayo-Polynesian] contact language families. This is because historical data for MPSEA contact languages is relatively scarce, due to pervasive diglossia, as a result of which the nascent field will continue to depend heavily on plausible reconstruction. Ultimately, comparative synchronic work among contact languages in MPSEA, as well as comparative work involving other contact language families will both contribute to future progress in this area of inquiry.

CHAPTER 19

# Heritage languages and the study of Malayo-Polynesian diasporas

FRANCESCA R. MORO AND PETER SLOMANSON

## 19.1 Introduction

Heritage linguistics is a new linguistic subdiscipline primarily concerned with the study of heritage languages and heritage speakers (Benmamoun, Montrul, and Polinsky 2013; Scontras, Fuchs, and Polinsky 2015). Generally speaking, heritage languages are immigrant minority languages spoken in diaspora contexts. The 'minority 'and 'immigrant' properties are not inherent in any language, therefore the status of a language as a heritage language is to be defined on a case-by-case basis depending on the local context and on sociohistorical factors (Montrul 2016: 14). Heritage speakers are unbalanced bilinguals, who grew up acquiring their heritage language and the majority language of their society (either simultaneously or the latter in early childhood), and who are dominant in the majority language. Even though the degree of language maintenance in heritage language communities varies, a general pattern has been observed such that the heritage language tends to decline with each generation, following the pattern G1 > G2 > G3. First generation speakers are dominant in the heritage language, second generation speakers have relatively strong skills in both the heritage and the majority languages, whereas third generation speakers are dominant in the majority language. Beyond the third generation, few heritage speakers retain a functional command of their heritage language. There are, however, heritage languages that are transmitted for a longer span of time, such as Javanese in Suriname which is spoken today by the fifth generation of heritage speakers (Villerius 2019: 5).

The main goal of heritage linguistics is to describe and analyse the differences between heritage languages and their baseline counterparts (homeland language, first generation immigrant language, etc.), and to identify the sources or causes of divergence. The major factors accounting for such divergence are cross-linguistic influence, incomplete acquisition, attrition, the different type of input heritage speakers are exposed to, and universal principles of language acquisition in contact settings (Benmamoun, Montrul, and Polinsky 2013: 166ff; Moro 2016: 10ff). In the case of heritage languages, the unequal status of the dominant languages and the heritage languages in terms of prestige and functional domains mostly leads to transfer from the dominant language to the heritage language, while the intense contact situation is conducive to both lexical and structural transfer. Typically, cross-linguistic influence proceeds from individual expressions and constructions to more general syntactic schemata or patterns, so that lexical–semantic calques open the door for further structural changes, leading to grammatical convergence between the languages. Heritage languages also offer us the opportunity to study how new linguistic forms are innovated and diffused in a speech community and how processes such as contact-induced grammaticalization unfold (Backus, Doğruöz, and Heine 2011).

Heritage speakers can be an invaluable source for language documentation and description projects, as in diaspora communities it is possible to find minority local languages or dialects that are no longer spoken in the homeland. This happens because, being farther away from the homeland, the language of first generation speakers is less influenced by the national language (e.g. Standard Indonesian). For example, a research project by Florey and van Engelenhoven (2001) among the community of Moluccan migrants in the Netherlands uncovered remaining speakers of approximately twenty-five languages indigenous to the Moluccas, some of which are highly endangered. As documentation fieldwork in the homeland might be impractical or even dangerous, due to violent conflicts, "the presence of remaining speakers in the immigrant setting may provide the only opportunity to undertake salvage work" (Florey and van Engelenhoven 2001: 197).

Among the Austronesian languages, there are at least a dozen languages spoken by diaspora communities, among these are Cham in Hainan (China; Thurgood, Thurgood, and Fengxiang 2014), Malay in Sri Lanka (Nordhoff 2009), Malay in the Cocos (Keeling) Islands (Australia; Lapsley 1983; Adelaar 2010a), Malay in South Africa (den Besten 2000),

Francesca R. Moro and Peter Slomanson, *Heritage languages and the study of Malayo-Polynesian diasporas*. In: *The Oxford Guide to the Malayo-Polynesian Languages of Southeast Asia*. Edited by: Alexander Adelaar and Antoinette Schapper, Oxford University Press. © Francesca R. Moro and Peter Slomanson (2024). DOI: 10.1093/oso/9780198807353.003.0019

Javanese in Suriname (Villerius 2019), Javanese in New Caledonia (Subiyantoro 2014; Subiyantoro, Marsono, and Udasmoro 2017), Javanese in Malaysia (Mohd Jan 2011), Ambon Malay in the Netherlands (Tahitu 1989), Amahai (and other Moluccan indigenous languages) in the Netherlands (Florey 2013), Indonesian in the US (Wijaya 2006), and Tagalog in the US (Tanaka et al. 2019). Some of these are prototypical heritage languages, such as Ambon Malay in the Netherlands, Indonesian in the United States, and Javanese in Suriname. Others, such as Cham in Hainan, Sri Lankan Malay, and Cocos Malay only loosely fit the definition of heritage languages, as the duration of contact is much longer, to the point that some of them underwent a deeper level of grammatical restructuring, yielding what are known as 'mixed' languages (Slomanson, this volume, §18.2.2). Cham in Hainan, especially, falls outside the scope of heritage language studies as contact with the dominant languages (Mon-Khmer languages and Sanya Mandarin), has been going on since 986–988AD, thus for about 1,000 years (Thurgood, Thurgood, and Fengxiang 2014: 2).

In this contribution we focus on five of these Austronesian heritage languages by providing a historical and sociolinguistic background, together with selected salient linguistic features showing syntactic convergence on the grammars of the majority language(s). The heritage varieties, which are presented in chronological order from the oldest varieties to the most recent ones, are Sri Lankan Malay (§19.2), Cocos Malay (§19.3), Javanese in Suriname (§19.4), Javanese in New Caledonia (§19.5), and Ambon Malay in the Netherlands (§19.6).

## 19.2 Malay in Sri Lanka

Sri Lankan Malay, an overseas heritage variety since the mid-seventeenth century, is spoken by an unknown number of people in various urban communities throughout Sri Lanka, as well as a relatively small number of rural ones. The ethnic population is estimated at approximately forty thousand people, however due to ongoing language shift to Sinhala, Tamil, and English, the population statistic does not match the number of native or second language speakers in the country.

The first non-sporadic Malay settlement on the island was in the Dutch colonial period in the middle of the seventeenth century, at the same time as the Netherlands East Indies Company was establishing control over the Cape of Good Hope in southern Africa. Throughout this period, only coastal Sri Lanka came under foreign control, whereas the interior of the island remained politically free and actively opposed the Dutch presence. In urban coastal areas, especially—but not limited to—Colombo, the Moorish (Tamil-speaking Muslim) presence was proportionally very strong, in spite of Dutch hostility to that population as commercial competitors. The need for Sinhala in those areas was consequently not great, though it was strong for those Malays who escaped Dutch control by aligning themselves with the Kandyan kingdom in the interior. As a non-Muslim transactional language, it is likely that Asian contact Portuguese was of greater utility in coastal areas than Sinhala, since Portuguese was used by members of the Dutch administration, even as a home language. The linguistic culture of the community was characterized by diglossia, familiar also from the western Austronesian world.

In Sri Lankan society, religious process and teaching always involve an additional highly differentiated register. In the Sri Lankan Muslim community, this process language was an Arabicized variety of Tamil, called 'Arwi'. Historically, there was a certain amount of intermarriage between Malay-speaking and Tamil-speaking Muslims. This was documented in Slomanson (2012), with fragments from the thombos, communal records of households kept by Dutch administrators. In these thombos, onomastic evidence as well as actual descriptors attest to the presence of Tamil-speaking Muslims in Malay households, as family members, but in some cases also as servants. This and other varieties of evidence from the British period attest to the significance of Malay–Tamil bilingualism in a territory in which the majority of the rural population outside the colonial plantations was Sinhala-speaking. With the exception of the southeast, which had specifically Malay rural settlements, the Malay presence has historically been most closely associated with towns, in which interaction with the more numerous Tamil-speaking Muslims was a matter of course. This is not to say that there has been no influence from Sinhala on Sri Lankan Malay, however the historical evidence favours the position of Tamil as a primary model language. There is linguistic evidence for this as well (Slomanson 2011), most strikingly in the form of a constraint blocking the co-occurrence of negation morphology with tense morphology, which is one of the morphosyntactic processes that continues to strongly differentiate Dravidian languages from Sinhala. Although Sinhala (Indo-Aryan) and Tamil (Dravidian) are typologically close, there are still marked grammatical differences between them. We can see from the following examples that negation cannot co-occur with other bound verbal morphology, a pattern well known in the major Dravidian languages, including Tamil. Sinhala does not have a similar constraint, and negation does not block the expression of past tense morphology in Sinhala verbs. The verb in (1a) is marked for past tense, whereas the verb in (1b) is negated, but with no tense morphology. The ungrammaticality of concatenating tense and negation markers is demonstrated in (1c), illustrating the parallel with Tamil.

Sri Lankan Malay

(1) a. *Miflal pe tumman Java si-tau.*[1]
Miflal POSS friend Malay PST-know.
'Miflal's friend knew Malay.'

b. *Miflal pe tumman Java tara-tau.*
Miflal POSS friend Malay NEG-know
'Miflal's friend did/does not know Malay.'

c. **Miflal pe tumman Java tara-si-tau.*
Miflal POSS friend Malay NEG-PST-know
'Miflal's friend did not know Malay.'

This constraint blocks sequences of negation and tense markers. However, it could be argued that the negative particle *tara* is fused and bears a (past) tense feature, since it carries a past tense interpretation with most verbs. Nevertheless, stative verbs (such as *tau* 'know' and *suka* 'like'[2]), other classes of predicate (such as *kemauan* 'want', a predicate nominal that can be negated), and predicate adjectives are all negated with *tara*, regardless of tense interpretation.

Sri Lankan Malay stands out in many ways among heritage varieties of Austronesian languages, in the extent to which it has diverged from its Malay lexical source language. Sri Lankan Malay also stands out among heritage languages generally in the fact that there have long been rural communities in which the heritage language is spoken by a local (rural) majority in which no other Austronesian language is spoken, a sociological fact which also applies to Javanese in Suriname. The most striking of these communities, both in terms of settlement density and vernacular (heritage) language maintenance, is the village of Kirinda in coastal southeastern Sri Lanka. The two other Malay-speaking villages in the region that are smaller and somewhat more linguistically mixed, are the inland communities of Badagiriya and Bolana. All three communities are located in the Hambantota region. The diminutive urban centre of this region is the town of Hambantota. It has a proportionally large ethnic Malay population, although there has recently been a considerable shift there to (Muslim) Tamil as the language of the home. Malay inhabitants of the rural communities travel frequently to Hambantota for a broad range of reasons, sometimes including marriages with Tamil-speaking Muslims. Although there are exceptions, ethnic Malay children raised in Hambantota nowadays only infrequently speak Malay as a home language. Slomanson (2011, 2012, 2013, 2018a) draws primarily on data collected in the southeastern area, including Kirinda. Its dialect is, to some extent, different from the varieties spoken elsewhere in the country, for instance in the local forms of its functional morphology and in parts of its lexical inventory. Most noteworthy to the casual observer is the fact that the number of recent borrowings from Tamil is higher than elsewhere in the country, due to the prominence of Tamil-medium Muslim education for children and teenagers. The availability of government-subsidized Tamil-medium Muslim schools in the rural villages has meant that the traditional pattern of Tamil–Malay diglossia, in which Muslim Tamil is the language of writing and religion, has been perpetuated in those communities. This is what has led in some places to an increase in Tamil words at the expense of Malay vocabulary, but it is also an open-ended resource for new terms. Passive knowledge of the Malay items is still present, however linguistic informants under fifty years of age typically associate their use with older speakers.

By far the majority of Sri Lankan Malays live in the vicinity of the capital, Colombo. However that has also been the area with the most extensive language shift for over sixty years, primarily to Sinhala and English. The shift to Sinhala follows from the spread of mass media in that language, the rapidly increasing multiplexity of the networks that transcend religious and ethnolinguistic boundaries, and the Sinhalization of the educational system since the 1950s. Nevertheless, there are still urban and suburban pockets in Colombo and its surroundings in which stable concentrations of L1 Malay speakers live. Among these are Slave Island (*Kartel* in Sri Lankan Malay and *Kompana Vidiya* in Sinhala) and Maradana in Colombo, as well as a cluster of suburban communities adjacent to each other, including Hunupitiya, Wattala, Hendala, and Akbar Town, just north of Colombo. In a cross-section of small towns elsewhere in the country, there are small communities in which there is still a fair degree of cross-generational language transmission and maintenance, however the linguistic repertoire of the younger generation is contracting relative to middle-aged and older community members. This weakening has generally taken place in favour of Sinhala, but, for example, in Trincomalee on the east coast, as in Hambantota town on the southern coast, the primary beneficiary is Tamil. Trincomalee is situated in a predominantly Tamil-speaking area, and Hambantota is not. However, in both areas, an important catalyst for this shift to Tamil is the fact that is the traditional language of the larger Muslim community on the island. That community is well represented in the Tamil-speaking region of coastal eastern Sri Lanka, as it is in Hambantota town. In Muslim schools in those areas, Tamil, as one of the two official languages of the

[1] The term for Sri Lankan Malay in the Kirinda variety is Java. The speakers know they are speaking Malay, and they know the word Melayu, but do not generally use it to refer to their language. The usage may have been borrowed from Sri Lankan Tamil, in which Java is the ordinary descriptor.

[2] Nordhoff (2009) refers to these verbs as 'defective' rather than stative, a reference to their inability to take the otherwise productive temporal prefix *a(rə)-*.

country, is also the publicly funded medium of education, as it is in the villages.

Throughout the history of Sri Lankan Malay, the relationship of Malay speakers to Sinhala and Tamil has shifted, and cannot be regarded as static. Ultimately, for a traditional religious community, the prestige of Tamil as a process language for religious and community affairs and learning has been great, as it continues to be in the southeastern and eastern areas. In spite of their relatively small numbers in the general population, Malay speakers have long inhabited a wide range of localities throughout the island, and community bonds are maintained through a network of organizations, locally as well as over considerable distances. Historically, these localities are socially, ethnically, economically, and politically differentiated from each other. These factors have determined to a great extent which non-Malay language was most salient for Malay speakers in a given community.

## 19.3 Malay in the Cocos Islands

Cocos Malay is spoken natively, though not indigenously, in a remote Australian-controlled territory in the Indian Ocean. It is reasonably characterized as a heritage variety because it is spoken in an island territory to which no variety of Malay or a related language is native. Adelaar and Prentice (1996: 686) describe it as "basically a form of Java Malay with an admixture of English and Javanese loanwords". A recent population estimate for the area (Adelaar 1996b) is 400 individuals, rendering this homeland dramatically less populous than the Malay-speaking village of Kirinda in Sri Lanka, consisting of 400 *families*. This is due in part to emigration, as there are more than 3,000 Cocos Malays in eastern Sabah in Malaysian Borneo, as well as smaller groups living in Singapore and western Australia. In addition to demography, another contrast with the situation in Sri Lanka is the fact that no language at all is native to the area in which Cocos Malay is spoken, because the Cocos islands remained uninhabited until 1826. After that time, slaves were brought there from different regions in the Indonesian archipelago. As was the case in other non-voluntary labour migrations from the archipelago (i.e. to Sri Lanka and southern Africa), those who came were from diverse ethnolinguistic backgrounds, but varieties of Malay performed a lingua franca function, as they did in the homeland. Since varieties of Malay constituted the only intergroup vernacular, this did not lead to influence from a competing community language in which the Malay-speaking community would become bilingual (as in the case of Muslim Tamil in Sri Lanka), and the substrate (L1) languages were predominantly related Austronesian languages.[3] For this reason, in spite of the subsequent decline in contact with Indonesia and Malaysia, Cocos Malay still has much vocabulary in common with Jakartanese, and in other respects with Java Malay generally, in which *di-* and *-kan* map in their functionality to the way they are used in Cocos Malay (Adelaar 1996b). As in Sri Lankan Malay, the pronominal system is based on forms used in the contact varieties, including the Baba Malay of the Malayan peninsula (Adelaar 2005b) and Jakartanese (see Table 19.1).

**Table 19.1** Pronouns in Cocos Malay

| | Singular | Plural |
|---|---|---|
| 1st person | *gua* | *kita* |
| 2nd person | *lu* | *dorang*, *dong* (< *dia orang) |
| 3rd person | *dia* | *ong* (< *orang), *dorang* |

The relative pronoun is *nang*, possibly from Java Malay *nyang*.

Cocos Malay

(2) *Orang pulu nang pigi semua...*
person island REL go all
'All the islanders who went...' (Lapsley 1983: 66)

Cocos Malay

(3) *Tapi nang paling kena ma orang kita gambar Melayu.*
but REL most fit with people 1 picture Malay
'But the ones we like most are Malay films.' (Lapsley 1983: 83)

The extent to which Cocos Malay has failed to diverge from varieties of Malay spoken in more populous areas, as it has diverged in Sri Lanka and as, to a much lesser extent, Javanese has done in Suriname, is paradoxically what may be most intriguing about this language. The other heritage languages discussed here diverged through contact with unrelated languages. Cocos Malay is just as much a heritage variety, but one in which there has been koineization in the absence of non-Austronesian languages within the speech community. The isolation of the language in the Cocos Islands yielded a conservative outcome, rather than

[3] A substantial population of indentured Javanese speakers arrived relatively late in the history of the community. Though the presence of a cohesive Javanese-speaking community might have exerted a lasting linguistic influence, the founder effect (in which a founding linguistic system sets the tone for the linguistic behaviour associated with later migrations) nevertheless prevailed.

divergence. In addition to that conservatism, the distinctive character of Cocos Malay that has developed is currently at risk. This is due, again in contrast with Sri Lankan Malay, to considerable recent exposure to Indonesian. Welsh (2015), based on recent fieldwork, rejects the view that increased proficiency in English in the territory spells the death of Cocos Malay in the near future. Welsh (2015: 65) writes that:

> The resilience of Cocos Malay language is demonstrated through its viability associated with a cultural identity position that has endured huge social, political, and economic change in recent decades. Cocos Malay language has been shown as resisting the assimilative forces exerted by English in the Cocos Islands. . .

At the same time, English has exerted extensive influence on the lexicon of Cocos Malay, a fact that follows from the political status and affiliation of the community.

## 19.4 Javanese in Suriname

Suriname is a highly multilingual country where about twenty-one languages are spoken (Simons and Fennig 2017). With its 60,000 members, the Javanese community is the third largest ethnic group, and Surinamese Javanese is the fourth most widely spoken language (Carlin and Arends 2002). The two majority languages are Dutch, the official language, and Sranantongo, an English-based creole used for inter-ethnic communication. Among the major in-group languages, we find Maroon creoles (the languages of the Afro-Surinamese people whose ancestors fled the plantations), and Sarnami (the language of the Indo-Surinamese community).

The Javanese were brought by the Dutch to Suriname as temporary contract labourers (a similar immigration policy was applied in New Caledonia (see §19.5). The migration of workers from Java to Suriname started toward the end of the nineteenth century. After the abolition of slavery in 1863, there was a labour shortage on the plantations, and the Dutch started to import workers from Indonesia. Between 1890 and 1939, 33,000 Javanese were shipped to Suriname mainly from Central and East Java (Derveld 1982).

Most Javanese labourers chose to settle permanently in Suriname. To encourage their stay in Suriname, the Dutch regime offered them some money and a piece of land. The Javanese became farmers and lived in small communities in the countryside. Until quite recently, many Javanese still lived relatively isolated in village communities. This isolation and the limited assimilation into Surinamese mainstream society aided cultural preservation and the maintenance of the Javanese language, which was the only language spoken at home. This situation is similar to that of Ambon Malay in the Netherlands, where the lack of integration into Dutch mainstream society and housing policies have contributed to the preservation of Ambon Malay as a heritage language (see §19.6). As is the case with Ambon Malay in the Netherlands, Surinamese Javanese is more strongly maintained in the families living in districts outside large cities (Villerius 2017: 155). In many households in the capital Paramaribo, heritage Javanese is losing ground in favour of Dutch (Hagoort and Schotel 1982).

Unlike prototypical heritage languages, but like Malay in Sri Lanka, heritage Javanese is in contact not with one, but with two dominant languages: Sranantongo and Dutch. As for the duration of contact, we can distinguish between two main 'layers': whereas Sranantongo has been in contact with Javanese from the very beginning of immigration up until now, the influence of Dutch began later, after World War II. Bilingualism in Sranantongo probably started as early as the arrival of the Javanese contract labourers in Suriname, where they learnt Sranantongo to communicate with other non-Javanese workers on the plantations. At that time, Dutch was probably not yet used in everyday contexts. The influence of Dutch began later, as a consequence of urbanization and the increasing importance of education (Vruggink 2001: xxvii).

Today, most Surinamese Javanese speak three languages: Javanese—their heritage language, Dutch, and Sranantongo, the two majority languages of the speech community. Javanese is usually spoken at home and at cultural and religious events, Dutch is learnt at school and spoken at work, and Sranantongo is the informal language learnt 'on the street' and used with friends and peers (Villerius 2017: 155). Due to the intense contact with Sranantongo and with Dutch, and to the limited domains of use (typically the home), Surinamese Javanese has come to diverge significantly from its homeland variety, Indonesian Javanese. Major linguistic research on Surinamese Javanese includes a dictionary by Vruggink (2001), a sociolinguistic investigation on speech levels by Wolfowitz (1991, 2002), and a doctoral thesis by Villerius (2019), which systematically compares Indonesian Javanese and Surinamese Javanese with respect to a number of morphosyntactic features. Language contact effects on Surinamese Javanese include lexical borrowings, phonological simplification, morphosyntactic transfer, and reduction of speech registers.

As for lexical borrowings, both Sranantongo and Dutch function as donor languages for Surinamese Javanese. According to Villerius (2017: 158), the Surinamese–Javanese dictionary by Vruggink (2001) contains a total of 469 lexical items of Sranantongo origin, and 548 items of Dutch origin. The Sranantongo loanwords are related to semantic fields such as natural habitat, technology, or tools, while the Dutch loanwords are related to government and law. An example of a Dutch loanword or insertion is presented in (4), where the Dutch word *geluid* 'sound' has been suffixed with the Javanese definite marker *è*. Examples of Javanese morphology attached to dominant language nouns also occur in the heritage Javanese variety of New Caledonia (see example (8)).

Surinamese Javanese

| (4) | *mèn* | *ora* | *metu* | *geluid-è* |
|---|---|---|---|---|
| | so.that | NEG | go.out | sound-DEF |

'so that the sound doesn't come out.'
(Villerius 2017: 159)

Sranantongo and Dutch are also involved in the frequent code-switching practices of Surinamese Javanese speakers. Dutch is the preferred source for multi-word switches among older and younger speakers, although older speakers use relatively more Sranantongo items. According to Villerius (2017: 156), this preference reflects a longer and more profound contact with Sranantongo, and less proficiency in Dutch. An example of code-switching is presented in (5), which includes multiple word insertions from Dutch (underlined) and a single word insertion from Sranantongo (in bold).

Surinamese Javanese

| (5) | *Eh* | *lha* | *sing,* | *wong* | *sing* | *manggon,* |
|---|---|---|---|---|---|---|
| | EXCL | EXCL | REL | person | REL | live |
| | *<u>dus</u>* | *<u>behalve</u>* | ***famiri**-né* | *dhéwé,* | *sing* | *manggon apa,* |
| | so | except | family-DEF | own | REL | live or |
| | *<u>die</u>* | *<u>buren</u>* | *<u>toch,</u>* | *ora* | *tau* | *omong-omong-an?* |
| | ART | neigh-bours | right | NEG | ever | speak.to.each.other |
| | *<u>Of</u>* | *eh,* | *<u>over</u>* | *kok* | *ora,* | *nganu ora* |
| | or | ehm | about | INTERJ | NEG | something NEG |
| | *terus* | *ya,* | *ora* | *tau* | *omong-omongan?* | |
| | then | yes | NEG | ever | speak.to.each.other | |

'And those, those who lived there, so except for your own family, who lived or, the neighbours right, they never spoke [about it]? Or eh, about, not, well that it did not go through, they never spoke [about it]?'
(Villerius, p.c.)

An example of phonological simplification is the loss of retroflex consonants. Villerius (2017: 160–1) reports the case of the word *kodhok* 'frog', which contains a retroflex [ɖ] in Standard Javanese. A comparison of Surinamese Javanese and Indonesian Javanese speakers reveals that Indonesian speakers realized the *dh* as retroflex [ɖ] in 100% of the cases, while Surinamese speakers did so only in 67% of the cases. In the remaining 33%, they realized it as dental [d̪]. Furthermore, there is a relationship with age: younger speakers more often produced the non-retroflex occlusive [d̪] than older speakers, who still produced the retroflex [ɖ]. This change is likely due to contact with Sranantongo and Dutch, which do not have retroflex consonants.

Morphosyntactic transfer manifests itself as an increase in the frequency of the constructions which are shared with Sranantongo (and Dutch). For instance, Surinamese Javanese speakers have a stronger preference for using Serial Verb Constructions (SVCs) to describe motion events (Lestiono 2012; Villerius 2019: 117ff), compared with Indonesian speakers. The higher frequency of SVCs is argued by the authors to be due to language contact with Sranantongo, in which SVCs are highly productive. Another example of transfer, is the increase of Double Object (DO) constructions in the description of *give*-events, as illustrated in the pair in (6). Homeland Javanese speakers prefer the Prepositional Object (PO) construction in (6a), while heritage Javanese speakers in Suriname prefer the DO construction, as in (6b).

(6) a. Indonesian Javanese: PO Construction

| *Ibu* | *nge-kèk-ké* | *dhuwit* | *nèng* | *aku* |
|---|---|---|---|---|
| mother | AV-give-APPL | money | LOC | 1 |

'Mother gives money to me' (Arps et al. 2000: 435)

b. Surinamese Javanese: DO Construction

| *Wong* | *lanang* | *nge-wènèh-i* | *wong* | *wadon* | *dhus* |
|---|---|---|---|---|---|
| person | male | AV-give-APPL | person | female | box |

'A man gives a woman a box.'
(Villerius, Moro, and Klamer 2019: 793)

According to Villerius, Moro, and Klamer (2019), Surinamese Javanese speakers prefer the DO construction to the more homeland-like PO construction, because the DO construction is also the preferred option among speakers of Sranantongo. The increase in the frequency of DO constructions in Surinamese Javanese reflects similar findings for heritage Ambon Malay in the Netherlands, but in the latter case transfer from Dutch is the main force at work (see §19.6).

Finally, similarly to what happens in other heritage language settings (Chevalier 2004), we observe a narrowing of speech registers in Surinamese Javanese. Since the heritage language is mostly confined to the home and used with familiar interlocutors, younger speakers only learn the casual (conversational) speech style. According to Wolfowitz (1991), the differentiation in speech levels in Suriname is reduced in comparison to Indonesia, and the low level *ngoko* is used regardless of the status of the interlocutors. A similar development is found among heritage speakers of Javanese in New Caledonia, who are reported to address any Javanese speaker using the *ngoko* level, a choice that may create discomfort in Indonesian Javanese speakers (see §19.5).

## 19.5 Javanese in New Caledonia

The other major diaspora of Javanese outside the Malay world is New Caledonia, a French-administered territory in the South Pacific. After French annexation in 1853, large-scale plantations and mining industries needed manpower to grow coffee and extract nickel (Lockard 1971). The French turned first to Vietnam, another French colony, and later to the densely populated Java to recruit labourers. As a consequence, between 1896 and 1955, approximately 19,400 Javanese arrived in New Caledonia to work as indentured labourers (Maurer 2010: 867, 873). While the Vietnamese were mostly recruited in the mining sector, the Javanese were absorbed in the agricultural sector, mostly on coffee plantations, or worked as domestic servants. After World War II and Indonesia's independence, the great majority of Javanese (about 12,000) decided to be repatriated to Java, but a few thousand remained and integrated successfully into multicultural New Caledonia.

Unlike in Suriname, where the Javanese make up a major segment of the population and the majority still lives in rural areas, in New Caledonia the Javanese are a relatively small group mostly centred in an urban area (Lockard 1971: 55). The 1996 Census counted 5,003 people of Indonesian descent (approximately 2% of the total population), while in the 2009 Census the number decreased to 3,985 (Subiyantoro 2014: 46). The Javanese are highly concentrated in the Greater Nouméa urban area (3,364 persons), with some others living in Koné, where they work as public or private company employees, workers in industries or in the craft sector, teachers, nurses, technicians, foremen, craftsmen, independent traders and engineers.

Not all New Caledonian Javanese-speaking individuals are of Javanese ancestry. Some are of Batak or Sundanese origin, but their parents lived in Java when they were recruited. The suggestion of replacing the term Javanese with Indonesian has been accommodated in the names of several associations that have been established, such as the *Association Indonésienne de Nouvelle-Calédonie* (AINC), the Indonesian Association of New Caledonia, created in 1984 to maintain and promote Javanese cultural heritage by offering language and dance courses, as well as organizing events and celebrations. Subiyantoro (2014: 47), who has attended several meetings organized by the AINC in February 2013, reports that, quite ironically, all speeches were delivered in French. The closing prayers were delivered in Arabic for the Muslims and in French for the Catholics. In non-formal sessions, like coffee breaks, many Javanese of the older generation spoke in Javanese while the younger Javanese spoke in French.

Culturally and linguistically, the Javanese community in New Caledonia is in the process of shifting to French. According to Lockard (1971: 58), urbanization and the small size of the community has made the Javanese in New Caledonia more open to change than the Javanese in Suriname. Despite encouraging exceptions, most teenagers of Javanese origin who belong to the third or fourth (or even fifth) generation in New Caledonia, are not very concerned or even interested in their origins. In contrast, their grandparents and many of their parents continue to be very attached to the Javanese customs and try to maintain their heritage language (Maurer 2002). As suggested above, heritage language maintenance is stronger among first and second generation speakers, as they often did not learn to speak French correctly. Maurer (2002: 83) reports that, in 1996, among the population aged fourteen years old and over, nearly a hundred people still had no knowledge of French, two-thirds being over sixty years old.

Heritage Javanese in New Caledonia has evolved in very interesting ways, however there are only two studies, one on code-switching (Subiyantoro 2014), and one on French loanwords (Subiyantoro, Marsono, and Udasmoro 2017) that focus on linguistic aspects. Both studies are based on the linguistic fieldwork, in the form of interviews, carried out by Subiyantoro in Nouméa and in Koné in 2013.

One of the most obvious differences between New Caledonian Javanese and homeland Javanese is that New Caledonian Javanese only uses the low register *ngoko*, the other registers *madyò* (intermediate) and *kròmò* (high) being virtually absent. In New Caledonia, the *ngoko* register is used by all members of the community, while in Java it is used among peers or with someone who is younger or of lower social status. This difference is due to the nature of the input heritage speakers in New Caledonia received. The first generation speakers, who provided the input for the future generations of heritage speakers, were labourers mostly using *ngoko* in their daily lives. The lack of knowledge of the intermediate and high registers poses some problems for New Caledonian Javanese when they visit Java, or when they interact with diplomats at the Consulate General in Nouméa (Maurer 2002: 83; Subiyantoro, Marsono, and Udasmoro 2017: 92).

Code-mixing (within a clause), and code-switching (across clauses) with French is very common, as illustrated in example (7), from Subiyantoro (2014: 48).[4] In it, a New Caledonian Javanese (S1) is talking with a homeland Javanese, Subiyantoro (S2). Code-mixing is often motivated by lexical retrieval difficulties, while code-switching is related to prestige and politeness. Note also that S1 (the New Caledonian speaker) uses the *ngoko* register, and that S2 (the homeland speaker) aligns with his interlocutor by replying in *ngoko*.

[4] The transcription of the examples (7) and (8) follows the original where no diacritics are present. The English translation of the examples has been slightly revised.

New Caledonian Javanese (French is underlined)

(7) S1: *Bonjour* *Pak* *Toro.* *Comment*
good.morning Mr Toro how
*allez* *vous?* *Aku* *pak* *Toukiman,*
go.2PL 2PL 1SG Mr Toukiman
*iki* *bojo-ku.* *Njenengan*
DEM.PROX wife-1SG.POSS 2SG
*neng* *kene* *voyage?*
LOC here trip
'Good morning, Mr Toro. How are you? I'm Toukiman, this is my wife. Are you on vacation, here?'

S2: *Yo* *iso* *di-sebut* *vayage* [sic], *aku*
Also can UV-call trip 1SG[5]
*di-undang* *Pak* *Kon.* *Jen.* *di-kon*
UV-invite Mr Consulate General UV-ask
*ngisi* *sarasehan.*
fill seminar
'You can call it voyage, I am invited by Mr Consulate General to speak at a seminar.'

S1: *C'est* *pour ça* *que* *vous* *venez?* *Pour*
it.is for.that that 2PL come.2PL for
*combien* *de* *jours* *vous* *êtes* *là?*
how.much of days 2PL be.2PL there
'You came here for that? How long will you stay here?'

Regarding (7), Subiyantoro (2014: 49) explains that the French word *voyage* was inserted in the Javanese clause because the speaker (S1) might not have known the Javanese equivalent forms, *plesir* or *dolan*, which are used by wealthy Javanese in Java. This lack of knowledge relates to the fact that his ancestors who came to New Caledonia came from a lower socioeconomic background and were not familiar with these terms. The switch to French in the third utterance by S1, who was using the *ngoko* register, was done with the purpose of raising prestige after he heard that Pak Toro was invited by the consul general to speak at a seminar.

Some innovations on the lexical level involve forms such as *lafetan* 'party' created by adding the Javanese nominal suffix *-an* to the French word *la fête* 'the party' on analogy with the Javanese word *slametan* 'ceremony asking safety from God' (*slamet* 'safe' + nominal suffix *-an*). Interestingly, the word *slametan* has undergone a restriction of meaning in New Caledonia, where it only refers to death-related ceremonies, while *lafetan* is used for ceremonies related to birth, wedding, and circumcision (Subiyantoro, Marsono, and Udasmoro 2017: 90).

Native Javanese morphology can be added to French loanwords or insertions. The definite suffix *-é* is attached to French nouns, like *salairé* 'the salary' (< French *salaire* 'salary' + Javanese definite *-é*), or to verbs, like *gagnerné* 'the salary' (< French *gagner* 'to earn' + Javanese definite *-é*). Incidentally, affixation of the Javanese definite marker *-é* also occurs in Javanese in Suriname, where it is suffixed to Dutch or Sranan nouns (cf. example (4)).

The following interaction between a New Caledonian Javanese (S1) and Subiyantoro (S2) presents an example of the abovementioned phenomena, marked here in bold (from Subiyantoro 2014: 52).

New Caledonian Javanese

(8) S1: *Yen* *supit* *biye* *ana* *bong*
If circumcise formerly EXIST bong
*sekon* *Jawa.* *Saiki* *kudu* *neng*
from Java now must LOC
*hôpital.* *Yo* *nganggo* ***lafet-an.***
hospital Also use party-NMLZ
*Kebeh* *di-undang,* *ana* *sing* *ngeneh-i*
All UV-invite EXIST REL give-APPL
*envelope* *kanggo* *bocah-e.*
envelope for child-DEF
'When we were going to circumcise our child, there used to be bong (a physician specialized in circumcision) from Java, but now we have to go to hospital. We also hold a lafetan. All neighbours are invited, some give some money in the envelope to the child.'

S2: *Ketok-e* *wong* *Jawa* *padha* *seneng* *urip*
visible-DEF person Java same happy live
*neng* *NC* *yo?*
LOC NC yes?
'It seems that the Javanese enjoy living in New Caledonia, don't they?'

S1: *Yo, parce.que* *enak* *neng* *NC,* *ana*
Yes because good LOC NC EXIST
*sing* ***gagnern-é*** *gedhe.* *Guru* *neng*
REL salary-DEF big teacher LOC
*kene* ***salair-é*** *dhuwur.*
here salary-DEF high
'That's right. It's because living here is good. Some of us earn well. Teachers here are well paid.'

Unfortunately, nothing can be said about other grammatical changes or transfer from French on the morphosyntactic

[5] The singular number attributed to first and second pronouns in these sample sentences is uncertain, given the fact that Javanese varieties spoken in Java do not usually distinguish number in pronouns.

level, as these issues have so far not been studied. They could be an interesting direction for future research, and also an urgent one, considering that the Javanese community in New Caledonia is in the process of shifting to French.

## 19.6 Ambon Malay in the Netherlands

Ambon Malay or *Melaju Sini* 'Malay from here' is the heritage language of Moluccans living in the Netherlands (Tahitu 1989; Moro 2016). They are the descendants of soldiers in the former Dutch East Indian colonial army (KNIL), who were originally stationed with their families in camps on Java after Indonesia's Independence in 1949. After a rebellion broke out in the Moluccas in 1950, they risked being associated with this event. In what was meant to be a temporary measure, they were moved to the Netherlands for their own protection. Some 12,500 Moluccans were brought over in 1951. The community never returned to Indonesia and has grown considerably since. Their current number is in excess of 58,000 (Oostindie 2012: 101).

After their arrival in the Netherlands, the Moluccans were housed in thirty-four camps spread throughout the country. The camps were situated in rural and isolated areas, where the Moluccans lived segregated until the 1960s, when the Dutch government decided to close the camps and to move the Moluccans to newly built wards on the outskirts of small towns. This situation is changing. Nevertheless, Vermeulen and Penninx (2000: 9) report that, although the Moluccans increasingly disperse from these areas, they are still the least likely of all migrant groups to be found in large Dutch cities. As in the case of heritage Javanese in Suriname, the isolated housing situation and slow integration strengthened mutual links and facilitated heritage language maintenance. Today, after almost seventy years, heritage Ambon Malay is still spoken in the community, although its domains of use are becoming limited.

The main source of heritage Ambon Malay is Tangsi Malay or Barracks Malay, a divergent form of Ambon Malay spoken by Moluccan soldiers which was heavily influenced by Javanese and Dutch. All Ambon Malay heritage speakers are bilingual in Dutch and Ambon Malay. For second and third generation speakers, Dutch is the functionally dominant language, while heritage Ambon Malay is used to communicate with elders, at weddings, funerals, parties, or other Moluccan events and in church. Some heritage speakers still speak it with their parents, friends, and neighbors. Generally speaking, heritage Ambon Malay is preserved more strongly among those families living in Moluccan wards, such as Wierden, while the variety spoken by heritage speakers who live in big cities is more heavily influenced by Dutch (Moro 2018). A similar development is attested for heritage Javanese in Suriname, which is maintained more strongly in families living in rural districts than in the capital Paramaribo (see §19.4).

Heritage Ambon Malay has been investigated in a number of doctoral dissertations: among others, Tahitu (1989) describes the phonology, morphology, and some basic syntactic features of the heritage language; Huwaë (1992), and Voigt (1994) focus on code-switching patterns; while Moro (2016) systematically compares heritage Ambon Malay to homeland Ambon Malay to detect contact-induced changes in the heritage variety.

In the heritage variety of Ambon Malay, a number of changes have occurred, which are due to intense contact with Dutch, unbalanced bilingualism, and restricted domains of usage (typically the home). As for the lexicon, Huwaë (1992) is the only study that investigates lexical knowledge by means of translation tasks. Her findings show that older heritage speakers score higher in Dutch–Ambon Malay translation tasks than younger speakers. The results also show that words can be divided into five groups according to their translation likelihood: common verbs and nouns such as 'sleep' and 'chair' are likely to be known by every informant, while the equivalents for adjectives and adverbs such as 'bitter' and 'suddenly' are known only by the older ones. Code-switching is very frequent, as shown in example (9) illustrating Ambon Malay–Dutch code-switching with Malay as the matrix or base language. The absence of an overt subject in both clauses is typical for Malay, but ungrammatical in Dutch.

Heritage Ambon Malay in The Netherlands
(Dutch is underlined)

(9) *Want* *continu* *omong* *maar*[6] *omong* *leuk*
for continuously talk but talk nice
'For she talks continuously but she talks nice.'
(Huwaë 1992)

Morphosyntactic innovations mainly involve the frequency with which certain constructions that exist in the homeland variety occur in the heritage language. If Ambon Malay has two (or more) equally possible options, heritage speakers prefer the option also present in Dutch, therefore increasing its frequency. One example is the higher frequency of DO constructions in the description of *give*-events (Moro and Klamer 2015). To express *give*-events, Ambon Malay allows both PO constructions and DO constructions, as illustrated in (10a) and (10b), respectively.

[6] The Dutch conjunction *maar* 'but' was borrowed in homeland Ambon Malay as *mar* 'but' (Tjia 1992: 51). In her code-switching example, Huwaë (1992) gives the Dutch form, and therefore *maar* is underlined in example (11).

(10) a. Homeland Ambon Malay: PO Construction
*Cowo kasi tas par cewe*
boy give bag to girl
'A boy gives a bag to a girl.'
(Moro and Klamer 2015: 268)

b. Homeland Ambon Malay: DO Construction
*Tadi ada om satu, kasi dia*
just.now EXIST uncle one give 3SG
*pung tamang tas*
POSS friend bag
'There was a man, (he) gave his friend a bag.'
(Moro and Klamer 2015: 268)

The use of the DO construction, however, is rare and mostly limited to constructions in which the Recipient argument is a pronoun. Dutch also allows both constructions, but PO constructions are more frequent in elicited data, while DO constructions dominate in corpora (Colleman and Bernolet 2012). Heritage speakers of Ambon Malay in the Netherlands use DO constructions significantly more than homeland speakers, an increase likely due to Dutch influence (Moro and Klamer 2015). A similar development is attested in heritage Javanese in Suriname, where, as a consequence of bilingualism in Sranantongo, we also observe an increase in the frequency of DO constructions (see §19.4).

Another example is the decrease in the use of SVCs to express resultative events. Homeland speakers prefer resultative SVCs, as shown in (11). Heritage speakers in the Netherlands tend to favour more Dutch-like strategies, such as Prepositional Phrases (PP) (Moro 2014, 2016), as illustrated in (12) and (13).

Homeland Ambon Malay: SVC
(11) *Parampuang robe kaeng jadi dua*
girl tear cloth become two
'A girl tears a piece of cloth into two (lit.: tears a piece of cloth becomes two).' (Moro 2016: 189)

Heritage Ambon Malay in the Netherlands: PP
(12) *Nona ada robe kaeng dalam dua bagean*
girl PRS tear cloth in two part
'A girl tears a piece of cloth in two parts.'

Dutch: PP
(13) *Een vrouw scheur-t een doek*
ART.INDEF woman tear-3SG ART.INDEF cloth
*in tweeën*
in two
'A woman tears a piece of cloth into two.'
(Moro 2016: 194)

Interestingly, while in the Netherlands, contact with Dutch (a non-serializing language) has led to a decrease in the use of SVCs among heritage speakers of Ambon Malay, in Suriname, contact with Sranantongo, (a serializing language) has led to an increase in the use of SVCs among heritage speakers of Javanese (see §19.4).

Finally, the increase in the frequency of some morphemes seems to be a symptom of incipient contact-induced grammaticalization. The existential marker *ada*, which functions as a marker of progressive aspect, is used by heritage speakers in a fashion that resembles the Dutch present tense marker. In other words, there is evidence that, in the heritage language, *ada* is changing into a marker of present tense (possibly also encoding finiteness; see Moro 2017). Interestingly, this shift in temporal status and frequency of *ada* is consistent with a similar change in Sri Lankan Malay, in which the original progressive marker *ada* has become an obligatory present tense marker for non-stative verbs under the influence of the languages of Sri Lanka (see Slomanson, this volume, §18.2.2). Another example is the increase in the frequency of the definite marker *=nya*, which is arguably due to contact with Dutch. Since the category of definiteness is highly salient in Dutch and definiteness marking is obligatory, it is expected that heritage speakers will try to replicate this linguistic category with the available material. Some heritage speakers, in fact, consistently use *=nya* to mark already mentioned nouns, following a pattern typical of Dutch (Moro 2016: 122).

## 19.7 Conclusion

We find grammatical influence in Sri Lankan Malay, Surinamese Javanese, and Ambon Malay in the Netherlands, the best documented heritage varieties, while significant grammatical influence has not been identified for Cocos Malay, because it lacks a dominant non-Malay source language, and for Javanese in New Caledonia, because there is insufficient data to determine the type and extent of change. In the oldest varieties (including Sri Lankan Malay), this influence manifests as restructuring, with the addition of functional categories, such as tense and finiteness. In more recent heritage varieties, this manifests as an increase in the frequency of already available structures, but also embryonic contact-induced grammaticalization, possibly leading to grammatical elaboration.

An important direction for future research will involve determining the extent to which MPSEA heritage languages have followed predictable developmental paths in heritage contexts, comparable with what we find in heritage contexts involving languages in other language families. Is the development of 'new' functional categories and frequency changes in the expression of existing ones to be expected, and to what extent is it influenced by cultural and contextual factors, such as the appropriateness of the heritage language in peer group networks outside of the domestic sphere? To what extent is it influenced by reduced language input due to a loss of sociolinguistic domains?

An additional goal for future research is the investigation of a greater range of language pair combinations, in order to differentiate between the relative roles of factors such as cross-linguistic influence. For instance, data from heritage languages such as New Caledonian Javanese, in contact with French and the indigenous languages of the Kanaks, could test previous hypotheses on the role of dominant language influence in the domain of *give*-constructions. It has been argued that Ambon Malay in the Netherlands and Javanese in Suriname display a higher frequency of DO constructions due to the influence of Dutch and Sranan, respectively. If this is true, one would not expect an increase in DO constructions in New Caledonian Javanese, as French does not allow DO, but rather has a stronger preference for PO constructions. If dominant language transfer is the strongest force at work, one would expect an increase in the frequency of PO constructions in New Caledonian Javanese. At the same time, grammatical phenomena such as negation, as well as pragmatic phenomena marked by intonation and information structuring conventions have proven sensitive to external influence in heritage language contexts. These phenomena also await systematic comparative research.

CHAPTER 20

# Language contact in Mainland Southeast Asia

## *Historical impacts on Malayo-Polynesian languages*

PAUL SIDWELL

## 20.1 Introduction

This chapter takes a historical perspective on the issues of how languages of the Asian mainland have impacted on Malayo-Polynesian in prehistoric and early historic periods (Map 20.1 shows the languages discussed in the chapter). The dominant consensus view among linguists places the homeland of the Austronesian language in Taiwan more than 5,000 years ago (Gray et al. 2009; Blust 2013a), with subsequent pulses of expansion through insular Southeast Asia and out into the Pacific. While much of this movement was to islands to the south and east, taking speakers further away from the Asian mainland, some communities did end up settling on the mainland, or among networks in regular contact with mainland peoples. The history of these mainland interactions extends back into the first millennium BCE, and perhaps significantly earlier,[1] yet the dating of various linguistic splits, migrations, and arrivals in this period is necessarily imprecise, and we must rely on interdisciplinary insights to fill out the picture further.

Mainland Southeast Asia is home to several language families. They are: Austroasiatic, Tai, Tibeto-Burman, and Hmong-Mien. With the exception of Burmese, which is a large national language, the languages of the latter two groups are spoken by inland communities and consequently have had no effective opportunity to interact with Malayo-Polynesian speakers historically. The Tai family, which is these days dominated by modern Thai, is also something of a latecomer to Mainland Southeast Asia, spreading south from Guangxi and into Indo-China through the second half of first millennium CE. During this time the Austroasiatic speaking kingdoms, the Mon Dvaravati and Khmer Angkor, controlled the coastal regions of the Gulf of Thailand, from the Mekong Delta to the Isthmus of Kra, and also dominated over various smaller Austroasiatic groups of the region. At the geographical extremes of this coastal range Austroasatic speakers ran up against Malayic speaking peoples on the Malay Peninsula, and the closely related (and strongly Indianized, and later Islamicized) Chamic peoples living along the Vietnam coast. The Vietnamese, also partly Austroasiatic in origins, were still largely confined to the Chinese controlled Red River region in the north of Indo-China, and their interactions with outsiders during this period were substantially moderated by their functioning as a southern granary for Tang Dynasty China. Mons were also a dominant presence in southern Burma, the ethnic Burmese only beginning to migrate into the Upper Irrawaddy valley in the early ninth century from Yunnan, eventually establishing the Pagan kingdom in the eleventh century. The interior of the Malay Peninsula was (then and now) inhabited by the Austroasiatic speaking Aslian peoples, and although they do not appear to have ever established a state, there was clearly some interaction with coastal Malays and perhaps other Austronesian speakers.

Thus, it is clear that at least as far back as the middle of first millennium BCE, the coastal regions, roughly from modern day Yangon to Hanoi, were home to various Austroasiatic and Malayo-Polynesian speaking peoples. We also know that, from late in the first millennium BCE, and probably much earlier, there were extensive maritime trading networks along these coasts, mediating trade in goods such as spices, ceramics, precious stones and metals, and textiles, to and from India, China, and the Indonesian archipelago (e.g. Gupta 2007; Hung et.al. 2007; Nguyen 2017). These networks mediated contact and migration about the region for many centuries, ultimately driving linguistic change as various western Malayo-Polynesian and Austroasiatic speakers interacted, borrowing from each other and even shifting language according to demographic and dominance dynamics.

[1] The upper limit appears to indicate a calibrated dating estimate of the Moken separation (presumably somewhere in Philippines or Borneo) during the second millennium BCE (Gray et al. 2009), and we can assume their migration to the region of the Kra Isthmas to have been at some unknown time after that.

Paul Sidwell, *Language contact in Mainland Southeast Asia*. In: *The Oxford Guide to the Malayo-Polynesian Languages of Southeast Asia.* Edited by: Alexander Adelaar and Antoinette Schapper, Oxford University Press. © Paul Sidwell (2024). DOI: 10.1093/oso/9780198807353.003.0020

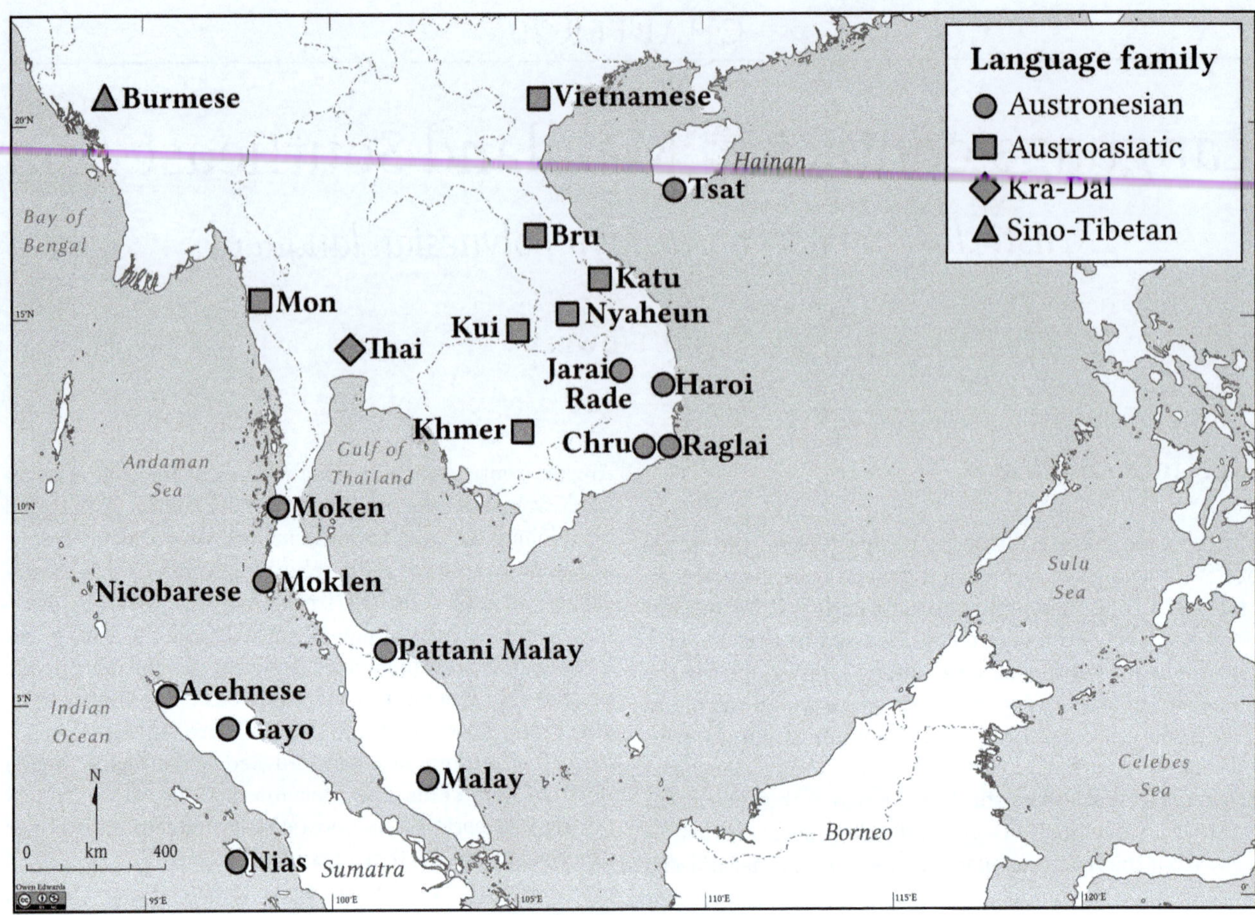


**Map 20.1** Languages of Mainland Southeast Asia and Sumatra mentioned in this chapter.

An outcome of this ancient period is that we observe an old stratum of Austroasiatic loans into Malay, and more speculatively this may also explain the broad tendency for verb-medial word order in both the languages of Mainland Southeast Asia and Malay and other western Malayo-Polynesian tongues.

As the second millennium CE dawned there began a major social realignment on the mainland, particularly as Tai and Burmese populations absorbed and/or displaced large numbers of Mon, Khmer, and other Austroasiatic speakers. Additionally, Vietnam—after throwing off Chinese rule—began a long push southward that would eventually conquer all of the Indo-Chinese lowlands east of the Annamite range and the Mekong Delta. Consequently, the second millennium saw Siamese influence on the Moken/Moklen and Pattani Malay on the Peninsula, and Vietnamese related changes in coastal Cham. The Vietnamese expansion also provoked centuries of Cham diaspora, with migrations to Hainan, inland Cambodia, Sumatra, and into the hills of the Annamite range. As a result, many Chamic languages that exist today show a diverse range of language contact effects, with restructuring in their lexicon, phonology, and morphology so thoroughly that, for many decades, linguists classified them as either Austroasiatic or mixed Austroasiatic-Austronesian.

Contact also went in the other direction, with centuries of Malayic and Chamic influence on the Austroasiatic languages of Khmer, the Bahnaric and Katuic languages of the Vietnam central highlands, and the Aslian languages of the Malay Peninsula. Additionally, the Nicobarese languages (located in the Andaman Sea), were apparently profoundly affected by an unknown Malayo-Polynesian language or languages (perhaps spoken by substrate populations). Nicobarese varieties display morphosyntactic features reminiscent of the Sumatran language Nias and languages of the Philippines (such as VOS order and subject agreement marking on verbs) that are quite unknown among its relatives on the mainland.

## 20.2 Emergence of mainland features in MP languages

Geography figures heavily in the varying extents to which we can identify the signs of mainland language contacts on affected Malayo-Polynesian languages. On the mainland of Southeast Asia the most profound areal features are the shift to iambic word structure, the frequent emergence of breathy register and even lexical tone in the case of at least one Chamic language (which is strongly connected with iambicity) and preference for SVO (verb medial) word order. There is also a strong tendency for isolating morphology to replace inflexional morphology, while derivational affixation persists rather robustly, and has even been borrowed into Chamic and Acehnese from Austroasiatic (especially the nominalizing instrumental *<ən> infix, see discussion later in this section). Some mainland languages even reduced all historical lexemes to monosyllables (e.g. Vietnamese, Nyaheun) and lost all historically productive affixation. Other characteristically mainland features include the presence of implosive and aspirated syllable onsets, palatal codas, and complex vowel inventories (see Enfield and Comrie 2015; Enfield 2018 for detailed expositions on mainland areal features). How this convergence among mainland languages has come about is complex and yet to be properly understood, although clearly it cannot have been a simple process of social dominance and language shift. It is apparent that in addition to metatypical change mediated by multilingualism, there are strong tendencies for directionality in internal change relating to shifts in speech rhythm and word shape (Donegan and Stampe 2004) and these have played out across the region.

The Malayo-Polynesian language groups demonstrably affected by mainland contact, in order of geographical proximity, are Chamic, Achenese, Moken-Moklen, and Malayic, and we can see a cline of contact effects across these groups. At the same time we need to recognize that Malay itself has exerted a strong influence over the region, and has probably played a role as both recipient of mainland features and secondary vehicle for their transmission.

The effect on Malay is immediately seen in lexical borrowings (e.g. *kətam* 'crab', *prak* 'silver', and others from Austroasiatic, discussed further below), understandably matched by a substantial cohort of Malay words taken into Khmer, or mediated via Malay (e.g. អ្នក *neak* 'you' cf. Malay *anak* 'child', ផ្សារ *psa:* 'market' ultimately from Persian, and others). Less obvious, but still related to the question of mainland influence, Malay and various western Malayo-Polynesian relatives show a tendency for verb-medial word order that conflicts with the assumed verb-initial preference of Proto-Austronesian (Donohue 2007). Verb-medial order is overwhelmingly dominant in Indo-China and southern China (see Map 46.1 in Donohue, chapter 46, this volume), yet verb-final order is reconstructed for Sino-Tibetan (LaPolla 2015) and it is an emerging consensus (since Jenny 2015) that Austroasiatic was verb-initial. Thus it is likely that the dominant word order pattern in Mainland Southeast Asia is an emergent effect of typologically divergent families coming into contact on the mainland and among coastal trade networks. This broad areal convergence has developed over many centuries and continues into the present.

A similar preference for verb media order also extends from Southeast Asia across Indonesia to the western edge of New Guinea, as do various other linguistic and cultural features, prompting Gil (2015a) to propose a larger and chronologically deeper 'Mekong-Mamberamo' linguistic area, although this particular proposal remains controversial.[2] For the reasons given above, this writer favours the view that verb-medial order in Malay and western Indonesia is emergent and related to mainland contact rather than a historical remnant. It is striking that verb medial order is not dominant in Sumatran languages, including Acehnese, a close relative of Chamic. This is consistent with a lack of specific evidence for mainland influence in Sumatra beyond the arrival of the Acehnese themselves, and one can suggest that Acehnese lost dominant verb-medial order in contact with languages such as Gayo and Nias after arrival in Sumatra.

Roughly coinciding with the convergence in word order is also a shift to final stress at the word level (or iambic stress pattern) which has had powerful effects in the phonological and morphological restructuring of mainland languages, and is at the heart of the long-term trend to monosyllabicism. It is apparent that Proto-Austroasiatic was strongly iambic (Shorto 2006) and this underlies the strength of the tendency on the mainland. Chamic, Acehnese, Moken-Moklen, and various vernacular Malayic languages in Sumatra and Borneo have adopted fixed final stress (see Brunelle and Jensen, this volume, §30.2.1; McDonnell, Wu, McKinnon, and Adelaar, this volume, §29.2.2.1) as have Land Dayak and some other Bornean languages (see Kroeger and Smith, this volume, §27.2.3). In the case of Aceh-Chamic, reconstruction (Thurgood 1999) suggests that this shift was early and occurred in conditions of close contact with Austroasiatic. In the other cases it is apparent that the shift is later and part of a broader areal trend that may in part be independent and in part catalysed by historical contact.

[2] Other writers have also drawn attention to cultural features shared across the region from Papua to Mainland Southeast Asia (e.g. Urban 2010; Schapper 2019) but this writer finds unconvincing any suggestions arising that the facts support an ancient culture area. See also Blust (2011) for a rebuttal of Urban (2010).

There are indications that derivational morphology has been borrowed from Austroasiatic into Aceh-Chamic. The Austroasiatic nominalizing instrumental infix *<ən> is found throughout Chamic and is characterized as productive in Acehnese (Durie 1985), and is potentially reconstructable to Proto-Aceh-Chamic. By contrast, the labial infix—Acehnese <ɯm>, Cham <əm>, Malay <əm> (fossilized only)—derives from an Austronesian voice-marking infix *<um>, and is not related to the similar Nicobarese causative <um> as otherwise suggested by Reid (1994b). The Nicobarese infix is an allomorph of the Austroasiatic *p- causative prefix, perhaps better reconstructed *ɓ- (as it has also glottal stop and vocalic reflexes).

The same Austroasiatic causative *p- is coincidentally paralleled by Austronesian *pa- causative.[3] Aymonier and Cabaton (1906: xxiii) suggested that Chamic had borrowed this prefix from Khmer, but there is no evidence for this. Thurgood (1999: 242–3) has suggested that the coincidence of such similar prefixes in languages in contact has reinforced their use, mitigating against historical loss, but this is rather speculative. Thurgood (1999) also proposes that the Acehnese and Chamic negative imperative morpheme reconstructed as *bɛʔ was borrowed from Austroasiatic due to its presence in North Bahnaric languages, but this is probably a loan from Cham. The same form with meanings 'small; short; low; a bit', etc. is found throughout Bahnaric and Katuic, and may point to a local word that grammaticalized as a negator in Aceh-Chamic. Beyond these examples there are no clear indications of mainland morphosyntactic influence on other Malayo-Polynesian languages such as Moken-Moklen or Malay.

## 20.3 Chamic

Chamic is a group of about ten languages[4] that form a sister branch with Malayic within Malayo-Chamic, the Malayo-Chamic homeland is assumed to be in Western Borneo (Thurgood 1999; Adelaar 2005a). While the ancient Malays spread westward to Sumatra and the Malay peninsula (and elsewhere) the early Chams settled on the Indo-Chinese coastline from the mid first millennium BCE and, by the early first millennium, had begun to establish a network of small Hinduized states that eventually left an impressive legacy of monumental architecture, and a diaspora of Chamic communities in Cambodia, Hainan, and beyond. It is also apparent that throughout Chamic history the social elite maintained contact with the Malay world and wider trade and social networks, and a Cham state persisted in southern Vietnam into the 1830s (for a recent discussion of Cham history see Vickery 2005).

The long period of Chamic presence in Indo-China led to prolonged and intimate contact with Austroasiatic speaking peoples, such as the Bahnaric, Katuic, Khmer, and Vietnamese, (Collins 1975; Thurgood 1999; Sidwell 2005). Consequently, Chamic replaced a substantial proportion of native vocabulary with Austroasiatic lexicon (some Highland Chamic lects ultimately replacing more than 40% of their basic lexicon in this way, see Grant 2005b and discussion below), assimilating also the phonological structures associated with the borrowed lexicon, as well as aspects of morphosyntax. The changes are so profound that it appears likely that early Chamic history was marked by significant language shift by indigenous Indo-Chinese who were assimilated into the emerging Chamic society during its first millennium.

Thurgood's breakthrough (1999) study relied upon a rather narrow range of data, and the problem remains insufficiently understood. It is very much open to question which language(s) actually contributed to the early relexification and restructuring of Chamic during its first millennium on the mainland, although the general assumption is that it was Austroasiatic. Approximately half of the early Chamic lexicon identified as loans of non-Austronesian origin actually lack apparent Austroasiatic etymologies, and the mass of early lexicon shared between Chamic and Bahnaric is almost entirely absent from the West Bahnaric and Austroasiatic more generally. Thus, one can suggest that an unidentified Austroasiatic language, or an entirely unknown language, contributed significantly to the early relexification of Chamic (Sidwell and Jacq 2003; Sidwell 2005).

It is clear that with the Vietnamese drive southward—which played over the millennium following independence from China in 938CE—Chamic splintered socially, with numerous migrations resulting in a regional diasporas finding themselves in new and complex language contact situations. This has seen diverse and specifically locally driven contact induced change that includes lexical borrowing, phonological reconstruction, and syntactic assimilation.

### 20.3.1 Lexical borrowing

The most important study of borrowing into Chamic remains Thurgood (1999), although various subsequent studies (e.g. Grant 2005a, b; Sidwell 2005, 2007, 2008) permit

[3] Reid (1994b) also cited the coincidence of the labial stop causative prefix in Austroasiatic and Austronesian as supporting the Austric hypothesis.

[4] Brunelle and Jensen (this volume, §30.1) mention "seven attested Chamic languages", yet Thurgood (1999: vii) lists some fifteen named languages. This author's estimate of ten is based on unpublished lexical analyses.

**Table 20.1** Adaptation of Grant (2005a: 51, Figure 1), counts by strata of basic lexicon (combined Swadesh 100 and 215 lists) from the Appendix to Thurgood (1999)

| | Acehnese | Ede | Jarai | Haroi | Chru | Cham | Raglai |
|---|---|---|---|---|---|---|---|
| Austronesian | 93 | 93 | 95 | 97 | 94 | 94 | 99 |
| Early Mon-Khmer | 13 | 48 | 56 | 44 | 47 | 46 | 43 |
| Unknown - MK? | 6 | 14 | 12 | 17 | 19 | 17 | 13 |
| Other | 1 | 3 | 1 | 3 | 3 | 3 | 3 |
| Later Mon-Khmer | 3 | 23 | 18 | 17 | 18 | 13 | 19 |
| **Total items** | **116** | **181** | **182** | **178** | **181** | **173** | **177** |

a more nuanced interpretation of the data. In Table 20.1 is Grant's (2005a) tabling of counts of indigenous and borrowed vocabulary in the basic lexicons of various Highland Chamic languages (plus Acehnese) based on Thurgood's (1999) appendices. The identification of Austroasiatic (=Mon-Khmer) as a source is Thurgood's, although in some cases these are speculative and lack specific support. The main point to note here is that in regard to these Chamic languages, between 44% and 49% of the basic lexicon (based on items found in the combined Swadesh 100 and 215 lists) is of non-Austronesian origin, predominantly identifiable as Austroasiatic.

A very high proportion of basic vocabulary has been replaced by borrowing in Highlands Chamic languages; items borrowed include body parts and functions, animal and plant names, kin terms, verbs (active and stative), and grammatical(ized) terms such as negators and aspect markers. Note also that Thurgood identified approximately three quarters of the Austroasiatic loans as early borrowings, meaning they were taken into Proto-Chamic during the first millennium or earlier. Thurgood's thesis, which has broadly been well received, is that this heavy early borrowing brought so many foreign sounds and new contrasts into Proto-Chamic, that it changed the character of the segmental inventory and syllable template, and catalysed a restructuring of the word shape.

## 20.3.2 Phonological convergence

The Malayo-Polynesian language that arrived on the Indo-China coast sometime in the first millennium BCE, let us call it pre-Proto-Chamic, would have been an immediate daughter of Malayo-Chamic, and hardly distinguishable from Malayo-Chamic.[5] This further implies that pre-Proto-Chamic is at most a few hundred years separated from Proto-Malayic (if differentiated at all, it is not obvious that this is the case) so we can reasonably use Proto-Malayic as a proxy for Proto-Malayo-Chamic for the purposes of modelling phonological change. See Brunelle and Jensen, this volume, §30.2 for an overview of Chamic phonologies.

Table 20.2 compares the segmental inventory of Proto-Malayic (following the reconstruction of Adelaar 1992a) with that of Proto-Chamic (Thurgood's 1999), without phonotactic context which would clutter the presentation and only increase the degree of overall difference. Proto-Chamic is modelled as reflecting the last stage of approximate linguistic unity of Chamic achieved some time in the first millennium CE, after already undergoing contact induced change. Comparison reveals that Proto-Chamic had a much richer segmental inventory than its immediate antecedent, adding multiple phonation types among oral stops and a more complex vowel inventory that includes diphthongs within closed syllables, short and long contrasts, and new timbre distinctions.

The phonological transition to Proto-Chamic was also marked by a shift to fixed iambic word stress, accompanied by various cluster reductions that partially transformed the Malayic preference for disyllabic roots, creating sesquisyllabic and monosyllabic forms; some examples are given in Table 20.3.

The Proto-Chamic of the first millennium had taken in phonological oppositions embodied within newly borrowed lexicon rather than simply adapting new forms by reduction of contrasts to fit the Malayo-Chamic template. By

[5] The calibrated dating estimates of Gray et al. (2009) place the break-up of Malayo-Sumbawan beginning early in the first millennium BP, implying Malayo-Chamic separation only a few hundred years later.

**Table 20.2** Proto-Malayic and Proto-Chamic segments

| Proto-Malayic segments | | | | | Proto-Chamic segments | | | | |
|---|---|---|---|---|---|---|---|---|---|
| p | t | c | k | ʔ | p | t | c | k | ʔ |
| b | d | ɟ | g | | $p^h$ | $t^h$ | $c^h$ | $k^h$ | |
| m | n | ɲ | ŋ | | b | d | ɟ | g | |
| | s | | | h | $b^h$ | $d^h$ | | $g^h$ | |
| w | l | j | ʀ | | ɓ | ɗ | ʔj | | |
| i | | u | | | m | n | ɲ | ŋ | |
| | ə | | | | | s | | | h |
| | a | | | | w | l, r | j | | |
| | | | | | i | | | u | uː |
| | | | | | | ə | | | |
| | | | | | ɛ | a | aː | ɔ | ɔː |
| | | | | | ia | | | ua | uə |

**Table 20.3** Chamic phonological reduction illustrated with comparison to Malay

| PMP | Malay | Proto-Chamic | |
|---|---|---|---|
| *pahit | *pahit* | *phit | 'bitter; bile' |
| *tahun | *tahun* | *thun | 'year' |
| *buhuk | – | *ɓuk | 'head hair' |
| *nahik | *naik* | *ɗiʔ | 'to climb' |

this means the language had come to strongly resemble conservative Austroasiatic languages such as contemporary Bahnar and Katu (which themselves became recipients of Chamic influence).

The timing of the Chamic diaspora, occurring largely through the second millennium,[6] has interesting consequences for the phonological restructuring of the languages. It is recognized that through East Asia and Mainland Southeast Asia, approximately from the twelfth to the seventeenth centuries, a wave of devoicing of voiced stops spread over the region, variously affecting all language families and giving rise to all manner of phonological complexities, especially complex tonologies and voice quality contrasts (Matisoff 1973).[7] As residents of the Southeast Asian Linguistic Area, Chamic languages were also affected by this. Brunelle and Jensen (this volume, §30.2) discuss the phonology of Cham in detail, here I will touch on two other Chamic varieties.

#### 20.3.2.1 *Hainan Cham/Tsat*

Hainan Cham (HC henceforth) is described recently by Thurgood et al. (2014) and the discussion here follows that work as well as Thurgood (1999), unless otherwise marked. HC is remarkable in that since its migration from Indo-China, the biggest linguistic influence seems to have been the local Chinese in Hainan, with minimal contribution by the Li, Hlai, and Mien of the island. Thurgood et al. (2014) report that the HC are a relatively closed and homogenous group, and it is speculated that the main source of contact over time has been the in-marriage of Chinese women. The most notable feature of HC is that the di- and sesquisyllabic morphemes of Proto-Chamic have become compact monosyllables with a five tone system, and there is a richness of diphthongs[8] and creaky phonation. Much of this phonological restructuring is due to natural evolution within the inherited Chamic system rather than to outright borrowing from Chinese. Nevertheless, much borrowing has occurred, so a degree of mimicking of Chinese structures is reasonably assumed.

The HC onsets restructured completely away from clusters and presyllables to monosegmental onsets (treating aspirates and affricates as monosegments). The mechanisms include both segmental elision and fusion of segmental features, in some cases yielding segments that are not commonly found in other Chamic languages (examples in Tables 20.4 and 20.5).

The pattern of tonogenesis in HC follows well understood principles, paralleling in most respects historical tonal development in Vietnamese, although this follows mainly from general principles rather than from specific contact with Vietnamese. It appears that there was an initial split into modal (tense) and breathy (lax) syllables, the latter associated with voiced obstruent onsets (subsequently lost

[6] The Hainan Cham probably migrated from Indo-China in the late 900s directly fleeing Vietnamese conquest. Over later centuries many Cham took refuge by sailing up the Mekong and into Tonlesap, establishing many communities in Cambodia. This seems to have occurred off and on into the 1700s (Vickery 2005).

[7] Matisoff (2003) correlates this process in East Asia with the period of the Mongol invasions (twelfth and thirteenth centuries), although the mechanism for the spread of this change is not clear.

[8] It should be noted that, in practice, scholars of Austroasiatic and Austronesian languages have a very different operating notion of 'diphthong'. The former tend to regard diphthongs as entities only when they are unambiguously functioning as syllable peaks, and syllables with glide codas are treated as closed syllables, so such glides are not counted as components of diphthongs. Austronesianist practice, especially influenced by Robert Blust, does not distinguish between nuclei and coda, so glide codas are characterized as components of diphthongs or even triphthongs. Common Austroasiatic usage is followed here.

**Table 20.4** Elision of Hainan Cham initial syllables/segments

| Malay | Proto-Chamic | Hainan Cham | |
|---|---|---|---|
| nipis | *lipih | *pi55* | 'thin (material)' |
| habis | *ʔabih | *phi55* | 'all; finished' |
| tanah | *tanah | *na55* | 'earth; soil' |

**Table 20.5** Cluster reduction with fusion of segments in Hainan Cham

| Malay | Proto-Chamic | Hainan Cham | |
|---|---|---|---|
| turun | *trun | *tsun33* | 'descend' |
| – | *bara | *phia11* | 'shoulder' |
| balay[a] | *palɛj | *piai33* | 'village' |

[a] Malay *balay* 'community hall'.

with general devoicing of egressive obstruents), and the voice quality features yielded insipient high and low tones respectively. Final oral stops generally became glottal stops, and within each high and low tone class there was a three way split relating to glottal stop, fricative (/h/) or sonorant codas. All syllables with etymological coda *-h merged to tone 55, so the Sonoran outcome is a five-tone system. The tonal inventory is similar to that found in Hainanese (Southern Min) Chinese varieties, such as the five tone system described for the Tan-Chou dialect by Ting (1980).

Although HC has come to resemble Chinese, the evidence suggests that the bulk of Chinese influence has been relatively late historically, and thus much of the change within HC that has contributed to the apparent convergence with Chinese is grounded in universal tendencies plus dynamics of change that were already in play due to much earlier language contact on the mainland. HC began its independent development not greatly dissimilar to other Chamic lects spoken in Indo-China a thousand years ago, and yet has taken tendencies nascent within Chamic to a much greater extent than other Chamic varieties. It has not taken in new phonemes by direct borrowing as Proto-Chamic previously did, but it did continue to develop new distinctions based on its native resources, paralleling structures among its unrelated neighbours, specifically Hainanese Chinese.

#### 20.3.2.2 *Haroi*

Haroi is spoken by about 25,000 speakers in Bình Định and Phú Yên provinces, in central Vietnam. It is one of the Northern Chamic languages and is spoken in proximity to Bahnar, a large and important Austroasiatic language of the Central Highlands. It has been discussed by various scholars (e.g. Goschnick 1977; Lee 1977; Mundhenk and Goschnick 1977), and a synthesis of Haroi historical phonology is offered by Thurgood (1999).

Like HC, Haroi, lost voicing in onset obstruents, but the consequences have been somewhat different. Resembling much more phonological developments of Khmer and the Kui and Bru of Katuic (Huffman 1985), Haroi has undergone a partial two-way split of its vowel system, resulting in a very un-Austronesian vocalism. The analysis of Mundhenk and Goschnick (1977) yields twenty-two simple vowels (eleven short, eleven long), ten glided vowels, and ten nasalized vowels, making a total of forty-two vowel phonemes. The glided vowels (diphthongs) are attested in closed syllables, so they cannot be simply decomposed into monophthong plus glide sequences as the so-called Austronesian 'diphthongs' can.

Broadly, the long–short distinction among the vowels is due to extensive lexical borrowing, and to some reorganization of length values correlating with specific syllable types. Overlaying this is a tendency for vowels to acquire raised or lowered on-glides correlating with the historical voicing values of the initial consonants. This creates new centring diphthongs that add to the overall inventory of nuclei. Nasalization is also a feature of syllables, but it is not discussed further here. Consequently, we ultimately arrive at the situation that the ancient four-vowel Austronesian inventory has evolved into one analysed as having forty-two distinct units, see Table 20.6.

**Table 20.6** The Haroi vowels, adapted from Mundhenk and Goschnick (1977)

| i | iː | ia | iːa | ɨ | ɨː | ɨa | ɨːa | u | uː | ua | uːa |
|---|---|---|---|---|---|---|---|---|---|---|---|
| ɪ | ɪː | | | | | | | ʊ | ʊː | | |
| e | eː | ea | eːa | ə | əː | | | o | oː | oa | oːa |
| ɛ | ɛ | | | a | aː | | | ɔ | ɔː | | |
| | | | | | | | ɨ̃ːa | | | | ũːa |
| | | ẽa | ẽːa | ə̃ | | | | | | õa | õːa |
| ɛ̃ | | | | | ãː | | | | ɔ̃ː | | |

**Table 20.7** Haroi vowel innovations

| Gloss | Proto-Chamic | Haroi | Austroasiatic comparisons | Commentary |
|---|---|---|---|---|
| to eat | *ɓəŋ | *ɦiŋ* | Cf. Mlabri *ɓoŋ* 'to eat' | *ə > ɨ unconditioned change |
| to stand | *ɗua | *ɗoa* | Cf. Ksing-Mul *cəldu:* 'carry on head' | *ua > oa, lowered vowel onset |
| narrow | *ganiat | *tapak* | Cf. Khmer *caŋgiət* 'narrow' | *ia > ea, lowered vowel onset (Chamic form by infixation) |
| handle | *gər | *kʰʊl* | Cf. Bahnar *gər* 'handle' | *ə > ʊ before (secondary) lateral |
| near | *ɟɛʔ | *sɪʔ* | Cf. Bahnar *ɟɛʔ* 'near' | *ɛ > ɪ raised after palatal |
| to tread | *ɟuaʔ | *sʊʔ* | Cf. Khasi *juʔ* 'to tread' | *ua > ʊ shortened before glottal |
| to scold, talk | *puac | *poaiʔ* | Cf. Surin Khmer *rpoc* 'talkative' | *ua > oa lowered vowel onset |
| to bring, carry | *ba: | *pʰɨauʔ* | Cf. Stieng *ba:* 'to carry on back' | *a: > ɨa lowered vowel onset, plus *-p > -uʔ |

Table 20.7 examples give some indications of how vowels have been introduced via loans and/or restructured (Chamic data from Thurgood 1999).

What is particularly interesting about the secondary vowel developments in Haroi is that they correlate primarily to the devoicing of onsets, yet this devoicing is not shared by the immediate neighbours Bahnar, Vietnamese, Ede (also Rhade or Rade), and Jarai. Therefore, they cannot simply be explained as a contact effect, but rather as an internal development by general linguistic tendency. These changes have acted equally upon both the native Malayo-Polynesian vocabulary and the various loan strata.

## 20.4 Acehnese

Acehnese is a Malayo-Polynesian language spoken in Northern Sumatra by more than three million people. However, the classification of Acehnese, and how and when it came to Sumatra, is a matter of unresolved dispute among scholars. Although essentially surrounded by other Malayo-Polynesian languages, it is not closely related to any of its neighbours and shows numerous lexical and structural oddities that suggest a historical connection to Chamic and influence from mainland Austroasiatic. As Blust notes:

> Acehnese has a number of other consonant segments that are unusual from a general AN [Austronesian] standpoint, including postploded medial nasals (called 'funny nasals'), automatically glottalised labial and dental stops word-finally, voiced allophones of the glottal fricative h, and a laminal alveodental fricative [...].
>
> (Blust 2013a: 190)

To this list we can add a moderately large vowel inventory of ten monophthongs and six diphthongs that occur in closed syllables, essentially reflecting an older set of long monophthongs, and fixed word final stress. This adds up to a very mainland-like phonological typology, although the evidence that this typology is directly related to mainland contact is limited. Such observations have motivated a history of attempts by scholars to identify an Austroasiatic stratum within Acehnese. The most extensive study of this type is the PhD thesis of Collins (1975), although that effort is of very mixed quality and later work has not significantly added to the small number of reasonable lexical comparisons embodied in that thesis.[9]

The broad consensus among western scholars[10] is that Acehnese originated in Indo-China as a Chamic lect or sister of Chamic, who migrated to Sumatra no later than the mid-second millennium. Thurgood (1999) suggests that Acehnese reached Sumatra as refugee populations some time after the Vietnamese conquest of Indrapura in 968BP, since he specifically regards Acehnese as having been a Northern Chamic language (although without making the reasons for this clear). Blust appears to support Sidwell's (2005) claim that the separation of Chamic and Acehnese must have been much earlier, since there are additional

[9] This writer is also in possession of several drafts of an unpublished etymological dictionary of Acehnese prepared by Harry Sorto (SOAS London) in the mid 1970s, testimony to the interest that this subject held for linguists at that time.

[10] Native Acehnese linguists that this writer has visited in Banda Aceh variously express resentment and scepticism at suggestions that Acehnese originated outside of Sumatra.

Chamic structural changes that are not manifested in Acehnese:

> The first change apparently was a shift of the primary stress from the penultimate to the final syllable. With final stress the penultimate vowel then tended to weaken. Apart from Acehnese, which evidently returned to insular Southeast Asia before this tendency had progressed far [...] all other Chamic languages show vowel neutralisations in the penult.
> Blust (2013a: 157)

Dyen (2001) voiced scepticism about the Aceh-Chamic hypothesis; he counted only forty-four Acehnese reflexes among the hundreds of Chamic words of apparent Austroasiatic origin, and discounting those that are also shared with Malay leaving only "twenty-eight entries, perhaps better reduced to twenty-six, then appear to constitute the basis of the hypothesis that Acehnese is a Chamic immigrant" (Dyen 2001: 393). Sidwell (2005, 2007, 2008) confirmed that the direct evidence of Austroasiatic lexical influence on Acehnese is modest, but offers a different interpretation: Acehnese split from Chamic before the Proto-Chamic phase reconstructed by Thurgood. Furthermore, on general grounds we can expect that some early Austroasiatic borrowings were erased once the Acehnese settled in Sumatra and the language was relexified from Malay(ic).

Additionally, there is small body of Acehnese words with specifically Khmer parallels—apparently absent from Chamic—and these may provide a hint about the route taken to Sumatra, or may be indicative of later contacts as the Acehnese are accomplished maritime traders (see Table 20.8).

**Table 20.8** Acehnese words with cognates in Khmer

| Acehnese | Comment |
|---|---|
| tət 'to burn' | Cf. Old Khmer *tut*, Modern Khmer ដុត *dot* 'to burn' |
| cɔp 'to sew' | Cf. Khmer *kcɨp* ខ្ជិប 'to mend' |
| sɯʔɯəm 'warm' | Cf. Khmer *sʔɔm* ស្អុំ 'warm' |
| sɯmɯŋɯp 'yawn' | Cf. Khmer *samŋa:p* សំងាប 'yawn'; all Chamic reflexes lack /ŋ/ (apparently borrowed independently from another Austroasiatic language) |

There are suggestions of apparent Aslian loans and influence on Acehnese; for example Blench (2006: 7) tables some seven putative Aslian-Acehnese isoglosses. However, under close examination four of these appear to be independent Austronesian loans, and one is a poor phonological match, while two are potentially viable, see Blench's comparisons and my commentary in Table 20.9.

**Table 20.9** Aslian-Acehnese lexical comparisons offered by Blench (2006)

| English | Aslian | Acehnese | Commentary |
|---|---|---|---|
| 'sand' | *aney* | *anoy* | < PAN *qənaj 'sand', loan into Aslian |
| 'rattan' | *awe* | *awe* | < PAN *quay 'rattan variety', loan into Aslian |
| 'finished' | *telas* | *teles* | < Malay *təlah* 'already' (cf. Proto-Malayic *laØas 'finished, used up', Adelaar 1992a: 94) |
| 'riverbank' | *terbis* | *tərbis* | Cf. Malay *tərbis* 'slipping down at the side (as earth after a landslip)' |
| 'sleepy' | *lebod* | *lebui* | main syllable rhymes do not agree |
| 'tame' | *lagi* | *raghoi* | the *l:r* correspondence is problematic, so may be from a third (unknown) source |
| 'very' | *tehet* | *tehat* | |

Thus there seems to be little evidence of a significant Aslian substrate in Acehnese; more likely some Acehnese loans have found their way into Northern Aslian due to trading contacts. Thurgood (1999: 23–4) suggests that there was a Cham or Acehnese presence in Kelantan on the peninsula based on various place names with the base *Cepa* (< Champa?), although he agrees that this "looks to have been quite late" so it is not clearly linked to an Austroasiatic contact.

On balance, it would appear that, while Acehnese shares various characteristics with mainland languages, these have emerged overwhelmingly within the etymologically Malayo-Polynesian vocabulary (including in Malay borrowings) and mostly after emigrating from Indo-China at an unknown date possibly well before the tenth century CE. An early shift to fixed final stress—which is shared with Proto-Chamic—was an important initial conditioning factor that set in train a long process of restructuring. Given that the outcomes of this shift included uniquely shared innovations with Chamic (such as pre-aspirated initial liquids), it likely predates a similar move to iambicity in various languages of Sumatra and West Borneo, including various vernacular Malayic languages.

## 20.5 Moken-Moklen

The languages of the Moken-Moklen group form three clusters of dialects which are spoken by sea-oriented communities (sometimes known as 'Sea Gypsies') living along the Myanmar and Thailand coasts of the Andaman Sea. For the sake of convenience, the languages of this group will simply be referred to as Moken here. Various descriptive works are available, including useful grammars and lexicons (e.g. Lewis 1960; Chantanakomes 1980; Makboon 1981; Swastham 1982; Naw Say Bay 1995; Larish 1999, 2005). It is evident from the descriptive and comparative studies that Moken languages have restructured towards a strikingly Mainland type in their phonology, although the lexicon remains overwhelmingly Malayo-Polynesian. Explaining this restructuring has been a source of disagreement among scholars.

The thesis by Larish (1999) includes an extensive comparative-historical analysis and commentary, and substantially informs much of the related discussion in the secondary literature (such as Pittayaporn 2005; Blust 2013a: 189). Larish confidently concludes that Moken restructured specifically due to close contact with Austroasiatic. By contrast, Pittayaporn argues that the main drivers of change within Moken have been internal, with general linguistic tendencies acting upon the Austronesian structures. While various Austroasiatic, Thai, and Burmese loanwords are apparent, specific indications of intensive borrowing or some sort of influential substrate are lacking.

### 20.5.1 Lexical borrowing

Overall, a critical examination of the available data suggests that there has been some lexical borrowing into Moken from Austroasiatic, and also quite recently from Thai and Burmese. The most extensive published set of lexical comparanda for Moken remains the 1199 page thesis of Larish (1999). Larish proposes a large number of Austroasiatic loans in his thesis, yet most of these comparisons provide poor phonological or semantic matches and must be discarded. Table 20.10 aggregates the fullest set of convincing loans I could extract from the thesis.

This is a meagre list of loans; a fuller examination of the published lexicons of Moken languages might reveal more possible borrowings, but any results are unlikely to overturn the general impression that lexical borrowing into Moken has been modest, undermining any strong claims of Austroasiatic or another language stratum being a significant factor in conditioning restructuring.

### 20.5.2 Phonological convergence

From a phonological viewpoint, it is striking how much Moken resembles mainland languages, especially Austroasiatic. Moken has developed a strictly iambic word template: the canonical word shape is disyllabic CVCV̀(:)(C), and monosyllabic forms are rare and mostly limited to function words. In Table 20.11 the segments of Moken are tabled according to the analysis of Pittayaporn (2005). The segmental inventory is immediately similar to what is found in Thai and many Austroasiatic languages, especially the multiple stop series, the length contrast among the vowels, and the presence of centring diphthongs.

Additionally, some scholars have analysed Moken varieties as having tense vs. lax contrasts in their vowel systems. For example, both Chantanakomes (1980) and Naw Say Bay (1995) analyse Rawai and Dung Moken respectively as having contrasts between tense and lax vowels, with tense nuclei tending to have a central on-glide. However, Pittayaporn (2005) analyses the data provided by Chantanakomes as indicating a three-height distinction without a robust register distinction.

The register distinction reported by Naw Say Bay seems robust based on her data, and she speculates that it is due to "Mon-Khmer (Old Mon?) influence." (1995: 205). Certainly Moken registers remain insufficiently investigated and historically unexplained, but they may not be very old. Larish projects the tense–lax distinction back to Proto-Moken-Moklen (PMM), reconstructing a tense–lax distinction for each of the long vowels, although not for the short vowels, which is typologically odd. While Larish argues that this reconstruction is reasonable in light of attested expansions of vowel systems in Chamic languages and their widespread occurrence in Austroasiatic languages, it is immediately clear that it cannot be older than the vowel length distinction itself, which is not a primitive feature in Malayo-Polynesian. Generally such kinds of phonation contrasts are historically quite late in Austroasiatic, correlating with the wave of devoicing of voiced stops spread over the region. The latter emerged in Mon and Khmer through the middle of the second millennium, and only became complete by the eighteenth century. This is well established by loanword phonology (e.g. Jenner 1976; Headley 1998). In light of this known linguistic history, it is difficult to see how ancient contact with Austroasiatic could be related to tense–lax distinctions.

**Table 20.10** Convincing Moken lexical borrowings from mainland languages extracted from Larish (1999)

| Language (Larish) | Form | English | Comment |
|---|---|---|---|
| Moken-BDC | *mək* | 'fog' | Cf. Thai *mɔ̀:k* 'fog' |
| Moken-KS | *ʔəda:* | 'duck' | Cf. Mon *ʔətɛ̤a* < Proto-Monic *(ʔa)da: |
| Moken-KS | *pɛ:t* | 'knife' | Cf. Pear *pe:t*, Old Khmer *kmɓiət* 'knife' |
| Moken-LWS | *po:t* | 'lung' | Cf. Thai *pɔ̀:t* 'lungs' |
| Moken-RW | *ɲam* | 'to eat' | Cf. Khmer *ɲam* 'to eat' (baby word) |
| Proto-MM | *ʔa:k | 'crow' | Widespread imitative form in AA |
| Proto-MM | *kəta:m | 'crab' | Cf. Malay *kətam* borrowed from AA |
| Proto-MM | *phəlɔ:k | 'brain' | Cf. Pear *prəlo:k̥* 'brain' (?< Khmer) |
| Proto-MM | *ɲi: | 'uncle' | Cf. Bahnar, Katu, Khasi *ɲi:* 'uncle' |
| Proto-MM | *chiplu: | 'betel leaf' | Cf. Proto-Mon *həplṳʔ |
| Proto-MM | *kala:ŋ | 'eagle; hawk' | Cf. Khmer *khlaeŋ* 'kite', Malay *həlaŋ* < AA |
| Proto-MM | *cicum | 'bird' | Cf. Mon *hacem* 'bird', also resembles the unrelated Nicobarese form, cf. Nancowry *ceco:n* 'bird' |
| Proto-MM | *mɯcɛ:m | 'to feed; raise' | Cf. Proto-Monic *[ɲ]cim 'to feed' |
| Proto-MM | *ci:/cəj | 'I; me' | Cf. Nancowry *cə~cɯə* 'I; me' |
| Proto-MM | *kamɔ(:)n | 'nephew' | Cf. Old Mon *kmøn* 'nephew' |
| Proto-MM | *pɪn | 'to be' | Cf. Thai *pen* 'to be' |
| Proto-MM | *pɔthaw | 'old people' | Cf. Thai *pù:tʰâw* 'old man' |
| Proto-MM | *kho:ŋ | 'things' | Cf. Thai *kʰɔ̌:ŋ* 'things' |
| Proto-MM | *kɯb(ə)lɔk | 'coconut shell' | Cf. Thai *kalò:k* 'coconut shell' |
| pre-Moken | *lawaʔ | 'gibbon' | Cf. Old Mon *lwaʔ* 'gibbon' |

**Table 20.11** Moken segmental inventory based on Pittayaporn (2005)

| | | | | | | | |
|---|---|---|---|---|---|---|---|
| p | t | c | k | (ʔ) | i, i: | | u, u: |
| pʰ | tʰ | cʰ | kʰ | | | ə | |
| b | d | ɟ | g | | ɛ, ɛ | a, a: | ɔ, ɔ: |
| m | n | ɲ | ŋ | | iə | | uə |
| | s | | | h | | | |
| w | l, r | j | | | | | |

Note: 1. The glottal stop ʔ is regarded as predictable by Pittayaporn.
2. /ə/ is restricted to unstressed pre-syllables.

Probably a limited long/short distinction in stressed syllable vowels is indicated for PMM. Larish speculates that this arose either by direct borrowing from Austroasiatic or inheritance from Proto-Moken-Moklen-Aceh-Chamic-Malayic, but both of these ideas are untenable. Pittayaporn (2005) demonstrates that the most robust length distinction arises from the historical Austronesian opposition between *a (> *a:) and *ə (> *a), with other cases arising variously from conditioned positional lengthening and some borrowing. The observation supports the claim that much of the mainland character of Moken is an emergent result of internal tendencies over which there is a veneer of Austroasiatic and other lexical borrowings of no great antiquity.

## 20.6 Malay

The history of mainland linguistic influence on Malay discussed here focuses on lexical borrowing as the most obvious form of contact influence, with special attention to apparent lexical signature of early Austroasiatic contact with Malay. Additionally, there is more recently Thai influence on Pattani Malay spoken in southern Thailand, although this is only touched upon briefly here.

### 20.6.1 Early Malay-Austroasiatic contact

Malay, in its various varieties as the standard languages of Malaysia and Indonesia, and numerous local varieties in insular Southeast Asia, is these days spoken by upwards of 300 million people as a first or second language. As an important national language, scholarly discussion of lexical borrowing has emphasized important lexifier languages in the context of religion and national development, particularly the contributions of Sanskrit, Arabic, Persian, Hindi, Tamil, Chinese, and various European languages (especially Dutch and English). This is reflected in, for example, Jones (2007) *Loan-words in Indonesian and Malay* and the study of Old Malay generally. Mahdi (2008: 322) in his review of Jones, points out that, "Mon-Khmer borrowings have been altogether neglected" in that volume, and one can say that this is indicative of a broader disinclination to discuss the topic among scholars.

Among historical linguists, particularly since Schmidt (1905), lexical similarities between Malay and Austroasiatic are occasionally mentioned, often in the context of a hypothetical Austric superphylum supposed to underlie both Austroasiatic and Austronesian. The Austric idea enjoyed some support into the 1970s (e.g. Shorto 1976), but was largely abandoned as the Taiwan Austronesian homeland hypothesis emerged, and progress in Proto-Austronesian reconstruction indicated increasing dissimilarity between the families rather than convergence (notwithstanding later studies such as Reid 1994b; Hayes 1992, 1997, 1999; and others). Shorto's *Mon-Khmer Comparative Dictionary*, although published in 2006, was compiled in the 1960s and 1970s, and includes some 279 proposed Austric etymologies, based on comparing Dempwolff's Proto-Austronesian to Austroasiatic.

The problem remains, however, that once the putative Austric comparisons are subjected to close scrutiny and the great bulk are rejected as unconvincing, there remains a stubborn core of words restricted to Malay (and some languages under Malay influence, although this is not explored further here) that lack Austronesian etymologies and are apparently borrowed from or via Austroasiatic, in many cases clearly via Khmer. Among these, animal terms are especially abundant, in addition to some traded goods, and even some body part terms. Some thirty of these items are listed in Table 20.12, with etymological commentary (Shorto 2006 reconstructions indicated with §), for the sake of the present discussion.

How are we to explain lexical similarities such as these? Animal terms such as *kətam* 'crab', *səmut* 'ant', *dəkan* 'bamboo rat' are particularly striking; the distributions of these and other Austroasiatic loans are so widespread that they strongly confirm their origins on the mainland. At the same time, the Malayic homeland is generally assumed to have been in Western Borneo around 3000BP (Adelaar 1992a), with subsequent migrations to Sumatra, the Malay Peninsula, and elsewhere. Some isoglosses and typological parallels between Bornean languages and Austroasiatic have been pointed to (Adelaar 1995b; Blench 2010c) with Blench (2010) in particular hypothesizing an Austroasiatic (AA) presence in Borneo. Ancient maritime movement of Austroasiatic speakers may have occurred, perhaps as mainlanders drafted into Malay(ic) mediated trade networks, but there is no clear evidence that Austroasiatic was established in Borneo, or elsewhere in insular Southeast Asia, east or south of the Malay Peninsula.

Perhaps a reasonable hypothesis is that as early sailors set out from Borneo, they established trading relations with Austroasiatic speakers of the Indo-Chinese mainland, perhaps in cooperation with the early Chams, hence some common loan vocabulary. Mahdi writes:

> [...] archaeological studies (Solheim 1980: 334) and other data (Mahdi 1994: 188–91, 1995: 162–5) suggest that Malay-speaking seafarers became involved in sea trade with China, India, and the Near East between 200BC and 200AD [2150 to 1750BP]. (Mahdi 2005: 183)

This is approximately the same period in which the early Indianized states of Indo-China were emerging, such as the pre-Angkorian Funan kingdom, which according to Chinese sources controlled not just the Mekong delta, but maritime trade along the Isthmus of Kra and much of the peninsula during the first half of the first millennium (Çoedès 1968; Vickery 2003). In such circumstances it seems likely that the early Malays encountered and formed close relations with the Funanese, before turning attentions to the peninsular and Sumatra, and more extensive trade networks of the kind mentioned by Mahdi. The Angkorian period (circa 1150BP onwards) saw the Khmers orient inland, moving their capital from the lower Mekong to the far side of Tonle Sap much further from the sea. They apparently did so in a

**Table 20.12** Malay lexical items with apparent Austroasiatic etymologies

| Gloss | Malay | Commentary |
|---|---|---|
| *Body parts* | | |
| neck | *taŋkok* | §17 *kɔ(:)k, cf. Riang Lang *kok*[1] 'neck' |
| palm, sole | *tapak* | §349 *tpa:k, cf. Sora *dapa:-n* 'step' |
| belly | *pərut* | §844 *ruəc, cf. Sre *prɔ:c* 'intestine' (also Acehnese, Cham) |
| wart | *kətuat* | §1009 *ktuəc, cf. Nyah Kur *kətuac 'wart' |
| *Animal terms* | | |
| ox | *ləmbu* | §119 *ln(b)(o)ʔ, cf. Kammu-Yuan *ləmpò* 'ox' |
| peacock | *mərak* | §416 *mraik(), cf. Old Mon *mrek* 'peacock' (also Javanese, Acehnese, Cham) |
| hawk | *lang, həlang* | §714 *la:ŋ, cf. 'khlaeŋ kite' (also Javanese, Acehnese, Cham) |
| starling | *cəmperliŋ* | §757 *rli:ŋ, cf. Khmer *krəlì:ŋ-krəlò:ŋ* 'starling' |
| ant | *səmut* | §873 *su(:)t 'to sting', cf. *srəmaoc* 'ant' (also Javanese, Acehnese, Cham) |
| bamboo rat | *dəkan* | §1129 *dkan, cf. Khasi *dkhan* 'hill-rat; mole' |
| crab | *kətam* | §1348 *kta:m, cf. Khmer *kda:m* 'crab' (also Iban, Acehnese, Cham) |
| rabbit | *tapai* | §1468 *bta:j, cf. Bahnar *təpa:j* 'hare' (also Cham) |
| squirrel | *tupai* | §1481 *(t)pu:j, cf. Nyah Kur *mpuj* 'mole, bamboo rat' |
| gnat | *kəmus* | §1496 *mu:js, cf. Khmer *muh* 'mosquito' |
| imperial pigeon | *pərgam* | §1319 *prgəm, cf. Mon *həkɜ̀m* 'imperial pigeon' |
| mouse deer | *napoh* | §1911 *pus, cf. Riang Lang *pos*[1] 'barking deer' |
| tusk | *taring* | §699 *draŋ, cf. Kharia *ɖɛ'rɛŋ* 'boar tusk' |
| *Plant terms* | | |
| sesame | *lənga* | §34 * lŋa:ʔ, cf. *ŋaʔ*[1] 'sesame' (> Javanese, Bugis, Tagalog, etc.) |
| ginger | *bonglai* | §216 *bnli(:ʔ), cf. Old Khmer *vanli* 'ginger' |
| millet | *səkoi* | §1447 *skuəj, cf. Kammu-Yuan *həŋkɔ:j* 'millet' (also Cham) |
| bran; chaff | *dədak* | §1313 *ska:mʔ, cf. Riang Lang *kham*[1] 'chaff; husks' (also Acehnese, Cham) |
| stump | *tuŋgal* | §1719 *dgə(:)l, cf. Bahnar *dəŋəl* 'stump' |
| cotton | *kapas* | §1915 *pka:s, cf. Khmer *krəpa:h* 'cotton' (via (?) Sanskrit *karpāsa*) |
| *Other items* | | |
| gold | *əmas* | §1873 *ʔa:s 'to shine', cf. Old Mon *jimās* 'shining (gold)' (also Acehnese *məjh*, Cham *muɯh*) |
| silver | *perak* | Old Khmer *prak* 'silver' |
| canoe | *bidok* | §336 *ɗu(:)k, cf. Khmer *tù:k* 'boat' |
| solid | *kəjap* | §1248 *gɟap, cf. *khcɔ̀əp* 'solid; enduring' (also Cham) |
| small hill | *tompok* | §350 *tpu:k 'heap', cf. Khmer *dəmbo:k* 'hillock; mound; anthill' |
| thick | *təbal* | §1768 *[t]ɓəl, cf. Kammu-Yuan *həmpul* 'thick' (note voicing conflict with PAN *kaS(e)pal) |

Note: the empty space between brackets indicates ambiguity about presence of a glottal stop, as no Vietnamese cognate is known.

deliberate strategy to distance themselves from the Austronesian world, and consequently the circumstances for close Khmer–Malay contact dramatically declined.

There may also have been some first millennium Malay contact with the Aslian languages of the peninsula, but there is little indication that this had impact upon Malay. The Aslians are historically interior dwellers rather than navigators or traders, and the strong presence of Malay loans in Aslian seems to be a predominantly recent phenomenon. Kruspe (2009) discusses some phonological indications that the early Austronesian loans into Aslian do not come from Malay, but some unknown other Austronesian language(s). Nonetheless the indications are not sufficient to suggest a specific contact history, and we are left with speculations.

### 20.6.2 Pattani Malay and Thai

Pattani Malay, known as Yawi or Jawi, is spoken mainly in the three most southerly Thai provinces by both ethnic Malays and many local Thais; additionally a closely related dialect is used in the neighbouring Malaysian state of Kelantan. The southern dialect of Thai, which is quite distinctive compared to the national standard, is reported to have a strong influence on Pattani Malay, particularly in respect of lexicon, reportedly to such an extent that it can hamper intelligibility with Kelantan Malay. There are various studies that examine this influence (e.g. Chaiyanara 1983; Yupho 1986; Saleh 1986; Umar 2010; Iamdanush and Pittayaporn 2014), and as yet Chaiyanara's thesis is apparently the only linguistic grammar of vernacular Pattani Malay. The thesis on English borrowing in Pattani Malay by Benjasmith (2016: 48) found a wide range of foreign influence on the language, "It is found that PM is filled with many foreign words from languages such as Mon, Khmer, Sanskrit, Arabic, English, Chinese, Portuguese, and Thai." although this was not discussed in an extensive or especially systematic manner.

Iamdanush and Pittayaporn (2014) suggest that Pattani Malay is converging structurally with Thai (and mainland languages generally), pointing to features such as the eight-member vowels inventory (compared to five or six in most Malay varieties), a shift to monosyllables, and a reduction in the use of derivational morphology. Their study focuses on the *waʔ* 'do' construction, *wi* 'give' construction and *waʔwi* causative construction, which appear to parallel the Thai *tham*$^{1}$ 'do', *haj*$^{3}$ 'give', and *tham*$^{1}$ *haj*$^{3}$ constructions in syntax and semantics, rather than following the typical Malay pattern. They also point out that, in classifier phrases in Pattani Malay, the numeral and classifier follow the noun as in Thai, and do not precede it as in standard Malay. It is clear that Pattani Malay speakers are calquing Thai word orders in their speech, not just code-switching, with Thai increasingly providing the matrix for Pattani Malay constructions.

The shift to monosyllables sits within a broader tendency to consolidate and simplify non-final syllables (including phrasal forms), one of the consequences being the emergence of geminate onsets in mono- and disyllabic words. For example *nna.yu* 'Malay' cf. Malay *məlayu*, *ddiɣi* 'to stand', cf. Malay *bərdiri*, and this can also apply to loans: *llɔpʰaʔ* < Thai *lo:ŋ pʰák* 'police station'. From the phonological perspective, it is apparent that Pattani Malay speakers are not modelling their speech after Thai phonotactics, but have independently developed a phonological template that superficially shares features with the Mainland Southeast Asian Linguistic Area.

## 20.7 Conclusion

The so-called mainland Austronesian languages—Chamic, Acehnese, Moken—do show remarkable typological similarities with the Southeast Asian Linguistic Area, but only the first of these groups—Chamic—has a significant presence on the mainland and can be shown to have restructured under the effects of massive lexical borrowing and metatypical convergence. By contrast, Acehnese and Moken, although both heavily restructured, remain Malayo-Polynesian lexically, having taken in very few actual lexical borrowings from mainland languages, and much of their restructuring can be explained as long term outcomes of an early shift to final stress, which while probably related to early mainland contacts, although the timing and circumstances of this early contact are not known. Malay shows evidence of lexical borrowing from Austroasiatic, and this may partly extend back to a common Malayo-Chamic period when the protolanguage or early forms of Malay and Chamic were integrated into a trade network that spanned the South China Sea in the first millennium BCE.

Looking forward, several potentially fruitful lines of research present themselves: (i) toponym analysis—a thorough survey and analysis of place names, in insular regions suspected of mainland influence, may shed light on the (pre)historic linguistics landscape. However, any such studies need to be solidly grounded in knowledge of local linguistic histories and philological methods; (ii) better documentation of language diversity: comparative studies are generally based on the best documented lects, and necessarily neglect lesser-known language varieties that may retain archaisms in structure or lexicon. Thus, better data—or better utilization of existing data—for lesser-known Acehnese, Malayic, and other languages should significantly enrich investigations of historical language contact; (iii) more diachronic typological comparison: analyses that link the qualitative identification of shared features with the origins of the specific structures that bear them should yield more grounded results. Typological comparisons that focus on aggregating similarly labelled features without etymological considerations risk placing undue reliance on superficial parallels and may confuse emergence with retention in language history. Such lines of research arguably hold real prospects of revealing historical linguistic connections between mainland and insular Southeast Asia alongside the constantly emerging advances in other fields such as archaeology and genetics.

CHAPTER 21

# Language contact in Africa

Alexander Adelaar

## 21.1 Introduction

This chapter is about linguistic contact between Austronesian and Bantu languages. Languages involved on the Austronesian side are Malagasy and, to a much lesser extent, Malay. On the Bantu side, the languages that have played a role in this contact are mainly Comorian languages and Swahili (see Map 21.1), and, it seems, an older form of Bantu which cannot be more precisely identified at this stage.

Contacts between the Austronesian world and Africa are much older than the settlement history of Madagascar. The introduction of the banana, water yam, and taro testify to this, as do the introductions of the outrigger canoe and chickens and the spread of elephantiasis (cf. Blench 2010a). These early contacts, which are largely shrouded in mystery, must have started around 2300BP (ibidem). They have left no detectable linguistic traces, and for some transfers it is not always certain that Austronesian speakers were directly involved.

Malagasy is a Southeast Barito (SEB) language, and its original homeland is in the southern (Indonesian) part of Borneo Island. Other SEB languages are Ma'anyan, Dusun Witu, Bayan, Dusun Malang, and Samihim. They are spoken in the central, south, and east Kalimantan provinces of Indonesia which are located on Borneo Island. Most SEB speakers live in central Kalimantan along the eastern shores of the Barito River (see also Smith, this volume, Chapter 8; and Kroeger and Smith, this volume, Chapter 27).

The time of the migrations of speakers of an early form of Malagasy from Borneo to East Africa is estimated at the seventh century CE and the subsequent settlement of Madagascar at the eighth century CE. It was in this period that Malagasy must have acquired a Bantu substrate. Afterwards, cultural and trade contacts between Africa and Island Southeast Asia (ISEA) continued until shortly after the arrival of the Portuguese in the Indian Ocean in the sixteenth century CE.

This chapter focuses on a period starting with the migration (seventh century CE) until the end of precolonial contacts with ISEA (sixteenth century CE), as there is no linguistic evidence of an Austronesian presence in Africa in times previous to that.

The chapter is organized as follows. §21.2 discusses some of the ways Malagasy migration history has been approached, including suggestions of multiple migrations and the presence of an earlier population in Madagascar. §21.3 explains the need to distinguish two Malagasy protolanguages, one representing the language as it was just before the migrations, and the other representing it after it had acquired a Bantu substratum. §21.4 is an account of the actual Bantu linguistic influence on Malagasy, including the presence of a Bantu substratum and its effects on the lexicon, phonology, and grammar. §21.5 describes the influence of Malagasy and Malay on Bantu languages. Some concluding remarks are presented in §21.6.

Unless otherwise indicated, lexicographical and grammatical sources used in this chapter are as follows: Shindzuani—Ahmed-Chamanga (1997, 1992); Malagasy—Beaujard (1998); Dahl (1951); Malay—Wilkinson (1959); Shimaore—Blanchy (1996); Shingazidja—Lafon (1991); PMP—Blust and Trussel (2020); Proto-Bantu, Proto-Northeast Bantu, Sabaki—Nurse and Hinnebusch (1993); Dahl (1988); Proto-Southeast Barito (PSEB)—Hudson (1967); Adelaar (nd); Swahili—Sacleux (1939).

## 21.2 Migration history: Interpretations and issues

As already stated, the early Malagasy language hails from the East Barito region in southern Borneo. However, at the time of the migrations it had already undergone much influence from other parts of Indonesia: today, Malagasy has a high proportion of Malay loanwords, both from the Malay of Banjarmasin in southern Borneo and from a variety of Sumatran Malay, as well as loanwords from Javanese and from a language of South Sulawesi that cannot be further identified. These languages have also had a morphological influence on Malagasy. It is likely that Malays organized the voyage(s) to East Africa rather than the SEB speakers from southern

Alexander Adelaar, *Language contact in Africa.* In: *The Oxford Guide to the Malayo-Polynesian Languages of Southeast Asia.* Edited by: Alexander Adelaar and Antoinette Schapper, Oxford University Press. © Alexander Adelaar (2024). DOI: 10.1093/oso/9780198807353.003.0021

Borneo, who were likely transported as passengers or crew (Adelaar 2016b).

Meanwhile, human genetics has shown that people across Madagascar share ISEA as well as East African genes in both their Y-chromosomes (inherited from father to son) and mitochondrial DNA (inherited from the mother), although there is a preponderance of SEA genes in their mitochondrial DNA (Kusuma Pradiptajati 2017; see also Ricaut, Brucato, and Cox, this volume, §5.5.4). It has also shown that the Asian DNA of the current Malagasy population has an important (but regionally not very specific) eastern Indonesian mitochondrial DNA component, indicating that many eastern Indonesian women must have been among the early migrants.

Several scenarios have been proposed for the migration route followed by the early Malagasy.

Dahl (1951) thought that they migrated from Borneo directly to Madagascar, and that this island was already settled by speakers of an early form of the kind of Bantu spoken in the Comoros. His idea has largely been abandoned. (The Comoros form a string of islands between northwest Madagascar and the coast of Mozambique. Its current population speaks several very closely related Bantu languages which belong to the Sabaki subgroup, a subdivision of Northeast Coast Bantu which also includes Swahili).

Murdock (1959) and Deschamps (1960) concluded that the SEB speakers in question first travelled to East Africa, where they mixed with local Bantu language speakers. Afterwards, this new, ethnically mixed community crossed over to Madagascar. An 'out-of-Africa' scenario is also supported by Adelaar (2016a), who argues on the basis of linguistic homogeneity, including a Bantu substratum shared in all Malagasy dialects, that the basis for modern Malagasy must have been laid in a mixed Bantu–SEB environment outside Madagascar. It is further supported by Blench (2007) on the basis of evidence from plants and animals that have Bantu names despite also existing in South Borneo (see the terms for 'chicken' and 'banana' in §21.4.2), and based on typology of musical instruments.

Simon (2006) proposes a settlement of Madagascar by SEB speakers from the Comoros rather than from the African mainland. Beaujard (2012: 565) also believes that SEB speakers sailed directly from ISEA to the Comoros and North Madagascar, although they may have had contacts with Bantu speakers on the African mainland before their arrival in Madagascar. Crowther et al. (2016), on the basis of archaeological investigations, discovered that the rice, mung beans, and cotton found in Madagascar and the Comoros have a common source in Southeast Asia and must have been introduced in the eighth century CE at the earliest. They are part of an agricultural zone which is different from the one predominating in East Africa, although it marginally includes some Swahili islands (such as Pemba) along the East African coast.

Adelaar (2016a) observes that while the Comoros served as a springboard for SEB speakers to migrate to Madagascar, settlement in either of these regions is unlikely to have been the initial purpose of their travels. The African mainland must have been more attractive to them because of what it had to offer in terms of trade commodities. They may have used the Comoros islands, which were unoccupied prior to their arrival (Crowther et al. 2016), as a safe haven from which to engage in trade with the African mainland.

The above scenarios are not mutually exclusive and may be combined in an integrated migration history.

The idea of multiple migration waves has been a persistent motif in theorizing about the settlement history of Madagascar. It concerns both multiple waves from ISEA (usually involving later groups who were not SEB speakers, e.g. Deschamps [1960]; Beaujard [2012]) and separate waves of SEB and Bantu speakers (Beaujard 2012). See Adelaar (2016b) for a critical evaluation of this scenario.

Finally, the question of whether Madagascar had a population before the arrival of SEB speakers remains unresolved to date (see Bellwood and Huong, this volume, §6.11). This is a question that is unlikely to be solved based on linguistics (Adelaar 2016a). Blench (2010b) analysed lexical evidence from Beosy and Mikea (spoken by hunter-gatherers in Madagascar) and from Vezo (the dialect of a fishing community on Madagascar's southwest coast) in an attempt to demonstrate that these dialects have a pre-Bantu and pre-Austronesian substratum. However, it is basically impossible to relate the vocabulary that he highlights to any identifiable language.

## 21.3 Malagasy before and after the migrations: Two different historiolects

At the time of the migration, Malagasy must have undergone some rapid and far-reaching structural change. In agreement with Simon (2006), two protolanguages are distinguished. The language of the Asian ancestors of the Malagasy just prior to their migration to eastern Africa is referred to as 'Proto-Malagasy$_1$' (PMLG$_1$). Phonologically, it may not have been very different from the SEB languages today, although there are clear indications that it had already become a dialect or sociolect in its own right (Adelaar 2017). However, it must have been quite different from what it would become after its speakers had reached East Africa and had integrated Bantu speakers into their speech community, a development which caused a Bantu substratum in Malagasy. Important phonological features of the substratum from those Bantu speakers are loss of *h and lenition of *k and *p and of clusters involving *k. These are discussed in §21.4.5. This post-migratory stage, which will be referred to as 'Proto-Malagasy$_2$' (PMLG$_2$), must have been the hypothetical stock language of modern Malagasy dialects.

## 21.4 Bantu influence on Malagasy

### 21.4.1 The languages involved

Of the languages in Africa, only Bantu languages have left identifiable traces in Malagasy. Cushitic (Afroasiatic) languages were formerly more widespread in East Africa than they are today. It is also possible that the Khoisan languages once extended all the way to Africa's northeast coast (Güldemann 1999). Nevertheless, although some Bantu loanwords in Malagasy can ultimately be traced back to other African language families, including Cushitic, there seem to be no direct loanwords from any family other than the Eastern Bantu languages.

Bantu influence betrays multiple borrowing events which differ in terms of source and period of borrowing (Dahl 1988; Simon 2006; Adelaar 2007b, 2009a, 2009b, 2016a), although many borrowed elements do not signal that information, and there is some doubt about lexical influence from non-Sabaki languages (Nurse 1988). Simon (2006: 151–2) distinguishes as many as nine Sabaki source languages from different periods and regions that may have influenced Malagasy. This may be an over-differentiation and needs further testing, but at the very least, it underscores Dahl's observation that there were distinct periods of Bantu–Malagasy contact and that the earliest of these concerned a Bantu language (or several Bantu languages) other than Swahili or Comorian.

Bantu languages that have exerted influence on Malagasy belong to four categories.

Dahl (1988) identified some old Bantu words with no satisfactory counterpart in either Swahili or Comorian. They included domestic animal names such as *ùndri*[1] 'sheep' and *ùsi* 'goat'. Dahl argued that some of these words, such as *ùndri*,[2] bear more similarity with cognates found in Bantu languages spoken away from the East African coast (and towards Lake Victoria).

Swahili loanwords may be seen as evidence of contacts between Madagascar and Swahili-speaking coastal areas. However, Swahili was also a literary language and an official court language in the Comoros in the nineteenth century (Nurse and Hinnebusch 1993:18: 18), leaving open the possibility that some Swahili influence was exercized via these islands and was therefore a relatively local affair. Swahili is also generally believed to be a vehicular language for Arabic influence in Madagascar's northwest. Some Swahili was previously spoken on Nosy Be Island on Madagascar's

[1] Foreign words in this chapter are spelled as in their sources. However, velar nasal is written as *ŋ*, and schwa as *ə*. Moreover, in Malagasy words, stress is indicated, 'o' is written as *u*, 'y' as *i*, and whispered final 'a' as *ă*.

[2] He also mentioned *akùndru* 'sweet banana', but according to Rossel (1998: 121), this form also has cognates in Sabaki Bantu languages, including Shingazidja in the Comoros. In these languages, the word has the primary meaning 'red', but it is also the name of a ripe *musa* (banana).

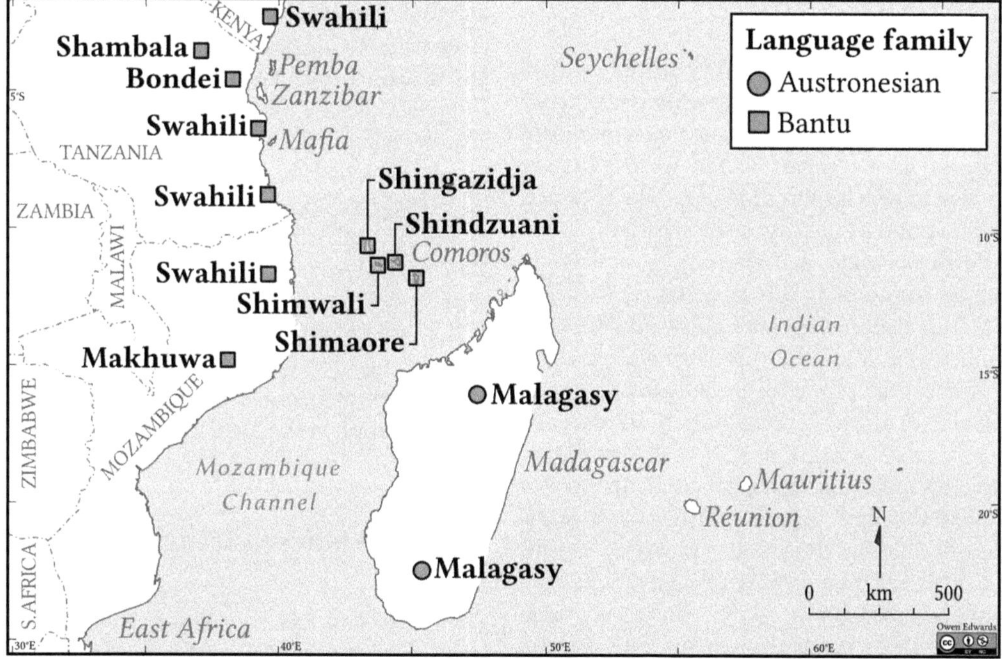


**Map 21.1** Languages in Madagascar, Comoros, and African East Coast referred to in this chapter.

northwest coast, but is now dormant or about to become dormant.

The phonological histories of the Comorian languages (Shingazidja, Shindzuani, Shimaore, and Shimwali, see Map 21.1) are intimately related to that of Malagasy. While the pathways of phonological change in Comorian and in Malagasy were not the same, the changes themselves had some converging effect on the phonologies of these languages. These phonological changes, some of which are atypical in their respective language families, include the tendency to spirantize *y and *w, the fricativization of *p and *k, the change from an SEB (loan) *d and East Bantu *t to a retroflex affricate *tr*, the development of *-ndr-* in Comorian, and widespread vowel paragoge in Malagasy. Comorian languages and Malagasy have borrowed much vocabulary from one another. In Mayotte, where Shimaore is the majority language, a third of the population speaks local dialects of Malagasy (Gueunier 1986; Serva and Pasquini 2021).

A fourth Bantu language that has played a role in Madagascar is Makhuwa (see Map 21.1), the mother tongue of many enslaved people who were brought to Madagascar from Mozambique. This language also became a lingua franca and a mother tongue of other enslaved people from mainland Africa. It mainly left traces in regional Malagasy (Gueunier 2003).

### 21.4.2 Bantu lexical influence from Swahili and Comorian languages

The list of possible cognates in Table 21.1 (based on Dahl 1988) is neither exhaustive nor definitive in its assessments. It reflects the preliminary level of analysis that Bantu loanwords in Malagasy have received so far. Word pairs are grouped according to which source language seems to best match the structure of the Malagasy counterparts.

Note that north Malagasy dialects have several Bantu loanwords that do not occur in Official Malagasy (which is based on the Merina dialect, see Howe, this volume, §40.1): compare Tsimihety *antsùva*, (other northern dialects) *zùva* 'sun', and Tankarana *tsiùta* 'six' with *jua* and *sita* (ultimately from Arabic *sittah* 'six'), which occur in both Swahili and Comorian. Compare also *ndzìa* 'path; road' in the list above.

Bantu lexical borrowing is conspicuous in names for plants and (domestic and other) animals, as in *ùmbi* 'cow', *ùndri* 'sheep', *ambùa* 'dog', *akùhu* 'chicken', *ampàha* 'wild cat', and in terms related to rice cultivation, such as *akùfa* 'chaff' (< Proto-Bantu *-kup- 'shake off', Dahl 1988: 102).[3] It sometimes created synonyms with original MPSEA names, for example, *màmba* vs. *vuài* (< Malay *buaya*) 'crocodile'; *akùndru* vs. *ùntsi* (< South Sulawesi *unti* < PMP *punti) 'banana'. The contact situation also caused various MPSEA terms to become semantically unstable. For instance, Ma'anyan, Banjar Malay *lambu* 'cattle' has generally become Malagasy *làmbu* 'pig', and PMP *pajey 'paddy' has become *fàri* 'sugarcane'; however, the original meanings of 'cattle' and 'rice' still turn up in regional Malagasy or in set environments and expressions, as in Tandroy Malagasy *lambuhàmba* 'twin cattle' (*hàmba* 'twin(s); similar'), or Merina Malagasy *kifarifàri* 'rice-like weeds' (for *ki-* see §21.4.3). In other semantic fields (including grammatical function words), early Bantu lexical influence is limited. It should also be distinguished from the considerable number of more recent Bantu loanwords, which are often traceable to Swahili or the Comorian languages Shimaore, Shingazidja, and Shindzuani, and which entered Malagasy after it had already diverged into various dialects.

### 21.4.3 Bantu morphological influence

Bantu prefixes appear non-systematically in individual lexical items. It is often unclear whether they are the result of the Bantu substrate or due to recent Swahili and Comorian influence.

The future tense markers *hu*, *h-* are discussed more extensively in §21.4.6b.

The prefixes *ki-* and (less frequently) *tsi-* form inanimate nouns. Neither is productive, although they must have been at some stage as they occur with *tràŋu* 'house' which derives from Malay *daŋaw* 'field hut' (Adelaar 2010b: 166–7). Examples are Sakalava *kitràŋu*, Merina *kitranu~trànu*, also *tsitranu~trànu* 'miniature house', *kiràru* 'shoe(s)', Sakalava *kilùluke* 'butterfly' (related to Merina *lùlu* 'ghost') (< Swahili *kilulu* 'butterfly'), *kifàfa* 'broom' (cf. *fàfa* 'sweeping'), *kilalàu* 'toy' (*lalàu* 'playing').

*mu-* is another nominalizer; it is not productive, and instances are few: *musàvi* 'witchcraft', *musàri* 'famine', *mulùlu* 'rice-straw'.

*va-* marks plural in nouns with human reference. It occurs with various roots but is no longer productive (if it ever was), for example, *vahùakă* 'the people; citizens', *vazìmba* 'original population in the highlands', *vahìni* 'stranger; foreigner; guest'.

### 21.4.4 A Bantu substratum in $PMLG_2$

Thomason and Kaufman (1988) consider a substratum a form of 'shift-induced interference'; it is due to imperfect

[3] Dahl also gives *sa-hàfa* 'winnowing pan', which he traces to Proto-Bantu *-kapa 'to spill moving to and fro' (Dahl 1988: 109). However, the first syllable *sa/-* is problematic. Dahl explains it as an Austronesian prefix which is no longer productive in Malagasy, but this leaves its meaning unexplained and it does not account for the fact that *s regularly became Malagasy Ø in inherited vocabulary.

**Table 21.1** Bantu lexical influence from Swahili and Comorian languages

| Malagasy/English | Swahili | Shimaore | Shingazidja | Shindzuani |
|---|---|---|---|---|
| Comorian seems to be the source: | | | | |
| *akànga* 'guinea fowl' | *kanga* | *kanga* | *ŋkanga* | *ŋkanga* |
| *ampundra* 'donkey' | *punda* | *pundra* | *mpundra* | *mpundra* |
| *akuhu* 'chicken' | *kuku* | *kuhu* | *ŋkuhu* | *ŋkuhu* |
| *ampàha* '(wild) cat' | *paka* | *paha* | *paha* | *mpaha* |
| *papàngu* 'vulture (sp.)' | *pungu* | *papangu* | - | — |
| *làsa*, 'leave; abandon' | *acha* | *-latsa* 'to lose; throw away' | *-latsa* 'to lose; throw away' | *latsa* 'to lose; throw away' |
| An older form of Comorian may be the source: | | | | |
| *kiràru* 'shoe; sandal' | *kiatu* | — | - | *shilarú* |
| *kiànja* 'open place' | *kiwanja* | — | *shandza* | - |
| Swahili (or an older form of Comorian?) seems to be the source: | | | | |
| *màmba* 'crocodile' | *mamba* | (*mamba* 'scale') | (*mamba* 'scale') | (*mamba* 'scale') |
| *musàvi* ('witchcraft') | *mchawi* 'witch' | *mutsayi* | - | *mchwai* 'witch' |
| *kilèma* 'deformity' | *kilema* | — | - | - |
| *vahìni* 'strangers; guests' | *wageni* | *wadjeni* | *wadjeni* | *wadjeni* |
| *kùnguna* 'bedbug' | *kunguni* | *kunguni* | *ŋkunguni* | *ŋkunguni* |
| Both Comorian and Swahili could be the source: | | | | |
| *ndzìa** 'path; road' | *njia* | *ndzia* | *ndzia* | *ndzia* |
| *ambùa* 'dog' | *mbwa* | *mbwa* | *mbwa* | *mbwa* |
| Neither Comorian nor Swahili are an obvious immediate source: | | | | |
| *ùsi* 'goat' | *mbuzi* | *mubuzi* | *mbuzi* | *mbuzi* |
| *ùndri, aŋùndri*† 'sheep' | — | — | *gondzi* | *gondzi* |
| *akùndru* 'banana' | - | — | *zinkudu* | - |
| *tungùlu* 'onion' | *kitunguu* | *shirungu* | *itrungu baswara* | *shirungu, shurungu* |

* A Northwest Malagasy word (Dahl 1988: 100).
† A Sakalava form (Dahl 1988: 100). Note South Swahili *ng'undi* [ŋundi] as a possible source of this word (Walsh p.c.).

target language learning and affects phonology and syntax more than lexicon. This characterization fits the development of Malagasy, which appears to have such a substratum from a Bantu language, as will be demonstrated below. (Recall that only part of the lexical borrowing discussed so far happened early enough to be substratum vocabulary). Some Bantu speakers must have shifted to $PMLG_1$, a language which apparently had more prestige than their own. In the process, they must have learned it imperfectly, affecting the structure of their version of $PMLG_1$. When some effects of this imperfect L2 learning were adopted by mainstream speakers, they eventually ended up in the language of all Malagasy speakers, and $PMLG_2$ gradually evolved. According to Thomason and Kaufman, substrata affect languages very differently from borrowing, and the presence of a substratum often co-occurs with low incidence of borrowing rather than high. In the Malagasy case, lexical borrowing from Bantu languages in early times was present but restricted. Although we see many Bantu loanwords in Malagasy today, a large number of them are attributable to recent (post PMLG$_2$) borrowing. Their sources (Swahili, Comorian languages) can often be identified, and in contrast to earlier Bantu loanwords, they are spread unevenly among the modern dialects.

The impact of a Bantu substratum is shown in phonology, some early loanwords, and morphosyntax.

### 21.4.5 Bantu substratum effects on phonology

Phonological changes from PMLG$_1$ to PMLG$_2$ involve lenition and loss of the consonants shown below. The changes also affected early Bantu loanwords. The first three were sequentially dependent, that is, *h had become Ø before *k and *g became h, and *k had become h before *kk, *ŋk, *ʔk became k:

| PMLG1 | | PMLG2 |
|---|---|---|
| *h | > | Ø |
| initial or intervocalic *k, *g | > | *h |
| final *k, *k with prenasalization (or other forms of fortition) | > | *k |
| initial or intervocalic *p | > | *f |

Examples: in MPSEA vocabulary: PSEB *huŋey 'river' > *ùni*; PSEB *aku 'I' > *àhu*; ML *gasiŋ* 'toll' > *hàsină*; Malay *taŋkap* 'gripping; clasping; capture (esp. in the hand)' > PMLG2 *takaT 'reached; understood; perceived' > *tàkatră*; *si *kita + *kam 'we (INCL)' > (with regular metathesis) *si *tik(V) + *kam > *hi *tikkaN > *itsìka* (Adelaar and Kikusawa 2014: 507); PMP, PSEB *epat 'four' > *èfatră.*

In Bantu vocabulary: Proto-East-Bantu *-kup- 'shake off' > MRN *hùfa* 'shake; winnow'; Proto-Bantu *-pû 'stomach' > Malagasy *vava-fù* 'pit of the stomach' (MLG *vàva* 'mouth' < PMP *baqbaq); Proto-Bantu *Wa- 'plural marker' + Common Bantu *-gènì 'stranger' > *vahìni* 'stranger(s); guest(s)'; Proto-Sabaki *-nkaŋga 'guinea-fowl > Malagasy *akàŋga*; Proto-Sabaki *nkunguni 'bedbug' > Malagasy *kuŋgùna*; Proto-Sabaki *-nkundru 'banana' > *akùndru.*

Other phonological changes from SEB to modern Malagasy dialects happened only after PMLG$_2$ had begun to diverge into the present-day Malagasy dialects. Typical changes such as *w > *v*, *y > *z*, final *T > *-tr* and *-ts*, and the addition of paragogic vowels, had not yet taken place. They still have not taken their full course in all the dialects, except for *w > *v* (although in Houtman's (1603) wordlist *w is still written as both 'w' and 'v').

### 21.4.6 Substratum effects on grammar

*a. Effects on the deictic system.* Malagasy has a deictic pronoun *ao* referring to any enclosed space (not occupied by the speaker). While absent in SEB languages (and generally atypical for MPSEA languages), this deictic notion is also present in Sabaki languages (see Howe, this volume, §40.3.3, for an illustration).

*b. The development of morphological tense.* In present tense, verbs are not marked, and the AV verb form has kept the inherited *maN- and *mi- prefixes. However, they have been re-analysed as sequences of a tense prefix (*m-*, *n-*, *h-*) and an AV prefix (*aN-*, *i-*). In present tense, derived verbs are marked with *m-* or *Ø-*, in past tense, with *n-* or *nu-*, and in future tense, with *h-* or *hu*. See the AV verbs in (1) and the UV verb in (2):

(1) *m-angàlatră Paùli / n-angàlatră Paùli / h-angàlatră Paùli* 'Paul steals/stole/will steal'
(*angàlatră* -> *aN-* + *hàlatră*
*m-i-àkatră àhu / n-i-àkatră àhu / h-i-àkatră àhu*
'I lift/lifted/will lift'

(2) *Ø-umènă àzi ni vùla* (give-PASS 3SG.OBL ART money)
'the money is given to him'
(*umèna* -> [ùme + -inà]
*n-umènă àzi ni vùla* (n-ume-nă 'PST-give-PASS) 'the money was given to him'
*h-umènă àzi ni vùla* (h-ume-nă 'FUT-give-PASS) 'the money will be given to him'

Most root verbs only mark future tense:

(3) *tùnga izàu ìzi* (arrive now 3SG) 'she's arriving now'
*tùnga umàli ìzi* (arrive yesterday 3SG) 'she arrived yesterday'
*hu tùnga rahampìtsu ìzi* (FUT arrive tomorrow 3SG)
'she'll arrive tomorrow'

(Past tense is also expressed by the non-Agent voice marker *<in>* in southern and western dialects, see Howe, this volume, §40.4.2).

Dahl (1988: 123–4, 1954: 355–60) traced the development of this three-way tense distinction to Bantu influence.

He also explained that in Sabaki Bantu languages, verbs combine a future tense marker *-ta- with an infinitive marker *-ku-. When Malagasy adopted this future tense there was no need for the combination. However, in an attempt to rationalize this complex marking *-ta- was dropped whereas *-ku- was kept, becoming the default future tense marker *hu*. It became further reduced to a prefix *h-* when occurring before the AV prefix *aN-* or before verbs with no prefix and starting with a vowel.

*c. A contrast between reciprocal causative and causative reciprocal derivations.* The causative marker *amp-* and the reciprocal marker *if-* occur after tense prefixes. Both derive from SEB and are cognates of *ampi-* and *ip-* respectively in Ma'anyan (Dahl 1951: 171–5).

Examples of causative verbs:

(4)

| | | |
|---|---|---|
| *tàhutră* 'fear' | *ma-tàhutră* 'to be afraid' | *m-amp-a-tàhutră* 'to inspire fear' |
| *ànatră* 'instruction' | *mi-ànatră* 'to learn' | *m-amp-i-ànatră* 'to teach' |
| *tùhi* 'what is added' | *mi-tùhi* 'to be added; to continue' | *m-amp-i-tùhi* 'to link up' |

Examples of reciprocal verbs:

(5)

| | | |
|---|---|---|
| *àtrikă* 'face; front' | *man-àtrikă* 'to be present; assist' | *m-if-an-àtrikă* 'to confront each other' |
| *vàli* 'answer' | *mamàli* 'to answer' | *m-if-amàli* 'to answer each other; to argue' |

A causative and reciprocal affix may combine to form a causative reciprocal, that is, a causative that has a reciprocal derivation in its scope (e.g. 'they cause them to eat each other'), as in the following examples:

(6)

| | |
|---|---|
| *m-if-an-atrikă* 'to confront one another' | *m-amp-if-an-àtrikă* 'set people up against each other' |
| *m-if-an-àrakă* 'to agree' | *m-amp-if-an-àrakă* 'to make agree' |
| *m-if-amàli* 'to answer each other; argue' | *m-amp-if-amàli* 'to make answer to each other; cause to argue' |

Interestingly, they can also be combined to form a reciprocal causative, that is, a reciprocal that has a causative derivation in its scope (e.g. 'they caused each other to eat'). Examples:

(7)

| | |
|---|---|
| *m-amp-a-tàhutră* 'to inspire fear' | *m-if-amp-a-tàhutră* 'to scare each other' |
| *m-amp-i-ànatră* 'to teach' | *m-if-amp-i-ànatră* 'to teach each other' |
| *m-amp-i-tùhi* 'to link up' | *m-if-amp-i-tùhi* 'to link up with one another' |

The opposition between causative reciprocals and reciprocal causatives is unusual in Austronesian languages (although it marginally occurs in Makasar, Jukes (2020: 294–5, 323–4)). It does, however, occur relatively frequently in Bantu languages (Hyman 2002). That Malagasy causative and reciprocal affixes can have one another in their scope depending on how they are ordered is a typologically highly marked situation. The fact that it is also found in various Bantu languages but almost never in the Austronesian context suggests a Bantu source for this phenomenon.

*d. Bantu substrate influence on the development of the circumstantial voice?* In the following discussion PMP is taken as a historical reference point rather than PSEB, as the PMP voice system is well established, whereas the grammar of PSEB remains unstudied. From a formal perspective, the Malagasy voice system is very conservative, having retained reflexes of all original PMP voice affixes in their non-past form. Blust (2013a: 69–70) and Dahl (1976: 118) considered it a textbook example of a PMP core grammar feature that remained well preserved in the Austronesian periphery. This preservation is the more remarkable given that other SEB languages have lost almost all traces of it and have adopted a more Malay-like morphosyntax. In contrast, Malagasy is considered to be a typical 'Philippine-type' language. Compare the following three historical stages shown in Table 21.2:

**Table 21.2** Historical adaptations in the Malagasy voice system

| | Proto-Austronesian | $PMLG_1/PMLG_2$ | (Merina) Malagasy |
|---|---|---|---|
| Voice: | Non-past | Present | Present |
| Agent Voice | *<um>, | *<um>, | (unproductive) *<um>* |
| | *maN-, *maR- | *maN-, *mi- | *m-aN-, m-i-* |
| Undergoer Voice | *-ən | *-en† | *-ină* |
| Locative Voice | *-an | *-an | *-ană* |
| Theme Voice | *i- | *i- | *a-*†† |
| Circumstantial Voice | — | *aN- -an, *i- -an | *aN- -ană. i- -ană* |

† Note that in Merina Malagasy, *ə in last syllables before the paragogic vowel is realized as *i*. However, western and southern Malagasy dialects have maintained *e* in this position.

†† In most Malagasy dialects, antepenultimate vowels became *a* except in Tandroy Malagasy (in southern Madagascar), which has maintained *i-* (alongside *a-*) as a Theme Voice (or Instrument Voice) marker.

However, this formal similarity belies the fact that the Malagasy system has been undergoing some far-reaching systemic changes. Keenan (1976); Paul (2000a); Pearson (2001) and others report that (i) *-ină* and *-ană* are in an advanced stage of merging as goal voice markers, (ii) the Intermediary Theme voice marker (*a-*) (used for displaced theme and instrument subjects) has a tendency to be replaced by the CIRCV, and (iii) in general, verbs tend to take only one of the non-agent voice forms. Himmelmann (2005a: 113) does not consider Malagasy to be a Philippine-type language as it lacks non-local phrase marking clitics for nominal expressions as well as pronominal second position clitics (see Kroeger and Riesberg, this volume, §47.4.1.4, for a summary of the literature).

So it appears that the traditional PMP non-agent voice categories tend to lose their mutual distinctions and to become allomorphs. A main question now becomes how the CIRCV came into being, and why. The CIRCV circumfix consists of a combination of an agent voice prefix without *m-* and a Locative Voice suffix, for example, *manùratră* 'to write' (AV) gives *anuràtană* (CIRCV), misàutră 'to thank' gives *isaùrană*, *mahafàly* 'to make happy' gives *ahafalìană*, etc. (See Howe, this volume, §40.4.2 for further discussion). CIRCV constructions can raise a wide variety of noun phrases to subject position, which not only includes goal, location, instrument, etc. but also time, manner, reason, comitative, and various other phrases. It would be tempting to explain the emergence of this category in Malagasy as a form of repair, as it is able to raise all sorts of phrases that cannot, or can no longer, be handled by the historical voices; as such, it would compensate for the semantic bleaching of *a-*, *-ină*, and *-ană*. However, that explanation makes little sense because formally there is no reason for a new category: why create a new voice affix when all old voice affixes are still formally intact? Another explanation is that its emergence was due to contact with Bantu languages, or at least, was triggered by it. These languages also have a 'circumstantial' category which is semantically similar to the CIRCV in Malagasy, although it is not expressed through a voice marker but an applicative (early Bantu *-ɪl-), which raises the non-core arguments of beneficiary, location (including time, cause, reason), and instrument to object position (Schadeberg 2003: 74). In other words, whereas Malagasy has a *circumstantial voice* which promotes a whole range of arguments to subject, Bantu languages have a *circumstantial applicative* promoting a similarly large range of arguments to object. Furthermore, there is also some similarity in the way both categories came into being: the CIRCV in Malagasy is a circumfix built on a locative affix *-ană*; and the Bantu circumstantial applicative *-ɪl- originally only raised benefactive and locative arguments to object position.

Malagasy seems to have adapted to the Bantu pattern in a way that fits metatypical change as described by Ross (2006). Both this semantic similarity and parallel evolution call for further investigation: to what extent were these caused by contact with East Bantu languages at around the time Madagascar became settled?

Explaining the emergence of the CIRCV in Malagasy as due to Bantu contact and not to a tendency to compensate for the reduced functionality of other voice affixes also fits in with what happened to the original Philippine system in the SEB languages of Borneo. The latter have lost a Philippine-type morphosyntax and acquired a typologically much more West Indonesian one, and the northern SEB languages have even lost all original non-agent voice affixes (§3). There may have been a common stage in the early history of SEB languages (including Malagasy) in which the original Philippine system was becoming affected by semantic bleaching. This trend must have continued among the SEB languages in Borneo, which remained under influence of Malay and Javanese, both of which are West Indonesian type languages that have had an enormous impact on the southern Borneo region. In Malagasy, however, this influence was stemmed after the language became isolated from other Indonesian languages (some 1,300 years ago) and came into contact with eastern Bantu languages.

The several features attributed to a Bantu substratum in this chapter are more typical of the structure of east Bantu languages than they are of Austronesian ones. Nevertheless, among the more than 700 MPSEA languages there are admittedly a few that do have such features. As already mentioned, reciprocal prefixes having the causative in their scope, and causative prefixes having the reciprocal in their scope may also sporadically occur in Makasar (Jukes 2020). CIRCV constructions also occur in some languages in northern Borneo (see Kroeger and Smith, this volume, §27.3.1.1). Various other languages have a tense system. However, in Malagasy, these features are best explained as manifestations of a Bantu substratum given that (i) they are not shared with other SEB languages, (ii) for more than a millennium, Malagasy has been in contact with eastern Bantu languages, which do share them, and (iii) the configuration of these features as found in Malagasy is matched by similar configurations in eastern Bantu languages, whereas in MPSEA these features are spread individually and disparately over many areally discontinuous and genetically distantly related languages.

## 21.5 Austronesian influence on Bantu languages

*a. Austronesian loanwords in Comorian languages* There has been frequent borrowing between Malagasy and Comorian languages. Ahmed-Chamanga (1992) indicates the original forms of what he considers Malagasy loanwords in his Shindzuani dictionary. Many of them are names for plants and animals.

The sets in Table 21.3 must have Malagasy or Malay as their source language:

Note that the word *landa* in Comorian was apparently not borrowed from Malagasy but from Malay, as it does not share the (unexpected) phonological adaptations from *l* to *tr* and from *nd* to *ndr* shown in Malagasy *tràndrakă*. On the other hand, the *tenrec* (Tenrec ecaudatus) was introduced in the Comoros from Madagascar (Walsh 2007). (Incidentally, *tràndrakă* must also be borrowed from Malay as the other SEB languages agree in having *tetuŋ* for 'porcupine' [Hudson 1967]).

*b. Austronesian influence on Swahili.* This influence is much more difficult to spot, although there is evidence. One term often mentioned in the literature is Swahili *kiazi* 'tuber sp.; potato', which was traced to Malay *kəladi* 'taro (colocasia)' (cf. Schadeberg 2009: 82; Walsh 2019) with the implication that its first syllable was re-analysed as a nominal prefix *ki-*. Schadeberg furthermore assumes that it must have been borrowed early because it preceded the Swahili loss of *l and shift from *di to *zi*. The etymology makes sense from a formal point of view. However, it is rather striking that *kəladi* does not have cognates in other Austronesian languages, raising doubts about its directionality: if it has no Austronesian history, where did Malay obtain it from, and could it have been borrowed from (early) Swahili into Malay? Or did both languages borrow it from another common source? Philippe Beaujard (2017: 166) refers to *(hu)ti* 'banana', which is found in Shambala and Bondei (in Tanzania, see Map 21.1), as a possible loanword reflecting PMP *punti. (However, the implied etymology was refuted previously by Rossel [1998: 107–8]). Other sources for loanwords from Malay as well as from Malagasy into Swahili are discussed in Walsh (2019); Adelaar (2007b, 2016a); and Hoogervorst (2013). The loanwords in question clearly illustrate contacts between Sabaki speakers and speakers of Malay (and sometimes Malagasy) that must have persisted over a long period. Some must be very old; others cannot be dated or are demonstrably recent. The loanwords in (8), (9) and (10) are supposedly old:

**Table 21.3** Austronesian influence on Comorian languages

| Origin | Malagasy | Comorian |
|---|---|---|
| Malay *daŋau* 'field hut' | *trànu* 'house' | *dago* (Shimaore, Shindzuani), *daho* (Shingazidja) 'house' |
| PMP *pali 'taboo' | *fàdi* | *fadi* (Shingazidja) |
| Malay (< Sanskrit) *kala* '1. scorpion; 2. spider' | *hàla* | *kala* (Shimaore), *hala* (Shindzuani) 'scorpion' |
| Iban (Borneo) *laŋkan* 'keel' | *làkană* | *laka* (Shimaore, Shingazidja) 'dug-out' |
| Malay *landak* 'porcupine' | *tràndrakă* 'tenrec' | *landrá* (Shindzuani), *landa* (Shimaore, Shingazidja) 'tenrec' |
| PMP *kali 'to dig' | *aŋgàdi* 'spade' | *ngadí* (Shindzuani) |
| Malay *salubuŋ* 'cover; veil; wrapper' | *salùvună* | *saluva* (Shimaore, Shindzuani) 'kind of women's dress' |
| *sudu 'spoon' | *sùtru* | *sutrù* (Shimaore, Shingazidja, Shindzuani) 'spoon' |
| *buqaya 'crocodile' | *vuày* | *vwayi* (Shindzuani), *vwai* (Shimaore, Shingazidja) 'crocodile' |
| PSEB *uŋkɛ, PMLG2 *i-uke 'older sibling' | *zùki* | *zuki* (Shimaore, Shingazidja) |
| Bugis *wala*, South Toraja, Mandar *bala* 'palisade; fence' | *vàla* 'palisade; corral' | *vala* (Shimaore, Shindzuani) 'ox pen; stable'[a] |

[a] Also Shingazidja *vala* 'cabin for young men who no longer live with their parents'.

From Malay:

(8) Malay *tuba* 'fish poison', Swahili *u-tupa*
Malay *kəladi* 'taro (colocasia)', Swahili *kiazi* 'tuber; potato' (Walsh 2019; Schadeberg [2009: 82])
Malay *kota* 'fortified place; town', Swahili *u-kuta* 'stone walls of a house' (ultimately from Dravidian; Adelaar 2007b; Hoogervorst 2013)

From Malagasy or Malay:

(9) Malagasy *sàmbu* 'ship', Ma'anyan *sambaw* 'celestial ship', Old Malay *sambaw*, 'ship', dialectal Swahili *sambo* (same meaning) (Adelaar 2007b; Walsh 2019, 2021);
Malagasy *farìhi* 'lake', Malay *pərigi* 'well; spring', and Swahili *m-fereji* 'ditch; furrow' (ultimately from Dravidian)
Malagasy *sùratră*, Malay *surat* 'writing; letter; document', Swahili *chora* 'to carve; draw' (see Adelaar (1989) for the Malay origin of *sùratră*)

From Malagasy:

(10) Malagasy *tùrakă* 'to launch (spear, etc.); throw', Swahili *tora* 'fishing spear'
Malagasy *vàri* 'rice (in general)', Swahili *wali* 'cooked rice' (ultimately from Dravidian)

See Walsh (2019) for more recent Malay loanwords in Swahili (including boat terms). This source also provides alternative interpretations about the origins of Swahili *u-tupa*, *u-kuta*, *m-fereji*, *chora*, *tora*.

## 21.6 Concluding remarks

The impact of Bantu languages on Malagasy has been considerable. The influence from Sabaki languages is easiest to identify, although it is often difficult to differentiate between Comorian and Swahili influence. In spite of these influences, Malagasy has remained a unified language with a predominantly Austronesian vocabulary and grammar. There are also many traces of lexical influence from Malay and Malagasy in Comorian languages, and to a much lesser extent in Swahili. However, influence of Malagasy in other African languages is absent or has remained undetected. The history of Malagasy has garnered much attention in the context of Austronesian comparative-historical linguistics. Sadly, the same cannot be said about the history of contact between African and Austronesian languages. This is clearly an area in need of further research best conducted in collaborative projects between Austronesianists and Africanists.

## Acknowledgements

My gratitude goes to Penelope Howe, Noël Gueunier (Paris), Antoinette Schapper, Martin Walsh (Cambridge, UK), and Erik Zobel for their extremely valuable comments on an earlier draft of this chapter.

CHAPTER 22

# Papuan contact and its impact on Malayo-Polynesian languages of Island Southeast Asia

ANTOINETTE SCHAPPER

## 22.1 Introduction

This chapter looks at the impact of Papuan languages on the Malayo-Polynesian languages of Southeast Asia. 'Papuan' (alternatively, 'non-Austronesian') languages are the genealogically diverse languages spoken on and around the island of New Guinea at the eastern perimeter of the area covered by this volume. Interactions between speakers of Papuan and Austronesian languages extend back to the initial dispersal of speakers of Austronesian languages across Island Southeast Asia in the mid-Holocene. As early Austronesian speakers moved south out of the Philippines, they are thought to have encountered pre-existing populations speaking what we believe were Papuan languages throughout much of the eastern MPSEA area. Here Austronesian speakers settled in areas or among networks in regular contact with speakers of Papuan languages. It is widely acknowledged that this contact with Papuan speakers and, in some cases, likely shift from the Papuan languages has given rise to many of the features that characterize eastern Austronesian languages and set them apart from their relatives in the northern and western parts of the MPSEA area.

The geographical area containing Papuan languages and the inferred zone of their influence on Austronesian languages has been referred to as the "New Guinea region" (Ross 2017) and "Linguistic Melanesia" (Schapper 2020b). The western portion of the wider Melanesian area, corresponding to the eastern MPSEA region with which this chapter is concerned, bears various names in the literature, including "East Nusantara" (Klamer, Reesink, and van Staden 2008) and "Linguistic Wallacea" (Schapper 2015a). Blust (1993a) posits that the Austronesian languages found within Linguistic Melanesia all belong to a single subgroup - Central Eastern Malayo-Polynesian (CEMP), which takes in the Central Malayo-Polynesian (CMP), South Halmahera-West New Guinea (SHWNG), and Oceanic subgroups. The languages of CMP and SHWNG fall within the MPSEA area (Zobel, this volume, chapter 13; Kamholz, this volume, chapter 14) and are the exclusive object of this chapter, even though many of the features that will be discussed are also present in members of the Oceanic subgroup, particularly those spoken on or very near to New Guinea.

Numerous Papuan language families are located within the MPSEA area (Map 22.1). They can be divided geographically into those spoken on the mainland of New Guinea and those languages which are 'outliers', that is, spoken on islands offshore from New Guinea. On the New Guinea mainland, we find multiple families and language isolates (essentially, one-language families). On the Bird's Head there are the East Bird's Head family, the West Bird's Head family, the South Bird's Head family, as well as three isolates. On the Bomberai Peninsula we find members of the West Bomberai family and two isolates, Mor and Tanahmerah, while on the Bird's Neck we find members of the Mairasi family. There are three outlier families: (i) the Timor-Alor-Pantar family, consisting of around twenty-five languages scattered among Austronesian languages in eastern and central Timor, and dominating on the islands of Alor and Pantar; (ii) the North Halmahera family, encompassing around a dozen languages on Halmahera Island and some small satellite islands in north Maluku; and (iii) the Yawa family, comprising a series of closely related lects spoken in central Yapen, an island in Cenderawasih Bay. A fourth language, Kalamang, is spoken just off the coast of Bomberai peninsula. All outlier families west of New Guinea are hypothesized to be related to Papuan languages on mainland New Guinea. Kalamang and the Timor-Alor-Pantar languages form a family with Mbaham and Iha spoken on Bomberai peninsula, known as the 'Greater West Bomberai' (GWB) family (Usher and Schapper 2022). The North Halmaheran languages are likely relatives of the West Bird's Head languages (Voorhoeve 1989, 1994a), and may even be part of a wider 'West

Antoinette Schapper, *Papuan contact and its impact on Malayo-Polynesian languages of Island Southeast Asia.* In: *The Oxford Guide to the Malayo-Polynesian Languages of Southeast Asia.* Edited by: Alexander Adelaar and Antoinette Schapper, Oxford University Press. © Antoinette Schapper (2024). DOI: 10.1093/oso/9780198807353.003.0022

Papuan' family together with the Papuan outliers of Yapen (Donohue 2008a). Aside from the Papuan languages that are extant today, the reasoned assumption of linguists is that Papuan languages were spoken by people all across the eastern MPSEA area before the Austronesian arrival.

Whilst Austronesian influence on Papuan languages is certainly important for understanding the prehistorical interactions between the speakers of the different groups, this chapter will deal exclusively with influence from Papuan languages on Austronesian ones. I discuss transfer of features that are either widely associated with Papuan languages across Linguistic Melanesia, or that are more restricted, being associated with one or more Papuan family within the eastern MPSEA area. Most of the Papuan features discussed in detail will be drawn from the Papuan outlier families as these tend to be more completely described, thus allowing for inferences to be made about the histories of lexemes and structures with greater certainty.

The structure of this chapter is as follows. §22.2 addresses issues of lexical transfer from Papuan languages to eastern MPSEA languages. §22.3 looks at some of the many structural features in eastern MPSEA languages that are thought to have originated in Papuan languages. §22.4 deals with the issue of determining directionality of transfer for structural features that are not typical of Papuan or Austronesian languages. §22.5 overviews debates surrounding the timing of Papuan features entering the Austronesian languages and the validity of their use in subgrouping. §22.6 presents an outlook for future studies into Papuan influence on Austronesian languages of the MPSEA area.

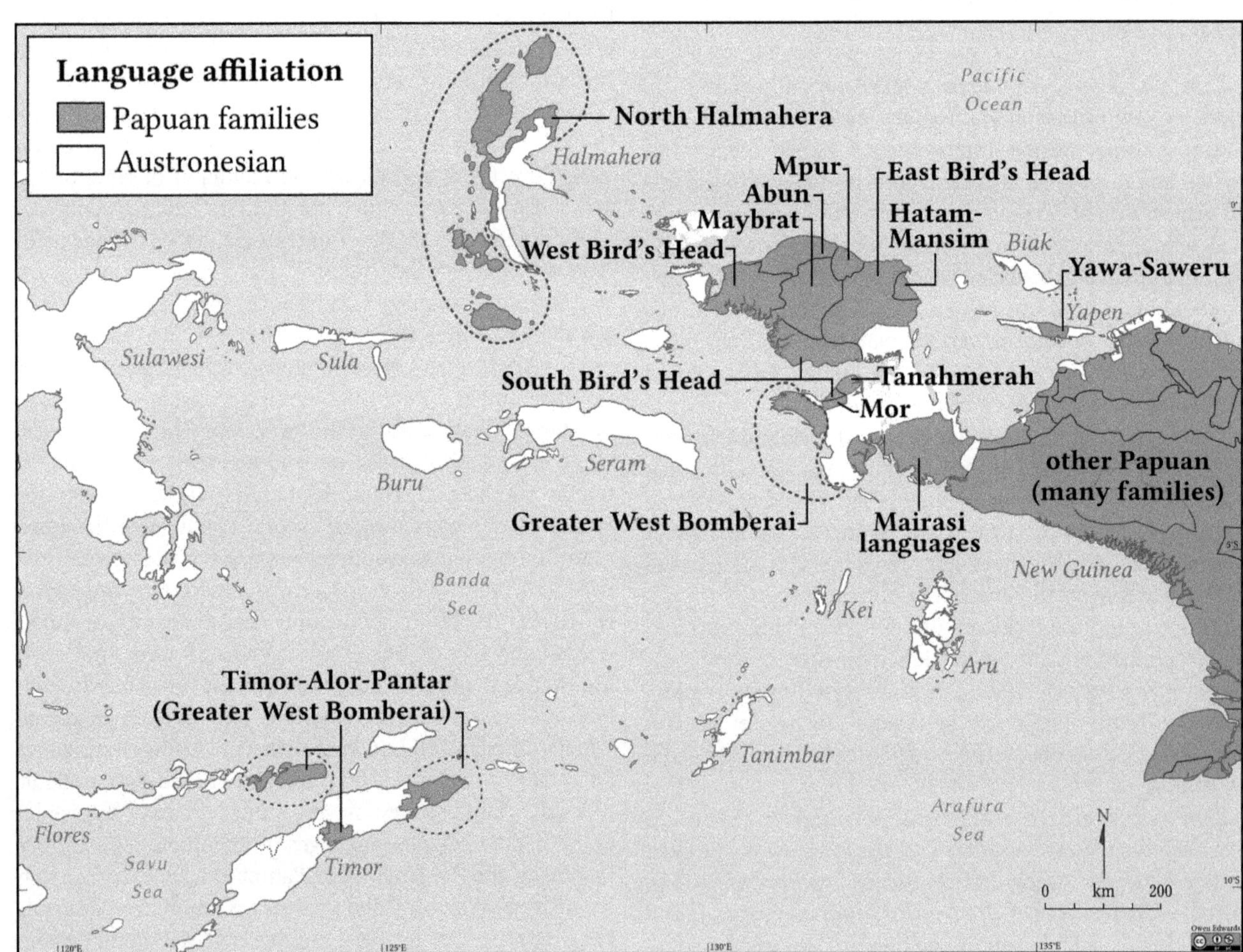


**Map 22.1** Papuan language families on and around the Bird's Head of New Guinea.

Based on an original map © Antoinette Schapper.

## 22.2 Lexical transfer

The presence of lexical borrowings from Austronesian languages in Papuan languages in the MPSEA area is well known (see, e.g. Gasser 2017b, 2019a; Reesink 1998: 610–14; Schapper and Huber 2019; Schapper and Wellfelt 2018; Usher and Schapper 2018). By contrast, the converse situation, lexical items that originate in Papuan languages being found in Austronesian languages, is scarcely represented in the literature on language contact west of New Guinea.

It is often suggested, or at least implied, in the literature (e.g. Gasser 2019a is a recent example) that the skewed directionality of lexical transfer from Austronesian to Papuan languages points to the highly influential place which speakers of Austronesian languages occupied in the past. In general terms, the Austronesians certainly were responsible for the introduction of new items and technologies into the New Guinea region, and Austronesian speaking groups likely played key roles in coastal trade networks. However, it cannot be assumed that speakers of Papuan languages occupied an inferior social or technological position. While the languages of other pre-existing populations of Island Southeast Asia were lost in the face of the Austronesian expansion, the fact that many Papuan languages persist attests to the ability of Papuan peoples to put up significant resistance to replacement, not only in the highlands, but also in coastal areas on and around New Guinea. The strength of this resistance has been attributed to the peoples of New Guinea possessing agriculture, and therefore having developed dense populations (Bellwood 1998); New Guinea is home to a suite of plant domestications that made the island a centre of vegecultural innovation (see, e.g. Denham 2011). Donohue and Denham (2009) argue that there are two widespread banana terms in Austronesian languages in eastern Indonesia that reflect originally Papuan lexemes for indigenous banana cultivars. The existence of terms with such wide projections into Island Southeast Asia points to a sphere of Papuan influence that in the past extended well beyond the areas where Papuan languages are spoken today. See Denham and Donohue (2009), Donohue and Denham (2010), and Schapper (2017a) for more discussion of Papuan agriculture and elements of its linguistic expression. Assumptions about the low status or lack of influence of Papuan speakers should therefore be put aside in future studies of lexical transfer between Papuan and Austronesian languages.

The apparent paucity of Papuan lexical items identified in Austronesian languages around western New Guinea is in no small part a reflection of the poor state of historical linguistic reconstruction of Papuan language families in comparison to that of the Austronesian family. Austronesian languages have been subject to serious historical comparison for at least 100 years; we have a well-developed picture of many Austronesian lexical histories and a significant lexicon reconstructed for Proto-Malayo-Polynesian (PMP). As a result, loanwords with Austronesian etymologies are, for the most part, easily spotted in Papuan languages. Conversely, the phonological history of most Papuan languages is unknown and lexical reconstructions are either non-existent or, in the case of the more heavily studied families, are limited to a few dozen items. The dearth of historical work on Papuan languages around western New Guinea cannot be put down to a lack of documentation. Ample material exists for many groups of Papuan languages, but there is a trope in the literature that New Guinea may be one of the parts of the world which present potentially insurmountable problems for the comparative method (Thomason 1999). In particular, apparently high rates of lexical replacement, variously attributed to word tabooing (see, e.g. Foley 1986: 42–6; Comrie 2000) and to processes resulting from small group size (see, e.g. Thurston 1987: 66–7) and from frequent bi- and multilingualism (see, e.g. Laycock 1982; Foley 1986: 9, 27; Kulick 1992), seem to have turned linguists away from attempting bottom-up historical work on, and lexical reconstructions of, Papuan families.

This is not to say that Papuan lexemes are unknown in Austronesian languages. Many words from Ternate, the Papuan language traditionally spoken on the island of the same name, have found their way into the variety of Malay spoken on Ternate today (examples in Table 22.1).[1] However, this situation is not one of borrowing, but rather reflects relatively recent, and to some extent still ongoing, language shift from Ternate to Malay. As such, it is unsurprising for Ternate words of this kind to be readily identifiable.

Given the significant historical position of their speakers, we should be able to identify loanwords from the Papuan languages, Ternate and Tidore, across much of the northern Moluccas and adjacent areas such as Raja Ampat and northern Sulawesi. Ternate and Tidore were at the centre of powerful indigenous polities and trading networks between the fifteenth and eighteenth centuries. Descriptions of Austronesian languages in Halmahera and adjacent areas often mention loanwords from one of these two being present in the language, but almost never with illustration or discussion (see Voorhoeve 1994b for a preliminary study of Papuan loanwords in Halmahera). The fact that so little is known about Ternate and Tidore loanwords in Halmahera, one of the best documented groups of Papuan languages, underlines the lack of concerted effort to identify and study the loanwords from Papuan languages that can be observed across much of the western Papuan contact area. Tracking the semantic domains and geographical extent of loanwords from Ternate and Tidore would offer a unique perspective

[1] Manado Malay and, to a lesser extent, Papuan and Ambonese Malay have all been influenced by Ternate Malay. Numerous words ultimately from Ternate can thus be identified in these three vehicular varieties of Malay orbiting the North Moluccas.

**Table 22.1** Ternate words in Ternate Malay (Betty Litamahuputty p.c.)

| | | | |
|---|---|---|---|
| *amo* | 'breadfruit' | *ŋafi* | 'anchovy sp.' |
| *balacai* | 'castor oil plant' | *ŋana* | 'you (singular)' |
| *balakama* | 'basil sp.' | *ŋoni* | 'you (plural)' |
| *bifi* | 'ant' | *ɲoɲoke* | 'to grumble' |
| *cahi* | 'carry on the back' | *ofu* | 'bee' |
| *dusu* | 'to chase' | *pala-pala* | 'thigh' |
| *fofoki* | 'eggplant' | *pasugo* | 'asthma' |
| *foro* | 'to brood' | *poha* | 'to be able to do' |
| *foya* | 'to lie' | *poloso* | 'to pinch' |
| *gai* | 'bug' | *poŋo* | 'deaf' |
| *ganemo* | 'plant sp., gnemon' | *riki* | 'to catch' |
| *guraka* | 'ginger' | *sugili* | 'eel' |
| *guraŋo* | 'shark' | *tobo* | 'to swim' |
| *holo* | 'to sting' | *totofore* | 'to shiver' |
| *kokehe* | 'to cough' | *tusa* | 'cat' |

on indigenous trade in the early modern period that could be offset against evidence from documentary sources.

In more remote contact situations where the past relationships between different linguistic groups is unknown, a sound knowledge of the phonological and lexical histories of Papuan families is essential for our ability to establish the directionality of transfer of lexemes shared between neighbouring Papuan and Austronesian languages. However, the complexity and longevity of many Papuan-Austronesian contact situations means that lexicons can become deeply entangled. The languages of Yapen illustrate this point well. Here we can observe that there are many lexical forms shared between the closely related Papuan languages Yawa and Saweru and their Austronesian neighbours belonging to the West Yapen subgroup, such as those presented in example (1). It is often not possible to determine with any certainty whether these forms were innovations in some common ancestor of the Austronesian languages that were then borrowed into the Papuan languages, or vice versa. Because the lexemes in the modern languages may not show indicative sound changes, we can, in many cases, only conclude with unsatisfying vagueness that forms shared between West Yapen languages and the Yawa-Saweru languages appear to reflect contact between their respective protolanguages, as in (1a). In other cases, the apparent loss of phonological material such as in (1b) suggests borrowing from Papuan into Austronesian, but this is by no means certain. See Gasser (2017b, 2019a) for more discussion of this contact situation.

(1) a. Proto-Yawa-Saweru (Papuan) *mamu 'snot' > Yawa *mamu*, Saweru *mamu* 'snot; nasal mucus'
Proto-West Yapen (Austronesian) *mamu 'snot' > Wamesa *(suo) mamu*, Wooi *mamu*, Ambai *mamu*, Serui-Laut *mamu* 'snot; nasal mucus'

b. Proto-Yawa-Saweru (Papuan) *kaŋkunam 'caterpillar; beetle; bug' > Yawa Central *kaŋkunam* 'caterpillar', Yawa Mantembu *kaŋkuna* 'caterpillar; beetle', Yawa Turu *kaŋunamɛ* 'bug; caterpillar'
Proto-West Yapen (Austronesian) *kaŋkuna 'caterpillar; beetle; bug' > Pom *kaŋkuŋ* 'beetle', Wamesa *kakuna* 'maggot', Serui-Laut *kauna* 'caterpillar'

In the small number of cases where we do have more detailed phonological histories and reconstructions of Papuan protolanguages, we are able to detect loanwords into Austronesian languages. For example, three sibling terms in Kemak and Mambae, two Austronesian languages of the Central Timor subgroup, have robust Proto-Timor-Alor-Pantar (PTAP) etymologies, as given in (2). Bunaq is the only extant Papuan language in central Timor; its relatives in the Timor-Alor-Pantar family are spoken several hundred kilometres either to the north or east. The older sibling term in Kemak in (2a) could represent a relatively recent Bunaq borrowing as Bunaq has a near identical form; although given that the root takes a no-longer productive form of inalienable possessive suffixing in Kemak, it is likely an older borrowing. The younger sibling term in (2b) cannot have been borrowed from modern Bunaq, because the forms of the loan in the Austronesian languages do not show the metathesis of the glottal stop to word final position which is typical of Bunaq. Finally, Bunaq does not have a reflex of the sister term in (2c). This means that either this term was borrowed into Kemak and Mambae from pre-Bunaq before its loss in modern Bunaq or it was borrowed from another, now no longer extant TAP language in Central Timor. Such forms in Austronesian languages would not be possible to identify as borrowings without the higher-level PTAP reconstructions. Some of the PTAP reconstructions go back further to Proto-Greater West Bomberai, the ancestral language of the West Bomberai and TAP languages.

(2) a. Kemak *nana-* 'older sister' < PTAP *nana 'older sibling' (Bunaq *nana* 'older sister', Makalero *nana*, Sawila *na:na*, Wersing *-naŋ* 'older sibling', Abui *na:na*, Nedebang *-naŋ* 'older sibling') < Proto-Greater West Bomberai *nana 'older sibling'

b. Kemak *kaʔu* 'young (of a baby)', Mambae *kau* 'younger sibling' < PTAP *kaku 'younger sibling' (Bunaq *kauʔ* 'younger sibling', Makalero *kaʔu* 'younger, junior relative', Blagar *kaku* 'sibling of same gender; friend', Reta *kaku* 'friend', Kamang *-kak* 'younger relative', Wersing *kaku*, Sawila *ka:ku* 'younger sibling')

c. Kemak *topor-* 'sister; female cousin (male speaking)', Mambae *topo* 'younger sister' < PTAP *tubur 'woman; sister' (Makasae *tufu* 'man's older sister; man's mother's sister's daughter; man's father's brother's daughter; man's father's sister's daughter', Makalero *tufur* 'sister; (female) cousin', Fataluku *tupur(u)* 'woman', Oirata *tuhur(u)* 'woman') < Proto-Greater West Bomberai *tumbur 'woman; sister'

Loss of lexemes from Papuan languages after they have been borrowed into Austronesian languages may represent a widespread problem for the identification of loans from Papuan languages. For example, reflexes of Proto-Greater West Bomberai *mandel 'bat' have been borrowed into Austronesian languages both on Timor and Bomberai peninsula on New Guinea (see Usher and Schapper 2022 for specific phonological arguments about the directionality of borrowing here), as given in (3). But the immediate Papuan neighbours of the Austronesian languages on Timor with this term, Makasae and Makalero, as well as the immediate Papuan neighbours of several of the Austronesian languages on Bomberai, Kalamang, and Mbaham, do not attest reflexes of PGWB *mandel 'bat'. This highlights the point that simply comparing vocabularies of neighbouring Austronesian–Papuan languages will not necessarily be revealing of loanwords, particularly in the direction of Papuan to Austronesian. What is more, the example illustrates that we must be cautious about assuming the cognacy of lexemes without established Malayo-Polynesian etymologies that are found in Austronesian languages in disparate parts of the Papuan contact area. Parallel borrowings from related, but geographically removed, Papuan languages, as in this case, can easily be mistaken as having reconstructive value in the Austronesian family.

(3) a. Proto-Greater West Bomberai *mandel 'bat':
Proto-Timor-Alor-Pantar *madel 'bat': Fataluku *matsa*, Oirata *maṯa*, Teiwa *madi*, Nedebang *marra* 'bat', Western Pantar *madde* 'kind of bat', Klon *mdɛl*, Kafoa *marel*, Abui *marel*, Kamang *matei* 'bat'
Proto-Iha-Mbaham *manda 'bat': Iha *manda* 'bat'

b. Austronesian
Timor: Waima'a *mada*, Naueti *mada*, Midiki *mada* 'bat'
Bomberai: Sekar *mada* 'fruit bat', Onin *mad-mada* 'flying fox', Uruangnirin *mada* 'bat', Kowiai *mada-mada* 'small bat'

Another cautionary note for identifying loanwords from Papuan languages is not to exclude a lexeme from examination just because it has a known Austronesian etymology. Given that many Papuan languages have substantial amounts of Austronesian loanwords, it is possible for Austronesian lexemes borrowed into a Papuan language to then be borrowed back into an Austronesian language again. Precisely this can be seen to have occurred in the Austronesian languages, Naueti and Waima'a. Both have multiple borrowings of Papuan and Austronesian etyma from their large Papuan neighbour, Makasae. The tell-tale sign of Makasae being the immediate source for a loanword in Naueti or Waima'a is the presence of an additional, unetymological final vowel. Examples are given in (4). In Makasae paragoge of a vowel echoing the final vowel of the root is a productive morphophonological process that affects all consonant final roots including assimilated loanwords. The echo vowel is dropped when the root is marked by a suffix or enclitic. Echo vowels are not known in Naueti or Waima'a phonology, and the final vowel on these loans cannot be dropped in Naueti and Waima'a. See Schapper and Huber (2023) for more discussion and illustration of lexical entanglement between these neighbouring Papuan and Austronesian languages.

(4) a. Naueti *naili* < Makasae *nail-i* 'to fish; to hook' < borrowing of reflex of a voice form of PMP *kawil 'fishhook' (cf. Blust's PWMP *ma-ŋawil 'to fish with hook and line')

b. Naueti *neluku* < Makasae *neluk-u* 'turtle' < Tetun *lenuk* 'turtle'

c. Waima'a *daduru* 'inmate; prison' < Makasae *dadur-u* < Tetun *dadur* 'imprison; hold captive'

All the cases of lexical transfer discussed thus far have involved transfer between individual languages or small groups of closely related languages. Yet, Papuan contact is likely to have occurred quite early in the history of some Austronesian subgroups in the eastern MPSEA area. Whilst structural support for this abounds (see following sections), lexical evidence in the form of reconstructable protoforms with clear Papuan etymologies has not yet been forthcoming for likely older subgroupings of Austronesian languages in the eastern MPSEA area. However, with more lexical reconstructive work being undertaken in the area (e.g. Edwards 2021), there is perhaps reason to be optimistic about the possibility of detecting such lexemes in the future. An example would be the related lexemes in the Papuan languages belonging to the Greater West Bomberai family and in the Austronesian languages belonging to the Timor-Babar subgroup presented in (5). Here we see that a reflex of Proto-Greater West Bomberai *saŋgara 'search' has been borrowed into Proto-Timor-Babar, the common ancestor of a large number of Austronesian languages extending in an arc through the Babar Islands in southern Maluku to the island of Rote at the western end of Timor. An alternative scenario in which the Papuan languages have multiple parallel borrowings from Proto-Timor-Babar *saŋga 'search' is less well supported by the data for two reasons. First, Kalamang is far from any extant Timor-Babar language from which a reflex of Proto-Timor-Babar *saŋga could have been borrowed. Whilst it may have been that, in the past, languages had quite a different geographical arrangement, there is at this stage no reason to think that Timor-Babar languages once extended to New Guinea. I also do not know of cognates of Proto-Timor-Babar *saŋga in other Austronesian languages in the area around Kalamang. Second, the reflexes of the final syllable/segment in several Papuan languages (Bunaq *l*, Abui *i*, and Kalamang *ra*) would be unexplained in a scenario where they were borrowed from the Austronesian languages, whereas they are entirely accounted for as regular reflexes of PGWB final *ra.

(5) a. Proto-Greater West Bomberai *saŋgara 'search'
Proto-Timor-Alor-Pantar *sagara 'search': Bunaq *sagal*, Abui *tahai* 'search', Fataluku *haʔa* 'look; see'
Kalamang *saŋgara* 'search'

b. Proto-Timor-Babar: *saŋga 'search'
Rote: Ba'a *saŋga*, Bilba *saŋa* 'search'
East Timor: Hresuk *saŋa*, Dadu'a *sana*, Galolen *saga* 'search'
Southwest Maluku: Ili'uun *haga*, Tulun *haga*, Leti *(βa-)saka*, Luang *(wa-)haka*, Wetan *aka*, Serua *(wa-)saka*, Daweloor *(ma-)ake* 'search'

Identifying such early borrowings from Papuan to Austronesian can be difficult, again, because of borrowing back and forth between groups. For example, two TAP languages have borrowed a reflex of Proto-Timor-Babar *saŋga 'search' from Austronesian languages: Makasae *saga* 'look for; go after', Makalero *haka* 'search; look' are the result of borrowing from Galolen *saga* 'search' (or a predecessor of that language), into Proto-Maka, the common ancestor of Makasae and Makalero. This is apparent because PGWB *ŋg should be reflected as ʔ in Makasae and Makalero. This etymon, thus, serves to highlight a point that has been underestimated in much of the existing literature, namely, that contact between Austronesian and Papuan languages has occurred at different times in different places and, most importantly, with different directions of influence.

In sum, insufficient attention has been paid by linguists to the identification of Papuan loanwords in the Austronesian languages west of New Guinea. Whilst it is likely that many Papuan etymologies will never be identified as such because their Papuan source is lost, the examples adduced here show there is scope for careful comparative work to uncover lexemes with ultimately Papuan etymologies in the eastern MPSEA area. The complex dynamics of borrowing back and forth between Papuan and Austronesian languages means that it will often be difficult for the researcher to decide on whether lexical sets of related words are Austronesian or Papuan in origin.

## 22.3 Structural transfer

Numerous studies of the Austronesian languages of the eastern MPSEA area have pointed out structural changes that align with features found in Papuan languages. Whilst Papuan languages are structurally diverse and cannot easily be regarded as representing a single linguistic type (Ross 2017), there are multiple broad structural features that are found very widely across Papuan languages in (parts of) Linguistic Melanesia (Schapper 2020b). The recurrent appearance of these features in eastern MPSEA languages and their typical absence in Austronesian languages in other parts of the MPSEA area have been argued to point to Papuan languages as the ultimate source of those features.

Table 22.2 provides an overview of the features in the eastern MPSEA languages which have been suggested to be the result of Papuan influence. The list is not complete, but covers the most robust and widely agreed upon claims in the literature. The reader is referred to the works cited in the table for more information about the features, their distribution in Austronesian and Papuan languages, and the specific arguments concerning their Papuan origins. I will mention a few other cases of structural transfer that are less widespread than those listed in Table 22.2. In §22.5 I also treat several features in Austronesian languages west of New Guinea that are agreed by scholars to be the result of Papuan contact, but whose reconstructive value within the Austronesian family is disputed. In the remainder of this section, I discuss some of the general issues surrounding arguments of Papuan origins for structural features in Austronesian languages.

The transfer of structural features from Papuan languages to Austronesian ones in eastern MPSEA region is consistent

**Table 22.2** Papuan features appearing in eastern MPSEA languages

| | Austronesian: Philippines and western Indonesia | Austronesian: eastern Indonesia and East Timor | Papuan: Bird's Head and western outliers | |
|---|---|---|---|---|
| Velar nasal phoneme | Typically present | Sporadic | Typically absent | Schapper 2015a: 116–17 |
| Phonemic lexical tone contrasts | Typically absent | Sporadic | Common | Kamholz 2017; Arnold 2018b; Schapper 2020b: 483–4 |
| Clause final negators | Typically absent | Sporadic | Common | Reesink 2002b; Klamer, Reesink, and van Staden 2008: 130–4 |
| Split intransitivity | Typically absent | Sporadic | Common | Donohue 2004b; Klamer 2008; Schapper 2015a: 124–8 |
| Basic preposed possessor | Absent | Common | Common | Donohue 2007; Schapper and McConvell, this volume, §48.2 |
| Possessive classification | Absent (except Borneo) | Common | Common | Klamer, Reesink, and van Staden 2008: 116–22; Schapper with McConvell, this volume, §48.4 |
| Neuter gender | Absent | Common | Common | Schapper 2010b |
| Numeral bases | Decimal | Quinary, Decimal Vigesimal | Quinary, Decimal Vigesimal | Schapper and Hammarström 2013; Schapper 2020b: 490–1 |

with contact situations in which speakers of Papuan languages shifted to speaking Austronesian languages. Given how widespread some of the innovative features are, these shift events most likely lay a long way back in time, dating probably in some instances to the earliest contacts between speakers of Austronesian and Papuan languages in the region. As such, actual documented cases of shift from Papuan languages to Austronesian ones are almost non-existent. As mentioned in the previous section, the case of the ongoing shift from Ternate to Malay on the island of Ternate is one of the few clear cases, although it is in some ways unique in that we know that shift was preceded by several centuries of bilingualism in Ternate and Malay. Nonetheless, the contact has resulted not only in lexical, but also structural transfer. For example, in the Papuan language Ternate, locative prepositions take different forms depending on the semantic properties of the nominal referent: *se* is used with nouns with human referents and *toma* with nouns with non-human referents (Hayami-Allen 2001: 72–5). This structural distinction is paralleled in Ternate Malay in that the locative preposition *pa* 'to; at' is used exclusively with nouns that have a human referent, while the preposition *di* is typically (but not exclusively) used with nouns that have non-human referents (Litamahuputty 2012: 161–5).

Shift-induced interference presents problems for the linguist in the eastern MPSEA area, in that in almost all cases, we have no certainty about the identity of the languages which were shifted from. Where there are neighbouring Papuan languages with the same feature, we might infer that the feature is the result of speakers shifting from that Papuan language or a relative or ancestor of it. However, often the features that are argued to be the result of Papuan shift are not specific to one Papuan language or language family, such that it is difficult to convincingly attribute the structural changes to any specific Papuan language(s). This is, for example, the case with the Austronesian languages of the Flores-Lembata subgroup (see Zobel, this volume, §13.2.1.4) examined by Fricke (2019). She attributes the emergence of Papuan features in the group to language mixing based on long-term bilingualism with code-switching practices, followed by eventual shift to Austronesian languages (or Austronesian-dominant codes, i.e. languages with more Austronesian than Papuan features). However, she concedes that it is not possible to definitively lay the structural innovations in Flores-Lembata languages at the door of the neighbouring Papuan languages of the Timor-Alor-Pantar family (2019: 417–18). Whilst some of the innovative structures, like preposing of possessors, are found in the neighbouring TAP languages, that feature is actually present in almost all Papuan languages in the eastern MPSEA area as well as the majority of them in Linguistic Melanesia. Other innovations that Fricke (2019) suggests are the result of a Papuan substrate, like plural-marking affixes, are not found in neighbouring Papuan languages (see Nagaya, this volume, §34.9, for discussion of other features). Such issues, along with a lack of lexemes with clear TAP etymologies in the Flores-Lembata languages, mean that Fricke (2019) is forced to the vague conclusion that the Papuan substrate language(s) that influenced the Flores-Lembata languages were typologically similar to the Timor-Alor-Pantar languages, but not necessarily members of that family.

In other cases, we have no descriptions of the Papuan languages from which shift is most likely to have occurred and so we are left with appeals to Papuan generalities. This is the case, for example, with the appearance of lexical tone in the Austronesian languages of southern Cenderawasih Bay. Kamholz (2017) shows that independent tonogenetic innovations occurred in the proximal Austronesian languages, Moor, Yerisiam, and Yaur. He points out that tone is widespread in New Guinea (Donohue 1997b), but that it is not known whether lexical tones are present in the Mairasi languages which neighbour the three Austronesian languages. Kamholz (2017) concludes that it is not sufficient to attribute the strikingly parallel, but independent tonogenesis in these languages to chance, and that contact with, and likely shift from, one or more unknown Papuan languages still provides the best explanation for the phenomenon.

The cross-linguistic rarity of a feature is also often appealed to in positing contact- or shift-induced change from Papuan languages. That is to say, whilst a feature could have emerged in eastern MPSEA languages on their own without Papuan influence, such a scenario is less likely for uncommon linguistic features. The repeated emergence of clause-final negation in Austronesian languages in the eastern MPSEA area is one such case. Papuan languages in the region mostly have free negators occurring in a clause final position in both verb medial and verb final languages (i.e. VONeg or OVNeg). In Austronesian languages in the western and northern parts of the MPSEA area, free negators typically precede the verb. By contrast, numerous Austronesian languages in the Papuan contact zone have clause final negators. Natural processes of historical change, known as Jespersen cycles, whereby originally pre-verbal markers of negation are replaced by postverbal ones, could be used to explain the shift in word order in Austronesian languages west of New Guinea without recourse to contact. However, because VONeg, rather than simply VNegO, is such a cross-linguistically unusual word order, contact is extremely likely to have played a role in inducing VONeg in multiple Austronesian languages (Ross 2017: 794–5). See van der Auwera, Van Olmen, and Vossen (this volume, §60.2) for discussion of the different historical pathways along which such remodelling could have taken place. Similar arguments of rarity are used by Gil (2017) in his study of the transfer of do/give colexification patterns in the northwest New Guinea area.

The number of times an innovation occurs in the Austronesian languages of the eastern MPSEA area is also often taken to be indicative of contact- or shift-induced transfer. For example, Papuan languages in the eastern MPSEA area display different configurations of numeral systems involving base-5 and base-20. Although both these bases have good physiological motivations and can therefore emerge spontaneously, the concentration of eastern MPSEA languages with these bases is striking. Schapper and Hammarström (2013) observe that languages with base-5 and base-20, either replacing or being taken on alongside the Austronesian decimal base, number around fifty in the eastern MPSEA area and can be associated with over a dozen separate innovation events. Elsewhere in the MPSEA languages, only a few innovations of base-5 and base-20 are known. For Schapper and Hammarström (2013), the sheer number of parallel innovations of structural features in eastern MPSEA numerals corresponding to features that are also present in nearby Papuan languages precludes these being independent innovations, and strongly points to Papuan interference.

Skewing in the geographic distribution of features within eastern MPSEA languages can also be adduced as evidence for a Papuan origin. More specifically, a clustered, rather than an evenly spread, distribution of a feature can arguably be read as a result of contact with and/or shift from Papuan languages, where that feature is also found in Papuan languages. For example, the lexical association of 'leaf' and 'head hair' discussed in §22.5 is found in eastern MPSEA languages clustered around Papuan languages with the same feature. In such a situation, one could posit a sphere of Papuan influence in which multiple transfer events occurred, for example, with the feature diffusing from language to language and/or being transferred to different Austronesian languages at various stages as a result of contact with speakers of no longer extant Papuan languages.

Finally, it is not legitimate to attribute simply any innovation in the eastern MPSEA languages to a Papuan substrate or contact with a Papuan language. The edible/general possessive distinction, for example, is innovative in eastern Austronesian languages, but it cannot, on current knowledge, be put down to Papuan substrate/contact; there are no known Papuan languages that have such a semantic contrast in their possessive structures. We see in Blevins (this volume, §41.2.1) the temptation to ascribe the unusual consonant inventories of Waima'a and Naueti to contact with their Papuan neighbours, even though the segments are not present in them and an internal mechanism for their emergence has been pointed out (Schapper 2020a: 401–3; see also Schapper and Zobel, this volume, §35.2.2). Specific argumentation is required as in order to posit a Papuan origin for a feature. This issue is taken up further in the following section.

## 22.4 Directionality of transfer

The previous section looked at structural features where the arguments for the directionality of transfer from Papuan languages to Austronesian ones are reasonably well developed. Yet, for many features in the eastern MPSEA area, these arguments do not exist. In fact, there are multiple shared features in localized sets of Papuan and Austronesian languages for which the directionality of transfer is not at all certain. By way of example, I will discuss two of these features here: (i) possessive marking of adjectival attributes; and (ii) synchronic root alternations based on a final/non-final distinction (often referred to in the Austronesian literature as simply "metathesis").

It is a recurrent but not universal feature of the TAP languages that adjectival attributes can be optionally constructed with the morphosyntax of possession (Schapper accepted). That is, the noun denoting the referent acts as if it were a possessor, while the attribute is marked as if it were a possessed noun. Thus, in the TAP language Teiwa, the basic attribute construction for adjectives has the adjective following the head noun with no morpheme marking the relationship (6a). A second, more marked, attribute construction includes the possessive marker *ga* between the head noun and the adjectival attribute (6b), paralleling an adnominal possessive construction (6c).

Teiwa (Pantar, Timor-Alor-Pantar)

(6) a. *yaf* *uaad*
house big
'a/the big house'

b. *yaf* ***ga*** *uaad*
house 3SG.POSS big
'the big house (of a group)'

c. *Amos* ***ga*** *yaf*
Amos 3SG.POSS house
'Amos' house' (Amos Sir p.c.)

This feature is clustered in the TAP languages of eastern Timor, northern Pantar, and western Alor. What is notable is that several proximal Austronesian languages on Timor and in the Solor archipelago exhibit analogous structures (see Schapper and Zobel, this volume, §35.4.6.1). For example, Naueti, spoken next to Makasae and Makalero on Timor, similarly uses a possessive marker to optionally mark an attributive adjective:

Naueti (East Timor, Austronesian)

(7) a. *asukai* *riku*
man rich
'rich man'

b. *asukai* *riku-**na***
man rich-POSS
'rich man'

c. *asukai* *bui-**na***
man cat-POSS
'man's cat' (Veloso 2016: 52–4)

In Kedang, an Austronesian language spoken on Lembata just west of Pantar, possessive marking of attributes was clearly present at an earlier stage of the language. Possessive suffixes have been lost in favour of a possessive pronoun structure (see Schapper and McConvell this volume, §48.5), but a reflex of the earlier possessive suffix *-n*, cognate with Naueti *-na*, is still used in Kedang as an optional marker of attribution on adjectives ending in a vowel (Samely 1991: 84).

The second feature is synchronic root alternations based on whether an item occurs in a final or non-final position of a phrase or clause (see Schapper and Zobel, this volume, §35.3.4 and Edwards 2020: 19–89 for an overview of these phenomena in the region and beyond). Root alternations involving metathesis of a consonant and a vowel are characteristic of many Austronesian languages in the Timor area. Consonant final forms are preferred in non-final syntactic positions, while vowel-final forms are preferred in final syntactic positions, as illustrated with Helong in (8).

Helong (Austronesian, West Timor, Indonesia)

(8) a. *Auk* ***mail*** *lahin.*
1SG smile:NONFIN yesterday
'I smiled yesterday.'

b. *Auk* ***mali.***
1SG smile:FIN
'I smile.' (Bowden 2010)

Similar processes are found in a small number of Papuan languages in the East Alor group of the Timor-Alor-Pantar family. Wersing, for instance, has a synchronic metathesis involving final unstressed syllables containing a high vowel whereby the consonant-final form is used in non-final positions (9a), while the vowel-final form is used in final positions (9b).

Wersing (East Alor, Timor-Alor-Pantar)

(9) a. *mei* *pok=a* *ge-nimbat*
female small=SPEC 3-headhair
*le-**kuir*** *tuk~tuk*
APPL-comb:NONFIN keep.on
'The girl kept combing her hair.'

b. *mei* *pok=a* *ge-nimbat*
female small=SPEC 3-headhair
*le-**kuri***
APPL-comb:FIN
'The girl combed her hair.' (Schapper fieldnotes)

Not all languages use metathesis to create their final/non-final distinctions of consonant-final vs. vowel-final forms. In two closely related Papuan languages, Sawila and Kula, roots with a final open syllable historically show loss of the final vowel in their non-final forms, while phrase-final forms retain the vowel. For roots historically with a final closed syllable, final forms have a vowel *-a added, while non-final forms retain the historical closed syllable (Schapper 2017b: 29–31).

Cross-linguistically, both possessive-like attribute constructions and final/non-final root alternations are highly unusual linguistic features. It seems unlikely that these two features would occur by chance in unrelated languages in proximity to one another. Especially when the diversity of formal manifestations involving the use of language- and family-specific devices to achieve similar structures is also considered, it seems much more likely that language contact is responsible for these features being transmitted across families. However, because neither feature is typical of Austronesian or Papuan languages, no obvious directionality for the transfer of the features presents itself.

Although Papuan languages have undoubtablely had a significant impact on Austronesian languages in the eastern MPSEA area, indeterminate Papuan substrates or Papuan contact cannot be assumed to be the source of all innovative features in those languages. Only where specific argumentation can be presented to support the directionality of transfer should innovations in Austronesian languages of the eastern MPSEA area be ascribed to transfer from Papuan languages.

## 22.5 Inheritance vs. diffusion of Papuan features

We have a reasonable picture of the structural states of the Austronesian family at several points in its history, including outside of the Papuan contact zone. However, there is a major gap in our understanding of the Austronesian family when it first enters the area where Papuan languages are spoken or are inferred to have been spoken in the past. In the time intervening between Proto-Malayo-Polynesian and Proto-Oceanic, the two clearest and best understood major nodes of the Austronesian family tree outside of the Formosan homeland, speakers of Papuan languages were encountered and their influence is agreed to be responsible for many of the differences in these two reconstructed languages. In the western Papuan contact zone, the timing of the introduction of Papuan features into the Austronesian family is contested.

Four features proposed by Blust (1993a) as defining Proto-Central Eastern Malayo-Polynesian are suggested by Donohue and Grimes (2008) to have been the result of contact with Papuan languages. Whilst originating in contact with a Papuan language is not a reason to doubt the subgrouping value of an innovation *per se*, Donohue and Grimes (2008) argue that the only sporadic attestation of some features and the lack of clearly cognate morphology for others point to erratic diffusion rather than a single innovation in a common protolanguage. The features of disputed entry in PCEMP are: (i) verbal person-number prefixes/proclitics; (ii) the distinction between alienable and inalienable possession; (iii) semantic extension of PMP *dalem 'inside; interior' to PCEMP *dalem 'mind; feelings'; and (iv) innovation of PCEMP *daun ni qulu 'leaf of the head' for 'head hair'. The first three of these will be discussed briefly in turn, before a more in-depth discussion of (iv), an agreed Papuan feature whose reconstructive value is particularly contested.

Blust (1993a: 258–9) tentatively reconstructs a paradigm of verbal person-number prefixes/proclitics for PCEMP, but Donohue and Grimes (2008: 131–2) cast doubt on whether the different forms, particularly in CMP languages, can convincingly be treated as a single innovation such as would characterize an ancestral protolanguage. Following Wolff (1996), Blust (2009a: 59) concedes that in the Austronesian family "the use of prefixal/proclitic agreement markers on the verb has arisen independently through multiple historical changes. This obviously weakens it as subgrouping evidence, although it is still noteworthy that systems of this type are extremely common in eastern Indonesia, and are found in a number of the languages of western Melanesia." The unelaborated implication of Donohue and Grimes' (2008: 152) treatment is that the concentration of Austronesian languages with prefixal/proclitic agreement on verbs in the western Papuan contact zone is due to diffusion from Papuan languages in the region where similar agreement markers are the norm. See Zobel (this volume, §13.5.2) for further discussion of the agreement prefixes, their functions, and reconstruction in CMP languages.

Blust (1993a: 259) observes that the contrast between direct possession for inalienable nouns and indirect possession for alienable nouns is unique to CMP, SHWNG, and Oceanic languages and suggests that it could be reconstructable to his PCEMP node. Donohue and Grimes (2008: 142) contend that, although distinctions between alienable and inalienable possession are found widely across Austronesian languages of the eastern MPSEA area, "it is only in [Eastern Malayo-Polynesian] that they become the norm, and where cognate morphology can regularly be found" and that the feature can readily be ascribed to Papuan contact, given the widespread presence of this feature in the Papuan languages. Blust (2009a: 59) again concedes, writing "[t]his point is well taken, since without cognate morphology the comparison relies on typological data for subgrouping, and it is well known that this is unreliable." Van den Berg (2009) further agrees that Papuan contact was likely responsible for the feature entering Austronesian languages, but he argues for seeing the distinction between alienable and inalienable possession as entering the Austronesian language family in PEMP, the hypothetical ancestor of PSHWNG and POc spoken in the vicinity of West New Guinea. He agrees with Donohue and Grimes (2008) that the contrast between alienable and inalienable possession in CMP languages is best explained as due to diffusion from Papuan languages. Donohue and Schapper (2008) point out that the contrast between direct possession for inalienable nouns and indirect possession for alienable nouns can be reconstructed to Proto-Timor-Alor-Pantar and that the presence of such a feature at an early time in a Papuan family in the vicinity of where Austronesian languages first begin to display such typologically unusual systems is hardly likely to be chance. See Schapper and McConvell (this volume, §48.4) for further discussion of possessive contrasts and their distribution in MPSEA languages.

The third of Blust's (1993a) PCEMP developments, argued by Donohue and Grimes (2008: 148–9) to be of Papuan origin, is the semantic extension of PMP *dalem 'inside; interior' to PCEMP *dalem 'mind; feelings'. Donohue and Grimes (2008: 148–9) point out that the extension semantically mirrors the situation found in Timor-Alor-Pantar languages, whereby a locative noun 'inside' is also used with sense of 'seat of character, emotions, and values'. Blust (2009a: 66) does not make any comment on the appearance of the same lexico-semantic association in Papuan languages of the area. This silence could be taken to indicate concession of the point that remodelling on the basis of Papuan languages is the likely source of the semantic extension. Nonetheless, Blust (2009a) makes clear that he maintains the subgrouping value of the semantic change within the Austronesian language family.

The final point of Papuan influence in PCEMP is what Blust (1993a: 262) calls a "striking semantic innovation" in several Austronesian languages of the Papuan contact zone whereby a lexeme 'leaf' is used to denote 'head hair', often as part of a compound with 'head'. He argues that the form *daun ni qulu 'leaf of head' was an alternative term for 'head hair' in PCEMP alongside *buhek 'head hair' continued from PMP. As it is common in Papuan languages to use words meaning 'leaf' also in the sense of 'hair', Blust (1993a) recognizes that the innovation may be a product of contact with Papuan languages, but he notes that it is known principally from languages that are not in contact with Papuan languages. The spotty appearance of the innovation west of New Guinea led Donohue and Grimes (2008: 148) to view expressions 'leaf of the head' for 'head hair' as calqued from Papuan languages: "The very scarcity of the expression in the Austronesian languages lends to the argument that this was a contact-induced change affecting some, but not all, of the languages proposed to be CEMP, and not an innovation defining the group." Blust (2009a: 65) restates that "the point at issue is whether it reflects a single historical change in a language community ancestral to the languages of eastern Indonesia and Oceanic, or is a product of multiple contact induced changes that produced similar outcomes" and concludes that "there appears to be no obvious way to settle this issue on present evidence". Because it is agreed to be of Papuan origin, but its value for subgrouping within the Austronesian family is openly contested, it is worth reviewing the data for this feature in greater detail so that the reader can come to their own conclusions.

Table 22.3 presents the languages of the western Papuan contact zone that use a lexeme denoting 'leaf' also as (part of) an expression for 'head hair'. The reader can see that the forms and word orders used in the constructions using 'leaf' for 'head hair' are diverse. In addition to expressions for 'head hair' transparently involving a generic lexeme for 'leaf', there are numerous cases of more obscure forms where we are in essence dealing with historical compounds in which the second element reflects PCEMP *daun 'leaf' (e.g. Ambai *nu**randaun*** 'head hair' is segmentable with an unexplained medial consonant, thus *nu-ra-C-**raun*** lit. 'hair-LOC-C-leaf'). Because of the initial consonant mutations that occur in compounds (so-called VRK mutation, see Gasser, Arnold, and Kamholz, this volume, §37.2.4), the forms in West Yapen languages are not identical to generic lexemes 'leaf' and I annotate them apart here.

The data assembled in the table is the result of a wide-ranging areal study of lexico-semantic constructions in Melanesia (Schapper 2017c). It includes many more

**Table 22.3** Austronesian languages west of New Guinea with lexico-semantic constructions in which 'leaf' = 'head hair'

| | 'head hair' | 'leaf' | 'head' | *Notes* | *Source* |
|---|---|---|---|---|---|
| Arguni | *árug**náno*** | ***náno*** | *árug* | | Narfafan 2011 |
| Sekar | *unin **fakin*** | *ka**fakin*** | *unin batin* | | Donohue 2010 |
| Masiwang | *-ulin **lan*** | *ai **lan*** | *-ulin katin* | | Collins 1986b |
| Ili'uun (Erai) | *kuru(n)**rōn*** | *ai**rōn*** | *kuru(n)* | | Josselin de Jong 1947 |
| Waima'a | *ulu-**rae*** | *kai-**rae*** | *ulu* | | Belo et al. 1999 |
| Naueti | *ulu-**rae*** | *kai-**rae*** | *ulu* | | Veloso 2016 |
| Idate | *huhu **ron*** | ***ron*** | *huhu* | | Purwa et al. 1994 |
| Dadu'a | *ulu **roo*** | *ai **roo*** | *ulu-n (fatuk)* | | Penn 2006 |
| Hresuk | *ulu **ron*** | ***ron*** | *ulu* | | Boarccaech 2013 |
| Central Mambae | *ulu **nora*** | ***nora**-n* | *ulu* | | Fogaça 2017 |
| Welaun | *ulut **loon*** | ***loon*** | *ulut* | | da Silva 2012 |
| Dhao | ***rəu** kətu* | ***rəu*** | *kətu* | | Balukh 2020 |
| Hawu | ***ru**-kətu* | ***rou**, ro- ~ ru-* | *kətu* | ***ru**-aju* 'leaf', ***ro**-muʔu* 'banana leaf' | Walker 1982 |
| Hewa | *loʔe **roun*** | ***roun*** | *loʔe-n* | | Fricke 2014 |
| Biak | *bu**ram*** | ***ram*** | *bu-kor* | | Anceaux 1961 |
| Kurudu | *du**koi*** | ***koi*** | *du* | | Anceaux 1961 |
| Moor | *u**rànu*** | ***rànu*** | *vàru* | | Kamholz online |
| Ambai | *nur**andaun*** | *rau* | *nu* | *nu-ra-C-**raun*** (lit. 'hair-LOC-leaf') | Silzer 1983 |
| Ansus | *du**andauŋ*** | *werauŋ* | *dukami* | *du-na-C-**rauŋ*** (lit. 'hair-LOC-leaf') | Rayewai, Worabai, Donohue 2002 |
| Wamesa | *ru**nandau*** | *rau* | *ru* | *ru-na-C-**rau*** (lit. 'hair-LOC-leaf') | Gasser 2014 |
| Wooi | *riu**andauŋ*** | *ariuŋ* | *riukami* | *r<i>u-na-C-**rauŋ*** (lit. 'hair-LOC-leaf') | Sawaki 2016 |

languages displaying the semantic association of head hair and leaf than given in either Blust (1993a, 2009a) or Donohue and Grimes (2008) and, unlike the data in those works, can be taken to represent a fairly complete distributional picture of the feature in the Austronesian languages in the eastern MPSEA region. The fact that the association of head hair and leaf is more numerous in Austronesian languages in the eastern MPSEA region than previously clear could be taken to support Blust's reconstruction to PCEMP. However, if the feature was present in PCEMP, we would expect to see the feature dotted widely across the CMP and SHWNG languages. Instead, we find a strong geographical skewing of the feature into clusters of proximal Austronesian languages from diverse subgroups within CMP and SHWNG. The clusters are found in three fairly compact regions: (i) on and around Timor; (ii) on and around the Onin peninsula of Bomberai; and (iii) on and around Yapen island in Cenderawasih Bay.

What is striking about this distribution is that the clusters form around what we can infer were prehistorical contact regions because in each case there are extant Papuan languages at their core. In the case of the Timor region, Donohue and Grimes (2008) already noted that 'leaf' is found in expressions for 'head hair' in the Papuan languages of Pantar (e.g. Teiwa *-oʔon waʔ* 'head hair' < *-oʔon* 'head' and *waʔ* 'leaf'). The same pattern is attested in three of the four Papuan languages in Timor, for example, Makasae *daʔe-asa* 'head hair' < *daʔe* 'head' and *asa* 'leaf'. On the Onin peninsula, the Papuan languages also display the pattern associating leaf and head hair, for example, Iha *kanda-ten* 'head hair' < *kanda* 'head' and *ten* 'leaf'. On Yapen, the Papuan languages are not well documented and it is not clear whether they display the pattern: Yawa *akarivuin* 'head hair' and Saweru *nayaribn* 'head hair'. In both languages the lexemes are transparently compounds with an initial element 'head' (Yawa *akari* 'head', Saweru *nayari* 'head'), but the second elements (Yawa *vuin*, Saweru *bin*) are not known outside of these compounds.

For the present author, the diversity of forms and constructions as well as the skewed geographical distribution of the lexico-semantic association of 'head hair' with 'leaf' in Austronesian languages of the eastern MPSEA area speaks much more to multiple calquing events from Papuan languages than inheritance. However, as Blust (2009a) points out, different interpretations are possible. The authors of the Proto-Oceanic lexicon seemingly agree with Blust's view, reconstructing POc *raun 'leaf; head hair' alongside POc *puRu- 'head hair; feather' (Ross, Pawley, and Osmond 2016: 91–2), even though the distribution of the languages with the extension 'leaf' > 'head hair' in Oceanic is also consistent with multiple calquing events from Papuan sources east of New Guinea.

In short, decisions about how to deal with Papuan influence on Austronesian languages can come down to the disposition of the treating linguists. Reconstructively minded linguists often prefer an analysis of inheritance of Papuan features within the Austronesian family tree, while areally minded linguists tend to see multiple diffusion events for features commonly found in Papuan languages. Whilst the features discussed here are not essential to the maintenance of the CEMP and CMP nodes in the Austronesian family tree (see Zobel, this volume, Chapter 13 for discussion of the most important phonological evidence), they do illustrate the complicating role that Papuan contact has had in the history of the Austronesian family.

## 22.6 Concluding discussion

The existing literature provides ample evidence of Papuan linguistic features having entered the Austronesian languages of the eastern MPSEA area. This evidence and its significance for understanding the manner in which the Austronesian expansion progressed in the eastern MPSEA area has been downplayed by some scholars (e.g. Hung and Bellwood, this volume, Chapter 6). The widespread presence of Papuan structural features, but comparatively few (known) lexical borrowings, strongly suggests imperfect learning of a target language by a group of shifting speakers. Casual, fleeting contacts between languages are not under normal circumstances sufficient to cause structural transfer. What is more, structural influence is not typical where the shifting population is small (Thomason 2009). Given these typological observations, 'shift-induced' or 'substrate' interference occasioned by large groups of Papuan-language speakers shifting relative to the original Austronesian-language speaking populations provides the best explanation for the significant changes we observe in the Austronesian languages of the eastern MPSEA area. The idea that the Austronesian expansion involved substantial interaction with Papuan languages and cultures in the eastern part of the MPSEA area is put most forcefully by Donohue and Denham (2010).

Observations of contact phenomena between Papuan languages and Austronesian languages of the Oceanic subgroup to the east of New Guinea have been important in the development of linguistic theory, with a number of the canonical contact situations described in the literature originating there (e.g. Thurston 1987; Ross 1996). To the west of New Guinea in the eastern MPSEA area, by contrast, there has been comparatively little study of contact between extant Papuan and Austronesian speaking groups. There are still no detailed case studies of the many ongoing contact situations of Papuan and Austronesian languages in the MPSEA area. In-depth case studies of Papuan–Austronesian contact, such as Saweru–Ambai, West Makian–Taba, Mbaham–Sekar, Kisar–Oirata, or Bunaq–Kemak, would be desirable for the light that they could shed on the contact dynamics between the different language groups, both now and in the past.

As witnesses of the languages of human populations in New Guinea prior to the Austronesian language dispersal, the importance of Papuan languages for understanding changes in the Austronesian family tree cannot be underestimated. Yet, there has been little work to unpick the sources of hypothesized Papuan features in Austronesian languages and the timing of their introduction into the Austronesian family. Contact between speakers of Austronesian languages and pre-existing populations in the MPSEA area was not a single, uniform process, but rather involved different processes with "different starting points, different trajectories, and different time spans in different societies (even those in the same local area)" (Donohue and Denham 2020: 449). One of the major problems with reconstructing Papuan influence in the Austronesian family tree is the fact that there has been little historical reconstructive work on key Papuan language families around the Bird's Head of New Guinea. With reconstructions of these Papuan families in hand, linguists would be better able to illuminate the various points of contact between speakers of Austronesian and Papuan languages, when Austronesian speakers moved into the eastern MPSEA area around 3000 years ago.

## Acknowledgements

Many thanks to Sander Adelaar, David Gil, Betty Litamahuputty, and Erik Zobel for comments on various portions of this chapter at different stages. Research funding has come from the Netherlands Organisation for Scientific Research VENI project "The evolution of the lexicon. Explorations in lexical stability, semantic shift and borrowing in a Papuan language family", the Volkswagen Stiftung DoBeS project "Aru languages documentation", the Australian Research Council project (ARC, DP180100893) "Waves of words", and the European Research Council "OUTOFPAPUA" project (grant agreement no. 848532). All errors are my own.

CHAPTER 23

# Non-areal contact

Tom Hoogervorst

## 23.1 Introduction

This chapter discusses non-areal contact between MPSEA languages and other families found in four regions: South Asia, West Asia, East Asia, and Europe. These contact situations are outlined in four separate sections. Attention is given to lexical borrowing, typological convergence, and influence through language planning policies. In most non-areal contact situations, Austronesian languages have adopted more features from non-Austronesian sources than vice versa, yet lexical and grammatical borrowing in the opposite direction will be addressed as well. Language contact with the non-Austronesian languages of Mainland Southeast Asia (see Sidwell, this volume, Chapter 20) and near Oceania (see Schapper, this volume, Chapter 22) falls beyond the scope of this chapter, as do the Austronesian languages spoken in Taiwan and Oceania.

South Asian languages, especially Sanskrit, represent the earliest and most enduring layer of non-areal contact in MPSEA languages. Most lexical influence from West Asia comes from classical Arabic, although connections with the region predate Islamization. Contacts with East Asia predominantly took place through speakers of Southern Min (Min Nan), in particular the Hokkien variety. The role of European languages largely reflects colonial expansion, with Portuguese, Spanish, Dutch, English, and French being the most important donors of loanwords and typological influence. Historically, Malay was the main vector of direct and indirect borrowings in Southeast Asia and—in early times—also in Madagascar, so that it merits slightly more attention in the present chapter than other Austronesian languages. That being said, Javanese, the languages of South Sulawesi, and possibly other languages also played significant roles (Adelaar 1994a; Mahdi 1994; Hoogervorst 2013). In terms of geographical distribution, pre-modern loanwords from Sanskrit are attested in Island Southeast Asia (including what is now the Philippines and eastern Indonesia), Mainland Southeast Asia, and Madagascar. Arabic loanwords are equally widespread and were also chiefly transmitted through Malay. Most Arabic loans entered Malagasy directly from the Middle East or through East Africa, although the Antaimoro Muslims on Madagascar's east coast also exhibit some likely Southeast Asian links (Adelaar 1995a, 2009b). Lexical influence from Southern Min is strongest in what is now the Philippines and western Indonesia. Spanish and Portuguese were the earliest vehicles of European concepts and commodities. Later European influence, including from Dutch, English, French, and Portuguese (in the case of Timor Leste), is palpable in all the national languages of the regions discussed here. Some policies of post-independence language planning have sought to replace such loanwords by neologisms—in many cases loan translations—consisting of indigenous or at least non-European elements.

Some of the historical layers of lexical borrowing identified in this chapter have been revitalized in modern times. A cross-linguistic comparison of some modern coinages illustrates this point. Tetun, the national language of Timor Leste, designates the concept of 'human rights' with the Portuguese-inspired *direitu umanu* (< *direitos humanos*). Tagalog and Malagasy exhibit loan translations—respectively *karapatáŋ pantao* and *zon'olombelona*—consisting of the segments 'right' + 'human'. Indonesian, Indonesia's standardization of the Malay language, has opted for the loan translation *hak asasi manusia*, consisting of two loans from Arabic (*hak* 'right' < *ḥaqq* + *asasi* 'basic' < *asāsī*), and one from Sanskrit (*manusia* 'human' < *manuṣya*). Indeed, it is not uncommon for Indonesian to draw from pre-European phases of language contact to 'indigenize' foreign concepts, or to combine multiple layers. The loan translation *warisan non-bəndawi* 'intangible heritage' consists of *waris* 'heir' (< Arabic *wāriṯ*) in combination with the Malay suffix *-an*, the Dutch and ultimately French prefix *non-*, and *bənda* 'object; matter' (< Sanskrit *bhāṇḍa* 'goods; wares') in combination with the Arabic adjectival suffix *-wi* (see §23.3.4). In Malaysia, which exhibits a slightly different Malay standardization, the word *siswazah* 'graduate' combines *siswa* 'pupil' (< Sanskrit

Tom Hoogervorst, *Non-areal contact.* In: *The Oxford Guide to the Malayo-Polynesian Languages of Southeast Asia.* Edited by: Alexander Adelaar and Antoinette Schapper, Oxford University Press. © Tom Hoogervorst (2024). DOI: 10.1093/oso/9780198807353.003.0023

*śiṣya*) and *ijazah* 'diploma' (< Arabic *iǧāza*). Henceforth, I use 'Indonesian' and 'Malaysian' for the present-day Malay standardizations of Indonesia and Malaysia respectively (see Hoogervorst, this volume, §17.2.2), and 'Malay' in reference to the pre-standardized language from which both are derived.

Non-areal language contact offers valuable insights into a region's history and the role of different ethnolinguistic communities contributing to it. Nevertheless, etymology alone is rarely adequate to identify the ethnolinguistic community responsible for the introduction of a borrowed concept. Contact situations often involve multiple layers of borrowing and processes of semantic specialization. Malay literature, for example, exhibits several indigenous words for 'shipmaster', but tended to use *naxoda* (< Persian *nāḫudā*) if the captain in question was of West Asian descent, *taikoŋ* (< Southern Min 舵公 *tāi-kong*) if he was Chinese, and *kapitan* (< Portuguese *capitão*) if he was of European ancestry. Along the same lines, it exhibits at least four competing words for 'ink': *maŋsi* (< Sanskrit *maṣi*); *dawat* (< Arabic *dawāt*); *baʔ* (< Southern Min 墨 *bák*); and *tinta* (< Portuguese *tinta*), reflecting overlapping contact situations. Personal pronouns, especially the first and second person singular, are also liable to be borrowed and replaced (Wallace 1983). Several Spanish loanwords in Philippine languages have likewise replaced pre-existing vocabulary, some of which of Malay/Javanese and ultimately Sanskrit origins. Tagalog *diyos* 'god' (< Spanish *dios*) and *armas* 'weaponry' (< Spanish *armas*), for example, have rendered obsolete *bathalaʔ* (< Malay *bətara*, Old Javanese *bhaṭāra* < Sanskrit *bhaṭṭāra* 'noble lord') and *sandata* (< Malay *sənjata* 'weapon', Old Javanese *sañjata* < Sanskrit *saṁyatta* 'come into conflict; being on one's guard') with the same meaning.

It is difficult to the point of futility to quantify the number of non-areal loanwords in MPSEA languages. Notwithstanding some lexicographical and etymological studies on the sources of Javanese, Tagalog, Cham, Malagasy, and other Austronesian languages, nothing surpasses the scope and breadth of scholarship assembled in *Loan-words in Indonesian and Malay* (Jones 2007). The loanwords cited in most studies are not necessarily established or known to modern-day speakers. In fact, the majority tend to be restricted to archaic speech styles and arcane literature. In addition, numerous loans from European languages are confined to the multilingual elites of a country, who often use them to showcase their cultural capital. In doing so, it is not uncommon for acrolectal speakers to also superimpose the phonology of European languages onto their Austronesian mother tongues.

## 23.2 South Asian languages

### 23.2.1 History of contact

Contacts between South and Southeast Asia can be traced archaeologically to the late first millennium BCE. They were predominantly of a commercial and cultural nature, eventually culminating in the introduction in Southeast Asia of literacy and 'Indic' notions of statehood, social organization, and religion. Cham, Malay, Javanese, and Balinese epigraphy contains innumerable loanwords and multiple-word segments in Sanskrit, which by the first century CE had become South Asia's chief language of elite expression. The epigraphical record thus contains the first solid evidence of language contact, leaving the preceding centuries, for which we have no written evidence, poorly understood. It is likely that some knowledge of Sanskrit was common among the literati from the abovementioned speech communities.

The majority of Sanskrit-derived loanwords in Austronesian languages comprise abstract concepts, such as terms related to religion, law, scholarship, art, and numerals. However, they also include a number of distinctly quotidian things and materials such as Malay *kaca* 'glass' (< *kāca*), *kota* 'fort; city' (< *koṭṭa*), and *mərica* 'black pepper' (< *marīca*), which spread across a large number of Austronesian languages. Several Sanskrit loanwords complemented or ousted existing vocabulary. The Malay first-person singular polite pronoun *saya* goes back to Sanskrit *sahāya* 'companion; follower'. Other 'luxury loans' include parts of the body: *kəpala* 'head' (< *kapāla* 'skull'), *muka* 'face' (< *mukha*), and *roma* 'body hair' (< *romā*); or natural phenomena: *gajah* 'elephant' (< *gaja*), *gərhana* 'eclipse' (< *grahaṇa*), and *goa* 'cave' (< *guha*). A Sanskritized register of Old Malay seems to have been responsible for the introduction of Sanskrit loanwords into Madagascar, the Philippines and elsewhere in Island Southeast Asia. Some Sanskrit loans in especially Tagalog evolved from a phonologically and semantically conservative form of Malay or Javanese (Table 23.1).

It is impossible in this chapter to go into great depths regarding the influence of Sanskrit on Austronesian languages. In general, the quantity of Sanskrit loanwords in Old Javanese, Old Sundanese, Old Malay, and Old Cham was considerably larger compared to their present-day equivalents. Best studied is the influence of Sanskrit on Malaysian/Indonesian (Sharma 1985; de Casparis 1997; Jones 2007; Collins 2009), Malagasy (Dahl 1951; Bernard-Thierry 1959; Adelaar 1994a, 2009a), Toba Batak (Parkin 1978), and the Philippine languages (Kern 1880, 1881; Francisco 1964; Wolff 1976), while the most exhaustive comparative study has been undertaken by Gonda (1973). Conversely, much less

**Table 23.1** Distribution of Sanskrit loanwords

| Sanskrit | Old Javanese | Malay | Toba Batak | Tagalog |
|---|---|---|---|---|
| *doṣa* 'offence; sin' | *doṣa* 'offence; sin' | *dosa* 'sin; offence against law' | *dosa* 'sin' | *dusa* 'suffering' |
| *kathā* 'story; narration' | *kathā* 'story; narration' | *kata* 'speech; utterance; word' | *hata* 'word; speech; language' | *kathá?* 'literary composition' |
| *sama* 'the equal of; likeness' | *sama* 'equal; same' | *sama* 'sameness; with' | *sama* 'together' | *ka-sama* 'companion' |
| *sūtra* 'thread; yarn' | *sutra* 'silk' | *sutəra* 'silk' | *sutora* 'silk' | *sutlá?* 'silk' |
| *vaṁśa* 'lineage; dynasty' | *vaṅśa* 'lineage; dynasty' | *baŋsa* 'decent; people' | *baŋso* 'people; nation' | *bansá?* 'nation' |
| *vr̥tta* 'happened; an event' | *vr̥tta* 'event' | *bərita* 'news; report' | *barita* 'rumour; message' | *balita?* 'news; information' |

is known about the role of South Asian languages other than Sanskrit, as will be discussed next.

## 23.2.2 Beyond Sanskrit

Across a number of 'Indianized' parts of pre-modern South and Southeast Asia, Sanskrit was the chief vehicle of proclamatory politics, religious liturgy, and literary aesthetics, yet it never served as a medium of everyday oral communication. The earliest South Asian merchants in contact with Austronesian speech communities would have spoken Dravidian or Middle-Indo-Aryan (henceforth MIA) languages or 'Prakrits', depending on their regional origins. Only two studies (known to me) deal with MIA influence on Old Javanese and other Austronesian languages (de Casparis 1988; Hoogervorst 2017). Unlike the more abstract Sanskrit loans, MIA and Dravidian borrowings often include items of practical use, such as weapons and other metal objects, structures, and construction techniques (Hoogervorst 2016a). They can be found, alongside Sanskrit loanwords, in the earliest Malay inscriptions (seventh century CE) and in Javanese inscriptions and other texts (ninth century CE). During the latter centuries of the first millennium CE, the MIA languages evolved into New-Indo-Aryan languages (henceforth NIA), such as Hindustani, Gujarati, Marathi, Oriya, and Bengali. As this took place when contact with Southeast Asia was still regular, some archaic NIA forms (*Apabhraṁśa*) must have entered Malay and neighbouring Austronesian languages (Hoogervorst 2017: 423–31), for example, *sərapah* 'curse' (< **śrāpa* < Sanskrit *śāpa*, cf. Hindustani *srāp*) and *unta* 'camel' (< **uṇṭa* < Sanskrit *uṣṭra*, cf. Hindustani *uṇt*).

Direct contact between Austronesian languages and Pali appears to have been limited. In Island Southeast Asia, all words previously identified as Pali could equally well come from a different MIA source (Hoogervorst 2017). To my knowledge, the only unequivocal attestations of Pali loanwords are in Austronesian languages situated within the Daic (i.e. Thai and related languages), Burmese, and/or Mon-Khmer influence sphere, such as Moken and Cham. In these instances, they are all indirect borrowings. In the case of Cham, a number of postulated Indic loanwords are reconstructable to the level of Proto-Cham (Thurgood 1999: 346–47). Their phonological shape would suggest borrowing from Pali through Old Khmer (Table 23.2).

**Table 23.2** Pali loanwords in Cham

| Pali | meaning | Old Khmer | Proto-Cham |
|---|---|---|---|
| *assa* | 'horse' | *'aseḥ* /seh/ | *ʔasɛh |
| *ratha* | 'vehicle' | *radeḥ* /rᵊdeh/ | *radɛh |
| *visa* | 'poison; venom' | *bisa* /bɪh/ | *bih |

Language contact between South and Southeast Asia exhibits multiple layers. Sanskrit *vajra*, for example, can denote a variety of hard objects including diamonds, thunderbolts, and types of steel. This Sanskrit word has been borrowed directly into Javanese as *bajra*, denoting a jewel, a type of weapon, and a flash of lightning. The early-MIA counterpart of Sanskrit *vajra* is *vajja*, which entered Malay and some surrounding languages as *baja* 'steel'. This early-MIA form developed into late-MIA *vaïra*, which was borrowed into Tamil as *vayiram* and eventually entered the Malay literature as *biram* 'red diamond'. Various other loanwords in especially Malay and Old Javanese have undergone sound changes pointing to MIA rather than Sanskrit as their donor (Table 23.3). Phonological irregularities often reflect indirect borrowing. For example, Sanskrit *hasta* 'forearm (a measure of length)' was borrowed directly into Malay as *hasta*, whereas Moken *hat* in the same meaning was probably borrowed from Pali *hattha* through a Mon-Khmer language.

Among the Dravidian languages, most loanwords into MPSEA languages have been taken from Tamil. Medieval inscriptions and early European accounts attest to the long historical presence of Tamil speakers in some parts of Sumatra and the Malay Peninsula. Many more arrived in colonial times, chiefly but not exclusively as labour migrants. Etymological scholarship on Tamil loanwords has been carried out for Malay (van Ronkel 1902a, 1903a; Asmah Haji Omar 1966; Jones 2007), Philippine languages (Francisco 1966; Arokiaswamy 2000), and comparatively (Hoogervorst 2015). Some of the most widespread Tamil loans in Malay and, hence, other Austronesian languages relate to manufactured items, for example, *bədil* 'firearm' (< *veḍil* 'explosion'), *bələŋgu* 'fetters' (< *vilāṅgu*), and *kapal* 'ship' (< *kappal*). Other examples are found in the realm of food preparation, for example, *apam* 'rice flour pancake' (< *appam*), *kari* 'curry' (< *kaṟi*), and *putu* 'kind of confectionery' (< *puṭṭu*). The Tamil word *tamaṉ* 'male friend' became Malay *təman* 'friend', which serves as the first person singular pronoun in the Malay dialect of Perak. Less studied are Tamil loanwords unattested in Malay but found in other Austronesian languages. Examples from Javanese include *baṭi* 'profit' (< *vaṭṭi*), *roṇḍe* 'k.o. ball-shaped snack' (< *uruṇḍai* 'mouthful of food in the shape of a ball'), and *tir* 'chariot (in chess)' (< *tēr* 'chariot'). Karo Batak exhibits among others *metu* 'unable to move (in chess)' (< *māttu* 'checkmate'), *patam* 'a forehead ornament' (< *paṭṭam* 'plate of gold worn on the forehead'), and *sore* 'k.o. arrow' (< *curai* 'head of an arrow'). Beyond Tamil, some words in Malay and other Austronesian languages appear to come from Malayalam, including *pərmadani* 'carpet' (< *paravadāni*), *sərambi* 'veranda' (< *saṟāmbi* 'k.o. pavilion'), and *tandas* 'latrine' (< *taṇḍās*). Malay *cəlana* and Javanese *clana* 'trousers' might reflect Kannada *callaṇa* 'short breeches'. No loanwords of unambiguously Telugu origin are known to me, although some might be identified upon further study. Based on their phonological characteristics, a number of loanwords of ultimately non-Dravidian origins appears to have entered Austronesian languages through speakers of Dravidian languages (Tadmor 2009: 694; Hoogervorst 2015: 80–3), including Malay *kuda* 'horse' (< **koḍa* < Sanskrit *ghoṭa*), and *pasar* 'market' (< **pasār* < Persian *bāzār*).

Loanwords of a likely NIA provenance, although the precise donor language remains to be identified, include Malay *kətumbar* 'coriander', *kunci* 'key', *pandai* 'expert; specialist', *patəri* 'to solder', and *sundal* 'whore'. More specifically, several NIA loanwords in Austronesian languages seem to be from an early form of Hindustani (van Ronkel 1902b; Winstedt 1917; Jones 2007). Such loans are most numerous in Acehnese and Malay, particularly in the Malay dialect of Penang. Common examples include Malay *baŋsal* 'shed' (< *bhansāl* 'storehouse'), *biri-biri* 'sheep' (< *bheṛī* 'ewe'), and *cap*

**Table 23.3** MIA loanwords in Old Javanese and Malay (based on Hoogervorst 2017)

| Sanskrit | meaning | MIA | Old Javanese | Malay |
|---|---|---|---|---|
| *kañcuka* | 'dress; armour' | *kañcuga | *kañcuga* | |
| *prage* | 'early in the morning' | *page | | *pagi* 'morning' |
| *prastaraṇa* | 'a seat' | *pattharaṇa | *paṭāraṇa* 'ceremonial seat' | *pətarana* 'ceremonial seat' |
| *sakala* | 'entire; all' | *sagala | *sagala* | *səgala* |
| *tāmraka* | 'copper' | *tambaga | *tambaga* | *təmbaga* |
| *trika* | 'triple' | *tiga | | *tiga* 'three' |
| *utpatti* | 'production' | *uppatti | *upəti* 'production; tribute' | *upəti* 'tribute' |
| *vāṇijaka* | 'merchant' | *vāṇiyaga | *baṇyaga, baṇyāga* | *bəniaga* |

**Table 23.4** NIA loanwords in Malay (data largely taken from Turner 1966)

| Malay | meaning | Bengali | Oriya | Hindustani | Marathi | Gujarati |
|---|---|---|---|---|---|---|
| *basi* | 'stale' | *bāsi* | *bāsi* | *bāsī* | | *vāsī* |
| *bəndahari* | 'treasurer' | *bhāṇḍārī* | *bhaṇḍāri* | *bhāḍārī* | *bhaṇḍārī* | *bhāḍārī* |
| *bəndi* | 'okra' | | *bhẽḍi* | *bhiṇḍī* | *bheṇḍī* | |
| *curi* | 'theft; to steal' | *curi* | *cori* | *corī* | *cōrī* | *corī* |
| *cuti* | 'vacation' | *chuṭi* | *chuṭi* | *chuṭṭī* | | *chuṭṭī* |
| *pəti* | 'box; chest' | *peṭi* | | *peṭī* | *peṭī* | *peṭī* |
| *roti* | 'bread' | *ruṭi* | *ruṭi* | *roṭī* | *roṭī* | *roṭī* |
| *topi* | 'hat' | *ṭupi* | *ṭopi* | *ṭopī* | *ṭopī* | *ṭopī* |

'stamp; seal' (< *chāp*). For other NIA loanwords, the precise source is less clear (Table 23.4). No research known to me has been published on loanwords that can be identified as uniquely Gujarati, notwithstanding the historically attested importance of traders from Gujarat in early modern times. The same holds true for Bengali, although colonial era dictionaries tend to erroneously mark generic NIA loanwords as 'Bengali'.

The NIA word *beṭā* 'son; boy' entered Malay as *beta* 'servant', which is used as a first person singular pronoun in Kupang Malay, Ambon Malay, and literary Malay. Acehnese exhibits some NIA loanwords not attested in Malay, including *pacih* 'k.o. board game' (< *pacīsī*), *panaih* 'breadfruit' (< *panas*), and *patisah* 'k.o. sweet' (< *patīsā*). A more recent borrowing is Indonesian *bajaj* (pronounced as *bajai*), a three-wheeled vehicle named after its Indian manufacturer Bajāj Auto.

A number of MIA, NIA and Tamil loans—some of which of ultimate Sanskrit origins—have found their way into Malagasy and a number of Sumatran and Philippine languages (Table 23.5), presumably through Malay and/or Javanese.

## 23.2.3 Borrowings into South Asian languages

A small number of probable Malay loanwords can be found in the Sanskrit and Pali literature, although the directionality of borrowing is conventionally assumed to have been reverse. These loans presumably first entered the vernacular languages of South Asia, after which they were artificially hypercorrected using the known sound correspondences between Sanskrit and MIA (Table 23.6).

A number of Malay loanwords entered some of South Asia's modern languages (Table 23.7). It remains to be determined whether these words were borrowed during precolonial or colonial times. In addition, some Karo Batak words have been documented in the slang of nineteenth-century Tamil merchants (cf. Hoogervorst 2013: 17–18, 27–8).

## 23.2.4 Typological influence

The presence of consonant clusters ending in /h/ in languages such as Old Javanese, Tagalog, and presumably also historically in Old Malay reflects phonological influence from Sanskrit, which displays aspirated consonants. South Asian influence may also have reinforced the contrasts in Malay between the voiced palatal stop /j/ [ɟ] and palatal approximant /y/ [j] and between the voiced labial stop /b/ and labial approximant /w/, and in Javanese and Madurese between dental stops and alveolar stops (traditionally known as retroflexes). Borrowing between neighbouring languages, however, seems to have been equally important to these phonological developments (Blust 2013a: 189–93).

On a grammatical level, the morphophonological phenomenon known in Sanskrit linguistics as *sandhi* has been adopted in Old Malay and Old Javanese: the optional merger of the word-final vowel of one segment with the word-initial vowel of the next (van der Molen 2015: 2–3), for example, *bhinna ika* 'it is different' > *bhinneka*. Another example of South Asian influence is the possibility in a number of Austronesian languages of gender assignment through the formation of secondary bases ending in /i/, corresponding to feminine *ī*-stems in Indo-Aryan languages (Hoogervorst 2016b). Modern-day Indonesian also exhibits this option

**Table 23.5** Geographical distribution of South Asian loanwords

| source | meaning | Malay | Javanese | Malagasy | Toba Batak | Tagalog |
|---|---|---|---|---|---|---|
| *buddhu* (MIA) | 'stupid' | *bodoh* | *bodo* | *bodo* | *bodo* | |
| *cukka* (MIA) | 'vinegar' | *cuka* | *coka?* | *tsoha* ('lemon', dial.) | | *suka?* |
| *jagga* (MIA) | 'waking' | *jaga* | *jaga* | *zaha* ('to examine') | *jaga* | |
| *parigai* (Tamil) | 'ditch; moat' | *pərigi* | *prigi* | *farihy* | | |
| *talāga* (MIA) | 'pool; pond' | *təlaga* | *tlaga* | | *talaga* | *talaga?* |

**Table 23.6** Malay loanwords in Sanskrit and Pali (based on Hoogervorst 2013: 103–4)

| Malay | meaning | MIA | Pali backformation | Sanskrit backformation |
|---|---|---|---|---|
| *buah* | 'areca nut' (← 'fruit') | *pūa | *pūga* | *pūga* |
| *halia* | 'ginger' | *allaya | *adda* | *ārdraka* |
| *kapur* (< *kapur Barus*) | 'camphor' | *kappūra | *kappūra* | *karpūra* |
| *kəcur, kəncur* | 'aromatic ginger' | *kaccūra | | *karcūra* |
| *lawang* (< *buah lawang*) | 'clove (spice)' | *lavaṅga | *lavaṅga* | *lavaṁga* |
| *layar* | 'sail' | *layara | *lakāra* | |
| *limau* | 'lime (fruit)' | *?limū | | *nimbū* |
| *timah* (← *timərah) | 'tin (metal)' | *?tīmara | | *tivra* |

**Table 23.7** Malay loanwords in modern South Asian languages (based on Hoogervorst 2013: 106–16)

| Malay | meaning | Hindustani | Tamil | Sinhala | Dhivehi |
|---|---|---|---|---|---|
| *damar* | 'resin; torch' | *ḍāmar* | *kaṟuppu-t-tāmar* | *dummala* | *danmaru* |
| *gudaŋ* (? < Tamil *kiṭṭaṅgi*) | 'storehouse' | *gudām* | *kutām* | *gudama* | *gudan* |
| *kakatua* | 'cockatoo' | *kākātūā* | *kākkattuvāṉ* | | *takatuvā* |
| *kəmənan* (← *?kəmənjan) | 'benzoin; incense' | | *kumañcāṉ* | *kaṭṭa-kumancal* | *kumunzāni* |
| *kəris* | 'k.o. dagger' | | *kiṟicu* | *kiriccaya* | *kiris* |
| *nuri* (< Ternatan *luri*) | 'k.o. parrot' | *nūrī* | | | *nūrī* |

with a limited amount of non-Indic vocabulary, for example, *pəmuda* 'young man' vs. *pəmudi* 'young woman', and *plonco* 'freshman' vs. *plonci* 'female freshman'.

A considerable number of grammatical particles in Malay are derived from Sanskrit and Tamil (Tadmor 2007: 318–20), including *tətapi* 'but' (< Sanskrit *tathāpi* 'but still'), *bila* 'when' (< Sanskrit *velā* 'period'), and *cuma* 'just; only' (< Tamil *cummā* 'leisurely; freely'). Compound forms also exist, for example, *andaikata* 'assuming that' (< Tamil *aṇḍai* 'nearness' + Sanskrit *kathā* 'talk') and *bagaimana* 'how' (< Tamil *vagai* 'sort' + Malay *mana* 'which'). Javanese particles from Sanskrit include *nalika* 'when (in the past)' (< *nālika* 'a period of twenty-four minutes'), *upama-ne* 'supposing that' (< *upama* 'similarity' < *upamā*), and *utawa* 'or' (< *atha vā*). While the adjective typically follows the noun in Austronesian languages, some Sanskrit loans in Malay maintain the Indo-Aryan word order: *pərdana məntəri* 'prime minister' (< *pradhāna* 'chief' + *mantrī* 'minister'), and *pərtama kali* 'first time' (< *prathama* 'first' + Malay *kali* 'time' < Sanskrit *kāla*).

### 23.2.5 Language planning

Modern language engineering has yielded numerous Indonesian neologisms consisting of Sanskrit elements (Gonda 1973; de Casparis 1997; Adelaar 1996a). Examples of such neo-Sanskritisms include: *beasiswa* 'scholarship' (< *vyaya* 'expense' + *śiṣya* 'scholar'), *dwiwarna* 'bicolour, the Indonesian flag' (< *dvi* 'two' + *varṇa* 'colour'), *mahakarya* 'masterpiece' (< *maha* 'great' + *kārya* 'result'), *pancasila* 'The Five Principles of National Ideology' (< *pañca* 'five' + *śīla* 'moral conduct'), and *warganəgara* 'citizen' (*varga* 'group' + *nagara* 'town'). A large number of productive affixes are also inspired by Sanskrit. Table 23.8 lists a number of common derivations so formed.

Sanskrit plays a less prominent role in Malaysia's language planning policy. Several Sanskrit-inspired neologisms in Indonesian exhibit an Arabic counterpart in Malaysian (cf. §23.3.5). For example, 'condolences' is *belasuŋkawa* (< Sanskrit *velā* 'hour of death' + Javanese *suŋkawa* 'sad') in Indonesian and *taʔziah* (< Arabic *taʿziya* 'consolation') in Malaysian, and 'penal' is *pidana* (< Sanskrit *pīḍana* 'torture') in Indonesian and *jənayah* (< Arabic *ǧināya* 'crime') in Malaysian. Conversely, 'victim' is *korban* (← 'sacrifice' < Arabic *qurbān*) in Indonesian and *maŋsa* (← 'prey' < Sanskrit *māṁsa* 'meat') in Malaysian. Some orthographical differences exist for Sanskrit loanwords, such as Indonesian *karəna* 'because' vs. Malaysian *kərana* (< *kāraṇa* 'cause'). Finally, a number of novel concepts exhibit different Sanskrit inspired neologisms; 'astronaut' is *antariksawan* (< *antarīkṣa* 'atmosphere' + *-van*) in Indonesian and *aŋkasawan* (< *ākāśa* 'ether' + *-van*) in Malaysian. Their corresponding female forms are *antariksawati* and *aŋkasawati* respectively.

**Table 23.8** Indonesian neologisms formed through Sanskrit-derived affixes

| Sanskrit element | Indonesian affix | Example |
|---|---|---|
| *antar* 'within' | *antar-* | *antarpulau* 'inter-island' (← *pulau* 'island') |
| *maha* 'great' | *maha-* | *mahabintaŋ* 'superstar' (← *bintaŋ* 'star') |
| *nara* 'man' | *nara-* | *narasumbər* 'informant' (← *sumbər* 'source') |
| *nir* 'without' | *nir-* | *nirkarat* 'stainless (metal)' (← *karat* 'rust') |
| *paścā* 'after' | *pasca-* | *pascabayar* 'postpaid' (← *bayar* 'to pay') |
| *pra* 'before' | *pra-* | *prasaŋka* 'prejudice' (← *saŋka* 'expectation') |
| *sva* 'one's own' | *swa-* | *swalayan* 'self-service' (← *layan* 'service') |
| *-van* 'endowed with; being engaged in (m.)' | *-wan* | *gərilyawan* 'male guerrilla fighter' (← *gərilya* < Spanish *guerrilla*) |
| *-vatī* 'endowed with; being engaged in (f.)' | *-wati* | *gərilyawati* 'female guerrilla fighter' (← *gərilya* < Spanish *guerrilla*) |

## 23.3 West Asian languages

### 23.3.1 History of contact

The vast majority of lexical influence from West Asia is from classical Arabic and consists of innumerable religious, legal, and scholarly terms. Unlike parts of the Mediterranean and West Asia, Southeast Asia and Madagascar were never part of an Arabized empire characterized by large-scale bilingualism. While some Islamic scholars from these regions wrote in Arabic, it was never a widespread language of spoken communication. In addition to Arabic, a smaller yet still considerable quantity of loanwords in Austronesian languages comes from Persian (§23.3.2). Influence from Turkish has been extremely limited and historically entered the region indirectly, typically through Arabic and Persian. Examples in Malay literature include *baʃah* 'Pasha' (< Arabic *bāšā* < Turkish *paşa*), and *bokca* 'wallet' (< Persian *buqča* < Turkish *buqça* 'a bundle'). Malay *opau* and Ilokano *upáw* 'men's purse; money pouch' go back to Southern Min 荷包 *hô-pau*, which ultimately reflects Turkish *kap* 'pouch' (Serruys 1968: 138).

Almost all Arabic loanwords in Austronesian languages are based on their written rather than spoken forms, although it is likely that early colloquial pronunciations were erased in processes of religiously inspired re-Arabization. This has severely complicated the ongoing debate on the ethnolinguistic origins of Southeast Asia's earliest proselytizing Muslims (see §23.3.2). Best studied is the Arabic lexical influence on Malay (Beg 1979; Jones 1978, 2007; Kasimin 1987; Versteegh 2003; Campbell 2009), Javanese and Sundanese (Juynboll 1883, 1894; Machali 2008), and Malagasy (Dez 1967; Versteegh 2001a; Rajaonarimanana 2009). Several Arabic loanwords entered Malagasy through maritime trade networks linking Madagascar with eastern Africa, for example, *hatra* 'up to' (< Swahili *hatta* < Arabic *ḥattā*), and *zomà* 'Friday' (< Swahili *juma*, *ijumaa* < Arabic *jumʿa*), yet an earlier layer transmitted through Malay has been proposed by Adelaar (1995a, 2009b). In Southeast Asia, Malay appears to have been the main vector of intraregional transmission, as can sometimes be seen from the morphology. For example, Tagalog *sapakát* 'intrigue; conspiracy' reflects Malay *sə-pakat* 'to agree' (< *pakat* 'agreement' ← *mupakat*, *muapakat*, *muafakat* < Arabic *muwāfaqa*). Javanese *kasuwur* 'famous' seems to go back to Malay *kə-sohor*, *tər-sohor*, *sohor*, *məsohor*, ultimately from Arabic *mašhūr* but given a native prefix in Malay.

As with Sanskrit, it is often said that Arabic chiefly donated words for abstract concepts, particularly in the realm of religion, rather than concrete objects to the Austronesian languages. Nevertheless, some of the most widespread borrowings pertain to the latter domain, including Malay *arak* 'distilled liquor' (< *ʿaraq*), *kalam* 'pen' (< *qalam*), and *kursi* 'chair' (< *kursī*). Arabic was also the language through which a number of originally European commodities first entered Southeast Asia, including Malay *kərtas* 'paper' (< *qirṭas* < Greek *khártēs*), *kopiah* 'skullcap' (< *kūfiyya* < Italian *scuffia*), and *sabun* 'soap' (< *ṣābūn* < Greek *sápōn*). A number of widespread Arabic loans may have replaced pre-existing vocabulary, including *dunia* 'world' (< *dunyā*), *kuat* 'strong' (< *qūwa* 'strength'), and *pikir* 'to think' (< *fikr*). In Malay-speaking Muslim circles, the ongoing use of Arabic loanwords instead of co-existing vocabulary is often religiously motivated, for example, *ahad* 'Sunday' (< *aḥad* ← *miŋgu* < Portuguese *domingo*), *idulfitri* (Indonesian), *aidilfitri* (Malaysian) 'holiday marking the end of Ramadan' (< *ʿīd al-fiṭr* ← *hari raya*), *iftar* 'breaking fast' (< *ifṭār* ← *buka puasa* < Malay *buka* 'to open' + Sanskrit *upavāsa* 'fast'), *milad* 'birthday' (< *mīlād* ← *hari ulaŋ tahun*, *hari jadi*), and *salat* 'to pray' (< *ṣalāh* ← *səmbahyaŋ*). The Malay word *badan* 'body' (< *badan*) became *aden* in some varieties of Minangkabau, a first person singular pronoun. The Betawi (Jakarta Malay) pronouns *ane* 'I' and *ente* 'you' reflect Arabic *ana* and *anta* 'you (m.)' respectively. As Malay and other Austronesian languages generally do not distinguish between singular and plural words beyond personal pronouns, some Arabic loanwords were adopted in their plural forms, for example, *huruf* (< *ḥurūf* (pl.) ← *harf* (sg.)), and *ulama* 'theologian' (< *ʿulamāʾ* (pl.) ← *ʿalīm* (sg.)).

### 23.3.2 Beyond Classical Arabic

As mentioned previously, the phonological characteristics of most Arabic loanwords in Austronesian languages do not unambiguously reveal regional origins. The Hadhrami subdialect—spoken in southern Yemen and historically by the majority of ethnic Arabs in Indonesia and Malaysia—has been of negligible influence to the standard language. In fact, Hadhrami Arabic has undergone more influence from Malay than the other way around (see §23.3.3). In Malay dialects such as Betawi (Jakarta Malay), however, we do find some examples of Hadhrami loanwords (van Dam 2010: 223). This is presumably similar in coastal, urban varieties of other MPSEA languages. The Javanese dialect of Gresik, for example, exhibits a number of culinary borrowings including *kaʔak* 'k.o. cake' (< *kaʿāk*), *maraʔi* 'k.o. honey' (< *marāʿī*), and *marak* 'k.o. soup' (< *maraq*). The Malay word for 'Wednesday', *rabu* (cf. Javanese *rəbo*, Acehnese *rabu*), is another rare example of a vernacular borrowing, reflecting Yemeni Arabic *rabūʿ* rather than standard Arabic *al-arbaʿāʾ* (van Dam 2010: 223). The latter form, however, has yielded the competing form *arbaʔa* attested in archaic Malay texts (cf. Minangkabau *rabaʔa*, Maranao *arbaʔa*).

Several loanwords in Austronesian languages are of Persian origin (Bausani 1964; Beg 1982; Jones 2007). As medieval Javanese texts reveal, many of these early loans were pre-Islamic in nature, for example, *dastar* 'headcloth' (< Persian *dastār*), *kəmar* 'a girdle' (< Persian *kamar*), and *rəbab* 'a kind of violin with two strings' (< Persian, Arabic *rabāb*). The earliest attested Persian loans entered Southeast Asia indirectly through MIA languages, for example, Old Javanese *palana* 'saddle' (< *pallāṇa* < Persian *pālān* 'pack-saddle'), and *peka* 'foot soldier' (< *pāikka* < Persian *paik* 'running footman'). Modern Persian emerged around the tenth century and some of its loanwords were widely adopted across Southeast Asia (Table 23.9). The majority, however, are found exclusively in the literary domains of such languages as Malay, Acehnese, and Javanese. Since Persian was the language of administration and aesthetic expression in Mughal India, it is not unlikely that many of these loanwords entered Southeast Asia via South Asia rather than directly from Iran. As with Arabic, no particular Persian dialect can be identified as the source of these loans; borrowing seems to have been based on their written rather than spoken forms. It is also noteworthy that a number of common and widespread Islamic terms are of Persian rather than Arabic provenance, including Malay *abdas* 'ablution (before prayer)' (< *āb-dast*), *baŋ* 'call to prayer' (< *bāng* ← *bāng-i namāz*), and *laŋgar* 'building for religious purposes' (< *langar* 'alms-house'). The

**Table 23.9** Distribution of Persian loanwords

| Persian | meaning | Old Javanese | Cham | Malay | Tagalog |
|---|---|---|---|---|---|
| *pingān* | 'bowl; cup' | *piṅgan* | | *piŋgan* | *piŋgan* |
| *šalwār* | 'trousers' | | | *səluar* | *salawál* |
| *sūrnāy* | 'trumpet; clarion' | *surune* | *śāranai* | *sərunai* | |
| *tarāzū* | 'a balance' | *taraju, traju* | *taraju* | *təraju* | *taláró?* |

archaic Malay word *məsəgit* (< Arabic *masǧid*) 'mosque'—borrowed either through Persian *mazgit* or a colloquial variety of Arabic which has /g/ for <ǧ>—is now commonly replaced by its re-Arabized equivalent *masjid*.

Arabic-derived vocabulary in Malay consists of multiple layers, reflecting various levels of phonological integration (Bausani 1964; Campbell 1996, 2009; Versteegh 2003). While Malay itself exhibits a number of lexical doublets reflecting an early and a late borrowing, other MPSEA languages are less prone to re-Arabization and thus retain older stages of phonological integration (Table 23.10). Some of the attested phonological characteristics cannot be explained through Austronesian linguistics alone, giving room for ample speculation on the intermediate source through which a number of Arabic loanwords reached Southeast Asia. The discussion typically involves three parameters: (i) the pronunciation of the Arabic letter *tāʾ marbūṭa* (ة) in the word-final position as either *-at* or *-ah*; (ii) the pronunciation of the Arabic letters *ḍād* (ض) and *ẓāʾ* (ظ); and (iii) the addition of /u/ or /i/ following a word-final consonant cluster. These phenomena will be discussed below.

As regards the first phenomenon, most *-at* pronunciations seem to predate *-ah* pronunciations, although the latter are structurally preferred for religiously embedded concepts such as Malay *fatihah* 'opening chapter of the Qurʾān' (< *fātiḥa*), *Makkah* 'Mecca' (< *Makka*), and *sədəkah* 'alms' (< *ṣadaqa*). Very sporadically, two doublets exist in different meanings, for example, *sunat* 'to circumcize' and *sunah* 'usage sanctioned by tradition' (< *sunna*). The distribution of *-at* and *-ah* endings in Malay has been attributed to Persian intermediacy (Campbell 1996), where a comparable dichotomy (*-at* vs. *-ā*) exists. A transmission via Persian (or a NIA language) might certainly be plausible for specific words, yet on a structural level this hypothesis is troubled by ample contradictory evidence (cf. van Dam 2010) and a scarcity of additional sound changes corroborating Persian transmission. Furthermore, Malay has several words ending in *-at* whose Persian and NIA counterparts have *-ā*; for example, Malay *filsafat* 'philosophy' vs. Persian *falsafā* (< Arabic *falsafa*), *martabat* 'rank' vs. *martabā* 'time' (< *martaba* 'step; degree'), and *tarekat* 'religious order' vs. *tarīqā* (< *ṭarīqa*).

In addressing the second and third phenomena together, it is worth pointing out foremost that the *ḍād* (ض) and *ẓāʾ* (ظ) have merged in almost all vernacular varieties of Arabic. Both sounds are realized as /z/ in Persian and a number of NIA languages, which is not typically the case in Malay. Interestingly, they are both realized laterally in Tamil (as well as in a number of southern Arabic varieties) and occasionally also in Malay (Tschacher 2009), for example, *lafal* 'to pronounce' (< *lafẓ* 'to enunciate; to articulate'), and *lahir* 'manifest; external' (< *ẓāhir*). The irregular attestation of *u*-endings and, less commonly, *i*-endings in an early layer of Arabic loanwords in Malay has been taken as additional

**Table 23.10** Early and late Arabic loanwords

| Arabic | meaning | Malay (early borrowing) | Acehnese | Maranao | Malay (late borrowing) |
|---|---|---|---|---|---|
| *ḍarūra* | 'emergency' | *lorat* | *lalurat* | | *darurat* |
| *farḍ* | 'religious duty' | *pərlu* | *puɯrulɛə* | *parlo* | *fardu* |
| *fatwā* | 'formal legal opinion' | *pətuah* | *puɯtua* | *pitua* | *fatwa* |
| *ḥaḍra* | 'presence' | *halarat* | *halarat* | *halarat* | *hadirat* |
| *ramaḍān* | 'ninth month of the Islamic calendar' | *ramalan* | *ramuɯlan* | *ramalan* | *ramadan* |
| *ziyāra* | 'pilgrimage' | *jirat* | *juɯrat, jirat* | | *ziarah* |
| *ẓuhr* | 'afternoon prayer' | *lohor* | *luɯho* | *lohor* | *zuhur* |

evidence for a transmission through speakers of Dravidian languages, in which epenthetic vowels are common (Gonda 1973: 59; Tschacher 2009: 434; Tadmor 2009: 696). In Malay, word-final epenthesis (*paragoge*) is only attested in a very limited quantity of examples, and always after a phonotactically inadmissible consonant cluster. The more common way to incorporate such words is through the insertion of an echo vowel, for example, *asal* 'origins' (< *aṣl*), *sihir* 'sorcery' (< *siḥr*), and *umur* 'age' (< *ʿumr*). Theories of Tamil interference are therefore likewise complicated by a paucity of positive examples as well as an absence of additional sound changes expected with a Tamil transmission (van Dam 2010: 232–3), although the pronunciation of Arabic loanwords in colloquial Tamil varieties remains understudied. More data are needed to take this discussion further.

Finally, a small quantity of tentative Arabic loans in Malay and other Austronesian languages display unexpected vowel changes, for example, *filsafat* 'philosophy' (< *falsafa*), *gizi* 'nutrition' (< *ġiṣāʾ*), *judul* 'title' (< *jadwal* 'table, schedule'), Indonesian *naskah*, Malaysian *nasxah* 'manuscript' (< *nusḫa*), and *šair* 'poetry; poem' (< *šiʿr*). Such irregularities are not easily accounted for; were the borrowings transmitted through a regional variety of Arabic, an intermediate language along the way, or simply in their written rather than spoken forms? Some attestations may even reflect phonosemantic conflation, for example, Malay *muhibah* 'love; goodwill' (< *muḥibba* 'female friend', but *maḥabba* 'love; affection'), *muhrim* 'too closely related to be marriageable' (< *muḥrim* 'Mecca pilgrim', but *maḥram* 'too closely related to be marriageable'), and *mukənah* 'veil' (*muqannaʿ* 'veiled', but *miqnaʿa* 'veil'). In other cases, borrowing may have taken place through a North Indian vernacular, where similar pronunciations are observed in unofficial speech (Table 23.11).

### 23.3.3 Borrowings into West Asian languages

Malay loanwords in Arabic are predominantly confined to Yemeni Arabic, for example, *biliǧ* 'cabin of a ship' (< *bilik* 'compartment') and *manǧa* 'mango' (< *maŋga*; see §23.5.1). The largest number of Malay loans exists in the Hadhrami subdialect of Yemeni Arabic (van Ronkel 1903b; Al-Saqqaf 2006), including words that Malay itself borrowed from other sources, for example, *blēg* 'big tin' (< *blek* < Dutch *blik*), *kwēh* 'cake' (< *kue* < Southern Min 粿 *kóe*), and *sfattū* 'shoes' (< *səpatu* < Portuguese *sapato*).

### 23.3.4 Typological influence

Arabic introduced a number of phonemes into Malay and some other Austronesian languages: /f/, /x/, /q/, /ʃ/, and /z/. These tend to be used interchangeably with their closest inherited equivalents, respectively /p/, /k/~/h/, /k/, /s/, and /j/. Some of these borrowed phonemes also occur in pseudo-Arabic forms, for example, Malaysian *beza* 'difference' (← *beda* < Sanskrit *bheda* 'separation, difference'), Indonesian *fihaq* 'side' (← *pihak*, but alternatively and without firm verification explained as < Arabic *fī ḥaqq* 'concerning'), and Malaysian/Indonesian *furga* 'heaven' (← *surga* < Sanskrit *svarga*).

**Table 23.11** Possible Arabic borrowings via North India

| Arabic | meaning | colloquial Hindustani | Malay | Malay (late borrowing) |
|---|---|---|---|---|
| *baraka* | 'blessing' | *barkat* | *bərkat* | *barakah* |
| *bāṭil* | 'null' | *bātal* + verb ('to annul') | *batal* ('to annul') | |
| *ḍamīn* | 'guarantor' | *jamīn* | *jamin* | |
| *ḫalāʾiq* | 'creation; created being' | *ḫalāyaq* | *xalayak* | |
| *lāʾiq* | 'worthy' | *lāyaq* | *layak* | |
| *muʿāf* | 'forgiveness' | *maʿāf, māf* | *maʔaf* | |
| *muʿallim* | 'religious teacher' | *mālim* | *malim* | *mualim* |
| *mayyit* | 'corpse' | *mayyat* | *mayat* | *mait* |
| *nafaqa* | 'expenses for daily living' | *nafqa* | *nafkah* | |
| *tawakkul* | 'trust in God' | *tawakkal* | *tawakal* | *tawakul* |

Grammatical influence from Arabic is strongest in the Malay idiom of religious books (*kitab* < Arabic *kitāb* 'book'), which were often translated sentence-for-sentence from Arabic (van Ronkel 1899). In addition, a number of Arabic loanwords underwent grammaticalization in Malay (cf. Tadmor 2007: 318–20), including *asal* 'so long as' (← 'origin' < *aṣl*), *pasal* 'concerning' (← 'subject; section' < *faṣl* 'division; section'), and *saʔat* 'at the moment that' (← '(short) time; hour' < *sāʿa*). The grammaticalized use of Malay *səbab* 'because' (← 'cause' < *sabab*) is also attested in a number of languages spoken in Africa and might reflect a form of conventionalized Arabic foreigner talk (Versteegh 2001b: 501). Standard Arabic typically uses *bi-sabab* or *liʾanna*. It is commonly believed that Malay *agar* 'so that' goes back to Persian *agar* 'if', although the tentative semantic shift needs further explanation.

It is often claimed that Malay has borrowed a series of suffixes from Arabic, including the singular feminine suffix *-ah* (< *-a*), the plural masculine suffix *-in* (< *-īn*), the plural feminine suffix *-at* (< *-āt*), and the derivative suffixes *-i* (< *-ī*) and *-iah* (< *-iyya*). Given that these would-be suffixes are only attested with Arabic loanwords, a better explanation would be that all so-derived forms have been borrowed wholesale from Arabic, for example, *harfiah* 'literal' (< *harfiyya*), *ilmiah* 'scientific; learned' (< *ʿilmiyya*), and *logawiah* 'linguistic' (< *luġawiyya*). As the above attestations show, the morphophonological rules of Arabic rather than Malay were applied. The only Arabic-derived suffix with some productivity is *-wi*, for example, *gərejawi* 'ecclesiastical' (< *gəreja* 'church' < Portuguese *igreja*), *kimiawi* 'chemical' (< *kimia* 'chemistry' < Arabic *kīmiyāʾ*), and *surgawi*, *ʃurgawi* 'heavenly' (< *surga*, *ʃurga* 'heaven' < Sanskrit *svarga*).

### 23.3.5 Language planning

As mentioned previously, the influence of Arabic on modern language engineering is stronger in Malaysia than in Indonesia, for example, Malaysian *daʔyah* 'propaganda' (< *dāʿiya* [same meaning]), *ixtisas* 'professional' (< *iḫtiṣāṣ* 'duly qualified'), *rasuah* 'corruption' (< *rašwa* 'bribe; corruption'), and *siasah*, *siasat* 'politics' (← 'management' < *siyāsa* 'administration'). This also involves the re-Arabization of Arabic loanwords that entered Malaysian through English, such as *aljabar* instead of *algəbra* (< *al-ǧabr*). Some Arabic loanwords are pronounced and spelled differently in the two countries; Arabic *daraǧa* 'grade; rank' is *dərajat* in Indonesian and *darjah* in Malaysian, *kursī* 'chair' is *kursi* in Indonesian and *kərusi* in Malaysian, and *mušāwara* 'deliberation' is *muʃawarah* in Indonesian and *məʃuarat* in Malaysian. Other loanwords have different meanings; *ahli* (< *ahl* 'relatives; people') is 'expert' in Indonesian and 'member' in Malaysian, and *logat* (< *luġa* 'language') is 'accent' in Indonesian and 'dialect' in Malaysian. Occasionally, different Arabic loanwords are preferred to cover the same concept, for example, 'general; common; (the) public' is *umum* (< *ʿumūm* 'the general public') in Indonesian and *am* (< *ʿāmm* 'public; general') in Malaysian, and 'sentence (grammar)' is *kalimat* (< *kalima* 'word; utterance') in Indonesian and *ayat* (< *āya* 'passage; utterance') in Malaysian. A small number of words in Indonesian and Malaysian consist of a Sanskrit and an Arabic element: *praʃarat* 'precondition' (< Sanskrit *pra* 'pre-' + Arabic *šarṭ* 'condition'), *sukarela* 'voluntary' (< Sanskrit *sukha* 'happy' + Arabic *riḍāʾ* 'consent'), and *tatatərtib* 'discipline' (< Sanskrit *tata* 'extended' + Arabic *tartīb* 'order').

## 23.4 East Asian languages

### 23.4.1 History of contact

East Asian contacts with Southeast Asia are of considerable antiquity, predominantly involving the coastal varieties of southern China. The present-day prominence of Mandarin throughout the region is a relatively novel development. It is often said that Chinese lexical influence on Malay chiefly consists of concrete rather than abstract items, typically of commercial and/or culinary value and specific to China. This strongly depends on the Malay variety being researched. The Malay varieties spoken natively by the *Peranakan*—Southeast Asia's acculturated Chinese communities—naturally contain numerous additional loanwords in the domains of culture, religion, philosophy, and kinship terms. This is also the case in other Chinese ethnolects of Austronesian languages. Chinese varieties are not considered as a potential source for enrichment in the official language planning policies of any MPSEA language.

Early Chinese loanwords are attested in some parts of Southeast Asia yet are absent in Malagasy. This suggests that structural language contact between Chinese and Austronesian languages post-dates the migrations to Madagascar. The quantity of Chinese loanwords in literary Cham is also relatively low, with attestations different from those found in the languages of Island Southeast Asia, for example, *ḍav* 'sword' (< 刀 *dāo*), *hauv* 'family' (< 戶 *hù*), *liuv* 'silk' (< 縷 *lǚ* 'thread'), *pauv* 'k.o. game of chance' (< 寶 *bǎo*), *phav* 'gun' (< 砲 *pào*), and *phok* 'shop' (< 舖 *pù*). Only the Chamic variety of Hainan, Tsat, exhibits large-scale lexical and grammatical influence from

**Table 23.12** Distribution of Southern Min loanwords

| Southern Min | meaning | Malay | Javanese | Tagalog |
|---|---|---|---|---|
| 木屐 *bak-kiah* | 'wooden clogs' | *bakiaʔ* | *bakiaʔ* | *bakyáʔ* |
| 蝦米 *hê-bí* | 'dried prawns' | *ebi* | *ebi* | *híbi* |
| 膏藥 *ko-io̍h* | 'medicinal plaster' | *koyoʔ* | *koyuʔ* | *koyo* |
| 韭菜 *kú-chhaì* | 'Chinese chives' | *kucai* | *kucai* | *kutsáy* |
| 新客 *sin-kheh* | 'recent immigrant' | *siŋkeʔ* | *siŋkeʔ* | *siŋkíʔ* ('greenhorn; beginner') |
| 豆醬 *tāu-chiò*$^{n}$ | 'k.o. sauce' | *tauco* | *taoco* | *totso* |

Chinese (Zheng 1997) and is to be considered as the most Sinicized Austronesian language. In the languages of Island Southeast Asia, the vast majority of Chinese loanwords are from Southern Min varieties (Table 23.12). The relatively small quantity of Cantonese loanwords in Malay tend to be of relatively recent acquisition, regionally confined (e.g. Jakarta, Kuala Lumpur, and Sabah), and not known to all speakers, for example, *ceoŋsam* 'k.o. gown' (< 長衫 *coeng*$^{4}$ *saam*$^{1}$), *ŋam* 'just right' (< 啱 *ngaam*$^{1}$), and *siham* 'cockles' (< 蜆蚶 *si*$^{1}$ *ham*$^{1}$).

Within the Southern Min dialect continuum, most loanwords borrowed into Malay and other Austronesian languages can be traced specifically to the Zhangzhou subdialect of Hokkien (Table 23.13). Some other loans must have entered through a Southern Min variety that realizes the historical word-final /n/ as a velar /ŋ/, e.g. *giwaŋ* 'earrings' (← 耳環 *ngí-hoân*), *joŋ* 'junk (ship)' (← 船 *chûn*), and *uaŋ* 'money' (← 元 *oân* 'k.o. coin'). Chaozhouhua ('Teochew') is a contemporary example of a Southern Min variety that does so, yet the historical situation is less clear. A small number of tentative early Chinese loans in Malay cannot be identified specifically with any of the modern Chinese varieties and might partly predate their divergence, for example, *daciŋ* 'scales' (< 大秤 *dàchèng* 'big scale') and *pisau* 'knife' (< 匕首 *bǐshǒu* 'dagger'). The Old Javanese words *guci* 'jar' and *tampo* 'k.o. alcoholic beverage' are also of likely Chinese origins, the latter possibly from *tām-po̍h* 淡薄 'not strong (of wine)'. The Old Javanese word *taŋ* 'tub', attested in the *Rāmāyaṇa* (22.11), goes back to Southern Min 桶 *tháng* 'cask, barrel' (Robson 2015: 597).

Most research has been published on Southern Min loanwords in Malay (Schlegel 1891; Kong 1986; Jones 2009) and Tagalog (Manuel 1948; Chan-Yap 1977). Some of these loanwords became part of the Malay core vocabulary and feature in the earliest available dictionaries. The first person and second person pronouns *gua* 'I' (< 我 *góa*), and *lu* 'you' (< 汝 *lú*) have been adopted into several Malay varieties, including Sri Lankan Malay. Others remain restricted to Malaysian/Indonesian slang, e.g. *kepo* 'nosy person' (< 雞婆 *ke-pô*) and *lihai* 'excellent' (< 厲害 *lī-hāi*). To my knowledge, no comprehensive study has been undertaken on Chinese loanwords in Javanese or other Austronesian languages. Javanese exhibits some Southern Min loanwords that are unattested in Malay and Tagalog, including *baʔmoe* 'k.o. porridge' (< 肉糜 *bah-môe*), *jiʔit* 'twenty-one (card game)' (< 二一 *jī-it*), and *lupai* 'k.o. brooch' (< 鈕牌 *liú-pâi* 'button'). In addition, as with colloquial Arabic influence (see §23.3.2), a focus on particular urban dialects may yield interesting results. The Malay variety of Jakarta exhibits several Chinese loans not attested in other Malay varieties (Leo 1975). Several more can undoubtedly be identified in the Javanese dialects of port cities such as Surabaya, Semarang, and Lasem.

**Table 23.13** Zhangzhou loanwords

| Malay | meaning | characters | Zhangzhou | Amoy, Quanzhou |
|---|---|---|---|---|
| *gincu* | 'lipstick' | 銀朱 | *gîn-chu* | *gûn-chu* |
| *huncue* | 'tobacco pipe' | 煙吹 | *hun-chhoe* | *hun-chhe* |
| *kecap* | 'k.o. sauce' | 鮭汁 | *kê-chiap* | *koê-chiap* |
| *kue* | 'cake' | 粿 | *kóe* | *ké* |
| *swipoa* | 'abacus' | 算盤 | *sùi*$^{n}$*-pôa*$^{n}$ | *sǹg-pôa*$^{n}$ |

Loanwords from Japanese are relatively few in number and mostly of recent acquisition. Although *Loan-words in Indonesian and Malay* (Jones 2007) lists 296 Japanese loanwords in Indonesian, almost all of these date to the Second

World War and are no longer used nor understood. Some relatively well-known examples are *bakero* 'idiot' (< *bakayarō*), *Kempetai* 'Military Police Corps' (< *Kenpei-Tai*), and *romusya* 'forced labourer during the Second World War' (< *rōmusha* 'labourer'). Indonesian and Tagalog both display *geisha* (spelled *geysha* in Tagalog), *kimono*, and *sakura* 'cherry-blossom flower'. The Japanese loan *karaoke*, also borrowed in both languages, has yielded *videoke* 'video karaoke' in Tagalog and other Philippine languages. The brand name *ajinomoto* is used as a generic term for 'monosodium glutamate' in Malaysia, Indonesia, and the Philippines, whereas the Japanese slang term *shabu* 'methamphetamine' is also commonly used in all three countries. In Indonesia, *honda* can refer to either a motor cycle or a minibus, depending on the region. In the Philippines, *katol* 'mosquito coil' reflects Japanese *katori senkō* in the same meaning. Tetun *katana* 'sword' must have been borrowed through Portuguese *catana* (< Japanese *katana*).

### 23.4.2 Borrowings into East Asian languages

A small number of Malay words has been adopted into Chinese. Some only existed in the nautical slang of Chinese seafarers (Salmon 2019). In general, the characters of Malay loans match the Southern Min pronunciation, suggesting that they entered Chinese writing through that variety (Table 23.14). Certain early Malay borrowings are difficult to recognize as such, as they are typically abbreviated in modern speech, for example, 蘇木 *sūmù* 'sappanwood' (← 蘇枋木 *sūfāng mù* < *səpaŋ*) and 西米 *xīmǐ* 'sago grains' (← 西谷米 *xīgǔ mǐ* < *sagu*). The former also entered Japanese as 蘇芳 *suō*. Other Malay loanwords in Chinese have been matched phonosemantically with pre-existing elements, for example, 芒果 *mángguǒ* 'mango' (← 芒 *maŋga*; see §23.5.1 + 果 *guǒ* 'fruit') and 紅毛丹 *hóngmáodān* 'rambutan' (← 紅毛 *hóngmáo* 'red-haired, Caucasian' + 丹 *dān* 'crimson').

**Table 23.14** Malay loanwords in Chinese

| characters | meaning | Mandarin | Southern Min | Malay |
|---|---|---|---|---|
| 檳榔 | 'areca nut' | *bīnláng* | *pin-nn̂g* | *pinaŋ* |
| 吉貝 | 'tree cotton' | *jíbèi* | *ka-pók* | *kapok* |
| 蓮霧 | 'Java apple' | *liánwù* | *liám-bū* (← *jiám-bū*) | *jambu* |
| 榴槤 | 'durian' | *liúlián* | *liû-liân* | *durian* |

Naturally, most Malay loanwords can be found in the varieties of Southern Min, Hakka, and Cantonese spoken in Southeast Asia (Chen 2003). Some of these Malay borrowings can be written in Chinese characters, for example, Southern Min 甘榜 *kam-póng* 'village' (< *kampuŋ*), 馬打 *má-tâ* 'police officer' (< *mata-mata*), and 沙爹 *sa-te* 'satay' (< *sate*). A small number of these loans have also entered the Southern Min varieties of China, including 擔缸 *tam-kong* 'to bail out' (< *taŋguŋ*) and 洞葛 *tōng-kat* 'stick' (< *toŋkat*). In addition, certain loanwords from other languages entered Southern Min through Malay (Table 23.15).

**Table 23.15** Loanwords that entered Southern Min through Malay

| | meaning | Malay | ultimate source |
|---|---|---|---|
| 峇峇 *bābā* | 'Peranakan man' | *baba* | Hindustani *bābā* ('Sir') |
| 鐳 *lui* | 'money' | *duit* | Dutch *duit* |
| 舺舨 *kap-pán* | 'ship' | *kapal* | Tamil *kappal* |
| 巴刹 *pa-sat* | 'market' | *pasar* | Persian *bāzār* |
| 雪文 *sap-bûn* | 'soap' | *sabun* | Arabic *ṣābūn* |

Postulations of Austronesian loanwords into Japonic languages have not been broadly accepted. Speakers of Ryukyuan dialects were historically in contact with Southeast Asia, but even here, little unambiguous evidence of borrowing has been presented as yet. One exception might be the Ryukyuan stir-fry dish *tʃampuruu* (< Malay *campur* 'to mix') (Lawrence 2015: 169).

### 23.4.3 Typological influence

Grammatical influence from Southern Min is strongest in the pidginized varieties of Malay, sometimes designated as 'Bazaar Malay' or 'Pasar Malay'. One pidgin-derived variety, Baba Malay, became the mother tongue of the Peranakan communities in the Straits Settlements in colonial times, although it is now fast disappearing (Lee 2014). Aside from loanwords, typical features revealing Chinese influence include the possessive and attributive use of the Malay particle *puɲa* 'have' and the causative use of such auxiliary verbs as *kasi* 'give' and *kəna* 'hit' (Lim 1981; Pakir 1986; Ansaldo and Matthews 1999). The origins of this same set of features in non-Chinese contact varieties of Malay remains a matter of discussion (Adelaar and Prentice 1996; Paauw 2008).

In the opposite direction, it may be pointed out that Chinese varieties spoken in Island Southeast Asia tend to display reduced tonal systems as a likely result of Austronesian influence. The Southern Min spoken in Malaysia, for example, is heavily influenced by Malay and other languages in contact. In the Hokkien variety spoken in Penang, Malay influence is primarily lexical although it includes a number of grammatical particles (Teoh and Lim 2003). The variety of Kelantan also exhibits typological influence from Malay as manifested in its word order (Teo 2003). Similar regional differences are found in Indonesian Teochew, where the variety spoken in Sumatra has undergone more syntactic influence from Malay than the variety spoken in Borneo (Peng 2012). The same may hold for Hakka varieties but needs further investigation. Typological cross-fertilization involving Javanese, Malay, and Southern Min is also found among the Chinese-descended communities of Java (Wolff and Poedjosoedarmo 1982; Oetomo 1987).

## 23.5 European languages

### 23.5.1 History of contact

Spanish, Portuguese, Dutch, English, and French have all asserted influence on MPSEA languages. The first Europeans to arrive in numbers in Southeast Asia, also frequently calling at Madagascar, were the Portuguese. Lexical borrowing from Portuguese has influenced Malay and the languages of eastern Indonesia. The Spaniards, meanwhile, established themselves around the archipelago now known as the Philippines. Together, Spanish and Portuguese facilitated the introduction of several European (and New World) concepts into the languages of Island Southeast Asia (Table 23.16). In addition to a multitude of concrete objects, the Catholic religion and much of its associated terminology also entered the region through these Iberian languages (and in Madagascar through French). As Austronesian languages typically do not mark plurality on lexical items, some nouns from European languages were adopted in their plural form, for example, Tagalog *sapatos* 'shoe' (< Spanish *zapatos* 'shoes'), Malay *kubis* 'cabbage' (< Portuguese *couves* 'cabbages'), and Malagasy *gisy* 'goose' (< English geese).

A relatively small quantity of Portuguese loans also entered Malagasy (Table 23.17), but the lexical influence was considerably stronger in Southeast Asia. Some eastern regions of Island Southeast Asia exhibit Portuguese loanwords unattested in standard Malay (cf. Santa Maria 1967; da França 1985), for example, Tetun *apitu* 'whistle' (< *apito*), *aradu* 'plough' (< *arado*), and *kanudu* 'cigarette' (< *canudo* 'straw'), and Manado Malay *leŋso* 'handkerchief' (< *lenço*), *milu* 'maize' (< *milho*), and *pombo* 'pigeon' (< *pombo*). As is clear from the phonology, several of the lexical items attested in Malay entered the language not directly through European Portuguese but through a local creolized variety, for example, *algojo* 'executioner' (< **algozo* < *algoz*), *nona* 'young lady' (< **nona* < *dona*), and *rodi* 'order' (< **ordi* < *ordem*). Meanwhile, Spanish loanwords entered every imaginable domain of Tagalog (Wolff 2001), Cebuano (Quilis 1976), and other Philippine languages (Steinkrüger 2008b). In Indonesia, Spanish influence is restricted to speech communities in close proximity to the Philippines. In Manado Malay, for instance, we find *barba* 'sideburns' (< *barba* 'beard'), *kompania* 'politeness' (< *compañía* 'companionship'), and *panada* 'a fried pastry with filling' (< *empanada*). Examples from Sangir

**Table 23.16** Distribution of Portuguese and Spanish loanwords

| meaning | Portuguese | Malay | Tetun | Spanish | Tagalog | Cebuano |
|---|---|---|---|---|---|---|
| 'ball' | *bola* | *bola* | *bola* | *bola* | *bola* | *búla* |
| 'butter' | *manteiga* | *məntega* | *manteiga* | *mantequilla* | *mantikilya* | *mantikilya* |
| 'cheese' | *queijo* | *keju* | *keiju* | *queso* | *keso* | *kísu* |
| 'flag' | *bandeira* | *bəndera* | *bandeira* | *bandera* | *bandilaʔ* | *bandura* |
| 'fork' | *garfo* | *garpu* | *garfu* | *tenedor* | *tinidór* | *tinidur* |
| 'school' | *escola* | *səkolah* | *eskola* | *escuela* | *iskuwela* | *iskuyla* |
| 'shirt' | *camisa* | *kəmeja* | *kamiza* | *camiseta* | *kamiseta* | *kamisíta* |
| 'table' | *mesa* | *meja* | *meza* | *mesa* | *mesa* | *mísa* ('billiard table') |
| 'wheel' | *roda* | *roda* | *roda* | *rueda* | *ruweda* | *ruyda* |
| 'window' | *janela* | *jəndela* | *janela* | *ventana* | *bintanaʔ* | *bintánaʔ* |

**Table 23.17** Portuguese introductions in Malagasy and Malay

| Portuguese | Meaning | Malagasy | Malay |
|---|---|---|---|
| *batata* (< Taíno *batata*) | 'sweet potato' | *batata* | *batata* (more commonly: *ubi jalar*) |
| *espingarda* | 'musket; flintlock gun' | *ampingaharatra* | *istiŋgar* |
| *manga* (< Malayalam *māṅṅa*) | 'mango' | *manga* | *maŋga* (or directly from South India) |
| *marca* | 'mark (distinctive feature; arithmetic)' | *marika* | *marka* |

include *baraŋka* 'ditch; ravine' (< *barranca* 'canyon'), *kawal̪o* 'horse' (< *caballo*), and *liwirə* 'free' (< *libre*). In a number of cases, it is unclear whether a loanword originates from Spanish or Portuguese, as in Manado Malay and Ambon Malay *fresko* 'fresh' (< *fresco*), *gargantaŋ* 'throat' (< *garganta*), and *oras* 'time' (< *horas* 'hours').

Lexical influence from Dutch is the strongest in Java, parts of eastern Indonesia, and other localities where Dutch colonialism has had a relatively old pedigree (de Vries 1988; van der Sijs 2010). As Dutch language education for Indonesians was typically discouraged, these loanwords were adopted despite, rather than due to, colonial governance. Examples of relatively widespread Dutch loanwords in Malay include *balak*, *balok* 'large piece of timber' (< *balk*), *buncis* 'green beans' (< *boontjes*), *duit* 'money' (< *duit* 'k.o. coin'), *kantor* 'office' (< *kantoor*), and *laci* 'drawer' (< *laatje*). Mostly restricted to Ambon Malay and Manado Malay are *donci* 'melody' (< *deuntje*), *flur* 'floor' (< *vloer*), and *sondər* 'without' (< *zonder*). Sri Lankan Malay likewise exhibits several Dutch loans not attested as such in other Malay varieties, such as *baiskop* 'film' (< *bioscoop* 'cinema'), *iskol* 'school' (< *school*), and *orlos* 'watch' (< *horloge*). Unique (provincial) Javanese loans from Dutch include *bruwəre* 'brewery' (< *brouwerij*), *ḍirənten* 'zoo' (< *dierentuin*), and *rolak* 'weir; dam' (< *rollaag* 'soldier course (architecture)'). Malay and Javanese also adopted a number of archaic words now uncommon in Dutch, for example, *kakus* 'toilet' (< *kakhuis*), *sənapaŋ* 'rifle' (< *snaphaan*; spelled *sənapan* in Indonesian), and *sopi* 'strong alcoholic drink' (< *zopie*). Some words have undergone interesting semantic shifts from their Dutch precursors, for example, Malay *bui* 'prison' (< *boei* 'chain'), *labrak* 'to thrash' (< *radbraak* 'to break on the wheel'), and *səloki* 'shot glass' (< *slokkie* 'a sip'). A number of Dutch loanwords must have entered Malay and Javanese through a Portuguese-based creole (Adelaar 1996a: 699–700; Tadmor 2009: 690–1), accounting for otherwise unexpected sound changes such as the epenthetic *-u* and/or syncope, for example, *buku* 'book' (< *boek*) and *taplak* 'tablecloth' (< *tafellaken*).

As a relatively late arrival in the region, the English language lent a number of words to Malagasy in the nineteenth century, including *dokotra* 'duck', *hareza* 'razor', and *sekoly* 'school' (Adelaar 2009a). In addition, English asserted itself on both sides of the Straits of Malacca by the same time. Examples of English loans in Bengkulu Malay include *blaŋkit* 'blanket', *kabit* 'cupboard', *pakit* 'pocket', *sasar* 'saucer', and *stakin* 'stockings' (M.A.J. 1972). For a number of Malay loanwords, it is not clear whether the direct source of acquisition was English, Dutch, or both, for example, *bistek* 'beefsteak' (← Dutch *biefstuk*), *gəlas* '(drinking) glass' (← *glas*), and *kopi* 'coffee; copy' (← *koffie*; *kopie*). Sri Lankan Malay exhibits some English loanwords not found in other Malay varieties, such as *gelan* 'gallon', *leṭar* 'letter', and *re:san* 'prison' (Paauw 2004). Some English loanwords in Malaysian have Dutch-derived 'false friends' in Indonesian, for example, Malaysian *klasikal* 'classical' vs. Indonesian *klasikal* 'whole-class' (< Dutch *klassikaal*), *polis* 'police' vs. *polis* '(insurance) policy' (< *polis*), and *polisi* '(insurance) policy' vs. *polisi* 'police' (< *politie*). While British English gradually grew more influential in the linguistic landscape of Malaysia, American English gained foothold in the Philippines from the late nineteenth century as a result of shifting colonial occupations. No comprehensive publications on the adoption of English loanwords in any of the Philippine languages are known to me.

As the language of global power, the influence of English on most modern Austronesian languages is extensive and ongoing. In contemporary Indonesian, Dutch loanwords are often replaced by newer English ones, for example, *faktur* 'invoice' (< *factuur*), *kortiŋ* 'discount' (< *korting*), *prahoto* 'truck' (< *vrachtauto*), *rekəniŋ* 'bill' (< *rekening*), and *stanplat* 'terminal' (< *standplaats*) by *invois*, *diskaun*, *truk*, *bil*, and *terminal*. English words also prevail in youth slang throughout the region. Interestingly, some widespread examples are shared by Tagalog, Malaysian/Indonesian, and several other Austronesian languages, for example, *lobat* (< low battery; pronounced as *lobet*) and *miskol* (< missed call). Recent

Indonesian slang features a number of very popular English loanwords used in ways that would be ungrammatical in the donor language, for example, *boriŋ* 'boring' (but also 'bored'), *fens* 'fans' (but also 'fan'), and *merit* 'married' (but also 'to marry; marriage'). Hybrid English–Indonesian creations, such as *so what gitu loh* 'so what, who cares' (2000s) and *kids jaman now* 'kids nowadays' (2010s), tend to be pervasive for relatively short time spans, after which they slowly sink into oblivion. In Tagalog slang, English loans—often with new, localized meanings—are also ubiquitous (Zorc et al. 1993).

French has directly influenced Malagasy from the late nineteenth century—where it had to compete with English—and remains firmly established in Madagascar to this day. French loanwords encompass concrete objects as well as technical, scientific, and Catholic terms (Dez 1965; Adelaar 2009a), for example, *eglizy* 'church' (< *église*), *forosety* 'fork' (< *fourchette*), and *lalàna* 'law' (< *la loi*). No studies are known to me on French borrowings into modern Cham varieties, which were under some degree of French colonial influence from the late nineteenth century. As a rule, French lexical influence on the languages of Island Southeast Asia has taken place indirectly. A modern example is Indonesian *kudeta* 'coup d'état' (presumably through English). The French word 'chauffeur' ended up in Indonesian as *sopir* and Tagalog as *tsupér* (< Spanish *chófer*), although the English word 'driver' (spelled *drayber* in Tagalog) is currently preferred in both languages. In Malagasy, conversely, the same concept is designated with the locally coined term *mpamily* (< *vily* 'to turn'). A number of French-derived loanwords have become obsolete in Dutch, yet remain in use in Indonesian, including *gaji* 'salary' (< *gage*), *koran* 'newspaper' (< *courant*, modern Dutch *krant*), and *səpeda* 'bicycle' (< *vélocipède*; modern Dutch *fiets* > Javanese *pit*).

## 23.5.2 Borrowings into European languages

As Southeast Asia's main lingua franca, Malay was often the first language to acquaint speakers of European languages with the animals, plants, commercial products, food items, and other concepts specific to Southeast Asia. Long inventories of loanwords from Malay have been compiled for Portuguese (Dalgado 1919), Dutch (van der Sijs 1996), and English (Scott 1897), although most of these words disappeared from the general consciousness of the respective speech communities in post-colonial times. Examples of Malay words still in popular use in English include cootie (< *kutu* 'louse'), rattan (< *rotan*), and sarong 'k.o. garment' (< *saruŋ*). Commonly understood by most Dutch speakers are *bakkeleien* 'to quibble' (< *bər-kəlahi* 'to quarrel' < Sanskrit *kalaha* 'quarrel'), *kroepoek* 'prawn crackers' (< *kərupuk*), and *senang* 'happy' (< *sənaŋ*). Other loanwords from Malay have undergone semantic shifts in Dutch, for example, *nasi* 'fried rice' (< *nasi* 'cooked rice'), *piekeren* 'to worry, ponder' (< *pikir* 'thinking' < Arabic *fikr*), and *soebatten* 'to plead' (< *ṣobat* 'friend' < Arabic *ṣuḥba*). Furthermore, a number of Southern Min loanwords entered Dutch through Malay, including *bami* 'noodles' (< *baʔmi* 'k.o. noodle dish' < 肉麵 *bah-mī*), *taugé* 'beansprouts' (< *taoge* < 豆芽 *tāu-gê*), and *toko* 'store (for Asian products)' (< *toko* 'store' < 土庫 *thó·-khò·* 'storeroom').

Next to Malay, a number of Javanese words are still used in Dutch, including *amok* 'furious attack' (< *amuk*), *laos* 'k.o. spice (galangal)' (< *laos*), and *pienter* 'smart' (< *pintər* 'smart, skilled'). Alternatively, these forms may all go back to a colloquial Malay variety spoken on Java. Common English loans from Philippine languages include boondock (< Tagalog *bundók* 'mountain') and yo-yo (< Ilokano *yóyo*). Loanwords from Malagasy are limited to the island's unique ecology, for example, aye-aye 'k.o. lemur' (< *aiay*), raffia 'k.o. tree' (< *rofia*), and tenrec 'k.o. mammal' (< *trandraka*).

While not technically a European language, Afrikaans has also received several loanwords from Malay. Examples attested in Afrikaans but not in Dutch include *akkerwanie* 'k.o. fragrant grass' (< *akar waŋi*), *baie* 'many' (< *bajak*), and *borrie* 'turmeric' (< *boreh* 'yellow cosmetic made from turmeric'). Through Afrikaans, a small number of Malay words ended up in Nguni languages. In some varieties of Xhosa, we find *umbara* 'inexperienced person' (< *baar* < *(oraŋ) baru* 'new person'), and *ipiringi* 'plate' (< *piering* < *piriŋ*). Examples in Shona include *bhachi* 'jacket' (< *baatjie* < *baju*) and *chamboko* 'whip' (< *sjambok* < *cambuk*). Ultimately, the latter three words are from Persian: *piring* 'copper; copper plate', *bāzū* 'upper arm', and *cābuk* 'whip'.

## 23.5.3 Typological influence

Many MPSEA languages have undergone phonological expansion to accommodate large numbers of European loans. One of the most extreme instances is Tetun, which adopted no less than eleven phonemes from Portuguese (Williams-van Klinken et al. 2002: 8–9). Sociolinguistically, the 'correct' pronunciation of these phonemes typically signifies erudition. In both Malay and Tagalog, the pronunciation of /f/ as /p/ (its closest inherited counterpart) in recent English loanwords tends to be food for comedy. It has also given rise to common hypercorrections such as Indonesian *fasfoto* 'passport photo' (← *pasfoto* < Dutch *pasfoto*) and *nasif* 'fate' (← *nasip* < Arabic *naṣīb*).

A number of European-derived grammatical particles have been widely adopted. Malay *məski*, Tetun *maski*, Tagalog *maskí*, and Cebuano *maski*, *maskin* 'although; even if' reflect a common creole Portuguese and early Spanish usage of respectively *mais que* and *más que* (Veiga and Fernández 2012). Other Spanish-derived grammatical particles in Tagalog include *pero* 'but' (< *pero*), *sige* '(particle) go ahead!' (< *sigue* 'follow'), and *siyempre* 'of course' (< *siempre* 'always'). Examples of common Portuguese loans in Tetun include *depois* 'then; afterwards' (< *depois* 'after'), *komesa* 'since' (← 'to start' < *começar*), and *komu* 'as; because' (< *como* 'as; since'). Dutch introductions in Indonesians are *pas* 'exactly; when' (< *pas* 'fit; just now') and *pərsis* 'precisely' (< *precies*) (Tadmor 2009: 319). Both in Indonesian and Malaysian, the English second person pronoun 'you' is frequently used, whereas the first-person pronoun 'I' is mostly restricted to Malaysian. The Dutch-derived *ekə* 'I' (< *ikke*), and *ye* 'you' (< *jij*) are in use among Indonesia's Peranakan Chinese community. Portuguese *você* 'you (sg.)' has been borrowed into Ambon Malay as *ose*.

Several European affixes can be combined with inherited roots. For example, Tetun *hemudór* 'drunkard' consists of *hemu* 'to drink' and the Portuguese agentive suffix *-dór*. Austronesian languages of a relatively complex morphological type tend to borrow more European suffixes (Hajek and van Klinken 2019). Tagalog, for example, has adopted several suffixes from Spanish which can also be combined with inherited vocabulary (Table 23.18). In many cases, however, the productivity of these borrowed affixes and the quantity of words to which they can be attached are limited (cf. Baklanova and Bellamy 2023). The Indonesian suffix *-is* can be traced to two separate Dutch suffixes: *-isch* ('-ic') and *-ist* ('-ist') (de Vries 1998). In the first sense, it competes with the English-inspired suffix *-ik* ('-ic'), yielding lexical doublets such as *diatermis* vs. *diatermik* (*diathermisch* vs. 'diathermic'), and *realistis* vs. *realistik* (< *realistisch* vs. 'realistic'). In the latter sense, it can also be applied to Indonesian stems, for example, *ganjais* 'pot smoker' and *suhartois* 'Suharto supporter'. The English suffix *-er* provides a more contemporary alternative to do so, for example, *mabukər* 'drunkard' (← *mabuk* 'drunk') and *ahokər* 'supporter of (the politician) Ahok'. The most productive Dutch-derived Indonesian suffix is *-(n)isasi* (< *-(n)isatie* '-(n)ization'), for example, *daerahisasi* 'regionalization' (← *daerah* 'region' < Arabic *dāʾira* 'periphery'), *iklanisasi* 'commercialization' (← *iklan* 'advertisement' < Arabic *iʕlān* 'advertising'), and *swastanisasi* 'privatization' (← *swasta* 'private' < Sanskrit *svastha* 'self-sufficient').

**Table 23.18** Tagalog neologisms formed through Spanish-derived suffixes

| Spanish suffix | Tagalog suffix | example |
|---|---|---|
| *-eña/o* | *-enya/o* | *Kotabatenyo* 'from Kotabato' |
| *-era/o* | *-era/o* | *baŋkero* 'canoer' (< *baŋka* 'canoe') |
| *-illa/o* | *-ilya/o* | *binatilyo* 'teenager' (< *binata* 'adolescence') |
| *-ista* | *-ista* | *Ilokanista* 'specialist on the Ilokano language' |
| *-ita/o* | *-ita/o* | *dalagita* 'young girl' (< *dalaga* 'girl') |

In terms of grammatical influence, it is sometimes argued that the increased frequency of the SVO word order and the use of copula in contemporary standard Malay reflect European influence (Tadmor 2007: 320–1). Since the former is also observed in Javanese, Sundanese, and other Austronesian languages, much more research on textual corpora is needed to chart the precise features and timeframe of these changes. In pidginized Malay trade varieties, the genitive use of *dari* 'of; from' and the preposition of the demonstratives *ini* 'this; these' and *itu* 'that; those' may also point to European influence or—in the latter case—possibly to Chinese influence (ibid.). More straightforward are a number of European-inspired loan translations in Malay that neatly reflect colonial-era boundaries: 'half one, 13:30' is *satu sətəŋah* in Malaysian but *sətəŋah dua* (< Dutch *half twee* '13:30') in Indonesian, while 'more or less' is *ləbih kuraŋ* in Malaysian but *kuraŋ ləbih* (< Dutch *min of meer*) in Indonesian, although *ləbih kuraŋ* is attested as well.

Deep-level grammatical convergence is encountered in extensive contact situations. The moribund Portuguese-based creoles of Tugu (Indonesia; now extinct), Malacca (Malaysia), Bidau (Timor Leste), and Macau (China) exhibit substratal influence from Malay (Baxter 1996), whereas the Spanish-derived Chabacano varieties display Philippine influences (Steinkrüger 2008b; Grant 2011). The basilectal varieties of English spoken in Malaysia and Singapore exhibit lexical and grammatical influence from Malay as well as Southern Min, while Petjok—an almost extinct Dutch-lexified language of Indonesia's Eurasian community—is influenced lexically and grammatically by Malay and Javanese (van Rheeden 1995). Conversely, Ambon Malay as spoken in the Netherlands displays lexical as well as grammatical influence from Dutch (Tahitu 1989) and the Javanese variety of Suriname exhibits structural influence from Dutch and Sranan Tongo, an English-lexified creole (Villerius 2017).

### 23.5.4 Language planning

European languages continue to have an impact on language planning policies in different ways. Tetun consciously draws from Portuguese to reduce the influence of Indonesian, which is associated with a more recent episode of colonial occupation (1975–1999). In Madagascar, with its enduring tensions between standard Malagasy and French (see Hoogervorst, this volume, §17.2.1), indigenous neologisms are normally preferred over French loanwords, for example, *fahitalavitra* 'television' (< *hita* 'to see' + *lavitra* 'far'), *fifindra-monina* 'immigration' (< *findra* 'change locations' + *monina* 'to reside'), and *fomba fahandro* 'recipe' (< *fomba* 'way' + *handro* 'to cook'). Indonesian has accepted several Dutch loanwords to designate novel concepts. English fulfils this role for Malaysian and Tagalog (Table 23.19), in the latter case replacing Spanish. To some degree, however, all language planning bodies have made at least some attempts to replace loanwords with equivalents deemed more indigenous. Such top-down coinages do not always find traction in the actual spoken vernaculars.

## 23.6 Concluding remarks

Non-areal contact in the MPSEA linguistic area, to the extent it can be known from historical sources, involves two millennia and multiple layers of lexical and grammatical cross-fertilization. In addition to the 'usual suspects', Sanskrit, Arabic, Chinese, and European languages, I have attempted to shed some light on some lesser known languages involved, including Tamil, Japanese, Middle-Indo-Aryan, and a number of regional subvarieties. To better contextualize these contact situations, two factors must be taken into account. Firstly, lexical borrowing often involved donor languages that are themselves poorly documented. For example, certain loanwords have evident Chinese or New-Indo-Aryan origins, but the particular variety from which they were acquired often remains unclear. Secondly, the phonological characteristics of some loanwords point to borrowing through a third source, such as a colloquial Dravidian language or a variety of creole Portuguese, yet in the absence of scholarship on such varieties, little more can be said about the matter.

As this chapter has substantiated, Malay was the main vector through which South Asian and West Asian loanwords entered other MPSEA languages. In the opposite direction, Malay also lent the largest number of borrowings to non-Austronesian languages, comprising both inherited and borrowed words. In general, lexical influence from MPSEA languages on the languages of South Asia, West Asia, East Asia, and Europe chiefly pertained to regionally specific products, concepts, and inventions. Expectedly, nouns comprise the majority of borrowed items in both directions. They have occasionally been adopted into MPSEA languages in their plural form. Prestigious languages such as Sanskrit and Arabic were responsible for the introduction of several abstract concepts into Malay and Javanese, whereas the Philippine languages have mostly drawn from Spanish and English for this purpose, Tetun from Portuguese, and Malagasy from French and English. These source languages continue to inspire language users, particularly in the realm of post-independence language engineering. They often show up as part of contemporary neologisms, even though many concepts so coined are in fact loan translations from English (or, in Malagasy, from French). Mundane objects have generally been borrowed from vernacular languages, including European languages. External origins are also evident in a plethora of grammatical particles in the

**Table 23.19** European loanwords designating introduced concepts

| English | Malaysian | Tagalog | Dutch | Indonesian | Portuguese | Tetun |
|---|---|---|---|---|---|---|
| *automatic* | *automatik* | *awtomatik* | *automatisch* | *otomatis* | *automático* | *automátiku* |
| *bag* | *beg* | *bag* | *tas* | *tas* | *saco* | *saku* |
| *billion* | *bilion* | *bilyon* | *miljard* | *milyar* | *trilhão* | *triliaun* |
| *cancer* | *kansər* | *kanser* | *kanker* | *kankər* | *cancro* | *kankru* |
| *garrison* | *garison* | *garison* | *garnizoen* | *garnisun* | *guarnição* | *guarnisaun* |
| *immigration* | *imigreʃən* | *imigrasyon* | *immigratie* | *imigrasi* | *imigração* | *imigrasaun* |
| *police* | *polis* | *pulis* | *politie* | *polisi* | *polícia* | *polísia* |
| *recipe* | *resəpi* | *resipi* | *recept* | *rəsep* | *receita* | *reseita* |
| *stadium* | *stadium* | *istadyum* | *stadion* | *stadion* | *estádio* | *estádiu* |
| *television* | *televiʃən* | *telebisyon* | *televisie* | *teləvisi* | *televisão* | *televizaun* |

languages researched here, some of which were not used grammatically in their donor languages.

In several MPSEA languages, lexical borrowing displays a cyclical character in which loanwords from new prestige languages tend to replace those taken from older ones. The tendency in Malay to adopt personal pronouns from external sources is an example of such 'luxury' borrowings. Lexical replacement is generally a good indicator of a speech community's contact situation and sociolinguistic hierarchies in a given period in time. Sanskrit, for example, has replaced several pre-existing lexical items in Malay, Javanese, and other languages, illustrating the social prestige of 'Indianized' registers in parts of pre-modern Southeast Asia. At a later stage of language development, many of these borrowings were in turn replaced by Arabic and/or European ones. This process of cyclical borrowing is still ongoing. Today, for example, English loanwords often replace Spanish ones in Tagalog and Dutch ones in Indonesian.

## Acknowledgements

I am grateful to the editors of this volume and to Arlo Griffiths for their valuable comments, which have improved this chapter significantly. They do not necessarily agree with all my findings.

## Languages referred to

IPA is used to represent Austronesian languages. In line with common practice, the following exceptions apply: <j> is used for the voiced palatal stop /ɟ/, and <y> is used for the palatal approximant /j/. In Malagasy, <y> represents /i/. Word stress in Philippine languages is indicated with diacritics. For Tamil and Malayalam, (unorthographical) voiced consonants are indicated. If not specified, Pinyin is used for Chinese characters. The Pe̍h-ōe-jī romanization is used for Southern Min and Jyutping for Cantonese. European words are spelled orthographically.

I draw upon my personal knowledge of the following languages cited from in this chapter: Afrikaans, Ambon Malay, Bengali, Dutch, English, French, Gujarati, Hadhrami Arabic, Japanese, Kupang Malay, Manado Malay, Marathi, Middle-Indo-Iranian, Old Khmer, Oriya, Pali, Portuguese, Sanskrit, Shona, Spanish, Turkish, Xhosa.

For other languages I use the following dictionaries:

Acehnese (Djajadiningrat 1934), Arabic (Wehr 1994), Cebuano (Wolff 1972), Cham (Aymonier and Cabaton 1906, Moussay 1970), Dhivehi (Reynolds 2003), Hindustani (Platts 1884; McGregor 1993), Ilokano (Rubino 2000), Javanese (Robson and Wibisono 2002), Karo Batak (Prinst 2002), Malagasy (Richardson 1885; Diksionera 1992), Malay (Wilkinson 1932; Noresah 2005), Maranao (McKaughan and Al-Macaraya 1996), Minangkabau (Moussay 1995), Moken (Lewis 1960), Old Javanese (Zoetmulder 1982), Persian (Steingass 1892), Proto-Cham (Thurgood 1991), Sangir (Steller and Aebersold 1959), Sinhala (Clough 1892), Southern Min (Douglas 1899; Zhang 2009), Sri Lankan Malay (Saldin 2007), Tagalog (Ferrer 2003), Tamil (Tamil 1924-36), Tetun (Hull 1999; Manhitu 2007), Toba Batak (Warneck 1977), Yemeni Arabic (Piamenta 1990).

# PART III

# Areal Overviews

CHAPTER 24

# Languages of the northern Philippines

HSIU-CHUAN LIAO AND LAWRENCE A. REID

## 24.1 The language scene

This chapter provides a linguistic typology of the northern Philippine languages. These are the languages that have been subgrouped into Bashiic, Northern Luzon, and Central Luzon languages, consisting of about seventy of the total number of Philippine languages (Eberhard et al. 2020). The south-central Philippine languages, consisting of the Greater Central Philippine languages and other groups are discussed in Chapter 25 by Kaufman, this volume.

Bashiic languages (also known as 'Batanic languages' (Tsuchida et al. 1987, 1989, etc.) or 'Vasayic languages' (Moriguchi 1983)) are a discrete, non-controversial group of Malayo-Polynesian languages spoken on islands in the Luzon Strait between Taiwan and the island of Luzon of the Philippines. Northern Luzon (also known as Cordilleran) languages are widely distributed through the mountains, valleys, and coastal strips of the northern portion of Luzon. Northern Luzon languages are composed of five subgroups: (i) Arta; (ii) Ilokano; (iii) Northern Cordilleran languages; (iv) Northeastern Luzon languages; (v) Meso-Cordilleran languages (Reid 1989, 1991, 1994c, 2006b; Himes 1996: 102; Robinson and Lobel 2013). Central Luzon languages are composed of three subgroups of languages: (i) Kapampangan (or Pampango); (ii) Remontado; and (iii) Sambalic (Himes 2012: 490, 527; Lobel and Surbano 2019: 3). See Map 24.1, for the languages of the northern Philippines.

The subgrouping of northern Philippine languages has developed primarily on the basis of different reflexes of Proto-Malayo-Polynesian (PMP) *R and developments in the pronominal system (Reid 2006b). PMP *R developed into *y* [j] in both Bashiic and Central Luzon languages (Conant 1911; Zorc 1974b; Himes 2012), which leads Zorc (1986) to consider that they and northern Mangyan languages might form a larger genetic unit. PMP *R has three different reflexes in Northern Luzon languages: it became *g* in both North Cordilleran languages and Northeastern Luzon languages; *l* in Meso-Cordilleran languages; and *r* in both Arta and Ilokano.

As a result of the Spanish and English periods of influence in the Philippines, many lexical items were borrowed from these languages either directly or via the trade languages in the area. Subsequently, Tagalog was chosen as the national language and taught in the schools under the rubric Filipino, which has influenced the lexicon and to some extent the morphology and syntax of some of these languages. The major trade language of the area is Ilokano, although in some areas Filipino/Tagalog is used as such. Most languages are direct developments from Proto-Malayo-Polynesian, while other languages, spoken by Negrito groups, are presumably the result of a shift to the language of their neighbours (Reid 1987).

## 24.2 Phonology

Most northern Philippine languages have a relatively simple native phonology (that is, excluding phonemes that are the result of borrowing), with four voiceless stops /p/, /t/, /k/, and /ʔ/, three voiced stops /b/, /d/, and /g/, three corresponding nasals /m/, /n/, and /ŋ/, one voiceless fricative /s/, one lateral /l/, and two semi-vowels /w/ and /j/. In some languages a vibrant occurs, either a trilled or tapped /r/ (in many languages the result of the lenition of an intervocalic /d/). In a number of northern Philippine languages, an inherited *s has become /h/ either in all forms, such as some of the Ifugao languages (Newell and Poligon 1993; Lambrecht 1978; Hohulin and Hohulin 2014), or in some forms, such as pronouns and case markers (Fukuda 1997; Shetler 1976). In addition, some of the Sambalic Negrito languages and Itbayat supposedly maintained an original PMP *-h (Blust 2018c). Kapampangan (Central Luzon) is the only Philippine language reflecting the PMP palatal nasal *ɲ (Blust 2013a: 175).

Most northern Philippine languages have a four-vowel system; some have four vowels /a/, /i/, /u/, and /ə/ (or /ɨ/). Some other languages have either fronted *ə to /e/ or backed it to /o/ or /u/. Other languages again have developed up to eight vowels by various typological and phonological processes, such as monophthongization of diphthongs and vowel splitting (Reid 1973: 490–500).

Hsiu-chuan Liao and Lawrence A. Reid, *Languages of the northern Philippines*. In: *The Oxford Guide to the Malayo-Polynesian Languages of Southeast Asia*. Edited by: Alexander Adelaar and Antoinette Schapper, Oxford University Press. © Hsiu-chuan Liao and Lawrence A. Reid (2024). DOI: 10.1093/oso/9780198807353.003.0024

**Map 24.1** Northern Philippine languages.

All northern Philippine languages have distinctive lexical stress, which is sometimes labelled as vowel length.[1] In languages with phonemic lexical stress, it falls on one of the last two syllables, but it cannot be predicted beyond that, for example, Ayta Mag-antsi (Central Luzon) /ˈha.lo/ 'mix' vs. /ha.ˈlo/ 'throat', /ˈʔa.po/ 'grandparent' vs. /ʔa.ˈpo/ 'grandchild' (Storck and Storck 2005: xiv); Kankanaey (Northern Luzon) /ˈʔo.tot/ 'rat' vs. /ʔo.ˈtot/ 'flatulence', /man.ˈba.lin/

[1] In orthographies, stress is indicated with an acute accent on the vowel of the stressed syllable.

'to travel' vs. /man.ba.'lin/ 'to become' (Allen 2014: 348). In the Bashiic languages Itbayat and Ibatan, vowel length is phonemic, whereas stress is not phonemic and always falls on the final syllable of a word (Yamada 2014: 13, 14; Maree 2007: 20), for example, Itbayat /to:.'kod/ 'a kind of yam' vs. /to.'kod/ 'support; vertical support', /ni:.'ni/ 'personified doll' vs. /ni.'ni/ 'sap or wax of tree', /mit.ta:.ta.'ja/ 'boat-shaped' vs. /mit.ta.ta.'ja/ (< /tata'ja/ 'boat') 'build a boat'.

The most common syllable patterns of native words in all northern Philippine languages are CV and CVC. Some Central Luzon languages also allow VC, but in non-initial syllables only (Antworth 1979: 3; Yamashita 1992: 9–10). Syllable-initial and syllable-final consonant clusters are found only in loanwords in most, if not all, northern Philippine languages. Heterosyllabic geminates occur in most, if not all, northern Philippine languages. Some northern Philippine languages have a complete set of geminate clusters, including geminate glottal stops (see §24.2.6).

Distribution of segments within a word has one constraint. Some Northern Luzon languages, such as Bontok, Kankanaey, and Tuwali Ifugao, do not allow the glottal stop to occur in a syllable-final position when the following syllable begins with a different consonant (Reid 2005; Allen 2014: 349; Hohulin and Hohulin 2014: 13). This is avoided by metathesis, producing consonant–glottal stop combinations, Central Bontok /na-/ + /ʔə.'fər/ 'wet' becomes [nabʔər] 'to be wet' (in Bontok /b/ typically occurs in syllable-final position, while /f/ is its equivalent in syllable-initial position, Reid 2005).

The following subsections describe widespread phonological processes found in northern Philippine languages.

### 24.2.1 Vowel syncope

Vowel syncope has been a tendency in the history of all northern Philippine languages and is typically observed when a vowel occurs in the environment VC_CV after affixation. When disyllabic roots are suffixed with reflexes of PMP *-an or *-ən, which typically attract stress to move one syllable to the right in resultant forms, the vowel in the final syllable of some roots gets syncopated, for example, Kakilingan Sambal (Central Luzon) [dak'pən] 'to catch' (</da'kəp/ + /-ən/), [lob'tan] 'to make a hole into. . .' (< /lo'bot/ + /-an/) (Yamashita 1992: 11); Kankanaey (Northern Luzon) [kɨd'ŋɨn] 'finish' (< /kɨ'dɨŋ/ + /-ɨn/), [liŋ'ban] 'hide' (< /li'ŋɨb/ + /-an/), but /ʔɨdda'san/ 'attain' (Allen 2014: 357). When disyllabic roots are prefixed or infixed, for example with *<om>*, the first vowel of some roots get syncopated, for example, Kakilingan Sambal (Central Luzon) [ʔil'bəŋ] 'to bury' (</i-/ + /lə'bə́ŋ/), [lom'pad] 'to fly' (from /<om>/ + /lə'pad/) (Yamashita 1992: 11).

Vowel syncope interacts with other processes. For example, in Botolan Sambal, vowel syncope triggers metathesis of *h*-C (e.g. [mah'laj ~ mal'haj] 'large' (< /ma-/ + /hə'laj/) and [pabhu'lɨn] (< /hu'bul/ + /pa-...-ɨn/) 'to cause to spring forth'). Following vowel syncope there is a metathesis of *n*-*m*, for example, [ti'namnan] (< /<in>/ + /ta'nam/ + /-an/) 'planted' (Antworth 1979: 4–5). In Dupaningan Agta (Northern Luzon), in words in which vowel syncope occurs, it triggers degemination; specifically, geminate consonants become singletons, for example, [matnog]/ 'noisy' (< /ma-/ + /tannog/) (Robinson 2011: 24, 26, 27).

### 24.2.2 Vowel raising

In Bugkalot and all Negrito languages along the eastern coast of northern Luzon, from Dupaningan in the north to as far south as Manide, PMP *a is raised to /ɨ/, /e/, or /i/, following voiced stops /b/, /d/, and /g/ (and sometimes also following /w/ and /j/), for example, Casiguran Agta /bisa/ 'wet' (< PMP *basəq), /dinom/ 'water' (< *daNum), /gimot/ 'root' (< *Ramut) (Healey 1974; Himes 1998; Lobel 2013a; Robinson 2011). This could be the result of palatalization before /a/ following voiced stops, for example, Kadaclan Bontok /baboj/ [ɓʲafoj] 'pig', /danom/ [tᶴanom] 'water', /gasot/ [kʲasot] 'hundred' (Fukuda 1997), see §24.2.4 about voiced stop palatalization below.

### 24.2.3 Voiced stop allophony

While the term allophony is used here (see Reid 1963; Himes 1984/1985), in all languages that formerly exhibited voiced stop allophony, the variants have become phonemic as a result of education in English and borrowing from other languages, such as Ilokano, Tagalog, and English (for examples and explanation, see Reid 2005). The variants described here occur in most of the Central Cordilleran languages, except Kankanaey and Kiangan Ifugao. In the other Central Cordilleran languages, voiced stops [b], [d], and [g] occur only as the codas of syllables, while before vowels, in syllable onset position, there are a variety of aspirates, fricatives or affricates, either voiced or voiceless, depending on the language. In some Kalinga languages, [g] occurs in all positions of the syllable, while in most Bontok languages, the syllable initial variant of /g/ is a fronted, aspirate [k̟ʰ], contrasting with a backed [k̠] or [q], which is the regular reflex of PMP *k, for example, Central Bontok *nakhakkhak* [nak̟ʰak̟k̟ʰak̟] 'to have small holes; to have caries'. Ibaloi, alone among the Southern Cordilleran languages, has apparently been influenced by Central Cordilleran languages. It has a very complex phonology, with variants depending on word position and word stress (see Ballard 2011: 864 et seq.).

### 24.2.4 Palatalization

Despite the rarity of palatalization of a voiceless velar [k] before [i] in Austronesian languages (Blust 2013a: 236), it does occur in the Bashiic languages—Yami, Ivatan, Ibatan (Babuyan), and Itbayat. These languages have added three consonant phonemes, for example, /t͡s/, /d͡ʒ/, and /ɲ/ in Ibatan (Maree and Tomas 2012: 6). The added /t͡s/ phoneme (written as Ibatan *ch*) is a result of palatalization of *k before *i, for example, Ibatan /mat͡si-/ < PMP *maki- 'social action' (Liao 2011a), Yami /t͡sita/ < PMP *kita 'see'. The added /d͡ʒ/ (written as Ibatan *dy*) and /ɲ/ (written as Ibatan *ny*) are results of the widespread palatalization of *d and *n before *iya.

In a number of languages, syllable-initial variants of voiced stops are palatalized before /a/. For example, Eastern Bontok communities (Reid 1974: 514), Barlig (/fʲallig/), and Kadaclan palatalize syllable-initial variants of voiced stops before /a/, for example, Kadaclan Bontok /baboj/ [fʲafoj] 'pig', /danom/ [tᶴanom] 'water', /gasot/ [kʲasot] 'hundred' (Fukuda 1997). In Balbalasang, the language name is *Vyanaw* (often written *Banao*), and only syllable-initial /b/ [v] is palatalized, for example, Banao *mavyalin* [mavʲalin] (cf. Ilokano /maˈbalin/) 'possible', *vuvya-i* [vuvˈʲaʔi] (cf. Ilokano /baˈbai/) 'woman'. Himes (2002: 278) notes that in some communities in Rizal province, palatalization occurs in both inherited and borrowed forms (e.g., *bʲato* 'stone' and *bʲaŋka* 'boat').

### 24.2.5 Homorganic stopping and assibilation

In the Cagayan Valley languages, Ibanag, Yogad, Itawis, Gaddang, etc. (but not in Malaweg), as well as Negrito languages of the area (Atta Pamplona and Central Cagayan Agta), these processes have affected a number of reflexes of PMP *s > /t/ except before *i, for example, PMP *ʔasa:wa and PMP *ʔa:su are reflected as Ibanag /ʔatawa/ 'spouse' and /ʔatu/ 'dog', respectively. In the same languages, PMP *t before /i/ has become /s/. These changes have been borrowed in Bugkalot and from Bugkalot into the Bambang dialect of Isinay, but have not spread into the other dialects of Isinay, such as in Dupax del Sur, for example, Bambang Isinay /ʔapsijoʔ/ 'short; of horizontal length', Dupax del Sur Isinay /ʔaptijoʔ/; Bambang Isinay /ʔatawa/ 'spouse', Dupax del Sur Isinay /ʔaˈsawa/ (Reid 2019; Blust 2013a: 237).

### 24.2.6 Gemination and degemination

Gemination can occur root-internally or at morpheme boundaries. Gemination is often associated with the reflex of PMP *ə. For example, in Dupaningan Agta, /a/ from PMP *ə triggered the consonant immediately after it to geminate (e.g. *tallo* 'three' and *laddap* 'dive in water', but when /a/ from PMP *ə becomes medial (i.e. in the environment VC_CV) due to affixation, it is sometimes syncopated and the following geminate becomes a singleton (§24.2.1).

In some of the Central Cordilleran languages, such as Batad Ifugao and Isinay, geminate glottal stops are the result of a sequence of voiceless velar stops at the end of a word and a following singular genitive pronoun /ʔu/ (< *=ku) 'my' (e.g. Isinay /ʔanaʔʔu/ (< *ʔanak=ku) 'my child'). In other Northern Luzon languages, such as Ibanag and other Cagayan Valley languages, many geminate consonants are the result of regressive assimilation (e.g. *maglu:tu > Ibanag *mallutu* 'to cook', *magsu:su > Ibanag *massusu* 'to suck').

### 24.2.7 Lateral allophony

Many languages have variants of /l/ (see §24.2.3 about voiced stop allophony). Those that do not are Ilokano and the Central Luzon languages (apart from light and dark variants in the usual environments). In many Central Cordilleran languages, for example, it is reflected as [l] initially in citation forms (e.g., Central Bontok /ˈlarəg/ [la:ɹ̣əg] 'fly (insect)'), adjacent to a high front vowel (/ˈʔali/ [ʔa:li] 'come', /ˈʔila/ [ʔi:la] 'see'), or a high front vowel in a preceding closed syllable (/ʔomiblaj/ [ʔumiblaj] 'to tire'), or following an alveolar consonant (/katlo/ [katlu] 'third') (Reid 2005). In other environments (in some dialects of Central Bontok, Eastern Bontok and Batad Ifugao) /l/ occurs as /r/, a retroflex [ɹ̣] (not flapped or trilled, similar to an English *r*), for example, Central Bontok /ˈʔara/ [ʔa:ɹ̣a] 'get', /ˈʔoro/ [ʔu:ɹ̣u] 'head'. In other languages, the allophones of /l/ range from an interdental or lateral approximant in some Kalinga languages [ð̥] (Olson et al. 2010), to zero or a velar fricative in Northern Kankanay (Reid 1973), Bashiic languages and some Cagayan Valley languages, for example, Ibatan, Isnag /ʔahad/ 'fence'. For some languages, such as Kiangan Ifugao, variants of /l/ are not reported; this may be due to influence from languages such as Ilokano. In Southern Bontok (Talubin), the sequences /al/, /ul/, and /əl/ became /o/ (for data, see Kikusawa and Reid 2003: 90). Isinay maintains /l/ in almost the same environments discussed above.

In forms in which these conditions are not met (that is, in non-high positions) the /al/ sequence became /ej/, /e/, /w/, or /j/, depending on the phonological environment, for example, PMP *ʔa:lad 'fence' is Dupax del Sur Isinay /ʔe:jar/ (Reid 2019).

### 24.2.8 Lenition

Apart from voiced stop allophony, which may be seen as lenition, many Northern Luzon languages have intervocalic variants of voiceless stops /p/, /t/, and /k/, respectively [f], [θ], and [x]. The dialect of Isinay spoken in Dupax del Sur is unique among Northern Luzon languages in having a lenited set of variants of historically voiced stops in word final position. These are still maintained as voiced stops in the Bambang dialect of Isinay, e.g., Dupax del Sur Isinay /u'wav/, Bambang Isinay /uwab/ 'yawn', Dupax del Sur Isinay /'ejar/, Bambang Isinay /ejad/ 'fence', Dupax del Sur Isinay /o'roh/, Bambang Isinay /orog/ 'back of a person'. Intervocalic *-b- and *-d- appear as *-v-* and *-r-* in all dialects of Isinay, but intervocalic **-g-* occurs as a velar fricative *-h-* in Dupax del Sur Isinay and as *-k-* in Bambang Isinay (Reid 2019).

## 24.3 Morphological profile

In terms of the classic morphological typology of isolating vs. synthetic, and agglutinative vs. fusional, northern Philippine languages can be characterized as synthetic–agglutinative. Northern Philippine languages are synthetic in that they make a robust use of affixation (including reduplication) in word building; they are agglutinative in the sense that morpheme boundaries are usually clear. However, they differ from ideal agglutinative languages like Turkish because morphemes do not always exhibit 'one form–one meaning/function'.

Examples (1)–(5) demonstrate synthetic–agglutinative properties of northern Philippine languages. Specifically, lexical verbs in northern Philippine languages are typically composed of a root morpheme and affixes that encode various sorts of information, for example, *<in>* for 'perfective aspect', (1) and (4), $C_1V_1C_2$- reduplication, that is, the repetition of the first vowel and the first two consonants of a base (2) or *ʔan-* (3) for progressive or imperfective aspect, *pa-* for 'causative' (5), *pachi-* for 'social/joint action', *paN-* for 'distributive action' (1), *<om>*/*<um>* 'actor voice in the indicative mood' or 'inchoative action' and *nag-* for 'perfective aspect form of actor voice in the indicative mood', (2), (4), and (5), respectively, *-en* (/ən/) for 'patient voice in the indicative mood', (3) and (5), *-an* for 'locative voice in the indicative mood' (1). Moreover, when multiple morphemes co-occur, it is typically not difficult to posit a morpheme boundary among them. Note that although morpheme boundaries are generally clear, some affixes (e.g. so-called 'voice affixes' like *<um>*, *-en* (/ən/), *-an*, etc.) actually encode information about both voice and mood. In the case of *nag-*, it encodes information about voice, mood, and aspect simultaneously.

Southern Ivatan

(1) *Pinachipanlakatan=ku=sira* *su* *kabayu.*[2]
*p<in>achi-paN-lakat-an=ku=sira*
<PFV>SOC-DISTR-chase-LV= OBL horse
GEN.1SG=NOM.3PL[3]
'I joined them chasing a horse.'
(Hidalgo and Hidalgo 1971: 197)

Kankanaey

(2) *G<om>oy~goyang* *si* *Baby.*
<AV>REDUP~play PERS Baby
'Baby is playing (not with objects).' (Allen 2014: 55)

Botolan Sambal

(3) *ʔan-ʔetʔet-en* *nin* *bakiʔ* *ya* *taʔen.*
IPFV-chew-PV GEN rat SPEC trap
'The rat is chewing the trap.' (Antworth 1979: 53)

Botolan Sambal

(4) *T<in><um>abaʔ* *ya* *baboy.*
<PFV><INCH>fat SPEC pig
'The pig got fat.' (Antworth 1979: 43)

Botolan Sambal

(5) *Nag-pa-tabaʔ* *hi* *Jose* *nin* *baboy*
PFV.AV-CAUS-fat PERS Jose OBL pig
*ta* *patyen [pati-in]* *ha* *pista.*
because kill-PV LOC fiesta
'Jose fattened a pig because he will kill it for the fiesta.'
(Antworth 1979: 43)

[2] Data cited from published materials reflect the actual spelling conventions of the original with the following exceptions. First, clitics are indicated with an equals sign whether or not they are written with a space between them or joined to their host in the original. Second, the glottal stop symbol 'ʔ' is used for any q, apostrophe, grave accent mark, or hyphen that occurs in the original, since it is assumed that these are various ways of marking a glottal stop. Literal and free translations reflect, wherever possible, that of the original, although these have also been changed at times to more accurately reflect the syntax of the example. Grammatical labels are changed in accordance with our theoretical assumptions.

[3] Even though we analyse northern Philippine languages as ergative, we choose not to use the term 'absolutive', preferring instead the typologically more general term 'nominative' for the foregrounded phrase of a basic predication, and the one that is most likely to undergo deletion under conditions of coreference in a relative clause, whether transitive or intransitive. Similarly, since in most, if not all, northern Philippine languages the actor of transitive constructions and the possessor in a possessive phrase have identical forms, we choose to use the more general term genitive as the label for both of these noun phrases.

Although morpheme boundaries are generally clear in northern Philippine languages, exceptions to the agglutinative profile are found with reflexes of PMP *maN-/*paN- (or *maŋ-/*paŋ- in Blust 2004b). Generally, the default form of the final nasal is considered to be a velar nasal in northern Philippine languages; however, the default final nasal is *n* in Itbayat [Bashiic] and Kapampangan (Central Luzon) (Yamada 2002, 2014; Forman 1971). The final nasal of *maN-/*paN- typically changes its point of articulation to that of the initial consonant of the base to which it is attached. That is, PMP *maN-/*paN- is reflected as *mam-/pam-* before labial consonants, *man-/pan-* before alveolar and dental consonants, and as *mang-* (/maŋ/)/ *pang-* (/paŋ/) before velar and glottal consonants. Following assimilation, the initial consonant of the base is deleted (see Newman 1984–1985; Blust 2004b; Liao 2004 for details).

Special attention is needed to distinguish reflexes of PMP *maN-/*paN- from reflexes of PMP *maR-/*paR- in some Northern Luzon languages. In the Meso-Cordilleran subgroup of Northern Luzon languages, the reflex of *R is *l*; thus, reflexes of PMP *maR-/*paR- are expected to appear as **mal-/*pal-*. However, all Meso-Cordilleran languages, including South-Central Cordilleran languages, Northern Alta and Southern Alta, show the innovated form *man-*, or a further development, such as *mon-*, *mun-*, *men-* (/mən/ or /mɨn/), *min-*, *ʔan-*, *ʔin-*, *ʔen-* (/ʔən/). The form *man-* occurs in most of the West Southern Cordilleran languages and in some Central Cordilleran languages. The /n/ in *man-* does not undergo nasal assimilation in most of the West Southern Cordilleran (such as Karao, Ibaloi, etc.), but it does undergo it in some Central Cordilleran languages (such as Balangao, Limos Kalinga, etc.) and in Keley-i Kallahan (Southern Cordilleran).

In cases where *man-* undergoes homorganic nasal assimilation, the reflex of *maR- (*man-* with nasal assimilation) and the reflex of *maN- (*mang-* with nasal assimilation and consonant deletion) are sometimes hard to distinguish. The only key that one can use to distinguish their reflexes is to check whether the base-initial consonant is retained after nasal assimilation. If it is, as in (6), then the prefix attached to the base is a reflex of *maR-. If it is deleted after assimilation, as in (7), the prefix attached to the base is a reflex of *maN- (see Liao 2004 for a detailed discussion of reflexes of PMP *maN- and *maR- in Philippine languages).

Limos Kalinga
(6) *Man-dalus si Malia=t danat palatu.*
AV.DUR-wash PERS Maria=OBL PL.SPEC plate
'Maria washed some plates (plates are partially, not fully, affected).' (Ferreirinho 1993: 39)

Limos Kalinga
(7) *Mananum=ak. [maN-danum=ak]*
AV.DISTR-water=NOM.1SG
'I am fetching water.' (Ferreirinho 1993: 29)

In terms of the relative position between affixes and bases, northern Philippine languages can be described as predominantly prefixing. All northern Philippine languages have a large inventory of prefixes but a relatively limited number of suffixes and infixes. For example, Rubino (2000: xviii–xxi) lists 419 prefixes, fourteen suffixes, and nine infixes in the Introduction section of his *Ilocano Dictionary and Grammar*. In addition to prefixes, suffixes, and infixes, many northern Philippine languages also have circumfixes, for example, benefactive voice (BEN) is typically marked by the circumfix *ʔi- -an* in Northern Luzon languages (8), cf. *ʔi-* for theme voice (TV)/instrumental voice (IV) (9) and *-an* for locative voice (LV) (10).

Limos Kalinga
(8) *ʔin-dalus-an ʔud Malia si*
PFV.BEN-wash-BEN GEN Maria PERS
*ʔina=na=t nat palatu.*
mother=GEN.3SG=OBL SPEC plate
'Maria washed some plates for her mother.'
(Ferreirinho 1993: 39, 58)

Limos Kalinga
(9) *ʔin-dalus ʔud Malia nat sabun sinat*
PFV.IV-wash GEN Maria SPEC soap OBL
*palatu.*
plate
'Maria washed plates with the soap.'
(Ferreirinho 1993: 58)

Limos Kalinga
(10) *D<in>alus-an ʔud Malia danat palatu.*
<PFV>wash-LV GEN Maria PL.SPEC plate
'Maria washed the plates' (Ferreirinho 1993: 39)

## 24.4 Reduplication

Reduplication is a morphophonological process in which some phonological material is repeated within a single form for semantic or grammatical purposes. It is very pervasive in northern Philippine languages. Formally, a wide variety of patterns, such as *Ca-*, CV-, *Caw-*, $C_1V_1C_2$-, $C_1V_1C_2V_2$- (or foot reduplication), full reduplication, etc., are found to be associated with the inflectional and derivational functions mentioned in Himmelmann (2005a: 121). Moreover, lexicalized reduplication can also be observed in most, if not all, northern Philippine languages. In what follows, we discuss functions/meanings associated with the various patterns of reduplication found in northern Philippine languages.

### 24.4.1 *Ca*- reduplication

*Ca*- reduplication refers to the repetition of the initial consonant of a base plus a fixed vowel, which is usually (but not necessarily) /a/. Although it has been reconstructed to Proto-Austronesian (Blust 1998a, 1999c), it is rarely used in northern Philippine languages (or other Austronesian languages spoken in the Philippines). In a restricted number of Northern Luzon languages, it is associated with the following functions: (i) with verbs, it indicates 'plural actors involved in an action', Central Cagayan Agta *magbabída kid* (AV.PL.talk.about they) 'they are talking together' implies that 'both or all of the actors are actually involved in the action'. (The matching unreduplicated form is *magbída* 'talk about'); (ii) with kin terms, it creates a multiple, Dupaningan Agta (with the prefix *pat-*) *papatwadi* 'sibling set (more than two)' (cf. *patwadi* 'pair of siblings' and *wadi* 'younger sibling (either sex)'); and (iii) as part of a special affix *Ca*- -$V_2$- in a few onomatopoeic forms, it expresses sounds that are 'loud and prolonged or iterative', Ilokano *kakreeb* 'sound of crashing waves' (cf. *kireb* 'wave crash') (Healey 1960: 9; Robinson 2011: 79; Rubino 2001: 309).

### 24.4.2 CV- reduplication

CV- reduplication, the repetition of the first consonant and the first vowel of a base, is probably the most commonly used pattern of reduplication in most northern Philippine languages. A wide range of functions and meanings can be associated with it (Antworth 1979; Hidalgo and Hidalgo 1971; Rubino 2000; Vanoverbergh 1955; Yamashita 1992; Reid 2006c; Yamada 2014).

With verbs, it has at least the following functions: (i) it expresses habitual aspect, Southern Ivatan (with the circumfix *ma-. . .-en*) *machichimuyen* 'usually rain' (cf. *chimuy* 'rain'); (ii) it expresses recent perfective aspect, for example, Ilokano (with the prefix *ka-*) *kasasangpét* 'just arrived' (< *sangpét* 'arrive') or an intensification of a state, Central Bontok /kakamáŋan/ 'to hurry a lot' (< /kamáŋan/ 'to hurry'); and (iii) forming verbs of collection, Southern Ivatan (with the prefix *man-*) *manbabaka* 'collect (rustle or buy) cows' (< *baka* 'cow').

With numeral bases, it predominantly forms: (i) restrictive numerals, Botolan Sambal *lolowa* 'only two' (< *lowa* 'two'); and (ii) distributive cardinal numbers, Ilokano (with the prefix *sag-*) *saglilimá* 'five each' (cf. *limá* 'five).

With nouns, it has at least the following functions: (i) it expresses facsimile, as in Southern Ivatan *vavahay* 'playhouse' (< *vahay* 'house'); (ii) it expresses 'something is similar to the olfactory feature possessed by the referent of the predicative stem', for example, Southern Ivatan (with the prefix *maya-*) *mayakakadin* 'smell like goat' (< *kadin* 'goat'); (iii) it designates 'a person who is associated with or performs the action specified by the base', Botolan Sambal (with the prefix *mang-*) *mananapon* 'a thrower' (cf. *tapon* 'to throw'); (iv) it forms instrumental nouns, Itbayat *kokoyta* 'tool for catching large octopus' (< *koyta* 'large octopus'); (v) it forms abstract nouns, for example, Ilokano (with the prefix *ka-*) *kababagás* 'meaning, essence' (cf. *bagás* 'rice'); and (vi) plurality, for example, Southern Ivatan /babaŋku/ 'benches' (< /baŋku/ 'bench'). With the reciprocal relation prefix *mi-* or *mita-* in Central Luzon languages, it indicates 'more than two people in an intimate kinship or social relationship', for example, Botolan Sambal /mitataʔanak/ 'parent and children' (cf. /mitaʔanak/ 'parent and child' (< /ʔanak/ 'child')).

In Northern Luzon languages, it is a major means for forming plurals of human nouns (Reid 2006c: 49, 67). Examples of it are widely found in different branches of Northern Luzon languages, such as, Ilokano /ʔiʔikit/ 'aunts' (cf. /ʔikit/ 'aunt'); Central Bontok /ʔaʔalitáʔu/ 'uncles' (cf. /ʔalitáʔu/ 'uncle'); Balangao /sosnod/ 'brothers' (cf. /sonod/ 'brother'); Pangasinan /kukúja/ 'older brothers' (cf. /kúja/ 'older brother'); Gaddang /bababbáj/ 'women' (cf. /babáj/ 'woman'). In many Northern Luzon languages, it also forms plural non-human nouns, Central Bontok *lilíma* 'arms' (cf. *líma* 'arm'); Balangao *babali* 'typhoons' (cf. *bali* 'typhoon'); Ibaloi *mamanuk* 'chickens' (cf. *manuk* 'chicken'); Pangasinan *niniógニ* 'coconuts' (cf. *nióg* 'coconut').

### 24.4.3 $C_1V_1C_1$- reduplication and -$C_2$- reduplication?

In addition to CV- reduplication, plurality of a limited number of human nouns can be marked by $C_1V_1C_1$- reduplication or -$C_2$- reduplication in Ilokano. $C_1V_1C_1$- reduplication refers to the repetition of the first two segments and the gemination of the first consonant of a base. This pattern of reduplication can indicate plurality of high-frequency forms having an initial syllable, either *ba* or *la*, which is identical to the initial syllable in the terms for 'woman' and 'man' respectively', Ilokano *babbalásang* 'young women' (*balásang* 'young woman'), *lallakáy* 'old men' (cf. *lakáy* 'old man'). These plural forms, as well as *tattáu* 'people' (cf. /táʔu/ 'person') are probably results of analogy with forms such as *babbái* 'women' and *lalláki* 'men', which superficially looks like the gemination of the second consonant of the singular forms *babái* 'woman' and *laláki* 'man' or -$C_2$- reduplication (Rubino 2000: xvii). However, *babbái* 'women' and *lalláki* 'men' are probably the results of the application of two processes: (i) prefixing CV- reduplication to a singular form *babái* 'woman' and *laláki* 'man'; and (ii) the loss of an unstressed *a* vowel (i.e. *babbái* (< **bababáʔi* < /babbáʔi/) 'women' and *lalláki* (< **lalaláki* < /lalláki/) 'men') (Reid 2006c: 54–5).

### 24.4.4 *Caw-* reduplication

*Caw-* reduplication, the repetition of the initial consonant of a base plus a fixed vowel-glide sequence /aw/, is found only in Central Luzon languages and Tausug (Central Philippines). Its sole function appears to indicate plurality in some nouns,[4] as in Botolan Sambal *lawlapis* 'pencils' (cf. *lapis* 'pencil'); Kakilingan Sambal *bawbakolaw* 'monkeys' (cf. *bakolaw* 'monkey'). In Kakilingan Sambal, it not only occurs with common nouns, but also with nominative demonstratives, as in *hawhábaycí* 'these' (cf. *hábaycí* 'this') (Antworth 1979; Yamashita 1992; Rubino 2006).

### 24.4.5 $C_1V_1C_2$- reduplication

$C_1V_1C_2$- reduplication refers to the repetition of the first three segments of a base. Because syllable structures in northern Philippine languages are either CV or CVC, $C_1V_1C_2$- reduplication can be either (i) the repetition of an initial light syllable plus the onset of the second syllable or (ii) the repetition of an initial heavy syllable.

With numerals, quantity expressions, and pronouns, it expresses limitation in number or quantity, as in Ilokano *taltalló* 'only three' (cf. *talló* 'three'), *siksika* 'only you (SG)' (cf. *sika* '2SG') (Rubino 1997, 2000). With nouns, it has at least two functions. First, in some Northern Luzon languages (Ilokano, Pangasinan, Central Cagayan Agta, Isnag, etc.), it expresses plurality of some human nouns and/or nouns closely associated in some way with humans, as in Ilokano *am-amma* /ʔamʔamma/ 'fathers' (cf. *ʔama* 'father'), *balbaláy* 'houses' (cf. *baláy* 'house'); (with the prefix *ka-*) Southern Ivatan *kaykayvan* 'friends' (cf. *kayvan* 'friend'). Second, it indicates facsimile or resemblance, as in Central Bontok *an-annak* 'doll (like a child)' (cf. /ʔanák/ 'child') (Reid 1976, 2006c; Hidalgo and Hidalgo 1971: 47).

With verbs, it has at least the following functions: (i) marking continuative or imperfective aspect, as in Ilokano *lakláko* 'selling' (< *láko* 'sell') and Central Bontok *kawkawkaw* 'is making a hole' (< *kawkaw* 'make a hole'); (ii) expressing a repetitive or distributive meaning, as in Ilokano *gimmatgatang* (< *g<imm>at-* + *gatang* 'kept on buying' (cf. *gatang* 'buy')); and (iii) expressing the recent perfective aspect, as in Ilokano (with the prefix *ka-*) /kaʔitʔitlúg/ 'freshly laid; just laid' (< /ʔitlúg/ 'egg'). With stative verbs, it expresses the following functions in Northern Luzon languages: (i) the comparative degree of a stative, as in Ilokano *narugrugít* 'dirtier' (cf. *narugít* 'dirty'); and (ii) intensification of a condition or state, as in Ilokano (with the prefix *naka-*) *nakaragragsak* 'quite happy' (cf. *ragsak* 'happy') (Reid 1992, 2006c; Rubino 2000; Vanoverbergh 1955).

### 24.4.6 CV:- reduplication

This is a variant pattern of $C_1V_1C_2$- reduplication (with its multiple functions). It occurs with roots that have a medial glottal stop or glide, regardless of the stress pattern of the root, as in Ilokano *agsasao* [ʔagsa:saʔó] 'speaking' (< *agsao* [ʔagsaʔó] 'speak'), *agdadait* [ʔagda:dá:ʔit] 'sewing' (< *agdait* [ʔagdá:ʔit] 'sew'). Reid (1992: 71, 2006c: 54) considers the presence of a long vowel in these examples "as resulting from a phonotactic constraint that does not permit consonant clusters with initial glottal stop".

### 24.4.7 $C_1V_1C_2V_2$- reduplication (or foot reduplication)

This reduplication refers to the repetition of the first two syllables except the coda of the second syllable. With nouns, it indicates plurality in Bashiic and Northern Luzon languages, as in Southern Ivatan /ʔatəʔatəp/ 'roofs' (cf. /ʔatəp/ 'roof')[5] and Pangasinan /ʔutúʔutút/ 'rats' (cf. /ʔutút/ 'rat'). In Dupaningan Agta, it indicates a distributive plural, as in *sikasikaw* '(scattered) swidden fields' (cf. *sikaw* 'swidden field') (Hidalgo and Hidalgo 1971: 47; Reid 2006c: 62; Robinson 2011: 70).

[4] In Tausug, *Caw-* reduplication appears with kin terms to form collectives, for example, *maglawlahasiya'* 'all the relatives' (cf. *maglahasiya'* 'relatives'); *magtawtaymanghud* 'entire family' (cf. *magtaymanghud* 'siblings') (Rubino 2006: 275).

[5] Hidalgo and Hidalgo (1971) do not list glottal stops, they give the form as *ateatep*. Other works (e.g. Persons 1979) usually do not list glottal stops. Examples from here will be given as they list them, although glottal stop will be inserted where there is a pattern with other consonants. Some works have various methods such as a hyphen or an apostrophe for marking glottal stops (see also fn2).

With verbs, it indicates at least the following functions: (i) repetitive or habitual aspect, as in Central Bontok *ʔanaʔánap* 'keep on looking for fish' (< /ʔánap/ 'look for fish'); and (ii) intermittent action, as in Southern Ivatan (with the prefix *ka-*) *kasavusavu:ng* 'go on blossoming' (cf. *kasávung* 'has just blossomed' and *kasavu:ng* 'go on blossoming'). With stative verbs, it indicates the comparative degree in Bashiic languages, as in Southern Ivatan *matalatalakak* 'lazier' (cf. *matalakak* 'lazy') (Hidalgo and Hidalgo 1971).

### 24.4.8 Full reduplication

Full reduplication refers to the repetition of an entire disyllabic root. With nouns, it expresses facsimile in Central Luzon languages, Botolan Sambal *tawotawo* 'scarecrow' (cf. *tawo* 'person'). With numerals, it indicates grouping numerals, Botolan Sambal *tatlotatlo* 'three by three' (cf. *tatlo* 'three') (Antworth 1979: 11,14).[6] It derives new words in Northern Luzon languages and Central Luzon languages, as in Ilokano *bangabánga* 'skull' (cf. *bánga* 'pot'); Ayta Mag-antsi /ʔaŋgaʔaŋga/ 'forever, eternity' (cf. /ʔaŋga/ 'until, end') (Storck and Storck 2005: 18).

### 24.4.9 Lexicalized reduplication

Lexicalized reduplication refers to the repetition of a fossilized root that is synchronically bound; typically, the root is a monosyllable of the shape CVC, although it is also possible to find fossilized roots that are disyllabic. Lexicalized reduplication is commonly found in floral and faunal terms, as in Ayta Mag-antsi *pakpak* 'wings', *digidig* 'small cicada'; (with the prefix *kali-*) *kalibangbang* 'kind of fire-resistant tree'; *kalidakdak* 'varieties of black ants', (with the infix *<al>*) *galudgod* 'elephant's ear', (with the prefix *ka-*) *kalubi-lubi* 'kind of yam' (Storck and Storck 2005). In addition to floral and faunal terms, lexicalized reduplication is also commonly found with some action verbs that show sound symbolism, as in Ibatan *gisgis* 'to rub together' (Maree 2007: 23).

## 24.5 Syntax

### 24.5.1 Word order

Northern Philippine languages are strongly right-branching. In the most common and basic type of clause, words or phrases that express predicates typically occur at the beginning of a clause.

#### 24.5.1.1 *Phrasal-level order*

In numeral phrases, the numeral appears first and is followed by a ligature and then the noun (phrase) that it enumerates (11)–(12). Note that the ligature used to link between a numeral and a noun (e.g. *=y* in Bolinao and *aka* in Southern Ivatan) might not be identical to the ligature used to link a noun with a non-numeral element (e.g. *a* in both Bolinao and Southern Ivatan).

Bolinao
(11) *Main saya=y anak a lalaki.*
EXIST one=LIG child LIG male
'There was a male child. (lit. 'Exists one who is a child who is a male.')' (Persons 1979: 34)

Southern Ivatan
(12) *u dadwa sa awri aka manganak ñi*
SPEC two 3PL MED LIG children GEN
*Kwan a ma-ha~hakay*
John LIG NMLZ-REDUP~boy
'those two boys of John (lit. 'those two who are children of John who are boys')'
(Hidalgo and Hidalgo 1971: 244)

In possessive constructions, the possessed noun appears before the genitive-marked possessor (12)–(13).

Kankanaey
(13) *Babaʔi [din ʔanak=da].*
girl/female SPEC child=GEN.3PL
'Their child is a girl.' (Allen 2014: 41)

In noun phrases with a relative clause or other modifying elements, the head noun typically precedes the relative clause or modifying elements (14)–(16). In Itbayat, Yamada (2014: 108) observes that *vaxay a vato* (house LIG stone) 'a house made of stone' is considered a better expression than *vato a vaxay* (stone LIG house) which means practically the same. Like numeral phrases, a ligature (e.g. *ya* in Kakilingan Sambal and *a* in Itbayat) is required to occur between the head noun and its following modifying elements.

Kakilingan Sambal
(14) *Maʔín ʔari [ya ʔampanga-ʔilangan nin*
EXIST king LIG IPFV-need OBL
*magʔin man-lo~lotoʔ]*
become DISTR-REDUP~cook
'There was a king who needed a cook.'
(Yamashita 1992: 23)

[6] Without examples with a coda consonant in the second syllable, these examples might be interpreted as instances of full reduplication or of foot reduplication. This chapter follows Antworth's (1979: 14) analysis in treating these examples as instances of full reduplication.

Itbayat
(15) *tawo [a aʔbo so aktokto]*
man LIG NEG OBL thought
'person without thought (lit. 'a man who has no thought')' (Yamada 2014: 109)

Itbayat
(16) *K<om><in>an=ta so vinivex [a rakox].*
<AV><PFV>eat=NOM.1PL.INCL OBL banana LIG big
'We ate big bananas. (lit. 'We ate bananas that were big.')' (Yamada 2014: 131)

Note that northern Philippine languages do not have a distinctive form class of adjective, although many descriptions of these languages use the term and some have argued for its existence (e.g. Rubino 2000: liv). Words that are translated as adjectives in English syntactically function as either nouns or verbs. When they function as nouns, they are typically unmarked (16), although they might be marked by *ma-* in Southern Ivatan (18)–(19).

In phrases containing a descriptive term ('adjective') (16)–(19) or relative clause, the form preceding the ligature acts as the syntactic head of the construction because it may stand alone, without the following modifying element or relative clause.

Southern Ivatan
(17) *u mavid [a metdeh [a anak nu tau aw]]*
SPEC beautiful LIG child LIG child GEN person MED
'the beautiful child who is a child of that person (lit. 'the beautiful one who is a child, who is a child of that person')' (Hidalgo and Hidalgo 1971: 244)

Southern Ivatan
(18) *u maistra [a ma-vakes]*
SPEC teacher LIG NMLZ-female
'the teacher who is a female'
(Hidalgo and Hidalgo 1971: 242)

Southern Ivatan
(19) *u ma-vakes [a maistra]*
SPEC NMLZ-female LIG teacher
'the female who is a teacher'
(Hidalgo and Hidalgo 1971: 242)

In prepositional phrases, the preposition functioning as head of its construction appears before its dependent noun phrases (20)–(21).

Botolan Sambal
(20) *[Para koni Jose] ya libro.*
for LOC Jose SPEC book
'The book is for Jose.' (Antworth 1979: 35)

Botolan Sambal
(21) *[Tongkol ha pagʔong] ya kowinto.*
about LOC turtle SPEC story
'The story is about the turtle.' (Antworth 1979: 36)

Note that not all words that are translated as prepositions in English are prepositions in northern Philippine languages. Specifically, forms expressing meanings such as 'inside', 'outside', 'above', 'below', etc., are syntactically nouns (22). As for the locative marker *ha* (21)–(22), it is not clear whether it should be analysed as a determiner, a preposition, or an extension noun (Reid 2002a: 306).

Kakilingan Sambal
(22) *Nací=hila=yna baydó [ha laleʔ nin ʔabong].*
PFV.die=3PL=COS DIST LOC inside GEN hut
'They already died inside the hut. (lit. 'They already died in the inside of the hut.')' (Yamashita 1992: 21)

### 24.5.1.2 *Clausal-level order*

In clauses with an auxiliary verb, the auxiliary verb will function as the main predicate of the clause and will occur clause-initially and attract all clitic elements (including clitic pronouns and clitic adverbs) (23)–(24).

Botolan Sambal
(23) *Maʔarìʔ=na=n i-takel ya damowag=ko.*
can=GEN.3SG=LIG IV-tie SPEC carabao=GEN.1SG
'He can tie my carabao.' (Antworth 1979: 71)

Bolinao
(24) *Baʔyo=na=ya=yna k<in>alap a daga=na.*
then=GEN.3SG=NOM.3SG=COS <PFV>take SPEC knife=GEN.3SG
'Then he took his knife.' (Persons 1979: 36)

In clauses without any auxiliary verb, the main lexical predicate occurs initially and attracts all clitic elements. Clauses with non-verbal predicates can be headed by either a noun or a preposition. In non-verbal clauses, no copula is used. Thus, nouns or prepositions that head nominal clauses or prepositional clauses typically occur initially and are then followed by the nominative noun phrase.

Non-verbal clauses headed by a nominal predicate are of two types: (i) classificational (also referred to as proper inclusion (Payne 1997: 114) or descriptive) nominal clauses; and (ii) identificational (also referred to as equative or equational) nominal clauses. These two types of nominal clause differ in the following ways. First, the predicate nominal in classificational nominal clauses simply classifies the entity expressed in the nominative noun phrase of the clause, so the predicate nominal is non-specific and is typically expressed by a bare common noun without any nominal specifier (25). By contrast, the predicate nominal in identificational nominal clauses provides specific identification for the entity expressed in the nominative noun phrase, so the nominal predicate is specific and/or definite and is typically expressed by a specific or definite common noun (usually accompanied by a specific or definite nominal specifier) (26), a possessive noun phrase (27), a personal noun phrase (28), or a personal pronoun (29), or a demonstrative pronoun (30).

Kankanaey
(25) *Baba?i din ?anak=da.*
girl/female SPEC child=GEN.3PL
'Their child is a girl.' (Allen 2014: 41)

Botolan Sambal
(26) *Hay Amirikano ya doktor.*
PRED.SPEC American SPEC doctor
'The doctor is the American.' (Antworth 1979: 35)

Dupaningan Agta
(27) *Ilay=ko ni Lubak.*
friend=GEN.1SG PERS Lubak
'Lubak is my friend.' (Robinson 2011: 164)

Southern Ivatan
(28) *Si Kwana ya.*
PERS Jean PROX
'This is Jean.' (Hidalgo and Hidalgo 1971: 241)

Limos Kalinga
(29) *Sakon ?ud mang-?adok.*
1SG SPEC AV-dance
'The one who will dance is me.' (Ferreirinho 1993: 19)

Botolan Sambal
(30) *Habayto ya bali.*
that.DIST SPEC house
'The house is that (one).' (Antworth 1979: 35)

In addition to nominal clauses, non-verbal clauses can be headed by a preposition (31).

Kakilingan Sambal
(31) *?obat ha Kakilingán hi Picáy.*
from LOC Kakilingan PERS Picay
'Picay is from Kakilingan.' (Yamashita 1992: 37)

Verbal predicates can lack a core argument, have a single core argument, or have two core arguments. Verbal clauses headed by an avalent verb (such as a meteorological verb) can have a verb occurring alone (32) or a verb followed by adverbs (33).

Southern Ivatan
(32) *Ma-chimuy.*
IPFV.STAT-rain
'It is raining.' (Hidalgo and Hidalgo 1971: 185)

Kakilingan Sambal
(33) *Nang-?odan nin biglá?.*
PFV.INTR-rain OBL suddenly
'It rained suddenly.' (Yamashita 1992: 39)

Verbal clauses headed by a monadic verb consist of a verb followed by a core argument (34)–(35).

Southern Ivatan
(34) *Ma-tava u ma-vakes.*
STAT-fat SPEC NMLZ-female
'The girl is fat.' (Hidalgo and Hidalgo 1971: 214)

Botolan Sambal
(35) *Mog-?alih=?ako ha Lonis.*
AV-leave=NOM.1SG LOC Monday
'I will leave on Monday.' (Antworth 1979: 53)

Verbal clauses headed by a dyadic verb can be either intransitive or transitive. Dyadic intransitive verbal clauses consist of a verb followed by two arguments: a nominative-marked actor argument and an oblique-/locative-marked undergoer argument, the latter is typically indefinite or non-specific. If the actor argument is a clitic pronoun, the pronoun must occur immediately after the verb and is followed by the (indefinite/non-specific) undergoer argument (36). If no clitic pronoun is involved, the relative order between the two arguments (and additional adjuncts) is relatively free (37)–(39).

Limos Kalinga
(36) *Nammula=?ak [nan-mula=?ak] si kantila.*
PFV.AV-plant=NOM.1SG OBL sweet.potato
'I planted sweet potatoes.' (Ferreirinho 1993: 82)

Southern Ivatan
(37) *Manarip [maN-tarip] si ina su*
AV.DISTR-pare PERS mother OBL

*wakay* *du* *gagan.*
sweet.potato LOC outside
'Mother pares sweet potatoes outside.'
(Hidalgo and Hidalgo 1971: 223)

Southern Ivatan
(38) *Manarip [maN-tarip]* *su* *wakay* *si*
AV.DISTR-pare OBL sweet.potato PERS
*ina* *du* *gagan.*
mother LOC outside
'Mother pares sweet potatoes outside.'
(Hidalgo and Hidalgo 1971: 223)

Southern Ivatan
(39) *Manarip [maN-tarip]* *su* *wakay* *du*
AV.DISTR-pare OBL sweet.potato LOC
*gagan* *si* *ina.*
outside PERS mother
'Mother pares sweet potatoes outside.'
(Hidalgo and Hidalgo 1971: 223)

Dyadic transitive verbal clauses consist of a verb followed by two arguments: a genitive-marked actor argument and a nominative-marked undergoer argument (e.g. patient/goal, location, theme, instrument, benefactive, etc.), the latter is typically definite or specific. If one of the arguments is a (clitic) pronoun, the clitic pronoun (regardless of whether it is an actor or an undergoer) typically occurs immediately after the verb (40)–(41). If no clitic pronoun is involved, the genitive-marked actor must precede the nominative-marked undergoer (42)–(43), or the genitive-marked phrase will receive a possessor reading (44).

Kankanaey
(40) *Pa-kan-en=da* *si* *Doligen.*
CAUS-eat-PV=GEN.3PL PERS Doligen
'They fed Doligen.' (Allen 2014: 78)

Southern Ivatan
(41) *Ryus-en=sya* *ñi* *ina* *du* *bañu.*
bathe-PV=NOM.3SG GEN mother LOC bathroom
'Mother bathes him in the bathroom.'
(Hidalgo and Hidalgo 1971: 224)

Southern Ivatan
(42) *Ñi-rutung* *ñi* *Kwana* *du* *gagan* *u* *manuk.*
PFV-cook GEN Jean LOC outside SPEC chicken
'Jean cooked the chicken outside.'
(Hidalgo and Hidalgo 1971: 173)

Southern Ivatan
(43) *Ñi-rutung* *ñi* *Kwana* *u* *manuk* *du* *gagan.*
PFV-cook GEN Jean SPEC chicken LOC outside
'Jean cooked the chicken (which is) outside.'
(Hidalgo and Hidalgo 1971: 174)

Southern Ivatan
(44) *Ñi-rutung* *u* *manuk* *ñi* *Kwana* *du* *gagan.*
PFV-cook SPEC chicken GEN Jean LOC outside
'Jean's chicken was cooked outside.'
(Hidalgo and Hidalgo 1971: 174)

If both the actor argument and the undergoer argument of a dyadic transitive clause are personal pronouns, the following co-occurrence restrictions are observed.

In languages such as Central Cordilleran (Northern Luzon) and Bashiic languages, despite having two sets of clitic pronouns, two clitic pronouns are not allowed to co-occur in the same clause. To avoid violating this co-occurrence restriction, in transitive clauses with two core pronominal arguments, the actor argument will be expressed by a genitive clitic pronoun whereas the undergoer argument will be expressed by a full form Nominative pronoun (45).

Itbayat
(45) *Ni-tawag-an=ko* *imiyo.*
PFV-call-LV=GEN.1SG NOM.2PL
'I called you.' (Yamada 2014: 27)

In languages such as Central Luzon languages and most Northern Luzon languages, two clitic pronouns are allowed to co-occur in the same clause. In these languages, the relative order of the two clitic pronouns is conditioned by two factors: (i) case/grammatical relations and (ii) politeness. More specifically, an actor argument typically precedes an undergoer argument (46)–(48). One thing to be noted is that syllable weight, although often considered a major factor that conditions pronominal ordering in some south-central Philippine languages, such as Tagalog (Schachter 1973), does not seem to play any role in determining pronominal ordering in northern Philippine languages. For example, the Botolan Sambal example (48) shows that a disyllabic genitive actor pronoun can precede a monosyllabic nominative undergoer pronoun. Moreover, unlike some south-central Philippine languages, such as Cebuano and Manobo languages (Payne 1994; Brainard and Van der Molen 2005), the semantic factor 'person' or the Nominal hierarchy (1 > 2 > 3) does not seem to condition pronominal ordering in northern Philippine languages either (46)–(47).

Casiguran Agta
(46) *ʔ<in>agum-an=de=ka?*
<PFV>help-LV=GEN.3PL=NOM.2SG
'Did they help you?'
(Headland and Headland 1974: xxxiv)

Pangasinan
(47) *ʔanengnéng=da=kamí.* [*ʔaN-nengnéng=da=kamí*]
PFV.AV-see=GEN.3PL=NOM.1PL.EXCL
'They saw us.' (Benton 1971a: 86)

Botolan Sambal
(48) *T<in>ambay-an=nawen=ya.*
<PFV>help-LV=GEN.1PL.EXCL=NOM.3SG
'We helped him.' (Antworth 1979: 40)

However, when a clause involves a first-person singular genitive pronoun and a second-person singular or plural nominative pronoun, politeness also seems to be at work. Specifically, Northern Luzon languages and Central Luzon languages do not allow the occurrence of the following sequence(s): predicate=GEN.1SG=NOM.2SG (and sometimes also predicate=GEN.1SG=NOM.2PL). In most Northern Luzon languages and Bolinao (Central Luzon), the first-person agent is replaced by a first-person dual form (or a first-person plural form in languages with no distinct set of dual pronouns) (49)–(50). In Kapampangan (Central Luzon) and Gaddang (Northern Luzon), the first-person agent is replaced by a third-person plural form (51)–(52). In Ilokano (Northern Luzon), the first-person agent is left unexpressed (53). In some Central Luzon languages (Ayta Mag-antsi, Botolan Sambal, Kakilingan Sambal, and Halitaq Baytan), special portmanteau forms *=katá* 'NOM.2SG+GEN.1DU' (< *=ka* 'NOM.2SG' + *=ta* 'GEN.1DU') and *=katáw* 'NOM.2PL+GEN.1DU' (< *=kaw* 'NOM.2PL' + *=ta* 'GEN.1DU') are used (54)–(55) (Liao 2009).

Bugkalot
(49) *ʔi-piya-ʔan=ta=ka nu sulat.*
BEN-write-BEN=GEN.1DU=NOM.2SG OBL letter
'I am writing a letter for you.' (Liao, fieldnotes)

Bugkalot
(50) *ʔi-piya-ʔan=ta=ki nu sulat.*
BEN-write-BEN=GEN.1DU=NOM.2PL OBL letter
'I am writing a letter for you.' (Liao, fieldnotes)

Kapampangan
(51) *Ka-lugur-án=da=ká.*
STAT-love-LV=GEN.3PL= NOM.2SG
'I/We/They love you.' (Gonzalez 1981: 178)

Kapampangan
(52) *Ka-lugur-án=da=kayú.*
STAT-love-LV=GEN.3PL= NOM.2PL
'I/We/They love you.' (Gonzalez 1981: 178)

Ilokano
(53) *Ma-kita=ka=nto.*
POT.TR-see=NOM.2SG=FUT
'I will see you.' (Rubino 2000: 230)

Ayta Mag-antsi
(54) *Haglap-an=katá.*
help-LV=NOM.2SG+GEN.1DU
'I will help you.' (Storck and Storck 2005: 146)

Ayta Mag-antsi
(55) *Haglap-an=katáw.*
help-LV=NOM.2PL+GEN.1DU
'I will help you.' (Storck and Storck 2005: 146)

In negative constructions, most northern Philippine languages treat negators as the main predicate of a clause, so negators occur clause-initially and attract all clitic elements (56)–(61).

Botolan Sambal
(56) *Aheʔ p<in>ati nin tawo ya*
NEG <PFV>kill GEN person SPEC
*damowag=ko.*
carabao=GEN.1SG
'The person didn't kill my carabao.'
(Antworth 1979: 51)

Botolan Sambal
(57) *Alwa=n ma-hipeg ya tatay=ko.*
NEG=LIG STAT-ambitious SPEC father=GEN.1SG
'My father is not ambitious.' (Antworth 1979: 51)

Botolan Sambal
(58) *Ag=ko naka-ka-toloy na-yabi.*
NEG=NOM.1SG PFV.POT-STAT.DEP-sleep PST-night
'I couldn't sleep last night.' (Antworth 1979: 51)

Botolan Sambal
(59) *Ayin=ʔako=n anak.*
NEG.EXIST=NOM.1SG=LIG child
'I have no child.' (Antworth 1979: 52)

Botolan Sambal
(60) *Ayin nin haʔa.*
NEG.EXIST LIG banana
'There are no bananas.' (Antworth 1979: 52)

Botolan Sambal
(61) *Ag=mo=ko i-tapon ha lanom.*
NEG=GEN.2SG=NOM.1SG TV-throw LOC water
'Don't throw me into the water.' (Antworth 1979: 51)

Bashiic languages, however, differ from other northern Philippine languages in placing negators after lexical predicates (62)–(64).

Southern Ivatan
(62) *Ma-gulang ava si Teresa.*
STAT-thin NEG PERS Theresa
'Theresa is not thin.' (Hidalgo and Hidalgo 1971: 226)

Itbayat
(63) *Ma-yayoh=ah si Pidro.*
AV-run.up=NEG PERS Pidro
'Pidro does not run.' (Yamada 2014: 128)

Itbayat

(64) *Ihñit=mo [ʔi-ʔahŋit=mo] alih.*
CV-laugh=GEN.2SG NEG
'Don't laugh at [him].' (Yamada 2014: 126)

Northern Philippine languages allow the occurrence of a marked construction, commonly referred to as 'inversion' in Philippine literature. That is, a non-predicate element, if topicalized, can be fronted to a clause-initial position. In sentences with inversion, typically the fronted phrase is followed by a topic linker (e.g. *ay* in Botolan Sambal; *am* in Bashiic languages) and then the predicate and other elements (65)–(66); cf. their corresponding unmarked basic clauses (67)–(68).

Botolan Sambal

(65) *Hi Pedro ay h<in>iyaw-an=na*
PERS Pedro TOP.LNK <PFV>saddle-LV=GEN.3SG
*ya kabayo.*
SPEC horse
'Pedro saddled the horse.' (Antworth 1979: 53)

Botolan Sambal

(66) *Hi Elem ay alwa=n malháy [ma-huláy].*
PERS Elem TOP.LNK NEG=LIG STAT-large
'Elem is not large.' (Antworth 1979: 53)

Botolan Sambal

(67) *H<in>iyaw-an ni Pedro ya kabayo.*
<PFV>saddle-LV GEN Pedro SPEC horse
'Pedro saddled the horse.' (Antworth 1979: 53)

Botolan Sambal

(68) *Alwa=n malháy hi Elem.*
NEG=LIG STAT.large PERS Elem
'Elem is not large.' (Antworth 1979: 53)

## 24.5.2 Noun phrases and noun phrase marking systems

Noun phrases can be of three types: full noun phrases, demonstrative pronouns, and personal pronouns. Full noun phrases are typically introduced by one of a series of short, often monosyllabic forms which specify semantic features of the lexical head of the phrase, whether it is a personal or a common/non-personal noun, whether it is singular or plural, whether it is specific/definite or non-specific/indefinite, and in some languages, they indicate the spatial or temporal relationship to the speaker. These forms, referred to as 'nominal specifiers' (Reid 2006b: 9), can also indicate grammatical functions or case of the lexical head. Demonstrative pronouns and personal pronouns are case-marked.

Most northern Philippine languages have at least three sets of nominal specifiers. For example, Guinaang Bontok (Northern Luzon) distinguishes three sets: nominative, genitive, and locative. Botolan Sambal and other Central Luzon languages distinguish four sets: nominative (minimal), predicate/topic (referred to as 'nominative (full)'), genitive, and locative (referred to as 'oblique'). Ivatan [Bashiic] and Kabayan Ibaloi (Northern Luzon) distinguish five sets: nominative, genitive, locative, oblique, and topic. The genitive set of nominal specifiers typically has two functions: (i) introducing the attribute (i.e. the possessor) in a possessive construction; and (ii) introducing the actor of a non-actor voice clause. Strictly speaking, what have been referred to as 'nominative' case markers actually function as specific or definite markers and do not mark 'case' because it is possible to find two noun phrases being marked by so-called 'nominative' case markers in identificational clauses.

Ilokano (Northern Luzon), however, distinguishes only two sets of nominal specifiers: core vs. locative (referred to as 'oblique'). The core set of nominal specifiers (*ti* 'NPERS.CORE.SG', *dagití* 'NPERS.CORE.PL', *ni* 'PERS.CORE.SG', and *da* 'PERS.CORE.PL') are used to introduce core arguments of a predicate (69); that is, they subsume functions of genitive and nominative nominal specifiers in other northern Philippine languages.

Ilokano

(69) *K<inn>aán dagití babbái ti*
<PFV.PV>eat CORE.PL girls CORE.SG
*baradibód.*
sweet.potato.porridge
'The girls ate the sweet potato porridge.'
(Rubino 2000: liii)

Full noun phrases introduced by a core nominal specifier can be replaced by genitive enclitic pronouns or nominative enclitic pronouns. The locative set of nominal specifiers (*ití* 'NPERS.LOC.SG', *kadagití* 'NPERS.LOC.PL', *kenní* 'PERS.LOC.SG', and *kadá* 'PERS.LOC.PL') are used to introduce a locative phrase (70) or a non-specific patient phrase of an actor voice construction (71). Full noun phrases introduced by a locative nominal specifier cannot be replaced by genitive enclitic pronouns or nominative enclitic pronouns (Rubino 2000: lii–liii).

Ilokano

(70) *Na-kíta ti babái ti laláki*
PFV.PV.POT-see CORE.SG girl CORE.SG boy
*iti madióngan.*
LOC.SG mahjong.parlour
'The girl saw the boy at the mahjong parlour.'
(Rubino 2000: liii)

Ilokano

(71) *Nangán ti babái iti pariá.*
PFV.AV.eat CORE.SG girl LOC.SG bittermelon
'The girl ate bittermelon.' (Rubino 2000: lii)

In many Northern Luzon languages, nominal specifiers distinguish postconsonantal and postvocalic variants. For example, in Bugkalot (also in Isinay) *si* 'PERS.SG' and *ni* 'PERS.GEN.SG' occur postconsonantally (72), whereas *=t* 'PERS.SG' and *=n* 'PERS.GEN.SG' occur postvocalically (73).

Bugkalot

(72) *Bugkalut si Madiya.*
Bugkalot PERS.SG Maria
'Maria is a Bugkalot.' (Liao, fieldnotes)

Bugkalot

(73) *ʔun-ʔupu=t Madiya nitu.*
AV-talk=PERS.SG Maria now
'Maria is talking now.' (Liao, fieldnotes)

Most northern Philippine languages have three (or more) sets of demonstrative pronouns: (i) genitive, (ii) nominative, and (iii) locative. Demonstrative pronouns typically consist of a case-marking element plus a deictic base and distinguish singular from plural and at least three distances: proximate ('close to the speaker'), medial ('close to the hearer'), and distal ('distant from both the speaker and the hearer'), as shown in Table 24.1. Forms beginning with =*n* and =*d* in the Genitive and Locative columns (e.g. *=n jay* 'PROX.SG' and *=d man* 'DIST.SG') occur postvocalically, whereas forms that occur before the slash (e.g. *niyay* 'PROX.SG' and *chiwan* 'DIST.SG') occur postconsonantally.

Personal pronouns typically consist of a case-marking element plus a pronominal base. In Northern Luzon and Central Luzon languages they distinguish minimal forms from non-minimal forms. Minimal forms are first-person singular, first-person plus second-person singular (often referred to as 'first-person dual'), second-person singular, and third-person singular. Non-minimal forms are first-person plural exclusive, first-person plural inclusive, second-person plural, and third-person plural (Liao 2008a; Reid 1971). A similar situation is also found in the Bashiic language Yami (Reid 2009b). Other Bashiic languages, however, do not have a distinct first-person dual form.

Northern Philippine languages typically distinguish four sets of personal pronouns: (i) genitive; (ii) nominative; (iii) independent neutral; and (iv) locative. Bashiic languages, however, distinguish five sets of personal pronouns: (i) genitive; (ii) nominative; (iii) neutral; (iv) locative; and (v) associative, as shown in Table 24.2. Associative pronouns are used to express instrument, cause, benefactive, comitative, etc. (74) (Yamada 2002: 10).

Itbayat

(74) *Nawi o ni-sorih-an=da aya*
DIST SPEC PFV.STAT-angry-LV=GEN.3PL PROX
*ñaken.*
ASSOC.1SG
'That is why they were angry with me.'
(Yamada 2002: 10)

In general, genitive and nominative sets of pronouns are enclitics, whereas other sets of pronouns are free pronouns. Many Northern Luzon languages have two variants of singular genitive pronouns: a postconsonantal variant (e.g. *=ku* 'GEN.1SG'; *=mu* 'GEN.2SG') and a postvocalic variant (e.g. *=k* 'GEN.1SG'; *=m* 'GEN.2SG') (75).

Central Cagayan Agta

(75) *Nag-tappan=ãk, t<in>appan-ãn=ku*
PFV.AV.REFL-cover=NOM.1SG <PFV>cover-LV=GEN.1SG
*matã=k.*
eye=GEN.1SG
'I covered myself; I covered my eyes.' (Liao 2004: 405)

**Table 24.1** Demonstrative pronouns in Karao (adapted from Brainard 1997: 147)

| | Neutral | Nominative | Genitive | Locative |
|---|---|---|---|---|
| PROX.SG | *sejay* | *ʔiyay/jay* | *niyay/=n jay* | *chiyay/=d jay* |
| MED.SG | *setan* | *ʔithan/tan* | *nithan/=n tan* | *chithuan/=d tan* |
| DIST.SG | *seman* | *ʔiwan/man* | *niwan/=n man* | *chiwan/=d man* |
| PROX.PL | *sejay ʔira* | *ʔira jay/cha jay* | *ʔiren jay/chen jay* | *ʔired jay/ched jay* |
| MED.PL | *setan ʔira* | *ʔira tan/cha tan* | *ʔiren tan/chen tan* | *ʔired tan/ched tan* |
| DIST.PL | *seman ʔira* | *ʔira man/cha man* | *ʔiren man/chen man* | *ʔired man/ched man* |

**Table 24.2** Personal pronouns in Itbayat (adapted from Yamada 2002: 9–10)

| | Genitive | Nominative | Neutral | Locative | Associative |
|---|---|---|---|---|---|
| 1SG | *ku* | *ako* | *yaken* | *jaken* | *ñaken* |
| 2SG | *mo* | *ka* | *imo* | *dimo* | *nimo* |
| 3SG | *na* | – | – | *dira* | *niya/ña* |
| 1PL.EXCL | *namen* | *kami* | *yamen* | *jamen* | *ñamen* |
| 1PL.INCL | *ta* | *ta* | *yaten* | *jaten* | *ñaten* |
| 2PL | *miyo* | *kamo* | *imiyo* | *dimiyo* | *nimiyo* |
| 3PL | *da* | *sira* | *sira* | *dira* | *nira* |

The nominative set of pronouns substitutes for foregrounded noun phrases in both intransitive clauses (i.e. 'actor voice' constructions) (76) and transitive clauses (i.e. 'non-actor voice' constructions) (77).

Central Cagayan Agta
(76) *Mag-burung=kãm teyak.*
AV-worry=NOM.2PL LOC.1SG
'Maybe you are also worrying about me.'
(Liao 2004: 412)

Central Cagayan Agta
(77) *ʔatad-an=mi=kid ta baggat=en.*
give-PV=GEN.1PL.EXCL=NOM.3PL OBL rice=DIST
'We supplied them with some of the rice.'
(Liao 2004: 414)

### 24.5.3 Verbal clause structure

In northern Philippine languages, verbal clauses consist of a verb followed by one or more arguments. The verb typically contains an affix—which may be a prefix, an infix, a suffix, or a circumfix—that indicates the semantic role of the foregrounded noun phrase. The foregrounded phrase, commonly referred to as a nominative phrase, is typically unmarked for case when it is a full noun (79)–(80), but is case-marked when it is a pronoun (78).

Based on the morphosyntactic patterning of noun phrases and/or verb marking, three major verbal clause patterns are observed. Pattern 1 typically consists of a monadic verb that contains a reflex of PAN *<um> or its probably historically related forms PMP *maN- or *maR- and expects only one nominative NP (78).[7] Pattern 2 typically consists of a dyadic verb that also contains a reflex of PAN *<um>, PMP *maN- or *maR- and expects both a nominative-marked agent/actor and a locative/genitive/oblique-marked patient or theme. Typically, the patient or theme in Pattern 2 is non-specific or indefinite (79)–(80). The choice of one form over the others is determined by verb class and the meaning that one intends to convey, and it may vary from one language to another. In general, *<um> verbs are typically used to express either punctual events (81)–(82), or inchoative events (83), *maR- verbs are typically used to describe reciprocal (84), reflexive, or durative events (85), and *maN- verbs are typically used to describe distributive events (i.e. events that imply multiple activities, actions, or actors over time or space) (78)–(80). Pattern 1 and pattern 2 clauses are commonly referred to as 'actor voice (AV)' or by some linguists as 'actor/agent focus (AF)' because the actor is the foregrounded phrase in both patterns of clauses. Both patterns are considered intransitive by some linguists.

Southern Ivatan
(78) *Nanutung=aku [naN-rutuŋ=aku] su naypidwa.*
PFV.AV-cook=NOM.1SG OBL twice
'I cooked twice.' (Hidalgo and Hidalgo 1971: 227)

Limos Kalinga
(79) *Nam-bayu si Juan ʔutdit pagoy.*
PFV.AV-pound PERS John OBL rice
'John pounded some rice.' (Ferreirinho 1993: 67)

Southern Ivatan
(80) *Nanrip [naN-tarip] u tau du wakay.*
PFV.AV-pare SPEC man LOC sweet.potato
'The man pared sweet potato.'
(Hidalgo and Hidalgo 1971: 178)

[7] Since a wide range of forms are found across northern Philippine languages, the non-completive forms of the reconstructed Proto-Austronesian (PAN) and/or Proto-Malayo-Polynesian (PMP) verbal affixes *<um>, *-ən, *-an, *Si-, and PMP *maR- and *maN- are used in this chapter to represent the verbal clause patterns found in northern Philippine languages.

Botolan Sambal
(81) *Nilomateng [ni-l<om>ateng]*[8] *hi* *Juan.*
PFV-<AV>arrive PERS Juan
'Juan arrived.' (Antworth 1979: 45)

Kankanaey
(82) *S<om>aliktoto* *din* *ʔinnapoy.*
<AV>boil SPEC cooked.rice
'The rice boils.' (Allen 2014: 55)

Kankanaey
(83) *Ng<om>ato* *din* *blood pressure=ko.*
<AV.INCH>high SPEC blood pressure=GEN.1SG
'My blood pressure is rising.' (Allen 2014: 263)

Isnag
(84) *Mag-singan=kami* *kala:wa.*
AV.RECP-see=NOM.1PL.EXCL tomorrow
'We will see each other tomorrow.' (Barlaan 1999: 53)

Isnag
(85) *Nag-languy* *ya* *ʔanʔanaʔ.*
PFV.AV-swim SPEC child
'The child swam (for a long time).' (Barlaan 1999: 40)

Pattern 3 concerns non-actor voice verbs. It consists of three subtypes: (a) dyadic *-ən verbs, (b) dyadic *-an verbs, and (c) dyadic *Si- verbs. Patterns 3(a)–3(c) are considered transitive and are often collectively referred to as 'non-actor voice (NAV)' because the foregrounded phrase in these three subtypes of clause patterns is not an actor and they share the same case frame; that is, they all expect a genitive-marked agent and a nominative NP. However, they differ from each other in the interpretation of the nominative NP. In dyadic *-ən clauses, often referred to as patient voice (PV), the nominative NP is usually interpreted as a directly affected patient (86). In a dyadic *-an clause, often referred to as locative voice (LV), the nominative NP is usually interpreted as a location, or a less directly affected patient (87). In dyadic *Si- clauses, often referred to as circumstantial voice or conveyance voice (CV), the nominative NP is usually interpreted as an instrument (88)/transported theme (89)/ benefactive (90). Depending on whether the foregrounded phrase is an instrument, transported theme, or benefactive, pattern 3(c) can also be referred to as instrumental voice (IV), theme voice (TV), or benefactive voice (BEN), respectively.

[8] In Botolan Sambal, Tagalog, and many other Philippine languages, when *<in>* is affixed to a base beginning with *l*, *y* [j], or *w*, it can metathesize and become a prefix *ni-*.

Southern Ivatan
(86) *Ryus-en* *ñi* *ina* *u* *metdeh* *du* *bañu.*
bathe-PV GEN mother SPEC child LOC bathroom
'Mother bathes the child in the bathroom.'
(Hidalgo and Hidalgo 1971: 224)

Southern Ivatan
(87) *Tarip-an* *nu* *tau* *u* *wakay.*
pare-LV GEN man SPEC sweet.potato
'The man is paring the sweet potato.'
(Hidalgo and Hidalgo 1971: 178)

Southern Ivatan
(88) *I-tarip* *nu* *tau* *anchi* *su* *wakay* *u* *tatari.*
CV-pare GEN man FUT OBL sweet.potato SPEC paring.tool
'The man will pare sweet potato with the paring tool.'
(Hidalgo and Hidalgo 1971: 179)

Southern Ivatan
(89) *I-sun* *ñi* *Marya* *u* *alat* *anchi* *ji* *Chanaryan.*
CV-carry.on.head GEN.PERS Mary SPEC basket FUT LOC Chanaryan
'Mary will carry (on her head) the basket in Chanaryan.' (Hidalgo and Hidalgo 1971: 178)

Southern Ivatan
(90) *Ipangamung [ʔi-paN-ʔamuŋ]* *ñi* *Kwan* *si* *Kusi.*
CV-DISTR-fish GEN.PERS John PERS Jose
'John catches fish for Jose.'
(Hidalgo and Hidalgo 1971: 180)

Benefactive voice verbs often carry reflexes of PAN *Si- (with or without *paN-/*paR-) in Bashiic languages, Central Luzon languages, and a few Northern Luzon languages. However, in most Northern Luzon languages and in Ibatan, a Bashiic language with heavy influence from Ilokano (Northern Luzon), benefactive voice verbs carry either a reflex of PAN/PMP *-an or a reflex of Proto-Northern Luzon *ʔi- . . .-an (Liao 2008b). The choice of one form over the others is determined by the meaning that one intends to convey, and it may vary from one language to another. For example, in Yogad (Northern Luzon), the use of *-an* and *ʔi-. . .-an* with the same lexical root encodes the following subtle differences. First, the use of *-an* suggests that there is no prior communication between the individuals who performs the act (e.g. counting) and the beneficiary (91). By contrast, the use of *ʔi-...-an* suggests there is a communication (i.e. a request of some sort is involved) between the beneficiary and the person who carries out the activity (92). Second, the use of *-an* suggests that the beneficiary and the direct recipient of the activity is the same person (*Walter* in (91)), whereas the use of *ʔi-...-an* suggests the act is performed in place of the beneficiary (*Walter* in (92)) but the recipient of the activity is a third party, not the beneficiary (Davis et al. 1998: 248).

Yogad
(91) *B<in>ilang-án=ku* *si* *Walter* *tu*
<PFV>count-BEN=GEN.1SG NOM Walter OBL
*manók.*
chicken
'I counted chickens for Walter.' ('I counted chickens and gave them to Walter.') (Davis et al. 1998: 247)

Yogad
(92) *Ni-bilang-án=ku*[9] *si* *Walter* *tu*
PFV.BEN-count-BEN=GEN.1SG NOM Walter OBL
*manók.*
chicken
'I counted chickens for Walter.' ('I counted chickens in Walter's stead.') (Davis et al. 1998: 248)

Northern Philippine languages are generally analysed as having an ergative actancy structure; that is, the actor of intransitive clauses has the same form or morphological marking as the foregrounded phrase in transitive clauses. Moreover, the affixes which are said to mark instrument, locative, and benefactive focus are often treated as applicative affixes. However, it is controversial as to whether the grammatical subject should be the actor phrase or the foregrounded noun phrase in both intransitive (i.e. actor-voice constructions) and transitive clauses (i.e. non-actor-voice constructions) (Brainard 1996).

Unlike Austronesian languages spoken in other parts of the Philippine archipelago, agreement has been reported in a number of northern Philippine languages. Central Luzon languages, such as Bolinao and Kapampangan, are reported to require agreement marking for both a third-person genitive actor phrase and a third-person nominative phrase in transitive clauses (93), or for the third-person nominative phrase in intransitive clauses (Persons 1979; Mithun 1994; Kitano 2005). Similarly, Ivatan (Bashiic) textual data also shows that agreement marking is allowed for both a third person genitive actor phrase and a third person nominative phrase in transitive clauses (94).

Bolinao
(93) *Awit=na=ya* *ni* *Nanay=ra=y*
carry=GEN.3SG=NOM.3SG GEN mother=GEN.3PL=SPEC
*panis.*
broom
'The broom is carried by their mother.'
(Persons 1979: 31)

Ivatan
(94) *Oyod=na=sira* *a* *chinasi* *ni* *ina*
truly=GEN.3SG=NOM.3PL LIG pity GEN mother
*o* *manganak=na=ya.*
SPEC children=GEN.3SG=that
'Mother truly pitied her children.' (Larson 1986: 11)

In Central Cagayan Agta and Eastern Cagayan Agta (Northern Luzon), agreement marking is found to cross-reference only a third person genitive actor phrase in transitive clauses (Liao 2004, 2005; Nickell 1985) (95)–(96); no such marking is found to cross-reference a third person nominative phrase in either intransitive clauses or transitive clauses.

Central Cagayan Agta
(95) *...k<in>agăt=na* *hapa* *na* *taggam* *ya*
...<PFV>bite=GEN.3SG also GEN ant SPEC
*huli* *na* *ʔatu.*
rump GEN dog
'... the ant bit the rump of the dog.' (Liao 2004: 406)

Eastern Cagayan Agta
(96) *Awan=na* *hidi* *ma-buno* *na* *ngayaw.*
NEG=GEN.3SG 3PL PV.POT-kill GEN raider
'The raider is not able to kill them.' (Nickell 1985: 136)

In addition to affixes that are commonly referred to as voice markers (e.g. *<um>*, *maN-*, *mag-/man-/may-/mi-*, *-ən/-un*, *-an*, etc.), verbs also carry mood and aspectual information. Typically, at least three aspectual distinctions are made in northern Philippine languages (as illustrated in Table 24.3): (i) contemplated aspect—denoting an action that has not yet begun, such as future events and imperatives; (ii) imperfective/progressive aspect—denoting an action begun but not yet completed; it is typically marked by partial reduplication in Bashiic languages and Northern Luzon languages, but it

[9] The form *nibilaŋán* developed from affixation of *<in>* 'PFV' and *ʔi-...-an* 'BEN' to *biláng* 'count'.

is marked by the prefix *ʔan-* in Central Luzon languages;[10] and (iii) perfective aspect—denoting a completed action; it is typically marked by *<in>*.

**Table 24.3** Aspect in Botolan Sambal (adapted from Antworth 1979: 28)

| Contemplated | Imperfective | Perfective |
|---|---|---|
| *ma-* + Base | *ʔang-* + *ka-* + Base | *na-* + Base |
| *mag-* + Base | *ʔam-* + *pag-* + Base | *nag-* + Base |
| *mang-* + Base | *ʔam-* + *pang-* + Base | *nang-* + Base |
| *mangi-* + Base | *ʔam-* + *pangi-* + Base | *nangi-* + Base |
| *maka-* + Base | *ʔam-* + *paka-* + Base | *naka-* + Base |
| *maki-* + Base | *ʔam-* + *paki-* + Base | *naki-* + Base |
| *mi-* + Base | *ʔam-* + *pi-* + Base | *ni-* + Base |
| *<om>* + Base | *<om>* + Base | *<in>* + *<om>* + Base |
| Base + *-ən* | *ʔan-* + Base + *-ən* | *<in>* + Base |
| *ʔi-* + Base | *ʔan-* + *ʔi-* + Base | *ʔi-* + *<(i)n>* + Base |
| Base + *-an* | *ʔan-* + Base + *-an* | *<in>* + Base + *-an* |
| *pag-* + Base + *-an* | *ʔam-* + *pag-* + Base + *-an* | *<in>* + *pag-* + Base + *-an* |

Northern Philippine languages typically do not allow tense distinctions. Sentences translated as past tense in English actually express perfective aspect (97).

Southern Ivatan
(97) *Na-gulang* *si* *Teresa* *kaminsawan.*
PFV.STAT-thin PERS Theresa last.year
'Theresa was thin last year.'
(Hidalgo and Hidalgo 1971: 227)

In addition to the abovementioned three-way aspectual distinction, northern Philippine languages are also described as having a special construction known as 'recent perfective construction', 'recent past construction', 'recent completive construction', or 'recent construction' in the literature. This unique construction is reserved specifically for events completed just prior to the speech event. Most commonly, the predicate in a recent perfective construction is marked by the prefix *ka-*, which may occur alone, or be followed by some form of reduplication (usually CV-, CVC-, C-, or full reduplication) (98)–(103). The predicate in such a construction is marked by the prefix *paʔi(C)-* or *paʔa(C)-* in Batad Ifugao, or by the prefix *kapi-* in Ayta Mag-antsi and Halitaq Baytan (101) (Liao 2011b: 862–6).

In most northern Philippine languages with a recent perfective construction, this construction does not take any nominative phrase. More specifically, if it is a monadic recent perfective construction, the sole argument of the sentence will be in the genitive case form (98)–(100). If it is a dyadic (or triadic) recent perfective construction, NONE of the two (or three) arguments of the sentence will be in the nominative case form (101) (Liao 2011b: 863–5).

Southern Ivatan
(98) *Ka-wára* *namen* *pa...*
RCT.PFV-arrive GEN.1PL.EXCL already
'We have just arrived....'
(Hidalgo and Hidalgo 1971: 160)

Ilokano
(99) *Ka-sa~sangpét=ko.*
RCT.PFV-REDUP~arrive=GEN.1SG
'I just arrived.' (Rubino 2000: lxvii)

Kapampangan
(100) *Ka-lákad~lákad=na=pá*
RCT.PFV-REDUP~walk=GEN.3SG=still/yet
*mu=ŋ* *Pédru.*
just=PERS.GEN Pedro
'Pedro has just now walked.' (Gonzalez 1981: 75, 184)

Halitaq Baytan
(101) *Kapi-pa-kan* *nin* *aho* *nin* *dalaga.*
RCT.PFV-CAUS-eat GEN dog GEN maiden
'The maiden has just fed the dog.' (Malicsi 1974: 66)

However, not all languages exhibit special case marking for arguments in the recent perfective construction. In Batad Ifugao and Central Bontok (both belong to the Central Cordilleran group of Northern Luzon languages), the case marking for arguments in the recent perfective construction is not different from that in other aspectual constructions.

That is, in a monadic construction, the sole NP of the sentence will still be in the nominative form (102); in a dyadic construction, the foregrounded non-actor phrase will still be in its regular form (103). Similarly, Ayta Mag-antsi, a Central Luzon language, also exhibits a regular case-marking pattern. More specifically, the sole argument in an intransitive clause is encoded as nominative.

Central Bontok
(102) *Ka-ʔil~ʔíla=ʔak.*
RCT.PFV-REDUP~come=NOM.1SG
'I just came.' (Waterman 1932: 133)

[10] The prefix *ʔan-* has the final 'n' assimilating to the place of articulation of the following consonant.

Central Bontok
(103) *Ka-ʔil~ʔíla=k* *nan* *ʔaso=cha.*
RCT.PFV-REDUP~see=GEN.1SG SPEC dog=GEN.3PL
'I just saw their dogs.' (Lawrence Reid, fieldnotes)

In addition to the recent perfective construction, a construction known as the 'potentive' construction (Rubino 1997) is also commonly found in many northern Philippine languages. It is commonly used to express the following meanings: (i) the internal, innate ability of an actor to perform a certain action; (ii) an actor has the opportunity to perform an action, that is, that external circumstances (not innate ability) permitted the actor to perform the action; and (iii) an actor involuntarily, unintentionally, or accidentally performs an action. In general, *maka-* forms are considered to be 'actor voice' (intransitive) verbs in the potentive mood (104). Typically, they have transitive counterparts with the forms *ma-* ('patient voice') (105), *maʔi-* (or *ʔika-*) ('circumstantial voice') (106), and *ma-* *-an* (or *ka-* *-an*) ('locative voice') (107) (Liao 2011b: 857–9).

Limos Kalinga
(104) *Maka-bayu=ʔak.*
AV.POT-pound=NOM.1SG
'I am able to pound.' or 'I will be able to pound.'
(Ferreirinho 1993: 19)

Limos Kalinga
(105) *Ma-sugat=na* *sika.*
PV.POT-hurt=GEN.3SG NOM.2SG
'He can hurt you.' (Ferreirinho 1993: 46)

Limos Kalinga
(106) *Na-ʔi-ngina=mi* *dit* *bolok.*
PFV.POT-CV-sell=GEN.1PL.EXCL SPEC pig
'We were able to sell the pig.' (Ferreirinho 1993: 50)

Ilokano
(107) *Na-puʔór-an=na* *ti* *baláy.*
PFV.POT-burn.down-LV=GEN.3SG SPEC house
'He accidentally burned down the house.'
(Rubino 2000: lxvi)

## 24.5.4 Multipredicate constructions, compound sentences, and complex sentences

Multipredicate constructions are "constructions which involve two or more phonologically independent predicate expressions within a single clause" (Himmelmann 2005a: 159). Multipredicate constructions in northern Philippine languages have the following structural properties. First, clitic elements (including personal pronouns, aspectual adverbs, etc.) are attracted to the first predicate (108)–(111). Second, a ligature (e.g. *nin* (108)–(110) or *=n* (111) in Botolan) is required to link the second predicate with the first predicate. Third, an argument of the second predicate is not overtly expressed. For example, *hila* 'NOM.3PL', the undergoer of the first clause, conditions the interpretation of the actor in the second predicate in (108); *ya* 'NOM.3SG', the actor of the first clause, conditions the interpretation of the actor in the second predicate in (109)–(111). Note that the use of different aspectual forms of the second predicate can result in slight semantic differences, as contrasted in (109)–(110). The use of a contemplated form of the second predicate results in a purpose reading (109); however, the use of a perfective form of the second predicate gives a result reading (110).

Botolan Sambal
(108) *T<in>oroʔ-an=na* *hila* *nin* *mang-gawaʔ*
<PFV>teach-LV=GEN.3SG NOM.3PL LIG AV-make
*nin* *taʔen.*
OBL trap
'He taught them to make a trap.' (Antworth 1979: 95)

Botolan Sambal
(109) *Nako=ya* *nin* *mangonaʔ [maN-konaʔ].*
PFV.AV.go=NOM.3SG LIG AV.DISTR-fish
'He went to fish.' (Antworth 1979: 96)

Botolan Sambal
(110) *Nako=ya* *nin* *nangonaʔ [naN-konaʔ].*
PFV.AV.go=NOM.3SG LIG PFV.AV.DISTR.fish
'He went fishing.'/'He went and fished.'
(Antworth 1979: 97)

Botolan Sambal
(111) *Nanandaliʔ=ya=n [naN-dandaliʔ=ya=n]* *nag-lako*
PFV.AV-hurry=NOM.3SG=LIG PFV.AV-go
*ha* *pagʔong.*
LOC turtle
'Hurrying, he went to the turtle.' (Antworth 1979: 98)

In addition to multipredicate constructions, compound sentences and complex sentences are also found in northern Philippine languages. Compound sentences are sentences with two (or more) coordinate main clauses. A conjunction is required to link two clauses of equal syntactic status in a compound sentence. The choice of conjunctions depends on the meaning one intends to express. For example, in Botolan Sambal, the coordinating conjunction *boy* 'and' links two equally important statements with no logical or temporal sequence (112), *ʔo* 'or' indicates an alternative relation between the statements expressed in the clauses (113), and *piro* 'but' and *baleʔ ta* 'but' link statements with a contrastive relationship (114).

Botolan Sambal
(112) *Nang-ʔangin nin makhaw [ma-hukaw] boy*
PFV.AV-wind LIG STAT-strong and
*biglaʔ nang-ʔoran.*
suddenly PFV.AV-rain
'The wind blew strong and it suddenly rained.'
(Antworth 1979: 77)

Botolan Sambal
(113) *Mag-ʔaral=ka ʔo mag-paʔinawa=ka*
AV-study=NOM.2SG or AV-rest=NOM.2SG
*hapaʔeg ʔalloʔ*
today/now day
'Will you (SG) study or will you (SG) rest today?'
(Antworth 1979: 77)

Botolan Sambal
(114) *Hi Lawin ʔay ma-yaman, piro hi*
PERS Hawk TOP.LNK STAT-rich but PERS
*Manok ʔay ma-ʔirap.*
Chicken TOP.LNK STAT-poor
'The Hawk was rich, but the Chicken was poor.'
(Antworth 1979: 78)

By contrast, complex sentences are sentences with one main clause and one or more subordinate clauses. When the subordinate clause is a complement clause, it is headed by a complementizer (e.g. Botolan Sambal *ya* in (115)); when it is an adverbial or relative clause, it is headed by a subordinator (e.g. Botolan Sambal *no* 'if' in (116)).

Botolan Sambal
(115) *H<in>alitaʔ=na=et ya*
<PFV>ask=GEN.3SG=also COMP
*ʔag=na=ya ʔan-labi-yen.*
NEG=GEN.3SG=NOM.3SG IPFV-love-PV
'She also said that she didn't love him.'
(Antworth 1979: 92)

Botolan Sambal
(116) *No tadtar-en=mo=ko, sigorado=n*
if chop-PV=GEN.2SG=NOM.1SG surely=LIG
*l<om>akeʔ=ʔako.*
<INCH>many=NOM.1SG
'If you chop me up, I will surely become many.'
(Antworth 1979: 86)

## 24.6 Conclusion

This chapter has provided an overview of the phonological, morphological, and syntactic typology of northern Philippine languages. Due to space limitations, only some salient phonological phenomena have been touched upon. Our discussion of the nominal marking system and of the verbal clause structure is necessarily concise. Although only a relatively few select examples are provided in this chapter; these examples are (unless otherwise noted) usually typical of a fairly broad range of languages.

Northern Philippine languages are typologically unique and exhibit the following features that distinguish them from other Philippine languages (and other Malayo-Polynesian languages).

First, although palatalization of *k* is rare in Austronesian languages (Blust 2013a: 236), it is observed in Bashiic languages.

Second, palatalization of syllable-initial voiced stops occurs only before the low vowel *a* in some Central Cordilleran languages.

Third, low vowel raising, in which PMP *a is raised to /ɨ/, /e/, or /i/ following voiced stops /b, d, g/ (and sometimes also following glides /w/ and /j/), is observed in northeastern Luzon languages and Bugkalot (Northern Luzon). This process resembles low vowel fronting found in some Austronesian languages spoken in northern Sarawak (Blust 2000c: 287), but differs from it in the following way. Blust (2000c: 287) considers "raising is an incidental by-product of vowel fronting in the languages of northern Sarawak", whereas in Northern Luzon languages low vowel raises, but does not always front, for example, PMP *a is raised to /ɨ/ after voiced stops in Bugkalot.

Fourth, a wide variety of reduplication patterns is observed in northern Philippine languages, including *Ca-*, CV-, *Caw-*, $C_1V_1C_1$-, $C_1V_1C_2$-, CV:-, $C_1V_1C_2V_2$- (or foot reduplication), full reduplication, and lexicalized reduplication. Among productive reduplication patterns, only $CV_1$-, $C_1V_1C_2$-, and full reduplication are commonly found in other Austronesian languages. As for *Ca-* reduplication, although it is reconstructed to PAN (Blust 1998a, 1999c), it is only attested in a few northern Philippine languages.

Fifth, northern Philippine languages, especially Northern Luzon languages, exhibit more complex morphophonology than other Philippine languages. Reflexes of PMP *maR- and *maN- are not easily distinguished due to irregular developments of reflexes of *maR- in Meso-Cordilleran languages and the application of regressive assimilation in some Northern Luzon languages.

Sixth, benefactive voice verbs carry either a reflex of PAN *Si- (with or without *paN- or *paR-) or a reflex of PAN/PMP *-an in other Philippine languages. Although these affixes are also found in northern Philippine languages, benefactive voice verbs in Northern Luzon languages often carry a reflex of Proto-Northern Luzon *ʔi-. . .-an.

CHAPTER 25

# The languages of the central and southern Philippines

Daniel Kaufman

## 25.1 Introduction

This chapter provides a typological overview of the languages of the central and southern Philippines (henceforth, CSP languages). Despite not forming a discrete phylogenetic group, the CSP languages share certain morphosyntactic retentions from Proto-Malayo-Polynesian which make them a useful unit for typological generalizations. Like other Philippine languages, almost all the CSP languages maintain the full PMP voice system. On the other hand, the voice system mutates in interesting ways in the southernmost CSP languages, specifically, in the Bilic languages, covered here, and Sama-Bajaw languages, covered in Kaufman (this volume, Chapter 26).

The languages within the scope of this chapter (Map 25.1) are those of the Greater Central Philippine subgroup (see Blust 1991b; and Zorc, Lobel, and Hall, this volume, §7.2.7), Kalamian (consisting of Agutaynen and Calamian Tagbanwa) and the Bilic subgroup (consisting of Tboli, Blaan, and Teduray). All these subgroups are argued to belong to a larger Philippine family by Blust (2019b).

Several members of the putative Philippine group are located outside of the Philippines, namely, the Sangiric, Minahasan, and Gorontalic subgroups. These are excluded here on geographical grounds but are covered in Van den Berg and Mead (this volume, Chapter 33). It should be noted that these languages have been influenced by distinct contact scenarios over the last several centuries, which have made them diverge morphosyntactically from their more northern relatives.[1] The Bilic languages, especially outside of Tboli, are still not sufficiently documented. Tboli thus serves here as a representative of this subgroup for present purposes with brief mention of Teduray. Giangan, a language often classified as Bilic, is argued by Zorc (2019) to be an independent branch of a higher-level subgroup. Giangan and Inati, potentially important witnesses, are too sparsely documented to be discussed here.

A series of work from the 1970s through the 1990s (Gallman 1983; Burton 1996; Elkins 1986; Savage 1986; Fleischman 1981) greatly improved our understanding of the languages of Mindanao and their interrelations. Two landmark dissertations cited frequently here, McFarland (1974) and Zorc (1977), provide comprehensive overviews of the Bikol and Bisayan languages, respectively, and include a wealth of comparative data on their morphological and syntactic structure. Gallman (1983); Burton (1996); and especially Pallesen (1985), show how contact effects have given shape to the vocabulary, phonological history and typology of several regions within the southern Philippines.

## 25.2 Phonology

### 25.2.1 Segment inventories

Vowel inventories in the CSP zone are relatively simple, often of the type shown in Table 25.1, where the mid vowels in parentheses represent common allophones of the high vowels. The Central Philippine languages typically either preserve the Proto-Austronesian four vowel system (*i, *u, *a, *ə) or conflate it to a three-vowel system by merging *ə with one or more of the other vowels. In the languages of Mindanao, *ə is often preserved as a high central vowel (ɨ), and this was clearly the case in the not-so-distant past for many of the Central Philippine subgroups, as well. In rare cases, the inherited vowel inventory has been expanded

[1] I have reglossed the functional morphology in many of the examples here so that the terminology employed is as uniform as possible throughout. I do not mean to impose a particular analysis on the data by the use of 'nominative' and 'genitive' case, nor do I mean to imply that all forms glossed as 'actor voice' are syntactically identical across languages. I transcribe examples of nasal substitution (triggered by the PMP prefixes *paŋ-/*maŋ-) with deleted consonants in square brackets (e.g. *maŋ-[k]u:ha*). I have also aimed to represent all the data presented here in a broad IPA transcription to avoid confusion across orthographies, although I maintain the symbol <y> for the palatal glide, as opposed to IPA [j]. Finally, any numbered examples whose language is not specified in the first line are Tagalog.

Daniel Kaufman, *The languages of the central and southern Philippines.* In: *The Oxford Guide to the Malayo-Polynesian Languages of Southeast Asia.* Edited by: Alexander Adelaar and Antoinette Schapper, Oxford University Press. © Daniel Kaufman (2024). DOI: 10.1093/oso/9780198807353.003.0025

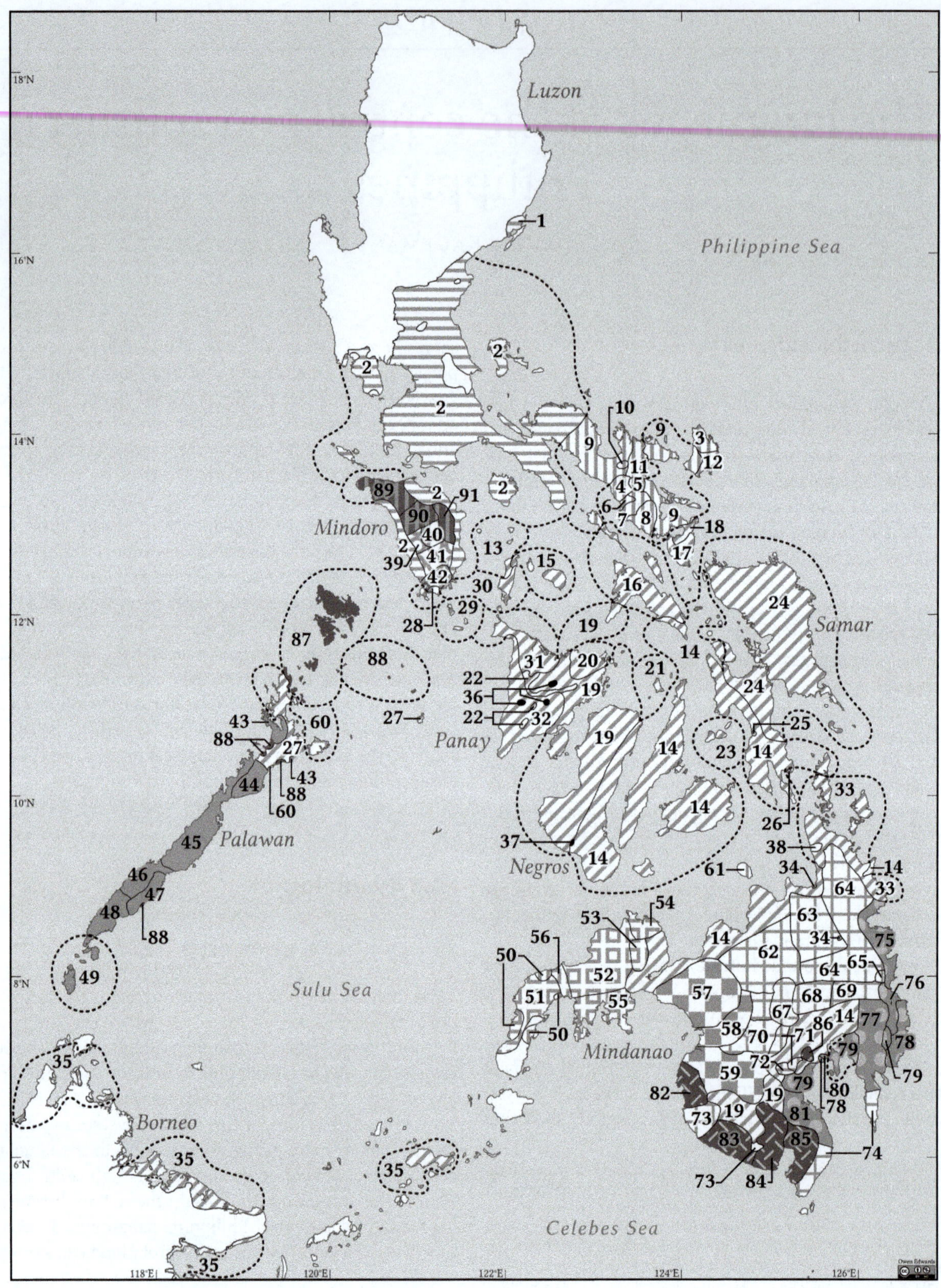


**Map 25.1** Languages of central and southern Philippines.

**GREATER CENTRAL PHILIPPINE**

***Central Philippine***

**Tagalic**
1. Kasiguranin
2. Tagalog

**Bikol**
3. Northern Catanduanes Bikol (Pandan)

**Inland Bikol**
4. Rinconada

**Albay Bikol**
5. Buhinon
6. Libon
7. West Albay Bikol
8. Miraya Bikol

**Coastal Bikol**
9. Central Bikol
10. Isarog Agta
11. Partido Bikol
12. Southern Catanduanes Bikol

**Visayan**
13. Asi
14. Cebuano

**Central Visayan**
15. Romblomanon
16. Masbatenyo
17. Southern Sorsogon
18. Central Sorsogon

**Peripheral**
19. Hiligaynon
20. Capiznon
21. Bantayanon
22. Ati
23. Porohanon

**Warayan**
24. Waray
25. Baybayanon
26. Kinabalian

**West Visayan**
27. Kuyonon
28. Ratagnon
29. Caluyanon
30. Inonhan
31. Aklanon
32. Kinaray-a

**South Bisayan**
33. Surigaonon
34. Butuanon
35. Tausug

**Unclassified** *(within Central Philippine)*
36. Sulod
37. Southern Binukidnon
38. Mamanwa

**GREATER CENTRAL PHILIPPINE (contd.)**

***Southern Mindoro***
39. Western Tawbuid
40. Eastern Tawbuid
41. Buhid
42. Hanunoo

***Palawan***
43. Central Tagbanwa
44. Palawan Batak
45. Aborlan Tagbanwa

Palawano (dialect continuum)
46. Brooke's Point Palawano
47. Central Palawano
48. Southwest Palawano

49. Molbog

***Mindanao***

**Subanon** *(dialect continuum)*
50. Kolibugan Subanon
51. Western Subanon
52. Central Subanon
53. Eastern Subanon
54. Northern Subanon
55. Southern Subanon
56. *dialectal boundary*

**Danao**
57. Maranao
58. Iranun
59. Maguindanao

**Manobo**

**North Manobo**
60. Kagayanen
61. Kinamigin
62. Binukid
63. Higaonon

**Central Manobo**
64. Agusan
65. Rajah Kabungsuwan
66. Western Bukidnon
67. Matigsalug
68. Ata
69. Dibabawon
70. Ilianen
71. Obo

**South Manobo**
72. Tagabawa
73. Cotabato Manobo
74. Sarangani

***Mansakan***
75. Kamayo
76. Mandaya
77. Mansaka
78. Davawenyo
79. Kalagan *(dialect continuum)*
80. Kagan Kalagan
81. Tagakaulo

**BILIC**
82. Teduray
83. Tboli
84. Koronadal Bla'an
85. Sarangani Bla'an
86. Giangan

**KALAMIAN**
87. Calamian Tagbanwa
88. Agutaynen

**NORTH MANGYAN**
89. Iraya
90. Alangan
91. Tadyawan

in complex ways (e.g. Tboli, with its seven-vowel system, Porter 1977; Forsberg 1992).

Several languages have developed an allophonic relationship between the high vowels and their mid counterparts. In Tagalog, a generally word-final process of vowel lowering turns *i* and *u* into *e* and *o*, respectively. Kapampangan of the Central Luzon group (outside the purview of this chapter) has innovated a new set of mid vowels not from lowering of high vowels but rather through monophthongization of *ay > *e* and *aw > *o*, but this is vanishingly rare in the CSP zone. A large monophthongization zone begins just southeast of the CSP languages in Sulawesi and includes the Sangiric languages.

**Table 25.1** Typical Central Philippine vowel inventory

| | | |
|---|---|---|
| i | ɨ | u |
| (e) | | (o) |
| | a | |

Consonant inventories are also relatively simple and do not vary much across the area surveyed here. A typical inventory of phonemic consonants for the Central Philippine group is shown in Table 25.2. The tap ɾ can have several historical sources. Most typically, it is an intervocalic allophone of /d/.

We also find palatal obstruents at various stages of phonemicization, typically resulting from the combination of alveolars preceding /ij/ (e.g. Tagalog 3SG.NOM /sija/ → [ʃ(j)a], 'there' /dijan/ → [dʒ(j)an], 'stomach' /tijan/ → [tʃ(j)an]). In a rarer development, Boholano has developed a voiced alveopalatal affricate from a historical palatal glide (i.e. PMP *y > dʒ).

**Table 25.2** Typical Central Philippine consonant inventory

| | Labial | Alveolar | Palatal | Velar | Laryngeal |
|---|---|---|---|---|---|
| Voiceless stop | p | t | | k | ʔ |
| Voiced stop | b | d | | g | |
| Nasal | m | n | | ŋ | |
| Fricative | | s | | | h |
| Lateral | | l | | | |
| Tap/trill | | ɾ | | | |
| Glide | w | | j | | |

Unusual segments in CSP languages include the fortis/heavy stops of Maranao, described by Lobel and Riwarung (2009), and the aspirated stops of Subanen, described by Lobel and Hall (2010). As Lobel and Hall (2010: 336–7) note, these form part of a larger set of unusual reflexes of consonant clusters in the languages of Mindanao and northern Borneo, a fact that they tentatively attribute to language contact.

### 25.2.2 Phonotactics

The canonical lexical root in Philippine languages is a disyllable with the following template: CV(C).CV(C). On one analysis, there are no true vowel-initial syllables in lexical roots (Zorc 1977: 52). Roots that appear to be vowel-initial (and are treated as vowel-initial orthographically) begin with a glottal stop.[2] Relatedly, there is a general lack of vowel hiatus in most CSP languages, as vowel hiatus relies on the possibility of onsetless syllables.[3] Root initial glottal stops, whether they are underlying or epenthetic, surface predictably with prefixation, as in /mag-(ʔ)abut/ (AV-reach) → [magʔabot], rather than **magabot*. On the most transparent analysis, all syllables in lexical roots begin with a consonant while codas are optional.

Monosyllabic lexical roots are both rare and a relatively recent innovation in Central Philippine languages, having entered through loans and various processes of reduction. In several languages of the Sulu archipelago, the deletion of intervocalic /l/ has created monosyllables with long vowels. Tboli shows another pattern of historically truncated monosyllabic roots, e.g., PMP *epat > *fat* 'four', PAN *kaen > *ken* 'eat'.

Affixes do not have the same constraints as lexical roots; they are often monosyllabic and need not contain onsets. Onsetless affixes are typically provided with an onset either through epenthesis or infixation, the latter which only applies at the left edge of the base. When onsetless suffixes attach to stems that end in a vowel, either deletion or epenthesis avoids vowel hiatus. This latter process can be seen in Tagalog and Tagakaulo in (1a) and (b), respectively. The fricative /h/ is often used in this epenthetic capacity as it is not phonemic in root final position but glides also fulfil this role as in Tagakaulo.

[2] Central Tagbanwa is apparently the only language in the CSP zone that is described as contrasting vowel initial syllables with glottal initial syllables (Scebold 2003: 30). Merely to simplify transcription, I omit the initial glottal stop in orthographically vowel-initial roots here, as it is predictable.

[3] Words that are written with two vowels orthographically in languages such as Tagalog (e.g. *bait* 'goodness'), are pronounced with an intervening glottal stop (e.g. [baʔit]). Zorc (1977: 54) mentions Kuyonon and certain dialects of Tausug as exceptional in allowing vowel hiatus.

(1) a. *bagu-h̲in* b. *bagu-w̲un*
new-PV new-PV (Burton 2018)

Infixes typically are of a VC shape but obtain an onset from the stem, as shown again for Tagalog and Tagkaulo in (2).

(2) a. *s<um>agot* b. *t<um>ubag*
<AV>answer <AV>answer (Burton 2018)

Gemination is relatively rare in the CSP zone but is attested in Bagobo, Mansakan, Kagayanen, and at least one dialect of Bikol (Blust 2013a: 229). Phonemic glottal stop arises from the historical change PMP *q > ʔ which took place widely throughout the Philippines but the synchronic distribution of the glottal stop varies by language and region. For instance, PMP *baqeRu 'new', reduced historically to a disyllable, yields Naga Bikol *baʔgo*, Cebuano *bagʔo* (with metathesis), and Tagalog *ba:go* (with deletion and compensatory lengthening). These changes follow a general pattern as Cebuano does not allow ʔC clusters and Standard Tagalog does not allow either Cʔ or ʔC clusters. Similar cases of metathesis are triggered by syncope when the resulting cluster is excluded by the general phonotactics of a language. Some of these clusters are universally absent in certain subgroups. For instance, Zorc (1977) cites **nm* as an unattested cluster in Bisayan roots and one that is actively avoided in forms that undergo syncope, as in /inum-an/ drink-LV which yields [imnan] with metathesis of the nasal consonants after deletion of medial /u/.

There appears to be a gradated loss of root final glottal stop from south to north. In southern CSP languages, glottal stop is highly salient phonetically and does not appear to undergo (synchronic) deletion. In many languages of the northern Philippines, root final glottal stop has been lost completely. In Tagalog, which lies on the border, word final glottal stop is less phonetically salient than in the south and it is often lost in phrase medial position, occasionally with compensatory lengthening. But even within a single subgroup, we find variation in the distribution of glottal stop. In the three members of the Danao languages, Maranao allows stem/word final glottal stop but Iranun and Maguindanao have both eliminated it in this position.

To summarize the status of the glottal stop in CSP languages: (i) there is only one language that possibly shows a contrast between V and ʔV at the beginning of roots (Central Tagbanwa); (ii) root internally, some languages allow ʔC, others Cʔ, while others allow neither; and (iii) most but not all CSP languages contrast root-final ʔ with root-final V.

In most CSP languages, glides pattern like any other consonant in the native vocabulary, but in some languages, glides can form consonant clusters at the syllable edge. For instance, in the Jolo dialect of Tausug, we find monosyllables such as *awn* EXIST and *lawŋ* 'inside'. In onset position, we find languages such as Maranao and Tagkaulo where the historical perfective infix *<in> has been reduced to a single glide <y>. In these languages, onset clusters with *y* as a second member are commonly derived through infixation. Tagalog shows a historical pattern of intervocalic *l* deletion which occasionally gives rise to similar clusters (e.g. PMP *bulan > Tagalog *buwan ~ bwan*).

The Bilic languages of Southern Mindanao are exceptional with regard to the typically simple syllable margins of Philippine languages. Tboli allows for a large number of typologically rare onset clusters that violate the principle of sonority sequencing with regard to manner and voicing (e.g. /btaŋ/ 'fall', /tboli/ 'Tboli').[4]

Complex tautosyllabic clusters have also entered CSP languages through Spanish and English borrowings (e.g. Tagalog *plato* 'plate', *preno* 'brake'). An illustrative example is seen in the Spanish loan *sombrero*, which enters Tagalog at a very early stage as *sambalilo*, fully adapted to native Tagalog phonotactics, and again at a later stage as *sombrero*, with the non-native *br* cluster and free distribution of mid-vowels, which were originally word final allophones of high vowels.

All Philippine languages allow heterosyllabic clusters although each language exhibits its own constraints and tendencies. Interestingly, such clusters may be innovative and do not generally reconstruct to PMP (Blust 2013a: 62). The only clusters found at the PMP level as reconstructed in Blust and Trussel (2020) are either nasal+stop sequences (e.g. *simbuR 'to sprinkle'), or the result of reduplicated monosyllables (e.g. *taktak 'to fall, of many things at once'). However, there are many apparently reconstructable lexemes in Philippine languages which contain clusters that do not fit into either of the above patterns. It should be noted that gradient phonotactic patterns have not been examined systematically for languages of the CSP area and present a rich area for further study.[5]

### 25.2.3 Phonological processes

The phonology of most CSP languages is relatively transparent in that surface forms do not differ substantially from what would be posited as underlying forms. Attested processes include palatalization, lenition, fortition, metathesis, and compensatory lengthening, exemplified below.

[4] While these can be broken up with a schwa, according to Awed et al. (2004), schwa insertion is optional. Whether this schwa should be analysed as underlying or epenthetic has not been addressed in the literature.

[5] Zorc (1977: 53) notes the existence of phonotactic constraints in heterosyllabic clusters but laments the lack of data to address its nature. For Austronesian languages outside the CSP area, see Coetzee and Pater (2008) for Muna (Southeast Sulawesi) and Benton (1971b) for Pangasinan (Northern Luzon) for examples.

#### 25.2.3.1 *Lenition*

Tapping, a type of lenition, takes place in Tagalog morpheme internally, between a prefix–stem boundary as well as between a word-enclitic boundary. Tapping does not occur in Tagalog between proclitics and their following hosts, as seen in (3), although other languages show tapping in these contexts, too, as shown in (4) for Matigsalug Manobo.

(3) a. /daː~datiŋ/ → [daːɾatiŋ]
IPFV~arrive

b. /aku=din/ → [ako ɾin]
1SG.NOM=also

c. /maŋa=dagaʔ/ → [maŋa=dagaʔ], **maŋa=ɾagaʔ*
PL=rat

Matigsalug Manobo, tapping
(4) /me=datuʔ/ → [me ɾatuʔ]
PL=chief (Wang et al. 2006: 3)

Other types of lenition can be found in Western Bukidnon Manobo (Blust 2013a: 236), where it applies productively with affixation (e.g. *baləy* 'house', *bə-valəy* 'build a house', *guraŋ* 'old', *mə-ɣuraŋ* 'old person; old'). Deletion of intervocalic /l/ is also common across the area and was clearly a historical process in Tagalog, as well, although it was not carried out to completion.

#### 25.2.3.2 *Palatalization*

A palatalization processes takes place in Tagalog with the alveolar obstruents /t/, /s/, and /d/ before /j/, as shown in (5a)–(5b). A phonetically less natural palatalization process also takes place with the sequence /ts/, transforming it to [tʃ], as in (5c).

(5) a. /sija/ → [ʃja] ~ [ʃa]
3SG.NOM

b. /tijan/ → [tʃjan] ~ [tʃan]
stomach

c. /at saka/ → [tʃaka]
and then

In Central Tagbanwa, we find a similar but more circumscribed palatalization rule: /t/ → [tʃ]/__i. A similar pattern, although less advanced, is found in other Central Philippine languages like Cebuano. Despite allophonic rules that create palatal or alveopalatal segments, very few CSP languages have phonemicized a palatal or post-alveolar series of obstruents.

#### 25.2.3.3 *Syncope and metathesis*

The canonical Austronesian root is disyllabic and trisyllabic stems are reduced to disyllables through an active rule of syncope in many CSP languages, exemplified by Agutaynen in (6).

Agutaynen, syncope
(6) a. /balet-en/ → [balten]
respond-PV

b. /b<in>etaŋ/ → [bintaŋ]
<PFV>put (Quakenbush et al. 2010: 41)

In rarer cases, syncope has been attested across clitic boundaries, as described by Lobel and Riwarung (2009, 2011) for Maranao clitics, such as *səka* 2SG.NOM and *səkano* 2SG.NOM, shown in (7).

Maranao
(7) [dɤ.ʔɤ.mɪs.ka.no.ma.ɪ.lay]
/daʔ=ami=səkano ma-ilay/
NEG=1PL.EX.GEN=2PL.NOM PV.POT-see
'We didn't see you (pl.)' (Lobel and Riwarung 2011: 41)

When syncope creates a cluster that is otherwise unattested, a phonological process typically repairs the output. In Agutaynen, a debuccalization process (C → ʔ) repairs certain clusters, as shown in (8), while in other cases, metathesis is employed, as in (9).

Agutaynen, syncope + debuccalization
(8) /te~teled/ → tetled → [teʔled]
PROG~enter (Quakenbush et al. 2010: 42)

Agutaynen, syncope + metathesis
(9) a. /pa-belag/ → pablag → [palbag]
CAUS-separate

b. /pa-belet/ → pablet → [palbet]
CAUS-borrow (Quakenbush et al. 2010: 41)

Neither syncope nor metathesis are productive in Tagalog but both processes are richly attested in allomorphy, as seen in (10) (see Blust 1971 for the complex interaction of metathesis and assimilation in this pattern).

Tagalog, metathesis
(10) a. /atip-an/ → atpan → [aptan]
roof-LV

b. /silid-an/ → sildan → [sidlan]
room-LV (Bloomfield 1917: 391)

#### 25.2.3.4 *Vowel reduction and harmony*

Vowel reduction is not common in Central Philippine languages, but found in several languages of Mindanao and Sulu, for example, Sindangan Subanen (Arms 1996: 5), as well as Bornean languages south of the Philippines. Lobel and Riwarung (2009, 2011) describe a rare and intriguing case of harmony in Maranao where two complementary sets of vowels have developed, a 'lax' set, [ɪ, ə, o, a], and a corresponding 'tense' set, [i, ɨ, u, ɤ]. They show that the set of consonants they term 'heavy', represented as /p', t', k', s', h/, obligatorily trigger the tense allophones of the following vowels. The voiced stops /b, d, g/ optionally trigger the tensing of the following vowel, and all other consonants condition the lax set. Because the heavy/light distinction on consonants plays an important role in the morphology, there are minimal pairs for every verb, as exemplified in (11). The 'future' is signalled by the change of a light stem initial consonant to its heavy counterpart, and the consequent vowel harmony.

Maranao
(11) a. [t̪a.ʔa.man] b. [t̪'ɤ.ʔɤ.man]
/taʔam-an/ /t'aʔam-an/
taste-LV FUT/taste-LV
(Lobel and Riwarung 2011: 40)

Central Tagbanwa shows a rightwards vowel harmony process with prefixes, as in (12). Unlike Maranao, this process does not affect lexical stems and is restricted to the change /a/→[u] immediately following a syllable bearing /u/.

Central Tagbanwa
(12) a. [pupuŋaralan] b. [pugputabas]
/pu-paŋ-aral-an/ /pug-pa-tabas/
IPFV-DISTR-study-LV AV.IPFV-CAUS-prune
(Scebold 2003: 35)

## 25.2.4 Morphophonology

### 25.2.4.1 *Infixation*

Two productive infixes inherited from PAN, *<um> ACTOR VOICE and *<in> PERFECTIVE/BEGUN ASPECT, continue to play an important role in CSP languages and Philippine languages, more generally (Reid 1992). They are positioned after the first consonant of the stem, as shown in (13) for Tagalog. Historically, both of these infixes could co-occur as shown in Bikolano (14), although this is only found in a small number of living languages (Lobel 2004).

(13) a. *k<in>u:ha-Ø* b. *k<um>u:ha*
<BEG>take-PV <AV>take
'taken' 'take'

(14) *k<um><in>u:ha*
<AV><BEG>take
'consequently took'

Infixation is often externalized altogether in a process which turns *<um> into *mu-* and *<in> into *ni-*, as found in Cebuano. Reflexes of *<in> have also been reduced to a single segment in Danao languages (e.g. Maranao *t<i>abas* <PFV>cut), Tboli, Mansakan, and elsewhere in Mindanao.

Other minor infixes occur, as well, in a large number of CSP languages. For instance, in Bikolano and several Bisayan languages we find a plural infix <Vr>, whose vowel harmonizes with the first vowel of the stem. Another widespread *<aŋ>* infix marks a different type of plurality.

### 25.2.4.2 *Reduplication*

Philippine languages tend to make heavy use of various types of reduplication for a vast number of purposes. Tagalog has two types of CV reduplication, one with and one without vowel length, as well as foot reduplication. CV reduplication without vowel length is found in agentive nominalization, shown in (15a), intensive formation, and elsewhere. CV reduplication with vowel length, shown in (15b), is used chiefly for imperfective/progressive aspect.

(15) a. *mag-na~na:kaw* b. *mag-na:~na:kaw*
AV-NMLZ-steal AV-IPFV-steal
'thief' 'will steal'

Foot reduplication in many cases is indistinguishable from full reduplication of the root, as shown in (16a), as most roots are disyllabic. However, larger stems, as in (16b), demonstrate that no process of reduplication in Tagalog copies more than a foot.

(16) a. *ma-ganda~ganda=sila* b. *bali:~bali:taʔ*
ADJ-MODER~beauty=3PL.NOM MODER~news
'They are moderately beautiful.' 'gossip'

Other languages, such as Central Tagbanwa, possess full word reduplication without such a maximality constraint, as seen in (17).

Central Tagbanwa
(17) a. *naka-tohod* b. *naka-tohod~naka-tohod*
LOC-forest LOC-forest~LOC-forest
'in the forest' 'deep in the forest'
(Scebold 2003: 42)

Multiple processes of reduplication can take place in the same word, as shown in Tagalog (18a), where (aspectual) CV reduplication applies to a stem that has already undergone (iterative) foot reduplication and in (18b), where (imperfective) CV: reduplication has applied to a stem that has undergone (intensive) CV reduplication.

(18) a. *mag-ha:~hanap~hanap*
AV-IPFV~ITER~search
'will keep searching'

b. *p<in>ag-sa:~sa~sabi*
<BEG>TR-IPFV~INTNS~search
'what is being said (intensively)'

Whereas Tagalog reduplication simply truncates a base that has more than two syllables, Cebuano and Bikol employ reduplication with fixed segmentalism for the same aim.

Thus, for a trisyllabic Cebuano stem like *padala* 'send' we find *p<ulu>~padala*, where the first consonant of the stem has been copied and the following *ulu* is infixed, instead of **padala~padala* or **pada~padala* (see Mattes 2014: 76 for additional complications).

Word-based reduplication should be differentiated from a robustly syntactic process of reduplication which employs the linker or genitive case marking. These types of reduplication, shown for Central Tagbanwa in (19) and Tagalog in (20) (cf. Schachter and Otanes 1972: 398), usually indicate repetitive action and are never affected by maximality constraints. Such constructions typically allow pronominal and other clitics to intervene between the base and the reduplicant, as in (20).

Central Tagbanwa
(19) *t<um>umpok* *a* *t<um>umpok*
<AV>pile LNK <AV>pile
'kept piling up' (Scebold 2003: 57)

(20) *k<um>a:ʔin=ako* *naŋ=k<um>a:ʔin*
<AV.BEG>eat=1SG.NOM GEN=<AV.BEG>eat
'I kept eating and eating.'

### 25.2.4.3 *Nasal substitution*

Languages of the CSP zone, like many other Malayo-Polynesian languages, display a morphophonological process termed 'nasal substitution' with cognates of the sister prefixes PMP *paŋ- 'DISTRIBUTIVE' and *maŋ- 'ACTOR VOICE + DISTRIBUTIVE' (§25.3.3.2). Nasal substitution refers to assimilation of the final nasal of these prefixes to the place of articulation of the stem-initial consonant accompanied by deletion of the latter, as in Tagalog (21).[6]

(21) /maŋ-baril/ → [mamaril]
AV.DISTR-gun
'shoot'

The deletion of the stem onset after nasal assimilation is not entirely predictable in Tagalog and other Central Philippine languages. Zuraw (2000) proposes a multifactorial analysis of this deletion for Tagalog, which must take into account the features of the first segment of the stem, as well as the stem's semantics and frequency. In other CSP languages, nasal substitution patterns are completely predictable on the basis of phonology alone, typically with stem-initial voiceless segments undergoing deletion and voiced segments being maintained (Blust 2004b).

[6] The nasal coda of the prefixes that trigger nasal substitution are often represented by N, a placeless nasal with special morphophonological properties. Blust (2004b) reviews nasal substitution patterns across Malayo-Polynesian languages.

## 25.2.5 Stress and prosody

The vast majority of Philippine languages have a phonemic stress/prominence distinction on roots which has long posed a challenge for reconstruction. As discussed in Kaufman and Himmelmann (this volume, §42.4.3), the basic feature that underlies the Philippine penultimate vs. final (aka paroxytone vs. oxytone) stress distinction is probably a vowel length contrast in the penultimate syllable. Central Philippine languages differ in whether closed penultimate syllables attract stress in the same way. In Tagalog, penultimate closed syllables do not attract pitch prominence nor can they co-occur with a long vowel and are thus predictably unaccented. In the Bisayan languages, on the other hand, closed penultimate syllables do attract pitch prominence on par with syllables containing a long vowel. Thus, a root like /dakdak/, in isolation, would surface as [dak'dak] in Tagalog but ['dakdak] in Cebuano.

As noted by Blust (2013a: 251) and Kaufman and Himmelmann (this volume, §42.4.3), prosody is not phonemic in several languages of the southern Philippines. Revel-Macdonald (1979: 63) describes a general absence of phonemic accentual distinctions in Palawan while noting the presence of final syllable lengthening, which gives the impression of final stress. The lack of contrastive prosody (penultimate long vowels) appears to be a contact feature in this area. Pallesen (1985) observes that the Tausug of Sulu lacks the prosodic distinctions found in Central Philippine languages but that the Tausug of Palawan, which originated in nineteenth-century Sulu, maintains the distinctions found in other Central Philippine languages, concluding that the loss of this distinction in Sulu is a relatively recent phenomenon that came about through contact with Sama-Bajaw languages, which show predictable penultimate word stress.

Other languages of the CSP zone without contrastive accent include Central Tagbanwa, which shows variable stress (Scebold 2003: 27), Agutaynen, described by Quakenbush et al. (2010: 40) as having penultimate phrase-based stress, Matigsalug Manobo, which shows regular penultimate word based stress (Wang et al. 2006: 3), Maranao (Lobel and Riwarung 2011), and Tboli, which shows regular word final stress (Forsberg 1992).

CSP languages often employ vowel length, generally referred to as 'contrastive stress' or 'accent' in the literature, as a prosodic morpheme. Zorc (1977: 64–7) discusses three types of morphological accent in the Bisayan languages which he takes to be part of the exponence of certain affixes. He notes, for instance, that in the Warayan subgroup of Bisayan, a prefix *ha-*, which derives adjectives indicating dimension and distance, co-occurs with penultimate stress.

Thus, a root like *ra'yuʔ* 'distance' which shows final stress in isolation surfaces with penultimate stress with this prefix: *ha-'rayuʔ* 'far'. This apparent accent shift is likely due to the addition of vowel length to the penultimate syllable of the prefixed form (e.g. /ha-ra:yuʔ/). Other Bisayan affixes co-occur with final stress and Zorc terms these "ultima-accent affixes", for instance, the prefix *manog-* 'on the verge of'. When attaching to a stem with penultimate stress like *'tapus* 'finish', the derived form *ma,nog-ta'pus* has final stress. Finally, Zorc discusses affixes that appear to flip the stress of the stem with final stress stems taking penultimate stress and vice versa.

The morphological use of vowel length and stress in the Central Philippine languages is still largely uncharted territory. Even for Tagalog, the best studied language of the CSP region, the facts remain elusive and not well understood. Little progress has been made since Zorc 1977 and some following work may have obscured these matters by ignoring the crucial role of vowel length in favour of a purely stress based analysis.

## 25.3 Morphology

The morphology of most Philippine languages is highly complex along several dimensions: (i) a large proportion of morphemes are multifunctional and take on distinct meanings in different morphological contexts; (ii) much of the morphology is portmanteau, yielding a prototypical 'fusional' language in Sapir's (1921) classic typology; and (iii) the exponence of a morpheme, that is, how a set of features are expressed on the surface, is often dependent on what other morphemes are present in the word. Below, I discuss aspect morphology (§25.3.1), voice morphology (§25.3.2), a variety of common derivational functions that typically fall under the heading of 'mode' (§25.3.3), the causative (§25.3.4), and negation (§25.3.5).

### 25.3.1 Aspect

Although often described in terms of tense in the literature (e.g., McKaughan 1958; Wolff 1973; Zorc 1977 *inter alia*), the temporal inflections of Philippine languages uniformly indicate aspect rather than tense, with the possible exception of Iraya (Reid 2017). Voice and aspect are grammatically prominent and paradigmatically interconnected in most Philippine languages (cf. Reid 1992; Ross 2002b; Himmelmann 2005a). This can be seen in the Tagalog voice/aspect paradigm shown in Table 25.3, where the voice marker disappears unexpectedly in the prospective aspect of the actor voice paradigm and in the perfective and progressive of the patient voice paradigm.

**Table 25.3** Fragment of the Tagalog voice aspect paradigm for *ba:sag* 'break'

| | Actor <um> | Patient -in | Locative -an | Conveyance i- |
|---|---|---|---|---|
| NEUT | *b**<um>**a:sag* | *basa:g-**in*** | *basa:g-**an*** | ***i**-ba:sag* |
| PRF | *b**<um>**a:sag* | *b<in>a:sag* | *b<in>asa:g-**an*** | ***i**-b<in>a: sag* |
| PROG | *b**<um>**a: ~ba:sag* | *b<in>a: ~ba:sag* | *b<in>a:~basa: g-**an*** | ***i**-b<in>a: ~ba:sag* |
| PROS | *ba:~ba: sag* | *ba:~basa:g-**in*** | *ba:~basa:g-**an*** | ***i**-ba:~ba: sag* |

A subset of Central Philippine languages display three primary aspects which can be termed perfective, progressive, and prospective.[7] The three way distinction may arise from two atomic features corresponding to reflexes of *<in> and *CV reduplication, as in (22).

(22)

| atomic features | | compositional meanings | |
|---|---|---|---|
| <in> | BEGUN | <in> | **PERFECTIVE** |
| CV~ | IMPERFECTIVE | <in>CV~ | **PROGRESSIVE** |
| | | CV~ | **PROSPECTIVE** |

The feature combination [+begun, -imperfective] is interpreted as perfective, [+begun, +imperfective] as progressive, and [-begun, +imperfective] as prospective. Thus, while none of the surface aspects are indicated uniquely by a morpheme, they are derived in a compositional manner (see Otanes 1966; De Guzman 1978; and Reid 1992 for different feature based approaches to this paradigm).[8]

Aspect marking is most often obligatory on finite verbs although in some languages, such as Cebuano and Agutaynen, a single form will be used for the imperfective/prospective and the infinitive thus yielding a two-way distinction. Such languages can be said to conflate the historical unmarked and prospective aspects into a general 'unrealized' inflection (Reid 1992: 74).

[7] The prospective, which is used for unbegun action, is also referred to as 'contemplated', 'future', and 'irrealis', all of which are, strictly speaking, inappropriate labels. 'Contemplated' suggests cognition on the part of an agent; 'future' designates a tense rather than an aspect; 'irrealis' suggests that the form would be obligatory in negated and counterfactual contexts, although this is not the case.

[8] PAN *CV~ may have originally marked the imperfective or durative while *<in> appears to have marked the perfective (Wolff 1973; Zorc 1977; Reid 1992; Ross 1995b, 2002b). Reid (1992) argues that *<in> innovatively spreads into the progressive in Central Philippine languages, where it comes to signal [+begun].

In addition to the major aspects shown in the above tables, most languages also possess minor aspects like Tagalog's recent perfective and immediate prospective, shown in (23).

(23) a. *ka-ra~ratiŋ=ko=laŋ*
RCT.PFV$_1$-RCT.PFV$_2$~arrive=1SG.GEN=only
'I just arrived.'

b. *pa-ratiŋ=na=ako*
IMM.FUT-arrive=already=1SG.NOM
'I'm about to arrive.'

They are minor both in their frequency and in their emphatic interpretation, in contrast to the basic aspect categories. The syntax of the recent perfective is also distinct from the major aspects. In Tagalog and other Central Philippine languages, voice is neutralized and genitive case is assigned to what would normally be the nominative case marked argument. The recent perfective cannot be negated and may also show additional syntactic restrictions.

Other languages of the CSP area appear to have expanded this system more dramatically using the PMP mode prefix *paR- as a durative (e.g. Aklanon, which Zorc 1977 analyses as having six aspects). The use of a *paR- reflex as a durative can also be seen in Cotabato Manobo (Kerr 1988: 8), where *eg-* (< PMP *paR-) indicates the progressive and CV reduplication no longer plays any role in the aspect paradigm (i.e. √*-en* 'PROSPECTIVE', *eg-*√*-en* 'PROGRESSIVE' and *<in>*√'PERFECTIVE'). The neighbouring Danao languages also use a reflex of *paR- (*pe-*) for what is signalled by reduplication in Tagalog, as seen in Table 25.4.

**Table 25.4** Maranao voice aspect paradigm (McKaughan 1958)

| | Actor | Patient | Locative | Conveyance |
|---|---|---|---|---|
| NEUT | *t<om>abas* | *tabas-en* | *tabas-an* | *i-tabas* |
| PRF | *t<omi>abas* | *t<i>abas* | *t<i>abas-an* | *i-ni-tabas* |
| PROG | *pe-t̲ebas* | *pe-t̲ebas-en* | *pe-t̲ebas-an* | *i-pe-t̲ebas* |
| PROS | *t̲ebas* | *t̲ebas-en* | *t̲ebas-an* | *i-t̲ebas* |
| IMPRT | *tabas* | *tabas-a* | *tabas-i* | |

In many languages, disyllabic reduplication indicates repetitive action and can be considered an aspectual category as well, although it is rarely included as part of the basic aspect paradigm in the descriptive literature and perhaps rightly so; unlike CV imperfective or progressive reduplication, disyllabic repetitive reduplication is never seen to interact with mood, negation, or voice.

The combination of *<in> with the composite actor voice markers beginning with *m-* (i.e. PMP *maŋ- 'AV.DISTR', *maki- 'AV.SOC', *maR- 'AV.MID', *maka- 'AV.POT') typically yields *n-* initial forms without infixation (e.g. *naŋ-*, *naki-*, *nag-*, *naka-*). This 'externalization' of *<in> postdates PMP, as we also find CSP languages that reflect *m<in>aR- as *mig-* rather than *nag-*, showing that the full historical form was reduced in diverse ways after the break-up of the major Philippine subgroups.

In negated clauses, aspect is often indicated by the choice of negator and the verb is left unmarked or marked with an aspect neutral inflection. An example of this is seen in Sarangani Manobo, where aspect is marked on the verb in (24a)–(24b) but through negation in (24c)–(24d). Similar examples could also be produced for most Bisayan languages.

Sarangani Manobo

(24) a. *t<om>edogi se bayi*
<AV>sleep NOM woman
'The woman will sleep.'

b. *t<im>edogi se bayi*
<AV.PFV>sleep NOM woman
'The woman slept.'

c. *edek tedogi se bayi*
NEG sleep NOM woman
'The woman will not go to sleep.'

d. *weda? tedogi se bayi*
NEGEXIST sleep NOM woman
'The woman didn't sleep.' (Dubois 1976: 20)

A more holistic understanding of aspect in Philippine-type languages must take into account both 'inner aspect', that is, perfective, progressive, prospective, as marked with bound morphology, together with 'outer aspect', as marked by enclitics, typically descendants of PMP *=dena 'already' (almost always reduced to a monosyllable) and *=pa 'still'. Aspectual clitics in Philippine languages play a larger role than might be gleaned from their English glosses and are near obligatory in certain types of contexts. Outer aspect markers are both morphologically external to perfective, progressive, and prospective morphology and also involve higher level pragmatics. Reflexes of PMP *=dena 'already' place a situation before an *expected* time while PMP *=pa 'still' places a situation after such a time.

### 25.3.2 Voice

Voice is a pivotal feature of the morphosyntax of all Philippine and Philippine-type languages.[9] The Philippine-type alignment system is generally understood to select a particular participant as the nominative argument (or absolutive, depending on the analysis) using one of several voice morphemes. This argument is typically interpreted definitely and can stand alone without an associated predicate. It is in some sense a privileged argument but its cross-linguistic status vis a vis subject and topic remains debated.

Agents of non-actor voice verbs are uniformly expressed in the genitive case in Philippine languages. Notional objects, when not selected by the voice morphology to become nominative arguments, are either expressed as genitives (as in Tagalog), as obliques (as in Cebuano), with a dedicated object case (as in Maranao and Ivatan), or with the linker (as in the Bikol example below and more generally in Kapampangan).

The four primary voices are the actor voice, patient voice, locative voice, and conveyance voice, as seen earlier in Table 25.5.[10] The exponence of these voice markers in CSP languages do not differ drastically from their PMP reconstructions.

**Table 25.5** Common CSP reflexes of PMP voice markers

| Voice | PMP reconstruction | Common CSP reflexes |
|---|---|---|
| Actor voice | *<um> | <um>, m-, mu- |
| Patient voice | *-en | -in, -un, -ɨn |
| Locative voice | *-an | -an |
| Conveyance voice | *(h)i-[a] | ʔi-, hi-, Ø |

[a] The PMP cognate of the PAN conveyance voice marker *Si- is predicted to be *hi-, but this form only surfaces as such in Tausug and Samarenyo. Everywhere else, the initial *h* seems to have been eliminated in favour of a (possibly epenthetic) glottal stop. Nonetheless, because *h* is expected and these two languages were not in close contact with each other, the more common form *ʔi-* is thought to have come about through parallel innovation.

The basic use of the voice markers is very consistent across the CSP range with the exception of the Sama-Bajaw languages and, to a lesser extent, the Bilic languages. The system can be illustrated with the Naga Bikol examples in (25).

Naga Bikol

(25) a. *nag-bakal=aku=ŋ* *bagas*
AV.BEG-buy=1SG.NOM=LNK rice
'I bought rice.'

b. *b<in>akal-Ø=ko* *an=bagas*
<BEG>buy-PV=1SG.GEN NOM=rice
'I bought the rice.'

c. *b<in>akal-an=ko* *si=hwan* *ki=bagas*
<BEG>buy-LV=1SG.GEN NOM=Juan OBL=rice
'I bought some rice from Juan.'

d. *i-b<in>akal=ko* *si=hwan* *ki=bagas*
CV-<BEG>buy=1SG.GEN NOM=Juan OBL=rice
'I bought some rice for Juan.'
(McFarland 1974: 104–5)

As can be seen, one participant is selected by the predicate to be the nominative argument while other participants are expressed in non-nominative cases. The actor voice selects the prototypical agent as the nominative argument; the patient voice typically selects an affected patient; the locative voice selects a locative, directional or other type of oblique argument as well as an unaffected object; the conveyance voice selects a theme moving away from the agent as well as an instrumental or benefactee as the nominative argument.

The proper treatment of these voice markers remains an area of endless theorization and major debate in Austronesian linguistics. The earliest published analyses carried out by Spanish linguists and inherited by Bloomfield (1917) treated the patient, locative, and conveyance voices as types of passive (e.g. direct passive, locative passive, etc.). It was recognized from the earliest point, however, that the putative 'passives' of Philippine languages, which are fully transitive, were not equivalent to the Indo-European passive, a marked detransitive construction used primarily to background the agent. In the symmetrical analysis of Philippine-type voice (Foley 2008; Himmelmann 2005a; Riesberg 2014), the system represents a unique type of alignment where all voices are equally marked, standing in natural opposition to accusative and ergative languages, which typically display unmarked transitive and intransitive clauses. For the vast majority of CSP languages, it also holds true that there is no morphologically unmarked voice, just as in the Tagalog paradigm seen earlier. Proponents of an ergative analysis of the Philippine voice system (Starosta et al. 1982; De Guzman 1988; Gerdts 1988; Aldridge 2004; Liao 2004) argue that the actor voice appears less transitive than its

[9] On the Bornean side, Lobel (2013a: 150) locates the southern border of the full voice system in the area of "Brunei Dusun, Kolod, Tingalan, Abai Sembuak/Tubu, Bulusu, and Tidung languages, although a handful of non-Philippine-type languages exist north of this hypothetical line." In Sulawesi, the full voice system seems to be continued only in the Mongondow-Gorontalo (or 'Gorontalic') languages, as well as the Minahasan and Sangiric subgroups.

[10] What is termed here conveyance voice, following Wolff 1973, goes by several other names as well: circumstantial, instrumental, benefactive, secondary object, and theme voice, among others. See Blust (2002c) and Ross (2002b) for a review of the terminology and its history.

non-actor voice counterparts. Although this is not the place to review the arguments for one analysis over another (but see Kaufman 2017), the principles of voice selection require basic explication.

There is widespread agreement that some type of referentiality largely determines voice selection (see Wolfenden 1961; Wolff 1966; Schachter 1976; McFarland 1978 for early treatments). Table 25.6, based on Tagalog but applicable more widely, abstracts away from many complications, additional factors, and cross-linguistic variation (Schachter 1976; Naylor 1986a; Adams and Manaster-Ramer 1988; McFarland 1978; Latrouite 2011; Nolasco 2003) but captures the core basis for the alternation. When the agent is definite and the theme/patient is indefinite or absent, the predication will be expressed in the actor voice. When the theme/patient is definite, there is a strong tendency to employ the patient voice, regardless of the definiteness of the agent. With a verb of transfer and similar predicates, the locative voice will be selected when the theme is indefinite but the recipient is definite. When a conveyed theme of such predicates is definite, the conveyance voice will be selected, regardless of the definiteness of the agent and recipient.

**Table 25.6** Voice selection in a typical CSP language

| Agent | Theme/Patient | Locative | Preferred Voice |
|---|---|---|---|
| def | (indef) | – | Actor voice |
| def/indef | def | – | Patient voice |
| def/indef | (indef) | def | Locative voice |
| def/indef | def | def | Conveyance voice |

Definite referents can always be expressed as genitive agents and nominative arguments, while directional arguments are felicitously expressed in the oblique case regardless of their definiteness. What the pattern in Table 25.6 conspires to avoid is the expression of a definite undergoer as a non-nominative object.[11] If a previously introduced or otherwise familiar argument does surface as a non-nominative object, it typically receives a partitive interpretation or is understood to be less affected by the action (Nolasco 2003).

[11] This pattern holds throughout the CSP languages but some languages, such as Cebuano (Bell 1978), are argued to have a more flexible correspondence between the syntactic status of an argument and its definiteness.

In an intransitive predication with an indefinite subject, the subject is typically introduced with the use of an existential, as shown in (26a) (Schachter and Otanes 1972: 279, but see Adams and Manaster-Ramer 1988 and Bell 1978 for additional wrinkles). The same holds for a bivalent predication in which neither argument has been previously introduced, as seen in (26b). This strategy is necessary to avoid the ordinarily definite interpretation of the nominative phrase.

(26) a. *may* *d<um>atiŋ*
EXIST <AV.BEG>arrive
'Someone arrived.'

b. *may* *k<um>a:ʔin* *naŋ=sa:giŋ*
EXIST <AV.BEG>eat GEN=banana
'Someone ate a banana.'

It should not be assumed that the patient voice is restricted to semantically bivalent predicates. Examples of the type in Tagalog (27) show that patient voice also selects affected subjects of monadic and even entity denoting predicates.

(27) a. *la:~laŋgam-in* *aŋ=asu:kal*
IPFV~ant-PV NOM=sugar
'The sugar will be "anted".'

b. *s<in>i:~sipon-Ø=ako*
<BEG>IPFV~flu-PV=1SG.NOM
'I have the flu.' ('I'm being "flued".')

Similarly, the locative voice can select a recipient or location that we would consider part of the lexical semantics of the verb, as in (28), but it can just as easily 'promote' an adjunct to become the nominative argument, as in (29).

(28) *b<in>igy-an* *ni=rori* *naŋ=pe:ra* *si=pe:peŋ*
<BEG>give-LV GEN=Rory GEN=money NOM=Pepeng
'Rory gave Pepeng money.'

(29) *in-iyak-an* *ni=rori* *si=pe:peŋ*
BEG-cry-LV GEN=Rory NOM=Pepeng
'Rory cried to Pepeng.'

The locative voice can also alternate with the patient voice to indicate that the nominative argument is less affected by the action than would normally be assumed, as seen in the minimal pair in (30).

(30) a. *k<in>a:ʔin-Ø* *ni=maria* *aŋ=isdaʔ*
<BEG>eat-PV GEN=Maria NOM=fish
'Maria ate the fish.'

b. *k<in>aʔi:n-an* *ni=maria* *aŋ=isdaʔ*
<BEG>eat-LV GEN=Maria NOM=fish
'Maria ate from/at the fish.'

The conveyance voice (PAN *Si-) is difficult to characterize semantically in a unified manner. It selects benefactees, instrumentals, and objects conveyed away from the agent as the nominative argument. These seemingly disparate functions can be disambiguated in a number of CSP languages with an emergent marker for each function (e.g. Tagalog *i-pag-* BENEFACTIVE, and *i-paŋ-* INSTRUMENTAL), although the bare *i-* prefix in Tagalog is still as polysemous as its historical source.

In addition to the indicative/independent voice forms, there also exists a non-indicative/dependent paradigm. Wolff (1973: 88) reconstructs this paradigm for the imperative and after certain 'preverbs' while later work by Ross (2002b) reconstructs it with a slightly wider range of functions. The CSP languages are crucial in understanding the role of the non-indicative forms in PMP, as they are preserved more faithfully here than in languages of the northern Philippines. In most MP languages outside the Philippines, the distinction between the indicative and non-indicative forms are also merged. In the northern and central Philippines, the paradigms are generally merged in favour of the indicative paradigm and are reduced in various ways south of the CSP zone.[12] Wherever the non-indicative paradigm is preserved, it is used in the imperative. This is seen in Batangas Tagalog (31) and Maranao (32). The dependent paradigm imperatives are distinguished from independent paradigm imperatives in most languages by the obligatory omission of a second person singular addressee pronoun, as in Batangas Tagalog, although there are rare exceptions to this, like Maranao.

Batangas Tagalog

| (31) | *buks-i=(*mo)* | *aŋ=pintuʔan* |
|---|---|---|
| | open-LV.DEP=2SG.GEN | NOM=door |
| | 'Open the door!' | |

Maranao

| (32) | *tabas-a=ŋka* | *so=dinis* |
|---|---|---|
| | cut-PV.DEP=2SG.GEN | NOM=cloth |
| | 'Cut the cloth!' | (McKaughan 1958: 25) |

In many Central Philippine languages, the dependent paradigm is also used in the negated perfective, as shown by Wolff (1973) for Samarenyo (33). This paradigm does not co-occur with imperfective reduplication or the perfective/begun *<in> infix (although they can occur in the recent perfective, see below).

[12] In the majority of Austronesian languages, the independent locative voice *-an* survives with a nominalizer function and some remnant of *<um>* (typically melded with one of the mode prefixes as *m-*) survives in the actor voice. On the other hand, patient voice *-en and conveyance voice *Si- are widely lost as productive voice markers south of the Philippine languages, although the distinction may be carried out through different morphological means.

Samarenyo (Waray)

| (33) | a. | *waraʔ* | *lakaw-Ø* | *a=ba:taʔ* |
|---|---|---|---|---|
| | | NEGEXIST | go.away-AV.DEP | NOM=child |
| | | 'The child did not go away.' | | |
| | b. | *waraʔ=ku* | *balik-a* | *a=sibi:sa* |
| | | NEGEXIST=1SG.GEN | return-PV.DEP | NOM=beer |
| | | 'I did not go back after the beer.' | | |
| | c. | *waraʔ=ku* | *hiŋalimt-i* | *a=isturya* |
| | | NEGEXIST=1SG.GEN | forget-LV.DEP | NOM=story |
| | | 'I did not forget the story.' | | |
| | d. | *waraʔ=niya* | *pilak-an* | |
| | | NEGEXIST=3SG.GEN | throw.away-CV.DEP | |
| | | *an=basu:ra* | | |
| | | NOM=garbage | | |
| | | 'He did not throw the garbage away.' (Wolff 1973) | | |

The dependent forms are also employed in temporal adjuncts, as seen in (34) and (35) (Stevens 1969; Zorc 1977) and the recent perfective (not shown here). These contexts are particularly interesting as the voice morphology selects a particular argument to promote, *kanya suwildu* in (34) and *baŋku* in (35), but no argument actually surfaces with nominative case.

Samarenyo (Waray)

| (34) | *pag-ta-tág-an=niya* | *[sa=kanya suwildu]* |
|---|---|---|
| | SBJV-ASP-give-CV.DEP=3SG.GEN | OBL=3SG.GEN earning |
| | *[kanya nanay]...* | |
| | 3SG.GEN mother | |
| | 'When he gives all of his earnings to his mother. . .' (Zorc 1977: 139) | |

Samarenyo (Waray)

| (35) | *pag-liŋkur-i=niya* | *han=baŋku,* |
|---|---|---|
| | SBJV-sit-LV.DEP=3SG.GEN | GEN.DEF=bench |
| | *na-rubaʔ* | |
| | STAT.PFV-break | |
| | 'When he sat on the bench, it broke.' (Zorc 1977: 139) | |

The Tboli voice system has been reshaped by the general loss of suffixes and case marking on full noun phrases. Here, there exists a general actor voice marked by *me-/<em>* and a general undergoer voice marked by *ne-/<en>*, while the conveyance voice is left unmarked morphologically but still considered distinct. Tboli agent voice, undergoer voice, and instrumental voice clauses are exemplified in (36).

Tboli

| (36) | a. | *s<m>akay=le* | *owoŋ* | *yo* | *ken ŋaʔ* |
|---|---|---|---|---|---|
| | | <AV>ride=3PL | airplane | that | PL child |
| | | 'The children rode in the airplane.' | | | |
| | b. | *gel* | *n-boʔ* | *maʔ* | *ɔu* |
| | | always | UV-carry_on_back | Father | me |
| | | 'Father always carried me on his back.' | | | |

c. *Ø-əfək* *Walan* *du* *asay*
cv-chop_down Walan it axe
'Walan chopped it down with an axe.'
(Awed et al. 2004: 79, 25)

We can also speak of composite minor voices that target adjuncts such as purposive clauses for promotion to pivot. These appear to have been innovated more recently, often from combinations of inherited morphemes. The Tagalog prefix *ika-* (< PMP *(h)i- CONVEYANCE VOICE + *ka- STATIVE) and its cognate Sarangani Manobo exemplify this in (37) and (38).

(37) *ano* *aŋ=ik<in>a-pu:~punta=niya* *duʔun?*
what NOM=<BEG>RV-IPFV~go=3SG.GEN there
'What's his reason for going there?'

Sarangani Manobo
(38) *yan* *se* *iŋke-opal=ko*
that NOM RV-anger=1SG.GEN
'That's why I became angry.' (Dubois 1976: 67)

The CSP languages typically allow only one voice marker per word, but this is not the case in the languages of the northern Philippines. In many languages of North Luzon, reflexes of conveyance voice *(h)i- combine with locative *-an to form an unambiguous benefactive voice (Reid and Liao 2004: 460). Such combinations are vanishingly rare in the CSP languages but may not be entirely absent, if the Hiligaynon example in (39) is representative of a wider pattern.[13]

Hiligaynon
(39) *i-lutu:ʔ-an=ko=kamo* *sang=paniʔudto*
CV-cook-LV=1SG.GEN=2PL.NOM GEN=lunch
'I will cook lunch for you all.' (Wolfenden 1975: 95)

## 25.3.3 Mode

There are several common verbal morphemes in CSP languages that are often treated under the somewhat vague header of 'mode', a practice I continue here. These include the potentive, which subsumes both accidental and abilitative meanings (§25.3.3.1), the sociative (§25.3.3.2), the distributive (§25.3.3.3), as well as reflexive and reciprocal marking (§25.3.3.6).

### 25.3.3.1 *Potentive*

Nearly all CSP languages have a potentive paradigm, which is used to indicate both possible and unintentional action. This polysemy, which is remarkably stable across Austronesian languages, can be seen in the Tboli sentences in (40) and (41) with the *g(e)-* prefix, a reflex of PMP *ka- (cf. Bennásar 1892: 38–9 for the Teduray cognate).

Tboli
(40) *nə* *g-tutuk* *kulu* *nib*
and POT-nail head Nib
'And Nib accidentally bumped his head.'

(41) *g-uŋəl-u* *udɛl* *sdoʔ* *fatu* *ləm* *law*
POT-hear-1SG.GEN voice pig across in cane
'I was able to hear the squeal of a pig in the cane across (the river).' (Forsberg 1992: 92)

The potentive in CSP languages does not simply provide a way of emphasizing the accidental or unintentional nature of an action. It is obligatory in such contexts and as a corollary, the unmarked (non-potentive) form unambiguously denotes intentional action when there is an animate agent. This paradigm, which is contrasted with the unmarked 'dynamic' voice paradigm in Table 25.7 for Tagalog, has a very distinct history involving the PAN prefix *ka-, whose original function may have involved possession (Kaufman 2011a).

**Table 25.7** The Tagalog potentive paradigm

| | Dynamic | Potentive |
|---|---|---|
| Actor voice | *<um>* | *maka-* |
| Patient voice | *-in* | *ma-* |
| Conveyance voice | *i-* | *ma-i-* |
| Locative voice | *-an* | *ma- -an* |

The Tagalog potentive is transparently derived from the basic voice paradigm in the conveyance and locative voices with the addition of *ma-* but the actor and patient voices do not show clear correspondences. The potentive patient voice does not include a reflex of patient voice *-en and the potentive actor voice is not obviously related to other forms in the paradigm. This somewhat confusing picture,

[13] Apparent combinations of voice markers do occur in the CSP languages when one voice marker derives the stem for the true voice marker. For instance, a Tagalog stem can be formed with locative nominalizer/voice marker *-an* and then go on to take the *mag-* actor voice prefix. Combinations of voice markers can also take on seemingly non-compositional functions, such as Tagalog *mag-tulug-tulug-an* AV-PRETEND~sleep-PRETEND 'to pretend to sleep', where both the reduplication and the *-an* suffix constitute multiple exponence of the 'pretendative'. But here there is no clear link between the pretendative function of *-an* and its more common locative voice function. Such cases are markedly different from *maŋ-i-* AV-CV- in Cordilleran languages, in which both the actor voice markers and the conveyance voice marker are playing a voice related role, the first determining the voice of the entire predicate and the second functioning as an applicative for objects moving away from the agent.

typical for Central Philippine languages, has a straightforward historical explanation. The *ma- prefix was originally a reduction of stative *ka- combined with actor voice *<um>, as a general *non-actor voice* potentive (Ross 1995b: 741). Historically, there was an opposition between an active clause such as (42a) and a passive-like stative clause, as in (47b), where the logical object would be the nominative argument. The latter is derived with the stative prefix *ka-* combined with the actor voice *<um>* followed by apheresis of the first syllable.

(42) a. *ʔ<um>u:bos* b. *k<um>a-ʔu:bos → ma-ʔu:bos*
<AV>finish <AV>STAT-finish
'to finish' 'to get finished'

In all CSP languages that show a reflex of this *ma-, an agent can be introduced just as in a regular dynamic transitive clause, yielding oppositions like that in (43).

(43) a. *na-ʔu:bos ni=bo:boy aŋ=pagka:ʔin*
STAT.BEG-finish GEN=boboy NOM=food
'Boboy finished the food (accidentally)'

b. *<in>u:bos-Ø ni=bo:boy aŋ=pagka:ʔin*
<BEG>finish-PV GEN=boboy NOM=food
'Boboy finished the food (purposefully)'

The use of the genitive in (43a) was most likely an innovation, one which has apparently not taken place in many Cordilleran languages of the northern Philippines, which treat the paradigm derived from *ma- more along the lines of a passive than a transitive clause (cf. Reid and Liao 2004: 462–4). The reanalysis of *ma- from its original actor voice stative function to a potentive undergoer voice marker goes hand in hand with its appearance in other voices. The spread of *ma- can be seen clearly in the comparison between Ratahan (also known as Toratán, a Sangiric language of North Sulawesi, Himmelmann and Wolff 1999), Naga Bikol, and Tagalog (both Central Philippine), shown in Table 25.8. Note that *ma-* is labelled as a patient potentive in Table 25.8 due to sharing a case frame with the patient voice in CSP languages, as seen above in (48), but it is historically an intransitive actor voice form and can still be considered so in many languages outside the CSP zone.

Ratahan shows the most conservative paradigm, with *ka-* still used in both the conveyance and locative voices. It is innovative in having lost the *i-* in the potentive conveyance voice, but this is a recurring change seen to take place in Mindanao, as well. The *ma-* prefix has spread to the locative in Naga Bikol and additionally to the conveyance voice in Tagalog.[14]

**Table 25.8** Potentive paradigms for three Philippine-type languages

| | Ratahan | Naga Bikol | Tagalog |
|---|---|---|---|
| Actor voice | *maka-* | *maka-* | *maka-* |
| Patient voice | ***ma-*** | ***ma-*** | ***ma-*** |
| Locative voice | *ka- -an* | ***ma-*** *-an* | ***ma-*** *-an* |
| Conveyance voice | *ka-* | *i-ka-* | ***ma****-i-* |

The other oddity of the potentive paradigm is the actor voice counterpart to *ma-*, namely, *maka-*, which is derived from the combination of PMP *<um> with the PMP causative *pa- and the stative *ka-. The original opposition between today's patient and actor voice potentive was thus not one of voice but one of causation.

### 25.3.3.2 *Distributive*

Many CSP languages express a distributive or pluractional meaning with a reflex of the PMP prefix *paŋ- and its actor voice counterpart *maŋ-. For certain predicates, this is obligatory. For instance, the act of fishing, by its nature, involves repeated action and does not have a single fish as its target. The use of the pluractional has thus become obligatory for forming the predicate 'to fish' in several CSP languages, including Tagalog. For other predicates, such as Tagalog *kuha* 'take', shown in (44), it is optional and adds a meaning ranging from repeated action, action on plural generic objects, and unwanted persistence (De Guzman 1978).

(44) a. *k<um>u:ha* b. *maŋ-[k]u:ha*
<AV>take AV.DISTR-take
'to take' 'to take (many)'

Although the distributive most often occurs in the actor voice form with a cognate of *maŋ-, it is not restricted to the actor voice. As exemplified by Tagalog (45) and Sarangani Manobo (46), the distributive can co-occur with any voice in most CSP languages.

(45) *i:log na la:bis na p<in>aŋ-isdaʔ-an*
river LNK overly LNK <BEG>DISTR-fish-LV
'an over-fished river'

[14] The replacement of *ka-* with *ma-* in the locative and conveyance voices appears to have been a gradual and messy process in the Central Philippine languages. In many languages, including Tagalog, the conservative *ka- -an* and *i-ka-* coexist alongside the innovative *ma- -an* and *ma-i-* but are used with innovative meanings or with a limited set of roots.

Sarangani Manobo
(46) *i-m-pem-[b]egay=dan* *se* *libro*
CV-PFV-DISTR-give=3PL.GEN NOM book
'They gave out books.' (Dubois 1976: 76)

South of the Philippines, the distributive takes on new functions, such as that of a dedicated anti-passive in certain South Sulawesi languages (Kaufman 2017), as well as the default marker of actor voice, as in Malayic languages.

### 25.3.3.3 *Sociative*

A morphological category found most commonly among Philippine languages is the so-called 'sociative', expressed with a reflex of PMP *paki- or its actor voice counterpart, *maki-. In most cases, this morpheme can be translated into English as 'with others', as in Tagalog (47), although this often does not capture the relation between the agent and the others.

(47) a. *maki-hiŋiʔ*
AV.SOC-request
'to request'
b. *maki-ta:wa*
AV.SOC-laugh
'to laugh with others'
c. *maki-upoʔ*
AV.SOC-sit
'to sit with others'

The sociative often connotes copying the action of others for social purposes, a meaning which is more salient for certain predicates, such as (47b). The predicate *makita:wa* denotes laughing along because other people are laughing whereas the predicate *makiupoʔ* is simply to sit among others. The sociative need not denote a social activity in a positive sense. For instance, 'to fight' is often expressed with the sociative in CSP languages: Tagalog *maki-pag-a:way* (AV.SOC-TR-fight), Cebuano *makig-a:way* (AV.SOC-fight). The difference between the sociative mode vs. the unmarked mode in such cases is subtle but the sociative appears to foreground an aspect of social exchange, even with predicates like 'fight'.[15]

### 25.3.3.4 *Plural agent marking*

It appears possible to reconstruct a PMP marker *si- which necessitated a plural subject (reconstructed by Kitada 2021 as a sociative and by Liao 2011b as simultaneous aspect). In Central Philippine languages, we find a reflex in such forms as Tagalog *mag-si-takbo* (AV-PL-run), where it serves to mark plurality. In the Bisayan languages, a reflex of this prefix indicates individuated action over a group, translated with 'each (subject)' (Zorc 1977: 143).

Although it is rare for CSP languages to show obligatory number agreement with any argument, plural marking can be indicated simultaneously by several morphemes for emphasis, as in Tagalog (48), where the matrix clause predicate takes both the *si-* prefix as well as the *<aŋ>* infix, both independently indicating agent plurality. The subordinate verb again takes the plural marker *si-*, in addition to the pluractional marker *paŋ-*.

(48) *n<aŋ>ag-si-handa=ŋ* *mag-si-pam-[b]aril*
AV.BEG<PL>-PL-prepare=LNK AV.BEG-PL-DISTR-shoot
'they prepared to go shooting' (Venago 1929: 62)

Similarly, in Agutaynen (49), we find that the distributive *maŋ- prefix has been reinterpreted as a plural agent prefix, which can co-occur with another plural marker *<Vr>*, commonly found in nearby Central Philippine languages, and the locative voice *-an* suffix used in its reciprocal function.

Agutaynen
(49) *mam-[p]ag-s<or>oay-an*
AV.PL-TR-<PL>fight-LV
'They will fight each other.' (Quakenbush et al. 2010: 43)

Plural marking is often not uniform across word classes. In Tagalog, Agutaynen, and elsewhere, adjectives with the uninflectable *ma-* prefix indicate plurality via CV-reduplication (without vowel length), for example, Tagalog *ma-tabaʔ* (ADJ-fat), *ma-ta~tabaʔ* (ADJ-PL-fat). In Maranao, plurality on adjectives is marked with the *<aŋ>* infix, and in Cebuano, the *<g>* infix carries out the same function on dimension adjectives, for example, *mu<g>boʔ* (<PL>short), *da<g>koʔ* (<PL>large).

### 25.3.3.5 *Multifunctional* *paR-/*maR-

Reflexes of *paR- (*maR-, in the actor voice) can be found in almost all CSP languages although the range of functions associated with these morphemes differs from language to language. As Pittman (1966) first noted, Tagalog *mag-* has apparently contradictory functions, in some cases increasing valency, for example, *<um>akyat* 'to ascend' vs. *mag-akyat* 'to bring something up', and in other cases, for example, *<um>ahit* 'to shave others' vs. *mag-ahit* 'to shave one's self', decreasing valency. Kaufman (2018) derives the apparently contradictory functions of this affix by viewing it as a historically complex combination of two components: the well attested causative prefix *pa- and a middle voice prefix *R-, which fused with the former. With some roots and paradigms, it is the causative *pa-* function which is meaningful while in other cases it is the middle voice whose interpretation prevails. The middle function of *R- is also implicated in the durative, reciprocal, and reflexive

[15] It appears that the imperative of the sociative, *paki-, has developed in another direction, now signalling a polite request in a number of Philippine languages. Liao (2011b) argues that there need not be a derivational relationship between *paki- and *maki- although the pragmatic link between the sociative function and polite requests is unlikely to be accidental.

functions found with the *paR-/*maR- prefix. A typically mixed paradigm showing both the putative middle function and causative function of *paR- is found in Palawano (Zorc 1971b), shown in Table 25.9. Here, a reflex of *maR- is found in the progressive of both intransitive and transitive actor voice paradigms but in other aspects it signals transitivity. Progressive aspect is often associated with decreased transitivity (Hopper and Thompson 1980) and thus appears to derive from middle voice *R-. On the other hand, causative *pa- is clearly responsible for the increased transitivity of the forms in the right hand column.

**Table 25.9** Partial Palawano actor voice paradigm (Zorc 1971b: 70, with PMP etymologies added)

| | Intransitive AV | Transitive AV |
|---|---|---|
| Progressive | *məg$C_1$ə-* | *məg$C_1$ə-* |
| | (*p<um>a-R-REDP~) | (*p<um>a-R-REDP~) |
| Perfective | <*umin*> (*<um><in>) | *nəg-* (*p<um><in>a-R-) |
| | <*um*> (*<um>) | *məg-* (*p<um>a-R-) |
| Habitual | | |
| Participle | *pəg-* (*pa-R-) | *pəg-* (*pa-R-) |

In many CSP languages south of Tagalog, the 'plain' actor voice *<um> paradigm increasingly gives way to a *maR- paradigm, as discussed by Liao (2004: 106) and Lobel (2004, 2013a: 46–7). This prefix also appears to have been borrowed in several areas in the Philippines as the reflex of *R often does not match regular sound correspondences (Liao 2004: 107–12; Reid and Liao 2004: 457).

### 25.3.3.6 *Reciprocals and reflexives*

There are two recurring strategies for forming reciprocals in CSP languages. The first, shown in Tagalog (50a), involves an apparent circumfix formally consisting of the actor voice prefix together with the locative nominalizer/voice suffix, that is, *maR-√-an, a formation which is also found in Malay (e.g. *bər-təŋkar-an* AV-fight-RECP). The second, exemplified by Samar-Leyte (50b), involves the *maR- prefix together with the *ka- prefix, one of whose functions is similar to English *co-*, deriving a partner in sharing something denoted by the stem. This later formation may only happen to overlap semantically with the reciprocal proper in (50a), as it more often refers specifically to two agents sharing in an activity.

(50) a. Tagalog
*nag-patay-an=sila*
AV-kill-RECP=3PL.NOM
'They killed each other.'

b. Samarenyo (Waray)
*nag-ka-du:rug=hira*
AV-co-sleep=3PL.NOM
'They slept together.' (Zorc 1977: 144)

In some cases, the *maR- prefix appears to express a reciprocal on its own, as in Tagalog *mag-kitaʔ* AV-see 'to meet'. There are other reciprocal markers whose etymologies are not so clear. For instance, Tboli marks reciprocals with an *s-* prefix (likely derived from PMP *si- discussed above), for example, *tagak* 'to leave behind', *s-tagak* 'to leave each other'; *toboŋ* 'to help', *s-toboŋ* 'to help each other' (Forsberg 1992: 91). In Western Bukidnon Manobo, as well as several Bisayan languages, the reciprocal is expressed with a circumfix whose first part is the <*in*> infix and the latter part is *-aʔ* or *-ay* (with *-ay* also appearing in the Bisayan languages), as seen in (51). Although both components of this circumfix occur in other derivations, they do not seem to be semantically related.

Western Bukidnon Manobo
(51) *m<i>g-b<in>ulig-aʔ*
<PFV>AV.DUR-<RECP$_1$>help-RECP$_2$
'They helped each other.' (Post and Gardner 1992: xxiv)

Reflexives are also commonly expressed with a descendant of *maR- and stative reflexives are expressed with a reflex of PMP *maR-pa-ka- 'AV.TR-CAUS-STAT-' in certain CSP languages among other areas (Blust 2003b). Tagalog (52) exemplifies a remnant of this construction although it is not entirely productive as a reflexive.

(52) a. *mag-pa-ka-bu:lag*
AV.TR-CAUS-STAT-blind
'make oneself blind'

b. *mag-pa-ka-matay*
AV.TR-CAUS-STAT-die
'kill oneself'

c. *mag-pa-ka-ta:ʔo*
AV.TR-CAUS-STAT-person
'be humane' ('make self a person')

### 25.3.3.7 *Inchoative*

The inchoative, termed by Zorc (1977: 142) "essive", has barely been investigated from a comparative perspective. In many languages, it is signalled with a unique prefix, as shown in (53).

Aklanon

(53) a. *nagiŋ-rayna* *si=neli*
AV.PFV.INCH-queen NOM=Neli
'Nellie became a queen.' (Zorc 1977: 142)

Teduray

b. *mente-eteu*
AV.INCH-person
'to become a person' (Bennásar 1892: 40)

The inchoative form also allows for non-actor voice derivations. These were still current in the Tagalog of the early twentieth century, as seen in (54), but are now obsolete.

(54) *aŋ=maynila* *aŋ=p<in>agin-pari:ʔ-an=niya*
NOM=Manila NOM=<BEG>INCH-priest-LV=3SG.GEN
'It was in Manila where he was ordained a priest.' (Lendoyro 1909: 256)

Maranao uses a periphrastic construction, as in (55a), or a simple reflex of *maR-, as in (55b), to express change of state.

Maranao

(55) a. *mim-baloy* *a* *ator*
AV.DISTR-change LNK stone
'changed into a rock'

b. *m<iy>ag-ator*
AV<PFV>-rock
'became a rock'

### 25.3.4 Causative

The PAN causative prefix *pa- is perhaps the most stable affix in the entire PMP morphological inventory and is found in some form in all the CSP languages. The causative introduces a causer into the argument structure and can co-occur with any voice, mode, and aspect. Abstracting away from various complications, Table 25.10 shows the canonical mapping of roles to arguments in a causative clause.

**Table 25.10** Canonical role/case correspondences in the causative

| | GEN | NOM | OBL |
|---|---|---|---|
| Actor voice | theme | causer | causee |
| Patient voice | causer | causee | theme |
| Conveyance voice | causer | theme | causee |

In an actor voice causative clause, as in (56), the nominative argument is the causer while the theme is expressed just as an actor voice object would be expressed. The causee, on the other hand, is expressed as an oblique argument.

(56) *nag-pa-su:lat=ako* *naŋ=li:ham*
AV.BEG-CAUS-write=1SG.NOM GEN=letter
*sa=estudya:nte*
OBL=student
'I had a student write a letter.'

In a patient voice causative clause, as in (57), it is always the causee that is selected as the nominative argument rather than the theme. The agent is assigned genitive case, as expected, and the theme, if expressed, is assigned genitive or objective case.

(57) *p<in>a-su:lat-Ø=ko* *naŋ=li:ham*
<BEG>CAUS-write-PV=1SG.GEN GEN=letter
*aŋ=estudyante*
NOM=student
'I had the student write a letter.'

The conveyance voice consistently selects causative themes as the nominative argument, regardless of what voice is used to 'promote' the notional object to nominative in a non-causative clause. The example in (58) shows how the causer is expressed as a genitive agent, as in the other non-actor voices, the causee is expressed as an oblique, and the theme or 'notional object' becomes the nominative argument.

(58) *i-p<in>a-su:lat=ko* *sa=estudya:nte*
CV-<BEG>CAUS-write=1SG.GEN OBL=student
*aŋ=li:ham*
NOM=letter
'I had the student write the letter.'

### 25.3.5 Negation

CSP languages are relatively rich in negators; distinct functional negators exist for perfective events, prospective events, prohibitives (imperatives), identification, and existential predication. Few if any languages possess five distinct negators for each of these functions, but many languages show three- and four-way distinctions. The negation inventories of five CSP languages are shown in Table 25.11.

What is termed here 'event' vs. 'identification' negation is often framed in terms of lexical categories (e.g. verbal, nominal, and adjectival negation). Non-verbal negation can often be traced to a word meaning 'different'. For instance, Blust and Trussel (2020) reconstruct both PWMP *beken 'negator

**Table 25.11** Negation in CSP languages

| | Tagalog | Aklanon | N. Subanen | Maranao | Tboli |
|---|---|---|---|---|---|
| Perfective event | *hindiʔ* | *ʔuwaʔ* | *ʔəndaʔ* | *diʔ* | *laʔ* |
| Prospective event | *hindiʔ* | *ʔindiʔ* | *ʔəndiʔ* | *diʔ* | *laʔ* |
| Prohibitive | *huwag* | *ʔayaw* | *ʔəndiʔ* | *diʔ* | *béʔ* |
| Identification | *hindiʔ* | *bukon* | *gənnaʔ* | *kenaʔ* | *sundu* |
| Existential | *walaʔ* | *ʔuwaʔ* | *ʔəndaidun* | *daraʔ* | *(laʔ wən)* |

of nominals, other, different' as well as PWMP *laqin 'different', which also comes to function as a general negative marker in Central Sorsogon.

The distinction between perfective and prospective negation is uncommon, occurring mostly in Bisayan languages that employ the negative existential in perfective event-denoting contexts.

It is a common feature of Malayo-Polynesian languages outside the Philippines to combine the event negator with the existential to derive a negative existential (e.g. Malay *tidak ada* NEG EXIST and *ti-ada* NEG-EXIST), but most Philippine languages employ distinct unanalysable roots for the existential and negative existential. As seen in Table 25.11, Tboli employs an analytic combination, as commonly found further south. There is a degree of fluidity between these functions, as shown by McFarland (1974: 254–6). Nonetheless, there are several generalizations that can be made:

i. If a language has distinct negation for perfective events, it will be the same as the negative existential. (Subanen *ʔəndaidun*, above, exceptionally adds the formant *idun* in the negative existential.)
ii. If a language does not have a distinct prohibitive, this function will be carried out by the same form employed in the prospective.
iii. If a language does not have a distinct identification/non-verbal negator, this function will be carried out by the eventive/verbal negator.
iv. If a language does not have a distinct negative existential marker, this function will be carried out by the eventive negation in combination with the (positive) existential.

In a large number of CSP languages, certain negative contexts require the dependent verbal paradigm, as discussed by Wolff (1973) and Zorc (1977).

## 25.4 Elements of syntax

In this section, I present the basic word order across various phrase types (§25.4.1), and then take a closer look at word order within the noun phrase (§25.4.2) and the clause (§25.4.3). Finally, I look at the syntax of referential expressions: pronouns, demonstratives, case markers, and the positioning of pronominal clitics (§25.4.4).

### 25.4.1 Basic word order relations

All the CSP languages are robustly head initial, as can be seen in the basic ordering relations exemplified by Tagalog in (59).

(59) a. **Pred > Subj**
*matali:no* *si=bo:boy*
smart NOM=Boboy
'Boboy is smart'

b. **Noun > Possessor**
*aŋ=na:nay* *ni=keŋkoy*
NOM=mother GEN=Kengkoy
'Kengkoy's mother'

c. **Adj > Noun**
*mataŋkad* *na* *baba:ʔe*
tall LNK woman
'tall woman'

d. **Verb > Adv**
*t<um>akbo* *naŋ=mabilis*
<AV>run GEN=fast
'to run fast'

e. **Adposition > Noun**
*ga:liŋ* *sa=gu:bat*
from OBL=jungle
'from the jungle'

f. **Title > Name**
*ginoʔo=ŋ* *reyes*
mister=LNK Reyes
'Mister Reyes'

g. **Complementizer > Clause**
*aka:laʔ ni=dodoŋ na matali:no=siya*
thought GEN=Dodong COMP smart=3SG.NOM
'Dodong thinks he's smart.'

h. **Noun > Relative Clause**
*daga=ŋ p<in>atay-Ø ni=kengkoy*
rat=LNK <BEG>kill-PV GEN=Kengkoy
'a rat killed by Kengkoy'

i. **Aux > Verb**
*da:pat mag-madali:=ka=na!*
must AV.TR-hurry=2SG.NOM=already
'You should hurry up!'

j. **Comparative > Adjective > Standard**
*lalo=ŋ mataŋkad sa= kanya*
more=LNK tall OBL=3SG.OBL
'taller than him/her'

k. **Negation > Verb**
*hindiʔ s<um>ayaw*
NEG <AV.BEG>dance
'didn't dance'

However, not all these relations are equal. Some, such as (e), (f), (g), (i), (j), and (k) are relatively strict or invariable. Others, such as (a), (b), and (d), allow for alternatives but with different semantic or pragmatic implications. A third category, which includes (c) and (h), represent tendencies but co-exist with equally unmarked alternative orders. We examine these in the following subsections.

## 25.4.2 Word order within the noun phrase

The vast majority of CSP languages are both head and dependent marking and possess a set of case marking determiners. While the order of case markers in relation to the noun phrase is strict, the order of certain modifiers within the noun phrase can be relatively flexible. The canonical order of elements in the Tagalog noun phrase is shown in (60). The elements in square brackets do not co-occur but rather represent two options for expressing possessors.

(60) **CASE PRE-POSS NUM ADJ**
*aŋ [kanya=ŋ] maŋa ma-ga~ganda=ŋ*
NOM 3SG.OBL=LNK PL ADJ-PL~beauty=LNK
**ADJ N POST-POSS**
*pula=ŋ bulaklak [niya]*
red=LNK flower 3SG.GEN
'his/her beautiful red flowers'

The case marker is in absolute initial position, as is the rule in Philippine languages, and this is followed by the position of the preposed possessor. The more common position for possessors is after the possessum, as shown on the right edge of the sequence although in rare cases (e.g. Hanunoo (Epo 2014)), the preposed position appears to have become the norm. The preposed position only hosts pronominals in modern Tagalog although in earlier Tagalog, we find full NP possessors in this position, too, although stylistically marked. When possessors are preposed, they are always in the oblique case and never in the 'pure' (typically *n-* initial) genitive case in CSP languages. Furthermore, they are typically connected to the following material in the phrase by the linker, as shown for Central Tagbanwa in (61a) (Scebold 2003: 60), Tagalog in (61b), and Naga Bikol in (61c).

(61) Central Tagbanwa
a. *kanimi a bavoy*
2PL.OBL LNK pig
'your (pl.) pig'

Tagalog
b. *inyo=ŋ ba:boy*
2PL.OBL=LNK pig
'your (pl.) pig'

Naga Bikol
c. *sa=indo=ŋ urig*
OBL=2PL.OBL=LNK pig
'your (pl.) pig'

In some languages, preposed oblique possessors have been described as inherently focused, as in Matigsalug Manobo (62). A better description for Tagalog would be that they are *focusable*, as opposed to the unfocusable enclitic pronominals.

(62) Matigsalug Manobo
a. *ka anak=ku*
NOM child=1SG.GEN
'my child'

b. *ka keddì ne anak*
NOM 1SG.OBL LNK child
'my child (not his)'
(Wang et al. 2006: 41)

Following this position we find the ubiquitous plural marker.[16] It is only the position of the case marker and the plural marker which are in a truly fixed position preceding the head noun. Following the plural marker, the canonical order of elements is adjective followed by noun, but this is variable in most CSP languages. In Tboli, where order appears to be more rigid, some adjectives must precede the noun, for example, *tehe kimu* (former property), *dumu lan* (other path) (Forsberg 1992: 39) but most follow the noun, for example, *lan mahil* (path easy), *koyu lembaŋ* (tree large). For at least some adjectives, the position with regard to the noun is variable. As discussed by Donohue (2007: 359–63), a rigid Noun–Adjective order emerges south of the CSP area and is common to languages of the Southeast Asian mainland. There is a marked difference between Central Philippine languages and those of the southern periphery in

[16] Zorc (1977: 103) claims that the plural marker (or "diversity marker") *maŋa* is found in all the Bisayan languages. Blust and Trussel (2020) reconstruct PMP *maŋa as a prenominal plural marker. See Lynch et al. (2002: 90–1) for its history in Oceanic and Wu (2017) for a general look at plural markers in Austronesian, including the distribution of *maŋa.

this regard, where the Bilic and Sama-Bajaw groups pattern similarly to languages of Indonesia.[17]

Demonstratives were left out of the template in (66) above because they are somewhat more difficult to generalize over in the CSP languages. Case is often marked syncretically on demonstratives (e.g. Tagalog *ito* 'this (neutral)', *nito* 'this (GEN)', *di:to* 'this/here (OBL)'). In Tagalog, a prenominal demonstrative takes the place of the case marker and is connected to the following material via the linker. It can also occur on the right edge of the noun phrase and here the argument is preceded by the expected case marker. Demonstratives can also sandwich the noun phrase for emphasis, as in (63).

(63) *ito=ŋ* *malaki=ŋ a:so=ŋ* *ito*
this=LNK big=LNK dog=LNK this
'this big dog'

In Northern Subanen (Daguman 2004: 148), demonstratives are described as occurring only on the right edge of the noun phrase, but followed by relative clauses, as in (64).

Northern Subanen
(64) *s<in>aak-an su d-libun kətu nə*
<RLS>ask-LV NOM ART-woman that LNK
*mig-bələdyaʔ ice cream*
AV.RLS-sell ice cream
'... he asked that lady who was selling ice-cream.'
(Daguman 2004: 159)

Obligatory classifiers are very rare in the CSP zone although they seem to exist in certain languages on the southern periphery. Daguman (2004: 87) describes both sortal (e.g. *buuk* 'non-flat', *laad* 'flat', *tawan* 'human') and mensural (e.g. *dipa* 'arm span', *daŋaw* 'hand span') classifiers in Northern Subanen. These follow numeral modifiers and precede adjectives in the pre-head domain, as shown in (65).

Northern Subanen
(65) *... k=sala buuk g=əm-bagəl nə d=liun...*
ART=one CLF:non.flat ART=ADJ-big LNK ART=lion
'one big lion' (Daguman 2004: 158)

The linker, which signals all types of modification, is common to the vast majority of Philippine languages but far rarer south of the CSP zone, even among Philippine-type languages and those of Blust's (2019b) Philippine subgroup. The presence of the linker correlates with freer word order within the noun phrase. For instance, languages with linkers can typically place a relative clause before or after the phrase being modified. As the linker disappears towards the southern range of the CSP area, the order within the noun phrase becomes more rigid. The Bilic and Sama-Bajaw languages again pattern with their southern neighbours in lacking the linker and word order flexibility within the noun phrase (including the position of relative clauses in relation to their head noun).

### 25.4.3 Word order within the clause

As with all conservative MP languages, the CSP languages are almost without exception predicate initial across lexical category and clause type. Beyond the simple predicate-initial generalization, the question of the basic order of phrases within the clause has never been answered definitively. Furthermore, as Himmelmann (2005a: 143) notes, there have been unwarranted claims of total freedom of phrasal order in the post-predicate domain. Nearly all CSP languages show the basic order shown in (66) for undergoer voice (i.e. non-actor voice) clauses and actor voice clauses.

(66) a. Undergoer voices b. Actor voice
$V\ A_{GEN}\ P_{NOM}$ $V\ (P_{OBL/GEN})\ A_{NOM}\ (P_{OBL/GEN})$

In the undergoer voices, there is a very strong tendency for the genitive marked agent to immediately follow the predicate head. In languages with impoverished case marking, this tendency becomes a rule. In the actor voice, the ordering relations appear to be less fixed although, if there is an unmarked order, it tends to be one in which the nominative argument follows the patient.

The preverbal domain is typically reserved for pragmatically marked arguments and adjuncts (see Naylor 1975; Kroeger 1993a; Kaufman 2005; Nagaya 2007 for Tagalog). All languages discussed here allow for topicalization of the nominative/absolutive argument to a preverbal position (Reid and Liao 2004: 447). Typically, the fronted topic is followed by a dedicated topic marker, but in languages like Cebuano, there is topic fronting without a topic marker. In the unique case of Iraya, a language of northern Mindoro, most pronominal arguments must appear clause-initially, as exemplified in (67).

[17] Even languages of northern Sulawesi belonging to Blust's Philippine subgroup appear to show Donohue's (2007) southern pattern, for example, Buol *botu moitomo* stone black (Zobel 2005: 633). On the Bornean side, Kroeger (2005a: 411) describes the Kimaragang order of elements within the NP as: Determiner (Number) N (Possessor) (Modifier). It is only the unmarked position of the modifier that has shifted to the right edge when compared with the Central Philippine languages.

Iraya
(67) a. *Nay* *ʔinəm-en* *ʔag* *sapaʔ* *ŋuna*
1SG.GEN drink-PV DEF water now
'I'm drinking the water now.'
b. *kawu* *nay* *malyag.*
2SG.NOM 1SG.GEN like
'I like you.' (Reid 2017: 27, 34; cf. Or 2020)

Zorc (1974b) and Lobel (2013a: 188–93) also describe the shift to a pure actor voice, SVO syntax in main clauses in the Buhid language of southern Mindoro.

Oblique phrases, prepositional phrases, and adjuncts can be topicalized in all the languages surveyed here. Genitive arguments and certain types of adjuncts cannot be topicalized so easily. The least extractable phrase is generally the actor voice object, which must occur post-verbally, as shown in (68). This restriction extends to relativization and cleft-like constructions in addition to topicalization. The constraint holds in much the same way across all CSP languages.

(68) a. *aŋ=ba:taʔ* *ay* *k<um>a:ʔin* *naŋ=maŋga*
NOM=child TOP <AV.BEG>eat GEN=mango
'The child, ate the mango.'
b. * *naŋ=maŋga* *ay* *k<um>a:ʔin* *aŋ=ba:taʔ*
GEN=mango TOP <AV.BEG>eat NOM=child
(For, 'A mango, the child ate.')

The Central Philippine languages appear to have innovated a special focus position for fronted oblique arguments and adjuncts shown in (69).

(69) $_{\text{Foc}}$[*sa= mayni:la*]*=na=kami* *nag-a:~a:ral*
OBL=Manila=already=1PL.EX.NOM AV.BEG-IPFV~study
'We already study *in Manila.*'

The focus fronted oblique phrase attracts second-position clitics and receives a cleft-like 'exhaustive list' interpretation, that is, 'It's in Manila (and nowhere else) that we study'. This construction is generally uncommon, if attested at all, in languages of the northern Philippines and most likely represents an innovation that took place in some subset of the CSP languages. In several Bisayan languages, focus fronting of an oblique phrase in this manner requires using the dependent paradigm of the verb.

## 25.4.4 Referential expressions

### 25.4.4.1 *Pronouns*

There are almost always distinct pronominal paradigms for the nominative, genitive, and oblique cases. A typical example in this respect can be seen in the Maranao pronouns in Table 25.12 (McKaughan 1958; Kaufman 2010b). As is typical, clusivity is distinguished in the first person plural but relatively few languages have a distinct dual form, as Maranao does.

**Table 25.12** Maranao pronoun paradigm (Kaufman 2010b)

| | NOM (bound) | NOM (free) | GEN (bound) | OBL (free) |
|---|---|---|---|---|
| 1SG | *(a)ko* | *sakən* | *akən ~ ko* | *rakən* |
| 1PL.EXCL | *kami* | *səkami* | *(a)mi* | *rəkami* |
| 1+2 DUAL | *ta* | *səkta* | *ta* | *rəkta* |
| 1PL.INCL | *tano* | *səktano* | *tano* | *rəktano* |
| 2SG | *ka* | *səka* | *(ŋ)ka* | *rəka* |
| 2PL | *kano* | *səkano* | *(n)iyo* | *rəkano* |
| 3SG | *səkaniyan* | *səkaniyan* | *(n)iyan* | *rəkaniyan* |
| 3PL | *siran* | *siran* | *(i)ran* | *kiran* |

### 25.4.4.2 *Demonstratives and deictics*

Demonstratives and deictics in CSP languages typically distinguish three types of proximity: speaker proximate, hearer proximate, and distal. Some languages, such as Matigsalug Manobo, shown in Table 25.13, distinguish four grades of proximity in deixis, although even in this language, the demonstratives only show the canonical three-way distinction. Remarkably, Western Subanon is described as having six grades of proximity as reflected in both deictics and demonstratives (Estioca 2020: 60, 74).

**Table 25.13** Matigsalug Manobo locative pronouns (Wang et al. 2006: 28)

| | |
|---|---|
| *kayi, dini* | here |
| *due* | there (within reach) |
| *dutu* | there (beyond reach but within sight) |
| *diyeʔ* | way over there (nonspecific/out of sight) |

Deictics are in most languages derived transparently from demonstratives with one of the PAN locative/directional markers *sa, *ka, *di (see Ross 2006 and Blust and Trussel 2020 for the reconstruction of these morphemes).

### 25.4.4.3 *Case markers*

Case markers have received ample attention from a historical perspective (Reid 2002a, 2007; Blust 2005d, 2015a;

Ross 2006). I focus here on some salient features of typological interest. In the Central Philippine languages, case is often expressed syncretically with other referential and even temporal features. For instance, Waray employs three types of nominative and genitive case markers for full noun phrases: *ʔin* NOM indefinite, *ʔan* NOM past definite, and *ʔit* NOM non-past definite, with genitive counterparts *hin*, *han*, *hit*, respectively (Zorc 1977: 85). McFarland (1974) discusses similar specific/non-specific distinctions in the Legazpi Bikol case markers shown in (70) and (71). The (a) examples show that indefinite possessors and genitive agents are introduced by *ki* while definite ones are introduced by *kan*.

Legazpi Bikol

(70) a. *aruŋ ki=lala:ki*
house GEN.INDEF=man
'a man's house'

b. *aruŋ kan=lala:ki*
house GEN.DEF=man
'the man's house'
(McFarland 1974: 161)

Legazpi Bikol

(71) a. *pig-bakal ki=lala:ki.*
PV.BEG-buy GEN.INDEF=man
'bought by a man'

b. *pig-bakal kan=lala:ki*
PV.BEG-buy GEN.DEF=man
'bought by the man' (McFarland 1974: 161)

Other varieties of Bikol make a subtle three-way distinction in referentiality, as seen for the Buhi dialect in Table 25.14. From the object marking in the examples in (72), we see that a generic object is marked by *nin*; a definite, but not yet 'realized' object is marked by *nya*; and a definite, identifiable or 'realized' object, is marked by *nyu*. As in Tagalog, the nominative phrase does not lend itself to an indefinite interpretation but still distinguishes what McFarland calls "definite" from "specific" arguments. In (72), because the action has not yet been realized, the subject receives the *a* marker. In (24a) and (24c), because the action has been realized, the subject receives the specific *yu* marker.

**Table 25.14** Buhi Bikol case markers (McFarland 1974: 164)

| | Nominative | Genitive | Oblique |
|---|---|---|---|
| Indefinite | - | *nin* | |
| Definite | *a* | *nya* | *sa* |
| Specific | *yu* | *nyu* | |

Buhi Bikol

(72) a. *aku yu nag-kaʔin nin adu:bu*
1SG.NOM NOM.SPEC AV.PFV-eat GEN.INDEF adobo
'I'm the one who ate adobo.'

b. *aku a magi-kaʔin nya adu:bu*
1SG.NOM NOM.DEF AV.IPFV-eat GEN.DEF adobo
'I'm the one who will eat the adobo.'

c. *aku yu nag-kaʔin nyu adu:bu*
1SG.NOM NOM.SPEC AV.PFV-eat GEN.SPEC adobo
'I'm the one who ate the adobo.'
(McFarland 1974: 165)

In other languages which do not mark definiteness or specificity explicitly via case marking, the basic referentiality of an argument is largely predictable on the basis of grammatical function. There is some debate about whether these morphemes are inherently case markers or whether they have inherent referentiality related functions.[18]

In Table 25.15, we see case markers for common nouns (all nouns but personal names) in six CSP languages and in Table 25.16 we see their counterparts for personal names. It is immediately clear that Tboli diverges from the others in its reduced case system. All other languages make at least a three-way distinction between nominative case, genitive/ergative case, and an oblique case.

**Table 25.15** Common noun case markers in six CSP languages

| | Tagalog | Aklanon | Subanen | Maranao | Tboli |
|---|---|---|---|---|---|
| NOM/ABS | *aŋ* | *ro* | *su* | *so* | Ø |
| GEN/ERG | *naŋ* | *it* (indef) *ku* (def) | *nə* *nu* (anaphoric) | *o* | Ø |
| OBL | *sa* | *sa* | *sə* (local) *nə* (non-local) | *sa* (indef) *ko* (def) | *beʔ* |

[18] Himmelmann (2016) and Reid and Liao (2004: 466) treat the Tagalog phrase marker *aŋ*, glossed NOMINATIVE here, as a definiteness marker of sorts without any inherent case features. Collins (2018), on the other hand, treats the same morpheme as a case marker without any inherent semantics at all. The fact that NP fragments with the nominative case marker always receive a referential interpretation (e.g. *dagaʔ!* 'a rat!' vs. *aŋ dagaʔ!* 'the rat!') favours an analysis in which the case markers at least have some semantic features.

**Table 25.16** Personal case markers in six CSP languages

| | Tagalog | Aklanon | Subanen | Maranao | Tboli |
|---|---|---|---|---|---|
| NOM/ABS | *si* | *si* | *si* | *si* | Ø |
| GEN/ERG | *ni* | *ni* | *ni* | *i* | Ø |
| OBL | *kay* | *kay* | *ni* | *ki* | Ø |

On the southern periphery of the CSP zone, as well as in Mindoro (Zorc 1974b: 577), word order becomes increasingly important in indicating grammatical relations. The example in (73) shows how actor voice objects and obliques may remain completely unmarked despite the existence of case markers in the language.

Cotabato Manobo
(73) *h<um>ated=a* *sagiŋ* *kaut* *ta*
<AV>take=1SG.NOM banana kaut DET
'I will take some bananas to Kaut.' (Kerr 1988: 13)

In Tboli, case is only distinguished on pronouns and the order of arguments in multi-argument clauses such as (74) is thus rigid.

Tboli
(74) *Ø-oguh-en* *tum* *libun* *tum* *kun*
CV-hand.to-3SG.GEN that girl that 3SG.OBL
*namak*
betel.nut.quid
'He hands his own quid of betel nut to the girl.'
(Forsberg 1992: 78)

While the rich case marking system of Bikol languages shows that subtle referentiality distinctions can be made in the markers themselves, the basic definiteness distinction typical to Philippine type voice systems remains even in languages that have lost their case markers.

We can make the following generalizations about case marking in CSP languages:

i. There is a common three-way case system involving NOMINATIVE/ABSOLUTIVE, GENITIVE/ERGATIVE, and OBLIQUE cases.
ii. The OBLIQUE case is employed for a wide range of directional/locative functions, as well as for marking definite objects of actor voice clauses, when this is allowed.
iii. The case of non-actor voice agents is always the same as that of possessors, hence labelled GENITIVE/ERGATIVE.
iv. Common noun phrases and personal names have distinct but morphologically related case markers.
v. Case marking is typically obligatory on all arguments.
vi. Case marking persists in accordance with the following hierarchy: pronouns > personal names > common nouns, such that it is lost first on common nouns and last on pronouns.

#### 25.4.4.4 *The positioning of clitics*

All Philippine languages possess clitics whose positioning differs from full phrases. Pronominal and adverbial clitics are typically second position (aka Wackernagel) clitics following the first word and occasionally the first phrase within a clause-like syntactic domain (Kaufman 2010a). In languages such as Maranao and Tagalog, pronominal arguments are in complementary distribution with full phrasal arguments, as seen in (75). When a potential clitic host precedes the predicate (in this case the progressive marker *diʔi*), a bound pronoun must typically attach to it, as shown in (76a), but this position is not available for full noun phrases, as shown in (75b).

Maranao
(75) a. *diʔi[=ako]* *ma-matiya[*=ako]* *sa* *kitab*
PROG=1SG.NOM AV-read=1SG.NOM OBL book
'I'm reading a book.'

b. *diʔi* *[*so* *wataʔ]* *ma-matiya* *[so* *wataʔ]*
PROG NOM child AV-read NOM child
*sa* *kitab.*
OBL book
'The child is reading a book.' (Kaufman 2010b: 136)

In languages of this type, free pronouns are only used in predicate position, as independent fragments or as fronted topics. In other Central Philippine languages, such as Cebuano, long forms of the genitive and nominative pronouns show more syntactic freedom (Wolff 1966).

There are many co-occurrence constraints on pronominal clitics in the CSP languages with a fascinating variety of repair mechanisms and ordering patterns which cannot be discussed fully here (see Kaufman 2010a and references therein). The relative ordering of clitics is determined by up to three factors: prosody (shorter precedes longer), case (genitive precedes nominative), and person (first person precedes second person precedes third person). Different constraints are active in different languages, but if a particular domain is active, it will always follow the above scales.

Clitic doubling, which is found occasionally in the northern Philippines, is rare in the CSP zone. Tboli, however, does show clitic doubling with certain preverbal elements, as seen in (76), where the second position clitic *le* doubles the nominative argument *kem dumu*.

Tboli
(76) *deŋ=le* *ma* *koyu* *kem* *dumu*
already=3PL.NOM AV.fetch wood PL companion
'The others already fetched some wood.'
(Forsberg 1992: 63)

## 25.5 Complex constructions

### 25.5.1 Finite complement clauses

All CSP languages allow for finite clause complements, as in (77). The embedded clause is generally introduced with the linker and has all the hallmarks of a main clause predicate.

(77) *s<in>a:bi-Ø=ko* *sa=iyo* *na*
<BEG>say-PV=1SG.GEN OBL=2SG LNK
*ga:~gaw-in=niya* *bu:kas.*
IPFV~do-PV=3SG.GEN tomorrow
'I told you that s/he will do (it) tomorrow.'

### 25.5.2 Questions and interrogative complements

When the interrogative phrase is a noun phrase, a cleft-like construction is required where the interrogative is in the predicate position and the remainder of the clause is embedded in a nominative phrase, as shown in (78).

(78) *ano* *aŋ=s<in>a:bi-Ø=niya?*
what NOM=<BEG>say-PV=3SG.GEN
'What did s/he say?'

Interrogative complements are used in subordinate clauses as complements to matrix predicates of cognition as well as subjunctive type complements. These complements are typically identical to questions except that the interrogative phrase is introduced by a conditional marker, as in (79)–(81).

Central Tagbanwa
(79) *pog-tuʔma* *iŋ* *kali=ka* *nag-giʔit.*
IPFV.AV-ask HYP where=2SG.NOM PFV.AV-depart
'He is asking where you came from.' (Scebold 2003: 73)

Matigsalug Manobo
(80) *su mig-inse=sikandan* *ke hendei=key*
so AV.PFV-ask=3PL.NOM if where=1PL.EX.NOM
*eg-pa-bulus*
AV.PROG-CAUS-continue
'So they asked where we were going...'
(Wang et al. 2006: 112)

Hanunoo
(81) *sabi-hun=nimu* *sa=kaŋku* *nu* *hayga*
tell-PV=2SG.GEN OBL=1SG.GEN COND why
'Tell me why (it's) that way.' (Epo 2014: 22)

### 25.5.3 Nonfinite complement clauses

Clausal complementation with verbs of wanting, trying, and certain non-verbal predicates are typically non-finite and appear in a neutral form that does not indicate aspect, as shown in (82) and (83).

Cebuano
(82) *kinaháŋlan* *ni=tibúʔ* *ŋa* *táwg-un* *aŋ=páriʔ*
need GEN=Tibo LNK call-PV NOM=priest
'It is necessary for Tibo that a priest be called.'/'Tibo needs to call a priest.'

Agutaynen
(83) *mambeŋ* *aŋ* *mag-pa-layog* *ta* *boradol*
fun LNK AV-CAUS-fly OBL kite
'It's fun to fly a kite.' (Quakenbush et al. 2010: 13)

Note that voice marking is still present in most non-finite subordinate clauses. Other morphosyntactic categories discussed above, including the potentive, causative, reflexive, etc. can also appear in such contexts. In a small number of CSP languages, including Agutaynen, as seen in (84), aspect in the subordinate clause agrees with the matrix predicate in what are typically non-finite contexts for other CSP languages.

Agutaynen
(84) a. *nam-[p]ag-t<ar>abaŋ-an* *tanira=ŋ*
AV.PFV-PL-TR-<PL>help-LV 3PL.NOM=LNK
*naŋ-ayeg*
AV.PFV.DISTR-harvest
'They helped one another to harvest.'

b. *mam-[p]ag-t<ar>abaŋ-an* *tanira=ŋ*
PFV.PL-TR-<PL>help-LV 3PL.NOM=LNK
*maŋ-ayeg*
AV.DISTR-harvest
'They will help one another to harvest.'
(Quakenbush et al. 2010: 20)

A less common type of complementation pattern attested in Central Philippine languages involves treating the subordinate predicate as a case marked complement, as shown in (85)–(86).

(85) *b<in>ilis-an=ko* *aŋ=pag-ka:ʔin*
<BEG>fast-LV=1SG.GEN NOM=GER-eat
'I sped up my eating.'

Cebuano

(86) *nag-si:ge* *ug* *sunod sa* *iya=ŋ*
AV.BEG-continue OBJ follow OBL 3SG.GEN=LNK
*bukog*
bone
'He continues following his bones.'

#### 25.5.3.1 *Control patterns*

Control refers to coreference between an argument in a matrix clause and a missing argument in a non-finite subordinate clause. Most CSP languages pattern as in (87), where an embedded agent co-referring with a matrix argument must be null.

(87) *gusto=ko=ŋ* *tawa:g-an(*=ko)* *si=bo:boy*
want=1SG.GEN=LNK call-LV=1SG.GEN NOM=Boboy
'I want to call Boboy.'

Conversely, the agent of a subordinate non-finite clause must be overt when it does not co-refer with a matrix clause argument, as in (88).

(88) *gusto=ko=ŋ* *tawa:g-an=mo=ako*
want=1SG.GEN=LNK call-LV=2SG.GEN=1SG.NOM
'I want you to call me.'

As has been noted (Cena 1977; Kroeger 1993a; Schachter 1976), the volitionality of the subordinate predicate determines which argument can be controlled, as seen in the minimal pair in (89).

(89) a. *gusto=ko=ŋ* *tawa:g-an*
want=1SG.GEN=LNK call-LV
'I want to call (someone).'
b. *gusto=ko=ŋ* *ma-tawa:g-an*
want=1SG.GEN=LNK STAT-call-LV
'I want to be called.'

This seems to hold true for at least the Central Philippine subgroup although this type of data is generally lacking for other subgroups.

#### 25.5.3.2 *The actor voice restriction*

A more unusual phenomenon whose presence in Philippine languages has not received any notice is found in the Danao languages. For fully biclausal sentences, Maranao and Maguindanao show structures similar to Tagalog and other Central Philippine languages, as seen in Maguindanao (90), where the embedded verb is an infinitive in the locative voice.

Maguindanao

(90) *kalinian=neŋka* *tawag-an=ko=seka?*
want=2SG.GEN call-LV=1SG.GEN=2SG.NOM
'Do you want me to call you?'

However, the Danao languages have a reduced complement clause structure that requires the subordinate verb to appear in the actor voice, as in Maranao (91). Here, the undergoer of 'call' appears to obtain case from the matrix verb and is positioned in the matrix clause.

Maranao

(91) *t<in>ekaw-an=ko=seka* *t<em>awag!*
<PFV>try-LV=1SG.GEN=2SG.NOM <AV>call
'I tried to call you!'

This corresponds to the so-called 'actor voice constraint' discussed by Aldridge (2004) and Chang (2017) for Formosan languages and Kroeger (2014) for Kimaragang, a Dusunic language of Sabah, whereby certain types of subordinate clauses must be in the actor voice.

### 25.5.4 Adjunct clauses

Temporal adjuncts are most often formed via nominalization in CSP languages (Kaufman 2011a). A typical structure is shown in Sarangani Manobo (92), which displays the combination of the gerundive *peg-* with the lack of a nominative case on either of the arguments.

Sarangani Manobo

(92) *peg-dineg* *te* *amay=din* *kenyan*
GER-hear GEN father=3SG.GEN that.OBL
'When his father heard that...' (DuBois 1976: 94)

## 25.6 Conclusion

This chapter has attempted to give a broad overview of the phonology, morphology, and syntax of the CSP languages while focusing on several phenomena of interest that are characteristic of the region. I have also attempted to highlight areas in need of further research. In the phonology, gradient phonotactic generalizations have largely gone unexplored beyond Tagalog and the study of word prosody and intonation is also a rich and relatively untouched area. The CSP languages have played a large role in our understanding of PMP morphosyntax but we still have an incomplete understanding of how the dependent paradigm was deployed as well as various types of subordination. The actor voice constraint has been presented here for the first time as a

Philippine phenomenon, in addition to its presence in Sabah and Formosan languages.

Finally, a note on the general typology of the region. Himmelmann (2005a) defines Philippine-type languages as having symmetric voice in addition to the following three characteristics:

(a) at least two formally and semantically different undergoer voices
(b) at least one non-local phrase marking clitic for nominal expressions
(c) pronominal second position clitics

These features, all of which are understood to be retentions from PMP, have eroded to various extents in the Bilic languages, the Sama-Bajaw languages (Kaufman, this volume, Chapter 26), and several languages of Mindoro, thereby opening a typological rift within the CSP region. Thus, while the core of the CSP region, represented by familiar Central Philippine languages such as Tagalog and Cebuano, is typologically homogeneous, the outliers present fascinating departures from the norm.

Despite progress, there is still much work to be done in the description of CSP languages outside the Central Philippine group. While contact relations have been studied in Mindanao (see references in §25.1.1), no major effort has been made for other areas within the region. The Bilic languages, in addition to the languages of Palawan and Mindoro are in special need of further work with an eye towards contact relations. Blust (1992a), examining the Teduray lexicon, has already shown that the emerging picture is complex and multilayered. As Blust (2019b) presents a new argument for the unity of a Philippine subgroup based on shared lexical innovations, it becomes even more urgent to understand the dual roles of contact and inheritance in the historical formation of Philippine languages.

CHAPTER 26

# Sama-Bajaw languages

DANIEL KAUFMAN

## 26.1 Introduction

The Sama-Bajaw (henceforth SB) languages (Map 26.1) comprise one of the most remarkable subgroups of the Austronesian family. Despite being scattered throughout the Sulu archipelago, coastal areas of Borneo (including Pulau Laut in southern Borneo), Kangean Island (facing Madura), Sulawesi, the Timor area, and the Moluccas, the SB languages clearly display a phylogenetic unity suggesting descent from a single language. Equally remarkable is the fact that speakers of SB languages, to a large extent, maintain a common way of life as sea-nomads, with many present-day sedentary communities having settled down within historical memory.[1] It is very difficult to know the full geographical range of SB communities, even those that have been long established. For instance, Pallesen (1985) mentions several communities of Luzon in the Philippines but there is scant information confirming their existence and no information on their language. The more prominent SB communities are mapped out by Pallesen (1985) and Mead and Lee (2007) provide a comprehensive mapping of SB communities of Sulawesi, but those further east are not well documented.

There exist other sea-nomads speaking non-SB Austronesian languages closer to the Southeast Asian mainland, most notably the Moken of Thailand (Larish 1999; Pittayaporn 2005) the Urak Lawoi' (Hogan 1988, 1999), and Malayic-speaking *orang laut* (sea people) populations around the Malaysian peninsula (Anderbeck 2012), but the majority of sea-nomads in the MPSEA region speak SB languages. This makes for a clear parallel between the Sama-Bajaw and the Roma 'Gypsy' people of Europe who share both a historically nomadic lifestyle and a widely dispersed language family that, despite many layers of contact-induced changes, can be traced to a single ancestral tongue. Given the obvious similarity in nomadic lifestyle, Sama-Bajaw peoples are often referred to as the 'Sea Gypsies' in both the scholarly and popular literature. Endonyms often employ a reflex of Proto-Sama-Bajaw (PSB) *saməh. In areas of Sulu, the term Bajaw has a stronger association with sea nomadism while Sama implies a degree of sedentarism, but Bajaw has become an endonym of more general use among the Indonesian communities regardless of whether they are sedentary or nomadic.

As elsewhere in the Austronesian world, it is not easy to distinguish independent SB languages from dialects of a single language. Pallesen's (1985) careful study of SB subgrouping, suggests the family tree in Figure 26.1, which has been adopted by the Ethnologue (Eberhard et al. 2020) and Glottolog (Hammarström et al. 2020).

The Sama languages of the Philippines are relatively well described, with comprehensive dictionaries existing for Mapun (Hashim, Collins, and Collins 2001), Yakan (Behrens 2002), Proto-Sama-Bajaw (Pallesen and Pallesen 2019) and smaller dictionaries for Sama-Pangutaran (Walton and Walton 1992), Sama Bangingi' (Diment and Gault 1980; Diment 1995), as well as word lists for Abaknon (Jacobson 1999). Descriptive grammars and grammar sketches exist for Southern Sinama (Akamine 1996, 2005), West Coast Bajau (Miller 2007), Sama Bangigi' (Gault 1999), Central Sinama (James 2017), Pangutaran Sama (Walton 1986), Yakan (Brainard and Behrens 2002), and eastern Indonesian varieties (Verheijen 1986), although thorough descriptions of the SB languages of eastern Indonesia are completely lacking. Abaknon (also known as Inabaknon) is an SB outlier within the Philippines. It is the northernmost documented variety, whose speakers have a long history of settlement in the eastern Visayas region. Unlike most other SB communities, the Abaknon have assimilated in lifestyle to their non-SB (Visayan) neighbours and appear to have separated from other SB groups before Islamization (and consequently lack the Arabic loans found in other SB varieties).

The phylogeny and contact-induced developments of the SB languages of Sulu are dissected in exquisite detail by

[1] Notwithstanding the surprising correspondence between language and lifestyle, it should be stressed that modern SB groups represent "a wide range of economic and cultural types," in the words of Sopher (1965: 54). Groups like the Yakan, Jama Mapun, and Abaknon are thoroughly sedentary and have engaged in farming for many generations.

Daniel Kaufman, *Sama-Bajaw languages.* In: *The Oxford Guide to the Malayo-Polynesian Languages of Southeast Asia.* Edited by: Alexander Adelaar and Antoinette Schapper, Oxford University Press. © Daniel Kaufman (2024). DOI: 10.1093/oso/9780198807353.003.0026

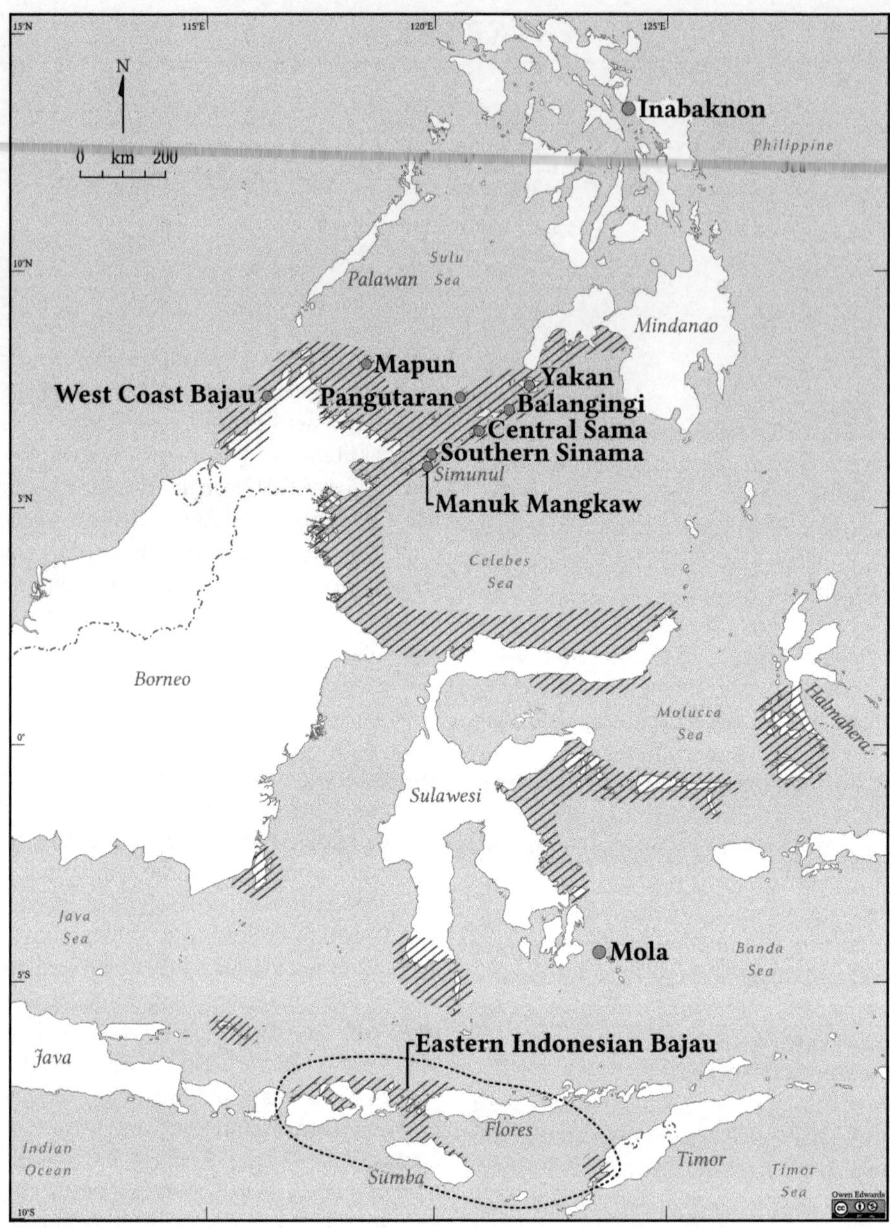


**Map 26.1** The Sama-Bajaw languages.

Pallesen (1985). Pallesen demonstrates how contact led to bidirectional influence between Tausug, a Central Philippine language, and the SB languages of the Sulu archipelago. He furthermore locates the centre of greatest phylogenetic diversity in the Sulu archipelago (specifically, the Sulu-Sibuguey Bay area). As seen in Figure 26.1, he identifies Abaknon as a first order branch of the family followed by Yakan. The place of Abaknon in the family tree may, however, be obscured by its heavy contact with Central Philippine languages and its relative isolation from other SB languages for far longer than any other variety. Blust (2007c: 78), in fact, notes several diagnostic sound changes suggesting Yakan as the first SB language to branch off, rather than Abaknon. On the basis of lexicostatistics, Pallesen proposes that PSB began to diversify in the area of Sulu circa 800CE. He notes, however, on the basis of typology,

Sama-Bajaw
 **Abaknon** [abx]
 **Sulu-Borneo** (7)
  Borneo Coast Bajaw (3)
   *Indonesian Bajau* [bdl]
   (Jampea, Jaya Bakti, Kajoa, Matalaang, Poso, Roti, Same', Sulamu, Togian 1, Togian 2, Wallace)
   *Mapun* [sjm]
   *West Coast Bajau* [bdr] (Banggi, Kawang, Kota Belud, Papar (West Coast Bajau), Pitas Bajau, Putatan, Sandakan Bajau)
  Inner Sulu Sama (3)
   *Balangingi* [sse] (Daongdung, Kabinga'an, Lutangan, Nuclear Balangingi, Sibuco-Vitali)
   *Central Sama* [sml] (Dilaut-Badjao)
   *Southern Sama* [ssb] (Bajau Banaran, Bajau Darat, Bajau Laut, Bajau Semporna, Balimbing, Bongao, Laminusa, Languyan, Obian, Sama, Sapa-Sapa, Sibutu', Sikubung, Simunul, Sitangkai, Tandubas, Ubian)
  Pangutaran Sama [slm]
 **Yakan** [yka]

**Figure 26.1** A Sama-Bajaw family tree (Pallesen 1985).

that SB shows closer connections to the south rather than the Philippines:

> A number of distinctive characteristics (e.g., the *h* reflex of PAN *R, the semantic features of the phrase marking particles or prepositions, the lack of verbal inflection to mark the action-begun vs action-not-begun contrast, a 7-vowel system, a uniquely marked agentive phrase) suggest an Indonesian origin rather than any close relationship to the Central Philippine languages with which many SB daughter languages are currently in geographical proximity.
> (Pallesen 1985: 245)

In the next major work on the history of the subgroup, Blust (2007c) demonstrates a more specific link between PSB and the Barito languages of southeast Borneo and claims that the speakers of PSB emerged from the Barito river basin at around the same time that the Proto-Malagasy left Borneo for the east African coast. He infers from borrowed maritime vocabulary that the PSB communities were "an originally landbound population drawn out of southeast Borneo by trade contacts with a more maritime people" (Blust 2007c: 103), similar to the Malagasy (Adelaar 1989, 1995a). Blust (2007c: 91–5) sums up all the correspondences between PMP and PSB and presents novel evidence for his argument involving both sound changes and lexical replacements.[2]

In contrast to the high diversity of Sulu, the area with the least internal diversity seems to be Sulawesi and eastern Indonesia. Verheijen (1986), based on informal comprehension tests with the eastern varieties, suggests that they are in a dialect relation to each other. Mead and Lee (2007) tentatively confirm this with a lexical similarity score of around 90% across the varieties of Sulawesi, Moluccas, and the Lesser Sunda Islands.

The remainder of this chapter is organized as follows. I review the salient phonological features of the SB languages in §26.2 and examine questions of lexical category in the better described SB varieties in §26.3 and grammatical relations in §26.4. I turn to SB syntax through a comparative lens in §26.5 and sum up in §26.6 with notes on the role of language contact and suggestions for further research.

## 26.2 Phonology

Pallesen reconstructs PSB with a seven-vowel system: /a, e, o, i, u, ə, ʉ/ although *ʉ and *ə are not contrastive with each other in all positions and their independence is still open to question.[3] Typical vowel systems of Sulu either show a six-vowel system (/a, e, o, i, u, ə/) or a five-vowel system (/a, e, o, i, u/), where *ə has merged with one or more other vowels. Abaknon has reduced the system even further to a three-vowel system (/a, i, u/), as found in many Central Philippine languages.

[2] The following changes, among others, distinguish the SB languages from all their Philippine neighbours: PMP *R > *h*, gemination of onsets following PMP *e, vowel lowering before *ʔ, and final devoicing. Blust (2007c) shows that lexical replacements, such as PMP *qulu 'head' > PSB *takuluk, PMP *qudip 'living; alive' > PSB *belum, betray SB's Bornean origins.

[3] The only attested SB languages to show a full seven-way vowel distinction are Sama Batuan and Sama Pangutaran. Pallesen (1979, 1985: 74) argues that PSB *ə and *ʉ result from "a phonemic split of PAN *ə, probably conditioned by stress."

In the native stratum, SB languages show final devoicing, merger of historic *l and *r, as well as post-schwa gemination. Additionally, pre-tonic vowel neutralization and intervocalic /l/ deletion are commonly found in the SB languages of Sulu. Both of these processes are seen in Yakan (1), where vowels are reduced to [ɛ] in pre-stress (pre-penultimate) positions and a productive rule of intervocalic /l/ deletion operates on the root onset.

Yakan, vowel reduction
(1) /mag-pa-ˈlaboʔ-an/ → [mɛg-pɛːˈboʔan]
AV-CAUS-drop-LOC 'repeatedly drop something'
(Pallesen 1985: 76; Brainard and Behrens 2002: 7)

The native stratum also shows a simpler phonotactic template, only allowing a limited range of consonant sequences (nasal-stop clusters and geminates). Contact with Central Philippine languages has led to more complex phonotactics while contact with languages of Sulawesi has, in some cases, led to further simplification. For instance, the varieties of eastern Indonesia only allow /l, r, s, ŋ, ʔ, h/ as word-final codas, with historical oral stops (both voiced and voiceless) having gone to ʔ in word-final position and word-final nasal stops merging with the velar nasal, as found commonly in Sulawesi.

In almost every SB language, there exists a minor degree of vowel harmony, typically occurring with suffixes that harmonize with their stem. This can be seen in West Coast Bajau /pogos-an/ force-APPL → [pəgoson] where the suffix has assimilated to the final root vowel and the first vowel of the root has been neutralized to [ə] (in pre-tonic position).

No SB language shows the phonemic vowel length distinction in penultimate syllables characteristic of Philippine languages. Rather, most SB languages have been described as having a right-aligned trochaic stress pattern. Some varieties, such as Pangutaran Sama, have been further described as having iterative secondary stress preceding the primary stress on the penultimate syllable (Pallesen 1979: 192). The stress window includes suffixes and genitive pronominal enclitics, as shown in (2).[4]

Central Sinama
(2) a. *bónoʔ* b. *bonóʔ-un* c. *pag-bonoʔ-án-bi*
kill kill-UV.IMP GER-kill-NMLZ-2PL.GEN
'to kill' 'Kill it!' 'the cause of your act of fighting together'
(Pallesen 1985: 94)

All SB languages possess a reflex of the PMP prefixes *maŋ- and *paŋ-, which are used for various derivational functions and which trigger a range of different morphophonological behaviours depending on the type of segment the stem begins with (Blust 2004b). The most common pattern in SB languages, found both in Sulu and eastern Indonesian varieties, involves assimilation to, and deletion of, stem-initial /p, b, t, s, k, ʔ/. However, with nasals, liquids, and the voiced obstruents /d, dʒ, g/, we find the allomorph /ŋaŋ-/ (followed by assimilation or deletion of the affixal coda), for example, *ŋan-doleʔ* 'to anger' (Akamine 1996: 40). Blust's (2004b) survey shows that the pattern of vowel epenthesis with stem-initial voiced stops (e.g. /ŋ-t. . ./ vs. /ŋa-d. . ./) is strongly centred in Borneo (with the exception of Sundanese), and is found across different subgroups (e.g. Tombonuwo *moŋod-*, Kadazan *momod-*, Timugon Murut, *mamad-*, Kayan *ŋed-*). SB languages are unusual in that, despite the vowel epenthesis, a nasal stop cluster still occurs. In the Bornean languages, epenthesis serves to separate the prefix-final nasal from the stem-initial voiced stop.

## 26.3 Lexical categories and basic ordering relations

On the level of full words, descriptive grammars of SB languages have defined lexical categories on the basis of semantics (e.g. Miller 2007: 95) or by voice and person morphology, although morphological criteria have not been applied rigorously. I thus adopt a standard, uncritical view of lexical categories in the following, with a notional categorization of nominal, verbal, and adjectival roots.

Nouns are most often underived roots but can also be derived from verbal roots with a reflex of PMP *-an in combination with PMP *ka- and *paŋ-. Brainard and Behrens (2002: 11) treat the Yakan suffixal determiner *-in* as deriving nouns in forms like Yakan *ma-hāp-in* (ADJ-good-DET) 'the good one' and *mag-belli-hin* (AV-buy-DET) 'the one who buys', but such data also easily support an analysis where the general determiner *-in* simply does not discriminate with regard to the category of its host. Because there exist event-denoting roots that function as predicates without voice, aspect, or agreement morphology, there is an ambiguity with roots such as *uran* in (3), just as we find in Malay.

West Coast Bajau
(3) a. *ai uran.* b. *uran pan duwai. . .*
PFV Rain rain also fell
'It's begun to rain.' '. . . the rain fell. . .'
(Miller 2007: 178)

James (2017: 59) notes a more general difficulty in distinguishing between verbal and non-verbal predicates in Central Sinama, as putative nouns function as predicates

[4] To facilitate comparison, the glossing and presentation of examples from various sources has made to conform with a relatively neutral analysis (e.g. with reference to voices instead of their purported morphosyntactic functions).

without a copula and putative verbs can function as arguments to a certain extent. He notes that evidence for a noun–verb distinction may, however, also be found in TAM marking; while the tense/aspect markers very commonly precede verbal predicates, they only rarely precede nominal ones, although such combinations may not be completely ungrammatical.

As in nearly all Austronesian languages, entity-denoting roots can take voice morphology and thus become event-denoting words, as in (4).

(4) Yakan
*sinna-ku* *mag-luma?* *dem* *puweblo*
like-1SG.GEN AV-house in town
'I like to live in town.'
(Brainard and Behrens 2002: 236)

Adjectives are argued by Miller (2007: 101–5) to not constitute an independent morphosyntactic class in West Coast Bajau but rather to be a subtype of an intransitive verb. Verbs and putative adjectives can be modified by the same aspectual markers, intensifying adverbs, and form predicates in their bare form. They also share the same morphological potential. Property-denoting words in most SB languages are also bare roots, again as in Malay. Exceptions to this include Yakan and Sama Bangingi', where a stative prefix *ma-/a-* is commonly found on adjectives (e.g. *a-ha:p* STAT-good 'good', *a-bottoŋ* STAT-stomach 'pregnant') and Abaknon, where we find a *ma-* prefix in the same function, a likely borrowing from a Central Philippine language rather than a direct retention of PMP *ma-. Similarly, in Bajau Mola (southeast Sulawesi), we find occasional use of an adjectival *ma-* but these are apparent loans from Bugis (e.g. *marannu* 'happy'). James (2017: 33) notes that not all 'adjectives' require the *a-* prefix in Central Sinama and that event denoting predicates like *lahi* 'flee', *həlliŋ* 'say' also take this prefix.

Manner adverbs are formed with adjectival bases using the *pa-* prefix in a number of SB languages, such as Mapun (5), even if the roots are unaffixed when used as adjectival modifiers.

(5) Mapun
*lay ya* *sonse* *pa-taŋkas*
PFV 3SG.NOM run ADV-quick
'She ran quickly.' (Hashim et al. 2001: 32)

Negation offers evidence for a two-way split across lexical categories in most SB languages. Typically, one negator is used for verbal and adjectival predicates (e.g. Abaknon *ga?i*, Yakan *ga?*, Manuk Mangkaw *maha*, Sama Dilaut *mbal*) while another is used for nominal and prepositional phrase predicates (e.g. Abaknon *ma?in*, Yakan *duma?in* [both derived from PWMP *laqin 'different; another', Blust and Trussel 2020], Manuk Mangkaw *sikeyya*, Sama Dilaut *halam*).

Unlike most languages of the Philippines, there exists a class of bound roots in many SB languages, which are claimed to not occur without stem-forming voice or valency affixes. Miller (2007: 97) argues that bound roots in West Coast Bajau (e.g. *pule? 'return') are inherently verbal, based on their morphological behaviour. In Philippine-type languages, valency is typically determined by voice in combination with valency changing morphology with great flexibility on the part of the roots. Transitivity in SB languages may not be as flexible. For instance, monovalent roots (e.g. *teko* 'arrive') generally resist taking the passive/undergoer voice (Miller 2007: 98; Donohue 1996: 785).

SB languages have a richer inventory of true prepositions when compared to the languages of the Philippines. Akamine (2005: 385) enumerates five for Simunul Island Sama: *le?* AGENT/REASON, *ma* LOCATION, *ni* GOAL, *min* SOURCE, and *maka* INSTRUMENT, COMITATIVE. Unlike the prepositions of other CSP languages, these take noun phrase complements directly rather than as oblique case phrases. The origin of some but not all of these prepositions can be traced to earlier sources. The agent marker *le?* and its many SB cognates descend transparently from PMP *uliq 'get; obtain' (see §26.4.4 below). A common goal marker *pa*, as seen in (6), most likely represents a degrammaticalization of PMP *pa- in one of its common non-causative functions (cf. Cebuano *pa-iŋun sa gawaŋ* DIR-toward OBL door).

(6) Pangutaran Sama
*t<um>uju* *a?a* *pa* *luma?* *saupak*
<AV>toward person OBL house Saupak
'The man is headed for Saupak's house.'
(Walton 1986: 87)

On the other hand, the instrumental preposition *maka*, appears to be a grammaticalization of Malay *makai* < *memakai* (/məŋ-pakai/) 'use', as a fuller form can still be seen in the same function in (7).

(7) West Coast Bajau
*boi_jo* *Ø-tata?=ni* *anak* *makay*
after UV-pour.water=3SG.I child AV.use
*gayuŋ...*
bucket
'Just after he poured water on the child using a bucket...' (Miller 2007: 235)

Pallesen (1985) reconstructs PSB pronouns as in Table 26.1. Note that the nominative pronouns, which are second position clitics in some SB languages, only differ minimally from the independent pronouns. SB pronouns differ from

Table 26.1 PSB pronouns (Pallesen 1985: 103)

| | | Set I NOMINATIVE | Set II GENITIVE | Set III INDEPENDENT |
|---|---|---|---|---|
| Minimal | 1 | *aku, *ku | *-ku | *aku |
| | 2 | *kaa, *kaw | *-nu | *kaʔa, *kaʔaw |
| | 1+2 | *kitəh | *-təh | *kitəh |
| | 3 | *iəh | *-nəh | *iəh |
| Augmented | 1 | *kami | *-kami | *kami |
| | 2 | *kaam | *-bi(i) | *kaʔam |
| | 1+2 | *kitəh | *-təh | *kitəh |
| | 3 | *iəh | *-dəh | *iəh |

most surrounding languages in having lost the number distinction in the third person nominative and independent sets. The distinction is reasserted through a number of independent innovations, for example, Abaknon *maŋa iya* (a 3sg pronoun preceded by a common Central Philippine plural marker), Central Sinama *sigala* (via Malay *segala* 'all' ultimately from Sanskrit *sakala* 'complete; entire; all', see Pallesen 1985: 201), and Bajau Mola *disiʔ iru* (via a demonstrative meaning 'those over there', see Donohue 1996: 784).

Pronominal objects of actor voice verbs are avoided in Philippine varieties but when there is no choice, SB languages vary in which set they employ for this function with the independent set (Set III) enjoying preferred status. Note also that, in accordance with a widespread Philippine pattern, a first person singular agent acting on a second person patient is often expressed with a reflex of *-təh rather than the expected *-ku (James 2017: 25). In contrast, Bajau Mola has adopted an areal pattern of south Sulawesi in using the first person plural inclusive as a polite second person pronoun.

Besides the above major categories, there are a number of TAM markers and adverbial clitics which cannot be reviewed fully here. The independent aspect markers supplant PMP syllable reduplication marking progressive (not to be mistaken with full reduplication marking continued action, cf. Miller 2007: 78) and the PMP perfective marker *<in> on verbs. As discussed below, the reflex of *<in> survives as a marker of passive voice or a resultative.

The basic word order relations in the SB languages appear similar to Malay. These can be exemplified with West Coast Bajau (Miller 2007):

(i) Possessors and adjectives must follow the phrases they modify (e.g. *moto Deli* (eye Deli) 'Deli's eye', *beriu daras* (wind strong) 'strong wind').
(ii) Complementizers (e.g. *eŋkoʔ*) and adpositions uniformly precede their complements.
(iii) Relative clauses tend strongly to follow the head noun they modify (see §26.5.1).
(iv) Negation and auxiliaries precede verbs (e.g. *nyaʔ buli s<in>egir* (NEG can <PASS>touch) 'must not be touched').
(v) The comparative marker precedes the adjective which precedes the standard of comparison (e.g. *lagi laŋa man kam* (more tall than 2PL.II) 'taller than you').

The ordering relations that are more difficult to generalize over involve adverbs and the relative order of subject and predicate. The northern SB languages are more thoroughly predicate initial while a subject initial order is claimed to be unmarked for actor voice clauses in West Coast Bajau and certain SB languages of Indonesia. The positioning of adverbs depends on adverb type and discourse factors but has not been described in any detail.

## 26.4 Grammatical relations

### 26.4.1 Voice and valency

An unexpected feature of Philippine SB languages is their apparent maintenance and even elaboration of the basic four-way PMP voice system, despite the simplification of the case system and total loss of verbal aspect morphology. The five-way voice distinction of Central Sinama is shown in (8).

Central Sinama

(8) a. *amonoʔ=aku* *edoʔ* *maka* *lahut* *itu*
AV:kill=1SG.NOM dog with knife this
'I will kill the dog with this knife.'

b. *bonoʔ-ku* *edoʔ* *maka* *lahut* *itu*
kill-1SG.GEN dog with knife this
'I will kill the dog with this knife.'

c. *pamonoʔ-ku* *edoʔ* *lahut* *itu*
IV:kill-1SG.GEN dog knife this
'I will kill the dog with this knife.'

d. *bonoʔ-an-ku* *kaʔa* *edoʔ*
kill-BEN-1SG.GEN 2SG.NOM dog
'I will kill the dog for you.'

e. *pamonoʔ-an-ku* *edoʔ* *lantay* *itu*
LV:kill-LV-1SG.GEN dog floor this
'I will kill the dog on the floor.' (Pallesen 1985: 96–7)

The actor voice is expressed with a reflex of PMP *maŋ- in (8a) (usually *ŋ*- with nasal substitution), originally a pluractional/distributive actor voice prefix. In SB languages, it has been analysed as an antipassive/intransitive marker (Gault

1999; Trick 2008; Brainard and Behrens 2002) as well as an inchoative (Walton 1986) but is most commonly glossed as actor voice/focus. The patient voice in (8b), on the other hand, is expressed with the bare verb stem. The morphology of both voices thus resembles Malay and languages of Indonesia that have replaced PMP *-en PATIENT VOICE with a bare verb stem and widened the function of PMP *maŋ- to become a default actor voice, subsuming PMP *<um>.

Whereas the PAN voice marker *Si- was polysemous in selecting an instrumental, beneficiary, and conveyed object as the pivot, these functions are cleaved apart in SB. The instrumental voice is marked uniquely by *paŋ-* < PMP *paŋ- INSTRUMENTAL, as seen in (8c), while beneficiaries, recipients, and kindred roles are selected by *-an* < PMP *-an LOCATIVE, as in (8d).[5] The use of *paŋ-* to mark instrumental voice is also found in Central Philippine languages and elsewhere, which may either indicate parallel innovation or a function that was already present in PMP (perhaps to derive instrumental nouns), but not fully incorporated into the voice system. The locative (which corresponds to true location, rather than directional or oblique roles) is expressed with a combination of PMP *paŋ- and *-an, as seen in (8e).

Pallesen reconstructs the PSB voice markers as shown in Table 26.2, with two moods and two aspects in the indicative. What Pallesen terms "perfective" really derives from the PMP potentive paradigm, which is often used to mark accomplishment, ability, and accidental action, functions that are also continued in SB languages. Note also that while the PMP *-en patient voice has been eliminated in the indicative voice, it survives in the imperative as *-un (as in modern Javanese). Where we might expect a reflex of PAN *Si- in the instrumental (Pallesen's "accessory"), we again find a reflex of *-en. Finally, PSB shows a unique innovation in the imperatives of the benefactive/referent and locative voice, which appears to be a blend of the PMP dependent mood locative *-i (used commonly for locative imperatives in Philippine languages) and the final *-n* found in all the other suffixes in the voice paradigm.

The presentation of Pallesen's paradigm in (8) and Table 26.2 perhaps misleadingly makes SB appear as a Philippine-type language. In reality, SB languages may be more amenable to a two-voice (actor vs. undergoer) analysis with the other voices in the paradigm being applicatives. All SB languages allow 'referent voice' to combine with either undergoer voice (unmarked) or actor voice. For instance, in West Coast Bajau, we find *beli-an* 'to buy for X' but also with the actor voice stem, yielding *meli-an* 'X buys for Y', as well as

[5] The benefactive use of the locative voice is also found in Philippine languages as an option under certain conditions.

**Table 26.2** Verbal affixes (Pallesen 1985: 99)

| VOICE | MOOD | | |
|---|---|---|---|
| | INDICATIVE | | IMPERATIVE |
| | IMPERFECTIVE | PERFECTIVE | |
| Actor | *N- | *maka- | *N- |
| Patient | *∅ | *ta- | *-un |
| Accessory | *paN- | (*)tapaN- | (*)paN- -un |
| Referent | *-an | *ka- -an | *-in |
| Locative | *paN- -an | (*)kapaN- -an | (*)paN- -in |

the passive stem, yielding *b<in>eli-an* 'X is bought something (by Y)' (Miller 2007: 274). The promotion of a prepositional object to a direct object in this manner is shown in (9).

West Coast Bajau

(9) a. *endo=ku muan peraŋgiʔ e m-aku*
wife=1SG.I AV:give pineapple DEM PREP-1SG.II
'My wife gave the pineapple to me.'

b. *endo=ku muan-an aku peraŋgiʔ e*
wife=1SG.I AV:give-APPL 1SG.II pineapple DEM
'My wife gave me the pineapple.' (Miller 2007: 282)

Walton (1986: 87–94) argues explicitly that Pangutaran Sama *-an* should be treated as a valency increaser (i.e. applicative), rather than its own voice. Note that Pangutaran Sama, like all other SB languages, has an applicative use of *-an*, similar to Malay, but at the same time resembles Philippine languages in its verb-initial syntax and strong tendency for an indefinite interpretation of actor voice objects and definite interpretation of the pivot (see §26.4.3). In (10a), we see a plain undergoer voice clause with a benefactive adjunct expressed as an oblique phrase (*ma si Andi*). In (10b), we see the promotion of the benefactive to the pivot of the undergoer clause with the help of *-an*. In (10c), we see an actor voice clause where the actor is the pivot and the benefactive is again an oblique phrase. So far, the facts abide by typical the Philippine pattern. But in (10c) we see an actor voice clause co-occurring with *-an* and the former oblique phrase promoted to object. This divergence from the Philippine pattern is another typological feature which points to a southern origin for SB languages.

Pangutaran Sama

(10) a. *Ø-bəlli-ku taumpaʔ ma si andi*
UV-buy-1SG.GEN shoes OBL PERS Andy
'I bought the shoes for Andy.'

b. *Ø-bəlli-an-ku si andi taumpaʔ*
UV-buy-LOC-1SG.GEN PERS Andy shoes
'I bought Andy some shoes.'

c. *məlli=aku taumpaʔ ma si andi.*
AV:buy=1SG.NOM shoes OBL PERS Andy
'I bought some shoes for Andy.'

d. *məlli-an=aku si andi taumpaʔ*
AV:buy-LOC=1SG.NOM PERS Andy shoes
'I bought Andy some shoes.' (Walton 1986: 88–9)

The status of the instrumental and the locative is even less clear. There is little evidence from any SB variety that actor voice ever co-occurs with the instrumental derived from *paŋ- and the locative voice circumfix *paŋ- -an (cf. James 2017: 66). The possibility of recent convergence with the cognate Malay nominalizations, *pəŋ-* AGENT NOMINALIZER and *pəŋ- -an* GERUND, is unlikely, as the semantics of these in Malay/Indonesian and SB have drifted apart considerably (cf. Miller 2007: 296–8). If Pallesen is correct in the reconstruction of an imperative mood for all voices, as in Table 26.2, then Indonesian varieties must have simplified this part of the paradigm. This, however, remains to be worked out, because imperatives for the instrumental and locative voices are also lacking in Philippine varieties (Walton 1986: 10; Akamine 2005: 389). More likely is a scenario in which nominalizations derived with *paŋ- have been incorporated into the voice system to a greater extent in SB languages of Sulu through contact with Philippine languages.

Pallesen also reconstructs what he terms "secondary verbal affixes" related to valency and aspect. These include PSB *si- 'RECIPROCAL' and *pa- 'CAUSATIVE' whose forms and functions are inherited directly from PMP. There are also several uses of a *pa-* prefix that are not, strictly speaking, causative but which probably descend from the same PMP morpheme. In many SB varieties, *pa-* forms motion verbs from deictics, location words, and body positions (Walton 1986: 75). Several SB languages have the unusual property of combining causative *pa-* with the actor voice prefix to yield an active causative prefix *ma-*. There is little need to avoid homophony with widespread stative *ma-* as the stative prefix is highly marginal in SB and has been reduced to *a-* in several languages.

A prefix cognate to PMP *ka- is also commonly found and plays a role in the potentive paradigm, typically cancelling out an agentive interpretation (Walton 1986: 83). The undergoer counterpart of this prefix is *ta-*, whose distribution is robustly southern and only rarely found in the Philippines, despite being reconstructable to PAN *taR- (Blust and Trussel 2020). Actor voice and undergoer voice potentive clauses are shown in (11).

Pangutaran Sama
(11) a. *ka-kəlloʔ si mmaʔ daiŋ*
AV.POT-get PERS father fish
'Father was able to get some fish.'

b. *ta-kəlloʔ aʔa daiŋ kuhapu*
UV.POT-get PERS father fish
'A man was able to catch the grouper fish.'
(Walton 1986: 101)

Most SB languages differ from Malay in making a clearer distinction between undergoer voice, with an unmarked verb, and passive voice, with a reflex of PMP *<in> (although see van den Berg and Mead, this volume, §33.5.1 for parallels in Sulawesi). In the Yakan undergoer voice, neither agent nor patient are case marked but the agent must be adjacent to the verb, as seen in (12a). In (12b), we see what is often considered a passive; the verb is marked with *<in>*, which, unlike Philippine languages, has no association with aspect. With the use of *<in>*, the agent must take the agentive marker *weʔ* and can appear in a wider range of positions in the clause. This appears to be equally true for Pangutaran and other SB languages of Sulu.

Yakan
(12) a. *pogpog [aʔa] sawe-hin [*aʔa]*
hit person snake-DEF person
'A person hit the snake.'

b. *p<in>ogpog [weʔ aʔa] sawe-hin [weʔ aʔa]*
<PASS>hit AGT person snake-DEF AGT person
'A person hit the snake.'
(Brainard and Behrens 2002: 113)

Prepositionally marked agents are also used for non-agentive causers but in this case, the predicate is typically not marked with a reflex of *<in>, as shown in (13).

Pangutaran Sama
(13) *tutuŋ uk lətteʔ kabbun-kami*
burn AGT lightning plantation-1PL.EXCL.GEN
'Our plantation was burned by lightning.'
(Walton 1986: 62)

While (13) shows a passive agent without a passive-marked verb, we also find a passive marked verb with a bare agent in Mola Bajau (14c), where it can also be introduced by the oblique markers *ma* or *aleh*.[6] The actor voice and undergoer voice are shown in (14a) and (b) for comparison. It is not

[6] A bare agent with a passive marked verb appears to be rare in SB languages and the Mola construction may be a recent calque from Indonesian which allows both bare agents of passive verbs as well as those marked by the agentive preposition *oleh*. Note also that the Mola passive is uniquely (among SB varieties) marked with *di-*, as in Malay.

clear how the undergoer and passive voice differ syntactically in Mola Bajau or to what extent (14c) represents a real passive.

Mola Bajau
(14) a. *ŋ-ita uggoʔ aku*
AV-see pig 1SG
'I saw the pig.'

b. *kita-ku uggoʔ*
see-1SG.GEN pig
'I saw the pig.'

c. *di-kita-ku uggoʔ*
PV-see-1SG.GEN pig
'The pig was seen by me.' (Donohue 1996: 784)

Actor voice clauses show more flexibility in the ordering of arguments in the postverbal domain. This can give rise to ambiguity in some languages, as in (15).

Manuk Mangkaw Sinama
(15) *Bey nipaʔ kambiŋ kuda*
already AV:kick goat horse
'The goat kicked a horse.' OR 'The horse kicked a goat.' (Akamine 1996: 73)

Akamine (1996: 73) shows that definiteness disambiguates the relations in the Manuk Mangkaw actor voice. If one of the arguments in (15) is marked as definite (with a following demonstrative), it must also be interpreted as the subject, abiding by a common tendency in Austronesian languages for the pivot to be definite and actor voice undergoers to be indefinite. We examine the relation of this constraint to transitivity and alignment below in §26.4.3.

## 26.4.2 Pronominal arguments

In all documented SB varieties, genitive/ergative pronominal arguments are verb-adjacent enclitics (Set II) while nominative pronouns are either free (Set III) or found in second position (Set I). Unlike most languages of the Philippines, second-position clitics in SB languages of Sulu can be hosted by complementizers like *baŋ* 'if', as in (16).

Sama Bangingi'
(16) *baŋ=aku iŋgaʔi pa-billi-nu...*
if=1SG.NOM NEG CAUS-buy-2SG.GEN
'If you won't sell to me...' (Gault 1999: 78)

This type of split in positioning between genitive and nominative clitics recurs in various areas of Indonesia (Haaksma 1933; Billings and Kaufman 2004; Himmelmann 2005a; Kikusawa 2003) but the second-position condition on nominative clitics is stronger in SB languages of the Philippines than those of Indonesia. Free pronouns play an expanded role in Indonesian varieties, which tend to place the pivot in clause-initial position, as in (17). Free pronouns are generally used only for emphasis or as predicates in Philippine varieties.

Eastern Indonesian Bajau
(17) *kau korobbaŋ-ku*
2SG slaughter-1SG.GEN
'I will slaughter you.' (Verheijen 1986: 21)

Clitic doubling has gone unexamined in SB languages although its existence is clear from published texts and other examples. Verheijen analyses the ergative clitics in (18) as object clitics, but the interpretation in (18b) would be impossible on his view. Interestingly, the clitics are doubling an agent introduced by the preposition *alé* rather than an unmarked ergative argument.

Eastern Indonesian Bajau
(18) a. *baraʔ-an-**na** né **alé enda-na** ka...*
tell-APPL-3.GEN already AGT wife-3.GEN to
'His wife told it to...'

b. *soho-**na** lagi **alé anaʔ-ku** ka kita*
command-3.GEN again AGT child-1SG.GEN to 2.POL
'(I) was again ordered by my son to (go) to you.' (Verheijen 1986: 21)

Ergative clitic doubling and agreement are ubiquitous in Sulawesi and other parts of eastern Indonesia but it should be pointed out that Abaknon (19) also shows this pattern, despite being geographically embedded in the Central Philippine subgroup where clitic doubling is absent.

Abaknon
(19) *ag-laklak-**na** **si** **idoʔ** i luhoʔ*
ASP-drink-3.GEN OBL dog NOM soup
'The dog drinks the soup.' (Jacobson 1999)

## 26.4.3 Transitivity, definiteness, and alignment

Recent work on SB languages has focused on questions of alignment type and transitivity. In this regard, the SB languages are more conservative than Malay, despite the two subgroups sharing several morphosyntactic innovations enumerated earlier. Definiteness correlates strongly with grammatical relations in Philippine varieties but much less so in Indonesian varieties, which appear more symmetrical in the sense of Himmelmann (2005a), that is, having "at least two voice alternations marked on the verb, neither of which is clearly the basic form" (cf. Foley 2008). The resistance of actor voice clauses to definite undergoers in

Philippine varieties has led many analysts to treat these languages as ergatively aligned rather than symmetric, with the actor voice as an antipassive (Gault 1999; Akamine 1996; Trick 2008). A concrete example from Yakan is seen in (20).

Yakan

(20) a. *kehet* *dende-hin* *kenna-hin*
Cut woman-DEF fish-DEF
'The woman cut up the fish.'

b. *ŋehet* *kenna* *dende-hin*
AV:cut fish woman-DEF
'The woman cut up fish.'
(Brainard and Behrens 2002: 160)

Uniquely in Yakan, the pivot argument must be suffixed with the definite marker *-in*. In a transitive clause, such as (20a), the agent can also be suffixed with *-in* and interpreted definitely. However, in a canonical matrix clause such as (20b), the undergoer argument of an actor voice verb cannot be marked with the definite marker. A similar situation holds for Pangutaran Sama, although here the definite interpretation of the pivot comes 'for free' without the use of determiners, as shown in (21).

Pangutaran Sama

(21) a. *Ø-tauʔ-ku* *kahawa* *ma* *siliʔ*
UV-put-1SG.GEN coffee OBL teapot
'I put the coffee in the teapot.'

b. *nauʔ* *aku* *kahawa* *ma* *siliʔ*
AV:put 1SG.NOM coffee OBL teapot
'I put some coffee in the teapot.' (Walton 1986: 7)

Even when the undergoer takes a definite possessor, it is interpreted with lower transitivity in the actor voice, as shown in (22).[7]

Pangutaran Sama

(22) a. *Ø-bonoʔ* *sultan* *bantaʔ-na*
UV-kill king enemy-3SG.GEN
'The king killed his enemy.'

b. *monoʔ* *sultan* *bantaʔ-na*
AV:kill king enemy-3SG.GEN
'The king kills/fights some of his enemies.'
(Walton 1986: 120)

As suggested by (23), this is not the case for West Coast Bajau, which allows definite actor voice objects more freely, as in Malay.

[7] I maintain Walton's glossing of the null prefix as a marker of undergoer voice although this can just as well be applied to other SB languages described here.

West Coast Bajau

(23) *dela* *e* *pan* *nambut* ***iyo*** *taʔ*
man DEM TOP AV:receive 3SG.II PREP
*beluang...*
door
'The man welcomed him at the door...'
(Miller 2007: 163)

In West Coast Bajau, and presumably other varieties of western Indonesia that have been under the constant influence of Malay, we see two concomitant changes; the actor voice allows for definite objects more freely and takes on SVO as the unmarked word order. The asymmetric word order change in the actor voice but not the undergoer voice, which remains largely predicate initial, also reflects the historical development of Malay, as detailed by Cumming (1991).

The status of the 'passive' vs. the undergoer voice remains an open question for most SB languages. Trick (2008) shows that clefting, relativization, and question formation in Southern Sinama are all restricted to the pivot argument, as is true for all SB languages and, more generally, nearly all syntactically conservative Austronesian languages. But there is a clear contrast in control constructions between Philippine-type patient voice clauses and what Trick (2008) treats as a plain transitive clause in Southern Sinama. He presents the data in (24) suggesting that the controllee (the null argument in the lower clause that must corefer with an argument in a higher clause) is restricted to the pivot.

Southern Sinama

(24) a. *ka-bilahi-an-ku* *ni-liŋan-an* *leh*
NMLZ-want-NMLZ-1SG.GEN UV-call-APPL AGT
*si* *Ben*
PERS Ben
'I want Ben to call [me].'

b. *ka-bilahi-an* *si* *Ben* *ni-liŋan-an*
NMLZ-want-NMLZ PERS Ben UV-call-APPL
*aku.*
1SG.NOM
'Ben wants me to be called [by someone].'
NOT: 'Ben wants to call me.' (Trick 2008)

Trick (2008) thus analyses the Sama control pattern as following an ergative system in that only the absolutive argument can be controlled, whereas the Central Philippine pattern has been analysed as being sensitive to a number of factors including thematic role and grammatical function (Schachter 1996). The behaviour we see in (24) does, however, correspond to how control operates in Malay/Indonesian clauses with *di-* marked verbs and agents introduced by *oleh*. Unfortunately, Trick (2008) does not compare prefixed forms like *ni-liŋan-an* to *liŋan-an*, in the unmarked undergoer voice, and suggests that such a distinction is not at play with full noun phrases in this variety. If the expected opposition between the two types of undergoer voice does exist here, it may be that the *ni-* marked verbs are simply more passive-like than their bare undergoer counterparts, as suggested by other descriptions. This is clearly an area that requires further exploration.

## 26.4.4 The *leʔ* actor voice construction

Akamine (1996, 2002, 2003, 2005) describes a highly peculiar perfective construction involving the agentive marker *leʔ* introducing a verb with ACTOR VOICE prefix *ŋ-*, followed by an agent also introduced by *leʔ*, seen in (25).

Manuk Mangkaw Sinama

| (25) | *leʔ* | *ŋ-ajal* | *leʔ* | *ku* | *manuk* |
|---|---|---|---|---|---|
| | ? | AV-cook | AGT | 1SG.GEN | chicken |

'I have cooked the chicken.' (Akamine 2005: 391)

This is odd on four counts: (i) *leʔ* does not introduce verbs in any other context; (ii) the verb is marked with the actor voice but behaves as an undergoer voice verb in expressing the agent with *leʔ* and giving a definite interpretation to the patient (Akamine 2002: 361); (iii) the construction has a perfective meaning whose source is unclear; and (iv) the agent can be fronted in this construction, as in (26), but here, only one instance of *leʔ* can appear.

| (26) | *leʔ* | *ku* | *(*leʔ)* | *ŋ-ajal* | *manuk* |
|---|---|---|---|---|---|
| | AGT | 1SG.GEN | ? | AV-cook | chicken |

'I have cooked the chicken.' (Akamine 2005: 391)

I would like to briefly pursue Akamine's (2002: 363) suggestion that "The *leq-* prefix and the *leq* preposition are possibly both derived from an earlier verb via different grammaticalisation paths" and attempt an explanation of these puzzling features that departs from previous proposals (Akamine 1996; Ross 2002a). It appears all of the above anomalies obtain a natural solution by taking the above pattern to be a remnant of a serial verb construction based on PMP *uliq 'get; obtain' (Blust and Trussel 2020), serving in two distinct but related functions. The use of reflexes of *uliq to introduce an agent are widespread in Malayic and even found to some extent in eastern Indonesia (e.g. Bima, Manggarai), and are thus rather straightforward. In contrast, the first instance of *leʔ* is unusual but can be understood as an auxiliary based on the verbal meaning of 'get'. It is similar to a 'get' passive of the type commonly found in Mainland Southeast Asia in its resultative and perfective semantics, although it appears freely with an agent. I propose that the structure in (25) represents restructuring (or 'clause union'), in which the oblique agent is really an argument of the initial verbal *leʔ* but appears after the lexical verb in the actor voice. We have already seen earlier that oblique agents occur not only with passives in SB languages but also with certain stative predicates, as in (13), above. As seen for several Philippine and Formosan languages in Kaufman (this volume, §26.5.3.2), actor voice plays a dual role as both a voice marker and a voice-neutral infinitive marker. Actor voice is required on the lexical verb in this construction due to its subordinating function rather than its voice function. Finally, in (26), restructuring has not taken place and the agent is in the expected position of an argument of the verbal auxiliary *leʔ*. On this account, we do not expect an additional *leʔ* to follow the agent in (26) and we predict both the semantics of the construction and the apparent anomalous voice on the lexical verb.[8] Further descriptive work on the details of this construction should support or disconfirm this analysis.

## 26.5 The noun phrase

The typical linear order of elements within an SB noun phrase is shown in (27):

(27) Case | Plural | **Num** | **Class** | <u>Noun</u> | Poss | Adjective | Relative | **Num** | **Class** | Dem

Note that post-nominal adjectives and demonstratives are a southern feature among Malayo-Polynesian languages and are not reflected by most languages of the Philippines (Donohue 2007). The absolute final position of demonstratives (following the relative clause) is typologically unusual but common to languages of Indonesia and possibly an effect of Malay contact.[9] Note also that there are two positions for numeral-classifier constituent, one before the head noun and one after. In Yakan, the choice between these positions depends on the definiteness of the entire NP. As seen in (28), prenominal numerals correspond to indefinite interpretations and postnominal ones with definite interpretations.

Yakan

| (28) a. | *ŋite* | *ku* | *lime* | *manuk* |
|---|---|---|---|---|
| | AV:see | 1SG.NOM | five | chicken |

'I saw five chickens.'

| b. | *kite-ku* | *(meʔ)* | *manuk-in* | *lime* |
|---|---|---|---|---|
| | see-1SG.GEN | PL | chicken-DEF | five |

'I saw the five chickens.'
(Brainard and Behrens 2002: 30–1)

[8] As pointed out in Adelaar (2005e), a similar construction exists in Salako. This constellation of properties is so unusual that it is unlikely to have arisen multiple times independently and may be another piece of evidence linking the SB languages to Borneo (Kaufman 2007: 629).

[9] Pallesen (1985: 180) observes that the strictly postnominal order of demonstratives and possessors in Sama languages has entered Tausug, a Central Philippine language, via contact, while its closest relatives in the Eastern Mindanaoan subgroup show the same flexibility found in Tagalog.

Other SB languages also show multiple positions, as in (29) (see also Verheijen 1986: 20), but the semantic correlates, if any, have not been described.

West Coast Bajau

(29) a. *duo em-bua? belud oyo*
two CNT-CLF hill large
'two large hills'

b. *enselan di-kau? tin*
gasoline one-CLF can
'one can of gasoline'
(Miller 2007: 313)

SB classifier systems are relatively simple. Eastern Indonesia Bajau employs *kau* for both animate and inanimate objects of various types. West Coast Bajau uses *-aŋan* for people, *-kau?* for animals and non-round objects, and *-bua?* for fruits, round objects, and very large objects (Miller 2007: 109). Some SB languages of the Philippines, like Yakan, only have a vestigial use of classifiers.

SB languages only show a remnant of the linker found ubiquitously in Philippine languages which mediates between modifiers and their complements. This is almost always restricted to numeral modifiers in SB languages. The general loss of the linker and presence of classifiers puts the SB languages closer to Austronesian languages outside of the Philippines typologically.

### 26.5.1 Relative clauses

Only pivots can be relativized in SB languages without a resumptive pronoun. Relative clauses follow the head noun but are introduced in a variety of ways. West Coast Bajau allows relative clauses to follow the head noun without the mediation of any overt functor, as seen in (30).

West Coast Bajau

(30) a. *uwa? nguma e pan beranti.*
dog bark DEM TOP stop
'The dog that was barking (or 'the barking dog') stopped.'

b. *enselan Ø-boo azam kemuap e*
gasoline UV-bring Azam afternoon DEM
'the gasoline that Azam bought yesterday'
(Miller 2007: 392–3)

Some SB languages of the Philippines make use of *ya* or *iya*, a relativizer derived from the third singular pronoun. In Southern Sinama, we find relative clauses introduced with a combination of *ya* and the linker *na*, parallel to the etymology of Malay *yaŋ* (Adelaar 1992a).[10]

Southern Sinama

(31) *si Ben* ***ya*** ***na*** *bey nengge*
PERS Ben NMLZ LNK PFV AV:stand
'Ben is who stood.'
(Trick 2008: 191)

Intriguingly, Yakan employs a prefix *ma-* specifically for agent oriented relative clauses, as seen in (32), but not for other types of relatives. This use of *ma-* does not exist in surrounding languages (but see Klamer 1998: 316–34 for a parallel in Kambera).

Yakan

(32) a. *Iyan sawe* ***ma****-pa-diyalem luma?-in*
that snake ACT.REL-VBLZ-inside house-DEF
'That is the snake that went into the house'

b. *Iyan naknak* ***ma****-molong buwa?buwa?-in*
that child ACT.REL-AV:break toy-DEF
'That is the child who broke a toy.'
(Brainard and Behrens 2002: 165–6)

## 26.6 Conclusion: Internal diversity, contact, and convergence

Just like the Roma languages of Europe and Asia, the SB languages provide a unique view into language contact across a family of dispersed communities in various stages of sedentarization. Recent descriptive grammars and dictionaries have shed much light on several SB languages of the Philippines but Pallesen's (1985) study remains the only in-depth investigation of language contact in the SB family. As this work focused primarily on the bidirectional contact effects between Tausug and the SB languages of the Sulu area, there still remain large gaps in our understanding of SB languages of Indonesia, Malaysia, and the central Philippines. Certain SB languages, in particular, beg for attention. Abaknon has barely been described in published work and, next to Chavacano, is the closest thing to a true mixed language (in the sense of Bakker 1997) in the Philippines. The diverse influences are plain to see in the typical Abaknon utterance shown in (33), where native morphemes are in plain italics without particular marking, morphemes with a Central

[10] James (2017: 75) notes that the use of *ya* in Sinama Dilaut is obligatory with resumptive pronouns but not typically found with the gap strategy. Several authors note variation in this area among the SB languages of Sulu.

Philippine origin are in bold, English-origin morphemes are underlined, and Spanish-origin elements are bolded and underlined. (Note that *baligyaʔ* may have its ultimate source in a language of South Asia, although its immediate source is a Central Philippine language.)

Abaknon

(33) *I*=***maŋa***=*ismaglir* ***pirmi*** *hamok* *ag-tago*
NOM=PL=smuggler always only VBLZ-hide
*si* ***maŋa*** ***baligyaʔ****-na* ***kon*** *niyaʔ* ***sundalo***
OBL PL goods-3S.GEN if EXIST soldier
'The smugglers always hide their goods for sale whenever there is a soldier.' (Jacobson 1999)

The SB languages are clearly a fruitful area for further study, both for Austronesianists and those interested in language contact more generally. As discussed earlier, the SB languages also possess syntactic puzzles that provide interesting evidence of grammaticalization and that may shed additional light on the Bornean origins of the SB subgroup.

CHAPTER 27

# Non-Malayic languages of Borneo

Paul Kroeger and Alexander D. Smith

## 27.1 Introduction

This chapter presents a brief typological survey of non-Malayic Bornean languages (Map 27.1; see Anderbeck, Chapter 9, this volume, for a discussion of Malayic languages). Rather than attempting a comprehensive typology, we have selected certain features which seem to provide an interesting basis for comparison among the Bornean languages, including both phonological features (phoneme inventories, nasality, word shape, stress systems, etc.) and morphosyntactic features (word order, voice systems, case marking, clitics, NP structure, pronoun inventories, etc.).

Based on their phonological features, we suggest that the languages of Borneo can be divided into two general types: (i) an 'Island Southeast Asian' (ISEA) type, which shares features commonly found in Austronesian languages throughout Insular Southeast Asia; and (ii) a less common 'Mainland Southeast Asian' (MSEA) type, which shares with languages of MSEA many features that are not typically found in western Austronesian languages.

Morphosyntactic properties support a three-way partitioning similar to typological classifications that have been proposed in earlier work: (i) Philippine-type; (ii) Indonesian-type; and (iii) Central Bornean type. Of course, we (like many other authors) recognize the limitations of such classifications: there are quite a few languages that do not fit neatly into any of these types. Nevertheless, the classification is useful because it reflects widespread patterns of grammatical structure in terms of generalizations that do hold, by and large, for a significant number of languages.

As discussed below, based on the available evidence there appears to be a limited correlation between the phonological and grammatical typologies: MSEA phonology implies Central Bornean grammar. Apart from this, however, the two typologies are largely independent of each other.

## 27.2 Phonology

In this section we provide an overview of the phonological typology of Borneo. Basic concepts such as word and syllable shape are discussed first, followed by a discussion of consonantal typology, and finally vowel typology. We find that languages with an ISEA type phonology tend to have phonological features that are similar to other, more well-known western Austronesian languages, and that MSEA type languages have phonological typologies that are sometimes substantially different. Geographically, we note that ISEA-type languages are found spread throughout the island and do not form a distinct linguistic area. MSEA-type languages, on the other hand, are found concentrated in the central latitudes roughly between 0° and 3° N; they are not present in northern or southern Borneo. Smith (2017c) had earlier named this area the Central Bornean Linguistic Area. Here we do find a correlation between geographic location and phonological typology.

### 27.2.1 Word shape

Word shape in Borneo tends to follow straightforwardly from that reconstructed for Proto-Malayo-Polynesian, especially for ISEA type languages. Content words are disyllabic in uninflected forms. Syllables are not typically more complex than CVC, and may consist of a single vowel. The canonical word-shape is thus CV(C)CV(C), and longer words of three or more syllables are usually derived through morphological affixation.

Exceptions to the two-syllable canonical word shape typology are not uncommon, however. MSEA-type languages have moved away from a two-syllable basic word shape towards sesquisyllabic and monosyllabic word shapes and have simultaneously complexified syllables. Sesquisyllabic words contain "one and a half" syllables (Matisoff 1973; Thomas 1992) and in MSEA, as well as in Borneo, this means

Paul Kroeger and Alexander D. Smith, *Non-Malayic languages of Borneo*. In: *The Oxford Guide to the Malayo-Polynesian Languages of Southeast Asia*. Edited by: Alexander Adelaar and Antoinette Schapper, Oxford University Press. © Paul Kroeger and Alexander D. Smith (2024). DOI: 10.1093/oso/9780198807353.003.0027

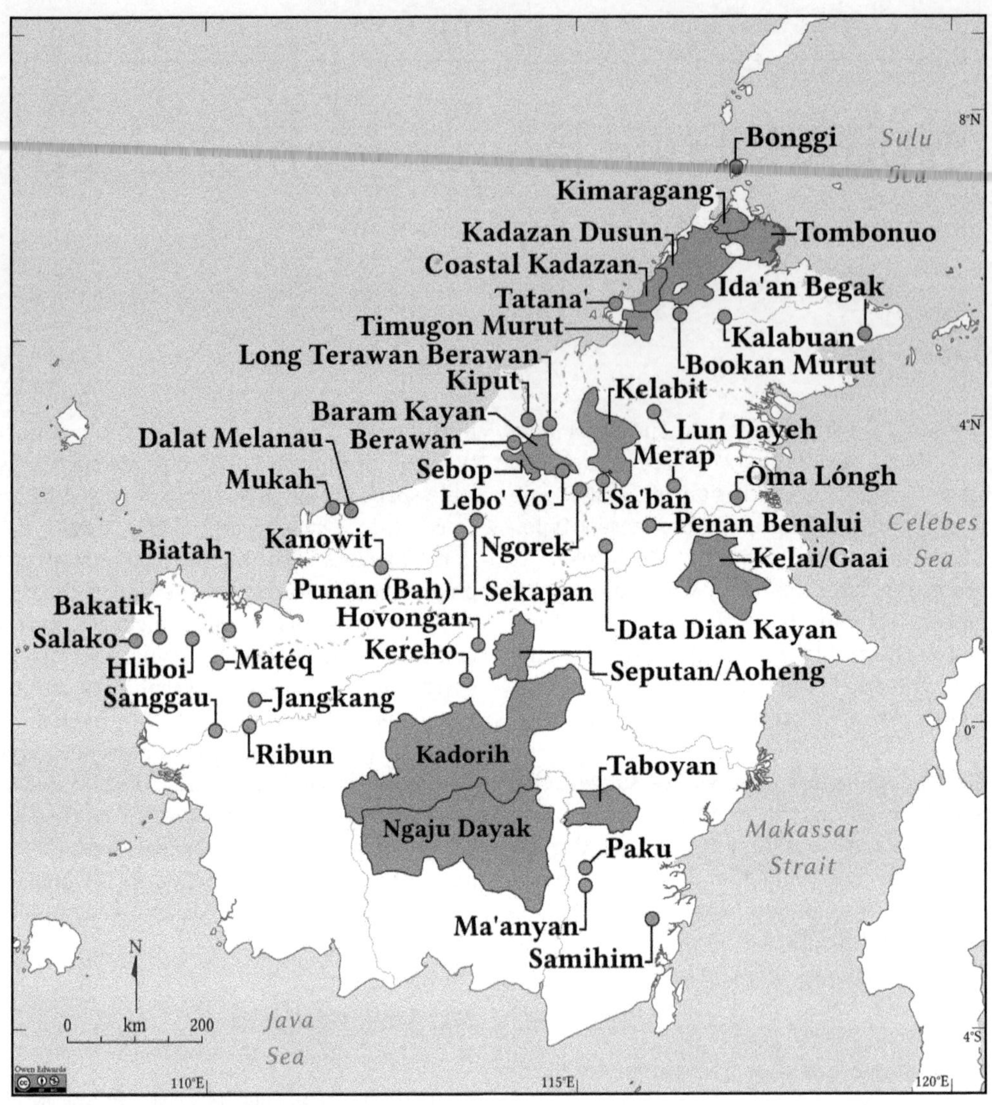


**Map 27.1** The non-Malayic languages of Borneo.

an initial 'minor' syllable followed by a word-final 'main' syllable. Minor syllables are unstressed, short, and allow only a restricted set of vowels, whereas main syllables are stressed, long, and typically allow for the full range of vowel contrasts. Languages may have different levels of sesquisyllabicity. Some, such as various Modang dialects, permit only schwa in the penultimate minor syllable. Others, such as Kiput, may permit several different vowels in the penult, but permissible penultimate vowels are always a fraction of permissible final-syllable vowels.

Most of the MSEA-type languages contain both sesquisyllabic and monosyllabic words and a system of strict word-final, rather than penultimate, stress. Languages of this type tend to have a preference for either sesquisyllabic or monosyllabic word shapes. Modang (Long Gelat and Woq Helaq) and Kiput, for example, are largely sesquisyllabic, while Kelai, Sa'ban, and Hliboi are mostly monosyllabic. In Table 27.1, languages are ordered from more monosyllabic languages (Hliboi, Kelai, Sa'ban) on the left to more sesquisyllabic languages (Woq Helaq, Long Gelat, Kiput) on the right, with examples of words illustrating their preference.

Regarding syllable shape, some languages of the MSEA type can have quite complex syllable structures. Most languages in this type allow for two-consonant onsets (Kiput is an exception, a MSEA-type language that avoids all consonant clusters), but others have greater syllable complexity. Merap, for example, can have three-consonant onset

**Table 27.1** Example languages demonstrating monosyllabic and sesquisyllabic word shapes

| Hliboi | Kelai | Sa'ban | Woq Helaq | Long Gelat | Kiput | |
|---|---|---|---|---|---|---|
| *bitotn* | *mtæn* | *atəh* | *məteə̯n* | *mətiə̯n* | *matəh* | 'eye' |
| *glaʔ* | *klæʔ* | *iliʔ* | *tələa̯ʔ* | *təleʔ* | *dələyʔ* | 'tongue' |
| *d:iə̯s* | *kol* | *t:ay* | *tayh* | *tayh* | *bəti* | 'calf' |
| *blatn* | *uluə̯n* | *blin* | *wəlun* | *ulun* | *bulin* | 'moon' |
| *blutn* | *bloə̯n* | *bləw* | *bəluə̯n* | *bələn* | *buləw* | 'body hair' |
| *jatn* | *ciə̯n* | *din* | *sin* | *sun* | *pəra:ʔ* | 'rain' |
| *klug* | *təlæŋ* | *hloə̯ŋ* | *təluə̯ŋ* | *təlua̯ŋ* | *tula:ŋ* | 'bone' |
| *d:utn* | *ptao̯* | *təw* | *to* | *toə̯* | *kutəw* | 'louse' |

clusters paired with complex nuclei: *ŋkraw̯əʔ* 'to snore'[1] and *hŋki̯ət* 'every'. Hliboi also has rather complex syllables, including syllables of the shape CCVCC, CCCVC, and CCCVCC: *ntitn* 'to remember', *ŋglap* 'to overflow', *ŋglupm* 'to set, of the sun'. These types of complex syllable shapes are unattested in languages with ISEA type phonologies in Borneo, which, as stated earlier, tend to have greater restrictions on syllable shape.

## 27.2.2 Consonant inventories

Most languages of Borneo, regardless of phonological type, follow a typical western Austronesian typology of consonants. A 'prototypical' consonant inventory contains oral stops with a voicing contrast, a set of nasals, two to three fricatives, and typical sonorants. An additional feature that is found throughout Borneo is the presence of implosive stops, a feature that cuts across the ISEA and MSEA phonological typologies. Some languages also have less typologically common consonants, such as lateral fricatives (Kajang) and voiceless sonorants (Sa'ban, Merap, and Hliboi), but these are rare overall.

### 27.2.2.1 *Implosive stops*

Implosive consonants can be found in all parts of Borneo in a diverse group of languages. A preference for implosive consonants at forward places of articulation, labial and alveolar, is well established, although some languages have attested implosive consonants at palatal and velar positions as well. An example of the preference for implosives at forward places of articulation comes from Kadazan Dusun, where Blust (2010b: 60) states that "the voiced bilabial and alveolar stops in most native words of Kadazan Dusun are implosives, and non-implosive *b* and *d* are generally confined to loanwords."

In the Lebo' Vo' language, implosive consonants are found at all places of articulation: labial, *ɓ*; alveolar, *ɗ*; palatal, *ʄ*; and velar, *ɠ*. In the case of Lebo' Vo', the palatal and velar implosives form contrasts with regular voiced stops at the same place of articulation, *ʄ* vs. *j* and *ɠ* vs. *g*. Contrasts in similar environments between plain and imploded stops can be seen between *məjam* 'smart' and *pəʄap* 'to count' and between *təgan* 'floor' and *məɠaʔ* 'to shake off dust from s.t.' The Lebo' Vo' data is even more interesting when the phonemics of implosives are considered. The bilabial and alveolar implosives are in variation with the regular stops, so the only *phonemic* implosives in this language are at the palatal and velar places of articulation. Bintulu, spoken on the coast of Sarawak, also allows implosives in multiple places of articulation, although they are not phonemic. In Bintulu, the implosive stops ɓ, ɗ, and ɠ appear only in the onsets of final syllables and are allophones of the regular stops b, d, and g.

### 27.2.2.2 *Voiced aspirates*

Borneo is also home to typologically rare "true voiced aspirates" as described by Blust 2006. True voiced aspirates are described as consonants that begin voiced, end voiceless, and have an extended voice onset time. Phonetically, such consonants may be transcribed as [b͡pʰ], [d͡tʰ], and so forth, depending on place of articulation. Such consonants are

[1] Merap is known for having triphthongs which, although complex, represent single syllable nuclei. Smith (2017c) discusses why these words are monosyllabic, rather than disyllabic, with phonological evidence.

found in the Long Semadoh, Long Lellang, and Bario dialects of Kelabit. They arose after voiced consonants lengthened, resulting in an extended period of voicing during full oral closure, which presented a phonetic difficulty that was eventually eliminated through terminal devoicing of the stop: [b] > [b:] > [b͡pʰ] (see Blust 2018b for more).

#### 27.2.2.3 *Gemination*

Consonant gemination is fairly common in Borneo, and a large number of languages have either phonemically long consonants which form a contrast with singleton consonants, or phonetically long consonants which lengthen under predictable conditions. Phonetically conditioned consonant lengthening in the onset of a final syllable is common throughout Borneo in words with a schwa in an open penult. Such systems were likely inherited from a common ancestor. For example, in the dialect of Kayan spoken in Data Dian, Indonesia, phonetic gemination was recorded in Smith (2017a). It is observed after a penultimate schwa but not after other vowels: *təpaʔ* [təp:áʔ] 'to pound rice'; *mətaŋ* [mət:áŋ] 'to ask'; and *məjuʔ* [məj:úʔ] 'to lift; carry'. An identical pattern is observed in Sekapan, spoken in central Sarawak, Malaysia: *bəbaw* [bəb:áw] 'tall'; *pətəbeə̯* [pətəb:éə̯] 'to meet'; *məjat* [məj:át] 'to pull'; and *məgəm* [məg:ə́m] 'strong'.

Phonemic geminate consonants (those which form meaningful contrasts with singleton consonants) are also common and are often analysable as arising from historically conditioned lengthening triggered by schwa that was subsequently phonemicized through sound change. Not all cases of geminate consonants are analysable in this way, however. Phonemic geminate consonants can be observed in Begak, a language of Sabah. In Begak, Goudswaard (2005) records gemination after a penultimate schwa in words like *dəl:ay* 'job's tears' and *rəp:a* 'a fathom' but also after other vowels and in unpredictable environments as in *sərag:aʔ* 'to fight' and *bid:aʔ* 'different'.

Begak also permits word-initial geminate clusters in monosyllabic words. Initial geminates, although typologically quite rare, are found in several Bornean languages. In Idaan Begak, the following words occur with initial geminates: *b:oŋ* 'a skin disease'; *p:aʔ* 'thigh'; and *d:aʔ* 'blood'. Other languages with initial geminates include Sa'ban, with examples such as *b:əh* 'derris root'; *d:əuʔ* 'seven'; and *t:ay* 'calf of the leg' (Blust 2001b), Hliboi with examples such as *b:akŋ* 'hole'; *m:uk* 'soft'; *d:is* 'calf of the leg' (Smith 2017a), and Kiput,[2] with examples /lay/ [l:ay] 'dry season' and /say/ [s:ay] 'meat; flesh' (Blust 2002b: 388).

[2] In Kiput, word-initial geminates are conditioned allophones of singleton consonants. If a monosyllabic word has a short vowel, then the initial consonant automatically lengthens.

### 27.2.3 Vowels

We now turn our attention to the typology of vowels in Borneo. A clear majority of languages in Borneo maintain a stable inventory of between four and six vowels, most commonly the vowel triangle, /a, u, i/ with the addition of mid vowels, /e, o/ and schwa /ə/ in some languages. An example of a language with relatively few vowel contrasts is Mukah Melanau, which Blust describes as having four vowel phonemes, /i, a, u, ə/. This type of system is also common in Sabah, although the mid-central vowel *ə* is often written *o*, and pronounced with a backed articulation. Slightly larger inventories are quite common, including five and six vowel systems which make up the majority of vowel inventories in the languages of Borneo. A five-vowel system of /i, e, a, o, u/ has been recorded in Kendayan/Salako (Adelaar 2005e), Punan, Hovongan/Kereho, various Barito languages, and many more (Smith 2017a). Six vowel systems, /i, e, a, o, u, ə/, include those found in Kenyah (most varieties), Kayan, Kajang, Kanowit, Malayic, Land Dayak, various Barito languages, and some Sabahan languages (e.g. Begak; Goudswaard 2005).

Among the MSEA-type languages, there is a tendency for vowel inventory expansion. Some of the more dramatic cases are Merap and Sa'ban, two languages which have expanded their vowel inventories to an extreme degree. (When discussing vowel inventories, we take both simple and complex syllable nuclei as constituting vowel contrasts, which includes diphthongal and triphthongal realizations.) In Sa'ban, for example, Blust (2001b) reports twenty-six distinctions, which includes ten monophthongal vowels (i, ɪ, e, ɛ, a, u, ʊ, o, ɔ, ə), nine diphthongs (iə̯, eə̯, əy, əw, ay, aw, uə̯, oə̯, oy), and seven triphthongs (iə̯w, eə̯w, aə̯y, aə̯w, oə̯y, oə̯w, uə̯w). Smith (2017c) also reports twenty-six distinctions in Merap, including the seven monophthongs i, u, ɛ, ə, o, a, aː plus fifteen diphthongs, ĩə̯, iə̯, iw, ũə̯, uə̯, uy, ɛy, əw, oy, ãə̯, aə̯, ao̯, au̯, ai̯, ae̯, and four triphthongs, oyə̯, ɛyə̯, awə̯, ayə̯. Honourable mentions for languages with large vowel inventories include Kiput, with twenty-four, Kelai, with seventeen, Long Terawan Berawan, with sixteen, and Gaai, with fifteen.

Vowel inventory expansion beyond the typical four to six vowels is not restricted to MSEA-type languages, nor is it guaranteed that languages of this type will undergo expansions in vowel inventory. Land Dayak languages are stress-final and many have sesquisyllabic or monosyllabic word shapes, but Land Dayak languages have so far not undergone the types of dramatic vowel inventory expansions seen in some other languages. Hliboi, for example, is of the MSEA type with a preference for monosyllabic content words but a vowel inventory of *i*, *e*, *a*, *o*, *u*, and *ə* (Smith

2019a). Biatah, a dialect cluster within Land Dayak, is another example. Kroeger (n.d.) reports up to eight vowels, seven well-attested vowels (*i, e, a, o, u, ə, ɯ*), and minimal attestation for the eighth vowel (ɤ). Although Biatah has a slightly larger vowel inventory than most other Land Dayak languages, it has not undergone the type of expansion found in many other MSEA-type languages of Borneo.

There are also examples of vowel inventory expansion in ISEA type languages. For example, Òma Lóngh has innovated a lax–tense distinction in the mid vowels, resulting in an eight-vowel inventory: i, e, ɛ, a, u, o, ɔ, ə, and Seputan innovated two additional high vowels resulting in a seven-vowel inventory: i, ɪ, e, a, o, ʉ, u (Soriente 2006 and Smith 2017a respectively). What differentiates these examples from those of the MSEA type are a lack of diphthong and triphthong contrasts, and overall fewer distinctions.

#### 27.2.3.1 *Vowel length*

Vowel length distinctions are not common in Borneo, but are nevertheless found in some languages. Often, length distinctions are restricted to final syllables. In Merap, for example, there is a distinction between /a/ and /a:/ which occurs only in the final syllable, for example, *prah* 'sick; painful' and *lata:h* 'flat'. Some Kayan languages have a length distinction between /a/ and /a:/ that is even more restricted, occurring only before a word-final glottal stop. An example is Data Dian *m-ata:ʔ* 'raw' and *mataʔ* 'eye'.

Another example of a length distinction found only in final syllables is from Biatah (Land Dayak), where vowel length is contrastive only in closed word-final syllables. Examples of vowel length contrasts in final syllables in Biatah are *bas* 'bus' vs. *ba:s* 'great; big'; *juʔ* 'seven' vs. *ju:ʔ* 'juice'; *buʔan* 'drop; throw down' vs. *buʔa:n* 'bearing fruit'; and *səgan* 'cram; pack down' vs. *səga:n* 'downstairs'. Length is not contrastive in open syllables (a situation that is paralleled in the other languages already discussed). Instead, word-final (open-syllable) vowels are predictably lengthened in Biatah when they appear in phrase-final position; they do not form lexical contrasts.

#### 27.2.3.2 *Velar-conditioned vowel breaking*

A process of vowel breaking and fronting in final syllables, conditioned by the presence of a velar consonant in word-final position, is widespread in Borneo. Numerous cases have been recorded, including in Ngorek (Blust 1974b), Mukah Melanau (Blust 1988a), Uma Juman and Data Dian (Blust 1977b; Smith 2017a), Kiput (Blust 2002b), Merap (Smith 2017c), Kajang languages and Punan Bah (Smith 2017a). In Mukah Melanau, for example, /i/ is realized as [iə̯], /u/ as [uə̯], and /a/ as [eə̯] before word-final velars *-k* and *-ŋ* (but not before *-g*) and also before word-final -h (from earlier *-R) but not before other word-final consonants. In Data Dian and Balui Liko, /i/ is realized as [iə̯] in *utiə̯ŋ* 'domestic pig' and *masiə̯k* 'fish', and Data Dian further fronts /a/ in *lufeə̯ŋ* 'hole' and *aneə̯k* 'child' (from earlier *lubaŋ and *anak). In Punan Bah, four vowels, *a, i, u,* and *o* undergo velar-conditioned breaking: *luveə̯ŋ* 'hole' (underlying /luvaŋ/), *bəruə̯ʔ* 'pig-tailed macaque' (from earlier *bəruk), *ikiə̯ŋ* 'pinky', and *masoə̯ʔ* 'to enter' (from earlier *masək). In all known cases of velar-conditioned vowel breaking, *g* does not act as a trigger.

### 27.2.4 Nasals and nasality

Nasality is an interesting topic in Borneo, since the island is the centre of a large, diffuse linguistic area where nasals in word-final position are often pronounced with a secondary homorganic oral stop immediately preceding the nasal (for example, /am/ may be pronounced [a$^{p}$m]). These are named pre-ploded word-final nasals, and are common in western Borneo as well as in the far north in Bonggi, to the east in some Barito and Modang languages, and outside of Borneo in Aslian (Mon-Khmer) and Chamic languages of Mainland Southeast Asia and Sumatra as well as in Urak Lawoi', a Malayic language of southern Thailand. Phillips (2005); Blust (1997b); and Adelaar (1995b) describe the scope and motivations for this phenomenon, and a brief overview will be given here. Pre-plosion occurs in Southeast Asia only in nasal consonants in historically word-final position, and only when preceded by a phonetically oral (non-nasal) vowel. The oral stop may be pronounced as voiced or voiceless, depending on the language, and there are no known conditioning factors which can predict the emergence of voiced vs. voiceless plosives in pre-ploded nasals. The following examples illustrate word-final nasal pre-plosion in two Land Dayak languages (Banyaduq and Bakatik (/Bekati')), two Barito languages (Benuaq and Taboyan), Bonggi (northeast Sabah), and Woq Helaq (Kayanic). Note that in Bakatik the non-nasal element has come to totally replace the inherited nasal. Total replacement of the nasal is also observed in Urak Lawoi', and some Chamic languages (not shown in example (1)).

(1)

| | |
|---|---|
| Banyaduq: | *rubakŋ* 'hole', *idukŋ* 'nose', *anapm* 'sick', *gaatn* 'name' |
| Bakatik: | *rubak* 'hole', *duduk* 'nose', *anap* 'sick', *gaut* 'name' |
| Benuaq: | *liakŋ* 'hole', *urukŋ* 'nose', *atetn* 'liver', *ayapm* 'pangolin' |
| Taboyan: | *luagŋ* 'hole', *aradn* 'name', *maləbm* 'night' |
| Bonggi: | *idukŋ* 'nose', *ŋaardn* 'name', *siabm* 'nine' |
| Woq Helaq: | *ŋəlẹədn* 'name', *ŋəndabm* 'dark', *təkəwgŋ* 'helmeted hornbill' |

Blust (1997b) pointed to the directionality of nasalization as motivation for word-final nasal pre-plosion. Austronesian languages of the area typically have rightward-spreading (or onset-driven) nasality. Nasality spreads from a nasal onset onto a following vowel, but coda nasals do not similarly nasalize the preceding vowel. Early closure of the velum helps prevent leftward nasal spread and under this view, may have motivated the appearance of final-nasal pre-plosion in languages throughout Borneo. See Jardine et al. (2015) for more on this phenomenon in Banyaduq.

A second, and less widespread, consequence of onset-driven nasality in Borneo is the pre-nasalization of previously oral word-final stops. Pre-nasalization was recorded in Land Dayak languages of western Borneo in Smith (2017a), where nasality spreads from the onset onto the vowel, but the velum remains open during the initial closure of the word-final stop. The result is pre-nasalization. Reflexes of Proto-Land Dayak *amut 'ghost; spirit' show this development in Jangkang, Ribun, and Sanggau, where *amut became *munt*, with the addition of pre-nasalization before the word-final stop.

Prenasalization of oral stops clearly originates in the rightward spread of nasality from nasal onsets. Rightward nasal spreading also motivates a third type of nasal phenomenon, namely the nasalization of intervocalic glides. This phenomenon is found concentrated in languages of south and southeastern Borneo, including Modang, Central Sarawak (Smith 2017a), and Barito languages such as Ngaju Dayak and Ma'anyan (Rubay et al. 1997). In the root *kayaw* 'headhunting', for example, the intervocalic *y* may alternate with the nasal *ñ* when the root is prefixed with a nasal: Ngaju Dayak *ŋañaw*, Long Gelat Modang *ŋəñu*, Kajaman *ŋañaw*, Punan Bah *(ma)ŋañuow*. In Punan Bah specifically, the root *kayaw* is independently attested, meaning that the alternation is a part of the synchronic phonology. Less common, but still attested, is the alternation of intervocalic *w* with *ŋ*, which can be seen in Sekapan *məŋah* 'second person dual', which is formed from the second person prefix *m-* attached to the bound root *-əgwah*, itself from Proto-Central Sarawak *dua [duwa] 'two'.

### 27.2.5 Stress systems

There are two main types of stress systems in Borneo: systems where stress falls exclusively or mainly on the penultimate syllable (associated with ISEA-type phonologies), and systems where stress falls on the final syllable (associated with MSEA-type phonologies). Both types are found throughout the island, but penultimate stressed languages are more common. Wherever descriptions are available, penultimate stressed languages follow a right-bound trochaic pattern, where primary stress falls on the penultimate syllable, with secondary stress falling on every other syllable to the left.

Many examples of a strict penultimate stress are found in Sabah. For example, Prentice (1971) lists several examples from various Murutic languages. Pekkanen (1993), Hurlbut (1993), Harris and Chapple (1993), Spitzack (1993), and King (1993) describe the same type of system for Tatana', Labuk-Kinabatangan Kadazan, Tagal, Kalabuan, and Tombonuo respectively. Similar strict penultimate systems are also found in Barito, with Paku having a penultimate-only stress system (Diedrich 2018). A few Sabahan languages, such as Kimaragang Dusun (Kroeger 1993b) and Coastal Kadazan (Miller 1993), are reported to have stress systems that are not fully predictable but at the same time not contrastive (there are no cases where stress alone is responsible for distinguishing between otherwise homophonous lexemes).

Elsewhere, there is still a preference for penultimate stress, although many languages have an additional constraint that prevents stress from falling on the penultimate syllable if its vowel is schwa. In the Long Wat language, part of the Kenyah subgroup, Blust (n.d.) recorded penultimate stress in *lúəh* from *duha 'two' and *búlun* from PMP *bulu(-n) 'body hair' but final stress in *təláw* from PMP *təlu 'three' and *təbə́w* from PMP *təbuh 'sugarcane'. In these cases, stress is final because penultimate schwa cannot hold stress on its own. In some languages, schwa in the penultimate syllable may hold stress, but only after the following consonant lengthens. This is the case in the Bario dialect of Kelabit (Blust 2006, 2018b). In Bario Kelabit stress falls on the penultimate syllable like most languages of Borneo. If the penultimate-syllable vowel is schwa, stress remains on the penult, but the following onset lengthens. If the following onset is /r/, however, consonant lengthening does not occur and stress shifts to the final syllable. Note that gemination does not render penultimate schwa capable of holding stress in all languages. For example, in Data Dian, stress shifts to the final syllable after a penultimate schwa even though consonants simultaneously lengthen in words like *təp:áʔ* 'pound rice', *mət:áŋ* 'ask', and *məj:úʔ* 'lift; carry' (Smith 2017a).

Languages with a fixed word-final stress system are found mostly in central Borneo, but the Ida'an languages in Sabah represent a small group in the north with final stress (Goudswaard 2005). Word-final stress is found in Kiput (Blust 2002b), in all recorded Segai-Modang languages (Smith 2019b), in Land Dayak (Smith 2019a), and in many Malayic languages such as Iban and Kendayan, amongst others. All languages with an MSEA typology also have word-final stress, although not all languages with word-final stress have an MSEA typology. For example, many Land Dayak and Malayic languages in western Borneo have word-final stress but a more ISEA-type phonology in other respects.

## 27.3 Clause structure

In terms of grammatical typology, we can classify the languages of Borneo into three prototypes, as noted in the introduction to this chapter. Philippine-type languages are found in northeastern Borneo. The Indonesian type includes, but is not restricted to, the Malay varieties of coastal Borneo and Malayic languages such as Iban and Kendayan of western Borneo. The third type, in its grammatical features, exhibits some similarity to languages of Mainland Southeast Asia; but it is probably more useful to speak of a 'Central Borneo type', as described by Beatrice Clayre (1996, 2014). Of course, the boundaries between these types are somewhat fuzzy, and a number of languages will be seen to be transitional in various respects between two types.

Himmelmann (2002a) states that "the presence of both pronominal prefixes and applicative suffixes is held to be the crucial characteristic" that defines Indonesian-type languages. (Core Central Borneo languages have neither of these features.) Other commonly assumed features of Indonesian-type languages include SVO as basic word order and a simple two-way voice contrast, active vs. passive. In fact, as noted in Kroeger and Riesberg (this volume, §47.2), many Indonesian-type languages have three distinct voice categories: active (typically marked with a nasal prefix), inflected passive, and zero-marked (and non-demoting) Undergoer Voice. Since the properties of these languages are discussed in some detail in that chapter, we focus here on the Philippine-type (as represented in northeastern Borneo) and the Central Borneo type.

### 27.3.1 Core Sabah languages

The boundary between Philippine- and non-Philippine-type languages in Borneo roughly follows the southern border of the Malaysian state of Sabah.[3] All of the indigenous Philippine-type languages of Sabah belong to one of three related subgroups (Prentice 1971): Dusunic, Paitanic, and Murut-Tidung.[4]

Himmelmann (2005a: 113) offers the following criteria for identifying Philippine-type languages:

> Philippine-type languages are symmetrical voice languages which have:
>
> a) at least two formally and semantically different undergoer voices. . .;
> b) at least one non-local phrase marking clitic for nominal expressions. . .;
> c) pronominal second position clitics.

The term 'symmetrical voice' refers to a non-demoting voice alternation, in contrast to passive or antipassive which select a new subject by demoting the underlying subject to oblique status; see Kroeger and Riesberg (this volume, §47.1–2) for discussion. In addition to complex voice systems, case marking, and second position clitic pronouns, Philippine-type languages are known to have strongly verb-initial word order, a fairly rich inventory of derivational morphology, and an ergative bias (or 'patient preference') in voice selection. In other words, the active voice is dispreferred for transitive verbs, except when the patient or Undergoer is indefinite, or when the Actor is the target of some syntactic operation such as extraction, Raising, or control. This preference is true to varying degrees among the languages of Sabah. All of these Philippine-type features are most strongly attested in northern Sabah, and become progressively weaker or less consistent the farther south one looks.

#### 27.3.1.1 *Voice*

As discussed in Kroeger and Riesberg (this volume §47.3), the verb in a typical Philippine-type language is inflected for one of several voice categories (typically between four and six), which identify the semantic role of the subject.

[3] The indigenous Philippine-type languages of Sabah comprise a subgroup which has been referred to as the Northeast Borneo group (Wurm 1983) or the Southwest Sabah group (Blust 2010b). The label 'Northeast Borneo' reflects the current distribution of the language groups, while 'Southwest Sabah' refers to the proposed location where the protolanguage for this group was spoken.

[4] Recent work by Jason Lobel (2013b) makes a strong case for some revision in this sub-classification, but we use the traditional sub-grouping labels for convenience in the present chapter.

NP arguments are case-marked, with nominative case identifying the subject NP. Among the core Sabah languages, northern Dusunic and northern Paitanic varieties preserve quite strongly the classic Philippine voice and case patterns, as illustrated in (2) with examples from Kimaragang Dusun (adapted from Kroeger 2005a). The Murut and Tidung languages to the south, occupying the border areas between Sabah and northern Kalimantan, are more innovative.

Kimaragang Dusun

(2) a. Active Voice

*Mangalapak*[m-poN-lapak] *oku* *do*
AV-TR-split 1SG.NOM GEN
*niyuw.*
coconut
'I will split a coconut/some coconuts.'[5]

b. Objective Voice

*Lapak-on* *ku* *it* *niyuw.*
split-OV 1SG.GEN NOM coconut
'I will split *the coconut(s)*.'

c. Dative Voice

*Lapak-an* *ku* *do* *niyuw* *it* *wogok.*
split-DV 1SG.GEN GEN coconut NOM pig
'I will split some coconuts for *the pig(s)* (to eat).'

d. Instrumental Voice

*Tongo* *ot* *pangalapak*[Ø-poN-lapak]
what NOM IV-TR-split
*nu* *dilo?* *niyuw?*
2SG.GEN that coconut
'*What* will you split those coconuts with?'

e. Conveyance Voice ('affected instrument' usage)

*Nokuro.tu* *n-i-lapak* *nu* *do*
why PST-CV-split 2SG.GEN GEN
*niyuw* *ino* *dangol* *ku?*
coconut that(NOM) bush.knife 1SG.GEN
'Why did you use *my bush knife* to split coconuts?'

f. Circumstantial Voice

*Sera/Siombo* *pangalapakan[poN-lapak-an]*
when/where CIRCV-split-CIRCV
*kito* *diti* *niyuw?*
1DU.INCL this coconut
'*When/Where* shall we split these coconuts?'

Geographically there is a clear trend toward simplification in the voice systems as one travels from north to south and (for Dusunic) from east to west. This simplification involves a reduction in the number of voice categories, beginning with the loss of the Conveyance Voice prefix (*i-*), the reflex of Proto-Austronesian *Si-. A striking exception to this generalization is Tatana', a language in the southwest corner of Sabah that preserves the full six-voice system illustrated in (2) (Dillon 1994).

Conveyance Voice can also be marked with a circumfix *po-*ROOT*-on* (or *pa-*ROOT*-on*) in all of the core Sabah languages, and apparently only in these languages (Kroeger 2011).[6] In languages where *i-* is no longer productive, including those represented in (3), this circumfix is the only or primary means of marking Conveyance Voice. In languages where *i-* is retained, the circumfix occurs in free variation with *i-*, as illustrated in (4).

(3) a. Bundu Tuhan Dusun

*Po-tokon-on* *ku* *i* *tandus* *do*
CV-throw-CV 1SG.GEN NOM spear PART
*hilo* *id* *gouton.*
there DAT jungle
'I will throw *(your) spear* into the bush.'
(Harrison 2007)

b. Bookan Murut

*Pa-sungug-o* *timug* *da* *pariuk* *ino.*
CV-pour-CV.IMP water DAT pot that
'Pour *the water* into the pot.'
(adapted from Doi and Doi 2003: 83)

c. Kalabuan (Southern Paitanic)

*Pa-atag-o?* *nai* *so?* *baladi* *no.*
CV-put-CV.IMP there DAT bucket that
'Put (*it*) there in the bucket.' (Spitzack 1988: 144)

(4) a. Tombonuo (Northern Paitanic)

*I-siit/po-siit-on* *bo* *ono* *baai-o* *so*
CV-hang PART that bag-that DAT
*lansang-o.*
nail-that
'Hang up *that bag* on that nail.'
(King and King n.d.: 657)

b. Tatana'

*I-taak/pa-taak-on* *ku* *ani?* *dokou*
CV-give 1SG.GEN only 2SG.DAT
*bua?* *diti.*
fruit this
'I am just giving *this fruit* to you (no price).'
(Dillon 1994: 48)

[5] In exx. 2–4, the English phrase corresponding to the subject (nominative argument) is italicized.

[6] As Kroeger (1988) points out, the circumfix is formally identical to a morphological causative in Objective Voice with intransitive or ingestive roots. Synchronically, the circumfix is clearly not part of the morphological causative paradigm. This can be seen from the inherent transitivity of the roots in examples (3)–(4), and from the fact that morphological causatives allow permissive and indirect causation interpretations, whereas the Conveyance Voice circumfix allows neither. See Harrison (2013) for a proposal concerning the diachronic development of this circumfix, based on Dusunic evidence.

#### 27.3.1.2 *Case marking*

In these Philippine-type languages, all NP arguments are case-marked, with three cases being distinguished: nominative, genitive, and dative/locative. Case is marked by the use of suppletive forms for the pronouns (and, in Dusunic, demonstratives), and by clitic particles on lexical NPs, with distinct forms of the case clitics for personal names vs. common noun phrases. The use of the personal vs. common noun forms of the genitive marker in Timugon Murut is illustrated in (5). Representative samples of the case marking clitics are presented in Table 27.2. As this table shows, all of the core Sabah languages have "at least one non-local phrase marking clitic for nominal expressions" (Himmelmann 2005a: 113), namely the genitive case marker, thus satisfying the second of Himmelman's criteria as listed above.

Timugon Murut
(5) a. *Lapak-on* *ru=maayo* *ku=no*
split-OV GEN=older.sibling my=there
*Ø=luton* *no.*
NOM=firewood that
'The firewood was split by my big brother.'

b. *Lapak-on* *ri=apa?* *Ø=luton*
split-OV GEN=father NOM=firewood
*no.*
that
'The firewood was split by Father.'
(adapted from Brewis 2004)

**Table 27.2** Case marking clitics in four Sabah languages

| | | NOM | GEN | DAT/ LOC |
|---|---|---|---|---|
| Kimaragang | Personal name | *i* | *di* | *sid+i* |
| (Dusunic) | Common nouns | *i(t)~o(t)* | *di(t)~do(t)*[a] | *sid* |
| Tombonuo | Personal name | *si* | *ni* | *so* |
| (Paitanic) | Common nouns | *Ø* | *nu* | *so* |
| Timugon | Personal name | *i* | *ri* | *ra* |
| (Murutic) | Common nouns | *Ø* | *ru* | *ra* |
| Tatana' | Personal name | *i* | *ni* | *di* |
| (mixed) | Common nouns | *Ø* | *nu* | *do* |

[a] The /i/ forms occur with definite NPs, the /o/ forms with indefinites

Nominative case marks the subject. The genitive case is used not only for possessors but also for the agent of a non-active clause, as seen in examples (2b)–(2f), (3a), and (4b). Pronominal direct objects normally get dative case, while lexical NP direct objects get genitive case in Dusunic and Paitanic languages, but dative in Murutic and Tatana'. The case marker which is used for direct objects is also used for a variety of other arguments and adjuncts, as illustrated in (6) with uses of the dative case in Timugon and Tatana'. We might refer to this as the 'general' case marker for the language. The common noun form of the general case marker is, in many languages, also used as a linker, relativizer, and/or complementizer, marking various types of subordinate clauses, etc.

(6) a. Timugon Murut
*Mangiru?*[m-paN-iru?] *aku* *ra=tana?*
AV-TR-becomes.loose 1SG.NOM DAT=earth
*ra=kinandoi* *ti.*
DAT=machete this
'I'll remove the earth with this machete.'
(Brewis 2004)

b. Tatana'
*Popo-taak* *isio* *do=usin* *do=anak*
AV.TR-give 3SG.NOM DAT=money DAT=child
*no.*
3SG.GEN
'He gives money to his child.' (Dillon 1994: 48)

#### 27.3.1.3 *Order of clausal constituents and special clitics*

As is frequently observed in case-marking languages, the order of lexical NP arguments after the verb is somewhat flexible. In non-active clauses the genitive agent tends to come first in a number of languages (e.g. Kimaragang, Tatana'), and NP arguments tend to come before PPs. Several authors report that where there is potential ambiguity, for example, if two or more NP arguments bear the same case marker, then the order of constituents is fixed. In Tatana' this most basic ordering is: V–Actor–Subject–Undergoer–other core argument–Locative–Time (Dillon 1994: 65ff.). Brewis (2004) describes the basic ordering of NPs in Timugon Murut as V–agent–patient–recipient–instrument–locative, but states that the subject NP normally precedes all other full NP arguments. Hurlbut (1988: 6) states that the basic word order in Labuk Kadazan is V–Actor–Subject–other, but does not describe an ordering for arguments after the subject NP. These patterns, and in particular the order described by Dillon for Tatana', are very reminiscent of the basic word order pattern in a number of Philippine languages: V–Actor–Subject–other (ordered by semantic role); see Kroeger and Riesberg (this volume §47.3.3) for discussion.

In discussing constituent order, it is important to distinguish lexical NPs from pronouns. First, it appears that in most, if not all, core Sabah languages, there is a general preference for pronouns to precede lexical NP arguments. Second, certain pronoun forms are special clitics, which always appear near the verb. In many Sabah languages these clitic pronouns are Wackernagel, or second position (2P), clitics, which immediately follow the verb in basic, verb-initial word order, but precede the verb when negation or some other element appears in clause initial position. This is Himmelman's third criterion for identifying Philippine-type languages: "pronominal second position clitics."

Aside from the clitic pronouns, it seems that most core Sabah languages have other types of 2P clitics as well, typically including particles that mark aspect, mood (sentence type), and a wide range of other functions such as miratives, frustratives, quotatives (hearsay markers), etc.[7] Wackernagel clitics of these types are also a common feature of languages of the Philippines.

Second position pronominal clitics are most common in northern Sabah, and become more sporadic as one moves farther south. In Kimaragang, all genitive pronouns are 2P clitics, as are first and second person nominative pronouns.[8] Third person nominative pronouns may optionally function as second position clitics. Together with the aspectual and other classes of second position particles mentioned above, these forms occur immediately after the verb in verb-initial clauses like (7), and immediately before the verb when a negation marker or some other focused element precedes the verb, as in (8)–(9) (examples from Kroeger 2020).

Kimaragang

(7) *N-o-dindi* ***nu*** ***no*** ***gaam*** *i=wogok?*
PST-NVOL-hog.call 2SG.GEN IAM Q NOM=pig
'Have you called the pigs?'

(8) *Sid=tana* ***ya*** *n-odop-on.*
DAT=earth 1PL.EXCL.GEN PST-sleep-LV
'It was on the ground that we slept (after the house burned down).'

(9) *Amu* ***oku*** ***po*** ***dati*** *ko-guli*
NEG 1SG.NOM yet probably NVOL.AV-return
*dot* ...
COMP
'I probably cannot return (to work here tomorrow).'

Dillon (1994: 73ff.) states that in Tatana', first and second person genitive pronouns are 2P clitics. First and third person nominative pronouns are optional 2P clitics, while there are two forms for the second person nominative singular and plural pronouns, one clitic and the other not. Prentice (1971: 157ff) describes a slightly more complex situation in Timugon Murut. Aspectual and discourse particles appear to be 2P clitics, occurring before the verb when it is preceded by the negation marker. Nominative and genitive pronouns appear to be verb-adjacent clitics, in the sense of Billings and Kaufman (2004) and Lee and Billings (2005): they always occur immediately after the verb, with genitive Actor pronouns preceding nominative subject pronouns.[9] When the verb is the first element of the clause, both types of clitics follow the verb, with the 2P clitics following the verb-adjacent clitics.

The north–south distinction in prevalence of 2P clitic pronouns can be seen in the following contrast between Tombonuo (Northern Paitanic) and Kalabuan (Southern Paitanic; Upper Kinabatangan river). In the Tombonuo example (10a), we see the clitic pronoun in second position, following NEG but preceding the verb. In the Kalabuan example (10b), we see the aspectual clitic in second position, but the clitic pronoun follows the verb.

(10) a. Tombonuo
*Dai* *aku* *noko-oyang.*
NEG 1SG.NOM AV.PST.POT-find
'I didn't find it.' (King 1988: 154)

b. Kalabuan
*Daa* *po* *raiton* *ku* *ong* *ada?*
NEG ASP say.OV 1SG.GEN COMP what
*inaal* *mu...*
PST.do.OV 2SG.GEN
'I do not yet mention what you did...'
(Spitzack 1988: 117)

### 27.3.2 Languages of central Borneo

Beatrice Clayre (1996, 2014) identifies a number of grammatical features which are shared by central Borneo languages such as Berawan, Melanau, Penan, Kayan, and Kenyah, and which distinguish these languages from the Philippine-type languages of northeastern Borneo. The central Borneo languages she discusses are spoken in Sarawak and adjacent areas of Kalimantan. She identifies the following distinctive characteristics of these languages:

[7] See Kroeger (2017, 2020) for a description of the Kimaragang Dusun clitics, Prentice (1971: 150ff) for a listing of 2P clitics in Timugon Murut.

[8] The second person nominative pronouns have two forms, one used when the pronoun is the first element of the clitic cluster, and the other when it is not.

[9] Certain adverbials can optionally function as clausal predicates, in which case nominative and genitive pronouns occur immediately after the adverbial predicate.

(11) Distinctive characteristics of central Borneo clause structure (based on Clayre 1996):
a) Just two voice categories, Actor Voice vs. Undergoer Voice/passive;
b) Actor Voice is the more normal or preferred form for transitive verbs;
c) Correlation between voice and tense-aspect, with morphological UV occurring only or primarily in past tense or completive aspect (the old non-past UV suffix *-en* occurs in nominalizations and fossilized verb forms);
d) Complex allomorphy in the voice morphology;
e) A periphrastic Undergoer Voice (or passive?) marked by an auxiliary verb is attested in a number of languages, which competes with, or replaces, UV verbal morphology;
f) Absence of case marking in common noun phrases;
g) No contrast between subject and object pronominal forms, but distinctive genitive pronouns used for actors and possessors, at least in the first person;
h) Fairly rigid word order, in which the non-subject core argument immediately follows the verb; preference for subject to precede verb in many of these languages, especially in Actor Voice;
i) Absence of applicative suffixes (dative and benefactive shift are possible in at least some of these languages, but not morphologically marked).

Table 27.3 summarizes the voice-marking affixes in four central Borneo languages. In all four of these languages, past tense or completive aspect is indicated by an auxiliary with AV forms; the AV verb itself is not inflected for tense-aspect. The productive UV markers are portmanteau morphemes expressing both voice and tense-aspect.

The choice of allomorph for the voice markers is partially predictable from the phonological shape of the root, but in some languages there seems to be a high degree of idiosyncratic (irregular and/or lexically determined) allomorphy. The *-i-* and *-u-* allomorphs listed for Melanau in Table 27.3 represent ABLAUT, a pattern of vowel alternation in which an underlying schwa is replaced by *-i-* or *-u-*. Blust (1997c) reports that ablaut is attested in Kelabitic (including Lun Bawang, Kelabit, and Sa'ban) and several varieties of Melanau, as well as Berawan, Kiput, Miri, Narum, and Bintulu. Ablaut occurs as an allomorph of the infixes *-ən-* 'UV.past', and (more rarely) *-əm-* 'AV'. It generally applies to some but not all verb roots whose first vowel is a schwa, changing the schwa to /i/ to indicate 'UV.past', and (in certain languages) to /u/ to indicate 'AV'.[10] As noted by Clayre (1996: 65, fn. 17) ablaut is also attested in some Sabah languages, including Begak and, to a limited extent, Bonggi. Examples of Ablaut in Mukah Melanau are shown in Table 27.4, and additional examples from Begak in Table 27.5.

Examples of Central Borneo-type clause structure are presented in (12), with data from Penan Benalui, and in (13), with data from Dalat Melanau. Notice the SVO word order, lack of case marking on common nouns, and non-clitic pronoun ordering.

Penan Benalui

(12) a. Actor Voice
*kuyat* *k<um>an*
longtail.macaque <AV>eat
*parai=kéq*
rice.plant=1SG
'the macaque eats my rice plants'

b. Undergoer Voice
*aseu=kéq* *p<en>orah* *tamen=kéq*
dog=1SG <UV>hit father=1SG
'my dog is/was hit by my father' (Soriente 2013)

Dalat Melanau

(13) a. Actor Voice
*Akou* *m-atuʔ* *teluh.*
1SG AV-pick.up egg
'I pick up an egg.'

b. Undergoer Voice
*Teluh* *n-atuʔ* *kou.*
egg UV.PST-pick.up 1SG.GEN
'I picked up the egg.'

c. Verb focus
*Atuʔ* *kou* *gaʔ* *teluh.*
pick.up 1SG.GEN at egg
'I picked up the egg.' (I. Clayre 1972: 338–41)

The alternation between Actor Voice and Undergoer Voice is illustrated in (12a–b) and (13a–b).[11] Notice that, at least in Melanau, the UV marker also indicates tense (or aspect). Example (13c) illustrates a construction that Iain Clayre (1972) refers to as "Verb Focus". Based on the marking of the

[10] Iain Clayre (1972) refers to the class of verbs which undergo ablaut as UIE verbs. Ablaut is sometimes accompanied by consonantal changes, a pattern which Blust refers to as "compound ablaut".

[11] The distinction between a symmetrical Undergoer Voice vs. a (demoting) passive voice is discussed in Kroeger and Riesberg (this volume, §47.1–2). The data needed to make this distinction are not available for most of the Central Borneo languages, so for the most part we will follow Clayre (1996) in referring to the non-active voice in these languages as Undergoer Voice. However, one must bear in mind that in some or all of these languages, the constructions in question could turn out to be true passives.

**Table 27.3** Voice-marking affixes in four central Borneo languages (Clayre 1996)

| LANGUAGE | ACTOR VOICE | UNDERGOER VOICE | |
|---|---|---|---|
| | | PAST | NON-PAST |
| Sa'ban | *n-, la-,* gemination | *i-* | (not productive) |
| Berawan | *N-, k-, p-* | *n-, -ən-, i-* | (none recorded) |
| Melanau | *m-, mə(N)-, -əm-, -u-* | *n(ə)-, -ən-, -i-* | bare root (infrequent) |
| Penan | *m-, N-* | *n(ə)-, -ən-, kə-* | bare root (infrequent) |

**Table 27.4** Examples of ablaut in Mukah Melanau (Blust 1997c; *e* = schwa)

| ROOT | GLOSS | AV | UV.past |
|---|---|---|---|
| *geget* | 'gnaw' | *guget* | *giget* |
| *kekut* | 'excavate' | *kukut* | *kikut* |
| *lepew* | 'pick' | *lupew* | *lipew* |
| *ngenget* | 'gnaw' | *ngunget* | *nginget* |
| *puput* | 'spray from mouth' | *memuput* | *piput* |
| *seleg* | 'burn' | *suleg* | *sileg* |
| *seput* | '(shoot with) blowpipe' | *suput* | *siput* |

**Table 27.5** Examples of ablaut in Begak (Goudswaard 2005: 46–8)

| ROOT | GLOSS | AV.dependent | UV.completive |
|---|---|---|---|
| *səgkow* | 'call' | *sugkow* | *sigkow* |
| *təssong* | 'stuff' | *tussong* | *tissong* |
| *səmmuʔ* | 'command' | *summuʔ* | *simmuʔ* |
| *dalud* | 'wait' | *dolud* | *delud* |
| *dagang* | 'buy' | *dogang* | *degang* |

arguments, this looks like it might be an impersonal (subjectless) construction, with the Actor pronoun appearing in the genitive and the Undergoer marked with a preposition. Note also the verb-initial (V-A-U) word order, in contrast to the normal subject-initial (S-V-O) word order. However, Beatrice Clayre (1996: 73) identifies this construction as a non-completive UV form. Some support for this suggestion comes from the fact that this is the form that is used when the Undergoer is relativized, as seen in (14). On the other hand, based on the English translations, it is not clear how the examples in (13c) and (14) can be interpreted as non-completive.

Dalat Melanau

(14) a. *kapak beʔ belei kou.*
axe REL buy 1SG.GEN
'the axe that I bought' (I. Clayre 1975: 229)

b. *teluh atuʔ nyin.*
egg pick.up 3SG
'the egg that he picked up' (I. Clayre 1972: 148)

Kanowit is an example of a language whose default word order is SVO in AV clauses, but verb initial in UV clauses (15). (Subject-initial order is possible in UV clauses, but less common in spontaneous speech.) Verb-initial order is also preferred in imperatives, in Kanowit and in a number of other languages which otherwise have SVO order.

Kanowit

(15) a. Actor Voice
*akoʔ ŋitin(N-gitin) ña*
1SG AV-pinch 3SG
'I pinched him.'

b. Undergoer Voice
*gənitin(<ən>gitin) ku ña*
<UV>pinch 1SG.GEN 3SG
'I pinched him.' (A. Smith, fieldnotes)

The periphrastic Undergoer Voice construction seems to be fairly widely attested. It is not restricted to central Borneo, but ranges from Land Dayak in the west to Bonggi and Begak in the northeast. Examples from Seputan, Matéq, and Begak are presented in (16)–(18). Notice that the main verb in this construction appears in the AV form, even though the clause as a whole functions as a kind of Undergoer Voice.[12] In all of the Lun Bawang examples cited by Clayre, the Undergoer-subject occurs at, or near, the end of the clause, following the main verb; but in many of the languages that have this

[12] In Begak the main verb appears in the Dependent form, which Goudswaard analyses as UV. We treat it as an AV form, based on case marking and word order patterns.

construction, the subject may occur in either clause-initial or final position, as seen here. In most languages there seems to be at least a preference, if not a requirement, for the auxiliary to precede the main verb, but some languages allow the opposite order. In either order, the actor NP in all languages must immediately follow the auxiliary. (The Undergoer-subject NP is italicized in the English translations for these examples.)

Seputan
(16) *ane nan tori inun ho mosu?*
child that PASS mother 3SG AV.breastfeed
'*the child* is being fed by her mother'
(A. Smith, fieldnotes)

Matéq Lun Dayeh: Undergoer Voice
(17) a. *pingat aiq yoh ni koq moruh*
plate that DET AUX 1SG AV.smash
'I smashed *the plate*.'
(lit: 'The plate was smashed by me.')

b. *ni ular aiq degeq nyora*
AUX snake that constantly AV.attack
*ruba turuaq=ng*
hole dibbling.stick=3
'The snake kept on attacking *their dibbling holes*.'
(lit: 'Their dibbling holes were constantly attacked by the snake.') (Connell 2013)

Begak: Undergoer Voice
(18) a. *Nong ku dumus(<u>dəmus) gulo anak*
AUX 1SG <AV.DEP>bathe first child
*ku te.*
1SG this
'I will/have to bathe my child first.'

b. *Suku assak no nong kəmmi*
all ripe that AUX 1PL.EXCL
*m-iang*
AV.DEP-separate
'All the ripe (rice) has to be/is usually separated by us.' (Goudswaard 2005: 191)

In some Bornean languages, the UV auxiliary is a form of the verb which means 'make' or 'do'. In Lun Bawang, for example, the verb for 'make' is *ng-anau* (AV), *ruen* (UV-nonpast), *i-nau* (UV-past). The verb can be used alone, as in 'they made a cooking tripod', or in a periphrastic causative construction, as in 'I will make her ready'. The UV forms of this same verb are used as the auxiliary in the periphrastic UV construction, illustrated in (19).

(19) a. Lun Bawang
*I-nau ku ng-egkar tarob di. . .*
AUX.PST 1SG.GEN AV-shake blanket DEF
'I shook *the blanket*, (but . . .)' (B. Clayre 1996: 77)

b. Lun Dayeh
*Ruen muh ngubuk iyeh...*
AUX.NPST 2SG.GEN AV.console 3SG
'Comfort *her*, (to make her stop crying.)'
(Ganang et al. 2008)

Actors tend to be expressed as pronouns in the majority of cited examples, but proper names and bare nouns are also not uncommon in this position. There does not seem to be any grammatical constraint requiring that the Actor in this construction consist of a single word, as in the UV constructions of Malay and Balinese. Clayre and Cubit (1974) cite the following example (see also (17b) above):

Kayan
(20) *En [lake? buta atih] ala na?.*
AUX man blind that(DIST) take it
'*It* was taken by that blind man.'
(Clayre and Cubit 1974: 67)

As this example illustrates, the auxiliary which marks UV in Kayan is reduced to a single invariant syllable, *en*, and the same is true for Murik (Ngorek). Clayre (1996: 76–80) states that this periphrastic Undergoer Voice is the only productive UV construction remaining in Kayan and Murik.

## 27.3.3 Some problem cases

Kroeger and Riesberg (this volume, §47.4.1.3) discuss several languages of northern Borneo which appear to be transitional between the Philippine and Central Borneo types. The Barito languages of southern Borneo are also difficult to assign to any of the three grammatical types we have posited. In fact, different members of the Barito linkage (Smith 2018a) seem to belong to different types. Malagasy fits best into the Philippine type, while most of the Sama-Bajaw languages fit fairly well into the Indonesian type.

Gudai (1985) describes a voice inventory for Ma'anyan (Southeast Barito) that is quite similar to that of Indonesian and Balinese: Active Voice marked by the prefix N-, an inflected passive marked by the prefix *na-*, and a zero-marked Undergoer Voice. Ma'anyan also resembles Indonesian in terms of its word order and lack of case marking. On the other hand, Ma'anyan lacks applicative suffixes, which are generally considered a defining feature of the Indonesian type.

Like Ma'anyan, Paku (Central-East Barito) has an Active Voice marked (for most verbs) by the prefix N-, and a passive marked by the prefix *na-* (Diedrich 2018). Diedrich identifies the *na*-V construction as passive when the agent is expressed as a PP or is omitted entirely, and as a symmetrical Undergoer Voice when the agent is expressed as a NP with no preposition. But since no other syntactic difference is reported between the two, we will assume that *na*-V construction is always a passive construction whose agent is optionally marked with the preposition *daya*, as in Ma'anyan.[13]

Diedrich does not identify a zero-marked UV construction in Paku like that which Gudai (1985) describes for Ma'anyan, but her data suggest that such a construction does exist. She describes "pronominal undergoer voice constructions" as follows: "Whenever the [UV] construction has a pronominal actor the morphosyntactic features of the clause change. While the undergoer still occurs in pre-verbal position, the verb occurs in its root form with the actor pronoun either cliticised to the verb ... if singular or following the verb as a free morpheme if plural" (Diedrich 2018: 142; see also page 178). These pronominal undergoer voice constructions also allow variation between SVO and verb-initial word order.

The examples in (21) illustrate Paku's voice inventory, with an active voice (21a), passive (21b), and zero-marked undergoer voice (21c):

Paku

(21) a. *setuwa* *iro* *ŋ-(k)ikit* *iyaŋ=ku*
animal DEM.MED AV-bite friend=1SG.GEN
'The animal bit my friend.'

b. *iyaŋ=ku* *na-kikit* *(daya)* *setuwa* *iro*
friend=1SG.GEN PASS-bite by animal DEM.MED
'My friend was bitten by the animal.'

c. *pea* *iro* *Ø-popok=ku* *pita* *inre*
child DEM.MED UV-hit=1SG.GEN morning earlier
'I hit the child earlier this morning.'
(Diedrich 2018: 139–47)

The preference for a zero-marked UV construction over a true passive when the actor phrase is a pronoun is reminiscent of patterns observed in some Malayic and Sama-Bajaw languages. As with Ma'anyan, the voice inventory of Paku is quite similar to that of Indonesian and Balinese, but the lack of applicative suffixes makes it problematic to assign Paku to the Indonesian type, which would otherwise seem quite natural.

[13] Passive agents in Paku can also be marked by the preposition *ulah*.

Both Ma'anyan and Paku have a transitivizing prefix *sVN-* (Diedrich 2018: 154). Gudai (1985: 74) identifies this prefix as an allomorph of the causative morpheme in Ma'anyan, and with many roots it does have a causative meaning, as illustrated in (22). But as Diedrich points out, the prefix has a number of other uses as well. When combined with the active voice prefix *N-*, it can change non-volitional semi-transitives into fully transitive volitional predicates, as in Ma'anyan *rengey* 'hear' > *N-saN-rengey* 'to listen to' (Gudai 1985: 261).[14] The transitivizing prefix is also used to derive transitive verbs from nouns, as in Paku *walah* 'slave' > *nyamalah* (*N-saN-walah*) 'enslave' (Diedrich 2018: 154).[15]

Ma'anyan causatives

(22) *tumbang* 'fall' — *santumbang* 'to fell'
*riqet* 'close' — *sanriqet* 'to bring (something) close'
*rengey* 'hear' — *sanrengey* 'to let hear'
*lawit* 'far' — *sanawit* 'to remove; to keep something at a distance'
*lawuq* 'fall' — *sanawuq* 'to cause to fall'
*fare* 'good' — *samare* 'to cure'. (Gudai 1985: 74–5)

In some uses this transitivizing prefix may be similar to an applicative marker, if it increases transitivity by adding a direct object. And some of its other uses (e.g. causative and derivational) are also associated with the Indonesian applicative suffix *-kan*. However, it appears to lack core applicative functions such as benefactive, instrumental, or locative object, and to be less productive than the typical Indonesian-type applicative.

In contrast to Ma'anyan and Paku, which exhibit primarily Indonesian-type grammatical patterns, Kadorih (Ot Danum; Northwest Barito; Inagaki 2010, 2013) exhibits some features which are more characteristic of the Central Borneo type. Active Voice is marked by the N- for some verbs and by zero for others. The Undergoer Voice is marked by an infix *<an>* ~ *<on>*. The Actor of the UV clause, which is optionally marked with the postposition *kai*, must immediately follow the verb, but the Undergoer subject may either precede the verb or follow the Actor. Inagaki (2010) indicates that UV verbs are normally interpreted with perfective aspect, whereas in AV clauses perfective aspect can only be marked with an auxiliary.

The Tamanic languages, which are descended from South Sulawesi languages, have a different type of voice system. In Embaloh, for example, Adelaar (1995e) describes the language as having an ergative alignment and corresponding active and antipassive voice; see Kroeger and Riesberg (this volume, §47.2.2).

[14] Sander Adelaar (p.c.) cites an additional example: *ri?et* 'be near' > *N-saN-ri?et* 'to approach'.

[15] Sander Adelaar (p.c.) cites the following Ma'anyan example: *wulu* 'hair; feather' > *nyamulu* 'to pluck'.

## 27.4 Noun phrases

### 27.4.1 Noun phrase structure

As the previous section demonstrated, Borneo languages exhibit a significant degree of variation in terms of their clause structure (voice systems, case marking, word order, etc.). In contrast, the structure of the noun phrase in Borneo appears to be relatively uniform, and in many ways quite similar to that of Malay/Indonesian. However, all of the generalizations offered in this section must be viewed as tentative, because detailed information about NP structure is available for only a relatively small number of languages.

The following structural description of the Malay noun phrase seems to work fairly well as a template for most Borneo languages, at least those for which information is available. It shows that the NP is generally head-initial, as expected, apart from quantifiers and cardinal numerals, which occur before the head.

(23) NP → (Q/NUM) N (A) ($\text{NP}_{\text{GEN}}$) (RELCL) (DEM)

A Kayan example illustrating most of these constituents is presented in (24).

Kayan
(24) *telo? buhup nyanyi kui aleng dekaya? lelan*
three book singing 1SG REL big very
'my three very big song books' (lit: 'my three song books that are very big')
(Clayre and Cubit 1974: 60)

In at least some of the Dusunic languages of Sabah, including Kimaragang, demonstratives may occur at the beginning or the end of the NP, or both at the same time. (Reid and Liao 2004: 472 say that the same is true in most Philippine languages.) Initial demonstratives replace the case markers, and appear in distinct nominative vs. non-nominative forms. However, in most Borneo languages, as in Malay, the demonstrative is the final element of the NP.[16] NP-final demonstratives in many of these languages may occur as full, independent words, or in a shortened clitic form.

Possessive NPs in Borneo languages occur almost universally in the order Possessum–Possessor, for example, *uma? ke?* 'my house' (house-1SG.GEN) or *meja la?iŋ* 'La'ing's table' from Lebo' Vo'. Possessor–Possessum orderings, if they appear at all, are always marked relative to Possessum–Possessor. In Kimaragang Dusun, the Possessor–Possessum ordering is possible with pronominal possessors, but requires that the possessive pronoun occur in the dative case rather than the genitive, as illustrated in (25a). Lexical NP possessors can also appear in pre-nominal position, preceded by the particle *dang* as seen in (25b), but this is relatively rare (see Schapper and McConvell, this volume, §48.2 and §48.5 for further discussion).

Kimaragang Dusun
(25) a. *tanak ku*
child 1SG.GEN
=
*dogon do tanak*
1SG.DAT LNK child
'my child'

b. *tanak do raja*
child LNK king
=
*dang raja do tanak*
PART king LNK child
'a king's child' (P. Kroeger, fieldnotes)

Many Philippine languages allow modifying adjectives and relative clauses to appear either before or after the head noun. This kind of freedom seems to be quite rare in Borneo. Clayre and Cubit (1974: 60–1) state that modifiers can optionally precede the head noun in Kayan, but most of their examples of prenominal modifiers are actually quantifiers ('some', 'much', 'a little') rather than adjectives.[17] We are not aware of a Borneo language that allows pre-nominal relative clauses.

Cardinal numerals can be immediately followed by a classifier or measure word. The classifier inventories of Borneo languages seem to be generally smaller than that of Malay. Iain Clayre (1972: 108–11) reports twelve classifiers in Dalat Melanau: one for humans, one for non-human animate creatures, and ten for inanimate things. (These same classifiers also function as relative pronouns in Melanau.) Goudswaard (2005: 101) lists eleven classifiers in Begak, but states that only five of them are frequently used in everyday speech. Clayre and Cubit (1974: 76) list nine classifiers in Kayan, and Prentice (1971: 176) identifies eight classifiers in Timugon Murut. Connell (2013: 71) states, regarding Matéq, "Four classifiers were frequently attested in the data, although further research may reveal that the Matéq classifier system is more complex." Only two classifiers seem to be in common use in Kimaragang Dusun: one for people and another one for animals and solid physical objects.

[16] Timugon Murut appears to be a partial exception to this general pattern. As mentioned below, the short clitic forms of the demonstratives can optionally occur before a relative clause.

[17] They do present one example of what appears to be a pre-nominal adjective, in the phrase 'my two sore legs'.

In a number of languages, the numeral + classifier complex may occur either before or after the head noun. Begak is one such language, as illustrated in (26).

Begak
(26) a. *təllu tassaʔ asu gayo no*
three CLF dog big DEM
'those three big dogs'

b. *asu gayo təllu tassaʔ no*
dog big three CLF DEM
'those three big dogs' (Goudswaard 2005: 272)

In Dusun and Murut, classifiers and measure words are connected to the numeral by a linking clitic, as illustrated in (27a–b). The same clitic is used to connect the words for 'tens', 'hundreds', and 'thousands' in large cardinal numbers (27c).

Timugon Murut
(27) a. *tulu nga=inan ra kalabaw*
seven LNK=CLF LNK buffalo
'seven buffaloes'

b. *onom ngang=gilin ra binjin*
six LNK=gallon LNK petrol
'six gallons of petrol'

c. *limo nga=ribu (am) siyam*
five LNK=thousand (and) nine
*nga=atus*
LNK=hundred
'five thousand nine hundred'
(Prentice 1971: 174–6)

One interesting, and typologically somewhat unusual, fact about the Malay NP structure shown in (23) is that the Adjective position allows just a single word, and not a phrase. If the adjective is modified by an intensifier ('very big'), or coordinated ('big and heavy'), it must be expressed as a relative clause, marked with the relativizer *yang* and occurring after the possessor phrase; and the same holds for a second modifying adjective within a single NP. This issue is not explicitly addressed in most work on Borneo languages, but Prentice (1971: 188) says that any modifier which occurs before the possessor NP in Timugon Murut must be just a single word. Clayre and Cubit (1974: 60–1) state that the same is true in Kayan. The Timugon example in (28) illustrates the use of two modifying adjectives within a single NP; notice that the second of these must be expressed as the predicate of a relative clause. (This example also illustrates the fact that the clitic short forms of the Timugon demonstratives can optionally occur before a relative clause, rather than in strict NP-final position.)

Timugon Murut
(28) *apol toojo na=li ra masalag*
rice.chaff real 3SG.GEN=DEM REL coarse
'its real chaff which is coarse' (Prentice 1971: 192)

Similarly, in Lebo' Vo', an adjective modified by an intensifier cannot occur in the same post-nominal slot as a bare adjective (29a–b); it must be expressed as a relative clause, as illustrated in the constructed example (29c).

Lebo' Vo'
(29) a. *ñəmulay biyoʔ*
snake big
'a big snake'

b. **ñəmulay nara biyoʔ*
snake very big
(intended: 'a very big snake')

c. *ñəmulay yaʔ nara biyoʔ* (constructed)
snake REL very big
'a snake that is very big' (A. Smith, fieldnotes)

## 27.4.2 Pronoun systems

Pronominal systems in Borneo can be divided into two major types. Pronouns in most Sabahan languages closely resemble Philippine-type systems, with at least three distinct pronoun forms (nominative, genitive, and oblique). In other languages pronoun systems have been altered through two main developments: (a) the elimination of the oblique set and the expansion of the nominative set so that 'nominative' pronouns appear in multiple grammatical positions; and (b) the loss of all case distinctions for many of the pronouns. Another typologically rare phenomenon, the innovation of complex number distinctions in the pronouns, is prevalent throughout Borneo. In such cases, pronouns distinguish not only between singular and plural, as most Austronesian pronominal systems do, but between dual, trial, and sometimes paucal numbers. We discuss both the pronominal form paradigms and the number categories in this section.

### 27.4.2.1 *Philippine-type pronouns in core Sabah languages*

As discussed in §27.3.1.2–§27.3.1.3, the majority of the core Sabah languages retain a pronominal system that distinguishes three cases, nominative, genitive, and dative/oblique. Lobel (2016b) lists pronominal paradigms for dozens of languages in Sabah, noting that most languages have the three-way distinction just mentioned, and a further distinction between long-form (topic/emphatic) nominative pronouns and short-form nominative pronouns. The system listed for Kadazan Kimanis in Table 27.6 is representative of the pronominal systems in many other Sabah languages.

**Table 27.6** Kadazan Kimanis pronouns (Lobel 2016b)

| | Nom/Top | Nom-Short | Genitive | Oblique |
|---|---|---|---|---|
| 1SG | *joʔo* | *oku* | *ku* | *dojoʔ* |
| 2SG | *jiʔaw* | *ko* | *nu* | *diʔaw* |
| 3SG | *(j)isido* | *(i)sido* | *nisido* | *disido* |
| 1PL.EXCL | *jiʔoy* | *ojiʔ* | *ja* | *dajan, dajay* |
| 1DU.INCL | *(j)ikito* | *kito* | *kito* | *dikito* |
| 1PL.INCL | *itokow* | *tokow* | *tokow* | *ditokow* |
| 2PL | *jioju* | *kow* | *ju* | *dioju* |
| 3PL | *josido* | *(josido)* | *nosido* | *dosido* |

### 27.4.2.2 *Central Bornean pronouns*

Central Bornean languages have reduced the number of pronominal case distinctions, while increasing grammatical number contrasts. In contrast to the Sabahan languages, most Central Bornean languages have only two pronoun sets: a default 'long-form' (nominative) pronominal set, used for subjects and a variety of other functions, and 'short-form' (genitive) pronouns used for possessors as well as for non-subject agents. The two sets typically contrast only in the singular and/or in the first and (perhaps) second persons, although some languages (e.g. Sa'ban) have contrasts between long and short pronouns even for the third person plural.

In the Lebo' Vo' language, only the singular pronouns maintain a distinction between nominative and genitive. In the plural (as well as the dual, trial, and paucal, not shown) the default (nominative) forms are used in all contexts. In some other Kenyah languages even the plurals may appear with a distinct genitive form (Clayre 2014). The system recorded for Lebo' Vo' is shown in Table 27.7.

In some languages, including Kayan, Murik, and Punan Tubu', the singular genitive pronouns have alternate reduced forms consisting of a single consonant (cf. Clayre 1996: 57–8; Soriente 2013: 51). The paradigm recorded in the Data Dian dialect is shown in Table 27.8.

These reduced genitive forms, which appear to be phonologically conditioned allomorphs, replace the final consonant of the root to which they attach, and may also cause vowel allomorphy. The pattern of phonological conditioning can be summarized as follows: for words ending in a

**Table 27.7** Lebo' Vo' pronouns (Smith 2017d)

| | Nominative | Genitive |
|---|---|---|
| 1SG | *akeʔ* | *-keʔ* |
| 2SG | *ikoʔ* | *-koʔ* |
| 3SG | *yə* | *-ñə* |
| 1PL.INCL | *ilu* | *ilu* |
| 1PL.EXCL | *ameʔ* | *ameʔ* |
| 2PL | *ikəm* | *ikəm* |
| 3PL | *irə* | *irə* |

**Table 27.8** Data Dian pronoun inventory (A. Smith, fieldnotes)

| | Nominative | Genitive | Reduced genitive |
|---|---|---|---|
| 1SG | *akuy* | *-kuy* | *-k* |
| 2SG | *ikaʔ* | *-kaʔ* | *-m* |
| 3SG | *ihaʔ* | *-naʔ* | *-n* |
| 1PL.INCL | *itam* | *itam* | |
| 1PL.EXCL | *kamiʔ* | *kamiʔ* | |
| 2PL | *kəloʔ* | *kəloʔ* | |
| 3PL | *dahaʔ* | *dahaʔ* | |

glottal stop, the glottal is replaced with *-k*, *-m*, and *-n* for the first, second, and third person singular respectively. Words ending in *-n* have the original *-n* replaced with *-k*, *-m* for the first and second persons, while in the third person the regular genitive form *naʔ* appears. Roots ending in other consonants have so far been recorded only with the regular (unreduced) genitive forms. This pattern is illustrated in Table 27.9. (The reduced forms also appear on vowel-final roots, in the dialects described by Clayre and Cubit.)

In addition to the phonological conditioning, there may be lexical conditioning factors as well. Clayre and Cubit (1974: 58) state that in the Uma Pu and Uma Peliau dialects of Kayan (Baram River), the nouns which take the reduced genitive clitics "all have to do with parts of the body or some personal thing," suggesting that inalienable possession may be relevant. They provide (1974: 87–8) a list of roots that take reduced genitive forms, which includes twenty-seven nouns

**Table 27.9** Data Dian genitive pronoun alternations (A. Smith, fieldnotes)

| ROOT | 1SG.GEN | 2SG.GEN | 3SG.GEN |
|---|---|---|---|
| *mataʔ* 'eye' | *mateə̯-k* | *mata-m* | *mata-n* |
| *aran* 'name' | *areə̯-k* | *ara-m* | *aran naʔ* |
| *tieə̯ŋ* 'friend' | *tieə̯ŋ kuy* | *tieə̯ŋ kaʔ* | *tieə̯ŋ naʔ* |

and nine verbs. In addition, they list six roots that take the reduced form only in the third person, and one root that takes the reduced form only in the first person.

Inagaki (2010, 2013) reports a similar pattern in Kadorih (Northwest Barito). Pronouns may occur either as free words or as enclitics. The singular enclitics have a reduced form (Table 27.10) whose distribution is phonologically conditioned, appearing only on base forms that end in /n/.

**Table 27.10** Kadorih pronominal forms (Inagaki 2010)

| | FREE | CLITIC | REDUCED CLITIC |
|---|---|---|---|
| 1SG | *ahku* | *=ku* | *=k* |
| 2SG | *ihko* | *=ko* | *=m* |
| 3SG | *io* | *=ah/=oh* | *=i/=u* |
| 1PL.INCL | *ihto* | *=to* | |
| 1PL.EXCL | *ihkai* | *=kai* | |
| 2PL | *ihkam* | *=kam* | |
| 3PL | *iroh* | *=(n)do* | |

### 27.4.2.3 *Pronominal number*

Borneo is well known for the prevalence of complex pronominal number systems, with as many as five number distinctions in some languages. Historically, pronominal number distinctions arose through a coalescence of pronouns plus numeral modifiers, but many modern languages have completely lost any formal morphological division between the pronoun and the numeral, innovating complex forms for dual, trial, and paucal numbers. Smith (2017d) provides numerous examples of such cases. The pronoun system of one such language, Punan Bah, is shown in Table 27.11.

The Punan Bah system is one of the several maximally complex 5-number pronoun systems in Borneo (along with

**Table 27.11** Punan Bah 5-number pronominal system (Smith 2017d)

| | SG | DU | TRI | PCL | PL |
|---|---|---|---|---|---|
| 1INCL | *oa̯ʔ* | *tou* | *tolu* | *topat* | *to* |
| 1EXCL | | *kuo* | *ko tolu* | *kipat* | *kai* |
| 2 | *kou* | *komo* | *komo tolu* | *kopat* | *kom* |
| 3 | *en* | *duo* | *do tolu* | *dopat* | *do* |

many Kenyah languages). We can observe in the Punan Bah system that dual, trial, and paucal pronouns were formed through the fusion of pronouns plus numeral modifiers. The trial series, *tolu*, *ko tolu*, *komo tolu*, and *do tolu*, for example, contains the numeral *tolu* 'three' and the paucal series, *topat*, *kipat*, *kopat*, and *dopat*, contains the numeral *pat* 'four', now fused with the pronominal element. Other systems include 4-number systems (singular, dual, trial/paucal, plural) like those found in Kayan, Berawan, and Kelabit, and 3-number systems (singular, dual, plural) like those found in Bintulu, most Melanau dialects, Penan, and Sebop. A number of other languages, including most of the core Sabah languages, have a distinct dual form only for the first person inclusive, to refer to the speaker and hearer. In such languages (those with dual number on the first person inclusive only) the pronoun tends to reflect PAN *kita, which (in other branches of Malayo-Polynesian) is typically utilized for the first person plural. For example, Sabah Bisaya, Rungus Dusun, Dumpas, and Tatana', among others, have *kito* 'first person dual inclusive', and another, innovative form for its plural counterpart.

## 27.5 Conclusion

Adelaar (1995b) has described the island of Borneo as "a crossroads for comparative Austronesian linguistics". The typological diversity of the languages of Borneo, as we have described it, is consistent with this characterization.

Both in their phonology and in their morphosyntax, Bornean languages are divisible into different types that are often associated with different geographical areas. In terms of phonological structure, we identified two types: the more common ISEA-type, dispersed throughout the island, and the MSEA phonological type, which occurs mainly in the central latitudes and which defines a Central Bornean linguistic area.

Certain correlations are observable in the phonological typology of these languages. For example, languages with word-final stress often have MSEA typological features such as sesquisyllabic and monosyllabic word shapes, vowel length, complex syllable structure, and large vowel inventories. Conversely, languages with penultimate stress (either strict penultimate stress or penultimate stress that shifts under certain conditions), tend to have ISEA-type features such as disyllabic word shapes, vowel inventories of four to six vowels, syllable structures that are maximally CVC or in some cases CCVC, and fewer overall diphthongs and triphthongs. However, other phonological features cut across typological groups. These include the presence of onset-driven nasality and associated phenomena such as word-final nasal pre-plosion, pre-nasalized stops, and nasalization of glides, velar-conditioned vowel breaking in final syllables, and consonant gemination.

Grammatically we distinguished between the Philippine-type, found mostly in the Malaysian state of Sabah and areas just to the south; the Indonesian-type, found throughout the remainder of Borneo; and the Central Bornean grammatical type, which, like the MSEA phonological type, occurs mostly in the central latitudes. There is thus a measure of truth in the traditional view of Borneo as a zone of transition between the grammatical patterns of the Philippines, to the northeast, and those of the Indonesian-type languages to the south and west. But in the centre of the island we find languages of the Central Bornean type, with features that do not fit neatly into either of the larger prototypes. The changes which produced these distinctive features seem to be independent of any changes which affected non-Bornean languages.

The extent to which phonological and grammatical typologies overlap varies to some extent, but we may nevertheless make a few observations. First, languages with a Philippine-type grammar are exclusively of the more ISEA-type phonology. That is, we have not yet observed a language with a MSEA-type phonology that maintains the Philippine-type grammatical system. Similarly, all MSEA-type languages that have so far been described appear to be of the Central Bornean grammatical type, with a lack of applicative suffixes and pronominal prefixes, and the emergence of two-way voice distinctions marked often by a periphrastic, rather than morphological, passive. Beyond these observations few correlations exist between phonological and grammatical typologies. For example, the majority of languages of Borneo have an ISEA-type phonology, and languages of this phonological type may belong to any of the grammatical types discussed in this chapter.

CHAPTER 28

# Non-Malayic languages of Sumatra and the Barrier Islands

BRADLEY MCDONNELL AND CHRISTINA L. TRUONG

## 28.1 Introduction

This chapter covers the non-Malayic Malayo-Polynesian languages of Sumatra and the Barrier Islands (henceforth referred to as the non-Malayic languages of Sumatra or NMLS). This area is comprised of one apparent expansive subgroup (i.e. Barrier Islands-Batak, Nothofer 1986), several languages or language clusters that have not yet been found to form a larger subgroup with other Malayo-Polynesian languages (i.e. Lampung, Nasal, Rejang, Enggano, Gayo), and Acehnese, which subgroups with Chamic languages outside the region (see Brunelle, chapter 11, this volume).[1] NMLS are spoken in regions located on the periphery of Sumatra. This includes the north and south ends of Sumatra as well as the Barrier islands off the western coast of Sumatra (see Map 28.1). NMLS are extremely diverse. They share few typological features other than those due to their shared Austronesian inheritance, their general geographic position, and the contact they have all had with Malayic languages. The most divergent of the NMLS, Enggano, is perhaps the most aberrant Austronesian language altogether. Some scholars have even questioned its status as an Austronesian language (Capell 1982; see also Nothofer 1991: 394 for discussion), although now it is fairly widely accepted to be Austronesian (see Edwards 2015).

This chapter is organized as follows. §28.2 describes the consonant and vowel inventories, stress, and phonological processes. §28.3 presents an overview of common affixes and morphological processes in the languages. §28.4 covers basic syntactic properties including grammatical relations, case, agreement, word order, and noun phrase structure. §28.5 describes some aspects of tense, aspect, modality, and mood in NMLS. §28.6 summarises the chapter and describes directions for further research including the need for more documentation and description of NMLS. Unless mentioned otherwise, we draw on the following sources for our typological generalizations and examples: Acehnese (Durie 1985), Gayo (Eades 2005), Karo Batak (Woollams 1996), Toba Batak (Nababan 1981; Adelaar 1995d), Devayan (also called Simeulue; Kähler 1955), Sigulai (also called Sikule; Kähler 1955), Nias (Brown 2001), Mentawai (Morris 1900; Pampus 1989), Enggano (Kähler 1940; Crowley n.d.), Rejang (McGinn 1982, 2005), Nasal (McDonnell fieldnotes), and Lampung (Walker 1976).[2]

## 28.2 Phonology

NMLS present diverse phonological properties at almost every level. This section aims to describe these phonological systems, noting similarities and differences across languages in phonemic inventories and allophonic variation (§28.2.1), stress and prosodic prominence (§28.2.2). and phonological processes (§28.2.3).

### 28.2.1 Phoneme inventories

#### 28.2.1.1 *Consonants*

The consonant inventories of the NMLS are comprised of anywhere from ten to twenty-two consonant phonemes. The median inventory size for NMLS is nineteen consonant phonemes, with the majority of languages contrasting somewhere between sixteen and nineteen consonant phonemes. One language, Enggano, has a much smaller inventory. The most comprehensive study lists twelve consonant phonemes, but of these, two—/r/ and /l/—are extremely rare outside of loanwords (Yoder 2011/2014: 21–4). Two other Barrier Islands languages, Devayan and Nias,

[1] In a recent paper, Billings and McDonnell (in revision) propose that Gayo, Enggano, Nasal, and Barrier Islands-Batak languages comprise a single subgroup, Sumatran (cf. also Smith 2017b).

[2] It was not possible to provide an exhaustive discussion of all NMLS. We chose to focus on the better described Batak languages. Leukon and Haloban are also not discussed because they lack descriptions see §28.6.

Bradley McDonnell and Christina L. Truong, *Non-Malayic languages of Sumatra and the Barrier Islands.* In: *The Oxford Guide to the Malayo-Polynesian Languages of Southeast Asia.* Edited by: Alexander Adelaar and Antoinette Schapper, Oxford University Press. © Bradley McDonnell and Christina L. Truong (2024). DOI: 10.1093/oso/9780198807353.003.0028

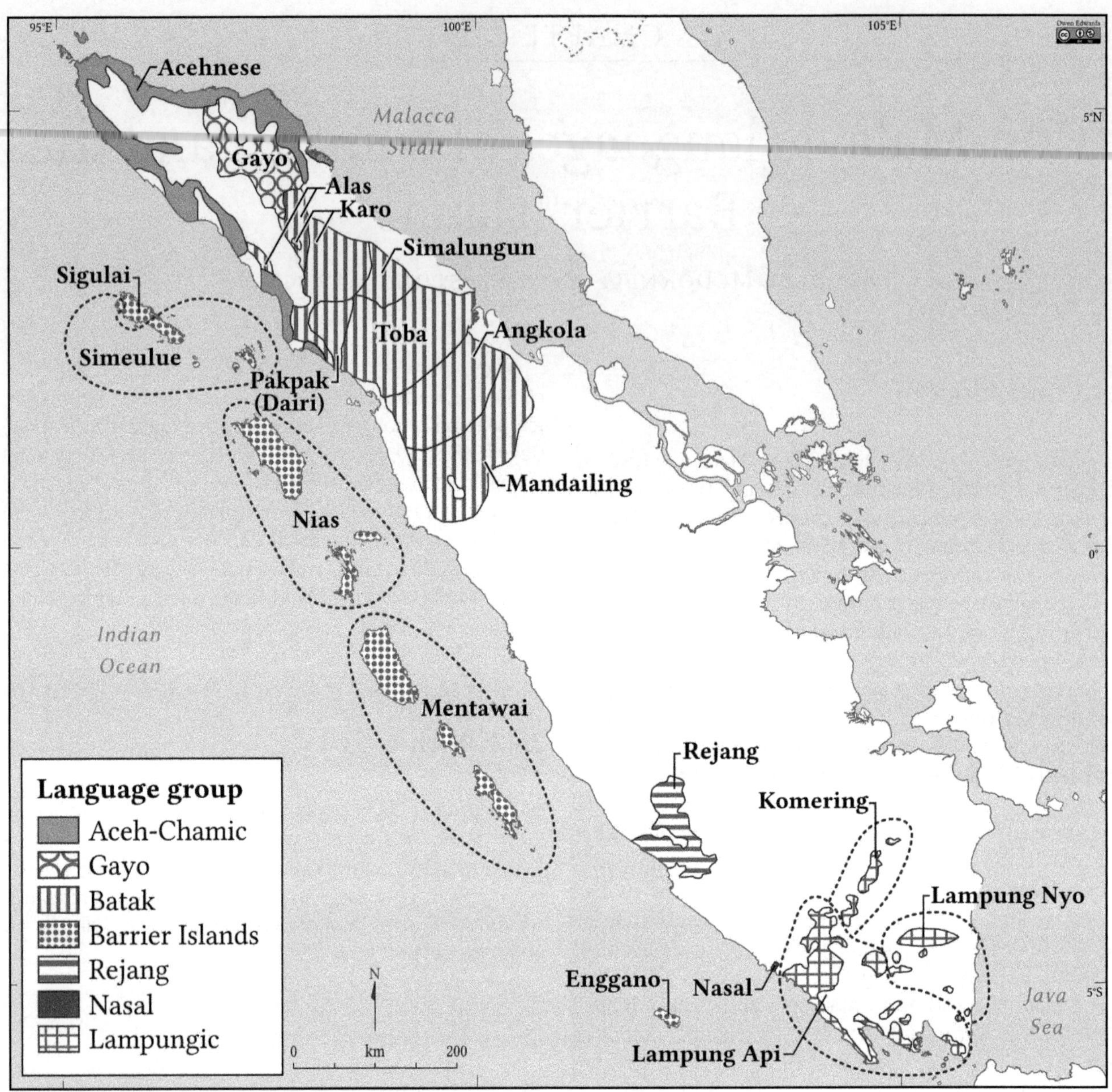


**Map 28.1** Location of NMLS in Sumatra and the Barrier Islands.

*Sources*: Language data from SIL International (R) (c) 2020. Includes geodata from Natural Earth (public domain) and Badan Pusat Statistik (licensed under CC BY-SA 4.0, https://creativecommons.org/licenses/by-sa/4.0).

have larger inventories with twenty-one and twenty-two consonants, respectively.[3] In some cases, the size of the inventory depends upon the analysis of a series of postploded nasals as either phonemes or allophones, which is discussed below.

Table 28.1 presents the consonant phoneme inventory of Gayo.[4] This inventory is representative of the majority of NMLS and exemplifies many common features of such consonant systems. The majority of these languages contrast voiced and voiceless stops at the labial, dental/alveolar, and

[3] These numbers do not include phonemes that only occur in loanwords. Such phonemes, however, are discussed below.

[4] In tables showing phonemic inventories, we have given orthographic representations in angled brackets.

**Table 28.1** Gayo consonant inventory (Eades 2005)

| | Bilabial | | Alveolar | | Post-alveolar | | Palatal | Velar | | Glottal | |
|---|---|---|---|---|---|---|---|---|---|---|---|
| Stop | p | b | t | d | | | | k | g | (ʔ) | (') |
| Nasal | | m | | n | | | ɲ ⟨ny⟩ | | ŋ ⟨ng⟩ | | |
| Tap/Trill | | | | r | | | | | | | |
| Fricative | | | s | | | | | | | h | |
| Affricate | | | | | tʃ ⟨c⟩ | dʒ ⟨j⟩ | | | | | |
| Approximant | | w | | | | | j ⟨y⟩ | | | | |
| Lateral | | | | l | | | | | | | |

velar places of articulation as well as alveopalatal affricates /tʃ/ and /dʒ/. There are several exceptions. Nias lacks a voiceless labial stop /p/ but instead has a labiodental fricative /f/. Enggano lacks a voiced velar stop /g/ and any affricates. Toba Batak lacks a phonemic voiceless alveopalatal affricate /tʃ/. According to Adelaar (1995d), it is only found in recent loanwords and was absent from van der Tuuk's (1971 [1864-1867]) grammar. Acehnese lacks any affricates but has voiced and voiceless alveopalatal stops /c/ and /ɟ/. The majority of NMLS have a phonemic glottal stop. Only the Batak languages, Sigulai, and the Kebanagung dialect of Rejang lack one. As for Gayo, the glottal stop is somewhat marked as it occurs only in recent loanwords.

In some languages, the voiceless apical stop is dental [t̪] (e.g. in Toba Batak and Karo Batak) or alveo-dental (e.g. in Gayo), while its voiced counterpart is alveolar [d]. This asymmetry is common throughout languages in western Indonesia (Blust 2013a: 172). Furthermore, in Acehnese, voiceless stops are aspirated [$p^h$, $t^h$, $c^h$, $k^h$] and voiced stops are 'murmured' with a 'whispery voice' phonation [$b^h$, $d^h$, $ɟ^h$, $g^h$] in onset position (Durie 1985: 26). As is the case for other NMLS, Acehnese stops are unreleased word-finally.

The majority of NMLS distinguish four nasal stops: labial, alveolar, palatal, and velar. Exceptions include Batak and Sigulai, which lack a palatal nasal and thereby distinguish only three nasals, and Enggano and Nias, which distinguish only two nasals, labial and alveolar. Acehnese, Rejang, and older speakers of Gayo additionally have a series of four postploded (or 'funny' nasals)—a consonant with nasal airflow through the closure followed by a brief plosive release—at labial, alveolar, palatal, and velar places of articulation.[5] Historically, these postploded nasals transparently come from nasal + voiced stop sequences. However, synchronic analyses of postploded nasals vary, which has consequences for the size of the consonant and even vowel inventories. Durie (1985), for example, analyses postploded nasals in Acehnese as allophones of their plain nasal counterparts. In his analysis, allophonic variation is triggered by the presence or absence of a immediately following nasal vowel in a stressed syllable: plain nasals occur before nasal vowels, while postploded nasals occur before oral vowels. As a result, Acehnese is analysed as contrasting nineteen rather than twenty-two consonant phonemes. Simplicity in the consonant inventory, however, results in complexity in the vowel inventory, where two sets of phonemes—nasal vowels and oral vowels—must be included under this analysis (see §28.2.1.2 for details). McGinn (2005) analyses postploded nasals in Rejang as phonemic. Nasalized vowels are the result of nasal spreading and are thus allophonic: vowels following plain nasals are nasalized (e.g. /maʔaʔ/ [mãʔaʔ] 'approach'), while vowels following postploded nasals are not (e.g. /$im^bo$/ [$im^bo$] 'forest') (McGinn 1982: 63). This results in a larger consonant inventory with twenty-two consonant phonemes. An alternate analysis of the postploded nasals as allophonic would mean that Rejang has only eighteen consonant phonemes. On a conceptual level, both Durie and McGinn's analyses are equally defensible for either language. There is no apparent advantage to analysing the postploded nasals as phonemic and vowel nasalization as allophonic versus analysing vowel nasalization as phonemic, with postplosion of nasals as allophonic.

Cohn and Riehl (2016), however, argue that postploded nasals in Acehnese and Sundanese ought to be analysed phonologically as nasal-stop clusters rather than unary segments. They show that the distribution of postploded nasals is the same as clusters of nasal + voiceless stop. They also provide phonetic evidence that the duration of Acehnese postploded nasals is more consistent with a cluster analysis

[5] These postploded nasals have also been referred to as "barred" nasals in Rejang (Coady and McGinn 1982).

than a unary one. Of course, the analysis of postploded nasals is language dependent, as Cohn and Riehl themselves point out, so without further research, the status of Rejang postploded nasals remains an open question. In Gayo postploded nasals are only contrastive for older speakers of the language (Eades 2005). Apparently, younger speakers of Gayo have collapsed plain and postploded nasals. In addition to postploded nasals in word-medial position, word-final nasals following oral vowels are optionally preploded in Rejang. Word-final preploded nasals are also apparently found in some dialects of Mentawai (Blust 1997b: 169, 2013a: 241).

The number of fricative phonemes in NMLS ranges from one to five. With the exception of Enggano, NMLS have at least the fricative /s/, and many languages, like Gayo, also have a glottal fricative /h/ (i.e. Acehnese, Kebanagung and Rawas dialects of Rejang, Batak languages). Among the Barrier Islands languages, Devayan and Sigulai have a series of four fricatives /f, s, x, h/ and Nias has a fifth phoneme /v/. In this regard, Mentawai diverges from the other Barrier Islands languages as it has only a single fricative /s/. The Pesisir, Lebong, and Musi dialects of Rejang also have a single fricative /s/.

Several languages have a back (i.e. velar or uvular) fricative or approximant, which alternates with an alveolar trill /r/ either in loanwords or between dialects. In Nasal, the alveolar tap/trill /r/ only occurs in some recent loanwords, while the uvular fricative /χ/ occurs in inherited vocabulary and older Malay loans where Malay has an alveolar trill /r/ (e.g. Malay *perang* 'war' is pronounced [pəχaŋ]). Lampungic languages have been described similarly (Walker 1976: 3). In Acehnese, Durie (1985) describes the orthographic <r> as a uvular approximate [ʁ] in the northern dialect, but in other dialects, it is realized as an alveolar trill [r]. The Barrier Islands languages have an alveolar trill /r/ and all but Mentawai also have a voiceless velar fricative /x/. However, these velar fricative phonemes do not appear to have the same relationship to the alveolar trill as seen in Nasal, Lampung, and Acehnese. Interestingly, Rejang is the only language in this region to lack both an alveolar trill and any sort of back fricative or approximant. All other languages have an alveolar trill, and all have a lateral approximant phoneme, however in Enggano, /l/ is found only rarely.

The phonemic status of labiovelar /w/ and palatal /j/ approximants is questionable in several languages. One common issue is that it is difficult to know how to analyse instances of [w] and [y]. In some cases, these glides are predictable between two vowels, where they break up vowel hiatus. In other cases, /w/ and /j/ are best analysed as vowels which fill an onset or coda position in the syllable, as in a tier-based analysis such as Hayes (1989). In Nasal, /w/ occurs in a number of words that are not predictable (e.g. *watu* 'stone'), while /j/ is much more rare. The most extreme case is Toba Batak. Adelaar (1995d) points out that /w/ and /y/ were not included in van der Tuuk's (1971 [1864–1867]) grammar and are only present in recent loanwords. Karo Batak, however, shows evidence of both labiovelar and palatal phonemic approximants. Finally, Sigulai lacks /w/ but apparently has /y/.

The Nias consonant inventory presented in Table 28.2 diverges from the other languages in significant ways. With twenty-two consonant phonemes, it is the largest inventory. It has several marked sounds. Most famously, Nias has the bilabial trill /ʙ/, which is especially remarkable because it can occur before any vowel; Ladefoged and Maddieson (1996) found that in other languages the bilabial trill only occurred before rounded vowels such as [u]. Nias also has an alveolar stop with trilled release /$d^r$/ and a labiodental approximant /ʋ/. Yoder (2018) reports that Nias /ʙ/ and /$d^r$/

**Table 28.2** Nias consonant inventory from Brown (2001)

| | Bilabial | Alveolar | Post-alveolar | Palatal | Velar | Glottal |
|---|---|---|---|---|---|---|
| Stop | b | t d | | | k g | ʔ ⟨'⟩ |
| Trilled release | | $d^r$ ⟨ndr⟩ | | | | |
| Nasal | m | n | | | | |
| Tap/Trill | ʙ ⟨mb⟩ | r | | | | |
| Fricative | f v | s | | | x ⟨kh⟩ | h |
| Affricate | | | tʃ ⟨c⟩ dʒ ⟨j⟩ | | | |
| Approximant | ʋ ⟨β⟩ | | | j ⟨y⟩ | w | |
| Lateral | | l | | | | |

vary in phonetic realization between plain stop, stop with trilled release, and stop with fricative release.

### 28.2.1.2 *Vowels*

Most NMLS have average to moderately large sized vowel inventories (Maddieson 2013b) of five to eight vowel phonemes. A typical vowel inventory includes two front unrounded vowels /i/ and /e/, two back rounded vowels /u/ and /o/, the low central vowel /a/, and one mid or high central vowel. Table 28.3 shows the vowel phonemes of Lampung Api, which exemplifies a typical inventory. Walker (1976: 4) notes that realizations of the high vowels /i, u/ is varied across speakers, but they are frequently lowered to mid-high allophones [e, o] in unstressed open syllables and following certain consonants.

**Table 28.3** Lampung Api vowel inventory

| | Front | Central | Back |
|---|---|---|---|
| High | i | | u |
| Mid | ɛ ⟨é⟩ | ə ⟨e⟩ | ɔ ⟨o⟩ |
| Low | | a | |

A few NMLS contrast fewer than six vowel qualities. Nasal has five vowel phonemes (/a, i, u, ə, o/), lacking a mid front vowel /e/. Pampus (1989) lists Mentawai with only five vowel qualities (/a, i, u, e, o/). A number of languages, including Karo Batak, Toba Batak, Gayo, and Acehnese, have more than six vowel qualities because they distinguish two levels of mid vowels. Among NMLS, Acehnese, as shown in Table 28.4, has the greatest number of vowel qualities for monophthongs, with ten contrastive qualities for oral vowels (including four heights for central vowels) and seven contrastive qualities for nasal vowels. Enggano and Acehnese have also both been analysed as having phonemic nasal vowels (Durie 1985; Yoder 2011/2014), though not all scholars are in agreement on how to account for the nasalization patterns in these languages (see discussion of postploded nasals above and word-level nasalization below).

Some NMLS, such as Karo Batak, Toba Batak, and Nias, are reported not to contrast diphthongs phonemically, while other languages have a large number of contrastive diphthongs. For example, Rejang and Acehnese contrast five diphthongs (see Table 28.4 below), while Enggano contrasts six (/ai, aɨ, au, ei, əi, oi/) (Yoder 2011/2014: 32).[6] Others, like Lampung (Anderbeck 2007b) and Nasal, contrast just three diphthongs (/au, ai, ui/). Gayo contrasts diphthongs in some dialects and in poetic speech.

**Table 28.4** Acehnese vowel inventory

| | Front | Back | |
|---|---|---|---|
| | Unrounded | Unrounded | Rounded |
| Oral Monopthongs | | | |
| High | i | ɯ | u |
| Mid-high | e | ɤ | o |
| Mid-low | ɛ | ʌ | ɔ |
| Low | | a | |
| Nasal monophthongs | | | |
| High | ĩ | ɯ̃ | ũ |
| Mid-low | ɛ̃ | ʌ̃ | ɔ̃ |
| Low | | ã | |
| Oral Diphthongs | | | |
| High | iə | ɯə | uə |
| Mid-low | ɛə | | ɔə |
| Nasal Diphthongs | | | |
| High | ĩə | ɯ̃ə | ũə |
| Mid-low | ɛ̃ə | | ɔ̃ə |

Enggano evinces an unusual word-level nasal harmony, in which a word has either all nasal vowels (e.g. [kãʔĩʔ] 'strong', [kũkũ] 'follow', [nõʔo̤ẽ] 'spilled') or all oral vowels (e.g. [kudi] 'belt', [ʔɨaʔ] 'tie') (Yoder 2011/2014: 33). What is more, these nasal/oral vowel patterns do not appear to be the result of a single process. Yoder (2011/2014) proposes two nasal spreading processes that account for these patterns. First, in words containing nasal consonants, vowels are always nasalized, which can be attributed to spreading of nasalization from nasal consonants to underlyingly oral vowels in the same word. Second, in words with only oral consonants, either all vowels are oral, or all are nasalized. Nasalization in such words is attributed to phonemically nasalized vowels and subsequent spreading. Spreading of nasalization can be observed for oral vowels in prefixes when attached to a stem that contains a [+nasal] feature. For example, the /a/ in the Enggano adjectival prefix remains oral in words

[6] Diphthongs in Rejang vary significantly across different dialects, see McGinn (2005: 19).

like /kaʔ-pix/ [kaʔə̆piç] 'sudsy', but is nasalized in words like /kaʔ-kĩh/ [kãʔə̆kĩh] 'dry' (in which the root vowel is phonemically nasal) and /kaʔ-man/ [kãʔə̆mãn] 'fragrant' (in which the root contains a nasal consonant). For a diachronic account, see Smith (2020).

### 28.2.2 Stress and prosodic prominence

NMLS represent a diversity of stress and prosodic prominence systems. Among these, Acehnese stands out, as it reflects the sesquisyllabic word structure of the Chamic subgroup (see Brunelle, chapter 11, this volume). Acehnese words consist of one or two syllables, of which the ultimate is most prominent. All Acehnese vowels, including diphthongs and nasal vowels, are contrastive in the final syllable, as opposed to the penult, which is characterized by fewer contrasts, and shorter and less distinct vowel pronunciation (Durie 1985). Only the final syllable of a word can bear stress, which is assigned at the phrase level to the penultimate or final word of the phrase.

The majority of NMLS have been described as possessing a predictable stress system. Of these Gayo, Sigulai, Enggano, Lampung, and Rejang (in addition to Acehnese as mentioned above) are reported to exhibit fixed final stress, while Karo Batak, Nias, and Mentawai are reported to show predictable penultimate stress with some exceptions. However, Toba Batak, has been described as a distinctive stress system. While stress in Toba Batak falls on the penultimate for most nouns and verbs, some words have final, lexical stress (van der Tuuk 1971 [1864–1867], Nababan 1981). Stress also has a derivational role: adjectives used predicatively bear final stress, while adjectives used attributively and related abstract nouns bear penultimate stress, as shown below in (1).

| | Toba Batak | | |
|---|---|---|---|
| (1) | *tibó* | 'high' | Predicative adjective |
| | *na tíbo* | 'which is high' | Attributive adjective |
| | *tíbo* | 'height' | Noun |
| | | | (Roosman 2007: 93) |

Many of the descriptive accounts of stress in these languages have relied on researcher perception, and further research is needed to identify the correlates of stress and to distinguish word stress from phrasal prominence (see Kaufman and Himmelmann, chapter 42, this volume). Roosman (2007) stands out as an exception to the general state of research on prosody for NMLS. Her study shows that word-level stress in Toba Batak is marked by rising pitch and that this pitch movement is influenced by prosodic boundaries and intonation. In general, however, further detailed phonetic study of prosody for these languages is needed.

### 28.2.3 Phonological processes

This section presents some characteristic phonological processes in NMLS, including nasal substitution, consonant gemination, and reduplication. In addition, we also include discussion of the distinctive morphophonemic process in Nias known as nominal mutation.

Like other western Indonesian languages, most NMLS exhibit a morphophonemic processes known as nasal substitution and nasal accretion. These processes have been reported for Gayo, Karo Batak, Toba Batak, Devayan, Sigulai, Nias, Mentawai, Rejang, Lampung, and Nasal. In most of these languages, the morpheme that triggers the process is a verbal prefix with the shape *mang-*, *maN-*, or even *N-* where *N* represents a nasal unspecified for place (see §28.3.1 for discussion of the function of this prefix). There is also frequently a corresponding nominal prefix, *pang-*, *paN-*, or similar, that also triggers the process. The initial stem consonants which are subject to substitution vary slightly from language to language; these generally include voiceless obstruents but can exclude /h/ and other back consonants such as /x/ and /k/ (e.g. Lampung, Nias). In the case of initial /s/ and alveopalatal consonants, the substituting nasal is usually palatal if the language has a palatal nasal phoneme, and alveolar otherwise, but some variation for /s/-initial stems has been reported for Toba Batak, Gayo, and Rejang (see Toba Batak examples in Table 28.5 below).

A number of NMLS show a process of consonant gemination, though the underlying motivations are not always similar. In Toba Batak, a nasal assimilates completely to a following stop, resulting in a geminate stop. This is an active synchronic process that occurs at a morpheme boundary with some exceptions, including environments which trigger nasal substitution as discussed above. Table 28.5 presents a paradigm for the Toba Batak prefix *mang-* that includes examples of both nasal substitution and consonant gemination using data from Percival (1981) and Nababan (1981). Some lexical items show exceptional behaviour compared to the general pattern for stems of the same shape; examples of these are indicated by asterisks in the table. Consonant gemination in Toba Batak can also be shown to have occurred diachronically for PMP nasal–stop sequences *mp, *nt, and *ŋk (Blust 1995c). In Karo Batak and Lampung, consonant gemination has a different trigger (Anderbeck 2007b). When a schwa in an open syllable appears in the stressed penult of a word, the initial consonant of the following syllable undergoes gemination, as in Karo Batak /təbu/ [təb.bu] 'sugarcane' (Woollams 1996: 30). This process appears to be motivated by a preference for longer duration in stressed syllables.

**Table 28.5** Morphophonemic behaviour of Toba Batak *mang-*

| Stem | /maŋ-/ + Stem | Gloss | Process |
|---|---|---|---|
| *pukkul* | *mamúkkul* | 'to beat' | nasal substitution |
| *bolos* | *mamólos* | 'to pass' | nasal substitution |
| *boan* | *mabbóan* | 'to bring' | gemination* |
| *taru-hən* | *manaruhən* | 'to convey' | nasal substitution |
| *duda* | *maddúda* | 'to stamp rice' | gemination |
| *cubo* | *maccúbo* | 'to try' | gemination |
| *jalɔ* | *majjálɔ* | 'to receive' | gemination |
| *karejo-hən* | *makkarejóhən* | 'to do' | gemination |
| *gadis* | *maŋgadis* | 'to sell' | nasal accretion |
| *mata-hən* | *mamatáhən* | 'to supervise' | nasal substitution |
| *nipuran-i* | *maŋanipuráni* | 'to hand round betel nut' | V-insertion |
| *suru* | *manuru* | 'to sell' | nasal substitution |
| *siamun* | *maŋiamun* | 'to turn left' | nasal substitution* |
| *hɔna* | *maŋɔ́na* | 'to be efficacious' | nasal substitution |
| *huliŋ* | *makkuliŋ* | 'to speak' | gemination* |
| *lɛan* | *maŋalɛán* | 'to give' | V-insertion |
| *rippu* | *maŋarippu* | 'to guess' | V-insertion |
| *usuŋ* | *maŋúsuŋ* | 'to carry' | — |

Reduplication is a very common morphological process in NMLS. In almost every one of them, two types of reduplication are active: single syllable reduplication and disyllabic or total reduplication. Examples of the two types from Toba Batak include *ta~tangis-an* (HAB~cry-NMLZ) 'that about which one cries' (van der Tuuk 1971 [1864–1867]: 395), and *poso~poso* (NMLZ~young) 'a newly born young (of animals)' (van der Tuuk 1971 [1864–1867]: 395).

While the reduplicant is commonly an exact copy of all or part of the base, sometimes phonological variation exists between the form of the base and the reduplicant. Certain reduplicated forms in Acehnese, for example, show variation in quality of the stressed vowel, as in *muda~mudi* 'young people', from base *muda* 'young' (Durie 1985: 43). The vowel in the reduplicant may also be systematically reduced. For instance, in western dialects of Karo Batak, initial-syllable reduplicants often are pronounced with a schwa instead of the full quality of base vowel, as in *pə~pagi* 'tomorrow', from base *pagi* 'morning; tomorrow' (Woollams 1996: 92). Consonant alternation may also occur, as in Gayo *sakit~**m**akit* 'very sick; difficult', from the base *sakit* 'sick', where the substitution of /m/ for the initial consonant is reported to have an intensifying function (Eades 2005: 55).

As the examples in this section show, reduplication has a variety of functions. For nouns, it indicates plurality or variety. For verbs, it can indicate multiple actors, distributive action, iterative, habitual, or progressive aspect, or more intense state or action. Reduplication is also used to form words indicating manner and similitude or imitation, as in Karo Batak *pe-ganjang~ganjang-ken* (CAUS-SIM~tall-APPL) 'to put on airs and graces' (Woollams 1996: 95). Reduplication can also be used to form nouns, such as instruments associated with the base action, as in Nias *raʔu~raʔu* 'small net for catching fish', from the base *raʔu* 'catch'.

Nias exhibits a striking morphophonemic process known as nominal mutation. The case-marking functions of nominal mutation are discussed in §28.4.1.2. Nominal mutation occurs on nouns (including pronouns), classifiers, and the prefix *ira-* which indicates plurality. Phonologically, nominal mutation is marked by alternations in the initial consonant of consonant-initial words, the addition of initial /g/ or /n/ to vowel-initial words, or irregular changes for pronouns and *ira-*. Examples of nominal mutation are shown in Table 28.6 below. Note that a similar nominal mutation process has been reported for Sigulai (Kähler 1955: 11–12), but details about its application and function are much less clear (see discussion in §28.4.1.2). No other NMLS display a similar phenomenon. In examples below, nominal mutation is indicated by the glossing convention MUT.

## 28.3 Morphology

The NMLS are mildly synthetic with both prefixes and suffixes. Acehnese and Rejang are exceptions as they have no suffixes. In some languages, a base may only take a single prefix (e.g. Nasal), while in others several prefixes can stack (e.g. Nias). The use of infixes and circumfixes is also quite common, as is reduplication (see §28.2.3 above). The remainder of this section discusses some of the most common affixes and morphological processes in NMLS, but it is by no means exhaustive.

**Table 28.6** Nias nominal mutation

| Base item | Mutated form | Alternation |
|---|---|---|
| *fakhe* 'rice' | *vakhe* | f → v |
| *kefe* 'money' | *gefe* | k → g |
| *ciʔaciʔa* 'gecko' | *ziʔaciʔa* | c → z [dʒ] |
| *baβi* 'pig' | *mbaβi* | b → mb [ʙ] |
| *doi* 'thorn; fishbone' | *ndroi* | d → ndr [dʳ] |
| *oβo* 'boat' | *noβo* | ∅ → n |
| *oβoto* 'small dike' | *goβoto* | ∅ → g |
| *yaʔo* 1SG | *ndrao* | irregular |
| *yaʔia* 3SG | *ya* | irregular |
| *ira-* COLL | *ndra-* | irregular |

### 28.3.1 Verbal morphology

#### 28.3.1.1 *Agreement*

Three NMLS mark some form of agreement on verbs: Nias, Acehnese, and Enggano.[7] In all three languages, the bound affixes or clitics commonly occur without any cross-referenced lexical NP, meaning that they represent a fairly non-canonical form of agreement (Corbett 2006).

In Nias, agreement is marked by prefixes that distinguish number and person. These appear on verbs in transitive clauses, in which case they agree with the actor argument (A), and on irrealis verbs in intransitive clauses, in which case they agree with the single argument (S). Realis verbs in intransitive clauses take no agreement prefixes. Table 28.7 below shows the paradigm for Nias agreement prefixes.

**Table 28.7** Pronominal prefixes in Nias by mood (Brown 2001: 124)

| | Realis | Irrealis | | Realis | Irrealis |
|---|---|---|---|---|---|
| 1SG | *u-* | *gu-* | 1PL.INCL | *ta-* | *da-* |
| | | | 1PL.EXCL | *ma-* | *ga-* |
| 2SG | *ö-* | *gö-* | 2PL | *mi-* | *gi-* |
| 3SG | *i-* | *ya-* | 3PL | *la-* | *ndra-* |

In Enggano, subject agreement is marked on the verb, but is limited to particular clauses (see §28.4.1.2 for details). It distinguishes number (singular, dual, plural) and person, and is indicated by means of a prefix or circumfix. Common forms used for subject agreement are presented in Table 28.8, however, other morphophonological changes may apply, resulting in surface forms that differ from those shown here (Crowley n.d.).

**Table 28.8** Enggano subject agreement prefixes (Crowley n.d.: 21)

| Singular | | Dual or Plural | |
|---|---|---|---|
| 1SG | *ʔu-* | 1DU.INCL | *ka-* |
| | | 1PL.INCL | *ka- -aʔa* |
| | | 1DU/PL.EXCL | *ʔu- -ʔai* |
| 2SG | *u-* | 2DU/PL | *u- -aʔa* |
| 3SG | *i-* | 3DU/PL | *da-* |

In Acehnese, agreement and/or argument cross-reference is marked on the verb by means of clitics, which, like other Acehnese pronominals, distinguish person, but not number (singular/plural) in most cases. Proclitics mark agreement for person with the Actor arguments in intransitive ($S_A$) or transitive (A) clauses, and enclitics optionally mark agreement with the Undergoer in intransitive ($S_P$) or transitive (P) clauses (see §28.4.1.3 for further discussion and examples). A paradigm is shown in Table 28.9.[8]

#### 28.3.1.2 *Affixation on verbs*

This section describes some common affixes used on verbs in NMLS. These affixes mark transitivity, verb subclass (stative vs. dynamic), voice, valency, and other dimensions of the verbal action, such as aspect and volitionality.

Almost all NMLS make use of a verbal prefix that triggers the morphophonemic process of nasal substitution (see §28.2.3 above). These prefixes can be considered reflexes of PMP *maŋ- 'active verb' (Blust 2013a: 242). Only Acehnese and Enggano do not make use of such a verbal prefix. In Karo Batak, Lampung, and Nasal the prefix has been shortened to *N-* or *ng-*. In Gayo it is *mun-*, in Rejang it is *meng-*, and in all others the form is represented either as *mang-* or *maN-*, with phonological variation of the vowel quality in some cases. In languages with two basic transitive voices (see §28.4.1.1 below), this prefix typically marks what we are

[7] Sigulai may also exhibit verbal agreement, but see §28.4.1.2 below for a discussion of complicating factors.

[8] For simplicity, we exclude some pronominal forms listed as "very polite" or "reverential" by Durie (1985).

**Table 28.9** Acehnese agreement clitics (Durie 1985: 117)

| | Proclitic | Enclitic |
|---|---|---|
| 1SG familiar | *ku=* | *=ku(h)* |
| 1 polite | *lôn=, lông=* | *=lôn, =lông* |
| 1PL.INCL neutral | *ta=* | *=teu(h)* |
| 1PL.EXCL neutral | *meu=* | *=meu(h)* |
| 2 familiar | *ka=* | *=keu(h)* |
| 2 neutral | *ta=* | *=teu(h)* |
| 2 polite | *neu=* | *=neu(h)* |
| 3 familiar | *ji=, di=, i=* | *=ji(h), =i* |
| 3 polite | *geu=* | *=geu(h)* |

calling Actor Voice (AV); in other languages it commonly marks transitive and dynamic verbs. In a few languages, the function of the prefix is quite diminished, as with Nias *maN-/mo-*, which only marks intransitive dynamic verbs denoting an action associated with the base noun, as in *adulo* 'egg', *man-adulo* 'lay egg' (Brown 2001). In Rejang, *meng-* is restricted to intransitive verbs expressing durative action (McGinn 1982: 58).

In addition to reflexes of *maŋ, almost all NMLS have a reflex of the PMP infix *-um- which is associated with intransitive verbs (see Kroeger and Riesberg, chapter 47, this volume). Functions and forms of this affix vary across NMLS. One common function is to mark progressive, habitual, or durative aspect, as with Acehnese *meu-/-eum-*, Nias *m-/-um-*, and Mentawai *mu-*. In Devayan and Sigulai, the infix *-um-* marks verbs denoting processes. In Gayo, the prefix *mu-* marks intransitive verbs with various functions, including speaking verbs and inchoatives, while the infix *-em-* is used with verbs of motion. In Toba Batak, *(u)*m- or *-um-* forms intransitive dynamic verbs and verbs expressing comparison of state. In Rejang, *m(e)-/-em-* marks transitive (AV) verbs. In other languages, the function of this affix is narrow. In Karo Batak, *-um-* is not very productive and means to do an action 'erratically or unsteadily' (Woollams 1996: 77). In Enggano, *b(u)-/-ub-* is used in narratives to advance the action of the plot (Kähler 1940: 107). This affix appears to be used less frequently than the Enggano verbal prefix *ki-*, which simply marks the verbal predicate in a clause (see §28.4.1.2). An example is shown below in (2). In Nasal, the infix *-em-* occurs with a very limited number of roots and functions as a detransitivizing prefix that results in a meaning of 'do ROOT completely', as in (3).

Enggano
(2) *pãhũmãnã-hũmãnã ʔ<ub>ahadɔ, ʔ<ub> ahiudi*
morning-morning 1SG-BU-get.up, 1SG-BU-whistle.for
*e-bɛɔ, da-b-i e-bɛɔ ʔadiba.*
CORE-dog, 3DU/PL-PROG-come CORE-dog five
'I get up early in the morning, I whistle for the dogs, they come, five dogs.' (Kähler 1940: 107)

Nasal
(3) *iyo kak khadu s<em>uah di lahan=nyo.*
3 PFV finish <DETRANS>burn LOC field=3
'He burned his (entire) field.' (McDonnell fieldnotes)

Many NMLS contain a reflex of the Proto-Austronesian (PAn) infix *-in- (or its allomorph *ni-). In some NMLS, such affixes are used to indicate passive or Undergoer Voice (UV), as with Rejang *n(e)-/-en-*, Toba Batak *di-* and *ni-*, and Enggano *d(i)-* (see §28.4.1 below for a discussion of voice in these languages). Similar functions have also been reported for the prefix *ni-* in Sigulai and Devayan. In other cases, this affix forms nouns rather than verbs, especially deverbal nouns which result from the action indicated by the stem. For example, Gayo has *t-en-emak* 'rocks to channel water to a paddy' cf. *i-temak* 'to block irrigation' (Eades 2005: 69). In Acehnese, the infix *-eun-* is very productive and may form abstract properties, nouns expressing events, nouns denoting undergoers of an action, and instruments and locations associated with an action. In a few languages, such as Karo Batak, Sigulai, and Mentawai the affix appears only infrequently or is fossilized.

Many NMLS mark stative verbs with adjectival meanings by means of a verbal prefix derived from PAn *ma- 'stative prefix' (Blust 2013a: 376). This is the case for Batak languages and the Barrier Islands languages except for Enggano. Examples from Toba Batak are shown in (4). In some other NMLS, this affix is less productive, and may be associated with intransitives more widely, rather than stative verbs only. In Lampung Api, the prefix *ma-* is found on a subset of intransitive verbs which can have both dynamic and stative meanings as in (5).

Toba Batak
(4) a. *rara* 'red'
*ma-rara* 'to be red'
b. *bubu* 'fish trap (with an oblong bag)'
*ma-bubu* 'having a pot belly'
(van der Tuuk 1971 [1864–1867]: 87–8)

(5) Lampung Api

a. *esaq* 'ripe' root
*ma-esaq* 'to be ripe' INTR verb
*ng-esaq-ko* 'to ripen s.t.' TR verb
(Walker 1976: 37, 41)

b. *impix* 'return' root
*m-impix* 'to return' INTR verb
(Walker 1976: 21, 40)

Like other western Indonesian languages, NMLS make use of a number of verbal affixes that can change the valency of the verb. Reflexes of the PMP prefix *pa- have a causative function in Acehnese, Gayo, Batak languages, and the languages of the Barrier Islands.

Other applicative affixes commonly found in NMLS include reflexes of PMP verbal suffixes *-i, *-an, and *-aken (Blust 2003b). The functions of applicative suffixes derived from these forms vary across languages, with polyfunctionality of individual suffixes being very common. Common valency-increasing functions of these suffixes in NMLS include the introduction of a causer, patient, location, or beneficiary argument. However, non-valency increasing functions are also common, such as indicating iterative aspect (see §28.5 below), increased affectedness of the patient, or higher intensity, as well as lexicalized changes in meaning. For example, the Gayo suffix *-(n)en* signals a causative meaning when affixed to intransitive bases, signals a causative meaning or "an increase in volition or intention" when added to transitive bases, and allows addition of an affected P argument when affixed to nominal bases (Eades 2005: 186). Some examples of applicative affixes and their functions in Karo Batak are shown in Table 28.10.

### 28.3.2 Nominal morphology

For the most part, nouns in NMLS require no explicit marking for grammatical category such as number, gender, or animacy. Enggano is an exception; number, human vs. non-human, and proper vs. common noun are distinguished on nouns by means of prefixes. A paradigm is shown in Table 28.11. Some of these prefixes have another function in marking case. In general, case marking on nouns is rare among NMLS (see §28.4.1.2 for further discussion). The remainder of this section describes some common noun-forming affixes in NMLS.

Some NMLS make use of a nominal prefix derived from PMP *paŋ- which forms nouns that express an instrument or agent of the base action, or in some cases deverbal nouns in general. These include Karo Batak *peN-*, Toba Batak *paŋ-*, Gayo *pen-*, Lampung Api *paN-*, and Rejang *peng-*. Like reflexes of *maŋ, these prefixes trigger nasal substitution and accretion (e.g. Karo Batak *pengkawil* 'fisherman' from *kawil* 'to fish' (Woollams 1996: 77), and Gayo *penengkam* 'trap (n.)' from *tengkam* 'to catch' (Eades 2005: 38)).

Other nominal prefixes found in the NMLS include reflexes of the PMP nominalizing prefix *paR-. Examples include the Rejang deverbal noun prefix *pe-* (e.g. *pe-tulung* 'assistance', *tulung* 'to help') as well as noun-forming prefixes in Nias (*fa(ʔa)-*), Lampung Api (*pa-*), and Karo Batak (*per-*), which have more varied functions. Other affixes can also be used to form abstract nouns, especially those indicating abstract states. Examples include the circumfixes *ka- -an* in Lampung Api (e.g. *ka-xabay-an* 'fear', *xabay* 'afraid' (Woollams 1996: 95)), and *ke- -en* in Karo Batak (e.g. *ke-dung-en* 'conclusion', *dung* 'finished' (Woollams 1996: 86)). As discussed above, affixes derived from PMP *-in- may also play a role in noun formation.

A number of suffixes also function to form nouns, especially deverbal and locative nominalizations, in many NMLS. Some of these appear to be derived from PMP *-an, which as mentioned above also forms locative applicatives (§28.3.1). For example, Toba Batak *-an* may form nouns indicating the location of an action, as in *páŋan* 'eat', *paŋán-an* 'dish, plate' (Nababan 1981: 96). Lampung Api *-an* is very productive and often derives nouns indicating the result or object of an action, as in *aji* 'to chant', *aji-an* 'the chant' (Walker 1976: 26). In Nias, the suffix *-(C)a* forms nouns denoting the place or time of an action, as well as deverbal nouns and nouns denoting the object or result of an action. A similar suffix *-Ca* in Enggano forms "locational nouns" (Edwards 2015: 73).

## 28.4 Syntax

This section covers some basic syntactic properties of NMLS, including voice, case, agreement, and grammatical relations (§28.4.1), word order (§28.4.2), and the structure of the noun phrase (§28.4.3).

### 28.4.1 Voice, agreement, case, and grammatical relations

NMLS can be grouped into two basic types based upon whether the voice system is considered symmetrical or asymmetrical. Languages with symmetrical voice systems have multiple basic transitive constructions and are common throughout western Indonesia (see Kroeger and Riesberg, chapter 47, this volume). Languages with asymmetrical voice systems, on the other hand, have a single basic transitive construction with valency-changing alternations

**Table 28.10** Causative and applicative affixes in Karo Batak

| Affix | Function | Root | | Affixed form | |
|---|---|---|---|---|---|
| *pe-* | causative | *galang* | 'big' | *pe-galang* | 'expand' |
| *-ken* | causative | *keri* | 'depleted' | *keri-ken* | 'deplete; use up' |
| *-ken* | theme applicative | *rukur* | 'think' | *rukur-ken* | 'think about' |
| *-i* | locative applicative | *kendul* | 'sit' | *kendul-i* | 'sit on; occupy' |
| *-i* | iterative aspect | *pekpek* | 'hit' | *pekpek-i* | 'hit repeatedly' |
| *pe-...-i* | causative, intensive | *kitik* | 'small' | *pe-kitik-i* | 'make smaller' |
| *pe-...-ken* | causative, intensive | *ganjang* | 'high' | *pe-ganjang-ken* | 'put up even higher' |

**Table 28.11** Enggano noun prefixes (Crowley n.d.: 11)

| | Singular | Plural |
|---|---|---|
| human | *e-* | *ka-* |
| kinship term | *Ø-* | *kahə-* |
| proper | *Ø-* | — |
| common, non-human | *e-* | *e-* |

(i.e. active–passive, ergative–antipassive) and are common among the world's languages. Symmetrical voice NMLS include all but Acehnese on mainland Sumatra (i.e. Nasal, Lampung, Rejang, Gayo, and Batak) and two languages of the Barrier Islands, Devayan and Mentawai.[9] Asymmetrical voice NMLS include most other Barrier Islands languages (Sigulai, Nias, and Enggano).[10] These two groups of languages have different strategies for marking grammatical relations. In symmetrical voice NMLS, grammatical relations are closely tied to voice, while in asymmetrical voice NMLS (i.e. Nias, Enggano), they are marked through case, agreement, and word order. Acehnese is in an uncertain position. It arguably has two transitive constructions, one in which the actor is unmarked and another in which it is marked by an agent case-marker *lé*. According to some studies, the latter is a passive, and Acehnese falls into the asymmetrical voice group (Legate 2012, 2014). However, because its position is still unclear, we provide a separate discussion of Acehnese.

[9] Based on descriptions of Devayan (Faridan 1981) and Mentawai (Morris 1900), these langauges appear to make use of AV and UV constructions that are consistent with those in the other symmetrical voice languages.

[10] However, we note that Nias maintains an alternation in relative clauses that is similar to symmetrical voice (see Brown 2001: 417 -21).

#### 28.4.1.1 *Voice and grammatical relations in symmetrical voice languages*

Symmetrical voice NMLS have a two-way distinction between Actor Voice (AV), in which the transitive actor (A) argument is the subject, and Undergoer Voice (UV), in which the transitive undergoer (P) is the subject. In both constructions, the non-subject argument is not demoted, which distinguishes it from asymmetrical voice systems, which have a passive construction (Riesberg 2014; Chen and McDonnell 2019).[11] In NMLS the single (actor or undergoer) argument of an intransitive verb (S) is also considered a subject. The examples from Nasal in (6) below demonstrate these patterns of symmetrical voice and grammatical relations: (6a) is an intransitive construction where the verb is unmarked, (6b) is an AV construction in which the verb is prefixed with a homorganic nasal *ng-*, and (6c) is a UV construction in which the verb is prefixed with *di-*. In these constructions, the preverbal argument is the subject: S in (6a), A in (6b), and P in (6c). In transitive constructions, the post-verbal argument is considered a non-subject core argument, since they are unmarked and do not appear to be demoted. This includes P in (6b), and A in (6c).

Nasal

(6) a. *watang sijo masih hukhik.*
tree DEM.PROX still live
'This tree is still alive.'

b. *iyo kak ny-(s)uah lahan.*
3SG PFV AV-burn field
'He burned the field.'

[11] In some of the symmetrical voice languages, there is also a true passive construction in addition to AV and UV (see Kroeger and Riesberg, chapter 47, this volume).

c. *lahan* *ni* *kak* *khadu*
field that PFV finish
*di-suah* *Anton.*
UV-burn Anton
'Anton already burned the field.'
(McDonnell fieldnotes)

Evidence for a subject grammatical relation in symmetrical voice NMLS primarily comes from behavioural—as opposed to coding (Keenan 1976a)—properties. That is, subjects have the ability to raise, relativize, and/or float quantifiers (see Kroeger and Riesberg, chapter 47, this volume). Eades (2005) states that only subject arguments in relative clauses may be relativized. Examples are shown in (7) below: S is relativized in (7a), A is relativized in (7b), and P is relativized in (7c). The relative clause is within brackets, and the head noun, which is co-referential with the so-called 'gap' in the relative clause, is bolded.

Gayo
(7) a. ***jema*** *[si* *gintes* *kin* *aku]*
person REL surprised DAT 1SG
'the people who were surprised by me'

b. ***urang*** ***tue*** *[si* *mu-lahir-en*
person old REL AV-be.born-CAUS
*tubuh=leu=ni]*
body=1SG.POSS=this
'the parent who gave birth to me.'

c. ***kurik*** *[si* *i-geléh=è=a]*
chicken REL UV-slaughter=3SG.NSBJ=that
'the chicken that he slaughtered' (Eades 2005: 277–8)

Similar restrictions are found in other symmetrical voice NMLS such as Karo Batak (Woollams 1996; Norwood 2002), Toba Batak (Schachter 1984), and Nasal (McDonnell fieldnotes), but whether these hold in other symmetrical voice NMLS, such as Rejang, Devayan, and Lampung remains unclear because these languages lack descriptions of grammatical relations.

Non-subject arguments are more challenging to pin down. However, the discussion surrounding non-subject arguments in symmetrical voice NMLS concerns their core (or oblique) status (see Kroeger and Riesberg, chapter 47, this volume for a detailed discussion of the issues). The clearest evidence for the core status of non-subject arguments come from the strict position within the clause (see §28.4.2 below) and their lack of additional marking by prepositions. These properties are found in all of the symmetrical voice NMLS and demonstrated in the Nasal examples in (6b) and (6c), in which the non-subject arguments occur post-verbally and do not receive any additional marking.

### 28.4.1.2 *Case, agreement, and grammatical relations in asymmetrical voice NMLS*

Grammatical relations in asymmetrical voice NMLS are primarily marked by coding—as opposed to behavioural—properties, such as case marking and agreement but also word order (see §28.4.2). However, no clear patterns emerge for case and agreement across the two languages for which we have adequate descriptions, namely, Nias and Enggano. With limited descriptions of the remaining asymmetrical voice NMLS, Sigulai, our generalizations are limited.[12] Thus, we describe case and agreement in Nias and Enggano in this section.

Nias presents a particularly interesting situation because agreement and case-marking show two different patterns of grammatical relations, reinforcing the idea that grammatical relations are both language and construction specific (Bickel 2010). Agreement in Nias is obligatorily marked on the verb. It encodes person and number of S and A arguments in irrealis mode, as in (8) below. In realis mode, only A arguments show agreement, as in (9). Thus, agreement shows fairly straightforward evidence of a subject relation with nominative–accusative alignment.

Nias
(8) a. ***Ya**-ma-nana* ***nono-nia*** *ba*
3SG.IRR-DYN-hand child:MUT-3SG.POSS LOC
*va-a-lio.*
[NMLZ-STAT-quick]:MUT
'Her child will be crawling soon.'

b. ***Ya**-mbalö* *gefe* ***Ama*** ***Dali***
3SG.IRR-repay:IRR money:MUT Ama Dali
'Ama Dali wants to borrow (lit. 'repay') some money.' (Brown 2001: 502)

Nias
(9) ***I**-fa-tene* *ga* *ndrao*
3SG.RLS-DO-messenger here 1SG.MUT
*khö-mi* ***ama-gu.***
DAT-2PL.POSS father-1SG.POSS
'My father sent me here to you.' (Brown 2001: 355)

Case in Nias is marked via a phonological process of nominal mutation (see S28.2.3). In general, A arguments do not undergo nominal mutation, as in (9), while S and P arguments do, as in (10). This apparent ergative–absolutive pattern in case-marking is exceedingly rare among the world's languages as the absolutive argument in Nias is marked (Comrie 2013). There are a some exceptions to this pattern. For example, clauses that contain one of several mental state

[12] Sigulai appears to have limited case marking via nominal mutation (see §28.2.3) and limited agreement (see discussion below).

verbs (e.g., 'like', 'fear') take two mutated arguments. There is also variation based on aspect (e.g. A is mutated when the verb is marked imperfective but not mutated when it is marked as perfective) or the (in)dependant status of a clause (e.g. A is mutated in some dependant clauses but unmutated in most independent clauses). For more details on these exceptions see Brown (2001: Ch. 7).

Nias
(10) a. *Aukhu* ***nidanö***
STAT:hot water:MUT
'The water is hot.' (Brown 2001: 342)

b. *La-bunu* ***mbaβi.***
3PL.RLS-kill pig:MUT
'They killed a pig.' (Brown 2001: 345)

Sigulai shows similar albeit more limited patterns of nominal mutation, for example, a subset of lexical nouns mutate but pronouns do not (Kähler 1955). However, these patterns do not clearly provide evidence for grammatical relations. While Kähler notes that nominal mutation occurs on subject arguments, which would presumably be S and A arguments, the only examples of noun mutation in Kähler (1955) involve S arguments (see (26a) in §28.4.2). A arguments are either realized as pronouns, as in (27a), or some sort of left-dislocated topicalization that apparently does not undergo noun mutation, as in (27b) below.[13] Given the limited description we have in Kähler (1955), patterns of nominal mutation in Sigulai are still unclear. Furthermore, Sigulai shows very limited evidence of agreement. It is only found in a very limited number of examples where the enclitic A argument cross-references a pre-verbal argument (see (27b) in §28.4.2).

Enggano marks case and agreement but such marking is much more limited than Nias. Person and number agreement only occur in a subset of clause types, and what might be considered case-marking prefixes are also noun classifiers, distinguishing human from non-human nouns (see §28.3.1.1). These hybrid case-marking/classifier prefixes do not distinguish grammatical relations but core arguments from several types of oblique or otherwise dependent arguments (Edwards 2015). That is, the case-marking prefixes *e-* (for non-human nouns, singular human nouns) and *ka-* (for plural human nouns) mark core arguments.[14] Other case-marking prefixes include the locative case-marker *i-* and a dependent prefix *u-*, which marks the possessor in nominal possession, nouns following the oblique marker *iʔiɔə/ʔɔ-* or the locative case-marked noun, among others (Crowley n.d.).

[13] Note that the example in (27b) is not evidence against nominal mutation of A. Brown (2001: 78–9) notes that when an argument is fronted before the verb in Nias, it is always unmutated.

[14] Proper names and kinship terms are unmarked for case.

The example in (11) demonstrates the functions of these three case-marking prefixes in Enggano.

Enggano
(11) *e-kɛʔɛpa* *eʔana* *ki-hɛkũ* *i-tɛbɛ* *u-kuɔ.*
CORE-bird that VERB-sit LOC-top DEP-tree
'The bird is sitting on top of the tree.'
(Kähler 1940: 182 cited in Crowley n.d.: 16)

Person and number agreement prefixes in Enggano only occur on verbs in a subset of clause types, including negative and subordinate clauses (Edwards 2015: 61). The examples in (12) demonstrate agreement with S and A arguments. In (12b), the third singular agreement prefix *i-* agrees with the subject *e-kaka eʔana* 'that person'. However, in (12a), the third singular agreement marker is prefixed to the verb, and here realized as *y-* before a vowel-initial root, but Kähler (1940) does not provide any examples where there is a lexical subject.

Enggano
(12) a. *kɛabaʔa* ***y**-ɛdɔ.*
NEG 3SG.AGR-cry
'He does not cry.' (Kähler 1940: 104)

b. ***e-kaka*** ***eʔana*** *kɛabaʔa* ***i**-pudu*
CORE-person that NEG 3SG.AGR-kill
*e-kɔyɔ.*
CORE-pig
'That person did not kill the pig.'
(Crowley n.d.: 41)

As case marking and agreement are limited, grammatical relations in Enggano are primarily evidenced in word order patterns. S and A arguments occur before the verb and P occurs after the verb (see §28.4.2 for more details).

#### 28.4.1.3 *Agreement, case, and grammatical relations in Acehnese*

Acehnese grammatical relations have sparked controversy. Some have claimed that Acehnese has an active–passive alternation with subject and object grammatical relations (Lawler 1988; Legate 2012, 2014). Durie (1988) and others have argued that Acehnese does not have any grammatical relations since agreement patterns of arguments can be explained by semantic macroroles, Actor and Undergoer (Van Valin and LaPolla 1997: 255*ff*). According to Durie (1985, 1987), Acehnese distinguishes two macroroles, Actor (analogous to A) and Undergoer (analogous to P), in both transitive and intransitive clauses. Thus, S is split and could be represented as $S_A$ for Actors and $S_P$ for Undergoers (see Himmelmann 2005a: 133*ff*). These macroroles are primarily distinguished by the manner in which they are cross-referenced on the verb: Actors are proclitics, while Undergoers are enclitics (see §28.3.1.1). Examples of this system are presented in (13).[15]

Acehnese

(13) a. *geu=jak gopnyan*
3.POL=go 3.POL
'(S)he goes.'

b. *gopnyan rhët(=geuh)*
3.POL fall=3.POL
'(S)he falls.'

c. *kèe h'an geu=patéh=kuh gopnyan*
1SG.FAM NEG 3.POL=believe=1SG.FAM 3.POL
'(S)he doesn't believe me.' (Durie 1987: 370)

In most cases, the Actor proclitic is obligatory, while the Undergoer enclitic is optional. When a lexical Actor argument is present, it agrees with the proclitic, either $S_A$ or A, as in (13a) or (13c), respectively. Likewise, when a lexical Undergoer argument is present, it agrees with the enclitic (if present), either $S_P$ or P, as in (13b) or (13c), respectively.

Acehnese has a single case marker *lé*, which marks transitive Actor (A) arguments, as in (14). These case-marked Actors still agree with the obligatory proclitic on the verb. When an Undergoer enclitic is present, the case-marker is optional. Thus, the lexical Actor argument in (13c) above is not case-marked.

Acehnese

(14) *raja ji=kap lé uleue*
king 3.FAM=bite AGT snake
'A snake bit the king.' (Durie 1987: 371)

Durie (1987) shows that syntactic processes apply to either Actors (e.g. control), Undergoers (e.g. resultatives), or equally to Actors and Undergoers (i.e. core arguments). Based on this evidence, Acehnese does not appear to have any grammatical relations since the behaviour of arguments can be explained by these semantic macroroles. For alternative views on Acehnese, see Legate (2014).

## 28.4.2 Word order

NMLS are largely head-initial. They all have prepositions or case markers that occur before the noun (see discussion of Enggano case in §28.4.1.2 above). Standard negators occur before the predicates they negate and nouns occur before their modifiers with the exception of numerals and quantifiers, which commonly occur before the noun (see §28.4.3).

[15] Glossing has been updated to reflect the fact that these pronouns are clitics and not affixes.

The examples from Lampung Api below demonstrate head-initial word order in prepositional phrases (15) and negation (16).

Lampung Api

(15) *Holon hina lagi cecok* ***di*** *xangoq.*
person that continue stand at door
'That man is standing in the doorway.'
(Walker 1976: 11)

Lampung Api

(16) *Holon Lampung biasa=ni* ***maq*** *jadi padagang.*
person Lampung usual=3SG NEG become trader
'Lampung people usually don't become traders.'
(Walker 1976: 11)

In terms of clausal word order, NMLS are either verb-initial or verb-medial. However, in describing the particulars of clausal word order in these languages, it is again useful to treat asymmetrical voice NMLS separate from symmetrical voice NMLS because of the complications introduced by having two basic transitive constructions. We first discuss symmetrical voice NMLS.

### 28.4.2.1 *Word order in symmetrical voice NMLS*

Word order in symmetrical voice NMLS can be summarized as follows. The position of the non-subject argument is relatively constrained; it is, with very few exceptions, adjacent to the verb, forming a constituent that we refer to as the *predicate complex.* Subject arguments are less constrained and either occur before or after the predicate in intransitive clauses or the predicate complex in transitive constructions, resulting in the two patterns in (17). For our purposes, the notion of predicate complex subsumes predicates in intransitive constructions and the verbal predicate and non-subject argument in transitive clauses.

(17) a. Subject-initial order: Subject – Predicate complex
b. Subject-final order: Predicate complex – Subject

In symmetrical voice NMLS, both orders are possible. However, in two languages, Nasal and Lampung, the basic word order is subject-initial. To illustrate subject-initial word order, the Nasal examples in (18) are repeated from (6) in the previous section.

Nasal

(18) a. *watang sijo masih hukhik.*
tree DEM.PROX still live
'This tree is still alive.'

b. *iyo kak ny-(s)uah lahan.*
3SG PFV AV-burn field
'He burned the field.'

c. *lahan ni kak khadu di-suah*
field that PFV finish UV-burn
*Anton.*
Anton
'Anton already burned the field.'
(McDonnell fieldnotes)

In Batak languages, there is strong preference for subject-final word order (Cumming 1984), as in the Toba Batak examples in (19).

Toba Batak
(19) a. *Di-jahar si Poltak buku.*
UV-read PN Poltak book
'Poltak read the book.'

b. *Man-jahar buku si Poltak.*
AV-read book PN Poltak
'Poltak read the book.' (Erlewine 2016: 82)

In Gayo and Rejang, the basic word order differs based upon voice: intransitive and UV constructions prefer subject–final order, while AV constructions must be in subject-initial order, as in the Gayo examples in (20).

Gayo
(20) a. *I-jerang ine sine kerô=ni.*
UV-cook mother earlier cooked.rice=this
'Mother cooked this rice earlier.'

b. *Ine pora mi mu-jerang*
mother a.little more AV-cook
*gule=ni.*
edible.fish=this
'In a little while mother will cook this fish.'
(Eades 2005: 104)

As mentioned above, however, word order varies in all symmetrical voice NMLS. Subjects in Nasal and Lampung can appear after the predicate complex, and subjects in Batak can occur before the predicate complex. Only the AV construction in Gayo appear to be strictly subject initial, as demonstrated in the examples in (21). Crucially, the subject-final word order in (21b) is considered ungrammatical.[16]

Gayo
(21) a. *Aku mun-emah=è.*
1SG AV-make=3.NSBJ
'I made/am making it.'

b. * *Mun-emah=è aku.*
AV-make=3.NSBJ 1
'I made/am making it.' (Eades 2005: 174)

[16] Note that the predicate complex initial order in (21b) is possible when the AV construction is considered intransitive with a P argument that has a non-individuated reference, which Eades considers an incorporated noun. This may also be true for Rejang, but there is no evidence from ungrammatical examples. Interactions of voice and word order in Mentawai are unclear.

28.4.2.1.1 Order of non-subject arguments within the predicate complex

As mentioned above, non-subject arguments in all but a few cases are adjacent to the verb. While non-subject P arguments (in AV constructions) occur after the verb in canonical transitive clauses, non-subject A arguments (in UV constructions) in all symmetrical voice NMLS—with the exception of Rejang—are variable, occurring before or after the verb. The variable position is based on the person of the non-subject A argument. In Nasal, for example, first and second person non-subject A arguments occur before the verb while third person arguments occur after the verb, as in the examples in (22). However, in Gayo and Toba Batak, first person non-subject A arguments occur before the verb, while second and third person arguments occur after the verb.

Nasal
(22) a. *lahan ni kak khadu ku=suah.*
field that PFV finish 1SG=[UV]burn
'I already burned the field.'

b. *lahan ni kak khadu mu=suah.*
field that PFV finish 2SG=[UV]burn
'You already burned the field.'

c. *lahan ni kak khadu (di-)suah=nyo.*
field that PFV finish UV-burn=3SG
'He already burned the field.'
(McDonnell fieldnotes)

These non-subject A arguments are typically realized as clitics and in a number of cases differ in form from free pronouns (e.g. the Nasal first person singular free pronoun is *nyak* while the non-subject A form is *ku=*). If this argument is a proclitic it occurs without any UV prefix, but if it is an enclitic, it commonly combines with the UV prefix *di-*, as in (22c).

### 28.4.2.2 *Word order in asymmetrical voice NMLS*

In asymmetrical voice NMLS, the basic word order is either V(O)S (Nias, Sigulai), as in (23), or SV(O) (Enggano), as in (24).

Nias
(23) a. *Anakhö sibai ndrao.*
STAT.tired INT 1SG.MUT
'I'm very tired.' (Brown 2001: 190)

b. *I-rino vakhe ina-gu.*
3SG.RLS-cook rice:MUT mother-1SG.POSS
'My mother cooked rice.' (Brown 2001: 571)

Enggano
(24) a. *E-keʔepa ẽʔãnã kĩ-hãhãmõ.*
CORE-bird that VERB-fly
'That bird flies/Those birds fly.'
(Kähler 1940: 86 cited in Edwards 2015: 61)

b. *Kia* *ki-pudu* *e-koyo* *ẽʔãnã* *iʔioo*
3SG VERB-kill CORE-pig that PREP
*u-bohe.*
OBL-spear
'He kills that pig with a spear.'
(Kähler 1940: 196 cited in Edwards 2015: 61)

While word order appears to be fairly strict in asymmetrical voice languages, there is variation under certain conditions. For example, Brown (2001) notes that in Nias when the clause contains a clausal complement, it follows the verb and the subject argument.[17] In Enggano, variation from the basic SV(O) word order pattern occurs under two conditions. First, if the predicate is stative, the subject follows the verb, that is, it shows VS word order (Crowley n.d.: 32). The second condition is a bit more complicated. In Enggano, the verb is marked by either verbal agreement (see §28.4.1.2 above) or a verbal prefix *ki-* in basic SV(O) clauses, as in (24) above. However, there is a prefix *ka-* that when attached to the verb triggers a change in the word order to VS(O), as in (25). Other than triggering a change in word order, the semantic and/or pragmatic functions of *ka-* are not clear.[18]

Enggano

(25) a. *Kã-kõkõnã-hã* *e-koʔeʔe* *kude*
VERB-come.out-EMPH CORE-demon from
*i-hoo* *u-kuehi.*
LOC-inside DEP-forest
'The demon came out from inside the forest.'
(Kähler 1940: 203 cited in Edwards 2015: 61)

b. *Ka-nũkĩ* *e-kaka* *eʔana* *e-kihi.*
VERB-pull CORE-person that CORE-rattan
'That person pulled the rattan.' (Kähler 1940: 203)

Word order in Sigulai appears to be primarily verb-initial (Kähler 1955), as in (26b). However, in many examples in Kähler (1955), S appears before the predicate without any differences, as in (26a) below.

Sigulai

(26) a. *naitə̃* *mə=la* *mate.*
fire:MUT CMPL=EMPH die
'The fire has gone out.'

b. *löntuʔ* *bəlöŋ-bölöŋ*
come beetle
'The beetle came.' (Kähler 1955: 17)

In transitive constructions, the vast majority of examples are verb-initial with A and P arguments occurring after the predicate. However, in these cases, the A argument appears to be a clitic pronoun, as in (27a). In the few examples where there are two lexical arguments, the lexical A argument appears before the verb but is set off with a comma, as in (27b), which likely means that it is prosodically marked. Whether these constructions represent word order variation or some sort of topicalization requires further research.

Sigulai[19]

(27) a. *maŋ-inu=do* *idanö.*
AV-drink=1SG water
'I drink water' (Kähler 1955: 28)

b. *baeliŋ,* *maŋ-ili=di* *bebiʔ-ni*
crab AV-molt=3SG shell-3SG.POSS
'The crab changes its shell.' (Kähler 1955: 28)

### 28.4.2.3 *Word order in Acehnese*

According to Durie (1985, 1988), Acehnese word order is relatively free, but the majority of clauses are predicate-initial and all arguments may follow the predicate in any possible order as long as A is marked by the case-marker *lé*, as in (28).

Acehnese

(28) a. *Geu=jak* *gopnyan*
3.POL=go 3.POL
'He goes.' (Durie 1988: 107)

b. *Ka* *geu=côm* *lôn* *lé* *gopnyan*
already 3.POL-kiss 1.POL AGT 3.POL
'She kissed me.'

c. *Ka* *lôn=pateh* *lé* *lôn* *aneuk*
already 1.POL=believe AGT 1.POL child
*miet* *nyan*
small that
'I believe that child.' (Durie 1988: 107)

The clearest constraint on word order is that only a single argument can precede the predicate, which Durie (1985) refers to as the 'Core Topic'. This argument can be S, A, or P, as in the examples in (29).

Acehnese

(29) a. *Gopnyan* *geu=jak*
3.POL 3.POL=go
'He goes.' (Durie 1988: 107)

17 A similar pattern also occurs in Karo Batak AV constructions (Woollams 1996: 189).

18 The *ka-* prefix presents a number of challenges. Edwards (2015) first notes that the *ka-* may be the combination of the verbal *ki-* prefix and a separate *a-* prefix, which triggers elision of the high vowel *i*. This means that *ka-* is not alternating with *ki-*, but represents an additional *a-* prefix. Furthermore, Edwards (2015: 61) summarises the only clue that Kähler provides to understand the function of *(k)a-*: "Verbs marked with the prefix *ki-* are described by Kähler (1940: 192–4) as having more nominal characteristics, while those with the prefix *ka-* are described as having more verbal characteristics."

19 Since Sigulai is an asymmetrical voice language, *maŋ-* may be analysed as a marker of active voice.

b. *Gopnyan* *ka* *geu=côm* *lôn*
3.POL already 3.POL=kiss 1.POL
'She kissed me.'

c. *Lôn* *ka* *geu=côm* *lé* *gopnyan*
1.POL already 3.POL-kiss AGT 3.POL
'She kissed me.' (Durie 1988: 104–5)

### 28.4.3 Noun phrases

NMLS show a fair degree of similarity in regard to noun phrase (NP) structure. Across these languages, most elements of the NP occur after the head noun, including possessors, adjectival and nominal modifiers, relative clauses, and demonstrative determiners. Quantificational elements, which include numerals, numeral classifiers, and (non-numeral) quantifiers, are an exception and most commonly occur before the head noun. For some languages, such as Enggano and Sigulai, the position of some elements in the NP is not fully clear from available descriptions. The most typical NP structure in NMLS is shown in (30) with corresponding examples from Toba Batak (31) and Karo Batak (32).

(30) QUANT/NUM – Noun – PSR – Modifier – DEM

Toba Batak
(31) *sudé* *hálak* *húta* *(na)* *mɔra* *í*
all person village REL rich DEM.DIST
'all the rich villagers' (Nababan 1981: 109)

Karo Batak
(32) kenna kerbo bapa enda
all water.buffalo father DEM.PROX
'all these water-buffalo of Father's'
(Woollams 1996: 106)

Possessors most commonly occur immediately following the head noun. However, in some languages, including Acehnese, the possessor may either precede or follow an attributive modifier, as in (33a) and (33b) below, respectively.

Acehnese
(33) a. *sa-boh* *keubeue=**neuh*** *nyang* *ji=cu*
one-CLF buffalo=2.POL REL 3.FAM=steal
'one of his buffaloes that were stolen'

b. *bak* *pisang* *manyang=**lôn***
tree banana tall=1.POL
'my tall banana tree' (Durie 1985: 108)

Possessors may be either pronominal or lexical, with the former typically marked by a set of pronominal enclitics. Lexical possessor NPs often appear immediately following the head noun with no overt marking, but in some languages, possessors are grammatically marked. In Nias, possessor NPs and other nominal modifiers are marked with mutation, for example, *telau mbuaya* 'head of the crocodile', where the possessor noun *buaya* 'crocodile' is mutated (Brown 2001: 373), see §28.2.3. In Sigulai, this nominal mutation also marks nominal modifiers including possessors in a few nouns (Kähler 1955: 24). Particles may also be used to mark possessors as discussed below. Adjectival modifiers, nominal modifiers, and relative clauses typically occur after the possessor. In almost all NMLS, demonstrative determiners occur after the head noun and any possessors, modifiers, and relative clauses. However, Nias differs from this pattern. In Nias, a series of up to two demonstratives occurs after the head noun and any possessor as in (34), but Brown (2001: 372) notes that demonstratives can precede any number of other modifiers, which are analysed as relative clauses with verbal or numeral predicates.

Nias
(34) *Ba* *siʔulu=wa=e*
CONJ village.leader=that=Q
***nama-da***
ancestor:MUT-1PL.INCL.POSS
***andre*** ***noemaʔe***!?
DEM.DIST DEM.RECOG
'And you mean that ancestor you've been talking about was a village leader!?' (Brown 2001: 411)

In some languages, the possession relationship, as well as other types of semantic relationships between the head noun and a following nominal modifier are marked with an intervening particle, which has been described as a 'ligature' or 'linker'. For example, in Gayo, full NP possessors are marked with the particle *ni=*, which often cliticises to the possessor NP, as in *kôrô ni ama* ~ *kôrô n=ama* 'father's buffalo.' The linker particle *ni=* is also said to mark kin relationships, part–whole relationships, and 'componential' relationships, in which the head noun is made up of the type of object expressed by the nominal modifier, as in *empus ni awal* (garden LNK banana) 'banana garden/plantation' (Eades 2005: 219). As mentioned above in §28.4.1, the prefix *u-* in Enggano similarly appears to mark dependent nouns including possessors and certain nominal modifiers (see (11) above). In Mentawai, *n=* (or allomorph *=t*) appears between a modifying nominal and the preceding head noun, as in *ūma n=abak* (house LNK=boat) 'boat house', and *mata=t ukui* (face=LNK father) 'face of father' (Morris 1900: 16).[20] Kähler (1955: 21) also mentions that attributive relationships can be marked by *-n* between the head noun and modifying nominal in Devayan as in *luma-n ana='u* (house-LNK child=1SG) 'my child's house'. In Toba Batak, some attributive modifiers are marked

[20] Morris (1900) does not distinguish clitics from affixes, but the behaviour of *n=* is more consistent with that of a clitic.

with *ni-* or *na-* (Nababan 1981: 108), while in Karo Batak, similar markers *ni* ~ *nu* ~ *u* are found before a possessor or nominal modifier only in archaic expressions (Woollams 1996: 137–8). As some of the preceding examples indicate, in many of these languages, there is no clear distinction between possessor NPs and nominal modifiers.

Of the NP elements discussed in this section, it appears that only quantificational elements canonically appear before the head noun. These include non-numeral quantifiers and their modifiers (such as degree words) or a numeral, sometimes together with a noun classifier. As an apparent exception, Enggano examples show that numerals and numeral classifiers follow the head noun (see (39) below). Additionally, descriptions of Nias, and Gayo show that some quantificational elements can 'float', that is, they may appear separated from the head noun, or entire NP, by another constituent (Brown 2001: 427; Eades 2005: 89). For example, in Gayo, a quantifier or numeral element most commonly appears immediately preceding the head noun, as in (35a) and (36a). These quantificational elements can also float, as shown in (35b) and (36b).

Gayo

(35) a. *Kahè i sien* ***delé*** *kule.*
later LOC here ***many*** tiger
'Later there will be many tigers here.'
(Eades 2005: 214)

b. ***Delé pedih*** *leu-engon kutu=mu.*
***many very*** UV.1SG-see louse=2.POSS
'I see your many lice.' (Eades 2005: 89)

Gayo

(36) a. ***sara*** *belanga kôl jantar-dengké*
***one*** pot big vegetable-meat
'a big cooking pot of vegetables' (Eades 2005: 215)

b. *Aku mun-osah emas kin tengku*
1SG AV-give gold DAT sir
***sara bongkil.***
***one lump***
'I will give you a lump of gold, sir.'
(Eades 2005: 216)

Besides cases of quantifier float mentioned above, variable position for quantificational elements has been described in a few other languages. For example, in both Acehnese and Mentawai, elements such as numerals and classifiers usually precede the head noun, but may also follow it (see Mentawai contrast between (38a) and (38b) below).

In NPs containing numerals, numeral classifiers are commonly used. Numeral classifiers are typically a small, closed class that are transparently derived from nouns. When classifiers are used, the common order is numeral–classifier, with the exception of Nias, where it is classifier–numeral. In a few languages, a ligature intervenes between numeral and classifier. In Lampung Api, this ligature is *nga*, as in (37). In Mentawai, it is *ṅa* (which is pronounced [ŋa] and is optional), as in (38). In Enggano, it is *h* (< PMP *ŋa), as in (39) (Crowley n.d.).

Lampung Api

(37) *telu ngam-biji manuq*
three LIG-COUNTER chicken
'three chickens' (Walker 1976: 17)

Mentawai

(38) a. *lima-ṅa munäṅ djō-djō*
five-LIG ANIM dog-PL
'five dogs'

b. *inu pulu šara tära bā̈*
bead ten one remainder COUNTER
'eleven beads' (Morris 1900: 23)

Enggano

(39) *e-ʔitə ʔakədu h-apɛ̃a*
CORE-banana three LIG-CLF
'three bananas' (Crowley n.d.)

## 28.5 Tense, aspect, and mood (TAM)

Tense, aspect, and modality (TAM) are marked in NMLS by a variety of strategies. These include the use of a special set of TAM markers, reduplication, and affixation directly on the verb—often with a portmanteau morpheme that signifies both aspect and voice. Most NMLS make use of more than one of these strategies. Additionally, Nias makes use of grammatical mood, which is described below. Aspectual meanings of reduplication are mentioned above (§28.2.3) and will not be discussed further here.

NMLS commonly make use of a closed set of morphemes that function as markers of tense, aspect, and/or modality. These markers are never obligatory, and their syntactic status varies across languages. Some TAM markers must be situated close to the verb and pattern like auxiliary verbs, while others are less integrated into the predicate complex and pattern like adverbs or other particles; many languages make use of more than one type. Some TAM markers are clitics (e.g. Nias, Sigulai), some are verbs (e.g. Acehnese, Toba Batak), and some are adverbials with a freer distribution (e.g. Gayo). Further discussion of these types of TAM markers follows.

The Acehnese preverbal TAM markers, which Durie (1985: 47) treats as complement-taking verbs, show close integration with the predicate. They can attach to the pronominal clitic that appears on the verb, and are "pronounced as one phonological unit" with the predicate (Durie 1985: 248). Such preverbal TAM markers express tense and aspect including future, iamitive (meaning 'already'), and completive, as well as modality, such as probability and ability. The examples below show that the absence of a TAM marker, as in (40a), can indicate an intended action, while using the existential verb *na=* alongside a verbal predicate, as in (40b), indicates that the predicate is a fact (not merely an intention). In (40c) the iamitive marker *ka=* 'already' indicates that the event has happened; this morpheme also marks states that have already begun.

Acehnese

(40) a. *lön* *lön=jak* *u=kende*
1SG.POL 1SG.POL=go to=town
'I am going to town.' (expressing intention)

b. *lön* *na=lön=jak* *u=kende*
1SG.POL exist=1SG.POL=go to=town
'I go to town (habitually).' or 'I went to town.'

c. *ka=geu=jak*
already=3.POL=GO
'He has gone.' (Durie 1985: 248)

In Toba Batak, one set of TAM markers is treated by Nababan (1981) as a type of auxiliary verb. These are quite closely integrated with the predicate complex, as they must immediately precede or follow the head of the predicate. Toba Batak also makes use of particles which express aspectual or modal meaning. These are less closely integrated with the predicate; they occur either in clause-initial position or between the predicate and subject. The examples in (41) show the TAM marking auxiliaries *íkkən* 'must' and *musɛ* 'again' occurring in positions adjacent to the head verb *láo* 'go'.[21] The examples also show modal particles occurring between the predicate and subject, namely the affirmative particle *dɔ*, the narrative particle *ma* 'and so', and the distinct (but homophonous) hortative particle *ma*, respectively.

Toba Batak

(41) a. ***íkkən*** *láo* ***dɔ*** *hɔ* *tu* *húta*
must go AFF 2SG to village
'You must go to the village.'
(Nababan 1981: 85)

b. *láo* ***musɛ*** ***ma*** *ibána*
go again and.so 3SG
'(And so) he went again.' (Nababan 1981: 86)

c. *láo* ***ma*** *hɔ*
go HORT 2SG
'Please, go now!'
(van der Tuuk 1971 [1864–1867]: 360)

In Gayo, the set of aspectual markers include the progressive *tengah*, perfect *nge*, and immediate perfect *ben* or *teku*. These are treated as a type of adverb; they must precede the predicate they modify, but it is possible for a subject NP to intervene, suggesting that these are less tightly integrated with the predicate complex than the Acehnese preverbal TAM markers and Toba Batak auxiliaries.

In Nias, the proclitic *ma=* expresses perfective aspect. It occurs in realis clauses, either on the verb, as in (42a), or on one of a set of auxiliary verbs that express aspectual meanings, as in (42b) below. Sigulai appears to make use of a similar completive marker *mɔ=* (Kähler 1955: 17).

Nias

(42) a. *Ma=a-buso* *ndrao.*
PFV=STAT-replete 1SG.MUT
'I'm full. (I have become replete.)'

b. *Ma=aβai* *i-fazökhi* *zagö.*
PFV=finished 3SG.RLS-fix roof:MUT
'He has finished fixing the roof.' (Brown 2001: 478)

In addition to the use of special TAM markers, aspectual meaning in NMLS can be marked by affixation directly on the verb, and in particular has been tied to portmanteau functions of voice and applicative affixes (see §28.3.1). In

**Table 28.12** Partial paradigm for voice and aspect in Toba Batak (Nababan 1981: 70–1)

| Form | Gloss | Description |
|---|---|---|
| *jóu* | 'call!' | imperative |
| *joú-i* | 'call repeatedly!' | iterative, imperative |
| *mad-jóu* | 'to call' | simple aspect, AV |
| *mad-joú-i* | 'to call repeatedly' | iterative, simple aspect, AV |
| *j<um>óu* | 'have called' | completive, AV |
| *j<um>oú-i* | 'have called repeatedly' | iterative, completive, AV |
| *hu-jóu* | 'called by me' | simple aspect, UV (inflected for 1SG actor) |
| *j<in>óu* | 'have been called' | completive, UV |
| *joú-ən* | 'will be called' | future, UV |

[21] Spelling in these examples has been altered so that all conform to the same orthographic conventions.

Toba Batak, a rich system of verbal affixes are used to indicate TAM. There are two AV prefixes: *mang-* marks AV and simple aspect, while *-um-* marks AV and completive aspect. In UV clauses, simple aspect is indicated by *di-* and completive aspect by *ni-/-in-*, except for first person singular and first person plural inclusive actors, which take pronominal proclitics instead of these verbal prefixes. Nababan (1981: 70) also notes that the suffix *-ən* can be used to mark future action or to express a promise or duty. Batak languages also make use of the suffix *-i* to indicate iterative aspect. A partial paradigm showing voice and aspect in Toba Batak is given in Table 28.12. Despite the fact that they are correlated in some NMLS, few studies on the relationship between voice and aspect have been carried out for these languages, so this relationship is not well understood.

Nias is unique among NMLS for its use of grammatical mood. Nias verbs are obligatorily marked for realis or irrealis mood. Examples of irrealis mood in Brown (2001) show that it is used to express future, potential, hypothetical, and desiderative actions, among others. Grammatically, the distinction between irrealis and realis mood in Nias is indicated by the set of pronominal agreement prefixes that appear on the verb, as shown in Table 28.7 in §28.3.1.1 above. As mentioned earlier, realis verbs take no such prefix in intransitive clauses. This is shown in (43) where the realis verb is unmarked in (43a), but the irrealis verb is marked with *ya-* (3SG.IRR) in (43b).

Nias

(43) a. *Göna ya teu.*
be.struck 3SG:MUT rain
'She got caught in the rain.'

b. *Na mofanö ya mana*
if leave 3SG:MUT at.this.time
***ya**-göna teu.*
3SG.IRR-be.struck rain
'If she leaves now she will get caught in the rain.' (Brown 2001: 498)

A secondary indicator of mood is found in the presence of the infix *-um-*.[22] An example is shown in (44) where the realis verb is marked with the prefix *la-* (3PL.RLS) in (44a), and the irrealis verb is marked with both the prefix *ndra-* (3PL.IRR) and the infix *-um-* (IRR) in (44b).

Nias

(44) a. ***La**-ohe*
3PL.RLS-carry
'They carried (it).'

b. *Lö tola lö?ö **ndra-m-ohe.***
NEG can NEG 3.PL.IRR-IRR-carry
'They will have to carry it.' (Brown 2001: 504)

## 28.6 Conclusion and future directions for research on NMLS

This chapter represents the first of its kind to describe the typological features of NMLS. In doing so, we demonstrate that NMLS comprise a diverse group of languages with very little that unites them. Many NMLS exhibit features found in western Indonesian languages, such as an articulated voice system marked by several verbal affixes, applicative suffixes, reduplication, among other properties. Some NMLS contain more marked features, such as postploded nasals in Acehnese and Rejang, agreement in Acehnese, Nias, and Enggano, and case-marking in Enggano, Nias, and Sigulai. One typological parameter that is particularly informative is the distinction between asymmetrical and symmetrical voice languages. While Acehnese appears to fall somewhere between the two groups, the other NMLS can be classified in one group or the other. This division is significant because the symmetrical voice languages do not mark case or agreement, while many of the asymmetrical voice languages do. There are likely other relevant typological features that unite (some portion of) NMLS, but much more research into individual languages is needed in order to develop further cross-linguistic generalizations.

Despite a relatively long history of linguistic research in the region (e.g. Hazeu 1907; van der Tuuk 1971 [1864–1867]), many NMLS lack any in-depth description, including Nasal, Mentawai, Devayan, Leukon, Haloban, and Sigulai. Aside from Nasal, which the first author has a project to document and describe, the other languages have limited descriptions that vary in quality, reliability, and comprehensiveness. For the remaining NMLS much more description is still needed, especially Enggano, Lampungic languages, Rejang, and Batak languages such as Alas, Simalungun, and Dairi-Pakpak. These languages have little in terms of detailed, accessible descriptions. Furthermore, documentation in the form of archived collections of audiovisual recordings, transcriptions, and annotations of various speech events is even more rare.[23] In some sense, this is expected since much of the research done in Sumatra and the Barrier Islands was done before modern documentary linguistics was widely

[22] The infix *-um-* is obligatory for one verb class when the clause is irrealis. In this case, *-um-* does not indicate progressive aspect (as it may in realis clauses).

[23] Currently, there are closed collections of Mark Durie's materials on Acehnese (Durie 1980, 1982, n.d.), an open collection of Gayo audio recordings (Eades 1998), a collection of transcribed conversations of Mentawai (Gil 2015b), and a collection of Leukon audio and video recordings (Lubis and Williams 2019). The first author is also working on a project to document Nasal, which is archived with the Pacific and Regional Archive for Digital Sources in Endangered Cultures (McDonnell 2019).

practised. Thus, basic documentation and description of the NMLS listed above is the highest priority for this region.

Aside from the documentation and description of individual languages, there are many outstanding questions that we were unable to answer in this chapter. We list a few of these questions in (45).

(45) a. Are postploded nasals in Rejang and Acehnese unitary segments or nasal–stop sequences?
b. What is the nature of agreement and nominal mutation in Sigulai? How similar are they to Nias?
c. What is the nature of voice and grammatical relations in Mentawai, Sigulai and Devayan? How do they fit into the typology of voice systems (i.e. symmetrical vs. asymmetrical voice) in NMLS?
d. Other than triggering differences in word order, what are the functions of Enggano verbal prefixes *ki-* and *ka-*?

These questions represent just some of the specific outstanding issues in NMLS that deserve further detailed study.

Finally, we are also able to identify three broad areas of linguistic research on NMLS that ought to be prioritized. First, as descriptions of stress do not reliably separate word-level stress from phrase-level prominence(s), detailed phonetic studies on the interaction of word- and phrase-level prominence of individual languages are important for understanding prosody in NMLS. Second, grammatical voice and its relationship to grammatical relations, case, agreement, and word order is crucial to unlocking the grammars of NMLS. More studies that illuminate the defining properties of grammatical subjects and distinguish core arguments from obliques are needed. Third, as grammars of many NMLS (especially those of mainland Sumatra) appear to have undergone significant changes as a result of contact with Malayic languages (see e.g. Blust 1984 for Rejang; Adelaar 1995d for Toba Batak; and Anderbeck 2007b for Lampungic languages), further research on language contact may explain a number of the typological patterns we observed in NMLS.

## Acknowledgements

We would like to thank Sander Adelaar, Antoinette Schapper, and Blaine Billings for valuable feedback on an earlier version of this chapter. We would also like to thank Owen Edwards, Mary Dalrymple, and I Wayan Arka for providing access to unpublished Enggano materials. Map 28.1 is used by permission and redistribution is not permitted. Special thanks to SIL International for permission to use language data displayed therein. The first author would also like to acknowledge Johan Safri, Wawan Sahrozi, and Anton Supriyadi, all of whom are collaborating on the documentation and description of Nasal. He is also grateful to his research counterpart in Indonesia, Yanti (Atma Jaya Catholic University of Indonesia), and to the Ministry of Research and Technology in Indonesia for allowing him to conduct research on Nasal. Discussion of the Nasal data is based upon work supported by the National Science Foundation under Grant BCS–1911641. Any opinions, findings, and conclusions or recommendations expressed in this material are those of the author(s) and do not necessarily reflect the views of the National Science Foundation.

CHAPTER 29

# Malayic languages

BRADLEY MCDONNELL, JIANG WU, TIMOTHY MCKINNON, AND ALEXANDER ADELAAR

## 29.1 Introduction

Malayic languages (Map 29.1) are languages that are sufficiently closely related to Malay to form a direct subgroup with it (see Introduction in Adelaar 1992a). The *Ethnologue* distinguishes in excess of forty Malayic varieties, most of which are spoken in Indonesia and Malaysia with a few others being spoken in southern Thailand, Brunei Darussalam, Singapore, Timor Leste, Cambodia, Sri Lanka, and the Netherlands (Eberhard, Simons, and Fennig 2021). This source mentions 81,578,326 first language speakers of Malayic languages, and the actual number is probably in excess of that. Many varieties are in a dialect relationship to one another; others are genetically more distantly related (such as Iban and Kendayan in western Borneo) or have typologically diverged from mainstream Malay(ic) varieties to the extent that they are recognized as languages in their own right (such as Minangkabau, Kerinci, and possibly Banjar Malay [henceforth Banjar]). Malayic languages are traditionally spoken in Sumatra including its satellites, the Malay Peninsula, and Borneo. Through its frequent use as a means of interethnic communication, Malay has also developed into a multitude of contact languages, some of which are spoken far outside the MPSEA region. Many of these mixed languages share elements of the same structure, which is fundamentally different from the structure of other Malayic varieties, and some of them (e.g. Ternate Malay and Ambon Malay) have become first languages. See Collins 1998; Sneddon 2003b; and Slomanson (this volume, chapter 18) for an overview of the diversity and the social and linguistic history of Malayic languages.

Adelaar and Prentice (1996) and Adelaar (2005b) distinguish three basic sociolinguistic categories of Malayic varieties: vernacular Malay, literary Malay, and vehicular Malay (initially referred to as Pidgin Derived Malay, see Anderbeck, this volume, §9.1). This division is per force a schematic one, which does not always take areal issues and other categorical crossover factors into account. Gil (2020a) and Paauw (2008) discuss some of the limitations of this categorization. Among others, they point out the need to recognize regional koinés and colloquial varieties as additional categories. These issues are also discussed in Chapters 9, 16, 18, and 19, in this volume.

The goal of this chapter is to provide a short overview of the typological features displayed by members of the Malayic subgroup, focusing on areas of typological interest rather than on the sociolinguistic status of Malayic languages or the genetic distance between them. An earlier overview of typological variation in Malayic is found in Adelaar (2005b). The present chapter goes beyond that publication by providing data from a broader range of Malayic varieties and more thorough analyses of the typological features that occur in them. Although other varieties will be mentioned, the languages chosen for this overview best capture the typological diversity of the Malayic subgroup, including Banjar (Nirmala Sari [1984] and Abdul Djebar Hapip [2006]), Besemah, a dialect of South Barisan also known as Central Malay (McDonnell 2016b), Jakarta Malay (Muhadjir 1981), Kelantan and Ulu Terengganu (Wu 2023), Kerinci (Mckinnon 2011), Mualang (Tjia 2007), Salako (Adelaar 2005e), Standard Malay/Indonesian (Sneddon 2010), and Ternate Malay (Litamahuputty 2012).[1]

The chapter is organized as follows. §29.2 gives a phonological typology of Malayic varieties. §29.3 deals with the morphology of these varieties; §29.4 is about their syntax; §29.5, about TAM and negation. Concluding remarks follow in §29.6.

## 29.2 Phonology

Malayic varieties show similarities in many aspects of their phonology, but they also present considerable diversity. In

[1] Unless mentioned otherwise, Kerinci refers to the Tanjung Pauh Mudik variety (Mckinnon 2011). Kelantan refers to the variety spoken in the Tanah Merah district, and Ulu Terengganu refers to the variety spoken in Kampung Dusun. Banjar has two sub-dialects, Banjar Hulu and Banjar Kuala. The main difference between these is that Banjar Hulu has three phonemic vowels (/a, i, u/), whereas Banjar Kuala has six (/a, e, ə, i, o, u/) (Nirmala Sari 1984). In this chapter the two sub-dialects will only be distinguished where this is relevant.

Bradley McDonnell, Jiang Wu, Timothy Mckinnon, and Alexander Adelaar, *Malayic languages.* In: *The Oxford Guide to the Malayo-Polynesian Languages of Southeast Asia.*
Edited by: Alexander Adelaar and Antoinette Schapper, Oxford University Press. 
DOI: 10.1093/oso/9780198807353.003.0029

**Map 29.1** The Malayic languages.

**Table 29.1** Consonant inventory of Banjar

| | | Labial | Dental/Alveolar | Palatal | Velar | Glottal |
|---|---|---|---|---|---|---|
| Stops | Voiceless | p | t | c | k | |
| | Voiced | b | d | j | g | |
| Nasals | | m | n | ɲ | ŋ | |
| Fricatives | | | s | | | h |
| Liquids | | | l, r | | | |
| Glides | | w | | y | | |

§29.2.1, we show that the consonant inventory is mostly comparable across the subgroup, whereas the size of vowel inventory varies to a great extent. In the prosodic domain (§29.2.2), Malayic varieties have diverse patterns in the stress system, and some varieties demonstrate remarkable patterns of phrasal allophony. Some common phonological processes are discussed in §29.2.3.

## 29.2.1 Segmental inventories

### 29.2.1.1 *Consonants*

Consonant inventories of most Malayic varieties have eighteen to twenty consonant phonemes. Table 29.1 presents the consonant inventory of Banjar, which has eighteen consonant phonemes including four sets of stops, four nasals, two fricatives, two liquids, and two glides.[2] This is the same consonant inventory as Standard Indonesian, and Proto-Malayic (PM) is reconstructed with these eighteen consonant phonemes (where *r is realized as velar and not alveolar) plus a disputable *-ʔ (Adelaar 1992a, also see Anderbeck, this volume, §9.2).

These eighteen consonant phonemes are commonly found in other varieties as well, with divergence in the realizations of the palatal obstruents *c*, *j*, and the rhotic *r*. In some varieties, *c* and *j* are described as stops (IPA /c/ and /ɟ/, as in Banjar), in others, as palato-alveolar affricates /t͡ʃ/ and /d͡ʒ/ (e.g. Besemah and Kerinci) or palatal affricates /c͡ç/ and /ɟ͡ʝ/ (e.g. Kelantan and Ulu Terengganu).[3] The realization of *r* varies from a dental or alveolar tap/trill, as in Salako and Kerinci, to a velar or uvular fricative in many other varieties, such as Mualang and most peninsular varieties. Kaur (southwest Sumatra) even has a pharyngeal fricative /ʕ/ (McDonnell fieldnotes). There is, as a rule, an asymmetry in the place of articulation between a dental /t̪/ and an alveolar /d/ across Malayic varieties, and more broadly in MPSEA languages (Henderson 1965; Adelaar 1983; Donohue 2009). Another phonotactic rule is that voiced obstruents and palatals do not occur root- or word-finally, although in a few varieties such as Jakarta Malay, root-final voiceless obstruents can be voiced when followed by a suffix with an initial vowel, for example, [jawabin] 'to answer' (← /jawap-in/) and [parudin] 'to grate' (← /parut-in/).

Many Malayic varieties have an additional phonemic glottal stop or an extra liquid, expanding the size of consonant inventory to twenty. A phonemic glottal stop is common throughout the Malayic-speaking area, as can be found in Salako, Besemah, Kerinci, and Kelantan, among many others. In some varieties it is the result of debuccalization of final stops; for example, in Besemah root-final /ʔ/ originated from an earlier velar stop *-k, and in Kelantan and Ulu Terengganu, all earlier final stops have merged to /ʔ/. Ibanic and various Sumatran varieties have /ʔ/ with different origins, which corresponds to Ø or /r/ in other varieties (Adelaar 1992a: 62–9; Blust 2013a: 568–9; Anderbeck, this volume, §9.2). Besemah and all other South Barisan Malay dialects also stand out as they distinguish an alveolar tap/trill and a velar fricative /ɣ/ or /x/. Kelantan and Ulu Terengganu also have a velar fricative /x/, although it is only marginally phonemic, and is the result of reciprocal assimilation from earlier *kɣ- clusters, for example, Kelantan /xxɛtɔ/ 'car' < Standard Malaysian *kəreta*.

An inventory with more than twenty consonant phonemes is found in Urak Lawoi', Mualang, and Jambi Malay. Urak Lawoi' aspirated stops /pʰ, tʰ, cʰ, kʰ/ are probably due to contact with Thai (Hogan 1988: 15). In Mualang and some dialects of Jambi Malay (Yanti et al. to appear), a set of postploded nasals /mᵇ, nᵈ, ɲʲ, ŋᵍ/ is described as phonemic alongside four plain nasals, which apparently

[2] Nirmala Sari (1984) does not include a glottal stop in the phoneme inventory, but we suggest that a glottal stop might be phonemic in Banjar, see §29.2.3.4.

[3] It is unclear whether these differences represent different articulations or different analyses of the same articulations of *c* and *j*.

developed from earlier word-medial homorganic nasal + voiced obstruent sequences. Sequences as such are usually considered strings of two segments in other varieties (Cohn and Riehl 2016); the number of consonant phonemes therefore depends on the language-dependent analysis of these consonant sequences (see McDonnell and Truong, this volume, §28.2.1.1, for a discussion of the consequences of these factors in the non-Malayic languages of Sumatra).

Many Malayic varieties have preploded nasals [ᵖm, ᵗn, ᵏŋ] which typically occur in final position, but their phonemic analyses differ across the subgroup. Preploded nasals in Mualang are in variation with plain nasals, as in /malam/ 'night' → [mãlaᵖm] ~ [mãlam] and /ujuŋ/ 'tip; end' → [ujuᵏŋ] ~ [ujuŋ]. Here, nasal preplosion is clearly a synchronic phonetic process. In Salako, however, preploded nasals are phonemic, as justified by (near-)minimal pairs like /muaᵏŋ/ [muɔᵏŋ] 'go back' (← *N-puàkŋ* 'AV-go.back') vs. /muaŋ/ [muaŋ] 'throw away' (← *N-buàkŋ* 'AV-throw.away').[4] Preploded nasals in Salako also appear word-medially in suffixed forms, for example, /ŋiɲaᵖmiʔ/ [ŋiɲaᵖmiʔ] 'lend out to' (← *ŋ-iɲapm-iʔ* 'AV-lend-APPL') and /puaᵏŋaʔ/ [puaᵏŋɔʔ] 'go home' (← *puàkŋ-aʔ* 'go.home-SBJV'). Therefore, they are best treated as single complex phonemes. Diachronically, preploded nasals have been further reduced to their obstruent components in certain varieties, including Belangin (a Kendayan variety, Adelaar 2006), Urak Lawoi' (Hogan 1988), some subvarieties of Duano (Seidlitz 2007), and Satun Malay (Uthai 2007). Original nasals became homorganic stops, as shown in Urak Lawoi' /kirip/ 'to send', /turot/ 'to descend', and /bitak/ 'star' (cf. Standard Indonesian *kirim*, *turun*, and *bintang*). Nasal preplosion (or traces thereof) is also a widespread phenomenon outside Malayic, as has been reported in Blust (1997b) and in Blevins (this volume, Chapter 41). Smith (Chapter 8) and Kroeger and Smith (Chapter 27) discuss the phenomenon in Bornean languages, and Brunelle and Jensen (Chapter 30) in Chamic languages. There are also varieties where the reverse pattern is observed. That is, final oral stops can be pronounced as prenasalized in several Kerinci varieties (e.g. /sakat/ 'sick.AB'→ [sakat] ~ [sakaⁿt]).

On the left edge of words, Kelantan and Ulu Terengganu have developed word-initial clusters of various shapes, some of which appear as geminates at the phonetic level. All consonants except for glottals and glides can appear geminated in Kelantan, and initial geminates can be either monomorphemic (e.g. /nnatɛ/ 'animal' and /ttinɔ/ 'female'), or morphologically complex (e.g. /jjalɛ/ 'to walk' (← *j-jalɛ* 'INTR-road') and /ggadiʔ/ 'to thicken' (← *g-gadiʔ* 'CAUS-thick')). The morphological aspect of initial geminates will be discussed in §29.3.3.

#### 29.2.1.2 *Vowels*

The size of vowel inventory varies considerably across Malayic varieties. Some have as few as three vowel phonemes, while many others have retained the original four vowels /a, i, u, ə/ from PM and acquired a set of mid vowels. Some more innovative varieties have expanded the inventory size up to twelve.

Varieties with a small vowel inventory are typically found in Borneo. Brunei, Berau, and Banjar (Hulu variety) all have three monophthongs /a, i, u/. Most Sumatran varieties have developed a set of mid vowels therefore having five or six monophthongs, with the exception of Besemah. In Besemah, a four-vowel system /a, i, u, ə/ can be established, with /a, i, u/ showing predictable allophonic variations depending on the presence or absence of a coda consonant and the position of the vowel within the root (McDonnell 2008a). Standard Indonesian also has six monophthongs /a, i, u, ə, e, o/, but the mid vowels are only contrastive with high vowels in non-final syllables.

Kelantan and Kerinci are more innovative in the vowel system; both have developed a four-way distinction in vowel height. In Kelantan, in addition to eight oral vowels /a, i, u, e, o, ɛ, ɔ, ə/, there are four phonemic nasal vowels /ã, ũ, ɛ̃, ɔ̃/. These nasal vowels occur independent of nasal contexts and can be contrasted with their oral counterparts, as in /ɛsɔʔ/ 'tomorrow' vs. /ɛsɔ̃ʔ/ 'to scoot over' and /busuʔ/ 'ant hill' vs. /busũʔ/ 'smelly'. The genesis of nasal vowels in Kelantan mostly reflects rhinoglottophilia (Matisoff 1975), that is, oral vowels are nasalized adjacent to laryngeals (also see Brunelle and Jensen, this volume, §30.2.3, for a similar phenomenon in Chamic). However, not all nasal vowels in Kelantan have such a clear origin (e.g. /ɛ̃/ in /matɔ kaɛ̃/ 'fishhook', cf. Standard Indonesian *mata kail*).

While diphthongs can be found in the descriptions of many Malayic varieties, we suggest that there is a distinction between vowel–glide sequences and true diphthongs. Final *ay* and *aw* in Standard Indonesian, as in *pantai* [pantay] 'beach' and *pulau* [pulaw] 'island', as well as their equivalents in other varieties and PM *-ay and *-aw, are often referred to as diphthongs. Combinations of vocoids as such are common in Austronesian languages, but they typically only occur root-finally and cannot be followed by a coda consonant. The label 'diphthongs' has thus been questioned (Clynes 1997, 1999), and an alternative analysis is to treat them as vowel–glide sequences and to analyse the second component as a syllable coda. Diachronic evidence

[4] Orthographically *à* represents [ɔ], an allophone of /a/ (Adelaar 2005e).

within Malayic supports this analysis. In Ulu Terengganu, for instance, final-syllable *a is raised to /ɔ/ before all back consonants (*-k, *-h, *-ŋ, *-r [ɣ]) and retained as /a/ before non-back consonants, and all final approximants are deleted. The diachronic paths of *-aw and *-ay well fit into the pattern: *-aw > /ɔ/ and *-ay > /a/, which suggest that *-w in *-aw behaved just like a back coda, whereas *-y behaved like a non-back coda. True diphthongs are single phonemes, that is, they are complex vowel units that can be analysed as syllable nuclei. Ulu Terengganu has two diphthongs /ɛi/ and /əʊ/; they can be followed by a coda, and they have similar distributions as other monophthongs in final syllables. It has to be conceded that the demarcation between vowel–glide sequences and true diphthongs is not always clear-cut, and the phonological analysis of vocoid sequences is ultimately language-dependent. In Kerinci, for instance, seven types of vocoid sequences are attested in final syllables, namely /ɨy, ɨw, əe, ʌe, əo, ae, ao/. These vocoid sequences behave like single phonemic units as they can be followed by a coda, but the following coda must be glottal (monophthongs may be followed by dental and velar stops /t, k/, and alveolar and velar nasal /n, ŋ/). In order to capture the constraints on rimes, one could propose an alternative analysis and treat the second component in these vocoid sequences as a glide-like component, which has a competing place feature with the following non-glottal coda (see more details in Mckinnon 2011). In various other Sumatran varieties including Minangkabau and some varieties of South Barisan Malay, diphthongs are well attested at the phonetic level (Zainul Arifin Aliana et al. 1979; Adelaar 1995c), but their phonological analyses require further study.

### 29.2.2 Prosody

#### 29.2.2.1 *Stress*

Most Malayic varieties do not have phonemic stress in the sense that stress does not differentiate otherwise identical pairs. However, many vehicular varieties have minimal pairs that contrast stress location (e.g. Ternate Malay /ˈaŋka/ 'lift up' vs. /aŋˈka/ 'a kind of cake', /ˈbarat/ 'west' vs. /baˈrat/ 'heavy'). In other varieties, word stress is often reported to be predictable. Banjar is said to have fixed penultimate stress, whereas Besemah, Kerinci, and Salako have regular final stress. Mualang stress is described as generally falling on penultimate syllables (e.g. [ˈuma] 'field', [kəːmua] '1DU.EXCL'), but it shifts to final syllables when the penultimate has a schwa or the final syllable has a preploded nasal, as in [təmˈpaʔ] 'to forge', [tuˈhaᵗn] 'Lord'.[5] Kelantan also has penultimate stress, but if the penultimate syllable has a schwa or the final syllable has a final glottal stop, stress tends to shift to the final syllable. Exceptions are found in words with initial geminates, in which cases stress always falls on the initial syllable even if it has a schwa, for example, [ˈssəjeʔ] 'mosque' and [ˈjjəlah] 'to explain' (cf. [jəˈlah] 'clear').

The descriptions of stress assignment in many varieties are based on rather impressionistic generalizations, and acoustic correlates of stress are usually not clear. In more recent phonetic studies, Besemah is shown to have final-syllable stress associated with a higher fundamental frequency and increased intensity (McDonnell 2016a), and word stress in Papuan Malay is most strongly indicated by longer duration (Kaland 2019). Detailed phonetic studies as such are often lacking for other varieties. However, whether there are fixed patterns for stress assignment or whether there is stress at all is a subject of controversy in Malayic languages. Standard Indonesian is a notable case in point (see Kaufman and Himmelmann, this volume, §42.4(1), for a detailed summary of these issues).

#### 29.2.2.2 *Phrasal allophony*

Phrase-level allophony occurs in several Malayic varieties. The observed processes occur at the end of a prosodic phrase and affect the nucleus or coda of a final syllable. There is considerable variability in the conditioning environments for the processes described here. §29.3.4 distils some generalizations about the phrasal-phonological and morphological conditioning environments found in varieties spoken in Jambi; however, like stress and intonation, variation in Malay phrasal allophony is yet poorly understood. We discuss three processes found in Sumatran varieties: oralization of final nasals, excrescent nasals, and changes to vowels in the final rime. Additional phenomena not discussed here include the presence of a final glottal stop phrase-finally in Jakarta Indonesian (e.g. *duaʔ* 'two' vs. *dua kaliʔ* 'two times'), metathesis in Kupang Malay (e.g. *satu* 'one' vs. *saut kali* 'one time'), and phrase-final lengthening among others (see Gil and Mckinnon 2015).

One particularly common pattern involves oralization of word-final nasal stops in phrase-final position (see Yanti et al. 2018 for a fuller discussion). Muaro Sipongi, a variety spoken in the Mandailing Natal Regency of north Sumatra near the border of west Sumatra exemplifies this.[6] In word-final position, segments /m/, /n/, /ŋ/ become [p], [t], and [k] respectively; however, underlying nasal forms surface when the closest preceding consonant is nasal or when a nasal appears in certain phrase-medial positions. The following pairs from Puspawati and Laili (2013), all of which

[5] Note that preploded nasals in Mualang are variable realizations of plain nasals, and the difference in stress location between [ˈtuhan] and [tuˈhaᵗn] 'Lord' is secondary and pragmatic, with the latter bearing more emphasis.

[6] This variety is spoken on the periphery of the Minangkabau area, but yet to be classified.

underlyingly end with a nasal stop, illustrate the phrase-medial ~ phrase-final pattern: [malom] ~ [malop] 'night', [maken] ~ [maket] 'eat', [pasaŋ] ~ [pasak] 'pair'. The following forms fail to alternate as the result of a preceding nasal: [dɛmum] 'fever', [hŏlamen] 'yard', and [bənaŋ] 'thread'. Oralization fails to apply when a stem is followed by a suffix or a word within a sufficiently 'tight' syntactic relation, including the nominalizing suffix /-et/ (a cognate of Standard Indonesian *-an*, which surfaces as [-en] with nasal-final stems) and phrases like numeral–numeral, numeral–classifier, and less consistently, noun–noun and noun–attributive adjective, as in Table 29.2.

**Table 29.2** Phrase-final oralization in Muaro Sipongi[a]

| | Final | | | Medial | |
|---|---|---|---|---|---|
| Suffix /-et/ | *kirip* | 'send' | → | *kirimen* | 'a package' |
| Numeral-numeral | *lapet* | 'eight' | → | *lapen bɛlɛh* | 'eighteen' |
| Numeral-classifier | *lapet* | 'eight' | → | *lapen ori* | 'eight days' |
| Noun-modifier | *gorek* | 'to fry' | → | *gorek/goreŋ pisak* (free variation) | 'fried banana' |

[a] Puspawati and Laili (2013)

A second pattern of phrasal allophony involves the appearance of an excrescent nasal. This is a historical process wherein a nasal segment surfaces in a phrase-final position after a final high vowel. This pattern is illustrated by two varieties spoken in the Sarolangun Regency of Jambi: Lubuk Kepayang and Dusun Baru. In both varieties, the nasal stops [n] and [m] appear after word-final /i/ and /u/, respectively, in phrase-final forms: for example, Lubuk Kepayang [taum] 'to know' (cf. Standard Indonesian *tahu*) and [talin] 'rope' (cf. Standard Indonesian *tali*), see wordlist in Anderbeck (2008: 49). Dusun Baru shows the same pattern with an additional complication: the excrescent nasal variably undergoes partial preoralization (nasal preplosion), for example, [bejupm] or [bejum] 'clothes' (cf. Standard Indonesian *baju*). The excrescent nasal does not appear in forms that correspond to those with a suffix or a third person enclitic pronoun in other varieties, as in (1). It also does not appear in medial forms within certain syntactic phrases (e.g. a noun followed by an attributive adjective, or a verb followed by a direct object), as in (2).

Dusun Baru Sarolangun, pronominal cliticization

(1) Final form    Medial form
*talin*   'rope'   *tali:*$^{a}$*h* 'his/her/the rope'
(cf. Standard Indonesian *tali=nya*)
*tumum*   'guest'   *tamo*$^{a}$*h* 'his/her/the guest'
(cf. Standard Indonesian *temu=nya*)
(Mckinnon fieldnotes)

Dusun Baru Sarolangun, nominal modification

(2) a. *ɲo mli beju*$^{p}$*m*
3 AV.buy.MED clothes.FIN
'He/she bought clothes.'

b. *ɲo mli beju biʁu*$^{p}$*m*
3 AV.buy.MED clothes.MED blue.FIN
'He/she bought blue clothes.' (Mckinnon fieldnotes)

Another common form of phrasal allophony involves changes in the quality of the vowel in the root final syllable, either via a change of place of articulation or the formation of a vowel–glide sequence from a historical monophthong. A hallmark of so-called strongly alternating varieties of Kerinci (Yanti et al. 2018) is that vowels in final syllables, especially *i and *u, historically underwent complex vowel chain shifts that led, among other things, to the formation of vowel–glide sequences (also analyzed as diphthongs by Steinhauer 2002, *inter alia*). Jambi Ulu varieties, such as the Jernih dialect of Sarolangun Regency, provide a relatively straightforward illustration of this phenomenon. (Incidentally, Jernih Sarolangun also exhibits oralization of phrase-final forms, as illustrated by examples in §29.3.4). Root-final *i and *u developed an off-glide in citation/phrase-final forms but are lowered in certain syntactically 'tight' phrase-medial positions (e.g. [api$^{y}$] 'fire' ~ [apɪ ʊnggʊt] 'campfire' (lit. 'woodstack fire'), [nʊŋgu$^{w}$] 'AV.wait' vs. [nʊŋgʊ nɪneʔ] 'AV.wait.for grandma'). However, not all sentence-medial positions trigger the medial form.

### 29.2.3 Phonological processes

#### 29.2.3.1 *Vowel raising*

Vowel shifts triggered by voiced obstruents (henceforth phonation-driven vowel shifts or PDVS), are prevalent in Malayic varieties in several regions but have received limited attention. These changes affect vowels to the right of the triggering voiced obstruent, but in some varieties may trigger changes non-locally, skipping intervening vowels (e.g. Kerinci *anaʔ* 'child' → *b-aniʔ* 'have children'), spread across vowels in more than one syllable (e.g. Jernih Sarolangun *anaʔ* 'child' → *bə-ɒnɒʔ* 'have children'), or even across words (e.g. Kerinci *(nəŋ) mala* '(six) night(s)' vs. *tujiwh mali* 'seven nights'). Moreover, voiced obstruents preceded by a homorganic nasal stop in some varieties fail to act as triggers (e.g. Kerinci *paɲja* 'long' vs. *taji* 'sharp' but Jernih Sarolangun *paɲjɒkᵑ* 'long' and *tajɒpᵐ* 'sharp'). In most cases, PDVS only affects the low vowel *a and may be restricted to penults, for example, in the Barok variety of Orang Laut *a > *e* in *dehan* 'branch' but *a > *a* in *panas* 'hot'.[7] In a few cases of final syllable PDVS, the final coda conditions vowel quality, for example, in Lubuk Kapayang, a Jambi Malay variety, non-local PDVS affects *a in root-final syllable and is conditioned by a non-local trigger, *a > *e* or *ɛ* before a final coronal coda (e.g. *kəbɛt* 'tether', *tiŋᵍel* 'to stay', cf. Standard Indonesian *kəbat*, *tinggal*) and *a > *o* before a final rhotic or labial coda (e.g. *tajom* 'sharp', *liboʁ* 'wide', cf. Standard Indonesian *tajam*, *lebar*). In many Kerinci varieties and a handful of Jambi Malay varieties, PDVS affects non-low vowels. In Jernih Sarolangun, *a raises to *ɒ*, and *i and *u in closed final syllables remain high following voiced obstruents (e.g. *diŋin* 'cold' and *bunuh* 'to kill', cf. Standard Indonesian *dingin*, *bunuh*), but lower to mid vowels elsewhere (e.g. *kuneŋ* 'yellow' and *minom* 'to drink', cf. Standard Indonesian *kuning*, *minum*). Kerinci varieties, despite the complexity of their historical phonological changes, show stratification of vowel reflexes whereby higher exponents of proto-vowels occur following a voiced obstruent trigger. Numerous variants of the same process can be found across the Malayic varieties of western Indonesia.

#### 29.2.3.2 *Nasalization*

Nasalization in Malayic varieties is allophonic and generally progressive, which is a common feature of MPSEA (see Blevins, this volume, §41.3.2). Vowels following nasal consonants may be nasalized, and nasality often spreads rightwards and affects more than one vowel until it is blocked by consonants other than glottals or glides. This pattern is observed in Salako, Mualang, and Ulu Terengganu, as shown in the following examples: Salako *muhà* [mũhɔ̃] 'face', *ɲahit* [ɲãhĩt] (← *N-jahit*) 'AV-sew' and Ulu Terengganu *naiʔ* [nãĩʔ] 'to go up', *ŋŋuwaʔ* [ŋŋũwãʔ] 'to yawn'. A by-product of nasalization is the (historical) final nasal accretion in some varieties. In Kelantan and Ulu Terengganu, original final open syllables consisting of a nasal onset and a high vowel have acquired a final nasal as a result of the carryover of nasality: *bini 'wife' > Kelantan *bini* ~ *biniŋ*, *kamu '2SG' > Kelantan *moŋ*, Ulu Terengganu *məʊŋ*.

Regressive nasalization can be found in Kelantan, but it only operated as a historical process which left some traces. PM root-final sequences *-aN and *-əN are reflected as *ɛ̃* or *ɛ* depending on the sub-variety (Ajid Che Kob 1997) (e.g. *hayam 'domestic animal' > *ayɛ* ~ *ayɛ̃* 'chicken', *jalan > *jalɛ* ~ *jalɛ̃* 'road'). The sound changes presumably started with the regressive nasalization of *a preceding final nasals, followed by the raising of *ã* to *ɛ̃* and subsequent loss of vowel nasality in some subvarieties of Kelantan.

#### 29.2.3.3 *Nasal assimilation and nasal substitution*

As is the case for other MPSEA languages, Malayic varieties have morphophonemic processes involving nasal assimilation and nasal substitution, triggered by the prefixation of morphemes with a nasal *N* which is underspecified for place of articulation. In Standard Indonesian, for example, the general rules for the morphophonemic alternations of *N-* in the verbal prefix *məN-* 'AV' and the nominal prefix *pəN-* 'NMLZ' are as follows: (i) *N* appears as a velar nasal [ŋ] when preceding vowel-initial stems or stems with an initial *h*; (ii) *N* is 'deleted' when the stem-initial consonant is a nasal, a liquid, or a glide; and (iii) when preceding obstruents, *N* takes up the place feature of the stem-initial consonant, and voiceless obstruents are substituted by the nasal. Exceptions to the rules are found when *N* is prefixed to stems with an initial *c* or *s*: *N* appears as [ɲ] and does not trigger substitution before *c*, and *s* is substituted by a palatal nasal [ɲ] instead of an expected alveolar nasal (see also Donohue, this volume, §43.2).

Similar morphophonemic rules can be attested in Malayic in general, but the class of consonants affected by nasal substitution is not always exactly the same. Unlike Standard Indonesian, in most other varieties an initial *c* is substituted by a homorganic nasal, as in Salako *N-cocok* 'AV-drink' → *ɲocok*, Kelantan *NN₁-cɛtəʔ* 'NMLZ-print' → *ɲɲɛtəʔ* 'printer'. Stem-initial voiced obstruents also undergo nasal substitution in some varieties, as shown by the examples from Salako *N-bareʔ* 'AV-give' → *mareʔ* and Kerinci *N-dəŋə͡o* 'AV-listen.AB' → *nəŋə͡o*. In Besemah, there is variation in whether *N* triggers assimilation or substitution (e.g. *N-beli* 'AV-buy' → *mbeli* or *meli*).

In Banjar, it has been described that *N* in *maN-* or *paN-* is deleted before vowel-initial stems, and a non-phonemic glottal stop is inserted between two vowels after *N* deletion, for example, *maN-ukur* 'AV-measure' → *maukur* [maʔukur] and *maN-ambil* 'AV-take' → *maambil* [maʔambil] (Nirmala Sari 1984: 14). From this analysis it appears that a rule of glottal stop insertion applies between any two vowels, but it is nevertheless contradicted by the suffixation of *-i* 'APPL', which does not trigger glottal insertion, as shown in *maN-bawa-i* 'AV-bring-APPL' (to invite) → [mambawai] and *maN-bumbu-i* 'AV-spice-APPL' (to put spices on) → [mamumbuwi] (Nirmala Sari 1984: 17). An alternative analysis which can better account for *N* deletion in *maN-ukur* 'AV-measure' → [maʔukur] is to posit that the stem has an initial phonemic glottal stop (i.e. *ʔukur* instead of *ukur*), and *N-* is deleted

[7] The original source (Kadir et al. 1986) does not specify whether *e* is [e] or [ə].

**Table 29.3** Full reduplication in Mualang and Ternate Malay

| | Mualang | Ternate Malay |
|---|---|---|
| Root | *sikit~sikit* 'little by little' (← *sikit* 'few') | *ana~ana* 'children' (← *ana* 'child') |
| Stem | *pəmulaʔ~mulaʔ* 'big liar' (← *bulaʔ* 'lie') | *ta-guling~guling* 'unintentionally rolling over repetitively' (← *guling* 'roll over') |
| Word | *pəɲcuri~pəɲcuri* 'thieves' (← *pəɲcuri* 'thief') | *bacarita~bacarita* 'to keep talking all the time' (← *bacarita* 'to be talking') |

preceding *ʔ* rather than a vowel. Following this reasoning, we suggest a phonemic glottal stop to be included in the consonant inventory of Banjar.

#### 29.2.3.4 *Reduplication*

Reduplication in Malayic languages expresses a number of conceptually related meanings and performs conceptually related functions, including distributivity, iterativity, pluractionality, reciprocality among others. While Mattes and Schwaiger (this volume, chapter 45) present an extensive list of reduplicative patterns in MPSEA languages, Malayic varieties present only some of these patterns, and they are not uniform across varieties.[8] This section is organized according to the formal properties of reduplication.

Perhaps the most common form of reduplication across Malayic varieties is root-, stem-, or word-reduplication, which is shown in Table 29.3.

In some cases, root-reduplication is lexicalized, for example, Standard Indonesian *mata-mata* 'spy' (← *mata* 'eye') or Salako *gabu-gabu* 'kapok' (there is no root †*gabu*). When stem- or word- reduplication involves nasal substitution with prefix *N-* (or the nasal part of the prefix), the prefixed form appears in both the reduplicant and stem or word. For example, when the Besemah root *tetak* 'to chop' is prefixed with *N-* forming *netak* 'AV.chop', the entire word is reduplicated *netak~netak* 'chop repeatedly', but when it is prefixed with *di-* forming *ditetak* 'UV.chop', only the root is reduplicated *ditetak~tetak* 'chop repeatedly' (see also Mualang stem-reduplication in Table 29.3). In some varieties these patterns of reduplication involve the loss of a final coda consonant in the reduplicant, for example, Besemah *ala~alap* '(various) good (things)' ← *alap* 'good' or Jambi Malay *diki~dikit* 'little by little' ← *dikit* 'a little' (Yanti and Raimy 2010). Finally, Mckinnon (2011) reports that Kerinci has foot reduplication where the final two syllables (or sesquisyllable) of the root are reduplicated (e.g. *ŋariteʔ~riteʔ* 'active' (← *N-kariteʔ* 'AV-active.AB')).

First syllable reduplication is common among Malayic varieties. In general, this reduplication only occurs in words with an initial consonant, and the antepenultimate vowel as a rule is neutralized to schwa, effectively yielding Cə-root. This is common in Besemah (e.g. *me~minum* 'drink (coffee) as a habit'). Roots beginning with a vowel have full reduplication instead (e.g. ala~alap '(various) good (things)'). In Banjar (Kuala dialect) first syllable reduplication, the antepenultimate vowel is neutralized to *a* (e.g. *ra~rumah-an* 'toy house' ← *rumah* 'house'), and vowel-initial roots may be reduplicated with *a* (e.g. *a~itik*an 'toy duck' ← *itik* 'duck'). In the Hulu dialect, the original vowel is maintained in both cases, compare *ru~rumah-an* 'toy house' and *i~itik-an* 'toy duck' to the examples above. In Jambi Malay, first syllable reduplication has all three options: no neutralization (e.g. *bu~budaʔ* 'children'), neutralize to schwa (e.g. *sə~sobor* 'very fertile'), or neutralize to *a* (e.g. *pa~potoŋ* 'to cut').

Affixation interacts with reduplication in several ways. First, there is reduplication that is formed with another affixal element, for example, in Banjar, first syllable reduplication combines with a suffixal element *-an*, resulting in forms such as *ga~gilaan* 'somewhat crazy' (← *gila* 'crazy'). Second, in eastern Indonesian varieties, the affix (and not the root) can be reduplicated, for example, Ternate Malay *ba~ba-dara* 'bleed severely' (← *ba-dara* 'to bleed'). Third, full reduplication sometimes occurs with a linking element (e.g. Mualang *səmak ka səmak* 'come closer and closer').

Finally, there are two types of reduplication that are fairly lexicalized. Echo reduplication results in the variation in an initial consonant (e.g. Standard Indonesian *sayur~mayur* 'all sorts of vegetables' ← *sayur* 'vegetables'), a vowel

[8] Mattes and Schwaiger (this volume, chapter 45) often take Jambi Malay as an example. Many of their observations about this variety apply to all Malayic languages.

(e.g. Jakarta Malay *orak~arik* 'to confuse') or both (e.g. Jakarta Malay *səluk~bɛluk* 'complicated' (← *bɛluk* 'bend; curve')). The second is root-prefix-root reduplication, which expresses reciprocality, for example, Mualang *bantu~ba-bantu* 'be engaged in helping each other' (← *bantu* 'helping').

## 29.3 Morphology

Malayic languages vary in their morphological complexity. Some have limited morphology, while others have fairly large inventories of affixes. This section covers some of the most common nominal (§29.3.1) and verbal (§29.3.2) affixes found among Malayic languages. In §29.3.3 and §29.3.4, we discuss typologically unusual patterns found in Kelantan initial gemination and Kerinci phrasal alternations, respectively. §29.3.5 describes free and clitic pronouns.

### 29.3.1 Nominal morphology

Following Adelaar (1984, 1992a, 2004b), Anderbeck (this volume, §9.3) lists seven nominal affixes from PM. Three of these affix forms—*pAr-, *kA- -an, and *-an—have identical forms that also function as verbal affixes.[9] Some languages, such as Standard Indonesian and Banjar, still make use of all seven affixes with varying levels of productivity, while others have retained only one, such as Kelantan and Ulu Terengganu *NN*$_1$-, or Ternate Malay *paN-*, which is now unproductive. Most other Malayic varieties fall somewhere in between. Malayic varieties exhibit no infixes, although infixes sometimes appear in fossilized form, as in Banjar *turun~timurun* 'descendant' (← *turun* 'to go down') reflecting the PMP actor voice (AV) marker *<um> (which was also used in nominalizations), or in Banjar, Salako *minantu*, Standard Indonesian *menantu* 'child-in-law' reflecting the PMP non-AV marker *<in> (see Kroeger and Riesberg, this volume, §47.3.5).

Nominal affixes were originally in a paradigmatic relationship with certain verbal derivations, but that relationship has, to a varying extent, been lost in individual varieties. For instance, *pəN-* and *pəN- -an* are usually derived from transitive verbs historically prefixed with *məN*$_1$- (or one of its cognates), whereas *pə(r)-* and *pə(r)- -an* have intransitive verbal or nominal roots that have *bə(r)-* or *pə(r)-* (or one of their cognates) as a prefix.

[9] Antepenultimate PM *A stands for undecided *a or *ə (Adelaar 1992a: 51). This differs from Salako *A*, which stands for *a* before a plain nasal and *à* before a preploded one.

#### 29.3.1.1 *Nominal prefixes*

In many Malayic varieties, derivations of the prefix *pəN-* (or *paN-*) often refer to the agent of an act (e.g. Jakarta Malay *pənonton* 'watcher' ← *tonton* 'to watch'), the instrument with which the act is performed (e.g. Salako *panutup* 'cover' ← *tutup* 'to shut; a cover, lid') or the meaning of the root as a tendency or characteristic (e.g. Salako *paŋaloʔ* '(someone) prone to lying' ← *alok* 'a lie'). In Banjar and Mualang, this prefix has derivations with broader meanings (e.g. Banjar *pandangar* 'hearing' ← *dangar* 'to hear' and Mualang *pəmayuh* 'amount' ← *mayuh* 'much; many'), especially in Mualang, where it is the only productive nominal affix. This results in polysemy in Mualang, for example, *pəmbəri* 'gift; giver; giving' (← *bəri* 'to give'). Finally, Kelantan and Ulu Terengganu have an unproductive nominalizing prefix *NN*$_1$- that corresponds to *pəN-*; it derives instruments, as in Kelantan *mməgɛ* 'handle' (← *pəgɛ* 'to hold').

There is also a *pə(r)-* prefix that has similar functions but is often unproductive (as in Mualang) or no longer occurs. It frequently occurs in Standard Indonesian but usually without the (historical) final (*r*)- segment, for example, *pekerja* 'worker' (cf. *bekerja* 'to work').

#### 29.3.1.2 *Circumfixes forming abstract nouns*

Malayic varieties have up to three circumfixes that express abstract nouns: *pəN- -an*, *pə(r)- -an*, and *kə- -an*. Some languages have all three, but they do not typically show the same level of productivity. The circumfix *pəN- -an* (and its cognates) forms abstract nouns from transitive and dynamic verbs, as in Salako *pamintaʔan* 'requesting; request' ← *mintàʔ* 'to beg, request'. It is common among Malayic varieties. In some varieties this circumfix has other functions, for example, in Besemah *peN- -an* also expresses a locative meaning, as in *pe-langkah-an* 'threshold' ← *langkah* 'to step'. Banjar *paN- -an* derivations have wider meanings, which include, among others, 'to have an inclination towards what is expressed by the root', as in *pamilihan* 'choosing all the time' (← *pilih* 'to choose'). Jakarta Malay *pəN- -an* derivations are even less semantically constrained, expressing the meanings above and others, such as *pəŋgoreŋan* 'frying pan' (← *goreŋ* to fry') and *pəncarian* 'livelihood' (← *cari* 'to look for').

Forms with the *pə(r)- -an* circumfix (and its cognates) are derived from roots that are typically prefixed with the intransitive *bə(r)-* or causative *pə(r)-* or other dynamic intransitive verbs, for example, Besemah *peghagihan* 'portion' (cf. *beghagih* 'to share') or Salako *pajaanan* 'journey' (cf. *bajààtn* 'to walk; go').

The *kə- -an* circumfix (and its cognates) forms nouns referring to the quality expressed by the stative root in many varieties, for example, Banjar *kapintaran* 'cleverness' (← *pintar* 'clever') and Salako *kagagasàtn* 'beauty' (← *gagas* 'good; beautiful'). However, this circumfix is not very productive in a number of varieties. For example, in Besemah, it only occurs with a limited number of roots, for example, *keghaseghan* 'feeling' (← *ghase* 'feel'), *kepacakan* 'ability' (← *pacak* 'be able to'), and it shows some evidence of lexicalization in cases like *kadan* 'situation' (← *ade* 'exist'). In a few cases, only the prefixal element is present, for example, *kegalak* 'delight' (← *galak* 'want'), *kepacak* 'knowledge' (← *pacak* 'be able to'). Furthermore, Mualang has a corresponding unproductive prefix *kə-* with the same function (e.g. *kəkaya* 'wealth' ← *kaya* 'rich').

#### 29.3.1.3 *The nominal suffix -an*

The suffix *-an* has many functions. One that is often mentioned in the literature is that of object nominalizer forming nouns denoting the goal or result of an action or the patient argument associated with the root. While this description matches the use of *-an* derivations in Banjar (e.g. *ulahan* 'make; product' ← *ulah* 'to make') and Salako (e.g. *uihàtn* 'catch; yield' ← *puih* 'to obtain'), it is too narrow for other varieties with this suffix. For example, in Besemah, it also derives locations (e.g. *mandian* 'bathing place' ← *mandi* 'to bathe') and instruments (e.g. *ayakan* 'sifter' ← *ayak* 'to sift'), and it is even added to nominal roots resulting in various meanings (e.g. *kaweghan* 'coffee field' ← *kawe* 'coffee').

#### 29.3.1.4 *Other nominal morphology*

There are two other nominal affixes that need mention. Salako has a vocative suffix *-à*, for example, *Kàʔ-à* 'Hey Sister!' (← *(ka)kàʔ* 'older sibling'). There is also an inclusive prefix *mi-* for relational terms in Salako (*mi-*), as in (3). Besemah and Iban have similar constructions, expressed by the prefixes *be(gh)-* and *meny-*, respectively.

Salako
(3) *ià talu mi-adiʔ*
3 three INCL-younger.sibling
'them three siblings' or 'he with his two siblings'
(Adelaar 2005e: 69)

### 29.3.2 Verbal morphology

Anderbeck (this volume, §9.3) lists ten verbal affixes from PM and two prepositions that have developed into applicative suffixes in many varieties. As with nominal morphology, Malayic languages vary in regards to the number of the verbal affixes present in the language and the productivity of the affixes that are present.

#### 29.3.2.1 *Causative and applicative affixes*

Many Malayic languages have two applicative suffixes, one that serves a benefactive among other functions and another that serves a locative or goal function among others. These suffixes have several disparate functions, which often represent lexicalized meanings. The argument that is licensed by the applicative suffix can be a subject or a non-subject (core) argument depending on the voice marking (see §29.4.1), and in a limited number of cases can even be marked as an oblique (see Cole and Son 2004). In addition to these productive suffixes, some Malayic languages have a non-productive causative prefix *(məm)pə(r)-* (or equivalents in other varieties). It occurs with various roots and can co-occur with applicative suffixes. In Standard Indonesian and other varieties, it is in competition with *-kan*, which seems to have largely replaced it. In Kelantan, however, there is only a causative prefix *pɣ-* (a cognate of *pə(r)-*) without any applicative suffixes, whereas Ulu Terengganu lacks both causative and applicative affixes. The causative function can also be realized by geminating the initial consonant of the root in Kelantan (see §29.3.3), and is more typically expressed periphrastically in Ulu Terengganu.

The applicative suffix *-i(ʔ)* occurs in a number of varieties and generally forms transitive verbs that take on a goal or location argument. It also often adds plurality to this argument or iterativity to the action, and in some varieties, it regularly acts as a causative. An example of these functions is presented in Table 29.4 below.

**Table 29.4** Functions of *-i(ʔ)* in Banjar (in AV)

| | | |
|---|---|---|
| Locative/goal | *manduduki* 'to sit on' | ← *duduk* 'to sit' |
| Plurality/iterativity | *manjamuri* 'to dry (many clothes)' | ← *manjamur* 'to dry (clothes)' |
| Causative | *maisii* [maʔisiʔi] 'to fill' | ← *isi* 'content' |

In Salako, the applicative and plurality marking functions can always be distinguished because of their complementary distribution, and Adelaar (2005e: 44, 49) treats applicative *-iʔ* and plural *-iʔ* as homonymous affixes. The former only appears in transitive verbs and never co-occurs with the other applicative suffix *-AN*, whereas the latter occurs with intransitive verbs and transitive verbs that are suffixed with *-AN*, as in *baukaʔatniʔ* 'to be covered with wounds' (← *ba-ukaʔ-AN-iʔ* 'INTR-wound-APPL-PL') and *ŋapasatniʔ* 'to set free (many)' (← *ŋ(a)-apas-AN-iʔ* 'AV-loose-APPL-PL').

Many Malayic varieties also have a suffix that is functionally equivalent to Standard Indonesian *-kan* and has various forms in other varieties: Banjar *-akan*, Besemah *-ka*, Jakarta Malay *-in*, and Salako *-AN*. It acts as a benefactive, causative, or category-changing suffix that derives transitive verbs from various roots. Except in Salako, it also acts as an instrumental applicative. Examples of these functions with Banjar *-akan* are shown in Table 29.5.

**Table 29.5** Functions of *-akan* in Banjar

| | | |
|---|---|---|
| Benefactive | *mambawaakan* 'to bring for someone' | ← *bawa* 'to bring' |
| Instrumental | *mamukulakan* 'to hit with' | ← *pukul* 'to hit' |
| Category-changing | *manarusakan* 'to continue something' | ← *tarus* 'continuously' |

Jakarta Malay *-in* has an even wider application, encompassing the functions associated with both applicative suffixes. However, the instrumental applicative function is restricted to UV constructions (Muhadjir 1981: 50–6).

In general, applicatives cannot be suffixed to the same root, but in Banjar, *-akan* can also be suffixed to a verb which already has *-i*, in which case it is always benefactive, for example, *mandudukiakan* 'save a seat for someone' (← *man-duduk-i-akan* 'AV-sit-LOC.APPL-BEN.APPL' ← *manduduki* 'sit on' ← *duduk* 'to sit'). Similar combinations of *-i* and *-kan* are used in Brunei Malay (Clynes 2001: 29). It is noteworthy that most applicative suffixes—including *-kan*, *-akan*, *-ka*, and *-in*—are relatively recent and have replaced an older applicative **-An* (Adelaar 2021).

### 29.3.2.2 *Voice prefixes*

Most Malayic varieties have productive actor voice (AV) and undergoer voice (UV) prefixes. AV prefixes are expressed by *N-* (e.g. Salako) or contain this nasal element (e.g. Banjar *maN-*). The UV counterpart of these AV prefixes is *di-* and its cognate forms. In Salako *di* is not bound. Some varieties, such as Kelantan and Ulu Terengganu, no longer mark voice morphologically. They have a cognate form of AV prefix $NN_2$-, but it does not function as a voice marker, and there is no UV counterpart. See §29.4.1 for a description of voice.

Many Malayic varieties have a prefix with the same form as the AV prefix that forms dynamic intransitive verbs (e.g. Banjar *manaŋis* 'to cry' ← *taŋis* 'crying') and/or forms inchoative verb from stative ones (e.g. Banjar *mamucat* 'to become pale' ← *pucat* 'pale'). In Iban, this intransitive prefix does not have the same form as the AV prefix: *əN-* is dedicated to dynamic intransitive verbs (e.g. *ənsəput* 'to breathe' ← *səput* 'breath'), while *N-* acts as an AV prefix (Steinmayer 1999: 60). A similar—albeit less clearly delineated—distinction is found between an intransitive *məN-* and a transitive prefix *N-* in Jakarta Malay (Muhadjir 1981: 45–7). The fact that Iban and to a lesser extent Jakarta Malay distinguish two nasal prefixes and that, in many other Malayic languages, the nasal prefix has these distinct functions has led some to analyse them as homonymous (see e.g. Prentice 1987), while others make no such distinction because these prefixes are never contrastive (see e.g. McDonnell 2016b: 45–51 who attributes the different functions of *N-* to the root to which the prefix attaches).

### 29.3.2.3 *Intransitive and middle prefixes*

The prefix *bə(r)-* (or its cognates) is often prefixed to intransitive verbs (e.g. Besemah *be-rupuk* 'to think') and also yields middle verbs (e.g. Salako *ba-cukur* 'to shave') or expresses reciprocity (e.g. Jakarta Malay *bə-dame* 'to make peace' ← *dame* 'peace'). With nominal roots it results in verbs expressing various meanings, the most common of which are found in Table 29.6.

For the varieties where *bə(r)-* is productive, the meanings mentioned thus far are common. However, in some varieties, this prefix expresses particular meanings. For example, in Banjar *ba-* derivations often can have an inchoative meaning (e.g. *bahabaŋ* 'to become red' ← *habaŋ* 'red'), and in Ternate

**Table 29.6** Examples of *ber-* + nominal root in Standard Indonesian

| Meaning | Root | Derived form |
|---|---|---|
| to have or produce [root] | *buah* 'fruit' | *berbuah* 'to bear fruit' |
| to have, use or wear [root] | *sepatu* 'shoe' | *bersepatu* 'to wear shoes' |
| to cultivate [root] | *ladang* 'field' | *berladang* 'to work a field, farm' |
| to use amount of time (for a time unit root) | *tahun* 'year' | *bertahun(~tahun)* '(do/take) for years' |
| to be in the relationship expressed in the root | *kawan* 'friend' | *berkawan* 'to be friends' |

Malay, it often expresses a habit (e.g. *baminoŋ* 'to be an alcoholic' ← *minoŋ* 'to drink'). Finally, a common characteristic of verbs prefixed with *bə(r)-* across Malayic varieties is that they may also take an indefinite complement, as in Mualang *ba-bunuh babi* 'to hunt pigs' (← *bunuh* 'to hunt', *babi* 'wild pig').

In many varieties, there is also a middle prefix, which varies in productivity and the form(s) it takes (often related to a combination of *bə(r)- and the reciprocal prefix *si-).[10] The Minangkabau middle prefix *basi-* is perhaps the most productive (Moussay 1981: 197–9). Derivations based on it are realized as middle verbs with various meanings, some of which overlap with those in Table 29.6: verbs expressing using [noun] (e.g. *basisarawa* 'wear trousers'), doing [verb] habitually (e.g. *basilupo* 'often forget'), reciprocity (e.g. *basiidu* 'to hug o.a.'), doing with many (e.g. *basipulang* 'go away together'), show/act/play [stative verb] (e.g. *basirancak* 'show one's beauty', *rancak* 'beautiful'). It also combines with the suffix *-an*, expressing meanings like 'to rival or compete in being [stative verb]' (e.g. *basimaluan* 'to compete being shy' (← *malu* 'shy')) and 'to precipitate in doing [intransitive verb]' (e.g. *basipaian* 'to go in a rush', (← *pai* 'to go')). Other varieties have less productive middle voice prefixes, such as Standard Indonesian *be(r)si-* (see Sneddon 2010: 64). The Salako prefix *siN-* forms middle verbs, which are sometimes preceded by *ba-* (e.g. *basimuhà* 'to wash one's face' ← *muhà* 'face'; *basiŋkomor* 'to rince once's mouth' <- *-komor* [unbound form not attested]). Finally, vehicular varieties share a prefix *baku-* that expresses similar meanings of reciprocity or intensified action (e.g. Ternate Malay *bakulia* 'to look at each other ← *lia* 'to see', *bakucari* 'to search everywhere' ← *cari* 'to look for').

### 29.3.2.4 *Non-volitional prefixes*

Non-volitionality is expressed in all varieties by a verbal prefix *tə(r)-* (or its cognates). It indicates that an act is performed without the actor intending it to happen. In Standard Indonesian, non-volitional constructions derived from transitive verbal stems have a passive meaning, as in (4), but in other varieties this is not a precondition, as demonstrated in Mualang in (5).

Standard Indonesian

| (4) | *imel-nya* | *ter-baca* | *oleh* | *umum* |
|---|---|---|---|---|
| | email-3POSS | NVOL-read | by | general |

'His email was accidentally read by everyone.' (Sneddon 2010: 122)

Mualang

| (5) | *ia* | *tə-təguk* | *ka* | *ipuh* |
|---|---|---|---|---|
| | 3SG | NVOL-swallow | PREP | poison |

'He accidentally swallowed the poison.' (Tjia 2007: 169)

In many varieties, the non-volitional prefix expresses other notions, such as ability, stativity, and, with stative verbs, comparative or superlative degree. In Jakarta Malay, *tə-* has largely been replaced by *kə-* and only occurs in a few residual forms and in loanwords from Standard Indonesian (Muhadjir 1981: 36).

### 29.3.2.5 *Affixes indicating plurality, reciprocity, and continuous action*

The suffix *-an* (or the circumfix *bə(r)- -an*) has several meanings, but they all involve plurality of actors that is repeated or continuous. They also frequently involve reciprocity, iterativity, and reflexivity, notions which are often encoded in the same way more universally (see e.g. Nedjalkov 2007). In the languages that have *-an*, plurality is most clearly expressed in Banjar where it is suffixed to transitive, dynamic, and stative verbs, including verbs that have been prefixed with *maN-* or *ba-*, for example, *tulakan* 'many go' (← *tulak* 'to go'), *mamutikan* 'many pick' (← *mamutik* 'to pick'), *basandaran* 'many lean' (← *basandar* 'to lean'). With stative and dynamic verbs without *ba-* the suffix can also indicate an ongoing process, for example, *layuan* 'withering' (← *layu* 'faded') or a continuous process, for example, *badarahan* 'to keep bleeding' (← *badarah* 'to bleed', *darah* 'blood'). With some nouns it expresses action with reduced purpose, for example, *basapedaan* 'to cycle for fun; go biking' (← *basapeda* 'to cycle', *sapeda* 'bike'). In other varieties, *-an* is often part of the circumfix *bə(r)- -an*, which express reciprocity and/or diffuse action, as in the Salako examples *basamakàtn* 'to be close to one another' (← *samak* 'nearby') and *baʔamparàtn* 'to be spread out all over, of many things' (← *baʔampar* 'to be spread out', *ampar* 'to spread out').

### 29.3.2.6 *The adversative affixes*

There are two adversative affixes in Malayic varieties, a suffix and a circumfix. In Jakarta Malay and Salako, the suffix *-an* expresses that one is suffering from a bodily affliction, for example, Jakarta Malay *panoan* 'suffer from a skin disease' (← *pano* 'skin disease'). In Besemah, the suffix *-an* is productive and has a broader adversative meaning in examples such as *getahan* 'get sap all over oneself' (← *getah* 'sap') and *kutuan* 'be afflicted with lice' (← *kutu* 'lice'). In other varieties, the adversative circumfix, *kə- -an* (or its cognates) has the broader meaning and is used more often than *-an*, for example, Banjar *kamalaman* 'overtaken by night' (← *malam*

[10] Adelaar (1992a: 394–6) discusses the history of *bərsi-* as a combination of *bər- and a reciprocal prefix *si-. Kitada (2021) gives a detailed history of *(maR-)si- and how it expresses the notions of plurality, reflexivity, and reciprocality etc. in western Indonesian, Sulawesi, and Philippine languages.

'night'). Salako differentiates between derivations with *-AN* referring to a state or tendency and derivations with *ka--AN* referring to being affected momentarily by the condition expressed by the root (e.g. *saŋehan* 'suffer from asthma' and *kasaŋehan* 'have an asthma attack'). Finally, in Kerinci, the adversative is marginal and expressed only by a prefix *k(a)-*, such as, *k-ujʌn* 'ADVS-rain.OB' (get caught in the rain). Mualang, Ternate Malay, Kelantan, and Ulu Terengganu only express adversity with a periphrastic passive construction (see §29.4.1).

#### 29.3.2.7 *A subjunctive suffix*

Salako is the only variety still spoken to have a subjunctive marker *-àʔ*, as in (6). It is a reflex of the PMP subjunctive marker *-a and has a cognate (*-a*) in Old Malay. It is suffixed to predicates denoting intention or purpose, approaching events, conceivable danger, and so on.

Salako

(6) *Aku dah baiʔ ba-lawakŋ-àʔ kau!*
1SG already not.want INTR-marry-SBJV 2SG
'I don't want to marry you anymore!'
(Adelaar 2005e: 52)

### 29.3.3 Initial gemination in Kelantan

Kelantan only has a small number of prefixes with a restricted distribution. *Bɣ-* 'INTR', *pɣ-* 'CAUS' and *tɣ-* 'NVOL' (cognates to *bə(r)-*, *pə(r)-*, and *tə(r)-* mentioned above) typically occur before vowel-initial stems, that is, *bɣ-ae* 'contain water' (← *ae* 'water'), *pɣ-ilɛ* 'make disappear' (←*ilɛ* 'to disappear'), and *tɣ-iŋaʔ* 'to miss' (← *iŋaʔ* 'to think'). Allomorphs *b-*, *p-*, and *t-* appear before stems with certain initial consonants, with the allomorphic alternation conditioned by the relative sonority between the initial consonant of the prefix and that of the stem. For instance, *b-* and *p-* are found before stems with initial liquids (which rank higher in the sonority hierarchy than the initial stops in prefixes), as in *b-ɣacoŋ* 'poisonous' (← *ɣacoŋ* 'poison'), and *p-lumaʔ* 'to crush' (← *lumaʔ* 'crushed'), and *t-* is also found before stems with an initial voiced stop, for example, *t-baka* 'burn (accidently)' (← *baka* 'to burn'). The other two prefixes *$NN_1$-* 'NMLZ' and *$NN_2$-* 'IPFV' occur before stems with initial vowels and voiceless obstruents, in the latter cases triggering the substitution of obstruents by homorganic nasals, for example, *ɲɲakoʔ* 'hanger' (← *$NN_1$-sakoʔ* 'NMLZ-hang'), *ŋŋakaʔ* 'lifting' (← *$NN_2$-akaʔ* 'IPFV-lift'), and *mmaŋge* 'calling' (← *$NN_2$-paŋge* 'IPFV-call').

In other environments, the functions of all these prefixes are replaced by the gemination of a stem-initial consonant, as in (7).

Kelantan

(7) a. *jalɛ* 'road' vs. *jjalɛ* 'walk' (← *j-jalɛ* 'INTR-road')
b. *siyaʔ* 'finished' vs. *ssiyaʔ* 'finish' (←*s-siyaʔ* 'CAUS-finished')
c. *kəjuʔ* 'to startle' vs. *kkəjuʔ* 'be startled' (← *k-kəjuʔ* 'NVOL-startle')
d. *bilɛ* 'to count' vs. *bbilɛ* 'counting' (← *b-bilɛ* 'IPFV-count')
e. *basoh* 'to wash' vs. *bbasoh muloʔ* 'dessert' (← *b-basoh muloʔ* 'NMLZ-wash mouth')

Historically these geminated segments and prefixes have the same origin, all resulting from the phonological reduction of original prefixes (Wu 2019, 2023). Initial geminates with similar morphological functions and a similar history are also found in Ulu Terengganu and Coastal Terengganu.

### 29.3.4 Kerinci and Jambi Ulu phrasal alternations

In many Kerinci varieties, especially those spoken near Sungai Penuh and to the south, most lexical items exhibit two morphological forms differing in the phonological form of the root-final syllable rime. The two forms are referred to as absolute and oblique [henceforth AB and OB respectively] by Prentice and Usman (1978), which is exemplified in Table 29.7.

The oblique form has multiple functions. For a limited set of roots, it acts as derivational morphology, for example, with the same functions as the nominalizer *-an and verbal suffix *-An that were lost historically, or marking sundry lexicosemantic oppositions enumerated in Steinhauer and Usman (1978), *inter alia*. For a much larger set of roots, the distribution of absolute/oblique forms is morphosyntactic, with oblique forms surfacing within specific structures and the absolute appearing elsewhere as a default form. The following is a simplified discussion of these forms based on Mckinnon (2011).

When the alternating root is a noun, it occurs in the oblique form in the following environments: (i) when followed by an attributive adjective (8a), a nominal possessor (8b), or a demonstrative (8c); or (ii) when a third person possessive pronoun *=ɲəh* is encliticized to root (e.g. *umə͡oh=ɲəh* 'the/his/her house') or even unrealized but understood (e.g.

**Table 29.7** Kerinci absolute and oblique forms[a]

| Absolute | | Oblique | |
|---|---|---|---|
| *umah* | 'house' | *umə͡oh* | 'the/his/her house' |
| *kanta͡e* | 'friend' | *kantiy* | 'the/his/her friend' |
| *tidə͡o* | 'to sleep' | *tidiw* | 'put to sleep' |
| *manda͡e* | 'to bathe' | *mandiy* | 'bathe someone' |
| *maka* | 'to eat' | *makən* | 'eat it' |
| | | *makən rutiy* | 'eat bread' |

[a] Mckinnon 2011

*umə͡oh* 'the/his/her house'). Absolute forms occur elsewhere (e.g. followed by relative clauses and adjunct modifiers).

Kerinci, noun roots in oblique form

(8) a. *umə͡oh* *gdi* [Attributive adjective]
house.OB big.AB
'a big house'

b. *umə͡oh* *kanta͡e* [Nominal possessor]
house.OB friend.AB
'a friend's house'

c. *kantiy* (*ŋən* *tiŋga͡e*) *itə͡oh* [Demonstrative]
friend.OB REL tall.AB that
'that (tall) friend' (Mckinnon 2011: 242–4)

When the alternating root is a verb, the oblique form occurs in AV and UV constructions when it is followed by non-subject P arguments (in AV) or non-subject A arguments (in UV), as in (9), whether these arguments are overt or unrealized but understood. Absolute forms occur elsewhere (e.g. intransitive verbs, imperatives with *di-* UV prefix, or when followed by non-verbal complements or adjuncts).

Kerinci, verb roots

(9) a. *ka* *ndə͡oʔ* *makən* *nasa͡e* *minin* *lah.* [Non-subject P (overt or understood)]
1SG FUT AV.eat.OB rice.AB now just
'I am going to eat rice now.' (Mckinnon 2011: 202)

b. *kakiy* *ɲəh* *di-gigit* *hah.* [Non-subject A (overt or understood)]
leg.OB 3 UV-bite.OB person.AB
'His leg was bitten by someone.'
(Mckinnon 2011: 222)

When the root is an adjective, the oblique form occurs when it is followed by a nominal possessor or it occurs in an emphatic or comparative construction. See Mckinnon (2011) and Mckinnon et al. (2011) for a unified morphosyntactic analysis that argues for a single morphophonological rule, deriving all oblique forms from corresponding absolute forms.

Until recently, Kerinci alternations were seen as a sui generis morphological phenomenon in Malayic, but recent work shows closely related phenomena in varieties spoken well outside of Kerinci. Steinhauer (2002) posits that the Kerinci alternation derives historically from phrasal phonological alternations, with the absolute and oblique forms corresponding to historical phrase-final and phrase-medial forms, respectively. Mckinnon et al. (2018) and Yanti et al. (2019) draw on evidence from other varieties in the region to argue that the absolute/oblique alternation comprises the remnant of two merged processes.

The first process is a pattern of phrasal allophony found in geographically non-contiguous regions of Jambi. The conditioning environment for phrasal allophony varies considerably across dialects (see §29.2.2.2); however, Jambi Malay varieties spoken in Jangkat, Jernih Sarolangun, and Gunung Masurai all show roughly the same pattern, outlined in abridged form in Table 29.8. (See Yanti et al. 2019 for a thorough discussion of these phenomena).

The second process involves final syllable morphological ablaut forms reflecting the third person clitic pronoun and the verbal suffix *-An. Jernih Sarolangun and Jangkat varieties, for example, exhibit separate morphophonological processes affecting root-final syllables, which is exemplified by the third person clitic pronoun *=ah*. In Jangkat, this alternation results in: (i) vowel shifts wherein the vowel in the clitic *=ah* assimilates to the final vowel in roots ending with glottal codas /ʔ/ and /h/ and [ah] elsewhere (see Figure 29.1); (ii) metathesis of final nasal–glottal sequences derived historically from the obstruent stop series, for example, *ɲo(ʔ)mah* 'his/her silence' (← *ɲamʔ* 'silent' + *=ah*, cf. Standard Indonesian *senyap*); and (iii) an alternation whereby underlying ʁ surfaces, for example, *ancʊʁah* 'destruction' (← *ancʊ* 'destroy' + *=ah*, cf. Standard

**Table 29.8** Phrasal allophony

| | Phrase-medial | Phrase-final |
|---|---|---|
| Verb | Followed by NP argument (P in AV, A in UV) | Elsewhere (e.g. phrase-finally, followed by adjunct) |
| Noun | Followed by adjacent attributive adjective, nominal possessor, demonstrative | Elsewhere (e.g. phrase-finally, followed by PP or numeral-classifier modifier) |

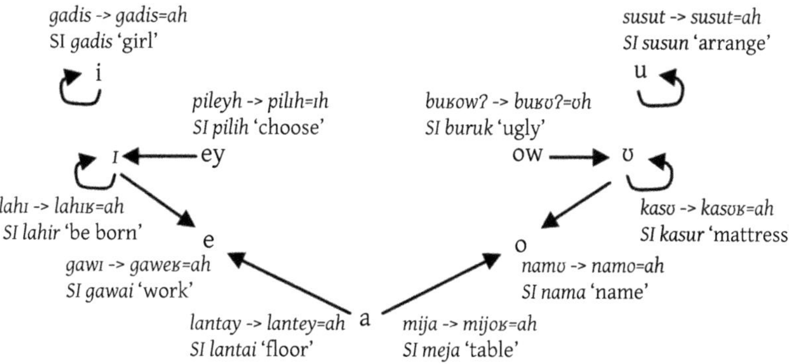


**Figure 29.1** Jangkat vowel changes triggered by cliticization of the third person pronoun *=ah*.
SI stands for Standard Indonesian. Mckinnon et al. (2015) describes a similar pattern in Lempur Kerinci where the third person pronoun assimilates to the final V of glottal-final stems.

Indonesian *hancur*), *mijoʁah* 'his/her table' (← *mija* 'table' + *=ah*, cf. Standard Indonesian *meja*).[11]

Mckinnon et al. (2015) discuss these and related phenomena in several Sumatran varieties, wherein the functions of an apparent verbal suffix *-An and the third person enclitic pronoun are reflected as a chain shift in vowels (see Figure 29.2).

Yanti et al. (2018) propose that these two processes merged historically in Kerinci varieties. That is, Kerinci oblique forms correspond to the union of phrase-medial phonological forms *and* morphophonological forms appearing in enclitic/suffix environments (see Yanti et al. [2018: 453] for a detailed summary).

## 29.3.5 Pronouns and pronominal clitics

Allowing for the many replacements of individual pronouns in each of the Malayic languages, as a group these languages retained the original Proto-Malayo-Polynesian (PMP) pronoun system rather well, both in structure and in terminology. Many of them have kept the original first, second, and third persons, the singular vs. plural as well as the inclusive vs. exclusive distinctions, which distinguish between first person plural pronouns that include the hearer (*kita* 'we and you together') and those that do not (*kami* 'we but not you'). However, the use of pronouns is also sensitive to politeness, and some basic pronouns are replaced in hierarchically sensitive situations. Historically, the most vulnerable pronoun is the third person plural: the original PMP pronoun *sida was lost everywhere with that meaning except in Ibanic languages (e.g. Mualang and Iban), which have maintained the original *sidaʔ* '3PL'. In other Malayic varieties *sida was taken over by other lexical forms or by the third singular pronoun *ia (see also Adelaar and Hajek, this volume, §52.3.(1)).

PMP made seven pronominal distinctions, and many of these were maintained in Malayic languages, which is exemplified with Salako in Table 29.9. In addition to full pronouns, Malayic languages typically have a series of clitic forms that act as either possessive forms (see §29.4.3) or the A argument in UV constructions (see §29.4.1). Not all full pronouns have a corresponding clitic, as Table 29.9 clearly shows. Vehicular Malay varieties as well as Kelantan and Ulu Terengganu do not have clitic forms.

**Table 29.9** Basic pronouns in Salako

| | 1 | | | 2 | | 3 |
|---|---|---|---|---|---|---|
| | SG | PL | | SG | PL | |
| | | INCL | EXCL | | | |
| Free | *aku, ku* | *diriʔ* | *kami* | *kau* | *kitàʔ* | *ià, se* |
| Possessive | *=ku* | *=tàʔ* | | *=(ŋ)u* | | *=ne, =e* |
| A in UV | *ku=* | | | | | |

One common property not exemplified in Salako is the preponderance of forms that express social stratification. Consider first and second person pronouns in Banjar in Table 29.10.

While first and second person forms more commonly express social stratification, there are some third person polite forms as well (e.g. Standard Indonesian *beliau*, Kerinci *sidu*).

[11] ʁ in the latter case appears to be a backformation.

Closed final syllables:

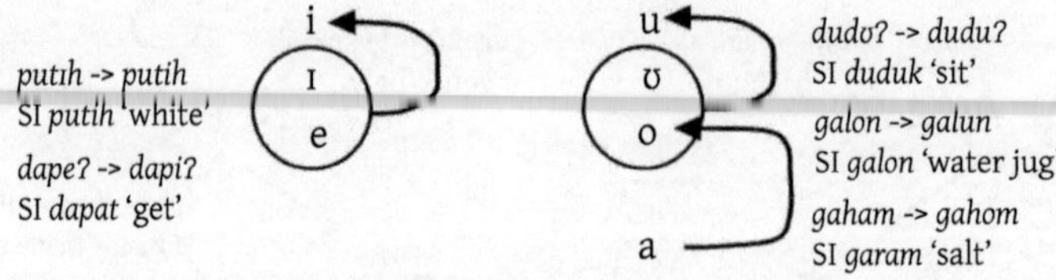


Open final syllables:

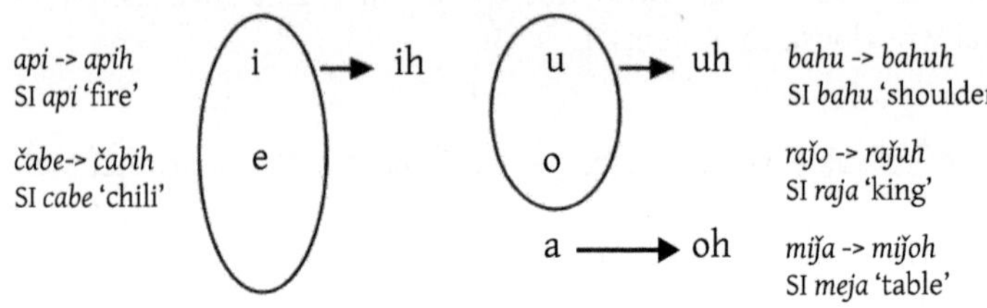


**Figure 29.2** Rantau Panjang vowel shifts marking functions associated with the verbal suffix *-An and third person pronoun in other varieties.

**Table 29.10** Social stratification in Banjar

| | First person | Second person |
|---|---|---|
| Familiar | *aku* | — |
| Talking to a younger person | *unda* | *ikam*<br>*nyawa* (Kuala dialect) |
| Showing respect | *ulun*<br>*sorang* (Kuala dialect)<br>*saurang* (Hulu dialect) | *pian* (< Javanese *sampéan*)<br>*andika* (Kuala dialect) |

While number is commonly lost in third person, it is also lost in second person in some varieties. In Banjar, for example, second person pronouns in Table 29.10 are number neutral. In addition to neutralizations in number, several varieties, such as Jakarta Malay, Kelantan, and vehicular Malayic varieties, have lost clusivity distinctions. Lack of number and clusivity is part of a more general areal feature (see Adelaar and Hajek, this volume, §52.4).

Malayic languages use several strategies to refer to plural referents. In Jakarta Malay, the third person pronoun *diè* (and enclitic form =*ñè*) is used for both singular and plural, but plural is made explicit by adding *padè* after the pronoun. In vehicular Malay varieties, the plural is morphologically expressed by a grammaticalized form of *oraŋ 'person, people', for example, Ternate Malay *toraŋ* 'we' (< *kita + *oraŋ*), *doraŋ* 'they' (< *dia + *oraŋ*). Finally, in Salako, in addition to the general third person pronoun *ià*, other forms used for third person plural include *uràkŋ* 'people', *daŋan* 'people, they (people outside one's family circle)', and *neʔ idàʔ* (a reference to the deceased, consisting of *neʔ* 'grandma, grandpa', 'older person' + *idàʔ*, a reflex of PMP *sida '3pl').

A number of Malayic varieties make distinctions not present in PMP. Ibanic languages have developed pronouns that express dual number, which have transparent etymologies of a combination of the pronoun and the PM numeral *dua 'two' (e.g. Mualang *kəmua* < *kami + *dua* '1DU.EXCL'). Furthermore, some varieties have developed forms based on gender. Mualang has dedicated second person singular references for male addressees *m'ih* and for female addressees *diʔ*, and Besemah has a form *dengah* '2SG' that is a familiar form used between a speaker and an addressee of a different gender.

## 29.4 Syntax

The syntax of Malayic languages has been relatively well described for a number of varieties. In this section, we describe the basic syntactic structures in Malayic languages, including voice and grammatical relations, word order, and the structure of the NP.

### 29.4.1 Voice and grammatical relations

Voice systems in Malayic languages fall somewhere on a cline where, at one extreme, there is a grammaticalized symmetrical voice system with multiple transitive constructions, none of which is clearly the 'basic' one, and, at the other extreme, a single unmarked transitive construction with a marginal periphrastic passive. In between these two extremes are systems where voice marking appears to be optional, resulting in a widespread use of a bare transitive construction. We treat each of these three groupings in turn.

Malayic languages with a symmetrical voice system are typically described as Indonesian-type languages (see Chen and McDonnell 2019, Kroeger and Riesberg, this volume, §47.2). They have a two-way opposition between AV and UV, as in the examples from Sarang Lan Malay (South Sumatra) in (10) and (11), respectively. In AV constructions the transitive actor (A) is the subject, while in UV constructions the transitive undergoer (P) is the subject. What makes symmetrical voice different from an (asymmetrical) active–passive voice system, however, is the fact that the non-subject argument is not demoted but maintains its core status. The AV construction is marked with the so-called nasal prefix often represented as *N-* (see §29.3.2.2). The UV construction that is marked with a prefix has simply been referred to as UV or type one passive. In most varieties it is marked by a UV prefix *di-* or *ni-* and an A argument that immediately follows the verbal predicate, as in (11a). However, Sarang Lan Malay is quite different from other varieties because UV constructions can also be marked by gemination of the initial consonant of the verbal predicate, as in (11b). Sarang Lan Malay examples have been slightly altered for consistency in glossing and presentation.

Sarang Lan Malay
(10) *uwəŋ itu ɲ-jompot-i ana?=ɛ di*
man that AV-pick.up-APPL child=3 LOC
*səkola.*
school
'The man picked up his child at school.'
(Cole et al. 2008: 1524)

Sarang Lan Malay
(11) a. *di-tanəm=ɛ padi.*
UV-plant=3 rice
'He planted rice.'

b. *bbəli=ɛ ruma joni.*
UV.buy=3 house Joni
'He bought Joni's house.' (Cole et al. 2008: 1525)

One notable exception to this general pattern of verbal marking is Salako, wherein the AV prefix *N-* may be combined with the UV proclitic *di=* or *i=*. When Salako *N-* occurs in a UV construction, it marks completed actions, but in AV constructions, there is no such restriction (Adelaar 2005e: 57–61).

For many of these Malayic varieties, there is a second UV construction that lacks any UV prefix and the non-subject A argument is immediately adjacent to the verbal predicate, as in (12) below. This construction has been referred to as a type of UV construction (i.e. the *pro-V* or bare UV construction) or a third voice category (e.g. type two passive, or Object Voice). The A argument is often considered a clitic pronoun, even though, in many cases, the pronoun is not in a reduced form.

Sarang Lan Malay
(12) *buku ini la aku bəli di siŋapura.*
book this PFV 1SG UV.buy LOC Singapore.
'I bought this book in Singapore.'
(Cole et al. 2008: 1525)

In some symmetrical voice systems, the position of the A argument is restricted depending on the person. This restriction is well known in standard varieties, but occurs in other Malayic languages as well. For example, in Besemah and Sarolangun Malay (Cole et al. 2008), spoken in Jambi, first and second person A arguments occur before the verb, while third person arguments occur after the verb. In other Malayic languages no such restrictions occur. In Salako, A arguments in UV constructions always occur before the verb despite the person of A, and in Mualang, A arguments occur immediately before or after the verb without any restriction on person (see §29.4.2 for examples).

In addition to the UV construction(s), most Malayic languages with a symmetrical voice system also have what looks to be a passive construction, which is fairly typical for languages with the so-called Indonesian-type voice system (Kroeger and Riesberg, this volume §47.2).

In many of these languages it has proven difficult to determine which constructions are passives and which are UV (see Chen and McDonnell 2019). In prototypical passive constructions (see e.g. Shibatani 1985), the A argument is demoted by either being omitted or occurring in an oblique-marked phrase, as in (13).

Sarang Lan Malay
(13) a. *padi di-tanəm.*
rice UV-plant
'Rice was planted.'

b. *padi di-tanəm əlɛ uwəŋ itu.*
rice UV-plant by man that
'Rice was planted (by that man).'

However, based on evidence from reflexive binding, Arka and Manning ([1998] 2008) in an influential paper using data from Standard Indonesian propose that a lexical A is oblique whether or not it occurs in an oblique-marked phrase. That is, for Arka and Manning, Standard Indonesian constructions with a structure like the (Sarang Lan Malay) sentence in (14) are all considered passive constructions, while those with structures like the (Sarang Lan Malay) sentences in (11) and (12) are not.

Sarang Lan Malay

(14) a. *padi di-tanəm uwəŋ itu.*
rice UV-plant man that
'Rice was planted (by that man).'

b. *padi ttanəm uwəŋ itu.*
rice UV.plant man that
'Rice was planted (by that man).'

In Standard Indonesian examples with the same structure as those in (14), a subject antecedent does not bind the lexical A, but in Standard Indonesian examples with the same structure as those in (12), it does bind the pronominal A argument. While many studies of Malayic languages have followed Arka and Manning's lead (e.g. Aldridge 2008; Cole et al. 2008), Kroeger (2014) shows quite convincingly that this binding property is not a grammatical restriction in Standard Malay but a pragmatic one, thus calling into question Arka and Manning's distinction between passive and UV constructions. For Kroeger, the lack of distinction demonstrates that all UV constructions with the prefix *di-* in Standard Indonesian are true passives.

Chen and McDonnell (2019), however, propose an alternative analysis where passive constructions are those where A is unrealized or marked by a preposition, as in (13). UV constructions, on the other hand, are transitive constructions whether or not the A argument is a pronominal or lexical argument, as in (11), (12), and (14). While the majority of these types of Malayic languages allow for a passive construction to either omit the actor (e.g. agentless passive) or express A in a by-phrase, there are Malayic languages where these options are not available. For example, Salako appears to only have an agentless passive (see below), while the Tanjung Pauh Kerinci does not allow agents to be expressed in an oblique phrase. In fact, Yanti et al. (2019) argue that the A argument in all UV constructions is obligatory as in (15).

Kerinci

(15) a. *kakɨy ɲəh di-gigit hah/alɨy.*
leg.OB 3 UV-bite.OB person.AB/Ali.
'His leg was bitten by someone/Ali.'

b. **kakɨy ɲəh di-gigit.*
leg.OB 3 UV-bite.OB
'His leg was bitten.' (Yanti et al. 2019: 35)

They state that while the example in (15b) is technically acceptable without an overt A argument, it must reference a third person argument, and thus should be considered an instance of 'pro-drop'. No such requirement is found in Besemah or even Standard Indonesian. In these languages, the unexpressed A in passives could be interpreted as any person (see Mckinnon et al. 2011).

One area where Malayic varieties with symmetrical voice systems vary is in the marking of A arguments in UV constructions. For most, the A argument that is adjacent to the verb in UV constructions is unmarked. However, in Salako, A arguments may be marked by the preposition *di*, as in (16).

Salako

(16) a. *Rajà uràkŋ ŋ-unak-iʔ.*
king person TR-wake.up-LOC
'They woke up the king.' (Adelaar 2005e: 77)

b. *Ià di kayo tatak: anàʔ ukàʔ*
3 by enemy chop not wounded
*karana ià kabà.*
because 3 invulnerable
'The enemy tried to cut him to pieces but he was not wounded because he was invulnerable.' (Adelaar 2005e: 59)

In (16a), A occurs before the verbal predicate and is unmarked, but in (16b), the A argument *kayo* 'enemy' is marked by the preposition *di*. This marking appears to be completely optional. However, when the verb is marked by the passive proclitic *di=*, this A argument is never expressed. Thus, it appears that Salako has a UV construction, where A occurs immediately before the verb and an agentless passive construction is marked by the proclitic *di=*. The fact that the A argument appears to be a core argument but nonetheless can be marked by the preposition *di*, raises several questions about its status as a core argument.

For the varieties that fall on the far end of the symmetrical voice end of the cline, it is important to note that the unprefixed (or bare) transitive verbal predicates have a P subject. The only exceptions include a closed class of verbs. In Besemah, for example, these include *ghulih* 'get', *keruan* 'know', *endak/dindak* 'want/not want', *galak* 'want', *ade* 'have', and *jadi* 'become', which are transitive verbal predicates that do not take voice-marking *and* do not have the structure of the bare UV construction.

In other Malayic languages, voice-marking on transitive verbal predicates appears to be optional. That is, varieties with these types of systems have an AV, UV, and a bare construction, as in the examples in (17) from Mudung Darat dialect of Jambi Malay. For some, this bare construction is analysed as a subset of AV constructions; the AV prefix is 'dropped' (see e.g. Cole et al. 2008).[12] Others, beginning with Gil (2002), refer to such a system as Sundic-type voice. Under this analysis, bare constructions are neutral (i.e. neither A nor P is the subject), and even apparent AV and UV constructions are analysed as generalized active and passive markers because A and P arguments are not considered to be the subject.

Mudung Darat

(17) a. *Mariana neŋo? pilem ktun*
M. AV.look film cartoon
'Mariana watches a cartoon movie.'

b. *Mariana teŋo? pilem ktun*
M. look film cartoon
'Mariana watches a cartoon movie.'

c. *pilem ktun di-teŋo? mariana*
film cartoon UV-look M.
'The cartoon movie was seen by Mariana.'
(Cole et al. 2008: 1537–8)

Another feature of these languages is that the UV constructions are limited to the UV construction marked by *di-*. They do not have the bare UV construction with pronominal A argument. This is the case in Mudung Darat in (17) above (Cole et al. 2008). Finally, languages appear to differ in how frequent bare constructions are in discourse. Yanti et al. (to appear), for example, find that in Jambi Malay the *N-* prefix in AV construction is not strictly obligatory, but is strongly preferred and far more frequent in discourse. Crouch (2020), on the other hand, finds that bare constructions are frequent in Colloquial Minangkabau.

Treatment of such Malayic languages has varied. Many descriptions have assumed (often implicitly) that these voice systems are impoverished varieties of the symmetrical voice systems described above (Ross 2002b). Explicit arguments for this position propose that these varieties arise due to language contact (McWhorter 2007). Gil (2015a) and others have pointed out that the assumption that colloquial varieties with Sundic-type voice systems are impoverished forms of standard varieties with a Indonesian-type voice is unwarranted. In recent work (Gil 2015a, 2020a), he argues that these Sundic-type voice systems are more widespread than previously thought, and that it is likely that they have developed from Sundic-type to Indonesian-type. He further argues that the descriptions of Malayic languages as having Indonesian-type voice is likely due to an overrepresentation of elicited data, which by the nature of the activity is heavily influenced by Standard Indonesian. Leaving aside the diachronic explanations, it is important to note that there are Malayic languages that have a symmetrical voice system other than Standard Indonesian and Standard Malaysian. For example, McDonnell (2016b), which is largely based upon a corpus of everyday conversations, has shown that Besemah has a symmetrical voice system.

There are a number of Malayic languages without a grammaticalized voice system, including Ternate Malay (Litamahuputty 2012: 116) and Ambon Malay (van Minde 1997: 323–6), among vehicular Malay varieties. These languages lack a morphologically marked passive like we saw in other Malayic languages above.[13] They typically have one or more periphrastic passives, such as an adversative passive or a 'get' passive construction, which are also common in both vehicular and non-vehicular Malayic languages, even those that mark voice alternations morphologically. Consider an example of the periphrastic get passive in Ternate Malay in (18).

Ternate Malay, periphrastic passive

(18) *padahal selama hidup kita tara parna*
whereas as.long.as live 1SG NEG ever

*dapa holo deng ofu bagitu macang.*
get sting with bee like.that kind
'whereas as long as I've lived I've never been stung by bees in such a way.'
(Litamahuputty 2012: 116)

In this example, *dapa* 'get' precedes the verb *holo* 'sting' and the single undergoer argument *kita* 1SG is the subject. A is then optionally expressed in a prepositional phrase *deng ofu* 'by bees' after the verb.

In addition to the periphrastic passive, some varieties have an apparent passive construction that is marked by word order and oblique marking on A. In Coastal Terengganu Malay, transitive clauses typically have AVP word order (see §29.4.2), but in the example in (19), P *ikaŋ* 'fish' appears before the verb *makaŋ* 'eat' while A *di kuciŋ* 'by the cat' is marked by a preposition and occurs after the verb. This structure, on the surface, appears to be quite similar to passive constructions in the languages of eastern Indonesia described by Arka and Kosmas (2005).

[12] Cole et al. (2008) use active and passive to describe these constructions instead of AV and UV, so they consider this bare construction to be active.

[13] Languages that lack a grammaticalized voice system may have additional passive-like constructions expressed by the non-volitional prefix. In some cases, the subject in these clauses is the undergoer, but in other cases it is not (see §29.3.2.4).

Coastal Terengganu Malay, passive

(19) *abih ikaŋ hɔʔ bəli p=pasɔ taʔdi*
finish fish REL buy LOC=market just.now
*makaŋ di kuciŋ.*
eat A cat
'The fish I bought at the market was eaten by the cat.' (Wu fieldnotes)

### 29.4.2 Word order

By and large, Malayic languages are head-initial. With few exceptions, they have prepositions. Modifiers generally follow the head noun, and standard negators precede the verb. While word order within the clause is typically described as verb medial, there is considerable variation, which also depends upon where the Malayic variety falls on the cline of voice systems discussed above. In the vast majority of these languages, the non-subject argument is relatively constrained, occurring adjacent to the verb and forming a constituent with it. We refer to this constituent as the *predicate complex*.

The majority of symmetrical voice languages have two word order patterns: a subject-initial order where the subject occurs before the predicate (or predicate complex) and subject-final order where the subject occurs after an intransitive predicate or in the case of transitive clauses the predicate complex. Consider the examples from Mualang in (20) and (21) below.

Mualang, subject-initial order

(20) a. *Kitaʔ datay kituʔ.*
2PL come here
'You all came here.' (Tjia 2007: 218)

b. *Apay Aluy N-igaʔ jabaw.*
father A AV-look.for bamboo.shoots
'Aluy's father was looking for bamboo shoots.' (Tjia 2007: 147)

c. *Tajaw nyaʔ Aji Melayu temu da sabar*
k.o.jar that Haji Melayu find LOC fence
*bubu ia.*
k.o.fishtrap 3SG
'That jar Haji Melayu found at the fence leading to his fishtrap.' (Tjia 2007: 153)

Mualang, subject-final order

(21) a. *"Datay kitaʔ kituʔ!" Datay sidaʔ iaʔ*
come 2PL here come 3PL that
*jaraʔ.*
so.it.is
'Come here you all!" (And) come they did.' (Tjia 2007:218)

b. *Agiʔ N-pulah jimut sidaʔ.*
still AV-make k.o.snack 3PL
'They ARE still making snacks/Still making snacks, they are.' (Tjia 2007:154)

c. *Kuʔ kuʔ ting'iʔ rumah tuʔ.*
FUT 1SG heighten house this
'I'm going to raise this house/MAKE this house higher.' (Tjia 2007: 155)

In the intransitive, AV and UV constructions shown in (20), the subject occurs before the predicate complex, while in (21) the subject in the same constructions occurs after the predicate complex. In varieties with a symmetrical voice system, the non-subject P argument in AV constructions follows the verb, as in (20b) and (21b). However, Malayic languages vary in regards to the position of non-subject A arguments in UV constructions. For example, in Salako, the non-subject A arguments must occur before the verb, while in Mualang they can either occur before the verb, as in (20c) and (21c), or immediately following the verb, as in (22). See Tjia (2007: 154–6) for discussion of possible word order patterns in Mualang.

Mualang

(22) *Kayit sidaʔ antu. Mati antu tuʔ.*
hook 3PL ghost die ghost this
'They hooked the ghosts. The ghosts died.' (Tjia 2007: 155)

In other varieties this position is based upon the person of the non-subject A argument. In Besemah, for example, first and second person occur before the verb but third person arguments occur after the verb (see McDonnell 2016b: 116–21). This is also the case in Standard Indonesian. In many cases, some portion of these pronominal forms is reduced.

Non-subject A arguments in Brunei Malay show the same restrictions and similar clitic forms as Besemah and Standard Indonesian. However, unlike any other Malayic varieties, Brunei Malay also has clitic S and A subject arguments that occur in intransitive or AV constructions, respectively (Clynes 2001: 23). These forms appear to be second position clitics that encliticize to the first word in the clause whether it be a negative particle (23a), an auxiliary verb (23b), or a main verb (23c).

Brunei Malay

(23) a. *inda=ku pacaya.*
NEG=1SG believe
'I don't believe (it).'

b. *mau=ku ba-karaja lagi bah.*
like=1SG INTR-work again PART
'I want to work again.'

c. *mam-bali=ku kain ampat mitar kan*
AV-buy=1SG cloth four meter to
*anak=ku.*
child=1SG
'I bought four meters of cloth for my child.'
(Clynes 2001: 23)

For Malayic languages where the voice-marking on transitive verbal predicates is optional, word order has been described to be extremely flexible. Gil's Sundic-type voice model (Gil 2005) for Riau Indonesian has been applied by Conners et al. (2015) to Jakarta Indonesian, and by Crouch (2020) for Colloquial Minangkabau. For example, Conners et al. show the flexibility of word order in Jakarta Indonesian. For intransitive verbs, SV and VS are attested in their corpus, and for transitive verbs (e.g. *suka* 'like') all six orders are attested in their corpus: AVP, VPA, VAP, PVA, APV, and PAV. However, when looking at two transitive verbs *beli* 'to buy' and *makan* 'to eat', they found that the vast majority of clauses were AVP order (Conners et al. 2015: 952–3).

In Malayic languages that lack voice marking, such as Kelantan and Ulu Terengganu, word order is typically subject-initial (i.e. SV or AVP), but some varieties have been described to be extremely flexible. In Ternate Malay, for example, the typical word order is SV or AVP, as in (24), but Litamahuputty (2012: 116) states that there are alternative orders to draw attention to other elements in the clause. The examples in (25) demonstrate orders where the verb (a) or the P argument (b) are highlighted in the initial position.

Ternate Malay
(24) a. *de pe kaki sake.*
3SG POSS leg painful
'His feet hurt.' (Litamahuputty 2012: 205)

b. *dong kase bengkok itu triplek bagini*
3PL CAUS bent that plywood like.this
'They bent the plywood like this'
(Litamahuputty 2012: 209)

Ternate Malay
(25) a. *gaga bufet.*
stylish cupboard
'The cupboard was stylish.'
(Litamahuputty 2012: 197)

b. *peda kita pegang.*
machete 1SG hold
'I was holding the machete.'
(Litamahuputty 2012: 200)

### 29.4.3 Noun phrase structure

Noun phrases (NP) in Malayic varieties display a relatively uniform structure. Most elements in an NP follow the head noun, including attributive modifiers, possessors, and demonstratives. Quantifiers, numerals, and classifiers, on the other hand, generally precede the head noun. The typical constituent order in an NP can be schematized in (26), illustrated by Besemah in (27):

(26) Quantifier/numeral – classifier – noun – modifier – possessor – demonstrative

Besemah
(27) *due ikuk kucing kecik=ku tu be-laghi*
two CLF cat small=1SG that MID-run
'My two small cats ran away.' (McDonnell 2016b: 99)

While numeral classifiers are not ubiquitous in Austronesian languages, they are prevalent throughout Malayic varieties, Standard Indonesian being one variety that makes the most extensive use of classifiers. The exact number of classifiers in Standard Indonesian is not clear; Sneddon (2010) lists eighteen classifiers which are relatively common, but only three would be considered frequent: *orang* (for humans), *ekor* (for animals), and *buah* (for inanimate objects). Most other varieties have a small number of common classifiers, but the conceptual categorization of nouns may differ. For instance, Salako has one classifier *ekoʔ* for all animate beings including human and animals, and Kelantan differentiates fruits and small objects (*bute*) from big objects (*buwɔh*). Classifiers are usually not strictly obligatory. Numerals can directly precede the head nouns in many varieties, as shown in Besemah *se-dusun* 'one village' and *se-mubil* 'one car'. When classifiers do occur, they almost always follow numerals. An exception is found for the classifier for human beings in Besemah, which exhibits the alternation between a free form *ughang* and a proclitic form *gha=* with the free form following the numeral and the proclitic form preceding the numeral (e.g. *due ughang* vs. *gha=due* 'two people'). Variation is also attested for the position of numeral + classifier, which may appear before or after the head noun, as can be seen from the following Kelantan examples.

Kelantan
(28) a. *s-kilɔ satɛ maʔnɔ [ppaʔ bute]*
one-kilo coconut.milk meaning four CLF
*ɲɔ.*
coconut
'One kilo coconut milk means four coconuts.'

b. *diyɔ buwi=lah buwɔh pɛ [tigɔ bute].*
3 give=EMPH fruit pear three CLF
'He gave away three pears.' (Wu, fieldnotes)

Attributive modifiers usually occur immediately after the head noun. In many varieties, there is preference for a single modifier, with additional modifiers placed in relative clauses.

Possessors can be either nominal or pronominal. Nominal possessors are typically unmarked, and pronominal possessors often appear as enclitics. A few varieties such as Kelantan and Ulu Terengganu lack clitic pronouns altogether, and there is no distinction between possessive pronouns and personal pronouns (see §29.3.5).

Most Malayic varieties only make a two-way distinction in the demonstrative pronouns, for example, Standard Indonesian *ini* 'this' and *itu* 'that', Besemah *tini* 'this' and *titu* 'that' (also shortened clitic forms *=ni* and *=tu*), Kelantan *ni* 'this' and *tu* 'that'. Iban makes a three-way distinction, as in *tuʔ* 'this', *ɲaʔ* 'that', and *ɲin* 'yonder', which reflects a more conservative system that can be traced back to PM (Adelaar 1992a: 127). A still more elaborate four-way distinction is found in Salako *ɲian, aŋ=ɲian* 'this (proximal)', *koà, aŋ=koà* 'that (medial)', *naʔan, an=naʔan* 'that, yonder (distant)', and *naʔun* 'yonder (distant+)'.[14]

## 29.5 TAM and negation

### 29.5.1 TAM markers

Tense, aspect, and mood (TAM) markers are expressed in various ways in Malayic languages. Most commonly, they are made up of a closed class and optionally expressed as auxiliary verbs, adverbs, or particles. In only a few cases is TAM expressed as an affix. In Malayic languages, TAM is expressed as auxiliary verbs that precede the verbs they modify, although the Mudung Darat dialect of Jambi Malay also allows post-verbal TAM markers (see the discussion of post-verbal negation below). Consider examples from Besemah, which show a future tense marker in (28a), a completive aspect marker in (28b), and an inferential mood marker in (28c).

Besemah

(28) a. *misal=nye kampung kerbai ka*
example=3 group woman FUT
*m-(p)eghut-i ikan tu.*
AV-gut-LOC fish that
'for example (when) a group will gut fish.'
(McDonnell 2016b: 103)

b. *Sate udim makan=nye, lemak aku.*
after COMPL AV.eat=3 pleasant 1SG
'After (I) finished eating it, I felt satisfied.'
(McDonnell 2016b: 101–2)

c. *Cengki ade jeme kecelakaan.*
INFR exist people accident
'There must have been people who got in accidents.'
(McDonnell 2016b: 105)

In addition to these TAM markers, Besemah has other tense markers (i.e. *empai* 'RCT.PST' and *nak* 'FUT'), aspect markers (i.e. *dang* 'IPFV', *la* 'already', *masih, gi=* 'still', *belum* 'not yet', *ade* 'ever', *kelah* 'never'), and modal markers (i.e. *pacak* 'can', *endak* 'want; need', *galak* 'want', *bulih* 'may'). In recent years, aspectual forms expressing notions 'already', 'still', 'not yet', and 'no longer' have been analysed as an expression of phasal polarity (see Veselinova, Vander Klok, and Asplund, this volume, chapter 51).

Tense is commonly described as being expressed by adverbs that occur in various places in the clause. For example, in Ternate Malay, the recent past adverb *tadi* 'earlier' occurs at the beginning of the clause (i.e. before the subject) or immediately after the subject and before the verb, respectively, in the examples in (29). The remote past adverb *dulu* 'before' and the distant future adverb *nanti* 'later' also occur in the same positions (Litamahuputty 2012: 233–7).

Ternate Malay

(29) a. *Ya Allah ampong, tadi kita tau,*
EXCLAM Allah mercy earlier 1SG know
*jang angka suda.*
don't lift.up COMPL
'Goodness gracious, if I had realised this before, I wouldn't have carried this.'

b. *Kita me tadi karja paya*
1SG PART earlier work troublesome
*skali.*
very
'I did a lousy job today.'
(Litamahuputty 2012: 235)

Many Malayic languages have a wide variety of adverbs (or adverbial phrases) that express tense, see, for example, Mualang examples in Tjia (2007: 193). In other Malayic languages, tense can be expressed by the combination of a particle and a demonstrative. The particle *embak* in Besemah can mean 'like; as' when followed by an NP or a distal demonstrative *itu* 'that', but when it is followed by a proximal demonstrative in *embak ini*, it means 'now'. Finally, some tense markers act as auxiliary verbs, immediately preceding the verb. This is the case of the recent past marker *empai* in Besemah or *baru* in Standard Indonesian.

Affixes that express tense, aspect, or mood are extremely limited. Salako and Old Malay express subjunctive mood

[14] There is nevertheless a mismatch in the demonstrative adverbs, which lack the medial category.

with the suffix *-àʔ* and *-a* respectively, see §29.3.2.7. The nasal prefix *N-* in Salako also displays aspectual and modal properties. This prefix attaches to verbs to express AV, but unlike other Malayic languages, it also attaches to UV constructions in which case, it marks that the action of the verb as complete, as in (30). The completive meaning in this example is not present in AV constructions. Furthermore, in UV constructions the prefix *N-* cannot co-occur with the subjunctive suffix *-àʔ*.

Salako
(30) *Uma-e* *akàʔ* *di=ŋa-rumput.*
field-3.POSS done UV=TR-weed
'Her field was already weeded.' (Adelaar 2005e: 57)

## 29.5.2 Negation

In accordance with what generally applies to languages in the western fringes of the MPSEA region, Malayic languages typically have five kinds of negators, examples from Mualang and Besemah are presented in Table 29.11.

**Table 29.11** Types of negators in Malayic languages

| | Mualang | Besemah |
|---|---|---|
| Standard 'no, not' | *naday* (long form), *nday* (short form) | *dide* (long form), *dik* (short form) |
| Prohibitive 'don't' | *naŋ* | *jangah, jangan* |
| Contrastive | *ukay* | *bukane, bukan, kane, kan* |
| 'Aspectual' 'not yet' | *bədaw* | *belum, lum* |
| Negative existential 'there is not' | *nisiʔ, naday* | — |

Standard negation in Malayic languages is typically expressed as a preverbal particle and typically has long and short forms. In Besemah, the long and short forms are generally interchangeable except that the long form can occur on its own (e.g. when answering a yes–no question) whereas the short form cannot. In Kelantan, it does not appear to be an issue of long or short, but the form *dɔʔ* is used on its own whereas *tɔʔ* negates a verbal predicate.

The contrastive negator (also known as a nominal negator) in Malayic languages typically contradicts or provides an alternative, which is implied in the Standard Indonesian example in (31).

Standard Indonesian
(31) *bukan* *di* *sini* *(mungkin* *di* *pantai=lah)*
NEG LOC here maybe LOC beach=EMPH
'not here ([but] maybe at the beach!)'
(Novi Djenar, p.c.)

In other cases, this same negator is used to negate predicate nominals as in (32).

Standard Indonesian
(32) *Dia* *bukan* *orang* *jahat.*
3SG NEG person bad
'He's not a bad person.' (Novi Djenar, p.c.)

The Kerinci negator has two forms: *sidʲɨʔ* (absolute) and *sidʲɨwʔ* (oblique). The absolute form functions as a contrastive negator, much like the Standard Indonesian *bukan*, whereas the oblique form exhibits a distribution similar to the standard negator.

Prohibitive negators occur at the beginning of imperative clauses and are commonly followed by a UV construction, as in (33). In Besemah, the UV prefix *di-* is also commonly used, despite the fact that *di-* is restricted to third person A arguments. Apparently, since the second person A argument is not overtly realized, it is possible for the verb to be prefixed with *di-*. The same applies to Standard Indonesian.

Besemah
(33) *radang* *tu,* *jangan* *di-makan.*
potato that NEG.IMP UV-eat
'(as for) potatoes, don't eat (them).' (McDonnell 2018)

Negative existential markers follow the universal trend to become standard negators which then combine again with existential markers (see van der Auwera, Van Olmen, and Vossen, this volume, §50.2). There are various other lexicalized negative verbs and modal forms in several varieties. Mualang and Besemah have an extended series of negators, which are historically derived with *ni- and *di-, respectively (Tjia 2007: 240; McDonnell and Tadmor 2015). For example, this prefix appears in Mualang *nisiʔ*, *naday*, and *nday* (possibly also in *naŋ*) mentioned above, and also in Mualang *nikala* 'never', *nitaw* 'not know; can't; may not', *nusah* 'needn't' (< *ni + *usah 'need'), *nupa* 'not as; not like' (< *ni + *upa* 'as; like'). In Besemah, this prefix is found in *dimak* 'not pleasant' (< *di + *lemak* 'delicious'), *dindak* 'not want' (< *di + *hendak 'want'), *digik* 'not any longer' (< *di + *agi* 'again').

Several Malayic languages have a post-verbal negative construction. In Besemah, there is a special construction wherein the negator *adak* occurs after the predicate or predicate complex and negates a situation that is more likely, which translates to 'not even' in English, as in (34).

Besemah

(34) *Die me-lekat adak.*
3 AV-stick NEG
'They (i.e. rice plants) won't even stick.'
(McDonnell 2018)

In Salako, the negator *anàʔ* can be used as a negative existential verb meaning 'not exist' or 'not have' when it occurs after the nominal argument (Adelaar 2005e: 40–1). Finally, in Jambi Malay, the standard negator can occur before or after the predicate. This order is also possible for auxiliaries such as TAM markers (see Yanti et al. to appear, Chapter 3).

## 29.6 Concluding remarks

The previous pages represent the phonological and morphosyntactic variety that exists within Malayic. While the Malayic languages form a well-defined and close-knit genetic subgroup, they also show an enormous typological diversity even within the context of MPSEA languages in general. Such diversity can be observed at almost all levels of the grammar, and it is often in direct contrast with the relative transparency of corresponding levels in standard forms of Malay. The size of phoneme inventories varies considerably, and some varieties exhibit cross-linguistically very marked features such as preploded nasals, initial geminates, and nasal vowels. There is also remarkable variation in the morphological complexity. While many varieties such as Salako and Banjar preserved original affixes to a large extent, vehicular Malay and the Kelantan and Ulu Terengganu varieties have rather reduced morphological inventories. At the level of syntax, voice shows variation, and the systems fall on a cline: on one end, varieties such as Besemah have a grammaticalized symmetrical voice system, and on the other, varieties such as Ternate Malay lack a grammaticalized voice system altogether. Perhaps the most typologically unusual features are manifested in the absolute and oblique distinction in Kerinci and variation in morphophonological processes and phrasal phonology in other varieties in the region.

The typological overview in this chapter was based on the systematic comparison of a group of nine Malayic varieties (Banjar, Jakarta Malay, Mualang, Kelantan, Ulu Terengganu, Besemah, Kerinci, Ternate Malay, and Standard Indonesian) which were selected with an eye on maximal regional and typological representativeness and availability of data. However, in the process of selecting and sourcing these varieties, it also became clear that there are still many other varieties for which there is hardly any material available, and which remain seriously understudied. They include those spoken on Bangka Island (off the coast of Southeast Sumatra), in Aslian Malay areas (on the Malay Peninsula) and in southwestern Borneo, to mention a few. Furthermore, some grammars of regional varieties (especially older grammars) are based on what seem to be regional standards, or regional literary varieties, rather than on vernacular speech (compare for instance the grammars of Minangkabau by van der Toorn 1899 and Moussay 1981). There are also varieties that are converging with neighbouring languages or are developing into koiné and standard forms, processes that often happen at the cost of a loss of their original structure and flavour. The typological variation that has resulted from sustained contact is closely related to sociolinguistic issues that have hitherto remained underresearched and need further investigation. More attention needs to be given to these varieties and these neglected aspects in the direct future.

CHAPTER 30

# Chamic languages

Marc Brunelle and Joshua Jensen

## 30.1 Introduction

Chamic languages are primarily spoken in Viètnam and Cambodia (Map 30.1). It is currently believed that the forebears of modern Chamic speakers first came from northern Borneo and settled the coast of modern central Vietnam in the seventh century BC (Bellwood 1985; Bronson and White 1992; Blust 2010b). The ancestors of Chamic speakers formed a string of politically decentralized states on the coast of central Vietnam from the first to the fifteenth century (Hall 2011: 67–101). These states were gradually conquered by the Vietnamese starting from the tenth century, leading to the development of a significant Chamic diaspora in Cambodia from the seventeenth century onward. The last autonomous Cham state, Panduranga, centred around modern-day Phan Rang in south-central Vietnam, was absorbed by the Vietnamese Nguyễn dynasty in 1832 (Po 1987, 1991).

There are currently seven attested Chamic languages (see Map 30.1).[1] The largest is Jarai, spoken by about 410,000 speakers in Highlands Vietnam and 25,000 in Cambodia. In this chapter, we will distinguish the eastern (Vietnamese) and western (Cambodian) dialects of Jarai, as they are phonologically and lexically rather distinct. Cham proper comes next: its western dialect has about 250,000 speakers (mostly in Cambodia), while its eastern dialect has more than 100,000 speakers on the coast of south-central Vietnam. Ede (also Rade or Rhade) is spoken by about 350,000 speakers in the central Vietnamese Highlands, including a handful of speakers of Bih, a dialect of Ede that may actually be a different language (Nguyễn 2013b). Raglai (120,000 speakers) and Chru (20,000 speakers), two closely related varieties of what seems to be the same language or dialectal continuum, are spoken on the slopes of the Annamite cordillera, from Khánh Hòa to Lâm Đồng provinces. Haroi is spoken by about 25,000 speakers in Bình Định and Phú Yên provinces, in central Vietnam. Finally, Tsat, a Chamic language that is typologically very divergent from the rest of the family, is spoken in two villages in Hainan (Thurgood et al. 2014 use "Hainan Cham"; on the autonym we use here, see Pang 1998). It has also been argued that Acehnese is a Chamic language (Cowan 1991; Blust 1994; Thurgood 1999). As it has not been shown to share innovations with a specific Chamic language, we adopt the more conservative view that it is a sister to Chamic and that it split from the rest of Chamic very early (Durie 1985; Dyen 2001; Sidwell 2005; Brunelle 2019). See Brunelle, this volume, Chapter 11 for an overview of Chamic historical linguistics.

This overview of Chamic phonology and morphosyntax provides a description of the most interesting characteristics of the subgroup, with a focus on what sets it apart from the rest of Austronesian. We used all available literature on the language family, but favoured examples from Cham and Jarai, the two largest languages in the subgroup and those with which we have the most first-hand experience. Transcriptions of spoken languages are given in IPA (even if the original materials were not), while reconstructed forms follow the conventions used in Thurgood (1999). The only departure from IPA is that we note short vowels with [˘] rather than using [ː] for long vowels, as long vowels are more common. In order to facilitate cross-linguistic comparison, we have opted for a level of transcription that represents phonemic contrasts, but avoids abstract analyses. Vowel length, for instance, is not marked in contexts where it is not contrastive (as in minor syllables), and coda palatal stops are represented as /-ʲʔ/ even if they could be analysed as positional allophones of onset /c/. Data cited without reference to a source comes from our own fieldwork. Readers interested in detailed reconstructions of Proto-Chamic (henceforth PC) are referred to the seminal work of Ernest Lee (1966) and Graham Thurgood (1999).

## 30.2 Phonology

The phonology of Chamic languages is in many ways more Austroasiatic than Austronesian, probably because

[1] All populations figures are extracted from the Cambodian 2008 census and the Vietnamese 2009 census. Most Chamic groups in Vietnam have since grown by about 20% according the 2019 Vietnamese census, but we do not have more recent official figures for Cambodia. For more details, see Brunelle and Thurgood (2015). 'Commune' is the official English designation for an administrative level smaller than the province and the district in both Vietnam and Cambodia.

Marc Brunelle and Joshua Jensen, *Chamic languages*. In: *The Oxford Guide to the Malayo-Polynesian Languages of Southeast Asia*. Edited by: Alexander Adelaar and Antoinette Schapper, Oxford University Press. © Marc Brunelle and Joshua Jensen (2024). DOI: 10.1093/oso/9780198807353.003.0030

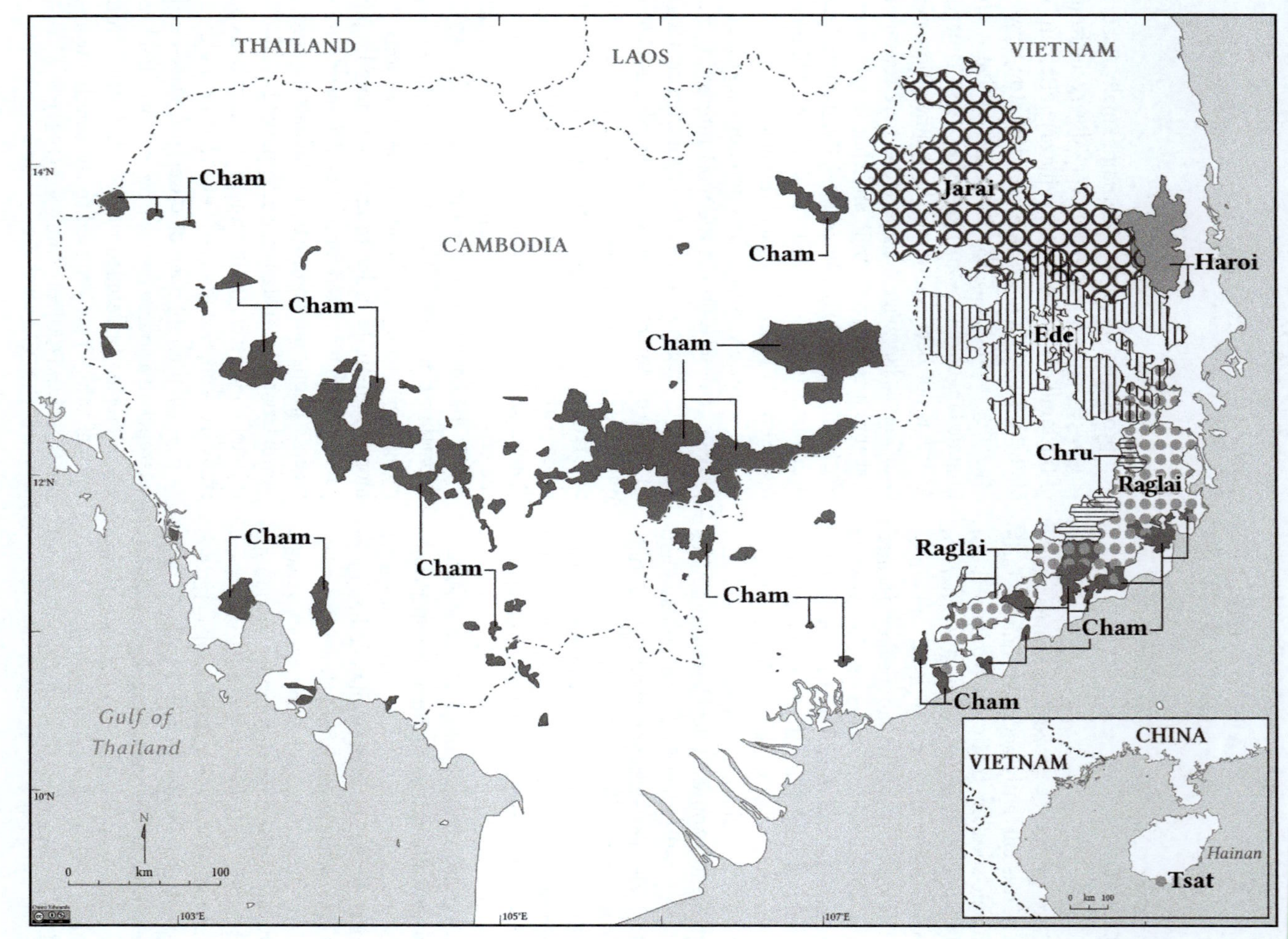


**Map 30.1** Current distribution of Chamic languages in communes with more than 200 speakers.

Based on map by Marc Brunelle, using data from Cambodian census 2008 and Vietnamese census 2009.

of prolonged contact between Chamic and neighbouring Mon-Khmer languages (Thurgood 1999; Sidwell 2007, 2008; see Sidwell, this volume, §20.3 on Austroasiatic influence on Chamic languages). In this section, we first describe the typical word template of Chamic languages and then present inventories of their consonants and vowels in various phonotactic contexts. We then discuss the development of lexically contrastive prosody in a number of Chamic languages and close the section with an overview of some phonological processes that are common in the family.

### 30.2.1 Sesquisyllabicity

Like many Mainland Southeast Asian languages, Chamic languages have developed a **sesquisyllabic** structure (Matisoff 1973; Thomas 1992; Butler 2014; see Donohue, this volume, §43.3.1 for more on sesquisyllabicity in MPSEA languages). This means that Chamic words consist of a **main** (or **major**) stressed syllable that can optionally be preceded by one (or more rarely two) unstressed **minor** syllables. While the full segmental inventory can appear in the main syllable, only a subset of consonants, vowels, and phonotactic structures are found in minor syllables. The canonical word template of formal Eastern Cham,[2] which is representative of Chamic in general, is given in (1).

(1) Canonical Chamic word template (G = glides and L = liquids)
(C V) . (C V) (C) .ˈ**C (G/L) V (C)**

A typical example of a sesquisyllable is the Proto-Chamic word *kakay 'foot' (formal Eastern Cham /tăˈkaj/, Jarai /tə̆ˈkaj/) in which the main stressed syllable contains a contrastive long vowel and a glide, while the minor syllable has a reduced short vowel (stress and minor syllable vowel duration will not be marked in examples below). The segmental inventories of minor and major syllables are discussed at greater length in the following section.

### 30.2.2 Consonants

In contrast to typical Austronesian languages, the consonant inventories of Chamic languages are characterized by the presence of implosives and aspirated consonants, including voiced aspirated consonants (or their modern reflexes). This is illustrated with the formal Eastern Cham consonant inventory in (2).

² Eastern Cham is characterized by a diglossic situation in which a prestigious conservative formal variety closely related to the written language coexists with a dramatically restructured colloquial variety that is the main code of communication in everyday life. For more details, see Brunelle (2008).

(2) Formal Eastern Cham consonant inventory

| | Lab. | Dent. | Pal. | Vel. | Lar. |
|---|---|---|---|---|---|
| Plain stops | p, -ʷʔ | t | c-, -ʲʔ | k | ʔ |
| Low register plain stops (< voiced stops) | p̥ | t̥ | ç̥ | k̥ | |
| Aspirated stops | pʰ | tʰ | cʰ ~ s | kʰ ~ x | |
| Low register aspirated stops (< voiced stops) | p̥ʰ | t̥ʰ | ç̥ʰ | k̥ʰ | |
| Implosives | ɓ | ɗ | ʄ | | |
| Fricatives | | s-, -ʲh | | | h |
| Nasals | m | n | ɲ | ŋ | |
| Liquids | | l, r | | | |
| Semi-vowels | | | j | w ~ ʋ | |

In Eastern Cham, as in several other Chamic languages, non-implosive onset obstruents have been devoiced. The functional role of voicing has been replaced with a register contrast, or a bundle of acoustic properties including pitch, voice quality, and vowel quality that are realized on the whole syllable, but that seem to remain associated to the onset at the phonological level (Brunelle 2005a). This will be discussed in detail in §30.2.4, but for the moment, it suffices to say that the low register is marked with a subscript circle, which is an adaptation of the subscript dot used in Moussay (1971) and Thurgood (1999).

For the most part, differences between the consonantal inventories of Chamic languages are limited. Common departures from the inventory in (2) include the merger of voiced aspirated stops (or their reflexes) with voiceless aspirated stops in Chru (Fuller 1977), Haroi (Lee 1977), Jarai (Dournes 1976), and Northern Raglai (Lee 1966); the merger of /cʰ/ with /s/ (e.g. Jarai, Chru, colloquial Eastern Cham); and the realization of /r/ as [ɣ] (Western Cham, Western Jarai). The Chamic language with the most divergent consonant inventory is Tsat: it has developed voiced fricatives and an affricate, and has lost palatals and /r/, but nevertheless remains fairly Chamic-looking (Thurgood et al. 2014).

Eastern Cham is representative of Chamic languages as a whole in that, while all of the consonants in (2) are attested in main syllable onsets, only plain voiceless stops, fricatives, nasals, and glides can be found in main syllable codas. Moreover, a strong diachronic trend towards debuccalization of coda obstruents has affected most Chamic languages (with more limited effects in Jarai and Ede), resulting in stops and *s being realized as laryngeal codas, often combined with glides. For instance, PC *hudip 'alive' is /hədĭp/ in Jarai and Ede, but /hədiʷʔ/ in Chru and /hat̥iʷʔ/ in formal Eastern Cham. Likewise, PC *pusat 'navel', has the modern reflexes /săt/ in Jarai and /msăt/ in Ede, but /pəsăʔ/ in Chru and /p̥atʰăʔ/ in formal Eastern Cham. Although debuccalization is quite systematic in the Austronesian lexicon, it had a more limited effect on loanwords, as illustrated by post-PC *sap 'sound; language', which has preserved its final /-p/ even in Chru and formal Eastern Cham as /săp/.

In general, Chamic languages only tolerate tautosyllabic consonant clusters in main syllable onsets. Clusters can only be composed of an onset plus a liquid and/or a semi-vowel. Note that the clusters /ʔj-/ and /ʔw-/ typically contrast with plain semi-vowels, as in the colloquial Eastern Cham minimal pair /ʔwa/ 'to plough' and /wa/ 'parent's older sibling'. The maximal possible cluster is attested, for example, in the Chru words /kəbrwəj/ 'yesterday' and /brwăʔ/ 'work; business'. The only language that departs dramatically from this pattern is colloquial Eastern Cham, where a process of monosyllabization has led to the development of a wider array of possible clusters (see §30.2.5).

Minor syllables have a more restricted consonant inventory than main syllables. Implosives and aspirated stops are typically unattested in minor syllable onsets. Voiced stops (or their modern reflexes) also have a restricted distribution as they were diachronically devoiced in minor syllable onsets preceding a main syllable with a voiceless onset (Thurgood 1999). Other patterns of mergers and reduction are attested in different languages, the most extreme case being Ede, a language that underwent a dramatic reduction of its minor syllable onset inventory and now preserves only /m-, k-, h-/. Minor syllable codas are usually limited to homorganic nasals, although /-h/ is also possible in Eastern Cham and Raglai (Brunelle 2005b; Tạ 2009).

### 30.2.3 Vowels

Chamic languages have much larger vowel inventories than the typical Austronesian language. Most of them have vowel systems with three contrastive vowel heights and a contrast between front unrounded vowels, central unrounded vowels, and back rounded vowels. Distinctive length is also found in most vowels, but it is neutralized to long vowels in open syllables (and in other contexts in individual languages). Diphthongs that cannot be decomposed into sequences of medial glides and vowels, or vowels and final glides exist in Western Cham, Eastern Cham, Northern Raglai, Western Jarai, and Haroi, but are not attested in Chru (Lee 1966; Fuller 1977; Mundhenk and Goschnick 1977; Headley 1991; Brunelle and Phú 2019). Their status is unclear in other languages, but they seem to be frequently reanalysed as monophthongs or rising diphthongs. For instance, Eastern/Western Cham /hap̥iᵉn/ 'when' corresponds to Ede and Jarai /habin/, and Western Cham /juᵒn/ 'Vietnamese' corresponds to Chru /jwə̆n/ and Jarai and Ede /jwăn/.

The colloquial Eastern Cham vowel inventory in (3) is fairly representative of Chamic vowel systems. Formal Eastern Cham also preserves the two diphthongs /iᵉ/ and /uᵒ/ (Moussay 1971; Bùi 1996), but these diphthongs tend to merge with long monophthongs in colloquial speech, a form like /hap̥iᵉn/ being realized as /p̥in/ in colloquial speech (Brunelle and Phú 2019). The apparent absence of (near)-minimal pairs with the nuclei e/ĕ and o/ŏ makes it difficult to establish the existence of a contrast in front and back high-mid vowels in Eastern Cham, but at least the o/ŏ contrast is attested in other Chamic languages (e.g. Western Jarai /soŋ/ 'brush (teeth)' vs. /sŏŋ/ 'mortar').

Colloquial Eastern Cham vowel inventory (monophthongs)

| (3) | ĭ/i | ɨ̆/ɨ | ŭ/u |
|---|---|---|---|
| | e | ə̆/ə | o |
| | ɛ̆/ɛ | ă/a | ɔ̆/ɔ |

Many Chamic languages also have either a marginal nasalization contrast in vowels or synchronic remnants of nasality. Nasal vowels were at best marginal in Proto-Chamic (Lee 1966; Thurgood 1999), but it is difficult to do away with them. While nasalization in modern Chamic languages mostly occurs on vowels adjacent to nasal consonants and in rhinoglottophiliac contexts (near laryngeals h and ʔ), it also occurs in words that contain no such environments. Chru for instance, has nasal vowels in words like /hənĩ/ 'bee' and /hã/ '2SG.INFRM', but also in /ɟrãw/ 'medicine'. Even in Eastern Cham, a language that no longer has nasal vowels, raising of *a to /ɨ/ as in /ʔanɨʔ/ 'child' (< PC *ʔana:k) and /hɨ/ '2SG.INFRM' (< PC *hã) suggests previous nasalization. According to available materials, the only Chamic varieties that preserve robust and non-marginal nasalization to this day are Western Jarai and Raglai dialects (Lee 1966; Nguyễn 2003). Western Jarai retains a large number of minimal pairs like /cɛ̃/ 'stag beetle' vs. /cɛ/ 'tea; to sing' and /dã/ 'immature (fruit)' vs. /da/ 'duck'.

Three Chamic languages depart significantly from the inventory given in (3). The first one is Haroi, which, as we will see in §30.2.4, has undergone a partial two-way split of its vowel system as a result of losing voicing in onset obstruents (Lee 1977; Mundhenk and Goschnick 1977; Thurgood 1999; Đoàn 2009). The second one, Raglai, lacks high-mid vowels and /ɨ/ (Lee 1966; Awơi-hathe et al. 1977). The third one, Tsat, has undergone major restructuring and now has a vowel system composed of seven monophthongs, with a length contrast limited to /ă-a/ (Thurgood et al. 2014). Thurgood et al. also describe nine diphthongs and three triphthongs, but these seem to be largely decomposable into combinations of vowels and medial/coda glides.

In minor syllables, vowels are always short. Some languages, such as Jarai, Chru, and some Southern Raglai dialects, allow a single possible vowel, which is either /ə/, or an allophonic variant thereof (e.g. in Chru and Jarai, there is an [a] allophone after /ʔ-/) (Dournes 1976; Fuller 1977; Tạ 2009). In Ede, a three-way contrast is maintained after /ʔ-/, but there is otherwise neutralization to /ĕ/ (Tharp and Đuôn-Ya 1980). Finally, in Cham, most Raglai dialects, and Bih, up to five vowel qualities, /i, ɨ, u, ə, a/, are maintained in minor syllables, but in a non-contrastive manner: although minor syllables tend to have a fixed vowel quality, there are no minimal pairs, variation is frequent, and the use of a different minor syllable vowel does not seem to be noticed by listeners (Lee 1966; Tạ 2009; Nguyễn 2013b; Brunelle and Phú 2019).

### 30.2.4 Register/tonal developments

Several Chamic languages have developed lexical prosodic contrasts, ranging from two-way register contrasts based on pitch or restructured vowel systems to full tone systems. A systematic assessment of the resources accumulated since the 1960s suggests that most Chamic languages have developed Mon-Khmer-type **register** systems, that is, simple prototonal contrasts resulting from the loss of voicing in onset obstruents (unrelated to speech levels or sociolinguistic registers). In Cham, for instance, syllables previously headed by voiced obstruents have taken on a relatively low pitch, a breathy or lax voice quality, and have slightly raised vowels, while syllables with voiceless obstruent onsets have preserved a relatively higher pitch, a clear (modal) voice quality, and slightly lower vowels or diphthongs with a relatively low onglide (Friberg and Hor 1977; Headley 1991; Brunelle 2005b, 2009a). By default, sonorants tend to pattern with voiced obstruents in Western Cham, but with voiceless obstruents in Eastern Cham (Blood 1967; Friberg and Hor 1977; Headley 1991).

Eastern Cham can be used to illustrate this. The word /pa/ 'to cross', which is produced with a high pitch, contrasts with /p̥a/ 'to carry', which is produced with a lower pitch and a lax/breathy vowel. Several authors have proposed that Eastern Cham is in the process of developing a more complex tone system as codas affect the realization of the two registers (Hoàng 1987; Phú et al. 1992; Thurgood 1993), but synchronic evidence suggests that these coda-conditioned effects are still allophonic (Brunelle 2005a, b).

Comparison of three Cham dialects (Western Cham as spoken in Kompong Chhnang, Cambodia, Western Cham as spoken in Châu Đốc, in the Vietnamese Mekong Delta, and Eastern Cham as spoken in Ninh Thuận) reveals that speakers of all three dialects rely mostly on the pitch (f0) cue for register production and perception, but that Eastern Cham, the dialect most in contact with Vietnamese, seems to have a slightly greater pitch difference (Brunelle 2009a, 2012). There is also good evidence that Western Cham has stronger register-conditioned vowel quality differences than Eastern Cham (Friberg and Hor 1977; Headley 1991). In the Western Cham dialect spoken in the Phnom Penh area for example, the high-register word [tɔʔ] 'bottom' contrasts with the low-register word [tọ̤ʔ] (< PC *dɔːk) 'to be at' (Friberg and Hor 1977).

The other Chamic languages in which register is documented are Haroi (Lee 1977; Mundhenk and Goschnick 1977; Thurgood 1999; Đoàn 2009) and Chru (Brunelle et al. 2020). Haroi devoiced its voiced stops just like Cham, but the phonetic outcomes of this change are quite different. First, Haroi voiced obstruents did not merely devoice, but became aspirated. Secondly, several vowels diphthongized after former voiced stops, leading to a partial split in the vowel system. For instance, the *a of PC *mata 'eye' remained stable in Haroi /məta/, whereas the *a of PC *muda 'young' diphthongized, yielding Haroi /mətʰɨə/. While Mundhenk and Goschnick (1977) report no voice quality or pitch distinctions in the vowel system, Đoàn (2009) reports breathiness and treats the diphthongization as secondary. Chru register is also mostly based on vowel quality, but a non-negligible minority of its speakers preserve stop voicing as an optional secondary property (Brunelle et al. 2020).

Although all other Chamic languages have been described as preserving the voicing contrast in onset obstruents, there is mounting evidence that many of them actually have some form of register. Detailed phonetic work is still needed, but both preliminary published evidence and recordings of minimal pairs suggest that Western Jarai and at least some dialects of Raglai do not consistently exhibit vocal fold vibrations during 'voiced' obstruents and might have phonologized vowel and voice quality differences (Lee 1998; Tạ 2009; Brunelle et al. 2022; our own recordings of Western Jarai). Preliminary observations also suggest that Eastern Jarai may have redundant voicing and register (Jensen 2014).

The most radical tonal developments in Chamic have occurred in Tsat. In this language, a five-tone system has developed out of a typical transphonologization of the laryngeal properties of onsets and codas (Maddieson and Pang 1993; Thurgood et al. 2014). This is summarized in (4).

(4) Tsat tonogenesis (adapted from Thurgood 1993)

| Original onset | Original coda | Tone |
|---|---|---|
| Voiceless obstruent<br>Sonorant | -h | 55 |
| | Voiceless stop | 24 |
| | None or sonorant | 33 |
| Voiced obstruent | -h | 55 |
| | Voiceless stop | 42 |
| | None or sonorant | 11 |

As pointed out in Thurgood (1993), there are similarities between Tsat tonogenesis and registral developments in the rest of Chamic: Tsat tones were partly conditioned by the voicing of onset obstruents, just like Cham and Haroi registers.

### 30.2.5 Phonological processes

A small number of phonological processes, synchronic or diachronic, are prevalent enough in Chamic languages to be worth mentioning. The first one, **monosyllabization** of sesquisyllables, has reached its fullest extent in colloquial Eastern Cham and Tsat (Blood 1961; Hoàng 1989; Alieva 1994;

Brunelle 2009b; Thurgood et al. 2014), but is also attested as a variable phenomenon in Jarai (Dournes 1976), Haroi (Lee 1977), Western Cham (Headley 1991), and Southern Raglai (Nguyễn 2007; Tạ 2009).

In Eastern Cham, minor syllables are systematically dropped in daily life, making the colloquial variety of the language almost entirely monosyllabic. For instance, formal Eastern Cham words like /limɔ/ 'cow' and /tamɨ/ 'to enter' are reduced to /mɔ/ and /mɨ/ in colloquial speech. Eastern Cham monosyllabization has even led to the development of consonant clusters that, although they mostly satisfy sonority sequencing, are quite atypical of Chamic (Bùi 1996; Brunelle 2009b). These include stop + stop clusters, as in /kte/ 'new year festival' (formal EC /kate/), obstruent + nasal clusters, as in /snɨŋ/ 'to think' (formal EC /sanɨŋ/), and nasal + nasal clusters as in /mnoʲʔ/ 'word; speech' (formal EC /panoʲʔ/). Nasal + stop clusters apparently violating sonority sequencing are even attested, as in /mta/ 'eye' (formal EC /mɨta/) and /ŋkĕj/ 'male' (formal EC /likĕj/), although their nasal could be argued to form a minor syllable.

Monosyllabization in colloquial Eastern Cham (Brunelle 2009b), Haroi (Lee 1977), and some Western Cham dialects (Headley 1991) led to the **extension of the register contrast** to onset sonorants. This happened in two steps, as illustrated with the Eastern Cham example in (5). There was first a regular process of register spreading from minor syllables to the sonorant onsets of following syllables. Then the process of monosyllabization elided the minor syllable, creating non-predictable environments.

(5) Register spreading and the extension of contrastive register to sonorants in Eastern Cham

| Proto-Chamic | Register with spreading (reconstructed) | Current forms (after monosyllabization) | |
|---|---|---|---|
| *ʔinĭ | *ʔini* | *ni* | 'this' |
| *bini (post-PC) | *p̥an̥i* | *n̥i* | 'follower of syncretic Islam' |
| *klas ? | *tlah* | *lah* | 'lost' |
| *dilah | *t̥al̥ah* | *l̥ah* | 'tongue' |

Finally, a number of diachronic and synchronic processes attested in Chamic involve nuances in the synchronization of **oral and nasal gestures**. The most common one, discussed above in §30.2.3, is that many Chamic languages tend to nasalize vowels before nasal codas (and near laryngeals), a process that has even contributed to the development of contrastive vowel nasalization in some Chamic varieties. However, many Chamic languages also exhibit evidence of instability in the phasing of nasal gestures in codas. The most mundane type consists in a diachronic shift of coda nasality onto the preceding vowel. For instance, in the Phước Trung dialect of Northern Raglai, PC *dalam 'inside' became /dalə̃p/ and PC *thun 'year' became /tʰũt/ (Nguyễn 2003: 73). Other Northern Raglai dialects fully denasalized nasal codas after oral vowels as in /lubak/ 'hole; pit' from PC *luba:ŋ, but preserved their nasality in syllables with a nasal onset, as in /canãŋ/ 'furniture; bed' from post-PC *cana:ŋ (Lee 1966; Thurgood 1999). More complex phasing patterns have also been reported, but will require detailed phonetic studies. Many speakers of Western Jarai have systematic nasal preplosion (or prestopping), a process in which a delayed realization of nasalization causes the initial portion of nasal codas to be oral after oral vowels. For instance, PC *thun 'year' and *tula:ŋ 'bone' can be realized as [tʰŭᵈn] and [kəlaᵍŋ] in Western Jarai, while PC *kanam 'dark' is always /kənə̃m/ without preplosion because nasality has spread from the main syllable onset /n-/ onto the vowel. There are also reports of post-glottalized nasals in Raglai dialects spoken in northern Ninh Thuận, in forms like /cĭmʔ/ 'bird' from post-PC *cim (Tạ 2009). Interestingly, similar processes are reported in Tsat, where post-glottalized nasal codas are attested in words like /nanʔ$^{33}$/ 'six' from PC *nam and /tɕʲoŋʔ$^{33}$/ 'eggplant' from post-PC *trɔŋ. Thurgood (1999) used these similarities to reconstruct preploded nasals in a Tsat-Northern Raglai subgroup. However, preliminary data recently collected by the first author on the Phước Đại (PĐ) variety of Northern Raglai in Ninh Thuận reveals that at least some varieties of Northern Raglai have much less regular final nasal correspondences than previously reported. Some PC forms now have post-glottalized nasals like Tsat, such as PC *cim 'bird' > PĐ Raglai /cĭmʔ/, but others have undergone denasalization and debuccalization, such as PC *thun 'year' > PĐ Raglai /tʰŭʔ/, have lost their final nasal altogether, such as PC *hadum 'how many; several' > PĐ Raglai /hadu/, or have kept their nasals, such as post-PC *cum 'kiss' > PĐ Raglai /cŭm/. The status of the Tsat-Northern Raglai subgroup may thus need to be revised when better descriptive data is available.

## 30.3 Morphology

### 30.3.1 Derivational affixation

Chamic languages have no inflectional morphology. They share a number of derivational affixes, which are primarily prefixes, but include at least one productive infix (Lee 1966; Dournes 1976; Bùi 1996; Thurgood 1999; Moussay 2006). The only exceptions are Tsat and colloquial Eastern Cham, in which affixes were lost because of monosyllabization. In both of these languages, the functional role of affixation has been taken over by syntactic devices (Thurgood et al. 2014; Brunelle 2020), a trend also observed in some dialects of Western Jarai. Where affixation is retained, it is generally only present in frozen forms.

The large majority of Chamic affixes are Austronesian, and none is more pervasive than causative *pə-, illustrated in (6). Across Chamic languages (and reaching back to Cham manuscripts from the seventeenth to the nineteenth centuries), it is affixed primarily to verbs, both active and stative (i.e. adjectives, see §30.4.1), but there are a few examples of affixation to nouns and perhaps other word classes (Aymonier 1889; Aymonier and Cabaton 1906; Moussay 2006).

Causative *pə- (Moussay 2006: 63; Headley p.c.; Jensen 2014: 158)

(6) Formal Eastern Cham<br>
V *$t^h$ɔ̆w* 'to know' *pa$t^h$ɔ̆w* 'to inform'

Ede (*pa- > m-)<br>
V *fe* 'to die' *mfe* 'to kill'

Eastern Jarai<br>
N *hjăp* 'sound; voice' *pəhjăp* 'to talk'

The derivational prefix *mə-, which combines with either verbs or nouns, lacks a single core semantic contribution (see examples in (7)) and is less productive than *pa- (Aymonier 1889; Aymonier and Cabaton 1906; Moussay 2006).

Versatile *mə- (Dournes 1964: 596–7, 622; Moussay 2006: 160–1)

(7) Eastern Jarai<br>
*bɔh* 'egg; fruit' *məbɔh* 'to produce fruit'<br>
*jaŋ* 'deity' *məjaŋ* 'supernatural'

Formal Eastern Cham<br>
*tjan* 'belly' *mɨtjan* 'pregnant'<br>
*kɛ̆ʔ* 'to bite' *mɨkɛ̆ʔ* 'to get angry'

Another prefix, *tə-, illustrated in (8), is most likely the reflex of Proto-Malayo-Chamic *tAr-. This prefix, too, has come to have a range of meanings, with an underlying idea (at least historically) of unintentionality (Aymonier 1889; Aymonier and Cabaton 1906; Adelaar 1992a; Moussay 2006).

Inadvertent *tə- (Dournes 1964: 999; Moussay 2006: 164; Headley p.c.)

(8) Eastern Jarai<br>
*pɛ̆ʔ* 'to pluck; pinch' *təpɛ̆ʔ* 'to break off'

Formal Eastern Cham<br>
*lap̥uh* 'to fall' *talap̥uh* 'to abort'

Western Cham<br>
*ləh* 'naked' *taləh* 'to fall off'

Finally, Chamic has borrowed from Mon-Khmer the nominalizing infix *-an-, illustrated in (9).

Nominalizing *-an- (Dournes 1976: 51; Moussay 2006: 63; Headley p.c.)

(9) Eastern Jarai<br>
*kih* 'to sweep' *kənih* 'broom'

Formal Eastern Cham<br>
*t̥ɔʔ* 'to stay' *t̥anɔʔ* 'shelter'

Ede<br>
*kăm* 'to forbid' *knăm* 'prohibition; taboo'

Affixes found in classical Cham inscriptions but not attested in contemporary Chamic languages are not discussed here (Aymonier 1889; Aymonier and Cabaton 1906; Brunelle 2020). Note, too, that the complex voice and agreement morphology found in many Austronesian languages is entirely absent in Chamic.

### 30.3.2 Compounding and reduplication

The other type of morphology that is pervasive in Chamic is compounding (Dournes 1976; Bùi 1996; Brunelle and Phú 2019). Here we distinguish four compound structures: coordinative, subordinative, elaborative, and reduplicative. Only the final type is productive. Coordinative compounds, illustrated in (10), are not obviously right- or left-headed and typically have a meaning to which both parts contribute equally.

Coordinative compounds (Brunelle and Phú 2019: 531; second author)

(10) Colloquial Eastern Cham<br>
N+N *plĕj k̥an* 'village'+'country' 'hometown'

Western Jarai<br>
V+V *kətĭʔ ɟwăʔ* 'wrestle'+'trample' 'to abuse'<br>
V+V *pəʔjăʔ gəhŭl* 'sunny'+'muggy' 'sultry'

Subordinative compounds, shown in (11), are left-headed and often have an idiomatic meaning.

Subordinative compounds (Brunelle and Phú 2019: 531; second author)

(11) Colloquial Eastern Cham<br>
V+N *sam kɛ̆j* 'beautiful'+'male' 'handsome'<br>
V+N *wăn k̥laj* 'forget'+'forest' 'confused'

Western Jarai<br>
V+V *sɛm ɓɔ̆ŋ* 'search'+'eat' 'to earn a living'

Elaborative compounds are illustrated in (12): these involve a meaningful base that can occur outside the compound, and a second element with no independent meaning but which exhibits sound correspondence to the base (not always rhyming). This second element is not phonologically predictable, so it is not strictly a form of reduplication. Elaborative compound nouns are interpreted as plurals. A sub-type of elaborative compounds is composed of two or four elements, neither of which has a meaning independent of the other, as shown in the last example in (12). Many elaborative compounds are members of the category of expressives, discussed in §30.4.1.

Elaborative compounds (Pawley and Kim 2017: 46–7; Brunelle and Phú 2019: 533)

(12) Western Jarai
*cɛm* 'to feed' *cɛm caʲʔ* 'to feed'
*naʔ* 'child' *nuʔ buʔ* 'children'

Colloquial Eastern Cham
*lin pin lan pan* 'pell-mell; meaningless'

The final type of compounds are full reduplicants, in which a lexical item is copied, as exemplified in (13). Reduplicated stative verbs are either attenuated or have a distributive meaning (that is, they are interpreted as applying to plural referents), and reduplicated nouns typically have a plural interpretation.

Reduplicative compounds (Brunelle and Phú 2019: 533; second author)

(13) Colloquial Eastern Cham
*sam* 'beautiful' *sam sam* 'cute'
*p̥ʰoŋ* 'red' *p̥ʰoŋ p̥ʰoŋ* 'reddish'

Western Jarai
*ɗahkəj* 'male; man' *ɗahkəj ɗahkəj* 'males; men'

## 30.4 Syntax

### 30.4.1 Parts of speech

Rather than give an exhaustive account of Chamic lexical categories, we here highlight only a few noteworthy parts of speech. We begin with **pronouns**, for which we note a few peculiar features. First, as with Austronesian languages generally (Himmelmann 2005a: 149), Chamic languages distinguish two types of first person plural: inclusive (of addressee) and exclusive, as exemplified by Jarai /ta/ vs. /gəməj/, respectively. Second, many Chamic languages incorporate some degree of politeness into their pronoun system, like Eastern Cham and Chru, which contrast informal/unmarked and formal first person singular pronouns (Cham /kǒw/ vs. /t̥ahl̥aʔ/; Chru /kəw/ vs. /dəlhaʔ/). Finally, Chamic languages, like their Mon-Khmer neighbours and Austronesian languages more generally (see Adelaar and Hajek, this volume, §52.7), use kinship terms and other nouns as terms of address and substitutes for pronouns, as in (14).

Eastern Cham, kinship terms

(14) **təcɔ** *lǝ̆j* *t̥ɔʔ* *tʰǒŋ* **muʔ** *mɛ̆ʔ*
grandchild VOC stay with grandmother IMP
'O granddaughter, stay with me!' (Blood 1978: 126)

Chamic '**adjectives**' behave like a subclass of verbs on standard tests, as in many other Austronesian languages, as illustrated below for Western Jarai. Adjective-like verbs such as 'big' and prototypical verbs like 'come' both head the predicate without a copula (15); both immediately follow verbal auxiliaries such as future/prospective (16); and both can directly modify a noun in a noun phrase (17).

Western Jarai, diagnostics for verbal status

(15) a. *ɲu* **pɣŏŋ** *bɔʲh*
3SG big already
'He's already big.'

b. *ɲu* **ɣaj** *bɔʲh*
3SG come already
'He already came.'

(16) a. *ɲu* *ti* **pɣŏŋ** *jəh*
3SG FUT big ACHIEV
'He will be big (soon enough).'

b. *ɲu* *ti* **ɣaj** *jəh*
3SG FUT come ACHIEV
'He will come (soon enough).'

(17) a. *mənɯʲh* **pɣŏŋ** *nŭn*
person big that
'that big person'

b. *mənɯʲh* **ɣaj** *nŭn*
person come that
'that person who came'

Nevertheless, Chamic languages, like other languages of Southeast Asia, do distinguish among verb types. For example, Eastern Cham distinguishes *stative* from *active* verbs: the intensifier /p̥jăʔ/ 'very' can occur before stative verbs such as /sĭt/ 'short' (for the meaning 'very short'), but not before active verbs such as /ɓăŋ/ 'eat' (for the meaning 'eat very much') (Brunelle and Phú 2019: 533fn). Eastern Jarai distinguishes between two classes of intransitive verbs: *unaccusative* (including state, directed motion, and psych verbs) and *unergative* (agentive verbs). Many unaccusative verbs can combine with the causitive prefix /pə-/, for example, /pə-ɓuh/ 'show' from psych verb /ɓuh/ 'see', and /pə-glaʲʔ/ 'return (smt.)' from directed motion verb /glaʲʔ/ 'return'; in contrast, unergative verbs never combine with causitive /pə-/ (note the impossibility of such forms as */pə-swaŋ/ 'cause to dance' and */pə-rəbat/ 'cause to walk') (Jensen 2014: 158–60). Furthermore, in clauses headed by an unaccusative verb, the universal quantifier meaning 'all' can modify the subject from one of two positions: before the subject or after the verb (18). However, with clauses headed by unergative verbs, a subject-modifying universal quantifier can appear only before the subject (19).

Eastern Jarai, unaccusative clause

(18) *(ʔabih-baŋ)* *boh* *pənɛh* **lĕʔ** *trŭn*
all fruit papaya fall go.down
*(ʔabih-baŋ)* *mŏŋ* *kəjəw*
all from tree
'All the papaya fell from the tree.' (Jensen 2014: 166)

Eastern Jarai, unergative clause

(19) *(ʔabih-baŋ)* *dra* **swaŋ** *(*ʔabih-baŋ)*
all girl dance all
'All the girls danced.' (Jensen 2014: 167)

Chamic languages tend to have a relatively small set of dedicated **prepositions**, typically including at least source 'from' (/mɨ̆ŋ/ in both Western Jarai and Eastern Cham), accompaniment 'with' (Western Jarai /hɣɔ̆m/, and Eastern Cham /tʰɔ̆ŋ/), and a preposition meaning 'in(side)' (Western Jarai /tăm/, Eastern Cham /t̪ələ̆m/). Chamic languages all possess a general locative preposition: Jarai /pə/, Eastern Cham /pă/. And most Chamic languages also have a dative-marking preposition: Eastern Jarai /kə/, Eastern Cham /ka/, which also precedes the subject in non-finite embedded clauses (Jensen 2014: 77–91; Thurgood 2005: 505). In Chru, however, /tə/ marks both locative and dative (Fuller et al. 1974), and Western Jarai has largely lost dative /kə/, sometimes using the locative to mark indirect objects. In some Chamic languages, the locative and dative prepositions may have the properties of clitics, but we lack the evidence to make a judgement. Many functions served by prepositions in other languages are served by serial verbs in Chamic (especially path prepositions; see §30.4.5 on SVCs). Additionally, Chamic languages regularly use locative nouns for place relations, often preceded by a dedicated preposition, as in Western Jarai /mɨ̆ŋ ɣɔ̆ŋ/ (from back) 'behind' (see also Thurgood 2005: 506 on Eastern Cham).

Like their Southeast Asian neighbours, Chamic languages rely primarily on pre-verbal **auxiliaries** for explicitly marking tense and aspect (especially future, prospective, and progressive), and nearly all such auxiliaries are derived from verbs. For example, progressive action is typically marked in Chamic languages with reflexes of PC *dɔːk 'sit; stay; live', occurring immediately before the main verb. (Reflexes of *dɔːk retain their primary meaning 'sit' when used as the main predicate.)

Unlike future and progressive, past or perfective meanings are often indicated with a post-verbal **adverb** (such as Eastern Jarai /laʲh/ 'already', Jensen 2014: 143) or **particle** (such as Eastern Cham /paçə~jə/ 'already', Doris Blood 1977: 41). In fact, post-verbal particles are pervasive in Chamic languages, as is generally the case in Southeast Asia. Such particles are often characterized as clause- or sentence-final particles, but many are not restricted to final position, though they most often appear there. The role of particles and adverbs in questions and commands is illustrated in §30.4.3.

A final word category quite common to Chamic languages is **expressives** (also called ideophones), which vividly depict sensory information. The Tsat example in (20) illustrates sound symbolism; the two examples in (21) are visually or kinetically symbolic: /ŋut ŋut/ depicts the aspect of a person nodding off to sleep, while /ku-kil ku-kil/ expresses the (back-and-forth?) effort of a person trying to dislodge an object. Expressives may be used adverbially or independently (as exclamations).

Tsat, expressive

(20) *ʔja*$^{33}$ *ljo*$^{21}$ ***phja*$^{21}$*-phja*$^{21}$**
water flow gurgle-gurgle
'Water flows gurgling.' (Zheng 1997: 92; cited in Thurgood et al. 2014: 190)

Colloquial Eastern Cham, expressive

(21) a. *hɨ tɔ̆ʔ-wah* ***ŋut ŋut*** *naw*
2SG.INFRM nod IDEO go
'You nod as if you're falling asleep.' (Brunelle and Phú 2019: 32)

Eastern Jarai, expressive

b. *ɲu swaʲʔ lăŋ* ***ku-kil ku-kil***
3SG remove try IDEO
'She tried to pull it out.' (Dournes 1974: 80)

This category contains expressions that do not fall into any other part of speech, but there are also many nouns and verbs in Chamic languages that are mimetically expressive, or at least aurally artful, especially when they occur as similar-sounding word pairs (e.g. Eastern Cham /sup lup/ 'pitch dark' from /sup/ 'dark', or /mi măn/ 'very fast' from /măn/ 'fast', Brunelle and Phú 2019: 533). Detailed descriptions of expressives and other sound symbolic expressions in Bih and Jarai can be found in Nguyễn (2013a) and Williams and Siu (2013).

## 30.4.2 Word order

All Chamic languages have basic unmarked subject–verb–object word order, with prepositions preceding objects (on the status of subjects see §30.5). In ditransitive clauses, the default position of indirect objects is after the object, but indirect objects are typically permitted before the object, as well. Both word order possibilities are shown for Ede in (22). Intransitive clauses may be headed by an active or stative verb, with unmarked subject–verb order.

Ede, ditransitive clause

(22) *ʔaduᵒn cʰĭʔ (kə kɔ̆w) sa pɔ̆k*
grandmother sell DAT 1SG one CLF
*hədruᵒm hərăʔ (kə kɔ̆w)*
study word DAT 1SG
'She sells me a book.' (Nguyễn 2006: 13)

## 30.4.3 Clauses and sentences

We now turn to clause types other than simple verbal clauses. For **nominal** (equative) **clauses**, three languages have borrowed a copula—Chru /la/ and colloquial Eastern Cham /l̥a/ from Vietnamese, and Tsat /si$^{21}$/ from Mandarin

(Fuller et al. 1974: 16; Thurgood et al. 2014: 205–6; Brunelle and Phú 2019: 21). Ede (along with Bih) and Eastern Jarai optionally use /ɟiŋ/ 'become' as a copula, as illustrated in (23) (Nguyễn 2013b: 110–12; Jensen 2014: 116). Only in Tsat is the copula obligatory. Western Cham, Western Jarai, and apparently Haroi lack a copula altogether (Goschnick 1977: 116–17; Baumgartner 1998: 3).

Eastern Jarai, nominal clause with optional copula
(23) *ɲu ʔanŭn (ɟiŋ) ɗah-kəməj twãj*
3SG that COP female visitor
'She's a foreign woman.' (Jensen 2014: 116)

With the exception of Tsat, Chamic languages for which we have data use reflexes of PC *dɔ:k to head **locative predicates**, typically followed by a prepositional phrase, as illustrated for Western Jarai in (24a); in Western Cham /ţɔʔ/ may be followed by either a prepositional phrase or, as in (24b), simply a noun phrase. In Tsat, locative clauses are non-verbal (Thurgood et al. 2014: 207), as in (25), and Haroi appears to have the option of omitting the verb in locative clauses (Y-Lách and Mundhenk 1976: 12).

(24) a. Western Jarai, locative clause
*ʔəj dɔʔ mĭŋ saŋ*
grandfather stay at house
'My grandfather is at home.'

b. Western Cham, locative clause
*ķŏt ţɔʔ saŋ*
3SG stay house
'He is at home.'
(Ko 2018: 14)

Tsat, non-verbal locative clause
(25) *ʔa²¹ma³³ tsiaŋʔ³³ ko⁵⁵lu²¹*
mother at kitchen
'Mother is in the kitchen.' (Zheng 1997: 87 cited in Thurgood et al. 2014: 207)

Chamic **existential** (presentational) **clauses** all follow the same basic pattern: a word meaning 'have; there is' (a reflex of either PC *ʔada or *hmu, depending on the language) followed by an indefinite noun phrase (the pivot); this noun phrase often includes a numeral phrase or a relative clause, or both. Example (26) from Western Cham illustrates the presence of both a numeral phrase and a relative clause.

Western Cham, existential clause
(26) *maţa căm ha raŋ nŏn trah*
have Cham one CLF that cast.net
'There was a Cham man casting fish-nets.'
(Baumgartner 1998: 4)

**Possessive clauses** in Chamic languages are mostly unexceptional verbal clauses in the form of the Chru example in (27).

Chru, verbal possession clause
(27) *kəw hũ sra*
1SG have salt
'I have salt.' (Ministry of Education 1972: 11)

At least two non-verbal possessive structures are also attested alongside the verbal construction: Eastern Jarai can make a nonverbal possessive clause with a dative prepositional phrase as the predicate, as in (28), and Western Cham sometimes uses a nominal clause, as in (29).

Eastern Jarai, dative (prepositional) possession clause
(28) *mənŭʔ ʔanaj kə kəw*
chicken this DAT 1SG
'These chickens are mine.' (Jensen 2014: 79)

Western Cham, nominal possession clause
(29) *tənih ʔea ni ţrăp hɨ*
land water this thing 2SG
'This land is yours.' (Baumgartner 1998: 10)

Note however that the verbal vs. nonverbal clauses have distinct information structures: in the verbal clause, (27), the object possessed (or the fact of possession) is in focus and the possessor is the topic under discussion, whereas in the nonverbal clauses, (28) and (29), the object possessed—now in subject position—is topical, while the possessor—in the predicate NP or PP—is the new information.

Most Chamic languages encode **negation** discontinuously, with the first negator (NEG1) before the verb (or subject) and the second negator (NEG2) after the verb (or clause-final). Exceptions are colloquial Eastern Cham, which marks negation only clause-finally, and Tsat, which has only preverbal negation (Lee 1996; Thurgood et al. 2014). Among the languages that use both pre- and post-verbal negators, Raglai, Jarai, and perhaps Ede (for which data is sparse) use both as a matter of course in standard, unmarked negative clauses (Lee 1996; but see Nguyễn 2006: 14, which does not mention post-verbal negators in Ede). In the remaining languages, one or the other is optional, or there are particular conditions determining which will be used. Only in Bih does NEG1 occur canonically before the subject (Nguyễn 2013b), though pre-subject negation appears as a marked structure in at least Raglai, Ede, and Chru (Lee 1996). Example (30) illustrates discontinuous negation in Northern Raglai, with both the marked (pre-subject) and unmarked (post-subject) positions for NEG1 shown.

Northern Raglai
(30) ***(ɓuh)*** *ʔamã* ***(ɓuh)*** *nãw paʔ ʔapu* ***ʔoh***
NEG1 father NEG1 go LOC rice.field NEG2
'Father didn't go to the rice field.' (Lee 1996: 293–4)

Although NEG2 is most commonly sentence-final, in some Chamic languages it can also occur immediately after the negated verb (at least in Jarai, Raglai, and Chru), perhaps for information structuring purposes. As in much of the rest of Austronesian (Polinsky and Potsdam nd.), negative quantified expressions like 'no one' and 'nothing' are absent from Chamic languages, expressed instead with negative existential constructions, as illustrated for Bih in (31).

Bih, negative existential
(31) *ɓuh məw ʔadɔ̆ʔ kəw cjɛŋ ʔoh*
NEG1 have thing 1SG want NEG2
'There is nothing I want.' (Nguyễn 2013b: 206)

All three classic types of **subordinate clauses** are present in Chamic languages: relative (discussed in §30.4.4 along with noun phrases), complement, and adverbial. Complement clauses are often marked only by word order (typically occurring immediately after the matrix verb), though most Chamic languages—the one certain exception is Tsat (Thurgood et al. 2014: 242–4)—have at least one complementizer. This complementizer is usually a reflex of post-PC *lac 'say', which optionally introduces complement clauses after verbs of speaking, as in (32), or (sometimes) perception. Adverbial clauses for time, condition, and purpose (among others) are also common across Chamic languages; a conditional subordinate clause is illustrated in (33).[3]

Northern Raglai, complement clause
(32) *cəw drɔ̃ **[la$^j$ʔ** cəw ɓuh fɔ̆ʔ*
1SG answer COMP 1SG NEG1 true
*ʔita ʔoh]*
nurse NEG2 [ʔita < Vietnamese *y tá* 'nurse']
'I answered that I wasn't a nurse.'
(Cobbey et al. 1969: 16)

Formal Eastern Cham, adverbial conditional clause
(33) *[**mɨjah** hɨ təŋ kɔ̆w] năn*
if 2SG.INFRM beat 1SG then
*kɔ̆w təŋ hɨ wɔ̆ʔ*
1SG beat 2SG.INFRM again
'If you hit me, then I'll hit you back.'
(David Blood 1977: 59)

Unlike many Western Austronesian languages, where grammatical **voice** plays a prominent role, Chamic languages have no voice marking on verbs (or any other marking, for that matter), and no strictly syntactic strategies for promoting or demoting arguments. However, the order and prominence of core arguments may be modified within limits by focus and topic constructions (including zero anaphora), discussed below in §30.5. Two other factors may affect the presence and position of arguments in a clause: causative morphology and zero-marked causative–inchoative alternations. Causative morphology, discussed above in §30.3.1, takes a state-denoting verbal root which can be predicated of a subject, as in (34a), and adds an external causer, so that the argument of which the state holds is now in object rather than subject position, as in (34b).

Eastern Jarai, morphological causative
(34) a. *baj ʔanŭn **băʔ***
basket that full
'That basket is full.'

b. *kəw **pə-băʔ** baj ʔanŭn*
1SG CAUS-full basket that
'I fill the basket.' (Jensen 2014: 159)

Causative–inchoative alternations have a similar pattern but with no overt causative morphology. For example, in Eastern Jarai, /pŏk/ 'open' and /krĭʔ/ 'close' can be used inchoatively, where the affected theme is in subject position and no agent is present, (35a), or causatively, where the affected theme is in object position and a causing agent is in subject position, (35b).

Eastern Jarai, causative-inchoative alternation
(35) a. *boh-ʔamăŋ glăk krĭʔ*
door PROG close
'The door is closing.'

b. *ɲu (*pə-)krĭʔ boh-ʔamăŋ*
3SG CAUS-close door
'She closed the door.' (Jensen 2014: 159)

Discussion so far has dealt primarily with declarative sentences. We turn now to questions. **Polar** (yes–no) **questions** are signalled primarily by marked intonation, though they often include a final particle as well (Phạm and Brunelle 2014). Example (36) illustrates both a final particle (/jəh/) and the role of intonation in Jarai. The Chru particle /pəɟə/ has parallel uses (Fuller et al. 1974).

Western Jarai, question/statement intonation
(36) *ɲu ɓɔ̆ŋ jəh*
3SG eat ACHIEV
'He has already eaten.' [high-falling intonation on final syllable]
'Has he eaten yet?' [high intonation on penultimate syllable, low-rising on final syllable]

[3] Even for the best documented Chamic languages, there are no explicit tests to identify particular subordinate clauses as adverbial. In the case of example (33), we adduce the following arguments for an adverbial analysis (the first two drawn from David Blood (1977: 58–9): first, /mɨjah/ 'if' is obligatory but /năn/ 'then' is not, suggesting that the first clause is subordinate, but the second is not. Second, the two clauses are reversible, which is most compatible with an analysis in which one of them is adverbial. Third, a clause introduced by /năn/ 'then' can stand alone in Eastern Cham. And fourth, 'if' clauses are amenable to an adverbial analysis across languages.

Additionally, clause-final adverbs meaning ‘also’ are regularly used in polar questions (e.g. Eastern Cham /rĕj/, Western Jarai /mɨ̆n/), and at least Eastern Cham and Jarai have dedicated question particles, illustrated for Eastern Cham in (37).

(37) Eastern Cham, question particle

| | | | |
|---|---|---|---|
| *ʔoŋ* | *naw* | *puh* | *lɛ̆j* |
| grandfather | go | field | Q |

‘Are you going to (your) field?’ [rising intonation on final syllable] (David Blood 1977: 68)

Chamic languages have two basic patterns for **content** (*wh*-) **questions**: in Cham (Eastern and Western) and Tsat, the questioned word or constituent remains *in-situu*, illustrated for Eastern Cham in (38a) (Baumgartner 1998: 17; Thurgood 2005: 498; Thurgood et al. 2014: 225); all other Chamic languages have movement of the *wh*-word or phrase to the left edge of the sentence, illustrated for Eastern Jarai in (38b). In at least Jarai, this movement is fully optional with no apparent change in meaning (Jensen 2014: 92); in Haroi movement is a marked option used for emphatic questions (Goschnick 2018: 119–20). Only Bih appears to have obligatory movement (Nguyễn 2013b: 140–3). When a moved *wh*-word is a modifier or quantifier inside a noun phrase or the object of a prepositional phrase, the entire NP or PP is pied-piped along with it, as illustrated in (38b) by the PP /mɨ̆ŋ pă ʔ/ ‘from where’ for Eastern Jarai. Chamic languages with movement show no extraction restrictions: all arguments, along with obliques, are eligible for fronting.

(38) a. Colloquial Eastern Cham, *in-situ* questioned phrase

| | | | |
|---|---|---|---|
| *t̥ɛ̆j* | *ʔaj* | *maj* | ***taw*** |
| yng.sibling | eld.sibling | come | where |

‘Where have you come from?’ (Blood 1981: 54)

b. Eastern Jarai, left-displaced questioned phrase

| | | | | |
|---|---|---|---|---|
| *mɨ̆ŋ* | ***păʔ*** | *ɲu* | *rəbat* | *raj* |
| from | where | 3SG | walk | come |

‘Where did he walk from?’ (Jensen 2014: 184)

**Commands** and **requests** are typically marked with post-verbal particles, as illustrated for Haroi in (39) (see also the Eastern Cham example in (14)). Chamic languages possess a range of such particles which are appropriate under different conditions (see especially Doris Blood 1977: 45–7 for various particles and combinations of particles used in Eastern Cham for simple imperative, coaxing, and invitation, among many others).

(39) Haroi, command particle

| | | | | |
|---|---|---|---|---|
| *ni* | *ʔɔ̆ŋ* | *ɓɨ̆ŋ* | ***pɛ̆ʔ*** | *ni* |
| this | 2SG.INFRM | eat | IMP | this |

‘Here, eat this!’ (Goschnick p.c.)

## 30.4.4 Noun phrases

Noun phrases in Chamic languages can contain the elements schematized in (40). None of these elements is obligatory.

(40) Typical noun phrase constituent order in Chamic languages
Quantifier – Numeral – Classifier – Plural – Generic – Noun – Modifier – Possessive – Demonstrative

**Attributive modifiers** typically occur immediately after the head noun. The examples in (41) illustrate, in (41a), a head noun modified by a verbal modifier; in (41b), a head noun modified by a prepositional phrase specifying location; and in (41c), a nominal attributive modifier.

(41) a. Formal Eastern Cham

| | | |
|---|---|---|
| *ʔanɨʔ* | ***talɨ̆$^{j}$ʔ*** | *pataw* |
| child | lastborn | king |

‘the king’s youngest child’ (Blood 1981: 54)

b. Western Cham

| | | | |
|---|---|---|---|
| *p̥oh* | *kajăw* | *t̥i* | ***p$^{h}$ŏn*** |
| fruit | wood | at | trunk |

‘fruit on the tree’ (Ko 2018: 38)

c. Bih

| | | |
|---|---|---|
| *ɓăŋ* | ***ʔubej*** | *năn* |
| hole | tuber | that |

‘that tuber hole’ (Nguyễn 2013b: 314)

Observe that the **possessive** noun /pataw/ ‘king’ in (41a) follows the verbal modifier, though in some Chamic languages a possessor phrase can occur before other modifiers (at least Western Cham, Baumgartner 1998: 11–12; and Jarai, Jensen 2014: 25–6; Pawley and Kim 2017: 29). Chamic languages do not distinguish direct and indirect possession. Demonstratives—like the medial /năn/ in the Bih example (41c)—almost always follow all other modifiers and possessives.

In most Chamic languages, **demonstratives** encode a three-way distinction going back to Proto-Chamic: *proximal* *ʔinɛy/*ʔinĭ ‘this’,[4] *medial* (or *near-distal*) *ʔanan ‘that’, and *distal* *dih ‘that (far)’. Three-way distinctions of this sort are not uncommon in Austronesian languages (Himmelmann 2005a: 174). Reflexes of *ʔanan are especially important in discourse, where they mark topical referents and often serve as interclause transitions (with the meaning ‘then’ or ‘so then’). Two Chamic languages do not distinguish between

[4] Thurgood (1999) reconstructs the form *ʔinɛy for Ede and Jarai (as well as Acehnese), and *ʔinĭ (where the breve indicates absence of stress) for other Chamic languages.

medial and distal: Tsat has a simple two-way distinction between proximal /ni[33]/ 'this' and distal /năn[33]/ 'that' (Thurgood et al. 2014: 200); and Northern Raglai has two distal demonstratives, /ʔuhjã/ 'that (specific)' and /ʔut̥ih/ 'that (non-specific)', in addition to proximal /ʔunĩ/ 'this' (Lee 1966: 65).

All Chamic languages have **numeral classifier** systems, with both *sortal* (count) and *mensural* (measure) classifiers. Enumeration of countable nouns usually requires a sortal classifier which is selected based on semantic properties of that noun, especially animacy and shape (Bisang 1999). A typical classifier construction is illustrated in (42a), where a new character is introduced to the story with a full NP including a numeral and sortal classifier. Mensural classifiers, illustrated in (42b), measure out the noun rather than individuate it.

Formal Eastern Cham, classifiers

(42) a. *ɓoh tʰa* ***t̥rĕj*** *tapa prŏŋ*
see one CLF turtle big
'(He) saw a big turtle.'

b. *hu t̥wa* ***ç̥əʔ*** *mɨh*
have two jar gold
'There were two jars of gold!' (Blood 1981: 58, 60)

Some nouns, such as those for time and money, can be directly enumerated (e.g. Western Jarai /ha hɣəj/ 'one day'). Most Chamic languages have only a small number of attested sortal classifiers (in the range of five to fifteen), and even in Tsat, for which Thurgood et al. 2014 list twenty-five, only two classifiers occur at high frequency, one a classifier used generally for animate nouns (a reflex of PC *drɛy 'body'), and one for inanimate nouns (from PC *bɔh 'fruit') (159–61).

A noun phrase with no noun head but only a numeral, classifier, and demonstrative (almost always a reflex of PC *ʔanan 'that') is commonly used to track a topic that has already been introduced into the discourse, as in (43a), where the headless noun phrase refers to two characters just introduced (with full noun phrases) in the preceding discourse. Numerals with classifiers are regularly used with pronouns, too, as in (43b). (With pronouns, the classifier is sometimes omitted, as in Western Jarai /dwa gəməj/ 'us two (excl)'.)

(43) a. Western Cham
*t̥wa ɣaŋ nŏn kăn lo*
two CLF that poor much
'Those two were very poor.' (Ko 2018: 29)

b. Chru
*dwa ʔaraŋ gu drəj naw wŏʔ*
two CLF PL 1PL.INCL go return
'Let's us two go home!' (Fuller et al. 1974: 5)

Some Chamic languages also have a **plural**-marking word for humans that precedes nouns or pronouns, such as /gu/ in Chru /gu drəj/ 'us (INCL)', illustrated in (43b), and /labŭʔ/ in Northern Raglai /labŭʔ ʔadəj/ 'younger siblings' (Lee 1966: 63–4), but no Chamic language has obligatory plural-marking.

The unmarked position for numeral + classifier is immediately before the head noun for most Chamic languages (as in Vietnamese), but in the Cambodian varieties of Cham and Jarai, the numeral + classifier typically follows the noun and precedes the demonstrative. This split among Chamic languages reflects the region more generally: classifiers precede the noun in languages of Vietnam, but follow it in languages of Cambodia. Kenneth Gregerson suggests (p.c.) that classifier–noun order in Chamic may date back to Malayo-Chamic, as Malay also has this order.

Chamic languages all possess another word type sometimes grouped with classifiers: **generic nouns**. Generic (or *class*) terms are similar to classifiers in that they refer to classes of entities, such as 'plant', 'fruit', or 'liquid', and many generic nouns can also serve as classifiers. Unlike classifiers, however, they are not used for enumeration. Instead, generic terms occur with a following noun which specifies the type, as in Bih /bɔh dŭŋ/ 'coconut' (with the class term /bɔh/ for fruit and other three-dimensional objects) and Tsat /pʰun[33]pa[33]/ 'kapok tree' (with the plant-building class term /pʰun[33]/) (Nguyễn 2013b: 50–2; Thurgood et al. 2014: 162–71). It is especially common (as in the preceding examples) for specific plant and fruit types to be preceded by a generic noun, and it is unusual for plant (and fruit) names to occur as bare nouns. Sometimes a numeral classifier and identical generic term will appear in the same noun phrase, as in (44).

Western Jarai, generic noun

(44) *bɔh ʔɔʔ ha bɔh*
GENR mango one CLF
'one mango' (lit. 'one mango fruit')

**Relative clauses** occur late in the noun phrase, but generally before the demonstrative. Two Chamic languages have an optional relativizer: Western Cham /kŏŋ/ (Baumgartner 1998: 6; Ko 2018: 60) and colloquial Eastern Cham /lac/ 'say; > that' (rare and possibly calqued from Vietnamese; Brunelle and Phú 2019: 14). Relativized positions are signalled by gapping, as in (45), and, in contrast to many other Austronesian languages, there are almost no restrictions on which grammatical positions can be relativized (whether arguments or obliques).

Western Cham, relative clause with relativizer and gapping

(45) *ʔoŋ* *nə̆n* *khɨ̆n* *miʔ* *lanŭŋ* ***[kŏŋ***
grandfather that want take eel REL
*cɔ* *k̥ət* *ɣŏŋ* *_]*
grandchild 3SG raise *gap*
'The grandfather wanted to take the eel which his grandchild raised.' (Ko 2018: 60)

### 30.4.5 Serial verb constructions (SVCs)

Chamic languages all have **serial verb constructions** (SVCs), multi-verb constructions distinct from coordinate and subordinate clauses.[5] As noted above, directional verbs in SVCs routinely function like prepositions in Chamic languages, as illustrated in (46), where directional /naw/ 'go' follows manner of motion verb /ɗoʲʔ/ 'run'. Nevertheless, the position of the directional verb in (47)—before the object—suggests that these verbs have not fully grammaticalized as prepositions.

Formal Eastern Cham, directional SVC

(46) *məkam…* ***ɗoʲʔ*** ***naw*** *$t^h$aŋ* *t̥ahlŏw*
NAME run go house before
'Kam … ran home ahead.' (Blood 1978: 122)

Western Jarai, directional SVC

(47) *kəw* *dĭʔ* *məto* ***ba*** ***naw***
1SG ride motorbike transport go
*cɔ* *kəw* *poʔ* *saŋ* *pɛt*
grandchild 1SG LOC house doctor
'I drove my motorbike and took my grandchild to the doctor.'

Result states, too, are routinely encoded by the second verb of an SVC, as in (48).

Western Cham, result SVC

(48) *sp̥ŏp* *ŋăʔ* *ha* *tăʔ* *ʔĕŋ* ***k̥lɛh***
because work one only self tire
***mataj*** *jə*
die ACHIEV
'Because of working alone, (I) will die of tiredness.' (Ko 2007: 28)

Finally, the verb meaning 'give' can occur as V2 in an SVC to mark the beneficiary in most Chamic languages, as in (49).

However, Eastern Cham and Chru mark beneficiaries simply with a preposition.

Eastern Jarai, beneficiary SVC with 'give'

(49) *bənaj* ***swaŋ*** ***brəj*** *kə* *pətaw*
female dance give DAT king
'The girls danced for the king.' (Jensen 2014: 192)

## 30.5 Information structure

We have taken for granted in this chapter that Chamic languages, which lack the sort of morphology common in many Western Austronesian languages for marking **grammatical relations**, have bona fide subjects, objects, and indirect objects, marked primarily by their order in relation to the verb and each other (and in the case of indirect objects, by dative-marking prepositions). An alternative analysis is that the left edge of a clause is reserved for topics, and the right edge of the clause (after the verb) is reserved for focused items. We reject this analysis for a few reasons. First, Chamic languages do not have free word order in the absence of discourse constraints: instead, before the verb we almost always find the theme of stative verbs and the agent of active verbs; after the verb we almost always find the object and indirect object of active verbs. Second, the exceptions to the normal patterns can be attributed to information structuring; that is, as we will see below, unexpected constituents at the left edge of the clause are clearly participating in topic or focus constructions. Third, when constituents have moved to the left edge of the clause, the expected subject position to the left of the verb is still occupied by a subject. Nevertheless, as we discuss below, there is a strong correlation between the left edge of the clause (and thus subjecthood) and topicality, and the right edge of the clause and focus. We know of no specificity or definiteness requirement for subjects in any Chamic language.

We now turn to topic and focus in Chamic. We take a **topic** to be any entity in the common ground (or which can be accommodated to the common ground) which a sentence is about. As is common across languages, pre-verbal subjects are typically topical, as are most occurrences of pronouns, non-realized noun phrases (zero anaphora), and noun phrases that have the demonstrative 'that' (from PC *ʔanan). In addition to these ordinary topic devices, most or all Chamic languages also have special topic-marking constructions. Left-edge (pre-subject) topical phrases are attested quite generally, illustrated in (50) for Haroi. In this

[5] Diagnostics distinguishing SVCs from other multi-verb construction types are applied to Chamic languages by Ko (2007: 19–23; Western Cham), Jensen (2014: 196–205; Eastern Jarai), and Nguyễn (2013b: 186–8; Bih).

example, a new topic is introduced by a left-edge topic phrase co-referent with an explicit subject pronoun.

| | Haroi, left-displaced topic phrase | | | | |
|---|---|---|---|---|---|
| (50) | *[ʔɔ̆j* | *ləmuŋ* | *ni]* | *hədɑ̆ʷʔ* | *ɲăw* |
| | grandfather | tiger | this | formerly | 3SG |
| | *ɓɨ̆ŋ* | *mnɔ̆ŋ* | *cʰəsăʔ* | | |
| | eat | meat | well.done | | |

'This grandfather tiger, formerly he ate cooked meat.' (Goschnick p.c.)

Chamic languages also have left-displacement of topical object phrases (with or without a coreferential noun phrase after the verb), and several Chamic languages have specialized topic markers that can follow a topic, whether the topic occurs at the left edge of the clause or *in-situ* (e.g. Eastern Cham uses /năn/ 'that; > TOP' for this function, Brunelle and Phú 2018: 22). It is likely that both left-edge topics and particle-marked topics serve special functions, such as introducing a new topic (as in (50) above) or indicating a choice between topics (contrastive topic).

Whereas topics are typically part of the common ground, **focus** marks information selected from a set of alternatives that updates the common ground (Krifka 2008; Matic and Wedgwood 2013). Special focus constructions have been described for only two Chamic languages, Bih and Jarai. In Jarai, focused constituents may remain *in-situ* (marked by intonation), or they may front to the left edge of the clause, as in (51), where the right edge of the focus item is also delineated by a focus particle:

| | Eastern Jarai, left-displaced focus phrase | | | | |
|---|---|---|---|---|---|
| (51) | *[kətʰŭŋ* | *ʔja* | ***jəh]*** | *tam* | *kɔ̆n* |
| | bucket | water | FOC | NAME | weigh |

'It was a *bucket of water* that Tam weighed.' (Jensen 2014: 110; 106–15)

This left-displacement (present also in Bih; Nguyễn 2013b: 238–46) is distinct from left-edge topics, which appear to occur more generally in Chamic. Jensen (2014) suggests that there may be a correlation between the presence of focus-movement and *wh*-movement in any particular language, but at present we lack the data to make a certain judgement. Whatever the case, detailed study of information structure is a field wide open for further research.

## Acknowledgements

We are indebted to Robert Headley and Hella Goschnick for providing additional data on Western Cham, Ede, and Haroi. Thanks to Phạm Thị Thanh Hiền for her cartographic advice.

CHAPTER 31

# Languages of Java

Jozina Vander Klok

## 31.1 The language scene

While the number of languages spoken on the island of Java is quite low compared to other areas within Indonesia, Java certainly makes up for it in terms of speaker numbers: With a population density of 1100 people per km$^2$, Java is home to some 145 million people, almost 57% of the total population of Indonesia. Javanese, Sundanese, and Madurese speakers together comprise 58.75% of the Indonesian population, and Javanese alone 40.22%. **Javanese** is spoken by over 68 million speakers in east and central Java as well as in parts of west Java. **Sundanese** is spoken by about 32 million speakers in West Java, and **Madurese** is spoken by almost 8 million people on the island of Madura and in coastal regions of northeast Java.[1] **Balinese**, the language of Bali Island to the east of Java (see Shiohara and Arka, this volume, Chapter 32), is also spoken in Banyuwangi and Surabaya, East Java. Beyond Java Island, Javanese, Madurese, and Sundanese are all spoken in pockets on other Indonesian islands, partly due to government policy of transmigration to reduce the population density on Java. Outside of Indonesia, Javanese is also spoken in Malaysia, Singapore, the Netherlands, New Caledonia, and Suriname.[2]

There are also other languages or language varieties spoken on Java. **Baduy** is spoken in the interior of west Java in the Kendeng mountains of Banten province. **Osing** in Banyuwangi, East Java; **Tengger** in the highlands around Mt. Bromo near Malang, East Java; **Banyumas** in southwestern Central Java; **Cirebon** on the north coast of West Java near the Central Java border; and **Banten** west of Jakarta in Banten, West Java, are all varieties of Javanese, although some consider them as separate languages.[3] Although not included in this chapter, the national language **Indonesian** also needs mention. It is presently also spoken by most of the population of Java and particularly in the capital Jakarta (Sneddon 2003b). Varieties of Malay are also spoken on Java, including **Betawi** (spoken in and around Jakarta); **Peranakan Malay** (spoken throughout by mixed Chinese/Malay); and **North Coast Malay** (spoken along the north of Java).

Map 31.1 illustrates where Sundanese, Madurese, Javanese, Betawi (Jakarta Malay), Tengger, and Osing are spoken. It also indicates the three main Javanese dialect groups.

The languages of Java belong to the Malayo-Polynesian branch of Austronesian. Nothofer (1975) placed Javanese within a Malayo-Javanic subgroup which also includes Madurese, Sundanese, and Malay. Other scholars argue that Javanese is less closely related to the latter three than they are to one another (Adelaar 2005c; Smith 2017b); see Adelaar, this volume, §10.6 for more on these relationships).

The modern languages of Java are characterized typologically by SVO default word order, no case marking, and a reduced number of voice marking distinctions.

While the focus of this chapter is on the languages of Java today, it is worth noting that Javanese boasts one of the oldest literary traditions within Austronesian, with epigraphs and classical literature dating from the ninth century, and a written tradition using three main different scripts throughout its history. Javanese scholars identify three partly overlapping periods, Old, Middle, and Modern (though 'Middle Javanese' is controversial as a separate stage). See Ogloblin (2005) on the history of Javanese and Zoetmulder (1982, 1983) on Old Javanese. Sundanese has a literature going back to the fourteenth century.

[1] Many Madurese left Madura island due to its arid conditions (Davies 2010: 3). Of the 7,179,356 Madurese people, 6,520,403 reportedly live in East Java (Na'im and Syaputra 2011: 38).

[2] Among the diaspora Javanese varieties, see for example, Vruggink (2001) and Villerius (2019) on Suriname Javanese.

[3] The Indonesian census does not include the speaker population of these varieties. Conners (2020) estimates that Tengger has a speaker population of about 600,000, Banyumasan 15 million, and Banten 5 million. Iskandar and Iskander (2016) report that the ethnic population of the Baduy is 11,620. Arps (2004) estimates that while the ethnic population of Osing is 300,000, there is a significantly larger group of speakers of about 500,000–750,000.

Jozina Vander Klok, *Languages of Java*. In: *The Oxford Guide to the Malayo-Polynesian Languages of Southeast Asia*. Edited by: Alexander Adelaar and Antoinette Schapper, Oxford University Press. © Jozina Vander Klok (2024). DOI: 10.1093/oso/9780198807353.003.0031

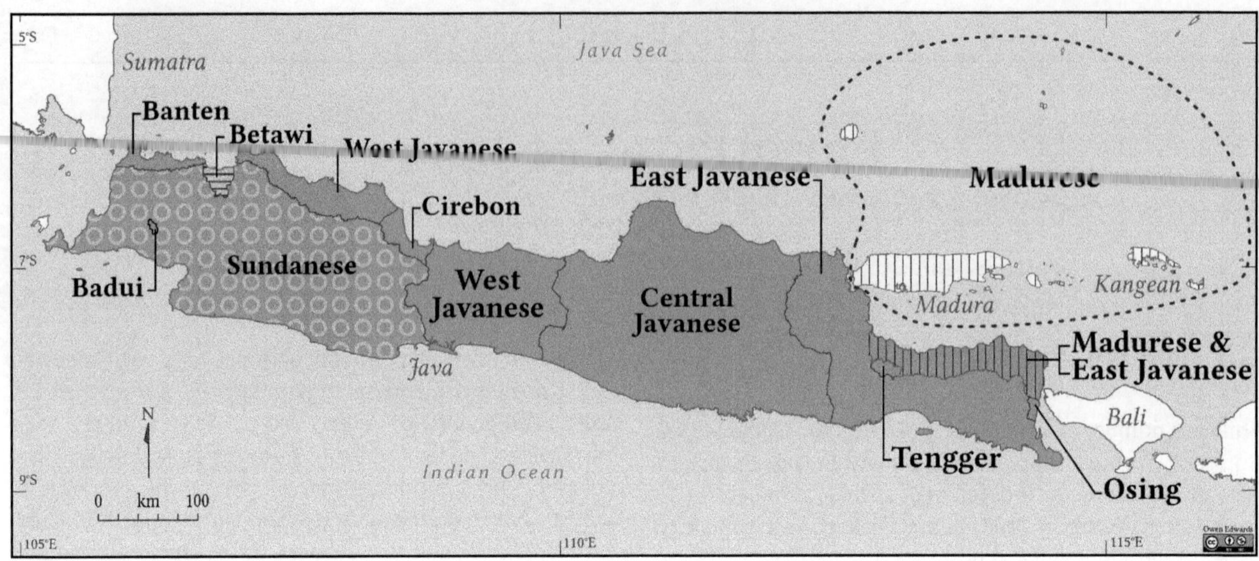


**Map 31.1** The languages of Java and dialect groups of Javanese.

### 31.1.1 Dialects/varieties of the languages of Java

This chapter focuses on the typological features of the languages of Java; however, where possible, an effort has been made to bring to light relevant dialectal features since many dialects are quite distinct from each other across all areas of grammar, including morphosyntax.

Some erstwhile dialects are today recognized as separate languages, such as **Baduy** vis-à-vis Sundanese. The Baduy people went into seclusion in the sixteenth century to pursue a life in accordance with traditional Sundanese values.

**Madurese** has two main dialects, Western Madurese and Eastern Madurese (Sutoko et al. 1998). Eastern Madurese in Sumenep regency, Madura, is considered the standard due to historical royal prestige. Most Madurese speakers live on Java, and there, Western Madurese is prevalent in the Surabaya area, whereas Eastern Madurese is common in the *Tapal Kuda* 'horseshoe' region in East Java. In addition, the Kangean dialect spoken on the Kangean islands northeast of Madura Island, appears to be quite distinct.

The Parahiangan or Priangan (Southern) dialect of **Sundanese**, considered the standard, is spoken in south-central West Java in Bandung City and surrounding areas (Kurniawan 2013: 6). This variety is the basis for the school curriculum (Rosidi 1984). Other Sundanese dialects include a Western variety in Banten province (where Javanese, Betawi (Jakarta Malay), and Jakarta Indonesian are also spoken), a Northern variety in and around Bogor; and various Eastern varieties.

**Javanese** dialects divide into three broad groups: West Javanese (spoken on the eastern and northern edges of West Java), Central Javanese, and East Javanese (Nothofer 1980), as shown in Map 31.1. Within Central Javanese, the dialect in and around the courtly cities of Yogyakarta and Surakarta/Solo is considered the ideological standard (Errington 1988: 22). It is used in the Javanese school curriculum. Within East Javanese, other groupings are the *Pesisir Lor* dialectal continuum along the northeast coast of Java directly west of Semarang, Central Java (e.g. Jepara, Blora, Rembang) to Surabaya, East Java; the *Tapal Kuda* dialects in the east peninsula; and the *Malang-Pasuruan* dialects (Hoogervorst 2008: 17–20). Osing, Tengger, Banyumasan, Cirebon, and Banten have quite different linguistic features and are considered by many scholars to be distinct varieties of Javanese; while others place them within the three main groupings above (see Krauße 2017 on the latter). **Peranakan Javanese** is spoken by ethnic Chinese–Javanese throughout Java; the lexicon is mainly Indonesian but also includes Chinese and Dutch vocabulary, while functional words are Javanese (Wolff 1983, 1997). Some of the considerable lexical differences across Javanese dialects are illustrated in (1); *Pesisir Lor* here refers to the variety spoken in Pemalang, Tegal, and Pekalongan cities along Central Java's north coast (Conners 2020: 270). See Krauße (2017: 6–9) for detailed classification of Javanese varieties.[4]

[4] For consistency and transparency across languages, the glottal stop is represented as [ʔ] in this chapter. This differs from the current orthographic practice and the cited examples, where the glottal stop is represented as [k] in Javanese and ['] in Madurese.

Javanese varieties

| (1) | a. *Aku* | *arep* | *teko* | *karo* | *kanca-ne.* |
|---|---|---|---|---|---|
| | b. *Kite* | *pen* | *teke* | *karo* | *batur-e.* |
| | c. *Nyong* | *pang* | *teka* | *karo* | *batir-e.* |
| | d. *Inyong* | *pan* | *teka* | *karo* | *kanca-ne.* |
| | e. *Eyang* | *kate* | *teka* | *karo* | *rewang-e.* |
| | f. *Isun* | *kate* | *teko* | *ambe* | *konco-ne.* |
| | 1 | FUT/*want* | *come* | *with* | *friend*-DEF |

'I'm going to come with a friend.'
(Conners 2020: 254–5, *gloss adjusted*) (1a - Central Javanese; 1b - Banten, 1c - Banyumasan, 1d - Pesisir Lor, 1e - Tengger, 1f - Osing)

This linguistic variation is on the whole understudied with the focus almost exclusively on the 'standard' dialects, but this is changing (e.g., Davies' (2010) grammar of Western Madurese).[5]

## 31.2 Speech levels of the languages of Java

Speech levels—a system of politeness distinctions across all grammatical categories—are common to all the larger languages of Java as well as neighbouring languages Balinese and Sasak (see Shiohara and Arka, this volume, §32.5). This feature originally stems from the influence from the Javanese, when the Mataram empire ruled over the area. The levels are suggested to have arisen in the late fourteenth century (Clynes 1994; Conners 2008: 41). This feature spread to the Sundanese aristocracy in the sixteenth century and then spread to all Sundanese speakers with the advent of schooling in the early twentieth century (Rosidi 1984).

There are three main speech levels in Javanese, *krama* (or *basa*) 'high', *madya* 'mid', and *ngoko* 'low'. While *ngoko* is productive, *krama* has around 1,600 words and *madya* has about sixty words (Robson and Wibisono 2002). There are also two vocabulary sets which can be applied over and above the default distinctions expressed by any of these levels (see further below): they are used to raise and honour the addressee (*krama inggil*, about 445 words) or to lower and humble the speaker (*krama andhap*, which comprises only around fifteen words). Having been borrowed into the other languages of Java, three levels are also recognized in Madurese: *biyasa/kasar* 'regular; coarse', *tengngaʔan* 'mid', and *alos* 'smooth; polite' (Davies 2010). Sundanese has a basic distinction between *basa kasar* 'rough language' and *basa lemes* 'refined language', and there are as many as 400 word pairs (Cohn 2000: 694). Anderson (1993) also identifies a set of humble vs. respectful vocabularies within *basa lemes* in Sundanese.

The use of these levels indicates the type of relationship the speaker has with their addressee. To illustrate with Javanese, *krama* gives respect, but is also more socially distant and formal; *ngoko* indicates a closer, intimate relationship, but can be viewed as *kasar* 'coarse'. Poedjosoedarmo (1968: 60–1) explains that by uttering the *krama* sentence in the first line of (2), the speaker can indicate that she does not know her addressee very well, but also that her addressee has some higher social status. In contrast, by uttering the same meaning in *ngoko* in the last line of (2), the speaker could be an employer speaking to her employee, highlighting their different social status, or the speaker could be talking to a friend, highlighting their close relationship. The *madya* counterpart in the middle line of (2) serves as a middle ground to indicate that the speaker is addressing someone neither close nor of low social status, such as a student talking with an older market-seller.[6] Thus, the degree of formality between the speaker and addressee, their royal ties, their social status, kinship, and age all play a role in the choice of speech level, and further, of which additional vocabulary sets may be required. Further, gender and the topic under discussion also can play a role (cf. Anderson 1993 for Sundanese). For instance, a young Javanese nobility, or *priyayi*, would address an older *priyayi* with the *krama* sentence in (2) plus *krama inggil* words. Because of these complexities, Uhlenbeck (1978: 307) and Errington (1988: 11) prefer the term 'speech style'; see also Wolff and Poedjosoedarmo (1982).

Javanese speech levels *(krama, madya, ngoko)*

| (2) | *Menika* | *anaʔ* | *kula* | *Tini* | *éngkang* | *kula criyos-aken* | *wau.* |
|---|---|---|---|---|---|---|---|
| | *Niki* | *anaʔ* | *kula* | *Tini* | *séng* | *kula criyos-aké* | *wau.* |
| | *Iki* | *anaʔ* | *ku* | *Tini* | *séng* | *taʔ= kandhaʔ-aké* | *mau.* |
| | here | child | my | Tini | REL | 1=tell-CAUS | just |

'Here is my child Tini about whom I told you just now.'
(Poedjosoedarmo 1968: 62, *gloss adjusted*)

The Javanese examples in (2) show that the differences in speech levels cut across both lexical and functional word classes, beyond just within the pronominal system such as

[5] See Conners and Vander Klok (2016) for an overview of the research on colloquial varieties of Javanese.

[6] Both Robson (2002: 12) for Javanese and Davies (2010: 480) for Madurese raise the question whether the mid-level is a separate speech level, as it has a much lower number of distinct vocabulary items and is largely composed of high-level words plus low-level affixes.

**Table 31.1** Pronouns in Standard Javanese *ngoko/krama*, Madurese *biyasa/alos*, and Tengger

| | Javanese *ngoko* | Madurese *biyasa* | Javanese *krama* | Madurese *alos* | Tengger |
|---|---|---|---|---|---|
| 1 | *aku* | *sengkoʔ* | *kula* | *kaula* | *(ı)eyung* (male)<br>*isun* (female) |
| 2 | *kowé,*<br>*awaʔmu* | *baʔna* | *sampéyan,*<br>*panjenèngan* | *sampeyan,*<br>*panjennengngan* | *sira*<br>*rika* (distant) |
| 3 | *dhéwèʔé* | *abaʔna* | *piyambakipun* | | *dhéwèʔ(n)é* |

the French *tu/vous* distinction. Further, three *ngoko* affixes have *krama* counterparts: the passive prefix *di-/dipon-*; the definite clitic *-(n)e/-(n)ipon*; and the causative/applicative suffix *-aké/-aken* (see (2)) (Poedjosoedarmo 1968: 58). The speech levels are more than mere vocabulary choices. Many words are argued to be derivationally related across speech levels. Uhlenbeck (1978: 288–93) and Poedjosoedarmo (1968: 65–6) show that a number of words in *krama* can be derived from their *ngoko* counterparts through phonological stem changes (primarily word-final). For example, for *ngoko* words ending in *-i*, their *krama* counterparts often use *-os*: *ganti* → *gantos* 'to change'; *wadi* → *wados* 'secret' (Poedjosoedarmo 1968: 65).

The pronominal systems themselves (unspecified for number) are extensive in the different word forms across speech levels, as shown in Table 31.1 for Javanese and Madurese, where the pronouns for high terms of address are identical. Table 31.1 also contrasts these forms with Tengger, showing how this system is employed and varies across dialects in Javanese. In general, the more distant a speech community is from the royal courts in Yogyakarta/Solo, the less speakers know or use the full speech levels; nevertheless, this system remains ideologically important (e.g. Ewing 2005a: 7; Vander Klok 2019). Tengger lacks this system altogether (Conners 2008: 40), except for having a more formal second person pronoun (*rika*). This variation, due to geographical distance and historic separation from the cultural centre, is also at play across dialects in Sundanese, and Baduy lacks this system like Tengger (Müller-Gotama 2001: 2).

Another point of variation is the change over time in how the speech levels are used, documented in particular for Javanese. In the description of (2), many of the uses are asymmetric; that is, the speaker would use *krama*, while the addressee responds in *ngoko*, and vice-versa, indicating different degrees of formality and social status (Poedjosoedarmo 1968). Errington (1988, 1998a) documents that in the courtly city of Surakarta/Solo, the *krama* speech level and honouring/humbling vocabulary sets are no longer used in an exclusively asymmetric manner in the *priyayi* circles and beyond; this was particularly noticeable in the use of pronouns. Goebel (2002) also observes more symmetric uses in Semarang, central Java. He notes that Semarang speakers indicate their close relationship by both using *ngoko*, regardless of their ethnicity; whereas to indicate social distance *krama* is used symmetrically, or more commonly, Indonesian, which has no speech levels. More recent sociolinguistic studies have also shown this trend in central and east Java cities, where Indonesian is used as the default alternative instead of *krama* (Smith-Hefner 2009; Setiawan 2012; Nurani 2015). These studies show an ongoing change in the use of speech levels throughout Java, where speakers no longer emphasize past social hierarchy.

## 31.3 Phonology

### 31.3.1 Vowels and related phonological processes

Table 31.2 outlines the phonemic inventory of vowels for **Central Javanese**, **Sundanese**, and **Madurese**. Their symmetrical vowel systems are considered more complex within Austronesian, wherein most languages have between three and five phonemes (Himmelmann 2005a: 115–16); whereas across the world's languages, they have an 'average' or 'large' size, defined as five to six or seven to fourteen phonemes respectively, according to Maddieson (2013b).

The **Central Javanese** vowel inventory has six phonemes and four allophonic pairs /i/-/ɪ/, /u/-/ʊ/, /e/-/ɛ/, /o/-/ɔ/ (Dudas 1976; Hayward 1999; Wedhawati et al. 2006).[7] The low vowel /a/ is laxed in word-final position, /sutʱa/ → [sutʱɔ] 'decrease'. Mid and high vowels are laxed in closed syllables (e.g. /kakuŋ/ → [kakʊŋ] 'male'; /oleh/ → [olɛh] 'to.get'). Vowel harmony occurs with penultimate low and mid vowels when they are identical with the ultimate vowel

[7] Although Hayward (1999) argues that /ɛ/ and /ɔ/ are the underlying phonemic mid vowels instead of /e/ and /o/.

**Table 31.2** Phonemic vowel inventories of Central Javanese, Sundanese, and Madurese

| | Central Javanese | | | Sundanese | | | Madurese | | |
|---|---|---|---|---|---|---|---|---|---|
| | Front | Central | Back | Front | Central | Back | Front | Central | Back |
| High | i | | u | i | ɨ | u | i | | u |
| Mid | e | ə | o | e | ə | o | ɛ | ə | ɔ |
| Low | | a | | | a | | | a | |

(e.g. /pala/ → [pɔlɔ] 'nutmeg' or /leren/ → [lɛrɛn] 'to.rest'). The trigger for harmony of the penultimate vowel is the realization of the final vowel in CVC syllables for mid vowels and in CV syllables for low vowels as laxed (Dudas 1976; see also Adisasmito-Smith 2004: 53–8).

Different from Central Javanese, **East Javanese** extends vowel harmony with low and mid vowels to high vowels (e.g. /sisiʔ/ → [sɪsɪʔ] 'fish.scale' (compared to [sisɪʔ] 'fish.scale' in Central Javanese) (Adisasmito-Smith 2004; Hoogervorst 2008)). **Tengger**, on the other hand, does not have vowel harmony (Conners 2008: 52). A unique feature of **Osing**, which has the same vowel inventory as Javanese, is word-final diphthongization of /i/ as [ai] and /u/ as [au], such as the demonstratives [ikai] > [iki] and [ikau] > [iku] (Herusantosa 1987). No other Javanese dialect has diphthongization; instead concurrent vowels are treated as separate nuclei of syllables (e.g. *rai-mu* 'your face' is parsed as [ra.i.mu]).

**Sundanese** has seven vowel phonemes (Robins 1953; Sudaryat et al. 2007). The additional phoneme compared to Javanese, /ɨ/, is written as *eu* (*henteu* 'not') and is uncommon across Austronesian as well as cross-linguistically (Cohn 2000: 693). Its phonemic status is, however, controversial: Perwitasari et al. (2017) argue that /ɨ/ is better analysed as /ɣ/ on the basis of acoustic measurements, while Müller-Gotama (2001) proposes that it is /ɤ/, following Robins (1953). There are also no diphthongs in Sundanese: vowel-glide sequences are treated as two phonemes since glides block nasalization (Müller-Gotama 2001: 9).

The size of the phonemic vowel inventory in **Madurese** is not completely clear. Stevens (1968) and Cohn and Lockwood (1994) consider Madurese to have eight phonemic vowels based on the system of vowel harmony with paired high~non-high alternating vowels that match in backness: [ɛ]~[i], [ɔ]~[u], [a]~[ɤ], [ə]~[ɨ]. Thus, in addition to the six phonemes in Table 31.2, the central vowels [ɨ] and [ɤ] would also be included for Madurese, although no other work recognizes the status of [ɨ] as a surface vowel (Davies 2010: 37). The vowel harmony or vowel raising affects 95% of Madurese vocabulary (Stevens 1968), where the phonation of the consonant conditions the height of the following vowel: high vowels occur following voiced and aspirated stops, and non-high vowels elsewhere. For example, the [ɛ]~[i] complementarity is shown with bilabial stops: [pʰikʰɤl] 'rob' and [bilɤ] 'when' vs. [pɛkkɛr] 'think' (Davies 2010: 30). However, exceptions are noted for [l], [r], [ʔ], and [s]. This phenomenon has been well documented since Kiliaan (1897) and Stevens (1968).

As a final note, there is no word-final schwa in Sundanese (Müller-Gotama 2001: 6–7) or Central Javanese. However, word-final schwa occurs regularly in Banten Javanese and sporadically in Pesisir Lor Javanese varieties where Central Javanese has underlying /a/ (Conners 2020: 267, 270). In Madurese, schwa only occurs in closed syllables (e.g. [sənnəŋ] 'happy').

## 31.3.2 Consonants and related phonetic and phonological processes

The consonant inventories—Javanese with twenty-one segments, Sundanese with eighteen, and Madurese with twenty-three—fall within the average worldwide size of between nineteen and twenty-five consonants (Maddieson 2013a), but are large within Austronesian, where sixteen to twenty segments is common (Himmelmann 2005a: 115).

**Javanese** consonants show a five-way place distinction for stops (see Table 31.3, based on Wedhawati et al. 2006: 74).[8] Stops [ʈ] and [ɖ], written as *th* and *dh*, are also de-

[8] Based on phonetic and phonological properties (nasal substitution), <h> is considered a glide (Ladefoged 1990; Garellek et al. 2021). Although based on its phonological property with nasal substitution, <s> behaves like an alveolo-palatal, it is articulatorily produced as a dental/alveolar fricative (Archangeli et al. 2017P.20).

**Table 31.3** Inventory of Javanese consonants

| | Labial | Dental/Alveolar | Post-alveolar | Palatal/Alveolar-palatal | Velar | Glottal |
|---|---|---|---|---|---|---|
| Stop | p b̥ | t̪ d̪̥ | ʈ ɖ̥ | | k g̊ | ʔ |
| Affricate | | | | c ɟ̥ | | |
| Nasal | m | n | | ɲ | ŋ | |
| Fricative | | s | | | | |
| Liquid | | l r | | | | |
| Glide | | | | j | w | h |

scribed as 'apical-palatal' (Wolff and Poedjosoedarmo 1982). Hayward and Muljono (1991) show using palatography that [ʈ] and [ɖ̥] are articulated by raising the tip of the tongue to touch the back of the alveolar ridge (with [ʈ] more retracted than [ɖ̥]). [f] and [z] are loan phonemes. Yannuar (2019) argues that [ʔ] is not phonemic in Malang Javanese (East Java), but allophonic to /k/ word-finally.

A particularly well-studied feature of Javanese consonants is the difference between voiceless stops (tensed) and their so-called 'heavy', 'breathy', or 'slack-voiced' (lax) counterparts (e.g. Fagan 1988; Hayward 1993, 1995; Thurgood 2004).[9] Acoustically, the contrast is realized primarily in changes to the following vowels of the lax stop relative to their tensed counterpart; in other words, both stops can be considered as voiceless. Brunelle (2010) summarizes that vowels following lax stops in Javanese are breathy and have a lower pitch and F1, while those following tense stops are modal and have higher pitch and F1. These differences, he argues, are due to the articulatory change of larynx lowering with lax stops.

**Osing** is unique in that it has palatalization, induced with any voiced consonant before [a] and [ɛ], such as *Byanyuwangi* [bʲaɲuwaŋi] (Herunsantosa 1987). Palatalization can also interact with diphthongization, for example, *gedigu* [g̊əɖ̥ig̊ʲau] 'like.that' or *gedigi* [g̊əɖ̥ig̊ʲai] 'like.this' (Witke 2019).

The inventory of **Sundanese** consonants is slightly less than Javanese, lacking /ʈ, ɖ, ʔ/. The voice contrast of stops is voiced vs. voiceless, unlike in Javanese. All consonants can occur in any position except the palatal affricates and palatal nasal which cannot occur word-finally. The alveolar [r] can be trilled or flapped. A glottal stop is phonetically predictable: it occurs by default before initial vowels, after final vowels, and between identical vowels, for example, /tuur/ → [tuʔur] 'knee' (Müller-Gotama 2001: 11); it also occurs in some unpredictable environments in some Arabic loanwords (Müller-Gotama 2001: 8). [f], [v], and [z] occur in loanwords.

A phenomenon in Sundanese that has inspired theoretical work is progressive nasalization of vowels, [ʔ] and [h] (Robins 1953, 1957; Cohn 1990). Nasal spreading is blocked by obstruents, liquids and glides, as shown by [ŋãjak] 'to sift' and [mãro] 'to halve'. It also interacts with the plural *-ar/al-*: when the infix occurs following a nasal, its vowel is nasalized, but a following vowel is not, blocked by the consonant of the infix as expected. However, any subsequent vowels *remain* nasalized, as in [m-ãr-ahãl] 'expensive:PL' vs. [mãhãl] 'expensive' (Robins 1957).

**Madurese** has the same articulation places for oral stops as Javanese (Table 31.4, Davies 2010: 12) but is unique among the languages of Java in that it has a three-way stop contrast: voiceless, voiceless aspirated, and voiced. In addition, [f] and [h] are found in loanwords. Glides between vowels are largely the result of epenthesis, but word-final glides are not (Davies 2010: 16–18). Glide epenthesis between different vowels in Madurese is conditioned by backness (not height, as is commonly found; cf. Himmelmann 2005a: 116). Thus [w] is inserted after a back vowel and [j] after a front vowel, as illustrated with two actor voice verb stems both combining with the benefactive suffix, which differ in their stem-final vowel: [məllɛ + akʰi] → [məllɛjakʰi] 'buy for' vs. [ŋataɔ + akʰi] → [ŋataɔwakʰi] 'convince' (Davies 2010: 41–2).

Another noteworthy feature of Madurese consonants is gemination, which is contrastive except after schwa (Cohn and Lockwood 1994: 68). Gemination is most productive

9 Based on their phonological properties, Javanese <c, ɟ> function as stops, in that they contrast in terms of "tense vs. lax" register, but based on their phonetics, Javanese <c, ɟ> sound alveolar-palatal [t͡ɕ]. It may be for typographical reasons that previous literature on Javanese use the IPA stop symbols to stress that these sounds don't function phonologically as clusters of t+ɕ. These comments also apply to Madurese (Table 31.4) and Sundanese.

**Table 31.4** Inventory of Madurese consonants

| | Labial | Dental/alveolar | Retroflex | Palatal | Velar | Glottal |
|---|---|---|---|---|---|---|
| Stop | p pʰ b | t tʰ d | ʈ ʈʰ ɖ | | k kʰ g | ʔ |
| Affricate | | | | c cʰ ɟ | | |
| Nasal | m | n | | ɲ | ŋ | |
| Fricative | | s | | | | |
| Liquid | | l r | | | | |

where it ensures that schwa remains in a closed syllable: [ma.ɲəs.səl + -a] 'regret+IRR' entails gemination of [l] in [ma.ɲəs.səl.la], thus maintaining the Madurese phonotactic schwa constraint (Davies 2010: 43).

### 31.3.3 Syllable structure

Syllable structure as described for the languages of Java are common to Austronesian languages as a whole: consonant clusters are restricted to onset position and also have restricted shapes (Himmelmann 2005a: 115). The permitted syllable structures are V, VC, CV, CVC, CCV, and CCVC, and the majority of roots are disyllabic consisting of CV and CVC syllables (85% for Javanese; Uhlenbeck 1949: 31). In Madurese, consonant clusters are predominantly the result of vowel deletion (e.g. /paraɔ/ → [praɔ] 'boat') or borrowing (e.g. [ɛs.trɛ] 'wife' from Indonesian *istri*) (Davies 2010: 25). In the languages of Java, consonant clusters are restricted to two phonemes, but some words, mostly Dutch loanwords, allow up to three ([spri.tus] 'spirit', [skrip.si] 'thesis', Wedhawati et al. 2006: 97). The shape of two-consonant clusters is largely restricted to an obstruent followed by a liquid in all three languages. In the case of nasal + stop clusters, the question arises whether they consist of one segment with prenasalization or two segments. Yannuar (2019) revisits these phonotactics in Javanese using data from *Walikan*, a segment-based reversal language based on Malang Javanese with Indonesian input. The reversal process of *Walikan* reveals that the phonotactics of nasal + stop clusters are two segments because in word-final position either segment can undergo deletion depending on the word. For instance, in one case, the stop is deleted in *Walikan*, as in /mbah/ ['mbah] > /ham/ ['ham] 'grandparent'; while in another case, the nasal is deleted: /mbaʔju/ ['mbaʔ.ju] > /ujab/ ['ʔu.jap] 'older sister'.

### 31.3.4 Stress—or lack thereof

Recent work on prosody in Indonesian languages has shifted from the assumption that these languages have stress to the proposal that stress plays no prosodic role; instead, these languages use intonation wherein boundary tones may be associated with a prosodic boundary (see Kaufman and Himmelmann, this volume, §42.4.1). Indeed, stress has been reported to be non-contrastive in the languages of Java, but with various generalizations. In Madurese, word stress can fall on any syllable in the root; as such, it is "not a salient feature" (Davies 2010: 51). In Sundanese, stress occurs on the penultimate syllable, but if it has schwa, it will fall on the final syllable (Müller-Gotama 2001: 10). This same distribution was stated for Javanese (Ras 1985). More recently, Stoel (2006) concludes that Javanese (Banyumasan) has no stress. Using an autosegmental metrical approach, he argues that the seven intonation patterns described in Uhlenbeck (1941) can be generalized to an HL% tone associated with the end of the focus domain.

## 31.4 Morphology

### 31.4.1 Reduplication

Reduplication is considered the most widespread morphophonological process across western Austronesian languages (Himmelmann 2005a: 121); it also plays an important role in the grammars of the languages of Java. Reduplication occurs across all grammatical categories, and includes all types between full vs. partial and simple (reduplicant copies material from base) vs. complex (reduplicant alters material from base).

**Simple full base reduplication** generally conveys a range of meanings associated with this process across the world's languages including multiplicity, intensity, and duration. These are illustrated with Javanese in (3) and (4).[10] An example of emphasis is with temporal nouns, such as *esuʔ* 'morning' → *esuʔ~esuʔ* 'early in the morning' (East Javanese; Author's notes).

Javanese, full reduplication of nouns or adjectives indicating plurality

(3) a. *omah* 'house' → *omah~omah* 'houses'

b. *pelem-é gedhé* 'the big mango' → *pelem-é gedhé~gedhé* (mango–DEF big–RED) 'the big mangos'
(Wedhawati et al. 2006: 197, 234)

Javanese, full reduplication of verbs indicating repetition or continuation

(4) a. *neluʔ* 'call [someone] from afar' → *neluʔ~neluʔ* 'to keep on calling [someone]'

b. *mlaku* 'walk' → *mlaku~mlaku* 'to keep on walking'
(Uhlenbeck 1978: 100, 107)

Uhlenbeck (1978: 100) notes that full reduplication of verbs in Javanese also has an intensive or conative reading besides a repetitive one as in (4); these are dependent on the predicate type, the syntactic construction, or the discourse context (see also Wedhawati et al. 2006: 145–6).

Madurese also uses simple full reduplication of verbs to indicate the same family of readings as in Javanese. Likewise, full reduplication of nouns can indicate plurality and that of adjectives can indicate emphasis, but Madurese more pervasively uses **simple partial reduplication** of the final syllable of the base for these functions (Davies 2010). Partial reduplication of a verb can also be used for iteration, as in (5). Across Austronesian, copying the base-final syllable is less common than the initial syllable of the base (Himmelmann 2005a: 123).

Madurese

(5) a. Reduplication of noun: plurality
*prao* 'ship' → *o~prao* 'ships'

b. Reduplication of adjective: emphasis
*penter* 'smart'→ *ter~penter* 'very smart'

c. Reduplication of verb: iteration
*mokol* 'hit' → *kol~mokol* 'hit a bunch of times'

d. Reduplication of verb: plurality
*maen* 'play' → *en~maen* 'play (PL)'
(Davies 2010: 130)

An example of **complex partial reduplication** is Cə-reduplication in Javanese. It derives verbs from non-verbal roots and adds a causative, intensive, or repetitive reading to verbal roots. Some examples of these functions are given in (6) (glosses translated from Indonesian):

Javanese

(6) a. *putu* 'grandchild' → *pe~putu* 'have a grandchild'
b. *nangis* 'to cry' → *ne~nangis* 'to cause to cry'
c. *muji* 'to pray' → *me~muji* 'to pray intensely'
d. *nyolong* 'to steal' → *nye~nyolong* 'to steal habitually'
(Wedhawati et al. 2006: 147)

Ca-reduplication is also found in Madurese (e.g. *tolong* 'help'→ *ta~tolong* '(really) help'), which seems to allow for plurality, emphasis, or iteration readings depending on the root and context. In comparison, final-syllable reduplication is more common (Davies 2010: 131).

**Complex full reduplication** is common in Javanese verbs, combining full reduplication with additional vowel changes: the final vowel of the reduplicant is replaced with [a], but in case it is already [a], the base may also have vowel differences, in some cases associated with vowel harmony, as shown in (7). This type has been termed 'habitual-repetitive' reduplication and has been analysed in different ways (Dudas 1976; Uhlenbeck 1978: Chapter 5; Kenstowicz 1986).

Javanese

(7) a. *tuku* 'to buy' → [tuka~tuku] 'to buy repeatedly'
b. *udan* 'to rain' → [udan~udɛn] 'to keep on raining'
c. *lali* 'forget' → [lola~lali] 'to keep on forgetting'
d. *salah* 'wrong' → [solah~salah], [salah~sɛlɛh], or [solah~sɛlɛh] 'all messed up'

Reduplication can interact with additional morphology, depending on the type. For instance, Madurese nominal reduplication include all affixes to indicate plurality (e.g. *pang-asel-an* 'income' → *pangaselan~pangaselan* 'incomes'), while verbal reduplication only includes the root (e.g. *a-caca* 'AV-talk' → *a-caca~caca* 'AV-REDUP-chat') (Davies 2010: 130).

### 31.4.2 Affixation

Western Austronesian languages are considered to be 'agglutinative', but as Himmelmann (2005a: 126) notes, this needs to be more deeply investigated, as there are also a few fusional morphophonological processes such as nasal substitution, and most affixes are multifunctional. This multifunctionality is seen across the languages of Java. For example, the suffix *-an* in Javanese can derive intransitive verbs (e.g. *kalung* 'necklace' → *kalung-an* 'to wear a necklace'); nominalize the root (e.g. *ukur* 'measure' → *ukur-an* 'size'); or can form the comparative manner of adjectives (e.g. *resiʔ* 'clean' → *resiʔ-an* 'cleanly') (Robson 2002). In Sundanese, *-an* can also derive nouns or verbs, and form the comparative degree of

[10] While full reduplication in (3) overtly indicates plurality, a bare noun itself is unspecified for number in all of the languages of Java. Note also that (3b) is ambiguous between an attributive reading (shown in the translation) or a predicational reading (e.g. 'the mango is big').

adjectives (e.g. *kolot* 'old' → *kolotan* 'older'). Madurese *-an* has all of these functions (Davies 2010).

In 'nasal substitution' the stem-initial oral obstruent of the predicate is replaced by a homorganic nasal (with the same place of articulation); for example, *kopi* 'coffee' → *ngopi* 'drink coffee', *baca* 'read' → *maca* 'read' in Javanese. In some cases, the homorganic status is not clear, such as with an [s]-initial root, an alveolar fricative, which is replaced with a palatal nasal, for example, *sabun* 'soap' → *nyabun* 'wash with soap' in Sundanese. Based on acoustic analysis of nasal substitution in Javanese and Sasak, Archangeli et al. (2017) conclude that [s] and [ɲ] do not share place of articulation, but are only abstractly related. Nasal substitution occurs with all oral obstruents in Madurese and Javanese, whereas in Sundanese it is restricted to voiceless obstruents. With vowel initial roots in all languages, the velar nasal is prefixed, for example, *ilang* 'chase away' → *ngilang* 'chase away' in Sundanese. Other examples of fusional morphology are sandhi processes in Javanese, where identical vowels across a morpheme boundary merge (Conners 2008: 54).

Infixes are very limited in the contemporary languages of Java, and are inserted before the first vowel. Sundanese has the plural infix *-ar-* (allomorph *-al-* with *l*-initial roots, see (21)); Javanese has the intensifier infix *-u-*, common in East Javanese varieties (Nurhayani and Cohn 2016). Madurese *-al-* serves as an intensifier with adjectives, *-am-* is a nominalizer with some verbs, but other infixes do not seem to have identifiable semantic functions (Davies 2010). All languages have non-productive vestiges of PAN **-um-* (e.g. *s-um-aur* 'to answer' in Javanese); Sundanese and Javanese also have fossilized occurrences of *-in-* (e.g. Sundanese *sareng* 'together' → *s-in-areng* 'together with').

These languages are sparsely head marking. Head marking is only found on the possessed noun for varieties of Javanese, Sundanese, and Madurese; or on the verb, shown only in Sundanese with plural actors and third person agreement. Neither the head nor the dependent is marked in attributive adjectival modification or prepositional phrases (see §31.5).

### 31.4.3 Morphological typology of the languages of Java

Javanese, Sundanese, and Madurese are generally considered to be synthetic. However, much more variation of synthesis is revealed upon closer observation of language varieties. Conners (2020) presents one such study on Javanese and related language varieties including Osing, Banten, Banyumasan, and Tengger. He proposes that the latter are actually closer to the analytic languages of Mainland Southeast Asia with primarily isolating morphology (Enfield 2005), while Standard Javanese is less analytic, exhibiting more properties of concatenative morphology. For example, with possessive modification, Conners (2020: 269) shows that Standard Javanese requires concatenation with the suffix *-(n)e* as in *buku*(-**ne**) Singgih* 'Singgih's book', while simple parataxis is possible in Banyumasan (e.g. *buku Singgih*). See also a distinction along the same lines with relativization in (12). Interestingly, Sundanese allows both simple parataxis or the possessor marked by the definite suffix (Müller-Gotama 2001: 36).

The number and form of affixes also varies greatly across language varieties. For example, Standard Javanese has four distinct moods (indicative, propositive, imperative, and subjunctive), with formal variation across voice type, such as the imperative mood *n-jupuk-a* 'AV-pick-IMP' in actor voice vs. *jupuk-en* 'pick-IMP' in passive (Robson 2002: 82). Other varieties such as Tengger only distinguish between three moods, with imperative and subjunctive mood sharing the same suffix (*-a* in actor voice, called 'optative' in Conners 2008).

## 31.5 Word order

The basic word order of the languages of Java is SVO, as in other West Indonesian languages. These languages are also head-initial. In a basic declarative, the verb precedes its object, auxiliaries precede the verb phrase, and sentential negation precedes the verb phrase, as in (8).

Madurese
(8) *Red-mored-da ta? bisa maca buku reya.*
REDUP-student-DEF NEG can AV.read book this
'The students can't read this book.'
(Davies 2010: 274, (106))

The contemporary languages of Java all have distinct markers for predicational, nominal, and imperative negation, as in Table 31.5. Madurese and Sundanese have a negative existential marker in addition to a dedicated existential verb (*badha* in Madurese; *aya* in Sundanese). Some Javanese varieties also have a negative existential marker, such as *gano?*, *geno?* in Malang Javanese, although Standard Javanese does

**Table 31.5** Types of negative forms

| Type of Negation | Javanese | Madurese | Sundanese |
|---|---|---|---|
| Predicational | *ora/ra?/ga?* | *ta?, lo?* | *(hen)teu* |
| Nominal | *dudu* | *banne* | *lain* |
| Imperative | *aja/ojo(?)* | *ja?* | *ulah; (mon)tong* |
| Existential | - | *(t)adha?* | *euweuh* |

not, and uses a periphrastic strategy in which the existential verb *ònò/ene* is negated with predicational negation. Madurese also uses this strategy, but less frequently than the negative existential verb *(t)adhaʔ* (Davies 2010: 156).

Predicational negation can precede or follow most auxiliaries, and the different positions correlate with semantic effects on the scope of negation. Double negation is also possible with some auxiliaries, yielding a positive sentence (see, e.g. Vander Klok 2012: 119 for Javanese; Müller-Gotama 2001: 53 for Sundanese). A Javanese example demonstrates this phenomenon in (9) with the past tense auxiliary *tau*:

Javanese

(9) Context: *Mr. Agus smokes every day.*
*Mas Agus ora tau ora nge-rokoʔ.*
Mr. Agus NEG EXIST.PST NEG AV.smoke
'Mr. Agus did not ever not smoke.'
(Chen et al. 2020: 18)

Within the **noun phrase**, the basic word order in Javanese is [N–Adj–Num–Dem], while in Sundanese and Madurese, the basic nominal word order differs with respect to number as prenominal as [Num–N–Adj–Dem]. Beyond these basic nominal word orders, other word orders are possible concerning numerals, adjectives plus a definite marker, or other types of modifiers such as quantifiers: some have semantic differences, while in other cases, there is apparently no interpretational difference. In general, the noun phrase is understudied.

Each language allows for alternate word orders with numerals, but with different outcomes. In Javanese, while numerals in the default postnominal position have a count interpretation and are bare, numerals in prenominal position can quantify mass nouns and can also occur with a classifier (Ishizuka 2008). Further, prenominal numerals from one to nine are morphologically complex in that they obligatorily occur with a velar nasal linker (e.g. *pitong menit* 'seven.LNK minutes' vs. *pitu* 'seven'). In Sundanese, the unmarked position for numerals is prenominal (e.g. *lima desa* 'five villages'), while a postnominal position is possible and appears to indicate (contrastive) focus (e.g. *desa lima* 'five villages instead of six') (Müller-Gotama 2001: 38). In Madurese, the prenominal position can host cardinal numerals in a full (citation), abbreviated or clitic form; in the clitic form, prenominal numerals seven to nine have a velar nasal linker (e.g. *pettong* 'seven.LNK + HEAD'). There does not seem to be any semantic difference between pre- vs. postnominal position in Madurese with bare numerals, numerals plus *ka-* (indicating a coherent group), Ca-reduplicated numerals, or even numerals plus a measure phrase—unlike in Javanese (Davies 2010: 200–6). However, there are some distributional differences: only prenominal position allows for the clitic form, while only the postnominal position allows for numerals suffixed with *-an* (indicating a collective meaning) in Madurese.

As for quantifiers, in Madurese, *kabbi* 'all' and *bannyaʔ* 'many' can occur in either position with no interpretational difference, for example, *kabbi mored* or *mored kabbi* 'all the students' (Davies 2010: 194–5). Javanese *(sa-)kabeh(-ane)* 'all' also allows either position (Davies and Dresser 2005: 58). For other quantifiers in Madurese, however, semantic distinctions arise based on their position; these include *sakoneʔ* 'a few', *pan-barampan* 'several', and *sabban* 'each; every' (e.g. Davies 2010: 194–9). The syntactic distribution of quantifiers in Sundanese has not been discussed.

All other modifiers must occur postnominally in these languages. Thus, all adjectives are postnominal, although alternative word orders are found in conjunction with the definite clitic in Javanese and Madurese in their attributive use with no interpretational differences. That is, one or two adjectives can either follow the head noun marked with the definite [N=DEF ADJ1 ADJ2] or the noun-phrase complex including one or maximally two adjectives can be marked with this clitic [[N ADJ1 ADJ2]=DEF], as in (10). The definite marker cannot cliticize to phrasal modifiers, such as prepositional phrases, intensified adjectives, or relative clauses (Davies and Dresser 2005: 67–8).

Javanese

(10) *Aku ketemu* ***wong*** *Jawa tuwa=****ne.***
1 meet person Javanese old=DEF
'I met the old Javanese person.' (Ishizuka 2008: 12)

Adjectives can be used attributively or predictively in the languages of Java. One restriction in Javanese is that attributive adjectives cannot be intensified with degree markers such as *banget* 'very' or *tenan* 'very'. If there is more than one adjective, speakers tend to prefer a limit of two attributive adjectives; any additional adjectives are introduced as relative clause markers with an overt relativizer (shown in (14)) (see Davies 1999, 2010 on Madurese; Vander Klok 2013b on Javanese). Adjectives in Javanese follow the semantic ordering restrictions as discussed in Cinque (2010) (see Ishizuka 2008; Vander Klok 2013b).

The order in possessive constructions is [POSSESSUM–DEF POSSESSOR]. In Javanese and Madurese, the possessum can be modified by an adjective to which the definite marker attaches, resulting in the word order [POSSESSUM ADJ–DEF POSSESSOR], parallel to the distribution in (10). Alternatively, the adjectival modifier occurs in a relative clause following the possessive construction, as in (11).

Madurese

(11) a. ***Koceng*** *koros-**sa*** ***Nabun*** *ngeco?* *juko?.*
cat skinny-DEF Nabun AV.steal fish
'Nabun's skinny cat stole the fish.'
(Davies 2010: 215, 159)

b. ***Koceng-nga*** ***Nabun*** *se* *koros* *ngeco?*
cat-DEF Nabun REL skinny AV.steal
*juko?.*
fish
'Nabun's skinny cat stole the fish.'
(Davies 2010: 214, 157)

Relative clauses are marked by a relativizer *nu* in Sundanese; *se* in Madurese (see (14)); and *sing* in Standard Javanese, (12). In Banyumasan, simple parataxis is allowed, (13). Note also that the relativized noun is the object of the relative clause and the verb remains in AV form, whereas in other varieties only subjects can be relativized (and only the verb in PV or passive form would be possible in examples like (12)–(13)); see also §31.6.

Central Javanese

(12) *Buku-ne* ***sing*** *aku* *wis* *maca*
book-DEF REL 1 already AV.read
'the book I read' (Conners 2020: 266)

Banyumasan

(13) *Buku* *nyong* *maca* *wingi*
book 1 AV.read yesterday
'the book I read yesterday' (Conners 2020: 269)

If there is both an attributive adjective and a relative clause modifier, they must follow the head noun in that order, as in (14). A relativizer is optional when the relative clause is adjectival and immediately follows the head noun (15), but obligatory otherwise, such as following the determiner, adjective, (14), or possessors, (11).

Madurese

(14) *Koceng* ***celleng*** ***se*** ***koros*** *juwa* *lo?* *tedhung.*
cat black REL thin that not sleep
'The skinny black cat is not asleep.'
(Davies 2010: 217, 170b)

Preposition phrases must also occur postnominally, and can be introduced in a relative clause.

When the relativizer is non-overt, the question arises whether the relative clause structure is still present. That is, given that a noun plus an adjective seems to have apparent optionality of the relativizer as in Madurese *koceng (se) celleng* 'cat (REL) black', is the adjective always introduced in a relative clause? Vander Klok (2011, 2013b) argues that comparatives in Javanese still have a relative clause structure even when the relativizer is non-overt because of the lack of the clausal interpretation, illustrated in (15).

Javanese

(15) *Tomo* *nulis* ***makala*** ***(sing)*** ***luwih***
Tomo AV.write paper REL more
***dawa*** *tinimbang* *Amina.*
long than Amina
'Tomo wrote a paper that is longer than [the height of] Amina.'
# 'Tomo wrote a longer paper than Amina did.'
(Vander Klok 2013b: 7, 21)

## 31.6 Grammatical relations

Grammatical relations are marked by **voice**—one of the hallmark features of Austronesian languages. Compared to the symmetrical voice of Philippine-type languages such as Tagalog with a four-way distinction, these Indonesian-type languages have a reduced voice system with a two-way distinction between actor voice (AV) and patient voice (PV). As illustrated in (16) for Sundanese, in actor voice, the predicate is marked by a homorganic nasal prefix via nasal substitution, the actor generally precedes the verb, and the theme/patient follows. In patient voice, the predicate is marked by the prefix *di-* and the theme/patient generally precedes the verb whereas the actor follows and is optionally introduced by a preposition. However, as detailed below, the analysis of *di-* as a patient voice marker in the languages of Java is contested with the alternative analysis as a passive.

Sundanese

(16) a. *Ujang* ***n****ajong* *éta* *korsi.* **(najong > ŋ-tajong)**
Ujang AV.kick DEM chair
'Ujang kicked that chair.' (Kurniawan 2013: 15, 7a)

b. *Éta* *korsi* ***di****-tajong* *(ku)* *Ujang.*
DEM chair PV-kick by Ujang
'That chair was (deliberately) kicked by Ujang.'
(Kurniawan 2013: 19, 13a)

Most transitive non-stative verbs take the actor voice prefix, while a small class of verbs do not, such as *gawe* 'to make', *tuku* 'to buy', or *entu?, oleh* 'to get' in Standard Javanese (Robson 2002: 45). Other Javanese varieties vary, such as Malang Javanese *nggawe* 'to make', *nuku* 'to buy' while Tengger has a larger class of unmarked transitive verbs compared to Standard Javanese (Conners 2008: 139). An unmarked class is also noted for Sundanese (Hanafi 2001: 2).

Intransitive verbs are split between those that take the AV prefix and those that do not. This split has been proposed

**Table 31.6** Voice constructions in Javanese, Madurese, and Sundanese

| Language | 'Actor Voice' | 'Patient Voice' or 'Passive' |
|---|---|---|
| Javanese | A (aux) *N*-V Th | Th (aux) A1/2=V |
| | | Th (aux) *di*-V ((Prep) A3) |
| Madurese | A (aux) *N*-V Th | Th (aux) *e*-V ((Prep) A) |
| Sundanese | A (aux) *N*-V Th | Th (aux) *di*-V ((Prep) A3) |
| | | Th (aux) *di*-V *(Prep) A1/2 |

to reflect the distinction between unergatives (underlying agentive subject; AV) and unaccusatives (underlying object; no voice); see Davies (1999) for Javanese; Hanafi (2001) for Sundanese; Davies (2010) for Madurese. Madurese is unique in having two AV forms: most intransitives occur with *a-* such as *a-lako* 'AV-work' and *a-tare* 'AV-dance'; but a limited number take the nasal AV prefix (which occurs primarily with transitives) including *nangdang* (> *tangdang*) 'AV.dance' and *ngabber* (> *abber*) 'AV.fly' (Davies 2010: 254).

While there is agreement among scholars for the analysis of the nasal prefix marking a transitive actor voice construction in these languages, 'patient voice' has been analysed as either transitive (the agent is an argument) or intransitive as a passive construction (the agent is an oblique/adjunct). On the one hand, Indonesian-type languages behave like symmetrical voice languages in that the distribution of 'patient voice' is much higher than passives in English (Davies 2010: 257 for Madurese) and 'patient voice' is marked overtly with a prefix just like actor voice. On the other hand, the realization of the agent in 'patient voice' is optionally or obligatorily introduced by a preposition (see (16b)) or it is simply not realized if the antecedent is recoverable from the discourse, behaving like a canonical passive construction (cf. Jeoung 2020); see Table 31.6. The Indonesian-type languages are of theoretical interest since they show characteristics of both symmetrical voice (where both constructions are basic) as well as an active–passive distinction (where one construction is derived from another).

In Sundanese and Javanese, there is a person distinction between first/second vs. third person, which also feeds into how patient voice vs. passive constructions may be distinguished. In Sundanese, this distinction is realized by whether or not the preposition *ku* is obligatory: for first/second person it is, while for third person *ku* is optional (as in (16b) but in both cases, the prefix *di-* is obligatory; see Hanafi (2001)). In Javanese, the distinction is manifested morphologically by different verb forms and syntactically by different positions of the agent. That is, first/second person agents must be indicated by a pronominal clitic or a kinship term which obligatorily precedes a bare verb stem, while the third person is indicated on the verb by *di-* and the agent is optionally indicated following the verb, illustrated here with Tengger in (17) with the agents underlined. In (17a), the presence of the aspect marker *wis* 'already' shows that the first person clitic indicating the agent strictly precedes the verb and, further, the verb stem must be bare. The restriction of *di-* marked verbs to third person agents is shown in (17b); in the latter, the intended interpretation 'I already planted the fields' is not possible. Because of these distinctions, some Javanese scholars treat the *di-* prefix as a passive construction and the bare form as the unmarked patient voice (e.g. Davies 1995), while others call these as two types of passive (e.g. Sudaryanto 1991; Ogloblin 2005; Wedhawati et al. 2006; Conners 2008).

Tengger

(17) a. *Gaga iku wis* ***ta?****={semprot /*nyemprot}.*
field DEM already 1=spray/AV.spray
'I already sprayed that field.'
(Conners 2008: 153, 15, *gloss adjusted*)

b. *Gaga wis* ***di****-panja {réwang-é / *isun}*
field already PV-plant friend-DEF / 1
'The fields have already been planted by my husband/*me.' (Conners 2008: 150, 12)

Table 31.6 compares the voice constructions in Javanese, Madurese, and Sundanese, showing the different word orders of the agent (A) and theme (Th), optionality or not of the preposition, as well as person restrictions. (*N* refers to the homorganic nasal prefix.) It is notable that only Javanese has a bare form of the verb with a pre-verbal theme, like Indonesian (Chung 1976).

In Madurese, the patient voice/passive constructions are argued to differ across speech levels. 'Familiar' Madurese only has the construction with prefix *e-*, which typically has *patient > verb > (prep) agent* word order and no person restrictions (Davies 2010: 256–9). Jeoung (2017) argues that *alos* 'polite' Madurese also has a construction with a bare verb stem with word order *patient > agent-verb* (parallel to Javanese

**Table 31.7** Two types of applicative suffixes across languages of Java

| Sundanese | Madurese | Central Javanese/ Standard | East Javanese/ Pesisir Lor | West Javanese/ Cirebon | Tengger | Osing |
|---|---|---|---|---|---|---|
| (a) *-keun* | *-agi* | *-aké, -ké*<br>*-aken* (krama) | *-no* [nɔ(ʔ)] | *-aken* [akən]<br>*-nang* | *-en/-na* [na] | *-aken* [(k)aʔən] |
| (b) *-an* | *-e* | *-i* | *-i* | *-i* | *-i* | *-i* |

first/second person patient voice) that familiar Madurese does not have. This discovery suggests that a grammar can differ across speech levels, which in this case, I suggest is due to a syntactic borrowing from Javanese *krama*. Another example is the different use of the imperative that exists between high and low Javanese (Poedjosoedarmo 1968: 61).

Beyond the two-way actor/patient voice distinction in Indonesian-type languages, the arguments of other types of undergoer voices in Philippine-type languages such as locatives, instruments, or beneficiaries are instead incorporated as applicativized arguments through the means of an obligatory suffix. Across the languages of Java, there are two main applicative suffixes, as illustrated in Table 31.7. The suffixes in (a) serve to applicativize benefactives, instrumentals (or displaced themes), and themes. The suffixes in (b) serve primarily to applicativize a locative or goal argument. In Madurese and Javanese, the locative applicative suffix has a different form, *-an*, in certain environments: In Madurese, *-an* is restricted to following the irrealis suffix *-a* (Davis 2010: 106), while in Javanese, *-an* is found in a wider range of grammatical contexts, including with passives formed with *ka-* or *-in-*, adversative passives formed with *ke-*, and with verbs in the subjunctive mood (see Robson 2002; Conners 2008).

To give an example from Madurese, in (18b), the applicativized recipient/goal argument is *Ebuʔ* 'mother' and is the direct object, located adjacent to the verb suffixed with *-e* (compare to (18a)). With this suffix, the theme *paket* 'package' is no longer accessible for syntactic operations like passivization or relativization that target the direct object (Davies 2010: 285). Similarly, the suffix *-agi* in (19b) indicates that *naʔ-kanaʔ* 'children' is the applicativized benefactive argument. The semantic role of the applicativized argument is often dependent on the semantics of the predicate (e.g. Suhandono 1994: 57 for Javanese). Note that in actor voice constructions, applicative suffixes must co-occur with the nasal prefix.

Madurese, 'locative' applicative

(18) a. *Embuk* *ngerem* *paket* ***ka*** ***Ebuʔ.***
elder.sister AV.send package to mother
'Big Sister sent a package to Mother.'

b. *Embuk* *ngerem-**e*** ***Ebuʔ*** *paket.*
elder.sister AV.send-LOC mother package
'Big Sister sent Mother a package.'
(Davies 2010: 283, 1a, b)

Madurese, 'benefactive' applicative

(19) a. *Saʔdiyah* *melle* *permen* ***kaangguy*** ***naʔ-kanaʔ.***
Saʔdiyah AV.buy candy for REDUP-child
'Saʔdiyah bought candy for the children.'

b. *Saʔdiyah* *melle-**yagi*** ***naʔ-kanaʔ*** *permen.*
Saʔdiyah AV.buy-AGI REDUP-child candy
'Saʔdiyah bought the children candy.'
(Davies 2010: 299, 74a, b)

In addition to the applicative function, these suffixes can also be used with a causative function, such as with intransitives in Javanese: *dadi* 'to become' → *ndadèʔaké* 'to make; to appoint' or *mlebu* 'to go in' → *ngleboʔaké* 'to put in, send in' (Robson 2002: 50). How the causative is related to the applicative function is debated (see e.g. Hemmings (2013) and Nurhayani (2014)). Across the languages of Java, these morphemes also have extended semantic uses, such as pluractionality with the locative suffix. Vander Klok and Evans (2022) propose that the semantic extensions arose from features of high transitivity.

A noteworthy feature of Sundanese is the case of double AV marking with benefactive morphology. The benefactive applicative can occur with the prefix *pang-* in combination with the suffix *-keun* (Hanafi 2001: 137; Kurniawan 2013: 19–21). When this construction is in actor voice, both the verb root and the benefactive prefix are marked for actor voice, (20a); in contrast, in patient voice, the verb root is still marked for actor voice, but not the benefactive prefix, (20b):

Sundanese

(20) a. *Bapa* ***mang-maca-keun*** *anak-na* *surat.*
father AV.BEN-AV.read-APPL child-DEF letter
'The father reads the letter to his child.'
(Robins 1968: 357)

b. *Anak-na* **di-pang-***maca*-**keun** *surat* *ku*
child-DEF PV-BEN-AV.read-APPL letter by
*bapa.*
father
'The father reads the letter to his child.'
(Robins 1968: 357)

A final voice type is the so-called 'accidental' or 'adversative' voice marker *ke-. . .(-an)* in Javanese, such as in *keblasu?* 'got lost' and *kegawa* '(accidentally) got taken'. Schwa is lost with vowel initial roots, according to sandhi rules retained from Old Javanese (Conners 2008), as seen in *kodanan* (*ke-udan-an*) 'got rained on'.

As is evident from the above examples, noun phrases are not morphologically marked for case, in contrast to Philippine-type languages (see Liao and Reid, this volume, §24.5.2 on Northern Philippine languages, and Kaufmann, this volume, §25.4.4.3 on Central and Southern Philippine languages). These languages also have no obligatory verbal/predicational agreement. Only plural is optionally marked, agreeing with a plural actor, by an auxiliary *padha* in Javanese (Hayward 1998), or by the infix *-ar-/-al-* in Sundanese (Müller-Gotama 2001: 20–1), see (21). In Madurese, the adverbs *saleng* and *pateng* optionally occur with plural subjects, and they also seem to imply pluractionality (Davies 2010: 428). These markers are independent of voice marking.

Sundanese
(21) *Masarakat* *keur* *n-***ar***-éang-an* *kapal* *nu*
community PROG AV-PL-seek-ITER plane REL
*ragrag* *téa.*
fall PART
'The people are searching for the falling plane.'
(Kurniawan and Davies 2015: 6, 20)

Sundanese additionally has optional third person subject agreement, realized by the suffix *-eun*, which only occurs with a limited set of predicates including *nyaho* 'know', *haying* 'want', *poho* 'forget', or *bisa* 'capable' (Kurniawan and Davies 2015: 7).

The voice system has consequences for other grammatical constructions in these languages, such as relativization and question formation. Keenan and Comrie (1977) has noted that for many Austronesian languages such grammatical processes are restricted to the subject. This also holds for Sundanese, where relativization is restricted to subjects and possessors. Thus, in order to relativize the object of a clause, it must first be promoted to subject position with passivization. Without this step, relativization is ungrammatical:

Sundanese
(22) a. *Buku-buku* *nu* *kudu* *di-jual*
book-REDUP REL must PASS-sell
'books that must be sold'
(Müller-Gotama 2001: 33, 45)

b.* *Buku-buku* *nu* *kudu* *nga-jual*
book-REDUP REL must AV-sell
('books that I/you/etc. must sell')
(Müller-Gotama 2001: 33, 46)

In some varieties of Javanese such as Paciran Javanese, this restriction also holds, while in others, object extraction is possible, such as in Banyumasan (see (13); see also Cole et al. 1999; Conners 2020).

## 31.7 Tense, aspect, modality, and evidentiality

In the languages of Java, the predicate does not carry any overt marking of tense, aspect, modality, or evidentiality. For instance, the predicate in (23) can have past, present, or future reference time. To indicate these notions, adverbs or auxiliaries optionally modify the predicate.

Sundanese
(23) *Ujang* *neunggeul* *kuring.*
Ujang AV.hit 1
'Ujang hit/hits/will hit me.'
(Kurniawan and Davies 2015: 1, 1a)

A plausible hypothesis is that these languages are tenseless. However, recent research on Javanese proposes that the auxiliary *tau*, which has dominant experiential readings as in (24), is in fact a past tense marker (Chen et al. 2020), and not an aspectual marker such as an experiential or perfect aspect (Dahl 1985).

Javanese
(24) *Sopo* *sing* ***tau*** *munggah* *gunung?*
who REL EXIST.PST AV.ascend mountain
'Who has ever climbed a mountain?'
(Chen et al. 2020: 2)

To overtly indicate a future reference time, Madurese, Sundanese, and Central Javanese all have the future auxiliary *bakal*. Sundanese also uses *baris* 'FUT', *(a/é)rék* 'FUT; will', as well as a dedicated negative future marker, *moal* 'will.not' (Kurniawan 2013: 358). In Central Javanese, the future marker *arep* seems to additionally express volitionality, suggested by the gloss 'want, will' (Robson 2002: 54). Many dialects have their own future markers (see e.g. (1) for Javanese).

The languages of Java do not seem to have dedicated perfective or imperfective aspect markers, although some markers express a subset of the readings associated with perfective vs. imperfective. Markers indicating progressive or inceptive aspect are found in Javanese (e.g. *lagi* 'PROG', *mentas/entas/tas* 'just now', *wae/bae* 'just') or Madurese (e.g. *buru* 'just'). Under the perfective umbrella, telicity is also a common marker in these languages: *(bu)bar* 'finish', *rampung* 'finish' in Standard Javanese or *mare* 'finish' in Madurese. Sundanese *geus* is glossed as perfective (Müller-Gotama 2001).

A prominent feature of these languages in the aspectual domain is that they have grammaticalized markers indicating phasal polarity, expressing 'already' and 'still' (see also Veselinova, Asplund, and Vander Klok, this volume, §52.2.1 and §52.2.3 for a wider typological perspective). Vander Klok and Matthewson (2015) provide diagnostics to tease apart the perfect aspect from an analysis of 'already', and analyse Javanese *wis* as 'already' (previously described as a past tense, perfect, or perfective). Phasal polarity markers interact with negation as dual pairs, where the external negation of one is truth-conditionally equivalent to the internal negation of the other (e.g. Löbner 1989). The external negation of 'still' is transparently encoded in both Madurese (*la loʔ* '[already NEG] > no longer') and Javanese (*wis ora* '[already NEG] > no longer'), lexically expressed by the internal negation of 'already'. Additionally, the external negation of 'already' is transparently encoded in Madurese, lexically expressed by the internal negation of 'still' (having *giʔ+taʔ* or *giʔ+loʔ* '[still.NEG] > not yet'), whereas Javanese has a dedicated word *durung* 'not.yet'.

Another prominent feature of these languages is their rich number of grammaticalized modal expressions. Modal markers vary across languages in the grammatical strategies used to indicate possibility or necessity, different grades of necessity and possibility, or whether the type of modality is relative to the law (e.g. deontic), or to someone's knowledge (e.g. epistemic), or other types.

In Javanese, most modals lexically specify for modal force (possibility or necessity) as well as the type of modality. In the Paciran Javanese dialect, these include *paleng* 'maybe', an epistemic possibility modal; *mesthi* 'must', an epistemic necessity modal; and *oleh* 'may', a deontic possibility modal. The modals *iso* 'can' and *kudu* 'have to' are lexically specified for modal force, but not for the type of modality: *iso* 'can' allows for ability and goal-oriented types of modality, and *kudu* 'have to' allows for all types of root modality (Vander Klok 2013a). Madurese and Sundanese probably have similar typological profiles of their modal system, but their semantics has not been formally studied. The languages of Java thus contrast with most Indo-European languages in which modal expressions only lexically specify for force, such as *must* in English, (e.g. Palmer 2001). To illustrate, Javanese *mesthi* 'must', which lexically specifies for necessity force, is only compatible in an epistemic context, (25a),[11] but not in a deontic context, (25b)[12] (while the free translation suggests that English *must* is compatible with both types of modality).

Javanese

(25) a. Context: *'They can't be hiding in the box', says the policeman. 'It's too small. And they can't be hiding under the bed. It's too low. . . .'*

*cah* *loro* *iku* *{**mesthi** /* *#kudu}* *sengidan*
child two DEM EPIS.NEC ROOT.NEC hide
*neʔ* *ngguri-ne* *selambu.*
at behind-DEF curtain
'Those two kids must be hiding behind the curtain!' (Vander Klok 2013a: 353, 9)

b. Context: *A while later, Mary recovers from her cold. Her friends come over and ask her to come play outside. Mary says, 'Sorry, I can't come out to play. . .'.*

*PR-ku* *<uw>akeh* *yo*
homework-my <INTNS>many yes
*{kudu/* ***#mesthi}*** *taʔ=kerjaʔ-no.*
ROOT.NEC EPIS.NEC 1=work-APPL
'I have so much homework, I must work on it!' (Vander Klok 2013a: 353, 10)

Javanese also brings to light a different way to express the type of modal strength indicating 'weak necessity', in contrast to a number of Indo-European languages which use the same morphology as for counterfactuality (von Fintel and Iatridou 2008). In Javanese, weak necessity is transparently composed of a necessity modal plus the suffix *-(n)e* and derives an adverb (Vander Klok and Hohaus 2020): these include *kudu-ne* 'ought' and *mesthi-ne* 'should'. This strategy seems to also be used in Madurese with the adverb *saongguna* 'apparently', composed of the root *onggu* 'definite' plus the prefix *sa-* and the definite suffix (Davies 2010: 393). While the suffix has the same form as the present-day definite marker in these languages, it is not obvious from a semantic perspective whether this is the same suffix or simply homophonous. The strategy of using the suffix *-(n)e* in Javanese can also derive adverbs expressing evidentiality. Examples from Paciran Javanese are *ketoʔ-e* 'apparently', *koyoʔ-e* 'likely', *wataʔ-e* 'characteristically', *jeke-ne* 'based.on.my.thinking', and *bonaʔ-e* 'apparently' (Vander Klok 2012).

## 31.8 Multipredicate constructions

Multipredicate constructions, defined as "constructions which involve two or more phonologically independent predicates within a single clause" (Himmelmann 2005a: 159), seem to be widely attested in the Javanic languages but

[11] Context from the storyboard 'On the Lam' (TFS Working Group 2011a).

[12] Context from the storyboard 'Sick Girl' (TFS Working Group 2011b).

remain understudied. One of the main concerns of this research is the syntactic size of the second predicate within a single clause. While these languages do not have serial verb constructions, they do have a rich number of TAM auxiliaries which can co-occur, some only in a strict relative order, while other markers allow for different orders, some with interpretational differences, and others, seemingly not; see Vander Klok (2012, 2015) for Paciran and Standard Javanese, Cole et al. (2008) for Peranakan Javanese, and Davies (2010) for Madurese. Cole et al. (2008) propose that some TAM markers in Peranakan Javanese (*pernah* 'PERF', *isa* 'can', and *gelem* 'want') are more predicate-like than others and can occur in multipredicate constructions.

## 31.9 Question constructions

In forming content/informational questions, the languages of Java show an argument~adjunct asymmetry. Argument questions are formed wherein the question word remains *in-situ* (i.e. in the canonical position of the argument) or by using a cleft construction, while the question word in adjunct questions can occur sentence-initially or finally, as illustrated by Madurese in (26). In a cleft construction, the question word is the predicate and the headless relative clause is the NP subject (e.g. Paul 2001). Further, the clefted question word corresponds to the subject (or possessor) of the relative clause; adjunct questions can never be formed using a cleft.

Madurese

(26) a. *Siti maca* ***apa?***
Siti AV.read what
'What did Siti read?' (Davies 2003: 239)

b. ***Apa*** *se e-baca Siti?*
what REL OV-read Siti
'What did Siti read?/What is it that was read by Siti?' (Davies 2003: 239)

c. *[**Arapa**] Ita me? mole, [**arapa**]?*
why Ita EMPH go.home why
'Why did Ita go home? (Davies 2010: 449–50)

In embedded clauses, argument questions have three different strategies according to the position of the question word, as illustrated in (27) with Sundanese: *in-situ*, in its canonical position in the embedded clause; at the beginning of the embedded clause where the embedded clause is a cleft construction; or sentence-initially. See Davies and Kurniawan (2013) on Sundanese, and Davies (2003, 2010) on Madurese.

Sundanese

(27) a. *Ali ng-anggap [Hasan kakara meuli* ***mobil naon*** *]?*
Ali AV-assume Hasan recently AV.buy car what
'What car did Ali assume Hasan had recently bought?'

b. *Ali ng-anggap [**mobil naon** nu kakara di-beuli ku Hasan]?*
Ali AV-assume car what REL recently PV-buy by Hasan
'What car did Ali assume Hasan had recently bought?'

c. ***Mobil naon*** *nu di-anggap ku Ali [(nu) kakara di-beuli ku Hasan]?*
car what REL PV-assume by Ali REL recently PV-buy by Hasan
'What car did Ali assume Hasan had recently bought?' (Davies and Kurniawan 2013: 111)

Polar questions in Javanese, Sundanese, and Madurese are formed using all three typologically attested strategies as well as combinations thereof: intonation, word order, and particles. First, the intonation of polar questions for Sundanese and Madurese is described as rising at the end of a declarative sentence (Müller-Gotama 2001: 54; Davies 2010: 441). Javanese is reported to have a rise–fall–rise pitch contour, where the first rise is optional and the fall occurs at the left edge of the final syllable before rising at the right edge boundary (Rahyono 2007; Vander Klok 2017).

Second, 'subject–auxiliary inversion' is possible with a subset of auxiliaries in Javanese to form polar questions (Cole et al. 2008). In Paciran Javanese, these licit auxiliaries include *tau* 'EXIST.PST', *iso* 'CIRC.POS', *oleh* 'DEON.POS'; while illicit auxiliaries are *ape* 'FUT', *wis* 'already', *lagek* 'PROG', and *kudu* 'ROOT.NEC' (Vander Klok 2015).

Paciran Javanese

(28) ***Tau*** *ca? Khuluq bel-ajar no? Kanada?*
EXIST.PST Mr. Khuluq INTR-learn at Canada
'Did Mr. Khuluq once study in Canada?'
(Vander Klok 2015: 150, 5)

Third, all languages of Java can use affirmative/negative particles to form polar questions, and all have one particle which has the same form as a content question word; in Javanese *apa/opo* and Madurese *apa* are used, which have the same form as 'what', while in Sundanese *naha* is used, which has the same form as 'why'. The latter particles occur sentence-initially (unless it is preceded by a topicalized or focused constituent, which is typically a subject or sentence-level adverb):

Sundanese

(29) a. ***Naha*** *anjeun* *geus* *pernah* *ngasa-an*
Q you PERF ever AV.taste-DER
*rujak* *petis?*
rujak petis
'Have you ever tried *rujak petis?*'

b. *Isukan* *mah* ***naha*** *maneh* *rek* *balik?*
tomorrow FOC Q you will go.home
'Tomorrow, will you go home?'
(Müller-Gotama 2001: 54)

Beyond question word and affirmative/negative particles, Madurese has a second position clitic *baʔ* forming polar questions, which can co-occur with question words for some speakers (Davies 2010: 465). Javanese also uses the particle *ta*, and some East Javanese varieties use *toh* or *leh*. Vander Klok (2017) describes *toh* as a focus particle which can indicate different focus depending on its syntactic position: in sentence-final position, it indicates broad focus across the whole sentence or narrow focus on the final constituent. Elsewhere, it indicates narrow focus on the constituent it follows: in (30), *toh* has narrow focus either on the object or the verb phrase.

Paciran Javanese

(30) *Tutus* *tuku* *rujaʔ* ***toh*** *ndeʔ* *pasar?*
Tutus buy k.o.salad FOC at market
'Was it ***rujaʔ*** that Tutus bought at the market?'
'Was it **buying *rujaʔ*** that Tutus did at the market?'
(Vander Klok 2017: 21, 39)

## 31.10 Future outlook

The languages of Java have benefitted from a rich history of scholarly attention to many grammatical phenomena including vowel harmony and control in Madurese, nasal spreading and complementation in Sundanese, or the tense/lax contrast in stops and modality in Javanese. But much remains to be investigated, such as TAM markers, discourse particles, quantifiers, or their prosodic system. Beyond the standard varieties, dialects are still understudied. Linguistic research and further documentation of these languages and their dialects is all the more important considering that Indonesian language policy has put all indigenous languages under pressure, even those with many speakers like Javanese, Sundanese, and Madurese (e.g. Zentz 2015b; Abtahian et al. 2016).

## Acknowledgements

Thank you to Thomas J. Conners, Marc Garellek, Tom Hoogervorst, and Nurenzia Yannuar for fruitful discussion, as well as the editors Sander Adelaar and Antoinette Schapper for helpful and detailed comments. Any errors are my own.

CHAPTER 32

# Balinese, Sasak, and Sumbawa

ASAKO SHIOHARA AND I WAYAN ARKA

## 32.1 Introduction

This chapter covers Balinese, Sasak, and Sumbawa. Balinese has approximately 3,300,000 speakers inhabiting the Island of Bali and Nusa Penida, but also western Lombok and Balinese transmigration sites in Sumatra and Sulawesi. Sasak has 2,100,000 speakers on the island of Lombok, and Sumbawa has 300,000 speakers in the western part of Sumbawa. Map 32.1 show the locations in which these languages are spoken.

It is generally accepted that these languages form a distinct subgroup within Malayo-Polynesian, as shown in Esser (1938); Dyen (1965a, 1982); and Mbete (1990), who labels the group "Bali-Sasak-Sumbawa" (henceforth BSS). However, there is no consensus about the relation of BSS to other Malayo-Polynesian languages (see Adelaar, this volume, §10.7).

All three languages exhibit varying degrees of dialectal variation. Beginning with Balinese, dialects are primarily divided into two large groups called Plains Balinese and Aga (Mountain) Balinese, with the latter retaining older features of Balinese, such as word-medial *h*, word-final *a*, and Austronesian first and second pronouns (*aku* and *engko*) (Sedeng 2007; Arka and Sedeng 2018: 140–1). Plains Balinese has lost almost all Austronesian pronouns, except the third person *ia*. In addition, Both Mountain and Plains Balinese pronouns no longer show number distinction and clusivity. Regarding Sumbawa, Mahsun (1999) distinguishes four dialects, which primarily differ on phonological and lexical grounds: Sumbawa Besar, Tongo, Taliwang, and Jereweh. Finally, Sasak exhibits the greatest dialectal variation (Teeuw 1951, 1958; Jacq 1998) and is traditionally divided into five dialects: (i) Ngeno-Ngené (Eastern and Western Lombok); (ii) Ngeto-Ngeté (Eastern Lombok); (iii) Meno-Mené; (iv) Meriaq-Meriku (Central and Southern Lombok); and (v) Kuto-Kuté (Northwest and Northern Lombok). Relatively recent works, such as Austin (2001, 2004, 2014); Asikin-Garmager (2017); and Shibatani (2008), account for its dialectal variation based on morphosyntax. Notable variations include number and clusivity in pronouns. Number has been lost in the second and third persons across all Sasak varieties, but it is retained in the first person in Mataram Ngeno-Ngené dialect, in which clusivity (*kami* vs. *ite*) is also retained. Other dialects, such as Meriaq-Meriku, have lost clusivity, and use the inclusive form *ite* for the general plural.

In this chapter, the following dialects will constitute the main focus of the ensuing comparative discussion: the Plain dialect in Balinese (following Kersten 1984; Barber 1977; Clynes 1995b; Artawa 1994; and Arka 2003b); the Ngeno-Ngené and Meno-Mené dialects in Sasak (NN-Sasak and MM-Sasak hereafter); and finally, the Sumbawa Besar dialect for Sumbawa (following Shiohara 2006, 2013a, b; and Riester and Shiohara 2018).

## 32.2 Phonology

### 32.2.1 Sound inventory

The BSS languages exhibit almost identical phoneme inventories, and these are, in turn, broadly similar to those of other languages of western Indonesia.[1] A crucial point of difference lies in their consonant inventories (e.g. eighteen in Balinese and Sumbawa, nineteen in Sasak), which are smaller compared to neighbouring languages to the west, such as Madurese or Javanese (each with twenty-six consonants). The BSS languages have four pairs of voiced and voiceless stops, /p, b/, /t, d/, /c, j/, and /k, g/; four nasals homorganic to these stops, /m, n, ɲ, ŋ/; two fricatives, alveolar /s/ and glottal /h/; two liquids, /l/ and /r/; and two glides, /w/ and /y/. The differences among these languages are briefly captured by the following features:

a) The apical stops, /d/ and /t/, are realized as retroflexes in some dialects of Balinese, but not in Sasak and Sumbawa.
b) The glottal stop [ʔ] is phonemic in Sasak (Clynes 1995c: 512) and Sumbawa, but not in Balinese.

[1] The notation conventions in this chapter are as follows: The International Phonetic Alphabet (IPA) is employed in section 32.2, whereas starting from section 32.3, the prevalent orthography based on Indonesian conventions is primarily employed for both Balinese and Sumbawa. As for Sasak, the original source notation is employed throughout this chapter.

Asako Shiohara and I Wayan Arka, *Balinese, Sasak, and Sumbawa*. In: *The Oxford Guide to the Malayo-Polynesian Languages of Southeast Asia*. Edited by: Alexander Adelaar and Antoinette Schapper, Oxford University Press. © Asako Shiohara and I Wayan Arka (2024). DOI: 10.1093/oso/9780198807353.003.0032

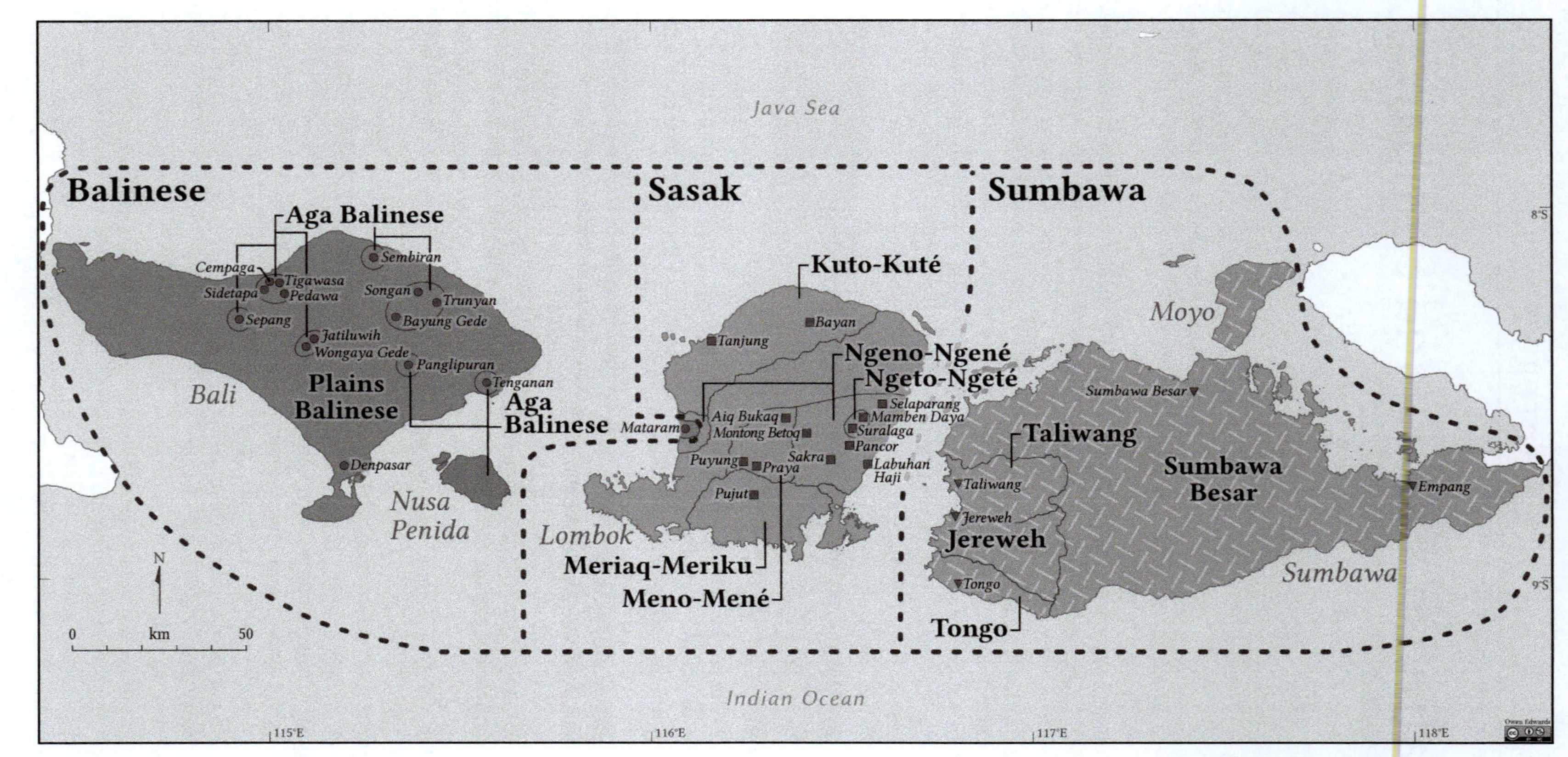


**Map 32.1** The languages of Bali, Lombok and Sumbawa.

c) Balinese has six vowels (/i/, /e/, /ə/, /a/, /o/, /u/) while Sumbawa has eight, including split-middle vowels (/i/, /e/, /ɛ/, /ə/, /a/, /ɔ/, /o/, /u/), where parenthesized forms represent their orthographic representation. Minimal pairs for the mid-close and mid-open vowels in Sumbawa include *mɛ* 'rice' vs. *me* 'which' and *tɔ* 'know' vs. *to* 'this'.

There is no solid consensus on the Sasak vowel inventory based on previous studies, at least partly because of its dialectal variation (see Teeuw 1951; Jacq 1998; Asikin-Garmager 2017).

### 32.2.2 Syllable structure and phonotactics

All BSS languages have the syllable structure (C)(L)V(C), where L stands for a liquid, and V alone is obligatory. Although L does not occur in monosyllabic roots in Balinese and Sasak (Clynes 1995b: 499), it does occur in Sumbawa (e.g. *krɛ* 'whittle', *blɛ* 'snake'). In syllable-initial positions, all consonants in BSS may occur except /h/ and /ʔ/. Note that, as mentioned above, /ʔ/ is phonemic only in Sasak. In syllable-final position, none of the BSS languages have palatals or semivowels. Further, voiced stops do not occur syllable-finally in Sasak and Sumbawa; the latter also does not have /h/ in final position.

The majority of root morphemes are disyllabic with the preferred structures CVCV(C) and CVNCV(C), where N stands for a nasal which is homorganic to a following oral stop, for example, *bambaŋ* 'hole' in Balinese, *lantar* 'clash into' in Sumbawa. Moreover, disyllabic morphemes of the structure (C)VV(C) are common. All these syllabic possibilities can be summed up in the formula: $[(C_1)(L)V_1(N)(C_2)(L)(V_2)(C_3)]$, where only $V_1$ is obligatory.

A second possible disyllabic structure, which is observed in Balinese and Sasak, is a reduplicated $C_1(L)V_1C_2$ sequence, where L, if any, may only occur in the first syllable, such as *sluksuk* 'weave in and out of a crowd' in Balinese and *blukbuk* 'roast; burn' in Sasak (Clynes 1995b: 500, 1995c: 514).

Acceptable intervocalic consonant clusters are thus usually either NC or NCL, for example, *paŋkriŋ* 'cage' in Balinese. However, in a reduplicated sequence in Balinese and Sasak, any consonants that are acceptable in the syllable-final position and the syllable-initial position can cluster medially, for example, *kis~kis* 'thresh' in Sasak (Clynes 1995b: 500, 1995c: 514).

### 32.2.3 Stress

In BSS languages, stress falls by default on the last syllable of a word, see the following example in which the default stress is represented in bold, for example, *mla**li*** 'go sightseeing' (Balinese). Derivational suffixes attract stress by shifting the stress to the right, for example, *be**li*** 'buy' → *beli-**aŋ*** [buy-APPL] 'buy for' (Balinese). Further, clitics do not typically attract stress, for example, *ba**le*** 'building' → *ba**le**=(n)e* [building=DEF] 'the building' (Balinese). However, it is worthwhile noting that clitics in BSS languages may vary in terms of their prosodic properties since certain clitics, such as the Balinese third person actor *=a/-a*, may have been morphologicalized and grammaticalized, to such a point that they function doubly as a suffix and a clitic (see Arka 2008).

Monosyllabic functional words often form a phonological word with their semantic host (e.g. *ka=tu**kad*** [to=river] 'to (the) river' in Balinese, *kanak=**nó*** [child=that] 'that child' in Sasak (Austin 2004: 6), *ka=ku=da**taŋ*** [PST=1SG=come] 'I came' in Sumbawa). In Sumbawa, when an adjective modifies the head noun, the NP always forms a phonological unit with only one (primary) stress, which falls on the last syllable of the whole prosodic phrase (e.g. *lamong=mi**ra*** 'red clothes', *tau=ba**loŋ*** 'good person'). However, when the modifying element is a noun, both the head noun and the modifier have their own primary stress (e.g. *ba**le** ba**tu*** 'stone houser') (Shiohara 2006: 18ff).

Sumbawa has a small set of pairs of homonymous words, which are distinguished only by their prosodic property of stress, with one form having heavier stress than the other. Hence, strong(er) stress in these pairs of words distinguishes lexical meaning. This (heavy) lexical stress is indicated by the word-final high vertical line (ˈ) (e.g. *si**oŋ*** 'fry without oil'/*si**oŋ**ˈ* NEG and *sa**pu*** 'bloom'/*sa**pu**ˈ* 'male hair ornament'). The heavy stress in Sumbawa can be functionally derivational, such as in the derivation of denominal verbs (e.g. *jagir* 'fist' → *jagirˈ* 'to punch' and *kubir* 'tomb' → *kubirˈ* 'to bury').

### 32.2.4 Phonology–morphosyntax interface

While phonology, morphology, and syntax are distinct domains in grammar, they are interconnected in a complex and non-trivial way. The following section provides examples that demonstrate the interfaces of these domains, whose patterns and underlying principles are actually not unique to BSS languages. In the interest of space, only one affix is discussed here: the actor voice prefix N- 'AV', which is a widespread Austronesian feature. The allomorphy of N- is discussed first to show the complex interplay of phonology with other domains in the grammars of BSS languages. Its morpholexical and morphosyntactic significance in BSS languages is discussed in further detail in §32.3.2 and §32.4.4.

The realization of the prefix N- involves homorganic nasal assimilation, possibly with segment substitution of the stem (e.g. *tulis* → *nulis* 'N-write' (Balinese)). The absence of nasal segment substitution provides evidence for the complex interaction of morphophonology, morphosyntax, and pragmatics. Phonologically, the absence of the segment substitution is conditioned by the prosodic structure of the base, namely the number of syllables forming the stem: a monosyllabic stem does not allow the nasal segment substitution. In this case, N- is realized in its default form [ŋ-] typically with a schwa epenthesis [ŋə] (e.g. *bel* → *ŋəbel* (not **mel*) 'to produce car.horn' and *gas* → *ŋəgas* (not **ŋas*) 'to accelerate' (Balinese)).

Similarly, the retention of the initial segment of the stem in Sasak reveals an important interface between phonology, morphosyntax, and discourse pragmatics. This is exemplified in (1) where the verb is part of a pragmatically marked predicate focus structure in Sasak. In this structure, the verb is morphologically marked by N- and is also assigned focus, which is structurally marked by verb fronting to a sentence-initial position. Crucially, the initial segment of the base is retained (i.e. there is no nasal substitution), irrespective of the voice feature of the initial segment. Hence, the base *pantók* 'hit', which would typically become ***m**antok* 'AV.hit' (when it is not focused), becomes *m**p**antok* in this predicate focus construction.

Sasak

(1) *m-pantòk=nei* *begang* *inó* *(isiʔ* *lóʔ* *Musi)*
PRED.FOC-hit=3 rat that (by ART.M Mus)
'Mus HIT the rat (he finally got it!)' (emphasis added) (Asikin-Garmager 2017: 29)

The existence and distribution of doublets like ***m**antok/m**p**antok* in Sasak highlights constraint interactions in the morphophonology–syntax–pragmatics interface. While these two phonological rules (*N* substitution and *N* accretion) compete with each other (among other rules), only the latter form is used in the predicate focus construction. This kind of constraint interaction and competition, which is nicely captured by Optimality Theory (McCarthy 2001; Sells 2006), reveals the nature and role of prominence in the overall grammar (Latrouite 2011). In other terms, when constraints interact, they show their relative significance: one outweighs another with a less prominent constraint possibly violable for the satisfaction of a higher-ranked constraint. In the case of Sasak, nasal substitution does not apply even though its phonological condition is met, because its violation is necessary (and acceptable) to satisfy a higher-ranked constraint of focus marking.

Another case showing the phonology–morphosyntax interface is the allomorphic realization of what Asikin-Garmager (2017: 37) calls antipassive marking in Sasak. The surface form is the output of the N- prefixation with partial *Cə*-reduplication (e.g. *tiup* → *niup* → *nəniup* 'blow'). This pattern illustrates the classic idea that phonological rules are ordered in their application (i.e. N substitution comes before *Cə*-reduplication). For additional discussion on reduplication, refer to §32.3.3.

## 32.3 Morphology

BSS languages are agglutinative with a relatively small number of affixes, especially Sumbawa, which only exhibits prefixes. However, Sumbawa, like its neighbouring Austronesian languages in western Flores and Sumba, has developed clitics (see §32.4.2). In this section, morphological features of BSS languages are highlighted in the context of shared Austronesian traits and related issues. The issue of word class as a category is considered first before a discussion of derivational affixes and reduplication.

### 32.3.1 Roots and word class

There has been a debate whether bare forms (or roots) in Austronesian languages have grammatical categories. Verhaar (1984a, b); and Himmelmann (2005a: 129), among others, adopt the 'precategorial' analysis for bound forms, arguing that Indonesian roots such as *-ajar* do not belong to a particular grammatical category or word class. These morphemes lack category information, rendering them absent in syntax without further affixation or without being outside a compound structure. Based on evidence from Riau Indonesian and Jakarta Indonesian, Gil (2001, 2009a, 2010a) argues for 'monocategoriality' and claims that all open lexical classes in Indonesian are indistinguishable for their parts of speech. Recent studies by Yoder (2010) reassess this monocategoriality analysis.

As for morphological level classification, Clynes (2010) argues against a precategorial analysis for bound roots. He shows that there is good evidence (e.g. from nominalization with *-an*) that bound roots in Balinese like *-tegak* 'sit' and -*siram* 'bathe (high register)' are verbal. The evidence for the verbal category of these bound roots comes from their morphosyntactic behaviour: just like free verbal roots, like *pules* 'sleep', the bound roots receive the same affixation when derived to become nouns (e.g. *tegak-an* 'the place to sit on' and *pules-an* 'the place to sleep on'). Other evidence comes from recent studies that apply the three criteria (equivalent combinatorics, compositionality, and bidirectionality) proposed by Evans and Osada (2005). Mistica et al. (2011) is one such study, undertaking a corpus-based quantitative analysis of different root/stem combinations to demonstrate the distinction between verbs and nouns based on morphological features.

### 32.3.2 Derivational morphology

BSS morphology is mainly derivational and mostly associated with the formation of verbs and nouns. The following three subsections discuss verbal morphology, and revolve around issues associated with transitivity, voice marking, and semantically related properties, such as even conception and agentivity/patientivity.

#### 32.3.2.1 *Actor-oriented middle-related intransitivizing morphology*

BSS languages have reflexes of PMP *maR-, an actor-oriented middle-related marker. It is realized as *ma-* in Balinese, *bə(r)-* in Sasak, and *bar-* in Sumbawa.[2] Reflexes of *maR- express meanings which are the hallmarks of the middle (MID) voice. These meanings are typically associated with the conception of the 'unitary' of events, which include such meanings as natural reciprocal, reflexive, or self-instigated actions, like grooming, body posture, and manner of motion (Klaiman 1992; Kemmer 1993; Shibatani and Artawa 2007; Arka 2003b). Examples of the middle voice *ma-* in Balinese are evident from the verbal roots such as *ma-siat* 'MID-fight (reciprocal)', *ma-sugi* 'MID-wash: wash self's face (reflexive)', *ma-jujuk* 'MID-stand (body posture)', *ma-suah* 'MID-comb=comb own hair (grooming)', and *ma-jalan* 'MID-walk (manner of motion).

The middle prefix derives an intransitive verb. It may highlight the self-instigating and actor-oriented property of the root, which gives rise to the backgrounding, demotion, or suppression of the patient-like participant. It therefore has a valency-decreasing effect, much like an antipassive, and possibly takes a bound or precategorial root. Examples of this include *-takon* 'ask' → *ma-takon* 'MID-ask' (Balinese), and *garu'* 'disturb' → *ba-garu'* 'make a disturbance' (Sumbawa).

#### 32.3.2.2 *Patient-oriented intransitivizing morphology*

Sasak and Sumbawa have a prefix deriving potentive intransitive verbs. It denotes events that involve an agent not in full control of the action (Himmelmann 2005a: 165ff.). This is exemplified by *kə(r)-* in Sasak (e.g. *kə-səkuʔ* 'hiccough'). The counterparts in Sumbawa are *ka(N)-* (N = homorganic nasal substitution) and *gəN-* (N = homorganic nasal accretion) (e.g. *ka-ningin* '(animates) feel cold' (< *dingin* '(the climate or an entity is) cold'); *gəm=panas* '(animates) feel hot' (< *panas* '(the climate of an entity is) hot')). These prefixes formally contain an element of *ka* and invoke adversative passive-like meaning, and they appear to be related to the PMP adversative passive *ke- -an. The *ka-* formative also appears related to the PAN stative marker *ka-, which contrasts against the middle (actor-oriented) *ma(R)-. This contrast is shown in the following Balinese phrases: *ke-clekut-an* 'hiccough uncontrollably' vs. *ma-clekut-an* 'hiccough controllably'.

It should be noted that Balinese and Sasak also have passive prefixes (without the suffix *-an)*, *ka-* and *te-* respectively. They productively derive passive verbs from transitive stems. In these passives, the underlying P argument becomes the derived S argument. The Balinese passive *ka-* carries no adversative meaning. It is unclear whether it originated from the same source as *ke-* in its *ke- -an* counterpart in Balinese, or *kə(r)-* in Sasak and *ka(N)-* in Sumbawa. Finally, Sasak *te-* appears to be a cognate of the Indonesian passive *ter-*, which both originate from PAN *taR- and express 'accidental or uncontrolled action'.

#### 32.3.2.3 *Transitivizing causative/applicative affixes*

Balinese and NN-Sasak share two transitivizing suffixes, *-ang* and *-in*, which have no counterparts in Sumbawa. Formally, *-ang* is invariable across Balinese dialects, but it varies in Sasak dialects, with MM-Sasak shortened forms showing fusion with an incorporated object clitic (e.g. *-angk* 'APPL.1SG' and *-at* ~ *-ant* 'APPL.1PL') (Austin 2001: 69). While Balinese and Sasak *-ang/-in* suffixes are reflexes of the PMP undergoer benefactive and locative applicatives, *-akən and *-i respectively, *-in* is unusual in that the locative suffix is *-in* rather than *-i* as found in other Western Indonesian languages (Ross 2002b: 466). Importantly, both *-in* and *-ang* are polysemous, functioning as causative and applicative suffixes. They function as causatives when affixed to patientive intransitive stems (including nominal stems), and as applicative suffixes when affixed to agentive stems (e.g. *ulung* 'fall' → *ulung-ang* 'fall-CAUS; drop' vs. *ngeling* 'cry' → *ngelingang* 'cry-APPL; cry for' (Balinese)) (Clynes 1995b: 503, 516; Arka 2003b). Such polysemy is common cross-linguistically in Western Indonesian languages, for example, in Indonesian (Arka et al. 2009; Arka and Yannuar 2016) and Madurese (Davies 2010).

However, with transitive stems, *-ang* and *-in* typically result in applicativization. Causativization is also possible only with restricted stems with specific coercive causative meaning. For example, the transitive stem *jemak* 'take' gives rise to the applicative *jemak-ang* 'X take Y for Z' and *jemak-in* 'X takes Y from Z'; these verbs cannot mean 'X makes Z take Y'. A small set of transitive stems allowing causativization include *diman* 'kiss' for *-ang*, deriving *diman-ang* and meaning 'X makes Y kiss Z coercively (e.g. holding body/his head

[2] Sumbawa *bar-* has four allomorphs: *barə-* is used with mono-syllabic bases (e.g. *tə'* 'know something (vt)' → *barə-tə'* 'know (vi)'); *ra-* is prefixed to bases with the initial bilabials /p/ and /b/ (e.g. *bɛtak* 'pull (vt)' → *ra-betak* 'pull (vi)'); *ba-* is used with other consonant-initial bases (e.g. *kemang* 'a flower' → *bakemang* 'bloom'); *bar-* occurs before initial vowels (e.g. *anak* 'a child' → *bar-anak* 'having a child').

such that kissing is possible)'. Likewise, *tegen-in* 'carry (on the shoulder)-CAUS' means 'X makes Y carry something on Y's shoulder coercively (e.g. by helping to put the thing on his/her shoulder)'.

#### 32.3.2.4 *Nominalization: pə- and -an*

Both Balinese and Sasak have two nominalizing affixes, *pə-* and *-an*, which are very likely reflexes of PMP *paR- and *-en respectively. Sumbawa, however, only has a lone nominalizer, *pa-*. Independently, each of the two can convey the same meaning: 'product of an action' or 'thing affected by an action'. Hence, the derived noun referentially bears a patient role in relation to the verbal stem (e.g. *pə-baang* 'gift', *dum-an* 'share' in Balinese, *pə-nyesek* 'loom', *kakən-an* 'food' in Sasak (Clynes 1995b: 503–4, 1995c: 517), and *pa-kakan* 'snack' in Sumbawa).

The two affixes, *pə- -an*, can co-occur as a nominalizing circumfix in Balinese. The circumfix conveys an abstract nominal meaning, 'the act as depicted by the verbal stem', typically associated with plural reciprocal meaning (e.g. *temu* 'meet' → *pe-temu-an/patemon* 'the act of meeting').

### 32.3.3 Reduplication

All BSS languages have reduplication as one of their word deriving processes. Balinese appears to have the most complex reduplicative forms among these three languages by showing three types of reduplication: full reduplication, partial reduplication, and foot reduplication (Clynes 1995d: 149–75; Arka and Dalrymple 2017). Neighbouring Austronesian languages, such as Javanese, show comparable complexity in reduplication (see Vander Klok, this volume, §31.4.1 on the languages of Java). The reduplication types are presented in the following sub-section, followed by their complex semantics.

In full reduplication, the entire base morpheme is copied (e.g. Balinese *umah* 'house' → *umah~umah* house~REDUP 'houses' (Balinese)). In partial reduplication, part of the base morpheme, such as the CV material, is copied, possibly with an invariable vowel (V) substitution. For example, in Balinese, the initial CV of the stem *pineh* 'thought' is copied, but the vowel is substituted with /ə/, resulting in the reduplicative form *pepineh* 'different kinds of thought'. Included in this partial reduplication is a situation where almost the whole stem's material is copied, but one V segment is the V of the second syllable of the stem is replaced with /a/ (e.g. in Balinese, *angguk* 'node' → *anggak~angguk* 'to nod in different ways', and *kecog* 'jump' → *kecag~kecog* 'jump in different ways'). Partial reduplication of different kinds with vowel substitution is also observed in Sasak (e.g. *kepəntang~kepanting* 'flap-flip' in Thoir et al. 1986: 24), and in Sumbawa (e.g. *kaməri~kəmərɛ* 'feel very happy'). See Mattes and Schwaiger (this volume, §45.2.4) for more discussion of such non-prototypical reduplication patterns.

Foot reduplication copies the material of the prosodic unit called 'foot', which can consist of the stem and some following material. For example, the noun *oka* 'child' is the stem of the possessive noun *oka-n-ne* 'fish-LIG-3SG.POSS=his/her child'. The reduplicated form expressing plural 'his children' is *okan~okan-ne* 'child.LIG~REDUP-3SG.POSS', in which the ligature (LIG) *-n* is part of the foot and included in the reduplicated form.

Reduplication applies across main lexical categories (i.e. nouns, verbs, adjectives, and adverbs) and minor categories such as numerals. They primarily express plurality of entities or events. Full reduplication encodes homogenous plurality, which involves a set of entities of the same types (e.g. *batu* 'stone' → *batu~batu* 'multiple stones of similar type'). On the other hand, partial reduplication typically expresses heterogeneous plurality, which is related to a 'kind' or 'type' plural meaning (e.g. *batu* 'stone' → *bebatuan* 'different kinds of stones') (Arka and Dalrymple 2017: 286). Reduplicated verbs, or categories exhibiting predicative functions, exhibit more complex meanings termed pluractionality (PLURACT) or verbal number (Wood 2007). The following examples demonstrate this semantic complexity in Balinese, where the fuller reduplication of material correlates to the encoding of larger temporal gaps (see Arka and Dalrymple 2017 for further discussion). Further research is needed to confirm whether similar semantic complexity is attested in Sasak and Sumbawa.

Balinese

(2) a. *ma-ke-plug*
MID-PUNC-explode
'X (singular or plural) explode (once)'

b. *pa-ke-plug*
PLURACT-PUNC-explode
'X (plural) explode more or less simultaneously'

c. *pa-ke-plug~plug*
PLURACT-PUNC-explode~REDUP
'X (plural) explode more or less simultaneously, each of X also repetitively exploding successively without clear pauses'

d. *pa-ke-plag~plug*
PLURACT-PUNC-REDUP~explode
'X (plural) explode in different ways more or less simultaneously, each of X also repetitively exploding successively without clear pauses'

e. *pakeplug~pakeplug*
explode~REDUP
'X (plural) repetitively explode more or less simultaneously, without recognized pauses'

f. *pakeplag~pakeplug*
REDUP~explode
'X (plural) repetitively explode more or less simultaneously in different manners, without recognized pauses'

## 32.4 Morphosyntax

### 32.4.1 Noun phrases

This section focuses on nominal structures and provides comments on certain aspects of their nominal phrasal syntax, which characterize BSS as a group, but also broadly in the context of Austronesian linguistics. See Arka (2003b) for a more detailed analysis of Balinese phrase structure. Clausal syntax is discussed in §32.4.4.

The internal structure of noun phrases in BSS languages is similar and is schematized in (3). Of interest are their salient structural features in terms of headedness, possessive expression, definiteness, and attributive modification. Each is briefly discussed in turn below.

(3) NP structure in BSS languages
(Personal ART) HEAD (attributive) (possessor) (NUM/QUANT) (PP/ relative clause) (DEM)

*Definiteness.* Definiteness plays a critical role in BSS languages and is expressed by more than one element with different structural properties: an article (ART), DEM, and a DEF clitic. This is shown in Table 32.1. Balinese articles, when used for names, also carry gender (GEND) information, for example, *i* for male (M) and *ni* for female (F). The equivalent articles are *nya* (M) and *si* (F) in Sumbawa. Note that Balinese *i* may be used with a common noun indicating a definite referent or role in some social domains, with no M gender information implied (e.g. *i Bapa* '(our/your) father', *i Guru* '(the) teacher', *i meme* '(our/your) mother'). Each language also has some other articles indicating social status or property (e.g. *endɛ* 'uncle' or *dɛa*, a noble title in Sumbawa).

Demonstratives structurally occur in NP final position and express definiteness with additional deictic information (as in Table 32.1). They differ in terms of spatial categories, with a two-way distinction in Balinese and Sasak, but a three-way distinction in Sumbawa. Furthermore, the forms in Balinese and Sasak, unlike those in Sumbawa, carry social deixis and form part of the speech level systems in those languages. Additionally, the medial or distal forms often exhibit anaphoric and situational use. Sumbawa also has an anaphoric marker *ita*.

Finally, Balinese has a bound form, =*e*, to express definiteness. While often analysed as a suffix, it shows properties of a clitic (see §32.4.2). Given its form, =*e* may have originated from the demonstrative *əne*, undergone some morphologicalization during this process and became a clitic. This kind of clitic-like suffix is reported elsewhere as 'final-marking' in Australian languages (Dench and Evans 1988: 5).

*Possession.* All BSS languages have postposed possessors; for example, *balɛ =ode guru* 'a small house of (the) teacher' (Sumbawa). In Balinese, a ligature *-n* appears on the head noun when the head noun is vowel final; for example, *buku-n Bapa=e* 'book-LIG father=DEF; father's book'. There is no distinct possessive pronoun in Balinese, except for the third person (invariable) =*ne*, which is homonymous with the allomorph of the DEF =*e* and realized as =*ne* for a vowel-final host.

*Attributive modification.* Attributive modification typically shows two patterns. The first pattern shows a simple but tight structure, in which the noun head is immediately followed by a bare modifier, either a noun or an adjective; for example, ***balɛ batu*** 'stone house' and *balɛ=ode* 'small house' (Sumbawa). The second pattern is a complex attributive structure with multiple modifiers. In Balinese, there is a restriction in this case whereby only one simple modifier is typically allowed to appear immediately after the noun head. The other modifiers should appear as (postposed relative) clauses, as in (4b), or prepositionally flagged modifiers, as in (5b). The acceptability of NPs with the second modifiers appearing in bare forms, as in (4a) and (5a), is downgraded. However, Sumbawa does not have such a constraint, as in (6).

Balinese

(4) a. *?celeng selem* ***gede*** *tiang=e nto*
pig black big 1=DEF that
'that black big pig of mine'
(Arka, own knowledge)

b. *celeng selem tiang=e* ***ane gede*** *nto*
pig black 1=DEF big big that
'that black pig of mine which is big'

Balinese

(5) a. *?/*pintu kuning* ***besi*** *nto*
door yellow iron that
'the yellow iron door' (Arka, own knowledge)

b. *?/*pintu kuning* ***aji/uli besi*** *nto*
door yellow from iron that
'the yellow door made out of iron'

**Table 32.1** Definiteness in BSS languages, including articles, deictic systems (demonstratives), and clitics

| | ART | | DEM | | | DEF CLITIC |
|---|---|---|---|---|---|---|
| | MALE | FEMALE | PROXIMAL | MEDIAL | DISTAL | |
| Balinese | *i* | *ni* | *əne* (LR)/*niki* (HR) | *ənto* (LR)/*niku* (HR) | | *=e* |
| Sasak | *loʔ* | *leʔ*[a] | *ine* ~*ni* (LR) /*niki* (HR) | *ino* ~ *no* (LR)/*nike* (HR) | | *=ne* ~ *=ni*[b] |
| Sumbawa | *nya* | *si* | *ta/dεta* | *nan/dεan* | *ana/dεna* | - |

[a] These markers only occur in NN and MM dialects of Sasak (Ika Rama Suhandra, p.c.).

[b] These clitics only occur in MM and NN dialects (Ika Rama Suhandra, p.c.)

Sumbawa

(6) *lawang puti batu ta*
door white stone this
'the white stone door' (Shiohara's field notes, elicited)

*Quantification.* The term 'quantifier' here covers quantifying words, such as universal quantifiers (e.g. *onya/makejang* 'all') and numerals. Numerals often appear with classifiers in Balinese, for example, *bidang* for leaves *diri* for people, *lembar* for cloth, *ukud* (for animals (see Kersten 1984: 87–9 for a more comprehensive picture).

A salient property of quantifiers in BSS languages is that they may float away from the default position. Quantifier float (QF) is highly constrained, however. It can be motivated pragmatically by information structure considerations. In Sumbawa, for example, a quantifier precedes the head noun when the quantified referent is newly introduced to the discourse, but it appears in its default position following the head noun when the referent is given.

Sumbawa

(7) *ada pitu' tau dadara*
exist [seven person young (of.girls)]

*tau dadara pitu nan sarεa*
person young (of.girls) seven that all

*basanak-sɔai*
be.sisters

'There are seven girls. The seven girls are all sisters.' (Shiohara 2014: 22).

In Balinese QF is a syntactic property of core arguments. Readers are directed to Arka (2003b, 2019) for a detailed discussion of the semantic and grammatical constraints of QF in this language and in other Austronesian languages of Indonesia.

### 32.4.2 Clitics

BSS languages possess two of the typologically known classes of clitics: simple and special clitics (Zwicky 1985). Balinese, however, appears to have fewer clitics than Sasak and Sumbawa.

Simple or 'peripheral' clitics are those that serve as reduced forms and occur in the same syntactic positions as corresponding full forms, but attached to adjacent constituents, for example, English auxiliary clitics *'s* and *'d* are the simple clitics of their full forms *has/is* and *would/had* respectively (Zwicky 1985). In BSS languages, simple clitics include certain (reduced) forms of function words. These include TAM clitics in Sumbawa (Shiohara 2013b) and demonstratives in Sasak, such as *=nó*, which is often cliticized to the adjacent noun, as in *kanak=nó* [child=that] 'that child' (Austin 2004: 6). The third person possessive clitic in Balinese *=ne* is also a simple clitic, as it occupies the same syntactic position as other possessors in the NP (e.g. *poh=ne/tiang/cai* [mango=3/1/2] 'his/her/their/my/your mango'). Pronominal object clitics in Sasak also belong to the class of simple clitics.

Special clitics have a 'special' distribution in that its position is not determined by the normal rules of syntax (Kroeger 2005b: 322–3). In BSS languages, this includes the second position clitic in Sasak and Sumbawa and the definite marker *=e*, and verbal clitic *=a* in Balinese. Each of these is briefly discussed in order.

Second position clitics are shown in the MM-Sasak example in (8). Sumbawa also has a set of second position clitics—the discourse particles *si*, *mɔ*, and *pɔ*—which convey various discourse functions. The clitics in Sasak, like *=k* '1SG' and *=n* '3', are subject second position clitics; that is, they are 'special' in that they appear in the second position of the core clause structure, clearly seen with *=k* in (8a, b).

Sasak

(8) a. *Laló=k jok peken*
go=1SG to market
'I am going to the market.'

b. *Iaʔ=k laló jok peken*
FUT=1SG go to market
'I will go to the market.' (Austin, 2004: 11)

The Balinese definite marker, has a distribution which does not follow the usual syntactic rule. In particular, it does not occupy the same position as the demonstrative that also expresses definiteness in Balinese. It may appear like a second position clitic within the NP domain and hence, it is hosted by the first noun (i.e. the head of the NP) (e.g. *anak=e ento* [person=DEF that] 'that person', *anak=e jegeg* 'beautiful person', and *anak=e ane teka mai* [person=DEF REL come to.here] 'the person coming to here'). However, it may also appear in other positions. When the head noun is modified by a noun, such as a compound formation or possessive specification, the clitic *=e* is attached to the second modifying noun (e.g. *montor jepang=e* [car Japan= DEF] 'the Japanese car', *sebun kedis=e* [nest bird= DEF] 'the bird's nest') (Shiohara and Artawa 2014: 143). The clitic *=e* can also be hosted by the last word of a phrase, such as a pronominal possessor like *kunci montor kuning tiang=e* [key car yellow 1=DEF] 'the key of my yellow car', or an adjective as in *umah paling cenik=e nto* [house very small= DEF that] 'that smallest house'.

Finally, the third person pronominal actor *=a* in Balinese is a special clitic in that it only appears on the head verb and has no corresponding full form in the expected syntactic slot, even though it has arguably originated from the free pronoun form *ia*. Furthermore, *=a* has been morphologicalized and grammaticalized to become a passive suffix in Balinese (see Arka 2008 for further details). This special clitic will be detailed in §32.4.4.2.

## 32.4.3 Negators and tense-aspect-modal (TAM) markers

The structural position of negators is a crucial typological property characterizing symmetrical voice languages (Himmelmann 2005a: 175). This property will be briefly discussed in BSS languages, including its connection to tense-aspect-modal (TAM) markers. The generalization is that while negation and TAM broadly show similar structural properties, there are differences in their specific expressions, with Sasak and Balinese appearing more similar to each other than Sumbawa.

Structurally and by default, all BSS show negators and TAM markers in the position before the predicate (i.e. in pragmatically unmarked contexts). This is in line with the head-initial structural property of BSS languages. Relevant examples from Balinese and Sasak are given in (9) and (10) below. When both NEG and TAM markers co-occur, the left NEG/TAM element has scope over the right one, which is further discussed below.

Balinese
(9) *Wayan* ***sing*** *pules.*
Wayan NEG sleep
'Wayan is not sleeping.' (Arka's own knowledge)

MM-Sasak
(10) *muʔ ndég araʔ masih=n*
PART NEG exist still=3
'(but) still there was nothing.' (Jordan 2002: 41)

The grammar of negation among BSS languages shows variation. Formally, Sumbawa is like Indonesian in that it distinguishes two negators depending on the category of the unit being negated: *no* is used for verbal negations (equivalent to Indonesian *tidak*) as in (11a), and *siɔng'* is for non-verbal negations (equivalent to Indonesian *bukan*) as in (11b). Balinese and Sasak do not make such a distinction. Instead, the speech registers have different negators, which is not the case in Sumbawa (e.g. *sing* 'NEG, low register' vs. *tan* 'NEG, high register' in Balinese).

Sumbawa
(11) a *no ku=sadu' kau*
NEG 1SG=believe 2SG
'I don't believe you.' (Shiohara 2013b: 187)

b. *siɔng' guru nya*
NEG teacher 3
'He/she is not a teacher' or 'They are not teachers.' (Shiohara 2013b: 176)

Among the BSS group, Balinese is the only language showing double marked negation, which is exemplified in (12) below. Double negation does not deliver a logical double-negation meaning (i.e. which would be 'positive'). Instead, it encodes a complex emphatic and communicative meaning associated with evidentiality (Aikhenvald 2018) and engagement (Evans, Bergqvist, and San Roque 2017). It highlights the speaker's authority and knowledge regarding the truth-value of events and is highlighted by the complex meaning provided in the free translation in (12). However, Balinese is not unique. Out of the 409 languages surveyed in Vossen and van der Auwera (2014), double-negative marking is encountered in eighty-one (20%) languages; see van der Auwera, Van Olmen, and Vossen, (this volume, §50.2) for a further survey on negation in MPSEA.

Balinese
(12) *Wayan* ***sing*** *pules* ***sing.***
Wayan NEG1 sleep NEG2
'Wayan is (indeed) not sleeping (but doing something else; I know this, e.g. I saw it with my own eyes).'
(Arka, own knowledge)

In BSS languages, tense, as well as aspect and mood, are only optionally marked. This means that in the absence of overt TAM elements, TAM is inferred from the context. In terms of formal marking, Balinese and Sasak exhibit similarities that contrast with Sumbawa: TAM is consistently expressed through independent auxiliary words in Balinese and Sasak, while Sumbawa expresses TAM through simple/peripheral clitics. Consider the sentences in (13), which show the usage of Balinese TAM markers. Specifically, some auxiliaries, such as *konden* 'not yet', may stand alone in question–answer pairs, without the main verb.

Balinese
(13) A: ***Suba*** *mandus?*
already have.shower
'Have you had a shower?'

B: ***Konden,*** *jani* ***lakar*** *mandus.*
not.yet now will have.shower
'Not yet, (I) am going to have a shower now.'
(Ardana and Suzuki 1998: 42)

Examples in (14) below demonstrate the expression of TAM markers through simple clitics in Sumbawa:

Sumbawa
(14) a. *ka=datang nya*
PST=come 3
'He/she/they came.'

b. *ya=datang nya*
FUT=come 3
'He/she/they will come.'
(Shiohara field notes, elicited)

Finally, there is evidence that the co-occurrence of negative and TAM marking may form a construction which undergoes morphologicalization and lexicalization over time and gives rise to a form that is not always semantically transparent or compositional. Thus, the past tense clitic *ka=* in Sumbawa may form a combination with the negator *no* and/or discourse particles, giving rise to a new meaning (e.g. *no=mong=ka* (← *no mo ka*) NEG=necessary=PST 'not any more (negative present perfective)'), as exemplified in (15) (see Shiohara, 2013b: 160 for further details). Another example is the NEG word *tuara* in contemporary Plains Balinese, and *ngara* in Aga Balinese. Historically, both appear to have originated from the NEG+V structure involving two morphemes, the PMP negator *taq and probably the Old Javanese *wara* (rather than the PMP verb *wada) 'exist'.[3]

[3] We thank Sander Adelaar who pointed out to us about this possible source and the sound changes involved. In Balinese, PMP *w became Ø, and PMP *d stayed *d*; PMP **d* > *r* happened in Javanese, but not in Balinese or Malay.

Sumbawa
(15) *no mɔngka datang kota nya.*
NEG DP.PAST come to.here 3
'He will not come here anymore.'
(Shiohara 2013b: 190)

## 32.4.4 Clause structure and grammatical relations

The following section discusses three salient and interrelated properties of BSS clausal morphosyntax: grammatical relations, word order, and voice systems. The discussion is contextualized in the typological context of Austronesian linguistics. Before beginning this discussion, there are two points worthwhile highlighting. First is the linear order of realizations of core arguments, which shows that all BSS languages share the same [A/S]–V–P order. Second, Balinese and NN-Sasak exhibit robust evidence for grammatical SBJ/PIVOT, where systematic alternative argument realizations are made possible by the functional presence of Austronesian verbal voice selectors. For example, the Balinese voice system makes Balinese typologically aligned with other Indonesian-type languages (Himmelmann 2005a; Arka and Ross 2005). Sumbawa, on the other hand, shows semantically transparent grammatical relations with limited or no verbal (voice) morphology. Its grammatical system, therefore, allows for rather limited alternative argument realizations. Each of these general patterns is discussed in order below.

### 32.4.4.1 *Subject and [S/A]–V–P order*

There is strong morphosyntactic evidence for the notion of subject, represented here as $[S/A]_{SBJ}$, as the most generalized argument in BSS languages. This evidence comes from two kinds of coding properties: linear order and verbal morphological selectors. There are other behavioural properties, such as equi- (or control) structures, which will be discussed in §32.4.6.

The default linear order of core clausal syntax in Balinese and Sasak is schematized in (16) and exemplified in (17)–(18). The $[S/A]_{SBJ}$ (shown in bold in these examples) canonically comes before the head verb. Other arguments (P/G/T) that are identified as objects or obliques, if any, come after the verb. The $[S/A]_{SBJ}$ preverbal position is the position for the most generalized argument; that is, it can be associated with any role, such as the patientive/agentive S in (17a) or A (17b) in Balinese. The same pattern holds in Sasak (18). There has been some corpus-based research supporting this default $[S/A]_{SBJ}$-V order in Balinese and Sasak (Pastika 1999; Wouk 2002).

(16) $[S/A]_{SBJ}$ VERB P/G/T

Balinese

(17) a. ***Ida*** *labuh/nangis*
3 fall/ AV.cry
'S/he fell off.'

b. ***Ketut*** *numbas-ang* *tiang* *bawi*
Ketut AV.buy-APPL 1 pig
'Ketut bought a pig for me.'
(Arka, own knowledge)

NN-Sasak

(18) a. *kenyengken=**ne*** *tokol.*
PROG=3 sit
'They were sitting.'

b. *[kanak meme inó]i* ***nei=malé?*** *bèmbé? inó*
child male that 3=AV.chase goat that
'The boy chased the goat.'
(Asikin-Garmager 2017: 63)

However, the actual realization of linear order may vary for independent reasons. For instance, because of the subject status of Sasak's special second position clitic, it can appear as an enclitic (i.e. after the verb) when the verb is the first constituent in the clause (as seen in (8a). Further, a verb may be pragmatically focused and therefore fronted, resulting in an inverted V–[S/A] order, as exemplified in (1) in §32.2.4.

Unlike Balinese and Sasak, it is difficult to set a default linear order in Sumbawa. Corpus-based research shows that verb-initial clauses, as in (14a–b) above, most frequently occur in narratives (Shiohara 2013a). However, a focal argument may also occur in pre-predicate position, as in (19), in response to a question such as 'Who paid for that table?'.

Sumbawa

(19) ***Helmi*** *ka=bayar* *mɛjang* *ta*
Helmi PST=pay table that
'Helmi paid for that table.' (Wouk 2002: 300)

### 32.4.4.2 *Voice and transitivity*

Like other languages of western Indonesia, voice and transitivity are two interrelated salient features characterizing the clausal morphosyntax of BSS languages. This sub-section begins by discussing these features in Balinese and NN-Sasak to show how symmetrical voice plays out in these languages (see Kroeger and Riesberg, this volume, §47.2.2, for symmetrical voice in other Malayo-Polynesian languages). In the symmetrical system, any argument role (A, P/T, and G) can be equally selected and appear in the SBJ position without demoting the underlying core A/P to Oblique. This is seen in the AV–UV alternation, exemplified from Balinese in (20) and Sasak in (21). The argument selected as subject and the associated verbal selector are indicated in bold. In AV (20a) and (21a), A is selected as subject with the verbal AV selector being the AV prefix N-. In the UV examples of (20b) and (21b), P is selected as subject with the UV verbal selector being the zero prefix.[4] Crucially, syntactic transitivity in this voice AV–UV alternation remains the same; both structures are transitive, with A and P maintaining their core status and neither is demoted to Oblique in the voice alternation. This makes the AV–UV alternation fundamentally distinct from the passive alternation, in which A is demoted to Oblique.

Balinese

(20) a. ***Tiang*** ***ng**-adep* *siap-e*
1 AV-sell chicken-DEF
SBJ: A P
'I sold the chicken.'

b. *Siap-e* *Ø-adep* *tiang*
chicken-DEF UV-sell 1
SBJ:P A
'I sold the chicken.' (Arka 2019: 261)

Pancor NN-Sasak

(21) a. ***kanak meme inó*** ***malé?*** *bèmbé? inó*
child male that AV.chase goat that
'The boy chased the goat'
(Asikin-Garmager 2017: 24)

b. ***bèmbé? inó*** *palé?* *kanak meme inó*
goat that UV.chase child male that
'The boy chased the goat'
(Asikin-Garmager 2017: 26)

Like in Balinese, the AV N- morphology in NN-Sasak is the A-SBJ selector. Importantly, however, the Sasak data indicates the significance of distinguishing the basic clause-internal subject (so far abbreviated [S/A]SBJ) from the clause-external prominent function, variously called TOPIC (Shibatani 2008) or PIVOT (Foley and Van Valin 1984). These different notions of 'subject' were first recognized in Schachter (1977) and their interconnection has been made explicit in the more recent theoretical works of Lexical Functional Grammar. These works by Falk (2000, 2009) and Arka (2021) are adopted here to define the term PIVOT as an overlay syntactic function of a highly prominent discourse function (typically contrastive FOCUS/TOPIC) and a grammatical function (typically subject, but possibly object). Taking PIVOT into account, we can revise the BSS clausal structure previously shown in (16) as (22) below:

[4] Asikin-Garmager (2017) labels this construction NAV (Non-Actor Voice).

(22) [TOPIC/FOCUS [[S/A]$_{SBJ}$ Verb [P/G/T]$_{OBJ}$ ]BASIC-CLAUSE ]EXTENDED-CLAUSE

[PIVOT]

The connection line in (22) shows the selection of the overlay function of PIVOT. PIVOT is needed for clause-external purposes, such as complex clause formation, or discourse information structure purposes, as in (contrastive) TOPIC/FOCUS selection. See §32.4.6 for data points reflecting the significance of PIVOT in BSS languages/Sasak.

Voice is related to, and may affect, transitivity. In AV–UV alternations like those discussed earlier, both AV and UV clauses are equally transitive; that is, the core status of A and P remains unchanged. This shows symmetricality in voice alternation in BSS languages. However, voice alternations in BSS languages also result in, or require, A and P asymmetry: argument demotion to oblique status, argument suppression, or referential indefiniteness of A/P (see example (26b)).

Balinese also has an AV–MID voice alternation resulting in intransitivization, which is shown in (23). The passive-like *ma-* 'MID' totally suppresses A from the argument structure of the base verb. Note that overtly expressing the oblique agent, as in (23b), is ungrammatical.

Balinese

(23) a. *Nyoman suba ng-adep celeng-ne*
Nyoman PERF AV-sell pig-3POSS
'Nyoman has sold his pig.'

b. *Celeng-ne suba ma-adep (*teken Nyoman)*
pig-3.POSS PERF MID-sell by Nyoman
'His pig has been sold.' (Arka, own knowledge)

The relative definiteness of A/P appears to play a role in constraining voice selection/alternation in BSS languages. The pervasive pattern is that the argument selected as PIVOT (i.e. being contrastive TOPIC/FOCUS and typically linked to the prominent core status of SBJ) must be definite, and the non-PIVOT/non-SBJ argument (if it is non-pronominal) is often constrained to be indefinite and/or unspecified. In Balinese, the UV Actor, if non-pronominal, should be indefinite, as exemplified in (24). However, making the non-pronominal A definite (e.g. with the presence of the demonstrative 'that') is ungrammatical. This indefiniteness A constraint is intriguing and has attracted different analyses, such as agent incorporation (Clynes 1995d).[5]

Balinese

(24) *Nyoman ejuk polisi/*polisi nto*
Nyoman UV.arrest police/police that
'Nyoman was arrested by the police.'
(Arka, own knowledge)

It should be noted that verbal voice morphology in BSS languages is multifunctional. In one function, it is an argument selector that can be clearly seen when it appears with the verbal base selecting either A or P as SBJ/PIVOT. This semantic role coding of voice morphology gives rise to a split-S/fluid-S alignment system, as seen in Balinese (Arka 2003b).

Voice marking also has a derivational function and so it is more than just an argument selector, but also an argument-structure creator. For example, the AV *N-* prefix introduces an argument structure with A in it. This is particularly clear in its derivational function to create a verb out of a non-verbal stem (e.g. *roko* 'cigarette' (N) > *ngroko* 'smoke' (V) in Balinese).

Turning to MM-Sasak and Sumbawa, this *N-* morphology does not function as AV selector. These languages lack (verbal) voice opposition in transitive constructions. The symmetrical voice feature, as seen in Balinese and NN-Sasak, also disappears in these languages, or alternatively, its existence is somewhat elusive and is possibly only observable in certain behavioural properties. They have only one type of transitive construction with invariably bare verbs; this is exemplified in (25a–b) from Sumbawa. Of interest is the structure in (25b), which is still syntactically transitive, as A (*ya=*) and P 'Amin' appear in their subject and object positions, respectively. The A argument is cross-referenced by the postposed PP (flagged by *ling*).

Sumbawa

(25) a. *Polisi bau nya Amin*
police catch ART Amin
'The police caught Amin.'

b. *ya=bau nya Amin ling Polisi*
3=catch ART Amin by Police
'The police caught Amin.'
(Shiohara's field note, elicited)

In MM-Sasak and Sumbawa, *N-* morphology derives intransitive verbs. It therefore functions like an anti-passive marker, as exemplified by the Sumbawa sentences in (26a–b). The verb without *N-* in (26a) is transitive with the definite P argument appearing postverbally. This contrasts to the

[5] See Arka (2003b) for arguments against this analysis.

clause with the N- verb in (26b), where the P argument must be suppressed; that is, the P which occurs in the corresponding transitive clause (26a) may not occur.

Sumbawa

(26) a. *ka=ku=inum* *kawa* *nan* *ling* *aku.*
PST=1SG =drink coffee that by 1SG
'I drank the coffee.'

b. *ka=ku=ng-inum* *aku* (*kawa).
PAST=1SG=N-drink 1SG (coffee)
'I drink (something).' (Shiohara 2013a: 148)

Finally, the set of pronominal clitics in Sumbawa have developed into a full system with the exception of the third person proclitic *ya=*, which only occurs in transitive clauses; see Table 32.2. These pronominal clitics express the core grammatical relation of subject ([S/A]). Unlike their Sasak counterparts, there is evidence these clitics are only hosted by verbs, suggesting a morphologicalization process where they are becoming tightly part of the verbal morphology. This is evidenced in the structural property of the subject clitic (e.g. *ku=* '1SG') exemplified in (27). The free pronoun subject *aku* in (27a) is in the subject position whereas the bound form *ku=* after the auxiliary particle *ka=* in (27b) is part of the verbal structure. Since this clitic occurs closer to the verb stem than the tense marker *ka=*, this may indicate a structural change taking place in Sumbawa where it is moving towards a full-fledged head-marking cross-referencing system. Additional evidence for this change comes from attestations like (27c), which are perceived to be ungrammatical among some speakers.

**Table 32.2** Free and clitic pronouns in Sumbawa

| PERSON & NUMBER | FREE FORM | CLITIC FORM |
|---|---|---|
| 1SG | *aku* | *ku=* |
| | *kaji* (humble) | |
| 1PL.INCL | *kita* | *tu=* |
| PL.EXCL | *kami* | |
| 2SG | *kau* | *mu=* |
| | *sia* (honorific) | |
| 2PL/3PL | *nɛnɛ* | |
| 3 | *nya* | *ya=* |

Sumbawa

(27) a. *aku/kau* *ka=təri'*
1SG/2SG PST=fall
'I/you fell.' (Riester and Shiohara 2018: 288)

b. *ka=ku=təri'*
PST=1SG=fall
'I fell.' (Riester and Shiohara 2018: 286)

c. *Aku* *ku=inum* *kawa=nan*
1SG 1SG=drink coffee=that
'I drink the coffee.' (Shiohara field notes, elicited)

## 32.4.5 Serial verb constructions (SVCs)

Serial verb constructions (SVCs) are the hallmarks of Austronesian languages of the isolating type, as seen in the neighbouring languages of Flores (see Nagaya, this volume, §34.8), however, they remain understudied in BSS languages. There is evidence of SVCs in Balinese and Sumbawa. In Balinese, they express a range of semantic relations such as comitative, benefactive, and instrumental relations; see Shiohara and Artawa (2012) and Indrawati (2014) for further details.

The distinction between SVCs and adverbial subordination is, however, not always clear cut. A typical diagnostic test for SVCs is negation: since SVCs are monoclausal the criterion of single negatability applies (Durie 1997). In this section, we discuss one language-specific criterion in Balinese which can be used to distinguish SVCs from multi-verb constructions in coordinate and subordinate clauses: this is neutralization of the voice in the second verb of the SVC structure. The second verb can appear in its bare form, without the N- 'AV' or the A clitic *=a* in the UV form of the verb. The ordinary coordination/subordination would have verbs with alternating voice morphology, depending on the argument role selected and whether it is elided or controlled in the second/subordinate clause. Consider examples (28a–b), with attention to the contrast of verbal voice on the second verb *ngajak/ajak* and the associated meaning differences. In the comitative SVC (28a), the second verb can have its prefix N- 'AV' elided (indicated in parentheses). In contrast, the elision is not possible in (28b) because of the syntactic coordination requirement in (b). That is, the A argument of the transitive verb *ajak* is a separate clause and co-referential with the S of the preceding clause (*tiang*). Such S/A coreference is only possible when A is selected as grammatical subject; hence, the obligatory presence of the subject selector morphology on the verb.

Balinese

(28) a. *tiang* ***malajah*** *kelompok* ***(ng-)ajak***
1SG MID.study group (AV-)invite
*timpal~timpal-e*
friend~REDUP=DEF
'I studied in group together the friends.'

b. *tiang* *malajah* *kelompok* *[tan*
1SG MID.study group NEG
*ngajak/*ajak* *Ketut]*
AV.invite/invite Ketut
'I studied in group, (but) I didn't invite Ketut (to join).' (Arka's own knowledge)

Likewise, the verb *baang* 'give' can be the second verb in the benefactive SVC in Balinese, and in such constructions, it appears without the AV morphology, such as the A clitic =*a* in (29a). The verb *baang* in the second VP is part of the SVC and its A clitic =*a* can be elided (indicated parenthetically). Note that the A clitic in the UV structure of coordination cannot be elided, as seen in (29b).

Balinese
(29) a. *Ni* *Sari* ***[meli*** *baju]*$_{VP}$ ***[baang(=a)***
ART Sari AV.buy clothes give=3
*adi-n=né]*$_{VP}$*]*$_{SVC}$
sister-LIG=3POSS
'Sari bought clothes for her sister.'

b. *Baju* *nto* *jemak=a* *lantas* *baang=a/*
shirt that AV.take=3 then UV.give=3/
**baang* *adi-n=ne*
give sister-LIG=3POSS
'The shirt s/he took (it), then she gave it to his/her sister.' (Arka's own knowledge)

## 32.4.6 Subordinate clauses

This section highlights salient features of two types of subordination in BSS, complement clauses and adverbial clauses. Complement clauses are object-like arguments of the matrix clauses although for certain matrix verbs, the complements may be syntactically peripheral or oblique-like. Formally, they can be realized as finite and non-finite clauses.

Finite complement clauses in BSS languages are characterized by the overt expression of the subject and a TAM auxiliary element. They often occur without an overt complementizer in BSS languages, as seen in the Balinese example in (30). There is no dedicated complementizer marker like English *that* in Balinese. Sumbawa optionally uses the complementizer *luk* with the quotative or cognitive verb, as in shown in example (31).

Balinese
(30) *wentan* *timpal* *bapa-n-tiang-e* *ngortaang*
exist friend father-INS-1-DEF tell
*[memen* *tiange* *memitra* *jak*
mother 1 have.an.affair with
*nak* *len]*$_{COMP.CL}$
person different
'A friend of my father told that my mother had an affair with a different guy.'
(Arka's Balinese SCOPIC data, SocCog-ban-04-badung3-task_4)

Sumbawa
(31) *datang* *dəngan,* *bada* ***[luk*** *soai* *ada* *main*
come friend tell COMP wife exist play
*kɛ* *tau* *lin* *pang* *dɛsa* *ana]*$_{COMP.CL}$.
with person other in village over.there
'A friend came (and) told that the wife played with someone else in the village over there.'
(Shiohara's Sumbawa SCOPIC data, SocCog-smw-01_task6_sya-032)

Generally speaking, adverbial clauses typically have no fixed position and possibly precede or follow the matrix clause. The following examples exemplify a temporal (finite) adverbial clause in Balinese, a conditional clause in Sumbawa.

Balinese
(32) *dugas* *tiang* *teka,* *tusing* *ada* *nyen* *jumah.*
when 1 come NEG exist who house
'When I came, no one was at home.'
(Arka's own knowledge)

Sumbawa
(33) *lamin* *satɛ* *mu=tutit* *aku,* *mu=datang* *mɔ.*
if want 2SG=follow 1SG 2SG=come PART
'If you like to follow me, just come.'
(From the folktale *Lalu Kurekkure*)

Relative clauses are introduced by the relativizers *ane* in Balinese, *(i)siq* in Sasak, and *adɛ* in Sumbawa. Balinese and NN-Sasak contrast with MM-Sasak and Sumbawa in that the latter pair typically lack a verbal morphology contrast with regards to encoding AV vs. UV, while in all the languages, the relativized argument must be pragmatically highly prominent, providing evidence for the existence of PIVOT in BSS languages. For example, the contrast in Balinese relativization in (34) is due to the restriction that only the selected SBJ-PIVOT argument can be relativized. The relativization of A in (34a) is fine because A is selected as SBJ-PIVOT by the AV verb. The structure in (34b) is unacceptable because it attempts to relativize A when the verb is in UV (i.e. A is not SBJ-PIVOT).

Balinese: Relativization of A:
(34) a. *Anak-e* *ane* *[_* *nunas* *kopi].*
person-DEF REL $A_{SUBJ}$ AV.take coffee
'The person who took the coffee.'

b. **Anak-e* *ane* *[kopi* *tunas* *_ ].*
person-DEF REL coffee UV.take $A_{NON\text{-}SBJ}$
'The person who took the coffee.'
(Arka's own knowledge)

## 32.5 Speech levels

Balinese and Sasak show an elaborate speech-level system that is otherwise absent in Sumbawa. The speech-level system in Sasak is historically due to Balinese influence, which is in turn due to Javanese influence (Clynes 1989, 1995d; Nothofer 2000; Arka 2005). The speech-level systems in these languages exhibit similar characteristics and underlying principles. They differ in terms of their lexicon and complexity, with Sasak showing the least elaborate system.

As in Javanese (see Vander Klok, this volume, §31.2), these speech-level systems are characterized by different registers encoded by suppletive paradigmatic forms of words across major and minor categories; see Table 32.3 below for different forms in major categories. The forms encode different social information associated with speech participants and/or the entity being talked about. The low (or *lumrah*) register is used with reference to an addressee/referent who is socially equal or low(er) than the speaker. This usage of speech levels is complex and is further discussed below in the context of linguistic politeness.

**Table 32.3** Examples of high and low registers in major categories in Balinese

| | CATEGORY | *lumrah* LOW REGISTER | *alus* HIGH REGISTER | |
|---|---|---|---|---|
| a. | Noun | *bok* | *rambut* | 'hair' |
| b. | Adjective | *gelem* | *sungkan* | 'ill' |
| c. | Verb | *mati* | *seda* | 'die' |
| d. | Adverb | *jani* | *mangkin* | 'now' |

The speech levels differ mainly in the lexicon, not in morphosyntax. For example, the sentence pair in (35) show high and low registers in Balinese. They show parallel morphosyntax, but all of the words are formally distinct. Note that the sentences logically share identical meaning, as seen in the English translation. They differ in terms of the social relations of the speech participants. The addressee is socially superior to the speaker in (35a), but socially inferior/equal in (35b).

Balinese

(35) a. *Tiang numbas bawi-ne ageng punika*
1 AV.buy pig-DEF big that
*ring pasar.* (HR)
at market
'I bought the big pig at the market.'

b. *Cang meli celeng-e gede ento di*
1 AV.buy pig-DEF big that at
*peken.* (LR)
market
'I bought the big pig at the market.' (Arka 2005)

The usage of speech levels is complex and skilful speakers can exploit speech-level lexical recourses to express rich and subtle sociopragmatic meanings in the context of linguistic politeness and verbal arts. For instance, third person pronouns in Balinese differ along two social dimensions or indices: (a) the absolute or fixed social status of the referent, and (b) the speaker–addressee relative social relation in a given context. The usage of *ia* and *ipun* in Table 32.4 below is more complex than that of *dane/ida* because both social indices (a) and (b) have to be accounted for in their proper usage.

**Table 32.4** Balinese third person pronouns

| | (a) Social status of the referent (REF) | (b) Social relation of the Speaker and Addressee (ADDR) |
|---|---|---|
| *ia* | 'ordinary, low caste, commoner' | 'equal' (Speaker=Addressee), 'informal' |
| *ipun* | 'ordinary, low caste, commoner' | 'superior' (Speaker<Addressee), formal' |
| *dane* | 'middle caste' | |
| *ida* | 'high caste' | |

In addition, similar conditioning is observed among suppletive verb forms, which correlate with the relative social relation of their arguments. For example, the variants of 'give' in Balinese/Sasak are: *bang/bèng* where the giver and recipient are the same status, *atur/atur* where the giver is lower in status than recipient, and *icen/ican* where the giver is higher in status than the recipient. With these verbs, the relative social status of the addressee is irrelevant for the choice of the form of the 'give' verb.

Finally, it is worthwhile noting on the 'grammar' of a speech level system: it is essentially a constraint of sociopragmatic consistency operating along the two indices mentioned above, namely the speaker–addressee and/or referent indices (Arka 2005). Hence, it is not a 'hard' constraint of the types found in grammatical subject selection or voice alternation (as seen earlier in §32.4.4.2). The speech-level related constraint is a 'soft' one where a violation of the expected rule would lead to infelicity and this is indicated by a hash (#) in (36b) below. Sentence (36a) is appropriately used to report the death of a socially high-ranked person (*ida*) to any addressee, irrespective of the social rank. Replacing the subject *ida* with *ia*, as in (36b), results in a sociopragmatically inappropriate utterance because *ia* carries a L referent index (cf. Table 32.4). The L referent index of the subject *ia* is in clash with the referent's index required by the verb *seda*. Alternatively, if the rule violation is done deliberately, then it leads to a pragmatic implicature of (im)politeness. Politeness/impoliteness in the Balinese speech-level system is explainable in terms of pragmatic co-operative principles and implicatures (Levinson 1983; Brown and Levinson 1987), as well as Morgan's (1978) distinction between convention of language vs. convention of usage (see Arka 2005 for a more detailed discussion). It is important to note that the so-called HR and LR forms can co-occur in a sentence, as seen in (35a) (see Arka (2005) for precise solutions to this challenge).

Balinese

(36) a. *Ida* *suba* *seda*
HR LR HR
$3_{\text{[REF:HIGH; ADDR:LOW]}}$ $\text{already}_{\text{[ADDR:LOW]}}$ $\text{die<PT}_{\text{[REF:HIGH]}}\text{>}$
'He has passed away' (context: talking about a high caste person; the speaker–addressee relation is equal and informal).

b. *#ia* *suba* seda
LR LR HR
$3_{\text{[REF:LOW; ADDR:Low]}}$ $\text{already}_{\text{[ADDR:LOW]}}$ $\text{die< PT}_{\text{[REF:HIGH]}}\text{>}$
'He has passed away' (context: talking about a commoner with the verb *seda*)

## 32.6 Conclusion: Typological remarks

By way of concluding the discussion on BSS languages, the following section situates BSS in terms of morphological typology, while also indicating areas for future linguistic research.

Himmelmann (2005a) proposed two broad defining properties for classifying the Austronesian languages—symmetricality in voice system and preposed possessor construction—each of which displays multiple characteristic features. In terms of the first criterion, BSS languages show a continuum: from clear symmetrical voice morphosyntax and sporadic person marking in Balinese to Sumbawa with its lack of voice system, but pervasive person indexing on verbs. Sasak dialects show properties in between the two, with particular dialects exhibiting various degrees of attrition in Austronesian voice morphology and the emergence of argument/person indexing. In this respect, NN-Sasak is more like Balinese, whereas MM-Sasak is more like Sumbawa.

In terms of Himmelmann's (2005a) second criterion and related properties, the BSS languages share the following same typological features: postposed possessors, no alienable/inalienable distinction, negators in pre-predicate position, and V-initial or SVX, rather than V-second of V-final, constituent order. On a broader note, the varying degrees of attrition and disappearance of AV voice morphology in certain dialects of Sasak and a total loss of it in Sumbawa indicates that Lombok and Sumbawa are transitional zones towards a full-fledged subject (S/A) person marking/indexing system as typically found in the Austronesian languages of Sumba in eastern Indonesia.

In terms of their clausal and phrasal syntax, the BSS languages are head-initial with most of the structural implications that follow from this property. They exhibit grammatical relations with robust morphosyntactic evidence for syntactic SBJ/PIVOT, particularly in Balinese and NN-Sasak. All BSS languages are not case-marking languages. However, the distinction between core and non-core or oblique arguments is typically straightforward, with core arguments occurring in unmarked forms (i.e. bare NPs). On the other hand, non-cores or obliques, which typically express peripheral semantic roles, appear with prepositional flagging. Alternations of argument status can therefore be assessed through this flagging, which also often correlate with verbal marking, such as applicative morphology.

While this discussion has provided a succinct overview of BSS languages at various linguistic interfaces, there are many areas that would benefit from additional research. For instance, it remains unclear whether similar bare stems like *lalo* 'go' in Sasak and Sumbawa, and *teri*? 'come' in Sasak/*teri'* in Sumbawa are indeed verbs; or whether the bound roots such as *-rari* 'run' in Sasak and Sumbawa are also verbs, or precategories. Thus, similar research to Clynes (2010) and Mistica et al. (2011) is needed in Sasak and Sumbawa to settle the issue on roots and word classes in these two languages. Further, while Sumbawa has types of serial verb constructions as seen in Balinese, more research is needed to uncover their properties and distinguish them from ordinary bi-clausal coordination/subordination structures. Finally, the distinction of finite and non-finite clauses is well studied in Balinese (Natarina 2018), but could benefit from additional investigation and comparative analysis in Sasak and Sumbawa.

## Acknowledgements

For helpful comments, we are grateful to the volume editors Antoinette Schapper and Sander Adelaar. We also thank Charbel El-Khaissi for editing the earlier version of the draft. Wayan Arka gratefully acknowledges the support of the NSF grant (BCS-0617198), while Asako Shiohara, the support of JSPS KAKENHI Grant Number 15K02472, 20K00599, and LingDy3 project of the Research Institute for Languages and Cultures, Tokyo University of Foreign Studies. Thanks are also due to native speakers for their help with the data: Ika Rama (Sasak) and Dedy Mulyadi (Sumbawa).

CHAPTER 33

# Languages of Sulawesi

René van den Berg and David Mead

## 33.1 Introduction

The strangely shaped island of Sulawesi, with its four arms and legs pointing north, east, southwest, and southeast, is home to 111 indigenous Austronesian languages (according to *Ethnologue* 22nd ed. 2019). This introduction briefly discusses the number and location of the various Sulawesi subgroups, number of speakers, language vitality and documentation status.

Present-day scholarship parcels the languages of Sulawesi into ten low-level, relatively non-controversial groupings for which the term 'microgroup' has been used (Sneddon 1989, 1993), a term which we also adopt here. The South Sulawesi microgroup, the largest in terms of both geographic area, number of languages and number of speakers, occupies the southwestern quadrant of the island and comprises more than thirty languages.[1] Three microgroups, traditionally considered to be 'Philippine' languages on typological grounds, are spread across Sulawesi's northern peninsula and stretching into islands further north. These are: (i) the Sangiric group, spoken in the Sangir-Talaud archipelagoes north of the Sulawesi mainland (though one of the Sangiric languages, Sangil, is actually spoken in the Philippines, in the far south of Mindanao); (ii) the Minahasan group, at the tip of the northern arm; and (iii) the Gorontalo-Mongondow group, west of the Minahasan group, also in the northern arm.

The remaining six microgroups occupy a broad swath across central and southeastern Sulawesi. Following van den Berg (1996a) and Mead (2003a), these six microgroups are assigned to the large Celebic supergroup. Celebic comprises: (i) Tomini-Tolitoli, located in the 'neck' of Sulawesi, north of the city of Palu; (ii) Kaili-Pamona, located in the very centre of the island; (iii) Saluan-Banggai, on the eastern arm; (iv) Bungku-Tolaki, on the southeastern mainland; (v) Muna-Buton, on the islands off the southeastern leg; and (vi) Wotu-Wolio, in scattered locations at the northern tip of the Gulf of Bone, on Buton Island, and islands in the Flores Sea. In addition, Sulawesi is home to numerous scattered Bajau-speaking communities (see Mead and Lee 2007), as well as a 'homegrown' variety of Malay, Manado Malay.[2] These Bajau and Malayic varieties are not considered further in this typological overview. See Kaufman, this volume, Chapter 26 for a treatment of the Sama-Bajaw languages.

Table 33.1 shows the ten microgroups, the number of languages in each group and the better-known languages of each group, many of which figure in this chapter.

Map 33.1 shows the ten numbered Sulawesi microgroups, while Map 33.2 shows the location of individual languages.

It should be noted that this classification is still preliminary and several uncertainties remain. The status of Celebic as a bona fide supergroup, for example, is tentative, awaiting a solid historical-comparative reconstruction of its phonology, morphology, and lexicon. The position of the Badaic languages within a Greater South Sulawesi group is provisional. It is also unclear whether the Tomini-Tolitoli microgroup is a valid entity. For a discussion of these and other subgrouping issues see further Mead, this volume, Chapter 12.

The **number of speakers** of the languages of Sulawesi varies enormously, from several million to a few dozen (data from *Ethnologue* 22nd edition and updates in progress). However, such numbers must be treated with great care, since accurate figures are hard to obtain and are often based on older census data and estimates made several years, or even decades, ago. Population growth, language shift, migration to cities, and determining who counts as a (fluent) speaker all contribute to making the following figures rather imprecise. But the general picture is clear. On the one hand there are large languages like Bugis (over 4 million speakers), Makasar (around 2.5 million), Gorontalo (1 million), and Toraja Sa'dan (750,000). Several other languages have over 300,000 speakers, including Mandar, Kaili Ledo, Tae' (Luwu'-Rongkong), Tolaki, and Muna. On the other hand there are small languages with very few speakers such as Lolak (fifty

[1] It also includes the Tamanic languages (Taman, Embaloh) of interior Borneo (Adelaar 1994b). The Tamanic languages are not further considered in this chapter.

[2] Another variety, Makassar Malay or Makassar Indonesian, is also listed in the *Ethnologue* as a separate language, but this is apparently just a regional variant of standard Indonesian.

René van den Berg and David Mead, *Languages of Sulawesi*. In: *The Oxford Guide to the Malayo-Polynesian Languages of Southeast Asia*. Edited by: Alexander Adelaar and Antoinette Schapper, Oxford University Press. © René van den Berg and David Mead (2024). DOI: 10.1093/oso/9780198807353.003.0033

**Table 33.1** Sulawesi microgroups

| Microgroup | Nr of lgs | Sample languages |
|---|---|---|
| 1. South Sulawesi | 30 | Aralle-Tabulahan, Bada, Bambam, Behoa, Bugis, Konjo, Makasar, Mamasa, Mamuju, Mandar, Napu, Seko, Selayar, Toraja Sa'dan, Tae' (Luwu'-Rongkong), Ulumanda' |
| 2. Sangiric | 5 | Bantik, Ratahan, Sangil, Sangir, Talaud |
| 3. Minahasan | 5 | Tondano, Tonsawang, Tontemboan |
| 4. Gorontalo-Mongondow | 9 | Buol, Gorontalo, Mongondow, Ponosakan |
| *Celebic:* | *(62)* | |
| 5. Tomini-Tolitoli | 10 | Dampelas, Lauje, Pendau, Tajio, Totoli |
| 6. Kaili-Pamona | 13 | Kaili Da'a, Kaili Ledo, Pamona, Rampi, Uma |
| 7. Saluan-Banggai | 6 | Balantak, Banggai, Bobongko |
| 8. Bungku-Tolaki | 15 | Bungku, Kulisusu, Mori Bawah, Padoe, Tolaki |
| 9. Muna-Buton | 12 | Cia-Cia, Muna, Tukang Besi |
| 10. Wotu-Wolio | 6 | Barang-Barang, Wolio, Wotu |
| Total | 111 | |

speakers in 2017), Budong-Budong (seventy speakers in the late 1980s), and Taje (200 speakers in the late 1990s). Most of the languages of Sulawesi lie somewhere in the middle, with a median size of around 15,000 speakers.

In terms of **language vitality**, several languages appear to be healthy and are passed on to the next generation. These are put at level 6a (vigorous), or even level 5 (developing), on the EGIDS scale.[3] This is true for large languages such as Toraja Sa'dan, but also for medium-sized and smaller languages such as Balantak, Bambam, Talaud, and Bada (6,800 speakers in the late 1980s). A majority of languages in Sulawesi, however, show clear signs of decline, though so far only one language (Ponosakan) has actually become extinct. Young people, notably those living in or close to urban areas, are shifting to Indonesian, or Manado Malay in the case of the Minahasan languages. These languages are listed as 6b (threatened), 7 (shifting), 8a (moribund), 8b (nearly extinct), or 9 (dormant) on the EGIDS scale. This decline is not only noticeable in smaller languages, but also for medium-sized and large languages like Tolaki and Gorontalo. For the Tomini-Tolitoli languages, Himmelmann (2010a) sketches various 'endangerment scenarios'.

Table 33.2 summarizes the vitality information.

A final sociolinguistic point to be made is that a few Sulawesi languages have traditional **writing systems**, predating colonial contact. The best-known cases are Bugis and Makasar (and to a limited extent Mandar), which were written with a script usually referred to as *lontara*, an alphasyllabary of Indian origin. It was used for Bugis and Makasar myths (including the famous Galigo creation myth), court history, genealogies, as well as personal correspondence. Wawonii, off the coast of southeastern Sulawesi, also had an Indian-based script, distinct from *lontara*, which has received almost no scholarly attention (a list of characters can be found in Manyambeang et al. 1982/1983: 107). The other language with a written tradition is Wolio, the court language of the Buton sultanate, which was written in an adapted form of the Arabic script. These writing systems are only rarely used nowadays.

Sulawesi has a relatively strong **research history** (see Noorduyn 1991a for details) which started in the middle of the nineteenth century. The first survey of Sulawesi linguistics was published in Dutch over a century ago (Adriani and Kruyt 1914), and thanks to the work of Matthes, Adriani,

[3] EGIDS stands for Expanded Graded Intergenerational Disruption Scale, a tool developed to grade language status and language vitality. See http://www.ethnologue.com/about/language-status for details and literature.

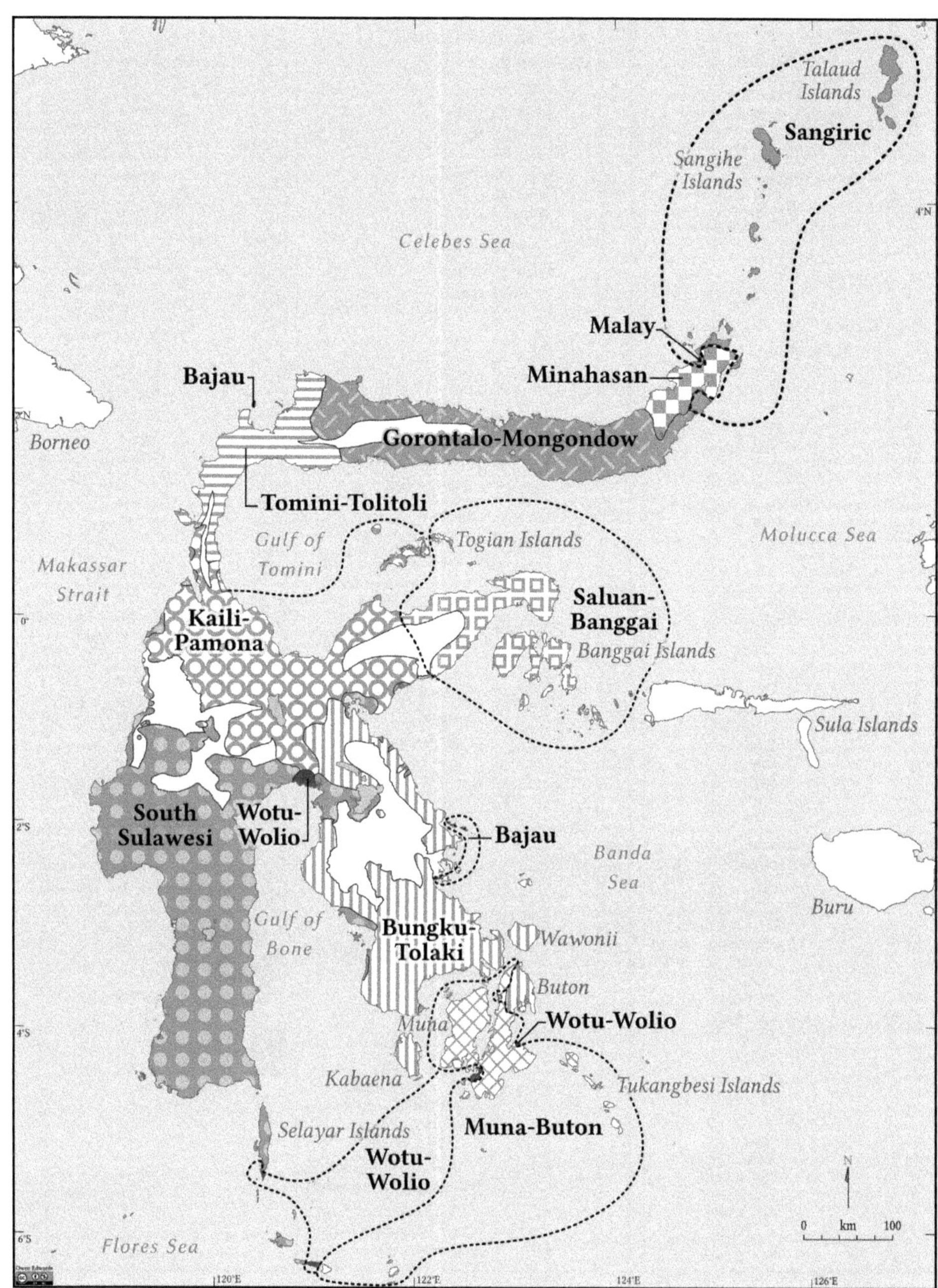


**Map 33.1** Sulawesi microgroups.

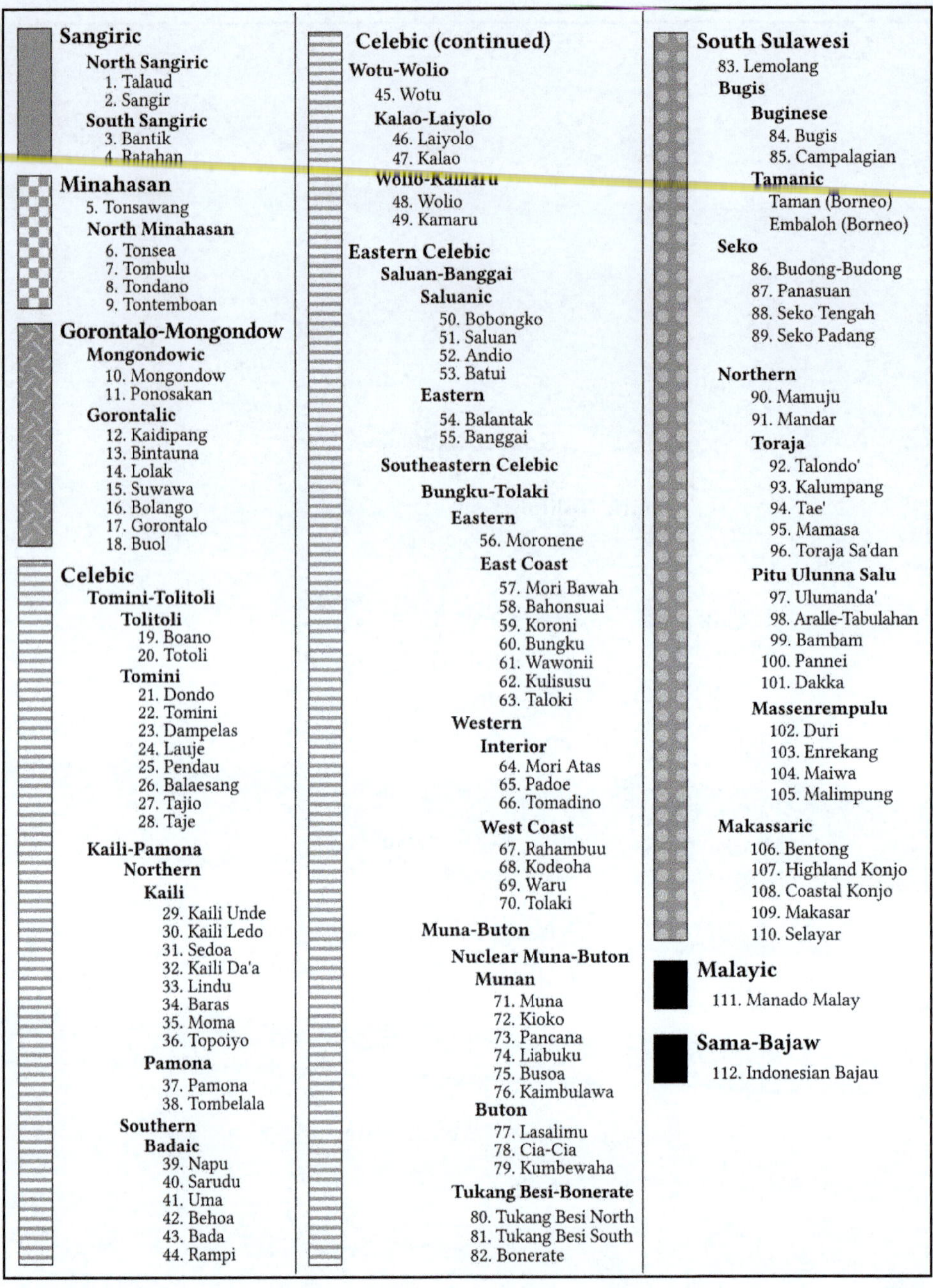


and Schwarz, published grammars and/or dictionaries were already available for Bugis, Makasar, Sangir, and Tontemboan around 1900. In the first half of the twentieth century, further work was done by various Dutch missionary linguists, notably Adriani himself (on Pamona, then called Bare'e) and Esser (on Mori and Uma). After an interval of several decades, fresh descriptive and especially comparative ground was covered by Sneddon in the 1970s–80s (see references), while the work of SIL linguists led to an outburst of activity and publications in the 1980s–90s. Due to extensive survey trips, the language map of Sulawesi could finally be drawn up with a fair degree of certainty. In addition, detailed phonologies, many grammatical studies and some dictionaries became available. The last two decades have seen various

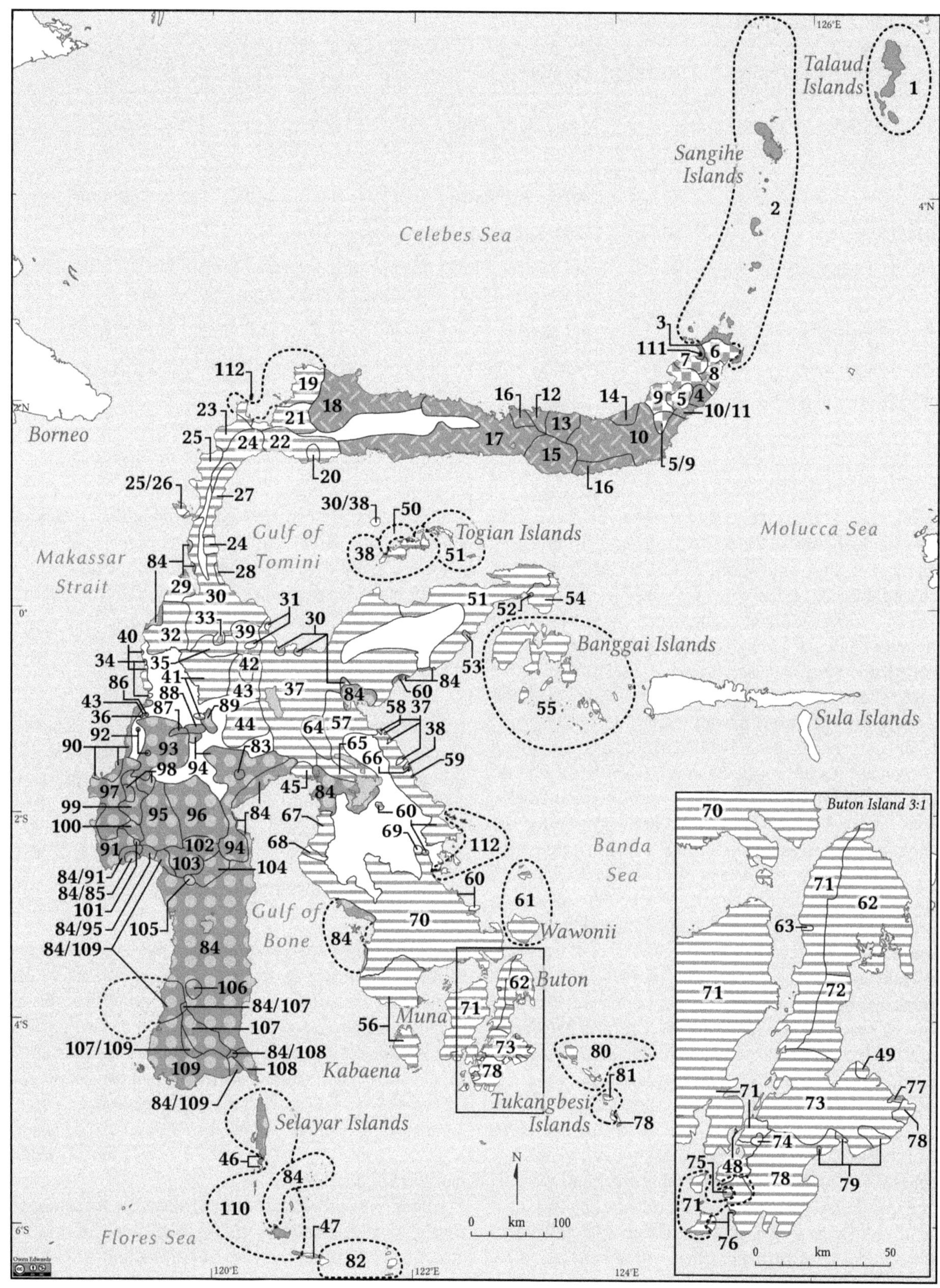


**Map 33.2** Sulawesi languages.

**Table 33.2** Language vitality in Sulawesi

| EGIDS level + description | | Nr of lgs | Examples |
|---|---|---|---|
| 3 | (Wider communication) | 2 | Bugis, Kaili Ledo |
| 4 | (Written) | – | |
| 5 | (Developing) | 14 | Balantak, Bambam, Kaili Da'a, Napu, Sangir, Toraja Sa'dan, Uma |
| 6a | (Vigorous) | 16 | Buol, Kulisusu, Mamasa, Seko Padang, Talaud, Tukang Besi |
| 6b | (Threatened) | 48 | Duri, Gorontalo, Konjo, Makasar, Mandar, Mongondow, Mori Bawah, Moronene, Muna, Pamona, Pendau, Rampi, Tolaki, Wolio |
| 7 | (Shifting) | 17 | Banggai, Tajio, Totoli, Wotu |
| 8a | (Moribund) | 7 | Bantik, Tondano |
| 8b | (Nearly extinct) | 3 | Lolak, Ratahan, Taje |
| 9 | (Dormant) | 1 | Ponosakan |

new grammars, and an increasing number of Indonesian students and scholars working on languages of Sulawesi, though most of these studies are written in Indonesian and remain unpublished and largely inaccessible.

Currently, eleven Sulawesi languages have something that approaches a comprehensive grammar. These are, in chronological order: Makasar (Matthes 1858; Jukes 2006), Bugis (Matthes 1875; Sirk 1983), Sangir (Adriani 1893), Pamona (Adriani 1931), Mori Bawah (Esser 1927, 1933; Mead 2005), Muna (van den Berg 1989), Tukang Besi (Donohue 1999a), Pendau (Quick 2007), Balantak (van den Berg and Busenitz 2012), Tajio (Mayani 2013), and Tondano (Brickell 2014). Comprehensive dictionaries are available for the following languages: Bugis (Matthes 1874), Tontemboan (Schwarz 1908), Pamona (Adriani 1928), Sangir (Steller and Aebersold 1959), Makasar (Cense 1979), Wolio (Anceaux 1987), Muna (van den Berg 1996b, 2000), Balantak (Bradbury 2000), and Kaili Ledo (Evans 2003). The first five of these are in Dutch. Balantak, Muna, and Tajio have also entered the electronic age with searchable online dictionaries, available at webonary.org. Various dictionaries can also be downloaded from internet play stores, including Bugis, Makasar, Muna, and Tolaki. Only a few Sulawesi languages have significant text collections. Notable from the Dutch era are the collections for Tontemboan (141 texts with Dutch translations; Schwarz 1907) and Pamona (150 texts and translations; Adriani 1932–1933). The only comparable compilation in the post-independence era are the 112 Uma stories published in Laua et al. (2001). Language documentation projects have resulted in a number of archived collections of language data, including audio and video. These include Ratahan (Jukes 2005–2007), Tolitoli (Leto et al. 2005–2010), Tondano (Brickell 2016a), and Tonsawang (Brickell 2016b).

In spite of almost 150 years of linguistic research on Sulawesi and many excellent descriptions, huge gaps remain. Virtually nothing is published or known about some twenty-eight languages, representing about one fourth of the languages of Sulawesi.

## 33.2 Phonology

From a MPSEA perspective, the languages of Sulawesi are phonologically not particularly striking or deviant, with the possible exception of the presence of prenasalized consonants. The most conspicuous phonological features are summarized in the following sections.

### 33.2.1 Consonant inventory

Most languages have a relatively modest consonant inventory, ranging from fourteen to thirty. Numbers on the higher end are usually caused by the unitary interpretation of prenasalized obstruents (discussed in §33.2.3), as well as the presence of marginal loan phonemes. A lower end consonant inventory is Bantik with fourteen consonants: /p t k ʔ b d g m n ŋ s h r j/, whereas Wolio represents a high end inventory with thirty consonants: /p t c k ʔ b d ɟ g ɓ ɗ m n ɲ ŋ f s z h w l r $^{m}$p $^{n}$t $^{ɲ}$c $^{ŋ}$k $^{m}$b $^{n}$d $^{ɲ}$ɟ $^{ŋ}$g/, five of which are marginal phonemes.

Palatal consonants are typically absent in Sulawesi, including the Minahasan languages, Buol, Gorontalo, Mongondow, Behoa, Bada, and a majority of the Bungku-Tolaki and Muna-Buton languages, but they do occur in the South Sulawesi group, while some Kaili-Pamona languages have a single prenasalized palatal consonant (Uma /$^{ɲ}$c/, Kaili Ledo

/$^{\text{ɲ}}$ɟ/). Bungku-Tolaki, Muna-Buton, and several other languages are described as not having approximants (except in recent loanwords), and /i/ retains its syllabic nature even between vowels (e.g. Kulisusu [meˌieˈie] 'play Chinese jump rope'). Banggai and certain Saluan dialects do not make a phonemic contrast between /l/ and /r/.

Typically lacking in Sulawesi consonant inventories are fricatives such as /z/, /v/, /f/ (but present in Muna and Busoa), and /x/ (present in Kumbewaha). A contrast between voiced and voiceless fricatives at the same point of articulation is rare (but Talaud and Tombulu contrast /s/ with a voiced retroflexed fricative /ʐ/). Two common patterns are for fricatives to be all voiceless (e.g. Bungku /ɸ s h/), or voiceless except for the labial fricative (e.g. Bambam /β s h/), but other patterns also occur (e.g. Muna /f s ʁ h/).

**Typologically rare consonants** include the following. Implosives contrasting with regular plosives are prevalent in all of the Muna-Buton languages (extending to neighbouring Wolio and Kulisusu as an areal feature of Buton), and also in Gorontalo (though not all sources agree). Implosives also occur as free variant allophones of /b/ and /d/ in Bugis and Tolaki. The retroflexed lateral [ɭ] is quite common, found either as a distinct phoneme in addition to a regular /l/, as in Sangir, or as a conditioned allophone of /l/, as in Tonsawang, Mongondow, Buol, Pendau, Uma, the Badaic languages (Bada, Behoa, Napu), and Rampi. Moronene has a phonemic contrast between /r/ and /ɽ/, a retroflex flap. Other unusual phonemes include a voiceless dental affricate /θ/ in Tonsawang, a voiced retroflexed fricative /ʐ/ in Talaud and Tombulu, and, in Kaimbulawa, a voiced pharyngeal fricative /ʕ/ which corresponds to /r/ in related languages.

**Glottal stop** is phonemic in almost all the languages of Sulawesi. Exceptions are Bambam Kambowa, Napu, Sarudu, and Muna, where glottal is absent, as well as Gorontalo, Topoiyo, and Cia-Cia, where its phonemic status is not completely clear. Various phenomena show that glottal stop has a unique status among the consonants.

(i) It is the only consonant not to occur morpheme-initially in Tondano, Balantak, Pamona, Konjo, Uma, Padoe, and possibly also Bobongko. There may be an audible glottal stop before initial vowels, but it is non-phonemic and usually optional, as in Padoe *uma* 'father' [*uma* ~ *ʔuma*].

(ii) Medial consonants usually syllabify to the next syllable (see also §33.2.3), but in languages with syllable-final glottal stops but no initial phonemic glottal stops, an intervocalic glottal stop does not. This is reported for Balantak (e.g. *reʔ.es* 'fed up with'), as well as for Konjo (*teʔ.eŋ* 'tea'), Mamasa and Tondano. Compare Southern Muna *ta.ʔu* 'year', where glottal stop syllabifies in the expected way.

(iii) Balantak has unique allomorphy for *-Vm* '2SG.POSS', in which a syllable-final glottal stop is not treated as a consonant (which triggers infixation), but is ignored. Compare *tama* > *tama-am* 'your father' (final vowel, so a suffix), *sarat* > *sara<a>t* 'your foot', *wewer* > *wewe<e>r* 'your lip' (final consonant, so an infix), with *aleʔ* > *aleʔ-em* 'your garden' (final glottal, and a suffix, not the expected infix **ale<e>ʔ*).

(iv) Glottal stop is often automatically inserted to break up vowel sequences both within and across morphemes (see below for examples).

(v) Glottal stop is the only consonant to occur in monomorphemic CC clusters (in addition to NC clusters), as in Tondano *tuʔmər* 'catch'.

(vi) In Pendau and Dampelas an intervocalic glottal stop may manifest itself phonetically as creaky voice on the neighbouring vowels.

(vii) In Lindu and Moma /ʔ/ may occur word-finally when words are spoken in isolation (e.g. in eliciting wordlists).

(viii) Uma has no sequences #Vʔ and ʔVʔ, but two intervening Vs are allowed: *kiʔouʔ* 'pine tree'. Uma also has 'glottal hopping' with affixation (see §33.2.5).

Many language descriptions include **marginal consonant phonemes** in parentheses in the phoneme inventory, as these phonemes have low frequency (sometimes a single item). They are typically, but not always, limited to loanwords, onomatopoeia, and functor words, and usually do not participate in morphophonemic processes. Regularly recurring marginal phonemes across Sulawesi are palatal consonants and /h/. Examples from ten languages are: (a) Ratahan /b d ɟ g c h ɲ w/; (b) Buol /h s ɟ ʔ/; (c) Gorontalo /c ɲɟ ɲ r/; (d) Mongondow /ɟ ɲ h/, where /ɲ/ is found only in the morpheme *-ɲa* '3SG.POSS'; (e) Pendau /c h/, but also /k/ which is defective in many Tomini-Tolitoli languages. (It is present, but much less common initially, medially, and finally than /p t/, but very common in the cluster /ŋk/); (f) Dampelas /h/, which fluctuates with /r/, e.g. *hano* ~ *rano* 'lake'; (g) Ledo /c h/; (h) Napu /c, ɲɟ/; (i) Muna /c ɟ y/; and (j) Wolio /b d f z ɲ/.

## 33.2.2 Vowel inventory

Over 90% of Sulawesi languages have a five-vowel system /i ɛ ɑ ɔ u/, but several have six vowels, three have seven, and one (Ulumanda') has eight. A six-vowel system with /ə/ is found in Sangil and Sangir (but not Talaud), the five

Minahasan languages, Bugis, Barang-Barang, and possibly Wotu. Bambam and Aralle-Tabulahan also have six vowels, but in these languages the sixth vowel is /æ/. Two Badaic languages reportedly have seven vowels. In Bada and Behoa the two additional vowels are a back low rounded /ɒ/ and a mid-high /o/. A dialect of neighbouring Rampi also has seven vowels for some speakers, including a central vowel /ə/ and, very unusual for Western Austronesian, a high front-rounded vowel /y/, as in /ylɛ/ 'snake'. Detailed phonetic descriptions are still lacking for these three languages. Ulumanda' has eight vowels: /i, e/ and the front-back pairs /æ/ - /a/, /ø/ - /o/, and /y/ - /u/. The fronted vowels developed as allophones before velar consonants, but became phonemic when consonant contrasts were lost (a similar process gave rise to the vowel /æ/ in Bambam and Aralle-Tabulahan).

In most languages of Sulawesi, phonetically long vowels can be analysed as underlying sequences of two like vowels because of stress patterns and pattern symmetry. Tolaki [te'goː] 'to burp', for example, is phonemically /tegoo/. However, contrastively long vowels occur in ultimate syllables in Seko (where they reflect former *-Vq sequences) and Saluan and Batui (where they reflect former *-Vy, *-Vj, and *-VR sequences) (Mead and Pasanda 2015). In Seko historical schwa in penultimate syllables harmonized with the following vowel but retained short timing, resulting in contrastively quick vowels (T. Laskowske 2007).

In the languages that have the phoneme /ə/, it often occupies a special position, comparable to /ʔ/ among the consonants. In Bugis, for example, /ə/ does not occur word-finally, unlike the other vowels. Likewise in Sangir, /ə/ does not occur word-finally, nasals and laterals geminate following /ə/, it is never followed by certain consonants, and it is the vowel in paragogic syllables (see §33.2.3.5).

### 33.2.3 Syllable structure and phonotactics

There is an overwhelming preference for syllables of the shape CV or V among the languages of Sulawesi (see Sneddon 1993). Codas and hence CVC syllables are less common, often with restrictions. These coda restrictions on CVC syllables often differ between medial and final syllables. For final syllables the following distinctions can be made.

(a) **No coda consonants.** Roughly half of the languages of Sulawesi allow only open syllables. This is true for Gorontalo, most of the Kaili-Pamona, all of the Bungku-Tolaki and Muna-Buton and most of the Wotu-Wolio microgroups.

(b) **A very limited coda set.** Examples: Uma has only /ʔ/, Sangil only /ŋ ʔ/, Mamasa only /n ŋ k ʔ/.

(c) **A relatively large coda set.** Non-occurring final consonants are often voiced stops, palatals, /h/, and the glides /w j/. Examples from selected languages include Tondano: all twenty-two consonants except /b d g/; Buol: all eighteen except /h ʔ ɟ s ß/; Pendau: all nineteen except /c ɟ ɲ v h/; Dampelas: all nineteen except /c ɟ ɲ h j w (k)/; Balantak: all fifteen except /b d g w j/; Bobongko: all nineteen except /ɓ, h, j, ɲ, w/; Banggai: all twenty-one except /b d g w j/. Tonsawang is unusual in that of its seventeen consonants it only disallows final /p t k/. When final voiceless stops do occur, they are typically unreleased, as in Dampelas and Balantak.

(d) **No coda restrictions:** Tonsea allows for all fourteen consonants in coda position, and Bolaang-Mongondow for all sixteen (not counting three marginal consonants). This includes voiced stops.

CVCV is always syllabified as CV.CV, except with medial glottal stop in languages such as Balantak and Konjo, as illustrated in §33.2.1. Initial V(C) syllables often have a non-phonemic initial glottal stop. Apart from (C)V(C), there are the restricted syllable types NC (nasal and homorganic obstruent) and N̩ (syllabic nasal), discussed below.

Several languages have **onset restrictions.** For example, Sangil has no initial /w ɣ r ɭ ŋ/, Tontemboan lacks initial /b d j ʔ/, and many languages, including Balantak and Tonsawang, have no initial phonemic glottal stop. Initial non-phonemic glottal stop, however, is very common throughout Sulawesi, but occasionally glottal stop and zero (and /h/) are contrastive, as in Dampelas *api* 'fire', *ʔapi* 'wing', *hapi* 'spouse', and Southern Muna *ato* 'accompany', *ʔato* 'roof', *hato* 'arrive'.

#### 33.2.3.1 *Nasal-obstruent clusters*

Most languages of Sulawesi allow for a sequence of a nasal followed by a homorganic obstruent (hereafter NC). The number of allowed combinations varies from three to nine. Some languages only have a voiceless series (Uma /mp nt ɲc ŋk/), others only a voiced series (Tolaki /mb nd ŋg/), but most have a double set. Kaili (both Ledo and Da'a) has four voiced prenasalized stops /mb nd ɲɟ ŋg/, but only two voiceless ones /mp nt/, though Ledo has /ŋk/ in a few loans. On the other hand, Tado-Lindu has four voiceless prenasalized stops /mp nt ɲc ŋk/, but only two voiced ones /mb nd/. Kodeoha is exceptional in having no NC sequences, or other consonant combinations for that matter.

Languages which allow word-medial NC clusters differ as to whether these sequences can also occur word initially. Pamona has nine NC combinations, all of which can occur word initially. Balantak has four initial NC combinations (of a possible seven), as in *ndaiŋ* 'dried meat' and *ŋgeaak* 'saliva'. These initial clusters occur infrequently, and initial *nt* is only found in one word: *ntuʔu* 'that'. In Bobongko, initial NCs are even more limited. Banggai sometimes shows free variation between initial C and NC: *(n)duangan* 'boat'. In Buol initial

NCs are only found in proper names (e.g. *Ndubu*). Word-initial nasals in NCs in both Pendau and Dampelas have been analysed as syllabic nasals, with N constituting a separate syllable, as in Pendau *ntolu* /n.'tɔ.lu/ 'egg'. In Tondano, initial NCs are tautosyllabic, but bimorphemic: the N of an initial NC cluster is an inanimate noun class marker: *n-tali* 'rope', *m-poʔpoʔ* 'coconut'.

In some languages, NC sequences have been analysed as clusters of two phonemes, but in others they have been analysed as unary segments, that is prenasalized stops. Arguments thought to favour a unary analysis for a particular language include (i) absence of other types of CC sequences; (ii) absence of non-homorganic NC sequences; (iii) absence of a nasal coda word finally; (iv) presence of NC sequences word initially; and (v) native-speaker intuitions for dividing syllables before the nasal. Pendau does have word-final nasals, and hence Quick analyses medial NC sequences as clusters (e.g. *maŋ.ge* 'uncle'). Riehl (2008) argues, however, that even when all five criteria are met, one still cannot conclude that NC sequences are unary, only that they are tautosyllabic. A case in point: where Adriani analysed Pamona *wombu* 'door' as CV.CV (*wo.ᵐbu*), Riehl analyses it as CV.CCV. We are inclined to favour a unary analysis, giving credit to pattern symmetry, but the matter is not settled.

### 33.2.3.2 *Other consonant clusters*

Apart from NC sequences, other monomorphemic clusters are fairly rare, but /ʔC/ is found in Tondano and Tontemboan (and the South Sulawesi languages), while /hC/ occurs in Tombulu and Aralle-Tabulahan. Word-medial bimorphemic clusters are limited to (i) reduplicated monosyllables, as in Tombulu *səpsəp* 'to suck' and (ii) cases of affixation and cliticization, where C-initial morphemes meet stem-final consonants, as in Balantak *atop-ta* 'our roof', *utus-ku* 'my sibling', and *malom-si* 'later, at night'. Several languages avoid such sequences by either consonant deletion or vowel epenthesis. See §33.2.5 for examples of these morphophonemic processes. Word-final consonant clusters are universally disallowed in Sulawesi, with Tontemboan providing a rare exception: *kilauʔmb* 'to dig' (and variants).

### 33.2.3.3 *Diphthongs and vowel sequences*

Diphthongs appear to be absent from Sulawesi. Sequences of vowels are typically analysed as belonging to different syllables, as evidenced by pattern symmetry. In many languages most of the twenty-five (5x5) different vowel sequences are allowed, though some have restrictions. A diphthong analysis for these sequences would need to posit an additional fifteen to twenty phonemes, while other evidence against a diphthong analysis comes from stress patterns and reduplication. In CV-reduplication, for example, it is the first vowel of a sequence that gets copied, as in Dampelas *sae* 'long time' > *sa-sae* 'very long time'. Monomorphemic sequences of three vowels are present in many languages (e.g. Napu *boea* 'village', *raoa* 'weather'), but absent elsewhere (e.g. Mamasa). Mori has a rare sequence of four vowels in *buaea* 'crocodile'.

### 33.2.3.4 *Geminate consonants*

Geminate consonants are common in the South Sulawesi microgroup (except Badaic), but rare elsewhere. They are not analysed as single phonemes, but as sequences of identical consonants, often the result of assimilation. They typically occur stem-internally and at morpheme boundaries, although, in Bugis, geminate consonants also occur word initially due to aphaeresis of an initial vowel (Noorduyn 1990). In most Bugis dialects, geminated continuants and voiceless stops are true geminates, but voiced stops are preglottalized (e.g. Bugis *tabbukka* [taʔbuk:a] 'open'). Mamasa is similar but maintains a contrast between geminate lateral /ll/ and preglottalized /ʔl/. In Makasar, geminate nasals, *ll* and *rr* all contrast with corresponding preglottalized sequences *ʔm, ʔn, ʔɲ, ʔŋ, ʔl, ʔr*. In Tabulahan voiceless obstruents are preaspirated, where surrounding languages have geminates (e.g. Toraja [ap:aʔ], Tabulahan [uhpaʔ] 'four'). From the South Sulawesi group, geminates spread areally into Limola, Wotu, and Laiyolo, small languages located on the fringes of the South Sulawesi group. They are also reported for Talaud, where they are in free variation with preglottalized single consonants (e.g. *pap:uso ~ paʔpuso* 'heart'). Doubling also occurs before the paragogic vowel /a/ in Talaud (e.g. /laŋit:a/ 'sky'). Neighbouring Sangir geminates all nasals and laterals following /ə/: /əl:o/ 'day', /tən:iʔ/ 'mosquito'. Bimorphemic geminate consonants occur in Bobongko, where they result from the assimilation of consonant clusters at morpheme boundaries, for example, /tiŋkod+ku/ 'my heel' [tiŋkod:u] (Mead 2001a).

### 33.2.3.5 *Paragogic syllables*

Sneddon (1993) was the first to point out that various Sulawesi languages have added an additional vowel (a paragoge) to avoid word-final consonants, which through resyllabification of the original final consonant results in a paragogic syllable. This phenomenon is part of a general drift towards final open syllables in Sulawesi. Paragogic syllables are found in Sangir, Talaud, Buol, Gorontalo, most Tomini-Tolitoli languages, as well as in a variety of other Sulawesi languages where they are limited to borrowed words. A few points can be noted about these paragogic syllables.

(a) The quality of the paragogic vowel is not identical across these languages. It is /a/ in Talaud, /ə/ in Sangir (obligatorily followed by a final /ʔ/, e.g. *kəndagəʔ* 'love'), /o/ in Pendau, /o/ in Buol (but /u/ after voiced consonants), /e/ in Lauje, /i/ in Pamona (restricted), and an echo vowel in Bantik (again, followed by /ʔ/) and also in Dampelas.
(b) This paragogic syllable is often extrametrical: stress stays on the original penultimate syllable (e.g. Dampelas *ˈbuluru* 'mountain', Pamona *ˈlindugi* 'earthquake').
(c) The paragogic vowel may disappear when a suffix or enclitic is added: Sangil *laedəʔ* 'foot' + *-e* '3SG.POSS' > *laede* 'his foot'.
(d) There are various degrees of variability, stability, and integration into the larger phonological system. This is especially true for the Tomini-Tolitoli languages and Buol, where there appears to be considerable variation within a speech community, and even for a single speaker. In Buol the paragogic vowel is often dropped in connected speech before consonants, and younger speakers tend to drop it even before vowels or pause. In Dampelas, paragogic vowels tend to occur at prosodic breaks, especially during storytelling performances, but again there is substantial variation.

### 33.2.4 Stress

Taking as our starting point the prosodic typology suggested by Kaufman and Himmelmann (this volume, Chapter 42), the languages of Sulawesi are split between the Philippine type and the Eastern type. The Philippine type, characterized by a phonemic prominence distinction on roots, appears to be limited to the three northern microgroups (Sangiric, Minahasan, Gorontalo-Mongondow). However, clear examples of monomorphemic minimal pairs distinguished solely by stress are often hard to find, detailed prosodic studies are not available, and the interplay between word stress and phrasal stress is largely unexplored in these languages.

In the Eastern prototype, stress regularly falls on the penultimate syllable and hence is not phonemic. Even under affixation, word stress remains penultimate, for example, Muna *ˈfotu* 'head' and *foˈtuno* 'his/her head' (with *-no* '3SG.POSS'). This appears to be the norm for all the Celebic languages, as well as for the South Sulawesi languages, though the Tomini-Tolitoli languages may have features of the Java-prototype, which is stressless.

In many languages, however, there are various rule-governed exceptions to the rule of penultimate stress.

(a) In a number of languages certain clitics are extrametrical. In Kaili Da'a these include the enclitics *=ku* '1SG.POSS', *=mu* '2SG.POSS', *=na* '3SG.POSS'. Compare *ˈana* 'child' and *ˈanamu* 'your child'. (In neighbouring Kaili Ledo these morphemes are suffixes and hence the root undergoes stress shift: *aˈnamu* 'your child'.) In Uma the absolutive pronouns are extrametrical: compare *ˈkeni* 'carry', *ˈkenia* 'carry me' (with *=a* 1SG.ABS) and *keˈnia* 'baggage' (with *-a* NMLZ). Napu is similar.
(b) Paragogic syllables (see §33.2.3) are typically extrametrical.
(c) With sequences of like vowels, the whole long vowel is stressed as a unit, rather than just the section of the vowel in the penultimate syllable; compare Balantak *ˈkaan* 'eat' and *ˈkaanon* 'will be eaten'.
(d) With sequences of non-high vowels followed by high vowels (such as *ai, au, ou, oi, ei, eu*), in which the high vowel occurs in the penult, stress shifts to the antepenult, presumably because the lower vowel is more sonorous: Tolitoli *ˈtaipaŋ* 'mango', Dampelas *ˈndoumo* 'not again', Uma *ˈdaeoʔ* 'grave', Moronene *ˈbaura* 'skin'.
(e) Sangil has an unusual rule that blocks the shift of stress to the penultimate syllable which normally occurs under affixation. The rule is triggered when the suffix is a single phoneme (*ˈtemaŋe* 'his field' < *ˈtemaŋ* + *-e* '3SG.POSS'), or when any *k*-initial suffix is added to a C-final stem: *liˈmaku* 'my arm/hand' (< *ˈlima* + *-ku* '1SG.POSS'), but *ˈanaʔku* 'my child' (< *ˈanaʔ* + *-ku).*

**Secondary stress** on words is not often mentioned in descriptions, but it appears to be rhythmically based, with secondary stress occurring on alternating syllables preceding the stressed penultimate syllable. Dampelas shows an unusual pattern whereby words with final glottal stop often receive secondary stress on the ultimate syllable: *mbureʔ* [m̩.ˈbu.ˌreʔ] 'to go south', compare *m-bure* [m̩.ˈbu.re] 'scared'.

### 33.2.5 Morphophonemics

The morphophonemic phenomena typically associated with Western Austronesian—such as nasal assimilation, nasal deletion, and nasal substitution related to the active prefix *moN-* —are also widespread in Sulawesi and illustrated by Tolaki *moN-kaa* > *moŋgaa* 'to burn', Pendau *moN-rampuŋ* > *morampuŋ* 'to burn' and Gorontalo *moN-putu* > *momutu* 'to cut'. Though the exact details differ from language to language, the overall picture is relatively uniform. Other morphophonemic processes which occur in various languages include the following.

(a) **Deletion** of consonants across morpheme boundaries occurs in Buol (e.g. *utat* + *-ku* > *utatu* 'my sibling'). Balantak deletes the medial nasal in sequences of three consonants (*wuruŋ* + *-nta* > *wuruŋta* 'our language') and also degeminates identical CC sequences: *naan* + *-na* > *naana* 'his/her name', *wuuk* + *-ŋku* > *wuuku* 'my hair'. Balantak also has a very complex set of rules governing the deletion of base-initial *p*, determined by the meaning and shape of the prefix, as well as the presence of another *p* in the base.

(b) **Vowel epenthesis** is a second repair mechanism to avoid CC clusters arising through affixation. Tondano inserts /ə/, as in *wuʔuk* + *-ku* > *wuʔukəku* 'my hair', while Dampelas inserts an echo vowel: *bisol* + *ʔu* > *bisoloʔu* 'my calf'. (In many languages, including Dampelas, such epenthetic vowels do receive stress when found in penultimate position.)

(c) **Lenition** of certain medial consonants is found in Sangir and Tontemboan. In Sangir the following alternating pairs are found: /b-w, g-ɣ, d-r, r-ɭ/, as in *baeʔ* 'to troll' and *bawaeʔ* 'trolling line'; *geliʔ* 'to give', and *maɣeli* 'generous'.

(d) **Vowel harmony** is relatively common in Sulawesi. The clearest example of complete vowel harmony is Balantak, which has an irrealis agent voice prefix *mVŋ-* (with twenty allomorphs), as well as a second person possessive suffix *-Vm* (also with twenty allomorphs). For the latter suffix this large number is due to vowel harmony in combination with the choice between suffix *-Vm* (with final vowels and glottal stop) or infix *-V-* (with final consonants), as well as *w*-insertion in both cases to break up sequences of three identical vowels, hence *-wVm* and *-wV-*. Examples are *tama-am* 'your father', *suloo-wom* 'your heart', *wewe<e>r* 'your lip', and *tuu<wu>r* 'your knee'. Muna also shows full vowel harmony in the 1PL.INC and 2PL suffix *-Vmu* on verbs. Other languages have partial or incomplete vowel harmony, where only a subset of vowels participate in the process. Examples are Buol (vowel raising *a* > *o*) and Pendau, where prefixes of a specific set with underlying *o* change to *a* before a low vowel or to *e* before front vowels. An example is the prefix *so-* 'one': *so-mpulu* 'ten', *so-ndouŋ* 'one evening', *sa-gatus* 'one hundred', *se-ribu* 'one thousand', *se-eleo* 'one day'. Banggai has the same three resulting vowels, but a different system: *maN-* with *a*, *meN-* with *e*, *moN-* with *o*, *i*, and *u*: *mang-ampal* 'seek', *men-tembel* 'slaughter', *moŋ-kita* 'seek', *moŋ-umbas* 'hit'. High vowels seem less inclined to participate in vowel harmony processes than mid and low vowels.

(e) **Glottal insertion.** When a vowel-final prefix or proclitic meets a vowel-initial root Balantak inserts a glottal stop: *ni* + *ala* > *niʔala* 'was taken'. Southern Muna inserts a glottal stop across morpheme boundaries to break up a sequence of three vowels: compare *hako* + *-e* > *hakoe* 'catch it' with *humaa* + *-e* > *humaaʔe* 'eat it' and *tei* + *-e* > *teiʔe* 'put it'.

Below follows a sample of less commonly found morphophonemic processes, often limited to one or two languages.

(a) ***moN-* allomorphy.** Gorontalo shows the regular pattern where N is deleted before most consonants /c d ɟ g h l m n ŋ r s/, and nasal substitution occurs with initial /p b k/: *moN-putu* > *momutu* 'to cut', *moN-bilohu* > *momilohu* 'to see', *moN-kaluhu* > *moŋaluhu* 'to scratch'. However, initial *t* changes to *l* (*moN-tuladu* > *moluladu* 'to write'), some *h*-initial roots change to *m* (*moN-huluto* > *momuluto* 'to husk a coconut'), and some root-initial *w* and *y* change to *h*: *moN-wulato* > *mohulato* 'to wait', *moN-yilapito* > *mohilapito* 'to chase'.

(b) ***k-ʔ* alternation.** In Pendau root-initial *ʔ* alternates with *k* before *moN-*: *ʔai*, *moŋkai* 'to call', *ʔolog*, *moŋkolog* 'cut; break'.

(c) ***ol/ul*-deletion** in Gorontalo. The suffix *-lio* '3SG.POSS' has the variant *-io* with most roots ending in *o/u*, where this back vowel is also deleted. Compare the regular *depula-lio* 'her kitchen' with *biihu-lio* > *biihio* 'his/her lip(s)'.

(d) **Nasal fronting** changes final *ŋ* to *n* in Pendau before certain affixes (e.g. *ni-* + *tambiŋ* + *a* > *nitambina* 'extended', *ni-* + *tuuŋ* + *-i* > *ni-tuun-i* 'ordered').

(e) **Unusual prenasalization alternations.** Obstruents and their corresponding prenasalized counterparts show various deviant patterns. In Pamona *s* and palatal *nc* alternate: *susu* 'breast', *mancusu* 'to suck'. In Kaili Ledo the alternations are between *s* and *nɟ*, and *k* and *ŋg* (there is no *ns* or native *ŋk*): *sala* 'wrong' and *naN-* + *sala* + *-i* > *nanɟalai* 'criticize'; *kava* 'come', *naN-* + *kava* > *naŋgava* 'find s.t. you were searching for'. In Uma *h* and *nc* alternate: *N-hilo* > *ncilo* 'to see'; *pitu* + *haluʔ* > *pitu-ncaluʔ* 'seven streams'.

(f) Napu shows what can be called **deprenasalization**: when a root containing a prenasalized stop is followed by a suffix containing a voiceless prenasalized stop, the second one loses its prenasalization. Compare the regular *ana-ŋku* 'my child' with *dimba-ku* 'my sheep', and *sou-nta* 'our house' with *hampi-ta* 'our clothes'. Interestingly, voiced prenasalized stops are immune to this rule: *dimba-nda* 'their sheep'. In Kulisusu, deprenasalization occurs only to prevent two voiceless prenasalized stops in sequence: compare *wembe-ŋku* 'my goat' with *sinsi-ku* 'my ring'. Regressive deprenasalization occurs with the Mori Bawah prefix *moN-*, also to prevent a sequence of two voiceless prenasalized stops: *mom-paho* 'plant', *mon-tunu* 'roast', *mong-keke* 'dig' (regular assimilation) but *mo-pingko* 'finish off', *mo-tampele* 'slap', *mo-kungku* 'clench' (deprenasalization).

(g) Balantak has **w-insertion**, to avoid sequences of three identical vowels: *see* + *-Vm* > *see-wem* 'your odour', *tuur* + *-V-* (an allomorph of *-Vm*) > *tuuwur* 'your knee'.

(h) Bobongko shows **total assimilation** of the 1SG.POSS *-ku* (*-ŋku* after vowels) following obstruents. Compare regular *gianan-ku* 'my house', *kapara-ŋku* 'my machete' with *tingkod-du* 'my heel' and *kilit-tu* 'my skin'.

(i) **Glottal assimilation.** A glottal stop assimilates fully to a following voiceless consonant in Selayar: *appaʔ balo* 'four holes', but *appap pao* 'four mangoes' and *appas sapo* 'four houses'.

(j) ***-um-* allomorphy.** Instead of the regular irrealis infix *-um-* (*kala* > *kumala* 'to go'), Muna has the prefix *m-* before vowel-initial roots (*ala* > *mala* 'to take'), nasal substitution with initial *p* and *f* (*punda* > *munda* 'to jump', *foni* > *moni* 'to go up'), and zero with initial *b ɓ m mp mb*. This final allomorphic rule is shared with Tolaki and Padoe.

(k) Uma has '**glottal hopping**'. A root-final /ʔ/ moves to word-final position following derivational affixes. Compare *mo-niuʔ* 'to bathe' and *po-niu-aʔ* 'bathing place'. With enclitics glottal hopping does not occur: compare *anaʔ* 'child' with the two verbs *moʔanaiʔ* 'to have children' (with derivational *-i*; the first /ʔ/ is automatically inserted), and *moʔanaʔi* 'she gave birth' (with enclitic *=i* '3SG.ABS'). How this unusual phenomenon is best analysed prosodically is an open question.

### 33.2.6 Reduplication

Reduplication is heavily exploited in the languages of Sulawesi. Most languages have at least the following two reduplication patterns: monosyllabic CV-reduplication and bisyllabic reduplication. The first type is illustrated by Buol *ko~kait* 'broom'; (cf. *moŋait* 'to sweep'). Bisyllabic reduplication is usually without the coda C (in languages which allow codas), as in Dampelas *ales* 'slow' > *ale~ales* 'quite slowly', and similarly in Buol, Tajio, and Balantak. Some other languages do allow coda Cs to be reduplicated, as in Pendau *orop* 'hungry' > *nong-orop~orop-omo* 'starving'. Banggai has a variant where the medial consonant is dropped in the sequences *CaCi*, *CaCu*, and *CoCi*: *malu* > *mau~malu* 'tame', *sobit* > *soi~sobit* 'for a little while'. Minor reduplication patterns include CVV-reduplication (Balantak *memel* 'cold', *mee~memel* 'almost cold'), and infixing reduplication (Tukang Besi *koruo* 'many', *koruʔuo* 'certainly many', *amai* 'they', *amaʔai* 'certainly them', where the stressed vowel of the word is reduplicated).

Chapter 6.9 of Blust (2013a) provides a general overview of reduplication in Austronesian, including a discussion of Ca-reduplication in Sangir and Bolaang-Mongondow.

## 33.3 Word order

Compared to the enormous diversity in grammatical systems and morphosyntax (as discussed in §33.5), the languages of Sulawesi are relatively uniform with respect to word order. The areas where there is diversity are limited to the order of nouns and article-like elements, nouns, and demonstratives and, to a lesser degree, the basic word order within the clause.

### 33.3.1 Clausal order

The notion of basic word order in the languages of Sulawesi is not straightforward. Most transitive clauses in natural discourse do not have two full NPs, there is no consensus on the grammatical role labels for the NPs, and many word order permutations are allowed, usually for pragmatic reasons. In addition, very few statistically based descriptions are available. Given these caveats and limitations, the following characteristics appear to be shared by all of the languages of Sulawesi.

(a) VO order is the dominant order, both for agent voice in symmetrical languages, as well as for transitive clauses in non-symmetrical languages.

(b) The position of S in transitive clauses is relatively free. SVO appears to be the dominant order in a few languages (Balantak, Muna, and possibly others), but Tukang Besi is described as VOS, whereas for other languages there is essentially no fixed position for S (Buol, Ratahan, Wolio, Makasar). Riesberg et al. (2019) show that in symmetrical voice languages in Sulawesi the position of S is flexible, whether or not S is agent or patient, though there are various deviations. In Tondano actor voice constructions, for example, only <u>A</u>VP is allowed, not VP<u>A</u>.[4]

[4] Riesberg et al. (2019) use A(ctor), P(atient) and V(erb), with the underlining indicating the subject.

(c) The position of S in intransitive clauses also varies, with both VS and SV occurring widely, though SV appears to be the dominant order in Tondano, Bobongko, and others. Note, however, that not all descriptions distinguish between the position of S in transitive and intransitive clauses. VS is reported to be basic for Muna (VS 69%, SV 31%, n=115), while for Balantak it is undeterminable (VS 46%, SV 54%, n=55). The same holds true for Buol.

### 33.3.2 Adpositions

Sulawesi languages only have prepositions, and their number is typically rather small, ranging from three (Mori Bawah) to a dozen or so. Postpositions are not reported.

When a language employs a generalized preposition (such as Tolaki *i* 'at'), its meaning can be enriched through the use of relator nouns (part–whole relationships) within the complement of the prepositional phrase, or through directional verbs or nouns preceding the generalized preposition. Compare Tolaki *i* ***aa*** *laika-no* (at interior.part house-3SG.GEN) 'inside his house', ***butu*** *i kota* (go.toward at city) 'to the city', ***ari*** *i* ***une*** *benggi* (from at inside.part earthen.pitcher) 'from inside a pitcher'.

An unusual word order within prepositional phrases is reported for Moronene and Aralle-Tabulan (Andersen and McKenzie 2008). When a demonstrative is present in a PP, the normal order is Dem–Prep–N (rather than the expected Prep–N–Dem or Prep–Dem–N), thus involving discontinuous constituency, as the preposition breaks up the noun phrase. Examples include Moronene *koie hai landa* (DEM at veranda) 'on the veranda' and Aralle-Tabulahan *yato di kahpala?* (DEM at vessel) 'onto that airplane'.

### 33.3.3 Noun-modifiers

(a) **Articles.** Many Sulawesi languages have article-like elements, variously labelled as determiners, particles, noun markers, or case markers (see §33.5.1 for a discussion). Where they occur, they almost always precede the noun they modify, sometimes procliticizing. In various South Sulawesi languages, however, article-like elements are suffixes or enclitics that follow the head noun. These indicate definiteness, as Bugis *-e* in *nanre-e* 'the rice', and Makasar *-a* in *batu-a* 'the stone', where *-a* is an affixal clitic, having properties of both affixes and clitics.

(b) **Possessive NPs.** In all of the languages, possessive pronouns are suffixed to the head noun, as illustrated by Mori Bawah *ana-ku* 'my child', *nee-no* 'his/her name', *ue-do* 'their grandparent'. Similarly, full NP possessors follow the head noun, typically linked by a third person possessive suffix or a linker, as in Mori Bawah *nee-no torokuno* (name-3SG.POSS mountain) 'the name of the mountain', *ue-do ana-ni Sinongi* (grandparent-3PL.POSS child-3SG.POSS:PERS Sinogi) 'the grandfather of Sinongi's children'. (See §33.4.4 for more details on possession and head-dependent marking.) This pattern of postnominal possession is found throughout Sulawesi, with one notable exception. Banggai, the easternmost language of Central Sulawesi in the Saluan group, has regular suffixal possessive pronouns, but NP possessors usually precede the head noun. This unusual feature was already noted by Adriani in 1914, and is probably due to influence from neighbouring Maluku languages to the east. Examples are *ko tomusi mata-no* (ART bird eye-3SG.POSS) 'the bird's eye' and *ko tama-nggu ulu-no* (ART father-1SG.POSS head-3SG.POSS) 'my father's head'. Interestingly, Banggai also makes an alienable–inalienable distinction in its possessive system, a feature that is found nowhere else on Sulawesi: *ko mata-nggu* (ART eye-1SG.POSS) 'my eyes' vs. *ko-nggu bonua* (ART-1SG.POSS house) 'my house', where the article *ko* hosts the possessive suffix to signal alienable possession.

(c) **Adjectives.** In most Sulawesi languages, property concepts such as 'big', 'new', and 'amazed' are verbs, albeit with stative semantics. Hence there is no separate category 'adjective'. Within a noun phrase, such stative verbs always follow the head noun, either directly, as in Balantak *kuda pate* (horse dead) 'a dead horse', or in a relative clause, as in Buol *botu moitomo* (stone STATIVE:black) 'a black stone'.

(d) **Demonstratives.** In regards to the order of demonstrative–noun, there appears to be a dichotomy between South Sulawesi languages and the rest of Sulawesi. In virtually all of the Sulawesi languages outside of the South Sulawesi group, demonstratives follow the head noun, as in Ratahan *watu teqé* (stone DEM) 'that rock', Dampelas *pae 'ua* (rice DEM) 'that rice', and Tukang Besi *kalambe ana* (girl DEM) 'this girl'. However, many languages in the South Sulawesi subgroup show the reverse order: demonstratives typically precede the head noun. This is illustrated by Makasar *anjo tedong-a* (DEM buffalo-DEF) 'that buffalo', Duri *joq bola* (DEM house) 'that house', and Bambam *indo änäq* (DEM child) 'that child'.

However, exceptions to this geographic dichotomy are not hard to find. On the one hand Bugis, the largest language of the South Sulawesi group, has suffixed (possibly encliticized) demonstratives, e.g., *lopi-e-wé* (ship-DEF-DEM) 'this ship', and *bulu'-ro* (mountain-DEM) 'that mountain'. A posthead position is also found in Makasar as an alternative order: *tedong-a anjo* 'that buffalo'. On the other hand, Moronene, a Bungku-Tolaki language, has prenominal demonstratives: *die haratia* (DEM word) 'this word', *koie ato* (DEM roof) 'that roof'. A further anomaly is Banggai (the language with prenominal possessive NPs, see above), which normally has the expected posthead demonstratives: *lipu doo* (land DEM) 'that land'. Somewhat surprisingly, the language also allows for the demonstrative to occur twice, both preceding and following the head noun: *nia lipu nia* (DEM land DEM) 'this land/soil'.

(e) **Numerals.** The main pattern for Sulawesi seems to be that the numeral precedes the head noun, with or without an accompanying classifier. However, there are also languages for which the reverse order is given as basic. Examples of prehead numerals include Balantak *tolu' rondom* (three night) 'three nights', Kaili *lima mbaa manu* (five CLF chicken) 'five chickens' and Ratahan *ere roá kapuna* (unit two dog) 'two dogs'. An example of a language with (only?) posthead numerals is Sangir: *kalu ḷima-n-pədi* (stick five-LIG-CLF) 'five sticks'.

For a considerable number of languages both orders are reported, with the difference related to focus, definiteness, or the presence of other prehead modifiers. An example of both orders is Wolio with *rua angu banua* (two CLF house), 'two houses' (no emphasis) vs. *loka sa-puu* (banana one-CLF) 'one banana tree' (emphasis on the number).

Another example is Makasar, where the difference correlates with definiteness: *rua tau Parancisi'* (two person France) 'two French people' (indefinite), vs. *anjo anaʔ-na karaeng-a tallu-a* (DEM child-3.POSS king-DEF three-DEF) 'those three children of the king' (definite). Bambam normally has a prenominal numeral: *mesa hante* (one flat.area) 'one flat area', but when a numeral and a demonstrative co-occur, the numeral is found in postnominal position: *indo änäq mesa* (DEM child one) 'that one child'.

### 33.3.4 Negator

Negators in Sulawesi are typically invariant particles or adverbs which precede the verb or the noun they negate. In many Bungku-Tolaki languages negators attract subject indexing, as in Moronene *na=i po-turi* (NEG=3SG.NOM INTR-sleep) 'he did not sleep'. In Seko the negator is a proclitic on the verb, accompanied by a change in pronominal marking. Compare *ku=m-anne:* (1SG.REAL=INTR-eat) 'I'm eating' with *ha=m-anne:-kaʔ* (NEG-INTR-eat-1SG.IRR) 'I'm not eating' (see also §33.5.2). Negative imperatives are also preverbal. There are no known cases of unmarked clause-final negation in Sulawesi.

## 33.4 Morphological profile

The languages of Sulawesi are generally rich in morphology, showing a wide array of prefixes and suffixes, as well as circumfixes and infixes. Reduplication (discussed in §33.2.6) is found everywhere, while compounding, incorporation, and zero-derivation (word-formation without an overt formal change) are less frequent. Subtraction (the deletion of a part of a form) appears to be even rarer, but is reported for names in Muna and Wolio (e.g. *Wia* for *Dawia*). Non-linear morphology involving tone, stress, nasalization, or ablaut appears to be absent in Sulawesi.

Arriving at a satisfactory morphological typology for the languages of Sulawesi is complicated by various factors. First of all, many languages have a variety of non-productive or fossilized morphemes, such as *-in-* in Uma, which is found in a handful of nouns (e.g. *pinuʔai* 'dried rice', cf. the verb *puʔai* 'dry s.t. in the sun'). Since it is unclear whether such affixes should be included in various counts, we have excluded them. A second complication is the question of affix or clitic. Clitics are found throughout Sulawesi and while some enclitics can be unambiguously identified as such (mainly due to their non-participation in stress shifts), this is more difficult for proclitics. The presence of intermediate categories, such as affixal clitics (in Makasar), and clitic particles (imperative *le* and nominalizing *to* in Ratahan), as well as the occurrence of optional cliticization, complicate matters further and are indicators that the distinction between word and affix is a continuum, rather than a dichotomy. For further discussion of clitics in Sulawesi (and the Philippines), see Kaufman (2008, 2010a). A final point is that the distinction between inflection and derivation does not appear to be adequate for the languages of Sulawesi. While some affixes are clearly inflectional (e.g. person markers on the verb) and others are obviously derivational (e.g. nominalizations, causatives), there is a large number of affixes for which the distinction appears to be inadequate and possibly irrelevant. These include voice and TAM affixes, and various verbal derivations such as requestives. Given these caveats, the following statements outline the morphological profile of the languages of Sulawesi.

### 33.4.1 Synthesis

In the traditional morphological typology of analytic (or isolating), fusional, and agglutinative languages (seen as a continuum), the languages of Sulawesi can be located somewhere between fusional and agglutinative: many words are made up of more than one distinct morpheme, but fusion is not uncommon. Table 33.3 shows the morpheme-per-word ratio for eight representative languages, based on the first 150 words taken from the first lines of two published texts.[5]

These numbers are only suggestive, as orthographic conventions, analytical decisions on the status of morphemes as affix, clitic, or particle, as well as the genre of the text all play a role. Given the perceived complexity of verbal morphology in various Sulawesi languages, the numbers listed in Table 33.3 are not high (and they would be lower still if all clitics were removed). Numbers on the higher end, including Tondano, are due to extensive person and TAM marking on the verb. The low number for Ratahan appears to be a combination of relatively few affixes (see below), and the fact that clitics and clitic particles are written as separate words. This happens, for instance, with possessive enclitics: *walei nu* (house 2SG.POSS) 'your house'. These low counts should not obscure the potential for complex words containing several affixes and clitics. As these are not uncommon in texts and in daily use, examples (1) to (4) illustrate such complex words (with roots bolded):

**Table 33.3** Morpheme-per-word ratio in selected Sulawesi languages

| Language | Morphemes per word |
|---|---|
| Ratahan | 1.27 |
| Balantak | 1.51 |
| Makasar | 1.64 |
| Pendau | 1.66 |
| Kaili | 1.75 |
| Muna | 1.76 |
| Tondano | 1.85 |
| Konjo | 2.07 |

[5] For this table, the word breaks and interlinear morphemic analysis in the source texts were followed. This meant that the distinction between affixes and clitics could not be incorporated in this table, as it is only overtly coded for the texts in Makasar, Pendau, and Tondano. Hence 'word' represents a grammatical word in some languages, a phonological word in others, and a mixture in most. To ensure some consistency in the tabulation, prepositional proclitics in Pendau and Konjo were counted as separate words, circumfixes were counted as two separate morphemes, and zero morphemes were ignored.

Tondano

(1) *Sè=pa-**ketor**-en=na=mow.* (Pronouned as *èpaketorenamou*)
3SG.PIV-DYN-cut-PV=3SG.NPIV.A=COMPL
'She slices them (the bats) up.' (Brickell 2014: 469)

Tajio

(2) *Ni-pe-**valung**-i=nya=mo.*
UV.REAL-SF-carry.food-APPL=3SG.GEN=COMPL
'She/he has carried the food already.' (Mayani 2013: 87)

Muna

(3) *Ka-ti-feka-**mate**-ha-no-mo.*
NMLZ-PASS-CAUS-die-NMLZ-3SG.POSS-PFV
'And that was the reason he got killed.'
(van den Berg fieldnotes)

Mori Bawah

(4) *Mem-p<in>o-**ʔisa**-ako-kami* *inisa.*
PL.SBJ-<PASS>AP-pestle-APPL-1PL.EXCL.ABS pestled.rice
'We were pestled some rice (rice was pestled for us).'
(Esser 2011: 459)

### 33.4.2 Suffixing vs. prefixing

The ratio of prefixing vs. suffixing morphology for five Sulawesi languages (from five different microgroups) is displayed in Table 33.4, further split between person-marking morphology and other morphology. For the purposes of this table (and to make things simple and comparable), distinct affixes were counted only once, even when they are clearly polysemous. Combinations of prefixes are ignored, and so are circumfixes. Most clitics are excluded in this count, but clitic person markers are included.[6]

It is clear that prefixing morphology outnumbers suffixing morphology in each case, and that person-marking morphology is responsible for the very high number of affixes in Muna. Ratahan probably represents the low end of morphological complexity in Sulawesi, though further research is needed to corroborate this claim. Interestingly, the nominative person-markers in Bungku-Tolaki languages are ambidirectional: they are normally proclitics, but in some contexts they act as enclitics.

The distribution of infixing across Sulawesi is scattered. Most of the three northern Sulawesi microgroups appear to have the infixes *-um-* and *-in-* (as well as combinations such as *-inum-*), but in the rest of Sulawesi their distribution is scattered. The infix *-um-* is completely absent in a large number of languages (including Uma, Makasar, Wolio), restricted to a subset of locomotive verbs in Pendau (e.g. *l<um>eap* 'to

[6] The Tondano value is based on the phonological word. If all clitics are removed in Tondano (person markers, noun phrase markers, TAM enclitics), the number drops to 1.38 morphemes per grammatical word.

**Table 33.4** Affix count in selected Sulawesi languages

| Language | Prefixes | | | Suffixes | | | Infixes |
|---|---|---|---|---|---|---|---|
| | total | person-marking | Other | total | person-marking | other | |
| Muna | **53** | 21 | 32 | **26** | 16 | 10 | **1** |
| Balantak | **33** | 1 | 32 | **17** | 6 | 11 | **1** |
| Makasar | **21** | 4 | 17 | **13** | 10 | 3 | – |
| Kaili Da'a | **20** | 3 | 17 | **12** | 6 | 6 | – |
| Ratahan | **15** | – | 15 | **4** | 1 | 3 | **3** |

fly') and to some thirty intransitive verbs in Balantak (e.g. *l<um>ango* 'to swim'), but in other languages it is productive. In Muna-Buton languages, it typically marks irrealis, as for example, in Muna: *a-leni* (1SG-swim) 'I swim', *a-l<um>eni* (1SG-<IRR>swim) 'I will swim'.

### 33.4.3 Exponence

Though most morphemes express a single grammatical category, cumulative exponence, in which one morpheme encodes more than one category at the same time, is very common in Sulawesi. In most cases such portmanteau affixes encode a combination of voice, TAM and/or person-marking on verbs. Examples are Ratahan *na-* in *na-oman* 'I said', which encodes both agent voice and past tense; Balantak *-on* in *ili-on* 'will buy/will be bought', which encodes both patient voice and irrealis; Muna *nae-* in *nae-lagu* 'he/she will sing', which encodes a third person subject as well as irrealis, and Kaili *ku-* in *ku-kande* 'I will eat/will be eaten by me' which encodes three categories: first person (agent), patient voice, and irrealis. Portmanteau morphemes appear to be less common or absent in languages which lack both voice and the realis-irrealis distinction, such as Wolio.

### 33.4.4 Head-dependent marking

The following section describes head-dependent marking in two areas of the grammar of Sulawesi languages: within possessive phrases (part of the NP), and in clauses.

#### 33.4.4.1 *Within possessive phrases*

Most of the languages of Sulawesi have an explicit marker that encodes the relationship between a head (the possessed noun) and the dependent (the possessor noun). The locus of this marking can be on the head or on the dependent, but some languages have intriguing mixed systems. A caveat is in place here. This summary is provisional, as many sources are not explicit about the exact nature of the linking elements (affixes, clitics, or particles). Nor do they indicate the criteria by which they choose between competing analyses.

(a) **Marker on the head noun.** The use of the 3SG possessive suffix on the head noun appears to be the main pattern for many Celebic and South Sulawesi languages, as in Wolio *o bake-na loka* (ART fruit-3SG.POSS banana) 'the fruits of the banana tree', and Padoe *ana-no dahu* (child-3SG.POSS dog) 'puppy'. Various languages make a distinction in the possessive suffix between a following common noun and a following personal noun, as illustrated by Balantak *sina-na* 'his/her mother', *sina-na anak* 'the child's mother' and *sina-ni Aman* 'Aman's mother'.

(b) **Marker on the dependent noun.** Typically, a genitive/possessive marker (different from the 3SG possessive affix) procliticizes to the dependent noun, as in Pendau *bau nu=dagat* (fish GEN=ocean) 'the ocean fish' and *siama ni=Eko* (father GEN.PERS=Eko) 'Eko's father', again making a distinction between common and proper nouns. Tondano is similar: *wale ni=Tim* (house ANIM.SG.GEN=Tim) 'Tim's house', as is Bantik *i-maʔ nu-anaʔ* (NOM-mother GEN-child) 'the mother of the child', where *nu* is probably also a proclitic. Ratahan *ni=* (with proper nouns) is more complex. It procliticizes to the dependent possessor: *walei ni=tonaqas* (house GEN=shaman) 'the shaman's house', but the variant *i* is triggered by a possessor head which ends in *n* or *ng*: *long i=tonaqas* (hut GEN=shaman) 'the shaman's hut'.

(c) **Mixed system.** Sangir has a mixed system: there is no marker following consonants, as in *ahus i David* (son PERS David) 'son of David' (*i* is not a linker but a proper noun marker, possibly a proclitic), but when the head noun ends in a vowel, it is marked with the suffix *-n* and the proper name marker is dropped: *wale-n Simon* (house-GEN Simon) 'house of Simon' (Adriani 1893: 219–20). A slightly more complex mixed system is illustrated by Kaili Ledo. Before common nouns there is a particle *nu* (which is written separately, but is possibly a proclitic): *banua nu roa-na* (house GEN friend-3SG.POSS) 'the house of his friend'. When the possessor starts with the voiceless consonants *s*, *p*, *t*, or *k*, the particle is absent, but the consonant is prenasalized: *koya n-tovau* (leg GEN-goat) 'a goat's leg'. When the possessor is a personal name, the linking element is absent and only the person marker *i* is found: *banua i Rina* (house PERS Rina) 'Rina's house'.

Given these mixed systems (and various uncertainties surrounding the analysis), it is not immediately clear whether the head-dependent dichotomy is actually a relevant typological concept for the morphosyntax of NPs in Sulawesi. It seems more satisfactory to establish an area-specific typology of 'possessive linking' which does justice to the distinct morphophonemic, grammatical, and prosodic features of the various types of linkers, and correlates them with the presence of noun phrase markers on the clausal level (see §33.5).

#### 33.4.4.2 *In clauses*

On the clause level, the verb is defined as the head, while the arguments are dependents. In this section subjects are explicitly included in the typology (cf. Nichols and Bickel 2013b in WALS, where subjects are excluded). Case marking is defined as the presence of morphemes that unambiguously indicate the grammatical function of the NP in question. For the sake of convenience proclitics are treated as being part of the head. In clauses, most of Sulawesi is head-marking, though double marking is also common. There do not seem to be examples of dependent marking only in Sulawesi.

(a) Two types of **head marking** in clauses can be distinguished. The first is found in languages which make heavy use of person marking on verbs, and no case marking on nouns. This is a large group (possibly some sixty to seventy languages), consisting of all the non-symmetrical voice languages of Sulawesi, including the South Sulawesi group, several Kaili-Pamona languages (such as Uma), and all the languages in the Bungku-Tolaki, Muna-Buton, and Wotu-Wolio groups. A second type of head-marking is exemplified by languages with voice morphology on the verb (and little or no person marking), but again no case marking on nouns. Examples are Tondano, Tajio, Pendau, and Kaili (but see below).

(b) **Double marking** covers the languages where there is symmetrical voice marking on the verb, as well as syntactic case marking on the NPs (these markers are usually proclitics, though often written as separate words). However, in all cases this double marking is limited to various degrees. In Buol only personal nouns take the nominative *ti* (common nouns are unmarked). In Balantak only common nouns functioning as post-predicate subjects are case-marked by *a* (pre-predicate subjects are unmarked). Another type of double marking is Tukang Besi, which has both person marking on the verb and case marking on NPs (nominative *na* and core *te*). Ratahan, Tajio, Pendau, and Kaili could also be marginally classified as double-marking, as agents in patient voice are case-marked by *nu* (common nouns) or *ni* (proper nouns), but all other grammatical roles are unmarked.

### 33.4.5 Meaning categories

We end this section by listing semantic categories that are typically encoded morphologically. Apart from case marking, **nouns** have limited morphological possibilities, often only possession and occasionally definiteness (as with Makasar *-a*) or plurality (as with Muna *-hi* and Tolaki *=hako*). **Verbs**, on the other hand, show a wide range of morphological potential. Ignoring voice morphology, transitivity (including passives and detransitives), as well as TAM marking, the following meaning categories are found in Sulawesi, ranging from very common to rare.

(a) Found in virtually all the languages of Sulawesi are the following meaning categories expressed by verbal affixes: stative aktionsart, causative action, non-volitional or accidental action, reciprocal or mutual action, verbalization (to have or to use N), as well as one or more nominalizations (action, agent, object, instrument, location).
(b) Frequently found are the following meaning categories on verbs: various applicatives, including beneficiary and locative (present in all Celebic and South Sulawesi groups, but absent in the northern Sulawesi groups), iterative or repetitive action, pretence or simulated action, requestive action, attemptive action (try to do X), diffuse action (engaged at length in activity X, but without giving it proper attention), plural subject, and affected subject. Various languages have a suffix indicating 'affected by discomfort (including disease)' (e.g. Tukang Besi *no-kesu-ʔo* (3SG.REAL-ant-INFEST) 'full of ants, ant-infested'). Numerals regularly have the following derivational possibilities: ordinal

number (xth), frequentative (x times), and distributive (each x). Various languages also have unproductive morphology on numeral bases indicating 'x days ago' or 'in x days' (see Mead 2001b).

(c) Rare or unique categories are illustrated in the following non-exhaustive list (with relevant affixes bolded). Mori Bawah has a plural (non-dual) subject prefix *(me)N-*: *ka=do* ***m****-pekule* (and=3PL.NOM PL.SBJ-return) 'and they (three or more) returned'. Balantak has a verbal circumfix *poo-...(i)kon* meaning 'less than ideal': *tatapi* 'wash' > *mom-****poo****-tatapi-****kon*** 'to wash as best as one can (given less than ideal circumstances such as little water and no soap)'. Tukang Besi has a 'social activity' prefix *hopo-* which indicates that the action is done for a social or ceremonial function: *waa* 'tell, inform' > ***hopo****-waa* 'announce'. Muna has a circumfix *sao-. . .hano* 'to a minimal degree': ***sao****-meko-****hano*** 'barely sweet enough' (*meko* 'sweet').

Finally, though functor words in closed classes typically allow for little or no derivation, mention should be made of two exceptional cases. Moronene has a staggering array of some sixty derivations on number bases, including causative quantity verbs such as *mom-poko-'opaa* 'make it four' and distributive adverbs such as *te-'opa-opaa (wula)* 'every four (months)'. In Balantak the seven basic demonstrative roots can all undergo affixation, reduplication, and compounding, generating some 250 possible demonstrative forms. An example of an extreme derivation is *ka-ndaʔa-mbaa-tuʔu* (DEIC-DEM.ADV6-ALL.REAL-DEM4) 'from somewhere up there to the front'.

## 33.5 Basic morphosyntax

Within Western Austronesian, Sulawesi is perhaps the area with the greatest amount of variation in basic morphosyntax. Moving from north to south there is a gradual decrease of the number of symmetrical voices, as well as a loss of TAM (tense and realis-irrealis encoding). This is offset by an increase in the role of pronominal indexing on the verb, showing absolutive–ergative, nominative–accusative, and fluid–S alignments, as well as an increase in transitive clause constructions, specifically semi-transitive clauses. In Himmelmann's (2005a) typology, the languages of Sulawesi are either symmetrical voice languages (the three northern microgroups, as well as Tomini-Tolitoli and Saluan) or transitional (the South Sulawesi, Bungku-Tolaki, Muna-Buton, and Wotu-Wolio microgroups). Himmelmann's third category, preposed possessor languages, is not found in Sulawesi, with the possible exception of Banggai. Banggai has preposed possessors and an alienable/inalienable distinction, but also has symmetrical voice.[7] Capturing all this diversity is challenging. This section concentrates on voice, case marking, transitivity, and person-marking. TAM marking, though included in Table 33.5, is discussed in 33.6.

### 33.5.1 Overview

Table 33.5 shows the most salient parameters of variation in Sulawesi, illustrated by six languages which are more or less representative of the total range of morphosyntactic variation found in Sulawesi.

The following examples illustrate the essential features of each of these six languages, concentrating on voice and transitivity, using relatively simple clauses, and ignoring various complications and alternative word orders. Glossing mostly follows the sources; non-agent voices are translated with both English actives and passives, following the sources. Surface forms are presented in parentheses. The examples from each language are followed by a brief paragraph explaining the main features illustrated. Following the six languages is a discussion of the main parameters of morphosyntactic variation across Sulawesi.

1. Tondano[8]

intransitive

(5) *Ku=r<um>uber=mow (kurumuberou)*
1SG.PIV<AV>sit=COMPL
'I will sit.'

agent voice

(6) *Si=okiʔ=ku t<um>eles raaren.*
ANIM.SG=small=1SG.POSS <AV>buy vegetables
'My child would buy some vegetables.'

patient voice

(7) *Raaren teles-en ni=okiʔ=ku.*
vegetables buy-PV ANIM.SG.NPIV.A=small=1SG.POSS
'The vegetables would be bought by my child.'

locative voice

(8) *N=pasar (empasar) teles-an*
INAN=market buy-LV
*ni=okiʔ=ku.*
ANIM.SG.NPIV.A=small=1SG.POSS
'At the market my child would buy something.'

[7] The statement that Banggai has symmetrical voice is somewhat tentative. It is based on a reading of van den Bergh's (1953) grammar of Banggai (especially §8.6), but this needs to be confirmed by a modern, typologically informed description.

[8] Examples (6)–(9) are elicited; the modal element ('would') is irrelevant for the discussion of the voice system.

**Table 33.5** Morphosyntactic variables in six Sulawesi languages

| Language | Symmetrical voice and transitive clause types | Case marking on subject NP | TAM marking | Person-marking on the verb |
|---|---|---|---|---|
| 1. Tondano | 4 symmetrical voices: agent/patient/locative/conveyance | none | 2 tenses: past/non-past<br>2 moods: realis/irrealis | proclitic subjects; agent in non-agent voices (suffix) |
| 2. Balantak | 3 symmetrical voices: agent/patient/locative | article *a* (only post-predicate) | 3 modes: re-alis/irrealis/gerund | agent in non-agent voices (suffix) |
| 3. Kaili Ledo | 2 symmetrical voices: agent/patient | none | 2 moods: realis/irrealis | agent on realis patient voice (suffix),<br>agent on irrealis patient voice (prefix) |
| 4. Uma | no symmetrical voice; 3 transitive clause types; no passive | none | aspectual enclitics (no realis/irrealis) | intransitive S, transitive A O, erg-abs system |
| 5. Makasar | no symmetrical voice; 2 transitive clause types; agented passive | none | TAM clitics (no realis/irrealis) | intransitive S, transitive A O, erg-abs system |
| 6. Wolio | no symmetrical voice; 1 transitive clause type; agentless passive | none | aspectual enclitics (no realis/irrealis) | intransitive S, transitive A O, nom-acc system |

conveyance voice
(9) *N=loit (eloit)* *i-teles*
INAN=money CV-buy
*ni=oki?=ku.*
ANIM.SG.NPIV.A=small=1SG.POSS
'With the money my child would buy something.'
(Brickell 2014)

Example (5) illustrates an intransitive verb with a proclitic subject pronoun. Sentences (6)–(9) show the four basic voices on the verb *teles* 'buy'. In the three non-agent voices the post-verbal agent is introduced by the clitic *ni=* which marks an animate singular non-pivot. In (9) the conveyance voice marks the instrument as the subject (or pivot).

2. Balantak

agent voice, irrealis
(10) *Kita* *ming-ili* *loka?.*
1PL.INCL AV.IRR-buy banana
'We will buy bananas.'

patient voice, irrealis
(11) *Loka?* *ka-ni?i* *ili-on-ta*
banana DEIC-DEM1 buy-PV.IRR-1PL.INCL.POSS
'We will buy these bananas.'

patient voice, irrealis
(12) *Loka?* *ka-ni?i* *ili-on-na*
banana DEIC-DEM1 buy-PV.IRR-3SG.POSS
*sina-ngku.*
mother-1SG.POSS
'My mother will buy these bananas.'

locative voice, realis
(13) *Pasar* *men* *ning-ili-an-na* *pae...*
market REL REAL-buy-LV-3SG.POSS rice
'The market where she bought rice...'

patient voice, realis, postverbal subject
(14) *ka?* *yaku?* *kolon* *a* *basung-ku.*
and 1SG carry.on.back ART basket-1SG.POSS
'...and I put my basket on my back.' (van den Berg and Busenitz 2012)

Example (10) is basic agent voice clause with SVO word order in irrealis mode. In (11), the patient is definite, which triggers patient voice, with the agent indexed as a possessive suffix on the verb. (12) is similar to (11), but the agent is now a full NP, introduced by the 3SG possessive suffix *-na.* (13) illustrates locative voice in realis mode on the same verb *ili* 'buy', with the pronominal agent coded by the 3SG possessive suffix *-na.* (14) illustrates realis patient voice, again triggered by a definite patient. The pronominal agent *yaku?*

'I' occurs preverbally, and the postverbal subject shows the use of the article *a*, limited to post-predicate subjects.

3. Kaili Ledo

agent voice, realis

(15) *Soso naN-kande (nangande) loka*
gecko AV.REAL-eat banana
'The gecko ate (the) bananas.'

patient voice, realis, nominal agent

(16) *Loka ni-kande nu soso*
banana PV.REAL-eat GEN gecko
'The gecko ate the bananas.'

patient voice, realis, pronominal agent

(17) *Nuapa ni-kande-mu?*
what PV.REAL-eat-2SG.POSS
'What did you eat?'

patient voice, irrealis, nominal agent

(18) *Nuapa ra-kande nu asu?*
what PV.IRR-eat GEN dog
'What will the dog eat?'

patient voice, irrealis, pronominal agent

(19) *Nuapa mu-kande?*
what 2SG.PV.IRR-eat
'What will you eat?' (Evans 2003)

Example (15) is a basic agent voice clause in realis mode with SVO word order. Its patient voice counterpart is (16), which has a nominal agent introduced by the genitive marker *nu*. (17) shows realis patient voice, indicated by *ni-*, with a pronominal agent, indexed by a possessive suffix, a structure which is open to all person–number combinations. In (18), irrealis patient voice is marked by the prefix *ra-*, and the agent is a full NP, again introduced by *nu*. Irrealis voice with a pronominal agent is marked with a pronominal prefix, as in (19), but this is limited to 1SG *ku-*, 2SG *mu-*, and sometimes 2PL *nu-*. Other persons take *ra-* and a possessive suffix (e.g. *ra-kande-na* (PV.IRR-eat-3SG.POSS) 'he will eat (it); (it) will be eaten by him').

4. Uma

intransitive with absolutive S

(20) *Mo-lengiʔ=ko.*
INTR-cold=2SG.ABS
'You are cold.'

semi-transitive with absolutive A

(21) *M-po-hilo=i ro-mehaʔ sakaea.*
AV-TR-see=3SG.ABS two-CLF boat
'He saw two boats.'

agent voice

(22) *Tuama-ku m-po-ʔoli once.*
father-1SG.POSS AV-TR-buy rice
'My father bought rice.'

patient voice with ergative A

(23) *Na-hilo ro-mehaʔ sakaea toe.*
3SG.ERG-see two-CLF boat that
'He saw the/those two boats.'

patient voice with ergative A and absolutive O

(24) *Hiapa lokaʔ-kuʔ? Ku-kuniʔ=mi.*
where banana-1SG.POSS 1SG.ERG-eat=PFV.3SG.ABS
'Where are my bananas?' 'I already ate them.'
(Martens 1988a, b)

Example (20) shows an intransitive verb with an absolutive subject pronoun. In (21) and (22) the indefinite patients trigger agent voice. In (21), clearly a transitive construction, the pronominal A is indexed by an absolutive pronoun, hence the term 'semi-transitive'. In (23) and (24), a definite patient is responsible for the patient voice, marked by ergative pronouns for A and an absolutive pronoun for O.

5. Makasar

intransitive with absolutive S

(25) *Aʔ-jarang=aʔ.*
INTR-horse=1SG.ABS
'I ride a horse.'

semi-transitive with absolutive A

(26) *AN-kanre=aʔ (angnganreaʔ) taipa.*
TR1-eat=1SG.ABS mango
'I eat mangoes.'

transitive with ergative A and absolutive O

(27) *Na-kokkoʔ=aʔ (nakokkokaʔ) miong-ku.*
3.ERG-bite=1SG.ABS cat-1SG.POSS
'My cat bit me.'

passive with absolutive S

(28) *Miong-a ni-buno=i (ri kongkong-a).*
cat-DEF PASS-kill=3.ABS by dog-DEF
'The cat was killed (by the dog).' (Jukes 2005)

Makasar is similar to Uma, though the terminology used by Martens and Jukes is different. Again, the absolutive pronoun marks an intransitive S, as in (25). The absolutive marks A with indefinite patients in semi-transitive clauses, as in (26), and it marks O in transitive clauses with definite objects, as in (27). Contrary to Uma, Makasar also has a real passive, illustrated in (28), in which S is indexed by an absolutive, and the agent is optionally present in a PP.

6. Wolio.

intransitive with nominative S

(29) *Ku-lingka i dhaoa.*
1SG.NOM-go LOC market
'I go to the market.'

transitive with nominative A

(30) *A-kande bhae o ama-ku.*
3SG.NOM-eat rice ART father-1SG.POSS
'My father eats/ate rice.'

transitive with nominative A and accusative O

(31) *A-kemba-aku.*
3SG.NOM-call-1SG.ACC
'He called/invited me.'

passive with nominative S

(32) *Ingkomiu harusu u-to-gagari.*
2PL must 2.NOM-PASS-count
'You (= the total number of you all) must be counted.' (Anceaux 1988; Alberth 2000)

Wolio has a nominative–accusative system with only one transitive clause type. The nominative marks S in (29) and (32) and A in (30) and (31), while the accusative marks O in (31). Wolio also has an agentless passive, marked by *to-*, as in (32).

The main parameters of morphosyntactic variation between these and other languages of Sulawesi are as follows.

### 33.5.1.1 *The number of symmetrical voices: 4, 3, 2, or none*

Symmetrical voice is here defined as a system of voice opposition in which all voices are morphologically marked, none of the voices can be considered basic, and the voices appear to be syntactically equivalent, not involving detransitivization and argument demotion, as is the case with passives in European languages (see also Riesberg 2014). **Four** symmetrical voices are found in the three northern Sulawesi microgroups (Sangiric, Minahasan, Gorontalo-Mongondow): agent voice, patient/undergoer voice, locative/dative/local voice, and instrument/conveyance voice (the actual labels used vary considerably). Voice is marked in two ways in these languages: primarily by affixes on the verb, including infixes, that closely interact with TAM; and to a limited extent by case markers on the noun phrases (see below). Four voices are reported for Tondano, Ratahan, and Buol, and presumably also occur in the other languages in these three subgroups (though, somewhat surprisingly, large languages like Sangir, Gorontalo, and Bolaang-Mongondow still await a modern typologically informed description). It is possible that Bobongko (in the Saluan group, outside of North Sulawesi) also has four voices, though the analysis is tentative. **Three** symmetrical voices (agent voice, patient voice, and locative voice) are reported for Balantak. It should be pointed out that in languages with three or four voices, intransitive verbs participate in the voice system and can receive agent voice as well as locative voice. An example from Balantak is *ilio men no-taka-an-ku* (day REL REAL-arrive-LV-1SG.POSS) 'the day when I arrived', with locative voice, marked by *-an* on the intransitive verb *taka* 'arrive'. **Two** symmetrical voices (agent and patient voice) are reported for Kaili Da'a, Kaili Ledo, Tajio, Dampelas, and Pendau (Quick 2007 uses the term 'inverse' for patient voice).

Finally, symmetrical voice is **lacking** in the southern half of Sulawesi, roughly south of the line running from Palu to the Tomori Bay. None of the South Sulawesi languages and none of the Bungku-Tolaki, Muna-Buton, or Wolio-Wotu microgroups have it. Notice that this division only partially corresponds with recognized subgroups: the dividing line between symmetrical and non-symmetrical voice cuts across the large Celebic group, roughly splitting it in two.

### 33.5.1.2 *The number of transitive clause constructions*

Many of the languages in the southern half of Sulawesi, all of which lack symmetrical voice, have multiple clause constructions with pronominal indexing, as illustrated by Uma above. We adopt the neutral term *transitive clause constructions*, in which *transitive* is to be understood as semantic transitivity, a state of affairs involving an A (roughly an agent) and a P (roughly an undergoer/patient). Many descriptions use voice terminology (and we follow those here), but whether these transitive clause constructions can be considered true voice alternations is a theoretical question that is beyond the scope of this chapter. Uma is illustrative in showing three major alternations for transitive clauses (agent voice, patient voice, semi-transitive)[9] and two minor ones (detransitive and incorporation, the latter illustrated below). Various South Sulawesi languages show similar patterns, including Bambam which has the same five alternations as Uma. Mori Bawah has only two major types: transitive and antipassive (or semi-transitive). Makasar also has two major alternations: transitive and semi-transitive. Similarly, Tukang Besi has two major transitive alternations, labelled actor voice and undergoer voice. In each case the selection for a particular transitive clause construction is determined by a combination of syntactic and pragmatic factors, including topicality of A, definiteness and referentiality of P, and the status of the clause as main or dependent. Muna and Wolio have only one transitive clause type, though both allow for a voice distinction in relative clauses.

[9] The terminology used in Martens (1988a, b) is Actor Focus, Goal Focus, and Antipassive.

### 33.5.1.3 *Passive clause type*

Several Sulawesi languages with non-symmetrical voice have a distinct passive clause type, defined as a construction in which the patient functions as the subject of an intransitive clause, with unique verbal morphology, and with the agent optionally present in an oblique NP or, more commonly, obligatorily absent. (Non-volitional or accidental passives such as Uma *te-* and Bambam *ti-* are disregarded, as their semantics is too specific.) Bambam has an agentless passive marked by the verbal prefix *di-*: *mala dukaq di-paq-baju* (can also PASS-TR-shirt) '(The sarong) can also be used as a shirt.' Seko has an agentless passive marked by *ni-*, Mori Bawah by *-in-*, while in Wolio and Tukang Besi it is marked by *to-*. Makasar has an agented passive marked by *ni-*, the optional agent appearing in an oblique NP introduced by the preposition *ri*, as in example (28). However, in many non-symmetrical voice languages basic passives are lacking, including Uma, Napu, Pamona, and Muna (where passives are limited to relative clauses and nominalizations). In these languages, the pragmatic function of backgrounding the agent is accomplished through fronting the patient and using a vague third person agent (e.g. Muna *o kasibu do-rako-e* (ART thief 3PL.REAL-catch-3SG.OBJ) 'the thief was/got caught').

### 33.5.1.4 *NP marking*

So far, no language in Sulawesi has been reported that combines a symmetrical voice system with unique case marking for subject NPs headed by a common noun, typical of Philippine-type languages. In other words, there are no languages with case markers structurally similar to Tagalog *ang*. To our knowledge, this fact has not been noted before. There is, however, a bewildering variety of case markers (variously labelled as phrase markers, noun markers, and articles), but rarely is there a straightforward correlation with a grammatical function.

Languages with symmetrical voice typically have several NP case markers, differentiated for common and personal or proper nouns. With four voices there are theoretically eight case markers, but once again Sulawesi shows remarkable variety in a number of unexpected directions. Tondano, for example, has five phrase-marking proclitics, but only two are obligatory: the genitive (non-pivot actor) singular-plural pair *ni=/nè=*. The other three markers, the animate SG/PL pair *si=/sè=* and the inanimate *N=*, occur on NPs irrespective of their grammatical function, as *si=* does in (6) above. In Ponosakan, subjects and possessors are both marked by *in*. In Ratahan and Buol, subject NPs headed by common nouns are unmarked. In Tajio the marker *te=* occurs on nouns in subject and object roles, whereas *si=* gives an honorific reading in those roles. Balantak does mark common nouns functioning as subject with the enclitic article *=a* (written as a separate word), but it only occurs in post-predicate position, as in (14).

In languages without symmetrical voice, NP markers are limited to personal nouns in any grammatical role, such as Makasar *i*. Articles are also found in many Bungku-Tolaki and Muna-Buton languages, as well as in Wolio, but in most cases they have no syntactic function, apart from marking the following word as a common noun. In Mori Bawah the article *io* may have a pragmatic function of focusing attention. In Tolaki the article *o* is found only with disyllabic common nouns. Muna has a different prosodic restriction in that the article *o* only occurs after a prosodic break (van den Berg 2010). Tukang Besi is exceptional in that it has two articles *te* and *na*, both marking grammatical roles, labelled core and nominative by Donohue (1999a). The Bungku-Tolaki and Muna-Buton languages also have articles for personal nouns (names). In Wolio and the Muna-Buton languages, these are differentiated for gender and have the form *la* (for men) and *wa* (for women).

Table 33.6 shows the case marking of subject NPs again (with a few additional languages) and also shows the marking of the agent in patient voice and how this relates to the genitive/possessive linker in NPs, restricted to common nouns. From this table it is clear that the case marking of the agent in patient voice (as well as other non-agent voices) is much more common than the case marking of the subject NP. It is also clear that the marking of the agent in patient voice is almost always identical to the linker in possessive NPs, with the exception of two languages that do not have symmetrical voice.

### 33.5.1.5 *Person marking*

This section focuses on person marking on verbs; for pronominal systems as a whole, see §33.5.3 below. We first discuss person marking in symmetrical voice languages, followed by a discussion of person marking in non-symmetrical voice languages of Sulawesi.

(a) In symmetrical voice languages such as Tondano, Balantak, Pendau, and Kaili, the major (and sometimes only) pronominal marking on verbs is the presence of possessive suffixes indexing the agent in non-agent voices, as in Balantak *loka men ni-ili-ngku* (banana REL PV.REAL-buy-1SG.POSS) 'the banana that I bought'. Within Western Austronesian this is a common pattern. Tondano is unusual among the symmetrical voice languages in that it allows free pronouns to procliticize to verbs, including stative verbs:

**Table 33.6** Morphosyntactic parameters in ten Sulawesi languages

| Language | Number of symmetrical voices | Case marking of subject NP | Marking of agent in patient voice | Possessive linker in NPs [N of N] |
|---|---|---|---|---|
| Ratahan | 4 | None | *nu=* | *nu=* |
| Tondano | 4 | None | *ni=* (sg) | *ni=* (sg) |
| Buol | 4 | None | *no=* | *no=* |
| Balantak | 3 | post-predicate *a* | 3SG.POSS *-na* | 3SG.POSS *-na* |
| Pendau | 2 | None | *nu=* | *nu=* |
| Tajio | 2 | None | *nu=* | *nu=* or *N-* |
| Kaili | 2 | None | *nu* or *N-* | *nu* or *N-* |
| Muna | 0 | None | (3SG.POSS *-no*, only in relative clauses) | 3SG.POSS *-no* |
| Tukang Besi | 0 | *na* or *te* | – | 3SG.POSS *-no* |
| Makasar | 0 | None | *ri* | 3SG.POSS *-na* |

*ko=ma-arem=mow* (2SG.PIV=EV.STAT-hungry=COMPL) 'you are already hungry'.

(b) A typologically unusual feature found in some symmetrical voice languages is that the agent/possessive suffixes are also attached as prefixes or proclitics to verbs in patient voice, though the resulting paradigm is typically defective. A clear example is Kaili Ledo (illustrated in §33.5.1 above), where for the 1SG, 2SG, and 2PL patient voice irrealis the portmanteau prefixes *ku-*, *mu-*, and *nu-* are in use. Compare realis *ni-povia-miu* (PV.REAL-do-2PL) 'you did' and irrealis *nu-povia* (2PL.PV.IRR-do) 'you will do'. For the remaining persons the general PV irrealis prefix *ra-* is used: *ra-peinta=kami* (PV.IRR-see=1PL.EXCL) 'we will see'. Other Kaili languages show slightly different constraints: Kaili Da'a only permits 1SG and 2SG prefixes in the patient voice irrealis (not 2PL), but Kaili Ija allows for an additional 1PL inclusive with prefix *ta-*. Pendau shows a similar pattern: next to the general irrealis prefix *ro-* with a possessive suffix, we find prefixes for 1SG and 2SG as a variant in irrealis patient voice. So, next to *ro-oli=ʔu* (PV.IRR-buy=1SG) 'I will buy' there is *ʔu-oli* (1SG.PV.IRR-buy) 'I will buy', and similarly for 2SG with *=mu* and *mu-*. Interestingly, for 1SG realis Pendau also has two options: the regular *ni-oli=ʔu* (PV.REAL-buy=1SG) 'I bought' and the variant *noʔu-oli* (1SG.PV.REAL-buy). It is obvious that this is an area where a considerable degree of restructuring and analogical formation has taken place (and probably still is taking place). Tajio is very similar to Pendau, having 1SG and 2SG prefixes in irrealis. Dampelas allows only for a 1SG preclitic *nu-* ~ *u-* on patient voice, but this is apparently found in realis mode, not in irrealis as is the case with Kaili, Tajio, and Pendau. Balantak, finally, has a lone 1SG *ku=* in narrative conversational style, both realis and irrealis.

(c) In languages with non-symmetrical voices we find at least three rather different systems of person marking.

1. Person marking is organized on an **ergative–absolutive basis**, whereby the S of intransitive verbs and the P of transitive verbs is marked identically by a set of absolutive enclitics, while the A of transitive verbs is marked by ergative proclitics. This is the case in Uma and Makasar, as illustrated in §33.5.1, examples (20)–(28). This is the pattern in virtually all the languages of the South Sulawesi group (Bugis, Toraja, Bambam Napu), as well as a few Kaili-Pamona languages (including Uma). There are, however, a number of environments where the proclitic no longer has an ergative function. These include 'consecutive linking' (see §33.5.2 and §33.7.3) and the 'double ergatives' of Konjo with aspectual *-mi* (see §33.6.2).
2. The Muna-Buton languages show a **nominative–accusative** pattern, whereby S and A are encoded by preclitics or prefixes, and P by suffixes/enclitics. This is true for Tukang Besi, Muna, Cia-Cia, as well as non-Muna-Buton languages spoken on the island of Buton such as Wolio (illustrated above) and Kulisusu.

3. A third system is reported for Wotu and various Bungku-Tolaki languages such as Mori Bawah and Tolaki, showing a **fluid-S system.** A is marked by a so-called nominative proclitic set, O by an absolutive enclitic set, but S (the intransitive subject) can be marked by either set, depending on various syntactic factors—not on the meaning of the verb. The default for S is the absolutive, as in Mori Bawah *me-ʔaiwa=ʔira* (PL.SBJ-arrive=3PL.ABS) 'they arrived', but nominative indexing is required in various syntactic contexts, including imperative mood, negated clauses, following certain conjunctions and in various subordinate clauses. An example of a nominative 1SG (triggered by the negator) is *ongkue nahi ku=memee* (1SG NEG 1SG.NOM=afraid) 'Me, I'm not afraid.'

Not every language in Sulawesi fits in this system. Seko, for example, shows a unique mixed system of person marking (T. Laskowske 2001). The main opposition here is between realis and irrealis, with irrealis defined as the mood of negative, conditional, and imperative clauses. Somewhat simplified, Seko has three basic pronominal sets for marking core arguments on the verbs, called realis, irrealis, and inverse. Realis proclitics mark S in intransitives, passives, and semi-transitives (or antipassives): *ku=mu-toleʔ* (1SG.REAL-INTR-smoke) 'I smoke', *ku=ni-kiniʔ* (1SG.REAL-PASS-pinch) 'I'm being pinched'. Irrealis enclitics mark S in irrealis mood: *ha=mu-toleʔ=ka?* (NEG=INTR-smoke=1SG.IRR) 'I don't smoke.' In transitive clauses with pronominal indexing, P is a realis proclitic, while A is drawn from the third set of inverse proclitics, the order being normally P–A–Verb: *ku=na=kiniʔ* (1SG.REAL-3SG.INV-pinch) 'he pinches me'. However, with first person P and second person A, the order of the proclitics is reversed: *u=mi=kiniʔ* (2SG.REAL-1.INV-pinch) 'You pinch me/us (excl).' It is likely that more variety in the area of person marking will surface when more grammatical descriptions become available.

## 33.5.2 Further complications and expansions

Various factors which complicate this basic picture can only be briefly touched upon.

### 33.5.2.1 *Verb classes*

Many languages have underived morphological **verb classes**, including Pendau, Balantak, Kaili Ledo, and Muna. Often these verb classes correlate with meaning categories such as stative, dynamic, postural, factive, volitional, locomotion, involuntary action, etc. Muna, which has three verb classes (class *a-*, *ae-*, and *ao-*), shows an unusual correlation between verb class and definiteness of the object. Verbs in class *ae-* move to class *a-* when the object is definite: *ae-bhasi mie* (1SG.REAL-call person) 'I called people' vs. *a-bhasi La Aso* (1SG.REAL-call ART A.) 'I called La Aso'.

### 33.5.2.2 *Additional verbal modes*

So far, all the examples have illustrated indicative verb forms. Several languages have one or two other 'modes' (a term covering tense, mood, and other categories such as nominalizations). Ratahan, for example, has an imperative mode next to its past and non-past verb forms, while Buol distinguishes imperative and prohibitive, next to past and neutral. Balantak has an atemporal mode labelled gerund, in a tripartite system with realis and irrealis. The gerund, which is mostly marked by initial *p*, is used for imperatives and nominalizations. Compare the following three forms of the root *soop* 'enter': *nin-soop yaku'* (INTR.REAL-enter 1SG) 'I entered', *min-soop yaku'* (INTR.IRR-enter 1SG) 'I will enter', *pin-soop kuu!* (INTR.GER-enter 2SG) 'Come in, you!' Another gerund is found in the locative nominalization *na ping-ili-an oli* (PREP GER-buy-LV oil) 'at the place for buying oil'. Muna and Wolio have an additional verbal category of participles, uninflected for subject and used in relative clauses. Examples of Wolio active and passive participles: *mia be-mo-gora-akea* (person FUT-ACT.PTCP-call-APPL.3SG) 'someone who should call to him', *kambakamba i-tobe-na i dala* (flower PASS.PTCP-pick-3SG LOC road) 'flowers picked along the roadside'.

### 33.5.2.3 *Valency-changing derivations*

Valency-changing derivations are found in all the Sulawesi languages. Causatives and applicatives are treated in more detail in §33.5.3. In addition, there are also locatives, reciprocals, and detransitivizers (see also §33.4.5).

### 33.5.2.4 *Stem formers*

Semantically empty formatives of the shape *pV(C)-* occur in a number of languages to 'prepare' a root for further derivation. In Tajio, for instance, the verbal root *turu* 'to sleep' can be affixed with the locative applicative suffix *-i* or the causative prefix *pe-*, but in both cases a (homophonous) stem former *pe-* is needed first: *no-pe-turu-i* (AV.REAL-SF-sleep-APPL) 'to sleep at' and *no-pe-pe-turu* (AV.REAL-CAUS-SF-sleep) 'to make s.o. sleep'. Similar examples are found in Ratahan: *p<in>a-pa-tere* (<PAST>CAUS-SF-run) 'was made to run', where a stem former *pa-* is needed to derive a causative verb by means of a (homophonous) causative prefix *pa-*. For Pendau, Quick (2007) extends the analysis of stem formers in such a way that they occur on virtually every verb in agent voice. Realis and irrealis forms with initial *nong-* and *mong-* are analysed as combinations of the stem former *pong-* with an abstract floating autosegment N (realis) or M (irrealis) which docks on the phoneme *p* of the stem former. For example, the surface form *monatap* 'to wash' (irrealis) is then underlyingly *M-pong-tatap* (IRR-SF.TR-wash). Similar analyses have been proposed for Mori by Barsel (1994) and for Lauje by Himmelmann (2002b), but whether these abstract analyses actually contribute towards an understanding of the morphology of these languages or present an unnecessary level of complication remains to be seen.

#### 33.5.2.5 *Noun incorporation*

Noun incorporation is found in various languages (e.g. Uma *ng-koni? loka?-a* (AV-eat banana-1SG.ABS) 'I am banana-eating'), where the absolutive pronoun on the patient (rather than on the verb) shows that the noun is incorporated in the verb phrase.

#### 33.5.2.6 *Pronoun hopping*

Pronoun hopping (or pronoun clitic movement) from verbs to preverbal negators and conjunctions is common in languages with an ergative–absolutive or a fluid S pronominal system, such as many South Sulawesi languages, but also Uma, Mori Bawah, Padoe, and Moronene. An example from Uma is *hilou=a* (go=1SG.ABS) 'I go', and its negated counterpart *uma=a hilou* (NEG=1SG.ABS go) 'I don't go'. In example (33), the subject prefix of the Padoe verb *nahu* 'cook' (with antipassive prefix *poN-*) 'hops back' to the preceding conjunction *ba* 'if'.

Padoe
(33) *Amba~amba-no* **ba=to** *po-nahu*
REDUP~first-3SG.POSS if=1PL.INCL.SBJ AP-cook
*boka...*
oil
'First, if we make coconut oil...' (Vuorinen 1995: 109)

#### 33.5.2.7 *Consecutive linking*

Fluidity in person marking due to syntactic factors is common in languages with ergative–absolutive indexing. 'Consecutive linking' is a term used to indicate ergative marking of the subject of the consecutive clause, irrespective of its semantic role. This is reported for various South Sulawesi languages, including Bugis, Duri, and Mamasa. Example (34) is from Mamasa, where the first clause has the regular 2SG absolutive *=ko* on a passive verb for the patient subject, but the second clause (also passive) has the 2SG ergative *mu=* for exactly the same role, triggered by the consecutive proclitic *an=* (*am=* before bilabials).

Mamasa
(34) *Dako? di-pe-ala-i=ko*
later PASS-TR-take-LOC=2SG.ABS
*am=mu=di-tarungkun.*
CONSEC=2SG.ERG=PASS-imprison
'Later you will be captured and then you will be imprisoned.' (Matti 1994: 79)

### 33.5.3 Causatives and applicatives

Many Sulawesi languages have two types of causatives: one for adjectives or stative verbs, and another one for dynamic intransitive verbs and transitive verbs. This constrast is illustrated by Makasar *paka-* on adjectives: *paka-baji?* (CAUS-good) 'improve', *paka-lompo* (CAUS-big) 'enlarge', but *pa-* on verbs: *pa-lari* (CAUS-run) 'put to flight', *pa-kanre* (CAUS-eat) 'feed'. Such causative verbs are also open to passivization, as illustrated in (35).

Makasar
(35) *Ni-pa-kanre=i bembe=a (ri Ali).*
PASS-CAUS-eat=3 goat=DEF PREP A.
'The goat was fed (by Ali).' (Jukes 2006: 278)

Tukang Besi has a similar contrast (factitive *hoko-* vs. causative *pa-*), but presents an interesting twist on this contrast. In addition to the more usual *hoko-*, *pa-* can also be used as causative prefix on non-dynamic (stative) verbs, but with the implied meaning that the degree of effort was not very high and the results not permanent. This is illustrated in the contrast between *hoko-mobela* (FACT-wound) 'hurt; seriously damage' and *pa-mobela* (CAUS-wound) 'hurt, but not too badly' (Donohue 1999a: 207).

Applicatives are widespread in the Celebic languages and the South Sulawesi microgroup. Most languages have two verbal suffixes which allow a peripheral argument to become the object. The suffix *-i* or *-Ci* (where C is a lexically specified thematic consonant) typically attaches to intransitive verbs and marks a location, goal, or direction. The locative NP directly follows the verb, as in (36), and can also be passivized, as in (37).

Bambam
(36) *La-lako-kam-**i*** *banua-nna Ani*
IRR-go.over-1PL.EX.ABS-LOC house-3S.POSS A.
'We're going over to Ani's house.' (Campbell 1989: 112)

Dampelas
(37) *U-garang-**i*** *ʔoo.*
1SG.UV.REAL-care-DIR 2SG
'I care for you.' (Moro 2010: 88)

In the second type of applicative, the semantic role of the peripheral argument varies considerably: beneficiary, recipient, instrument, accompaniment, source, reason, purpose, and others. In Celebic languages this applicative is marked by a variety of forms, including *-kon* (Balantak, Banggai), *-ako* (Bungku-Mori, Tukang Besi), *-aʔo* (Dampelas), *-aʔ* (Pendau), *-aka* (Pamona), *-ka* (Kaili Ledo), *-ghoo* (Muna), and Busoa *-ho*, ultimately from Proto-Austronesian *akən. In South Sulawesi this applicative is marked by *-an*, *-ang*, or *-am* (though Seko has *-ing*) and appears to be limited to the role of benefactive and recipient. Examples (38) to (40) illustrate benefactive *-ing* and two general applicatives, with (40) showing the applicative instrument as a subject.

Seko
(38) *Yeni mang-ala=**ing*** *adi-nna*
Yeni TR-get=BEN younger.sibling-3.POSS
*k<in>anne:.*
<NMLZ>eat
'Jenny is getting rice for her brother.' (T. Laskowske 2001: 75)
(The order *k<in>anne: adi-nna* is also possible.)

Tukang Besi
(39) *No-bose=**ako*** *te kawi-ʔa.*
3.REAL-paddle=APPL CORE marry-NMLZ
'They are paddling for the wedding.'
(Donohue 2001: 221).

Pendau
(40) *Piso uo ni-pong-sambale-**aʔ*** *(niponyambaleaʔ)*
machete that IV/REAL-SF-butcher-APPL
*ni=Yusup japing uo.*
PERS/GEN=Yusup cow that
'Joseph used the machete to butcher the cow.'
(Quick 2007: 295)

Some languages have three applicatives: Tukang Besi has an additional comitative applicative marked by *-ngkene*, as in *no-wila-ngkene* X (3.REAL-go-COM) 'he went with X'; see Donohue (2001) for a detailed study of the use of applicatives in Tukang Besi discourse. In addition to locative *-i* and applicative *-kon*, Balantak has an additional benefactive marked by *-ii* (e.g. *mang-ala-ii* (AV.IRR-get-BEN) 'get s.t. for s.o.'). In Totoli, voice and applicative morphology interact in various complex ways (Himmelmann and Riesberg 2013), beyond the scope of this chapter.

### 33.5.4 Pronoun systems

The pronominal systems of seven representative Sulawesi languages are presented below. The labels are generally taken from the original sources and are short-hand notations, as most pronoun sets are multifunctional. For an earlier classic study of pronominal systems in the languages of Indonesia, see Haaksma (1933), Chapter 4 of which contains a discussion of synchronic and diachronic aspects of eleven languages of Sulawesi.

Ratahan (Table 33.7) has a simple system of nominative and genitive pronouns, which are only distinct in the singular. The genitive set is used as possessor on nouns and as agent on non-actor voice verb forms.

**Table 33.7** Ratahan pronouns

| Person/Num | | Nominative | Genitive |
|---|---|---|---|
| SG | 1 | *yaq* | *=ku* |
| | 2 | *(i) kau* | *=nu* |
| | 3 | *(i)sé* | *=ne* |
| PL | 1INCL | *(i) kite* | *ni kite* |
| | 1EXCL | *(i) kami* | *ni kami* |
| | 2 | *(i) kumú* | *ni kumu* |
| | 3 | *(i) mangasé* | *(nu) mangasé* |

Balantak (Table 33.8) has a system of free pronouns, possessive suffixes, and oblique pronouns, which occur, inter alia, following prepositions (e.g. *na koʔona* (LOC 3SG.OBL) 'to/at him'). The 3PL form *(i)raayaʔa* is actually a demonstrative.

**Table 33.8** Balantak pronouns

| Person/Num | | Free | Possessive | Oblique |
|---|---|---|---|---|
| SG | 1 | *yakuʔ* | *-(ng)ku* | *koʔongku ~ ingkuʔ* |
| | 2 | *koo* | *-Vm* | *koʔoom* |
| | 3 | *ia* | *-na* | *koʔona* |
| PL | 1INCL | *kita* | *-(n)ta* | *koʔonta* |
| | 1EXCL | *kai* | *-mai* | *koʔomai* |
| | 2 | *kuu* | *-muu* | *koʔomuu* |
| | 3 | *(i)raayaʔa* | *-na i raayaʔa* | *koʔona i raaya'a* |

Kaili Ledo (Table 33.9) has a free and a possessive suffix set, as well as a defective prefix set for the agent in irrealis patient voice, illustrated for *mu-* in (19).

**Table 33.9** Kaili Ledo pronouns

| Person/Num | | Free | Possessive | Irrealis patient voice |
|---|---|---|---|---|
| SG | 1 | *(y)aku* | *-ku* | *ku-* |
| | 2 | *iko* | *-mu* | *mu-* |
| | 3 | *ia* | *-na* | - |
| PL | 1INCL | *kita* | *-ta* | - |
| | 1EXCL | *kami* | *=kami* | - |
| | 2 | *komiu* | *-miu* | *nu-* |
| | 3 | *(ge)ira* | *-ra* | - |

Uma (Table 33.10) has a free and a possessive suffix set, as well as an ergative prefix set (used for A in patient voice) and an absolutive suffix set, used for S in intransitives, A in semi-transitives, and P in patient voice. These are illustrated in (20)–(24).

**Table 33.10** Uma pronouns

| Person/Num | | Free | Possessive | Ergative | Absolutive |
|---|---|---|---|---|---|
| SG | 1 | *akuʔ* | *-ku* | *ku-* | *-a* |
| | 2 | *iko* | *-nu* | *nu-* | *-ko* |
| | 3 | *hiʔa* | *-na* | *na-* | *-i* |
| PL | 1INCL | *kitaʔ* | *-ta* | *ta-* | *-ta* |
| | 1EXCL | *kaiʔ* | *-kai* | *ki-* | *-kai* |
| | 2 | *koiʔ* | *-ni* | *ni-* | *-koi* |
| | 3 | *hiraʔ* | *-ra* | *ra-* | *-ra* |

The pronominal system of Makasar (Table 33.11) is unusual. Typically there are seven number–person categories in Sulawesi, but Makasar (and also Seko) only have five, due to the conflation of 1PL.INCL and 2PL, and the absence of a number contrast for third person. Makasar lacks 1PL.EXCL ergative. Functionally, the Makasar system is similar to Uma.

Tolaki (Table 33.12) has five pronominal sets, adding a dative set (for beneficiaries and recipients; in the plural

**Table 33.11** Makasar pronouns

| Person/Num | Free | Possessive | Ergative | Absolutive |
|---|---|---|---|---|
| 1SG | *(i)nakke* | *-ku* | *ku=* | *=aʔ* |
| 1PL.INCL/2PL | *(i)katte* | *-ta* | *ki=* | *=kiʔ* |
| 1PL.EXCL | *(i)kambe* | *-mang* | - | *(=kang)* |
| 2SG | *(i)kau* | *-nu* | *nu=* | *=ko* |
| 3 | *ia* | *-na* | *na=* | *=i* |

only distinct from the absolutive set in third person). The nominative pronouns are ambidirectional: they are normally proclitics, but in some contexts they act as enclitics.

Muna (Table 33.13) probably has the most complex pronominal system of all the Sulawesi languages, though the functions are quite straightforward. Like Tolaki, it has five basic sets, including an indirect object (or dative) set. Muna has polite/honorific forms for 2SG and 2PL (identical to 1DU.INCL and 1PL.INCL). It does not have a dual morpheme, but the absence of the plural morpheme *-Vmu* on the first person non-singular inclusive set encodes duality. The subject set is divided into three classes, and for most person–number combinations there is a contrast between realis and irrealis. Muna lacks a first person dual/plural inclusive object suffix. (In the table $\surd$ stands for the verb stem).

Some general comments on pronominal systems.

(a) All languages make an inclusive–exclusive distinction for 1PL except for Tukang Besi, which has a paucal–plural distinction instead: *ikami* 'we (paucal)', *ikita* 'we (plural)'.

(b) Dual pronouns are rare, though they are reported for several Gorontalo-Mongondow languages (Lobel 2011). Mongondow and Lolak even distinguish a trial and a paucal form. Outside of this subgroup, Ratahan has a dual *(i) kará* 'we two (excl)', fused from *kami-ruá* (1PL.EXCL-two).

(c) None of the languages makes a gender distinction among the pronouns.

(d) Honorifics are quite common, though only rarely are there separate forms. In South Sulawesi languages the 1PL inclusive forms do double duty: Makasar *(i) katte* means both 'we (inclusive)' and 'you (SG polite)'. The same is true for various non-South Sulawesi languages, possibly influenced through Bugis or Makasar, including Kaili, Tajio, Muna, Wolio, and Tukang Besi,

**Table 33.12** Tolaki pronouns

| Person/Num | | Free | Genitive | Nominative | Absolutive | Dative |
|---|---|---|---|---|---|---|
| SG | 1 | *inuku* | *nggu* | *ku* | *-aku* | *-kona* |
| | 2 | *inggoʔo* | *-mu* | *u* | *-ko* | *-koʔo* |
| | 3 | *ieʔi ~ iee* | *-no* | *no* | *-ʔi, -e, -o* | *-kee* |
| PL | 1INCL | *inggito* | *-ndo* | *to* | *-keito* | *-keito* |
| | 1EXCL | *inggami* | *-mami* | *ki* | *-komami* | *-komami* |
| | 2 | *inggomiu* | *-miu* | *i* | *-komiu* | *-komiu* |
| | 3 | *ihiro* | *-ro* | *ro* | *-ʔiro, -ero, -oro* | *-kehero, -keero* |

though in some of these 2PL is also commonly used as a (lesser) honorific. In Tajio *siami* '1PL.EXCL' is used as a humble form for 1SG, and *sisia* '3PL' as a polite form of 3SG.

(e) Various paradigms are defective, showing gaps or being asymmetrical, as in Kaili Ledo, Makasar, and Muna. Another example is Tukang Besi, which has a 3PL free pronoun *amai*, but no distinction is made between 3SG and 3PL in the affixes.

Additional pronoun sets not illustrated above include the following: (i) a future nominative set: Mori Bawah *ta* '3SG.FUT' vs. *i* '3SG.NOM'; (ii) an additive set: Mori Bawah *ngkuda(ʔa)* 'I also', also found in Padoe; (iii) a commiserative set in Uma and Napu, indicating pity for someone in a lowly or pitiable state: Uma: *mai-ko=kowo* (come-2SG.ABS=2SG.COMS) 'Come here (poor you).'; and (iv) a veridical set in Seko to emphasize the veracity of the statement: *ku=boro=mo=ko* (1SG.REAL=full=PFV=1SG.VER) 'I really am full; I'm full, I am.'

## 33.6 Tense, aspect, and mood (TAM)

Languages of the northern half of Sulawesi, covering both the three Philippine groups and several Celebic languages, mark a 'realized' and 'unrealized' tense–aspect distinction on the verb. In addition, two aspectual enclitics (perfective *mo* and imperfective *pa*) occur widely across nearly the whole of Sulawesi. In some languages distinctions have shifted to the pronoun sets. Beyond these, tense, aspect, and mood are commonly expressed through verbs, auxiliaries, verbal affixation, and adverbs.

### 33.6.1 Realized vs. unrealized tense

The difference between what we call realized and unrealized tense has been variously described as realis vs. irrealis, past vs. non-past, past vs. neutral, realis vs. neutral, and factual vs. non-factual, and is often referred to as mood or mode. In Tondano (Sneddon 1975; Brickell 2014), the realized category (past) is marked by the infix *-in-* or one of its allomorphs, while the unrealized category (non-past) is unmarked. This pattern is illustrated in Table 33.14 on the verb *tələs* 'to buy' in four different voices.

The surface realization of *-in-* varies. Table 33.14 illustrates three of its allomorphs: the replacement of *-um-* with *-im-* in actor voice (historically a coalescence of **-inum-*), the infix *-in-* (patient and locative voice) and the prefix *na-* (instrumental voice). In the form *t<in>ələs* the infix *-in-* acts as a portmanteau affix, combining patient voice and realized tense.

Table 33.15 presents the voice system of another language, Kaili Da'a, following Barr (1988b). Although this language only has actor and patient voice forms, it maintains a contrast between realized and unrealized tense, here illustrated on the verb *koni* 'eat'. Note here two other allomorphs of *-in-*: the prefix *ni-* (patient voice) and the replacement of an initial *m* with *n* (actor voice; historically *na(N)-* is a reduction of **m<in>a(N)-*, with loss of the first syllable *mi*; the voicing assimilation of /ŋ+k/ > /ŋg/ is regular).

A distinction between realized and unrealized tense along these lines is found in the Sangiric, Minahasan, and Gorontalo-Mongondow languages (with sometimes a third category, e.g. the imperative, recognized by some authors). It has also been preserved in the Tomini-Tolitoli languages, in the Saluan-Banggai languages except Banggai, and in a

**Table 33.13** Muna pronouns

| Person/Num | | Free | Possessive | Subject | | | | | | Object | Indirect object |
|---|---|---|---|---|---|---|---|---|---|---|---|
| | | | | class a- | | class ae- | | class ao- | | | |
| | | | | 1. realis | 2. Irrealis | 3. realis | 4. irrealis | 5. realis | 6. irrealis | | |
| SG | 1 | *inodi* | *-ku* | *a-* | *a-* | *ae-* | *ae-* | *ao-* | *ao-* | *-kanau* | *-kanau* |
| | 2 | *(i)hintu* | *-mu* | *o-* | *o-* | *ome-* | *ome-* | *omo-* | *omo-* | *-ko* | *-angko* |
| | 2POL | *intaidi* | *-nto* | *to-* | *ta-* | *te-* | *tae-* | *to-* | *tao-* | *-kaeta* | *-kaeta* |
| | 3 | *anoa* | *-no* | *no-* | *na-* | *ne-* | *nae-* | *no-* | *nao-* | *-e* | *-ane* |
| DU | 1INCL | *intaidi* | *-nto* | *do-* | *da-* | *de-* | *dae-* | *do-* | *dao-* | – | – |
| PL | 1INCL | *intaidi-imu* | *-nto-omu* | *do-*√*-Vmu* | *da-*√*-Vmu* | *de-*√*-Vmu* | *dae-*√*-Vmu* | *do-*√*-Vmu* | *dao-*√*-Vmu* | – | – |
| | 1EXCL | *insaidi* | *-mani* | *ta-* | *ta-* | *tae-* | *tae-* | *tao-* | *tao-* | *-kasami* | *-kasami* |
| | 2 | *(i)hintu-umu* | *-Vmu* | *o-*√*-Vmu* | *o-*√*-Vmu* | *ome-*√*-Vmu* | *ome-*√*-Vmu* | *omo-*√*-Vmu* | *omo-*√*-Vmu* | *-ko-omu* | *-angko-omu* |
| | 2POL | *intaidi-imu* | *-nto-omu* | *to-*√*-Vmu* | *ta-*√*-Vmu* | *te-*√*-Vmu* | *tae-*√*-Vmu* | *to-*√*-Vmu* | *tao-*√*-Vmu* | *-kaeta-amu* | *-kaeta-amu* |
| | 3 | *andoa* | *-ndo* | *do-* | *da-* | *de-* | *dae-* | *do-* | *dao-* | *-da* | *-anda* |

**Table 33.14** Tondano voice and tense illustrated with the stem *tələs* 'buy'

| | Past | Non-past |
|---|---|---|
| **Actor voice** *-um-* | *t<im>ələs* | *t<um>ələs* |
| **Patient voice** Ø/*-ən* | *t<in>ələs* | *tələs-ən* |
| **Locative voice** *-an* | *t<in>ələs-an* | *tələs-an* |
| **Instrumental voice** *i-* | *na-i-tələs* | *i-tələs* |

**Table 33.15** Kaili Da'a voice and tense illustrated with the stem *koni* 'eat'

| | Realis | Irrealis |
|---|---|---|
| **Actor voice** | *nang-goni* | *mang-goni* |
| **Patient voice** | *ni-koni* | *ra-koni* |

subset of the Kaili-Pamona languages (Kaili, Lindu, Moma, and Topoiyo, but not Sedoa, Uma, or Pamona). There is, in other words, an isogloss line which runs from west to east through the Kaili-Pamona and Saluan-Banggai microgroups, south of which a realized–unrealized distinction marked by distinct verbal prefixes has been lost. The Muna-Buton languages occupy a special place in this respect, in that the realis–irrealis distinction has been retained, but irrealis is coded by a different set of subject markers, as well as the infix *-um-* (see §33.6.4). Striking though this isogloss is across Sulawesi, it is clearly untenable as a subgrouping argument (see also Noorduyn 1991b: 140).

Another important observation is that the absence of this realized–unrealized distinction on verbal prefixes in Celebic seems to correlate with the absence of a symmetrical voice system and the presence of more widespread pronominal marking on the verb (see also §33.5.2). It is only south of this isogloss line that we find *-in-* or its cognates functioning as a 'real' passive marker. Thus Banggai, Bungku-Tolaki *-in-*; Muna *ne-*; Cia-Cia, Rampi, Makasar, Konjo, Seko *ni-*; Panasuan, Budong-Budong, Limola, Wotu, Wolio *i-*; Bugis, Selayar, Laiyolo *ri-*. South Sulawesi languages spoken in the northern area of that microgroup use mostly *di-*. Regarding *ri-* and *di-* passive forms in Malay and Sulawesi, see van den Berg (2004b).

Although the semantics of the realized–unrealized distinction is straightforward at first blush (past vs. non-past tense), the languages of Sulawesi show an interesting pattern of variation in the actual use of the contrast when it is extended to other domains, including imperative, negative polarity (in past contexts), conditional clauses, and procedural discourse, as shown by Table 33.16 for a sample of eight languages.

Particularly striking is the variation for the present tense. Muna is unusual in that negated clauses use an unrealized verb form, making this a prototypical irrealis category. Other points of variation are the treatment of imperatives (which in various languages is a distinct verb form), and the verb forms found in habitual or procedural discourse (e.g. texts on house-building, preparing sago, etc.).

### 33.6.2 Aspectual enclitics

Apart from the Sangiric group, languages across Sulawesi reflect two aspectual formatives with the original forms **mo* and **pa*. The widespread distribution of these two morphemes (often enclitics) and their similar meanings across nine of the ten Sulawesi microgroups is striking.

Reflexes of **mo* have the sense of 'already' and in present-day grammars are typically described as perfective or completive markers (e.g. Balantak *no-taka-mo* (INTR.REAL-arrive-PFV) '(X) have/has already arrived'). With stative verbs it is typically inchoative, denoting a new current state (e.g. Tukang Besi *no-meha-mo* (3.REAL-red-PFV) '(it) has become red, it is red now'). In many cases they are probably best regarded as **iamitive** markers as defined by Olsson (2013). Reflexes of **pa* have the meaning 'still' and in present-day grammars are described as imperfective, incompletive, or continuative/sequential markers (e.g. Tukang Besi *-ho* (from **pa*) in *no-homoru-ho te wurai* (3.REAL-weave-yet CORE sarong) 'she is still weaving a sarong').

The phonological shape of these two aspectual particles differs only slightly across Sulawesi, but grammatically they vary between particles, enclitics, and regular suffixes. In Pamona, Kaili, Lindu, Duri, Mamasa, and Toraja Sa'dan they have the (original) forms *mo* and *pa*. In other languages the vowels have harmonized, as in Makasar *ma*, *pa*; Mori Bawah, Bungku, Wawonii, Kulisusu, Moronene, Cia-Cia *mo*, *po*; Muna, Tukang Besi *mo*, *ho*. Tonsawang has *əm* and *peʔ*, other Minahasan languages generally *mo* and *peʔ*. In scattered languages the completive member of this pair begins with an alveolar consonant. Bugis has *na*, *pa*; Mandar and Mamuju have *do*, *po*; while Tolaki, Mori Atas, and Padoe have *to*, *po*. In Mongondow these clitics have the forms *don* and *pa*; in Buol *lon*, *po*; in Gorontalo *lo*, *po*.

In some languages the post-verbal order is person marker followed by aspectual marker, as in Kulisusu *ndo-onto-**ho-mo***

**Table 33.16** Use of realized (R) and unrealized (U) verb forms in selected Sulawesi languages

| Language | Past | Present | Future | Conditional | Negation | Positive imperative | Negative imperative | Adhortative | General, habitual, procedural |
|---|---|---|---|---|---|---|---|---|---|
| Tondano | R | R | U | U | R | U | U | U | U |
| Tajio | R | R | U | U | R | (other) | U | U | U |
| Pendau | R | U | U | U | R | (other) | U | U | U |
| Balantak | R | U | U | U | R | U | U | U | U |
| Kaili Ledo | R | R | U | U | R | U (+ other) | U | U | R |
| Kaili Da'a | R | R | U | U | R | U (+ other) | U | U | U |
| Tukang-Besi | R | R | U | R? | R | (other) + R | R | R | R |
| Muna | R | R | U | U | U | (other) | (other) | R | R |

(3PL.NOM-see-3SG.ACC-COMPL) 'they saw it'. In other languages we find the reverse (e.g. Wolio *a-ala-**m-ea*** (3.NOM-take-COMPL-3.ACC) 'they took it'), while a few languages exhibit both orders. Moma, for example, has *natua-**mo-ko*** (old-COMPL-2SG.ABS) 'you are already old', but the reverse order with all other persons and numbers: *natua-**ʔa-mo*** (old-1SG.ABS-COMPL) 'I am already old'. In some languages the aspectual clitics interact phonologically with post-verbal person markers, as in Uma *rata=a=ma* (arrive=1SG.ABS=PFV) 'I arrived', *rata=i=mi* (arrive=3SG.ABS=PFV) 'he arrived'. In Uma and Bambam the unmarked forms are now *mi*, *pi*. Wotu is similar with *me*, *pe*. Konjo is unusual in that the presence of completive =*mo* triggers a pronominal shift in the marking of the patient: from postverbal absolutive it moves to become a preverbal 'ergative' (resulting in a double 'ergative'). Compare *na=peppe=aʔ* (3.ERG=hit=1.ABS) 'he hit me' and *ku=na=peppe=mo Ali* (1.ERG=3.ERG=hit=COMPL Ali) 'Ali hit me'.

In most languages these particles combine with the negator to produce forms meaning respectively 'not any more' and 'not yet', such as Mongondow *diaʔ-don*, *diaʔ-pa*; Pendau *ndau-mo*, *ndau-po*; Toraja Sa'dan *taeʔ-mo*, *taeʔ-pa*. However, there are a few exceptional cases, such as Uma *uma* 'no', *uma-pi* 'no longer', but *koʔia* 'not yet'; Seko Padang *ha-* 'not', *ha-hura:* 'not anymore', *ha- -mo* 'not yet'.

As for meaning, apart from its aspectual iamative meaning, completive *mo* is also commonly employed in narratives to mark mainline events and advance the storyline. This is reported for Balantak, Kaili Da'a, Konjo, Uma, Bambam, and Muna, though this discourse function of *mo* has been little studied (Gregerson and Martens 1986 on Uma is an exception). In languages that have a realized–unrealized distinction, the combination of unrealized aspect with perfective *mo* (or its variants) usually signals imminent action, as in Muna *a-k<um>ala-mo* (1SG-<IRR>go-PFV) 'I am about to go'. Tukang Besi, Balantak, Tajio, and Pendau, among other languages, are similar. The clitic *mo* (or what corresponds to it) is also widely used in imperatives, usually to strengthen them, but occasionally to soften, depending on intonation. In a variety of languages it can also be found as a predicative clitic on nouns and pronouns (e.g. Balantak *yakuʔ-mo* (1SG-PFV) 'I am the one').

The meanings of incompletive *pa* (or its correspondent forms) are also very diverse. Apart from its typical meaning 'still; yet' and its use as sequential marker in discourse, various other uses are reported. These include temporal 'since' (Balantak *-po*), 'again or more of something' (Kaili Da'a *-pa*, Tajio =*po*), comparative degree (Kaili Da'a *-pa*, Pendau =*po*), optative (Muna *-ho*), and concessive (Makasar =*pa*).

### 33.6.3 Aspectual proclitics

The use of proclitics to express tense, aspect, or mood is rare. Various southern Sulawesi languages have a single-syllable future particle that is clitic in nature. Examples include Kulisusu *be/bo*, Wolio *be*, Moronene *nta*, Pamona *da*, Mamuju *na*, and Tae', Mamasa, Bambam, Duri, and Konjo *la*. The following example is from Mamasa.

Mamasa

(41) *La=na=riwa=ko* *ambe-mu.*
FUT=3SG.ERG=hold=2SG.ABS father-2SG.GEN
'Your father will hold you.' (Matti 1994: 73)

### 33.6.4 Tense on person markers

In some languages a tense distinction is found among the pronominal sets. Realis vs. irrealis nominative subject prefixes are characteristic of the entire Muna-Buton group, where irrealis markers are usually paired with *-um-* marking on the verb. Compare the following Cia-Cia subject-marking prefixes (where an initial labial blocks *-um-*).

(42) Cia-Cia

| | Realis | Irrealis | |
|---|---|---|---|
| a. | *no-hende* | *na-h<um>ende* | 'he goes up' |
| b. | *ka-sampu* | *cu-ka-s<um>ampu* | 'you all go down' |
| c. | *o-ʔala-ʔe* | *a-m-ala-ʔe* | 'I take it' |
| d. | *no-mbule* | *na-mbule* | 'he returns' |
| e. | *no-pongko* | *na-pongko* | 'he kills' |

Future nominative pronouns are limited to a subset of Bungku-Tolaki languages, namely Padoe, Mori Atas, Mori Bawah, and Bungku. In all four languages there is a distinct resemblance (in some persons and numbers identity) between future nominative pronouns and the absolutive markers, but the former occur in preverbal position while the latter are postverbal. Recall also from §26.5.2 that these languages have fluid subject marking. The following examples from Mori Bawah illustrate the use of *kami* as a future pronoun in (43), and as an absolutive marker in (44); they are homophonous, but they differ in distribution: preverbal free word vs. postverbal suffix.

Mori Bawah

(43) *Kami* *mem-pongu-ko.*
1PL.EXCL.FUT PL.SBJ-tie-2SG.ABS
'We will tie you up.' (Esser 2011: 152)

Mori Bawah

(44) *Me-doito-kami* *me-ʔompeda.*
PL.SBJ-afraid-1PL.EXCL.ABS PL.SBJ-nearby
'We are afraid to approach.' (Esser 2011: 280)

### 33.6.5 Other TAM marking

Various other ways of encoding TAM are (a) aspectual verbs, (b) auxiliaries, (c) verbal prefixes, (d) reduplication, and (e) TAM adverbs or TAM markers.

(a) Aspectual verbs are common in Sulawesi. Tolaki has an inflected existential verb *laa* 'be', that encodes progressive aspect when serialized with another verb, as in (45). Moronene uses the verb *ari* 'finish' to indicate the perfect, as in (46).

Tolaki

(45) *Laa-ʔi=to* *lako* *tekura, ...*
be-3SG.ABS=PFV go distressed
'While he was going around distressed...'
(Mead and Youngman 2008: 113)

Moronene

(46) *Ari-aku-mo* *mon-totapi.*
finish-1SG.ABS-COMPL PTCP:AP-wash
'I've washed (clothes).' (S. Andersen 1995: 18)

Tolaki has three other aspectual verbs that pattern similarly: *hori* 'be near, beside' (always in negative contexts to express 'not near; not yet; never before'); *ari* 'finish; over; after' and *ndee* 'habitually' (or after a negative, 'ever'). Similar patterns exist in many other languages.

(b) Auxiliaries differ from aspectual verbs in that they are deficient in some way. In Tukang Besi, for example, auxiliaries are defined as verbs without subject affixation. Auxiliaries in Tukang Besi include *ane(-ho)* 'is currently; is still'; *mina(-mo)* 'ever' and *poʔoli(-mo)*, 'after; finished', as in (47) and (48).

Tukang Besi

(47) *Ane-ho* *no-wande.*
exist-yet 3.REAL-rain
'It is still raining.' (Donohue 1999a: 191)

Tukang Besi

(48) *Mina-mo* *no-wila* *i* *Tomia.*
ever-PFV 3.REAL-go OBL Tomea
'They have been to Tomea before.'
(Dononue 1999a: 177)

Tondano has five modal auxiliaries: *toro* 'can; be able'; *poʔar* 'want; desire; like'; *musti* 'must; have to'; *siaʔ-sighaʔ* 'can; be capable; expect to' and *soʔo* 'don't want' (with inherent negation). Bambam has two modal auxiliaries: *melo* 'want to' and *mala* 'can; may'.

(c) A number of verbal prefixes indicate something about the temporal profile of an event, and could thus also be considered aspectual in nature. Included are the durative, the iterative, the habitual, and the diffuse action.

For example, habitual aspect in Bambam is marked by the prefix *si-*, as in (49).

Bambam
(49) *Si-ma-heaq* *sia-m-äq.*
HAB-STAT-afraid really-PFV-1SG.ABS
'I was really afraid (the whole time).'
(Campbell 1989: 138)

Some prefixes with a plural meaning, particularly distributive, can imply that an action is carried out over time. An example is Sangir *pam-* 'diversive action affix' (the action is diverse, independent, individualized, and thus of necessity requires a plurality of agents). The number of recognized aspectual prefixes varies from language to language, and many descriptions do not explicitly identify them as such.

(d) Reduplication is widely used across Sulawesi to mark continuous or repetitive action, as in (50).

Kaili Da'a
(50) *Ni-kita~kita* *daʔa* *ria* *sou.*
PV.REAL-REDUP~see not be house
'He looked and looked (but) there was no house.'
(Barr 1988a: 38)

(e) A very common strategy for marking aspect, and especially mood, is through a series of words that are variously analysed as adverbs or simply TAM or mood markers. These words are typically uninflected and occur in preverbal or clause-initial position. They cover a wide range of aspectual and modal categories, including ability, possibility, permission, and necessity. Bambam, for example, has a modal marker *dotam* 'should', as in (51).

Bambam
(51) *Dotam* *um-papia-m-kiaq*
should AV-make-PFV-1PL.INCL.ABS
*onge-am.*
occupy-LOC.NMLZ
'We should make ourselves a place.'
(Campbell 1989: 149)

The following preverbal aspect and mood markers are listed for Wotu (Mead 2013): *pura* 'finish; already'; *melo* 'will; want'; *waddi* 'permitted; able; can'; *poli* 'possible; capable; can'; *harusu* 'must'; *bulli* 'unnecessary; do not'; and *tuli* 'always; regularly'. It is not unusual for loanwords to be found in this category (Wotu *harusu* is from Indonesian *harus* 'must'), and to find very specific modal meanings (e.g. Balantak *somo* 'be forced to; have no choice but; have to').

## 33.7 Multipredicate constructions and clause combining

In this section we describe a variety of multipredicate constructions and clause combinations that are found in Sulawesi languages. This is an area that has barely been studied for Sulawesi; many descriptive grammars do not treat the topic in much detail (some do not treat it at all), and the terminological variation is also considerable. For these reasons we propose a tentative classification here, based on a limited number of structural criteria, but going beyond the traditional coordination–subordination dichotomy. Multipredicate constructions are best seen as a continuum from very tight to very loose linking of predicates, with compounding on the one end, and conjoining on the other. Different languages segment this continuum at different points using a set of similar criteria. For Sulawesi we propose the following tentative divisions, while also allowing for overlap, fuzzy boundaries, and some indeterminacy: compounding and complex predicates (§33.7.1); serial verb constructions (§33.7.2); juxtaposition and compressed clauses (§33.7.3); non-finite clauses (§33.7.4); and conjoining, which includes adverbial clauses and a discussion of conjunctions (§33.7.5). Note that relative clauses are not treated here, except for some non-finite relative clauses in §33.7.4. Issues of control and raising have not been studied in much detail in Sulawesi (but see Finer (1997) on Selayar from a theory-specific perspective), and are therefore also left for another occasion.

### 33.7.1 Compounding and complex predicates

In this section we first consider verbal compounds in which a verb head is immediately followed by another verb. Together they form a single phonological word, sometimes with an intervening linking element. The combination expresses a single event, usually with the head determining the overall transitivity of the construction. The following two examples are from Tukang Besi; in (52) the second verb expresses manner, in (53) the resultant state.

Tukang Besi
(52) *No-wila-lolaha.*
3.REAL-go-search
'They went searching.' (Donohue 1999a: 195)

Tukang Besi
(53) *No-tobo-mate-ʔe* *na* *sanggila.*
3.REAL-stab-dead-3.OBJ NOM pirate
'He stabbed the pirate dead.' (Donohue 1999a: 199)

Donohue (1999a: 194) treats these constructions as instances of 'contiguous serial verbs' under a single VP, but they can also be considered compounds. Parallel constructions are Muna *do-gaa-bughou-mo* (3PL.REAL-marry-new-PFV) 'they are newly married' and *do-po-mai-n-suli* (3PL.REAL-RECP-come-LIG-return) 'they go back and forth'. Verbal compounds appear to be relatively rare in Sulawesi; nominal compounding is much more widespread.

Mori Bawah and Tolaki have variations on these compounds, which we call complex predicates. In Mori Bawah both verbs, not just the first verb, can take a plural subject prefix; thus next to *mong-kaa me-ntade* (eat stand) 'eat standing up' there is also *i-meng-kaa m-pe-ntade-o* (2PL.NOM-PL.SBJ-eat PL.SBJ-INTR-stand-3SG.ABS) 'you all eat it standing up'; although possibly two phonological words, here again (as in (53)) O indexing follows the second (intransitive) verb. In Tolaki the second verb can be negated and in some cases it even brings along a non-pronominal argument, as in (54); nonetheless indexing (in this case for S) still follows the second verb.

Tolaki
(54) *Mate* *n-daa* *mo-naa-ʔi=to* *(ona)*
die LIG-NEG PTCP:AP-have-3SG.ABS=PFV EMPH
*o* *ana.*
ART child
'He died without having children.'
(Mead and Youngman 2008: 131)
(**Mateʔito ndaa monaa (ona) o ana.*)

## 33.7.2 Serial verb constructions (SVCs)

Serial verb constructions (SVCs) are probably found throughout Sulawesi, but only more recent and comprehensive grammars (such as those of Pendau, Tajio, and Tukang Besi) actually describe them as such, and we follow the analysis presented there. Examples from the South Sulawesi group are lacking in this section. SVCs are less tight than compounds or complex predicates. In Sulawesi languages they exhibit many of the characteristics described in general for serial verb constructions: (i) two or more verbs linked without conjunction, linking element, or intonational pause; (ii) the verbs cannot be separately negated and share the same tense, aspect, and mood; and (iii) the two predicates typically describe a single event. However, the verbs are two distinct words, not a single phonological unit with a ligature. Verbs commonly encountered in serial verb constructions include verbs of motion, manner verbs, aspectual and modal verbs, and various others. Examples (55) to (57) show motion verbs in SVCs. Notice that in (56) two verbs of motion follow the main verb, both indicating the direction of the action.

Tajio
(55) *Siaʔu* ***mao*** ***mo-leler*** *paame* *ini*
1SG go AV.IRR-draw at.the.moment PROX
'I will go to draw (rattan) a moment later.'
(Mayani 2013: 203)

Pendau
(56) ***Bagi-i*** ***nyau*** ***mai*** *aʔu* *loka* *nao!*
give-DIR go.down come 1SG banana that
'Bring down to me that banana!' (Quick 2007: 306)

Moronene
(57) *Meʔasa* *tempo* *koie* *koe* ***leu***
one time that stork come
***titia****-ho* *dahu.*
invite-3SG.ABS dog
'Once upon a time the stork came and invited the dog.' (S. Andersen 1995: 13)

As for the other usages of SVCs, Tolaki has five aspectual verbs that participate in SVCs. The aspectual use of *laa* 'be' in a SVC is illustrated in (45) in §33.6.5.

Since most of these aspectual verbs are dependent on the main verb and cannot be used by themselves to assert events or states, they are sometimes analysed as auxiliary verbs. In Tukang Besi, for example, Donohue (1999a) distinguishes between: (i) preverbal auxiliaries, which are not indexed for subject; (ii) serial verbs that are invariantly indexed with third person subject prefixes; and (iii) serial verbs that are indexed with the clausal subject. Examples of auxiliaries are given in §33.6.5. Examples of the other two categories are the third person-indexed serial verb *mura* 'likely; maybe', illustrated in (58), and the clausal-subject indexed serial verb *hematuu* 'begin', shown in (59). (Under an alternative analysis, these would be analysed as complement constructions.)

Tukang Besi
(58) ***O-mura*** *ku-rato* *ʔuka* *ilange.*
3.REAL-maybe 1SG-arrive also tomorrow
'I might come over tomorrow as well.'
(Donohue 1999a: 190)

Tukang Besi
(59) ***Ku-hematuu-mo*** *ku-henahenai* *te* *pogau*
1SG-begin-PFV 1SG-learn CORE language
*Wanse.*
Wanci
'I have begun to learn Wanci.' (Donohue 1999a: 192)

In addition to motion and aspectual verbs, various other verbs can appear in serial verb constructions. These include phasal verbs, illustrated in (59), degree adverbial notions such as 'very' and 'extremely' (Tukang Besi *saori* and *harai*), and a variety of other verbs, traditionally called complement-taking verbs, such as 'learn' and 'refuse'. The last two are illustrated in (60) and (61).

Tondano
(60) *Sè=ma-ajar* *ma-siwo* *cucur.*
3PL.PIV=AV.DYN-learn AV.DYN-make k.o.cake
'They learn to make *cucur* cake.' (Brickell 2014: 425)

Wolio
(61) *A-mendeu* *a-sapo.*
3SG-refuse 3SG-go.down
'He refused to go down.' (Anceaux 1987: 44)

### 33.7.3 Juxtaposition

Juxtaposition, the simple linking of two or more verbal clauses without any conjunction, and often (but not always) without a noticeable intonation break, is common in Sulawesi. However, distinguishing SVCs from juxtaposition is far from straightforward in many languages, and more research is needed to arrive at language-specific criteria that clarify and validate this distinction for the languages of Sulawesi. A case in point is (62).

Muna
(62) *Ao-nea* *ae-rimba* *a-kala.*
1SG.REAL-usual 1SG.REAL-fast 1SG.REAL-go
'I usually go fast.' (van den Berg 1989: 242)

This sequence of three verbs is analysed as juxtaposition by van den Berg, but it could arguably be considered an SVC as well, with an aspectual and a manner verb preceding the main verb. In the following section we will therefore focus on unambiguous cases of predicate juxtaposition, where the verbs can be non-contiguous; can differ in subject, TAM, and polarity; and the two predicates clearly do not constitute a single event. Semantically juxtaposition covers a large area, including object complementation, a variety of adverbial notions (e.g. purpose), and clauses following certain adjectives. These three categories are illustrated in examples (63) to (65) from Balantak.

Balantak
(63) *Yaku?* ***rongor*** *ia* *sian-po* ***mule?kon.***
1SG hear 3SG NEG-IMPFV return
'I heard he has not returned yet.' (van den Berg and Busenitz 2012: 229)

Balantak
(64) ***No-mae?-mo*** *na* *bengkel* ***mon-totobo?i***
INTR.REAL-go-PFV LOC repair.shop AV.IRR-repair
*oto-na.*
car-3SG.POSS
'(He) went to the repair shop to repair his car.'
(van den Berg and Busenitz 2012: 227)

Balantak
(65) *Ia* ***ma-male*** ***ba-limang.***
3SG INTR.IRR-tired INTR-work
'She is tired of working.'
(van den Berg and Busenitz 2012: 232)

A subtype of juxtaposition is what could be called the compressed clause. This is neither a serialized verb construction nor a typical clause juxtaposition. The defining features of the compressed clause are: (i) the clauses have shared ellipsed arguments; (ii) an intonational pause is allowed (and often present); (iii) clauses can have different TAM and be separately negated; and (iv) they describe two or more distinct events or states. From a semantic perspective, compressed clauses express a series of temporally related (simultaneous or subsequent) events. Compressed clauses exist in many languages of Sulawesi, though they are not always described as such. Examples (66) to (68) are illustrative, with the relevant verbs bolded.

Tolaki
(66) *. . . a=no* ***ina?u*** ***pe?ula*** *i* *pu?u*
and=3SG.NOM go.over get.on at base
*ndawa-no* *uewai,* ***me-kopu***
LIG:leaf-3SG.GEN k.o.rattan PTCP:INTR-grasp
*mope~mopee.*
INTENSE~tight
'. . . and he went over and got on at the base of the rattan's leaves, holding on very tightly.'
(Mead and Youngman 2008: 133)

Pendau
(67) *Ito* ***me-lampa=mo,*** ***ma'o***
1PL.INCL.ABS IRR:INTR-travel=COMPL go
*mang-angka.*
IRR:TR-steal
'Let's leave now, and we will go steal.' (Quick 2007: 358)

Tae' (Luwu'-Rongkong)
(68) *Pa?anu* ***di-alli~alli*** ***la=di-bawa.***
things PASS-REDUP~buy FUT=PASS-bring
'Things were bought in order to be brought along.'
(*Carita Pangkep* 009, unpublished text)

Another subtype of juxtaposed clause is the phenomenon of consecutive linking that is found in the South Sulawesi languages, already mentioned in §33.5.2.7. What is striking about this construction is that in the second clause, which marks a temporal sequence, a logical conclusion or a purpose, the subject of an intransitive verb is indexed with the 'ergative' set of prefixed pronouns (rather than the expected absolutive suffix). This is illustrated in (69) for Bugis and in (70) for Duri.

Bugis

(69) *Aléng=ngaʔ duiʔ* ***u****=lésu matuʔ.*
give=1SG.ABS money 1SG.ERG=return later
'Give me money that I might return later.'
(D. Laskowske 2016: 45)

Duri

(70) *Ia tee ambeq-na ma-lajaq tongan-m-i,*
3 this father-3.POSS STAT-afraid truly-PFV-3
***na****-mes-suun...*
3.ERG-INTR-come.out
'His father was afraid and therefore came out...'
(K. Valkama 1995: 59)

In Duri, the second verb can also be preceded by the clitic conjunction *an=*, and in those cases is therefore better treated as conjoining (see §33.7.5).

A final type of juxtaposition is the combination of two distinct main clauses without an overt conjunction. Example (71), from Tukang Besi, describes two parallel simultaneous events. In sentence (72), from Balantak, the first clause provides the temporal setting of the second, but there is no sign of subordination. These two patterns appear to be quite common across Sulawesi.

Tukang Besi

(71) *Te La Kolokolopua no-hembula te*
CORE ART Tortoise 3.REAL-plant CORE
*huʔu-no, te La Kandokendoke*
trunk-3.POSS CORE ART Monkey
*no-hembula te umbu-no*
3.REAL-plant CORE extremity-3.POSS
'Tortoise planted the trunk, (and) Monkey planted the top.' (Donohue 1999a: 425)

Balantak

(72) *Potoʔ-oruang i kai,*
MULT-sit PERS 1PL.EXCL
*no-taka-mo i ia.*
INTR.REAL-arrive-PFV PERS 3SG
'While all of us were sitting (there), he arrived.'
(van den Berg and Busenitz 2012: 234)

### 33.7.4 Non-finite clauses

A slightly different type of linking is the use of non-finite clauses. Non-finite clauses, where the verb lacks person and/or TAM marking, are the only unambiguous example of dependent clauses in Sulawesi. They appear to be rare, possibly due to the fact that many languages do not distinguish finite and non-finite verb forms, and seem to be limited to relative clauses and temporal adverbial clauses. Muna, where verbs are normally inflected for person and realis-irrealis mood, has both types, as does Tukang Besi. A non-finite active participle form is found in relative clauses where the subject is the relativized constituent, as in (73).

Muna

(73) *Ae-faraluu dahu so*
1SG.REAL-need dog FUT
*me-dhaga-ni-no lambu.*
ACT.PTCP-guard-TR-ACT.PTCP house
'I need a dog that will guard the house.'
(van den Berg 1989: 232)

There is also a specific type of temporal adverbial clause where the verb is marked by the prefix *sa-* 'when; as soon as', or *paka-* 'when first; when just'. In these cases, the agent is marked by a possessive suffix, as in (74).

Muna

(74) *Paka-gaa-ndo sadhia do-pogira.*
FIRST-marry-3PL.POSS always 3PL.REAL-fight
'When they were first married, they were always fighting.' (van den Berg 1989: 250)

Mori Bawah also has a number of elements that are formally verbs in that they attract indexing (in genitive/possessive case) for the clausal subject, but in function act like subordinating conjunctions. Compare *inso* and *kontongaa* in examples (75) and (76).

Mori Bawah

(75) *Inso-mu kode~kodei...*
be.from-2SG.GEN REDUP~small
'Since you were small...' (Esser 2011: 112)

Mori Bawah

(76) *Kon-tonga-a-do me-kutui*
at.stage.of-middle-LOC-3PL.GEN PTCP:INTR-delouse
*andio...*
this
'While they were thus delousing each other...'
(Mead 2008: 170)

### 33.7.5 Conjoining and conjunctions

Conjoining is the 'loosest' of the multipredicate constructions. Typically, there is a clear intonational break between the two clauses, and normally a conjunction is present as well. Each clause may have its own TAM, polarity, and participants. Semantically, two (or more) distinct states or events are described.

Semantically, conjunctions signal a wide range of temporal and logical connections between clauses, including simultaneity, sequence, alternative, condition, concession, purpose, contrast, conclusion, result, and clarification. Syntactically, most conjunctions are free words that are found clause-initially (either at the beginning of the first clause, or at the beginning of the second clause, depending on various factors). A few languages have second-place conjunctions (e.g. Muna *kaawu* 'after') or clitic conjunctions. In Bambam the additive conjunction *am=* procliticizes to the verb, while Balantak has an enclitic sequential conjunction *=si* meaning 'only when', often in combination with the temporal adverb *kasi* 'then'. Examples (77) to (82) are illustrative.

Tajio

(77) *Sisia* *no-po-mbosi* *te=ato?* ***sono***
3PL AV.REAL-CAUS-good ART=roof with
*no-pa-pacing* *te=vombong.*
AV.REAL-CAUS-clean ART=door
'They fixed the roof and cleaned the door.'
(Mayani 2013: 194)

Pendau

(78) *?u-jamin,* ***maumpo*** *a?u* *ndau*
1SG.INV.IRR-guarantee although 1SG NEG
*mu=?ito.*
2SG.INV.IRR=see
'I guarantee it, even though you cannot see me.'
(Quick 2007: 523)

Kaili Da'a

(79) ***Ane*** *ma-uja* *ma-romba,* *mo-wia* *jumu*
if IRR-rain IRR-hard IRR-make bed
*rampimpi.*
in.grass
'If it rains hard, he makes a bed in the grass.'
(Barr 1988b: 109)

Muna

(80) *No-mate* ***kaawu*** *ghule* *amaitu,* *andoa*
3SG.REAL-die after snake that 3PL
*do-suli-mo.*
3PL.REAL-return-PFV
'When the snake was dead, they went home.'
(van den Berg 1989: 148)

Bambam

(81) *Tamba-i-äq,* ***am****=ku-bali-i-ko.*
call-LOC-1SG.ABS and=1SG.ERG-help-LOC-2SG.ABS
'Call me and I will help you.' (Campbell 1989: 113)

Balantak

(82) *Doi?-an=****si*** *kasi* *bayar-on.*
money-HAVE-SEQ then pay-PV.IRR
'Only when you have the money, then you pay for it.' (van den Berg and Busenitz 2012: 238)

Deverbal conjunctions are common in Sulawesi. Examples include Mori Bawah *insono* 'since', from the verb *inso* 'be from' as in (75), as well as Balantak *daa*, Muna *pada*, Tukang Besi *po?oli*, all with the meaning 'when; after' and derived from verbs meaning 'to finish'. The historical origin of conjunctions has been discussed for Mori Bawah (Mead 2001c) and for Sangir (Maryott 1990). Many Sulawesi languages have borrowed conjunctions. Pendau is described with no less than twenty-five conjunctions, five of which are borrowings from Malay/Indonesian. Tajio has the loan conjunctions *sementara* 'while', *waktu* 'when', *supaya* 'so that', and *karna* 'because'. Other examples are Wolio *sababuno* and *karana* 'because' (next to native *roonamo* and *madaakana*), Kaili Ledo *lantara* 'because', Balantak *tempo* 'when; while' and Tukang Besi clarificatory *berarti* 'I mean to say; that is'.

## 33.8 Deixis and directionals

Sulawesi shows considerable variation within the area of deixis and directionals. All languages have a basic demonstrative system which distinguishes at least three degrees of distance (proximal-medial-distal), illustrated by Makasar *anne* 'this (near speaker)', *antu* 'that (near hearer)' and *anjo* 'that (away from speaker and hearer)'. Many languages have additional demonstratives, further refining degrees of distance, but especially related to elevation, distinguishing lower and higher and sometimes level locations, as seen from a deictic centre. (This deictic centre is normally the speaker, but it can also be the narrator or the protagonist in a story.) Mori Bawah has five basic terms: *andio* 'near speaker', *atuu* 'near hearer', *arau* 'remote; level', *atahu* 'remote; higher', and *alou* 'remote; lower'. Wolio and Moronene are similar, but Moronene has six terms, distinguishing two proximal forms: *diie* 'at speaker' and *soie* 'by speaker'. Other semantic distinctions among demonstratives include laterality, visibility, and cardinal direction. Balantak has seven basic terms, four of which are distal terms: *tu?u* 'not close to either speaker or hearer, somewhat vague or indistinct', *le?e* 'not close to speaker and hearer and on the speaker's side', *ra?a* 'that (to the front and/or higher than the speaker)', and *ro?o* 'that (lower than the speaker)'. Muna also has seven basic terms, including four distals: *watu* 'that (level or lower than speaker, or to the west)', *tatu* 'that (higher or to the east)', *nagha* 'that (invisible or earlier referred to)', and *waghaitu* 'that (which was in view but is no longer in view)'. In Bantik medial *ene* is also used for invisible referents. In many languages the demonstratives are not only used for locative deixis, but also for temporal deixis and as referent tracking devices.

Several languages have special presentative demonstratives, including Bantik and Bobongko *kaʔa* 'here is'. Kulisusu distinguishes deictic discoveratives *ai-ho-mo poɗa!* (here-3PL.ABS-COMPL) 'here's the knife!' (after searching) from corresponding presentatives *kaʔai poɗa* 'here's the knife' (e.g. offering it).

Muna has two sets of demonstratives, one referential (to refer to known entities), and one identifying (with initial *a*), to signal one unique referent among many. An example is *ne Raha ini* (LOC Raha this) 'here in Raha' vs. *ne Raha a-ini* (LOC Raha ID-this) 'in this Raha' (implying that there are other places called Raha). Mori Bawah has deictic verbs which predicate existence/location: *da lou-o mboʔu* (still be.down.there-3SG.ABS again) 'it was still down there'. Kulisusu has deictic verbs of arrival: *ndo-teusoa-mo* (3PL.NOM-arrive.over.there-COMPL) 'they arrived over there'. See Holton and Pappas, this volume, §49.5.1 for more on spatial systems in Eastern Celebic.

A number of languages also have grammaticalized directional systems. Buol has two directional enclitics: *=agi* 'towards speaker' and *=ako* 'away from speaker'. Dampelas has eleven directional verbs, partly to make up for the lack of specific prepositions. But the most complex directional systems are found in the Sangir-Talaud microgroup. Bantik, for example, has twelve adverbs that mark relative height (up and down) as well as degree of distance, and they are also differentiated for stationary and moving (dynamic) entities. Examples are the stationary terms *daya* 'somewhat upwards' and *daŋ* 'considerably upwards', and the dynamic terms *tanao* 'considerably downwards, moving away from speaker' and *nsao* 'somewhat downwards, towards speaker'. In Sangir, Talaud, and Ratahan, similar terms exist which interact in complex ways with cardinal directions. In Sangir, for example, *taraiʔ* 'go up', also means 'go south' (including on level ground), but in closely related Sangil, spoken by people who have lived in southern Mindanao for a long time, the cognate form *tallaiʔ* 'go up' refers to going north. See Holton and Pappas, this volume, §49.5.3 for more on Sangiric systems.

Several South Sulawesi languages also have complex directional systems. Mamuju has near-obligatory deictic agreement on verbs of motion, for example, *me-lampa=ʔ sao di Jawa* (AV-go=1.ABS SEAWARD PREP Jawa) 'I went overseas to Jawa' (this cannot be expressed as **melampaʔ di Jawa*). Aralle-Tabulahan distinguishes six directions, three of which are related to geographical contour (*daiʔ* 'upwards', *naung* 'downwards', and *pano* 'level(wards)'), and a further three related to river: *tama* 'upstream/inwards', *sau* 'downstream/outwards', and *beteʔ* 'across(wards)'. The exact choice of directionals is complex, especially when summarizing longer trips, and determined by a hierarchy of factors. River, for example, takes precedence over contour, and the ultimate feature is critical: a final descent overrides an initial ascent. But extralinguistic factors also play a role. A trip to the coastal town of Makassar, for example, is always described as *daiʔ* 'upwards', because of its social and political prestige.

## 33.9 Conclusion and outlook

This concludes our overview of Sulawesi. Even though the basic contours of the typological variety found in Sulawesi are clear, much remains to be done before the island will give up all its linguistic secrets. Some of the more urgent research issues include the following.

(a) Some twenty-five to thirty languages of Sulawesi are still completely undescribed. Given the rate of language shift in Sulawesi, documenting and describing these speech varieties should be a high priority.
(b) Even though information is available on a number of the larger languages, they lack a modern typologically informed comprehensive description. This includes Sangir, Gorontalo, Mongondow, Toraja, Tolaki, and Pamona, as well as Banggai, which is a typological oddity in Sulawesi.
(c) The extent of morphosyntactic variation needs focused attention. Especially in the area of pronoun systems, voice marking, transitive clause types, and TAM marking, Sulawesi shows great diversity, probably even more than has been covered in this chapter. This has implications for areal typology, reconstruction, and subgrouping.
(d) Analytically and terminologically, there are still some open questions. For example, does Uma really have a voice system (see §33.5.1)? And can certain clause types better be characterized as antipassive, rather than as semi-transitive (as is done in this chapter)?
(e) Specific topics that should be on the research agenda are the status of nasal–obstruent clusters (see §33.2.3), the status and function of stem-formers (see §33.5.2), as well as intonation patterns (mostly ignored or treated cursorily in descriptions), and deixis and demonstratives.

# Appendix: Sources

Aralle-Tabulahan: McKenzie (1991); Andersen and McKenzie (2008)
Badaic languages: Martens (1989)
Balantak: van den Berg and Busenitz (2012)
Bambam: Campbell (1989, 1991)
Banggai: van den Bergh (1953)
Bantik: Utsumi (2013a, 2014)
Barang-Barang: Laidig and Maingak (1999); Belding et al. (2001); Smith (2002)
Batui: Mead and Pasanda (2015)
Bobongko: Mead (2001a)
Budong-Budong: Manda et al. (2002)
Bugis: Sirk (1983); Macknight (2012); D. Laskowske (2016)
Buol: Zobel (2005)
Bungku-Tolaki microgroup: Mead (1998)
Busoa: van den Berg (2020)
Cia-Cia: van den Berg (1991c)
Coastal Konjo: Friberg (1991, 1996)
Dampelas: Moro (2010)
Duri: K. Valkama (1993, 1995), S. Valkama (1995)
Gorontalo: Little (1978, 1989); Badudu (1982); Pateda (1986); Steinhauer (1991a)
Kaili Da'a: Barr (1988a, b, c); Barr and Barr (1988)
Kaili Ledo: Esser (1934); Evans (2003)
Kaili-Pamona microgroup: Martens (1997)
Kaimbulawa: van den Berg fieldnotes
Kodeoha: Mantasiah (2007)
Kulisusu: Mead fieldnotes
Lauje: Himmelmann (1991a, 2002b)
Makasar: Jukes (2005, 2006, 2013); Macknight (2012)
Mamasa: Matti (1991, 1994)
Mamuju: Strømme (1994); Kaufman (2011b)
Mandar: Ba'dudu et al. (1985); Lee (2008)
Minahasan group: Adriani (1925); Sneddon (1978)
Moma: Adriani and Esser (1939)
Mongondow: Dunnebier (1929–1930)
Mori Bawah: Esser (1927, 1933, 2011); Barsel (1994); Mead (2005, 2008)
Moronene: D. Andersen (1999a, b); S. Andersen (1994, 1995); Andersen and Andersen (2005); Andersen and McKenzie (2008).
Muna: van den Berg (1989, 1997); Southern Muna: van den Berg (2004a).
Napu: Hanna and Hanna (1991); Hanna (2004)
Padoe: Karhunen (1991); Vuorinen (1995)
Pamona: Adriani (1931)
Panasuan: Manda et al. (2002)
Pendau: Quick (2007)
Ponosakan: Lobel (2015)
Rampi: Christensen (1990)
Ratahan: Himmelmann (2002b); Himmelmann and Wolff (1999)
Saluan: Gobée (1929)
Sangil: Maryott (1974); Sneddon (1984)
Sangir: Adriani (1893); Maryott (1990)
Sangiric microgroup: Sneddon (1984)
Sarudu: M. Martens (p.c.)
Seko Padang: Payne and Laskowske (1997); K. Laskowske (1994); T. Laskowske (2001, 2007)
Selayar: Mithun and Basri (1986); Ceria (1993); Jackson (2008)
South Sulawesi microgroup: Mills (1975a)
Tae' (Luwu'-Rongkong): Ibrahim (2002)
Tajio: Mayani (2013); Derek Harman p.c.
Talaud: Utsumi (2013b)
Tolaki: Gouweloos (1936); Edwards (2012); Mead and Youngman (2008)
Tomini-Tolitoli microgroup: Himmelmann (2001)
Tondano: Sneddon (1975); Brickell (2014)
Tontemboan: Sneddon (1978)
Tonsawang: Utsumi (2018)
Topoiyo: Martens fieldnotes
Toraja Sa'dan: Sande (1997)
Totoli: Himmelmann (1991a); Himmelmann and Riesberg (2013)
Tukang Besi: Donohue (1999a)
Uma: Martens (1988a, b, c); Martens and Martens (1988)
Wolio: Anceaux (1988); Alberth (2000)
Wotu: Mead (2013)
Wotu-Wolio microgroup: Mead and Smith (2015).

CHAPTER 34

# Languages of Flores and its satellites

Naonori Nagaya

## 34.1 Introduction

This chapter provides a typological overview of the Austronesian languages of Flores and its satellites, namely, the Central Malayo-Polynesian languages of the islands of Flores, Palu'e, Komodo, the Solor Archipelago, the Alor Archipelago, Sumba, Sabu, and Sumbawa. The languages dealt with in this chapter are listed in (1), (2), and (3). Note that there are many other languages in this region not listed here. They are not discussed here due to the lack of materials for them.[1]

(1) Bima

(2) Sumba-Flores languages:
  a. Sumba-Hawu: Laboya, Kambera, Hawu,[2] Dhao
  b. Western Flores: Manggarai, Rembong
  c. Central Flores: Rongga, Ngadha, Keo, Ende, Lio, Palu'e

(3) Flores-Lembata languages:
  a. Sika, Hewa
  b. Lamaholot varieties: Lewotobi, Lewoingu, Solor, Central Lembata, Alorese
  c. Kedang

These islands are part of the Lesser Sunda Islands of eastern Indonesia. The island of Sumbawa is included in the West Nusa Tenggara province, while the other islands politically belong to the East Nusa Tenggara province, together with the western part of Timor Island and Roti Island. See Map 34.1 for the approximate locations of these languages.

The Austronesian languages of Flores and its satellites belong to the Central Malayo-Polynesian subgroup (Blust 1993a).[3] Subgrouping within Central Malayo-Polynesian is controversial. Traditionally, languages of this region have been classified as belonging to the Bima-Sumba subgroup (languages in (1) and (2)) or the Ambon-Timor subgroup (those in (3)) (Esser 1938). This traditional classification is disputed by Blust (2008), who instead proposes the Sumba-Hawu subgroup (2a) and offers some evidence for subgrouping the languages in (2). Elias (2018) proposes the Central Flores subgroup (2c) but excludes Palu'e from it. Fricke (2019) provides evidence for the Flores-Lembata subgroup (3) as an innovation-defined subgroup and argues that it further forms the Bima-Lembata subgroup with (1) and (2) (see Zobel, this volume, §13.2.1, for an overview of the current subgrouping proposals and their basis). In this chapter, I refer to the languages in (1)–(3) using the geographical term "languages of Flores and its satellites".

The languages of Flores and its satellites play a significant role in understanding the typology and history of the Malayo-Polynesian languages of Southeast Asia (MPSEA languages) for at least two reasons. First, the languages of this region represent a transitional stage between symmetrical voice languages and preposed possessor languages, the two typological types proposed for MPSEA languages by Himmelmann (2005a). According to Himmelmann's (2005a) typology, symmetrical voice languages tend to show the following features: (i) symmetrical voice alternations; (ii) postposed possessor; (iii) no alienable/inalienable distinction; (iv) few or no differences between narrative and equational clauses; (v) person marking only sporadically attested; (vi) numerals/quantifiers precede head; (vii) negators in pre-predicate position; and (viii) V-initial or SVX word order. In contrast, preposed possessor languages are likely to have the

[1] Linguistic studies on the languages of Flores and its satellites have a long history since the early work done by Dutch and German researchers and missionaries, such as J. C. G. Jonker; P. Arndt; and J. A. J. Verheijen. Descriptive work on the languages of this region used to be spotty, but fortunately the situation has been improving over the last decade. Data are mainly from the following sources: Bima (Owens 2000), Laboya (Verdizade 2019), Kambera (Klamer 1998), Hawu (Walker 1982), Dhao (Balukh 2020), Manggarai (Semiun 1993), Rongga (Arka 2016), Ngadha (Arndt 1933; Djawanai 1983), Keo (Baird 2002), Lio (Elias 2018), Sika (Lewis and Grimes 1995), Hewa (Fricke 2014), Lamaholot (Nishiyama and Kelen 2007; Nagaya 2011; Kroon 2016; Fricke 2019), Kedang (Samely 1991), and Alorese (Klamer 2011).

[2] The Hawu language is called 'Savu', 'Sawu', or 'Sabu' in the older literature, and the name of the island where Hawu is spoken is written as Sabu (Grimes 2010b).

[3] Technically, non-CMP languages are also spoken in this region, including varieties of Malay, such as Standard Indonesian and Larantuka Malay (Steinhauer 1991b; Dietrich 1997), and other non-Austronesian languages. Descriptions of these languages are beyond the scope of this chapter.

Naonori Nagaya, *Languages of Flores and its satellites*. In: *The Oxford Guide to the Malayo-Polynesian Languages of Southeast Asia*. Edited by: Alexander Adelaar and Antoinette Schapper, Oxford University Press. © Naonori Nagaya (2024). DOI: 10.1093/oso/9780198807353.003.0034

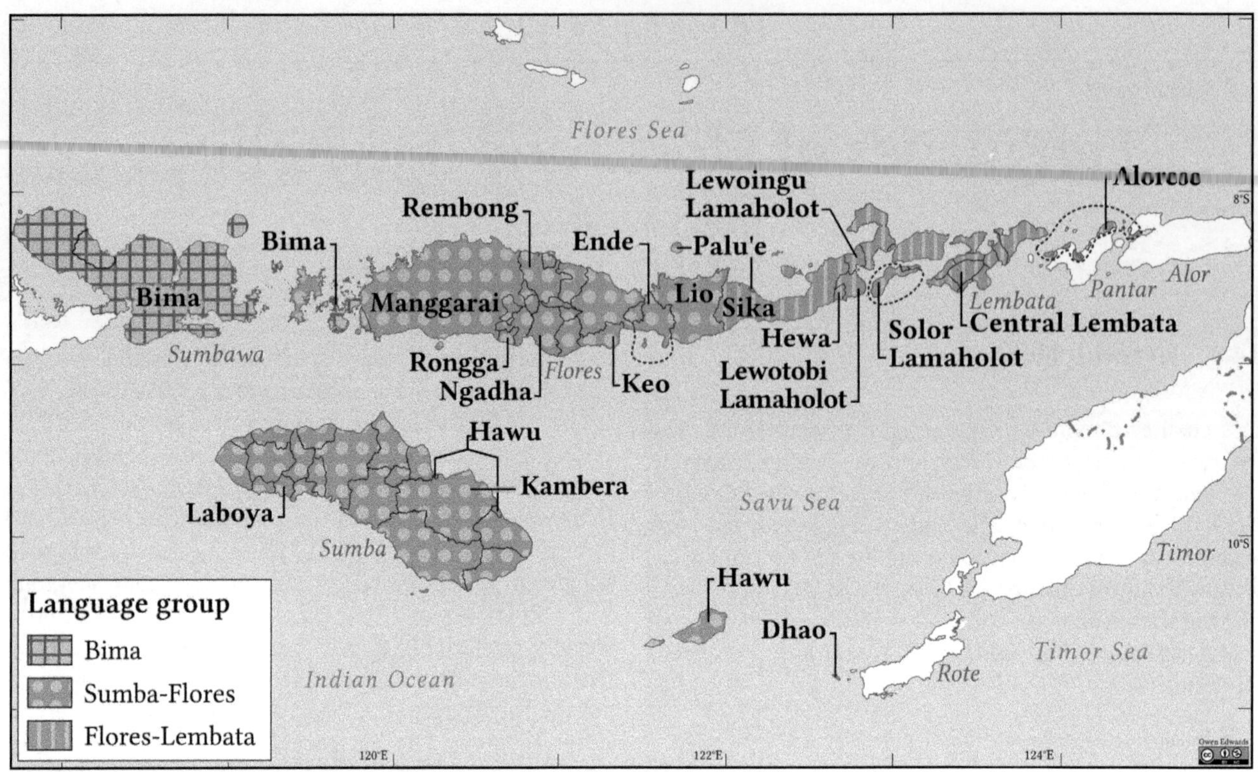


**Map 34.1** Languages of Flores and its satellites.

following characteristics: (i) no or asymmetrical voice alternations; (ii) preposed possessor; (iii) alienable/inalienable distinction; (iv) clear-cut differences between narrative and equational clauses; (v) person-marking prefixes or proclitics for S/A arguments; (vi) numerals/quantifiers follow head; (vii) clause-final negators; and (viii) V-second or V-final word order. As will be seen later, Flores-Lembata languages tend to show typical correlates of preposed possessor languages, but languages of Sumbawa, Sumba, Sabu, and Western/Central Flores do not, showing more properties indicative of the transition from symmetrical voice to preposed possessor languages. In other words, the line delineating the boundaries of the two major types of MPSEA languages can be drawn in this geographic area. Thus, a good understanding of the typological variations in this area is required to get a better picture of the typology of MPSEA languages.

Second, since the intrusion of Austronesian-speaking populations into this region already inhabited by speakers of non-Austronesian (or 'Papuan') languages, Austronesian languages and non-Austronesian languages have co-existed and influenced each other for about 3,500 years (Klamer 2019). This contact between Austronesian and non-Austronesian languages has led to a series of contact-induced changes in Austronesian languages to the extent that this contact area has been labelled "East Nusantara" (Klamer 2004; Klamer, Reesink, and Staden 2008; Klamer and Ewing 2010: 1–25) or "Wallacea" (Schapper 2015a). Recently, it has been proposed that the "East Nusantara"/"Wallacea" linguistic area is part of a larger linguistic area, the Mekong-Mamberamo linguistic area (Gil 2015a), encompassing Mainland Southeast Asia, the Nusantara archipelago, and western parts of New Guinea. In the following sections, we will see such contact-induced characteristics in the languages of Flores and its satellites, especially the Flores-Lembata languages.

The purpose of this chapter is to provide an overview of typological variations in the languages of Flores and its satellites, paying attention to structural diversity rather than affinity. The linguistic features examined in this chapter are phonology (§34.2), morphological profile (§34.3), word classes (§34.4), word order (§34.5), grammatical relations and voice (§34.6), tense, aspect, mood, and evidentiality (§34.7), and serial verb/multipredicate constructions (§34.8). Taken together, it will be shown that this region is an area of great linguistic diversity.[4]

[4] Throughout the chapter, some transcriptions and glosses are modified for the sake of consistency and readability. In Kambera, short (lax) /a/ and /i/ are represented with a grave accent (à and ì); long /u:/ is marked with an acute accent (ú).

## 34.2 Phonology

This section discusses the basic phonological characteristics of the languages of Flores and its satellites: consonants, vowels, syllable structures, and stress assignment. First, let us consider consonant phoneme inventories. Here we can see a contrast between Flores-Lembata languages and the other languages. On the one hand, Flores-Lembata languages have a small (fourteen or fewer consonants) or moderately small inventory (from fifteen to eighteen consonants), by Maddieson's (2013a) criterion, in which the mean of the number of consonant phonemes for the 562 languages is 22.7: Sika, Hewa, Lewoingu Lamaholot, and Lewotobi Lamaholot each have sixteen consonants, Central Lembata fourteen, Alorese eighteen, and Kedang twenty. These languages have a system of oral stops, distinguishing three places of articulation (labial, coronal, and velar) and a two-way voicing contrast (unvoiced and voiced), as in the Central Lembata system in (4).

(4) Central Lembata

| p | t̪ | k |
|---|---|---|
| b | d | g |

By contrast, the number of consonant segments among the languages of Sumbawa, Sumba, Sabu, and Western/Central Flores is either average (22 ± 3 consonants) or larger (from twenty-six to thirty-three consonants): Bima and Manggarai each have twenty-six consonants, Laboya twenty, Kambera nineteen, Hawu twenty, Dhao twenty-three, Rongga twenty-three, Ngadha twenty-one, Keo and Lio twenty-three, Ende twenty-four, and Palu'e nineteen. The larger inventories are due to the presence of prenasalized, implosive, and/or preglottalized consonants in these languages (Klamer 2002b: 367; Himmelmann 2005a: 116), as shown in (5).

(5) a. Rongga

| p | t | k |
|---|---|---|
| b | d | g |
| ᵐb | ⁿd | ᵑg |
| ɓ | ɗ | ɠ |

b. Keo

| p | t | k |
|---|---|---|
| b | d | g |
| ʔb | ʔd | |
| ᵐb | ⁿd | ᵑg |

c. Kambera

| p | t | k |
|---|---|---|
| ɓ | ɗ | |
| ᵐb | ⁿd | ᵑg |

d. Manggarai

| p | t | k |
|---|---|---|
| ᵐp | ⁿt | ᵑk |
| b | d | g |
| ᵐb | ⁿd | ᵑg |

For example, Rongga has full sets of both prenasalized voiced stops and implosive consonants /ᵐb, ⁿd, ᵑg, ɓ, ɗ, ɠ/, making a four-way manner distinction between stops: voiceless, voiced, prenasalized, and implosive stops. Keo also makes a four-way distinction, but between voiceless, voiced, prenasalized, and preglottalized stops. Some languages such as Kambera, Lio, and Ende have full sets of prenasalized voiced stops but lack /ɠ/ in the implosive series. Ngadha, Hawu, and Dhao lack prenasalized voiced stops and have implosive consonants only: Ngadha has /ɓ, ɗ/ but lacks /ɠ/, while Hawu and Dhao have bilabial, alveolar, alveopalatal, and velar implosives /ɓ, ɗ, ʄ, ɠ/. Manggarai is exceptional in that it does not have implosive consonants but has both voiced and voiceless prenasalized stops (Verheijen and Grimes 1995). In terms of Himmelmann's (2005a) typology, these languages with a large consonant inventory are transitional languages, while those with a small consonant inventory are preposed possessor languages.

Some languages of Flores and its satellites show what Donohue (2009) calls "dental discrepancies": the unvoiced coronal stop is dental, while the voiced coronal stop is alveolar, as in (4). Such languages include Lio, Palu'e, Ngadha, Hewa, Lewotobi Lamaholot, and Central Lembata. Interestingly, dental discrepancies are found in the Austronesian languages of Indonesia and New Guinea, but not of the Philippines (see also Blevins, this volume, §41.2.3). Donohue (2009) argues that this is due to a substrate influence from pre-Austronesian languages. Gil (2015a) considers it to be one of the defining characteristics of the Mekong-Mamberamo linguistic area.

Little diversity is observed among the vowel phoneme inventories. The languages of Flores and its satellites have vowel phoneme inventories of average size (five to six vowels) according to Maddieson's (2013b) criterion. Most have a five- or six-vowel system /i, e, a, o, u/ with or without the schwa /ə/. Exceptional in this respect are Kambera with ten vowels, Laboya with eleven, and Kedang with twelve. Kambera has /i, iː, e, ai, a, aː, o, au, u, uː/, distinguishing long and short vowels and including diphthongs. Laboya has a similar inventory: /i, iː, e, ai, a, aː, o, oː, au, u, uː/. Interestingly, Kedang makes a contrast between modal and breathy vowels (Samely 1991: 13): /a, a̤, ɛ, ɛ̤, æ, æ̤, a, a̤, o, o̤, u, ṳ/. This is "highly unusual" for this region (Hajek 2010: 27). Also worth mentioning is Lewotobi Lamaholot, which has contrastive nasalized vowels in addition to six oral vowels (e.g. *miʔi* 'urologic disease' vs. *miʔĩ* 'taboo in food', Nagaya 2011: 68), although they may be analysed as derived from an underlying /Vn/ sequence.

As for syllable structures, languages of this region prefer open syllables and simple CVCV roots (Klamer 2002b: 368). Some languages, such as Bima, Hawu, Dhao, Keo, Lio, Ngadha, and Ende, only allow open syllables (Elias 2018). Other languages permit closed syllables, but, even in such cases, the number of consonants that can appear as codas is restricted. For example, in Hewa, only six out of sixteen consonants (/t̪ k ʔ n ŋ r/) are allowed in codas (Fricke 2014: 21). The exception is Manggarai, which freely allows final consonants. Thus, PMP *anak 'child', *epat 'four', and *bulan 'moon' are reflected as *ana*, *upa*, and *vura* in Bima but as *anak*, *pat*, and *wulaŋ* in Manggarai (Blust 2008: 99–101).

In the languages of Flores and its satellites, stress usually falls on the penultimate syllable and is non-distinctive. In some languages like Keo, Sika, and Central Lembata, stress cannot occur on the penultimate syllable when it contains a schwa. In such cases, it falls on the last syllable.

## 34.3 Morphological profile

Most MPSEA languages show a moderate inventory of affixes and have been considered to be agglutinative (Himmelmann 2005a: 125–6). The languages of Flores and its satellites are known as exceptions to these generalizations. Most of them are nearly isolating, with few affixes, if any at all. Almost all lexical roots can appear as free words. The extreme cases are Alorese and the Central Flores languages. Alorese has virtually no inflectional or derivational morphology (Klamer 2011: 27). Keo is "a highly isolating language with no inflectional or derivational morphological affixation" (Baird 2002: 165). Native reduplication is not productive, either. This is also the case with other Central Flores languages, such as Rongga (Arka 2016: 52, 67) and Lio (Elias 2018).

The Flores-Lembata languages are also more or less isolating languages, but they have affixes for agreement, possession, nominalization, and other derivational purposes. For example, Lewoingu Lamaholot (Nishiyama and Kelen 2007) has several derivational processes, such as *N*-nominalization, as in (6) (cf. Blust 2004b).

Lewoingu Lamaholot

(6) a. *pet* 'bind' ***met*** 'belt'
b. *poe* 'redeem' ***moe*** 'things redeemed'
c. *pota* 'add' ***mota*** 'things added'
d. *bitu* 'catch animal and fish' ***mitu*** 'trap'
e. *dira* 'use a fan' ***nira*** 'fan'
(Nishiyama and Kelen 2007: 48)

The Bima and Sumba-Hawu languages are a bit more morphologically complex. Bima seems relatively rich in morphology. It has two passive prefixes and multifunctional agreement affixes, among others (Arka 2009b). Kambera has a handful of affixes: one productive prefix *pa-*, six unproductive prefixes *ha-*, *ka-*, *la-*, *ma-*, *ta-*, and the homographic nasal prefix (see (76)), one productive suffix (or enclitic) *-ŋ*, and one unproductive suffix *-k* (Klamer 1998: 46). Hawu has two valency-changing prefixes and agreement morphology (Walker 1982: 23). Dhao has agreement prefixes (but only for eight verbs) and one multifunctional derivational prefix *pa-* (Balukh 2020).

In addition to affixation, vowel alternations are found in Hawu and Dhao. Some verbs in Hawu have two alternating forms, singular forms and plural forms, as in (7). Singular forms are used when an absolutive NP is singular, but plural forms when it has a plural, generic, or mass interpretation (Walker 1982: 23). In Dhao, two alternating forms are employed for semantic, valency-changing, or category-changing purposes (Balukh 2020: 185–91), as in (8).

Hawu

(7) a. *təɓo* 'pierce; stab (SG)' ***təɓu*** 'pierce; stab (PL)'
b. *ɓuje* 'touch; feel (SG)' ***ɓuju*** 'touch; feel (PL)'
c. ***ele*** 'disappear (SG)' ***ila*** 'disappear (PL)'
(Walker 1982: 23)

Dhao

(8) a. *base* 'wash (SG)' ***basa*** 'wash (PL)'
b. *bəɓβe* 'fall (SG)' ***bəɓβa*** 'fall (PL)'
c. *afa* 'teach (verbally)' *afe* 'teach (through exercises)'
d. *tapa* 'be adhered' *tape* 'adhere'
e. *oka* 'garden (noun)' *oke* 'fence (verb)'
(Balukh 2020: 187, 189, 190, 191)

Thus, the languages of Flores and its satellites display different degrees of morphological complexity, although they have a general tendency to be isolating. Interestingly, when they have affixes, they tend to have prefixes rather than suffixes, like many other MPSEA languages (Himmelmann 2005a: 125–6). This is against the strong preference for suffixes observed across the world's languages (Dryer 2013n).

### 34.3.1 Common functions of affixes

Since the languages of Flores and its satellites are more or less isolating languages, grammatical categories that are often morphologically marked in other MPSEA languages are not expressed by affixes. Lexical nouns do not inflect for person, gender, number, or case, and verbs do not change their form for tense, aspect, mood, or evidentiality (see §34.7). Still, several functions that are commonly found in the affixes of these languages are agreement, adnominal possession, nominalization, and valency-changing operations. Among them, agreement is the most widely observed across these languages (see §34.6.1 as well as Schapper and Zobel, this volume, §35.3.1 for similar agreement markers in Timor and southern Maluku languages). Consider (9) and (10).

Central Lembata

(9) *Go ka=ləbo-ka kia.*
1SG 1SG=bathe-1SG INCEP
'I will take a shower now.' (Fricke 2019: 94)

Lewotobi Lamaholot
(10) *Srinu r-enũ tua neku nokõʔ.*
Srinu 3PL-drink tuak last night
'Srinu *and his friends* drank tuak last night.'
(Nagaya 2011: 294)

In the Central Lembata example in (9), the person and number of the subject are indexed on the verb by the proclitic *ka=* and the suffix *-ka*. Likewise, in the Lewotobi Lamaholot example in (10), the verb has the agreement prefix *r-* '3PL', coercing an associative plural reading on the subject.

In most languages of this region, adnominal possession is often expressed by means of juxtaposition of the possessor and possessum NPs (see §34.5.2). In the Flores-Lembata languages, it is not only syntactically expressed, as in (11), but can also be morphologically marked, as in (12).

Central Lembata
(11) *goe kajor*
1SG.POSS wood
'my wood' (Fricke 2019: 287)

Central Lembata
(12) *(go) najan-ga*
1SG.POSS name-1SG.POSS
'my name' (Fricke 2019: 287)

The contrast between the two adnominal possessive constructions in (11) and (12) represents an important characteristic of the Flores-Lembata languages (and other preposed possessor languages), namely, the distinction between alienable and inalienable possession (Himmelmann 2005a: 163ff). In Central Lembata and other Lamaholot varieties (Nishiyama and Kelen 2007; Nagaya 2011; Kroon 2016), different types of possession are expressed by different constructions. In Lewotobi Lamaholot, for example, inalienable possession is marked by the suffix *-N*, and alienable possession by the enclitic *=kə̃*. See Grangé (2015) and Fricke (2019) for a comparative study of adnominal possessive constructions in these languages. See also Schapper and Zobel (this volume, §35.4.7) for the expression of adnominal possession in the languages of Timor and southern Maluku.

Nominalization is also found across the languages of Flores and its satellites. The Lamaholot varieties have rich nominalization morphology, such as *N*-nominalization in Lewoingu Lamaholot (6). See Fricke (2019: 79ff) for an inventory of Central Lembata nominalizing affixes. In Kambera, the subject relative clause marker *ma=*, as in (13), acts as a nominalizing prefix, as in (14) (Klamer 2005: 731).

Kambera
(13) *Niŋu ma=rara.*
PROX.APPL REL=be.red
'There are ripe ones.' (Klamer 2005: 725)

Kambera
(14) a. *rara* 'be red, ripe'
*ma-rara* 'gold' (which is red)
b. *mbowa* 'hole; gap'
*ma-mbowa* 'something with gaps/holes'
(Klamer 1998: 262)

Lastly, the Bima and Sumba-Hawu languages have valency-changing operations such as causatives, reciprocals, and applicatives. For example, Bima has the causative prefix *ka-* (Owens 2000). See §34.6.3 and §34.6.4 for valency-changing operations.

## 34.3.2 Reduplication and compounds

Himmelmann (2005a: 110) considers reduplication to be one of the three characteristics that can be found across MPSEA languages; the other two are the distinction between inclusive and exclusive pronouns and morphological causatives (see §34.6.4). Somewhat surprisingly, however, this generalization does not always apply to the languages of Flores and its satellites. The Sumba-Hawu languages, such as Kambera, Dhao, and Hawu, have productive reduplication. For example, Kambera distinguishes several types of reduplication, such as CV-reduplication, foot reduplication, reduplication of one prosodic word, and reduplication of more than one word (Klamer 1998: 34ff). Dhao has (C)a~ reduplication, full reduplication, lexical reduplication, and rhyming reduplication (Balukh 2020). In Hawu, reduplicated verbs express a repetitive or continuous action, as in (15).

Hawu
(15) a. *wəbe* 'hit' *wəbe~wəbe* 'hit again and again'
b. *pedute* 'follow' *pedute~dute* 'keep on following'
(Walker 1982: 25)

However, reduplication is not necessarily very productive in Flores languages except in Indonesian borrowings. On the one hand, in Ngadha, reduplication is used for marking plurality with nouns, and progressive aspect with verbs (Djawanai 1983). Manggarai has CV-reduplication, CVCV-reduplication, and other types of reduplication (Semiun 1993; Verheijen and Grimes 1995). In Alorese, reduplicated verbs are employed to indicate iterative or intensive activity, as in (16), while reduplicated nouns denote plural diversity.

Alorese
(16) *No geki~geki sampai no neiŋ aliŋ bola.*
3SG laugh~laugh until 3SG POSS back break
'He laughed and laughed till his back broke.'
(Klamer 2011: 24)

On the other hand, some reference grammars of Flores languages, such as Keo (Baird 2002: 177), Lewoingu Lamaholot (Nishiyama and Kelen 2007: 60), and Lewotobi Lamaholot (Nagaya 2011: 129), clearly state that reduplication is not productive in these languages. Descriptions of other languages, such as Rongga (Arka 2016), Hewa (Fricke 2014), and Central Lembata (Fricke 2019) do not have an entry for reduplication in the table of contents.

By contrast, compounding is widely observed across the languages of Flores and its satellites. Both nominal and verbal compounds occur. In some languages like Rongga, compounding is the only morphological process for creating new lexemes because of the lack of affixes (Arka 2016: 91). Although reduplication is not productive in Keo, it has a variety of types of compounds, as in (17).

Keo
(17) a. *meke-sune*
cough-sniffle
'flu' (Baird 2002: 168)

b. *daʔe-dondo*
place-place
'space' (Baird 2002: 168)

c. *ʔae-ŋasi*
water-angry
'conversation; warning; advice' (Baird 2002: 169)

d. *ʔadu-aʔi*
pounding.stick-leg/foot
'shin' (Baird 2002: 169)

Thus, compounding is very productive but reduplication is not necessarily so in the languages of Flores and its satellites. The frequent use of compounding is no surprise, as it is widely observed in isolating languages in and out of Southeast Asia. However, it remains unclear why reduplication is uncommon in some Flores languages. It is a bit puzzling in light of the fact that there are quite a few isolating languages with productive reduplication such as Thai, Vietnamese, and Khmer (Dryer 2013n; Rubino 2013). The lack of reduplication cannot be ascribed to the isolating nature of these languages.

## 34.4 Word classes

It is well known that, in western Indonesian and Philippine languages (i.e. symmetrical voice languages), lexical bases are often difficult to categorize into either nouns or verbs (Himmelmann 2005a). Unlike these languages, the languages of Flores and its satellites tend to show a relatively clear-cut distinction between nouns and verbs. In Kambera, for example, lexical bases can be identified as nouns if they can occur with articles, if they can be modified by emphatic or demonstrative pronouns, and if they can occur with an underived numeral and may have a classifier (Klamer 1998: 92; 2005). By contrast, only verbs can have a nominative subject and can be modified by adverbs (Klamer 1998: 94; 2005). There are also two affixes that can only be used with verbs. Similarly, nouns and verbs in Hawu can be distinguished in several ways: on syntactic-distributional grounds, by their relative position to the negation marker *ɗo*, by the types of words and particles with which they can co-occur, and so on (Walker 1982: 9). Descriptions of Lamaholot dialects also assume that such a distinction is clearly made (Nishiyama and Kelen 2007; Nagaya 2011; Kroon 2016; Fricke 2019). These languages have a set of morphology for nominalizing non-nominal lexical bases.

However, in the Central and Western Flores languages, the noun–verb distinction cannot be clearly made. In these languages, lexical roots are often multifunctional: they can occupy both a nominal slot and a verbal slot (Baird 2002; Elias 2018). Furthermore, they lack affixes or clitics that mark category change (e.g. nominalization). For instance, the root *petu* expresses a property concept as an intransitive predicate in (18), but in (19) it is a transitive predicate expressing an action that induces a change of state of the object NP *ʔae* 'water'.

Keo, intransitive predicate
(18) *Minu te* ***pətu*** *reʔe-reʔe.*
drink this **hot** very
'This drink is very hot.' (Baird 2002: 134)

Keo, transitive predicate
(19) *Rəkə ha goʔo ŋaʔo* ***pətu*** *ʔae.*
wait a little 1SG **heat** water
'Wait a moment while I heat the water.'
(Baird 2002: 134)

Note that, since the languages of Flores and its satellites are not rich in morphology, evidence for nouns and verbs in these languages is distributional in most cases. Nouns are not marked for person, number, case, or gender, and neither are verbs for tense, aspect, mood, or evidentiality. In addition, the possibility of a lexical word taking a predicate position is not a good indicator of verbhood in these languages. Most lexical words can occupy a predicative position without a copula. See the Keo intransitive clause with a predicate nominal in (20). It consists of the simple juxtaposition of a subject and a predicate nominal.

Keo
(20) *ʔimu ʔata nua Ndai.*
3SG person hamlet Ndai
'She is a Ndai hamlet person. (She is from the Ndai hamlet.)' (Baird 2002: 264)

Most descriptions of the languages of Flores and its satellites agree that there is no morphosyntactic evidence for postulating adjectives as a separate word class. In these languages, lexemes expressing property concepts often appear in the same distribution as those expressing actions. In his description of Hawu, for example, Walker (1982: 23) distinguishes two types of verbs, A-verbs and B-verbs. They share the same distributional properties, such as word order and relative position to the negator *ɗo* and other particles (Walker 1982: 9). The difference is that the A-verbs denote an action, while the B-verbs express a property concept. This semantic difference becomes clearer when A-verbs and B-verbs are reduplicated: reduplicated A-verbs indicate a repetitive or continuous action, as in (15), but reduplicated B-verbs express an intensified degree of a property concept, as in (21) and (22). Thus, lexemes for property concepts are only a subclass of verbs in Hawu.

Hawu
(21) a. *ɗida*
'be high'
b. *ɗida~ɗida*
'be very high' (Walker 1982: 25)

Hawu
(22) a. *ɓəku*
'be rotten'
b. *ɓəku~ɓəku*
'be very rotten' (Walker 1982: 25)

Such "verby adjectives" are common across the languages of the Mekong-Mamberamo linguistic area (Gil 2015a). But, as Fricke (2019) points out, the Flores-Lembata languages have "nouny adjectives" as well as "verby adjectives". Thus, Nagaya (2011) distinguishes two kinds of property concept words in Lewotobi Lamaholot, adjectival nouns and adjectival verbs. Adjectival nouns, such as *wuʔũ* 'new', *okĩ* 'old', *ləmeʔ* 'deep', and *gehə̃* 'odd', cannot only modify an NP but can also appear in the argument position without additional morphological modification, as in (23). In contrast, adjectival verbs, such as *blega* 'wide', *knipu* 'narrow', *beləʔ* 'big', and *kreʔ* 'small', need to be nominalized to appear in the argument position, as in (24).

Lewotobi Lamaholot
(23) a. *Go hope honda wuʔũ.* (modification)
1SG buy motorbike new
'I bought a new motorbike.' (Nagaya 2011: 176)
b. *Go hope wuʔũ.* (referential)
1SG buy new
'I bought a new one.' (Nagaya 2011: 176)

Lewotobi Lamaholot
(24) a. *Go hope pao blega=kə̃.* (modification)
1SG buy mango wide=NMLZ
'I bought a wide mango.' (Nagaya 2011: 179)
b. *Go hope blega (*=kə̃).* (referential)
1SG buy wide =NMLZ
'I bought a wide one.' (Nagaya 2011: 179)

Other word classes that are often recognized in the languages of Flores and its satellites include pronouns, demonstratives, classifiers, numeral, adverbs, prepositions, conjunctions, interjections, and discourse particles,[5] among others. All of the languages have a closed word class of pronouns, but the size of the inventory differs from language to language. Presumably the most complex system is represented by the Kambera system, shown in Table 34.1 (Klamer 2005: 716). This system includes both free pronouns and pronominal clitics. It distinguishes person, number (SG/PL), and case (NOM, GEN, ACC, and DAT). Like other Austronesian languages, in/exclusiveness is distinguished, and pronouns are not marked for gender.

**Table 34.1** Kambera pronouns and pronominal clitics

| | Pronoun | NOM | GEN | ACC | DAT |
|---|---|---|---|---|---|
| 1SG | *nyuŋga* | *ku=* | *=ŋgu* | *=ka* | *=ŋga* |
| 2SG | *nyumu* | *(m)u=* | *=mu* | *=kau* | *=ŋgau* |
| 3SG | *nyuna* | *na=* | *=na* | *=ya* | *=nya* |
| 1PL.INCL | *nyuta* | *ta=* | *=nda* | *=ta* | *=nda* |
| 1PL.EXCL | *nyuma* | *ma=* | *=ma* | *=kama* | *=ŋgama* |
| 2PL | *nyimi* | *(m)i=* | *=mi* | *=ka(m)i* | *=ŋga(m)i* |
| 3PL | *nyuda* | *da=* | *=da* | *=ha* | *=nja* |

Not all languages have such an elaborated system. Lamaholot varieties only distinguish nominative and possessive cases, in addition to person and number. Rembong has regular vs. honorific possessive pronouns (e.g. *ᵑgaku* '1SG.POSS' (regular) vs. *ᵑgɛʔ-ŋ* '1SG.POSS' (honorific)) but only has a nominative–possessive distinction. The simplest systems

[5] The term "discourse particle" is used here as a cover term for invariable linguistic items that are used to express the speaker's epistemic attitude toward the propositional content of an utterance or to manipulate discourse coherence. It has been given different names in the literature of the languages in this chapter: "particles" (Arka 2016: 139), "sentence-final particles" (Nagaya 2011: 431), and "tags" (Klamer 1998: 144).

are found in Rongga, Keo, Ende, and Lio. These Central Flores languages only have free pronouns and do not distinguish case relations. See Table 34.2 for the Rongga pronominal system.

**Table 34.2** Rongga pronouns (Arka 2016: 69)

| | SG | PL |
|---|---|---|
| 1 | *jaʔo* | *kami* (EXCL) *kita* (INCL) |
| 2 | *kau* | *meu* |
| 3 | *kaɹi* | *siɹa* |

Demonstratives are another word class that is found across the languages of Flores and its satellites. Simple demonstratives in Flores languages such as Hewa, Rongga, Lewoingu, and Lamaholot often make a two-way spatial distinction between proximal and distal, although complex demonstratives may code further minute meaning differences. By contrast, demonstratives in the Sumba-Hawu languages make a finer distinction. In Kambera, there are four simple demonstratives: *ni* 'at/near speaker', *na* 'at hearer', *nu* 'remote from both speaker and hearer', and *nai* 'near speaker (further away than *ni*)'. Hawu even makes a five-way distinction, as detailed in Table 34.3.

**Table 34.3** Hawu demonstratives (Walker 1982: 11)

| SG | PL | *Meaning* |
|---|---|---|
| *oni* | *(uhi)* | zero distance from speaker (who is referring to a part of the speaker's own body, or something the speaker is holding or touching) |
| *(na(pu))ne* | *nahe* | near the speaker (i.e. specified point near the speaker) |
| *(na)ɗe* | *(na)heɗe* | near the speaker (i.e. immediate vicinity of the speaker) |
| *(na(pu))nəne* | *(na(pu))həre* | near the addressee |
| *(na)ni/naɗo* | *(na)hiɗe* | distant from speaker and addressee |

The languages of Flores and its satellites often have a relatively large inventory of numeral classifiers. For example, Keo has a closed class of approximately forty sortal numeral classifiers and an open class of mensural numeral classifiers with many potential members (Baird 2002: 245–6).[6] Numeral classifiers play an important role in nominal syntax of these languages. In particular, in Central Flores languages such as Lio, the use of numeral classifiers is obligatory in a numeral-noun construction, as in (25) (Elias 2020) (see also §34.5.3). For example, the numeral classifier *əsa* in (25) cannot be left out even when the preceding noun is countable.

(25) Lio
*saʔo* *əsa* *təlu*
house CLF three
'three houses' (Elias 2020: 306)

This is also the case with other Central Flores languages (Ngadha and Keo) and Sumba-Hawu languages (Hawu and Kambera) and is typical of other isolating languages in Southeast Asia (but not in the Austronesian languages of Taiwan and the Philippines). The obligatory use of numeral classifiers is considered to be characteristic of the Mekong-Mamberamo linguistic area by Gil (2015a) (see also Elias 2020).

Some Flores languages often have a closed-class category of directionals. Directionals are those grammatical elements that are used to describe the location of an entity or its direction of movement relative to environmental landmarks such as a mountain or the sea. For example, Lewotobi Lamaholot has five directionals: *rae* 'mountainward', *lau* 'seaward', *wəli* 'parallel with the coast', *teti* 'upward', and *lali* 'downward' (Nagaya 2011: 263). Other Flores languages like Keo, Hewa, and Lewoingu Lamaholot also have this word class.

Articles are often identified in descriptions of the Sumba-Hawu and Western Flores languages. Articles are words that precede NPs to indicate features like definiteness and number. For example, Kambera has three articles: *na* 'definite, singular', *da* 'definite, plural', and *i* 'proper names' (Klamer 1998: 141). Indefinite NPs have no article and are not specified for number. See (39), for example. Hawu has only one article, *ne*. It marks common nouns in absolutive case or common nouns in non-verbal clauses. It does not convey any information about definiteness or number but only marks common NPs (Walker 1982: 12).

[6] Note that other Flores languages such as Lewotobi Lamaholot do not have sortal numeral classifiers, such as the Lio *əsa* in (25), but only mensural numeral classifiers, which are used with noun phrases of low countability as a unit of measure (e.g. *nuro* 'spoon', *mala* 'slice', and *karaʔ* 'bunch'; Lewotobi Lamaholot, Nagaya 2011: 169). See Gil (2013) for the distinction between sortal and mensural numeral classifiers.

## 34.5 Word order

As in many other Austronesian languages of Indonesia, the languages of Flores and its satellites tend to have basic SV/AVP word order and employ prepositions rather than postpositions. See examples of transitive clauses with two NPs and one prepositional phrase in Bima (26) and Hewa (27). Although some word order flexibility in these languages is observed due to voice-related word order changes (§34.6.3) and discourse-pragmatic considerations, Flores languages generally adhere to this clausal word order pattern (Himmelmann 2005a: 141).

Bima
(26) *Nahu mbako=ku uta laɓo Rao.*
1SG cook=1SG fish with Rao
'I cooked fish with Rao.' (Owens 2000: 19)

Hewa
(27) *Rimu ʔəle blaʔur ʔia sepatu une-n.*
3PL 3PL.search frog LOC shoe inside-POSS
'They look for the frog in the shoe.' (Fricke 2014: 41)

The Sumba-Hawu languages, by contrast, do not always follow this generally observed pattern. To begin with, Kambera has an unmarked word order of AVP, as in (28), but also has relatively free word order (Klamer 1998: 85; 2005: 718). VPA and VAP are used frequently, as in (29). One of the reasons for this is that Kambera does not rely on the order of noun phrases but rather employs the pronominal clitics shown in Table 34.1 for the purpose of marking grammatical relations.

Kambera
(28) *(Na tau wútu) na=palu=ka*
ART person be.fat 3SG.NOM=hit=1SG.ACC
*(nyuŋga).*
1SG
'The big man hit me.' (Klamer 2005: 720)

Kambera
(29) *Roŋu=nanya=ka [ana ŋilu]$_{NPobj}$ [yena na*
hear=3SG.CONT=PFV DIM wind DEIC.3SG ART
*ina-na]$_{NPsubj}$.*
mother-3SG
'His mother heard a breeze (approaching)'
(Klamer 1998: 86)

In addition, Hawu has a verb-initial basic word order, as in (30).

Hawu
(30) *Huba ke ø noo ri ama.*
forgive PART ABS 3SG ERG father
'Father forgave him.' (Walker 1982: 36)

In the rest of this section, word order variations of other constituents are discussed: negation (§34.5.1), adnominal possession (§34.5.2), and numerals (§34.5.3). A clear contrast between the Flores-Lembata languages and others is observed, corresponding to the typological distinction between preposed possessor languages and transitional languages.

### 34.5.1 Negation

In the languages of Flores and its satellites, clausal negation is marked by a negative particle, but there is considerable variation with regard to the position of the negator relative to the predicate. In Kambera and Keo, negative particles appear preverbally, as in (31) and (32), respectively.

Kambera
(31) *Nda ku=hili beli=ma=nya=pa.*
NEG 1SG.NOM= again return=EMPH=3SG.DAT=IPFV
'I am not going back to him again.' (Klamer 1998: 77)

Keo
(32) *ʔimu mona nai nio.*
3SG NEG climb coconut
'He didn't climb the coconut tree.' (Baird 2002: 333)

By contrast, negative particles directly follow the predicate in Hawu, as in (33), and appear in clause-final position in Lewotobi Lamaholot, as in (34).

Hawu
(33) *Piɗe do ri ubu naba ø ne*
pick.up(SG) NEG ERG Ubu Naba ABS ART
*nalehu pune.*
handkerchief DEM.SG
'Ubu Naba did not pick up the handkerchief.'
(Walker 1982: 47)

Lewotobi Lamaholot
(34) *Hugo brea=aʔ n-ə̃ʔə̃ mo həlaʔ.*
Hugo happy=3SG 3SG-do 2SG NEG
'Hugo is not happy with you.' (Nagaya 2011: 420)

Intralinguistic as well as cross-linguistic variation is observed with regard to the position of negators: different types of negators occupy different clausal positions. To begin with, in Hawu, negators directly follow the predicate in main clauses, as in (33), but can immediately precede it in subordinate clauses, such as relative clauses, as in (35).

Hawu

(35) *ne* *hubi* *due* *do* *ɗo* *jaɗi* *ta*
ART blossom lontar REL NEG become NPST
*ŋape*
squeeze(SG)
'the lontar blossoms which cannot be squeezed'
(Walker 1982: 47–8)

Lewotobi Lamaholot also has the negative imperative particle *ake* in addition to the basic negative partive *həlaʔ*. Although the basic negator appears clause-finally as in (34), the negative imperative particle occurs directly before the predicate, as in (36).

Lewotobi Lamaholot

(36) *Mo* *ake* *pana* *ka.*
2SG NEG.IMP walk EMPH
'Don't leave!' (Nagaya 2011: 430)

Another interesting feature about the position of the negator is found in Hewa. In (37), for example, double negation is used to negate the predicate *puas* 'satisfied'. Note that either negator can be omitted. Double negation is also possible in Kambera, as in (38). See Fricke (2017) for more detailed descriptions of double negation in Hewa and related languages.

Hewa

(37) *Dediʔ* *anak* *eʔon* *puas* *iwa.*
child small NEG satisfied NEG
'The small child is not satisfied.' (Fricke 2014: 9)

Kambera

(38) *Nda* *niŋu* *ndoku.*
NEG be NEG.EMPH
'There are none at all'/'I have none at all.'
(Klamer 1998: 143)

## 34.5.2 Adnominal possession

The order of possessor and possessum has been one of the important typological features that divide the languages of this region into transitional languages and preposed possessor languages (Himmelmann 2005a).[7] On the one hand, the Bima and Sumba-Hawu languages and the Western and Central Flores languages consistently show a possessum-possessor order, as in (39)–(43).

[7] Another important typological feature related to adnominal possession is the contrast between inalienable and alienable possession. See (11) and (12) again.

Bima

(39) *ŋgaro* *Rao*
garden Rao
'Rao's garden' (Owens 2000: 22)

Kambera

(40) *na* *uma=na* *na* *ama=ŋgu*
ART house=3SG.GEN ART father=1SG.GEN
'My father's house' (Klamer 2005: 725)

Hawu

(41) *əmu* *duae*
house king
'king's house' (Walker 1982: 48)

Keo

(42) *ʔae* *koʔo* *kami*
water POSS 1PL.EXCL
'our water' (Baird 2002: 204)

Ende

(43) *ɹima* *yu*
hand 2SG.POSS
'your hand' (McDonnell 2008b: 114)

On the other hand, the Flores-Lembata languages display a possessor–possessum order, as in (44) and (45).

Lewotobi Lamaholot

(44) *Hugo* *laŋoʔ=kə̃*
Hugo house=NMLZ
'Hugo's house' (Nagaya 2011: 24)

Kedang

(45) *koʔ* *huna*
1SG.POSS house
'my house' (Samely 1991: 76)

Note that there are some intralinguistic variations in the order between possessor and possessum. Sometimes, more than one order is acceptable in the same language. For instance, in Sika, possessors precede possessums when they are lexical nouns, as in (46), but they follow them when they are pronominal, as in (47).

Sika

(46) *wawi* *waʔi-ŋ*
pig leg-POSS
'pig's leg' (Arka 2016: 300)

Sika

(47) *taʔi* *aʔu-n*
stomach 1SG-POSS
'my stomach' (Arka 2016: 299)

### 34.5.3 Numerals

The order of numerals and nouns is another word order feature that divides the languages of this chapter into two major categories. The Bima, Sumba-Hawu, and Western Flores languages tend to show a numeral–noun order. See (48) and (49).

Kambera
(48) *ha-kambulu ŋiu kamambi*
one-ten CLF goat
'ten goats' (Klamer 1998: 139)

Manggarai
(49) *sua ləso*
two day
'two days' (Semiun 1993: 42)

By contrast, the Central Flores and Flores-Lembata languages show a noun–numeral order, as in (50)–(52).

Keo
(50) *nio puʔu dima rua*
coconut CLF five two
'seven coconut trees' (Baird 2002: 244)

Hewa
(51) *kursi wərun təman rua ʔia*
chair new CLF two DEM.DIST
'those two new chairs' (Fricke 2014: 7)

Alorese
(52) *ni niŋ aho rua*
3SG POSS dog two
'his two dogs' (Klamer 2011: 45)

Like possessor–possessum order, there are intralinguistic variations in the order between numeral and noun. In Rongga, for instance, when the numeral is *sa* 'one', the numeral can either follow or precede the noun, as in (53) and (54). When the numeral is two or greater, however, it can only precede the noun, as in (55).

Rongga
(53) *manu sa=eko*
chicken one=CLF
'a chicken' (Arka 2016: 189)

Rongga
(54) *sa=eko manu*
one=CLF chicken
'a chicken' (Arka 2016: 189)

Rongga
(55) *esa ɹua mbo ito ndau*
CLF two house small this
'these two small houses' (Arka 2016: 189)

## 34.6 Grammatical relations and voice

This section looks into alignment phenomena in the languages of Flores and its satellites, namely, how grammatical relations are grouped and marked and how they are rearranged for pragmatic purposes. By grammatical relations, I mean S (the single argument of a one-place predicate), A (the agent argument of a transitive verb), and P (the patient argument of a transitive verb). The languages of Flores and its satellites vary considerably in the grouping of these grammatical relations and in their rearrangement.

Note that, in addition to S, A, and P, we can identify T (the theme argument of a ditransitive verb) and R (the recipient argument of a ditransitive verb) to examine the alignment of the coding of T and R in ditransitive clauses. Unfortunately, few studies of the languages of Flores and its satellites look into alignment in ditransitive clauses, except for Nagaya (2013, 2014), which analyse Lewotobi Lamaholot as displaying secundative alignment, in which P and R behave alike, and differently from T (Haspelmath 2015).

### 34.6.1 Alignment: Case-marking, agreement, and word order

Cross-linguistically, there are three major ways of marking grammatical relations: case-marking, agreement, and word order. Few languages of Flores and its satellites employ case-marking for this purpose, because in most languages lexical noun phrases do not inflect for case or take case markers (§34.3). The exception is Hawu, which has a rich inventory of case markers or "case prepositions" in Walker's (1982: 13) terminology. Thus, in this language, S and P are marked by the absolutive marker *ø*, whereas A is marked by the ergative marker *ri* (or *ø* in some cases). Consider (56) and (57), for example. Hawu is also exceptional among the languages of this region because it has a clear ergative-absolutive system.

Hawu
(56) *Ta ɓuke ø huri ri noo.*
NPST write(SG) ABS letter ERG 3SG
'He is writing a letter.' (Walker 1982: 13)

Hawu

(57) *Ta* *bui* *ke* *ø* *noo.*
NPST fall PART ABS 3SG
'He is failing.' (Walker 1982: 14)

Agreement (or "argument indexing"[8]) also plays an important role in the coding of grammatical relations in the languages of Flores and its satellites. For example, Central Lembata has three different sets of indexing markers, S/A proclitics, S/A prefixes, and S/P suffixes. See examples of S/A proclitics and S/P suffixes in (58)–(60).

Central Lembata

(58) *Kopo* *lame* *tune* ***na****=tobe-ŋa.*
child male one **3SG**=sit-3SG
'A boy sits.' (Fricke 2019: 112)

Central Lembata

(59) *Nəpo* ***na****=supəŋ-****u****.*
later **3SG**=pick.up-**2SG**
'Then she will pick you up.' (Fricke 2019: 98)

Central Lembata

(60) *Nəpo* *mo* *tue-****gu****.*
later 2SG return-**2SG**
'Then you will return home.' (Fricke 2019: 98)

As illustrated in (58) and (59), S and A are marked alike with the S/A proclitic *na=*; in contrast, as shown in (59) and (60), P and S are indexed on the verb by the S/P suffix *-(g)u*. Importantly, proclitics indicate accusative alignment (S/A), but suffixes ergative alignment (S/P). Other Flores languages also have such markers. For example, Manggarai has a set of enclitics indexing core arguments (S/A/P) (Arka and Kosmas 2005). Lewotobi Lamaholot has enclitics for S in addition to prefixes for S/A. Note that indexing is often optional in these languages. For example, in (58), the subject *kopo lame tune* is indexed on the verb by the S/A proclitic *na=* and the S/P suffix *-ŋa*, but neither of them is obligatory (Fricke 2019: 112–13).[9]

Last, word order is also important, especially in isolating Flores languages (e.g. Keo), as is often the case in other isolating languages of the world. They often have AVP and SV basic word order, with a nominative-accusative system (preverbal S/A and postverbal P). An interesting pattern is observed in Palu'e (Donohue 2008b). This language has a canonical pattern of AVP for transitive clauses, as in (61), and SV for intransitive clauses, as in (62).

Palu'e

(61) *Kami* *phote* *nio.*
1PL.EXCL pick.coconut coconut
'We picked some coconuts.' (Donohue 2008b: 38)

Palu'e

(62) a. *Ia* *phana-ʔu.*
3SG go-PFV
'She's gone.' (Donohue 2008b: 38)

b. *Ia* *molu-ʔu.*
3SG fall-PFV
'She's fallen over.' (Donohue 2008b: 38)

Interestingly, intransitive clauses in Palu'e also allow postverbal S, but this order is only possible for non-agentive predicates. Compare sentences (a) and (b) in (63). Agentive S always appears preverbally in the same position as A, while non-agentive S can optionally occupy the postverbal position, like P.

Palu'e

(63) a. **Phana* *ia-ʔu.*
go 3SG-PFV
'She's gone.' (Donohue 2008b: 38)

b. *Molu* *ia-ʔu.*
fall 3SG-PFV
'She's fallen over.' (Donohue 2008b: 38)

### 34.6.2 Semantic alignment

Some languages of Flores and its satellites show semantic alignment, also referred to as split S, split intransitives, or active/agentive. This is a phenomenon whereby S can align with either A or P (Donohue and Wichmann 2008). According to Klamer's (2008) analysis, Kambera and Kedang have such a system (see also Schapper and Zobel, this volume, §35.5.3 on semantic alignment in the languages of Timor and southern Maluku). Let us illustrate this with the Kambera pronominal clitics (given in Table 34.1). In most cases, Kambera shows a nominative-accusative system: in transitive clauses, A is realized in the nominative case, and P in the accusative case, as in (64), while S is marked with a nominative, as in (65). S and A are thus marked alike, differently from P.

Kambera

(64) *Na=palu=ka.*
3SG.NOM=hit=1SG.ACC
'He hit me.' (Klamer 1998: 63, 2008: 228)

[8] In descriptions of the languages of Flores and its satellites, the term 'agreement' has sometimes been used to refer to a phenomenon in which arguments are indexed on verbs, whether indexing markers are affixes or clitics. The term 'argument indexing' (Haspelmath 2013) would be more appropriate.

[9] Klamer (2002b: 371) characterizes many Central/Eastern Indonesian languages as "pronominal argument" languages (cf. footnote 8). Klamer (2002b: 372) also notes that if a language has such indexing markers for S and A they often show formal relations with Proto-Central Malayo-Polynesian *ku- '1SG', *mu- '2SG', *na- '3SG', *ta- '1PL.INCL', *ma- '1PL.EXCL', *mi- '2PL', and *da- '3PL' (Blust 1993a: 269).

Kambera
(65) *Na=mbana* *na* *tau* *Jawa.*
3SG.NOM=be.hot/angry ART person Java
'The stranger is angry.' (Klamer 1998: 118, 2008: 228)

However, in nonverbal predicate clauses, like (66), S is obligatorily marked with an accusative enclitic. See Klamer (2005: 721–2) for other contexts where the accusative marking of S is obligatory.

Kambera
(66) *[Mbapa=ŋgu* *nyuŋga]=ya.*
husband=1SG.GEN 1SG=3SG.ACC
'He is MY husband.' (Klamer 1998: 156, 2008: 229)

Furthermore, S can be optionally marked with an accusative enclitic when it is presented as explicitly non-volitional and out of control. Compare (67) and (68) (Klamer 2008: 229).

Kambera
(67) *...hi* ***na****=hí=ma=a=ka* *i* *Mada* *una...*
and **3SG.NOM**=cry=EMPH=MOD=PFV ART Mada EMPH.3SG

Kambera
(68) *...hi* *hí=ma=a=****ya****=ka* *i* *Mada* *una...*
and cry=EMPH=MOD=**3SG.ACC**=PFV ART Mada EMPH.3SG

The examples in (67) and (68) mean that Mada cried, but the S is marked in the nominative case in (67) while it is marked as accusative in (68). The interpretations of the two examples are slightly different. The accusative S in (68) is interpreted as less volitional than the nominative S in (67). Thus, Kambera has volitionality-based semantic alignment.

### 34.6.3 Passive with and without passive morphology

The alignment patterns discussed in §§34.6.1 and 34.6.2 can be rearranged in various ways. These valency-changing operations include passives, in which the original P is promoted to S and the original A turns into an adjunct or is left out. In some languages of Flores and its satellites, passive voice is marked on the verb either morphologically or analytically. For example, Bima has two morphological passives, realis passive in (69) and irrealis passive in (70) (Jauhary 2000) (see also Arka 2009b: 255), and Palu'e has an analytical passive with the verb *coma* '(be) affect(ed)', as in (71) (Donohue 2005c).

Bima
(69) *Sia* *ra-haʔa* *ba* *ŋao* *ede.*
3SG PASS.REAL-bite by cat that
'(S)he has been bitten by the cat.' (Jauhary 2000, cited in Arka and Kosmas 2005: 105)

Bima
(70) *Wela* *ede* *di-weli* *ba* *La* *Amir.*
kite that PASS.IRR-buy by ART Amir
'The kite will be bought by Amir.' (Jauhary 2000, cited in Arka and Kosmas 2005: 106)

Palu'e
(71) *Vavi* *vaʔa* *coma* *cube.*
pig that affect shoot
'That pig was shot.' (Donohue 2005c: 83)

In addition to these morphological and analytical passives, it has been proposed that the Flores languages have word order-based passives, namely, passive voice without passive marking on the verb. For example, the Manggarai passive is indicated by marking the agent argument with the preposition *le* (or *l=*) (Arka and Kosmas 2005). To illustrate this, consider the contrast between (72) and (73).

Manggarai
(72) *Aku* *cero* *latuŋ=k.*
1SG fry corn=1SG
'I fry/am frying corn.' (Arka and Kosmas 2005: 88)

Manggarai
(73) *Latuŋ* *hitu* *cero* *l=aku=i.*
corn that fry by=1SG=3SG
'The corn is (being) fried by me.' (Arka and Kosmas 2005: 88)

The example in (72) is a canonical transitive clause with AVP word order. The agreement enclitic *=k* agrees with the preverbal subject *aku*. By contrast, in (73), the patient appears preverbally, and the agent pronoun is marked as an adjunct by means of the preposition *l=*. Syntactically, in this sentence, the preverbal patient is the subject because it agrees with the enclitic pronoun *=i* and can be a pivot in control phenomena (e.g. purpose clauses) and relativization. However, the *l=* agent is only an adjunct because it cannot agree with the agreement enclitic, can appear with relatively free positioning in a clause like other adjuncts, cannot be a pivot in control phenomena or relativization, and cannot bind a patient reflexive argument (Arka and Kosmas 2005). For these reasons, Arka and Kosmas (2005) argue that the sentence in (73) is best analysed as passive. See Arka (2016: 216ff) for a similar passive construction in Rongga.

In Palu'e, there are two competing word orders for transitive clauses, the unmarked AVP construction and the marked PAV construction (Donohue 2005c). See (74) and (75), respectively.

Palu'e
(74) *Ia cube vavi vaʔa.*
3SG shoot pig that
'He shot that pig.' (Donohue 2005c: 60)

Palu'e
(75) *Vavi vaʔa ia cube.*
pig that 3SG shoot
'That pig was shot by him.' (Donohue 2005c: 60)

Donohue (2005c) analyses the sentence in (75) as passive, like the Manggarai sentence in (73). His evidence comes from the floated quantifiers, conjunction reduction, and purposive clauses. These tests show that, in PAV constructions, P is the subject and A is an adjunct, supporting the passive analysis of the example in (75). It is reported that Sika and Lio have an alternation of the same kind (Arka and Wouk 2014: 318–20).

Thus, some languages of Flores and its satellites have passive voice: morphological passives, analytical passives, and word order-based passives. Before closing this section, two notes are in order regarding the word order-based passives. First, the existence of passive voice without passive morphology is highly controversial. In their typology of grammatical voice, Zúñiga and Kittilä (2019) consider formal coding on the predicate complex to be a defining feature of voice. Thus, in this view, the contrast between (72) and (73) in Manggarai and the one between (74) and (75) in Palu'e do not constitute a voice opposition due to the lack of verbal morphology (Zúñiga and Kittilä 2019: 4–5, 188–9). Second, Arka and Wouk (2014: 318–20) insist that the Palu'e construction in (75) is best analysed as Undergoer or Objective Voice rather than passive, because A is not clearly demoted to adjunct status in terms of the diagnostic tests for core argument status (see Nagaya 2013 for a topicalization analysis of similar alternations in Lewotobi Lamaholot). For a description of similar PAV constructions in Timor and southern Maluku languages, see Schapper and Zobel (this volume, §35.5.1).

As is often the case with other grammatical categories, different definitions of voice result in different views of its typology in the languages of this region. Taking a traditional definition of voice as involving verbal morphology, some authors including Arka and Ross (2005) and Himmelmann (2005a) conclude that most languages of this region either display no grammaticized voice contrasts or show asymmetrical voice alternations if they do. By contrast, adopting Shibatani's (2006) conceptual framework for voice phenomena, Arka and Wouk (2014) demonstrate that the Flores languages show rich voice oppositions, such as active voice, passive voice, undergoer voice, middle voice, (anti)causatives, and dative shift, without making use of verbal marking. See Kroeger and Riesberg, this volume, §47.5.2 for further information and discussion of voice in the languages of Flores and its satellites with the MPSFA context.

### 34.6.4 Other valency-changing operations

The languages of Flores and its satellites have several valency-changing operations, which can be either morphological or analytic. We have already considered the passive in §34.6.3. Other valency-decreasing operations include: anticausatives, reflexives, and reciprocals. First, I will consider anticausatives, which derive noncausal (intransitive) verbs from causal (transitive) ones. In some languages of this region, they are marked morphologically. In Kambera, for example, the homorganic nasal prefix (i.e. prenasalizing word-initial stops) is used for deriving intransitive verbs or what Klamer (1998: 262) calls "non-controlled achievement" from transitive verbs, as in (76).

Kambera
(76)

| Transitive | | Intransitive | |
|---|---|---|---|
| *pata* | 'break' | ***mb**ata* | 'be broken' |
| *pana* | 'heat up' | ***mb**ana* | 'be warm/hot' |
| *pàda* | 'extinguish' | ***mb**àda* | 'have gone out' |
| *pinu* | 'fill' | ***mb**inu* | 'be full/filled' |
| *kuŋguluŋ* | 'roll' | ***ŋg**uŋgul* | 'roll over' |

(Klamer 1998: 263)

In most languages of Flores and its satellites, however, such causal/noncausal verb pairs are not morphologically marked but rather are syntactically expressed by 'labile' alternations (Haspelmath 1993: 92), as in the Rongga examples in (77) and (78). The same verb *ŋgoli* 'roll' is employed either transitively or intransitively.

Rongga, transitive
(77) *Jaʔo ŋgoli watu ndau.*
1SG roll stone that
'I rolled the stone.' (Arka and Wouk 2014: 327)

Rongga, intransitive
(78) *Watu ndau ŋgoli.*
stone that roll
'The stone rolled (or was rolled).'
(Arka and Wouk 2014: 327)

Second, reflexives are often marked analytically by means of a reflexive noun/pronoun. In the Manggarai sentence in (79), for instance, the reflexive expression *wəki run* indicates that A and P are coreferential with each other.

Manggarai
(79) *Hia mbəle wəki ru-n.*
3SG kill body self-3SG.GEN
'S/he killed himself/herself.'
(Arka and Kosmas 2005: 99)

Last, reciprocals can be morphologically marked, as in the Hawu reciprocal prefix *pe-* in (80), but in other languages reciprocity is also analytically expressed. For example, it is marked by *papa* in Ngadha, which also means 'side', as in (81).

Hawu
(80) *Ta pe-təɓu ø roo ri tuɗi.*
NPST RECP-stab(PL) ABS 3PL ERG knife
'They are stabbing each other with knives.'
(Walker 1982: 24)

Ngadha
(81) a. *papa ɗekke*
RECP ascend
'marry each other'
b. *papa sabu*
RECP meet
'meet each other' (Djawanai 1983: 175)

Next, let us consider two valency-increasing operations, causatives and applicatives. Morphological causatives are widely found in the Bima and Sumba-Hawu languages, marked with *pe-* in Hawu (82) and with *pa-* in Kambera (83).

Hawu
(82) a. *tobo*
'be full'
b. *pe-tobo*
'make full'
c. *puru*
'descend'
d. *pe-puru*
'lower' (Walker 1980: 56)

Kambera
(83) *Da=pa-katuda=ya na anakeda.*
3PL.NOM=CAUS-sleep=3SG.ACC ART child
'They put the child to sleep.' (Klamer 1998: 180)

The existence of such morphological causatives is considered to be one of the three common features of MPSEA languages (Himmelmann 2005a: 110). However, in isolating Flores languages, only analytical causatives are available, as in causative serialization in Keo, exemplified in (108) below. Since morphological and analytic causatives are both productive, the languages of Flores and its satellites can be analysed as strongly causativizing languages. In this way, they contrast with western Indonesian languages, which employ equipollent derivation (e.g. Indonesian *ter-isi/meng-isi* 'fill') as well as causative derivation (e.g. Indonesian *mulai/memulai* 'begin') (Haspelmath 1993: 116).

Applicatives are common valency-increasing processes in the Bima and Sumba-Hawu languages. Let us consider the Kambera *-ŋ* in (84) and (85) (Klamer 2005) and the Bima *kai* in (86) and (87) (Wouk and Arafiq 2016). Note that the applicative suffix *-ŋ* (as in *ŋàndi-ŋ*) disappears when it is followed by a dative enclitic.

Kambera
(84) *Da=ŋàndi=ya na uhu.*
3PL.NOM=take=3SG.ACC ART rice
'They take/bring the rice.' (Klamer 2005: 729)

Kambera
(85) *Da=ŋàndi=nya na uhu i Ama.*
3PL.NOM=take:APPL=3SG.DAT ART rice ART father
'They bring father the rice.' (Klamer 2005: 730)

Bima
(86) *ɗari=na foʔo ake kai tiso=na.*
cut=3SG mango DEM KAI knife=3SG
'He cut the mango with his knife.'
(Wouk and Arafiq 2016: 323)

Bima
(87) *ɗari=kai=na tiso=na foʔo ake.*
cut=KAI=3SG knife=3SG mango DEM
'He cut the mango with his knife.'
(Wouk and Arafiq 2016: 323)

The sentence in (84) is a monotransitive clause, in which the theme *uhu* 'rice' is cross-referenced with the accusative pronominal enclitic *=ya*. By contrast, the verb in (85) is applicative, although the applicative suffix *-ŋ* disappears here because of the dative enclitic *=nya* '3SG.DAT'. Importantly, this sentence can additionally take the recipient *Ama* 'father', and this recipient is cross-referenced on the verb by means of *=nya*. Similarly, the particle *kai* in Bima is a valency-increasing device (Owens 2000: 19ff). It is a preposition for an instrument when it appears outside the verb complex, as in (86). But it is a marker for an instrumental applicative when it is used as part of the verb complex, as in (87).[10] The instrument *tiso na* 'his knife' is only an adjunct in (86) but a direct object in (87). Note that *-ŋ* and *kai* are not only employed for applicatives but also for other functions. See Klamer (1998, 2005); and Wouk and Arafiq (2016), respectively, for details.

By contrast, in isolating Flores languages, applicative morphology is absent. Instead, argument alternations are

[10] Cross-linguistically, the same morpheme is often used for marking an applicative verb and an instrumental participant, and the morphology that marks applicative constructions tends to come from adpositions and verbs (Peterson 2007: 123ff).

employed to achieve applicative-like functions (see also §34.8 on serial verb constructions with similar functions). For example, consider the Rongga dative alternation in (88) and (89) and the Lewotobi Lamaholot benefactive alternation in (90) and (91).

Rongga
(88) *Ardi indi ndoi pe ndia ne jaʔo.*
Ardi bring money to here to 1SG
'Ardi brought money to me.' (Arka 2016: 235)

Rongga
(89) *Ardi indi jaʔo ndoi.*
Ardi bring 1SG money
'Ardi brought me money.' (Arka 2016: 235)

Lewotobi Lamaholot
(90) *Go biho lama neĩ Ika.*
1SG cook rice give Ika
'I cooked rice for Ika.' (Nagaya 2014: 228)

Lewotobi Lamaholot
(91) *Go biho Ika lama.*
1SG cook Ika rice
'I cooked Ika rice.' (Nagaya 2014: 228)

The examples in (88) and (89) have much the same meaning, but the syntactic status of *jaʔo* '1SG' is different between them. It is only an adjunct marked by the preposition *ne* 'to' in (88) but is an argument following the verb *indi* 'bring' in (89) (Arka 2016: 104). Likewise, the beneficiary-recipient *Ika* is only an adjunct introduced by the serialized verb *neĩ* 'give' in (90) but is an argument in (91). In both cases, the different constructional patterns change the number of arguments, although there is no morphological marking on the verb.

## 34.7 Tense, aspect, mood, and evidentiality

Grammatical meanings related to tense, aspect, mood, and evidentiality, collectively referred to as TAME, tend to be realized as grammatical categories of verbs in morphologically complex languages. In the languages of Flores and its satellites, however, reflective of their isolating nature, such information is not morphologically marked. Thus, verbs have no morphological distinction such as finite/non-finite clauses, perfective/imperfective, realis/irrealis mood, and so on. Such TAME-related information is expressed instead by separate words, particles, or sometimes formulaic expressions. When such elements are missing, clauses can be interpreted either way depending on the context. An exception to this generalization is Bima, which is reported to have affixes carrying TAME-related meanings (Owens 2000; Arka 2009b).

One of the most common strategies for specifying the TAME-related information of a clause is the use of adverbs and adverbials. Klamer (1998: 102, 119ff) lists a number of adverbials that express such information in Kambera. In Keo, temporal adverbs such as *ndəwe* 'earlier (same day)', *nembu* 'a long time ago', *napa* 'later', and *numai* 'yesterday' serve this purpose. See (92).

Keo
(92) *Arno ŋgəʔde naŋu numai.*
Arno NEG swim yesterday
'Arno didn't swim yesterday.' (Baird 2002: 158)

In some languages of Flores and its satellites, TAME-related information is marked on pronominal clitics (or argument-indexing clitics). In Kambera, a clitic cluster with a combination of genitive and dative is used for marking continuative aspect, as in (29), (104), and (106) (Klamer 1998: 151–8; 2000). In Central Lembata, a subset of S/A proclitics can only appear in irrealis contexts (Fricke 2019: 88–90). In Laboya, different sets of pronominal clitics are employed in non-modal and modal constructions, as in (93) and (94), respectively.

Laboya
(93) *Daŋa=gu=ni hape=gu.*
forget=1SG.SBJ=3SG.OBJ phone=1SG.POSS
'I forgot my phone.' (Verdizade 2019: 33)

Laboya
(94) *Nauwa aŋta=wa hawai ɗau=yi*
1SG can=1SG.SBJ dry self=OBJ
*kalabe=gu.*
cloth=1SG.POSS
'I can dry my own clothes.' (Verdizade 2019: 48)

The first person singular subject is indexed on the verb by *=gu* in the non-modal construction in (93), but by *=wa* in the modal construction in (94). Such modal constructions include the *aŋta* 'can' abilitative construction, the *da=ho* 'must' obligative construction, and standard negation (Verdizade 2019: 47–8). Note that, as in (93) and (94), *=gu* is also used for marking the first person singular possessor and that *=yi* in (94) serves to index objects in complement/subordinate and imperative clauses (Verdizade 2019: 50–5).

In addition, the languages of Flores and its satellites have a relatively rich inventory of TAME particles. For example, Keo has seven aspect particles, as in (95), differentiated in terms of very subtle semantic distinctions (Baird 2002: 307).

Keo

(95)

| | | |
|---|---|---|
| a. | *nexa* | 1. Persistent perfect when placed before predicate<br>2. Perfective, completive when clause final |
| b. | *ka* | Persistent perfect with expectation |
| c. | *daʔe* | Imperfective, incompletive |
| d. | *ma* | Progressive |
| e. | *ʔdatu* | Imperfective, continuative |
| f. | *moʔo* | Prospective aspect |

TAME particles in the languages of Flores and its satellites often exhibit quite complex multifunctional patterns, as in (96)–(100).

Keo

(96)

| *Aʔi* | *ŋaʔo* | *nexa* | *poʔi.* | *ŋaʔo* | *mbana* | *tado.* |
|---|---|---|---|---|---|---|
| leg | 1SG | NEXA | break | 1SG | walk | unable |

'My leg is broken. I can't walk.' (Baird 2002: 308)

Keo

(97)

| *Aʔi* | *ŋaʔo* | *poʔi* | *nexa.* | *ŋaʔo* | *ʔbia* | *poʔi* | *wadi!* |
|---|---|---|---|---|---|---|---|
| leg | 1SG | break | NEXA | 1SG | not.want | break | again |

'My leg has been broken. I don't want it broken again!' (Baird 2002: 308)

Lewotobi Lamaholot

(98)

| *Go* | *kə̃* | *morə̃.* |
|---|---|---|
| 1SG | eat.1SG | MORE |

(a) 'I am still eating.'
(b) 'I haven't eaten yet.' (Nagaya 2011: 416)

Lio

(99)

| *Aku* | *boʔo* | *dowa.* |
|---|---|---|
| 1SG | full | IAM |

'I am already full.' (Elias 2020: 313)

Lio

(100)

| *Aku* | *ka* | *dowa.* |
|---|---|---|
| 1SG | eat | IAM |

'I have eaten.' (Elias 2020: 313)

The Keo examples in (96) and (97) show that the particle *nexa* has either a perfect or perfective interpretation. The pre-predicate *nexa* in (96) conveys that the event of breaking the leg started in the past but continues into the present, while the clause-final one in (97) expresses the same event as a whole. The aspect/modal particle *morə̃* in Lewotobi Lamaholot in (98) has either a factual (progressive) interpretation or a non-factual (not yet realized) interpretation, depending on the context. Last, the contrast between (99) and (100) in Lio represents an 'iamitive' aspect category (Olsson 2013). Like Indonesian *sudah* 'already', *dowa* in Lio can be used for marking both "the notion of a 'new situation' that holds after a transition" (cf. English *already*) and "the consequences that this situation has at reference time for the participants in the speech event" (cf. "perfect") (Olsson 2013: 43).

Unfortunately, almost nothing is known about the marking of evidentiality, or the nature of the evidence that speakers have for their statements, in the languages of this region. It seems that these concepts are not expressed by TAM particles or other particles that appear in the same slot as TAM particles. Rather, they are conveyed through formulaic strategies, such as (101) in Lewotobi Lamaholot.

Lewotobi Lamaholot

(101)

| *Marĩ* | *na* | *mata* | *kaeʔ.* |
|---|---|---|---|
| say | 3SG | dead | IAM |

'(They say) He or she is already dead.' (author's fieldnotes)

## 34.8 Serial verb/multipredicate constructions

The use of more than one independent verb in a single clause without a linking element is widely observed across the languages of eastern Indonesia. Such constructions have been referred to as 'serial verb constructions' or 'multi-verb/multipredicate constructions' in descriptions of these languages. But (descriptions of) the languages differ significantly in terms of (i) what can count as such a construction, and (ii) how such constructions should be identified. To illustrate this point, let us compare two representative descriptions of serial verb constructions, Kambera (Klamer 1998) and Keo (Baird 2002).

On the one hand, in Klamer's (1998) description of Kambera, serial verbs are considered to be combinations of two verbs that jointly constitute a single predicate. They consist of two verbs, transitive or intransitive, in any combination, as in (102).

Kambera, serial verbs

(102)

a. V1 intransitive, V2 intransitive:

| *ma-ndapu hàpa* | *hei puru* |
|---|---|
| 'sit+ chew betelnut' | 'go up + go down' |
| 'sit chewing betelnut' | 'go up and down' |

(Klamer 1998: 275)

b. V1 intransitive, V2 transitive

| *palài ŋàndi* | *tama ŋàndi* |
|---|---|
| 'run + take X' | 'go in + take X' |
| 'bring X running' | 'go in with X' |

(Klamer 1998: 276)

c. V1 transitive, V2 transitive:
*hiku puha* 'lever up X+ drop X'
*tila wàruŋ* 'kick X + dispose off X'
'lever X (out) off'
'kick X away'
(Klamer 1998: 278)

d. V1 transitive, V2 intransitive:
*hema ha-dàŋgit* 'answer + be out of breath'
*hema hoput* 'answer + be disappointed'
'answer curtly'
'answer disappointed'
(Klamer 1998: 278)

Klamer (1998) uses the term "serial verb" "in its traditional descriptive sense" (Klamer 1998: 421), noting that Kambera serial verbs may be analysed as verbal compounds (i.e. single complex verbs). The formal properties of serial verbs in this language include serial verbs that behave like simple verbs with regard to (i) subject and object marking, (ii) modal and aspectual marking, (iii) the scope of adverbs and negators, and (iv) stress assignment patterns. See (103) and (104).

Kambera
(103) [*Na*=[***palài*** ***wàru***]$_V$=*nja*]$_S$.
3SG.NOM=run dispose.of=3PL.DAT
'He ran leaving them behind' (Klamer 1998: 281)

Kambera
(104) [[***Dedi*** ***meti***]$_V$=*ma*=*a*=*nanya*$_k$ [*na* *ana*=*na*]$_k$]$_S$.
be.born die=EMPH=MOD=3SG.CONT ART child=3SG.GEN
'Her child died at birth' (Klamer 1998: 281)

In (103) and (104), two verbs form a complex verb, yielding a serial verb construction. In (103), the two verbs *palài* and *wàru* operate as one unit and cannot be separated by an object or another element. The subject is marked only once with *na*=, and the object with =*nja*. In (104), the two verbs *dedi* and *meti* have the same aspectual and modal specification as simple verbs would. In both examples, serial verbs have the same prosodic properties as nominal compounds: the V2 has primary stress, while the V1 has secondary stress.

These serial verbs are distinguished from juxtaposed clauses, as in the two conjoined clauses separated by a pause (,) in (105) and (106).

Kambera
(105) [*Na*=***palài***]$_S$, [*na*=***wàru*** *hàla*=*nja*]$_S$.
3SG.NOM=run 3SG.NOM=dispose.of he.complete=3PL.DAT
'He ran (and) he left them all behind'
(Klamer 1998: 281)

Kambera
(106) [***Dedi***]$_S$, [***meti***=*ma*=*a*=*nanya*$_j$ [*na* *ina*=*na*]$_j$ ]$_S$.
be.born die=EMPH=MOD=3SG.CONT ART child=3SG.GEN
'(When he) was born, his mother died'
(Klamer 1998: 281)

In (105), the two verbs *palài* and *wàru*, separated by a pause, have their own subject marker. In (106), the particles =*ma* and =*a* do not have scope over the verb *dedi*, which is in a separate clause. In both examples, both verbs in the conjoined clauses have main stress.

On the other hand, in her description of Keo serial verb constructions, Baird (2002: 286–292) employs the following diagnostic tests: (i) a serial verb construction contains two or more verbs, which occur in the same clause describing a single event; (ii) the whole serial verb complex is negated by a negator preceding the first verb; (iii) all verbs come under the scope of one aspect or mood particle which precedes the verb complex; (iv) all verbs share a single subject, at the surface level; and (v) the construction falls under one intonation contour. A wide range of verb serialization passes these diagnostic tests: benefactive serialization in (107), causative serialization in (108), cause-effect serialization in (109), motion serialization in (110), synonymic serialization in (111), and manner serialization in (112).

Keo
(107) *Jaʔo* ***təndo*** *jawa* ***tiʔi*** *ʔine.*
1SG **plant** corn **give** mum
'I'm planting corn for Mum.' (Baird 2002: 293)

Keo
(108) *ʔine* ***tau*** ***iso*** *ʔuwi jawa.*
mum **make** **half.cook** sweet potato
'Mum half-cooked the sweet potato.' (Baird 2002: 295)

Keo
(109) *Taku* *ʔata* *podo* ***poŋga*** ***mata*** *kau.*
afraid person sorcerer **hit** **die** 2SG
'I'm afraid the sorcerer will beat you to death.'
(Baird 2002: 296)

Keo

(110) *ʔimu* ***nuka*** ***wado*** *rede* *saʔo,* *nambu* *dəra*
3SG **go.up** **return** up house when sun
*pətu-keʔe.*
very.hot
'He returned up to his house when the sun was very hot.' (Baird 2002: 297)

Keo

(111) *ʔimu* ***kai*** ***mbana*** *pasa* *rede* *Soʔa.*
3SG **go** **go** market east So'a
'She went to the market in So'a.' (Baird 2002: 301)

Keo

(112) *"Modo* *miu* ***pake*** ***dama,"*** *ʔembu ŋembu*
alright 2PL **dress** **be.fast** whale
*ʔdəwo.*
answer
'"Alright dress her quickly," the whale answered.' (Baird 2002: 302)

Importantly, serial verbs in Keo are not verb compounds. They can be separated by an object, as in (107). By and large a similar observation is made for other Flores languages such as Lio (Elias 2018: 14), Rongga (Arka 2016), and Lewotobi Lamaholot (Nagaya 2011).

Thus, in descriptions of the languages of Flores and its satellites, the term 'serial verb' refers to structurally and conceptually diverse phenomena. There are several understandable reasons for this. To begin with, in the literature of linguistic typology, the term 'serial verb' has been used for describing quite a diverse range of phenomena (Foley and Olson 1985; Durie 1997; Aikhenvald 2006; Bisang 2009; Haspelmath 2016). In particular, there has been debate over how broadly the term should be defined for cross-linguistic comparison. On the one hand, Aikhenvald (2006: 1) understands serial verb constructions broadly as "a sequence of verbs which act together as a single predicate, without any overt marker of coordination, subordination, or syntactic dependency of any other sort."[11] In her broad definition, all the Kambera examples in (102)–(104) and all the Keo examples in (107)–(112) are considered instances of serial verb constructions. Furthermore, her definition of serial verb constructions also includes the Lewotobi Lamaholot examples that function like auxiliaries in (113) and (114).

Lewotobi Lamaholot

(113) *Nia* *gə̃* *waha.*
Nia eat.3SG finish
'Nia finished eating.' (Nagaya 2011: 476)

[11] In their typological study of serial verb constructions in East Nusantara, Staden and Reesink (2008) adopt much the same broad definition.

Lewotobi Lamaholot

(114) *Go* *k-enũ* *tua* *teʔẽ*
1SG 1SG-drink tuak DEM.PROX.NMLZ
*k-waro.*
1SG-be.capable
'I can drink this tuak.' (Nagaya 2011: 478)

In (113) and (114), a closed set of aspectual and modal verbs, such as *waha* 'finish' and *k-waro* 'can', are serialized with another verb, adding aspectual and modal meanings. In these types of verb serialization, serialized verbs can be separated by an object, as in the Keo example in (107).

In contrast, Haspelmath (2016) proposes a stricter definition: a serial verb construction is "a monoclausal construction consisting of multiple independent verbs with no element linking them and with no predicate–argument relation between the verbs" (Haspelmath 2016: 296). Under this narrow definition, causative serialization in (108) in Keo and possibly the Lamaholot auxiliary serial verb constructions in (113)–(114) are excluded from the scope of serial verb constructions, because they present a predicate–argument relation between two verbs.

In addition to this terminological/conceptual debate, there is a methodological issue that makes it difficult to compare the structural properties of serial verb constructions in the languages of Flores and its satellites. That is, these languages vary in terms of morphological complexity. As a consequence, different structural properties are recruited to identify serial verb constructions in different languages. In Kambera, which has a relatively rich morphological system, word-level diagnostics such as subject/object marking and word stress are available. But this is not the case with Keo serial verb constructions, where only clause-level tests such as argument sharing, scope phenomena, and intonation can be applied.

Languages also differ with regard to how heavily they have to rely on verb serialization. Isolating Flores languages employ verb serialization intensively for adjusting the valency of verbs and introducing new participants into a clause. Refer, once again, to benefactive serialization in (107) and causative serialization in (108) in Keo. Such uses of verb serialization are not well motivated in Kambera, for example, which maintains the causative *pa-* in (83) and the applicative *-ŋ* in (85).

To conclude, it remains unsettled what definition is the most suitable to understand the diversity of the construction types in question in this region and how they should be compared. Sometimes different phenomena are lumped under the same name, while very similar phenomena are given different names, which makes it impossible to make a meaningful cross-linguistic comparison between them.

## 34.9 Conclusions: Typology and language contact

This chapter has presented a bird's eye view of typological variations in the languages of Flores and its satellites, ranging from phonology to serial verb constructions. In the literature on the languages of this region, such typological variations have been repeatedly claimed to be results of contact with and shift from languages of people who had inhabited this area before the arrival of speakers of Austronesian languages in this region.

By way of conclusion, let us briefly review such contact-based accounts of the linguistic variations in this region with two illustrative phenomena, morphological simplicity and word order variations. First, as mentioned in §34.3, Alorese and the Central Flores languages, such as Keo, Lio, and Ende, are extremely isolating languages even in comparison with other relatively isolating Flores languages. This fact has been drawing attention in the context of language contact and creole languages. On the one hand, the morphological simplicity of Alorese has been attributed to simplification resulting from language contact between Alorese and Papuan languages (Klamer 2012, 2020; Moro 2019). On the other hand, there is also evidence to suggest that the simplicity of the Central Flores languages is due to simplification resulting from language contact, but the nature of the contact remains to be disputed. McWhorter (2019) claims that morphological simplification in the Central Flores languages is the result of the extensive non-native acquisition of a language of Sulawesi, brought by groups migrating from Sulawesi to Flores in the relatively recent past. By contrast, Elias (2020) insists that the Central Flores languages show a lack of morphology as well as other Mekong-Mamberamo features because of a strong substrate influence from a now-extinct isolating language with Mekong-Mamberamo linguistic features.

Second, in addition to morphological simplicity, word order variations have long been at the centre of contention. In §34.5, it was shown that there are cross-linguistic and intralinguistic variations with regard to word order phenomena in the languages of Flores and its satellites. The Bima and Sumba-Hawu languages tend to have relatively unrestricted word order, clause-medial negation, postposed possessors, and preposed numerals. In contrast, Lamaholot and other Flores-Lembata languages have basic SVO word order, clause-final negation, preposed possessors, and postposed numerals, as typical examples of preposed possessor languages. The Central and Western Flores languages are somewhere in between the two types: they behave like Flores-Lembata languages in some aspects but like Bima and Sumba-Hawu languages in others. Such word order variations have been considered to be the result of language contact between Austronesian languages and Papuan languages in the East Nusantara area including the Flores-Lembata region (Klamer 2002b, 2004; Donohue 2007; Klamer, Reesink, and Staden 2008; see also Fricke 2019 for other possibly contact-induced changes that occurred to the Flores-Lembata languages, such as the existence of "nouny adjectives" (§34.4) and the occurrence of deictic motion verbs in clause-final position).

To conclude, the languages of Flores and its satellites show great linguistic diversity. They not only play an important role in understanding the typology and history of Austronesian languages but also offer a testing ground for theories of linguistic description, linguistic typology, historical linguistics, and contact linguistics.

## Acknowledgements

I am thankful to Alexander Adelaar, Antoinette Schapper, and Kyosuke Yamamoto for valuable comments and criticism that have helped in improving the manuscript. I also acknowledge my gratitude to I Wayan Arka, Jermy Balukh, Hanna Fricke, and Marian Klamer for sharing their work and knowledge of the languages in this chapter with me. Any errors that remain are my responsibility. This work was supported by JSPS KAKENHI Grant Numbers JP19H01264, JP21H00528, and JP21K00522.

CHAPTER 35

# Languages of Timor and southern Maluku

ANTOINETTE SCHAPPER AND ERIK ZOBEL

## 35.1 Introduction

This chapter offers a typological overview of the Austronesian languages at the southeastern fringe of the MPSEA area, extending from the Kei and Aru Islands in the north through the Tanimbar and Southwest Moluccan Islands to Timor and the island of Rote off the western tip of Timor (henceforth, the whole will be referred to as 'Timor-SMaluku'). According to the *Ethnologue* (Eberhard, Simons, and Fennig 2021), there are sixty-eight Austronesian languages spoken in this region. Detailed grammars exist for only half a dozen languages. The information presented here is necessarily limited by this lack of documentation, and the failure of a given pattern to appear in the attested data does not necessarily entail its absence. The languages for which data is presented in this chapter are marked in Map 35.1. Note that there are many other languages in this region that are not discussed here due to the lack of materials available.

The classification of the Malayo-Polynesian languages of Timor and southern Maluku is only slowly being developed. Several small-scale subgroups are uncontroversial, such as the Aru, Tanimbar-Kei, Babar, Teun-Nila-Serua, Kisar-Leti, Wetar-Galolen, Kawaimina, Central Timor, and Rote-Meto subgroups, but the closer links between these microgroups still need to be established. They are classified by Blust as part of the Central Malayo-Polynesian linkage, but this proposal is problematic and not widely accepted (see Zobel, this volume, chapter 13). Throughout this chapter, we refer to Southwest Maluku languages not as a genealogical unit, but as a typological sub-area among the Timor-SMaluku languages. This group comprises two island chains between Timor and the Tanimbar Islands. The northern chain stretches from Wetar to Serua, the southern chain stretches from Kisar to the Babar Islands. Selaru, in the south of Tanimbar, lies geographically outside of this area, but partially aligns with these languages in its typological features. A genealogical relation of Selaru to the Southwest Maluku languages has been proposed (see Zobel, this volume, §13.3.2).

This chapter outlines key elements of phonology (§35.2), morphology (§35.3), noun phrases (§35.4), grammatical relations (§35.5), negation (§35.6), and serial verb constructions (§35.7) in the languages of Timor-SMaluku. Our description seeks to make generalizations over (sets of) languages in the region, but at the same time highlights unusual features presented by Timor-SMaluku languages in the wider MPSEA context.

## 35.2 Phonology

### 35.2.1 Vowels

Most languages in the Timor-SMaluku area have a simple five-vowel system /a, e, i, o, u/[1]. An extended inventory distinguishing between mid-high /e, o/ and mid-low vowels /ɛ, ɔ/ is found in West Tarangan and Leti. In a few languages of Southwest Maluku, vowels in final syllables have a reduced inventory because they are always unstressed. In Leti, Luang, and Roma, only three vowels /a, i, u/ are allowed in this position.

A few languages in southern Maluku have a phonemic length contrast, for example, Leti and Southeast Babar in Southwest Maluku as well as Ujir and Kola in the Aru islands. In Leti, this contrast has arisen through compensatory lengthening after the loss of certain medial consonants (e.g. PMP *hikan > *iʔan > *iʔna (with metathesis, see §35.3.4) > Leti *iːna* 'fish'; PMP *qapuR > *ahur > *ahru > Leti *aːru* 'lime'). In Ujir, loss of reflexes of medial PMP *j and *R has resulted in compensatory lengthening of the preceding vowel (e.g. PMP *qaləjaw > Proto-Aru *laRaw > Ujir *laːu* 'sun'). In Kola, long vowels have arisen through monophthongization of vowel–glide–vowel sequences (e.g. PMP *wai > Proto-Aru *waya > Kola *weː* 'mango').

[1] In this chapter, examples from natural languages are rendered in a broadly phonemic IPA transcription. For instance, while most orthographic conventions in the area transcribe the palatal glide as <y>, it will be represented with [j] here. The spelling of PMP reconstructions follows Blust (2013a), except for *ə which is used instead of *e for the PMP central vowel.

Antoinette Schapper and Erik Zobel, *Languages of Timor and southern Maluku.* In: *The Oxford Guide to the Malayo-Polynesian Languages of Southeast Asia.* Edited by: Alexander Adelaar and Antoinette Schapper, Oxford University Press. © Antoinette Schapper and Erik Zobel (2024). DOI: 10.1093/oso/9780198807353.003.0035

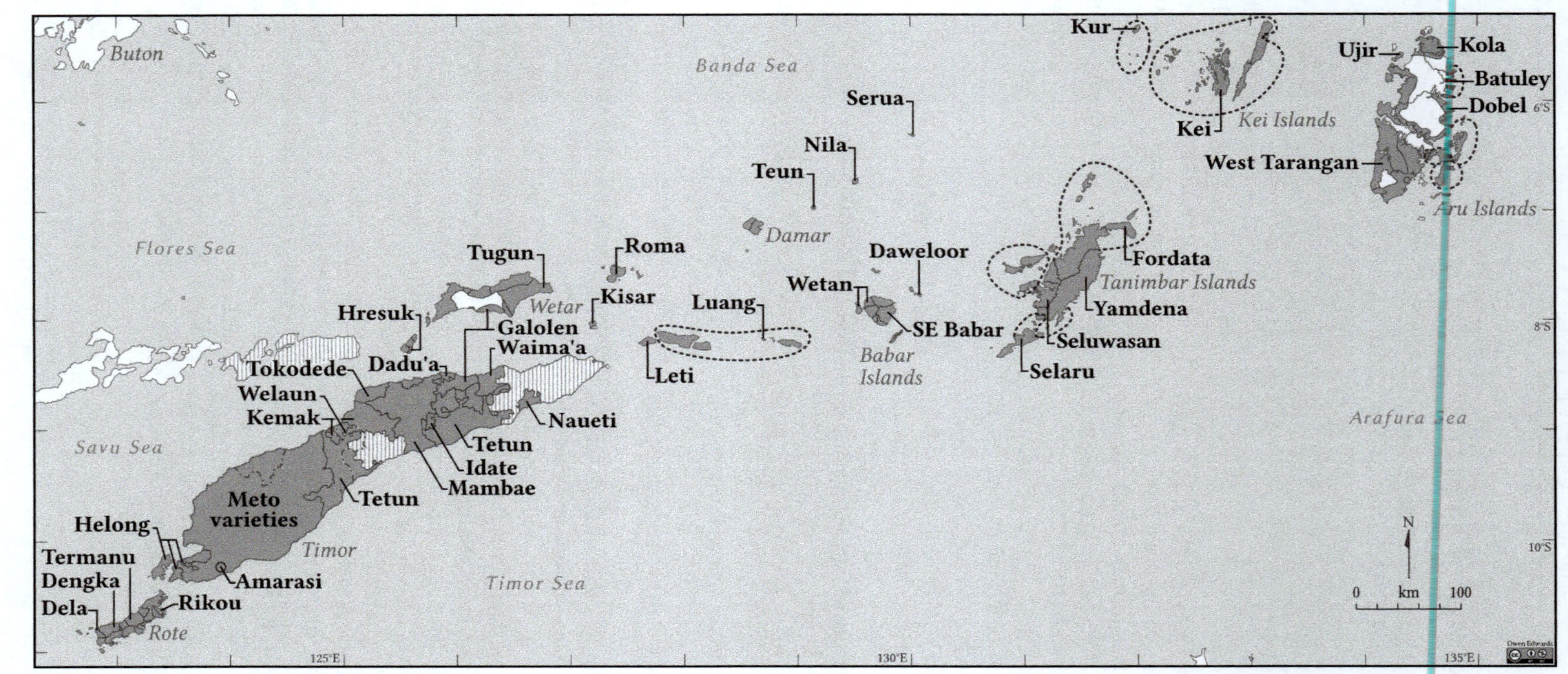


**Map 35.1** Languages of Timor and southern Maluku discussed in this chapter.

Phonetic long vowels occur in most Timor languages, but they are best analysed as sequences of like vowels, see, for example, descriptions of Amarasi (Edwards 2020: 96–100), of Tetun (van Klinken 1999: 30–1), and of Naueti (Veloso 2016: 24). A similar analysis of Fordata is made by Marshall (2000: 193–5).

### 35.2.2 Consonants

Most languages of Timor and southern Maluku have small consonant inventories of between ten and fifteen consonant phonemes (marginal sounds that have entered via recent borrowing from Indonesian and local vehicular Malays will not be considered here). It is difficult to characterize a 'prototypical' consonant inventory for this region beyond broadly applicable observations such as there are generally two liquids /l, r/, two glides /j, w/, minimally a bilabial and alveolar nasal, and two fricatives (one of which is always /s/).

In most languages, the contrast between voiceless and voiced stops is weakly developed. At least one language, viz. Kisar in Southwest Maluku, even entirely lacks voiced stops. Distinct /b/ and /p/ are only found in the western and central Timor area (e.g. Rote-Meto lects, Helong, and Kemak). In a long stretch that comprises eastern Timor and almost all of southern Maluku, only one labial stop occurs. In Tetun, Central and Southern Mambae, Idate, and the languages of Aru, Kei, and Tanimbar, this is voiced /b/, while the languages of Southwest Maluku only have voiceless /p/. This reduced contrast is due to a sound change which shifted earlier *p and *b to fricatives: *p > *ɸ*, *f*, *h* (or further to zero); *b > *β*, *v*, *f*. The bilabial stop in the modern languages represents earlier prenasalized *$^{m}$b (see Zobel, this volume, §13.4.1.3). Only Yamdena has not been affected by this shift. It retains plain /b/ and prenasalized /$^{m}$b/ as distinct labial stops.

The most robust voicing contrast is that between /t/ and /d/. But even here we find gaps, with /d/ lacking in Uab Meto, Kisar and Southeast Babar to name a few. A dental discrepancy in the place of articulation of dental /t/ and alveolar /d/, as commonly observed in MPSEA, is reported for Welaun, Fordata, Dobel, and Leti. In Kisar, the dental discrepancy is realized as alveolar /t/ vs. retroflex /ʈ/. The latter corresponds to /d/ in other Kisar-Luangic languages.

In velar position, almost all languages have a plain voiceless stop /k/. Voiced /g/ is less common; it occurs in Central Timor languages (Kemak, Mambae, Tokodede), Aru languages (Batuley, Kola), Wetar languages (e.g. Tugun), and Luang.

Languages in the western and central area of Timor and on Wetar Island as a rule have a phonemic glottal stop. So do southern Maluku languages, although some of them lack this phoneme, including Roma, Leti, Daweloor, Southeast Babar, Yamdena, Kola.

In the Timor-SMaluku area, prenasalized stops are rare and only occur in certain Rote lects and in Yamdena. The largest inventory among the Rote lects is found in western variants like Dela or Tii, which have three prenasalized stops /$^{m}$b, $^{n}$d, $^{ŋ}$g/; Termanu has /$^{n}$d, $^{ŋ}$g/, while Rikou only has /$^{n}$d/. Yamdena has /$^{m}$b/ and /$^{n}$d/. Prenasalized stops played an important role in the phonological history of all languages in the area, but shifted to stops everywhere except in the two abovementioned relic areas (see Zobel, this volume, §13.4.1.3 for more on the history of prenasalized stops).

Implosive stops are only found in a few languages on Rote at the western extreme of the Timor-SMaluku region. Dela has /ɓ, ɗ/ and Dengka has /ɗ/. These languages also have prenasalized voiced stops, but they lack plain voiced stops. The appearance of implosives in Rote languages is likely due to contact with circum-Savu Sea languages to the west, which very commonly have them (see Nagaya, this volume, §34.2).

Post-alveolar affricates /tʃ/ and /dʒ/ are not common. Both are found in Wetar languages (Tugun) and Makuva, whereas the languages of Aru (West Tarangan, Ujir, Batuley) and Uab Meto only have voiced /dʒ/. In Roma, post-alveolar affricates appear as realizations of phonemic /tj/ and /dj/.

Labialized velar stops are found in Uab Meto /g$^{w}$/ and Dobel /k$^{w}$/ (which lacks a plain velar stop); in both cases, these sounds have historically arisen through fortition of the glide /w/.

Many languages in the area have three or more fricatives. The most common fricative is /s/ followed by /h/. The phoneme /s/ is absent only in the languages of southern Babar, while /h/ is lacking in languages such as Leti, Southeast Babar, as well as many Aru languages. Labial fricatives are widespread due to spirantization of earlier *p and *b. The phoneme /f/ is found in the western Timor area, much of southeastern Maluku, and in pockets of central Timor (Tetun, Welaun) and southwestern Maluku (Wetar languages). In the Aru languages, /ɸ/ is common, and even appears alongside /f/ in Kola. The contrast between /ɸ/ and /f/ is unique in the whole MPSEA area. A voiced labial, /β/ or /v/, occurs widely in southern Maluku. Non-labial fricatives other than /s/ and /h/ are rarely found. They include [ʒ] as an allophone of /j/ in Kola, and [x] as an allophone of /k/ in Southeast Babar.

As a rule, there are two glides /j, w/ and two liquids /l, r/ (flapped or trilled), although some Rote-Meto lects only have one liquid. Leti has been analysed as lacking phonemic glides; phonetic glides only occur as non-syllabic allophones of /i/ and /u/.[2]

From western Timor to southwestern Maluku, most languages only have two nasals /m, n/; /ŋ/ is typically absent (Schapper 2015a: 116–17). In this region, a velar nasal phoneme only appears in the Rote languages, Helong and Hresuk. Further to the east, the languages of Tanimbar, Kei, and Aru, all have three nasals /m, n, ŋ/, except for Selaru, which only has /m, n/.

Unusually large inventories are found in the Kawaimina languages of eastern Timor. This is due to the additional features of glottalization, aspiration, and devoicing. For example, Waima'a has ejective /p', t', k'/, aspirated /pʰ, tʰ, kʰ/, glottalized /sˀ, mˀ, nˀ, lˀ, rˀ, wˀ/ and devoiced /m̥, n̥, l̥, w̥/ (Schapper 2020a: 401). These are unique in the Timor-SMaluku area,[3] and also—with the exception of aspirated stops—in the MPSEA area as a whole. Most likely, these unusual segments are reflexes of earlier initial consonant clusters which are commonly found in the area (see §35.2.3). Schapper (2020a: 402–3) suggests that aspirated plosives and voiceless sonorants reflect an earlier prefix *pa-, while glottalized consonants reflect earlier *ka-, via the pathways *pa-C- > *ha-C- > *hC- > Cʰ/C̥- and *ka-C- > *ʔa-C- > *ˀC- > Cˀ-. Some words with an innovative consonant can indeed be related to existing protoforms in this manner. For instance, Waima'a *l̥ai* 'quick' goes back to earlier *hlai < *halai < *pa-laRiw 'to run' (cf. Dadu'a *hlai*, Tetun *halai*). Other prefixes—such as the stative prefix *ma- or person agreement prefixes—may also have played a role here, as can be seen in the case of Waima'a *tʰaku* 'afraid', which goes back to *matakut (cf. Galolen *mtaʔuk*) and indicates that a nasal element may also have triggered the aspiration of stops. This is supported by Waima'a *tʰede* 'heavy' (cf. Kemak *mdedan*), and *tʰelu* 'egg' (cf. Tetun *mantolun*).

### 35.2.3 Syllable and word structure

The languages of the Timor-SMaluku area show a great diversity with regards to their syllable structure, but we can observe a prototypical pattern that is found in most languages of Timor, and also in Kisar and Fordata. Here, the basic word type is CCVCVC: consonant clusters are only allowed preceding the penultimate (= stressed) vowel (e.g. Tetun *ktodan* 'heavy', Fordata *fnebuŋ* 'braid'). Closed CVC-type syllables are allowed in final (and in antepenultimate position), but not in penultimate position.

In the phonological history of some languages of southwestern Maluku (e.g. Leti and Serua), ultimate V and final C swap their order in phrase-final position through metathesis (see §35.3.4.1), resulting in an unusual CCVCCV root type which allows initial and medial clusters, but no final consonants (e.g. Leti *smakra* 'spirit'). Roma displays a mixed type, allowing both CCVCCV and CCVCVC, but not **CCVCCVC. Final consonant clusters are rare but occur in Selaru (where they consist of only C plus glide, e.g. *asʷ* 'dog', *tasʲ* 'rope'), Daweloor (*watk* 'stone', *mers* 'beautiful'), and Southeast Babar (*mexm* 'black', *lalk* 'sky'). These clusters have arisen through vowel loss from earlier ultimate syllables (*laŋit > *lalik > *lalk*) or desyllabification (*batu > *watw > *watk*).

CCC-clusters are generally not allowed. Where they would have come up as a result of a morphological process such as metathesis (see §35.3.4), they are broken up with an epenthetic vowel (e.g. Leti *ternu* + *-nV* > ***tern-nu* > *teran-nu* (egg-3SG.POSS) 'its egg').

In the languages of Aru, closed CVC syllables can occur in all positions, therefore they allow both medial clusters *and* final consonants (e.g. Kola *kenkoɸ* 'grip'). This is unlike what happens in most other languages in southern Maluku and Timor.

### 35.2.4 Stress

In the languages of Timor and also in many languages of southern Maluku (Roma, Leti, Fordata), stress is predictable and falls on the penultimate syllable of the word. Selaru has predictable stress which always falls on the root; if the latter is polysyllabic, the penultimate syllable is stressed. Stress does not shift under affixation, which may lead to minimal pairs with contrastive stress on the word level (Coward and Coward 2000: 29):

Selaru
(1) /t-ala/ ['tala] 'we (incl.) take'
/ta-la/ [ta'a] 'we (incl.) run'
/amana/ [a'mana] 'octopus'
/ama-na/ ['amana] 'his/her father'

In the languages of Aru, stress is not predictable. As a rule, it falls on the penultimate syllable of a root (e.g., Dobel *da-'tabaj* 'they carry (on shoulder)'), but in around 30% of cases falls on the ultimate syllable (e.g., *da-ta'baj* 'they hit', Hughes 2000: 135, see also Takata 1992: 40 for Kola; Daigle 2015: 31 for Batuley). Some deviations from this penultimate stress pattern in Aru can be explained historically as a result of desyllabification or loss of the vowel in the final syllable (e.g. Kola *ɸa'nis* < PMP *paniki 'bat').

[2] These are transcribed as <ï> and <ü> by van Engelenhoven (2004), but will be indicated here with IPA [i̯] and [u̯].

[3] Devoiced sonorants are found in Roma as surface realizations of initial clusters with /h/ (e.g. [m̥-] /hm-/) (Steven 1991: 30).

## 35.3 Morphology

The languages of Timor and southern Maluku generally have little affixal morphology. Inflectional affixation is largely restricted to person agreement (§35.3.1). Derivational affixes are commonly found, but in most languages, few of these are productive (§35.3.2). A special case is represented by the languages of central and eastern Timor, which are well known for being near isolating, with several languages having little to no productive inflectional or derivational affixes. Reduplication (§35.3.3) and metathesis (§35.3.4) are present as productive morphological processes in many languages in the region.

### 35.3.1 Inflectional morphology

Most Timor-SMaluku languages have some inflectional morphology. The typical pattern involves verbal agreement prefixes for subjects and nominal agreement suffixes for possessors. Languages do, however, differ widely in (i) the number of agreement paradigms they have, (ii) the number of affixes in each agreement paradigm, and (iii) what proportion of their verbal and nominal lexicons permit inflectional affixes. A relatively small number of languages concentrated exclusively in the eastern half of the island of Timor lack these affixes: Tokodede has neither agreement prefixes nor suffixes; Kemak lacks agreement prefixes on verbs, but retains the agreement suffixes for the possessor on a class of nouns; sister languages Waima'a and Naueti have no verbal agreement prefixes and only maintain a remnant of the third person possessive suffix on some nouns. A few languages elaborate on the typical pattern, adding—or in some cases substituting—verbal agreement suffixes and nominal agreement prefixes to their inventories of inflectional affixes.

**Table 35.1** Ujir agreement prefixes (Schapper fieldnotes)

| | Paradigm I<br>/_#'CVCV | Paradigm II<br>/_#V, CV'CV |
|---|---|---|
| 1SG | *ku-* | *ko-* |
| 2SG | *m-* (~ Ø/_#m) | *mo-* |
| 3SG | *a-* | *a-* |
| 1PL.INCL | *ta-* | *ta-* |
| 1PL.EXCL | *ma-* | *ma-* |
| 2PL | *mi-* | *me-* |
| 3PL | *da-* | *da-* |

**Table 35.2** Amarasi agreement prefixes (Edwards 2020: 439)

| | Paradigm I<br>/_#V | Paradigm II<br>/_#C |
|---|---|---|
| 1SG | *ʔ-* | *u-* |
| 2SG | *m-* | *mu-* |
| 3SG | *n-* | *na-* |
| 1PL.INCL | *ta-* | *ta-* |
| 1PL.EXCL | *m-* | *ma-* |
| 2PL | *n-* | *mi-* |
| 3PL | *n-* | *na-* |

#### 35.3.1.1 *Agreement on verbs*

The pattern with the widest distribution across the region is for verbal agreement to be marked by prefixes on all lexical verbs occurring as the main verb in a clause. In these languages, there are typically two paradigms of phonologically conditioned agreement prefixes. We illustrate this with two languages at the extremes of the area, Ujir in northern Aru (Table 35.1) and Amarasi in far western Timor (Table 35.2).

Fordata presents a more elaborated picture than the standard with four phonologically conditioned paradigms of verbal agreement prefixes (Marshall 2000: 205). Tugun is also unique in the area, having separate prefixal paradigms for realis and irrealis, each with two phonologically conditioned paradigms (Table 35.3). The realis/irrealis distinction is more commonly found in Oceanic languages (Lichtenberk 2016). Realis agreement prefixes are used in past and present contexts and in resultative clauses, while irrealis agreement prefixes are used in future time contexts, as well as in imperatives, hortatives, and purpose clauses (Hinton 1991: 93–4, 98–100). Diachronically, the irrealis prefixes can at least partially be analysed as a fusion of an earlier aspect marker *ma with the prefixes of the realis paradigm, as can be best seen from the first person singular and the third person singular and plural forms.

As mentioned already, several languages in eastern Timor have no verbal agreement prefixes. These languages represent the end stage of a process of prefixal attrition that is still in progress in other languages in eastern Timor. In

**Table 35.3** Tugun verbal agreement prefixes (Hinton 1991: 75–6)

| | Irrealis | | Realis | |
|---|---|---|---|---|
| | /_#C | /_#V | /_#C | /_#V |
| 1SG | *mu-* | *mu-* | *u-* | *v-* |
| 2SG | *om-* | *om-* | *o-* | *m-* |
| 3SG | *ma-* | *man-* | *Ø-* | *n-* |
| 1PL.INCL | *ka-* | *kat-* | *it-* | *itt-* |
| 1PL.EXCL | *am-* | *amʔ-* | *am-* | *amʔ-* |
| 2PL | *mar-* | *marr-* | *mi-* | *mir-* |
| 3PL | *mar-* | *marr-* | *ra-* | *r-* |

**Table 35.4** Batuley verbal agreement suffixes (Daigle 2015: 36–7).

| | Paradigm I | Paradigm IIa | Paradigm IIb | Paradigm III |
|---|---|---|---|---|
| 1SG | *-iŋ* | *-uŋ* | *-uŋ* | *-aŋ* |
| 2SG | *-ig* | *-ug* | *-ug* | *-eg* |
| 3SG.AN | *-in* | *-un* | <e> | *-en* |
| 1PL.INCL | *-sit* | *-sit* | *-sit* | *-sit* |
| 1PL.EXCL | *-kom* | *-kom* | *-kom* | *-kom* |
| 2PL | *-kem* | *-kem* | *-kem* | *-kem* |
| 3PL | *-i* | *-uj* | *-uj* | *-ej* |

multiple languages here, there is only a single paradigm of agreement prefixes and not all person–number feature specifications receive prefixation. What is more, the prefixes are typically limited to appearing on vowel- and sometimes /h/-initial verb roots (often replacing initial *h*, Hull 2001a: 153–4). See Schapper (2020a: 397–400) for an extensive picture of the stages of prefixal attrition that can be perceived across the eastern Timor languages, both in the number of verbal agreement prefixes within a paradigm and in the verbs on which they are able to appear. Languages close to eastern Timor show the beginnings of prefixal attrition, for example, Tugun *la* 'go' does not always take agreement prefixes when it is the main clausal verb. See Blood (1992) for the description of rules of prefixal occurrence in Kisar.

Agreement suffixes, rather than prefixes, are found on a subset of intransitive verbs in the northern languages of Aru. The suffixes divide into multiple, minimally different, paradigms the choice of which appears to be lexical synchronically, but likely goes back to phonological differences in root shape. Table 35.4 lays out the complex forms in agreement suffixes on the basis of Batuley, a language of eastern Aru. Note that the paradigms include a singular infix: third person singular animate <e> replaces unstressed /a/ in a small number of roots with a final closed syllable, for example, /ka'nawar/ 'hungry' > /ka'naw<e>r/ 'hungry<3SG.AN>' (see Daigle 2015: 42–3 for more details on this phenomenon).

Languages in central and southern Aru do not have agreement suffixes, but rather enclitics on members of the stative intransitive verb class. In Dobel (2) we see that where a verb such as *soba* 'good' is followed by an intensifier, the enclitic occurs on the intensifier. Like the verbal suffixes in Batuley, the Dobel enclitics are agreement markers and are required for grammaticality with all non-third person inanimate Ss in clauses with a verb of the relevant class.

Dobel

(2) a. *tamatu ne soba=**ni***
person DEM good=3SG.AN
'That person is good.'

b. *tamatu ne soba juʔu=**ni***
person DEM good very=3SG.AN
'That person is very good.' (Hughes 2000: 143)

Beyond Aru, verbal suffixes have a limited and only sporadic appearance in the languages of Timor-SMaluku. These suffixes and similar enclitics or postverbal agreement markers for S are discussed further in §35.5.3 on alignment.

### 35.3.1.2 *Agreement on nouns*

The main nominal inflection in the languages of Timor-SMaluku concerns affixes on possessed nouns that agree with the person and number of the possessor. Such possessive affixes only occur on small, closed lexical classes of nouns denoting 'inalienables'. The exact membership of the class differs from language to language, but typically includes body parts, locative nouns, and some kin terms.

The most widespread pattern is for possessors of these inalienably possessed nouns to be marked by a paradigm of agreement suffixes. The number of suffixes in the possessive paradigm varies: languages at the northern and southern extremes of the area typically have distinct suffixes for most cells in the paradigm, while languages in eastern Timor often have greatly reduced paradigms (Table 35.5; see Schapper 2020a: 406–7 for more discussion of paradigm reduction).

**Table 35.5** Possessor suffixes

| | Kei | Yamdena | Tetun Fehan | Kemak Atsabe | Amarasi | Termanu |
|---|---|---|---|---|---|---|
| 1SG | *-ŋ* | *-ŋ* | | *-gV* | *-k* | *-ŋ* |
| 2SG | *-m* | *-m* | *-n* | *-mV* | *-m* | *-m* |
| 3SG | *-n* | *-n* | | *-V* | *-n* | |
| 1PL.INCL | *-d* | *-nindar* | | | *-m* | *-n* |
| 1PL.EXCL | *-b* | *-mamyar* | *-n/-r* | *-rV* | | *-m* |
| 2PL | | *-mir* | | | | |
| 3PL | *-r* | *-nir* | | | *-k/-r* | *-n* |

While one suffixal set is typical, a few languages have multiple phonologically conditioned paradigms of possessive suffixes on inalienable nouns. For example, Welaun has two sets of phonologically conditioned possessive suffixes, one for roots with a final vowel and another for roots with a final consonant (Edwards 2019: 39). Languages in Aru have the most complicated paradigms, with numerous vocalic forms depending on the last vowel of the historical root and some infixation. At least one language has a minor lexically specified split in the form of its possessive suffixes: in Fordata the first person singular possessive suffix is *-ŋ* for most inalienable nouns, but two kin term nouns (*yana-* 'child' and *ina-* 'mother') take *-k*. (Splits of this kind are more common in SHWNG languages, see Gasser, Arnold, and Kamholz, this volume, §37.3.6).

In a cluster of languages in far eastern Timor, the alienability distinction in possession has broken down, but one or more possessive suffixes are retained for nouns of particular types. In Idate, nouns ending in a vowel take possessor suffixes, while nouns ending in a consonant take free possessive markers (Alcantara 2015: 135–6). In Waima'a and Naueti, only one possessive suffix (Waima'a *-n*, Naueti *-na*) is preserved and can be used for encoding third person possessors on any noun (and marking attributes, see §35.4.6).

Languages in Southwest Maluku and nearby show a cline of movement away from possessive suffixes towards prefixes. This is part of a more general process associated with the loss of alienability contrasts in adnominal possession. Consider the possessive markers in Table 35.6. In Selaru, Leti, and Luang, several possessive suffixes have become conflated and are disambiguated by a preposed, either free or proclitic, possessive marker. In Selaru, the first person plural exclusive and inclusive suffixes are identical to the second and third person plural suffixes, respectively (1PL.INCL, 3PL *-t*; 1PL.EXCL, 2PL *-mj*) and must co-occur with the free possessive pronoun *irj* and *ara*, respectively (Coward 2005: 48). This pattern is continued in Leti and Luang where the suffix *-nV* serves as possessive marker for the first person plural and the third person singular and plural. In Leti, the default value is third person singular, while all others meanings have to be expressed by an additional free possessive pronoun. Luang has extended the obligatory use of a free possessive marker even to the first person singular slot where no ambiguity exists (Coward 2005: 109). Tugun has moved further away from possessive suffixes, with only one suffix *-n* '3SG' still used on a small number of originally inalienable nouns where they have a non-human possessor (Hinton 1991: 70–1). Otherwise, nouns in Tugun have their possessor

**Table 35.6** From possessive suffixes to possessive prefixes

| | Selaru | Leti | Luang | Tugun | Dadu'a |
|---|---|---|---|---|---|
| 1SG | *-kw* | *-ku* | *a= ~ -ʔu* | *au / u=* | *a-* |
| 2SG | *-mw* | *-mu* | *(o=) ~ -mu* | *o* | *o-* |
| 3SG | | *-nV* | *(e=) ~ -ni* | *ni/ni-/-n* | *ni-* |
| 1PL.INCL | *ity ~ -t* | *ita= -nV* | *it= / ita= ~ -ni* | *ita / it=* | *ita-* |
| 1PL.EXCL | *ara ~ -mj* | *ami= -nV* | *a= ~ -mamni* | *ami / am=* | *ami-/am-* |
| 2PL | *-mj* | *-mi* | *mi= ~ -mi* | *mi* | *mi-* |
| 3PL | *-t* | *ira= -nV* | *ir= ~ -ni* | *hira / hi(r)=* | *sia- / si-* |

encoded with a free possessive pronoun preceding the head noun, some of which have enclitic or prefixal forms (Hinton 1991: 67–8). Dadu'a represents the logical end point of the loss of inalienable suffixes and the move to prefixal possessive marking, with all nouns having their possessor encoded with a possessive prefix.

The expression of adnominal possession is discussed further in §35.4.7.

## 35.3.2 Derivational morphology

Whilst rather impoverished in terms of inflectional morphology (which is largely restricted to person-marking), many Timor-SMaluku languages have retained at least some affixes from PMP with a derivational function. Depending on the language, these affixes may be fossilized, productive or have, in some cases, even fused with inflectional morphology. Innovative affixes are also found, which shows that derivational morphology has remained a stable feature in many languages of the area. We limit our discussion to relatively productive derivational affixes, while recognizing that fossilized forms are found in almost every language in the region.

Since most affixes in PMP were prefixes, it is no surprise that Timor-SMaluku languages mostly have derivational prefixes. A few derivational suffixes are found in the Timor area, all of which are innovations. None of the suffixes of PMP (all of which were inflectional) were retained, and only the PMP inflectional infix *<in> survived in a few languages of southern Maluku as a derivational affix.

### 35.3.2.1 *Valency-changing verbal derivation*

In many languages of the Timor-SMaluku area, two prefixes have been retained: causative *pa-, stative *ka- (and its inflected form *ma-).

Reflexes of the PMP causative prefix *pa- are widely found in the area (e.g. Yamdena, Fordata *fa*-; Amarasi, Tetun *ha*-; Termanu, Mambae, Welaun, Idate, Galolen, Dadu'a *a*-). The prefix is lacking in some languages of central and eastern Timor (e.g. Kemak or Naueti), and in the Aru languages. These languages employ a periphrastic causative construction (see §35.7). Since PMP *p has undergone lenition to *h* or zero in most languages of Timor and Southwest Maluku, the causative prefix is often fused with the person agreement prefixes, as can be seen in the Table 35.7 with examples from Galolen, Tetun, and Leti (based on Schapper 2020a: 405; van Klinken 1999: 59, 172; van Engelenhoven 2004: 135). In Galolen, the causative element is regularly *-a-* due to complete loss of *p, while in Tetun, *ha-* is only preserved in absolute initial position, but drops its *h* where it is preceded by another prefix. In Leti, the fused causative person agreement prefix has the same syllabic shape as the basic person prefix before a consonant cluster. This can be interpreted as an indirect reflex of earlier *pa-. For example, the second person singular prefix went through the following stages: *mu-pa-CV- > *mu-h-CV- > *mu*-CV-. Earlier *h* (< *p) thus blocked external metathesis of the high vowel *u* which is observed in the basic form of the prefix (*mu-CV- > *m*-Cu̯V-). The use of syllabic agreement prefixes is however not restricted to causative function. They also appear in derivations of verbs from nouns (*vua* 'fruit' > *na-vua* 'it bears fruit') and often, their use is lexically determined (*na-keni* '(s)he puts').

**Table 35.7** Basic and fused causative person agreement prefixes

| | Galolen | | Tetun | | Leti | |
|---|---|---|---|---|---|---|
| | Basic | Causative | Basic | Causative | Basic | Causative |
| 1SG | *ʔ-* | *ʔa-* | *k-* | *ka-* | <u̯> | *u-* |
| 2SG | *m-* | *ma-* | *m-* | *ma-* | *m-* <u̯> | *mu-* |
| 3SG | *n-* | *na-* | *n-* | *na-* | *n-* | *na-* |
| 1PL.INCL | *t-* | *ta-* | ø | *ha-* | *t-* | *ta-* |
| 1PL.EXCL | *r-* | *ra-* | ø | *ha-* | *m-* | *ma-* |
| 2PL | *r-* | *ra-* | ø | *ha-* | *m-* <i̯> | *mi-* |
| 3 PL | *r-* | *ra-* | *r-* | *ra-* | *r-* | *ra-* |

Waima'a entirely lacks person agreement and has the prefix *ra-* as invariant causative marker. This is a fossilized fused third person plural form (< *da- + *pa-).

The PMP stative prefix *ka-/*ma- is commonly retained in the Timor–Southwest Maluku area. In several languages, this prefix is employed to derive anticausative verbs from transitive verb roots, which was among its original functions in PMP (Table 35.8). These languages include Amarasi (Edwards 2020: 446–7), Tetun (van Klinken 1999: 86), Tugun (Hinton 1991: 102), Fordata (Drabbe 1926a, 1932a), and Yamdena (Drabbe 1926b, 1932b).

Reflexes of three inherited prefixes make a more limited appearance in the region's languages. First, the accidental prefix *taR- is retained in Yamdena (*labar* 'to lay' > *t-labar* 'to lie prone'; Drabbe 1926b) and Kei (*fee* 'to cut (a rope)' > *t-fee* 'to snap'; Geurtjens 1921: 29). Innovative accidental or anticausative prefixes include Idate *si-/di-* (Alcantara 2015: 133) and Tugun *p-* (Hinton 1991: 102).

**Table 35.8** Anticausative derivations

| | | Transitive | Anticausative |
|---|---|---|---|
| Amarasi | *m- -ʔ* | *sopu* 'finish' | *m-sopu-ʔ* 'be finished' |
| Tetun | *k- -k* | *sira* 'tear' | *k-sira-k* 'torn' |
| Tugun | *k-* | *soan* 'pour' | *k-soan* 'spilt' |
| Fordata | *m-* | *kusa* 'melt (tr.)' | *m-kusa* 'melt (intr.)' |
| Yamdena | *m-* | *tetak* 'cut (a rope)' | *m-tetak* 'snap' |

Second, the reciprocal prefix *si- is present in Fordata *si-* (e.g. *si-raning* 'praise each other'; Drabbe 1926a: 43) and probably also in Tugun *ihi-* (e.g. *ihi-dʒago* 'fight each other'; Hinton 1991: 104). Some languages have affixes marking reciprocal action which do not reflect *si-. These include the prefixes *ma(k)-* in Meto varieties (Middelkoop 1950: 433; Edwards 2020: 441), *va-* in Leti (van Engelenhoven 2004: 146) or the circumfix *hak- -k* in Tetun (van Klinken 1999: 68–9). Analytic reciprocal constructions are rare; for example, Helong uses a construction with a noun meaning 'body', for example, *tuuk afaʔ* 'punch each other (= fight)' (Edwards 2018c: 22). In Tetun, an alternative construction with a dedicated reciprocal pronoun *malu* is also available, for example, *sia mós n-usu malu* (3PL also 3-request RECP) 'they asked each other (questions)' (van Klinken 1999: 234).

Third, the intransitivizer *maR-/*paR- is retained in the Aru languages as Proto-Aru *R-, with reflexes as *r-* in Dobel (Hughes 2000: 149) and Batuley (Daigle 2015: 90), *h-* in Kola (Takata 1992: 62), or *i-* in Ujir (Schapper, fieldnotes). This intransitivizing prefix forms antipassives (Dobel *r-ʔara* 'to bite (habitually, intr.)') and reflexives/reciprocals (Dobel *r-d~dayar* 'to hit oneself/each other'). It is also lexically required with many intransitive verbs (e.g. Dobel *r-tir* 'to bathe'). In the Timor area, reflexives are typically formed analytically, using a noun 'body', such as Luang *inon-* (3), as is cross-linguistically common (cf. Adelaar and Hajek, this volume, §52.5.4).

Luang reflexive

(3) *rij* *jatjat* *de* *nalaharia* ***inon-ni***
person evil DIST 3SG:reveal body-3SG.POSS
'That evil man will reveal himself.' (Taber and Taber n.d.)

In some languages, the 'body' noun has been captured to the verb as a suffix (e.g. Meto *-oo-n* 'him/herself' < *ao-n* 'his/her body'). Or it is retained as a free form but only with the specialized function as a reflexive marker (e.g. Tetun *aan* < *awak-n 'his/her/its body'), but no longer with its original lexical meaning.[4]

Termanu has a derivational prefix *a-*, always fused with a person agreement prefix, that is striking for the wide array of its functions, including causative, antipassive, reciprocal, and also denominal derivations meaning 'to have/carry X' (Jonker 1915: 147–58). Since PMP *p has weakened to *h* in initial and zero in medial position, the causative function clearly reflects the prefix *pa-, for example, *mate* 'dead' > *na-mate* '(s)he kills' (< *na-ha-mate < *na-pa-matay). For the remaining functions, we can assume that these reflect the intransitivizing prefix *paR-, since *R has a zero reflex in Rote lects: *ka* 'to bite' > *na-ka* 'to bite (habitually, intr.)' (< *na-paR-kaRat), *fali* 'to help' > *la-fali-ao* 'they help e.o.' (< *da-paR-bali, with an additional suffix *-ao* meaning 'body'), *boak* 'fruit' > *na-boa* 'it bears fruit' (< *na-paR-buaq).

### 35.3.2.2 *Deverbal nominalization*

Deverbal nominalizations are common in Timor-SMaluku languages. Two nominalizing strategies are inherited from PMP: partial reduplication, which will be discussed in §35.3.3, and the infix *<in>. PMP *<in> was an inflectional past/perfective TAM marker, but has changed in many languages outside of the conservative area of the Philippines and satellites into a derivational affix forming deverbal nouns. While it originally referred to the undergoer of the action described by the verb root (e.g. Fordata *vuat* 'to load' > *v<n>uat* 'cargo'), it has increasingly acquired a wider function of forming nouns that describe the action itself (e.g. Fordata *tabar* 'to stomp' > *t<n>abar* 'dance (lit., stomping)').

The nominalizing infix is retained only in Southwest Maluku and the Tanimbar Islands (Table 35.9). It appears as *<ini>* in Wetan (de Josselin de Jong 1987: 167), as *<nj>* with metathesis in Roma (Steven 1991: 79–81), Leti (van Engelenhoven 2004: 140), Luang (Taber and Taber 2015: 31–2) and Yamdena (Drabbe 1926b: 21), and as *<n>* in Fordata (Marshall 2000: 211).

Innovative nominalizers are also found. For example, there is the non-finite nominalizer *yeR- in the Aru languages (Nivens n.d. a), which appears as *ser-* in Dobel (Hughes 2000: 151), *jeh-* in Kola (Takata 1992: 56–7), *jer-* in (Daigle 2015: 93–4), and *dʒer-* in West Tarangan (Nivens n.d. a). In Amarasi (Edwards 2020: 442, 445), agent nouns are formed with the circumfix *a- -t* (*mepu* 'to work' > *a-mepu-t* 'worker'), while the circumfix *ʔ- -ʔ* forms deverbal nouns

[4] In the South Maluku languages Tugun and Leti, and in the languages of the Tanimbar Islands (Selaru, Yamdena, Fordata), reflexive clauses can be formed without any special marking at all (Hinton 1991: 87; van Engelenhoven 2004: 194; Drabbe 1926a: 28; Drabbe 1926b: 41). A coreferential object in a reflexive construction is expressed in the same way as a non-coreferential object (e.g. Yamdena *jakbwabal jak* (1SG:hit 1SG) 'I hit myself'). Some languages can optionally use a reflexive marker (e.g. *koko* in Yamdena).

**Table 35.9** Deverbal nominalizations with reflexes of *<in>

| | | Verb | Nominalization |
|---|---|---|---|
| Roma | *<nj>* | *sinin* 'to sing' | *s<nj>inin* 'song' |
| Wetan | *<ini>* | *wali* 'to answer' | *w<ini>ali* 'answer' |
| Yamdena | *<nj>* | *tasiŋ* 'to cry' | *t<nj>asiŋ* '(act of) crying' |

that mostly refer to instruments (*sapu* 'to sweep' > *ʔ-sapu-ʔ* 'broom').

### 35.3.3 Reduplication

Reduplication is a common morphological process in MPSEA languages. Partial reduplication is attested widely across the Timor-SMaluku languages, but is associated with different functions and frequencies in different languages. Partial reduplication has a particularly high functional load in many of the languages of southern Maluku. Comparatively little use is made of reduplication in eastern Timor languages. Full reduplication is rare in the region.

#### 35.3.3.1 *Form*

The overwhelming majority pattern is for a reduplicant to occur initial to the base, for example, Idate *mo~mor* 'calm', *maru~marun* 'slowly' (Alcantara 2015: 113). The base for reduplication is typically limited to the root and excludes affixes. For the vast majority of languages, this means that the reduplicant occurs to the immediate left of the root, for example, Luang *na-p-lo~lola* 3SG-STAT-REDUP~straight 'very true' (Taber and Taber 2015: 75). The languages of Aru form a major exception; the base for reduplication is the stressed syllable, but stress can be initial or final. Where the stressed syllable is non-initial, reduplicants appear root internally, much like an infix, in these languages (West Tarangan, Nivens 1993; Dobel, Hughes 2000: 167–8; Batuley, Daigle 2015: 53–5). For example, in West Tarangan the stressed syllable of a root is the base and the copy is attached to the immediate left of the base, resulting in initial reduplication with monosyllabic and initially stressed disyllabic roots (e.g. *təp* 'short' > *təp~'təp*, *da-'ɛla* '3PL-go' > *da-ɛl~'ɛla*, *'suar* 'pole' > *su~'suar*) and in internal reduplication with non-initially stressed roots (e.g. *ɛ-ta'il* '3SG-bounce' > *ɛ-ta<il~>'il*, *ɛ-la'dʒir* '3SG-white' > *ɛ-la<dʒir~>'dʒir*).[5] Outside of Aru, the only languages in the region with clearly described internal reduplication are in west Timor, Amarasi (Edwards 2020: 116–17) and Helong (Balle 2017b). In several cases where the reduplicant might appear to be internal, it is due to the presence of historical prefixes. For example, Tetun *krakat* 'angry; wild' reduplicates as *kr**a**rakat* (van Klinken 1999: 79); the initial segment does not participate in the reduplication because it is a (partially fossilized) derivational prefix *k-* (cf., Tetun *ha-rakat-an* 'to get angry').

The examples in the preceding paragraph illustrate the most common shapes for a reduplicant in the region, namely CV, CVC, and CVCV, even though the rules for determining the reduplicant's shape may be complex. A few rarer copying patterns are attested. In Kola the initial consonant of the base is never copied, only the coda consonant either with or without a vowel (e.g. *nar* 'long' > *ar~nar*, *da-talah* '3PL-sit' > *da-l~'talah*, Takata and Takata 1992: 45). Dobel only copies a single segment, the initial C of the base (Hughes 2000: 167).[6] Luang allows copying of CCVC on bases with initial consonant cluster (e.g. *pleta* 'quickly' > *plet~pleta*, Taber and Taber 2015: 29). A fixed segment /a/ in the reduplicant, typically in combination with a copied consonant, is found sporadically throughout the region, including in Tugun (e.g. *hopan* 'to order' > *ha~hopan* 'request'), Fordata (e.g. *folat* 'to close' > *fal~folat* 'door'), Kola, and Tetun.

Many languages in Timor and Southwest Maluku have more than one reduplication type, with different functions associated with each. Leti, for instance, has CV- and CVCV-reduplication (van Engelenhoven 2004: 102). Luang has C(C)VC-reduplication and full reduplication (Taber and Taber 2015: 28–9). Naueti has CV- and full reduplication (Veloso 2016: 31–3). Dadu'a has CV- and CVCV-reduplication (Penn 2006: 41–2). Tetun has reduplication with a generalized vowel *Ca-* next to CVCV-reduplication (van Klinken 1999: 44). Helong has distinct CV-initial (word based) and CV-internal (foot based) reduplication (Balle 2017a: 95–6). In the following section, we discuss the functions of reduplication.

#### 35.3.3.2 *Function*

Reduplication is sporadically but widely associated with iconically motivated meanings involving plurality (e.g. Kei *manut* 'bird' > *man~manut* 'poultry', Geurtjens 1921: 71; Luang *leta* 'village' > *leta~leta* 'villages', Taber and Taber 2015: 29; Tugun *haru* 'shirt' > *haru~haru* 'shirts', Hinton 1991: 39; Dadu'a *seluk* '(an)other' > *selu~seluk* 'others', Penn 2006: 41) and intensity (e.g. Naueti *ita* 'black' > *ita~ita* 'very black, dark', Veloso 2016: 33; Idate *waʔik* 'much' > *wa~waʔik* 'very

[5] West Tarangan roots shaped CVCV(C) are reduplicated by copying the initial CVCV (e.g. *da-kɛru* '3PL-scrape' > *da-kɛru~kɛru*, *i-tubuk* '3SG-punch' > *i-tubu~tubuk*).

[6] Jock Hughes (p.c.) says this is true of the Koijabi variety of Dobel. He suggests that this is a reduction of earlier CV that can still be observed in other Dobel dialects (cf. Hughes 2000: 167 fn 49).

much', Alcantara 2015: 112; Dadu'a *lala* 'good' > *la~lala* 'really good', Penn 2006: 41), or repetition (e.g. Naueti *muni* 'kiss' > *muni~muni* 'kiss repeatedly', Veloso 2016: 33; Helong *ninu* 'drink' > *ni~ninu* 'drink repeatedly, continuously, habitually', Balle 2017a: 72–4). The last of these kinds of iconic reduplication is often described as shades of imperfective aspect. For example: Roma "durative", Steven 1991: 83; Leti "atelic", van Engelenhoven 2004: 194–7; Luang "iterative", Taber and Taber 2015: 75; Selaru "iterative", Coward 2005: 121; Batuley "progressive" and "iterative", Daigle 2015: 242, and some dialects of West Tarangan "progressive" aspect, Nivens 1993: 378.

Iconically motivated forms of reduplication are never grammatically required and, where frequency statements exist, are often observed to be only occasionally used. For example, Carpenter (1996: 110) writes of Wetan: "[a]lthough de Josselin de Jong provides examples of verb reduplication to indicate iterative and durative aspect, emphasis, and plurality, in the texts the incidence of all of these is actually quite low". In eastern Timor languages such as Idate, Dadu'a, and Naueti, iconic forms of reduplication are the main type reported and here we also find relatively little reliance on reduplication.

In non-iconic uses, reduplication is frequently described as having derivational functions. The most widespread derivational function is for deriving nouns from verbs. South Maluku examples include: Roma *kudi* 'crush' > *kud~k<j>udi* 'mortar' (Steven 1991: 85); Leti *sapu* 'sweep' > *sap~s<u̯>apu* 'broom' (van Engelenhoven 2004: 140); Selaru *lakut* 'to walk' > *lak~lakut* 'gait' (Coward and Coward 2000: 44); Yamdena *bare* 'to swell' > *ba~bare* 'swelling' (Drabbe 1926b: 21); Kola *rein* 'clever' > *ra~rein* 'cleverness' (Takata 1992: 64), and Kei *suban* 'to swear' > *sub~suban* 'oath' (Geurtjens 1921: 71). In Timor, derivational reduplication is typically combined with a suffixal morpheme: Termanu with *-k*: *soda* 'to sing' > *so~soda-k* 'song' (Jonker 1915: 199–201); Tetun, often with *-n* or *-k*: *fofe* 'to paddle' > *fa~fofe-n* 'paddle', but not always (*fiar* 'believe' > *fa~fiar* 'faith', van Klinken 1999: 78–81); Waima'a with *-n*: *$k^h$aa* 'to eat' > *$k^h$a~$k^h$aa-n* 'food' (Bowden et al. n.d.: 10–11).

In southern Maluku languages, reduplication is often also described as deriving adjectives and adverbs from verbs and, less commonly, nouns. An example is Kei where reduplication is said to derive adjectives from verbs, for example, *ro~roor* 'roasted' < *roor* 'to roast', *wat~watun* 'opened' < *watun* 'to open' (Geurtjens 1921: 72). Given that it is doubtful a distinct adjectival class exists for most languages in the region, it is debatable whether this is truly a derivational process. Arguably, this kind of reduplication could be seen as the first stage in the grammaticalization of what is a wider, more thoroughgoing grammatical device used in other languages of southern Maluku to indicate syntactic dependency on another constituent (for more on this, see Carpenter 1996). The use of reduplication to mark dependency to a noun (i.e. attribution of verbal/nominal modifiers and relative clauses) in southern Maluku is discussed extensively in §35.4.6.2–§35.4.6.3. Reduplication marking dependency to a verb (i.e. adverbial use), is found in languages from Wetar to Aru. An example from Tugun is provided in (4). Outside this southern Maluku region 'adverbial' notions are denoted either by dedicated lexemes or by serial verbs.

Tugun reduplicative dependency to a verb
(4) *n-a* *ga~gale*
3SG-eat REDUP~stand
'He's eating standing up.' (Hinton 1991: 132)

The use of reduplication as an obligatory device to form syntactic dependents is a unique and striking feature of languages in southern Maluku.

### 35.3.4 Metathesis

Metathesis is a common synchronic phenomenon in the languages of the Timor-SMaluku area. Although it is in itself a phonological process, it plays an important part in the morphosyntax of these languages, since wherever it occurs, it is not solely phonologically motivated, but also depends on grammatical context in the widest sense.

Two types of metathesis are observed. *Internal* metathesis occurs within a morpheme and results in many words appearing in two phonetic shapes which are distinguished by the order of phonemes in the final syllable (e.g. Amarasi *fatu* ~ *faut*; Leti *kapal* ~ *kapla* 'ship'). *External* metathesis operates across morpheme boundaries in syntactically tight constructions and causes the final high vowel of a morpheme to swap its place with the initial consonant of a following word or clitic (e.g. Leti *sivi* 'chicken' + *ternu* 'egg' > *siv-ti̯ernu* 'chicken's egg').

On Timor, only internal metathesis occurs, while in southeastern Maluku, there is only external metathesis. In Southwest Maluku, both types are found. In both areas, metathesis has a high functional load, with many bound and free morphemes having an unmetathesized and a metathesized form.

Where internal metathesis occurs, there is much variation among individual languages concerning which among the two forms of a word is marked or unmarked. For consistency, the terms 'unmetathesized' and 'metathesized' will be used here from an etymological viewpoint. Thus, the form that represents the historically original segment order will be called *unmetathesized*, regardless of its synchronic markedness. For example, the Amarasi pair *fatu* ~ *faut* goes back to

PMP *batu; consequently, *fatu* is unmetathesized, while *faut* is metathesized.

#### 35.3.4.1 *Internal metathesis*

In the Timor area, the basic formula for internal metathesis is $\mathrm{CVC}_{\alpha}\mathrm{V}_{\beta}$(C) (unmetathesized) vs. $\mathrm{CVV}_{\beta}\mathrm{C}_{\alpha}$(C) (metathesized). The outcome of metathesis shows some variation depending on language, especially with the final consonant, which is often dropped, or with the second member of the vowel sequence, which may undergo total or partial assimilation. Table 35.10 give examples of unmetathesized and metathesized forms of words in Amarasi (Kotos dialect, Edwards 2020: 159).[7]

**Table 35.10** Unmetathesized and metathesized forms in Amarasi

| | Unmetathesized | Metathesized | |
|---|---|---|---|
| 'stone' | *fatu* | *faut* | |
| 'house' | *ume* | *uim* | height assimilation |
| 'five' | *nima* | *niim* | total assimilation |
| 'animal' | *muʔit* | *muiʔ* | loss of final C |

Other languages on Timor that display the same type of internal metathesis are Helong, which is an immediate neighbour of Amarasi (and other Meto languages), and Mambae, which is not spoken in the direct vicinity of other metathesizing languages. Helong largely agrees with Meto, and also shows the same width of dialectal variation with regards to vowel assimilation and the treatment of final consonants (for details, see Steinhauer 1996: 471–8; Balle 2017a: 91–8; Edwards 2020: 68–75). In Mambae, only vowel-final words metathesize (Edwards 2020: 60).

In the Southwest Maluku languages Leti, Luang, Roma, and Serua, internal metathesis is found with words ending in $\text{-CV}_{\alpha}\text{C}_{\beta}$ ~ $\text{-CC}_{\beta}\text{V}_{\alpha}$ (e.g. Leti *terun* ~ *ternu* 'egg'). Historically, the consonant-final form -CVC is original, while -CCV has arisen through metathesis. In Leti, the process is fully active for all word classes. The citation form always ends in -CCV, with the CVC-form occuring in certain morphological contexts if followed by another morpheme beginning in a single consonant: Leti *llarna* 'fly' + *məta* 'blue/green' > *llaran-məta* 'house fly'. In Luang, this alternation only occurs with verbs (*n-ernu* ~ *n-erun* '(s)he descends'), while nouns invariantly have the CCV-form (e.g. Luang *ternu* 'egg'). The opposite is observed in Roma (Steven 1991: 63–9): here, only nouns display metathesis (*hurta* ~ *hurat* 'letter', while verbs do not alternate and only occur in the CVC-form (*-hurat* 'to write'). Metathesis in nouns is also reported for Serua (*letna* ~ *letan* 'forest'; van Engelenhoven 2003: 53).

#### 35.3.4.2 *External metathesis*

External metathesis is found in Leti, Luang, Roma, and Southeast Babar in Southwest Maluku (van Engelenhoven 2004: 89–92; Taber and Taber 2015: 24–7; Steven 1991: 93–7; Steinhauer 2009: 97), and further to the east in Selaru, Yamdena, and Fordata (Coward 2005: 29; Mettler and Mettler 1990: 65–6; Marshall 2000: 206). It operates when a word ending in a high vowel (or a glide in Southeast Babar and Selaru) combines with a word or clitic beginning with a single initial consonant. The high vowel/glide is then metathesized into the following morpheme as a non-syllabic vowel or glide:

| (5) | Leti | ***asu*** 'dog' + *mata* 'eye' | > *as m**u̯**ata* 'dog's eye' |
|---|---|---|---|
| | SE Babar | *lmox**j*** '3SG.die' + *tel* 'PFV' | > *lmox-t**j**el* '(s)he has died' |
| | Selaru | *as*$^{w}$ 'dog' + *-ke* 'definite' | > *ask*$^{w}$*e* 'the dog' |
| | Yamdena | ***ku***- '1SG' + *ti* 'to go' | > *kt**w**i* 'I go' |

Often, there are phonotactic constraints against the occurrence of a non-syllabic high vowel or glide in the target syllable. In this case, there is apocope instead of external metathesis:

| (6) | Leti | ***asu*** 'dog' + *nisa* 'tooth' | > *as nisa* 'dog's tooth' |
|---|---|---|---|
| | Yamdena | *buti* 'ten' + *lim* 'five' | > *butlim* 'fifty' |

Evidence from Leti, Luang, and Yamdena shows that historically, high-vowel metathesis also operated word-internally. These languages have a nominalizing infix <ni̯> which goes back to earlier *<in>, for example, Leti *v<ni̯>alsa* 'answer, retaliation' from *b<in>aləs (from *valsa* 'to answer, retaliate' < *baləs). Here, the antepenultimate vowel *i has shifted into the following syllable in the same way as observed with external metathesis across word boundaries.

#### 35.3.4.3 *The function of metathesis*

Metathesis is a morphological tool for marking phrasal constituency and grammatical function. Occurrence or lack of metathesis can determine the function of a word in a phrase. For instance, in the Meto construction NOUN + ADJECTIVE, the function of the adjective is determined by the shape

[7] No metathesis takes place in Amarasi with words of the shape CVVC, CVVCV, CVVCVC. When a metathesized form is required, then a truncated form of the word occurs: CVV, CVVC, CVVC (e.g. *kaut* → *kau* 'papaya', *naena* → *naen* '(s)he runs', *kaunaʔ* → *kaun* 'snake').

of the noun: if the noun is metathesized, the adjective is a modifier to the noun (e.g. *faut koʔu* (stone.METATHESIS big) 'big stone'), if the noun is unmetathesized, the adjective is a predicate (e.g. *fatu koʔu* (stone big) 'stones are big'). In Leti, lack of metathesis is an allomorph of the 'indexer' enclitic *=e*.[8] This enclitic is only visible with words ending in *-a* (*kuda* 'horse' + *=e* > *kude*). With words ending in a high vowel, the presence of the clitic is manifested only indirectly by the lack of metathesis even in environments where metathesis occurs per default. For example, *toli* 'to see' can undergo metathesis when followed by an object (*a-tu̯ol-ki̯aptɛɛnera* (1SG-see captains) 'I (kind of) see the captains'), but is not metathesized when it takes an indexer (*a-tu̯oli kaptɛɛnera* (1SG-see:DEX captains) 'I see the captains'). In Southern Mambae, deverbal nouns and adjectives can be formed by obligatory unmetathesis, for example, *mori~moir* 'to live' > *mori* 'life', *domi~doim* 'to love' > *domi* 'love (n.)' (Fogaça 2017: 136).

The extent of metathesis is further dependent on word class. Next to full restrictions on certain word classes as in Luang or Roma, there are also word class-related preferences. In Meto, nominals are by default unmetathesized (including in their citation form), while the metathesized form is marked; for all other word classes, the metathesized form is the unmarked default form. Table 35.11 lists the preferences for internal metathesis for nouns and verbs in selected languages.

**Table 35.11** Markedness of metathesized and unmetathesized nouns and verbs

| | | **Unmetathesized** | **Metathesized** |
|---|---|---|---|
| | | CVCV | CVVC |
| **Meto** | NOUN | unmarked | marked |
| | VERB | marked | unmarked |
| **Mambae** | NOUN | marked/derived | unmarked |
| | VERB | marked | unmarked |
| | | **Unmetathesized** | **Metathesized** |
| | | CVCVC | CVCCV |
| **Leti** | NOUN | marked | unmarked |
| | VERB | marked | unmarked |
| **Luang** | NOUN | — | invariant |
| | VERB | marked | unmarked |
| **Roma** | NOUN | marked | unmarked |
| | VERB | invariant | — |

### 35.3.4.4 *The origin of metathesis*

The emergence of internal metathesis in the Timor area and high vowel metathesis in the southern Maluku area can be explained as a result of regressive and progressive co-articulation of unstressed vowels into the neighbouring syllable (Edwards 2020: 82). In Timor-type metathesis, the unstressed vowel first spread into the preceding syllable as a non-syllabic vowel [V̯], and was then lost in its original position:

(7) ˈCVC$_{\alpha}$**V**$_{\beta}$(C) > ˈCV**V̯**$_{\beta}$C$_{\alpha}$**V**$_{\beta}$(C) > ˈCV**V**$_{\beta}$C$_{\alpha}$(C)
(e.g. Amarasi *ˈfat**u*** > *ˈ*fa**u̯**t**u*** > *ˈfa**u**t* 'stone')

The intermediate stage of regressive co-articulation without vowel loss is found in Ro'is Amarasi (e.g. *hu͡**i**nik* 'turmeric') (cf. Kotos Amarasi *hunik*).

High-vowel external metathesis in southern Maluku operates in the opposite direction: here, the unstressed vowel moved into the following syllable and then underwent apocope in its original position:

(8) ˈCVC**V**$_{\alpha}$ + C$_{\beta}$VC- > ˈCVC**V**$_{\alpha}$ + C$_{\beta}$**V̯**$_{\alpha}$VC- > ˈCVC + C$_{\beta}$**V̯**$_{\alpha}$VC-
(e.g., Leti *as**u** mata* > **as**u** m**u̯**ata* > *as m**u̯**ata* 'dog's eye')

The intermediate stage is still visible in Wetan where apocope is optional: *iw**i** + terni* > *iw**i** t**i**erni* 'chicken's egg' (cf. Leti *siv-ti̯ernu*).

Southwest Maluku internal CVC/CCV-metathesis has a different but related origin. Here, an original unstressed final syllable -CVC added an echo vowel before a pause and before consonant clusters, with subsequent loss of the unstressed vowel (Edwards 2020: 79):

(9) a. -C**V**$_{\alpha}$C$_{\beta}$# > -C**V**$_{\alpha}$C$_{\beta}$**V**$_{\alpha}$# > -CC$_{\beta}$**V**$_{\alpha}$#
or
b. -C**V**$_{\alpha}$C$_{\beta}$ + CC- > -C**V**$_{\alpha}$C$_{\beta}$**V**$_{\alpha}$ + CC- > -CC$_{\beta}$**V**$_{\alpha}$ + CC-
(e.g. Leti ˈ*ter**u**n* > *ˈ*ter**u**n**u*** > ˈ*tern**u*** 'egg')

The original shape of the syllable remained unchanged phrase-internally before a single consonant.

(10) -C**V**$_{\alpha}$C$_{\beta}$ + CV- > -C**V**$_{\alpha}$C$_{\beta}$ + CV-

This resulted in the synchronic CVC/CCV-alternation found in Leti, Luang, Wetan, Roma, and Serua.

As we can see, the occurrence of metathesis in the Timor-SMaluku area is the result of natural phonological processes. Yet, metathesis is extremely rare in MPSEA languages. One

[8] The indexer enclitic is a pervasive feature of Leti. Its presence usually indicates certainty about the identity of a referent or event (Engelenhoven 2004: 159–61).

case of external metathesis is found in the Cendrawasih Bay languages, where metathesis is however restricted to the second and third person singular subject agreement markers (Gasser 2015). The widespread occurrence of metathesis in the Timor-SMaluku area thus calls for an explanation and further study.

## 35.4 Noun phrases and their elements

### 35.4.1 NP word order

Within the noun phrase, the default order of elements is Noun–Attribute–Numeral–Demonstrative. Relative clauses, numeral classifiers, and plural words also appear between the noun and demonstrative. The typical position of a nominal possessor is preceding the head noun. The small number of variations on these orders are mentioned where they exist in the following sections.

### 35.4.2 Demonstratives

Adnominal demonstrative systems are varied in the Timor-SMaluku area. A few languages make a two-way (e.g. Kemak *nua* 'this' and *nogo* 'that', Schapper fieldnotes) or three-way (e.g. Selaru *ne* 'this', *desj* 'that', *so* 'that over there (out of sight)') distinction in their demonstrative systems. The most common pattern is a four-way distinction, but the semantics of the systems do not appear very similar based on the available descriptions, particularly for the fourth demonstrative. Compare the following descriptions: Amarasi *=ii* is used for entities close to first person, *=ana* for entities close to the second person, *=ee* for entities close to third person, and *=aa* for entities distal to all persons (Edwards 2020: 264); Naueti: *eti* is used for entities close to the speaker, *ini* for entities close to the addressee, *eto* for entities distal to speaker and addressee, and *emo* for entities that are not present in the speech situation and are, by extension, unknown to the addressee (Veloso 2016: 49); Dobel: *naj/wa* is used for entities close to the speaker, *ne/re* for entities at a middle distance or close to the addressee, *nno* for entities distal to speaker and addressee, and *niʔa/riʔa* for entities that are in focus, but not visible (Hughes 2000: 140).

In some languages, demonstratives must also agree with features of the head noun. A few languages have demonstratives marked for number (e.g. Luang *di* 'PROX.SG', *ri* 'PROX.PL', *de* 'DIST.SG', *re* 'DIST.PL', Taber and Taber 2015: 89). In the languages of Aru, demonstratives are marked for number and grammatical gender. Batuley has a four-way demonstrative system distinguishing singular and plural forms, with additional forms for animate and inanimate in the singular. The result is a total of twelve demonstratives (Table 35.12). Plural marking of Batuley demonstratives appears to go back to a prefix *di-*, which has now become fused with the demonstrative root. Plural marking morphemes that only attach to demonstratives are found in several languages of the region, for example, Mambae *-gar* (Hull 2001b: 13) and Fordata *av-* (Marshall n.d.).

**Table 35.12** Batuley demonstratives (Daigle 2015: 112)

| | Singular | | Plural |
|---|---|---|---|
| | INANIMATE | ANIMATE | |
| Proximal | *onen* | *nanen* | *dini* |
| Medial | *enon* | *nenon* | *dinon* |
| Distal | *eregen* | *neregen* | *dieregen* |
| Non-visible | *er* | *ner* | *dir* |

Finally, a recurrent feature of demonstratives in eastern Timor languages is that they can appear suffixed to the numeral 'one' (e.g. Kemak *sia-nua* 'this one', *sia-nogo* 'that one', Schapper fieldnotes). These demonstratives are focused, functioning to highlight a specific referent.

### 35.4.3 Plural marking

Nouns are not obligatorily marked for number in MPSEA languages, but nominal plurality can be optionally marked by means of a free form expressing plural in the NP or an enclitic to the NP. We already saw in the previous section that languages in southern Maluku frequently have demonstratives that are marked for number. Beyond these, there are several common means of plural marking to be observed across the region. Many languages have more than one plural marking strategy; the availability of different strategies typically has to do with properties such as animacy, definiteness, and individuation.

Plural-marking enclitics with similar forms are found from Southwest Maluku (e.g. Leti *=ra*, Engelenhoven 2004: 115–16; Serua *=rV*, Chlenov and Chlenova 2004) to Tanimbar (Selaru *=(a)re*, Coward 2005: 39–40); Yamdena *=ar*, Drabbe

1926a: 9; Fordata *=ra*, Marshall 2000: 198). Amarasi in western Timor has an unrelated plural-marking enclitic showing complex patterns of conditioned allomorphy (Edwards 2020: 234). In the Southwest Maluku–Tanimbar languages, enclitic plural markers attach to the right of an NP demonstrative, as for example in Kisar in (11a), while in Amarasi the plural enclitic is to the left of the demonstrative (11b).

Position of plural enclitics with respect to determiners

(11) a. Kisar
*tatan=en=**he***
child=DEM=PL
'the children' (Christensen and Christensen n.d.)

b. Amarasi
*aanh=**ein**=aa*
child=PL=DEM
'the children' (Edwards 2020: 247)

Reduplication as a means to mark plurality is attested in several languages of southern Maluku. Leti uses its enclitic plural for NPs with human referents, and full reduplication of nouns for signalling plurality of non-human referents (Engelenhoven 2004: 116). In Luang full reduplication is used with nouns of all types "indicating plurality but a vagueness of exact number" (Taber and Taber 2015: 51). See examples in §35.5.3.2.

In the languages of eastern Timor and Wetar, plurality can be optionally indicated by means of a third person pronoun alongside a head noun in the NP, for example, Naueti *phulitiku sira* politican 3PL 'the politicians' (Veloso 2016: 42, see also Tetun *sira*, van Klinken 1999: 124; Dadu'a *sia*, Penn 2006: 51; Tugun *hira*, Hinton 1991: 50; Mambae *sɛr*, Hull 2003a: 11; Kemak *roo*, Schapper fieldnotes). This is a widespread strategy for marking plurality across MPSEA languages. Use of such a plural-marking pronoun is often restricted to humans or higher animates and may bear a range of additional semantic connotations beyond simple plurality, including definiteness and topicality.

Across the languages of Timor, it is common for lexical nouns meaning 'name' and a reduplicated form of 'face' to be used in adnominal constructions denoting plurality in which the group of referents has internal diversity. This is illustrated for Tetun and Amarasi in eastern and western Timor respectively in (12) and (13).

Tetun

(12) a. ***naran*** *bibi*
name goat
'various sorts of goats'

b. *bibi* ***oiʔ~oik***
goat REDUP~face
'various goats, all sorts of goat'
(Schapper fieldnotes)

Amarasi

(13) a. *areʔ* ***kana-n*** *bibi*
every name-3SG goat
'various sorts of goats'

b. *bibi* ***humaʔ~humaʔ***
goat REDUP~face
'various goats, all sorts of goats'
(Charles Grimes p.c.)

## 35.4.4 Numerals and classifiers

### 35.4.4.1 *Numeral inflection*

A striking feature of several languages from eastern Timor to Aru is the presence of obligatory inflectional morphology on numerals used in referential counting. Here we do not refer to morphology that frequently occurs on numerals to derive frequentatives or group numerals (e.g. Fordata *lima* 'five' > *fa-lima* 'five times' and *lam~lima-n* 'in fives'), but rather inflectional morphology that is required for the numeral to be well formed when used attributively. Numeral inflection of the type described here is notably absent from western and central Timor, but is known in a few languages of Cenderawasih Bay (see Gasser, Arnold, and Kamholz, this volume, §37.4.2).

The most widely attested morphological pattern—extending from eastern Timor to Babar and Tanimbar—is a single, semantically empty prefix that occurs on the basic numerals 'two' through 'nine'. Blust (2013a: 284–5) describes such phenomena as "onset runs", implying that they are fixed, analogy motivated phonological material. However, for the languages in this region where data is sufficient, these initial elements on numerals are demonstrably separable prefixes. For example, in Tugun, basic numerals above one are always prefixed with *fa-* when used attributively (e.g. *leo matan* ***fa-telu*** sun eye AGR-three 'three days'), but this is dropped where the numeral attaches to another morpheme, such as a numeral base (e.g. *fele-**telu*** 10-3 'thirty') or a pronoun (*am-**telu*** 1PL.EXCL-three 'we three'). Similar behaviour is evident with Hresuk *he-* (Boarccaech 2013), Dadu'a *wa-* (Penn 2006: 48–50), Kisar *wo-* (Christensen n.d.), Leti *vo-* (van Engelenhoven 2004: 163–5), and Fordata *i-* (Marshall n.d.), to name a few.

A few languages have a more complicated pattern involving two contrasting numeral prefixes triggered by different properties of the nominal referent. In Waima'a (and its sister language Naueti), a numeral takes a prefix that must agree with the head noun for human/non-human (14). In Selaru, a numeral has different agreement forms depending on the specificity of the NP (15). But like the languages discussed above this agreement is limited to basic numerals between 'two' and 'nine'.

Waima'a numeral agreement

(14) a. HUMAN
*anu-ata* ***wuo**-hitu*
woman HUM-seven
'seven women'

b. NONHUMAN
*kumu* ***kai**-hitu*
pigeon NHUM-seven
'seven pigeons'
(Bowden et al. n.d.)

Selaru numeral agreement

(15) a. SPECIFIC
*aro* ***de**-ru* *desike*
boat SPEC-two DEM
'those two boats'

b. NONSPECIFIC
*aro* ***ena**-ru*
boat NSPEC-two
'two boats'
(Coward 2005: 45)

Schapper (2020a: 413) suggests that such agreement markers on numerals likely represent grammaticalizations of semantically bleached numeral classifiers.

Aru languages display a different pattern of numeral agreement from languages elsewhere in the region. In Aru attributive numerals from 'one' to 'nine' are marked by agreement suffixes, similar or identical in form to the agreement suffixes on stative verbs (compare: Ujir *rua-da* two-1PL.INCL 'we two' and *dʒami-da* quick-1PL.INCL 'we are quick'). Numerals quantifying nouns with inanimate referents do not inflect, while numerals quantifying nouns with animate referents take agreement suffixes. This pattern is illustrated in (16) on the basis of Ujir. With *set* 'one', the suffix *-na* is used for animate agreement, while on other numerals *-si* is used.

Ujir numeral agreement

(16) a. INANIMATE
*tul* *set*
bone one
'one bone'

b. ANIMATE
*woitau* *set-**na***
bird one-3SG.AN
'one bird'

c. INANIMATE
*tul* *dubu*
bone six
'six bones'

d. ANIMATE
*woitau* *dubu-**si***
bird six-3PL.AN
'six birds' (Schapper fieldnotes)

### 35.4.4.2 *Numeral classifiers*

In contrast to MPSEA languages to the west, some of which have quite large inventories of sortal numeral classifiers, the languages of this region have very few, if any, numeral classifiers. Where they do exist, they appear to have a marginal status, since they are rarely used and are seemingly never obligatory. Numeral classifiers are not mentioned in the descriptions of Amarasi (Edwards 2020), Leti (Engelenhoven 2004), Selaru (Coward 2005), Yamdena (Drabbe 1926b) and are explicitly noted to be as absent for Galolen (Hull 2003a: 18). Descriptions of many languages record a small number of numeral classifiers, for example, one in Mambae (Hull 2001b: 15), two in Dadu'a (Penn 2006: 50), three in Tugun (Hinton 1991: 65), six in Tetun Fehan (van Klinken 1999: 105) and Dobel (Hughes 2000: 158). In all these languages, the classifier occurs between the head noun and the numeral (17).

(17) a. Dadu'a
*ana-barane* ***lolo*** *wa-rua*
child-male TRUNK:CLF AGR-two
'two sons' (Penn 2006: 50)

b. Dobel
*nor* ***fatin*** *ro*
coconut BODY:CLF two
'two coconut trees' (Hughes 2000: 158)

The only language with more than a handful of numeral classifiers is Kei in the north of the region, with around two dozen sortal numeral classifiers listed in Geurtjens (1921: 14–16).

## 35.4.5 Grammatical gender and animacy contrasts

The languages of Aru all display a grammatical gender contrast in which nouns belonging to the animate and inanimate classes trigger different agreement forms on verbs, numerals, and demonstratives. Gender assignment is not entirely semantic: whilst all entities that are biologically animate belong to the animate gender, many nouns denoting inanimate reference belong to the animate class (Schapper 2015b; Daigle 2015: 101–11). This pattern is unusual in Timor-SMaluku but is more common in languages of Central Maluku and further north (Schapper 2010b).

Purely semantic animacy contrasts are known for a handful of other languages in Timor-SMaluku. Kawaimina languages have a human/nonhuman contrast marked by prefixes on numerals (see §35.4.4.1). In Selaru, an animate/inanimate distinction is indexed by verb prefixes, with *i-* '3SG.AN' and *ra-* '3PL.AN' contrasting with *ki-* '3.INAN'. With non-verbal predicates, animates are coindexed with an enclitic =*i*, while inanimates are unmarked.[9]

## 35.4.6 Attributes and relative clauses

Simple verbal and nominal attributes are often unmarked in the languages of Timor; only word order signals the relationship between head noun and attribute. For example, in Tokodede, as in other languages in the region, an attribute always follows the head noun it modifies. Additionally, in

[9] Coward (2005: 67) notes that *sew* 'sun' is grammatically animate, but no other nouns with inanimate referents seem to be grammatically animate in Selaru.

Tokodede there is no morph that signals the head–attribute relationship.

Tokodede
(18) a. Verbal attribute
*malae* **buti**
foreigner white
'white foreigner'

b. Nominal attribute
*sao* **mane**
friend man
'male friend'
(Schapper fieldnotes)

In many other languages in Timor-SMaluku, however, attributes are morphologically marked, either obligatorily or optionally. In this section, we deal with the various non-possessive attribute constructions, including relative clauses, which involve explicit morphological marking (see §35.4.7). Languages in the region exhibit several typologically unusual patterns in this domain. We focus on these in the following sections.

#### 35.4.6.1 *Optional possessive marking of attributes*

Multiple languages in eastern Timor have "possessive-like attribute constructions", similar to those found in many Oceanic languages (Ross 1998). These are marked attribute constructions which display the typologically unusual phenomenon of having adjectival attributes encoded in the same way as possessions. That is, the noun denoting the referent of the NP acts as if it were a possessor, while the attribute looks as if it were a possessed noun. Thus, in Welaun, the basic attribute construction for simple adjectival attributes has the attribute following the head noun with no morpheme marking the relationship (19a). A second, more marked, attribute construction includes the third person possessive marker *-aan* '3.POSS' on the attribute (19b), paralleling the encoding of a possessed noun in an adnominal possessive construction (19c). Such constructions are known in Naueti (Veloso 2016: 52–4), Waima'a (Bowden et al. n.d.), Kemak, and Idate (Schapper 2020a: 408–9).

Welaun
(19) a. *taku naruk*
bean long
'long beans'

b. *taku naruk-aan*
bean long-3.POSS
'beans which are long' (Edwards 2019: 40)

c. *mota hasan-aan*
river cheek-3.POSS
'branch of a river' (lit. cheek of a river)
(da Silva 2012: 133)

At present, possessive-like attribute constructions are poorly described in the Timorese languages, but cross-linguistic evidence suggests that they mark selective focus, that is, they selectively identify the referent from among a set on the basis of its possessive-marked attribute, as illustrated by the difference between (19a) and (19b) above (see Schapper, this volume, §22.4, for more on this feature).

#### 35.4.6.2 *Reduplicative attributes*

Across the languages of southern Maluku from Wetar to Kei and Aru, verbs are obligatorily partially reduplicated when used attributively.[10] Languages across this region, however, differ in their treatment of (non-possessor) attributive nouns.

In Tugun a non-reduplicated verb is interpreted predicatively (20a), while a reduplicated one is attributive (20b). Attributive nouns are not reduplicated in Tugun (Hinton 1991: 53–4).

Tugun
(20) a. Predicative – no reduplication
*otur ge* ***metʃu***
mountain DEM tall
'This mountain is tall.'

b. Attributive – reduplication
*otur* ***ma~metʃu***
mountain REDUP~tall
'tall mountain' (Hinton 1991: 56)

In Leti, both verbs and nouns show partial reduplication when used attributively (21). This pattern is also found in nearby languages such as Wetan (Carpenter 1996), Roma (Burquest and Steven 1992 cited in Carpenter 1996) and in the languages of Aru, such as Dobel (Hughes 2000: 172–4) and Batuley (Daigle 2015: 129–31).

Leti
(21) a. Attributive verb
*asu la~lavna*
dog REDUP~big
'big dog'

b. Attributive noun
*sop uer~uera*
soup REDUP~water
'watery soup' (Aone van Engelenhoven p.c.)

Fordata has a different pattern again. Compare the phrases in (22). We see that both attributive verbs and nouns show partial reduplication, but nouns additionally have a third person possessive suffix marking their dependency to the head (cf. §35.4.6.1 on possessive marking of attributes).

10 The exception is Luang; based on Taber and Taber (2015), reduplication does not appear to have an attributive marking function.

Fordata

(22) a. Attributive verb

*ŋuur* ***ŋa~ŋiar***
sand REDUP~white
'white sand'

b. Attributive noun

*ia* ***sar****~sira-n*
fish REDUP~salt-3SG.POSS
'salted fish' (Marshall 2000: 225)

The difference in the treatment of nominal attributes in these languages probably has to do with the source of the attributive construction. In all these languages, the same pattern of partial reduplication that is used for attribution as described here is used for nominalization. In all likelihood, partial reduplication began as a nominalization strategy that then grammaticalized into an attribute-marking feature for verbs and then relative clauses (§35.4.3.6). In only some languages has this construction been further extended to attributive nouns.

#### 35.4.6.3 *Reduplicative relative clauses*

The pattern of reduplication of an attribute extends to the verbal predicates of relative clauses in some languages of SW Maluku and Aru that have attributive reduplication as described in the previous section. Languages with this feature differ with respect to whether they include an explicit relative clause marker and what arguments can be relativized with reduplication.

Reduplication as a relative marker is most widely employed in Tugun. Here the main verb of a relative clause is always reduplicated, no matter the argument that is relativized on (Hinton 1991: 57–60). The relative clause marker *naha* is optional following the nominal head (compare examples in (23)).

Tugun

(23) a. No relative clause marker

*lalaik eha* ***na~nai*** *Leti*
man INDEF REDUP~from Leti
'a man who was from Leti' (Hinton 1991: 58)

b. Relative clause marker

*ankoca eha* ***naha na~nai*** *leo*
captain INDEF REL REDUP~from sun
'a captain who was from the east' (Hinton 1991: 151)

In the languages of Aru, the use of a relative clause marker and reduplication of the main verb of the relative clause is obligatory for most arguments, see details of Kola (Takata 1992: 63), West Tarangan (Nivens 1993: 375–8), Batuley (Daigle 2015: 131–4). Dobel has a restriction on reduplication in relative clauses where relativization is on A. While relativization on S always triggers reduplication of the verb in the RC (24a), relativization on A does not trigger reduplication where P is expressed by free (pro)nominal elements (24b). However, where P is expressed by an enclitic, reduplication of the verb does occur with relativization on A (24c). This structure parallels that found in situations where P is relativized on; there is reduplication of the verb in the RC and a resumptive enclitic pronoun for P (24d).

Dobel

(24) a. Relativization on S – reduplication

*tamatu ne ʔa-****l~la*** *re*
person REL 3SG.AN-REDUP~run LOC
*ʔa-mul ti*
3SG.AN-return PFV
'The person who ran (away) has returned'

b. Relativization on A – no reduplication

*kʷojar ne ʔa-****ʔara*** *tamatu de re*
dog REL 3SG-bite person DEM LOC
*ʔa-kʷoj ti*
3SG-die PFV
'The dog that bit those people has died'

c. Relativization on A, with enclitic pronoun for P – reduplication

*kʷojar ne ʔa-****ʔ~ʔara****=je re*
dog REL 3SG-**REDUP**~bite=3PL LOC
*ʔa-kʷoj ti*
3SG-die PFV
'The dog that bit them has died'

d. Relativization on P, with enclitic resumptive pronoun – reduplication

*siʔa ne ʔa-****k~ka****=ni*
fish REL 3SG-REDUP~eat=3sg.ANIM
*loʔar=ni*
good=3SG.ANIM
'The fish which he is eating is good'
(Hughes 2000: 175–7)

Further south, Leti also uses partial reduplication of verbs to mark relativization, but only with arguments other than S/A (P in 25a and oblique in 25b). Where reduplication is used, no relative clause marker appears. When relativization is on S/A, there is no reduplication. The verb then takes the prefix *k(a)-* instead of a person agreement prefix, and there is a relative clause marker *ma(k)* (25c). Wetan follows the same pattern as Leti (Carpenter 1996).

Leti

(25) a. Relativization on P – reduplication

*vɛtra=e kɔkkɔi ra-**kdi̯o~dori**=la*
maize=DEX child:DEX 3PL-REDUP~steal=DIR
*pni̯ɛpan-ku*
garden-1SG.POSS
'the maize which the children stole from my garden' (van Engelenhoven and Williams-van Klinken 2005: 762)

b. Relativization on Obl – reduplication

*Nus=e n-**sə~səpal**=la=e*
island=DEX 3SG-REDUP~sail=DIR=DEX
*n-vava Malai=o*
3SG-carry.name Timor=IND
'The island he sails to is called Timor.' (van Engelenhoven 2004: 275)

c. Relativization on S/A – no reduplication

*kokkoi **mak** ta **ka**-mdud=mu̯aate=ra.*
kokkoi [mak ta ka-mdud~maata=e]=ra
child:DEX REL NEG REL-sleep~IPFV=DEX=PL
'the children who do not yet sleep'

The variety of structures found in Leti is echoed in its near relatives, Luang and Selaru discussed in the next section.

### 35.4.6.4 *Non-reduplicative relative clauses*

The majority pattern in Timor-SMaluku languages is for no reduplication of the verb of the RC. The languages do differ, however, in terms of the obligatoriness of a relative clause marker, the appearance of traces of the extracted constituent in the RC, and the relativization strategies used for S, A, and P.

The languages of Timor have the simplest relative clauses: a free relative clause marker follows the head noun and no trace of the relativized constituent is left in the RC. There is no difference between the structures used for S, A, or P. For example:

Dadu'a

(26) a. Relativization on S/A

*rare-obu isa **namee** Ø titi nii la*
land.owner one REL send 3SG go
*n-eni wawi*
3SG-wait pig
'a landowner who sent him to tend pigs . . .'

b. Relativization on P

*kuda sia **namee** ami Ø rouh*
horse PL REL 1PL.EXCL buy
'the horses which we bought' (Penn 2006: 81–3)

In Fordata and Yamdena, relative clauses are simply juxtaposed to the right of the head, or can optionally take a clause linking particle *ma* that appears between the head and relative clause (Drabbe 1926a: 30; 1926b: 43). Subject agreement is always retained in the relative clause, including subject relative clauses. In non-subject relative clauses, the coreferent of the head leaves an overt pronominal trace in the relative clause, as in the following example, where the object *i* in the relative clause *ko mu-fngal i* is coreferential to the head *tomwate*:

Yamdena

(27) a. Relativization on S/A

*tomwate **(ma)** maniap Ø n-ma nbal*
person REL yesterday 3SG-come also
'the man who was also here yesterday'

b. Relativization on P

*tomwate **(ma)** ko mu-f-gnal **i***
person REL 2SG 2SG-CAUS-wound 3SG
'the man whom you have injured' (Drabbe 1926b: 43–4)

Luang has an obligatory relative clause marker *maka* that follows the head noun of all relative clauses (28). Where an S/A is relativized on, a trace of the relativized noun is left in Luang relative clauses in the form of a prefix *k-*, replacing the normal subject agreement prefix on the verb. This structure parallels that found in Leti subject relativization, but lacks the reduplication in its other structures.

Luang

(28) a. Relativization on S/A

*hadi **maka** **k**-ala uli-a Lgona*
PRO REL REL-take before-OBJ Luang
'this one who went ahead of Luang'

b. Relativization on P

*maʔnu **maka** ira r-waʔal-nana*
bird REL 3PL 3PL-threw-ABIL
'the bird which they had knocked down' (Taber and Taber 2015: 119)

Selaru relative clause structures have several similarities to the Leti and Luang structures. When relativization is on S/A, we find a prefixal trace *ma-* replacing the agreement prefix on the verb (29a). Consistent with the pattern shown by other Tanimbar languages, however, there is no free relative clause marker in Selaru. When relativization occurs on P, the verb always takes a syllabic person agreement prefix (29b). Because this syllabic prefix normally occurs on roots with initial consonant clusters, the appearance of this prefix here suggests that historically a reduplicated C occurred on these roots.

Selaru

(29) a. Relativization on S/A

*Kw-naik* *nam* ***ma**-haw* *lwau-kw-ke*
1SG-pull.out thing REL-prick foot-1SG-ART
'I pulled out the thing which was pricking my foot'

b. Relativization on P

*hahj* *Nico* ***i**-tabahunw-ke* *lan=i*
pig Nico 3SG-kill-ART big=3SG
'The pig Nico killed is big.' (Coward 2005: 94, 99)

The replacement of the person agreement marker with a special prefix in S/A-relative clauses which occurs in Leti, Luang, and Selaru is also found in other MPSEA languages such as Bima (Jonker 1896: 67), Kambera (Klamer 1998: 318), and Wolio (Anceaux 1988: 25).

### 35.4.7 Adnominal possession

Most languages of the Timor-SMaluku region have suffixes encoding the possessor of an inalienable noun. This is also known as 'direct' possession and it contrasts with so-called 'indirect' possession where the possessor of an alienable noun is encoded by a free possessive marker preceding the possessed noun. This is illustrated with Kei in (30). Languages on and around eastern Timor which have lost the direct/indirect contrast and the associated direct possessive suffixes are discussed in §35.3.1.2.

Kei

(30) a. Direct (inalienable) possession

*jana-**m***
child-2SG
'your child'

b. Indirect (alienable) possession

***mu*** *kubaŋ*
2SG.POSS money
'your money' (Geurtjens 1924)

The broad parameters of variation in adnominal possessive typology in the MPSEA area, including that of Timor-SMaluku languages, are discussed in detail in Schapper and McConvell, this volume, chapter 48. Here we focus on some of the less frequently treated properties of adnominal possessive structures in Timor-SMaluku languages.

Many, but not all, languages in the region show some identity between free personal pronouns and free possessive markers. Table 35.13 gives examples of languages which have fully or partially distinct sets of free possessive markers; forms in parentheses are identical to free personal pronouns. In the Central Timor languages Tokodede and Kemak, there do not appear to be separate paradigms of personal pronouns and free possessive markers, but their close relative Welaun derives possessive forms by affixing *-n* to personal pronouns, for example, *haʔu-n kaʔa* 1SG-POSS sister-in-law 'my sister-in-law' (Edwards 2020: 39). In Waima'a, the distinction between personal pronouns and free possessive markers appears to be weakening. In the Waima'a corpus, there is a marginal construction in which a personal pronoun can be used to encode a possessor in combination with the third person possessive suffix appearing on the possessed noun (e.g. ***kamu*** *ruo kele-**n*** 2PL two foot-3.POSS 'your (DU) feet').

Neither free nor bound possessive markers are described here as pronominal, because—although referential—they do not typically block other free nominal or pronominal elements expressing the possessor. In other words, possessive markers are referential agreement markers. For example, while a possessive suffix is sufficient to express the possessor of *jama-* 'father' in (31a), Geurtjen's (1924) Kei texts attest an array of combinations of free forms with the same person number specification, both preposed (31b)–(31d) and postposed (31e)–(31f), that can co-occur with the inalienable possessive suffix. These are marked structures, but they are by no means infrequent in the Kei data.

Kei

(31) a. *jama-**b***
father-1PL.EXCL
'our father'

b. ***am*** *jama-**b***
1PL.EXCL father-1PL.EXCL
'our father'

c. ***mam*** *jama-**b***
1PL.EXCL.POSS father-1PL.EXCL
'our father'

d. ***am*** ***mam*** *jama-**b***
1PL.EXCL 1PL.EXCL.POSS father-1PL.EXCL
'our father'

e. *jama-**b*** ***am***
father-1PL.EXCL 1PL.EXCL
'our father'

f. *jama-**b*** ***mam***
father-1PL.EXCL 1PL.EXCL.POSS
'our father' (Geurtjens 1924)

In §35.4.1, it was stated that the unmarked ordering of elements in an adnominal possessive construction sees the possessor precede the possessed noun. The Kei constructions in (31e)–(31f) show that marked constructions where the possessor is postposed to the possessed noun are also found. Marked postposed possessive structures have the greatest concentration in the languages of eastern Timor. Schapper and McConvell (this volume, §48.2) illustrate a

**Table 35.13** Free possessive markers

| | Kei | Yamdena | Serua | Kisar | Dobel | Ujir | Waima'a |
|---|---|---|---|---|---|---|---|
| 1SG | *niŋ* | *niŋu* | *saʔu* | *ainuʔu* | *ʔana* | *kanaŋ* | *au* |
| 2SG | *mu* | *nime* | *mu* | *num* | *ʔamu* | *kanam* | *ga* |
| 3SG | *ni* | *niye* | *ni* | *nin* | *ʔani* | *na* | *(-n)* |
| 1PL.INCL | *did/din* | *ninde* | *tita* | *iknik* | *ʔitada* | *(tita)* | *(kite)* |
| 1PL.EXCL | *am* | *mami* | *sama* | *ainim* | *(ʔama)* | *(kama)* | *(hire)* |
| 2PL | *bir* | *mire* | *mira* | *minim* | *ʔami* | *(tem)* | *gamu* |
| 3PL | *rir* | *nire* | *rira* | *rir* | *ʔada* | *ida* | *(-n)* |

postposed possessor in Kemak and argue that it denotes a prospective possessor relationship. Penn (2006: 47–8) writes that preposed possessors in Dadu'a are more referential and used for possessive relationships that are more prototypical or ownership-like, while postposed possessors are de-emphasized and are more like descriptive attributes than possessors. Waima'a and Naueti also have postposed possessive structures, but it is not known what their functions are (cf. Veloso 2016: 57).

## 35.5 Grammatical relations

Grammatical relations are the morphosyntactic behaviours of the S (the single argument of a one-place predicate), A (the agentive argument of a transitive verb), and P (the patientive argument of a transitive verb) with respect to one another. This section examines the grouping of grammatical relations and the possibility of their rearrangement for pragmatic purposes in the languages of Timor-SMaluku.

### 35.5.1 Word order

Most languages in the area have a basic SV/AVP word order. Word order follows a nominative–accusative alignment pattern, with S/A preceding the verb, and P following it. This is illustrated in examples (32a)–(32b) on the basis of Luang.

Luang
(32) a. $[$*aʔ=apn-u*$]_S$ *na-mehra.*
1SG=stomach-1SG.POSS 3SG-sick
'My stomach hurts.' (Taber and Taber 2015: 58)

b. $[$*Seri*$]_A$ *n-tutu* $[$*boneka de*$]_P$.
Seri 3SG-point.at doll DEM
'Seri points at the doll.' (Taber and Taber 2015: 101)

The alignment pattern of word order is often matched by nominative–accusative person agreement, especially in the languages of Timor. However, many languages in southern Maluku have split-S person marking with postverbal agreement for certain predicates, yet their word order for NPs is aligned on a nominative–accusative pattern: full NPs as S/A-argument always appear in preverbal position (see the Selaru examples (48a) and (48c) in §35.5.2).

In transitive clauses, many languages allow the alternative word order PAV as in examples (33), (34), and (35), or PV in the absence of an overt A, as in the Tetun and Kei examples (36) and (37). This word order is employed for the topicalization of the patient, or to place contrastive emphasis on it.

Termanu
(33) $[$*au hehelu-ŋ-a*$]_P$ *sɛ* $[$*au*$]_A$
1SG promise-1sg.POSS-DEF FUT 1SG
*tao-atetu-n.*
do-be.right-3SG.POSS
'I shall fulfil my promise.' (Jonker 1915: 469)

Tugun
(34) $[$*mu*$]_P$ $[$*laku*$]_A$ *n-a rehi me.*
banana cuscus 3SG-eat all COMPL
'The cuscus ate all the bananas.' (Hinton 1991: 89)

Selaru
(35) $[$*Tulisama Botan ne*$]_P$ $[$*irj-ke*$]_A$ *j-tabahunwa=i.*
Tulisama Botan DEM man-ART 3SG-kill=3SG
'Tulisama Botan was killed by the man.'
(Coward 2005: 68)

Tetun

(36) [*oa* *ne?e*]$_P$ *k-atene*
child DEM 1SG-know
'This child I know.' (van Klinken 1999: 180)

Kei

(37) [*habo*]$_P$ *er-duk* *er-ut* *ma,* *ra:t* *en-ba*
boat 3PL-sit 3PL-make CONJ king 3SG-go
*en-hamoniŋ*
3SG-view
'[While] they were making the boat, the king went to have a look.' (Geurtjens 1924: 260)

Note that in examples (33) and (35) from Termanu and Selaru, fronting of P results in the addition of a pronominal trace following the verb (*-n* in Termanu, *=i* in Selaru). This construction can often be translated as a passive (cf. anticausative formations described in §35.3.2.1; these resemble agentless passives but are actually derivational processes). True syntactic passives, however, are lacking in the Timor-SMaluku area. This sets Timor-SMaluku languages apart from the languages of the Flores area in the west (see Nagaya, this volume, §23.6.3).

In Tetun, verb-final APV word order is possible in very restricted contexts. In these cases, the patient is always non-referential, and the statement is in irrealis mood.

Tetun

(38) a. [*ha?u*]$_A$ [*kopi*]$_P$ *k-enu* *ha?i,* [*kaŋkuŋ*]$_P$
1SG coffee 1SG-drink NEG water.spinach
*k-aa* *ha?i*
1SG-eat NEG
'I don't drink coffee, and I don't eat water spinach.' (van Klinken 1999: 181)

b. [*nia*]$_A$ [*inan*]$_P$ *lalek,* [*aman*]$_P$ *lalek...*
3SG mother lack father lack
'She has no mother, no father...' (van Klinken 1999: 190)

This word order is obligatory with the verb *lalek* 'to lack', as in example (38b).

Verb-initial word order is reported for some languages, but almost exclusively with intransitive verbs. In Tugun, VS order is occasionally used as an alternative word order in clauses which reintroduce previously established participants to the foreground of the discourse (Hinton 1991: 90). In Termanu, VS order is regularly found with intransitive verbs of 'annihilation' expressing the semantic range of 'to die; to disappear; to be gone; to break; to be consumed', etc. (Jonker 1915: 449–50), as in examples (39a) and (39b). VS order is also found with serial verb constructions in which the second verb belongs to this semantic class (39c).

Termanu

(39) a. *fɔ* *mɔpo* [*au* *ana*
because disappear 1SG child
*susue-ŋ-a*]$_S$ *sɔ*
beloved-1SG.POSS-DEF PFV
'...because my beloved child has disappeared.'

b. *bɔe-ma* *mate* [*kɔde-a*]$_S$
CONJ-CONJ die monkey-DEF
'...and the monkey died.'

c. *tuda* *heni* [*pa-a*]$_S$
fall be_gone meat-DEF
'The meat fell down.' (Jonker 1915: 450)

Since all other intransitive verbs trigger SV order, and transitive clauses have basic AVP order, Termanu word order displays semantic alignment.

### 35.5.2 Alignment of case marking on personal pronouns

Nouns and noun phrases are unmarked for case in Timor-SMaluku languages. Most languages in the region also have no marking for case on their pronouns. That is, the same personal pronouns are used for S, A, and P. An example is Naueti: in (40) *ka* '2SG' appears in the S (40a), A (40b), and P roles (40c). Only word order distinguishes P from S and A, as discussed in the previous section.

Naueti

(40) a. ***ka*** *kiri=n* *da?*
2SG urinate=or NEG
'Have you weed?'

b. ***ka*** *daha* *muni* *eto*
2SG not.yet kiss 3SG
'You haven't kissed him yet.'

c. *sira* *ru?a* ***ka*** *la* *p*$^h$*esta-na* *raha?*
3PL invite 2SG LOC party-POSS DUB
'Did they invite you to their party?' (Veloso 2016)

In some languages of southern Maluku (Leti, Luang, Yamdena), there is an incipient distinction between subject pronouns and pronouns in all other functions. In these languages, pronouns usually appear in a shortened cliticized form when used as subject preceding a verb with a person-agreement prefix. This shortening is the result of haplology, whenever the medial consonant of the pronoun is identical to the initial consonant of the agreement prefix. While this process is phonologically motivated, its outcome is irregular and thus has resulted in the emergence of a distinct set of subject pronouns. For example, in Leti, the first person plural exclusive clitic subject pronoun is *a=* when appearing before the agreement prefix *mi-* (e.g. *a=m-k~i̯~ari* (1PL.EXCL=1PL.EXCL-work) 'we work'), instead of expected ****ami m-k~i̯~ari*. When used as object or in other functions, the pronoun invariably has its full form *ami*.

Case-marked pronouns are limited to two clusters, namely, the languages of Western Timor-Rote and the languages of Aru. In both clusters, the pattern is the same: subject pronouns encoding S and A are distinct from object pronouns encoding P. For example, Amarasi has one pronominal paradigm for S and A such as *au* '1SG' (41a)–(41b) and another for P such as *=kau* '1SG' (41c).

Amarasi
(41) a. *au* *ʔ-nao...*
1SG 1SG-go
'I'll go...'

b. ***au*** *u-hana* *minaʔ* *taus* *meseʔ* *mes...*
1SG 1SG-cook oil wok one but
'I cooked a single wok of oil but...'

c. *mama* *na-tuinaʔ=**kau**=ma,...*
mum 3-follow=1SG=and
'Mum agreed with me and...' (lit., 'mum followed me and...' (Edwards 2020: 263)

The reader will notice that there is a difference in Amarasi between subject and object pronouns in terms of their morphophonological independence: whilst subject pronouns are independent words, object pronouns are enclitic. This is also true of the languages of Aru. Interestingly, the languages with a distinction between subject and object pronouns in Timor-SMaluku all have additional uses of their object pronouns as agreement markers for certain kinds of non-active S argument. This is discussed in §35.5.3.

### 35.5.3 Alignment of agreement markers

The dominant pattern across Timor-SMaluku is for languages to have nominative–accusative alignment of agreement markers. This manifests itself, for example, in verbal agreement patterns where the S argument of an intransitive verb is prefixed on the verb in the same way as the A of a transitive verb. The examples from Kei in (42) illustrate the pattern: both S and A are indexed by an obligatory verbal agreement prefix on the verbs *-duk* 'sit' and *-tai* 'enter' respectively, while the P of *-tai* is unmarked on the verb.

Kei
(42) a. Agreement with S
*hir-ru* ***er**-duk,...*
3PL-two 3PL-sit
'The two of them sat,...'

b. Agreement with A
*hir-ru* ***er**-tai* *habo* *u-ru,...*
3PL-two 3PL-enter boat CLF-two
'The two of them entered the two boats,...' (examples from Guertjens 1924, cited in Villa-Rikkers 2014: 55, 85)

Split-S alignment—also known as split intransitive, stative-active, or semantic alignment—refers to a situation in which an S argument shows variable morphosyntactic properties, aligning sometimes with A and other times not. As is the case in other parts of eastern Indonesia where it occurs sporadically (see Nagaya, this volume, §34.6.2), split-S is a recurrent, but not a universal feature of the verbal agreement systems of the Timor-SMaluku languages. It is concentrated in two clusters, (i) languages of Aru, and (ii) the languages of Southwest Maluku extending from Selaru in southern Tanimbar to Kisar and Leti off the eastern tip of Timor. Remnants are also evidenced in a few Timorese languages.

The Split-S pattern in Aru is very similar across all languages of the subgroup: intransitive verbs are divided into two lexicalized agreement classes, those taking agreement prefixes for S and those taking agreement enclitics or suffixes for S. The former pattern is typical for verbs with 'active' semantics (43a) and the same prefixes are used for indexing the A argument of a transitive verb (43b). The latter pattern tends to occur with verbs with 'stative' semantics (43c) and the enclitics/suffixes are used also for encoding the P argument of a transitive verb (43d).[11] Enclitics for S and P do, however, differ in that an enclitic marking S is an agreement marker and can co-occur with free nominal elements co-indexing the argument, while an enclitic marking P is pronominal and does not permit the argument to be expressed with co-occurring free elements.

Dobel
(43) a. *tamatu* *s~soba=ni* *ne* ***ʔa**-kʷoj* *ti*
person REDUP~good=3SG.ANIM DEM 3SG-die already
'That good person has died already.'

b. *Wursin* ***ʔa**-tara* *Ilafi* *s~sel*
Wursin 3SG-call Ilafi REDUP~continue
'Wursin kept on calling Ilafi.'

c. *tamatu* *ne* *soba=**ni***
person DEM good=3SG.ANIM
'That person is good.'

[11] Hughes (2000) describes Dobel as having proclitics and enclitic agreement markers. Jock Hughes (p.c.) states that the 'proclitics' do not attach to a phrase, but always to the verb itself, hence the adjusted analysis of proclitics as prefixes here. This change brings Dobel into line with other languages in the region.

d. *ʔa-jokʷa=**ni***
1SG-see=3SG.ANIM
'I see him/her.' (Hughes 2000)

In Southwest Maluku languages, split-S patterns are more varied. Leti and Luang have broadly similar systems of verbal agreement prefixes, but have some notable differences in the use of agreement suffixes/enclitics. Leti and Luang have two paradigms of agreement prefixes, for example, Luang paradigms given in Table 35.14. Both paradigms of prefixes can index the S argument of an intransitive verb or the A argument of a transitive verb. The availability of a prefixal paradigm for any one lexical root is governed by a combination of phonological, lexical, and semantic factors (cf. §35.3.2.1; for Leti, see van Engelenhoven 2004: 134ff; for Luang, see Taber and Taber 2015: 56ff).

**Table 35.14** Luang agreement prefixes

| | Paradigm I | Paradigm II |
|---|---|---|
| 1SG | *u-* (*g-* /_#V) | *u-* (*g-* /_#V) |
| 2SG | *mu-* | *m(u)-* |
| 3SG | *na-* | *n-* |
| 1PL.INCL | *ta-* | *t-* |
| 1PL.EXCL | *ma-* | *m-* |
| 2PL | *mi-* | *m(i)-* |
| 3PL | *ra-* | *r-* |

On intransitive verbs, the interaction of these factors gives rise to complex split-S patterns. For Luang, Taber and Taber (1995) argue that intransitive verbs which take prefixes of Paradigm I typically denote less active, volitional events (44a, 44b), while those taking prefixes of Paradigm II tend to denote more active, volitional events (44c, 44d).

Luang
(44) a. ***na**-nina*
3SG-sleep
'S/he sleeps'

b. ***na**-mau*
3SG-tired
'S/he is tired'

c. ***n**-nem*
3SG-sleep
'S/he sleeps'

d. ***n**-maha*
3SG-exhausted
'S/he is exhausted (panting)'
(Taber and Taber 1995: 91)

Leti and Luang show more divergence from one another in the use of verbal agreement markers other than prefixes. In Leti, there is a class of intransitive verbs with stative semantics which can host either agreement prefixes or suffixes (van Engelenhoven 2004: 139–40). The choice of affix affects the dynamicity of the event: with a verbal agreement prefix, the event is a dynamic one (45a), while with a suffix, it is stative (45b). Agreement suffixes occurring on predicative verbs in Leti are identical to the possessive suffixes on nouns (see Table 35.6).

Leti
(45) a. Agreement prefix: dynamic event
*kokodie* *nvitano*
*kokoi=de* ***n-vitan**=o*
child=DET 3SG-fat=IND
'The child gets fatter.'

b. Agreement suffix: stative event
*kokodie* *vitanne*
*kokoi=de* ***vitan-ne***
child=DET fat-3SG
'The child is fat.' (Aone van Engelenhoven p.c.)

In Kisar and Luang there is no alternation between suffixes and prefixes such as occurs in Leti, but each language does have a small class of intransitive verbs that obligatorily mark S with agreement suffixes. In Kisar, just two verbs *mai* 'come' and *ki* 'go' have a suffixal inflection for S (46a). Other verbs either take no inflection (as in the case of *la* 'go') or a prefixal inflection for S/A (46b).

Kisar
(46) a. Suffix for S
..., *ik* *musti* *ki-k* *kaʔar*
1PL.INCL must go-1PL.INCL visit
'..., we must go visit

b. Prefix for S/A
*ik* *la* *k-apali ai*
1PL.INCL go 1PL.INCL-cook
'We'll go cook.' (Blood 1992: 12–14)

In Luang, a small set of verbs take both agreement prefixes and enclitics. These verbs denote self-directed 'middle' events, like 'defecate' illustrated in (47). Such 'middle' intransitive verbs represent a kind of semantic alignment that is also found in some languages in Cenderawasih Bay (see Gasser, Arnold, and Kamholz, this volume, §37.4.2).

Luang middle verb
(47) *a-lia* *pa* ***g-omi=aʔu***
1SG-go to 1SG-defecate=1SG
'I am going to go defecate.' (Taber and Taber 2015: 45)

Selaru represents a different system of split-S again, but like Leti an altogether more productive one: the S of an intransitive verb is encoded with an agreement prefix (48a) in the same manner as the A of a transitive verb (48b), but the arguments of non-verbal predicates are with an enclitic (48c) in the manner of a P of a transitive verb (48d). In Coward's (2005) description, the coding split is described as being between verbs and non-verbs. However, it is worth noting that Selaru's adjectives are simply described as intransitive verbs in other nearby languages. Thus, an alternative analysis of Selaru as having different classes of stative and active verbs with different agreement properties is conceivable.

Selaru

(48) a. *ama-ku* ***i**-ris*
father-1SG 3SG-bathe
'My father is bathing.'

b. *naman-ke* ***j**-oban* *asw-Vre*
child-ART 3SG-hit dog-PL
'The child hit the dogs.'

c. *sew-ke* *manas=**i***
sun-ART hot=3SG
'The sun is hot.'

d. *kete* *mj-ala=**i***
PROH 2PL-bother=3SG
'Don't bother him.' (Coward 2005: 66–7)

Similar to Selaru, Amarasi in West Timor is described as having a split between the coding of S in verbal and non-verbal clauses. The S of a verbal predicate is normally marked with an agreement prefix, but a first and second person S of a non-verbal predicate (what Edwards 2020: 311 calls a "pronominal equative clause") has S coindexed by an enclitic identical in form to the object pronoun (49)[12]:

Amarasi

(49) a. ... *au* *a-mon~mono-t=**kau**!*
1SG NMLZ-REDUP~stupid-NMLZ=1SG
'... I was a real idiot!'

b. ... *natuin* *au* *kninu?=**kau***
because 1SG clean=1SG
'... because I am holy.' (Edwards 2020: 312)

Traces of split-S systems are to be found in a small number of languages in Timor. Helong and Galolen both have S agreement suffixes on one verb (Helong *lako* 'go', Balle and Cameron 2014; Galolen *gosta* 'like', Correira 2017).

What is common across the languages of Timor-SMaluku with elements of split-S is the emergence of different strategies for encoding a stative/undergoer S, chiefly by means of a post-verbal agreement marker, be it in the form of an independent pronoun, enclitic or suffix.

[12] Property words such as *kninu?* 'clean' are part of the broader noun word class in in Amarasi. Elsewhere in eastern Indonesia, property words are verb-like.

## 35.6 Negation

Standard negation is typically marked by a free-standing negator in Timor-SMaluku languages. In most languages, the standard negator is preverbal (examples in 50, see also Fordata, Drabbe 1926a: 47; Yamdena, Drabbe 1926b: 62; Selaru, Coward 2005: 138–40; Luang, Taber and Taber 2015: 95). In Southwest Maluku languages, negators are either prefixal (e.g. Tugun *ta-*) or proclitic (e.g. Kisar *ka=*). Clause-final negators are found at the extremes of the area (51).

Preverbal negation

(50) a. Kemak
*ua* ***tai*** *hutan* *ikan*
3SG NEG get fish
'He didn't get fish.' (Mandaru et al. 1998: 78)

b. Fordata
*ami* ***wel*** *am-dapa* *ian* *dawan* *amarini*
1PL.EXCL NEG 1PL.EXCL-get fish big today
'We didn't get a big fish today.' (Marshall n.d.)

Clause-final negation

(51) a. Helong
*un* *da~dake* *mo* *haup* *duit* ***lo***
3SG REDUP~work but get money NEG
'He kept working but didn't get any money.'
(Balle 2017b: 74)

b. Kei
... *bet* *am-ut* *er-waeit-il* *hir*
if 1PL.EXCL-cause 3PL-recover-REFL 3PL
***waeid**, ...*
NEG
'... if we can't bring them back to life, ...'
(Geurtjens 1924, cited in Villa-Rikkers 2014: 49)

In parts of Timor, double 'embracing' negators are near-obligatory in standard negation. A typical example is Galolen where a preverbal negator *ta* can be used on its own (52a), but is more commonly used in combination with a second negator *ene* which occurs postverbally, either before (52b) or after an object (52c). Similar highly frequent double negation patterns are described for several neighbouring languages in eastern Timor (Dadu'a *ta-... (ene)*, Penn 2006: 66–7; Idate *bi ... (dar)*, Ferreira 2005: 15–17; Naueti *da ... (ho?o)*, Veloso 2016: 77–8) and for some Meto varieties of western Timor (Amarasi *ka= ... (=fa)*, see examples in Edwards 2020).

Galolen

(52) a. Preverbal negation

*sia* ***ta*** *bluri tun nai huhun*
3PL NEG can descend from mountain
'They can't come down from the mountain'

b. Double-negation: non-final postverbal negator

*sia* ***ta*** *bluri tulun* ***ene*** *mii*
3PL NEG can help NEG 2PL
'They can't help you.'

c. Double-negation: final postverbal negator

*gami* ***ta*** *bluri tulun nii* ***ene***
1PLEXCL NEG can help 3SG NEG
'We can't help him.' (Hull 2003a: 7, 25, 36)

Like most MPSEA languages (see van der Auwera, Van Olmen, and Vossen, this volume, §50.5), Timor-SMaluku languages have prohibitive negators that are distinct from those used in standard negation. In a few languages, the standard negator and the prohibitive negator are clearly related to one another, but they are never identical. For example, Waima'a has the standard negator *de* and the prohibitive negator *deme?e*, an apparently compositional form of *de* and *me?e* 'strong; force' (Schapper 2017d). The standard negator *waeid* in Kei looks to be a reduced form of the prohibitive negator *waheid* (Geurtjens 1921: 36). Where a language has a preverbal standard negator, the prohibitive negator is also preverbal (53). Similarly, in languages where the standard negator is postverbal, the prohibitive negator is also postverbal (54).

Kemak

(53) ***isi*** *mala!*
PROH enter
'Don't enter.' (Mandaru et al. 1998: 81)

Helong

(54) *nadidingun* ***deen...***
forget PROH
'Don't forget. . .' (Balle and Cameron 2014: 8)

To express existential negation, the majority pattern is for the existential verb to simply be negated by the standard negator, as *lema* 'NEG' does with *kika* 'EXIST' in Selaru (55).[13]

Selaru negative existential

(55) ***lema*** *kika wer*
NEG EXIST water
'There isn't any water.' (Coward 2005: 38)

In some languages, standard negators can, in certain contexts, act independently as negative existential verbs. For example, Tokodede existential negation is expressed with the standard negator *tai* plus the existential verb *bel* (56a), while negative possession is expressed simply with *tai* (56b).

Tokodede

(56) a. Negative existential

*dueke* ***tai*** *bel=se*
frog NEG EXIST=ASP
'There wasn't a frog.'

b. Negative possessive

*ferik los katuas os* ***tai***
old.woman with old.man money NEG
'The parents didn't have money.'
(Schapper fieldnotes)

In other languages, even when not identical in form, the standard and existential negators are likely related to one another. For example, Waima'a can express existential negation with the standard negator plus the existential verb, *de do?e* NEG EXIST 'not exist; there is not'. However, a second, dedicated negative existential negator *da* is used where no other verb is expressed in a clause (57a) or where there is a locative predicate (57b).

Waima'a

(57) a. *tuo* ***da*** *lo*
palm.wine NEG.EXIST ASP
'The wine is finished.' (lit., 'palm wine already doesn't exist')

b. *mau rui-n* ***da*** *le ne?i*
anger-POSS NEG.EXIST LOC PROX
'There are no grudges here.' (Schapper 2017d: 4)

A relatively small number of languages have a negative existential that is completely distinct from the standard negator. For example, in Naueti, *dii* 'EXIST' has the negative verbal counterpart *ma?a* 'NEG.EXIST', which is not related to the language's standard negator *da* 'NEG'.

## 35.7 Serial verb and related constructions

Serial verb constructions (SVCs) are monoclausal constructions involving sequences of verbs which act together as a single predicate and occur without any overt marker of syntactic dependency. Serial verbs are widespread in Timor-SMaluku, but in many languages they have grammaticalized

[13] This verb is unusual for Selaru in that it does not permit a preverbal subject NP. Coward (2005) occasionally glosses it as *ki-ka* '3AN-exist', suggesting that the verb has a dummy subject encoded by the prefix.

and cannot be considered to be serial verbs synchronically. Productive serialization is most common in languages spoken on Timor and its nearest satellites. It appears to be less common in Kei-Tanimbar languages. In this section, we will discuss recurrent types of serial verbs by their semantics and, where they are known to exist, grammaticalizations out of them.

The most common SVCs in the region involve motion verbs. These are of several types. Motion–action SVCs involve a motion verb serialized with a following action verb, with the first usually being done in order to do the second (58). See also Tetun (van Klinken 1999: 262) and Naueti (Veloso 2016: 102–3).

Motion–action SVCs

(58) a. Waima'a

*mai*$_{V1}$ *buni*$_{V2}$ *aku* *loo*
come look 1SG make
'Come and see me make (it).'
(Bowden et al. n.d.: 29)

b. Batuley

*kam* *ma-ban*$_{V1}$ *ma-jol-un*$_{V2}$
1PL.EXCL 1PL.EXCL-go 1PL.EXCL-ask-3SG.AN
'We will go and propose to her.' (Daigle 2015: 228)

Directional SVCs involve an action verb followed by a motion verb, with the first denoting an action and the second the direction in which it occurred (59).

Directional serialization

(59) a. Tokodede

*ana-ana* *ni* *asu* *blasi*$_{V1}$ *dara* *dʒanela* *du*$_{V2}$
child 3.POSS dog fall from window descend
'The child's dog fell down from the window.'
(Schapper fieldnotes)

b. Yamdena

*m-al*$_{V1}$ *kelar* *m-ti*$_{V2}$
2SG-take box 2SG-go
'Take the box away!' (Drabbe 1926b: 80)

In many languages in the region, directional verbs that originally occurred as $V_2$ in an SVC have grammaticalized into directionals, no longer taking verbal inflections as a serial verb would (e.g. Ujir, Tugun) and/or occurring in a distinct syntactic slot that is different from where a serial verb would be expected to occur (e.g., Naueti, Veloso 2016: 93–4, 103–4; Luang, Taber and Taber 2015: 97).

Across the region, motion verbs have widely grammaticalized into prepositions introducing NPs denoting locations, goals, sources, recipients, to name the most common. Verb-derived prepositions typically arise out of transitive uses of motion verbs that then have their verbal properties—in particular agreement inflection—reduced. For example, Ujir *bana* can be an intransitive motion verb denoting 'walk; depart' (60a). Like other motion verbs in Ujir, *bana* as a main verb can be followed by a locative prepositional phrase denoting a goal (60b). *Bana* can also appear in a transitive frame, where the second argument denotes a source (60c). This transitive use is the basis of the prepositional use of *bana* for sources; in this use, where appearing with another verb in the clause, *bana* occurs without an agreement prefix (60d).

Ujir

(60) a. *ku-**bana***
1SG.ACT-walk
'I walked/left.'

b. *ku-**bana*** *ana* *bel* *tuti*
1SG.ACT-walk LOC coast top
'I walked to/left for the beach.'

c. *ku-**bana*** *dʒuma*
1SG.ACT-walk house
'I walked out of/left the house.'

d. *ku-fan* ***bana*** *kai*
1SG.ACT-fall walk tree
'I fell from a tree.' (Schapper 2011a: 101)

Most languages have only one or two serial verb-derived prepositions, typically reflexes of PMP *lakaw 'walk' (e.g. Leti *la* 'to', Luang *laʔa* 'in, at, on, to', Naueti *la* 'in, at, by, for, to', Dadu'a *la* 'to'), and, to a lesser extent, PMP *panaw 'go' (e.g. Tetun *baa* 'to', Ujir *bana* 'from'), and PMP *maRi (e.g. Dadu'a *ma* ~ *na* 'to, towards'). The languages of Aru stand out for having large inventories of prepositions derived from verbs; see, for example, Dobel (Hughes 2000: 160–1) and Batuley (Daigle 2015: 211–28).

On and around Timor, verbs meaning 'bring; use; carry' are widely found introducing instruments. This is illustrated on the basis of Tugun *otʃi* in (61). In many Timor languages, the 'bring' verb shows limited or no inflection and can be regarded as a preposition synchronically (e.g. Kemak *odi* 'with', Dadu'a *no(ro)* 'with').

Instrumental SVCs

(61) a. Tugun

*ni* *ʔedʒa* *ika* *n-otʃi* *nufa*
3SG kill fish 3SG-use poison
'He kills fish with poison.' (Hinton 1991: 26)

b. Tetun

... *haʔu* *la* *k-are* *k-odi* *matan*
1SG NEG 1SG-see 1SG-use eye
'... I didn't see (it) with (my) eyes.'
(van Klinken 1999: 274)

A further common grammaticalization of these verbs in Timor is as purposive clause conjoiners. Van Klinken (2000) details the grammaticalization path of Tetun *hodi* 'carry;

bring' into an instrumental preposition and clause conjoiner 'to; and'.

Resultative SVCs are also widely found in the region. They involve the serialization of two verbs, the first of which denotes an action and the second its result, as in (62). See also Tetun (van Klinken 1999: 257–8), Naueti (Veloso 2016: 102–103) and Batuley (Daigle 2015: 232–3).

Resultative SVCs

(62) a. Tugun
*mu-tutu,* *tutu*$_{V1}$ *koha*$_{V2}$ *gean* *o*
1SG.IRR-pound pound split finally 2SG
'I'm going to pound, pound you open finally.' (Hinton 1991: 137)

b. Amarasi
*au* *ʔ-oat*$_{V1}$ *ʔ-iis* *ʔ-aan*$_{V2}$
1SG 1SG-cut 1SG-completely 1SG-result
'I'll cut him dead.' (Edwards 2020: 315)

Causation is most commonly expressed synthetically with a verbal prefix (§35.3.2.1). However, for those languages in Timor where this prefix is lost, an analytic strategy using a serial verb meaning 'make' is found. Examples are provided in (63). Notice the difference in word orders between Naueti and Mambae with respect to the S/A of $V_2$: in Naueti the word order of the SVC is much as it would be in a monoverbal clause, with *dihaana* 'child' occurring as an A before $V_2$, *ose* 'wash'. In Mambae, however, *xave* 'key' follows the verb *lako* 'disappear' for which it is the S, with the result that $V_1$ and $V_2$ occur alongside one another in a structure that suggests possible grammaticalization away from a SVC.

Causative SVCs

(63) a. Naueti
*boʔo* *onaata* *seto* *loo*$_{V1}$ *dihaana*
old.person woman DEM make child
*ose*$_{V2}$ *kele-na*
wash foot-3.POSS
'That lady makes the child wash his feet.' (Veloso 2016: 105)

b. Mambae
*au* *pun*$_{V1}$ *lako*$_{V2}$ *tel* *xave* *kuartu* *ni*
1SG make disappear ASP key room POSS
'I lost (lit., made disappear) the key for the room.' (Hull 2001b: 30)

Luang has an unusual construction which combines a causative serial verb *-hiʔa* 'make; do' and a causative prefix *a-* on the verb denoting the caused event (Taber and Taber 2015: 98). In the languages of Aru, a dedicated verb not found outside of serial verb constructions is used as the causative serial verb (e.g. Batuley *nam*, Daigle 2015: 233ff.).

Comparative SVCs using a verb '(sur)pass' to introduce the standard of comparison are also common in the languages of Timor and its satellites, (64).

Comparative SVCs

(64) a. Tugun
*ni* *metʃu* ***sari*** *au*
3SG tall pass 1SG
'He's taller than me.' (Hinton 1991: 138)

b. Naueti
*Noba-Gine* *heba* ***wai-ʔliu*** *Timoro*
New.Guinea big surpass Timor
'New Guinea is bigger than Timor.' (Veloso 2016: 110)

Elsewhere in Timor-SMaluku prepositions tend to be used to introduce the standard of comparison.

## 35.8 Summary and outlook

This chapter has presented a view of typological variation in a number of domains in the languages of Timor and southern Maluku. Despite some broad typological similarities, we have underlined the many divisions that are present in the languages. Kei is noticeable for often having patterns distinct from those of the other languages in the region, particularly in southern Maluku (e.g. many numeral classifiers, no semantic alignment, little use of reduplication for dependency marking, final negation). Southwest Maluku languages have a divided profile, patterning in some respects like Timor languages (e.g. use of exceed verbs in comparative serialisations, internal metathesis, breakdown of alienability contrasts in adnominal possession) and in others like Tanimbar languages (e.g. plural enclitic on nouns, external metathesis, productive infixation) and to a lesser extent Aru (e.g. reduplication as a marker of syntactic dependency, some semantic alignment of agreement markers). There is also a clear split in Timor, with central-eastern Timor languages showing several patterns in common with one another that are often absent in West Timor and nearby islands (e.g. significant attrition of inflectional morphology, possessive-like attribute constructions, 3PL pronoun rather than enclitic to mark plurality, pre- and post-posed possessive orders). Many of these structural parallels will be due to prolonged and intense contact between the languages in the region, but very little attention has been paid to this in the literature. Much of the scholarly focus has instead been on features attributed to contact with Papuan languages. While that undoubtably plays a role in this region (see Schapper, this volume, chapter 22), this chapter has shown that there is much more scope for understanding regional patterns in these languages, likely, as the result of contact between speakers of the many Austronesian languages in the region.

Many languages in the region of Timor-SMaluku have been largely omitted from this survey due to the absence of documentation. For example, very little is available beyond basic vocabulary wordlists for the languages of Damar and Babar (Taber 1993), while for Seluwasan on Tanimbar not even a wordlist has been published. For Kur, no data is available except for a wordlist that was collected in the 19th century (Wallace 1962[1869]). Another set of languages excluded from our discussion due to a lack of documentation are the four languages spoken in the Bomberai peninsula at the western coast of Papua: Arguni, Sekar, Onin, and Uruangnirin. Little is known about these languages, again with the exception of a few wordlists. Based on this material, Blust argued that they are most closely related to Yamdena (Blust 1993a: 276–9). The assumption of an especially close relationship to the latter is somewhat premature, given the limited amount of data, but a connection to the languages of the wider southern Maluku area appears likely. Future work on the Timor-SMaluku languages would do well to focus on these near undocumented language regions.

## Acknowledgements

Schapper's research was supported by the Netherlands Organisation for Scientific Research VENI project 'The evolution of the lexicon. Explorations in lexical stability, semantic shift and borrowing in a Papuan language family', the Volkswagen Stiftung DoBeS project 'Aru languages documentation', and the European Research Council 'OUTOFPAPUA' project (grant agreement no. 848532).

CHAPTER 36

# Languages of central Maluku

CHARLES E. GRIMES

Around sixty-one Austronesian languages in geographical central Maluku are severely under-documented, with less than a handful of grammars and phonologies available, along with a few topic-specific papers in additional languages. This chapter surveys issues such as active/non-active orientation in the verbs, subjecthood, human/non-human marking in pronominal systems, predicative vs. attributive marking on verbs, possession and the 'reversed genitive', pre-verbal vs. clause-final negation, and directional systems.

Given the lack of data, favoured examples are from Buru (a *Sula-Buru* language); Asilulu, South Nuaulu, and Yalahatan (all *Ambon-Seram* languages); and Kowiai off the coast of Papua, whose closest linguistic relative is Geser-Gorom (Walker and Walker 1991: 120). Kowiai is a *Seram Laut* language (far eastern Seram and nearby islands, including Banda).[1] Buru and Sanana are the largest local languages in the region with around 45,000 speakers each, followed by Alune (17,000), and Wemale (around 8,000 combining both North and South Wemale). Ambon Malay, a Malay-based contact creole (B. Grimes 1991), has significantly more first and second-language speakers than any of them. The location of languages spoken in central Maluku is shown in Map 36.1.[2]

While the literature names over seventy-five languages spoken in the region in the past, many indigenous languages on Ambon-Lease and coastal west and south-central Seram are recently extinct, near extinct, or spoken only by the older generation in one or two villages. Collins (2003b, and various); Florey (various); B. Grimes (1994); C. Grimes (2000b, 2010a) have all written about language endangerment issues, many set in motion in the 1600s by forced resettlement and some genocide by European powers and companies attempting to gain a monopoly in the spice trade. A common pattern today is that historically displaced communities outside their traditional homelands and in intense contact with other languages are more likely to have shifted to Malay or another language. Larger communities still in their traditional heartlands are more likely to have maintained their language. The popular view that Muslim villages have maintained their languages and Christian villages have lost their languages has too many counter-examples to be useful (Musgrave and Ewing 2006).

## 36.1 Phonology and morphophonemics

### 36.1.1 Consonants

Consonant inventories in central Maluku tend to be relatively simple, with three to five place grades of voiceless obstruents, often a simpler grade of voiced obstruents, and two to three fricatives. Table 36.1 presents consonant inventories of three languages, moving from west to east. South Nuaulu has merged several protophonemes to /n/, and has no voiced obstruents. Semivowels, affricates, and [ŋ] are sometimes due to morphophonemic processes, rather than full phonemes in the native inventory or historical retentions.

Apical *t* is typically slightly more fronted or dental than *d*. Fricative *s* often groups phonemically with the apicals.

In the *nasal* series, labial *m* and alveolar *n* are found in all languages. Palatal *ɲ* is rarely found phonemically in central Maluku, and often reflects a phonetic expression of a 3SG genitive *-ni* or *-in* at the end of nouns. For example: Kayeli *biti-ɲ* ~ *biti-ni* 'leg; foot'; *nee-ɲ* ~ *nee-ni* 'nose; snout'. Soboyo *buhi-ɲ* 'rear'; *n-oyu-ɲ* 'gall'; *ŋaa-ɲ* 'name'. PMP *ŋ is retained as *ŋ* in Sula-Buru and Seram Laut languages, but merges *ŋ/*n/*ñ > *n* in Ambon-Seram languages. Phonetic

[1] *Buru* data are from C. Grimes (1991, 2000b); Grimes and Lesnussa (1995); Grimes and Grimes (2020). *Kayeli* data are from Grimes (2000b, in process). Other sources include: *Taliabu*, *Soboyo*, *Kadai*, *Mangole*, *Sanana* (Bloyd 2015, 2020; Blust 1981d [based on Fortgens 1921]; Collins 1981, 1989); *Ambelau* (Collins 1981; Ed Travis n.d.); *Alang* (Ewing 2005b); *Asilulu* (Collins 2003a); *Sou Amana Teru* (Musgrave 2010); *Manusela* (MacDonald 2015); *Banda* (Collins 1986b); *Kowiai:* (Walker and Walker 1991). The following people kindly supplied data by filling in Grimes (1990): *South Nuaulu*: Rosemary Bolton (also Bolton 1990). *Larike*: Wyn and Carol Laidig (also Laidig and Laidig, 1990, 1991; C. Laidig 1992; W. Laidig 1993); *Alune*: Yushin and Takako Taguchi; *Yalahatan*: Carrie Beckley (also Beckley, n.d.); *Liana-Seti*: Frank McCollum; *Geser-Gorom*: Russel Loski. Two non-English resources of note are Stresemann (1918) on *Paulohi*, and Fortgens (1921) on *Soboyo*. Subgrouping classification follows Edwards and Grimes (2021).

[2] My thanks to Owen Edwards for collaborating on this map.

Charles E. Grimes, *Languages of central Maluku.* In: *The Oxford Guide to the Malayo-Polynesian Languages of Southeast Asia.* Edited by: Alexander Adelaar and Antoinette Schapper, Oxford University Press. © Charles E. Grimes (2024). DOI: 10.1093/oso/9780198807353.003.0036

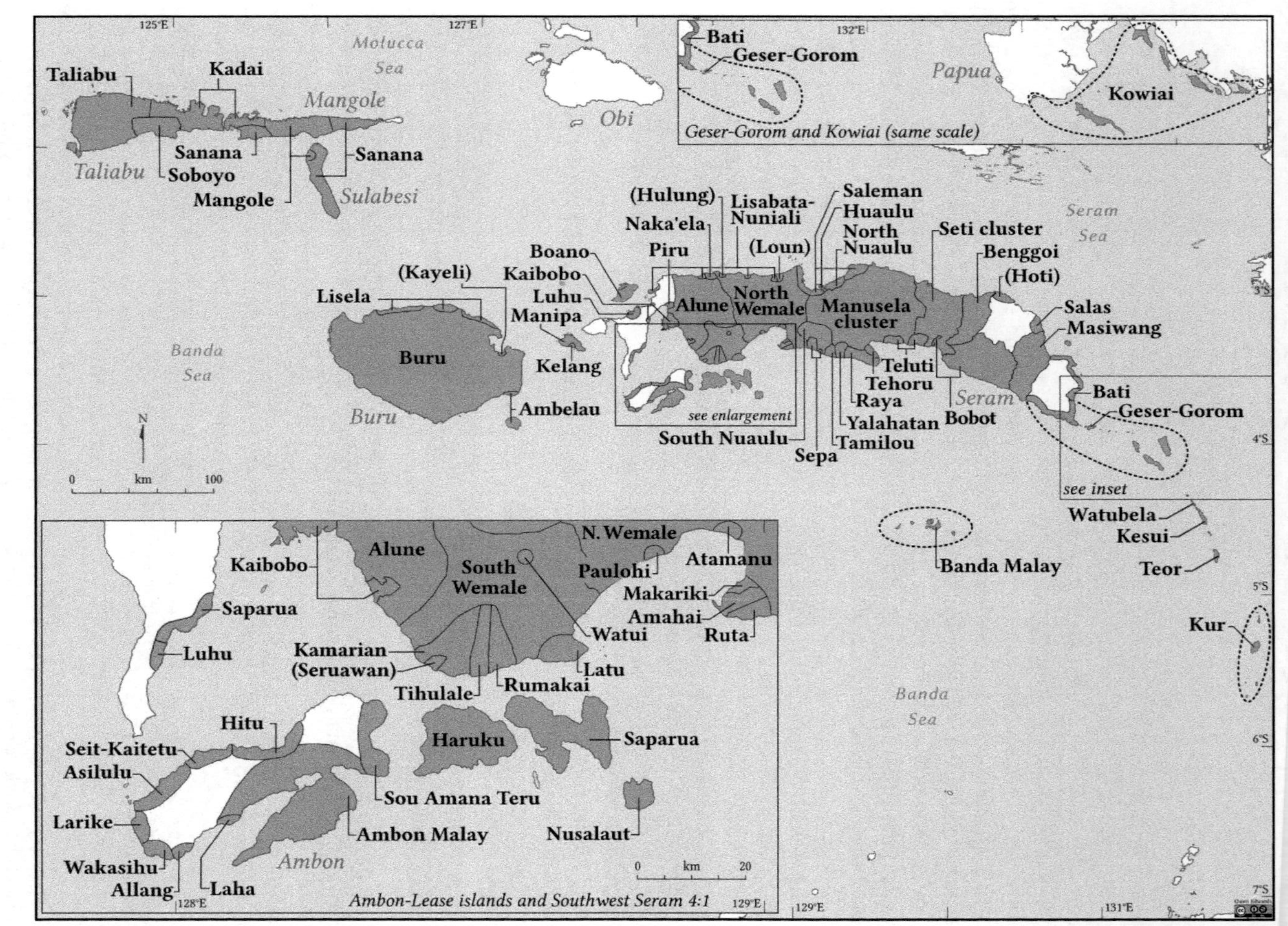


**Map 36.1** Languages in the central Maluku region.

**Table 36.1** Consonant inventories of three central Maluku languages

| | Buru (C. Grimes 1991: 48) | | | | Asilulu (Collins 2003a: xxvii) | | | | | South Nuaulu (Bolton 1990: 14) | | |
|---|---|---|---|---|---|---|---|---|---|---|---|---|
| Obstruent (vless) | p | t | tʃ | k | p | t | tʃ | k | ʔ | p | t | k |
| Obstruent (voiced) | b | d | | g | b | d | dʒ | g | | | | |
| Fricative | f | s | | h | | s | | | h | | s | h |
| Nasal | m | n | | ŋ | m | n | ɲ | ŋ | | m | n | |
| Lateral | | l | | | | l | | | | | l | |
| Flap/trill | | r | | | | r | | | | | r | |
| Semivowel | w | | y | | w | | y | | | w | y | |

[ŋ] can be found in Ambon-Seram languages where the nasal assimilates to point of articulation, and in loans.

Alune has a labialized stop $k^w$ regularly reflecting PMP *w, and in certain items reflecting historical *-aw, and *-aq. Laminal affricates [dʒ] and [tʃ] are not widespread, often have limited distribution, and are most commonly found in loans, onomatopoeia, or as a result of morphophonemic processes.

There are phonemic *homorganic prenasalized stops* in some languages, but these can also be easily confused with various affixes such as stative prefixes, subject indexes, preposed genitives, and the like. Example (1) illustrates phonemic homorganic prenasalized stops.

(1) phonemic

| | | | |
|---|---|---|---|
| Kayeli | *mbano* | 'wake up; get up' | (< PMP *baŋun) |
| | *embina* | 'female' | (< PMP *b<in>ahi) |
| Larike | *undaha* | 'rat' | (< PMP *balabaw) |
| | *undana* | 'male' | (< PMP *maRuqanay) |
| Sepa | *ntun* | 'dry up' | |
| Banda | *umbo* | 'grandparent' | (< PMP *umpu) |
| | *rindin* | 'cold' | (< PMP *diŋdiŋ) |
| Kowiai | *raŋgit* | 'sky' | (< PMP *laŋit) |

Example (2) illustrates homorganic prenasalized stops resulting from combining productive morphemes.

(2) morphological

| | | | |
|---|---|---|---|
| Soboyo | *m-fataŋ* | 'GEN-tree trunk' | (< PMP *bataŋ) |
| | *ŋ-kuli* | 'GEN-skin' | (< PMP *kulit) |
| Kadai | *n-tala* | 'GEN-bone' | |
| Buru | *(e)m-pei* | 'STAT-hurt; sting; sick' | (< PMP *hapəjiq) |
| | *(e)m-pait* | 'STAT-bitter; poisonous' | (< PMP *paqit) |
| Kayeli | *en-dane* | '3SG-bury' | (< PMP *tanəm) |

## 36.1.2 Vowels, vowel sequences, and word stress

Languages of central Maluku typically have *five canonical vowels*. Phonetic schwa [ə] may be an allophone of /a/ in unstressed (typically open final, or pretonic) syllables, but this is not widespread. High vowels *i* and *u* may have allophones [ɪ] and [ʊ] in unstressed closed syllables. [ɛ] may be an allophone of /e/. [ɔ] may be an allophone of /o/. A number of observers note that the distinction between *o/u* and *i/e* is sometimes obscured by variant pronunciations and shared allophones.

*Vowel sequences* warrant discussion with wide discrepancies in descriptions and analyses. The main issues are: (i) are there true diphthongs?; (ii) are phonetically long vowels to be analysed as single units, or as phonemic sequences of like VV, with each V being a syllable nucleus?; and (iii) are intervocalic semi-vowels phonemic? phonetic? or simply transcription variants? For example, words like *sawan, dawe, tewa* are straightforward. But what about *duwe ~ due, ua ~ uwa, leya ~ leiya ~ lea*? These three issues are relevant to all languages in the region, yet many investigators do not address them.

Analysing VV sequences is inherently linked to *word stress*. Stress is usually non-contrastive and falls on the penultimate syllable of the root. Epenthetic or paragogic V, clitics and cliticized roots may be extrametrical, that is not participating in or not shifting lexical stress from the root. This gives the superficial impression in many Ambon-Seram languages that there is contrastive or antepenultimate stress in some words—almost always nouns (see examples in Tables 36.2 and 36.3). To understand VV sequences it helps to first understand norms for VCV sequences. Example (3) uses a metrical grid to mark syllable peaks, stress, and extrametrical syllables in South Nuaulu (Bolton 1990: 11). A similar pattern is described for Buru (C. Grimes 1991: 52).

South Nuaulu, south central Seram

```
(3)          x
      (x)    x    x   (x)
     (CV-) C  V  C  V(-CV)
      ||   | | | |  ||
             r a n a          'grate (v)'
      ka-    r a n a -te      'grater (n)'
             s a n i -ku      'shoulder-1SG.GEN'
```

Secondary stress in polymorphemic forms and compounds is cyclical on every preceding second syllable working backwards from the penultimate syllable that takes primary stress, as in (4).

South Nuaulu

```
(4)              x
            x    x
     x      x x x x   (x)
     V-CVCVCVCV-CV)
     | |||||||| ||
        karatupa       'chili'
        kupanaha-ne    'clove'
     i-  amaha  i-ki   'he's alive (3SG.A-live-3SG.U)'
```

Sequences of like VV often occur as a result of the loss of a historical consonant. Word stress is on the penultimate V of the root. Several Ambon-Seram languages add vowels after the historical final C that are extrametrical and do not participate in the stress on the root. Table 36.2 provides a comparative context for seeing how VV sequences can be derived historically in some languages.

Regardless of whether or not VV sequences are like or unlike, word stress falls on the penultimate syllable, which for Buru and many other languages is the penultimate V on the root. Depending on the speaker and the language, measured instrumentally these VV sequences (both like and unlike) average 20–45% longer in duration than a single V. Single V and like VV sequences are contrastive, as illustrated by Buru data in example (5).

Buru

(5) *lee-t* 'sieve (noun)-NMLZ' *laa* 'sail (n)'
*leta* 'rest one's back against something' *la* 'irrealis marker'
*tuu-k* 'lift up, appoint-APPL'
*tuke* 'give'
*maa* 'presently at'
*ma* '1PL pronominal proclitic'
*baa* 'only, exclusive (post-predicate TAM)'
*ba* 'durative (pre-verbal TAM)'
*paa* 'four'
*pa* 'realis connector, so then'

**Table 36.2** VV sequences from loss of historical consonants

| PMP<br>gloss | *qazay<br>'chin, jaw' | *tazəm<br>'sharp' | *layaR<br>'sail' | *Raya<br>'big, large' | *ŋajan<br>'name' |
|---|---|---|---|---|---|
| Taliabu | *n-ade* | | *laya* | *haya* | *ŋaa-ɲ* |
| Sanana | *n-aya* | | | *aya* | |
| Buru | *aa-n* | *em-tae* | *laa* 'sail (n)'<br>*laa-n* 'dorsal fin' | *haa* 'grow'<br>*haa-t* 'big, important'<br>*ep-haa-k* 'enlarge (vt)'<br>*eb-haa-n* 'increase (vi)' | *ŋaa-n* 'name'<br>*ŋaa-t* 'rank'<br>*em-ŋaa* 'titled' |
| Ambelau | *ala-mu* | | *haa* | *ehea* | *nea-mo* (2SG.GEN) |
| Kayeli | *aa-ni* | | *laa-ni* | *lei* | *naa-ni* |
| Larike | *ala-hehe* | | *laed-u* | *(ida)* | *nala* |
| Alune | *ala-mu* | | *lael-e* | *(ela)* | *nan-e* |
| S. Nuaulu | *ana nohu-e* | | *nan-e* | | *nana-i* |
| Manusela | *aha-nia* | | | | *lala-ni* |
| Liana-Seti | *ala-k* | | *laiyal-a* | | *nala-k* (1SG.GEN) |
| Geser | *ʔar* | *ma-tarin* | *laar* | | *ŋasa-n* |

For the Asilulu dictionary, Collins (2003a) explains his orthographic approach to what I see as a phonemic sequence of like vowels, "The colon (:) marks long vowels, which contrast phonemically with short vowels." (p. xxvii) "perhaps a more consistent orthography would have represented these long vowels as double vowels (*aa, ii,* and so forth)." (p. xxxvi) Sequences of unlike VV "do not constitute diphthongs" (p. xxvii). For South Nuaulu, Bolton (1990: 24–6) notes "In sequences of two vowels, all 5 vowels can co-occur in any combination. Each vowel is a syllable nucleus." This includes like VV. Sequences of like VV are widespread in eastern Indonesia, and it has been repeatedly demonstrated that native speakers of many languages have better success both in reading and writing their own languages if the orthography handles these as double vowels: *aa, ee, ii, oo, uu* where they occur. Comparative linguists get better results as well.[3]

There are wide discrepancies of transcription in distinguishing true V-initial words from glottal ʔ-initial words, often making comparative work difficult, and sometimes underrepresenting 1SG prefixes. In Ambon-Seram languages is it *eu* 'I go'? Or *ʔ-eu* '1SG-go'? Is it *ai* 'tree, wood'? Or *ʔai* (reflecting the historical *k of PMP *kahiw)? These examples illustrate that orthographies used for linguistic resources should perhaps be different on some points from the practical orthographies for popular consumption. Some central Maluku languages have sporadic y-insertion, w-insertion, h-insertion, or l-insertion before #a on some nouns, which makes it clear those words are not glottal initial for those languages. Lexically specific initial y-insertion from North Wemale is illustrated from a variety of historical sources in example (6).[4]

| | PMP | Wemale | |
|---|---|---|---|
| (6) | *hapuy | *yahu* | 'fire' |
| | *qatəp | *yate* | 'thatch' |
| | *asu | *yasu* | 'dog' |
| | *kahiw | *yai* | 'wood' |
| | *kasaw | *yasa pul* | 'rafter' |
| | PECM *kabil | *yapil-e* | 'fish hook' |

[3] Unfortunately, this very common and significant feature of the vowel systems of eastern Indonesia was only mentioned in passing by Hajek (2010).

[4] Suggestions that these irregular onsets are sporadic reflexes of historical *h, *q, or retentions of PAN articles/noun markers *si or *(s)u in the protolanguage (Collins 1982b, 1983a: 6, 120–8, 130–1), do not account for all the forms encountered, the many exceptions in the data, nor inconsistencies with regular sound correspondences. And the claim that these have implications for subgrouping also fails to recognize similar lexically specific and sporadic occurrences in the nearby Tanimbar-Bomberai, Aru, and Timor-Babar subgroups (Edwards and Grimes 2021).

## 36.1.3 Syllable structure

*Content words* such as nouns and verbs tend to be overwhelmingly disyllabic in their roots, with a small number of monomorphemic trisyllables. Grammatical *functors* may be single phoneme, monosyllabic, disyllabic, polymorphemic, or phrasal. *Precategorials* (bound roots) are common, in which the root does not occur except in combination with other morphemes, and often without clear evidence that the root is inherently nominal or verbal until morphemes are added and it is put in the context of a sentence. Disyllabic roots commonly have the monomorphemic structures illustrated from Buru in example (7).

| | Buru | | |
|---|---|---|---|
| (7) | ˈCVCVC | *fulan* | 'moon' |
| | ˈCVCV | *heta* | 'recede (e.g. tide)' |
| | ˈVCV | *eta* | 'until' |
| | ˈCVV | *wea* | 'move s.t. back-and-forth; shake' |
| | ˈVV | *ea* | 'minuscule' |

To account for Buru patterns of CVC-reduplication (as in example (16)), or *compounding* such as *fatu* 'rock' + *hese-t* 'wall' → *fat.hese* 'cliff' or *heka* 'flee' + *tata-k* 'drop s.t.' → *hek.tatak* 'abscond with', the intervocalic C is defined as being *ambisyllabic*—affiliated with both the preceding and following syllable. This approach simplifies explaining morphophonemic processes for many other languages as well.

Among the Seram Laut languages, *Liana-Seti* appears to have a few content words with monosyllabic CVC roots that are disyllabic CVCV(C) historically or in other languages:

| | Liana-Seti | |
|---|---|---|
| (8) | *lah-e* | 'blood' |
| | *al* | 'dig' |
| | *u-kin* | '1SG-drink' |
| | *ul-e* | 'maggot-NMLZ' |
| | *is-na* | 'meat-3SG.GEN' |
| | *tun* | 'burn' |
| | *fal* | 'stingray' |
| | *rak* | 'go' |
| | *au-ran* | '1SG-cry' |
| | *au-rul* | '1SG-descend' |
| | *en-tol* | 'NUM-three' |
| | *en-hit* | 'NUM-seven' |
| | *en-wal* | 'NUM-eight' |

Some CVCVC words (particularly roots ending in n# or l#) are restructured to CVCC(V), as in *timuR > *timl-a* 'east monsoon-NMLZ'. Masiwang, Geser, and Kowiai also have a few monosyllables of this sort where we find equivalent disyllabic roots in other languages.

For historical *CVCVC roots, the most obvious phonotactic issue is whether there are root-final consonants, and what historical consonants are retained in root-final position. While many historical *final consonants* are lost in central Maluku, PMP final consonants *n, *t, *R, *k are often retained on some nouns (often relating to nature), as illustrated in Table 36.3. Retentions of final *l, *m, *p, *s, *j, *q are also found, but much less widely.

There seems to be phonotactic pressure to lose historical root-final consonants to make way for pronominal enclitics, genitive enclitics, nominalizers, noun markers, and applicatives, which often take the shape of *-n*, *-ɲ*, *-ni*, *-i*, *-e*, *-t(e)*, and *-k*. Seram Laut languages retain more historical final consonants than do Sula-Buru or Ambon-Seram languages. Investigators are easily confused about which are historical retentions, and which are productive suffixes.

There is a broad tendency for a *weakening of antepenultimate V* (pre-tonic) across the region. In several languages the historical V is replaced by a fixed vowel supplied in a certain slot, regardless of the historical V. In Buru, this is accompanied by metathesis *CV → VC, often resulting in a CC cluster following the epenthetic /e/ (C. Grimes 1991: 59–60). (See Table 36.7 for the same phonotactic metathesis in Buru verbal prefixes.) In some other languages the antepenultimate V is /a/. In Buru, CC clusters occur only between the penultimate and antepenultimate syllables. The epenthetic /e/ can also be omitted in Buru, often following a vowel in normal speech. Some languages preserve the historical CV structure of the antepenultimate syllable, but may regularize the weakened V. Or they may reduce *CVCVCV(C) to CCVCV(C). Weakening of the historical antepenultimate V is shown in Table 36.4.

**Table 36.3** Retention of historical final consonants in selected words

| PMP<br>local gloss | *quzan<br>'rain' | *aŋin<br>'wind' | *bulan<br>'moon' | *layaR<br>'sail' | *timuR<br>'east monsoon' | *habaRat<br>'west monsoon' | *laŋit<br>'sky' |
|---|---|---|---|---|---|---|---|
| Taliabu | *uyaɲ* | *aŋin* [a] | | *laya* | *timu* | | *laŋi* |
| Buru | *(dekat)* | *aŋin* | *fulan* | *laa* | *ful timo* | *ful fahat* | *laŋit* |
| Ambelau | *ulan* | *ani* | *hula* | *haa* | | | *lanir-e* |
| Larike | *udan-u* | *anin-u* | *hudan-u* | *laed-u* | *timud-u* | *halat-a* | *lanit-a* |
| Alune | *ulan-e* | | *bulan-e* | *lael-e* | *timur-e* | *balat-e* | *lanit-e* |
| S. Nuaulu | *uan-e* | | *hunan-e* | *nane* | | *hanat-e* | *nant-e* |
| Liana-Seti | *roa* | | | *laiyal-a* | *timl-a* | *farat-a* | |
| Banda | | *anin* | *ϕulan* | | | | |
| Geser | *uran* | *aŋin* | *ulan* | *laar* | *timur* | *warat* | |

[a] Taliabu *aŋin* means 'sea current'

**Table 36.4** Weakening of antepenultimate V

| PAn/PMP | Buru | Larike | S. Nuaulu | Liana | Geser | Local Gloss |
|---|---|---|---|---|---|---|
| *taliŋa | *etliŋa-n* | *tedina* | *(tina-i)* | *(tina-k)* | *teli'ŋaa* | 'ear' |
| *kuRita | *ekhita* | *kuriga* | *urita* | *uwita* | *gurita* | 'octopus' |
| *maRuqanay | *emhana* | *undana* | *hanai-e* | *mulaina* | *urana* | 'male' |
| *ma-putiq | *boti-t* | *pute-te* | *puti-e* | *but:a* | *futi* | 'white' |
| *ma-tuqaS | *em-tua-t* | *n-tua* | *mtua-ne* | | | 'old; respected' |
| *ma-takut | *em-tako* | *n-taʔu* | *kaitau* | *muta* | *mataʔut* | 'STAT-afraid' |
| *ka-wanan | *eʔwana* | | *wanan-e* | *amuwaina* | *uwanan* | 'right side' |
| *bulawan | *eflawa* | | *halawan-u* | | | 'gold; majestic' |

### 36.1.4 Morphophonemic processes

Processes such as truncation, epenthesis, vowel harmony, deletion, lowering, raising, metathesis, neutralization of contrast, assimilation, palatalization, and resyllabification are all attested in the region (Bolton 1990; Collins 2003a; C. Grimes 1991; Laidig and Laidig 1991). In Buru, morphophonemic palatalization occurs with V-initial roots (C. Grimes 1991: 65–6), as illustrated in example (9).

Buru, palatalization

```
(9)       [+front]
     e    [+high]
                                x
     |     |           x        x     x
     V C- + C V C V →  V C C V C V-C
       |      | | |    | | | | | | |
       p-     o s o    e p y o s o-k  'enter → put s.t. into s.t.'
       n-     o l i    e n y o l i-t  'return (vi) → return (fare)'
       n-     i n o    e n y i n u-t  'drink (vt) → drinking (water)'
       n-     e g o    e n y e g u-n  'take (vt) → taken (goods), harvest'
```

Himmelmann (2005a: 126) says, "In terms of the formal concatenation of formatives, in particular transparent segmentability and phonological cohesion, many Austronesian languages indeed show few signs of fusion." Yet a number of Ambon-Seram languages have bundles of processes happening which make discrete boundaries difficult to ascertain. For example, Collins (2003a: xxx) provides the "verbal conjugation" paradigms for Asilulu verbs illustrated in Table 36.5.

**Table 36.5** Subject indexing in Asilulu showing morphophonemic fusion

| | Emphatic pronoun | Neutral 'swim' (PMP *naŋuy) | s-verbs, t-verbs 'ascend' (PMP *sakay) | k-verbs 'stand' (PMP *kədəŋ) |
|---|---|---|---|---|
| 1SG | *aʔu* | *u-nanu* | *u-saʔa* | *wele* |
| 2SG | *ale* | *a-nanu* | *araʔa* | *a-kele* |
| 3SG | *ali* | *i-nanu* | *iraʔa* | *i-kele* |
| 1PL.EXCL | *ami* | *ma-nanu* | *ma-saʔa* | *maʔele* |
| 1PL.INCL | *ite* | *nanu* | *saʔa* | *ele* |
| 2PL | *imi* | *(i)-nanu* | *(i)raʔa* | *(i)-kele* |
| 3PL | *sini* | *si-nanu* | *si-saʔa* | *si-ʔele* |

Laidig (1992: 87) shows similar fusional processes with Larike where verbs beginning with *p* or *k* show one pattern

**Table 36.6** Subject indexing in Larike showing morphophonemic fusion

| | p-verb 'work' | k-verb 'bite' | s-verb 'ascend' (PMP *sakay) | t-verb 'know' (PCM *tewa) |
|---|---|---|---|---|
| 1SG | *au-ʔese* | *au-ʔiʔi* | *au-saʔa* | *au-tiwa* |
| 2SG | *ai-pese* | *ai-kiʔi* | *ai-raʔa* | *ai-riwa* |
| 3SG | *mei-pese* | *mei-kiʔi* | *mei-raʔa* | *mei-riwa* |
| 3SG.NHUM | *i-pese* | *i-kiʔi* | *i-raʔa* | *i-riwa* |
| 1PL.EXCL | *ami-ʔese* | *ami-ʔiʔi* | *ami-saʔa* | *ami-tiwa* |
| 1PL.INCL | *ite-ʔese* | *ite-ʔiʔi* | *ite-saʔa* | *ite-tiwa* |
| 2PL | *imi-ʔese* | *imi-ʔiʔi* | *imi-saʔa* | *imi-tiwa* |
| 3PL | *mati-ʔese* | *mati-ʔiʔi* | *mati-saʔa* | *mati-tiwa* |
| 3PL.NHUM | *iri-pese* | *iri-kiʔi* | *iri-raʔa* | *iri-riwa* |

involving *ʔ*, while verbs beginning with *t* or *s* show another involving *r*. (in Table 36.6, NHUM = non-human).[5]

A different morphophonemic process is found in Buru that makes discrete boundaries difficult to identify, even though the process is clear. The process is easier to see by starting with examples in which the boundaries are easily identifiable. Buru *eg-* marks a middle (agentless) passive, as illustrated in examples (10)–(11).

Buru, Subject=Actor; Object=Undergoer

(10) ***Da*** ***huda*** ***huma.***
3SG dismantle house
'She <u>tore apart</u> the house.'

Buru, Subject=Undergoer; (no Actor)

(11) *Huma* *di* ***eg-huda-k.***
house DIST BE[6]-dismantle-APPL
'The house <u>fell apart</u> (e.g. from the wind, age, people taking pieces over time, etc.).'

C. Grimes (1991: 77–9, 118–19) also shows how the feature [+voice] can function as an allomorph of *eg-* before voiceless obstruents, as in examples (12)–(15):

Buru, Subject=Actor; Object=Undergoer

(12) *Da* ***tata-k*** *fua* *dii.*
3SG drop-APPL betelnut DIST
'He <u>dropped</u> the betelnut.'

[5] Both Asilulu and Larike are West Piru Bay (Ambon-Seram) languages. Similar fusional processes are found with subject indexing in other Piru Bay languages as well. Similar fusional processes are also found to a lesser degree in the Seram Laut language of Banda.

[6] BE here is shorthand for 'agentless passive'. See discussion and examples in §36.2.1.

Buru, Subject=Undergoer; (no Actor)

(13) *Fua di* ***data-k*** *gam pa rahe.*
*eg-tata-k pao*
betelnut DIST BE-drop-APPL ALL down ground
'The betelnut fell to the ground.' (non-agentive)

Buru, Subject=Actor; Object=Undergoer

(14) *Da* ***kesu-k*** *enhero mae-n.*
3sg break-APPL spear handle-GEN
'He broke the spear shaft.'

Buru, Subject=Undergoer; (no Actor)

(15) *Mae-n di* ***gesu-k*** *haik.*
*eg-kesu-k*
handle-GEN DIST BE-break-APPL PFV
'That (spear) handle is already broken.' (resulting state, agent irrelevant)

### 36.1.5 Reduplication

Various forms and functions of reduplication are found throughout the region for many parts of speech. Some languages have a small number of adverbs that occur only in reduplicated form. The functions of reduplication include: distribution, variety; habitual, repeated, or on-going activity; intensity and emphasis; increase or decrease of size or amount. See C. Grimes (1991: 75–7, 194, 206, 297) and Bolton (1990: 46, 55, 57, 65), as well as examples scattered though Collins (2003a) and Laidig and Laidig (1991). All of the examples in (16) are from Buru.

Buru

(16)

| | | |
|---|---|---|
| full reduplication | *emsian~em-sia-n* | 'each' (distributive); *emsian* 'one (numeral)' |
| | *emŋesa~em-ŋesa* | 'together' (plural); *emŋesa* 'on an even plane' |
| redup. of root | *geba~geba* | 'various people' (variety); *geba* 'person' |
| | *gao~gao* | 'grasp at' (repeated); *gao* 'hold' |
| | *boho~boho* | 'very' (intensity, lexicalized); *boho* 'bad; rotten; evil' |
| root-stem redup. | *gosa~gosa-n* | 'well-being' (manner); *gosa* 'good' |
| | *sup~supa-k* | 'do early in the morning' (degree); *supan* 'morning' |
| CVC-redup. | *bal~bala* | 'long ago' (degree); *bala* 'before' |
| CV-redup. (various) | *gi~giwe* | 'forcefully' (intensity, manner); *giwe* 'hard' |
| | *ro~roi-n* | 'a bit' (decrease); *roin* 'small' |
| | *emsi~em-sika-n* | 'alone' (emphatic); *emsikan* 'alone' |
| template driven | *fe~folo* | furred (cuscus, not yet plucked) [HAVE X]; *folon* 'hair, fur' |
| | *pe~pani* | 'winged (ship = airplane) [HAVE X]; *panin* 'wing' |
| phrasal redup. | *fi doo~fi doo* | 'everywhere, anywhere' (distributive); *fi doo* 'where' |

## 36.2 Clause level typology

The basic clause structure with NP arguments or free pronouns is SUBJECT + PREDICATE. There are verbal predicates and non-verbal predicates. A few TAM modifiers may be used with both verbal and non-verbal predicates. Most can be used only with verbal predicates. Most languages have some *pre-verbal* (pre-predicate) TAM modifiers, and some languages also have *clause-final* (post-predicate) TAM modifiers (see §36.8). Both have sentential scope—the one by being in the clause nucleus, and the other by being at the clause margin. As discussed in §36.9, the pre-predicate or post-predicate position of *standard negation* in languages of central Maluku is of interest.

The typical unmarked order of a transitive clause with NP arguments is S V O X. X can be fronted for pragmatic prominence when it marks a paragraph-level (or event level) shift or discontinuity in time or location in the discourse. The order remains the same with pronominal arguments—with some complications summarized below. All kinds of arguments can be omitted. The languages of central Maluku appear to have both prefixes and suffixes, but many 'affixes' function at the phrase or clause level and are grammatically clitics. The grammatical Subject may be marked by an NP, a free pronoun, or pronominal clitic, and some Ambon-Seram languages take inflection on certain verbs. Different investigators variously treat the 'inflection' or 'conjugation' as clitics or affixes, and there are arguments both ways. I use the neutral term of 'index' to cover both. Where both an NP and pronoun or index marking co-occur, the NP tends to convey discourse level reference-related information, and the pronoun or index marks clause-level role-related information. Because of the multiple expressions of 'Subject', the syntactic status of the subject clitics and index marking is of interest. The distinctions are not always clear-cut as illustrated in the section below, and different investigators have differing views on similar data. Subtle prosodic differences may distinguish whether the NP is treated as a left-dislocated Topic, or as clause-internal Subject.

A discussion of the notion of Subject is interwoven with various topics through the next sections, beginning with the simpler case of Buru, and adding complexity moving eastward. Example (17) illustrates a Buru active transitive S V O X clause with an NP Subject and NP Object. Example (18) shows the same clause with a pronominal proclitic Subject. Example (19) illustrates a left-dislocated clause-external Topic, with a trace pronoun in the main clause. The syntactic Subjects are bolded.

Buru, verbal predicate, NP subject, transitive
(17) ***Geba di*** *kaa tonal lebetu.*
[person DIST]$_{SBJ}$ [eat]$_{V}$ [Phalanger]$_{O}$ [yesterday]$_{X}$
'That person ate cuscus yesterday.'

Buru, pronominal subject, transitive
(18) ***Da*** *kaa tonal lebetu.*
[3SG]$_{SBJ}$ [eat]$_{V}$ [Phalanger]$_{O}$ [yesterday]$_{X}$
'She ate cuscus yesterday.'

Buru, left-dislocated Topic with trace pronominal subject
(19) *Geba dii,* ***da*** *kaa tonal*
[person DIST]$_{Topic}$ [3SG]$_{SBJ}$ [eat]$_{V}$ [Phalanger]$_{O}$
*lebetu.*
[yesterday]$_{X}$
'That person, she ate cuscus yesterday.'

Example (20) illustrates pragmatic fronting of a peripheral argument from a Buru text, with a dummy subject.

Buru, topicalized X as Source
(20) *Fi di wae bula-t,* ***da***
[LOC DIST water hex-NMLZ]$_{X:Topic}$ [3SG]$_{SBJ}$
*poda fah raha-t.*
[crest]$_{V}$ [hand blood-NMLZ]$_{O}$
'From the poisoned water source, it spilled over into bloodshed.'

Examples (21)–(22) illustrate non-verbal predicates from Buru. Example (21) has a noun predicate, while example (22) has a PP predicate. Again, the syntactic Subjects are bold, showing the consistent pattern of the clause for Buru being SUBJECT + PREDICATE.

Buru, non-verbal noun predicate
(21) ***Geba dii,*** *Porwisi.*
[person DIST]$_{SBJ}$ [clan.head]$_{Predicate}$
'That man [is] a Porwisi (title of leader of the Mual origin group).'

Buru, non-verbal PP predicate
(22) ***Feten dii,*** *fi sak lufe.*
[millet DIST]$_{SBJ}$ [LOC up storehouse]$_{Predicate}$
'That foxtail millet [is] up in the storehouse (with a sliding roof for drying grain).'

The following two examples from South Nuaulu (23) and Yalahatan (24) begin to illustrate increased complexity in the notion of Subject. The Subject NPs are not fronted topics, and the proclitics are obligatory.

South Nuaulu, NP subject, transitive
(23) ***Senet-a ra****=oto ruka.*
[hornet-PL 3PL.NHUM]$_{SBJ}$=[bite]$_{V}$ [monkey]$_{O}$
'The hornets stung the monkey.'

Yalahatan, transitive
(24) ***(Tumata) i****=ahelie iane.*
[person 3SG]$_{SBJ}$=[sell]$_{V}$ [fish]$_{O}$
'Someone is selling fish./He is selling fish.'

In Kowiai, there must be either a noun or pronoun in addition to the subject index as in examples (25)–(26).

Kowiai, proper noun subject; transitive
(25) ***Miwara na****-ϕawas niur.*
[Miwara 3]$_{SBJ}$-split]$_{V}$ [coconut]$_{O}$
'Miwara split coconuts.'

Kowiai, pronominal subject, transitive
(26) ***I na****-ϕawas niur.*
[3 3]$_{SBJ}$-split]$_{V}$ [coconut]$_{O}$
'He/they split coconuts.'

As mentioned above, the subject index provides grammatical role-related information including person and number which indexes the discourse level referential-related information provided by the NP. Subject indexes, when they co-occur with subject NPs or pronouns within the clause may jointly constitute the subject argument. See Dixon (2010: 210ff.) and Haspelmath (2013: 224) for a broader discussion about double expression of subject arguments.

### 36.2.1 Semantic opposition and Split-S systems

While there are wide discrepancies in descriptions and terminology, there is a broad pattern of verbal semantics and verbal prefixes dividing along an active/non-active distinction, which distinguishes the Subject in the macrorole of

Actor (DO) from the macrorole of Undergoer (BE).[7] This may also be reflected in the pronominal systems. This Active/non-Active distinction is of fundamental importance to all languages in the region. Many Ambon-Seram languages also have a Split-S system of pronominal marking in which the single argument $S_A$ of Active intransitive verbs takes a different set than the $S_U$ of non-Active verbs. In languages like Yalahatan, $S_A$ is marked *before* the verb with the Actor set of pronouns, whereas $S_U$ is marked *following* non-Active verbs with the Undergoer set of pronouns. And, as Pawley (1973) noted for Oceanic languages, some languages in the central Maluku region, such as Sou Amana Teru (Musgrave 2010) and Yalahatan also have *intradirective* verbs of motion, posture, or bodily function which are semantically intransitive, but grammatically transitive, with Actor and Undergoer coreferential—the one doing the action is also the one undergoing or experiencing the action or quality of the verb, or the one whose location is being changed. This sort of semantic alignment found in Ambon-Seram languages is relatively uncommon in the languages of the world and therefore noteworthy (Siewierska 2013), although it is not uncommon in the wider context of eastern Indonesia.

Yalahatan active transitive clauses have the subject:Actor *preceding* the verb, and the object:Undergoer *following* the verb as in (27) and (28).

Yalahatan, active transitive clause with NP Object

(27) *Si=hita* *ulu-si.*
3PL.A=chop head-3PL.GEN
'They$_i$ cut off their$_j$ heads.'

Yalahatan, active transitive clause with pronominal Object

(28) *Yaʔu* *waru=i.*
1SG hit=3SG.U
'I hit him.'

The single $S_U$ argument of a non-active intransitive verb is marked by subject indexing *following* the verb, indicated here in bold.

Yalahatan, non-active intransitive clause with pronominal Subject

(29) *... lau* *mata=**ʔu**.*
until die=1SG.U
'... until I die.'

[7] Some in the general literature refer to this as *stative-active*, or *dynamic-stative* systems. I reserve the term 'stative' at a lower level, to distinguish *states* (BE, BE-at) from *processes* (BECOME; change-of-state) of non-Active verbs. Collins (2003a) describes this broad distinction for Asilulu as "agentive" verbs, and "agentless" verbs (p.xxix), and adds "only statives belong to the agentless category" (p.xxxvii). Walker and Walker (1991: 122) say, "Kowiai clause types can be defined as either STATIVE or ACTIVE in terms of the characteristic arguments they take." (Emphasis in the original.)

Intradirective verbs of motion and posture are syntactically transitive, although the Subject and Object are *coreferential*, as in example (30).

Yalahatan, intradirective verb of posture, syntactically transitive

(30) *Amite* ***yaʔu*** *tue=**ʔu**...*
last.night 1SG sit=1SG.U
'Last night I was sitting...'

Many experiencer verbs are marked like intradirective verbs, being syntactically transitive with coreferential Subject and Object, as in example (31). The agency of the Subject:experiencer is low.

Yalahatan, experiencer verb, syntactically transitive

(31) ***Yaʔu*** *atere=**ʔu**.*
1SG afraid=1SG.U
'I'm afraid.'

These should not be seen as causative or reflexive (i.e. 'I made myself afraid', 'I frightened myself'), as those would take morphological or periphrastic causatives or explicit reflexive pronouns. Compare the following Buru examples.

Buru, experiencer verb with coreferential Subject and Object

(32) ***Yako*** *sei* ***kono*** *haik fi di nani*
1SG weary 1SG.U PFV LOC DIST 1PL.INCL.POSS
*fina emsawan rua naa.*
female child-in-law two PROX
'I am fed up with these two daughters-in-law of ours.'

Buru, reflexive construction

(33) ***Yako*** *la ep-toke* ***emhewak*** ***kono***, ...
1SG IRR CAUS-show self 1SG.U
'I want to teach myself, [how to read and write the Buru language].'

Sou Amana Teru is similar to Yalahatan in marking intradirective verbs of motion as syntactically transitive. Example (34) shows a transitive verb in which the Subject and Object are not coreferential. Examples (35) and (36) show intradirective verbs of motion that are syntactically transitive, but in which the Subject and Object are coreferential.

Sou Amana Teru, transitive; not coreferential

(34) *Jadi ruʔa* ***e****=supu=**i**.*
then monkey 3SG=catch=3SG
'Then Monkey caught him.'

Sou Amana Teru, intradirective, syntactically transitive, coreferential

(35) *Sori* *bombonu* *e=kecewa* ***e=oi=ʔi.***
then turtle 3SG=disappointed 3SG=go=3SG
'Then turtle was sad and he took himself off.' (= and he left)

Sou Amana Teru, intradirective, syntactically transitive, coreferential

(36) ***Ike*** *reu=**ka!***
1PL.INCL go=1PL.INCL
'We want to go home!'

The recently extinct Ambon-Seram language of Kayeli shows a similar but simpler pattern in example (37), with the single Actor pronoun *preceding* the active intransitive verb, and the single Undergoer pronoun *following* the non-active intransitive verb.

Kayeli, active intransitive and non-active intransitive

(37) ***A*** *stea* *hene* *tu* *mate* ***ko.***
1SG.A rest first with tired 1SG.U
'I'll rest now, because I'm tired.'

South Nuaulu (Bolton 1990: 93–109) and many other Ambon-Seram languages work similarly to the Yalahatan examples above, including intradirective verbs. See Ewing (2010) for additional examples and discussion further illustrating this semantic alignment system. As one can see above from the semantic alignment of the Split-S Ambon-Seram languages, the notion of Subject becomes a bit more complicated. Modern Buru (C. Grimes 1991: 149–59) is fairly simple, with the Subject usually defined simply as "the pre-verbal core argument," with much of the morphosyntax pivoting around the interpretation of Subject as Actor or Undergoer. Buru still has traces of an older distinction between pre-verbal Actor pronouns and post-verbal Undergoer pronouns, but is developing an incipient switch-subject system driven by pragmatic factors that is also a bit more accusative in its modern syntax. Musgrave (p.c. 2019) describes issues around Subject for Sou Amana Teru, "The argument of an intransitive verb and the more agent-like argument of a transitive precede the verb even if they are only represented by a reduced pronoun. The patient-like argument of a transitive verb follows the verb; some exponent of the argument must be present." But as example (29) shows for Yalahatan, and example (37) for Kayeli, the single $S_U$ pronominal argument of a non-active intransitive verb for some languages can be marked *following* the verb.

C. Grimes (1991: 362) also describes a situation for Buru in which the normal role interpretation of Actor and Undergoer by position is reinterpreted from the extralinguistic context—a *fluid interpretation.* Example (38) shows the normal interpretation with the subject: Actor *preceding* the verb, and the object: Undergoer *following* the verb.

Buru, normal interpretation

(38) *Asu* *saŋa* *tonal.*
$[\text{dog}]_A$ bite $[\text{cuscus}]_U$
'The dog bit a cuscus.'

Yet this sentence was uttered while hunting in the jungle in response to a question, "Why does your dog have a bloody wound on its haunch? What happened?" Pragmatic focus is now on the dog. I heard no subtle prosodic differences, and quizzed the speaker's understanding of his own statement.

Buru, reinterpretation from pragmatic context

(39) *Asu* *saŋa* *tonal.*
$[\text{dog}]_U$ bite $[\text{cuscus}]_A$
'The dog was bitten by a cuscus.'

### 36.2.2 Verb morphology and role interpretation of Subject

Buru (C. Grimes 1991: 113–21) has many productive *verbal prefixes* that pivot around valence, volition, and semantic role of Subject (see Table 36.7). There are also many verbal prefixes listed for Asilulu (Collins 2003a: xxx) and South Nuaulu (Bolton 1990: 42–6), but most of those are described as unproductive or their functions are "difficult to ascertain" (Collins 2003a: xxx). *Statives* involving *m* (< PMP **ma*–) or another nasal (as in example (2)) are widely identifiable, and flag the Subject as Undergoer.

There are both *morphological causatives* (e.g. Buru *ep-*, Kayeli *he-*, Asilulu *pa-*, Larike *pa-*, Alune *a-*, Manusela *pa-*, South Nuaulu *a-*, *apu-*, Yalahatan *a-*, Liana-Seti *ba-*), and *periphrastic causatives* often involving a secondary sense of the verb 'do; make' or 'give'. Where both can be found on the same verb there is a tendency for morphological causatives to reflect more direct causation, and periphrastic causatives to reflect more indirect causation (C. Grimes 1991: 113–14, 211–12). Example (41) illustrates a morphological causative applied to the non-active verb in (40), indicating a direct cause-result.

Buru, non-active verb

(40) *Da* ***gosa.***
$[\text{3SG}]_U$ good
'It is good/right/beautiful.'

**Table 36.7** Buru verbal prefixes

| Historical | Buru | Buru function |
|---|---|---|
| *pa- | ep-$_1$ | causative (active; SBJ=A) |
| *paRa- | ep-$_2$ | reciprocal with multiple actors (active; SBJ=A/U) |
| *ka- (?) | ek- | agentive passive (causative, volitional; SBJ=U) |
| | eg- | agentless passive (middle passive, accidental; SBJ=U) |
| | ef- | many involve bodily action (active; SBJ=A/U) |
| | es- | many involve contact of surfaces (active; SBJ=A) |
| *ma- | em- | stative (non-active; SBJ=U) |
| | eb- | stative (non-active; SBJ=U) |

Buru, morphological causative – direct causation
(41) *Da* ***pe-gosa*** *riŋe.*
*ep-gosa*[8]
[3SG]$_A$ CAUS-good [3SG]$_U$
'He$_i$ healed him$_j$ (with medical treatment or spiritual power).'

The periphrastic causative in (42) indicates the Actor set things in motion that achieved the desired result. The serial verb construction in (43) has a similar force to (42), or can be even more indirect.

Buru, periphrastic causative – indirect causation
(42) *Da* ***pun gosa*** *riŋe.*
[3SG]$_A$ do good [3SG]$_U$
'He$_i$ [did something which] made him$_j$ well.'

Buru, core-layer serial verb construction – indirect causation
(43) *Da* ***puna*** *riŋe* ***gosa.***
[3SG]$_A$ do [3SG]$_U$
[3SG]$_U$ good
'He$_i$ [did something which] made him$_j$ well.'

Several languages in central Maluku have an *applicative* reflecting *-kV that repackages the role structure in various ways, including transitivizing intransitive verbs (both active and non-active), changing activity verbs into accomplishment verbs, dative raising, deriving verbs from nouns, marking argument incorporation. and other functions. C. Grimes (1991: 108–12, 230, 276) describes these in detail for Buru *-k*. Comparable forms are Asilulu *-k* "yielding transitive verbs" (Collins 2003a: xxx); Larike *-ku* "transitivizer" (Laidig and Laidig, p.c. in Grimes 1990); Alune *-(k)e* "valence changer" (Taguchi and Taguchi, p.c. in Grimes 1990). Similar functions of applicatives are found in SHWNG languages (Gasser, Arnold, Kamholz, chapter 37, this volume), although the forms vary widely.

Examples (44)–(45) show how Buru applicative *-k* can make a non-active intransitive verb function as an active transitive verb. Many active intransitive verbs can also be made transitive through similar use of applicative *-k*. Example (46) shows similar transitivization for Kayeli using *heer*.

Buru, non-active intransitive
(44) *Toho-n* ***maŋi.***
descend-GEN dry
'The trail is dry/getting dry.'

Buru, derived active transitive
(45) *Du* ***maŋi-k*** *tonal* *isi-n.*
3PL dry-APPL marsupial meat-3SG.GEN
'They're drying cuscus meat.'

Kayeli
(46) *kela* 'go up; rise; ascend; stand up; get up'
*kela heer* 'erect s.t.; put s.t. up; raise s.t.'

Examples (47)–(48) show how Buru applicative *-k* can repackage the role structure of an already transitive verb to flag that the syntactic object is in a different semantic role than expected.

Buru, active transitive; expected object
(47) *An-rua* *dii,* *du* ***sai*** *waga* *dii.*
offspring-two DIST 3PL paddle boat DIST
'Those two kids, they're paddling that canoe.'

Buru, object repackaged; not the expected 'boat'
(48) *Geba=r* *telo* ***sai-k*** *kami* *gam*
person=PL three paddle-APPL 1PL.EXCL ALL
*pa* *Leksula.*
down (town)
'Three men paddled us down the coast to Leksula.'

Examples (49)–(50) show a common aspectual function of Buru applicative -k, narrowing a broad and ambiguous reading (activity or accomplishment) to a narrower accomplishment reading. There is no change to transitivity. See Foley and Van Valin (1984: 36ff.) for a broader discussion of aspectual differences between activities and accomplishments.

[8] Buru *ep-* → *pe-* before CC onsets or voiced obstruents, which are seen as internally complex (see examples (12)–(15)).

Buru, active transitive; activity interpretation

(49) *Da* ***ali*** *warahe.*
3SG hand.peel peanut
'He husked/is husking peanuts.'

Buru, accomplishment interpretation

(50) *Da* ***ali-k*** *warahe.*
3SG hand.peel-APPL peanut
'He husked/is husking the peanuts.'

### 36.2.3 Pseudo copula

While the languages of central Maluku do not have true *copula*, there may be other words that have a secondary sense used like a copula. Without a verb, as in the Buru example (51), there are limited possibilities for TAM modifiers, and pronominal proclitics or prefixes cannot be used as subject. With a copular-like verb there are many more nuances available, as in examples (52)–(53) (see C. Grimes 1991: 373–4).

Buru, non-verbal noun predicate

(51) *Riŋe* *guru.*
$[\text{3SG}]_{\text{SBJ}}$ $[\text{teacher}]_{\text{Predicate}}$
'She is a teacher.'

Buru, copular use of *puna* 'do; make'

(52) *Da* ***puna*** *guru.*
$[\text{3SG}]_{\text{SBJ}}$ $[\text{make teacher}]_{\text{Predicate}}$
'She is a teacher./She became a teacher.'

Buru, TAM modifiers with copula-like verb

(53) *Da* ***puna*** *guru* ***hede.***
$[\text{3SG}]_{\text{SBJ}}$ $[\text{make teacher still}]_{\text{Predicate}}$
'She is still a teacher.'

Bolton (1990: 109–11) notes that the demonstrative *rei* 'this; that' in South Nuaulu in the form of *(a)-rei-mo* "does often seem to function like the English copula 'to be'." This use is illustrated in example (54). Neither Buru *puna* 'do; make', nor South Nuaulu *rei* can be used existentially as 'there is. . . '.

South Nuaulu, deictic as copula

(54) *Ina-i* *na* *ama-i,* ***o-rei-mo,***
mother-3SG.POSS and father-3SG.POSS ?-DEM-TOP
*sio* *aia-u.*
3PL king-PL
'His mother and father were kings.'

### 36.2.4 Presentational clauses

*Presentational clauses* (also known as 'existential' or 'presentative' clauses) are often used to introduce main or major participants with ongoing relevance into the discourse. Some languages in the broader region may use a secondary sense of a common verb (e.g. 'have; get') or a preposition (e.g. 'in; at') with an existential meaning (Grimes 2018), but other languages like Buru tend to use neither. Cross-linguistically, when presentational clauses introduce single individuals with ongoing relevance, it is quite common for there to be the use of some form of the numeral 'one' in association with a generic category (Grimes 2018; Payne 1997: 123–5). This is certainly true in central Maluku, as illustrated in the next three examples.

Buru, a Sula-Buru language; presentational clause

(55) *Anafina* ***sa*** *ŋaa-n,* *Yane.*
female one name-3SG.GEN Yane
'[There was] a girl/woman named Jane.'

Yalahatan, an Ambon-Seram language; negative existential clause

(56) *Kepen* ***sa*** *taʔm.*
money one NEG
'[There was] no money.'

Kowiai, a Seram Laut language; presentational clause

(57) *Timet* *muana* ***sa*** *nesa* *Achmad.*
child male one name Achmad
'[There was] a boy named Achmad.'

South Nuaulu can use relativizers *(w)ai* 'REL; there is (human)' and *(w)a* 'REL; there is (non-human)' in an extended existential function (Bolton 1990: 69, 103–5, 164–70).

South Nuaulu, an Ambon-Seram language; relativizer as existential

(58) *Sio* *umau* ***a-so-n*** *su* *nau.*
3PL some REL-PL-PROX toward sea
'There are some people down by the sea.'

## 36.3 Pronominal systems

The languages of central Maluku all seem to include at least one series of pronominal prefixes or proclitics. Many free pronouns have both long forms and short forms (also referred to as 'truncated', 'reduced', or 'cliticized' forms), with limited distribution for the truncated set. Pronominal systems in this region are best understood together, as with the Buru forms in Table 36.8. As in most Austronesian languages, *inclusive/exclusive* distinctions are made for 1PL

**Table 36.8** Buru pronominal systems

| | Free pronouns | Cliticized Actor pronouns | Pronominal proclitics | Possessive word 'have, own, associated' | *Genitive enclitics* [a] | Archaic Undergoer |
|---|---|---|---|---|---|---|
| 0 | | | | *nuin* | -t | |
| 1SG | *yako* | *yak, yaʔ, ya* | *a* | *naŋ(o)* | -ŋ | *kon(o)* |
| 2SG | *kae* | *ka* | *ku* | *nam(o)* | -m(o) | |
| 3SG | *riŋe* | *riŋ, rin* | *da* | *nak(e)* | -n | |
| 1PL.EXCL | *kami* | *kam* | *ma* | *nam(i)* | -nam | |
| 1PL.INCL | *kita* | *kit* | *ma* | *nan(i)* | -nan | |
| 2PL | *kimi* | *kim* | *ku* | *nim(i)* | -nim | |
| 3PL | *sira* | *sir* | *du* | *nin(i)/nun(u)* | -nin | |
| 3DU | *siro* | | | | | |

[a] In the Masarete dialect the genitive system has collapsed to the 3SG *-n* form for all person and number combinations. Collins (1980b) describes a similar collapse of the genitive system for Laha, spoken around the airport on Ambon.

**Table 36.9** Kowiai pronominal systems

| | Free pronouns | Active verb subject prefixes | Inalienable prefixes | Inalienable suffixes | Alienable possessive |
|---|---|---|---|---|---|
| 1SG | *laʔ* | *u-* | *nuŋgu-* | *-yoŋ* | *laʔo* |
| 2SG | *au* | *mu-* | *mu-* | *-yom* | *aɸo* |
| 3SG | *i* | *na-* | *ni-* | *Ø* | *i-ɸo* |
| 1PL.EXCL | *ʔam* | *a-* | *ʔam nuŋgu-* | *-mam* | *ʔambo* |
| 1PL.INCL | *ʔita* | *ta-* | *ʔita nuŋgu-* | *-nina* | *ʔita-ɸo* |
| 2PL | *o* | *mu-* | *mu-* | *-yom* | *o-ɸo* |
| 3PL | *si* | *na-* | *ni-* | *Ø* | *si-ɸo* |

in the pronominal systems of central Maluku. While Buru maintains the distinction in full pronouns *kita* (1PL.INCL) and *kami* (1PL.EXCL), and their cliticized variants *kit* and *kam*, it neutralizes the INCL-EXCL distinction in the pronominal proclitic *ma* (1PL), and the SG-PL distinction in second person *ku*. The short form of the possessive word also neutralizes the distinction between 2SG and 1PL.EXCL *nam*. The *-t* is more broadly a nominalizer with many functions, including where one would expect a genitive for generics, amputated body parts, things whose possessor has already been established in the discourse, or almost like a definite article 'the' which is neutral between 'proximal' *naa*, or 'distal' *dii* (some functions of *-t* are illustrated in examples (59), (66), (71), (73), (98), (99), (106)). The neutral possessive word *nain* is used in a fixed phrase with some inanimate objects, as in *aki rana nain kaha-n* 'across to the other side of the lake (lit: across lake has side-3SG.GEN)', or *wae nain kaha-n* 'other side of the river (lit: water has side-3SG.GEN)'.

Kowiai (a Seram Laut language) similarly neutralizes the SG-PL distinction for second and third person forms in several categories, as shown in Table 36.9.

As described in §36.2.1 and §36.2.2 discussing semantic alignment in the syntax, Ambon-Seram languages additionally distinguish *Actor* proclitics from *Undergoer* enclitics. Tables 36.5 and 36.6 illustrate some fusional processes that happens with subject indexing in some Piru Bay languages (a branch of Ambon-Seram).

**Table 36.10** Human/non-human marking in Ambon-Seram languages

| | Larike | | Asilulu | | Sou Amana Teru | | Alune | | S. Nuaulu | | Yalahatan | |
|---|---|---|---|---|---|---|---|---|---|---|---|---|
| | A | U | A | U | A | U | A | U | A | U | A | U |
| 3SG | *mei-* | | *i-* | *-ni* | *e-* | *-i* | *(e)i-* | *-(n)i* | *i-* | *-(k)i* | *i-* | *-i* |
| 3SG.NHUM | *i-* | *-a* | *a-* | *-ne* | | *-re* | *e-* | *-(l)e* | *(e)re-* | *Ø* | *e-* | *-e* |
| 3PL | *mati-* | | *si-* | *-si* | *si-* | *-si* | *si-* | *-si* | *o-* | *-so* | *si-* | *-si* |
| 3PL.NHUM | *iri-* | | *ru-* | *-ru* | | | *u-* | *-(l)u* | *(e)ra-* | *-re* | *ru-* | *-ru* |

### 36.3.1 Human/non-human distinctions in Ambon-Seram languages

In the morphosyntax, Ambon-Seram languages further distinguish *human* from *non-human* in 3SG and 3PL pronominal marking, as well as making the Actor (A) vs. Undergoer (U) distinction discussed in §36.2.1. In Table 36.10, the Actor proclitics and Undergoer enclitics marked for Asilulu reflect the pattern in the other languages as well. Sula-Buru languages do not seem to make this human/non-human distinction,[9] although Ambelau (a Sula-Buru language) and recently extinct Kayeli (an Ambon-Seram language) data are too sparse to be definitive on this point. Collins (1983a: 28) provides additional data for Ambon-Seram languages. Human/non-human distinctions are also fairly widespread in SHWNG languages (Gasser, Arnold, Kamholz, chapter 37, this volume). See Schapper (2010b) for broader discussion.

### 36.3.2 Plural markers

Many languages have a dedicated *plural* marker. For example, Buru plural =*ro* (with allomorphs =*r*, =*o*, =*oro*) can attach to the head, or to the modifier, and give contrastive meaning. So *kau omo-n=o 'the leaves (pl) of a tree', but kau=r omo-n 'the leaves of various trees (pl)'.*

Most languages also use the 3PL pronoun as an *associative* plural. Buru 3PL pronoun *sira* after a name or rank is interpreted by context. So *Ben sira* could refer to Ben and his family, Ben and his clan, Ben and his playmates, Ben and his office mates, Ben and those hunting with him, etc. See C. Grimes (1991: 62, 147, 159–61), and Bolton (1990: 51).

[9] Bloyd (2020: 233, 417, 568) gives contradictory information for the Sula (Sanana) language. He says there is a human/non-human distinction in Sula. But in terms of form, function, and distribution, the "pronominal prefix" (i-) is identical for 3SG human, 3SG non-human, and 3PL.

### 36.3.3 Dual and trial pronouns

There are a few *dual* and *trial* pronominal forms reported in Central Maluku, such as for Larike (Laidig and Laidig 1990). Traditional Alune has *inimi* for '2DU' (which is not a combination of *imi* '2PL' and *lua* 'two'). Buru has an archaic *siro* '3DU' sometimes still heard in remote mountain communities, whereas the productive modern pattern is *sira rua* or truncated *sir rua* 'they two, the two of them' following the widespread pattern of PRONOUN + NUMBER (C. Grimes 1991: 153).

### 36.3.4 Kin terms in place of pronouns for respect and avoidance

In most languages of central Maluku, referring to or addressing someone by kin term or political rank is more respectful than using pronouns. *Kin terms* are often used from the point of reference of the youngest person present, rather than necessarily the speaker. So the speaker might refer to someone as *meme* 'mother's brother', which is the relationship of the youngest child present, whereas the speaker themself may be in a different kin relationship with that individual. It is a way of training the younger generation in proper and respectful relationships and their associated behaviours. *Teknonyms* are common in the region to show respect and to avoid using names, in which the person is referred to as the father or mother of the oldest (sometimes living) child. So people all over Buru know about *Ben-tama* 'Ben's father', whereas very few know me as 'Charles'. *In-law taboos* are common, in which the names of certain in-laws—and words sounding like their names, cannot be uttered by certain individuals. Fines may be paid for the rights to use high frequency words that cannot be avoided, which are similar to taboo names. In Larike, the 2PL pronoun *imi* is sometimes used for 2SG in formal occasions. Politeness rules vary.

## 36.4 Noun phrases

In central Maluku languages, the canonical order of the noun phrase is HEAD + MODIFIER.

Buru, Head + Attribute
(59) *Da* *ep-kere* ***huma*** ***haa-t.***
3SG CAUS-stand house big-NMLZ
'He built a **large house**.'

Buru, Head + Number[10]
(60) *Da* *ep-kere* ***huma=r*** ***paa.***
3SG CAUS-stand house=PL four
'He built **four houses**.'

Buru, Head + Quantifier
(61) *Da* *ep-kere* ***huma*** ***eʔdeme-n.***
3SG CAUS-stand house many-3SG.GEN
'He built **many houses**.'

The general pattern is to limit an NP to a single (non-plural, non-deictic) modifier. Stacking multiple modifiers is possible, but is not commonly found in natural text. If additional modifiers are needed, a second one might be put in a relative clause. Otherwise they are made separate propositions. The plural marker and spatial-temporal-referential deictics can co-occur with all other categories of modifiers. Deictics occur on the outer layer of the NP, as in examples (62)–(63).

Buru, Head + PL + Number + Deictic
(62) *Da* *ep-kere* ***huma=r*** ***paa*** ***dii.***
3SG CAUS-stand house=PL four DIST
'He built **those four houses**.'

Buru, Head + Attribute + PL + Deictic
(63) *Da* *ep-kere* ***huma*** ***haa-t=o*** ***dii.***
3SG CAUS-stand house big-NMLZ=PL DIST
'He built **those large houses**.'

### 36.4.1 Attributive marking and the notion of 'adjectives'

What are traditionally labelled as *adjectives* in Indo-European languages tend to have many properties of verbs in languages of central Maluku, and a few may have properties associated with nouns. Words conveying DIMENSION (small, big), VALUE (good, bad), COLOUR (reddish-brown, black, white, yellow, blue-green) tend to be verbal. To put this in perspective, in my searchable Buru text corpus, the noun *huma* 'house' occurs 676 times. Of those, 409 have attributive modifiers. 341 instances of attributive modifiers are verbs or built around verb roots (=83%); fifty instances are underived nouns (12%); thirteen are loans (3%); five are of indeterminate status as nouns or verbs. Example (64) illustrates some noun modifiers, (65) some loan modifiers; (59), (61), (66) some verbal modifiers.

[10] The pattern in western AN languages is NUMBER + HEAD, as in Malay *tiga (buah) rumah* 'three (COUNTER) house'. But Ambon Malay often follows the eastern (local) order of HEAD + NUMBER. I lived for several years in the village of Rumah Tiga on Ambon Island.

Buru, noun modifiers
(64) *huma fatu* 'cement house'; *fatu* 'rock'
*huma nitu* 'grave (roof over a burial site)'; *nitu* '1) spirit of a dead person, 2) corpse'
*hum hawa* 'garden hut'; *hawa* 'garden'
*huma fena* 'village house'; *fena* '1) village, 2) origin group'

Buru, noun (loan) modifiers
(65) *huma sikit* *'mosque'*
*hum puji* 'house for implements of traditional worship'

Buru, verbal modifiers
(66) *huma ebraut* 'meeting house'; *ebrau* 'gather people together'
*huma emkele* 'tall house; pile house (on stilts)'; *emkele* 'STAT-high'
*huma endefut* 'residential house'; *defo* 'stay; dwell'
*huma esnilit* 'rented house'; *sili* 'pay' (regular metathesis with *en-s*)
*huma remat* 'dormitory (police, logging company)'; *rema* 'be long'
*huma tanheit* 'shelter; lean-to'; *tanhei* 'be temporary, fleeting'

Kowiai requires a subject index on most verbs (see Table 36.9). Example (67) shows this on an active intransitive verb used predicatively.

Kowiai, active intransitive verb; predicative
(67) *Udu* ***na-ɸarar.***
Udu 3-run
'Udu ran.'

Example (68) shows the same subject index on a non-active intransitive verb used *predicatively* along with a perfective modifier. Example (69) shows the same subject index on the same non-active intransitive verb used *attributively* in an NP, along with a distal deictic 'that'.

Kowiai, non-active intransitive verb; predicative
(68) *Musa* ***na-beʔ*** *roʔa.*
Musa 3-big PFV
'Musa is already big.'

Kowiai, attributive use of verb in NP

(69) ***Biyer na-beʔ*** *iɸamu nai na-taɸur.*
[boat 3-big DIST]$_{\text{NP}}$ almost 3-sink
'That **big boat** almost sunk.'

Many languages of central Maluku have a multifunctional *nominalizer* reflecting a form *-te. In Buru this is *-t* (C. Grimes 1991: 102, 143–5). In Ambelau this is *-re* ~ *-ri*. In the Taliabu, Soboyo, Kadai languages this is *-ts*, *-ti*, *-it*. In many Ambon-Seram languages it is *-t(e)*, *-e*, or *-ke*. This nominalizer can derive nouns from precategorials or verbs, such as in example (3) for South Nuaulu. Or Buru *flehe* 'the action of hoeing, or pounding sago to pulp' → *flehe-t* 'hoe, bamboo adze used to pound sago'. The *-t* is also used to distinguish whether a verb is being used *predicatively* or *attributively* as part of a nominal constituent. (There is also a discourse function of Buru *-t* relating to the genitive enclitics described in §36.5.2.)

The predicate 'big' in (70a) is verbal, and can take verbal modifiers in examples (70b)–(70c) that cannot be used to modify nouns.

Buru, non-active intransitive verb; predicative

(70) a. *Da* ***haa.***
3SG big
'She is big.' [STATE]/'She is getting big.' [PROCESS]

b. *Da* ***ba haa.***
3SG DUR big
'She is getting big.' [PROCESS]

c. *Da* ***haa haik.***
3SG big PFV
'She is already big.' [RESULTING STATE]

Example (71) shows that the same verb root, when used *attributively* within an NP, is marked as being part of the nominal constituent with the nominalizer *-t*.

Buru, attributive marking on verb in NP

(71) *Da dufa* ***fafu haa-t*** *saa.*
3SG get [pig big-NMLZ one]$_{\text{NP}}$
'He got a **large pig** (on the hunt).'

Active verbs (both intransitive and transitive) can also be nominalized or marked as being used attributively with *-t*, often in concert with participial prefix *en-*, as illustrated in examples (72)–(73). Additional examples are seen in (66), including that not all stative *em-* verbs take *-t* when used attributively.

Buru, active intransitive verb; predicative

(72) *Da* ***oli*** *(gam di huma).*
3SG return ALL DIST house
'She returned home.'

Buru, attributive marking on verb in NP

(73) *Riŋ tuke yako tu* ***oŋkos eny-oli-t.***
3SG give 1SG with fare PTCP-return-NMLZ
'She gave me **return fare**.'

## 36.5 Possession

There is wide variation in structures, terminology, description, and analysis in languages of this region, and the terminology is often used in conflicting ways between different investigators. To try and bring some clarity to the confusion, it is helpful to define terms as follows:

- 'Alienable' and 'inalienable' refer to a noun class system.
- 'POSSESSIVE' and 'GENITIVE' describe two different grammatical constructions.
- *Alienable* nouns tend to be an open class, and often correlate with the POSSESSIVE construction. The idea of *alienability* implies the possibility of disassociating the possessed item from its possessor. This can also be thought of as general possession and is sometimes referred to as 'indirect' possession.
- *Inalienable* nouns tend to be a closed class, reflect physical or conceptual part–whole relationships, including body parts and some kin terms. The idea of *inalienability* suggests the possessed item is an inherent or obligatory part of something, and cannot be disassociated from its whole, or its possessor. It is obligatorily possessed. *Inalienable* nouns in Ambon-Seram languages tend to be bound roots and must use the GENITIVE construction to become fully formed words. If the GENITIVE clitic is absent from an *inalienable* noun, it is often ungrammatical. This is sometimes referred to as 'direct' possession.
- In some languages there is widespread crossover between which nouns can occur with either the GENITIVE or the POSSESSIVE construction, while in other languages there is little or no crossover.
- The order of POSSESSOR–POSSESSED or POSSESSED–POSSESSOR is of typological interest for both the GENITIVE and the POSSESSIVE constructions.
- The GENITIVE enclitics in languages of central Maluku can be thought of semantically as similar to English 'of', as in 'jaw of pig', or the 's as in 'pig's jaw'. But to force the English, note that structurally the GENITIVE enclitic in central Maluku is marked on the POSSESSED, rather than the POSSESSOR, something like 'pig jaw-its' The Sula and Taliabu languages have GENITIVE proclitics as in example (2).
- The POSSESSIVE word when used predicatively is similar to transitive-like verbs 'have; own; possess', with

the Subject having no agency, and the Object having no effectedness. The POSSESSIVE word can also be used phrasally within an NP.

- English possessive pronouns such as *my*, *your*, *his*, *hers*, *ours*, *theirs*, can be equally used to translate both the GENITIVE (*my head*) and the POSSESSIVE (*my house*) constructions. I distinguish them in the abbreviations, for example, as '1SG.POSS' (first person singular POSSESSIVE) and '1SG.GEN' (first person singular GENITIVE).

For a more detailed language-specific discussion of the semantic relationships mapped by POSSESSIVE and GENITIVE constructions, see Ewing (2005b) for Alang, Laidig (1993) for Larike, Bolton (1990: 52) for South Nuaulu, and C. Grimes (1991: 277–8) for Buru.

There are several interconnected issues at play. What are the structures? What goes with what? What is the order of the parts? Is there a grammatical class system relating to possession, or do different grammatical constructions simply map different semantic relationships?

In some languages the GENITIVE affixes/clitics are preposed (rarer), in others postposed (widespread), and still others have both. Taliabu uses proclitics (*n-ade* '3SG.GEN-chin, jaw'; *ŋ-ama* '1SG.GEN-father') for cognate words for which Buru uses enclitics (*aa-n* 'chin, jaw-3SG.GEN'; *ama-ŋ* 'father-1SG.GEN'). Donohue and Schapper (2008) show links between the preposed POSSESSIVES of central Maluku with the pattern found in many Papuan languages in eastern Indonesia. They also posit a possessive stem *nV in independent POSSESSIVE pronouns.

### 36.5.1 Word order in the genitive construction

For well over 100 years, investigators in eastern Indonesia have noticed that the *order in the genitive construction* with a preposed possessor, is opposite to the order found in Austronesian languages to the west, which has a postposed possessor as illustrated in the Malay example (74), presented here for typological comparison. The head of the construction is bold in the examples below.

Malay, western pattern; postposed possessor
(74) ***kəpala*** *babi.*
head pig 'pig's head'

Examples (75)–(76) illustrate the order in the GENITIVE construction found throughout central Maluku and much of eastern Indonesia and Timor-Leste. The Buru example in (75) shows the GENITIVE construction as the juxtaposition of two nouns, with the GENITIVE enclitic on the POSSESSED. The Kowiai example in (76) shows one of its GENITIVE constructions simply as the juxtaposition of two nouns.

Buru, a Sula-Buru language; preposed possessor
(75) *fafu* ***olo-n.***
pig head-3SG.GEN
'pig's head'

Kowiai, a Seram Laut language; preposed possessor
(76) *oi* ***riɸut.***
shark tooth
'shark's tooth'

Both Greenberg (1966) and Comrie (1981) observe that it is rare in their databases of languages in the world to find prepositional SVO languages in which modifiers follow their nouns but which have the genitive preceding the head noun in the GENITIVE construction. That, however, is precisely the pattern found in central Maluku and most other Austronesian languages of eastern Indonesia and Timor-Leste. Examples (77)–(78) are from Buru.

Buru
(77) *fafu* ***kada-n***
[pig]$_{\text{GENITIVE}}$ [foot-3SG.GEN]$_{\text{HEAD}}$
'pig's foot/foot of a pig'

Buru
(78) *huma* ***tea-n***
[house]$_{\text{GENITIVE}}$ [post-3SG.GEN]$_{\text{HEAD}}$
'house post/post of a house'

The order in a POSSESSIVE NP in Buru (discussed more fully in §36.5.2) is similar, with the POSSESSOR preceding the head noun, as in the next two examples.

Buru
(79) *naŋ* ***huma***
[1SG.POSS]$_{\text{POSSESSOR}}$ [house]$_{\text{HEAD}}$
'my house'

*nak* ***ina***
(80) [3SG.POSS]$_{\text{POSSESSOR}}$ [mother]$_{\text{HEAD}}$
'his mother'

Givón (1984: 221) observes that the order of the GENITIVE or POSSESSIVE to its head noun has "the most consistent" correlation with such things as the noun–modifier order within an NP. The languages in eastern Indonesia with the 'reverse genitive' are clearly exceptions to this pattern, since the modifier in the POSSESSIVE and GENITIVE constructions *precede* the head noun, whereas the modifiers of other types of NPs *follow* the head noun. The distinction is significant enough to be the defining typological feature of Himmelmann's (2005a) *preposed possessor* type, as opposed to his *symmetrical voice* type of Austronesian languages.

The explanation for the order in the Buru POSSESSIVE NP is most easily dealt with. Earlier it was noted that the possessive word may be used predicatively much like a transitive verb (examples in §36.5.2). When used predicatively it is the nucleus of the clause. When the distribution is shifted to function as a POSSESSIVE NP, as in examples (79)–(80), the ordering of the clausal constituents is maintained, with POSSESSOR *before* POSSESSED in both clausal and phrasal uses.

Although the *order* of other Buru NPs has the modifier following the head, it is consistent with being a predominantly head-marking language to have the GENITIVE enclitic *marked* on the second nominal as the head of the construction (the POSSESSED), rather than on the first nominal as the dependent (the POSSESSOR). The first noun of the GENITIVE construction is a pre-head modifier; its presence is optional, often either referring back to a previous referent in the discourse or merely implied from the external context or general knowledge (examples in §36.5.2); the first noun distinguishes the type of whole (i.e. 'pig's HEAD' rather than 'dog's HEAD'; 'DIGIT of a foot' rather than 'DIGIT of a hand'). The first nominal of the GENITIVE construction may be modified separately from the whole, and it is shown in §36.5.2 that the first nominal can be absent altogether. The second nominal cannot be modified independently of the entire construction. Thus, when two nominals are juxtaposed in a GENITIVE construction, the second is the head, and the first is the dependent (modifier).

An explanation for the anomalous ordering of the preposed GENITIVE is not immediately recoverable from the central Maluku (or eastern Indonesian) data itself. The most likely explanation is to be found from contact-induced change between Austronesian and SOV non-Austronesian languages, with the AN languages calquing on the order of the GENITIVE construction of languages spoken in the region prior to the arrival of the Austronesians (Donohue and Grimes 2008; Grimes 2000a, in press; Klamer et al. 2008; Schapper 2015a). Preposed possessors in the GENITIVE construction are the result of contact-induced change, and as such should not be used for claims about genetic subgrouping.

## 36.5.2 Structures and functions relating to possession

Writers on Oceanic languages long held the view that there was a noun class system at work distinguishing 'alienable' and 'inalienable' (and sometimes 'eatable' and 'drinkable') nouns. However, Lynch (1973, 1982), Pawley (1973), and others have effectively shown that actual usage in text indicates that *many* nouns in Oceanic languages can appear in more than one construction, in effect indicating the inadequacy of the notion of a strict noun class system for those languages, and perhaps better characterized as different grammatical constructions reflecting different semantic and pragmatic relationships. Pawley and Sayaba (1990) point out that neither extreme position of noun classes nor no noun classes adequately accounts for the Fijian data, and this approach provides insight for addressing the complexities found in the languages of central Maluku.

Collins (1983a: 27–9) argues for an *alienable/inalienable* noun class distinction for all Central Maluku languages, although closer inspection shows that generalization applies best if limited to Ambon-Seram languages. Collins (2003a: xxviii-xxix) discusses the noun class distinction for Asilulu and illustrates the two different grammatical constructions associated with them, illustrated in Table 36.11. He also notes, "In general, there is no crossover from one category to another. A few exceptions to this generalization include loanword kinship terms, usually classed in the alienable category, but occasionally appearing with inalienable marking" (p.xxvi). The occurrence of the 'full emphatic pronouns' is optional, in what I call the GENITIVE construction associated with *inalienable* nouns.

**Table 36.11** Asilulu alienable and inalienable nouns

| Alienable | | Gloss | Inalienable | | Gloss |
|---|---|---|---|---|---|
| *aʔu* | ***ku**-haku* | my boat | *(aʔu)* | *ulu-**ku*** | my head |
| *ale* | ***mu**-buku* | your(sg) book | *(ale)* | *wali-**mu*** | your(sg) younger sibling |
| *ali* | ***na**-luma* | his house | *(ali)* | *nala-**ni*** | his name |
| *ami* | ***ma**-tipil* | our(excl) basket | *(ami)* | ***ma**-tuku* | our(excl) knees |
| *ite* | ***ra**-pikal* | our(incl) plate | *(ite)* | *mata* | our(incl) eyes |
| *imi* | ***mi**-lapun* | your(pl) shirt | *(imi)* | ***mi**-meme* | your(pl) uncle (MB) |
| *sini* | ***ri**-kata* | their pants | *(sini)* | ***ri**-lima* | their arms |

Bolton (1990: 52–5, 107–8) similarly describes South Nuaulu as having an *alienable/inalienable* noun class distinction marked by two different constructions. The GENITIVE enclitics follow the POSSESSED *inalienable* noun (as in example

(81)), whereas the POSSESSIVE proclitics precede the *alienable* noun (as in examples (82)–(83)).

South Nuaulu, GENITIVE NP; *inalienable* noun
(81) *asu* *neni-e.*
dog incisor-3SG.NHUM.GEN
'dog's incisor'

South Nuaulu, POSSESSIVE NP; *alienable* noun
(82) ***au*** ***we*** *topi.*
1SG 1SG.POSS hat (Malay)
'my hat'

South Nuaulu, POSSESSIVE NP; *alienable* noun
(83) ***noa*** *momo.*
3PL.POSS grandmother
'their grandmother'

The POSSESSIVE words in South Nuaulu can also be used as the nucleus of the POSSESSIVE clause, as in example (84).

South Nuaulu, POSSESSIVE clause; *alienable* noun
(84) *Ami* *rua-ma* ***mani***
1PL.EXCL self-1PL.EXCL.GEN have:1PL.EXCL.POSS
*akama* *wa-n.*
religion EXIST-PROX
'We have our own religion.'

Seram Laut language Kowiai diverges from a two-way noun class system that maps cleanly into two grammatical constructions. Walker and Walker (1991: 137–41) give Kowiai examples (see the forms in Table 36.9) that show certain kin terms are prefixed (*ni-mema* '3SG.POSS-mother's brother'); other kin terms and many body parts are suffixed (*riʔi-yoŋ* 'sibling-1SG.GEN'; *siʔai-yoŋ* 'nose-1SG.GEN'); *alienable* possession uses the POSSESSIVE word 'have' which follows the head noun (*san iɸo* 'house 3SG.POSS'); and some part–whole relationships are simply juxtaposed as whole + part (*biyer tena* 'canoe keel'; *oi riɸut* 'shark's tooth').

Sula-Buru language Buru diverges even further. All nouns can be used with the POSSESSIVE construction, either clausally or phrasally. And many nouns that would be considered *inalienable* nouns with bound roots in other languages can be found in natural texts without their expected GENITIVE enclitics. As expected, Buru has the two different syntactic constructions relating to possession, but it does not have a noun class system. The forms of the Buru GENITIVE enclitics and POSSESSIVE word are found in Table 36.8. C. Grimes (1991: 190, 277–92, 330–3) shows natural texts in Buru indicate that many roots can be used in more than one construction where the semantics allow, and can be used with either the GENITIVE or the POSSESSIVE construction, or both (as in (85)–(88)), thus arguing against characterizing the Buru data as a noun class system. Example (85) has a 'head' of a physical body in a POSSESSIVE construction with no GENITIVE enclitic. Example (86) has a 'head' of a social body in a POSSESSIVE construction with no GENITIVE enclitic.

Buru, POSSESSIVE - no genitive
(85) *Susana* ***nak*** ***olo*** ***em-hapu.***
Susana 3SG.POSS head STAT-tie
'Susana had her (own) head tied up (in a cloth).' (Showing her working hard in a Cinderella-like story.)

Buru, POSSESSIVE - no genitive
(86) *Da* *iko* *tu* ***nak*** ***olo.***
3SG go with 3SG.POSS head
'He went with his (social/political) head.' (comitative)

In example (87), however, the 'head' is in a part–whole relationship with an anaphoric referent (a pig), and hence is marked with the GENITIVE enclitic *olo-**n***.

Buru, GENITIVE - no possessive
(87) *Da* *iko* *tu* ***olo-n.***
3SG go with head-3SG.GEN
'He went with its (the pig's) head.' (accompanied possession that may belong to someone else)

In example (88) below, a POSSESSIVE relationship and a part–whole GENITIVE relationship are both indicated in reference to the head.

Buru, both POSSESSIVE and GENITIVE
(88) *Da* *iko* *tu* ***nak*** ***olo-n.***
3SG go with 3SG.POSS head-3SG.GEN
'He went with his (pig's) head.' (accompanied possession that he owns)

Many Buru roots can occur with the kind of flexibility illustrated above. So, for example, *faha-n* 'his/her hand, arm' occurs 183 times in my text corpus with a GENITIVE enclitic (80%), and forty-six times without a GENITIVE enclitic (20%) as *faha eʔwana* '1) right hand, 2) assistant, 3) husband'; *faha eʔbali* '1) left hand, 2) wife'; *faha rema-t* 'long sleeve'; *faha sahe-t* 'the other hand'; *faha sia-k* 'one-armed'; *faha eʔnaka* 'thieving hand' and so forth. Many of these can occur with a genitive enclitic, so we also get *faha-m eʔwana* 'your right hand', depending upon context in discourse.

It is quite common for the referent of the whole to be remote in the discourse or to be assumed cultural knowledge known from the context of what is being talked about. In the Buru examples (89)–(90) below, the anaphoric or exophoric referent (not expressed) is supplied in square brackets [].

Buru, assumed cultural knowledge
(89) *Da toho pao [wae] lopi-**n.***
3SG descend down water bed-GEN
'He (the pig) went down to the [stream] bed.'

Buru, redundant information
(90) *Sapa-n di [kae] olo-**m** dii?*
what-GEN DIST 2SG head-2SG.GEN DIST
'What's that there on your head?'

When GENITIVES are concatenated in Buru, there are differences among different speakers in how they are marked. In example (91), the speaker is referencing both 'hand' and 'digit' to the POSSESSOR 'you (sg)'. In (92) 'hand' is referenced to 'you', whereas 'digit' is referenced to its whole, which is 'hand'.

Buru
(91) *Tu sapkoko naa bet~beta di ka*
with ring PROX REDUP~connect LOC 2SG
*faha-**m** waŋa-**m**.*
hand-2SG.GEN digit-2SG.GEN
'And this ring fits perfectly on your finger.'

Buru
(92) *...ka faha-**m** waŋa-**n***
2SG hand-2SG.GEN digit-3SG.GEN
'your finger/the finger of your hand'

In its full form the Buru POSSESSIVE construction mirrors the structure of an active transitive clause with a pre-verbal Actor, the possessive word (≈ verb 'have, own, possess, associated with') and a post-verbal Undergoer—but there is no action, and no state of being affected. It can be interpreted either clausally or phrasally. The paired examples below are considered to be equivalents, with the difference being stylistic. There appears to be no semantic or pragmatic difference between them. Both occur frequently in recorded natural texts, and both are used by the same speakers. Example (93) can function either clausally or phrasally.

Buru
(93) *Ya **naŋo** todo saa.*
1SG 1SG.POSS machete one
'I have/own a machete.'/'one of my machetes.'

Example (94) shows a POSSESSIVE NP in the Object slot of a clause. The pronominal possessor is optional, with no pragmatic difference.

Buru, POSSESSIVE NP as Direct Object
(94) *Da kala-k **(ya) naŋ** ama.*
3SG call-APPL [1SG 1SG.POSS father]$_{NP}$
'He summoned **my** father.'

Example (95) shows a POSSESSIVE NP in a Subject slot. The pronominal possessor is optional, with no pragmatic difference.

Buru, POSSESSIVE NP as Subject
(95) ***(Ya) naŋ** fafu mata haik.*
[1SG 1SG.POSS pig]$_{NP}$ die PFV
'**My** pig died.'

The applicative *-k* in Buru can yield POSSESSIVES with an assumed definite Undergoer, or a response to questions like *san nake-k?* 'whose is it?', as in (96).

Buru
(96) *(Todo naa), ya **naŋu-k.***
machete PROX 1SG 1SG.POSS-APPL
'(This machete), it is mine.'

The Buru POSSESSIVE word not only functions as the nucleus of the possessive clause, it can also take additional verbal morphology, as in (97).

Buru
(97) *Kawasan **p-em-nake-k** geba rua*
head CAUS-STAT-3SG.POSS-APPL person two
*ute riŋe eta dena la masi.*
DAT 3SG until arrive downstream sea
'The village head **put** two people **at his disposal** until they should reach the coast.' (i.e. caused him to be in possession of)

In §36.4.1 a multifunctional nominalizer *-te was introduced that is found widely in languages of central Maluku. It (i) makes nouns from precategorials and verbs; (ii) marks verbs as being used attributively as part of a nominal constituent in the syntax; and (iii) in Buru this *-t* also interacts with the GENITIVE enclitics in discourse almost like a *zero genitive* to pragmatically indicate nouns that are general, not associated with a whole, already understood, or whose identity is already established or irrelevant to the discourse. It has the force more like an article 'the' than a genitive 'its' or demonstrative 'this' or 'that'. In example (98) below, not only are *-n* and the *-t* attached to the same precategorial root *rohi-* 'bone', but the resulting forms (i.e. *rohi-n* and *rohi-t*) below refer to the same real world referent (i.e. the pig bone). In my Buru text corpus, there are twenty instances of *rohi-n* and 5 of *rohi-t*, all meaning 'bone'.

Buru, GENITIVE construction with -n → -t once identity is established

(98) *Asu di ba hada* ***fafu rohi-n*** *saa,*
dog DIST DUR bite pig bone-3SG.GEN one
*petu riŋ spel-yaha-k fi dii, pa*
SEQ 3SG throw-evict-APPL LOC DIST REAL
*heka eta breman, petu da hada saki*
flee until far SEQ 3SG bite return
***rohi-t*** *fi saka huma mori-n,*
bone-NMLZ LOC up house behind-3SG.GEN
*fi saka kawaan lahi-n.*
LOC up bamboo sp. root-3SG.GEN
'The dog$_i$ was gnawing on a **pig bone**, so then he$_j$ (the dog's master) chased him$_i$ away from there (by throwing a rock) so that (result) (he$_i$) fled far away, and then he$_i$ resumed gnawing on **the bone** up behind the house up by the stand of *kawaan* bamboo.'

Similarly, *uha-t* and *uha-n* (< PMP *uRat 'vein; tendon') have the same real world referent in the Buru example (99) below. The background for this was that I returned to the village of Wae Katin after several months and was told that an acquaintance had died. He, his companion and their dog had been running in pursuit of a deer. His companion yelled for him to watch out for some sharp bamboo spike traps hidden in the grass. He did not hear the warning and ran into the spikes.

Buru, assumed identity

(99) NARRATOR: *Da beta* ***uha-t,*** *petu*
3SG connect vein-NMLZ SEQ
*da mata.*
3SG die
'It (the bamboo spike) punctured **the vein**, so he died.'

GRIMES: *Uha-t teni-k?*
vein-NMLZ which-APPL
'Which vein?'

NARRATOR: *Da beta* ***kada-n***
3SG connect leg-3SG.GEN
***uha-n.***
vein-3SG.GEN
'It punctured his **leg vein**.' (i.e. femoral artery; clarify identity).

## 36.6 Deictics and directional systems

Although data are sparse, two-way 'proximal, distal' spatial-temporal-referential *deictic* systems (a.k.a. demonstratives) are common. Some Ambon Seram languages hint at three-way 'proximal, distal, remote' distinctions, such as Asilulu *au le* 'this one', *au mani* 'that one', *au wise* 'that one over there' (Collins 2003a). The deictics tend to be definite and anaphoric in space, time, or reference in the discourse.

*Directional* systems and *locatives* can be complex and interact with the deictics. There are two underlying systems found in central Maluku languages. The first is the *island system* 'landward-seaward, up the coast-down the coast (plus added complexities)'. The second is oriented around the *drainage pattern of the watershed* (see C. Grimes 1991: 167–75 for the latter system in Buru). Both systems are relative to shifting points of reference and scope. The Buru system is simplified in Table 36.12. (The interplay of the two systems is illustrated in examples (13), (20), (22), (32), (48), (72), (89), (90), (91), (97), (98).)

South Nuaulu (Bolton 1990: 66–9) has different twists in the system, summarized in Table 36.13 and the discussion below.

**Table 36.12** Buru deictics and directionals (simplified)

| Full form (final) | Cliticized form (non-final) | Gloss/function |
|---|---|---|
| *saa* | *sa* | indefinite (specific or non-specific) |
| *naa* | *na* | definite proximal (near in space, time or reference) |
| *dii* | *di* | definite distal (non-proximal) |
| *saka* | *sak/saʔ* | up, upward |
| *pao* | *pa* | down, downward |
| *dae* | *da* | upstream; toward emic centre |
| *lawe* | *la* | downstream; away from emic centre; far, dative |
| *aki* | *ak/aʔ* | across (stream, valley, ridge) |

**Table 36.13** South Nuaulu deictics and directionals (simplified)

| Full form | Cliticized form | Gloss/function |
|---|---|---|
| *rei* | | definite, anaphoric; this, that |
| | *-ni* | close |
| | *-no* | far away |
| *nau* | *nau* | seaward |
| *ria* | *ra* | inland |
| *poe* | *po* | downward |
| *roe* | *ro* | upward |
| *pani* | *pa* | across |
| *kua* | *kua* | in the area/vicinity of |
| *mai* | *mai* | here, towards speaker |
| *noi* | *noi* | unspecified direction |
| *hahae* | *hae* | on the side of |
| *suru* | *su* | toward |

Location at, or referential focus tends to be indicated by the demonstrative *rei* combined with a proximity clitic, as in (100).

South Nuaulu
(100) *Au we korobou unte* ***rei-ni.***
1SG 1SG.POSS cow skin DEM-PROX
'This is my belt.'

Motion toward a goal is indicated with the cliticized form of *suru* 'toward' with the full form of other directionals as in example (101).

South Nuaulu
(101) *Au u-eu* ***su-roe.***
1SG 1SG.A-go toward-upward
'I am going up.'

## 36.7 Prepositions

Dative and benefactive functions are often conflated in the region, as is common cross-linguistically. The Buru prepositions in (102)–(103) are often interchangeable.

Buru
(102) *Da puna-h* ***ute*** *riŋe.*
3SG do-3SG.O DAT/BEN 3SG
She$_i$ did it **to/for** him$_j$.

Buru
(103) *Da puna-h* ***la*** *riŋe.*
3SG do-3SG.O DAT/BEN 3SG
She$_i$ did it **to/for** him$_j$./She$_i$ made it **for** him$_j$.

Kowiai uses the verb 'give' in a serial construction to mark benefactive, as in example (104).

Kowiai
(104) *I na-ʔardʒaŋ* ***na-maŋg*** *i laʔ.*
3 3-work 3-give 3 1SG
'He works **for** me.'

Other constructions can have a similar force as a dative 'to', as in Buru examples (105)–(106). There is an ellipted verb *tuke* 'give' in (105). The POSSESSIVE *nam* 'your' (see §36.5.2) in example (106) indicates who is to receive the reward/wage; change the possessive word, the recipient is changed.

Buru, dative-like construction
(105) *[tuke] yako* ***tu*** *proi.*
give 1SG with small
'[Give] some to me.'/'Give me some.'

Buru, dative-like construction
(106) *Ramak riŋe tuke* ***nam*** *emloo-t.*
later 3SG give 2SG.POSS tired-NMLZR
'Later he will give the reward/wages to you.'

Instrumental, comitative, manner, and other functions are often conflated, as is also common elsewhere. Additional functions of Buru *tu* are discussed in C. Grimes (1991: 251–3). Examples (107)–(108) illustrate *tu* indicating accompanying person and accompanying possession.

Buru, comitative, accompanying person
(107) *Da iko tu riŋe.*
3SG go with 3SG
'He$_i$ went **with** him$_j$.'

Buru, accompanying possession
(108) *Da iko* ***tu*** *enhero.*
3SG go with spear
'He went **with** his spear.'

Example (109) shows *tu* indicating means (vehicle); (110) manner; and (111) time.

Buru, means/vehicle
(109) *Da iko* ***tu*** *waga.*
3SG go with boat
'He went **by** boat.'

Buru, manner

(110) *Da iko* ***tu*** *em-taku-t.*
3SG go with STAT-fear-NMLZ
'He went **with** fear (i.e. fearfully).'

Buru, time

(111) *Da iko* ***tu*** *beto.*
3SG go with night
'He went **by** night.'

There are *verbal prepositions* (or prepositional verbs) moving along the grammaticalization chain in many languages. See C. Grimes (1991: 265–71) for a description of verbal prepositions in Buru, and Bolton (1990: 160) for South Nuaulu. The assumption for both languages is that serial verb constructions are the mechanism by which verbs become prepositions. Verbal prepositions can function as full verbs, or they can encode a case role for oblique or peripheral arguments in a clause (see Kowiai example (104) above). In South Nuaulu, the verb 'leave' can indicate SOURCE 'from', as in example (112) and still retain its verbal indexing.

South Nuaulu

(112) *Ia muie i-hoka mansia*
3SG behind 3SG.A-come person
***re-rihoni ai.***
3SG.NHUM-leave tree
'The younger one caused a person to come **out from a tree.**'

Prepositions may be simple or complex, often interacting with the deictics and directionals (see Bolton 1990: 81, 112–19; C. Grimes 1991: 249–76). Occasionally repetition of a preposition can be used as a rhetorical device to indicate *extended duration* of an action in the sense of 'do something on-and-on-and-on'. The greater the number of repetitions, the longer the length of time indicated by the speaker. This has been recorded for many speakers in many different texts.

Buru

(113) *Sira epkiki* ***et-et-et-et-et-et-et-et-eta*** *lea*
3PL dance REDUP———until sun
*tau-n dii.*
full-3SG.GEN DIST
'They danced on-and-on-and-on all day long.'

## 36.8 TAM and other pre-verbal and post-predicate modifiers

Some languages have mostly *pre-verbal TAM* modifiers, some have *post-predicate TAM* modifiers. Pre-verbal TAM modifiers come after subject NPs, pronouns, subject proclitics (but not subject indexing) before the main verb. Post-predicate TAM modifiers follow the verbs, adverbial modifiers, core, peripheral, and oblique arguments. Some languages like Buru, South Nuaulu, and Kowiai have both. Some are polymorphemic. No pattern has yet been identified indicating an organizing principle for what is pre-verbal and what is post-predicate.

*Pre-verbal modifiers* in South Nuaulu are discussed in Bolton (1990: 82–8). Buru pre-verbal TAM markers (C. Grimes 1991: 210–23) are often non-stress bearing CV clitics and include: *ba* 'durative (is X-ing)', *ka* 'habitual (characterized by X)', *te* 'abilitative (can, able to)', *la* 'irrealis (is about to, is going to, will, in order to)', *ma* 'presently at', *puna* 'periphrastic causative', *iak* 'debitive (must)', *bara* 'prohibitive (don't, shouldn't)', *peltanek* 'inceptive (begin to)', *barisuk* 'permissive (allow, let)', *bamba* 'immediate past (just now)', *mamba* 'presently occurring', *lamba* 'immediate (is about to). Their use is illustrated briefly for Buru in examples (114)–(115), and for South Nuaulu in example (116).

Buru

(114) *Da* ***ba*** *iko.*
3SG DUR go
'He was/is going.'/'He was/is leaving.'

Buru

(115) *Kita* ***te*** *kaa-h moo.*
1PL.INCL ABIL eat-3SG.O NEG
'We can't eat it.'

South Nuaulu

(116) *Au rua-ku* ***maha*** *nana numa.*
1SG self-1SG able make house
'I can build a house by myself.'

*Post-predicate modifiers* in South Nuaulu are described in Bolton (1990: 88–9). Buru post-predicate TAM modifiers (C. Grimes 1991: 231–43) are all stress bearing and include: *haik* 'perfective (already)', *sepo* 'completive (finish)', *hede* 'continuative (still)', *moo* 'standard negation (no, not)', *mohede* 'incompletive (not yet)', *tehuk . . . moo* 'non-continuative (no longer)', *deduk* 'repetitive (again)', *saki(-k)* 'shift orientation (instead, rather)', *salak* 'dubitive (maybe, uncertain)', *suek* 'thorough (completely)', *selek* 'to its full conclusion'; *tirin* 'emphatic (very)', *eʔdemen* 'frequentive (often)', *toŋi* 'also, as well', *rahek* 'mitigative (just)', *baa* 'restrictive (only, just)', *leuk* 'prior (previous, before, earlier)', *temak* 'first-time experience (ever)', *beka/peni/tagahak* 'imminent (first, right away)', *aŋa* 'immediate (now, right away)', *holik* 'momentarily', *heik* 'temporary', *ledak* 'thoughtlessly, in vain, without thought to the consequences', *penegak* 'ready for use, ready for the taking'. Buru examples (117)–(119) show post-predicate TAM modifiers following a variety of other modifiers and constituents.

Buru

(117) *Da mata oma-k* ***haik.***
3SG die long-APPL PFV
'She's already been dead for a long time.'

Buru
(118) *Da kaa mansari luke-n dii* ***sepo.***
3SG eat hunt tip-3SG.GEN DIST finish
'He has finished eating what was obtained on the hunt.'

Buru
(119) *Da em-pei boho~boho* ***hede.***
3SG STAT-hurt REDUP~bad CONT
'He is still very sick.'

Example (120) shows a post-predicate TAM modifier in South Nuaulu encompassing the whole serial verb construction.

South Nuaulu
(120) *I-sohu-i i-ai-ki* ***pusi.***
3SG-bathe-3SG 3SG-eat-3SG COMPL
'He finished bathing and eating.'

## 36.9 Negation

Many different kinds of negation are found in central Maluku languages. The primary focus here is on *standard negation*, the negation of simple declarative clauses. Florey (2010) shows that (a) some preposed possessor languages in Central Maluku have *pre-predicate* standard negation, (b) many others have *post-predicate* (clause final) standard negation, and (c) at least one has *embracing* (bipartite, split, double) negation. For typological comparison, example (121) shows the pre-predicate standard negation commonly found in western Austronesian languages.

Malay
(121) *saya* ***tidak*** *tahu*
1SG NEG know
'I don't know.'

Examples (122)–(124) show that pre-predicate standard negation is also found in Central Maluku, with all three of these being Piru Bay languages in or near the Ambon-Lease region.

Amahai
(122) *ama-ʔu* ***aya****-ñ i-supu ia-no*
father-1SG.POSS NEG-3SG 3SG-get fish-NMLZ
'My father didn't catch any fish.' (Florey 2010: 232)

Sou Amana Teru
(123) *ire hose* ***taha****-u berani*
3SG say NEG-1SG brave
'She said, "I'm not brave."' (Florey 2010: 233)

Alang
(124) *nalisa ite* ***ta*** *supu luma-nu*
tomorrow 1PL.INCL NEG meet RECP-NMLZ
'We won't meet each other tomorrow.'
(Florey 2010: 233)

Post-predicate (clause final) negation is widespread in Central Maluku. Example (125) is the Sula-Buru language Buru; (126)–(127) the Ambon-Seram languages of South Nuaulu and Yalahatan; and (128) the Seram Laut language of Kowiai.

Buru
(125) *Ya liŋa-h* ***moo****, petu ya tewa* ***moo.***
1SG see-3SG.O NEG so 1SG know NEG
'I didn't see it, so I don't know.'

South Nuaulu
(126) *ne munata i-amanaku* ***tewa****, au tentene* ***tewa.***
but if 3SG-agree NEG 1SG force NEG
'But if she doesn't agree, I won't force (her).'
(Bolton 1990: 126)

Yalahatan
(127) *yaʔu nia-i mo mosa-i* ***tam.***
1SG look.for-3SG but find-3SG NEG
'I looked for her but didn't find her.' (Beckley n.d.)

Kowiai
(128) *I bot na-mata* ***tei.***
3 still 3-die NEG
'He still had not died.' (Walker and Walker 1991: 130)

At least one Ambon-Seram language in Central Maluku has embracing (bipartite) standard negation.

Haruku
(129) *au* ***taʔ*** *ane* ***sa*** *hahu*
1SG NEG1 eat NEG2 pig
'I don't eat pork.' (Florey 2010: 233)

Reesink (2002b), and Schapper (2015a) point out that post-predicate negation correlates with the SOV typology associated with Papuan languages in eastern Indonesia and Timor-Leste (West Papuan Phylum and Timor-Alor-Pantar languages). Grimes (in press) also argues that embracing (bipartite) negation, which is also found widely in the Rote-Meto languages around Timor, where NEG2 follows post-verbal arguments, provides a transitional mechanism to shift from pre-predicate negation to post-predicate negation. Post-predicate negation is also fairly widespread in SHWNG languages (Gasser, Arnold, Kamholz, chapter 37, this volume).

Buru has a fuller range of negative lexemes (both lexical and phrasal) than what has been documented for other languages in the region, summarized in (130):

| | | |
|---|---|---|
| | Buru | |
| (130) | *moo* | 'no, not' (standard negation; *post-predicate*/clause final) |
| | *mohede* | 'not yet' (*hede* 'still'; post-predicate/clause final) |
| | *sa moo* | 'are none' (negative existential; *saa* 'one'; can be split; post-predicate/clause final) |
| | *tehuk moo* | 'no longer (can be split; post-predicate/clause final) |
| | *sa tehuk moo* | 'no longer are any' (can be split *sa ... tehuk moo*; post-predicate/clause final) |
| | *bara* | 'don't, shouldn't' (prohibitive, negative imperative; *pre-predicate*) |
| | *bara ... moo* | 'no way, don't in any way (emphatic prohibitive; pre-predicate ... post-predicate)' |
| | *mel(e)* | 'lest, so that not (negative irrealis; *pre-predicate*)' |

Tables 36.14 and 36.15 are adapted and expanded from Florey's (2010) survey of negation in Central Maluku. The languages in the table progress from west to east. Note the three positional categories (post-pred = post-predicate; pre-pred = pre-predicate; pre- + post- = split in two positions).

One can see from the available data that *pre-predicate* standard negation (commonly associated with the languages of western Indonesia) is restricted to the Piru Bay languages (a branch of Ambon-Seram), whereas *post-predicate* standard negation (commonly associated with SOV Papuan languages) is more widespread across the whole region, including Sula-Buru, Ambon-Seram, and Seram Laut languages (as in the Kowiai example (128)).

## 36.10 Complex sentences and discourse issues

Bolton (1990) and C. Grimes (1991) have entire chapters describing many complexities of interclausal relations and discourse issues for South Nuaulu and Buru respectively. As mentioned in §36.2, various arguments may be fronted for discourse pragmatic reasons as a sentence-level Topic. Left dislocation of Object and other non-core arguments leaves a trace pronoun in the position of the topicalized argument as in example (131), and in a relative clause in (132).

Buru, Topic with trace pronoun as Object

(131) ***Geba oko em-gihi-n dii,***
[person skin STAT-gross-3SG.GEN DIST]$_{\text{TOPIC}}$
*bara gau-**h** moo.*
PROH hold-3SG.O NEG
'That person with the gross skin disease, don't touch **her**.'

Buru, trace pronoun in REL clause

(132) *Yako sale haik* ***kae nam surat*** *ha*
1SG receive PFV 2SG 2SG.POSS letter REL
*di Yamo tu Ber egu-**h**.*
DIST Yamo with Ber get-3SG.O
'I have received your letter which Yamo and Bert took/brought (it).'

While there are many types of simple and complex connectors, many logical and temporal interclause relationships can be also carried by intonation with no overt connector

**Table 36.14** Survey of negation in Central Maluku (part 1)

| | Standard NEG 'no, not' | 'not yet' | NEG existential 'are none' |
|---|---|---|---|
| Buru (Sula-Buru) | post-pred *moo* | post-pred *mohede* | post-pred (or split) *sa moo* |
| Alang (Ambon-Seram) | pre-pred *ta* | 1) pre-pred *tau* 2) pre- + post- *tau* (*sala*) | pre-pred *tahi* |
| Sou Amana Teru | pre-pred *taha* | pre-pred *taha* X *sala* | pre-pred *taha* |
| Kouro (Amahai) | pre-pred *aya* | pre-pred *aya* X *kala* | pre-pred *aya* |
| Haruku | pre- + post- *taʔ* V *sa* | pre-pred *taʔu sa* | pre-pred *taha* |
| Alune | post-pred *mo* | post-pred *mo sa* | post-pred *sae* X *mo* |
| S. Nuaulu | post-pred *tewa* | post-pred *tewa si* | post-pred *isa* X *tewa* |
| Yalahatan | post-pred *tam, taʔm* | post-pred *tamaʔuru* | post-pred *tam* |

**Table 36.15** Survey of negation in Central Maluku (part 2)

| | 'no longer' | PROHIBITIVE 'don't' | Emphatic PROH 'no way' |
|---|---|---|---|
| Buru (Sula-Buru) | post-pred (or split) *tehuk moo* | pre-pred *bara* | pre- + post- *bara ... moo* |
| Alang (Ambon-Seram) | pre-pred *tahi mana* | pre-pred *naka* | pre-pred *yaʔa naka* |
| Sou Amana Teru | pre-pred *taha* X *ea* | pre-pred *eheʔe* | pre- + post- *eheʔe* X *eheʔe* |
| Kouro (Amahai) | pre-pred *aya* X *nya* | pre-pred *hakai* | pre- + post- *hakai* X *hakai* |
| Haruku | pre-pred *taʔ seiya* | pre-pred *eheʔe* | |
| Alune | post-pred *mo neʔa* | post-pred *yaʔe* | |
| South Nuaulu | post-pred *tewa nea* | post-pred *pene* | |
| Yalahatan | post-pred *tamnii* | post-pred *yaʔe* | |

(asyndesis) and are interpreted from the inferential framework, as illustrated in (133) for South Nuaulu and (134) for Buru.

South Nuaulu
(133) *Marae eu hae-nau, au hita-i.*
Marae go side-long 1SG hit-3SG.U
'[If] Marae goes far, [then] I hit her.'

Buru
(134) *Da iko mansari, da dufa saa moo, da oli hama saa.*
3SG go hunt 3SG get one NEG 3SG return look for one
'[When] he goes hunting, [if] he doesn't get anything, [then] he comes home looking for something.'

Overt connectors are found at clause margins in various combinations. These include conjunctions, complementizers, aspect markers, and time phrases. Example (135) shows an irrealis complementizer introducing a purpose clause in Buru. Example (136) shows the connector marking a Kowiai purpose clause coming at the end.

Buru, purpose clause
(135) *Da ego gomi* ***la*** *ya pake-k.*
3SG get axe IRR 1SG use-APPL
'She fetched an axe **for** me to use.'

Kowiai, purpose clause
(136) *Sena na-maŋgur boʔan na-maŋg-ita ta-paʔ* ***rom.***
Sena 3-buy axe 3-give-1PL.INCL 1PL.INCL-use for
'Sena bought an axe and gave it **for** us to use.'

## 36.10.1 Information questions

In information questions, the question word is typically in the position of the argument being interrogated. Example (137) is interrogating the direct object. Examples (138)–(139) are interrogating the complement clause of 'do'.

Buru
(137) *Sira flal-mata-k* ***sane*** *pa fena dii?*
3PL beat-die-APPL who down village DIST
'**Who** did they beat to death down at that village?'

Buru
(138) *Da puna* ***sapan****?*
3SG do what
'**What** did he do?' (lit: he did **what**?)

South Nuaulu
(139) *Sio una* ***sae*** *nau nuae?*
3PL do what seaward sea
'**What** did they do by the sea?'

Example (140) is interrogating the object of a preposition. Example (141) is asking to clarify the object.

South Nuaulu
(140) *Ano rue na* ***sea****?*
2SG live with who
'**Who** do you live with?'

Kowiai
(141) *Au mu-saʔa biyer* ***niŋ****?*
2SG 2SG-ascend boat which
'**Which** boat did you take/ride/embark on?'

### 36.10.2 Quote formulae and complementizers

Quote formulae precede the quote content in central Maluku languages. Schachter (1985b: 50) observes cross-linguistically, "A good many languages have a complementizer that is rather transparently derived from the verb meaning 'say'." This is common with speech act verbs in central Maluku languages, as in examples (142)–(144).

South Nuaulu
(142) *Sio o-asau* ***ata****, "Pene roma nione*
3PL 3PL-say say PROH pick up coconut
*unte."*
skin
'They said, "Don't pick up the coconut skin."'

Buru, as main verb
(143) *Sira* ***fen****, "Ama-n, kami nam*
3PL say father-VOC 1PL.EXCL 1PL.EXCL.POSS
*suka la kam kita-h."*
like IRR 1PL.EXCL see-3SG.O
'They said, "Father, we'd like to see that."'

Buru, as complementizer
(144) *Kami prepa* ***fen,*** *"Kae la kae ep-mata*
1PL.EXCL say say 2SG IRR 2SG CAUS-die
*geba, ..."*
person
'We said, "You (are intending) to kill someone, ..."'

In both South Nuaulu and Buru, once two protagonists are established in a conversation, change of speaker can be indicated with the complementizer alone, with no subject or other speech-act verb.

South Nuaulu
(145) ***Ata,*** *"Upu, au u-aman-ku u-kani tau*
say master 1SG 1SG-agree-1SG 1SG-dig with
*tuamane rei."*
soil PROX
'[He] **said**, "Master, I agree to dig this soil."'

Buru
(146) ***Fen,*** *"Ego tase naa la sapan?"*
say get bag PROX IRR what
'[He] **said**, "Why are you taking this bag?"' (lit: for what [purpose])

In eastern Indonesia these same complementizers used with verbs of speech are often also used with verbs of perception or cognition, functioning like a realis complementizer 'that' (Grimes 2018), as in (147)–(148).

Buru
(147) *Eta da tʃaan* ***fen*** *yako emŋaha tu*
when 3SG hear say 1SG shout with
*iŋa-ŋ haa-t, ...*
voice-1SG.GEN big-NMLZ
'When she heard **that** I was shouting with a loud voice,...'

Buru
(148) *Ya odo* ***fen*** *kimi kita yako tehuk moo.*
1SG think say 2PL see 1SG again NEG
'I think **that** you will not see me again.'

### 36.10.3 Serial verb constructions (SVCs)

Both nuclear-layer and core-layer serial verb constructions are attested (Bolton 1990: 158–60; C. Grimes 1991: 207–10, 399–402). In *nuclear layer serialization* the combined clauses function as a single unit syntactically and prosodically. The core arguments are shared by the verbs with both Subject and Object functioning for the combination of verbs. Examples (149)–(150) illustrate shared Subjects when one-argument intransitive verbs combine with two-argument transitive verbs.

South Nuaulu, intransitive + transitive; nuclear layer serialization
(149) *Au* ***u-eu keta*** *manue isa.*
1SG 1SG.A-go shoot bird one
'I'm going to go shoot a bird.'

Sou Amana Teru, intransitive + transitive; nuclear layer serialization
(150) *Nina e=paʔanusi yau:* ***"Oi apai=si."***
mother 3SG=order 1SG go call=3PL
'Mother told me: "Go call them."' (Musgrave 2010: 3)

Examples (151)–(152) illustrate shared Subjects and Objects when two two-argument transitive verbs combine.

South Nuaulu, transitive + transitive; nuclear layer serialization
(151) ***I-hita hunu-i,*** *poe re-mata-i.*
3SG.A-hit kill-3SG.U down 3SG.NHUM-die-3SG.U
'He hit it, killing it so it died.'

Buru, transitive + transitive; nuclear layer serialization
(152) *Du* ***amo hama*** *foki-t sak loteŋ.*
3PL grope look for wrap-NMLZ up loft
'They were groping searching for the bundle up in the loft.'

Examples (153)–(154) illustrate complexities when transitive and intransitive verbs combine in a nuclear serial verb construction.

Buru, transitive + intransitive; nuclear layer serialization

(153) *Geba* *di* *heka,* *emrimo* *iko* *la*
person DIST flee constable go IRR
***kala-k*** ***oli.***
call-APPL return
'[If] the person flees, the *emrimo* goes to call [him] back.'

Buru, shared core arguments; nuclear layer serialization

(154) *Da* ***kala-k*** ***oli*** *riŋe.*
3SG.A call-APPL return 3SG.U
'He$_i$ called him$_j$ back.'

The semantic relationship between the clauses as realis or irrealis, *purpose* or *result* is drawn from the inferential framework of the discourse as illustrated in (155).

Buru, intransitive + transitive; nuclear layer serialization

(155) *Riŋe* ***oli*** ***taga*** *ana-t=o.*
3SG return meet child-NMLZ=PL
'He returned **to** meet [his] children.' (irrealis, purpose)
'He returned **and** met [his] children.' (realis, result)

In nuclear-layer serialization, verbal modifiers such as the pre-verbal TAM modifiers and negation are shared by the combination of the verbs as a unit as in (156).

Buru, shared scope of verbal modifiers

(156) *Sira* ***te*** ***keha*** ***bage*** *saka* *huma*
3PL ABIL [ascend sleep] up house
*lale-n* ***moo.***
inside-3SG.GEN NEG
'They **can't** go up [and] sleep inside the house.'

In *core-layer serialization*, the verbs maintain their separate roles for core arguments, so the Object of the first verb can be the Subject of the second verb. Compare core-layer example (157) with nuclear-layer example (154) above.

Buru, core-layer serialization

(157) *Da* ***kala-k*** *riŋe* ***oli.***
3SG.A call-APPL 3SG.U
3SG.A return
'He$_i$ called him$_j$ [for him$_j$ to] return.' [purpose]
'He$_i$ called him$_j$ [and he$_j$] returned.' [result]

## 36.10.4 Relativization and relative clauses

Relative clauses are clausal modifiers of a head noun embedded within an NP argument of the main clause. Relative clauses add background information to a text, rather than event-line information. Bolton (1990: 61–3, 77–8, 164–70) and Grimes (1991: 183, 429–36) discuss a number of structures and functions relating to relativization for South Nuaulu and Buru respectively. Some are more nominal, describing *characteristic roles.* In example (158), South Nuaulu uses various forms of a nominalizing relativizer. In example (159), Buru uses the HABITUAL relativizer *ka* with the noun *geba* 'person' for similar constructions.

South Nuaulu

| (158) | *rahu* | 'plant (v)' | *ia* ***mam****-rahu-e* | 'farmer' |
|---|---|---|---|---|
| | *akarota* | 'lie' | *ia* ***m****-akarota-ne* | 'liar' |
| | *atanunu* | 'cook (v)' | *ia* ***m****-atanunu-e* | 'a cook (n)' |
| | *ehu* | 'smoke (v)' | *ia* ***mam****-ehu-e* | 'smoker' |

Buru

| (159) | *ruba* | 'treat' | *geba* **ka** *ruba geba*<br>'healer; medical practitioner' |
|---|---|---|---|
| | *epmata* | 'kill' | *geba* **ka** *epmata geba*<br>'murderer; killer of people' |
| | *fasa* | 'cut; decide' | *geba* **ka** *fasa perkara*<br>'judge; decider of disputes' |
| | *lata* | 'cut' | *geba* **ka** *lata hawa*<br>'farmer; cutter of fields'<br>*geba* **ka** *lata kau*<br>'carpenter; cutter of wood' |
| | *toto* | 'pound' | *geba* **ka** *toto momol*<br>'blacksmith; pounder of iron' |
| | *enilik* | 'exchange' | *geba* **ka** *enilik liet*<br>'translator; interpreter; exchanger of language' |

In addition to the mechanisms in the previous two examples, both South Nuaulu and Buru have other mechanisms for more verbal or clausal relativization, for example describing events. In both languages a RELATIVE CLAUSE modifier in an NP follows the HEAD, just like other NP modifiers (except the GENITIVES and POSSESSIVES described in §36.5). South Nuaulu can use the pronoun *saho(ro)* 'who' for human referents, as in (160).

South Nuaulu, RC in Object NP

(160) *Au* *u-ationa* *Hukala* ***sahoro*** *i-una*
1SG 1SG.A-know Hukala who 3SG.A-make
*sona* *osi* *Wanto.*
sago for Wanto
'I know Hukala **who** made sago for Wanto.'

More commonly in South Nuaulu the relativizers *(w)ai* with human referents, and *(w)a* with non-human referents are used. These also function as existentials (see example (58)), and can interact with the deictics and directionals (see Table 36.13). Subjects are the most common argument relativized in natural text, but relativization of Direct Objects and oblique arguments are also found. The use of the relativizer *(w)ai* is illustrated in (161).

South Nuaulu, RC in Object NP

(161) *Ere-kati* *na~nana-ke* *Hunahane*
3SG.NHUM-replace REDUP~name-? Hunahane
***ai-ni*** *sio* *hunu-i.*
REL-PROX 3PL kill-3SG.U
'She replaces [the person] named Hunahane **whom** they killed.'

Example (160) can substitute the relativizer *ai-ni* for *sahoro* with the same meaning. It can also have no overt relativizer, but there is a non-final intonation break added, marked by the comma in (162).

South Nuaulu, RC with no RELATIVIZER

(162) *Au* *u-ationa* *Hukala,* *i-una*
1SG 1SG.A-know Hukala 3SG.A-make
*sona* *osi* *Wanto.*
sago for Wanto
'I know Hukala, [**who**] made sago for Wanto.'

For Buru, *ha* is a general relativizer which identifies information assumed to be already known by the addressee to enable the addressee to *identify* the correct referent. Because the information in the *restrictive relative clause* is assumed to be known, the relative clause with *ha* is often bracketed with a definite deictic *dii* 'distal' or *naa* 'proximal'. The head noun of the argument in the main clause has a coreferential generic noun or pronoun within the relative clause. This was illustrated in example (132) in a relativized Object NP, and also here in (163). The relative clause identifies the two brothers that got burned as those that were killed, in contrast with the two brothers that did the killing.

Buru, RC in Object NP

(163) *Petu* *du* *pefa* *hum-tapa* *dii*
SEQ 3PL burn house-smoke DIST
*ep-sia-k* *tu* *kaka-wai-t* *rua*
CAUS-one-APPL with [elder-younger-NMLZ two
***ha*** *dii* *du* *ba* *ep-mata* ***dii.***
REL DIST 3PL DUR CAUS-die $\text{DIST}]_{\text{NP}}$
'Then they burned down the hunting lodge together with **those two brothers whom they had killed.**'

The Buru relativizer is marked according to the plurality of the referent, as *ha* 'singular referent' or *ha-r* 'plural referent', as in example (164).

Buru, plural REL in Subject NP

(164) *Petu* *yebu* ***ha-r*** *dii,* *ha* *poto*
SEQ person REL-PL DIST DUR burn
*nunu-r* *cengke-r* ***dii,*** *...*
3PL.POSS-PL clove-PL DIST
'Then those people whose cloves got burned, ...'

The *non-restrictive relative clause* in Buru mirrors the restrictive relative clause described above, but has no explicit relativizer (i.e. no *ha* (... *dii*) phrase). There is no phonological juncture between the head noun and the descriptive relative clause. The relative clause introduces a new participant in discourse with no definite or anaphoric markers, but expands the information to locate the new participant geographically (adding backgrounded information). Example (165) begins with the widespread narrative pattern of tail-head linkage, continuing from the previous sentence.

Buru, non-restrictive RC with no REL

(165) *Rohi* *eta* *suba* *di* *geba*
stalk until cross threshold DIST [person
*boho-n* *da* *ba* *eptea* *di*
bad-3SG.GEN [3SG DUR sit DIST
*koltelo* *lahi-n.*
tree sp. root-$\text{3SG.GEN}]_{\text{RELATIVE}}]_{\text{NP}}$
'[He kept] stalking [the pig in the rain] until he came to **a bad man [who was] living at the *koltelo* tree.**'

## 36.11 Summary and future directions

Moving eastward from Sulawesi and Sumbawa we begin to see trace evidence of Austronesians who spoke VSO and SVO languages coming in *contact* with pre-Austronesian populations, most likely speaking SOV Papuan languages.[11] There is evidence of Austronesian languages adapting structurally and typologically to work more like Papuan languages, and Papuan languages adapting to work more like Austronesian languages (Donohue and Grimes 2008; C. Grimes 2000a, in

[11] The Papuan substrate is assumed, based on multiple trace evidence in the grammars, phonologies, and lexicons. Timor-Alor-Pantar languages and West Papuan languages still spoken around Timor, Halmahera, and the Bird's Head of Papua are SOV and manifest the many features that have been attributed to contact-induced change in the region. While there are no Papuan languages currently spoken in central Maluku, the Austronesian languages exhibit the same features found where Papuan languages are still spoken.

press; Klamer et al. 2008; Schapper 2015a). B. Grimes (2010) also identified traces in the present-day cultures of such early contact-induced change. Recognizing that these SVO, HEAD before MODIFIER, prepositional, predominantly head-marking Austronesian languages of central Maluku have a *preposed possessor* and other features associated with SOV languages is typologically significant. These Austronesian languages of central Maluku are largely what delineates Himmelmann's (2005a) *preposed possessor* type, in contrast to his *symmetrical voice* type.

More comprehensive grammars based on natural texts, and lexicographically informed corpus-based dictionaries are essential to improving our understanding of this severely under-documented region.

CHAPTER 37

# The languages of Halmahera and West New Guinea

EMILY GASSER, LAURA ARNOLD, AND DAVID KAMHOLZ

## 37.1 Introduction

There are forty to forty-five Austronesian languages spoken in and around Halmahera and west New Guinea in east Indonesia. This region may be usefully divided into several geographic subregions: the island of Halmahera; the Raja Ampat islands and western Bird's Head; the Bomberai peninsula; Cenderawasih Bay, including the islands of Biak and Yapen; and the Mamberamo delta. The Austronesian languages are generally associated with individual ethnic groups, and speakers are concentrated near the coasts. Elsewhere in the region, genealogically diverse non-Austronesian languages are spoken.

The majority of the Austronesian languages of this region belong to the South Halmahera–West New Guinea (SHWNG) subgroup (Kamholz 2014). The languages spoken on the Bomberai peninsula, however, do not (Blust 1993a; Edwards and Grimes 2021). This chapter includes data from SHWNG and from Irarutu, but not from the other Bomberai languages, which are not well described. Farther east, Oceanic languages are spoken along the Sarmi coast; these are not addressed in this chapter. Nor are the Austronesian languages of Nusa Tenggara and Maluku (outside of southern Halmahera) to the west, or the regional varieties of Malay.

SHWNG contains two high-level subgroups: Raja Ampat–South Halmahera (RASH) and Nuclear Cenderawasih Bay (see Kamholz, this volume, §14.4). The RASH subgroup comprises all of the SHWNG languages spoken in Halmahera and Raja Ampat, as well as As, spoken on the Bird's Head peninsula. Within RASH, the languages of Halmahera (including Gebe) belong to the South Halmahera subgroup. Most languages of Cenderawasih Bay belong to the Cenderawasih Bay subgroup; notable exceptions include Moor and Waropen, which are likely family-level isolates. Within the Cenderawasih Bay subgroup, Biak, Roon, Dusner, and Meoswar belong to the Biakic subgroup, and the languages of Yapen Island plus Wamesa belong to the Yapen subgroup. Umar, Yaur, and Yerisiam make up the Southwest Cenderawasih Bay subgroup. Yoke and Warembori are spoken at the mouth of the Mamberamo river to the east, but do not constitute a subgroup—both are family-level isolates.

The largest languages are Biak, reported to have up to 70,000 speakers (Eberhard et al. 2019; van den Heuvel 2006), and Taba, with perhaps 30,000–40,000 speakers (Bowden 2001). Most languages have several hundred to a few thousand speakers, and all are endangered to some degree, under pressure from Indonesian and local varieties of Malay, particularly in coastal areas and towns. Several are moribund: for example, Dusner is down to its last three fluent speakers (Dalrymple and Mofu 2012), there are only five or six fluent speakers of As (Laura Arnold fieldwork 2020), and Tandia has only a handful of semi-speakers left. Historically, Biak has served as a lingua franca throughout Cenderawasih Bay, as has Wamesa in the southwest of Cenderawasih Bay and the Bird's Neck area, and Ma'ya in Raja Ampat; multilingualism is common (see Clouse et al. 2002; Gasser 2017b; Sawaki 2016, inter alia).

The languages are generally under-described, with few accessible documentary corpora. Detailed grammars now exist for Ambai, Ambel, Biak, Irarutu, Taba, Waropen, and Wooi; a handful of additional languages are documented by short sketch grammars or dissertations addressing only a part of their grammar. For the rest, resources vary from individual articles and conference handouts to collected wordlists or unpublished fieldnotes, of varying reliability. The information presented here is necessarily limited by the lack of documentation available, and the failure of a given pattern to appear in the attested data does not necessarily mean that it is actually absent. Because of the lack of reliable data, we do not discuss all Austronesian languages of the region here; those we do address, and the sources consulted, are listed at the end of this chapter. Map 37.1 shows the Austronesian languages of Halmahera and West New Guinea.

The earliest linguistic documentation in the region was done by Dutch missionaries and government functionaries in the late 1800s (van Balen, de Clerq, and Fabritius), with

Emily Gasser, Laura Arnold, and David Kamholz, *The languages of Halmahera and West New Guinea.* In: *The Oxford Guide to the Malayo-Polynesian Languages of Southeast Asia.* Edited by: Alexander Adelaar and Antoinette Schapper, Oxford University Press. © Emily Gasser, Laura Arnold, and David Kamholz (2024). DOI: 10.1093/oso/9780198807353.003.0037

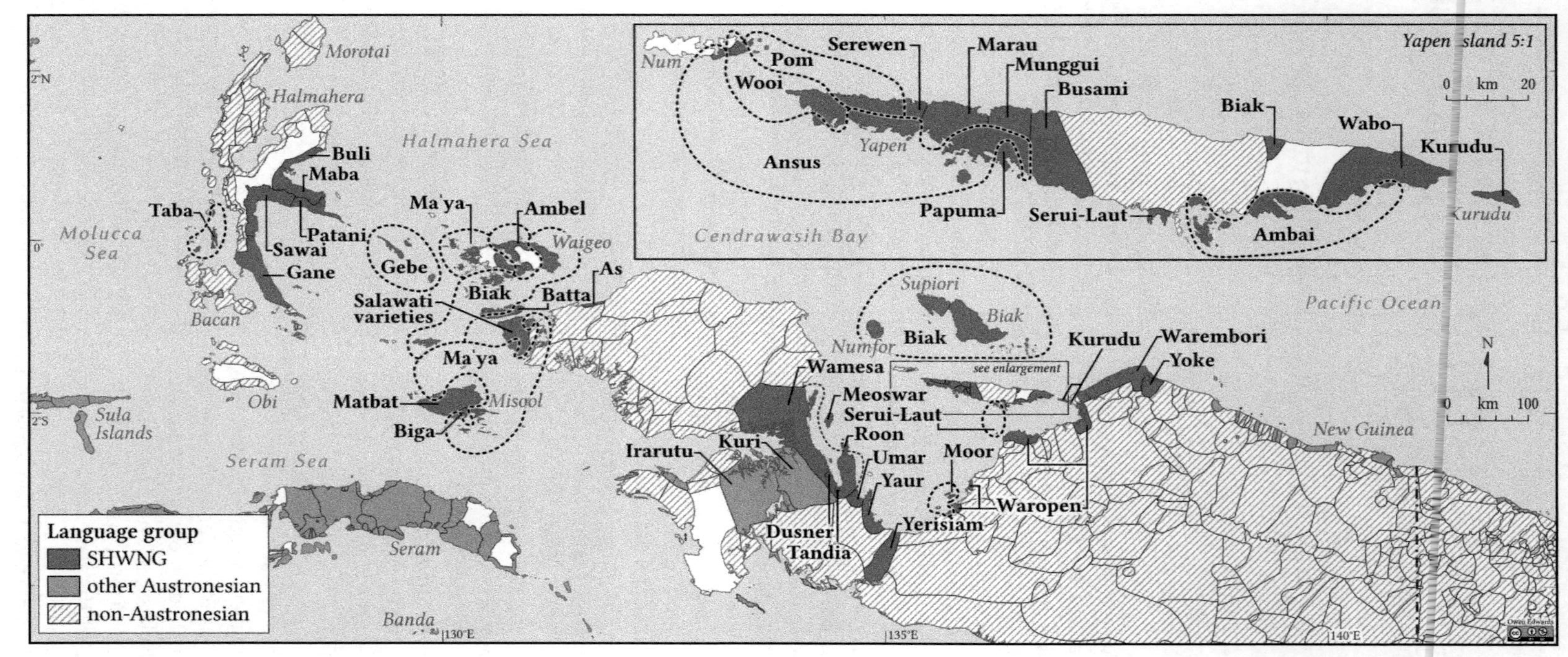


**Map 37.1** The Austronesian languages of Halmahera and West New Guinea.

a peak of interest in the early/mid-twentieth century (see work by Esser, Adriani and Kruyt, Holle, Kijne, Cowan, Anceaux, Slump, Maan, Peski, and Grace). Recently, interest in the region has renewed, with a spate of new dissertations, sketch grammars, and conferences in the 2010s (Arnold 2018a; Dalrymple and Mofu 2012; Gasser 2014; Jackson 2014; Kamholz 2014; Sawaki 2016), and others currently underway.

Since Austronesian speakers settled in west New Guinea and the nearby islands some 3,500 years ago, they have been in close contact with speakers of neighbouring non-Austronesian languages. As mentioned, these non-Austronesian languages are genealogically very diverse, with languages from several different families as well as a number of isolates spoken in the area. Multilingualism and intermarriage are common, and the effects are seen in the grammar and lexicon. Klamer (2002b), Klamer et al. (2008), and Schapper (2015a) describe some areal features of eastern Indonesia that cross-cut familial boundaries; several of these, including post-verbal negation and alienability distinctions, are common in the languages discussed here. Contact with non-Austronesian languages has additionally resulted in the adoption of additive quinary-decimal numeral systems in a number of languages (Gasser 2017b); may have instigated the development of tone in Raja Ampat and south Cenderawasih Bay (Arnold 2018b; Kamholz 2017); and has had an extensive impact on the lexicons of both the Austronesian and non-Austronesian languages of the region (Gasser 2019a; Usher and Schapper 2018; inter alia).

Throughout this chapter, orthography is used in cases where phonology is not the focus; we follow the spelling practices of the original authors and regional conventions (e.g. *v* for [β], *ng* for [ŋ], *y* for [j], *c* for [t͡ʃ], *j* for [d͡ʒ] or [ɟ]), with the exception of glottal stop which we always render with *ʔ*. Superscript numerals and diacritics denote tone, except in Biak, where an acute accent denotes a long vowel; lexical stress is additionally marked in Maˈya.

## 37.2 Phonology and morphophonology

### 37.2.1 Segment inventories

Phonemic inventories are relatively small, especially when compared to some Austronesian languages further west (Blust 2013a). Most of the surveyed languages use a standard five-vowel system: '/i e a o u/'. The RASH languages can exceed this: Biga adds /ɪ/, while Matbat, Buli, Maba, Sawai, and Patani add lax /ɛ/ and /ɔ/. Irarutu contrasts the basic five vowels plus /ɪ/ and /y/. Biak, Yerisiam, Yaur, and (marginally) Moor have contrastive vowel length.

Most languages have consonant inventories of ten to fifteen segments. All have a basic set of voiced, voiceless, and nasal stops, and at least one fricative. Glides also appear, although in some languages, such as Wamesa, these are derived from underlying high vowels (Gasser 2014). Beyond this, consonant inventories follow strong geographic patterns. The smallest are found at the eastern end of the subgroup, in the languages of the Mamberamo delta: Warembori has only ten contrastive segments, /p t k b d s m n w j/. All of the Yapen and Biakic languages add /β/ and /r/ to the Warembori set. Some languages also include /ŋ/, /h/, and /ɸ/ or /f/; /ɲ/, /c/, and /t͡ʃ/ are rarer. In Moor and the Yapen and Biakic languages, /g/ tends to have a limited distribution; elsewhere it is widespread. Biak is unusual in that /t/ is marginal; historically, *t became /k/ in Biakic languages other than Dusner. The Pom inventory, shown below as Table 37.1, is typical of the Yapen languages.

Elsewhere in Cenderawasih Bay, Yaur (see Table 37.2), Yerisiam, and Moor include /gʷ/ (also found in the Wondama dialect of Wamesa), and these languages plus Umar also use /d͡ʒ/ and /h/. Contrastive glottal stops are found in Moor and Yaur, and /ɣ/ appears in Waropen.

The largest consonant inventories, with up to nineteen consonants, again appear in the RASH languages. The fricatives /f/ and /h/ are commonly found across RASH, and most languages of South Halmahera additionally include /t͡ʃ d͡ʒɲŋ/. Irarutu's inventory of thirteen consonants is unusual in its inclusion of /ɟ/ and its prenasalization of voiced plosives. Table 37.3 gives the phoneme inventory of Patani, a South Halmahera language.

The liquids /r/ and /l/ show strong areal tendencies in their distribution. Irarutu and the languages spoken around Cenderawasih Bay and the Mamberamo delta use only /r/ except in recent loans; earlier *r and *l merged to /r/ in these languages. Several languages of Raja Ampat and South Halmahera distinguish /r/ and /l/, although /r/ tends to have a limited distribution. For those RASH languages without this distinction, /l/ is found.

The prevalence of bilabial fricatives is also noteworthy. Most Cenderawasih Bay languages have phonemic /β/, several have phonemic /ɸ/, and both surface allophonically in the Raja Ampat and Mamberamo languages. These segments are an areal feature: though globally rare, one or both fricatives are present in a number of nearby non-Austronesian varieties, including Yawa (Jones et al. 1989), Tause (Clouse 1997), and Hatam (Donohue 1997a; Reesink 1999).

### 37.2.2 Phonotactics

Phonotactic structure is quite variable across the region. Waropen, Moor, and the West Yapen and Mamberamo languages tend towards simpler phonotactics and fewer permitted clusters. In these languages, all clusters are word-medial and heterosyllabic. Warembori, Waropen, and Wamesa, for example, limit their clusters to a nasal plus homorganic voiced stop. Others allow the second member of the cluster to be a voiceless stop (Pom, Ansus, Wabo), or any homorganic obstruent (Ambai).

**Table 37.1** The Pom phoneme inventory

| | Labial | Alveolar | Palatal | Velar | Glottal | | | |
|---|---|---|---|---|---|---|---|---|
| Stops | p b | t d | | k | | | | |
| Nasals | m | n | | | | i | | u |
| Fricatives | β | s | | | h | e | | o |
| Tap/trill | r | | | | | | a | |
| Approximants | w | | j | | | | | |

(Gasser fieldnotes)

**Table 37.2** The Yaur phoneme inventory

| | Labial | Alveolar | Velar | Glottal | | | |
|---|---|---|---|---|---|---|---|
| Stops | p b | t d | g gʷ | ʔ | i | | u |
| Nasals | m | n | | | e | | o |
| Fricatives/affricates | β | d͡ʒ | | h | | a | |
| Tap/trill | | r | | | | | |

(Kamholz fieldnotes)

**Table 37.3** The Patani phoneme inventory

| | Labial | Alveolar | Palatal | Velar | Glottal | | | |
|---|---|---|---|---|---|---|---|---|
| Stops | p b | t d | | k g | | | | |
| Nasals | m | n | (ɲ) | ŋ | | i | | u |
| Fricatives | f | s | | | (h) | e | | o |
| Affricates | | t͡ʃ d͡ʒ | | | | ɛ | | ɔ |
| Taps/trills | | r | | | | | a | |
| Approximants | w | l | j | | | | | |

(Linn Iren Sjånes Rødvand, p.c.; Kamholz fieldnotes)

Kurudu, Yaur, Umar, Taba, Patani, Sawai, and the Biakic languages (excluding Roon) allow a wide variety of clusters in various positions within the word, many of which violate the Sonority Sequencing Principle (SSP), which governs the ordering of segments within a syllable (Kenstowicz 1994). Patani, Biak, and Umar allow triconsonantal clusters; Taba, Patani, and Umar also permit geminates.

Biak
(1) *rmomn* 'angry', *srepk* 'short', *fnder* 'forget'
(van den Heuvel 2006: 39–41)

Kurudu
(2) *kmi* 'seed', *sorm* 'sea', *mandukri* 'younger sibling'
(Xavier Bach p.c.)

Taba
(3) *amseh* 'be drunk', *ddáwa* 'grass', *npoglak* 'he or she holds something with something'
(Bowden 2001: 39, 49)

Umar
(4) *mdirke* 'you move', *ehher* 'disturb', *mgre* 'destroyed'
(Kamholz fieldnotes)

Patani
(5) *gbu* 'grandchild', *mfyan* 'you go', *lollo* 'inside; content' (Linn Iren Sjånes Rødvand p.c.)

Irarutu allows up to five consonants in a row, although more than three is uncommon. The SSP is maintained in onsets by resyllabification, but is not necessarily respected in codas. Almost any consonant may be a syllable nucleus in Irarutu; the language also permits sequences of two identical consonants, which Jackson (2014) describes as being each separately released.

Irarutu, consonant clusters and syllabification
(6) [kkor] 'chicken', [sr̩.fufn] 'top of head', [tf̩.tfrie] 'dragonfly', [n̩.fn̩.taᵑg.re] 'regarding' (Jackson 2014: 65, 67, 72)

Most of the languages surveyed here place restrictions on which consonants may appear word-finally. No attested Yapen language allows final voiced plosives, and several limit final Cs to only nasals or a subset thereof (as does Warembori). Yapen word-final nasals often neutralize to [ŋ], and in some cases they may assimilate to the place of articulation of a following clitic (e.g. Ansus, where [waruŋ] 'fence' appears with a determiner as [warum pai]). Yaur and Yerisiam do not permit final consonants at all. Roon allows a wide range of final Cs, as do Umar and the RASH languages (although the voicing distinction in plosives tends to be neutralized syllable-finally in Raja Ampat). As noted above, Biak, Dusner, and Irarutu allow a range of final clusters.

In the Yapen languages, glides may appear in a nucleus adjacent to a consonant cluster, but are always vowel-adjacent. All attested languages of the region allow sequences of two vowels, vowel plus glide, or diphthongs. In some cases, these vowel sequences may be lengthy, as in Dusner /βeβeiu/ 'good' and Pom /tauaua/ 'short'.

Words tend to be disyllabic. Languages with historical syncope, like Biak, have a higher proportion of monosyllabic words. In Wamesa, roots can be up to five syllables long (*aparapiri* 'gnat'), and morphological processes may further enlarge words (*sematitiotap* 'they (human) destroyed', with affixation and reduplication of *matiotap* 'break').

Epenthetic vowels occur across the region. Commonly, epenthetic [e] or [ə] is inserted to break up consonant clusters in some environments (e.g. Taba, Irarutu, and Biak). A word-final epenthetic vowel is described in Wamesa, Biak, Matbat, Ma'ya, Salawati, Biga, Batta, Ambel, and Moor, appearing as [-e], [-i], [-a], or [-o] depending on the language; often this is prosodically conditioned or optional. In Patani, an epenthetic vowel is inserted before an initial consonant cluster when the preceding word ends in a consonant; this vowel copies the quality of the vowel of the preceding syllable. Waropen inserts an obligatory (synchronically) epenthetic 'supporting vowel' after any word-final C except nasals and [r].

Biak
(7) /bakn/ → [bakn] ~ [baken] 'body' (van den Heuvel 2006: 28)

Biga
(8) /kanun/ → [kanuno] 'feather' (Remijsen 2001a: 142)

Waropen
(9) /ran/ → [rana] 'song' (Held 1942: 20)

### 37.2.3 Stress and tone

Stress across the region tends to be penultimate, but it is rarely entirely predictable. Taba and Sawai, for example, are both described as having generally penultimate stress, with a handful of exceptions in which stress is final. Warembori words generally get penultimate stress, which, in most cases, shifts rightwards with the addition of suffixes. In Wamesa, primary stress is penultimate in roughly 60% of the lexicon, with the rest split between final and antepenultimate stress; secondary stress is usually word-initial. For Biak, van den Heuvel (2006) argues that lexical stress is underlyingly unspecified, and surface stress patterns arise from the interaction between vowel length and rhythmic stress assignment.

Tone, an unusual feature in Austronesian, is found in several languages. At least seven languages in and around Raja Ampat (Ambel, As, Ḃatta, Biga, Matbat, Ma'ya, and Salawati) and three languages in Cenderawasih Bay (Moor, Yerisiam, and Yaur) have lexical tone (Arnold 2018b, c; Kamholz 2017; Remijsen 2001a, b, 2007; Arnold fieldwork 2019–2020).[1] Limited grammatical tone is also reported in Roon (Gil 2019, 2023) and possibly Waropen (van Velzen n.d., 1994). The systems themselves, however, are very diverse. For example, while Ambel has a comparatively simple system, in which High syllables contrast with toneless syllables, Matbat has a very rich system, distinguishing Low, High, Extra-High Fall, Low Fall, Low Rise, and Rise-Fall syllables. The Ma'ya tone system is relatively straightforward: word-final syllables can be High, Rise, or toneless. However, in addition to lexical tone, Ma'ya also has lexical stress; the combination of lexical tone with lexical stress is highly unusual cross-linguistically. Moor has a word-tone system with four primary tonal patterns; tone is neutralized except in phrase-final position. Yerisiam and Yaur have two tones, High and Low, which associate with morae; surface contour tones can appear on long vowels and diphthongs.

[1] Himmelmann (2018: 370 fn. 19) reports that Wooi may also have lexical tone.

### 37.2.4 VRK mutation

Most of the Austronesian languages of Cenderawasih Bay show a process that Gasser (2023) calls VRK mutation after the triggering sounds, although the details vary considerably language to language. In the prototypical case, clusters in which the second member is /β/ (orthographic *v*), /r/, or /k/ will surface as [mb], [nd], and [ŋg], respectively—all other clusters behave differently, usually undergoing deletion or coalescence, or simply surfacing as-is. VRK mutation is a typologically unexpected pattern, as the set of segments it targets are not a natural class, and there is often no phonetic motivation (e.g. in example (11) below). VRK mutation in most languages is triggered only when the first consonant in the cluster is a nasal; in many Yapen varieties, the process has generalized and any $C_1$ may trigger mutation. Even Biak and Umar, generally very permissive of consonant clusters, specifically disallow nasal plus /β, r, k/ in surface forms. The examples in (10)–(12) show VRK mutation in three eastern SHWNG languages; the word *fama* in the Waropen example includes what Held calls a "supporting vowel", /a/, which only surfaces word-finally, yielding a cluster in the morphologically complex surface form.

Umar
(10) /mbre**n**-**β**ie/ → [mbre**mb**ie] 'my tongue'
(Kamholz fieldnotes)

Wamesa
(11) /su**r**-**r**a/ → [su**nd**a] 'they two go' (Gasser 2014: 47)

Waropen
(12) /fa**m**a + **k**i/ → [fa**ŋg**i] 'he strikes them' (Held 1942: 24)

### 37.2.5 Reduplication

Reduplication is attested across the region. Full root reduplication is attested in several languages, but is never productive. It may take as its base nouns, verbs, or numerals, typically contributing either an iterative function (e.g. Ma'ya *ma'no*$^3$ 'move' → *ma'no*$^3$*~ma'no*$^3$ 'move continuously') or an intensifying function (e.g. Taba *kutu* 'small' → *kutu~kutu* 'very small, cute'). Full reduplication without the independent attestation of the base is additionally reported for some languages (e.g. Wamesa *kowokowo* 'kind of bird', Irarutu *rabirabi* 'kind of knife'). In other languages, full reduplication is not attested (e.g. Wooi and Ambai).

Ca(C)-reduplication is more common, typically taking the first CV(C) sequence of verbal roots, and creating a prefix in which /a/ is substituted for the V.[2] This type of reduplication is particularly common in RASH, where it has a nominalizing function (e.g. Taba *bulaj* 'to wind/coil something' → *bal~bulaj* 'device for winding rope, cord onto'). Patani has Ci(C)-reduplication, directly analogous to Taba's Ca(C)- pattern. Two similar patterns, aC- and (a)Ca(C)-reduplication, are reported in Biak, where they either have a nominalizing function (e.g. *kenm* 'live' → *kan~kenm* 'life'), or serve to mark iterativity or durativity (e.g. *kavr* 'return' → *kav~kavr* 'come back again and again').

Several other reduplication patterns are sporadically attested, for example: (C)aC(C)a-reduplication in Taba, which contributes a 'plurality of action' meaning (e.g. *k-sung um* 1SG-enter house 'I entered the house' → *k-sang~sung um* 1SG-REDUP~enter house 'I entered many houses'); CC-reduplication in Irarutu, which marks plurality and distributivity on nouns (e.g. *bar* 'lung' → *br~bar* 'lungs'; *met* 'half, part' → *mt~met* 'little by little'); and reduplication of the first or second root syllable of adjectives, verbs, and adverbs in Wamesa, which functions as an intensifier (e.g. *saira* 'quickly' → *sa~saira* 'very quickly'; *matiotap* 'broken' → *ma~ti~tiotap* 'destroyed')

### 37.2.6 Infixation

As described in §37.3.4, person, number, and sometimes animacy of the clausal subject are marked on verbal predicates in all of the surveyed languages. In many languages across the region, infixation is used to mark the subject on certain, usually consonant-initial verbs, though the patterns differ by subgroup. In the Cenderawasih Bay subgroup, infixes mark 2SG and 3SG subjects; in RASH, 1SG and 2SG subject markers are infixed.

Although the details vary, infixation is attested in all Cenderawasih Bay languages for which data are available. In Yapen, subject marking affixes appear as a CV prefix if the root is vowel-initial, and as a V infix if the root is consonant-initial. In Biakic, the forms are similar, but the divide between infixing and prefixing verb roots is more arbitrary: while all V-initial roots take prefixes, some C-initial roots do as well, thus the distinction is not fully predictable. In Roon, for example, the root *ve* meaning 'want; say' is prefixing, but shifts to the infixing class when used with the meanings 'do; give; become' (Gil 2017). The forms in Umar, Yaur, and Yerisiam are more complex, with combinations of prefixes and infixes on the same root, as shown for Yerisiam in Table 37.4.

In Yaur, the infixing class includes both V- and C-initial verbs, although this surfaces synchronically only as vowel alternations in the root, shown in Table 37.5. It is

[2] Ca(C)-reduplication is likely derived from Proto-Austronesian Ca-reduplication, which functioned to derive nouns referring to instruments from verbs (Blust 1998a).

**Table 37.4** Verbal infixation

| Language | | Root | 1SG | 2SG | 3SG |
|---|---|---|---|---|---|
| Wamesa | prefixing | *ena* 'sleep' | ***y**-ena* | ***bu**-ena* | ***di**-ena* |
| | infixing | *pera* 'cut' | ***i**-pera* | *p‹**u**›era* | *p‹**i**›era* |
| Roon | prefixing | *ve* 'want, say' | ***ya**-ve* | ***wa**-ve* | ***i**-ve* |
| | infixing | *ve* 'do, give, become' | ***i**-ve* | *v‹**w**›e* | *v‹**y**›e* |
| Yerisiam | prefixing | *áréekí* 'see' | ***né=j**-áréekí* | ***á=gú**-áréekí* | ***í=dí**-áréekí* |
| | infixing | *rá* 'go' | ***nè**=rá* | ***à**=r‹**ú**›a* | ***ì**=r‹**í**›a* |

(Wamesa: Gasser 2014: 197, fieldnotes; Roon: Gil 2017: 45; Yerisiam: Kamholz 2011: 4)

accompanied by sporadic vowel harmony in the root, unusual for SHWNG (see Gasser 2024).

**Table 37.5** Yaur verbal subject marking

| Root | 1SG: *igw-* | 2SG: *agw-‹u›* | 3SG: *‹i›* |
|---|---|---|---|
| *údàarè* 'arrive' | *igw-úd**àa**rè* | *agw-úd**èe**rè* | *úd**èe**rè* |
| *jàgwné* 'hit' | *i-j**à**gwné* | *a-j**ù**gwné* | *j**à**gwné* |
| *méemèjè* 'laugh' | *i-m**ée**m**è**jè* | *a-m**íi**m**ì**jè* | *m**íi**m**ì**jè* |
| *hòdàaré* 'go up' | *i-h**ò**d**àa**ré* | *a-h**ù**d**èe**ré* | *h**ù**d**èe**ré* |

(Kamholz fieldnotes)

Affixation may trigger a range of phonological processes on the verb root, frequently involving vowel alternations, although rarely as extensive as the Yaur patterns. In Wamesa and Wooi, the high vowel of the affix will replace or coalesce with an /a/ in the initial syllable of some verb roots, yielding, for example, Wamesa *didiava* and *biba* as the 3SG forms of *adiava* 'to hear' and *baba* 'big', respectively. In Wooi, infixed /i/ may trigger palatalization of a preceding /t/, as in *cuva* '3SG-put on' from /t‹i›uva/. Similarly, *t*-initial verbs in Moor are regularly *s*-initial in 1SG and 3SG. In Ambai, infixes rarely actually surface unchanged, as shown in Table 37.6. Their presence frequently can only be inferred from their assimilatory effect on the first segments of the root, and that effect is variable, stress-related, and not always visible.

A different pattern of infixation appears in RASH: a *‹y›* infix marking a first or second singular subject is one of the defining features of the subgroup (Kamholz 2014). For example, in Ambel, verbs are divided semi-arbitrarily into

**Table 37.6** Ambai verbal subject marking

| | Root | 1SG | 2SG | 3SG |
|---|---|---|---|---|
| Prefixing | *adai* 'to be tall' | *yadai* | *bodai* | *dedai* |
| Infixing | *tanam* 'to plant' | *itanam* | *tanam* | *sanam* |
| | *sai* 'to weep' | *isai* | *wai* | *sai* |
| | *roki* 'to sing' | *iroki* | *roki* | *yoki* |
| | *matai* 'be afraid' | *imatai* | *mutai* | *mitai* |

(Silzer 1983: 143; see Gasser 2015; Kamholz 2014 for further discussion of infixation in eastern SHWNG)

morphological classes. One group of C-initial verbs, designated Class III by Arnold (2018a), receives a *‹y›* infix with 1SG subjects and a *N-‹y›* prefix/infix combination with a 2SG subject, as in Table 37.7. Similar patterns are reported in Patani and Gebe; and Ma'ya, Salawati, Biga, and Batta extend infixation to 3SG forms (see Table 37.8).

**Table 37.7** Ambel verbal infixation

| | Root | 1SG | 2SG | 3SG animate |
|---|---|---|---|---|
| Class I (prefixing) | *gón* 'promise' | *ya-gón* | *nya-gón* | *na-gón* |
| Class III (infixing) | *tum* 'follow' | *t‹**y**›um* | ***n**-t‹**y**›um* | ***n**-tum* |

(Arnold 2018a: 180)

### 37.2.7 Clitics

Clitics are widespread, and a number of items described as particles in the literature are likely best analysed as clitics. In Yapen and Biakic, articles, directional markers, additives, and negators tend to be phrasal enclitics; other clitics include topic markers, intensifiers, aspect and mood markers, and some pronouns. Many of these are phrase- or clause-final, and cannot bear lexical stress. Biak emphatic pronominals are composed of *mankun* 'self' plus an encliticized pronoun.

Wamesa
(13) *Yau=**ma*** *i-vori* *kavaru* *maki=**pa**-i=**va**.*
1SG=TOP 1SG-buy bean mung=DET-SG=NEG
'I don't buy mung beans.' (Gasser fieldnotes)

Biak
(14) *E-ro* *vor-ri=**s**-ya* *si-bór*
REL-LOC side-out=3PL.ANIM-SPEC 3PL.ANIM-much

*syadi* *nko=**n**=**ri**.*
more 1PL.EXCL=SEP=IRR
'...Let the ones outside not outnumber us.'
(van den Heuvel 2006: 128)

In the Wamesa and Biak sentences above, and similarly in other Yapen languages, some affixes attach directly to the clitics themselves, not to their lexical hosts. In (13), for example, the singular marker *-i* is affixed to the determiner clitic *=pa*, not the root *kavaru maki* 'mung bean'; *pai* then encliticizes to its nominal host (see Gasser 2014 for further discussion). This is rarely attested in the cross-linguistic literature for most parts of the world.

In RASH, clitics are mainly pronominal, although Ambel has an expressive proclitic *ki=*, and Taba uses the enclitic plural marker *=si*. In Matbat, pronouns appear as proclitics when appearing as subjects or possessors and as enclitics when appearing as objects and following prepositions; a similar pattern is described for Sawai.

Ambel
(15) *Kátin* *kapyu* ***ki**=wa-pa*
stone fruit EMO=DEM.CONTR-MID
***aN=ki**=bu.*
3SG.IN AN=EMO=white
'That small stone is white.' (Arnold 2018a: 124)

## 37.3 Morphology and syntax

### 37.3.1 Morphological type

The languages of the region tend to be isolating/analytic to lightly agglutinating. Monomorphemic words are common across subgroups. The RASH languages are more isolating, with perhaps three morphemes as the per-word maximum in Ambel. Irarutu lands firmly in agglutinative territory; Jackson (2014) gives the verb template as Habitual-Agreement-ActiveMarker(=)Agreement-IncidentalStative-Verb-Detransitivizer, although it is unclear whether all of these can co-occur simultaneously.

Warembori stands apart from the rest of the documented Austronesian languages of the region in its extensive use of compounding and even noun incorporation. Some Warembori constructions thus appear polysynthetic, with multiple roots combined into a single complex word.

Warembori
(16) *E-tire-pue-na-a'ne-pa-ta-o.*
1SG-see-pig-APPL-jungle-big-PRF-IND
'I saw some pigs in the heavy bush.'
(Donohue 1999b: 13)

### 37.3.2 Parts of speech

These languages generally make a clear morphosyntactic distinction between nouns and verbs. In addition, most of the languages have a small, closed set of adjectives, which typically share morphosyntactic features with verbs. In some cases, the distinction between adjectives and verbs can be seen when the adjective functions as a predicate: for example, in Ambai, predicatively used adjectives (e.g. *fuba* 'large', *reifofa* 'tiny') do not take subject-marking morphology, unlike verbs. In other cases, predicative adjectives are morphosyntactically indistinguishable from predicative verbs, and the difference between the two word classes can only be seen when the forms are used attributively. For example, Ambel is analysed with a class of 'adjectival verbs' (e.g. *bábo* 'young, new' and *bálu* 'raw'). When occurring predicatively, these roots take subject-marking morphology, just like non-adjectival verbs. However, when occurring attributively, adjectival verbs can directly modify a head noun (see example (17a)); this is opposed to non-adjectival verbs, which must first be subordinated in a relative clause construction (see example (17b)). A similar pattern is described in Wooi, Dusner, and Wamesa.

Ambel

(17) a. *Láp* **lál** *wa-pa* *aN=mát.*
fire big DEM-MID 3SG.INAN=die
'...That big fire went out.'

b. *Mét* **wa** **n-ól** *apa* *ni-k*
person REL 3SG-stand DEM.MID POSS-1SG
*mám* *wa-pa.*
father DEM-MID
'The person who is standing is my father.'
(Arnold 2018a: 127, 503)

In at least some languages of Halmahera, there is no distinction between adjectives and verbs: in Taba and Sawai, all adjectival notions are communicated with verbs. Biak is analysed by van den Heuvel (2006: 108–10) without a separate class of adjectives, although Mofu (2009: 131–4) argues for a small, closed class of adjectives in the language.

It is common for these languages to have very small inventories of manner adverbs: for example, six manner adverbs are attested in Ambel, eight in Biak, and only two in Wamesa (*nanaria* 'slowly' and *saira* 'quickly').

## 37.3.3 Grammatical relations

### 37.3.3.1 *Subject and object marking*

The order of the basic verbal clause in all of the attested languages of the region is SVO. All of the surveyed languages have verbal prefixes, infixes, and/or proclitics marking subjects (henceforth 'subject markers'), although the precise form of subject markers varies considerably (Kamholz 2014: 123; see §37.2.6 for more on infixation). Many of these languages allow pro-drop, with no overt independent subject, but some require a pronominal clitic in the absence of a full NP. Multiple inflection classes, in particular for consonant- vs. vowel-initial roots, are common. Table 37.8 shows a representative sample of singular subject markers (see also Table 37.4).

Independent pronouns generally appear in subject position only for disambiguation or emphasis. In Ambai and Biak, independent pronouns cannot appear as subjects at all.

Depending on the language, third person subject markers may or may not co-occur with full NP subjects. For example, in Yerisiam, the 3.ANIM clitic *i=* cannot co-occur with a full NP subject, but is obligatory without it; in Umar, the 3SG prefix *i-* is obligatory whether or not a full NP subject is present.

**Table 37.8** Verbal subject marking

| | | 1SG | 2SG | 3SG (animate) |
|---|---|---|---|---|
| Moor | *verá* 'go' | ***i***=*verá* | ***a***=*verá* | *verá* |
| | *enâ* 'lie (down)' | ***i=gw***-*enâ* | ***a***=*enâ* | ***j***-*enâ* |
| Waropen | *muna* 'kill' | ***ra***-*muna* | ***a***-*muna* | *muna* |
| | *ano* 'eat' | ***r***-*ano* | ***agh***-*ano* | ***i***-*ano* |
| Kurudu | *ra* 'go' | ***i***-*ra* | *r‹**u**›a* | *r‹**i**›a* |
| | *en* 'sleep' | ***(ay-)****en* | ***b***-*en* | ***d***-*en* |
| Ma'ya | *a*$^{12}$*p* 'row' | '***y***-*a*$^{12}$*p* | '***my***-*a*$^{12}$*p* | '***ny***-*a*$^{12}$*p* |
| | '*sapa*$^{3}$*n* 'go outside' | '*s‹**y**›apa*$^{3}$*n* | ***m***-'*s‹**y**›apa*$^{3}$*n* | ***n***-'*s‹**y**›apa*$^{3}$*n* |
| Taba | *unak* 'know' | ***k***=*unak* | ***m***=*unak* | ***n***=*unak* |

(Moor: Kamholz fieldnotes; Waropen: Held 1942: 97; Kurudu: Kamholz fieldnotes; Ma'ya: van der Leeden n.d.: 51; Taba: Bowden 2001: 223)

Yerisiam

(18) a. *Ì=r‹í›a.*
3.ANIM=‹3SG›go
'He left.'

b. *Dáî̂* *r‹í›a.*
father ‹3SG›go
'Father left.'

c. **Dáî̂* *ì=r‹í›a.*
father 3.ANIM=‹3SG›go
(Kamholz fieldnotes)

Umar

(19) a. *I-r‹i›a.*
3SG-‹3SG›go
'He left.'

b. *Tatai* *i-r‹i›a.*
father 3SG-‹3SG›go
'Father left.'

c. **Tatai* *r‹i›a.*
father ‹3SG›go
(Kamholz fieldnotes)

Unlike subject marking, object marking is much less common. It is unattested in RASH. Ambai and Wamesa have a suffix *-i* which occurs with transitive verbs when the object is not overt. In Wooi, object markers vary by person and number.

### 37.3.3.2 *Alignment*

While case marking is not attested in the surveyed languages, alignment can be observed in other ways. Most languages have nominative–accusative alignment: the sole argument of intransitive verbs is marked on the verb in the same way as the Agent of transitive verbs. The following examples from Moor illustrate the pattern:

Moor

(20) a. ***Ti***-*vera.*
3PL-go
'They went.'

b. ***Ti***-*ha* *ijan-o.*
3PL-carry fish-DET
'They carried the fish.'
(Kamholz fieldnotes)

Semantic alignment (Donohue 2008b) has been observed in Moor and Umar: a class of intransitive predicates, all stative in meaning, are marked as reflexive or objective. Membership in this class is lexically determined; not all stative predicates are in it, and there is no clear semantic commonality among class members. In Moor, the single argument of a predicate in this class is always marked on the verb as an object. It can optionally additionally be marked as a subject, in which case the construction takes the same form as a reflexive.

Moor

(21) a. ***(Ti-)****emeva-****ti****.*
(3PL-)large-3PL
'They are large.'

b. ***Ti****-vavo-****ti****.*
3PL-hit-3PL
'They hit themselves'
(Kamholz fieldnotes)

In Umar, the argument of a predicate in this class is marked as an object.

### 37.3.4 Person, number, and animacy

In all of the attested languages, first, second, and third person are distinguished in the main morphosyntactic paradigms (viz. the pronominal, verbal subject marking, and possessive paradigms), and a clusivity distinction for first person is made in non-singular numbers.

Grammatical number in Halmahera is limited to a bipartite distinction between singular and plural; in Irarutu, a singular/plural distinction is made in the pronominal and possessive paradigms, but no number distinction is made in the subject marking morphology. Elsewhere, a three-way singular/dual/plural distinction in the pronominal, subject marking, and/or possessive paradigms is common (e.g. Dusner, Kurudu, Ma'ya, Roon, Warembori, and Wooi). Languages with a four-way number distinction in these paradigms, adding a trial or paucal, are also attested (e.g. Ambel, Biak, Yerisiam, Moor, and Wabo); at least the Kawe and Wauyai dialects of Ma'ya make a five-way distinction (singular/dual/trial/paucal/plural) in their pronominal paradigms.

In addition to person and number, many languages distinguish two levels of animacy, usually human/non-human or animate/inanimate—although where in the grammatical system this distinction is instantiated varies (see Schapper 2010b; Grimes, this volume, §36.3.1 discusses a similar distinction for Central Maluku languages). Ambai is perhaps unique in making a three-way distinction: when determiners are marked for agreement with count nouns, inanimates can only be marked singular, non-human animates are limited to singular or plural, and human referents have additional dual and trial marking available.

Animacy distinctions are limited to third person forms. In Wamesa, Dusner, Biak, As, and Sawai, animacy is distinguished only in the plural; in Ma'ya, the distinction is limited to the singular. The most common loci for animacy marking are in the possessive and verbal subject marking paradigms, concord between nouns and determiners or demonstratives, and numerals. Ambai is again unusual within SHWNG in that different allative prepositions and *wh*-words are used depending on animacy.

Ambai

(22) a. *I-wo* ***to*** *Urui.*
1SG-paddle to Serui
'I paddle to Serui. (inanimate goal)'

b. *M‹i›to* ***we*** *Tom-i.*
‹3SG›run to Tom-PERS
'He runs to Tom. (animate goal)'
(Silzer 1983: 202–3)

The boundaries between animate and inanimate categories can be somewhat semantically arbitrary and language-specific. In Ambai, humans, spirits, and animals are animate, except shellfish, which are inanimate. In Roon, whole animals and plants are animate, whereas animal and plant parts and products are inanimate; *sarai* for example can mean 'coconut tree' or 'coconut fruit' depending whether it appears with animate or inanimate markers, respectively. In Biak, alcoholic drinks, dry coffee grounds, macaroni, and metal objects are considered animate (van den Heuvel 2006: 100–4). In Waropen and Taba, 'month' is animate, as are Ambel 'moon', 'star', and 'sun'.

### 37.3.5 The noun phrase

#### 37.3.5.1 *NP word order*

The default order of elements within the noun phrase in these languages is Noun–Adjective–Numeral/Quantifier–Determiner/Demonstrative, with possessors preceding the noun and relative clauses, classifiers, linkers, and other constituents appearing somewhere between the noun and determiner. An example from Wooi is given below.

Wooi

(23) *Agus tamani cong [manu baba*
Agus father.3SG.POSS 3SG.make house big
*koru wampa]$_{NP}$.*
two there.DIST.NSG
'Agus' father built those two big houses.'
(Sawaki 2016: 116)

Wamesa, Wooi, Dusner, and Warembori have a much more cross-linguistically rare word order: Noun–Adj–Dem/Det–Num/Quant (henceforth NADQ) (Cinque 2005; Dryer 2018; Gasser 2019b). Wooi also uses NADQ in limited environments, otherwise defaulting to the (cross-linguistically very common) NAQD order found elsewhere in SHWNG, exemplified above. In Warembori, the adjective is compounded to the noun and followed by a determiner suffix, making it rather different from the Wamesa/Wooi/Dusner case; it may well have a very different phrase structure as well.

Wamesa

(24) N Adj Det Quant
*anggadi* *pimasa* *=pa* *toru*
coconut big =DET three
'the three big coconuts' (Gasser 2014: 177)

Warembori

(25) a. N Adj Dem
*nu* *-pa* *-ni*
man -big.ATTR -this
'this big man'

b. N Dem Quant
*mani* *-yave* *wonti*
bird -DEF three
'the three birds' (Donohue 1999b: 20, 22)

### 37.3.5.2 *Determiners*

Most languages surveyed have at least one definite article, often synchronically or diachronically related to a demonstrative. For example, the Warembori distal demonstrative *-yave* also functions as a marker of definiteness; in Sawai, the form *ne* is used both as a generic distal demonstrative and as a definite article. In Ambai, definite, specific NPs are marked with elements that encode a three-way distance contrast (*ne* 'near speaker', *wa* 'near hearer', and *fo* 'far from speaker or hearer'), which take further affixes to mark singular, dual, trial, and plural number. Finally, in Biak, the main opposition is not between definite and indefinite NPs, but rather specific and non-specific. Specific NPs are marked with complex pronominal specificity markers, which agree with the head noun in terms of person, animacy, and number, and which can additionally be marked for givenness. A similar system of marking is found on Roon definite articles.

Indefinite articles are less commonly attested. Wamesa is one exception, with the indefinite *pe*, as is Ambai, which has an article *-fea* to mark indefinite, specific NPs. In Ambel, two originally deictic articles *ne* and *pa* can be used to mark indefinite, specific NPs. In some languages, words from other classes can be used to mark indefinite NPs—for example, the numeral 'one' in Taba and Biak.

Demonstratives are discussed in §37.3.13 on spatial orientation below.

### 37.3.5.3 *NP number marking*

As well as the number marking on the verb described in §37.3.4, many of the surveyed languages additionally mark number within the NP, most commonly on determiners. In Irarutu, the determiner roots *ad* and *wen* are used for singular and plural NPs, respectively; these roots may take additional affixes to mark specificity or deixis. In Wamesa, number-marking suffixes attach to the determiners: the singular is marked by *-i*, non-human plurals are marked with *-si*, and human non-singulars are marked by suffixes which agree in animacy, person, and number with the head noun. In Biak, the form of number marking depends on whether the NP is specific or non-specific: whereas there is a two-way singular/plural distinction for articles marking non-specific NPs, the complex pronominal markers of specificity make a four-way number distinction (singular/dual/paucal/plural).

In some languages, there is number marking both on the determiner and elsewhere in the NP. For example, in Ambel, number marking has several loci within the NP: non-singular specific NPs are optionally marked with the particle *i*; on the demonstrative prefix (*wa-* 'DEM.SG' vs. *we-* 'DEM.NSG'); and on the definite article (*wana* 'DEF.SG' vs. *wena* 'DEF.NSG'). An example of an NP with multiple plural marking—with both the particle *i* 'NSG' and the demonstrative prefix *we-* 'DEM.NSG'—is given in (26).

Ambel

(26) *Uma-bangun* *now* ***i*** ***we**-ne.*
1DU.EXCL-build house NSG DEM.NSG-PROX
'... The two of us built these houses.'
(Arnold 2018a: 252)

Finally, in some languages, number is solely expressed within the NP by a dedicated marker. In Taba, for example, the number-marking enclitic *=si*, which is obligatory for plural human NPs, attaches to the final element in an NP.

### 37.3.5.4 *Relative clauses*

Relative clauses follow the head noun and generally precede the determiner; headless relatives are also common. In eastern SHWNG, the relative marker is *ve-* or similar. In Wamesa, subject relatives get *ve-* but no subject marking on the verb; if the object is extracted, the verb marks the subject of the relative clause and no *ve-* is used. In Wooi, object and oblique relatives use a non-singular object marker on the verb of the relative clause, regardless of the number of the relativized object. In Moor, certain verbs receive an *-u* suffix when used in object relatives.

Wamesa

(27) Subject extraction

a. [Sinitu [_ **ve**-rora Uli]$_{REL}$ pa-sia]$_{NP}$
person _ REL-hit U. DET-3PL.HUM
se-nda vera wana.
3PL.HUM-go towards there
'The people who hit Uli went over there.'

Object extraction

b. [Kue [i-nunu _ kausapa]$_{REL}$ pa-si]$_{NP}$
cake 1SG-bake _ yesterday DET-PL
si-ate to diadiva.
3PL.NHUM-good until can't
'The cakes I baked yesterday are delicious.'
(Gasser fieldnotes)

Moor, object extraction

(28) toitoʔo manita j-orar-**u** _.
child friend 3SG-look.for-U _
'the child that the friend is looking for'
(Kamholz fieldnotes)

In RASH and Irarutu, a different set of relativizers appear, and can vary based on definiteness, specificity, and givenness. In Ambel and Maꞌya, NPs may be subordinated to a head noun in the same way as clauses. In Ambel, these constructions function to communicate the location of, an attribute of, or a relationship of affiliation with the head noun; an example of a relativized NP expressing location is given in (29).

Ambel

(29) [Áy [**wa** sórom]$_{REL}$ a-ne]$_{NP}$, mum-íy
tree REL middle ART-PROX 2DU-eat
an are.
3SG.INAN PROH
'...As for the tree in the middle [of the garden] here, don't you two eat [fruit from] it!' (Arnold 2018a: 579)

### 37.3.6 Possession

Compared with other areas of their grammar, possessive constructions in these languages have attracted a fair bit of attention—see van den Berg (2009), Kamholz (2014), and Gasser and Schapper (2023). (See also Schapper and McConvell, this volume, chapter 48 for more on how SHWNG languages fit into the broader areal patterns.) With two exceptions (Taba and Gane), the languages of the region all have more than one morphosyntactic possessive construction, reflecting to varying degrees a semantic distinction between alienable and inalienable possession.

The range of nouns that can enter into morphosyntactically inalienable possessive constructions varies from language to language. In all languages with an alienability distinction, at least some body parts and/or kin terms are possessed in the inalienable construction. Many languages additionally treat associative nouns ('name', 'breath', 'shadow', 'feeling'), locational nouns (e.g. 'top', 'side'), and parts of wholes (e.g. 'edge', 'fruit') as inalienable. In some languages, culturally important items are also inalienable (e.g. Warembori 'house', 'canoe', and 'net bag').

In most of the languages, inalienable possession is marked by a construction in which the possessor occurs before the possessed noun, and the person and number of the possessor is marked directly on the possessed noun with affixes. These may be prefixes, suffixes, or a combination of the two, as shown in Table 37.9 for Ambai.[3] In at least three languages (Irarutu, Matbat, and Ambel), some inalienably possessed nouns are infixed, probably as a result of the fossilization of a former compound.

**Table 37.9** Inalienable morphology in Ambai

| | SG | PL |
|---|---|---|
| 1INCL | — | *ta-...-mi* |
| 1EXCL | *-ku* | *ame-...-mi* |
| 2 | *-mu* | *me-...-mi* |
| 3 | *-n, -na* | *e-...-mi* |

(Silzer 1983: 88)

Some languages make a further distinction in their inalienable paradigms depending on the semantics of the possessed noun (Arnold 2023). For example, in Ambel, when an inalienably possessed noun is a body part, a 3SG possessor is unmarked (e.g. *nyai* 'stomach.3SG'); but when it is a kin term, 3SG is marked with *i-* (e.g. *i-nu* '3SG-same.sex.sibling').

There is more morphosyntactic variation in the way alienable possessive constructions are formed. In many languages, the possessor NP occurs before the possessed NP, and the possessor and possessed are separated by a prenominal possessive particle or verb (typically of the form *nV*, where V is a vowel), which is inflected to mark the person and number of the possessor.[4] An example from Ambel is given in Table 37.10.

[3] Only singular and plural possessors are shown throughout this section; many languages additionally distinguish dual possessors, and some also distinguish trial/paucal possessors.

[4] Possession in Taba, which does not have an alienability distinction, is expressed with a similar construction.

**Table 37.10** Alienable morphology in Ambel

| | SG | PL |
|---|---|---|
| 1INCL | — | *t-ni-n* |
| 1EXCL | *ni-k* | *áma-ni-n* |
| 2 | *ni-m* | *mim-ni-n* |
| 3 | *i-ni* | *la-ni-n* |

(Arnold 2018a: 294)

Several other alienable constructions are attested. For example, in Irarutu and Warembori, the possessor NP precedes the possessed NP, and the possessor is marked directly on the possessed noun, similar to inalienable constructions but using a different paradigm. The Biakic languages have innovated possessive markers built on the form *ve* (see §37.3.2), which occur after the possessed noun and agree with both the possessor and the possessed NPs. An example from Biak is given in (30): the possessive marker is inflected to mark both the 3SG possessor NP and the 3PL.AN possessed NP.

Biak
(30) *[romawa inai]*$_{\text{POSSD NP}}$ *[Manseren]*$_{\text{POSSR.NP}}$
son daughter Lord
***[v‹y›e=s-ya.]***$_{\text{POSS}}$
‹3SG›POSS=3PL.ANIM-SPEC
'the Lord's sons and daughters'
(van den Heuvel 2006: 232)

Finally, some languages (Buli, Patani, Sawai, and Waropen) make a further distinction in alienable possessive constructions between edible and inedible possession. In Sawai, whether a possessed noun is considered edible depends on context: for example, *in* 'fish' is considered edible when the fish has been caught but inedible when still in the water; *meja* 'table' is edible when it refers to a dining table but inedible when it refers to a school table (David Kamholz fieldwork 2018). This distinction, familiar from the Oceanic languages to the east (Lynch et al. 2002: 41), has been reconstructed to Proto-SHWNG (van den Berg 2009).

## 37.3.7 VE-morpheme

The VE-morpheme appears in most languages, whether by common descent or borrowing (Gil 2017). The exact phonological form of the morpheme varies somewhat, appearing as *ve(-)*, *we(-)*, *be*, *pe*, *fi*, and *fa*, among other (arguably) related forms. Within the eleven Austronesian varieties of northwest New Guinea that Gil surveys—a subset of those in which it is attested—he finds VE- used as a verb meaning 'do', 'give', 'say', 'become', and 'want', and as an affix or grammatical particle as a verbalizer, reifier, relativizer, and possessive, causative, dative, allative, purposive, future tense, or passive marker. VE- can often be analysed as a linker (cf. den Dikken 2006) or $P_{\text{HAVE}}$ (cf. Harley 2012).

Wamesa
(31) *S‹i›sera* *aiku* ***ve-ve****-rawana=pa-i.*
‹3SG›watch box REL-ESS-sea=DET-SG
'He watches the box that is blue.' (Gasser fieldnotes)

Ambel
(32) *Monkoné* *N-**be*** *guru* ***be***
say.3SG.ANIM 3SG.ANIM-become teacher BEN
*sia.*
3PL.ANIM
'He said he [would] become a teacher for them.'
(Arnold 2018a: 452)

VE- is used with the broadest range of functions in Biakic, and is most restricted in Taba, where it has only the 'do' meaning. Given its ubiquity, VE- can probably be reconstructed to Proto-SHWNG with some subset of those functions listed above, likely including meanings of doing, giving, and becoming.

Gil points out that a number of neighbouring non-Austronesian languages, such as Yawa, Meyah, Inanwatan, and Hatam, also include VE-like words with similar phonological forms and ranges of meaning, suggesting multiple borrowing events. One of the more unusual features of VE- is its use for both 'do' and 'give' meanings. This coexpression is present in several languages, even without the use of VE-: several Yapen languages, for example, have adopted *ong* in this function.

## 37.3.8 Valency-changing strategies

### 37.3.8.1 *Reflexives and reciprocals*

For most of the languages for which data are available, reflexives and reciprocals are expressed by an unmarked transitive construction, with an object pronoun coreferent with the subject of the clause.

Dusner reflexives
(33) ***Ndo****-man* ***ndoen*** *ro* *cermin*
1PL.INCL-see 1PL.INCL at mirror
*i-ne.*
3SG-DEM.PROX
'We saw ourselves [lit. we saw us] in this mirror.'
(Dalyrymple and Mofu 2012: 14)

Wooi reciprocals

(34) ***Hu**-r-mung* ***hura*** *na* *ramdempe.*
3DU-DU-fight 3DU LOC yesterday
'Those two fought each other [lit. those two fought those two] yesterday.' (Sawaki 2016: 312)

In several languages, reflexivity is optionally additionally marked or emphasized using a dedicated reflexive particle. This occurs either between the subject and the predicate, as shown for Taba in (35); or, more commonly, between the predicate and the object pronoun, as shown for Biak in (36).[5]

Taba

(35) *I* ***do*** *n=wet* *i.*
3SG REFL 3SG=hit 3SG
'He hit himself.' (Bowden 2001: 189)

Biak

(36) *F‹y›arwe* ***mankund***=*i.*
‹3SG›change REFL=3SG
'He changed himself.' (van den Heuvel 2006 : 81)

In at least Biak, Ambel, and Irarutu, reciprocals are optionally additionally marked with a dedicated affix or particle. In the Biak example in (37), the reciprocal suffix *-yáe* attaches to the verbal predicate.

Biak

(37) *S-faduru-**yáe*** *si.*
3PL.ANIM-care-RECP 3PL.ANIM
'They took care of each other.'
(van den Heuvel 2006: 82)

In Halmahera, Taba and Sawai have obligatory reciprocal marking. For example, in Taba, a reciprocal particle *maka* occurs between the subject and the predicate, and is marked for the person and number of the subject. (Compare Meto *ma(k)*-; Schapper and Zobel, this volume, §35.3.2.1.)

Taba

(38) *Si* *l=**maka*** *tala* *la-we.*
3PL 3PL=RECP meet sea-ESS
'They are meeting each other in a seawards location.'
(Bowden 2001: 192)

### 37.3.8.2 *Passives and detransitivizers*

Passive constructions are rare, but they are attested. Sawai has a passive-like involuntary action marker *te-*, and Biak forms passives with the prefix *veve-*, although it is rarely used.

Biak

(39) *Ankriabon* *an-ya* ***v‹y›eve**-pów.*
orange.fruit GIV-3SG.SPEC ‹3SG›PASS-peel
'The orange is being peeled.' (van den Heuvel 2006: 296)

In most cases, alternative strategies are used to convey passive-like meaning. Topicalization is described in Wamesa, Biak, Ambel, and Ma'ya as one such strategy, with the object given prominence and the subject NP generally omitted or realized with a generic, rather than specific, noun (e.g. 'people').

Wamesa

(40) a. *Yau* *i-nunu* *kokori=pa-i.*
I 1SG-cook chicken=DET-SG
'I cook the chicken.'

b. *Kokori=pa-i* *i-nunu.*
chicken=DET-SG 1SG-cook
'The chicken is cooked by me.' (Gasser fieldnotes)

Some languages have morphological detransitivizers. For example, Irarutu has a detransitivizing suffix *-fe*, resembling an antipassive; Taba has a detransitivizing prefix *ta-*; and Warembori has detransitivizing prefixes *a-* and *ke-*.

Irarutu

(41) a. *It-ga* *uce.*
1PL.INCL-eat papeda
'We eat papeda.'

b. *It-ga-**fe**.*
1PL.INCL-eat-DETRANS
'We eat (food).' (Jackson 2014 : 107)

### 37.3.8.3 *Applicatives*

A number of languages have applicative affixes which target an instrumental noun. In Wamesa, the verb continues to mark the agentive subject of the sentence, but this subject is not overtly mentioned, and the instrument appears pre-verbally. Only non-humans can be Instruments with the Wamesa applicative. The Biak applicative *k-* has expanded to also function as a verbalizer, attaching to the Instrument itself to form a verb meaning 'use X'.

Wamesa

(42) *Wai=ne-i=ma* *set-**it**-avakire* *sasu.*
rope=DET-SG=TOP 3PL.HUM-APPL-hang clothing
'They use the rope to hang up clothing.'
(Gasser 2014: 201)

[5] The default reflexive particle in Biak is *mankun(d)*, which can be used with either a male or a female referent; there is additionally a dedicated reflexive particle for female referents, *vinkun*.

Biak

(43) *Vín an-i-ne d-úf*
female GIV-SPEC-this 3SG-pick.up
*kamkam=ya fa i-**k**-kam*
hammer=3SG.SPEC CONJ 3SG-APPL-hammer
*diwr ben an-ya.*
smash plate GIV-3SG.SPEC
'This woman takes a hammer to hammer the plate into pieces.' (van den Heuvel 2006: 186)

In Ambel, instrumental applicatives are morphologically unmarked, but the adjunct becomes a core argument through word order (44b). This is similar to the Wamesa pattern, but without the prefix.

Ambel

(44) a. *Ine ce dún mi tátul pa.*
1SG spear.1SG fish INSTR spear ART
'I spear fish with a spear.'

b. *Ine ce tátul pa mi dún.*
1SG spear.1SG spear ART INSTR fish
'I use a spear to spear fish.' (Arnold 2018a: 464)

Patani applicatives are marked by a -V suffix, which changes to match the quality of the vowel of the root-final syllable, as in *faisib-**i*** 'tell someone something' from *faisib* 'tell something', and *ut-**u*** 'bring something for someone' from *ut* 'bring something'.

Warembori has the broadest range of applicative constructions, with three suffixes *-(u)na*, *-ta*, and *-tane* used (somewhat idiosyncratically) to mark direction, instrument, and source. An object targeted by the applicative can be topicalized as well, by moving it to the front of the clause, which is not possible otherwise.

Warembori

(45) a. *E-keoi-**na** anta ina kee-ro.*
1SG-fish-APPL fish INSTR fish.hook-IND
'I fish for fish with a fish-hook.'

b. *Nana karapesa iwi o(n)-**na**.*
OBL chair 1SG sit-APPL
'I sat on a chair.' (Donohue 1999b: 30–1)

### 37.3.8.4 *Causatives*

Causatives in Yapen, Biakic, and Warembori are most often formed periphrastically, with a verb meaning 'cause', 'make', 'give', or 'do'. In Biak these form two clauses linked by the conjunction *fa*; in Yapen serial verb constructions may be used. Wamesa is unusual in that it does have a causative prefix *on-*, clearly derived from the verb *one* 'give', although its use is rare.

Biak

(46) ***V‹y›e*** *motor an-ya fa i-mnai.*
‹3SG›give motor GIV-3SG.SPEC CONJ 3SG-stop
'He made/let the motor stop.'
(van den Heuvel 2006: 392)

Wamesa

(47) *Sur-**on**-rama. [surondama] ~ Sur-one r‹i›ama.*
3DU-CAUS-come ~ 3DU-give ‹3SG›come
'They two make (him) come here.'
(Gasser 2014: 206, fieldnotes)

Roon also has a zero-marked causative. Compare (48a) and (48b), where the addition of a causer Agent is enough to create causative meaning.

Roon

(48) a. *Ven-i-ya s‹y›un*
pig-3SG.ANIM-DEF ‹3SG.ANIM›enter
*ar-ri-ya.*
fence-3SG.INAN-DEF
'The pig entered the pen.'

b. *Lorens-i s‹y›un*
Lorens-PERS ‹3SG.ANIM›enter
*ven-i-ya ve ar-ri-ya.*
pig-3SG.ANIM-DEF to fence-3SG.INAN-DEF
'Lorens put the pig into the pen.' (David Gil p.c.)

Morphological causatives are more common in RASH, where they are described for Ambel, Ma'ya, Patani, Taba, and Sawai with the prefix *ha-*, *fa-*, or *fi-*. Periphrastic causatives are possible here as well; in Ambel these are formed with the verbs *úku* 'endanger', *in* 'make', or *alén* 'do' followed by a complement clause. Irarutu has the prefix *fi-*, which, while glossed as an active marker, can also contribute causative meaning.

Taba

(49) *In=**ha**-mot paramalam.*
3SG 3SG=CAUS-die lamp
'He turned the lamp out.' (Bowden 2001)

### 37.3.8.5 *Fossilized valency-changing morphology*

Valency-changing morphology inherited from an earlier stage of Austronesian is reported throughout the region. In some cases, this morphology is still productive: for example, the Sawai passive prefix *te-* discussed above. In many cases, however, it has fossilized to the root. For example, many languages have a fossilized element *m(a)-*, which typically occurs on intransitive verb roots referring to properties, changes of state, and human sentience (e.g. Biga *mtat* 'afraid' and Taba *makwai* 'be hot/feverish'). In some of these languages, a semantically related non-*m(a)*-initial root is occasionally attested, creating pairs such as Biak *mriwr* 'smashed' vs. *riwr* 'smash' and *msawk* 'be torn' vs. *sawk* 'tear' (van den Heuvel 2006: 172–3). Similarly, many *ta*-initial verbs in Ambel and *ka*-initial verbs in Biak have an inchoative meaning (e.g. Ambel *támje* 'break (intr.)' and Biak *kpéf* 'shatter').[6] Finally, in Ambel, many *ka*-initial verbs are transitive, denoting a causative action or process (e.g. *kapáw* 'chop' and *kájiw* 'pierce'), suggesting this segment formerly had a valency-changing function.

## 37.3.9 Tense, aspect, and mood (TAM)

Tense and aspect are most commonly marked in these languages with particles and adverbs, although some affixation is described as well. Wooi, Ambai, Biak, and Dusner are described as using only adverbs to mark functions such as completive, durative, habitual, and recurrent aspect; necessity/future, likelihood, and possibility, irrealis and conditional mood; and a range of tenses. This is largely the case in Wamesa as well, although the applicative prefix *it-* can have aspectual readings. Yerisiam is unusual in Cenderawasih Bay for using prefixes for aspect and irrealis mood.

Ambai
(50) *Anto-wo* *Urui* ***kiai*** ***ampa.***
1TRI.EXCL-paddle Serui COMPL PRF
'We already finished paddling to Serui.'
(Silzer 1983: 161)

Biak
(51) *Indya* *ya-mkák* *imbude* *ko-mnis* *si=n=**ri.***
so 1SG-fear let.it.not.be.that 1PL.INCL-be.like 3PL.ANIM=SEP=IRR
'So I am afraid that we are like them.'
(van den Heuvel 2006: 377)

Yerisiam
(52) *Í=**kóo**-h-rá.*
3.ANIM-PROG-PL-go
'They are going.' (Kamholz fieldnotes)

In Yaur, there is a distinct paradigm of irrealis subject prefixes which contrast with the realis prefixes. (See Schapper and Zobel, this volume, §35.3.1.1 for a similar pattern in Tugun.) Irrealis can indicate desire, but is not limited to this meaning.

Yaur
(53) a. *I-ráavúrè.*
1SG.REAL-go
'I go. (realis)'
b. *Ja ráavúrè*
1SG.IRR-go
'I want to go. (irrealis)' (Kamholz fieldnotes)

In Ambel and Matbat, aspect and mood are marked with particles, which are generally clause-final. Ma'ya and Sawai leave tense unmarked and express aspect with affixes.

Ambel
(54) *Ny-íy* *yáy* *pa* ***kada,*** *aN=máre* ***to.***
2SG-eat mango ART should 3SG.INAN=be.ripe IAM
'You should eat the mango, it's ripe.'
(Arnold 2018a: 417)

Taba and Warembori use serialization to express some aspectual meanings. In Taba, the verb *yoa* 'to search' appears in aspectual SVCs meaning 'almost', while the verb *okik* 'be finished', which does not show subject agreement in these cases, gives a completive meaning.

Taba
(55) *Au* *m=**yoa*** *m=han.*
2SG 2SG=search 2SG=go
'You've almost gone.' (Bowden 2001: 165)

Irarutu uses the productive prefix *m-* to mark stative aspect, and Jackson (2014) describes a single prefix *na-* with a range of meanings including infinitival, habitual, inchoative, and causative. Elsewhere aspect and mood are marked with what are referred to as preverbal 'auxiliaries'.

Irarutu
(56) *Ja* ***du**-kka=ti.*
1SG already-showered=NEG
'I haven't yet showered.' (Jackson 2014: 148)

Finally, several languages express future tense meanings using the VE-morpheme (discussed in §37.3.7). Gil (2017) argues that this use is a grammaticalization from an earlier allative function.

## 37.3.10 Negation

Clause- or phrase-final negation is widespread. This contrasts with the more general Austronesian pattern, where negation tends to occur clause-initially or pre-verbally (Clark 1990; Klamer 2002b), and is likely the result of contact—Klamer describes final negation as typical of the

[6] As mentioned in §37.2.1, note earlier Biak *t > *k*.

non-Austronesian languages of New Guinea and Halmahera. The shape of the negator varies between languages, but its placement is consistent.

Ambai
(57) *Y-okon* *dian* *we* *Yan-i* ***kaka.***
1SG-give fish to Yan-PERS NEG
'I didn't give any fish to Yan.' (Silzer 1983: 215)

Waropen
(58) *Rairumagha* *afa* *rasirana* *aka* ***ewomo.***
my.house ?? I.cover.it.with nipah.palm NEG
'I do not decorate my house with nipah palm.'
(Held 1942: 81)

In some languages, final negation co-occurs with initial negation in negative imperatives (see §37.3.12.1; Schapper and Zobel, this volume, §35.6 describe double negation on declaratives in languages of Timor). In Moor and Yerisiam, final negation co-occurs with optional pre-verbal negation in declarative clauses.

Moor
(59) *I=**ku*** *gw-anani* ***va.***
1SG=NEG 1SG-know NEG
'I don't know.' (Kamholz fieldnotes)

Other negators may also be available. Forms meaning 'not yet', sometimes built from the basic negator plus additional morphology, are common. Several Yapen languages distinguish a form (Wamesa/Wooi *pivai* and Ambai *bireri*) which negates an entire proposition, as well as one which expresses frustrated intent (Wamesa *diadiva* and Ambai *pari*).

In some languages, monomorphemic verb roots specifically communicating negated desire ('not want') are attested, for example Wamesa *kambarai*, Ambel *mséw*, and Moor *ogwé*. In Umar, negated desire is expressed via the inalienable noun *nae*, the relevant possessive suffix, and *-ri* (e.g. *nae-vua-ri* not.want-2SG-RI 'you don't want to').

## 37.3.11 Non-verbal clauses

### 37.3.11.1 *Existential clauses*

Existential constructions are generally marked with a dedicated existential particle, which does not take subject marking. The particle may occur clause-initially, as in the Wooi example in (60), or clause-finally, as in the Dusner example in (61).

Wooi
(60) ***E*** *anti* *ti-ra* *ma* *ne.*
EXIST 3SG.FOC 3SG-go hither PROX:NSG
'There is someone coming.' (Sawaki 2016 : 221)

Dusner
(61) *Riari* *ya-ve* *ah* *berkat* *ri-**ra.***
so 1SG-say ah blessing EVID-EXIST
'So I said: "Oh, it's a blessing!"'
(Dalrymple and Mofu 2012: 35)

In at least five RASH languages (Ambel, As, Biga, Sawai, and Taba), existential constructions are unmarked, and simply consist of an NP, as in (62). This clustering is significant: cross-linguistically, unmarked existentials are highly unusual (Dixon 2010: 161).

Sawai
(62) *Ay* *isə.*
tree one
'There is one tree.' (J. Whisler 1996: 11)

Special forms marking negative existential constructions are sporadically reported. For example, in Ambai, there is a negative existential particle *bireri*; in Matbat, there is a similar marker *mo³n*.

Ambai
(63) *Dian* ***bireri.***
fish NEG.EXIST
'There are no fish.' (Silzer 1983: 216)

Matbat
(64) *Yi¹n* *i-**mo³n**-paro.*
fish 3SG-NEG.EXIST-IMM
'There is no fish left now.' (Remijsen 2010: 308)

### 37.3.11.2 *Nominal clauses*

In Irarutu and some languages of Cenderawasih Bay, nominal clauses are marked with a copula, often marked to agree with the head NP. For example, in Wooi, a copula *ti-* follows the two NPs, and agrees with the head. In Ambai, a copula *dino* occurs unmarked between the two NPs.

Wooi
(65) *Ya* *pandita* ***ti**-ya.*
1SG pastor COP-1SG
'I am a pastor.' (Sawaki 2016: 71)

Ambai
(66) *Ne* *guru* ***dino*** *Yan-i.*
POSS.3SG teacher COP Yan-PERS
'His teacher is Yan.' (Silzer 1983: 194)

Nominal clauses are unmarked in most RASH languages, consisting instead of two juxtaposed NPs. This is shown for Taba in (67).

Taba
(67) *Mapin* *i.*
woman 3SG
'She's a woman.' (Bowden 2001: 148)

Finally, in Wamesa, constructions communicating the same notions as those expressed by nominal clauses in other languages require the use of the *ve-* prefix, which converts the noun into a verb.

Wamesa
(68) *Yau* *i-**ve**-guru.*
1SG 1SG-ESS-teacher
'I'm a teacher.' (Gasser fieldnotes)

#### 37.3.11.3 *Possessive clauses*

Predicative possessive constructions are identical to, or derived from, their adnominal counterparts in most of the surveyed languages (viz. Ambel, As, Batta, Biga, Ma'ya, Salawati, Taba, Wamesa, Wooi, and possibly Dusner). In those languages where there is no morphosyntactic distinction between attributive and predicative possessive constructions, an example such as the one in (69) is ambiguous as to whether the possessive construction is functioning as an object argument, or as a complement predicate.

Ambel
(69) *Y-ém* ***i-ni*** ***we*** *to.*
1SG-see 3SG-POSS child already
'I have seen her children.' ~ 'I see she already has children.' (Arnold 2018a: 354)

In Biak and Matbat, predicative possessive constructions are formed with verbal roots distinct from the markers found in attributive possessive constructions (the 'Have-Possession' of Stassen 2013). In Biak, the root is *na*, which marks the subject of the clause using the verbal subject marking paradigm; and in Matbat, the root is *ni*[21], which marks the subject of the clause using the same paradigm found in attributive inalienable constructions.

Biak
(70) ***Ya-na*** *in=s-ya* *si-bór.*
1SG-have fish=3PL.ANIM-SPEC 3PL.ANIM-much
'I have a lot of fish.' (van den Heuvel 2006: 253)

## 37.3.12 Non-declarative speech acts

#### 37.3.12.1 *Imperatives*

In several languages, imperatives are morphosyntactically unmarked—that is, imperative constructions are morphosyntactically identical to their declarative counterparts (e.g. Ambel, As, Batta, Dusner, Sawai, Wamesa, and Wooi). In some of these languages, imperatives are distinguished from declaratives by intonation: for example, in Wooi, imperatives are marked with a rising intonation contour across the utterance. In a handful of cases, there are optional dedicated clause-final imperative markers, such as *lo* in Taba, and *to* in Ambai. Several languages optionally use aspect and other clause-final particles to strengthen or soften a request: for example, the continuative particle *hu* is used in Taba to strengthen a request, whereas in Wooi the perfective particle *to* is used to make a request more polite.

All languages for which data are available have a dedicated negative imperative marker. In most cases, this marker is clause-final, as shown in (71) for Ambai. In some, it is clause-initial but co-occurs with a negator later in the clause, as in (72) for Wooi.

Ambai
(71) *Bu-matai* *fiawera* *wa-i* ***fanai!***
2SG-fear dog WA-SG PROH
'Don't be afraid of the dog!' (Silzer 1983: 230)

Wooi
(72) ***Remuho*** *r‹u›obang* *aim* ***pe!***
PROH ‹2SG›cut tree PROH
'Don't cut the tree!' (Sawaki 2016: 236)

#### 37.3.12.2 *Questions*

In Irarutu, Ambel, Taba, and Sawai, neutral polar interrogatives (i.e. yes/no questions where the speaker does not have a bias towards one answer or the other) do not receive any morphosyntactic marking, and are distinguished from their declarative counterparts only by intonation. This is shown for Taba in (73), where the clause has the same structure of the equivalent declarative statement.

Taba
(73) *Iswan* *n=ha-hag-ak* *i?*
Iswan 3SG=CAUS-fool-APPL 3SG
'Is Iswan kidding him?' (Bowden 2001: 76, 353)

In most other languages of the area (excluding those on Halmahera), neutral polar interrogatives are morphosyntactically marked with clause- or sentence-final question tags, typically of the form *e*, *te*, or *re*. An example from Wamesa is given in (74).

Wamesa

(74) *Sasu-sama=pa-i* *v‹i›e-mahal=te?*
clothing-buttocks=DET-3SG ‹3SG›ESS-expensive=Q
'Are the trousers expensive?' (Gasser 2014: 254)

Final particles or tags marking biased polar interrogatives are also attested, particularly positively biased interrogatives. An example showing a question tag marking a positively biased polar interrogative in Ambel is given in (75).

Ambel

(75) *Awa* *ny-áp* *ido* *n-d‹y›ók*
2SG 2SG-paddle when 2SG-‹2SG›meet
*lenkawáy,* ***ni?***
crocodile POS.Q
'...When you were travelling by sea, you met a crocodile, right?'(Arnold 2018a)

*Wh*-words generally appear *in situ*, although raising to clause-initial position is sometimes possible. In Dusner, *wh*-words may appear either initially or finally in the clause; if initial, the evidential determiner *rya* must appear clause-finally. 'Where' and 'how many' always appear clause-finally in Dusner, as in (76).

Dusner

(76) a. *Vemow* *snoman* *i* *ve-ro* ***vemundi?***
child male 3SG REL-at which
'Where is the boy?'

b. ***Rosai*** *w-ut* *i* *ro* *mandirndya*
what 2SG-take 3SG at yesterday
***r-ya?***
EVID-DET.3SG
'What did you take yesterday?'
(Dalrymple and Mofu 2012: 43, 45)

In a few Cenderawasih Bay languages, including Dusner, Ambai, Wamesa, and Yerisiam, the word meaning 'why' appears pre-verbally and marks the subject of the interrogative clause, as would a verb. This may in fact be analysable as a serial verb construction.

Wamesa

(77) *Wona=pa-i* *di-**otopi*** *s‹i›aire?*
dog=DET-SG 3SG-why ‹3SG›smell.bad
'Why does the dog stink?' (Gasser fieldnotes)

Dusner

(78) ***V‹w›eveso****=o* *w-arsai* *r-ya?*
‹2SG›which=FILL 2SG-angry EVID-DET.3SG
'Why are you angry?' (Dalrymple and Mofu 2012: 46)

### 37.3.13 Spatial orientation

Demonstrative systems typically make a three-way distance distinction. The systems are either anchored to the speaker, or to both the speaker and the addressee. For example, Dusner has three demonstrative roots in a speaker-anchored system: *ne* for entities near the speaker, *ya* for entities relatively close to the speaker, and *wa* for entities far from the speaker. The Irarutu demonstrative system is anchored to both the speaker and the addressee: *-ini* is used for entities near the speaker, *-ei* for entities near the addressee, and *-mai* for entities near neither the speaker nor the addressee.

While a three-way distal distinction is the norm, there are some exceptions. In Warembori and the languages of Halmahera, only two distinctions are made, proximal and distal. Ambel has three demonstratives used for static entities, and adds a fourth, *hana*, for entities moving away from the speaker. In Wooi, there is a three-way horizontal distinction anchored to the speaker and the addressee, and a fourth elevational demonstrative *pe* marking entities that are above eye-level.

Biak and all of the surveyed RASH languages have rich systems of grammatical directionals. These directionals integrate with demonstratives or other units to give more fine-grained information about the location of an entity relative to the wider environment. Examples include the Taba directionals *ya* 'up', *po* 'down', *la* 'sea', *le* 'land', and *no* 'across', to which are attached affixes indicating the position or motion of an entity. These directionals can be used on a small, local scale (for example, for orientation within a house); on an intermediate scale (for example, for orientation within a village); or on a wider, more global scale (for example, for orientation between villages or between islands; see Holton 2017 on the development of directionals in Halmahera).

When directionals are used on a local scale, they typically take their coordinates from a nearby entity in an intrinsic frame of reference. When used on an intermediate or global scale, they are used in an absolute frame of reference; they are also often geocentric, in that they take their coordinates from concrete geographical or topographical phenomena. An example of the Ambel directional *ta(y)-* 'FRONT' used at the intermediate scale of the village is given in (79a); in Ambel, the area around the pier (where visitors to the village usually arrive) is conventionally referred to as the 'front'. An example of the Ambel directional *mu-* 'IN' used on a wider scale to refer to travel between villages is given in (79b). This example uses geocentric island-level coordinates: Kabare, the settlement to which the speaker is referring, is located inside a bay.

Ambel
(79) a. ...*Ido* *la-buka* *jalan*
...so.then 3PL.ANIM-open road
***wa-tay-a.***
DEM-FRONT-AND
'...So then they built [lit: 'opened'] that road at the front [of the village].'

b. *Atúma-mayál* *asi* *be* *lo*
1PL.EXCL-sell 3NSG.INAN.OBJ LOC place
*Kabáre* ***a-mu-a.***
Kabare DEM-IN-AND
'We will sell them [the sea cucumbers] in Kabare inside [the bay] there.' (Arnold 2018a: 492, 495)

Languages tend to have a small closed subclass of nouns that are used specifically for spatial orientation. The Yapen languages differentiate between two sets of what Gasser (2014) calls "locational nouns". Members of the first set refer to parts of an object, and are similar to English words like 'top', 'bottom', and 'side'. They often appear possessed; in at least Wamesa, they usually fail to trigger number agreement on a determiner if one appears, making them similar to mass nouns in that sense.

Wamesa
(80) *Kerakera=pa-i* *n‹i›ai* *na* *meja=pa*
spider=DET-SG ‹3SG›be.at LOC table=DET
***vavo****=pa.*
top=DET
'The spider is on top of the table.' (Gasser fieldnotes)

The second set consists of geographical nouns, which denote salient geographical areas and features of the landscape, and describe direction/location relative to land, sea, and elevation. These are often cognate with the grammatical directionals described above. Geographical nouns are distinguished from other classes of noun in that they are never possessed, and they are specified to co-occur with a special set of adpositions that cannot occur with other nouns. For example, in Wamesa, *so* 'to' is used with most goals; but either *do* 'to', *ra* 'to there', or *ma* 'to here' must be used with geographical nouns.

Languages with geographical nouns, like those with grammatical directionals, use the 'land/sea' and 'up/down' axes at both an intermediate and a wider scale. For both languages with geographical nouns and those with grammatical directionals, at the intermediate scale, the 'up/down' axis refers geocentrically to vertical elevation or an incline. On the larger scale, however, most languages employ the 'up/down' axis in a more conventionalized way: 'up' (or 'upriver') is typically used to refer to locations to the east, such as Cenderawasih Bay and Jayapura, whereas 'down' (or 'downriver') is used to refer to locations in the west, such as Halmahera. On several of the islands off the coast of Halmahera, 'up' is used to refer to an anti-clockwise direction (i.e. leftwards along the coast while facing the sea), while 'down' is used to refer to a clockwise direction (see Holton 2017).

### 37.3.14 Adpositions

Adpositions are generally prepositional, although, unusually for SVO languages, some postpositions do occur. Moor, Waropen, and several Yapen languages have a cognate general locative adposition *na* 'on/at/in/from' which expresses a wide range of locative relationships, alongside more specific adpositions meaning 'to', 'with', etc. Several of these languages also use a related verb meaning 'to be at', 'to live at', or 'to stay'.[7]

Wooi
(81) *He-****na*** ***na*** *manu* *ne-i* ***na*** *ramdempe.*
3PL-stay LOC house PROX-SG LOC yesterday
'They stayed at this house yesterday.'
(Sawaki 2016: 94)

Moor
(82) *I=kariʔa* *bola* *sia* *ruma* ***na.***
1SG=throw ball enter house LOC
'I threw the ball into the house.' (Kamholz fieldnotes)

In some cases, such as Moor *na* 'LOC' and Wamesa *kasau* 'between', postpositions appear to be related to verbs. In the Raja Ampat languages Ambel and Biga, a postposition *lo* 'inside' has grammaticalized from a noun meaning 'place'. Elsewhere, locational nouns, directional adverbs, and directional enclitics resemble postpositions but are not the same (see §37.3.13).

### 37.3.15 Serial verb constructions (SVCs)

Serial verb constructions (SVCs) are monoclausal strings of two or more verbs which act together as a single predicate, usually describing a single event, without coordination, subordination, or other syntactic dependency, within a single intonational phrase (Aikhenvald 2006). These constructions are common across the region. In Ambai, SVCs are limited to statements of volition and ability; in other languages, they are less constrained.

Ambai
(83) *Tom-i* ***di-aitawan*** ***m‹i›un*** *dian.*
Tom-PERS 3SG-able ‹3SG›kill fish
'Tom is able (knows how) to catch (kill) fish.'
(Silzer 1983: 197)

[7] The Biak verb *na* 'to have' (see example (70)) is probably not cognate.

Dusner
(84) *Ko* *rimnau* *me* *kaka*
until having.completed.st then elder.sib
***i-ve*** *a* ***r‹i›a*** *s‹i›apnap.*
3SG-say FILL ‹3SG›move ‹3SG›hunt
'After finishing, (my) older brother said that he wanted to go hunting.'
(Dalrymple and Mofu 2012: 37)

In Wamesa, Wooi, Ambai, and Dusner, all verbs in an SVC take subject marking, although that subject may switch between verbs (see Senft 2004b). In Biak, the most common type of SVC is one in which only the first verb takes subject marking, and the rest appear as bare stems; these may be somewhat lexicalized.

Biak
(85) ***V‹y›ark*** ***wáf*** *romá* *v‹y›e=d-ya* *ro*
‹3SG›stay wait son ‹3SG›POSS-3SG-SPEC LOC
*rumahsakit.*
hospital
'He stays and guards his son at the hospital.'
(van den Heuvel 2006: 189)

For Warembori, Donohue describes contiguous and non-contiguous serialization. His contiguous serialization appears to be indistinguishable from verb compounding.

Warembori contiguous serialization
(86) *Make-yave* ***matim-pase****-ta-o* *nana* *ipa-yave.*
boy-DEF wash-finish-PRF-IND OBL river-DEF
'The boy has finished washing in the river.'
(Donohue1999b: 35)

Serialization in RASH is more restricted in function than in the languages further east. In Matbat, SVCs may express manner, aspect, and instrumental functions; in Ambel they convey direction of transfer, change of state, manner, and purposive motion. Taba is freer, making use of serialization for motion, cause–effect, causative, instrumental, and adverbial (including manner, mode, and aspect) meanings. Sawai is unusual in that SVCs are not attested. Irarutu patterns more closely with RASH than Cenderawasih Bay in that SVCs express purposive motion, causatives, and adverbials, and are used in double-object constructions.

Ambel direction of transfer
(87) *Kiranya* *ny-ále* *be* ***ny-ut-ále***
beseech 2SG-descend PURP 2SG-carry-descend
*ni-m* *roh* *pa.*
POSS-2SG holy.spirit ART
'[I] beseech [you], descend in order to bring down your holy spirit.' (Arnold 2018a: 538)

Ambel purposive motion
(88) ***N-tán*** ***na-kút*** *a,* *bey* *kánu* *máy.*
3SG.ANIM-go 3SG-cut HES sago leaf cooked
'He went to cut, umm, dry sago leaves.'
(Arnold 2018a: 553)

Structures similar to SVCs, but where one of the roots is not independently attested, are found in Ambel and Biak, in constructions referred to as 'compound verbs'. As described by van den Heuvel, the dependent elements in compound verbs are "like suffixes, in that they are bound to roots of a fixed lexical category. On the other hand, they resemble roots in that they have a richer lexical content than is usual for affixes" (2006: 190). An example of a compound verb from Biak is given in (89), where the bound element is *wark* 'block', which is not independently attested; and example from Ambel is given in (90), where the bound element is the suffix *-wop* 'help'.

Biak
(89) *...Ikák=ya* ***v‹y›ark*** ***wark*** *i.*
...snake=3SG.SPEC ‹3SG›lie block 3SG
'[He went inside the cave, but] a snake, it was lying on the ground and blocking it.'
(van den Heuvel 2006: 192)

Ambel
(90) *Ya-tabón* *awa* *be* *nya-mánin* *be*
1SG-wait.for 2SG PURP 2SG-to.here PURP
***nya-mát-wop*** *ana.*
2SG-extinguish-help 3SG.INAN
'I am waiting for you to come here to help extinguish it [a big fire].' (Arnold 2018a: 558)

## 37.4 Other phenomena

### 37.4.1 Tail–head linkage

Tail–head linkage is a cross-linguistically common phenomenon, most frequently found in procedural and narrative texts, in which clause chains are connected by partially or completely repeating material from the previous clause at the beginning of the next (Thompson et al. 2007: 272–5).[8] Tail–head linkage has been reported in Biak and Ambel. An example from an Ambel procedural text is given in (91); the repeated material is highlighted in bold, and phrase-final intonation is marked with full stops.

[8] Among other places, tail–head linkage is found in many non-Austronesian languages of west New Guinea (de Vries 2005), as well as Austronesian languages spoken elsewhere, for example, in the Philippines (Longacre 1968).

Ambel

(91) *Kalo* *pimám,* *ido* *antanane*
if sea.cucumber then later
***la-bót*** ***si.***
3PL.ANIM-boil 3PL.ANIM.OBJ
'If there are sea cucumbers, then later they boil them.'

***la-bót*** ***si*** *beposa,* *ido*
3PL.ANIM-boil 3PL.ANIM.OBJ after then
***la-suy*** ***si.***
3PL.ANIM-smoke 3PL.ANIM.OBJ
'After they boil them, then they smoke them.'

***la-suy*** ***si*** *be*
3PL.ANIM-smoke 3PL.ANIM.OBJ PURP
*la-mán* *beposa,* *ido* *gányul*
3PL.ANIM-dry after then sunshine
*ido* *la-ha* *si.*
if 3PL.ANIM-dry 3PL.ANIM.OBJ
'After they smoke them so they are dry, then if there is sunshine, they dry them.'
(Arnold 2018a: 367–8)

### 37.4.2 Numerals and classifiers

Most languages have base-ten number systems which descend transparently from Proto-Malayo-Polynesian. A number of the languages of Cenderawasih Bay have shifted from a decimal to a quinary-decimal system, where the numbers six through nine are composed by adding to five; these additive forms are then used to build the numerals sixteen to nineteen, and so forth. In most cases these are formed with the word order 'five plus X', but in Serui-Laut this is reversed. Gasser (2017b) suggests that the quinary-decimal systems arose as a result of contact with non-Austronesian languages in the region, many of which use them as well. Where higher numerals are documented, the Yapen languages, Dusner, and Irarutu use twenty as a base, while other languages continue to count in multiples of ten. In these languages, the word for 'twenty' often comes from the word for 'person'. In Yerisiam, the word for 'five' is the inherited form *rîmà*, with no further meaning, and there are two ways to express 'ten': *rîmà ìngkànà rîmà*, literally 'five plus five', and *bàkí rúuhí*, literally 'two arms'. (See Schapper and Hammarström 2013 for more on numeral systems in the region.)

The numeral system of Ambai, shown in Table 37.11, stands out from the others for two reasons. First, it uses a partially quinary system. The numerals one through seven are monomorphemic (plus an animacy classifier), but 'eight' and 'nine' have two possible realizations: they may be formed by adding three or four to a base not found elsewhere in the system, or by subtracting from ten. Ambai also uses an alternative base four number system for counting large fish.

**Table 37.11** Ambai numerals (inanimate)

| | | | |
|---|---|---|---|
| **1** | *bo-siri/bo-wei/bo-yari* | **6** | *wonan* |
| **2** | *bo-ru* | **7** | *itu* |
| **3** | *bo-toru* | **8** | *indea-toru* or *bo-ru kondarai sura* |
| **4** | *bo-a* | **9** | *indea-tan* or *bo-yari kondarai sura* |
| **5** | *rin* | **10** | *sura* |

(Silzer 1983: 113, 116)

Many of the languages use some sort of classifier system with their numerals. In Cenderawasih Bay, this is generally just an animate/inanimate distinction, if it exists at all. Ambai, for example, marks numerals with *bo-* if they modify inanimate count nouns, and *man-* if they modify animate ones; classifiers are generally cognate in the other languages that use them. These languages also vary in which numerals require classifiers: in Ambai, for example, only numbers under five get classifiers, whereas in Ansus classifiers only appear on numbers three through nine. (See also Schapper and Zobel, this volume, §35.4.4.1 for similar systems in eastern Timor and southern Maluku.)

More elaborate, and more diverse, classifier systems are found in RASH and Irarutu. Taba has a very well developed system, differentiating twenty-two categories including grains, skewers, armspans, and groups of ten animals. Sawai has only ten classifiers, but also has three additional words for 'ten', used specifically for counting coconuts (*giet-*), trees (*floten-*), and fish (*wəlen-*). Jackson (2014) lists fifteen classifiers in Irarutu.

## 37.5 Conclusion

Now is an exciting time for work on the Austronesian languages of Halmahera and west New Guinea: improvements in telecommunications and transport links across the region mean that these languages are becoming more accessible to researchers. On the other hand, however, these improvements in infrastructure have facilitated the very rapid spread of local varieties of Malay, which are used as *lingua francas* at the expense of the local languages. As mentioned above, many of these languages are endangered, some of them severely so. Documentation and description of the lesser-known languages of the region should therefore be a priority. While some progress has been made in recent years, there is still a great deal of latitude for further work. In particular, we recommend research on the under-documented languages of the Mamberamo and eastern Yapen areas, which appear to be typologically divergent from the other languages in the area; an up-to-date description of Waropen; and further work on the under-documented languages of Raja Ampat.

In this chapter, we have hoped to show both the typological similarity and the structural diversity of the Austronesian languages of Halmahera and west New Guinea. For example, while the vast majority of the languages in the area have an alienability distinction in adnominal possessive constructions, the morphosyntactic manifestation of this distinction is diverse. Similarly, while complex word-prosodic systems are found in several languages, the systems themselves are quite various. Much of this structural variation is due to prolonged and intense contact with the non-Austronesian languages of the region. Further research will thus not only be valuable for furthering our understanding of the Austronesian migrations from insular Southeast Asia into the Pacific, which are at present poorly understood, but will also help us to begin to address some of the many unanswered questions regarding the timescale and nature of contact between Austronesian and non-Austronesian speakers across the area.

## Data sources

Unless otherwise cited, the data in this chapter come from the following sources: Ambai: Silzer (1983); Ambel: Remijsen (2001a); Arnold (2018a); Laura Arnold's fieldwork (2014–17); Ansus: Rawejai, Worabai, and Donohue (2002); Emily Gasser's fieldwork (2016); As: David Kamholz's fieldwork (2015); Laura Arnold's fieldwork (2020); Batta: Laura Arnold's fieldwork (2019); Biak: van Hasselt and van Hasselt (1947); van den Heuvel (2006); Biga: Remijsen (2001a); Laura Arnold's fieldwork (2019–2020); Buli: Maan (1951); Dusner: Dalrymple and Mofu (n.d., 2012); Fiat: Remijsen (2001a); Gebe: David Kamholz's fieldwork (2015); Irarutu: Matsumura and Matsumura (1991); van den Berg and Matsumura (2008); Jackson (2014); Kurudu: Smits and Voorhoeve (1992); Xavier Bach (p.c.); David Kamholz's fieldwork (2015); Maba: David Kamholz's fieldwork (2015); Matbat: Remijsen (2001a, 2007, 2010, 2015); Maˈya: Remijsen (2001a, b); van der Leeden (n.d., 1993); Laura Arnold's fieldwork (2023); Meoswar: Smits and Voorhoeve (1992); Xavier Bach (p.c.); Moor: Kamholz (2011); David Kamholz's fieldwork (2008–2019); Patani: David Kamholz's fieldwork (2015); Linn Iren Sjånes Rødvand (p.c.); Pom and Serewen: Emily Gasser's fieldwork (2016); Roon: Gil (2010b, 2017); Emily Gasser's fieldwork (2016); David Gil (p.c.); Salawati varieties: Laura Arnold's fieldwork (2019); Sawai: Whisler (1996, 1992); Whisler and Whisler (1995); Serui-Laut: Slump (1924); Smits and Voorhoeve (1992); Taba: Bowden (2001); Tandia: Smits and Voorhoeve (1992); Umar: Kamholz (2011); David Kamholz's fieldwork (2010–2015); Wabo: David Kamholz's fieldwork (2015); Wamesa: Gasser (2014); Emily Gasser's fieldwork (2011–2019); Warembori: Donohue (1999b); Waropen: Held (1942); Wooi: Smits and Voorhoeve (1992); Sawaki (2016); Yaur: Kamholz (2011); David Kamholz's fieldwork (2010–2015); Yerisiam: Kamholz (2011); David Kamholz's fieldwork (2010–2015); Yoke: David Kamholz's fieldwork (2015).

## Acknowledgements

We would like to thank Antoinette Schapper, Sander Adelaar, David Gil, and an anonymous reviewer for their very helpful feedback, all the linguists and speakers who shared their data with us, and Ceci Williamson and Martin Rakowszczyk for their help in assembling this manuscript.

# CHAPTER 38

# Chamorro

Erik Zobel

## 38.1 Introduction

Chamorro is the indigenous language of the Mariana Islands, which are politically divided into the territory of Guam and the Commonwealth of the Northern Mariana Islands. It is spoken by ca. 40,000 speakers in the Mariana Islands,[1] and ca. 20,000 speakers abroad.[2] The major descriptive reference works for Chamorro are Topping (1973) and Chung (2020).[3]

Together with Palauan, it is one of the non-Oceanic Malayo-Polynesian outliers in Micronesia. Like Palauan, Chamorro is morphologically quite conservative. It has, for example, preserved *maN-, *<um>, *<in>, *ma-, and *-i as productive inflectional affixes. Its position among the Malayo-Polynesian languages remains controversial. It was grouped with the Philippine languages by Topping (1973) based on morphological and superficial syntactic similarities. Zobel (2002) proposed that Chamorro can be grouped with certain languages of western Indonesia based on shared morphological innovations, such as preposed actor pronouns, or innovative affix combinations such as *<um> + *-i, which have resulted in a significant restructuring of the inherited Austronesian alignment system. These potential subgrouping arguments were rejected by Blust (2000a) and Reid (2002b), but tentatively accepted by Ross (2002a). Smith (2017b) classifies Chamorro as a primary branch of Malayo-Polynesian based on lexical and phonological evidence.

Apart from the geographical outlier position and a certain degree of morphological conservatism, Chamorro has little in common with Palauan. There are hardly any shared features between Chamorro and Palauan which are not inherited from PMP. It is therefore safe to assume that the migration of Malayo-Polynesian speakers from insular Southeast Asia to the Marianas and Palau occurred independently.

The Mariana Islands were subject to Spanish colonial rule for more than three hundred years, which had a major impact on the Chamorro population and their language. Much of modern Chamorro vocabulary was borrowed from Spanish, including functors such as prepositions, conjunctions, and even numerals (Rodríguez-Ponga 1995). The latter have completely replaced the inherited Austronesian numerals, which were already obsolete at the time when Chamorro was first systematically studied (Safford 1903, 1904a, b). This has even led to proposals that Chamorro represents a case of a mixed language or creole (Rodríguez-Ponga 2001). However, in spite of the massive influx of Spanish lexicon, which altered the phonological structure of Chamorro, much of the basic inherited Austronesian vocabulary was retained, and moreover, the grammatical core of the language was largely unaffected, neither of which is compatible with the concepts of language mixing and creolization in the proper sense (Stolz 2003; Pagel 2018).

In the following parts, §38.2 treats the phonology, §38.3 is about nouns and pronouns, §38.4 about basic clause structure; §38.5 and §38.6 cover valency-reducing/-increasing and focus constructions. §38.7 closes with a discussion of the historical relationship of Chamorro to other MP languages.

## 38.2 Phonology

In the inherited lexical layer of Chamorro, only four vowels are distinguished: /i/, /u/, /a/, and /æ/.[4] With the borrowing of Spanish lexicon, the vowel system was extended by the mid vowel phonemes /e/ and /o/.

Stress is phonemic in Chamorro, with minimal pairs such as *mohon* /ˈmohon/ 'desire' vs. *mohón* /moˈhon/ 'boundary'. In inherited vocabulary, stress mostly falls on the penultimate syllable (e.g. *gumaʔ* /ˈgumaʔ/ 'house', *håfa* /ˈhafa/ 'what', *nigap* /ˈnigap/ 'yesterday'). Antepenultimate stress regularly occurs with certain prefixes such as *á-* 'reciprocal', *é-* 'look for', *mí-* 'have plenty of' (e.g. *apacha* /ˈapatsa/ 'touch each other', *míchigoʔ* /ˈmitsigoʔ/ 'have lots of juice'), and in words with reduplication (e.g. *húhungok* /ˈhuhuŋok/

[1] Census data from 2010 gives 25,800 speakers in Guam and 12,900 speakers in the Northern Mariana Islands.

[2] The US Census Bureau lists 19,780 Chamorro speakers (based on counts collected in 2009–2013).

[3] Chung's grammar appeared when this chapter was already completed.

[4] In common spelling, the low vowels are not distinguished. When the distinction is made explicit in conventional orthography, /a/ is spelled *å*, while /æ/ is spelled *a*.

Erik Zobel, *Chamorro.* In: *The Oxford Guide to the Malayo-Polynesian Languages of Southeast Asia.* Edited by: Alexander Adelaar and Antoinette Schapper, Oxford University Press.
 DOI: 10.1093/oso/9780198807353.003.0038

**Table 38.1** Consonants

| | Labial/Labiodental | Alveolar | Palatal | Velar | | Glottal |
|---|---|---|---|---|---|---|
| | | | | plain | labialized | |
| Voiceless stop | p | t | | k | | ʔ |
| Voiced stop | b | d | | g | gʷ <*gu*> | |
| Voiceless affricate | | ts <*ch*> | | | | |
| Voiced affricate | | dz <*y*> | | | | |
| Fricative | f | s | | | | h |
| Nasal | m | n | ɲ <*ñ*> | ŋ <*ng*> | | |
| Lateral | | l | | | | |
| Tap/Trill | | r | | | | |

'hear (continuative)'). In text samples in this chapter, stress will be indicated by an acute (e.g. *ápacha, húhungok*) unless it falls on the penultimate syllable (e.g. *gumaʔ, nigap*), following the convention used in earlier descriptions (e.g. Topping 1973; Cooreman 1987).

Penultimate vowels in trisyllabic words are often subject to syncope (e.g. *mafunot* > *mafnot* 'tight').

The high vowels /i/ and /u/ are lowered to /e/ and /o/ in closed syllables, and also in final open syllables which are preceded by a closed syllable. Prefixation and syncope can result in vowel lowering as a synchronic process. For example, the prefix *mí-* combines with the noun *hutu* 'louse' to form *míhutu* 'lousy', which is usually syncopated to *mehto*, with regular lowering in both the vowel of the prefix and the final vowel of the root (Topping 1973: 55).

A common morphophonological rule is progressive vowel fronting, by which stressed root vowels /u/, /o/, /a/ change to /i/, /e/, /æ/ if the preceding bound morpheme[5] contains a front vowel (/i/, /e/, /æ/).

The consonant inventory of Chamorro is quite unsurprising for a conservative Malayo-Polynesian language, the only unusual segments being /f/ and /gʷ/ (Table 38.1).

However, Chamorro actually has undergone quite significant sound shifts from Proto-Malayo-Polynesian (Blust 2000a). These changes include:

- Devoicing of voiced obstruents: *b > /p/, *z > /ts/, *j (probably via intermediate *g and *k) > /ʔ/.
- Spirantization of voiceless obstruents: *p > /f/, *k > /h/ (zero in final position).
- Fortition of resonants: *w > /gʷ/, *y > /dz/, *R > /g/.

Spirantization was a push chain result of devoicing. Note that *t remains unchanged, since *d did not devoice, but shifted to /h/ (probably via an intermediate *r).

These changes created gaps for *b, d, k,* and *r*. The occurrence of these sounds in Chamorro cannot be accounted for by straightforward regular sound shifts from PMP. The stops *b, d, k* often occur as medial geminates.[6] Many words with *b, d, k*, and *r* are loanwords from known sources (e.g. *babui* 'pig' from Tagalog (or another Philippine language); *kada* 'each' from Spanish *cada*; *tres* 'three' from Spanish).

## 38.3 Nouns and personal pronouns

### 38.3.1 Case marking

Chamorro has three case forms: unmarked case, oblique case, and locative case. Unmarked case is zero-marked with common nouns, while all other case forms have an explicit case marker (Table 38.2).

**Table 38.2** Case markers

| | Unmarked | Oblique | Locative |
|---|---|---|---|
| Common noun | Ø | *nu* | *gi* |
| Personal name | *si* | *as* | *gi as* |

[5] These include the case markers *i/ni/gi*, the pronominal prefixes *en-/in-*, and the affixes *mi-/sæn-/<in>*.

[6] Some of these can be derived from earlier clusters (e.g. *godde* < PMP *həRət-i 'tie' (with syncope), *oddaʔ* < PMP *buRtaq 'soil' (irregular loss of *b)).

Common nouns are obligatorily headed by a determiner when used as core arguments. The most commonly used determiner is the article *i* (see examples in §38.4.2). Place names take the article *iya* (*maolek iya Saipan* 'Saipan is good').

The oblique marker *nu* is not only used with common nouns, but also used with free pronouns (e.g. *nu guahu* '1SG.OBL'). The combination of oblique case marker and article *nu I* is often merged to *ni i*, *niʔ*, or *ni*. The locative case marker *gi* merges with the articles *i* and *iya* to *gi* (*gi gimaʔ* 'at home' or 'at the house') and *giya* (*giya Saipan* 'in Saipan').

## 38.3.2 Free and bound pronouns

**Table 38.3** Personal pronouns

| | Free | Absolutive | Genitive | Realis ergative | Irrealis S=A |
|---|---|---|---|---|---|
| 1SG | *guåhu* | *yoʔ* | *-hu/-ku* | *hu-* | *hu-* |
| 2SG | *hågu* | *hao* | *-mu* | *un-* | *un-* |
| 3SG | *guiya* | *gueʔ* | *-ña* | *ha-* | Ø |
| 1PL.INCL | *hita* | *hit* | *-ta* | *ta-* | *ta-* |
| 1PL.EXCL | *hami* | *ham* | *-måmi* | *in-* | *in-* |
| 2PL | *hamyo* | *hamyo* | *-miu* | *en-* | *en-* |
| 3DU | *siha* | *siha* | *-ñiha* | *ha-* | *ha-* |
| 3PL | | | | *ma-* | *Ø/ma-* |

Free pronouns are used in isolation, with oblique and locative case markers, and in focus clauses (Table 38.3). The absolutive pronouns are enclitics that appear directly following the predicate.[7] Together with the prefixed pronoun sets, they appear in a system of split-ergative alignment which is described in §38.4.1 below. Genitive pronouns are used to mark possessors (see §38.3.3), agents with *IN*-passives in focus constructions (see §38.6.3), and experiencers with a small number of words.

The person affixes cannot be coindexed by free pronouns (i.e. they are bound pronouns). However, third person genitive, ergative and irrealis pronouns can co-occur with overt noun phrases as cross-referencing person markers.

[7] Note that unlike in conservative Philippine-type languages, the absolutive enclitics are not second-position enclitics (cf. Kaufmann, this volume, §25.4.4).

## 38.3.3 Possession

Chamorro has two types of possessive constructions: direct possession and possession expressed by means of possessive classifiers (Safford 1903: 508ff.; Topping 1973: 221ff.).

Direct possession is obligatorily used with body parts and terms for human relationships, and is also the most common way of expressing possession with inanimate nouns. If the possessor is a pronoun, it is represented by a genitive suffix directly following the verb (e.g. *i asagua-mu* (ART spouse-2SG.GEN) 'your spouse'). With nouns as possessors, two constructions are available. The first construction employs third person genitive suffixes, with the possessor being expressed by a coreferential noun phrase directly following the genitive suffix (e.g. *i gimaʔ-ña si Rosa* (ART house-3SG.GEN PERS Rosa) 'Rosa's house'; *i malagoʔ-ñiha i taotao* (ART wish-3PL.GEN ART people) 'the people's wish'). In the second construction, the possessed noun takes the suffix *-n* if vowel-final, and remains unchanged if ending in a consonant, while the possessor immediately follows the possessed noun without any article or case marker: *i håga-n rai* (ART daughter-POSS king) 'the king's daughter'; *i gimaʔ Rosa* (ART house Rosa) 'Rosa's house'.

Possessive classifiers are obligatorily employed with nouns for living animals and food (e.g. *i gaʔ-hu mannok* (ART CLF-1SG.GEN chicken) 'my (pet) chicken'; *i naʔ-hu guihan* (ART CLF-1SG.GEN fish) 'my fish (to eat)'). A noun as possessor follows the possessed noun (e.g. *i naʔ-ña guihan si Maria* (ART CLF-3SG.GEN fish PERS *Maria)* 'Maria's fish (to eat)').

The use of the possessive classifiers *iyo* (inanimate noun) and *gimen* (drinkable things) is optional (e.g. *i iyo-ña kareta* (ART CLF-3SG.GEN car) or *i kareta-ña* (*art* car-3SG.GEN) 'his car'). Forms headed by *iyo* can also function as absolute possessives (e.g. in predicate position: *iyo-ku i lepblo* (CLF-1SG.GEN ART book) 'the book is mine').

Possessive classifiers are rare in western Malayo-Polynesian, and represent one of the few features which Chamorro may have been taken over from neighbouring Oceanic languages (cf. §38.7).

## 38.3.4 Modified noun phrases

In noun phrases with modifiers (i.e. adjectives, numerals, deictics), the modifier precedes the noun with the linking particle *na* (e.g. *i dánkolo na taotao* (ART big LNK person) 'the big person'; *kuatro na mangga* 'four mangos'; *ayu na lebplo* 'that book') (cf. Topping 1973:138ff.).

### 38.3.5 Plurals of noun phrases

There are three ways to express plural number of a noun phrase. The productive and most common way is to add *siha* after the noun phrase (e.g. *i niyok siha* 'the coconuts', *i amigu-hu siha* (ART friend-1SG.GEN PL) 'my friends'). A limited set of nouns for humans form their plural by means of the prefix *maN-* (e.g. *mañeʔlu* 'siblings' (< *cheʔlu*), *mamaleʔ* 'priests' (< *paleʔ*)). A few nouns have unproductive plural formations: *hahåga* 'daughters' (< *håga*), *lalåhi* 'men sons' (< *låhi*), *famalaoʔan* 'women' (< *palaoʔan*). An exeptional suppletive plural form is *famaguʔon* 'children' (singular: *patgun*).

## 38.4 Basic clause structure

Basic word order is predicate initial; the order of arguments following the predicate depends on the clause type (see §38.4.2 and §38.5.1). Transitive and intransitive predicates are strictly distinguished by means of patterns of person marking, case marking of overt NPs, and number agreement.

### 38.4.1 Split-ergative alignment

Person marking follows a split-ergative pattern. In transitive clauses, the actor is obligatorily marked by a prefixed pronoun, while a pronoun undergoer is represented by the absolutive set. This pattern is observed in realis (1) as well as in irrealis clauses (2).

(1) ***Hu**-guaiya* *hao*
1SG.ERG-love 2SG.ABS
'I love you.' (Cooreman 1987: 132)

(2) *Lao* *bai* ***hu**-lalatde* *hao*
CONJ FUT 1SG.IRR-scold 2SG.ABS
'But I will scold you.' (YSB Salmo 50: 20)[8]

For the subject of intransitive verbs, we find a split pattern determined by mood: in realis mood, we have ergative alignment, that is, the subject expressed by an absolutive pronoun (3), whereas in irrealis mood, there is nominative alignment with a prefixed pronoun expressing the subject (4).

(3) *Man-hanao* ***ham*** *gi* *tenda*
PL-walk 1PL.EXCL.ABS LOC store
'We went to the store.' (Cooreman 1987: 40)

(4) *Para* ***in**-fan-hanao* *gi* *tenda*
FUT 1PL.EXCL.IRR-PL-walk LOC store
'We are going to the store.' (Cooreman 1987: 40)

### 38.4.2 Clauses with overt noun phrases

In the most basic clause type, overt NPs follow the predicate. If common nouns or personal names are used as core arguments, they take the articles *i* (common nouns) or *si* (personal names). The basic word order in active transitive clauses with two overt arguments is VSO. Unlike in most Philippine-type languages, the role of the two core arguments is not expressed by case markers.

(5) *Pues* *h<um>anao* [*i* *haggan*]$_{S}$
CONJ <SG>walk ART turtle
'Then the turtle went.' (Stolz 2019: 542)

(6) *Ha-sakke* [*i* *patgun*]$_{A}$ [*i* *kareta*]$_{O}$
3SG.ERG-steal ART child ART car
'The child stole the car.' (Cooreman 1987: 158)

Note that the obligatory occurrence of an actor person marker in transitive clauses results in the cross-referencing of the actor NP in example (6), where the prefix *ha-* is co-referential to the actor *i patgun*.

Basic VSO word order is changed to VOS if the actor is a noun and the undergoer an enclitic absolutive pronoun.

(7) *Ha-guaiya* [*yoʔ*]$_{O}$ [*si* *Juan*]$_{A}$
3SG.ERG-love 1SG.ABS PERS Juan
'Juan loves me.' (Cooreman 1987: 124)

Next to basic verb initial word order, SVO word order is also frequently employed. Cooreman (1987) observes that SVO word order correlates with thematic discontinuity in narratives.

NPs marked for locative or oblique case always follow unmarked core NPs. This also holds for oblique undergoers in antipassive clauses (cf. §38.5.1), and oblique actors in passive clauses (see §38.5.2).

### 38.4.3 Number agreement

Intransitive clauses are characterized by number agreement. With singular and dual subjects, number is unmarked, while plural number is marked by the prefix *maN-* (irrealis *faN-*).

(8) *Mataʔchong* *yoʔ*
sit 1SG.ABS
'I sat down.' (Topping 1973: 226)

[8] YSB refers to *Y Santa Biblia*, a 1908 translation of the Psalms, Gospels, and Acts by the American Bible Society which was republished in the early 2000s on the website ChamorroBible.org.

(9) *Man-mata?chong* *siha*
PL-sit 3PL.ABS
'They sat down.' (Topping 1973: 226)

If an intransitive verb takes the intransitive infix *<um>*, this infix is dropped in the plural form, for example, *s<um>aga* 'stay (sg.)' vs. *mañaga* 'stay (pl.)'.

### 38.4.4 Negation

In basic clauses, negation is expressed by *ti*, which directly precedes the predicate. Unlike in Palauan or many languages of the Philippines and Sulawesi (cf. Zobel, this volume, §39.7.6.2), verbs in predicate position do not undergo a morphological change in negative clauses (e.g. *ti tumanges si Maria* [NEG cry PERS Maria] 'Maria didn't cry', cf. *tumanges si Maria* 'Maria cried').

Specialized negators include *taya?* (negative existential, cf. *guaha* 'there is'), *munga* 'don't!' (vetative) and *ni*, which forms negative indefinites (*ni un taotao* 'not even one person') (cf. van der Auwera, Van Olmen, and Vossen, this volume, §50.4).

## 38.5 Voice and applicatives

Since transitive and intransitive clauses are clearly distinguished in Chamorro, this allows for identifying passive and antipassive voice as valency-reducing verb alternations. For example, the transitive clause in (10) with two core arguments can be 'transformed' into the corresponding passive (11) and antipassive clause (12), each of which only has one core argument, while the other argument is marked by oblique case (all three examples taken from Chung 2014).

(10) *Ha-guaiya* [*si* *Julia*]$_{A}$ [*si* *Vicente*]$_{O}$
3SG.ERG-love PERS Julia PERS Vicente
'Julia loves Vicente.'

(11) *Gu<in>aiya* [*si* *Vicente*]$_{S}$ [*as* *Julia*]$_{OBL}$
PASS-love PERS Vicente OBL Julia
'Vicente is loved by Julia.'

(12) *Mang-guaiya* [*si* *Julia*]$_{S}$ [*as* *Vicente*]$_{OBL}$
ANTIP-love PERS Julia OBL Vicente
'Julia loves Vicente.'

The transitive form of the verb will be called *active voice* in the further discussion.

### 38.5.1 Antipassive

The antipassive is formed by adding the prefix *maN-/faN-* to transitive verb bases. It follows the rules of intransitive verbs for person marking and number agreement. Antipassive verbs differ from underived intransitive verbs in that they can be expanded by a plain noun (not headed by an article) to express an indefinite object.

The antipassive prefix *maN-/faN-* is homophonous to the plural agreement prefix *maN-/faN-* and historically, they are clearly derived from the PMP prefix *maN-/*paN-. Synchronically, there is a significant difference between the two in the ordering of nasal replacement and progressive reduplication. With the plural agreement prefix, nasal replacement only applies to the first consonant of the reduplicated verb (e.g. *manútunok* 'desend (pl.) (< *tunok*)). On the other hand, with the antipassive prefix, progressive reduplication operates after nasal replacement (e.g. *mañúñule?* 'carry (antip.)' (< *chule?*)).

The antipassive is mostly used with indefinite objects, which are always unmarked in antipassive clauses, and always directly follow the verb (13), unless the subject is an enclitic pronoun, in which case the pronoun intervenes between the verb and the indefinite object (14).

(13) *Man-li?e?* *lepblo* *si* *Juan*
ANTIP-see book PERS Juan
'Juan saw a book' (Topping 1973: 240)

(14) *Man-li?e?* *yo?* *lahi*
ANTIP-see 1SG.ABS man
'I saw a man' (Topping 1973: 107)

When the antipassive appears with definite objects, the latter have to be marked for oblique or locative case. Pragmatically, the antipassive here indicates reduced transitivity, that is, the undergoer is less affected than in the corresponding active construction, as exemplified in example (15), where *mamatek* is in antipassive voice, which contrasts with *un-patek* in example (16) in active voice.

(15) *Mamatek* *hao* *gi* *ga?lagu*
ANTIP:kick 2SG.ABS OBL dog
'You kicked at the dog' (Cooreman 1987: 124)

(16) *Un-patek* *i* *ga?lagu*
2SG.ERG-kick ART dog
'You kicked the dog' (Cooreman 1987: 124)

Unlike with the passive, the selection of the antipassive is not governed by a person–animacy hierarchy (cf. §38.5.3 below).

### 38.5.2 Two types of passive

Chamorro has two types of passive voice, called IN-passive and MA-passives here, following Cooreman (1987).

#### 38.5.2.1 *The IN-passive*

The IN-passive is formed by adding the infix *<in>* to transitive verbs. It can be employed as predicate and in focus constructions.

If employed as predicate, the IN-passive formally behaves like a canonical passive: the O-argument of the transitive verb becomes the S-argument of the IN-passive, which latter triggers intransitive person marking and number agreement, while the A-argument is either unexpressed or demoted to oblique case. In (17), the S-argument of *k<in>enne?* is expressed by the intransitive irrealis person marker *un-*. Number agreement is visible in (18) and (19), where *hamyo* and the plural noun *i famagu?on* (S) of the prefix *man-*.

(17) *Un-k<in>enne?*
2SG.IRR-PASS-take
'He will take you.' (YSB, Salmo 52:5)

(18) *Man-h<in>engge hamyo*
PL-PASS-believe 2PL.ABS
'He believed you (pl.).' (Cooreman 1987: 97)

(19) *Man-l<in>alatde i famagu?on ni maestro-n-ñiha*
PL-PASS-scold ART children OBL.ART teacher-LNK-3PL.GEN
'The children were scolded by their teacher.' (Topping 1973: 257)

Both person marking and number agreement is realized in (20).

(20) *Para in-fan-l<in>i?e*
FUT 2PL.IRR-PL-PASS-see
'so that you may be seen [by them]' (YSB, Mateo 6:1)

The IN-passive is used if the actor is definite, and by preference employed with singular actors (see §38.5.3. below).

#### 38.5.2.2 *The MA-passive*

The MA-passive also features intransitive characteristics. In example (21), the plural undergoer-turned-subject *mañaina-n-ñiha* 'their parents' triggers number agreement expressed by the plural prefix *man-*.

(21) *Man-ma-li?e? i mañaina-n-ñiha ni famagu?on*
PL-PASS-see ART parents-LNK-3PL.GEN OBL.ART children
'The parents were seen by the children.' (Cooreman 1987: 83)

As with the IN-passive, we observe both person marking and number agreement in irrealis clauses.

(22) *Ya in-fan-ma-chatli?e? ni todo i taotao*
CONJ 2PL.IRR-PL-PASS-hate OBL.ART all ART person
'And all people will hate you.' (YSB, Luca 21:17)

The MA-passive is employed if the actor is indefinite, or definite and plural (see §38.5.3 below).

### 38.5.3 Person–animacy hierarchy

One of the most peculiar features of Chamorro is the distribution of active and passive clauses based on a person–animacy hierarchy. While passive clauses are formally intransitive, functionally they serve as a counterpart of active clauses in what is quite similar to an *inverse-direct* system. The following combinations of agents and undergoers are disallowed in active transitive clauses due to hierarchy constraints (Cooreman 1987; Chung 2014).

| Actor | | Undergoer |
|---|---|---|
| third person | → | second person |
| overt NPs | → | animate third person pronoun or zero |
| inanimate | → | animate |

In such agent-undergoer constellations, use of the passive is obligatory. As a general rule, the IN-passive is employed if the agent is singular, whereas the MA-passive is used when the agent is plural or completely suppressed.

Clauses in obligatory passive voice with second person undergoers have already given above in examples (17), (18), and (20). Example (23) illustrates the obligatory use of the passive with an overt NP (*taotao*) acting on a pronoun undergoer (*gue?*). The corresponding active clause **Ha-galuti gue? i taotao* is ungrammatical.

(23) *G<in>aluti gue? nu i taotao*
PASS-hit 3SG.ABS OBL ART man
'The man hit him.' (Cooreman 1987: 85)

First person actors and undergoers are unaffected by person–animacy hierarchy constraints and therefore do not trigger the use of passive voice. First person undergoers can appear in active clauses with third person actors (even including overt NP actors, as in example (24)); at the same time second person undergoers *do* appear in active clauses if the actor is first person (25).

(24) *Ha-guaiya yo? si Juan*
3SG.ERG-love 1SG.ABS PERS Juan
'Juan loves me.' (Cooreman 1987: 124)

(25) *Hu-guaiya hao*
1SG.ERG-love 2SG.ABS
'I love you.' (Cooreman 1987: 132)

### 38.5.4 The applicative suffix *-i*

A frequently used valency-increasing construction is formed with the applicative suffix *-i*. The applicative suffix can combine with nouns and intransitive verbs to form transitive verbs, or with transitive verbs to form ditransitive verbs. The undergoer of a verb with the applicative suffix is a goal or beneficiary, as in example (26), where the transitive verb *hanagui* 'go to' is derived from intransitive *h<um>anao* 'go'.

(26) *Hu-hanagu-i si Pedro*
1SG.ERG-go-APPL PERS Pedro
'I went to Pedro' (Topping 1973: 250)

## 38.6 Focus

Focus constructions are used in *wh*-questions, relative clauses, and cleft clauses. Focus can, in many cases, be realized by the simple gap strategy, but there are notable exceptions that trigger special morphologically marked verb forms.

### 38.6.1 Simple gap strategy

In basic realis clauses, the simple gap strategy can be applied to the subject of intransitive clauses, and to the undergoer of transitive clauses. The latter is illustrated in example (27), a *wh*-question focusing on the undergoer.

(27) *Hafa ha-fahan si Maria gi tenda?*
what 3SG.ERG-buy PERS Maria LOC store
'What did Maria buy at the store?' (Dukes 1993: 179)

The gap strategy cannot be applied to the actor of realis transitive clauses; instead, a specialized verb form has to be used here (see §38.6.2 below).

In irrealis clauses, there are no constraints against the gap strategy with transitive actors. The transitive clause appears in active or passive voice, depending on the person–animacy hierachy status of the undergoer. In example (28), the undergoer ranks lower than the actor, triggering active voice.

(28) *Hayi para u-kacha? i niyuk?*
who FUT IRR-husk ART coconut
'Who will husk the coconut?' (Chung 2014)

The passive is obligatory in example (29) with a second person undergoer. Note that it is the oblique actor that is raised in this construction.

(29) *Hayi para un-<in>ayuda?*
who FUT 2SG.IRR-PASS-help
'Who is going to help you?' (Chung 2014)

Literally, this clause translates as 'Who are you going to be helped by?'

### 38.6.2 Transitive actor focus

The most important exception to the simple gap strategy in focus constructions is found with agents in realis active clauses. Here, the verb takes the infix *<um>* in place of a realis ergative person marker (30).

(30) *I patgun s<um>akke i kareta*
ART child AF-steal ART car
'The child was the one who stole the car.' (Cooreman 1987: 158)

It is important to note that the focus construction overrides the person–animacy hierarchy. In (31), we have a second person object, yet the verb does not have to take passive voice as in the corresponding irrealis question above (29):

(31) *Hayi <um>ayuda hao?*
who AF-help 2SG
'Who helped you?' (Chung 2014)

The infix *<um>* is not restricted to focus constructions, but also appears in infinitive-like function in same-subject embedded clauses.

(32) *Malago? si Juan h<um>atsa i lamesa*
want PERS Juan AF-lift ART table
'Juan wanted to lift the table.' (Cooreman 1987: 152)

Transitive actor focus has been discussed in the literature as "subject WH-agreement" (Dukes 1993) and "anti-agreement" (Richards 2001).

### 38.6.3 Transitive undergoer focus

As noted above in §38.6.1, the undergoer of transitive realis clauses can be focused by means of the simple gap strategy. There is however an alternative construction in which the verb takes the infix *<in>*, thus being superfically identical to the IN-passive. In such undergoer focus constructions, the actor is expressed by a genitive phrase.

(33) *Hafa* *l<in>iʔeʔ-ña* *si* *Maria?*
what PASS-see-3SG.GEN PERS Maria
'What did Maria see?' (Cooreman 1987: 47)

Note that genitive marking of the actor is only allowed in this specialized focus construction. In main clauses with the IN-passive, the actor is always expressed by an oblique phrase.

## 38.7 Chamorro's position among the Malayo-Polynesian languages

It is an oft-repeated claim that Chamorro has a Philippine-type voice system (e.g. Blust 2013a: 445). Superficially, the passive/antipassive clause pair in examples (34) and (35) could be taken for a typical symmetric voice alternation, with the antipassive corresponding to actor voice and the passive to undergoer voice.

(34) *Gu<in>aiya* [*si* *Vicente*]$_{S}$ [*as* *Julia*]$_{OBL}$
PASS-love PERS Vicente OBL Julia
'Vicente is loved by Julia.'

(35) *Mang-guaiya* [*si* *Julia*]$_{S}$ [*as* *Vicente*]$_{OBL}$
ANTIP-love PERS Julia OBL Vicente
'Julia loves Vicente.'

This approach has been adopted in several grammatical descriptions of Chamorro (e.g. Topping 1973; Donohue and Maclachlan 2000). However, as we have seen, passive and antipassive clauses are intransitive in their surface syntactic properties. On the other hand, the genuine transitive construction (i.e. active voice) cannot be integrated into a Philippine-type voice system.[9]

Functionally, actor voice in Philippine-type languages is matched by two distinct constructions in Chamorro. In main clauses, the antipassive marked by *maN-* corresponds to pragmatically triggered actor voice in Philippine-type languages, with indefinite or less-affected undergoers. The syntactic trigger for Philippine-type actor voice in focus constructions is covered by transitive actor focus in active voice marked by *<um>*.

Philippine-type undergoer voice is matched by both active and passive voice in Chamorro, the distribution of which is largely governed by the person–animacy hierarchy.

Applicative derivations with *-i* in active and passive voice functionally correspond to locative–subject undergoer voice in Philippine-type languages (see Kaufman, this volume, §25.3.2,), and are also historically related to the latter (Zobel 2002). Yet, they cannot be interpreted in a Philippine-type fashion, since they also can combine with the actor voice-derived affixes *maN-* and *<um>* (e.g. *man-aft-e* 'to thatch [a house]' or *s<um>angan-i* '[the one] who tells [it]').

All this clearly shows that Chamorro does not have a classical Philippine-type alignment system (cf. also Kroeger and Riesberg, this volume, §47.6.1). This does not mean, however, that Chamorro is typologically *sui generis*. Many of its characteristics have formal matches in languages of western Indonesia,[10] as was proposed by Zobel (2002). The most important feature shared with many of these languages are the ergative realis person markers. These correspond formally and functionally to similar and historically related pronoun sets which are likewise preposed to the plain verb base, and which are used in clauses that express undergoer voice, or other high-transitivity clause types (cf. van den Berg and Mead, this volume, §33.5.4). As was shown by Wolff (1996) and further elaborated by Zobel (2002), constructions of the type *hu-konneʔ* 'I take (it)' are derived from atemporal undergoer voice forms in Proto-Malayo-Polynesian. Other recurrent features linking Chamorro to the languages of western Indonesia include the combination of actor voice-derived affixes with the suffix *-i*, and the shift of past undergoer voice forms marked by *<in>* to a valency-reducing passive.

The exact implications of these innovative correspondences between Chamorro and the languages of western Indonesia for the subgrouping of the MPSEA still remain to be established. However, it is likely that these innovations point towards a direct genealogical link of Chamorro to these western Indonesian languages.[11]

The use of possessive classifiers (shared with Palauan) is an uncommon feature in conservative western Malayo-Polynesian languages. It is however common in the eastern Wallacea and Oceania, and might be the result of Oceanic influence. Apart from this, Chamorro shows little traces of typological convergence to Oceanic languages, in spite of its location in Micronesia, and long-standing contact with

[9] In fact, even Topping (1973) referred to the basic transitive clause type as 'non-focus', thus neither 'Actor focus' (= actor voice in current standard terminology) nor 'Goal Focus' (= undergoer voice).

[10] More specifically, this includes the languages of Sumatra and neighbouring islands, Java, Madura, Bali, and Sulawesi (excluding the Philippine-type of North Sulawesi).

[11] Note that these features shared by Chamorro and the languages of western Indonesia are not found in the other non-Oceanic outlier in Micronesia, Palauan.

the Carolinians, who speak a Micronesian language of the Chuukic branch.

Finally, one particular feature that sets Chamorro apart from most if not all Malayo-Polynesian languages (including Palauan), is the person–animacy hierarchy, especially the constraints with regards to second person undergoers. While many languages of western Indonesia have verb alternations that are formally equivalent to active and passive voice in Chamorro, the functional distribution as outlined in §38.5.3 above is unique.

CHAPTER 39

# Palauan

ERIK ZOBEL

## 39.1 Introduction

Palauan (*təkoi ər a Belau*) is spoken on the Palau Islands in the Republic of Palau in Micronesia. The number of speakers is approximately 14,000, not counting Palauan migrants who reside in Guam and the Northern Mariana Islands. (Nuger 2010: 13). Language use is vigorous among all generations (Nuger 2010: 14).

Palauan is classified as a primary branch of Malayo-Polynesian (Blust 2009b: 307; Smith 2017b: 477). The inclusion of Palauan within the Malayo-Polynesian subgroup is generally agreed upon, as it reflects the characteristic PMP consonant mergers of PAN *C/*t and *N/*n, and also the 2SG genitive suffix *-mu. There is also general consensus that Palauan—in spite of its location in Micronesia—does not belong to the Oceanic subgroup, since it does not display the phonological and lexical innovations that characterize the latter (Blust 2009b). Palauan is morphologically quite conservative. For example, it has retained PMP *<um> and *maN- as fully productive affixes, a feature shared with the western Malayo-Polynesian languages, while CEMP languages only display fossilized reflexes of these affixes. A highly conservative feature is the retention of the PMP tense distinction with past tense being marked by the infix *<in>, which is only found in the Philippines, in the northern parts of Sulawesi and Borneo, and in southwestern Malagasy dialects.

But in spite of many retentions shared with western Malayo-Polynesian languages, there are no innovations that would link Palauan to a specific subgroup of Malayo-Polynesian. Attempts to group Palauan with the languages of the Philippines or Indonesia led to inconclusive results (Pätzold 1968; Zobel 2002). There is also no evidence that would link Palauan to Chamorro, the other non-Oceanic MP in Micronesia. They apparently share no common features which are not inherited from PMP (cf. also Smith 2017b). This indicates that Palau and the Marianas were settled independently from insular Southeast Asia; based on archaeological evidence, this occurred at least 3,000 years ago.

## 39.2 Phonology

Palauan has six vowels, /a, e, i, o, u, ə/ (Josephs 1975: 16ff.). The schwa is spelled *e* in the Palauan standard orthography, but it will be spelled with IPA *ə* in this description. The five cardinal vowels have no positional restrictions, whereas schwa only occurs in unstressed syllables.

The consonant inventory in native Palauan words (Table 39.1) is highly asymmetrical (Josephs 1975: 3ff.). In the labial and velar positions, the only contrast is stop vs. nasal. With /b/ and /k/, voice is a non-contrasting feature which depends on the phonetic environment: in absolute initial position, we find [b] and [k]. Both are voiced between two vowels, and voiceless in final postion or when preceding a consonant. Lack of the voiced velar /g/ is common among MP languages, but lack of /p/ is rather unusual and is the result of the shift of PMP *p to non-syllabic *u* or *o* (Blust 2009b: 313).

**Table 39.1** Consonants (native only)

| | Labial | Dental | Alveolar | Velar | Glottal |
|---|---|---|---|---|---|
| Voiceless stop | | t | | k | ʔ <*ch*>[a] |
| Voiced stop | b | | | | |
| Voiceless fricative | | | s | | |
| Voiced fricative | | đ <*d*> | | | |
| Nasal | m | | | ŋ <*ng*> | |
| Lateral | | | l | | |
| Tap/Trill | | | r | | |

[a] The glottal stop is written *ch* which reflects a German-based spelling convention from the early twentieth century when this phoneme reportedly was pronounced [x] (Nuger 2010: xviii).

Erik Zobel, *Palauan.* In: *The Oxford Guide to the Malayo-Polynesian Languages of Southeast Asia.* Edited by: Alexander Adelaar and Antoinette Schapper, Oxford University Press. © Erik Zobel (2024). DOI: 10.1093/oso/9780198807353.003.0039

Two obstruents are distinguished in dental position, but there is no matching dental/alveolar nasal. This lack of /n/ is a very unusual gap among MP languages. This gap is due to the sound change from PMP *n to Palauan *l* (Blust 2009b: 318). Shift of *n of /l/ is an areal feature shared with the Oceanic Trukic languages Ulithian and Woleian, which are spoken halfway between Palau and Yap.

Stress is phonemic in Palauan, as can be seen from near-minimal pairs such as *nguíl* 'his/her fire' vs. *búil* 'moon'. As a general rule, stress falls on the rightmost full vowel (i.e. all vowels except for schwa) in a word (e.g. *ngálək* 'child', *miləngá* 'eat (antipassive, past tense)', *bəsós* 'paddle', *olík* 'flying fox'). Exceptions to this are: (i) many roots with vowel sequences, in which case the first vowel of the sequence is stressed (e.g. *cháus* 'lime', *blái* 'house', *líus* 'coconut', *ráel* 'road', *róis* 'mountain'); and (ii) a handful of words with final *o* and *u* (e.g. *chádo* 'roof', *omdásu* 'think'). Thematic vowels (see §39.3.4) and suffixes with a full vowel always carry stress, even in vowel sequences (e.g. *ngu-í-l* 'his/her fire', *chədo-**él*** 'its roof').

The root structure of Palauan is characterized by the common occurrence of monosyllabic roots, and consonant clusters in initial and final position, both of which emerged with the diachronic reduction of unstressed vowels to schwa or zero (e.g. *mad* < PMP *máta 'eye', *kard* < *káRat 'bite', *btachəs* < *bitáquR 'k.o. tree (*Calophyllum inophyllum*)'). Before this reduction occurred, stress lay on the penultimate syllable of a phonological word, which could shift to the right if a suffix or bound pronoun was added.[1] The effects of this vowel reduction are still visible in synchronic vowel reductions (cf. §39.3.2 below), and the insertion of thematic vowels (cf. §39.3.4). Full vowels in unstressed position are derived from contractions of a vowel with a consonant or even a full syllable (e.g. ***o**-sébək* < ***pa**-Rəbək 'make fly'; *chad**o*** < *qát**əp** 'roof'; *k**o**rd-íi* < *k**uma**Rat-ía 'will bite it').

## 39.3 Morphology and morphophonology

Palauan has many prefixes and suffixes. Like many other MPSEA languages, Palauan also has a small number of infixes, which are frequently used.

Palauan morphophonology is characterized by root-initial mutation, vowel reduction and ablaut in unstressed syllables, and the insertion of unpredictable thematic vowels with many roots when suffixes are added.

### 39.3.1 Root-initial mutation

The antipassive prefix *məN-* contains the element *N* which symbolizes mutation of the initial consonant of the verb root (Josephs 1975: 138ff.). Mutation affects all stops, *ng*, and (partially) *s*:

| | | |
|---|---|---|
| *b* > *m* | *məN-* + √***b**oes*[2] 'shoot' | > *o**m**oes* |
| *t, d, s, ng* > *l* | *məN-* + √***t**amk* 'shave' | > *mə**l**amk* |
| | *məN-* + √***d**aləm* 'plant' | > *mə**l**aləm* |
| | *məN-* + √***s**esəb* 'burn' | > *mə**l**esəb* |
| | *məN-* + √***ng**atəch* 'clean' | > *mə**l**atəch* |
| *k, ch* > *ng* | *məN-* + √***k**a* 'eat' | > *mə**ng**a* |
| | *məN-* + √***ch**uiu* 'read' | > *mə**ng**uiu* |

The liquids *l* and *r*, and with some roots also *s*, remain unchanged:

| | | |
|---|---|---|
| *l, r, s* | *məN-* + √***l**eng* 'borrow' | > *mə**l**eng* |
| | *məN-* + √***r**asm* 'sew' | > *mə**r**asm* |
| | *məN-* + √***s**ilək* 'wash' | > *mə**s**ilək* |

Palauan root-initial mutation is related to nasal replacement commonly found in western MP languages. The occurence of *l* as mutated consonant is a result of the sound shift PMP *n > *l* (e.g. *mə**l**aləm* (*məN-* + √***d**aləm*) < PMP *ma**n**anəm (*maN- + ***t**anəm)).

The prefixes *məN-* and *mə-* undergo *M*-dissimilation when combining with a root that begins with a labial consonant (Josephs 1975: 147). The prefixes *məN-* and *mə-* then change to *oN-* and *o-* (e.g. *məN-* 'antipassive' + √*boes* 'shoot' > ***o**moes* (not: **məmoes*), *mə-* 'passive' + √*boes* 'shoot' > ***o**boes* (not: **məboes*)).

### 39.3.2 Vowel reduction

Suffixation triggers a stress shift to the right. As a result, the vowels and diphthongs which carry stress in the corresponding unsuffixed forms now become reduced (Josephs 1975: 20, 56ff.). As a general rule, simple vowels are reduced to schwa or zero, for example:

| | |
|---|---|
| *rásəch* 'blood' + *-l* '3SG.POSS' | > *rsəch-él* 'his/her blood' |
| *bad* 'stone' + *-l* '3SG.POSS' | > *bəd-ú-l* 'his/her stone' |
| √*leng* 'borrow' + *-r* '3SG.O' | > *ləngír* 'borrow it' |
| √*lúchəs* 'write' + *-ii* '3SG.O' | > *ləchəsíi* 'write it'. |

In the case of diphthongs, it is usually the stressed vowel that is deleted, while the non-syllabic component becomes syllabified, for example:

[1] Note that in pre-Palauan, penultimate stress also applied to *ə, which is reflected as *e* and *o* (e.g. *deb* < *tə́bu, *dort* < *tə́Ras) (Blust 2009b: 311).

[2] Verb roots are indicated by a root-symbol (√). For most verbs, the root is an abstraction, since they are always realized with at least one affix.

*oách* 'leg' + *-l* '3SG.POSS' > *och-i-l* 'his/her leg'

*eólt* 'wind' + *-l* '3SG.POSS' > *elt-el* 'its wind'.

### 39.3.3 Realizations of the infix <*m*>

The infix <*m*> has several allomorphs. The basic allomorph <*m*> is found in stressed syllables in combination with roots that contain no labial consonant:

<*m*> + √*leng* 'borrow' > *l***m***eng* 'borrow them'

<*m*> + √*dul* 'roast' > *d***m***ul* 'burn them'

If the root begins with *b*, <*m*> is realized as the change of *b* to *m*, which is even retained with the active past-tense infix <*il*> (Josephs 1975: 167):

<*m*> + √***b****oes* 'shoot' > ***m****oes* 'shoot them'

<*il*> + √***b****oes* 'shhot > ***m****iloes* 'shot them'

The realization of *<um> as mutation to *m- with bases beginning in *b- (with apheresis of expected regular *b<um>-) is also found in many other MP languages.

In roots that contain a labial consonant in non-initial position, the infix <*m*> is replaced by <*u*> (Josephs 1975: 157):

<*m*> + √*daləm* 'plant' > *d***u***aləm* 'plant them'

<*m*> + √*kimd* 'cut (hair)' > *k***u***imd* 'cut them'

In unstressed syllables, the infix <*m*> is realized as ablaut (Josephs 1975: 157ff.). Originally unstressed schwa changes to *o* (rarely also to *u*):

<*m*> + √*səngóes* 'cook' > *s***o***ngóes* 'cook them'

<*m*> + √*kətmókl* 'clean' > *k***u***tmókl* 'clean them'.

With full vowels that become unstressed due to addition of a suffix, <*m*> is realized as blocking of vowel reduction. The vowels *i*, *o*, and *u* remain unchanged:

<*m*> + √*kimd* 'cut (hair)' + *-ii* '3SG.OBJ' > *k***i***mdíi* 'cut it'

<*m*> + √*dóbəch* 'chop' + *-ii* '3SG.OBJ' > *d***o***bəchíi* 'chop it'

<*m*> + √*lúchəs* 'write' + *-ii* '3SG.OBJ' > *l***u***chəsíi* 'write it'

The vowels *a* and *e* are changed to *o*, for example:

<*m*> + √*leng* 'borrow' + *-r* '3SG.OBJ' > *l***o***ngír* 'borrow it'

<*m*> + √*tamk* 'shave' + *-ii* '3SG.OBJ' > *t***o***mkíi* 'shave it'.

The corresponding forms without <*m*> are *kəmdíi*, *dəbəchíi*, *ləchəsíi*, *ləngír*, *təmkíi*.

The realization of PMP *<um> (which became Palauan <*m*>) as ablaut is also found in a number of languages in northern Borneo, and in the Philippine language Kapampangan.

### 39.3.4 Thematic vowels

Many roots add a stressed vowel of unpredictable quality when an unstressed suffix is added. This *thematic* vowel can either follow the final consonant, or is inserted preceding the final consonant, depending on the root structure.

The thematic vowel is added *after* the final consonant if the root ends in a stressed vowel followed by a consonant. This happens with nouns that take the non-syllabic possessive suffixes *-k*/*-m*/*-l*/*-d* (e.g. *mad* 'eye' + *-k* '1SG.POSS' > *məd-***a***-k* 'my eye', requiring the addition of the thematic vowel *a*. Diachronically, the quality of this thematic vowel is a continuation of original final vowels which were dropped in the phonological history from PMP to present-day Palauan: *mad* < *mata, *məd-***a***-k* < *mata-ku.

With verbs, we find final thematic vowels in conjunction with the suffixes *-əl* and *-r*,[3] for example:

<*m*> + √*chat* 'smoke (fish)' + *-r* '3SG.OBJ' > *chot-***u***-r* 'smoke it'

√*chat* 'smoke (fish)'+ *-əl* 'PASS' > *chət-***u***-ul* 'to be smoked'

Note that with such roots, the vowel of the suffix *-əl* undergoes complete assimilation to the inserted thematic vowel (e.g. *-ul* in *chət-***u***-ul*). Both forms are inherited from PMP: *chət-u-r* < *q<um>asu ya (< PMP *ia '3SG'), *chət-u-ul* < *qasu-ən), derived from *chat* < *qasu 'smoke'.

Thematic vowels are inserted *before* the final consonant if the root ends in a consonant cluster, or if the vowel in the final syllable is unstressed. This only occurs in conjunction with the suffix *-əl* (Josephs 1975: 183). The thematic vowel is either inserted before the final consonant of the root (√*kimd* 'cut' > *km***u***d-əl* 'to be cut', √*báil* 'wrap' > *bi***u***l-l* 'to be wrapped'), or replaces schwa in that position (√*silək* 'wash' > *səl***o***k-əl* 'to be washed'). While thematic vowels are synchronically unpredictable, historically, they represent inherited PMP vowels which were reduced to schwa or zero in ultimate position, but were not subject to reduction in the suffixed form due to stress-shift to the right: *ng<m>atəch* 'clean' < *h<um>ásaq, but: *ngət***a***ch-əl* 'to be cleaned' < *haság-ən; *d<u>aləm* 'plant' < *t<um>ánəm, but: *dəl***o***m-əl* 'to be planted' < *tanə́m-ən.

Loss of final vowels and the retention of these as thematic vowels is virtually absent from MPSEA languages, but it represents an areal feature shared with other languages of Micronesia (e.g. Yapese, Ulithian). These thematic vowels have been described in a generative model as underlying root vowels which are reduced to schwa or zero in unstressed position (Wilson 1972; Josephs 1975).

[3] The suffix *-r* is an allomorph of the 3SG.OBJ-suffix *-ii*: *-r* only is employed with verb roots that take a final thematic vowel.

## 39.4 Personal pronouns and person markers

Palauan has one set of free pronouns, and four sets of bound pronouns.

**Table 39.2** Palauan pronoun sets

| | Free | Possessive | Subject | | Object |
|---|---|---|---|---|---|
| | | | I | II | |
| 1SG | *ngak* | *-ek/-k* | *ak-* | *k(ə)-* | *-ak* |
| 2SG | *kau* | *-em/-m* | *kə-* | *(cho)m(ə)-* | *-au* |
| 3SG/ 3PL.NHUM | *ngii* | *-el/-l* | *ng-* | *l(ə)-* | *-ii/-r ø* |
| 1PL.INCL | *kid* | *-ed/-d* | *kədə-* | *d(ə)-* | *-id* |
| 1PL.EXCL | *kəmam* | *-am/-mam* | *aki-* | *kim-* | *-əmam* |
| 2PL | *kəmiu* | *-iu/-miu* | *kom-* | *(cho)m(ə)-* | *-əmiu* |
| 3PL.HUM | *tir* | *-ir/-rir* | *tə-* | *l(ə)-* | *-tərir* |

Free pronouns are used in topicalized position (§39.7.5), as predicates in basic clauses (§39.7.3), and in oblique phrases with the case marker *ər* (§39.7.2). Subject prefixes and object suffixes are obligatory person markers in basic clauses; the choice between the two subject sets, which are respectively called "non-emphatic" and "hypothetical" pronouns in Josephs (1975: 79, 103), is discussed in §39.7.

(1) ***Ng***$_{S}$*-məkələkolt* [***a ralm***]$_{S}$
3SG.SBJ$_{1}$-cold DET water
'The water is cold.' (Josephs 1994: 88)

Third person prefixes and suffixes are cross-referencing agreement markers, that is, they are also employed when the corresponding argument is expressed by an overt noun phrase, as in example (1), where the person prefix *ng-* cross-references the subject argument *a ralm* '[the] water' (cf. also §39.5).
Person-marking affixes cannot co-occur with a corresponding free pronoun, unlike in many other Malayo-Polynesian languages with obligatory person marking.

## 39.5 Possession

With native Palauan vocabulary, possession is indicated by means of possessive suffixes (e.g. *ngkl-ek* (name-1SG.POSS) 'my name'). If the possessor is expressed by a full noun phrase, it immediately follows the possessed noun with a cross-referencing possessive suffix (e.g. *chim-a-**l*** [*a Toki*] (hand-TH-3SG.POSS *a* Toki) 'Toki's hand') (Josephs 1975: 66).

Many nouns take an unpredictable nasal element *-ng-*, or a thematic vowel *-a-*, *-i-*, or *-u-*, when a possessive suffix is added (Josephs 1975: 53ff.). With nouns that take *ng*, the possessive suffixes have the same shape as with nouns that do not add a thematic vowel. The thematic vowels *a*, *i*, and *u* appear as full vowels with the non-syllabic suffixes *-k/-m/-l/-d*, but are reduced to schwa preceding the stressed suffixes *-mam/-miu/-rir* (Table 39.3).

Some nouns obligatorily appear in the possessed form (Josephs 1975: 63). These nouns include certain body parts (*bud-* 'skin'), kinship terms (*dəm-a-* 'father'), and part–whole relations (*bk-u-* 'corner; joint').

On the other hand, the great majority of loanwords cannot take possessive suffixes at all. With these nouns, the possessor is expressed by an oblique phrase (e.g. *sensei ər ngak* (teacher OBL 1SG) 'my teacher') (Josephs 1975: 69), with *sensei* being a loanword from Japanese.

Palauan makes use of a construction with possessive classifiers in certain contexts, primarily with nouns for animals, food and drinks (Josephs 1975: 74) (e.g. *chərm-ek əl babii* 'my pig' (CLF *charm* 'animal'), *odim-ek əl babii* 'my pork' (CLF *odoim* 'side-dish'), *iləm-el a Droteo əl biang* 'Droteo's beer' (CLF *iluməl* 'drink')). Possessive classifiers are an areal feature shared with other languages of Micronesia, both Chamorro and the Oceanic languages.

## 39.6 Verb morphology

### 39.6.1 Basic verb alternations

Many Palauan verbs appear in two different forms, viz. the independent form and the bound form. The bound form always takes a subject pronoun of the second set (Table 39.2), while the independent form in most contexts appears with a subject pronoun of the first set, but also occurs without subject-marking in certain constructions. The choice between these two forms is governed by the syntactic context and will be described in detail in §39.7.

Palauan verbs can be further divided into **action** and **state** verbs. Action verbs are morphologically marked for tense, distinguishing between **non-past** and **past** tense. This results in maximally four distinct forms of the verbs (not counting valency-reducing and causative derivations).

Stative intransitive verbs cannot be morphologically marked for past tense, but appear in a periphrastic serial construction (cf. §39.7.5.1 below) with *mle* (past tense of the directional verb *me* 'come') to express past tense (e.g. *ak mle smechər* 'I was sick').

The morphologically marked distinction between past and non-past tense, and the alternation between prefixes with and without the formative element *M* are typical

**Table 39.3** Posessive paradigms

| | *ngakl* 'name' | *iis* 'nose' | *mad* 'eye' | *bad* stone' | *buch* 'spouse' |
|---|---|---|---|---|---|
| 1SG | *ngkl-ek* | *is-**ng**-ek* | *məd-**a**-k* | *bəd-**u**-k* | *bəch-**i**-k* |
| 2SG | *ngkl-em* | *is-**ng**-em* | *məd-**a**-m* | *bəd-**u**-m* | *bəch-**i**-m* |
| 3SG 3PL.NHUM | *ngkl-el* | *is-**ng**-el* | *məd-**a**-l* | *bəd-**u**-l* | *bəch-**i**-l* |
| 1PL.INCL | *ngkl-ed* | *is-**ng**-ed* | *məd-**a**-d* | *bəd-**u**-d* | *bəch-**i**-d* |
| 1PL.EXCL | *ngkl-am* | *is-**ng**-am* | *məd-ə-mam* | *bəd-ə-mam* | *bəch-ə-mam* |
| 2PL | *ngkl-iu* | *is-**ng**-iu* | *məd-ə-miu* | *bəd-ə-miu* | *bəch-ə-miu* |
| 3PL.HUM | *ngkl-ir* | *is-**ng**-ir* | *məd-ə-rir* | *bəd-ə-rir* | *bəch-ə-rir* |

**Table 39.4** Basic verb alternations – intransitive verbs

| | Non-past | | Past | |
|---|---|---|---|---|
| | independent | bound | independent | bound |
| Action | <m> | ø | <il> | <il> |
| | *mə-* | *o-*† | *mil(ə)-* | *ul(ə)-* |
| State | <m> | ø | — | — |
| | *mə-* | *mə-* | — | — |

† Appearing as *u-* with the 1SG subject marker *k-*.

**Table 39.5** Basic verb alternations – transitive verbs

| | Non-past | | Past | |
|---|---|---|---|---|
| | independent | bound | independent | bound |
| Active | <m> | ø | <il> | <il> |
| Antipassive | *məN-* | *oN-*† | *mil(ə)N-* | *ul(ə)N-* |
| Passive | *mə-* | *mə-* | *mil(ə)-* | *mil(ə)-* |

† Appearing as *uN-* with the 1SG subject marker *k-*.

features of conservative MPSEA languages and can also be reconstructed for PMP (Zobel 2002: 419). The *mə(N)-/o(N)* alternation corresponds to the *ma(N)-/pa(N) alternation found in many of the latter.[4] The past tense infix *<il>* is related to the past tense infix *<in> found in the languages of the Philippines, northeastern Borneo and northern Sulawesi.

[4] *Palauan initial *o-* and *ulə-* are regular reflexes of PMP *pa- and *pina-.

## 39.7 Syntax

### 39.7.1 Word order

The word order in basic clauses is **VOS** (see also §39.7.3 below).

(2) *Ng-silsəb-ii* [*a blai*]$_{\text{O}}$ [*a rədil*]$_{\text{S}}$
3SG.SBJ$_1$-PAST:burn-3SG.OBJ DET house DET woman
'The woman burned down the house.'
(Josephs 1994: 253)

Fronting of one selected noun phrase before the predicate is very common in topicalized clauses (cf. §39.7.5), yielding SVO and OVS as marked alternative word order.

The basic constituent order in noun phrases is *modifier + head*, connected with the linker *əl*. This is obligatory for numerals and demonstratives as modifiers (e.g. *teru əl chad* (two LNK person) 'two people', *tia əl hong* (DEM LNK book) 'this book'). Intransitive verbs can also be used as modifiers (e.g. *bəches əl blai* (new LNK house) 'a new house' (Josephs 1975: 462), *məngitakl əl chad* (sing LNK person) 'a man who is singing' (Josephs 1975: 464)), although they can also follow the noun (*blai əl bəches, chad əl məngitakl*), which is the general position for relative clauses (cf. §39.7.5.1).

As already mentioned in §39.5, the order of full NPs in basic possessive constructions is *possessed + possessor* (*chimal a Toki* 'Toki's hand'), whereas the order in possessive constructions with a classifier is *classifier + possessor + possessed* (*iləm-el a Droteo əl biang* 'Droteo's beer'). In the latter construction, the classifier followed by the possessor behaves like a modifier to the possessed object.

### 39.7.2 Case marking

All noun phrases in Palauan except for pronouns and demonstratives are headed by the NP marker *a* (Josephs

1975: 44ff.). Unlike in conservative MPSEA languages, common nouns and proper nouns are not distinguished: *a blai* '(the) house', *a Belau* 'Palau', *a Droteo* 'Droteo (personal name)'. The NP marker *a* also heads the predicate in topicalized clauses, see §39.7.5 below.

Palauan only distinguishes two overt cases, viz. unmarked case and oblique case. Nouns in unmarked case only take the NP marker *a*, while pronouns and demonstratives are completely unmarked. Core noun phrases (i.e. the subject and the object of transitive verbs) are in unmarked case (see §39.7.3), and so are indefinite undergoers in connection with antipassive verbs, and possessors in head marking possessive constructions such as *bəch-i-l* [*a Droteo*] (wife-TH-3SG.POSS DET Droteo) 'Droteo's wife'.

In all other functions, noun phrases are headed by the oblique case marker *ər*, which expresses various grammatical relations such as location, source, instrument, possessor (mainly with loanwords), and definite undergoers of antipassive verbs (Josephs 1975: 70, 278ff.). Common nouns and personal names take the NP marker *a* (e.g. *ər a skuul* 'to school', *ər a Toki* 'to/from/with (etc.) Toki'), while pronouns and demonstratives are directly preceded by *ər* (e.g. *ər ngak* 'to/from/with (etc.) me') (Josephs 1975: 84).

The zero case-marking of core NPs and possessors is clearly innovative, since PMP and modern Philippine-type languages distinguish two or three case forms here, which are explicitly expressed by case markers preceding the NP. This loss of overt noun case-marking is shared with many Malayo-Polynesian languages outside of the Philippine-type area.

### 39.7.3 The basic clause

A basic clause in Palauan minimally consists of a predicate with a subject person marker of the first set.

(3) *Ng$_S$-smechər*
3SG.SBJ$_1$-sick
'She is sick.' (Josephs 1975: 83)

The predicate can be a verb, noun (*ak-sensei* 1SG.SBJ-teacher 'I am a teacher'), or even a pronoun (*ng-ngak* 3SG.SBJ-1SG 'it's me'). Furthermore, transitive predicates obligatorily take an object-marking suffix.

(4) *Tə$_S$-chilləbəd-ii*
3PL.SBJ$_1$-PST:hit-3SG.OBJ
'They hit him/her/it.' (Georgopoulos 1991: 43)

Verbs which alternate between bound and independent forms take the **independent** form in the basic clause type (e.g. *s<m>echər* in example (3)).

Person marking is strictly **nominative–accusative**, not distinguishing subjects of intransitive and transitive predicates in any context. Subject person-marking of predicates is obligatory except in certain clauses with subject pivot, which include clauses with subject topicalization and non-finite dependent clauses (§39.7.5.1).

When the basic clause includes overt NPs, these always **follow** the predicate. Undergoers and appositional phrases appear between the predicate and the subject (i.e. basic word order is **VOS**).

(5) *Ng$_S$-silsəb-ii$_O$* [*a blai*]$_O$ [*a rədil*]$_S$
3SG.SBJ$_1$-PAST:burn-3SG.OBJ DET house DET woman
'The woman burned down the house.'
(Josephs 1994: 253)

(6) *Ng$_S$-silebək ər a kərrəkar a bəlochəl*
3SG.SBJ$_1$-PAST:fly OBL DET tree DET pigeon
'The pigeon flew out of the tree.' (Josephs 1994: 254)

Full person marking is obligatory, as can be seen in examples (5) and (6), where the subject prefix *ng-* is co-referential to the bracketed subject NPs *a rədil* and *a bəlochəl*; in example (5), the object suffix *-ii* is co-referential to the undergoer NP *a blai*.

The basic verb-initial word order is superficially similar to the basic word order in many Philippine-type languages. The major innovative feature is person agreement of the type **s-V-o**, with person-markers obligatorily framing the verb. This is an areal feature which Palauan shares with the Oceanic languages of Micronesia (e.g. Yapese and the Trukic languages). It is very uncommon in western Indonesia (one example with ergative–absolutive alignment is Simeulue (formerly Simalur) in the Barrier Islands), but is predominantly found in MP languages of the eastern part of the Indonesian archipelago. Examples of languages with full nominative–accusative person agreement include Wolio and Muna on Sulawesi, and Kambera in the Lesser Sunda Islands.

### 39.7.4 Valency-reducing operations

#### 39.7.4.1 *Antipassive*

The antipassive is formed by adding the prefix *məN-/oN-* to transitive verb bases (Zobel 2002: 416). Antipassive verbs cannot take object suffixes and are thus formally intransitive. Nevertheless, the undergoer can still be overtly expressed by a noun phrase. An unmarked noun will always have a non-specific reading, such as *a ngikəl* in example (7).

(7) *Ng-mənga a ngikəl*
3SG.SBJ$_1$-ANTIP:eat DET fish
'(S)he is eating fish.' (Josephs 1975: 40)

Specific undergoers must be expressed by an oblique phrase (cf. §39.7.2). In example (8), *ər a hong* is definite.

(8) *Ng-mənguiu ər a hong a Droteo*
3SG.SBJ$_1$-ANTIP:read OBL DET book DET Droteo
'Droteo is reading the book.' (Josephs 1994: 252)

Without the oblique case marker *ər*, the clause would translate as 'Droteo is reading a book/(some) books.'

The antipassive has been described as an imperfect aspect form of the transitive verb (Josephs 1975, 1997; Georgopoulos 1991; Nuger 2010). The label 'imperfect' describes one major aspect of the function of the antipassive. Based on case marking and agreement patterns, however, the antipassive is clearly intransitive (Lemaréchal 1991; Josephs 1994).

Pragmatically, the Palauan antipassive corresponds to actor voice in Philippine-type languages, and occurs, for example, with generic, indefinite, or partially affected undergoers as in example (7), or when emphasizing the action rather than the result (cf. the imperfective meaning in example (8)). However, syntactic triggers such as NP fronting or *wh*-questions, which are crucial for voice selection in Philippine-type languages, do not play any role in the selection of the antipassive in Palauan (see §39.7.5).

### 39.7.4.2 *Passive*

Palauan distinguishes three types of passive formations[5]:

| | | |
|---|---|---|
| general: | *mə-chat* | 'is smoked' |
| resultative: | *ch<əl>at (ch<əl>t-uul)* | 'smoked' |
| future: | *chət-uul* | 'will be smoked' |

The general passive is a regular verb that can be marked for tense (non-past: *mə-*; past: *mil(ə)-*). Emphasis is on the event that the subject undergoes.

(9) *A blai a milsesəb*
DET house TOP PASS:burn
'The house was burned down.' (Josephs 1975: 65)

The agent is usually not expressed. When it exceptionally occurs, it is marked by oblique case.

The general passive prefix *mə-* is a straightforward reflex of the PMP stative prefix *ma-. Many Philippine-type languages have expanded the use of this prefix to include marking of undergoer voice in an alternative 'potentive' paradigm (see Kaufman, this volume, §25.3.5.1), which freely allows the inclusion of the agent as a core argument. Such a paradigm is completely lacking in Palauan. The restricted use of the general passive with *mə-* in Palauan is thus a conservative feature directly inherited from PMP.

The resultative passive is expressed by the infix *<(ə)l>* or by the affix combination *<(ə)l> -əl*. The future passive is formed by the suffix *-əl* (and assimilated allomorphs, see §39.3.4), or its variant *-all*. The resultative passive focuses on the result of the action, while the future passive indicates that the action still has to be performed on the subject. Both resultative and future passive are often used as nouns (e.g. *səlok-əl* '1. to be laundered; 2. laundry', *ch<əl>at* '1. smoked; 2. smoked fish').

The resultative and future passives are derived from PMP undergoer voice affixes:

| | |
|---|---|
| *<(ə)l>* | < *<in> |
| *<(ə)l> -əl* | < *<in> -an |
| *-əl* | < *-ən, *-an |

These have acquired a much more restricted function when compared to their original functional range in PMP, which is still reflected in Philippine-type languages. Major functions of undergoer voice in Philippine-type languages are served by other constructions in Palauan:

- Where Philippine-type languages has undergoer voice clauses in unmarked clause constructions, Palauan uses active transitive clauses (cf. example (5)).
- Whereas Philippine-type languages obligatorily use undergoer voice clauses to front the undergoer in topicalized, relative and *wh*-clauses, Palauan achieves this by a change in the person marking pattern that is not related to voice marking (see §39.7.5.2 below).

Note also that unlike with undergoer voice in Philippine-type languages, the agent cannot be expressed with the resultative and future passives.

## 39.7.5 Subject and non-subject raising in focus and embedded clauses

One of the best-studied aspects of Palauan syntax is the 'raising' of arguments out of the basic clause in constructions like topicalization, *wh*-questions, relativization, cleft, and pseudo-cleft sentences (Georgopoulos 1991). Such constructions can be summarized under the header 'focus clauses'. Unlike Philippine-type languages and also many other MPSEA languages, Palauan does not employ voice alternations in the formation of focus clauses, but rather employs two distinct strategies for subject and non-subject raising.

Subject raising constructions are not restricted to focus clauses, but also appear in embedded clauses in which

[5] In Josephs (1975), the following terms are employed: "ergative" (= general passive), "resulting state verbs" (=resultative passive), "anticipating state verbs" (= future passive).

the subject of the embedded clause is co-referential to an argument in the matrix clause.

#### 39.7.5.1 *Subject raising*

In constructions with subject raising, the subject agreement pronoun is simply dropped. If the predicate is a verb which has distinct bound and independent forms, the independent form is employed, as in the basic clause type.

In topicalized clauses, the subject or the possessor of the subject is fronted and the predicate is headed by *a* (which here serves as a topicalizer), for example, in (10) and (11) with topicalization of the subject NPs *a bəchik* 'my wife' and *a malk* 'the chicken'.

**Basic**
(10) *ng-smechər a bəchik* →
3SG.SBJ$_1$-sick DET wife:1SG.POSS

**Topicalized**
*a bəchik a smechər*
DET wife:1SG.POSS TOP sick
'My wife is sick.' (Josephs 1975: 38)

(11) *ng-kol-ii a bəras a malk*
3SG.SBJ$_1$-eat-3SG.OBJ DET rice DET chicken
*a malk a kol-ii a bəras*
DET chicken TOP eat-3SG.OBJ DET rice
'The chicken is about to eat the rice.'
(Josephs 1975: 258)

In example (12), it is the possessor in the possessive phrase *chim-a-l a Droteo* 'Droteo's hand' which is topicalized.

(12) *A Droteo a məringəl a*
DET Droteo TOP hurt DET
*chim-a-l*
hand-TH-3SG.POSS
'Droteo's hand hurts.' (Josephs 1975: 339)

Predicates headed by *a* in topicalized clauses can also appear as arguments, equivalent to headless relative clauses. In example (13), the headless relative expression *a mlo ər a stoang* 'the one who went to the store' is the undergoer NP of the verb *kə-mədəngəl-ii*.

(13) *Kə-mədəngəl-ii [a mlo ər a*
2SG.SBJ$_1$-know-3SG.OBJ DET PST:go ər DET
*stoang]*
store
'Do you know [the one] who went to the store?'
(Georgopoulos 1991: 65)

Cleft sentences are a special case where the headless relative clause appears as subject of a nominal predicate.

(14) *Ng-chobəkuk [a mla mərng-ii*
3SG.SBJ$_1$-brother:1SG.POSS DET PST hit-3SG.OBL
*a səchəlik]*
DET friend:1SG.POSS
'It is my brother who has hit my friend.'
(Georgopoulos 1991: 66)

Relative clauses employ the same construction which is found in topicalization. The verb is linked to the head noun phrase with the linker *əl*.

(15) *a rədil əl silsəb-ii$_0$ a blai*
DET woman LNK PST:burn-3SG.OBL DET house
'the woman who burned down the house'
(Josephs 1975: 453)

Another type of subject raising is found with non-finite complement clauses in which the subject is co-referential to a controlling argument in the matrix clause. As in focus clauses, there is no subject agreement, and the verb retains the independent form. The non-finite complement clause is linked to the matrix clause with the linker *əl*. In example (16), the raised subject is co-referential to the subject of the matrix clause.

(16) ***Ak**-uləba a sebəl əl*
1SG.SBJ$_1$- ANTIP:PST:use DET shovel LNK
***məngiis** ər a kliokl*
ANTIP:dig OBL DET hole
'I was using a shovel to dig the hole.'
(Josephs 1975: 306)

A special case of non-finite complement clauses is serialized constructions with the motion verbs *mo* 'go' (example (17) with the past tense form *mlo*), *eko* 'go', *me* 'come', and the auxiliary *mla* 'was/were'. These do not employ the linker *əl*.

(17) ***Ak**-mlo məchiuaiu*
1SG.SBJ$_1$-PST:go sleep
'I went to sleep.' (Josephs 1975: 448)

#### 39.7.5.2 *Non-subject raising*

Non-subject raising can apply to undergoers and appositional phrases. Subject agreement is then expressed by the **second set** of subject markers, and the verb appears in the **bound** form (e.g. *kəl-ii, onguiu, ongaus*[6] in examples (18), (19), and (20)).

[6] The corresponding independent forms are *kol-ii, mənguiu, məngaus*.

(18) *A bəras a* ***lə-kəl-ii*** *a malk*
DET rice TOP 3.SBJ$_2$-eat-3SG.OBJ DET chicken
'The chicken is about to eat the rice.'
(Josephs 1975: 405), cf. example (11).

Any noun phrase marked for oblique case will leave a pronominal trace in post-verbal position. Based on the basic antipassive clause in example (8'), the oblique undergoer *a hong* can be fronted to topicalized position, but leaves a trace *ər ngii* following the predicate in example (19).

(8') *Ng-mənguiu ər a hong a Droteo*
3SG.SBJ$_1$-ANTIP:read OBL DET book DET Droteo
'Droteo is reading the book.' (Josephs 1994: 252)

(19) *A hong a* ***l-onguiu*** *ər ngii*
DET book TOP 3.SBJ$_2$-ANTIP:read OBL 3SG
*a Droteo*
DET Droteo
'Droteo is reading the book.' (Josephs 1994: 252)

Note that the verb is still marked for antipassive voice, which clearly shows that voice selection is independent from syntactic operations such as topicalizaion.

Analogous to the case of subject raising, non-subject raising also appears in headless relative clauses and cleft sentences (20), and relative clauses linked with *əl* (21).

(20) *Ng-sualo [a* ***l-ongaus*** *ər ngii*
3SG.SBJ$_1$-basket DET 3.SBJ$_2$-ANTIP:weave ər 3SG
*a rəchəmas]*
DET women
'It is the basket that the women are weaving'
(Georgopoulos 1991: 66)

(21) *a delmərab əl* ***l-osuub*** *ər ngii*
DET room LNK 3.SBJ$_2$-study ər 3SG
*a Droteo*
DET Droteo
'the room that Droteo is studying in'
(Josephs 1975: 455)

## 39.7.6 Irrealis clauses

In §39.7.5.2, we have seen that the second set of subject markers (in combination with predicates that appear in the bound form) is employed in non-subject focus clauses. This construction is however not restricted to the latter, but also occurs in non-focus contexts, viz. irrealis clauses. These comprise finite dependent clauses, negative clauses, and optative clauses.

### 39.7.6.1 *Finite dependent clauses*

Finite dependent clauses are headed by *a* and are primarily used in conditional clauses.

(22) *A k-isa a John ər a*
CONJ 1SG.SBJ$_2$-see:3SG.OBJ DET John OBL DET
*klukuk...*
tomorrow
'if I see John tomorrow...' (Josephs 1975: 384)

(23) *A k-udənge a təkoi ər a*
CONJ 1SG.SBJ$_2$-PST:know DET word OBL DET
*Siabal...*
Japan
'if I knew Japanese...' (Josephs 1975: 384)

In serialized constructions, each component takes a subject person marker.

(24) *A* ***k****-ble* ***k****-udənge a*
CONJ 1SG.SBJ$_2$-come 1SG.SBJ$_2$-PST:know DET
*təkoi ər a Siabal...*
word OBL DET Japan
'if I had known Japanese...' (Josephs 1975: 385)

Other contexts in which finite dependent clauses are used include non-same-subject complement clauses.

(25) *Ng-soam a k-ungəsbrebər*
3SG.SBJ$_1$-wish:2SG.POSS CONJ 1SG.SBJ$_2$-PST:ANTIP:paint
*ər a kbokb*
OBL DET wall
'Do you want me to paint the wall?' (Josephs 1975: 392)

### 39.7.6.2 *Negative clauses*

Negative clauses are formed with the negative verb *diak* followed by the predicate with a second set-subject marker.

(26) *Ng-diak l-sensei a*
3SG.SBJ$_1$-NEG 3SG.SBJ$_2$-teacher DET
*dəmak*
father:1SG.POSS
'My father is not a teacher.' (Josephs 1975: 378)

The independent past tense form is *dimlak*:

(27) *Ng-dimlak k-bos-ii a babii*
3SG.SBJ$_1$-PST:NEG 1SG.SBJ$_2$-shoot-3SG.OBJ DET pig
'I did not shoot the pig.' (Josephs 1975: 376)

In finite dependent clauses, the negative verb takes the bound form *-ak* (past tense *-mlak*):

(28) *A l-ak l-osuub a Toki...*
CONJ 3.SBJ$_2$-NEG 3.SBJ$_2$-study DET Toki
'If Toki does not study...' (Josephs 1975: 386)

**Table 39.6** Philippine-type and Palauan clause types

| Clause type | Transitivity | Philippine-type | Palauan |
|---|---|---|---|
| Basic clause | low | actor voice | Antipassive |
| | high | undergoer voice | active |
| Focused actor | low | actor voice | non-finite antipassive |
| | high | | non-finite active |
| Focused undergoer | low | undergoer voice | bound finite antipassive |
| | high | | bound finite active |

#### 39.7.6.3 *Hortative clauses*

Hortative clauses minimally consist of a predicate with subject person-marker of the second set. With first and third person subjects, hortative clauses express obligation.

(29) *K-urael* *əl* *mo* *ər* *a* *blik*
1SG.SBJ$_2$-go LNK go OBL DET house:1SG.POSS
'I'd better go home.' (Josephs 1975: 397)

With inclusive and second person objects, hortative clauses have an imperative meaning.

(30) *D-orael*
1PL.INCL.SBJ$_2$-go
'Let's go!' (Josephs 1975: 399)

(31) *M-osilək* *ər* *a* *bilem*
2.SBJ$_2$-ANTIP:wash OBL DET clothes:2SG.POSS
'Wash your clothes!' (Josephs 1975: 394)

(32) *M-kəl-ii* *a* *ngikəl*
2.SBJ$_2$-eat-3SG.OBJ DET fish
'Eat up the fish!' (Josephs 1975: 395)

## 39.8 Conclusion

Palauan is only superficially aberrant (from conservative MPSEA languages), largely as a result of drastic phonological reductions. Otherwise, the language reflects many conservative MP features. Morphologically, it still has retained a large number of prefixes from PMP, next to a small number of infixes and suffixes. It also shares some typical features of Philippine-type languages, especially the weak distinction between nouns and verbs at the clause level: nouns can appear as predicates in the same position as verbs, while verbs can appear as arguments without explicit relative head.

On the other hand, as described in §39.7.3 to §39.7.5, Palauan shows major syntactic differences when compared with Philippine-type languages. The latter have a system where discourse prominence and syntactic prominence are coded by a single parameter (voice), with syntactic triggers outranking discourse triggers. In Palauan, these two are strictly kept apart. Table 39.6 lists the major differences for transitive verbs. Discourse prominence is tabulated as 'transitivity', with 'low' transitivity referring to clauses with suppressed, indefinite, or partially affected undergoer, and 'high' transitivity referring to clauses with definite and fully affected undergoer.

The radical restructuring of the voice system is reflected in the historical origin of Palauan clause types. The independent form of the verb which is employed in basic clauses is marked by affixes that are related to the same affixes that express actor voice in Philippine-type languages (cf. *<m>* < *<um>, *məN-* < *maN-, *mə-* < *ma(R)- in Table 39.4 and Table 39.5 above). This means that **all** basic clauses in Palauan are derived from what were actor voice clauses at an earlier stage. This includes active transitive clauses with a definite and completely affected undergoer as in example (5). Pragmatically, such clauses correspond to undergoer voice clauses in Philippine-type languages. This universal use of actor voice-derived verb forms in all basic clauses is a unique feature of Palauan.[7]

The origin of irrealis and non-subject focus clauses is less well understood, but most constructions can also be derived from special PMP actor voice forms (Zobel 2002: 430). With the extension of the function of PMP actor voice, PMP undergoer voice verb forms in turn have acquired a very restricted function in Palauan. While some parallels are found in other Malayo-Polynesian languages which have also voice and focus as distinct constructions (e.g. Chamorro, Southeast Celebic languages), the restructuring of the voice/focus system as summarized in Table 39.6 renders Palauan quite *sui generis* among Malayo-Polynesian languages.

[7] It is however partially matched by Nias and several Southeast Celebic languages, where the generalized use of actor voice-derived verb forms is restricted to irrealis clauses.

CHAPTER 40

# Malagasy

Penelope Howe

## 40.1 Introduction

Malagasy is spoken by more than 26 million people (INSTAT 2020) in Madagascar, an island country off the east African coast, as well as on the Comorian island Mayotte. It belongs to the Southeast Barito subgroup based in Kalimantan (South Borneo), within which it is most closely related to the southernmost languages (Maˈanyan, Samihim, Dusun Witu) (Adelaar, this volume, §21.2). Malagasy also shows much linguistic influence of Bantu.

Malagasy has a variety of regional dialects. Although their number is commonly cited as eighteen, this count is based on ethnopolitical divisions rather than on linguistic reality (Raharinjanahary 2004; Adelaar 2013). The modern Roman orthography was developed in 1823 to transcribe the dialect of the Merina ethnic group. Following independence of Madagascar from French colonization, a standard based largely on this dialect was designated in 1973 as Official Malagasy (henceforth OM).

The genetic relationships among Malagasy dialects are not well established, but Adelaar (2013) argues for a high-level division between groupings of the Southwestern and Western dialects and of the Central, Northern, and Eastern dialects (Map 40.1).

Descriptions of Malagasy structure are numerous (e.g. Cousins 1897; Rajaona 1972; Keenan and Polinsky 1998; Fugier 1999), so this information is not repeated in depth here. This discussion focuses instead on typologically interesting features investigated in recent work.

Among Austronesian languages, Malagasy is often noted for its apparent morphosyntactic conservatism (Dahl 1986, 1996; Adelaar 1995a; Blust 2013a). Despite the physical distance between Malagasy and the rest of the Austronesian world, much of its morphosyntax can be clearly traced to Austronesian roots. Most notably, the four distinct voice forms of a classic Philippine-type system can still be identified. A focus in the literature on this formal conservatism, however, as well as a tendency to consider data only from OM, belies significant functional evolution and other innovations among the Malagasy dialects. The current discussion employs dialectal data to highlight these ongoing changes. Dialect names other than OM/Merina are given in examples, which appear in the standard orthography and/or IPA where necessary. Where no source is cited, examples are from the author's fieldwork.

## 40.2 Phonology

The phonology of Malagasy has diverged from that of the Barito languages and has been described extensively in the literature. This section summarizes these innovations as well as recent research findings, including the development of contrastive tone in Central Malagasy.

### 40.2.1 Phoneme inventories

The Malagasy consonant inventory differs from a typical Austronesian inventory in having many fricatives and affricates (Blust 2013a: 186). The inventory for OM/Merina appears in Table 40.1; some dialectal variants in parentheses are discussed in the following text.

OM/Merina has merged /ŋ/ and /n/ to /n/, but most dialects maintain /ŋ/ (orthographic *gn*) (Dez 1963). The palatal nasal /ɲ/ has phonemic status only in the Kibushi dialect of Mayotte (Gueunier 2004). A glottal stop occurs in limited contexts in the Vezo and Tandroy dialects, though its phonemic status is unclear (Rajaonarimanana and Fee 1996), while North Betsimisaraka has bilabial fricatives /ɸ/ and /β/ rather than labio-dental ones (Kikusawa 2006). The historical changes *j > /z/ and *w > /v/ have both gone to completion in Merina/OM, but /j/ is maintained in individual lexical items in some dialects. The retroflex affricates are represented orthographically as *tr* and *dr* and the dental affricates as *ts* and *j*.

Dialects such as Eastern Bara and Betsileo merge the prenasalized voiceless segments to their oral counterparts, as in /aˈ$^{n}$t͡sasani/ [aˈt͡sasanɪ] 'half of it', while in Betsileo, Tanala, Tanosy, and others, the alveolar affricates /t͡s, d͡z/ are produced as simple fricatives [s, z], as in /ˌhat͡saˈraina/

Penelope Howe, *Malagasy*. In: *The Oxford Guide to the Malayo-Polynesian Languages of Southeast Asia*. Edited by: Alexander Adelaar and Antoinette Schapper, Oxford University Press.
 DOI: 10.1093/oso/9780198807353.003.0040

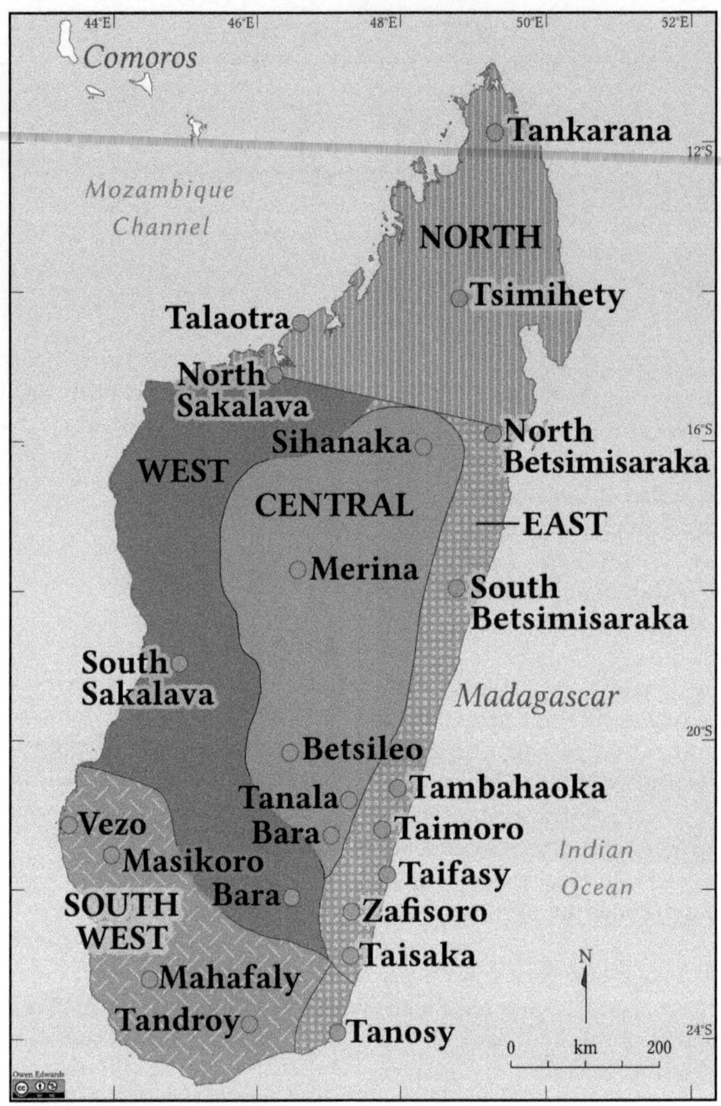


**Map 40.1** Boundaries of Malagasy subgroupings according to Adelaar (2013).

[ˌhasaˈraina] 'improve.UV' (Dahl 1952; Howe 2021: 111). In the latter case, place distinctions preserve the contrast with the phonemes /s, z/, which are retracted to retroflex [ʂ, ʐ] or palatal [ç, ʝ], for example, Betsileo /miˈsasa/ [miˈʂaʂə̥] 'wash.AV' (Howe 2021: 112).

Some Central dialects exhibit allophonic palatalization on all velar consonants following the high front vowel [i] (e.g. /ˈbika/ [ˈbikʲa] 'shape'), a relatively rare phenomenon in Austronesian (Blust 2013a: 237). Adelaar (2012: 140) relates this to a similar process in Comorian; however, it is not universal across modern Malagasy dialects (Howe 2021: 107).

Historically, Austronesian prenasalized obstruents occurred only in word-medial position and have been analysed as consonant clusters rather than single phonemes (Blust 2013a: 223ff). However, the common analysis for most dialects of Malagasy is that they allow only (C)V structure and that prenasalized sounds are separate phonemes (e.g. O'Neill 2015; Howe 2021); they are presented as such in Table 40.1. Prenasalized consonants exhibit the same duration as their oral counterparts (Howe 2017: 202, 230) but pattern differently from the oral obstruents in terms of phonological tone development (see §40.2.3).

OM/Merina and many other dialects have only four true phonemic monophthongs, /i, e, a, u/, with no contrastive length or nasality. Northern dialects (NMLG) have an additional /o/ (orthographic *ô*) (Thomas-Fattier 1982; Kikusawa

**Table 40.1** OM/Merina Malagasy consonant inventory (and dialectal variants)

| | Bilabial | Labio-dental | Dental | Alveolar | Retro-flex | Palatal | Velar | Glottal |
|---|---|---|---|---|---|---|---|---|
| Stops | p | | t | | | | k | (ʔ) |
| Low-tone (voiced) stops | b | | d | | | | g | |
| Pren. stops | $^{m}$p $^{m}$b | | $^{n}$t $^{n}$d | | | | $^{ŋ}$k $^{ŋ}$g | |
| Affricates | | | t͡s | | ʈ͡ʂ | | | |
| Low-tone (voiced) affr. | | | d͡z | | ɖ͡ʐ | | | |
| Pren. affr. | | | $^{n}$t͡s $^{n}$d͡z | | $^{n}$ʈ͡ʂ $^{n}$ɖ͡ʐ | | | |
| Fricatives | (ɸ) | f | | s | | | | h |
| Low-tone (voiced) fric. | (β) | v | | z | | | | |
| Nasals | m | | n | | | (ɲ) | (ŋ) | |
| Trills/Flaps | | | | r/ɾ | | | | |
| Approximants | | | | l | | (j) | | |

2006), and Tsimihety has /o/ as well as /ɔ/ and /ɛ/ (Tsimilaza 1981). In all dialects, orthographic *o* represents /u/, *y* word-final /i/, and an apostrophe (') marks a deleted final vowel. Allophonic vowel devoicing is extremely common cross-dialectally, primarily in unstressed syllables between voiceless obstruents and in word-final position. Howe (2017), however, suggests that vowels reduce less in unstressed syllables in Central dialects due to the development of tone (see §40.2.3).

The status of diphthongs in Malagasy is contested (see Andrianasolo 1993). In colloquial speech, diphthongs or vowel sequences are often 'coalesced' to a monophthong that lies between the two endpoints in terms of height and backness. For example, /au/ and /ua/ coalesce to [o] in Merina and other Central dialects (e.g. /ˈlauka/ [ˈloka] 'rice accompaniment'; /maˈ$^{n}$ɖ͡ʐauka/ [maˈ$^{n}$ɖ͡ʐoka] 'to collect'; /ˈtuaka/ [ˈtoka] 'alcohol'), and in many dialects, /ai/ and unstressed /ia/ coalesce to [e] (/maˈnaikiʈ͡ʂa/ [maˈnekiʈ͡ʂa] 'to bite'; /fiaˈnaɾana/ [feˈnaɾana] 'studies'). In some dialects, certain sequences also undergo monophthongization, in which only the first of the two vowel qualities is pronounced. For example, stressed /ia/ may monophthongize to [i] (/aˈ$^{m}$piana/ [aˈ$^{m}$pina] 'added to'), and word-final stressed /ua/ to [u] (/tuˈkua/ [tuˈku] 'truly' (O'Neill 2015).

In the Central dialects, [e] is not licensed after the primary stressed syllable. Underlying /e/ has allophone [i] in this position, with the underlying phoneme emerging in affixation processes. Thus, Central dialects have *faty* [ˈfati] 'corpse' but *fahafatesana* [ˌfahafaˈtesana] 'death', whereas Sakalava, for example, has *fate* [ˈfate] 'corpse' (Adelaar 2013: 474). In NMLG, unstressed /e/ always surfaces as [i] and stressed /u/ as [o] (Botouhely 2007: 8).

Distribution restrictions on both vowels and consonants are also found in the so-called 'weak final syllables', so named due to their distinct morphophonological behaviour, which includes frequent elision. Word-final consonants, common in the Barito languages, are not licensed in most dialects of Malagasy, a development which Adelaar (2012: 130ff) attributes to Bantu contact. Most Malagasy dialects developed paragogic vowels to achieve open final syllables (e.g. Proto-Malagasy *wuruŋ > Merina /ˈvuruna/ 'bird' [Adelaar 2012]). Due to pre-existing restrictions, the consonants in these weak final syllables are limited to /n, k, ʈ͡ʂ/ in OM; some dialects also maintain /ŋ/. Southern and Western dialects deleted nasals word-finally (e.g. South Sakalava /ˈvuru/ 'bird'), so that only [k, t͡s] occur in the weak final syllables, while in North Sakalava, final nasals are still present in some lexical items (e.g. /ˈvuruŋ/ 'bird' [Thomas-Fattier 1982: 368]). In the South Betsimisaraka dialect, paragogic vowels were not introduced at all (Dahl 1952; Ruud 1955: 35). The paragogic vowel in weak final syllables is [a] in Merina, while it is [a], [e], or [i] in other dialects (Adelaar 2012: 130). In NMLG, a vowel harmony rule requires that the paragogic vowel match the vowel of the preceding syllable (Botouhely 2007; Adelaar 2012). Examples are presented in Table 40.2.

**Table 40.2** Paragogic vowels in weak final syllables[a]

| English | Proto-Malagasy | Merina | S. Sakalava | Bara | N. Sakalava |
|---|---|---|---|---|---|
| 'wind' | *riwut | /ˈrivuʈ͡ʂa/ | /ˈrivuʈ͡ʂe/ | /ˈrivut͡ɕi/ | /ˈrivuʈ͡ʂu/ |
| 'path' | *lalan | /ˈlalana/ | /ˈlala/ | /ˈlala/ | /ˈlalaŋa/ |
| 'penis' | *latak | /ˈlataka/ | /ˈlatake/ | /ˈlataki/ | /ˈlataka/ |

[a] Examples from Adelaar (2012: 130)

Consonant alternations that emerge in affixation sometimes reveal historical final consonants that otherwise merged to the licensed final-syllable consonants. For example, the root /ˈlelaka/ 'licking' < *lelap becomes /leˈlafina/ with undergoer voice suffix *-ina* (see §40.4.2).

### 40.2.2 Word structure and stress

Many Malagasy lexical roots were originally disyllabic, but the addition of paragogic vowels has produced a large number of trisyllabic roots. There are also a few monosyllabic roots (e.g. /ra/ 'blood', /fe/ 'thigh', /vi/ 'iron', /zu/ 'civil rights'; see Cousins 1897: VIII).

In the Southeast Barito languages, stress is noncontrastive, falling regularly on the penultimate syllable (Gudai 1985). In Malagasy, however, innovation and borrowing have introduced unpredictable, contrastive stress, and primary stress may fall on any of the final three syllables of a word. Stress minimal pairs in both tri- and disyllabic roots occur, for example, /ˈtanana/ 'hand' (< Malay *taŋan) vs. /taˈnana/ 'village'; /ˈati/ 'liver' (< Proto-Malayo-Polynesian *qatay, Blust and Trussel 2020) vs. /aˈti/ 'here'. Borrowings may also have final stress, for example, /lakiˈle/ 'key' (< French *la clef*), /zavuˈka/ 'avocado' (< French *les avocats*). Stress can be marked orthographically with a grave accent. In conversation, particularly in the Central dialects, final vowel devoicing and elision of /h/ can also produce effective final stress, as in, for example, /aˈkuhu/ > [aˈku] 'chicken' and /haˈⁿdeha/ > [aˈⁿde] 'FUT.go.AV'.

When root stress is neither penultimate preceding a paragogic vowel nor final, suffixation causes it to shift to the right such that it falls on the final non-paragogic syllable of the original root (Howe 2021). For example, stress shift occurs in /ˈtsaku/ 'chewing action' vs. /tsaˈku-ina/ 'to chew-UV' and in /ˈlavaka/ 'hole' vs. /laˈvah-ana/ 'to dig a hole in-LV', but not in /ˈla/ 'refusal' vs. /ˈlav-ina/ 'to refuse-UV', which has final stress in the root, or in /ˈfuka/ 'act of smoking' vs. /i-ˈfuh-ana/ 'CIRCV-to smoke cigarettes-CIRCV', which has a paragogic vowel.

### 40.2.3 Tonogenesis in Central dialects

Traditional discussions of Malagasy, in any dialect, describe phonological voicing contrasts in all obstruent series (e.g. Rakotofiringa 1982; Poirot 1998; Kikusawa 2006; O'Neill 2015). In what appears to be a recent innovation, however, Central dialects have largely replaced the voicing contrast in the oral obstruent series with pitch distinctions over the syllable (Howe 2017, 2021). Although all dialects exhibit lower fundamental frequency (f0) at vowel onset following voiced as opposed to voiceless obstruents, this contrast is significantly enhanced in magnitude and persistence through the vowel in Central dialects (Howe 2017: 144ff). Moreover, it is accompanied by near-neutralization of the voicing contrast, such that formerly voiced obstruents are often entirely devoiced (Howe 2017: 167ff), and f0 is the primary consistent cue, a fact which is mirrored in perception (Howe 2017: 304ff). (Near-)minimal tonal pairs exist for all oral obstruents (Howe 2017, 2021); for example, *dombo* [ˈtùᵐbu̥] 'blunt' vs. *tombo* [ˈtúᵐbu̥] 'profit' and *bika* [ˈpìkʲḁ] 'shape' vs. *pika* [ˈpíkʲḁ] 'click'. (For illustration, tone diacritics are added and voice distinctions omitted in these examples only.) Dialects outside the Central group maintain a clear phonetic voicing contrast, often with pre-voicing on voiced stops. Voicing neutralization has not occurred in the prenasalized obstruents, where it still bears significant functional load in both production and perception. However, f0 contrasts following these segments are also enhanced in Central dialects and seem more developed among younger speakers, indicating a possible change in progress (Howe 2017).

## 40.3 Nouns and pronouns

### 40.3.1 Noun phrase structure

A schematic of noun phrase structure for OM is provided in (1) (Ntelitheos 2006: 93; Paul 2009) and exemplified in (2) and (3). Additional explanation is given in the text of §40.3.1 to §40.3.3.

(1) AN= DET/DEM NOUN [POSS] ADJ [POSS] NUM QUANT REL_CLAUSE (DEM)

(2) *ny alika keli=n'ny nama=ko*
DET dog small=GEN'DET friend=1SG.GEN
*anakiroa vao no-vid-i=ny*
two recent PST-buy-UV=3SG.GEN
'my friend's two small dogs that s/he just bought'

(3) *ome=ko an= ireo olona mahantra*
give=1SG.GEN OBL= DEM person poor
*maromaro ireo*
many.REDP DEM
'I am giving (it) to those many poor people.'

Common nouns do not inflect for number, and Malagasy does not have noun classes or genders. Number can be indicated in articles for personal names and with demonstrative determiners/pronouns (see §40.3.3). A singular personal name is preceded by *i* (for exceptions see Rasoloson and Rubino 2005: 466), while *ry* can precede a family or group name to indicate all of its members or can precede a singular name to imply an associated group, as in *Tonga ry Onja* (arrive ART.PERS Onja) 'Onja and her family have arrived'. The article *ry* is also used in singular or plural direct address with proper names or epithets, as in *Tongava ry nama=ko* (arrive.IMP ART.PERS friend=1SG.GEN) 'Come here, my friend(s)'.

The common noun articles are *ilay* and *ny*: *ilay* marks definiteness and referentiality; *ny*, though often termed a 'definite article', no longer entails either feature (Fugier 1999: 17; Paul 2009), and Fugier suggests it functions simply as a noun marker or nominalizer. It appears in (4) because a determiner is syntactically required with pivot arguments (see §40.4.1), but the noun phrase *ny olona roa* 'two people' is clearly neither definite nor specific.

(4) *H-ah-azo loka tsara ny olona roa*
FUT-AV-receive prize nice DET person two
'Two people (whose identity is not yet known or determined) will receive a nice prize.'

When *ny* is not syntactically required, it rarely occurs with indefinite, non-referential entities in spontaneously produced language (Paul 2009).

In OM and many dialects, demonstrative determiners often frame the entire noun phrase, replacing any preposed article and appearing again at the end of the phrase, as in (5).

(5) *An'iza io akanjo io?*
POSS='who that shirt that
'Whose is that shirt?'

In the Tandroy dialect, demonstrative articles and determiners surround the noun phrase, but the pre- and postposed elements are not identical, and in some cases, vowel harmony occurs between the second element and the final vowel of the preceding noun; a brief sketch is provided by Rajaonarimanana and Fee (1996: 25). In NMLG, demonstrative determiners appear only in final position, for example, *Ninjôvy akanjo io?* (whose shirt that) 'Whose is that shirt?'; with a proper name, the preposed article remains (Botouhely 2007: 31, 34).

## 40.3.2 Pronouns and case marking

Three pronoun cases are contrasted in OM and most other dialects: nominative, oblique, and genitive. Their forms in OM are presented in Table 40.3 and exemplified in (6).

**Table 40.3** Pronouns in OM/Merina Malagasy

| | Nominative | Oblique | Genitive |
|---|---|---|---|
| 1SG | *aho, izaho* | *ahy, anahy* | *=(k)o* |
| 2SG | *ianao* | *anao* | *=(n)ao* |
| 3SG | *izy* | *azy, anazy* | *=ny* |
| 1PL.INCL | *isika* | *antsika* | *=(n)tsika* |
| 1PL.EXCL | *izahay* | *anay* | *=(n)ay* |
| 2PL | *ianareo* | *anareo* | *=(n)areo* |
| 3PL | *izy ireo* | *an'izy ireo* | *=n'izy ireo, =ny* |

(6) a. *Ma-hita azy aho*
AV-see 3SG.OBL 1SG.NOM
'I see him/her.'

b. *Ma-hita ahy izy*
AV-see 1SG.OBL 3SG.NOM
'S/he sees me.'

c. *Ma-hita anao ny naman=ao*
AV-see 2SG.OBL DET friend=2SG.GEN
'Your friend sees you.'

The first person singular nominative pronoun *izaho* is used in constructions with pragmatically marked, pivot-initial word order (see §40.4.1). In colloquial speech, the first and third person singular oblique pronouns *anahy* and *anazy* often replace *ahy* and *azy* on analogy with the other oblique forms. In NMLG, nominative rather than oblique pronouns are used for objects, for example, *Mahita izy aho* (AV-see 3SG.NOM 1SG.NOM) 'I see him/her' (Botouhely 2007: 11). Genitive pronouns are enclitics and attach directly to the noun or to a modifying adjective following the noun; this placement variability is indicated by the square brackets in (1). Parentheses in the genitive series in Table 40.3 indicate morphophonological variation dependent on the form of the host. Genitive pronouns also serve as agent enclitics on verbs in non-actor voice clauses (see §40.4.1), though in NMLG, the genitive series has distinct forms for nominal vs. verbal uses in the first and third person singular (Botouhely 2007: 12).

Genitive marking on common nouns involves encliticization of the possessor and insertion of a nasal between it and its host, as in *kely* + *=n(a)* in (3) (with variations if the host ends in weak *-ka* or *-tra*). Oblique case, however, is often unmarked on common nouns, so that word order may be the only distinction between actor and undergoer, as shown in (7).

(7) a. *Man-enjika ny saka ny alika*
AV-chase DET cat DET dog
'The dog is chasing the cat.'

b. *Man-enjika ny alika ny saka*
AV-chase DET dog DET cat
'The cat is chasing the dog.'

Oblique case is sometimes marked on direct and indirect object common nouns by proclitic *aN=*, which also marks locatives (see §40.3.3) and possessives, as in (5), and which always appears in first position in the noun phrase. When no determiner is present, *aN=* attaches to the head noun, as in *Tia am=badiny i Jao* (love OBL=spouse.3SG.GEN ART.PERS Jao) 'Jao loves his wife'; otherwise, it attaches to the determiner or demonstrative, as in *mihinana an=ilay poara* (eat.AV OBL=DET.DEF pear) 'eating the pear'. Howe (2022) observes that objects in actor voice clauses tend to be *aN=*-marked when they denote highly individuated referents.

Endocentric compound nouns are often formed from indefinite genitive constructions, which are head-initial, as in *tranon-tantely* 'bee hive' < *trano* 'dwelling' + *=n(a)* 'GEN' + *tantely* 'bee'. Some compounds are formed through noun–noun juxtaposition with no nasal insertion, as in *solovolo* 'wig' < *solo* 'substitute' + *volo* 'hair'. When a head can be identified in these cases, it also occupies initial position (see Keenan and Polinsky 1998: 574ff).

### 40.3.3 Demonstrative systems

Malagasy has elaborate adverbial (locative) and adnominal demonstrative systems, which are presented in Table 40.4; the two bolded terms have additional properties discussed in the text.

As shown in §40.3.1, adnominal demonstratives in OM frame the noun phrase. Adverbial demonstratives precede or frame a prepositional phrase or place name in OM, as in (8a), but follow it in NMLG and Tandroy, as in (8b). All demonstratives can also act as pro-forms.

(8) a. *Mi-tsangana eo amin'io*
AV-stand MED.OPN.VIS at'DEM.MED.OPN.VIS
*tokontany io (eo)*
yard DEM.MED.OPN.VIS (MED.OPN.VIS)
*izy*
3SG.NOM
'S/he is standing there in that yard.'

b. *Mi-toboke (*ao) an=tragno ao*
AV-stay LOC=house MED.OPN.INVS
*re*
3SG.NOM
'S/he is staying at home.'
(Rajaonarimanana and Fee 1996: 24)

Rasoloson and Rubino (2005: 470) claim seven distinctions of distance but present the forms in the standard Austronesian three-tiered system (Blust 2013a: 305) of proximal, medial, and distal. Close observation suggests that the system in fact specifies four gradations of distance from speaker, with two distinctions within the general distal category; this is shown in Table 40.4. Additional terms in the paradigm indicate the 'precision' with which a space can be delimited (see (11a) and (11b)). The adnominal demonstrative system, derived from the adverbials, also marks number, though the plural series lacks one form.

The 'visibility' noted in Table 40.4 is not always literal. For instance, *eny* 'DIST.OPN.VIS' may refer to a distant place that is in fact invisible from the speaker's position but whose location is reasonably identifiable or familiar (Rasoloson and Rubino 2005: 472), as in (9a). When a location is neither visible nor identifiable, as in (9b), use of *eny* is often unnatural.

(9) a. *ka n-an-ontanintany azy*
SO PST-AV-ask.REDUP 3SG.OBL
*t-eny an=dalana*
PST-DIST.OPN.VIS LOC=road
'...so (he) asked him en route.' (path known)
(Rasoloson and Rubino 2005: 472)

b. *(?Eny) an=dalana ho aiza ianareo?*
DIST.OPN.VIS LOC=road IRR where 2PL.NOM
'Where are you on the way to?' (path unknown)

Similarly, visibility in the adnominal demonstratives can mark accessibility of a referent (Rasoloson and Rubino 2005: 472). In such cases, distance relates to time rather than space, as shown in (10), and the demonstrative placed only at the end of the noun phrase indicates the speaker's

**Table 40.4** Adverbial (locative) and adnominal demonstratives in OM/Merina Malagasy

| | Proximal | | Medial | | Distal | | |
|---|---|---|---|---|---|---|---|
| **ADVERBIAL** | PRECISE | OPEN | PRECISE | OPEN | PRECISE (CLOSER) | OPEN | PRECISE (FURTHER) |
| INVISIBLE | ***àto*** | *atỳ* | *àtsy* | ***ao*** | *aròa* | *àny* | *arỳ* |
| VISIBLE | *èto* | *etỳ* | *ètsy* | *eo* | *eròa* | *èny* | *erỳ* |
| **ADNOMINAL** | | | | | | | |
| INVISIBLE | *izàto* | *izatỳ* | *izàtsy* | *izào* | *izaròa* | *izàny* | *izarỳ* |
| VISIBLE | *ìto* | *itỳ* | *itsỳ* | *io* | *iròa* | *ìny* | *irỳ* |
| VISIBLE.PL | *irèto* | — | *irètsy* | *irèo* | *ireròa* | *irèny* | *irerỳ* |

uncertainty concerning accessibility of the referent for the other interlocutor(s).

(10) *Tadidi=nao ve ilay fety*
remember.UV=2SG.GEN Q DET.DEF party
*t-amin' ny herin-taona iny?*
PST-in DET return-year DEM.DIST.OPN.VIS
'Do you remember that party last year?'
(which was significant to us for some reason, but which we haven't necessarily been discussing recently)

There is also a conceptual and physical overlap between visibility and enclosure: as shown in (11a), a distant and non-visible location may nonetheless be marked by *eny* 'DIST.OPN.VIS' if it is not enclosed. The contrast between (11a) and (11b) illustrates the notion of 'precision'.

(11) a. *Mi-petraka eny an=tendrombohitra*
AV-reside DIST.OPN.VIS LOC=mountain_top
*eny izahay*
DIST.OPN.VIS 1PL.EXCL.NOM
'We (but not you) live at the top of a mountain.'
(precise location not specified)

b. *Mi-petraka ery an=tendrombohitra*
AV-reside DIST.PRCS.VIS LOC=mountain_top
*ery izahay*
DIST.PRCS.VIS 1PL.EXCL.NOM
'We (but not you) live at the top of that mountain there.' (pointing)

Locations marked as invisible tend to be either literally enclosed or conceptually bounded. The notion of boundedness is particularly imparted by the two bolded terms in Table 40.4, *ato* and *ao*, which usually have the meaning 'inside'. In (12), speaker and addressee are together in an enclosed location, visible to them but invisible from the outside.

(12) *Ato an=trano isika*
PROX.PRCS.INVS LOC=house 1PL.INCL.NOM
'We are here inside (our) house.'

Whereas *ato* fits into the distance schema, as it can only mark the speaker's location, Adelaar (2012: 150) notes that *ao* lies outside this scale, referring to any enclosed space not occupied by the speaker, as in (13). He attributes this function to contact with Bantu languages.

(13) *Ao am=piangonana ny olona*
MED.OPN.INVS LOC=church DET person
'The people are in church (nearby or on the other side of the world).'

Another unusual feature of the adverbial demonstratives is their ability to take the prefix *t*-, argued by Pearson (2008) to mark time-'boundedness'. With past tense verbs, *t*-marking indicates the truth condition of the locative at the time of speaking, as in (14a) vs. (14b).

(14) a. *N-i-ditra tao an=trano*
PST-AV-enter T-MID.OPN.INVS LOC=house
*ilay vehivavy*
DET.DEF woman
'The woman went into the house (and may be, but is likely not, still there).'

b. *N-i-ditra ao an=trano*
PST-AV-enter MID.OPN.INVS LOC=house
*ilay vehivavy*
DET.DEF woman
'The woman went into the house (and is still there).'
(Pearson 2008: 5, ex. 8c, d)

Despite Pearson's statement to the contrary, *t-* can also occur in present and future clauses, at least in colloquial speech; this further supports his claim that it marks a kind of aspect or 'present relevance' of the goal point (Pearson 2008: 6). This is exemplified in (15), where the speaker wishes for a future in which the current location 'here' is no longer relevant.

(15) *Tena te h-i-ala t-eto*
really want FUT-AV-leave T-PROX.PRCS.VIS
*mafy dia mafy aho*
strong then strong 1SG.NOM
'I really strongly want to leave here.'

## 40.4 Clausal syntax

### 40.4.1 Simple clause structure

All dialects of Malagasy allow a basic predicate-initial structure. Clauses with non-verbal predicates do not use a copula, as seen in (16a)–(16d).

(16) a. *Azy ilay trano*
3SG.OBL DET.DEF house
'The house is his/hers.'

b. *Telo fotsiny ny zana=ny*
three only DET child=3SG.GEN
'His/her children are only three (in number).'

c. *Eto ny toerana*
here DET place
*h-i-petrah-an=tsika*
FUT- CIRCV-stay-CIRCV=1PL.INCL.GEN
'Here is the place where we will stay.'

d. *Mp-i-hira ma-laza ny*
NMLZ-AV-sing AV-famous DET
*vadi=ko*
spouse=1SG.GEN
'My spouse is a famous singer.'

Simple clauses display a major constituent break between the predicate phrase and a nominal argument in final position, for which I use the theoretically neutral term 'pivot' (see Kroeger and Riesberg, this volume, §47.3–5). This constituent structure is reflected in intonation patterns (Aziz 2020; Howe 2021). The predicate phrase includes all non-pivot arguments of a predicate and often adverbial adjuncts, as in (17a)–(17b), although time and location adjuncts may also appear after the pivot, as in (17c). In this case, they can modify the pivot rather than the predicate (Rasoloson and Rubino 2005: 464; Randriamasimanana 2006), so that example (17c) has two possible meanings; these are indicated by the two translations, in which the full pivot phrase is bracketed, and can be distinguished by intonation.

(17) a. *N-an-ofa fiara omaly t-amin'ny*
PST-AV-rent car yesterday PST-at'DET
*telo tolak'andro izy*
three afternoon 3SG.NOM
'S/he rented a car yesterday at three in the afternoon.'

b. *Efa n-a-veri=ny t-amin'ny*
already PST-TV-return=3SG.GEN PST-at'DET
*telo tolak'andro ilay fiara*
three afternoon DET.DEF car
*no-hofa-i=ny*
PST-rent-UV=3SG.GEN
'S/he already returned, at three in the afternoon, the car that s/he rented.'

c. *Efa n-a-veri=ny ilay*
already PST-TV-return=3SG.GEN DET.DEF
*fiara no-hofa-i=ny t-amin'ny*
car PST-rent-UV=3SG.GEN PST-at'DET
*telo tolak'andro*
three afternoon
'S/he has already returned [the car that s/he rented at three in the afternoon].'
'At three in the afternoon, s/he already returned [the car that s/he had rented].'

The pivot argument in most dialects must be preceded by a determiner, but it is not necessarily definite, as seen in §40.3.1. The Tankarana dialect allows pivots with no determiner (Potsdam and Polinsky 2014: 6), but it is common in OM and other dialects to use an existential with no overt pivot argument to introduce indefinite, non-specific entities.

The majority of morphological activity in Malagasy occurs on verb-forming roots, which take affixes marking tense, aspect, mood, voice, and nominalization, but which exhibit no inflection for person or number agreement. Past and future tense prefixes *n(o)-* and *h(o)-* are exemplified in (2) and (4) above, and (16d) exemplifies actor nominalization with prefix *mp-*. Imperative mood suffixes are shown in (18), and the comparison of (17a) with (19) demonstrates the absence of person and number agreement between the verb (i.e. *nanofa*) and pivot. Voice and aspect are discussed in detail in §40.4.2 and §40.4.3.

(18) a. *Ma-tori-a fa alina ny andro*
AV-sleep-IMP for night DET day
'Sleep, for it is night time.'

b. *Mba* *a-veren-o* *amin'izao* *ilay* *fiara*
please TV-return-IMP at'now DET.DEF car
'Please return the car now.'

(19) *Tokony* *ho* *n-an-ofa* *fiara* *ianareo*
should IRR PST-AV-rent car 2PL.NOM
'You should have rented a car.'

Verbs occur in first position in the predicate phrase unless preceded by a negator or modal verb, as in (19), or an adverbial particle, as in (17b, c) and (18b). Objects usually immediately follow the verb, as in (17a). Prepositional phrases, such as *tamin'ny telo tolak'andro* in (17), are head-initial, and prepositions, like locative demonstratives, take *t*-marking (see §40.3.3).

Predicate-initial basic word order is one of Malagasy's oft-touted conservative traits (e.g. Keenan 1976; Paul 2000a; Rasoloson and Rubino 2005: 462). In OM and many dialects, pivot-fronting is possible only in a variety of pragmatically marked constructions that serve functions such as focusing, question formation, topicalization, and contrast. For example, the particle *no*, placed between fronted pivot (in bold) and predicate, as in (20), focuses the pivot (Pearson 2009: 166–7). It must also be used in content questions in OM when the argument being questioned is the pivot (Potsdam 2006a), as in (21a); insertion of *iza* 'who?' directly into final pivot position is not possible, as shown in (21b).

(20) ***ity*** ***boky*** ***ity*** [*no*] *no-sorat-a=ko* *malaky*
**this** **book** **this** [FOC] PST-write-LV=1SG.GEN quick
'This book (not some other one) is (the one) I wrote quickly.'

(21) a. ***Iza*** [*no*] *n-an-oratra* *boky?*
who [FOC] PST-AV-write book
'Who wrote/was writing a book?'

b. **Nanoratra boky iza?*

Fronting of pivot arguments can also serve to topicalize them; in this case, either the particle *dia* 'TOP' is inserted between pivot and predicate (Keenan 1976: 271–3; Rasoloson and Rubino 2005: 465), or an adverb such as *indray* 'again' is inserted, as in (22).

(22) *Fa* ***ilay*** ***alika*** [*indray*] *variana* *mi-lalao*
but **DET.DEF** **dog** [again] distracted AV-play
'But the dog, meanwhile, is distracted playing.'

Fronting of the pivot in other cases produces an 'emphatic construction' (Rasoloson and Rubino 2005: 465), marked with the emphatic particle *ange* or by a rising intonation and/or pause between fronted pivot and predicate. Keenan (1976: 270–1) and Pearson (2007) also discuss other limited constructions in which fronting can occur or is syntactically required.

In contrast to OM, NMLG appears to allow pivot-initial order as an alternative to predicate-initial order in basic clauses (Potsdam and Polinsky 2014: 6). Like OM, the Tankarana dialect requires fronting of a content question-word in pivot position, as in (21a); however, use of *no* in Tankarana is not required and is extremely rare: *Azôvy namono aomby?* (who PST.kill.AV zebu) 'Who killed the zebu?' (Potsdam and Polinsky 2014: 7–8, ex. 27a). Pivot-initial word order without *no* or other particles or prosodic cues is also very common in this dialect in declarative clauses, as exemplified in (23).

(23) *i* *magnangy* *n-an-orat-an'* *i* *lelahy* *taratasy*
ART.PERS woman PST-CIRCV-write-CIRCV ART.PERS man letter
'The woman was written a letter by the man.'

Whether there is a functional contrast in use of pivot-initial vs. predicate-initial order in Tankarana requires further exploration. Howe (2019) confirms that NMLG uses pivot-initial order in narratives about 45% of the time, with a preference for this order in two-argument and AV clauses, a pattern also observed in other Austronesian languages that have shifted from verb-initial to verb-medial order or that allow both pivot-initial and verb-initial basic orders (Hemmings 2016; Riesberg, Malcher, and Himmelmann 2019).

Whereas word order changes in other Austronesian languages have been attributed to contact, the cause of the shift in NMLG is less clear, as it is not spoken in a linguistic areal border zone. Code-switching with French (the former colonial language) is a hallmark of Northern speech, however, so contact cannot be ruled out as an explanation. But French influence is also significant in the capital city in the Central dialect region, where this change is not observed. Further investigation into the history of this word order change is needed.

### 40.4.2 Voice system

Another aspect of Malagasy often cited for its conservatism (e.g. Dahl 1986) is the voice system. The morphology of this system in OM is presented in Table 40.5 and exemplified in (24), where pivots are in bold. Some dialectal variants

**Table 40.5** OM/Merina voice-marking affixes

| Voice | Pivot argument role | OM affix |
|---|---|---|
| Actor (AV) | agent, experiencer | *(m)aN-*,[a] *(m)i-*, *(m)a-* |
| Undergoer (UV) | patient | *-i(na)* |
| Locative (LV) | location, goal, recipient | *-a(na)* |
| Theme (TV) | theme, instrument | *a-* |
| Circumstantial (CIRCV) | time, place, reason, instrument, beneficiary, and other | *aN- -a(na)*, *i- -a(na)* |

[a] *N* here indicates a generic nasal, subject to classic MPSEA nasal substitution and accretion rules (*cf.* Blust 2013a: 242ff); it is alveolar in Merina and OM but velar in other dialects.

are discussed in the following text. Parentheses indicate morphophonological variation.

(24) a. *Mam-etraka sakafo ambony vilia* ***ny***
AV-put food on plate DET
***mpivarotra***
salesperson
'The salesperson puts food on (a) plate(s).'
(AV, externally directed)

b. *Mi-petraka ambony seza* ***ny olona***
AV-sit on chair DET person
'The person is sitting on a chair.'
(AV, self-directed)

c. *Vono-in'ny mp-i-ompy* ***ny***
kill-UV'DET NMLZ-AV-raise_livestock DET
***akoho***
chicken
'The farmer kills the chicken(s).' (UV)

d. *No-zer-a=ny vato* ***ny***
PST-throw_down-LV=3SG.GEN rock DET
***lohan'ilay ankizy***
head.GEN'DET.DEF child
'S/he threw a rock down on the child's head.' (LV)

e. *H-a-tsipi=ko* ***ny kilalao***
FUT-TV-throw=1SG.GEN DET toy
'I will throw the toy.' (TV)

f. *N-an-osor-an'ny ankizy fotaka*
PST-CIRCV-smear-CIRCV'DET child mud
*t-amin'ny boky* ***ny kitay***
PST-on'DET book DET stick
'The child smeared mud on the book with the stick.' (CIRCV)

In Southern and Western dialects, an infix <*in*>, a reflex of the Proto-Malayo-Polynesian perfective marker *<*in*>, has developed into a (still productive) portmanteau marking both past tense and UV. Compare the following examples from the author's fieldnotes on the Mahafaly dialect: *soratse* 'writing' (root) vs. *sorat-ana* 'being written (by someone)' and *s*<*in*>*oratse* 'written (by someone) in past'. In OM and other dialects, <*in*> occurs unproductively in only a few lexical items in which it has been reanalysed as part of the root.

The morphological similarity of the Malagasy voice system to Philippine-type systems is clear (see Kroeger and Riesberg, this volume, §47.4.1.4), but the Malagasy paradigm has become less systematic (*cf.* Keenan 1976; Paul 2000a; Pearson 2001). Although five morphological forms can be identified, most roots form only three or at most four distinct voices. A single root rarely has both UV and LV forms. Instead, occurrence of these forms is highly lexicalized, with semantic properties partially guiding the choice, such that UV is more common when the pivot changes state and LV when the pivot is a goal or location. In some cases, a pivot may be both patient and location/goal, so one might expect either form to be available according to the role emphasized within the utterance. For example, root *lavaka* 'hole' forms the AV verb *man-davaka* 'AV-to dig; make a hole in'. When the location/entity in which the hole is dug is pivot, the form *lavah-ana* 'make_hole-LV' is used in OM, whereas Tsimihety has *lavah-igny* 'make_hole-UV' < *lavaka* 'hole' + *-igny* 'UV' (Tsimilaza 1981: 233; author's fieldnotes); the choice is therefore both lexically determined and dialectally variable.

Verb roots that denote movement of something towards a goal often allow both LV and TV but not UV forms. For example, the root *toraka* 'throwing' forms *torah-ana* 'throw_at-LV' (pivot is goal/person at which something is thrown) and *a-toraka* 'TV-throw_at' (pivot is thing thrown). The form **torah-ina* is not possible.

If the change of state of a pivot involves movement, however, a UV verb form may exist that has the same meaning and syntactic function as the TV form. For example, from root *velatra* 'spreading; unrolling', UV *velar-ina* and TV *a-velatra* forms are interchangeable, as seen in (25a). LV and CIRCV forms from this root can both take a locative pivot, as in (25b, c), but the meanings are different:

the LV clause describes a particular, ongoing event, while the CIRCV clause is habitual. This root thus occurs in all five morphological voice forms (including AV form *mame-latra* not exemplified here) but functionally has only four distinctions.

(25) a. *(Velar-in' / A-velatr')* *i* *Tojo* *ny* *tsihy*
spread-UV / TV-spread ART.PERS Tojo DET mat
'Tojo is spreading out the mat.'

b. *Velar-an'* *i* *Tojo* *tsihy* *eto*
spread-LV ART.PERS Tojo mat PROX.PRCS.VIS
'Tojo is spreading out a mat here (right now).'

c. *Am-elar-an'* *i* *Tojo* *tsihy* *eto*
CIRCV-spread-CIRCV ART.PERS Tojo mat PROX.PRCS.VIS
'This is where Tojo spreads out mats (in general, but not necessarily right now).'

The CIRCV is an innovation in Malagasy rather than an inheritance from Austronesian. As indicated in Table 40.5, its pivots are non-core adjuncts or prepositional elements such as time, place, reason, instrument, or beneficiary (see Paul 2000a). Adelaar (this volume, §21.4.6(*d*)) suggests that its development may have been stimulated by contact with Bantu languages, which must also have been a factor in changes in the demonstrative system described in §40.3.3 and in development of tense marking (Dahl 1988; Adelaar 2012: 149–50; Adelaar, this volume, §21.4.6(*b*)).

Fugier (1999) presents evidence that the CIRCV creates verbal nouns rather than a voice form on par with the other forms in the paradigm but that it is becoming integrated into the voice system due to its ability to function like, and substitute for, other voice forms (177ff). Indeed, despite the difference between LV and CIRCV forms in (25b, c), with some roots, the CIRCV form is apparently replacing or has already replaced the related LV form in common usage. For example, Malzac (1960[1]: 149, cited in Fugier 1999: 179) provides an example in which he claims the forms *ater-ana* 'bring-LV' and *an-ater-ana* 'CIRCV-bring-CIRCV' are interchangeable; however, a consultant in 2020 rejects the LV form in that example as nonsensical. Similarly, whereas generally more conservative Tandroy has an LV form *lefas-agne* 'send-LV' (author's fieldnotes) for use with a recipient pivot, OM uses CIRCV form *an-defas-ana* for this purpose.

[1] This was the fourth edition; the first edition appeared at least fifty years earlier, so the relevant example is quite old.

### 40.4.3 Aspect

Malagasy has a primary telicity contrast marked by morphology. The voice affixes in Table 40.5 form atelic verbs (Paul 2000a: 22; Travis 2005), as in (26), taken from natural conversation.

(26) *Mam-elona* *moto* *aho* *eto* *dia* *tsy* *mety* *velona*
AV-start scooter 1SG.NOM here then NEG possible alive
'I am starting the scooter here, and (it) won't start.'

Table 40.6 shows the corresponding telic affixes, which indicate non-volitionality of any overt or implied agent in addition to telicity.

**Table 40.6** OM/Merina atelic and telic voice-marking affixes

| Voice | Atelic affix | Telic affix |
|---|---|---|
| Actor Transitive | *(m)aN-*, *(m)i-* | *(m)aha-* |
| Actor Unaccusative[a] | *(m)i-* | *tafa-* |
| Undergoer | *-i(na)* | |
| Locative | *-a(na)* | *voa-* |
| Theme | *a-* | |
| Circumstantial | *aN- -a(na)*, *i- -a(na)* | *aha- -a(na)* |

[a] Term used by Travis (2005)

The prefix *tafa-* typically describes weakly agentive, intransitive processes (Fugier 1999: 142) in which there is an element of accident, suddenness, or success through great effort or chance. This is evident in the difference between (27a) and (27b).

(27) a. *N-i-tsangana* *izy*
PST-AV-stand_up 3SG.NOM
'S/he stood up (of own volition without difficulty).'

b. *Tafa-tsangana* *izy*
TAFA-standing 3SG.NOM
'S/he achieved standing (despite some condition which may have inhibited it).'

In contrast to *tafa-*, *voa-* occurs primarily in transitive contexts (Paul 2000a: 22), emphasizing the role of an external force or agent in effecting an action or state (Fugier 1999: 145). Clauses with *voa-* have an implicit agent, even if unexpressed (Travis 2005: 6), as in (28).

(28) *Voa-tsangana* *izy*
VOA-standing 3SG.NOM
'S/he was stood up (by someone or something).'

The telic prefix *aha-* combines with a preceding *m-* (or a tense marker) to produce AV forms or with the LV suffix to produce CIRCV forms. Verbs with this prefix carry abilitative and causative meaning. Thus, *voky* 'full; satisfied' > *maha-voky* 'make full'; *vita* 'completed' > *aha-vita-(a)na* 'circumstance in which (something) is completed'. An example in AV appears in (29). Elision of /h/ (see §40.2.2) often reduces *aha-* to [a] or [aː] in Central dialects.

(29) *Tsy* *maha-tsangana* *trano* *ny* *olona* *iray*
NEG MAHA-standing house DET person one
'One person (alone) cannot erect a house.'

Among the atelic voice forms there are also aspectual contrasts. UV, LV, and TV impart punctual and resultative readings, whereas CIRCV is durative and partitive; TV also contributes inchoative aspect (Randriamasimanana 2006: 81, 84). Pearson (2012) shows that AV clauses favour durative or progressive readings when a time expression is present in the utterance.

Howe (2022) studied the functional relation of voice forms in narratives to semantic transitivity characteristics in the sense of Hopper and Thompson (1980). A preference was found for non-AV over AV in clauses describing perfective and punctual events, and non-AV also scored more highly in other measures of semantic transitivity, including foregrounding of events and affectedness and individuation of objects. Transitivity is an important determiner of voice form in conservative Austronesian systems (Huang 2002). However, Howe suggests that the influence of transitivity factors on speakers' choice of verb form in Malagasy is weaker than in those most conservative languages.

## 40.5 Conclusion

This discussion has highlighted various topics in recent work on Malagasy that need further investigation. Although linguists have studied Malagasy for several hundred years, the scope of research was formerly limited, with much work in the second half of the twentieth century exclusively treating formal syntax. According to Randriamasimanana (2006), some analyses have also suffered from a reliance on false or misunderstood data or on examples taken out of context. Future work should incorporate a wider variety of research techniques, moving beyond elicitation and grammaticality judgements of OM to explore spontaneously produced language in context and deepen our functional understanding of all Malagasy varieties. Paul (2015) has recognized the need to examine dialectal syntactic variation, but much remains un- or under-documented. Work in areas other than syntax, such as phonetics, prosody, and sociolinguistic variation, is also scarce; these topics deserve further exploration.

# PART IV

# Featural Overviews

CHAPTER 41

# Segment inventories

JULIETTE BLEVINS

## 41.1 Introduction

The forces that shape segment inventories in spoken human languages are the focus of much research and debate. Some argue that global teleological factors such as symmetry, feature economy, and segmental markedness principles are at work, while others take the view that natural phonetic developments coupled with a deeper understanding of categorization and nuanced models of contact-induced change are sufficient to account for typological generalizations and distributions. In this chapter, I examine the segmental inventories of the Malayo-Polynesian languages of Southeast Asia (henceforth referred to as MPSEA) with this dichotomy in mind. What forces can be seen to shape the consonant and vowel inventories of MPSEA languages? Is there evidence of preferences for symmetry, economy, and unmarked sounds? Do systems of contrast appear to evolve on the basis of local phonetic properties, modulated by contact? What features are strong and constant in these systems, and which others are most liable to change? This chapter covers the MPSEA area languages including Malagasy, Chamorro, and Palauan, but excludes the South Halmahera–West New Guinea languages (see Gasser, Arnold, and Kamholz, this volume, §37.2, for a phonological overview of SHWNG languages).

Blust's (2009c, 2013a) monumental book, *The Austronesian Languages*, provides an extensive view of the sound systems of Austronesian languages from synchronic and diachronic perspectives, including those of many MPSEA languages. The purpose of this chapter is to provide further details of some of the interesting properties of MPSEA phoneme inventories discussed in that volume, and to offer notes, where relevant, on how typological features of MPSEA segmental phonologies illuminate our understanding of general phonological typology, and suggest explanations for skewed typological distributions.

In many ways, the segmental phonology of the average MPSEA language can be viewed as typologically frequent, unremarkable, or 'unmarked', from a cross-linguistic perspective. Take, for example, the overall size of the sound inventory. Based on the UCLA Phonetic Segment Inventories Database (UPSID) sample of 317 languages, Maddieson (1984: 7) estimated that the typical size of a segment inventory (excluding length and secondary vowel features like nasalization and voice quality) ranges between twenty and thirty-seven segments. Most MPSEA languages have segment inventories in this range as well. Or, consider, from the same study, the fact that 291 of the 317 languages, or 91.8%, have a series of plain voiceless stops, while 212, or 66.9%, have a series of plain voiced stops. Here again, MPSEA languages fit the norm, since most show both a series of plain voiceless stops and a series of plain voiced stops as well. The fricative inventory of most MPSEA languages also matches that of the average language: 74.5% of all sibilants in UPSID are voiceless, and the most common fricative cross-linguistically is a coronal sibilant, /s/. Most MPSEA languages show at least one voiceless fricative, and this fricative is a coronal sibilant. Of course, many of these properties are inherited properties of the protolanguage, Proto-Malayo-Polynesian (PMP). The Proto-Malayo-Polynesian vowel system is reconstructed as *i, *a, *u, *ə (with final diphthongs *-ay, *-aw, *-uy, *iw), while the consonant system for PMP has twenty-two distinct segments (where [ ] enclose approximate IPA values distinct from the symbols used): *p, *t, *c=[t͡ʃ], *k, *q, *b, *d, *z=[d͡ʒ], *D=[ɖ], *j=[gʲ], *g, *s, *m, *n, *ñ=[ɲ], *ŋ, *l, *R=[r], [ʀ], *r=[ɾ], *h, *w, *y=[j] (Blust 2009c: 594–5). Since many MPSEA languages are conservative in preserving these basic segmental contrasts, the overall gestalt is one of unremarkable phonology. On the other hand, MPSEA languages that diverge radically from this segmental norm offer insights into typological diversity, and the distribution of rare or unusual segments or contrasts outside of the Austronesian language family. In the sections that follow, I attempt to illustrate how both the unremarkable and remarkable aspects of MPSEA segmental phonology can inform our general understanding of sound patterns.

Juliette Blevins, *Segment inventories.* In: *The Oxford Guide to the Malayo-Polynesian Languages of Southeast Asia.* Edited by: Alexander Adelaar and Antoinette Schapper, Oxford University Press. © Juliette Blevins (2024). DOI: 10.1093/oso/9780198807353.003.0041

## 41.2 Consonant inventories

Consonant systems can be examined from many different perspectives. Here, we deconstruct the consonant systems of MPSEA languages in terms of natural classes of sounds defined in terms of articulatory, aerodynamic, acoustic, and perceptual properties. In examining each potential dimension of contrast, robust, common, and rare features of MPSEA languages are identified, examined in a broader typological context, and, where possible, assessed with respect to factors that might explain their presence.

### 41.2.1 Airstream mechanism

Proto-Austronesian and Proto-Malayo-Polynesian are reconstructed with only a single airstream mechanism, pulmonic egressive. In the great majority of MPSEA languages, all sounds are also produced with basic pulmonic egressive airflow. However, at least two other airstream mechanisms are found in a small number of MPSEA languages and used contrastively: glottalic ingressive (implosives) and glottalic egressive (ejectives).

At least a dozen MPSEA languages are reported to have implosive sounds. In implosives, the airstream is controlled by a downward movement of the glottis, in concert with pulmonic egressive airflow. Because implosion reduces intraoral airpressure, it allows voicing to be maintained, and is often an allophonic property of voiced plosives. At the same time, the percept associated with implosion is most salient for bilabials, less so for coronals, and even less so for velars, resulting in cross-linguistic asymmetries: bilabial implosives are most common; then coronals; and dorsal implosives are relatively rare. In at least three southern Philippine languages with voiced stops /b d g/, implosion is allophonic: Central Sama with allophones [ɓ ɗ ɠ] (Reid 1971); Sindangan Subanun with allophones [ɓ ɗ] only (Reid 1971); and Maranao, with allophones [ɓ ɗ ɠ] in initial position only (Lobel 2013a: 287).

In other MPSEA languages, implosives contrast with their plain egressive pulmonic voiced counterparts. Contrastive implosives are described for at least four languages of southeast Sulawesi: Muna, Kulisusu, Wolio, and Tukang Besi. In Muna (van den Berg 1989), /ɓ/ is the only contrastive implosive in the language, in contrast with /p/, /b/, /m/, /mp/, and /mb/. Interestingly, the same airstream mechanism is used non-contrastively in Muna too: implosive allophones of apico-alveolar /d/ are described for vocalic contexts (e.g. before /i/ and /ɛ/) where /d/ may be produced as post-alveolar or retroflex (van den Berg 1989: 19). In Wolio (Grimes, Anceaux, and van den Berg 1995: 575), Kulisusu (Mead 1998: 22) and Tukang Besi (Donohue 1999a), there are voiced implosives /ɓ ɗ/, but only minimal contrast with non-implosives /b/ and /d/, which are found only in loans.

Another group of languages with implosives are in the western Lesser Sundas and include (roughly from west to east): Bima (eastern half of Sumbawa Island), Kambera (eastern Sumba), Komodo (Komodo Island), Ngadha (Flores), Hawu (Savu Island), and Ndao (aka Dhao, Ndao Island, just west of Roti). Kambera has segments /ɓ ɗ/ and these contrast with voiceless /p t/, and pre-nasalized /$^{m}$b $^{n}$d/, but not with /b d/, which do not exist in the language (Klamer 1998: 10–11). Klamer's central argument that pre-nasalized stops function as plain voiced stops is from loan phonology: when words are borrowed from Indonesian or Dutch into Kambera, /b d g dz/ are always substituted with the pre-nasalized series, not with the implosive series: Indonesian *bangku* > Kambera *mbangku* 'bench'; Indonesian *bebas* > Kambera *mbembah(u)* 'free'; Indonesian *duit* > Kambera *ndui* 'money', etc. A stronger case for contrastive implosives is found in Hawu (Walker 1982: 5–8). In Hawu, there is a clear contrast between the plain voiced plosives /b d dʒ g/ and the four implosive voiced stops /ɓ ɗ ɗʸ ɠ/ as in: *bara* 'side; direction', *ɓara* 'goods; clothing'; *dəlu* 'egg', *ɗəlu* 'stomach'; *gili* 'roll', *ɠili* 'tickle'. Further, loans with plain voiced plosives, are replaced by the same: Hawu *doi* 'money' < Indonesian *duit*; Hawu *kedera* 'chair' < Portuguese *cadeira*; Hawu *gapa* 'easy' < Indonesian *gampang*. Ndao (aka Dhao) sound patterns are similar to those in Hawu (Walker 1982: 57–8; Balukh 2020). If implosion is an areal feature in the Lesser Sundas, it appears to have moved from east to west: in both Hawu and Ndao, there is a full set of implosives at labial, alveolar, palatal, and velar points of articulation that contrasts with plain voiced plosives, while as one moves west (or north), the number of implosives is reduced, and the contrastive status moves from clear to marginal to non-contrastive.

In recent work, Edwards (2018b) suggests *ɓ and *ɗ as protophonemes of Proto-Rote-Meto (West Timor). Under his account, implosion in Proto-Rote-Meto is "not attributable to regular inheritance from PMP" and is "an areal feature of the region ... in a triangle between (and including) southeast Sulawesi, Sumbawa, and western Timor. . ." (Edwards 2018b: 399; see also Nagaya, this volume, §34.2; van den Berg and Mead, this volume, §33.2.1; Schapper and Zobel, this volume, §35.2.2).

A final group of languages with contrastive implosion is found in Borneo. In Bintulu, a North Sarawak language, /ɓ ɗ/ contrast with voiced /b d/ (Blust 2013a: 184; Smith 2017a: 251). Implosives are also described for Lowland Kenyah dialects, where they are conditioned allophones of the plain voiced series, but where recent sound changes giving rise to new voiced stops have created an incipient contrast (Blust

2013a: 183–4; Smith 2017a: 253, 342). See Kroeger and Smith, this volume, §27.2.2.1 for a wider survey of implosives in the non-Malayic languages of Borneo.

In most MPSEA languages with implosives, there is evidence that implosion arose as a natural development of plain voiced stops, sometimes in conditioned environments (before certain vowels, in stressed positions, etc.). For example, in Hawu, we find *ɓare*, *ɓari* 'change; repent' < *baliw, *ɗara* 'in; within' < *dalem, and *ʄara* 'path; way' < *zalan. There is no evidence in the languages discussed in this section that implosion arose from clusters of glottal stop + voiced stop (or voiced stop + glottal stop). Indeed, some of the languages with full series of implosives, like Muna, lack a synchronic glottal stop, and show no historical evidence of glottal stop either.

A much rarer airstream mechanism in MPSEA languages is the glottalic egressive one, used in the production of ejective consonants. In ejectives, the glottis is closed, creating a body of air in the vocal tract that is then put in motion by an upward movement of the glottis. The typical ejective is voiceless (due to closed vocal folds), with a strong release burst due to the heightened intra-oral air pressure created by the raising of the glottis. The acoustic intensity of release in ejectives is inversely proportional to the volume of air trapped within the oral cavity: velar ejectives have high amplitude bursts, due to higher compression, while labial ejectives, with more intra-oral air volume, have the weakest bursts. These phonetic factors help explain why, cross-linguistically, ejectives are more common with dorsal place of articulation than labial.

Contrastive ejectives have been described for only one MPSEA language, Waima'a, spoken by about 3,000 people living on the northeastern coast of East Timor (Hajek and Bowden 2002), though some preglottalized consonants are also described for closely related Naueti (Veloso 2016). Waima'a has five vowels /i u e o a/ and thirty-one consonants /p t k ʔ $p^h$ $t^h$ $k^h$ p' t' k' b d g f s h s' m n $m^h$ $n^h$ m' n' l $l^h$ l' r r' w $w^h$ w'/ (where [$^h$] marks stop aspiration and sonorant voicelessness) making it one of the biggest overall inventories in the Lesser Sundas (Blust 2013a: 194–5). Since ejectives had only been reported for one other Austronesian language, Yapese (Blust 1980d; Hsu 1969; Jensen 1977), and since Hull (2002) described the Waima'a sounds as preglottalized, the acoustic, articulatory, and aerodynamic aspects of the Waima'a sounds were carefully studied (Hajek and Bowden 2002). The resulting analysis is that ejectives are contrastive sounds in Waima'a: "They are articulated clearly and in a manner that is consistent with the phonetic description provided by Ladefoged and Maddieson (1996) and Laver (1994), among others. While there is complete closure of the oral cavity, there is simultaneous closure and raising of the larynx. The latter results in compression in the oral cavity. Oral closure is then released, triggering a stop burst that is markedly louder and stronger than that found in other kinds of stops. The acoustic effect is of a loud pop on release." (Hajek and Bowden 2002: 223). Subsequent work on acoustic properties of ejectives in Waima'a, including their status as tense vs. lax, includes Stevens and Hajek (2004, 2008); and Hajek and Stevens (2005).

Of the 567 languages included in the survey of glottalized consonants in the World Atlas of Language Structures (WALS) (Maddieson 2013a), 409 had no glottalized consonants at all, while ninety-five had ejectives (17%). What is curious, and demanding of explanation, is why ejectives, which occur in about 17% of the world's languages, are not more common within the Austronesian family.

Two known sources of ejective evolution are conditioned or context-free Tʔ > T', ʔT > T', or T > T' (T a plosive), where, in most cases, there is evidence of contact with another language that has ejectives (Blevins 2017). Since many MPSEA languages have phonemic /ʔ/, and many have derived Tʔ or ʔT clusters, ejectives might be expected. However, there is no known contact between any Austronesian language and other languages that have ejectives. While it is tempting to attribute the evolution of ejectives in Waima'a to contact with a non-Austronesian language which might have these sounds, no such languages are known in the geographic area. Makasae, the closest non-Austronesian neighbour shows the same five vowel system, but a simple (native) consonant system /f t k b d g s h m n l ɾ w ʔ/, with loan phonemes /p v z ʃ ʒ ɲ ʎ r/ (Correia 2011: 7–8). Casting a wider geographic net, with the exception of Waima'a and Yapese, ejectives appear to be absent throughout the Austronesian speaking world: there are no ejectives in the Austroasiatic languages of the Southeast Asia mainland, nor are there any in Papuan languages of New Guinea and surrounding islands. Given this, the historical origin of Waima'a ejectives is of great importance to typologists. If these sounds evolved without exposure to ejectives in other languages, what internal factors gave rise to the change? Did contact play a less direct role? Could it be that the majority of the 17% of the world's languages with ejectives have them as a consequence of contact-induced change, and that the Austronesian language family, with 2/1,000+ instances represents the true low frequency of ejective evolution as an internal change? Further study of Waima'a synchronic and diachronic phonology, as well as the phonology of closely related Naueti, Kairui, and Midiki, may lead to answers to some of these questions. Indeed, a recent study by Schapper (2020a) presents evidence that at least some of the aspirates and ejectives in Waima'a arose from historical *h-C and *ʔ-C clusters respectively, where *h- < *pa- and *ʔ- < *ka- (see also Schapper and Zobel, this volume, §35.2.2 on Waima'a consonants).

In sum, MPSEA languages show three distinct airstream mechanisms: pulmonic egressive, glottalic ingressive (implosive), and glottalic egressive (ejective). There are no known velaric ingressive (click) sounds in these languages.

### 41.2.2 Laryngeal contrasts

Proto-Austronesian and Proto-Malayo-Polynesian are reconstructed with two series of obstruents: a voiceless unaspirated series and a voiced series. Unsurprisingly, the majority of MPSEA languages that inform these reconstructions show the same two types of oral stops: voiceless unaspirated and voiced. Given the many ways that voicing contrasts can be phonetically realized, it is important to observe that the majority of MPSEA languages are true 'voicing' languages, not 'aspiration' languages: in true voicing languages, plain voiceless fortis plosives (e.g. [p, t, k]) contrast with lenis plosives (e.g. [b, d, g]) that are generally prevoiced across phonetic contexts (Jansen 2004: 1–2). The classification of MPSEA languages as true voicing languages is important for several reasons.

First, it has been argued by Ohala (1983, 2011, 2018) and others that preferences for voiceless obstruents (especially fricatives) are due to the greater articulatory effort necessary for the production of actively voiced obstruents. Under these accounts, obstruent voicing requires some sort of active articulatory enhancement that is absent in the production of voiceless obstruents: enhancing gestures serve to augment the size of the oral cavity behind the constriction, thereby lowering supraglottal air pressure that would otherwise inhibit vocal fold vibration. The classification of MPSEA languages as true voicing languages, then, allows us to understand why some MPSEA languages show tendencies for voiced obstruents to become implosives, as discussed in §41.2.1: larynx lowering is one active articulatory strategy used to facilitate obstruent voicing.

A second feature of actively voiced stops is that they are typically accompanied by $F_0/F_1$ lowering (Jansen 2004: 53). This property allows us to better understand several unusual sound patterns involving voiced obstruents in MPSEA languages. Since breathy phonation is consistently associated with lower $F_0$ in many languages (Hombert et al. 1979), the development of breathy phonation as an enhancement of typical $F_0$ lowering associated with active voicing might be expected. And since active voicing is accompanied by $F_1$ lowering as well, enhancement of this feature could result in effects on the quality of a following vowel. In Javanese and Madurese, patterns of this kind are in evidence. In Javanese, the voiced obstruents /b, d, ḍ, j, g/ are produced with breathy voice or murmur, and/or 'slack voice' in the following vowel (Ladefoged and Maddieson 1996: 63), while in Madurese, historically voiced stops developed into 'voiced aspirates' (Stevens 1968: 16), sounds that are phonetically voiceless aspirated stops. In both languages there are vowel splits, with at least some apparently triggered by the historically voiced series (Cohn 1993b). Another sound pattern that may be explained in terms of the phonetics of actively voiced stops are conditions of vowel breaking in Dalat Melanau, and other languages of the Melanau dialect chain of Sarawak with similar sound patterns. As described by Blust (2013a: 265–6) the vowels /i/ and /u/ are pronounced with mid-central offglides before final /k/ and /ŋ/, but not before /g/. For example, we find Dalat Melanau *titik* [titíjək] 'drop of liquid', *buk* [búwək] 'head hair', but *lilig* [lilíg] 'tree resin', *tug* [tug] 'heel'. According to Blust (op cit.) "A similar limitation on breaking with a mid-central offglide before final *k* and *ŋ* but not before final *g* is found in all known languages of Sarawak that preserve a voicing distinction in final stops." In this case, coarticulatory effects of a final velar include raising of $F_1$, resulting in the centralized offglide. The absence of breaking before /g/ can be attributed to $F_1$ lowering associated with active voicing. Finally, the somewhat mysterious process of low vowel fronting (Blust 2000c, 2013a: 670–2) may also relate to the phonetics of MPSEA obstruent voicing. In some languages of northern Sarawak and the Pacific coast of Luzon, voiced stops trigger a shift of /a/ to /e/ or /i/. While the non-local features of these sound patterns are puzzling, the $F_1$ lowering effect of obstruent voicing could be one phonetic factor in the raising of /a/.

A third reason to recognize active voicing in MPSEA languages is for its apparent strength across time. Of the hundreds of MPSEA languages described to date, at least twenty-one exhibit evidence of word-final obstruent devoicing (Blust 2013a: 620–6), but only one, South Nuaulu, seems to have lost the voicing contrast altogether. South Nuaulu, spoken in south central Seram, has eleven consonants /p t k s h m n r l w y/, with a single series of voiceless unaspirated obstruents (Bolton 1990: 14–17). (But even in South Nuaulu, there is no evidence that the voiced series merged with the voiceless. Rather, for *b and *d, there is evidence of extreme lenition, as e.g. *ua* < *dua 'two', *haka* < *baŋkaq 'canoe'.) Languages like South Nuaulu, without obstruent voicing contrasts, have a great deal to offer to our understanding of laryngeal sound patterns. Based on broad typological surveys, it is widely believed that the default laryngeal setting for obstruents is voiceless unaspirated. However, Kakadelis (2018) demonstrates that other default settings are possible, including active voicing and mixed systems (voiced bilabial, voiceless non-bilabial oral stops). In this context, an interesting feature of South Nuaulu is the limited distribution of contextual allophonic voicing: word-medially after /n/, /p/ is variably voiced to [b], where this voiced stop "often has an implosive quality" (Bolton 1990: 33), while /k/ and /t/ fail to voice in the same context. This is exactly the expected pattern given the aerodynamics of voicing (Ohala 1983, 2011, 2018). However, South Nuaulu is a rare exception among sister languages.

Another remarkable property of some MPSEA languages is consonant systems with more voiced plosives than voiceless ones: in the Philippines, Atta Pamplona, Isinai, Samal, Tausug, Surigao Manobo, and Sama Bangingi, have three voiceless stops /p t k/ and four voiced stop /b d j g/ (Reid 1971). The same is true of Bintulu of northern Sarawak (Blust 2013a: 182), and Toba Batak of northern Sumatra (Nababan 1981).

In at least one MPSEA language, Malagasy, an incipient tonal contrast is analysed as a consequence of fundamental frequency effects of obstruent voicing (Howe 2017). Acoustic and perceptual evidence suggests that low tones develop after voiced obstruents, while high tones develop after voiceless obstruents in Central dialects of Malagasy (Howe 2017). Since tone is not a segmental feature, this sound pattern is not discussed further in this chapter.

Finally, some highly unusual allophonic patterns are found for voiced obstruents in some languages of northern Luzon. In Guinaang Bontok, /b d g/ are pronounced as voiced stops [b], [d], [g] in syllable coda position, but as [f], [ts] and [k$^{h}$] respectively in syllable onset position, and a similar pattern is found in Balangao, but with /d/ produced as [t͡ʃ] in the onset. In Kalinga /b d g/ are also produced as [b], [d], [g] syllable-finally, but /b/ has allophones [p$^{y}$] (/_a), [p͡ɸ] in the onset, while /d/ is pronounced as [t͡ʃ] or [d͡ʒ] and /g/ as [g] or [k] in the same position.

Overall, the obstruent voicing contrast in MPSEA languages is robust. It has been maintained for thousands of years in nearly all languages, and has been enhanced in some by implosion, breathiness, and perhaps also adjacent vowel quality.

Additional laryngeal series, including aspirated obstruents, voiceless sonorants, glottalized (but non-implosive, non-ejective) obstruents, glottalized sonorants, and breathy voiced (or murmured) obstruents and sonorants have also been described for some MPSEA languages. I begin with instances which appear to be primarily internal developments, and not the result of obvious contact. The extraordinary ejectives of Waima'a, discussed in §41.2.1, occur with a full series of glottalized sonorants, aspirated stops, and voiceless sonorants: /p t k ʔ p$^{h}$ t$^{h}$ k$^{h}$ p' t' k' b d g f s h s' m n m$^{h}$ n$^{h}$ m' n' l l$^{h}$ l' r r' w w$^{h}$ w'/. Given the absence of any of these segment types in languages of the region, the innovative laryngeal series may constitute an internal development, with the most likely potential source being clusters with /ʔ/ or /h/ (Donohue 2003; Schapper 2020a). Southern Subanen, a language of the Philippines, also has a full series of aspirated obstruents, with consonants /p t k ʔ p$^{h}$ t$^{h}$ k$^{h}$ b d g s s$^{h}$ h m n ŋ l r w y/. In Southern Subanen, aspirates contrast with their plain voiceless counterparts, except for /k/, which occurs in the coda, in complementary distribution with /k$^{h}$/, which is always prevocalic (Lobel and Hall 2010). As detailed in Lobel and Hall (2010), all aspirates derive from historical *CC clusters. While intermediate stages can be debated, Proto-Subanen *kp, *kt, *ks, and *kk/*gk > /p$^{h}$/, /t$^{h}$/, /s$^{h}$/, and /k$^{h}$/ respectively. Since an independent sound change of *k > h/_V is proposed, and all clusters have *k as a component, it is tempting to see the development of aspiration as a consequence of fusion in *hT or *Th clusters, where T is a voiceless obstruent. Lobel and Hall (2010) take a different view, where the Proto-Subanen clusters undergo total assimilation, yielding voiceless geminates which then shift to post-aspirated consonants. While the development appears to be wholly internal, Lobel and Hall (2010) raise an important typological question: since many related languages have similar cluster types, why is this the only known development of aspirated stops among the almost 190 Philippine languages? The authors suggest that this is just one of a group of unusual developments for consonant clusters in an area including western and southern Mindanao and northern and western Borneo (Lobel and Hall 2010: 336–7). Since this area is notable for an early trading port with ties to China, Borneo, Malaka, and other parts of Mainland Southeast Asia, it is possible that contact played a major role in this development (op cit.). In one other Philippine language, Maranao, clusters give rise to a consonant series with distinct laryngeal properties. The 'heavy' consonants of Maranao, /p' t' k' s'/, derive from Proto-Danaw *bp, *dt, *gk, and *ds, respectively and have phonetic realizations similar to the aspirated stops of Madurese (Lobel and Riwarung 2009; Lobel 2013a): these heavy consonants have a stronger release than their light counterparts, show aspiration in certain contexts, and, like the Madurese aspirates, result in obligatory tensing and raising of following vowels. Here again, we see the potential force of obstruent voicing: though the heavy series itself is voiceless, the obstruent voicing of the initial members of the protoclusters may persist in lowering effects on following vowels. Southern Subanen aspirates and Maranao heavy consonants both occur word-initially in languages which disallow initial consonant clusters, and hence, are arguably single segments. The 'voiced aspirates' /b$^{h}$ d$^{h}$ g$^{h}$/ described for several Kelabit dialects (Blust 2006, 2016), on the other hand, only occur word-medially following stressed vowels, are about twice as long as /b d g/, correspond to *-bp-*, *-dt-*, *-kg-* in related Begak, and appear to reflect earlier *-bb-, *-dd-, and *-gg- respectively (Blust 2013a: 675–6).

Kelabit voiced aspirates begin voiced and end voiceless, with voicelessness continuing into the following vowel for some speakers. Though Blust (2006, 2013a: 67, 183–4, 256–7, 674–6; 738–9; 2016) provides several arguments for a unit-phoneme analysis of Kelabit voiced aspirates, including high-vowel laxing which does not take place before voiced aspirates, stress patterns could be seen to argue for a cluster analysis. Kelabit stress regularly falls on the penultimate vowel. If the penult is schwa, and the post-tonic consonant is a flap, stress shifts to the final syllable; if the post-tonic consonant is anything but a voiced aspirate, it geminates; and if the post-tonic consonant is a voiced aspirate, no change occurs (Blust 2013a: 256–7). However, whether one adopts a unit phoneme analysis for Kelabit voiced aspirates, or a cluster analysis, the pattern seen above for obstruent voicing holds true: despite the aerodynamic effort involved in maintaining obstruent voicing for significant duration, obstruent voicing in MPSEA languages is strong, persistent, and often enhanced by phonetic developments related to the $F_0/F_1$ lowering effects of actively voiced stops.

In contrast to the seeming internal developments discussed above, some MPSEA languages have additional laryngeal series that are arguably the result of contact. The most striking examples of this are in Chamic languages that have had extensive contact with Mon-Khmer languages, developing aspirated stops, (pre)glottalized stops, and breathy voiced stops (Thurgood 1999). For example, Phan Rang Cham has five distinct laryngeal series: plain voiceless /p t c k/; aspirated /pʰ tʰ cʰ kʰ/; voiced /b d j g/; breathy voiced /bʰ dʰ jʰ gʰ/; and glottalized /ɓ ɗ ʔj/. More subtle effects on laryngeal contrasts can also be seen. Though Durie (1985: 10) describes Acehnese as having voiceless unaspirated /p t c k/ and voiced /b d j g/ series of stops, allophones of the first series include aspirated stops, while allophones of the second include murmured stops. Since this kind of allophony is rare outside of the Mon-Khmer contact zone, it is attributed to contact effects. Developments of voiced obstruents into Javanese breathy murmured stops and Madurese voiced aspirates were mentioned above. They appear to be enhanced instances of the historically voiced series and could be due to the influence of the breathy voiced or murmured series of stops in Sanskrit.

Recall from the general discussion above that preference for voiceless obstruents, especially fricatives, is due to the greater articulatory effort necessary for the production of actively voiced obstruents (Ohala 1983, 2011, 2018). In this context, it is noteworthy that, outside of loanwords, very few MPSEA languages have developed a voiced /z/ to pair with inherited /s/. Exceptional cases include /z/ < (*dz) < *y in: Ngadha and Riung; Kadazan Dusun, Bintulu, and Òma Lóngh (Blust 2007b); Malagasy; and Agta, Ibanag, Mamanwa, and Western Bukidnon Manobo; though /z/ may have other historical sources in these languages as well. The majority of MPSEA languages preserve the single sibilant system of PMP. It has long been thought that speech sounds tend to be organized by a principle of feature economy according to which languages maximize the combinatory possibilities of a few phonological features to generate large numbers of speech sounds (de Groot 1931; Martinet 1955; Clements 2003a, b). If this were the case, languages with isolated contrastive segments should show a diachronic tendency to eliminate these isolated segments, or to acquire additional segments making use of the same contrast. MPSEA /s/ is an isolated segment in many languages: whether treated as a contrastive continuant or strident, it is often the only fricative (Blevins 2005a). Yet, despite the robust role of voicing in the oral stop series, /z/ is not a common addition to these inventories, nor is there a tendency to eliminate /s/. At least where sibilants are concerned, phonetic accounts invoking the additional articulatory effort needed to voice these sounds are better able to explain the frequency of /s/ and rarity of /z/, where principles of feature economy incorrectly predict more languages with /s/ vs. /z/ contrasts.

In sum, the great majority of MPSEA languages have a single laryngeal contrast between voiceless unaspirated and actively voiced plosives. This laryngeal contrast is maintained, often with enhancement, in almost every known MPSEA language. Despite this, most of these same languages have a single voiceless sibilant /s/ with no voiced counterpart. Additional laryngeal series are the consequence of internal developments, as well as contact-induced change, and cover all known laryngeal contrasts.

### 41.2.3 Place contrasts

Proto-Malayo-Polynesian is reconstructed with consonants at eleven distinct places of articulation: labial *p, *b, *m; dental/post-dental *t; alveolar *d, *n, *l, *r; alveopalatal/palatal *c, *z; retroflex *D (limited to word-final position); palatal *ñ, *y; palatalized velar *j; velar *k, *g, *ŋ; labiovelar *w; uvular *q, *R; and glottal *h (Blust 2009c, 2013a). (PMP *s is not included as its place of articulation is unclear: it was some kind of coronal sibilant, but may have been pronounced anywhere in the dental-to-alveopalatal area.) While it is not surprising that MPSEA languages show most of the same points of articulation, two aspects of the distribution of place contrasts are typologically remarkable.

First, the typologically rare contrast between a dental/post-dental /t̪/ and an alveolar /d/ is a feature found widely dispersed among MPSEA languages, with Henderson (1965: 420–1) suggesting it as an areal feature common to many Southeast Asian languages. It should be stressed here that what makes the MPSEA system unusual is not the place contrast alone: dozens of Australian Aboriginal languages have a laminal vs. apical contrast in the dental–alveolar region. Rather, it is the alignment of this place contrast with the voicing contrast that is unusual. In the case of coronal stops /t/ and /d/, the voicing contrast is coupled with a difference in place of articulation: /t/ is dental/postdental but /d/ is alveolar, or /t/ is dental/alveolar and /d/ is post-alveolar (Blust 2013a: 172). In most languages showing this difference, /d/ patterns together with /n/ and /l/, which are also retracted with respect to /t̪/, leaving /t̪/ as the only dental/postdental in the language. For example, in Malay /t/ and /d/ are described by Alieva et al. (1972: 34) as "... voiceless and voiced apical stops... produced by raising the tongue-tip, which for *t* is pressed against the upper teeth, whereas for *d* it is pressed against the alveolar ridge", with /n/ "an alveolar nasal... homorganic with *d*... which becomes supradental when prenasalized to *t*" (op cit, p.36). Since the IPA has no standard symbols for these differences with both /t/ and /d/ able to represent dental, alveolar, or post-alveolar stops, and since the differences may not be salient to those writing grammatical descriptions, we may imagine that these contrasts are underreported. Nevertheless, there is an indication from several distinct areas and subgroups of MPSEA languages that the pattern is widespread. Blust (2013a) mentions Javanese, two languages of South Sulawesi, and two languages of Timor. Javanese has a voiceless postdental /t̪/ and a voiced alveolar /d/, but (possibly due to the influence of Sanskrit retroflexion) has added a voiced postdental stop and a voiceless alveolar so that, for each place of articulation, there is both a voiced and voiceless stop (Blust 2013a: 191). From South Sulawesi there are also descriptions of postdental /t/ but alveolar /d/ for Selayarese (Mithun and Basri 1986: 214), and Barang-Barang (Laidig and Maingak 1999: 80). Solor Lamaholot is described with /t/ a dental stop, and /d/ an alveolar stop (Kroon 2016: 38). Uab Meto has dental /t/ with alveolar /n/ and /l/ (there is no /d/) (Steinhauer 1993: 131). And in East Timor, Hajek and Bowden (2002: 223, fn.3) note for Waima'a that "As in many other East Timorese languages, e.g. Tetun, voiced *d* tends to be retracted to post-alveolar place, in contrast to the dental for alveolar articulation of voiceless coronals." To these languages, we can add several others. On Sabu Island, just west of Timor, the Hawu language is described with /t/ a voiceless dental stop, /d/ a plain voiced alveolar stop, and alveolar /n/, /l/, and /r/, though a phoneme chart collapses these into one column labelled "alveo-dental" (Walker 1982: 5). In Muna, /t/ is described as apico-dental and /d/ as apico-alveolar, neither to be confused with /d̪/ written, a voiced lamino-dental plosive that is only found in loanwords (van den Berg 1989: 19).

In an areal and typological study of these and other coronal contrasts, Donohue (2009: 278) remarks that "reports of this contrast are lacking for languages in the Philippines", and on the same page, in a footnote, quotes a reviewer's note that "[t]he picture for the Philippines may be largely a result of under-reporting". This same reviewer mentions Aklanon as a language with a dental /t/ vs. alveolar /d/ contrast. Another Philippine language with a similar contrast is Maranao of the Danaw group, as described by Lobel (2013a: 285–6). Maranao consonant phonemes include dental /t, t'/ and alveolar /d s s' n r l/, where /t'/ and /s'/ are members of the 'heavy' consonant series described in §41.2.2. To date, at least one palatographic investigation has been carried out on a Northern Philippine language. Santiago (2010) used static palatography to describe Kalanguya coronals, where this technique involves painting the upper surface of the tongue, having the speaker produce words with coronals, and then, taking pictures of the upper surface of the mouth. Static palatograms of intervocalic /t/, /d/, /n/, and /l/ show clear differences in both place and apical/laminal contact. Together, palatograms and linguograms result in classification of /t/ as apico-laminal denti-alveolar, /d/ and /l/ as apical alveolar, and /n/ as apical denti-alveolar. In terms of standard phonological features, /t/ would appear to be laminal, while /d, l, n/ are apical. Tausug (Suluk) also has a dental /t/, but alveolar /d n l s/ (Soderberg, Ashley, and Olson 2012). A slightly different subcategorization of coronals is found in Capiznon (aka Kinapisnon, Western Bisayan), where /t/ and /d/ are both described as dental, but /s, n, r, l/ are classified as alveolar (Pototanon and Rosero 2012), and in Arta (Kimoto 2017a: 33), where /t/ is alveolar but /d, l, n/ are post-alveolar. Contrasts between lamino-dental and apico-alveolar consonants are widespread in Australia, and may be appropriate categories for distinguishing common contrasts between interdental fricatives and dental/alveolar sibilants. The unique aspect of MPSEA languages is the occurence of this place contrast in systems where only one segment, usually /t/, has the laminal specification. Recall that under Feature Economy, languages with isolated contrastive segments should show a diachronic tendency to eliminate these isolated segments, or to acquire additional segments making use of the same contrast. Javanese appears to have acquired additional segments, but the Philippine data above suggest that /t/ may be the only consonant with a lamino-dental place of articulation in these inventories. Finally, there is some evidence that the dental /t/ vs. alveolar /d/, /n/ contrast may be reconstructable as far back as Proto-Malayo-Polynesian. Chrétien's (1965) study of PMP disyllabic lexemes includes a constraint against homorganic consonants: an initial stop was not followed by a homorganic nasal or a homorganic stop which did not agree in voicing. Adelaar (1983, 1992a) points out that this constraint did not apply to combinations involving *t and *n/*d. He also notes that Malayic varieties distinguish different articulation places for reflexes of *t and *n/*d, suggesting that Proto-Malayic must have had similar dissociations. The lack of homorganicity constraints can be accounted for by reconstructing distinct places of articulation: PMP *t as dental and PMP *d, *n as alveolar. In some languages, such as Malagasy and Ma'anyan, /t/, /d/, and /n/ have the same place of articulation, denti-alveolar for Malagasy (Howe 2017) and alveolar for Ma'anyan (Gudai 1985), suggesting a historical place merger. This merger may be related to allophonic distribution: Thomas-Fattier (1982: 28–9, 31) reports that, at least for North Sakalava, /t, d, n/ are produced as dentals before /i, e, a/ but as alveolars before /o, u/.

The second remarkable feature of MPSEA languages is the near-absence of uvular reflexes of *q, and, as a consequence, the absence of a velar/uvular place contrast for oral stops, despite its retention in all major subgroups. There is widespread agreement that PMP had a contrast between *k and *q in all positions: *qaCay 'liver' vs. *kaCu 'send'; *taq(a,e)n 'set trap' vs. *kaen 'eat'; *utaq 'vomit' vs. *aNak 'child'. There is also consensus that PAN *q is continued as *q in Proto-Malayo-Polynesian, Proto-Central/Eastern Malayo-Polynesian, Proto-Central-Malayo-Polynesian, Proto-Eastern-Malayo-Polynesian, Proto-South-Halmahera–West New Guinea, and Proto-Oceanic. However, among the approximately 800 MPSEA languages, there appears to be only one with a uvular reflex of *q. The language is Muna, of the Muna-Buton group of southeast Sulawesi (van den Berg 1989, 1991b, 1996b, 2003). In Muna, the reflex of PMP *q, is a voiced uvular fricative [ʁ]: Muna *ʁate* < PMP *qatay 'liver' (cf. Paiwan *qatsay*); Muna *ʁabu* < PMP *qabu 'ash' (cf. Paiwan *qavu*); Muna taʁi 'dregs' < PMP *taqi 'faeces' (cf. Paiwan *tsaqi*). As a consequence, Muna continues an ancient place contrast between velar and uvular stops, modulated by manner differences of voicing and continuancy as in ***ʁ**ulu* 'body' vs. *kuli* 'skin' (cf. PMP *qulu 'head', *kulit 'skin') or *ta**ʁ**i* 'dregs' vs. *saki* 'sick' (cf. PMP *taqi 'feces', *sakit 'sick'). Uvulars are not common segments, but they are found in about 16–20% of the world's languages (Maddieson 2013e). Further, in Maddieson's survey of uvular consonants, of the ninety-seven (of 576) languages that had contrastive uvulars, eighty-six had uvular stops. Given that uvular reflexes of PAN *q occur in Formosan languages, there is a conundrum: why do fewer than 1% of MPSEA languages have a uvular reflex of *q? Or, in synchronic terms, why are there no MPSEA languages with a /k/ vs. /q/ contrast, when this contrast occurs in at least 16% of the world's languages, and is thought to have existed in all the languages ancestral to these? For further discussion, see Blevins (2021).

In this context, it is important to note that some MPSEA languages do have a class of voiceless uvular stops, though, they typically do not contrast with velars. Jacobson (1979) finds so-called 'velar' stops quite regularly produced as uvulars in some Philippine languages, Reid (2005) confirms this, noting that uvular [q] is "the usual point of articulation of /k/ in many Philippine languages", and Reid (2020: 376) repeats this in highlighting the uvular or backed quality of /k/ in a range of Philippine languages, including Tboli, Tagbanwa, Tagalog, Hiligaynon, and Ibaloi. Jacobson (1979) reports a regular voiceless uvular stop (or 'backed velar') for Batad Ifugao, Balangao, Guinaang Kalinga, Keley-i Kallahan, Pangasinan, Tausug, and Blaan. Recent phonetic work supports basic /q/ for Kalanguya. Santiago (2010) uses acoustic data to show that Kalanguya /k/ is produced as a uvular [q] in all vocalic environments examined. Reid (2005) adds that in Guinaang Bontok, there is a clear difference between the point of articulation of the prevocalic allophone of /g/, which is a fronted velar or palatal stop, and its voiceless counterpart /k/, which is always [q]. This is interesting in the context of the earlier discussion of dental /t/ vs. alveolar /d/, since uvular /k/ vs. palatal/velar /g/ may also be seen as enhancing the voicing contrast. But, by far, the most perplexing typological fact in this area is Jacobson's (1979) report that /k/ and /q/ contrast in Ibaloi. Two pieces of evidence support this. First, 'Writing in my own language Inibaloi' (The Inibaloi Scripture Translation Project, no date), highlights the /k/ vs. /q/ contrast, stating that the two are separate phonemes as indicated by minimal pairs: *kapkap* 'to slice something' vs. *qapqap* 'to grope' (cf. PWMP *kapkap 'grope'); *kalkal* 'to chew something' vs. *qalqal* 'to search through something' (cf. PWMP *karkar 'scratch up the earth, as a fowl'). (In their orthography, they represent the velar /k/ as <kh> and uvular /q/ as /k/). Second, in a recent phonetic study Talavera, Matsushita, and Pelagio (2013) provide initial acoustic support for a /k/ vs. /q/ contrast in Ibaloi. At present, the /k/ vs. /q/ contrast in Ibaloi is the only known instance of a pure velar vs. uvular place contrast for oral stops among MPSEA languages. However, it should be emphasized that this contrast does not continue an earlier velar vs. uvular contrast: from the evidence available, it appears that Ibaloi *q* < *k, while PMP *q has been lost (Blust and Trussel 2020). Another MPSEA language with a reported voiceless uvular stop is Embaloh (aka Maloh), a South Sulawesi language of West Kalimantan, where PMP *k is continued as <k> which is realized as a uvular before /i/, but /g/ is velar (Adelaar 1995e). (In Embaloh, PMP *-q is continued as glottal stop or became Ø.)

Compared to uvulars, found in at least 16% of the world's languages, coronal retroflex sounds are rare, with /ʈ/ occurring in only 8.4 % of the UPSID 317 language sample, /ɖ/ occurring in 7.2%, and other retroflex sounds in less than 6% of the database (Maddieson 1984). Though PAN and PMP are reconstructed with *D, thought to represent a voiced retroflex stop, this sound is limited to final position, found in a small number of lexemes (some with doublets), and unpaired with any other retroflex phoneme. If it was a retroflex, it was carrying a low functional load, so it is not surprising that it merged with other coronals in all MPSEA languages (see Blust 2013a: 575–6 for further discussion). The only MPSEA language reported to have a retroflex contrast in coronal stops (outside of clear borrowings) is Javanese, with voiced and voiceless dental vs. retroflex stops; retroflex segments in Balinese and Madurese are likely due to Javanese influence (Blust 2013a: 78, 192). Whether Javanese retroflexion is attributed wholly to Sanskrit contact, a natural development of the dental /t/ vs. alveolar /d/ precursor, an extension of earlier sound symbolism, or some combination of these factors, continues to be debated (Blust 2013a: 191–2, 567, 575–7). What seems clear, given the rarity of retroflexion elsewhere in MPSEA languages, is that Sanskrit contact played some role. Though Blust (2013a: 191) concludes that "the hypothesis of an Indic origin for Javanese ṭ and ḍ is not convincing", Blevins' (2017) model of contact-induced regular sound change under perceptual magnet effects may provide an explanation for many features of the Javanese sound pattern. Within the model, salient phones in a contact language—in this case the Indic retroflexes—act as external perceptual magnets, drawing native Javanese sounds that are similar towards them. The outcome can look like regular sound change, but, in a typological context, can be distinguished from it, since such sound changes never (or rarely) occur as natural internal developments. Purely internal developments leading to retroflex/non-retroflex contrasts in coronals are rare: in Sangiric languages a contrastive retroflexed lateral flap originated as a conditioned allophone of *l in the context of back vowels (Sneddon 1984: 41–2). In Talaud, one of the Sangiric languages, /s/ contrasts with a voiced retroflex fricative /ʐ/ (< PMP *R), a sound that is also described for Tombulu (Sneddon 1978: 20) and for Western Bukidnon Manobo. In many languages where /d/ is realized as a voiced implosive, the articulation is retracted to post-alveolar or retroflex, as described for Bima, Ngadha, and Wolio (Blust 2013a: 88, 194).

Labio-dentals /f/ and /v/ are rare in MPSEA languages. Where /f/ occurs, it is sometimes a lenited *p, as in Blaan (Koronadal and Sarangani) and Tboli (Reid 1971), but in other cases a lenited *b or a strengthened *w. Northern Sarawak languages show both developments: Kiput has /$f^w$/ (< *w), while Narum, Miri, and other Lower Baram languages show /f/ (< *$b^h$), where Bintulu has /v/ (Blust 2013a: 182, 185, 556, 612, 675–6). Languages with /v/ but no /f/ (or /f/ limited to loans) include Isinai, Itbayaten, Ivatan, and Western Bukidnon Manobo (Reid 1971). Ibanag and Agta are exceptional in having an /f/ vs. /v/ contrast (Reid 1971), and the same contrast is found in Malagasy, where /f/ vs. /v/ (< *w) continues lenited Proto-Malayo-Polynesian *p vs. *b.

To date, there is no known reported case of a contrastive pharyngeal place of articulation in a MPSEA language, though some Malay dialects have non-contrastive pharyngeal fricatives where other varieties have /h/.

In contrast to their common occurrence in Oceanic, contrastive secondary features of labialization, palatalization, or velarization across a series of consonants are not found in MPSEA languages, though the occasional segment is labialized, labiovelarized, or palatalized. Alune and Dobel of the Moluccas have /$k^w$/; Kejaman and Beketan of south-central Sarawak have /$g^w$/; Chamorro has /$g^w$/; Kiput in northern Sarawak has /$f^w$/; and Yamdena of the southern Moluccas has /gb/, a labio-velar stop in place of /g/. Non-contrastive palatalization is also uncommon. Enggano, the language of Enggano island (the southernmost of the Barrier Islands that extend along the western coast of Sumatra), has consonants /p b t d k x ʔ m n r l h/. In Enggano, glottal stop is optionally palatalized after /i/, as in /ki-ʔu/ [kiʔu] ~ [kiʔ$^j$u] 'say', /ʔi-ʔõʔ/ [ʔĩʔõʔ] ~ [ʔĩʔ$^j$õʔ] 'there', though palatalization is not reported for any other consonant in the language (Yoder 2014). And in Malagasy, velars are described as palatalized after /i/ in Merina (Rajaonarimanana 1995), but not in Betsimisaraka (O'Neill 2015: 204–5, 235–6). The absence of palatalization as a common secondary feature may be related to the high frequency of palatal stop series, at least in the languages of Western Indonesia. Pharyngealized liquids and nasals may be variants of glottalized sonorants in Uab Meto (aka Atoni, West Timor) though Edwards (2016a) analyses glottalized consonants as consonant clusters, and word-final pharyngeal fricatives are reported as variants of laryngeals in some Malay dialects (Blust 2013a: 87, 189).

A note is in order regarding the unusual place–manner–voicing distribution of consonants in Palauan. Palauan is generally recognized as having only ten consonants: /t k ʔ b d [ð] m ŋ s l r/. This inventory is remarkable in lacking /n/, and for having only one place of articulation (/t/ vs. /d/) at which voicing is distinctive.

Finally, while most MPSEA languages continue PMP *ŋ as /ŋ/, this phoneme is strikingly absent in many languages of eastern Indonesia, and has been argued to be just one of several areal features of Wallacea as a linguistic area (Schapper 2015a).

Overall, the majority of MPSEA languages are conservative with respect to place of articulation. With the exception of the velar/uvular contrast discussed above, the place contrasts which carried the highest functional load in PAN have been maintained in most of these languages, and few new place contrasts have been introduced.

### 41.2.4 Manner contrasts

Proto-Malayo-Polynesian is reconstructed with voiceless and voiced series of oral stops (*p, *t, *k, *q, *b, *d, *D=[ɖ], *j=[gʲ], *g), two affricates (*c=[t͡ʃ], *z=[d͡ʒ]), a single sibilant fricative (*s), nasal stops (*m, *n, *ñ=[ɲ], *ŋ), a trill (*R=[r],[ʀ]), a flap (*r=[ɾ]), a lateral approximate (*l), two glides (*w, *y=[j]), and a laryngeal *h (Blust 2009c: 594–5).

In at least one language, Malagasy, the affricate and fricative inventories have increased dramatically, with four affricates written as <ts>, <tr>, <dz>, and <dr> (where <r> indicates retroflexion) and four fricatives, /s/, /z/, /f/, and /v/. Some of these innovations may be due to Bantu influence (Dahl 1954).

In Acehnese, a remarkable fricative is found in place of the garden-variety alveolar /s/. Acehnese <s> is described as a "laminal alveolar fricative with a wide channel area" (Blust 2013a: 190), produced by "holding the tongue tip in the position for English \θ\ and then, without moving the tip, raising the back part of the blade until it forms a constriction against the alveolar ridge" like a mix between English "/s/ with dental wake-turbulence but a narrow channel area (at the alveolar ridge) and /θ/ which has a wide channel area (at the teeth)" (Almurashi 2016: 49). Despite the dental articulation of /t/ in many MPSEA languages, contrastive interdental fricatives are rare. The only other known language with a contrastive sound of this type is Palauan /ð/, written <d> from PMP *t.

Several languages of the Aru islands have a voiceless bilabial fricative /ɸ/. In Dobel, /ɸ/ continues PMP *b, and contrasts with /s/, /b/, and /m/ (there is no /p/) (Blust 2014b), and in Kola (Takata and Takata 1992) /f/ (orthographic <p>) contrasts with /ɸ/ (orthographic <f>). In the Philippines, Kalagan, Cotabato Manobo, and Teduray continue *p as /ɸ/. In Biak /f/, a voiceless labiodental fricative, varies freely with [ɸ], and contrasts with /p/ and /v/ (a voiced bilabial fricative) (van den Heuvel 2006: 22).

A notable development in at least two MPSEA languages is the development of unusual trills, distinct from the standard simple alveolar [r] or uvular [ʀ]. In Muna, /bu, pu, mbu, mpu/ have trilled allophones [ʙu, ʙ̥u, mʙu, mʙ̥u] in stressed position, while Nias, a language of the Barrier Islands west of Sumatra has prenasalized bilabial and alveolar trills (Catford 1988).

Unusual flaps are the retroflexed laterals in many Sangiric languages, some Gorontalo-Mongondic languages and Tonsawang (Blust 2013a: 193).

An (inter)dental approximant, /ð̞/, occurs in at least nine languages of the Philippines, in Kalinga varieties of Northern Luzon, in Kalagan, Mandaya, and Central Bontok of the Central Philippines, and in Kagayanen of Manobo (Olson et al. 2010). Based on video and audio recordings from six of these nine languages, including five Kagayanen speakers, phonetic analysis confirms that these sounds are, indeed, central (inter)dental approximants, similar to [ð], but with much less constriction. At the phonological level, Kagayanen /ð̞/ contrasts with /d/, /t/, /l/, /r/, /n/, /y/, and /w/, and is found in native vocabulary, where it is often the reflex of PWMP *l, as in Kagayanen *ð̞að̞a* < PWMP *laja 'to weave', and *wað̞ð̞u* < PWMP *walu 'eight'. Indeed, Olson et al. (2010) suggest that, at an earlier stage of the language, dental [l̪] and [ð̞] were in complementary distribution, as they still are in the Guinaang variety of Lubuagan Kalinga, where [l] occurs in what we might call 'strengthening' environments (word-initially, in geminate clusters, in VC_V where C is a coronal consonant, and preceding [i]), while the dental approximant occurs elsewhere.

In addition to manner contrasts manifest on what are generally considered 'simple' consonants, 'complex' segments with multiple values of a single phonological feature have also been suggested for some MPSEA languages. Complex segments include prenasalized stops, post-stopped or postploded nasals, and pre-stopped or preploded nasals. Prenasalized stops as unit phonemes have been suggested for Malagasy, Javanese, Uma, Muna, Manggarai, Bima, Termanu, Kambera, and Yamdena, though it is only in the languages of Sulawesi that structural arguments for these as single segments, not clusters, are tenable (Blust 2013a: 224–8). The rare prenasalized bilabial and alveolar trills of Nias, unique to western Malayo-Polynesian languages were mentioned earlier (Catford 1988). Acehnese is reported to have medial postploded nasals (Durie 1985: 15), as is Narum of Northern Sarawak, where the segments "reflect prenasalised voiced obstruents in which the duration between velic closure and oral release is shortened until the obstruent is barely perceptible, if at all" (Blust 2013a: 242). Though typically non-contrastive with plain nasals, word-final preploded nasals are also reported for languages of Western Indonesia, mostly in Borneo, Sumatra, and Mainland Southeast Asia (Blust 2013a: 184–5, 241). In Rejang (Voorhoeve 1955: 21), preploded nasals are variants of final nasals, while in Land Dayak and other languages of Borneo they are allophones of final nasals in oral contexts (Smith 2017a: 142, 284). In Kendayan (aka Salako), the same stem-final preploded nasals occur intervocalically under suffixation (Adelaar 2005e).

### 41.2.5 Length contrasts

Proto-Malayo-Polynesian is reconstructed with limited types of medial consonant clusters, and with no consonant length contrasts. Nevertheless, many western Malayo-Polynesian languages show contrasts between short/singleton consonants and their long/geminate counterparts in medial position, and more rarely, in initial position as well. As argued by Blevins (2004a, 2005b), geminate consonant inventories typically reflect recurrent pathways of geminate evolution, mediated by phonetic aspects of production and perception, rather than universal markedness hierarchies giving preference to some types of geminates over others. Common pathways of geminate evolution include local assimilation in consonant clusters, post-tonic (or, in MPSEA languages, post-schwa) gemination, and vowel syncope between identical consonants, usually as a result of historical *CV-reduplication (Blevins 2004a: 170–83). MPSEA languages show all of these pathways, resulting in both small and large geminate inventories.

For the first pathway mentioned, where geminates evolve from local assimilation in consonant clusters, small or mid-size inventories can arise. One of the smallest geminate inventories for MPSEA languages is found in Palauan, where singletons /p t k ð s m n ŋ l r w ʔ/ are coupled with only two geminate consonants: /r:/ and /l:/. In this case, the geminates result from regressive manner assimilation in liquid clusters: *rl > ll and *lr > rr. Bigger geminate inventories as a consequence of local assimilation are found as well. In Ammacian, a Kalinga-Itneg language of northern Luzon, total assimilation of the lateral in *Cl > CC, results in voiceless geminate stops (*pikkat* < *piklat 'scar'), voiced geminate stops (*nabbaŋ* < *nablaŋ 'hard'), geminate nasals (*doŋŋon* < *doŋlon 'to hear'), and geminate laterals (e.g., *mallaŋoy* < *man-laŋoy 'to swim' (Himes 1997: 109, 132). In a few languages of Borneo, including Hliboi (Smith 2017a: 164–5) and Sa'ban (Blust 2001b), loss of an unstressed vowel in a word-initial syllable results in initial consonant clusters which then undergo total assimilation, yielding geminates in initial position only.

Tonic gemination is also a common source of contrastive gemination in MPSEA languages, especially in those languages where PMP *ə was preserved. Since *ə could not carry stress alone, a following C would be lengthened. An early stage of development can be observed in Konjo, a language of South Sulawesi (Friberg and Friberg 1991). Konjo singletons are /p t k b d g ʧ ʤ s m n ɲ ŋ r l h ʔ/, with post-tonic phonetic geminates [p: t: k: s: m: n: ɲ: ŋ: r: l:] and clusters [ʔb]~[pb], [ʔd]~[td], [ʔg]~[kg], where voiced geminates might be expected. Though Friberg and Friberg (1991: 79–80) choose to analyse all clusters as underlying /ʔC/, with total assimilation giving rise to surface geminates, they sketch an alternative analysis where geminates are underlying, subject to later pre-glottalization. Historically, ˈəCV > ˈəC:V, followed by a partial merger of *ə and *a, giving rise to geminates. Synchronically, /a/ now triggers gemination in some contexts, while geminates trigger lowering of central /ə/ to [a]: "This brings to light an interesting circularity, or rather, mutually conditioning environments. /a/ conditions gemination; gemination conditions /a/ . . . This is interesting in that historically and synchronically geminate sequences give rise to centralized [a]. Now in certain environments /a/ is geminating certain following consonantal segments" (Friberg and Friberg 1991: 92). Note that the absence of [b:], [d:], and [g:] may be related to phonetic factors: where these sounds are expected, partially voiced, or pre-glottalized segments occur, attesting to the well-known difficulty of maintaining obstruent voicing without greater articulatory effort (Ohala 1983, 2011, 2018 and related discussion in §41.2.2). See Blust (2018b) where the same aerodynamic voicing constraint is used to explain the evolution of voiced aspirates in the Kelabit and Lun Dayeh languages of Borneo.

A final common pathway of geminate evolution is that where an unstressed vowel is lost between identical consonants (Blust 2007a). Again, incipient contrasts are evident in languages where the sound change is in progress, as in Iban, where there is variation between schwa and no-schwa when abutting consonants are identical, as in *tətawak* ~ *ttawak* 'large gong' or *gəgudi* ~ *ggudi* 'a kite' (Scott 1956: vii; Blust 2007a, 2013a: 230).

MPSEA languages with geminate contrasts for every singleton are not uncommon. Languages of this type are of great interest to typologists, as investigation of phonetic properties of the geminate contrast can be assessed for different place, manner, and laryngeal features. Guinaang Bontok, with singleton consonants /p t k ʔ b d g m n ŋ l s w y/ has geminate contrasts for every singleton (Reid 1963; Aoyama and Reid 2006), allowing for an investigation of potential durational differences across manner contrasts. In an acoustic study of Guinaang Bontok geminates, Aoyama and Reid (2006) find that mean duration of singleton vs. geminate is: highest for nasals where geminates are 2.08 times longer than singletons; almost as high for liquids (1.90) and stops (1.87); and significantly lower for fricatives (1.67) and glides (1.56). Findings such as these support the view that cross-linguistic dispreferences for geminate fricatives and geminate glides may be due, in part, to perceptual factors: since the short–long ratio is smaller, there is a greater chance that length will be misperceived, with long fricatives and glides heard as short segments, or short fricatives and glides heard as long, with consequent degemination (Blevins 2004b).

While the majority of geminate consonants in MPSEA languages occur word-medially in intervocalic position, initial geminates are also attested. Languages with full series of initial geminates include Dobel of the Aru Islands (Hughes 1995), Sa'ban, and Iban of Sarawak (Blust 2007a), and Kelantan (Hamzah, Fletcher, and Hajek 2016, 2018) and Pattani Malay (Abramson 1986); in most instances, these initial geminates are the result of unstressed vowel loss between identical consonants (Blust 2007a). Since phonetic cues for the onset of stop closure duration are absent in utterance-initial position, MPSEA languages with initial geminates have been the subject of acoustic analysis and perception studies, with significant results. For example, a recent perception experiment by Hamzah, Hajek, and Fletcher (2016) manipulated length of closure duration for initial /k/ vs. /k:/, /b/ vs. /b:/, and /l/ vs. /l:/ pairs in Kelantan Malay, finding that closure duration is a robust acoustic-perceptual cue to word-initial geminate contrasts.

Given the great diversity of geminate inventories in MPSEA languages, their many historical sources, their robust attestation across time and space, and the numerous phonetic studies on them that have already informed our understanding of phonological geminate/singleton contrasts, it is striking that, in the fourteen chapters of Kubozono's (2017) edited volume, *The Phonetics and Phonology of Geminate Consonants*, there is not a single chapter focused on geminates in one or more MPSEA languages. See the following chapters in this volume for in-depth overviews of gemination in different MPSEA groups: Liao and Reid, this volume, §24.2.6 on Northern Philippine languages; Kroeger and Smith, this volume, §27.2.2.3 on non-Malayic languages in Borneo; van den Berg and Mead, this volume §33.2.3 on South Sulawesi languages.

### 41.2.6 Summary remarks on consonant inventories

Within the size classes suggested by Maddieson (2013a), consonant inventories of MPSEA languages are generally of average (22 ± 3) size, reflecting properties of the protolanguage, but range from small (6–14) to moderately large (26–33). In general, they adhere strongly to Lindblom and Maddieson's (1988) size principle which states that smaller consonant inventories will tend to include only those consonants which are inherently simpler, while more complex consonants will only be found in larger inventories. Maddieson (2013a, d) categorizes uvulars, clicks, labial-velar plosives, pharyngeals, glottalized consonants (including ejectives and implosives), and dental or alveolar non-sibilant fricatives as complex consonants, with clicks, labio-velars, pharyngeals, and dental or alveolar fricatives absent in approximately 80% of the world's languages. As we have seen in the survey above, clicks and pharyngeals are not contrastive sounds in any known MPSEA language, while contrastive uvular stops (Ibaloi only?), labial velar plosives (Yamdena only?), and dental/alveolar non-sibilant fricatives (Acehnese and Palauan only?) are extremely rare, reported for less than one percent of this language group. This last observation is perhaps surprising: given that many MPSEA languages have a dental /t/, lenition of this sound might be expected to yield an interdental non-sibilant fricative. However, as discussed by Blust (2013a: 604), despite common lenition of *p and *k to voiceless fricatives, *t "generally did not change, and when it did change it rarely lenited." As with our understanding of implosive frequency, here again, the phonetics of the PMP stop system may be of great importance. Perhaps the dental *t of PMP was not only lamino-dental, but also involved a longer closure duration than *p or *k. Segments with longer closure durations, including geminates, often resist lenition to fricatives, becoming shorter in lenition environments, but maintaining a closure duration equivalent to that necessary for plosive production. For glottalized consonants, there is a clear asymmetry in MPSEA languages: ejectives are extremely rare (Waima'a only?), but implosives are more common than expected. In §41.2.1 and §41.2.2, I suggest that the higher frequency of implosives is related to the robust property of true plosive voicing in MPSEA languages.

One final property of MPSEA consonant systems not yet mentioned are instances of phonesthemes, or submorphemic, segmental sound-meaning associations. Across the Austronesian language family, there is ample evidence for an inherited association between morpheme-initial /ŋ/ and the nasal/oral or snout region of the body, and sounds made with these bodyparts (Blust 2003a). Some Proto-Malayo-Polynesian reconstructions with initial *ŋ include *ŋek 'grunt', *ŋerŋer 'growl', *ŋijuŋ 'nose', *ŋipen 'tooth', *ŋuhuR 'nasal mucus', *ŋusuq 'nasal area; snout' (ACD, Blust and Trussel 2020).

## 41.3 Vowel inventories

Like consonant systems, vowel inventories can be studied from many different perspectives. Here we deconstruct the vowel systems of MPSEA languages in terms of traditional segmental features of quality, nasality, and length (with autosegmental features covered in Kaufman and Himmelmann, this volume, chapter 42) In examining each potential dimension of contrast, robust, common, and rare features of MPSEA languages are identified, examined in a broader typological context, and, where relevant, assessed with respect to factors that might explain their presence.

### 41.3.1 Vowel quality

Proto-Austronesian and Proto-Malayo-Polynesian are reconstructed with a four-vowel system consisting of two high vowels, *i and *u, one low vowel, *a, and one central extra-short vowel, *ə, considered unstressable. Many vowel systems of MPSEA languages are conservative in preserving this system, and Blust (2013a: 175) estimates that about half of all Philippine languages maintain the PMP four-vowel system /i u ə a/ (where the central vowel is mid-to-high, and often written /ɨ/), and many languages of Borneo maintain the system as well, while others have gone from four to six vowel systems /i u e o ə a/ with a change of PMP *-ay and *-aw > -e and -o respectively. (Massive expansion of this system occurs in some languages of Borneo, like Kelai, with nine monophthongs and nine diphthongs (Smith 2017a: 78–80) or Sa'ban with ten monophthongs (Blust 2001b).) A rare shift to three-vowel /a i u/ is found in Hulu Banjar, spoken in Banjarmasin, southern Borneo, where PMP *a merged with ə; see McDonnell et al., §29.2.1.2 this volume. In Reid's (1973) study of Philippine vowel systems based on seventy-three distinct languages/dialects, a natural evolution from Proto-Philippines *i *ɨ *u *a to /i u a/ via *ɨ > u merger appears to occur only once in the Visayan Islands, continued as the /i u a/ systems of Abaknon, Aklanon, and Cebuano (with /e, o/ developing later via Spanish contact), and the same development is found in Tausug. And in a survey of forty-three minor languages of the Philippines, only one had gone from a four-vowel /i u ə a/ to a three-vowel system (Blust 2013a: 174). Reid (1973) highlights many other important typological features. In a small number of Philippine languages, there is maintenance of the four-vowel system with peripheralization (but not neutralization) of the central vowel: in Guinaang Kalinga and Ata Manobo *ɨ > o, contrasting with u < *u; and in some Ilokano dialects and Keley-i Kallahan, *ɨ > e, contrasting with i < *i. The shift from four- to five-vowel systems is less common than expected under theories of Adaptive Dispersion (see later in this section). In the Philippines, the /i u e o a/ five-vowel systems of Atta Pamplona, Central Bikol, Ibanag, Isnag, Itawis, Kapampangan, Malaweg, and Tagalog derive from three-vowel /i u a/ systems after merger of *ɨ with a peripheral vowel. Subsequently, /e o/ develop from a combination of internal monophthongization of diphthongs and external influence of Spanish (Llamzon 1969: 14; Yap 1967: 30; Reid 1973). The only known language in the Philippines where a five vowel /i u a e o/ system appears to have developed without external influence is Ifugao as spoken in Amganad and Bayninan. In Subanon of Siocon, where o < *ɨ, and /e/ evolved from minor context-sensitive raisings and lowerings of the peripheral vowels, the *ɨ > o change is relatively recent, and could be related to Cebuano contact (where Cebuano /e o/ are due to Spanish contact.) Overall, the picture one sees in the Philippines is a fairly stable inherited MPSEA /i u a ə/ vowel quality system, where /ə/ is a central short vowel of variable quality. Where rare expansions or contractions of this system are in evidence, contact-induced change can often be seen to play a role.

The robustness of the inherited /i u a ə/ system, and its evolution, is of particular interest in the context of the theory of Adaptive Dispersion (Liljencrants and Lindblom 1972; Lindblom 1986, 1990a, b). This theory attempts to explain the structure of vowel inventories, and, more specifically, the observation that vowels tend to be evenly dispersed within the acoustic–perceptual space. The central claim is that vowels are evenly dispersed to facilitate communicative efficiency: if vowels are too close, they will be confused with each other and communication will be impaired. The theory of Adaptive Dispersion makes concrete predictions about preferred vowel systems, which should maximize distinctiveness: triangular /i u a/, peripheral five vowel /i u e o a/, and seven vowel /i u e o ɛ ɔ a/ systems should be preferred, while poorly dispersed systems like /i u a ə/ and /i u e o ə a/ should be dispreferred (Indeed, Liljencrants and Lindblom 1972 predict that an interior vowel like schwa should only appear when a system has ten or more vowels.) However, given the durational differences between /ə/ and other vowels in the system, including duration in addition to formant values would bring the model closer to making correct predictions. Further, in the context of the Philippines, one must be careful in identifying internal vs. external forces of change. As pointed out by Wolff (1968), Samar-Leyte Bisayan (aka Waray) shows what he refers to as a 'Stage I dialect' with the inherited /i u a ə/ vowel system, and a 'Stage II dialect' with an innovative /i u a/ vowel system. While an advocate of Adaptive Dispersion might jump to analyse this as an instance of internal change, spurred by forces of communicative efficiency, Wolff demonstrates that the 'Stage II dialect' is a consequence of contact with Cebuano of Cebu City, a language with an /i u a/ system. In the 'Stage II dialect' Samar-Leyte /ə/ has been replaced with /u/, and this replacement has all the hallmarks of a sociolinguistic feature, not a regular sound change.

Despite the overall conservatism of vocalism in the Philippines, and MPSEA languages more generally, three developments are relatively common in terms of expanding the number of vowel qualities. First, as already noted above, monophthongization of PMP *-ay and *-aw to *-e* and *-o* respectively give rise to contrastive mid vowels /e/

and /o/. This has occurred in languages of the Philippines (e.g. Ifugao, Kapampangan), Borneo (e.g. Kelabit, Embaloh), Sulawesi (e.g. Pamona, Wolio), Flores and its satellites (e.g. Bima), and languages of Sumatra, Bali, and Java among others. Second, vowel shifts triggered by consonant phonation, typically result in raising of /a/, and often give rise to one or more newly contrastive central vowels. Vowel changes triggered by consonant phonation include those in Madurese (Stevens 1968; Cohn 1993b), and Javanese (Fagan 1988) mentioned in §41.2.2, as well as similar splits of /a/ in Chamic (Thurgood 1999), Berawan-Lower Baram languages of Northern Sarawak (Blust 2000c), Minangkabau, and a wide range of Malay dialects, including Kerinci Malay, Tioman Malay, Kutai Malay, Natuna Malay, Bangka Malay, Sambas Malay, Orang Laut, Akit, Jambi Ulu Malay, Kubu, Tanah Tumbuh, Lubuk Kepayang, Inland Sumatra Seletan, and Bengkulu (McKinnon 2012) (see also McDonnell et al., this volume, §29.2.1.2). Third, in cases of contact with non-Austronesian languages with larger vowel systems, MPSEA languages may expand, matching vowel qualities in neighbouring languages. For example, Pang Ram Cham has eleven vowels, /i, ɨ, u, e, ĕ, ə, o, ŏ, ɛ, a, ɔ/, with this great expansion from the original four vowel system attributed to Mon-Khmer influence, and, more specifically contact with Bahnaric languages and their register differences of breathy vs. clear vowels (Thurgood 1999; Blust 2013a: 188–9).

Finally, it is worth mentioning typologically rare vowel quality systems that are found in some MPSEA languages. In Sarangani Manobo, there are three central vowels /ɨ/ written <u>, /ə/ written <e>, and /a/, but only two non-central vowels /i/ and /o/ (Reid 1973; DuBois 1976). For a five-vowel system, /i ɨ ə o a/ is highly unusual for having three central vowels, and for lacking /u/. The Agusan and Surigao varieties of Manobo are also rare five-vowel systems with two front vowels /i æ/, two central vowels /ɨ a/, and one back vowel, /u/, though, as Reid (1973) points out, it is only the addition of /æ/ (< a: < *ala, *al.) that distinguishes the /i ɨ u a æ/ system from Proto-Philippines *i *ɨ *u *a.

## 41.3.2 Vowel nasalization

Very few MPSEA languages have contrastively nasalized vowels, though many show allophonic nasalization of vowels after nasal consonants (Blust 2013a: 238–41, 267–8). Languages with allophonic nasalized vowels often show long-distance effects of a nasal consonant, with nasalization realized as a prosodic, rather than segmental, feature. In the few languages where nasalized vowels contrast with their oral counterparts, contact may be responsible. For example, Pattani Malay has twelve phonemic vowels, including four that are nasalized /i, ɨ, u, ũ, e, ɛ, ɛ̃, o, ɔ, ɔ̃, a, ã/, and is spoken in an area where Northern Aslian languages like Kensiu with fourteen oral vowels and twelve nasalized vowels, and Jahai with nine oral vowels and seven nasalized vowels are spoken. Further, nasalized vowels in Pattani Malay are often found in loanwords, suggesting they result from borrowing. A different situation is found in Flores of the Lesser Sundas. This is the only region where at least one MPSEA dialect continuum, Solor Lamaholot, shows evidence of the common sound change *VN# > Ṽ#, as in: PCMP *zalan, Solor Lamaholot *larã* 'path; road'; PCMP *hikan, Solor Lamaholot *ikã* 'fish'; PCMP *taqun, Solor Lamaholot *tũ* 'year' (Kroon 2016: 47). The same sound pattern is evident in Indonesian loans: Solor Lamaholot *sebayã* 'prayer' ≪ *sembayang*; Solor Lamaholot *dagĩ* 'meat; flesh' ≪ *daging*; *tuã* 'mister' ≪ *tuan* (Kroon 2016: 47). While Solor Lamaholot VN# > Ṽ# is generally viewed as a bizarre internal development in the context of MPSEA languages, Portuguese influence cannot be ruled out. The Lamaholot language area was one of the first places where Portuguese traders anchored in 1515 and a Portuguese presence remained in the area until the mid-nineteenth century (Kroon 2016: 7). Since Portuguese does not allow coda-nasals, and has nasalized vowels, acquisition of Solor Lamaholot by L1 speakers of Portuguese could have given rise to this sound pattern (Blevins 2017). One other language with contrastively nasalized vowels is Enggano, the language of Enggano island off the southwest coast of Sumatra. Enggano has seven oral vowels /i, e, ɨ, ə, u o, a/, and seven nasalized counterparts of these vowels (Yoder 2006/2014). Some nasalized vowels seem to continue a nasal consonant that has lenited to /h/ (or nasalized /h/) as in *dohõ-i* 'to hear' < PMP *deŋeR, while in other cases, /h/ may give rise to nasalization, as in *e-hũkũ* 'head louse' < PMP *kutu. This association between nasality and aspiration, sometimes known as rhinoglottophilia (Matisoff 1975), has been attributed to the perceptual similarity of these two features (Blevins 2004a: 135–6). A more limited case of rhinoglottophilia yields contrastive nasalized (vs. oral) vowels in Narum (Northern Sarawak), with *hããw* '2SG' < *kahu (Blust 2013a: 240) vs. *ihaw* 'elbow', *hayew* 'wood, tree', etc. Given that approximately one quarter of the world's languages show a contrast between nasalized and oral vowels (Hajek 2013), the rarity of contrastive nasalized vowels in MPSEA languages is striking, and deserving of some explanation. At present, the simplest explanation appears to be a phonetic one. Where nasal consonants occur, the tendency is for the lowered velum to persevere, not for it to be anticipated. This articulatory phonetic characteristic of MPSEA languages could be ancient, and would explain three distinct sound patterns observed: vowel nasalization after nasal consonants; pre-stopped nasals in oral contexts; and the absence of VN. > ṼN. > Ṽ sound change, the primary source of contrastive nasalized vowels cross-linguistically (cf. Blust 1997b on nasalization in languages of Borneo).

### 41.3.3 Vowel length

A contrast between short and long vowels is not reconstructed for Proto-Malayo-Polynesian. However, some MPSEA languages have developed contrastive vowel length through vowel coalescence, vowel lengthening, sound symbolism, borrowing, and contact. Just a few of these systems will be mentioned here. Before looking at these, however, it should be pointed out that in some cases, loss of a consonant between identical vowels does not result in a long vowel, but, rather, in a sequence of adjacent syllable peaks. Consider, for example, heterosyllabic Mukah Melanau *daaʔ* 'blood' (with two syllable peaks) < PMP *daRaq, where loss of *R gives rise to a vowel sequence, not a long vowel (Blust 2013a: 651). We should also mention that in many languages of the Philippines, contrastive stress is associated with vowel length in the penult: Ilokano *bára* [ba:ra] 'hot' vs. *bará* [bara] 'lung'; Bikol *bága* [ba:ga] 'ember' vs. *bagá* [baga] 'truly', etc. Determining whether vowel length or stress is contrastive in many of these languages is difficult (though see Kaufman and Himmelmann, this volume, chapter 42). In contrast, some Philippine languages, such as Arta of Northern Luzon, do have true vowel length contrasts (Kimoto 2017a, d). The Arta vowel system consists of short vowels /i a u ə/ and long vowels /i: a: u: ə: e: o:/ (though /ə:/ is found in only one word), providing a clear counterexample to the claim that there are never more long vowels than short vowels within a vowel system. Long vowels in Arta have multiple sources, and are independent of Proto-Philippine accent/length, which was lost in Arta. In some words, intervocalic consonants were lost, resulting in coalescence of sequential vowels into one long vowel: *aa > a:, *uu > u:, *ai > e:, and *au > o:. Some examples are: *sa:y* 'ride on' < *sakay, *du:t* 'fire' < *dukut, and *dita:w* 'outside' < *di tahaw (Kimoto 2017d). Long vowels in Arta have also become contrastive through a historical process of compensatory lengthening. When a final consonant was lost, the vowel preceding that consonant was lengthened, as in: Arta *manu:* 'bird' < *manuk; Arta *ana:* 'child' < *anak; Arta *buyu:* 'bad-smelling' < *buyuk; Arta *buli:* 'buttocks' < *buliq. Another source of long vowels in Arta is sound symbolism. Long vowels are found in sound symbolic words like *tattara:kot* 'cock-a-doodle-doo' (cry of rooster), *ku:tak* 'cluck' (cry of hen), and *be:w* 'cry of deer'. Finally, Arta has numerous words that appear to be borrowed from Yogad (*i:lug* 'egg', *le:but* 'walk around', *u:bi* 'violet/purple yam', etc.), Ilokano (*inda:yun* 'hammock', *tu:luy* 'continue', *bi:lin* 'order', etc.), and other languages, where the stressed vowel is taken into Arta as a contrastively long vowel.

We have already seen how the vowel quality systems in Chamic were extended by contact, and the same is true for quantity contrasts. Chamic languages have contrastive vowel length which is thought to be a feature that developed through contact with Mon-Khmer languages (Thurgood 1999). Contrastive vowel length is also found in Moken of the Mergui archipelago, a language with sesquisyllabic syllable structure, and where vowel length contrasts are limited to major syllables. Since Austroasiatic languages of the mainland have all of these features, including contrastive vowel length, they are also believed to have developed through contact.

### 41.3.4 Summary remarks on vowel inventories

Within the size classes suggested by Maddieson (2013b), vowel inventories of MPSEA languages are generally of small (2–4) to average (5–6) size, reflecting properties of the protolanguage, but can be in the large category (7–14) where contact with languages with larger vowel systems has occurred. Maddieson (2013a) notes that there is no overall correlation between consonant inventory size and number of vowel qualities. Nevertheless, he suggests (Maddieson 2013b, f) that examining the two aspects together may provide a more nuanced picture of their interaction. Maddieson's C–VQ ratio is calculated by dividing the number of consonants by the number of distinct vowel qualities, with number ranging from a low of just over one to a high of twenty-nine. Since the majority of MPSEA languages have small-to-average size vowel systems and small-to-average size consonant systems, their consonant-to-vowel ratios are moderately low (> 2, < 2.75)-to-average (> 2.75, < 4.5), like the majority of the world's languages. An interesting area of study for those looking for correlations between consonant inventory size and vowel quality inventory size would be in languages of the Philippines where expansions of the original four-vowel system to seven or eight vowels can be due to internal developments alone, but where no significant increase in consonant inventory is in evidence (Reid 1973). Alternatively, one could look at languages like Waima'a, where the explosion of the consonant system to thirty-four contrastive segments, including rare ejectives, is not accompanied by any significant change in the vowel system, which includes five vowel qualities.

CHAPTER 42

# Suprasegmental phonology

DANIEL KAUFMAN AND NIKOLAUS P. HIMMELMANN

## 42.1 Introduction

In this chapter, we investigate stress, tone, and intonation as it relates to Malayo-Polynesian languages of Southeast Asia and their outliers in Madagascar and the Pacific (MPSEA) and offer a typological overview of the region's prosodic systems. A major focus of the chapter is on the difficulties posed by MPSEA languages for canonical analyses of stress systems (cf. §42.2 and §42.4). Although the stress systems of many MPSEA languages have been described and most grammars contain a short note on stress, these descriptions have been almost entirely impressionistic. It is now clear that perception biases have coloured these impressions and, as a result, wide swaths of the descriptive literature. A small body of work examines this problem with regard to Malay varieties and concludes that several of these varieties, contrary to traditional descriptions, show no word stress at all (§42.4.1). On this analysis, common correlates of stress (i.e. prominence in pitch, duration, and intensity) originate on the phrase level rather than the word level. §42.3 provides a summary of the comparatively little that is known about phrase-level prosody and intonation in MPSEA languages. Lexical tone is not frequently attested in MPSEA languages and often, but not always, appears to result from language contact (§42.5). In short, the MPSEA area shows an impressive diversity of prosodic patterns and the current chapter seeks to bring some order to the descriptive landscape.

## 42.2 Typological overview

The typology of stress systems has been investigated rather vigorously over the last decade and a half. Work on prosodic typology, on the other hand, has gotten a later start and is, comparatively speaking, still in its nascence (see the papers in Hirst and DiCristo 1998 and Jun 2005, 2014, and the chapters in Gussenhoven 2004 and Ladd 2008), with very little work as of yet dealing with Austronesian languages. We thus first discuss how Austronesian languages have been described in the stress typology literature and introduce what appears to be a more appropriate typology.

The StressTyp database (Goedemans and van der Hulst 2009) together with the four chapters by Goedemans and van der Hulst in the World Atlas of Linguistic Structures (Goedemans and van der Hulst 2013a, b, c, d) are the first to provide a wide-scale typological overview of the Austronesian family. Van Zanten and Goedemans (2007); van Zanten et al. (2010); and Goedemans and van Zanten (2014) offer surveys and summaries specifically targeting Austronesian languages based on this database.

Van Zanten and Goedemans (2007: 78), in their review of the Austronesian and Papuan data in the StressTyp database, note that 80% of Austronesian languages within their sample show fixed penultimate stress, noting that for "the Western M[alayo-]P[olynesian] sub-group this percentage is even higher" (2007: 80). Very few Austronesian languages in the StressTyp database are said to use stress distinctively. Finally, they note that "Austronesian languages basically follow the main global patterning in that stress is located at the right-hand side of the word, mostly on the penultimate syllable" (van Zanten and Goedemans (2007: 87). Given that there is a strong preference for disyllabic roots in Austronesian, this means that unaffixed words typically show prominence on the first syllable.

Unfortunately, the impressions gleaned from the works listed above are somewhat misleading in several respects.[1] First, there are numerous cases where a language's prosodic system appears to have been misrepresented.[2] Second, the category 'no fixed stress', to which some MPSEA languages

[1] The developers realize the inherent weaknesses of such a far-reaching survey. StressTyp is presented as a guide to the literature and a tool for finding languages of interest for further investigation. "[U]sers of StressTyp are recommended to always consult the primary sources (if not speakers) before making hard-and-fast claims about a certain language." (Goedemans and van der Hulst 2014: 120). But see also the brief remarks on the problematic nature of stress descriptions found in the literature in this section.

[2] Teduray, for instance, is classified as being an antepenultimate outlier in the Philippines but is not described by the relevant sources as such. Tagalog is categorized as a trochaic language with penultimate stress, neither of which are correct. Bikol, which is nearly identical to Tagalog in relevant respects, is described as trochaic with no fixed stress. Cebuano and Aklanon which crucially do show minor evidence for trochaic patterning are conversely categorized as iambic languages. §42.4 below provides further details for these assessments. Acehnese is treated as a trochaic language by Goedemans and van der Hulst (2013d) but, based on the same sources, its stress pattern is summarized by van Zanten et al. (2010) as "Primary

Daniel Kaufman and Nikolaus P. Himmelmann, *Suprasegmental phonology.* In: *The Oxford Guide to the Malayo-Polynesian Languages of Southeast Asia.* Edited by: Alexander Adelaar and Antoinette Schapper, Oxford University Press. © Daniel Kaufman and Nikolaus P. Himmelmann (2024). DOI: 10.1093/oso/9780198807353.003.0042

are assigned, is problematic as it conflates languages with mobile stress (e.g. to avoid stressed schwa) together with languages that have phonemic stress distinctions. These properties are unrelated to each other and grouping them together occludes an important pattern in the MPSEA area. Namely, phonemic prominence distinctions on the root level are common in the Philippines but very rare in Indonesia. Third, the geographic distribution of final syllable stress tilts strongly towards the western edges of the MPSEA area, although this does not emerge clearly from the sample.

Thus, the generalization that MPSEA systems mostly have penultimate stress must be qualified carefully.[3] In order to make better sense of the typological landscape, we tentatively propose to classify MPSEA languages into the following prosodic prototypes:

**Western Rim prototype:** Final prominence either on the word or phrase level.

**Philippine prototype:** Phonemic vowel length distinction in open penultimate syllables. Both initial and final phrase edges are tonal targets, with long vowels in penultimate position in a phrase attracting (intonational) edge tones. Suffixes but not clitics shift length rightwards.

**Java prototype:** No length distinctions and no other type of word-level prominence. Prominence in pitch, duration, and intensity is inherited from higher prosodic levels (prosodic phrase and intonational phrase). Effects of suffixes and enclitics on prominence are highly variable and often difficult to discern.

**Eastern prototype:** No phonemic length/stress distinctions. Predictable penultimate prominence on the phrase level in unmarked declarative statements, commonly shifting to final position if penult contains schwa. Word-level penultimate prominence is attested to highly different degrees, ranging from barely noticeable to very regular and conspicuous prominences on the penultimate syllable of every phonological word. Suffixes and possibly certain enclitics included in the stress window.

Good exemplars of these types include Acehnese (Western Rim prototype), Tagalog (Philippine prototype), Javanese (Java prototype), and Kulawi (Eastern prototype). As areal prototypes, we of course find many exceptions. In fact, while the designations for the Eastern and Java prototypes are also geographical, these prototypes form the opposite poles of a continuum. One pole is formed by the languages of Java and surrounding islands where there appears to be no evidence for any kind of word-level prominence and where the segmental anchoring of intonational edge tones is very flexible. On the opposite pole we find Kulawi with very regular penultimate prominences on both the word and the phrase levels. Most languages of Indonesia, excepting the ones belonging to the Western Rim prototype, appear to belong to this continuum. While the languages clearly belonging to the Java prototype are mostly confined to western Indonesia, it is not the case that the languages belonging to the Eastern prototype show an areal distribution such that, the further east one gets, the stronger the prototypical features are manifested. In many instances, the presently available evidence does not allow us to clearly position a given prosodic system on the continuum just proposed, as further detailed in §42.3 and §42.4.

While the Philippine and Western Rim prototypes are more clearly areally delimited and the languages belonging to them overall form fairly coherent groups, there are also exceptions. Many, if not most, of the indigenous languages of Mindanao in the Philippines have no length distinction on roots and thus appear more compatible with the Eastern or Java prototype. Tboli and Blaan, on the southern coast of Mindanao, pattern with the Western Rim prototype. In some cases, closely related Philippine languages appear to differ in whether they have phonemic length/stress contrasts. As Lobel (2013a: 287) notes, Maranao does not appear to have stress contrasts but its sister language, Maguindanao does (Sullivan 1986: 11). Lobel further notes the loss of phonemic stress/length in Rinconada Bikol while Zorc (1978) and Himes (1998) discuss the same phenomenon in the South Cordilleran of Philippine languages. The exact delimitation of the Eastern and Java prototypes, both in their phenomenology and their geographic extent, is complex, as further discussed below.

The Western Rim prototype is likely the result of contact with Mon-Khmer languages, in Mainland Southeast Asia where final prominence is the norm. Jenny et al. (2015: 38) summarize the Austroasiatic situation, "The vast majority of AA [Austroasiatic] languages, which are sesquisyllabic, are strongly iambic, i.e., the first minor syllable is weak and unstressed and followed by a strong stressed main syllable. This pattern is not confined to AA languages in Mainland Southeast Asia but is also found in other languages of the area, e.g., in Thai (Bennett 1994), or Burmese (Green 2005)."[4] This has been well documented for those MPSEA languages

stress on the final syllable. Secondary stress on the first syllable, unless this syllable contains the vowel /ɯ/."

[3] See Tadmor (2000); Zorc (1978, 1993); Wolff (1993); and Blust (2013a: 175–80) for further discussion.

[4] Note that this holds true for Austroasiatic languages that have been in heavy contact with Austronesian, as with the Aslian languages of Malaysia. Kruspe (2004: 40) states that in Semelai, "the domain of word stress is the final syllable and there is no secondary stress. Only phonological words bear stress. In the case of words bearing suffixes, stress shifts from the root to the suffix." Burenhult (2005: 38) describes a similar pattern for Jahai.

that have had the heaviest contact, namely, the Chamic languages (Thurgood 1999), Moken (Larish 1999, 2005), and Acehnese (Durie 1985), all of which show strong final syllable prominence. In the case of the Chamic languages, the adoption of a Mon-Khmer prosodic template has even led to canonical sesquisyllabic words and the development of register and tone (Thurgood 1999; Brunelle 2005b). The distribution of this pattern in Austronesian, however, is not simple. In addition to the languages just mentioned, final syllable prominence is also found in western and northern Borneo, for example, Salako (Adelaar 2005e: 21), Bidayuh (Rensch 2006: 48–9), Begak (Goudswaard 2005: 35), as well as Sumatra, for example, Sigulai (Kähler 1955), Gayo (Eades 2005: 31), Besemah (McDonnell 2016a), Lampung (Walker 1976), but exceptions abound. For instance, two languages of the Barrier Islands, Nias and Mentawai, are described with penultimate prominence despite being located on the far Western Rim of the MPSEA area. Batak languages appear to have a predominantly penultimate pattern (cf. Woollams 1996 for Karo Batak, Nababan 1981 for Toba Batak) although, as first noted by van der Tuuk (1971), Toba Batak also employs a rightward stress shift for morphological purposes in addition to cases of unpredictable stress.

Thus, there is no solid area of final syllable prominence in Indonesia in the same way that we find large penultimate zones throughout eastern Indonesia. Nonetheless, the centre of gravity clearly sits on the border of the Southeast Asian mainland and this is likely to have developed through contact. This corresponds to another areal feature first noted by Skeat and Blagden (1906: 773) and discussed further by Adelaar (1995b: 93–8): the presence of word-final preploded nasals found in Malayic languages (e.g. Salako, Kendayan, Mualang), Land Dayak languages, and in the Austroasiatic Aslian languages of Malaysia. Lacking essential information and first-hand experience, we will have nothing more to say on prosodic characteristics of the Western Rim languages in the remainder of this chapter and all generalizations we offer should be understood *not* to include these languages.

The distribution of the Java prototype has yet to be investigated systematically, as it has only recently gained acceptance as an independent type. On Java itself, Javanese, Sundanese, Madurese, and local varieties of Malay all appear to lack a consistent pattern of word stress (cp. Goedemans and van Zanten 2014: 90; Stoel 2006 and references therein). Davies' (2010: 51) description of the Madurese state of affairs seems to hold equally for other languages of Java:

> Word stress is not a salient feature of Madurese, and receives little mention in the literature, e.g. Stevens (1968) mentions it only in passing. As pointed out by Ogloblin (1986), it is likely that the intonation group is the lowest relevant phonological unit in Madurese (which roughly coincides with what Uhlenbeck (1975) refers to as the 'sentence segment' in Javanese). Words uttered in isolation exhibit stress on almost any syllable in the root; in consecutive repetitions of single words stress may fall on the first syllable in the first instantiation and on the second in the next and vice versa.

It is unclear whether many Malayic languages of Borneo and Sumatra also belong to this type. Ngaju Dayak in Central Kalimantan, impressionistically, at least, appears to show remarkably even prominence across syllables and Tjia (2007: 37) describes sentence intonation as regularly 'overriding' whatever might be posited as word level stress in Mualang, an Ibanic language. Tadmor (2000) posits that lack of lexical stress is a general western feature that extends through Sumatra and Borneo. Similarly, Goedemans and van Zanten (2014: 87) list the following as "likely candidates for reclassification as no-stress languages": Betawi (Jakarta Malay) (Ikranegara 1988; Roosman 2006), Indonesian, Javanese (Ras 1985), Kulamanen (Dubois 1976), Malay (Malaysia: Winstedt 1927; Wehl 1961), Minangkabau (Adelaar 1995c), Mongondow (Dunnebier 1929–1930), Sundanese (Clynes 1995a), Wetan (de Josselin de Jong 1987). It seems, however, that Sumatra and Borneo show considerable variation, in addition to ongoing changes induced by contact with varieties of Malay. It is relatively clear that the Java prototype is very rare in the Philippines, with Central Tagbanwa, perhaps, being the best candidate based both on Scebold's (2003) description and our own auditory impressions.

We have opted to use 'Eastern prototype' rather than 'Sulawesi prototype' based on the speculation that it stretches as far east as the Oceanic languages (and actually includes most of these). The basic and largely undisputed observation is that east of Java/Madura there is a strong tendency towards penultimate prominence on the phrase level. What is not clear is to what extent there is also regular penultimate prominence on the word level. Some languages such as Waima'a (Himmelmann 2010b, 2018), the Tomini-Tolitoli languages (Himmelmann 2018; Bracks 2020), as well as Ambon Malay (Maskikit-Essed and Gussenhoven 2016) have explicitly been claimed to lack such word-level prominences (i.e. stress), in this regard showing one of the defining features of the Java prototype. On the other hand, these languages do not show the highly flexible anchoring of intonational tones that is the other major characteristic of the Java Prototype. §42.4 further expounds this problem.

Many Indonesian languages belonging to the Eastern prototype including, for example, Manggarai, Ngadha, Lamaholot, Leti, Selaru, Wolio are classified as 'no fixed stress' in the StressTyp database because they avoid stressed schwa and thus show 'variability'. However, all of them are otherwise described as displaying penultimate prominence and thus fall squarely within the Eastern prototype (see further §42.4.1). Even Dobel, a rare example of an eastern Indonesian language that shows distinctive lexical stress, as shown in (1), is described as having penultimate stress as its basic pattern (Hughes 2000: 135).

Dobel
(1) /da-ˈtabay/ 'they carry (on shoulder)'
/da-taˈbay/ 'they hit'
/ˈʔala-y/ 'its/his skin'
/ʔaˈla-y/ 'kind of lemon' (Hughes 2000: 135)

We have introduced here a tentative geographic typology of prominence patterns in MPSEA languages which hopefully begins to further clarify the picture emerging from previous surveys. Further work in filling out the geography of prosody in Sumatra, Borneo and many parts of eastern Indonesia should reveal if the prototypes discussed above represent valid areal generalizations. Before taking a closer look at the details of the Philippine, Java, and Eastern prototypes, it will be useful briefly to summarize the basic observations on intonation available to date as it is the interaction between lexical and phrasal prominences that is at the heart of the distinction between these prototypes.

## 42.3 Intonation

Stoel (2005, 2006) has proposed analyses of the intonation of Manado Malay and Banyumas Javanese, the essential features of which have also been found for Malaysian Malay (Zuraidah et al. 2008), Waima'a (Himmelmann 2010b), Ambon Malay (Maskikit-Essed and Gussenhoven 2016), and Totoli (Bracks 2020). These languages belong to the Eastern and Java prototypes. No specialist investigations are available for the other two prototypes, but some of the features mentioned below appear to be attested there as well. Importantly, however, to date there is no well established standard analysis for intonational contours in MPSEA languages. Consequently, much of what is reported here is still tentative.

The only truly obligatory part of an intonational contour in the MPSEA languages investigated so far is a pitch excursion marking the right edge of intonational phrases (IP). This typically involves a rise to a prefinal H target followed by either a further rise (H%) or a fall (L%), as in example (2). There also tends to be a second pattern where the prefinal target is L(ow), continuation rises being a typical example. Throughout this section we will refer to the combination of the two tonal targets as edge tones, the final pitch excursion as a boundary tone (T%) and the target preceding it simply as 'prefinal target'. The core issue regarding the analysis of the prefinal target is the question of how it is linked to the segmental string. We will return to this issue below.

Waima'a (elicited)
(2) *ne* *de* *kara* *haru* *lumu*
3SG NEG like shirt green
'S/he doesn't like the green shirt.'

Note that while the penultimate syllable of the phrase in Figure 42.1 obtains strong durational and intonational

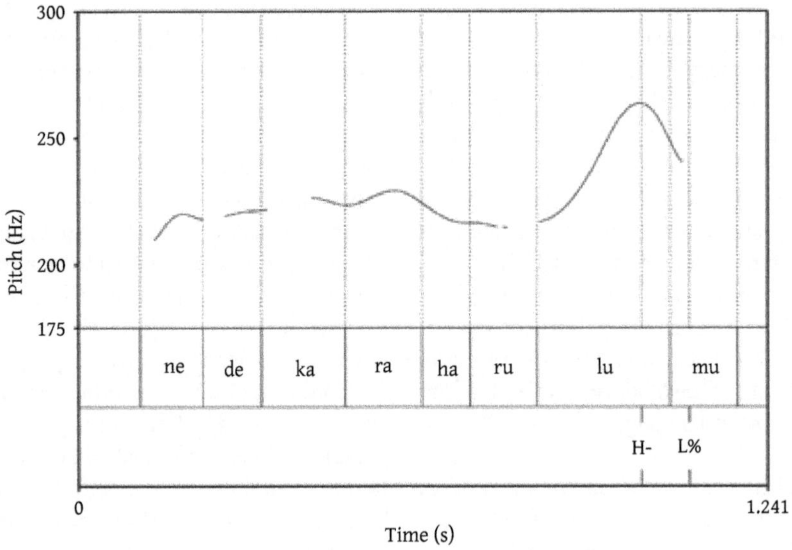


**Figure 42.1** Pitch track for (2).

prominence (by virtue of the phrasal H tone), the penultimate syllable of the preceding word, *haru* 'shirt', which is incidentally the head of the noun phrase, receives no durational or intonational prominence whatsoever. It is this type of data that crucially separates out the role of word-based prosody and phrase-based prosody.

While it is widely acknowledged that in the national standard varieties Indonesian and Malaysian Malay, IP edge tones are not systematically associated with either of the two unit-final syllables, this appears to be more systematic in many other varieties including Toba Batak, Waima'a, as well as eastern varieties of Malay (Manado, Ambon, Papuan). Here, rising prefinal targets appear to be regularly associated with the penultimate syllable and the final boundary tone with the final syllable, as seen in Figure 42.2 depicting the pitch tracks for examples (3a) and (3b), from Papuan Malay. It is this type of example of a word spoken 'in isolation' (i.e. as a short IP) which has given rise to the widely made claim that all these languages have regular penultimate stress.

Papuan Malay (elicited)

(3) a. *baju* b. *baju* *mera*
shirt shirt red

However, as seen in (3a) and (3b), signs of prosodic prominence typically disappear when a given word does not appear in IP-final position, major pitch changes being limited to the final word of the phrase. Compare the preceding two examples with (4) from Kulawi, a Pamona-Kaili language exemplifying the Eastern prototype. As seen in Figure 42.3, every phonological word is associated with a prosodic prominence (indicated by ' in example 4), not only the last one in the unit.

Kulawi (from a spoken narrative)

(4) *nam-pe'gika* *'dike=na* *no-pa-'dapa*
REAL.TR-wait dog=3SG.GEN REAL.INTR-CAUS-hunt
*hi'noko=ra*
prey=3PL.GEN
'... his dog was waiting while he was hunting their prey.'

The lack of prosodic prominence on units not occurring at the right edge of an IP constitutes a conspicuous similarity between languages such as Totoli, Waima'a, and Papuan Malay, and the Java prototype proposed in the preceding section. But they differ from the Java prototype in that pre-final H targets systematically occur on the penultimate syllable (but see the next paragraph for an important qualification). In languages belonging to the Java prototype, the association of the prefinal target is highly variable within a three-syllable window. Furthermore, as discussed in §42.4, there may also be weak indications for word-based prominence in the more eastern languages, at least in the case of Papuan Malay (Kaland 2019). They therefore are preliminarily classified as belonging somewhere in the transitional space on the continuum between the Java and Eastern prototypes.

Regarding the association of the prefinal target with the penultimate syllable in languages such as Waima'a and Papuan Malay, Maskikit-Essed and Gussenhoven's (2016) claim in their careful investigation of Ambon Malay that the f0 peak of the prefinal rise does not clearly align with either the final or the prefinal syllable. Instead, the best

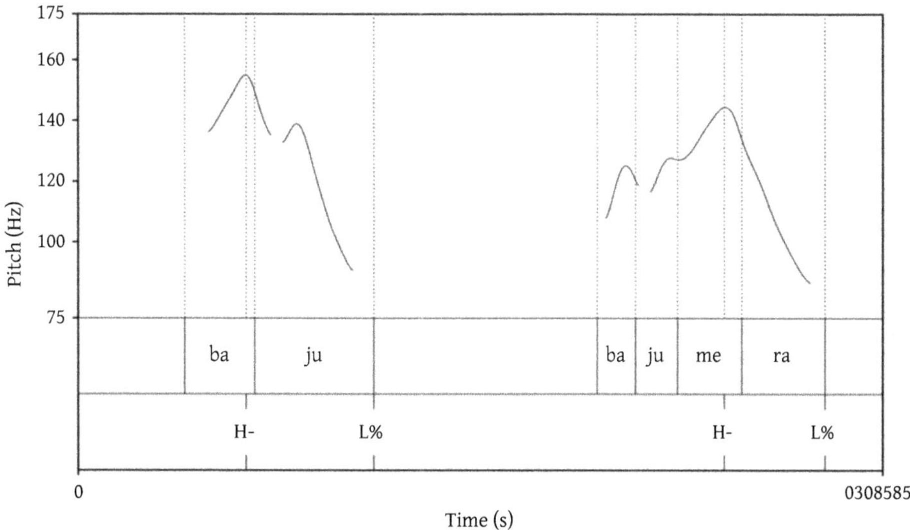


**Figure 42.2** Pitch tracks for (3).

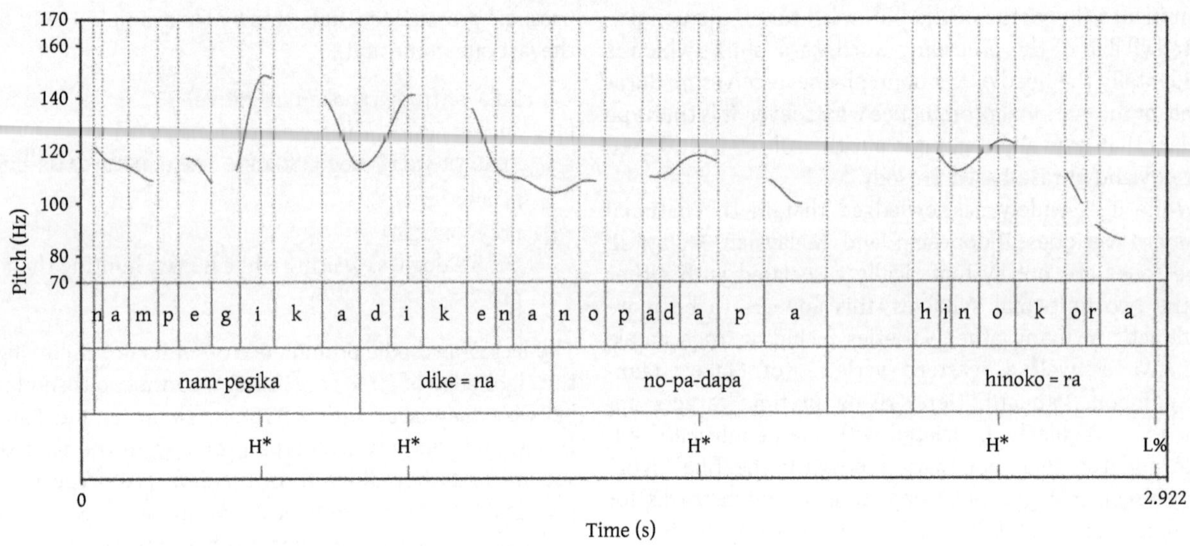


**Figure 42.3** Pitch track for (4).

predictor for its placement is the duration of the IP-final rhyme, syllable, or word, with a strong tendency for it to occur in the final syllable the longer these constituents are. They therefore propose an analysis of the IP-final edge tone combination as 'floating boundary tones' (HL%).

In this regard, it is important to note that the exact alignment of the prefinal L(ow) target in the second pattern mentioned above is also in need of further study. While Himmelmann (2010b) for Waima'a and Bracks (2020) for Totoli hypothesize that this target is also aligned with the penultimate syllable, it is rarely the case that this syllable shows other signs of prominence such as increased duration. Compare the prefinal syllable *ni* in Figure 42.4 (example (5)) with *lu* in Figure 42.1 or *me* in Figure 42.2. That is, it may be the case that the edge tone combinations with a prefinal L target are differently aligned from the ones with a prefinal H target, an issue that needs further scrutiny.

Totoli

(5) *daan tooka nemenek isia lau memenek naasyik lau monipu*

daan tooka noN-penek isia lau
later finished AV.REAL-climb 3SG presently

moN-penek no-asyik lau moN-tipu
AV-climb STAT.REAL-busy presently AV-pick

'after he climbed; eagerly picking (pears)' (Bracks 2020)

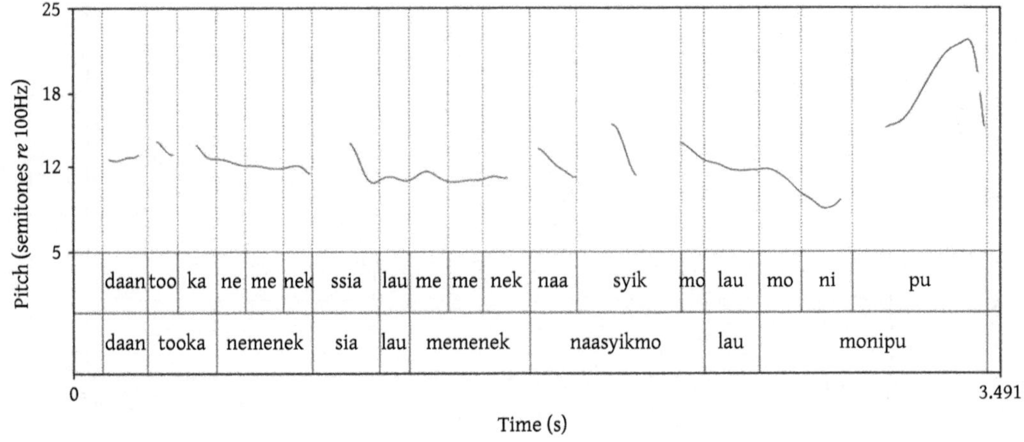


**Figure 42.4** Pitch track for (5).

In addition to the bitonal target at the right edge, it has also been noted for many MPSEA languages belonging to the Eastern, Java, and Philippine prototypes that IPs often begin with a rise on the initial word, starting from an onset position typically in the middle of the speakers range. This rise is usually followed by a fall back to mid-range, the rest of the pitch trajectory in the IP being relatively level until the major excursion marking the right edge. The details of the initial rise vary across languages and types both with regard to its extent and its alignment. In Philippine languages, IP-initial H tones typically involve a major rise and dock to the first or second syllable in the domain regardless of whether this syllable belongs to a lexical word or function word. The placement of domain-initial tones appears less strict than the positioning of domain-final tones in Philippine languages. An example can be seen in (6), where the initial H tone is located on the second syllable of the plural marker proclitic *maŋa*.

Tagalog (elicited)
(6) [maŋa ba:ta: ŋa: pala sila]
/maŋa=ba:taʔ=ŋaʔ=pala=sila/
PL=child=EMPH=MIRA=3PL.NOM
'They are really children!'

In (7), the initial rise is associated only with the first syllable of the verb *binili*. Note that no further prominence is associated with this verb, the final edge tone combination occurring on the question marking clitic *ba*.

Tagalog (elicited)
(7) *b<in>ili=mo=ba?*
<PFV.PV>buy=2SG.GEN=Q
'Did you buy (it)?'

Initial rises are also attested in Waima'a (Himmelmann 2010b) and Totoli (Bracks 2020) and probably many other languages belonging to the Eastern prototype.

As also illustrated by Figures 42.5 and 42.6, Philippine-type languages differ from the Eastern and Java-type languages in their association of the IP-final edge tones. In Philippine-type languages, these are regularly associated with the final syllable, unless the penultimate syllable contains a long vowel. In the latter case, the prefinal target is typically reached on the long vowel. Importantly, penultimate closed syllables do not attract edge tones in Tagalog. As noted by Zorc (1993: 19), this seems to be an important locus of variation in Central Philippine languages. Languages like Cebuano contrast here in that a closed penult may carry prosodic prominence, for example, ['tan.ʔaw] (Wolff 1972: x). Segementally identical forms such as /basbas/ thus appear to have final prominence in Tagalog [bas.'bas] but penultimate prominence in Cebuano ['bas.bas], as discussed further below in §42.4.3.

Languages belonging to the Eastern and Java prototypes typically show a layer of prosodic structure in addition to the initial rise and the bitonal target at the right edge. Longer IPs are often (but not necessarily) divided into smaller prosodically marked phrases, which we call phonological phrases

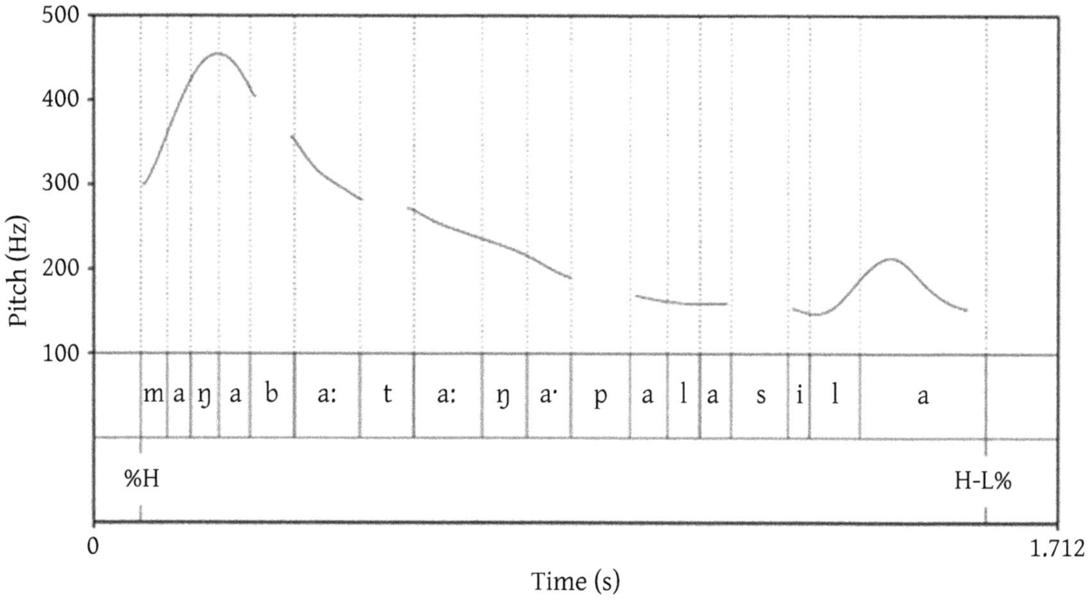


**Figure 42.5** Pitch track for (6).

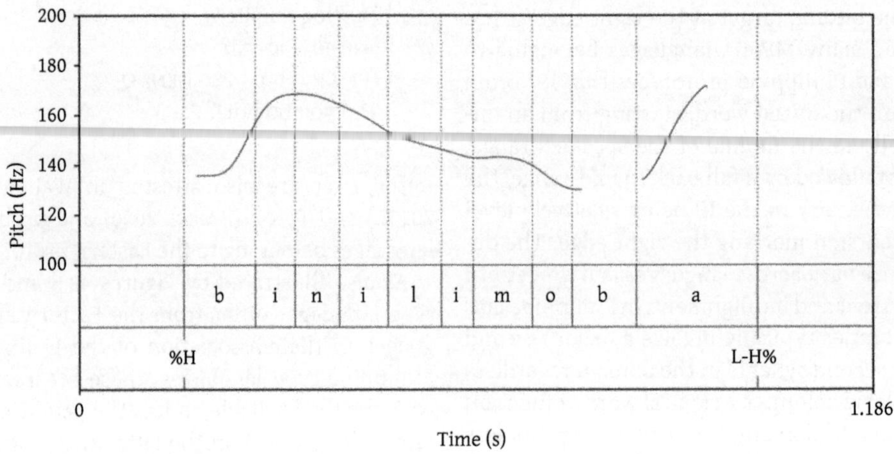


**Figure 42.6** Pitch track for (7).

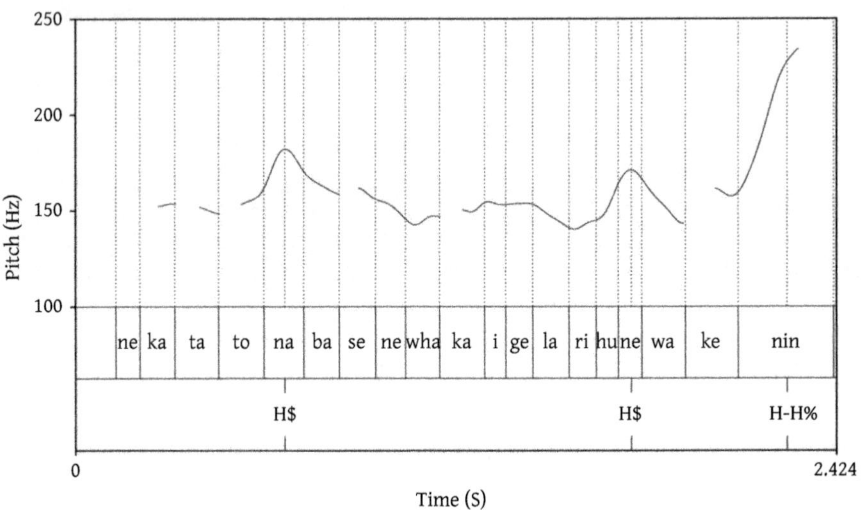


**Figure 42.7** Pitch track for (8).

(PhP) here (a widespread alternative term is *intermediate phrase*). The example in (8) from Waima'a contains two PhPs where H$ in Figure 42.7 represents the PhP boundary tone.[5]

Waima'a (from a narrative)[6]

| (8) | *ne* | *kara* | *data* | *naha* | *barse* | *ne* | *whaka* |
|---|---|---|---|---|---|---|---|
| | 3SG | want | alight | if | seem | 3SG | fly |
| | *ige* | *la* | *rihu* | *neʔi* | *wake* | *nin(i)* | |
| | PART | 3SG | fog | PROX | below | POSS | |

'If it were about to land, then it should fly below the clouds.'

As also seen in example (8), no pauses or other rhythmic boundary markers occur at PhP boundaries. Similarly, there is no interruption of the overall pitch contour (i.e. no offset–onset phenomena). The beginning of the following unit always involves a (consecutive) fall to a lower pitch level. This PhP-initial low(er) target is often reached within the first syllable of non-initial PhPs, but it may also occur somewhat later (second or even third syllable).

PhPs are of variable size but they are usually larger than a single phonological word and may span complete (subordinate) clauses, as in the first PhP in (8) where *na(ha)* is

[5] This is an ad-hoc device as we do not want to commit ourselves at this point how this tonal target relates to the tonal targets on the IP level. We also do not commit ourselves to a specific analysis for the last bit of this example (*wake nini*) which in most ToBI-style analyses would also be interpreted as a PhP where the PhP boundary tone is overwritten by IP-level tones.

[6] Elision of syllables is common in natural Waima'a discourse. In (8), for example, the initial conditional clause *ne kara data naha* is shortened to *ne katatona*. The regularities of syllable elision and concomitant sound changes are, however, not yet understood.

a clause-final subordinator. The boundary marker for PhPs is a H(igh) tone on the unit-final syllable, its peak usually being located at the very end of it. This syllable is not markedly lengthened or otherwise prosodically highlighted aside from hosting the boundary tone. In case there are two or more consecutive PhPs in an IP, the unit-final Hs tend to be downstepped. However, downstepping does not regularly include the IP-final edge tones, that is, the prefinal H target or the final boundary tone of an IP are often (but not necessarily) higher than any of the preceding H targets marking PhPs, as again illustrated by (8).

In his detailed analysis of Totoli, Bracks (2020) proposes a different analysis for the IP-internal prosodic units described as PhPs here. He argues that they are better analysed as recursively embedded intonational phrases, following Ladd (2008), who proposes that intonational phrases may form what he calls *compound intonation units*. Bracks' main argument for this analysis in Totoli is that the right boundaries of putative PhPs essentially allow for the same three edge-tone combinations also found at major IP boundaries.

Returning to the more general discussion of intonation in MPSEA languages, it is very likely that the prosodic framework sketched here is not sufficient to capture all the relevant intonational contrasts. Thus, for example, it has been noted for Manado Malay and the Javanese Palace language (see chapters in van Heuven and van Zanten 2007) that questions may involve a (more or less) continuous rise across most of an IP, usually after a minor initial drop. Furthermore, echo questions may have specific features such as being produced on a higher pitch level than the preceding statement. In fact, there appear to be various ways to expand the IP at the right edge, after the IP-marking edge tone combination. Stoel (2005), for example, reports the option for Manado Malay to add a single further phrase after the IP-edge tones which tends to be flat and involves a highly compressed pitch range. But there are also various options for what may be termed intonational clitics, often determiners or conjunctions, which may occur after the IP-marking edge tone combination (Bracks 2020 provides examples from Totoli).

Similarly, systematic durational effects on the higher prosodic levels remain largely unexplored although it is a potentially rich area for uncovering the mapping of syntactic structure to PhPs. One recent exception is Hsieh (2016) who examines Tagalog verb durations in two conditions and shows evidence for closer prosodic integration of genitive agents with preceding verbs when compared with nominative (pivot) arguments. Richards (2010: 165–82) also explores the structure of higher prosody in Tagalog with a view towards syntactic analysis and suggests an algorithm for locating edge tones associated with PhP. The prosodic typology of focus across MPSEA languages is also still poorly understood but see Stoel (2005, 2007); Kaufman (2005); Maskikit-Essed and Gussenhoven (2016); and Himmelmann (2005a) for some discussion.

## 42.4 The problematic nature of word stress in MPSEA languages

As discussed above, it has only been recently that the notion of word-stress in Indonesian languages has come under critical scrutiny, with the result that several languages are now generally analysed as not making use of word-level stress at all. However, languages that appear to show phonemic use of word-level prominence distinctions, as in the Philippines, also present serious challenges to traditional notions of stress and prominence. In §42.4.1, we review the literature on stresslessness as characteristic of the Java prototype and in §42.4.2 we provide a few more details regarding the Eastern prototype where clitics play an important role in determining the boundaries of the stress window. §42.4.3 discusses prominence patterns in Philippine languages.

While these issues are in part specific to the MPSEA languages, it will be well to take note of the fact that 'stress' is a highly problematic notion in most parts of the world. Until very recently, little effort has been made in the descriptive, typological, and theoretical literature to distinguish between bona fide stress (i.e. word-based prominence) and phrase-based prominence (cp. Hyman 2014; Roettger and Gordon 2017; among others). The problems result at least in part from the fact that stress in West Germanic languages, which has served as the primary example for stress in the literature, shows a systematic correlation of at least five different phenomena: (i) acoustic prominence (often involving increased duration and intensity); (ii) phonotactic structure (e.g. constraints on vowel distributions) and phonological alternations caused by stress; (iii) metrical structure (largely regular alternations of strong and weak syllables); (iv) a special function in text-tune alignment (stressed syllables function as anchors for intonational tones); and (v) marking of (information) focus. This correlation, however, appears to be rare in the languages of the world. Therefore, it is important to be clear as to what exactly one is referring to when talking about 'stress'. Our discussion here mostly pertains to (i) acoustic prominence and (iv) the function of serving as an anchor for intonational tones.

### 42.4.1 Stressless languages of Indonesia (Java prototype)

The bulk of the specialist work on stress in MPSEA languages relates to Standard Indonesian, the variety of Malay serving as the national language of Indonesia. As many other varieties of Malay, Indonesian has widely been claimed to have penultimate (primary) stress, unless the penultimate syllable contains a schwa, stress then shifting to the ultima. See Halim (1981: chap. 2) for a summary of the early literature and Cohn (1989, 1993) for a formalization of such an analysis. Beginning with Odé (1994), however, a group of Leiden phoneticians and phonologists has questioned this view in acoustic and perceptual investigations of presumed stress phenomena in Indonesia.

Van Heuven and van Zanten (2007) contains a detailed report on this work, which also extends to other Malayic varieties.[7] Their main findings can be summarized as follows:

- Strong L1 effects exist for the production and perception of potentially stress-related parameters in Indonesian, with L1 Javanese speakers having the least clear evidence for stress.
- Speakers of Manado Malay and L1 Toba Batak speakers of Indonesian are more consistent in rendering a fixed (typically penultimate) syllable within words more prominent.
- Perceptually, speakers rate examples where one of the final three syllables is made acoustically prominent by manipulating pitch, duration, or overall intensity as roughly equivalent. Using a different methodology, Riesberg et al. (2020) find that speakers of Papuan Malay are unable to agree on which syllables are prominent in short excerpts of spontaneous narrative Papuan Malay speech. Surprisingly, however, they perform significantly better when asked to identify prominences in German excerpts of a similar type, hence clearly not being 'stress-deaf'.
- Prominence distinctions among syllables and words appear to lack a communicative function in Indonesian. Thus, in gating experiments Indonesian speakers were unable to make use of prominence differences in the initial syllables. They were also unable to understand contrastive stress on the subword level (e.g. 'cof[FER] not cof[FIN]') as shown by their inability to judge the pragmatic appropriateness of examples involving such contrasts (van Heuven and Faust 2009).

Much of this work argues that what has been analysed as word stress in Indonesian has no functional relevance for native speakers and that Indonesian and other varieties of Malay have no word-based prominence. These empirical studies build on older observations in the literature to the effect that Indonesian has phrasal rather than word-based accent (Halim 1981; Wallace 1976). In fact, even older descriptive work during the Dutch colonial period work had already noted the weakness of stress in many languages of Indonesia. Goedemans and van Zanten (2014) propose a set of diagnostics for suspicious stress claims, noting that these apply to a broad range of Austronesian languages. At the same time, they posit that "the absence of stress might well be a family trait of the Malay languages, but that this feature has been introduced in the family through regional influences, be it in the distant past, or more recently" (Goedemans and van Zanten 2014: 90). As noted earlier, the geographical centring of this pattern around Java suggests that regional influences may indeed be at play.

It is likely that word-based prominence does not play a major role in the grammar of many of the languages belonging to the Eastern and Java prototypes. However, it is far from clear that all these languages completely lack evidence for stress-like distinctions. Kaland (2019), for example, finds that most disyllabic words in Papuan Malay show a consistent prominence difference between the penultimate and ultimate syllables in terms of duration (prominent syllables longer than non-prominent ones), formant displacement (prominent syllables more displaced than non-prominent ones), and spectral tilt (prominent syllables have more energy in higher frequency bands than non-prominent ones), and in this sense can be regarded as stressed. Importantly, this difference is found in non-phrase-final position. That is, the increased prominence of the penultimate syllable cannot be simply due to its association with the prefinal target of the edge-tone combination discussed in §42.3. Furthermore, Kaland (2020) discusses evidence for the claim that the prominence difference between penultimate and ultimate syllables may have a minor role to play in word recognition, a function that has been ascribed to stress in the psycholinguistic processing literature. Finally, Kaland and Baumann (2020) propose that the rising edge-tone combination at the end of IPs in Papuan Malay may have a (minor) highlighting function in addition to a purely demarcating function. In short, there are good reasons for the view that 'stress or no stress' is not a simple yes–no issue. The overall grammatical structure and relevance of word-level prominence distinctions varies significantly across languages. Therefore, a proper typological classification scheme for prominence distinctions needs to provide not only for an insightful classification of the different ways of grammatically structuring them, but also for different levels of relevance of such distinctions.

[7] See van Heuven et al. 2008 for Betawi (Jakarta Malay), Manado Malay, and Kutai Malay, as well as Toba Batak; Zuraidah et al. 2008 on Malaysian Standard Malay; Maskikit-Essed and Gussenhoven 2016 on Ambon Malay. Further experimental and theoretical work in this area includes van Zanten, Goedemans, and Pacilly 2003; van Zanten and van Heuven 1994, 1998; Goedemans and van Zanten 2014; van Zanten and Goedemans 2007; and van Heuven and Faust 2009.

One issue that stands out in this regard because it is widely attested in MPSEA languages is the avoidance of 'stressed' schwa. Many MPSEA languages have been analysed as making use of phonemic stress distinctions because words with schwa in the penultimate syllable tend to show prosodic prominence on the final syllable as in Standard Indonesian *kə'bun* 'field'. The evidence for prominence here mostly pertains to the anchoring of the phrase-final edge tone combination H–L% discussed in §42.3, which usually involves a clearly observable rise on the penultimate syllable unless this syllable contains a schwa. In the latter case, the rise typically comes later and often fully coincides with the final syllable. Importantly, this distinction persists even in many languages and varieties where historical *ə has merged with other vowels (often /a/ but also /e/ and /o/). In these cases, the syllable with historical schwa still avoids prominence as in Manado Malay *kobong* [ko'boŋ] 'field' (Stoel 2007) and similarly in Kupang Malay (Steinhauer 1983), North Moluccan Malay (Taylor 1983), and Papuan Malay (Kluge 2017). While this is a later development, as noted by Goedemans and van Zanten (2014), it clearly stems from the phonology of the Malayic parent language.[8]

Smith (2023) shows that schwa in penultimate open syllables is associated with a variety of phonological changes in almost all branches of the Austronesian family. Apart from the prominence shift just described for Malay this includes in particular the gemination of final syllable onsets. Smith advances the hypothesis that all attested changes relating to open penultimate schwa syllables can be explained by assuming that these syllables were mora-less in Proto-Austronesian and are still mora-less in many daughter languages. Of particular interest in the present context is the further claim that the intonational tones do not dock to penultimate schwa syllables because they are weightless. A similar argument is made by Maskikit-Essed and Gussenhoven (2016) with regard to word-level prosody in Ambon Malay, which was previously described by van Minde (1997) as having developed contrastive stress via the same process as the other Malay varieties cited above. They treat the /a/ derived from *ə as a mora-less vowel which they call "a-caduc" (on analogy with French *e-caduc*).[9]

Inasmuch as stress is often weight sensitive, the schwa avoidance of phrasal tones in MPSEA languages may be considered stress-like. But it must be kept in mind that there is only a small overlap between this and the phenomenon called 'stress' in West Germanic languages. Note also that the phenomena cited by Kaland (2019, 2020) to support the presence of word-level prominence distinctions in Papuan Malay, which may very well apply to other Eastern and Java-type languages as well, are not clearly correlated with schwa-conditioned prosodic changes.

### 42.4.2 The stress window in the Eastern prototype

Languages of the Eastern prototype have word-based prominence, as already briefly exemplified above with (4) from Kulawi. The hypothesis here is that stress in these languages is generally penultimate. However, as already shown in (4), surface prominence sometimes occurs on the penultimate syllable (*nampe'gika* and *nopa'dapa* in (4)), sometimes on the antepenultima (*'dikena* and *hi'nokora* in (4)). This can be explained as variation as to which clitics are included in the stress window. In Kulawi, both adverbial enclitics and possessor enclitics are excluded from the stress window (e.g. *bóne* 'field', *bóneku* 'my field') (Adriani and Esser 1939: 9) in addition to *'dikena* and *hi'nokora* in (4). Enclitics in Kulawi do not attract prominence even when they are disyllabic (e.g. *hóu=kami* 'our house' and *momúli=komi* in (9)). Function words such as *padena* 'then' in (9) do not attract prominence even when they appear to form a prosodic word of their own, as seen in Figure 42.8.

(9) Kulawi (from a spoken narrative)
*padena* *mo-'muli=komi*
then IRR.AV-create=2PL.NOM
'you (go) create'

In Ledo, a neighbouring Pamona-Kaili language, the stress window includes both possessor enclitics as well as second position adverbial clitics such as =*mo*, which is seen shifting the stress rightwards from what would be [na'kuya] 'why' in (10). Descriptions of Balantak (van den Berg and Busenitz 2012), Tukang Besi (Donohue 1999a), and Muna (van den Berg 1989) also fit this pattern.

(10) Ledo (from a spoken narrative)
*Naku'ya=mo* *'ledo* *ne-'guru* *'ia?*
why=COMPL NEG AV.BEG-study 3SG
'Why is he not studying anymore?'
(Kaufman 2010a: 43)

In other Pamona-Kaili languages, there are two classes of adverbial clitics, those which are included in the stress window and those which are not. Such a case is described by Martens

[8] This is not a feature of all Malay dialects that have lost the schwa. Soderberg (2014: 204), for instance, notes that words with unstressed penultimate schwa in Malay (e.g. [lə'suŋ] 'mortar') correspond to stressed penultimate /a/ in Kedayan (e.g. ['lasuŋ]).

[9] There is a morphological analogue to this in languages where lexical roots are privileged over affixes for purposes of stress. Bowden (2001: 51) describes Taba as having a general penultimate stress pattern with exceptions such as *magún* 'silent' and *makót* 'red', due to a maintained avoidance of stress on the frozen *ma-* prefix.

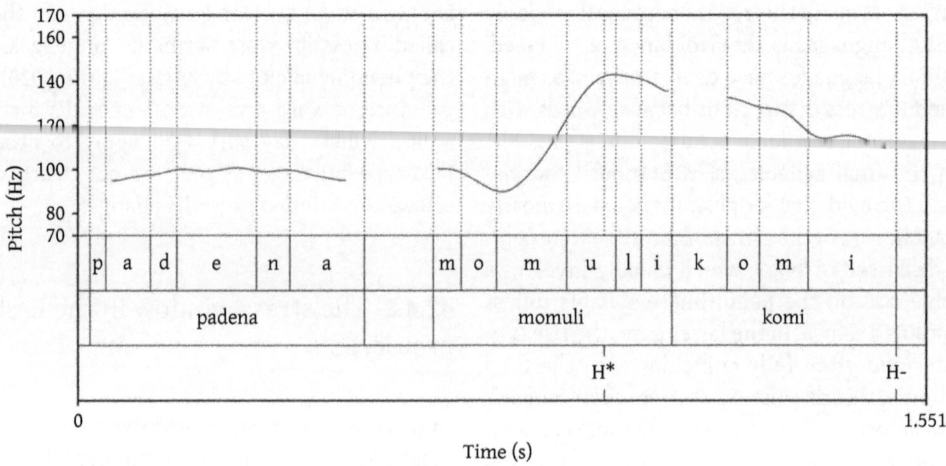


**Figure 42.8** Pitch track for (9).

(1988b: 172) for Uma where a small number of adverbial clitics such as *mpu'u* 'really' and *oa'* 'anyway' are included in the stress window. Excluded from this window is a large number of other types of clitics including those with pronominal, aspectual, and adverbial functions.

In the South Sulawesi languages, possessor clitics, which attach to the right edge of noun phrases, are included in the stress window but second-position subject clitics and adverbial are excluded. We thus find accentual contrasts like that in (11).

Makasar

(11) a. *te'doŋ=ku*
buffalo=1SG.GEN
'my buffalo'

b. *'tedoŋ=ko*
buffalo=2.FAM.NOM
'you are a buffalo'
(Jukes 2006:91)

As shown by Jukes (2006), clitic stacking yields the expected results in Makasar. Prominence remains penultimate within the prominence window and is unaffected by additional adverbial or absolutive clitics.

Makasar

(12) *(ka-gassing~gassing-án=na)=mo*
NMLZ-SUPER~strong-NMLZ=3SG.GEN=COMPL
'already at the peak of his strength' (Jukes 2006: 90)

Tukang Besi shows what may be a unique development in Sulawesi, where, in addition to the prosodic incorporation of all enclitics, a prepositional case marker *te* (marking a core non-nominative argument) is parsed prosodically with preceding material, as seen in (13a). This contrasts with the nominative case marker, as shown in (13b), which does not pull a preceding penultimate stress rightwards. (Note the close parallel to Hsieh's (2016) observation that nominative arguments in Tagalog are more loosely integrated to preceding material than genitive arguments.)

Tukang Besi

(13) a. [ˌnɔʔi'ta te kɛ'nɛno]
*no-ita te kene-no*
3.REAL-see CORE friend-3SG.GEN
'He saw his friend.'

b. [ˌnɔ'ʔita na kɛ'nɛno]
*no-ita na kene-no*
3.REAL-see NOM friend-3SG.GEN
'His friend looked.' (Donohue 1999a: 31)

In languages that avoid codas through the use of paragogic vowels, such as Lauje and Selayarese, among others, these vowels are ignored for purposes of assigning stress (Makasar) or the association of edge tones (Lauje). Thus, we find that epenthesis creates the appearance of antepenultimate prominence in words with an underlying word-final coda as in Lauje *lúbaʔe* 'hair' which consists of the base *lubaʔ* and paragogic *e* (Himmelmann 2005a: 118; Mithun and Basri 1986; Broselow 2000).

### 42.4.3 The Philippine challenge to universal stress

Philippine languages present different problems for stress typology as the majority of these languages have a phonemic distinction in prosodic prominence on the root level.[10]

[10] See Zorc (1978, 1993); Ross (1992: 47–54); Wolff (1993); Blust (1997a); and Smith (2023) for attempts to understand the history and proper reconstruction of this phonemic prosodic distinction in Austronesian.

In Tagalog, the best studied language of the Philippines, this prominence has been alternatively analysed either as the outcome of underlying stress or vowel length. Official Tagalog orthographic conventions for indicating stress (unduly influenced by Spanish orthography) imply that final stress is word based: <tangá> 'stupid' and that penultimate stress is unmarked <basag> 'break'. Both of these assumptions are likely wrong. Firstly, what has been analysed as word-final stress is most likely a right-aligned edge tone. Secondly, it has been noted that roots with apparent 'final stress' in Tagalog and other Philippine languages with distinctive prosody are significantly more common than those with 'penultimate stress' (Blust 2013a: 178–80). Penultimate prominence should thus be considered the marked case for most Philippine languages.

The situation becomes clearer when we examine words in non-final positions, as shown in the examples below, where all syllables would be typically pronounced with even duration, intensity, and pitch except the final one. The provisional stress marks in (14) simply indicate some form of perceived prominence.

Tagalog
(14) a. [ta'ŋa] b. [aŋ ta~taŋa ni'la]
stupid DET PL~stupid 3PL.GEN
'stupid' 'How stupid they are!'

The 'final stress' shown in (14a) is an artefact of the word's phrase-final position. When enclitics are added, as in (14b), there is no special prominence on any syllable of the lexical word, including the last one. It is therefore fair to say that 'final stress' in Tagalog and many related languages is not word-based. Unlike this final prominence, penultimate prominence in the Tagalog word does *not* disappear in non-final contexts such as (14b). It does, however, shift with suffixation or, alternatively, is positioned according to word boundaries rather than root boundaries. For instance, ['basag] 'break' becomes [ba'sagin] 'break (patient voice)' with the *-in* suffix. Again, unlike final prominence, penultimate prominence does not shift when the word is followed by clitics or other lexical material (e.g. [ba'sagin mo!] (break-PV=2.SG.GEN) 'break it!'). This, prima facie, looks like a proper stress system.

Treating Tagalog and similar Philippine languages as inherently stress-based (as French 1988 does), leads to a paradox in which closed syllables repel stress.[11] While roots with an open penult allow for penultimate (trochaic) or final (iambic) prominence, no possibility exists for a trochaic pattern when the penultimate syllable is closed, as shown schematically in (15).

[11] As Blust (2013a: 168–9) notes, the same is true for Ilokano, and other languages of the Philippines.

(15) Tagalog syllable structure with word-level stress analysis

| | | |
|---|---|---|
| open penult | 'CV.CV(C) | CV.'CV(C) |
| closed penult | *'CVC.CV(C) | CVC.'CV(C) |

This suggests strongly that length is the phonemic category that underlies penultimate prominence (following Schachter and Otanes 1972: 15–18; Wolff et al. 1991: 12; Wolff 1993: 1; Zorc 1993; and contra Bloomfield 1917: 141f; French 1988: 63). The penultimate syllable of native roots can bear a long vowel, as in /ba:sag/ 'break' or a short vowel, as in /taŋa/ 'stupid'. Long vowels can only occur in the penultimate syllable when it is open, a cross-linguistically common pattern in which 'super-heavy' syllables are avoided. The paradox of heavy syllables repelling stress is thus illusory. It must be stipulated that long vowels cannot occur in final syllables, but this is also common cross-linguistically due to the neutralizing effects of final lengthening.[12]

Evidence from loanword phonology in Tagalog also suggests that vowel length is the key underlying feature. Spanish words with penultimate stress in open syllables, such as ['bala] 'bullet', retain prominence on the penultimate syllable via vowel length in Tagalog (i.e. [ba:la]). On the other hand, loanwords with penultimate stress on closed syllables in the source language, such as Spanish ['libɾo] 'book' and ['basta] 'enough; only', lose their penultimate prominence in Tagalog, becoming [lib'ɾo] and [bas'ta] (with final prominence in isolation).

An unusual aspect of Philippine prosodic systems is that they instantiate 'length shift', a phenomenon far more familiar from stress. That is, the forms cited above as ['basag] 'break' and [ba'sagin] 'break (patient voice)' are underlyingly /ba:sag/ and /basa:g-in/. This can be explained as a structure preservation effect in light of the fact that long vowels never appear in (native) roots earlier than the penultimate syllable. Length shift thus preserves this generalization over suffixed words.

Length also plays an active morphological role in most Philippine languages and multiple long vowels can exist in morphologically complex words as a result. A minimal pair can be seen in (16), where reduplication without length yields a deaspectual nominalization and reduplication with length produces a form in the imperfective aspect. In both forms, however, a final edge tone docks within a disyllabic window aligned to the end of the phrase. If a long vowel exists within that window it serves to host the prefinal tonal target in the unmarked case.

[12] Barnes (2006: 260) notes in his typological survey that, "[l]anguages in which there is contrast between phonologically long and short vowels in all positions save word-final are extremely common cross-linguistically."

Tagalog
(16) a. *mag-na~'na:kaw* b. *mag-na:~'na:kaw*
AV-NMLZ~steal AV-IPFV~steal
'thief' 'will steal'

The fundamental prosodic distinction in Philippine roots thus boils down to the possibility of long vowels in open penultimate syllables. The attraction of edge tones to long vowels gives the impression that some roots are inherently trochaic while others are inherently iambic but the reality is that in both instances phrasal tonal targets are associated with the final syllables of an IP, the association rules taking into account weight differences between penultimate and ultimate syllable. To apply this to our initial examples [ta'ŋa] 'stupid' and ['ba:sag] 'break', in [ta'ŋa] both syllables are short, hence the phrasal edge tone aligns to the final syllable when this word occurs at the end of a phrase, giving the impression that it is stressed on the ultima. In ['ba:sag], on the other hand, the phrasal edge tone is attracted to the long vowel in penultimate position, contributing to the impression that this word is stressed on the penultima.

Some Philippine languages to the north of Tagalog also allow phonemically long vowels in *closed* syllables, at least on the word level if not the root level. Kapampangan, for instance, distinguishes between short /mag-/ and /pag-/ prefixes and their long counterparts to indicate aspectual distinctions, as shown in (17). This type of length distinction in closed syllables is generally impossible in Central Philippine languages.

Kapampangan
(17) a. *mag-doktor=ya*
AV.PROS-doctor=3SG.NOM
'is going to become a doctor'
b. *ma:g-doktor=ya*
AV.PROG-doctor=3SG.NOM
'is becoming a doctor' (Gonzalez 1981: 15–16)

As already briefly mentioned in §42.3, the Visayan languages of the Central Philippine group provide for an interesting minimal pair with Tagalog. Just as in Tagalog, when the penult contains a long vowel, it attracts the prefinal tonal target. Unlike Tagalog, the penult also attracts the prefinal target when it is a closed syllable. If both codas and long vowels are moraic, then the Visayan pattern can be described as in (18) (cp. Zorc 1972; Wolff 1972; van Zanten and Goedemans 2007: 69), where H represents a heavy syllable, L represents a light (short and open) syllable, and underlining represents the position of prosodic prominence.

(18) Visayan prominence patterns
<u>H</u>L <u>H</u>H L<u>H</u> L<u>L</u>

The difference between Visayan languages and Tagalog could *prima facie* be modelled as a difference in what types of syllables are considered heavy; Tagalog only treats syllables with long vowels as heavy whereas Visayan also includes closed syllables in this category.

In yet other Philippine languages, such as Itawis, Pangasinan, Hanunoo, and Palawan Batak, prominence is said to not be predictable on words with a closed penult at all (Blust 2013a: 177). The phonetics of prosodic prominence in these languages remains to be investigated and it is possible that this type of pattern will require a considerably different analysis.

### 42.4.4 Concluding remarks

We have seen in this section that MPSEA languages pose different problems to typical metrical stress analyses in accordance with the prominence prototype they belong to. In the case of languages of the Java prototype, it appears that prominence comes from the phrase level rather than the word level and is positioned rather freely. Some languages of the Eastern prototype are similar to the ones of the Java prototype in that evidence for word-level prominence is rather weak. But they differ from them in showing a strong preference for aligning (word- and phrase-level) prominences with the penultimate syllable. In other languages of the Eastern prototype, the penultimate stress pattern is much more robust and clearly obtains on the word as well as the phrase levels. Its robustness may occasionally be obscured by the fact that these languages differ quite significantly with regard to which (clitic) function words are included in the stress window. But all Eastern type languages agree in that at least some function words do not attract prosodic prominence quite unlike many of the languages belonging to the Java and Philippine prototypes where phrase-final function words may generally serve as anchors for edge tones in the same way as content words. In the case of Philippine languages such as Tagalog, the stress literature tends to obscure the true nature of the system by not distinguishing between phrase-level (edge tones) and word-level phenomena (phonemic length distinctions). A better analysis is that long vowels attract edge tones and the possibility of a long vowel in open penultimate syllables (and typically only in such syllables) is a defining feature of a Philippine prosodic template.[13] Finally, language of all three types

[13] Zorc (1993) discusses several sources of length but many of these are secondary and not directly relevant to the system described here, which underlies many Philippine languages. For instance, some languages have developed distinctive word-final vowel length from the loss of codas, although this is very rare. As with many of the generalizations over areas and subgroups made here, the precise distribution of this prosodic template has yet to be determined.

share the property of avoiding prominences on schwa syllables, though in no instance is this a property that holds true for all languages of a given type.

Segmental effects of prosodic prominence are scattered and irregular across MPSEA languages but may also help disentangle word-based phenomena from phrase-based effects. Kapampangan shows vowel centralization, as in (19). Here it seems that lexical or morphological vowel length blocks /a/→[ə], as in (19b), but the phrase final prominence that would obtain with a short penult is more variable in its blocking effects, as shown in (19a). This has not yet been well described and remains to be investigated further.

Kapampangan

| (19) | a. | [ənak] ~ [ənək] | b. | [a:nək] |
|---|---|---|---|---|
| | | /anak/ | | /a~anak/ |
| | | child | | PL-child |

Similarly, Kluge (2017: 91 passim) claims for Papuan Malay that some vowels may be centralized in unstressed syllables and the (rather rare) palatalization of /s/ is restricted to unstressed syllables but these appear to be very sporadic processes, possibly reflecting acrolectal usage rather than a regular phonological alternation. A clearer example of segmental effects is the stress dependent *ə/o* alternation in Begak described by Goudswaard (2005).

## 42.5 Lexical tone

Most Austronesian languages do not use tone to distinguish lexical items. Distinctive lexical tone patterns have only been reported for a few geographically widely separated language groups, for which see Edmondson and Gregerson (1993); Remijsen (2001a); Brunelle (2005b); Blust (2013a: 657–9). In most instances, distinctive lexical tone is transparently due to contact influences, a major exception being the Central Malagasy dialects discussed by Howe (2017). Tonal distinctions usually are restricted, either phonotactically (e.g. contrast only on final syllable) or with regard to permissible tone patterns per word (e.g. words bear either high or low tone). Tonogenesis often involves a shift from the strong preference for disyllabic words characteristic for the family to monosyllables as the most common word type. Edmondson and Gregersen (1993) contain specialist chapters for a number of the better studied Austronesian tone languages. Howe (2017, 2021) investigates a particularly interesting example of ongoing tonogenesis in Central Malagasy dialects where the voicing contrast in the oral obstruent series is largely replaced with pitch distinctions. With the notable exception of Arnold (2018a) briefly discussed below, none of the available literature discusses intonation, hence nothing is known as to whether and how lexical tone interacts with postlexical tonal targets.

The most widely quoted examples for Austronesian tone languages are the Chamic languages spoken in southern Vietnam, Cambodia and Hainan (see Brunelle, chapter 11, this volume). Here tonal distinctions are claimed to be emergent due to contact with Mon-Khmer languages (Tai-Kadai languages and Chinese in the case of Tsat on Hainan) and are heavily constrained by syllable structure and segment type, being closely correlated with voice quality distinctions (Thurgood 1999). In fact, it has recently been questioned whether the relevant contrast in some of these languages may properly be analysed as tonal or rather as involving register distinctions (Brunelle 2005b). Incipient tonal contrasts have also been claimed for varieties of Moklen spoken in Thailand (Larish 2005), but this is in need of further scrutiny.

The little that is known about the West New Guinea languages, which are mostly spoken on the islands along the Bird's Head and Cenderawasih Bay in eastern Indonesia, points to a bewildering variety of word-prosodic systems. These languages are part of the extended contact zone between Austronesian and Papuan languages along the island of New Guinea.

Monosyllabic words have a six-way tone contrast in Magey Matbat according to Remijsen (2007). From the few examples he gives, it appears that at least one syllable in polysyllabic words is toneless, but the position of tone-bearing syllables is not predictable. This contrasts with Moor, which is analysed by Kamholz (2014: 101–6) as having four tonal patterns, largely confined to the final two syllables. More importantly, and rather unusually for a tone language, "tones are realized only on phrase-final words" (Kamholz 2014: 102; 2017: 15). Kamholz (2014: 116 passim; 2017) also discusses Yerisiam and Yaur as languages with a complex word tone system plus contrastive vowel length.

A particularly complex—and cross-linguistically unusual—word-prosodic system is found in Ma'ya, spoken on the Raja Ampat Islands. Remijsen (2001a, 2002) makes a convincing case for an analysis in terms of both lexical stress and lexical tone. There are three tonal contrasts which are confined to the final syllable. In addition, lexical bases differ in whether they are stressed on the penultimate or ultimate syllable. That is, there are minimal pairs which differ only with regard to tone (e.g. *sa*$^{12}$ 'to sweep' vs. *sa*$^{3}$ 'to climb' vs. toneless *sa* 'one') (Remijsen 2002: 596). And there are minimal pairs differing only in stress (e.g. *'mana*$^{3}$ 'light (of weight)' vs. *ma'na*$^{3}$ 'grease') (Remijsen 2002: 600). Importantly, Remijsen (2002: 602–10) provides detailed acoustic evidence for the proposed stress difference, which includes not only duration measures, but also differences in vowel quality and spectral balance.

In Ambel, another Raja Ampat language, stress does not play a role according to Arnold (2018a) and the overall organization of the system appears to be very different again. Here, words may, but do not have to, carry a high lexical tone, and there is at most one such tone per lexical word. That is, lexical tone is not obligatory, but cumulative. The H tone may occur on any syllable of a polysyllabic word. It also occurs on monosyllables, including some monosyllabic function words. In addition, there is a complex interaction between the lexical tone and a HL% boundary tone marking the end of declarative and imperative IPs (there are slightly different boundary tones for questions and continuations). This boundary tone is in general associated with the final syllable of the phrase, but its realization depends on whether the final word is lexical or functional, whether the final syllable is toneless or bears a lexical H tone, and whether the final syllable is light or heavy (the rhyme consisting of a vowel and a sonorant consonant). The final L is generally truncated when the final syllable is monomoraic. In case the final word is a toneless polysyllabic function word, the HL% boundary combination is spread across the final two syllables, hence the H target occurs on the penult. See Arnold (2018a: 44–117, chapter 2) for further details.

Systems such as the one just reported for Ambel are widely known as 'lexical pitch accent' systems in the literature, a concept that has engendered controversy and confusion (cp. Hyman 2009; and Beckman and Venditti 2011 for very different views). In this regard, it is worth noting that inasmuch as word-based prominence in the languages belonging to the Eastern prototype manifests itself exclusively in a (typically high) pitch target, these languages would also be considered lexical pitch accent languages. Utsumi (2011) in fact uses a lexical pitch accent analysis for Bantik, a Sangiric language of northeastern Sulawesi.

## 42.6 Conclusion

As we have emphasized, the study of prosody in MPSEA languages is still in its infancy and many of the claims found in the literature, especially regarding the presence and placement of lexical stress, need further scrutiny, carefully combining evidence from production and perception and keeping phrase-level phenomena clearly separate from word-level ones.

The areal typology of prosodic systems sketched in §42.2 cannot be but a first hypothesis as to what kinds of prosodic systems to expect in the area. A major parameter of variation across the area appears to be the regularities of the association between phrase-marking edge tone combinations—so far found in all languages investigated—and the segmental string. This association may be highly variable as in the Java prototype or it may target the penultimate (Eastern) or the final syllable (Philippine and Western Rim prototype). A second parameter in this regard appears to be the role played by syllable weight, with vowel length distinctions being an important aspect in Philippine prosodic systems and open syllables with schwa being weightless. A third parameter that comes into play in various systems is the distinction between lexical and functional items, the latter often showing slightly different regularities for association rules.

CHAPTER 43

# Phonotactics and morphophonology

MARK DONOHUE

## 43.1 Introduction

The Malayo-Polynesian languages of Southeast Asia (henceforth MPSEA) show considerable variation in terms of phonological processes and conditions on well-formed structures, though we can identify clear areal tendencies in the deviations from these norms. In this chapter we will examine a number of processes that are found across many of the Austronesian languages of Southeast Asia, but which are much less common elsewhere. The resolution of nasal + plosive sequences varies across a number of languages, and has attracted considerable attention from phonologists (see Blust 2004b), which summarizes and extends much earlier work). Many languages have strict constraints on root shapes, including the extensive appearance of sesquisyllabic word shapes, matching their frequent occurrence in languages of mainland Southeast Asia, and in contrast to their rarity globally. Finally, against a background of globally modal CVC syllables, constraints against the appearance of codas are found in two areas, far western Island Southeast Asia (including Madagascar), and in and near southeast Sulawesi. At the other end of the syllable more elaborate onsets are permitted in a number of areas, though usually not as the modal setting for any area, nor as a categorical setting across most regions (other than Timor). The database examined includes 535 MPSEA languages. More languages are displayed in the maps included here, where languages of Taiwan and from the Oceanic subgroup are also displayed, as well as non-Austronesian languages from various families of New Guinea and (mainland) Asia. Details of the sample used for this chapter can be found at: https://doi.org/10.5281/zenodo.4915572. For details of different types of consonant and vowel inventories of the Malayo-Polynesian languages of Southeast Asia, see Blevins, this volume, chapter 41; for details of the different types of tone systems, see Kaufman and Himmelmann, this volume, chapter 42.

## 43.2 Nasal + plosive sequences

The behaviour of nasal + plosive sequences in Austronesian languages frequently shows complications, and has attracted considerable discussion in the academic literature. In Indonesian we see that root-internally voiceless and voiced plosives in all places can follow a nasal, as shown in (1).

| | | Indonesian | |
|---|---|---|---|
| (1) | a. | 'slap' | *ta**mp**ar* |
| | b. | 'jungle' | *ri**mb**a* |
| | c. | 'door' | *pi**nt**u* |
| | d. | 'miss' | *ri**nd**u* |
| | e. | 'fishing rod' | *pa**ntʃ**iŋ* |
| | f. | 'basket' | *kəra**ndʒ**aŋ* |
| | g. | 'circle' | *li**ŋk**a* |
| | h. | 'proud' | *ba**ŋg**a* |

When a nasal + plosive sequence would be created as the result of morphological processes, the possible combinations are not usually as rich. For instance, one inflection of Indonesian verbs involves the prefixation of *məŋ-*; on a vowel-initial root, such as *aɲam*, this prefix is realized without modification, seen in (2a).

With a plosive-initial root the nasal of the prefix assimilates in place to the place of the plosive, as can be seen in (2b) using a bilabial plosive. When the plosive is voiceless, the prefix is realized with a final bilabial nasal, but the initial *p* of the root is not realized, in (2c). The different possible phonological processes are outlined in (3); in Indonesian, only the first two are attested.

| | | Indonesian | | | |
|---|---|---|---|---|---|
| (2) | a. | 'weave' | *aɲam* | *mə**ŋ**aɲam* | |
| | b. | 'buy' | *bəli* | *mə**mb**əli* | |
| | c. | 'pluck' | *pəti?* | *mə**m**əti?* | (* *məmpəti?*) |

| | | | |
|---|---|---|---|
| (3) | a. | Nasal Assimilation | The nasal of the prefix assimilates in place |
| | b. | Nasal Substitution$_1$ | An initial voiceless stop is not realized |
| | c. | Nasal Substitution$_2$ | An initial voiced stop is not realized |

Different languages show different patterns of substitution (of the plosive), while all show assimilation (in place) as far as their phonologies allow. In (4a) we can see that in Balantak there is no substitution; *ŋ-* + *p-* is realized as [mp],

Mark Donohue, *Phonotactics and morphophonology*. In: *The Oxford Guide to the Malayo-Polynesian Languages of Southeast Asia*. Edited by: Alexander Adelaar and Antoinette Schapper, Oxford University Press. © Mark Donohue (2024). DOI: 10.1093/oso/9780198807353.003.0043

and *ŋ-* + *b-* is realized as [mb]; Nasal Assimilation applies, but there is no Nasal Substitution. Botolan Sambal allows the same pattern of Nasal Assimilation, but also allows for full nasal substitution with both the voiced and voiceless stops, so that *ŋ-* + *p-* can be realized as [mp] or [m], and *ŋ-* + *b* can be realized as [mb] or [m]. In addition to the pattern of Nasal Substitution$_1$ seen in Indonesian, we also see Nasal Substitution$_2$ in Malagasy and Iban and, in Makasar and Ilokano, Nasal Substitution with preservation of the C slot, resulting in a geminate nasal. Finally, Bolaang-Mongondow displays all of the processes in (3), but also allows the voiced, but not voiceless, stop to be completely lost.[1] Bolaang-Mongondow shows further complications, described below in Table 43.3.

| | | | *ŋ- + p-* | *ŋ- + b-* |
|---|---|---|---|---|
| (4) | a. | Balantak | *mp* | *mb* |
| | b. | Botolan Sambal | *mp/m* | *mb/m* |
| | c. | Indonesian | *m* | *mb* |
| | d. | Malagasy | *m* | *mb/m* |
| | e. | Makasar | *mm* | *mm* |
| | f. | Ilokano | *mm* | *m* |
| | g. | Iban | *m* | *m* |
| | h. | Bolaang-Mongondow | *m* | *m/Ø* |

In Ngaju Dayak and other languages, the degree to which Nasal Substitution applies depends on the shape of root which is inflected. In (5a) we can see that Nasal Assimilation applies to two roots with initial voiced plosives, but Nasal Substitution is not evidenced (Santoso et al. 1991). In (5b) two different roots with the same initial consonants do undergo Nasal Substitution. The difference is in the internal structure of the inflecting root; the forms in (5b) contain internal nasals. When the consonant following the ND sequence created by the affixation of *maN-* to a root is a nasal, then the oral stop is not realized. This is shown schematically in (6); the identities of the second, third and fourth consonants, in terms of nasality, determine whether or not a voiced oral stop will be preserved after nasal prefixation. It does not matter if the $C_4$ nasal consonant is in the same syllable as the $C_3$ or not, as shown in (7) (compare with (5b)).

| | | Ngaju Dayak | | |
|---|---|---|---|---|
| (5) | a. | *buwu* | 'wound' | *ma**mb**uwu* |
| | | *duhup* | 'help' | *ma**nd**uhup* |
| | b. | *buŋkus* | 'wrap up' | *ma**m**uŋkus* |
| | | *dindiŋ* | 'wall' | *ma**n**indiŋ* |

[1] We should note that these *synchronic* processes are not necessarily the same as the historical processes that have applied to a language. Kelantan Malay patterns with Indonesian in (4), but lexically shows the development of *-mp- > -p- (eg. Malay *kampoŋ* 'village', Kelantan *kapoŋ*), not *-mp- > -m- (Jaafar 2018). Modern loanwords in Kelantan Malay also attest the loss of the nasal before voiceless stops, but not before voiced stops: 'canteen' > *katin*, but 'attendant' > *itande* (Jaafar and Naziman 2017).

(6) a. $N_1VN_2\text{-}D_3VC_4\ldots;\quad C_{[+nas]}\,C_{[+nas]}\,C_{[-nas]}\,C_{[-nas]} \rightarrow N_1N_2D_3C_4\ldots$

b. $N_1VN_2\text{-}D_3VN_4\ldots;\quad C_{[+nas]}\,C_{[+nas]}\,C_{[-nas]}\,C_{[+nas]} \rightarrow N_1N_2\_N_4\ldots$

| | | | | |
|---|---|---|---|---|
| (7) | a. | *bunu* | 'kill' | *ma**m**unu* |
| | b. | *dawa* | 'accuse' | *ma**nd**awa* |

A pattern of what we might call Plosive Preservation is found in other languages, such as Itawis and Rejang, in which Nasal Assimilation and Nasal Substitution$_1$ apply, but a voiced plosive in the root is preserved in preference to the nasal of the prefix; in Itawis the C-slot is preserved, resulting in a geminate voiced plosive. In Nias both Nasal Substitution$_2$ and mutation to a bilabial trill are attested, in different roots.

| | | | | |
|---|---|---|---|---|
| (8) | a. | Itawis | *m* | *bb* |
| | b. | Rejang | *m* | *b* |
| | c. | Nias | *(m)* | *m/ʙ* |

Mori Bawah, from Sulawesi, shows evidence of Nasal Assimilation with voiceless stops, but the combination of *ŋ-* + *b-* results in the loss of both consonants. This second pattern is also attested in Mukah Melanau, from Borneo.

| | | | | |
|---|---|---|---|---|
| (9) | a. | Mori Bawah | *mp* | *Ø* |
| | b. | Mukah Melanau | *m* | *Ø* |

In addition to the differential patterns of Nasal Assimilation and Nasal Substitution, we also find that plosives in different places of articulation are differently subject to the phonological processes. We have seen in (2) that Nasal Assimilation and Nasal Substitution$_1$ apply in Indonesian, but from (10) we see that this is not true for the voiceless palatal plosive.

| | | Indonesian | | | |
|---|---|---|---|---|---|
| (10) | a. | 'pluck' | *pətiʔ* | *mə**m**ətiʔ* | (* *mə**mp**ətiʔ*) |
| | b. | 'certain' | *təntu* | *mə**n**əntu-kan* | (* *mə**nt**əntukan*) |
| | c. | 'bright' | *tʃərah* | *mə**ntʃ**ərah-kan* | (* *mə**ɲ**ərahkan*) |
| | d. | 'hard' | *kəras* | *mə**ŋ**əras-kan* | (* *mə**ŋk**əraskan*) |

Table 43.1 shows different patterns of nasal assimilation and nasal substitution with respect to plosives in a selection of MPSEA languages (the languages are organized in terms of increasing application of nasal substitution). We can see that, generally, the palatal series in most resistant to nasal substitution, and the labial series most susceptible.[2]

Numerous other languages mirror the behaviours seen here. In addition to Indonesian, the same patterns are reported for Banjar; the Javanese patterns are also found in

[2] Nasal Assimilation and Nasal Substitution also apply to roots beginning with segments other than plosives; Blust (2004b) provides a comprehensive survey and analysis going beyond what is presented here.

Chamorro; for Tagalog, we also have Tausug; for Itbayaten, Cebuano, Bikol, Palawano, and Casiguran Agta; for Iban, Kelabit, Katingan (Ngaju Dayak), Musi, Ogan, Sekak, Sanggau Malay, Sarangani Manobo, Western Bukidnon Manobo, Pangasinan, Ifugao, and Bontok.

In addition to the data in Table 43.1 we also find languages in which the prefix is syllabic for some places, but not for others. In Bajau languages (such as Mapun and Yakan) full Nasal Assimilation and Nasal Substitution applies to roots with bilabial onsets, or voiceless onsets, but roots beginning with *d*, *dʒ* or *g* see the nasal prefix *ŋ-* realized as *ŋan-* or *ŋaŋ-* (for instance, we see the alternation *busay*/*musay* 'paddle', but *dʒaggur*/*ŋandʒaggur* 'punch' in Southeast Sulawesi Bajau). Similar patterns are found in languages from western Java and southern Sumatra. These data are shown in Table 43.2, showing again the special status of the palatal series (in Lampung), the susceptibility of the labial place to nasal substitution (Sundanese), and the insulation of the nasal prefix from the verb root (Lampung, Sundanese, and Mukomuko).

In some languages we see Nasal Assimilation and Nasal Substitution applying to voiceless stops, but the nasal + voiced stop combination shows denasalization and, in some cases, the loss of the stop. In Bolaang-Mongondow the system is similar to Javanese, except for the optional loss of the *mb*/*nd*/*ŋg* outcomes. In Gorontalo only the voiced bilabial stop shows any preservation (Little Jr 1995), and in Mori Bawah and Mukah Melanau all of the original ND sequences are lost. Kadazan would fit in Table 43.1 were it not for the preservation of the oral plosives in all but the bilabial place. The irregular developments in Timugon Murut and Nias suggest a complicated (morpho)phonological history for these languages, while the Itawis and Rejang patterns (Suwawa has the same pattern as Rejang) resemble Kadazan and Timugon Murut in the preservation of the oral stop in preference to the nasal stop.

In Tables 43.1–43.3 we can see that while the manner (voiced vs. voiceless) of the initial stop is the primary determiner of the outcome of nasal prefixation, place is also important, and less principled.

**Table 43.1** Patterns of Nasal Assimilation and Nasal Substitution with plosives

| | *p* | *b* | *t* | *d* | *tʃ* | *dʒ* | *k* | *g* |
|---|---|---|---|---|---|---|---|---|
| Balantak | *mp* | *mb* | *nt* | *nd* | - | - | *ŋk* | *ŋg* |
| Botolan Sambal | *mp/m* | *mb/m* | *nt/n* | *nd/n* | - | - | *ŋk/ŋ* | *ŋg/ŋ* |
| Karo Batak | *m* | *mb/m* | *n* | *nd* | *ntʃ* | *ndʒ* | *ŋk* | *ŋg* |
| Indonesian | *m* | *mb* | *n* | *nd* | *ntʃ* | *ndʒ* | *ŋ* | *ŋg* |
| Javanese | *m* | *mb* | *n* | *nd* | *ɲ* | *ndʒ* | *ŋ* | *ŋg* |
| Tagalog | *m* | *mb/m* | *n* | *nd* | - | - | *ŋ* | *ŋg* |
| Malagasy | *m* | *mb/m* | *n* | *nd* | - | *ndʒ* | *n* | *ŋg* |
| Ngaju Dayak | *m* | *mb/m* | *n* | *nd/n* | *ɲ* | *ndʒ/ɲ* | *ŋ* | *ŋg/ŋ* |
| Sasak | *m* | *mb/m* | *n* | *nd* | *ɲ* | *ndʒ/ɲ* | *ŋk/ŋ* | *ŋg* |
| Balinese | *m* | *mb/m* | *n* | *nd/n* | *ɲ* | *ndʒ/ɲ* | *ŋ* | *ŋg/ŋ* |
| Makasar | *mm* | *mm* | *nn* | *nd* | *ttʃ* | *ndʒ* | *ŋŋ* | *ŋg* |
| Toba Batak | *m* | *m* | *n* | *nd* | *ttʃ* | *ddʒ* | *kk* | *ŋg* |
| Sangir | *m* | *m* | *n* | *nd* | - | - | *ŋ* | *ŋg* |
| Ilokano | *mm* | *m* | *n* | *nn* | - | - | *ŋŋ* | *ŋg* |
| Itbayaten | *m* | *m* | *n* | *n* | *ɲ* | *ndʒ* | *ŋ* | *ŋg* |
| Kapampangan | *m* | *m* | *n* | *nd* | - | - | *ŋ* | *ŋ* |
| Iban | *m* | *m* | *n* | *n* | *ɲ* | *ɲ* | *ŋ* | *ŋ* |

**Table 43.2** Augmented nasal prefixes

| | | | | | | | | |
|---|---|---|---|---|---|---|---|---|
| Mapun | *m* | *m* | *n* | *ŋand* | – | *ŋandʒ* | *ŋ* | *ŋaŋg* |
| Yakan | *m* | *m* | *n* | *ŋand* | – | *ŋadʒ* | *ŋ* | *ŋaŋg* |
| Lampung | *m* | *mb/ŋab* | *n* | *nd/ŋad* | *ɲ* | *ndʒ* | *ŋ* | *ŋg/ŋag* |
| Sundanese | *m* | *m/ŋab* | *n* | *ŋad* | *ɲ* | *ŋadʒ* | *ŋ* | *ŋag* |
| Mukomuko | *m* | *mab* | *n* | *mad* | – | *maɲ* | *maŋ* | *maŋ* |

**Table 43.3** Nasal preservation with voiceless plosives

| | | | | | | | | |
|---|---|---|---|---|---|---|---|---|
| Bolaang-Mongondow | *m* | *m/Ø* | *n* | *nd/Ø* | – | – | *ŋ* | *ŋg/Ø* |
| Gorontalo | *m* | *m* | *l* | *Ø* | – | – | *ŋ* | *Ø* |
| Mori Bawah | *mp* | *Ø* | *nt* | *Ø* | – | – | *ŋk* | *Ø* |
| Mukah Melanau | *m* | *Ø* | *n* | – | – | *Ø* | *ŋ* | *Ø* |
| Kadazan | *m* | *m* | *n* | *d* | – | *dʒ* | *ŋ* | *g* |
| Timugon Murut | *m* | *b* | *nt/n* | *d* | | *dʒ* | *ŋk/ŋ* | *g* |
| Itawis | *m* | *bb* | *n* | *n* | – | – | *ŋ* | *ŋg* |
| Rejang | *m* | *b* | *n* | *d* | *tʃ* | *dʒ* | *ŋ* | *g* |
| Nias | *(m)* | *m/ʙ* | *n* | *ndr/n/d* | N | *dʒ/n* | *g/n* | *g* |

## 43.3 Templaticity

A recurring theme in the phonologies of the MPSEA languages is the preservation of a target for root or word shapes. This is realized in various ways, described in this section.

### 43.3.1 Sesquisyllabicity

Sesquisyllabic patterns (Maps 43.1 and 43.2), also referred to as minor–major syllable patterns, are the phenomenon of the two syllables in a disyllabic word not having equal expansive possibilities, where the second syllable has a greater phonotactic range than the first syllable.

In (11) we can see six different disyllabic words in Indonesian, with different vowels in the first syllable. In the first five words, which have similar shapes, the lexical stress falls on the first syllable rather than the second (this may be overridden by phrasal stress). In the last word the stress falls on the second syllable, not on the first. These facts are summarized in (12), and this is a general principle when a schwa is found in the language: it cannot be stressed. Additionally, the schwa may not appear in a final syllable (this is violated in a number of non-standard varieties), and may not appear adjacent to a glide (*əj, *əw, *jə, *wə, *əh, *hə), in contrast to the other non-high vowels.

| | | Indonesian | | |
|---|---|---|---|---|
| (11) | a. | 'scar' | [ˈbirat̪] | (* [biˈrat̪]) |
| | b. | 'defecate' | [ˈbɛraʔ] | (* [bɛˈraʔ]) |
| | c. | 'west' | [ˈbarat̪] | (* [baˈrat̪]) |
| | d. | 'extravagant' | [ˈbɔrɔs] | (* [bɔˈrɔs]) |
| | e. | 'opaque' | [ˈburam] | (* [buˈram]) |
| | f. | 'heavy' | [bəˈrat̪] | (* [ˈbərat̪]) |

(12) a. ˈCV(N)CV(C)
b. Cə(N)ˈCV(C)

Similar facts can be found in other languages, such as Palu'e, where we find a degree of assimilation of quality of the erstwhile schwa to the following vowel, and the same assignment of stress to the final vowel in (13a)–(13j) in an

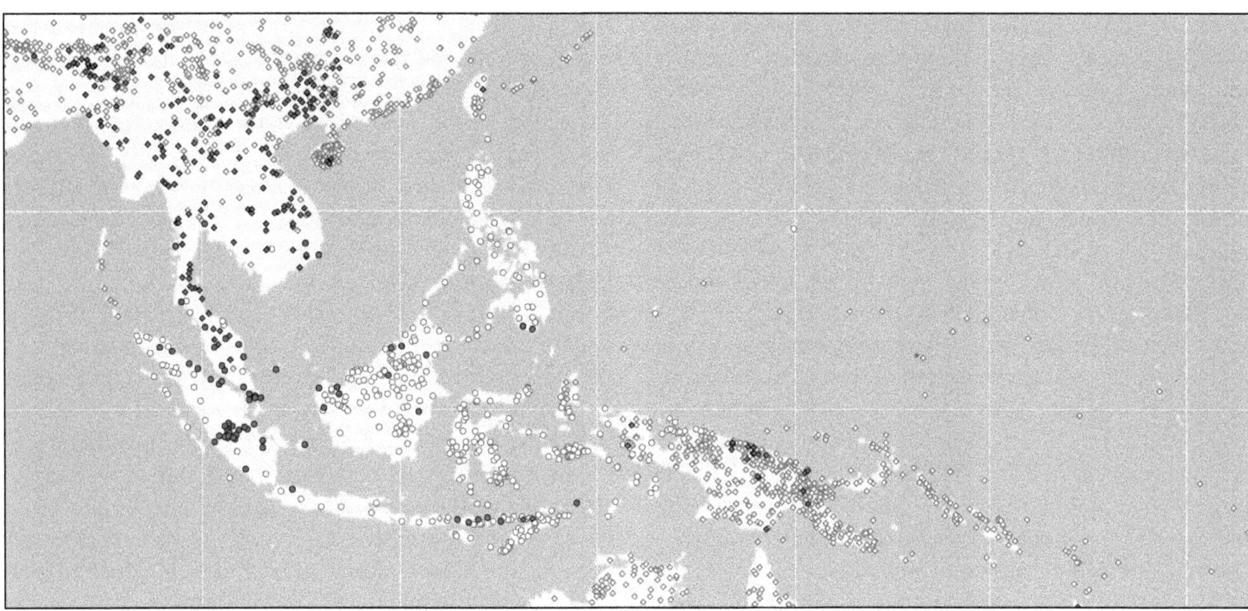

**Map 43.1** Sesquisyllabic word shapes.

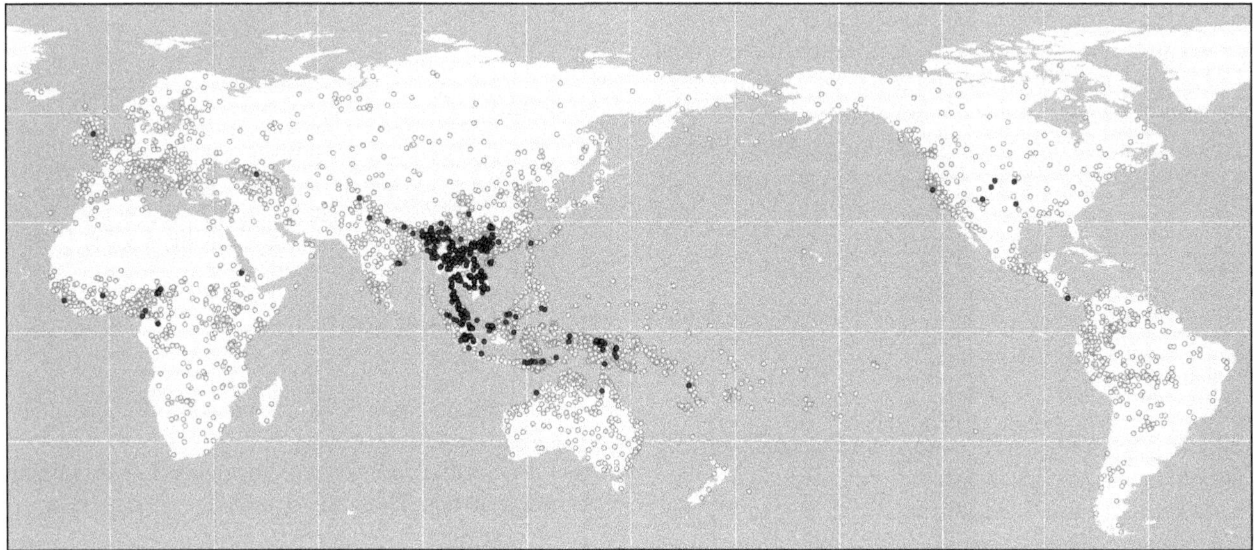

**Map 43.2** Sesquisyllabic word shapes globally.

otherwise trochaically footed language (as attested in (13a)–(13e)). In (13f)–(13j) we can see the optional partial assimilation of the vowel in the first syllable to the quality of the vowel in the second, implying that the vowel [ə] is not as stable phonologically as the other vowels.

|  |  | Palu'e |  |
|---|---|---|---|
| (13) | a. | 'tie' | [ˈt̪ikɛ] |
|  | b. | 'sell' | [ˈt̪ɛka] |
|  | c. | 'cook in earth' | [ˈt̪aki] |
|  | d. | 'cough' | [ˈt̪ɔkɔ] |
|  | e. | 'ascend' | [ˈt̪uka] |
|  | f. | 'tie' | [t̪əˈku] ~ [t̪ʊˈku] |
|  | g. | 'chew (hard)' | [t̪əˈgɔ] ~ [t̪ɵˈgɔ] |
|  | h. | 'sheathe' | [t̪əˈka] ~ [t̪ɐˈka] |
|  | i. | 'fill' | [nəˈgɛ] ~ [nɜˈgɛ] |
|  | j. | 'crammed' | [t̪əˈgi] ~ [t̪ɪˈgi] |

One solution to the question of stress assignment and variable vowel quality is to assume that stress is regularly penultimate, and that the underlying form of the words in (13f)–(13j) is not CVCV, but rather CCV, a stance which can be supported from various lines of evidence. Consonant clusters are not permitted in Palu'e, and the CC onset in (for instance) /t̪ku/ 'tie' is resolved via the addition of an epenthetic vowel; stress cannot be assigned to syllables not built from material in the underlying form, which means that *['t̪əku] is not a possible output for this form. A competing analysis, which assumes a more elaborate model of the phonological representations in the language, allows for two types of syllables, *major* and *minor* syllables. While major syllables in Palu'e can consist of any consonant and any vowel (eg. *vat̪u* 'stone', *t̪uva* 'fish poison'), a minor syllable can only include the vowels /a/ (shared with major syllables) or /ə/ (unique to minor syllables). Furthermore, a minor syllable cannot bear stress, and cannot be lengthened when assigned to a different foot, as shown in (14). With 'ascend' we can see that the addition of the perfective -*ʔu* results in the rightmost foot not including the initial syllable /t̪u/, which is then assigned to a foot of its own; foot binarity forces in the lengthening of the vowel, resulting in the form seen in (14b), which has the same prosodic structure as the monomorphemic form in (14e). With 'tie', on the other hand, we observe the same refooting of the syllables, but foot binarity does not apply to the schwa, and the resulting prosodic structure shows no evidence for two feet in the root.

| | | Palu'e | |
|---|---|---|---|
| (14) | a. | ['t̪uka] | 'ascend' |
| | b. | [ˌt̪uː'ka̯ʔu] | 'ascend-PERF' |
| | c. | [t̪ə'ku] | 'tie' |
| | d. | [t̪ə'ku̯ʔu] | 'tie-PERF' |
| | e. | [ˌpuː'lɔga] | 'whale' |

Finally, similarly to the restriction against schwa occurring adjacent to a glide in Indonesian, the schwa in Palu'e cannot occur adjacent to a vowel (there are no phonological glides in Palu'e). All of these facts indicate that schwas do not have the same phonotactic possibilities as other vowels. One final observation shows the divergence of Palu'e from Indonesian, and offers a strong suggestion for the analysis of schwas in Palu'e: schwa does not occur word-initially, whereas other vowels are found in this position.

| (15) | Palu'e vowel contrasts | i ɛ a ɔ u | ə |
|---|---|---|---|
| a. | Bear stress? | √ | × |
| b. | Non-initial syllable? | √ | × |
| c. | Lenthening? | √ | × |
| d. | #_C | √ | × |
| e. | _V, V_ | √ | × |
| f. | C_C | √ | √ |

If we analyse 'has tied' as /t̪kuʔu/ the lack of length on the surface schwa is not hard to explain, since it is not a footed vowel.

Languages with these patterns are common in Mainland Southeast Asia, and also dominate the linguistic ecologies of the islands closest to the mainland. Scattered attestation across Island Southeast Asia sees local concentrations around Flores and in the southern Philippines.

The epenthetic vowels in Palu'e are not eligible to bear stress, due to a constraint against the assignment of stress to material not in the input. A twist on the treatment of epenthetic schwas is found in Dhao. In Dhao CC sequences are again broken up by a schwa; in contrast to the Palu'e data, the schwa in Dhao may bear stress; the epenthetic status is apparent by the schwa not being able to be moraic. There are nonetheless conditions on foot binarity; and since the schwa only satisfies *CC, the extra mora is realized on the segment following the schwa, which is lengthened (this is the only environment in which long consonants occur).[3]

| | | Dhao | | |
|---|---|---|---|---|
| (16) | a. | /ŋutu/ | 'tooth' | ['ŋutu] |
| | b. | /ŋtu/ | 'agree' | ['ŋətːu] |

(17)

a. /ŋ u t u/ 'tooth' CVCV ['ŋutu]
(μ μ linked by vertical lines to the two V positions)

b. /ŋ t u/ 'agree' ŋətu CVCV ['ŋətːu]
(first μ linked diagonally to the second C, second μ linked to final V)

## 43.3.2 Root templates

The repair that is implicit in the analysis of sequisyllabicity in Austronesian languages points to a preference for particular (constrained) word shapes, and this or similar preferred root templates are attested in various ways in different languages.

| | Tagalog root templates | | |
|---|---|---|---|
| (18) | CVCVC | *putol* | 'cut' |
| | CVNTVC | *tumpok* | 'pile' |
| | $C_aVC_bC_{a'}VC_{b'}$ | *bukbok* | 'weevil' |

The Tagalog template is absolute; no roots begin with vowels, and no roots end with vowels. Written forms such as *akyat* 'climb' and *luto* 'cook' in fact include glottal stops ([ʔakjat], [lutoʔ]) which cannot easily be argued to be epenthetic, any more than any other segment could be.

[3] An alternative analysis treats the schwa as underlying, but defective in that it cannot bear the mora associated with the vowel position.

(In the absence of V-initial or V-final roots, any one segment could be selected to be analysed as epenthetic, and the justification would be equally weak for all such candidates.)

Indonesian allows more freedom, with the initial and final C-slots optional in the non-reduplicated templates.

(19) Indonesian

| | | |
|---|---|---|
| $C_aVC_bVC_c$ | *hitam* | 'black' |
| | *bawa* | 'carry' |
| | *alat* | 'tool' |
| | *isi* | 'contents' |
| $C_aVN_cT_cVC_b$ | *sombong* | 'proud' |
| | *rindu* | 'miss' |
| | *ambil* | 'take' |
| | *anda* | '2SG.H' |
| $C_{a'}VC_{b'}C_{a'}VC_{b'}$ | *dandan* | 'grooming' |

A disyllabic foot is still the preferred root shape in Tetun, but the freedoms found here extend to the inclusion of some extrametrical material at the left edge of the word (van Klinken 1999). Clusters are thus allowed, but only at the left edge.

(20) Tetun

| | |
|---|---|
| k(CVCVC) | *knosen* 'rib'; *metan* 'black'; *ain* 'leg; foot' |
| kCV(CVCVC) | *klalaras* 'average'; *falahok* 'indistinct'; *batane* 'campsite'[4] |
| (CVCV)(CVCVC) | *sibalebok* 'parsley'; *bibiliku* 'drum'; *liurai* 'noble' |

(21) *menta, *aklar, etc.

In Palu'e the familiar pattern of disyllabic feet dominates, and all roots with two vowels satisfy the need for a bimoraic foot. Some roots, however, do not contain two vowels. In (22) we can see two strategies to satisfy bimoraicity. In the first, as introduced in §43.3.1, roots with an underlying (but disallowed) CC sequence resolve the illicit structure through epenthesis of a schwa, which satisfies bimoraicity while not being visible for stress assignment. Roots that consist only of a V or CV sequence do not contain the environment that allows epenthesis, but satisfy bimoraicity through lengthened vowels.

(22) Palu'e

a. /kɔlɔ/ 'bird' [ˈkɔlɔ]
b. /kla/ 'thunder' [kəˈla] (* [kəˈlaː], * [klaː], etc.)
c. /la/ 'crow' [ˈlaː] (* [əˈla], * [ləa] etc.)

Evidence that the vowel in a word like [ˈlaː] in (22c) are not underlyingly long can be found when we examine verbs with the 1SG clitic, which contains its own vowel. In (23a) we can see that the verb root in isolation shows a long vowel; when this same verb is combined with the 1SG clitic there are two vowels in the phonological word, each of which contributes one mora. The two morae then satisfy bimoraicity and so removes the need (or possibility) for vowel lengthening.

(23)
a. /tʃi/ 'ask' [ˈtʃiː]
b. /aktʃi/ 'I ask' [ˈaktʃi]
c. * [ˈaktʃiː]

An interesting twist of these data is found in the treatment of three-syllable roots. The two forms in (24) clearly show different footing, made explicit in (25), since bimoraicity is resolved by vowel lengthening on different syllables in the different words presented.

(24)
a. /kululu/ 'rat sp.' [ˌkuluˈluː] (*[kuːˈlulu])
b. /puloga/ 'whale' [ˌpuːˈlɔga] (*[pulɔˈgaː])

(25)
a. (kulu) (lu)
b. (pu) (loga)

The languages of mainland southeast Sulawesi have elaborated the disyllabic template by preferring words to contain three syllables. With verb roots this is satisfied by the monosyllabic agreement prefix found in most inflected forms of the verb, or by the presence of a fossilized prefix, *moN-*, as seen in (26c); nonetheless *leu* in (26a) is licit, as an uninflected imperative form. With nouns we see the use of an article that is phonologically conditioned as much as it is morphosyntactically conditioned. In (27) we see that the article is strongly preferred with a disyllabic root, including in citation forms seen in (27a). The article is dispreferred with a root that is already trisyllabic (or longer), (27d–e), or which is trisyllabic due to possessive affixation, (27f–i).

(26) Tolaki

a. *leu* 'come' b. *no-leu* '3SG comes'
c. *moŋgii* 'see' d. *no-moŋgii* '3SG sees'

(27)
a. *ŋgituʔo* 'that' *o ruo* 'two' *o beka* 'cat'
b. *ŋgituʔo o ruo o beka*
that ART-two ART-cat
'those two cats'
c. */# ŋgituʔo o ruo beka*
d. *ŋgituʔo o ruo baŋgona*
that ART-two friend
'those two friends'
e. *# ŋgituʔo o ruo o baŋgona*
f. *No-leu beka-ŋgu.*
3SG-come cat-1SG.GEN
'My cat is coming.'
g. *# noleu o bekaŋgu*
h. *No-leu o beka.*
3SG-come ART-cat
'A/The cat is coming.'
i. *# noleu beka*

[4] We should note that the vowel in the first syllable of a trisyllabic word is always /a/.

### 43.3.3 Root length

In the MPSEA languages we find, as with Austronesian languages generally, words which are (slightly) longer than world norms. The languages are found between the area of the world with the most languages with small average words, Mainland Southeast Asia, and the area with the longest average words, mainland New Guinea (see maps 43.3 and 43.4). The Austronesian languages show a very low level of variation in average word length, compared to other language families.

Most of the MPSEA languages, like Austronesian languages generally, have disyllabic roots. In Tagalog, for instance, 88% of basic vocabulary words are disyllables, with monosyllables being found mostly as grammatical functors (eg. *ang* 'nominative'; *ba* 'question particle'; *huwag* ([hwag]) 'don't'). Similar facts are true for other MPSEA languages; although monosyllables are attested, they are only grammatical functors, and monomorphemic words of three or more syllables are very rare. In (28) we see examples of words of different syllable length in Indonesian. We should note that one of the trisyllabic forms is etymologically a disyllable, *bataŋ* 'corpse', with an infix *-in-*, and that the single quadrisyllabic form *manusia* is etymologically a loan from Sanskrit मनुष्य *manuṣyá* 'person' (similarly, *səmua* < Sanskrit समूह *samūha* 'assembly, collection'), indicative of the rarity of roots longer than two syllables in length. The longer words in (29) almost certainly represent (historical) compounds; *parantaea* can also be pronounced as *ntaea* (though no etymology for *para* is known), and *kalipopondaŋi* represents a word that is widespread across numerous languages of the southeast Sulawesi islands, *kali(m)popo*, compounded with *laŋi* 'sky' (and the genitive case, *n(u)*).

Indonesian roots of different sizes

| | | | | |
|---|---|---|---|---|
| (28) | a. | (1 syllable | *di* | 'at') |
| | b. | sesquisyllabic | *kəras* | 'hard' |
| | c. | 2 syllables | *karaŋ* | 'coral' |
| | d. | 2 syllables + | *səmua* | 'all' |
| | e. | 3 syllables | *binataŋ* | 'animal' |
| | f. | 4 syllables | *manusia* | 'human' |

Tukang Besi roots of different sizes

| | | | | |
|---|---|---|---|---|
| (29) | a. | (1 syllable | *nu* | 'genitive') |
| | b. | 2 syllables | *ompu* | 'grandparent/child' |
| | c. | 3 syllables | *oliha* | 'centipede' |
| | d | 4 syllables | *paŋkulela* | 'starfruit' |
| | e. | 5 syllables | *parantaea* | 'because' |
| | f. | 6 syllables | *kalipopondaŋi* | 'firefly' |

Figure 43.1 shows the proportion of words with a particular syllable count in different languages. All of the Austronesian languages in this (admittedly small) sample appear with more than 50% of roots being disyllabic, rising to 88% for Tagalog. The three languages with high numbers of monosyllables are external witnesses: Vietnamese, Thai, and English, all with mostly monosyllabic roots (on a basic word list). The more eastern languages, Tukang Besi and Ambai (Donohue 1999a; Silzer 1983), have more words with three or four syllables, and the Chamic languages (Lee 1966; Daud and Durie 1999), heavily influenced by Mainland Southeast Asian phonological and phonotactic norms (evidenced by Vietnamese and Thai in this chart), show a higher proportion of monosyllables than is normal for Austronesian languages,

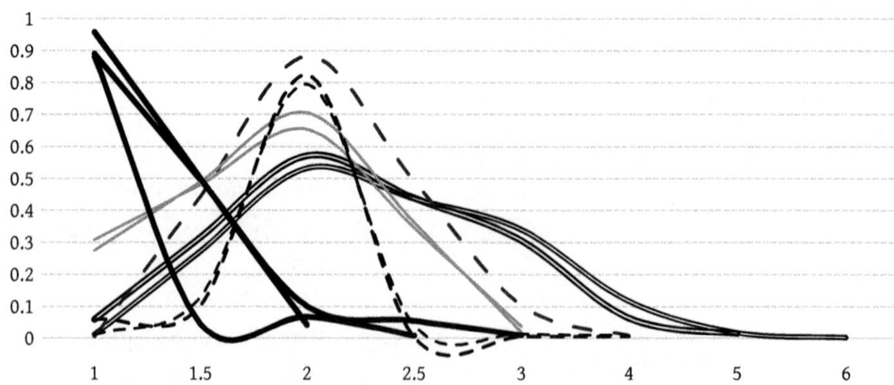


**Figure 43.1** Proportions of words of different size in different languages.

Key: Thick lines originating on the left are (top to bottom) Vietnamese, Thai, and English; grey lines originating at ~0.3 on the vertical axis are Raglai (/Roglai) and Acehnese; high dashed line: Tagalog; thin dashed lines: Indonesian and Palu'e; double lines are Ambai (higher) and Tukang Besi (lower).

but still have a majority of disyllabic roots in keeping with their Austronesian origins.

The different language families across southeast Asia show different average word lengths. In Figure 43.2 we can see different geographic groups of MPSEA languages in black, Taiwanese languages and Oceanic in speckled black, and six other language families in grey. The average word length for different Austronesian groups (shown as bars extending one standard deviation above and below the mean) is not significantly different, except for the languages of Mainland Southeast Asia. The languages of the Philippines conform most closely to a two-syllable canon (see the discussion of Tagalog above), and the level of variation in word lengths increases with proximity to New Guinea, where word lengths are on average longer, and more variable.

Map 43.3 shows the location of languages with smaller words than the global average (which is two syllables), while Map 43.4 shows where languages with longer than average words are found. As noted earlier, there is very little variation across the Austronesian languages, the exception being the Austronesian languages of Mainland Southeast Asia, where they have assimilated towards the other language families of the region. There is a slight (though not statistically significant) increase in average length towards New Guinea, indicating that at the other end of the MPSEA range, too, there is an accommodation to areal norms.

### 43.3.4 Metathesis

Perhaps the firmest evidence for the templatic treatment of words is found in western Timor, where productive syntactic metathesis is found (see Chapter 35). While metathesis is attested as a historical process in various forms in many languages, Austronesian and otherwise, it is rare as a productive synchronic process. In the representative data from Amarasi presented in (30) we see the unmetathesized and metathesized forms of four words of different shape from Amarasi (Edwards 2020). We have, respectively words that appear to have a CVCV, CVCVC, [ʔ]VCVC, CVV, CVVC, and CCVVC form. Note that while CC onsets are permitted in the language, CC codas are not, and that the initial glottal stop in 'cuscus' is phonetic, and not underlying.

| | | Amarasi | |
|---|---|---|---|
| (30) | a. | *fatu* | *faut* |
| | | 'rock' | |
| | b. | *tenuk* | *teun* |
| | | 'umbrella' | |
| | c. | [ʔ]*ukum* | [ʔ]*uuk* |
| | | 'cuscus' | |
| | d. | *hau* | *hau* |
| | | 'wood' | |

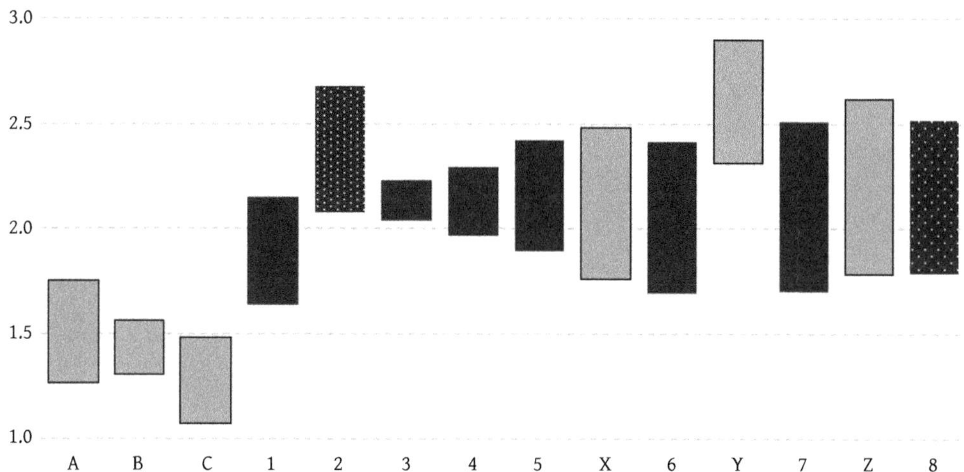


**Figure 43.2** Average word lengths in language groups relevant to Southeast Asia.

Key: A: Austroasiatic; B: Hmong-Mien; C: Tai-Kadai; 1: MPSEA languages of mainland SEA; 2: Taiwanese Austronesian languages; 3: MPSEA languages of the Philippines; 4: MPSEA languages of western Nusantara; 5: MPSEA languages of eastern Nusantara; 6: MPSEA languages of western New Guinea; 7: MPSEA languages of Cenderawasih Bay; 8: Oceanic Austronesian languages; X: Timor-Alor-Pantar languages; Y: West Papuan languages; Z: Trans New Guinea languages.

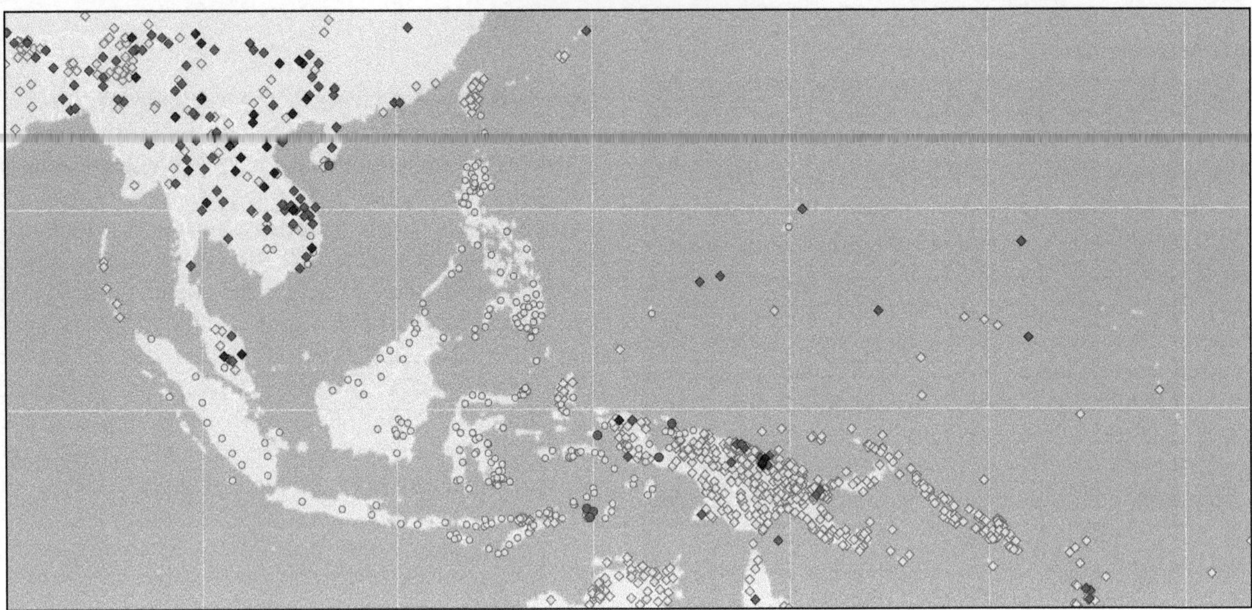

**Map 43.3** Languages with smaller words than the global average.

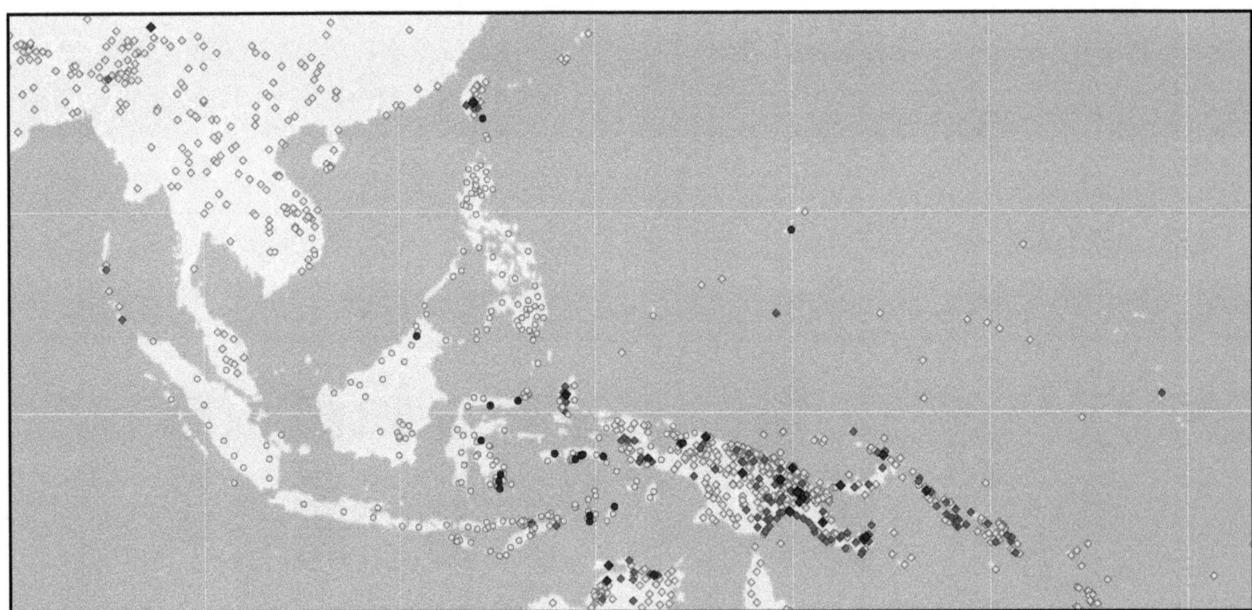

**Map 43.4** Languages with longer words than the global average.

e. *heum heu*
   'mango'

f. *knaaʔ knaa*
   'beans'

Based on apparent CVCV words such as *fatu* in (30a) we might propose that the alternations involve the swapping of the last two segments in the root, as schematized in (31).

(31) $X_1X_2\mathbf{X_3X_4} \rightarrow X_1X_2\mathbf{X_4X_3}$
     f a t u     f a u t

The data from CVCVC words, such as *tenuk* in (30b) show that when five segments are present it is the third and fourth segments that undergo metathesis; a general constraint in the language proscribing complex codas then results in the loss of the final consonant, which would otherwise be the second member of a -CC coda.

(32) $X_1X_2\mathbf{X_3X_4}X_5$ ➔ $X_1X_2\mathbf{X_4X_3}X_5$ ➔ $X_1X_2\mathbf{X_4X_3}$
t e n u k　　t e u n k　　t e u n

The data from an apparent VCVC word in (30c) show that the template that is manipulated specifies consonant and vowel positions, and not just generalized segments, and that the initial epenthetic glottal stop 'counts' as filling the root-initial C-position, indicating the obligatory nature of the initial C. The metathesized form corresponding to *ukum* is *uuk*, and not **ukmu*. Metathesis applies to the $C_3$ and $V_4$ slots, not the $X_3$ and $X_4$ slots. The absence of any underlying segment in the $C_1$ (or $X_1$) slot is not relevant to the selection of which part of the word template (namely, the first post-vocalic consonant and the vowel that follows that consonant) undergoes metathesis. An incorrect process, yielding the unattested form **ukmu*, is shown in (34).

(33) $C_1V_2\mathbf{C_3V_4}C_5$ ➔ $C_1V_2\mathbf{V_4C_3}C_5$ ➔ $C_1V_2\mathbf{V_4C_3}$
[ʔ]u k u m　　[ʔ]u u k m　　[ʔ]u u k

(34) *$X_1X_2\mathbf{X_3X_4}$ ➔ $X_1X_2\mathbf{X_4X_3}$
u k u m　　u k m u

With *hau* in (30d) we see that since only the $C_1$, $V_2$, and $V_4$ positions are filled, the putative swapping on the $C_3$ and $V_4$ positions is undetectable without further affixation (see Edwards 2020).

(35) $C_1V_2\mathbf{C_3V_4}C_5$ ➔ $C_1V_2\mathbf{V_4C_3}C_5$ ➔ $C_1V_2\mathbf{V_4C_3}$
h a　u　　h a u　　h a u

The data in (30e) and (30f) can *only* be explained by reference to the template. These forms are similar to those in (30d), lacking any segment occupying the $C_3$ position, except that metathesis is overtly visible because the final consonant is lost in the metathesized form. The process by which the $C_5$ consonant is lost reveals how strongly the template applies to Amarasi roots.

The same process of $C_3$ and $C_4$ metathesis applies that has been explanatory in the other root shapes. The loss of the final ($C_5$) segment can be explained by reference to the final $C_3C_5$ cluster that results from the metathesis: as seen earlier in (32) and (33), when two consonants are found finally, the second of those consonants is lost.[5] We have seen this with overt segmental consonants, but in the case of 'mango' and 'beans' there is not segmental consonant, only a templatic position. Again, the metathesis of positions in the template creates a CC sequence, even though segmentally only one of those C positions is filled by a segment.[6] With 'mango', this is shown explicitly in (36), with a less sophisticated, and infelicitous, process that does not specify the template in terms of Cs and Vs shown in (37). With 'beans' the process is the same, but the addition of the CC cluster in initial position further illustrates that whether the five segments of *knaaʔ* are treated as occupying five different slots in the template, or whether only the *knaaʔ* fits the template and the *k-* is extrametrical, the underspecified template without an empty, but present, $C_3$ position makes incorrect predictions about the outcome of metathesis. As with 'cuscus', the final consonants of the roots for 'mango' and 'beans' are lost because they occur in an illicit cluster *at the templatic level*, as final -CC for which only the second C corresponds to a segment.

(36) $C_1V_2\mathbf{C_3V_4}C_5$ ➔ $C_1V_2\mathbf{V_4C_3}C_5$ ➔ $C_1V_2\mathbf{V_4C_3}$
h e u　m　　h e u　m　　h e u

(37) *$X_1X_2\mathbf{X_3}$ $\mathbf{X_4}$ ➔ $X_1X_2\mathbf{X_4X_3}$
h e u　m　　h e m u

(38) $C_0C_1V_2\mathbf{C_3V_4}C_5$ ➔ $C_0C_1V_2\mathbf{V_4C_3}C_5$ ➔ $C_0C_1V_2\mathbf{V_4C_3}$
k-n a　a ʔ　　k-n a　a ʔ　　k-n a a

(39) *$X_1X_2\mathbf{X_3X_4}X_5$ ➔ $X_1X_2\mathbf{X_4X_3}X_5$
k n a a ʔ　　k n a a ʔ

(40) *$C_0X_1X_2\mathbf{X_3X_4}X_5$ ➔ $C_0X_1X_2\mathbf{X_4X_3}$
k-n a a ʔ　　k-n a ʔ a

### 43.3.5 Syllable shapes

The modal syllable in MPSEA languages is CVC, which is also modal globally. Some languages of the area are only found with CV syllables, and these languages typically also ban complex consonant clusters as well. Map 43.5 shows the languages without codas; in addition to a wide stretch of Sulawesi lacking codas, the languages to the south, not closely related, similarly share in the presence of prenasalized and/or imploded stops (Donohue and Whiting 2011). The synchronic productivity of NoCoda in these languages can be seen in the treatment of loanwords in Tukang Besi; the words in (41a) show the unsystematic treatment of -VC# in borrowed words, with some words showing the loss of the final consonant, and some words the addition of a paragogic vowel, the quality of which depends on the previous consonant and the previous vowel. In (41b) we can see the treatment of various root-internal clusters, which are all broken up by a copy of the preceding vowel, or /a/, or in some cases are lost altogether. Note that the homorganic

[5] Support for the productive avoidance of final -CC sequences can also be seen in the treatment of CC sequences in non-initial position in loanwords, where we find epenthesis: Dutch *mark* 'brand; stamp' > Amarasi *marak*, Dutch *dans* 'dance' > Amarasi *ranas*, Portuguese *festa* 'party' > Amarasi *fesat*, Malay *lampu* 'lamp' > Amarasi *ramup*.

[6] Unlike the case for initial empty C slots, there is not epenthesis of a glottal stop (or other consonant) into an empty $C_3$ or $C_5$ position.

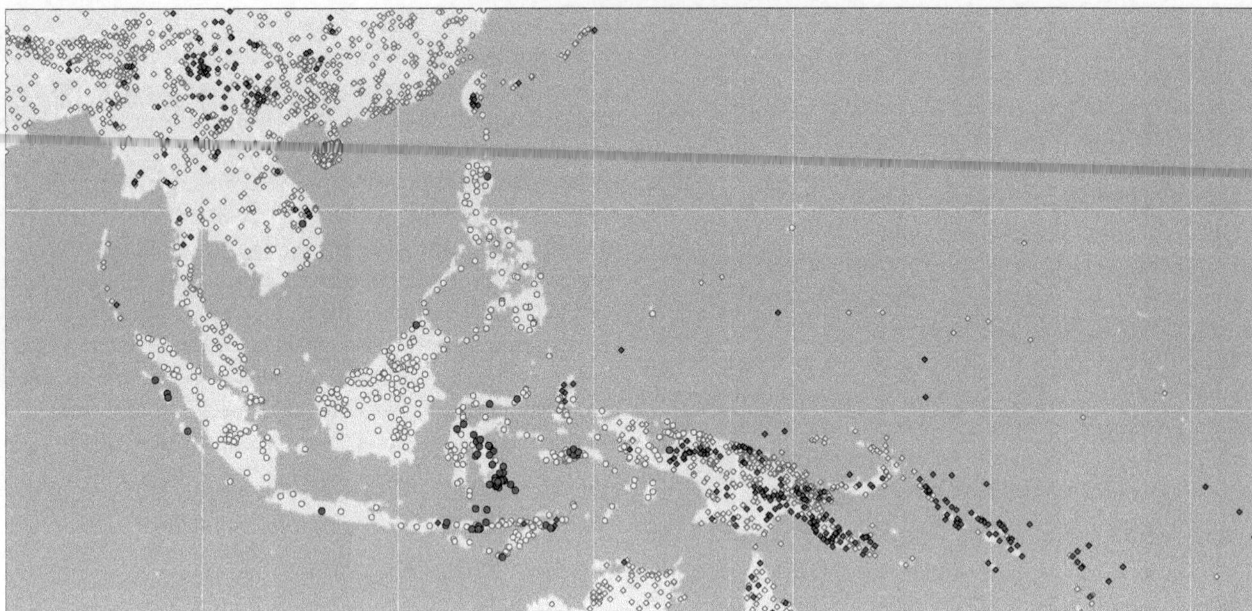

**Map 43.5** Languages with NoCoda dominant.

nasal + stop sequences in (41a) are not broken up, as they are reinterpreted as unit prenasalized complex segments, and so are not subject to paragogic vowel insertion.

(41) Tukang Besi loans from Indonesian and local Malay

| | | | |
|---|---|---|---|
| a. | *tonton* 'spectate' | > | *tonto* 'watch' |
| | *surat* 'letter' | > | *sura* 'letter' |
| | *waruŋ* 'stall' | > | *waru* 'stall' |
| | *garam* 'salt' | > | *gara* 'salt' |
| | *sumbaŋ* 'donate' | > | *sumbaŋa* 'donate' |
| | *taŋkap* 'catch' | > | *taŋkapu* 'capture' |
| | *senter* 'torch' | > | *sintere* 'torch' |
| | *ahad* 'Friday' | > | *ahadʒi* 'Friday' |
| b. | *blek* 'can' | > | *beleke* 'canned food' |
| | *harga* 'price' | > | *haragaa* 'price' |
| | *kərdʒa* 'work' | > | *karadʒaa* 'work' |
| | *komkomər* 'cucumber' | > | *komokomoro* 'cucumber' |
| | *pərlu* 'need' | > | *paraluu* 'need' |
| | *pəriksa* 'examine' | > | *parisa* 'examine' |
| | *potlot* 'pencil' | > | *potoloti* 'pencil' |
| | *plastik* 'plastic bag' | > | *pulasutii* 'plastic bag' |

The insertion of paragogic vowels in Tukang Besi is only found in modern loanwords; historical final consonants are lost, as can be seen in (42).

(42) Tukang Besi treatment of historical -C#

| Proto-Malayo-Polynesian | | Tukang Besi |
|---|---|---|
| *qudip | 'live' | *ʔiɗo* |
| *kulit | 'skin' | *kuli* |
| *anak | 'child' | *ana* |
| *daləm | 'deep' | *men-daro* |
| *ŋajan | 'name' | *ŋaa* |

In Malagasy, another language with a NoCoda constraint dominating the shape of words, historical final consonants show a split in terms of their preservation. In (43) we can see that final nasals (-N) are preserved, but with a paragogic vowel added, to maintain the strict CV syllable structure.[7] Stress, however, is (regularly for Malagasy) on the initial, antepenultimate, syllable, and not on the penultimate syllable, which is regular for most words that do not have a paragogic vowel (the final vowels also disappear in compounds, suggesting that even synchronically they are not underlying). Final fricatives (-S) are consistently lost, with

[7] For the sake of phonological transparency, orthographic *-y* is written as *-i* and *o* as *u* in the lexical examples in (32)–(35). Different varieties of Malagasy present a different picture; in western dialects, nasals are not realized word-finally, and in Merina there are many cases of the loss of a final nasal: PMP *ma-qitəm 'black' > *mainti*, 'PWMP' *balalaŋ 'grasshopper' > *valala* 'grasshopper'.

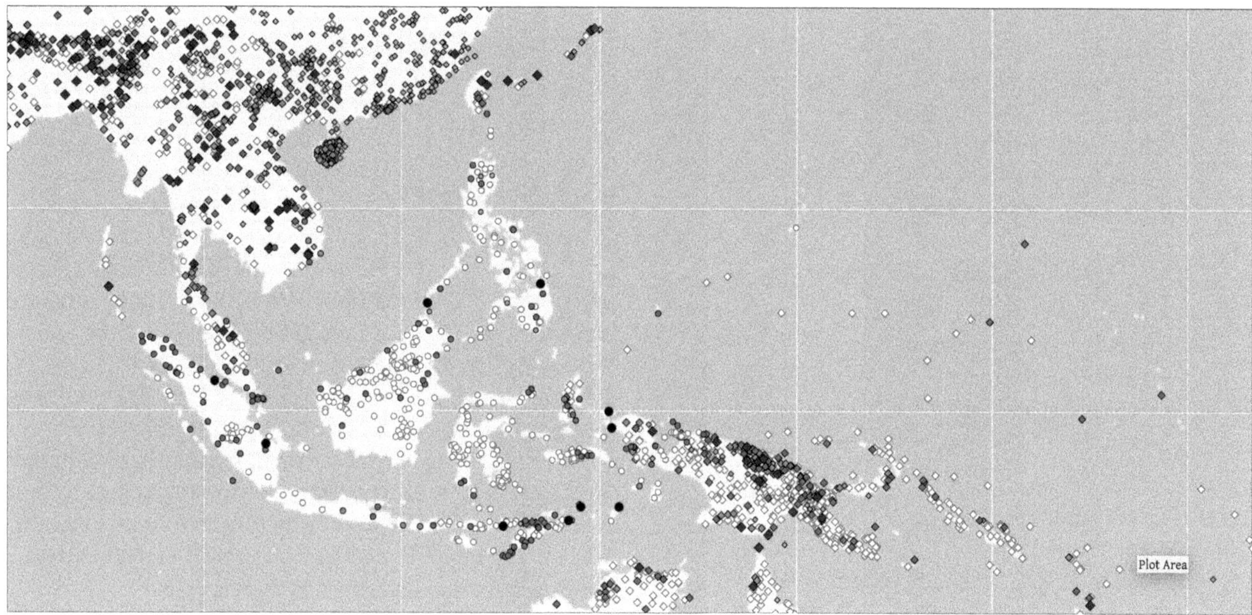


**Map 43.6** Languages with complex onsets.

*Notes*: circles: MPSEA language; diamond: non-MPSEA language; white: no complex onsets; grey: maximum onset CC; black: maximum onset CCC or larger.

no paragogy, and final plosives (-T) show variable treatment, as do final liquids (-R/-l).

Malagasy treatment of historical -N#

(43)

| Proto-Malayo-Polynesian | | Malagasy |
|---|---|---|
| *ənəm | 'six' | ***é**nina* |
| *daləm | 'deep' | ***lá**lina* |
| *haŋin | 'wind' | ***á**nina* |
| *quzan | 'rain' | ***ú**rana* |
| *apuŋ | 'float' | ***á**funa* |
| *duyuŋ | 'whale' | ***trú**zuna* |

Malagasy treatment of historical -S#

(44)

| Proto-Malayo-Polynesian | | Malagasy |
|---|---|---|
| *ləpas | 'release' | ***lé**fa* 'gone' |
| (Banjar: lamas | 'flexible; weak' | ***lá**ma*) 'smooth' |
| *dəpah | 'fathom' | ***ré**fi* |
| *talih | 'rope' | ***tá**di* |

Malagasy treatment of historical -T#

(45)

| Proto-Malayo-Polynesian | | Malagasy |
|---|---|---|
| *sisip | 'insert' | ***sí**sika* |
| *qambat | 'block' | ***á**mbatra* |
| *lipət | 'fold' | ***dí**fi* |
| *kunij | 'turmeric' | ***hú**nitra* |
| *pusej | 'navel' | ***fú**itra* |
| *lamak | 'mat' | ***lá**maka* |

Malagasy treatment of historical -R/-l#

(46)

| Proto-Malayo-Polynesian | | Malagasy |
|---|---|---|
| *dəŋəR | 'hear' | ***ré**ni* |
| *gatəl | 'itchy' | ***há**tina* |
| *paŋkal | 'root' | ***fá**ka* |

Complex onsets are not common in the MPSEA languages. The languages of Mainland Southeast Asia frequently allow complex onsets, though to the north those onsets are restricted to consonant + glide sequences (CG). In Island Southeast Asia we find that consonant + liquid (CL) is a more common allowed complex onset, and languages with this phonotactic possibility are found in Sumatra, eastern Java plus Bali and Lombok, and a concentration in the Timor area (Map 43.6), where we find other consonant–consonant complex onsets beyond those already discussed (CC). In general, however, onsets are simple. Acehnese examples of complex onsets are given in (47a); liquids are the most common second consonant in a complex onset, though /w/ is not completely unknown. In Roma the opposite is true, (47b), with glides being more common as the second consonant, but /l/ is also attested (Steven 1991). CG sequences are rare in Sarangani Manobo, (47c) and are mostly found in loans that are ultimately from Spanish, while Ambel is an example of a language that allows a wide range of complex onsets in (47d) (Arnold 2018a), including both CG sequences and CL sequences, and also allowing triconsonantal onsets (CCC).

(47) a. Acehnese

| | |
|---|---|
| *glaŋ* | 'worm' |
| *pla.wɯə* | 'smallpox' |
| *blɯə* | 'swamp; marsh' |
| *pɯ.trɯŋ* | 'brighten' |
| *drɔə* | 'self' |
| *dʒa.kwɔə* | 'return home' |

b. Roma

| | |
|---|---|
| *pwena* | 'his chin' |
| *lwina* | 'sword grass' |
| *pjaki* | '(place name)' |
| *rjaram* | 'inside' |
| *klodanna* | 'his shin' |
| *tlapirna* | 'his lungs' |
| *wledan* | 'mountain' |

c. Sarangani Manobo

| | |
|---|---|
| *kwani* | 'later' |
| *djèkəj* | 'right in that direction' |

d. Ambel

| | |
|---|---|
| *mnjaran* | 'diligence' |
| *tnjain* | 'our bellies' |
| *kris* | 'tree (sp.)' |

## 43.4 Summary

From a phonological viewpoint, the MPSEA languages can be statistically differentiated from the Oceanic languages and the Austronesian languages of Taiwan, but they do not form a consistent 'type'. This chapter has described the major ways in which languages diverge from the prototype described in (1), but does not pretend to exhaustively survey all of the peculiarities of the phonologies of individual languages. The areality of most of the phonological traits surveyed is remarkable, showing distinct areas within the MPSEA languages, or else including both Austronesian and non-Austronesian languages in their scope.

# CHAPTER 44

# Morphology

MARK DONOHUE AND DAVID GIL

## 44.1 Introduction

This chapter presents an overview of morphological structures in the Malayo-Polynesian languages of Southeast Asia, referred to here as MPSEA languages.

The morphology of MPSEA languages has been the object of numerous studies from a variety of perspectives, synchronic and diachronic, language-specific and cross-linguistic. A random sample of the numerous morphological phenomena that are commonly associated with MPSEA languages might include formal devices such as infixation and reduplication, and grammatical constructions such as nominal ligatures and verbal voice affixes. A variety of morphological phenomena form the focus of other chapters in this volume, for example Mattes and Schwaiger (this volume, chapter 45) on reduplication and Kroeger and Riesberg (this volume, chapter 47) on voice and transitivity. An overview of the morphology of Austronesian languages more generally is provided in Blust (2009c: 355–435).

This chapter presents a quantitative overview of the major morphological characteristics of MPSEA languages, drawing on a typological database compiled by the first author.[1] The main goal is to compare MPSEA languages to their non-MPSEA counterparts, the latter including Austronesian languages in Taiwan and the Pacific, non-Austronesian languages in the same regions as MPSEA languages, and non-Austronesian languages throughout the world. In addition, it highlights patterns of variation within MPSEA languages of different regions, from the Philippines through Madagascar and the Malay/Indonesian archipelago and into western New Guinea.

The data are presented in a series of tables, each representing a single morphological feature. All of the tables share a common format. Each table consists of two parts. In the top part, rows partition the Austronesian-speaking world into geographical regions, adding a final region for the rest of the world.[2] The final two rows of this part provide grand totals for all Austronesian languages, all non-Austronesian languages, and all of the world's languages. In the bottom part, consisting of the last four rows, the data from the top part are summarized and recapitulated with a specific focus on the category of MPSEA languages. The first three rows tell the story of the Austronesian expansion, beginning in Taiwan, continuing into MPSEA, and from there out into the Pacific, while the fourth and final row provides a grand total for non-MPSEA languages, both Austronesian and non-Austronesian, worldwide.[3] In each table, the columns specify the geographical region, the sample size

[1] The database contains data for 2,750 languages and varieties, of which 439 are Austronesian and 290 'Papuan'. (The 2,750 language sample is a subset of a larger database of phonological features, comprising 7,400 languages.) Languages are coded for 335 mostly binary features, of which many are based on features found in the *World Atlas of Language Stuctures* (Dryer and Haspelmath 2013), henceforth referred to as *WALS*; the overall coding rate stands at 82%. The database is accessible at https://doi.org/10.5281/zenodo.4910764.

[2] The regions are defined on the basis of a combination of geographical, cultural, and linguistic properties. *Taiwan* consists of the entirety of the island of Taiwan. *Philippines* comprises the Philippine archipelago south to Balabac and Tawi-Tawi islands, north to Orchard Island, and east including Palau and Guam but no other areas of Micronesia. *Mainland SEA* includes the languages of Mainland Southeast Asia as far west as the Irrawaddy River, plus the parts of Myanmar in which Tai languages are spoken (but not those west of the Patkai Hills). In the east the region extends as far north as Ningde in Fujian on the coast, inland to Nancheng (Jiangxi), Hengshan (Hunan), west to Xiangxi Tujia Miao Autonomous Prefecture and Yibin in Sichuan, then south to Qiannan Buyi Miao Autonomous Prefecture, and south of Kunming to Dehong Dai Jingpo Autonomous Prefecture, Shan State and the area occupied by speakers of Karen languages in Myanmar. Also included in Mainland SEA are the Mergui archipelago, the Nicobar Islands, and Hainan. *Indian Ocean* encompasses Sri Lanka, the Lakshwadeep archipelago, the Maldives, Seychelles, Mauritius, Réunion, the Comoros, and Madagascar. *SW Island SEA* consists of the Sunda islands from Sumatra and the Barrier Islands through Java to Bali, plus Borneo. *SE Island SEA* extends east from Lombok to the Aru islands, north to Sulawesi (including the Sangihe and Talaud islands), and also Halmahera and the Maluku islands. *West New Guinea* includes Raja Ampat and the Bird's Head and Bomberai peninsulas, down to Kaimana. *Cenderawasih Bay* includes the islands of the Cenderawasih Bay plus the maritime coastal regions up to and just beyond the Mamberamo river. *East New Guinea* includes locations east from West New Guinea and Cenderawasih Bay, on the New Guinea mainland plus off-shore islands, including the Bismarck archipelago up to and including Bougainville. Finally, *Remote Oceania* spans all the Pacific islands not included in the preceding areas, including also Takuu. It should be noted that while many of these regions represent synchronically and diachronically well-motivated areas in the linguistic sense, others, in particular the Indian Ocean region, are referred to purely as geographically contiguous groupings of languages, and are included here only in order to facilitate the exhaustive quantitative analysis of MPSEA languages that is presented here.

[3] In the bottom part of each table, the figures in the Taiwan AN row repeat the corresponding figures in the top part of the table, the figures in the MPSEA row are the sum of the figures for the seven MPSEA-speaking

Mark Donohue and David Gil, *Morphology*. In: *The Oxford Guide to the Malayo-Polynesian Languages of Southeast Asia*. Edited by: Alexander Adelaar and Antoinette Schapper, Oxford University Press. © Mark Donohue and David Gil (2024). DOI: 10.1093/oso/9780198807353.003.0044

(n), and then the 'score', that is to say, the relevant figures for the feature in question; a further distinction is made between Austronesian (AN) and non-Austronesian (non-AN) languages.[4] Within each table, the data for MPSEA languages is highlighted in boldface within shaded cells.

A total of twenty-four tables, each representing a single morphological feature, are presented below, organized as follows. §44.2 provides a general overview of the degree of morphological elaboration of MPSEA languages, §44.3 and §44.4 focus on formal types, including affixation and other processes, while §44.5 to §44.8 are concerned with functional types, grouped in accordance with nominal, tense-aspect-mood, causative-applicative, and other grammatical domains.

## 44.2 How much morphology is there?

Table 44.1 addresses the most basic of questions, namely, how much morphology there is in MPSEA languages; it does so by assigning to each language a numerical measure of morphological elaboration, ranging from 0 (low) to 1 (high), quantifying the cline between isolating and inflecting languages. The measure draws on a list of 125 different morphological processes, bound and derivational, presented in Donohue (to appear); these processes encompass the ones described in Tables 44.2–44.24 below, plus many others, such as, for example, tonal morphology, gender, evidentiality, and syncretism in case and agreement systems.

As evident from Table 44.1, the overall degree of morphological elaboration of MPSEA languages is substantially less than that of non-MPSEA languages, 0.23 vs. 0.42; a difference that is statistically significant at $p < 0.001$.[5] In particular, MPSEA languages exhibit a relatively high frequency of occurrence of languages with the lowest degree of morphological elaboration (i.e. isolating languages); see McWhorter (2008b); Gil (2015a); and a collection of case studies in Gil and Schapper eds. (2020).[6]

**Table 44.1** Morphological elaboration

| | *n* | | average | |
|---|---|---|---|---|
| | AN | non-AN | AN | non-AN |
| Taiwan | 10 | 2 | 0.30 | 0.13 |
| Philippines | **39** | 1 | **0.28** | 0.23 |
| Mainland SEA | **18** | 200 | **0.08** | 0.13 |
| Indian Ocean | **3** | 9 | **0.20** | 0.34 |
| SW Island SEA | **62** | 1 | **0.19** | 0.38 |
| SE Island SEA | **96** | 20 | **0.26** | 0.49 |
| W New Guinea | **14** | 17 | **0.22** | 0.47 |
| Cenderawasih Bay | **7** | 3 | **0.33** | 0.40 |
| E New Guinea | 77 | 247 | 0.34 | 0.45 |
| Remote Oceania | 102 | 3 | 0.33 | 0.64 |
| Rest of the World | - | 1780 | - | 0.45 |
| TOTAL | 428 | 2283 | 0.28 | 0.42 |
| | 2711 | | 0.40 | |
| Taiwan AN | 10 | | 0.30 | |
| MPSEA | **239** | | **0.23** | |
| Oceanic | 179 | | 0.33 | |
| non-MPSEA | 2472 | | 0.42 | |

Within those regions containing a substantial number of both MPSEA and non-Austronesian languages (over ten of each in the sample), the rate of morphological elaboration is consistently lower in the MPSEA languages than in their non-Austronesian neighbours: 0.08 vs. 0.13 in Mainland SEA, 0.26 vs. 0.49 in SE Island SEA, and 0.22 vs. 0.47 in West New Guinea. This pattern could be due to either or both of the following two factors. First, it could be an inheritance from Proto-Austronesian: note that the rate of morphological elaboration for the presumably conservative Austronesian languages of Taiwan is also significantly lower than of non-Austronesian languages worldwide, 0.30 vs. 0.42 ($p < 0.001$). Secondly, it could reflect contact-induced simplification undergone by the intrusive Austronesian languages in the course of their spread into regions where

regions, and the figures in the Oceanic row are the sum of those in the East New Guinea and Remote Oceania rows.

[4] In the bottom rows of each of the tables' two parts, the figures summarizing over both AN and non-AN languages are accordingly centred between the AN and non-AN columns.

[5] This figure is calculated with a two-tailed t-test with unequal variance. T-tests are used with the data in Tables 44.1, 44.2, 44.8, 44.12, 44.14, and 44.18, while chi-squared tests are used with the data in Tables 44.3–44.7, 44.9–44.11, 44.13, 44.15–44.17, and 44.19–44.24.

[6] Among MPSEA languages, the ones with the highest rate of morphological elaboration are from Southeast Sulawesi (e.g. Tolaki and Muna), while the ones with the lowest rate are from Mainland SEA (e.g. Nonthaburi Malay, Tsat, and Cham), central Flores (e.g. Ngadha and Rongga), and Timor (e.g. Naueti and Waima'a). Elsewhere in the Austronesian family, the languages with the highest rate of morphological elaboration are some belonging to the Oceanic subgroup (e.g. Nanggu, Sudest, and Southwest Tanna).

non-Austronesian languages were and, in many cases, still are spoken (Gil 2015a, 2020a; Donohue and Denham 2020).

The significance of language contact is further supported by the breakdown of the rate of morphological elaboration within the Austronesian language family. Following the out-of-Taiwan path of expansion of Austronesian languages, morphological elaboration drops from 0.30 in Taiwan to 0.23 in MPSEA languages ($p = 0.01$) before recovering to 0.33 in Oceanic ($p < 0.001$ compared to MPSEA languages). This pattern, which may be referred to as the 'MPSEA dip', is replicated in a handful of other, more specific morphological features, represented in Tables 44.13, 44.15 and 44.24 below. A closer look at the figures in Table 44.1 shows that the Philippines, at 0.28, is effectively on a par with Taiwan ($p = 0.49$), suggesting that the significant drop in morphological elaboration is associated with the spread of Austronesian languages southwards out of the Philippines and into the *Mekong-Mamberamo linguistic area*, spanning Mainland SEA, Southwest and Southeast Insular SEA, West New Guinea and the Cenderawasih Bay, where other languages with low levels of morphological elaboration are found (Gil 2015a; see also Donohue and Denham 2010). Additional more specific instantiations of the drop in morphological elaboration associated with the Austronesian expansion southwards out of the Philippines and into the Mekong-Mamberamo linguistic area are provided in Tables 44.3, 44.11, 44.15, 44.21, and 44.24 below. This drop in morphological elaboration is argued to reflect various processes of contact-induced simplification (McWhorter 2008b; Donohue and Denham 2020; Gil 2020a).

**Table 44.2** Prefixing vs. suffixing

| | *n* | | rate | |
|---|---|---|---|---|
| | AN | non-AN | AN | non-AN |
| Taiwan | 8/10 | 0/2 | 0.50 | -0.50 |
| Philippines | **32/38** | 0/1 | **0.70** | 0.00 |
| Mainland SEA | **5/18** | 35/162 | **0.06** | -0.02 |
| Indian Ocean | **1/3** | 2/8 | **0.00** | -0.13 |
| SW Island SEA | **23/62** | 0/1 | **0.10** | 0.00 |
| SE Island SEA | **55/97** | 10/20 | **0.27** | 0.25 |
| W New Guinea | **8/13** | 5/17 | **0.38** | -0.03 |
| Cenderawasih Bay | **5/8** | 1/2 | **0.25** | 0.50 |
| E New Guinea | 26/76 | 27/248 | 0.09 | -0.44 |
| Remote Oceania | 37/102 | 1/9 | 0.16 | -0.28 |
| Rest of the World | -/- | 273/1804 | - | -0.41 |
| TOTAL | 427 | 2274 | 0.22 | -0.38 |
| | 2701 | | -0.28 | |
| Taiwan AN | 8/10 | | 0.50 | |
| MPSEA | **129/239** | | **0.28** | |
| Oceanic | 63/178 | | 0.13 | |
| non-MPSEA | 362/2284 | | -0.37 | |

## 44.3 Formal types: Affixation

§§44.3 and 44.4 provide a breakdown of morphological processes in accordance with formal criteria.

Table 44.2 presents the relative predominance of prefixation and affixation, following the criteria laid out in WALS Chapter 26. In Table 44.2, the first two (n) columns show the proportion of languages with predominantly prefixing morphology, while the next two (rate) columns present the average values for individual languages, ranked on the following five-point scale: strongly prefixing +1.0; weakly prefixing +0.5; equal prefixing and suffixing *or* little morphology 0; weakly suffixing -0.5; strongly suffixing -1.0.

As evident from Table 44.2, MPSEA languages differ systematically from their non-MPSEA counterparts, exhibiting a stronger preference towards prefixation, 0.28 vs. -0.37 ($p < 0.001$). The propensity for prefixation in MPSEA languages is revisited further down in Tables 44.15 and 44.20.

While the greater-than-average propensity for prefixation is in evidence in each and every one of the Austronesian-speaking geographical regions, prefixation is strikingly more dominant in the two northernmost regions, Taiwan and Philippines. This suggests that the dominance of prefixation was associated with Proto-Austronesian and subsequently underwent attenuation in the course of the southward expansion of Austronesian languages out of the Philippines, through both the loss of some prefixal material and the acquisition of new suffixes. Still, it is worth noting that the preference for prefixation is higher than the global norm also among the non-Austronesian languages in all of the Austronesian-speaking regions for which there is a sufficiently large sample, pointing towards some kind of an areal effect.

Table 44.3 is concerned with infixation; following the definition in Anderson (1985), it shows the distribution of languages which have at least one morpheme whose primary realization is infixed into the root or stem to which it is attached.

**Table 44.3** Infixing

| | n | | rate | |
|---|---|---|---|---|
| | AN | non AN | AN | non AN |
| Taiwan | 10/10 | 0/2 | 1.00 | 0.00 |
| Philippines | **36/38** | 0/1 | **0.95** | 0.00 |
| Mainland SEA | **0/18** | 38/149 | **0.00** | 0.26 |
| Indian Ocean | **2/3** | 0/8 | **0.67** | 0.00 |
| SW Island SEA | **26/59** | 0/1 | **0.44** | 0.00 |
| SE Island SEA | **31/92** | 0/20 | **0.34** | 0.00 |
| W New Guinea | **4/13** | 2/17 | **0.31** | 0.12 |
| Cenderawasih Bay | **6/8** | 0/2 | **0.75** | 0.00 |
| E New Guinea | 6/43 | 20/248 | 0.14 | 0.08 |
| Remote Oceania | 4/90 | 0/8 | 0.04 | 0.00 |
| Rest of the World | -/- | 142/1754 | - | 0.08 |
| TOTAL | 374 | 2210 | 0.33 | 0.09 |
| | 2584 | | 0.13 | |
| Taiwan AN | 10/10 | | 1.00 | |
| MPSEA | **105/231** | | **0.45** | |
| Oceanic | 10/133 | | 0.08 | |
| non-MPSEA | 212/2220 | | 0.10 | |

**Table 44.4** Ablaut

| | n | | rate | |
|---|---|---|---|---|
| | AN | non AN | AN | non AN |
| Taiwan | 0/10 | 0/2 | 0.00 | 0.00 |
| Philippines | **0/38** | 0/1 | **0.00** | 0.00 |
| Mainland SEA | **1/18** | 7/162 | **0.06** | 0.04 |
| Indian Ocean | **0/3** | 0/8 | **0.00** | 0.00 |
| SW Island SEA | **4/62** | 0/1 | **0.06** | 0.00 |
| SE Island SEA | **6/97** | 0/20 | **0.06** | 0.00 |
| W New Guinea | **0/13** | 2/17 | **0.00** | 0.12 |
| Cenderawasih Bay | **0/8** | 0/2 | **0.00** | 0.00 |
| E New Guinea | 2/76 | 15/248 | 0.03 | 0.05 |
| Remote Oceania | 7/103 | 0/9 | 0.07 | 0.00 |
| Rest of the World | -/- | 180/1813 | - | 0.07 |
| TOTAL | 428 | 2283 | 0.05 | 0.07 |
| | 2711 | | 0.06 | |
| Taiwan AN | 0/10 | | 0.00 | |
| MPSEA | **11/239** | | **0.05** | |
| Oceanic | 9/179 | | 0.05 | |
| non-MPSEA | 204/2293 | | 0.07 | |

Although, as shown in Table 44.1 earlier, MPSEA languages tend to have little morphology in general, infixing is significantly more common in MPSEA languages than it is in non-MPSEA languages, at 0.45 vs. 0.10 ($p < 0.001$). In the Austronesian languages of Taiwan and the Philippines, infixation is nearly universal, at 1.00 and 0.95 respectively, with infixes *-um- and *-in- reconstructed for Proto-Austronesian (Blust 2009c: 382–9). As the Austronesian languages spread out of the Philippines, the prevalence of the original infixes drops off; however, in some cases, new infixes are innovated. One such case, involving the verbal agreement markers in South Halmahera–West New Guinea languages, is described in Gasser, Arnold, and Kamholz (this volume, §37.2.6); other cases include the attributive association marker in the Malayic dialect of Jernih, discussed in McKinnon et al. (2015), and the multifunctional process of consonantal affix insertion in Amfo'an Meto, described in Culhane (2018).

## 44.4 Formal types: Other

In addition to affixation, MPSEA languages exhibit various other kinds of morphological processes, including ablaut, metathesis, reduplication, and suppletion.

Table 44.4 presents the distribution of ablaut, in accordance with the definitions provided in WALS Chapter 20.

As suggested in Table 44.4, ablaut is relatively uncommon worldwide; however, it is even less common in MPSEA languages than in their non-MPSEA counterparts, at 0.05 vs. 0.07 ($p = 0.02$). Some instances of ablaut in the Malayic varieties of Rantau Panjang and Kerinci are discussed in Prentice and Usman (1978); Steinhauer and Usman (1978); McKinnon (2011); McKinnon et al. (2015); and Ernanda (2017).

Table 44.5 presents the distribution of metathesis, following the definitions provided in Edwards (2020).

As evident in Table 44.5, metathesis is significantly more common in MPSEA languages than in non-MPSEA languages,

**Table 44.5** Metathesis

| | *n* | | rate | |
|---|---|---|---|---|
| | AN | non-AN | AN | non-AN |
| Taiwan | 0/10 | 0/2 | 0.00 | 0.00 |
| Philippines | **0/38** | 0/1 | **0.00** | 0.00 |
| Mainland SEA | **0/18** | 1/162 | **0.00** | 0.01 |
| Indian Ocean | **0/3** | 0/8 | **0.00** | 0.00 |
| SW Island SEA | **0/62** | 0/1 | **0.00** | 0.00 |
| SE Island SEA | **14/97** | 2/20 | **0.14** | 0.10 |
| W New Guinea | **0/13** | 0/17 | **0.00** | 0.00 |
| Cenderawasih Bay | **0/8** | 0/2 | **0.00** | 0.00 |
| E New Guinea | 0/76 | 0/248 | 0.00 | 0.00 |
| Remote Oceania | 2/103 | 0/9 | 0.02 | 0.00 |
| Rest of the World | -/- | 15/1813 | - | 0.01 |
| TOTAL | 428 | 2283 | 0.04 | 0.01 |
| | 2711 | | 0.01 | |
| Taiwan AN | 0/10 | | 0.00 | |
| MPSEA | **14/239** | | **0.06** | |
| Oceanic | 2/179 | | 0.01 | |
| non-MPSEA | 18/2293 | | 0.01 | |

**Table 44.6** Reduplication

| | *n* | | rate | |
|---|---|---|---|---|
| | AN | non-AN | AN | non-AN |
| Taiwan | 8/8 | 1/1 | 1.00 | 1.00 |
| Philippines | **32/32** | 1/1 | **1.00** | 1.00 |
| Mainland SEA | **18/18** | 130/138 | **1.00** | 0.95 |
| Indian Ocean | **3/3** | 6/5 | **1.00** | 1.00 |
| SW Island SEA | **58/58** | 1/1 | **1.00** | 1.00 |
| SE Island SEA | **93/93** | 14/15 | **1.00** | 0.93 |
| W New Guinea | **8/9** | 12/12 | **0.89** | 1.00 |
| Cenderawasih Bay | **4/5** | 2/2 | **0.80** | 1.00 |
| E New Guinea | 61/61 | 114/135 | 1.00 | 0.84 |
| Remote Oceania | 88/88 | 4/5 | 1.00 | 0.80 |
| Rest of the World | -/- | 964/1205 | - | 0.80 |
| TOTAL | 375 | 1520 | 0.99 | 0.82 |
| | 1895 | | 0.86 | |
| Taiwan AN | 8/8 | | 1.00 | |
| MPSEA | **216/218** | | **0.99** | |
| Oceanic | 149/149 | | 1.00 | |
| non-MPSEA | 1257/1528 | | 0.82 | |

at 0.06 vs. 0.01; however, this difference is due entirely to the widespread occurrence of metathesis in SE Island SEA, at 0.14 ($p < 0.001$). Its relatively high rate of occurrence in the non-Austronesian languages of SE Island SEA, at 0.10, shows that the distribution of metathesis is of an areal nature, as argued by Schapper (2015a) and Edwards (2020). In actual fact, the distribution of metathesis within the SE Island SEA region is largely concentrated in a smaller region on and around the island of Timor, where its frequency is much higher. More detailed discussion of metathesis in Amarasi and other languages of the circum-Timor region is provided in Edwards (2020). See also Schapper and Zobel, this volume, §35.3.4 for a treatment of metathesis in the Timor area.

Table 44.6 presents the distribution of reduplication, encompassing both complete and partial varieties, in accordance with the definitions in WALS Chapter 27.

Although common worldwide, reduplication is, if anything, even more common in MPSEA languages than in non-MPSEA ones, at 0.99 vs. 0.82 ($p < 0.001$). This 0.99 figure is a joint product of genealogy, with a higher incidence of reduplication in the Austronesian language family, and of areality, with a greater prevalence of reduplication being associated with the languages of Mainland and Insular Southeast Asia. Further discussion of reduplication can be found in Mattes and Schwaiger (chapter 45, this volume).

Tables 44.7 and 44.8 present the distribution of morphological suppletion in the verbal domain, drawing upon WALS Chapters 79 and 80 which cover number, tense, aspect, imperatives, and hortatives, while adding an additional grammatical category, negation. Table 44.7 shows the proportion of languages that have morphological suppletion of any kind in the verbal domain, while Table 44.8 zooms in on the languages that have morphological suppletion in the verbal domain, and presents the number of grammatical categories that exhibit morphological suppletion.

**Table 44.7** Suppletion

| | *n* | | rate | |
|---|---|---|---|---|
| | AN | non-AN | AN | non AN |
| Taiwan | 0/10 | 0/2 | 0.00 | 0.00 |
| Philippines | 2/37 | 1/1 | 0.05 | 1.00 |
| Mainland SEA | 0/18 | 2/160 | 0.00 | 0.01 |
| Indian Ocean | 2/3 | 4/8 | 0.67 | 0.50 |
| SW Island SEA | 1/62 | 0/1 | 0.02 | 0.00 |
| SE Island SEA | 6/97 | 1/20 | 0.06 | 0.05 |
| W New Guinea | 0/13 | 2/13 | 0.00 | 0.15 |
| Cenderawasih Bay | 1/8 | 0/2 | 0.13 | 0.00 |
| E New Guinea | 16/76 | 122/182 | 0.21 | 0.67 |
| Remote Oceania | 37/103 | 1/9 | 0.36 | 0.11 |
| Rest of the World | -/- | 765/1507 | - | 0.51 |
| TOTAL | 427 | 1905 | 0.15 | 0.47 |
| | 2332 | | 0.41 | |
| Taiwan AN | 0/10 | | 0.00 | |
| MPSEA | 12/238 | | 0.05 | |
| Oceanic | 53/179 | | 0.30 | |
| non-MPSEA | 898/1915 | | 0.47 | |

**Table 44.8** Suppletion – number of categories

| | *n* | | average | |
|---|---|---|---|---|
| | AN | non AN | AN | non AN |
| Taiwan | 0 | 0 | n/a | n/a |
| Philippines | 2 | 1 | 1.0 | n/a |
| Mainland SEA | 0 | 2 | n/a | 1.0 |
| Indian Ocean | 2 | 4 | 1.0 | 1.0 |
| SW Island SEA | 1 | 0 | 1.0 | n/a |
| SE Island SEA | 6 | 1 | 1.2 | 1.0 |
| W New Guinea | 0 | 2 | n/a | 1.5 |
| Cenderawasih Bay | 1 | 0 | 1.0 | n/a |
| E New Guinea | 16 | 122 | 1.1 | 1.5 |
| Remote Oceania | 37 | 1 | 1.1 | 2.0 |
| Rest of the World | - | 765 | n/a | 1.4 |
| TOTAL | 63 | 898 | 1.1 | 1.5 |
| | 961 | | 1.4 | |
| Taiwan AN | 0 | | n/a | |
| MPSEA | 12 | | 1.1 | |
| Oceanic | 53 | | 1.1 | |
| non-MPSEA | 951 | | 1.5 | |

As evident from Table 44.7, morphological suppletion in the verbal domain is much rarer in MPSEA languages than in its non-MPSEA counterparts, at 0.05 vs. 0.47 ($p < 0.001$). In the larger Austronesian family, suppletion is also rare, in fact unattested, in the Taiwan languages in the sample; however, it increases in frequency as the Austronesian languages spread into the Pacific, reaching a near-average worldwide rate in Remote Oceania. Table 44.8 provides further support for the disfavouring of suppletion in MPSEA languages: even in languages with suppletion, the average number of categories exhibiting suppletion is lower than in non-MPSEA languages, 1.1 vs. 1.5 ($p = 0.01$). Notably, even in Remote Oceania, with its near-average rate of suppletion in Table 44.7, the average number of categories exhibiting suppletion remains low, on a par with MPSEA languages, at 1.1. In conjunction, then, Tables 44.7 and 44.8 suggest that the disfavouring of morphological suppletion in the verbal domain is a genealogically conservative feature characteristic of the Austronesian family in its entirety. In addition, however, the lower-than-average figures for the non-Austronesian languages of the region suggest that the disfavouring of morphological suppletion in the verbal domain may also be a characteristic feature of the Mekong-Mamberamo linguistic area.

## 44.5 Functional types: Nominal

§§44.5–44.8 are concerned with morphological process classified in terms of their functions, beginning, in this section, with those associated with the nominal domain.

Table 44.9 presents the distribution of morphological plural marking, combining plural prefixes, plural suffixes, plural stem changes, and plural tone, in accordance with the criteria formulated in WALS Chapter 33:

**Table 44.9** Morphological plural

| | *n* | | rate | |
|---|---|---|---|---|
| | AN | non-AN | AN | non-AN |
| Taiwan | 1/10 | 0/2 | 0.10 | 0.00 |
| Philippines | **4/38** | 0/1 | **0.11** | 0.00 |
| Mainland SEA | **1/18** | 25/157 | **0.06** | 0.16 |
| Indian Ocean | **1/3** | 5/8 | **0.33** | 0.63 |
| SW Island SEA | **3/62** | 0/1 | **0.05** | 0.00 |
| SE Island SEA | **25/97** | 3/20 | **0.26** | 0.15 |
| W New Guinea | **2/13** | 11/17 | **0.15** | 0.65 |
| Cenderawasih Bay | **3/8** | 0/2 | **0.38** | 0.00 |
| E New Guinea | 24/75 | 125/240 | 0.32 | 0.52 |
| Remote Oceania | 19/102 | 3/8 | 0.19 | 0.38 |
| Rest of the World | -/- | 1418/1789 | - | 0.79 |
| TOTAL | 426 | 2245 | 0.19 | 0.71 |
| | 2671 | | 0.63 | |
| Taiwan AN | 1/10 | | 0.10 | |
| MPSEA | **39/239** | | **0.16** | |
| Oceanic | 43/177 | | 0.24 | |
| non-MPSEA | 1591/2255 | | 0.71 | |

**Table 44.10** Obligatory morphological possessor

| | *n* | | rate | |
|---|---|---|---|---|
| | AN | non-AN | AN | non-AN |
| Taiwan | 0/8 | 0/2 | 0.00 | 0.00 |
| Philippines | **1/38** | 0/1 | **0.03** | 0.00 |
| Mainland SEA | **0/18** | 2/160 | **0.00** | 0.01 |
| Indian Ocean | **0/3** | 0/8 | **0.00** | 0.00 |
| SW Island SEA | **0/61** | 0/1 | **0.00** | 0.00 |
| SE Island SEA | **22/86** | 10/19 | **0.26** | 0.53 |
| W New Guinea | **5/13** | 13/17 | **0.38** | 0.76 |
| Cenderawasih Bay | **6/8** | 1/2 | **0.75** | 0.50 |
| E New Guinea | 55/57 | 101/190 | 0.96 | 0.53 |
| Remote Oceania | 69/83 | 2/8 | 0.83 | 0.25 |
| Rest of the World | -/- | 384/1478 | - | 0.26 |
| TOTAL | 375 | 1886 | 0.42 | 0.27 |
| | 2261 | | 0.30 | |
| Taiwan AN | 0/8 | | 0.00 | |
| MPSEA | **34/227** | | **0.15** | |
| Oceanic | 124/140 | | 0.89 | |
| non-MPSEA | 513/1894 | | 0.27 | |

Morphological plural marking is massively less common in MPSEA languages than in non-MPSEA ones, at 0.16 vs. 0.71 ($p < 0.001$). This difference is even greater than the corresponding difference across all functions, as represented in Table 44.1, thereby suggesting that there is a specific disfavouring of morphological plural marking in MPSEA languages.

Within regions containing a substantial number of both MPSEA and non-Austronesian languages, a somewhat more mixed picture presents itself: while the rate of morphological plural marking is lower in the MPSEA languages than in their non-Austronesian neighbours in Mainland SEA, 0.06 vs. 0.16, and in West New Guinea, 0.15 vs. 0.65, it is higher in the MPSEA languages than in their non-Austronesian neighbours in SE Island SEA, 0.26 vs. 0.15. This differential pattern probably says less about the distribution of morphological plural marking in MPSEA languages than it does about its distribution in the corresponding non-Austronesian languages in these three regions.

Table 44.10 presents the distribution of obligatory possessor inflection, as defined in WALS Chapter 58; an example of a language with obligatory possessor inflection is South Nuaulu, spoken on the island of Seram in the Maluku archipelago, in which certain words, such as *nesi-* 'tooth', can only occur in construction with a possessive suffix, for example *nesi-te* (tooth-SG.NH.POSS) 'its tooth' (Bolton 1990).

While the overall rate of obligatory possessor inflection in MPSEA is lower than in non-MPSEA languages, 0.15 vs. 0.27 ($p < 0.001$), this figure obscures its striking differential distribution across the various MPSEA- and other Austronesian-speaking regions. Within these regions, obligatory possessor inflection occurs almost exclusively to the east of the Wallace Line; moreover, within these regions it increases monotonically from west to east, with 0.26 in SE Island SEA, 0.38 in West New Guinea, 0.75 in Cenderawasih Bay and 0.96 in East New Guinea, before falling back to 0.83 in Remote Oceania—its frequency in the Cenderawasih Bay and eastwards being dramatically higher than the worldwide baseline. A similar pattern is in evidence also in the non-Austronesian languages of the same regions, suggesting that the distribution of obligatory possessor inflection is areally determined, and that its presence in the Austronesian languages is most probably the result of contact with the non-Austronesian languages that were in the region prior to the Austronesian expansion.

As argued by Haspelmath (2017) and others, obligatory possessor inflection is typically associated with semantic categories of possession commonly characterized as inalienable. The development of obligatory possessor inflection in Austronesian languages to the east of the Wallace Line is thus part and parcel of a larger typological shift in attributive possessive constructions that took place as Austronesian languages spread east, involving also the development of an alienable/inalienable-possession distinction and the switch in word order from Possessum–Possessor to Possessor–Possessum (Himmelmann 2005a; Klamer, Reesink, and van Staden 2008; Donohue and Schapper 2008; Schapper 2015a; Schapper and McConvell, chapter 48, this volume).

Tables 44.11 and 44.12 present the distribution of morphological case marking, in accordance with WALS Chapter 49. Table 44.11 shows the proportion of languages that have morphological case marking of any kind, while Table 44.12 focuses on the languages with morphological case and presents the number of cases that are distinguished in those languages.

As shown in Table 44.11, morphological case marking is significantly less common in MPSEA languages than in non-MPSEA ones, at 0.18 vs. 0.55 ($p < 0.001$). This difference is echoed by the corresponding figures in Table 44.12, which, restricting attention to the languages with case marking, shows the average number of case-marking distinctions to be lower in MPSEA languages than in non-MPSEA ones, at 3.0 vs. 4.8 ($p < 0.001$).

However, focusing on Table 44.11, the 0.18 figure for morphological case marking in MPSEA languages as a whole obscures the striking difference, within MPSEA languages, between Philippines, where the 0.80 rate of morphological case is significantly higher than the worldwide baseline, and the remainder of the MPSEA-speaking areas, where, with the exception of the Indian Ocean, the rate of morphological case is substantially lower than the world average: 0.00 for Mainland SEA, 0.08 for SW Island SEA, 0.11 for SE Island SEA, and 0.00, again, for both West New Guinea and Cenderawasih Bay. These figures thus provide a dramatic instantiation of the radical grammatical restructuring undergone by Austronesian languages as they spread south out of the Philippines and into the Mekong-Mamberamo linguistic area.

**Table 44.11** Case

| | *n* | | rate | |
|---|---|---|---|---|
| | AN | non AN | AN | non AN |
| Taiwan | 4/9 | 0/2 | 0.44 | 0.00 |
| Philippines | 24/30 | 0/1 | 0.80 | 0.00 |
| Mainland SEA | 0/18 | 11/151 | 0.00 | 0.07 |
| Indian Ocean | 1/3 | 4/7 | 0.33 | 0.57 |
| SW Island SEA | 5/60 | 0/1 | 0.08 | 0.00 |
| SE Island SEA | 10/95 | 5/19 | 0.11 | 0.26 |
| W New Guinea | 0/13 | 5/14 | 0.00 | 0.36 |
| Cenderawasih Bay | 0/8 | 0/1 | 0.00 | 0.00 |
| E New Guinea | 11/74 | 115/183 | 0.15 | 0.63 |
| Remote Oceania | 17/97 | 2/9 | 0.18 | 0.22 |
| Rest of the World | -/- | 895/1499 | - | 0.60 |
| TOTAL | 407 | 1887 | 0.18 | 0.55 |
| | 2294 | | 0.48 | |
| Taiwan AN | 4/9 | | 0.44 | |
| MPSEA | 40/227 | | 0.18 | |
| Oceanic | 28/171 | | 0.16 | |
| non-MPSEA | 1041/1896 | | 0.55 | |

Comparing MPSEA languages to their non-Austronesian neighbours in those regions where there is a substantial number of non-Austronesian languages, the prevalence of morphological case marking is lower in the MPSEA languages than in the non-Austronesian ones: this tendency is in evidence in Mainland SEA with 0.00 vs. 0.07 and West New Guinea with 0.00 vs. 0.36, though in SE Island SEA the 0.11 vs. 0.26 contrast is suggestive but not significantly different ($p = 0.06$). However, in these same regions, even the prevalence of case marking in the non-Austronesian languages is still lower than the worldwide average of 0.48: in Mainland and Island SEA the figures for the non-Austronesian languages, 0.07 and 0.26, are significantly lower than those of other non-AN languages ($p < 0.001$), while in West New Guinea, the 0.36 figure, while pointing in the same direction, is not significantly different ($p = 0.06$). The figures for these three regions are consistent with the antiquity of the Mekong-Mamberamo linguistic area, pre-dating the

**Table 44.12** Case – number of categories

| | *n* | | average | |
|---|---|---|---|---|
| | AN | non-AN | AN | non-AN |
| Taiwan | 4 | 0 | 2.8 | n/a |
| Philippines | **24** | 0 | **3.4** | n/a |
| Mainland SEA | **0** | 11 | **n/a** | 2.5 |
| Indian Ocean | **1** | 4 | **3.0** | 4.0 |
| SW Island SEA | **5** | 0 | **1.8** | n/a |
| SE Island SEA | **10** | 5 | **2.4** | 1.4 |
| W New Guinea | **0** | 5 | **n/a** | 4.8 |
| Cenderawasih Bay | **0** | 0 | **n/a** | n/a |
| E New Guinea | 11 | 115 | 3.0 | 4.6 |
| Remote Oceania | 17 | 2 | 3.2 | 2.0 |
| Rest of the World | - | 895 | - | 4.9 |
| TOTAL | 72 | 1037 | 3.0 | 4.8 |
| | 1109 | | 4.7 | |
| Taiwan AN | 4 | | 2.8 | |
| MPSEA | **40** | | **3.0** | |
| Oceanic | 28 | | 3.1 | |
| non-MPSEA | 1069 | | 4.8 | |

**Table 44.13** Morphological tense

| | *n* | | rate | |
|---|---|---|---|---|
| | AN | non-AN | AN | non-AN |
| Taiwan | 6/7 | 1/2 | 0.86 | 0.50 |
| Philippines | **7/37** | 1/1 | **0.19** | 1.00 |
| Mainland SEA | **1/18** | 12/160 | **0.06** | 0.08 |
| Indian Ocean | **2/3** | 8/8 | **0.67** | 1.00 |
| SW Island SEA | **3/59** | 1/1 | **0.05** | 1.00 |
| SE Island SEA | **9/97** | 0/19 | **0.09** | 0.00 |
| W New Guinea | **1/13** | 5/17 | **0.08** | 0.29 |
| Cenderawasih Bay | **0/8** | 0/2 | **0.00** | 0.00 |
| E New Guinea | 25/63 | 218/243 | 0.40 | 0.90 |
| Remote Oceania | 47/89 | 7/9 | 0.53 | 0.78 |
| Rest of the World | -/- | 1506/1709 | - | 0.88 |
| TOTAL | 394 | 2171 | 0.26 | 0.81 |
| | 2565 | | 0.73 | |
| Taiwan AN | 6/7 | | 0.86 | |
| MPSEA | **23/235** | | **0.10** | |
| Oceanic | 72/152 | | 0.47 | |
| non-MPSEA | 1765/2178 | | 0.81 | |

Austronesian intrusion, one of whose characteristic features is the scarcity or absence of morphological case marking (Gil 2015a: Section 2.16). However, the fact that the Austronesian languages exhibit an even lower rate of case marking than their non-Austronesian neighbours suggests that the radical restructuring of Austronesian languages as they spread south out of the Philippines cannot be accounted for exclusively in terms of assimilation to the mould of the non-Austronesian languages that were there before; in addition, it must, at least in part, be attributed to processes of contact-induced simplification (Donohue and Denham 2020; Gil 2020a).

## 44.6 Functional types: Tense–aspect–mood (TAM)

Tables 44.13 and 44.14 present the distribution of morphological tense marking, combining data for the past tense, in accordance with WALS Chapter 66, and the future tense, following the criteria of WALS Chapter 67. Table 44.13 shows the proportion of languages that have tense marking of either kind, while Table 44.14 zooms in on the languages with tense marking and presents the number of tense categories that those languages mark morphologically.

As evident in Table 44.13, tense marking is massively less common in MPSEA languages than in non-MPSEA ones, at 0.10 vs. 0.81 ($p < 0.001$). Further support for this difference is provided by Table 44.14, showing that even in languages with tense marking, the average number of tense categories marked is lower in MPSEA languages than in non-MPSEA ones, at 1.3 vs. 2.0 ($p < 0.001$).

Here too, the degree of morphological elaboration of MPSEA languages is also significantly lower than that of other Austronesian languages, with the MPSEA total of 0.10 contrasting dramatically with that of Taiwan, at 0.86, and Oceanic, at 0.47: an instantiation of the MPSEA dip ($p < 0.001$ in both cases). However, whereas with

**Table 44.14** Morphological tense – number of categories

| | *n* | | average | |
|---|---|---|---|---|
| | AN | non AN | AN | non-AN |
| Taiwan | 6 | 1 | 1.5 | 1.0 |
| Philippines | **7** | 1 | **1.1** | 2.0 |
| Mainland SEA | **1** | 12 | **1.0** | 1.3 |
| Indian Ocean | **2** | 8 | **1.5** | 2.0 |
| SW Island SEA | **3** | 1 | **1.3** | 1.0 |
| SE Island SEA | **9** | 0 | **1.3** | n/a |
| W New Guinea | **1** | 5 | **1.0** | 1.8 |
| Cenderawasih Bay | **0** | 0 | **n/a** | n/a |
| E New Guinea | 25 | 218 | 1.4 | 2.3 |
| Remote Oceania | 47 | 7 | 1.4 | 1.7 |
| Rest of the World | - | 1506 | - | 1.9 |
| TOTAL | 101 | 1759 | 1.4 | 2.0 |
| | 1860 | | 1.9 | |
| Taiwan AN | 6 | | 1.5 | |
| MPSEA | **23** | | **1.3** | |
| Oceanic | 72 | | 1.4 | |
| non-MPSEA | 1837 | | 2.0 | |

**Table 44.15** Tense–aspect–mood prefix

| | *n* | | rate | |
|---|---|---|---|---|
| | AN | non-AN | AN | non-AN |
| Taiwan | 7/8 | 0/2 | 0.88 | 0.00 |
| Philippines | **34/36** | 1/1 | **0.94** | 1.00 |
| Mainland SEA | **0/17** | 6/160 | **0.00** | 0.04 |
| Indian Ocean | **3/3** | 2/8 | **1.00** | 0.25 |
| SW Island SEA | **14/59** | 0/1 | **0.24** | 0.00 |
| SE Island SEA | **29/91** | 2/15 | **0.32** | 0.13 |
| W New Guinea | **1/12** | 3/16 | **0.08** | 0.19 |
| Cenderawasih Bay | **0/8** | 0/1 | **0.00** | 0.00 |
| E New Guinea | 36/65 | 41/241 | 0.55 | 0.17 |
| Remote Oceania | 48/89 | 0/9 | 0.54 | 0.00 |
| Rest of the World | -/- | 419/1745 | - | 0.24 |
| TOTAL | 388 | 2199 | 0.44 | 0.22 |
| | 2587 | | 0.25 | |
| Taiwan AN | 7/8 | | 0.88 | |
| MPSEA | **81/226** | | **0.36** | |
| Oceanic | 84/154 | | 0.55 | |
| non-MPSEA | 481/2207 | | 0.22 | |

regard to case marking, in Table 44.11 earlier, the big drop was between Philippines and regions to the south, in Table 44.11, for tense, the major decrease in frequency is between Taiwan, at 0.86, and Philippines, at 0.19 ($p < 0.001$).[7]

Table 44.15 broadens the functional scope to tense-aspect-mood (TAM) more generally, while narrowing the formal scope to prefixing; in accordance with WALS Chapter 69, it presents the distribution of languages that make use of prefixation to mark TAM categories:

As evident in Table 44.15, TAM-marking prefixes are more common in MPSEA languages than in non-MPSEA ones, at 0.36 vs. 0.22 ($p < 0.001$). These figures represent the interplay of the favouring of infixation in MPSEA languages as per Table 44.2, with the disfavouring of tense marking (as a major component of TAM marking) as per Tables 44.13 and 44.14, with the former factor proving to be the stronger of the two. Within the Austronesian language family, the figures for TAM-marking prefixes in Table 44.15 mirror those for tense marking in general, beginning with 0.88 in Taiwan, dropping off to 0.36 in MPSEA, before climbing back to 0.55 for Oceanic—another case of the MPSEA dip ($p < 0.01$ and $p < 0.001$ respectively). However, unlike for tense marking in general, the figure for Philippines, at 0.94, is much higher, with the dramatic drop off taking place in association with the Austronesian expansion out of the Philippines and southwards into the Mekong-Mamberamo linguistic area.

[7] Using different criteria, Gil (2015a: Section 2.17, 2021) presents the results of a cross-linguistic survey distinguishing between optional and obligatory marking of TAM categories. The overall picture that emerges is similar, with a lower rate of obligatory TAM marking in MPSEA languages than in other Austronesian ones, though in that survey, the most significant decrease is between the Philippines and locations further south, thereby replicating the pattern observable in Table 44.15 below.

**Table 44.16** Morphological causative

| | n | | rate | |
|---|---|---|---|---|
| | AN | non-AN | AN | non-AN |
| Taiwan | 9/9 | 1/2 | 1.00 | 0.50 |
| Philippines | **37/37** | 0/1 | **1.00** | 0.00 |
| Mainland SEA | **9/17** | 34/159 | **0.53** | 0.21 |
| Indian Ocean | **2/3** | 5/8 | **0.67** | 0.63 |
| SW Island SEA | **54/56** | 1/1 | **0.96** | 1.00 |
| SE Island SEA | **65/88** | 7/18 | **0.74** | 0.39 |
| W New Guinea | **3/12** | 3/14 | **0.25** | 0.21 |
| Cenderawasih Bay | **0/5** | 0/2 | **0.00** | 0.00 |
| E New Guinea | 48/62 | 50/196 | 0.77 | 0.26 |
| Remote Oceania | 69/91 | 6/9 | 0.76 | 0.67 |
| Rest of the World | -/- | 1117/1478 | - | 0.76 |
| TOTAL | 380 | 1888 | 0.78 | 0.65 |
| | 2268 | | 0.67 | |
| Taiwan AN | 9/9 | | 1.00 | |
| MPSEA | **170/218** | | **0.78** | |
| Oceanic | 117/153 | | 0.76 | |
| non-MPSEA | 1233/1897 | | 0.65 | |

**Table 44.17** Morphological applicative

| | n | | rate | |
|---|---|---|---|---|
| | AN | non-AN | AN | non-AN |
| Taiwan | 9/9 | 0/2 | 1.00 | 0.00 |
| Philippines | **38/38** | 0/1 | **1.00** | 0.00 |
| Mainland SEA | **3/18** | 3/161 | **0.17** | 0.02 |
| Indian Ocean | **2/3** | 2/8 | **0.67** | 0.25 |
| SW Island SEA | **40/51** | 0/1 | **0.78** | 0.00 |
| SE Island SEA | **41/88** | 12/18 | **0.47** | 0.67 |
| W New Guinea | **1/13** | 6/14 | **0.08** | 0.43 |
| Cenderawasih Bay | **3/7** | 0/2 | **0.43** | 0.00 |
| E New Guinea | 35/61 | 93/212 | 0.57 | 0.44 |
| Remote Oceania | 55/85 | 3/8 | 0.65 | 0.38 |
| Rest of the World | -/- | 643/1573 | - | 0.41 |
| TOTAL | 373 | 2000 | 0.61 | 0.38 |
| | 2373 | | 0.42 | |
| Taiwan AN | 9/9 | | 1.00 | |
| MPSEA | **128/218** | | **0.59** | |
| Oceanic | 90/146 | | 0.62 | |
| non-MPSEA | 771/2009 | | 0.38 | |

## 44.7 Functional types: Causatives and applicatives

The next four tables deal with causative and applicative constructions. Table 44.16 presents the distribution of morphological causatives, in accordance with the criteria of WALS Chapter 111A.

As evident in Table 44.16, morphological causatives are more common in MPSEA languages than in non-MPSEA ones, at 0.78 vs. 0.65 ($p < 0.001$); this figure is more significant given the general disfavouring of morphological elaboration in MPSEA languages.

Within Austronesian languages, morphological causatives are pretty much the rule in Taiwan and Philippines, both at 1.00, and in SW Island SEA, at 0.97, and also quite frequent elsewhere; however they are uncommon in West New Guinea, at 0.25, and absent from Cenderawasih Bay. In regions with a substantial number of both Austronesian and non-Austronesian languages, morphological causatives are consistently more common in the Austronesian than the non-Austronesian languages: 0.53 vs. 0.21 in Mainland SEA, 0.74 vs. 0.39 in SE Island SEA, and, collapsing the figures for West New Guinea, Cenderawasih Bay and East New Guinea, 0.65 vs. 0.25 in New Guinea as a whole ($p < 0.01$, $p < 0.01$, $p < 0.001$ respectively). In conjunction, these patterns suggest that the presence of a morphological causative is a relatively conservative feature associated with the Austronesian language family as a whole.

Tables 44.17 and 44.18 are concerned with morphological applicative constructions, drawing upon WALS Chapters 109A and 109B, but including additional semantic roles (the resulting set includes beneficiary, instrument, locative, associative, theme, reason, and malefactive).

As evident from Table 44.17, the distribution of applicatives largely follows that of causatives in Table 44.16 earlier.

**Table 44.18** Morphological applicative – number of categories

| | *n* | | average | |
|---|---|---|---|---|
| | AN | non-AN | AN | non-AN |
| Taiwan | 8 | 0 | 2.1 | n/a |
| Philippines | 37 | 0 | 2.3 | n/a |
| Mainland SEA | 1 | 3 | 1.0 | 1.0 |
| Indian Ocean | 2 | 2 | 4.5 | 2.5 |
| SW Island SEA | 39 | 0 | 1.6 | n/a |
| SE Island SEA | 36 | 3 | 2.3 | 2.0 |
| W New Guinea | 0 | 6 | n/a | 1.2 |
| Cenderawasih Bay | 2 | 0 | 3.0 | n/a |
| E New Guinea | 34 | 79 | 2.0 | 1.4 |
| Remote Oceania | 50 | 3 | 2.2 | 1.7 |
| Rest of the World | - | 564 | n/a | 1.8 |
| TOTAL | 209 | 660 | 2.1 | 1.8 |
| | 869 | | 1.8 | |
| Taiwan AN | 8 | | 2.1 | |
| MPSEA | 117 | | 2.1 | |
| Oceanic | 84 | | 2.1 | |
| non-MPSEA | 752 | | 1.8 | |

**Table 44.19** Causative/applicative syncretism

| | *n* | | rate | |
|---|---|---|---|---|
| | AN | non-AN | AN | non-AN |
| Taiwan | 0/9 | 0/2 | 0.00 | 0.00 |
| Philippines | 0/38 | 0/1 | 0.00 | 0.00 |
| Mainland SEA | 3/17 | 2/160 | 0.18 | 0.01 |
| Indian Ocean | 0/3 | 0/7 | 0.00 | 0.00 |
| SW Island SEA | 11/37 | 0/1 | 0.30 | 0.00 |
| SE Island SEA | 4/90 | 0/14 | 0.04 | 0.00 |
| W New Guinea | 0/12 | 0/13 | 0.00 | 0.00 |
| Cenderawasih Bay | 0/7 | 0/2 | 0.00 | 0.00 |
| E New Guinea | 8/58 | 3/185 | 0.14 | 0.02 |
| Remote Oceania | 15/74 | 1/6 | 0.20 | 0.17 |
| Rest of the World | -/- | 41/1204 | - | 0.03 |
| TOTAL | 345 | 1595 | 0.12 | 0.03 |
| | 1940 | | 0.05 | |
| Taiwan AN | 0/9 | | 0.00 | |
| MPSEA | 18/204 | | 0.09 | |
| Oceanic | 23/132 | | 0.17 | |
| non-MPSEA | 47/1604 | | 0.03 | |

Like causatives, applicatives are more common in MPSEA languages than in non-MPSEA ones, at 0.59 vs. 0.38 ($p < 0.001$), and once again, this figure is more significant given the relatively low overall rate of morphological elaboration in MPSEA languages. The favouring of applicative constructions in MPSEA languages is echoed by the average number of applicative categories, shown in Table 44.18, which, at 2.1 for MPSEA languages, is higher than the 1.8 for their non-MPSEA counterparts ($p < 0.001$).

The similarity to causatives extends also to their relative frequency across the various Austronesian-speaking regions. Applicatives are universal in Taiwan and Philippines, both at 1.00, and in SW Island SEA, at 0.97, and also widespread in several other regions; however they are uncommon in Mainland SEA, at 0.17, and West New Guinea, at 0.08. Comparing Austronesian languages to their non-Austronesian neighbours, a more mixed picture emerges. In several of the regions, applicatives, like causatives earlier, are somewhat more common in Austronesian than in non-Austronesian languages: 0.17 vs. 0.02 in Mainland SEA, 0.57 vs. 0.44 in East New Guinea, and 0.65 vs. 0.38 in Remote Oceania, though most of these contrasts are not statistically significant. In contrast, in two other regions, applicatives are less common in Austronesian than in non-Austronesian languages: 0.47 vs. 0.67 in SE Island SEA, and 0.08 vs. 0.43 in West New Guinea. In these two latter regions, then, the stories for causatives and applicatives seem to have diverged.

The overall similarity of patterning between causatives and applicatives is most dramatically expressed in those cases where causative and applicative constructions have actually converged, to the extent that they make use of one and the same construction, involving the same morphological marking. The distribution of such causative/applicative syncretism is presented in Table 44.19.

As evident in Table 44.19, causative/applicative syncretism is significantly more common in MPSEA languages, at 0.09, than it is in non-MPSEA languages, where it is at a scarce 0.03 ($p < 0.001$) Its relatively higher frequency in MPSEA languages is due mostly to its more widespread occurrence in Mainland SEA, at 0.18, and SW Insular SEA, at 0.30. An example of causative/applicative syncretism from the latter region, involving ablaut in Tanjung Pauh Mudik Kerinci, is discussed in McKinnon (2011). Interestingly, a second peak of causative/applicative syncretism is observable in East New Guinea and Remote Oceania, at 0.14 and 0.20 respectively; this most likely represents a retention of the patterns observable further to the west, which were largely lost in the east of the MPSEA area.

## 44.8 Functional types: Other

The remaining tables are concerned with various other kinds of morphological constructions.

Table 44.20 presents the distribution of languages in which verbal agreement with a nominative (S or A) argument is expressed by prefixation.[8]

As evident in Table 44.20, nominative verb-agreement prefixes are more common in MPSEA languages than in non-MPSEA ones, at 0.24 vs. 0.05 ($p < 0.001$). However, rather like in Table 44.15 earlier, these figures represent the interaction of the favouring of infixation in MPSEA languages as per Table 44.2, with the disfavouring of morphological elaboration in general, as per Table 44.1, with the balance tipping in favour of the former factor.

In the present case, the presence of nominative verb-agreement prefixes in Austronesian languages is almost exclusively limited to languages to the east of the Wallace Line, beginning with a 0.34 rate in SE Island SEA, increasing to 0.92 and 1.00 in West New Guinea and Cenderawasih, before decreasing again, beyond the MPSEA-speaking region, to 0.76 in East New Guinea and 0.61 in Remote Oceania. The widespread occurrence of nominative verb-agreement prefixes in the non-Austronesian languages of West New Guinea and Cenderawasih Bay suggests that their development in the more eastern Austronesian languages is due to contact with their non-Austronesian neighbours, in which verb-agreement prefixes are also present; for more general discussion of nominative verb-agreement prefixes in South Halmahera–West New Guinea languages see Gasser, Arnold, and Kamholz, this volume, §37.4.

**Table 44.20** Nominative verb agreement prefix

| | *n* | | rate | |
|---|---|---|---|---|
| | AN | non-AN | AN | non-AN |
| Taiwan | 0/10 | 0/2 | 0.00 | 0.00 |
| Philippines | **1/38** | 0/1 | **0.03** | 0.00 |
| Mainland SEA | **0/18** | 3/162 | **0.00** | 0.02 |
| Indian Ocean | **0/3** | 0/8 | **0.00** | 0.00 |
| SW Island SEA | **3/62** | 0/1 | **0.05** | 0.00 |
| SE Island SEA | **33/97** | 0/20 | **0.34** | 0.00 |
| W New Guinea | **12/13** | 6/17 | **0.92** | 0.35 |
| Cenderawasih Bay | **8/8** | 2/2 | **1.00** | 1.00 |
| E New Guinea | 58/76 | 14/248 | 0.76 | 0.06 |
| Remote Oceania | 62/101 | 0/9 | 0.61 | 0.00 |
| Rest of the World | -/- | 84/1809 | - | 0.05 |
| TOTAL | 426 | 2279 | 0.42 | 0.05 |
| | 2705 | | 0.11 | |
| Taiwan AN | 0/10 | | 0.00 | |
| MPSEA | **57/239** | | **0.24** | |
| Oceanic | 120/177 | | 0.68 | |
| all non-MPSEA | 109/2289 | | 0.05 | |

Table 44.21 presents the distribution of ability affixes on verbs, in accordance with the criteria in WALS Chapter 74:

As shown in Table 44.21, verbal ability affixes are less common in MPSEA languages than in non-MPSEA ones, at 0.15 vs. 0.33 ($p < 0.001$). However, this figure masks a big difference between the Philippines, where they are substantially more widespread than in the worldwide baseline, at 0.70, and other MPSEA-speaking regions, where they are significantly less common, thereby providing another example of morphological simplification associated with the spread of Austronesian languages south, out of the Philippines and into the Mekong-Mamberamo linguistic area. Further to the

[8] In Table 44.20, languages are counted as having a nominative verb-agreement prefix if it constitutes the only verb-agreement prefix in the language; however such languages may in addition have an accusative verb-agreement suffix. Excluded are languages with no agreement, such as Cham; a different alignment for agreement, e.g. Paulohi with active–stative alignment, or Makasar with an ergative–absolutive split; suffixal nominative agreement (e.g. Manggarai with VP-final clitics); fused or portmanteau agreement (e.g. the Papuan isolate Abinomn); languages with an additional agreement prefix (e.g. Swahili); and languages with various other mixed patterns.

**Table 44.21** Ability affix

| | *n* | | rate | |
|---|---|---|---|---|
| | AN | non-AN | AN | non-AN |
| Taiwan | 2/7 | 0/1 | 0.29 | 0.00 |
| Philippines | **14/20** | 0/1 | **0.70** | 0.00 |
| Mainland SEA | **1/18** | 3/147 | **0.06** | 0.02 |
| Indian Ocean | **2/3** | 2/7 | **0.67** | 0.29 |
| SW Island SEA | **8/53** | 0/1 | **0.15** | 0.00 |
| SE Island SEA | **5/87** | 1/5 | **0.06** | 0.20 |
| W New Guinea | **0/11** | 0/7 | **0.00** | 0.00 |
| Cenderawasih Bay | **0/4** | 0/1 | **0.00** | 0.00 |
| E New Guinea | 6/48 | 68/124 | 0.13 | 0.55 |
| Remote Oceania | 8/69 | 1/6 | 0.12 | 0.17 |
| Rest of the World | -/- | 397/1108 | - | 0.36 |
| TOTAL | 320 | 1408 | 0.14 | 0.34 |
| | 1728 | | 0.30 | |
| Taiwan AN | 2/7 | | 0.29 | |
| MPSEA | **30/196** | | **0.15** | |
| Oceanic | 14/117 | | 0.12 | |
| non-MPSEA | 474/1415 | | 0.33 | |

**Table 44.22** Negative affix

| | *n* | | rate | |
|---|---|---|---|---|
| | AN | non-AN | AN | non-AN |
| Taiwan | 0/10 | 0/2 | 0.00 | 0.00 |
| Philippines | **1/38** | 0/1 | **0.03** | 0.00 |
| Mainland SEA | **0/18** | 3/161 | **0.00** | 0.02 |
| Indian Ocean | **0/3** | 5/8 | **0.00** | 0.63 |
| SW Island SEA | **2/62** | 0/1 | **0.03** | 0.00 |
| SE Island SEA | **8/95** | 5/16 | **0.08** | 0.31 |
| W New Guinea | **1/12** | 7/17 | **0.08** | 0.41 |
| Cenderawasih Bay | **1/8** | 0/2 | **0.13** | 0.00 |
| E New Guinea | 10/74 | 92/225 | 0.14 | 0.41 |
| Remote Oceania | 21/99 | 2/9 | 0.21 | 0.22 |
| Rest of the World | -/- | 790/1699 | - | 0.46 |
| TOTAL | 419 | 2141 | 0.11 | 0.42 |
| | 2560 | | 0.37 | |
| Taiwan AN | 0/10 | | 0.00 | |
| MPSEA | **13/236** | | **0.06** | |
| Oceanic | 31/173 | | 0.18 | |
| non-MPSEA | 904/2151 | | 0.42 | |

east, a secondary rise in the distribution of verbal ability affixes is observed, with 0.13 in East New Guinea and 0.12 in Remote Oceania; this is probably due to contact with non-Austronesian languages of East New Guinea, where such verbal ability affixes are considerably more common, at 0.55.

Table 44.22 presents the distribution of negative affixes on verbs, in accordance with the criteria in WALS Chapter 112, including both languages where affixation is the sole way of expressing negation and languages in which affixation is used alongside a separate negative word.

As evident from Table 44.22, negative affixes on verbs are less common in MPSEA languages than in non-MPSEA ones, at 0.06 vs. 0.42 ($p < 0.001$). Again, this may largely reflect the general propensity for MPSEA languages to exhibit a low degree of morphological elaboration. A modest uptick in the occurrence of negative verbal affixes towards the east, beginning with SE Island SEA and West New Guinea at 0.08, continuing with Cenderawasih Bay and East New Guinea at 0.13 and 0.14, before culminating in Remote Oceania at 0.21, would seem to be due to contact with the neighbouring non-Austronesian languages, where negative verbal affixes are substantially more common.

Table 44.23 presents the distribution of noun incorporation following common definitions such as those of Mithun (1984, 1986); Sadock (1986); and Massam (2009).

As evident from Table 44.23, noun incorporation is less common in MPSEA languages than in non-MPSEA ones, at 0.03 vs. 0.13 ($p < 001$). This tendency is relatively consistent throughout the different regions, with the exception of Remote Oceania, where the rate of noun incorporation reaches the worldwide baseline.

Finally, Table 44.24 presents the distribution of morphological marking of subordination on the verb, as defined in WALS 125, 126, and 127; a language is considered to have such marking if it is available as an option in at least one of

**Table 44.23** Noun incorporation

| | *n* | | rate | |
|---|---|---|---|---|
| | AN | non-AN | AN | non-AN |
| Taiwan | 0/10 | 0/2 | 0.00 | 0.00 |
| Philippines | **0/38** | 0/1 | **0.00** | 0.00 |
| Mainland SEA | **0/18** | 3/162 | **0.00** | 0.02 |
| Indian Ocean | **2/3** | 0/7 | **0.67** | 0.00 |
| SW Island SEA | **1/62** | 0/1 | **0.02** | 0.00 |
| SE Island SEA | **2/94** | 0/20 | **0.02** | 0.00 |
| W New Guinea | **0/13** | 0/17 | **0.00** | 0.00 |
| Cenderawasih Bay | **1/8** | 0/2 | **0.13** | 0.00 |
| E New Guinea | 3/60 | 11/226 | 0.05 | 0.05 |
| Remote Oceania | 14/86 | 0/9 | 0.16 | 0.00 |
| Rest of the World | -/- | 219/1324 | - | 0.17 |
| TOTAL | 392 | 1771 | 0.06 | 0.13 |
| | 2163 | | 0.12 | |
| Taiwan AN | 0/10 | | 0.00 | |
| MPSEA | **6/236** | | **0.03** | |
| Oceanic | 17/146 | | 0.12 | |
| non-MPSEA | 233/1781 | | 0.13 | |

**Table 44.24** Subordinating morphology

| | *n* | | rate | |
|---|---|---|---|---|
| | AN | non-AN | AN | non-AN |
| Taiwan | 4/7 | 1/2 | 0.57 | 0.50 |
| Philippines | **24/24** | 1/1 | **1.00** | 1.00 |
| Mainland SEA | **2/18** | 11/157 | **0.11** | 0.07 |
| Indian Ocean | **1/3** | 6/7 | **0.33** | 0.86 |
| SW Island SEA | **8/59** | 0/1 | **0.14** | 0.00 |
| SE Island SEA | **27/87** | 1/11 | **0.31** | 0.09 |
| W New Guinea | **0/9** | 8/16 | **0.00** | 0.50 |
| Cenderawasih Bay | **2/4** | 0/1 | **0.50** | 0.00 |
| E New Guinea | 26/57 | 212/240 | 0.46 | 0.88 |
| Remote Oceania | 50/75 | 4/9 | 0.67 | 0.44 |
| Rest of the World | -/- | 1519/1679 | - | 0.90 |
| TOTAL | 343 | 2124 | 0.42 | 0.83 |
| | 2467 | | 0.77 | |
| Taiwan AN | 4/7 | | 0.57 | |
| MPSEA | **64/204** | | **0.31** | |
| Oceanic | 76/132 | | 0.58 | |
| non-MPSEA | 1767/2131 | | 0.83 | |

the following three types of subordinating clauses: purpose clauses, 'when' clauses, and reason clauses.

As shown in Table 44.24, morphological marking of subordination is significantly less common in MPSEA languages than in non-MPSEA ones, at 0.31 vs. 0.83 ($p < 0.001$). As in several previous tables, the overall MPSEA figure obscures the difference between the Philippines, which, at 1.00. is higher than the worldwide baseline, and all the other MPSEA-speaking areas, with much lower rates, thereby providing yet another example of morphological elaboration dropping off dramatically at the spread of Austronesian languages south, out of the Philippines and into the Mekong-Mamberamo area. Further to the east, the occurrence of morphological marking of subordination picks up once again, with 0.50 in Cenderawasih Bay, 0.46 in East New Guinea, and 0.67 in Remote Oceania; this effect may perhaps be due to contact with neighbouring non-Austronesian languages, as suggested by the higher rates of morphological marking of subordination, 0.50 in West New Guinea, and 0.88 in East New Guinea, though alternatively it could be construed as representing a default to a worldwide baseline. Whatever the historical explanation, the overall distribution of morphological marking of subordination provides yet another example of the MPSEA dip characterizing various aspects of morphological elaboration.

## 44.9 Conclusion

Although traditional terminology talks of morphology as being a clear and well-defined linguistic domain, the distinctiveness of morphology and the boundaries between it and other domains such as phonology and syntax, is actually quite problematical; see Haspelmath (2011) for discussion of some of the pertinent issues. On the one hand, the boundary between morphology and phonology is challenged by the existence of so-called *submorphemic* sound-meaning combinations. Indeed, Austronesian languages are renowned for the widespread presence of submorphemic roots, such as, for example, Malay *-pit* associated with the general meaning of 'approximation of two surfaces', as manifest in words such as *capit* 'pincers', *gapit* 'nipper', 'clamp', *jəpit* 'nip', 'catch between pincers', *kəmpit* 'carry under the arm' and many others (Blust 1988c). On the other hand, the purported boundary between morphology and syntax is also ridden with difficulties. Gil (2020b: 11–12) looks at alternative renditions of 'my father' into Papuan Malay: while Kluge (2014: 377) gives a periphrastic *sa pu bapa* (1SG POSS father), Donohue and Sawaki (2007: 260) provide *sa=pu=bapa*, representing the expression as a stem preceded by two proclitics and, in so doing, implying that the language might be endowed with a degree of morphological elaboration in the domain of possession. To a degree, then, morphology, or, more specifically, what counts as morphology as opposed to phonology or syntax, is in the eye of the beholder, dependent on the analytical assumptions of the individual linguist—a potentially serious confounding factor in any attempt to indulge in cross-linguistic comparisons drawing on descriptions of different languages offered by different scholars. Thus, the generalizations regarding the morphology of MPSEA languages presented in this chapter should be treated with due caution.

## Acknowledgements

This chapter has benefitted from comments and suggestions from Laura Arnold, Owen Edwards, and Tim McKinnon. The first author acknowledges funding received from the Australian Research Council under Future Fellowship award FT100100241 and Discovery Project award DP1093191. The second author is grateful to the Department of Linguistics at the Max Planck Institute for Evolutionary Anthropology and its director Bernard Comrie for the extensive and long-term support that facilitated some of the research represented in this chapter, and to the staff of the MPIEVA Jakarta Field Station and its Padang branch for their years and years of labour, some small fruits of which are represented here.

CHAPTER 45

# Reduplication

VERONIKA MATTES AND THOMAS SCHWAIGER

## 45.1 Introduction

This chapter provides a typological overview of the phenomenon of reduplication in the Malayo-Polynesian languages of Southeast Asia and its outliers (MPSEA). Generally, reduplication as a morphological device can be defined as "the systematically and productively employed repetition of words or parts of words for the expression of a variety of lexical and grammatical functions" (Schwaiger 2015: 468). Formally, the process can be divided into full reduplication and partial reduplication, depending on whether the exponent of a linguistic category, also called the reduplicant, is formed by repeating an entire morphological unit (including morphologically complex words like Indonesian *per-ubah-an~per-ubah-an* 'changes', from *ubah* 'to change' nominalized with *per-* and *-an*; Sneddon 1996: 15, 17, 41, 61) or a phonologically circumscribed part of it (e.g. syllables as in South Nuaulu *ha~hana-ne* 'carrying pole', from *hana* 'carry on shoulder' with a noun marker *-ne*; Bolton 1990: 65) as the respective base. Functionally, reduplicated forms are most commonly used to signal some nuance of plurality, intensity, or diminution with respect to their unreduplicated counterparts, but less frequently other intra-category and inter-category semantic effects of a grammatical or word-class-derivational nature may also be expressed through reduplication.

Morphological reduplication as confined to the domain of the word must be distinguished from syntactic repetition (e.g. constructions like *very, very old* in English) as well as from so-called parallelisms in ritual language (e.g. Grimes et al. 1997: 15–32). The distinction between full reduplication in morphology and repetition in syntax is not always trivial, but usually the latter is optional, less systematic, applicable to domains larger than the word (e.g. whole phrases) and can produce multiple iterations (e.g. "[u]p to 14" have been recorded in Buru according to Grimes 1991: 75, note 47). Repetition is moreover restricted to discourse-pragmatic uses like communicative reinforcement (e.g. Gil 2005: 43–4), text cohesion (e.g. Quick 2007: 563–6), non-grammaticalized iconic simulation of time duration (e.g. Gil 2005: 44–6; Quick 2007: 566–8), or concession (e.g. Miyake 2011: 51–2).

Since earlier theoretical research in modern linguistics like Wilbur (1973), reduplication is often treated as a special kind of affixation, while later developments like Inkelas and Zoll (2005) argue for an analysis in terms of a special kind of compounding (see also Larish 1999: 256 and Brunelle and Jensen, this volume, §30.3.2 on 'reduplicative compounds' in Moklen and Chamic, respectively). Cross-linguistic work in typology, by contrast, has always been more prone to viewing reduplicative exponents as a morphological device in their own right and thus as different from both affixes and compounds. In addition, there are also cases seemingly intermediate between affixation and reduplication. Many languages, among them several from the Austronesian family, display so-called fixed segmentism (Alderete et al. 1999), that is, full or partial reduplicants with pre-specified phonological material or, when described from the opposite angle, partly underspecified exponents in need of supplementary phonological material from the base. Fixed-segment full reduplication (e.g. Malaysian Malay *kuyup~k**a**y**a**p* 'to be drenched' from *kuyup* 'to be wet'; Abdullah Hassan 1974: 46) is typically known as echo-word formation in the reduplication literature and as rhyming/chiming or imitative reduplication in some Austroasiatic and Austronesian research traditions, but it is especially the partial variety of such morphemes that may indeed be viewed as a hybrid of reduplication and affixation (e.g. Gayo ***se**~sara* 'approximately one' from *sara* 'one'; Eades 2005: 55). Apart from productive reduplications, most languages also have numerous lexical reduplications, i.e. lexemes which exhibit a reduplicative structure in that they contain two identical strings of segments but, at least synchronically, cannot be morphologically related to corresponding unreduplicated forms in a regular fashion (e.g. Indonesian *tiba-tiba* 'suddenly'; Sneddon 1996: 16; Arta *ara-ara:pa* 'friend'; Kimoto 2017a: 94; Batuley *ur lala* 'sweet potato'; Daigle 2015: 26, 265).

Modern large-scale, macro-typological investigation into reduplication originated with the seminal study by Moravcsik (1978), which heavily informed more recent general typological contributions such as Stolz, Stroh, and Urdze (2011) and Rubino (2013) as well as several smaller-scale, micro-typological studies of reduplication in specific

Veronika Mattes and Thomas Schwaiger, *Reduplication.* In: *The Oxford Guide to the Malayo-Polynesian Languages of Southeast Asia.* Edited by: Alexander Adelaar and Antoinette Schapper, Oxford University Press.  DOI: 10.1093/oso/9780198807353.003.0045

language families, genetic subgroups or geographical areas. With respect to Austronesian in its entirety, Blust (2013a: 406) points out that "[n]o general survey of reduplication in A[ustro]N[esian] languages exists." But when zooming in, varyingly extensive and comprehensive surveys of reduplication across languages of the Philippines (Blake 1917), Indonesia (Brandstetter 1917; Gonda 1950), Micronesia (Harrison 1973), and Formosa (Zeitoun and Wu 2006) are found. Moreover, for the typologically rather variegated MPSEA languages, reduplication has been established as one of "only very few features which are sufficiently general and widespread to be considered typological characteristics of the group as a whole" (Himmelmann 2005a: 110). Himmelmann (2005a: 111; original emphasis) is actually talking about '*western Austronesian languages*' here, but even though for him this term "is strictly equivalent to *non-Oceanic Austronesian languages*" (i.e. also including the Formosan languages of Taiwan), his generalization similarly holds for the subset of MPSEA as identified in the present guide. Nevertheless, as the next sections illustrate, also within the latter genetic and geographical grouping the morphological process of reduplication may display very diverse properties, evinced by both a wide variety of reduplicative formal patterns as well as a considerable range of corresponding meanings and functions. At the same time, the following overview cannot, and does not, claim comprehensiveness of either data description or their analysis.

## 45.2 Forms

In presenting the manifold reduplicative forms found in MPSEA, we mainly follow the logical space set up by Pulleyblank (2009: 311) and expanded by Schwaiger (2017: 50–68). It covers the whole morphological and phonological spectrum from full reduplication of simple and complex words, stems, roots, and—more rarely—affixes, over several kinds of in-between cases, to the partial reduplication of feet, syllables, and single segments, also including all sorts of fixed-material reduplication as we go along. (See also Himmelmann's [2005a: 121–5] and Blust's [2013a: 418–31] surveys for reduplicative patterns in their respective wider samples.)

### 45.2.1 Word, stem, and root reduplication

The distinction between base and reduplicant is not always clear in full reduplication and needs language-specific arguments (see also Blust 2013a: 408–10), although providing these may not be possible in every case. Stress assignment can be one distinguishing feature between base and reduplicant, whereby the stressed constituent is usually assumed to be the base (e.g. Jackson 2014: 85 on Irarutu). Another, more general argument is to simply equate the position of the reduplicant in full reduplication with the most typical partial reduplication positions in a language, which in most cases turn out to be initial. A similar approach hypothesizes the position of reduplicants with respect to their bases to be predictable from the ordering of synonymous affixes in a language (see Moravcsik 1978: 328). However, this hypothesis rests on the not so self-evident assumption that reduplication is merely a special kind of affixation.

Similarly, distinguishing between words, stems, and roots is likewise not always easy or even relevant in a language, especially when it comes to some of the MPSEA languages spoken on the Southeast Asian mainland (e.g. Cham, Moken, and Moklen), in western Borneo (e.g. Land Dayak), and the Flores-Timor region (e.g. Alorese, Keo, and Waima'a), which are relatively poor in morphology or even nearly isolating (see Himmelmann 2005a: 126).

Word reduplication is frequently encountered and is clearest with bases that are themselves morphologically complex and may be used as full-fledged words on their own as well, as in the following example from West Coast Bajau, which includes an intransitivizing prefix *pe-*:

West Coast Bajau

(1) *pekar* 'to unfurl (transitive)'
*pe-pekar* 'to unfurl (intransitive)'
***pe-pekar~pe-pekar*** 'to unfurl repeatedly, (many) unfurl' (Miller 2007: 76)

The vowel-harmonic derivational suffix *-an* may be included or excluded (e.g. *sorong~sorong-on* or *sorong-on~sorong-on*, both from *sorong* 'to push' and "with no difference in meaning between the two forms"; Miller 2007: 76). Other affixes, among them the passive voice infix *<in>*, are not reduplicated (e.g. *p<in>isak~pisak* 'to be crushed repeatedly', not **p<in>isak~p<in>isak*; Miller 2007: 75, 76).

The difference between stem and root reduplication often appears to be merely one of terminology, for example when comparing Mamanwa 'full stem reduplication' in *tarak~tarak* 'toy truck' from *tarak* 'truck' (Miller and Miller 1976: 46) and Tondano 'full root reduplication' in *tou~tou* 'people' from *tou* 'person, man' (Brickell 2014: 73, 74). It would make sense, however, to speak of root reduplication when the central morphological part of a word is reduplicated without any affixes, and to designate as stem reduplication those patterns in which at least one affix is reduplicated along with the root but, crucially, not the entire word with all its affixes (see also Rubino 2005a: 11). Root reduplication in opposition to word reduplication is reported, for example, from Madurese, where, as in many other languages, 'whole-word reduplication' is distinguished from 'root only' reduplication (Davies 2010: 130). An example is the pluralization of derived nouns like *ka-rajaʔ-an~ka-rajaʔ-an* 'kingdoms' from *ka-rajaʔ-an* 'kingdom' (< *raja* 'king') or *pang-asel-an~pang-asel-an* 'incomes' from *pang-asel-an* 'income' (< *asel* 'succeed') vs. the pluralization of verbal roots like *berkaʔ~berkaʔ-an* 'run often (plural)' from *berkaʔ-an* 'run often' or *a-caca~caca* 'chat' from *a-caca* 'talk' (Davies 2010: 113, 130, 310).

In Kambera, full reduplication includes affixes, whereas partial reduplication does not (e.g. *ma-ˈramba~ma-ˈramba* 'various [kinds of] kings' vs. *ma-ra~ˈramba* 'various kings'; Klamer 1998: 36, 38).

In compounds, several languages confine reduplication to the head component, such as in Jambi Malay:

Jambi Malay
(2) ***alat~alat*** ***pancɪŋ*** *aku-ko...*
PL~tool fishing.rod 1SG-DEM.PROX
'My fishing tools...' (Yanti 2010: 618)

## 45.2.2 Affix reduplication

Full reduplication specifically targeting an affix is in general not very frequent in the languages of the world and normally implies the additional presence of fully reduplicated words, stems, or roots in a language (see Schwaiger 2017: 122). But, although MPSEA accordingly prefers full reduplication of especially stem or root bases, reduplicated affixes can be found in some instances. In Yami verbs, for example, reduplication of the perfective prefix *ni-* occurs (e.g. *ni~ni-akan* 'everything that has been eaten'; Rau and Dong 2006: 86). Verbs in Ternate Malay may reduplicate the verbalizer *ba-* or the reciprocal prefix *baku-*, as in *ba~ba-dara* 'bleed severely' from *dara* 'blood' and *baku~baku-susun* 'intensively stack on top of each other' from *susun* 'to stack' (Litamahuputty 2012: 138, 139). The Sawai language displays a curious case of pronominal prefix reduplication with an additional vowel *a* for expressing habitual or progressive (see Whisler 1996: 9):

Sawai
(3) ***ka~k-eyówe*** *ga* *k-duk* *pa*
PROG~1SG-look.for but 1SG-find NEG
'I looked all over for it but didn't find it.'
(Whisler 1996: 26)

In Arta, the adjective markers *me*C- (see also §45.2.11) and *ma-* are reduplicated in order to refer "to an intensified property, a much higher point than the norm on a particular scalar property scale" (Kimoto 2017a: 97), for example *mep~ep-pasu* 'very hot' (*me*C*e*C-) from *mep-pasu* 'hot' and, less transparently, *memem~ma-rakət* 'very bad' from *ma-rakət* 'bad' (Kimoto 2017a: 35, 97).

It should be pointed out that many instances showing a reduplicated affix are not really representing a rule for reduplication of an affix but result from a rule for reduplication of a specific syllable of the base word, which often simply coincides with an affix. In Bikol, for example, when stem-initial CV- reduplication for imperfective aspect applies, it is often the causative prefix *pa-* that gets reduplicated, as in *nag-pa~pa-kusog* 'making strong' (Mattes 2014: 49). In Ilokano CV-reduplication, it may be the left component of the derivational circumfix *ka-. . .-an* that is reduplicated to express plural, as in *ka~ka-ili-án* 'townmates' (Rubino 2005a: 12) from *ka-ili-án* 'townmate' (< *íli* 'town'; Rubino 2000: xlix). In Tajio, it may happen that a numeral prefix is attached to a root and subsequent reduplication yields a form which is ambiguous between monosyllabic reduplication of the whole base and 'prefix doubling' (the dots indicate syllable boundaries):

Tajio
(4) *e.le.o* 'day'
*se-e.le.o* 'one day'
***se~se.e.le.o*** 'every day' (Mayani 2013: 69)

But there are also languages that explicitly exclude affixes from reduplication, for instance Madurese (see §45.2.1) or Makasar:

Makasar
(5) a. ***aʔ-jappa~jappa***
INTR-DISTR~walk
'stroll'

b. ***ka-io~io-ang***
NMLZ-INTNS~yes-NMLZ
'someone who always agrees' (Jukes 2006: 105)

Nevertheless, phonological changes that are triggered by these affixes can influence the form of base and reduplicant (see also §45.2.11):

Makasar
(6) ***am-mekang~mekang***
aN(N)-pekang~pekang
TR-DIM~hook
'fishing (for fun)' (Jukes 2006: 105)

## 45.2.3 Full reduplication with linking elements

Full reduplications with dedicated linkers between their parts appear to be very rare in MPSEA, but they are frequent enough in other languages for Abbi (1992: 27) to use the term 'discontinuous word reduplication' for them. A possible MPSEA case might be found in Mualang so-called syntactic reduplication with a linking preposition *ka* 'to' conveying continuity or augmentation, as in *besay ka besay* 'become bigger and bigger', *tawʔ ka tawʔ* 'become more and more knowledgeable' and *ketawaʔ ka ketawaʔ* 'continue to laugh' (Tjia 2007: 191–2). However, since *ka* is a locative preposition not exclusive to this function (see Tjia 2007: 97–9), it may well be that the above examples are really cases of coordination or some other process in the syntax of the language that need to be kept apart from morphological reduplication proper.

Similar examples of reduplication (or repetition) with a linker *tu* 'too, also' are found in Begak, for instance *mə-ri-tu-mə-ri* 'DEP-tear to pieces repeatedly', from *ri* 'tear' inflected for the so-called dependent (Goudswaard 2005: 56, 57). Although they are in fact outcomes of a syntactic process, the construction shares phonological and semantic features with morphological reduplication (see Goudswaard 2005: 56) and also appears in sound-symbolic words which lack a simple base form, such as *gurung-tu-gurung* 'a few people crying loudly' (**gurung*) (Goudswaard 2005: 57; see §45.4 for more details).

A purely phonological linker is used in Ilokano, where an assimilating nasal is inserted between the components of fully reduplicated nouns (see Rubino 2000: xvii), for example *rupa-n~rupa* 'face to face' (from *rúpa* 'face'; Rubino 2000: xlix) and *gura-ng~gura* 'mutual hatred' (from *gúra* 'hate'; Rubino 2000: 207).

### 45.2.4 Echo-words

Although echo-word formations as a type of non-prototypical reduplication (see Urdze 2018) are a very widespread phenomenon in the languages of the world, Blust (2013a: 421) claims them to be "known from very few [Austronesian] languages. The best-known examples are found in Malay/Indonesian", for example *sayur~**mayur*** 'vegetables' from *sayur* 'vegetable' (Sneddon 1996: 22) or *asal~**ʊsʊl*** 'origin', the latter a variant of *asal* 'origin' in Tanjung Raden, a dialect of Jambi Malay (Yanti 2010: 623). Yet, Blust's statement seems a bit strong, especially with respect to MPSEA, where echo-words or, as they are sometimes also called, imitative or rhyming/chiming reduplications are also found in several languages other than Indonesian or Malay (see, e.g., Balinese-Sasak-Sumbawa discussed in Shiohara and Arka, this volume, §32.3.3 and the languages of Java discussed in Vander Klok, this volume, §31.4.1).

Echo-word formation combines full reduplication with fixed segmentism by replacing the sounds of the original in certain syllabic positions of the reduplicated part. The process is extraordinarily pervasive in Austronesian languages of the Southeast Asian mainland, very likely under the influence of neighbouring Mon-Khmer languages like Vietnamese, which abound in such patterns. The Chamic language Jarai serves to illustrate the possibilities of onset, nucleus, and coda replacement as well as the possibility for the changes to take place in the first or the second part of an echo-formation:

Jarai

| | | | | |
|---|---|---|---|---|
| (7) | *čim* | 'bird/s' | *čim~**brim*** | 'a grouping of different species of birds' |
| | *rang* | 'troubles, confusion' | ***rung**~rang* | 'problems' |
| | *arŏng* | 'insect/s' | *arŏng~**arot*** | 'all kinds of insects' |

(Williams and Siu 2013: 198, 199)

Still, the exact status of echo-words in MPSEA is far from settled, leading authors like Blust (2013a: 421) to point out that for some examples it can be difficult to answer "the question of where and how to draw the line between reduplication and compounding" (see also Brunelle and Jensen, this volume, §30.3.2 on 'elaborative compounds' in Chamic).

Some rare cases of productive echo-word formation with intensifying meaning are reported from Gayo:

Gayo

(8) a. *Mungôl-ni* *anak=é* *susah,*
A.FOC.raise-CAUS offspring=3.POSS difficult
***sakit~makit.***
sick~INTNS
'Raising their children was difficult, really difficult.'

b. *Enti* ***taring~maring*** *bèwèn=é* *turah* *beluh.*
don't remain~INTNS all=3.POSS must go
'Don't anyone stay behind at all, everyone must go.'
(Eades 2005: 56)

Various formal patterns of echo-reduplication are found in many MPSEA languages, yet—and this might be a typological feature of Austronesian languages in general—very often not in productive word formations but only in lexical reduplications. Examples are Bikol *burók-**busók*** 'sound of falling water', *kalóʔ-**kagóʔ*** 'to shake something (as water in a glass, a milkshake or cocktail)', *mayó-**payó*** 'the tip of a grain of rice', ***riwás**-**díwas*** 'to calm down or relax' (Mintz 2004: 505, 642, 740, 831) and many more (see also Mattes 2014: 165–9). In Keo, a language that does not have productive reduplication, there are lexical echo-words like *fingo-**fango*** 'dirty, red face from crying', *saké-**daké*** 'trousers', and ***gusu**-**gasa*** 'chaotic', referred to as 'rhyming jingle compounds' by Baird (2002: 175). See §45.4 for further details on lexical reduplication.

## 45.2.5 Borderline forms

Some forms can be subsumed either under full reduplication or under partial reduplication, depending on the phonological make-up of the base. These are already described by Moravcsik (1978: 306) as "cases where what appears to be a distinction between total and partial reduplication is actually a distinction between forms of different length whose reduplication, however, is governed by the same principle." Similarly, Blust (2013a: 407) observes that such "divergent surface patterns may be variants of a single reduplicative structure." Especially, since in many MPSEA languages the majority of roots are disyllabic, full reduplication and foot reduplication often look identical.

Mayani (2013: 67) describes such variations of partial and full reduplication in the MPSEA language Tajio, where "the syllable structure of the reduplicant may consist of (C)V(N).CV(C) combinations depending on the syllable structure of the base." The coda of the second syllable of a disyllabic base may appear in the reduplicant or not, without semantic difference (9a), while with (C)V(N).CV bases the pattern always looks like full reduplication (9b):

Tajio

(9) a. *pu.ras* 'to suffer from diarrhoea' **pu.ra~pu.ras** or **pu.ras~pu.ras** 'to suffer from intensive diarrhoea'

b. *ru.pa* 'kind of' **ru.pa~ru.pa** 'many kinds of'

(Mayani 2013: 68)

Similarly, Tagalog full-root reduplication appears as a disyllabic foot if the root is trisyllabic (e.g. *ma-sarap~sarap* 'rather tasty' from *ma-sarap* 'tasty' as opposed to *ma-sali~salita* 'rather talkative' from *ma-salita* 'talkative'; Schachter and Otanes 1972: 236). Liao and Reid (this volume, §24.4) also point out the ambiguity between full reduplication and foot reduplication in the Central Luzon language Botolan Sambal.

Conversely, in the Fehan dialect of Tetun (or Tetun Fehan), several truncation rules and their combinations (see van Klinken 1999: 45–7 for details) often make full reduplication look like partial reduplication:

Tetun Fehan

| (10) | *kmesak* | 'sole' | **kmesa~mesak** | 'very few' |
|---|---|---|---|---|
| | *ktomak* | 'whole' | **kto(ma)~tomak** | 'completely' |
| | *loron* | 'night' | **loro~loron** | 'nightly' |
| | *de?an* | 'scold' | **de~de?an** | 'scold for no reason' |
| | *bá* | 'go' | **bá~bá(n)** | 'go for no reason' |

(van Klinken 1999: 46, 93)

One reduplication type found in several languages can be interpreted as either prefixing CVCV- reduplication or as suffixing "full reduplication minus the coda" (Blust 2013a: 426). Examples are Ngaju Dayak *humo~humong* 'somewhat stupid' (< *humong* 'stupid') (Hardeland 1859: 183–4), Bolaang-Mongondow *ko-kuntu~kuntuŋ* 'being carried piggypack' (< *kuntuŋ* 'carry piggypack') (Dunnebier 1951, cited in Blust 2013a: 421) or Dupaningan Agta *maka-ngidi~ngidit* 'be laughing' (< *ngidit* 'laugh') (Robinson 2008: 168).

In Tanjung Raden (a dialect of Jambi Malay), there are three variants of full reduplication: full reduplication in the sense of two identical copies, for instance *jaram*[b]*a~jaram*[b]*a* 'bridges' or *mahal~mahal* 'expensive/very expensive' (Yanti 2010: 623), 'full reduplication with no final consonant', as in *sopa~sopan* 'very polite' or *diki~dikit* 'little by little' (Yanti 2010: 624), and 'full reduplication with a glottal stop'. In the latter case, the final, non-continuant non-sonorant consonant of the reduplicant is substituted by a glottal stop, such as *ɪkʊ?~ɪkʊt* 'imitate' or *diki?~dikit* 'little by little' (Yanti 2010: 624). The Helong language also has a 'word-no-coda' reduplication pattern, differing both from full-word reduplication as well as from partial CV- reduplication in that "each segment of a word is reduplicated except for the final coda at the end of the word" (Balle 2017b: iv), for example *duma~duman* 'during the night' as opposed to *duman~duman* 'during/in the dark night' and *du~duman* 'every night', all from *duman* 'night' (Balle 2017b: iv, 21, 58).

## 45.2.6 Foot reduplication

Partial reduplication as discussed in this and the following sections can be characterized "in reference to consonant–vowel sequences and absolute linear position" (Moravcsik 1978: 307), for example initial C-, final -CVC, or internal -CV- reduplication. When prosodic terms are also included, this amounts to partial reduplicants typically consisting of a two-syllable foot, a syllable of its own or merely a single sound, all of which may show a certain independence with respect to the phonological make-up and organization of their base. This often means that "although the reduplicant corresponds to a unit of prosody, it is not formed from a unit of prosody, or even from segments that are adjacent in the stream of speech" (Blust 2013a: 424). Reduplicants may furthermore be attached in front, in the middle or at the end of their base.

Foot reduplication in MPSEA may involve different degrees of syllable-internal complexity but in most instances does not exceed two syllables in length (see also Moravcsik 1978: 310). Trisyllabic reduplicative feet, as in Ibaloi *mariki~marikit* 'extremely pretty' from *marikit* 'pretty woman' (Ruffolo 2004: 98), are rather exceptional (but see also Keenan and Polinsky 1998: 571–3 for a more complex case in the outlier language Malagasy). In Ilokano, the maximal expansion of CVC(C)(V)V- reduplication (e.g. *buttua~buttuag* 'rocking chair'; Rubino 2000: xvii) apparently only occurs with bases in which the two word final vowels are syllabified together to really form just one syllable (see Rubino 2000: xxxix).

The much more frequent disyllabic foot reduplications in MPSEA languages may come with varyingly complex syllables and are at least partly dependent on the segmental make-up of the base, for example Tajio *lanta~lantap* 'floating for some time' (CVCCV-) from *lantap* 'to float' (Mayani 2013: 68), Makasar *baruʔ~barumbung* 'greyish' (CVCVC-, whereby the reduplicant always ends in a glottal stop) from *barumbung* 'grey' (Jukes 2006: 104), Begak *bəg-alud~galud* 'AV-go by boat for fun' (-CVCVC, whereby the final consonant of the prefix is copied into the reduplicant) from *alud* 'boat' (Goudswaard 2005: 55), Pendau *re-ingki~ingkit* 'nibbling' (VCCV-) from *ingkit* 'nibble' (Quick 2007: 91), Dampelas *ale~ales* 'very slow' (VCV-) from *ales* 'slow' (Moro 2010: 90) and Tausug *hambuuk~buuk* 'one and only, unique' (-CVVC) from *hambuuk* 'one' (Rubino 2006: 153).

Initial disyllabic foot reduplication with an open second syllable is typologically very widespread, thus Blust's (2013a: 422) remark that, in Austronesian as a whole, "reduplicative patterns which copy CVCV- are relatively hard to find" comes somewhat as a surprise. For MPSEA in particular, the list of rather complex fixed-segment $C_1eC_1V(C_2)$- examples from the outlier language Palauan adduced by Blust (2013a: 422–3), for instance *mę-sesu~saul* 'kind of tired' from *mę-saul* 'tired' (Josephs 1975: 267), can be readily extended by more canonical forms through languages like Northern Alta (e.g. *mudu~mudung* 'mountains' from *mudung* 'mountain'; García Laguía 2018: 74), Pangasinan (e.g. *manó~manók* 'chickens' from *manók* 'chicken'; Rubino 2005a: 11), Tondano (e.g. *pa-sèro~sèron* 'is being searched for' from *pa-sèron* 'search for'; Brickell 2014: 73), Yami (e.g. *ciri~ciring* 'words, language' from *ciring* 'word'; Rau and Dong 2006: 86) and many more. The mirror image, namely final foot reduplication of the form -CVCV, is rarely found in MPSEA languages. One isolated example is the adverb *sabole~bole* 'must; very much hoped' (< *sabole* 'definitely, certainly') in Balantak (van den Berg and Busenitz 2012: 19). Blust claims that such a reduplication type is common in the Austronesian family. If so, it might (in some cases at least) as well be interpreted as full reduplication, as it "requires bases of more than two syllables to distinguish it from full reduplication" (Blust 2013a: 423), and also because the roots in this family are typically disyllabic.

Especially with disyllabic reduplicative feet that attach in front of their bases, the second syllable often appears as open even when its base counterpart displays a coda consonant, as in the examples from Dampelas, Northern Alta, Pangasinan, Pendau, Tajio, Tondano, and Yami above. As a minor pattern, foot reduplication in which the second syllable consists solely of a vowel are also encountered, for example in Tajio *u.a~u.ar* 'to say repeatedly' from *u.ar* 'to say' (Mayani 2013: 68) and Yami *koi~kois* 'pigs' from *kois* 'pig' (Rau and Dong 2006: 83, 85).

### 45.2.7 Syllable reduplication

Reduplicants may also be formed by varyingly complex syllables attached before, within, or after the base. In MPSEA and elsewhere, syllable reduplication with a complex onset and a coda, as in the occasional CCVC- pattern in Luang, is rather exceptional (e.g. *plet~pleta* 'very quickly' from *pleta* 'quickly'; Taber and Taber 2015: 29). The same can be said about the codaless CCV- pattern in Yami reduplicated bound roots like *a-kdo~kdot-en* 'pinch a little' from *akdot-en* 'pinch out' (Rau and Dong 2006: 85, 112). However, both varieties can be found in a rather unusual pattern of Madurese, in which any final syllable is copied regardless of its make-up and attached to the left of the root, as in *sreng~assreng* 'frequently' from *assreng* 'frequent' and *tre~pottre* 'princesses' from *pottre* 'princess' (Davies 2010: 130).

So-called heavy syllables with a simple onset and coda are a widespread reduplicative type across the MPSEA languages. Usually, heavy syllable reduplication copies $C_1V_1C_2$- from the base, but in some very specific cases (reported from the Northern Philippine languages Arta and Ilokano; see also §45.3.1), the reduplicant copies $C_1V_1C_1$- (e.g. Arta *lal~lappul* 'dogs' from *lappul* 'dog'; Kimoto 2017a: 96). Amarasi offers a particularly instructive case, as in this language the first CVC sequence of the final foot of a root is copied and attached to the left of this foot, resulting in initial reduplication with disyllabic roots but in internal reduplication with roots that are longer than one foot (e.g. *baʔ~baʔuk* 'many' from the disyllabic base *baʔuk* vs. *tai<kob~>koib* 'fall down' from the trisyllabic base *taikobi* 'fall'; Edwards 2020: 116, 117, 497). (The form *tai<kob~>**koib*** from *taikobi* results from a metathesis process that occurs in addition to reduplication.) For bases without the necessary CVC structure, the second consonantal slot of the reduplicant is filled by the final consonant of the foot, as in *kas~kais* 'don't (prohibitive)' from *kais* (Edwards 2020: 117). Another type of heavy syllable reduplication is found when, instead of having a coda, the reduplicant vowel is lengthened, as in Tagalog *bi:~bilhin* 'will buy' from *bilhin* 'buy' (Schachter and Otanes 1972: 362, 376) or Ilokano (see Liao and Reid, this volume, §24.4). Moreover, mostly in dependence on whether the base offers an onset consonant or not, VC reduplication also occurs in several languages (e.g. Luang *ul~ulu* 'a long time ago' from *ulu* 'before'; Taber and Taber 2015: 29; Selaru *-ob~oban* 'hit repeatedly' from *-oban* 'hit'; Coward 2005: 121; Irarutu *esuem~em* 'various (ones)' from *esuem* '(just) one'; Jackson 2014: 86, 91). However, it is often the case in MPSEA that apparently vowel-initial roots are actually pronounced with an epenthetic glottal stop then appearing in both the reduplicant and the root, for example in Amarasi *an~anaʔ* 'small' pronounced as [ʔanˈʔanɐʔ] (Edwards 2020: 116). A less common mechanism occurs in Nias, where syllable reduplication of vowel-initial bases "copies the initial vowel and inserts /g/ between the copied vowel and the vowel of the stem" (Brown 2001: 95–6), as in *og~obou* 'rotten (plural argument)' from *obou* 'rotten' (Brown 2001: 96).

As elsewhere in the world, reduplication of the so-called core syllable, corresponding to the maximally unmarked CV-syllable type, is very common in the MPSEA languages. Most frequently, the initial CV sequence of a word, stem, or root is copied, as in Ilokano *ka-sa~sangpét* 'just arrive' (< *sangpét* 'arrive'), Central Bontok /la~lajdən/ 'to like very much' (< /lajdən/ 'to like') (both examples from Liao and Reid, this volume, §24.4) or Balantak *pe~penek* 'tree climber' (< *penek* 'climb') (van den Berg and Busenitz 2012: 20). However, non-initial syllables can also serve as the base for reduplication, especially when they are stressed, as in Chamorro *hu<gá~>gando* 'playing' from *hugándo* 'play' (Topping 1973: 259), Pangasinan *a<mi~>mígo* 'friends' from *amígo* 'friend' (Rubino 2005a: 11) or Wamesa *ka<si~>sio* 'furious' from *kasio* 'angry' (Gasser 2014: 56). Sometimes the CV sequence is reduplicated in final position (e.g. Irarutu [ˈ$^{n}$d$^{m}$be~$^{m}$be] 'he hit repeatedly' from /tbe/ 'hit'; Jackson 2014: 86; see also §45.2.11), a pattern judged to be "rare both diachronically and synchronically" by Blust (2013a: 429).

In the example above from the outlier language Chamorro, it can be seen that the drive towards an unmarked core-syllable reduplicant may be so strong as to be attained through not copying an available base coda. In languages like Kambera, only the first part of the nucleus of a diphthong is reduplicated for the same reason (e.g. *ha~haila* from *haila* 'saddle'; Klamer 1998: 35). Consonant clusters in the base onset may likewise be avoided through reduplicative reduction in order to yield the universally preferred CV-reduplicant structure in partial reduplication (see also Schwaiger 2017: 126). While this particular so-called emergence-of-the-unmarked effect (McCarthy and Prince 1994) is very common from a cross-linguistic perspective, MPSEA examples seem to occur mainly with loanwords in the Philippine subgroup, which are often the only vocabulary items allowing for complex onsets in these languages (e.g. Bikol *pig-da~drive* 'is riding' from *drive* 'drive'; Mattes 2014: 45; Pangasinan *pa~pláto* 'plates' from *plato* 'plate'; Rubino 2005a: 11; Tagalog *mag-ta~trabaho* 'will work' from *mag-trabaho* 'works'; French 1988: 60). A much rarer sort of mirror image can be found in the West Timor language Amarasi, where a root-initial consonant cluster (see Edwards 2020: 140–3) is simplified by not copying the first, pre-foot consonant and placing the reduplicant before the following foot "as a kind of infix", for example *na-b<re~>reo=n* from *na-breo=n* '3-grope.around=PL' (Edwards 2020: 117).

Whereas some languages clearly limit the base for reduplication to the root and exclude affixes, other languages ignore morpheme boundaries in the reduplicative process, for instance Ilokano (e.g. *mat~ma-turog* 'sleeping' from *ma-turog* 'sleep'; Rubino 2005a: 12). In Begak Cə- reduplication (see §45.2.9), the word-initial consonant is reduplicated irrespective of whether it is the $C_1$ of a root, as in *bə~buaʔ* 'various types of fruit' (< *buaʔ* 'fruit'), or of a prefix, as in *bə~b-iang* (RECP~MD-separate) 'separate from each other' (< *iang* 'separate') or *kə~k-uliʔ* (PL~AV.NVOL-go.home) 'go to and fro' (< *uliʔ* 'go home') (Goudswaard 2005: 52, 53).

However, on closer inspection, languages also differentiate between affixes in this respect. In Bikol, voice prefixes (*mag-*, *nag-*, *pig-*, *ma-*, etc.) are usually not included in the base for marking imperfective aspect by CV- reduplication, but with disyllabic voice/mood prefixes (e.g. abilitative or sociative *maka-*/*naka-*), the second syllable of the affix can be reduplicated (11a) or not (11b):

Bikol
(11) a. *permi-ng* *man* *siya*
always-LNK also 3SG.A
***naka~ka-bohe***
BEG.AV.ABIL~IPFV-escape
'he also always managed to escape'

b. *dai* *pa* ***naka-ta~tapos***. . .
NEG still BEG.AV.ABIL-IPFV~finish
'(she) was not yet able to finalize. . .'
(Mattes 2014: 48)

In Tukang Besi, disyllabic reduplication never includes material from the subject prefixes of a verb (12a), whereas other prefixes and infixes are part of the reduplication base, as in (12b) (see Donohue 1999a: 298–9). With adjectives, the base for reduplication depends on the allomorph of the adjectival prefix (see Donohue 1999a: 299–301).

Tukang Besi
(12) a. ***No-kede~ngkede.*** but: **Noke~no-kede.*
3.REAL-ATT~sit ATT~3.REAL-sit
'They are sitting around.'

b. ***No-heta~he-tade-ʔe.***
3.REAL-ATT~VBLZ-stand-3.OBJ
but: **No-he-tade~ntade-ʔe.*
3.REAL-VBLZ-ATT~stand-3.OBJ
'They are building it, sort of.' (Donohue 1999a: 299)

### 45.2.8 Single-segment reduplication

In general, reduplication of single consonants or vowels is also found in the languages of the world, and it appears to be a relatively frequent phenomenon in MPSEA. The Irarutu language in fact shows that sometimes even two consonants can be copied to form a consonantal-cluster reduplicant, as in [ᵑgr̩~ˈᵑgir] 'story' from /gir/ 'story-tell' and [fra~fr] 'wing' from /fra/ 'hand' (Jackson 2014: 85, 86; see also Gasser, Arnold, and Kamholz, this volume, §37.2.5).

Single-consonant reduplication is found initially (e.g. Kerinci *k~kantae͡* 'friends' from *kantae͡* 'friend'; McKinnon 2011: 85, 146) and internally (e.g. Ilokano *a<d~>di* 'younger siblings' from *ádi* 'younger brother or sister'; Rubino 2000: xvii, 10). In Kola, it is actually the second consonant of the stressed syllable that is copied and placed in front of this syllable, as in *bu<b~>ˈtebi* 'gentleness' from *buˈtebi* 'gentle' (Takata 1992: 61). In Dobel, C- is, rather unusually, even the only "true productive reduplication" (Hughes 2000: 167).

Single-vowel reduplication is likewise found initially (e.g. Chamorro *éʔ~eggaʔ* 'watching' from *éggaʔ* 'watch'; Topping 1973: 259) and internally (e.g. Arta *mal-la:gip* 'talk too much or to unnecessary extent' from *mal-lagip* 'talk'; Kimoto 2017a: 98, 445), though cases like the former may be complicated by the fact that "an excrescent glottal stop is always placed between the two succeeding vowels" (Topping 1973: 259), while cases like the latter may also be described and transcribed as vowel lengthening (see Kimoto 2017a: 98). Another alternative analysis of reduplicative vowels could involve treating them as the minimal form of syllable reduplication.

Both final single-consonant and final single-vowel reduplication may turn out to be infrequent, perhaps even non-existent, because of the inherent phonetic difficulty for the hearer to identify them at the end of words or to differentiate them in this position from phonologically or morphologically motivated consonant gemination and vowel lengthening, respectively (see also Schwaiger 2017: 64, 118).

### 45.2.9 Partial reduplication with fixed segments

Fixed-segment partial reduplication typically involves the expansion of reduplicated material by vocalic and/or consonantal units and is a very frequent phenomenon in MPSEA languages. As these exponents combine pre-specified material with reduplicative material, they constitute a hybrid category that merges features of both affixes and reduplicants.

The most common forms of this type copy a consonant in combination with the vowel /a/, *Ca-* being "by far the most common pattern of reduplication with fixed segmentism in [Austronesian] languages" (Blust 2013a: 427). In MPSEA the latter is used, for instance, in Balinese, Chamorro, Dupaningan Agta, Madurese, Ngaju Dayak, Yami, Tetun Fehan (but without extrasyllabic initial *k*, then looking like infixation; see van Klinken 1999: 44–5), and Arta (with a distinction between *Ca-* and *Ca:-*; see Kimoto 2017a: 98–9). Some examples are Dupaningan Agta *ma-sa~singgat=kan* (STAT-PL~sweet=EVID) 'she said they were sweet' (Robinson 2008: 178), Madurese *ba~buruk* 'advises (plural)' (< *buruk* 'advise') (Davies 2010: 131) and Yami *ra~roa* 'two (plural)' (< *doa* 'two') (Rau and Dong 2006: 86; see also §45.2.11 for the phonological changes). Other occurring variants copying a consonant with a pre-specified vowel are *Caa-* (e.g. Balantak *sianta no-baa~bubut* 'pull nothing' from *bubut* 'pull out'; van den Berg and Busenitz 2012: 21), *Cə-* (e.g. Begak *bə~bunuʔ* 'kill each other' from *bunuʔ* 'kill'; Goudswaard 2005: 52), *Ci-/Ce-* (e.g. Tondano *we~wolè* 'oar' from *wolè* 'row'; Brickell 2014: 73), *Co-/Cu-* (e.g. Tukang Besi reduplicated numerals like *lo~lima* 'five'; Donohue 1999a: 107) and *Caw-* (with a fixed vowel-glide sequence) in some Central and Northern Philippine languages (e.g. Botolan Sambal *daw~dowih* 'thorns' from *dowih* 'thorn'; Antworth 1979: 9; Tausug *mag-law~lahasiyaʔ* 'all the relatives' from *mag-lahasiyaʔ* 'relatives'; Rubino 2006: 275; see also Liao and Reid, this volume, §24.4). Sometimes such forms reflect a diachronic vowel change, for example in Cebuano, where *Cə-* reduplication (which in turn probably evolved from either CV- or *Ca-*; see also §45.5) became *Cu-* reduplication via the strengthening of reduced schwa to the full vowel /u/ (Sander Adelaar, personal communication).

More complex syllable reduplications with fixed /a/ or /e/ occur in several languages of the South Halmahera–West New Guinea region (see also Gasser, Arnold, and Kamholz, this volume, §37.2.5), for instance *CaC-* in Fordata (including *aC-*) or Taba and *CeC-* in Sawai. Examples are *lav~lova* (ATTR~fog) 'cloudy' and *am~umat* (REDUP~cook.salted.fish) from Fordata (Marshall and Marshall 1992: 27, 28), *bal~búlaj* (INSTR~to.wind/coil.something) 'device for winding rope, cord onto' from Taba (Bowden 2001: 72) and *tél~tolén* (NMLZ~sit) 'chair' from Sawai (Whisler 1996: 8). In some instances, even comprising two syllables, Taba *(C)aC(C)(a)-* reduplication takes "the first syllable of a verb, plus the onset and nucleus of its second syllable if there is one, then replacing any vowels with /a/" (Bowden 2001: 226):

Taba

(13) a. ***K-sang~sung*** *um.*
1SG-PL~enter house
'I entered many houses/I entered the house many times.' (Bowden 2001: 227)

b. ***N-sanga~sung-ak*** *wang* *lloci=si* *nik*
3SG-PL~enter-APPL child many=PL 1SG.POSS
*um.*
house
'He put lots of kids in the house.'
(Bowden 2001: 228)

Whereas all the examples listed so far are initial reduplications, Biak has patterns of consonant reduplication with fixed /a/ that are initially or internally *a*C or (*a*)C*a*(C), depending on the phonotactic structure of the root (see van den Heuvel 2006: 259–68). Illustrative instances are *as~usr* 'follow continually' (< *usr* 'follow'), *nya<ka~>ki* 'sowe always' (< *nyaki* 'owe'), *maw~mewr* 'refusal' (< *mewr* 'refuse'), *ma<ras~>risn* 'happiness' (< *marisn* 'happy'), *m<ana~>nis* 'similarity' (< *mnis* 'fit, similar'), and *p<adak~>dúk* 'beauty' (< *pdúk* 'beautiful') (van den Heuvel 2006: 263, 264, 265, 266). Another, rarer case of initial or internal *a*C reduplication is attested in Kola, where the second consonant of the stressed foot is copied and preceded by /a/, then attached to the left edge of that foot (e.g. *as~ˈtosi* 'short' from *ˈtosi* 'short' and *af<al~>ˈral* 'early morning' from *afˈral* 'morning'; Takata 1992: 61).

Extended fixed-segment reduplications yielding an entire foot of the form CVCV-, with a pre-specified VCV sequence and an initial C copying $C_1$ of the base, are possibly a development confined to certain parts of the Philippines (see Blust 2013a: 427). Examples for such patterns are C*ala*- in Central Cagayan Agta (e.g. *pala~pirák* 'a little money' from *pirák* 'money'; Healey 1960: 6), C*uru*- in Bikol (e.g. *huru~hapros* 'to touch gently and repeatedly' from *hapros* 'touch'; Mattes 2014: 76) and C*ulu*- in Hiligaynon (e.g. *tulu~táwo* 'puppet' from *tawo* 'person'; Wolfenden 1971: 73). As these reduplicants predominantly consist of fixed material, they could also be described as prefixes with a reduplicated initial consonant. In Tagalog and some other Philippine languages, such patterns are unknown and exact foot reduplication is used in corresponding contexts (e.g. Tagalog *ma-tali~talino* 'rather intelligent' from *ma-talino* 'intelligent'; Schachter and Otanes 1972: 236; see also §45.2.5).

Other forms of affix-reduplication hybrids are much rarer. A further example is the rather unusual *fa*C- pattern for reciprocals in Sawai, in which only the second consonant of the stem is reduplicated (e.g. *fal~gali* 'to help one another' from *gali* 'to help', *fat~pitno* 'to tie to something else' from *pitno* 'to tie' or *fak~duk* 'to meet one another' from *duk* 'to meet'; Whisler 1996: 8, 9). Some disagreement exists concerning a form of plurality infixation with a variable vowel and a uniform liquid consonant in some Central Philippine languages, such as <Vl> in Hiligaynon or <Vr> in Bikol and Inonhan. Examples are Bikol *pag-d<ir>ipan* (NMLZ-<PL>gather) 'gathering' from *dipan* 'gather' (Mattes 2014: 61), Hiligaynon *nag-p<al>a-lutoʔ* 'is always cooking' (Wolfenden 1971: 107) and Inonhan *nag-s<ur>úlat* 'PRS.PFV-<PL>read' from *súlat* 'read' (Goudswaard 2005: 51, note 15). For Hiligaynon, this pattern is described as "an infix consisting of a *reduplicated* $V_1$ of the stem and *l*" (Wolfenden 1971: 67; our emphasis; see also Wolfenden 1971: 101), while <Vr> in Bikol is explicitly analysed as fixed-segment reduplication by Mattes (2014: 58–69). However, many experts strongly opt for treating these forms as conventional affixes involving vowel assimilation instead (e.g. Sander Adelaar, Hsiu-chuan Liao, and Laurie Reid, personal communication). (See also Inkelas 2008 for a third, in-between possibility of analysis in terms of 'phonological duplication'.)

### 45.2.10 Reduplication and affixation

Blust (2013a: 406) observes that "reduplicative morphology in [Austronesian] languages often co-occurs with non-reduplicative affixes", and the present subset of MPSEA languages is no exception in this regard. In most non-isolating languages, reduplicated bases can undergo further affixation and the respective meanings are usually combined. Davies (2010: 131–7) describes in detail how Madurese reduplication interacts with all kinds of affixes (i.e. prefixes, suffixes, and circumfixes). For example, "[w]ith certain types of generic nouns, in combination with the suffix *-an*, reduplication serves not only to indicate plurality but also carries the additional meaning of indicating a variety of types" (Davies 2010: 143), as in *men~tamen-an* '(various kinds of) plants' from *tamen* 'plant' or *un~daun-an* '(various kinds of) leaves' from *daun* 'leaf' (Davies 2010: 132, 144). Further examples are temporal expressions where "in combination with other morphology, the plurality of the time units indicates frequency [. . .] or [. . .] duration" (Davies 2010: 144), as in *re~saʔ-are* 'every day/day after day' from *are* 'day' (with a prefix *sa-* denoting 'all') or *lan~bulan-an* 'for months and months' from *bulan* 'month' (with an adverbial suffix *-an*). In the words just cited as well as in the following example (14) of a reduplicated causative verb expressing pretence or fake (see also §45.3.3), the ultimate syllable is reduplicated and attached at the very beginning (see also §45.2.7), skipping any intervening prefix:

Madurese
(14) *Kanaʔ* *juwa* *loʔ* *labu* *tape* *coma*
kid that not fall but only
***bu~ma-labu.***
ATT~AV.CAUS-fall
'That kid didn't fall but only pretended to fall.'
(Davies 2010: 141)

By contrast, a prefix like *a-* is not skipped and the reduplicant attached directly to the root (e.g. *a-on~taon* 'for years' from *taon* 'year'; Davies 2010: 144). In a language like Ibaloi, intensive CVC- reduplication co-occurs with the superlative circumfix *ka-…-an*, as in *ka bak~baknang-an* 'the very richest' from *baknang* 'rich person' (Ruffolo 2004: 105).

There is also "reduplication that is obligatory in combination with another affix, and which does not add meaning by itself to the overall construction; the affix and reduplicated matter together are monomorphemic" (Rubino 2005a: 18). This 'automatic reduplication' is also very widespread in MPSEA languages. In Philippine languages, for example, various reduplications together with verbal prefixes or circumfixes express several aspectual meanings, such as continuative and completive in Dupaningan Agta by *maka-* + CVCV- reduplication (15a) and *naka-* + CVCV- reduplication (15b), respectively:

Dupaningan Agta

(15) a. ***maka-ngidi~ngidit*** *i* *wadi=ko*
CONT-CONT~laugh DEF younger.sibling=1SG.GEN
'My younger sibling is laughing.'

b. ***naka-taba~tabas*** *ni* *Garwet*
COMPL.CONT-COMPL.CONT~clear PERS Garwet
'Garwet kept on clearing the land.'
(Robinson 2008: 168)

In Southern Ivatan, habitual aspect is expressed by *ma-…-en* + CV- reduplication, as in *ma-chi~chimuy-en* 'usually rain' from *chimuy* 'rain' (see Liao and Reid, this volume, §24.4). The Ilokano combination *agin*CV-, on the other hand, expresses pretence of an action, for example *aginsi~singpet* 'to pretend to behave' (Rubino 2005a: 18). An instance of automatic reduplication from the Aru language Batuley is intransitivization by the prefix *r-* with the accompanying verb being reduplicated:

Batuley

(16) *kaig* ***mo-r-ka<lag~>lag-eg***
2SG 2SG.A-INTR-<INTR~>hide-2SG.P
'you hide (yourself)' (Daigle 2015: 90)

### 45.2.11 Reduplication and phonological processes

Reduplication often triggers phonological changes, such as assimilation, dissimilation, metathesis, epenthesis, elision, vowel lengthening, reduction, deletion, stress shift, or consonant gemination.

Probably the most widespread process involved in reduplication is assimilation, especially nasal assimilation. The latter occurs with prefixed and reduplicated roots, for example, in Makasar *am-mekang~mekang* 'fishing (for fun)' (aN(N)- + full reduplication of *pekang* 'hook'; Jukes 2006: 105; see also §45.2.2), Karo Batak *ngukur~ngukur-i* 'to think about, ponder' (N- + full reduplication of *ukur* 'mind'; Woollams 1996: 96), Bikol *na-nu~nublíʔ* 'going around borrowing' (*nang-* + CV- reduplication of *sublíʔ* 'borrow'; Mattes 2014: 9, 47), and many other MPSEA languages (Lewotobi Lamaholot appearing to be a notably restricted case; see Nagaya 2011: 18). Furthermore, nasal assimilation often applies simultaneously to base and reduplicant, even when the triggering conditions for assimilation are not fulfilled in one of the two strings. In addition to the examples just mentioned, this may also be found without any further affixation, for instance in Irarutu [ˈⁿdᵐbe~ᵐbe] 'he hit repeatedly' from /tbe/ 'hit' (Jackson 2014: 86; see also §45.2.7). The phenomenon in question lies at the heart of a broad theoretical discussion on the order of morphological processes in rule-based theories of reduplication (e.g. Wilbur 1973) as well as on principles of reduplication in Optimality Theory (e.g. McCarthy and Prince 1994).

Other assimilation processes also take place, for example in Taba CaC- reduplication, where the final consonant of the reduplicant often assimilates to the root-initial consonant, as in *dab~dóba* 'earth' from *dóba* 'garden', assimilated to *dad~dóba* and sometimes reduced to *d~dóba* (Bowden 2001: 51).

A phonological process that is related to reduplication, and sometimes appears in combination with it, is consonantal gemination. In Arta, prefixation of the adjective marker *me-* triggers gemination of the base-initial consonant (Hsiu-chuan Liao, personal communication), which becomes part of the reduplicant when intensified (e.g. *mel~el-layat* 'very wide, large' from *mel-layat* 'wide, large'; Kimoto 2017a: 196, 197). Less transparently, another Arta adjective marker, *ma-*, may also be reduplicated for intensification, as in *memem~ma-lala:ki* 'very nice, good' from *ma-lala:ki* 'nice, good' (Kimoto 2017a: 197, 198; see also §45.2.2).

The opposite process, dissimilation, occurs, for example, in Batuley CVC- reduplication, in which the base vowel /a/ changes to /e/ in the unstressed reduplicant, for example /ŋa<maj~>ˈmaj/ [ŋa.mej.ˈmaj] from /ŋaˈmaj/ [ŋa.ˈmaj] 'fragrance' or /tu<baj~>ˈbaj/ [tu.bej.ˈbaj] from /tuˈbaj/ [tu.ˈbaj] 'new' (Daigle 2015: 16, 17).

Another form of consonantal change can be observed in Buli, where initial /d/ is substituted by /r/ when preceded by a prefix or a reduplicant, for instance *dò~ror* 'attempt' (< *dòr* 'to try') (Maan 1951: 23). Similarly, in Yami, intervocalic /d/ is changed to /r/, but, unlike in Buli, this change also spreads to the reduplicated portion in order to maintain the identity of base and reduplicant, as in *ra~roa* 'two (plural)' (< *doa* 'two') (Rau and Dong 2006: 86, including note 7). In Matéq, initial nasals become stops during reduplication, for example *bedep~bedep* 'blink repeatedly' from *medep* 'blink' (Connell 2013: 140).

Phonological reductions and deletions are also common. In South Nuaulu, for instance, a 'high vowel deletion rule' is involved in full reduplication, as in *ere-sun~suni-ku* 'I'm very tired' (< *ere-suni-ku* 'I'm tired') (Bolton 1990: 46). In Karo Batak, there is a tendency for the vowel in a CV-reduplicant "to alternate freely with schwa", for example *pa~pagi* or *pe~pagi* 'tomorrow' (Woollams 1996: 101). In Batuley, "[g]eminate consonants formed through reduplication are always reduced so that the consonant coda of the reduplicant is elided" (Daigle 2015: 29), a condition which is met when CVC- reduplication applies to a base with identical $C_1$ and $C_2$, for instance /gag~ˈgagen/ [ga.ˈgag.ɛn] 'she is pretty' (as opposed to /ɸug~ˈɸugar/ [ɸugˈɸug.ar] 'REDUP~hill').

In contrast to deletion, epenthesis is also often triggered by reduplication, especially glottal stop insertion. For bases beginning with a vowel, a glottal stop is usually inserted when a reduplicant ending in a vowel precedes, as in Balantak *upa~upa* [upaʔupa] 'things; anything' from *upa* 'what' and *sianta noʔaa~ʔili* 'did not buy anything' from *ili* 'to buy' (van den Berg and Busenitz 2012: 18; the latter is a case of *Caa-* reduplication; see §45.2.8). In Amarasi, a glottal stop is not only added to the base but also to the reduplicant, for example *ok~ʔokeʔ* [ʔɔkˈʔɔkɛʔ] 'all' from *okeʔ* (Edwards 2020: 116).

Frequently, reduplication goes along with vowel lengthening, as in the Arta $C_1V_1C_1$- reduplicative pattern for human nouns like *bab~ba:bakat* 'old women' from *babakat* 'old woman' (Kimoto 2017a: 75, 96). In Balantak, lengthening of the base vowel occurs with CVV- reduplication, for instance *bee~beenteng* 'almost full' from *benteng* 'full, satisfied' (van den Berg and Busenitz 2012: 20).

In Luang, reduplication of bases ending in a high vowel creates the conditioning environment for high-vowel disyllabification and metathesis, for example *man~mwanu* 'masculine' from *manu* 'male' or *mai~myai* 'arrival' from *mai* 'come' (Taber and Taber 2015: 29).

In Helong, metathesis is a productive derivational process (e.g. *ˈma.na* 'place' vs. *ˈma.an* 'specific place' or *ˈni.ni* 'sleep' vs. *ˈni.in* 'sleeping'; Balle 2017b: 47, 48). When it co-occurs with full reduplication, only the second constituent undergoes the metathesis process, leading to rather unusual forms showing a non-identical base and reduplicant, for instance *ˈta.ma~ˈta.am* 'repeatedly entering' from *ˈta.ma* 'enter' or *ˈpa.lu~ˈpa.ul* 'eight by eight' from *ˈpalu* 'eight' (Balle 2017b: 49, 51, 117).

In Ibaloi, *Cə-* reduplication causes a stress shift as well as gemination, for example *te~too* /tə~toˈʔo/ [tətto ˈʔo] 'doll' from *too* /ˈtoʔo/ [ˈtoʔo] 'person' (Ruffolo 2004: 48).

## 45.2.12 Summary of reduplication forms

The subset of MPSEA languages more or less exhaustively represents all formal reduplication types that can be found in the languages of the world, that is, full root, stem, and word reduplication, reduplication of syllables, feet, and single phonemes, as well as reduplication with fixed segments. Partial reduplicants can be attached to their bases initially, finally, or internally, but there is a clear preference (universally and very clearly within MPSEA) for initial reduplication. All MPSEA languages that have partial reduplication possess the initial type. Only very few languages of the group use unambiguous final and rightward reduplication (e.g. Begak, Chamorro, and Irarutu). By contrast, internal reduplicative patterns targeting the first stressed syllable of a base's final foot seem to be a fairly frequent MPSEA phenomenon, as in Batuley /ŋa<maj~>ˈmaj/ '<REDUP~>fragrance' from *ŋaˈmaj* (Daigle 2015: 16), Tukang Besi *koru<~ʔu>o* 'certainly many' from *koruo* 'many' and *ama<~ʔa>i* 'certainly them' from *amai* 'they' (Donohue 1999a: 42; see also van den Berg and Mead, this volume, §33.2.6), West Tarangan (Coast dialect) *ta<kur~>kúr* 'sago/coconut mix' from *takúr* 'coconut shell' (Nivens 1993: 384), or Amarasi *maʔ<fen~>fenaʔ* 'very heavy' from *maʔfenaʔ* 'heavy' (Edwards 2020: 117). In Kola, the second consonant of the stressed foot is copied in front of the stressed syllable, for instance *bu<b~>ˈtebi* 'gentleness' from *buˈtebi* 'gentle' (Takata 1992: 61; see also Schapper and Zobel, this volume, §35.3.3.1).

Overall, the formal variability of reduplication is not only reflected between different languages of MPSEA as a whole but may also show up in closely related languages or even within dialects of a single language. The former state of affairs is exemplified by the South Halmahera–West New Guinea language Dusner having only very few and only fully reduplicated nouns (see Dalrymple and Mofu 2012: 11), whereas its close relative Biak uses partial reduplications on verbs very productively (see van den Heuvel 2006: 259). Cases in point for the latter situation are described by Nivens (1993) for reduplication in four West Tarangan dialects as well as by Woollams (1996: 101) for the Karo Batak language, of which only some dialects have partial reduplication. (See also §45.6 for differences between Indonesian and Malaysian Malay).

Individual MPSEA languages differ considerably with respect to their inventories of reduplicative patterns. Languages like Amarasi, Begak, Dobel, Makasar, Matéq, and South Nuaulu use only a small set of formal reduplication patterns. Others differentiate several forms, such as Ibaloi, Irarutu, Yami, or Arta, the latter two being extreme cases with up to eleven partial reduplication types (see Rau and Dong 2006: 84–7 and Kimoto 2017a: 92–101, respectively).

Most languages allow the combination of two or more reduplication patterns within one word. In Begak, *Cə-* reduplication is often combined with root reduplication, for example *bə~bunuʔ~bunuʔ* 'kill each other' from *bunuʔ* 'kill' (Goudswaard 2005: 54). In Bikol, imperfective reduplication is usually combined with any other type of reduplication within a word. In example (17), imperfective CV- reduplication occurs together with *Curu-* reduplication expressing object plurality:

Bikol

| (17) | ***pig-bu~buru~bulnot*** | *an* | *sanribo-ng* | *uban* |
|---|---|---|---|---|
| | BEG.UV-IPFV~PL~pull | ART | thousand-LNK | grey.hair |

'pulling thousands of grey hairs' (Mattes 2014: 97)

In the Gayo example *beberu~be~beru pong=é* (PL~GENR~girl friend=3.POSS) 'her girlfriends', "the noun *beru* 'girl' is partially duplicated, signalling a generic meaning" (Eades 2005: 58), and the result in turn undergoes full reduplication, adding the notion of plurality. Balle (2017b: iv) mentions some extreme examples from Helong of reduplications of already reduplicated forms, which she calls 'embedded reduplication', for instance the following based on *duman* 'night': *du~du~du~duman~du~du~du~duman* 'during each and every single night' or *duma~du~du~du~duman* 'during each and every night'. But not all MPSEA languages combine reduplication patterns. In Muna, for example, "[r]eduplication can not occur twice within words" (van den Berg 2013: 326).

To a certain extent different patterns are selected for functional differentiation, as in South Nuaulu, where CV- reduplication derives deverbal nouns, whereas CVCV- and CVN- reduplication intensifies the meaning of adverbs and verbs (see Bolton 1990: 46, 57, 65). More often, it is also the phonological structure, syntactic category, or semantic class of the base which selects a specific reduplication pattern (e.g. in Arta, Biak, Irarutu, Jambi Malay, Makasar, South Nuaulu, or Taba). Other times, patterns seem to be in free variation (e.g. Goudswaard 2005: 53 on Begak). In Madurese, for example, "*Ca* reduplication and initial-syllable reduplication are ostensibly in free variation" (Davies 2010: 131) and "both final-syllable and whole-word reduplication signals [sic] plurality" of nouns (Davies 2010: 143). In Buru, shortened variants of the more common full reduplications are recorded (see Grimes 1991: 76). In Karo Batak, some words are optionally reduplicated, "without any discernable variation in meaning" (Woollams 1996: 93).

It is very common in MPSEA for the phonological or phonotactic structure of the base to select a certain reduplication pattern (see also Himmelmann 2005a: 124). In Makasar, full and partial reduplication are in complementary distribution in that mono- and disyllabic roots are fully reduplicated, whereas partial reduplication is applied to bases longer than two syllables (see Jukes 2006: 104). In Ibaloi, the amount of material to be reduplicated depends on the syllable template of the root. The initial CVCV- pattern applies to roots beginning with an open syllable, while initial CVC- reduplication applies to roots that begin with a closed syllable (see Ruffolo 2004: 45–6). In Fordata, (C)VCV(C) roots select (C)*a*C- or full reduplication, whereas CVV(C) roots select *Ca-* reduplication (see Marshall and Marshall 1992: 26–7). In Bikol, full vs. *Curu-* reduplication is selected on the basis of the length of the root, so that bases with two syllables are fully reduplicated, while longer and shorter bases are prefixed with *Curu-* (see Mattes 2014: 74–6). Begak shows suppletive allomorphy of infixation and reduplication for reciprocals, depending on the stem-initial consonant: "Stems starting with a liquid or with a vowel or monosyllabic stems undergo prefixation with *gə-* followed by *Cə-* reduplication" (Goudswaard 2005: 50), all others are infixed with *<ər>* after the first consonant, for example *k<ər>ədtut* 'pinch each other' as opposed to *gə~gə-rakop* 'wrestle with each other'.

Some languages block certain reduplication patterns, if they would lead to sequences of three or more identical syllables: In Ngaju Dayak, full reduplication minus the coda is an alternative to *Ca-* reduplication, for example *ha~henda* or *henda~henda* 'yellowish' and *ma-na~nipis* or *ma-nipi~nipis* 'rather thin', and obligatory in words beginning with *b* that are combined with the stative prefix *ba-*, in order to avoid the sequence *ba-ba~bV*, such as *beha~behat* 'rather heavy' (**ba-ba~behat*) from *ba-behat* 'heavy' (Hardeland 1859: 60, 174, 348). The avoidance of sequences of too many identical syllables (usually three or four, languages differ in their tolerance in this respect) can be observed in several but not all languages (see also Blust 2013a: 422). In Bikol, "full reduplication is only allowed for bisyllabic $C_1V_1.C_2V_2(C_3)$-bases where the two syllables are not identical" (Mattes 2014: 74). For bases such as *sup.sop* 'suck' or *ra.ra* 'poisonous', the allomorphic pattern *Curu-* (see §45.2.9) is chosen (e.g. *suru~supsop* 'sucking continuously' or *ruru~rara* 'somewhat poisonous'; Mattes 2014: 75). In Cebuano, which also has allomorphic variation between full and *Culu-* reduplication, bases of two identical syllables are not a conditioning factor for *Culu-* but are fully reduplicated instead (e.g. *yap.yap~yap.yap* 'shake out playfully'; see Trosdal 1990: 468).

## 45.3 Meanings and functions

Although the repetitive formal nature and cross-linguistically recurring semantics of plurality and intensity in reduplication suggest a highly iconic motivation of the process in that "[m]ore of the same form stands for more of the same meaning" (Kouwenberg and LaCharité 2005: 534), other frequent reduplicative functions cannot be straightforwardly interpreted in terms of iconicity, such as diminution (except as a semantic extension of plurality via, inter alia, similarity) and word-class derivation. Indeed, as in languages all over the globe, the semantic categories and morphological functions of reduplication vary considerably also within MPSEA. Additionally, reduplicative forms are often polysemous (i.e. one pattern expresses different but related meanings) while, in other cases, the meanings expressed by the same reduplication form appear to be unrelated. Conversely, there can also be various formal alternatives for one and the same reduplicative function (e.g. in Kambera, where the different patterns are mostly "used as interchangeable forms"; Klamer 1998: 35).

Despite the relatively wide range of specific meanings expressed by reduplication in individual languages, from a cross-linguistic comparative view, typically general functions of reduplication can be discerned, as the process is most frequently associated with the broader semantic categories of plurality, intensity and diminution (see Schwaiger 2017: 69–74). Commonly, these can apply to all parts of speech and lexical classes, though often there are language-specific constraints and category-specific preferences (see also Fischer 2011: 59–63). In most MPSEA languages, all major lexical classes are subject to reduplication, and typically also minor lexical classes like numerals and pronouns, the latter mainly of the interrogative type. What Woollams (1996: 92–3) observes specifically for Karo Batak is more generally valid in many languages of MPSEA: "Words from different classes are often reduplicated with the same semantic effect; conversely, words of the same class may have entirely different functions and meanings when doubled" (see also Moro 2010: 94–5 on Dampelas).

In some instances, the function of reduplication extends beyond the domain of semantics and is more adequately described in terms of pragmatics (i.e. morphopragmatic functions in the sense of Dressler and Merlini Barbaresi 1994), such as emphasis of an utterance (an extension of intensity) or attenuation of a request or critique (an extension of diminution).

The iconicity of some reduplicative meanings is still a controversial issue and will not be dealt with in any theoretical detail here. It should be noted, though, that two influential early studies on iconic meanings of reduplication have rested upon Tagalog (Naylor 1986b) and on a larger sample of Malayo-Polynesian languages (Kiyomi 1995). By trying "to seek out the underlying common denominator that characterises the various and apparently divergent functions and meanings of reduplication" (Naylor 1986b: 178), these investigations have contributed to laying important groundwork for several later authors who assume a common cognitive source of all reduplicative functions (e.g. Fischer 2011). These authors argue in different ways for an ultimate grounding in iconicity also of those meanings of reduplication which at first glance do not seem to support an iconic analysis (see also Schwaiger 2017: 83–112).

### 45.3.1 Plurality

There exists a great variety of terms which refer to many kinds of plurality. Very basically, one can distinguish nominal and verbal plurality (see also Dressler 1968: 21, 52–3, 94), or, more generally, person, object, and event plurality. However, pluralizing reduplication occurs with all sorts of word classes, not only the putatively universal noun and verb categories.

Nominal plurality expressed by reduplication is usually not just marking a noun for simple plural in the sense of a general grammatical category that is obligatory in certain syntactic environments, but rather evokes more specific nuances like distributivity, totality, multiplicity, collectivity, numerousness, variety, diversity, and so on. This is underscored by an observation in Jambi Malay. Here, a noun reduplicatively marked for plural cannot "occur in conjunction with a numeral" (Yanti 2010: 617), for example *ruma~ruma* 'houses' vs. **mpat ruma~ruma* 'four houses', but is merely used for an unspecified number of entities (see Yanti 2010: 618). Furthermore, only count nouns but no mass nouns can be pluralized in Jambi Malay (see Yanti 2010: 483–4), the inherent semantics of the latter apparently excluding pluralization. Reduplicated nouns in MPSEA may pluralize both humans (e.g. *gambe~gambe* 'grandfathers' and *ina~ina* 'mothers' in Alorese; Klamer 2011: 39; *k~kantae͡* 'friends' in Kerinci; McKinnon 2011: 85) and objects (e.g. *vonua~vonua* 'houses' in Tajio; Mayani 2013: 68; *al~palaw* 'houses' in Kola; Takata 1992: 62). Often, pluralizing reduplication has a clear distributive meaning, as shown in Buru:

Buru

(18) ***Supak~supa-k,*** ***geba~geba*** *ik.linga*
DISTR~next.day-k DISTR~person go.look
***geba~geba*** *nake* *unet* *tu*
DISTR~person 3SG.POSS snare and
*sura-n.*
stake-GEN
'Each day early in the morning, each person goes and inspects each person's cuscus snares and (sharpened bamboo) stake traps.' (Grimes 1991: 194)

In other MPSEA languages, reduplicative plurality is sensitive to a distinction between human and non-human nouns. In Ibaloi, reduplication may express a proper plural only when applied to humans (e.g. *to~too* 'people' from *too* 'person'; Ruffolo 2004: 86) but yields a multiplicity or abundance interpretation with non-humans, sometimes with misleading English translations (e.g. *chon~chontog* 'mountains' from *chontog* 'mountain' and *chara~charat* 'lot of sand' from *charat* 'sand'; Ruffolo 2004: 95, 96). The Arta language selects different patterns for nouns denoting humans and non-humans, whereby CVC-, sometimes combined with lengthening of the second base syllable, only applies to human nouns (e.g. *bab~ba:bakat* 'old women' from *babakat* and *beb~bebbe:* 'aunts' from *bebbe:*; Kimoto 2017a: 96), while either CV:- or CVCV-, depending on the syllable structure of the base, is used with non-human nouns (e.g. *ba:~barowa:si* 'clothes' from *barowa:si* and *kuwa~kuwarto* 'rooms' from *kuwarto*; Kimoto 2017a: 95, 96). In Tondano, "full root reduplication is primarily used when nouns refer to inanimate/non-human entities. Alternatively, the number value of animate or human entities represented by nouns is usually encoded via different phrase markers" (Brickell 2014: 74).

There are also many different nuances for reduplicative verbal plurality, such as repetition, iterativity, continuity, duration, progressivity, frequency, habituality, imperfectivity, simultaneity, dispersion, reciprocity, plural arguments, and so on. This issue inevitably also touches upon the grammatical notions of aspect and pluractionality (Dressler 1968; Cusic 1981). In Madurese, reduplicated verbs express multiple action, that is, the distribution of an event over one of the arguments (plural) and/or over time (iteration):

Madurese
(19) a. *Aleʔ* **les~noles** *sorat* *dhaʔ* *bibbi-na.*
younger.sibling DISTR~A.write letter to aunt-DEF
'Little sister wrote letters to her aunt.'

b. *Hasan* **kol~mokol** *Ali.*
Hasan DISTR-A.hit Ali
'Hasan hit Ali a bunch of times.' (Davies 2010: 138)

Repetitive and frequentative meanings of verb reduplication can be adduced from Tajio, for example *go~gou* 'to shout repeatedly' from *gou* 'to shout' and *sau~saup* 'to rub frequently' from *saup* 'to rub' (Mayani 2013: 67, 68). A semantic extension of iterative and frequentative is the expression of habituality (see Bybee, Perkins, and Pagliuca 1994: 172), indicating, as in Nias, that an "action is 'always' done and is not done just on one occasion" (Brown 2001: 530):

Nias
(20) *Asese* **ma-be~be** *khö-nia* *gefe.*
often 1PL.EXCL.REAL-HAB~give DAT-3SG.POSS money
'We often give him money.' (Brown 2001: 531)

As event plurality may also refer to actions or states of affairs which are continuous (e.g. Muna *ne-tola~tola* 'he is calling' from *tola* 'call'; van den Berg 2013: 325) or progressive (e.g. Northern Alta *men-le~ledep* 'be swimming underwater' from *ledep* 'swim underwater'; García Laguía 2018: 74), reduplication is moreover often extended to mark imperfective aspect (see Bybee, Perkins, and Pagliuca 1994: 172). This is found especially in Philippine languages but also within other subgroups of MPSEA, for example in Chamorro (see Zobel, this volume, §38.2), Madurese (e.g. *sambi dang~tandang* 'while they were dancing' from *tandang* 'dance'; Davies 2010: 139, 140), Tondano (e.g. *ma-lèʔo~lèʔos* 'being good to someone/something' from *ma-lèʔos* 'be good'; Brickell 2014: 73), West Tarangan (under the name 'progressive aspect' in Nivens 1993: 378–9; see also Schapper and Zobel, this volume, §35.3.3.2), and others. Most of these more grammaticalized imperfective meanings seem to be expressed by some type of partial reduplication. This would lend support to the hypothesis for "the fullest, most explicit form of reduplication, total reduplication, to be the originating point for all reduplications, with the various types of partial reduplication as reductions and thus later developments from this fullest form" (Bybee, Perkins, and Pagliuca 1994: 166). Reciprocality is a further subcategory of plurality marked in many MPSEA languages, for example in Begak *tə~tiruʔ* 'teach each other' from *tiruʔ* 'teach' (Goudswaard 2005: 52), Tajio *li~livur-ong* 'to chase each other' from *livur* 'to chase' (Mayani 2013: 135), West Coast Bajau *si-ogo~ogo* 'to visit each other's homes' from *ogo* 'to visit' (Miller 2007: 251) and Kelabit:

Kelabit
(21) **Siwa~siwa** *teh* *diweh* *ngen* *sapaq* *diweh* *ih.*
RECP~exchange PTCP 3DU with shirt 3DU PTCP
'They exchanged shirts.' (Hemmings 2016: 149)

Adjectives can also be reduplicated for plurality, as in Tetun Fehan, where a large number of referents is not necessarily implied, however:

Tetun Fehan
(22) *Kabau* *aman* **bó~bót** *sia* *faʔen* *tiʔan.*
buffalo male PL~big PL sell already
'The large male buffaloes (whether few or many) have been sold.' (van Klinken 1999: 94)

Other word classes that may show reduplicative pluralization include pronouns (e.g. *misan hisiyu~siyu* 'anyone [plural]' from *misan hisiyu* 'whoever, anyone, no matter who' in Tausug; Rubino 2006: 294), adpositions (e.g. the preposition *so~sono* 'together with' from *sono* 'with' in Pendau; Quick 2007: 209), quantifiers (e.g. *tiap~tiap urang* 'each and every person' from *tiap urang* 'each person' in Mualang; Tjia 2007: 88) and numerals. The latter are very often marked specifically for distributivity, for example in Nias, where reduplication of a combination of numeral and classifier serves "to indicate that the entities referred to by the reduplicated form occur in a group" (Brown 2001: 534):

Nias
(23) ... *ira-matua* *ni-fa-taßi*
COLL-male PASS-CAUS-eat.ritual.meal
***daru~da-rua.***
DISTR~CLF-two
'... the boys who are fed their ritual meal two by two.'
(Brown 2001: 534)

### 45.3.2 Intensity

Some authors assume intensity to be a semantic extension of plurality with often a fuzzy boundary between the two meanings. For example, in Luang reduplication, "[w]hen occurring on stative verbs it intensifies the state. It also appears to intensify the action in action verbs and add a sense of iterativity to it" (Taber and Taber 2015: 74). In Dampelas, "when reduplication applies to verb [sic], it marks durative or progressive aspect. In addition, it may also indicate a high intensity of the action expressed by the verb" (Moro 2010: 89). In other languages, the semantics of the base may differentiate between an intensifying and a pluralizing meaning of the reduplicated form. In Buru, for example, reduplication yields intensity with stative verbs (24a) and iterativity with active verbs (24b):

Buru
(24) a. *Ringe* ***roho~roho*** *gam.la* *masi.*
3SG INTNS~slow ALL.downstream sea
'She (went) very slowly down to the coast.'
(Grimes 1991: 206)
b. *Da* ***iko~iko.***
3SG ITER~go
'He kept going (repeatedly).' (Grimes 1991: 207)

In general, reduplication may intensify, augment, specify, or limit the notion of entities, actions, events, states, and properties, and it may occur accordingly with all sorts of word classes. However, reduplicative intensity seems most common by far with stative verbs, as in (24a) above, and adjectives. The latter are often a subtype of verbs, as in Madurese:

Madurese
(25) *Pottre-na* ***din~raddin.***
princess-DEF INTNS~pretty
'The princess is very pretty.' (Davies 2010: 142)

In Ilokano, CV- reduplication together with *ka-* prefixation designates "actions completed just prior to the speech event" (Rubino 2000: lxvii), such as *ka-sa~sangpét* 'just arrived' from *sangpet* 'arrive'. A further intensive verbal meaning sometimes expressed through reduplication occurs in the context of imperatives or commands, for example in Karo Batak:

Karo Batak
(26) ***Pe-turah~turah*** *sitik* *ukurndu.*
CAUS-IMP~grow ATT mind.your
'Grow up a bit! (i.e. Act like an adult!)'
(Woollams 1996: 98)

With adjectives, reduplication can be used for gradation, such as the comparative degree (e.g. Ilokano *dak~dákes* 'worse' from *dákes* 'bad'; Rubino 2000: lvi; Yami *rako~rako* 'bigger' from *rako* 'big'; Rau and Dong 2006: 85) or the superlative degree (e.g. Madurese *ter~penterr-an* 'smartest' from *penter* 'smart' via *penterr-an* 'smarter'; Davies 2010: 117), as well as for total affectedness (e.g. Helong *perat~perat* 'completely wet' from *perat* 'wet'; Balle 2017b: 89) or equal quality, the latter for example in Kola:

Kola
(27) *Ni* ***at~eta-ni*** *ak.*
3SG.ANIM EQ~tall-3SG.ANIM 1SG
'He is as tall as I.' (Takata 1992: 65)

Ibaloi even distinguishes several degrees of intensification via different reduplication types in an obviously iconic manner, whereby "the more of the word is reduplicated the more strongly the gradable element is present in the meaning" (Ruffolo 2004: 96), for example *baknang* 'rich' > *be~baknang* 'little rich' > *bak~baknang* 'very rich' > *bakna~baknang* 'extremely rich'. Reduplicative intensity for adverbs is found, for example, in Luang (e.g. *plet~pleta* 'very quickly' from *pleta* 'quickly'; Taber and Taber 2015: 29).

With nouns, reduplication may also intensify their meaning, for instance in Kola *ab~loba* 'new-born baby' from *loba* 'baby' and *af<al~>ral* 'early morning' from *afral* 'morning' (Takata 1992: 62). The latter semantic relationship is also found in Moklen between *suwaŋ* 'morning' and *suwaŋ~suwa:ŋ* 'early morning' (Larish 1999: 256). Pendau reduplicates agentive nouns for specificity, as in *to~togoge* 'this elder, parent' from *togoge* 'elder, parent' (Quick 2007: 164). In Wamesa, also geographic locational nouns in phrases with a preposition *do* 'to' can be intensified, for example *do rau~rau* 'far out to sea' from *do rau* 'seawards' (Gasser 2014: 241–2).

Turning to minor word classes, many of them can likewise undergo intensifying reduplication. In Tausug, the reflexive pronoun *baran* 'self' can be reduplicated to *baran~baran* 'all by oneself' (Rubino 2006: 207). Similarly, other pronouns in Tausug may also express intensity with reduplication, for example *kamu~kamu* '(all/just) you guys' from *kamu* 'you (plural)' (Rubino 2006: 35, 330). Wooi reduplicates neutral demonstratives as in (28), where "*vavaw* is used to indicate the distance which is far but is still reachable in the sense of people have a capability to go there" (Sawaki 2016: 430–1):

Wooi

| (28) | *trus* | *he-t-vo* | *he-t-vo* | *na* | |
|---|---|---|---|---|---|
| | then | 3PL-PL-paddle | 3PL-PL-paddle | LOC | |
| | ***va~vaw*** | *he-t-vo* | *ra* | *he-t-mahi* | |
| | DEM~INTNS | 3PL-PL-paddle | tither | 3PL-PL-arrive | |

'Then, they paddled, paddled to there until they arrived...' (Sawaki 2016: 431)

Numerals are very prone to be intensified by reduplication for limitation purposes, for example in Balantak *toto~totoluʔ* 'only three', *papa~papaat* 'only four' and *lili~lilimaʔ* 'only five' (van den Berg and Busenitz 2012: 54) or in Tausug *hambuuk~buuk* 'one and only, unique' from *hambuuk* 'one' (Rubino 2006: 153).

### 45.3.3 Diminution

Diminution again subsumes several more specific notions, such as the small size of entities and the toning down of properties, actions, events, or states, which may all be extended to include the approximative imitation or pretence of certain appearances or performances.

Size diminution of nouns is, for example, found in Mamanwa *banig~banig* 'artefact, miniature sleeping mat' from *banig* 'sleeping mat' (Miller and Miller 1976: 46) and in Muna *ka-kontu~kontu* 'small stone' from *kontu* 'stone' (van den Berg 2013: 299). Typical reduplicative attenuation occurs with colour adjectives (e.g. Karo Batak *megara~megara* 'reddish' from *megara* 'red'; Woollams 1996: 95) and verbs like the following in Tukang Besi:

Tukang Besi

(29) ***No-heta~he-tade-ʔe.***
3.REAL-ATT~VBLZ-stand-3.OBJ
'They are building it, sort of.' (Donohue 1999a: 299)

Similarly, verb reduplication may "convey the meaning of an action done in a casual[1] or leisurely way" (Yanti 2010: 620 on Jambi Malay), "a sense of non-seriousness or lack of success/completion of the action" (Hemmings 2016: 149 on Kelabit) or "the meaning 'with no purpose'" (Takata 1992: 62 on Kola), thus "often signalling meanings such as approximation" (Eades 2005: 55 on Gayo).

It is therefore a very widespread phenomenon in MPSEA languages to extend the above reduplication meanings to all sorts of similarity, imitation, pretence, or the naming of toys and games. In Karo Batak, resemblance through reduplication is displayed in the derivation of body part terms, for example *berku~berku* 'skull' from *berku* 'coconut shell', *buluh~buluh* 'throat' from *buluh* 'bamboo' and many more (see Woollams 1996: 95). Imitation or pretence can be exemplified by Tagalog *pari~pari-an* 'pretence of being a priest' from *pari* 'priest' (Schachter and Otanes 1972: 357) as well as by Tukang Besi *no-heka-hawa~hawaa* 'pretend to be angry' (including an intensifier *heka-*) from *hawaa* 'angry' (Donohue 1999a: 282). In Toba Batak, verb reduplication in combination with *pa-* prefixation refers to an action that is performed repeatedly in an irresponsible or playful manner, showing a conceptual connection between plurality and diminution, as in *pa-dɔk~dɔ́k* 'chatter about (something)' from *dɔk* 'say' (Nababan 1981: 103). In a similar vein, toy and game-name reduplication can be argued to reflect this conceptual link between pluralization and diminutivization, "games essentially being repetitive and often imitative activities, typically played by more than one person and very frequently by children" (Schwaiger 2017: 96, note 6). Examples are Balantak *dua~duangan* 'toy boat' from *duangan* 'boat' (van den Berg and Busenitz 2012: 42), Ibaloi *ke~kebajo* 'horse figurine' from *kabajo* 'horse' (Ruffolo 2004: 105) or Tagalog *bahay~bahay-an* 'doll house/house (the game)' from *bahay* 'house' (Schachter and Otanes 1972: 100).

A further extension of reduplicative plural and diminutive meanings concerns different notions of diffuseness, aimlessness, and indefiniteness. This may be exemplified by verbs like Karo Batak *ter-daram~daram* 'looking here and there' from *daram* 'seek' (Woollams 1996: 96) or West Coast Bajau *main~main* 'to play around' from *main* 'to play' (Miller 2007: 79). The Kerinci formation of negative polarity items might also be listed here. In the following example, an indefinite meaning component is expressed on the verb:

Kerinci

| (30) | *ndiʔ* | ***maka~maka*** |
|---|---|---|
| | not.want | INDEF~eat |

'not want to eat anything' (McKinnon 2011: 85)

But more typical for MPSEA and several other languages of the world is that this type of reduplication occurs with question words to form indefinite pronouns. Some examples, among many more, are Luang *heʔa~heʔa* 'whoever' from *heʔa* 'who' (Taber and Taber 2015: 29), Tausug *kansiyu~kansiyu* 'anyone' from *kansiyu* 'whose' (Rubino 2006: 119), Keo *wengi~wengi* 'whenever' from *wengi* 'when' (Baird 2002: 178) and Buru *fi doo~fi doo* 'wherever (location)'. The latter is a language in which reduplicated "indefinite interrogative pronouns are often topicalised" (Grimes 1991: 166):

Buru

| (31) | ***Fi-doo~fi-doo*** | *sira* | *iko,* | *du* | *dufa* | *fafu.* |
|---|---|---|---|---|---|---|
| | LOC-where~LOC-where | 3PL | go | 3PL | get | pig |

'Wherever they went, they got pig.' (Grimes 1991: 76)

[1] Written as "causal" in Yanti (2010: 620), but this is a typo according to the author's own explanation.

## 45.3.4 Other reduplicative intra-category meaning changes

In addition to the three most frequent main functions of reduplication there also exist further intra-category changes, some of them fairly common all over the globe, others rather specific to the MPSEA group or to individual languages, although none of them can straightforwardly be subsumed under the umbrella terms of plurality, intensity, or diminution, at least not at first glance.

In Buru, *Ce-* reduplication can express a generic non-referential possessive relation between two nouns:

Buru
(32) *kapal* ***pe~pani***
ship POSS~wing
'airplane' (Grimes 1991: 77)

By contrast, Madurese reduplication of *kanaʔ* 'child' (the final syllable is copied to the left edge of the base) generalizes the reference of the noun phrase such that the child "is not the offspring of any of the participants being discussed" (Davies 2010: 145):

Madurese
(33) a. *Siti a-temmo anaʔ-eng e taman.*
Siti AV-meet child-DEF at park
'Siti met her child in the park.' [*anaʔ* = one's child, offspring]

b. *Siti a-temmo* ***naʔ~kanaʔ-eng*** *e taman.*
Siti AV-meet NPOSS~child-DEF at park
'Siti met the child in the park.' [*kanaʔ* = a child]
(Davies 2010: 145)

A frequent effect of reduplication found with verbs is a decrease of valency, that is, reduplicated "forms are lower in transitivity than non-reduplicated" forms (Hemmings 2016: 151 on Kelabit). Biak *fas~fas* 'write (intransitive)' from *fas* 'write (transitive)' (van den Heuvel 2006: 277) and Tajio *nom-balu~baluk* 'to go around to sell (products)' from *nom-baluk* 'to sell something' (Mayani 2013: 138, 139) are cases in point. Note that Kiyomi (1995: 1150) proposes to treat reduplicative valency decrease as a type of diminution, since intransitivity correlates with low affectedness of the patient (see also Schwaiger 2017: 73–4). Tagalog, on the other hand, may use this device to express accidental result (e.g. *magkang-hu~hulog* 'fall accidentally [as a result]' from *ma-hulog* 'fall'; Schachter and Otanes 1972: 342) by reduplicating verbs, while Tondano may use *Ce-* reduplication to mark irrealis mood, either for a "[h]ighly likely immediate future event (soon after utterance)" or a "[d]esired, hoped for future event" (Brickell 2014: 391), as in *me-we~wui* 'will ask' from *ma-wui* 'asks' (Brickell 2014: 73).

Stative verbs or adjectives may be reduplicated for attributive use as opposed to predicative use, for example in Kola:

Kola
(34) a. *Nuh ekin ahbut.*
coconut that hard
'That coconut is hard.'

b. *Ak kufah*ₗ *nuh* ***ah<at~>but.***
I look.for coconut <ATTR~>hard
'I look for a hard coconut.' (Takata 1992: 64)

This function could in fact be related to plurality and intensity, as "[a]ttributive adjectives, unlike predicative ones, express a more permanent state, a result, a more inherent feature of the noun it accompanies" (Fischer 2011: 74). A phenomenon possibly related to adjective reduplication for attributive modification purposes is the relativization of non-specific nouns in Tolaki, for which the first syllable of a relative clause is reduplicated:

Tolaki
(35) *Laa toono ikita* ***ku~k<um>ii****-ʔaku.*
there.is person there NSPEC.REL~<NFIN>see-1.ABS
'There are some people over there looking at me.'
(Edwards 2012: 44)

Next to numerals often being reduplicated to express limitation and thus intensification, cardinal numbers may also reduplicate to serve as ordinal numbers, as in Kola:

Kola
(36) *tamata* ***ra~rui*** *ne*
person ORD~two that
'the second person' (Takata 1992: 66)

In Batuley complex numerals, "only the final numeral in the numeral compound takes an agreement suffix and is reduplicated" (Daigle 2015: 124):

Batuley
(37) *tamata urfaef eng* ***ka~kau-ei***
person ten and ORD~four-3PL.ANIM
'the fourteenth person' (Daigle 2015: 125)

Yami *Ca-* reduplication as in *pa~pira* 'how many' otherwise "usually occurs in numbers" (Rau and Dong 2006: 86), apparently exclusively for the function of counting humans, a feature likely retained under the influence of the neighbouring languages of Formosa (see Liao and Reid, this volume, §24.4 on Northern Philippine languages; see also Adelaar 2011: 143).

In several languages, reduplication derives lexemes within the same word class, especially but not exclusively among nouns. These derivations are more or less unpredictably related in meaning to their bases, such as Kola *ang~tangan* 'ring' from *tangan* 'hand' (Takata 1992: 62), Madurese *ne~bine* 'seed rice' from *bine* 'wife' (Davies 2010: 145), Jambi Malay *mato~mato* 'spy' from *mato* 'eye' (Yanti 2010: 619) or Tukang Besi *mea~meanaʔe* 'lately' from *meanaʔe* 'now' (Donohue 1999a: 118). In Muna, animal and other terms can moreover be personified through reduplication to yield names, normally being preceded by an article, for example *a-kapo~kapoluka* 'Mr. Tortoise' from *kapoluka* 'tortoise' or *a-ware~ware-lima* 'Mr. Broadhand' from *ware* 'broad' and *lima* 'hand' (van den Berg 2013: 327).

## 45.3.5 Reduplicative word-class derivation

Austronesian languages are often mentioned as challenging the universality of word-class distinctions at the root level (e.g. Sasse 1993; Broschart 1997; Himmelmann 2008). However, at least in the morphologically richer languages of the family, different word classes can be established on the morphological level (i.e. word-class differences are often derived from unspecified roots). Reduplication is very often used to establish a word class or to derive one word class from another, whereby in the latter use the change in class is often accompanied by the more common semantic changes involving plurality, intensity, or diminution (see also Moravcsik 1978: 324–5).

Reduplicative word-class derivation is first and foremost a cross-linguistically widespread nominalization device (see Schwaiger 2017: 105), and this is also the major derivational direction served by reduplication in MPSEA languages. For instance, in Tausug, "[t]he prefixes *mag-* and *maN-* coupled with initial CV reduplication of the stem form actor nominalizations that designate habitual action" (Rubino 2006: 280), such as *mag-da~ragang* 'vendor' from *dagang* 'sell' and *mang-lu~lurup* 'diver' from *lurup* 'dive' (Rubino 2006: 280, 281). Kola and many other languages display instrumental nominalization, as in *ang~lang* 'language' from *lang* 'speak' or *ak~lakuh* 'broom' from *laku* 'sweep' (Takata 1992: 63). In addition to instruments, languages like Tetun Fehan show undergoer nominalizations, for example *da~dada-n* 'zip' from *dada* 'pull' or *sa~solok* 'gift' from *solok* 'send' (van Klinken 1999: 80). In Karo Batak, some terms for body parts are deverbal instrumental nouns like *kundul~kundul* 'buttocks' from *kundul* 'sit' or *tuduh~tuduh* 'index finger' from *tuduh* 'point' (Woollams 1996: 95). In Yami, animals can be named by reduplicating (with an additional prefix *ka-*) terms for certain of their features, for example *ka-la~lavi* 'cicada' from *lavi* 'cry' or *ka-goza~gozang* 'lizard' from *gozang* 'thin' (Rau and Dong 2006: 134).

Adjectives can also be derived from other word classes, for example Fordata *ia sar~sira-n* 'salted fish' from *sira* 'salt' and *afa fan~fonak* 'secret thing' from *n-fonak* '3SG-hide' (Marshall and Marshall 1992: 28) as well as Irarutu *tɪm~tɪm* 'closed' from *tɪm* 'close' (Jackson 2014: 91).

While reduplicative verbalization in general appears to be rare (see Schwaiger 2017: 103), adverbialization from all sorts of word classes is quite common also in MPSEA (e.g. Mualang *malam~malam* 'at [typical] night [time], late at night' from *malam* 'night'; Tjia 2007: 86), including a rather special instance in Gayo, which takes a preposition as its base for the adverb *urum~urum* 'together' from *urum* 'with' (Eades 2005: 54). Word-class derivation in turn proceeding from adverbs, however, seems to be very infrequent, perhaps even non-existent in the languages of the world (see Schwaiger 2017: 106).

Nouns, verbs, adjectives, and sometimes other word classes like numerals may be reduplicated in dependent position (i.e. when they are modifying another word class). Next to the Tolaki relativization example given in the preceding section, this is especially common in languages like Dobel, Fordata, Kola, and West Tarangan, most languages in the Southern Maluku area (see Schapper and Zobel, this volume, §35.4.6.2. and §35.4.6.3 for a full overview of the attributive- and relative-marking functions of reduplication in Southern Maluku languages). Dobel shows various types of this function that can be argued to involve a change of word class as well:

Dobel

(38) a. Ordinal numbers as modifiers within the noun phrase
*labun* *ne* ***r~ro***
garment REL ORD~two
'the second garment' (Hughes 2000: 171)

b. Non-active verbs as modifiers within the noun phrase
*tamatu* ***s~soba-ye*** *wadi*
person ATTR~good-3PL.P DEM
'these good people' (Hughes 2000: 172)

c. Nouns as modifiers within the noun phrase
*tamatu* ***s~siʔa***
person ATTR~fish
'fisherman' (Hughes 2000: 174)

Furthermore, Dobel also possesses relativizing reduplication, Hughes (2000: 174) seeing "a strong resemblance between this role of reduplication and that mentioned above where verbs act as modifiers in the noun phrase." While it is not clear whether for Dobel this also involves a change of word class, reduplication for subordination and complementation purposes in West Tarangan is explicitly analysed as a form of deverbal nominalization (see Nivens 1993: 379). Others might prefer to view these cases as expressing a dependency relation without word-class derivation necessarily being involved (see Schapper and Zobel, this volume, §35.3.3.2 for more on the dependency-marking view of reduplication in Southern Maluku languages).

## 45.3.6 Pragmatic uses of reduplication

Most languages use reduplication not only grammatically or lexically but also pragmatically or expressively in at least some of its forms and functions. Usually this is to express emphasis, an extension of reduplicative intensity, or to mitigate the literal force of an utterance (typically when voicing a critique or a request), an extension of the diminution meaning of reduplication.

Intensive reduplication "to signal emphasis in discourse" (Eades 2005: 58) is reported from Gayo, among many other languages:

Gayo
(39) *I* *Acéh=ni,* ***betul~betul*** *agama* *kuet.*
LOC Aceh=this INTNS~true religion strong
'Here in Aceh, truly religion is strong.'
(Eades 2005: 58)

In example (40) from Madurese, "reduplication of the verb *tolong* 'help' emphasizes the importance of the help of the addressee to the speaker" (Davies 2010: 140):

Madurese
(40) *Sakalangkong,* *abaʔeng* *se* *ella*
thank.you you REL already
***a-ta~tolong*** *dhaʔ* *engkoʔ.*
AV-INTNS~help to me
'Thank you, you are the one who really has helped me.' (Davies 2010: 140)

In Tukang Besi, vowel reduplication (with an inserted intervocalic glottal stop) "is used for pragmatic effect to emphasise the truth values of one word sentences" (Donohue 1999a: 42), for example *koru<~ʔu>o* 'certainly many' from *koruo* 'many' and *ama<~ʔa>i* 'certainly them' from *amai* 'they'. Moreover, it comes as no surprise that many emphatic reduplications come to be used for the expression of feelings in emotional contexts, such as Yami "depreciative intensification [...] to express a complaining attitude" (Rau and Chang 2015: 398):

Yami
(41) a. *ya* *ma-singat* *o* *napa.*
AUX ST-expensive NOM vegetable
'Vegetables are expensive.'

b. ***ka-singa~singat*** *naʔ* *tosia,*
INTNS-INTNS~expensive 3SG.GEN don't.want.it
*ji* *ko* *nazang-i.*
NEG 1SG.GEN buy-LOC.FOC
'That expensive? Never mind then, I'm not buying it.' (Rau and Chang 2015: 398)

Diminutives of all sorts can be generally used to weaken a potentially rude speech act, essentially making it politer and less obtrusive (see also Dressler and Merlini Barbaresi 1994). An example for politeness through reduplicative diminution is the following from Riau Indonesian, where a negative imperative is accordingly mitigated:

Riau Indonesian
(42) ***Teh-obeng~teh-obeng*** *tak* *usah*
tea-screwdriver~tea-screwdriver NEG NEG.IMP
*lah*
CONTR
[Group of people getting together an order for take-away food; speaker tries to cut down on size of order]
'No need for iced tea.' (Gil 2005: 57)

A further example of diminutive reduplication as a possible kind of politeness which "comes into operation through evaluative moments" (Kádár 2017) is found in the following compliment from Bikol:

Bikol
(43) ***Bagay~bagay*** *su* *bado* *saimo.*
ATT~fit SPEC.ART dress 2SG.LOC
'This dress suits you well!' (Mattes 2014: 72)

A possibly related but somewhat different politeness strategy might be the reduplication of personal pronouns in Karo Batak "accompanied by a sense of disparagement or self-effacement" (Woollams 1996: 101):

Karo Batak
(44) *Tapi* *adi* ***kami~kami*** *saja* *kerina* *anak*
but if we~we just all child
*sekolah* *la* *até* *kami* *melas.*
school not heart our warm
'But as for us, who are only school children, we don't feel keen about it.' (Woollams 1996: 101)

From polite self-belittling it is merely a small step into the generally pejorative expressive domain, as in the following expressions reduplicated for contempt in Muna: *ka-guru~guru* 'non-professional teacher, poorly performing teacher' from *guru* 'teacher' and *ka-pahu~pahulo* 'poorly performing hunter' from *pahulo* 'hunter' (van den Berg 2015: 368). On a level of maximal impoliteness, such uses of reduplication may be metaphorically extended to express outright insults, for example in the following from Makasar, where "*tai* 'shit' and *mea* 'piss' when reduplicated and possessed both have the meaning 'descendant, offspring, spawn'" (Jukes 2006: 224):

Makasar

(45) *toa-nu* *lagi* *ta=ngng-ew(a)=aʔ*
old-2.FAM.POSS even NEG=TR-oppose=1
*apa=pa* *seng* *i-kau=ntu*
what=IPFV again PERS 2.FAM=that
***mea~mea-na-ya***
PEJ~urine-3.POSS-DEF
'even your grandfather didn't dare oppose me, what (compared to him) are you who is his piss' (Jukes 2006: 224)

### 45.3.7 Summary of reduplication meanings and functions

In reduplication, a variety of forms expressing the same meaning are typically organized more systematically by clear phonological or grammatical conditions and restrictions than a variety of functions expressed by the same form, which can often only be disambiguated by the linguistic and/or situational context (e.g. Grimes 1991: 123 on Buru; Davies 2010: 142 on Madurese; Mattes 2014: 81–3 on Bikol).

Sometimes one and the same reduplication pattern can even produce quite opposite meanings, such as full reduplication in Bikol, which can express intensity or diminution in forms like *dangog~dangog* 'hear very clearly' or 'hear by gossip' from *dangog* 'hear' (Mattes 2014: 81). The following opposite poles of evaluation in Buru for the manner adverb formed from *boho* 'bad, ugly' could be a lexically restricted phenomenon (comparable to *terrific* and *awesome* in English or *c'est pas terrible* 'it's not that great/it's great' in French): *Da paha tuba* ***boho~boho*** 'he plays drums horribly' or 'he plays drums outstandingly well' (Grimes 1991: 123). In Madurese, final syllable reduplication of causative verbs can have a plural meaning as well as a pretence interpretation, for example *bu~ma-labu* (< *labu* 'fall'), which can mean either 'cause more than one to fall' (Davies 2010: 142) or "that the actor is only pretending or faking" to fall (Davies 2010: 141). In all these cases, disambiguation is guaranteed by the situation and/or the discourse, whereby certain adverbs, discourse particles or conjunctions can play a disambiguating role, especially in the latter case. Semantic analyses of reduplication like Kiyomi (1995) or Fischer (2011) interpret these varying and sometimes even opposite meanings as subcategories of more general, underspecified categories such as the consecutive (i.e. plurality) or cumulative (i.e. intensity) increase in quantity as opposed to the imagic character of child language and baby babbling (i.e. diminution) extended into adult language via semantic shifts.

In many languages, at least some reduplication types must be considered to be underspecified in their functioning. Consequently, the reduplicative meaning in a concrete utterance is usually the result of combining the semantics of the base, any additional morphological processes, the syntactic position and contextual information. A representative example is Ibaloi, where CVC(V)- reduplication "may take a durative, distributive, or iterative meaning when applied to a verbal root; or intensive ('very') meaning when applied to a root with a property-like meaning; or plural, multiplicative, or abundant meaning when applied to a root with a non-human referent" (Ruffolo 2004: 45). Respective examples are *beti~betik* 'continuously run' from *betik* 'run', *mate~ma-teba* 'very fat' from *ma-teba* 'be fat' and *chon~chontog* 'mountains, mountainous (place)' from *chontog* 'mountain' (Ruffolo 2004: 45–6). The meaning of a second type in Ibaloi, CV- reduplication, also depends on the semantics of the root: "It carries mainly a limitative meaning with property-like roots or quantifying roots, a plural meaning with roots referring to human entities, or conveys iterativity or the participantion [sic] of more than one actor with action roots" (Ruffolo 2004: 47). Illustrative examples are *di~dima* 'only five' from *dima* 'five', *bi~bii* 'women' from *bii* 'woman' and *man-ʔa~ʔsop* 'go near (to each other)' from *esop* 'near' (Ruffolo 2004: 110, 230).

However, there can also be differences in formal reduplication patterns that clearly correspond to a difference in meaning, as in Kambera, where CV:- reduplication expresses greater intensity than CV- reduplication, for example *ta~'tata* 'shaking a lot' vs. *'ta:~'tata* 'keep on shaking heavily all the time' (Klamer 1998: 36). In Gayo, partial reduplication expresses, among other meanings, plurality as a semantic notion, whereas full reduplication is used to put pragmatic emphasis on the pluralization (e.g. *ke~kiding* 'feet' vs. *kiding~kiding* 'those feet', both from *kiding* 'foot'; see Eades 2005: 55). Ibaloi, in addition to the two very polysemous patterns CVC(V)- and CV- above, has a third reduplication pattern, Cə-, that has only the very specific meaning of fake, pretence, or resemblance, as in *te~too* 'doll' from *too* 'person' (Ruffolo 2004: 48).

Sometimes incompatibilities between certain reduplicative forms and certain functions have been suggested, for example that "full reduplication apparently is never used to mark grammatical functions such as tense" (Blust 2013a: 419). Although this may correlate with the fact that tense is rather exceptional anyway in Austronesian languages, it corresponds to Stolz, Stroh, and Urdze's (2011: 194) more general list of functions which are cross-linguistically not expressed by full reduplication, and which next to tense includes such categories as gender, case, and person. Interestingly, many of these are also very unlikely to be expressed by partial reduplication (see Schwaiger 2017: 149), which ultimately may have to do with their strongly inflectional character and the fact that reduplication can be argued to fulfil largely, maybe even exclusively, derivational morphological purposes in the languages of the world (see Schwaiger 2015: 477, 2017: 133–53).

## 45.4 Lexical reduplication

Lexical reduplications are not related, at least synchronically, to corresponding unreduplicated forms. They are defined as a group of monomorphemic word forms with "inherently reduplicated" structure (Clynes 1995d: 77). Lexical reduplications are very widespread in the languages of the world, the MPSEA languages being no exception. On the contrary, lexical reduplications are found abundantly in basically all languages of the group. A part of these reduplicated structures are clearly lexicalized forms of former productive word formations now stored in the lexicon, but such an origin cannot be assumed for all of them. Lexemes with various reduplicative structures may have different diachronic sources, and these sources can only be reconstructed in some cases. Others might have come into the language as such. Synchronically, as argued by Klamer (2002a) and Mattes (2017), lexical reduplication is very often a fairly systematically structured part of a language's lexicon and, furthermore, may not only show considerable formal but also semantic overlap with productive reduplication, such as plurality, intensity, and diminution (see §45.3). Lexical reduplications can be considered a subtype of expressives (see Klamer 2002a) which systematically and cross-linguistically correspond to certain meanings (see Mattes 2017). They frequently refer to animals (typically to fishes and insects, but also other animals), plants, body parts, diseases and physical or mental abnormalities, inherently plural objects and actions, feelings, colours, small things, movements, sensations, and so on. Examples are found in nearly every MPSEA language, some representatives being Alorese *kapu-kapu* 'firefly' or *uli-uli* 'fable' (Klamer 2011: 39), Amarasi *kir-kiri* 'cricket', *mun-munu* 'kind of tree', or *ʔbak-bakan* 'monitor lizard' (Edwards 2016b: 110), Balinese *cadcad* 'criticize', *kedongdong* 'kind of fruit tree', or *lumbalumba* 'dolphin' (Clynes 1995d: 77), Bikol *gulingguling* 'kind of snail', *kawalkawal* 'hang loosely and move back and forth', or *saʔsaʔ* 'crushing metal' (Mattes 2017: 816), Begak *soksok* 'house lizard', *pakpak* 'drop something small', or *mənus-nus* 'stormy wind' (Goudswaard 2005: 58), Buli *dongdong* 'breastbone', *boboko* 'head', *dibdib* 'to bounce', or *bukbuk* 'to foam' (Maan 1951: 25, 62), Makasar *kongkong* 'dog', *bambang* 'hot', or *rinring* 'ceiling' (Jukes 2006: 104), as well as Toba Batak *lappuláppu* 'butterfly', *habahába* 'thunderstorm', or *saságun* 'delicacy made of rice flour, coconut, and sugar' (Nababan 1981: 93).

In some languages, there are also lexical reduplication patterns that reflect fossilized reduplications with fixed segments, such as *Ca-* in colour terms of Tanimbar-Kei, for instance ***ba**bul* 'red' or ***ta**tom* 'yellow' (Blust 2013a: 427).

In contrast to what occurs in many non-Austronesian language families, echo-words (see §45.2.4) are rarely found as a productive word-formation pattern in MPSEA languages. However, monomorphemic words with an echo-structure can be found in several MPSEA languages, for instance in Bikol *p**i**ringp**i**ting* 'to shake the head (indicating negation)' or *r**a**ʔand**a**ʔan* 'hold a grudge against someone' (Mattes 2017: 828), Keo *f**i**ngo-f**a**ngo* 'dirty, red face from crying', *sak**é**-d**a**ké* 'trousers', *g**u**s**u**-gasa* 'chaotic' (Baird 2002: 175) and Mualang *tek**a**k**a**k-tek**i**k**i*** 'laugh continuously with various sounds', *k**a**s**a**k-k**u**s**u**k* 'be restless with all kinds of busy movements', *l**i**c**a**k-l**a**c**i**k* 'very muddy and wet' (Tjia 2007: 191).

Begak has some lexical reduplications which involve a linking element. Besides transparently repeated forms with *tu* 'also, too' (see §45.2.3), "there is [sic] also a number of repeated forms with *tu* 'too' that lack a non-reduplicated equivalent. Most of these items are sound-symbolic words" (Goudswaard 2005: 57), for example *kərup-tu-kərup* 'eat something crispy noisily' (**kərup*), *bəligbid-tu-bəligbid* 'walk zigzagging' (**bəligbid*), *kisol-tu-kisol* 'turn around constantly in sleep' (**kisol*), and many more.

As these and many other examples serve to illustrate, lexical reduplications typically refer to a semantically very specific class like sound, movement, feeling, and the like. This is in clear contrast to the usually underspecified meanings of productive reduplication, which often can only be interpreted in context (see also Mattes 2017: 836 and §45.3).

## 45.5 Historical development

The historical development of some reduplication types that are widespread in MPSEA languages, such as *Ca-* or CV-, has been discussed, also controversially, by Blust (1998a, 2003b) and Reid (1992, 2009c; see also Liao and Reid, this volume, §24.4.1). Blust (1998a) assumes the CV- reduplications with a fixed vowel, which are very widespread in MPSEA languages (see §45.2.9), to have a Proto-Austronesian ancestor *Ca-*. He reconstructs the function of forming instrument nouns from verbs for this *Ca-* reduplicant. This meaning is still attested, for example CaC- and *Ca-* in many Maluku languages (see Bowden 2001: 51; Schapper and Zobel, this volume, §35.3.3.1) like Sawai *tél~tolén* 'chair' from *tolén* 'to sit' (Whisler 1996: 8), but in general *Ca-* and other CV-reduplications have a broader range of meanings, mainly comprising various subcategories of plurality and of nominalizations (see §45.2.9). Reid (2009c) proposes the reverse development, in which *Ca-* reduplication evolved from CV-reduplication.

For Proto-Philippine languages, also the typical fixed-segment CVCV- reduplication with the function of diminutive derivation is assumed to have existed (see Blust 2013a: 428; as well as Zorc, Lobel, and Hall, this volume, chapter 7; Kaufman, this volume, chapter 25; Liao and Reid, this volume, chapter 24).

A purely formal diachronic development is described for Biak, where the internal -*Ca-* or -*CaC-* reduplication pattern probably originated from a former base-initial reduplication, for instance in *masa~sór* from *msór* 'angry' or *kafa~frok* from *kafrok* 'strike hard', with *m(a)* or *k(a)* as petrified prefixes (see van den Heuvel 2006: 260). A similar developmental tendency may also be observed in several other languages, where there can be free variation of reduplicated forms that are either root-based or stem-based. One example is imperfective CV- reduplication in Bikol verbs derived by a disyllabic prefix, which can either reduplicate the second syllable of the prefix (e.g. *na**ka**~ka-aram* [BEG.ABIL.AV~IPFV-know] 'be knowing' from *aram* 'know/knowledge') or the first syllable of the root (e.g. *naka-ta~**ta**pos* [BEG.ABIL.AV-IPFV~finish] 'being able to finalize' from *tapos* 'finish/end') (Mattes 2014: 48; see also §45.2.7). These variations in Biak and Bikol point towards a development from an originally root-based reduplication to a more general word- or stem-based partial reduplication pattern.

Very few MPSEA languages are reported only to have borrowed reduplications from other languages. One case is Keo, which natively does not have reduplication but where some borrowed or calqued examples from Indonesian are used mainly by younger speakers, for example *mbana~mbana* 'go for a stroll' from *mbana* 'walk' and *saʔo~saʔo* 'houses' from *saʔo* 'house', calqued from Standard Indonesian *jalan~jalan* 'go for a stroll' and *rumah~rumah* 'houses', respectively (Baird 2002: 180, 181; see Nagaya, this volume, §34.3.2 on the limited appearance of reduplication in Central Flores languages). Another external influence on reduplicative patterns can be observed in some Philippine languages. In Northern Luzon languages, for example in Ilokano, the comparative is formed by reduplication of root-initial $C_1V_1C_2$- (e.g. *dákes* 'bad' > *dak~dákes* 'worse' or *na-kuttóng* 'thin' > *na-kut~kuttóng* 'thinner'; Rubino 2000: lvi, lvii). However, in other Luzon languages, the comparative is formed by the prefix *mas-*, which is originally derived from Spanish *mas* 'more' (e.g. Bikol *dakul* 'much' > *mas-dakul* 'more' or *ma-gayon* 'beautiful' > *mas-ma-gayon* 'more beautiful', where a former reduplication pattern might have been substituted by a borrowed affix; see Mattes 2014: 42). In Dupaningan Agta, a close neighbour of Ilokano, which also uses *mas* to express the comparative, a concatenation of *mas* with CVC- reduplication is found in Ilokano-influenced constructions (see Robinson 2008: 142–3):

Dupaningan Agta
(46) *mas* ***ap~apellak*** *ni* *Jon* *im* *ni* *Charles*
more COMPAR~short PERS Jon than PERS Charles
'Jon is shorter than Charles.' (Robinson 2008: 143)

## 45.6 Typological considerations

Overall, like Austronesian languages in general, MPSEA languages make up a typological area in which reduplication plays an essential role in morphology and where almost all known formal reduplication types and typically associated meanings are found. There are some MPSEA languages in which reduplication is even the only productive device of word formation, such as Alorese (see Klamer 2011: 63). Moreover, there are several languages in which reduplication is one of the most productive morphological processes, such as Arta (see Kimoto 2017a: 92), and only very few languages which have no (native) productive reduplication at all (e.g. Keo; see Baird 2002: 177 and §45.5).

There is a well-known typological implication that productive partial reduplication in a language implies the existence of productive full reduplication (e.g. Moravcsik 1978: 328; see also Rubino 2013). In MPSEA we find a lot of evidence for this implicational statement. There are several languages that only use full reduplication, whereas they lack partial reduplication as a productive process, such as Alorese, Standard Indonesian (as opposed to Tanjung Raden; see Yanti 2010: 622), Keo and Dusner. Nevertheless, the majority of languages in the MPSEA area display productivity in their use of both general formal patterns. However, some MPSEA languages also challenge the universality of the above implication, as they only use partial reduplication productively while they lack full reduplication. Examples are Batuley, Chamorro (see also Stolz, Stroh, and Urdze 2011: 107, note 105), Dobel, Wamesa, Wooi, and some of the Northern Luzon Philippine languages (e.g. Arta, Dupaningan Agta, and Ibaloi). The universality of the implication is also weakened by Biak and Buli. In these languages, full reduplication exists but, in contrast to partial reduplication, is extremely rare and may be the result of an influence from other languages such as Indonesian or local Malay (see van den Heuvel 2006: 256 for Biak).

What generally seems to be mostly lacking in MPSEA languages is triplication, that is, a pattern in which the same reduplicant is attached twice to the base for a different semantic effect from reduplication, reported elsewhere in the Austronesian family for some Micronesian languages (e.g. Mokilese; Harrison 1973) and Formosan languages such as Thao (Blust 2001c) or Siraya (see Adelaar 2011: 69). A few examples of double *Ca*(C)- reduplication are found in Biak, as in the following:

Biak
(47) ***i-daf~daf~dúfe***
3SG-REDUP~REDUP~ill
'He is ill all the time.' (van den Heuvel 2006: 268)

Within the MPSEA language group, there are some features of reduplication that seem to be further restricted to certain subgroups or areas. One example is the distribution of reduplication types with fixed segments (see §45.2.9), common in many West and East-Malayo-Polynesian languages but not in Central-Malayo-Polynesian. Although *Ca*-reduplication and its variants are very widespread in the MPSEA languages and have been reconstructed for Proto-Austronesian by Blust (1998a), there is one subarea in which it rarely appears, namely the Philippine languages (see Liao and Reid, this volume, §24.4.1 and Kaufman, this volume, §25.2.4.2).

On the other hand, a very specific feature shared mainly by MPSEA languages of the Northern Philippines is the differentiation of reduplication patterns with respect to the nominal categories of human vs. non-human (e.g. Arta, Ibaloi, and Ilokano; see also Reid 2006c), which is otherwise more widespread in the Formosan languages.

Finally, there are some reduplicative functions that can be considered very characteristic for MPSEA languages on the whole and thus are found in the majority of the latter. These especially include the imitative or pretence meaning for entities, actions, or states. Another typical domain of reduplication pertains to numerals, demonstratives, and interrogative pronouns, according to Himmelmann (2005a: 122) making up some of the most widespread uses of reduplication in the Austronesian languages in general.

CHAPTER 46

# Word order

MARK DONOHUE

## 46.1 Introduction

Word order, at the clause or noun phrase (NP) level, has been the object of perhaps more syntactic and typological research than any other subfield of morphosyntax. The order of the arguments in the clause, or modifiers in the noun phrase, or phrasal clitics/affixes, show a number of dependencies, but also significant freedoms. The Malayo-Polynesian languages of Southeast Asia (MPSEA) show considerable variation in terms of word order parameters, to the point that it is not meaningful to talk of 'modal' or 'common' patterns in this group of languages.

Rarely are the different orders of elements in a phrase completely independent of each other; much work has shown that principles of harmony are frequently found, such that one order of head and modifier strongly influences the order of the head and the modifier in another construction. For example, Greenberg's Universal 2 (Greenberg 1966: 73–113) discusses the order of the object of a clause and the verb, and the order of the adposition and the noun phrase it governs. The verb is the head of the verb and object construction, and the adposition is the head of the adposition and noun phrase construction. Taking data from Dryer (2013c, d) (restricting the count to languages with a fixed orders), we see a great preponderance of languages with postpositions and preverbal object, or prepositions and postverbal objects. These *harmonic* orders, in which the order of head and modifier are the same in both constructions, account for 95% of the languages taken from Dryer's sample; only 5% of the languages have a *disharmonic* order between the two constructions, as shown in (1). Here we can see that prepositions are very rarely found in languages with object-verb order in the clause; while postpositions in languages with verb-object order are more common, they are still not a dominant pattern. In (1) we can also see that, for this sample, there is no strongly modal (that is, most frequent) setting, with two contenders that are approximately equally frequent.

| (1) | NP postposition | preposition NP |
|---|---|---|
| Object Verb | 48% | 1% |
| Verb Object | 4% | 46% |

A number of word order parameters are examined in this chapter, drawing on work by Dryer (1992, 1997, 2013a-l, 2018). With respect to clausal-level word order settings, we examine the relative position of the subject, object, and verb (S, O, and V), the position of polar question particles in the clause (Q), the position of content question words in the clause (WH), the position of negation in the clause (NEG); with respect to NP-level word order settings, we examine the order of a demonstrative modifier and noun (Dem, N), the order of a genitive modifier and noun (Gen N), the order of numeral modifier and noun (Num, N), the order adjective modifier and noun (Adj, N), and the order of relative clause modifier and noun (RC, N). The maximally harmonic patterns are shown in (2); (2a) shows the orders expected with consistently head-final orders, having OV order of object and verb, final question particles, post-verbal negation, postpositions, no fronting of content question words, and all the modifiers of the NP preceding the head noun. The orders in (2b) are the mirror image of this, showing a maximally harmonic head-initial language.

(2) Maximally harmonic word order settings

a. OV & Clause=Q & V NEG & NP=POSTPOSITION & WH in situ &
Dem-N & Gen-N & Num-N & Adj-N & RC-N

b. VO & Q=Clause & NEG V & PREPOSITION=NP & WH initial &
N-Dem & N-Gen & N-Num & N-Adj & N-RC

While there are a number of MPSEA languages with completely harmonic word orders, we also find a great deal of variation, and a great deal of local disharmonic patterns. Most importantly, we find that geography, in a complex way, is a good predictor of word order, though it is not the case that different parameters of word order variation line up together. Rather, we find, for instance, that the preference for at least some of the different elements in the NP to show or allow prenominal or postnominal modification remains stable even when clausal word order changes away from the verb-initial setting that was original to the languages.

This chapter reports on a database that includes 204 MPSEA languages, being those languages in my

Mark Donohue, *Word order*. In: *The Oxford Guide to the Malayo-Polynesian Languages of Southeast Asia*. Edited by: Alexander Adelaar and Antoinette Schapper, Oxford University Press.
 DOI: 10.1093/oso/9780198807353.003.0046

database that are in the right genealogical units, and in the right geographic region, excluding intrusive creoles (see Donohue 2021 for details of the sample used). More languages are displayed in the maps included here since it is clear that it does not make sense to examine the distribution of word order types in Austronesian languages without simultaneously presenting the context in which they are found, and so surrounding (and surrounded) languages from other families are also displayed.

## 46.2 Clausal word order

Proto-Austronesian was spoken in what is now Taiwan, and has been reconstructed as showing a verb-initial word order at the clause level (Blust 2009c: chapter 7; Starosta et al. 1982). While the original verb-initial order is categorially present in the northern MPSEA languages, we see the widespread adoption of SVO orders when adjacent to those areas where SVO patterns predate the Austronesianization of the region (e.g. Donohue 2005a, 2007). Verb-final orders are not attested in the MPSEA languages, even in those languages in proximity to non-Austronesian languages with SOV word orders.[1] Given the preponderance of SVO orders in the non-Austronesian languages of far western New Guinea in the Bird's Head, this is not surprising. Map 46.1 shows the extension of verb-initial orders (at least as an (unmarked) option) through the centre of Island Southeast Asia, in regions removed from Mainland Southeast Asia or western New Guinea, and in languages spoken on the western (Acehnese, Batak and the Barrier islands, and Madagascar) and eastern (Chamorro and Palauan) peripheries (see examples (3) and (4)). Example (5) from the Malayo-Sumbawan language Jamee shows variation between SVO and VOS order, with the VOS order described as 'daily usage' (*pemakaian sehari-hari*), indicating that verb-initial orders are preserved in western Sumatra (the existence of nearby Austroasiatic languages preserving verb-initial orders is further evidence of areal support for this morphosyntactic trait, combined with the preservation of the original verb-initial trait on this edge of the Malayo-Polynesian spread). In Kambera, (6), from south-central Indonesia, SVO is described as the normal word order in clauses, but verb-initial orders are also possible, with a focused subject and a topicalized object. Close to the western shores of New Guinea the verb-initial order is not preserved; the dominant word order in the region is SVO, illustrated with South Nuaulu in (7).

Chamorro: verb-initial (VSO)
(3) *Ha-faʔgasi si Juan i kareta.*
3SG-wash PERS Juan ART car
'Juan washed the car.' (Chung 1998: 236)

Tukang Besi: verb-initial (VOS)
(4) *No-tolo te kadola na kumbou.*
3-swallow CORE chicken NOM monitor.lizard
'The monitor lizard swallowed the chicken.'
(Donohue fieldnotes)

Jamee: verb-initial ~ SVO
(5) *Malulue ayom ula.* (~ *Ula malulue ayom.*)
swallow chicken snake
'The snake swallowed the chicken.'
(Wamad Abdullah et al. 1991: 46)

Kambera: SVO ~ verb-initial
(6) *I Miri na-kataku-ya*
ART Lord 3SG.NOM-accept-3SG.ACC
*na hamayang.*
ART prayer
'The Lord accepted the prayer.'
(~ *Nakatakuya i Miri na hamayang.*) (Klamer 1996: 21)

South Nuaulu: SVO
(7) *Senet-a ra-oto ruka.*
hornet-PL 3PL-bite monkey
'Hornets bit the monkey.' (Bolton 1990: 98)

A complication in the description of word order is found in the order of elements in a non-verbal predicate in a few languages. In Tukang Besi (Donohue 1999a), which is consistently head-initial at the clause-level and in the NP (see (4)), non-verbal clauses have a subject-initial order as a default (8), indicating that the predicate-initial order is not as completely dominant as might be thought. The opposite case is found in South Nuaulu, where SVO order is normal in verbal clauses, (7), but Predicate–Subject order is found in non-verbal clauses, (9).

Tukang Besi (VOS, but $NP_{SUBJ}$ $NP_{PRED}$)
(8) *Te ana te topi-su.*
CORE this CORE hat-1SG.GEN
'This is my hat.' (Donohue fieldnotes)

South Nuaulu (SVO, but $NP_{PRED}$ $NP_{SUBJ}$)
(9) *Au we korobou unte rei-ni.*
1SG 1SG.AL.POSS cow skin this-PROX
'This is my belt.' (Bolton 1990: 68)

[1] An exception to this statement is found in Singapore Indian Malay, a pidgin with a Tamil matrix and evidence of SOV clausal order as an alternative to SVO for many speakers (Sasi 2007). Similar facts apply to Sri Lankan Malay (see Slomanson and Moro, chapter 19; and Slomanson, this volume, chapter 18). Verb-final orders are present at the extreme eastern end of Indonesia in Ormu and Tobati, two Oceanic languages of the Jayapura area, and in Oceanic languages of the Papuan Tip group, in the southeast of New Guinea.

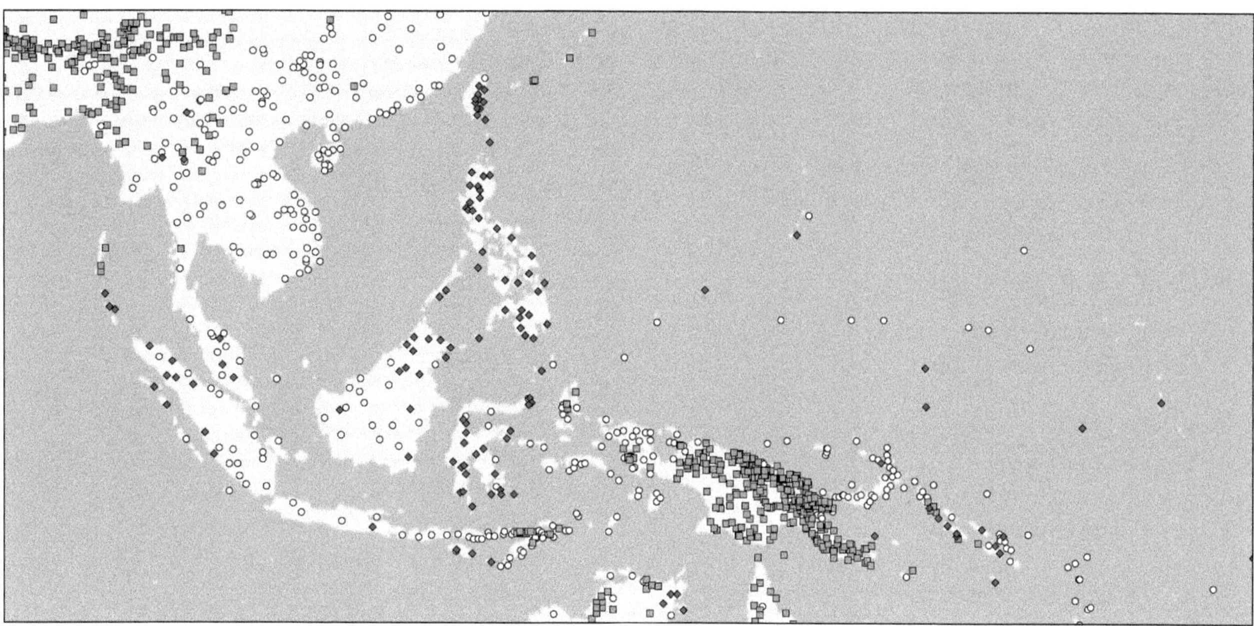

**Map 46.1** Main clausal word order types.

*Notes*: filled diamond: verb-initial (possible); white circle: SVO (verb-initial not possible); grey square: verb-final.

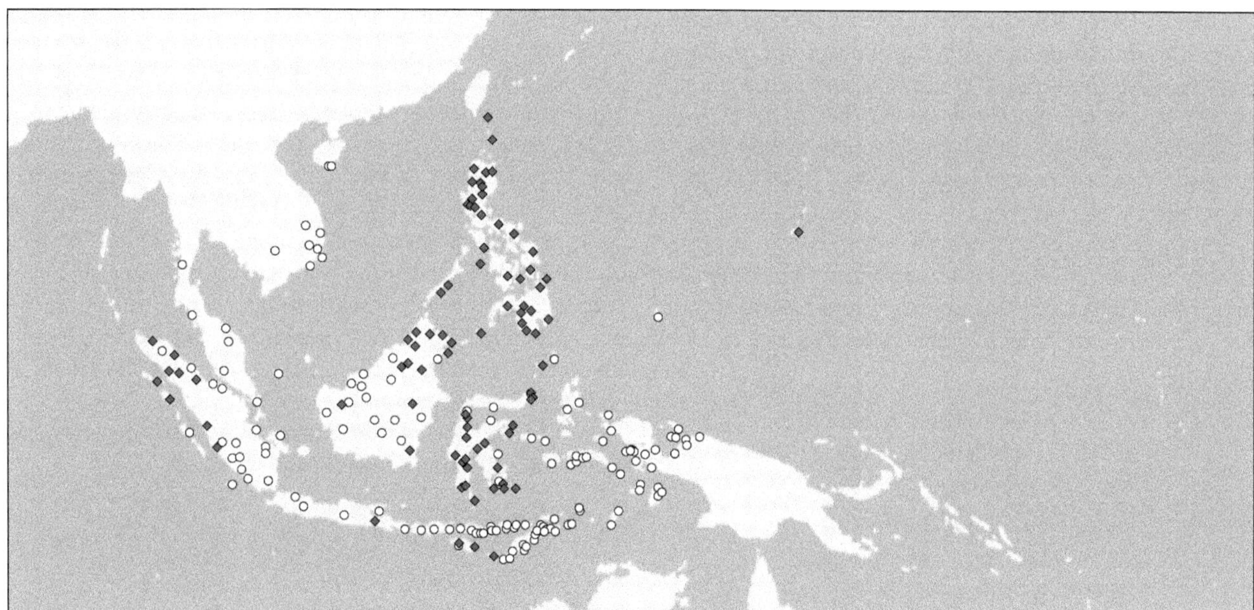

**Map 46.1'** Main clausal word order types among MPSEA languages.

*Notes*: filled diamond: verb-initial (possible); white circle: SVO (verb-initial not possible); grey square: verb-final.

It has been pointed out that most verb-initial languages allow the possibility of the subject appearing before the verb (e.g. Quakenbush 1992). This is true of Tukang Besi, where we can see different marking on the relevant NP, as seen in (10). In Begak there is no overt marking of the difference between verb-initial and subject-initial orders, but there are contextual contrasts: Goudswaard (2005: 382) reports that "initially only [a clause with an initial subject] was judged correct", but that "[t]he verb-initial word order with AV-verb is perfectly grammatical, but only as long as it is embedded in a discourse context", as shown in (11).

Tukang Besi
(10) a. *No-waliako-mo* ***na*** *ana~ana.*
3-return-PFV NOM REDUP~child
'The children have returned.'
b. ***Te*** *ana~ana* *no-waliako-mo.*
CORE REDUP~child 3-return-PFV
'The children have returned.'
(Donohue fieldnotes)

Begak
(11) a. *Lina bəg-arab (nong) niun.*
Lina AV-look.for OBL 2SG.ACC
'Lina is looking for you.'
b. *Bəg-arab Lina (nong) niun (...)*
AV-look.for Lina OBL 2SG.ACC
'(...) Lina is looking for you (...)'
(Goudswaard 2005: 382)

In other languages, variation in word order correlates with changes in voice (see Kroeger and Riesberg, this volume, chapter 47). Arka and Kosmas (2005) describe Manggarai passives as involving no verbal morphology, but having an overtly-marked by-phrase (the clitics *=k* and *=i* indicate subject agreement, marked not on the verb but on the VP), and a range of syntactic tests which demonstrate that (12b) is not just a word order alternative to (12a). Palu'e (Donohue 2005c) has a similar alternation, but without marking of the by-phrase, and without agreement. Again, a range of syntactic tests indicate that (13b) is a passive variant of (13a), with *keʔo* as the subject, and not just an alternative word order due to, for instance, topicalization of the object.

Manggarai
(12) a. *Aku cero latung=k.*
1SG fry corn=1SG
'I fry/am frying corn'
b. *Latung hitu cero l=aku=i.*
corn that fry by=1SG=3SG
'The corn is (being) fried by me'
(Arka and Kosmas 2005)

Palu'e
(13) a. *Aku seo keʔo.*
1SG fry corn
'I fry corn.'
b. *Keʔo aku seo.*
corn 1SG fry
'The corn was fried by me.'
(Donohue fieldnotes)

Similar data can be found in a restricted subset of Indonesian non-Active clauses. With verbs that do not take the active prefix *meng-*, and with a first- or second-person agent, the alternation in (14) appears to represent a voice alternation mediated only by word order. The structural differences between (14a) and (14b) run more deeply, however, with *saya* in (14b) being in tighter constituency with the verb than in (14a), and the initial NP in each sentence being the subject. The same is probably true of the Palu'e data in (13).

Indonesian
(14) a. Active
*Saya makan nasi itu.*
1SG eat rice that
'I ate the rice.'
b. Non-Active
*Nasi itu saya makan.*
rice that 1SG eat
'I ate the rice.' ~ 'I ate *the rice*.'
(Donohue own knowledge)

Passive constructions without verbal marking are attested elsewhere, but only rarely. The sort of passive seen in Manggarai is also present in the passives of Chinese and Tai-Kadai languages from mainland Asia, with an overtly marked by-phrase, if present. The data in (13) shows that voice alternations can be marked without any morphological changes.

Many languages allow pragmatically determined variation in word order, and the MPSEA languages are no exception to this. The Kupang Malay examples in (15) illustrate morphologically unmarked variation of the order of subject, verb, and object. The pragmatic differences, and corresponding required intonation changes, are dramatic. The P is more likely to be retrievable from recent discourse in structure similar to (15a), (15b), and (15e), and the P in (15d) and (15f) is likely to be generic. The constraints on topicality and focus described for Kambera most likely approximate those that pertain for Kupang Malay as well.

Kupang Malay
(15) a. Unmarked
*Beta suka nasi.*
1SG like rice
'I like rice.' ~ 'I would like some rice.'
b. Topicalized P
*Nasi, beta suka.*
rice 1SG like
'(Now, as for) rice, I like (it).'
c. Antitopic A
*Suka nasi, beta.*
like rice 1SG
'(I) like rice, me.'

d. Topicalized A, topicalized P
*Beta, nasi suka.*
1SG rice like
'Me, rice, (I) like (it).'

e. Topicalized P, antitopic A
*Nasi, suka, beta.*
rice like 1SG
'(Now, as for) rice, (I) like (it), I do.'

f. Antitopic A, antitopic P
*Suka beta, nasi.*
like 1SG rice
'(I) like (it), rice, me.' (Tom Therik p.c.)

Many languages of the Philippines are verb-initial, but allow a preverbal NP if marked with *ay*, (16). In constructions without *ay* pronouns are normally realized as second-position clitics, (17). The determination of word order is thus complicated; the (morphologically and pragmatically) unmarked clause is clearly verb-initial, but the relative position of the post-verbal NPs depends on word class (pronouns are clitics), the semantic role of the arguments and their position in the thematic hierarchy, and the grammatical function borne by the NP (subjects precede obliques and adjuncts). This is schematized in (18).

Tagalog
(16) a. *Um-alis ako.*
AV-leave 1SG.NOM
'I left.'

b. *Ako-(a)y um-alis.*
1SG.NOM-AY AV-leave
'I left.' (Donohue own knowledge)

(17) a. *K<um>ain ng tinapay ang aso.*
bite<AV> GEN bread NOM dog
'The dog ate some bread.'

b. *K<um>ain=ako ng tinapay.*
bite<AV>=1SG.NOM GEN bread
'I ate some bread.'

c. **k<um>ain ng tinapay ako*
bite<AV> GEN bread 1SG.NOM
'I ate some bread.'

Tagalog clausal word order
(18) Verb (clitics) Agent, . . ., Patient Subject Obliques/Adjuncts

Special mention must be made of the order of elements of the clause in Iraya, a Philippine language of Mindoro. Word order is not consistent with any of the main types described above; nominal arguments and adjuncts normally follow the verb, as seen in (19a), but pronominal arguments are frequently pre-verbal, as shown in (19b–c). Reid argues that these word order characteristics, along with other morphosyntactic traits, is evidence of the survival of a pre-Austronesian linguistic stratum in the northern Philippines.

Iraya
(19) a. *. . . batay mamahuy ʔag nay apu*
FUT visit SPEC 1SG.OBL grandfather
*sa kun kamutiyan.*
LOC 3SG.OBL sweet.potato.field
'. . . my grandfather was going to visit his sweet potato field.'

b. *Kawu nay malyag.*
2SG.NOM 1SG.OBL like
'I like you.'

c. *Kawu tuwaʔ tumuŋkaʔ.*
2SG.NOM here sit
'You sit here.' (Reid 2017: 30, 27)

Oblique arguments are typically located on the same side of the verb as are the objects in any given MPSEA language, though there are some exceptions to this pattern, as seen in the Palu'e data in (20). Similar word-order facts in Chinese languages have been argued to represent a retention of SOV typological traits in those languages (e.g. Dryer 2003), or the influence of neighbouring SOV languages (e.g. Yue 2003). In light of (19b) and (19c), this suggests the possible existence of a pre-Austronesian verb-final region extending over a large region, from the Philippines to Flores.

Palu'e
(20) *Kami noʔo ʔɓiu kti kadʒu.*
1PL.EXCL with axe cut wood
'We cut wood with an axe.' (Donohue fieldnotes)

Adpositions in the MPSEA languages are, as in the Palu'e example in (20), prepositional. Many prepositions are intermediate between adposition and verb; the Palu'e examples in (21) show that *lae* has an unproblematic prenominal use in (21a). It appears with the morphosyntax of a verb in (21b)–(21c). Since Palu'e allows serial verb constructions, as exemplified by the string *ladʒu phana lau* in (21d), the analysis of *lae* in (21a) as a preposition, and not a locational verb, is problematic.

Palu'e
(21) a. *Konen nodo lae nua-gu.*
3PL sit at house-1.GEN
'They're in our house.'

b. *Kami laʔe lae.*
1PL.EXCL not.yet be.at
'We weren't (there) yet (at that time).'

c. *Konen lae-ʔu.*
3PL be.at-PRF
'They were already there.'

d. *Kita* *ladʒu* *phana* *lau* *laŋa.*
1PL.INCL run go go.seawards beach
'We ran down to the beach.' (Donohue fieldnotes)

Ambiguities between verbs and prepositions are found in other languages; in Tukang Besi the locative oblique *di* corresponds to *dei* 'be left over'; *mina* 'from' to *mina* 'have ever been at'; *ako* 'benefactive' to *ako* 'do something for (someone)'; *kene* 'with' to *kene* 'accompany' (Donohue 1999).

In some languages closer to the western edge of New Guinea (though not the MPSEA languages in Cenderawasih Bay) we find postpositions, or preposition–postposition combinations, appearing in the languages. Kowiai has only postpositions, and South Nuaulu has constructions such as that in (22) in which *haha* and *sui* might be analysed as functioning as postpositions, used in conjunction with prepositions. Similar constructions are attested in Solor Lamaholot, Fordata, Banda, and Uruangnirin, as well as in Òma Lóngh, from Borneo, and possibly Isinay Dupax from the Philippines.

South Nuaulu

(22) a. *Rei-mo,* *on* ***roe*** *nian-a* ***haha(e)****-ya.*
this-TOP from up village-PL top-PL
'As for this, it was up in the villages up top.'

b. *I-eu* *tau* *ai-ni* ***roe*** *wae*
3SG-go with foot-3SG.POSS up water
*onate* ***hahae.***
big top
'He was walking on the surface of the lake.'

c. *Ne* *au* ***runa****-mo* ***sui*** *osa* *tewa.*
but 1SG with-2PL along one NEG
'But I will not always be with you.'
(Bolton 1990: 110, 71, 91)

## 46.3 Noun phrase word order

NP-internal word orders show a great range of variation in the MPSEA languages. Three major patterns, with two variants, account for the order of elements in the NP in 81% of the languages in the MPSEA language sample for which reliable data is available. The most frequent pattern sees all modifiers following the noun, except for numerals; this is found across most of the MPSEA area, apart from the east, where the prenominal element is the Genitive (Maps 46.2 and 46.7). The variants involve one of the major patterns with one modifier type that can appear both prenominally or postnominally. The only large and geographically coherent group of languages that do not fit into one of the schemas are those of the Philippines (as well as those in Taiwan); they are excluded from these dominant types due to the many languages in which at least some modifiers are prenominal or else may occur either prenominally or postnominally.

- Numeral–Noun–other modifiers 30%

  with variable position of Numeral 9%

- Genitive–Noun–other modifiers 26%

  with variable position of Genitive 2%

- Noun–all modifiers 14%

Other NP patterns found in the MPSEA languages include: Numeral–Noun–other modifiers, with variable position of Genitive (2%); Numeral–Noun–other modifiers, with variable position of Demonstrative (2%); Noun–modifiers, with variable position of Demonstrative (2%); Numeral–Noun–other modifiers, with variable position of Adjective (1%); and Demonstrative–Noun–other modifiers, with variable position of Numeral (1%). Another 11% of the MPSEA languages in the sample show minor patterns, or unique orders of the elements of the NP.

The variation allowed in the order of a noun and its modifiers in the northern languages of MPSEA area is shown for Tagalog, in (23). A demonstrative may appear prenominally or postnominally (or both), as shown in (23a). Similarly, adjective-like modifiers, genitive modifiers, and relative clauses can all appear both prenominally and postnominally. Only numerals show a preference for appearing on one side of the noun, as seen in the contrast between (23e) and (23f).

Tagalog

(23) a. *ang* *palasyo-ng* *iyan*
NOM palace-LNK that
'that palace'

a.' *ang* *iya(n)-ng* *palasyo*
NOM that-LNK palace
'that palace'

b. *ang* *palasyo-ng* *malaki*
NOM palace-LNK big
'the big palace'

b.' *ang* *malaki-ng* *palasyo*
NOM big-LNK palace

c. *ang* *palasyo* *ng* *pangulo*
NOM palace GEN president
'the president's palace'

c.' *ang* *sa* *pangulo-ng* *palasyo*
NOM DAT president-LNK palace
'the palace of the president'

d. *ang* *palasyo-ng* *nagustuhan*
NOM palace-LNK be.liked
'the palace which was liked'

d.' *ang* *nagustuha(n)-ng* *palasyo*
NOM be.liked-LNK palace
'the palace which was liked'

e. *# ang* *palasyo-ng* *isa*
NOM palace-LNK one
'one palace' ~ 'a palace'

f. *ang* *isa-ng* *palasyo*
NOM one-LNK palace
'one palace' (Donohue, own knowledge)

The last of the orders listed earlier, in which the noun precedes all modifiers, is surprisingly rare given the overwhelming prevalence of head-initial order at the clause level, but the Tukang Besi data in (24) shows this pattern; none of the modifiers may occur pre-nominally.

Tukang Besi

(24) a. *te* *wunua* *iso*
CORE house that
'that house'

b. *te* *wunua* *to?oge*
CORE house big
'big house'

c. *te* *wunua* *nu* *raja*
CORE house GEN king
'(the) king's house'

d. *te* *wunua* *di-niimati*
CORE house P.PTCP-enjoy
'the house which was enjoyed'

e. *te* *wunua* *sa-?asa*
CORE house one-CLF
'one house' (Donohue, fieldnotes)

(Standard) Indonesian presents an example of a (slightly) disharmonic language with the most common pattern found in the MPSEA languages: most modifiers follow the noun, as shown in (25a)–(25d), illustrating modifying demonstratives, adjectives, genitives, and relative clauses, respectively. As indicated above, the exception involves modifying numerals, which, together with their classifier, appear preverbally as an unmarked order.

Indonesian

(25) a. *istana* *itu*
palace that
'that palace'

b. *istana* *besar*
palace big
'big palace'

c. *istana* *Presiden*
palace president
'(the) President's palace'

d. *istana* *yang* *dinikmati*
palace REL be.enjoyed
'the palace which was enjoyed'

e. *# istana* *se-buah*
palace one-CLF

f. *se-buah* *istana*
one-CLF palace
'one palace' (Donohue, own knowledge)

The explanation for this disharmony lies in the treatment of numerals in Austronesian languages, which are accorded a more pragmatically prominent position than in most language families. The order in (25e) represents a floated numeral phrase that is outside the NP. (25f) might be represented as $[_{NP}$ NUM-CLF Noun], while (25e) is best viewed as $[[_{NP}$ Noun] NUM-CLF]. I return to the analysis of numeral modifiers in more detail in §46.3.1. Map 46.2 illustrates the distribution of the Major NP orders attested in the MPSEA.

The orders of the separate modifiers in the NP are shown in Maps 46.3–46.7. Comparing the patterns in the different maps, we can see that the most head-initial orders (in which the modifier follows the noun) are found in the southeast of the MPSEA area. The northern languages show more prenominal orders of modifiers, while the southwestern languages break the strict head-initially of the NP with prenominal numerals, as shown in (25), a trait that is both retained from earlier Austronesian, and supported areally by the numerous non-Austronesian languages in the southwest Southeast Asian region (which is not the case for the MPSEA languages to the east). In Map 46.3 we can see that postnominal demonstratives are normal, with prenominal demonstratives found mostly in the north, where they are often an option that is found along with postnominal demonstratives. This was earlier illustrated in (23).

Adjectival modifiers (in the sense of Dryer 2013f) follow much the same pattern as demonstratives in terms of position, as can be seen in Map 46.4. Very few MPSEA languages outside the Philippine area allow prenominal adjectives;

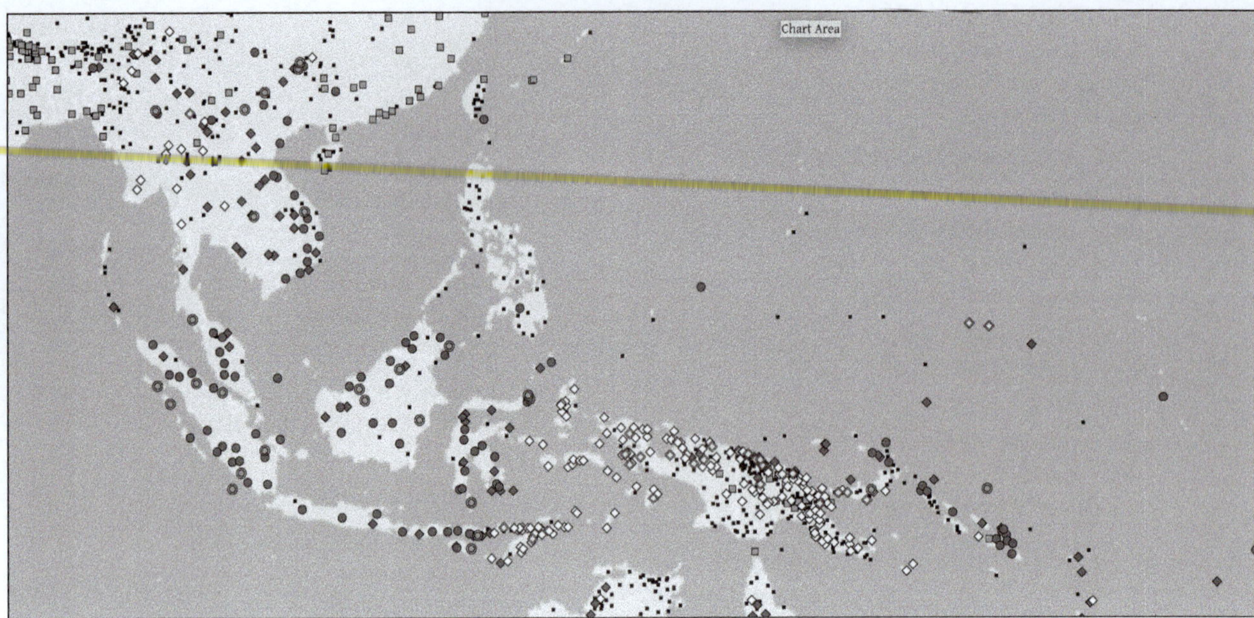


**Map 46.2** Major NP orders.

*Notes*: grey square: all modifiers prenominal; grey diamond: all modifiers postnominal; white diamond with double border: all modifiers postnominal, with the possibility of a prenominal genitive; grey circle with double border: all modifiers postnominal, with optionally prenominal numeral; grey circle: Num-N-Mod order; white diamond: Gen-N-Mod order; small black square: other NP modifier possibilities.

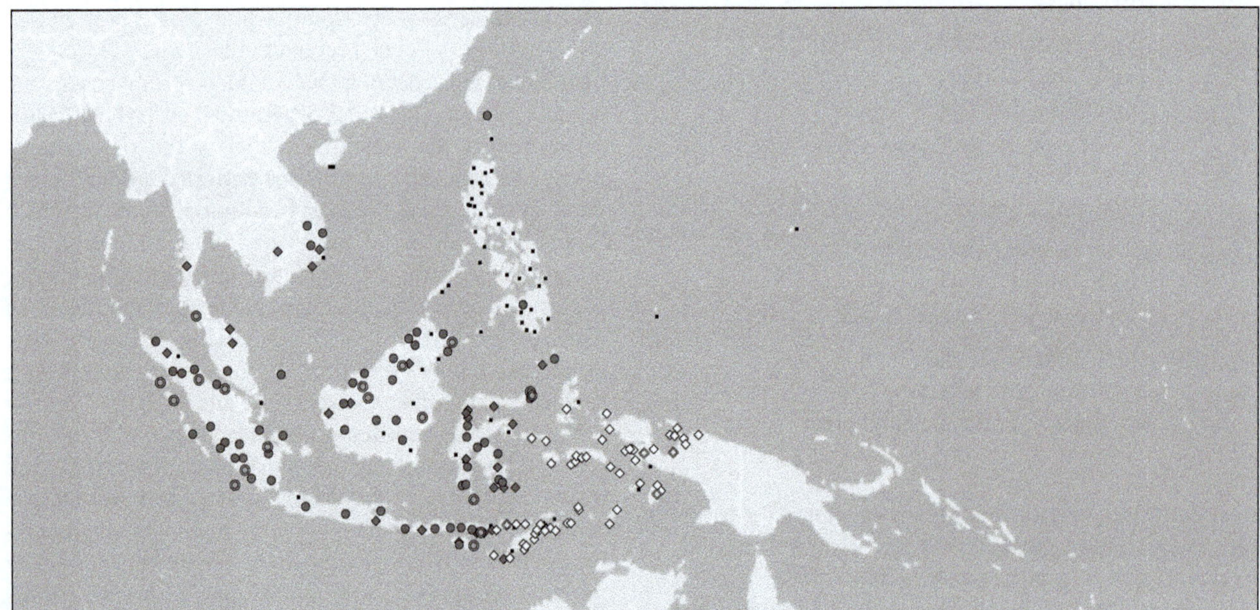

**Map 46.2′** Major NP orders among MPSEA languages.

*Notes*: grey square: all modifiers prenominal; grey diamond: all modifiers postnominal; white diamond with double border: all modifiers postnominal, with the possibility of a prenominal genitive; grey circle with double border: all modifiers postnominal, with optionally prenominal numeral; grey circle: Num-N-Mod order; white diamond: Gen-N-Mod order; small black square: other NP modifier possibilities.

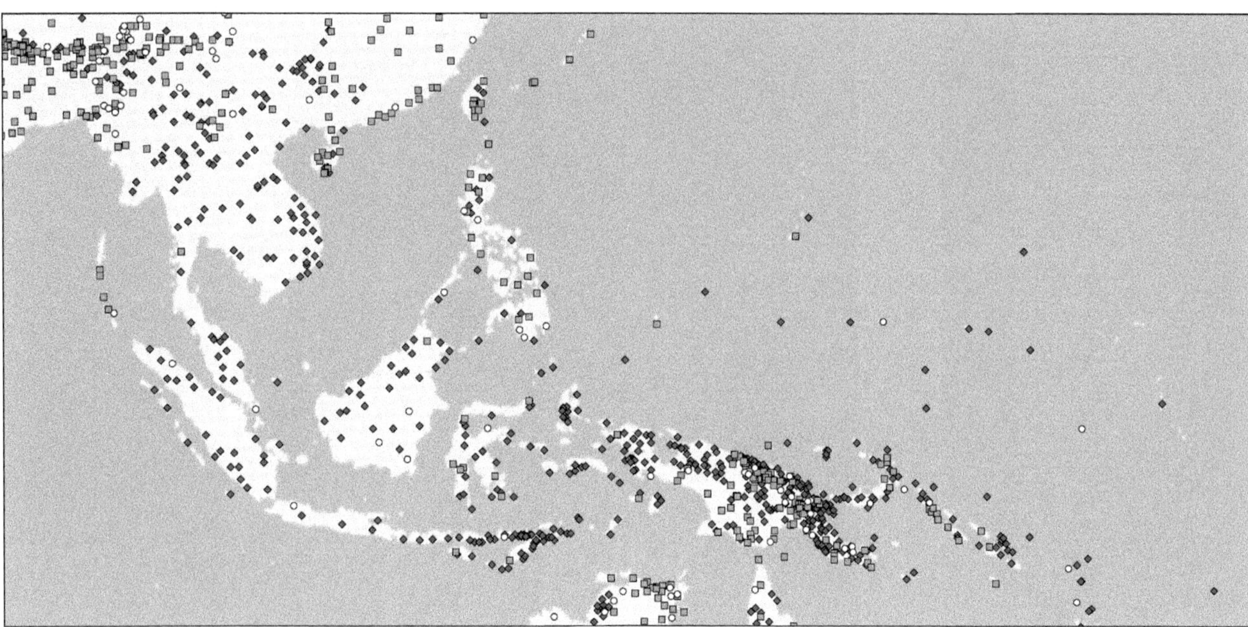

**Map 46.3** Order of demonstrative and noun.

*Notes*: filled diamond: noun precedes modifier; white circle: modifier can precede or follow the noun; grey square: modifier precedes noun.

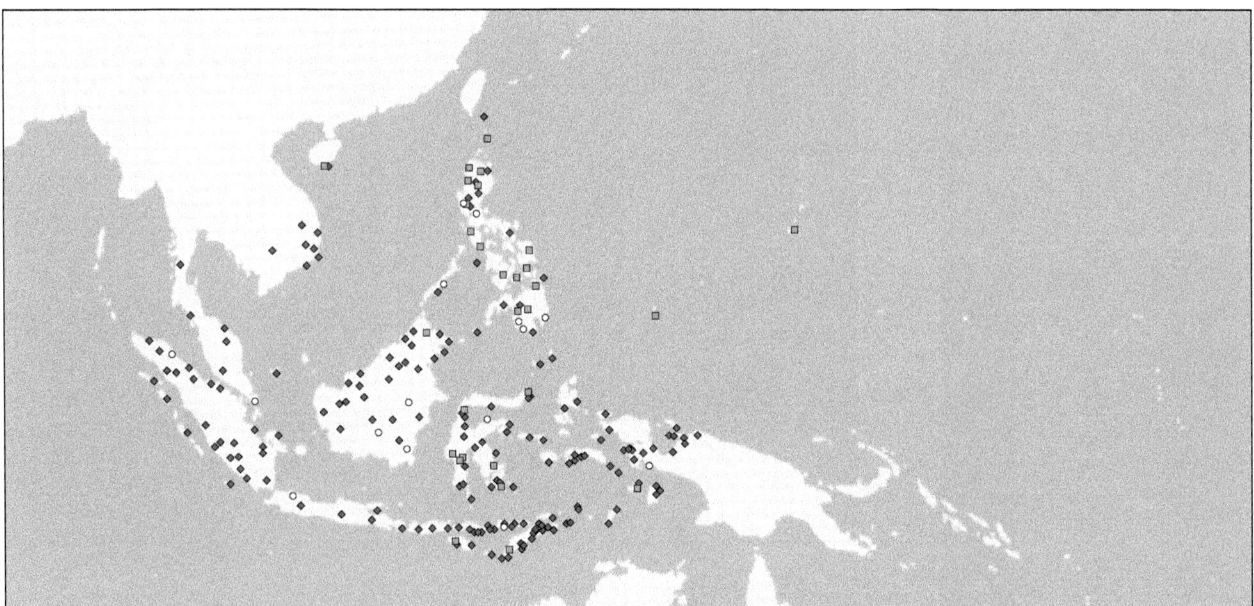

**Map 46.3'** Order of demonstrative and noun among MPSEA languages.

*Notes*: filled diamond: noun precedes modifier; white circle: modifier can precede or follow the noun; grey square: modifier precedes noun.

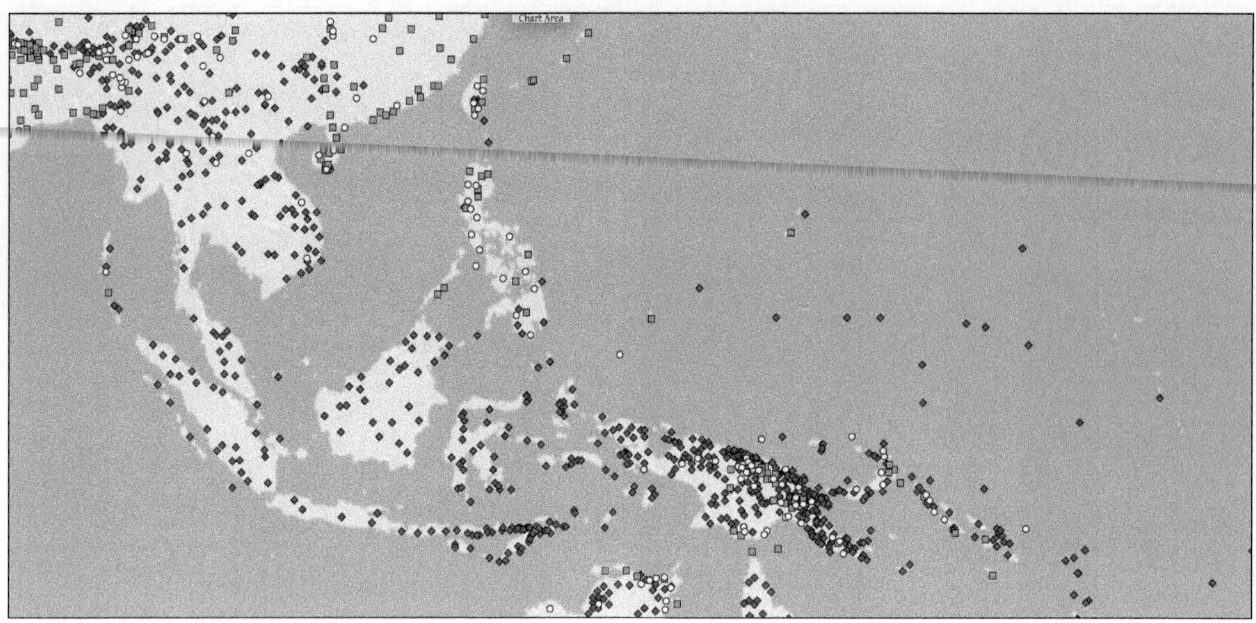


**Map 46.4** Order of adjective and noun.

*Notes*: filled diamond: noun precedes modifier; white circle: modifier can precede or follow the noun; grey square: modifier precedes noun.

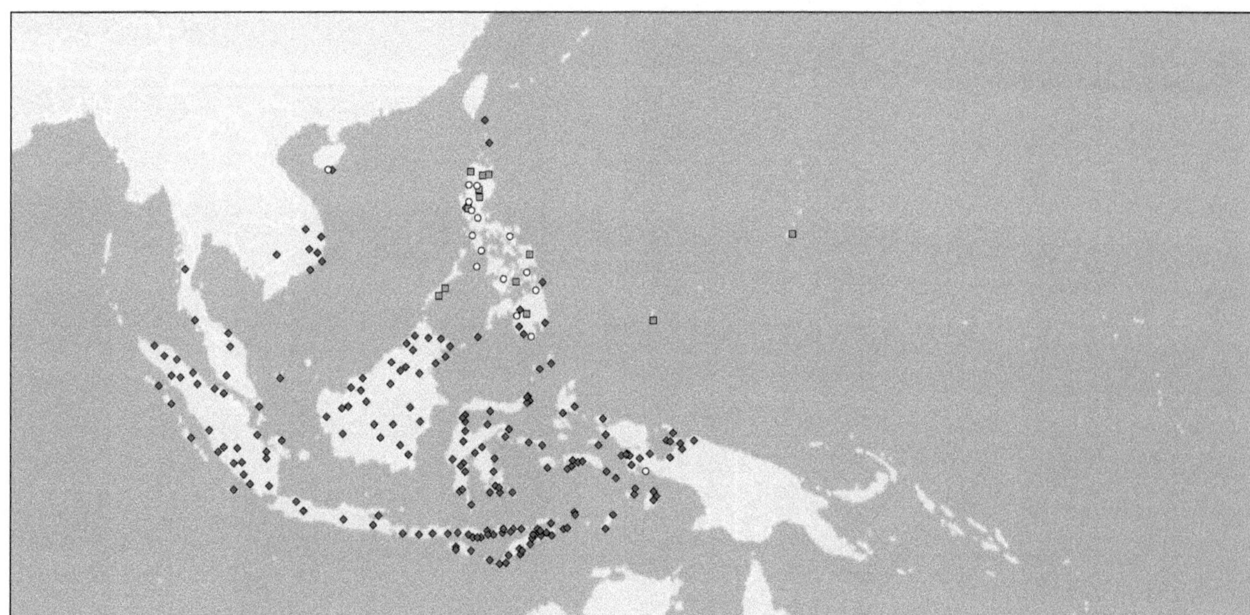

**Map 46.4'** Order of adjective and noun among MPSEA languages.

*Notes*: filled diamond: noun precedes modifier; white circle: modifier can precede or follow the noun; grey square: modifier precedes noun.

they are obligatorily prenominal in Singapore Indian Malay, and have this as an option in Matéq, Kowiai, and modern, but not older, Tsat (a result of contact with Chinese languages; Thurgood et al. 2014). In Tsat the normal (and conservative) order is for adjectives to be postnominal, as in (26a). Nonetheless, a number of prenominal adjectives are found, as shown in (26b); Thurgood et al. note that this is common in "more Mandarinized texts"; in (26b) the head nouns *sin*$^{33}$ and *pa:u*$^{33}$, are both Mandarin loans (心 *xīn* and 报 *bào*, respectively).

Tsat

(26) a. *na*$^{11}$*tsun*$^{33}$ *pioŋʔ*$^{32}$ *poiʔ*$^{24}$*:*
bird big say
'The big bird said:...'

b. *na:iʔ*$^{32}$ *sin*$^{33}$ *na:iʔ*$^{32}$ *pa:u*$^{33}$*,...*
good heart good reward
'...kind-hearted people will be rewarded...'
(Thurgood et al. 2014: 175, 176)

An additional construction sees adjectives in prenominal position, with the innovative genitive postposition *sa*$^{33}$ (structurally parallel to the postpositional genitive found in many Chinese languages, including Hainan *ke*$^{22}$ 嘅 and Mandarin *de* 的). This is seen in (27a), which parallels the structure of an innovative possessive phrase, shown in (27b) (compare to the conservative genitive construction in (27c), which is postnominal and does not employ *sa*$^{33}$).

Tsat

(27) a. *na:iʔ*$^{32}$ *sa*$^{33}$ *saŋ*$^{33}$*huat*$^{24}$
good GEN life
'(the) good life'

b. *ʔa*$^{11}$*ɓa*$^{11}$ *sa*$^{33}$ *sa:ŋ*$^{33}$
father's.elder.brother GEN house
'father's elder brother's house'

c. *ŋa:n*$^{33}$ *kau*$^{33}$ *kiʔ*$^{24}$
hand 1SG painful
'My hand hurts.'
(Thurgood et al. 2014: 177, 210, 213)

Relative clauses, which in many of the MPSEA languages are morphologically indistinguishable from adjectives, show a tendency to appear postnominally, even when adjectives can appear prenominally. This follows the well documented preference for heavier elements in the NP (those that are longer) to appear later in the phrase in which they are embedded, an instance of heavy shift that has become grammaticalized (Fox and Thompson 1990; Hawkins 1994; amongst others). Outside the Philippine area, only the Tsat varieties of Hainan Island show prenominal relative clauses (see Map 46.5). This is a clear result of contact with Jiamao and the Chinese languages of southern Hainan.

Numeral and Genitive modification both present additional complications, and they are discussed separately in the following sections.

### 46.3.1 Numerals and the NP

The position of numerals in the NP is often at variance from the position of other modifiers, frequently being found prenominally, even when all other modifiers are postnominal. Compared to the orders seen in Maps 46.3–46.5, the position of numerals in Map 46.6 shows a much broader area in which prenominal modification is found, with postnominal numerals only prevalent in the southeast of the region, matching their position in most of lowlands New Guinea, and in the MPSEA languages of Mainland Southeast Asia.

Numerals in Austronesian languages are treated as more predicative than is the case in most language families. Whereas lexemes with telic, active semantics are generally selected as clausal predicates, numerous cases are found in Austronesian languages of numerals being preferentially coded as clausal predicates, while highly transitive events are demoted. In Tukang Besi the example in (28a) was attested in the context of filling a motorbike. The sentence in (28b), in which the numeral is encoded as part of the NP, was offered as an explication, but would not be likely to be produced spontaneously.

Tukang Besi

(28) a. *To-tolu-ʔe?*
1PL-be.three-3
'Shall we (fill it with) three (bottles of petrol)?'
(literally, 'Shall we make (them) three?')

b. *To-neʔi-ke te botolu totolu?*
1PL-fill-3 CORE bottle three
'Shall we fill it with three bottles?'
(Donohue fieldnotes)

Similar data can be found elsewhere in the Austronesian world (e.g. Mosel and Hovdhaugen 1992: 115, describing Samoan, state that "the most common way to refer to a certain number of specific items is to employ the cardinal numeral as the predicate of an independent clause"). The Indonesian examples in (29) are both felicitous, unlike the literal translations into English.

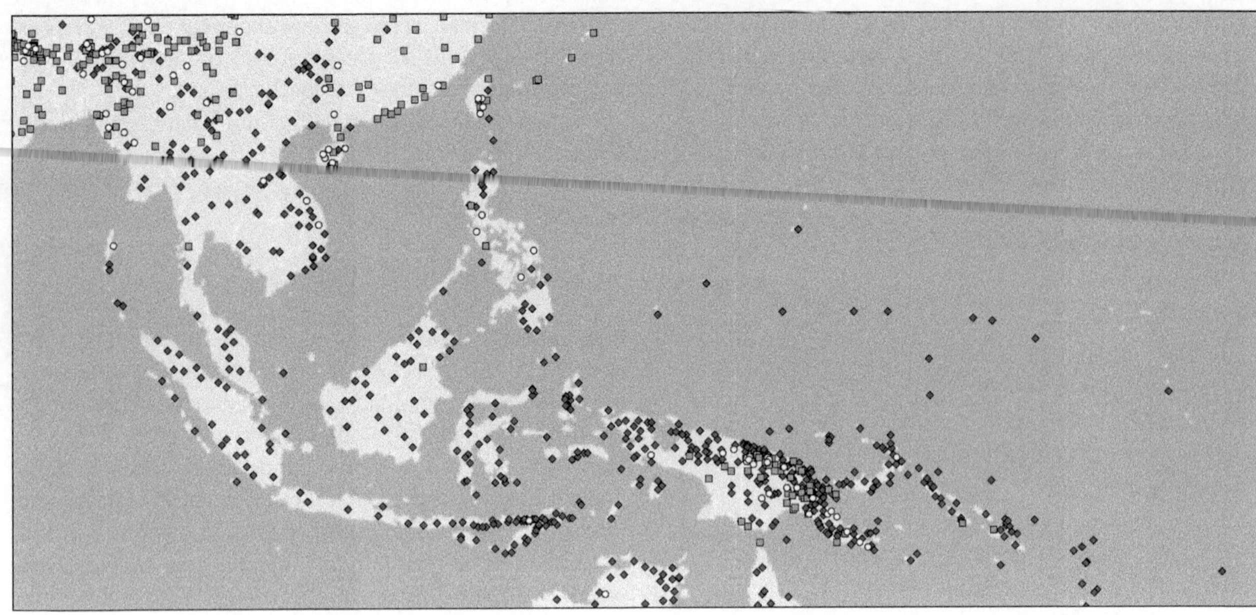

**Map 46.5** Order of relative clause and noun.

*Notes*: filled diamond: noun precedes modifier; white circle: modifier can precede or follow the noun; grey square: modifier precedes noun.

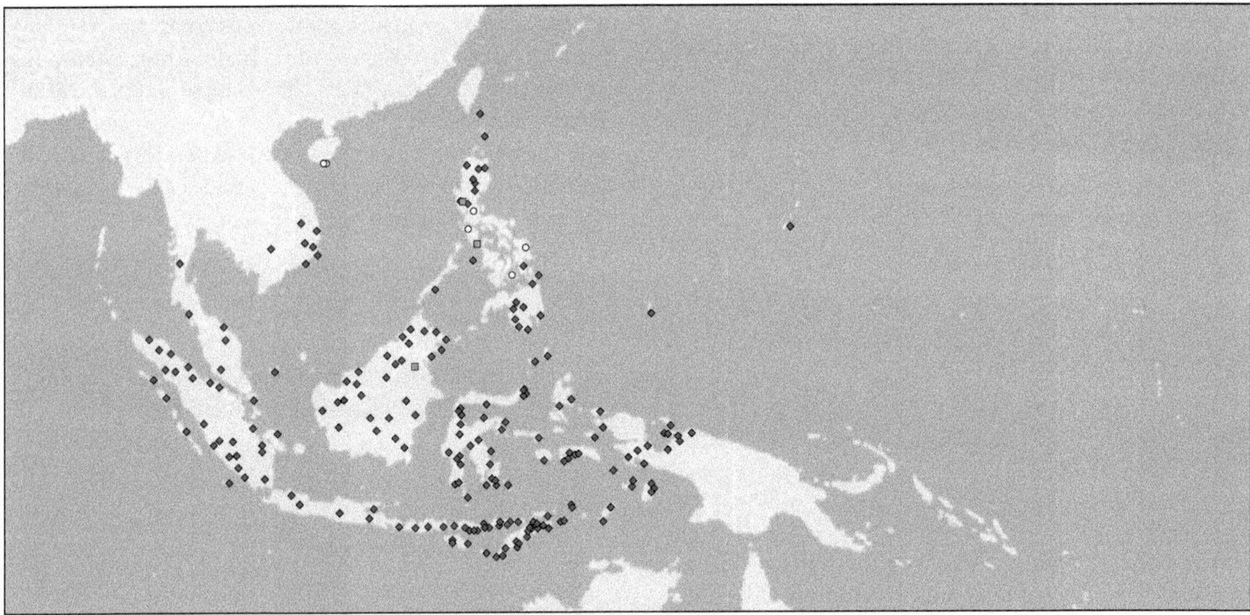

**Map 46.5'** Order of relative clause and noun among MPSEA languages.

*Notes*: filled diamond: noun precedes modifier; white circle: modifier can precede or follow the noun; grey square: modifier precedes noun.

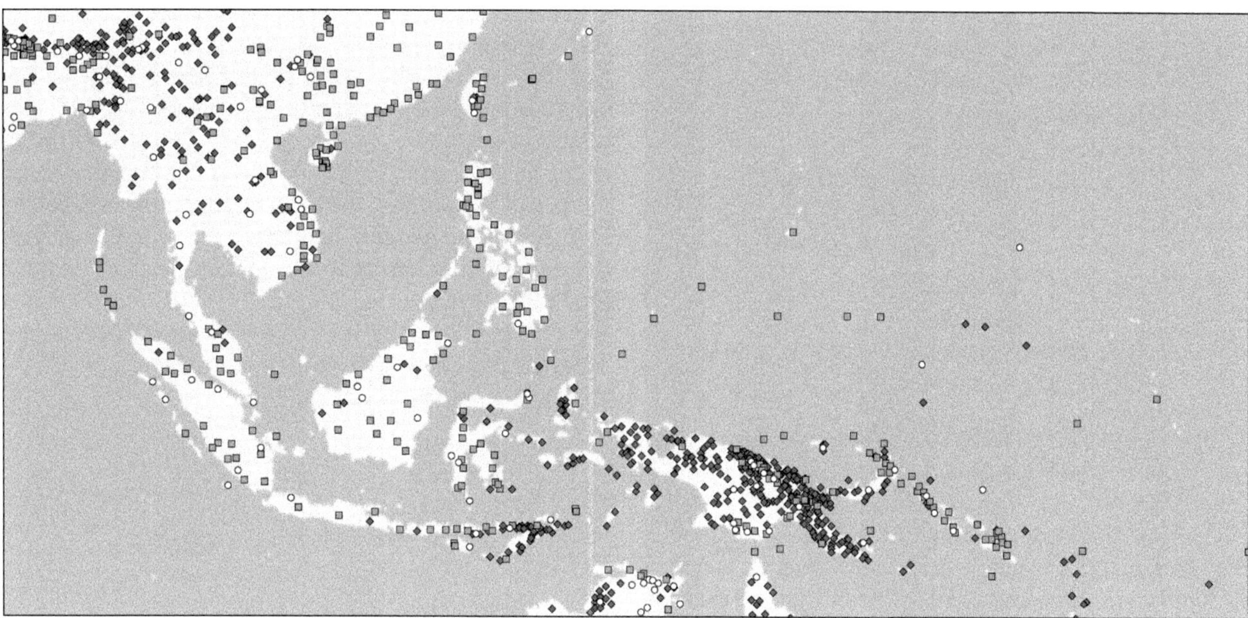

**Map 46.6** Order of numeral and noun.

*Notes*: filled diamond: noun precedes modifier; white circle: modifier can precede or follow the noun; grey square: modifier precedes noun.

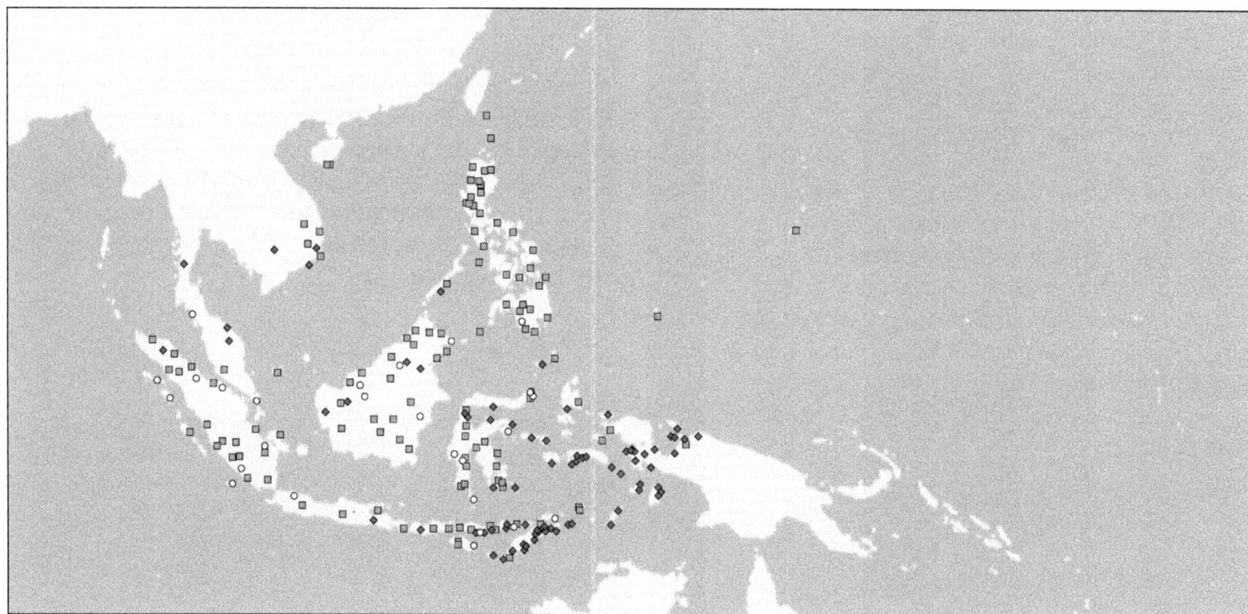

**Map 46.6'** Order of numeral and noun among MPSEA languages.

*Notes*: filled diamond: noun precedes modifier; white circle: modifier can precede or follow the noun; grey square: modifier precedes noun.

Indonesian

(29) a. [$_{NP}$ *Tiga-orang murid* ] *bermain di*
three-CLF student play OBL
*halaman.*
yard
'Three students are playing in the garden.'

b. [$_{NP}$ *Murid yang bermain di*
student REL play OBL
*halaman* ] *tiga(-orang).*
yard three-CLF
'The students playing in the garden were three.'
(Donohue, own knowledge)

Finally, a small class of verbs allows for numeral incorporation in the verb; in these constructions the serial verb takes the prefixes that show agreement with an S or A, as well as the suffixes that show agreement for P, as exemplified in (30a). Again, it is possible to code the numeral in an NP, as in (30b), but the numeral (and no other possible NP-internal modifiers) may appear in a 'higher' position.

Tukang Besi

(30) a. *No-tinti-totolu-ʔe.*
3-run-three-3
'The three of them ran.'

b. *No-tinti* [$_{NP}$ *na amai totolu* ].
3-run NOM 3PL three
'The three of them ran.'
(Donohue, fieldnotes)

The data from the three languages presented here, data which can be approximated in many other Austronesian languages, suggest that numerals are often afforded pragmatic and/or syntactic privileges that are not available to other potential NP-internal modifiers (cf. Donohue 2005b). Even when the numeral appears in a constituent with the noun, in many languages there is a position higher than the NP in which the numeral is the head, (31), consistent with a head-first syntax.

(31)

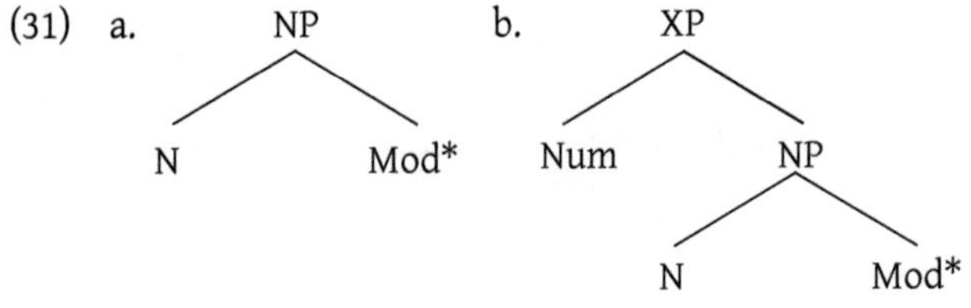


## 46.3.2 Genitives in the NP

Postnominal genitives are overwhelmingly common in Austronesian languages; the Indonesian example in (25c) is typical of many languages, as indicated in Maps 46.2 and 46.7 below. There are, however, languages in the east where we find prenominal genitives, as shown in the South Nuaulu examples in (32). The possessor in both alienable and inalienable possession constructions appears before the possessum, though the agreement on the possessum (in the inalienable construction) is by the suffix/enclitic *-te*, and not prefix, as seen in (32b). This misalignment between the order of a free genitive and the order of a bound genitive marker is common in the MPSEA languages west of New Guinea, where the conservative Austronesian N=GEN order is often found even when the nominal possessor precedes the possessum (see also Schapper and McConvell, this volume, chapter 48 on possession).

South Nuaulu

(32) a. *au we topi*
1SG 1SG.POSS hat
'my hat'

b. *puhaa nene*
crocodile 3SG.NHUM.POSS
*nesi-te*
tooth-3SG.NHUM.POSS
'the crocodile's teeth' (Bolton 1990: 124, 54)

In Palu'e the basic possessive structure is that seen in (33a). Example (33b) is a possibility that adds identification focus to the possessor by coding the possessor in a relative clause, which is postnominal and is marked by the use of the third person genitive, agreeing with *nua* 'house'. The structure seen in (33c) is attested, but only in the opening line of The Lord's Prayer as originally (poorly) translated from Indonesian/Malay without reference to Palu'e morphosyntax; a more felicitous rendering would be that shown in (33d), which matches (33a).

Palu'e

(33) a. *kami nua-gu*
1PL.EXCL house-1.GEN
'our house'

b. *nua kami-ne*
house 1PL.EXCL-3.GEN
'our house'
('the house which is our(s)')

c. *ama kami*
father 1PL.EXCL
'our father'

d. *ama kami-gu*
father 1PL.EXCL-1.GEN
'our father' (Donohue fieldnotes)

Prenominal genitives are possible in some of the MPSEA languages which have case marking, in what is better analysed as a (non-verbal) relative clause (the most 'basic' genitive construction is shown in (34a); compare the alternative in (34b) with the unambiguous relative clause in (34c), with which it shares the same structure). A more morphologically direct translation of (34b) would be 'the father who is mine'.

Tagalog

(34) a. *ang* *ama=ko*
NOM father=1SG.GEN
'my father'

b. *ang* *aki(n)-ng* *ama*
NOM 1SG.DAT-LNK father
'my father'

c. *ang* *nag-punta-ng* *tao*
NOM AV-go-LNK person
'the person who went' (Donohue, own knowledge)

See Schapper and McConvell, this volume, §48.2 for more discussion on the order of possessor and possessum and §48.5 for marked constructions in which the basic order of the possessor and possessum are reversed.

## 46.4 Word order in questions

The order of elements in both content questions and polar questions show areal patterns amongst the MPSEA languages. Approximately one quarter of languages show word orders like English, in which the questioned element is exceptionally placed initially in the clause, as shown in the contrast between the verb–object order in the statement *You ate a banana*, and the initial interrogative phrase in *What did you eat?* (Dryer 2013k). Amongst verb-initial languages the proportion is reversed, with only one quarter of these languages not displaying initial questioned elements. Since verb-initial orders are found in numerous MPSEA languages, we can expect to see this as a significant areal variable. With polar questions, which elicit a yes or no answer, the most common morphosyntactic strategy globally is to employ a question particle with a sentence that is otherwise identical to the equivalent statement, as if *You ate a banana, hey?* was the only way to code a question in English, employing *hey* as a sentence-final question particle Dryer 2013j; see also Zwicky 1985; Bailey 2013; Metslang et al. 2017).

In this section we examine the occurrence of question particles in the MPSEA languages, and the occurrence of the fronting of interrogative phrases in content questions, as well as discussing the correlation between these two strategies.

### 46.4.1 Order of polar question particles

Question particles are found in most of the MPSEA languages, with the exclusion of the languages near New Guinea. A mixture of second position and clause-initial question particles are common in the Philippines and western Island Southeast Asia (plus Malagasy, which originates in western Island Southeast Asia), exemplified in (35)–(39), with clause-final particles found in the Malayic and Chamic languages on Mainland Southeast Asia, as illustrated in the Jarai sentence in (38), and sporadically in languages spoken east of Lombok, such as Tetun in (39).[2]

Indonesian: clause-initial

(35) ***Apakah*** *dia* *belum* *tiba?*
Q 3SG not.yet arrive
'Hasn't she arrived?' (Donohue, own knowledge)

Tagalog: second position

(36) *Hindi* ***ba*** *siya* *dumating?*
not Q 2SG.NOM has.arrived
'Hasn't she arrived?' (Donohue, own knowledge)

Malagasy: second position

(37) *Miasa-loha* ***ve*** *i* *Soa?*
work-head Q ART Soa
'Is Soa preoccupied?' (Keenan 2008: 29)

Jarai: clause-final

(38) *Je* *pioh* *asơi* *ɓơi* *kơɓang* *hă?*
Je put cooked.rice on table Q
'Did Je put the rice on the table?' (Jensen 2014: 114)

Tetun: clause-final

(39) *ó* *la* *bá* *sekola* ***ká?***
2SG not go school Q
'Didn't you go to school?' (van Klinken 1999: 212)

The distribution of these different types is shown in Map 46.8; geographically the second-position particles are a subset of the clause-initial clitics, and both are good candidates for the original position of question particles in Austronesian languages. To the southwest of New Guinea and Cenderawasih Bay both clause-initial and clause-final particles are found, with the second of these orders clearly an extension of an areal norm found in much of lowland New Guinea. Similarly, clause-final particles are found in the languages of mainland Asia, and Hainan, which are in contact with Tibeto-Burman, Tai-Kadai, and Austroasiatic languages that show a similar word order. Based on their distribution, second position question particles appear to be the original Austronesian construction, being found on Taiwan and preserved through most of northern and western Island Southeast Asia, and as far east as Sulawesi, while the clause-initial pattern has a south(-west)ern origin. Clause-final particles originate in both Southeast Asia and in both

[2] In Malaysian, spoken on mainland Asia, a sentence-final *-kah* is also possible. An alternative to (42) would be *Dia belum tiba-kah?*

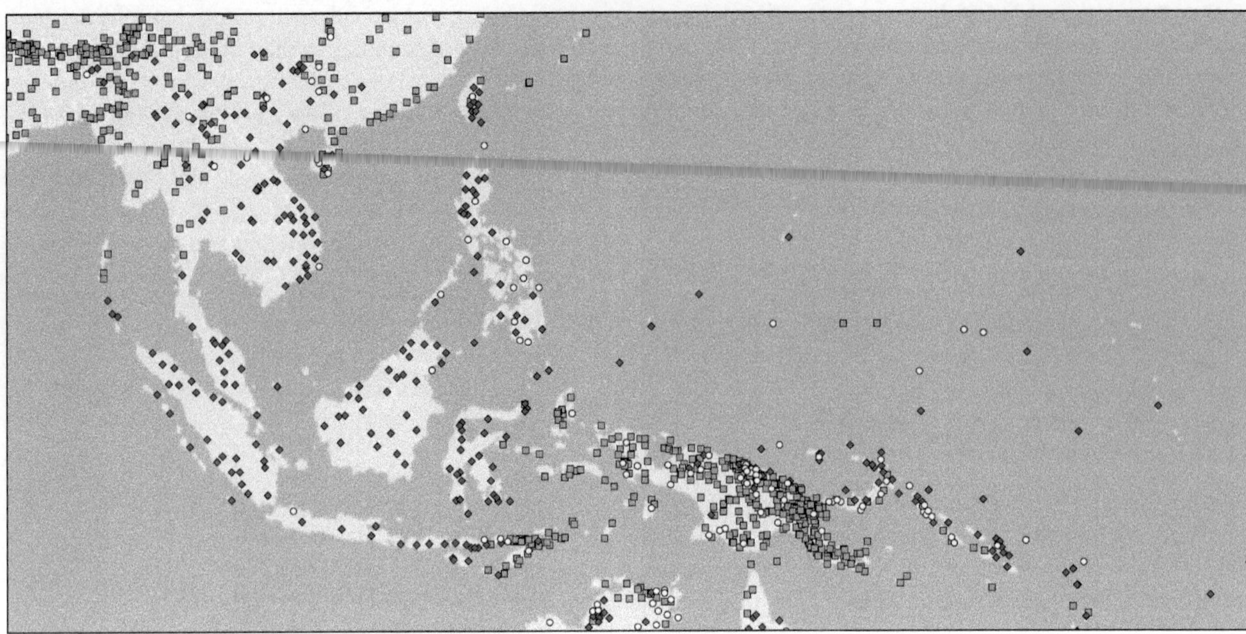

**Map 46.7** Order of genitive and noun.

*Notes*: filled diamond: noun precedes modifier; white circle: modifier can precede or follow the noun; grey square: modifier precedes noun.

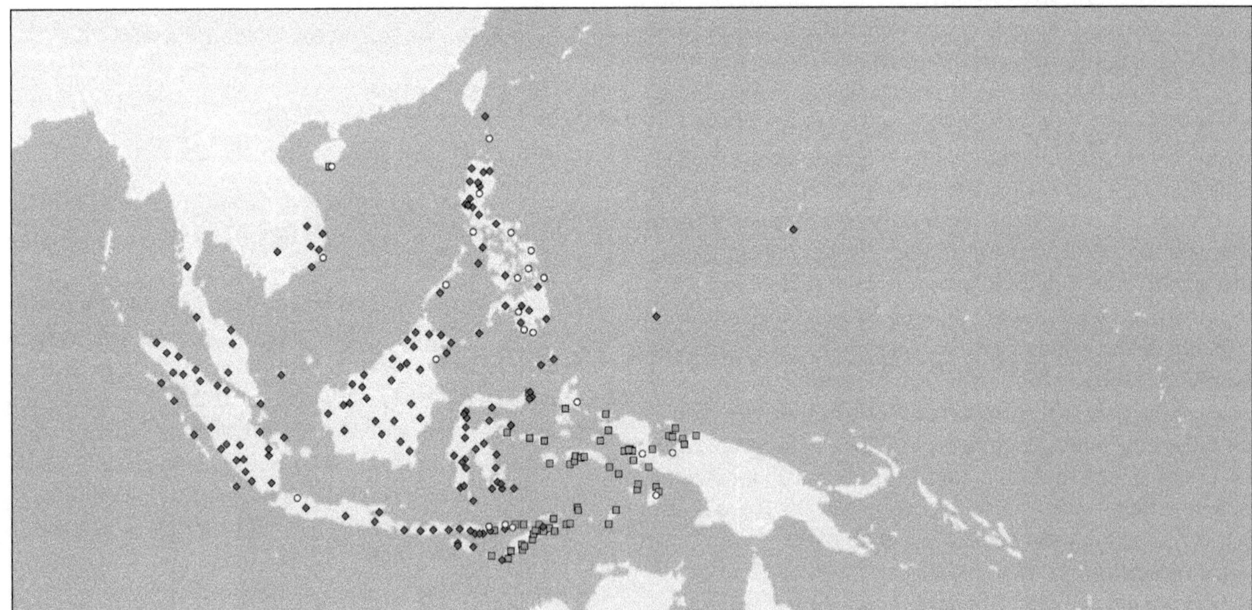

**Map 46.7'** Order of genitive and noun among MPSEA languages.

*Notes*: filled diamond: noun precedes modifier; white circle: modifier can precede or follow the noun; grey square: modifier precedes noun.

northwestern and eastern New Guinea, and they are found in many of the eastern MPSEA languages.

### 46.4.2 Order of questioned element in content questions

Globally the most common treatment of a questioned element in a content question is to have the question phrase appear in the position normally occupied by a participant with that particular grammatical function; the strategy of having the questioned element appearing initially, as in English and other northwestern European languages, is rare. Amongst verb-initial languages, however, it is much more frequent, and so we can expect it to be found as a strategy in many of the (verb-initial) MPSEA languages. Map 46.9 shows the position of question words in the languages of the region; initial content question words are the norm in the northern and southwestern languages of Island Southeast Asia, with the southwestern languages showing variability. Northern Island Southeast Asian languages, such as Tagalog in (40a–f), only allow initial content question words, in structures which have attracted much discussion (for example, see Dahl 1986; Paul 2001; Sabel 2002; Potsdam 2006b; Law 2007, and others). The initial content questions in (40a) and (40d) are in contrast to the post-verbal arguments seen in (40c) and (40f), which represent pragmatically unmarked statements; as seen in (40b) and (40e), the content question words cannot appear in post-verbal positions.

Tagalog

(40) a. *Ano ang k<in>ain-niya?*
what NOM eat<PV>-3SG.GEN
'What did she eat?' ('What she ate is what?'?)

b. * *k<in>ain-niya (ang) ano?*
eat<PV>-3SG.GEN NOM what

c. *K<in>ain-niya ang saging.*
eat<PV>-3SG.GEN NOM banana
'She ate the banana.'

d. *Sino ang k<um>ain?*
who NOM eat<AV>
'Who ate?'

e. * *k<um>ain sino?*
eat<AV> who

f. *K<um>ain siya.*
eat<AV> 3SG.NOM
'She ate.' (Donohue, own knowledge)

In verb-initial Tukang Besi (Donohue 1999) there are two possible positions for content question words depending on their grammatical function. A content question words with any syntactic function may appear *in situ*, as seen in (41a–c), unless the NP questioned is a subject (41d). Subjects may only be questioned in clause-initial position, using pseudo-cleft constructions (41e); a clause-initial construction is possible for any content question, though it is unusual for obliques or adjuncts, and requires a nominalized verb (41f–h).

Tukang Besi

(41) a. *ʔu-manga* ***te paira****?*
2SG-eat CORE what
'What are you eating?'

b. *No-manga-ʔe* ***te emai****?*
3-eat-3 CORE who
'Who is eating it?'

c. *ʔu-manga te kaujawa* ***di ʔumpa****?*
2SG-eat CORE cassava OBL.R which
'Where did you eat cassava?'

d. * *no-rato na emai?*
3-fetch NOM who
'Who arrived?'

e. ***Te emai*** *na r<um>ato?*
CORE who NOM arrive<SI>
'Who arrived?'

f. ***Te paira*** *na i-manga-ʔu?*
CORE what NOM P.PTCP-eat-2SG.GEN
'What are you eating?'

g. ***Te emai*** *na <m>anga?*
CORE who NOM eat<SI>
'Who is eating it?'

h. # ***Di ʔumpa*** *na manga-ʔa-(ʔ)u nu kaujawa?*
CORE who NOM eat-NMLZ-2SG.GEN GEN cassava
'Who is eating it?' (Donohue, own knowledge)

The languages of southeast MPSEA do not generally show fronting with content question words. C. Grimes (1991) states that "the queried argument occurs in its normal position" in Buru (42). This means that a queried subject will occur initially in SVO Buru, but this is not the same as the exceptional clause-initial position seen in Tagalog and Tukang Besi, since we expect the subject to be found in this position.

Buru

(42) a. *Sane tuke kepeng la nang ina?*
who give money DAT 1SG.POSS mother
'Who gave money to my mother?'

b. *Sira flal-mata-k sane pa fena dii?*
3PL beat-die-APPL who down village DIST
'Who did they beat to death down at that village?' (C. Grimes 1991: 456)

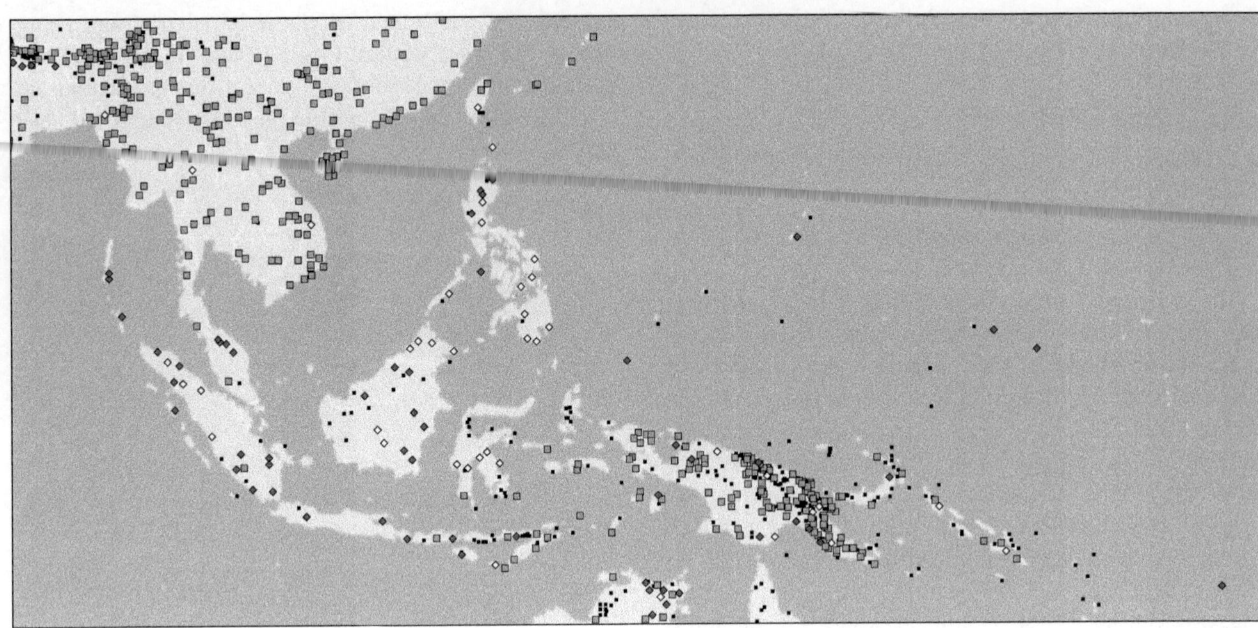

**Map 46.8** Position of polar question particles.

*Notes*: small black square: no question particles; grey square: final question particles; filled diamond: initial question particles; white diamond: second-position question particles.

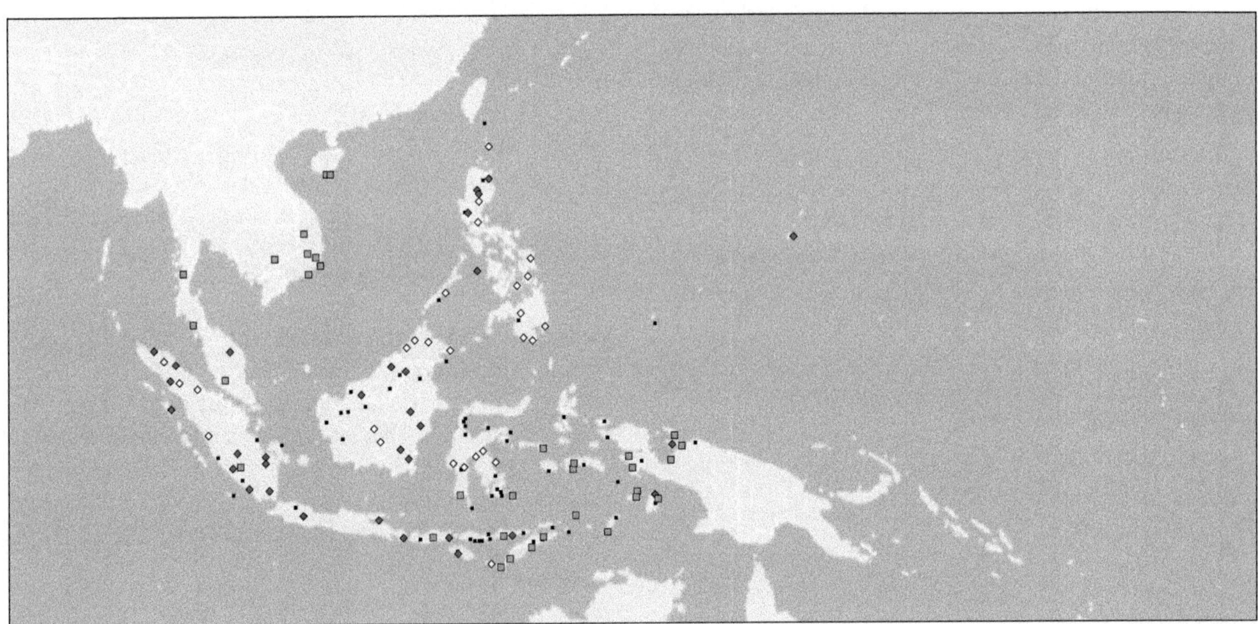

**Map 46.8'** Position of polar question particles among MPSEA languages.

*Notes*: small black square: no question particles; grey square: final question particles; filled diamond: initial question particles; white diamond: second-position question particles.

There is a strong correlation between a language having a clause-initial or second-position polar question particle, and the language having sentence-initial content questions; Rejang is one such language with both clause initial question words and polar question particles (43).

Rejang
(43) a. ***Jano*** *tun* *o* *camat?*
Q person that district.head
'Is he the district head?'

b. ***Moy*** ***ipe*** *si* *loq* *lalaw?*
to which 3SG want go
'Where does he want to go?'
(Syahrul Napsin et al. 1980/1981: 106, 107)

Comparing Maps 46.8 and 46.9 we can see that sentence-initial content question constructions extend further east than the non-final particles. There is an outpost of clause-initial content question constructions in the south-east of Mainland Southeast Asia, but these constructions do not persist close to New Guinea.

## 46.5 Order of negator in standard negation

Details of negation in the MPSEA languages are discussed in van der Auwera, Van Olmen, and Vossen, this volume, chapter 50; in this section we simply examine the word orders associated with negation. Three major patterns are found for the position of negators in MPSEA languages. None of these patterns involve affixal negation, such as is common in many languages of New Guinea, and only one language (Palauan; see Zobel, this volume, §39.7.6.2) has negative auxiliary verbs, which are found in many Oceanic languages. In the MPSEA languages the position of the negative particle is most commonly preverbal; in languages with verb-initial clausal word order this means that the negator will be clause-initial.

- Clause-initial 41%
- Pre-verbal 45%
  double: pre-verbal + clause-final 8%
- Clause-final 6%

Although clause-initial and pre-verbal negation strategies correlate closely with verb-initial vs. SVO constituent order, there are differences. Tukang Besi is a verb-initial language of Southeast Sulawesi, and we can see in (44c), reflecting the facts that we saw in (10), that it allows pre-verbal arguments in the right pragmatic circumstances. Even when there is a preverbal argument, the negator must still appear in absolute clause-initial position, as can be seen in (44b) and the contrast between (44d) and (44e) (a sentence-initial topic, on the other hand, will precede the negator).

Tukang Besi
(44) a. *No-wini* *te* *ika.*
3-reel.in CORE fish
'They caught fish.'

b. ***Mbeaka*** *no-wini* *te* *ika.*
NEG 3-reel.in CORE fish
'They didn't catch fish.'

c. *Te* *ika* *no-wini-ʔe.*
CORE fish 3-reel.in-3
'They caught the fish.'

d. ***Mbeaka*** *te* *ika* *no-wini-ʔe.*
NEG CORE fish 3-reel.in-3
'They didn't catch the fish.'

e. **te* *ika* ***mbeaka*** *no-wini-ʔe*
CORE fish NEG 3-reel.in-3
'They didn't catch the fish.'
(Donohue, own knowledge)

Palu'e has SVO order and pre-verbal negation, and allows for a pre-verbal P, (45a)–(45c). The sentences in (45d) and (45e) show that the negator is consistently pre-verbal, though in Palu'e it can be shown (Donohue 2005c) that clauses such as (45b) are syntactically passive, and not just word order variants.

Palu'e
(45) a. *Kami* *phote* *nio.*
1PL.EXCL pick coconut
'We picked coconuts.'

b. *Nio* *kami* *phote*
coconut 1PL.EXCL pick
'The coconuts were picked by us.'

c. *Kami* ***kaʔa*** *phote* *nio.*
1PL.EXCL NEG pick coconut
'We didn't pick coconuts.'

d. *Nio* *kami* ***kaʔa*** *phote.*
coconut 1PL.EXCL NEG pick
'The coconuts were not picked by us.'

e. * ***kaʔa*** *nio* *kami* *phote*
NEG coconut 1PL.EXCL pick
'The coconuts were not picked by us.'
(Donohue fieldnotes)

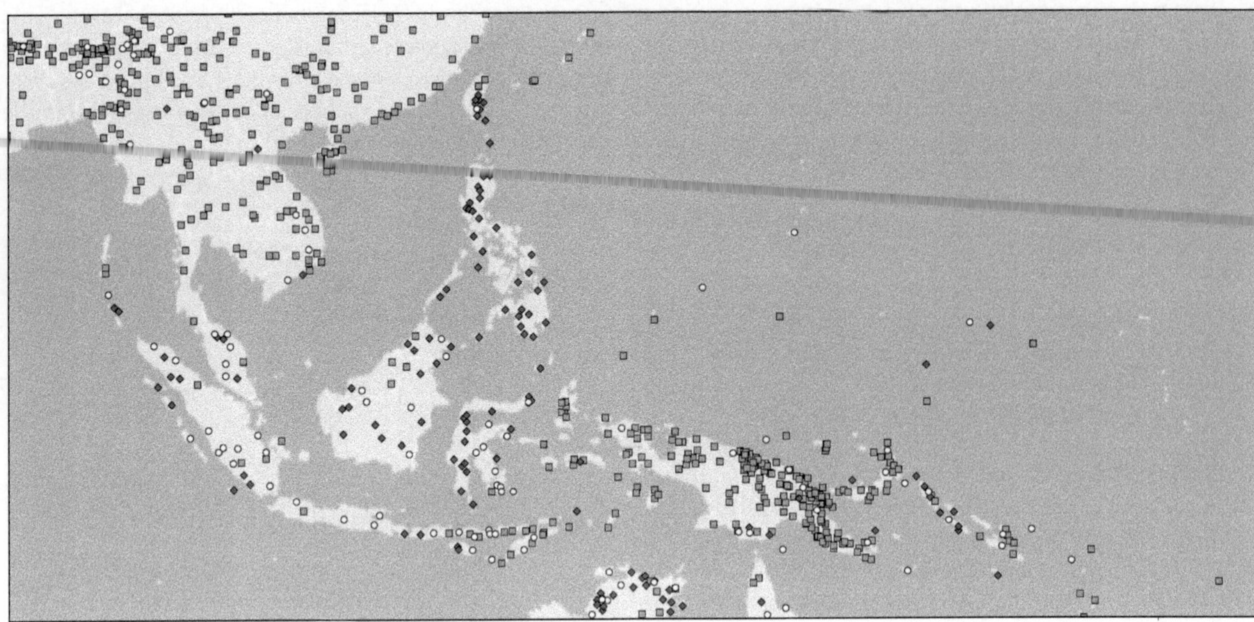

**Map 46.9** Position of content question words.

*Notes*: grey squares: content question words in situ; filled diamond: content question words in initial position; white circles: content question words either in situ or in initial position.

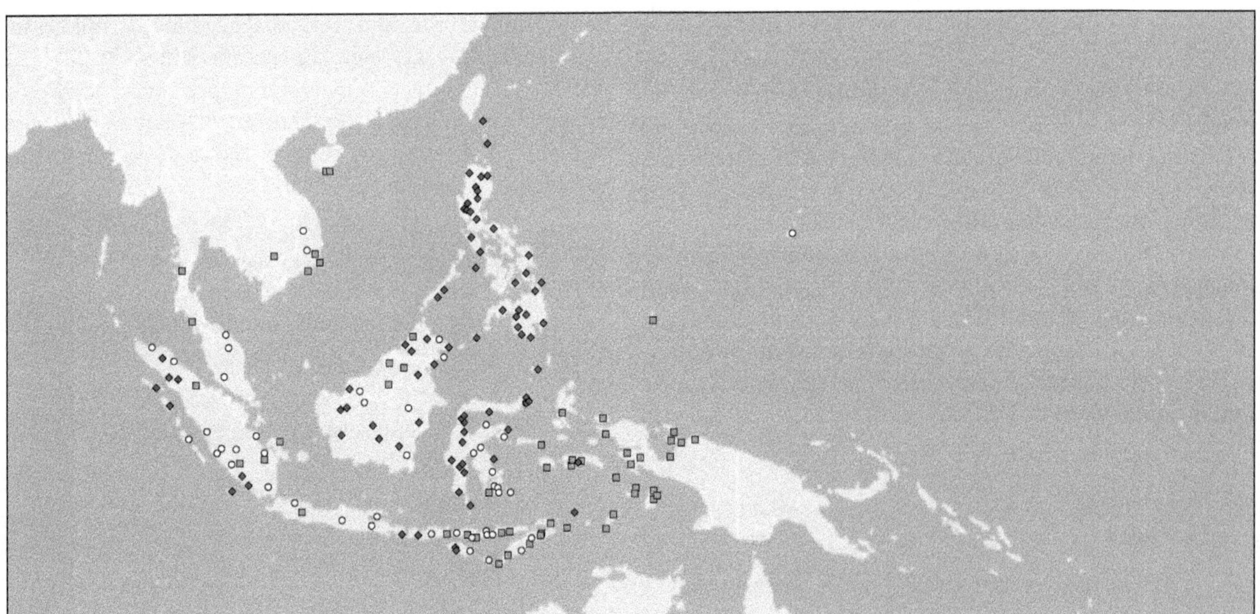

**Map 46.9'** Position of content question words among MPSEA languages.

*Notes*: grey squares: content question words in situ; filled diamond: content question words in initial position; white circles: content question words either in situ or in initial position.

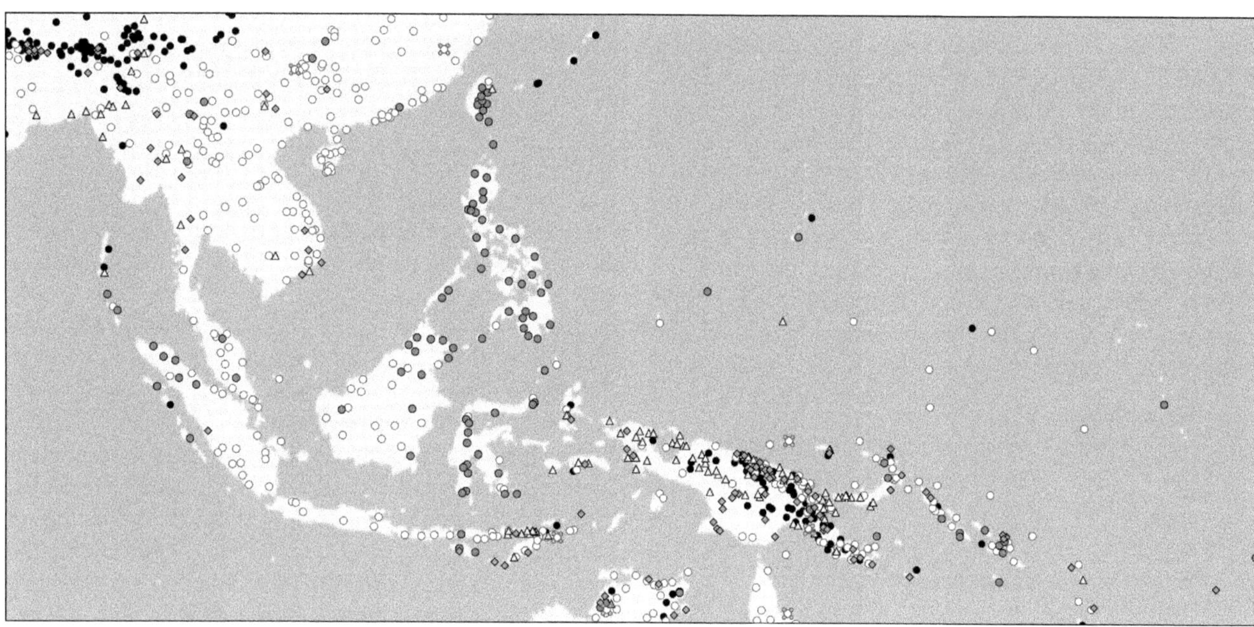

**Map 46.10** Position of negative particles.

*Notes*: white circle: preverbal negation; filled grey circle: clause-initial negation; triangle: clause-final negation; diamond: double negation; black circle: affixal negation.

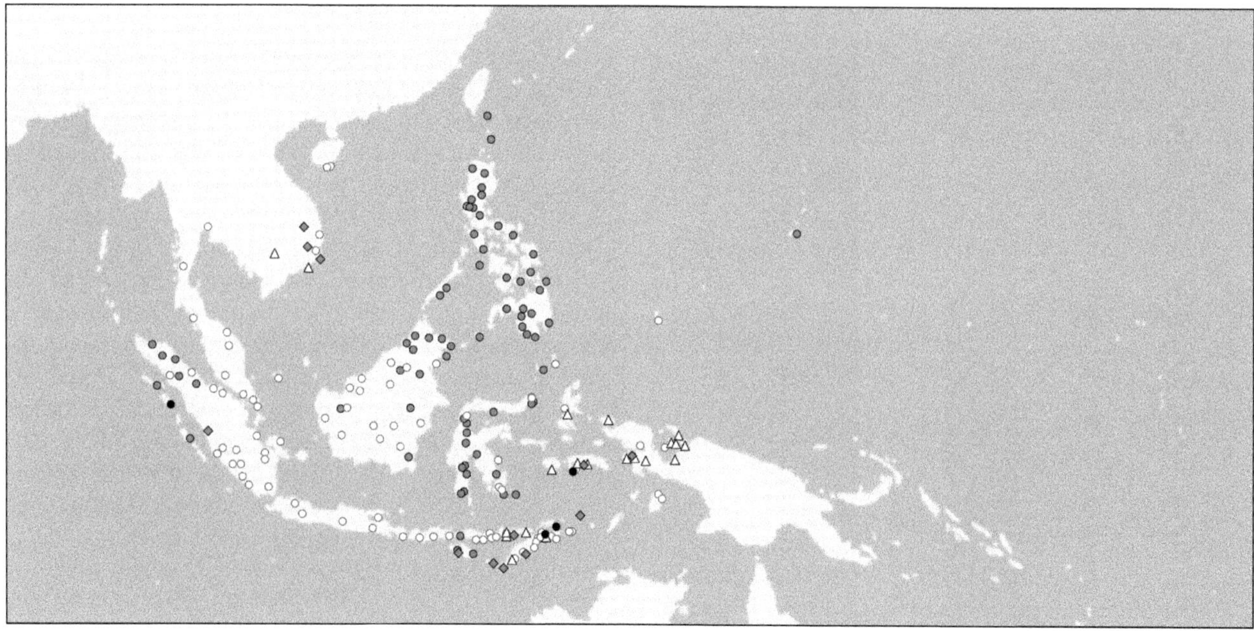

**Map 46.10'** Position of negative particles among MPSEA languages.

*Notes*: white circle: preverbal negation; filled grey circle: clause-initial negation; triangle: clause-final negation; diamond: double negation; black circle: affixal negation.

The other major pattern that we find is clause-final negation, such as in South Nuaulu (46). This is found with a number of SVO languages of eastern Indonesia, and represents the effect of influence from head-final languages on the clausal syntax of the Austronesian languages of the area (a similar position is used with non-Austronesian languages of western New Guinea, regardless of whether they are SVO or verb-final. Other MPSEA languages with final negation include Western Cham (Mainland Southeast Asia), Helong, Solor Lamaholot (Nusa Tenggara), Alune, Buru, Taba (Maluku), Ambai, Biak, Wooi (Cenderawasih Bay), and Irarutu, Onin (Bomberai).

South Nuaulu

(46) *Ne* *munata* *i-amanaku* ***tewa***, *au* *tentene*
but if 3SG-agree NEG 1SG force
***tewa***.
NEG
'But if she doesn't agree, I won't force her.'
(Bolton 1990: 126)

An additional pattern is found in a small number of languages on the western Island Southeast Asian periphery, and near Timor, in which clause-final negation is combined with preverbal negation, shown in Jarai from Mainland Southeast Asia in (47), and Dadu'a from northern Timor in (48). In some of the languages of Timor (Tugun, Dadu'a) we see prefixed negation on the verb, which can combine with clause-final negation to result in a double negative structure (see §35.6 for more examples). Other MPSEA languages with double negation patterns include Bih, Jarai, Minangkabau (western MPSEA), and Amarasi, Atadei, Dhao, Hawu (Timor area).

Phan Rang Cham

(47) *Plɔ̆h* *ɲu* ***oh*** *khin* *pà* *təkhəʔ* *tuy*
after 3SG NEG dare take shoe follow
*tra* ***o***.
again NEG
'After that she didn't dare take the (other) shoe with her anymore.' (Thurgood 2005: 504)

Dadu'a

(48) *Aʔu* ***ta****-woʔuk* ***ene***.
1SG NEG-lift NEG
'I didn't take them.' (Penn 2006: 67)

Map 46.10 shows the distribution of different negation patterns. Clause-final negation is also found in the islands west of New Guinea, to an extent not delimited by linguistic subgroups. Clause-initial negation strongly correlates with verb-initial order in the clause, and preverbal negation is a pattern found away from the periphery of southwest Island Southeast Asia, suggesting that the clause-initial pattern, preserved on the periphery of the range, was original.

## 46.6 Summary

The word order patterns we have discussed in this chapter show considerable variation across the MPSEA languages, with both north to south and west to east clines clearly apparent. With a verb-initial origin in Taiwan, we saw the retention of this option southwards in the centre through Philippines, Borneo, and Sulawesi, and also in the far west near the Austroasiatic languages which preserve verb-initial orders; the same regions, approximately, require content questions, and negative particles to be initial in the clause. Verb-medial orders dominate most of the southern range of Island Southeast Asia, reflecting the same preferences in the unrelated languages both to the west and the east (Donohue 2007). While the conservative order in the clause is preserved in a solid block in the south, the order of elements in the noun phrase is rarely preserved south of the Philippines, with the exception of genitives and numerals, which remain prenominal in the southwest, matching the norms in coastal mainland Asia. Genitives only appear prenominally in the southeast, showing the same modal order as is found in the non-Austronesian languages of eastern Indonesia and New Guinea, approximately the same area in which numerals follow the modified noun. Question particles are initial in the west, and final in the east, with a scattering of second-position particles down the middle. The final question particles in the east reflect both global norms, and the norms found in New Guinea, and their range roughly coincides with the appearance of clause-final negation.

The evidence from a study of word order in the MPSEA languages is that the Austronesianization of Island Southeast Asia was not a 'steamroller' event, as it has sometimes been portrayed, but that the morphosyntactic traits that are found in the north are only strongly preserved in the immediate south (Borneo/Sulawesi), and on the edges of the 'western Malayo-Polynesian' region (Sumatra/Micronesia, where early contact with speakers of non-Austronesian languages would have been with other verb-initial languages (Sumatra) or absent (Micronesia)). The south sees a number of word order traits that are not predicted from the typological profiles of the languages of the Philippines or Taiwan; it is easy to spot the extensive diffusion of mainland New Guinea traits into the islands west, but there is an equally dramatic assimilation of traits from Mainland Southeast Asia to the islands to its southeast.

CHAPTER 47

# Voice and transitivity

PAUL KROEGER AND SONJA RIESBERG

## 47.1 Introduction

This chapter explores the remarkable variety of voice systems attested among the Malayo-Polynesian languages of Southeast Asia (henceforth "MPSEA" languages). We understand the term VOICE to refer to a productive alternation that changes the identity of the grammatical subject but does not, in general, change the basic meaning of the clause, including the number and semantic roles of the arguments. A very similar definition is adopted by Shibatani (1988: 3): "Voice is . . . a mechanism that selects a grammatically prominent syntactic constituent — subject — from the underlying semantic functions (. . . thematic roles) of a clause."[1]

Identifying the semantic role of each argument (who did what to whom?) is critical for accurate communication of the speaker's intended meaning. Cross-linguistically three basic coding devices are available for indicating the role of each argument: case marking, agreement, and word order. However, apart from the semantically restricted case marking of oblique arguments in some languages, these three devices generally encode not semantic role but grammatical relation. Semantic roles are indicated indirectly, by way of the association (or 'linking') of semantic roles to grammatical relations. Voice, as Shibatani states, determines the semantic role associated with one particular grammatical relation, namely the subject.[2]

Partial correlations are also well documented between grammatical relations and discourse functions, in particular the widespread correlation between subject and topic. However, these correlations exhibit more language-specific variation than is commonly realized. This is true in particular for a number of MPSEA languages, in which agents are highly topical even though they are frequently not selected as subject. In this chapter we focus on grammatical and morphological aspects of voice systems and, to a lesser extent, applicativization pertaining to MPSEA languages. The interaction of voice and applicativization with the coding devices mentioned above (case marking, agreement, and word order) is an important part of this study.

The most common voice pattern cross-linguistically is the active–passive alternation, followed by the ergative–antipassive alternation.[3] Both of these alternations involve the selection of a new subject via the demotion of the basic or underlying subject (agent in the case of the passive, patient in the case of the antipassive). Both passive and antipassive are thus detransitivizing operations, because they reduce the number of core arguments in a basic transitive clause from two to one, changing transitive clauses into intransitive clauses.

Voice is a topic of recurring and ongoing controversy in Austronesian linguistics, because a substantial number of western Austronesian languages exhibit voice alternations which are not easily analysed as either passive or antipassive. (The term "western Austronesian" here refers to all Austronesian languages excluding those in eastern Indonesia, Timor Leste and the Pacific). In many of these languages there is little evidence of syntactic demotion or detransitivization; rather, the voice alternation seems to license two (or more) syntactically transitive clause patterns. A voice system of this type can be referred to as non-demoting or SYMMETRICAL.[4]

The concept of non-demoting voice alternations has proved challenging for both formal syntactic theories and typological-descriptive frameworks (see Chen and McDonnell 2019 for a recent overview and for arguments against a

[1] This definition is fairly restrictive as compared to that of Kulikov (2010), who (like a number of other authors) uses the term 'voice' to include any change in the mapping from semantic roles to grammatical relations.

[2] Applicative constructions may determine the semantic role of another grammatical relation, namely the primary object.

[3] There is some disagreement as to whether the antipassive counts as a voice alternation under our definition, because identifying the grammatical subject in ergative languages remains controversial. We follow Doron (2015) in assuming that for at least some ergative languages, the antipassive promotes the agent to surface subject position.

[4] Foley was the first to argue that symmetrical voice languages constitute "a distinct syntactic type" (2008: 42) in addition to accusative and ergative systems (cf. also Foley 1998; Himmelmann 2005a).

Paul Kroeger and Sonja Riesberg, *Voice and transitivity.* In: *The Oxford Guide to the Malayo-Polynesian Languages of Southeast Asia.* Edited by: Alexander Adelaar and Antoinette Schapper, Oxford University Press. © Paul Kroeger and Sonja Riesberg (2024). DOI: 10.1093/oso/9780198807353.003.0047

valency-changing approach to western Austronesian voice). Our goal in this chapter is not to develop a new analysis for such languages, but rather (i) to describe a representative sample of the Western and Central Malayo-Polynesian voice systems, and (ii) to summarize the major analytic approaches that have been proposed for these systems. The crucial empirical questions to be answered will be: (i) What is the grammatical subject for a particular clause type? and (ii) How do we distinguish core arguments from obliques?

The latter question, which is critical to the identification of non-demoting voice alternations, leads us to address certain issues related to syntactic valency, or transitivity. We define a syntactically transitive clause as one that contains two or more CORE (non-oblique) arguments. A significant number of Malayo-Polynesian languages have applicative affixes which increase syntactic transitivity by introducing a new primary object. The existence of applicative affixes is a key diagnostic in the traditional distinction between 'Indonesian-type' languages (in which applicatives are distinct from, and co-occur with, voice-marking affixes) vs. 'Philippine-type' languages (in which a putative distinction between applicatives and voice-markers remains controversial; see discussion in §47.2.2.3).

The remainder of this chapter is organized as follows. §47.2 provides an overview of some foundational issues. We begin by discussing the distinction just mentioned, between 'Philippine-type' vs. 'Indonesian-type' languages. We then consider in more detail what a symmetrical voice alternation looks like, and what evidence is required to support such an analysis. A defining property of a symmetrical system is that it includes at least two equally basic transitive voices. As noted in the preceding paragraph, we adopt a strictly syntactic definition of transitivity: a clause is transitive if it contains two or more core arguments, and the distinction between core vs. oblique arguments is based on syntactic properties. We then discuss the interaction of applicative affixes, which serve to increase the transitivity of a clause, with voice systems.

§47.3 discusses the typologically unique Philippine-type voice pattern and presents a summary of the various analyses that have been proposed to account for its special properties. §47.4 discusses the voice systems of two large, central Indonesian islands: Borneo and Sulawesi. In both islands we find Philippine-type systems in the far north and something closer to an 'Indonesian-type' in the south, with transitional patterns in between.

§47.5 discusses a similar cline along the east–west axis, from the core 'Indonesian-type' languages of western Indonesia to the languages of eastern Indonesia where voice is severely reduced or even non-existent. §47.6 discusses the voice systems of two languages of Micronesia, Chamorro, and Palauan, which preserve some features of Western Malayo-Polynesian voice.

## 47.2 Typology of Malayo-Polynesian voice systems

### 47.2.1 Traditional classification

Himmelmann (2002a: 8) notes that "it is common in the literature to assume a fairly rough and hardly ever explicitly discussed division of western Austronesian languages into the following two types: Philippine type languages and the rest (occasionally also called Indonesian-type languages)." He describes the most commonly cited criteria for distinguishing these two types as follows (footnotes omitted):

> [T]he presence of both pronominal prefixes and applicative suffixes is held to be the crucial characteristic that distinguishes Philippine-type languages from Indonesian-type languages. And while it appears to be true that none of the generally recognised Philippine-type languages exhibits both these features, it is not true that the languages of western Indonesia all exhibit both of them. Thus, for example, there are no pronominal prefixes or proclitics in Balinese. . .
> (Himmelmann 2002b: 139)

In later work, Himmelmann (2005a: 113) offers the following criteria for identifying Philippine-type languages. On the basis of these criteria, he excludes Malagasy, Chamorro, and a number of other languages which various other authors had previously identified as Philippine-type languages:

> Philippine-type languages are symmetrical voice languages which have:
>
> a) at least two formally and semantically different undergoer voices...
> b) at least one non-local [i.e. non-locative, PK&SR] phrase marking clitic for nominal expressions...
> c) pronominal second position clitics.

As detailed descriptions of more languages have become available, it is increasingly clear that many of the Malayo-Polynesian languages of Southeast Asia do not fit particularly well into either of these two classes. For the purposes of the current chapter our primary interest is with the classification of voice systems, rather than languages, but the two issues are closely related. The widely shared notion of a Philippine-type voice system is useful, if viewed as a prototype concept, even though the exact boundaries of this class are disputed and somewhat vague. The most common basis for identifying a voice system as belonging to this class is the presence of multiple (at least three, but usually four or more) contrastive voice categories. However, the term 'Philippine-type' usually also implies something about the special, non-demoting nature of the voice alternation, often indicated (especially in earlier work) by the use of the term 'focus' rather than voice (see §47.3.1 below). There is general agreement that such voice systems are found not only in the Philippines but also in certain languages of northeastern Borneo and northern Sulawesi, as well as some Formosan languages.

It is much harder to define an Indonesian-type voice system, for the same reasons that it is difficult to define an Indonesian-type language. As Himmelmann (2005a) points out, the presence of applicative suffixes is widely assumed as a defining feature of this class. A number of authors (e.g. Wolff 1996) have observed that Indonesian-type applicative suffixes provide information similar to that provided by Philippine-type voice affixes. This observation has led some authors (e.g. Pawley and Reid 1979; and Starosta, Pawley, and Reid 1982), to refer to the Indonesian-type system as "object-focus", and to the Philippine-type system as "subject-focus".

Another common assumption has been that Indonesian-type voice systems involve just two distinctive voice categories, in contrast to the richer Philippine-type inventories. However, it appears that languages with a two-way voice contrast plus applicative suffixes are not as common in western Austronesian as is often assumed. Toba Batak (Schachter 1984), Madurese (Davies 2010), and Sundanese (Kurniawan 2013) seem to be well documented examples, but a number of other western Indonesian languages actually have three distinct voices, as discussed in the following section. Many languages of central Borneo have a two-way voice contrast but no applicatives. Many eastern Indonesian languages do not have any voice morphology (Arka and Wouk 2014); some of these have a passive construction marked by word order alone, while others have no voice alternations at all.

While these labels are useful for certain purposes, the simple two-way classification of languages as either Philippine-type or Indonesian-type ignores the striking degree of diversity which is found among western Austronesian voice systems. As we show in the rest of this chapter, the range of voice patterns attested within this single language family is unusually rich and varied. Additional variations will undoubtedly be discovered as more research is devoted to thus far undocumented languages of the region.

### 47.2.2 Symmetrical voice

As stated above, symmetrical voice alternations involve alternations in the choice of grammatical subject without demoting either the actor or the undergoer to oblique status, producing an opposition between two (or more) transitive clause types. One of the clearest and best-documented examples of symmetrical voice comes from Balinese, as described by Wechsler and Arka (1998) and Arka (2003a). These authors demonstrate that Balinese distinguishes three voice categories: undergoer voice (UV), marked by *Ø-* (see discussion immediately below); actor voice (AV) marked by *N-*; and a true passive construction.

Balinese (high register)

(1) a. *Bawi-ne punika Ø-tumbas tiang.*
pig-DEF that UV-buy 1SG
'I bought the pig.'

b. *Tiang numbas bawi-ne punika.*
1SG AV:buy pig-DEF that
'I bought the pig.'

c. *Buku-ne ka-ambil (antuk i guru).*
book-DEF PASS-take by ART teacher
'The book has been taken (by the teacher).'
(Wechsler and Arka 1998: 388, 429)

A number of authors (e.g. Foley 1998; Himmelmann 2005a; Riesberg 2014) have adopted the position that in a symmetrical voice system, the verb is morphologically marked in all voices (i.e. that there is no unmarked voice category). Under this view, it is not clear that Balinese should be considered a symmetrical voice language, since UV seems to be unmarked. However, Arka (2003a, 2009b) argues that the UV form is zero-marked, and not just a bare stem:

> A zero prefix has no phonological material but is considered present on the basis of functional and paradigmatic opposition in a particular grammatical system... The bare form *palu* [(2)b] is used to express the undergoer voice (UV) in Balinese. It can be analysed as having a zero prefix, represented by *Ø-*, on the basis of systematic formal opposition with the other forms in [(2)].

Balinese

(2) a. *m-(p)alu* (<*N-palu*) 'AV-collide'
b. *Ø-palu* 'UV-collide'
c. *ka-palu* 'PASS-collide'
d. *ma-palu* 'MID-collide' (Arka 2009b: 247)

The distinction between unmarked vs. zero-marked forms is controversial but not crucial to the central concerns of this chapter. For current purposes, to distinguish symmetrical vs. asymmetrical voice alternations, we will depend primarily on the syntactic properties of the arguments in the different voice constructions. An alternation will be considered to be symmetrical if the relevant voice categories are all syntactically transitive, but select different arguments as grammatical subject.

In Balinese, the agent is the subject of an AV clause, while the patient is the subject in UV and passive clauses. Evidence for this identification is based on the subjecthood properties listed in (3). Evidence for the claim that both AV and UV are fully transitive comes from the fact that UV actors and AV undergoers share certain properties, listed in (4), which distinguish adjuncts and oblique arguments from core arguments.

**Subject properties in Balinese:**

(3) a. Only subjects can precede the verb in canonical, pragmatically unmarked word-order; all other arguments follow the verb.

b. Only subjects can be relativized using the gap strategy (although possessors of subjects can also be relativized using a resumptive pronoun strategy).

c. Only subjects can be raised in either the Raising to Subject or Raising to Object constructions.

d. Only subjects can be 'controllees', i.e., targets of 'Equi-NP deletion'.

e. Among the core (NP) arguments, only subjects can be extraposed to sentence-final position.

f. Only subjects can occur in the initial focus position marked with *anak*.

g. *Wh*-fronting applies only to question words that are subjects; non-subject question words remain *in situ*.

**Core-argument properties in Balinese:**

(4) a. Core arguments are expressed as NPs, while oblique arguments are expressed as PPs.

b. 'Floating quantifiers' can only be launched by core arguments.

c. Core arguments and possessors of core arguments can be topicalized, but obliques and possessors of obliques cannot. (The resumptive pronoun is obligatory when possessors are topicalized.)

d. Core arguments (but not oblique arguments) can be modified by certain predicative adjuncts, often referred to as 'depictive secondary predicates'.[5]

e. The addressee/agent of an imperative clause must be a core argument. A passive verb may not function as an imperative, unlike Malay/Indonesian where the passive is often used in polite or softened imperatives.

Recent work on Malay/Indonesian syntax (Guilfoyle, Hung, and Travis 1992; Arka and Manning 2008; Musgrave 2001; Arka 2003a, 2009b; Cole, Hermon, and Yanti 2008) has argued for the same three voice categories as Balinese: a symmetrical alternation between AV and UV, plus a true passive. Similar analyses have been proposed for Acehnese (Legate 2012, 2014) and various Sama-Bajaw languages (Miller 2007; James 2017). Examples from West Coast Bajau are presented in (5):

West Coast Bajau

(5) a. *iyang=ku masang suu? e kaang*
mother=1SG.GEN AV:turn.on light DEM later
'my mother turned on the light' [AV]

b. *sapi e pan sembali emma?=ni no*
COW DEM TOP UV:slaughter father=3SG.GEN FOC
'his father slaughtered the cow' [UV]

c. *belunang e pan b<in>uka no*
door DEM TOP <PASS>open FOC
***ole?*** *anak=ni sioko*
**PREP** child=3SG.GEN oldest
'the door was opened by the oldest child' [PASSIVE]
(Miller 2007: 154, 158, 168)

In Totoli (Central Sulawesi) we find another example of symmetrical alternation between actor voice and undergoer voice, but the system is different from Balinese, Indonesian, and West Coast Bajau in two significant ways. First, Totoli has no passive. Second, the voice system is not only *syntactically* symmetrical (valence-preserving), but also *morphologically* symmetrical, since the verb in both constructions carries overt voice marking. The subjecthood of the argument in preverbal position[6] is confirmed by a number of syntactic properties similar to those listed in (3). The core argument status of AV undergoer and UV actor are demonstrated by the lack of any preposition or special case marking; their fixed, post-verbal position; and their ability to launch floating quantifiers.

Totoli

(6) a. *I Budi nanako? buki? ana.*[7]
i Budi **noN**-tako? buki? ana
HON Budi **AV.REAL**-climb mountain MED
'Budi climbed that mountain.'

b. *Buki? ana nitako? i Budi.*
buki? ana **ni**-tako? i Budi
mountain MED **UV.REAL**-climb HON Budi
'Budi climbed that mountain.' (Leto et al. 2005–2010)

[5] Depictives, like resultatives, are secondary predicates. They differ from resultatives, in that they denote a state of affairs that holds at the same time as the event denoted by the main predicate. Resultatives, on the other hand, denote a consequence or a result of the event denoted by the main predicate. See (14) for an example of a depictive secondary predicate in Tagalog.

[6] As in many other Austronesian languages, the position of the subject argument is somewhat flexible. It can either occur in sentence initial position, as in (6), or follow the verb-non-subject complex.

[7] The base form for 'climb' and 'mountain' is *takol* and *bukil*, but word-final laterals after vowels are regularly replaced by vowel lengthening in Totoli (i.e. *takol* is [tako:]). Elided laterals are indicated by an apostrophe <'> in the practical orthography used here. See Himmelmann (1991a) and Bracks (2020) for more on Totoli phonology.

Of course, more familiar asymmetrical voice systems are also found in Western Malayo-Polynesian languages. Kurniawan (2013) presents a detailed analysis of Sundanese, which he describes as having a simple active–passive voice alternation. He notes, however, that the agentive PP of the Sundanese passive is different in certain respects from its counterpart in English and other European languages. For example, in Sundanese the agentive PP can serve as the antecedent for a reflexive pronoun that functions as the subject of the passive, something that is impossible in English.

Adelaar (1995e) describes an ergative–antipassive alternation in Embaloh, a Tamanic language of north-central Borneo.[8] In basic verbal clauses, both intransitive subjects (S) and transitive patients or undergoers (P) agree with the absolutive suffix on the verb (cf. (7a), (7b)). The actor argument (A) in a transitive clause agrees with an ergative prefix (cf. (7b)). Embaloh also has an antipassive construction (cf. (7c)), in which the verb carries special voice morphology (in this case the antipassive prefix *maN-*), the undergoer is demoted to oblique status and marked by a preposition or omitted, and the actor agrees with the absolutive suffix.[9]

Embaloh

(7) a. *A-naŋis-**ak***.
INTR-cry-**1SG.ABS**
'I cry.'

b. *Ai si naʔan* ***ku**-tiŋkam-**ko*** *bea*
how not **1SG.ERG**-catch-**2SG.ABS** in.fact
*balik ia ʔi-pa-tabeʔ-i-ko!*
then as ERG-CAUS-*tabeʔ*-TR-2SG.ABS
'Why shouldn't I catch you, after all [your mother] brought you into a state of *tabeʔ*!'[10]

c. *Da-iko* *indiʔ* *baru* *takir-a*
EMPH-you.SG this only measure-3SG.GEN
*unti* *kurabo* *suar-u-ʔan,* *toʔ*
banana *kurabo* fang-2SG.GEN-DEF intend
***maniŋkam-ko*** *namin* ***loʔ-kuʔ!***
**maN**:catch-**2SG.ABS** already **PREP-1SG.GEN**
'You on the other hand, with your fangs no bigger than *kurabo* bananas, you do want to catch me!' (Adelaar 1995e: 389, 390)

As discussed in §47.4.2 below, antipassive constructions are also reported in a number of Sulawesi languages, including Mori Bawah (Mead 2005), Bugis (Laskowske 2016), Uma (Martens 1988a, d), and Mamuju (Kaufman 2017). However, in at least some of these languages the antipassive is part of a voice system that also includes a symmetrical AV–UV alternation.

### 47.2.3 Transitivity

As noted in the introduction to this chapter, the question of transitivity is important in two respects when dealing with voice in Malayo-Polynesian languages. First, the question of whether an alternation is to be considered symmetrical or not will depend on whether it involves an opposition between two (or more) transitive clause types. Second, in many Austronesian languages, applicative marking is closely intertwined with voice marking, and distinguishing the two is sometimes not an easy task. We will discuss these two issues in turn.

#### 47.2.3.1 *Core arguments vs. obliques*

The labels CORE, NON-CORE, and OBLIQUE have been used in slightly different ways in different syntactic frameworks. We follow Musgrave (2001); Arka and Manning (2008); and Arka (2009a, 2017) in distinguishing between CORE ARGUMENTS, OBLIQUE ARGUMENTS, and ADJUNCTS.

Arguments (whether core or oblique) are selected by the verb and assigned a semantic role specified by the verb's argument structure. They are often (but not always) obligatory. Adjuncts are not selected, and hence are (almost) always optional. Oblique arguments and adjuncts are typically marked by adpositions or semantically restricted case marking, whereas core arguments typically require neither of these. Core arguments are also distinguished from oblique arguments and adjuncts by their syntactic properties. However, the specific properties which are relevant for making this distinction vary from one language to another. We have already mentioned some of the properties that distinguish core arguments from obliques in Balinese (see ex. (4)). Musgrave (2001); Arka and Manning (2008); and Arka (2009a, 2017) discuss similar core argument diagnostics for Indonesian. In a number of languages, however, it has proven difficult to identify such diagnostics, and the core vs. non-core distinction has been based primarily on coding properties, such as word order, verb agreement, case marking, and prepositional marking (or its absence).[11]

[8] He also argues that the Tamanic languages are genetically most closely related to Bugis and other languages of southern Sulawesi.

[9] The antipassive can also take a non-specific undergoer NP.

[10] *tabeʔ* translates as 'be susceptible to misfortune because of an offence one made against customary law' (Adelaar, p.c.).

[11] Arka (2017) demonstrates that some core arguments may satisfy only a subset of the diagnostic criteria for a particular language, and suggests that the core–oblique distinction should be viewed as gradient rather categorical. We cannot discuss this proposal in the current chapter, but it is

#### 47.2.3.2 Applicatives and voice

As noted above, many 'Indonesian-type' languages have applicative affixes, whereas such affixes are (apparently) not found in languages of the Philippine type. These valency-increasing affixes are typically distinct from the voice morphology, and can occur in all voices (actor voice, undergoer voice, and passive) to promote a non-core argument to core status. In (standard) Indonesian, there are two such applicative markers which usually derive transitive verbs from transitive or intransitive bases. The suffix *-kan* marks the primary object as a beneficiary, instrument, causee (as illustrated in (8b)), object of perception, etc., while the suffix *-i* marks the primary object as goal or location, as illustrated in (8c); it may also have an iterative meaning (Ewing 2005c: 352f).

Indonesian

(8) a. *Buku saya jatuh.*
book 1SG fall
'My book fell.'

b. *Dia men-jatuh-kan buku saya.*
3SG AV-drop-*kan* book 1SG
'He dropped my book.'

c. *Dia men-jatuh-i buku saya.*
3SG AV-drop-*i* book 1SG
'He fell on my book.' (Dardjowidjojo 1971)

It has often been observed that voice morphology in Philippine-type languages can have semantic functions which are very similar to those of applicatives in other languages. In fact, the distinction between applicative morphology and voice morphology in WMP languages has been challenged by a number of authors who have argued for a unified analysis of the Philippine-type and Indonesian-type voice systems. Davies (2005, 2010), for example, argues that the Madurese suffixes *-agi* and *-e*, which are cognate to Indonesian *-kan* and *-i* respectively, could be analysed as part of a Philippine-type voice system. The suffix *-e* usually adds directional and locative elements as core arguments, while *-agi* applies benefactives, causatives, instruments, and 'subject matter of communication'. Davies notes that these are precisely the semantic roles for which Philippine-type languages have distinct voices. So one might view examples like (9d), in which the goal argument ('mother') is selected as subject, as the analogue of locative/dative voice in Cebuano or Tagalog. The difference is that in Cebuano or Tagalog, locative voice marking involves only a single affix, whereas in Madurese or Indonesian it is marked by a combination of affixes.

Madurese

(9) a. *Embuk ngerem paket* ***ka ebuʔ.***
elder.sister AV.send package **to mother**
'Big sister sent a package to mother.'

b. *Paket rowa* ***e-kerem ka ebuʔ*** *biʔ embuk.*
package that **UV-send to mother** by elder.sister
'That package was sent to mother by big sister.'

c. *Embuk ngerem-e* ***ebuʔ*** *paket.*
older.sister AV:send-LOC **mother** package
'Elder sister sent mother a package.'

d. ***Ebuʔ*** *e-kerem-e paket biʔ embuk.*
**mother** UV-send-LOC package by elder.sister
'Mother was sent a package by big sister.'
(Davies 2010: 283f)

Naylor (1978) also proposes an analysis of the Indonesian applicatives in terms of a Philippine-type 'focus' system. Conversely, a number of authors have argued that some Philippine-type voice markers should be analysed as applicatives. Under the ergative analysis discussed in §47.3.4 below, UV is treated as the unmarked transitive ergative construction, AV as an antipassive, and the other voice markers (instrumental, benefactive, locative, etc.) as applicative affixes (Payne 1982; Gerdts 1988; De Guzman 1988; Blake 1988; Aldridge 2004, 2012). Arka and Ross (2005: 8–9) point out that this view suggests a way to unify the analysis of Philippine-type and Indonesian-type voice systems, namely:

> to treat both Indonesian- and Philippine-type languages as having a single undergoer/actor voice alternation (with undergoer as the default voice in many languages) enriched by applicative morphology which allows a location, instrument, or beneficiary noun phrase to be promoted to undergoer. The applicative morphemes would be the Madurese suffixes *e* and *agi* and their equivalents in other Indonesian-type languages, and the locative and instrument/beneficiary voice morphology of Philippine-type languages.

However, Arka and Ross go on to point out a fairly serious problem for this kind of proposal:

> Madurese (or any other Indonesian-type languages such as Indonesian, Javanese and Balinese) has three actor voice

important to remember that the core–oblique distinction is often not a trivial matter.

forms, one unsuffixed and two suffixed respectively with *e* and *agi*, whereas Puyuma and Tagalog have only one.

In other words, voice prefixes and applicative suffixes in Madurese and Indonesian co-occur productively in all possible combinations, and in a semantically and syntactically transparent system. The contrast between the putative locative voice form *e-kerem-e* in (9d) and the AV form *ngerem-e* in (9c) is entirely analogous to the contrast between the undergoer voice form *e-kerem* in (9b) and the AV form *ngerem* in (9a). Similarly, for each putative benefactive voice form *e-ROOT-agi* there is a corresponding AV form *N-ROOT-agi*. Subject selection is entirely determined by the prefixes, while object selection is entirely determined by the suffixes.

Now it is true that many Philippine-type languages have voice categories marked by a combination of affixes. It is also true for certain roots there may be more than one AV form (e.g. the *mag-* vs. *-um-* forms in Tagalog). However, neither of these patterns is as productive, transparent, or semantically regular as the Madurese and Indonesian system.

The apparent intertwining of voice and applicative functions is even more severe in languages like Totoli, where, at least on the formal level, the same set of formatives are used for these two functions (see Table 47.1). Without going into detail of the analysis, Table 47.1 illustrates that in Totoli, the suffixes *-i* and *-an* are part of the applicative paradigm, but they also occur in 'plain', non-applicative voice forms (UV2), in both realis and non-realis mood. Likewise, bare (i.e. non-suffixed) forms can be found in both functions, non-applicative undergoer voice (UV1) and applicative undergoer voice.

**Table 47.1** Voice and applicative morphology in Totoli

| | NON-REALIS | REALIS |
|---|---|---|
| AV | *moN-* | *noN-* |
| UV1 | *Ø* | *ni- -Ø* |
| UV2 | ***-i*** | *ni-* ***-an*** |
| AV.APPL1 | *moN-* ***-an*** | *noN-* ***-an*** |
| AV.APPL2 | *moN-* ***-i*** | *noN-* ***-i*** |
| UV.APPL1 | ***-an*** | *ni-* ***-Ø*** |
| | *poN-* ***-an*** | *ni-poN-* ***-Ø*** |
| UV.APPL2 | ***-i*** | *ni-* ***-an*** |

Himmelmann and Riesberg (2013) argue that in Totoli there is good evidence to keep the two paradigms apart, the main argument being that an applicative undergoer voice form, which links the applied argument directly to subject function, always stands in paradigmatic opposition to an actor voice form that also takes applicative marking, just as plain undergoer voice forms stand in opposition to plain actor voice forms (cf. also Riesberg et al., 2021). Consider the Totoli data in (10).[12]

Totoli

(10) a. *i* *Rinto* *manaip* *taipang*
HON Rinto AV:peel mango
'Rinto peels a mango'

b. *taipang* *ko-doong* *taip* *i* *Rinto*
mango POT-want peel:UV1 HON Rinto
'Rinto will peel a mango'

c. *i* *Rinto* *manaip-**an*** *aku* *taipang*
HON Rinto AV:peel-**APPL1** 1SG mango
'Rinto peels a mango for me'

d. *aku* *ko-doong* *panaip-**an*** *Rinto* *taipang*
1SG POT-want SF:peel-**APPL1** Rinto mango
'Rinto will peel a mango for me' (Himmelmann and Riesberg 2013: 414, 413)

## 47.3 Voice in 'Philippine-type' languages

Philippine languages exhibit a distinctive type of voice system which is also found in languages of northern Sulawesi and northeastern Borneo. Because similar systems are attested in various Formosan languages, a Philippine-type voice inventory is reconstructed for Proto-Austronesian which includes four basic voice markers (*<um>, *-ən, *-an, *Si-; Wolff 1973; Ross 2002b). However, the syntactic and typological character of the Philippine-type system remains a highly controversial issue. At the heart of the controversy is the identification of the grammatical subject in a transitive clause.

We begin by illustrating the basic pattern of case marking and voice alternations, using Tagalog data. Tagalog has three distinctive case categories, with the case markers also reflecting a distinction between proper names and other

[12] See Himmelmann and Riesberg (2013: 421) for a proposed list of diagnostics to distinguish between the symmetrical voice and applicative alternations.

**Table 47.2** Case markers in Tagalog

| | NOM | GEN | DAT/LOC |
|---|---|---|---|
| **Common noun markers:** | *ang* | *ng* | *sa* |
| **Personal name markers:** | *si* | *ni* | *kay* |

NPs as shown in Table 47.2. Each verbal clause must contain one and only one nominative argument, and the semantic role of the nominative element is reflected by the voice marker on the verb. All other NP constituents of the clause get genitive or dative case, depending on their semantic role (and sometimes animacy and/or definiteness).

The examples in (11) illustrate how the choice of voice marker on the verb reflects the semantic role of the nominative argument in each clause:

Tagalog

(11) a. *B<um>ili ang=lalake ng=isda sa=tindahan.*
<AV.PFV>buy NOM=man GEN=fish DAT=store
'The man bought fish at the store.'

b. *B-in-ili-Ø ng=lalake ang=isda sa=tindahan.*
<PFV>buy-PV GEN=man NOM=fish DAT=store
'The man bought the fish at the store.'

c. *B<in>ilh-an ng=lalake ng=isda ang=tindahan.*
<PFV>buy-DV GEN=man GEN=fish NOM=store
'The man bought fish at the store.'

d. *Ip<in>am-(b)ili ng=lalake ng=isda ang=pera.*
IV<PFV>buy GEN=man GEN=fish NOM=money
'The man bought fish with the money.'

e. *I-b-in-ili ng=lalake ng=isda ang=bata.*
BEN<PFV>buy GEN=man GEN=fish NOM=child
'The man bought fish for the child.' (Foley and Van Valin 1984: 135)

Early treatments of Tagalog grammar, including Bloomfield (1917); Blake (1925); Lopez (1937, 1965); and Aspillera (1969), identified the nominative argument as the subject, treating the non-active voices as passive constructions. Bloomfield, for example, refers to undergoer voice as the "direct passive", instrumental voice as the "instrumental passive", and dative/locative voice as the "local passive". Bell's (1976) analysis of Cebuano within the Relational Grammar framework is similar.

Under this analysis, Philippine-type voice systems exhibit a number of typologically unusual features, including the following:

Features of Philippine-type languages
(*ang*-phrase = subject)

(12) a. multiple voice categories (four or more);
b. preference for patients, rather than agents, to be selected as subject of transitive clauses;
c. symmetrical (i.e. non-demoting) voice alternations;
d. direct promotion of oblique arguments to subject, sometimes described as the merger of subject selection with applicativization in a single paradigm;
e. requirement (or strong preference) that subject NPs must be definite;
f. extraction limited to subjects only;
g. long-distance extraction possible only out of sentential subjects;
h. voice alternations do not affect the potential binding relationship between a reflexive pronoun and its antecedent.

These features, especially the non-demotion of the actor when some other argument is selected as the nominative NP, have led many authors to challenge the assumption that the nominative argument of a clause is its subject. Most of the alternative proposals over the past sixty years can be grouped into two broad classes: (a) the nominative argument is a topic, or something similar to a topic; (b) the nominative argument is the absolutive argument in an ergative system. Both kinds of analyses assume that the actor is always the subject, regardless of case and voice marking. We present here a brief overview of these competing analyses.

### 47.3.1 'Topic' and 'focus'

In the mid-twentieth century, a number of Philippine specialists became dissatisfied with the Bloomfieldian approach, apparently beginning with members of the Summer Institute of Linguistics. McKaughan (1958, 1962) proposed that NP markers corresponding to Tagalog *ang* mark not the subject of the clause but the TOPIC. At about the same time, various SIL linguists began to use the term FOCUS to refer to the voice-marking affixation on the verb (e.g. Thomas 1958;

Dean 1958).[13] These terminological innovations reflected an intuition that the non-active voices in Philippine languages should not be classified as passives, because passive constructions in English and most other European languages are pragmatically marked, and disfavoured in various ways (e.g. text frequency). In most European languages the preferred subject of a basic transitive clause corresponds to the actor, whereas in Philippine-type languages it is typically the undergoer (unless the undergoer is non-specific). This 'topic and focus' analysis marked a turning point in Philippine linguistics, and proved to be quite influential in wider Austronesian studies as well.

McKaughan's (1958) analysis implies that the voice system does not produce any change in grammatical relations: the actor is always the grammatical subject, and the undergoer is always the grammatical object. The function of the voice-marking affix is to indicate the syntactic relation of the topic, while the syntactic relation of the other NP arguments is indicated by their case markers. This is essentially the view of the Tagalog voice system found in the work of Wolfenden (1961); Schachter and Otanes (1972); Carrier-Duncan (1985); and many others.

In the 1950s, the terms TOPIC and FOCUS apparently had no fixed meaning in general linguistics. However, with the explosion of work on Information Structure in the 1970s and 1980s, the non-standard use of these terms within Austronesian (and in particular Philippine) linguistics became a source of endless confusion. While the old topic and focus terminology continues to be used in some work on Philippine and Formosan languages, several other terms have been proposed in recent decades to replace 'topic': PIVOT (Foley and Van Valin 1984), TRIGGER (Wouk 1984; Fox 1984: 68), and PRIVILEGED SYNTACTIC ARGUMENT (PSA; Van Valin and LaPolla 1997), among others. These terms are intended to reflect the fact that the nominative argument plays a uniquely active role in the syntax of the clause, while remaining agnostic concerning the identity or existence of a grammatical subject in these languages.

### 47.3.2 Identifying the subject: Actor, nominative argument, both, or 'none of the above'?

Schachter (1976, 1977, 1996) argued that no argument of a basic transitive clause in Tagalog can be uniquely identified as the grammatical subject. He pointed out that when the nominative argument is not the actor, the characteristic properties associated with subjects cross-linguistically are divided between the actor and the nominative argument. The split as he described it is shown in Table 47.3:

**Table 47.3** Split of properties in nominative and actor arguments in Tagalog

| Nominative argument | Actor |
|---|---|
| a. Obligatory element of every clause | a. Reflexive binding |
| b. Launches floating quantifiers | b. Equi (= control) target |
| c. Relativization | c. Imperative addressee |
| | d. Relevance to word order (Kapampangan, Cebuano) |

Kroeger (1993a: chapter 2) identified a number of additional subjecthood properties associated with the nominative argument in Tagalog, including raising (13), modification by depictive secondary predicates (14), and conjunction reduction (not illustrated here).

Tagalog

(13) a. *Inasah-an ko ang=pambansang.awit*
expect-DV 1SG.GEN NOM=national.anthem
*na [awit-in ni=Linda* ____NOM].
COMP sing-PV GEN=Linda
'I expected the national anthem to be sung by Linda.'

b. **Inasah-an ko si=Linda na*
expect-DV 1SG.GEN NOM=Linda COMP
*[awit-in ang=pambansang.awit* ____GEN].
sing-PV NOM=national.anthem
(intended: 'I expected Linda to sing the national anthem.') (Kroeger 1993a: chapter 2)

Tagalog

(14) a. *Naghain na lasing si=Maria*
AV.PFV:serve LNK drunk NOM=Maria
*ng=isda.*
GEN=fish
'Maria served the fish drunk.' (Maria was drunk.)

[13] See Blust (2002c); Quakenbush (2003); Ross and Teng (2005) for further discussion of the origins of this term.

b. *Inihain* *na* *hilaw* *ni=Maria*
IV.PFV:serve LNK raw GEN=Maria
*ang=isda.*
NOM=fish
'Maria served the fish raw.' (The fish was raw.)

c. # *Inihain* *na* *lasing* *ni=Maria*
IV.PFV:serve LNK drunk GEN=Maria
*ang=isda.*
NOM=fish
'Maria served the fish drunk.' (can only mean that the fish was drunk) (Kroeger 1993a: chapter 2)

Moreover, as noted by Dell (1981) and Schachter (1985a: 458), the Equi target (or controllee, often referred to as PRO) in a transitive complement clause is not always the actor. With some control predicates (e.g. *himukin* 'persuade' and *magpilit* 'insist on'), the controllee may be either the actor (regardless of case marking) or the nominative argument. And when the embedded verb is marked for potentive (=non-volitive) mood, the controllee must be the nominative argument (Kroeger 1993a: 95ff). These control facts are important because there is a strong cross-linguistic tendency for the controllee in control complements to be restricted to subject position.

Based on these observations, Kroeger argues that:

> . . . the syntactic evidence for subjecthood in Tagalog is less equivocal than most linguists, following Schachter, have assumed. Evidence for the grammatical subjecthood of non-nominative Actors is weaker than has been claimed, in light of the observation that neither reflexive binding nor Equi-deletion are exclusively properties of Actors. Conversely, the evidence for analysing the nominative argument as a grammatical subject is even stronger than Schachter implied. . .
> (Kroeger 1993a: 54–5)

Guilfoyle, Hung, and Travis (1989, 1992), working within the Principles and Parameters framework, argued that some western Austronesian languages have two structural subject positions, one for the actor and the other for the nominative argument. (They discussed four languages: Malagasy, Tagalog, Cebuano, and Indonesian; we focus here on their analysis of Tagalog.) Under their proposal, actors are base-generated in an 'internal subject' position (specifier of VP), as shown in (15). The voice affix on the verb changes the verb's syntactic properties (technically formulated in terms of Case assignment) in such a way that one particular argument is forced to move up to the 'external subject' position, as shown in (16). The argument in this position gets marked with nominative case.

(15) **D-structure**

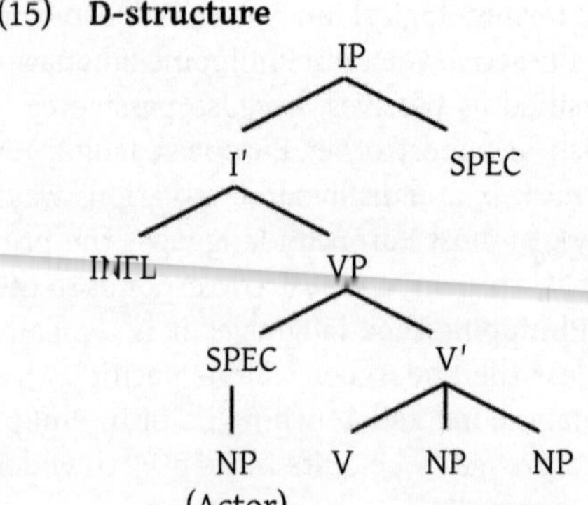


(16) **S-structure**

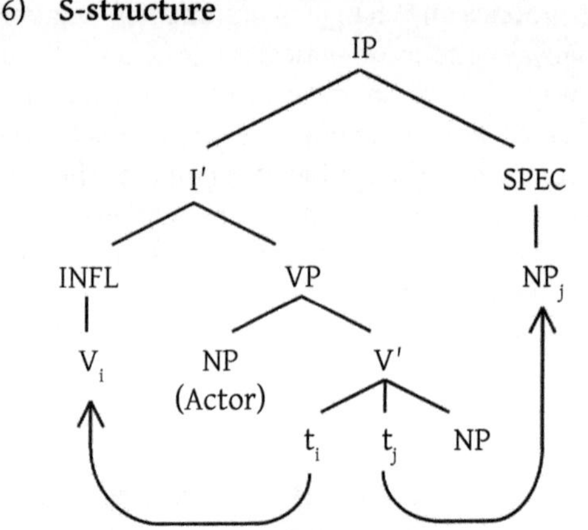


Subjecthood properties like raising, extraction, and quantifier float are associated with the 'external subject' position, and thus with the nominative argument. But because the actor is not demoted or otherwise affected when some other argument is selected as subject, it retains its core argument status in the syntax, as reflected in constraints on reflexive binding and control complements.

Guilfoyle, Hung, and Travis' proposal appears to be the first formal syntactic analysis of non-demoting voice alternations. Their proposal has been extremely influential in subsequent work on the formal syntax of western Austronesian languages.

### 47.3.3 Nominative as topic-like argument

Guilfoyle, Hung, and Travis treat Philippine-type voice alternations as changes in the assignment of grammatical relations, specifically the subject relation. An alternative formal approach makes use of similar structures, but treats 'pivot'-selection as something more like topicalization, which does not involve a change of grammatical relations. In other words, the nominative argument occupies a position of syntactic and pragmatic prominence, but is not the grammatical subject.

In support of this approach, Richards (2000) and Pearson (2005) point out that the grammatical properties of 'pivots' in Philippine-type languages are similar in many ways to those associated with the pre-verbal element in verb-second languages such as German and Icelandic.[14] The similarities include constraints on extraction (e.g. relativization and *wh*-fronting), zero anaphora, lack of relevance for reflexive binding, and a specificity requirement. Moreover, the pre-verbal constituent in German may be either a topic or a focused element, and the same is true for Tagalog pivots (Kroeger 1993a: chapter 3).

Under this type of analysis, as in McKaughan (1958) and much subsequent work, the actor is always the structural subject of the clause. As for the function of the voice morphology itself, Rackowski and Richards (2005) analyse it as a kind of Case agreement. Pearson (2001, 2005) and Chen (2017) suggest that Philippine-type 'voice' marking is actually a kind of *wh*-agreement, as described for Chamorro by Chung (1982, 1994, 1998).

One empirical challenge for this approach comes from word order. While the clause-final location of pivots in Malagasy is consistent with their occupying the kind of structural position this hypothesis requires, Richards (2000) notes that this is not the case in Tagalog. He suggests that the movement of pivots in Tagalog is covert (i.e. does not affect the visible syntax), in contrast to V2 languages like Icelandic where it is overt.

This challenge is more acute in other Philippine languages. Sells (2000) states that Tagalog is not a typical Philippine language in terms of word order: "By far the most common (and often quite rigid) requirements for the ordering of constituents within the clause most commonly put the subject effectively in THIRD position" (Sells 2000: 124). "Third position" refers to the requirement or strong preference for non-actor pivots to be the third constituent of the clause, following the verb and actor NP and preceding all other arguments (see also Riesberg et al. 2019). Sells states that this "nominative-third" (N3) order is the fundamental order in Pangasinan (Mulder and Schwartz 1981), Cebuano (Bell 1976/1979), Kalagan (Collins 1970; Travis 1991), Dibabawon (Forster 1964), Isnag (Barlaan 1986), and Balangao (Shetler 1976). The same is true for Limos Kalinga (Ferreirinho 1993; Travis 2010).

Of course, N3 order can be handled in various ways. For example, Travis (2010) proposes that a non-actor pivot occupies the structural position of the 'highest object' within the clause. But whatever view of the N3 pattern is adopted, accounting for it under the type of analysis discussed in this section adds another layer of complexity to an already fairly abstract proposal.

Another sort of challenge for this analysis comes from the pattern of control mentioned in §47.3.2, in which the controllee (or Equi target) must be nominative but need not be the actor. This pattern is possible with some Tagalog control predicates, such as *pilit* 'insist on' and *himok* 'persuade' (Ramos 1971: 132; Kroeger 1993a: 101). It is obligatory in some other languages. One such language is Kimaragang Dusun, a Philippine-type language of northeastern Borneo. As the following examples illustrate, the controllee can be a nominative patient (17a), (18a) but not a non-nominative actor (17b), (18b).

Kimaragang

(17) a. *Suu-on ku [it=tanak ku]$_i$*
order-UV 1SG.GEN NOM=child 1SG.GEN
*[gambar-on _$_i$ dit=tawkey].*
picture-UV GEN=merchant
'I will tell my son to have his picture taken by the merchant.'[15]

b. **Suu-on ku [it=tawkey]$_i$*
order-UV 1SG.GEN NOM=merchant
*[gambar-on _$_i$ it=tanak ku].*
picture-UV NOM=child 1SG.GEN
(intended: 'I will tell the merchant to take my son's picture.')

c. *Suu-on ku [it=tawkey]$_i$*
order-UV 1SG.GEN NOM=merchant
*[mangagambar _$_i$ dit=tanak ku].*
AV.TR:picture ACC=child 1SG.GEN
'I will tell the merchant to take my son's picture.' (P. Kroeger, fieldnotes)

(18) a. *Amu ko-bulun [it=tanak ku]$_i$*
not POT-dare NOM=child 1SG.GEN
*[suntik-an _$_i$ dit=dorisa].*
inject-DV GEN=dresser
'My child does not dare to be injected by the dresser.' (P. Kroeger, fieldnotes)

b. **Amu ko-bulun [it=tanak ku]$_i$*
not POT-dare NOM=child 1SG.GEN
*[patay-on _$_i$ it=wulanut].*
kill-UV NOM=snake
(intended: 'My child does not dare to kill the snake.')

[14] Erlewine et al. (2017) make similar arguments in support of this type of analysis by comparing Austronesian voice with Dinka, a V2 language of eastern Africa.

[15] For reasons discussed immediately below, the most common way to express the intended meaning in (17a) would be to use an AV complement verb form that means 'request a picture'.

c. *Amu ko-bulun [it=tanak ku]$_i$*
not POT-dare NOM=child 1SG.GEN
*[m-poN-patay _$_i$ dit=wulanut].*
AV-TR-kill ACC=snake
'My child does not dare to kill the snake.'

Cross-linguistically, there is a strong tendency for controllees to be the grammatical subject of their clause. In addition to this syntactic requirement, semantic constraints may also apply. Many control predicates impose selectional restrictions which require that their complement clause expresses a volitional action, and with these predicates there is a strong cross-linguistic preference for the controllee to be the actor of the complement clause. Since the grammar of Kimaragang requires the controllee to be the nominative argument of the complement clause, complement verbs in such constructions tend to appear in actor voice, as in (17c), (18c). But examples like (17a) and (18a) show that this is not syntactically required. With respect to the current discussion, the requirement for controllees to be the nominative argument of their clause is difficult to explain under any analysis which claims that the actor is always the grammatical subject.

### 47.3.4 Ergative–antipassive

An ergative analysis of the Philippine-type voice system is motivated by two primary factors: 'patient preference' and typological familiarity.[16] Cena (1977) and De Guzman (1992 [1979]) present morphological and syntactic arguments for the claim that, other factors being equal, the preferred voice marking in Tagalog is the one which selects the patient as pivot. This claim is supported by text frequency (Cooreman, Fox, and Givon 1984) and acquisition data (Tucker 1971; Segalowitz and Galang 1978; Galang 1982), which appear to show that active voice is more highly 'marked' than the non-active voices, for semantically transitive verbs.

If, based on these arguments, we accept the 'patient-voice' form in (19a) as the basic transitive clause pattern, the Tagalog case marking system can be seen as ergative. Ergativity is recognized by comparing transitive with intransitive clauses, as illustrated in the following examples:

[16] Several authors have proposed ergative analyses within the Relational Grammar framework, including De Guzman (1988) and B. Blake (1988) for Tagalog, and Gerdts (1988) for Ilokano. Payne (1982); Brainard (1994, 1997); and Liao (2004) argue for ergative analyses from a functional-typological perspective. Edith Aldridge argues for a Minimalist version of the ergative analyses in her 2004 dissertation and a series of subsequent papers.

Tagalog
(19) a. *B<in>ili-Ø ng=babae ang=isda.*
<PFV>buy-PV ERG=woman ABS=fish
'The woman bought the fish.'

b. *D<um>ating ang=babae.*
<AV.PFV>arrive ABS=woman
'The woman arrived.' (Aldridge 2012: 192)

We observe that the same marker *ang* is used for transitive undergoers (P) and intransitive subjects (S); so it must be analysed as marking absolutive case. The transitive actor (A) gets a distinctive marker, in this case *ng*, the marker of ergative case. The split in subjecthood properties described by Schachter, summarized in Table 47.3 above, is readily accounted for: Actor properties are held to be properties of syntactic subjects, while relativization and quantifier float are assumed to be properties of absolutive arguments (S or P).

Under the ergative analysis, 'actor focus' clauses like (20) are analysed as antipassive constructions, in which the patient is demoted to oblique argument status, creating an intransitive clause. The actor, as the single core argument of the clause (S), gets absolutive case, while the demoted patient takes oblique case marking. Since the infix *-um-* appears in both basic intransitive clauses like (19b) and derived intransitive (=antipassive) clauses like (20), it cannot be regarded as a marker of antipassive voice. Instead, it is analysed as a marker of intransitivity.

Tagalog
(20) *B<um>ili ang=babae ng=isda.*
<AV.PFV>buy ABS=woman OBL=fish
'The woman bought a fish.' (Aldridge 2012: 192)

The transitive verb form in (19a) is unmarked for voice, if we regard the infix *-in-* as marking perfective or realis aspect. The other voice markers, (e.g. *-an, i-, i-paN-*) are analysed as applicative affixes, which promote an oblique or adjunct to direct object. This applied argument, as object of a transitive clause, gets absolutive case. The 'patient focus' suffix *-in*, which appears in imperfective/irrealis clauses, is analysed by Aldridge (2004) as a marker of transitivity.

The great advantage of the ergative analysis is that it reduces the degree of typological 'strangeness' of Philippine-type voice systems, accounting for many of their distinctive characteristics in terms of linguistic features that are familiar from other language families:[17]

[17] See Payne (1982) and B. Blake (1988) for explicit comparisons of Tagalog with ergative + applicative systems in other languages.

> The strength of the ergative hypothesis lies in the fact that it offers an explanation of voice system behavior that does not require postulating mechanisms that are unique to Austronesian.
>
> (Erlewine et al. 2017: 379)

However, Erlewine et al. (2017) argue that many of these distinctive characteristics are shared by languages which cannot be analysed as ergative, both within the Austronesian family (e.g. Balinese) and in other parts of the world (e.g. Dinka). If the distinguishing features of Philippine-type voice systems are independent of ergativity, this would remove the strongest theoretical motivation for adopting the analysis.

The most serious empirical challenge for the ergative analysis is related to the claim that 'actor focus' clauses like (20) are antipassives. The defining feature of an antipassive construction is the demotion of the patient (underlying object) of a transitive verb (Polinsky 2017: 309). The demoted patient may either be expressed as an oblique argument or be left unexpressed. Thus, the crucial question is whether patients in 'actor focus' clauses are obliques or core arguments.

The evidence that is most frequently cited for identifying the patient in 'actor focus' clauses like (20) as an oblique argument is the strong tendency for *ng*-marked patients in these clauses to be interpreted as non-specific. The patient of an antipassive does tend to be interpreted as indefinite or non-specific in a number of languages, although as Polinsky (2017: 316) points out, this is by no means always the case.

Richards (2000) notes several contexts where an *ng*-marked patient may get a definite interpretation. These include clauses in which some constituent other than the agent or patient is extracted, and constructions such as gerunds and the recent past which do not allow voice-marking morphology on the verb. These observations suggest that the non-specific interpretation of 'actor focus' patients is not syntactically encoded, but the result of a pragmatic inference. Kroeger (1993a: 47–8) presents syntactic evidence which suggests that the patient of an AV clause is a core argument rather than an oblique.

## 47.3.5 Voice as nominalization

It is often pointed out that the distinction between nouns and verbs in Philippine-type languages is not clear cut. Three principal reasons for this are: (a) the use of genitive case for non-pivot actors, which makes actors and possessors formally identical; (b) the very productive use of headless relative clauses (21), which allows 'verbal' clauses (minus the pivot) to function as NPs in argument positions; and (c) the lack of a copula with nominal and adjectival predicates, which means that nouns and adjectives can function as clausal predicates in much the same way as verbs (22).[18]

Tagalog

(21) *ang* *mga* *b<in>ili-Ø* *ko*
NOM PL <PFV>buy-PV 1SG.GEN
'the ones/things that I bought' (Schachter and Otanes 1972: 151)

(22) a. *Maganda* *ang=babae.*
beautiful NOM=woman
'The woman is beautiful.'

b. *Bato* *ang=bahay.*
stone NOM=house
'The house is stone.' (Schachter and Otanes 1972: 61, 64)

Moreover, the Philippine voice markers also have lexically specific nominalizing functions in most if not all Philippine-type languages. Starosta, Pawley, and Reid (1982) suggest that the Proto-Austronesian voice markers (*<um>, *-ən, *-an, *Si-) were originally nominalizers specified for semantic roles, like the English suffixes *-er* for agent or instrument and *-ee* for patient or affected argument. Clauses involving these voice markers were originally equative in structure, consisting of two juxtaposed NPs. The nominalized forms were subsequently re-analysed as verbs, creating a 'normal' verbal clause structure, as illustrated in (23) using Tagalog examples:

Tagalog

(23) a. *[B<um>ili* *ng=isda]* *[ang=lalake].*
<AV.PFV>buy GEN=fish NOM=man
original: 'The man was the buyer of fish.'
reanalysis: 'The man bought fish.'

b. *[B<in>ili-Ø* *ng=lalake]* *[ang=isda].*
<PFV>buy-PV GEN=man NOM=fish
original: 'The fish was the purchased thing of the man.'
reanalysis: 'The man bought the fish.'

[18] In fact, Gil (1993) argues that on purely distributional grounds, there is no basis for distinguishing lexical categories N, V, A, or P; there is only a single category of content words. Himmelmann (1991b) cites Lemaréchal (1982) as making a similar claim. However, there are clear morphological grounds for distinguishing these categories, especially in the case of adjectives. Some distributional criteria for identifying verbs will be discussed below.

c. [*B<in>ilh-an* *ng=lalake* *ng=isda*]
<PFV>buy-DV GEN=man GEN=fish
[*ang=tindahan*].
NOM=store
original: 'The store was the place of the man's purchase of fish.'
reanalysis: 'The man bought fish at the store.'

d. [*I-b<in>ili* *ng=lalake* *ng=isda*]
BEN-<PFV>buy GEN=man GEN=fish
[*ang=bata*].
NOM=child
original: 'The child was the beneficiary of the man's purchase of fish.'
reanalysis: 'The man bought fish for the child.' (Tagalog examples from Foley and Van Valin 1984: 135)

A number of authors have adopted a similar approach to the synchronic analysis of Philippine-type languages. For example, Dahl (1951: 121) states that verbal clauses in Malagasy have the structure of an 'equation'. Capell (1964) provides an extended argument for identifying the non-active voice forms in Philippine languages as nouns derived from verbs, or 'verbal nouns'. Cecilio Lopez (1928, 1937) refers to the Tagalog verb forms used in (23) as "quasi-verbs", arguing that they are actually nominal in character:[19]

> The quasi-verb is not a real verb, for it is treated like a *nomen* ['noun'] in the sentence and the enlargements, according to their forms, are considered as attributes and not as objects. (Lopez 1928: 51)

More recently, Himmelmann (1991b, 2008) and Kaufman (2009a, b) have built a strong case for the nominalist analysis of Tagalog, and by extension of Philippine-type voice systems in general. This work has been extremely influential, and a full discussion is beyond the scope of the present chapter. Here we will just mention some empirical challenges for the nominalist proposal. Some of these have been addressed by Himmelmann and Kaufman, but (we believe) not fully resolved.

a) **Word order**: The nominalist hypothesis predicts that the most basic word order should place the pivot in clause-final position, as seen in (23). In fact, this order is attested in Malagasy, Toba Batak, and some Formosan languages including Seediq, Atayal, and Tsou (Chung 2006); but otherwise appears to be relatively uncommon among Philippine-type languages.[20] Languages like those discussed in §47.3.3, in which 'nominative-third' (N3) is the fundamental order of clausal constituents, present an even greater challenge.

b) **Control complements**: Richards (2009a, b) points out for Tagalog that control complements provide distributional evidence for distinguishing nouns from verbs. Only verbal clauses can occur as complements to control predicates; with all non-verbal clauses, the copula *maging* 'be, become' is obligatory. In main clauses the copula normally expresses a change of state, as in (24c); no copula is required for the stative reading in main clauses, as illustrated in (24b).

Tagalog
(24) a. *Nag-aaral* *ako.*
AV.IPFV-study 1SG.NOM
'I am studying.'

b. *Doktor* *ako.*
doctor 1SG.NOM
'I am a doctor.'

c. *Naging* *doktor* *ako* *noong* *1977.*
PFV.COP doctor 1SG.NOM when:LNK 1977
'I became a doctor in 1977.' (Richards 2009a: 181, 183)

In control complements, however, the copula can express either the stative or change of state reading. Example (25b) is designed to rule out the change of state reading. If *magaral* and *doktor* are both nouns, we would expect them to be interchangeable in this context. However, as the contrast in (25) demonstrates, the copula is impossible with *magaral* but obligatory with *doktor*.

Tagalog
(25) a. *Ayo=ko* *na=ng* [(**maging*)
don't.want=1SG.GEN now=COMP AV.INF:be
*mag-aral*].
AV-study
'I don't want to study any more.'

b. *Ayo=ko* *na=ng* [*maging*
don't.want=1SG.GEN now=COMP AV.INF:be
*doktor*].
doctor
'I don't want to be a doctor any more.'

c. **Ayo=ko* *na=ng* [*doktor*].
don't.want=1SG.GEN now=COMP doctor
cannot mean: 'I don't want to be a doctor any more.' (based on Richards 1982a:182)

[19] See Capell (1964); Himmelmann (1991b, 2005a: 140–1); and Kaufman (2009b) for further discussion of the history of the nominalist proposal.

[20] Himmelmann (1991b) discusses the relatively free word order observed in Tagalog, arguing that there is less variation in natural texts than in isolated examples, and that the dominant order observed in natural texts is consistent with the nominalist hypothesis.

Himmelmann himself (2005a: 141; 2009: 117–18) points out that apparently only voice-marked forms (i.e. those forms traditionally analysed as verbs) can occur as predicates of a control complement. He considers this fact "to be one of the two most difficult empirical challenges to the nominalist hypothesis."

c) **Island constraints**: Kaufman (2009a) argues that the structure of (26a) is the same as that of (24b), because the predicates *sumayaw* 'dance' and *doktor* 'doctor' are both nouns. In support of this analysis, he shows in (26b) that *sumayaw* can be modified by the normal range of NP dependents, including demonstratives and numerals.

Tagalog

(26) a. *S<um>ayaw* *diyan* *ang=mga=pinsan*
<AV.PFV>dance there NOM=PL=cousin
*ko.*
1SG.GEN
'My cousins danced there.'

b. *Iyo=ng* *dalawa=ng* *sumayaw*
that=LNK two=LNK <AV.PFV>dance
*diyan* *ang=mga=pinsan* *ko.*
there NOM=PL=cousin 1SG.GEN
'My cousins are those two who danced over there.' (Kaufman 2009a: 34)

In comparing the two sentences in (26), Kaufman states: "There is, as can be expected, a difference in the predicational vs. specificational reading between these two sentences but I am not aware of any evidence for substantial differences in their underlying structure" (2009a: 34, fn. 34). Richards (2009b) points out that one difference between the two sentences concerns extraction: the location can be questioned in (26a) but not in (26b):

Tagalog

(27) a. *Saan* *s<um>ayaw* *ang=mga=pinsan*
where <AV.PFV>dance NOM=PL=cousin
*mo?*
2SG.GEN
'Where did your cousins dance?'

b. **Saan* *iyo=ng* *dalawa=ng* *sumayaw*
where that=LNK two=LNK <AV.PFV>dance
*ang=mga=pinsan* *mo?*
NOM=PL=cousin 2SG.GEN
'*Where were those two who danced your cousins?' (Richards 2009b: 144)

Under traditional analyses, (26a) is a simple (monoclausal) verbal clause but (26b) begins with a headless relative clause. The contrast demonstrated in (27) is expected under the traditional analysis, because relative clauses (headless or not) are typically 'islands' (i.e. constituents from which nothing can be extracted). It is not clear how to explain these facts under the nominalist analysis.

## 47.4 Voice in Borneo and Sulawesi

### 47.4.1 Borneo (and Madagascar)

#### 47.4.1.1 *Sabah interior languages*

In Borneo, the boundary between Philippine-type voice systems and systems that are closer to the Indonesian-type, roughly follows the southern border of the Malaysian state of Sabah. The indigenous Philippine-type languages of Sabah include three primary subgroups: Dusunic, Paitanic, and Murut-Tidung (Prentice 1971; Wurm 1983; Blust 2010b). Languages of all three groups preserve the classic Philippine voice, case marking, and word-order patterns (including second position clitics), as discussed in more detail in Kroeger and Smith, this volume, §27.3.1. Northern Dusunic and Northern Paitanic varieties preserve the full inventory of Philippine voice categories. As an example, the voice markers of Kimaragang Dusun are in listed Table 47.4.[21] (Sentences illustrating the use of these forms are presented in Kroeger and Smith, this volume, §27.3.1.1.).

**Table 47.4** Kimaragang Dusun voice affixes

| Voice category | Affixation |
|---|---|
| ACTOR (AV) | R<*um*>OOT (intransitive)<br>*m-poN*-ROOT (transitive)<br>*Ø-po*-ROOT (transitive) |
| OBJECTIVE (OV) | ROOT-$on_1$ |
| DATIVE (DV) | ROOT-*an* |
| CONVEYANCE (CV) | *i*-ROOT |
| INSTRUMENTAL (IV) | *poN*-ROOT |
| LOCATIVE (LV) (INTRANS) | ROOT-$on_2$ |
| CIRCUMSTANTIAL (CIRCV) | *poN*-ROOT-*an* |

In languages located farther to the south and west we observe a simplification of the voice inventory. This simplification involves a reduction in the number of voice cat-

[21] The distinction between -$on_1$ vs. -$on_2$ is motivated by a difference in allomorphy. -$on_1$ is realized by a zero allomorph in past tense and in non-volitive (a.k.a. potentive) mood, whereas the form of -$on_2$ is unchanged in these contexts.

egories, beginning with the loss of the conveyance voice prefix (*i*-), the reflex of PAN *Si-. (Tatana', a language in the southwest corner of Sabah, stands as an exception to this generalization; it preserves six of the seven voices listed in Table 47.4.)[22]

Four semantic functions are reconstructed for PAN *Si (Wolff 1973). It was used to mark the subject of the clause as being (i) an instrument, (ii) a beneficiary, (iii) the displaced theme of verbs of transfer or conveyance, or (iv) the patient of a morphological causative. As far as we know, the benefactive use of *i*- is not attested in any Borneo language. This fact is consistent with a pattern reported by Liao (2008b), who shows that the benefactive use is largely restricted to Taiwan and the northern half of the Philippines; it is quite rare south of Manila.

The Murut and Tidung languages occupy the border areas between Sabah and northern Kalimantan. (We focus on the Murutic languages here, because relatively little information is available about Tidung syntax in general, and voice in particular.) All of the Murutic languages have lost the prefix *i*- entirely, but they have acquired a third voice-marking suffix (*-in*), which Prentice (1971) refers to as "referent focus". The contrast between referent focus and 'associate focus' is neutralized in past tense, atemporal, and non-volitive forms, as shown in Table 47.5.

**Table 47.5** Voice paradigms in Timugon Murut (Prentice 1971; R. Brewis 2004: 915)

| Voice Category | Non-past | Past | Atemporal |
|---|---|---|---|
| Actor | *m-/-um-* | *n-/-imin-* | *Ø-* |
| Objective | *-on* | R<*in*>OOT-Ø | *-oʔ* |
| 'Referent' | *-in* | R<*in*>OOT-*an* | *-iʔ* |
| 'Associate'/ Locative | *-an* | R<*in*>OOT-*an* | (n.a.) |
| Instrumental | *paN*-REDUP- | *p<in>aN*-REDUP- | (n.a.??) |

The existence of three contrastive voice suffixes (*-in*, *-an*, *-on*) in Murutic is unusual.[23] We are not aware of any other Austronesian language with three voice suffixes.

[22] Dillon (1994) states that the seventh, locative voice, does exist in Tatana', but no longer seems to be productive; the LV suffix occurs in a handful of verbal forms, but is used more often in nominalizations.

[23] Jason Lobel (p.c.) argues that the 'associate focus' suffix (*-an*) is not a productive voice marker but rather a nominalizer. We follow here the descriptions of Prentice, and Brewis (2004), but this is an issue that requires further investigation.

#### 47.4.1.2 *Languages of central Borneo*

Beatrice Clayre (1996, 2014) describes the voice system of Lun Bawang as being transitional between the Philippine-like voice systems of NE Borneo and the much simpler systems of central Borneo languages such as Berawan, Melanau, Penan, Kayan, and Kenyah, spoken in northern Sarawak and adjacent areas of Kalimantan. The distinctive typological characteristics of central Borneo languages are discussed in more detail in Kroeger and Smith (this volume, §27.3.2). In this section we focus on the issues of voice, transitivity, and coding properties.

In contrast to the multi-voice systems of the Philippines and NE Borneo, central Borneo languages generally exhibit a simple two-way contrast between AV vs. UV or passive, and actor voice is the more basic or preferred form for transitive verbs. (The issue of symmetrical or non-demoting voice has not been addressed for most of these languages, apart from Kelabit (Hemmings 2016) and Begak (Goudswaard 2005). For the others we will follow Clayre in referring to the non-active voice as undergoer voice, but recognize that in some or all of these languages the constructions could turn out to be true passives.)

Central Borneo languages generally lack case marking in common noun phrases and for third person pronouns. First and (for some languages) second person pronouns have distinct genitive forms for actors and possessors, but no distinction between subject and object forms. Because of this lack of case marking, word-order tends to be fairly rigid, with the non-subject core argument immediately following the verb. SVO order is preferred in many of these languages, especially in actor voice.

Although these two-voice systems are sometimes identified as 'Indonesian-type' languages, they are distinct from the Indonesian prototype in lacking applicative suffixes. Dative- and benefactive-shift are possible in at least some of these languages, but not morphologically marked. An example is presented in (28), with data from Dalat Melanau (Iain Clayre 1972). The AV–UV alternation is illustrated in (28a–b), and benefactive-shift is illustrated in (28c).

Dalat Melanau

(28) a. Actor Voice

*Akou melei ubat ʔih gim a pedih.*
1SG AV:buy medicine this for person sick
'I am buying this medicine for a sick person.'

b. Undergoer Voice
*Ubat ʔih b<en>elei kou gim*
medicine this <UV>buy 1SG.GEN for
*a pedih.*
person sick
'I bought this medicine for a sick person.'

c. UV with benefactive shift
*A pedih b<en>elei kou ubat*
person sick <UV>buy 1SG.GEN medicine
*ʔih.*
this
'I bought this medicine for a sick person.'
(I. Clayre 1972: 355)

The voice morphology in many Central Borneo languages exhibits complex allomorphy which is only partially predictable from the phonological form of the root. In some of these languages there is an interaction between voice inflection and tense-aspect, with UV inflection occurring only or primarily in past tense or completive aspect. (The old non-past UV suffix *-en* is retained in nominalizations and fossilized verb forms.)

In addition, a periphrastic undergoer voice is attested in a number of these languages, which competes with or replaces UV morphology. Beatrice Clayre (1996: 76–80) states that this periphrastic undergoer voice is the only productive UV construction remaining in Kayan and Murik. In these languages, the auxiliary which marks UV is reduced to a single invariant syllable, *en*. (In some other central Borneo languages, e.g. Lun Bawang and Lun Dayeh, the UV auxiliary is the UV form of the verb which means 'make' or 'do'.) The main verb follows the auxiliary, appearing in the AV form. The actor NP occurs after the auxiliary and before the main verb. The undergoer-subject may occur either before the auxiliary or following the main verb. A Kayan example is presented in (29). The undergoer-subject NP is underlined.

Kayan
(29) *Hiap atih en Anyiq ngaput(N-kaput)*
chicken that PASS Anyi AV-tie
*menaʔa di.*
a.little.ago PART
'The chicken was tied up by Anyi a while little ago.'
(Clayre and Cubit 1974; as cited by Soriente 2013)

As noted in the following section, similar constructions are also attested in at least two languages of Sabah, namely Bonggi and Begak. In fact, the periphrastic undergoer voice construction seems to be quite widely distributed in Borneo. It is found not only in Bonggi, at the extreme northeastern corner of the island, but also in at least some of the Land Dayak varieties in western Borneo.

### 47.4.1.3 *Transitional languages*

As noted above, Beatrice Clayre (1991, 1996, 2014) describes the Lun Dayeh voice system as transitional between the richer Philippine-type systems to the northeast and the simpler two-voice systems characteristic of central Borneo languages. Two other languages which might be seen as transitional in certain respects are Bonggi (spoken on Banggi and Balambangan islands, between Borneo and Palawan) and Begak (a dialect of the Ida'an language, spoken in southeastern Sabah).[24] The genetic classification of both of these languages has been somewhat controversial; see Smith (chapter 8, this volume) for discussion.

The transitional features of these languages are summarized in Table 47.6. As this table shows, Bonggi voice morphology preserves a fairly typical Philippine-type system of four contrastive voices, which in our terminology we refer to as AV, UV, DV, and IV. Boutin (2002) notes that IV (his instrumental passive) is extremely rare in natural speech. Clayre (1991, 1996, 2014) identifies three productive voice affixes in Lun Dayeh: AV, UV, and IV. She notes (1996: 60) that IV is less common than AV or UV. Hemmings (2016) states that in the closely related Kelabit language, IV is not fully productive as a voice marker; with some roots it has only a nominalizing function. However, Kelabit also has a periphrastic construction involving the auxiliary *inan* which can be used to promote oblique arguments (including instruments) to subject, much like an applicative. Begak has a typical Bornean two-voice system, AV vs. UV. On the other hand, Begak preserves the Philippine-type preference for UV over AV, whereas AV is the most frequent voice category in Bonggi and Lun Dayeh.

### 47.4.1.4 *Malagasy*

Malagasy is spoken on the island of Madagascar, but is genetically most closely related to Ma'anyan and the other Barito languages of SE Borneo (Dahl 1951). Unlike the Barito languages, however, Malagasy preserves many features of a Philippine-type voice system. The voice marking affixes of Malagasy seem to provide evidence of a change in progress from an earlier five-voice system, highly reminiscent of the NE Borneo voice systems discussed in §47.4.1.1, to a three-voice system similar to that of Lun Bawang.

Dahl (1986) recognizes five distinct voice-marking affixes, which he labels using traditional Philippinist terminology as shown in Table 47.7. Pearson (2001) recognizes the same five categories, but uses case-like labels to refer to them.

[24] Information about Bonggi is based on Boutin (2001, 2002). The information about Begak is from Goudswaard's (2005) dissertation.

**Table 47.6** Transitional features summary chart

| Language Feature | Kimaragang (Philippine-type) | Bonggi | Lun Dayeh/ Kelabit | Begak | Core Central Borneo pattern |
|---|---|---|---|---|---|
| # of morph. voice categories | 7 | 4 | ? | 2 | 2 |
| preferred/highest frequency voice | non-active | AV | AV | UV | AV |
| basic word order | V-initial | SVO | AV: SVO<br>UV: VOS[a] | AV: SVO<br>UV: VOS | SVO |
| case marking | all NPs: 3 cases | 1/2 pers: 3 cases<br>proper name: 2 cases<br>common NP: no case | sg & 3rd pl pro: 3 cases<br>all others: no case | 1/2 sg: 3 cases<br>1/2 pl: 2 cases<br>3rd pers: no case | pronouns: 2 cases<br>all others: no case |
| periphrastic UV | no | yes | yes | yes | yes |

[a] Based on frequency counts for Kelabit, from Hemmings (2016: 457).

Keenan (1976: 257) combines the suffixes *-ina* and *-ana* into a single category, which he labels goal voice. Paul (2000a: 23) and Pearson (2001) also treat these suffixes essentially as variant forms of a single morpheme, on the grounds that the choice between the two forms in modern Malagasy is lexically determined: it "appears to be an idiosyncratic feature of the verbs in question" (Pearson 2001: 48). However, there is a residual contrast between the two suffixes. At least thirteen roots have been identified which accept both *-ana* and *-ina*, with different semantic functions (Rahajarizafy 1960; Keenan and Polinsky 1998: 623; Pearson 2001: 50, fn. 14). Pearson (1998) notes that the *-ana* form tends to occur where NE Borneo languages would use *-an*, and *-ina* tends to occur where the NE Borneo languages would use *-on*.

**Table 47.7** Malagasy voice-marking affixes

| MARKER | Dahl (1986) | Pearson (2001) | Keenan (1976) |
|---|---|---|---|
| *maN-*, *mi-* | Actor Focus | Nominative-pivot | Active Voice |
| *-ina* | Object Focus | Accusative-pivot | Goal Voice |
| *-ana* | Referent Focus | Dative-pivot | |
| *a-* | Instrument Focus | Translative-pivot | Intermediary Voice |
| *aN*-ROOT-*ana* ~ *i*-ROOT-*ana* | Circumstantial Focus | Circumstantial-pivot | Circumstantial Voice |

While Keenan (1976) distinguishes goal voice vs. intermediary voice on semantic and morphological grounds, in his discussion of syntax he treats both of these as 'passive' forms, resulting in just three syntactic voices. Guilfoyle, Hung, and Travis (1992) adopt the same three-voice analysis for Malagasy, and this has become the standard view in most recent work on the formal syntax of the language. The basic intuition is that there is a single syntactic process which promotes underlying objects to the subject/pivot/trigger position. Goal voice and intermediary voice affixes select different classes of arguments as underlying primary objects; see Paul (2000a) for one version of this analysis.

Synchronically, the contrast between goal voice vs. intermediary voice seems to be productive enough to justify recognizing them as distinct morphological categories. Pearson (1998) and Paul (1999, 2000a, b) identify at least three classes of verb roots for which the prefix *a-* occurs in contrast to a 'suffixed passive' form. In such cases the semantic functions associated with the two forms are largely parallel with analogous forms (prefixed CV vs. suffixed OV and DV) in languages of northeastern Sabah: *a-* is used for displaced theme and instrument subjects, while *-Vna* is used for patient and goal subjects.

However, both Keenan (1976) and Paul (2000a) note a tendency for *a-* to be replaced by the goal or circumstantial voice forms with particular roots; and, more generally, "a growing tendency for verbs to take only one of the 'passive' forms" (Keenan 1976). If this tendency continues to the point that the contrast is no longer productive, the resulting voice inventory will be much like that of Lun Bawang: actor voice, undergoer voice, and circumstantial voice. The various markers of undergoer voice (*a-* vs. *-Vna*) would be best treated as lexically conditioned allomorphs, with a residual contrast preserved between prefixed vs. suffixed passive forms for a limited number of roots.

While the Malagasy voice paradigm preserves evidence of a rich Philippine-type voice system, this is not the case in modern languages of SE Borneo, and in particular the Barito languages, which are genetically the closest relatives of Malagasy. One such language, Ma'anyan, is discussed in the next section.

#### 47.4.1.5 *Ma'anyan*

Ma'anyan, a Barito language of SE Borneo, is closely related to Malagasy but preserves few if any traces of a Philippine-type voice system. In many ways, the grammar of Ma'anyan (as described by Gudai 1985) is quite Malayic in character.[25] NPs are not case marked, aside from distinct genitive forms of the singular pronouns (used for both possessors and passive agents). SVO appears to be the dominant word order in both active and passive clauses.

Gudai (1985: 213 ff) describes two types of passive construction, one marked by the prefix *na-* and the other marked by a null prefix. (Active transitive verbs generally bear the prefix N-.) With the prefixed passive, the agent is marked with the preposition *daya* (homophonous with the particle meaning 'because'). This agentive PP can optionally be omitted when it is understood from the context. When it is expressed, it can occur in various positions, including sentence-initial (before the subject) and sentence-final. When the agent phrase immediately follows the verb, the preposition may optionally be omitted, like *oleh* in the Malay *di-* passive.

With the zero passive, however, the agent is obligatory, is never marked with a preposition, and must always occur immediately after the verb. In these respects, it is similar to the UV construction in Balinese. The zero passive is preferred over *na-* when the agent is a pronoun, and only the zero passive is possible when the agent is first or second person. Proper names and common noun phrases can appear as agents in both types of passive. Gudai (1985: 228) states that for both types of passive, the subject NP must be definite or specific. However, it is not clear to what extent this might also hold for subjects of active clauses.

Gudai (1985: 225) describes a third type of passive, marked by the prefix *ta-*, which he labels the ACCIDENTAL passive. In fact, *ta-* has both active and passive uses, as illustrated in (30a–c).

Ma'anyan

(30) a. *Ijap ta-qalap sapidaq=ku.*
Ijap ACCIDENT-take bicycle=1SG
'Ijap has taken my bicycle by mistake.'

b. *Sapidaq=ku ta-qalap (daya) Ijap.*
bicycle=1SG ACCIDENT-take by Ijap
'My bicycle has been taken by Ijap by mistake.'

c. *Ulun yeruq ta-dinung daya=ku rahat manrus.*
person that ACCIDENT-see by=1SG PROG take.shower
'I accidentally saw the man taking a shower.'
(Gudai 1985: 225, 226)

We might be tempted to assume that the accidental passive is simply a zero passive formed from a stem that contains the accidental prefix. However, the constraints on the agent in the accidental passive construction are different from those in either of the other passive types. The agent is obligatory in the accidental passive, but can optionally be marked with the preposition *daya*, even when the agent is first or second person (30c).

The prefix *i-* also attaches to transitive roots, with an interesting range of detransitivizing functions. The derived intransitive formed with this prefix may occur with no object NP (31a), or with a bare non-specific object NP (31b). Gudai (1985: 188) describes this second pattern as being equivalent to noun incorporation in a language like English. This verb form cannot take an object NP that is definite (31c) or quantified (31d). In order to express these kinds of meanings, the normal transitive form must be used as in (31e).

Ma'anyan

(31) a. *Waweh yeruq i-wuwiq.*
woman that DETRANS-wash
'That woman is washing.'

b. *Waweh yeruq i-wuwiq lumbah.*
woman that DETRANS-wash dish
'That woman is dish-washing.'

c. **Waweh yeruq i-wuwiq lumbah yiti.*
woman that DETRANS-wash dish this
(intended: 'That woman is washing this dish.')

[25] It is likely that some of the similarities are the result of contact-induced change, since Gudai reports that virtually all Ma'anyan speakers are bilingual in Banjar (Malay).

d. **Waweh yeruq i-wuwiq dime*
woman that DETRANS-wash five
*kawuwaq lumbah.*
CLF dish
(Intended: 'That woman is washing five dishes.')

e. *Hi ineh muwiq(N-wuwiq) lumbah yiti.*
HON mother AV-wash dish this
'Mother is washing this dish/these dishes.'
(Gudai 1985: 187, 188, 114)

The prefix *i-* is also used to form reflexive verbs, and occurs optionally on reciprocals. It is also used to derive a wide range of intransitive denominal verbs. We do not know whether this prefix might be an inherited reflex of PAN *Si-. The form is identical to the conveyance voice prefix in the conservative NE Borneo languages, but its functions are quite different.

### 47.4.2 Sulawesi

In Sulawesi, as in Borneo, we find Philippine-type languages in the far north. The Minahasan languages preserve a Philippine-type voice system which may be in some ways even more conservative than the NE Borneo languages. For example, Sneddon (1978) reports that in Minahasan, the prefix *i-* is still used for benefactive as well as conveyance and instrumental functions. Totoli, spoken in northern Central Sulawesi, has been argued to constitute an intermediate type between the prototypical Philippine-type and the Indonesian-type systems (cf. Riesberg et al. 2021).

The predominant voice pattern of South Sulawesi languages is strikingly different from those found in the north of the island. We illustrate it here with examples from Bugis. Laskowske (2016) describes a symmetrical alternation between AV vs. UV, as illustrated in (32). The UV form is the most basic and frequent transitive construction, and is characterized by ergative and absolutive agreement clitics on the verb. In the AV form, the verb bears only an absolutive agreement clitic, which agrees with the actor rather than the undergoer. However, Laskowske argues that the AV clause is syntactically transitive, with the undergoer retaining its core argument status as indicated by the lack of preposition or oblique case marking, and the fact that it is obligatory.

Bugis
(32) a. Undergoer voice
*Na=uno=i ula-é Popi.*
3ERG=kill=3ABS snake-DEF Popi
'Popi killed the snake.'

b. Actor voice
*M-uno=i ula Popi.*
AV-kill=3ABS snake Popi
'Popi killed a snake.' (Laskowske 2016: 2)

In addition, Bugis has detransitivizing passive and antipassive constructions, as illustrated in (33a) and (33b).

Bugis
(33) a. Passive voice
*I-uno=i ula-é ku Popi.*
PASS-kill=3ABS snake-DEF OBL Popi
'The snake was killed by Popi.'

b. Antipassive voice
*Mabb-uno ula=i Popi.*
ANTIP-kill snake=3ABS Popi
'Popi was killing snakes.' (Laskowske 2016: 2)

In contrast to the AV undergoer, the undergoer of an antipassive cannot occur as an independent NP. It may be expressed as an oblique PP, as in (34a); it may be incorporated, occurring between the verb stem and the absolutive clitic as in (33b) and (34b); or it may be omitted entirely, as in (34c). None of these options is possible with the AV undergoer (cf. Laskowske 2016: 63).

Bugis
(34) a. *Mas-sémpeʔ=i Saénal lao ri asu-é.*
ANTIP-kick=3ABS Saénal OBL dog-DEF
'Saénal kicked at the dog (but didn't necessarily hit it).'

b. *Mas-sémpeʔ asu=i Saénal.*
ANTIP-kick dog=3ABS Saénal
'Saénal kicked dogs/a dog.'

c. *Mar-oki=kaʔ.*
ANTIP-write=1SG.ABS
'I'm writing.' (Laskowske 2016: 65, p.c., 85)

Similar voice systems are found in closely related languages such as Konjo and Makasar, although Jukes (2013) identifies the Makasar analogue of AV as a "semi-transitive" construction, rather than fully symmetrical.[26] Laskowske argues that the more distantly related Seko Padang also has the same voice inventory as Bugis.

Quick (2007) describes a Bugis-like voice inventory for Pendau, including a symmetrical alternation between AV (marked with *N-poN-*) and the "inverse voice" (our UV, marked with *ni-*). In addition, Quick describes detransitivizing passive and antipassive constructions, marked with *no-* and *N-pe-* respectively.

Many other Sulawesi languages can be seen as transitional between the Minahasan and Bugis prototypes. A number of languages exhibit a two-way symmetrical distinction

[26] Laskowske suggests that the reason for this difference in analysis is that Jukes uses a different definition of symmetrical voice from the one assumed by Laskowske (compare also with Jukes 2005, 2006).

between AV and UV. Often, these languages display a passive voice in addition to the two symmetrical voices. Balantak (van den Berg and Busenitz 2012), for example, appears to have a zero-marked UV that contrasts with a prefixed agentless passive. In languages where there are two distinct undergoer voice markers, such as Totoli, the choice between the two is lexically determined. In these languages Philippine voice affixes may be preserved, but with grammatical functions that are different from the functions found in Philippine languages.

In a Philippine-type language, every voice category has an associated voice marker (although UV is typically zero-marked in past tense or perfective aspect). In Bugis, UV verbs are identified only by the presence of the ABS and ERG agreement clitics; they do not bear a voice-marking affix. Pendau might be viewed as transitional in this respect. In irrealis verbs with a first or second person singular actor, the normal UV irrealis prefix *ro-* can optionally be replaced by an agentive clitic pronoun:[27]

Pendau

(35) a. ***ro**-oli=**ʔu*** ~ ***ʔu**-oli*
**UV.IRR**-buy=**1SG** **1SG**-buy
'I will buy (UV)'

b. ***ro**-oli=**mu*** ~ ***mu**-oli*
**UV.IRR**-buy=**2SG** **2SG**-buy
'you will buy (UV)' (Quick 2007: 371, 375)

In realis verbs with a first person singular actor, the normal UV realis prefix *ni-* can optionally be replaced by a portmanteau prefix that encodes information about voice, mood, and person.

Pendau

(36) ***ni**-oli=ʔu* ~ ***noʔu**-oli*
**UV.REAL**-buy=**1SG** **1SG.REAL.UV**-buy
'I will buy (UV)' (Quick 2007: 371, 375)

Pendau

(37) a. *paey* ***ni**-ʔito* *nu=too* ***aʔu***
and.then **UV.REAL**-see GEN=person **1SG**
'and then people saw me'

b. *apa sura butu baliung moo*
since only just axe this
***noʔu**-ʔomung~ʔomung apa ndau*
**1SG.UV.REAL**-carry~REDUP since NEG
*ʔe-piso*
HAVE-machete
'since I am only just carrying this axe, (and) since I don't have a machete' (Quick 2007: 371, 375)

[27] In a number of other languages this use of actor marking, restricted to first or first and second person singular, occurs only in non-realis mood (e.g. Da'a, Tajio, Totoli).

Similar portmanteau prefixes are obligatory in all persons in Tukang Besi, although the contrast between realis vs. irrealis is neutralized in the first person singular. Unlike Pendau, the prefixes in Tukang Besi do not encode voice. The prefix agrees with the single core argument of an intransitive clause (including passives), and with the actor in all transitive clauses. The contrast between AV vs. UV is indicated by the presence or absence of a pronominal enclitic which cross-references the undergoer in UV forms.

Example (38a) illustrates the AV pattern: the verb is marked only by the S/A prefix, the actor argument gets nominative case and functions as the subject of the construction, and the undergoer gets the non-subject core marker *te*. Example (38b) illustrates the UV pattern: both actor and undergoer are cross-referenced on the verb, with the nominative undergoer functioning as subject and the actor marked as a non-subject core argument.

Tukang Besi

(38) a. *no-kikiʔi te ikoʔo* ***na beka***
3.REAL-bite ART 2SG **NOM cat**
'the cat bit you'

b. *no-kikiʔi=**ko*** ***na*** ***ikoʔo*** *te beka*
3.REAL-bite=**2SG.U** **NOM** **2SG** ART cat
'the cat bit you' (Donohue 1999a: 53)

Grammatical subjects in Tukang Besi are identified on the basis of relativization, possessor ascension, and quantifier float. Donohue (2002: 87) argues that the AV–UV alternation is best analysed as symmetrical, rather than an ergative–antipassive or active–passive alternation.

Mori Bawah is another South Sulawesi language that makes use of portmanteau clitics which encode S/A indexing plus future vs. non-future aspect/mood. Examples (39a) and (39b) illustrate the 3SG non-future clitic *=i*. Object agreement enclitics are obligatory in transitive clauses, but do not occur in intransitive clauses, including the passive and antipassive constructions, marked with *-in-* and *poN-* respectively. The three-way voice contrast is illustrated in (39). The undergoer of the antipassive construction receives an indefinite/non-specific reading (39b). As in Tukang Besi, the passive in Mori Bawah is actor-deleting (i.e. the actor argument can never be overtly expressed in a passive construction (39c)).

Mori Bawah

(39) a. *...ka=i pepate=**ʔira*** *ana-o*
and=3SG.NOM kill=**3PL.ABS** child-3SG.GEN
'...and she killed her children'

b. *...ka=i* ***pom**-pepate singa*
and=3SG.NOM **ANTIP**-kill lion
'...and he killed a lion'

c. *ta* *p<in>epate*
3SG.FUT <PASS>kill
'he will/shall/must be killed' (Mead 2005: 698)

We have seen that some Sulawesi languages have symmetrical voice systems, whether these involve multiple voice categories (e.g. Minahasa) or just AV vs. UV, as in Bugis and Pendau. Other Sulawesi languages exhibit only asymmetrical voice alternations, like Mori Bawah. Finally, there are languages which don't exhibit any voice at all, and which use other means for foregrounding or backgrounding arguments. Muna is an example of this latter type.

Basic word order in Muna is SVO, as seen in (40a). There are two marked word orders that are functionally similar to passives. In both cases the subject is moved into sentence final position, with the object realized either by a pronominal suffix (40b), or as a full NP which then occurs in sentence initial position (40c).

Muna

(40) a. *ai-hi-ku* *minaho*
younger.sibling-PL-1SG.GEN not.yet
*da-[m]ande-ha-ane* *hula-no*
3PL.IRR-know-INTNS-it face-LNK
*ama-mani*
father-1PL.EXCL.GEN
'my younger siblings still did not know our father's face'

b. *no-wora-e-mo* *dahu*
3SG.REAL-see-him-PFV dog
'he was seen by a dog'

c. *dadi* *o* *karambau* *no-talo-e*
so ART buffalo 3SG.REAL-defeat-him
*o* *bhiku*
ART snail
'so the buffalo was defeated by the snail' (van den Berg 2013[1989]: 163, 166, 167)

Van den Berg notes that in the latter two constructions, the object is taken as "point of departure" and the subject is backgrounded, as in a passive. Native speakers usually translate these structures as passives in Indonesian (van den Berg 2013: 165). However, unlike a true passive construction, there is no re-linking of semantic roles to syntactic functions. In all three examples in (40), the actor is the subject, cross-referenced on the verb by the subject prefix, and the undergoer is the object, cross-referenced by the object suffix.[28] When both subject and object are third person and have the same number value, a structure like the one in (40b) is formally ambiguous, allowing the post-verbal NP to be interpreted either as subject or as object. In spoken speech, however, this ambiguity does not arise, as the two interpretations correlate with two different intonation patterns. If the post-verbal NP is the object, it carries the intonational nucleus. If the post-verbal NP is the subject, the nucleus is on the verb (van den Berg 2013: 167).

## 47.5 From west to east – a cline of voice in the Sundic Islands and beyond

### 47.5.1 Western Indonesia

Several languages in western Indonesia have been analysed as having the same basic inventory of voice categories as Balinese, illustrated in (1) in §47.2.2 above: an undergoer voice, typically marked by Ø-; an actor voice, typically marked by a nasal prefix; and a true passive. These languages include: Malay/Indonesian (Guilfoyle, Hung, and Travis 1992; Arka and Manning 2008; Musgrave 2001; Arka 2009a; Cole, Hermon, and Yanti 2008); various Sama-Bajaw languages (Miller 2007; James 2017); and Acehnese (Legate 2012, 2014).

The undergoer voice in these languages is fully transitive, because the actor is a core argument; but there are restrictions on the kind of NP that can be used to express the UV actor. James (2017) states that in Central Sinama, the actor in a UV clause is obligatory and must be expressed as an enclitic pronoun on the verb. This contrasts with the actor of a passive, which is an oblique argument marked by a preposition, is freely ordered within the clause, and may be omitted entirely. Miller (2014) cites Sama Bangingi' and Southern Sinama as examples of other Sama-Bajaw languages in which the actor in a UV clause is obligatory and must be expressed as an enclitic pronoun on the verb. In addition, he states that in Sama Bangingi' the UV actor is normally first or second person, and only rarely occurs as a third person pronoun.

In Indonesian, Sneddon (1996: 249–50) states that the UV actor must be expressed as a free pronoun form as in (41a), a clitic pronoun as in (41b), or a 'pronoun substitute' (i.e. a kinship term or proper name used with first or second person reference) as in (41c) and (41d). Moreover, the UV actor phrase is obligatory and must appear immediately before the verb, in contrast to the prepositional actor phrase in the true passive construction (in which the verb is marked with *di-*). The passive actor is flexible in its ordering and may

[28] The subject agreement marker on the verb is obligatory, whether or not the clause contains a free subject pronoun or lexical NP. The object pronominal suffix is optional. It can co-occur with a lexical NP object, as seen in (40a) and (40c), but not with a free object pronoun.

optionally be omitted when it is understood from context, or may simply remain unspecified.[29]

Indonesian

(41) a. *Mobil itu dapat* <u>*kita*</u> *Ø-perbaiki.*
car that get 1PL.INCL UV-repair
'We can repair the car.' (Chung 1976: 60)

b. *Buku ini harus* <u>*kau*</u>*=Ø-baca.*
book this must 2SG=UV-read
'You must read this book.' (Sneddon 1996: 249)

c. *Surat ini harus* <u>*adik*</u>
letter this must younger.sibling
*Ø-tandatangani.*
UV-sign
'You (younger sibling) must sign this letter.'
(Dalrymple and Mofu 2009)

d. *Buku itu sudah* <u>*Tini*</u>
book that already (speaker's name)
*Ø-kembalikan.*
UV-return
'I (Tini) have already returned the book.'
(Sneddon 1996: 250)

Person restrictions can be observed in Malay/Indonesian as well. First and second person pronouns are strongly disfavoured as the actor of a *di-* passive, and are considered ungrammatical in this function in the standard varieties, Malaysian and Indonesian.[30] Conversely, as Chung (1976: 60) points out, some authors have stated that UV actors must be a first or second person pronoun. Chung observes that this was true at an earlier stage of the language, and Safiah Karim et al. (1987: 91) seem to imply that this continues to be at least a preference in modern standard Malaysian. In modern Indonesian, however, third person pronouns are fully acceptable as UV actors.

The status of the passive construction in Acehnese has been a controversial issue. Lawler (1977) analysed the construction in (42b) as a passive, in spite of the fact that the verb agrees with its prepositional actor phrase. This proposal triggered much discussion, since agreement with oblique arguments seems to be vanishingly rare across languages.[31] Durie (1985, 1988) argued in reply that the so-called passive construction in (42b) is merely topicalization of the object NP, and does not involve any change in grammatical relations.

Acehnese

(42) a. *Uleue nyan di-kap lôn.* [AV]
snake DEM 3.FAM-bite 1SG
'The snake bit me.'

b. *Lôn di-kap lé uleue nyan.* [PASSIVE]
1SG 3.FAM-bite by snake DEM
'I was bitten by the snake.'

c. *Lôn uleue nyan kap.* [UV]
1SG snake DEM bite
'The snake bit me.' (Legate 2012: 497, 498)

In more recent work, Legate (2012, 2014) argues that Lawler was correct in analysing this construction as a passive. She uses evidence from control, weak crossover, and pronominal binding to argue that the sentence-initial patient is in fact the subject of (42b). The *lé*-marked actor in (42b) is argued to be an oblique PP based on the following properties: (a) it can be topicalized, occurring before the subject, unlike other core arguments; (b) it cannot be questioned with the *wh*-question pattern that makes use of the complementizer (or relativizer) *(n)yang*; (c) it cannot launch floating quantifiers; (d) it is freely ordered with respect to other prepositional phrases; and (e) it is omissible, unlike the UV actor in (42c), and when omitted receives a non-specific, existential reading rather than a specific, pro-drop reading.[32]

In addition to the three-voice systems discussed above, symmetrical two-voice systems (no passive) are attested in Toba Batak (Schachter 1984; Cole and Hermon 2008; Erlewine 2018), Besemah (McDonnell 2016b), and Madurese (Davies 2010). Recent work on Toba Batak has retained the traditional label 'passive' for the UV, but makes it clear that this construction is quite different from the English-type passive:

> Following previous literature. . . I refer to the prefix *maN-* . . . as 'active' and *di-* . . . as 'passive', though I should warn against conflation with Indo-European active/passive alternations. In particular, the passive is not valence-decreasing: for example, the agent . . . continues to be a nonoblique core argument in the passive. . . (Erlewine 2018)[33]

Such comments raise an important issue with respect to the numerous languages of western Indonesia that have

[29] The preposition that marks the passive actor, *oleh*, may optionally be dropped if the actor phrase immediately follows the verb.

[30] Sneddon (1996: 249) and Nomoto and Kartini (2014) state that such examples are attested in natural conversation, even among educated speakers. However, the corpus data in the study by Nomoto and Kartini indicate that first and second person actors occur in the *di-* passive with very low frequency, as compared to third person actors.

[31] Montana Salish has been cited as another instance of this; transitive subjects trigger verb agreement even when marked with the oblique particle (Baier 2013).

[32] Under the formal analysis that Legate proposes, the passive verb does not 'agree' with its actor in the technical Minimalist sense. However, Legate concedes that on a descriptive level, this does seem like agreement (2014: 33): "It is clear that in a broad sense the prefix may be termed agreement: it is a dependent morpheme that registers the features of an argument" [specifically, in this case, person and politeness — PK & SR].

[33] Similar comments are made by Cole and Hermon (2008).

been analysed as having the same basic voice inventory as English, namely active vs. passive. In many cases, a non-active voice may have been labelled 'passive' without ever considering the possibility of a symmetrical alternation or applying any diagnostics to distinguish passive from UV. A counterexample to this tendency is the careful study by Cole, Hermon, and Yanti (2008) comparing the voice systems of Jambi Malay dialects (south-central Sumatra). They demonstrate that the Sarolangun and Sarang Lan dialects have the same basic voice inventory as standard Indonesian: AV, UV, and passive. The Mudung Darat dialect, in contrast, lacks UV, and so instantiates a simple active vs. passive voice system.

However, in many grammatical descriptions of western Indonesian languages the term 'passive' continues to be used without consideration of the distinction between UV and passive. For this reason, it is probably impossible at the current time to estimate how widespread the Indonesian type of symmetrical voice system might be in this region.

### 47.5.2 Voice – and lack of voice – in eastern Indonesia

Turning east from Bali, we find that the use of voice morphology decreases and that languages become more isolating the further east we get. These tendencies are observed even in Sasak, Balinese's closest (geographic) neighbour to the east. In Sasak the matrix verb is frequently preceded by an auxiliary which hosts a pronominal clitic that cross-references the subject. An additional free subject NP is optional. Like Balinese, Sasak has verbal forms with nasal prefixes, and it has bare verb forms. The functional difference between these two, however, has been partly lost in some of the Sasak varieties, as illustrated in (43), where either *bace* or *mbace* 'read' can be used.[34]

Sasak Ngeno-Ngené
(43) ***aku*** *jengke-ng=**ku*** *bace* / *mbace* *buku=ni*
**1SG** PROG-LNK=**1** read N:read book=this
'I am reading this book' (Arka 2009b: 250)

As Arka (2009b) shows, however, there are certain contexts in which the difference between bare and nasal verb form is not neutralized. This is, for example, the case when an undergoer question word is fronted, as in (44). In this context, only a bare verb can be used. A parallel example to this can be found in Balinese, where clearly only the (bare) undergoer voice form, but not the actor voice verb can be used.

[34] Austin (2010: 96) notes that, depending on the verbal form, the non-subject argument receives either a specific (with nasal verb) or a non-specific (with bare verb) reading. The translation of (43) should thus be 'reading this book' for *mbace* and 'reading (some) books' for *bace*. He agrees, however, that the use of the two different verb forms does not mark a difference in voice.

Sasak Ngeno-Ngené
(44) *epe te Amir paleng* / **maleng rubin?*
what PART Amir steal N:steal yesterday
'what did Amir steal yesterday?' (Arka 2009b: 250)

Balinese
(45) a. *apa ane paling cai?*
what REL UV:steal 2
'what did you steal?'
b. **apa ane cai maling*
what REL 2 AV:steal (Arka 2009b: 250)

Comparing (44) and (45), it seems tempting to analyse the bare verb in Sasak, just like the Balinese bare verb, as an undergoer voice verb. However, the interchangeability of the bare verb and the nasal verb shown in (43) speaks against such an analysis. When the actor is third person, the order shown in (43) is possible, but strongly marked. Rather than (46a), speakers prefer the construction in (46b), where the actor occurs as a clitic in preverbal position, and can furthermore be optionally realized as a PP.

Sasak Meno-Mené
(46) a. ***inaq*** *mu-**n*** *kelor sebie odaq*
**mother** PST-**3** eat chili green
'mother ate green chili'
b. *mu-**n*** *kelor sebie odaq* ***isiq inaq***
PST-**3** eat chili green **by mother**
'mother ate green chili' (Musgrave 1998: 92)

This construction might at first sight constitute another candidate for an undergoer voice construction (because the verb occurs in its bare form) or for a passive (because the actor occurs as a PP). Musgrave (1998), however, argues that the preverbal pronominal clitic remains the subject of this construction (see also Arka 2009b). Shibatani (2008), on the other hand, argues that the two clauses in (46) constitute what he calls ACTOR FOCUS and PATIENT FOCUS, respectively, in the same way as Balinese AV and UV (which he also calls AF and PF), and shows that they exhibit different relativization properties:

Sasak Meno-Mené
(47) a. *dengan nine [saq Ø kelor sebie*
person female REL eat chili
*odaq]=no inaq=ku*
green=that mother=1
'the woman who ate the green chili is my mother'
b. **sebie odaq [saq inaq mu=n kelor*
chili green REL mother PST=3 eat
*Ø ] besar*
big
for: 'the green chili which my mother ate was big'

c. *sebie odaq [saq mu=n kelor* **Ø** *isiq*
chili green REL PST=3 eat by
*inaq] besar*
mother big
'the green chili that my mother ate was big'

d. **dengan nine [saq mu=n kelor sebie*
person female REL PST=3 eat chili
*odaq (isiq)* **Ø**] *=no inaq=ku*
green by =that mother=1
for: 'the woman who ate green chili is my mother' (Shibatani 2008: 885f)

The status of these constructions thus remains unclear. It is, however, clear that *if* (46a) and (46b) were to constitute a difference in voice, we would be dealing with a voice alternation without morphological marking on the verb.

Sasak does, however, have a canonical passive construction, in which the verb is marked by the passive morpheme *te-* and the actor argument is realized as an oblique, introduced by the preposition *isiq*.

Sasak Ngeno-Ngené
(48) *aku te-pantòk isiq lóq Ali*
1SG PASS-hit by ART Ali
'I was hit by Ali' (Austin 2013: 35)

Thus, even if the status of the alternation between constructions like (46a) and (46b) remains unclear, we find an alternation between an active (as in (43)) and a passive (as in (48)).

Turning further east and looking at Sumbawa, we find that (the use of) the nasal prefix is not only neutralized, but has been lost as a marker of transitive verbs altogether.[35] Sumbawa has an 'active' construction parallel to the one described for Sasak, that is, with an actor subject cliticized to an auxiliary and optionally realized as a free NP, if first or second person singular. Third person singular, however, remains unmarked, so in these contexts, clause structure will be simply NP V NP (see (49a)). The verb in this construction, as in Sasak, is morphologically unmarked, and just like Sasak, Sumbawa also displays a canonical passive, with a passivized verb and an oblique actor (see (49b)). In addition to that, however, a passive construction is also possible without morphological marking on the verb, as in (49c). Here the patient occurs in (preverbal) subject position, and the actor is demoted to oblique, but the verb remains in its bare form.

[35] The nasal form is only used when the verb is formally intransitive (Wouk 2002: 300).

Sumbawa
(49) a. *Helmi sapu kamar ta.*
Helmi sweep room DEM
'Helmi is sweeping the room.'

b. ***Ka**-ajak-ku* ***ling*** *dengan-ku lalo ko*
**PASS**-invite-1SG **by** friend-1SG go to
*Moyo.*
Moyo
'My friend invited me to go to Moyo.'

c. *Andi pikul* ***ling*** *Iwan.*
Andi hit **by** Iwan
'Andi was hit by Iwan.' (Wouk 2002: 301, 302, 303)

Bima (Sumbawa, Flores), like Sumbawa, has different passive constructions with and without verbal morphology. To the east on Flores, languages like Rongga and Manggarai have this 'bare' passive (as illustrated in (49c)) as the only means of voice alternation (for examples see Arka and Kosmas (2005); Arka (2009b); and Arka and Wouk (2014)). That is, in these languages there is no verbal morphology to indicate voice on the verb. There is, however, clear demotion of the actor argument to oblique status, signalled by post-verbal position and prepositional marking.

In eastern Flores we find further attrition, with languages that exhibit voice alternations in which there is neither voice marking on the verb, nor demotion of the actor argument to oblique status. In these languages, the change of linking is solely achieved by a change in word order. Consider the examples from Sika (Flores) in (50).

Sika
(50) a. *Petrus gita ilin ia.*
Petrus see mountain that
'Petrus saw the mountain.'

b. *Ilin ia Petrus gita.*
mountain that Petrus see
'The mountain, Petrus saw.'

c. **Ilin ia toma gita éʔi Petrus.*
mountain that can see by Petrus
(Arka and Wouk 2014: 318)

(50a) constitutes what Arka and Wouk (2014: 318) call the "active" construction in Sika, in which the actor occurs in subject function and directly precedes the verb. In (50b), the undergoer is fronted into sentence-initial position. Importantly, however, the undergoer in this P–A–V construction is not simply topicalized into pre-clausal position, but is actually promoted to be the grammatical subject. The actor remains obligatory and, as illustrated in (50c), cannot be demoted to oblique. Other languages reported to exhibit the kind of 'structural' voice alternation illustrated in (50) are Lio (Arka and Wouk 2014) and Palu'e (Donohue 2005c). For Palu'e, Donohue (2005c: 77ff) argues that the P–A–V construction should be analysed as a passive, because the actor cannot launch floating quantifiers, which is a core-argument property in Palu'e. Arka and Wouk, on the other hand, show that the actor in this construction actually does show a number of core properties, such as, among other things, the ability to bind core reflexive arguments (see Arka and Wouk (2014: 319) for more details). They therefore conclude that the P–A–V construction in Palu'e should better be analysed as a (symmetrical) undergoer voice, similar to the undergoer voice in Balinese or Totoli (see §47.2.2).

In other languages of this region, such as Keo (Flores), Kambera (Sumba), or Waima'a (East Timor), there is no evidence for canonical passives or any other kind of voice alternations. To achieve the pragmatic effect of different voice constructions (i.e. foregrounding or backgrounding of different arguments), these languages make use of different strategies, such as topicalization, cleft-like structures, or other word order options similar to those found in Muna, illustrated in (40) in §47.4.2. Some of these are illustrated for Kambera in the examples below, where the first example shows unmarked word order with the object following the verb, while in the second example the object is 'in focus' (Klamer 1998: 337) and occurs pre-verbally. Example (51c) is a cleft-like construction involving an object relative.

Kambera

(51) a. *na* *tau* *wútu* *na-palu-ka*
ART person be.fat 3SG.NOM-hit-1SG.ACC
*nyungga*
1SG
'the big man hit me'

b. *nyungga* *na-palu-ka* *tau*
1SG 3SG.NOM-hit-1SG.ACC person
*wútu*
be.fat
'I (was) hit by a big man'

c. *nyungga* [*pa-palu-na* *nyuna*]
1SG REL.O-hit-3SG he
'I (am) (the one who) (was) hit by him'
(Klamer 1998: 337)

A lack of voice alternations has also been reported for most of the Central Malayo-Polynesian (CMP) languages of the Moluccas and the South Halmahera–West New Guinea (SHWNG) subgroup (cf. Musgrave 2007 for a general survey). Many of these languages use word order alternations, as illustrated for Kambera in example (51), while others use impersonal constructions to de-emphasize the actor and to shift the focus to the undergoer argument. Consider the example in (52) from Ambel, a SHWNG language of the West New Guinea branch in Raja Ampat, a group of islands north of the Bird's Head.

Ambel

(52) a. *béle,* *y-asáw* *to,* *ape* *ni-k*
cross-cousin 1SG-marry IAM but GEN-1SG
*bísa* *pa,* *mé* *l-ál*
wife ART person 3PL.ANIM-take
*ki=i* *to*
EMO=3SG.ANIM.OBJ IAM
'Cousin, I'm married, but my wife has been taken'
(or: 'cousin, I'm married, but as for my wife, people have taken her')

b. *sehingga* *yé* *wa-lu-ma,*
so island DEM.CONTR-sea-DIST
*l-úl* *an* *be* *Maúrom*
3PL.ANIM-call 3SG.INAN OBL Maurom
*a-pa*
DEM.NCONTR-MED
'So that island at sea there is called Maurom'
(or: 'so as for that island at sea there, they call it Maurom') (Arnold 2018a: 362, 363)

In both Ambel examples above the undergoer argument—*nik bísa pa* 'my wife' in (52a), and *yé waluma* 'that island at sea there' in (52b)—occurs in pre-clausal position and is co-referential with the object pronoun of the clause. In (52a), the subject of the clause is the generic noun *mé* 'person', in (52b) the subject is unspecified. In both cases, however, the verb carries third person plural animate subject marking (cf. Arnold 2018a: 362). Other West New Guinea languages that, like Ambel, lack syntactic voice alternations, are Wamesa (Gasser 2014), Irarutu (Jackson 2014), and Wooi (Sawaki 2016). Biak, on the other hand, is reported to have a passive, but one which is rarely used. As van den Heuvel (2006) notes, not all Biak transitive verbs can be passivized. Furthermore, in his corpus of natural speech, passives only occur with third person singular subjects (cf. van den Heuvel 2006: 297). Much more widespread than this restricted passive construction are impersonal constructions, similar to the Ambel construction illustrated in (52b), in which the actor argument remains unexpressed but the verb is marked with an impersonal third person plural subject marker (cf. van den Heuvel 2006: 297).

Taba, on the other hand, which belongs to South-Halmahera branch of the SHWNG group, exhibits a detransitivizing prefix. This prefix marks non-volitionality when applied to intransitive verb stems, but it also removes the actor argument from transitive verbs and thus derives intransitive undergoer verbs (Bowden 2001: 218ff), as illustrated in (53).

Taba

(53) a. *I nbhes niwi.*
i n=bhes niwi
3SG 3SG=husk coconut
'She husked the coconut.'

b. *Niwi tabhes do.*
niwi ta-bhes do
coconut DETRANS-husk REAL
'The coconut has been husked.'
(Bowden 2001: 219)

To summarize this section, we can see a decrease in the use of voice morphology, and in the availability of voice alternations in general, the further east in the Indonesian archipelago we move. In the languages of Sumatra, Java, and Bali, we usually find an actor voice, an undergoer voice, and a passive. In Sasak (Lombok), the typical Austronesian nasal voice prefix is still part of the morphological inventory, even if its functional load is partly neutralized in some Sasak varieties. In Sumbawa (Sumbawa) this prefix has been lost. In addition to a prototypical morphological passive, Sumbawa displays a morphologically unmarked passive. Other languages, like Waima'a (East Timor) or Kambera (Sumba), have lost both the morphological and the syntactic means of voice alternation. Languages east of the Sundic Islands, that is, the languages of the Moluccas and the SHWNG languages of Halmahera and New Guinea, display an (almost) complete lack of voice alternations (both morphological and syntactic).

## 47.6 Voice in Chamorro and Palauan

Chamorro and Palauan, spoken on Palau, Guam, and the northern Mariana Islands east of the Philippines in the Pacific Ocean, are the easternmost outliers of the Western Malayo-Polynesian (WMP) linkage. Blust (2013a), who assumes a binary split of Malayo-Polynesian (MP) into Western- and Central-Eastern Malayo-Polynesian, considers both Chamorro and Palauan members of the former branch. Other, more recent approaches favour a 'diverse' model of MP, in which Chamorro and Palauan are two (of a number of) primary branches (Smith 2017b, this volume, chapter 2). Zobel (this volume, chapters 38 and 39) presents a third view.

This section provides some very basic information on the two languages, which have received contradictory treatment in the literature. In particular, it shows once again how any claim about alignment (nominative, ergative, symmetrical) crucially depends on transitivity and a detailed, language specific analysis of grammatical relations.

### 47.6.1 Chamorro

Chamorro can probably be best analysed as an asymmetrical voice language, similar to Mori Bawah described in §47.4.2. It has a morphologically unmarked active construction, a marked antipassive, and two passive constructions. The antipassive is syntactically intransitive and patterns with ordinary intransitive clauses in its use of pronouns: only in intransitive, but not in transitive clauses pronominals vary depending on the mood of the clause (i.e. realis vs. irrealis).

Chamorro

(54) a. *hu-liʔeʔ i lepblo*
1SG.ACTR-see ART book
'I saw the book'

b. ***man**-(t)aitai yoʔ lepblo*
**ANTIP.REAL**-read 1SG.ABS book
'I read a book'

c. ***mam**-(p)atek hao **gi** gaʔlagu*
**ANTIP.REAL**-kick 2SG.ABS **LOC** dog
'you kicked at the dog' (Zobel 2002: 412, 413)

Just as in the Mori Bawah example in (39b), the non-subject patient argument of the antipassive in (54b) has to be interpreted as indefinite or non-specific. However, with certain transitive verbs, a definite patient can be reintroduced, which then has to be marked by the locative marker *gi*, as in (54c). This rather unusual construction is discussed in more detail for Palauan in §47.6.2. The two Chamorro passives, one marked by the infix *-in-*, the other by the prefix *ma-*, distinguish between singular actors and plural or undefined actor arguments (for pragmatic differences between these two passive constructions see Cooreman (1987): chapter 5).

Chamorro

(55) a. *si nana-hu ch<**in**>atge **gias***
ART mother-1SG.GEN <**PASS**>smile **OBL**
*tata-hu*
father-1SG.GEN
'my mother was smiled at by my father'

b. *todu na taotao ni mang-gaige Guam*
all LNK people REL PL-be Guam
*guihi na tiempo man-**ma**-takpangi*
there LNK time PL-**PASS**-baptize
'all the people that were in Guam at that time were baptized' (Cooreman 1987: 50)

The passive and antipassive analysis of clauses like (55) and (54b) is probably the most widespread approach in the literature on Chamorro (e.g. Chung 1982, 1994; Gibson 1992; Zobel 2002, chapter 38, this volume). Topping (1973), on the other hand, and later more explicitly Donohue and Maclachlan (2000), argue that Chamorro is a Philippine type language with a (symmetrical) voice system similar to Tagalog (§47.3). Under their approach, the passive is analysed as an undergoer voice and the antipassive as an actor voice, while the transitive construction in (54c) is assumed to be an innovation without any Philippine-type voice morphology. Once again, much relies on the analysis of the non-subject argument. While Zobel and others argue that the undergoer in (54c) is a prepositionally marked oblique, and we are thus dealing with an antipassive, Donohue and Maclachlan claim that it is marked "as non-oblique (but not subject or object)" (Donohue and Maclachlan 2000: 123), and that this construction is therefore better analysed as actor voice.

## 47.6.2 Palauan

In many respects, Palauan is very similar to Chamorro, but there are a few morphosyntactic complexities that make the analysis of Palauan voice even less straightforward than that of Chamorro. Like Chamorro, Palauan distinguishes three different voice-like categories, but there has been little consensus as to how to interpret certain aspects of these constructions. In this section, we will contrast two approaches to Palauan verbal morphosyntax and briefly discuss them in light of our definition of voice given in the introduction to this chapter. Consider the following examples:

Palauan

(56) a. *ak* *kilisii* *a* *kiokl*
ak k<**il**>ios-ii a kiok-l
1SG.IRR <??>dig-3SG.OBJ ART dig-GER
'I (completely) dug the hole'

b. *ak* *milengiis* *a* *kiokl*
ak **mileN**-kios a kiok-l
1SG.IRR ??-dig ART dig-GER
'I was digging holes'

c. *ak* *milengiis* *er* *a* *kiokl*
ak **mileN**-kios **er** a kiok-l
1SG.IRR ??-dig ?? ART dig-GER
'I was digging the hole' (Zobel 2002: 418, 419)

The first example is a transitive clause, in which object agreement is obligatory. The second and third examples look parallel to the Chamorro antipassives illustrated in (54b) and (54c): both are unmarked for object agreement, and just as in Chamorro, the non-subject phrase is indefinite unless it is introduced by a preposition-like element. In contrast to Chamorro, however, the activity has to be interpreted as ongoing.

The two approaches we will discuss here differ (among other things) as to whether the difference between (56a) on the one hand, and (56b) and (56c) on the other hand, should be analysed as a difference in VOICE (active vs. antipassive), or as a difference in ASPECT (perfective vs. imperfective). Let's first consider the second option, that is, the approach that analyses *kilisii* and *milengiis* as perfective and imperfective forms of the verb *kios* 'to dig', respectively. This view is put forth in Josephs' *Palauan Reference Grammar* (Josephs 1975; see also Wilson 1972; Georgopoulos 1991). In this analysis a perfective verb obligatorily carries an agreement suffix that marks its objects, and it is marked by a 'verb marker' which is infixed after the initial consonant of the verb stem, if in realis mood.[36] Imperfective verbs also take this verb marker if in realis mood,[37] this time as a prefix, followed by the past tense marker (if past tense), followed by an imperfective marker. Imperfective verbs never take object agreement.

The alternative approach, represented by Zobel (2002; this volume, §39.7.4), analyses (56a) as the active construction, and (56b) and (56c) as antipassives, as we have seen for Chamorro. Under his analysis, *-il-* is the marker for active (past), and *mileN-* marks the antipassive (past). Both analyses agree that the construction which involves the presence of an object-indexing suffix is truly transitive. It has an actor subject and a (definite) undergoer object, and can thus be considered to be the 'active' construction. The second construction is (semantically) less transitive in that the non-subject argument is either absent, or receives an indefinite, non-specific reading, as in (56b). Interestingly, and rather unusually, this construction allows for the reintroduction of a definite non-subject phrase, marked by *er*, as in (56c). Its imperfective semantics, however, might still give reason to consider this construction (semantically) less transitive than the active, as does the fact that unlike the active object, the patient argument is not cross-referenced on the verb. These observations would justify an analysis of these two clauses as antipassive constructions, parallel to the Chamorro analysis in §47.6.1.

Again, the relevant question is, what is the *syntactic* status of the two non-subject phrases in (56b) and (56c)? For the latter, the answer to this question crucially depends on

[36] Note that this verb marker is replaced by the past tense and thus does not show in (56a).

[37] Georgopoulos analyses the verb marker as a realis marker, because a verb without this marker is irrealis (Georgopoulos 1991: 26f).

the analysis of the element *er*. And again, there is little consensus in the literature. Josephs (1975: 52) postulates two homonymous words, a specific article, as in *er a kikol* 'the hole' in (56c), and a preposition, as seen, for example, in a phrase like *er a Kuam* 'from Guam' (Georgopoulos 1991: 39). Georgopoulos (1991) and Zobel (2002, chapter 38, this volume) treat both instances as a preposition or oblique marker. This could be taken as evidence that the *er*-marked phrase in the apparent antipassive in (56c) is not a core argument, though neither Georgopoulos nor Zobel (2002) make this claim. Rather, Georgopoulos treats the use of *er* in (56) as an instance of differential object marking: definite objects are marked by the preposition *er*, other objects remain unmarked. She further notes that it also occurs in "various oblique phrases" (Georgopoulos 1991: 29). This view is also advocated by Nuger (2008, 2010, 2016), who offers the most detailed analysis of object marking in Palauan. Like Josephs, he distinguishes two homonymous elements: one preposition, which marks obliques, and one accusative marker, which marks direct objects (Nuger 2008: 20f). Nuger explicitly argues against the antipassive hypothesis and shows that both active and imperfective (apparent antipassive) verbs can equally well occur as matrix predicates in so-called *raising-to-object* constructions.

Palauan

(57) a. *ak=mo* *rul-leterir* *[a*
1SG=AUX.FUT make.PFV-3PL.HUMO DET
*re-chad* *er* *a* *Ekipten* $]_i$ *el*
PL-person PREP DET Egypt LNK
*mo* *mengull* *er* *a*
AUX.FUT respect.IPFV ACC DET
*re-ched-ak* $\_\_{}_i$.
PL-person-1SG.GEN
'I will make the Egyptians respect my people.'

b. *kom=mengiil* *[er* *a* *re-chad*
2PL=expect.IPFV ACC DET PL-person
*er* *a* *Ekipten*$]_i$ *el* *mo*
PREP DET Egypt LNK AUX.FUT
*oltobed* *a* *kuruma* *me*
take.out.IPFV DET chariots and
*a* *re-chad* *er* *a* *uos*
DET PL-person PREP DET horse
*el* *mei* $\_\_{}_i$!
LNK come
'You expect the Egyptians to send (you) chariots and cavalry!' (Nuger 2016: 120, 121)

Under an antipassive hypothesis, so Nuger argues, the raising verb should not be able to appear in the imperfective/antipassive form, as it does in (57b), because "if it cannot Case license a direct object, it should not be able to license the embedded subject of an infinitival clause complement either" (Nuger 2016: 120). Given that the non-subject arguments in (56) behave syntactically alike, the difference between (56a) and the examples in (56b) and (56c) would indeed be an aspectual one, rather than a difference in voice.

## 47.7 Summary

Our survey of voice systems among the Malayo-Polynesian languages of Southeast Asia reveals several interesting points. First, these systems exhibit a strikingly broad range of variation. Second, a substantial number of these languages exhibit some form of the typologically unusual pattern referred to as 'symmetrical' voice, which means that they are able to express semantically transitive eventualities in two (or more) different clause structures, both of which are syntactically transitive. Unlike more familiar voice alternations, such as active–passive or ergative–antipassive, these symmetrical voice systems are not valence decreasing.

We have made use of the widely cited distinction between Philippine-type and Indonesian-type voice systems, although, as discussed in §47.2.1, this dichotomy is not unproblematic. Especially for the latter category, it is difficult to provide a rigorous definition. Philippine-type voice systems are found not only in the languages of the Philippines but also in northern Sulawesi, northern Borneo, Taiwan, and (for some authors) Madagascar. These systems have a number of distinctive features, and for that reason have received a great deal of attention in both formal and typological literature. In both Borneo and Sulawesi we identified a cline along the north–south axis from (more) Philippine-type to (more) Indonesian-type voice systems.

We have also illustrated how voice morphology, and voice distinctions in general, become more sparse when moving across Indonesia from west to east. While many of the languages of Sumatra, Java, and Bali display Indonesian-type symmetrical voice systems, the languages east of Bali gradually seem to lose this feature. Most languages of the Moluccas and the Austronesian languages of Papua have no voice alternations at all, but make use of other means to encode the prominence of arguments, such as word order alternations and impersonal constructions.

Finally, we have briefly described the voice systems of Chamorro and Palauan, the two easternmost languages of the Western Malayo-Polynesian linkage. We note, however, that the data available for these languages, and even more so for the languages of eastern Indonesia, is sparse in comparison to the data and analyses available for major languages of the Philippines and western Indonesia.

CHAPTER 48

# Adnominal possession

ANTOINETTE SCHAPPER AND WILLIAM MCCONVELL

## 48.1 Introduction

This chapter deals with the structural characteristics of adnominal possessive constructions in the Malayo-Polynesian languages of Southeast Asia. The broad geographical patterns of word order in basic possessive constructions across the Austronesian family are well known (see, e.g., Donohue 2007). However, there are no wide-ranging surveys of the variable features of possessive constructions in the Austronesian languages of the MPSEA area. Much of the literature has been concerned with different aspects of possessive constructions in Oceanic languages (e.g. Lynch 1973, 1996, 2001; Lichtenberk 1985, 2005, 2009, inter alia). Even Blust (2013a: 488–97) in his otherwise wide-ranging treatment of Austronesian languages only looks at Oceanic, remarking "[i]n the AN languages of Taiwan, the Philippines and western Indonesia possessive relationships generally are simple and uninteresting" (2013a: 488). This chapter takes a different perspective; it lays out the features of both basic and marked possessive constructions with a view to bringing out the — often overlooked — diversity seen across the MPSEA area. The discussion concentrates on representing the often quite substantial differences between possessive constructions, many of which have been conflated descriptively under unduly broad typological labels. We also draw particular attention to divergent, subregional patterns in possessive constructions that are of typological interest. In many cases, we seek to understand these divergent constructions as arising from processes of language change.

Throughout this chapter we follow the standard practice in the linguistic literature in using the terms 'possessive' and 'possession' to refer to all kinds of adnominal possessive constructions regardless of whether the semantics is one of literal possession or not. We use the terms 'possessor' (PSR) for the entity that possesses and 'possessum' (PSM) for the entity that is possessed. The term 'genitive' is used in many different ways in the Austronesian and typological literature, but we reserve it here exclusively for possessive markers that are part of a wider system of nominal articles marking grammatical case.[1] Irrespective of their other functions or etymology, morphs marking a possessive relationship will be glossed with 'POSS'.

Our survey is based on a sample of 100 languages from the MPSEA area. Details of the languages sampled can be found in Schapper and McConvell (2021). The languages have been chosen as representative of the genetic and areal diversity found across MPSEA languages. The availability of adequate grammatical descriptions has also played a role in the compilation of the sample. In the text of this chapter, we refer to a small number of languages in addition to the map sample. For the most part, these additional languages are cited because they illustrate some further feature or an unproductive feature not found in our map sample.

We compare the following aspects of adnominal possessor constructions: order of possessor and possessum (§48.2), locus and marking of possessor (§48.3), patterns of differential possessive marking (§48.4), and pragmatic variation in possessive constructions (§48.5).

## 48.2 Order of possessor and possessum

Differences in the order of possessor and possessum are one of the most widely known typological divisions in the Austronesian family. The so-called 'Brandes Line', named after J. L. A. Brandes (1884: 20–2) who was among the first scholars to draw attention to the major geographical divide in Austronesian possessor–possessum ordering, is also the earliest major typological isogloss drawn within the family (see also van Hoëvell 1877: 15). It is such a defining feature within the family that Himmelmann (2005a) names one of his two

[1] In the typological literature, the term 'genitive' is, confusingly, used with two senses. In its original narrow sense, 'genitive' refers to a possessive flag (case-marker, adposition, etc.) which occurs on the possessor noun. In its broader sense, 'genitive' means any construction which encodes a possessive relationship, regardless of whether it is on the possessor, possessum or otherwise. The latter use seems to have been pioneered by the typologist Joseph Greenberg and is continued in some typological reference works like *The World Atlas of Language Structures* as well as Donohue, this volume, §46.3.2. In Austronesian linguistics, 'genitive' is typically used to characterize members of sets of case-marked articles and case-marked pronouns. In many languages in the eastern part of the MPSEA area, reflexes of the so-called genitive pronouns of Proto-Malayo-Polynesian become inalienable possessive suffixes (see §48.4.1). This etymology leads some Austronesianists to the use of 'genitive' for possessive constructions in which the flag occurs on the possessed noun (see, e.g. Grimes, this volume, §36.5), the precise opposite of the narrow sense of 'genitive' employed by typologists.

Antoinette Schapper and William McConvell, *Adnominal possession.* In: *The Oxford Guide to the Malayo-Polynesian Languages of Southeast Asia.* Edited by: Alexander Adelaar and Antoinette Schapper, Oxford University Press. © Antoinette Schapper and William McConvell (2024). DOI: 10.1093/oso/9780198807353.003.0048

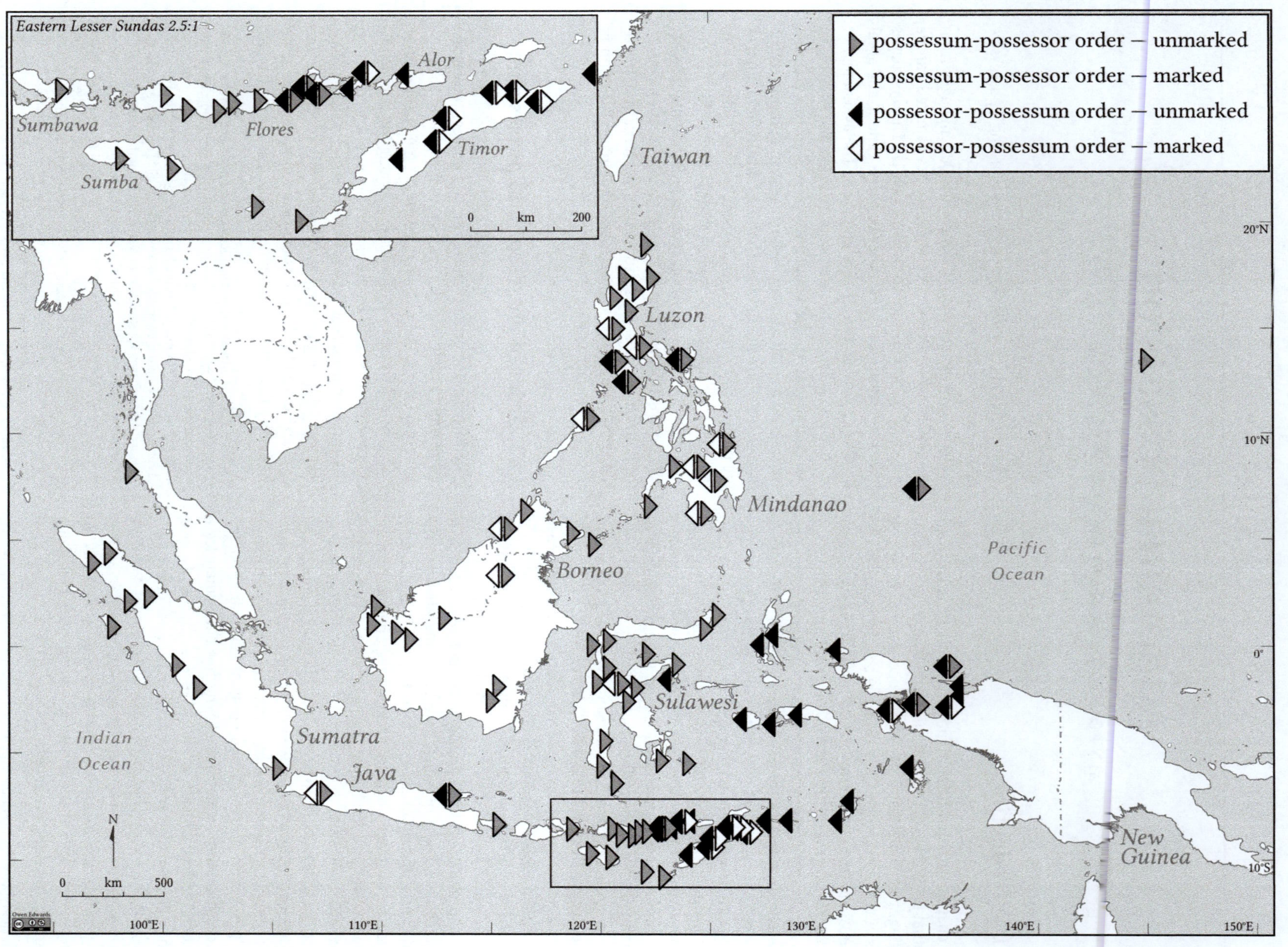


**Map 48.1** Order of possessor and possessum.

major types, that formed by the eastern Austronesian languages, 'preposed possessor languages'.

Map 48.1 sets out the variation in the order of possessor and possessum observed in MPSEA languages. Note that this map is only concerned with the position of free elements, either nominal or pronominal, that express the possessor (see §48.3.2 on bound markers in adnominal possessive constructions). As already noted, the broad geography of postposed vs. preposed possessors is well known. The conservative Austronesian word order of possessum–possessor (postposed possessor) is basic (i.e. the unmarked construction) in the north and west of the MPSEA area. Preposed possessors are basic throughout much of the eastern MPSEA region and beyond into Oceania.

Throughout the MPSEA area, we also find languages with marked constructions where the order of possessor and possessum is reversed: in languages where the basic possessive construction has possessum–possessor order, more marked possessive structures have possessor–possessum order; languages with a basic possessor–possessum order have marked possessive structures with possessum–possessor order. Pragmatically marked possessive constructions with reversed word order are illustrated and discussed in detail in §48.5. In the following subsections we focus on languages which show notable deviations and splits in the word order of possessive constructions with respect to the broad areal patterns found across the MPSEA area.

### 48.2.1 Lack of correspondence between genealogy and the reversal of the basic possessive order

It is important to emphasize that the emergence of basic possessor–possessum ordering in Austronesian languages in the eastern MPSEA area does not correspond to the putative genealogical boundary between Central-Eastern Malayo-Polynesian languages and westerly subgroups of the Austronesian family.

As pointed out by Himmelmann (2005a: 165, following Adriani and Kruyt, 1914: vIII 275, 281; Kanski and Kasprusch 1931: 883, 888), Banggai, of the Saluan-Banggai group in Sulawesi, belongs to a westerly genetic grouping and has completely reversed the order of possessor and possessum. In Banggai both nominal (1a) and pronominal (1b) possessors are preposed to the possessum in the unmarked possessive construction. Other 'eastern' features of Banggai possession are discussed in §48.4.1.2.

Banggai

(1) a. $N_{PSR}$ $N_{PSM}$ b. $PRO_{PSR}$ $N_{PSM}$

| | | | | |
|---|---|---|---|---|
| ***tomundo*** | *na* | *bonua* | ***ko-ŋgu*** | *bonua* |
| king | 3.POSS | house | ART-1SG.POSS | house |
| 'the king's house' | | | 'my house' | |

(van den Bergh 1953: 107, 49)

At the same time, not all languages belonging to the easterly Central Malayo-Polynesian subgroup have the preposed possessor (cf. Brandes 1884: 21, fn 2). Languages of the Sumba-Hawu subgroup display the conservative postposed possessor order, while the languages with which they subgroup on Flores are transitional between preposed and postposed possessors. Languages in western and central Flores have postposed possessors, while the languages to the east of Flores have consistently preposed possessors. Between these two sets, there are a group of languages in which a possessor expressed by a noun is preposed, and a possessor expressed by a pronoun is postposed (see §48.2.2).

### 48.2.2 Unmarked splits in possessor posing

Several clusters of languages in the MPSEA area show splits in the ordering of possessor and possessum depending on whether the possessor is encoded with a noun or a pronoun. These are languages where the preposed versus postposed possessors show no difference in markedness.

The first cluster occurs in eastern Flores and the Solor archipelago, the transition zone between the preposed and postposed possessor types (see inset in Map 48.1).

The languages with the pronominal vs. nominal split in possessor posing form a subgroup, known as

**Table 48.1** Progression of possessor leftwards in the languages of Flores and its satellites (arranged from west at the top to east at the bottom)

| | Possessor = Free pronoun | | Possessor = Lexical noun | |
|---|---|---|---|---|
| Bima | PSM | PSR | PSM | PSR |
| Manggarai | PSM | PSR | PSM | PSR |
| Rongga | PSM | PSR | PSM | PSR |
| Keo | PSM | PSR | PSM | PSR |
| Ende | PSM | PSR | PSM | PSR |
| Lio | PSM | PSR | PSM | PSR |
| Hewa | PSM | PSR | PSR | PSM |
| Lamaholot Lewotobi | PSM | PSR | PSR | PSM |
| Lamaholot Solor | PSM | PSR | PSR | PSM |
| Central Lembata | PSR | PSM | PSR | PSM |
| Kedang | PSR | PSM | PSR | PSM |
| Alorese | PSR | PSM | PSR | PSM |

Flores-Lembata, together with the languages with exclusively preposed possessors in Table 48.1.

The split pattern in possessor posing is found in Hewa, an independent branch of the Flores-Lembata subgroup (2), and in the western but not eastern Lamaholot varieties of the eastern Flores-Lembata subgroup (e.g. Lewotobi Lamaholot in (3)). This indicates that a split in possessor posing here cannot be regarded as a matter of shared inheritance. That the split is marked using different morphosyntactic resources further reinforces the picture of an areal rather than inherited pattern.

Hewa

(2) a. N$_{PSM}$ PRO$_{PSR}$
*me* ***nimu-n***
child 3SG-POSS
'his/her children'

b. N$_{PSR}$ N$_{PSM}$
***du?a*** *me-n*
woman child-POSS
'woman's children'
(Fricke 2013: 39–40)

Lewotobi Lamaholot

(3) a. N$_{PSM}$ PRO$_{PSR}$
*oto* ***go?ẽ***
car 1SG.POSS
'my car'

b. N$_{PSR}$ N$_{PSM}$
***Hugo*** *laŋo?=kə̃*
Hugo house=POSS
'Hugo's house' (Nagaya 2015)

Biakic is a second set of languages with an apparent split in their possessor posing. These closely related languages express possession using a possessive "pronoun" inflected for both the person/number of the possessum and the possessor. The possessive pronoun is postposed to the possessum, as in (4a). Where a noun is used to express the possessor, it is preposed, while the so-called pronoun stays in the postnominal position, (4b). The pronoun cannot be omitted from a possessive construction.

Dusner

(4) a. N$_{PSM}$ DET$_{PSR}$
*wak* ***yerya***
wak y-ve-rya
boat 1SG-POSS-DET.3SG
'my boat'

b. N$_{PSR}$ N$_{PSM}$ DET$_{PSR}$
***Nelwan*** *wak* ***vyerya***
Nelwan wak v<i>e-rya
Nelwa boat 3SG-POSS-DET.3SG
'Nelwan's boat' (Dalrymple and Mofu 2012: 24–5)

Whilst the sources on Biakic languages typically describe the postposed element in their possessive constructions as a possessive pronoun, the label is ill fitting. Crucially, they are not truly pronominal: they do not block the nominal expression of a possessor. Following observations in van den Heuvel (2006: 86), Bach (2021) argues that the unusual possessive markers in Biakic languages are the result of the grammaticalization of a verb *ve* in an object relative clause. A verbal source for the Biakic possessive markers explains the apparent word order split in Biakic possessive constructions as well as the typologically unusual double agreement of the possessive markers.

### 48.2.3 Marked splits in possessor posing

Splits in the order of possessor and possessum are found in other clusters of MPSEA languages, but these differ from the Biakic and eastern Flores situations in that here one order is typically more marked.

Many Philippine languages have two possessive structures, the basic structure typically involves a postposed possessor, while a second, pragmatically marked possessive structure involves a preposed possessor, most commonly pronominal, in an oblique case. For example, Tboli has two unmarked strategies, involving either a postposed nominal possessor (5a) or a pronominal suffix (5b). An additional marked strategy involves a preposed free oblique pronoun encoding the possessor (5c). Splits in possessor posing arising out of pragmatically marked possessive constructions in MPSEA languages are discussed further in §48.5.

Tboli

(5) a. N$_{PSM}$ N$_{PSR}$
*gunu* *ma*
house father
'father's house'

b. N$_{PSM}$-PRO$_{PSR}$
*libun-u*
sister-1SG.POSS
'my sister'

c. PRO$_{PSR}$ N$_{PSM}$
*dou* *libun*
1SG.OBL sister
'*my* sister.' (Forsberg 1992: 12)

The marked preposed possessor construction is noticeably absent from most languages of northern Luzon. Bontok, Isinay, Balangao, Batad Ifugao, Kankanaey, Ilokano, and the Batanic languages, for example, all appear to lack the preposed structure. The absence of the preposed possessor in these languages is at odds with Himmelmann's (2005a: 164) statement that the alternate preposed possessor construction is a regular feature of Philippine languages. Of the Philippines languages that do have a marked preposed possessor construction, a further division can be made. Whilst all allow a preposed pronominal possessor, only a subset allow a preposed nominal possessor. Languages that permit a preposed nominal possessor are clustered in the central Phillipines. Preposed nominal possessors appear to be entirely absent from the southern Philippines.

In most languages of Mindoro, suffixes/enclitics for possessors appear to have been lost (cf. Lobel 2013a: 146). The result is that the basic, unmarked possessive structure with a pronominal possessor is preposed, while possessive constructions with a nominal possessor are postposed. We illustrate this contrast with Iraya (6).

Iraya

(6) a. PRO$_{PSR}$ N$_{PSM}$ b. N$_{PSM}$ N$_{PSR}$

| a. PRO$_{PSR}$ | N$_{PSM}$ | b. N$_{PSM}$ | N$_{PSR}$ | |
|---|---|---|---|---|
| *kura* | *balay* | *awak* | *laki* | *Manhuŋ* |
| 3PL | house | back | MALE | Manhung |
| 'their house' | | 'Manhung's back' | | |

(Lawrence A. Reid p.c.)

Given that the languages of southern and northern Mindoro are not thought to subgroup with one another, it seems that the move towards preposing pronominal possessors represents an areal feature of those languages. The change from postposed to preposed possessor appears, however, to be ongoing: Hanunoo still has both postposed and preposed possessors, but the postposed ones seem to be relatively rare. According to David Zorc (p.c.), Tadyawan seems to be the only Mangyan language to not have, let alone prefer, preposed possessors.

Person-based splits in possessor posing are known from two languages of Java. In Madurese, second and third person possessors, be they nominal or pronominal, are postposed (7a), while a first person possessor is encoded with a preposed pronoun (7b). In Sundanese the unmarked position for a possessor is postposed to the possessum (8a), but first and second person possessors are preposed when they are encoded by dedicated honorific pronouns (8b).

Madurese

(7)

| a. N$_{PSM}$ | Pro$_{PSR}$/N$_{PSR}$ | b. Pro$_{PSR}$ | N$_{PSM}$ |
|---|---|---|---|
| *buku-na* | ***baʔeŋ / guru*** | ***taŋ*** | *buku* |
| book-POSS | 2SG / teacher | 1SG.POSS | book |
| 'your/the teacher's book' | | 'my book' | |

(Davies 2010: 163, 193–4)

Sundanese

(8)

| a. N$_{PSM}$ | Pro$_{PSR}$ | b. Pro$_{PSR}$ | N$_{PSM}$ |
|---|---|---|---|
| *paman* | ***kuriŋ*** | ***pun*** | *bojo* |
| uncle | 1SG | 1SG.POSS.HON | wife |
| 'my uncle' | | 'my wife' | |

(Müller-Gotama 2001: 36–7)

It seems likely that the unmarked first person preposed possessor in Madurese developed out of a marked, honorific structure such as found in Sundanese.

In eastern Timor languages, splits in possessor posing seem to be governed by semantics relating to the closeness of the possessive relationship. Here, the unmarked order is for the possessor to be preposed. Where a possessor is postposed, there is a semantic change in the relation between the possessor and the possessum. For example, in Kemak, the construction with the preposed possessor in (9a) represents a fairly standard possessive relationship, where the child is the owner of the maize. By contrast in (9b) where the possessor is postposed, the possessive relationship is more removed, with the child being the prospective possessor of the maize, but not the person to whom it necessarily belongs.

Kemak (Atsabe variety)

(9) a. Preposed possessor

| *au* | *tere* | *[anamugu* | *siana* | *no:]*$_{PSR}$ | *sele*$_{PSM}$ |
|---|---|---|---|---|---|
| 1SG | cook | child | DEM | 3SG.POSS | maize |

'I cook this child's maize (i.e. the maize belonging to the child).'

b. Postposed possessor

| *au* | *tere* | *sele*$_{PSM}$ | *[anamugu* | *siana* | *no:]*$_{PSR}$ |
|---|---|---|---|---|---|
| 1SG | cook | maize | child | DEM | 3SG.POSS |

'I cook corn for this child.' (Schapper 2009)

The use of the marked postposed possessor constructions in eastern Timor languages is governed by a complex interaction of lexical, semantic, and constructional factors, for example, as described for Tetun Fehan (van Klinken 1999: 151–2) and Tetun Dili (Williams-van Klinken, Hajek, and Nordlinger 2002: 35–6). See Schapper and Zobel, this volume, §35.4.7 for more examples.

The Moor language of southern Cenderwasih Bay has a unique form of split possessor posing. The most frequent possessive construction involves a preposed possessor and a suffix *-ío* on the possessum signalling the possessive relationship (10a). A second, less common structure has a postposed possessor marked with the suffix *-ìjo* and an obligatory article on the possessum (10b). The factors governing the choice of preposed vs. postposed possessors are not understood at present, but the semantics of the possessive relationship does appear to play a role: in elicitation, only preposed possessors were accepted with kin terms (David Kamholz p.c.).

Moor

(10) a. Preposed possessor

| ***kamuka*** | *gwoʔ-ío* |
|---|---|
| friend | canoe-3SG |

'friend's canoe'

b. Postposed possessor

| *gwoʔ-o* | ***kamuka****-ìjo* |
|---|---|
| canoe-ART | friend-3SG |

'friend's canoe' (David Kamholz p.c.)

Other kinds of variation in possessive constructions relating to the semantics of the possessive relationship are treated in §48.4.

## 48.3 Locus and marking of the possessive relationship

This section deals with the locus of possessor marking and the formal means by which a possessive relationship is marked. We are concerned in the first instance with the marking of the possessive relationship where the possessor and possessum are encoded by nouns. The major variables are as follows (examples of each given below): (i) no marker of possessive relationship (11); (ii) free possessive linker (not marked for person/number of the possessor) occurs between possessum and possessor (12); (iii) bound possessive linker not marked for person/number of the possessor (13); (iv) free possessive marker marked for person/number of the possessor (14); and (v) bound possessive marker marked for person/number of the possessor (15).

Dhao, no marker of possessive relationship
(11) *solo* *ana*
hat child
'child's hat' (Balukh 2020: 325)

Manggarai, free possessive marker without a person feature
(12) *baju* ***dé*** *amé*
shirt POSS father
'father's shirt' (Semiun 1993: 41)

Balinese, bound possessive marker without a person feature
(13) *tai-**n*** *sampi*
faeces-POSS horse
'horse's manure' (Clynes 1995d: 106)

Taba, free possessive marker with a person feature
(14) *Mado* ***ni*** *mtu*
Mado 3SG.POSS child
'Mado's child' (Bowden 2001: 230)

Balantak, bound possessive marker with a person feature
(15) *laigan-**na*** *wiwine*
house-3SG woman
'woman's house' (van den Berg and Busenitz 2012: 62)

Map 48.2 presents the distribution of these types broken down into the following features: (i) no possessive marker vs. possessive marker; (ii) free vs. bound possessive marker, as well as possessor-marking or possessum-marking of the bound possessive marker; and (iii) possessive markers with a person feature vs. without a person feature. As can be seen from the map, most languages evince more than one type of possessive marking. In many cases, this is due to the existence of possessive classification and distinct lexical classes of possessed nouns (see differential possessive marking in §48.4). In other cases, markers of the possessive relationship are optional or different possessive constructions are available with different types of possessors (some of these are discussed in §48.5). Making particular reference to geographic distribution, three topics will be discussed in the following sections: zero-marked possessive constructions (§48.3.1), possessive markers with a person feature versus without a person feature (§48.3.2), and possessum-marking vs. possessor-marking in possessive constructions (§48.3.3). The following discussion focuses on possessive relationships between nouns, but some reference is made to possessors expressed by pronominal elements where there are notable constructions.

### 48.3.1 Zero-marked possessive constructions

Possessive constructions in which there is no possessive marker between nouns for the possessor and possessum are referred to here as 'zero-marked possessor constructions'. Although found in scattered pockets throughout much of the MPSEA area, it is only in Borneo that zero-marked possessor constructions dominate. A few Borneo languages use alternative possessive constructions, but then only for small subsets of possessed nouns (see §48.4 on the various manifestations of differential possessive marking in Borneo).

The sporadic appearance of zero-marked possessive constructions in other MPSEA languages can usually be traced to loss of grammatical markers of possession in individual languages. For example, Karo Batak has a zero-marked possessive construction due to its loss of reflexes of PMP case markers, while its close relative and neighbour Toba Batak retains an historical case marker in possessive constructions (see §48.3.2 for more discussion of this). Similarly, in the Tominic group of Sulawesi, both Pendau (Quick 2007: 201–2) and Tajio (Mayani 2013: 156) show productive use of *ni*= and *nu*= as personal and non-personal genitive case markers. However, their sister Balaesang has lost these markers and instead uses a zero-marked possessive construction, as in (16).

Balaesang
(16) *navut* *Salim*
garden Salim
'Salim's garden' (Garantjang et al. 1985: 65)

Zero-marked possessive constructions are unusual in our sample of languages in the Philippines, being limited to Hanunoo, Iraya, Tboli and Yakan. The Tboli and Iraya constructions are already illustrated in examples (5) and (6) respectively.

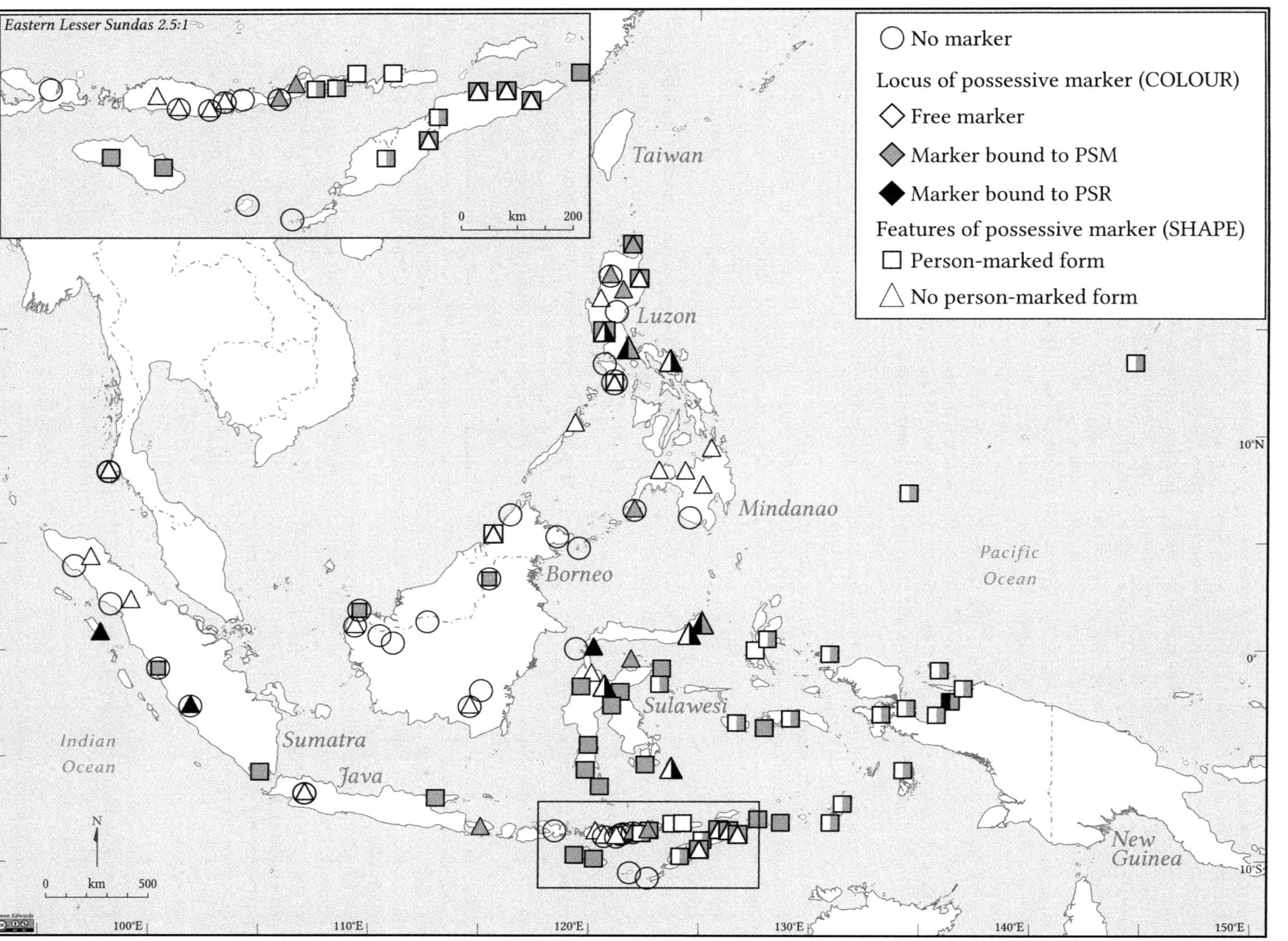


**Map 48.2** Locus and marking of possessive relationship where possessor and possessum are expressed with nouns.

Zero-marked possessive constructions are also noticeably absent in much of the east of the MPSEA area (see §48.3.2 on the person-marking possessive constructions that dominate there). Only the languages of Central Flores and the closely related Hawu and Dhao languages have zero-marked possessive constructions. The aberrant nature of these languages appears to have come about because both sets of languages have lost the person inflections found in their nearest relatives. All Central Flores languages with the exception of Lio have an optional possessive linker (discussed further in §48.4.2), while Hawu and Dhao do not.

There is an interpretative issue around the status of some juxtaposed noun–noun constructions that look much like zero-marked possessive constructions. For example, in Muna the unmarked possessive construction has a possessive suffix *-no* on the possessor, as in (17a), (17b). However, there are also noun–noun constructions where *-no* is not used, such as in nominal modifier situations with constituent materials (17c). Similar restricted marker-less constructions are found in Makasar, Padoe, and many other Sulawesi languages.

Muna

(17) a. *lambu-**no*** *ani*
house-3.POSS bee
'beehive' (lit. house of bees)

b. *galu-**no*** *pae*
field-3.POSS rice
'field of rice'

c. *siŋkaru* *bulawa*
ring gold
'golden ring' (van den Berg 2013: 86–9)

Constructions such as this where a possessive marker can be left off with nouns of certain types are not regarded as possessive constructions here. To qualify as a possessive construction, we require that a possessor noun in the construction can be a prototypical possessor (i.e. have a human or animate and/or definite referent). This is not the case here, and accordingly we regard these as possessive compounds (i.e. morphological) and not the syntactic possessive constructions that we are concerned with in this chapter. Languages such as Muna are coded as having an obligatory bound person marker for the possessor. To be regarded as having a zero-marking possessive construction, a language must display zero marking as the default possessive construction for at least a subset of nouns with animate or human posssessors.

## 48.3.2 Possessive markers with and without a person feature

Across the MPSEA area, strong geographical patterns can be observed in the distribution of possessive markers with a person feature versus those without.

Languages in the east almost all use possessive markers with a person feature. Exceptions are the already mentioned languages of Central Flores and the Hawu and Dhao languages, which have almost completely lost person inflections. The dominance of possessive markers with a person feature in the east can be seen as part of the development of bound pronouns into agreement markers in these languages. PMP had a set of enclitic pronouns that in the nominal domain could mark a possessor and these are continued very widely across MPSEA languages today. In the west and north, the PMP forms are continued as possessive pronouns. West Coast Bajau, for example, has enclitic possessive pronouns that cannot cooccur with a noun for the possessor (18a); where a possessor is encoded with a noun, a zero-marked possessive construction is used (18b). The enclitic pronoun *=ni* cannot be used between possessum and possessor nouns in (18b).

West Coast Bajau

(18) a. *rumaʔ=**ni***
house=3.POSS
'his house'

b. *rumaʔ* *emmaʔ=ni*
house father=3.POSS
'their father's house'
(Miller 2007: 120, 315)

From Sulawesi eastwards, continuations of the PMP possessive enclitics do not block nominal expression of the possessor. Thus, in Sulawesi languages like Muna (illustrated in (17a–b)), a bound possessive marker with a person feature cooccurs with a possessor noun as a matter of course.

East of Sulawesi, not only do bound possessive markers with a person feature allow coindexing of an independent nominal element in the third person, but also pronominal elements in non-third persons. For example, in Banggai a possessive suffix can denote a possessor on its own (19a), and for additional emphasis a free pronoun can coindex the person–number features of the suffix (19b).

Banggai

(19) a. *sambu-**ŋgu***
name-1SG.POSS
'my name'

b. ***iaku*** *sambu-**ŋgu***
1SG name-1SG.POSS
'*my* name'
(van den Bergh 1953: 55)

In the Moluccas, the movement towards obligatory person markers in possessive constructions is still more advanced in that the availability of coindexing free elements is not limited to bound markers. That is, even free person-marked possessive markers allow coindexing with pronominal elements of all persons, illustrated with Taba in (20).

Taba

(20) a. ***nik*** *mapin*
1SG.POSS wife
'my wife'

b. ***yak*** ***nik*** *mapin*
1SG 1SG.POSS wife
'*my* wife' (Bowden 2001: 230–1)

Possessive markers without a person feature often reflect PMP nominal case markers. These are scattered through the west and the north of the MPSEA area. Sulawesi is particularly interesting for the fact that it is divided: in the south, possessive markers with a person feature dominate, while in the north, possessive markers without a person feature are the norm. The latter pattern is areally consistent with the Philippines and is a reflection of nominal case systems being more fully intact in these languages. In the south of Sulawesi, case markers for possession are only found in fossilized forms and are not coded on the map here due to their non-productivity. Similar differences exist between Batak languages in Sumatra: Toba Batak uses the historical case marker *ni* as the marker of possession, while Karo Batak, as mentioned earlier, has a zero-marked construction for expressing possessive relations between nouns, but retains the case markers *(n)u* and *ni* only in archaisms (Woollams 1996: 165–6).

In the north of the Philippines, we often find hybrid systems where case markers and markers with a person feature combine in particular situations. For example, Ibatan uses case markers *=n(o)* (21a) and *=ni* (21b) in the singular, but combines the case marker with the person-marked form *=da* '3PL.POSS' in the plural (21c).[2]

Ibatan

(21) a. *saŋa=**n(o)*** *kayo*
branch=POSS tree
'branch of a tree'

b. *bahay=**ni*** *Mayor*
house=POSS.PRS Mayor
'The Mayor's house'

c. *ŋaran=**da=n*** *anak=da* *Marcelino*
name=3PL.POSS=POSS child=3PL.POSS Marcelino
'The names of the children of Marcelino and co.' (i.e. wife) (Maree 2007: 35, 119, 106)

In one Philippine language, double marking of the possessive relationship with a genitive case marker and possessive marker with a person feature is the default construction. As can be seen in (22), Kapampangan uses both the genitive case marker and a person marker in its possessive construction. Similar double-marked constructions can occasionally be observed in northern Philippine languages as marginal and largely non-obligatory possessive constructions (e.g., Dupaningan Agta *nagen=na na anak=mo* name=3SG.GEN GEN child=2SG.GEN 'your child's name', Robinson 2011:72).

Kapampangan

(22) *ing* *bale=**na*** ***niŋ*** *anak*
ART house=3SG.POSS GEN child
'the house of the child' (Gonzalez 1981: 295)

A further sort of possessive marker without a person feature is found in some Philippine languages with a secondary preposed possessive construction. In these, a so-called 'linker' (glossed 'LNK') marks the preposed possessor. Typically, these possessors are encoded by an oblique pronoun, but in a few cases by a noun. Only the linkers that occur on possessor nouns appear in Map 48.2 (see §48.3.3 for discussion and illustration of this type of possessive construction). The linkers are generally employed with several types of nominal modifiers, like oblique possessors, adjectives and so on, but *not* with possessors encoded by bound pronouns. For example, Cebuano has a basic pronominal possessive structure encoded simply by means of an enclitic possessive pronoun (23a). Cebuano's secondary, marked pronominal possessive structure involves a preposed free pronoun marked with a linker morpheme (23b).

Cebuano

(23) a. *aŋ* *amigo=**niya***
ART friend=3.POSS
'his friend'

b. *ang* ***iya-ŋ*** *amigo*
ART 3.OBL-LNK friend
'his friend'
(Tanangkingsing 2009: 83–4)

The linker is sporadically lost from the preposed possessor constructions in Philippine languages, including Mangyan (e.g. Iraya, Hanunoo), southern Mindanao (e.g. Tboli), and Central Philippine languages (e.g. Mansaka). Zorc (1977: 230–1), following Wolff and Wolff (1967: 72–4), remarks that the loss of the linker on preposed possessors is an areal feature found scattered through Bisayan and Mansakan dialects; the linker is maintained in preposed possessor constructions in many languages of the Central Philippines region, including Mamanwa (Miller and Miller 1976: 27, 31) Matigsalug Manobo (Wang et al. 2006: 41), Tagalog and Bikol. See §48.5 for more on secondary preposed constructions possessor constructions.

### 48.3.3 Possessum-marking vs. possessor-marking

In this section we are concerned with whether a bound possessive marker occurs on the possessum (i.e. 'possessum-marking') or the possessor (i.e. 'possessor-marking'). We avoid the terms 'head-marking' and 'dependent-marking' in

[2] The second instance of *=da* '3PL.POSS' on its own without the possessive marker in (21c) has become a kind of associative plural marking. It appears to be a recurrent grammaticalization pathway for possessum-marking third person plural possessor markers to, over time, become more associated with the plurality of the possessum rather than the possessor. Developments in this vein can also be seen in Tolaki (Donohue and Edwards 2014) and in Kemak on inalienably possessed nouns where *-r* has generalized (Schapper 2009).

our characterization of the locus of marking in possessive constructions. Whether the possessor or the possessum constitutes the head of a possessive construction is a matter of debate in Austronesian linguistics (see, e.g. Palmer and Brown 2007 vs. Lichtenberk 2009). The headedness of possessive constructions needs to be determined on a language-by-language basis, but that is not information that can be easily extracted from most grammatical descriptions. Classification of possessive constructions on the basis of headedness is therefore impossible at this stage.

Map 48.2 shows that the overwhelming majority of languages in the MPSEA area are possessum-marking. All but one language with bound person markers for possession in our sample is possessum-marking. For the most part, possessum-marking represents a continuation of the pattern from PMP whereby pronominal enclitics expressing a possessor bind to the possessum.[3] The one exception is Moor, already discussed in example (10) in §48.2. In Moor, there is both a possessum-marking construction with a preposed possessor and an alternate possessor-marking construction where the possessor is postposed. All other examples of possessor-marking in our sample involve possessive markers without a person feature. They are concentrated in enclaves in northern Sulawesi and in north-central Philippines.

In Sulawesi, the appearance of possessor-marking constructions has to do with cliticization patterns of genitive case markers. In some languages like Tajio, both the non-personal genitive case marker *nu=* (24a) and personal genitive case marker *ni=* (24b) have become proclitics.

Tajio

(24) a. *te=vonua* **nu**=*topo-meaŋ*
ART=house POSS=NMLZ-fish
'the fisherman's house'

b. *te=vonua* **ni**=*maŋgeʔ=u*
ART=house POSS=uncle=1SG.POSS
'my uncle's house' (Mayani 2013: 156, 158)

In others like Tondano, we find a split in the behaviour of genitive case markers. We see the non-personal genitive marker is an enclitic *=na* (25a), while the personal genitive marker is a proclitic *ni=* (25b).

Tondano

(25) a. Possessum-marking
*ŋaran=***na** *keluarga*
name=POSS family
'family's name'

b. Possessor-marking
*lawas* **ni**=*Kalo*
hand POSS=Kalo
'Kalo's hand'
(Brickell 2014: 112, 341)

Precursors of such cliticized genitive case markers are found in many languages in Sulawesi. Pamona, for instance, has a free genitive case marker *nu* used in possessive constructions (26a), but uses a procliticized allomorph *ŋ=* before voiceless obstruents (26b). Similar bound allomorphs of otherwise free genitive case markers are found in Ratahan (Himmelmann and Wolff 1999: 30) and Tukang Besi (Donohue 1999a: 338–9). Such cases are indicated by the half-black, half-white triangles on Sulawesi in Map 48.2.[4]

Pamona

(26) a. *pela* **nu** *garoŋgo*
skin POSS crocodile
'crocodile's skin'

b. *pela* **ŋ**=*kadʒu*
skin POSS=tree
'bark (skin of tree)'
(Adriani 1931)

In the Philippines, we saw already that possessor-marking constructions are found with preposed pronominal possessors that are marked with a linker. This is particularly common in the Central Philippines (see Cebuano construction in (23)). In three languages in our sample, the linker has been extended in function to also mark preposed nominal possessors. The Bikol and Kapampangan constructions with preposed nominal possessors marked by a linker are illustrated in (27) and (28). In both languages, the possessor noun is also preceded by an oblique case-marking article. See (41) for similar constructions in Tagalog.

Bikol

(27) *an sa maestro-***ŋ** *kotse*
ART LOC teacher-LNK car
'the teacher's car' (Mintz 1971: 70-1)

Kapampangan

(28) *ing kaŋ pedru-***ŋ** *bale*
ART LOC Pedro-LNK house
'Pedro's house' (Gonzalez 1981:166–7)

Bound possessive linkers in western Indonesia are rare, but where they do exist, they are typically possessum-marking suffixes (e.g. Balinese) and in some cases show grammaticalization into definiteness markers (e.g. Sundanese as well as other languages on Java, see §31.5). Nias, spoken in the Barrier Islands, displays an unusual pattern of consonant mutation which we treat as a form of possessor marking. Entering into a possessive construction triggers mutation of the initial consonant of the possessor noun. For example, Nias *buaja* 'crocodile' mutates to *ʙuaja* when possessed in Nias. This mutation in all likelihood goes back to an earlier prefix marking possession.

[3] As mentioned in the previous section, due to our focus on constructions where the possessor is encoded with a noun, many more languages have bound pronouns marking the person and number of the possessor on the possessum than are listed on the map.

[4] A significant complicating factor for the classification of possessive structures with respect to the boundness of their markers is the tendency to write clitics as independent words, particularly in older sources and for some languages with established orthographies.

Nias
(29) *telau* *BUAJA*
head crocodile:MUT
'head of the crocodile' (Brown 2001: 373)

The only other possessor-marking in western Indonesia appears to be found in Kerinci, spoken nearby on Sumatra. Here the form of the possessor noun alternates between an 'A-form' and an 'O-form' depending on the definiteness of the possessor (McKinnon 2011: 274–8).

## 48.4 Differential possessive marking

Differential possessive marking involves alternations in the morphosyntax of possessive constructions that are determined by the lexical identity of the possessed noun or by the semantics of the possessive relationship (expanding on the definition in Karvovskaya 2018).

We use 'differential possessive marking' as an umbrella term for what, in much of the literature, is described as 'inalienability'. (In)alienability—the perceived closeness of the relationship between possessum and possessor—frequently impacts on the choice and availability of different possessive constructions in languages worldwide (Chappell and McGregor 1996). In the Austronesian literature, however, distinct morphosyntactic types of possessive construction have often been conflated, even confused, by the terms 'alienable' and 'inalienable'. As such, we avoid these and instead draw a primary distinction between: the 'obligatory possessive inflection' type where certain nouns must occur with an inflection for a possessor (§48.4.1) and the 'free possessive linker' type, whose optional use is conditioned by the semantics of the possessive relationship (§48.4.2). A third type of differential possessive marking is the edible/general possessive contrast discussed in §48.4.3.

Map 48.3 presents an overview of the distribution of differential possessive marking in MPSEA languages. Two subtypes of obligatory possessive inflection are differentiated based on the inflectional forms taken by obligatorily and optionally possessed nouns. Languages where obligatorily possessed nouns take different inflections from optionally possessed nouns are clearly concentrated to the east of Sulawesi within the MPSEA area. Languages where obligatorily possessed nouns take the same inflections as optionally possessed nouns have no clear areal patterning. Similarly, differential possessive classification with optional possessive linkers is only spottily attested in Borneo and Flores. Finally, edible/general possessive contrasts are found in just a handful of languages scattered at the area's eastern perimeter.

### 48.4.1 Obligatory possessive inflections

A major point of variation in the possessive constructions of MPSEA languages is to be found in the (non-)existence of classes of noun which cannot stand alone and require possessive inflection. Obligatory possessive inflections are typically found with nouns referring to body parts and kin relations, that is, classic 'inalienables', although the precise lexical set varies from language to language. As mentioned above, we divide this type in two: (i) obligatory possession marked in the same way as non-obligatory possession; and (ii) obligatory possession marked in a different way to non-obligatory possession.

Lexical classes of obligatorily possessed nouns, while generally strict as to their membership, can have fuzziness at the edges. In each language with a lexical class of obligatorily possessed nouns, there is some leeway to be observed in the possessive marking of some nouns. In our experience, however, the flexibility is usually very limited and does not take away from the basically lexicalized nature of the possessive classes. This issue will be not be discussed further in this chapter.

#### 48.4.1.1 *Obligatory possessors = non-obligatory possessors*

In this type, the inflections used with nouns that are obligatorily possessed are the same as those used with those that are not obligatorily possessed. The only difference is that there is a class of nouns that must occur with an inflection for the possessor. For example, possession in Leti is expressed by means of a possessive suffix on the possessed noun. Body part nouns and other nouns denoting typical inalienables are always inflected for a possessor (30a), whereas other nouns such as *vatu* 'stone' are not required to (30b).

Leti
(30) a. Obligatorily possessed b. Optional possession
*iran-nu* *vat-nu*
nose-3SG.POSS stone-3SG.POSS
'his/her/its nose' 'his/her/its stone'
(van Engelenhoven 2004: 94–100)

This relatively minor pattern is a sporadic feature that is found in several small clusters of MPSEA languages, including some southern Moluccan languages, such as Leti exemplified above (see Schapper and Zobel, this volume, §35.3.1.2 for more examples), and several Central Cordilleran languages including Batad Ifugao, Bontok, Kankanaey and Isinay (Lawrence Reid p.c.). In the latter languages of the northern Philippines, the local obligatory possession phenomenon seems to mainly apply to kin and social category

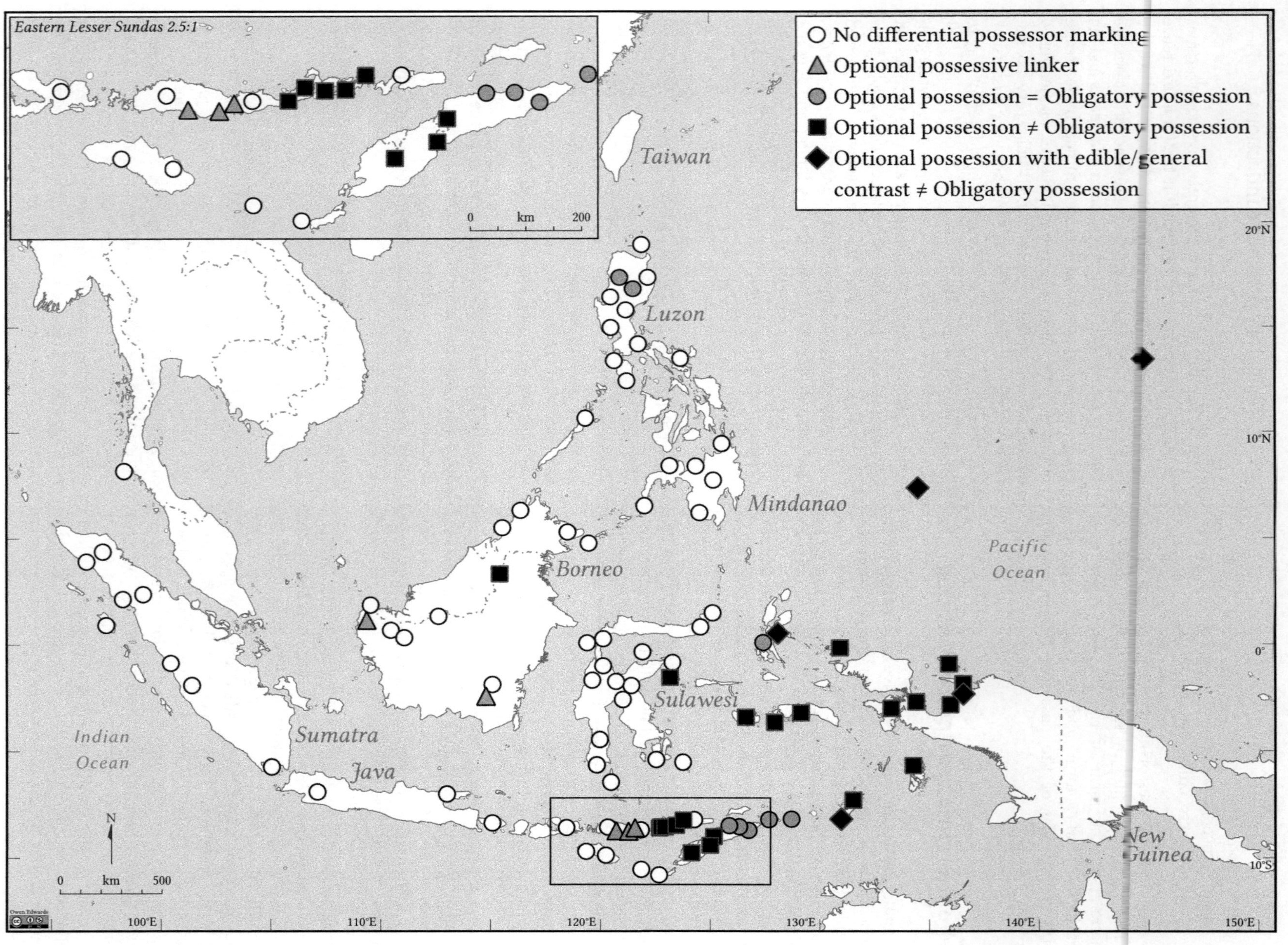
Eastern Lesser Sundas 2.5:1
0 km 200
No differential possessor marking
Optional possessive linker
Optional possession = Obligatory possession
Optional possession ≠ Obligatory possession
Optional possession with edible/general contrast ≠ Obligatory possession
Taiwan
Luzon
Mindanao
Pacific Ocean
Borneo
Sulawesi
Sumatra
Java
Indian Ocean
New Guinea
20°N
10°N
0°
10°S
100°E
110°E
120°E
130°E
140°E
150°E
N
0 km 500

**Map 48.3** Differential possessive marking.

terminology, and to some nouns denoting parts of inanimate objects. In addition, both MPSEA languages of Micronesia also have small classes of obligatorily possessed nouns that include certain body part, kinship, and relational nouns (see Zobel, this volume, §38.3.3 and §39.5 for overviews).

#### 48.4.1.2 *Obligatory possessors ≠ non-obligatory possessors*

The second type, obligatory possession marked distinctly from non-obligatory possession, dominates in eastern Indonesia. Of the languages with this type, the majority pattern is for obligatorily possessed nouns to be marked with possessive suffixes, while optionally possessed nouns take free, typically preposed possessive markers Precisely this pattern is found, for example, in the languages of Aru, as illustrated in (31) by Ujir. In the Austronesian literature, this kind of contrast is often referred to as 'direct' and 'indirect' possession: direct possession involves the person-number of the possessor being marked 'directly' on the noun expressing the possessum (31a), while indirect possession sees the person–number of the possessor marked 'indirectly' by means of a form independent of the possessor noun (31b).

Ujir
(31) a. Obligatory possession: Direct
*mata-ŋ*
eye-1SG.POSS
'my eye'

b. Optional possession: Indirect
*kanaŋ* *dʒuma*
1SG.POSS house
'my house' (Schapper fieldnotes)

The direct/indirect contrast has broken down in many languages. For example, preposed 'indirect' possessive markers have developed into possessive prefixes in languages like Asilulu. This means that possessors of nouns of the obligatorily possessed class are marked by a suffix (32a), while possessors of nouns of the optionally possessed class are marked by a prefix (32b). See Florey (2005a) for a description of further developments in the marking of the obligatorily possessed class that can be seen in other languages of central Maluku.

Asilulu
(32) a. Obligatory possession: Suffixal
*ulu-ku*
head-1SG.POSS
'my head'

b. Optional possession: Prefixal
*ku-haku*
1SG.POSS-boat
'my boat' (Collins 2003a: xxix)

In a small number of languages, the direct/indirect possessive contrast is maintained, but is no longer entirely lexically motivated. In Waima'a, the split is now in person: third person possessors of all kinds are encoded with a possessive suffix, while a free possessive marker is used for other persons (Bowden, Hajek, and Himmelmann nd: 29–31). In Idate, the split is at least partly morphophonological: nouns ending in a vowel take possessor suffixes, while nouns ending in a consonant take free possessive markers (Alcantara 2015: 134–5). See Schapper and Zobel (this volume, §35.4.7.) for an overview of the various ways in which the direct/indirect possessive contrast has broken down in the languages of Timor and southern Maluku.

For eastern Indonesian languages where obligatory possession is marked in a different way to non-obligatory possession, Arnold (2019) has recently drawn attention to a minor subtype in which obligatory possessed nouns are further divided between separate inflectional paradigms. Under the label of 'split inalienable coding', she identifies a cluster of SHWNG languages around the Bird's Head in which the possessors of kin terms are marked with one inflectional paradigm, while body parts are marked with another. The differences between paradigms are typically minimal and often only in the third person. For example, Ambai has *-na* for a third person possessor of obligatory possessed kin terms, but *-n* for a third person possessor of obligatory possessed body part nouns (Silzer 1983: 160–3). Such splits in the obligatorily possessed class, however, do not appear to be limited to SHWNG languages. At least some Seram Laut languages have an unusual system in which the possessors of kin terms are indexed with prefixes, but body-part nouns with suffixes (e.g., Kowiai *nugu-aʔa* [1SG.POSS-eSl] 'my older sibling', but *fifir-yoŋ* [cheek-1SG.POSS] 'my cheek', Schapper fieldnotes).

Blust (1993a: 259) observes that the direct/indirect possessive contrast is unique to CMP, SHWNG, and Oceanic languages, suggesting that it could be reconstructable to his PCEMP node. However, as with the order of possessor–possessum, the Sulawesi language Banggai blurs the clarity of Blust's east/west genealogical divide. Banggai has a class of obligatory possessed nouns marked by a suffix like most eastern Austronesian languages (33a), while optional possession is encoded with a suffix on the article preceding the possessum (33b).

Banggai
(33) a. Obligatory possession: Direct
*ko* *tama-ŋgu*
ART father-1SG.POSS
'my father'

b. Optional possession: Indirect
*ko-ŋgu* *bonua*
ART-1SG.POSS house
'my house' (van den Bergh 1953: 53, 49)

**Table 48.2** Examples of geographical terms with fossilized third person possessive suffixes (bolded) in Saluan-Banggai languages

| | Balantak *-na* | Andio *-no* | Saluan *-nyo* | Bobongko *-nyo* |
|---|---|---|---|---|
| 'mountain' | *buuʔ-**na*** | *babo-**no*** | *buŋkul-**nyo*** | *bulud-**nyo*** |
| 'hill' | *buŋkur-**na*** | – | *buŋkut* | *bulu~bulud-**nyo*** |
| 'summit' | *sampe-**na*** | *tomboulo?* | *tutubul-**nyo*** | *tudu* |
| 'valley' | *leok-**na*** | *limboŋa* | *hata:-**nyo*** | *lemba-**nyo*** |
| 'bay' | – | – | *ho:l-**nyo*** | *luok-**nyo*** |
| 'cape' | *tadu-**na*** | *tadu-**no*** | *tadu:* | *uruŋ-**nyo*** |

What is more, a direct/indirect possessive contrast is also documented for a number of languages of the North Sarawakan group of Borneo. Here the directly possessed classes are very small. Kelabit, for example, has only three kinship terms, 'mother', 'father', and 'grandparent', that occur with direct possessor suffixes (34a). All other nouns are possessed using the indirect construction in which the pronoun or noun expressing the possessor is postposed to the possessum (34b).

Kelabit

(34) a. Obligatory possession: Direct
*sina-ʔ*
mother-1SG.POSS
'my mother'

b. Optional possession: Indirect
*anak* *kudih*
child 1SG.POSS
'my child' (Hemmings 2016: 143, 154)

The description in Soriente (2008: 57) suggests that a similar distinction is to be found in Kenyah languages.

#### 48.4.1.3 *Fossilized possessive morphology on inalienable nouns*

Although not mapped in Map 48.3, fossilized possessive morphology on sets of nouns denoting typical 'inalienables' suggests obligatorily possessed noun classes were once present in several other parts of the MPSEA area.

Adelaar (2005a: 25) points out an apparently fossilized final *-n* is found on many vowel-final body-part and kinship nouns in various Land Dayak languages, including Sungkung and Bidayuh varieties. He suggests that this *-n* may, at least in part, be explained as a fossil of an earlier, now defunct possessor marking suffix for a class of obligatorily possessed nouns. The Kayan languages of Borneo also appear to have obligatory possessed classes, with lesser amounts of fossilization. Blust (1977b: 46–7, 120) reports obligatory possession on kinship terms in Uma Juman and points to the existence of a fossil *-n* on these and other items. Blust (1977b: fn20) also notes that Murik evidences semantic specialization of contrastive pairs of identical roots in unpossessed form vs. a fossilized obligatorily possessed form (e.g. Murik *buluq* 'feather; fur' vs. *bulu-n* 'body hair').

Fossilized obligatory possessive suffixes *-n* also show up in some of the most isolating languages of eastern Indonesia, such as Naueti (Veloso 2016: 57–9) or Alorese (Klamer 2011: 48–9). An example of the kind of lexicalization found with fossilized possessive suffixes in these languages is the Tetun Dili pair *bee* 'water' and *bee-n* 'juice; sap; bodily fluid'.

An unusual pattern is found across many languages of northern and eastern Sulawesi. Here, third person possessive suffixes are sporadically fossilized on certain nouns denoting geographical features. This is illustrated with a small sample of words from the Saluan-Banggai languages in Table 48.2. Even though they are fossils, these possessive suffixes still clearly originate in suffixes in that they give rise to C.C sequences that would not otherwise be allowed within a root in these languages, or alternately show phonotactic constraints unique among root forms. While the original motivation for this possessive marking is obscure, the pattern is one consistent with a fossilized obligatory possessive class.

#### 48.4.1.4 *Unpossession*

World-wide languages with obligatorily possessed nouns often provide a morphological means of using obligatorily possessed nouns without expression of a possessor. Yet, we have found very few instances of this among MPSEA languages.

One of the only cases is that of Uab Meto where, instead of a person–number suffix marking the possessor, the suffix *-f* is used when an obligatory possessed noun is unpossessed or the possessor is backgrounded (Edwards 2016b: 123). A bound determiner can be used instead of a possessor inflection in languages such as Buru and Termanu where the identity of the possessor has already been established in the discourse (Chuck Grimes p.c.). More common in MPSEA languages is that a particular person form, typically first person plural inclusive, is used with generic reference including often as citation forms in elicitation contexts. In the Eastern dialect of Banggai, the 'unpossessed' suffix *-ndo* on obligatorily possessed nouns has developed historically from a first person plural inclusive inflection (van den Bergh 1953: 54–7).

Kin terms often show unusual behaviour in respect to obligatory possessive inflections. Unpossessed vocative forms of nouns can be found alongside obligatorily possessed kinship nouns in some languages. For example, Bontok obligatorily possessed nouns *amá-* 'father', and *iná-* 'mother' are relationship terms, distinct from the initially stressed vocative forms *áma* 'father.VOC', and *ína* 'mother.VOC' (Reid 1976: xv). In languages around the Bird's Head, obligatorily possessed kin terms often show patterns of root suppletion whereby no morpheme for the possessor is easily identifiable. For example, the Biak paradigm for 'mother' has a suppletive form *awin* for a first person singular possessor, while a distinct root taking regular inflectional suffixes for the possessor is found with second and third person possessors, *sna-m* 'your mother' and *sna-r* 'his/her mother' (van den Heuvel 2006: 242–50). A second type of suppletion involving different parts of a paradigm using inflecting vs. non-inflecting roots is found in Raja Ampat and some Maluku languages. For example, Ambel has an indirectly possessed root *nén* 'mother' used with first and second person singular possessors, but a directly (obligatorily) inflecting root *-nya-* 'mother' for third person and non-singular possessors (Arnold 2018a: 315–17). The frequent special inflectional behaviour of kin terms is likely to go back to their use as terms of address.

### 48.4.2 Optional free possessive linkers

The optional use of a free possessive linker between (pro)nouns expressing a possessor and a possessum represents a distinct form of differential possessive marking in MPSEA languages. It is a minor pattern, only known from some Borneo and Central Flores languages. Optional possessor linkers are found in other languages, but we do not list these as differential possessive marking because there is either no semantic difference in the (non-)use of the possessive linker, or the description does not provide enough information for us to decide what motivates the (non-)use of the possessive linker.

The alternations seen in the use of possessive linkers are typical of semantically based distinctions correlating with the alienability of possessive relations. For example, Keo (like other Central Flores languages with the exception of Lio) uses no marker when a body part is possessed (35a), but can use a possessive linker when a noun is alienable (35b) (see Baird 2002: 204–17 for a more detailed description).

Keo

(35) a. No possessive linker
*ʔudu wawi*
head pig
'pig's head'

b. Possessive linker
*ʔae koʔo kami*
water POSS 1PL.EXCL
'my water'
(Baird 2002: 204, 210)

The semantic, rather than lexical, nature of (in)alienability contrasts encoded by such optional possessive linkers have engendered some confusing characterizations in the Austronesian literature. In outlining the optionality of the possessive linker *koʔo* in Keo, for example, Baird writes that "[a]lthough semantic alienability can be identified, the possessive constructions cannot be labelled as being 'alienable' or 'inalienable'" (2002: 31) and then again "there is not a clear-cut syntactically-realized inalienable versus alienable distinction as is found in many other languages in the world" (2002: 207). What is meant here is that Keo does not have the lexical classes of nouns with obligatorily inflection for a possessor so common in other languages in eastern Indonesia (§48.4.1). However, such constructions are considered to encode (in)alienability in languages in other parts of the world (Nichols 1988; Nichols and Bickel 2013a). They seen to accord with cross-linguistic trends in possessive constructions whereby a possessor and a possessum in conceptually close relationships, such as body-part and kinship relationships, are coded by formally less distance (i.e. no possessive marker occurs between possessor and possessum).

Different explanations have been proposed for the preference for zero-coding of 'inalienable' possession (see, e.g., Haiman 1983; Haspelmath 2017). However, language-specific differences in what is treated as inalienable have received less attention. Consider the contrastive possessive constructions from two only distantly related languages of Borneo, Bakatik (36) and Ma'anyan (37). Both languages have two possessive constructions: one where the possessor follows the possessum without any explicit marking of the possessive relationship, and another where the possessor is introduced by a possessive linker. The construction without the possessive marker is available for all nouns in Bakatik (36a, c, e) and Ma'anyan (37a, c, e). The construction with the possessive linker is not available with body part nouns in either Bakatik (36f) or Ma'anyan (37f). However, the languages differ in that the possessive linker can be used with nouns denoting kin relations in Bakatik (36d), but not in Ma'anyan (37d).

Bakatik

| (36) | a. *kasuk* | *Asoŋ* | | b. *kasuk* | ***(e)je*** | *Asoŋ* |
|---|---|---|---|---|---|---|
| | dog | Asong | | dog | POSS | Asong |
| | 'Asong's dog' | | | 'Asong's dog' | | |
| | c. *anakŋ* | *Amir* | | d. *anakŋ* | ***(e)je*** | *Amir* |
| | child | Amir | | child | POSS | Amir |
| | 'Amir's child' | | | 'Amir's child' | | |
| | e. *abok* | *ade* | | f. **abok* | ***(e)je*** | *ade* |
| | hair | 3SG | | hair | POSS | 3SG |
| | 'his hair' | | | (Sudarsono 2002: 168–70) | | |

Ma'anyan

| (37) | a. *lewuq* | *ambah* | | b. *lewuq* | *wat* | *ambah* |
|---|---|---|---|---|---|---|
| | house | father | | house | POSS | father |
| | 'father's house' | | | 'father's house' | | |
| | c. *wawey* | *ambah* | | d. **wawey* | *wat* | *ambah* |
| | wife | father | | wife | POSS | father |
| | 'father's wife' | | | | | |
| | e. *taŋan* | *warik* | | f. **taŋan* | *wat* | *warik* |
| | hand | monkey | | hand | POSS | monkey |
| | 'monkey's paw' | | | (Gudai 1985: 105–6) | | |

Language-specific differences in the availability of optional possessive linkers with nouns of different semantics are unexplained. Different semantic restrictions in the use of such optional possessive linkers may ultimately be attributable to the possessive linkers having different diachronic sources. For example, Bakatik *(e)je* seems to originate in a source preposition (Sudarsono 2002: 169), while Ma'anyan *wat* appears to be a reduced form of a noun meaning 'thing' (Sander Adelaar p.c.).

### 48.4.3 Edible/general possessive contrasts

A final pattern of differential possessive marking involves a two-way contrast between edible and general possession, typically, in the domain of indirect possession. This feature is prominently described in the literature on Oceanic languages (e.g. Lichtenberk 1985), but it is also present in a handful of languages in the eastern part of the MPSEA area. These are the SHWNG languages Sawai, Patani, Buli, and Waropen (van den Berg 2009) and the CMP language Selaru. A similar, but more elaborated, set of distinctions is found in the two MPSEA languages of Micronesia.

In the eastern Indonesian languages, an indirect possessive classifier precedes the possessed noun and hosts inflections for the person/number of the possessor. Typically, inflections for possessor are suffixal or involve a combination of suffixes and prefixes. Waropen is exceptional in that possessor inflections are prefixes. In addition, the Waropen general possessor classifier *-i-* has become bound to the possessum (38a), while the edible classifier remains free (38b).

Waropen general vs. edible possession

| (38) | a. ***ra-i-ruma*** | b. ***ra-na*** | *sabaku* |
|---|---|---|---|
| | 1SG-GENERAL-house | 1SG-EDIBLE | tobacco |
| | 'my house' | 'my tobacco' | |
| | | (van den Berg 2009: 11) | |

The choice of possessive classifier signals the intended use of the possessum by the possessor (Lynch 2001). In Selaru, for example, the general possessive classifier *wasi* indicates that the pig is not food, either still being alive or not yet prepared as food (39a), while the edible possessive classifier *hina* indicates that the pig is already considered food, that is, it has been killed and cooked (39b).

Selaru indirect possessive constrasts

| (39) | a. ***wasi-mw*** | *hahy* | *desike* | *lan=i* |
|---|---|---|---|---|
| | GENERAL-2SG | pig | DEM | big=3SG.ANIM |
| | 'Your pig there is big.' | | | |
| | b. ***hina-mw*** | *hahy* | *desike* | *mtelas* |
| | EDIBLE-2SG | pig | DEM | delicious |
| | 'Your pork (i.e. edible pig) there is delicious.' | | | |
| | (Coward 2005: 52) | | | |

Edibility is, however, only one factor governing the choice of indirect possessive classifiers. The use of a noun in association with eating is enough to trigger use of the edible possessive classifier in Sawai (Kamholz fieldnotes, cited in Gasser, Arnold, and Kamholz, this volume, chapter 37) and Patani (Rødvand 2023). Lexicalization also appears to play a role in such indirect possessive classification systems. Edible rather than general possession is still used in Selaru for cash crops which are not intended to be eaten and in some cases are not even edible (Coward 2005: 52). A corpus study of one or more of the eastern Indonesian languages with a general/edible distinction would be useful in illuminating the factors underlying indirect possessive classifier choice.

Both Chamorro and Palauan, the only two MPSEA languages of Micronesia, have systems of possessive classifiers broadly similar to the ones described above, but with more semantic elaboration. Chamorro has the following possessive classifiers, *naʔ-* 'EDIBLE', *gimen-* 'DRINKABLE', *gaʔ-* 'ANIMAL', and *iyo-* 'GENERAL' (Topping 1973: 164–6). Palauan has a larger set including *kall-* 'EDIBLE', *ilum-* 'DRINKABLE', *xarm-* 'ANIMAL', *xeləd-* 'INEDIBLE MEAT', *odoim-* 'EDIBLE MEAT', *xemaxel-* 'CHEWABLE', *inter alia* (Josephs 1975: 73–5). Derived from nouns, the Chamorro and Palauan possessive classifiers inflect for the person and number of the possessor and precede the noun denoting the possessum. See Zobel (this volume, chapters 38, 39) for more information.

## 48.5 Possessive constructions with pragmatically marked possessors

Many languages in our survey have multiple possessive structures, where one is less frequent and noted as 'marked' by the describing linguist. Although descriptions are often vague about these marked structures and examples few, it is in most cases clear that we are dealing with variation in possessive marking that is motivated by factors outside the possessive relationship. That is, the choice of a marked possessive structure is not governed by either the lexical class of the noun or the semantics of the possessive relationship between possessor and possessum (covered already in §48.4), but rather has to do with the discourse prominence or other pragmatic characteristics of the possessor.

As mentioned already in this chapter, many languages of the Philippines have a second, marked possessive structure in which the possessor is a preposed free oblique pronoun, often marked by a possessive linker. Compare Bikol (40a) and (40b). The type of pronoun that appears in this structure typically is also used independently as a possessive pronoun (e.g. '(it is) mine, my one'), as in (40c–d).

Bikol

(40) a. *an* *tataramon=**ta***
ART language=1INCL.POSS
'our language'

b. *an* ***satuya=ŋ*** *tataramon*
ART 1INCL.LOC=LNK language
'*our* language'

c. ***satuya*** *ito=ŋ* *libro*
1INCL.LOC DEM=LNK book
'That book is ours.' (lit. 'ours is that book')

d. *libro=ŋ* *ito* *an* ***satuya***
book=LNK DEM ART 1INCL.LOC
'That book is ours.' (Malcolm Mintz p.c.)

The oblique possessor construction is more commonly found with pronominal than nominal possessors across Philippine languages (see §48.3.3). Tagalog is one of the exceptional languages in that it allows postposed and preposed orders with both nominal and pronominal possessors. In Tagalog, the basic pronominal possessive structure has a bound enclitic (41a), while the marked structure involves a preposed dative pronoun marked with a linker (41b). In an alternative word order, the dative pronoun is postposed to the possessum and takes additional dative case marking, while the linker remains in second position (41c). With a nominal possessor, the basic word order involves a possessor postposed with genitive case marking (41d). Alternative, marked orders can also have a preposed nominal possessor with dative case and a linker (41e) or a postposed nominal possessor with dative case marking and the linker remains in second position (41f). Both (41c) and (41e) are highly unusual, marked constructions, but they are theoretically possible.

Tagalog

(41) a. *lapis=**ko***
pencil=1SG.POSS
'my pencil'

b. ***aki=ŋ*** *lapis*
1SG.DAT=LNK bag
'my pencil'

c. *lapis* ***na*** ***sa=akin***
pencil LNK DAT=1SG.DAT
'my pencil'

d. *lapis* ***ŋ=bata***
pencil GEN=child
'(a/the) child's pencil'

e. ***sa=bata=ŋ*** *lapis*
DAT=child=LNK pencil
'the child's pencil'

f. *lapis* ***na*** ***sa=bata***
pencil LNK DAT=child
'the child's pencil'
(Schachter and Otanes 1972: 135–6)

Descriptions often provide little information on the difference between such possessive constructions. Both Matigsalug Manobo and Tboli are described as using an oblique preposed pronoun to give 'negative contrastive' emphasis. For Mamanwa, a preposed possessive pronoun with a linker is described simply as an 'emphatic possessor', as opposed to the unmarked, postposed possessor. Similarly, Malcolm Mintz (p.c.) describes the Bikol preposed possessor construction as placing more emphasis on the possessor than the equivalent postposed structure. In Cebuano, the preposed possessive construction is said to be used where the possessor is topicalized (Tanangkingsing 2009: 84). The only mention we have found in the literature as to the difference in usage between the basic and marked constructions in Tagalog is that the use of the preposed possessor is described as being more formal (De Vos 2011: 57). However, Erik Zobel (p.c.) suggests to us that a different pragmatic markedness, such as contrastive, may better describe the function of the dative adnominal possessive in Tagalog. Daniel Kaufman (p.c.) argues that the Tagalog oblique case independent pronominal possessors do not have any inherent pragmatic marking but, unlike their clitic counterparts, they are compatible with pragmatic marking because as independent items they can be used with contrastive intonation. Clearly, the pragmatics of possessor coding in the Philippines needs more research.

Dedicated free 'emphatic' possessive pronouns (i.e. pronouns that are exclusively used in encoding possessors and have no further oblique functions) with similar semantics to possessive uses of oblique pronouns are found occasionally throughout the MPSEA region. In our sample, emphatic possessor pronouns are always independent, that is, unbound elements; they are able to function both adnominally (*my*, *your*, etc.) and pronominally (*mine*, *yours*, etc.). Although the descriptions are often vague on details, emphatic possessive pronouns typically seem to function to place contrastive focus on the identity of the possessor. One of the clearest statements of this is given by Maree (2007: 55–6) for Ibatan. He writes: "emphatic possessive pronouns are possessive forms that occur when contrast is implied, for example, 'this is his house, not anybody else's.'"

In our sample, the use of emphatic possessor pronouns is always associated with a change in the ordering of possessor and possessum. Where the unmarked ordering sees the possessor preposed to the possessum in eastern Indonesia, emphatic possessor pronouns are postposed to the possessum. This is illustrated by the Kedang examples in (42). The unmarked adnominal possessive construction involves an independent possessor pronoun preposed to the possessum (42a), while the marked adnominal possessive construction sees the emphatic possessor pronoun postposed to the possessum (42b). Example (42c) illustrates the additional pronominal function as well as contrastive meaning associated with the emphatic possessor pronouns. Donohue (this volume, §46.3.2) and Kroeger and Smith (this volume, §27.4.1) observe similar word order switches in Palu'e and Kimaragang Dusun, respectively.

Kedang

(42) a. ***koʔ*** *huna*
1SG.POSS house
'my house'

b. *labur* ***koʔo***
dress 1SG.POSS.EMPH
'my dress'

c. *labur* *nobe* *ohaʔ* ***moʔo****=ne,* *labur*
dress DEM NEG 2SG.POSS.EMPH=3SG dress
*nobe* ***koʔo****=ne*
DEM 1SG.POSS.EMPH=3SG
'That dress is not *yours*, that dress is *mine*.'
(Samely 1991: 76–7)

Conversely, in languages in the west and north of the MPSEA area where the possessor is normally postposed, the use of emphatic possessor pronouns, where they exist, is typically preposed to the possessum. This is illustrated by the Sulawesi language Pamona in (43), where an unmarked first person possessor is encoded by a pronominal enclitic attached to the possessum (43a). In the marked construction, the emphatic possessor pronoun is, however, preposed to the possessum (43b). Example (43c) shows the contrastive meaning of Pamona emphatic possessor pronouns, and demonstrates the adnominal as well as pronominal functions of them.

Pamona

(43) a. *pale=**ku***
hand=1SG
'my hand'

b. ***anuku*** *pale*
1SG.POSS.EMPH hand
'*my* hand'

c. ***anuku*** *kayuku* *mo-wua-mo,*
1SG.POSS.EMPH coconut HAVE-fruit-PRF
***anunya*** *bareʔe-pa*
3.POSS.EMPH NEG-IPF
'*My* coconut palm is already fruiting, but *his* is not yet.' (Adriani 1931: 343)

Given their ability to occur pronominally (e.g. *mine*, *yours*) including in predications of possession (e.g. *is mine*, *is yours*), it could perhaps be argued that adnominal emphatic possessive pronouns are actually truncated relativization structures (e.g. N *(that is) mine*, N *(that is) yours*). This idea finds some support in a few languages where descriptions explicitly state that a relativizer can be inserted between the possessum and possessive pronoun. For example, in Irarutu the basic possessive construction has a preposed possessor (44a). A second, marked construction makes uses of a postposed emphatic possessive pronoun (44b), which can be introduced by the relativizer *fi* (44c).

Irarutu

(44) a. *ja* *skripsi*
1SG.POSS thesis
'my thesis'

b. *skripsi* ***jari***
thesis 1SG.POSS.EMPH
'*my* thesis'

c. *motor* ***fi*** ***jari***
motorbike REL 1SG.POSS.EMPH
'motorbike which is mine' (Jackson 2014: 121, 177)

However, for most languages in our sample with emphatic possessor pronouns, it is unclear whether such relativization is possible.

There are clear parallels between the marked possessive constructions using preposed emphatic pronouns in western Indonesian languages and those using preposed oblique pronouns in Philippine languages. This may be taken to suggest that oblique pronouns are, at least in some cases, sources for emphatic possessive pronouns. The oblique pronouns that form marked preposed possessor structures are typically also used in an independent possessive function. Such independent possessive usages of a more general type of oblique pronoun is seen in several Philippine languages in which an adnominal use is not present, and beyond this in Sumatra (Gayo) and Sulawesi (Balantak). Another pattern to form an independent possessive is seen using some noun or pro-form, like the widely found indefinite pronoun *anu, with basic possessive marking, for example, in Andio *anu-ngku* 'my one', *anu-um* 'your one'. In one language, Pamona, such forms have also become preposed adnominal possessives, see example (43) above. Due to the predicative uses of such independent possessive (oblique) pronouns, it would seem that Philippine adnominal oblique possessives could have their origin in a type of possessive clause that was relativized.

## 48.6 Concluding discussion

This chapter has presented a comparative study of adnominal possessive constructions and their distribution in MPSEA languages. We focused on the following parameters: (i) word order of possessor and possessum; (ii) the marking, if any, of the possessive relationship, when possessor and possessor are expressed by nouns; (iii) the boundness of possessive markers to possessor or possessum; and (iv) the existence of differential possessive marking for different semantic and/or lexical classes of noun.

It is well known from the typological literature (e.g. Dryer 2013e) that MPSEA languages show a split in their word order correlations on account of changes in the basic order of possessor and possessum. The correlation between VO word order and basic possessum–possessor order in the northern and western MPSEA languages is expected. However, the appearance of possessor–possessum order together with VO word orders that is found in the east of the area is typically explained as the result of contact with Papuan languages with possessor–possessum order (see, e.g., Donohue 2007, Schapper and Gasser 2023). A contact explanation for this unusual eastern MPSEA correlation is supported by the fact that languages with VO and preposed possessors are substantially less common than languages with VO and postposed possessors, though the former are still attested in languages from many parts of the world.

A novel finding here is that across the MPSEA area there are marked possessive constructions in which the normal order of the possessor and possessum is reversed. That is, many MPSEA languages where the basic possessive construction has possessum–possessor order also present an additional, more marked structure in which possessor–possessum order is used. Conversely, where the basic possessive construction has possessor–possessum order, the marked structure displays a possessum–possessor order. Descriptions of marked possessive structures are often vague about their frequency and function, and we suspect that the marked possessive constructions with word order reversals may be more widespread than the literature makes clear. In addition, our study suggests more thorough investigation of marked possessive constructions would likely illuminate the pathways by which word order changes in possessive constructions take place. It was seen, for example, that several Mangyan languages had shifted to a preposed possessor by adopting what are in other languages pragmatically marked constructions using dative pronouns as the basic pronominal possessive construction.

Large differences across the MPSEA area were observed in how languages encoded a possessive relationship between possessor and possessum nouns. The true diversity of the marking of possessive constructions in the MPSEA area has not been appreciated in much previous work (e.g. Dryer 2013b) due to a focus on the position of any bound possessive markers, which are overwhelmingly suffixal/enclitic, irrespective of their ability to co-occur with free (pro)nominal elements. We saw that there was major variation in MPSEA languages with respect to whether a possessive construction with a nominal possessor involved a possessive marker with a person feature or not. The obligatory use of a person marked form, be it free or bound, in a possessive construction with a nominal possessor is the near universal pattern in the languages east of Sulawesi. Outside of this region, a person feature on a possessive marker was seen to be a minority pattern in possessive constructions with a nominal possessor, often limited to a particular constructional type. Zero-marked possessive constructions were concentrated in Borneo, but small patches were also found elsewhere in Indonesia and the Philippines. Typically, languages with these zero constructions showed erosion of their case- and/or person-marking systems. Finally, while the obligatory use of possessive markers with a person feature showed significant geographical variation across MPSEA languages, the overwhelming majority pattern was for a bound possessive marker to be hosted on the possessum, rather than the possessor. Possessor-marking is limited to small enclaves and is often only found in marked, that is non-basic, possessive constructions. From a cross-linguistic point of view, the MPSEA area is rather remarkable for the almost complete absence of possessor-marking, a common pattern in almost all other regions (see Nichols and Bickel 2013b).

Geographical skewings were also evident in the distribution of some, but not all, types of differential possessive marking. Obligatorily possessed nouns which are possessed in the same way as optionally possessed nouns were found scattered throughout the MPSEA area. The many places in which this particular type of differential possessive marking has independently arisen in the MPSEA languages suggests that it is extremely easy for these classes of nouns to arise due to the high frequency of their use with possessors (*pace* Haspelmath 2017). What is much less common is the indirect/direct possessive contrast (and further developments from it) found throughout much of the eastern Indonesian region. The appearance of inalienably possessed nouns here has been assumed to be the result of contact with Papuan languages with similar systems (e.g. Ross 2001: 138; van den Berg 2009). Donohue and Schapper (2008) go further and explicitly trace the indirect/direct possessive construction to Papuan languages in eastern Indonesia (see Schapper, this volume, §22.3). Outside eastern Indonesia, the only substantial concentration of differential possessive marking is in Borneo. Here the variety of systems, and the fact that many have become (near-)fossilized, makes generalization difficult, but it does appear to represent an areal feature there also.

Our survey also supports Aikhenvald's (2013: 45ff) claim that possessive classification systems are highly sensitive to the effects of contact situations. This is most strikingly seen in the MPSEA languages of western Micronesia, Chamorro, and Palauan, which have taken on possessive classifier systems paralleling, both in morphosyntax and semantics, the elaborate possessive classifier systems of their distant Micronesian relatives (Harrison 1988; Song 1997), while relatively little other Micronesian influence is detectable in their structures.

A desideratum for future research on possession in MPSEA languages would be more focused historical work, particularly, reconstruction of adnominal possessive constructions and their forms to low- and intermediate-level subgroups. This would be beneficial in understanding the significant processes of diversification and change that have occurred in MPSEA possessive constructions. Additionally, whilst this study has dealt exclusively with adnominal possessive constructions, our survey work suggested that MPSEA languages have a wide array of predicative possessive constructions, including contrastive predications for ownership proper and part–whole relations respectively, that would be worthy of closer investigation.

## Acknowledgements

This chapter has benefitted greatly from useful discussion and data from the following people: Sander Adelaar, David Kamholz, David Gil, Malcolm Mintz, Lawrence Reid, Erik Zobel, David Zorc, among others. Schapper's research was supported by the Netherlands Organisation for Scientific Research VENI project 'The evolution of the lexicon. Explorations in lexical stability, semantic shift and borrowing in a Papuan language family', the Volkswagen Stiftung DoBeS project 'Aru languages documentation', and the European Research Council 'OUTOFPAPUA' project (grant agreement no. 848532). It is with great sadness that I learned of the passing of Billy McConvell, my coauthor on this chapter, in October 2023. I got to know Billy while working on the Waves of Words project at Western Sydney University. Sadly, I never had the pleasure of meeting Billy in person, but for several years we chatted on Facebook, zoomed and emailed. As we discussed and worked together, I came to admire the depth and breadth of his knowledge on Austronesian and Australian languages. Billy always had something interesting to say. He is missed.

CHAPTER 49

# Spatial orientation

GARY HOLTON AND LEAH PAPPAS

## 49.1 Introduction

### 49.1.1 The study of space in Austronesian languages

The Austronesian languages are well known for the prevalence of geocentric systems of spatial orientation which use geography rather than ego as a reference point. The most common system of spatial orientation found in the Malayo-Polynesian languages of Southeast Asia and outliers (henceforth MPSEA) is the seaward–landward distinction, which minimally employs a single horizontal axis oriented transverse to the coast, distinguishing 'toward the sea/water' from 'toward the land/mountains'. This basic system has deep antiquity and can be reconstructed for Proto-Austronesian (PAN). As Blust remarks,

> the most general principle of macro-orientation in Austronesian languages is the land-sea axis, associated with the PAN terms *daya 'toward the interior' and *lahud 'toward the sea'. (Blust 2009c: 311)

Similarly, in a survey of MPSEA directional systems Adelaar concludes:

> The fundamental axis of orientation in Austronesian societies is the inland versus the sea. Proto-Austronesian *daya 'towards the interior' and *lahud 'towards the sea' have reflexes in a huge amount of daughter languages all over the Austronesian area. (Adelaar 1997: 43)

While in some languages the original PAN seaward–landward axis has been essentially maintained in its original function, in other languages one or both of the 'seaward' and 'landward' terms have lost their original directional meaning. In other cases, the seaward–landward axis has taken on the meaning of downriver–upriver or been adapted into an elevation system distinguishing LOW vs. HIGH. In still other cases the seaward–landward axis has become fixed, serving as a cardinal axis. And in yet other languages the original seaward–landward axis has been lost altogether and innovated terms are used for orientation purposes. Further, many languages have added a second axis of orientation, either a fixed cardinal axis or a geocentric axis determined by the orientation of the river or the coast, to the basic seaward–landward axis. The resulting possibilities for hybrid systems of spatial orientation yield an enormous diversity of systems.

The study of spatial orientation systems in the Oceanic subgroup of Austronesian languages is well advanced (François 2004, 2015; Palmer 2015; Bennardo 2002; Senft 2004a). And while the Oceanic subgroup includes more than one third of the languages of Austronesia, it is but a single subgroup and so doesn't begin to capture the range of diversity of spatial orientation systems attested in the family. In this chapter we propose a tentative typology of spatial orientation systems in Western Malayo-Polynesian languages, based on a survey of extant literature. We limit our focus to directional systems; demonstratives, motion verbs, and other forms of spatial language are beyond the scope of this study. In this effort we build on the pioneering work of Adelaar (1997), incorporating significant amounts of new data which have become available since that paper was published.

### 49.1.2 The data

One of the greatest challenges for understanding spatial orientation systems remains the paucity of available data. Because orientation systems are embedded within local geography, in order to understand their function it is necessary to know not just the forms of the orientation terms, but also their meaning across a range of geographic contexts. Without knowing how a system functions in different geographic contexts and at different scales, it can be difficult or impossible to disambiguate meanings. In a region with a mountain range that lies to the north, a term which indicates direction toward the mountains could be equally well interpreted as 'landward' or 'uphill' or 'upriver' or simply cardinal 'north'. Only by asking what happens on the other side of the mountains can we distinguish these potential meanings. Yet, all too often sources lack this information.

Gary Holton and Leah Pappas, *Spatial orientation.* In: *The Oxford Guide to the Malayo-Polynesian Languages of Southeast Asia.* Edited by: Alexander Adelaar and Antoinette Schapper, Oxford University Press. © Gary Holton and Leah Pappas (2024). DOI: 10.1093/oso/9780198807353.003.0049

Adelaar (1997) assigns the meanings 'north' and 'south', respectively, to Madurese *daya* and *lao?*, yet notes:

> The question remains whether the above directional terms are used in the same way in Madurese dialects spoken in the northern and north-western parts of Madura, which do not have the sea to the south or the interior to the north. In other words, are the directions still linked to local geography, or have they become independent from it so that the system now has a 'fixed' set of terms for cardinal directions? (Adelaar 1997: 57)

A similar statement is made by Brown (2001) regarding the cognate Nias terms *raya* 'south' and *löu* 'north':

> I have not yet checked whether the meanings of directional terms change depending on which part of the island the speaker is. (Brown 2001: 436)

A related problem concerns the scale of directionals, discussed in §49.1.4. Even where sources provide information about the geographic context of directional terms, they may fail to provide information about the scale of usage. For example, while a source may describe a seaward–landward system, it may not indicate whether that system operates at local, intermediate, or regional scales. Sometimes the relevant scales can be inferred from supplied examples, but where this is not possible we assume for the purposes of this survey that the system operates at the intermediate, or 'village' scale.

### 49.1.3 Spatial orientation systems

Spatial orientation systems locate referents by picking out a search domain radially at a particular angle from the deictic centre. In this chapter we limit our discussion to absolute systems of spatial orientation, as distinct from intrinsic and relative systems. Many, if not most, of the languages surveyed here also make extensive use of intrinsic orientation through systems of adpositions and positional verbs which locate a figure in relation to some intrinsic property of the referent (ground object) (e.g. 'front', 'top', etc). In contrast, egocentric relative systems ('left', 'right') are rarely used for spatial orientation in Western Malayo-Polynesian.

The diagnostic criterion we use for distinguishing absolute systems is invariance under rotation of both the viewer and the referent cf. Levinson (2003: 52). This should not be confused with the fact that the interpretation of the angle of the directional axis is *relative* to a particular location. These systems are absolute in the sense that for a given geographic location, the orientation of the directional axis remains fixed regardless of the orientation of the viewer and the referent. The apparent relativity of these systems arises only when viewed from the outside. For instance, if one compares a seaward–landward system to a cardinal system, the 'seaward' direction seems variable because it could point in several cardinal directions. From an emic perspective, however, the directions are fixed.

In spite of extensive work on absolute systems of spatial orientation (e.g. Haugen 1957; Brown and Levinson 1993; Levinson 2003; Burenhult 2008; Palmer 2015), there remains much confusion in the literature regarding just what is meant by the term *absolute* in reference to spatial orientation. Many authors are reluctant to step out of an etic grid in which the cardinal directions north-south-east-west are assumed to be fundamental. Statements like the following are typical, here referring to the apparently relative orientation of Solor Lamaholot *lau* 'seaward' (< *lahud) and *raé* 'landward' (< *daya) terms:

> Interestingly, although this orientation system is considered absolute, the direction to which this axis is pointing differs from village to village depending on which coastal side of the island the village is situated. For example ... for villages located on the north coast of the island, *lau* points to the north and *raé* to the south, but for villages on the opposite coastal side, *lau* points to the south and *raé* to the north. (Kroon 2016: 145)

From the perspective of a Solor Lamaholot speaker, one could just as easily construct such a statement about English 'north' and 'south'. Namely, English 'north' sometimes points in the *lau* direction and sometimes in the *raé* direction—and sometimes in neither direction. One could ask how 'north' can be considered to be an absolute directional if it points in so many different directions! Of course, the absurdity of this argument belies the fact that any absolute system of orientation will appear relative when interpreted within the context of a different absolute system. Even cardinal 'north' is not immune from this, as pointed out long ago by Haugen (1957) in his study of the use of Icelandic cardinal terms. In this survey we take an emic approach, describing directional systems in their own terms rather than attempting to align them with an etic cardinal grid.

Spatial orientation systems play a fundamental role in MPSEA, serving not only to locate referents in space but also providing an anchor for cosmology and ecological knowledge. As Nagaya observes for Lamaholot:

> Directionals are an important portion of the encyclopedic knowledge interwoven with culture and religion of Lamaholot-speaking communities. (Nagaya 2011: 261)

That is, spatial orientation systems do much more than simply locate referents in space. For many of the languages surveyed here, spatial orientation structures permeate everyday conversational language, providing a spatial lens through which culture, life, environment, and humanity is conceptualized. While this survey focuses on the structural aspects of spatial orientation, we acknowledge that these systems typically function at many levels.

### 49.1.4 Scale of orientation systems

Spatial orientation systems may operate at multiple scales, and languages differ as to which directional systems are used at each scale. Most languages differentiate at least three scales:

- local or small-scale, roughly the domain within and immediately surrounding a dwelling
- intermediate scale, roughly the domain of the village or island
- regional or worldwide scale, roughly the domain beyond the immediate group of villages or island

Local orientation is used within the immediate vicinity of the deictic centre; intermediate orientation is used across larger distances, such as within a village or between nearby villages; and worldwide orientation is used beyond the range of clear geographic reference points, such as at sea. However, the boundaries between these scales often overlap. Languages differ in terms of on which scales different directional terms are used. For example, a language which uses seaward–landward directionals at the intermediate scale may switch to using cardinal direction terms at the worldwide scale. Thus, Mapun makes use of the directional verbs *lūd* 'go downhill' and *tukad* 'go uphill' at the intermediate scale (1a) but relies on cardinal terms *uttaraʔ* 'north', *sātan* 'south', *timu* 'east', *balat* 'west' at the worldwide scale (1b).

Mapun

(1) a. *Pa-lūd* *ko* *pa* *lumaʔ* *kami* *sumawung.*
CAUS-go.DOWNHILL 2SG to house 1EXCL tomorrow
'Come down to our house tomorrow.'

b. *Bong* *ko* *lome* *pa* *Sandakan,* *mundaʔ* *nu* *tiluʔ* *pa* *sātan.*
when 2SG journey to Sandakan steer 2SG.POSS destination to south
'When you journey to Sandakan, head south.'
(Collins et al. 2001)

Also, even when the same lexical forms are used at all scales, their interpretation may differ. For example, Balinese *daja* means 'landward' at the local and intermediate scales but is conventionalized as 'north' at the worldwide scale, extending the intermediate scale pattern used in the more populous south coast of the island (Wassmann and Dasen 1998). Even where the same system is used at all scales, cross-linguistic variation in the lexicalization of earlier directional roots provides evidence of past variation across scales. For example, in languages spoken on the west coast of Luzon Island reflexes of *lahud 'toward the sea' have lexicalized as 'west', while in languages spoken on the east coast of the island reflexes of *lahud mean 'east'. Thus Ilokano has *laud* 'west' and Guinaang Kalinga has *lagud* 'east' (see §49.6 below on cardinal orientation).

### 49.1.5 Organization of this chapter

In the following sections we present a tentative typology of spatial orientation in MPSEA which recognizes five broad categories: seaward–landward (§49.2); riverine (§49.3); coastal (§49.4); elevational (§49.5); and cardinal (§49.6). Within each of these sections we provide prototypical and representative examples illustrating the spatial orientation category, along with examples of various subtypes within the category. For example, within systems that have a primary seaward–landward axis there exist subtypes that have a secondary 'across' axis and subtypes that have a secondary axis. Finally, we conclude in §49.7 by discussing the overall distribution of spatial orientation systems in the region.

## 49.2 Seaward–landward systems

The seaward–landward distinction is often viewed as fundamental to Austronesian spatial orientation, and seaward–landward systems are indeed common among the languages surveyed here, in languages such as Wooi (Sawaki et al. 2016), Kambera (Klamer 1998), and Yami (Gallego 2018). However, even when these systems originate from the same PAN source, there is quite a bit of diversity in their realization. In many cases the original seaward–landward axis has been conventionalized or fixed as a cardinal axis (see §49.6.1). In this section we consider those systems in which the seaward–landward axis maintains its geographic (non-cardinal) orientation. But even here there is significant variation. The seaward–landward axis typically occurs in conjunction with an additional, transverse axis. The transverse axis may be unoriented, often glossed 'across', or it may be oriented either as a fixed "cardinal" axis (in the sense of François 2004) or as a geocentric axis determined by the orientation of a geographic feature such as the coastline or a river.

Although a large number of Austronesian languages exhibit reflexes of the PAN directional terms *daya 'towards the interior' and *lahud 'towards the sea', these reflexes do not always form a geocentric directional axis. While the 'inland' meaning of *daya is generally retained in Philippine languages, reflexes of *lahud may be semantically bleached, losing their directional orientation (cf. Gallego 2018: 77). For example, Cebuano *laya* 'inland' but *lawud* 'toward town; open sea'. While the meaning 'toward town' can be seen to derive from an original 'seaward' meaning, it is not clear to what extent the 'seaward' meaning is still active in Cebuano (Blust and Trussel 2020). In Salako of northwest Borneo, *laut* no longer means 'seaward.' Instead, its meaning has changed to mean 'Malay' (i.e. the people who tend to live near the sea). *Dayà*, however, still means 'interior' (Adelaar 1997: 69). In other languages, including Aklanon, Bikol, and Binukid (Western Bukidnon Manobo), even the directional sense is lost and the reflex of *lahud simply denotes 'sea'. Though rarer, the inverse situation obtains as well. Mansaka has *lawud* < *lahud with the meaning 'downriver; seaward' but has no opposing term meaning 'inland' (and no reflex of *daya) (Blust and Trussel 2020). However, the term *agsaka* 'upriver' (derived from *saka* 'ascend; go upriver') can be apposed to *lawud* 'downriver', as in (2).

Mansaka

(2) a. *Kisurum dato ako lawud.*
tomorrow to.there 1SG DOWNRIVER
'I will be downriver tomorrow.'
(Svelmoe and Svelmoe 1990: 247)

b. *Olobang ko yaning opi na*
plant.taro 1SG this taro which
*sikun agsaka.*
come.from UPRIVER
'I will plant the taro seedlings that came from upriver.' (Svelmoe and Svelmoe 1990: 264)

Other languages have innovated terms to describe the opposition between land and sea. One such language that has maintained a seaward–landward distinction but has innovated terms is Pendau, a language of Central Sulawesi. Pendau lacks reflexes of *lahud and *daya and instead exhibits innovative terms *teriong* 'seaward' and *tebuat* 'inland'. These terms are used at a wide range of scales to refer to location along an axis perpendicular to the coast. The system is truly directional, not elevational, in that it can be used to distinguish the location of referents at the same level, depending on relative position with respect to the coast (49.3).

Pendau

(3) a. *Aʔu maʔo ri-teriong*
1ABS go LOC-SEA
'I am going towards the ocean' (Quick 2007: 88)

b. *Rapi-ʔu o unga-ʔu bengkel*
spouse-1SG/GEN and child-1SG/GEN female
*meneʔ joʔong ri-tebuat*
GO.UP garden LOC-landward
'My spouse and my daughter went inland up to the garden.' (Quick 2007: 157)

Innovative forms for the seaward–landward axis may differ even among closely related languages. Tajio, a Southern Tomini language spoken less than 10km across the narrow peninsula of Northern Sulawesi from Pendau, has a cognate form *ariong* 'seaward' but a distinct form *malae* 'landward' (Mayani 2013: 92).

Keo, a language of Flores, has innovated a seaward–landward system which distinguishes proximal and distal referents. Keo *dau* 'seawards a long distance' reflects *lahud, while the other terms have been innovated (Table 49.1). Keo proximal and distal terms can be used to distinguish local vs. more distant referents. The proximal term in (4a) indicates location within a house, while the distal term in (4b) refers to another village that lies on the shore.

**Table 49.1** Keo seaward–landward terms.

| | Proximal | Distal |
|---|---|---|
| Seaward | *ridi* | *dau* |
| Landward | *rédé* | *réta* |

Keo

(4) a. *Dako néʔé ʔoné ridi saʔo.*
dog exist in SEA.PROX house
'The dog is seaward in the house...'
(Baird 2002: 222)

b. *ʔAta Ndai biasa ndua kima*
people Ndai usual GO.DOWN mollusc
*dau Maundai.*
SEA.DIST Maundai
'Ndai people used to go down looking for molluscs seaward at Maundai.' (Baird 2002: 359)

Keo also exhibits traces of a coastal axis, as discussed in §49.4.4 below.

### 49.2.1 Seaward–landward plus 'across'

Kedang combines a seaward–landward axis lexified with *owe* 'seaward' and *oli* 'landward' with a unitary coastal directional *oyo* 'along the coast'. The coastal axis is always transverse, paralleling the coast but does not distinguish directions along the coast. Barnes (1974) interprets this as an elevation system distinguishing *oli* 'above', *owe* 'below', and *oyo* 'level'. However, more recent work by Samely (1991) reports that the terms are insensitive to local topography and are viewed by speakers as essentially horizontal. The association of the landward term *oli* with higher elevations is natural based on the tendency for higher elevations to occur inland. However, inland locations with no elevation difference are still considered to be *oli* 'landward' rather than *oyo* 'level' (Figure 49.1). The latter term is reserved for directions parallel to the coast. Both the seaward–landward and the unitary 'along the coast' axes are geographically determined (i.e. non-cardinal).

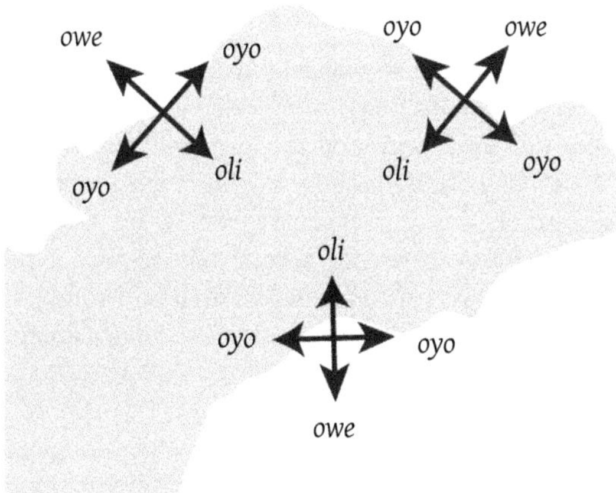


**Figure 49.1** Orientation of Kedang directional terms *owe* 'seaward', *oli* 'landward', and *oyo* 'along the coast' on eastern Lembata Island (after Samely 1991: 119).

Superimposed on the seaward–landward is an elevation system based on *ote* 'up' and *ole* 'down'. At larger navigational scales the vertical *ole-ote* axis can be used in a horizontal sense with *ole* 'down' indicating west and *ote* 'up' indicating east.

### 49.2.2 Seaward–landward plus cardinal

One of the most common extensions of the seaward–landward system is achieved via the addition of a second, transverse axis which is fixed or "cardinal" (in the sense of François 2004). This system tends to occur when the seaward–landward axis aligns primarily in the north–south direction and is thus well-suited to an island environment in which the dominant topographic features trend in an east–west direction. In these situations the path of the sun may serve as a salient feature intersecting the established seaward–landward axis.

Balinese and Sasak, spoken on the neighbouring islands of Bali and Lombok, respectively, both exhibit a seaward–landward axis intersected by a cardinal east–west axis. The seaward–landward axis is lexified with terms reflecting *daya and *lahud: Sasak *daya* 'landward', *lauʔ* 'seaward'; Balinese *kaja* 'landward', *kelod* 'seaward'. The origin of the east–west axis differs between the two languages. Sasak *timuʔ* 'east' and *baret* 'west' reflect PMP terms denoting monsoon winds, *timuR 'southeast monsoon' and *habaRat 'southwest monsoon' (Blust and Trussel 2020). Balinese *kangin* 'east' derives from PMP *haŋin 'wind' rather than for a name for a specific monsoon wind. In contrast, *kauh* is an innovation with uncertain etymology (cf. Old Balinese *karuh* 'west').

In both Bali and Lombok the seaward–landward axis is often conventionalized as a cardinal north–south axis. Sasak *daya* is often translated as 'north' by speakers located in the southern part of Lombok and as 'south' by those located in the northern part of the island (see Figure 49.2). In Bali, where the vast majority of the population is located in the south, *kaja* takes on the meaning of 'north' and plays an important role in Balinese cosmology as the direction toward the mountains, the dwelling place of the gods (Wassmann and Dasen 1998: 692–3). Moreover, intercardinal terms are

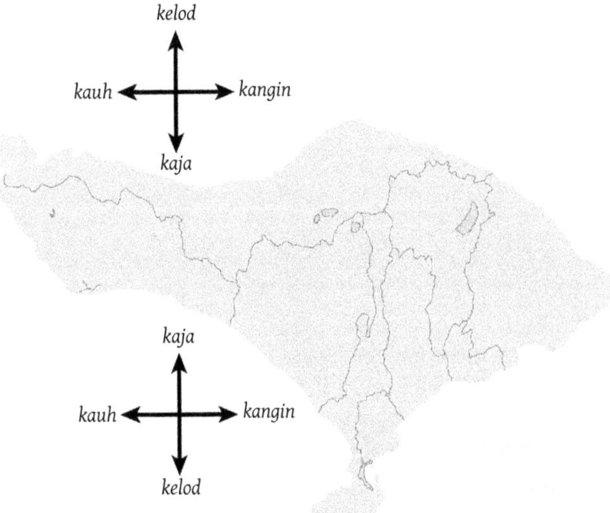


**Figure 49.2** Balinese directional terms on the north and south sides of Bali.

formed from the system as conventionalized by speakers on the south coast, resulting in an eight-point cardinal system. Thus, *kaja kangin* 'northeast', *kelod kangin* 'southeast', *kelod kauh* 'southwest', *kaja kauh* 'northwest'. While speakers in other regions of the island are aware of this conventionalized usage, the geocentric use of the points in areas outside of the south coast of the island.

Further, the so-called cardinal east–west axis also exhibits geocentric properties in regions where the coastline deviates significantly from the east–west direction. This occurs on both the east and west coast of Lombok and on the east coast of Bali. In these regions the orthogonality of the two axes breaks down, as the seaward direction lies roughly parallel to the east–west axis. As one moves along the east coast of Bali in an anticlockwise direction, the east–west axis is reinterpreted as a coastal one. The direction *kangin* 'east' shifts to follow the direction along the coast, that is, to the left when facing the water (see Figure 49.3). The opposing term *kauh* 'west' indicates direction along the coast in the opposite direction, that is, to the right when facing the water. Exceptions to this pattern can be readily seen as the result of historical migration. For example, as shown in Figure 49.3, the orientation of the east–west axis in the village of Bunutan is reversed from that in neighbouring villages. This apparently exceptional pattern can be explained by the fact that the people of Bunutan have migrated from the inland village of Bangle and in the process retained the original eastward direction of *kangin*.

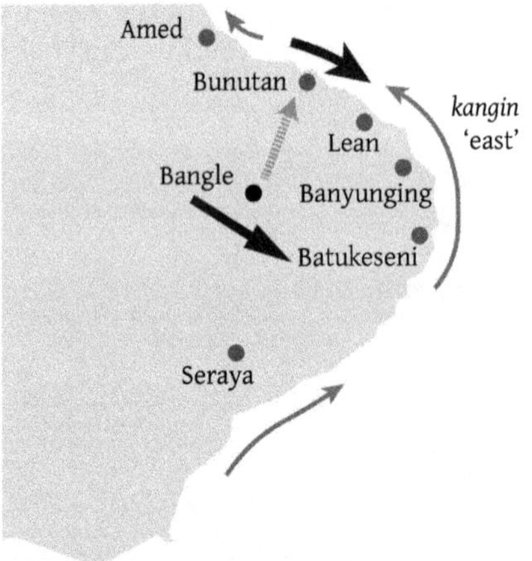


**Figure 49.3** Direction of Balinese *kangin* 'east' along the east coast of Bali. Wider arrows indicate 'reversed' direction in Bunutan, corresponding to usage in Bangle. The large grey arrow indicates historical migration from Bangle to Bunutan (after Wassmann and Dasen 1998: 698).

Given the behaviour of the Balinese system along the east coast of the island, we must conclude that the east–west axis is not, strictly speaking, cardinal. At least it is not cardinal in all locations. Perhaps systems like these could be labelled "partially cardinal." But it is also possible that systems which have been described as combining a seaward–landward axis with a cardinal axis may be less fixed than has been supposed, and the apparently exceptional status of Balinese is due to observational bias. That is, thanks to the work of Wassmann and Dasen (1998 2006) we are fortunate to have very detailed information about the usage of spatial orientation in villages across Bali, especially on the East Coast. This level of detail is often unavailable in the documentation for other languages. So it may well turn out that the cardinal axis in languages having a seaward–landward plus cardinal system is less fixed than has been supposed.

### 49.2.3 Seaward–landward plus coastal

A number of languages have augmented the seaward–landward system with a coastal axis co-lexified with the vertical up–down axis. We describe these under Coastal Systems in §49.4 below.

### 49.2.4 Seaward–landward plus elevation

Solor Lamaholot has a seaward–landward system which is used in conjunction with a two-term elevation system. Solor Lamaholot *raé* 'landward' and *lau* 'seaward' transparently reflect PMP *daya and *lahud, and their usage varies according to position along the coast (see Figure 49.4). Solor Lamaholot also has a vestigial 'across' axis *wéli* which refers to directions transverse to the seaward–landward axis but proximal to the deictic centre. In addition, Solor Lamaholot has an elevational axis distinguishing *téti* 'up' (HIGH) vs. *lali* 'down' (LOW). In most contexts the seaward–landward and elevational axes are aligned with each other, so speakers have a choice as to which system to use in any given context. The interaction between the two systems is subtle, but Kroon (2016: 146) suggests that the choice may depend on the steepness of the slope. At slopes below roughly 20% the seaward–landward system is preferred, while on steeper slopes the elevation system is preferred. This contrast is illustrated in (5). The reference to the river in (5a) makes use of the elevation system, indicating that the river is located steeply below the deictic centre. In contrast, the action of loading the canoe in (5b) involves little change in elevation and so employs the seaward–landward system.

Solor Lamaholot

(5) a. *Ema* *baha* *labu* *lali* *wai*
mother wash shirt DOWN water
'Mother is washing some clothes in the river.' (Kroon 2016: 243)

b. *R=eté* *bali* *lerã* *lau* *béro*
3PL=bring return load SEA canoe
'They loaded [beans] onto the canoe in a seaward direction.' (Kroon 2016: 296)

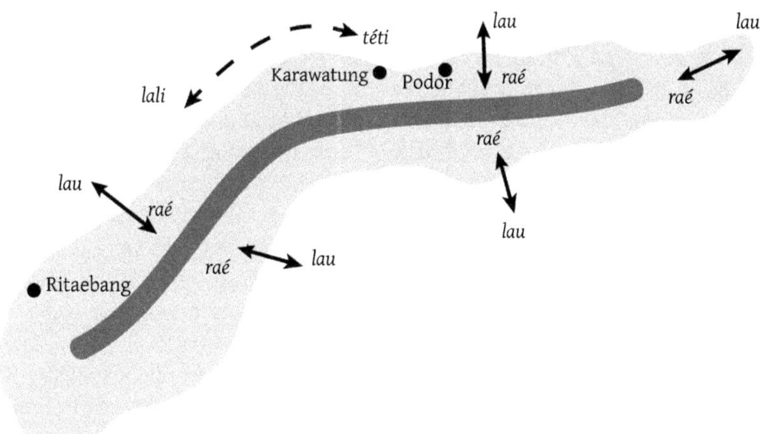


**Figure 49.4** Orientation of *lau* 'seaward' and *raé* 'landward' around the perimeter of Solor Island, with the interior mountain range indicated in dark grey (after Kroon 2016: 144). The dashed arrow indicates coastal usage of the elevation terms *lali* 'down' and *téti* 'up'.

At larger scales (greater than about two kilometres) the elevation system is conventionalized as a horizontal coastal axis, equating east with 'up' and west with 'down'. The example in (6) was uttered by a speaker near Podor (see Figure 49.4). This same conventionalized alignment of east with 'up' predominates in Eastern Indonesia.

Solor Lamaholot

(6) *Raʔé géré motor téti Podor nẽ r=ai*
3PL embark boat UP Podor and 3PL=go
*lali Ritaebang.*
DOWN Ritaebang
'They are boarding the boat in Podor and depart for Ritaebang.' (Kroon 2016: 146)

However, as can be seen from the map of Solor Island in Figure 49.4, the coastal usage of the elevational terms does not align entirely with cardinal east–west. The western half of the island follows a generally northeast–southwest axis.[1] As one moves further afield from Solor Island, all directions become *lali* 'down'. Thus, both Australia to the east and Singapore to the west are *lali*. Moreover, the coastal use of the elevational terms does not supplant the cardinal east–west axis borrowed from Malay, which is lexified as *wara* 'west' and *timu* 'east'.

Ambel, a SHWNG language spoken in the Waigeo Islands off the coast of the Bird's Head of New Guinea, has seaward–landward system augmented by an elevation system contrasting *i-* 'up' and *pu-* 'down'. The system also includes terms for 'front', 'side', and 'in, back', as shown in Table 49.2.[2] In addition, the elevational terms can be used as coastal directionals.

**Table 49.2** Directional terms in Ambel (Waigeo) (Arnold 2018a: 489).

| | Prefix | PROX | MID | DIST | AND |
|---|---|---|---|---|---|
| 'seaward' | *lu-* | *lune* | *lupa* | *luma* | *lua* |
| 'landward' | *li-* | *line* | *lipa* | *lima* | *lia* |
| 'up, out' | *i-* | *ine* | *ipa* | *ima* | *ia* |
| 'down' | *pu-* | *pune* | *pupa* | *puma* | *pua* |
| 'front' | *ta(y)-* | *tane* | *tapa* | *tama* | *taya* |
| 'in, back' | *mu-* | *mune* | *mupa* | *muma* | *mua* |
| 'side' | *pa(y)-* | *pane* | *papa* | *pama* | *paya* |

## 49.3 Riverine systems

Riverine systems include a primary axis which is oriented parallel to a river, distinguishing upriver and downriver directions. Riverine systems are most common in Borneo where sight of the coast is quickly lost and people instead rely on the rivers for food, water, and transportation, but

[1] It is not known how the elevational terms are used on the south coast of Solor Island, though presumably the same pseudo-alignment of east with 'up' and west with 'down' obtains.

[2] Arnold (2018a) uses AND as a glossing for a fourth demonstrative that means (i) The speaker is moving towards the addressee and away from the figure or moving away from both or (ii) The figure is moving towards the addressee and away from the speaker or moving away from both.

our survey has revealed that riverine systems are also common in Sumatra and the southern Philippines. Many of the languages with riverine systems have adapted the PAN seaward–landward axis (*lahud-*daya) as a downriver–upriver axis. This semantic extension is natural given the geographic tendency for rivers to flow down toward the sea and enter the sea at roughly a perpendicular angle to the coast. Thus in many cases 'toward the sea' or 'seaward' is directly aligned with 'downriver' (at least at the river mouth). However, in riverine systems the downriver–upriver meaning has been fully conventionalized and follows the local bends of the relevant river body. Moreover, the PAN seaward–landward axis is not the only source for lexifying riverine terms. Inati, a Malayo-Polynesian isolate of the Philippines, has *pamurik* 'upriver, toward the interior' (? < PWMP *pa- + *um-udahik 'go upstream') and *ribaba* 'downriver, toward the sea' (< PMP *babaq 'below'), with no relation to *daya and *lahud (Gallego 2018: 91). Sometimes only one of the terms is lexified with a reflex of the original seaward–landward axis, as in Mansaka, exemplified in (2). Because riverine orientation relies on reference to a particular river, the interpretation of riverine directionals may differ depending on which river is used for reference—for example, whether one is referring to a local tributary or the main river.[3]

In riverine systems the 'upriver' and 'downriver' directionals are not just used for locations on, and movement along, the river. Rather, they are general directional terms which locate referents at a variety of scales, as in the Mualang (Borneo) example (7).

Mualang
(7) *Dua ikuʔ... ti s-ikuʔ da iliʔ.*
two CLF REL one-CLF LOC DOWNRIVER
'Two (frogs) ... one of them was at the downriver side.' (Tjia 2007: 204)

Moreover, the 'upriver' and 'downriver' orientation terms typically co-exist with, and are distinct from, terms describing the river flow. For example, in addition to the upriver and downriver directional terms, Mansaka also has verbs *osaog* 'go with the current' and *songsong* 'go against the current'.

The strategy of adapting the original PAN seaward–landward axis for use as a downriver–upriver axis is so prevalent in Borneo that Adelaar proposes an implicational universal regarding the use of orientation terms in riverine contexts in Borneo. Namely,

> If a language has reflexes of the original terms *lahud and *daya, these have the meaning, respectively, of 'downriver area' and 'upriver area', rather than 'towards the sea' and 'towards the interior'. (Adelaar 1997: 69)

[3] See Brucks (2015) for a discussion of contextual interpretation of riverine orientation in a Dene language.

Almost all of the languages of Borneo follow this pattern, but riverine terminology is even further developed in most Borneo languages. In addition to the widespread use of reflexes of *daya and *lahud, PMP *qiliR 'to flow downriver' is often reflected as a directional meaning 'downriver', and PMP *udahik 'upriver part of a river' is often reflected with the meaning 'interior; headwaters; upriver'. In addition, at least three riverine terms were innovated in Proto-Greater North Borneo: *ajuʔ 'towards the interior; towards upriver areas', *uud 'the interior; upriver areas', *sabaʔ/*baʔay 'downriver' (Smith 2017a: 315).

A typical example of the way Borneo languages have innovated riverine systems is found in Begak, which has a simple two-way contrast between *akod* 'upriver' and *sarog* 'downriver', with corresponding verbs *kandik* 'go upriver' (probably < *ka *udahik) and *lau'* 'go downriver'. Only the verbal forms appear to be inherited from the Proto-Greater North Borneo forms, and there appear to be two distinct reflexes of *lahud: the directional verb *lau'* as well as a noun *laud* 'wind'.

At least one region of Borneo does provide counterexamples to Adelaar's generalization. The Melanau languages of North Borneo have innovated terms for 'upriver' and 'downriver'. However, the Melanau languages also exhibit reflexes of *daya and *lahud but with the meanings 'away from the river' and 'toward the river', respectively. See §49.3.2 below.

Outside of Borneo, varying meanings for reflexes of *daya and *lahud are found. For example, in Aralle-Tabulahan (discussed in §49.5.2), while the riverine term *tama* 'upriver' has been innovated, the term *sau* 'downriver/seaward' is a reflex of PMP *lahud (McKenzie 1997: 224). Matigsalug Manobo, spoken on the island of Mindanao Island in the southern Philippines appears to have innovated a term for 'downriver' but has retained *raya* < *daya for 'upriver' (Wang et al. 2006: 33). Irarutu of Papua has innovated terms for both 'upriver' and 'downriver' but shows no reflexes of *daya or *lahud (see §49.3.1).

As in seaward–landward systems, riverine systems may also employ a second axis, transverse to the axis defined by the flow of the river and other geographic features. This second axis may be cardinal, elevational, coastal, or may be explicitly defined as orthogonal to the river, that is, towards/away from the river or simply across the river. We discuss these compound systems in further detail below.

### 49.3.1 Riverine plus 'across'

A common extension of the basic riverine system is the addition of a transverse unidirectional axis referring to 'across the river' (i.e. neither upriver nor downriver). Buru, a Central Malayo-Polynesian language of Central Maluku, is one such language. Buru is spoken on Buru Island, a relatively large and roughly circular island with an area of approximately 1 million hectares. Most of the population traditionally resided in the interior along the rivers amid the steep and rugged mountains. Buru riverine directionals *dae* 'upriver' and *lawe* 'downriver' derive from PMP *daya and *lahud, respectively, as shown in (8a). The term *aki* 'across' defines an unoriented transverse axis, as in (8b). These terms are lexically distinct from the vertical directionals *saka* 'vertically up' and *pao* 'vertically down', as in (8c). In Buru it is also possible to combine the upriver–downriver terms with the across directional, as in (8d).

Buru

(8) a. *Anafina egalit ba roho lawe.*
female pregnant DUR slow DOWNRIVER
'The pregnant woman is moving slowly downriver.' (Grimes 1991: 98)

b. *Da puna huma aki.*
he make house ACROSS.RIVER
'He's making that house across [the river].' (Grimes 1991: 170)

c. *Ringe iko pao awe pao dii.*
3SG go DOWN water DOWN there
'He went down to that water there.' (Grimes 1991: 445)

d. *Du sai aki lawe.*
3PL paddle ACROSS.RIVER DOWNRIVER
'They are paddling across toward where the lake drains.' (Grimes 1991: 109)

Irarutu, spoken in the Bird's Neck region of New Guinea also employs a riverine system with an 'across' axis.[4] The Irarutu territory surrounds a large estuary which reaches far inland. Irarutu lacks the seaward–landward axis, but instead the distinction between 'up', 'down', and 'across' is "deeply woven into the language" (Matsumura and Matsumura 1991: 93). As in Halmahera, the horizontal up–down axis in Irarutu is colexified with vertically 'up' and 'down'. However, the region where Irarutu is spoken on the Bomberai Peninsula has almost no topographic relief, and it is likely that the riverine usage of the up–down axis is most salient.

Figure 49.5 shows the usage of Irarutu directionals from the perspective of the village of Gusimawa. For each location a pair of forms is cited separated by a colon. The first is the translocative form, indicating the direction from Gusimawa to that location; and the second is the cislocative form, indicating the direction to Gusimawa from that location (see Table 49.3). Gusimawa and the other Irarutu villages are located along an estuary which extends inland approximately

**Table 49.3** Irarutu directional terms (Matsumura and Matsumura 1991: 97).

| | Translocative | Cislocative |
|---|---|---|
| 'down(stream)' | *ro* | *bro* |
| 'up(stream)' | *iet* | *briet* |
| 'across' | *ri* | *bri* |
| non-riverine | *fa* | *ma* |

80km from the coast, narrowing in some places to a width of less than 500m. Though the estuary is technically not a river, the usage of the terms 'up', 'down', and 'across' appear to attribute riverine characteristics to it. These terms are used equally to refer to directions along and across a tributary river as well as along and across the estuary.

Notice that the translocative and cislocative forms are not necessarily reciprocal. For example, the direction from Gusimawa to nearby Burgerba is *ro* 'down', but the reciprocal direction returning from Burgerba uses the non-riverine form *ma* 'from' rather than the riverine *bro* 'from downriver'. Such distinctions are likely to be highly conventionalized. Nonetheless, there is a clear tendency for the 'up' terms to be used to refer to villages that are located up the estuary (further upriver) from Gusimawa, and 'down' to refer to those villages further downriver along the estuary toward the coast.

Systems contrasting 'upriver', 'downriver', and 'across' are common throughout the Subanen and Manobo languages of Mindano (Table 49.4). The 'downriver' terms in Table 49.4 show similarities with the 'downriver' terms *abaʔ and *baʔay reconstructed by Smith (2017a) for Proto-Greater North Borneo. Original PAN *lahud is reflected as *laud* 'deep sea' in Subanen but is completely lost in the Manobo languages, which both have *dagat* 'sea'. Both Agusan Manobo and Ata Manobo retain *daya with the meaning 'upriver', while Subanen has innovated the form *buid* 'interior;

**Table 49.4** Riverine directionals in three languages of Mindanao (Subanen: SIL Philippines 2011; Agusan Manobo: Gelacio et al. 2000; Ata Manobo: Hartung 2016).

| | 'upriver' | 'downriver' | 'across' |
|---|---|---|---|
| Central Subanen | *buid* | *dibabaʔ* | *dipag* |
| Agusan Manobo | *diraja* | *dibabà* | *yopà* |
| Ata Manobo | *diraya* | *dibabò* | *doipag* |

[4] Irarutu is sometimes classified as belonging to the South Halmahera–West New Guinea family, but this classification is controversial (see Blust 1978; Jackson 2014; Kamholz 2014).

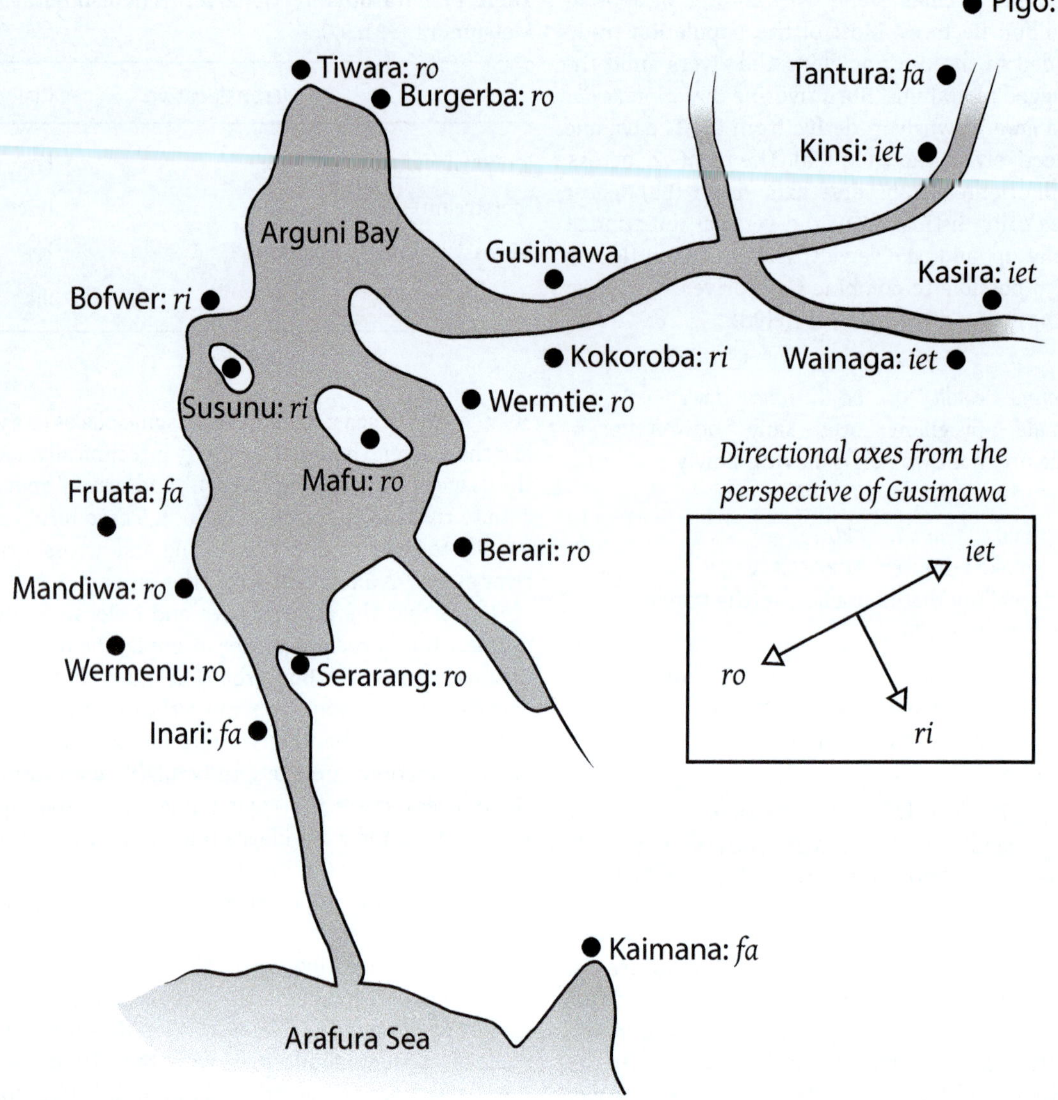


**Figure 49.5** Irarutu directional terms as viewed from the perspective of the village of Gusimawa (after Matsumura and Matsumura 1991: 97). Village names (in bold) are followed by the appropriate translocative form indicating direction from Gusimawa to that village.

upriver; inland' < PAN *bukij 'mountain; forested inland mountain areas' (SIL Philippines 2011).

## 49.3.2 Riverine plus towards/away from the river

In addition to a simple 'across' axis, riverine systems may also include terms indicating direction toward and/or away from the river, orthogonal to the direction of river flow. Thus, Embaloh, spoken in the northeastern part of West Kalimantan but belonging to the South Sulawesi language subgroup, has *urait* 'upriver' < *udahik, *kalaut* 'downriver' < *lahud, and *suali* 'across' (see Figure 49.6). The Embaloh system is further elaborated with *anait* 'toward the river', *indoor* 'away from the river to a nearby area' and *kandaa* 'away from the river beyond the village' (Adelaar 1997: 70).

Directionals indicating toward and away from the river are also found in the Melanau languages of North Borneo. The terms for 'upriver' and 'downriver' are innovated, while the terms for toward and away from the river may

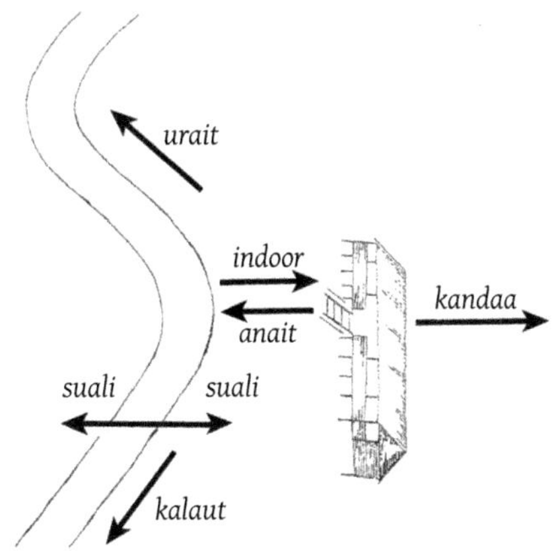


**Figure 49.6** Embaloh directionals (after Adelaar 1997: 70).

**Table 49.5** Riverine directionals in the Melanau languages Dalat, Kanowit, and Lahanan (Clayre 1973; Alex Smith, p.c.).

| | Dalat | Kanowit | Lahanan |
|---|---|---|---|
| 'upriver' | *ajuʔ* | *ajoʔ* | *najuʔ* |
| 'downriver' | *abaʔ* | *abaʔ* | *navaʔ* |
| 'away from river' | *dayeh* | *naya* | *nalem* |
| 'toward river' | *alud* | *win* | *nipa* |

reflect PAN *lahud and *daya, respectively (see Table 49.5). In Dalat Melanau the 'away from the river' and 'toward the river' terms reflect *daya and *lahud, but in Kanowit only the 'away from the river' term comes from PAN, while the 'toward the river' term has been innovated.

Melanau riverine directionals can be used at both intermediate and local scales. In (10) the directional *aba'* 'downriver' refers to the room on the downriver side of the house. While houses are conventionally located with the door facing the river, this downriver direction would be to the left or right as one enters, depending on which side of the river the house is located. The use of the directional *alud* 'toward the river' is interpreted to mean the first *kuden* 'jar' that the referent encounters, since the jar closest to the river would conventionally be nearest to the door of the house.

Dalat Melanau

(9) *A* *tama* *nyin* *agei* *dayeh*
person father her yet AWAY.FROM.RIVER
*juluh* *dagen* *guun*
AV.forage in forest
'Her father was still inland (away from the river) hunting in the woods.' (Clayre 1973: 74)

Dalat Melanau

(10) *Gaʔ* *bilit* ***abaʔ*** *bei* *kawaʔ* *telou* *ataʔ*
at room DOWNRIVER is also three CLF
*kuden* *ayeng.* *Besei* *in* *unei*
jar large spearhead that back-reference
*ninaʔ* *nyin* *dagen* *ataʔ* ***alud.***
PV.put 3SG in CLF TOWARD.RIVER
'In the room on the downriver side of the house there were in fact three large jars. He put the previously mentioned spearhead into the first one (i.e. one toward the river).' (Clayre 1973: 76)

In Ngaju, a West Barito language of Central Borneo, the directional roots *ngaju* 'upriver' and *ngawa* 'downriver' are paired with motion verbs *murik* 'go upriver' and *masuh* 'go downriver'. In addition, Ngaju has the static terms *hulu* 'headwaters' (< PAN *quluh 'head', Blust and Trussel 2020) and *tumbang* 'river mouth'. The name of the language itself derives from the upriver term, a reference to "upriver Dayak." The upriver–downriver axis is transected by a transverse axis determined by *ngambu* 'away from the river' and *ngiwa* 'toward the river', as illustrated in Figure 49.7. Ngaju also has an 'across river' term *dimpah*.

As illustrated in Figure 49.7, the riverine terminology in Ngaju has little if anything to do with elevation. The Ngaju region is transected by several major rivers, including the Kapuas, Kahayan, Katingan (Ngaju Dayak), and Mentaya Rivers, with little topographic relief. Thus, the toward and away from the river terms cannot readily be equated with downhill and uphill. Rather, they indicate directions toward and away from the river body itself, regardless of elevation. In a region with many rivers, the choice of directional term depends on the choice of reference river. In (11) the referent is travelling downriver along a tributary to access the main river. In order to avoid ambiguity, the speaker uses the non-riverine verb *muhun* 'go down' along with the riverine term *ngiwa* 'toward the river'. Even though the participant, Eter, might be travelling in the downriver direction along a tributary, the reference river is the main river, and the choice of directional term *ngiwa* reflects this.

Ngaju

(11) *Eter* *muhun* *ka* *ngiwa* *ka* *batang*
Eter GO.DOWN to TOWARD.RIVER to trunk
*danum.*
water
'Eter went down toward the main river to take water.' (Siwuh Binti 2015: 6).

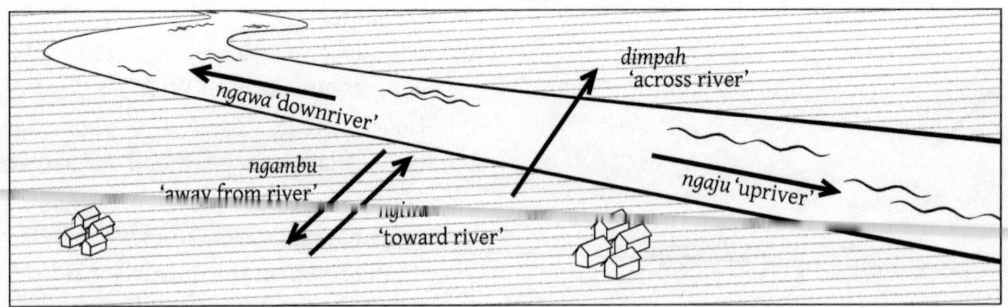


**Figure 49.7** Ngaju riverine directional terms *ngaju* 'upriver', *ngawa* 'downriver', *ngiwa* 'toward the river', *ngambu* 'away from the river', *dimpah* 'across river' (after Siwuh Binti 2015).

## 49.3.3 Riverine plus elevation

Gayo, spoken in a landlocked region of Northern Sumatra has a riverine system with innovated terms *uken* 'upriver' and *toa* 'downriver'. The riverine terms form part of a directional system which includes a transverse axis *palóh* 'downhill' and *atas* 'uphill, up'. The contrast between the riverine and elevational axes is shown in 12. While the uphill–downhill axis is not specifically described as indicating direction away from and toward the river, this much can be inferred from the nature of the geography of the region. Eades points out that, "as the Gayo region is a mountainous, inland region, the most useful directional terms refer to the uphill/downhill and upriver/downriver oppositions..." (2005: 213).

Gayo

(12) a. *Munyuen kepile kami i*
AV.plant sweet.potato 1EXCL LOC
*uken so.*
UPRIVER yonder
'We were planting sweet potatoes upriver.' (Eades 2005: 173)

b. *Kuneh pè [sangka ni akang],*
HOW also/even run POSS deer
*turun=é ku palôh.*
descend=3.POSS to DOWNHILL
'However the running of the deer (would be), it would go downhill.' (Eades 2005: 64)

A more explicit example of a riverine–elevational composite system is that in Kadorih, a Barito language of Borneo. This language uses the terms *juoi* 'upriver' and *booi* 'downriver' as one axis of the directional system. The transverse axis to the riverine upriver–downriver axis is elevational, defined by the terms *diang* 'upland, upward, over, above, away from the river' and *polih/pinda* 'downland, downward, under, down, beneath, below, low, towards the river.' The glossing for these words demonstrates their many uses, but generally, within the village, the words take on a 'towards/away from the river' meaning regardless of the elevation of the land (Inagaki 2014). Elsewhere they take on an elevational meaning (shown in 13).

Kadorih

(13) *Mahtan ondou=nai hila diang*
sun day=there direction/region UPLAND
*lowu=ndai, diang=ndai*
village=PFV UPLAND=PFV
'The sun is already going down in the upland direction' (Inagaki 2014: 74)

## 49.3.4 Riverine plus cardinal

In some areas, the axis running parallel to the river is intersected by one corresponding to the path of the sun. As such, like cardinal axes that are part of seaward–landward systems, those that are part of riverine systems tend to correspond to the cardinal directions 'east' and 'west' based on the path of the sun.

Toba Batak, a language of landlocked northern Sumatra, has a riverine system intersected by a cardinal axis. The riverine axis includes the terms *jae* 'upriver; upriver area; higher terrain, direction of the mountain' and *julu* 'downriver; downriver area; lower terrain; direction of the sea.' The transverse axis to this contains the terms *hapoltahan/habinsaran* 'direction of the sunrise; east' and *hasundutan* 'direction of the sunset; west' (Nababan 1981; Adelaar 1997).

The same type of system may also be found in Borneo. Timugon Murut, spoken in northern Borneo, has innovated the terms *relayo* 'upriver' *ra-bugus* 'downriver' for the riverine axis (Prentice 1981, cited in Adelaar 1997). The terms for the transverse axis derive from verbs describing the rising and setting of the sun and the moon which include *sirangon* 'east', from *s-um-irang* 'rise (sun)' and *kalasaan* 'west', from *l-um-asaʔ* 'set (moon, sun)' (Adelaar 1997).

## 49.4 Coastal systems

Coastal systems of spatial orientation include one axis which is oriented along, or parallel to, the coast, distinguishing directions to the left from directions to the right when facing the water. Typically these systems are lexified with terms meaning 'up' and 'down', though the ultimate orientation of the axis varies across and within languages. That is, the direction to the left when facing the water may be 'up' in some locations but 'down' in others. Coastal systems often include a second seaward–landward axis, which is naturally transverse to the coastal axis. Thus, these systems could be equally classified as seaward–landward. We choose to discuss coastal systems separately in this section, because they are functionally quite distinct from the single-axis seaward–landward systems prominent in many Austronesian languages. Because of the limited variation in the transverse axis, we instead categorize coastal systems by geography.

### 49.4.1 South Sulawesi

In the Makasar language, the coastal axis is lexified by *rate* 'up' and *rawa* 'down'. Makasar also has a transverse seaward–landward axis lexified by *lau'* 'seaward' (< *lahud) and *raya* 'landward' (< *daya) (Blust and Trussel 2020), but it is the coastal axis which is of most interest here. The 'up' and 'down' terms are paired with directional verbs *naiʔ* 'go up' and *naung* 'go down'. While all of these terms can have a vertical sense, they are commonly used by speakers in their horizontal, coastal sense (Liebner 2005: 271; Jukes 2006: 222). The town of Pare-Pare is located approximately 125km along the coast north of Makassar city. (14) reflects the conceptualization of this direction from Makassar city to Pare-Pare as 'down', even though both locations are on the coast at the same elevation.

Makasar

| (14) | *Ero-kaʔ* | *naung* | *ri* | *Pare-Pare.* |
|---|---|---|---|---|
| | want-1SG | GO.DOWN | LOC | Pare-Pare |

'I want to go down to Pare Pare.' (spoken in Makassar) (Liebner 2005: 271)

Similarly, the default interpretation of (15) is not vertical but horizontal along the coast. This example asks for news of a location up the coast, that is, to the south in the vicinity of Makassar city.

Makasar

| (15) | *Apa-ji* | *kabaraʔ-na* | *i-rateʔ* |
|---|---|---|---|
| | what-QUAL | news-3SG.POSS | LOC-UP |

'What is the news from above?' (Liebner 2005: 272)

Along the west coast of Sulawesi Island in the vicinity of Makassar city the direction *rate* 'up' aligns with south and *rawa* 'down' with north (see Figure 49.8). If this alignment were consistent, then this axis would be better viewed as cardinal, with the 'up' and 'down' terms serving merely as lexifiers of the axis. The geocentric nature of the axis becomes apparent as one moves south and east (i.e. anticlockwise) around the coast from Makassar. On the south coast, where the direction toward the sea is south, *rate* 'upcoast' and *rawa* 'downcoast' continue to be oriented parallel to the coast, so that *rate* 'upcoast' is aligned with east (to the left facing the water) and *rawa* 'downcoast' with west (to the right facing the water).

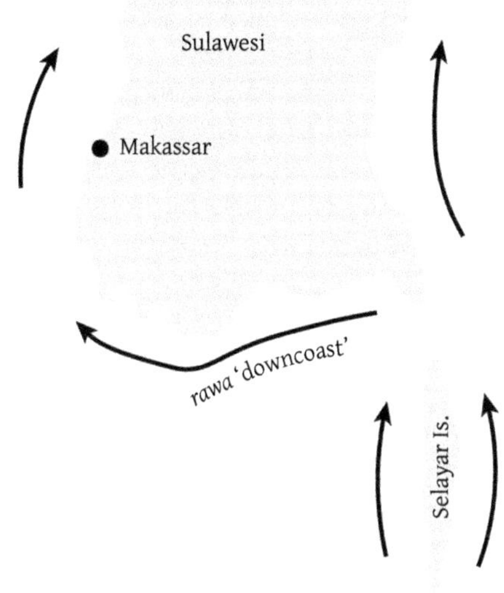


**Figure 49.8** Arrows indicate the direction of *rawa* 'downcoast' along the coast of South Sulawesi and Selayar Island; *rate* 'upcoast' is oriented in the opposite direction.

Curiously, Makasar has adapted the wind terms *baraʔ* 'southwest monsoon' and *timoroʔ* 'southeast monsoon', which it has regularly inherited (from *habaRat and *timuR), into this system as well, with *wara'* as an alternate term for *rawa* 'downcoast' and *timboroʔ* as an alternate term for *rate* 'upcoast' (Liebner 2005: 275). On the south coast these directions align with the expected west–east reflexes of the corresponding monsoon terms. Namely, *waraʔ* 'downcoast' aligns with 'west' and *timboroʔ* 'upcoast' aligns with 'east'. But on the more populated west coast in the vicinity of Makassar city itself *waraʔ* aligns with 'north' and *timboroʔ* aligns with 'south'. In other words, *timboro'* consistently retains the meaning of to the left when facing the water (i.e. anticlockwise along the coast).

Similar coastal systems are found throughout the languages of the South Sulawesi group. However, as one moves to the east coast of the island the orientation of the coastal axis shifts. Whereas on the west and south coasts the 'down' (*rawa*) direction is to the right and 'up' (*rate*) to the left when facing the water, on the east coast the 'down' direction is to the left and 'up' is to the right when facing the water. In other words, *rawa* indicates clockwise movement along the coast on the west and south coasts, but anticlockwise movement on the east coast. This shift introduces a discontinuity in the orientation of the axis. At some location between the south coast and the east coast the orientation of the coastal axis reverses. This reversal occurs at the point where Selayar Island lies just off the coast of the southeasternmost point of the peninsula of South Sulawesi. Selayar Island is approximately 80km long, varying in width between 5 and 10km. Its long axis is aligned in a north–south direction. The largest town, port, and airport are located on the west coast, approximately at the midpoint of the island. Due to the elongated shape of the island, travel between the west and east coasts is most efficiently achieved by transecting the island, rather than by following the coast. Along the west coast of the island the 'down' direction is to the north (i.e. to the right when facing the water), continuing the pattern established along the west and south coasts of Sulawesi. But on the east coast of Selayar 'down' remains oriented to the north (i.e. to the left when facing the water), following the same pattern as that attested along the east coast of Sulawesi (Yoshida 1980: 58). Figure 49.8 shows the orientation of the 'down' direction at various locations along the coast of South Sulawesi and Selayar Island. The relative orientation of 'up' and 'down' remains constant on both sides of Selayar Island. Departing the west coast heading east, the direction *rawa* 'down' remains constant to one's left side throughout the journey. Only upon reaching the east coast of the island does this give the appearance of a reversal. This reversal of the orientation of the coastal axis between the west and east coasts of Selayar has the effect of facilitating communication across the island. With the orientation of the coastal axis on the east coast of Selayar thus established, the extension to the east coast of the peninsula of South Sulawesi is readily explained.

### 49.4.2 Sangir: Coastal adaptation of an elevation system

While most of the Sangiric languages of North Sulawesi have elevation systems (§49.5.3), Sangir itself has adapted an original elevation system into a coastal system in which the 'up' and 'down' terms are used to refer to horizontal motion along the coast. This represents a natural adaptation of an elevation system to a coastal environment. Whereas the Sangiric languages Ratahan and Bantik are spoken in a mountainous region, Sangir is spoken on the island of Sangihe Besar and the surrounding archipelago consisting of roughly one hundred small islands located midway between Sulawesi and Mindanao. Travel is primarily by sea and thus across a horizontal surface with no change in elevation. The original Sangiric three-term elevation system has been augmented with the root *saeʔ* 'seaward' to a four-term directional system distinguishing LEVEL, HIGH, LOW, and SEA (see Table 49.6).

**Table 49.6** Sangir elevational terms, showing forms for a stationary entity (LOCATIVE), movement away from speaker (TRANSLOCATIVE), and movement toward speaker (CISLOCATIVE) (after Jukes and Utsumi 2015).

| | LOC | TRANS | CIS |
|---|---|---|---|
| similar level | *pai* | *tamai* | *damahi* |
| back-, inland-, somewhat upward | *dala* | *taraiʔ* | *ɨndaiʔ* |
| upward | *dasiʔ* | | |
| front-, coast-, somewhat downward | *dadeʔ* | *tanaeʔ* | *ɨnnaeʔ* |
| downward | *baβa* | | |
| seaward | - | *sasaeʔ* | *ɨnsaeʔ* |

As in other Sangiric languages, Sangir distinguishes static and dynamic forms, with the latter additionally distinguishing movement toward vs. away from the deictic centre. In the static paradigm the HIGH and LOW forms further distinguish proximal from distal; thus the locative form *dadeʔ* in (16) retains some of its original elevational characteristics in local usage, whereas the corresponding form *dasiʔ* 'upward' is a coastal directional.

(16) Sangir
*Dadeʔ* *kai* *piaʔ* *tau* *eseʔ*
DOWN.LOC.PROX is exist human male
*d<im> inta* *na-iaŋ...*
<PST.AV> arrive PST.STAT-seat
'There is a man down there who has come and seated…' (Jukes and Utsumi 2015)

At an intermediate scale within Sangihe Besar Island, the 'up' and 'down' terms form a circular system of orientation. As on Makian Island in the Halmahera region, the 'down' direction is clockwise in Sangir. Movement between Sangihe Besar and Sulawesi follows an up–down axis in which the direction toward Sulawesi is 'up'. Movement between Sangihe Besar and directions to the north and east, including Mindanao and Talaud may also follow an up–down axis, provided the distance is not so great. For longer distances the 'seaward' terms may replace 'down'. Thus, travel from Sangihe Besar to Mindanao might be considered *sasaeʔ* 'seaward', while travel to an island midway between Sangihe Besar and Mindanao might be *tanaeʔ* 'downward'.

## 49.4.3 Halmahera and beyond

Coastal systems are pervasive throughout the South Halmahera languages of North Maluku. As in Makasar and Sangir, the coastal axis in South Halmahera is co-lexified with terms meaning vertically 'up' and 'down', and the default meaning of these terms is always horizontal along the coast, not vertical. Thus, the Buli example (17) could only refer to motion in a direction parallel to or along the coast.

Buli
(17) *Ampea nap Bukumatiti*
3SG.go DOWN Bukumatiti
'He went downward along the coast to Bukumatiti.' (Maan 1951: 93)

Motion in a direction transverse to the coastline cannot be expressed using the 'up' and 'down' terms. Instead, as in Makasar, the South Halmahera languages employ a transverse seaward–landward axis reflecting *daya and *lahud. This yields a system with two orthogonal axes, seaward–landward and upcoast–downcoast. Thus in Buli motion down an incline toward the coast is expressed not with the term 'down' but rather with *lau* 'seaward', as in (18).

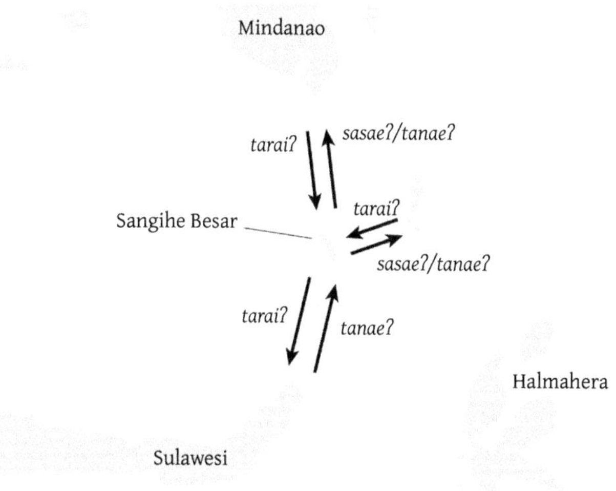


**Figure 49.9** Coastal usage of Sangir elevational terms *tanaeʔ* 'down', *taraiʔ* 'up', and *sasaeʔ* 'seaward' beyond Sangihe Island (translocative forms) (after Jukes and Utsumi 2015).

Buli
(18) *Fare namjaling la-lau olat i*
then drift to-SEA sea toward
'[He] drifted down toward the sea.' (Maan 1951: 92)

The South Halmahera directional roots are embedded within a larger deictic system which indicates direction of motion or absence of motion along the directional axis indicated by the directional root, as illustrated for Taba in Table 49.7.

**Table 49.7** Taba (South Halmahera) directional stems (Bowden 1997).

| | 'up' | 'down' | 'seaward' | 'landward' |
|---|---|---|---|---|
| Root | *ya* | *po* | *la* | *le* |
| Essive | *yase* | *pope* | *lawe* | *lewe* |
| Allative | *attia* | *appo* | *akla* | *akno* |
| Venitive | *yama* | *poma* | *lama* | *lema* |
| Partitive | *tabtubo* | *umpo* | *kla* | *kle* |

Although the coastal up–down axis is co-lexified with the vertical axis, the vertical sense of the 'up' and 'down' terms is restricted to situations of strict verticality, not geophysical elevation. The sense 'upslope' or 'up away from the coast' is always expressed with the landward term. Additionally, the vertical interpretation of the 'up' and 'down' terms typically requires additional grammatical material. Thus in (19) the location of the referent vertically 'down' is expressed by connecting the directional *umpo* 'down' to the noun referencing the ground object ('banana') using the linker *ni*. Thus, *loka ni umpo* references literally the vertically downward part of the banana tree. The directional form *lema* 'landward' requires no additional grammatical material in order to specify the location of the machete as landward from the banana tree.

Taba
(19) *Peda adia loka ni um-po le-ma*
machete there banana POSS PART-DOWN land-VEN
'The machete is there, landwards from the bottom of the banana tree.' (Bowden 2014: 88)

Directional terms are used frequently by South Halmaheran speakers. Bowden (2005: 789) estimates that at least 30% of narrative clauses in Taba include directional terms.

One of the most remarkable features of the coastal directional system found in the South Halmahera languages is that it is areal, extending across all of Halmahera and small islands off the west coast. While the terms used to lexify the 'up' and 'down' directions vary across the languages, the orientation of the coastal axis remains consistent across the languages. This usage extends to local Malay as well, so that Malay *ka atas* 'upward' and *ka bawa* 'downward' are interpreted by default as directions along the coast rather than along a vertical axis, even in regions of steep terrain (Taylor 1983). This usage is found in the non-Austronesian languages of the North Halmahera family as well (Holton 2017). The North Halmahera languages additionally distinguish a vertical up-down axis from the horizontal upcoast–downcoast axis, but the orientation of the latter is homologous to the upcoast–downcoast in the South Halmahera languages and local Malay. This shared regional alignment of the coastal axis allows multilingual speakers in the region to shift between languages without the need to shift orientation systems. Compare this to the situation in South Sulawesi, where the indigenous system employs coastal terms, while the Malay system makes use of cardinal directions. Thus, Malay *timur* is 'west', while the Makasar term *timboro'* 'upcoast' is 'south' in the vicinity of Makassar city. In South Sulawesi speakers must shift between a coastal plus seaward–landward system and a cardinal plus seaward–landward system, depending on which language they are using. In Halmahera no shift in orientation system is necessary.

In Halmahera the orientation of the upcoast–downcoast axis is fixed at each location, but it is not always possible to predict which way is 'up' and which way is 'down'. Some authors have proposed that the 'up' direction is oriented toward the social centre or area of higher social status (Bubandt 1997; Teljeur 1987), while other authors have proposed just the opposite, that the 'down' direction flows toward the social center (Bowden 1997; Allen and Hayami-Allen 2002). More recently, Holton (2017) has proposed that the coastal directional systems in Halmahera derive from an original riverine system. In small island environments—such as the small islands off the west coast of Halmahera—the polarity of the downcoast–upcoast axis is consistent: down is to the right facing the water, while up is to the left facing the water. In these environments the coastal system is 'circular', in that if one circumambulates the island in an upward (or downward) direction, the direction remains upward (or downward) for the entire journey until one arrives again at the starting point. Thus, on Makian Island the Taba directional *appo* 'downwards' indicates clockwise movement around the island. In this respect the Halmahera systems differ markedly from those in South Sulawesi and from those described for Oceanic languages. In most Oceanic languages small islands have a point of convergence, where the up directions come together, and a point of divergence where the upcoast terms points in two opposite directions along the coast (cf. François 2015).[5]

A second notable feature of the directional system in South Halmahera is that it is used at local, intermediate, and worldwide scales. Relative frames of reference (e.g. 'left' and 'right') are rarely used. Directional terms are used not only to indicate directions within a village or between islands, but also locally on a table within a house, as in (20).

Taba

(20) a. *Tabako* *a-dia* *kurusi* *ni* *la-we*
cigarettes DEM-DIST chair POSS sea-ESS
*la-ma*
see-VEN
'The cigarettes are there, in the space away from the seaward side of the chair' (Bowden 1997: 260)

b. *Jo-lo-so* *polo* *ni-im* *kuda*
good-and-one if POSS-1SG knight
*la-we*
sea-ESS
'Better (to move) your seawards knight' (said of a chess game move) (Bowden 1997: 261)

A coastal orientation very much like that found in Halmahera has been reported in Sula, spoken on Sula Island some 200km southwest of Halmahera. The directional terms are *fai* 'seaward', *tema* 'landward', *lepa* 'upward', and *neo* 'downward' (Yoshida 1980: 57).

As one moves east from Halmahera toward the Bird's Head of New Guinea, the use of the coastal orientation system at the intermediate scale is more or less retained, with the upward direction extending eastward from the Patani region of eastern Halmahera, through Gebe, the Raja Ampat Islands, and even as far as Biak. The neat system of two orthogonal axes, one parallel and one transverse to the coast, becomes further complicated with intrinsic terms 'in', 'front', and 'side', which may nevertheless also have absolute usages. In (21a) the meaning 'upriver' is conveyed with the proximal UP form *i-ne*, while in (21b) this meaning is conveyed with the andative 'in' form *mu-a*.

Ambel

(21) a. *Kira-kira* *lé* *wa-i-ne* *kórben*
REDUP-think thing DEM-UP-PROX dragon
*ke,* *ato* *ái*
may or dog
'Maybe this thing up [river] here is a dragon, or a dog.' (Arnold 2018a: 288)

[5] The one exception that we are aware of is found in the Oceanic language Manam, which exhibits a circular system similar to that found in Halmahera (Lichtenberk 1983).

b. *O,* *l-áp* *do* *welo* *i*
EXCL 3PL.ANIM-paddle along river NSG
*a-mu-a?*
DEM-inside-AND
'Oh, they paddle up the rivers inland there?'
(Arnold 2018a: 253)

The examples below show the coastal use of the UP term *i-*, in distal (22a) and andative (22b) forms.

Ambel
(22) a. *Ng-way* *po* *lo-i-ma*
3SG.ANIM-return from DEM-UPCOAST-DIST
*mansope...*
then
'He returned from upcoast [i.e. Jayapura]...'
(Arnold 2018a: 497)

b. *Gana* *wapa* *ya* *Waisai*
one DEM-MED 3SG.ANIM.PRED W.
*a-i-a?*
DEM-UPCOAST-AND
'Is that one upcoast in Waisai?'
(Arnold 2018a: 385)

The complete paradigm of Ambel directional stems includes seven directional roots which may combine with four deictic suffixes indicating proximal, medial, distal, and andative meaning, resulting in a total of thirty-five distinct stem forms (Arnold 2018a: 489).

On the geographic scale, the upward direction continues along the coast of the Bird's Head into Cendrawasih Bay, at least as far as Biak Island, some 800km from Halmahera (see Figure 49.10). As in Ambel, the upcoast–downcoast axis in Biak is also used to refer to an upriver–downriver axis. While these two axes may sometimes coincide, in principle, they are distinguished in cases when a river flows at an acute angle to the coast.

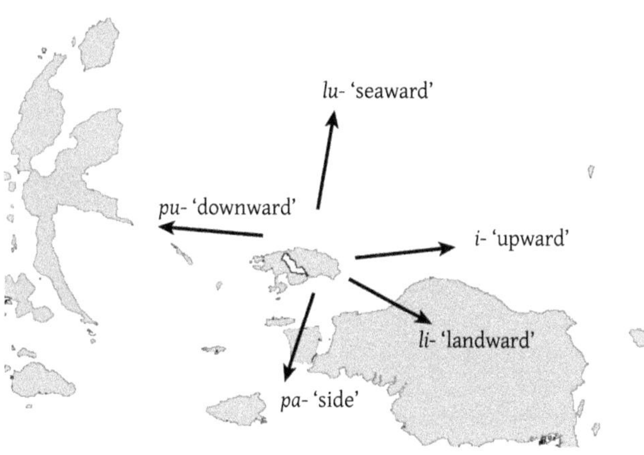


**Figure 49.10** Ambel directional usage on a geographic scale (after Arnold 2018a: 496).

Biak
(23) *Ramnai* *r<y>a* *m-pur* *ro* *di-ne*
afterwards <3SG> go ABL-down LOC place-this
*i-mrúr* *rar-vav*
3SG-go.underwater DIST-DOWN
'then it went downriver to here [and] dived downwards,' (van den Heuvel 2006: 356)

As in Halmahera, these directions are geographically motivated but highly conventionalized. Though at most places on Biak Island one can see neither a river nor the sea, van den Heuvel (2006: 349) reports that speakers are always aware of which direction is seaward, landward, downriver, and upriver, even in the absence of visible waterways. In contrast to Halmahera languages, in Biak the coastal directional *pur* 'downwards' is lexically distinguished from the vertical locational *vav* 'down', as in (23) (though 'upwards' and vertically 'up' are co-lexified, as in Halmahera).

### 49.4.4 Southeast Nusantara

Southeast Nusantara is a region of high linguistic diversity, encompassing East Timor and the Indonesian provinces of Central Maluku, Southeast Maluku, and East Nusa Tenggara. As in Halmahera, the region is home to both Austronesian and non-Austronesian languages; however, in contrast to Halmahera, there is no unified system of spatial orientation across this region. Instead, diversity prevails, and hybrid systems of orientation are common. Coastal systems are found in some languages of Flores, such as Lewotobi, part of the Lamaholot linkage in eastern Flores. Lewotobi has a typical seaward–landward plus 'across' system which has been further augmented by a coastal axis co-lexified with vertical up–down. The seaward and landward terms, *lau* and *rae*, reflect *lahud and *daya, respectively. The unoriented transverse term *wəli* is used in local contexts, such as within the village, as in (24a). The upcoast–downcoast axis is used at inter-village scales, as in (24b).

Lewotobi

(24) a. *Nia lewaʔ wəra wəli skola*
Nia GO.ACROSS sand coast school
*n-ai.*
3SG-go
'Nia went across the beach in the direction parallel with the coast (to) the school.'
(Nagaya 2011: 465)

b. *Ra teti Larantuka hau.*
3PL UPCOAST Larantuka come
'They came from upcoast in Larantuka.'
(Nagaya 2011: 526)

The upcoast direction lexified by *teti* is to the left along the coast when facing the water, while the downcoast direction *lali* 'down' is to the right. Thus, on the east coast of Flores *teti* aligns with north, but on the south coast it aligns with east. Hence, the general eastward trend of the 'up' direction is maintained in Lewotobi.

Traces of a coastal system can be found in Keo, a language spoken on the south coast of Flores. As discussed in §49.2, the primary orienation system in Keo employs a seaward–landward axis indicating direction toward vs. away from the coast, but Keo also makes use of two additional directional terms: *radé* 'westwards along the shore' and *mena* 'eastwards along the shore'. Although these terms are sometimes associated with the cardinal directions 'west' and 'east', respectively, in practice they are oriented along the coast. Flores is a narrow island some 350km in length, and in the region where Keo is spoken the coastline trends roughly northwest to southeast. Moreover, *radé* is co-lexified with the vertical directional 'down', so *radé* is literally 'downcoast', just as in the languages discussed earlier in this section. However, the opposing term, *mena*, is not co-lexified with *réta* 'up vertically', so it is not clear to what extent *mena* is conceptualized as 'upcoast'. However, *mena* is frequently used in constructions with the directional verb *nuka* 'go up', as in (25a), suggesting that *mena* is indeed associated with the upward direction. The coupling of the verb and directionals in *nuka mena* and *nuka radé* both meaning 'to go along' contrasts with directionals *réta* and *radé* indicating vertical movement. The latter co-occur with the verbs *nai* 'to climb' (25b) and *dhodho* 'to descend' (25c) to indicate movement along a vertical plane.

Keo

(25) a. *Imu mbana pau puʔu radé*
3SG walk EMPH from DOWNCOAST
*Mbawa nuka mena.*
Mbawa go.up UPCOAST
'She walked from downcoast (west) in Mbawa going east (up the coast).' (Baird 2002: 360)

b. *Bapa nai réta do nio*
father climb UP tree coconut
'Father climbed up the coconut tree.'
(Baird 2002: 369)

c. *Jaga nggoi dhodho radé puʔu*
careful fall GO.DOWN DOWN from
*ghumbu saʔo*
roof house
'Be careful climbing down from the roof of the house.' (Baird 2002: 369)

Moreover, Keo lacks distinct terms referring to other cardinal directions, suggesting that *radé* and *mena* are indeed coastal rather than cardinal terms.

Alune, spoken on Seram Island in Central Maluku, also exhibits traces of a coastal axis, defined by *ndi* 'parallel to the coast with ocean on the left' and *mpai* 'parallel to the coast with ocean on the right' (26). A transverse seaward–landward axis is defined by *mlau* 'seaward; downriver' (likely < *lahud) and *ndai* 'landward; upriver' (likely < *daya). An additional vertical axis is defined by *mlete* 'up' and *mpe* 'down'. Thus, in contrast to many of the previously described coastal systems, Alune coastal directions are lexically distinct from the vertical 'up' and 'down' terms. The etymologies of the coastal directional terms are obscure.

The six Alune directional terms are used at the local scale or what Florey and Kelly (2002) call the "zone of daily experience," as in travelling from the village to the garden (26).

Alune

(26) *Au lo-pai ʔeu dana manane*
1SG to-ALONG.COAST go fetch food
'I go along the coast to fetch food.'
(Florey and Kelly 2002: 33)

Beyond the local scale, directional usage is conventionalized. Locations beyond the local scale but still on Seram Island are conventionally *ndi* 'rightward along the coast', whereas locations beyond Seram Island but still in Central Maluku are conventionally *mpai* 'leftward along the coast'. For locations beyond Central Maluku, Alune speakers use *mlete* 'up vertically'.

Alune directionals may be used without reference to the location when that location can be inferred from the hearer's geographic knowledge. For example, in (26) the speaker indicates that the travel is 'leftward along the coast to fetch food'. Given local knowledge of the location of the speaker's garden, this can only mean that the speaker is going to her garden.

### 49.4.5 Other coastal systems

The Dalat Melanau directional system was described above in §49.3.2 as a riverine system with a transverse toward–away from the river axis. However, for coastal-dwelling Dalat Melanau, this system is further elaborated with coastal directional terms. Unfortunately, data on the coastal use of riverine directionals in Borneo is sparse; however, what data are available suggest that the terms used for coastal directions are not the same as those used for 'upriver' and 'downriver'. Dalat Melanau employs the notions up and down to refer to directions east and west along the north coast of Borneo, but these are lexified not as *ajuʔ* 'upriver' and *abaʔ* 'downriver' but instead with the distinct terms *wab* 'upcoast' and *laʔan* 'downcoast'.

## 49.5 Elevation systems

Elevation as a spatial orientation system distinguishes the elevation of a referent relative to the deictic centre. Elevation systems typically distinguish three levels: HIGH (above the deictic centre), LEVEL (at the same level as the deictic centre), and LOW (below the deictic centre). The spatial criteria which distinguish the levels can vary across languages. Burenhult (2008: 110) makes a distinction between vertical systems. Global elevation is irrespective of landscape, whereas geophysical systems are determined by the topographic relief of the landscape.[6]

Within the region, elevation systems are more common in the non-Austronesian languages of East Nusantara and New Guinea; however, they are found in several Malayo-Polynesian languages as well, often in combination with other systems. Austronesian languages with elevation systems are almost exclusively found in Sulawesi, especially within the Eastern Celebic and Sangiric branches, and thus may be an areal or a genetic feature, or both. For clarity of presentation we organize this section by genetic affiliation.

### 49.5.1 Elevation in Eastern Celebic

#### 49.5.1.1 *Muna*

Muna, a language of southeast Sulawesi, makes a two-way height distinction between HIGH and LOW/LEVEL (or non-HIGH). In some areas of grammar these terms occur alongside a third term which is unmarked for elevation, as in Table 49.8.

[6] Burenhult (2008) also recognizes an additional type of vertical system based on strict vertically ("verticality proper"); however, no examples of such systems were found in our survey.

**Table 49.8** Muna elevational prepositions (van den Berg 1997: 204)

| | |
|---|---|
| *te* | HIGH |
| *ne* | unmarked |
| *we* | non-HIGH |

The choice of appropriate elevation depends on the relative location of the deictic centre. Thus, in (27a) the deictic centre is located at the sea, where the machete is dropped, so the unmarked form *ne* is used. Elevation is simply not relevant to this situation. In (27b) the deictic centre is up away from the sea (e.g. in a house) so the non-HIGH term *we* is used to indicate the relatively lower position where the machete was dropped.

Muna

(27) a. *Kapulu-ku* *no-ndawu* *ne* *tehi.*
machete-my 3SG.REAL-fall LOC sea
'My machete fell into the sea.' (spoken at sea)

b. *Kapulu-ku* *no-ndawu* *we* *tehi.*
machete-my 3SG.REAL-fall LOC.DOWN sea
'My machete fell into the sea.' (spoken on land)
(van den Berg 1997: 207)

While *we* is interpreted as non-HIGH when used as a preposition, when used with the verb *kala* 'go' it is no longer neutral but has the meaning of descending. Thus, *kala we* 'go down to' contrasts with *kala te* 'go up to'.

The distinction between HIGH and non-HIGH is also found within the deictic system, distinguishing *tatu* 'higher' from *watu* 'that level or lower'. These two elevational deictics are embedded within a larger system of deictic demonstratives

**Table 49.9** Muna deictic demonstratives (van den Berg 1997: 199). This table shows just one set of demonstratives; an additional six sets can be derived from these.

| | | |
|---|---|---|
| PROX | *ini* | near speaker |
| | *itu* | near hearer |
| | *maitu* | near, but away from speaker and hearer |
| DISTAL | *nagha* | invisible |
| | *wagha* | past visible |
| | *watu* | level or lower |
| | *tatu* | higher |

which distinguishes proximity and visibility (see Table 49.9). The height distinction is relevant only in the distal sphere and when visibility is not relevant.

Muna has no terms meaning 'seaward' or 'landward'. Thus, elevational terms provide a primary means of spatial orientation. Where there is no difference in elevation, the elevational terms may take on a cardinal meaning, equating HIGH with west and south, and non-HIGH with east (and occasionally north).

#### 49.5.1.2 *Balantak*

Balantak is spoken in eastern Sulawesi and, like Muna, is also a member of the Celebic subgroup. Although the languages are rather distantly related, the Balantak elevation system is strikingly similar to that found in Muna, distinguishing HIGH and LOW elevational terms as part of a larger deictic system (Table 49.10), as exemplified in (28).

**Table 49.10** Balantak elevational demonstratives (Busenitz and Busenitz 1992: 132).

| | Demonstrative | Adverbial | |
|---|---|---|---|
| PROX | *niʔi* | *ita* | near speaker |
| | *nonoʔ* | *noʔo* | near hearer |
| | *yaʔa* | *mbaʔa* | near, but away from speaker and hearer |
| DISTAL | *tuʔu* | *ntuʔu* | front |
| | *leʔe* | *ndeʔe* | side |
| | *raʔa* | *ndaʔa* | HIGH |
| | *roʔo* | *ndoʔo* | LOW |

Balantak

(28) *I-roʔo* na *intu-na* *wooʔ*
extension-LOW PREP under-3SG:POSS areca
*i-yaʔa*
extension-DEM
'that person down there underneath that areca palm' (Busenitz and Busenitz 1992: 134)

Like Muna, Balantak also encodes three proximal deictic distinctions. However, rather than a visibility distinction, Balantak distinguishes two horizontal distal distinctions, 'front' and 'side'. In spite of the structural similarity between the systems, the forms show little phonological similarity.

#### 49.5.1.3 *Tukang Besi*

Tukang Besi, a language of southeast Sulawesi, has taken an an original seaward–landward system and reinterpreted it as an elevation system. The seaward–landward distinction has a natural semantic extension to elevation, based on the association of seaward locations as lower in elevation and landward locations as higher in elevation. However, in Tukang Besi the elevational distinction between LOW and HIGH has been further conventionalized so that *ito* 'landward; up' is now associated with cardinal east and with locations of higher social status (see Table 49.11).

**Table 49.11** Tukang Besi seaward–landward terms with extended meanings (Donohue 1999a: 139).

| | |
|---|---|
| *ito* | 'landwards, up, (north)east, in, higher social status' |
| *iwo* | 'seawards, down, (south)west, out, lower social status' |

As a result, it is possible for two locations in Tukang Besi to be located 'upward' from each other. For example, a village located at a higher elevation and to the west is considered *ito* because of its higher elevation, while the reverse direction is also *ito* because it lies to the east. Moreover, *ito* and *iwo* can even be used in contexts where there is no elevation difference. The four villages shown in Figure 49.11 are all at the same elevation. Pongo-Mandati is the social centre and is thus considered *ito* 'up' from the perspective of the other three villages. However, from the perspective of Pongo-Mandati itself, only the neighbouring villages of Wanse and Mola are *iwo* 'down'; the more distant village of Wandoka is *ito* 'up' because it is sufficiently far from the centre so that its location to the north of Pongo-Mandati takes precedence over social status in determining the orientation.

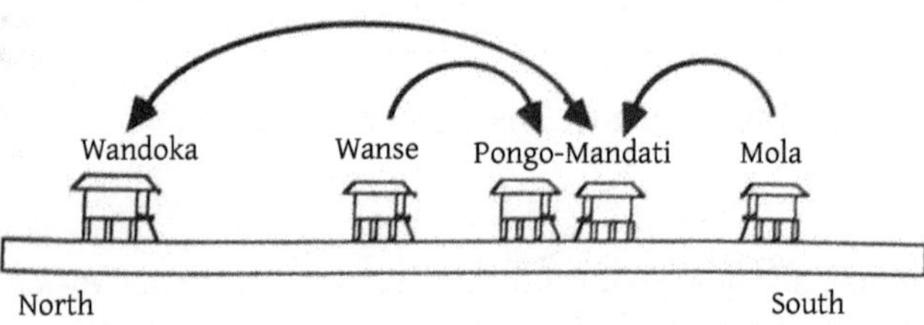


**Figure 49.11** Directional orientation between four Tukang Besi villages located at the same elevation. Arrows indicate direction of *ito* 'up' (Donohue 1999a: 141).

### 49.5.2 Aralle-Tabulahan (South Sulawesi): Elevation and riverine

Aralle-Tabulahan, a language of South Sulawesi, has a three-way elevational distinction between HIGH, LEVEL, and LOW. This system is used alongside a riverine system, forming a hybrid system of orientation which combines a traditional three-term riverine system with an elevation system. The 'upriver' and 'downriver' terms are co-lexified with 'landward' and 'seaward', respectively, with *sau* 'downriver/seaward'. However, as noted above, *daya is reflected in Aralle-Tabulahan not as 'upriver' but rather as *daiʔ* 'up vertically'. The two sets of riverine and elevational terms are shown in Table 49.12.

**Table 49.12** Aralle-Tabulahan directionals (McKenzie 1997: 224).

| | Directional | Locative | |
|---|---|---|---|
| ELEV | *daiʔ* | *yaho* | 'up' |
| | *naung* | *hoiʔ* | 'down' |
| | *panoʔ* | *hao* | 'level' |
| RIVER | *tama* | *yaling* | 'upriver' |
| | *sau* | *lauʔ* | 'downriver' |
| | *beteʔ* | *hipe* | 'across' |

Aralle-Tabulahan speakers choose between the riverine and elevation systems according to context. Thus, downward elevation *naung* (29a) is distinguished from riverine downriver *sau* (29b).

Aralle-Tabulahan
(29) a. *Me-pahe tau naung di Pikung*
INTR-rice people DOWN at Pikung
'They are going to harvest rice down at Pikung.'

b. *Maʔallo-ø sau sau*
go.church-3ABS friend-2SG.POSS DOWNRIVER
'Your friend is going to church DOWNRIVER.'
(McKenzie 1997: 226)

Where geography presents a potential ambiguity between the riverine and elevation systems, the conflict is resolved by convention. For example, where a river flows along a flat valley with little perceptible drop in elevation, the downriver direction could, in theory, be considered either *pano* 'level' using the elevation system, or *sau* 'downriver' using the riverine system, but only the latter term is used in this situation.

### 49.5.3 Sangiric: Elevation and seaward–landward

The Sangiric languages of Northern Sulawesi have hybrid systems of spatial orientation which combine an elevation system with a seaward–landward system. The simplest of these systems is found in Ratahan, spoken in the mountains above the south coast of the Minahasan peninsula. The system is comprised of four terms in two sets, one dynamic and one static (Table 49.13). Of note is the presence of two terms *na* and *sa* both glossed as LOW. In local settings an elevation system prevails, employing the three terms *neiʔ* HIGH, *mai* LEVEL, and *sa* LOW. In regional settings a seaward–landward system prevails, contrasting *neiʔ* 'landward' vs. *na* 'seaward' (Jukes and Utsumi 2015). In local settings the four terms together define a coordinate system, as suggested by the cardinal direction glosses in Table 49.13, specifying absolute reference within the domain of a house or village. However, this cardinal system is distinct from that employed at larger geographic scales. In that system the east–west axis is derived from terms referencing the path of the sun, while the north–south axis used on a local scale is derived from the elevational terms *neiʔ* and *sa*.

**Table 49.13** Ratahan (Toratán) elevational terms (after Jukes and Utsumi 2015).

| | Dynamic | Static |
|---|---|---|
| HIGH, landward (north) | *neiʔ* | *raya* |
| LEVEL, across (east) | *mai* | *pai* |
| LOW (south) | *sa* | *lar* |
| LOW, seaward (west) | *na* | *wa* |

The closely related Bantik language has only a single set of LOW terms, but it additionally has two paradigms of dynamic forms distinguishing translocative movement away from the deictic centre vs. cislocative movement toward the deictic centre (Table 49.14).

**Table 49.14** Bantik elevational terms, showing forms for a stationary entity (LOC), movement away from the deictic centre (TRANS), and movement toward the deictic centre (CIS) (after Utsumi 2014: 123).

| | LOC | TRANS | CIS |
|---|---|---|---|
| HIGH | *daŋ* | *tanaiʔ* | *naiʔ* |
| LEVEL | *raʔ* | *tansao* | *nsao* |
| LOW | *baba* | *tanao* | *nao* |

### 49.5.4 Other elevation systems

Elevation systems are rarely found in MPSEA outside of Sulawesi. However, there is some evidence of an elevation system much further afield in the Mariana Islands. Chamorro has been reported to use directionals to reference movement in an upwards or downwards direction. Topping (1980: 200) reports that the intrinsic locative terms *huloʔ* 'above' and *papä* 'below' can also be used to reference global elevation. In this usage *huloʔ* is used for places that are higher in elevation as compared to the deictic centre, regardless of whether this height difference is along the vertical axis (30a) or not (30b). Likewise, *papä* encodes lower global elevation. These terms can also be conventionally extended to use on a large scale where *huloʔ* refers to locations in the north and *papä* to locations in the south.

Chamorro

(30) a. *Ha hatsa i haluʔu huloʔ gi bote.*
3SG lift the shark UP to boat
'He lifted the shark up to the boat.'
(Topping 1980: 266)

b. *Ta hanao huloʔ asta i gimaʔ-hu*
1PL go UP to the house-1POSS
'We will go up to my house' (Topping 1980: 192)

Commonly throughout Austronesian languages the seaward–landward axis may also take on the meaning of 'up' (i.e. landward) and 'down' (i.e. seaward), thus functioning as a kind of elevation system. Chamorro has grammaticized this natural semantic extension to form an elevation system.

## 49.6 Cardinal systems

Cardinal systems of spatial orientation rely on fixed axes whose orientation is independent of local geography. Generally cardinal axes are determined by the path of the sun, thus corresponding roughly to the east–west axis in English, though the axes may be anchored by other non-geographic features, such as prevailing wind directions. Languages differ significantly in both when and where they employ a cardinal system, as well as in how the system has developed. Almost all of the languages in our survey discussed above make use of a cardinal system in some contexts. This occurs most commonly at the worldwide or navigational scale, where the lack of local geographic reference makes the use of riverine, coastal, elevational, and seaward–landward systems impracticable. We refer to this phenomenon as the secondary use of cardinal systems and discuss it separately in §49.6.2 below. Systems which use cardinal orientation in addition to other absolute systems can be distinguished from what we term *pure* cardinal systems, discussed in §49.6.1, which lack alternate systems of absolute orientation.

### 49.6.1 Pure cardinal systems

Given that most languages use cardinal systems at navigational scales, for the purposes of this survey we classify an orientation system as pure cardinal only if the cardinal system is the only absolute system of spatial orientation used in the language. In some sense then, the languages classified as having (pure) cardinal systems constitute a remainder category. Because nearly all languages have some sort of cardinal system, identifying pure cardinal systems can be challenging where the documentation is sparse. In particular, the mere existence of cardinal terms is not a sufficient diagnostic, since the language may also employ other non-cardinal systems of orientation. Similarly, as discussed in §49.1.2, a lack of data may result in the incorrect conclusion that a language employs a cardinal system when it is truly based on geography. Only in cases where relatively complete documentation exists can we be somewhat certain that a language employs a pure cardinal system without any alternate non-cardinal system. It may not be a coincidence that most languages with pure cardinal systems have relatively large speaker populations spread over a large area. In large, cosmopolitan speech communities speakers are more likely to have to orient themselves in unfamiliar terrain, making the application of geocentric systems of orientation more challenging. Since the cardinal system is the only absolute system of spatial orientation employed in these languages, orientation at small regional and local scales is accomplished using intrinsic and relative systems.

The sources/etymologies of the terms pertaining to the cardinal axes exhibit significant variation; common sources include: seaward–landward axis; path of the sun; wind terms; and locational terms.[7] Impressionistically, the most common system employs sun terms for the east–west axis and wind terms for the north–south axis (see Table 49.15).[8] In a region which largely straddles the equator, there is a natural equation of east with the rising sun and west with the setting sun. The sun terms are etymologically diverse but reference the direction of sunrise ('east') and sunset ('west'). The terms for 'north' reflect PAN *qamiS 'north wind', while the terms for 'south' reflect *timuR 'south or east wind', PMP *SabaRat 'south wind', and PWMP *salatan 'south wind'.

**Table 49.15** Cardinal systems based on sun and wind terms

| | North | South | East | West |
|---|---|---|---|---|
| Tagalog | *hilaga* | *timog* | *silangan* | *kanluran* |
| Hiligaynon | *amihan* | *timog/ habagatan* | *sidlangan* | *katundan* |
| Cebuano | *amihanan* | *habagatan* | *silangan* | *kasadpan* |

Another common type of cardinal system combines a wind axis with an original seaward–landward axis from *lahud-*daya (see Table 49.16). The determining feature in these systems is the orientation of the original seaward–landward axis. For instance, Ilokano is spoken primarily on the west coast of Luzon Island, where the seaward direction is to the west. Thus, *laud* has grammaticized as 'west' and *daya* as 'east'. Monsoon wind terms are used for the north–south axis. In contrast, Madurese is spoken primarily along the south coast of Madura Island, where the seaward direction is to the south. Hence, *lao?* has grammaticized as 'south' and *dhájá* as 'north'. Wind terms are used for the east–west axis.

[7] Gallego (2018) uses 'locational terms' and 'systems of location' as somewhat catch-all terms to refer to directional words that do not fit neatly into other geocentric system etymologies. Locational may derive from locatives such as Botolan *baba* < PMP *babaq 'lower surface; bottom; inside', general place terms such as Itbayat *sayid* which also means 'lower region', or body part terms such as Kapampangan *pangulu* < PAN *quluh 'head' (Gallego 2018: 85).

[8] Sun plus wind is the most common source in Gallego's (2018) survey of the etymology of cardinal terms in fifty-four languages of the Philippines. However, Gallego does not distinguish pure cardinal systems from secondary ones, so it is difficult to say how many of the sun-plus-wind systems are actually pure cardinal.

**Table 49.16** Cardinal systems based on sun and seaward–landward terms

| | North | South | East | West |
|---|---|---|---|---|
| Ilokano | *amianan* | *abagatan* | *daya* | *laud* |
| Ibatan | *ammyanan* | *abagatan* | *daya* | *laod* |
| Madurese | *dhájá* | *lao?* | *temor* | *bhárá?* |

Cardinal axes may also be lexified with original locational or riverine terms. Javanese, which employs both, provides a nice example of the often complex etymologies underlying cardinal systems. Javanese *lor* 'north' reflects *lahud 'seaward', while *kidul* 'south' is of uncertain etymology. Adelaar (1997: 65) speculates that *kidul* may come from the Tenggerese term referencing the direction of Mt. Bromo, which is located to the south of the majority of the Javanese-speaking population in East Java. Thus, a term originally denoting the direction toward a specific mountain may have generalized to a general 'landward' term, and from there conventionalized to the modern cardinal meaning 'south'. Javanese *wétan* 'east' derives from nominalization of *wwit* 'beginning; emergence', a reference to the sunrise (i.e. the east). On the other hand *kulon* 'west' derives from the nominalization of older Javanese *ulu 'head, headwaters' < PAN *quluh 'head'; This suggests that *kulon* originally meant 'upriver' and entered the language in a region where the upriver direction aligned with cardinal west. Curiously, Javanese also has the high register form *kilén* 'west', which derives instead from PAN *qiliR 'flow downriver'. Thus, both 'upriver' and 'downriver' are sources for modern Javanese words meaning 'west'. This suggests that the form *kilén* entered the language from a region where the downriver direction was aligned with west (Nothofer 1980, cited in Adelaar 1997).

**Table 49.17** Etymologies for Javanese cardinal terms

| | Term | Etymology | Type |
|---|---|---|---|
| 'north' | *lor* | < *lahud 'seaward' | SEA-LAND |
| 'south' | *kidul* | uncertain | ? |
| 'east' | *wétan* | < *wwit* 'emergence' | SUN |
| 'west' | *kulon* | < *quluh 'head' | RIVERINE |
| | *kilén* | < *qiliR 'flow downriver' | |

Standard Malay has an eight-point system whose terms also appear to reflect the topography of a historical population centre. The east–west axis is lexified with wind terms, *timur* (< PMP *timuR 'southeast monsoon') and *barat* (< PMP *habaRat 'northwest monsoon') (see Figure 49.12) (Blust and Trussel 2020). However the intercardinal points suggest an original system in which the north–south axis was aligned with a seaward–landward axis; *barat-laut* 'northwest' and *timur-laut* 'northeast' suggest that the original term denoting 'north' was *laut* (< *lahud). Similarly, *barat-daya* 'southwest' suggests that the original term denoting 'south' was *daya* (< *daya). Indeed, such a situation is geographically consistent with what we know of the location of the Srivijaya Kingdom, which was the centre of power of the Malay-speaking peoples until the fourteenth century. "In the Palembang area of South Sumatra (where Srivijaya was presumably located), the sea is in a northern direction, as opposed to the land, which is in a southern direction" (Adelaar 1992a: 115). The original seaward–landward terms were presumably replaced when the centre of power moved to Malacca on the Malay peninsula. There the sea lies to the south, potentially leading to some confusion with a term *laut* for 'north' which may have retained traces of its original semantics meaning 'seaward' (see Figure 49.13). The terms that replaced the seaward–landward items are also consistent with this explanation. The modern term *selatan* 'south' is derived from *selat* 'strait', and the Strait of Malacca would have been to the south from Malacca. The innovated term *utara* 'north' is a loan from Sanskrit *uttara* 'north(ern)', The term *tenggara* 'southeast' is ostensibly a loan, possibly from Tamil *ten kara* 'south bank' (Adelaar 1992a: 115).

As noted by Adelaar (1997), it is likely that this Malay eight-point cardinal system was adopted for its utility in maritime navigation. The Malays were powerful navigators and traders, who had widespread influence on navigation throughout the region. As a result, the Malay system has been borrowed by many other MPSEA, in some cases replacing original non-cardinal systems and in others serving as a secondary system. In Acehnese the Malay system has been superimposed upon an original seaward–landward system which itself has been largely conventionalized as cardinal. The borrowed cardinal terms *utara* 'north' and *selatan* 'south' co-exist with original *barôh* 'toward the sea; north' and *tunong* 'toward the hills; south' (Daud and Durie 1999: 87). The fact that the Malay terms were borrowed can be inferred because the indigenous terms reflect the local geography—the northern tip of the island of Sumatra—while the Malay terms do not.

Malagasy also borrowed the Malay system; however, the semantics of the 'north' and 'south' terms suggest that the system was borrowed before the Malay east–west axis had

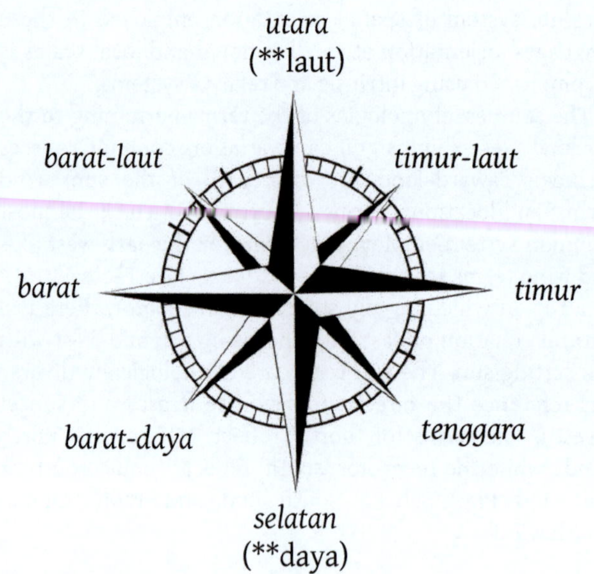


**Figure 49.12** Malay compass rose, with original terms indicated by asterisks.

been fully conventionalized. Malagasy *-varatra* 'north' and *-tsimo* 'south' correspond to Malay *barat* and *timur*, respectively. Presumably the terms were borrowed into Malagasy at a time when a polysemy with their original terms for the monsoon winds still existed, allowing them to be easily associated with local geographic and climatic patterns in Madagascar. The Malay term for the wet northwest monsoon, *barat*, was naturally associated with the wet northern monsoon in Madagascar (Adelaar 1997, citing Dahl 1951: 326). The Malagasy term *andrefana* 'west' is a Malay loan reflecting a non-cardinal notion which consists of a location marker *aN-* and a root *refana* that reflects Malay depan 'in front'." The term for 'east', *a-tsinanana*, consists of *aN-* and *tsinan-ana* 'place where the new moon appears'[9] (Adelaar 2020, personal communication).

Cham's eight-point cardinal system resembles that of Malay, but it has borrowed five of the terms directly from Sanskrit rather than Malay (Adelaar 1997: 66). Only the term *salatan* 'southeast' appears to have been borrowed directly from Malay. However, given that it was borrowed not as a cardinal term 'south' but rather as intercardinal 'southeast' suggests that it may have been borrowed in its original

[9] However, some Malagasy dialects still have *varatraza* 'east wind' or 'west wind', depending on the source dialect. For instance, Tanosy Malagasy has *simoulots* 'northeast' and *tsimilôtru* 'north wind' (spelling and meaning depending on source) (Adelaar 1989: 9–11). These wind names derive from Malay *barat-daya* and *timur-laut* respectively (Adelaar 2018, personal communication).

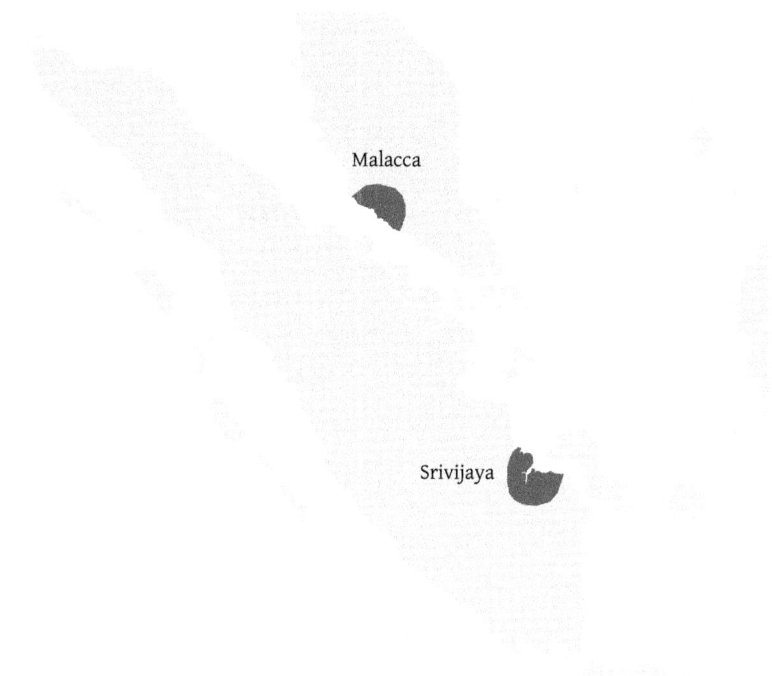


**Figure 49.13** Approximate locations of Srivijaya and Malacca kingdoms (dark grey), showing differing orientations toward the water.

sense of 'strait' rather than in its cardinal meaning. Further, the Chamic term ŭṭ exists as a doublet along with *piraʔ*, which directly reflects PMP *habaRat rather than Malay *barat*, with additional meanings 'north wind' and 'winter'. This last term may be an artefact of an earlier indigenous orientation system inherited directly from PMP.

Not all Malayic languages or Malay varieties reflect the cardinal system found in standard Malay. Often, the terms for 'east' and 'west' derive from terms referring to the path of the sun. The Malayic language Minangkabau has *puhun* 'east' from 'source' and *ujuəng* 'west' from 'end'. In Jakarta Malay, the terms *ilir* 'downriver; north' (< PWMP *qiliR 'flow downriver') and *udik* 'upriver; south' (< PWMP *udahik 'upriver part of river') are used alongside the standard Malay cardinal terms (Adelaar 1997). Vehicular Malay varieties may retain some or all of the standard Malay cardinal system or instead adopt the directional usage of their respective local regions. Papuan Malay retains the four standard Malay cardinal points (Kluge 2014: 214); in contrast, North Moluccan Malay shows no traces of a cardinal system but instead reflects the coastal system of orientation found in the local Austronesian (and non-Austronesian) languages of the region (see §49.4.3 above).

In contrast to Javanese and many Malay-type systems, some pure cardinal systems show signs of being recently innovated or only recently replacing former non-cardinal systems. As already discussed, one common lexical source for cardinal directions is the original PMP seaward–landward terms, *daya 'landward' and *lahud 'seaward'. The cardinal direction that they encode typically reflects local geography. Thus, when a reflex of *lahud is conventionalized as a cardinal direction, that direction is likely to coincide with the seaward direction in the region where the conventionalization took place, such as with Malay, Madurese, and Javanese. But the same pattern is also found across modern languages, especially in the Philippines (see Table 49.18).

Similar variation is found in terminology for the east–west axis based on the path of the sun. In her survey of cardinal orientation systems in fifty-four Philippine languages, Gallego (2018) identifies at least sixteen languages with full cardinal systems for which the east–west axis is encoded using terms referencing the path of the sun. Yet it is not possible to reconstruct a single term for 'east' or 'west'. Rather, terms for 'west' can be traced to at least five distinct historical sources; and terms for 'east' can be traced to eight different sources' (Table 49.19). The diversity of

**Table 49.18** Reflexes of *daya and *lahud as cardinal directions. Empty cells indicate that the language lacks a reflex or that the reflex is not a cardinal term.

| | *daya | *lahud |
|---|---|---|
| Bikol | – | west |
| Ibatan | east | west |
| Ilokano | east | west |
| Kankanaey | east | west |
| Yami | – | west/north |
| Gaddang | west | – |
| Lubuagan Kalinga | west | east |
| Guinaang Kalinga | – | east |
| Madurese | north | south |
| Javanese | – | north |
| Chamorro | south/east | north/west |
| Tae' | – | south |

**Table 49.19** Sources of terms encoding 'east' and 'west' in Philippine languages (Blust and Trussel 2020; Gallego 2018).

| | | | |
|---|---|---|---|
| West | PMP | *teɲej | 'sink, set (sun)' |
| | PMP | *-nej | 'submerge, sink, drown' |
| | PWMP | *len-ej | 'disappear underwater' |
| | PAN | *sejep/*selep | 'to enter, penetrate' |
| | PWMP | *salem | 'dive; immerse oneself' |
| East | PWMP | *siraŋ | 'dazzled, blinded by glaring light' |
| | PPh | *sebaŋ | 'to rise, of the sun, moon, or stars' |
| | PMP | *silaw | 'dazzling of light' |
| | PMP | *sila | 'outpouring of light' |
| | PMP | *silaq | 'outpouring of light' |
| | PMP | *silak | 'beam of light' |
| | PMP | *sirak | 'outpouring of light' |
| | PPh | *sikat | 'sunrise, rising sun' |

sources is evidence of the relatively recent emergence of cardinal direction terminology—a point noted for Philippine languages by Gallego (2018: 91) and more generally by Brown (1983).

While it is typical for the north–south cardinal axis to be oriented with distinct lexemes based on the wind or geographic features, there is some evidence of an indigenous cardinal system reflecting an axis perpendicular to the path of the sun, without a distinct north and south direction. In Ata Manobo the term *balabagan* < PPh *bala(R)báR 'crosswise; athwart' (cf. Tagalog *balagbág* 'crossbeam') is used to indicate the direction crosswise to the sun (Hartung 2016). This axis is not fully distinct from the original riverine system but rather entangled with it. Although the *balabagan* axis is unoriented, speakers may specify an orientation along this axis by using the riverine terms *dibabò* 'downriver' and *diraya* 'upriver'. Thus, *balabagan dibabò* denotes 'south', literally 'downriver along the axis transverse to the path of the sun', and *balabagan diraya* denotes 'north', literally 'upriver along the axis transverse to the path of the sun'.[10] This geographic specification is clearly motivated by the location of the Manobo-speaking region located upriver along the Libuganon River, which flows north to south across much of eastern Mindanao Island, emptying into the sea at the Gulf of Davao. In this geographic context, downriver is aligned with south, while upriver is aligned with north. The prevalence of this crosswise axis in other languages is not known, and cognates in other languages do not necessarily function to define a cardinal axis. For example, Bukidnon Manobo has *belavag* with the general meaning 'crosswise'.

There is, however, very little research into how and to what extent cardinal systems are used in everyday communication. Even the languages described here as having pure cardinal systems typically include a number of other spatial terms whose function is poorly understood. As shown in Table 49.20, even large languages like Tagalog and Kapampangan have what appear to be non-cardinal terms alongside the four main cardinal directions. Further study may reveal that some of the cardinal systems in these languages may actually be secondary, existing alongside non-cardinal systems of orientation.

## 49.6.2 Secondary cardinal systems

For languages which use a non-cardinal system at most scales, a commonly employed method for lexifying a secondary cardinal system is to conventionalize an existing

[10] Hartung (2016) also states that the direction of the *balabagan* axis can be clarified using the relative terms 'left' and 'right', though this of course requires knowing the orientation of the reference point from which 'left' and 'right' are specified—i.e. which way the speaker is facing.

**Table 49.20** Spatial orientation terms in three 'pure' cardinal languages of the Philippines (Storck and Storck 2005)

| | Tagalog | Kapampangan | Ayta Mag-antsi |
|---|---|---|---|
| east | *silágnan* | *aslagan* | *awahan allo* |
| west | *kanlúran* | *albugan* | *kanabuan allo* |
| north | *hilágà* | *paralaya* | *hilaga* |
| south | *tímog* | *mauli* | *timog* |
| downward | *pababâ* | *pakuldas* | *paaypa* |
| upward, uphill | *pataás/ paakyat* | *paukyat/ sakan* | *patag-ay/ palakat* |
| upriver | *pasalúnga* | *pasalunga* | *muntan hongêy* |
| downhill | *palusóng/ pababâ* | *pababa* | *palohan* |
| toward | *patúng* | *papunta* | *palako* |
| seaward | *papuntang dagat* | *palakon dagat* | *palakon dagat* |

system, essentially 'fixing' the axis of a system whose orientation in non-cardinal contexts would be determined by local geography. For example, the South Halmahera language Weda uses a coastal system of orientation at local and regional scales, contrasting an upcoast–downcoast axis with a seaward–landward axis. However, at larger navigational scales far from land these directions are fixed as 'landward' = 'north', 'seaward' = 'south', 'upcoast' = 'east', 'downcoast' = 'west'. This alignment of cardinal and coastal plus seaward–landward systems reflects the orientation in the main Weda speaking region along the south coast of the eastern peninsula of Halmahera Island. There the landward direction is indeed geographically north and downcoast is geographically west. Thus, the mapping between non-cardinal and cardinal systems in Sawai can tell us something about where the system arose. A similar alignment of cardinal and coastal plus seaward–landward systems is found in Makasar and Bugis (see Figure 49.14). In each case the particular alignment reflects the geographic orientation of the system in the main area where each language is spoken.

Many languages also have terms referring to the direction of sunrise and sunset, that can be used to delineate a cardinal axis—a common strategy for pure cardinal systems as well. Often these directions are spatially metonymous, in that the term for 'sunrise' and 'sunset' are used to denote the direction toward sunrise (i.e. 'east') and the direction toward sunset (i.e. 'west'), respectively. Gayo orientation uses a riverine system combined with elevational terms (see §49.3.3), but it also has indigenous cardinal terms based on the sun that refer to east and west (31).

Gayo

(31) a. *Mata* *n=ló* *m-urip*
eye POSS=day INTR-live
'east' (lit. the sun lives)

b. *Ilup-en*
set(sun)-NMLZ
'west' (literally, 'sunset') (Eades 2005: 213)

Similarly, Mansaka (discussed in §49.3 above) has a basic riverine system using the terms *lawud* 'downriver' vs. *agsaka* 'upriver', but it also has cardinal terms referring to the sun: *silatan* 'to rise (sun or moon); east' and *sallupan* 'sunset; west'

While sometimes the innovated terms for cardinal 'east' and 'west' may integrate into a geographic system, in many cases they exist alongside a riverine or seaward–landward system. This is true for example of the Mindanao languages discussed in §49.3.1 above. Central Subanen, Agusan Manobo, and Ata Manobo all exhibit a riverine system with an additional 'across' term, but they also have terms for 'east' and 'west'. Subanen *silangan*, Agusan *silatan*, Ata *silò* 'east'; and Subanen *sindep*, Agusan *sayopan* 'west'. (No term for 'west' is reported for Ata Manobo.) Although we lack sufficient data on the usage of directional terms, it is likely that spatial orientation at local and regional scales in these languages is accomplished using the riverine system while the cardinal directionals are used on the navigational scale.

Some languages have also innovated a north–south cardinal axis derived from the east–west solar axis. Busang uses the relative term *bèh* 'left' to derive cardinal terms for 'north' and 'south', as in (32).

Busang

(32) a. *Bèh* *ulé* *mata* *n* *dó* *muun*
side left eye GEN sun rise
'north' (literally, 'left of the rising sun')

b. *Bèh* *ulé* *mata* *n* *dó* *uli*
side left eye GEN sun return
'south' (literally, 'left of the setting sun')
(Barth 1910: 29)

However, it is not clear how frequently cardinal terms based on the sun are used in languages with secondary cardinal systems. The Gayo sun directions only appear in a single citation (31) in Eades's (2005) grammar. Giman also has indigenous cardinal terms based on the sun: *hawé ncapák li* 'place where the sun rises' and *hawé sisopu* 'bathing-place

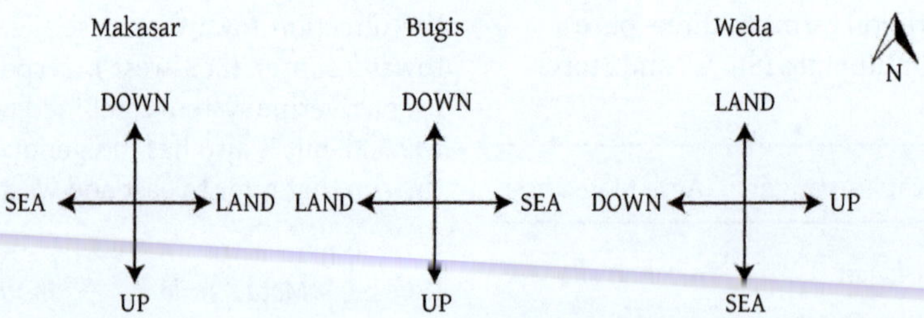


**Figure 49.14** Alignment of cardinal and non-cardinal axes at navigational scales in three languages which otherwise use coastal plus seaward–landward systems.

of the sun'; but Teljeur remarks that "these categories are hardly present in Giman culture" (1982: 361). Similarly, Adelaar notes that "the autochtonous peoples of Borneo do not make much use of cardinal directions" because of the forest blocking visibility and the meandering rivers going in various directions (1997: 68).

It is also important to bear in mind that most of the speakers of languages in this survey are multilingual and also speak a second language which has a pure cardinal system (e.g. Indonesian, Tagalog, Malaysian, English). Translanguaging is common, so speakers have, within their linguistic repertoires, the option to use pure cardinal terms from other languages. Taba generally uses a coastal system of orientation (see §49.4.3), but in the text excerpt in (33) the speaker freely mixes the indigenous coastal term *ya* 'upcoast' with the Malay cardinal term *barat* 'west'.

(33) Taba

| *Malai* | *no-ge* | *bagian* | *barat* | *ya-se* | *bagian* | *barat* |
|---|---|---|---|---|---|---|
| then | there-ESS | side | WEST | up-ESS | side | WEST |

'So over there on the western side, up there on the western side' (Bowden 2001: 419)

Moreover, there are often conventional associations between indigenous non-cardinal directions and cardinal directions within a language of wider communication. For example, in Gane the Indonesian cardinal term *kiblat* 'direction toward Mecca, approximately 25 degrees north of west' is conventionally equated with *po* 'down' (Teljeur 1987: 361).

## 49.7 Summary

In this survey of MPSEA spatial orientation systems, we have identified five primary types of spatial orientation systems used by languages throughout the region: seaward–landward, riverine, coastal, elevational, and cardinal. These five types may be combined in a hybrid fashion or used cooperatively, resulting in a large variety of different systems in use. Recall just a few of the many hybrids discussed in this chapter: seaward–landward systems may be augmented with cardinal axes, as in Balinese; riverine systems may be combined with transverse toward vs. away from water axes, as in Ngaju (Borneo); and elevation systems may be used in concert with riverine systems, as in Aralle-Tabaluhan (Sulawesi). Thus, while this initial typology is useful for understanding the diversity of spatial orientation systems in MPSEA, the actual picture is even more complex. Individual systems are uniquely adapted to address the spatial needs of the speakers of particular languages.

The distribution of orientation systems is largely areal (Map 49.1). Riverine systems prevail in Borneo and the southern Philippines. Borneo, in particular, initially provided the ideal landscape to nurture such systems as in many areas, the rivers, along which people tend to live, are the only geographic features to break up the forested landscape. Coastal systems are common in Halmahera but also found elsewhere in eastern Indonesia. Elevation systems are almost entirely restricted to Sulawesi. Languages which rely solely or largely on a cardinal system to the exclusion of other systems are localized to the northern Philippines and western Indonesia. It is possible that there is a correlation between this distribution and languages spoken by a large population across a large geographic area.

By far the greatest diversity of orientation systems is found in East Nusantara, where languages reflecting each of the five major types can be found. This pattern is consistent with the status of East Nusantara as a transitional zone between Austronesian and non-Austronesian languages, resulting in a shift from original Western Austronesian seaward–landward systems to more complex systems of spatial orientation (cf. Klamer et al. 2008). However, this region is also where almost all of the languages with seaward–landward systems are found. This finding is striking considering the long-standing assumption that the

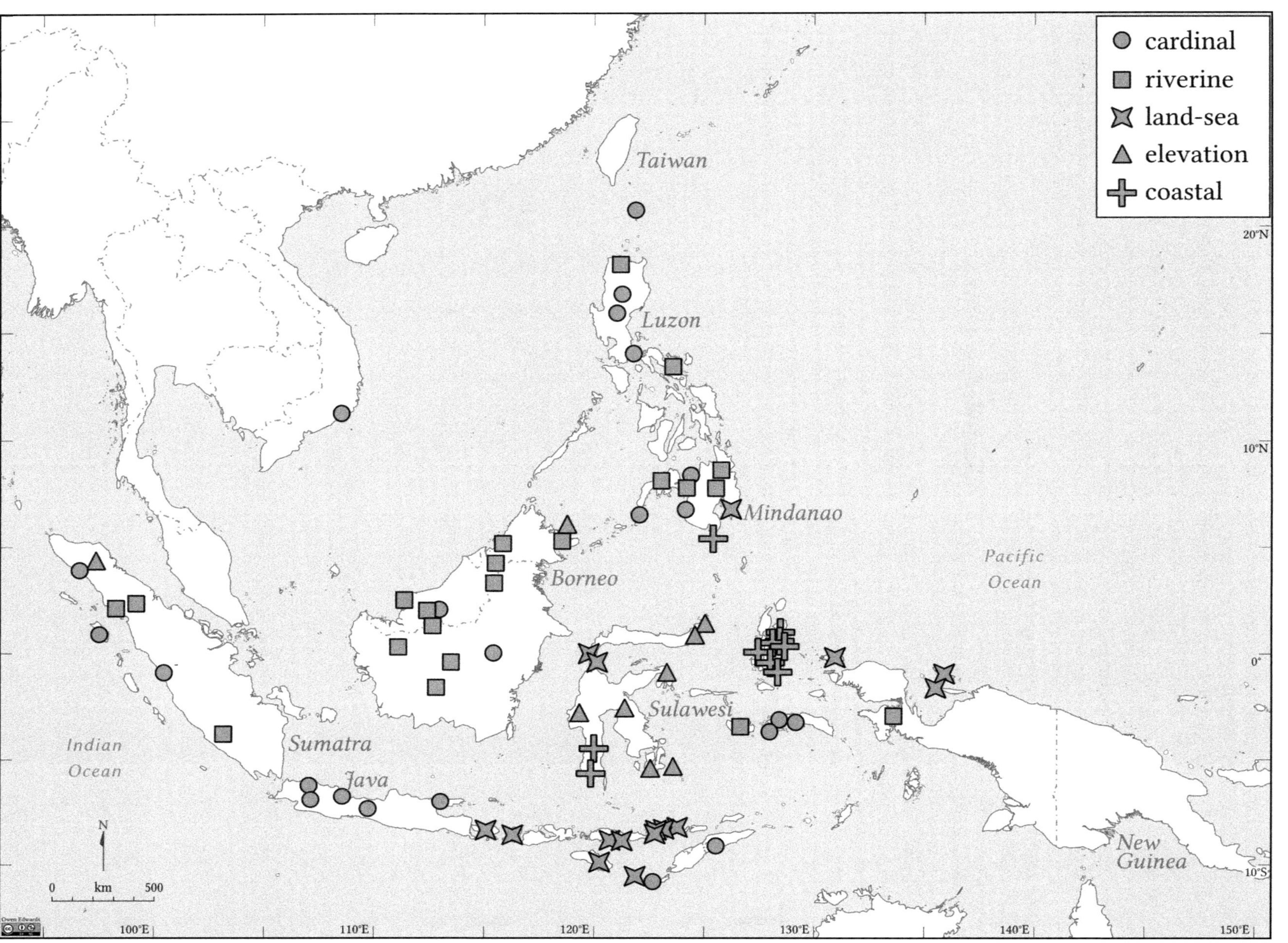


**Map 49.1** Locations of languages in the survey according to primary orientation system type.

seaward–landward axis is fundamental to Austronesian spatial orientation. As noted in the introduction to this chapter, the seaward–landward axis has been described as "the most general principle of macro-orientation" (Blust 2009c: 311) and "the fundamental axis of orientation" (Adelaar 1997: 43) among Austronesian languages. While this is clearly true historically, in our survey we find that languages employing a seaward–landward system are less common than those using riverine, coastal, and cardinal systems. In at least some cases vestiges of a former seaward–landward system remain. This is particularly true among the Philippine languages that we classify as cardinal (cf. Gallego 2018).

In other cases the original seaward–landward system has been drastically reshaped, and where reflexes of PMP *lahud 'seaward' and *daya 'landward' exist, they often behave in unexpected ways, functioning as part of a much more elaborate system of spatial orientation rather than as a simple seaward–landward system. Moreover, reflexes of *daya and *lahud may be incorporated in novel ways, as in Dalat Melanau *dayeh* meaning 'away from river', or Bantik *daya* indicating a location 'somewhat far; across the river'. The diversity of spatial orientation systems found across MPSEA in this survey suggests a much more complex picture, which clearly merits further study.

Finally, we acknowledge that there remain many gaps and potential errors of representation in the survey presented in this chapter. As noted at the outset, one of the greatest challenges for this work is the paucity of available data on the usage of spatial orientation in MPSEA. We hope that this brief survey—however imperfect—will inspire additional documentation of spatial orientation in the region.

## Acknowledgements

We acknowledge the very helpful input received from participants at the Austronesian and Papuan Languages and Linguistics conference in Leiden in June 2019, where an early version of this chapter was presented. We also received much helpful advice from the volume editors. Any remaining errors of fact or interpretation are of course our own. Funding for this research was provided in part by National Science Foundation grant BCS-1761223.

CHAPTER 50

# Negation

JOHAN VAN DER AUWERA, DANIËL VAN OLMEN, AND FRENS VOSSEN

## 50.1 Introduction

Negation is a multifaceted phenomenon. The sentences in (1), taken from Balantak, illustrate four types: (i) the negation of declarative main clause verbal negation, henceforth 'standard negation' (Miestamo 2005); (ii) existential negation; (iii) negative indefiniteness; and (iv) prohibitive negation.[1]

Balantak

(1) a. Standard negation
*Ia* ***sian(ta)*** *taka.*
3SG NEG arrive
'He has not arrived.'
(Van den Berg and Busenitz 2012: 193)

b. Existential negation
*Tama-ngku* ***sian(ta)*** *(isian)* *kaniʔi.*
father-1SG NEG EXIST here
'My father is not here.'
(Van den Berg and Busenitz 2012: 134)

c. Negative indefiniteness
***Saʔanguʔ-po*** ***mian*** ***sianta*** *yakuʔ* *piileʔ.*
one-even person NEG 1SG see
'I saw nobody.' (Van den Berg and Busenitz 2012: 194)

d. Prohibitive negation
***Alia*** *pan-sabak-ko!*
PROH INTR.GER-bite-2SG
'Don't you bite (me)!'
(Van den Berg and Busenitz 2012: 212)

In (1b) we see that the standard negator *sian(ta)* shows up in existential negation, and that it can even express existential negation by itself, for the existence marker *isian* is optional. (1c) illustrates that Balantak does not have a negative pronoun like *nobody*, but instead uses a generic noun *mian* 'person' preceded by the numeral 'one' and the scalar marker 'even', yielding what is literally 'even one person'. (1d) shows that Balantak has a prohibitive negator *alia*, which is different from the negator *sian(ta)* that appears in (1a–c). These aspects of negation have been prominent in the general theoretical and typological literature and these are also the ones we deal with for the Malayo-Polynesian languages of Southeast Asia (henceforth MPSEA).

Of course, there are many other interesting negation types that could be discussed. For example, ascriptive negation, where the ascription of a nominal or adjectival property often involves a negator different from the one used in standard negation, as illustrated with Tboli *là* versus *sundu* in (2). In Tboli, adjectives behave like verbs—so the ascriptive negator is only used with nouns (Forsberg 1992: 102—3).

Tboli

(2) a. Standard negation
***Là*** *munge.*
NEG AV.go.along.1SG
'I'm not going along.' (Forsberg 1992: 102)

b. Ascriptive negation
***Sundu*** *kumù* *Tboli* *du* *ni.*
NEG blanket Tboli it this
'This is not a Tboli blanket.' (Forsberg 1992: 103)

Similarly, prosentential negators—negators that are used as proform for a whole sentence—may be different from the standard negators. This is shown with Batuley *komo* and *foet* in (3).

Batuley, prosentential negation

(3) *Ja,* ***foet,*** ***komo*** *nal* *fusing…*
CONJ NEG NEG 3SG.ACT:get care
'So, no, he doesn't care…' (Daigle 2015: 170)

Phasal negators (corresponding to *not yet* and *no longer* in English, and to be studied together with their positive counterparts *already* and *still* (van der Auwera 2021, Veselinova, Vander Klok, and Asplund, this volume, chapter 51) are no less interesting. One might expect them to be clearly compositional constructs with a standard or ascriptive negator, but they may also have their own dedicated negators, like Tengger Javanese *urung*, different from the standard negator *ora*

[1] For the sake of uniformity, glossing has been standardized, but the orthography remains that of the original sources, except for glottal stop, which is rendered with ʔ.

Johan van der Auwera, Daniël Van Olmen, and Frens Vossen, *Negation.* In: *The Oxford Guide to the Malayo-Polynesian Languages of Southeast Asia.* Edited by: Alexander Adelaar and Antoinette Schapper, Oxford University Press. © Johan van der Auwera, Daniël Van Olmen, and Frens Vossen (2024). DOI: 10.1093/oso/9780198807353.003.0050

(or the ascriptive negator *dudu*) (Conners 2008: 120–1). See Vander Klok, this volume, §31.7 for more on negation in the languages of Java.

Tengger

(4) a. Standard negation
*Dhewek-e* ***ora*** *di-delok* *Amir.*
self-APPL NEG PV-see Amir
'He (himself) wasn't seen by Amir.'
(Conners 2008: 186, Th. Conners p.c.)

b. Phasal negation
*Balé* *desa* ***urung*** *di-jembar-né . . .,*
hall village not.yet PV-broad-APPL
'The village meeting hasn't been expanded yet . . .'
(Conners 2008: 113, Th. Conners p.c.)

These aspects—and others—fall outside the scope of this chapter. For some hypotheses on the standard—ascriptive—prosentential distinctions, see Blust (2009c: 467–71), and for phasal negation, see Florey (2010) and Veselinova, Asplund, and Vander Klok (this volume, chapter 51).

There are other restrictions. For this chapter, we have a database covering 207 languages. Our coverage is very uneven though. For instance, for Basap–Greater Barito we cover around one in four languages, whereas for South Sulawesi coverage is only one in ten languages. Our coverage is uneven in a second sense, going from reasonably satisfactory information on some aspects of standard and prohibitive negation to most unsatisfactory information for negative indefiniteness, with the coverage of existential negation in between. It is also important to stress that we are only dealing with a data set, not a balanced sample (Miestamo, Bakker, and Arppe 2016). Using a balanced sample would result in a sharp reduction of the number of languages. Since the data are suboptimal, we use all of the languages that we surveyed. In any case, the various restrictions add to the tentative nature of our generalizations.

## 50.2 Standard negation

MPSEA languages have an abundance of standard negators. The experts' opinions in the Austronesian Lexical Vocabulary Database and the Austronesian Comparative Dictionary allow us to recognize a fair number of cognates, spread in various branches. But what strikes the eye more is the great variation in forms which do not or not easily fall into cognate sets. This is not surprising; dispersal of MP languages across Southeast Asia occurred in the second millennium BC (Adelaar 2005a: 28). The great heterogeneity can be found even in rather small groups, maybe mostly in the ones involved in long-standing contact with non-Austronesian languages, like the Flores-Lembata languages, as shown by Fricke (2017, 2019).

Some of the standard negators originated from negators of other languages. Thus, Ambonese Malay *seng* comes from Portuguese *sem* 'without' (van Minde 1997: 274) and Kupang Malay *son(de)* from Dutch *zonder* 'without' (Paauw 2008: 138), and *pu*[33] in Hainan Cham is likely to have come from Sanya Mandarin *pu*[33] (Thurgood et al. 2014: 177). Also, the *ba/βa/(u)wa* negators of South Halmahera - West New Guinea (SHWNG) languages have been claimed to be borrowed from Papuan languages (Reesink 2002b: 247).[2] In a few cases one can invoke a 'Jespersen Cycle' (van der Auwera, Krasnoukhova, and Vossen 2021). In this process a negator is typically made emphatic with the repetition of the standard negator or with the addition of a non-negative element. These constructions then gradually lose emphasis, while the non-negative element also becomes a negative marker, resulting in a doubling structure with either identical or different standard negators. Finally, the 'old' negator disappears. Examples (5) to (7) illustrate three stages of a Jespersen Cycle: the emphatic stage in (5); the doubling stage in (6); and the 'undoubled' stage in (7), here resulting from a doubling with repetition. In Tetun the standard negator *la* can be strengthened by the word *ida*.

Tetun

(5) *Sira* ***la*** *tiru* ***ida.***
3PL neg shoot one
'They didn't shoot at us.' (Williams-van Klinken 2002: 89)

In Naueti the strengthener *hoʔo* suggests emphasis for some speakers. However, for most speakers it does not do so, but functions as a negator (Veloso 2016: 78).

Naueti

(6) *Onaata* *ˀnai* ***da*** *hia* ***hoʔo.***
women climb NEG be.good NEG
'Women don't climb well.' (Veloso 2016: 78)

Western Cham

(7) *Rean* *ngăk* *pap* *gah* *nuk* *matau* *non* ***ô.***
dare do evil direction child child.in.law that NEG
'He didn't dare do any more evil things to the son-in-law.' (van der Auwera and Vossen 2015: 28, based on Baumgartner 1998: 5)

Standard negators can also come from existential negators. Consider Tagalog and Tausug: in Tagalog, the standard negator is *hindi/di* and the existential one *wala*, and so the standard and existential negators are clearly different.

[2] Kamholz (2014: 36) agrees about the convergence with reference to the SHWNG and Papuan *ba/βa/(u)wa* negators, but abstains from a claim about the direction of borrowing. Vossen (2016: 157–61) found many more negators similar to *ba/βa/(u)wa* east of the SHWNG area, both in Austronesian and Papuan, and does not give up the Papuan to Austronesian borrowing hypothesis.

Tagalog

(8) a. ***Hindi*** *ko* *nakita* *si* *Rosa*
NEG 1SG PV.PFV.see P Rosa
'I didn't see Rosa.' (Schachter 1987: 947)

b. ***Wala**-ng* *bahay* *doon*
NEGEXIST-LIG house there
'There isn't a house there.' (Schachter 1987: 946)

By contrast, in related languages, such as Tausug in (9), we see cognates of *wala* sharing some of the functions of the standard negator, particularly where states of affairs in the past—and sometimes even the present—are concerned.

Tausug

(9) a. ***Way*** *siya* *miadtu* *pa* *Sūg.*
NEG 3SG.ABS AV.go to Jolo
'She didn't go to Jolo.' (Rubino 2006: 103)

b. ***Diʔ*** *umulank* *insum*
NEG AV.rain tomorrow
'It will not rain tomorrow.' (C. Rubino p.c.)

The rationale for this relationship between negation and tense is that the past can be taken to be real ('realis' in the terminology of Rubino 2006: 103)—it 'existed' and is unalterable—whereas the future does not exist and can unfold in multiple ways. In Acehnese there is a similar division of labour, with *h'an* for the future and *hana* (*han* 'NEG' + *na* 'EXIST'; Durie 1985: 247–8) for the past and the present. The latter is also used for an event in the future, but only if the event is considered inevitable (Durie 1985: 249).

Acehnese

(10) a. ***Hana**=lôn=jak.*
NEG=1SG=go
'I didn't go/I don't go.' (Durie 1985: 248)

b. ***H'an**=lôn=jak.*
NEG=1SG=go
'I won't go.' (Durie 1985: 249)

c. *Singöh* ***hana**=ta=meu-uroe=raya.*
tomorrow NEG=1PL.INCL=INTR-day=great
'Tomorrow we won't celebrate a festival.'
(M. Durie p.c.)

In this process the negative existential may become the sole exponent of standard negation and the language may create a new negative existential marker. Thus, the Standard Indonesian standard negator *tidak* is claimed to derive from a **ti* negator (Adelaar 1992a: 144; A. Adelaar p.c.) and the existence marker *ada*. For negative existence, Standard Indonesian now uses *tidak ada* 'not exist', adding the existence marker to the negator (McDonnell and Tadmor 2015). Note that the 'double existence' form *tidak ada*—'double' because *ada* is also part of *tidak*—can develop into a standard negator, too, as shown by the perfect negator *thraa* in Sri Lankan Malay. This negator must have combined a negator with a form of the existential *aada* (Nordhoff 2009: 254). The form *thraa* maintains negative existential uses, but we also get the 'double existence' constructions *thraada* and *thàrà-aada* (Nordhoff 2009: 297). For more information on Malayic negation, see McDonnell et al., this volume, §29.5.2 and Slomanson, this volume, §18.4ff.

In other cases, a negator may combine with something other than the default existence marker. In Mualang, the standard negator *naday* is taken to derive from *ni* 'NEG' and *aday* 'EXIST' (Tjia 2007: 240). For negative existence the language standardly uses *nisi*, from *ni* 'NEG' and *isiʔ*, the root of another existence marker (A. Adelaar, p.c.). *Isiʔ* combines with the antipassive prefix *ba-* to yield *bisiʔ*, a verb of expressing existence (Tjia 2007: 242). The root *isiʔ* ultimately derives from the PMP noun meaning 'flesh; content' (Blust and Trussel 2020).

Mualang

(11) a. *Ha!* *Aday* *s-ikuʔ* *geramaʔ* *besay!*
uh EXIST one-CLF crab big
'Uh! There is a big crab.' (Tjia 2007: 124)

b. *Sidaʔ* ***naday*** *ba-jalay* *lamaʔ.*
3PL NEG ANTIP-road long
'They did not walk long.' (Tjia 2007: 240, 242)

c. *Inay* ***nisiʔ*** *da* *dapur.*
mother NEGEXIST LOC kitchen
'Mother wasn't in the kitchen.' (Tjia 2007: 242)

These kinds of processes have been studied under the names of 'Croft Cycle' or 'Negative Existential Cycle' (Veselinova 2013, 2016; Hamari and Veselinova eds. 2020). There is an interesting twist here. The Negative Existential Cycle assumes that a language has a standard negator prior to the invasion of the existential one into the standard negation domain. This is not necessary: the starting point could be a language in which the negation of a verb is done existentially, with a construal of 'x does not V' as 'x Ving does not exist' (cf. Miestamo 2005: 206–8 for a motivation of this construal in terms of stativity).

The formal heterogeneity of standard negators contrasts with the great homogeneity in other respects: MPSEA standard negators are usually preverbal, standard negation usually has just one exponent and this is usually a syntactically unbound form, not an affix or a clitic or a verb. The fact that MPSEA negators are typically free forms aligns well with what we find in the world at large (Dryer 2013m), as does the fact that we typically have just one exponent of negation. Single exponence makes functional sense: clausal negation is a simple operation and why shouldn't a single clausal marker be sufficient? As to the preverbal position, this aligns MPSEA languages with what we find elsewhere too. And again, the explanation is functional. Already Jespersen (1917: 5) had the intuition that:

> [T]here is a natural tendency, also for the sake of clearness, to place the negative first, or at any rate as soon as possible, very often immediately before the particular word to be negatived [sic] (generally the verb).

Horn (1989) gave it the name 'Neg First' principle, although 'Neg Early' would have been a better choice, and later research showed this principle to be correct for the world at large (Dryer 2013l; Vossen 2016).[3] The principle is also relevant for Austronesian as a whole, as has been observed by many (e.g. Reesink 2002b: 244; Klamer et al 2008: 130; Vossen and van der Auwera 2014: 61; Schapper 2015a: 120) and no less so for MPSEA languages. The majority of the MPSEA languages surveyed here have a preverbal single negator. Note that the 'Neg Early' tendency does not only hold for standard negators, it also motivates the early position of existential negators. If the latter develop into standard negators, they may hold on to their erstwhile position, this being an additional motivation for an early and thus preverbal position of the standard negator.

Circumverbal and postverbal negators also occur, as already illustrated in (6) and (7). They may be due to the workings of a Jespersen Cycle, as has already been illustrated with (5) to (7). It is important to realize though that the Jespersen Cycle itself does not say anything about the position of a negator: it merely says that one can repeat a negator or that a negator can turn a non-negative element into a negator. What we need to add in order to explain that the second negator of the doubling construction follows the verb is the hypothesis that in MPSEA the starting point of the Jespersen Cycle is a single preverbal negator, which means that there is 'more space' on the other side of the verb. Also—and this takes us back to the relation of standard and existential negators—if the existential negator is the origin of the standard negator and if the existential negator goes to the right periphery of the clause, the standard negator may equally do that and be postverbal.

Circumverbal and postverbal negators are typical for languages that have been thought to be significantly altered by contact with non-MPSEA languages. In the eastern part of the region under investigation, the Malayo-Polynesian languages including those close to New Guinea's Bird's Head (Reesink 2002b; Klamer et al 2008: 130–4) and the Flores-Lembata languages (Fricke 2019) were, or are, in contact with Papuan languages (see Schapper, this volume, chapter 22 for more on the Papuan contact zone), and this has been claimed to have had an effect on the position of negation. Of course, contact itself does not explain why the MPSEA languages in question should have developed postverbal negators. We need to know how standard negation operates in the contact languages and what the direction of interference was. For the eastern languages the case seems fairly clear: the current or erstwhile coterritorial Papuan languages typically just have, or tend towards having, clause-final negation and the borrowing direction, at least for negation, as argued by Reesink (2002b); Klamer et al. (2008: 131–4); and Fricke (2017) (see also Ross 2017: 793–5), is from Papuan to MPSEA. Here the MPSEA languages arguably started from a preverbal negator and then underwent a contact-instigated Jespersen Cycle with their own material or even with a borrowed Papuan negator (Reesink 2002b: 247) or replaced their preverbal negator with a postverbal negator, again either of their own making or borrowed from a Papuan language. The scenario is all the more plausible when we realize that both the Papuan negators and the contact-instigated MPSEA ones are not just postverbal but more or less clause-final, which is the dominant order in Papuan languages. The hedge 'more or less' here is due to the fact there could be other contenders for the clause-final position. In Taba, for example, the continuous aspect marker is also clause-final and wins out when it occurs together with the negator (Bowden 2001: 335).

A similar scenario holds for the western contact zone on Sri Lanka. In Sri Lankan Malay the negative particle *thraa*, a negative existential used for perfect tenses, is postverbal and even clause-final (Nordhoff 2009: 257). Varieties of Malay interacted with Tamil and Sinhala since the mid-seventeenth century (Nordhoff 2009: 11–13) and both contact languages have postverbal and clause-final negators (Lehmann 1989: 228–31; Chandralal 2010: 13, 135).[4] There is also a western contact zone in Vietnam, where the Chamic family of Western Cham in (7) has been in contact for two millennia with Bahnaric languages of the Austroasiatic family (see Sidwell, this volume, §20.3 on this contact). The Bahnaric languages have preverbal, circumverbal, as well as postverbal standard negators, just like the Chamic languages (see Brunelle and Jensen, this volume, §30.4.3), and it is difficult to decide on the borrowing direction (van der Auwera and Vossen 2015).

On the western perimeter of the area under consideration, Moken and Moklen are also intriguing. They also have postverbal negators, viz. *ha* (Moken; Chantanakomes 1980: 7) and *hãh* (Moklen; Larish 2005: 7). These negators resemble the postverbal negator *oh/ô* in Chamic, illustrated in (7).

[3] The accounts by Dryer (2013l) and Vossen (2016) are not directly comparable as the former defines 'preverbal' relative to the lexical verb, whereas Vossen defines it as relative to the inflected verb, whether lexical or auxiliary. Still, they both support the Jespersen conjecture.

[4] This further relates to the fact that Sri Lankan Malay is SOV, distinguishing it strongly from other Malay vernaculars, as pointed out at least since Adelaar (1991). Interestingly, there are also two morphological standard negators (Nordhoff 2009: 297–301), which are prefixal and thus classified as 'preverbal'.

There is no evidence that they interacted with those of the surrounding languages (like Thai or Urak Lawoi'), yielding the conjecture that they developed their postverbal negation internally. Interestingly, Larish (1985: 523) reports a dedicated negative strengthener, which in a Jespersen perspective counts as a prelude to a doubling construction, like in Tetun (5) (Vossen 2016: 119). This strengthener obligatorily occurs preverbally—thus illustrating a right-to-left direction of the Jespersen Cycle.

Moklen
(12) *Cəy* ***laʔ*** *kutɛːn* ***hãh.***
1SG EMPH.NEG lie NEG
'I am not lying.' (Larish 2005: 523)

Just as postverbal negators may be more or less clause-final, preverbal negators can be more or less clause-initial. But there is a difference. The postverbal position of a negator is typically a trivial consequence of it taking up a clause-final position. For the clause-initial position, the dependency goes the other way. If the negator must be in front of the verb and the verb has a strong tendency to be close to the beginning of the sentence, as in the 'verb-initial' pattern typical for Philippine or northern languages, the negator may end up in clause-initial position. Of interest is also that the clause-initial negator need not be adjacent to the verb, in the sense that it may attract clitics, as in Yakan (13b), compared to (13a) (Brainard and Behrens 2002: 121–5, 127–31).

Yakan
(13) a. ***Gaʔi*** *belli-ne* *buwas-in.*
NEG buy-3SG rice-DEF
'She will not buy the rice.'
(Brainard and Behrens 2002: 124)

b. ***Gaʔ****=iye* *mag-bella* *ensiniʔ.*
NEG=ABS.3SG INTR-cook earlier
'She didn't cook earlier.'
(Brainard and Behrens 2002: 128)

## 50.3 Existential negation

A negative existential construction says that something or someone does not exist. One would expect such a construction to be compositional and simply combine a negator with a positive existential. However, from a cross-linguistic study of negative existentials, Veselinova (2013: 137), we know that it is common for negative existentials to bear no formal relation to positive existentials. Her study is based on a sample of ninety-five languages and non-compositionality is found in 40% of them. MPSEA languages have both compositional and non-compositional strategies, too, and we will see that the typology of MPSEA languages is more complicated than just a division between two types according to a [± compositional] parameter.

The first thing to note is that languages may have more than one positive and/or negative existential. This was already shown with Balantak and Mualang. In Balantak, for instance, the negative existential is the same as the standard negator and in the negative existential it may be accompanied by an existence marker (see (1)). Sri Lankan Malay offers an extreme example. It has two positive existential constructions and, depending on how one counts, six to eight negative ones. The positive ones are *aada* and *duuduk*. *Duuduk* is a normal verb, which also has the lexical senses 'sit' and 'stay', the ones from which the existential sense derived. *Aada* is often defective, that is, not taking the normal verbal morphology (Nordhoff 2009: 164–9). On the negative side, there are three counterparts to *duuduk*, viz. the compositional *thàràduuduk* for the past, and *thamaduuduk* for the non-past, but there is also *duuduk thraa* for the perfect (Nordhoff 2009: 672; S. Nordhoff p.c.), which is partially compositional, for *thraa* is itself already a negative existential, serving as the non-compositional *thraa* for *aada* in the present (Nordhoff 2009: 166–7). As counterparts for *aada* there are also the compositional forms *thàrà-aada*—for the past, less so for the present—and *thama-ada*—mainly for the non-past (Nordhoff 2009: 166–7, 297–300). *Thàrà-aada* also comes in a contracted form *thraada*, used for the present (Nordhoff 2009: 207). Tagalog also has several types, First, there is a pair formed by a positive existential *may* or *mayroon*, the latter containing a deictic *roon* 'there' element, and a non-compositional negative *wala*. Then there is a pair with a positive *magka* or *magkaroon* and its compositional negative *hindi magka* or *hindi magkaroon*. But there is also negative *wala roon*, which was "initially discovered through a web-search [. . .] never-mentioned in grammars or textbooks though the speakers [. . .] consulted will accept them (with some surprise) as grammatical" (Sabbagh 2009: 690). The 'ordinary' *wala* was already illustrated in (8b); (14a) shows its positive counterpart, and (14b) is the only recently 'discovered' *wala roon* construction.

Tagalog
(14) a. ***May(roon)*** *bigas* *na* *raw* *sa* *tindahan.*
EXIST rice now RPRT LOC store
'There's rice in the story now, they say.'
(Himmelmann 2005b: 355)

b. *[. . .] at* ***wala*** ***roo-ng*** *trabaho [. . .]*
and NEGEXIST there-LIG work
'[. . . because] there was no work [. . .]'
(Sabbagh 2009: 690)

We mention this 'discovery', because for most MPSEA languages there are no web-based searches followed by consultation of native speakers.

In the previous paragraph we have already started to illustrate the different (pairs of) existentials. The simplest type is the fully compositional one, as with Sri Lankan Malay *duduk – tham-duuduk*, Tagalog *magka(roon) – hindi magka(roon)* or with Cotabato Manobo *duen – yak duen* in (15).

Cotabato Manobo
(15) ***Yak duen*** *ini kawal amuk [...]*
NEG EXIST this shirt if
'There would (not) be this shirt if...' (Kerr 1988: 67)

A more complex compositional type is shown in Taliwang (16). The negative existential *nəña* has a clear negator *nə-*, but the second part is not the positive existential *loʔ*.

Taliwang
(16) a. ***Loʔ*** *pɨn kayuʔ niŋ buŋkak bale.*
EXIST tree wood at back house
'There is a tree at the back of the house.' (Hayami-Allen 1995: 55)

b. ***Nə*** *ku=rəa lalo lo amerika.*
NEG 1SG=want go to America
'I won't go to America.' (Hayami-Allen 1995: 33)

c. ***Nəña*** *pipɨs ku.*
NEGEXIST money 1SG
'I don't have any money.' (Hayami-Allen 1995: 35)

Another special compositional form is Tagalog *wala roon*. Its first part is already a negative existential, and the second 'there' part is neither positive nor negative, nor is it existential. Yet another intermediate subtype is found in Bonggi: the standard negator *nd(a')* is part of the negative existential *ndara*, but the positive existential is not just *ara*, but *kiara*, with *ki-* marking that the existence is positive (Boutin 1994: 76, 86). Note also that it is not always obvious to decide whether there is a relation between the positive and negative existential. In Buol the positive existential is *oulo*, the standard negators are *dia* and *diili* (Zobel 2005: 631), and the negative existential is *diauon* (E. Zobel p.c.). The form *diauon* easily betrays a negative morpheme *dia*, but that leaves us with *-uon*, which does not seem related to *oulo*. However, E. Zobel (p.c.) points to Usup (1986: 306, 373) for the hypothesis that both *-uon* and *oulo* derive from an existential protoform **oluʔon*.

In a third type, neither compositional nor non-compositional, the negative existential is just a negator, either one of the standard negators, as in Tausug (9) and Acehnese (10), or the only standard negator of the language, as in Dupaningan Agta.

Dupaningan Agta
(17) a. ***Atoy****=la i ruprup.*
EXIST=still DEF coffee
'There is still coffee.' (Robinson 2011: 171)

b. ***Awan****=ak nag=langoy.*
NEG=1SG.NOM COMPL.AV=swim
'I didn't swim.' (Robinson 2011: 173)

c. ***Awan****=kan dena=na.*
NEGEXIST-HSY PL.mother=3SG.GEN
'They say his mother and her companions aren't there.' (Robinson 2011: 172)

The fourth type is the non-compositional type: the negative existential contains neither a recognizable negator nor a positive existential. We have illustrated this with Tagalog (8b): the negative existential is *wala* and it bears no relation to any negator or to the positive existential *may(roon)*. Again, as illustrated with Buol, it is sometimes difficult to decide on the compositionality. The standard negator in Tukang Besi is *mbaeka*, the positive existential is *ane* and the negative existential is *mbeaʔe*. It seems possible that the latter is a contracted version of *mbaeka* and *ane*.

The fifth type involves the positive existential construction without an overt marker. Since one would assume that most if not all languages have some strategy to express existence, it will be difficult to decide whether this strategy is dedicated or not. Consider Ambel, for which Arnold (2018a: 351–3) states that the mere expression of a noun phrase can also express existence. Interestingly, negative existence does have an overt marker of the non-compositional type, but it alternates with the standard negator.

Ambel
(18) a. *Y-íy-a há* ***po.***
1SG-eat-PARA rice NEG
'I didn't eat rice.' (Arnold 2018a: 433)

b. *Kawé pu-ma mé ape [...]*
Kawe down-DIST people but
'Down from Kawe there were people, but...' (Arnold 2018a: 353)

c. *Korek* ***po, mámbayn.***
lighters NEG NEGEXIST
'There were no lighters, they didn't exist.' (Arnold 2018a: 354)

Taba represents a similar situation: its 'indigenous' positive existential uses no overt existential marker, although there is an alternative with an overt marker borrowed from North Moluccan Malay (Bowden 2001: 325). For the negative, however, there is an overt marker, viz. the standard negator (Bowden 2001: 336). Yet a third language with this kind of zero positive existential but an overt negative one is Ambai (Silzer 1983: 76, 183, 216). Interestingly these three languages are all SHWNG languages, spoken in the Papuan contact zone. It begs the question whether Papuan languages could have had an influence here. However, even if we do find a similar structure in a Papuan language, as in Tidore, this does not imply Papuan influence, and the contact interference could have gone from Austronesian to 'Papuan' (Van Staden 2000: 217).

Himmelmann (2005a: 138) considers the non-compositional strategy to be 'very common' in 'symmetrical voice' languages of the Philippine-type, and not common in the 'Malayic' languages. Our data seem to support this claim, but this does not mean that all Philippine-type languages have it—Cotaboto Manobo has the *duen* 'EXIST'—*endà duen* 'NEG EXIST' pair (Kerr 1988: 67–70) nor that Malayic languages cannot have it—Sri Lankan Malay has it, but then it has the compositional type too, reminding us that there is more to the classification than just [± compositional]. And, more generally, there is much more to be studied about (negative) existentials. Some of it will reappear in §50.4.

## 50.4 Negative indefiniteness

Negative indefiniteness concerns what English does with words like *nobody, nothing, never, nowhere*, or negative noun phrases like *no satisfaction*. MPSEA grammars treat this domain very poorly, so in what follows we cannot aspire to claims about what is frequent or rare. We also restrict the discussion to negative human indefiniteness corresponding to *nobody*, even though we know that other negative indefinites (such the ones corresponding to *nothing* or *no satisfaction*) do not have to function in the same way as *nobody* (see, e.g., van der Auwera and De Lisser 2019).

In order to convey what English does with *nobody*, MPSEA languages exhibit various strategies, but what immediately strikes the eye is that the MPSEA languages appear not to have one-word negative pronouns.[5] In Nias we get close. In Nias the interrogative 'who' is *hata* or *hanata*. It also has a so-called 'free choice' use—the use of *anybody* in *anybody can do that*—and there is a reduplicated form *hanata-nata* that Brown (2001: 231) has only found with negation. The interrogative and negative indefinite uses are shown in (19a), the free choice one in (19b).

[5] This is a good point to illustrate that not all negatives function the same way. Taba has no word for 'nobody' but there is one for 'nothing', viz. *nol* from a meaning 'zero' (Bowden 2001: 242), but, no less interesting, it is borrowed from Dutch, probably through Malay, which also has this *nol* use (John Bowden; A. Adelaar p.c.).

Nias

(19) a. - ***Hata*** *zi=fao* *khö-u?*
who REL=join DAT-2SG.POSS
'Who is going with you?'
- ***Löna*** ***hanata-nata.***
NEGEXIST who.who
'No one. I'm going alone'. (Brown 2001: 134)

b. ***Hata*** *ni* *anda* *z=o-okhöta,* *ande*
who 2PL PROX REL=have-possession DIST
*zi-talo-bali* *kafalo* *ba* *mbanua=nde.*
REL-RES-turn head LOC village=PROX
'Whoever amongst you has possessions, he is the one who will become the head of this village.' (Brown 2001: 134)

MPSEA languages make use of a range of strategies to express this. One strategy is to combine whatever construction the language uses for *somebody* (often just the word for 'person') with the clausal negator. This construction can be either pronominal or nominal. This is cross-linguistically the more frequent strategy (van der Auwera and Van Alsenoy 2016: 483, 2018: 113), but in MPSEA languages it is rare. Yamdena could be an example, with the numeral *sa* 'one' used either pronominally or adnominally with the noun *tomwat* 'person' for 'somebody' and together with the standard negator *to* for 'nobody'. When *tomwat* is present, the 'somebody' strategy is nominal.

Yamdena

(20) a. *Kam-keban* ***(tomwatar)*** ***sa.***
1PL.EXCL-see person one
'We have seen someone.' (Drabbe 1926: 45)

b. ***Sa*** ***to*** *ni* *brani* *ma* *nkafreje* *i.*
one NEG 3SG.POSS courage to quarrel 3SG
'Nobody had the courage to contradict him.' (Drabbe 1926: 45)

In Karo Batak the interrogative 'who' allows both free choice and negative polarity uses and in that case it is optionally followed by an emphasizer *pé*. It is the *pé* version that combines with the clausal negator to express a negative indefinite.

Karo Batak

(21) a. *Adi* *kin* ***isé*** *maba* *bunga* *encolé, [...]*
if EMPH who ACT.carry flower encolé
'If any were to be carrying encolé flowers, ...' (Woollams 1996: 231)

b. ***Isé*** ***pé*** *la* *meteh* *perjubana*
who EMPH NEG ACT.know marriage.their
*sumbang.*
incestuous
'Nobody knows their marriage was incestuous.' (Woollams 1996: 231)

The free choice strategy seems to be the more common one, as in Tagalog (22).

Tagalog
(22) a. ***Sino-man*** *ang* *narito,* *ma-ki~kita* *iyan.*
who-INDEF DET ST.PFV.here PV-IPFV~see that
'Whoever is here will see that.' (Schachter and Otanes 1972: 539; N. Himmelmann p.c.)

b. *Hindi* *ko* *ga~gaw-in* *iyon* *para* ***kaninu-man.***
NEG 1SG.GEN IPFV~do-PV that for whom-INDEF
'I won't do that for anyone.' (Schachter and Otanes 1972: 537; N. Himmelmann p.c.)

The third strategy is an existential one. We get a negative existence marker followed by a verb without a representation of the non-existent human (i.e. without a representation of an equivalent to *somebody*, *anybody*, or *nobody*). Thus in Belait (23) the negative existential *ndadeh* is immediately followed by a verb that says what nobody eats.

Belait
(23) *Waris* *kamay* ***ndadeh*** *k-uman* *kammal,* *aram* *[...]*
lineage 1PL.EXCL NEGEXIST AF-eat colugo pangolin
'In our lineage, nobody eats colugo, pangolin ...'
(Clynes 2005: 439)

This structure is most often treated as a headless relative clause or a nominalization and seen as a sign of a "lack of distributional differences between nouns and verbs" (Himmelmann 2005a: 138; Kaufman 2009b: 194). Another way of looking at this, not necessarily incompatible, is to say that at least some MPSEA languages prefer to construe a non-existent state of affairs to construing a non-existent participant in the state of affairs, leaving the non-existence of the participant implicit. What is negated in (23) is the eating of some animals, and when there is no eating of them, it is implied that nobody eats them. The ease to negate states of affairs also shows in the fact, described earlier, that the standard negators may derive from existential negators. In (9a), repeated below, there was no going of her to Jolo, hence she didn't go to Jolo.

Tausug
(9) a. ***Way*** *siya* *miadtu* *pa* *Sūg.*
NEG 3SG.ABS AF.go to Jolo
'She didn't go to Jolo.' (Rubino 2006: 103; C. Rubino p.c.)

(24) sketches the parallels.

(24) NEGEXIST [she go to Jolo]
↓
she didn't go to Jolo
NEGEXIST [eat colugo and pangolin]
↓
nobody eats colugo and pangolin

In some languages we find a negative existential serving to express standard negation (e.g. Tausug (9)). In others, they serve to express negative indefiniteness (e.g. Belait (23)). In still others, we find both, as in Cebuano (25).

Cebuano
(25) a. ***Walaʔ****=siya* *ni-adto.*
NEGEXIST=3SG.NOM AF-go
'He didn't go.'

b. *O* ***walaʔ-wa=y*** *mo-sugat* *sa* *ako.*
DISC NEGEX-NEGEXIST=NEUT AF-get OBL 1SG.POSS
'So, nobody will get me?'
(Tanangkingsing 2009: 213, 239)

The fourth and final strategy is a combination of the existential strategy with a representation of the non-existent entity. Thus, Bonggi uses the common noun *lama* for *somebody* and it combines this with a negative existential for 'nobody'.

Bonggi
(26) a. *Si* *Tereib teho-odn* ***lama.***
PIV Tereib steal-LOC person
'Someone stole from Tereib.' (Boutin 1994: 142)

b. ***Nd-ara*** ***lama*** *m-apit* *diaadn.*
NEG-EXIST person AF-stop.by 1SG.ACC
'Nobody stops by to see me.' (Boutin 1994: 107)

Included here are cases in which the verb following the existential marks its clause as relative.

Salako
(27) ***Anàʔ*** ***adà*** ***an****=nanaŋ* *ià.*
NEG EXIST REL=see 3
'Nobody saw him.' (Adelaar 2005e: 40)

Unsurprisingly, positive indefinites can also avail themselves of an existential strategy. We see this in Arta (28) and there is no other straightforward way to express positive indefiniteness—or negative indefiniteness for that matter.

Arta
(28) *Atti:* *n-inta=ku.*
EXIST PST.PV-see=1SG.ERG
'I saw someone.' (Y. Kimoto, p.c.)

Nias also uses existentials, except that for positive indefiniteness there is also a non-existential strategy.

Nias
(29) a. ***So*** ***(samösa/niha)*** *s/zi=möi.*
EXIST (one.some/person) REL=come
'Someone is coming.' (Brown 2001: 135)

b. *Na* *la-fa-bu?a* *darodaro*
if 3PL.REAL-CAUS-move seat.of.law
*mate* ***niha.***
die person
'If you move a seat of law, someone will die.' (Brown 2001: 234)

Thus we may conclude that the existential strategies are more strongly associated with negative indefiniteness. And probably not only in Nias.

We asked four speakers of Standard Malay (M-S; Malaysia) to translate both 'somebody called me' and 'nobody called you' into 'naturally occurring language'. Three of them also supplied judgements on regional or colloquial peninsular Malay varieties. We also consulted speakers of Standard Indonesian, Sundanese, Balinese, Banjar, and Kulisusu. For negative indefinites all of the twelve translations featured a negative existential strategy, like the one in (30).

Standard Malay
(30) ***Tiada*** *se-siapa* *meng-hubung-i* *kamu.*
NEGEX one-who ACT-connect-TR 2
'Nobody called you.'

For positive indefinites eight translations had an existential strategy as well, like the one in (31a), and four had non-existential ones, like the one in (31b).

Standard Malay
(31) a. ***Ada*** ***orang*** *panggil* *saya.*
EXIST person call 1SG

b. ***Se~se-orang*** *meng-hubung-i* *saya.*
REDUP-one-person ACT-connect-TR 1SG
'Someone called me.'

The 'experiment' illustrates another factor steering the choice between existential and non-existential strategies.[6] We also asked the native speakers to render 'I called nobody/I didn't call anybody' into 'naturally occurring language'. Nine of the twelve judgements showed a non-existential structure, such as the one in (32), two an existential strategy, and one had both an existential and a non-existential one.

[6] Yet another factor influencing the choice between existential and non-existential strategies concerns the occurrence of more than one indefinite, as in *he didn't say anything to anybody*. Haspelmath (1997: 54–5) claims that Tagalog can use the existential only for one of the indefinites.

Standard Malay
(32) *Saya* ***tidak*** *menghubungi* ***siapa~siapa.***
1SG NEG ACT.connect.TR REDUP~who
'I called nobody.'

We thus see a preverbal–postverbal parameter at play. We need this parameter for Indonesian: Sneddon et al. (2010: 178) point out that the reduplicated *siapa~siapa* cannot occur preverbally, a position only allowing *siapa pun* ('who even') or, as shown in (33), *se-orang pun* ('one-person even').

Standard Indonesian
(33) ***Tidak*** ***se-orang*** ***pun*** *mengenal* *saya* *di* *sini.*
NEG one-person even ACT.know 1SG LOC here
'Nobody knows me here.' (Sneddon et al. 2010: 178)

Note that (33) is a non-existential strategy, which appeared in none of the twelve judgements. In a final experiment we asked for 'He called somebody', with an indefinite that is positive as well postverbal, two properties that are not conducive to an existential strategy. We had eleven translations, ten of which were non-existential ones.

Interestingly, in the typological literature the preverbal–postverbal parameter shows up mostly in the analysis of 'negative concord', a term that usually refers to the phenomenon that a semantically single negation is expressed both on the clausal and the negative indefinite level (van der Auwera and Van Alsenoy 2018). Cross-linguistically negative concord is often obligatory when the negative indefinite follows the verb and impossible when it precedes the verb. In MPSEA this phenomenon has only been reported for Chamorro.

Chamorro
(34) a. ***Ti*** *hubisita* ***ni*** ***un*** ***taotao.***
NEG visited NEG one person
'I didn't visit even one person.' (Chung 1998: 142)

b. ***Ni*** ***unu*** *istaba* *guini* *gi* *paingi.*
NEG one was here LOC last.night
'No one was here last night.' (Chung 1998: 268)

The fact that we don't find it elsewhere is not surprising: MPSEA has few negative indefinites. Neither is it surprising that we find it in Chamorro: Spanish has the same kind of negative concord and Chamorro seems likely to have been influenced by Spanish here (Van Alsenoy 2014: 90–4).

## 50.5 Prohibitive negation

Prohibitive negation involves calling on the hearer(s) not to realize some state of affairs. In this section, we will focus on so-called 'canonical' cases, that is, cases with a(n implicit) second person subject, and exclude 'non-canonical' ones, which have meanings like 'let's not' and 'let them not' (see Aikhenvald 2010: 17 for the distinction). Moreover, we will only consider the canonical cases that are "suitable for the performance of the full range of [negative] directive speech acts" (Jary and Kissine 2016: 132)—thus not including those with just a preventive sense, for instance.[7] In other words, we are interested in the primary way(s) in which a language gets someone not to do something—excluding indirect expressions like 'you will not!' if there exists a construction expressing 'don't!' more directly. However, if such an indirect case constitutes a language's principal strategy to convey the meaning, it will be taken into account (cf. Schalley 2008: 24–35 on (in)direct primary imperative strategies).

Let us first address this final issue, that is, whether or not MPSEA possesses dedicated prohibitive constructions. Our survey suggests that the answer is, overwhelmingly, yes. Ambiguity between a directive and a non-directive/assertive interpretation in the primary prohibitive strategy is explicitly reported for just a few languages. The Kapampangan construction in (35) can serve as an example. For a handful of other languages, the information in grammars seems to point in the same direction, though it is not entirely conclusive.

Kapampangan
(35) ***É*** *ka* *púpunta* *kéni.*
NEG 2SG come.DUR here
'Don't come here!' or 'You aren't coming here.'
(Gonzalez 1981: 319)

Languages of this type are greatly outnumbered by those for which we have clear(er) evidence of specialized constructions for the expression of 'don't!'. MPSEA languages as a whole are probably not unique in this respect: preliminary research (see Van Olmen 2019) indicates that only approximately one sixth of the world's languages lack a dedicated prohibitive.

One way in which MPSEA prohibitives tend to be specialized is the use of distinct negators, not found in standard negation contexts. Balantak *alia* 'don't!' in (1d) is a case in point and so is South Nuaulu in (36). Its regular negator is *tewa* in (36a) but the prohibitive in (36b) features *pene* instead. The origins of such dedicated negators are mostly obscure. Still, two recurring sources in the data are 'not want' and 'lest, so that not', as (36c) and (37b) respectively illustrate. The pathway from negative volition or negative consequence to prohibition is well known in the typological literature (e.g. Aikhenvald 2010: 351–62).

South Nuaulu
(36) a. *Au* *neke* *munu* ***tewa.***
1SG sleep soundly NEG
'I didn't sleep soundly.' (Bolton 1990: 126)

b. ***Pene*** *o-ai* *ana* *rei-mo!*
PROH 2PL-eat rice this-PROX
'Don't eat that rice!' (Bolton 1990: 127)

c. *Mansia* *maina-ya* *o-**pene**-so.*
people elder-PL 3PL-not.want.to-3PL
'The elders didn't want to.' (Bolton 1990: 128)

Tukang Besi
(37) a. ***Bar(a)*** *ʔu-kede* *i* *atu!*
PROH 2SG.REAL-sit OBL there
'Don't sit there!' (Donohue 1999a: 454)

b. *No-wuju-ʔe* ***bara*** *no-wila*
3.REAL-persuade-3.OBJ lest 3.REAL-go
*peʔesa-no.*
own-3.POSS
'They persuaded him not to go on his own.'
(Donohue 1999a: 393)

There are obviously languages whose prohibitive strategy does not involve a distinct negator. In our data, the phenomenon is characteristic of—though not restricted to—North Luzon in particular. Consider Dupaningan Agta in (38) and (17), for instance, where *awan* is used across the board. If a language employs one of a number of standard negators differing in tense for its prohibitive, it will typically be the future one, as in Inati (Pennoyer 1986–1987: 36). The reason for this tendency is the future-oriented nature of directivity, of course. Another interesting case is Wamesa: standard negation is expressed by *=va* and prohibitive negation by *sa= . . . =va*, as in (39a) and (39b) respectively. However, the latter also appears in other contexts, namely for negation contrary to expectation. In (39c), for example, it serves to contradict the reasonable assumption that a dog pursuing a pig will seize it. One explanation for its usage in (39b) may be that telling someone not to do something is often done in situations when they were expected to behave differently.

Dupaningan Agta
(38) ***Awan****=mo* *alap-an!*
NEG=2SG.GEN get-PV
'Don't get it!' (Robinson 2011: 174)

Wamesa
(39) a. *Yau* *i-sayore* *mararea=wa-i=**va.***
1SG 1SG-see child=DET-SG=NEG
'I don't see the child.' (Gasser 2014: 187)

[7] The use of apprehensional morphemes, that is, grammatical markers of fear (see Vuillermet 2018: 256–60), as warnings (e.g. 'watch out, you might . . .!') will equally be left out of consideration. In fact, apprehensional morphology in general, including avertive 'lest, so that not', is beyond the scope of the present chapter for reasons of space—despite the fact that it seems quite common in Austronesian (e.g. Lichtenberk 1995) and MPSEA (e.g. (37b)).

b. ***Sa***=*r<u>a* *so* *sasi* *dire*=***va***!
NEG=2SG-go to salt edge=NEG
'Don't go to the beach!' (Gasser 2014: 188)

c. *Wona* *ve-usar* *pimuna-pa-i*
dog ESS-chase pig=DET-SG
***sa***=*t<i>pur-i*=***va***.
NEG=3SG-grasp-3SG=NEG
'The dog that is chasing the pig isn't catching it.' (Gasser 2014: 188)

In the present data, languages with a specialized prohibitive negator occur much more often than those without one. MPSEA seems to be similar to Austronesian in general (see Blust 2013a: 473–7) in this regard (and it perhaps even outdoes the world at large in the preference for non-standard negators in prohibitives; see van der Auwera and Lejeune 2013). A possible motivation for the cross-linguistic aversion to using a standard negator for 'don't!' is a clash between the stative character of standard negation and the illocutionary dynamicity of prohibitives (see van der Auwera 2006): 'he isn't singing' is typically 'stative' in some sense, conveying the idea 'it is not the case that he's singing', while 'don't sing!' is somehow always 'dynamic', expressing the notion 'make it the case that you're not singing'. As Devos and Van Olmen (2013) argue for Bantu, another reason could be the constant pressure on languages to come up with new prohibitive strategies, which may then grammaticalize. Telling people not to do something is particularly face-threatening as it usually implies some disapproval of their current behaviour or intentions. Appealing to their volition or presenting something as a negative consequence are ways of mitigating the risk. Such strategies can conventionalize over time and lose their original effect, giving rise to the South Nuaulu and Tukang Besi forms for 'don't!' in (36b) and (37a).[8]

In terms of exponence, prohibitive negation closely resembles standard negation in MPSEA. Of the languages for which we have the necessary information, practically all only ever employ one prohibitive negator at a time. This includes cases like Hainan Cham, whose prohibitive is marked by either dedicated *suŋ*$^{21}$ *vo*$^{21}$ 'don't!' or the standard negator *pu*$^{33}$ (Thurgood et al. 2014: 231). Moreover, only a handful of the exceptions are like the Wamesa in (39b), which requires the two verb-embracing negators to be present. In the remaining languages, there is some evidence of the initial stage of a Jespersen Cycle. In Amahai in (40), for example, adding the optional second negator is said to make the directive more emphatic.

Amahai
(40) ***Hakai*** *uʔu-mi* (***hakai***)!
PROH noisy-2PL PROH
'Don't you all be so noisy!' (Florey 2010: 241)

Note also that no correlation seems to exist between prohibitive and standard negation in multiple exponence. Most languages with a compulsory two-part negation in the prohibitive have just one obligatory marker in standard negation. One of them is Wamesa in (39). An exception is Ede (/Rhade, Rade; Tharp and Đuôn-ya 1980: 8, 165), with prohibitive *đăm . . . ôh* and standard negative *amâo . . . ôh*. Similarly, the majority of languages with multiple exponence in standard negation expresses 'don't!' with a single marker. West Damar (Chlenova 2008: 170) is a case in point, with standard negative *ke-. . .-we* and prohibitive *mani*. These facts are not surprising. The preponderance of specialized prohibitive negators suggests that MPSEA generally regards the two types of negation as distinct phenomena.

An unusual feature of MPSEA is that some languages possess multiple distinct prohibitive negators. There is, for instance, some evidence in our data that languages with different linguistic styles for different social contexts may (but need not) have one distinct negator for the high register and another one for the low register. Balinese is a case in point, with *sampunang* 'don't! (+high register)' and *da* 'don't! (-high register)' respectively (Artawa 2013: 19). It does not seem unlikely that the pragmatics of such register-dependent prohibitives differs greatly too but our sources do not allow us to say anything more about this. See Vander Klok, this volume, §31.2 on speech levels in the languages of Java, and Shiohara and Arka, this volume, §32.5 on speech levels in Balinese-Sasak-Sumbawa.

The comparison of the two-part prohibitive negation with the one-part standard negation in Western Cham is interesting. Example (7) showed that the latter is postverbal (and clause-final) whereas the former has a postverbal/clause-final marker as well as a preverbal one (which need not be clause-initial). A potential explanation for the difference is provided by Horn (1989: 450): "While Neg First is operative in both declarative and imperative contexts, there is a particularly strong motivation for avoiding postverbal negation in directive speech acts (imperatives and their functional equivalents)." The claim is illustrated with *kill him – oops – not!*. In Western Cham, any such confusion is averted by *di*'s place before the verb in (41).

Western Cham
(41) ***Di*** *đuaik* ***juai***!
PROH run PROH
'Don't run!' (Baumgartner 1998: 19)

[8] In Bantu as a whole, this politeness-driven pressure seems to have led to a more heterogeneous range of prohibitive negators, compared to the standard negators (see Devos and Van Olmen 2013: 24–43). For MPSEA, such a difference cannot be observed, mainly because standard negation itself is already extremely diverse (see §50.2).

There are a few more languages in our data where standard negation is entirely postverbal but prohibitive negation is (partially) preverbal. They are genetically and geographically quite diverse and include Moken, Wamesa, Dhao (Ndao), and South Nuaulu (see also Grimes, this volume, §36.9). The opposite situation is only really attested in Waropen: its standard negation in (42a) has a preverbal component but its prohibitive negation in (42b) is exclusively postverbal.

Waropen
(42) a. ***Afa*** *kikoaini* *nu* ***ewomo.***
NEG live.in.3PL village NEG
'They don't live in the village.' (Held 1942: 81)

b. *Aghaka* ***ewara!***
be.afraid PROH
'Don't be afraid!' (Held 1942: 82)

In other words, for MPSEA, there is some truth to Horn's (1989) idea that Neg First is stronger in prohibitive than in standard negation (but see Van Olmen 2010, 2021 for a typological perspective). On its own, prohibitive negation also clearly demonstrates the tendency to put the negative early (it tends to do so frequently even in clause-initial position). In our data, the majority of languages possesses a compulsory preverbal marker for 'don't!' (possibly with another marker following the verb), a few have the option of a preverbal prohibitive negator, and only a dozen or so lack any marking for 'don't!' before the verb. Examples of the former and latter types can be found above. For the second type, consider Bajau in (43). The language has two prohibitive constructions, one with preverbal *daqa* and another one with postverbal *dong*.

Bajau
(43) a. ***Daqa*** *gĕrô!*
PROH quarrel
'Don't quarrel!' (Omar 1983: 125)

b. *Tilow* ***dong!***
ask PROH
'Don't ask!' (Omar 1983: 125)

Note, finally, that nearly all of the languages with a postverbal prohibitive marker (which may be part of a circumverbal negation and need not be obligatory) come from the same areas and language groups mentioned for postverbal standard negation in §50.2. In the west, we have Moklen and the Chamic group. The latter appears to have affected Bahnaric in the prohibitive domain: several Bahnaric languages display postverbal marking for 'don't!', which may assume the Chamic form of *oh* 'don't' (see (41a); e.g. Rengao, Gregerson 1979: 54). In contrast to the former, Moken (Chantanakomes 1980: 150) has exclusively preverbal prohibitive negation, despite its postverbal standard negation but like many of the neighbouring languages (e.g. Urak Lawoi', Hogan 1999: 14). Another western language like Moken is Sri Lankan Malay. Its standard negation is postverbal, which must be due to the influence of Tamil and/or Sinhala. Its prohibitive marker, however, is mainly preverbal (see Nordhoff 2009: 253, 281), unlike those in the contact languages (e.g. Chandralal 2010: 254 for Sinhala). In the east, postverbal prohibitive negators are found in the MPSEA languages that have interacted with Papuan languages (see Schapper and Zobel, this volume, §35.6, which highlights a range of languages in the Timor–Southern Maluku region with post-verbal standard negation and post-verbal prohibitive negation, but not ones with known Papuan contact histories). An exploration of twenty Papuan languages neighbouring Austronesian languages in eastern Indonesia suggests that their prohibitive negation, like their standard negation, tends to be postverbal and has probably had an effect on a large number of the MPSEA languages spoken in the area. (In our data, no evidence exists of the borrowing of postverbal prohibitive markers, though). Nevertheless, in a substantial minority of these MPSEA *and* Papuan languages, prohibitive negation is marked preverbally, unlike standard negation. This fact can be attributed to the impact of 'Neg Early' discussed above and there is no need to appeal to contact to explain it. It is still interesting to observe, however, that the preverbal prohibitive marker *ʔake* in Papuan Blagar (Steinhauer 2014: 175) closely resembles the preverbal marker for 'don't!' *aké* in the neighbouring MPSEA language Solor Lamaholot (Kroon 2016: 192).

## 50.6 Conclusion

This chapter surveyed four types of negation, viz. standard, existential and prohibitive negation, and the negation of indefinites. The data set had a good size (ca. 200 languages), though the coverage was suboptimal. Much of what is known about MPSEA negation fits the general typology of negation. Thus, MPSEA standard and prohibitive negation usually require a preverbal single particle, prohibitive negation more so than standard negation, and the markers for both types of negation tend to be different. The origin of the negators is usually obscure. We find limited evidence of Jespersen Cycles and much more evidence of Negative Existential Cycles. Language contact affected MPSEA negation, especially on the western and eastern peripheries of the MPSEA area. What would appear to be most remarkable for MPSEA negation is that negative indefinites often avail themselves of an existential strategy. This is either the only indefiniteness strategy that the language has, or it is an alternative to nominal or pronominal strategies. There are also mixed existential (pro)nominal strategies.

## Acknowledgements

Thanks are due to John Bowden, Hanna Fricke, Nikolaus Himmelmann, Antoon De Rycker, Thomas Conners, David Mead, Sebastian Nordhoff, Carl Rubino, Uri Tadmor, René van den Berg, and Erik Zobel. For help with glossing of relevant examples, thanks goes to Ahmadiliman Ibrahim, Normaizura binti Md Zain, Nur Harizah Mohd Faiz, and Shazan Khan Omar (all Kuala Lumpur), Fachriah Syamruddin (Jakarta), Luh Annie Mayani (Jakarta), Euis Sumaryani (Bandung), and to Majanu J. (Butur, Sulawesi).

CHAPTER 51

# Phasal polarity

LJUBA VESELINOVA, LEIF ASPLUND, AND JOZINA VANDER KLOK

## 51.1 Introduction

This chapter describes how phasal polarity is encoded in the Malayo-Polynesian languages of Southeast Asia (MPSEA). Phasal meanings have to do with the existence or non-existence of a particular situation at specific points in time related to other points in time: ALREADY expresses that an (expected) situation has come to exist; NO LONGER expresses that a situation has ceased to persist; STILL expresses that a situation continues (despite expectations that it should have stopped); and NOT YET expresses that a situation has not come into existence (despite expectations that it would). These expressions are logically related via negation, where the negative expressions can be analysed as the internal or external negation of a positive expression (Löbner 1989). Indonesian illustrates each of these phasal polarity expressions in (1)–(2). The examples in (1) are affirmative and negative answers to a polar question *Does she talk?*, which was following the previous dialogue context (A: How old is your child now? B: She is 2 years old. A: Does she talk? B: . . . .).[1]

Indonesian

(1) a. *Ya, dia* ***sudah*** *bisa ber-bicara.*
yes 3SG already can INTR-speak
'Yes, she talks already.'

b. *Tidak, dia* ***belum*** *bisa ber-bicara.*
no 3SG not.yet can INTR-speak
'No, she does not talk yet.'
(Questionnaire data: Intan Fuji, twenty year old native speaker from Jakarta, 16 February 2017)

Indonesian

(2) a. *Dia* ***masih*** *makan.*
3SG still eat
'She is still eating.' (Sneddon et al. 2010: 206)

b. *Karena asap menara pengendali*
because smoke tower NMLZ.control
***sudah*** ***tidak*** *ter-lihat* ***lagi***
already NEG PASS-see again
'Because of the smoke the control tower could no longer be seen.' (Sneddon et al. 2010: 210)

In (1a), the marker *sudah* indicates the effectuation of an expected change; namely, when a child is two years old, she is expected to start talking. The use of *sudah* also indicates a change in polarity from negative to positive. Conversely, *belum* 'not yet' in (1b) encodes the non-realization of an expected situation. There is no change of polarity with *belum* in that it remains negative from one point in time to another point in time. However, there are, typically, expectations for the realization of the non-realized situation in the future. In (2a), *masih* 'still' indicates the persistence of an existing situation. Similarly to *belum* 'not yet', there is no change of polarity with *masih* 'still' but here we are dealing with positive polarity. Finally, when *sudah* 'already' scopes over a negated predicate as in (2b), the resulting sense is that the situation (action or state) referred to by the predicate has ceased to exist with a polarity change from positive to negative.

In this chapter, we distinguish between the phasal polarity concepts themselves and their specific expressions (since a language may have more than one expression for a given concept). In our notation, phasal polarity concepts appear in small capitals: ALREADY, STILL, NO LONGER, NOT YET.

The sample used in this chapter encompasses sixty-two languages; it is genealogically and geographically stratified in order to represent the diversity of MPSEA languages. The availability of data and the quality of the source have also influenced the inclusion of specific languages. The genealogical breakdown of the sample is shown on a map server, see Veselinova and Asplund (2020): twenty-six different Malayo-Polynesian branches are represented.

We investigate the synchronic distribution of phasal polarity expressions in MPSEA languages, while at the same time, we note plausible historical developments about the evolution, spread, (and demise) of these expressions. Our analysis builds on lexico-grammatical parameters developed by van der Auwera (1998); van Baar (1997); and

[1] These are Questions Nr 40 and 41 (Veselinova 2020), which is a translation questionnaire whereby speakers are provided with a context and asked to translate a sentence related to it.

Ljuba Veselinova, Leif Asplund, and Jozina Vander Klok, *Phasal polarity*. In: *The Oxford Guide to the Malayo-Polynesian Languages of Southeast Asia*. Edited by: Alexander Adelaar and Antoinette Schapper, Oxford University Press. © Ljuba Veselinova, Leif Asplund, and Jozina Vander Klok (2024). DOI: 10.1093/oso/9780198807353.003.0051

Kramer (2018). For the purposes of this chapter, we focus on a subset of the parameters: (i) expressibility; (ii) wordhood; (iii) coverage; and (iv) paradigmaticity. Expressibility is about whether or not all four concepts of a phasal polarity system are expressed in a language. Wordhood refers to the word class status of phasal polarity markers. Coverage refers to the range of phasal polarity concepts covered by specific expressions. Lastly, paradigmaticity concerns the oppositions that phasal polarity terms enter into. The oppositions can be internal, that is, within the phasal polarity system or external, within the more general grammatical system in the language. Expressions of phasal polarity can also be placed differently on the lexico-grammatical scale (van Baar 1997: 40). In many Indo-European languages, phasal polarity expressions are adverbials which modify the predicate. In the MPSEA languages, they are much closer to grammatical markers in their generality of function, scope, and frequency of use.

We illustrate these parameters briefly with the Indonesian phasal polarity expressions in (1) and (2). In terms of expressibility, all four phasal polarity concepts are expressed. Based on these data, Indonesian has flexible coverage regarding ALREADY and NO LONGER, since the latter is encoded by internal negation of ALREADY. On the other hand, the expressions for STILL and NOT YET show no overlap so the system is rigid in this regard. We will see that specific phasal polarity concepts may have more than one encoding and thus a system can be both flexible and rigid, depending on which expression is taken into account. For instance, Indonesian can also express NO LONGER by several different periphrastic expressions, only one of which was given in (2b); other encodings of this concept include *tidak lagi* or *sudah tidak* (formal register). Indonesian phasal polarity expressions are grammatical rather than lexical items, and are single morphemes except for NO LONGER. Concerning paradigmaticity, they are symmetric because each one of them can replace the other in otherwise similar contexts.

This chapter is organized as follows. In §51.2, we cover the encoding of each phasal polarity concept, and discuss the parameters of wordhood and paradigmaticity as well as their placement within the lexico-grammatical scale. The parameters of expressibility and coverage are examined in §51.3 and §51.4. The chapter closes with a summary and conclusions in §51.5.

## 51.2 Encoding of each phasal polarity concept in MPSEA

Our sample allows for several broad generalizations regarding the wordhood parameter, that is, the kinds of expressions used for the encoding of phasal polarity concepts. Expressions for ALREADY and STILL are typically single morphemes, as demonstrated with the Indonesian markers in (1a) and (2a). In contrast, the concept of NO LONGER is most commonly encoded by periphrastic expressions. The encoding of NOT YET shows greatest variation in that this concept can be expressed by periphrastic expressions, by univerbations with various degrees of transparency, or by single morphemes. These different strategies also show clear geographical patterning. We discuss the expressions of each phasal polarity concept separately, starting with STILL and NOT YET in §51.2.1 and §51.2.2, then ALREADY in §51.2.3 and NO LONGER in §51.2.4. Corpus data and frequency counts that highlight the grammaticalization status of phasal polarity markers are presented in §51.2.5.

### 51.2.1 Expressions for STILL

#### 51.2.1.1 *Formal characteristics*

In the MPSEA sample, the concept of STILL is commonly encoded by free markers, which tend to scope over the entire predication and are usually the only marker of continuity in the clause, such as in Indonesian in (2a). Furthermore, they occur with all kinds of predicates: active (see (2a) above) as well as stative, locative or nominal, as in (3).

Indonesian
(3) *Dia* ***masih*** *muda/di sini/pegawai*
3SG still young/here/an employee
'She is still young/here/an employee.'
(Sneddon et al. 2010: 206)

Free markers similar in distribution and function to Indonesian *masih* in (3) are better classified as grammatical rather than lexical expressions because of the generality of their meaning, their scope and frequency of use, as well as the fact that they build paradigmatic contrasts with other TAM markers. There are, however, languages where expressions for STILL come closer to the lexical scale and are better classified as adverbs. For instance, in Pendau, a language from Central Sulawesi, the adverb *mono* 'still' can be the only marker of persistence or continuity in the clause, (4). This adverb occurs with stative predicates in particular.

Pendau
(4) ***Mono*** *diang bau to=ni-tapa-i=mu*
still EXIST fish REL=IV.REALIS-smoke-DIR=2SG.GEN
*nimporongomo ʔuoʔ*
yesterday yonder
'Do you still have that fish you smoked yesterday?'
(Quick 2003: 437)

It is frequent for STILL to be encoded by several expressions in one and the same language (cf. a more theoretical discussion in §51.3). In Pendau, for instance, the adverb *mono* 'still' is far from the only option, typically co-occurring with other markers of continuity/imperfectivity of the situation such as a reduplicated verb in (5a) or with the continuative enclitic =*po* in (5b) (Quick 2003).

Pendau

(5) a. *saba?* *jimo* ***mono*** *bura~**bura***
because 3PL.ABS still speak~speak
*N-po-dua=mo* *si=Rante*
REAL-SF.FACTIVE-arrive=COMPL PERS=Rante
*Salaka*
Salaka
'Because they were still speaking when Rante Salaka arrived' (Quick 2003: 437)

b. *Watu=nyo* *?uo* *a?u* ***mono**=**po***
time=3SG.GEN yonder 1SG.ABS still=CONT
*kalas* *doruo*
class two
'[. . .]. At that time I was still in class two.' (Quick 2003: 498)

In Besemah, a language from Southwest Sumatra, STILL is expressed by the free-standing marker *masih* and by the enclitic *gi*=, shown in (6). There are no apparent differences in distribution and meaning between the two expressions (Bradley McDonnell, p.c.).

Besemash

(6) a. ***masih*** *pule* *sangi* *ghingge-ka*
PERSISTIVE also RECP [PV]greet-CAUS.APPL
'(we) still also greeted each other' (McDonnell 2016b: 160)

b. *aku* ***gi*** *nginak=(ny)e* *sawah*
1SG PERSISTIVE AV.see=3 rice.paddy
*ende* *ini*
LNK DEM.PROX
'I still see it, the rice paddy, that one' (McDonnell 2016b: 103)

Most expressions for STILL appear distinct on the synchronic level and postulating a common source does not seem possible. However, there are two groups where a historically common form can be postulated. There are eleven languages in our sample where the form *masi(h)* is used for the encoding of STILL, either as a sole expression or as an alternative. Most of these are Malayic or languages in close contact with them, such as Balinese, Sasak, Sundanese, Begak, and West Coast Bajau from Northern Borneo, and also Ambonese Malay and Papuan Malay. It may be motivated to conclude that expressions for STILL are easily borrowed (Antoinette Schapper, p.c.). There are fifteen languages where the expressions for STILL include enclitics such as *-po/-pa/-pe* which we assume most probably go back to Proto-Austronesian *-pa 'still, yet, till now, first' cf. (Blust and Trussel 2020). These languages are mostly spoken in Northern and Meso-Philippine as well as in Sulawesi. There also a couple of languages in the Southern parts of the MPSEA territory, such as Kambera and Lampung Api, where a cognate of *-po/-pa/-pe* is used.

### 51.2.1.2 *Functions*

Matéq, a language from West Kalimantan, Borneo, Indonesia, can be used to highlight formally distinct expressions for STILL, which are also semantically different. The Matéq data also illustrate uses of expressions for STILL outside the domain of continuity. Expressions of the concept STILL encode the persistence of an already existing situation. Some grammatical descriptions of Matéq also specify that the situation marked by STILL lasts longer than expected (Connell 2013: 137–8).

Matéq

(7) a. *onaq=ng* *diq* *binsu* *téq* ***mege***
child=3 REL youngest this still
*dicik* *rayo*
small very
'their youngest child was still very small' (Connell 2013: 137)

b. ***bayu*** *kurak~kurak* *tubiq*
still.only bubble~bubble rice
'the rice was bubbling' (Connell 2013: 138)

As indicated in (7), there are two expressions of persistence in Matéq, *mege* 'still' and *bayu* 'still.only'. Both are classified as aspect markers; they precede the predicate and are in paradigmatic contrast with other aspect markers. Both qualify as STILL phasal polarity markers since both encompass a sequence of stages (real or counterfactual/based on expectations) and a situation that continues through them. The TAM marker *mege* 'still' indicates imperfective aspect in contexts where there is an expected or possible change of state. Thus in (7a), the expected future change of state is the growing up of the youngest child. The TAM marker *bayu* 'still.only' ". . . signifies that the subject of the clause is about to be, or is currently engaged in another action which temporarily precedes another action or event" (Connell 2013: 137). The use of *bayu* in (7b) implies that the rice is still at the stage of bubbling but the expectation is that once it has bubbled, it will be eaten. In contrast to these phasal polarity expressions, Matéq also has a TAM marker *degeq* 'constantly' that indicates the constancy of a situation but without any implications about different points in time or speaker's expectations (Connell 2013: 137). Finally, *bayu* 'still.only' has another use which is worth mentioning since it falls in line with previous generalizations about phasal polarity markers: it can be used as a delimitative or restriction marker, as in (8).

Matéq

| (8) | **bayu** | *aroq=ng* | *panei* | *nyidoq* |
|---|---|---|---|---|
| | still.only | beginning=3 | clever | speak |

'He'd only just begun to speak well.' (Connell 2013: 138)

As noted by van Baar (1997: 110–11), the polysemy between the sense of persistence and a delimiting sense such as 'only' is observed in many unrelated languages which is why it can be safely described as a stable cross-linguistic tendency. In (7b), *bayu* 'still.only' occurs together with a reduplicated verb that refers to an atelic event, bubbling. In (8), *bayu* 'still only' scopes over a telic situation in that there is a clear point in time, its beginning; in addition, it appears to be encoded by a nominal construction. Thus, one and the same marker is interpreted as marking persistence with atelic predicates and as a marker of restriction with telic predicates and nominals. Expressions for STILL which also have a restrictive sense are observed in other languages in our data, including Acehnese. Heine et al. (1993: 60) also cite similar data on the development of adverbs expressing continuity into restrictive markers in African languages, with also the same distribution across atelic vs. nominals. Generally, phasal markers of continuity appear to be highly sensitive to context for their exact interpretation. We will return to this issue in the discussion on expressions of NOT YET in §51.2.2 as well as in §51.4 below.

Other senses expressed by STILL markers include iteratives such as 'again', 'more', 'also; too' and also futurity. Polysemy with an iterative sense is illustrated in (9) with data from Begak, a language spoken in Sabah, Malaysia. In this language the expression *masong* has both a continuative and an iterative meaning.

Begak

| (9) | *Sugaʔ* | *b<e>raʔ* | *duktur* | *apon* | *dan* |
|---|---|---|---|---|---|
| | but | <COM>say.UV | doctor | NEG | yet |

| *l<əm>uan* | *ngod* | *x-ray* | ***masong*** |
|---|---|---|---|
| <DEP>go.outside | because | x-ray | still.again |

'But the doctor said (that) he (can) not go out (of the hospital) yet, because he (needs) another x-ray/he still (needs) an x-ray.' (Goudswaard 2005: 322)

Polysemy that includes persistence of a situation and indication of future or obligation is illustrated by data from Mambae, a language from East Timor, in (10).

Mambae

| (10) a. | *Rom* | ***hei*** | *boe* |
|---|---|---|---|
| | 3PL | still | sleep |

'They are still sleeping'

| b. | *Orsíd* | *rom* | ***hei*** | *pun* | *sa* |
|---|---|---|---|---|---|
| | soon | 3PL | FUT | make | tea |

'Soon they will make tea' (Hull 2003b: 29)

To summarize, in the languages of the MPSEA area, expressions for STILL tend to be free, rather than bound, grammatical markers. Furthermore, STILL can be encoded by several different expressions in one and the same language, which may or may not differ semantically. Expressions that encode the notion of STILL commonly express the persistence of a situation, sometimes despite the expectations that it should have been discontinued. In addition, expressions of continuity are also related to other semantic domains such as universal quantification (e.g. *all*) and from there (temporal) restriction, iteration and finally futurity. See van Baar (1997: 110–11) on the polysemy of continuity and restrictive/delimiting function of STILL expressions as related to universal quantification.

When negation falls within the scope of STILL rather than vice-versa, these expressions come to express the continuation of a non-realized state, as in (11).

Matéq

| (11) | **bayu** | ***ka=ng*** | *rat* | *tauq* | *ngomong* |
|---|---|---|---|---|---|
| | still.only | NEG=3 | too.much | be.able | speak |

'He couldn't speak very well yet.' (Connell 2013: 145)

As indicated by the translation of (11), the continuation of a negative/non-realized state is in effect the concept NOT YET, which we discuss next.

## 51.2.2 Expressions for NOT YET

### 51.2.2.1 *Formal characteristics*

The concept of NOT YET can be encoded in a variety of ways, as summarized in Table 51.1.

The three most common ways of encoding NOT YET include periphrastic expressions in a solid one third of the sample, univerbations with various degrees of transparency in one fourth of the sample, and encoding by a single morpheme in close to one third of the investigated languages. These groups are illustrated by Matéq in (11) as well as by Tondano, a language spoken in Minahasa, North Sulawesi

**Table 51.1** Quantitative breakdown of different types of expressions for NOT YET

| | |
|---|---|
| Periphrastic | 18 |
| periphrastic or univerbation | 2 |
| transparent univerbation | 13 |
| semi-transparent univerbation | 4 |
| single morpheme | 17 |
| several possibilities | 5 |
| no information | 3 |
| Total | 62 |

Peninsula, (12); Madurese spoken on the island of Madura and in the province of East Java, (13); and Sundanese, spoken in West Java, (14).

Tondano: NOT YET encoded by a periphrastic expression

(12) *Ku* ***raiʔ=peʔ*** *kimaan*
1SG NEG-still/yet eat.SV.PST
'I haven't eaten yet.' (Sneddon 1975: 241)

Madurese: NOT YET encoded by a univerbation: *giʔ* 'still' and *taʔ* 'NEG'

(13) *Presiden* ***gitaʔ*** *dhapaʔ*
President not.yet arrive
'The president hasn't arrived yet.' (Davies 2010: 269)

Sundanese: NOT YET encoded by a single morpheme

(14) *Manehna* ***acan*** *kawin*
3SG not.yet married
'He is not yet married.' (Questionnaire data, Melania Tesa, 21-year-old native speaker, 1 March 2017)

As shown in (12), in Tondano, NOT YET is expressed by a single form rather than a phrase as in Matéq in (11); the form clearly consists of two morphemes *raʔ* 'NEG' and *=peʔ* 'still/yet', an enclitic which is hosted by the negator. Conversely, in Madurese, (13), the form *gitaʔ* 'not yet' is a fusion of *giʔ* 'still; yet' and the negator *taʔ*. Since the original morphemes can still be discerned, we have chosen to set such forms apart from others for which it is not possible to make any further morphological segmentation. For instance, *acan* 'not yet' in Sundanese, (14), can only be described as a single morpheme, similar to Indonesian *belum* 'not yet', (1b). We can see a progression from a phrase to univerbation where morpheme boundaries are gradually blurred to end up as a single morpheme.

The types of expressions identified above show a very clear geographical distribution, as shown in Map 51.1. Languages with periphrastic NOT YET expressions are consistently located in the northern parts of the MPSEA territory and are very common in Northern and Meso-Philippine languages. Transparent univerbations are observed on Sulawesi and the Halmahera islands, while languages where NOT YET is encoded by a single morpheme form an almost perfect belt on Sumatra and Java, Bali, and adjacent island groups to the east. We suggest that this is not an accident but is rather due to contact induced changes.

#### 51.2.2.2 *Functions*

NOT YET expressions encode the continuation of a non-realized state, often with the expectation that it will be realized in the future. Thus, there are two components to their sense: a continuative one and one about expectations. Via the continuative component they stand in a paradigmatic relationship with STILL markers. However, via the component of expectation, they come to be interpreted as negative counterparts of ALREADY which encode the realization of an expected change. In fact, the more consolidated a NOT YET marker becomes a part of the grammatical system of a language, the more it is paradigmatically linked to ALREADY and forms oppositions within the general domain of negation.

As demonstrated in (15) below, in Lamaholot (Central Malayo-Polynesian, Timor, Flores-Lembata), adverbs/grammatical markers such as *kae* 'already', *wati* 'not yet', and *ulin/dəra* 'still' are the sole indicators of the temporal-aspectual situatedness of a predication. They are all clause final and are in complementary distribution with each other. In addition, the marker *wati* 'not yet' can be said to form a contrast with *halaʔ* 'NEG', the general negator and thus form an opposition specific to the domain of negation. Finally, the markers *kae* 'already' and *wati* 'not yet' can be standalone answers to polar questions, cf. (16e), whereas no such uses are cited for *ulin/dəra* 'still' in Nishiyama and Kelen (2007). The uses as standalone answers come to strengthen the paradigmatic relationship between *kae* 'already' and *wati* 'not yet'. In fact, in many grammatical descriptions, monomorphemic NOT YET expressions like Lewoingu Lamaholot *wati* and Indonesian *belum* are suggested as corresponding negators to ALREADY markers. Because of this grammaticalization, the term NONDUM < Latin 'not yet' has been proposed by Veselinova and Devos (2020) for grammaticalized NOT YET expressions that are interpreted as negative counterparts to ALREADY.

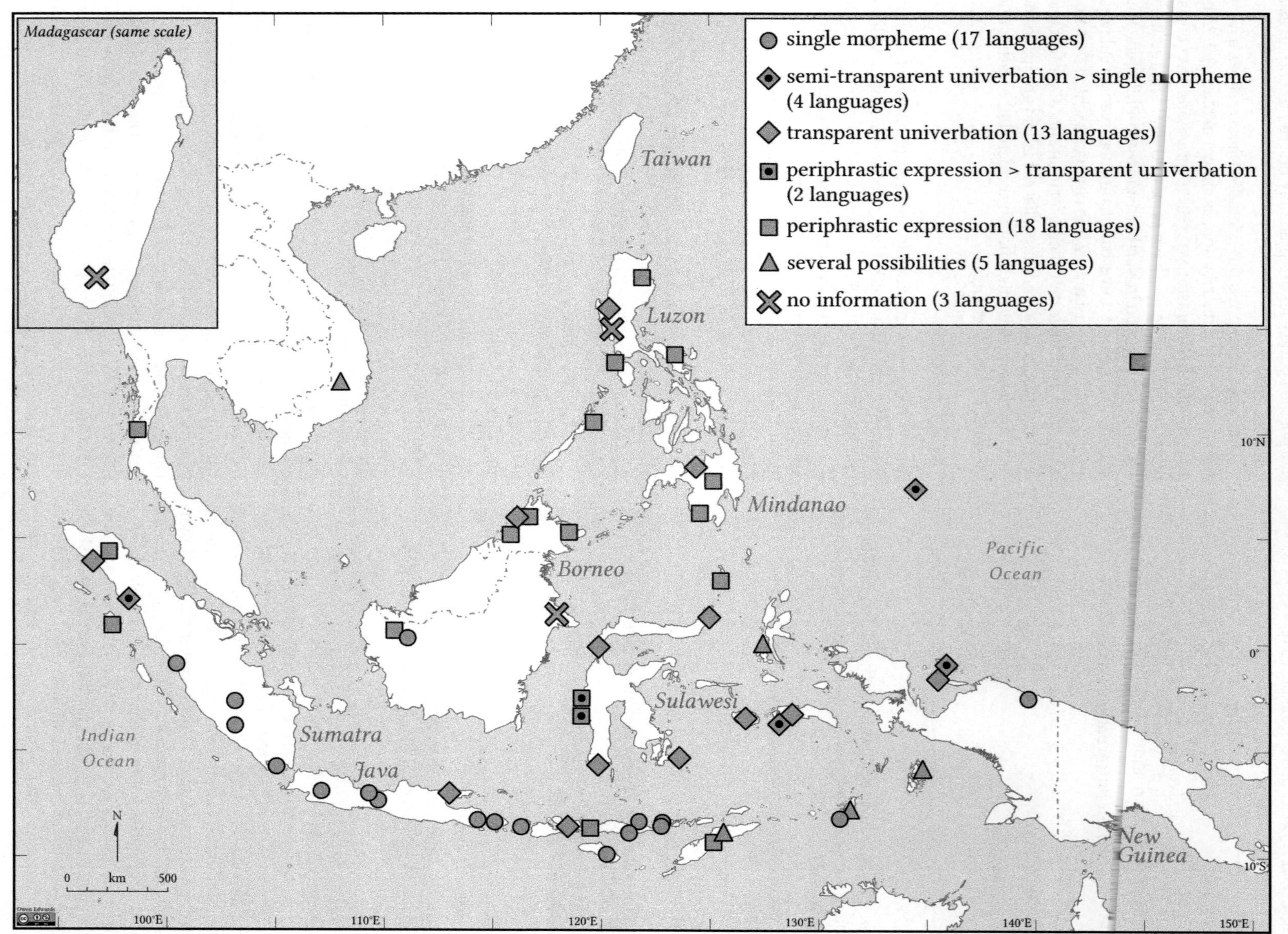


**Map 51.1** Encoding of NOT YET in MPSEA languages.

Lewoingu Lamaholot

(15) a. *go* *kawen* ***kae***
1SG married already
'I am (already) married.'
(Nishiyama and Kelen 2007: 86)

b. *go* *kawen* ***hala?***
1SG married NEG
'I am not married.'

c. *go* *kawen* ***wati***
1SG married not yet
'I am not married yet.'

d. *na* *tannin* ***ulin/dəra***
3SG cry still
'He is still crying.'

e. A: *mo* *kawen* ***kae?***
2SG married already
'Are you married?'

B: ***Kae/Wati***
Yes (already)/No (Not yet)
'Yes, I am/No, I am not'
(Nishiyama and Kelen 2007: 70)

Other uses of NOT YET markers include their uses as sentence tags, general markers of negation, and finally as a temporal subordinator (see (21)–(23)). They are discussed in §51.2.2.3 as we see them closely connected to the evolution/status of a NOT YET marker as lexico-grammatical, rather than as a purely lexical expression.

### 51.2.2.3 *Historical notes and the evolution of* NOT YET *as a grammatical marker*

Concerning the specific expressions used for the encoding of NOT YET within a historical-comparative context, we first discuss single morphemes. With the exception of Indonesian *belum* and its variants in most Malayic languages, most single morphemes that encode NOT YET appear to be completely unrelated, even in closely related varieties. For instance, in dialects of Lamaholot, Lewotobi Lamaholot has *morə* 'still/not yet' (Nagaya 2011: 414), while Lewoingu Lamaholot has *wati* 'not yet' (Nishiyama and Kelen, 2007: 32). Such facts indicate that these are not inherited forms but rather innovations which originate from different sources.

Periphrastic expressions of NOT YET, consisting of an internally negated 'still' cf. (11), are very common in MPSEA. They express the continuation of a non-realized situation and as such demonstrate the direct relation between the concepts of STILL and NOT YET as well as their encoding. In many languages what had initially been a periphrastic expression became fused into univerbations with various degrees of transparency.

NOT YET expressions stem often from two domains: persistence and iterativity. With regard to persistence, van der Auwera (1998) notes the association of expressions for STILL with contexts of negation leads in many cases to them being interpreted as negative polarity items. Thus, they remain into the negative domain while a new positive item is recruited for the positive continuative STILL. We observe such cases in our MPSEA data as well. For instance, in Iraya, a language from Mindoro, the Philippines, the word *dapu* is described to have several senses 'more; yet; still; last; past' (Tweddell 1958: 59). However, nowhere in the source is it used as a positive marker of persistence; the expression *bayuw* 'still' is used for that, while *dapu* is shown with iterative senses such as 'more; also' and as negative polarity item to express NOT YET, as shown in (16).

Iraya

(16) *ʔayuw* *tudlafen* ***dapu!***
PROH answer yet
'Don't answer yet!' (Tweddell 1958: 59)

Other languages highlight similar developments. In Pendau, the concept of NOT YET is encoded by a combination of the negator *ndau* and the continuative enclitic *=po*, (17), while a separate (probably diachronically younger) expression *mono* is used to express persistence of an existing situation (see (4)–(5) above).

Pendau

(17) *si=ina=nyo* ***ndau=po*** *sono*
PERS=mother=3SG.GEN NEG=CONT COM
*rapi=nyo*
spouse=3SG.GEN
'His mother was not yet with his spouse.'
(Quick 2003: 136)

Data from Acehnese, a language from northern Sumatra, are used to illustrate an iterative expression such as 'again' as a source for the encoding of NOT YET.

Acehnese

(18) a. *gopnyan* *h'an=geu=têm=jak=meulangue* ***lom***
3.HON NEG=3=want=go=swim again
'He doesn't want to go swimming again.'

b. *gopnyan* *h'an=geu=têm=jak=meulangue=**lom***
3.HON NEG=3=want=go=swim=again
'He doesn't want to go swimming yet.' (Durie 1985: 226)

As shown in (18a), when *lom* is used as a free form it means 'again', while when it is cliticized as in (18b) it expresses the continuation of a negative state, in this case the continued lack of desire to go swimming.

The data from Acehnese are instructive about the nature of NOT YET markers in many languages from MPSEA. Specifically, unlike NOT YET markers in the languages of Europe, NOT YET markers in MPSEA are of a much more general categorical character. In Acehnese, a NOT YET expression appears in a much tighter connection to the verb phrase formally as it is commonly cliticized. In other languages NOT YET expressions undergo phonological erosion, equally characteristic of grammaticalization. Finally, their frequency and functions are markedly different from those observed for NOT YET adverbials in the languages of Europe. For example, the Indonesian *belum* 'not yet' in (1b) appears in various contracted forms both in spoken Indonesian as well as in other Malayic languages, such as the data in (19) from Jambi Malay and in (20) from Besemah, both languages from Southern Sumatra.

Jambi Malay
(19) *bn$^d$o-tu* ***blʊm*** *caer*
thing-DEM.DIST not.yet diluted
'It hadn't melted yet.' (Yanti 2010: 407)

Besemah
(20) ***lum*** *m-buah* *anguk* *kate=ku* *kan*
not.yet AV-fruit intend word=1SG right
'(the cocoa plants) haven't yet bore fruit is what I intended to say, right.' (McDonnell 2016b: 82)

Compared to its counterparts in European languages, NOT YET expressions in MPSEA appear as markers with much more general scope. For instance, functions which they commonly cover include sentence tags (21), general negator (22), and finally temporal subordinator (23). Furthermore, NOT YET markers in MPSEA show markedly higher frequency than corresponding adverbials in European languages (cf. §51.2.5 for corpus counts from Jakarta Indonesian and English).

Jambi Malay
(21) *Eko* *nda?* *baraŋkat,* *apo* ***lʊm?***
Eko want leave.for or not.yet
'Does Eko want to leave, or doesn't he?' (Yanti 2010: 168)

Pendau
(22) *aʔu* ***ndau=po*** *mo-ate* *miu*
1SG.ABS NEG=CONT STAT.IRR-die 2PL.GEN
'I was not killed by/via you all.' (Quick 2003: 242)

Lewoingu Lamaholot
(23) *buʔa-te* *t-olo* *ətən* *ra*
eat.1PL.INCL 1PL.INCL-earlier while they
*səga* ***wati***
come not.yet
'Let's eat before they come.' (Nishiyama and Kelen 2007: 89)

The evolution from a sentence tag or standalone answer to a general marker of negation has been documented for other lexicalized expressions of negation as well (e.g. negative existentials (Veselinova 2016: 56)). We see these uses of NOT YET markers as part of their gradual generalization as grammatical markers of wider scope. In a similar vein, the use of NOT YET markers as temporal subordinators point to a generalization of meaning in a situation of a sequence of events. Specifically, when a non-realized, but expected, situation is part of an event chain/narrative, it is interpreted as bound to occur prior to other events in the narrative. Consequently, the marker of a non-realized, yet expected, situation becomes a marker of temporal priority or subordination.

### 51.2.3 Expressions for ALREADY

#### 51.2.3.1 *Formal characteristics*

The concept of ALREADY, the realization of an expected situation is typically encoded by free markers in MPSEA. They tend to scope over the entire predication, and they occur with all kinds of predicates, including dynamic, (24a), and stative predicates, (24b).

Jambi Malay
(24) a. *ʊntʊŋ-la* *dio?* ***la*** *nija?* *tana*
profit-EMPH 3 PRF ACT.step.on soil
*suci*
holy
'Fortunately she has gone to the holy land'

b. *Ka-duo* *oraŋ* *tuo* *awaʔ* ***la*** *tuo*
NUM-two person old 1/2/3 PRF old
'My parents are already old.' (Yanti 2010: 539)

While free markers such as those in Jambi Malay prevail in our dataset, more complex and variated expressions are also observed. For instance, in Tukang Besi, a language from Southeast Sulawesi, the concept of ALREADY can be encoded in several ways as in (25): by an enclitic *-mo*; by the adverbs, also dubbed auxiliaries, *mondo/monda*, *pasi* in combination with *-mo*; and finally, by the verb *poʔoli* 'finish' combined with *-mo*.

Tukang Besi

(25) a. *Te* *mia* *t<um>o-pa-manga* *nu*
CORE.ART person <PASS>CAUS-eat GEN
*sede* *no-bila-**mo**.*
taro 3.REAL-full-PRF
'The person who was made to eat some taro is already full.' (Donohue 1999a: 221)

b. *Ku-maʔeka* *kua* ***mondo-mo***
1SG-fear SW:COMP already-PRF
*no-wila* *ga*
3.REAL-go ILL
'I'm afraid that she's already gone…'
(Donohue 1999a: 400)

c. *Te* *wowine* ***pasi-mo*** *no-wila.*
CORE.ART woman already-PRF 3.REAL-go
'The women have already gone.'
(Donohue 1999a: 303)

d. ***ʔu-poʔoli-mo*** *ʔu-po-ʔawa* *ke*
2SG.REAL-finish-PRF 2SG-RECP-obtain and
*iai-su?*
younger.sibling-1SG.POSS
'Have you met my younger sister already?'
(Donohue 1999a: 92)

#### 51.2.3.2 *Functions*

Expressions of the concept ALREADY indicate a change of polarity in that a non-existent situation comes into existence, cf. (24)–(25). These expressions encode polarity change from negative to positive; they may also incorporate a sense of expectation on the part of the speaker, that is, situation X has come about as expected, earlier than expected or in some cases, later than expected (cf. van der Auwera 1998: 50), see also Löbner (1989) and Krifka (2000) for a discussion that these expectations arise from pragmatics. In (26) from Javanese, a language spoken in Central and East Java, the speaker expresses that time has passed quicker than expected, using *wes* 'already'. Since our material comes for the most part from grammars, detailed information about speakers' expectations is not always available.

Javanese

(26) Context: Someone passed away seven days earlier at the time of the speaker visiting.
*Ya Allah* ***wes*** *pitong* *ndino.* *Yo* *kok*
ya Allah already seven.LNK day yes PART
*cepet* *loh.*
fast PART
'Ya Allah, it's already been seven days. Wow, that's so fast!' (Vander Klok and Matthewson 2015: 200, 80)

The expressions of ALREADY in Southeast Asia, which includes MPSEA, have been widely discussed in both descriptive and theoretical work. Because of their function of expressing an effectuated change, they have been considered as (sub-)types of perfects, perfectives, or completives. A number of scholars have shown that expressions of ALREADY in Southeast Asia differ from the prototypical definitions of these categories in several respects; see Olsson (2013); Vander Klok and Matthewson (2015); and Dahl and Wälchli (2016). These authors show similarities in the functions they identify for ALREADY; they differ in their treatment of them as a separate gram type. The notion *gram type* is defined by Dahl and Wälchli (2016: 328) as a cluster of grams "whose members are highly similar in meaning and behaviour", building on the notion of a 'gram' by Bybee and Dahl (1989), which is "a grammatical item in a particular language with specific form and specific meaning and/or function". Olsson (2013) as well as Dahl and Wälchli (2016) consider many ALREADY expressions in the languages of Southeast Asia as a separate gram type and suggest the term *iamitive* (from Latin *iam* 'already') while Vander Klok and Matthewson (2015), discussing Javanese, do not share this view. We first review the functions which set ALREADY expressions apart from more established TAM categories and after that we turn to discussing their status as a separate gram type.

One of the most important differences between ALREADY expressions/iamitives and perfects is the interpretation of stative predicates marked by them, cf. (27).

Tukang Besi

(27) *No-meha-**mo*** *na* *watu* *iso*
3.REAL-red-PRF NOM rock yon
'That rock has become red.' (It was painted, or had red cloth draped over it; it is currently red)
(Donohue 1999a: 171)

When a stative predicate is marked by the perfect in English, as in *The house has been red*, the interpretation is that the house is currently not red. Rather, the use of the present perfect indicates that it was red at some past time and its non-redness now is relevant to the current state of affairs. In contrast, when a stative predicate is marked by an ALREADY/IAMITIVE, the only possible interpretation is that the state is a current one, and there was an effectuated change into that state that was expected, as indicated in (27). Dahl and Wälchli (2016: 328) put the sense of expectation in a more general perspective when they point out that iamitives often mark stative predicates they dub *natural development predicates*; that is, those which "become true sooner or later under normal circumstances". For instance, it is normal for parents to become old, cf. (24b).

Iamitives have a number of other functions which set them apart from perfects. These include their use as inceptive markers (28a), marking prospect and from there getting a future reading (28b), and showing ambiguity between ongoing activity and achieved result (28c). The latter ambiguity is completely impossible with a European-style perfect.

Tukang Besi

(28) a. Inceptive
*Na-b<um>sa-**mo*** *te* *sura.*
3.IRR-<SBJ FOCUS>read-PRF CORE.ART letter
'He's about to read the letter.'
(Donohue 1999a: 173)

b. Prospective → future
*Illange* *ku-ʔeka-**mo*** *i* *Wanse.*
tomorrow 1SG-climb-PRF OBL Wanci
'Tomorrow I'm going to Wanci.'
(Donohue 1999a: 139)

c. Activity with current relevance
*No-kili-**mo*** *te* *lante.*
3.REAL-clean-PRF CORE.ART floor
'She is cleaning the floor.'[2]/*'She (habitually) cleans the floor.'
'She has cleaned the floor.' (Donohue 1999a: 172)

Olsson (2013: 22–3) provides an insightful analysis of this seemingly puzzling polysemy, building on Comrie (1976: 64): these uses are possible because of the 'core function' of the iamitive to mark a new situation and its relevance to the current situation. Given appropriate context relating the present state to some future event may be interpreted as marking of the future. It is important to note, though, that iamitives do not mark future per se.

Iamitive markers are argued to be a separate gram type because it is possible to outline a semantic prototype of their functions, and they show scope of use and generality that set them in a completely different class from corresponding adverbs in European languages (Olsson 2013; Dahl and Wälchli 2016). Their high frequency of use lends further support to this statement: the marker *(u)dah* 'already/iamitive' in Jakarta Indonesian is in the same high frequency class as grammatical markers such as the verbal negator *nggak* and the nominal negator *bukan* (cf. Table 51.4 and Table 51.5 in §51.2.5 below).

The data from Tukang Besi are also very enlightening in this regard, as in this language, we observe a clear distinction between a clearly grammaticalized iamitive *-mo* and several emergent ALREADY adverbs. The enclitic *-mo* labelled perfect in the grammar shows all the prototypical uses of an iamitive. Since it is also a dependent rather than a morphologically free item, with many general functions and is very frequent, there is no doubt that it belongs to the grammatical rather than lexical core of the language. However, it is noteworthy that there are several adverbs that optionally co-occur with it, including *mondo/monda*, *pasi*, *poʔoli*, cf. (25). Among them, only *mondo/monda* are glossed with the sense 'already' throughout the grammar; *pasi* is also cited with the sense 'complete'; while *poʔoli* means also 'finish' (Donohue 1999a). So it looks like we observe a Jespersen-cycle type of development where the older iamitive marker is currently being 'reinforced' by several lexical items which are semantically congruent with it.

[2] Object incorporation in Tukang Besi has also a significant role for the aspectual interpretation of a predication but this is a complex issue which we do not delve into here. See Donohue (1999a: 167–70).

### 51.2.4 Expressions for NO LONGER

#### 51.2.4.1 *Formal characteristics*

Expressions for NO LONGER are periphrastic in close to half the investigated languages; other encodings such as by single morphemes or univerbations with various degrees of transparency amount to about 15% of the collected data, as shown in Table 51.2.

**Table 51.2** Quantitative breakdown of different types of expressions for NO LONGER

| | |
|---|---|
| periphrastic expression | 29 |
| periphrastic expression or a transparent univerbation | 2 (Karo Batak, Cebuano) |
| one word (univerbations with various degrees of transparency) | 8 |
| one word | 3 (Matigsalug Manobo, Sangir, Iraya) |
| no information | 20 |
| Total | 62 |

The geographical distribution of these different kinds of expressions is not random. Most of the univerbations are localized in the Sulawesi archipelago and the three languages where NO LONGER appears encoded by a single word are from Northern Sulawesi and in the Philippines.

The main types of expressions of NO LONGER are illustrated in (29)–(31): periphrastic with data from Sundanese, West Java; transparent univerbation from Tukang Besi; and a single word expression from Matigsalug Manobo, a language from the southern Philippines.

Sundanese

(29) *Teu, Sam* ***geus*** ***teu*** *gawe didieu*
No Sam IAM NEG work here
'No, Sam no longer works here'
(Questionnaire data, Melania Tesa, 21-year-old native speaker, 1 March 2017)

Tukang Besi

(30) ***Mbea-mo*** *no-sai kuikui.*
not-PRF 3.REAL-make cake
'S/he doesn't make cakes any more.'
(Donohue 1999a: 169)

Matigsalug Manobo

(31) ***Kenad*** *e ne masakit ka gettek ku.*
no.longer COMPLEMENTARY LNK sore F stomach my
'My stomach is no longer hurting.'
(Wang et al. 2006: 72)

As shown in (29), *geus* 'already/iamitive' is internally negated to encode NO LONGER. This is the case for most periphrastic expressions that include ALREADY and a negator—it is the phasal polarity term that scopes over the negator rather than vice-versa. With regard to the transparent univerbation *mbea-mo*, we note that it is the grammaticalized clitic *-mo* that combines with negation rather than any of the emerging adverbs that translate as 'already', cf. (25) above. This shows that similarly to the expressions for NOT YET, the older (grammaticalized expression) appears in negative contexts while new expressions for the positive concept emerge in the positive domain.

One-word expressions for NO LONGER are reported for three languages, Matigsalug Manobo (see (31)), Iraya *balen* (Tweddell 1958: 58), and Sangir *seng/sen* (Adriani 1893: 253–4). However, the descriptions of Iraya and Sangir do not provide any clear examples of these expressions for NO LONGER, and further research is required. On the other hand, *kenad* 'no longer' in Matigsalug Manobo appears with several grammatical functions, discussed further in §51.2.4.2.

We conclude our discussion of the formal properties of expressions for NO LONGER with an overview of their composition. One characteristic all of them appear to have in common is the presence of a negative element in the expression. Even *kenad* from Matigsalug Manobo cited in (31) most probably includes a negative marker *ké* or *kené*, cf. (Wang et al. 2006: 95). A breakdown of different kinds of elements used in NO LONGER expressions is presented in Table 51.3.

As summarized in Table 51.3, a negator typically combines with ALREADY or a completive marker (cf. (29) and (32)), found in about 50% of the languages for which NO LONGER expressions are reported. The next most common group covers NO LONGER expressions which include a temporal or an iterative expression, (33), accounting for about one fifth of the data. Finally, there are languages where the element which appears along with the negator is a negative polarity item, restricted to this construction. In (34), for example, the form *tehuk* is only found in a collocation with a negator (and is apparently completely dissociated from its source, as *tehuk* is said to derive from the verb *tehu* 'chase').

**Table 51.3** Quantitative breakdown of the composition of NO LONGER expressions

| | |
|---|---|
| ALREADY + NEG | 18 |
| completive + NEG | 2 (Mandar, Mamuju) |
| NEG + temporal/iterative | 8 |
| NEG +X (no identifiable sense) | 5 |
| NEG + still | 1 (Balinese) |
| Only/just + stative verb? | 1 (Palauan) |
| Multiple composition types | 3 (Indonesian, Palu'e, Basap) |
| Non-compositional (single morpheme) expressions | 3 (Matigsalug Manobo, Iraya, Sangir) |
| Total | 42 |

Mandar

(32) *Sukaq manarang-na mil-lamba kandiq-u,* ***andiang=m=i*** *meloq di-taqgalang.*
Since ADJ.clever-3GEN AV-walk little.sibling-1GEN, NEG=PFV=3 want PASS-held
'Since my little sibling learned to walk, he doesn't want to be held anymore.' (Dan Brodkin, p.c.)

Madurese

(33) *Tang leʔer* ***la*** ***taʔ*** *sakeʔ* ***pole.***
my neck already not hurt again
'My neck doesn't hurt anymore.' (Davies 2010: 475)

Buru

(34) *Da kaa gehu-t* ***tehuk*** ***moo.***
3SG eat taro-NOM longer NEG
'She doesn't eat taro any more.' (Grimes 1991: 236)

To summarize, NO LONGER expressions are overwhelmingly periphrastic and draw on a variety of sources. While ALREADY is clearly one of the most important ones, negation of temporal and iterative expressions is also frequently used for their encoding. A striking difference, when compared with the encoding of NOT YET is the fact that lexicalizations of NO LONGER expressions are rare. On the other hand, there is evidence for the formulation of stable constructions, such as those in Buru, a language spoken in Central Maluku, which means that there is sufficient frequency of use that leads to their creation.

#### 51.2.4.2 *Functions*

NO LONGER expressions encode the termination of an existing state. In the grammatical descriptions available to us, there is no information for any other functions of these expressions. The only exception is Matigsalug Manobo, already cited as one of the few languages where NO LONGER is expressed by a single word, *kenad*. In addition to the phasal polarity meaning, *kenad* is also used as a negative future marker (35a), as a sentence tag contrasting with the continuative marker *pad* 'still' (35b), and as a general negator (35c).

Matigsalug Manobo

(35) a. ***Kenad*** *egbehas se igpamula ney, ne*
won't fruit the plant our and
***kenad*** *langun ne kenè egbehas ne*
won't all of won't fruit and
*egpakaruma kahi se eg-aldew.*
other say the shine
'They said that our plants won't produce and everything won't give fruit if the sun shines (for a long time).' (Wang et al. 2006: 111)

b. *Egpabulus ki* ***pad*** *wey se* ***kenad****?*
continue we still or LNK not
'Shall we continue or not?' (Wang et al. 2006: 118)

c. *Su tenged te nekegsinug-ung*[3]
so since NONFOCUS met.on.trail
*key, ne* ***kenad*** *egkaayun ne*
1PL.EXCL then not possible that
*egpanalliya key.*
avoid.meeting we
'So since we met on the trail, it was not possible then, that we could have avoided meeting.' (Wang et al. 2006: 127)

It should be noted that all of the interpretations as a more general grammatical marker occur in contexts where a sequence of events is narrated. So even if *kenad* may be interpreted with broader functions, it very much remains in the phasal polarity domain. This puts it in sharp contrast with the other phasal polarity items which may evolve as gram types in their own right.

### 51.2.5 The status of phasal polarity items in MPSEA on the lexico-grammatical scale

We have shown that expressions for ALREADY, STILL, as well as NOT YET, frequently evolve into separate gram types in MPSEA. They occur with all kinds of predicates and are often the only TAM markers in a predication. In terms of form, many are prone to phonological erosions and in some cases, also cliticization. We relate this to their frequency of use but also to their more generalized semantics. Conversely, expressions for NO LONGER in the languages of MPSEA do not show such clear signs of grammaticalization and remain closer to the lexical end.

For the purposes of this chapter, we checked the Childes corpus of Jakarta Indonesian (Gil and Tadmor 2007) and for English (Braunwald 2015), cf. Table 51.4 and Table 51.5. As shown by the data below, the frequency of use of the markers discussed here is markedly different from the corresponding adverbials in European languages.

**Table 51.4** Frequencies in the Jakarta Indonesian Corpus

| *Indonesian expression* | *Number of hits* |
|---|---|
| *tidak* 'NEG.PRED' | 480 |
| *nggak* 'NEG.PRED' | 5947 |
| *bukan* 'NEG.NOM' | 6427 |
| *sudah* 'already/IAMITIVE' | 847 |
| *(u)dah* 'already/IAMITIVE' | 5688 |
| *belum/belom/lom* 'not yet/NONDUM' | 3255 |
| *lagi* 'again' | 2321 |
| *masih* 'still' | 1566 |

In both Jakarta Indonesian and English, grammaticalized expressions such as the different kinds of negators show very high frequencies. In Jakarta Indonesian, the marker *sudah* and especially its contracted variant *(u)dah* come on a par with the negators as regards their frequency. The marker *belum* 'not.yet' and its variants show half the frequency of the high frequency items such as *nggak, bukan,* or *(u)dah*. The positive continuative *masih* 'still' is half as frequent as *belum* 'not.yet'. In contrast, English *yet*[4] does not even come close half the frequency of grammatical markers

[3] The example is rendered exactly as it is presented in the source. The form -ung is cited without a gloss there as well.

[4] At this stage we were not able to search specifically for multiword strings such as *not yet*.

**Table 51.5** Frequencies in the Brauwald Corpus

| *English expression* | *Number of hits* |
|---|---|
| *n't* 'NEG' | 1468 |
| *not* 'NEG' | 1198 |
| *have* | 427 |
| *has* | 172 |
| *had* | 157 |
| *again* | 158 |
| *anymore* | 62 |
| *already* | 57 |
| *still* | 52 |
| *yet* | 44 |
| *longer* | 10 |

**Table 51.6** Number of phasal polarity expressions per language

| | NUMBER OF LANGUAGES |
|---|---|
| 4 phasal polarity expressions | 39 |
| 3 phasal polarity expressions NO LONGER missing | 19 |
| 3 phasal polarity expressions NOT YET missing | 2 (Bara Malagasy, Basap) |
| 3 phasal polarity expressions ALREADY missing | 1 (Palauan) |
| 2 phasal polarity expressions STILL & ALREADY only | 1 (Kapampangan) |
| Total | 62 |

such as the cliticized *n't* or *not*. This should be kept in mind when we define *belum* 'not.yet' as a grammatical or a lexical marker. Dahl and Wälchli (2016: 328) also bring up the fact that some Indonesian ID cards show the civil status of the owner as *sudah kawin* 'IAM married'. The opposite civil status, 'not married' is rendered by *belum kawin* 'not.yet married' (Östen Dahl, p.c.). Such facts go to show the generality of these markers as opposed to corresponding adverbs in many European languages.

## 51.3 Expressibility of phasal polarity concepts

Expressions of phasal polarity are found in all languages of the sample. As demonstrated in Table 51.6, there are two dominant groups. One includes languages where all four concepts are expressed, covering more than half of the languages (about 60%). The other includes languages where three phasal polarity concepts are expressed, wherein expressions for NO LONGER are missing in the source material, representing one third of the sample. The remaining groups cover a handful of languages only.

The geographical distribution of the groups in Table 51.6 is not random. Rather, languages with four phasal polarity expressions form an almost coherent pattern in the central parts of the MPSEA territory. 'Incomplete' phasal polarity systems are observed in the periphery; they can be also correlated with several Northern and Meso-Philippine languages, thus we can note a certain degree of genealogical dependence.

The MPSEA sample allows for the postulation of a lexicalization hierarchy (e.g. van der Auwera's 1998: 37 "Accessibility Hierarchy") for phasal polarity concepts in (36a). Specifically, the concepts which are expressed most commonly are STILL in all sixty-two languages of the sample, and ALREADY in sixty-one languages. Expressions for NOT YET are observed in fifty-nine languages and for NO LONGER in forty-two languages.

Within (36), we compare the MPSEA lexicalization hierarchy for phasal polarity concepts with similar hierarchies postulated for different samples. Using a stratified sample of forty languages with world coverage, van Baar (1997) finds that languages favour expressions for STILL and NOT YET, while ALREADY and NO LONGER would be frequently missing (36b). Based on an area-based study of forty-five European languages, van der Auwera (1998) posits that if a language has only one phasal polarity expression, it will be NO LONGER, followed by STILL/NOT YET and finally ALREADY, see (36c). Löfgren (2019) works on a sample of fifty-four Bantu languages, finding that expressions for NOT YET top the lexicalization hierarchy (36d).

Lexicalization hierarchies for phasal polarity expressions

(36) a. MPSEA (the current work)
STILL/ALREADY > NOT YET > NO LONGER
b. Worldwide (van Baar 1997: 132–3)
STILL/NOT YET > ALREADY > NO LONGER
c. Euroversal (van der Auwera 1998: 37)
NO LONGER > STILL/NOT YET > ALREADY
d. Bantu-versal (Löfgren 2019: 16)
NOT YET > STILL > ALREADY > NO LONGER

The hierarchies listed in (36) highlight Europe as the outlier in regard to expressibility of the phasal polarity domain: only in Europe does the terminative expression NO LONGER top the hierarchy and ALREADY is the least likely phasal polarity concept to be expressed in the sample. Furthermore, van der Auwera (1998: in passim) points out that expressions for ALREADY behave differently than other phasal polarity expressions in many European languages. Bantu languages are perhaps the phylum that falls best in line with van Baar's generalization that languages favour the continuative part of the system. MPSEA languages present a somewhat different picture since ALREADY tops the hierarchy on a par with the continuative STILL, closely followed by the negative continuative NOT YET. Both Bantu and MPSEA languages lend support to van Baar's observation that if there is non-expressed concept in the system, it will most likely be NO LONGER.

We conclude our discussion of the expressivity parameter by an overview of the number of expressions used for the encoding of specific phasal polarity concepts. Both van Baar (1997) and van der Auwera (1998) note that languages may have more than one expression for a single concept, termed 'allolexy' by van Baar. Allolexy is illustrated by three different constructional encodings of ALREADY in Makasar, South Sulawesi: The realization of an (expected) change/situation can be expressed either by the clitic *=mo* (37a), by a combination of this clitic and the auxiliary verb *le?ba?* 'finish, already' (37b), or by the auxiliary alone (37c).

Makasar

(37) a. *tallu-m-pulo=**mo**=i* *ang-annang* *taung* *umuru?=ku*
three-LNK-ten=PFV=3 LNK-six year age=1.POSS
'I'm already 36 years old (36 is my age)' (Jukes 2006: 200)

b. ***le?ba?=mo**=ko* *bunting* *di*
already=PFV=2F wedding TAG
'You're already married, aren't you?' (Jukes 2006: 209)

c. ***le?ba?**=i* *ku=baca* *sura?=nu*
finished=3 1=read letter=2F.POSS
'I already read your letter.' (Jukes 2006: 319)

Based on his own and also on van der Auwera's (1998) data, van Baar (1997) postulates a phasal polarity allolexy hierarchy, presented in (38). Specifically, this hierarchy states that the continuative concepts STILL and NOT YET are most likely to be encoded by different and variated expressions, while the least variation is likely to be found with expressions of ALREADY.[5]

(38) Phasal polarity allolexy hierarchy (van Baar 1997: 125)
STILL > NOT YET > ALREADY

Our data indicate that the languages of MPSEA are markedly different in this regard since the greatest variation in our sample is found exactly with expressions of ALREADY, as presented in (39). Furthermore, STILL and NOT YET show equal amount of variation while the least variation is observed with NO LONGER. The latter result should be taken with caution as it is directly amenable to the fact that many sources simply do not have information on NO LONGER.

(39) Phasal polarity allolexy hierarchy for MPSEA languages
ALREADY > STILL/NOT YET > NO LONGER

To summarize, unlike other parts of the world, in the MPSEA sample, ALREADY not only ranks high on the lexicalization hierarchy for this area but also shows the greatest amount of allolexy. Similar to other parts of the world, the languages of MPSEA give precedence to continuative concepts STILL and NOT YET in encoding the phasal polarity domain while the terminative NO LONGER is not only frequently missing, but when expressed, shows the least amount of allolexy.

## 51.4 Coverage

The parameter of coverage refers to the range of phasal polarity concepts covered by specific phasal polarity markers. Kramer (2018) distinguishes between two kinds of systems for this parameter, rigid and flexible. In rigid systems, one phasal polarity marker covers one phasal polarity concept; whereas in flexible systems, a single phasal polarity term may cover several phasal polarity concepts. That is, using the same positive phasal polarity expression (concepts ALREADY, STILL) with negation in the language to express a negative phasal polarity expression (concepts NOT YET, NO LONGER), as may be expected given that these expressions are logically related via duality (Löbner 1989).

[5] van Baar (1997) excludes NO LONGER order to be able to offer a generalized hierarchy that covers both his and van der Auwera's (1998) data. Expressions for NO LONGER show least variation worldwide and greatest variation in the languages of Europe.

A rigid system is illustrated in (40) by data from Biak, spoken in Western New Guinea.

Biak

(40) a. *e-ve-vín* *i-ne* *ma*
REL-VBLZ-female 3SG.SPEC-this TOP
*i-mnai* ***kwar*** *e-ve-snon*
3SG-stop already REL-VBLZ-male
*i-ne* *e-séwar* ***kaker****=i*
3SG.SPEC-this REL-seek still=3SG.SPEC
'The woman has stopped (studying) already, but the man is (the one who is) still studying.' (van den Heuvel 2006: 138)

b. *si-kaf~kif* *fa* *s-séwar*
3PL.ANIM-pick~pick CONSEC 3PL.ANIM-seek
*sarak* *i-ne* *ma* *si-srow*
bracelet 3SG.SPEC-this and 3PL.ANIM-find
*i* ***vanim***
3SG not.yet
'They (the chickens) pick to find this bracelet. And they have not found it yet.'

c. *S-ve-mnu* *ro* *di-ri-wu*
3PL.ANIM-VBLZ-village LOC place-out-over.there
*vo* *s-kavr* ***wer*** ***va***
SIMT 3PL.ANIM-return again not
'They became a village out there and did not come back any more.'
(van den Heuvel 2006: 131)

The system in Biak is rigid since completely different terms are used for the encoding of the four phasal polarity concepts: *kwar* 'already', *kakeri* 'still', *vanim* 'not yet', and *wer va* 'not anymore; no longer'.[6]

Data from Cebuano, a central Philippine language, are used to exemplify a flexible system in (41).

Cebuano

(41) a. Context: Interlocuter says that they have three children
*dako?<g>=****na****=sad*
big<PL>=already=also
'(They've) already (grown) big too.' (Tanangkingsing 2009: 50)

[6] We observe here, though it is not discussed by van den Heuvel (2006), that the *va* in *vanim* 'not.yet' seems to be a morphological negator (given its similarity with the free morpheme *va* in (40c)) that has fused with the morpheme *nim*, as *vanim* 'not.yet' is a stable word in Biak.

b. *pa-ka?on=nimo,* *init=****pa***
CAUS-eat=2SG.GEN hot=still
'You make (them) eat (it) (while it's) still hot.'
(Tanangkingsing 2009: 183)

c. *sauna* *puydi=man,* *karon*
at.first can=PART now
***di?=na=man*** *ma-himo?*
NEG=already=PART AV-do
'Before, it was allowed, (but) now it's not anymore possible.'
(Tanangkingsing 2009: 227)

d. *minimum* *sa* *ato?*
minimum.wage LOC 1PL.INCL.POSS
***wa?=pa=man*** *dos syentos*
NEG=still=PART two.hundred
'The minimum (wage) in our (country), (it's) not yet even two hundred.' (Tanangkingsing 2009: 227)

The phasal polarity system builds on essentially two terms, the clitics, *=na* 'already' and *=pa* 'still', which appear with a negator and the politeness particle *=man* to express the negative phasal polarity concepts NO LONGER and NOT YET respectively. Note that negators *di?-* and *wa?* in Cebuano have different functions within the negation system, see Tanangkingsing (2009).

Not all systems classified as flexible have both of the negative phasal polarity concepts expressed in terms of the positive ones. There are systems where either only NOT YET or only NO LONGER are expressed by some modification of the positive concept. We discuss different flexible systems below in Table 51.8.

Given the variation in the encoding of various phasal polarity concepts, there are also systems where more than one possibility is possible. For instance, in Batuley, a language spoken on the Aru islands, Maluku Province, Indonesia, NOT YET is expressed either by *narat* 'not yet' or by *komo ti* 'NEG already'. This makes the system either rigid (with *ti* 'already', *naotui* 'still', and *narat* 'not yet') or flexible since a negation of the term for ALREADY (external negation) is also used for NOT YET. Finally, there are also systems where the negative phasal polarity expressions combine aspect markers—distinct from the positive phasal polarity expressions—with negation. For instance, in Mandar, a language from South Sulawesi, STILL is expressed by a borrowed auxiliary *tattaq* (from Indonesian *tetap* 'still') while the negator *andiang* combines with the incompletive clitic *=pa* to express NOT YET, as shown in (42).

Mandar

(42) a. *Mau* ***andiang=pa**=i* *pole* *i=Dan,*
although NEG=yet=3 come PRS=Dan,
***tattaq**=i=tau* *na=min-daiq* *di* *oto.*
still=3=person FUT=AV-go.up in car
'Although Dan still hasn't come, we're still going up in the car.'

b. *Iyeq,* *diang,* ***andiang=pa**=i* *mala* *u-pau.*
yes exist NEG=yet=3 can 1.PV-say
'Yes, there's something, but I can't say it yet.'
(Dan Brodkin, p.c.)

Thus, with regard to coverage, the languages in our sample can be classified into four broad groups, as shown in Table 51.7: (i) rigid; (ii) flexible; (iii) languages with more than one possibility; and (iv) a group where an aspect marker is used for the encoding of the negative phasal polarity concepts.

**Table 51.7** Distribution of rigid and flexible systems in MPSEA

| TYPE OF SYSTEM | Number of languages |
|---|---|
| Rigid | 19 |
| Flexible | 31 |
| More than one possibility | 7 |
| Aspect-based phasal polarity expressions | 5 |
| Total | 62 |

**Table 51.8** Distribution of different patterns of flexibility in MPSEA

| PATTERN | Number of languages |
|---|---|
| 1. STILL > NOT YET and ALREADY > NO LONGER | 10 |
| 2. STILL > NOT YET, ALREADY | 11 |
| 3. STILL > NOT YET and ALREADY = NO LONGER | 1 (Sangir) |
| 4. STILL = NOT YET, ALREADY, and (NO LONGER) | 3 (Lewotobi, Palu'e, Southern Mambae) |
| 5. STILL > NOT YET, NO LONGER, ALREADY missing | 1 (Palauan) |
| 6. STILL > NO LONGER, ALREADY, and NOT YET distinct | 2 (Kambera, Balinese) |
| 7. ALREADY > NO LONGER, STILL, and NOT YET distinct | 8 |
| 8. ALREADY > NOT YET, STILL, and (NO LONGER) | 1 (Begak) |
| Total | 37 |

As indicated by the data in Table 51.7, the languages with rigid systems cover a solid one third of the sample but they appear scattered all over the territory under study. In contrast, the languages with flexible systems, which cover about half of the languages in the sample, appear concentrated on several locations: (i) the islands of Sumatra and Java; (ii) the easternmost parts of Indonesia, including East Timor; and (iii) the northern part of Borneo and the Southern Philippines. Aspect-based phasal polarity expressions are observed on Sulawesi where either NOT YET or NO LONGER or both are encoded by combining the negator with an aspectual marker rather than the positive phasal polarity expressions in their language.

The quantitative distribution of flexible systems is presented in Table 51.8. Clarification of the notation used in the table is in order: the sign > indicates that the term on its left side appears with a modifier—typically, though not always, a negator—to express the phasal polarity term on its right. The equal sign '=' indicates that one and the same term/construction is used for both concepts and context is the only disambiguator. Finally, the sum '37' indicates the number of observed patterns rather than the number of languages. Note that the brackets around NO LONGER indicate that an expression for this concept is missing in some of the languages in this group.

The patterns shown in Table 51.8 allow for several generalizations. First, there is a pronounced tendency for languages with flexible systems to use both of the positive phasal polarity concepts, typically with a negator to express the negative one, cf. (41). This is generally in line with van Baar (1997: 168).

With regard to phasal polarity expressions that cover multiple concepts, in this sample, STILL is demonstrably used for the encoding of NOT YET, as is ALREADY for the encoding of NO LONGER. It should be also pointed out that there is a tendency to preserve semantic cohesion, in that the continuative STILL is very seldom used for the encoding of the terminative NO LONGER while it is clearly the preferred option for derivation/encoding of NOT YET. Similarly, inchoative ALREADY, abundantly used for the encoding of NO LONGER, is only rarely used for the encoding of NOT YET.

We now come to the third property of coverage patterns, namely ways whereby (positive) phasal polarity expressions are modified to produce negative phasal polarity expressions in flexible systems. Since change of polarity is involved, the most frequent means is, of course, negation. Specifically, internal negation of the positive phasal polarity expressions is widely used for creating negative phasal polarity expressions, such as in (11) above for the forming a NOT YET expression by internal negation of STILL and (29) above for an illustration of NO LONGER yielded by internally negated ALREADY.

Using internal negation is, however, not the only means. For instance in Mambae, NOT YET is encoded by a reduplicating *hei* 'still/continuative'. The resulting form is described as a marker of incompletion which triggers a reading of either 'not yet X' or 'ongoing/still X' depending on the predicate it collocates with, cf. (43).

Mambae

(43) a. *Agora hela fe aan hina ruu kaben* ***hehei.***
now live FOC offspring feminine two marry IPFV
'Now there are still two daughters who have not yet married'

b. *Oo dega* ***hehei.***
2SG talk IPFV
'You were talking' (Fogaça 2017: 178)

Lewotobi Lamaholot, a language of southeastern Flores, illustrates another language with a general marker of incompletion, which effectively encodes both senses STILL and NOT YET. In this language, the word *morə̃* is described as an imperfective marker with two functions. When used with atelic predicates, either verbal or non-verbal, *morə̃* indicates the event/state to be in progress, (44a–b). When *morə̃* is used with telic predicates, it indicates that the event it marks is incomplete, which is why it is translated in English as 'not yet', cf. (44c–d).

Lewotobi Lamaholot

(44) a. *na həbo* ***morə̃***
3SG take.bath IPFV
'She is still taking a bath.' (Nagaya 2011: 414)

b. *wai? platẽ* ***morə̃***
water hot.NMLZ IPFV
'The water is still hot.' (Nagaya 2011: 414)

c. *go kriə̃ waha* ***morə̃***
1SG work finish IPFV
'I haven't finished working yet.' (Nagaya 2011: 415)

d. *Ale həkə oto* ***morə̃***
Ale stop car IPFV
'Ale hasn't stopped the car yet.'
(Nagaya 2011: 415)

Nagaya (2011: 416) points out that in most cases the distinction between telic and atelic events is less clear. Consequently, one and the same sentence can be interpreted either way; consider the data in (45).

Lewotobi Lamaholot

(45) a. *go kə̃* ***morə̃***
1SG eat.1SG IPFV
Progressive: 'I am still eating.'
Incomplete: 'I haven't eaten yet.'
(Nagaya 2011: 416)

b. *go kwukə̃* ***morə̃***
1SG drunk IPFV
Progressive: 'I am still drunk.' (The speaker has a hangover.)
Incomplete: 'I am not drunk yet.' (The speaker wants to drink more.) (Nagaya 2011: 416)

As indicated in (45), predications marked by *morə̃* become ambiguous between progressive/persistive and incomplete readings and the ambiguity can only be resolved by context. Generally, such data are very instructive about the close relation between the sense of persistence and the sense of incompletion. To put it differently, if a situation is ongoing, this also means that it is not completed or finished, hence markers such as Lewotobi Lamaholot's *morə̃* can allow both senses. In the current MPSEA sample, there are three languages with a general lexeme of incompletion. When analysed in terms of Kramer's (2018) coverage parameter, such general terms of incompletion are said to cover both STILL and NOT YET. This phenomenon has been discussed at length for a number of Bantu languages, cf. Veselinova and Devos (2020). Both van der Auwera (1998) and van Baar (1997) discuss this feature in diachronic terms; specifically, they outline the evolution of negative continuatives from positive ones. It is worth pointing out that the relation exists both on a synchronic and on a diachronic level.

A similar relation might exist between the inchoative and the terminative senses. In our sample, there is one language, Sangir, spoken in North Sulawesi, wherein the same term *seng/sen* covers both ALREADY and NO LONGER, cf. Adriani (1893, pp. 253–4). Unfortunately the source does not offer any detailed data of the kind we have seen for Lamaholot so at this stage it is not possible to offer informed hypotheses about the factors that would trigger the inchoative or the terminative reading. In any case, such a polysemy appears to be cross-linguistically less common and we leave it for future research.

In sum, the following generalizations emerge for the coverage parameter. Separate terms for each phasal polarity concept, in Kramer's terms 'rigid systems', are observed in a solid one third of the MPSEA sample. However, close to one half of the languages under study opt for flexibility, that is, use one and the same term to cover more than one phasal polarity concept. It is worth noting that internal, rather than external, negation of the positive terms is preferred for the expression of the negative ones. Typical scenarios of flexible coverage include the use of the term for ALREADY with internal negation to render NO LONGER and also the term for STILL with internal negation for the rendering of NOT YET. In addition, we highlight the close relationship between the sense of persistence, STILL, and the sense of incompletion, NOT YET, in both synchronic and diachronic perspectives. Thus, one and the same term can be used to cover both, without any mediation. This brings to light the context sensitive nature of expressions of continuity. Although this phenomenon does not appear to be very frequent in the current sample, it is still attested and falls in line with a general cross-linguistic tendency.

## 51.5 Summary and conclusions

The phasal polarity domain is very important for MPSEA languages as its expressions commonly evolve into lexico-grammatical markers with general content and scope. Expressions of phasal polarity concepts are observed in all languages of our sixty-two-language sample. Languages where all four concepts are expressed form an almost coherent pattern in the center of the MPSEA territory, while languages with 'incomplete' systems appear in the periphery. The concepts which are most frequently expressed include the positive inchoative ALREADY and continuative STILL, closely trailed by negative continuative NOT YET. On the other hand, the terminative NO LONGER is often missing in grammatical descriptions.

Expressions for ALREADY are on a par with continuative STILL as regards their importance for the phasal polarity domain. They commonly evolve into a gram type of its own right, the iamitive, a category that is close to the perfect but also distinct from it in several respects. The most important ones include the marking of stative predicates as current states resulting from an expected change, their prospective reading and also their ambiguity between indicating an achieved result and an ongoing activity. Expressions for ALREADY also frequently scope over negated predications to yield periphrastic expressions for terminative NO LONGER.

Expressions for STILL are omnipresent in the languages of the sample. They too develop into lexico-grammatical markers and are frequently subject to renewal.

The encoding of NOT YET shows the greatest variation among all phasal polarity concepts, with a clear geographical distribution. Periphrastic NOT YET expressions occur in the northern part of MPSEA, univerbations with various degrees of transparency are observed in the middle, and finally, monomorphemic NOT YET expressions form an almost uninterrupted belt across Sumatra, Java, and several island groups eastward of these islands. NOT YET expressions often originate in the continuative domain via STILL scoping over a negated predication. However, the more consolidated NOT YET becomes as a grammatical marker, the more it becomes paradigmatically linked to ALREADY, forming oppositions with it and within the domain of negation.

The encoding of NO LONGER, on the other hand, appears to be predominantly periphrastic. Even though stable collocations are observed, and occasionally also single words, these expressions rarely evolve as more general markers outside the phasal polarity domain.

As a final word, we would like to refer back the 'Duality Hypothesis' (Löbner 1989) whereby both external and internal negation are considered as possible relators between the positive and the negative phasal polarity concepts. In the languages of MPSEA, internal negation is demonstrably preferred for the encoding of the negative concepts. Furthermore, we note that negation—although the most common—is not the only possibility for yielding a negative phasal polarity concept. Continuative expressions show a very high context sensitivity and can be interpreted either as positive or a negative continuative depending on the kind of predicate they co-occur with. This context dependency has not been sufficiently discussed so far and should be highlighted more clearly in theoretical models of the phasal polarity domain.

## Acknowledgements

Thank you to the audience at APLL12 in June 2019 as well as to Robert Östling, Mar Santamaría Vaquer, and to the editors Sander Adelaar and Antoinette Schapper for their helpful comments. Ljuba Veselinova would like to acknowledge the financial support of the Swedish Research Council, Grant nr 2016-01045. Any errors are our own.

# CHAPTER 52

# Personal pronouns

ALEXANDER ADELAAR AND JOHN HAJEK

## 52.1 Introduction

This chapter provides a basic outline of free personal pronouns in Malayo-Polynesian languages of Southeast Asia and their outliers (henceforth MPSEA).

MPSEA pronoun systems show a fair degree of uniformity and diachronic stability. Many languages have seven underived pronouns reflecting first, second, and third person, singular and plural number, and clusivity (distinguishing between 1PL.INCL and 1PL.EXCL pronouns). Furthermore, MPSEA languages generally have various (morpho)syntactic series, for instance, free pronouns and possessive clitics, and many of them have additional series. These are recurrent features that can also be reconstructed for Proto-Malayo-Polynesian (PMP) and Proto-Austronesian (PAN) (see Blust's (2013a) reconstruction of PAN and PMP pronouns, §52.2 and Table 52.1). However, the multiple series of pronouns that exist in individual languages and the processes leading to their grammaticalization are not discussed here, as they are covered in the various typological chapters in this volume.

This chapter focuses on the semantic features of free pronouns (including their number, person and clusivity distinctions) and their arrangement into paradigms. It also discusses some other relevant pronominal features such as the effect of social register and the dual use of the historical 1PL.INCL pronoun. It follows the changes that these free pronouns have undergone over time, taking the PAN/PMP pronominal system as a reference point.

The organization of this chapter is as follows. §52.2 shows the reconstruction of PAN and PMP pronouns as proposed by Blust (2013a). §52.3 discusses number, §52.4, clusivity, and §52.5, person. §52.6 gives information about status, formality and pronoun avoidance. §52.7 is about the pronominal use of vocabulary belonging to other categories. §52.8 discusses the source of some pronouns. The chapter ends with summary conclusions in §52.9.

The information in this chapter has the entire MPSEA region in its scope. However, it also leans heavily towards the languages of Sumatra, Java, Borneo, and Madagascar, a focus hard to avoid given that the authors are most familiar with these languages and many of them have been studied more systematically than other MPSEA languages.

## 52.2 The original PMP pronoun system and prototypical MPSEA systems

Blust (2013a) reconstructed seven PMP pronouns along with earlier PAN ones that must have been very similar to them. The major changes that occurred from PAN to PMP were two so-called 'PAN/PMP politeness shifts'. One involved the loss of a politeness distinction in the 2SG free pronouns, which was due to an (unexplained) shift from the PAN 2SG form *i-Su to a 2PL form *i-hu in PMP, and the concomitant loss of politeness marking in the transition from PAN 2SG *(i)kaSu to PMP *(i)kahu which became a default 2SG pronoun as a result. The other involved the change in the second person genitive clitic *=mu from a default 2PL marker to a 2SG polite one (Blust 1977a: 11).[1] In many current MP languages reflexes of *i-kahu (and *=mu) have become default pronouns for the 2SG (see also Smith, this volume, §2.3.4).

Blust's (2013a) PMP and PAN pronouns (Table 52.1) are cliticized by a person marker (*i or *si):

As in many languages all around the world, pronouns in PMP and PAN are suppletive, that is, they are etymologically unrelated independent lexemes. This also applies to inclusive *i-(k)ita and exclusive *i-(k)ami: they are lexemes *sui generis* and are neither derived from one another nor from 1SG or 2SG pronouns.

As mentioned in §52.1, most MP languages have added at least one cliticized series to these free pronouns. They often have more than two pronominal series, and in some languages there are six series, as in Tukang Besi (Southeast Sulawesi; Donohue 1999a: 106) and Mori Bawah (East Sulawesi, Mead 2005: 686), or even more. However, these series are usually morphologically transparent.

[1] As indicated in §52.1, cliticized pronouns are not discussed further in this chapter.

Alexander Adelaar and John Hajek, *Personal pronouns*. In: *The Oxford Guide to the Malayo-Polynesian Languages of Southeast Asia*. Edited by: Alexander Adelaar and Antoinette Schapper, Oxford University Press. © Alexander Adelaar and John Hajek (2024). DOI: 10.1093/oso/9780198807353.003.0052

**Table 52.1** PAN and PMP personal pronouns

| | PAN | > | PMP |
|---|---|---|---|
| 1SG | *i-aku | | *i-aku |
| 2SG | *i-Su, *(i)kaSu (polite) | | *i-kahu |
| 3SG | *si-ia | | *si-ia |
| 1PL.INCL | *i-(k)ita | | *i-(k)ita |
| 1PL.EXCL | *i-(k)ami | | *i-(k)ami |
| 2PL | *i-kamu | | *i-kamu, *ihu |
| 3PL | *si-ida | | *si-ida |

## 52.3 Number

The general pattern for personal pronouns in MPSEA languages is to distinguish singular and plural, in contrast to nouns, which are typically unmarked for number. Moreover, MPSEA languages usually agree in that their plural pronouns are not derived from singular ones (see Table 52.1), with notable exceptions (see §52.3.3).

There are also many languages that have departed from this basic structure. Some, particularly in western Indonesia, have lost the pronominal number distinction (see §52.3.1). Other languages have extended the original number division with a dual category, and in some instances even with trial or quadral categories (see §52.3.2).

### 52.3.1 Loss of number

In modern Javanese pronominal number has been lost completely. If required, the plural is expressed periphrastically with *paḍa*, *kabɛh*, or another equivalent. Compare the following sentences in which *paḍa* marks plurality of Subject and Agent respectively:

Javanese
(1) *Anak-e paḍa g<um>uyu*
child-DEF PL <INTR>laugh
'The children laughed' (Novi Djenar p.c.)

Javanese
(2) *Aku paḍa di-tinggal*
I PL UV-leave
(Context: the parents were gone): 'I was left [by them]' (Ogloblin 2005: 607; original source Hayward 1998)

Number was also lost in neighbouring languages including Balinese (Arka and Dalrymple 2017: 262; Shiohara and Arka, this volume, §32.1), Madurese (Vander Klok, this volume, §31.2) and some varieties of Malay, where this has presumably happened under the influence of Javanese. Blust (2013a: 306) explains the loss of number in these languages to the fact that they are spoken in societies with extreme stratification (see §52.6).

In Old Javanese PMP, number may still have existed but it was in a state of erosion. In his analysis of the Old Javanese *Adiparwa*, Zoetmulder (1983: 17–18) shows that, at least in this prose text, number was no longer distinguished, although the pronouns signifying it were still extant. However, the third person pronouns *ya* (< PMP *ia '3SG') and *sira* (< PMP *sida '3PL') had instead become indicators of low and high position respectively. Furthermore, *kita* (a reflex of PMP *kita '1PL.INCL') had become a second person pronoun together with *kami* (originally '1PL.EXCL') and *ko* (< PMP *i-kau '2SG'). According to Kern (1918), which is based on a larger corpus of Old Javanese than the *Adiparwa* text, *kami* was no longer exclusively plural and had acquired a deferential meaning.

The trend towards loss of a number distinction is also observed in Merina Malagasy, a language spoken in the central highlands of Madagascar which was particularly affected by Hindu–Malay and Hindu–Javanese culture and associated social stratification in the past. In this language, PMP *sida '3PL' lost its pronominal function. It became a plural marker in combination with a following deictic element in Proto-Southeast-Barito *iu: *sida + *iu > *hire+iu > *irèu*. Modern Malagasy has essentially only one default third person pronoun *ìzi*, and *irèu* needs to follow it to make plurality explicit (Adelaar and Kikusawa 2014: 496). Furthermore, the 2PL pronoun *hianarèu* in Merina is the result of two successive attempts to mark plurality in a second person pronoun that had lost this notion several times in the history of Malagasy (see examples (3a) and (3b)):

Malagasy
(3) a. *ikam '2PL' > *iha '2SG' (compare *iha* '2SG' in west coast Malagasy dialects);
*iha + *nau(n) '2PL' > *ihanau '2PL'

b. *ihanau '2PL' > (with *i/*h metathesis) *hianàu '2PL'> *hianàu* '2SG';
*hianàu '2SG' + *irèu* (pluralizer) > *hianà(u)-(i)rèu > *hianarèu* '2PL' (Adelaar and Kikusawa 2014: 491–7)

The 1PL.INCL pronoun *isìka* is derived from a 1DU.INCL pronoun and has undergone a different development. But it too needed an element to be suffixed to in order to acquire plural meaning (see §52.4–4.2 fn.4). Of the Malagasy basic personal pronouns, only the 1PL.EXCL pronoun *izahài* cannot be shown to have gone through a stage in which the notion of plurality was missing (Adelaar and Kikusawa 2014).

The lack of a number distinction in a single person (as in English second person *you*) is more frequent. For instance, Malay *ia/dia* is historically a general third person pronoun; and although modern Malay and Indonesian have *məreka* '3PL', *ia/dia* (and particularly its genitive cliticized form -*nya*) is still used with plural reference. *məreka* is relatively new and derives from Old Javanese *mar-ika*, an emphatic particle with a deictic function (Adelaar 1992a: 125–6). Sambas Malay (in Semelagi Kecil, West Kalimantan) lacks a dedicated 3PL pronoun, using instead the number-neutral *die* or *oraŋ ito* (literally 'that person/those people') (Adelaar unpublished fieldnotes). In Mandailing, *halahí* (also *halaní*) 'those people' replaced an older *nasida* '3PL', part of which still reflects PAN/PMP *si-ida as a source (van der Tuuk 1971: 219). Colloquial Indonesian *kita*, Jakarta Malay *kitɛ* and, historically, Vehicular Malay *kita, all refer to any first person, with no number or inclusive/exclusive distinction (see further §52.4.3; for the notion of 'Vehicular Malay', see Anderbeck, this volume, §9.1). PMP *(si)ia '3SG' was generalized to a general third person pronoun *ia* in literary Malay (sixteenth to nineteenth centuries AD) and various other Malay varieties. As discussed previously, number distinction was lost in the Malagasy default third person pronoun *izy*. Sulawesi languages such as Makasar (Jukes 2005, 2020) and Busoa (van den Berg 2020), also make use a of single default third person pronoun.

## 52.3.2 Additional number categories

Most MP pronouns only distinguish singular and plural, but in various MPSEA regions it is not uncommon for languages to have an additional dual number distinction, especially in Borneo and eastern Indonesia.[2] Dual number is usually manifested throughout a dedicated dual pronoun series. In some MPSEA regions there is also a dual-like phenomenon which as a rule only involves reflexes of *kita. However, duality is not a semantic core element in these reflexes, which are discussed in §52.4 on clusivity. As a rule, dual pronouns are derived from plural ones and/or the numeral for 'two'.[3] A transparent example is Iban, a Malayic language in Sarawak, which has a full dual series based on such derivations (Richards 1981: xvi), as shown in Table 52.2:

**Table 52.2** Iban plural and dual personal pronouns

| | Plural | Dual |
|---|---|---|
| 1INCL | *kitay* | *tua* (< *kita(y) dua) |
| 1EXCL | *kami* | *kami dua* |
| 2 | *kitaʔ* | *kitaʔ dua* |
| 3 | *sidaʔ* | *siduay* (< *sidaʔ dua(y)) |

Various languages in eastern Indonesia and Borneo have trial number. Trial number also occurs in the Mongondow and Lolak languages in Sulawesi (van den Berg and Mead, this volume, Chapter 33). The example in Table 52.3 is from Larike (Central Maluku, Indonesia) (Laidig and Laidig 1990: 92). Parallel to the formation of dual series in Iban, the dual and trial series in Larike (Ambon Island, Moluccas) have evolved from compounds involving plural pronouns followed by the numbers *dua* 'two' and *tidu* 'three' respectively:

**Table 52.3** Larike plural, dual, and trial personal pronouns

| | Plural | Dual | Trial |
|---|---|---|---|
| 1.INCL | *ami* | *arua* | *aridu* |
| 1.EXCL | *ite* | *itua* | *itidu* |
| 2 | *imi* | *irua* | *iridu* |
| 3 | *mati* | *matua* | *atidu* |

Kenyah languages in Borneo have an additional quadral number, bringing the total number of categories up to five (singular, dual, trial, quadral, plural), the same unusually high number as in some Pacific languages, as Smith (2017d) points out. This is illustrated in the pronoun chart in Smith (2017d: 56); see also the Punan Bah five-number pronominal system presented in Table 27.11 by Kroeger and Smith (this volume, §27.4.2.3). In his demonstration of Lepo' Vo' (Kenyah, Borneo), Smith (2017d: 53–6) shows that the quadral is used for small numbers in general, not necessarily for only 'four', and therefore it is better described as a 'paucal'. This is not unlike other languages with more than three number distinctions. (Corbett shows that in Oceanic languages like Sursurunga (New Ireland), trial number is used as a 'lesser paucal', and quadral number as a 'greater paucal' (Corbett 2000)). In Biak, trial number is distinguished for the third person and functions practically as a paucal. However,

[2] Note also Chamorro which does not have dual pronouns but expresses dual number through verbal morphology (Topping (1973: 233) and Zobel, this volume, §38.4.3).

[3] Zobel (p.c.) makes the observation that number distinctions other than singular and plural are always derived from plural pronouns, never from singular ones.

the trial forms in Larike listed above unambiguously refer to a number of three (Laidig and Laidig 1990: 92).

Another feature shared by Lepo' Vo' and Sursurunga is that they use paucal number (not the plural) to refer to well defined groups such as a working team or a kin pair (one's uncles or one's siblings) (Smith 2017d: 52–4). Similarly, Biak uses the trial or paucal (rather than the plural) to refer to kinship members together.

Blust (2013a: 318) notes that in some Bornean languages which have no trial or quadral distinction, the plural is derived from original plural pronouns and a following numeral *telu 'three' or *epat 'four' respectively. This is demonstrated on the basis of Mukah Melanau in Table 52.4, the plural series of which is derived from reflexes of PMP plural pronouns followed by the word for three.

**Table 52.4** The origin of Mukah Melanau plural pronouns

| | Etymon | Mukah Melanau |
|---|---|---|
| 1PL.INCL | *kita *təlu | *tələw* |
| 1PL.EXCL | *kami *təlu | *mələw* |
| 2PL | *ikəm *təlu | *kələw* |
| 3PL | *ida *təlu | *(də)ləw iən* |

Blust speculates that this outcome may be due to the reduction of an originally more extended system which included trial number: at some point trial pronouns must have assumed the role of plural pronouns in general, whereas the original plural pronouns became superfluous (Blust 2013a: 318). In some languages with quadral number, a parallel development may have occurred (for an example in a Kenyah language of the shift from original quadral to plural number, see Smith (2017d: 62)).

A comparable phenomenon is observed in the history of Biak trial pronouns *sko* 'third person paucal', *ko* '2PL.INCL', *inko* '1PL.EXCL', and *mko* '2PL': the *-ko* component in these pronouns can be traced to the numeral *təlu 'three'; furthermore, van den Heuvel speculates that the *u* vowel in all dual pronouns may reflect the penultimate vowel of PAN *Du(S)a (> PMP *duha) 'two' (van den Heuvel 2006: 66–7).

### 52.3.3 Morphological marking of the plural

The dual, trial, and quadral (or paucal) number categories discussed above are morphologically marked in the pronoun systems of MP languages. As mentioned previously, as a rule, plural pronouns are not. Vehicular Malay languages are untypical in that they are historically singular pronouns with the word *oraŋ* 'person' cliticized to it. This is shown in Table 52.5 where we can also infer that *kita was a number-neutral pronoun in the early history of these languages.[4] In Manado Malay it subsequently became a singular pronoun.

## 52.4 Clusivity

Clusivity is defined by Filimonova as a "term denoting the phenomenon of inclusive-exclusive distinction and comprising simultaneously both members of the opposition" (Filimonova 2005: xii). It refers to the inclusion of more than one grammatical person in a pronominal reference and was discussed for the first time in Boas (1911) who was concerned with the phenomenon in North American languages.

Austronesian languages as a rule distinguish between 1PL.INCL and 1PL.EXCL pronouns. 'Inclusive' refers to the inclusion of both first person (self) and second person (addressee) in the use of a pronoun, and 'exclusive' to the exclusion of the second person in the use of the 1PL. The following Karo Batak sentences serve as simple examples: sentence (4) has *kita* 'we', which includes the addressee and translates as 'we (all)', whereas sentence (5) has *kami* 'we', which excludes the addressee and translates as 'we (but not you)':

Karo Batak (Sumatra)
(4) *Arus kita mə-hampat nandaŋi kalimbubu*
must 1PL.INCL STAT-respect towards in-law
'We must be respectful to our in-laws'
(Woollams 1996: 174)

Karo Batak (Sumatra)
(5) *Pitu garun dakan nakan kami!*
seven pot cook rice 1PL.EXCL
'Cook us seven pots of rice! (Woollams 1996: 134)

Clusivity is not limited to the first-cum-second person plural pronoun (see Boas 1911). In many languages in the Philippines, Borneo, and North Sulawesi, it also applies to the first-cum-second person singular. In these languages, reflexes of PMP *kita only refer to the first and second person singular combined and have lost their general plural meaning. Because of this narrowing of scope they are often identified as 'dual' pronouns, but they are more accurately defined as inclusive pronouns which have the 1SG and 2SG together as their reference (Thomas 1955: 205–8). The concomitant shift

[4] Jakarta Malay *kitɛ* (Abdul Chaer 1976) is also number-neutral, (see §52.4.3), although Jakarta Malay is not a Vehicular Malay variety.

**Table 52.5** Vehicular Malay pronouns

| | Sri Lankan Malay (Adelaar 1991) | Ambon Malay (van Minde 1997) | Manado Malay (Stoel 2005) | Standard Indonesian (Sneddon 2010) |
|---|---|---|---|---|
| 1SG | *go*, (polite) *se* | *beta* (with variants *bet, be*) | *kita* | *aku*, (polite *saya*) |
| 2SG | *lu* | *ose* (with variants *os, se*), *ale* | *nana* | (*əŋkaw*), *kamu* |
| 3SG | *de* | *dia* (with variants *di, de*) | *dia* | *dia* |
| 3SG | | (inanimate) *akaŋ* | | |
| 1PL | *kitaŋ* < *kita *oraŋ | *kat'oŋ, toŋ* (toraŋ) < *kita *oraŋ | *toraŋ* | *kita (incl), kami* (excl) |
| 2PL | *luraŋ* < *lu *oraŋ | *doraŋ, doŋ* < *dia *oraŋ | *ŋoni* | *(kamu), kalian* |
| 3PL | *deraŋ* < *dia *oraŋ | *doraŋ, doŋ* < *dia *oraŋ | *doraŋ* | *məreka (itu)* |

from plural to a dual-like meaning in *kita required a new 1PL.INCL pronoun as it potentially left a gap in the pronoun system. This gap is filled by a compound pronoun deriving from *kita + a cliticized 'extender'. The latter is usually a cliticized 2PL.GEN pronoun, but it can also be a quantifier. So, in Iraya (Mindoro, Philippines), PMP *kita '1PL.INCL' became *kita* '1SG+2SG', and the '1PL.INCL' slot was filled by an extended form *kita + -*mu '2PL.GEN', which in modern Iraya is reduced to *tamu* (Reid 2016: 155). Central Sinama *kita* is a 1SG+2SG.INCL pronoun, whereas the 1PL slot was filled by *kitabi* (which developed from *kita + a quantifier *qabis 'all').

**Table 52.6** Ilokano singular, dual, and plural pronouns

| | Singular | Dual | Plural |
|---|---|---|---|
| 1+2 | _ | *ta* | *tayo* |
| 1 | *co* | _ | *mi* |
| 2 | *mo* | _ | *yo* |
| 3 | *na* | _ | *da* |

## 52.4.1 Minimal vs. augmented number

The inclusive/exclusive opposition (in MPSEA languages—and in Austronesian languages in general) creates an irregular paradigm, as it only applies to the first person non-singular. In the Philippines, Borneo, and North Sulawesi, the imbalance is complicated further by the presence of a dual-like category, which is filled by *kita as its only member. This is shown in the many gaps (indicated by a hyphen) in the Ilokano pronominal paradigm in Table 52.6:

In order to get around this imbalance and to eliminate dual as a category in Ilokano, Thomas abandoned the notion of a singular vs. plural opposition and replaced it with one opposing 'limited' and 'generalized' number (Thomas 1955: 205–8; Cysouw 2003). Later on, Conklin (1962: 135) used the terms 'minimal' vs. 'augmented' for these same notions in Hanunoo (Philippines), which have since become the current labels in linguistics more widely. Through this change in vantage point, the rather 'lonely' 1DU.INCL pronoun can be arranged as a minimal pronoun along with what used to be called the singular pronouns but are now labelled as minimal pronouns (I with you [alone], she, he it). It is a 'minimal' pronoun because—although not singular—it can be classified together with the first, second, and third singular pronouns in a joint category. The members of this category refer to a minimal number of people (one individual in cases of first, second, and third person, and two individuals in the case of the 1DU.INCL). They contrast with the augmented pronouns, which are not limited in the number of people they may refer to. These minimal and augmented pronouns can be arranged into a simple binary classification. In Table 52.7, the inclusive pronoun *ta* refers only to speaker and addressee and contrasts with *tayo*, which refers to the speaker and an unspecified number of addressees.

The minimal/augmented arrangement shown in Table 52.7 is seen to be neater than the singular/plural one

**Table 52.7** Ilokano minimal and augmented pronouns

| | Minimal | Augmented |
|---|---|---|
| 1+2 | *tu* | *tayo* |
| 1 | *co* | *mi* |
| 2 | *mo* | *yo* |
| 3 | *na* | *da* |

in Table 52.6 when dealing with pronominal systems of languages in the Philippines, north Sulawesi, and north and central Borneo. For other MPSEA languages this arrangement is less relevant as it does not provide a more balanced description than the standard analysis identifying singular and plural pronouns.

### 52.4.2 The development of the first person 'dual' form *kita

Reflexes of PMP *kita are widespread among MP languages, and most of these refer to the 1PL. However, as noted above, in many Philippine languages and languages in northern Sulawesi and northern and central Borneo, they are a pronoun referring to the first and second person singular combined, and the only dual-like pronoun in their respective paradigms. Blust (2013a: 309) considers them dual pronouns and proposes that their 'dual' meaning is the result of a convergent development or 'drift', which happened in various languages independently. He concedes that the dual instances suggest that *kita originally had a dual meaning but explains that this is unlikely because if so, the protolanguage would have lacked a 1PL.INCL, a gap which would be difficult to account for. The shift from 1PL.INCL to 1DU.INCL is pragmatically predictable as contexts requiring a 1PL.INCL usually only involve a 1SG and a 2SG as participants. As for the subsequent development of a new 1PL.INCL based on *kita and cliticized pronominal extenders, Blust (2013a: 320) notes that these extenders seemed to be of first, second, or third person and could be singular or plural (a matter that he does not discuss any further). They almost always seem to derive from one of the following four forms:

> *=mu '2SG.GEN', *=ku '1SG.GEN', *=yu '2PL.GEN', and *=da '3PL.GEN'

In general outline, Blust's position (2013a) is supported by Liao (2008a). However, it is opposed by Reid (2016) who argues that, somewhere at a post-Proto-Austronesian stage (but prior to Proto-Malayo-Polynesian) *kita had become a 'dual' pronoun, and its meaning was maintained in Philippine and Bornean languages. The plural inclusive meaning in other languages is consequently the result of a semantic shift (or rather, a semantic U-turn). Reid points out that the suffixation of extenders was not a random process. The singular ones can be shown to derive historically from plural ones. *=mu and *=ku may look like singular forms today but are in fact derived from *=muyu, and *=kayu respectively, both 2PL.GEN clitics. In the course of time the latter became phonologically reduced and lost their plural meaning.[5] According to this analysis, extenders were originally all plural, and never first person, which would be more in line with general typological expectations than the assessment about their nature made by Blust. Reid furthermore claims that *=muyu was originally the only extender suffixed to *kita: after it was reduced to *-*mu* and had lost its plural meaning, some languages replaced it with other extenders which still had a plural meaning (*=yu, *=kayu, *=da).

In summary, Reid (2016) proposes that PMP had a 1DU.INCL pronoun *kita and had developed along with it an extended form *kita + *-muyu for the 1PL.INCL.

Reid's analysis is strengthened by recent evidence from languages outside the Philippines, north Sulawesi, and north and central Borneo. As mentioned above, languages within this region attribute 'dual' meaning to reflexes of *kita but usually do not distinguish dual number in other pronouns. Languages outside the region—provided they distinguish dual number—usually extend it to the entire pronominal series. However, a few languages are exceptional in that they are spoken outside the region delineated above and yet also limit dual meaning to *kita reflexes. These are the Southeast Barito languages (southern Borneo), Enggano, Mentawai (Enggano and Mentawai Islands east of Sumatra), Muna (Southeast Sulawesi), and (in historical hindsight) Malagasy. In the Southeast Barito languages, Ma'anyan *taruɛh*, Dusun Witu *uɛh* (Adelaar fieldnotes), and Bayan *tataruɛ* (Tjia fieldnotes), all derive from *(ki)ta- + *ruɛ(h) 'two', while other pronouns have no dual meaning. Moreover, Ma'anyan *takam* and Malagasy *(i)tsika*[6] '1PL.INCL' appear to be historically

[5] At a later stage*-kayu was also reduced and became formally identical to PMP *-ku '1SG' (see Reid 2009b: 472). As Reid points out, this 2PL pronoun -*ku* in the languages in question is unlikely to clash with reflexes of PMP *-ku '1SG' as these languages usually reflect the latter as -*k*.

[6] Compare Proto-Southeast-Barito *hi (topic marker) + *kita=kam > *i + *tik(a) (+ regular *k/*t metathesis) + *=kaN > *itsika* '1PL.INCL' (with loss of *N

derived from *(ki)ta '1SG+2SG' inclusive' combined with *=kam, a 2PL.GEN extender (Adelaar 2019: 420). Their history appears to be in alignment with that of the 1PL.INCL pronouns in Philippine, North Sulawesi, and North and Central Borneo languages.[7] Furthermore, Enggano has the pronouns *ʔika* '1DU.INCL' and *ʔikaʔa* '1PL.INCL'. The former is a regular reflex of PMP *kita, whereas the latter derives from *kita in combination with an unidentified post-clitic *-aʔa (Edwards 2015: 72). In Mentawai, the 1PL.INCL consists of *sita* (< *kita) and kam '2PL' and these two parts can move independently: *sita kam* (and *ta*-Verb *kam*) occurs in clause initial position, and *kam sita* follows a predicate (Zobel p.c.). Finally, in Muna (Southeast Sulawesi), *intaidi* is a 1DU.INCL, and *intaidi=imu*, 1PL.INCL (*=imu* is a plural marker).[8] With the exception of Malagasy, the number categories in these languages are described most adequately in terms of minimal vs. augmented.

### 52.4.3 Loss of clusivity

In Jakarta Malay (Betawi), the '1PL.INCL' pronoun *kita became a general first person *kitɛ* (Abdul Chaer 1976), which is neutral as to both clusivity and number. This also happened in Vehicular Malay varieties, although in most of these varieties *kita nowadays only occurs in derivations involving the plural marker *oraŋ* so that its initial lack of number became obscured (§52.3.3). In Indonesian there is a tendency to use *kita* for all first person plural reference, whereas *kami* keeps its basic meaning of '1PL.EXCL' but with a notion of emphasis added to it.[9]

The change from a clusivity opposition into one marking relative quantity in Tukang Besi (Southeast Sulawesi) is remarkable. In this language, *ikami* (< PMP *i-kami '1PL.EXCL'), became a first person paucal indicating numbers from two to four, and *ikita* (<*kita) a first person indicating numbers of four or more (Donohue 1999a: 114).

## 52.5 Person

Austronesian and Malayo-Polynesian languages generally distinguish first, second, and third person, although there is also variability in the manifestation of person in MPSEA languages. The following phenomena are addressed in this section: loss or reduction of pronominal distinction, change of pronominal referent, generic pronouns, reflexive pronouns, gender, and animacy.

### 52.5.1 Loss of pronominal distinctions

As mentioned in §52.2, various languages lack a dedicated 3PL pronoun (as in Sambas Malay, §52.3) or have created a new one after they lost PMP *sida (as in Malay and Merina Malagasy). Something similar no doubt also happened in Acehnese. The latter currently has a 3HON pronoun *gobñan*, which is number neutral and can still be analysed as *gop* 'other person' + *ñan* 'that' (Durie 1985: 118). Modern Javanese lost the original PMP third person pronouns, which are still extant in Old Javanese, although in the latter they lost their number distinction and differentiate social rank instead (§52.3.1). Modern Javanese now uses *ḍèwèʔé*, which is essentially a reflexive pronoun.

### 52.5.2 Change of original referent

A change of original referent often concerns reflexes of PMP *kita, the 1PL.INCL pronoun. In some languages this has led to a permanent shift, for instance, Old Javanese *kita* 'second person', dialectal Sundanese *kita* '2SG' (Eringa 1984), Mandar *itaʔ* '2SG.HON' (Abdul Muthalib 1977), Iban *kitaʔ* '2PL' (Richards 1981). In other ones, the first person inclusive pronoun has kept its original meaning but it can also be used as a second person polite. This is frequently the case in Timorese languages including Baikeno, Tokodede, Tetun, Idate, and Southern Mambae. In Naueti, *kita* has instead become a 1PL.EXCL pronoun and was replaced by *hira* as a 1PL.INCL pronoun. The latter pronoun is now also used as a second person (singular) polite form (Veloso 2016: 59–61), in agreement with the general tendency in Timor-Leste.

The use of the 1PL.INCL as a second person polite is also widespread in Sulawesi (see van den Berg and Mead, this volume, chapter 33). It is observed in the Dampelas, Totoli, and Amipibabo-Lauje languages of the Tomini-Tolitoli group (Himmelmann (2001: 90), and in Pendau (Quick 2003) (Central Sulawesi Province). It is also observed in Gorontalo (Gorontalo Province, Pateda 1977: 31), in Tompakewa (a variant form of Tontemboan, (North Sulawesi Province, Stokhof ed. (1983: 104)), in Tae' (van der Veen 1940), Makasar (Jukes 2020: 169), Bugis, Kajang (also known as Coastal Konjo), and Duri (Massenrempulu) (Sirtjo Koolhof p.c.) (in South

which is still extant in regional dialects; Adelaar and Kikusawa 2014: 492–3). In Ma'anyan, *kita=kam > *(ki)ta=kam > *takam*.

[7] However, Ma'anyan *tarueh*, Dusun Witu *ueh*, and Bayan *tatarue* are different from their Philippine, Sulawesi, and Bornean counterparts in that they are marked by the extender *-rueh* (/-rue/ueh) 'two'.

[8] The suffix *=imu* is a form of the plural marker *=Vmu*, also found on the 2PL pronoun *ihintu=umu* which is derived from the 2SG pronoun *ihintu*.

[9] Novi Djenar (p.c.).

Sulawesi), in Bangui (van den Bergh 1953) and Balantak (van den Berg and Busenitz 2012) (East Sulawesi), and in Muna (van den Berg 1989) (Southeast Sulawesi). Finally, Buol speakers (in Central Sulawesi) use *kito* when addressing elders, while referring to themselves as *kami ato-niu* [1PL.EXCL.NOM slave-2PL.GEN] 'we, your slave' (Zobel 2005: 633).

## 52.5.3 Generic pronouns

Personal pronouns can be used as generic pronouns. An instance of this is the following Colloquial Indonesian utterance (6) (made by someone laying out the conditions for hiring a rowing boat). According to Ewing (2005c: 245), here *kita* '1PL.INCL' is used without particular person affiliation:

Colloquial Indonesian

(6)

| *Tapi* | *kalau* | *kalau* | *ndak* | *bisa* | *ya,. . .* |
|---|---|---|---|---|---|
| but | if | if | not | can | yeah |

| *kita* | *nambah. . .* | *nambah* | *ongkos* |
|---|---|---|---|
| 1PL.INCL | increase | increase | payment |

'But if (one) can't [row], well one has to pay more [to hire an oarsman]' (Ewing 2005c: 245)

Some languages make use of the word for 'person' to express generic reference, for instance, Indonesian/Malay may use *oraŋ* as a general term for 'person'. This is seen in Indonesian expressions like *Kata oraŋ* [word; say + person] 'they say, it is said,. . .' and *baraŋ oraŋ* [thing, object + person] 'someone else's belongings' (Adelaar 1994c). Observe also the Colloquial Indonesian example in (7):

Colloquial Indonesian

(7)

| *Iya,* | *bisa* | *terjadi,* | *orang* | *nggak* | *tahu* | *kan!* |
|---|---|---|---|---|---|---|
| sure | can | happen | person | not | know | isn't.it |

| *Mana* | *orang* | *bisa* | *tahu!* |
|---|---|---|---|
| how | person | can | know |

'Sure, [these things] happen, one doesn't know, right? How's one to know?!' (Novi Djenar p.c.)

In Cocos Keeling Malay (West Australia) a reduced form of *oraŋ* has become a dedicated indefinite pronoun (Adelaar 1996b: 170, 183). See *oŋ* in (8):

Cocos Keeling Malay

(8)

| *ada* | *barat* | *kəncaŋ,* | *seklon* | *oŋ* |
|---|---|---|---|---|
| EXIST | westerly | strong | cyclone | someone.they |

| *bilaŋ,* | *dari* | *sana* |
|---|---|---|
| say | from | there |

'there is a strong westerly, a cyclone as they call it, coming from there' (Adelaar 1996b: 197)

## 52.5.4 Reflexive pronouns

Reflexive pronouns are "used to indicate that a non-subject argument of a transitive predicate is coreferential with (or bound by) the subject". They have to be distinguished from intensifiers, "which can be adjoined to either noun-phrases and verb-phrases, are always focused and thus are prosodically prominent" (König, Siemund, and Töpper 2013). Many MPSEA languages have reflexive pronouns, although notions like reflexivity and reciprocity[10] are also expressed through verbal morphology, especially in Philippine and Sulawesi languages (Kitada 2021; see also §§24.4.2, 24.5.3, 25.3.5.6, and 33.4.5). Conforming to what seems to be a universal tendency (König, Siemund, and Töpper 2013), reflexive pronouns are often derived from words for 'body' or '(something) standing upright'. In Phan Rang Cham, *-tray* is a 1PL.INCL as well as a reflexive pronoun, and it has also retained the original meaning 'body' (Thurgood 2005: 499). It is related to Indonesian *diri* 'self' (compare diri-ku 'myself', dirimu 'yourself' etc.)', and *səndiri* 'oneself' (for *səndiri* see further below). Note that Indonesian *diri* is also the root of the verbs *bər-diri* 'to stand' and *mən-diri-kan* 'to found; erect'. Related forms are Salako *diriʔ*, a default 1PL.INCL pronoun, and Acehnese *droe* 'self'. Cliticized to basic personal pronouns, the latter forms reflexive pronouns (*droe=ku* 'myself', *droe=neu(h)* 'yourself') but *droe=neu(h)* is also used as a polite second person or even a reverent third person (Durie 1985: 117–19). Even more obvious examples of polysemy involving 'body' and a reflexive pronoun are Makasar and Embaloh *kale* (Adelaar 1995e), Malagasy *tena*, Mentawai *tubu*, Minangkabau *awak*,[11] Manggarai *weki* (Nagaya, this volume, Chapter 34): all these words have a core meaning 'body' and serve as the basis of reflexive pronouns, for example, Makasar *kaleŋku* 'myself', *kalennu* 'yourself', *kalenna* 'her-, himself', etc. Note incidentally that such periphrastic constructions involving the word for 'body' are not only used as reflexives but have also other applications.[12]

[10] MPSEA languages generally express reciprocity morphosyntactically, although some of them additionally have lexical ways to do so (Kitada 2021: 7). Some languages use a personal pronoun (Gasser, Arnold, and Kamholz, this volume, §37.3.8.1) but that does not seem to be usual. As reciprocity in MPSEA languages is in any case still a poorly studied topic, the authors have made no attempt to include reciprocal pronouns in this survey.

[11] *Awak* is also used as a polite address term in Malaysian Malay.

[12] Zobel (p.c.) notes that, in some languages, prepositions cannot directly precede pronominals but need to combine with the term for 'body' in order to be able to do so, for example, Bugis *ri ale-ku* 'to/by me' and Mentawai *ka tubu-mu* 'to you' [both: PREP + body + PRO]. This is not unlike the Malay/Indonesian prepositions *kə* 'to and *dari* 'from' which need to be prefixed to *pada* 'at' before they can combine with a pronoun (*kə-pada-mu* 'to you' and so on). Although *pada* is currently a preposition, it derives from an (originally Sanskrit) noun meaning 'place; position' (Gonda 1973: 593).

Compare also High Balinese *tiaŋ*, Low Balinese *icaŋ* '1SG', Tanala Malagasy *itsìa*, *itsìana* < *i (topic marker) + *tiaN) '1PL.INCL'. These terms are related to the notion of 'mast' or 'post', compare Indonesian *tiaŋ* 'mast; post', Javanese *tiaŋ* 'mast; post; (high register) person; (generic pronoun)'.

Indonesian has *awak* 'body; trunk of body; self'. In regional Malay varieties and Minangkabau, *awak* 'person' is also a generic personal pronoun occurring separately as well as in combination with a pronominal suffix to express first, second, third person: *awak*-ku '1SG/1PL' *awak-mu* '2SG/2PL', *awak-nya* '3SG/3PL'. Javanese *ḍèwè'é* '3SG/3PL' in all likelihood derives from *awak (< *d(i)- + *awak 'body' + *-e* '3.POSS').

Toba Batak *iba* 'person; self' is also used as a generic pronoun and has the derivations *iba-ŋhu* [ibakku] 'my person; 1SG' and *iba-na*, the 3SG default form (Warneck 1977). Note the distinction between reflexive pronouns in dedicated reflexive constructions (e.g. Minangkabau *mambunuah badan/diri*, Malay *məmbunuh diri* 'to kill oneself'), and intensifiers expressing emphasis, for example, Minangkabau *awak* in *awak den* 'I myself', and Malay *səndiri* in sentence (9):

| | Indonesian | |
|---|---|---|
| (9) | *Lihat* | *sendiri!* |
| | see | self |
| | 'See for yourself!' (Novi Djenar p.c) | |

### 52.5.5 Gender and animacy distinctions

Gender, based on human male–female sex differentiation, is not usually distinguished in MPSEA languages, but there are various exceptions. These generally concern the 2SG, for example, Moken (*mɛ:* '2SG.FEMALE', *bɔ* '2SG.MALE') (Larish 2005), Mualang (di' '2SG.FEMALE', *m'ih* '2SG.MALE') (Tjia 2007). Punan languages from the Müller-Schwaner group in Indonesian Borneo have a three gender distinction for the third person (masculine, feminine, and neutral; Sellato 1981). In Minangkabau, gender distinction is only made with lower status pronouns: *aŋ* is to address a second person (singular) male of a lower position, and *kau* is the equivalent term to address a female (Moussay 1995). Besemah Malay (South Sumatra) has a 2SG pronoun to address someone of the same sex, *kaba*, and one to address someone of the opposite sex, *deŋa* (see McDonnell et al., this volume, §29.3.5).[13] In Tengger there are different first person pronouns for females (*isun*) and males (*(r)eyang*) (Conners 2008: 46).

[13] Helfrich (1904: 34) has *deŋan*, a 2SG pronoun used by young men when addressing young women.

An animacy distinction, (between animate and inanimate entities, or human and non-human entities), is expressed lexically more often than male and female gender in MPSEA languages. Ambon Malay *akaŋ* refers to a 3SG inanimate (van Minde 1997) (e.g. *akaŋ di atas meja* [it + on + top (of) + table] 'it's on top of the table'); this pronoun is derived from *akən, an object proposition. Note that, in many MPSEA languages, third person pronouns are only used with an animate reference (and sometimes only with a human one). For instance, Indonesian *dia* '(s)he' and *mareka* 'they' as a rule only refer to people.

Explicit animate vs. inanimate person marking is more pronounced in Austronesian-Papuan contact areas. SHWNG languages mark animacy only in plural pronouns, and in some of them (Biak, Wamesa, Dusner, As, and Sawai) only for the 3PL, as is the case with the animate *si/si-* and inanimate markers *na/na-* in Biak (van den Heuvel 2006: 64). As pointed out by Steinhauer (1985), this is counterevidence to some of the universals formulated by Greenberg (1966), who claimed that languages never have more gender categories in non-singular numbers than in the singular. Explicit animate vs. inanimate marking is also found in other languages in Austronesian/Papuan contact areas, and some of these languages also make this distinction in 3SG and even 3DU pronouns. For more details, see Schapper (2010b) as well as §35.4.5, §36.3.1, and §37.3.4 in this volume.

Schapper (2010b) points out that explicit animate/inanimate marking is untypical for MP languages in general. She also argues that in eastern Indonesian languages it is not an inherited feature but the result of contact with neighbouring Papuan languages. In eastern Indonesia different areas show varying patterns of animate/inanimate marking which are generally shared with similar patterning in neighbouring Papuan languages. These Papuan languages furthermore belong to various genetically distinct Papuan language groups, so a single shared origin of such marking is not likely.

## 52.6 Status, formality, and pronoun avoidance

Reference has already been made to changes that are linked to the pronominal expression of politeness (§52.5.2), but more detailed discussion of status and formality is merited here. (See also Vander Klok, this volume, §31.2 and Shiohara and Arka, this volume, §32.5, for the use of polite register in languages of Java, Bali, and Lombok). Polite language plays a particularly important role in western Indonesia, Malaysia, and Madagascar. These regions were, for centuries, subject to strong Indian influence, bringing with it the establishment of important polities (empires, kingdoms, city-states) under rulers with strong centralized power. The influence was also pervasive in Mainland Southeast Asia, including among Chamic speakers in Vietnam and (nowadays) Cambodia. It affected the Malagasy language and culture indirectly via contact with Malays and Javanese. An elaborate court culture developed in the polities affected, which was a decisive factor in the establishment of a strict social hierarchy. This hierarchy left clear traces in the languages involved, especially in Java and the wider Javanese sphere of influence. These languages include Javanese, Balinese, Madurese, Sundanese, Sasak, and Malagasy as well as Banjar and Palembang Malay, among others. They have seen the development of a socially stratified lexicon, a process which has gone furthest in Javanese but also left its mark in the other languages. Three parameters govern the use of a polite register in these languages: (1) relative age; (2) social status; (3) formal distance. An example of how the use of pronouns can express the extent of social layering in a speech community is Acehnese. According to Durie (1985: 120), the first person in this language has six different forms. These are shown in (10), organized in order of increasing formality from left to right:

Acehnese
(10) *lôŋ > ulôŋ > lôn > ulôn > lôntuwan > ulôntuwan.*
(Durie 1985: 120)

However, as Wolff and Poedjosoedarmo (1982: 44) point out, it is not only the choice of address forms, but also their frequent absence which is relevant in polite conversation. The high Javanese question in (11) lacks a subject pronoun, or indeed any subject argument, but to Javanese speakers the non-linguistic context leaves little doubt as to who is being addressed:

Javanese
(11) *Putra-né raq loro tô*
child-DEF one.assumes two isn't.it.so
'You have two children, don't you?'
(Wolff and Poedjosoedarmo 1982: 44)

Speakers of Indonesian may use the local deictics *sini* 'here', *situ* 'there', and *sana* 'yonder' for first, second, and third person respectively. Kaswanti Purwo (1984: 45) does not elaborate on the context or motivation for using these deictics in sentence (12), but it is likely that it involves the avoidance of a pronoun (or some other pronominal equivalent; Novi Djenar p.c.).

Indonesian
(12) *Sini sudah setuju, tinggal situ bagaimana.*
here already agree remain there how
*Tentang pendapat sana nanti bagaimana,*
about opinion yonder next how
*itu terserah kepada mereka.*
that left up to them
'We already agree, which leaves you to make up your mind. As to what they would think, that's up to them.'
(Kaswanti Purwo 1984: 45)

According to Blust (2013a: 306), the elimination of number distinction and the use of non-personal deictics and circumlocutions involving 'body' in these languages all serve to "de-activate individual deixis" and to "create a system of what might be called 'insinuative reference' rather than one of 'determinative reference'". In the highly stratified societies to which these languages belong, "hyper-sensitivity to social differences has made the inherited Austronesian pronouns unworkable" (ibidem). Clearly, the tendency to avoid any deictic form to address a second person, as discussed in Wolff and Poedjosoedarmo, should also be considered as a form of insinuative reference.

An interesting case of the status-sensitive use of pronouns is communication with God. Here, there seems to be competition between one's respect for divine beings and the intimate nature of one's communication with them. Whereas in many Malayo-Polynesian languages this communication requires the use of polite personal pronouns, in Indonesian and Malay the status-insensitive and intimate pronouns *aku/-ku* '1SG' and *əŋkau/kau/-kau/-mu* '2SG' are used. The same distinction exists in Tagalog, in which *kayo* '2PL' is also used as '2SG.HON' although *ikaw* (the non-honorific 2SG pronoun) is used when addressing God in prayers (Schachter and Otanes 1972: 433). That there is room for nuance is suggested in the case of Acehnese. In this language, *droe=neu(h)* '2SG.HON' is used to address God, but use of the first and second informal pronouns *kee* and *gata* respectively is also allowed in conversation with God (Durie 1985: 116–21). Note also Salako (West Borneo) which applies a special pronominal construction *ne' idà'* '3PL' to refer to the ancestors and the deceased: it consists of *(ne)ne'* 'grandparent' + *idà'*, a root which does not seem to occur in other contexts and derives from PMP *sida '3PL' (Adelaar 2005e: 78).

Specific patterns of polite speech linked to pronominal use are also found elsewhere in the MPSEA region and are apparently not limited to areas that have undergone more direct influence from the Indian subcontinent. As already indicated in §52.5.2, two areas stand out for expanding their use of the 1PL.INCL pronoun to include second person polite address, Timor and Sulawesi. While Tetun *ita* (< *kita) is also used as a polite 2SG form in an attempt to avoid direct address, an even more formal form of address is *ita boot* (lit. 'big you') which cannot be understood as a 1PL.INCL. In the plural we find formal *ita boot sira* (lit. 'big you (plural)' alongside informal *imi* 2PL. Williams-van Klinken and Hajek 2006). Insinuative reference is also very common in this area. The use of phrases without nominal arguments indicates the frequent tendency to avoid reference to any relative social standing, as seen in the two everyday greeting questions *Di'ak ka lae?* (lit. good or not?) 'How are you?', and *Ba nebee?* (lit. go where?) 'Where are you going?'. This type of ellipsed structure usefully allows speakers to address complete strangers without causing potential status-related offence.

## 52.7 Pronominal use of kinship terms, terms for professions, rank, and ethnicity, and proper names

Pronouns are not the only words that are used 'pronominally'. At least in the languages of Java, Sumatra, Borneo, and thereabout, pronominal reference can be done by: (1) dedicated pronouns; (2) kinship terms (especially those denoting a generational affiliation); (3) terms for professions, rank, and ethnicity; and (4) proper names. While many of these phenomena are also noted elsewhere in MPSEA languages (e.g. those of Timor-Leste), there is at present generally less information available about them.

Kinship terms are not only used to address or refer to kin but also to those in the same generation as the kin person mentioned. An Indonesian term like *ibu* 'mother' also refers to women of mother's generation and has become the term for 'Mrs'; *abaŋ* 'older brother' is also used for men in general who are older but still of the same generation as oneself etc.

The use of kinship terms by the speaker obliges the addressee to reciprocate with a socially appropriate terminological equivalent, for instance, someone addressed with 'older sibling' will reply in turn with 'younger sibling'; in Minangkabau, for instance, if a speaker uses a proper name, the interlocutor may do so too, and so on.

Among kin the choice of a kinship term is less governed by absolute age than by the kinship generation the referent is affiliated with. For instance, a parent's sister, if younger than oneself, will still be addressed as 'auntie' (and deserves polite treatment) because she belongs to an older kinship generation. This is demonstrated well by Tadmor (2015) on the basis of the Onya Darat address system, discussed further below.

Moussay (1981: 150–1) gives a detailed outline of the use of pronoun substitutes in Minangkabau. The following four lines in Table 52.8 all mean 'I can't go with you':

**Table 52.8** Pronoun substitutes in Minangkabau

| | | | | | | |
|---|---|---|---|---|---|---|
| (a) | Den | *indaʔ* | *dapeʔ* | *pai* | *jo* | *aŋ* |
| | I | not | can | go | with | you |
| (b) | uni 'older sister' | *indaʔ* | *dapeʔ* | *pai* | *jo* | *adiaʔ* 'younger sibling' |
| (c) | Eri (proper name) | *indaʔ* | *dapeʔ* | *pai* | *jo* | *Ida* (proper name) |
| (d) | awaʔ 'body' | *indaʔ* | *dapeʔ* | *pai* | *jo* | *uda* 'older brother' |

In Table 52.8, line (a) makes use of default pronouns for first and second person singular. Line (b) uses kinship terms, line (c) proper names, and line (d), the word for 'body' which also functions as a generic pronoun or as a substitute for a first, second, or third person pronoun. The use of *awaʔ* and *uda* in the last sentence suggests that it is uttered by a wife to her husband and implies intimacy. Moussay emphasizes that in each of these lines the terms for speaker and addressee are interdependent and not in free variation with those in the other lines. He also explains that some of the lines can vary in meaning, for example, line (b) can also be read as 'you can't go with me' or 'she can't go with him', depending on context. Such ambivalent instances also occur in various other languages in the region.

When other categories are used in place of pronouns the question arises whether they still function syntactically as other elements of the category they belong to or as pronouns. Categories used in this way are sometimes called 'imposters' (Collins and Postal 2012). While these imposters can be used as substitutes for the first and second person, in the case of hierarchically sensitive terms they can also end up as proper pronouns (see the Indonesian first person pronoun *saya*, originally meaning 'servant; slave' and borrowed from Sanskrit). However, this does not seem to happen to kin terms.

Kaufman (2014) shows that the notion of 'imposter' as defined in Collins and Postal is not adequate. In a sentence like 'Mommy needs her quiet time now' uttered by Mommy herself, 'Mommy' is an imposter which occurs instead of 'I'

(Kaufman 2014: 90). Kaufman (2014) explains that in contrast to English, in Indonesian such an imposter has a radically different syntactic representation from its plain noun phrases equivalent: in the above sentence, 'Mommy' triggers third person verb inflection (as in 'needs') and third person pronoun agreement ('her') even if it represents a first person. Taken on face value, this example might lead to a 'purely notional theory' of imposters, treating them syntactically the same as their homophonous non-imposter counterparts. However, there are problems with this theory and Kaufman shows that the syntactic behaviour of Indonesian imposters is particularly at odds with it.

For instance, Indonesian UV constructions require first and second person actors to immediately precede the verb whereas third person actors traditionally follow it,[14] and it is noticeable here that imposters must also precede the verb, in agreement with first and second person syntax. So, whereas English imposters follow the same agreement rules as their homophonous non-imposter counterparts would do, Indonesian imposters agree with the pronouns they replace, and they are clearly more integrated in the pronominal syntax than English imposters.[15] Consider the following three sentences: in (13), the 1SG pronominal clitic *ku-* precedes the UV verb, which is the conventional place for 1SG and 2SG agents; in (14), *ibu* 'mother' follows the UV verb, which is conventional for third person agents (whether they are nouns or pronouns). In (15), however, *ibu* precedes the UV verb, which (until recently) was considered incorrect unless interpreted as a 1SG pronominal imposter:

Indonesian

| (13) | *Nanti* | *ku-beritahukan* | *ke* | *dia* |
|---|---|---|---|---|
| | in.a.moment | 1SG.AV-tell | to | 3SG |

'I'll tell her' (Novi Djenar p.c.)

Indonesian

| (14) | *Nanti* | *di-beritahukan* | *ibu* | *ke* | *dia* |
|---|---|---|---|---|---|
| | in.a.moment | UV-tell | mother | to | 3SG |

'Mother will tell her' (Novi Djenar p.c.)

Indonesian

| (15) | *Nanti* | *ibu* | *beritahukan* | *ke* | *dia* |
|---|---|---|---|---|---|
| | in.a.moment | mother | tell | to | 3SG |

'I'll tell her' (Novi Djenar p.c.)

[14] In colloquial speech third person actors can also precede the verb, and there has been a tendency for this distinction to disappear.

[15] This use of imposters does not seem to be generally Austronesian. It would be worthwhile to investigate to what extent it is areal, and whether in western Indonesian languages it is the continuation of similar practices in Mainland Southeast Asian languages.

In relation to this, Mahdi (2001: 163–8) argues that the traditional (general linguistic) division of nominals into nouns and pronouns does not fit the morphological patterns in Indonesian. He proposes a different nominal classification for this language involving a class of non-personal nominals and one of personal nominals. Non-personal nominals include nouns (substantives) and non-personal (demonstrative and interrogative) pronouns.

Personal nominals include personal proper names, personal pro-names (i.e. personal pronouns) and relational pro-names (i.e. personalized kinship terms and honorific titles functioning as personal pronouns). Mahdi emphasizes that the division is a grammatical one and not one based on semantics. His distinction also fits the behaviour of nominals in Minangkabau and possibly also that of nominals in other MPSEA languages under discussion.

The pronoun system of the Onya Darat language in Ketapang (West Borneo) has grammaticalized one of the most basic values in the culture of its speakers (Tadmor 2015). Apart from distinguishing first, second, third, and 1+2 person as well as singular, dual, and plural number, it also encodes generational affiliation of pronominal referents. The latter is marked differently depending on person and number of a pronoun. *Maaʔ* '1SG' is used when addressing referents of a younger generation, *oko* '1SG' is used with referents of the same or older generation, *omo* '2SG' with referents of the same or younger generation, and *okam* '2SG' with referents of an older generation. Of the 3SG pronouns, *iyo* refers to someone of the same or younger generation, and *idoh* to someone of an older generation. However, the 'viewpoint' of *iyo* and *idoh* can be first person, second person, or another third person, that is, one refers to one's mother as *idoh*, but one also refers to one's spouse as *idoh* when talking to one's children. As to the 1DU, 2DU, 1PL, and 2PL pronouns as well as the 1DU.EXCL and 1PL.EXCL pronouns, they are differentiated as to whether their referents belong to one or more than one generation. The 1DU.INCL and 1PL.INCL pronouns do not mark generational affiliation. In this context, generational affiliation is defined genealogically rather than chronologically. Tadmor explains that Onya Darat communities are small enough that its members know each other intimately and are well acquainted with each other's generational affiliations. He speculates that the fact that these members used to live in a single longhouse in the past provided the environment that facilitated the development of such a pronoun system.

Finally, the Besemah Malay 2SG pronouns opposing same sex and opposite sex (§52.5.5) may also be indicative of the particular kinship organization of its speech community (a supposition in need of further investigation).

## 52.8 Source of personal pronouns

Personal pronouns may be inherited from PMP without showing major unexpected semantic or formal changes (see list of PMP pronouns in §52.1). In other instances, they are the result of lexical replacement, or they are inherited from PMP but have undergone considerable semantic and/or formal changes.

The changes that they have undergone in MPSEA languages (including lexical replacement and loss of meaning categories) often lack transparency. The histories of pronoun systems of most MPSEA languages still need to be worked out, and we often have no detailed insight in how these systems have developed from PMP. Such knowledge requires a systematic phonological and lexicosemantic comparison at genetic microgroup level which follows a bottom-up approach of pronouns and their paradigms and should be applied to as many language varieties as possible.

Given the large number of MPSEA languages involved and their preliminary state of research, the data presented here are limited and concentrated on the few languages that have been investigated more deeply. That said, personal pronouns not deriving from PMP have various origins. They can be derived from words denoting person, self, body, trunk, mast, or post (something erect) respectively, which are somehow semantically interrelated, as already discussed in §52.5.4. See also §52.5.3 for generic pronouns derived from the word for 'person'.

Other pronouns were adopted from foreign languages, a phenomenon which is usually due to the prestige yielded by the languages in question.[16] In Table 52.9, the marked pronouns are not general but show socially restricted use.

Other pronouns again were borrowed but were not pronouns in the lending language, in which they usually represent a hierarchically sensitive term. Pronouns in this category include Indonesian *sahaya* ~ *saya* '1SG' (§52.7) and Old Javanese *ŋhulun* '1SG'. The latter term literally means 'servant' and is originally a South Bornean and/or Lampung term referring to people living in the *qulu ('upriver area'); however, it can also be used by someone hierarchically higher than the addressee (Zoetmulder 1983: 18). Literary Malay *duli paduka* originally consists of Sanskrit words meaning 'the dust under the slipper [of the sovereign]', a Malay form of address to a sultan, or rather his feet, as he himself is too high to be addressed directly. Ambon Malay has *beta* '1SG'; it is also found in literary Malay; although originally a Hindi term for 'slave; servant' (Hoogervorst, this volume, §23.2.2), it is used between equals. High Javanese *sampeyan* literally means 'object hanging down'; it

[16] Although the Hokkien pronouns in some vehicular Malay languages in the Straits of Malacca and in Sri Lankan Malay may be explained more accurately as the result of a Hokkien substrate.

**Table 52.9** Foreign pronouns borrowed into varieties of Malay

| 1SG | 2SG | *Language* | *Status* | *Source* |
|---|---|---|---|---|
| *I [ay]* | *you [yu]* | Colloquial Malay[a] | (marked) | English |
| *ik (ikə)* | *(yɛ)* | Colloquial Malay | (marked, obsolete) | Dutch |
| — | *ose* | Ambon Malay[b] | (default) | Portuguese |
| *go* | *lu* | Sri Lankan Malay[c] | (default) | Hokkien Chinese |
| *guɛ* | *əlu* | Jakarta Malay[d] | (default) | Hokkien Chinese |
| *anɛ* | *ɛntɛ* | Colloquial Malay | (marked) | Arabic |

[a] Stevens and Schmidgall-Tellings
[b] van Minde (1997)
[c] Adelaar (1991)
[d] Abdul Chaer (1976)

refers to 'royal feet' and is used by extension as a second person pronoun (it is most likely derived from an originally Malay *sampay* 'hang; suspend'). An even more polite Javanese pronominal form of address is *pañjənəŋan sampeyan* (*pañjənəŋan* 'stand; established position; function').

Deictic elements also play a role in personal reference and the formation of pronouns. Muna *(i)hintu* '2SG' derives from an earlier *si-tu 'there (near you)' (René van den Berg p.c.). There are also various instances of combinations of personal pronouns with a deictic element. This element may be optional as in Indonesian *məreka* and *məreka itu* '3PL' (*itu* 'that'); in other cases it always co-occurs with a pronoun and has become a lexicalized unit with it, as in Acehnese *gobñan* 'third person' consisting of *gob* 'person' + *ñan* 'that' (§52.5.1), Malagasy *irè/u*, a plural marker reflecting *ire '3PL' (< PMP *sida) + *iu 'that' (Adelaar and Kikusawa 2014:496), and Balantak *(i)raaya'a* '3PL', deriving from PMP *sida '3PL' + *ya'a*, a demonstrative (van den Berg and Busenitz 2012: 35).

## 52.9 Concluding remarks

In MPSEA languages the distinctions between first, second, and third person, singular and plural, and 1PL.INCL and 1PL.EXCL, are firmly embedded, and they are typically expressed by lexically independent lexemes. *kita, *kami, and their clusive distinction can be reconstructed for PMP and

PAN. Their reflexes are remarkably widespread, often with no change of meaning. Semantically *kita and its reflexes combine the first and second person, which seems to have facilitated the ability of these reflexes to double as 2HON pronouns particularly in languages of Sulawesi and Timor-Leste, and to become dedicated 2SG.HON pronouns in some other languages. Another frequent change involving *kita is from a 1PL.INCL pronoun to one combining the 1SG and 2SG (see further below).

The languages of Java, Bali, Sumatra, the Chamic region, and some other areas under the influence of Java have a large array of (mainly) first and second person polite pronouns (often at several levels of stratification). In some of these languages (e.g. Javanese) these pronouns are integrated in more encompassing systems of speech registers that are typical for these languages. Blust (2013a) sees a correlation between these politeness registers and the tendency to lose pronominal number distinction. There may also be a correlation with other phenomena, such as the avoidance of pronouns and the use of imposters, which (at least in Indonesian) have become integrated in the verbal syntax. The languages mentioned above have some of these phenomena in common with the major languages in Mainland Southeast Asia. The interrelations between all these factors need further investigation. Further investigation is also needed to find out whether the use of dedicated pronouns in polite address in languages of Timor-Leste and Sulawesi are related to the same practice in the Java, Bali, Sumatra, and the Chamic region, or whether they are independent developments.

As far as pronominal number is concerned, most MPSEA languages conform to a simple singular/plural distinction in which plural pronouns are suppletive. Number tends to become lost in Javanese, Balinese, Sasak, Sumbawa, and Acehnese. Dual number (other than involving *kita only) occurs predominantly in Borneo and eastern Indonesia but is also sporadically spotted elsewhere. Trial number is found in some languages in Borneo, the South Halmahera–West New Guinea region, the Moluccas, and Sulawesi. Quadral number is found in a very few languages in Borneo and the South Halmahera–West New Guinea region. In practice, trial and more particularly quadral number may function as paucal number. Dual number comes in two forms. It may affect all persons and entail the integration of the number 'two' in all pronouns involved, as it does in eastern Indonesia and in western and central Borneo. Elsewhere, it only affects reflexes of *kita. These reflexes are usually considered dual pronouns but are more appropriately described as first-and-second person singular inclusive pronouns. They have first-and-second person plural inclusive counterparts which consist of *kita + a cliticized plural extender. This phenomenon involving *kita is widespread in languages of the Philippines, north Sulawesi, and north Borneo, and it is also observed in isolated instances elsewhere. It has led to the replacement of the singular/plural number contrast by a minimal/augmented one in the description of the pronominal paradigm in various Malayo-Polynesian languages. The origin of this use of *kita has been a subject of ongoing controversy.

As a rule, pronominal gender is not expressed in MPSEA languages. Where it is, it involves more often inanimateness (especially in South Halmahera and West New Guinea languages in Papuan contact areas) than female/male distinction.

On the other hand, in many languages, there is a particularly strong tendency to make pronominal use of kin terms, ethnic and professional terms, proper names, and deictics. However, it remains unclear how widespread and embedded this tendency is in MPSEA languages in general.

The discussion of free personal pronouns in this chapter is based on data obtained from the authors' own research and from the literature. Obviously, there is much more information to be sourced, both in the literature and even more so in the speech communities in the MPSEA region. Languages other than the standard versions of Malay, Javanese, Tagalog, and Malagasy need to be concentrated on, and certain regions such as central and eastern Indonesia, or parts of the Philippines, deserve much more attention. Another topic of future research is to investigate to what extent our current knowledge involving pronouns in MPSEA languages applies to these languages in general or is only of local interest and should not detract our attention from the existence of more general pronominal patterns in the entire MPSEA region.

## Acknowledgements

The authors would like to express their gratitude to Timothy Brickell, Novi Djenar, Nikolaus Himmelmann, Antoinette Schapper, René van den Berg, and Erik Zobel, for their valuable comments on earlier drafts of this chapter. All shortcomings and errors in the present version are the sole responsibility of the authors.

# REFERENCES


Abbi, Anvita (1992). *Reduplication in South Asian Languages: An Areal, Typological and Historical Study*. New Delhi: Allied Publishers.

Abdul Chaer (1976). *Kamus dialek Melayu Jakarta - Bahasa Indonesia.* [Jakarta (Betawi) Malay - Indonesian dictionary]. Jakarta: Nusa Indah.

Abdul Djebar Hapip (2006). *Kamus Banjar - Bahasa Indonesia.* [Banjar Malay - Indonesian dictionary]. Banjarmasin: PT Grafika Wangi Kalimantan.

Abdul Muthalib (1977). *Kamus Bahasa Mandar - Indonesia.* [Mandar - Indonesian dictionary]. Jakarta: Pusat Pembinaan dan Pengembangan Bahasa.

Abdulla M A, I Ahmed, A Assawamakin, J Bhak, S K Brahmachari, G C Calacal, A Chaurasia, et al. (2009). Mapping Human Genetic Diversity in Asia, *Science* 326: 1541–5.

Abdullah Hassan (1969). Bahasa Melayu Pasar di Malaysia Barat, [Bazaar Malay in West Malaysia] *Dewan Bahasa*, Xiii, 207–18.

Abdullah Hassan (1974). *The Morphology of Malay*. Kuala Lumpur: Dewan Bahasa dan Pustaka.

Abramson, Arthur S (1986). The Perception of Word-Initial Consonant Length: Pattani Malay, *Journal of the International Phonetic Association* 16: 8–16.

Abreu, Marvin M (2018). *A Reference Grammar of Southern Alta (Kabuloan Dumagat)*. PhD Dissertation, De La Salle University, Manila.

Abtahian, Maya Ravindranath and Abigail C Cohn (2018). Dynamic Multilingualism and Language Shift Scenarios in Indonesia, in Sebastian Drude, Nicholas Ostler and Marielle Moser (eds.), *Endangered Languages and the Land: Mapping Landscapes of Multilingualism, Proceedings of FEL XXII/2018 (Reykjavík, Iceland)*. London: FEL and EL Publishing, 106–12.

Abtahian, Maya Ravindranath, Abigail C Cohn and Thomas Pepinsky (2016). Modeling Social Factors in Language Shift, *International Journal of the Sociology of Language* 242: 139–79.

Adams, Karen L and Alexis Manaster-Ramer (1988). Some Questions of Topic/Focus Choice in Tagalog, *Oceanic Linguistics* 27(1/2): 79–101.

Adelaar, K Alexander (1981). Reconstruction of Proto-Batak Phonology, in Robert Blust (ed.), *Historical Linguistics in Indonesia Part 1.* Special issue of *NUSA* 11. Jakarta: Badan Penyelenggara Seri NUSA, Universitas Atma Jaya, 1–20.

Adelaar, K Alexander (1983). Malay Consonant-Harmony: An Internal Reconstruction, in James T Collins (ed.), *Studies in Malay* Dialects, Part I. Special issue of *NUSA* 16. Jakarta: Badan Penyelenggara Seri NUSA, Universitas Atma Jaya, 57–67.

Adelaar, K Alexander (1984). Some Proto-Malayic Affixes, *Bijdragen tot de Taal-, Land- en Volkenkunde* 140(4): 402–21.

Adelaar, K Alexander (1985). *Proto-Malayic: The Reconstruction of its Phonology and Parts of its Lexicon and Morphology*. PhD Dissertation. Leiden University.

Adelaar, K Alexander (1988). More on Proto-Malayic, in Mohd. Thani Ahmad and Zaini Mohamed Zain (eds.), *Rekonstruksi dan Cabang-Cabang Bahasa Melayu Induk* [Reconstruction and branches of Proto-Malay(ic)]. Kuala Lumpur: Dewan Bahasa dan Pustaka, 59–77.

Adelaar, K Alexander (1989). Malay Influence on Malagasy: Historical and Linguistic Inferences, *Oceanic Linguistics* 28(1): 1–46.

Adelaar, K Alexander (1991). Some Notes on Sri Lanka Malay, in Hein Steinhauer (ed.), *Papers in Austronesian Linguistics, No. 1.* Canberra: Pacific Linguistics, 23–37.

Adelaar, K Alexander (1992a). *Proto-Malayic: The Reconstruction of its Phonology and Parts of its Lexicon and Morphology*. Canberra: Pacific Linguistics.

Adelaar, K Alexander (1992b). The Relevance of Salako for Proto-Malayic and for Old Malay Epigraphy, *Bijdragen tot de Taal-, Land- en Volkenkunde* 148(3/4): 381–408.

Adelaar, K Alexander (1993). The Internal Classification of the Malayic Subgroup, *Bulletin of the School of Oriental and African Studies*, 56(3): 566–81.

Adelaar, K Alexander (1994a). Malay and Javanese Loanwords in Malagasy, Tagalog and Siraya (Formosa), *Bijdragen tot de Taal-, Land- en Volkenkunde* 150(1): 50–65.

Adelaar, K Alexander (1994b). The Classification of the Tamanic Languages, in Tom Dutton and Darrell T Tryon (eds.), *Language Contact and Change in the Austronesian World.* Berlin: Mouton de Gruyter, 1–42.

Adelaar, K Alexander (1994c). The history of thing, animal, person and related words in Malay, in Andrew K Pawley and Malcolm D Ross (eds.), *Austronesian Terminologies.* Canberra: Pacific Linguistics, 1–20.

Adelaar, K Alexander (1995a). Asian Roots of the Malagasy: A Linguistic Perspective, *Bijdragen tot de Taal-, Land-, en Volkenkunde* 151: 325–56.

Adelaar, K Alexander (1995b). Borneo as a Cross-Roads for Comparative Austronesian Linguistics, in Peter Bellwood, James J Fox and Darrell T Tryon (eds.), *The Austronesians: Historical and Comparative Perspectives.* Canberra: Australian National University Press, 75–95.

Adelaar, K Alexander (1995c). Minangkabau, in Darrell T Tryon (ed.), *Comparative Austronesian Dictionary: An Introduction to Austronesian Studies, Part 1.* Berlin/New York: Mouton de Gruyter, 433–42.

Adelaar, K Alexander (1995d). Toba Batak, in Darrell T Tryon (ed.), *Comparative Austronesian Dictionary: An Introduction to Austronesian Studies, Vol. 1.* Berlin/New York: Mouton de Gruyter, 421–32.

Adelaar, K Alexander (1995e). Problems of Definiteness and Ergativity in Embaloh, *Oceanic Linguistics* 34(2): 375–409.

Adelaar, K Alexander (1996a). Contact Languages in Indonesia and Malaysia Other Than Malay, in Stephen A Wurm, Peter Mühlhausler and Darrell T Tryon (eds.), *Atlas of Languages of Intercultural Communication in the Pacific*, Asia, *and the Americas.* Volume II.1: Texts. Berlin/New York: Mouton de Gruyter, 695–711.

Adelaar, K Alexander (1996b). Malay in the Cocos (Keeling) Islands, in Bernd Nothofer (ed.), *Reconstruction, Classification, Description; Festschrift in Honor of Isidore Dyen*. Hamburg: Abera, 167–98.

Adelaar, K Alexander (1997). An Exploration of Directional Systems in West Indonesia and Madagascar, in Gunter Senft (ed.), *Referring to Space: Studies in Austronesian and Papuan Languages*. Oxford: Oxford University Press, 53–82.

Adelaar, K Alexander (2000). Malay: A Short History, *Oriente Moderno* 19(2): 225–42.

Adelaar, K Alexander (2004a). À la recherche d'affixes perdus dans le malais, in Elizabeth Zeitoun (ed.), *Faits de Langues*. Paris: Ophrys, 3–53.

Adelaar, K Alexander (2004b). Where Does Malay Come From? Twenty Years of Discussions About Homeland, Migrations and Classifications, *Bijdragen tot de Taal-, Land- en Volkenkunde* 160: 1–30.

Adelaar, Alexander (2005a). The Austronesian Languages of Asia and Madagascar: A Historical Perspective, in Alexander Adelaar and Nikolaus Himmelmann (eds.), *The Austronesian Languages of Asia and Madagascar*. Routledge Language Family Series 7. London: Routledge, 1–43.

Adelaar, Alexander (2005b). Structural Diversity in the Malayic Subgroup, in Alexander Adelaar and Nikolaus P Himmelmann (eds.), *The Austronesian Languages of Asia and Madagascar*. London/New York: Routledge, 202–26.

Adelaar, Alexander (2005c). Malayo-Sumbawan, *Oceanic Linguistics* 44(2): 357–88.

Adelaar, Alexander (2005d). Much Ado About di-, *Bijdragen tot de Taal-, Land- en Volkenkunde* 161(1): 127–42.

Adelaar, Alexander (2005e). *Salako or Badameà: Sketch Grammar, Text and Lexicon of a Kanayatn Dialect in West Borneo*. Wiesbaden: Harrassowitz.

Adelaar, Alexander (2006). Where Does Belangin Belong?, in Fritz Schültze and Holger Warnk (eds.), *Insular Southeast Asia. Linguistic and Cultural Studies in Honour of Bernd Nothofer*. Wiesbaden: Harrassowitz. 65–84.

Adelaar, Alexander (2007a). Review of John Lynch (ed.) (2003). *Issues in Austronesian Historical Phonology*. Canberra: Pacific Linguistics. In *Bijdragen tot de Taal-, Land- en Volkenkunde* 163(1): 139–46.

Adelaar, Alexander (2007b). Language Contact in the Austronesian Far West. Presentation: 3rd Conference on Austronesian Languages and Linguistics, London: School of Asian and African Studies.

Adelaar Alexander (2008). On the Classifiability of Malayic, in Yury Lander and Alexander Ogloblin (eds.), *Language and Text in the Austronesian World: Studies in Honour of Ülo Sirk*. Munich: LINCOM, 1–22.

Adelaar, Alexander (2009a). Loanwords in Malagasy, in Martin Haspelmath and Uri Tadmor (eds.), *Loanwords in the World's Languages: A Comparative Handbook*. Berlin: de Gruyter Mouton, 717–46.

Adelaar, Alexander (2009b). Towards an Integrated Theory about the Indonesian Migrations to Madagascar, in Peter N Peregrine, Ilia Peiros and Marcus Feldman (eds.), *Ancient Human Migrations: A Multidisciplinary Approach*. Salt Lake City: University of Utah Press, 149–72.

Adelaar, Alexander (2009c). The Various Origins of the Passive Prefix di-, in Adelaar, Alexander and Andrew K Pawley (eds.), *Austronesian Historical Linguistics and Culture History: A Festschrift for Robert Blust*. Canberra: Pacific Linguistics, 129–41.

Adelaar, Alexander (2010a). Language Documentation in the West Austronesian World and Vanuatu: An Overview, in Margaret Florey (ed.), *Endangered Languages of Austronesia*. Oxford: Oxford University Press, 12–41.

Adelaar, Alexander (2010b). The Amalgamation of Malagasy, in John Bowden, Nikolaus P Himmelmann and Malcolm D Ross (eds.), *A Journey Through Austronesian and Papuan Linguistic and Cultural Space: Papers in Honour of Andrew K Pawley*. Canberra: Pacific Linguistics, 161–78.

Adelaar, Alexander (2011). *Siraya: Retrieving the Phonology, Grammar and Lexicon of a Dormant Formosan Language*. Berlin/Boston: de Gruyter Mouton.

Adelaar, Alexander (2012). Malagasy Phonological History and Bantu Influence, *Oceanic Linguistics* 51(1): 123–59.

Adelaar, Alexander (2013). Malagasy Dialect Divisions: Genetic versus Emblematic Criteria, *Oceanic Linguistics* 52(2): 457–80.

Adelaar, Alexander (2016a). A Linguist's Perspective on the Settlement History of Madagascar, *NUSA* 61: 69–88.

Adelaar, Alexander (2016b). Austronesians in Madagascar: A Critical Assessment of the Works of Paul Ottino and Philippe Beaujard, in Gwyn Campbell (ed.), *East Africa and Early Trans-Indian Ocean World Interchange*. London: Palgrave Macmillan, 77–112.

Adelaar, Alexander (2017). Who Were the First Malagasy, and What Did They Speak? In Andrea Acri, Roger Blench and Alexandra Landmann (eds.), *Spirits and Ships: Cultural Transfer in Early Monsoon Asia*. Singapore: Institute of South East Asian Studies, 441–69.

Adelaar, Alexander (2018). Dialects of Malay/ Indonesian, in Charles Boberg, John Nerbonne and Dominic Watt (eds.), *The Handbook of Dialectology*. Hoboken, NJ: Wiley-Blackwell, 571–82.

Adelaar, Alexander (2019). Dual *kita in the history of East Barito languages, *Oceanic Linguistics* 58/2: 414–25.

Adelaar, Alexander (2021). On the History of some verbal affixes in Malayic languages. Presentation: 15th International Conference of Austronesian Linguistics, June 2021, Palacký University, Olomouc.

Adelaar, Alexander (nd). Proto-Southeast Barito etymologies. Unpublished manuscript.

Adelaar, K Alexander and D John Prentice (1996). Malay: its History, Role and Spread, in Stephen A Wurm, Peter Mühlhausler and Darrell T Tryon (eds.), *Atlas of Languages of Intercultural Communication in the Pacific, Asia, and the Americas*. Volume II.2: Texts. Berlin/New York: Mouton de Gruyter, 673–93.

Adelaar, Alexander and Nikolaus P Himmelmann (eds.) (2005). *The Austronesian Languages of Asia and Madagascar*. (2nd edition 2011). London: Routledge.

Adelaar, Alexander and Ritsuko Kikusawa (2014). Proto-Malagasy Personal Pronouns: A Reconstruction, *Oceanic Linguistics* 53(2): 480–516.

Adisasmito-Smith, Niken (2004). *Phonetic and Phonological Influences of Javanese on Indonesian.* PhD Dissertation, Cornell University, Ithaca, New York.

Adriani, Nicolaus (1893). *Sangireesche spraakkunst.* [Sangir grammar]. PhD Dissertation, Rijksuniversiteit Leiden.

Adriani, Nicolaus (1894). *Sangireesche teksten, met vertaling en aanteekeningen.* [Sangir texts with translation and notes]. 's-Gravenhage: Martinus Nijhoff.

Adriani, Nicolaus (1898). Iets over de talen der to Sada en der to Wadu [Notes on the languages of the To Sada and To Wadu peoples in Sulawesi], *Mededeelingen van wege het Nederlandsche Zendelinggenootschap* 41: 111–50.

Adriani, Nicolaus (1925). De Minahasische talen [The Minahasan languages], *Bijdragen tot de Taal-, Land- en Volkenkunde van Nederlandsch-Indië* 81: 134–64.

Adriani, Nicolaus (1928). *Bare'e-Nederlandsch Woordenboek met Nederlandsch-Bare'e Register* [Bare'e-Dutch dictionary with a Dutch-Bare'e Finderlist]. Leiden: E J Brill.

Adriani, Nicolaus (1931). *Spraakkunst der Bare'e-taal* [Grammar of Bare'e]. Bandoeng: Nix.

Adriani, Nicolaus (1932–1933). *Bare'e-verhalen* [Bare'e Stories]. 2 Volumes. 's-Gravenhage: Martinus Nijhoff.

Adriani, Nicolaus and Alb C Kruyt (1914). *De Bare'e-sprekende Toradja's van Midden Celebes, Vol. 3: Taal- en letterkundige schets der Bare'e-taal en overzicht van het taalgebied Celebes-Zuid-Halmahera* [The Bare'e speaking Torajas of Central Sulawesi, Vol. 3: Language and literature sketch of the Bare'e language and overview of the language area of Sulawesi and South Halmahera]. Batavia: Landsdrukkerij.

Adriani, Nicolaus and Samuel J Esser (1939). *Koelawische Taalstudiën* [Kulawi language studies]. (Bibliotheca Celebica I, II, III). Bandoeng: Nix.

Ahmed-Chamanga, Mohamed (1992). *Lexique comorien (shindzuani) - français.* Paris: L'Harmattan.

Ahmed-Chamanga, Mohamed (1997). *Dictionnaire français-comorien (dialecte shindzuani).* Paris: L'Harmattan.

Aikhenvald, Alexandra Y (2006). Serial Verb Constructions in Typological Perspective, in Alexandra Y Aikhenvald and R M W Dixon (eds.), *Serial Verb Constructions: A Cross-Linguistic Typology.* Oxford: Oxford University Press, 1–68.

Aikhenvald, Alexandra Y (2010). *Imperatives and Commands.* Oxford: Oxford University Press.

Aikhenvald, Alexandra Y (2013). Possession and Ownership: A Cross-Linguistic Perspective, in Alexandra Y Aikhenvald and R M W Dixon (eds.), *Possession and Ownership: A Cross-Linguistic Typology.* Oxford: Oxford University Press, 1–64.

Aikhenvald, Alexandra Y (2018). Evidentiality: The Framework, in Alexandra Y Aikhenvald (ed.), *The Oxford Handbook of Evidentiality.* Oxford: Oxford University Press, 1–55.

Aikio, Ante (2006). Etymological Nativization of Loanwords: A Case Study of Saami and Finnish, in Ida Toivonen and Diane Nelson (eds.), *Saami Linguistics.* Amsterdam: John Benjamins, 17–51.

Ajid Che Kob (1997). Word Final Nasal in Malay Dialects, in Cecilia Odé and Wim Stokhof (eds.), *Proceedings of the Seventh International Conference on Austronesian Linguistics.* Amsterdam: Editions Rodopi B.V., 35–43.

Akamine, Jun (1996). *A Grammatical Analysis of Manuk Mangkaw Sinama.* PhD Dissertation, University of the Philippines, Diliman.

Akamine, Jun (2002). The Sinama Derived Transitive Construction, in Fay Wouk and Malcolm Ross (eds.). *The History and Typology of Western Austronesian Voice Systems.* Canberra: Pacific Linguistics, 355–66.

Akamine, Jun (2003). *A Basic Grammar of Southern Sinama.* Osaka: Osaka Gakuin University, Endangered Languages of the Pacific Rim, Faculty of Informatics.

Akamine, Jun (2005). Sama (Bajau), in Alexander Adelaar and Nikolaus P Himmelmann (eds.), *The Austronesian Languages of Asia and Madagascar.* London: Routledge, 377–96.

Al-Saqqaf, Abdullah Hassan (2006). The Linguistics of Loanwords in Hadrami Arabic *International Journal of Bilingual Education and Bilingualism* 9(1): 75–93.

Albalá, Paloma (2003). Hispanic Words of Indoamerican Origin in the Philippines, in *Philippine Studies* (Ateneo de Manila University) 51/1: 125–146.

Alberth (2000). A Grammar of the Wolio Language. MA Thesis, University of Western Australia.

Alcantara, Maressa Xavier (2015). *Descrição fonética e fonológica da língua idaté do Timor Leste* [Phonetic and phonological description of the Idate language of East Timor]. MA Thesis, Universidade de São Paulo.

Alderete, John, Jill Beckman, Laura Benua, Amalia Gnanadesikan, John McCarthy and Suzanne Urbanczyk (1999). Reduplication with Fixed Segmentism, *Linguistic Inquiry* 30: 327–64.

Aldridge, Edith (2004). *Ergativity and Word Order in Austronesian Languages.* PhD Dissertation, Cornell University.

Aldridge, Edith (2008). Phase-based Account of Extraction in Indonesian, *Lingua* 118: 1440-69.

Aldridge, Edith (2012). Antipassive and Ergativity in Tagalog, *Lingua* 122: 192–203.

Alieva, Natalia F (1994). The Progress of Monosyllabization in Cham as Testified by Field Materials, in Cecilia Odé and Wim Stokhof (eds.), *Proceedings of the Seventh International Conference on Austronesian Linguistics (ICAL).* Amsterdam: Rodopi, 541–9.

Alieva, Natalija F, Vladimir D Arakin and Aleksandr K Ogloblin (1972). *Grammatika indonezijskogo jazyka.* Moskow: Izdatel'stva Nauka.

Allen, Janet L (2014). *Kankanaey: A Role and Reference Grammar Analysis.* Dallas: Summer Institute of Linguistics International, Global Publishing.

Allen, Jr, R B and Rika Hayami-Allen (2002). Orientation in the Spice Islands, in M Macken (ed.), *Papers from the Tenth Annual Meeting of the Southeast Asian Linguistics Society.* Phoenix: Arizona State University, Program for Southeast Asian Studies, 21–38.

Allison, E Joe (1979). Proto-Danaw: A Comparative Study of Maranaw, Magindanaw and Iranun, in Andrew F Gallman, E Joe Allison, Carol W. Harmon, Jeannette Witucki (eds.), *Papers in Philippine Linguistics 10.* Canberra: Pacific Linguistics, 53–112.

Almurashi, Wael Abdulrahman (2016). Critical Reflection of Acehnese Language Phonology, *International Journal of English Language and Linguistics Research* 4: 43–55.

Amano, Noel, Philip Piper, Hsiao-Chun Hung and Peter Bellwood (2013). Introduced Domestic Animals in the Neolithic and Metal Age of the Philippines: Evidence from Nagsabaran, Northern Luzon, *Journal of Island and Coastal Archaeology* 8(3): 317–35.

Anceaux, Johannes C (1961). *The Linguistic Situation in the Islands of Yapen, Kurudu, Nau and Miosnum, New Guinea*. The Hague: Martinus Nijhoff.

Anceaux, Johannes C (1978). The Linguistic Position of South-East Sulawesi: A Preliminary Outline, in Stephen A Wurm and Lois Carrington (eds.), *Second International Conference on Austronesian Linguistics: Proceedings, Fascicle 1: Western Austronesian*. Canberra: Pacific Linguistics, 275–83.

Anceaux, Johannes C (1987). *Wolio Dictionary (Wolio-English-Indonesian); Kamus Bahasa Wolio (Wolio-Inggeris-Indonesia)*. Dordrecht: Foris.

Anceaux, Johannes C (1988). *The Wolio Language: Outline of Grammatical Description and Texts*. Dordrecht: Foris.

Anceaux, Johannes C (2016). *Southeast Sulawesi Word Lists*. Sulawesi Language Alliance. URL: http://sulang.org

Andaya, Leonard Y (2008). *Leaves of the Same Tree: Trade and Ethnicity in the Straits of Melaka*. Honolulu: University of Hawai'i Press.

Anderbeck, Karl (2007a). Haji: One Language from Twelve?, in Chong Shin, K Harun and Y Alas (eds.), *Reflections in Southeast Asian Seas: Essays in Honour of Professor James T Collins*. Pontianak: STAIN Pontianak Press, 51–91.

Anderbeck, Karl (2007b). An Initial Reconstruction of Proto-Lampungic: Phonology and Basic Vocabulary, in David Mead (ed.), *Studies in Philippine Languages and Cultures: 10-ICAL Sumatra Papers*. Manila: Linguistic Society of the Philippines and Summer Institute of Linguistics, 41–165.

Anderbeck, Karl (2008). *Malay Dialects of the Batanghari River Basin (Jambi, Sumatra)*. Dallas: Summer Institute of Linguistics International.

Anderbeck, Karl (2012). The Malayic-Speaking Orang Laut: Dialects and Directions for Research, *Wacana* 14(2): 265–312.

Anderbeck, Karl (2015). Portraits of Language Vitality in the Languages of Indonesia, in I Wayan Arka, Ni Luh Nyoman Seri Malini and Ida Ayu Made Puspani (eds.), *Language Documentation and Cultural Practices in the Austronesian World: Papers from 12-ICAL, Volume 4*. Canberra: Asia-Pacific Linguistics, 19–47.

Anderbeck, Karl (2018). *Mapping the Dialect Network of Western Bornean Malayic*. PhD Dissertation. Universiti Kebangsaan Malaysia.

Anderbeck, Karl (2019a). Rethinking Proto-Malayic Ultimate *ə: Geographical Evidence. *Twenty-Ninth Meeting of the Southeast Asian Linguistics Society (SEALS 29)*, Tokyo, 27 May.

Anderbeck, Karl (2019b). The Geographical Distribution of the Sound Change PM *r > ʔ, and What That Might Mean for Subgrouping Malayic. *Twenty-Third International Symposium of Malay/Indonesian Linguistics (ISMIL 23)*, Banyuwangi, East Java, 9 July.

Anderbeck, Karl and Doug Cooper (2017). Malayic Compiled Wordlist Database. Kuala Lumpur.

Anderbeck, Karl and Herdian Aprilani (2013). *The Improbable Language: Survey Report on the Nasal Language of Bengkulu, Sumatra. Summer Institute of Linguistics* Electronic Survey Report (2013)-012, August (2013). Summer Institute of Linguistics International.

Anderbeck, Karl and Tadmor, Uri (nd). Language Assimilation Among the Sea People of Belitung. Unpublished Manuscript.

Andersen, David (1999a). Moronene Numbers, in David Mead (ed.), *Studies in Sulawesi Linguistics, Part V*. Special issue of *NUSA* 50. Jakarta: Badan Penyelenggara Seri NUSA, Universitas Katolik Indonesia Atma Jaya, 1–72.

Andersen, David (1999b). Moronene Phonology, in Wyn D Laidig (ed.), *Studies in Sulawesi Linguistics, Part VI*. Special issue of *NUSA* 49. Jakarta: Universitas Katolik Indonesia Atma Jaya, 1–45.

Andersen, H (1988). Center and Periphery: Adoption, Diffusion, and Spread, in J Fisiak (ed.), *Historical Dialectology: Regional and Social*. Berlin: Mouton de Gruyter, 39–83.

Andersen, Suree (1994). *Moronene Noun Phrases*. Unpublished Manuscript.

Andersen, Suree (1995). *Moronene Person Marking: A Nominative Absolutive System*. Unpublished Manuscript.

Andersen, Suree and T David Andersen (2005). Semantic Analysis of the Moronene Verbal Prefix *Mon-*, in I Wayan Arka and Malcolm Ross (eds.), *The Many Faces of Austronesian Voice Systems: Some New Empirical Studies*. Canberra: Pacific Linguistics, 243–78.

Andersen, T David and Robin McKenzie (2008). Word Order of Prepositional Phrases in Aralle-Tabulahan and Moronene, in Yury A Lander and Alexander K Ogloblin (eds.), *Language and Text in the Austronesian World. Studies in Honour of Ülo Sirk*. München: LINCOM, 131–40.

Anderson, Atholl (2005). Crossing the Luzon Strait: Archaeological Chronology in the Batanes Islands, Philippines and the Regional Sequence of Neolithic Dispersal, *Journal of Austronesian Studies* 1(2): 25–45.

Anderson, Atholl, Geoffrey Clark, Simon Haberle, Tom Higham et al. (2018). New Evidence of Megafaunal Bone Damage Indicates Late Colonization of Madagascar, *PLOS One* 13 (10): E0204368.

Anderson, Edmund (1993). Speech Levels: The Case of Sundanese, *Pragmatics* 3(2): 107–36.

Anderson, Stephen R (1985). Inflectional Morphology, in Timothy Shopen (ed.), *Language Typology and Syntactic Description: Grammatical Categories and the Lexicon*. Volume 3. Cambridge: Cambridge University Press.

Anderson, Victoria B and James N Anderson (2007). Pangasinan—an Endangered Language? Retrospect and Prospect, *Philippine Studies: Historical and Ethnographic Viewpoints* 55(1): 116–44.

Andrianasolo, Fidèle Joseph (1993). Les diphtongues malgaches: problèmes d'identification et essai de définition vectorielle, in Øyvind Dahl (ed.), *Language - A Doorway Between Human Cultures. Tributes to Dr. Otto Chr. Dahl on His Ninetieth Birthday*, Oslo, Norway: Novus Forlag, 158–77.

Anggraeni, Truman Simanjuntak, Peter Bellwood and Philip Piper (2014). Neolithic Foundations in the Karama Valley, West Sulawesi, Indonesia, *Antiquity* 88(341): 740–56.

Anonby, Stan J (2020). *Prolonged Multilingualism Among the Sebuyau: An Ethnography of Communication*. PhD Dissertation, Simon Fraser University.

Ansaldo, Umberto and Stephen J Matthews (1999). The Minnan Substrate and Creolisation in Baba Malay, *Journal of Chinese Linguistics* 27(1): 38–68.

Ansyori, M Mirza (2016). Pottery from Harimau Cave, in Truman Simanjuntak (ed.), *Gua Harimau Cave and the Long Journey of Oku Civilization*. Yogyakarta: Gadjah Mada University Press, 226–46.

Antworth, Evan L (1979). *A Grammatical Sketch of Botolan Sambal*. Manila: Linguistic Society of the Philippines.

Aoyagi, Yoji, Melchor L Aguilera Jr., Hidefumi Ogawa and Kazuhiko Tanaka (1993). Excavation of Hill Top Site, Magapit Shell Midden in Lal-Lo Shell Middens, Northern Luzon, Philippines, *Man and Culture in Oceania* 9: 127–55.

Aoyama, Katsura and Lawrence A Reid (2006). Cross-Linguistic Tendencies and Durational Contrasts in Geminate Consonants: An Examination of Guinaang Bontok Geminates, *Journal of the International Phonetic Association* 36: 145–57.

Archangeli, Diana, Jonathan Yip, Lang Qin and Albert Lee (2017). Phonological and Phonetic Properties of Nasal Substitution in Sasak and Javanese, *Laboratory Phonology* 8(1): 1–27.

Ardana, Kuta and Rii Suzuki (1998). *Kuta Artana No Bali-Go Kaiwa* [Balinese Conversation by Kuta Ardana]. Tokyo: Mekong.

Arka, I Wayan (2003a). *Balinese Morphosyntax: A Lexical-Functional Approach*. Canberra: Pacific Linguistics.

Arka, I Wayan (2003b). On the Conceptual Basis of Voice Marking and the Split Middle in Indonesian. Presentation: International Symposium on Malay and Indonesian Linguistics, Nijmegen.

Arka, I Wayan (2005). Speech Levels, Social Predicates, and Pragmatic Structure in Balinese: A Lexical Approach. *Pragmatics* 15 (2/3): 169–203.

Arka, I Wayan (2007). Local Autonomy, Local Capacity Building and Support for Minority Languages: Field Experiences from Indonesia, in D Victoria Rau and Margaret Florey (eds.), *Documenting and Revitalizing Austronesian Languages*. Honolulu: University of Hawaiʻi Press, 66–92.

Arka, I Wayan (2008). Voice and the Syntax of =A/-A Verbs in Balinese, in Peter K Austin and Simon Musgrave (eds.), *Voice and Grammatical Relations in Austronesian Languages*. Stanford: CSLI, 70–89.

Arka, I Wayan (2009a). The Core-Oblique Distinction and Core Index in Some Austronesian Languages of Indonesia. Keynote Presentation: Fourth Association of Linguistic Typology Conference, Padang, Indonesia.

Arka, I Wayan (2009b). On the Zero (Voice) Prefix and Bare Verbs in Austronesian Languages of Nusa Tenggara, Indonesia, in Bethwyn Evans (ed.), *Discovering History through Language: Papers in Honour of Malcolm Ross*. Canberra: Pacific Linguistics, 247–70.

Arka, I Wayan (2013). Language Management and Minority Language Maintenance in (Eastern) Indonesia: Strategic Issues, *Language Documentation and Conservation* 7: 74–105.

Arka, I Wayan (2015). On the Dynamics of Glocalisation and Minority Language Conservation in Contemporary Indonesia, in Obing Katubi (ed.), *International Conference on Language, Culture and Society*. Jakarta: LIPI Press, 1–10.

Arka, I Wayan (2016). *Bahasa Rongga: Deskripsi, Tipologi dan Teori* [Rongga: Description, Typology and Theory]. Jakarta: PKBB, Universitas Katolik Atma Jaya.

Arka, I Wayan (2017). The Core-Oblique Distinction in Some Austronesian Languages of Indonesia and Beyond, *Linguistik Indonesia*, 35(2): 100–42.

Arka, I Wayan (2019). Grammatical Relations in Balinese, in Alena Witzlack-Makarevich and Balthasar Bickel (eds.), *Argument Selectors: A New Perspective on Grammatical Relations*. Amsterdam: John Benjamins, 257–99.

Arka, I Wayan (2021). Pivot selection and puzzling relativisation in Indonesian, in I Wayan Arka, Ash Asudeh and Tracy Holloway-King (eds.), *Modular Design of Grammar: Linguistics on the Edge*. Oxford: Oxford University Press, 181–202.

Arka, I Wayan and Mary Dalrymple (2017). Nominal, Pronominal, and Verbal Number in Balinese, *Linguistic Typology* 21(2): 261–331.

Arka, I Wayan, Mary Dalrymple, Meladel Mistica, Suriel Mofu, Avery Andrews and Jane Simpson (2009). A Linguistic and Computational Morphosyntactic Analysis for the Applicative *-i* in Indonesian, in Miriam Butt and Tracy Holloway King (eds.), *Proceedings of the LFG 09 Conference*. Stanford: CSLI Publications, 85–105.

Arka, I Wayan and Jeladu Kosmas (2005). Passive without Passive Morphology? Evidence from Manggarai, in I Wayan Arka and Malcolm Ross (eds.), *The Many Faces of Austronesian Voice Systems: Some New Empirical Studies*. Canberra: Pacific Linguistics, 87–117.

Arka, I Wayan and Christopher Manning (2008). Voice and Grammatical relations in Indonesian: A New Perspective, in Peter Austin and Simon Musgrave (eds.), *Voice and Grammatical Relations in Austronesian Languages*. Stanford: CSLI Publications, 45–69.

Arka, I Wayan and Malcolm D Ross (2005). Introduction, in I Wayan Arka and Malcolm D Ross (eds.), *The Many Faces of Austronesian Voice Systems: Some New Empirical Studies*. Canberra: Pacific Linguistics, 1–15.

Arka, I Wayan and I Nyoman Sedeng (2018). Information Structure in Sembiran Balinese, in Sonja Riesberg, Asako Shiohara and Atsuko Utsumi (eds.), *A Cross-Linguistic Perspective on Information Structure in Austronesian Languages*. Berlin: Language Science Press, 139–76.

Arka, I Wayan and Fay Wouk (2014). Voice-Related Constructions in the Austronesian Languages of Flores, in I Wayan Arka and

Ni Luh Ketut Mas Indrawati (eds.), *Argument Realisations and Related Constructions in Austronesian Languages: Papers from 12-ICAL*. Canberra: Asia-Pacific Linguistics, 313–33.

Arka, I Wayan and Nurenzia Yannuar (2016). On the Morphosyntax and Pragmatics of *-in* in Colloquial Jakartan Indonesian. *Indonesian and the Malay World* 44(130): 342–64.

Arms, D G (1996). Categories of the Sindangan Subanen Verb, in Hein Steinhauer (ed.), *Papers in Austronesian Linguistics, No. 3*. Canberra: Pacific Linguistics, 1–32.

Arndt, Paul P (1933). *Grammatik der Ngada-Sprache*. Bandoeng: A C Nix and Co.

Arnold, Laura (2018a). *A Grammar of Ambel: An Austronesian Language of Raja Ampat, West New Guinea*. PhD Dissertation, University of Edinburgh.

Arnold, Laura (2018b). A Preliminary Archaeology of Tone in Raja Ampat, in Antoinette Schapper (ed.), *Contact and Substrate in the Languages of Wallacea, Part 2*. Special issue of *NUSA* 64: 7–37.

Arnold, Laura (2018c). Lexical Tone in Metnyo Ambel, *Oceanic Linguistics* 57(1): 199–220.

Arnold, Laura (2020). Highs and Lows: A Previously Unattested Tone Split from Vowel Height in Metnyo Ambel. *Transactions of the Philosophical Society*, 118(1): 141–58.

Arnold, Laura (2023). Split Inalienable Coding in Linguistic Wallacea: Typology, origins, spread, *STUF - Language Typology and Universals*, 73(3): 331–68.

Arokiaswamy, Celine W M (2000). *Tamil Influences in Malaysia, Indonesia and the Philippines*. Manila: University of Michigan.

Arps, Bernard (2004). A Tour of Pantun Tracts: Planes of Movement in A Song from Banyuwangi, in Jan van der Putten (ed.), *Bahwa Inilah Tanda Kasih, Yaitu Persembahan Persahabatan Kepada Yang Termulia Prof Dr Muhammad Haji Salleh*. [Festschrift for Professor Muhammed Haji Salleh]. Leiden: Vakgroep Talen en Culturen van Zuidoost-Azië en Oceanië, Rijksuniversiteit Leiden, 79–97.

Arps, Bernard, Els Bogaerts, Willem van der Molen, Ignatius Surpriyanto and Jan van den Veerdonk (in collaboration with Betty Litamahuputty) (2000). *Hedendaags Javaans*. Leiden: Leiden University, Opleiding Talen en Culturen van Zuidoost-Azië en Oceanië.

Artawa, I Ketut (1994). *Ergativity and Balinese Syntax*. PhD Dissertation, La Trobe University.

Artawa, I Ketut (2013). The Basic Verb Construction in Balinese, in Alexander Adelaar (ed.), *Voice Variation in Austronesian Languages of Indonesia*. Special issue of *NUSA* 54: 5–27.

Asikin-Garmager, Eli Scott (2017). *Sasak voice*. PhD Dissertation, University of Iowa.

Asmah Haji Omar (1982). *Language and Society in Malaysia*. Kuala Lumpur: Dewan Bahasa dan Pustaka.

Asmah Haji Omar (1983). *The Malay Peoples of Malaysia and their Languages*. Kuala Lumpur: Dewan Bahasa dan Pustaka.

Asmah Haji Omar (2008). *Susur Galur Bahasa Melayu*. 2nd edition. Kuala Lumpur: Dewan Bahasa dan Pustaka.

Asmah, Haji Omar (1966). The Natural of Tamil Loan Words in Malay, in *Proceedings of the First International Conference of Tamil Studies, Kuala Lumpur. Vol. II*. Kuala Lumpur: International Association of Tamil Research, 534–58.

Aspillera, Paraluman (1969). *Basic Tagalog for Foreigners and Non-Tagalogs*. Rutland, VT: Charles E Tuttle Co.

Astar, Hidayatul, Buha Aritonang, Non Martis and Wati Kurniawati (2002). *Kosakata dasar Swadesh di Kabupaten Kutai* [Swadesh basic wordlist(s) in Kutai Regency]. Language Mapping Series, PT 2. Jakarta: Pusat Bahasa.

Athens, Stephen J and Jerome V Ward (2001). Palaeoenvironmental Evidence for Early Human Settlement in Palau: The Ngerchau Core, in Christopher Stevenson, F J Morin and Georgia Lee (eds.), *Pacific 2000: Proceedings of the Fifth International Conference on Easter Island and the Pacific*. Los Osos: Easter Island Foundation, 167–78.

Athens, Stephen J and Jerome V Ward (2005). *Holocene Palaeoenvironment of Saipan: Analysis of A Core from Lake Susupe*. Honolulu: International Archaeological Research Institute, Inc.

Atkinson, Quentin D and Russell D Gray (2005). Curious Parallels and Curious Connections—Phylogenetic Thinking in Biology and Historical Linguistics, *Systematic Biology* 54: 513–26.

Austin, Peter K (2001). Verbs, Valence and Voice in Balinese, Sasak and Sumbawan, *La Trobe Papers in Linguistics* 11: 47–71.

Austin, Peter K (2004). Clitics in Sasak, Eastern Indonesia. Unpublished manuscript. URL: https://www.researchgate.net/publication/252008136_Clitics_in_Sasak_eastern_Indonesia

Austin, Peter K (2010). Dialect Variation in the Voice System of Sasak: When is a Nasal-Verb Not a Nasal-Verb?, in *Proceedings of the Workshop on Indonesian-Type Voice Systems*. Tokyo: Research Institute for Languages and Cultures of Asian and Africa, Tokyo University of Foreign Studies, 93–9.

Austin, Peter K (2013). Too many nasal verbs: dialect variation in the voice system of Sasak, in Alexander Adelaar (ed.), *Voice Variation in Austronesian Languages of Indonesia*. Special issue of *NUSA* 54: 47–65.

Austin, Peter K (2014). Tense, Aspect, Mood and Evidentiality in Sasak, Eastern Indonesia, in John Bowden (ed.), *Tense, aspect, mood and evidentiality in languages of Indonesia*. Special issue of *NUSA* 55: 41–56.

Awed, Silin A, Lillian Underwood and Vivian M Van Wynen (2004). *Tboli-English Dictionary*. Manila: Summer Institute of Linguistics.

Awơi-Hathe, Aviong, A-Tý, A-Ly, Maxwell Cobbey and Vurnell Cobbey (1977). *Suraq Vungã Sanăp Radlai - Ngữ-Vựng Rơglai - Northern Roglai Vocabulary*. Saigon: Summer Institute of Linguistics.

Aye, Khin Khin (2013). Singapore Bazaar Malay, in Susanne M Michaelis, Philippe Maurer, Martin Haspelmath and Magnus Huber (eds.), *The Survey of Pidgin and Creole Languages, Volume 3: Contact Languages Based on Languages from Africa, Asia, Australia, and the* Americas. Oxford: Oxford University Press.

Aymonier, Étienne F (1889). *Grammaire de la langue chame*. Saigon: Imprimerie Coloniale.

Aymonier, Étienne F and Antoine Cabaton (1906). *Dictionnaire cam-français*. Paris: E Leroux.

Azis, Naszrullah, Christian Reepmeyer, Geoffrey Clark, Sriwigati and Daud A Tanudirjo (2018). Mansiri in North Sulawesi: A New Dentate-Stamped Pottery Site in Island Southeast Asia, in Sue O'Connor, David Bulbeck and Juliet Meyer (eds.), *The Archaeology of Sulawesi: Current Research on the Pleistocene to the Historic Period*. Canberra: Australian National University Press, 191–205.

Aziz, Jake (2020). Intonational Phonology of Malagasy: Pitch Accents Demarcate Syntactic Constituents, *Proceedings of the 10th International Conference on Speech Prosody 2020*. Tokyo, 201–4.

Bach, Xavier Cédric Alain (2021). 'Alienable' Possession in Biakic, *Transactions of the Philological Society* 119(3): 330–45. DOI: 10.1111/1467-968X.12221

Backus, Ad, Seza Doğruöz and Bernd Heine (2011). Salient Stages in Contact-Induced Grammatical Change: Evidence from Synchronic Versus Diachronic Contact Situations, *Language Sciences* 33(5): 738–52.

Badudu, Abd. Muis, Mustafa Abdullah, A M Yunus, Salahuddin Mahmud, Hady Abd. Hakim and Abdul Muthalib (1985). *Sistem Morfologi Kata Kerja Bahasa Mandar* [Verbal morphological system of Mandar]. Jakarta: Pusat Pembinaan dan Pengembangan Bahasa.

Badudu, J S (1982). *Morfologi Bahasa Gorontalo* [Morphology of Gorontalo]. Jakarta: Djambatan.

Bae, Christopher J, Katerina Douka and Michael D Petraglia (2017). On the Origin of Modern Humans: Asian Perspectives, *Science* 358: Eaai9067.

Baier, Nico (2013). Separating Case and Agreement in Montana Salish. Presentation: 18th Workshop on Structure and Constituency in the Languages of the Americas, UC Berkeley.

Bailey, D J S (1968). The Sru Dyaks (2[nd] Division), in Anthony Richards (ed.), *The Sea Dyaks and Other Races of Sarawak*. Kuching: Borneo Literature Bureau, 331–40.

Bailey, Laura Rudall (2013). *The Syntax of Question Particles*. PhD Dissertation, Newcastle University.

Baird, Louise (2002). *A Grammar of Kéo: An Austronesian Language of East Nusantara*. PhD Dissertation, Australian National University.

Bais, W J and A W Verhoef (1924). On the Biochemical Index of Various Races in the East Indian Archipelago, *Journal of Immunology* 9: 383.

Bakker, Peter (1997). *A Language of Our Own: The Genesis of Michif, the Mixed Cree-French Language of the Canadian Métis*. Oxford and New York: Oxford University Press.

Bakker, Peter (2000). Convergence Intertwining: An Alternative Way Towards the Genesis of Mixed Languages, in D G Gilbers, J Nerbonne and J Schaeken (eds.), *Languages in Contact*. Amsterdam: Rodopi, 29–35.

Baklanova, Ekaterina (2023). Spanish Borrowed Suffixes in Tagalog Nominative Derivation, in Marian Klamer and Francesca Moro (eds.), *Traces of Contact in the Lexicon: Austronesian and Papuan Studies*. Leiden: Brill, 307–47.

Balai Bahasa Yogyakarta (2006). *Pedoman umum ejaan Bahasa Jawa huruf Latin yang disempurnakan* [General guidelines for a standardised roman spelling of Javanese]. Yogyakarta: Kanisius.

Baldi, Philip, Ed (1990). *Linguistic Change and Reconstruction Methodology*. Berlin/New York: Mouton de Gruyter.

Ballard, Lee (Comp.) (2011). *Ibaloy Dictionary*. Baguio: Diteng, Inc. and the Cordillera Studies Center, University of the Philippines Baguio.

Balle, Misriani (2017a). Phonological Sketch of Helong, an Austronesian Language of Timor, *Journal of the Southeast Asian Linguistics Society* 10: 91–103.

Balle, Misriani (2017b). *Types of Reduplication in Helong, an Austronesian Language in Eastern Indonesia*. MA Thesis, Payap University.

Balle, Misriani and Cameron, Stuart (2014). The interplay of quantifiers and number in Helong grammar, in Marian Klamer and František Kratochvíl (eds.), *Number and Quantity in East Nusantara Papers from 12-ICAL, Volume 1*. Canberra. Asia-Pacific Linguistics.

Balukh, Jermy (2020). *A Grammar of Dhao: An Endangered Austronesian Language in Eastern Indonesia*. PhD Dissertation, Leiden University.

Bao, Zhiming and Khin Khin Aye (2010). Bazaar Malay topics, *Journal of Pidgin and Creole Languages* 25(10): 151–67.

Barber, Charles Clyde (1977). *A Grammar of the Balinese Language*. University of Edinburgh.

Barbian, Karl Josef (1977). *The Mangyan Languages of Mindoro: A Comparative Study on Vocabulary, Phonology, and Morphology*. MA Thesis, University of San Carlos.

Barker, Graeme, Lindsay Lloyd-Smith, Huw Barton, Franca Cole, Christopher Hunt, Philip J Piper, Ryan Rabett, Victor Paz, Katherine Szabo (2011). Foraging Farming Transitions at the Niah Caves, Sarawak, *Antiquity* 85(328): 492–509.

Barlaan, Rodolfo (1986). *Some Major Aspects of the Focus System in Isnag*. PhD Dissertation, University of Texas at Arlington.

Barlaan, Rodolfo R (1999). *Aspects of Focus in Isnag*. Manila: Linguistic Society of the Philippines.

Barnes, Jonathan (2006). *Strength and Weakness at the Interface: Positional Neutralization in Phonetics and Phonology*. Berlin/New York: Mouton de Gruyter.

Barnes, Robert H (1974). *Kedang: A Study of the Collective Thought of an Eastern Indonesian People*. Oxford: Clarendon Press.

Barr, Donald F (1988a). Da'a Verbal Affixes and Clitics, in Hein Steinhauer (ed.), *Papers in Western Austronesian Linguistics, No. 4*. Canberra: Pacific Linguistics, 11–49.

Barr, Donald F (1988b). Focus and Mood in Da'a Discourse, in Hein Steinhauer (ed.), *Papers in Western Austronesian Linguistics, No. 4*. Canberra: Pacific Linguistics, 77–129.

Barr, Donald F (1988c). The Functions of Reduplication in Da'a, in Hein Steinhauer (ed.), *Papers in Western Austronesian Linguistics, No. 4*. Canberra: Pacific Linguistics, 1–9.

Barr, Donald F and Sharon G Barr (1979). *Languages of Central Sulawesi: Checklist, Preliminary Classification, Language Maps, Wordlists*. Ujung Pandang: UNHAS-SIL.

Barr, Donald F and Sharon G Barr (1988). Phonology of Da'a, Central Sulawesi, in Hein Steinhauer (ed.), *Papers in Western Austronesian Linguistics, No. 4*. Canberra: Pacific Linguistics, 131–51.

Barron, Aleese, Ipoi Datan, Peter Bellwood, Rachel Wood, Dorian Q Fuller and Timothy Denham (2020). Sherds as archaeobotanical assemblages: Gua Sireh reconsidered, *Antiquity* 94(377): 1325–36.

Barsel, Linda A (1994). *The Verb Morphology of Mori, Sulawesi*. Canberra: Pacific Linguistics.

Barth, J P J (1910). *Boesangsch-Nederlandsch woordenboek* [Busang-Dutch dictionary]. Batavia: Landsdrukkerij.

Baumgartner, Neil (1998). A Grammar Sketch of Western (Cambodian) Cham, in David D Thomas (ed.), *Papers in Southeast Asian Linguistics No.15: Further Chamic Studies*. Canberra: Pacific Linguistics, 1–20.

Bausani, Alessandro (1964). Note sui vocaboli persiani in malese-indonesiano [Notes on Persian words in Malay/Indonesian], *Annali del Istituto Universitario Orientale di Napoli* 14: 1–32.

Baxter, Alan N (1996). Portuguese and Creole Portuguese in the Pacific and Western Pacific Rim, in Stephen A Wurm, Peter Mühlhausler and Darrell T Tryon (eds.), *Atlas of Languages of Intercultural Communication in the Pacific, Asia, and the Americas*. Volume II.1: Texts. Berlin/New York: Mouton de Gruyter, 299–338.

Baxter, Alan N (2013). Papiá Kristang, in Susanne M Michaelis, Philippe Maurer, Martin Haspelmath and Magnus Huber (eds.), *The Survey of Pidgin and Creole Languages*. Volume II. Oxford: Oxford University Press.

Bay, Naw Say (1995). The Phonology of the Dung Dialect of Moken, in David Bradley (ed.), *Papers in Southeast Asian Linguistics No. 13: Studies in Burmese Languages*. Canberra: Pacific Linguistics, 193–205.

Beaujard, Philippe (1998). *Dictionnaire malgache-français: dialecte tañala, sud-est de Madagascar, avec recherches étymologiques*. Paris: L'Harmattan.

Beaujard, Philippe (2005). The Indian Ocean in Eurasian and African World-Systems Before the Sixteenth Century, *Journal of World History* 16: 441–65.

Beaujard, Philippe (2012). *Les mondes de l'Océan Indien. Tome I: De la formation de L'état au premier système-monde afro-eurasien (4e millénaire av. J -C -6e siècle apr. J -C)*. Paris: Armand Colin. [English Edition: The *Worlds of the Indian Ocean. A Global History. Volume 1*. Cambridge University Press (2019)].

Beaujard, Philippe (2017). *Histoire et voyages des plantes cultivées à Madagascar*. Paris: Karthala.

Beckley, Carrie (nd). A Preliminary Yalahatan–English Dictionary: With English Finderlist. Unpublished Toolbox File.

Beckman, Mary E and Jennifer J Venditti (2011). Intonation, in John Goldsmith, Jason Riggle and Alan C L Yu (eds.), *The Handbook of Phonological Theory*. Oxford: Blackwell, 485–532.

Bedford, Stuart, Matthew Spriggs and Ralph Regenvanu (2006). The Teouma Lapita Site and the Early Human Settlement of the Pacific, *Antiquity* 80(310): 812–28.

Beg, Muhammad Abdul Jabbar (1979). *Arabic Loan-Words in Malay*. Kuala Lumpur: The University of Malaya Press.

Beg, Muhammad Abdul Jabbar (1982). *Persian and Turkish Loan-Words in Malay*. Bangi: Universiti Kebangsaan Malaysia.

Beguš, Gašper (2016). The Origins of the Voice/Focus System in Austronesian. Presentation: 42nd Annual Meeting of the Berkeley Linguistic Society, February 5, 2016. URL: https://scholar.harvard.edu/files/begus/files/begus_voice_system_of_austronesian_and_its_origins_handout.pdf

Behrens, Dietlinde (2002). *Yakan-English Dictionary*. Manila: Linguistic Society of the Philippines

Belding, Joanna L, Wyn D Laidig and Sahabu Dg. Maingak (2001). A Preliminary Description of Barang-Barang Morphology, in Wyn D Laidig (ed.), *Studies in Sulawesi* Linguistics, Part VII. Special issue of *NUSA* 49. Jakarta: Badan Penyelenggara Seri NUSA, Universitas Katolik Indonesia Atma Jaya, 1–57.

Bell, Sarah (1976). *Cebuano Subjects in Two Frameworks*. PhD Dissertation, University of California San Diego. Reprinted by Indiana University Linguistics Club (1979).

Bell, Sarah J (1978). Two Differences in Definiteness in Cebuano and Tagalog, *Oceanic Linguistics* 17(1): 1–9.

Bellwood, Peter (1976). Archaeological Research in Minahasa and the Talaud Islands, Northeastern Indonesia, *Asian Perspectives* 14(2): 240–88.

Bellwood, Peter (1984–1985). A Hypothesis for Austronesian Origins, *Asian Perspectives* 26(1): 107–17.

Bellwood, Peter (1985). *Prehistory of the Indo-Malaysian Archipelago*. Sydney: Academic Press.

Bellwood, Peter (1988). *Archaeological Research in South-Eastern Sabah*. Kota Kinabalu: Sabah Museum and State Archives.

Bellwood, Peter (1989). Archaeological Investigations at Bukit Tengkorak and Segarong, Southeastern Sabah, *Bulletin of the Indo-Pacific Prehistory Association* 9: 122–62.

Bellwood, Peter (1996). Hierarchy, Founder Ideology and Austronesian Expansion, in James J Fox and Clifford Sather (eds.), *Origins, Ancestry and Alliance*. Canberra: Australian National University Press, 18–40.

Bellwood, Peter (1997). *Prehistory of the Indo-Malaysian Archipelago*. Revised edition. Hawai'i: University of Hawai'i Press.

Bellwood, Peter (1998). From Bird's Head to Bird's Eye View: Long-Term Structures and Trends in Indo-Pacific Prehistory, in Jelle Miedema, Cecilia Odé and Rien A C Dam (eds.), *Perspectives on the Bird's Head of Irian Jaya, Indonesia*. Proceedings of the Conference, Leiden, 13–17 October 1997. Amsterdam/Atlanta: Rodopi, 951–75.

Bellwood, Peter (2005). *First Farmers: The Origins of Agricultural Societies*. Malden, MA: Wiley-Blackwell.

Bellwood, Peter (2007). *Prehistory of the Indo-Malaysian Archipelago*, Revised edition. Canberra: Australian National University Press.

Bellwood, Peter (2017). *First Islanders: Prehistory and Human Migration in Island Southeast Asia*. Hoboken, NJ: Wiley Blackwell.

Bellwood, Peter (ed.) (2019). *The Spice Islands in Prehistory*. Canberra: Australian National University Press.

Bellwood Peter, James J Fox and Darrell T Tryon (1995). *The Austronesians: Historical and Comparative Perspectives*. Canberra: Australian National University Press.

Bellwood, Peter and Colin Renfrew (eds.) (2002). *Examining the Language/Farming Dispersal Hypothesis*. Cambridge: McDonald Institute of Archaeological Research.

Bellwood, Peter and Eusebio Z Dizon (2008). Austronesian Cultural Origins. Out of Taiwan, Via the Batanes Islands, and Onwards to Western Polynesia, in Alicia Sanchez-Mazas, Roger Blench, Malcom D. Ross, Ilia Peiros, Marie Lin (eds.), *Past Human Migrations in East Asia Matching Archeology, Linguistics and Genetics*. London: Routledge, 23–39.

Bellwood, Peter and Eusebio Z Dizon (eds.) (2013). *4000 Years of Migration and Cultural Exchange: The Archaeology of the Batanes Islands, Northern Philippines*. Canberra: Australian National University Press.

Bellwood, Peter and Peter Hiscock (2018). Australia and the Indo-Pacific Islands during the Holocene, in Chris Scarre (ed.), *The Human Past*. London: Thames and Hudson, 261–302.

Bellwood, Peter and Peter Koon (1989). Lapita Colonists Leave Boats Unburned! the Question of Lapita Links with Island Southeast Asia, *Antiquity* 63(240): 613–22.

Belo, Maurício Da C A, John Bowden, John Hajek, Nikolaus P Himmelmann and Alexandre Vital Tilman (1999). *Glosáriu Waima'a Caisido* [Glossary of Waima'a Caisido]. Bochum: Ruhr-University Bochum, Department of Linguistics.

Benjamin, Geoffrey (1976). Austroasiatic Subgroupings and Prehistory in the Malay Peninsula, in Philip N Jenner, Laurence C Thompson and Stanley Starosta (eds.), *Austroasiatic Studies, Part I*. Honolulu: University of Hawai'i Press, 37–128.

Benjamin, Geoffrey (2009). Affixes, Austronesian and Iconicity in Malay, *Bijdragen tot de Taal-, Land- en Volkenkunde*, 165(2 and 3): 291–323.

Benjamin, Geoffrey and David Bradley (1983). Language Map with Notes: Peninsular Malaysia (Map 37), in Stephen Á Wurm and Shirô Hattori (eds.), *Linguistic Atlas of the Pacific Area*. Canberra: Pacific Linguistics. Australian Academy of the Humanities in Collaboration with the Japan Academy.

Benjasmith, Noorhayatee (2016). *A Study of English Borrowing in Patani-Malay*. MA Thesis, University of Malaya.

Benmamoun, Elabbas, Silvina Montrul and Maria Polinsky (2013). Heritage Languages and their Speakers: Opportunities and Challenges for Linguistics, *Theoretical Linguistics* 39(3–4): 129–181.

Bennardo, Giovanni (ed.) (2002). *Representing Space in Oceania: Culture in Language and Mind*. Canberra: Pacific Linguistics.

Bennásar, Guillermo (1892). *Observaciones gramaticales sobre la lengua tiruray* [Grammatical observations on Teduray]. Manila: Impresa y Litografía de M Pérez.

Bennett, J Fraser (1994). Iambicity in Thai, *Studies in the Linguistic Sciences* 24(1/2): 39–57.

Benton, Richard (1971a). *Pangasinan Reference Grammar*. Honolulu: University of Hawai'i Press.

Benton, Richard (1971b). *Phonotactics of Pangasinan*. PhD Dissertation, University of Hawai'i.

Benveniste, Émile (1973)[1969]). *Indo-European Language and Society*. Coral Gables, Florida: University of Miami Press (Original French Title: *Le vocabulaire des institutions indo-européennes*. Paris, 1969).

Bernard-Thierry, Solange (1959). À propos des emprunts sanskrits en malgache, *Journal Asiatique* 247(3): 311–48.

Bickel, Balthasar (2010). Grammatical Relations Typology, in Jae Jung Song (ed.), *The Oxford Handbook of Language Typology*. Oxford: Oxford University Press, 399–444.

Bickerton, Derek (1981). *Roots of Language*. Ann Arbor: Karoma Press.

Billings, Loren and Daniel Kaufman (2004). Towards a Typology of Austronesian Pronominal Clisis, in Paul Law (ed.), *Proceedings of AFLA 11 (ZAS Papers in Linguistics 34)*. Berlin: Zentrum für allgemeine Sprachwissenschaft, 15–29.

Bisang, Walter (1999). Classifiers in East and Southeast Asian Languages: Counting and Beyond, in J Gvozdanović (ed.), *Numeral Types and Changes Worldwide*. Trends in Linguistics Studies and Monographs. Berlin: Mouton de Gruyter, 113–85.

Bisang, Walter (2009). Serial Verb Constructions, *Language and Linguistics Compass* 3(3): 792–814.

Blagden, Charles O (1906). Language, in Walter W Skeat and Charles O Blagden (eds.), *Pagan Races of the Malay Peninsula. Vol. 2*. London: Macmillan and Co., 379–775.

Blagden, Charles O (1929). Achinese and Mon-Khmer, *Feestbundel, uitgegeven door het Koninklijk Bataviaasch Genootschap van Kunsten en Wetenschappen bij gelegenheid van zijn 150 jarig bestaan 1778-1928. Vol. 1*. Weltevreden: G Kolff, 35–8.

Blake, Barry (1988). Tagalog and the Manila-Mt Isa Axis, *La Trobe Working Papers in Linguistics* 1: 77–90.

Blake, Frank R (1917). Reduplication in Tagalog, *American Journal of Philology* 38: 425–31.

Blake, Frank R (1925). *A Grammar of the Tagalog Language*. New Haven, CT: American Oriental Society.

Blanchy, Sophie (1996). *Dictionnaire mahorais - français*. Paris: L'Harmattan.

Blench, Roger (2006). Why Are Aslian-Speakers Austronesian in Culture? Presentation: Preparatory Meeting for ICAL-3 EFEO, Siem Reap, 28–29th June (2006).

Blench, Roger (2007). New Palaeozoogeographical Evidence for the Settlement of Madagascar, *Azania* 42: 69–82.

Blench, Roger (2010a). Evidence for the Austronesian Voyages in the Indian Ocean, in Atholl Anderson, James H Barrett and Katherine V Boyle (eds.), *The Global Origin and Development of Seafaring*. Cambridge (UK): McDonald Institute for Archaeological Research, University of Cambridge, 239–48.

Blench, Roger (2010b). The Vocabularies of Vazimba and Beosi: Do They Represent the Languages of the Pre-Austronesian Populations of Madagascar? Unpublished Manuscript.

Blench, Roger (2010c). Was there an Austroasiatic Presence in Island Southeast Asia Prior to the Austronesian Expansion? *Bulletin of the Indo-Pacific Prehistory Association* 30: 133–44.

Blench, Roger (2014). The Enggano: Archaic Foragers and their Interactions with the Austronesian World. Unpublished Manuscript.

Blevins, Juliette (2004a). *Evolutionary Phonology: The Emergence of Sound Patterns*. Cambridge: Cambridge University Press.

Blevins, Juliette (2004b). Klamath Sibilant Degemination: Implications of a Recent Sound Change, *International Journal of American Linguistics* 70: 279–89.

Blevins, Juliette (2005a). Some Problems with Feature Economy: Labial Fricatives, Lone Fricatives, and Lost Labials. *Seoul Linguistics Forum 2005*. Seoul: Language Education Institute, Seoul National University, 211–30.

Blevins, Juliette (2005b). The Typology of Geminate Inventories: Historical Explanations for Recurrent Sound Patterns. *Seoul Linguistics Forum 2005*. Seoul: Language Education Institute, Seoul National University, 121–37.

Blevins, Juliette (2017). Areal Sound Patterns: From Perceptual Magnets to Stone Soup, in R Hickey (ed.), *The Cambridge Handbook of Areal Linguistics*. Cambridge: Cambridge University Press, 88–121.

Blevins, Juliette (to appear). Uvular Reflexes of Proto-Austronesian *q: Mysterious Disappearance or Drift Towards Oblivion? *Oceanic Linguistics*.

Blood, Cynthia (1992). Subject-Verb Agreement in Kisar, in Donald A. Burquest and Wyn D. Laidig (eds.), *Descriptive studies in languages of Maluku*. Jakarta: Universitas Katolik Indonesia Atma Jaya, 1–21.

Blood, David L (1967). Phonological Units in Cham, *Anthropological Linguistics* 9(8): 15–32.

Blood, David L (1977). A Three-Dimensional Analysis of Cham Sentences, in David D Thomas, Ernest W Lee and N Đ Liêm (eds.), *Papers in Southeast Asian Linguistics No.4: Chamic Studies*. Canberra: Pacific Linguistics, 53–76.

Blood, Doris E (1981). *Content and Structure in Cham Legends*. MA Thesis, University of Texas at Arlington.

Blood, Doris W (1961). Women's Speech Characteristics in Cham, *Asian Culture* 3: 139–43.

Blood, Doris W (1977). Clause and Sentence Final Particles in Cham, in David D Thomas, Ernest W Lee and N Đ Liêm (eds.), *Papers in Southeast Asian Linguistics No.4: Chamic Studies*. Canberra: Pacific Linguistics, 39–51.

Blood, Doris W (1978). Some Aspects of Cham Discourse Structure, *Anthropological Linguistics* 20(3): 110–32.

Bloomfield, Leonard (1917). *Tagalog Texts with Grammatical Analysis*. Volume 1–3. Urbana, Illinois: University of Illinois.

Bloomfield, Leonard (1925). On the Sound-System of Central Algonquian, *Language* 1(4): 130–56.

Bloyd, Tobias (2020). *Sula: its Language, Land, and People*. PhD Dissertation, University of Hawai'i.

Bloyd, Tobias (2015). Toward A Phonological Reconstruction of Proto-Sula, *University of Hawai'i Working Papers in Linguistics* 46(8): 1–23.

Blust, Robert (1971). A Tagalog Consonant Cluster Conspiracy, *Philippine Journal of Linguistics* 2: 85–91.

Blust, Robert (1974a). *The Proto-North Sarawak Vowel Deletion Hypothesis*. PhD Dissertation, University of Hawai'i.

Blust, Robert (1974b). A Murik Vocabulary, with a Note on the Linguistic Position of Murik, in Jérôme Rousseau (ed.), *The Peoples of Central Borneo*. Special Issue of *Sarawak Museum Journal* 22(43): 153–89.

Blust, Robert (1976). Austronesian Culture History: Some Linguistic Inferences and Their Relations to the Archaeological Record. *World Archaeology* 8 1: 19–43.

Blust, Robert (1977a). The Proto-Austronesian Pronouns and Austronesian Subgrouping: A Preliminary Report, *University of Hawai'i Working Papers in Linguistics* 9(2): 1–15.

Blust, Robert (1977b). Sketches of the Morphology and Phonology of Bornean Languages 1: Uma Juman (Kayan), in Hein Steinhauer (ed.), *Papers in Bornean and Western Austronesian Languages No. 2*. Canberra: Pacific Linguistics, 7–122.

Blust, Robert (1978). Eastern Malayo-Polynesian: A Subgrouping Argument, in Lois Carrington and Stephen A Wurm (eds.), *Second International Conference on Austronesian Linguistics: Proceedings*. Canberra: Pacific Linguistics, 181–234.

Blust, Robert (1980a). Early Austronesian Social Organization: The Evidence of Language, *Current Anthropology* 21: 205–47 (with Comments and Reply).

Blust, Robert (1980b). Notes on Proto-Malayo-Polynesian Phratry Dualism, *Bijdragen tot de Taal-, Land- en Volkenkunde* 136: 215–47.

Blust, Robert (1980c). Austronesian Etymologies, *Oceanic Linguistics*, 19: 1–181.

Blust, Robert (1980d). More on the Origins of Glottalic Consonants, *Lingua* 52: 125–56.

Blust, Robert (1981a). Dual Divisions in Oceania: Innovation or Retention? *Oceania* 52.1: 66–80.

Blust, Robert (1981b). Linguistic Evidence for Some Early Austronesian Taboos, *American Anthropologist* 83(2): 285–319.

Blust, Robert (1981c). The Reconstruction of Proto-Malayo-Javanic: An Appreciation, *Bijdragen tot de Taal-, Land- en Volkenkunde* 137/4: 456–69.

Blust, Robert (1981d). The Soboyo Reflexes of Proto-Austronesian *S, in Robert Blust (ed.), *Historical Linguistics in Indonesia, Part I*. Special issue of *NUSA* 10. Jakarta: Badan Penyelenggara Seri NUSA, Universitas Atma Jaya, 21–30.

Blust, Robert (1982). The Linguistic Value of the Wallace Line, *Bijdragen tot de Taal-, Land- en Volkenkunde* 138: 231–50.

Blust, Robert (1983/1984). More on the Position of the Languages of Eastern Indonesia, *Oceanic Linguistics* 22/23: 1–28.

Blust, Robert (1984). On the History of the Rejang Vowels and Diphthongs, *Bijdragen tot de Taal-, Land- en Volkenkunde* 140(4): 422–50.

Blust, Robert (1984/1985). The Austronesian Homeland: A Linguistic Perspective, *Asian Perspectives* 26: 45–67.

Blust, Robert (1986/1987). Language and Culture History: Two Case Studies, *Asian Perspectives* 27: 205–27.

Blust, Robert (1987). Lexical Reconstruction and Semantic Reconstruction: The Case of Austronesian House Words, *Diachronica* 4: 79–106.

Blust, Robert (1988a). Sketches of the Morphology and Phonology of Bornean Languages 2: Mukah Melanau, in Hein Steinhauer (ed.), *Papers in Western Austronesian Linguistics No. 3*. Canberra: Pacific Linguistics, 151–216.

Blust, Robert (1988b). Malay Historical Linguistics: A Progress Report, in Ahmad, Mohd. T and Zain, Z M (eds.), *Rekonstruksi dan Cabang-Cabang Bahasa Melayu Induk* [Reconstruction and branches of Proto-Malay(ic)]. Kuala Lumpur: Dewan Bahasa dan Pustaka, 1–33.

Blust, Robert (1988c). *Austronesian Root Theory: An Essay on the Limits of Morphology*. Amsterdam/Philadelphia: John Benjamins.

Blust, Robert (1991a). On the Limits of the Thunder Complex in Australasia, *Anthropos* 86.4 (6): 517–28.

Blust, Robert (1991b). The Greater Central Philippines Hypothesis, *Oceanic Linguistics* 30: 73–129.

Blust, Robert (1992a). On Speech Strata in Tiruray, in Malcolm Ross (ed.), *Papers in Austronesian Linguistics*, No. 1. Canberra: Pacific Linguistics, 1–52.

Blust, Robert (1992b). Tumbaga in Southeast Asia and South America, *Anthropos* 87: 443–57.

Blust, Robert (1993a). Central and Central-Eastern Malayo-Polynesian, *Oceanic Linguistics* 32(2): 241–93.

Blust, Robert (1993b). Austronesian Sibling Terms and Culture History, *Bijdragen tot de Taal-, Land- en Volkenkunde* 149: 22–76 (also published in A K Pawley and M D Ross [eds.] [1994]. *Austronesian Terminologies: Continuity and Change*. Canberra: Pacific Linguistics, 31–72).

Blust, Robert (1994). The Austronesian Settlement of Mainland Southeast Asia, in K L Adams and T J Hudak (eds.), *Papers from the 2nd Annual Meeting of the Southeast Asian Linguistic Society*. Tempe: Arizona State University, 25–83.

Blust, Robert (1995a). The Position of the Formosan Languages: Method and Theory in Austronesian Comparative Linguistics, in Paul Jen-Juei Li, Cheng-Hwa Tsang, Ying-Kuei Huang, Dah-an Ho and Chiu-Yu Tseng (eds.), *Austronesian Studies Relating to Taiwan*. Symposium Series of the Institute of History and Philology, Academia Sinica, No. 3. Taipei: Academia Sinica, 585–650.

Blust, Robert (1995b). The Prehistory of the Austronesian-Speaking Peoples: A View from Language, *Journal of World Prehistory* 9(4): 453–510.

Blust, Robert (1995c). Notes on Berawan Consonant Gemination, *Oceanic Linguistics* 34(1): 123–38.

Blust, Robert (1996a). Austronesian Culture History: The Window of Language, in Ward H Goodenough (ed.), *Prehistoric settlement of the Pacific*. Special issue of *Transactions of the American Philosophical Society* 86(5): 28–35.

Blust, Robert (1996b). Some Remarks on the Linguistic Position of Thao, *Oceanic Linguistics* 35: 272–94.

Blust, Robert (1997a). Rukai Stress Revisited, *Oceanic Linguistics* 36(2): 398–403.

Blust, Robert (1997b). Nasals and Nasalization in Borneo, *Oceanic Linguistics*, 36(1): 149–79.

Blust, Robert (1997c). Ablaut in Northwest Borneo, *Diachronica* 14: 1–30.

Blust, Robert (1998a). *Ca-* Reduplication and Proto-Austronesian Grammar, *Oceanic Linguistics* 37(1): 29–64.

Blust, Robert (1998b). The Position of the Languages of Sabah, in Maria Lourdes S Bautista (ed.), *Pagtanaw, Essays on Language in Honor of Teodoro A Llamzon*. Manila: The Linguistic Society of the Philippines, 29–52.

Blust, Robert (1999a). Subgrouping, Circularity and Extinction: Some Issues in Austronesian Comparative Linguistics, in Elizabeth Zeitoun and Paul J K Li (eds.), *Selected Papers from the Eighth International Conference on Austronesian Linguistics* (Symposium Series of the Institute of Linguistics, Academia Sinica 1). Taipei: Academia Sinica, 31–94.

Blust, Robert (1999b). Linguistics vs. Archaeology: Early Austronesian Terms for Metals, in Roger Blench and Matthew Spriggs (eds.), *Archaeology and Language III: Artefacts, Languages and Texts*. London/New York: Routledge, 127–43.

Blust, Robert (1999c). Squib: A Note on Covert Structure: *Ca-* Reduplication in Amis, *Oceanic Linguistics* 38(1): 168–74.

Blust, Robert (2000a). Chamorro Historical Phonology, *Oceanic Linguistics* 39: 83–122.

Blust, Robert (2000b). Why Lexicostatistics Doesn't Work: The Universal Constant Hypothesis and the Austronesian Languages, in Colin Renfrew, April McMahon and Larry M Trask (eds.), *Time Depth in Historical Linguistics*, Vol. 2. Cambridge, UK: McDonald Institute for Archaeological Research, 311–32.

Blust, Robert (2000c). Low-Vowel Fronting in Northern Sarawak, *Oceanic Linguistics* 39(2): 285–319.

Blust, Robert (2001a). Malayo-Polynesian: New Stones in the Wall, *Oceanic Linguistics* 40: 151–5.

Blust, Robert (2001b). Language, Dialect and Riotous Sound Change: The Case of Sa'ban, in G W Thurgood (ed.), *Papers from the Ninth Annual Meeting of the Southeast Asian Linguistics Society*. Arizona State University, Program for Southeast Asian Studies Monograph Series. Tempe: Arizona State University, 249–359.

Blust, Robert (2001c). Thao Triplication, *Oceanic Linguistics* 40: 324–35.

Blust, Robert (2002a). Formalism or Phoneyism? The History of Kayan Final Glottal Stop, in K Alexander Adelaar and Robert Blust (eds.), *Between Worlds: Linguistic Papers in Memory of David John Prentice*. Canberra: Pacific Linguistics, 29–37.

Blust, Robert (2002b). Kiput Historical Phonology, *Oceanic Linguistics* 41(2): 384–438.

Blust, Robert (2002c). Notes on the History of Focus in Austronesian Languages, in Fay Wouk and Malcolm Ross (eds.), *The History and Typology of Western Austronesian Voice Systems*. Canberra: Pacific Linguistics, 63–78.

Blust, Robert (2003a). The Phonestheme ŋ- in Austronesian Languages, *Oceanic Linguistics* 42: 187–212.

Blust, Robert (2003b). Three Notes on Early Austronesian Morphology, *Oceanic Linguistics* 42: 438–78.

Blust, Robert (2004a). *t to k: An Austronesian Sound Change Revisited, *Oceanic Linguistics* 43(2): 365–410.

Blust, Robert (2004b). Austronesian Nasal Substitution: A Survey, *Oceanic Linguistics* 43(1): 73–148.

Blust, Robert (2005a). The Linguistic Macrohistory of the Philippines: Some Speculations, in Hsiu-Chuan Liao and Carl R Galvez Rubino, eds., *Current Issues in Philippine Linguistics and Anthropology Parangal Kay Lawrence A Reid*. Manila: The Linguistic Society of the Philippines and Summer Institute of Linguistics Philippines, 31–68.

Blust, Robert (2005b). Borneo and Iron: Dempwolff's *besi Revisited, *Bulletin of the Indo-Pacific Prehistory Association* 25: 31–40.

Blust, Robert (2005c). Whence the Malays? in J T Collins and A Sariyan (eds.), *Borneo and the Homeland of the Malays: Four Essays*. Kuala Lumpur: Dewan Bahasa dan Pustaka, 64–88.

Blust, Robert (2005d). A Note on the History of Genitive Marking in Austronesian Languages, *Oceanic Linguistics* 44: 215–22.

Blust, Robert (2006). The Origin of the Kelabit Voiced Aspirates: A Historical Hypothesis Revisited, *Oceanic Linguistics* 45: 311–38.

Blust, Robert (2007a). Disyllabic attractors and Anti-antigemination in Austronesian Sound Change, *Phonology* 24: 1–36.

Blust, Robert (2007b). Òma Lóngh Historical Phonology, *Oceanic Linguistics* 46: 1–53.

Blust, Robert (2007c). The Linguistic Position of Sama-Bajaw, *Studies in Philippine Languages and Cultures* 15: 73–114.

Blust, Robert (2008). Is there a Bima-Sumba Subgroup? *Oceanic Linguistics* 47(1): 45–113.

Blust, Robert (2009a). The Position of the Languages of Eastern Indonesia: A Reply to Donohue and Grimes, *Oceanic Linguistics* 48: 36–77.

Blust, Robert (2009b). Palauan Historical Phonology: Whence the Intrusive Velar Nasal?, *Oceanic Linguistics* 48(2): 307–46.

Blust, Robert (2009c). *The Austronesian Languages*. Canberra: Pacific Linguistics.

Blust, Robert (2010a). Five Patterns of Semantic Change in Austronesian Languages, in John Bowden, Nikolaus P Himmelmann and Malcolm D Ross, (eds.), *A Journey Through Austronesian and Papuan Linguistic and Cultural Space: Papers in Honour of Andrew Pawley*. Canberra: Pacific Linguistics, 525–45.

Blust, Robert (2010b). The Greater North Borneo Hypothesis, *Oceanic Linguistics* 49: 44–118.

Blust, Robert (2010c). On Datus, Ancient and Modern, in Loren Billings and Nelleke Goudswaard (eds.), *Piakandatu Ami Dr. Howard P McKaughan*. Manila: Linguistic Society of the Philippines and Summer Institute of Linguistics Philippines, 36–51.

Blust, Robert (2011). Eye of the Day: A Response to Urban (2010), *Oceanic Linguistics* 50(2): 524–35.

Blust, Robert. 2012. The Marsupials Strike Back: A Reply to Schapper (2011), *Oceanic Linguistics* 51(1): 261–77.

Blust, Robert (2013a). *The Austronesian Languages*. 2nd edition. Canberra: Pacific Linguistics.

Blust, Robert (2013b). Formosan Evidence for Early Austronesian Knowledge of Iron, *Oceanic Linguistics* 52: 255–64.

Blust, Robert (2014a). Some Recent Proposals Concerning the Classification of the Austronesian Languages, *Oceanic Linguistics* 53: 300–91.

Blust, Robert (2014b). Dobel Historical Phonology, *Oceanic Linguistics* 53(1): 37–60.

Blust, Robert (2015a). The Case Markers of Proto-Austronesian, *Oceanic Linguistics* 54(2): 436–91.

Blust, Robert (2015b). Longhouses and Nomadism: Is There a Connection? *Borneo Research Bulletin* 46: 194–220.

Blust, Robert (2016). Kelabit-Lun Dayeh Phonology, with Special Reference to the Voiced Aspirates, *Oceanic Linguistics* 55: 246–77.

Blust, Robert (2017a). Historical Linguistics and Archaeology: An Uneasy Alliance, in Philip J Piper, Hirofumi Matsumura and David Bulbeck (eds.), *New Perspectives in Southeast Asian and Pacific Prehistory*. Canberra: Australian National Unviersity Press, 275–91.

Blust, Robert (2017b). The Linguistic History of Austronesian-Speaking Communities in Island Southeast Asia, in Peter Bellwood (ed.), *First Islanders: Prehistory and Human Migration in Island Southeast Asia*. Oxford: Wiley Blackwell, 190–7.

Blust, Robert (2017c). The Challenge of Semantic Reconstruction: Proto-Malayo-Polynesian *suku 'Lineage; Quarter'? *Oceanic Linguistics* 56: 247–58.

Blust, Robert (2017d). Regular Metathesis in Batanic (Northern Philippines), *Oceanic Linguistics* 56.2: 491–504.

Blust, Robert (2018a). The Challenge of Semantic Reconstruction 2: Proto-Malayo-Polynesian *kamalir 'Men's House', *Oceanic Linguistics* 57: 335–58.

Blust, Robert (2018b). Two Birds with One Stone: The Aerodynamic Voicing Constraint and the Languages of Borneo, *Journal of the Southeast Asian Linguistics Society* 11(2): 1–18.

Blust, Robert (2018c). The Mystery Aspirates in Philippine Languages, *Oceanic Linguistics* 57(1): 221–47.

Blust, Robert (2019a). The Austronesian homeland and dispersal, *Annual Review of Linguistics* 5: 417–34.

Blust, Robert (2019b). The Resurrection of Proto-Philippines, *Oceanic Linguistics* 58: 153–256.

Blust, Robert (nd). *Unpublished Fieldnotes from Borneo*. Unpublished Manuscript.

Blust, Robert and Alexander Smith (2014). *A Bibliography of the Languages of Borneo (and Madagascar)*. Phillips, Maine: Borneo Research Council.

Blust, Robert and Stephen Trussel (2013). The Austronesian Comparative Dictionary: A Work in Progress, *Oceanic Linguistics* 52(2): 493–523.

Blust, Robert and Stephen Trussel (2020). *Austronesian Comparative Dictionary*. Honolulu: Department of Linguistics, University of Hawai'i. Online at www.Trussel2.Com/ACD

Boarccaech, Alessandro (2013). *Dicionário Hresuk-Português* [Hresuk – Portuguese dictionary]. URL: https://issuu.com/kirstygusmao/docs/dicionario_hresuk_-_portugues

Boas, Franz (1911). *Handbook of the American Indian Languages*. Washington D C: Bureau of American Ethnology.

Bolton, Rosemary Ann (1990). *A Preliminary Description of Nuaulu Phonology and Grammar*. MA Thesis, University of Texas at Arlington.

Bondoc, Ivan Paul (2018). Revisiting relativization asymmetries in Philippine-type symmetrical voice languages, *University of Hawai'i Working Papers in Linguistics* 49(3).

Botouhely, Jean Lewis (2007). Le parler malgache du nord: Présentation des principales spécificités, Unpublished Manuscript, Antsiranana, Madagascar.

Boutin, Michael E (1988). Problems in Analyzing Focus in the Languages of Sabah, in Charles Peck (ed.), *Sabah Syntax Papers A: Borneo Language Studies I*. Dallas: Summer Institute of Linguistics, 53–80.

Boutin, Michael E (1994). *Aspect in Bonggi*. PhD Dissertation, University of Florida at Gainesville.

Boutin, Michael E (2001). Voice Alternations in Bonggi, in Karen Adams and Thomas Hudak (eds.), *Papers from the Sixth Annual Meeting of the Southeast Asian Linguistics Society 1996*. Tempe, AZ:

Program for Southeast Asian Studies, Arizona State University, 47–70.

Boutin, Michael E (2002). Nominative and Genitive Case Alternations in Bonggi, in Fay Wouk and Malcolm D. Ross (eds.), *The History and Typology of Western Austronesian Voice Systems*. Canberra: Pacific Linguistics, 209–39.

Bouwer, Leoni (2005). Towards a Sociolinguistic Profile of Madagascar: Issues of Diversity, *Language Matters* 36(1): 98–116.

Bowden, John (1997). The Meanings of Directionals in Taba, in Gunter Senft (ed.), *Referring to Space: Studies in Austronesian and Papuan Languages*. Oxford: Clarendon, 251–68.

Bowden, John (2001). *Taba: Description of A South Halmahera Language*. Canberra: Pacific Linguistics.

Bowden, John (2005). Taba, in Alexander Adelaar and Nikolaus P Himmelmann (eds.), *The Austronesian Languages of Asia and Madagascar*. London: Routledge, 769–92.

Bowden, John (2010). Metathesis in Helong, in Yassir Nasunius (ed.), *KOLITA* 8. Jakarta: Pusat Kajian Bahasa dan Budaya, Unika Atma Jaya, 59–63.

Bowden, John (2014). Mental Deixis in Taba, in Anthony Jukes (ed.), *Deixis and spatial expression in languages of Indonesian*. Special issue of *NUSA* 56: 79–100.

Bowden, John, John Hajek and Nikolaus P Himmelmann (nd). A Sketch Grammar of Waima'a. Unpublished Manuscript.

Boyer-Rossel, Klara (2014). From the Great Island to the African Continent Through the Western World: Itineraries of A Return to the Origins Through Hip Hop Music in Madagascar (2000–2011), in Msia Kibona Clark and Mickie Mwanzia Koster (eds.), *Hip Hop and Social Change in Africa: Ni Wakati*. Lanham: Lexington Books, 178–97.

Bracks, Christoph (2020). *Intonation Units and Grammatical Units in Totoli*. PhD Dissertation, Universität zu Köln.

Bradbury, Daniel (2000). *Kamus Balantak-Indonesia-Inggeris* [Balantak – Indonesian – English dictionary]. Luwuk: Pemerintah Daerah Kabupatan Banggai.

Brainard, Sherri (1994). Voice and Ergativity in Karao, in Tom Givón (ed.), *Voice and Inversion*. Amsterdam: John Benjamins, 365–402.

Brainard, Sherri (1996). Why the Focused NP Is Not the Subject in Philippine Languages: Evidence from Karao, *Philippine Journal of Linguistics* 27(1–2): 1–47.

Brainard, Sherri (1997). Ergativity and Grammatical Relations in Karao, in T Givón (ed.), *Grammatical Relations: A Functional Perspective*. Amsterdam/Philadelphia: John Benjamins, 85–154.

Brainard, Sherri and Dietlinde Behrens (2002). *A Grammar of Yakan*. Manila: Linguistic Society of the Philippines.

Brainard, Sherri and Ena Vander Molen (2005). Word Order Inverse in Obo Manobo, in Hsiu-Chuan Liao and Carl R Galvez Rubino (eds.), *Current Issues in Philippine Linguistics and Anthropology: Parangal Kay Lawrence A Reid*. Manila: The Linguistic Society of the Philippines and Summer Institute of Linguistics Philippines, 364–418.

Brandão A, K K Eng, T Rito, B Cavadas, D Bulbeck, F Gandini, M Pala, M Mormina, B Hudson, J White, T M Ko, M Saidin, Z Zafarina, S Oppenheimer, M B Richards, L Pereira and P Soares (2016). Quantifying the Legacy of the Chinese Neolithic on the Maternal Genetic Heritage of Taiwan and Island Southeast Asia, *Human Genetics* 1135(4): 363–76.

Brandes, Jan Laurens Andries (1884). *Bijdragen tot de Vergelijkende Klankleer der Westerse Afdeling van de Maleisch-Polynesische Taalfamilie* [Contributions to the phonology of the western division of the Malayo-Polynesian language family]. PhD Dissertation, Leiden University.

Brandes, Jan Laurens Andries (1894). *Taalkaart van de Minahasa* [Language map of Minahasa]. Batavia: Bataviaasch Genootschap van Kunsten en Wetenschappen.

Brandstetter, Renward (1906a). Die Stellung der minahassischen Idiome zu den übrigen Sprachen von Celebes einerseits und zu den Sprachen der Philippinen anderseits, in Fritz Sarasin, *Versuch einer Anthropologie der Insel Celebes*, Part 2. Wiesbaden: C W Kreidel, 34–8.

Brandstetter, Renward (1906b). *Ein Prodromus zu einem vergleichenden Wörterbuch der malaio-polynesischen Sprachen für Sprachforscher und Ethnographen*. Luzern: E Haag.

Brandstetter, Renward (1911). *Gemeinindonesisch und Urindonesisch*. Luzern: E Haag.

Brandstetter, Renward (1915). *Die Lauterscheinungen in den indonesischen Sprachen*. Luzern: Haag.

Brandstetter, Renward (1917). *Die Reduplikation in den indianischen, indonesischen und indogermanischen Sprachen*. Luzern: Beilage zum Jahresbericht der Luzerner Kantonsschule.

Braunwald, Susan R (2015). *Braunwald Corpus*. Irwine, CA: Computation of Language Laboratory Department of Cognitive Sciences.

Brewis, Richard (2004). Keterangan ringkas tatabahasa [A Brief Explanation of the Grammar], in Richard Brewis, Philippa Silipah Majius and Kielo Brewis, *Kamus Murut Timugon-Melayu: Dengan ikhtisar etnografi* [Timugon Murut – Malay Dictionary: with Ethnographic Sketch]. Kota Kinabalu: Kadazandusun Language Foundation, 899–935.

Brickell, Timothy C (2014). *A Grammatical Description of the Tondano (Toundano) Language*. PhD Dissertation, La Trobe University.

Brickell, Timothy C (2016a). Tondano, in Geoffrey Haig and Stefan Schnell (eds.), *Multi-CAST (Multilingual Corpus of Annotated Spoken Texts)*. Cologne: Language Archive Cologne.

Brickell, Timothy C (2016b). *Tonsawang: A Collaborative Multimedia Project Documenting an Endangered Language of North Sulawesi*. London: Endangered Languages Archive at the School of Oriental and African Studies University of London.

Brickell, Timothy C (2018). Tonsawang (Toundanow), North Sulawesi, Indonesia — Language Contexts, in Peter K Austin (ed.), *Language Documentation and Description, Vol. 16*. London: EL Publishing, 55–85.

Bronson, B and J C White (1992). Radiocarbon and Chronology in Southeast Asia, in R W Ehrich (ed.), *Chronologies in Old World Archaeology*. Chicago: Chicago University Press, 1–2.

Broschart, Jürgen (1997). Why Tongan Does It Differently: Categorial Distinctions in a Language without Nouns and Verbs, *Linguistic Typology* 1: 123–65.

Broselow, Ellen (2000). Stress, Epenthesis, and Segmental Transformation in Selayarese Loans, *Berkeley Linguistic Society* 25: 311–25.

Brosius, J P (1988). A Separate Reality: Comment on Hoffman's 'The Punan: Hunters and Gatherers of Borneo', *Borneo Research Bulletin* 20(2): 81–106.

Brown, Cecil H (1983). Where Do Cardinal Direction Terms Come from? *Anthropological Linguistics* 25(2): 121–161.

Brown, Lea (2001). *A Grammar of Nias Selatan.* PhD Dissertation, University of Sydney.

Brown, Penelope and Stephen C Levinson (1987). *Politeness: Some Universals in Language Use.* London: Cambridge University Press.

Brown, Penelope and Stephen C Levinson (1993). Uphill and Downhill in Tzeltal, *Journal of Linguistic Anthropology* 3(1): 46–74.

Brucato N, P Kusuma, M P Cox, D Pierron, G A Purnomo, A Adelaar, T Kivisild, T Letellier, H Sudoyo and F X Ricaut (2016). Malagasy Genetic Ancestry Comes from an Historical Malay Trading Post in Southeast Borneo, *Molecular Biology and Evolution* 33: 2396–400.

Brucato N, P Kusuma, P Beaujard, H Sudoyo, M P Cox and F X Ricaut (2017). Genomic Admixture Tracks Pulses of Economic Activity Over 2,000 Years in the Indian Ocean Trading Network, *Scientific Reports* 7: 2919.

Brucato N, V Fernandes, P Kusuma, V Černý, C J Mulligan, P Soares, T Rito, C Besse, A Boland, J F Deleuze, M P Cox, H Sudoyo, M Stoneking, L Pereira and F X Ricaut (2019). Evidence of Austronesian Genetic Lineages in East Africa and South Arabia: Complex Dispersal from Madagascar and Southeast Asia, *Genome Biology and Evolution* 11: 748–58.

Brucato N, V Fernandes, S Mazières, P Kusuma, M P Cox, J W Nganga, M Omar, M C Simeone-Senelle, C Frassati, F Alshamali, B Fin, A Boland, J F Deleuze, M Stoneking, A Adelaar, A Crowther, N Boivin, L Pereira, P Bailly, J Chiaroni and F X Ricaut (2018). The Comoros Shows the Earliest Austronesian Gene Flow in East Africa, *American Journal of Human Genetics* 102(1): 58–68.

Bruckmayr, Philipp (2019). *Cambodia's Muslims and the Malay World.* Boston and Leiden: Brill.

Brucks, Caleb (2015). *The Creation of Narrative Space: The Directional System of Upper Tanana.* PhD Dissertation, University of Regina.

Brugmann, Karl (1884). Zur Frage nach den Verwandtschaftsverhältnissen der indogermanischen Sprachen, *Internationale Zeitschrift für Allgemeine Sprachwissenschaft* 1: 228–56.

Brunelle, Marc (2005a). Register and Tone in Eastern Cham: Evidence from a Word Game, *Mon-Khmer Studies* 35: 121–32.

Brunelle, Marc (2005b). *Register in Eastern Cham: Phonological, Phonetic and Sociolinguistic Approaches.* PhD Dissertation, Cornell University.

Brunelle, Marc (2006). A Phonetic Study of Eastern Cham Register, in P Sidwell and A Grant (eds.), *Chamic and Beyond.* Canberra: Pacific Linguistics, 1–36.

Brunelle, Marc (2008). Diglossia, Bilingualism, and the Revitalization of Written Eastern Cham, *Language Documentation and Conservation* 2(1): 28–46.

Brunelle, Marc (2009a). Contact-Induced Change? Register in Three Cham Dialects, *Journal of Southeast Asian Linguistics* 2: 1–22.

Brunelle, Marc (2009b). Diglossia and Monosyllabization in Eastern Cham: A Sociolinguistic Study, in J Stanford and D Preston (eds.), *Variation in Indigenous Minority Languages.* Amsterdam: John Benjamins, 47–75.

Brunelle, Marc (2010). The Role of Larynx Height in the Javanese Tense~Lax Stop Contrast, in Ralph Mercado, Eric Potsdam, Lisa Travis (eds.), *Austronesian and Theoretical Linguistics.* Amsterdam: John Benjamins, 7–24.

Brunelle, Marc (2012). Dialect Experience and Perceptual Integrality in Phonological Registers: Fundamental Frequency, Voice Quality and the First Formant in Cham, *Journal of the Acoustical Society of America* 131(4): 3088–102.

Brunelle, Marc (2019). Revisiting the Expansion of the Chamic Language Family: Acehnese and Tsat, in A Griffiths, A Hardy and G Wade (eds.), *Champa: Territories and Networks of a Southeast Asian Kingdom.* Paris: Presses de l'École Française d'Extrême-Orient, 287–302.

Brunelle, Marc (2020). The Loss of Affixation in Cham: Contact, Internal Drift and the Limits of Linguistic History, in David Gil and Antoinette Schapper (eds.), *Austronesian Undressed: How and Why Languages Become Isolating.* Amsterdam: John Benjamins, 97–118.

Brunelle, Marc and Graham Thurgood (2015). The Historical Development of Chamic Languages, in J López Cortina and A Pérez Pereiro (eds.), *Rediscovering Cham Heritage in Cambodia.* Phnom Penh: Naga Editions, 46–97.

Brunelle, Marc and Phú Văn Hẳn (2019). Colloquial Eastern Cham, in A Vittrant and J Watkins (eds.), *The Mainland Southeast Asia Linguistic Area.* Berlin: de Gruyter Mouton, 522–57.

Brunelle, Marc, Tạ Thành Tấn, James Kirby and Đinh Lư Giang (2020). Transphonologization of Voicing in Chru: Studies in Production and Perception, *Laboratory Phonology: Journal of the Association for Laboratory Phonology* 11(1): 1–33.

Brunelle, Marc, Jeanne Brown & Phạm Thị Thu Hà. 2022. Northern Raglai voicing and its relation to Southern Raglai register: evidence for early stages of registrogenesis, *Phonetica* 79: 151–88.

Brzozowska M M, E Havula, R B Allen and M P Cox (2019). Genetics, Adaptation to Environmental Changes and Archaic Admixture in the Pathogenesis of Diabetes Mellitus in Indigenous Australians, *Reviews in Endocrine and Metabolic Disorders* 20: 321–32.

Bubandt, Nils (1997). Speaking of Places: Spatial Poesis and Localized Identity in Buli, in James J Fox (ed.), *The Poetic Power of Place.* Canberra: Australian National University Press, 131–62.

Buck, W S B (1933). Vocabulary of Land Dayak as Spoken in Kampong Boyan, Upper Sarawak, *Sarawak Museum Journal* 4(13): 187–92.

Budzhak-Jones, Svitlana (1998). Against Word-Internal Codeswitching: Evidence from Ukrainian-English Bilingualism, *International Journal of Bilingualism* 2: 161–82.

Bùi Khánh Thế (1996). Ngữ Pháp Tiếng Chăm [Cham Grammar]. Hà Nội: Nhà Xuất Bản Giáo Dục [Education Press].

Bùi Khánh Thế (1997). Problems of Compiling the Cham-Viet Dictionary, in Cecilia Odé and Wim Stokhof (eds.), *Proceedings of the Seventh International Conference on Austronesian Linguistics.* Amsterdam/Atlanta: Rodopi, 627–30.

Bulbeck, David (2000). Economy, Military and Ideology in Pre-Islamic Luwu, South Sulawesi, Indonesia, *Australasian Historical Archeology* 18: 3–16.

Bulbeck, David (2008). An Integrated Perspective on the Austronesian Diaspora: The Switch from Cereal Agriculture to Maritime Foraging in the Colonisation of Island Southeast Asia, *Australian Archaeology* 67: 31–51.

Bulbeck, David and Ian Caldwell (2000). *Land of Iron: The Historical Archaeology of Luwu and the Cenrana Valley*. Hull, UK: Centre for South-East Asian Studies, University of Hull.

Burenhult, Niclas (2005). *A Grammar of Jahai*. Canberra: Pacific Linguistics.

Burenhult, Niclas (2008). Spatial Coordinate Systems in Demonstrative Meaning, *Linguistic Typology* 12: 99–142.

Burnham, Eugene (1976). *The Place of Haroi in the Chamic Languages*. MA Thesis, University of Texas at Arlington.

Burquest, Donald A and Lee A Steven (1992). Prosodic Structure and Reduplication: Data From Some Languages of Maluku. Presentation: Second Annual Meeting of the Southeast Asian Linguistics Society, Tempe AZ.

Burton, Scott L (1996). *A Case Study of Lexical Borrowing Between Language Families: The East Mindanao and Manobo Languages*. MA Thesis, University of Texas at Arlington.

Burton, Scott L (2018). *Tagakaulo-English Dictionary*. Manila: Summer Institute of Linguistics Philippines.

Busenitz, Marilyn J and Robert L Busenitz (1992). Spatial Deixis in Balantak, *Pan-Asiatic Linguistics: Proceeding of the Third Intermediary Symposium on Language and Linguistics*, Vol. 1, 131–49.

Butler, Becky A (2014). *Deconstructing the Southeast Asian Sesquisyllable: A Gestural Account*. PhD Dissertation, Cornell University.

Butler, Brian M (1994). Early Prehistoric Settlement in the Mariana Islands: New Evidence from Saipan, *Man and Culture in Oceania* 10: 15–38.

Butler, Brian M (1995). *Archaeological Investigations in the Achugao and Matansa Area of Saipan, Mariana Islands*. Saipan: The Micronesian Archaeological Survey, Division of Historic Preservation, Department of Community and Cultural Affairs (Micronesian Archaeological Survey, Report No.30).

Bybee, Joan L and Östen Dahl (1989). The Creation of Tense and Aspect Systems in the Languages of the World, *Studies in Language* 13(1): 51–103.

Bybee, Joan, Revere Perkins and William Pagliuca (1994). The *Evolution of Grammar: Tense, Aspect, and Modality in the Languages of the World*. Chicago: University of Chicago Press.

Bynon, Theodora (1977). *Historical Linguistics*. Cambridge: Cambridge University Press.

Cabral, Estêvão and Marilyn Martin-Jones (2018). Paths to Multilingualism? Reflections on Developments in Language-in-Education Policy and Practice in East-Timor, in A P L Lim, C Stroud and D L Wee (eds.), *The Multilingual Citizen: Towards A Politics of Language for Agency and Change*. Bristol: Multilingual Matters, 120–49.

Calvet, Louis-Jean (2006). *Towards an Ecology of World Languages*. Cambridge: Polity. (Original title: *Pour une écologie des langues du monde*. Paris: Plon, 1999)

Campbell, Lyle (2013). *Historical Linguistics: An Introduction*. 3rd edition. Cambridge, MA: Massachusetts Institute of Technology Press.

Campbell, Lyle (2020). *Historical Linguistics: An Introduction*. 4th edition. Edinburgh: Edinburgh University Press, and Cambridge, MA: Massachusetts Institute of Technology Press.

Campbell, Philip J (1989). *Some Aspects of Pitu Ulunna Salu Grammar: A Typological Approach*. MA Thesis, University of Texas at Arlington.

Campbell, Philip J (1991). Phonology of Pitu Ulunna Salu, in René van den Berg (ed.), *Sulawesi Phonologies*. Ujung Pandang: Summer Institute of Linguistics in Cooperation with the Department of Education and Culture, 1–52.

Campbell, Stuart (1996). The Distribution of *-at* and *-ah* Endings in Malay Loanwords from Arabic, *Bijdragen tot de Taal-, Land- en Volkenkunde* 152(1): 23–44.

Campbell, Stuart (2009). Indonesian/Malay, in Kees Versteegh (ed.), *Encyclopedia of Arabic Language and Linguistics. Volume IV: Q-Z*. Leiden and Boston: Brill, 340–5.

Capell, Arthur (1964). Verbal Systems in Philippine Languages, *Philippine Journal of Science* 93: 231–48.

Capell, Arthur (1976). Austronesian and Papuan Mixed Languages: General Remarks, in Stephen A Wurm (ed.), *New Guinea Area Languages and Language Study, Vol. 2, Austronesian Languages*. Canberra: Pacific Linguistics, 527–80.

Capell, Arthur (1982). Bezirkssprachen im Gebiet des UAN, in Rainer Karle, Martina Heinschke, Peter Pink, Christel Rost and Karen Stadtlander (eds.): *GAVA: Studies in Austronesian Languages and Cultures Dedicated to Hans Kähler*. Berlin: Dietrich Reimer, 1–14.

Carlin, Eithne and Jacques Arends (2002). *Atlas of the Languages of Suriname*. Leiden: Koninklijk Instituut voor Taal-, Land- en Volkenkunde Press.

Carpenter, Kathie (1996). Subordination by Reduplication in Wetan, *Studies in Language* 20: 37–51.

Carrier-Duncan, Jill (1985). Linking of Thematic Roles in Derivational Word Formation, *Linguistic Inquiry* 16: 1–34.

Carson, Mike T (2008). Refining Earliest Settlement in Remote Oceania: Renewed Archaeological Investigations at Unai Bapot, Saipan, *Journal of Island Coast Archaeology* 3: 115–39.

Carson, Mike T (2014). *First Settlement of Remote Oceania- Earliest Sites in the Mariana Islands*. New York: Springer.

Carson, Mike T (2016). *Archaeological Landscape Evolution: The Marianas Islands in the Asia-Pacific Region*. Cham, Switzerland: Springer International.

Carson, Mike T (2017). *Rediscovering Heritage Through Artifacts, Sites, and Landscapes: Translating a 3500-Year Record at Ritidian, Guam*. Oxford: Archaeopress Access Archaeology.

Carson, Mike T (2018). *Archaeology of Pacific Oceania*. London/New York: Routledge.

Carson, Mike T (2020). Peopling of Oceania: Clarifying an Initial Settlement Horizon in the Mariana Islands at 1500 BC, *Radiocarbon*. Cambridge: Cambridge University Press (online publication).

Carson, Mike T and Hsiao-Chun Hung (2012). *Archaeological Research Excavations at the Landward Portion of House of Taga Site, Tinian, Commonwealth of the Northern Mariana Islands*. Report Prepared for Historic Preservation Office, Commonwealth of the Northern Mariana Islands. Mangilao: Archaeology Office, Micronesian Area Research Center, University of Guam.

Carson, Mike T and Hsiao-Chun Hung (2017). *Substantive Evidence of Initial Habitation in the Remote Pacific: Archaeological Discoveries at Unai Bapot in Saipan, Mariana Islands*. Oxford: Archaeopress.

Carson, Mike T and Hsiao-Chun Hung (2018). Learning from Paleo-Landscapes: Defining the Land-Use Systems of the Ancient Malayo-Polynesian Homeland, *Current Anthropology* 59(6): 790–813.

Carson, Mike T, Hsiao-Chun Hung, Glenn Summerhayes and Peter Bellwood (2013). The Pottery Trail from Southeast Asia to Remote Oceania, *Journal of Island and Coastal Archaeology* 8(1): 17–36.

Carson, Mike T and Hiro Kurashina (2012). Re-Envisioning Long-Distance Oceanic Migration: Early Dates in the Mariana Islands, *World Archaeology* 44: 409–35.

Carucci, James and Steven Mitchell (1990). Lime-Encrusted Shell Artifacts and the Prehistoric Use of Slaked Lime, *Micronesica Supplement* 2: 47–64.

Catford, J C (1988). Notes on the Phonetics of Nias, in Richard McGinn (ed.), *Studies in Austronesian* Linguistics. *Ohio University Monographs in International Studies, Southeast Asia* Series, *No. 76*. Athens, Ohio: Ohio University Center for International Studies, Center for Southeast Asian Studies, 151–200.

Cavalli-Sforza L L, A Piazza, P Menozzi and J Mountain (1988). Reconstruction of Human Evolution: Bringing Together Genetic, Archaeological, and Linguistic Data, *Proceedings of the National Academy of Sciences USA*, 85: 6002–6.

Cavalli-Sforza L L, P Menozzi and A Piazza (1994). *The History and Geography of Human Genes*. Princeton: Princeton University Press.

Cena, Resty M (1977). Patient Primacy in Tagalog. Presentation: Linguistics Society of America Annual Meeting, Chicago.

Cense, A A and E M Uhlenbeck (1958). *Critical Survey of Studies on the Languages of Borneo*. 's-Gravenhage: Martinus Nijhoff.

Cense, A A in collaboration with Abdoerrahim (1979). *Makassaars-Nederlands woordenboek, met Nederlands-Makassaars register en voorwoord door J Noorduyn* [Makasar-Dutch dictionary, with a Dutch-Makasar finderlist and foreword by J Noorduyn]. 's-Gravenhage: Martinus Nijhoff.

Ceria, Verónica Grondona (1993). Verb Morphology and Valency Change in Selayarese, *University of Pittsburgh Working Papers in Linguistics* 3: 76–185.

Chaiyanara, Paitoon Masmintra (1983). *Malay Dialect in Pattani and Malay Language: A Comparative Study-Phonology, Morphology and Syntax*. MA Thesis, University of Malaya.

Chambers, Geoffrey K and Hisham A Edinur (2021). Reconstruction of the Austronesian Diaspora in the Era of Genomics. *Human Biology Open Access Pre-Prints*. 182. https://digitalcommons.wayne.edu/humbiol_preprints/182

Chan-Yap, Gloria (1977). Hokkien Chinese Loanwords in Tagalog, *Studies in Philippine Linguistics* 1(1): 17–49.

Chan-Yap, Gloria (1980). *Hokkien Chinese Borrowings in Tagalog*. Canberra: Pacific Linguistics.

Chandralal, Dileep (2010). *Sinhala*. Amsterdam: John Benjamins.

Chang, Chi-Shan, Hsiao-Lei Liu, Ximena Moncada, Andrea Seelenfreund et al. (2015). A Holistic Picture of Austronesian Migrations Revealed by Phylogeography of Pacific Paper Mulberry, *Proceedings of the National Academy of Sciences of the United States of America* 112: 13537–42.

Chang, Henry Y (2017). The AV-Only Restriction and Locality in Formosan Languages, *Tsing Hua Journal of Chinese Studies* 47(2): 231–54.

Chang, Kwang-Chih (1995). Taiwan Strait Archaeology and Proto-Austronesian, in Li, Paul Jen-Kuei; Tsang, Cheng-Hwa; Huang, Ying-Kuei; Ho, Dah-an; Tseng, Chin-Yu (eds.), *Austronesian Studies Relating to Taiwan*. Taipei: Academia Sinica, 161–84.

Chang, Kwang-Chih and Goodenough H Ward (1996). Archaeology of Southeastern China and its Bearing on the Austronesian Homeland, in Ward H Goodenough (ed.), *Prehistoric Settlement of the Pacific*. Philadelphia: Independence Square, 36–56.

Chang, Kwang-Chih, George Grace and Wilhelm G Solheim II (1964). Movement of the Malayo-Polynesians, 1500 BC to AD 500, *Current Anthropology* 5: 359–406.

Chantanakomes, Veena (1980). *A Description of Moken: A Malayo-Polynesian Language*. MA Thesis, Mahidol University.

Chao, Yuen (1968). *A grammar of spoken Chinese*. Berkeley: University of California Press.

Chappell, Hillary and William McGregor (eds.) (1996). *The Grammar of Inalienability*. Berlin: de Gruyter.

Charles, Mathew (1974). Problems in the Reconstruction of Proto-Philippine Phonology and the Subgrouping of the Philippine Languages, *Oceanic Linguistics* 13: 457–509.

Chazine, Jean-Michel and Jean-George Ferrié (2008). Recent Archaeological Discoveries in East Kalimantan, *Bulletin of the Indo-Pacific Prehistory Association* 28: 16–22.

Chen J, R R Sokal and M Ruhlen (1995). Worldwide Analysis of Genetic and Linguistic Relationships of Human Populations, *Human Biology* 67: 595–612.

Chen, Chun-Mei (2004). Phonetic Structures of Paiwan, in Paul Law (ed.), *Proceedings of the 11th Meeting of the Austronesian Formal Linguistics Association (AFLA 11)*. Berlin: Zentrum für Allgemeine Sprachwissenschaft, Typologie und Universalienforschung (ZAS), 30–44.

Chen, Sihwei, Jozina Vander Klok, Lisa Matthewson and Hotze Rullmann (2020). The Experiential as an Existential Past: Evidence from Javanese and Atayal, *Natural Language and Linguistic Theory*. DOI: 10.1007/s11049-020-09488-6

Chen, Victoria (2017). *A Reexamination of the Philippine -Type Voice System and its Implications for Austronesian Primary-Level Subgrouping*. PhD Dissertation, University of Hawai'i.

Chen, Victoria and Bradley McDonnell (2019). Western Austronesian Voice, *Annual Review of Linguistics* 5(1): 173–95.

Chen, Xiaojin [陈晓锦] (2003). 马来西亚的三个汉语方言 [Three Chinese Dialects in Malaysia]. Beijing: China Social Sciences Press.

Chevalier, Joan (2004). Heritage Language Literacy: Theory and Practice, *Heritage Language Journal* 2(1): 1–19.

Chia, Stephen (2003). Prehistoric Pottery Production and Technology at Bukit Tengkorak, Sabah, Malaysia, in John Miksic (ed.), *Earthenware in Southeast Asia*. Singapore: Singapore University Press, 187–200.

Chia, Stephen (2008). Prehistoric Sites and Research in Semporna, Sabah, Malaysia, *Bulletin of the Society for East Asian Archaeology* 2: 1–5.

Chia, Stephen (2016). Austronesian Dispersal to Malaysian Borneo, in Bagyo Prasetyo, Titi Surti Nastiti and Truman Simanjuntak (eds.), *Austronesian Diaspora: A New Perspective*. Yogyakarta: Gadjah Mada University Press, 267–74.

Chlenov, M A (1980). Cultural Vocabulary as an Indicator of Interethnic Relations: Eastern Indonesian Evidence, *Bijdragen tot de Taal-, Land- en Volkenkunde* 136(4): 426–39.

Chlenov, M A and Chlenova, Svetlana (2004). Serua, a Vanishing Language in Eastern Indonesia, in Nataliya F. Alieva (ed.), *Malaysko-indoneziyskiye issledovaniya* [Malay-Indonesian studies], XVI. Moscow: Nusantara, 265–99.

Chlenova, Svetlana F (2008). Preliminary Grammatical Notes on Damar Batumerah or West Damar, A Language of Southwest Maluku, in Yury A Lander and Alexander K Ogloblin (eds.), *Language and Text in the Austronesian World: Studies in Honor of Ülo Sirk*. Munich: LINCOM, 163–77.

Chong, Shin, Ed (2008). *Bahasa Bidayuhik di Borneo Barat* [Bidayuhic languages in West Borneo]. Kuala Lumpur: Dewan Bahasa dan Pustaka.

Chou, Shu Hsiu (2002). *A Reconstruction of Proto-Melanau*. MA Thesis, Universiti Kebangsaan Malaysia.

Chrétien, C Douglas (1965). The Statistical Structure of the Proto-Austronesian Morph, *Lingua* 14: 243–70.

Christensen, John (nd). Kisar Dictionary. Unpublished Toolbox files.

Christensen, Pirkko (1990). *Rampi Phonology*. Unpublished Manuscript.

Christie, Emerson Brewer (1909). *The Subanuns of Sindangan Bay*. Manila: Bureau of Printing.

Chung, Sandra (1976). On the Subject of Two Passives in Indonesian, in Charles N Li (ed.), *Subject and Topic*. New York: Academic Press, 57–98.

Chung, Sandra (1982). Unbounded Dependencies in Chamorro Grammar, *Linguistic Inquiry* 13: 39–77.

Chung, Sandra (1994). Wh-Agreement and Referentiality in Chamorro, *Linguistic Inquiry* 25: 1–44.

Chung, Sandra (1998). *The Design of Agreement: Evidence from Chamorro*. Chicago: University of Chicago Press.

Chung, Sandra (2006). Properties of VOS Languages, in Martin Everaert, Henk van Riemsdijk, Rob Goedemans and Bart Hollebrandse (eds.), *The Blackwell Companion to Syntax (Syncom)*. Oxford: Blackwell, 685–720.

Chung, Sandra (2014). On Reaching Agreement Late, in Andrea Beltrama, Tasos Chatzikonstantinou, Jackson L Lee, Mike Pham and Diane Rak (eds.), *Chicago Linguistic Society* 48(1): 169–90.

Chung, Sandra (2020). *Chamorro Grammar*. Santa Cruz, University of California.

Cinque, Guglielmo (2005). Deriving Greenberg's Universal 20 and its Exceptions, *Linguistic Inquiry* 36(3): 315–32.

Cinque, Guglielmo (2010). *The Syntax of Adjectives: A Comparative Study*. Boston: Massachusetts Institute of Technology Press.

Clark, Geoffrey, Atholl Anderson and Duncan Wright (2006). Human Colonization of the Palau Islands, Western Micronesia, *Journal of Island and Coastal Archaeology* 1: 215–32.

Clark, Ross (1990). The Austronesian Languages, in Bernard Comrie (ed.), *The Major Languages of East and South East Asia*. London: Routledge, 173–84.

Clarkson C., Z Jacobs, B Marwick, R Fullagar, L Wallis, M Smith, R G Roberts, E Hayes, K Lowe, X Carah, S A Florin, J McNeil, D Cox, L J Arnold, Q Hua, J Huntley, H E A Brand, T Manne, A Fairbairn, J Shulmeister, L Lyle, M Salinas, M Page, K Connell, G Park, K Norman, T Murphy and C Pardoe (2017). Human Occupation of Northern Australia by 65,000 Years Ago, *Nature* 547: 306–10.

Clayre, Beatrice (1991). Focus in Lundayeh, *Sarawak Museum Journal* 63: 413–34.

Clayre, Beatrice (1996). The Changing Face of Focus in the Languages of Borneo, in H Steinhauer (ed.), *Papers in Austronesian Linguistics No. 3*. Canberra: Pacific Linguistics, 51–88.

Clayre, Beatrice (2014). A Preliminary Typology of the Languages of Middle Borneo, in Peter Sercombe, Michael Boutin and Adrian Clynes (eds.), *Advances in Research on Linguistic and Cultural Practices in Borneo*. Phillips, ME: Borneo Research Council, 123–52.

Clayre, Beatrice and Leah Cubit (1974). An Outline of Kayan Grammar, *Sarawak Museum Journal* 22(43): 43–91.

Clayre, Iain (1972). *A Grammatical Description of Melanau*. PhD Dissertation, University of Edinburgh.

Clayre, Iain (1973). Notes on Spatial Deixis in Melanau, *Anthropological Linguistics* 15(2): 71–86.

Clayre, Iain (1975). Grammatical and Semantic Groupings of Melanau Nouns, *Sarawak Museum Journal* 23(44): 221–41.

Clements, G N (2003a). Feature Economy in Sound Systems, *Phonology* 20: 287–333.

Clements, G N (2003b). Feature Economy as a Phonological Universal, in M J Solé, D Recasens and J Romero (eds.), *Proceedings of the 15th International Conference on Phonetic Sciences, Barcelona, 3-9 August 2003*. Rundle Mall (Adelaide): Causal Productions, 371–4.

Clough, Benjamin (1892). *Sinhala-English Dictionary*. New Delhi and Madras: Asian Educational Service.

Clouse, Duane (1997). Towards A Reconstruction and Reclassification of the Lakes Plain Languages of Irian Jaya, in Karl J Franklin (ed.), *Papers in Papuan Linguistics, No. 2*. Canberra: Pacific Linguistics, 133–236.

Clouse, Duane, Mark Donohue and Felix Ma (2002). Survey Report of the North Coast of Irian Jaya, Summer Institute of Linguistics, *Electronic Survey Reports*, 2002–078. URL: https://www.sil.org/resources/publications/entry/9028

Clynes, Adrian (1989). *Speech Styles in Javanese and Balinese: A Comparative* Study. MA Thesis, Australian National University.

Clynes, Adrian (1994). Old Javanese Influence in Balinese: Balinese Speech Styles, in Tom Dutton and Darrell Tryon (eds.), *Language*

*Contact and Change in the Austronesian World*. Berlin: Mouton de Gruyter, 141–80.

Clynes, Adrian (1995a). Sundanese, in Darrell T Tryon (ed.), *Comparative Austronesian Dictionary: An Introduction to Austronesian Studies, Part 1*. Berlin/New York: Mouton de Gruyter, 459–67.

Clynes, Adrian (1995b). Balinese, in Darrell T Tryon (ed.), *Comparative Austronesian Dictionary: An Introduction to Austronesian Studies, Part 1*. Berlin/New York: Mouton de Gruyter, 495–509.

Clynes, Adrian (1995c). Sasak, in Darrell T Tryon (ed.), *Comparative Austronesian Dictionary: An Introduction to Austronesian Studies, Part 1*. Berlin/New York: Mouton de Gruyter, 511–52.

Clynes, Adrian (1995d). *Topics in the Phonology and Morphosyntax of Balinese: Based on the Dialect of Singaraja, North Bali*. PhD Dissertation, Australian National University.

Clynes, Adrian (1997). On the Proto-Austronesian "Diphthongs", *Oceanic Linguistics* 36(2): 347–61.

Clynes, Adrian (1999). Rejoinder: Occam and the Proto-Austronesian "Diphthongs", *Oceanic Linguistics* 38(2): 404–8.

Clynes, Adrian (2001). Brunei Malay: an overview, in *Occasional Papers in Language Studies* 7. Department of English Language and Applied Linguistics, Universiti Brunei Darussalam, 11–43.

Clynes, Adrian (2005). Belait, in Alexander Adelaar and Nikolaus P Himmelmann (eds.), *The Austronesian Languages of Asia and Madagascar*. London: Routledge, 429–55.

Clynes, Adrian (2010). Bound Roots in Balinese and Indonesian—Precategorials or Verbs? in *A Journey Through Austronesian and Papuan Linguistic and Cultural Space: Papers in Honour of Andrew Pawley*. Canberra: Pacific Linguistics, 333–56.

Coady, James and Richard McGinn (1982). On the So-Called Implosive Nasals of Rejang, in Rainer Carle (ed.), *GAVA: Studies in Austronesian Languages and Cultures dedicated to Hans Kähler*. Berlin: Dietrich Reimer, 437–49.

Cobbey, Vurnell, Aviong and Awơihathe (1969). *Bài Học Tiếng Rơglai: Northern Roglai Language Lessons* Vol. 2 Tủ Sách Ngôn-Ngữ Dân-Tộc Thiểu-Số Việt-Nam 3 Manila: Summer Institute of Linguistics.

Cochrane, Ethan E, Timothy M Rieth, Darby Filimoehala (2021). The first quantitative assessment of radiocarbon chronologies for initial pottery in Island Southeast Asia supports multi-directional Neolithic dispersal, *PLOS ONE* DOI: 10.1371/journal.pone.0251407

Coedès, Georges (1930). Les Inscriptions malaises de Çrivijaya, *Bulletin de L'École Française d'Extrême-Orient* 30: 29–80.

Coedès, Georges (1968). *The Indianized States of Southeast Asia*. W F Vella (ed.), Translated by S B Cowing. Honolulu: East West Press (Translation of French 1964 Edition, Paris, Editions E de Boccard).

Coetzee, Andries W and Joe Pater (2008). Weighted Constraints and Gradient Restrictions on Place Co-Occurrence in Muna and Arabic, *Natural Language and Linguistics Theory* 26: 289–337.

Cohn, Abigail C (1989). Stress in Indonesian and Bracketing Paradoxes, *Natural Language and Linguistic Theory* 7: 167–216.

Cohn, Abigail C (1990). *Phonetic and Phonological Rules of Nasalization*. PhD Dissertation, University of California, Los Angeles.

Cohn, Abigail C (1993). The Initial Dactyl Effect in Indonesian, *Linguistic Inquiry* 24: 372–81.

Cohn, Abigail C (1993b). Voicing and Vowel Height in Madurese: A Preliminary Report, in J A Edmondson and K Gregerson (eds.), *Tonality in Austronesian Languages*. OLSP 24. Honolulu: University of Hawai'i Press. 107–21.

Cohn, Abigail C (2000). Sundanese, in Jane Garry and Carl Rubino (eds.), *Facts About the World's Languages*. New York: HW Wilson Press, 692–6.

Cohn, Abigail C and Anastasia K Riehl (2016). Are There Post-Stopped Nasals in Austronesian?, in Yanti and Timothy McKinnon (eds.), *Studies in Language Typology and Change*. Special issue of *NUSA* 60: 29–57.

Cohn, Abigail C and Katherine Lockwood (1994). A Phonetic Description of Madurese and its Phonological Implications, *Working Papers of the Cornell Phonetic Laboratory* 9: 67–92.

Cole, Franca (2012). *Communities of the Dead: Practice as an Indicator of Group Identity in the Neolithic and Metal Age Burial Caves of Niah, North Borneo*. PhD Dissertation, University of Cambridge.

Cole, Peter, Yurie Hara and Ngee Thai Yap (2008). Auxiliary Fronting in Peranakan Javanese, *Linguistics* 44: 1–43.

Cole, Peter and Gabriella Hermon (2008). VP Raising in a VOS Language, *Syntax* 11.2: 144–97.

Cole, Peter, Gabriella Hermon and Yanti (2008). Voice in Malay/Indonesian, *Lingua* 118: 1500–53.

Cole, Peter, Gabriella Hermon and Yassir Nasanius Tjung (2006). Is There *Pasif Semu* in Jakarta Indonesian?, *Oceanic Linguistics* 45: 65–90.

Cole, Peter, Elizabeth Jonczyk and Jason Lilley (1999). A Note on Extraction from Object Position in Javanese and Other Javanic Languages, *Toronto Working Papers in Linguistics* (*Proceedings of the Sixth Meeting of the Austronesian Formal Linguistics Association*) 16(2): 87–93.

Cole, Peter and Minjeong Son (2004). The argument structure of verbs with the suffix *-kan* in Indonesian, *Oceanic Linguistics* 43(2): 339–64.

Colleman, Timothy and Sarah Bernolet (2012). Alternation biases in corpora vs. picture description experiments: DO-biased and PD-biased verbs in the Dutch dative alternation, in Dagmar Divjak and Gries, Stefan Th. (eds.), *Frequency Effects in Language Representation*. Berlin/Boston: Walter de Gruyter, 87–125.

Collins, Chris and Paul M Postal (2012). *Imposters: A Study of Pronominal Agreement*. Cambridge (MA): Massachusetts Institute of Technology Press.

Collins, Grace (1970). *Two Views of Kalagan Grammar*. PhD Dissertation, Indiana University.

Collins, Ira V (1975). *The Austro-Asiatic Substratum in Acehnese*. PhD Dissertation, University of California, Berkeley.

Collins, James N (2018). Definiteness Determined by Syntax: A Case Study in Tagalog, *Natural Language and Linguistic Theory* 37: 1367–420.

Collins, James T (1980a). *Ambonese Malay and Creolization Theory*. Kuala Lumpur: Dewan Bahasa dan Pustaka.

Collins, James T (1980b). Laha, a Language of the Central Moluccas, *Indonesia Circle* 23: 3–19.

Collins, James T (1981). Preliminary Notes on Proto-West Central Maluku: Buru, Sula, Taliabo and Ambelau, in Robert Blust (ed.), *Historical Linguistics in Indonesia, Part I*. Special issue of *NUSA* 10. Jakarta: Badan Penyelenggara Seri NUSA, Universitas Atma Jaya, 31–45.

Collins, James T (1982a). Linguistic Research in Maluku: A Report of Recent Field Work, *Oceanic Linguistics* 21(1/2): 73–146.

Collins, James T (1982b). Prothesis in the Languages of Central Maluku: An Argument from Proto-Austronesian Grammar, in Amran Halim, Lois Carrington and Stephen A Wurm (eds.), *Papers from the Third International Conference on Austronesian Linguistics, Vol. 2: Tracking the Travellers*. Canberra: Pacific Linguistics: 187–200.

Collins, James T (1983a). *The Historical Relationships of the Languages of Central Maluku, Indonesia*. Canberra: Pacific Linguistics.

Collins, James T (1983b). *Dialek Ulu Terengganu* [Ulu Terengganu Malay]. Bangi: Penerbit Universiti Kebangsaan Malaysia.

Collins, James T (1986a). *Antologi kajian dialek daerah dan rekonstruksi bahasa purba* [Anthology of regional Malay dialects and the reconstruction of Proto-Malay]. Kuala Lumpur: Dewan Bahasa dan Pustaka.

Collins, James T (1986b). Eastern Seram: A Sugrouping Argument, in Paul Geraghty, Lois Carrington and Stephen A Wurm (eds.), *FOCAL II: Papers from the Fourth International Conference on Austronesian Linguistics*. Canberra: Pacific Linguistics, 123–46.

Collins, James T (1987). *Dialek Melayu Sarawak* [Sarawak Malay]. Kuala Lumpur: Dewan Bahasa dan Pustaka.

Collins, James T (1989). Notes on the Language of Taliabo, *Oceanic Linguistics* 28(1): 75–95.

Collins, James T (1990). *Bibliografi Dialek Melayu di Pulau Borneo* [Bibliography of Malay dialects in Borneo]. Kuala Lumpur: Dewan Bahasa dan Pustaka.

Collins, James T (1991). Chamic, Malay and Acehnese: The Malay World and Malayic Languages, in *Le Campā et le monde malais*. Paris: Publications du Centre d'Histoire et Civilisations de la Péninsule Indochinoise, 109–22.

Collins, James T (1995a). *Bibliografi Dialek Melayu di Pulau Jawa, Bali dan Sri Lanka* [Bibliography of Malay dialects in Java, Bali dan Sri Lanka]. Kuala Lumpur: Dewan Bahasa dan Pustaka.

Collins, James T (1995b). *Bibliografi Dialek Melayu di Pulau Sumatera* [Bibliography of Malay dialects in Sumatra]. Kuala Lumpur: Dewan Bahasa dan Pustaka.

Collins, James T (1996). *Bibliografi Dialek Melayu di Indonesia Timur* [Bibliography of Malay dialects in eastern Indonesia]. Kuala Lumpur: Dewan Bahasa dan Pustaka.

Collins, James T (1998). *Malay, World Language: A Short History*. Kuala Lumpur: Dewan Bahasa dan Pustaka.

Collins, James T (2001). Contesting Straits-Malayness: The Fact of Borneo, *Journal of Southeast Asian Studies*, 32(3): 385–95.

Collins, James T (2003a). *Asilulu-English Dictionary*. Jakarta: Badan Penyelenggaraan Seri Nusa, Universitas Katolik Indonesia Atma Jaya.

Collins, James T (2003b). Language Death in Maluku: The Impact of the VOC, *Bijdragen tot de Taal-, Land- en Volkenkunde* 159(2/3): 247–89.

Collins, James T (2004). Language Communities in the Sekadau River Basin, Kalimantan Barat: Three Viewpoints, *Suomen Antropologi*, 29(4): 2–21.

Collins, James T (2006). Homelands and the Homeland of Malay, in James T Collins and Awang Sariyan (eds.), *Borneo and the Homeland of the Malays: Four Essays*. Kuala Lumpur: Dewan Bahasa dan Pustaka.

Collins, James T (2009). *Bahasa Sanskerta dan Bahasa Melayu* [Sanskrit and Malay]. Jakarta: Kepustakaan Populer Gramedia and École Française d'Extrême-Orient.

Collins, James T (2019). Global Eras and Language Diversity in Indonesia: Transdisciplinary Projects Towards Language Maintenance and Revitalization, *Paradigma Jurnal Kajian Budaya* 9(2): 103–17.

Collins, James T and Awang Sariyan (eds.) (2006). *Borneo and the Homeland of the Malays: Four Essays*. Kuala Lumpur: Dewan Bahasa dan Pustaka.

Collins, James T and R Novotny (1991). Etymology, Entomology, and Nutrition: Another Word from Pigafetta, *Cakalele*, 2(2): 123–32.

Collins, James T and Timo Kaartinen (1998). Preliminary Notes on Bandanese Language Maintenance and Change in Kei, *Bijdragen tot de Taal-, Land- en Volkenkunde* 154(4): 521–70.

Collins, Millard A, Virginia R Collins and Sulfilix A Hashim (2001). *Mapun-English Dictionary*. Manila: Summer Institute of Linguistics. URL: https://philippines.sil.org/resources/online_resources/sjm

Coluzzi, Paolo (2011). Majority and Minority Language Planning in Brunei Darussalam, *Language Problems and Language Planning* 35(3): 222–40.

Coluzzi, Paolo (2017a). The Vitality of Minority Languages in Malaysia, *Oceanic Linguistics* 5(1): 210–25.

Coluzzi, Paolo (2017b). Language Planning for Malay in Malaysia: A Case of Failure or Success?, *International Journal of the Sociology of Language* 244: 17–38.

Coluzzi, Paolo (2020). Heritage Language Vitality Among University Students in Malaysia, *Journal of Modern Languages* 30: 142–57.

Comrie, Bernard (1976). *Aspect: An Introduction to the Study of Verbal Aspect and Related Problems*. Cambridge: Cambridge University Press.

Comrie, Bernard (1981). *Language Universals and Linguistic Typology*. Oxford: Blackwell.

Comrie, Bernard (2000). Language Contact, Lexical Borrowing, and Semantic Fields, *Studies in Slavic and General Linguistics* 28: 73–86.

Comrie, Bernard (2013). Alignment of Case Marking of Full Noun Phrases, in Matthew S Dryer and Martin Haspelmath (eds.), *The World Atlas of Language Structures Online*. Leipzig: Max Planck Institute for Evolutionary Anthropology.

Conant, Carlos Everett (1911). The RGH Law in Philippine Languages, *Journal of the American Oriental Society* 31.1: 70–85.

Conant, Carlos Everett (1912). The Pepet Law in Philippine Languages, *Anthropos* 7: 920–48.

Conant, Carlos Everett (1916). Indonesian "l" in Philippine Languages, *Journal of the American Oriental Society* 36: 181–96.

Conklin, H C (1962). Lexicographical Treatment of Folk Taxonomies, in E W Householder and S Saporta (eds.), *Problems in Lexicography*. Bloomington (IN): Indiana University, 119–42.

Connell, Timothy (2013). *A Sketch Grammar of Matéq: A Land Dayak Language of West Kalimantan, Indonesia*. MA Thesis, University of Canterbury.

Conners, Thomas J (2008). *Tengger Javanese*. PhD Dissertation, Yale University, New Haven (CT).

Conners, Thomas J (2020). Javanese Undressed: Peripheral Dialects in Typological Perspective, in David Gil and Antoinette Schapper (eds.), *Austronesian Undressed: How and Why Languages Become Isolating*. Amsterdam: John Benjamins, 253–86.

Conners, Thomas J., John Bowden and David Gil (2015). Jakarta Indonesian Valency Patterns, in Andrej Malchukov and Bernard Comrie (eds.), *Valency classes: a comparative handbook*, vol. 2. Leipzig: Max Planck Institute for Evolutionary Anthropology, 941–86.

Conners, Thomas J and Jozina Vander Klok (2016). On Language Documentation of Colloquial Javanese Varieties, in Lindsay Hrics (ed.), *Proceedings of 2016 Annual Conference of the Canadian Linguistics Association*, 1–12.

Cooreman, Ann M (1987). *Transitivity and Discourse Continuity in Chamorro Narratives*. Berlin: Mouton de Gruyter.

Cooreman, Ann M, Barbara Fox and Talmy Givón (1984). The Discourse Definition of Ergativity, *Studies in Language* 8: 1–34.

Corbett, Greville G (2000). *Number*. Cambridge: Cambridge University Press.

Corbett, Greville G (2006). *Agreement*. Cambridge: Cambridge University Press.

Correia, Adérito José Guterres (2011). *Describing Makasae: A Trans-New Guinea Language of East Timor*. PhD Dissertation, University of Western Sydney.

Correia, Marcelino Jose (2017). Subject-Marking on Galolen Verbs in Laleia, Manatuto municipality, in Michael Leach, Nuno Canas Mendes, Antero B. da Silva, Bob Boughton and Alarico da Costa Ximenes (eds.), *Peskiza foun kona-ba Timor-Leste/Novas investigações sobre Timor-Leste/New research on Timor-Leste/Penelitian baru tentang Timor-Leste*, Volume I: 179–85.

Cousins, W E (1897). A Concise Introduction to the Malagasy Language, Reproduced in Thomas P Jedele and Lucien Em. Randrianarivelo (1998), *Malagasy Newspaper Reader*. Kensington, Maryland: Dunwoody Press, I–LXXXII.

Covarrubias, Miguel (1937). *Island of Bali*. New York: Alfred A Knopf.

Cowan, Hendrik K J (1991). Achehnese Dialects in Connection with Chamic Migrations, in R Harlow (ed.), *VICAL 2 Western Austronesian and Contact Languages: Papers from the Fifth International Conference on Austronesian Linguistics*. Auckland: Linguistic Society of New Zealand, 53–83.

Coward, David Forrest (2005). *An Introduction to the Grammar of Selaru*. Dallas: Summer Institute of Linguistics International.

Coward, David Forrest and Naomi Coward (2000). A Phonological Sketch of the Selaru Language, in Charles E. Grimes (ed.), *Spices from the East: Papers in Languages of Eastern Indonesia*. Canberra: Pacific Linguistics, 9–54.

Cox, M.P (2019). Calibrating the Clock, in D.H. O'Rourke, *A Companion to Anthropological Genetics*. New Jersey: John Wiley & Sons, 47–66.

Cox, M P, M G Nelson, M K Tumonggor, F X Ricaut and H Sudoyo (2012). A Small Cohort of Island Southeast Asian Women Founded Madagascar, *Proceedings of the Royal Society B: Biological Sciences* 279: 2761–8.

Cox, M P, T M Karafet, J S Lansing, H Sudoyo and M F Hammer (2010). Autosomal and X-Linked Single Nucleotide Polymorphisms Reveal a Steep Asian-Melanesian Ancestry Cline in Eastern Indonesia and A Sex Bias in Admixture Rates, *Proceedings of the Royal Society B: Biological Sciences*, 277: 1589–96.

Craib, John L (1993). Early Occupation at Unai Chulu, Tinian, Commonwealth of the Northern Mariana Islands, *Bulletin of the Indo-Pacific Prehistory Association* 13: 116–34.

Craib, John L (1999). Colonisation of the Mariana Islands: New Evidence and Implications for Human Movements in the Western Pacific, in Jean-Christophe Galipaud and Ian Lilley (eds.), *The Pacific from 5000 to 2000 BP: Colonisation and Transformations*. Paris: Institut de Recherche pour le Développement, 477–85.

Cribb, Robert (2000). *Historical Atlas of Indonesia*. Honolulu: University of Hawai'i Press.

Crouch, Sophie (2020). Voice and bare verbs in Colloquial Minangkabau, in David Gil and Antoinette Schapper (eds.), *Austronesian Undressed: How and Why Languages Become Isolating*. Amsterdam: John Benjamins, 213–52.

Crowley, Terry (nd). Grammatical Sketch of Enggano. Unpublished Manuscript.

Crowley, Terry and Claire Bowern (2010). An *Introduction to Historical Linguistics*. 4th edition. Oxford: Oxford University Press.

Crowther, Alison, Leilani Lucas, Richard Helm, Mark Horton et al. (2016). Ancient Crops Provide First Archaeological Signature of the Westward Austronesian Expansion, *Proceedings of the National Academy of Sciences of the United States of America* 113(24): 6635–40.

Cruz, Celina Marie E (2010). The Revitalization Challenge for Small Languages: The Case of Isinai. Presentation: First Philippine Conference-Workshop on Mother Tongue-Based Multilingual Education. Capitol University, Cagayan De Oro City, 18–20 February.

Cruz, Priscilla Angela T and Ahmar Mahboob (2018). Mother-Tongue-Based Multilingual Education in the Philippines: Perceptions, Problems and Possibilities, in Julie Choi and Sue Ollerhead (eds.), *Plurilingualism in Teaching and Learning: Complexities Across Contexts*. New York: Routledge, 37–53.

Culhane, Kirsten (2018). *Consonant Insertions, A Synchronic and Diachronic Account of Amfo'an*. Honours Thesis, Australian National University.

Cumming, Susanna (1984). The Syntax and Semantics of Prepredicate Word Order in Toba Batak, in Paul Schachter (ed.), *Studies in the Structure of Toba Batak*. Berkeley: University of California Press, 17–36.

Cumming, Susanna (1991). *Functional Change: The Case of Malay Constituent Order*. Berlin/New York: Mouton de Gruyter.

Cusic, David Dowell (1981). *Verbal Plurality and Aspect*. PhD Dissertation, Stanford University.

Cysouw, Michael (2003). *The Paradigmatic Structure of Person Marking*. Oxford: Oxford University Press.

da Costa Cabral, Ildegrada (2019). As línguas têm de estar no seu devido lugar [Languages Have to Be in Their Proper Place]: Language Ideologies, Languagised Worlds of Schooling and Multilingual Classroom Practices in Timor-Leste, *Current Issues in Language Planning* 20(1): 33–49.

da França, Antonio Pinto (1985). *Portuguese Influence in Indonesia*. Lisbon: Calouste Gulbenkian Foundation.

da Silva, Eng. Guilherme Puru-Berliku (2012). *Disionáriu Wekais-Tetun* [Dictionary of Bekais-Tetun]. Dili: Secretaria de Estado da Cultura.

Daguman, Josephine S (2004). *A Grammar of Northern Subanen*. PhD Dissertation from La Trobe University.

Dahl, Östen (1985). *Tense and Aspect Systems*. Oxford/New York: Blackwell.

Dahl, Östen and Bernhard Wälchli (2016). Perfects and Iamitives: Two Gram Types in One Grammatical Space, *Letras de Hoje* 51(3): 325–48.

Dahl, Otto Christian (1951). *Malgache et maanjan. Une comparaison linguistique*. Oslo: Egede Instituttet.

Dahl, Otto Christian (1952). Étude de phonologie et de phonétique malgaches, *Norsk Tidsskrift for Sprogvidenskap* 16: 148–200.

Dahl, Otto Christian (1954). Le substrat bantou en malgache, *Norsk Tidsskrift for Sprogvidenskap* 17: 325–62.

Dahl, Otto Christian (1973). *Proto-Austronesian*. Oslo: Studentlitteratur.

Dahl, Otto Christian (1976). *Proto-Austronesian*, 2nd Revised Edition. London: Curzon Press.

Dahl, Otto Christian (1977). La subdivision de la famille barito et la place du malgache, *Acta Orientalia (Copenhagen)* 38: 77–134.

Dahl, Otto Christian (1986). Focus in Malagasy and Proto-Austronesian, in Paul Geraghty, Lois Carrington and Stephen A Wurm (eds.), *Proceedings of FOCAL 1*. Canberra: Pacific Linguistics, 21–45.

Dahl, Otto Christian (1988), Bantu Substratum in Malagasy, *Études Océan Indien* 9 (Paris: Institut National des Langues et Civilisations Orientales): 91–132.

Dahl, Otto Christian (1991). *Migration from Kalimantan to Madagascar*. Oslo: The Institute for Comparative Research in Human Culture.

Dahl, Otto Christian (1996). Predicate, Subject, and Topic in Malagasy, *Oceanic Linguistics* 35(2): 167–79.

Dahl, Øyvind (2011). Linguistic Policy Challenges in Madagascar, in Christina Thornell and Karsten Legère (eds.), *North-South Contributions to African Languages*. Cologne: Rüdiger Köppe, 51–79.

Daigle, Benjamin T (2015). *A Grammar Sketch of Batuley: An Austronesian Language of Aru, Eastern Indonesia*. MA Thesis, Leiden University.

Dalgado, Sebastião Rodolfo (1919). *Glossário Luso-Asiático* [A glossary of Asian Portuguese]. Coimbra: Imprensa da Universidade.

Dalrymple, Mary and Suriel Mofu (2009). Machine-Readable Grammatical Resources for Indonesian. URL: http://users.ox.ac.uk/~cpgl0015/indonesian/index.html

Dalrymple, Mary and Suriel Mofu (2012). *Dusner*. Munich: LINCOM.

Dalrymple, Mary and Suriel Mofu (nd). *Multimodal Language Documentation for Dusner, an Endangered Language of Papua*. URL: http://dusner.clp.ox.ac.uk/

Damsté, H T (1916). Simaloereesche texten [Simeulue texts], *Bijdragen tot de Taal-, Land- en Volkenkunde van Nederlandsch-Indië* 71(3/4): 584–638.

Dancause K N, C W Chan, N H Arunotai and J K Lum (2009). Origins of the Moken Sea Gypsies Inferred from Mitochondrial Hypervariable Region and Whole Genome Sequences, *Journal of Human Genetics* 54: 86–93.

Dardjowidjojo, Soenjono (1971). *The men-, men-kan* and *men-i* verbs in Indonesian, *Philippine Journal of Linguistics* 2: 71–84.

Datan, Ipoi (1993). Archaeological Excavations at Gua Sireh (Serian) and Lubang Angin (Gunung Mulu National Park), Sarawak, Malaysia, *Sarawak Museum Journal* 45: 1–192.

Datan, Ipoi and Peter Bellwood (1991). Recent Research at Gua Sireh (Serian) and Lubang Angin (Gunung Mulu National Park), Sarawak, *Bulletin of the Indo-Pacific Association* 10: 386–405.

Daud, Bukhari and Mark Durie (1999). *Kamus Basa Acèh/Kamus Bahasa Aceh/Acehnese-Indonesian-English Thesaurus*. Canberra: Pacific Linguistics.

Davies, William D (1995). Javanese Adversatives, Passives and Mapping Theory, *Journal of Linguistics* 31(1): 15–51.

Davies, William D (1999). Madurese and Javanese as Strict Word Order Languages, *Oceanic Linguistics* 38: 152–67.

Davies, William D (2003). Extreme Locality in Madurese *Wh*-Questions, *Syntax* 6: 237–59.

Davies, William D (2005). The Richness of Madurese Voice, in I Wayan Arka and Malcolm D. Ross (eds.), *The Many Faces of Austronesian Voice Systems. Some New Empirical Studies*. Canberra: Pacific Linguistics, 197–220.

Davies, William D (2010). *A Reference Grammar of Madurese*. Berlin: Mouton de Gruyter.

Davies, William D and Craig Dresser (2005). The Structure of Javanese and Madurese Determiner Phrases, *Proceedings of Austronesian Formal Linguistics Association XII*, University of California Los Angeles, 57–72.

Davies, William D and Eri Kurniawan (2013). Movement and Locality in Sundanese *Wh*-Questions, *Syntax* 16(2): 111–47.

Davis, Philip W, John W Baker, Walter L Spitz and Mihyun Baek (1998). *The Grammar of Yogad: A Functional Explanation*. LINCOM Studies in Austronesian Linguistics 01. München and Newcastle: LINCOM.

de Casparis, Johannes Gijsbertus (1988). Some Notes on Words of Middle-Indian Origin in Indonesian Languages (Especially Old Javanese), in Luigi Santa Maria, Faizah Soenoto Rivai and Antonio Sorrentino (eds.), *Papers from the III European Colloquium on Malay and Indonesian Studies, Naples, 2-4 June, 1981*. Naples: Istituto Universitario Orientale, 51–69.

de Casparis, Johannes Gijsbertus (1997). *Sanskrit Loan-Words in Indonesian: An Annotated Check-List of Words from Sanskrit in Indonesian and Traditional Malay*. Jakarta: Badan Penyelenggara Seri NUSA, Universitas Katolik Indonesia Atma Jaya.

De Guzman, Videa P (1978). *Syntactic Derivation of Tagalog Verbs*. Honolulu: University of Hawai'i Press.

De Guzman, Videa P (1988). Ergative Analysis for Philippine Languages: An Analysis, in R McGinn (ed.), *Studies in Austronesian Linguistics*. Athens, OH: Ohio University Center for Southeast Asia Studies, 323–45.

De Guzman, Videa P (1992)[1979]. Morphological Evidence for the Primacy of Patient as Subject in Tagalog, in Malcolm Ross (ed.), *Papers in Austronesian Linguistics, No. 2*. Pacific Linguistics, 87–96.

de Houtman van Gouda, Frederick (1603). *Spraeck ende Woord-Boeck inde Maleysche ende Madagaskarsche Talen*. [Malay and Malagasy textbook and dictionary]. Amsterdam: J E Cloppenburch.

de Josselin de Jong, J P B (1947). *Studies in Indonesian Culture II: The Community of Erai (Wetar) (Texts and Notes)*. Amsterdam: Noord-Hollandsche Uitgevers-Maatschappij.

de Josselin de Jong, J P B (1987). *Wetan Fieldnotes: Some Eastern Indonesian Texts with Linguistic Notes and a Vocabulary*. Dordrecht: Foris.

de la Torre, Amalia (2000). Archaeological Project: Clemente Irigayen Property Site (II-1995-O), Sta. Maria, Lal-Lo, Cagayan, *Journal of Southeast Asian Archaeology* 20: 67–110.

de Vos, Connie (2012). *Sign-Spatiality in Kata Kolok: How A Village Sign Language in Bali Inscribes its Signing Space*. PhD Dissertation, Radboud University Nijmegen.

de Vos, Fiona (2011). *Essential Tagalog Grammar*. 2nd edition. Self-Published Book.

de Vries, Jan W (1988). Dutch Loanwords in Indonesian, *International Journal of the Sociology of Language* 73: 121–36.

de Vries, Jan W (1997). Verbal Morphology in Javindo and Pecok, in Cecilia Odé and W Stokhof (eds.), *Proceedings of the Seventh International Conference on Austronesian Linguistics*. Amsterdam: Rodopi, 351–9.

de Vries, Jan W (1998). Adaptation of Loan-Words Ending in *-Is*/*-Ik* in Indonesian, in Mark Janse and Ann Verlinden (eds.), *Productivity and Creativity: Studies in General and Descriptive Linguistics in Honor of E M Uhlenbeck*. The Hague: Mouton de Gruyter, 393–400.

de Vries, Lourens (2005). Towards A Typology of Tail-Head Linkage in Papuan Languages, *Studies in Language* 29(2): 363–84.

Dean, James (1958). Some Principal Grammatical Relations of Bilaan, in Arthur Capell and Stephen A Wurm (eds.), *Studies in Philippine Linguistics by Members of the Summer Institute of Linguistics (Philippine Branch)*. Sydney: University of Sydney, 59–64.

Delfin F, J M Salvador, G C Calacal, H B Perdigon, K A Tabbada, L P Villamor, S C Halos, E Gunnarsdóttir, S Myles, D A Hughes, S L Xu, O Lao, M Kayser, M E Hurles, M Stoneking and M C A de Ungria (2011). The Y-Chromosome Landscape of The Philippines: Extensive Heterogeneity and Varying Genetic Affinities of Negrito and non-Negrito Groups, *European Journal of Human Genetics* 19: 224–30.

Delfin F, Ko AMin-Shan, M Li, E D Gunnarsdóttir, K A Tabbada, J M Salvador, G C Calacal, M S Sagum, F A Datar, S G Padilla, M C A De Ungria and M Stoneking (2014). Complete Mtdna Genomes of Filipino Ethnolinguistic Groups: A Melting Pot of Recent and Ancient Lineages in the Asia-Pacific region, *European Journal of Human Genetics* 22: 228–37.

Dell, François (1981). On Certain Sentential Complements in Tagalog, *Philippine Journal of Linguistics* 12: 11–28.

Dempwolff, Otto (1920). *Die Lautentsprechungen der indonesischen Lippenlaute in einigen anderen austronesischen Südseesprachen*. Berlin: Dietrich Reimer.

Dempwolff, Otto (1925). Die L-, R- und D-Laute in austronesischen Sprachen, *Zeitschrift für Eingeborenen-Sprachen* 15: 19–50, 116–38, 223–38.

Dempwolff, Otto (1926). Ivatan als Test-sprache für uraustronesisches *], *Zeitschrift für Eingeborenen-Sprachen* 16: 298–302.

Dempwolff, Otto (1927). Das austronesische Sprachgut in den melanesischen Sprachen, *Folia Ethnoglossica* 3: 32–43.

Dempwolff, Otto (1934). *Vergleichende Lautlehre des austronesischen Wortschatzes, 1: Induktiver Aufbau einer indonesischen Ursprache*. Berlin: Dietrich Reimer.

Dempwolff, Otto (1937). *Vergleichende Lautlehre des austronesischen Wortschatzes, 2: Deduktive Anwendung des Urindonesischen auf austronesische Einzelsprachen*. Berlin: Dietrich Reimer.

Dempwolff, Otto (1938). *Vergleichende Lautlehre des austronesischen Wortschatzes, 3: Austronesisches Wörterverzeichnis*. Berlin: Dietrich Reimer.

den Besten, Hans (2000). The Slaves' Languages in the Dutch Cape Colony and Afrikaans *Vir, Linguistics* 38(5): 949–71.

den Dikken, Marcel (2006). *Relators and Linkers: The Syntax of Predication, Predicate Inversion, and Copulas*. Cambridge (Massachusetts): Massachusetts Institute of Technology Press.

Dench, Alan and Nicholas Evans (1988). Multiple Case-Marking in Australian Languages, *Australian Journal of Linguistics* 8: 1–47.

Deng, Zhenhua, Hsiao-Chun Hung, Mike T Carson, Adhi Agus Oktaviana, Budianto Hakim and Truman Simanjuntak (2020). Validating Earliest Rice Farming in the Indonesian Archipelago, *Scientific Reports* 10: 10984.

Deng, Zhenhua, Hsiao-Chun Hung, Mike T Carson, Peter Bellwood, Shu-Ling Yang and Houyuan Lu (2018). The First Discovery of Neolithic Rice Remains in Eastern Taiwan: Phytolith Evidence from the Chaolaiqiao Site, *Archaeological and Anthropological Sciences* 10: 1477–84.

Denham, Timothy (2011). Early Agriculture and Plant Domestication in New Guinea and Island Southeast Asia, *Current Anthropology* 52(4): 379–95.

Denham, Timothy and Mark Donohue (2009). Pre-Austronesian Dispersal of Banana Cultivars West from New Guinea: Linguistic Relics from Eastern Indonesia, *Archaeology in Oceania* 44: 18–28.

Derveld, Ferdinand E R (1982). *Politieke mobilisatie en integratie van de Javanen in Suriname: Tamanredjo en de Surinaamse nationale politiek* [Political mobilisation and integration of the Javanese in Surinam: Tamanredjo and Surinamese national politics]. Groningen: Boumas Boekhandel.

Deschamps, Hubert (1960). *Histoire de Madagascar*. Paris: Éditions Berger-Levrault.

Devos, Maud and Daniël Van Olmen (2013). Describing and Explaining the Variation of Bantu Imperatives and Prohibitives, *Studies in Language* 37: 1–57.

Dewar, Robert E, Chantal Radimilahy, Henry T Wright, Zenobia Jacobs, Gwendolyn O Kelly and Francesco Berna (2013). Stone Tools and Foraging in Northern Madagascar Challenge Holocene Extinction Models, *Proceedings of the National Academy of Sciences of the United States of America* 110(31): 12583–8.

Dez, Jacques (1963). Aperçus pour une dialectologie de la langue malgache, *Bulletin de Madagascar* 204: 441–51; 205: 507–20; 206: 581–607; 210: 973–94.

Dez, Jacques (1965). Lexique des mots européens malgachisées, *Annales de L'Université de Madagascar (Série Lettres et Sciences Humaines)* 4: 63–86.

Dez, Jacques (1967). De l'influence arabe à Madagascar à l'aide de faits linguistiques, in Jean-Aimé Rakotoarisoa (ed.), *Arabes et islamisés à Madagascar et dans L'Océan Indien*. Antananarivo: Le Centre d'Archéologie de la Faculté des Lettres et des Sciences Humaines de l'Université de Madagascar, 1–20.

Diamond, Jared M and Peter Bellwood (2003). Farmers and their Languages: The First Expansions, *Science* 300: 597–603.

Diebold A Richard (1960). Determining the Centers of Dispersal of Language Groups, *International Journal of American Linguistics* 26: 1–10.

Diedrich, Daniela (2018). *A Grammar of Paku: A Language of Central Kalimantan*. PhD Dissertation, University of Melbourne.

Dietrich, Stefan (1997). Richtungsbegriffe im malaiischen Dialekt von Larantuka (Ostindonesien), *Anthropos* 92: 101–14.

*Diksionera Malagasy-Englisy* (1992). [Malagasy-English dictionary]. Antananarivo: Trano Printy Loterana.

Dillon, John (1994). *A Grammatical Description of Tatana*. MA Thesis, University of Texas at Arlington.

Diment, Eunice (1995). Bāngingi Sama: Introduction and Wordlist, in Darrell T Tryon (ed.), *Comparative Austronesian Dictionary: An Introduction to Austronesian Studies, Part 1*. Berlin/New York: Mouton de Gruyter, 375–80.

Diment, Eunice and Joann Marie Gault (1980). *Manga Bissara: Sama Bangingì-Filipino-English* [A Sama Bangingi Filipino English vocabulary]. Manila: Summer Institute of Linguistics.

Dixon, R M W (2010). *Basic Linguistic Theory, Volume 2: Grammatical Topics*. Oxford: Oxford University Press.

Dizon, Lino L (2000). *Amlat: Kapampangan Local History Contours in Tarlac and Pampanga*. Tarlac City: Tarlac State University.

Djajadiningrat, Hoesein (1934). *Atjèhsch-Nederlandsch woordenboek* [Acehnese – Dutch dictionary]. Batavia: Landsdrukkerij.

Djawanai, Stephanus (1983). *Ngadha Text Tradition: The Collective Mind of the Ngadha People, Flores*. Canberra: Pacific Linguistics.

Đoàn Văn Phúc (2009). Hế Thống Ngữ Âm Tiếng Chăm Hroi (Trong Sự So Sánh Với Hệ Thống Ngữ Âm Tiếng Chăm) [The Haroi vowel system (in comparison with the Cham vowel system)], in V T Tạ (ed.), *Tìm Hiểu Ngôn Ngữ Các Dân Tộc Ở Việt Nam* [Understanding minority languages in Vietnam]. Hà Nội: Nhà Xuát Bản Khoa Học Xã Hội [Social Science Press], 161–89.

Doi, Akira and Keiko Doi (2003). *Learn to Speak Bookan Murut: A Series of Twenty-Five Language Learning Lessons*. Kota Kinabalu: Sabah Museum.

Donegan, Patricia and D Stampe (2004). Rhythm and the Synthetic Drift of Munda, in R Singh (ed.), *The Yearbook of South Asian Languages and Linguistics*. Berlin/New York, Mouton de Gruyter, 3–36.

Donohue, Mark (1996). Bajau: A Symmetrical Austronesian Language, *Language* 72: 782–93.

Donohue, Mark (1997a). Hatam Phonology and Grammatical Notes, in Andrew Pawley (ed.), *Papers in Papuan Linguistics, No. 3*. Canberra: Pacific Linguistics, 37–57.

Donohue, Mark (1997b). Tone Systems in New Guinea, *Linguistic Typology* 1: 347–86.

Donohue, Mark (1999a). *A Grammar of Tukang Besi*. Berlin: Mouton de Gruyter.

Donohue, Mark (1999b). *Warembori*. Munich: LINCOM.

Donohue, Mark (2000). Tukang Besi Dialectology, in Charles E Grimes (ed.), *Spices from the East: Papers in Languages of Eastern Indonesia*. Canberra: Pacific Linguistics, 55–72.

Donohue, Mark (2001). Coding Choices in Argument Structure: Austronesian Applicatives in Texts, *Studies in Language* 25: 217–54.

Donohue, Mark (2002). Voice in Tukang Besi and the Austronesian focus system, in Fay Wouk and Malcolm Ross (eds.), *The History and typology of western Austronesian voice sytems*. Canberra: Pacific Linguistics, 81–99.

Donohue, Mark (2003). The Laryngeal Gesture in Austronesian Languages: A Terminological Quibble, *Oceanic Linguistics* 42: 213–17.

Donohue, Mark (2004a). The Pretenders to the Muna-Buton Group, in John Bowden and Nikolaus P Himmelmann (eds.), *Papers in Austronesian Subgrouping and Dialectology*. Canberra: Pacific Linguistics, 21–35.

Donohue, Mark (2004b). Typology and Linguistic Areas, *Oceanic Linguistics* 43: 221–39.

Donohue, Mark (2005a). Word Order in New Guinea: Dispelling A Myth, *Oceanic Linguistics* 44(2): 527–36.

Donohue, Mark (2005b). Numerals and Their Position in Universals, *Journal of Universal Language* 6 (2): 1–37.

Donohue, Mark (2005c). The Palu'e Passive: from Pragmatic Construction to Grammatical Device, in I Wayan Arka and Malcolm Ross (eds.), *The Many Faces of Austronesian Voice Systems: Some New Empirical Studies*. Canberra: Pacific Linguistics, 59–85.

Donohue, Mark (2007). Word Order in Austronesian from North to South and West to East, *Linguistic Typology* 11(2): 349–91.

Donohue, Mark (2008a). Bound Pronominals in the West Papuan Languages, in Claire Bowern, Bethwyn Evans and Luisa Miceli (eds.), *Morphology and Language History: In Honour of Harold Koch*. Amsterdam: John Benjamins, 43–58.

Donohue, Mark (2008b). Semantic Alignment Systems: What's What, and What's Not, in Mark Donohue and Søren Wichmann (eds.), *The Typology of Semantic Alignment*. Oxford: Oxford University Press, 24–75.

Donohue, Mark (2009). Dental Discrepancies and the Sound of Proto Austronesian, in Bethwyn Evans (ed.), *Discovering History Through Language: Papers in Honour of Malcolm Ross*. Canberra: Pacific Linguistics, 271–87.

Donohue, Mark (2010). Sekar Wordlist. Unpublished manuscript.

Donohue, Mark (2021). Database of Word order in the Malayo-Polynesian languages of Southeast Asia. DOI: 10.5281/zenodo.4911191

Donohue, Mark (to appear). Measuring and Mapping Morphology, and What It Tells Us About Language.

Donohue, Mark and Timothy Denham (2009). Banana (Musa Spp.) Domestication in the Asia-Pacific Region: Linguistic and Archaeobotanical Perspectives, *Ethnobotany Research and Applications* 7: 293–332.

Donohue, Mark and Timothy Denham (2010). Farming and Language in Island Southeast Asia, *Current Anthropology* 51(2): 223–56.

Donohue, Mark and Timothy Denham (2020). Becoming Austronesian: Mechanisms of Language Dispersal Across Southern Island Southeast Asia and the Collapse of Austronesian Morphosyntax, in David Gil and Antoinette Schapper (eds.), *Austronesian Undressed: How and Why Languages Become Isolating*. Amsterdam: John Benjamins, 447–82.

Donohue, Mark and Owen Edwards (2014). Number in Tolaki, in Marian Klamer and Frantisek Kratochvíl (eds.), *Number and Quantity in East Nusantara*. Canberra: Asia-Pacific Linguistics, 27–42.

Donohue, Mark and Charles E Grimes (2008). Yet More on the Position of the Languages of Eastern Indonesia and East Timor, *Oceanic Linguistics* 47: 114–58.

Donohue, Mark and Anna Maclachlan (2000). What Agreement in Chamorro? in Carolyn Smallwood and Catherine Kitto (eds.), *The Proceedings of the Austronesian Formal Linguistics Association VI*. Toronto Working Papers in Linguistics. Toronto: University of Toronto, 121–32.

Donohue, Mark and Yusuf Sawaki (2007). Papuan Malay Pronominals: Forms and Functions, *Oceanic Linguistics* 47: 253–76.

Donohue, Mark and Antoinette Schapper (2008). Whence the Indirect Possessor Construction?, *Oceanic Linguistics* 47(2): 316–27.

Donohue, Mark and Bronwen Whiting (2011). Quantifying Areality: A Study of Prenasalisation in Southeast Asia and New Guinea, *Linguistic Typology* 15: 101–21.

Donohue, Mark and Søren Wichmann (eds.) (2008). *The Typology of Semantic Alignment*. Oxford: Oxford University Press.

Doomkum, Lakhana (1984). *A Syntactical Study of the Malay Dialect in Taba Village*. MA Thesis, Mahidol University.

Doran, Edwin, Jr (1981). *Wangka: Austronesian Canoe Origins*. College Station: Texas A&M University Press.

Doron, Edit (2015). Voice and Valence Change, in Tibor Kiss and Artemis Alexiadou (eds.), *Syntax - Theory and Analysis: An International Handbook*. Berlin: Walter de Gruyter, 749–76.

Douglas, Carstairs (1899). *Chinese-English Dictionary of the Vernacular or Spoken Language of Amoy, with the Principal Variations of the Chang-Chew and Chin-Chew Dialects*. London: Publishing Office of the Presbyterian Church of England. New Edition.

Douglas, M T, M Pietrusewsky and R M Ikehara-Quebral (1997). Skeletal Biology of Apurguan: A Precontact Chamorro Site on Guam, *American Journal of Physical Anthropology* 104(3): 291–313.

Douglass, Kristina, Sean Hixon, Henry T Wright, Laurie R Godfrey, Brooke E Crowley, Barthelemy Manjakahery, Tanambelo Rasolondrainy, Zoe Crossland and Chantal Radimilahy (2019). A Critical Review of Radiocarbon Dates Clarifies the Human Settlement of Madagascar, *Quaternary Science Reviews* 221: 105878.

Dournes, Jacques (1964). *Ébauche de dictionnaire de la langue jörai*. Cheo Reo, Vietnam Marseilles: Maison Asie Pacifique.

Dournes, Jacques (1974). Ya Tok Bok (La Fée du figuier): Mythe jorai en texte et traduction avec commentaire, *L'Ethnographie* 68: 79–92.

Dournes, Jacques (1976). *Le parler des jörai et le style oral de leur expression*. Paris: Publications Orientalistes de France.

Drabbe, Peter (1926a). *Spraakkunst der Fordaatsche Taal* [Grammar of Fordata]. 's-Gravenhage: Martinus Nijhoff.

Drabbe, Peter (1926b). *Spraakkunst der Jamdeensche Taal* [Grammar of Yamdena]. 's-Gravenhage: Martinus Nijhoff.

Drabbe, Peter (1932a). *Woordenboek der Fordaatsche Taal* [Dictionary of Fordata]. Bandoeng: Nix.

Drabbe, Peter (1932b). *Woordenboek der Jamdeensche Taal* [Dictionary of Yamdena]. Bandoeng: Nix.

Dressler, Wolfgang U (1968). *Studien zur verbalen Pluralität: Iterativum, Distributivum, Durativum, Intensivum in der allgemeinen Grammatik, im Lateinischen und Hethitischen*. Wien: Hermann Böhlaus Nachf[olger].

Dressler, Wolfgang U and Lavinia Merlini Barbaresi (1994). *Morphopragmatics: Diminutives and Intensifiers in Italian, German, and Other Languages*. Berlin: Mouton de Gruyter.

Dryer, Matthew S (1992). The Greenbergian Word Order Correlations, *Language* 68: 81–138.

Dryer, Matthew S (1997). On the 6-Way Word Order Typology, *Studies in Language* 21: 69–103.

Dryer, Matthew S (2003). Word Order in Sino-Tibetan Languages from a Typological and Geographical Perspective, in Graham Thurgood and Randy J LaPolla (eds.), *The Sino-Tibetan Languages*. London: Routledge, 43–55.

Dryer, Matthew S (2013a). Against the Six-Way Order Typology, Again, *Studies in Language* 37: 267–301.

Dryer, Matthew S (2013b). Position of Pronominal Possessive Affixes, in Matthew S Dryer and Martin Haspelmath (eds.), *The World Atlas of Language Structures Online*. Leipzig: Max Planck Institute for Evolutionary Anthropology. URL: http://wals.info/chapter/57

Dryer, Matthew S (2013c). Order of Subject, Object and Verb, in Matthew S Dryer and Martin Haspelmath (eds.), *The World Atlas of Language Structures Online*. Leipzig: Max Planck Institute for Evolutionary Anthropology. URL: http://wals.info/chapter/81

Dryer, Matthew S (2013d). Order of Adpositions and Noun Phrases, in Matthew S Dryer and Martin Haspelmath (eds.), *The World Atlas of Language Structures Online*. Leipzig: Max Planck Institute for Evolutionary Anthropology. URL: http://wals.info/chapter/85

Dryer, Matthew S (2013e). Order of Genitive and Noun, in Matthew S Dryer and Martin Haspelmath (eds.), *The World*

*Atlas of Language Structures Online*. Leipzig: Max Planck Institute for Evolutionary Anthropology. URL: http://wals.info/chapter/86

Dryer, Matthew S (2013f). Order of Adjective and Noun, in Matthew S Dryer and Martin Haspelmath (eds.), *The World Atlas of Language Structures Online*. Leipzig: Max Planck Institute for Evolutionary Anthropology. URL: http://wals.info/chapter/87

Dryer, Matthew S (2013j). Position of Polar Question Particles, in Matthew S Dryer and Martin Haspelmath (eds.), *The World Atlas of Language Structures Online*. Leipzig: Max Planck Institute for Evolutionary Anthropology. URL: http://wals.info/chapter/92

Dryer, Matthew S (2013k). Position of Interrogative Phrases in Content Questions, in Matthew S Dryer and Martin Haspelmath (eds.), *The World Atlas of Language Structures Online*. Leipzig: Max Planck Institute for Evolutionary Anthropology. URL: http://wals.info/chapter/93

Dryer, Matthew S (2013l). Position of Negative Morpheme with Respect to Subject, Object, and Verb, in Matthew S Dryer and Martin Haspelmath (eds.), *The World Atlas of Language Structures Online*. Leipzig: Max Planck Institute for Evolutionary Anthropology. URL: http://wals.info/chapter/144

Dryer, Matthew S (2013m). Negative Morphemes, in Matthew S Dryer and Martin Haspelmath (eds.), *The World Atlas of Language Structures Online*. Leipzig: Max Planck Institute for Evolutionary Anthropology. URL: https://wals.info/chapter/112

Dryer, Matthew S (2013n). Prefixing vs. Suffixing in Inflectional Morphology, in Matthew S Dryer and Martin Haspelmath (eds.), *The World Atlas of Language Structures Online*. Leipzig: Max Planck Institute for Evolutionary Anthropology. URL: https://wals.info/chapter/26

Dryer, Matthew S (2018). On the Order of Demonstrative, Numeral, Adjective, and Noun, *Language* 94(4): 798–833.

Dryer, Matthew S and Martin Haspelmath (eds.) (2013). *The World Atlas of Language Structures Online*. Leipzig: Max Planck Institute for Evolutionary Anthropology.

Dubois, Carl D (1976). *Sarangani Manobo: An Introductory Guide*. Manila: Linguistic Society of the Philippines.

Dudas, K M (1976). *The Phonology and Morphology of Modern Javanese*. PhD Dissertation, University of Illinois.

Dukes, K M (1993). On the Status of Chamorro Wh-Agreement, in J Mead (ed.), *Proceedings of the Eleventh West Coast Conference on Formal Linguistics*. Stanford: Center for the Study of Language and Information, 177–90.

Dungcik, Masyhur (2015). Standardisasi sistem tulisan Jawi sebagai upaya menjadikan Bahasa Melayu sebagai bahasa internasional [Standardisation of the Jawi writing system in an effort to make Malay an international language], in Suhandano, Sudibyo and Saeful Anwar (eds.), *Kebersamaan Dalam Keragaman ASEAN: Perspektif Bahasa dan Sastra* [Similarity in the variety of ASEAN: a perspective from language and literature]. Yogyakarta: Jurusan Sastra Indonesia UGM, 117–26.

Dunnebier, W (1929–1930). Spraakkunst van het Bolaang Mongondowsch [A grammar of Bolaang-Mongondow], *Bijdragen tot de Taal-, Land- en Volkenkunde van Nederlandsch-Indië* 85: 297–468, 524–621; 86: 42–177.

Dunnebier, W (1951). *Bolaang Mongondowsch-Nederlandsch woordenboek: met Nederlandsch-Bolaang Mongondowsch register* [Bolaang-Mongondow – Dutch dictionary with Dutch – Bolaang-Mongondow index]. 's-Gravenhage: Martinus Nijhoff.

Durasid, Durdje (1980/1981). *Rekonstruksi Bahasa Proto Barito: fonologi dan daftar kata* The reconstruction of Proto-Barito: phonology and wordlist]. PhD Dissertation, Penataran Linguistic Kontrastif dan Historis Komparatif, Pusat Pembinaan dan Pengembangan Bahasa, Departemen Pendidikan dan Kebudayaan.

Durie, Mark (1980). Aceh (Indonesia) (MD5). Digital Collection Managed by PARADISEC.

Durie, Mark (1982). Aceh (Indonesia) (MD4). Digital Collection Managed by PARADISEC.

Durie, Mark (1985). *A Grammar of Acehnese on the Basis of a Dialect of North Aceh*. Dordrecht: Foris.

Durie, Mark (1987). Grammatical Relations in Acehnese, *Studies in Language* 11(2): 365–99.

Durie, Mark (1988). The So-Called Passive of Acehnese, *Language* 64(1): 104–13.

Durie, Mark (1990). Proto-Chamic and Acehnese Mid Vowels: Towards Proto-Aceh-Chamic, *Bulletin of the School of Oriental and African Studies* 53(1): 100–14.

Durie, Mark (1995). Acehnese, in Darrell T Tryon (ed.), *Comparative Austronesian Dictionary: An Introduction to Austronesian Studies, Vol. 1*. Berlin/New York: Mouton de Gruyter, 407–20.

Durie, Mark (1997). Grammatical Structures in Verb Serialization, in Alex Alsina, Joan Bresnan and Peter Sells (eds.), *Complex Predicates*. Stanford: CSLI Publications, 289–354.

Durie, Mark and Malcolm D Ross (eds.) (1996). *The Comparative Method Reviewed: Regularity and Irregularity in Language Change*. New York/Oxford: Oxford University Press.

Durvasula, K (2009). *Understanding Nasality*. PhD Dissertation, University of Delaware.

Dyen, Isidore (1956). Language Distribution and Migration Theory, *Language* 32: 611–26.

Dyen, Isidore (1962). The Lexicostatistical Classification of the Austronesian Languages, *Language* 36: 38–46.

Dyen, Isidore (1965a). *A Lexicostatistical Classification of the Austronesian Languages*. Baltimore: The Waverly Press.

Dyen, Isidore (1965b). Formosan Evidence for Some New Proto-Austronesian Phonemes, *Lingua* 14: 285–305.

Dyen, Isidore (1982). The Present Status of Some Austronesian Subgrouping Hypotheses, in Amran Halim, Lois Carrington and Stephen A Wurm (eds.), *Papers from the Third International Conference on Austronesian Linguistics, Vol.2: Tracking the Travellers*. Canberra: Pacific Linguistics, 31–5.

Dyen, Isidore (1990). Homomeric Lexical Classification, in Philip Baldi (ed.), *Linguistic Change and Reconstruction Methodology*. Berlin: Mouton de Gruyter, 211–30.

Dyen, Isidore (1995). Borrowing and Inheritance in Austronesianistics, in Paul Jen-kuei Li, Cheng-hwa Tsang, Ying-kuei Huang, Dah-an Ho and Chiu-yu Tseng (eds.), *Austronesian*

*Studies Relating to Taiwan* (Symposium Series of the Institute of History and Philology 3). Taipei: Academia Sinica, 455–520.

Dyen, Isidore (2001). Review of Graham Thurgood (1999). *From Ancient Cham to Modern Dialects: Two Thousand Years of Language Contact and Change. With an Appendix of Chamic Reconstructions and Loanwords*. Honolulu University of Hawai'i Press. In *Anthropological Linguistics* 43(3): 390–4.

Eades, Domenyk (1998). Gayo (Gajo, Indonesia) (DE1). Digital Collection Managed by PARADISEC. DOI: 10.4225/72/56e8248b2e370

Eades, Domenyk (2005). *A Grammar of Gayo: A Language of Aceh, Sumatra*. Canberra: Pacific Linguistics.

Eberhard, David M, Gary F Simons and Charles D Fennig (eds.) (2019). *Ethnologue: Languages of the World. Twenty-Second Edition*. Dallas, Texas: Summer Institute of Linguistics International.

Eberhard, David M, Gary F Simons and Charles D Fennig (eds.) (2020). *Ethnologue: Languages of the World. Twenty-Third Edition*. Dallas, Texas: Summer Institute of Linguistics International.

Eberhard, David M, Gary F Simons and Charles D Fennig (eds.) (2021). *Ethnologue: Languages of the World. Twenty-Fourth Edition*. Dallas: Summer Institute of Linguistics International.

Edmondson, Jerold A and Kenneth J Gregerson (eds.) (1993). *Tonality in Austronesian Languages*. Honolulu: University of Hawai'i Press.

Edwards McKinnon, Edmund (1985). Early Polities in Southern Sumatra: Some Preliminary Observations Based on Archaeological Evidence, *Indonesia* 40: 1–36.

Edwards, Owen (2012). *Grammatical Functions in Tolaki*. BA Thesis, Australian National University.

Edwards, Owen (2015). The Position of Enggano within Austronesian, *Oceanic Linguistics* 54: 54–109.

Edwards, Owen (2016a). Amarasi, *Journal of the International Phonetic Association* 46: 113–25.

Edwards, Owen (2016b). *Metathesis and Unmetathesis: Parallelism and Complementarity in Amarasi, Timor*. PhD Dissertation, Australian National University.

Edwards, Owen (2018a). Top-Down Historical Phonology of Rote-Meto, *Journal of the Southeast Asian Linguistics Society* 11(1): 63–90.

Edwards, Owen (2018b). Parallel Histories in Rote-Meto, *Oceanic Linguistics* 57(2): 359–409.

Edwards, Owen (2018c). Preliminary Report on Funai Helong, *NUSA* 65: 1–27.

Edwards, Owen (2019). Reintroducing Welaun, *Oceanic Linguistics* 58(1): 31–58.

Edwards, Owen (2020). *Metathesis and Unmetathesis in Amarasi*. Berlin: Language Science Press.

Edwards, Owen (2021). *Rote-Uab Meto Comparative Dictionary*. Canberra: ANU Press.

Edwards, Owen and Charles E. Grimes. 2021. *Revising the classification of the Austronesian languages of eastern Indonesia and Timor-Leste*. Paper: 15th International Conference on Austronesian Linguistics, Palacký University Olomouc, June 28 – July 2.

Effendy, Chairil, A R Muzammil, Firman Susilo, Dedy Ari Aspar, Agus Syahrani, Hangga Dwitika and Ediyanto (2006). *Kamus Bahasa Kayan-Bahasa Indonesia* [Kayan – Indonesian dictionary]. Pontianak: STAIN Pontianak Press Untuk Pusat Penelitian dan Kebudayaan Melayu (PPKM), Universitas Tanjungpura.

Elias, Alexander (2018). *Lio and the Central Flores Languages*. MA Thesis, Leiden University.

Elias, Alexander (2020). Are the Central Flores Languages Really Typologically Unusual?, in David Gil and Antoinette Schapper (eds.), *Austronesian Undressed: How and Why Languages Become Isolating*. Amsterdam: John Benjamins, 287–338.

Elias, Marie T (2020). *Focus and aspect in Iraya Mangyan verbs*. The Archive. 1(1–2): 35–74.

Elkins, Richard E (1974). A Proto-Manobo Word List, *Oceanic Linguistics* 13(1–2): 601–41.

Elkins, Richard E (1984). An Extended Proto Manobo Wordlist, in Andrew Gonzalez (ed.), *Panagani: Essays in Honor of Bonifacio P Sibayan on his Sixty-Seventh Birthday*. Manila: Linguistic Society of the Philippines, 218–29.

Elkins, Richard E (1986). *Manobo-English Dictionary*. Honolulu: University of Hawai'i Press.

Enfield, Nicholas (2003). Linguistic Epidemiology Semantics and Grammar of Language Contact in Mainland Southeast Asia. London: Routledge Curzon.

Enfield, Nicholas (2005). Areal Linguistics and Mainland Southeast Asia, *Annual Review of Anthropology* 31(1): 181–206.

Enfield, Nicholas (2018). *Mainland Southeast Asian Languages: A Concise Typological Introduction*. Cambridge: Cambridge University Press.

Enfield, Nicholas and Bernard Comrie (2015). Mainland Southeast Asian Languages, in Nicholas Enfield and Bernard Comrie (eds.), *Languages of Mainland Southeast Asia: The State of the Art*. Berlin: de Gruyter Mouton. 1–27.

Eng, Ken Kkong (2009). *Palaeoanthropological Study of Late Prehistoric Human Skeletal Remains in Semporna, Sabah*. MA Thesis, Penang: Universiti Sains Malaysia.

Epo, Yrrah Jane S (2014). *Discourse Analysis of Suyot: A Hanunuo-Mangyan Folk Narrative*. MA Thesis, Payap University.

Eringa, F S (1984). *Soendaas-Nederlands Woordenboek* [Sundanese – Dutch dictionary]. Dordrecht: Foris.

Erlewine, Michael Yoshitaka (2016). Multiple Extraction and Voice in Toba Batak, in Hiroki Nomoto, Takuya Miyauchi, Asako Shiohara and Takuya Miyauchi (eds.), *AFLA 23: The Proceedings of the 23rd Meeting of the Austronesian Formal Linguistics Association*. Asia-Pacific Linguistics, 81–95.

Erlewine, Michael Yoshitaka (2018). Extraction and Licensing in Toba Batak, *Language* 94(3): 662–97.

Erlewine, Michael Yoshitaka, Theodore Levin and Coppe van Urk (2017). Ergativity and Austronesian-Type Voice Systems, in Jessica Coon, Diane Massam and Lisa Travis (eds.), *The Oxford Handbook of Ergativity*. Oxford: Oxford University Press, 373–96.

Ernanda (2017). *Phrasal Alternation in Kerinci*. PhD Dissertation, Leiden University.

Errington, J Joseph (1988). *Structure and Style in Javanese: A Semiotic View of Linguistic Etiquette*. Philadelphia: University of Pennsylvania Press.

Errington, J Joseph (1998a). *Shifting Languages*. Cambridge: Cambridge University Press.

Errington, Joseph (1998b). Indonesian('s) Development: on the State of a Language of State, in Bambi B Schieffelin, Kathryn A Woolard and Paul V Kroskrity (eds.), *Language Ideologies: Practice and Theory*. New York: Oxford University Press, 271–84.

Esser, Samuel J (1927). *Klank- en vormleer van het Morisch* [Phonology and Morphology of Mori]. Part 1. Leiden: Vros.

Esser, Samuel J (1929). Nogmaals de vervoegde vormen [Once again on conjugated forms], in Walther Aichele (ed.), *Feestbundel Uitgegeven door het Koninklijk Bataviaasch Genootschap van Kunsten en Wetenschappen bij gelegenheid van zijn 150 Jarig bestaan 1778–1928, Volume 1*. Weltevreden: Kolff, 161–81.

Esser, Samuel J (1934). *Handleiding voor de beoefening der Ledo-Taal: inleiding, teksten met vertaling en aanteekeningen en woordenlijst* [Manual for learning Ledo: introduction and texts including translation, notes and wordlist]. Bandoeng: Nix.

Esser, Samuel J (1938). Talen, in *Atlas van Tropisch Nederland* [Atlas of tropical Netherlands]. Amsterdam: Koninklijk Nederlandsch Aardrijkskundig Genootschap, Sheet 9b.

Esser, Samuel J (1961). Naar aanleiding van I La Galigo [On the subject of I La Galigo], *Bijdragen tot de Taal-, Land- en Volkenkunde* 117: 384–5.

Esser, Samuel J (2011). *Phonology and Morphology of Mori*. Dallas: Summer Institute of Linguistics International.

Estioca, Sharon (2020). *A Subanon Reference Grammar*. PhD Dissertation, University of Hawai'i.

Estioca, Sharon Joy. 2020. *A grammar of Western Subanon*. PhD dissertation. University of Hawaii, Manoa.

Evans, Angharad (2017). *Phonology Essentials of Bagobo Klata, A Language of the Philippines*. MA thesis, University of Gloucestershire.

Evans, Donna (1991). *A Look at Proto-Kaili Phonology*. Unpublished Manuscript.

Evans, Donna (2003). *Kamus Kaili-Ledo - Indonesia - Inggris* [Kaili-Ledo – Indonesian - English dictionary]. Palu: Pemerintah Daerah Propinsi Sulawesi Tengah, Dinas Kebudayaan dan Pariwisata.

Evans, Nicholas (1998). Iwaidja Mutation and its Origins, in Anna Siewierska and Jae Jung Song (eds.), *Case, Typology and Grammar, in Honor of Barry J Blake*. Amsterdam: John Benjamins, 115–49.

Evans, Nicholas and Toshiki Osada (2005). Mundari: The Myth of a Language without Word Classes, *Linguistic Typology* 9(3): 351–90.

Evans, Nicholas, Henrik Bergqvist and Lila San Roque (2017). The Grammar of Engagement I: Framework and Initial Exemplification, *Language and Cognition* 10: 110–40.

Ewing, Michael C (2005a). *Grammar and Inference in Conversation: Identifying Clause Structure in Spoken Javanese*. Amsterdam: John Benjamins.

Ewing, Michael C (2005b). Diverging and Converging Patterns of Possession: Allang in its Central Maluku Context, *Monash University Linguistic Papers* 4: 45–64.

Ewing, Michael C (2005c). Colloquial Indonesian, in Alexander Adelaar and Nikolaus P Himmelmann (eds.), *The Austronesian Languages of Asia and Madagascar*. Routledge Language Family Series. London and New York: Routledge, 227–58.

Ewing, Michael C (2010). Agentive Alignment in Central Maluku Languages, in Michael Ewing and Marian Klamer (eds.), *East Nusantara: Typological and Areal Analysis*. Canberra: Pacific Linguistics, 119–41.

Fadlul Rahman, Fitri, Santi Kurniati, Yessy Prima Putri and David Gil (2013). Word-Internal Language Mixing: Borrowing, Code-Switching or Register-Switching. Presentation: Seventeenth International Symposium on Malay/Indonesian Linguistics, Padang, Indonesia, 9 June 2013.

Fagan, J (1988). Javanese Intervocalic Stop Phonemes: The Light/Heavy Distinction, in R McGinn (ed.), *Studies in Austronesian Linguistics*. Ohio: Ohio University Center for International Studies, Center for Southeast Asia Studies, 173–200.

Falk, Yehuda N (2000). Pivots and the theory of grammatical functions, in Miriam Butt and Tracy Holloway King (eds.), *Proceedings of LFG00*. Stanford: CSLI. URL: csli-publications.stanford.edu/LFG/5/lfg00.htm

Falk, Yehuda N (2009). *Subjects and Universal Grammar: An Explanatory Theory*. Cambridge: Cambridge University Press.

Faridan, Abdullah (1981). *Struktur Bahasa Simeulue* [The structure of Simeulue (Simalur)]. Jakarta: Pusat Pembinaan dan Pengembangan Bahasa.

Favereau, Aude and Bérénice Bellina (2016). Thai-Malay Peninsula and South China Sea Networks (500 BC- AD 200), Based on a Reappraisal of Sa Huynh-Kalanay-Related Ceramics, *Quaternary International* 416: 219–27.

Ferguson, Charles A (1959). Diglossia, *Word* 15: 325–40.

Fernandez, Inyo Yos (1990). Posisi Bahasa Komodo, Rembong, dan Paluqe dalam Kelompok Bahasa Flores [The position of Komodo, Rembong, and Palu'e in the Flores linguistic group], *Linguistik Indonesia* 8(1): 25–60.

Fernandez, Inyo Yos (1996). *Relasi Historis Kekerabatan Bahasa Flores: Kajian linguistik historis komparatif terhadap sembilan Bahasa di Flores* [Historical kinship relations of Flores languages: comparative historical research on the nine languages on Flores Island]. Ende: Nusa Indah.

Ferreira, Luísa (2005). *Ma Ta Su'ar Idate / Mai Ita Koalia Idate* [Let's speak Idate]. Dili: Timor Loro Sa'e-Nippon Culture Center.

Ferreirinho, Naomi (1993). *Selected Topics in the Grammar of Limos Kalinga, the Philippines*. Canberra: Pacific Linguistics.

Ferrer, Alicia S (2003). *Diksyunaryo Filipino - English* [Filipino – English dictionary]. Manila: MECS Publishing House.

Filimonova, Elena (ed.) (2005). *Clusivity: Typology and Case Studies of the Inclusive-Exclusive Distinction*. Amsterdam/Philadelphia: John Benjamins.

Finer, Daniel (1997). Contrasting Ā-Dependencies in Selayarese, *Natural Language and Linguistic Theory* 15: 677–728.

Finley, John Park and William Churchill (1913). *The Subanu: Studies of A Sub-Visayan Mountain Folk of Mindanao*. Washington, DC: Carnegie Institution of Washington.

Fintel, Kai von and Sabine Iatridou (2008). How to Say Ought in Foreign: The Composition of Weak Necessity Modals, in Jacqueline Guéron and Jacqueline Lecarme (eds.), *Time and Modality*. Berlin: Springer, 115–41.

Fischer, H Th (1957). Some Notes on Kinship Systems and Relationship Terms of Sumba, Manggarai and South Timor, *Internationales Archiv fur Ethnographie* 48: 1–31.

Fischer, Olga (2011). Cognitive Iconic Grounding of Reduplication in Language, in Pascal Michelucci, Olga Fischer and Christina Ljungberg (eds.), *Semblance and Signification*. Amsterdam: John Benjamins, 55–81.

Fishman, Joshua A (1978). The Indonesian Language Planning Experience: What Does It Teach Us?, in S Udin (ed.), *Spectrum: Essays Presented to Sutan Takdir Alisjahbana on His Seventieth Birthday*. Jakarta: Dian Rakyat, 333–39.

Fitzpatrick, Scott M (2003). Early Human Burial at Chelechol Ra Orrak: Evidence for a c.3000 Year Old Occupation in Western Micronesia, *Antiquity* 77(298): 719–31.

Fitzpatrick Scott M and R T Callaghan (2008). Seafaring Simulations and the Origin of Prehistoric Settlers to Madagascar, in G Clark, F Leach and S O'Connor (eds.), *Islands of Inquiry: Colonisation, Seafaring and the Archaeology of Maritime Landscapes*. Canberra: Australian National University Press, 47–58.

Fitzpatrick, Scott M and R T Callaghan (2013). Estimating Trajectories of Colonisation to the Mariana Islands, Western Pacific, *Antiquity* 87(337): 840–53.

Fitzpatrick, Scott M and G C Nelson (2011). Purposeful Commingling of Adult and Child Cranial Elements from the Chelechol Ra Orrak Cemetery, Palau, *International Journal of Osteoarchaeology* 21: 360–66.

Fleischman, Eric (1981). The Danao Languages: Magindanaon, Iranun, Maranao, and Illanun, *Philippine Journal of Linguistics* 12(1): 57–77.

Flenley, John (1988). Palynological Evidence for Land Use Changes in South-East Asia, *Journal of Biogeography* 15: 185–97.

Florey, Margaret (2005a). A Cross-Linguistic Perspective on Emergent Possessive Constructions in Central Moluccan Languages, *Australian Journal of Linguistics* 25(1): 59–84.

Florey, Margaret (2005b). Language Shift and Endangerment, in Alexander Adelaar and Nikolaus P Himmelmann (eds.), *The Austronesian Languages of Asia and Madagascar*. London: Routledge, 43–64.

Florey, Margaret (2010). Negation in Central Moluccan Languages, in Michael Ewing and Marian Klamer (eds.), *East Nusantara: Typological and Areal Analysis*. Canberra: Pacific Linguistics, 227–50.

Florey, Margaret (2013). Community Initiatives Towards Language Renewal Among Moluccan Migrants in the Netherlands, in David Bradley and Maya Bradley (eds.), *Language Endangerment and Language Maintenance: An Active Approach*. London/New York: Routledge, 257–71.

Florey, Margaret and Aone van Engelenhoven (2001). Language Documentation and Maintenance Programs for Moluccan Languages in the Netherlands, *International Journal of the Sociology of Language* 151: 195–219.

Florey, Margaret and Michael C Ewing (2010). Political Acts and Language Revitalisation: Community and State in Maluku, in Gunter Senft (ed.), *Endangered Austronesian and Australian Aboriginal Languages: Essays on Language Documentation, Archiving and Revitalization*. Canberra: Pacific Linguistics, 155–73.

Florey, Margaret and Barbara F Kelly (2002). Spatial Reference in Alune, in Giovanni Bennardo (ed.), *Representing Space in Oceania*. Canberra: Pacific Linguistics, 11–46.

Fogaça, Helem Andressa de Oliveira (2017). *O ecossistema fundamental da língua mambae: aspectos endoecológicos e exoecológicos de uma língua austronésia de Timor-Leste* [The basic ecology of the Mambae language: endoecological and exoecological aspects of an Austronesian language of Timor-Leste]. PhD Dissertation, Universidade de Brasília.

Foley, William A (1986). *The Papuan Languages of New Guinea*. Cambridge: Cambridge University Press.

Foley, William A (1998). Symmetrical Voice Systems and Precategoriality in Philippine Languages. Presentation: 3rd Lexical-Functional Grammar Conference, University of Queensland, 30 June – 3 July.

Foley, William A (2008). The Place of Philippine Languages in a Typology of Voice Systems, in Peter K Austin and Simon Musgrave (eds.), *Voice and Grammatical Relation in Austronesian Languages*. Stanford: Center for the Study of Language and Information Publications, 22–44.

Foley, William A and Mike Olson (1985). Clausehood and Verb Serialization, in Johanna Nichols and Anthony C Woodbury (eds.), *Grammar Inside and Outside the Clause: Some Approaches to Theory from the Field*. Cambridge: Cambridge University Press, 17–60.

Foley, William A and Robert D Van Valin (1984). *Functional Syntax and Universal Grammar*. Cambridge: Cambridge University Press.

Forestier, Hubert, Dubel Driwantoro, Dominique Guillaud, Budimull and Darwin Siregar (2006). New Data for the Prehistoric Chronology of South Sumatra, in Truman Simanjuntak, M Hisyam, Bagyo Prasetyo and Titi Surti Nastiti (eds.), *Archaeology: Indonesian Perspective: R P Soejono's Festschrift*. Jakarta: LIPI Press, 177–92.

Forman, Michael (1971). *Kapampangan Grammar Notes*. Honolulu: University of Hawai'i Press.

Forsberg, Vivian M (1992). A Pedagogical Grammar of Tboli, *Studies in Philippine Linguistics* 9: 1–110.

Forster, Jannette (1964). Dual Structure of Dibabawon Verbal Clauses, *Oceanic Linguistics* 3: 26–48.

Fortgens, J (1921). *Bijdrage tot de Kennis van het Sobojo (Eiland Taliabo, Soela groep)* [Contribution to the knowledge of Soboyo on Taliabo Island, Sula Archipelago)] The Hague: Martinus Nijhoff.

Fox, Barbara (1984). Participant Tracking in Toba Batak, University of California Los Angeles *Occasional Papers in Linguistics* 5: 59–79.

Fox, Barbara A and Sandra A Thompson (1990). A Discourse Explanation of the Grammar of Relative Clauses in English Conversation, *Language* 66(2): 297–316.

Fox, James J (1997). The Historical Position of Tetun among the Languages of the Timor Area. Unpublished Manuscript. Australian National University.

Fox, Robert (1970). *The Tabon Caves*. Manila: National Museum of the Philippines.

Francisco, Juan R (1964). *Indian Influences in the Philippines, with Special Reference to Language and Literature*. Diliman, Quezon City: University of the Philippines.

Francisco, Juan R (1966). Notes on Probable Tamil Words in Philippine Languages, in *Proceedings of the First International Conference of Tamil Studies, Kuala Lumpur. Vol. II*. Kuala Lumpur: International Association of Tamil Research, 572–9.

François, Alexandre (2004). Reconstructing the Geocentric System of Proto-Oceanic, *Oceanic Linguistics* 43(1): 1–31.

François, Alexandre (2011). Social Ecology and Language History in the Northern Vanuatu Linkage: A Tale of Divergence and Convergence, *Journal of Historical Linguistics* 1: 175–246.

François, Alexandre (2014). Trees, Waves, and Linkages: Models of Language Diversification, in Claire Bowern and Bethwyn Evans (eds.), *The Routledge Handbook of Historical Linguistics*. London and New York: Routledge, 161–89.

François, Alexandre (2015). The Ins and Outs of Up and Down: Disentangling the Nine Geocentric Space Systems of Torres and Banks Languages, in Alexandre François, Sébastien Lacrampe, Franjieh M and Stefan Schnell (eds.), *The Languages of Vanuatu: Unity and Diversity*. Canberra: Asia Pacific Linguistics, 137–95.

French, Koleen Matsuda (1988). *Insights Into Tagalog. Reduplication, Infixation, and Stress from Nonlinear Phonology*. Dallas: The University of Texas at Arlington.

Friberg, Barbara (1991). Ergativity, Focus and Verb Morphology in Several South Sulawesi Languages, in Ray Harlow (ed.), *Papers from the Fifth International Conference on Austronesian Linguistics: Western Austronesian and Contact Languages*. Auckland: Linguistic Society of New Zealand, 103–30.

Friberg, Barbara (1996). Konjo's Peripatetic Person Markers, in Hein Steinhauer (ed.), *Papers in Austronesian Linguistics, No. 3* Canberra: Pacific Linguistics, 137–71.

Friberg, Timothy (ed.) (1987). *UNHAS-SIL South Sulawesi Sociolinguistic Surveys 1983–1987*. Jayapura: Percetakan Universitas Cenderawasih.

Friberg, Timothy (ed.) (1991). *UNHAS-SIL: More Sulawesi Sociolinguistic Surveys, 1987–1991*. Ujung Pandang: Summer Institute of Linguistics.

Friberg, Timothy and Barbara Friberg (1991). Notes on Konjo Phonology, in James N Sneddon (ed.), *Studies in Sulawesi Linguistics, Part II*. Special issue of *NUSA* 33. Jakarta: Badan Penyelenggara Seri NUSA, Universitas Katolik Indonesia Atma Jaya, 71–115.

Friberg, Timothy and Kvoeu Hor (1977). Register in Western Cham Phonology, in David D Thomas, E W Lee and Đ L Nguyễn (eds.), *Papers in Southeast Asian Linguistics No.4*. Canberra: Pacific Linguistics, 17–38.

Friberg, Timothy and Thomas V Laskowske (1989). South Sulawesi Languages, in James N Sneddon (ed.), *Studies in Sulawesi Linguistics, Part I*. Special issue of *NUSA* 31. Jakarta: Badan Penyelenggara Seri Nusa, Universitas Katolik Indonesia Atma Jaya, 1–17.

Fricke, Hanna (2013). *Topics in the Grammar of Hewa*. MA Thesis. Leiden University.

Fricke, Hanna (2014). *Topics in the Grammar of Hewa: A Variety of Sika in Eastern Indonesia*. München: LINCOM.

Fricke, Hanna (2017). The Rise of Clause-Final Negation in Flores-Lembata, Eastern Indonesia, *Linguistics in the Netherlands* 34: 47–62.

Fricke, Hanna (2019). *Traces of Language Contact: The Flores-Lembata Languages in Eastern Indonesia*. PhD Dissertation, Leiden University.

Friedlaender J S, F R Friedlaender, F A Reed, K K Kidd, J R Kidd, G K Chambers, R A Lea, J H Loo, G Koki, J A Hodgson, D A Merriwether and J L Weber (2008). The Genetic Structure of Pacific Islanders, *PLOS Genetics* 4: 0173–90.

Fugier, Huguette (1999). *Syntaxe malgache*. Louvain-la-Neuve: Peeters.

Fukuda, Takashi (1997). *A Discourse-Oriented Grammar of Eastern Bontoc*. Manila: Linguistic Society of Manila, Summer Institute of Linguistics.

Fuller D Q, N Boivin, T Hoogervorst and R Allaby (2011). Across the Indian Ocean: The Prehistoric Movement of Plants and Animals, *Antiquity* 85: 544–58.

Fuller, Eugene (1977). Chru Phonemes, in David D Thomas, Ernest W. Lee and Đ L Nguyễn (eds.), *Papers in South East Asian Linguistics No. 4: Chamic Studies*. Canberra: Pacific Linguistics, 105–24.

Fuller, Eugene, Ja Wi and Ja Ngai (1974). *Bài Học Tiếng Chru: Pơnuaĭ Mơgru Ia Chru: Chru Language Lessons*, Tủ Sách Ngôn-Ngữ Dân-Tộc Thiểu-Số Việt-Nam. Manila: Summer Institute of Linguistics.

Galang, Rosita (1982). Acquisition of Tagalog Verb Morphology: Linguistic and Cognitive Factors. *Philippine Journal of Linguistics* 13(2): 1–15.

Galipaud, Jean-Christophe, Rebecca Kinaston, Sian Halcrow, Aimee Foster et al. (2016). The Pain Haka Burial Ground on Flores: Indonesian Evidence for a Shared Neolithic Belief System in Southeast Asia, *Antiquity* 90 (354): 1505–21.

Gallego, Maria Kristina S. (2014). *Tracing ancestry and descent: A reconstruction of the Proto-Batanic language*. MA thesis, University of the Philippines, Diliman.

Gallego, Maria Kristina (2018). Directional Systems in Philippine Languages, *Oceanic Linguistics* 57(1): 63–100.

Gallego, Maria Kristina (2020). Ibatan of Babuyan Claro (Philippines) – Language Contexts, in Peter K Austin (ed.), *Language Documentation and Description* 17. London: EL Publishing, 87–110.

Gallman, Andrew F II (1979). Proto-South-East Mindanao and its Internal Relationships. *Papers in Philippine Linguistics No. 10*. Canberra: Pacific Linguistics, 1–52.

Gallman, Andrew F II (1983). *Proto East Mindanao and its Internal Relationships*. PhD Dissertation, University of Texas at Arlington.

Gallman, Andrew F II (1997). *Proto East Mindanao and its Internal Relationships*. Manila: Linguistic Society of the Philippines.

Ganang, Ricky, Jay Crain and Vicki Pearson-Round (2008). *Kemaloh Lundayeh – English Dictionary and Bibliographic List of Materials Relating to the Lundayeh-Lun Bawang-Kelabit and Related Groups of Sarawak, Sabah, Brunei and East Kalimantan*. Borneo Research

Council Reference Series 1. Williamsburg, VA: Borneo Research Council.

Garantjang, Ahmad, Dahlan Kajia, Hasan Basri and Munir Salham (1985). *Struktur Bahasa Balaesang* [Linguistic structure of Balaesang]. Jakarta: Pusat Pengembangan dan Pembinaan Bahasa.

García-Laguia, Alexandro-Xavier (2018). *Documentation of Northern Alta: Grammar, Texts and Glossary*. PhD Dissertation, University of Barcelona.

Garellek, Marc, Yuan Chai, Yaqian Huang and Maxine Van Doren. 2021. Voicing of Glottal Consonants and Non-Modal Vowels. *Journal of the International Phonetic Association*, 1–28. DOI: 10.1017/S0025100321000116.

Garong, Ame (2002). Archaeological Exploration and Test Excavation in Cagayan Valley, Northern Philippines, in Hidefumi Ogawa (ed.), *Archaeological Research in the Lower Cagayan River: Study on the Historical Process of Hunter-Gather/ Farmer Interdependent Relationship*. Tokyo: Tokyo University of Foreign Studies, 33–68.

Gasser, Emily (2014). *Windesi Wamesa Morphophonology*. PhD Dissertation, Yale University.

Gasser, Emily (2015). The Development of Verbal Infixation in Cenderawasih Bay, in Malcolm Ross and I Wayan Arka (eds.), *Language Change in Austronesian Languages: Papers from 12-ICAL*, Vol. 3. Canberra: Pacific Linguistics, 1–17.

Gasser, Emily (2017a). The Right to Say Yes: Language Documentation in West Papua, *Australian Journal of Linguistics*, 37(4): 502–26.

Gasser, Emily (2017b). Papuan-Austronesian Language Contact on Yapen Island: A Preliminary Account, in Antoinette Schapper (ed.), *Contact and substrate in the languages of Wallacea, Part 1*. Special issue of *NUSA* 62: 101–55.

Gasser, Emily (2019a). Borrowed Color and Flora/Fauna Terminology in Northwest New Guinea, *Journal of Language Contact*, 12(3): 609–59.

Gasser, Emily (2019b). SHWNG Noun Phrases, and How They Got That Way. Presentation: 11th International Austronesian and Papuan Languages and Linguistics Conference, Leiden University, 13–15 June 2019.

Gasser, Emily (2023). VRK Mutation in West Papua: Phonological Variation Across Time and Space, in Lucas Fagen, Sam Gray, Quain, Stephanie Reyes and Irene Tang (eds.), *Proceedings of the Fifty-eighth Annual Meeting of the Chicago Linguistic Society* 119–139.

Gasser, Emily (To appear 2024). Vowel Harmony in Austronesian Languages, in Nancy A. Ritter and Harry van der Hulst (eds.), *The Oxford Handbook of Vowel Harmony*. Oxford: Oxford University Press.

Gasser, Emily and Antoinette Schapper (eds). (2023). Special issue on Possession in the Languages of Wallacea, *STUF - Language Typology and Universals*, 76(3).

Gault, Joann Marie (1999). *An Ergative Description of Sama Bangingi*. Manila: Linguistic Society of the Philippines.

Geerts, P (1970). *'Āre'āre Dictionary*. Canberra: Pacific Linguistics.

Gelacio, Teofilo E, Jason Lee Kwok Loong and Ronald L Schumacher (2000). *Manobo: Agusan Dictionary*. Dallas: Summer Institute of Linguistics.

Georgopoulos, Carol (1991). *Syntactic Variables: Resumptive Pronouns and A' Binding in Palauan*. Dordrecht: Kluwer.

Geraghty, Paul (1983). *The History of the Fijian Languages*. Honolulu: University of Hawai'i Press.

Gerdts, D B (1988). Antipassives and Causatives in Ilokano: Evidence for an Ergative Analysis, in Richard McGinn (ed.), *Studies in Austronesian Linguistics*. Athens, OH: Ohio University Center for Southeast Asia Studies, 295–321.

Geurtjens, Hendrik (1921). *Spraakleer der Keieesche taal* [Grammar of Kei]. 's-Gravenhage: Martinus Nijhoff.

Geurtjens, Hendrik (1924). *Keieesche legenden* [Kei legendary stories]. 's-Gravenhage: Martinus Nijhoff.

Gibson, Jeanne (1992). *Clause Union in Chamorro and in Universal Grammar*. New York: Garland.

Gil, David (1993). Syntactic Categories in Tagalog, in S Luksaneeyanawin (ed.), *Pan-Asiatic Linguistics: Proceedings of the Third International Symposium on Language and Linguistics, Chulalongkorn University, Bangkok, January 8-10, 1992*, Volume 3, 1136–50.

Gil, David (1994). The structure of Riau Indonesian, *Nordic Journal of Linguistics* 17: 179–200.

Gil, David (2000). Syntactic categories, cross-linguistic variation and universal grammar, in P M Vogel and B Comrie (eds.), *Approaches to the typology of word classes: empirical approaches to language typology*. Berlin: Mouton de Gruyter, 173–216.

Gil, David (2001). Creoles, Complexity, and Riau Indonesian, *Linguistic Typology* 5: 325–71.

Gil, David (2002). The prefixes di- and N- in Malay/Indonesian dialects, in Fay Wouk and Malcolm Ross (eds.), *The history and typology of Western Austronesian voice systems*. Canberra: Pacific Linguistics, 241–83.

Gil, David (2005). From Repetition to Reduplication in Riau Indonesian, in Bernhard Hurch (ed.), *Studies on Reduplication*. Berlin: Mouton de Gruyter, 31–64.

Gil, David (2006). Intonation and Thematic Roles in Riau Indonesian, in C M Lee, M Gordon and D Büring (eds.), *Topic and Focus, Cross-Linguistic Perspectives on Meaning and Intonation*. Dordrecht: Springer, 41–68.

Gil, David (2008). Why Malay/Indonesian Undressed: Contact, Geography and the Role of the Dice. Presentation: Twelfth International Symposium on Malay/Indonesian Linguistics, Leiden, the Netherlands.

Gil, David (2009a). Austronesian Nominalism and the Thinginess Illusion, *Theoretical Linguistics* 35: 95–114.

Gil, David (2009b). How Much Grammar Does It Take to Sail a Boat?, in Geoffrey Sampson, David Gil and Peter Trudgill (eds.), *Language Complexity as an Evolving Variable*. Oxford: Oxford University Press, 19–33.

Gil, David (2009c). Riau Indonesian: What Kind of a Language Is It?, *Kongres Internasional Masyarakat Linguistik Indonesia 2009*. Malang: Masyarakat Linguistik Indonesia and Universitas Negeri Malang, 29–61.

Gil, David (2010a). The Acquisition of Syntactic Categories in Jakarta Indonesian, in *Parts of Speech: Empirical and Theoretical Advances*. John Benjamins.

Gil, David (2010b). Word Classes in Roon. Presentation: Second TRIPLE International Conference. Word Classes: Nature, Typology, Computational Representations, Roma Tre University, 24–26 March 2010.

Gil, David (2013). Numeral Classifiers, in Matthew S Dryer and Martin Haspelmath (eds.), *The World Atlas of Language Structures Online*. Leipzig: Max Planck Institute for Evolutionary Anthropology. URL: https://wals.info/chapter/55

Gil, David (2015a). The Mekong-Mamberamo Linguistic Area, in N J Enfield and B Comrie (eds.), *Languages of Mainland Southeast Asia: The State of the Art*, Pacific Linguistics Series. Berlin: de Gruyter Mouton, 266–355.

Gil, David (2015b). Mentawai. A Joint Project of the Department of Linguistics, Max Planck Institute for Evolutionary Anthropology and Universitas Bung Hatta, Padang. URL: https://hdl.handle.net/1839/000000-0000-0022-5ac8-8

Gil, David (2017). Roon *ve*, DO/GIVE Coexpression, and Language Contact in Northwest New Guinea. Antoinette Schapper (ed.), *Contact and substrate in the languages of Wallacea Part 1*, Special issue of *NUSA* 62: 41–100.

Gil, David (2019). Attributive Possession in Roon. Presentation: Second Workshop on the Languages of Wallacea, Koninklijk Instituut voor Taal-, Land- en Volkenkunde, Leiden, 17 Jul 2019.

Gil, David (2020a). Dual Heritage: The Story of Riau Indonesian, in David Gil and Antoinette Schapper (eds.), *Austronesian Undressed: How and Why Languages Become Isolating*. Amsterdam: John Benjamins, 119–212.

Gil, David (2020b). What Does It Mean to Be an Isolating Language? The Case of Riau Indonesian, in David Gil and Antoinette Schapper (eds.), *Austronesian Undressed: How and Why Languages Become Isolating*. Amsterdam: John Benjamins, 9–96.

Gil, David (2021). Tense-Aspect-Mood Marking, Language Family Size, and the Evolution of Predication, in Antonio Benítez-Burraco and Ljiljana Progovac (eds.), *Reconstructing prehistoric languages*. Special issue of *Philosophical Transactions B* 376 (1824). DOI: 10.1098/rstb.2020.0194

Gil, David (2023). The grammaticalization and dissolution of High Extended Intonation: An inalienable possession paradigm in Roon. *STUF – Language Typology and Universals*, 76(3): 403–441.

Gil, David and Antoinette Schapper (eds.) (2020). *Austronesian Undressed: How and Why Languages Become Isolating*. Amsterdam: John Benjamins.

Gil, David and Timothy Mckinnon (2015). Phrasal Phonological Alternations in Malayic Languages. Presentation: 11th Meeting of the Association of Linguistic Typology, Albuquerque, NM, 1 August 2015.

Gil, David and Uri Tadmor (2007). *The MPI-EVA Jakarta Child Language Database*. Jakarta: Department of Linguistics, Max Planck Institute for Evolutionary Anthropology and the Center for Language and Culture Studies, Atma Jaya Catholic University.

Gil, David, Uri Tadmor, John Bowden and Bradley Taylor (2015). *Data from the Jakarta Field Station, Department of Linguistics, Max Planck Institute for Evolutionary Anthropology*, 1999–2015. URL: https://archive.mpi.nl/islandora/object/lat%3a1839_00_0000_0000_0021_10de_a

Gilks, W R, Sylvia Richardson and David J Spiegelhalter (1996). *Markov Chain Monte Carlo in Practice*. London: Chapman and Hall.

Givón, Talmy (1984). *Syntax: A Functional-Typological Introduction*, Vol. 1. Amsterdam: John Benjamins.

Glover, Ian (1976). Ulu Leang Cave, Maros: A Preliminary Sequence of Post-Pleistocene Cultural Development in South Sulawesi, *Archipel* 11: 113–54.

Glover, Ian (1977a). The Late Stone Age in Eastern Indonesia, *World Archaeology* 9: 42–61.

Glover, Ian (1977b). Prehistoric Plant Remains from Southeast Asia, with Special Reference to Rice, in M Taddei (ed.), *South Asian Archaeology*. Naples: Istituto Universitario Orientale, 7–37.

Gobée, E (1929). Een Loinansch verhaal [a Loinan story], in *Feestbundel uitgegeven door het Koninklijk Bataviaasch Genootschap van Kunsten en Wetenschappen bij gelegenheid van zijn 150-Jarig bestaan 1778-1928, volume 1*. Weltevreden: Kolff, 187–201.

Godfrey, Laurie R, Nick Scroxton, Brooke E Crowley, Stephen J Burns, Michael R Sutherland, Ventura R Perez, Peterson Faina, David McGee, Lovasoa Ranivoharimanana (2019). A New Interpretation of Madagascar's Megafaunal Decline: The Subsistence Shift Hypothesis, *Journal of Human Evolution* 130: 126–40.

Goebel, Zane (2002). Code Choice in Interethnic Interactions in Two Urban Neighborhoods of Central Java, Indonesia, *International Journal of the Sociology of Language* 158: 69–87.

Goebel, Zane, Anthony Jukes and Izak Morin (2017). Linguistic Enfranchisement, *Bijdragen tot de Taal-, Land- en Volkenkunde* 173: 273–95.

Goedemans, Rob and Harry van der Hulst (2009). StressTyp: A Database for Word Accentual Patterns in the World's Languages, in Martin Everaert, Simon Musgrave and Alexis Dimitriadis (eds.), *The Use of Databases in Cross-Linguistics Research*. Berlin: Mouton de Gruyter, 235–82.

Goedemans, Rob and Harry van der Hulst (2013a). Fixed Stress Locations, in Matthew S Dryer and Martin Haspelmath (eds.), *The World Atlas of Language Structures Online*. Leipzig: Max Planck Institute for Evolutionary Anthropology. URL: http://wals.info/chapter/14

Goedemans, Rob and Harry van der Hulst (2013b). Weight-Sensitive Stress, in Matthew S Dryer and Martin Haspelmath (eds.), *The World Atlas of Language Structures Online*. Leipzig: Max Planck Institute for Evolutionary Anthropology. URL: http://wals.info/chapter/15

Goedemans, Rob and Harry van der Hulst (2013c). Weight Factors in Weight-Sensitive Stress Systems, in Matthew S Dryer and Martin Haspelmath (eds.), *The World Atlas of Language Structures Online*. Leipzig: Max Planck Institute for Evolutionary Anthropology. URL: http://wals.info/chapter/16

Goedemans, Rob and Harry van der Hulst (2013d). Rhythm Types, in Matthew S Dryer and Martin Haspelmath (eds.), *The World Atlas of Language Structures Online*. Leipzig: Max Planck Institute for Evolutionary Anthropology. http://wals.info/chapter/17

Goedemans, Rob and Harry van der Hulst (2014). The Separation of Accent and Rhythm: Evidence from Stresstyp, in Harry van der Hulst (ed.), *Word Stress: Theoretical and Typological Issues.* Cambridge: Cambridge University Press, 119–48.

Goedemans, Rob and Ellen van Zanten (2014). No Stress Typology, in Johanneke Caspers, Yiya Chen, Willemijn Heeren, Jos Pacilly, Niels O Schiller and Ellen van Zanten (eds.), *Above and Beyond the Segments: Experimental Linguistics and Phonetics.* Amsterdam: John Benjamins, 83–95.

Gonda, Jan (1950). The Functions of Word Duplication in Indonesian Languages, *Lingua* 2: 170–97.

Gonda, Jan (1973). *Sanskrit in Indonesia.* 2nd edition. New Delhi: International Academy of Indian Culture (1st edition: published in 1952 by Oriental Bookshop, The Hague).

Gonzalez, Andrew (1981). *Pampangan: Towards a Meaning-Based Description.* Canberra: Pacific Linguistics.

Gonzalez, Andrew (1999). The Language Planning Situation in the Philippines, in Robert B Kaplan and Richard B Baldauf (eds.), *Language Planning in Malawi, Mozambique and the Philippines.* Clevedon: Multilingual Matters, 133–71.

Goschnick, Hella (1977). Haroi Clauses, in David D Thomas, Ernest W. Lee and Đang Liem Nguyễn (eds.), *Papers in South East Asian Linguistics No. 4: Chamic Studies.* Canberra: Pacific Linguistics, 105–24.

Goschnick, Hella (2018). *Haroi Grammar Sketch.* Unpublished Manuscript.

Goudswaard, Nelleke (2005). *The Begak (Ida'an) Language of Sabah.* PhD Dissertation, Vrije Universiteit, Amsterdam.

Gouweloos, M J (1936). *Spraakkunst der Toolaki-taal* [Tolaki grammar]. Unpublished Manuscript.

Grace, George (1971). Notes on the Phonological History of the Austronesian Languages of the Sarmi Coast, *Oceanic Linguistics* 10/1: 11–37.

Grangé, Philippe (2015). The Expression of Possession in Some Languages of the Eastern Lesser Sunda Islands, *Linguistik Indonesia* 33(1): 35–51.

Grant, Anthony P (2005a). The Effects of Intimate Multidirectional Linguistic Contact in Chamic, in Anthony Grant and Paul Sidwell (eds.), *Chamic and Beyond: Studies in Mainland Austronesian Languages.* Canberra: Pacific Linguistics, 37–104.

Grant, Anthony P (2005b). Non-Referenced Lexicostatistics and Chamic, in Anthony Grant and Paul Sidwell (eds.), *Chamic and Beyond: Studies in Mainland Austronesian Languages.* Canberra: Pacific Linguistics, 105–46.

Grant, Anthony P (2007). Admixture and After: The Chamic Languages and the Creole Prototype, in Umberto Ansaldo and Stephen J Matthews (eds.), *Deconstructing Creole: New Horizons in Language Creation*, Amsterdam: John Benjamins, 109–39.

Grant, Anthony P (2011). Substrate Influences in Mindanao Chabacano, in Claire Lefebvre (ed.), *Creoles, Their Substrates, and Language Typology.* Amsterdam/Philadelphia: John Benjamins, 303–24.

Gray Russell D, David Bryant and Simon J Greenhill (2010). On the Shape and Fabric of Human History, *Philosophical Transactions of the Royal Society of London. Series B, Biological Sciences* 365: 3923–33.

Gray, Russell D and Quentin D Atkinson (2003). Language-Tree Divergence Times Support the Anatolian Theory of Indo-European Origin, *Nature* 426: 435–39.

Gray, Russell D, Alexei J Drummond and Simon J Greenhill (2009). Language Phylogenies Reveal Expansion Pulses and Pauses in Pacific Settlement, *Science* 323: 479–83.

Green, Antony Dubach (2005). Word, Foot, and Syllable Structure in Burmese, in J Watkins (ed.), *Studies in Burmese Linguistics.* Canberra: Pacific Linguistics, 1–25.

Greenberg, Joseph H (1966). *Language Universals.* The Hague: Mouton (2nd edition: *Universals of Language.* Cambridge (MA): Massachusetts Institute of Technology Press, 1966).

Greenhill, Simon J (2016). Phylogemetric: A Python Library for Calculating Phylogenetic Network Metrics, *Journal of Open Source Software* 1(2): 26.

Greenhill, Simon J (in preparation). Are New Guinea Languages Unusual?

Greenhill, Simon J, Robert Blust and Russell D Gray (2008). The Austronesian Basic Vocabulary Database: from Bioinformatics to Lexomics, *Evolutionary Bioinformatics* 4: 271–83.

Greenhill, Simon J, Thomas E Currie and Russell D Gray (2009). Does Horizontal Transmission Invalidate Cultural Phylogenies? *Proceedings of the Royal Society B, Biological Sciences*, 276: 2299–306.

Greenhill, Simon J, Alexei J Drummond and Russell D Gray (2010). How Accurate and Robust Are the Phylogenetic Estimates of Austronesian Language Relationships? *PLOS One* 5: E(9573).

Greenhill, Simon J and Russell D Gray (2009). Austronesian Language Phylogenies: Myths and Misconceptions About Bayesian Computational Methods, in Alexander Adelaar and Andrew Pawley (eds.), *Austronesian Historical Linguistics and Culture History: A Festschrift for Robert Blust.* Canberra: Pacific Linguistics, 375–97.

Greenhill, Simon J and Russell D Gray (2012). Basic Vocabulary and Bayesian Phylolinguistics: Issues of Understanding and Representation, *Diachronica* 29: 523–37.

Gregerson, Kenneth (1979). *Predicate and Argument in Rengao Grammar.* Dallas: Summer Institute of Linguistics.

Gregerson, Kenneth and Martha Martens (1986). Perfective *mi* in Uma Discourse, in Benjamin F Elson (ed.), *Language in Global Perspective: Papers in Honor of the 50th Anniversary of the Summer Institute of Linguistics 1935–1985.* Dallas: Summer Institute of Linguistics, 163–76.

Grijns, C D (1991). *Jakarta Malay: A Multidimensional Approach to Spatial Variation* (2 Vols). Leiden: Koninklijk Instituut voor Taal-, Land- en Volkenkunde Press.

Grimes, Barbara Dix (1991). The Development and Use of Ambonese Malay, in Hein Steinhauer (ed.), *Papers in Austronesian Linguistics, No. 1.* Canberra: Pacific Linguistics, 83–123.

Grimes, Barbara Dix (1994). Cloves and Nutmeg, Traders and Wars: Language Contact in the Spice Islands, in Tom Dutton and Darrell T Tryon (eds.), *Language Contact and Change in the Austronesian World.* Berlin: Mouton de Gruyter. 251–74.

Grimes, Barbara Dix (2010). Eastern Indonesia as a Zone of Culture Contact in the Austronesian World. Presentation: Workshop on Critical Directions in Comparative Austronesian Studies, Australian National University, 27–28 January 2010.

Grimes, Barbara F (1988). *Ethnologue: Languages of the World*. Dallas: Summer Institute of Linguistics.

Grimes, Charles E (1990). *Comparative Wordlist for Austronesian Languages of Maluku, Nusa Tenggara and Irian Jaya*. Center for Moluccan Studies and Development, Pattimura University: Ambon.

Grimes, Charles E (1991). *The Buru Language of Eastern Indonesia*. PhD Dissertation, Australian National University.

Grimes, Charles E (2000a). Introduction: New Information Filling Old Gaps in Eastern Indonesia, in Charles E Grimes (ed.), *Spices from the East: Papers in Languages of Eastern Indonesia*. Canberra: Pacific Linguistics, 1–8.

Grimes, Charles E (2000b). Defining Speech Communities on Buru Island: A Look at Both Linguistic and Non-Linguistic Factors, in Charles E Grimes (ed.), *Spices from the East: Papers in Languages of Eastern Indonesia*. Canberra: Pacific Linguistics, 73–103.

Grimes, Charles E (2010a). Digging for the Roots of Language Death in Eastern Indonesia: The Cases of Kayeli and Hukumina, in Margaret Florey (ed.), *Endangered Languages of Austronesia*. Oxford: Oxford University Press, 73–89.

Grimes, Charles E (2010b). Hawu and Dhao in Eastern Indonesia: Revisiting Their Relationship, in Michael C Ewing and Marian Klamer (eds.), *East Nusantara: Typological and Areal Analyses*. Canberra: Pacific Linguistics, 251–80.

Grimes, Charles E (2018). Telling Stories in Eastern Indonesia and Timor-Leste: Patterns of Narrative Discourse in Austronesian Languages. Presentation: 7th International East Nusantara Conference on Language and Culture (ENUS-7), Universitas Kristen Artha Wacana, Kupang, Indonesia, 14–15 May 2018.

Grimes, Charles E (in press). Rethinking Austronesia—Again: Conflict and Convergences Between Assumptions, Methodologies, and the Data, in Greg Acciaioli, Thomas Reuter, Andrew McWilliam, Dedi Adhuri and Yunita Winarto (eds.), *The Ecopoetics of Social Life: Essays in Honour of Emeritus Professor James J Fox*. Canberra: Australian National University Press.

Grimes, Charles E (in process). Kayeli: Sketch and Vocabulary from a Recently Extinct Language.

Grimes, Charles E and Barbara Dix Grimes (1987). *Languages of South Sulawesi*. Canberra: Pacific Linguistics.

Grimes, Charles E and Barbara Dix Grimes (2020). *Encyclopedic Dictionary of the Buru Language of Eastern Indonesia*. Kupang: Unit Bahasa dan Budaya.

Grimes, Charles E and Wesly Lesnussa (1995). Buru Wordlist, in Darrell Tryon (ed.), *Comparative Austronesian Dictionary: An Introduction to Austronesian Studies*. Parts 2-4. Berlin/New York: Mouton de Gruyter, 623–37.

Grimes, Charles E, Johannes C Anceaux and René van den Berg (1995). Wolio: Introduction and wordlist, in Darrell T Tryon (ed.), *Comparative Austronesian Dictionary: An Introduction to Austronesian Studies, Part 1*. Berlin/New York: Mouton de Gruyter, 573–84.

Grimes, Charles E, Tom Therik, Barbara Dix Grimes and Max Jacob (1997). *A Guide to the People and Languages of Nusa Tenggara*. Kupang: Artha Wacana Press.

Groeneboer, Kees (1993). *Weg tot het Westen. Het Nederlands voor Indië (1600)–(1950): een taalpolitieke geschiedenis* [Gateway to the West. Dutch in the Dutch Indies (1600)–(1950): a history of language policy]. Leiden: Koninklijk Instituut voor Taal-, Land- en Volkenkunde.

Groot, Albert Willem de (1931). Phonologie und Phonetik als Funktionswissenschaften, *Travaux du Cercle Linguistique de Prague* 4: 116–47.

Gruiter, Miel de (1994). Javindo, A Contact Language in Pre-War Semarang, in Peter Bakker and Maarten Mous (eds.), *Mixed Languages. 15 Case Studies in Language Intertwining*. Amsterdam: Institute for Functional Research into Language and Language Use, 151–9.

Gudai, Darmansyah H (1985). *A Grammar of Ma'anyan: A Language of Central Kalimantan*. PhD Dissertation, Australian National University.

Guerreiro, Antonio J (1996). Homophony, Sound Changes and Dialectal Variation in Some Central Bornean Languages, *Mon-Khmer Studies. (Special Volume Dedicated to Professor André-Georges Haudricourt)* 25: 205–26.

Gueunier, Noël J (1986). *Lexique du dialecte malgache de Mayotte (Comores)*. Paris: Institut National des Langues et Civilisations Orientales.

Gueunier, Noël J (2003). Documents sur la langue makhuwa à Madagascar et aux Comores, *Études Océan Indien* 35–6: 149–223.

Gueunier, Noël J (2004). Le dialecte malgache de Mayotte (Comores): une discussion dialectologique et sociolinguistique, *Faits de Langues* 23: 397–420.

Guilfoyle, Eithne, Henrietta Hung and Lisa Travis (1989). SPEC of IP and SPEC of VP: Two Subjects in Malayo-Polynesian Languages, *McGill Working Papers in Linguistics* 6.1.

Guilfoyle, Eithne, Henrietta Hung and Lisa Travis (1992). SPEC of IP and SPEC of VP: Two Subjects in Austronesian Languages, *Natural Language and Linguistic Theory* 10(3): 375–414.

Güldemann, Tom (1999). Head-Initial Meets Head-Final: Nominal Suffixes in Eastern and Southern Bantu from A Historical Perspective, *Studies in African Linguistics* 28(1): 49–91.

Gupta, Sunil (2007). The Bay of Bengal Interaction Sphere (1000BC–AD500), *Bulletin of the Indo-Pacific Prehistory Association* 25: 21–30.

Gussenhoven, Carlos (2004). *The Phonology of Tone and Intonation*. Cambridge: Cambridge University Press.

Haaksma, Rémy (1933). *Inleiding tot de studie der vervoegde vormen in de Indonesische talen* [Introduction to conjugated forms in Indonesian languages]. Leiden: Brill.

Hage P and J Marck (2003). Matrilineality and the Melanesian Origin of Polynesian Y Chromosomes, *Current Anthropology* 44: S121–S127.

Hagoort, Pieter and Henk Schotel (1982). Teksten in Sranan, Sarnami en Javaans op school [Sranan, Sarnami and Javanese texts used at school], *Oso, Tijdschrift voor Surinaamse Taalkunde, Letterkunde en Geschiedenis* 1(1): 80–90.

Haiman, John (1983). Iconic and Economic Motivation, *Language* 59: 781–819.

Hajek, John (1996). The Mystery of the Kenaboi. Presentation: Workshop on the Study of Endangered Languages and Literatures of Southeast Asia, Royal Institute of Linguistics and Antropology, Leiden, 9–13 December 1996.

Hajek, John (2000). Language Planning and the Sociolinguistic Environment in East Timor: Colonial Practice and Changing Language Ecologies, *Current Issues in Language Planning* 1(3): 400–14.

Hajek, John (2002). Language Maintenance and Survival in East Timor: All Change Now? Winners and Losers, in D Bradley and M Bradley (eds.), *Language Endangerment and Language Maintenance: An Active Approach*. London: Routledge, 182–202.

Hajek, John (2010). Towards A Phonological Overview of the Vowel and Consonant Systems of East Nusantara, in Michael Ewing and Marian Klamer (eds.), *East Nusantara: Typological and Areal Analysis*. Canberra: Pacific Linguistics, 25–46.

Hajek, John (2013). Vowel Nasalization, in Matthew S Dryer and Martin Haspelmath (eds.), *The World Atlas of Language Structures Online*. Leipzig: Max Planck Institute for Evolutionary Anthropology. URL: http://wals.info/chapter/10

Hajek, John and John Bowden (2002). A Phonological Oddity in the Austronesian Area: Ejectives in Waimoa, *Oceanic Linguistics* 41: 222–4.

Hajek, John, Nikolaus P Himmelmann and John Bowden (2003). Lóvaia: An East Timorese Language on the Verge of Extinction, *International Journal of the Sociology of Language* 160: 155–67.

Hajek, John and Mary Stevens (2005). On the Acoustic Characterization of Ejective Stops in Waima'a, *INTERSPEECH-2005*: 2889–92.

Hajek, John and Catharina Williams-van Klinken (2019). Language Contact and Gender in Tetun Dili: What Happens When Austronesian Meets Romance? *Oceanic Linguistics* 58(1): 59–91.

Hakim, Budianto (2014). Archaeological Traces of Austronesian Ancestors at the Kamansi Site of the Karama River Valley in West Sulawesi, Indonesia, *Journal of Austronesian Studies* 5(1): 73–95.

Halim, Amran (1981). *Intonation in Relation to Syntax in Indonesian*. Canberra: Pacific Linguistics.

Hall, Kenneth R (2011). *A History of Early Southeast Asia: Maritime Trade and Societal Development, 100–1500*. Lanham, MD: Rowman and Littlefield.

Hall, Robert A (1969). *Pidgin and Creole Languages*. Ithaca: Cornell University Press.

Hall, William C (1987). *Aspects of Western Subanon Formal Speech*. Dallas: Summer Institute of Linguistics and the University of Texas at Arlington.

Hamari, Arja and Ljuba Veselinova (eds.) (2021). *The Negative Existential Cycle from A Historical-Comparative Perspective*. Berlin: Language Science Press.

Hammarström, Harald, Robert Forkel, Martin Haspelmath and Sebastian Bank (2020). *Glottolog 4.2.1*. URL: https://glottolog.org/

Hamzah, Mohd Hilmi, Janet Fletcher and John Hajek (2016). Closure Duration as an Acoustic Correlate of the Word-Initial Singleton/Geminate Consonant Contrast in Kelantan Malay, *Journal of Phonetics* 58: 135–51.

Hamzah, Mohd Hilmi, Janet Fletcher and John Hajek (2018). Non-Durational Acoustic Correlates of Word-Initial Consonant Gemination in Kelantan Malay: The Potential Roles of Amplitude and F0, *Journal of the International Phonetic Association* 50(1): 23–60.

Hamzah, Mohd Hilmi, John Hajek and Janet Fletcher (2016). The Role of Closure Duration in the Perception of Word-Initial Geminates in Kelantan Malay, in Christopher Carignan and Michael D Tyler (eds.), *Proceedings of the 16th Australasian International Conference on Speech Science and Technology*. Parramatta: Australian Speech Science and Technology Association, 85–8.

Hanafi, Nurachman (2001). A Description of Basic Clause Structure in Sundanese, in Peter Austin, Barry Blake and Margaret Florey (eds.), *Explorations in Valency in Austronesian Languages*. Special issue of *La Trobe Working Papers in Linguistics* 11(5): 121–42.

Hanna, Roger (2004). *An Introduction to the Grammar of Napu*. Unpublished Computer Files.

Hanna, Roger and Leanne Hanna (1991). Phonology of Napu, in René van den Berg (ed.), *Sulawesi Phonologies*. Ujung Pandang: Summer Institute of Linguistics in Cooperation with the Department of Education and Culture, 150–78.

Hansford, James, Patricia C Wright, Armand Rasoamiaramanana, Ventura R Pérez (2018). Early Holocene Human Presence in Madagascar Evidenced by Exploitation of Avian Megafauna, *Science Advances* 2018 (4): Eaat6925.

Hardeland, August (1859). *Dajacksch-deutsches Wörterbuch*. Amsterdam: Muller.

Harley, Heidi (2012). Lexical Decomposition in Modern Syntactic Theory, in Wolfram Hinzen, Markus Werning and Edouard Machery (eds.), *The Oxford Handbook of Compositionality*. Oxford: Oxford University Press, 328–50.

Harmon, Carol W (1977). *Kagayanen and the Manobo Subgroup of Philippine Languages*. PhD Dissertation, University of Hawai'i.

Harris, A Suzanne and Kristy Chapple (1993). Tagal Phonemics, in Michael E Boutin and Inka Pekkanen (eds.), *Phonological Descriptions of Sabah Languages*. Kota Kinabalu: Sabah Museum, 71–80.

Harrison, Sheldon P (1973). Reduplication in Micronesian Languages, *Oceanic Linguistics* 12: 407–54.

Harrison, Sheldon P (1988). A Plausible History for Micronesian Possessive Classifiers, *Oceanic Linguistics* 27: 63–78.

Harrison, Sheldon P (2007). *The Epiphenominal Nature of Affectedness Marking in Dusunic Languages*. Unpublished Manuscript.

Harrison, Sheldon P (2013). On the History of Conveyance Voice in Some Dusun Languages, in John Henderson, Marie-Eve Ritz and Celeste Rodríguez Louro (eds.), *Proceedings of the 2012 Conference of the Australian Linguistic Society*. Canberra: Australian Linguistics Society, 1–29.

Harrisson, Tom (1957). The Great Cave of Niah: A Preliminary Report on Borneo Prehistory, *Man* 57: 161–6.

Hartung, Pat (2016). *Ata Manobo - English Dictionary*. Webonary, Summer Institute of Linguistics. URL: https://atamanobo.webonary.org/

Hashim, Sulfilix, Virginia Collins and Millard Collins (2001). *Mapun-English Dictionary*. Manila: Summer Institute of Linguistics.

Haspelmath, Martin (1993). More on the Typology of Inchoative/Causative Verb Alternations, in Bernard Comrie and Maria Polinsky (eds.), *Causatives and Transitivity*. Amsterdam: John Benjamins, 87–120.

Haspelmath, Martin (1997). *Indefinite Pronouns*. Cambridge: Cambridge University Press.

Haspelmath, Martin (2011). The Indeterminacy of Word Segmentation and the Nature of Morphology and Syntax, *Folia Linguistica* 45: 31–80.

Haspelmath, Martin (2013). Argument Indexing: A Conceptual Framework for the Syntactic Status of Bound Person Forms, in Dik Bakker and Martin Haspelmath (eds.), *Languages Across Boundaries*. Berlin: de Gruyter Mouton, 197–226.

Haspelmath, Martin (2015). Ditransitive Constructions, *Annual Review of Linguistics* 1(1): 19–41.

Haspelmath, Martin (2016). The Serial Verb Construction: Comparative Concept and Cross-Linguistic Generalizations, *Language and Linguistics* 17(3): 291–319.

Haspelmath, Martin (2017). Explaining Alienability Contrasts in Adpossessive Constructions: Predictability vs. Iconicity, *Zeitschrift für Sprachwissenschaft* 36: 193–231.

Haugen, Eina (1957). The Semantics of Icelandic Orientation, *Word* 13: 447–60.

Hawkins, John A (1994). *A Performance Theory of Order and Constituency*. Cambridge: Cambridge University Press.

Hayami-Allen, Rika (1995). *A Descriptive Study of Taliwang*. MA Thesis, University of Pittsburgh.

Hayami-Allen, Rika (2001). *A Descriptive Study of the Language of Ternate, the Northern Moluccas, Indonesia*. PhD Dissertation, University of Pittsburg.

Hayes, Bruce (1989). Compensatory Lengthening in Moraic Phonology, *Linguistic Inquiry* 20(2): 253–306.

Hayes, La Vaughn (1992). On the Track of Austric, Part I: Introduction, *Mon-Khmer Studies* 21: 143–77.

Hayes, La Vaughn (1997). On the Track of Austric, Part II: Consonant Mutation in Early Austroasiatic, *Mon-Khmer Studies* 27: 13–41.

Hayes, La Vaughn (1999). On the Track of Austric, Part III: Basic Vocabulary Correspondence, *Mon-Khmer Studies* 29: 1–34.

Hayward, Katrina (1993). /P/ vs. /B/ in Javanese: Some Preliminary Data, *School of Oriental and African Studies Working Papers in Linguistics* 3: 1–33.

Hayward, Katrina (1995). /P/ vs. /B/ in Javanese: The Role of the Vocal Folds, *School of Oriental and African Studies Working Papers in Linguistics* 9: 1–11.

Hayward, Katrina (1998). The Verbal Auxiliary *Padha* in Contemporary Javanese, in M Janse, with A Verlinden (ed.), *Productivity and Creativity. Studies in General and Descriptive Linguistics in Honor of E M Uhlenbeck*. Berlin: Mouton de Gruyter, 317–35.

Hayward, Katrina (1999). Lexical Phonology and the Javanese Vowel System, *School of Oriental and African Studies Working Papers in Linguistics* 9: 191–225.

Hayward, Katrina and Muljono (1991). The Dental-Alveolar Contrast in Javanese, *Bulletin of the School of Oriental and African Studies* 54: 126–44.

Hazeu, G A J (1907). *Gajōsch-Nederlandsch woordenboek met Nederlandsch-Gajōsch register* [Gayo – Dutch dictionary with Dutch – Gayo index]. Batavia: Landsdrukkerij.

Headland, Thomas N (1975). Report of Eastern Luzon Language Survey, *Philippine Journal of Linguistics* 6(2): 47–54.

Headland, Thomas N (1986). *Why Foragers Do Not Become Farmers: A Historical Study of a Changing Ecosystem and its Effect on a Negrito Hunter-Gatherer Group in the Philippines*. PhD Dissertation, University of Hawai'i.

Headland, Thomas (2003). Thirty Endangered Languages in the Philippines, *Work Papers of the Summer Institute of Linguistics University of North Dakota Session* 47: 1–12.

Headland, Thomas (2010). Why the Philippine Negrito Languages Are Endangered, in Margaret Florey (ed.), *Endangered Languages of Austronesia*. Oxford: Oxford University Press, 110–18.

Headland, Thomas N and Doris E Blood (eds.) (2002). *What Place for Hunter-Gatherers in Millennium Three?* Dallas: Summer Institute of Linguistics International.

Headland, Thomas N and Janet D Headland (1974). *A Dumagat (Casiguran) - English Dictionary*. Canberra: Pacific Linguistics.

Headley, Robert K (1991). The Phonology of Kompong Thom Cham, in J H C S Davidson (ed.), *Austroasiatic Languages Essays in Honour of H L Shorto*. London: School of Oriental and African Studies, University of London, 105–21.

Headley, Robert K (1998). Cham Evidence for Khmer Sound Changes, in D Thomas (ed.), *Papers in Southeast Asian Linguistics No. 15: Further Chamic Studies*. Canberra: Pacific Linguistics, 21–9.

Healey, Alan (1974). Historical Development of Eight Vowels, in Thomas N Headland and Janet D Headland (eds.), *A Dumagat (Casiguran)-English Dictionary*. Canberra: Pacific Linguistics, xixx–xvii.

Healey, Phyllis M (1960). *An Agta Grammar*. Manila: Bureau of Printing.

Heine-Geldern, Robert Von (1932). Urheimat und früheste Wanderungen der Austronesier, *Anthropos* XXVII: 543–619.

Heine, Bernd, Tom Güldemann, Christa Kilian-Hatz, Donald A Lessau, Heinz Roberg, Mathias Schladt and Thomas Stolz (1993). *Conceptual Shift. A Lexicon of Grammaticalization Processes in African Languages*. Köln: Institut für Afrikanistik, Universität zu Köln.

Held, Gerrit Jan (1942). *Grammatica van het Waropensch (Nederlandsch Noord Nieuw-Guinea)* [Waropen grammar (Papua Province)]. 's-Gravenhage: Martinus Nijhoff; Bandung: A C Nix.

Helfrich, O L (1904). *Bijdragen tot de kennis van het Midden Maleisch (Besemahsch en Serawajsch Dialect)* [Contributions to the knowledge of Middle Malay (Besemah and Serawai dialect)]. Bandung: A C Nix.

Hemley, Robin (2003). *Invented Eden: The Elusive, Disputed History of the Tasaday*. New York: Farrar, Strauss and Giroux.

Hemmings, Charlotte (2013). Causatives and Applicatives: The Case for Polysemy in Javanese, *School of Oriental and African Studies Working Papers in Linguistics* 16: 1–28.

Hemmings, Charlotte (2016). *The Kelabit Language, Austronesian Voice and Syntactic Typology*. PhD Dissertation: *School of Oriental and African Studies*, University of London.

Henderson, Eugénie J A (1965). The Topography of Certain Phonetic and Morphological Characteristics of South East Asian Languages, *Lingua* 15: 400–38.

Hennig, Willi (1966). *Phylogenetic Systematics*. Urbana: University of Illinois Press.

Herusantosa, S (1987). *Bahasa Using di Kabupaten Banyuwangi* [The Osing language in Banyuwangi Regency]. PhD Dissertation, Universitas Indonesia, Jakarta.

Heydon, G and T Murphy (1924). The Biochemical Index in the Natives of the Territory of New Guinea, *Medical Journal of Australia Supplement* 1: 235–37.

Hidalgo, Cesar A and Araceli C Hidalgo (1971). *A Tagmemic Grammar of Ivatan*. Manila: University of the Philippines Press.

Higham, Charles (2014). *Early Mainland Southeast Asia: from First Humans to Angkor*. Bangkok: River Books Press.

Hildebrand, Hartmut K (1982). *Die Wildbeutergruppen Borneos*. München: Minerva Publikation.

Himes, Ronald S (1984/1985). Allophonic Variation and the Bontok-Kankanaey Voiced Stops, *Philippine Journal of Linguistics* 15 (2)/16(1): 49–56.

Himes, Ronald S (1996). Isinai: Reconstructions and Relations, *Philippine Journal of Linguistics* 27(1–2): 83–109.

Himes, Ronald S (1997). Reconstructions in Kalinga-Itneg, *Oceanic Linguistics* 36(1): 102–34.

Himes, Ronald S (1998). The Southern Cordilleran Group of Philippine Languages, *Oceanic Linguistics* 37(1): 120–77.

Himes, Ronald S (2002). The Relationship of Umiray Dumaget to Other Philippine Languages, *Oceanic Linguistics* 41(2): 275–94.

Himes, Ronald S (2005). The Meso-Cordilleran Group of Philippine Languages, in Hsiu-chuan Liao and Carl R. Galvez Rubino (eds.), *Current Issues in Philippine Linguistics and Anthropology Parangal Kay Lawrence A Reid*. Manila: The Linguistic Society of the Philippines and Summer Institute of Linguistics Philippines, 81–92.

Himes, Ronald S (2007). The Kalamian Microgroup of Philippine Languages, *Studies in Philippine Languages and Cultures* 15, *10-ICAL Historical Comparative Papers*, 54–72.

Himes, Ronald S (2012). The Central Luzon Group of Languages, *Oceanic Linguistics* 51(2): 490–537.

Himmelmann, Nikolaus P (1991a). Tomini-Tolitoli Sound Structures, in James N Sneddon (ed.), *Studies in Sulawesi Linguistics, Part II*. Special issue of *NUSA* 33. Jakarta: Badan Penyelenggara Seri Nusa, Universitas Katolik Indonesia Atma Jaya, 49–70.

Himmelmann, Nikolaus P (1991b). *The Philippine Challenge to Universal Grammar*. Arbeitspapier Nr. 15. Köln: Institut für Sprachwissenschaft.

Himmelmann, Nikolaus P (2001). *Sourcebook on Tomini-Tolitoli Languages: General Information and Word Lists*. Canberra: Pacific Linguistics.

Himmelmann, Nikolaus P (2002a). Voice in Western Austronesian: An Update, in Fay Wouk and Malcolm Ross (eds.), *The History and Typology of Western Austronesian Voice Systems*. Canberra: Pacific Linguistics, 7–16.

Himmelmann, Nikolaus P (2002b). Voice in Two Northern Sulawesi Languages, in Fay Wouk and Malcolm Ross (eds.), *The History and Typology of Western Austronesian Voice Systems*. Canberra: Pacific Linguistics, 123–42.

Himmelmann, Nikolaus P (2005a). The Austronesian Languages of Asia and Madagascar: Typological Characteristics, in Alexander Adelaar and Nikolaus P Himmelmann (eds.), *The Austronesian Languages of Asia and Madagascar*. London: Routledge, 110–81.

Himmelmann, Nikolaus P (2005b). Tagalog, in Alexander Adelaar and Nikolaus P Himmelmann (eds.), *The Austronesian Languages of Asia and Madagascar*. London: Routledge, 350–76.

Himmelmann, Nikolaus P (2008). Lexical Categories and Voice in Tagalog, in Peter Austin and Simon Musgrave (eds.), *Voice and Grammatical Functions in Austronesian Languages*. Stanford CA: CSLI, 247–93.

Himmelmann, Nikolaus P (2009). Notes on Tagalog Nominalism, *Theoretical Linguistics* 35: 115–23.

Himmelmann, Nikolaus P (2010a). Language Endangerment Scenarios: A Case Study from Northern Central Sulawesi, Margaret Florey (ed.), *Endangered Languages of Austronesia*. Oxford: Oxford University Press, 45–72.

Himmelmann, Nikolaus P (2010b). Notes on Waima'a Intonation, in Michael Ewing and Marian Klamer (eds.), *Typological and Areal Analyses: Contributions from East Nusantara*. Canberra: Pacific Linguistics, 47–69.

Himmelmann, Nikolaus P (2016). Notes on Noun Phrase Structure in Tagalog, in Jens Fleischhauer, Anja Latrouite and Rainer Osswald (eds.), *Explorations of the Syntax-Semantics Interface*. Düsseldorf: Düsseldorf University Press, 319–41.

Himmelmann, Nikolaus P (2018). Some Preliminary Observations on Prosody and Information Structure in Austronesian Languages of Indonesia and East Timor, in Sonja Riesberg, Asako Shiohara and Atsuko Utsumi (eds.), *Perspectives on Information Structure in Austronesian Languages*. Berlin: Language Science Press, 347–74.

Himmelmann, Nikolaus P and John Ulrich Wolff (1999). *Toratán (Ratahan)*. Munich: LINCOM.

Himmelmann, Nikolaus P and Sonja Riesberg (2013). Symmetrical Voice and Applicative Alternations: Evidence from Totoli, *Oceanic Linguistics* 52: 396–422.

Hinton, Bryan Douglas (1991). *Aspects of Tugun Phonology and Syntax*. MA Thesis, Arlington University of Texas.

Hirst, Daniel and Albert Di Cristo (1998). *Intonation Systems: A Survey of Twenty Languages*. Cambridge: Cambridge University Press.

Hirszfeld L and H Hirszfeld (1919). Essai d'application des méthodes sérologiques au problème des races, *Anthropologie* 29: 505–37.

Hoàng Thị Châu (1987). Hệ Thống Thanh Điệu Tiếng Chàm Và Các Kí Hiệu [The Cham tone system and diacritics], *Ngôn Ngữ* [Language] 1–2, 31–5.

Hoàng Thị Châu (1989). The System of Sounds in the Cham Language, *Vietnamese Studies* 22 92: 67–85.

Hocart, C H and B Fankhauser (1996). Betel Nut Residues in Archaeological Samples of Human Teeth from the Mariana Islands, *Experientia* 52: 281–85.

Hockett, C F (1960). *A Course in Modern Linguistics*. 3rd edition. New York: Macmillian and Co.

Hoëvell, G W W C van (1877). Iets over de vijf voornaamste dialecten der Ambonsche landtaal (Bahasa Tanah) [Some information on the five main dialects of the Ambonese language], *Bijdragen tot de Taal-, Land- en Volkenkunde* 4: 1–136.

Hoffman, Carl (1986). *Punan: Hunters and Gatherers of Borneo*. Ann Arbor, Michigan: University Microfilms International Research Press.

Hogan, D (1988). *Urak Lawoi': Basic Structures and a Dictionary*. Canberra: Pacific Linguistics.

Hogan, David (1999). *Urak Lawoi'*. München: LINCOM.

Hohulin, Richard M and E Lou Hohulin (2014). *Tuwali Ifugao Dictionary and Grammar Sketch*. Manila: Linguistic Society of the Philippines.

Holland, Barbara R, Katarina T Huber, Andreas W M Dress and Vincent Moulton (2002). δ Plots: A Tool for Analyzing Phylogenetic Distance Data, *Molecular Biology and Evolution* 19: 2051–9.

Holle, Karel Frederik (1894). *Schets-taalkaart van Celebes* [Linguistic sketch map of Sulawesi]. Batavia: Topografisch Bureau.

Holton, Gary (2017). A Unified System of Spatial Orientation in the Austronesian and non-Austronesian Languages of Halmahera, in Antoinette Schapper (ed.), *Contact and Substrate in the Languages of Wallacea (Part 1)*. Special issue of *NUSA* 62: 157–89.

Hombert, Jean-Marie, John J Ohala and W G Ewan (1979). Phonetic Explanations for the Development of Tones, *Language* 55: 37–58.

Honeyman, Tom and Laura Robinson (2007). Solar Power for the Digital Fieldworker, *Language Documentation and Conservation* 1: 17–27.

Hoogervorst, Tom G (2008). *Describing Surabaya's Linguistic Ecology*. MA Thesis, Leiden University.

Hoogervorst, Tom G (2009). Urban Dynamics: An Impression of Surabaya's Sociolinguistic Setting, *Wacana* 11(1): 39–56.

Hoogervorst, Tom G (2011). Some Introductory Notes on the Development and Characteristics of Sabah Malay, *Wacana* 13(1): 50–77.

Hoogervorst, Tom G (2013). *Southeast Asia in the Ancient Indian Ocean World*. Oxford: Archaeopress.

Hoogervorst, Tom G (2015). Detecting pre-modern lexical influence from South India in Maritime Southeast Asia, *Archipel* 89: 64–93.

Hoogervorst, Tom G (2016a). Problematic Protoforms: Some Hidden Indic Loans in Western-Malayo-Polynesian Languages, *Oceanic Linguistics* 55(2): 561–87.

Hoogervorst, Tom G (2016b). Lexical Influence from North India to Maritime Southeast Asia: Some New Directions, *Man in India* 97(1): 293–334.

Hoogervorst, Tom G (2017). The Role of Prakrit in Nusantara Through 101 Etymologies, in Andrea Acri, Roger Blench and Alexandra Landmann (eds.), *Spirits and Ships: Cultural Transfers in Early Monsoon Asia*. Singapore: Institute of Southeast Asian Studies, 375–440.

Hopper, Paul J and Sandra A Thompson (1980). Transitivity in Grammar and Discourse, *Language* 56(2): 251–99.

Horn, Laurence R (1989). *A Natural History of Negation*. Chicago: The University of Chicago Press.

Howe, Penelope Jane (2017). *Tonogenesis in Central Dialects of Malagasy: Acoustic and Perceptual Evidence with Implications for Synchronic Mechanisms of Sound Change*. PhD Dissertation, Rice University.

Howe, Penelope Jane (2019). Word Order and the Verb Voice System in Northern Malagasy Dialects. Presentation: Palacký University, 23 October: Olomouc, Czech Republic.

Howe, Penelope Jane (2021). Central Malagasy, *Journal of the International Phonetic Association* 51(1): 103–36.

Howe, Penelope Jane (2022). Semantics and Pragmatics of Voice in Central Malagasy Oral Narratives, *Oceanic Linguistics* 61(1): 68–117.

Howells W W (1976). Physical Variation and History in Melanesia and Australia, *American Journal of Physical Anthropology* 45: 641–49.

Hsieh, Henrison (2016). Prosodic Indicators of Phrase Structure in Tagalog Transitive Sentences, in Hiroki Nomoto, Takuya Miyauchi and Asako Shiohara (eds.), *Proceedings of AFLA 23rd Meeting of the Austronesian Formal Linguistics Association*. Canberra: Asia-Pacific Linguistics, 111–22.

Hsu, Robert Wen (1969). *Phonology and Morphophonemics of Yapese*. PhD Dissertation, University of California, Berkeley.

Huang, Shuanfan (2002). The Pragmatics of Focus in Tsou and Seediq, *Language and Linguistics* 3(4): 665–94.

Hublin J -J, A Ben-Ncer, S E Bailey, S E Freidline, S Neubauer, M M Skinner, I Bergmann, A Le Cabec, S Benazzi, K Harvati and P Gunz (2017). New Fossils from Jebel Irhoud, Morocco and the Pan-African Origin of Homo Sapiens, *Nature* 546: 289–92.

Hudjashov G., T M Karafet, D J Lawson, S Downey, O Savina, H Sudoyo, J S Lansing, M F Hammer and M P Cox (2017). Complex Patterns of Admixture Across the Indonesian Archipelago, *Molecular Biology and Evolution* 34: 2439–52.

Hudson, Alfred B (1967). *The Barito Isolects of Borneo: A Classification Based on Comparative Reconstruction and Lexicostatistics*. Ithaca, NY: Southeast Asia Program, Department of Asian Studies, Cornell University.

Hudson, Alfred B (1970). A Note on Selako: Malayic Dayak and Land Dayak Languages in Western Borneo, *Sarawak Museum Journal* 18(36–37): 301–18.

Hudson, Alfred B (1978). Linguistic Relations Among Bornean Peoples with Special Reference to Sarawak: An Interim Report, *Studies in Third World Societies* 3: 1–44.

Huebner, Thom (2019). Language Policy and Bilingual Education in Thailand: Reconciling the Past, Anticipating the Future, *LEARN Journal* 12(1): 19–29.

Huerta-Sánchez E, X Jin Z Asan Bianba, B M Peter, N Vinckenbosch, Y Liang, X Yi, M He, M Somel, P Ni, B Wang, X Ou, J Huasang Luosang, Z X Cuo, K Li, G Gao, Y Yin, W Wang, X Zhang, X Xu, H Yang, Y Li, J Wang, J Wang and R Nielsen (2014). Altitude Adaptation in Tibetans Caused by Introgression of Denisovan-like DNA, *Nature* 512: 194–7.

Huffman, Franklin (1985). Vowel Permutations in Austroasiatic Languages, in Graham Thurgood, James A Matisoff and David Bradley (eds.), *Linguistics of the Sino-Tibetan Area: The State of the Art. Papers Presented to Paul K Benedict for his 71st Birthday*. Canberra: Pacific Linguistics, 141–5.

Hughes, Jock (1987). The Languages of Kei, Tanimbar and Aru: A Lexicostatistic Classification, in Soenjono Dardjowidjojo (ed.), *Miscellaneous Studies of Indonesian and other languages in Indonesia*, Part IX. Special issue of *NUSA* 27. Jakarta: Badan Penyelenggara Seri NUSA, Universitas Atma Jaya, 71–111.

Hughes, Jock (1995). Dobel, in Darrell T Tryon (ed.), *Comparative Austronesian Dictionary: An Introduction to Austronesian Studies, Vol. 1*. Berlin/New York: Mouton de Gruyter, 637–50.

Hughes, Jock (2000). The Morphology of Dobel, Aru, with Special Reference to Reduplication, in Charles E Grimes (ed.), *Spices from the East: Papers in Languages of Eastern Indonesia*. Canberra: Pacific Linguistics, 131–80.

Hull, Geoffrey (1998). The Basic Lexical Affinities of Timor's Austronesian Languages: A Preliminary Investigation, in Geoffrey Hull and Lance Eccles (eds.), *Studies in Languages and Cultures of East Timor*. Campbelltown: University of Western Sydney Macarthur, 97–174.

Hull, Geoffrey (1999). *Standard Tetum-English Dictionary*. Crow's Nest: Allen and Unwin.

Hull, Geoffrey (2000). Historical Phonology of Tetum, *Studies in Languages and Cultures of East Timor* 3: 158–212.

Hull, Geoffrey (2001a). A Morphological Overview of the Timoric Sprachbund, *Studies in Languages and Cultures of East Timor* 4: 98–205.

Hull, Geoffrey (2001b). *Mambai Language Manual (Ainaro dialect)*. Dili: Sebastião Aparício da Silva Project.

Hull, Geoffrey (2002). *Waimaha*. Dili: Instituto Nacional de Linguística.

Hull, Geoffrey (2003a). *Galoli*. Dili: Instituto Nacional de Linguística.

Hull, Geoffrey (2003b). *Southern Mambai*. Dili: Instituto Nacional de Linguística.

Hung, Hsiao-Chun (2005). Neolithic Interaction Between Taiwan and Northern Luzon: The Pottery and Jade Evidence from the Cagayan Valley, *Journal of Austronesian Studies* 1(1): 109–34.

Hung, Hsiao-Chun (2008). *Migration and Cultural Interaction in Southern Coastal China, Taiwan and the Northern Philippines, 3000 BC to AD 100: The Early History of the Austronesian Speaking Populations*. PhD Dissertation, Australian National University.

Hung, Hsiao-Chun (2016). The Formation and Dispersal of Early Austronesian-Speaking Populations: New Evidence from Taiwan, the Philippines, and the Marianas of Western Micronesia, in Bagyo Prasetyo, Titi Surti Nastiti and Truman Simanjuntak (eds.), *Austronesian Diaspora: A New Perspective*. Yogyakarta: Gadjah Mada University Press, 125–44.

Hung, Hsiao-chun and Yoshiyuki Iizuka (2013). The Batanes nephrite artefacts, in Peter Bellwood and Eusebio Dizon (eds.), *4000 years of Migration and Cultural Exchange: The Archaeology of the Batanes Islands, Northern Philippines*. Canberra: Australian National University Press, 149–68.

Hung, Hsiao-Chun and Yoshiyuki Iizuka (2017). Nephrite and Mica Industries: A Link Towards the Austronesian World, in Bérénice Bellina (ed.), *Khao Sam Kaeo: An Early Port-City Between the Indian Ocean and the South China Sea*. Paris: École Française d'Extrême-Orient, 461–86.

Hung, Hsiao-Chun, Kim Dung Nguyen, Peter Bellwood and Mike T Carson (2013). Coastal Connectivity: Long Term Trading Networks Across the South China Sea, *Journal of Island and Coastal Archaeology* 8(3): 384–404.

Hung, Hsiao-Chun, Mike T Carson, Peter Bellwood et al. (2011). The First Settlement of Remote Oceania: from the Philippines to the Marianas, *Antiquity* 85(329): 909–26.

Hung, Hsiao-Chun, Yoshiyuki Iizuka, Peter Bellwood et al. (2007). Ancient Jades Map 3000 Years of Prehistoric Exchange in Southeast Asia, *Proceedings of the National Academy of Sciences of the United States of America* 104(50): 19745–50.

Hurlbut, Hope M (1988). *Verb Morphology in Eastern Kadazan*. Canberra: Pacific Linguistics.

Hurlbut, Hope M (1993). Labuk-Kinabatangan Phonemics, in Michael E Boutin and Inka Pekkanen (eds.), *Phonological Descriptions of Sabah Languages*. Kota Kinabalu: Sabah Museum, 47–58.

Huwaë, Rosita (1992). *Tweetaligheid in Wierden: Het taalgebruik van jongeren uit een Molukse Gemeenschap* [Bilingualism in Wierden: language use among young people in a Moluccan community]. PhD Dissertation, University of Amsterdam.

Hyman, Larry M (2002). Suffix Ordering in Bantu: A Morphocentric Approach. Unpublished Manuscript, U of California, Berkeley. URL: http://roa.rutgers.edu/files/506-(0302)/506-(0302)-hyman-0-0 pdf

Hyman, Larry M (2009). How (Not) to Do Phonological Typology: The Case of Pitch-Accent, *Language Sciences* 31: 213–38.

Hyman, Larry M (2014). Do All Languages Have Word Accent?, in Harry van der Hulst (ed.), *Word Stress: Theoretical and Typological Issues*. Cambridge: Cambridge University Press, 56–82.

Iamdanush, Jakrabhop and Pittayawat Pittayaporn (2014). Periphrastic Causative Constructions in Patani Malay, in Siaw-Fong Chung and Hiroki Nomoto (eds.), *Current Trends in Malay Linguistics*. Special issue of *NUSA* 57: 101–21.

Ibrahim, Gufran Ali (2002). *Keergatifan dan ketransitifan dalam wacana Bahasa Tae'* [Ergativity and transitivity in Tae' discourse]. PhD Dissertation, Universitas Hasanuddin.

Icban-Castro, Rosalina (1981). *Literature of the Pampangos*. Manila: University of the East Press.

Ikranegara, Kay (1988). *Tata bahasa Melayu Betawi* [Betawi Malay Grammar]. Jakarta: Balai Pustaka.

Inagaki, Kazuya (2010). Voice and Valency Alternations in Kadorih, in *Proceedings of the Workshop on Indonesian-Type Voice Systems*. Tokyo: Research Institute for Languages and Cultures of Asia and Africa, Tokyo University of Foreign Studies, 63–81.

Inagaki, Kazuya (2013). Argument Encoding and Voice in Kadorih of Central Kalimantan, in Alexander Adelaar (ed.), *Voice Variation in Austronesian Languages of Indonesia*. Special issue of *NUSA* 54: 47–65.

Inagaki, Kazuya (2014). The System of Spatial Reference in Kadorih, in Anthony Jukes (ed.), *Deixis and Spatial Expression in Languages of Indonesia.* Special issue of *NUSA* 56: 65–77.

Indrawati, Ni Luh Ketut Mas (2014). The Typological Perspective of the Balinese Serial Verb Constructions, in I Wayan Arka and Ni Luh Ketut Mas Indrawati (eds.), *Argument Realisations and Related Constructions in Austronesian Languages: Papers from 12-ICAL, Volume 2.* Canberra: Asia-Pacific Linguistics, 353–68.

Inibaloi Scripture Translation Project (nd). Writing in My Own Language Inibaloi. URL: http://www.inibaloi.com/en/working-orthography-0

Inkelas, Sharon (2008). The Dual Theory of Reduplication, *Linguistics* 46: 351–401.

Inkelas, Sharon and Cheryl Zoll (2005). *Reduplication: Doubling in Morphology.* Cambridge: Cambridge University Press.

INSTAT [Institut National de la Statistique de Madagascar]. (2020). *Madagascar en chiffre*, URL: https://www.instat.mg/accueil/madagascar-en-chiffre/

Ishizuka, Tomoko (2008). Deriving the Order of Constituents in the Javanese DP, University of California Los Angeles Unpublished Manuscript. URL: https://ling.auf.net/lingbuzz/000769

Iskandar, Johan and Budiawati S Iskandar (2016). Ethnoastronomy: The Baduy Agricultural Calendar and Prediction of Environmental Perturbations, *Biodiversitas* 17(2): 694–703.

Jaafar, Sharifah Raihan Syed and Sakinah Nik Muhammad Naziman (2017). The Phonological Behavour of Nasal Segment in English Loanwords in Kelantan Dialect, *Dialectologia* 18: 95–106.

Jaafar, Sharifah Raihan Syed (2018). Nasal Substitution and the Limited role of *NÇ in Malay Dialects, *Journal of the Southeast Asian Linguistics Society* 11 (1): 35–46.

Jackson, Jason (2008). A Comparison of Ergativity in Uma, Padoe and Selayarese, *Working Papers in Linguistics* 39(1): 1–33.

Jackson, Jason (2014). *A Grammar of Irarutu, a Language of West Papua, Indonesia, with Historical Analysis.* PhD Dissertation, University of Hawai'i.

Jackson, Jennifer (2013). *Political Oratory and Cartooning: An Ethnography of Democratic Processes in Madagascar.* Malden: John Wiley.

Jacobs G S, G Hudjasov, L Saag, P Kusuma, C C Darusallam, D J Lawson, M Mondal, L Pagani, F X Ricaut, M Stoneking, M Metspalu, H Sudoyo, J S Lansing and M P Cox (2019). Multiple Deeply Divergent Denisovan Ancestries in Papuans, *Cell* 177(4): 1010–21.

Jacobson, Marc R (1979). Phones in Philippine Languages, *Studies in Philippine Linguistics* 3: 138–64.

Jacobson, Marc R (1999). Inabaknon Wordlist. URL: https://www.trussel2.com/acd/acd-l_i.htm#Inabaknon

Jacq, Pascale (1998). How many dialects are there?, in Peter Austin (ed.), *Working Papers in Sasak* (Vol. 1). Melbourne: University of Melbourne, 67–90.

Jacques, Guillaume and Johann-Mattis List (2018). Save the Trees: Why We Need Tree Models in Linguistic Reconstruction (and When We Should Apply Them), *Journal of Historical Linguistics* 8: 1–32.

Jakobson, Roman (1960). Why Mama and Papa? in Bernard Kaplan and Seymour Wapner, (eds.), *Perspectives in Psychological Theory.* New York: International Universities Press, 21–9.

James, Jeremiah (2017). *Central Sinama Voice: A Symmetrical Analysis.* MA Thesis, Graduate Institute of Applied Linguistics, Dallas TX.

Jansen, Wouter (2004). *Laryngeal Contrast and Phonetic Voicing: A Laboratory Phonology Approach to English, Hungarian and Dutch.* PhD Dissertation, University of Groningen.

Jardine, Adam, Angeliki Athanasopoulou, Kristian and Peter Cole (2015). Banyaduq Prestopped Nasals: Synchrony and Diachrony, *Oceanic Linguistics* 54(2): 548–78.

Jary, Mark and Mikhail Kissine (2016). When Terminology Matters: The Imperative as a Comparative Concept, *Linguistics* 54: 119–48.

Jaspan, M A (1984). *Materials for A Rejang-Indonesian-English Dictionary.* Canberra: Pacific Linguistics.

Jauhary, Eddy (2000). *Pasif Bahasa Bima.* MA Thesis, Udayana University, Denpasar.

Jenner, P N (1976). The Relative Dating of Some Khmer CPA'PA*", in Philip N Jenner, Laurence C Thompson and Stanley Starosta (eds.), *Austroasiatic Studies.* Honolulu: University of Hawai'i Press, 693–710.

Jenny, Mathias (2015). Syntactic Diversity and Change in Austroasiatic Languages, in Carlotta Viti (ed.), *Perspectives on Historical Syntax.* Amsterdam: John Benjamins, 317–40.

Jenny, Mathias, Tobias Weber and Rachel Weymuth (2015). The Austroasiatic Languages: A Typological Overview, in Mathias Jenny and Paul Sidwell (eds.), *The Handbook of Austroasiatic Languages.* Leiden/Boston: Brill, 13–143.

Jensen, John Thayer (1977). *Yapese Reference Grammar.* Honolulu: University Press of Hawai'i.

Jensen, Joshua Martin (2014). *Jarai Clauses and Noun Phrases: Syntactic Structure in an Austronesian Language.* Berlin: de Gruyter Mouton.

Jeoung, Helen (2017). On the Number of Voices in Madurese, *Journal of Southeast Asian Linguistics* 10(1): 16–35.

Jeoung, Helen (2020). P-Drop Across Languages of Java: A Field Report, in Thomas J. Conners and Jozina Vander Klok (eds.), *Selected Papers of the Seventh International Symposium on the Languages of Java (ISLOJ 7).* Special issue of *NUSA* 69: 27–41.

Jespersen, Otto (1917). *Negation in English and Other Languages.* København: Høst and Søn.

Jinam T A, L C Hong, M E Phipps, M Stoneking, M Ameen, J Edo, HUGO Pan-Asian SNP Consortium and N Saitou (2012). Evolutionary History of Continental Southeast Asians: Early Train Hypothesis Based on Genetic Analysis of Mitochondrial and Autosomal DNA Data, *Molecular Biology and Evolution* 29: 3513–27.

Jones, Linda K, Yohanes Paai and Zet Paai (1989). *Ayao Yawa Mo Mona Nanentabo Ranugan = Perbendaharaan kata Bahasa Yawa = Yawa Vocabulary.* Publikasi Khusus Bahasa-Bahasa Daerah, Seri B 4. Jayapura: Cenderawasih University and Summer Institute of Linguistics.

Jones, Russell (1978). *Arabic Loan-Words in Indonesian; A Check-List of Words of Arabic and Persian Origin in Bahasa Indonesia and Traditional Malay, in the Reformed Spelling.* London: School of Oriental and African Studies.

Jones, Russell (2009). *Chinese Loan-Words in Malay and Indonesian.* Kuala Lumpur: University of Malaya Press.

Jones, Russell (ed.) (2007). *Loan-Words in Indonesian and Malay*. Leiden: Koninklijk Instituut voor Taal-, Land- en Volkenkunde Press.

Jonker, J C G (1918). Indonesische taalstam [Indonesian language family], in S de Graaff and D G Stibbe (eds.), *Encyclopædie van Nederlandsch-Indië (Tweede deel H–M)*. 's-Gravenhage: Martinus Nijhoff, 143–7.

Jonker, J C G (1932). *Lettineesche taalstudiën* [Linguistic studies of Letinese]. Bandoeng: A C Nix.

Jonker, J C G (1896). *Bimaneesche spraakkunst* [A grammar of Bima] 's-Gravenhage: Martinus Nijhoff.

Jonker, J C G (1915). *Rottineesche spraakkunst* [A grammar of Rotinese]. Leiden: Brill.

Jordan, Mary Ellen (2002). Discourse Strategies in Sasak, in Peter K Austin (ed.), *Working Papers in Sasak Vol. 2*. Melbourne: Department of Linguistics and Applied Linguistics, 25–48.

Josephs, Lewis (1975). *Palauan Reference Grammar*. Honolulu: University of Hawai'i Press.

Josephs, Lewis (1994). Review of Alain Lemaréchal (1991). *Problèmes de sémantique et de syntaxe en palau*. Paris: Presses du CNRS. In *Oceanic Linguistics* 33(1): 231–56.

Josephs, Lewis (1997). *Handbook of Palauan Grammar: Volume I*. Koror: Ministry of Education, Republic of Palau.

Jukes, Anthony (2005–2007). *Documentation of Ratahan, an Endangered Austronesian Language of North Sulawesi*. London: The Hans Rausing Endangered Languages Project.

Jukes, Anthony (2005). Makassar, in Alexander Adelaar and Nikolaus P Himmelmann (eds.), *The Austronesian Languages of Asia and Madagascar*. Routledge Language Family Series. London: Routledge, 649–82.

Jukes, Anthony (2006). *Makassarese (Basa Mangkasara): A Description of an Austronesian Language of South Sulawesi*. PhD Dissertation, University of Melbourne.

Jukes, Anthony (2010). Someone Else's Job: Externalizing Responsibility for Language Maintenance, in Hywel Glyn Lewis and Nicholas Ostler (eds.), *Reversing Language Shift: How to Re-awaken a Language Tradition: Proceedings of the Fourteenth Foundation for Endangered Languages Conference, Carmarthen, Wales*. Bath: Foundation for Endangered Languages, 44–50.

Jukes, Anthony (2013). Voice, Valence, and Focus in Makassarese, in Alexander Adelaar (ed.), *Voice Variation in Austronesian Languages of Indonesia*. Special issue of *NUSA* 54: 67–84.

Jukes, Anthony (2020). *A Grammar of Makasar, A Language of South Sulawesi, Indonesia*. Boston/Leiden: Brill.

Jukes, Anthony and Atsuko Utsumi (2015). Relative Height Terms in Sangiric Languages. Presentation: International Conference on Austronesian Linguistics, Taipei.

Jukes, Anthony, Asako Shiohara and Yanti (2017). Collaborative Project for Documenting Minority Languages in Indonesia and Malaysia, *Asian and African Languages and Linguistics* 11: 45–56.

Jun, Sun-Ah (2005). *Prosodic Typology: The Phonology of Intonation and Phrasing*. Oxford: Oxford University Press.

Jun, Sun-Ah (2014). *Prosodic Typology II: The Phonology of Intonation and Phrasing*. Oxford: Oxford University Press.

Juynboll, Abraham Wilhelm Theodorus (1883). Lijst van Javaansche en Soendaneesche woorden uit het Arabisch of het Perzisch afstammende [A list of Javanese and Sundanese words of Arabic and Persian origin], *Bijdragen tot de Taal-, Land- en Volkenkunde van Nederlandsch-Indië* (Special Issue Volume 2: Taal- en Letterkunde), 25–82.

Juynboll, Abraham Wilhelm Theodorus (1894). Vervolg van de lijst van Javaansche en Soendaneesche woorden, uit het Arabisch of het Perzisch afstammende [Continuation of the list of Javanese and Sundanese words of Arabic and Persian origin], *Bijdragen tot de Taal-, Land- en Volkenkunde van Nederlandsch-Indië* 44(1): 169–200.

Kaboy, Tuton (1974). The Penan Aput, in Jérôme Rousseau (ed.), *The Peoples of Central Borneo*. Special Issue of *Sarawak Museum Journal* 22 (New Series 43): 287–93.

Kádár, Dániel Z (2017). Politeness in Pragmatics, in Mark Aronoff (ed.), *Oxford Research Encyclopedia of Linguistics*. New York: Oxford University Press.

Kadir, Mohd Daud, M Yunus R and Sitti Syamsiar (1986). *Dialek bahasa Orang Laut* [Orang Laut Malay]. Jakarta: Pusat Pembinaan dan Pengembangan Bahasa.

Kähler, Hans (1940). Grammatischer Abriss des Enggano [Grammatical outline of Enggano], *Zeitschrift für Eingeborenen-Sprachen* 30. 81–117, 182–210, 296–320.

Kähler, Hans (1946). Ethnographische und linguistische Studien von den Orang Laut auf der Insel Rangsang an der Ostküste von Sumatra [Ethnographic and linguistic studies about the Orang Laut on Rangsang Island, Sumatra's east coast], *Anthropos*, 41/44(4/6): 757–85.

Kähler, Hans (1955). *Die Sichule-Sprache auf der Insel Simalur an der Westküste von Sumatra* [The Sigulai language on Simalur Island, Sumatra's west coast]. Berlin: Dietrich Reimer.

Kähler, Hans (1963). *Texte von der Insel Simalur* [Texts collected on Simalur Island]. Berlin: Dietrich Reimer.

Kakadelis, Stephanie (2018). *Phonetic Properties of Oral Stops in Three Languages with No Voicing Distinction*. PhD Dissertation, the Graduate Center, City University of New York.

Kakerissa, O et al. (1986). *Struktur Bahasa Gorom* [Grammatical structure of Gorom]. Jakarta: Pusat Pembinaan dan Pengembangan Bahasa.

Kaland, Constantijn (2019). Acoustic Correlates of Word Stress in Papuan Malay, *Journal of Phonetics* 74: 55–74.

Kaland, Constantijn (2020). Offline and Online Processing of Acoustic Cues to Word Stress in Papuan Malay, *the Journal of the Acoustical Society of America* 147(2): 731–47.

Kaland, Constantijn and Stefan Baumann (2020). Demarcating and Highlighting in Papuan Malay Phrase Prosody, *The Journal of Acoustic Society of America* 147(4): 2974–88.

Kamholz, David (2011). Moor, Yeresiam, Yaur, and Umar: Four Austronesian Languages of Southern Cenderawasih Bay. Presentation: Fieldwork Forum, University of California at Berkeley, 7 September 2011.

Kamholz, David (2014). *Austronesians in Papua: Diversification and Change in South Halmahera-West New Guinea*. PhD Dissertation. University of California, Berkeley.

Kamholz, David (2015). The Reconstruction of Proto-SHWNG Morphology. Presentation: 13th International Conference on Austronesian Linguistics, Academia Sinica, Taipei, May 2015.

Kamholz, David (2017). Tone and Language Contact in Southern Cenderawasih Bay, in Antoinette Schapper (ed.), *Contact and Substrate in the Languages of Wallacea* (Part 1). Special issue of *NUSA* 62: 7–39.

Kamholz, David (online). *Moor Dictionary*. URL: https://lexifier.lautgesetz.com/

Kanski, P and P Kasprusch (1931). Die indonesisch-melanesischen Übergangsprachen auf den kleinen Molukken, *Anthropos* 26: 883–90.

Karafet T M, B Hallmark, M P Cox, H Sudoyo, S S Downey, J S Lansing and M F Hammer (2010). Major East-West Division Underlies Y Chromosome Stratification Across Indonesia, *Molecular Biology and Evolution* 27: 1833–44.

Karhunen, Marjo (1991). Phonology of Padoe, in René van den Berg (ed.), *Sulawesi Phonologies*. Ujung Pandang: Summer Institute of Linguistics, 179–96.

Karvovskaya, Lena (2018). *The Typology and Formal Semantics of Adnominal Possession*. PhD Dissertation, Leiden University.

Kasimin, Amran (1987). *Perbendaharan kata Arab dalam Bahasa Melayu* [Arabic vocabulary in Malay]. Bangi: Penerbit Universiti Kebangsaan Malaysia.

Kaswanti Purwo, Bambang (1984). *Deiksis dalam Bahasa Indonesia* [Deixis in Indonesian]. Seri ILDEP. Jakarta: PN Balai Pustaka.

Kaufman, Daniel (2005). Aspects of Pragmatic Focus in Tagalog, in I Wayan Arka and Malcolm Ross (eds.), *The Many Faces of Austronesian Voice Systems: Some New Empirical Studies*. Canberra: Pacific Linguistics, 175–96.

Kaufman, Daniel (2007). Review of Alexander Adelaar (2005). *Salako or Badameà: Sketch Grammar, Text and Lexicon of a Kanayatn Dialect in West Borneo*. Wiesbaden: Harrassowitz. In *Oceanic Linguistics* 46(2): 624–33.

Kaufman, Daniel (2008). South Sulawesi Pronominal Clitics: Form, Function and Position, *Studies in Philippine Languages and Cultures* 17: 13–65.

Kaufman, Daniel (2009a). Austronesian Nominalism and its Consequences: A Tagalog Case Study, *Theoretical Linguistics* 35: 1–49.

Kaufman, Daniel (2009b). Austronesian Typology and the Nominalist Hypothesis, in Alexander Adelaar and Andrew Pawley (eds.), *Austronesian Historical Linguistics and Culture History: A Festschrift for Robert Blust*. Canberra: Pacific Linguistics, 179–226.

Kaufman, Daniel (2010a). *The Morphosyntax of Tagalog Clitics: A Typological Approach*. PhD Dissertation, Cornell University.

Kaufman, Daniel (2010b). The Grammar of Clitics in Maranao, in Loren Billings and Nelleke Goudswaard (eds.), *Piakandatu Ami Dr. Howard P McKaughan*. Manila: Linguistic Society of the Philippines and Summer Institute of Linguistics, 132–57.

Kaufman, Daniel (2011a). Exclamatives and Temporal Nominalizations in Austronesian, in Foong Ha Yap, Karen Grunow-Hårsta and Janick Wrona (eds.), *Nominalization in Asian Languages: Diachronic and Typological Perspectives*. Amsterdam: John Benjamins, 721–54.

Kaufman, Daniel (2011b). Deictic and Spatial Agreement in Mamuju (and Beyond). Presentation: Workshop on Deixis and Spatial Expressions in Indonesian Languages, Osaka, Japan, July 22–23.

Kaufman, Daniel (2014). The Syntax of Indonesian Impostors, in Chris Collins (ed.), *Cross Linguistic Studies of Imposters and Pronominal Agreement*. Oxford: Oxford University Press, 89–120.

Kaufman, Daniel (2017). Lexical Category and Alignment in Austronesian, in Lisa Travis, Jessica Coon and Diane Massam (eds.), *Oxford Handbook of Ergativity*. Oxford: Oxford University Press, 589–628.

Kaufman, Daniel (2018). Inner and Outer Causatives in Austronesian: A Diachronic Perspective, *McGill Working Papers in Linguistics* 25(1): 201–15.

Kayser M, O Lao, K Saar, S Brauer, X Wang, P Nürnberg, R Trent, M Stoneking (2008). Genome-Wide Analysis Indicates More Asian Than Melanesian Ancestry of Polynesians, *American Journal of Human Genetics* 82: 194–8.

Keenan, Edward (1976). Remarkable Subjects in Malagasy, in Charles Li (ed.), *Subject and Topic*. New York: Academic Press, 247–301.

Keenan, Edward L (2008). Voice and Relativization without Movement in Malagasy, *Natural Language and Linguistic Theory* 26: 467–97.

Keenan, Edward L and Bernard Comrie (1977). Noun Phrase Accessibility and Universal Grammar, *Linguistics Inquiry* 8: 63–99.

Keenan, Edward L and Maria Polinsky (1998). Malagasy (Austronesian), in Andrew Spencer and Arnold Zwicky (eds.), *The Handbook of Morphology*. Oxford: Blackwell, 563–623.

Kelly, Piers (2015). A Comparative Analysis of Eskayan and Boholano-Visayan (Cebuano) Phonotactics: Implications for the Origins of Eskayan Lexemes, *Journal of the Southeast Asian Linguistics Society* 8: iii–xiv.

Kemmer, Suzanne (1993). *The Middle Voice*. Amsterdam: John Benjamins.

Kenstowicz, Michael (1986). Multiple Linking in Javanese, in *Proceedings of the North East Linguistics Society (NELS)* 16. Amherst: Graduate Linguistics Students Association Publications, 230–48.

Kenstowicz, Michael (1994). *Phonology in Generative Grammar*. Oxford: Blackwell Publishing.

Kern, Hendrik (1880). Sanskritsche woorden in het Tagala [Sanskrit words in Tagalog], *Bijdragen tot de Taal-, Land- en Volkenkunde van Nederlandsch-Indië* 28: 535–64.

Kern, Hendrik (1881). Sanskritsche woorden in het Bisaya [Sanskrit words in Bisaya], *Bijdragen tot de Taal-, Land- en Volkenkunde van Nederlandsch-Indië* 29(1): 128–35.

Kern, Hendrik (1886). De Fidji-Taal vergeleken met hare verwanten in Indonesië en Polynesië [The Fijian language compared to related languages in Indonesia and Polynesia], *Verhandelingen der Koninklijke Akademie van Wetenschappen, Afdeling Letterkunde* 16: 1–242.

Kern, Hendrik (1906a). Bijdragen tot de spraakkunst van het Oudjavaansch [Contributions to Old Javanese grammar], *Bijdragen tot de Taal-, Land- en Volkenkunde* 59(2): 229–62.

Kern, Hendrik (1906b). Taalvergelijkende verhandeling over het Aneityumsch, met een aanhangsel over het klankstelsel van het Eromanga [Comparative linguistic treatise of Aneityum, with a phonology of Eromanga in an attachment]. *Verhandelingen der Koninklijke Akademie van Wetenschappen, Afdeling Letterkunde* 8(1): 1–146

Kern, Hendrik (1918). Spraakkunst van het Oud-Javaansch [Old Javanese grammar]. *Verspreide Geschriften*, 8: 136–324. (First Published in 1898 in *Bijdragen tot de Taal-, Land- en Volkenkunde* 49).

Kerr, Harland (1988). Cotabato Manobo Grammar, *Studies in Philippine Linguistics* 7: 1–123.

Kersten, J (1984). *Tata Bahasa Bali* [Balinese Grammar]. Ende, Indonesia: Arnoldus.

Kikusawa, Ritsuko (2003). The Development of Some Indonesian Pronominal Systems, in Barry J Blake, Kate Burridge and Jo Taylor (eds.), *Historical Linguistics 2001. Selected Papers from the 15th International Conference on Historical Linguistics*. Amsterdam/Philadelphia: John Benjamins, 237–69.

Kikusawa, Ritsuko (2006). A Malagasy (Northern Betsimisaraka) Text with Grammatical Notes, *Journal of Asian and African Studies* 71: 5–37.

Kikusawa, Ritsuko (2012). Standardization as Language Loss: Potentially Endangered Malagasy Languages and their Linguistic Features, *People and Culture in Oceania* 28: 23–44.

Kikusawa, Ritsuko and Lawrence A Reid (2003). A Talubin Text with Wordlist and Grammatical Notes, *Journal of Asian and African Studies* 65: 89–148.

Kiliaan, H N (1897). *Madoereesche spraakkunst* [Grammar of Madurese]. Batavia: Landsdrukkerij.

Kimoto, Yukinori (2017a). *A Grammar of Arta: A Philippine Negrito Language*. PhD Dissertation, Kyoto University.

Kimoto, Yukinori (2017b). *Arta (Edilod) Dictionary*. Webonary, Summer Institute of Linguistics. URL: https://www.webonary.org/arta/

Kimoto, Yukinori (2017c). Documentation and Description of the Arta Language. Endangered Languages Archive. URL: https://www.elararchive.org/dk0411/

Kimoto, Yukinori (2017d). Mora, Vowel Length, and Diachrony: The Case of Arta, A Philippine Negrito Language, in Liao Hsiu-Chuan (ed.), *Issues in Austronesian Historical Linguistics*. Journal of the Southeast Asian Linguistics Society Special Publication No. 1. Honolulu: University of Hawai'i Press, 1–22.

Kimoto, Yukinori (2019). Multi-CAST Arta, in Geoffrey Haig and Stefan Schnell (eds.), *Multi-CAST: Multilingual Corpus of Annotated Spoken Texts*. <multicast.aspra.uni-bamberg.de/>.

King, John Wayne (1988). Tambanua Clauses, in Charles Peck (ed.), *Borneo Language Studies 1: Sabah Syntax Papers*. Dallas: Summer Institute of Linguistics, 149–74.

King, John Wayne (1993). Tombonuwo Phonemics, in Michael E Boutin and Inka Pekkanen (eds.), *Phonological Descriptions of Sabah Languages*. Kota Kinabalu: Sabah Museum, 97–106.

King, John Wayne and Julie K King (nd). *Tombonuo Dictionary*. Unpublished Manuscript.

Kirch, Patrick Vinton (2002). On *the Road of the Winds: An Archaeological History of the Pacific Islands*. Berkeley: University of California Press.

Kirch, Patrick Vinton (2017). On *the Road of the Winds*. Revised Edition of Kirch (2000). Berkeley: University of California Press.

Kitada, Yuko (2021). *The Prefix *si- in Western Indonesian, Sulawesi and Philippine Languages*. PhD Dissertation, University of Cologne.

Kitano, Hiroaki (2005). Ergativity and Equational Structure in Kapampangan, in Hsiu-Chuan Liao and Carl R Galvez Rubino (eds.), *Current Issues in Philippine Linguistics and Anthropology Parangal Kay Lawrence A Reid*. Manila: Linguistic Society of the Philippines and Summer Institute of Linguistics, 338–45.

Kiyomi, Setsuko (1995). A New Approach to Reduplication: A Semantic Study of Noun and Verb Reduplication in Malayo-Polynesian Languages, *Linguistics* 33: 1145–67.

Klaiman, M H (1992). Middle Verbs, Reflexive Middle Constructions, and Middle Voice, *Studies in Language* 16 (1): 35–61.

Klamer, Marian (1996). Kambera Has No Passive, *NUSA* 39: 12–30.

Klamer, Marian (1998). *A Grammar of Kambera*. Berlin/New York: Mouton de Gruyter.

Klamer, Marian (2000). Continuative Aspect and the Dative Clitic in Kambera, in Ileana Paul, Vivianne Phillips and Lisa Travis (eds.), *Formal Issues in Austronesian Linguistics*. Dordrecht: Kluwer, 49–63.

Klamer, Marian (2002a). Semantically Motivated Patterns: A Study of Dutch and Kambera Expressives, *Language* 78: 258–86.

Klamer, Marian (2002b). Typical Features of Austronesian Languages in Central/Eastern Indonesia, *Oceanic Linguistics* 41(2): 363–83.

Klamer, Marian (2004). East Nusantara: Genetic, Areal, and Typological Approaches, *Oceanic Linguistics* 43(1): 240–4.

Klamer, Marian (2005). Kambera, in Alexander Adelaar and Nikolaus P Himmelmann (eds.), *The Austronesian Languages of Asia and Madagascar*. London: Routledge, 709–34.

Klamer, Marian (2008). The Semantics of Semantic Alignment in Eastern Indonesia, in Mark Donohue and Søren Wichmann (eds.), *The Typology of Semantic Alignment*. Oxford: Oxford University Press, 221–51.

Klamer, Marian (2011). *A Short Grammar of Alorese (Austronesian)*. München: LINCOM.

Klamer, Marian (2012). Papuan-Austronesian Language Contact: Alorese from an Areal Perspective, in Nicholas Evans and Marian Klamer (eds.), *Melanesian Languages on the Edge of Asia: Challenges for the 21st Century*. Honolulu: University of Hawai'i Press, 72–108.

Klamer, Marian (2019). The Dispersal of Austronesian Languages in Island South East Asia: Current Findings and Debates, *Language and Linguistics Compass* 13(4): E12325.

Klamer, Marian (2020). From Lamaholot to Alorese: Morphological Loss in Adult Language Contact, in David Gil and Antoinette Schapper (eds.), *Austronesian Undressed: How and Why Languages Become Isolating*. Amsterdam: John Benjamins, 339–68.

Klamer, Marian and Michael C Ewing (2010). The Languages of East Nusantara: An Introduction, in Michael C Ewing and Marian Klamer (eds.), *East Nusantara: Typological and Areal Analyses*. Canberra: Pacific Linguistics, 1–25.

Klamer, Marian, Ger P Reesink and Miriam van Staden (2008). East Nusantara as a Linguistic Area, in Pieter Muysken (ed.), *From Linguistic Areas to Areal Linguistics*. Amsterdam: John Benjamins, 95–149.

Kluge, Angela (2014). *A Grammar of Papuan Malay*. Utrecht: LOT Netherlands Graduate School of Linguistics.

Kluge, Angela (2017). *A Grammar of Papuan Malay*. Berlin: Language Science Press.

Ko Young Soo (2007). *Verb Serialization in Western Cham*. MA Thesis, Applied Linguistics, Charles Darwin University.

Ko Young Soo (2018). *Western Cham Grammar Sketch*. Unpublished Manuscript.

Ko, Albert Min-Shan, Chung-Yu Chen, Qiaomei Fu, Frederick Delfin, Mingkun Li, Hung-Lin Chiu, Mark Stoneking and Ying-Chin Ko (2014). Early Austronesians: Into and Out of Taiwan, *American Journal of Human Genetics* 94 (3): 426–36.

Kobari, Yoshihiro (2009). *The Current Status of the Butuanon Language and its Speakers in Northern Mindanao: Findings on Ethnic Identity, Language attitudes, Language Ability, Language Use, and Language Change*. PhD Dissertation, De La Salle University.

Kong, Yuanzhi (1986). *A Preliminary Study of Chinese Loanwords (from South Fujian Dialects) in the Malay-Indonesian Languages*. Leiden: Leiden University.

König, Ekkehard and Peter Siemund (with Stephan Töpper) (2013). Intensifiers and Reflexive Pronouns, in Matthew S Dryer and Martin Haspelmath (eds.), *The World Atlas of Language Structures Online*. Leipzig: Max Planck Institute for Evolutionary Anthropology.

Kouwenberg, Silvia and Darlene Lacharité (2005). Less Is More: Evidence from Diminutive Reduplication in Caribbean Creole Languages, in Bernhard Hurch (ed.), *Studies on Reduplication*. Berlin: Mouton de Gruyter, 533–45.

Kramer, Raija (2018). Position Paper on Phasal Polarity Expressions. Unpublished Manuscript.

Krauße, Daniel (2017). *A Description of Surabayan Javanese*. MA Thesis, Goethe Universität.

Kreemer, J (1912). De Loeboes in Mandailing [The Lubus in Mandailing Regency], *Bijdragen tot de Taal-, Land- en Volkenkunde* 66: 303–36.

Krifka, Manfred (2000). Alternatives for Aspectual Particles: Semantics of Still and Already, *Annual Meeting of the Berkeley Linguistics Society* 26(1). 401–12.

Krifka, Manfred (2008). Basic Notions of Information Structure, *Acta Linguistica Hungarica* 55: 3–4, 243–76.

Krigbaum J and Datan I (2005). The Deep Skull and Associated Human Remains from Niah Cave, in Z Majid (ed.), *The Perak Man and Other Prehistoric Skeletons of Malaysia*. Penang: Penerbit Universiti Sains Malaysia, 131–54.

Kroeger, Paul R (1988). Case Marking in Kimaragang Causative Constructions, in Hein Steinhauer (ed.), *Papers in Western Austronesian Linguistics No. 3*. Canberra: Pacific Linguistics, 241–76.

Kroeger, Paul R (1993a). *Phrase Structure and Grammatical Relations in Tagalog*. Stanford: CSLI Publications.

Kroeger, Paul R (1993b). Kimaragang Phonemics, in Michael E Boutin and Inka Pekkanen (eds.), *Phonological Descriptions of Sabah Languages*. Kota Kinabalu: Sabah Museum, 31–46.

Kroeger, Paul R (2005a). Kimaragang, in Alexander Adelaar and Nikolaus P Himmelmann (eds.), *The Austronesian Languages of Asia and Madagascar*. London and New York: Routledge, 397–428.

Kroeger, Paul R (2005b). *Analysing Grammar*. Cambridge: Cambridge University Press.

Kroeger, Paul R (2010). The Grammar of Hitting, Breaking, and Cutting in Kimaragang Dusun, *Oceanic Linguistics* 49(1): 1–20.

Kroeger, Paul R (2011). Instrumental Voice and the Loss of **Si-* in Northeast Borneo. Presentation: Austronesian Formal Linguistics Association (AFLA-18), Harvard University, March 2011.

Kroeger, Paul R (2014). An Affectedness Constraint in Kimaragang Restructuring, in Miriam Butt and Tracy Holloway King (eds.), *Proceedings of the 14th Lexical-Functional Grammar Conference (LFG14)*. Stanford, CA: CSLI Publications, 283–303.

Kroeger, Paul R (2017). Frustration, Culmination, and Inertia in Kimaragang Grammar, *Glossa: A Journal of General Linguistics* 2(1): 1–29.

Kroeger, Paul R (2020). Marking Accessible Information in Kimaragang, in Ileana Paul (ed.), *Proceedings of the Twenty-Sixth Meeting of the Austronesian Formal Linguistics Association (AFLA)*. University of Western Ontario, 142–58.

Kroeger, Paul R (nd). *Biatah (Land Dayak) Phonology*. Unpublished Manuscript.

Kroon, Yosep Bisara (2016). *A Grammar of Solor-Lamaholot: A Language of Flores, Eastern Indonesia*. PhD Dissertation, University of Adelaide.

Kruspe, Nicole (2004). *A Grammar of Semelai*. Cambridge: Cambridge University Press.

Kruspe, Nicole (2009). Loanwords in Ceq Wong, an Austroasiatic Language of Peninsular Malaysia, in Martin Haspelmath and Uri Tadmor (eds.), *Loanwords in the World's Languages: A Comparative Handbook*. Mouton de Gruyter, 659–85.

Kruyt, Alb C (1938). *De West-Toradjas op Midden-Celebes* [The West Toraja people in Central Sulawesi] 4 Volumes. Amsterdam: Noord-Hollandsche Uitgevers-Maatschappij.

Kubozono, Haruo (ed.) (2017). *The Phonetics and Phonology of Geminate Consonants*. Oxford: Oxford University Press.

Kulick, Don (1992). *Language Shift and Cultural Reproduction: Socialization, Self, and Syncretism in A Papua New Guinean Village*. Cambridge: Cambridge University Press.

Kulikov, Leonid (2010). Voice Typology, in Jae Jung Song (ed.), *The Oxford Handbook of Linguistic Typology*. Oxford University Press, 368–98.

Kurniawan, Eri (2013). *Sundanese Complementation*. PhD Dissertation, University of Iowa.

Kurniawan, Eri and Davies, William D (2015). Finiteness in Sundanese, *Oceanic Linguisics* 54(1): 1–16.

Kusmartono, P R Vida, Imam Hindarto and Eko Herwanto (2017). Late Pleistocene to Recent: Human Activities in the Deep Interior Equatorial Rainforest of Kalimantan, Indonesian Borneo, *Quaternary International* 448: 82–94.

Kusuma P, M P Cox, D Pierron, H Razafindrazaka, N Brucato, L Tonasso, H L SuryadI, T Letellier, H Sudoyo, F X Ricaut (2015). Mitochondrial DNA and the Y Chromosome Suggest the Settlement of Madagascar by Indonesian Sea Nomad Populations, *BMC Genomics* 16: 191.

Kusuma P, M P Cox, N Brucato, H Sudoyo, T Letellier and F X Ricaut (2016b). Western Eurasian Genetic Influences in the Indonesian Archipelago, *Quaternary International* 416: 243e248.

Kusuma P, N Brucato, M P Cox, D Pierron, H Razafindrazaka, A Adelaar, H Sudoyo, T Letellier and F X Ricaut (2016a). Contrasting Linguistic and Genetic Origins of the Asian Source Populations of Malagasy, *Scientific Reports* 6: 26066.

Kusuma P, N Brucato, M P Cox, T Letellier, A Manan, C Nuraini, P Grangé, H Sudoyo and F X Ricaut (2017). The Last Sea Nomads of the Indonesian Archipelago: Genomic Origins and Dispersal, *European Journal Human Genetics* 25: 1004–10.

Kusumaatmaja Pradiptajati (2017). *In Search of Asian Malagasy Ancestors in Indonesia.* PhD Dissertation, University of Toulouse III – Paul Sabatier.

Ladd, Robert D (2008). *Intonational Phonology.* 2nd edition. Cambridge: Cambridge University Press.

Ladefoged, Peter (1971). *Preliminaries to Linguistic Phonetics.* Chicago and London: The University of Chicago Press.

Ladefoged, Peter. 1990. Some Proposals Concerning Glottal Consonants. Journal of the International Phonetic Association 20.2: 24–25. DOI: 10.1017/S0025100300004217

Ladefoged, Peter and Ian Maddieson (1996). *The Sounds of the World's Languages.* Oxford: Blackwell.

Lafeber, Abraham (1922). *Vergelijkende klankleer van het Niasisch* [Comparative phonology of Nias]. PhD Dissertation, Leiden University.

Lafon, Michel (1991). *Lexique français-shingazidja.* Paris: L'Harmattan.

Lai, Regine, Emily Tynan and Yugyeong Park (2010). Stress Patterns in Kupangese. Presentation: The Fourteenth International Symposium on Malay/Indonesian Linguistics, Minneapolis, 2 May 2010.

Laidig, Carol (1992). Segments, Syllables, and Stress in Larike, in Donald A Burquest and Wyn D Laidig (eds.), *Phonological Studies in Four Languages of Maluku.* Dallas: Summer Institute of Linguistics International, University of Texas at Arlington, and Pattimura University. 67–126.

Laidig, Wyn D (1993). Insights from Larike Possessive Constructions, *Oceanic Linguistics* 32: 311–51.

Laidig, Wyn D and Carol J Laidig (1990). Larike Pronouns: Duals and Trials in A Central Moluccan Language, *Oceanic Linguistics* 29: 87–109.

Laidig, Wyn D and Carol J Laidig (1991). *Kamus Sou Rikedu/Kamus Bahasa Larike/Larike Dictionary.* Ambon: UNPATTI-SIL.

Laidig, Wyn D and Sahabu Dg. Maingak (1999). Barang-Barang Phonology: A Preliminary Description, in Wyn D Laidig (ed.), *Studies in Sulawesi* Linguistics, *Part VI.* Special issue of *NUSA* 46. Jakarta: Badan Penyelenggara Seri NUSA, Universitas Katolik Indonesia Atma Jaya, 46–83.

Lambrecht, Frans H (1978). *Ifugaw-English Dictionary.* Baguio City: The Catholic Vicar Apostolic of the Mountain Province.

Lansing J S, C Abundo, G S Jacobs, E G Guillot, S Thurner, SS Downey, L Y Chew, T Bhattacharya, N N Chung, H Sudoyo and M P Cox (2017). Kinship Structures Create Persistent Channels for Language Transmission, *Proceedings of the National Academy of Sciences USA* 114: 12910–5.

Lansing J S, M P Cox, S S Downey, B Gabler, B Hallmark, T M Karafet, P Norquest, J W Schoenfelder, H Sudoyo, J C Watkins and M F Hammer (2007). Coevolution of Languages and Genes on the Island of Sumba, Eastern Indonesia, *Proceedings of the National Academy of Sciences USA* 104: 16022–6.

Lape, Peter, Emily Peterson, Daud Tanudirjo, Chung-Ching Shiung, Gyoung-Ah Lee, Judith Field, Adelle Coster (2018). New Data from an Open Neolithic Site in Eastern Indonesia, *Asian Perspectives* 57(2): 222–43.

LaPolla, Randy (2015). Sino-Tibetan Syntax, in William S-Y Wang and Chaofen Sun (eds.), *The Oxford Handbook of Chinese Linguistics.* Online Publication May (2015). DOI: 10.1093/oxfordhb/9780199856336.013.0044

Lapsley, A D (1983). *Cocos Malay Syntax.* MA Thesis, Monash University.

Larena, Maximilian, Federico Sanchez-Quinto, Per Sjödin et al. (2021). Multiple migrations to the Philippines during the last 50,000 years, *Proceedings of the National Academy of Sciences USA*, March 30, 2021 118 (13) e2026132118. DOI: 10.1073/pnas.2026132118

Larish, Michael D (1999). The *Position of Moken and Moklen within the Austronesian Language Family.* PhD Dissertation, University of Hawai'i.

Larish, Michael D (2005). Moken and Moklen, in Alexander Adelaar and Nikolaus P Himmelmann (eds.), *The Austronesian Languages of Asia and Madagascar.* London: Routledge, 513–33.

Larson, Pier M (2009). *Ocean of Letters: Language and Creolization in an Indian Ocean Diaspora.* Cambridge: Cambridge University Press.

Larson, Virginia (1986). *Ivatan Texts.* Manila: Summer Institute of Linguistics.

Laskowske, Douglas (2016). *Voice in Bugis: An RRG Perspective.* MA Thesis, University of North Dakota.

Laskowske, Kathryn B (1994). Negation in Seko Padang, in René van den Berg (ed.), *Studies in Sulawesi* Linguistics, *Part III.* Special issue of *NUSA* 36. Jakarta: Badan Penyelenggara Seri NUSA, Universitas Katolik Indonesia Atma Jaya, 49–64.

Laskowske, Tom (2001). *A Grammar Sketch of Seko Padang.* Unpublished Manuscript.

Laskowske, Tom (2007). The Seko Languages of South Sulawesi: A Reconstruction, *Studies in Philippine Languages and Cultures* 15: 115–210.

Latip-Yusoph, Sorhaila (2016). Language Trends in Social Media: Manifestations of Meranaws' Use of English on Facebook, *US-China Foreign Language*, 14(7): 480–90.

Latrouite, Anja (2011). *Voice and Case in Tagalog: The Coding of Prominence and Orientation.* PhD Dissertation, University of Düsseldorf.

Laua, Johan, Martha Anne Martens and Michael P Martens (2001). *Ceritera rakyat dan kebudayaan Topo'uma: ceritera dalam Bahasa Uma, Sulawesi Tengah, Indonesia* [Folk tales and culture of the Topo'uma, told in the Uma Language, Central Sulawesi, Indonesia]. Jakarta: Yayasan Kartidaya.

Laver, John (1994). *Principles of Phonetics.* Cambridge: Cambridge University Press.

Law, Paul (2007). The Syntactic Structure of the Cleft Construction in Malagasy, *Natural Language and Linguistic Theory* 25: 765–823.

Lawler A (2014). Sailing Sinbad's Seas, *Science* 344: 1440–5.

Lawler, John M (1977). A Agrees with B in Acehnese: A Problem for Relational Grammar, in Peter Cole and Jerrold M Sadock (eds.), *Grammatical Relations.* New York: Academic Press, 219–48.

Lawler, John M (1988). On the Questions of Acehnese Passive, *Language* 64(1): 114–7.

Lawrence, Wayne (2015). Lexicon, in Patrick Heinrich, Shinsho Miyara and Michinori Shimoji (eds.), *Handbook of the Ryukyuan Languages.* Berlin: de Gruyter Mouton, 157–74.

Laycock, Donald C and W Winter (eds.) (1987). *A World of Language: Papers Presented to Professor S A Wurm on his 65th Birthday.* Canberra: Pacific Linguistics.

Laycock, Donald C (1982). Melanesian Linguistic Diversity: A Melanesian Choice?, in R J May and Hank Nelson (eds.), *Melanesia: Beyond Diversity.* Canberra: Pacific Linguistics, 33–8.

Lee, Celeste and Loren Billings (2005). Wackernagel and Verb-Adjacent Clisis in Central Philippines, in Jeffrey Heinz and Dimitris Ntelitheos (eds.), *Proceedings of the Twelfth Meeting of the Austronesian Formal Linguistics Association.* University of California Los Angeles Working Papers in Linguistics 12. Los Angeles: Department of Linguistics, University of California, 241–54.

Lee, Ernest W (1966). *Proto-Chamic Phonologic Word and Vocabulary*, PhD Dissertation (in Microform), Indiana University, Bloomington.

Lee, Ernest W (1977). Devoicing, Aspiration, and Vowel Split in Haroi: Evidence for Register (Contrastive Tongue-Root Position), in David D Thomas, Ernest W Lee and Nguyen Đang Liêm (eds.), *Papers in Southeast Asian Linguistics No.4.* Canberra: Pacific Linguistics, 87–104.

Lee, Ernest W (1996). Bipartite Negatives in Chamic, *Mon-Khmer Studies* 26: 291–317.

Lee, Ernest W (1998). The Contribution of Cat Gia Roglai to Chamic, in David D Thomas (ed.), *Papers in Southeast Asian Linguistics No.15: Further Chamic Studies.* Canberra: Pacific Linguistics, 31–54.

Lee, Jason Kwok Loong (2008). Transitivity, Valence and Voice in Mandar, *Studies in Philippine Languages and Cultures* 19: 55–66.

Lee, Nala Huiying (2014). *A Grammar of Baba Malay with Sociophonetic Considerations.* PhD Dissertation, University of Hawai'i.

Legate, Julie Anne (2012). Subjects in Acehnese and the Nature of the Passive, *Language* 88(3): 495–525.

Legate, Julie Anne (2014). *Voice and V: Lessons from Acehnese.* Cambridge, MA: Massachusetts Institute of Technology Press.

Lehmann, Thomas (1989). *A Grammar of Modern Tamil.* Pondicherry: Pondicherry Institute of Linguistics and Culture.

Lemaréchal, Alain (1982). Sémantisme des parties du discours et sémantisme des relations, *Bulletin de la Société de Linguistique de Paris* 77: 1–39.

Lemaréchal, Alain (1991). *Problèmes de sémantique et de syntaxe en palau.* Paris: Presses du CNRS.

Lendoyro, Constantino (1909). *The Tagalog Language.* Manila: Juan Fajardo.

Leo, Philip (1975). *Chinese Loanwords Spoken by the Inhabitants of the City of Jakarta.* Jakarta: Lembaga Research Kebudayaan Nasional.

Leow, Rachel (2016). *Taming Babel: Language in the Making of Malaysia.* Cambridge: Cambridge University Press.

Lestiono, Riski (2012). *Spatial Relations in Frog Story Narratives: A Comparative Study Between Surinamese Javanese and Java Javanese.* MA Thesis, Radboud University Nijmegen.

Leto, Claudia, Winarno S Alamudi, Nikolaus P Himmelmann, Jani Kuhnt-Saptodewo, Sonja Riesberg and Hasan Basri (2005–2010). *Dobes Totoli Documentation.* Dobes Archive MPI Nijmegen.

Lévi-Strauss, Claude (1969)[1949]. *The Elementary Structures of Kinship.* Boston: Beacon Press [1st edition 1949].

Levinson, Stephen C (1983). *Pragmatics.* Cambridge: Cambridge University Press.

Levinson, Stephen C (2003). *Space in Language and Cognition.* Cambridge: Cambridge University Press.

Lewis, E Douglas and Charles E Grimes (1995). Sika, in Darrell T Tryon (ed.), *Comparative Austronesian Dictionary: An Introduction to Austronesian Studies.* Berlin/New York: Mouton de Gruyter, 601–10.

Lewis, M Blanche (1960). Moken Texts and Word-List: A Provisional Interpretation, *Federation Museums Journal* 4: 1–102.

Li, Paul Jen-Kuei (2004). Origins of the East Formosans: Basay, Kavalan, Amis, and Siraya, in Paul Jen-Kuei Li (ed.), *Selected Papers on Formosan Languages.* 2 Vols. Taipei: Institute of Linguistics, Academia Sinica, 927–40.

Li, Paul Jen-Kuei, Elizabeth Zeitoun and Rik De Busser (in preparation). *Handbook of Formosan languages. The indigenous languages of Taiwan.* Leiden/Boston: Brill.

Liao, Hsiu-Chuan (2004). *Transitivity and Ergativity in Formosan and Philippine Languages.* PhD Dissertation, University of Hawai'i.

Liao, Hsiu-Chuan (2005). Pronominal Forms in Central Cagayan Agta: Clitics or Agreement Features, in Hsiu-Chuan Liao and Carl R Galvez Rubino (eds.), *Current Issues in Philippine Linguistics and Anthropology: Parangal Kay Lawrence A Reid.* Manila: Linguistic Society of the Philippines and Summer Institute of Linguistics, 346–63.

Liao, Hsiu-Chuan (2008a). A Typology of First Person Dual Pronouns and Their Reconstructibility in Philippine Languages, *Oceanic Linguistics* 47(1): 1–29.

Liao, Hsiu-Chuan (2008b). The Development of Benefactive Affect Verbs in Philippine Languages: Some Implications for Comparative Austronesian Linguistics. Presentation: 18th International Congress of Linguistics (CIL 18), Korea University, Seoul, South Korea, July 21–26, 2008.

Liao, Hsiu-Chuan (2009). When A First Person Participant Meets A Second Person Participant: Irregularities in Personal Pronoun

Systems in Philippine Languages. Presentation: Eleventh International Conference on Austronesian Linguistics, Aussois, France, June 22 –25.

Liao, Hsiu-Chuan (2011a). On the Development of Comitative Verbs in Philippine Languages, *Language and Linguistics* 12(1): 205–237.

Liao, Hsiu-Chuan (2011b). Some Morphosyntactic Differences Between Formosan and Philippine Languages, *Language and Linguistics* 12(4): 845–975.

Liao, Hsiu-Chuan (2020). A Reply to Blust (2019). The Resurrection of Proto-Philippines, *Oceanic Linguistics* 59: 426–49.

Lichtenberk, František (1983). *A Grammar of Manam*. Honolulu: University of Hawai'i Press.

Lichtenberk, František (1985). Possessive Constructions in Oceanic Languages and in Proto-Oceanic, in Andrew K Pawley and Lois Carrington (eds.), *Austronesian Linguistics at the 15th Pacific Science Congress*. Canberra: Pacific Linguistics, 93–140.

Lichtenberk, František (1995). Apprehensional Epistemics, in Joan Bybee and Suzanne Fleischman (eds.), *Modality in Grammar and Discourse*. Amsterdam: John Benjamins, 293–327.

Lichtenberk, František (2005). Inalienability and possessum individuation, in Zygmunt Frajzyngier, Adam Hodges and David S Rood (eds.), *Linguistic Diversity and Language Theories*. Amsterdam/Philadelphia: John Benjamins, 339–62.

Lichtenberk, František (2009). Oceanic Possessive Classifiers, *Oceanic Linguistics* 48: 379–402.

Lichtenberk, František (2016). Modality and Mood in Oceanic, in Jan Nuyts and Johan van der Auwera (eds.), *The Oxford Handbook of Modality and Mood*. URL: 10.1093/oxfordhb/9780199591435.013.15

Liebner, Horst H (2005). Indigenous Concepts of Orientation of South Sulawesian Sailors, *Bijdragen tot de Taal-, Land- en Volkenkunde* 161(2–3): 269–317.

Liljencrants, Johan and Björn Lindblom (1972). Numerical Simulation of Vowel Quality Systems: The Role of Perceptual Contrast, *Language* 48: 838–62.

Lim, Sonny (1981). *Baba Malay: The Language of the Straits-Born Chinese*. MA Thesis, Monash University.

Lindblom, Björn (1986). Phonetic Universals in Vowel Systems, in John J Ohala and Jeri J Jaeger (eds.), *Experimental Phonology*. Orlando (FL): Academic Press, 13–44.

Lindblom, Björn (1990a). Phonetic Content in Phonology, *PERILUS* 11: 101–18.

Lindblom, Björn (1990b). Explaining Phonetic Variation: A Sketch of the H&H Theory, in W Hardcastle and A Marchal (eds.), *Speech Production and Speech Modeling*, Dordrecht: Kluwer, 403–39.

Lindblom, Björn and Ian Maddieson (1988). Phonetic Universals in Consonant Systems, in C Li and L M Hyman (eds.), *Language, Speech and Mind*. London: Routledge, 62–78.

Lipson Mark, O Cheronet, S Mallick, N Rohland, M Oxenham, M Pietrusewsky, T O Pryce, A Willis, H Matsumura, H Buckley, K Domett, G H Nguyen, H H Trinh, A A Kyaw, T T Win, B Pradier, N Broomandkhoshbacht, F Candilio, P Changmai, D Fernandes, M Ferry, B Gamarra, E Harney, J Kampuansai, W Kutanan, M Michel, M Novak, J Oppenheimer, K Sirak, K Stewardson, Z Zhang, P Flegontov, R Pinhasi and D Reich (2018). Ancient Genomes Document Multiple Waves of Migration in Southeast Asian Prehistory, *Science* 361: 92–5.

Lipson, Mark, Po-Ru Loh, Nick Patterson, Priya Moorjani, Ying-Chin Ko, Mark Stoneking, Bonnie Berger and David Reich (2014). Reconstructing Austronesian Population History in Island Southeast Asia, *Nature Communications* 4689. DOI: 10.1038/ncomms5689.

List, Johann-Mattis, Simon J Greenhill and Russell D Gray (2017). The Potential of Automatic Word Comparison for Historical Linguistics, *PLOS One* 12: E(0170)046.

Liston, Jolie (2009). Cultural Chronology of Earthworks in Palau, Western Micronesia, *Archaeology in Oceania* 44: 56–73.

Litamahuputty, Betty (2012). *Ternate Malay. Grammar and Texts*. PhD Dissertation, Leiden University.

Little, Albert John Jr (1978). *An Outline of Gorontalo Morphology and Clause Structure*. PhD Dissertation (Draft), Cornell University.

Little, Albert John Jr (1989). *Gorontalo Phonology and Morphophonemics*. Fort Bragg, NC: Department of the Army.

Little, Albert John Jr (1995). Gorontalo, in Darrell T Tryon (ed.), *Comparative Austronesian Dictionary: An Introduction to Austronesian Studies, Part 1*. Berlin/New York: Mouton de Gruyter, 521–8.

Llamzon, Teodoro A (1969). *A Subgrouping of Nine Philippine Languages*. The Hague: Koninklijk Instituut voor Taal-, Land- en Volkenkunde.

Lloyd-Smith, Lindsay (2012). Early Holocene Burial Practice at Niah Cave, Sarawak, *Bulletin of Indo-Pacific Prehistory Association* 32: 54–69.

Lloyd-Smith, Lindsay (2013). The West Mouth Neolithic Cemetery, Niah Cave, Sarawak, *Proceedings of the Prehistoric Society* 79: 105–136.

Lobel, Jason W (2004). Old Bikol *-um-* vs. *mag-* and the Loss of a Morphological Paradigm, *Oceanic Linguistics* 43(2): 340–68.

Lobel, Jason W (2005). The Angry Register of the Bikol Languages of the Philippines, in Hsiu-Chuan Liao and Carl Rubino (eds.), *Current Issues in Philippine Linguistics and Anthropology, Parangal Kay Lawrence A Reid*. Manila: Linguistic Society of the Philippines and Summer Institute of Linguistics Philippines, 149–66.

Lobel, Jason W (2010). Manide: An Undescribed Philippine Language, *Oceanic Linguistics* 49(2): 480–512.

Lobel, Jason W (2011). Pronominal Number in Mongondow-Gorontalo, *Oceanic Linguistics* 50(2): 543–50.

Lobel, Jason W (2013a). *Philippine and North Bornean Languages: Issues in Description, Subgrouping, and Reconstruction*. PhD Dissertation, University of Hawai'i.

Lobel, Jason W (2013b). Southwest Sabah Revisited, *Oceanic Linguistics* 52: 36–68.

Lobel, Jason W (2015). Ponosakan: A Dying Language of Northern Sulawesi, *Oceanic Linguistics* 54(2): 396–435.

Lobel, Jason W (2016a). Notes from the Field: Ponosakan: The Sounds of a Silently Dying Language of Indonesia, with Supporting Audio, *Language Documentation and Conservation* 10: 394–423.

Lobel, Jason W (2016b). *North Borneo Sourcebook: Vocabularies and Functors*. Honolulu: University of Hawai'i Press.

Lobel, Jason W (nd. a). Notes on Vowel Fronting, Raising, and Backing in Luzon and Northeastern Sulawesi. Unpublished Manuscript.

Lobel, Jason W (nd. b). Proto-Manide-Alabat Reconstructions and Verb System. Unpublished Manuscript.

Lobel, Jason W (nd. c). Inagta Rinconada: An Undocumented Language of the Philippines. Unpublished Manuscript.

Lobel, Jason W (nd. d). The Mongondow-Gorontalo Subgroup of Languages. Unpublished Manuscript.

Lobel, Jason W (nd. e). Notes from the Field: Extinct or Extant? The Curious Case of Inata, Negros Island, Philippines. Unpublished Manuscript.

Lobel, Jason W, Amy J Alpay, Rosie S Barreno and Emelinda J Barreno (2020). Inagta Alabat: A Moribund Philippine Language, with Supporting Audio, *Language Documentation and Conservation* 14: 1–57.

Lobel, Jason W, Lubita Andrada, Salvador Cruz, Jennifer Nolasco Dela Cruz, Melona Torres, Juanita Ramos and Armando Ramos (nd). Umiray Dumaget: An Underdocumented Philippine Language. Unpublished Manuscript.

Lobel, Jason W and William C Hall (2010). Southern Subanen Aspiration, *Oceanic Linguistics* 49(2): 319–38.

Lobel, Jason W and Ade T Paputungan (2017). Notes from the Field: Lolak: Another Moribund Language of Indonesia, *Language Documentation and Conservation* 11: 328–63.

Lobel, Jason W and Labi H S Riwarung (2009). Maranao Revisited: An Overlooked Consonant Cluster and its Implications for Lexicography and Grammar, *Oceanic Linguistics* 48(2): 403–38.

Lobel, Jason W and Labi H S Riwarung (2011). Maranao: A Preliminary Phonological Sketch with Supporting Audio, *Language Documentation and Conservation* 5: 31–59.

Lobel, Jason W and Orlando Vertudez Surbano (2019). Notes from the Field: Remontado (Hatang-Kayi): A Moribund Language of the Philippines, with Supporting Audio, *Language Documentation and Conservation* 13: 1–34.

Löbner, Sebastian (1989). German *Schon-Erst-Noch*: An Integrated Analysis, *Linguistics and Philosophy* 12: 167–212.

Lockard, Craig A (1971). The Javanese as Emigrant: Observations on the Development of Javanese Settlements Overseas, *Indonesia* 11: 41–62.

Löfgren, Althea (2019). *Phasal Polarity Systems in Bantu Languages*. MA Thesis, Stockholm University.

Longacre, Robert E (1968). *Philippine Languages: Discourse, Paragraph and Sentence Structure*. Publications in Linguistics and Related Fields. Santa Ana, CA: Summer Institute of Linguistics.

Loofs-Wissowa, Helmut Hermann Ernst (1982). Prehistoric and Protohistoric Links Between the Indochinese Peninsula and the Philippines, as Exemplified by Two Types of Ear-Ornaments, *Journal of the Hong Kong Archaeological Society* IX: 57–76.

Lopez, Cecilio (1928). *Comparison of Tagalog and Iloko*. Hamburg: J J Augustin.

Lopez, Cecilio (1937). *Preliminary Study of the Affixes in Tagalog*. Manila: Publications of the Institute of National Language Bureau of Printing.

Lopez, Cecilio (1965). Contributions to a Comparative Philippine Syntax, in G B Milner and Eugénie J A Henderson (eds.), *Indo-Pacific Linguistics Studies II: Descriptive Linguistics, Lingua* 15: 3–16.

Los, Bettelou (2005). *The Rise of the to-Infinitive*. Oxford: Oxford University Press.

Loski, Russell A and Gail M Loski (1989). The Languages Indigenous to Eastern Seram and Adjacent Islands, in Wyn D Laidig (ed.), *Workpapers in Indonesian Languages and Cultures 6*. Ambon: Pattimura University and the Summer Institute of Linguistics, 103–41.

Lubis, Tasnim (2019). *Preliminary Documentation of Leukon Language*. Endangered Languages Archive. URL: http://hdl.handle.net/2196/00-0000-0000-0014-134E-C

Lynch, John (1973). Verbal Aspects of Possession in Melanesian Languages, *Oceanic Linguistics* 12(1–2): 69–102.

Lynch, John (1982). Towards a Theory of the Origin of the Oceanic Possessive Constructions, in Amran Halim, Lois Carrington and Stephen A Wurm (eds.), *Papers from the Third International Conference on Austronesian Linguistics: Currents in Oceanic*. Canberra: Pacific Linguistics, 243–68.

Lynch, John (1996). Proto-Oceanic Possessive Marking, in John Lynch and Faafo Pat (eds.), *Oceanic Studies: Proceedings of the First International Conference on Oceanic Linguistics*. Canberra: Pacific Linguistics, 93–110.

Lynch, John (2000). Reconstructing Proto-Oceanic Stress, *Oceanic Linguistics* 39(1): 53–82.

Lynch, John (2001). Passive and Food Possession in Oceanic Languages, in Andrew Pawley, Malcolm D Ross and Darrell Tryon (eds.), *The Boy from Bundaberg: Studies in Melanesian Linguistics in Honour of Tom Dutton*. Canberra: Pacific Linguistics, 193–214.

Lynch, John, Malcolm Ross and Terry Crowley (2002). *The Oceanic Languages*. London/New York: Routledge.

M A J (1972). A Note on English Loanwords in Bencoolenese Malay, *Berita Kadjian Sumatera* 1(2): 47.

Maan, G (1951). *Proeve van een Bulische spraakkunst* [Buli grammar]. The Hague: Martinus Nijhoff.

MacDonald, Alistair A (compiler) (2015). *Bahasa sehari-hari penduduk Nusaweleh (Seram Utara, Maluku, Indonesia)* [Daily language of the inhabitants of Nusaweleh, North Seram, Moluccas]. With Assistance from Boy Lekena, Ulis Mailisa, Alexander Lekena, Hendra Lilimau. Edinburgh: Royal (Dick) School of Veterinary Studies, University of Edinburgh.

Machali, Rochayah (2008). Cases of Linguistic Assimilation and Etymological Doublets in Javanese Words of Arabic Origin, in Paul Sidwell and Uri Tadmor (eds.), *SEALS XVI: Papers from the 16th Meeting of the Southeast Asian Linguistics Society (2006)*. Canberra: Pacific Linguistics, 47–63.

MacKnight, Charles Campbell (2011). The View from Marege: Australian Knowledge of Makassar and the Impact of the Trepang Industry Across Two Centuries, *Aboriginal History* 35: 121–43.

MacKnight, Charles Campbell (2012). *Bugis and Makasar: Two Short Grammars*. Canberra: Karuda Press.

MacLeod, Thomas R (1972). Verb Stem Classification in Umiray Dumaget, *Philippine Journal of Linguistics* 3: 43–74.

Maddieson, Ian (1984). *Patterns of Sounds*. Cambridge: Cambridge University Press.

Maddieson, Ian (2013a). Consonant Inventories, in Matthew S Dryer and Martin Haspelmath (eds.), *The World Atlas of Language Structures Online*. Leipzig: Max Planck Institute for Evolutionary Anthropology. URL: https://wals.info/chapter/1

Maddieson, Ian (2013b). Vowel Quality Inventories, in Matthew S Dryer and Martin Haspelmath (eds.), *The World Atlas of Language Structures Online*. Leipzig: Max Planck Institute for Evolutionary Anthropology. URL: https://wals.info/chapter/2

Maddieson, Ian (2013c). Glottalized Consonants, in Matthew S Dryer and Martin Haspelmath (eds.), *The World Atlas of Language Structures Online*. Leipzig: Max Planck Institute for Evolutionary Anthropology. URL: http://wals.info/chapter/7

Maddieson, Ian (2013d). Presence of Uncommon Consonants, in Matthew S Dryer and Martin Haspelmath (eds.), The World Atlas of Language Structures Online. Leipzig: Max Planck Institute for Evolutionary Anthropology. URL: http://wals.info/chapter/19

Maddieson, Ian (2013e). Uvular Consonants, in Matthew S Dryer and Martin Haspelmath (eds.), *The World Atlas of Language Structures Online*. Leipzig: Max Planck Institute for Evolutionary Anthropology. URL: http://wals.info/chapter/6

Maddieson, Ian (2013f). Consonant-Vowel Ratio, in Matthew S Dryer and Martin Haspelmath (eds.), *The World Atlas of Language Structures Online*. Leipzig: Max Planck Institute for Evolutionary Anthropology. URL: http://wals.info/chapter/3

Maddieson, Ian and Pang Keng-Fong (1993). Tone in Utsat, in J Edmondson and K Gregerson (eds.), *Tonality in Austronesian Languages*. Honolulu: University of Hawai'i Press, 75–89.

Mahdi, Waruno (1988). *Morphophonologische Besonderheiten und Historische Phonologie des Malagasy*. Berlin-Hamburg: Dietrich Reimer.

Mahdi, Waruno (1994). Some Austronesian Maverick Protoforms with Culture-Historical Implications, *Oceanic Linguistics* 33(1): 167–229, 33(2): 431–90.

Mahdi, Waruno (1995). Wie hießen die Malaien, bevor sie 'Malaien' hießen?, in A. Bormann, A. Graf, M. Voss (eds.), *Südostasien und Wir: Grundsatzdiskussionen und Fachbeiträge. Tagung des Arbeitskreises Südostasien und Ozeanien Hamburg 1993, Austronesiana. Studien zum austronesischen Südostasien und Ozeanien 1*. Hamburg: LIT-Verlag, 162–76.

Mahdi, Waruno (2001). Personal Nominal Words in Indonesian: An Anomaly in Morphological Classification, in Joel Bradshaw and Kenneth Rehg (eds.), *Issues in Austronesian Morphology: A Focusschrift for Byron W Bender*. Canberra: Pacific Linguistics, 163–93.

Mahdi, Waruno (2005). Old Malay, in Alexander Adelaar and Nikolaus P Himmelmann (eds.), *The Austronesian Languages of Asia and Madagascar*. London/New York: Routledge, 182–201.

Mahdi, Waruno (2008). Review of Russell Jones (ed.), (2007), *Loan-Words in Indonesian and Malay, Archipel* 76: 318–22.

Mahsun (1999). Variasi dialektal Bahasa Sumbawa – Kajian dialektologi diakronis [Dialect Variation in Sumbawa – A Study of Diachronic Dialectology]. Lombok, University of Mataram. Unpublished Manuscript.

Makboon, Sorat (1981). *Survey of Sea Peoples Dialects Along the West Coast of Thailand*. MA Thesis, Mahidol University.

Malicsi, Jonathan C (1974). *A Structural Sketch of Halitaq Baytan (A Sambal Aeta Dialect)*. MA Thesis, University of the Philippines—Diliman.

Malzac, Victorin (1960). *Grammaire malgache*. ($4^{th}$ edition; $1^{st}$ edition 1908] Paris: Société d'Éditions Géographiques, Maritimes et Coloniales.

Malinowski B (1922). *Argonauts of the Western Pacific*. London: G Routledge and Sons; New York: E P Dutton and Co.

Mallick S, H Li, M Lipson, I Mathieson, M Gymrek, F Racimo, M Zhao, N Chennagiri, et al. (2016). The Simons Genome Diversity Project: 300 Genomes from 142 Diverse Populations, *Nature* 538: 201–6.

Malmström H, A Linderholm, P Skoglund, J Stora, P Sjödin, M T Gilbert, G Holmlund, E Willerslev, M Jakobsson, K Lidén and A Götherström (2015). Ancient Mitochondrial DNA from the Northern Fringe of the Neolithic Farming Expansion in Europe Sheds Light on the Dispersion Process, *Philosophical Transactions of the Royal Society B: Biological Sciences* 370: 20130373.

Manda, Marthen L, Masao Yamaguchi and Hirotake Nakashima (2002). *Kosakata Dasar Bahasa Panasuan serta tata bahasa ringkas Bahasa Panasuan dan kosakata dasar Bahasa Tangkou serta tata bahasa ringkas Bahasa Tangkou* [Vocabularies and grammar sketches of Panasuan and Tangkou]. Kyoto: Endangered Languages of the Pacific Rim.

Mandaru, A. Mans, John W. Haan and Gomer Liufeto (1998). *Morfologi dan sintaksis bahasa Kemak* [Kemak morphology and syntax] Jakarta: Pusat Pembinaan dan Pengembangan Bahasa.

Manhitu, Yohanes (2007). *Kamus Indonesia - Tetun, Tetun - Indonesia* [Indonesian – Tetun and Tetun – Indonesian – English dictionary]. Jakarta: Gramedia Pustaka Utama.

Manlapaz, Edna (1981). *Kapampangan Literature*. Manila: Ateneo de Manila University.

Mantasiah R (2007). *Sintaksis Bahasa Kodeoha (Suatu kajian transformasi generatif)*. PhD Dissertation, Universitas Hasanuddin.

Manuel, Arsenio (1948). *Chinese Elements in the Tagalog Language, with Some Indication of Chinese Influence on Other Philippine Languages and Cultures, and an Excursion into Austronesian Linguistics*. Manila: Filipiniana Publications.

Manyambeang, A Kadir, Hamzah Mahmoed, Rabiana S Badudu, Tajuddin Maknun, A Kadir Mulya and Ambo Gani (1982/1983). *Struktur Bahasa Wawonii* [Wawoni structure]. Ujung Pandang: Proyek Penelitian Bahasa dan Sastra Indonesia dan Daerah Sulawesi Selatan.

Maree, Judith and Orland R Tomas (2012). *Ibatan to English Dictionary, with English, Filipino, Ilokano, Ivatan Indices*. Manila: Summer Institute of Linguistics Philippines.

Maree, Rundell D (2007). *Ibatan: A Grammatical Sketch of the Language of Babuyan Claro Island*. Manila: Linguistic Society of the Philippines.

Marsaja, I G (2008). *Desa Kolok - A Deaf Village and its Sign Language in Bali, Indonesia*. Nijmegen: Ishara Press.

Marshall, Craig (2000). A Phonological Description of Fordata, in Charles E. Grimes (ed.), *Spices from the East: Papers in Languages of Eastern Indonesia*. Canberra: Pacific Linguistics, 181–235.

Marshall, Craig (nd). *Fordata Dictionary*. Webonary, Summer Institute of Lingistics. URL: https://www.webonary.org/fordata/

Marshall, Craig and Sarah Marshall (1992). Reduplication in Fordata, in Donald A Burquest and Wyn D Laidig (eds.), *Descriptive Studies in Languages of Maluku*. Jakarta: Badan Penyelenggara Seri NUSA, Universitas Katolik Indonesia Atma Jaya, 23–30.

Martens, Michael P (1988a). Focus and Discourse in Uma, in Hein Steinhauer (ed.), *Papers in Western Austronesian Linguistics, No. 4*. Canberra: Pacific Linguistics, 239–56.

Martens, Michael P (1988b). Notes on Uma Verbs, in Hein Steinhauer (ed.), *Papers in Western Austronesian Linguistics, No. 4*. Canberra: Pacific Linguistics, 167–237.

Martens, Michael P (1988c). Phonology of Uma, in Hein Steinhauer (ed.), *Papers in Western Austronesian Linguistics, No. 4*. Canberra: Pacific Linguistics, 153–65.

Martens, Michael P (1988d). Focus or Ergativity? Pronoun Sets in Uma, in Hein Steinhauer (ed.), *Papers in Western Austronesian Linguistics, No. 4*. Canberra: Pacific Linguistics, 263–77.

Martens, Michael P (1989). The Badaic Languages of Central Sulawesi, in James N Sneddon (ed.), *Studies in Sulawesi Linguistics, Part I*. Jakarta: Badan Penyelenggara Seri Nusa, Universitas Katolik Indonesia Atma Jaya, 19–53.

Martens, Michael P (1997). *Proto Kaili-Pamona: Reconstruction of the Protolanguage of a Language Subgroup in Sulawesi*. Unpublished Computer File.

Martens, Michael P and Martha Martens (1988). Some Notes on the Inelegant Glottal: A Problem in Uma Phonology, in Hein Steinhauer (ed.), *Papers in Western Austronesian Linguistics, No. 4*. Canberra: Pacific Linguistics, 279–81.

Martinet, André (1955). *Économie des changements phonétiques*. Berne: A Francke.

Maryott, Kenneth R (1974). Sangil Elevationals and the Performative Analysis, *Work Papers of the Summer Institute of Linguistics, University of North Dakota Session* Vol. 18 Article 6: 139–98.

Maryott, Kenneth R (1990). Dari mana asal konjungsi Bahasa Sangir? [Where does the Sangirese conjunction come from?], in Husen Abas and T David Andersen (eds.), *Bahasa-Bahasa daerah Sulawesi dalam konteks bahasa nasional*. Ujung Pandang: UNHAS-SIL, 12–34.

Maskikit-Essed, Raechel and Carlos Gussenhoven (2016). No Stress, No Pitch Accent, No Prosodic Focus: The Case of Ambonese Malay, *Phonology* 33: 353–89.

Massam, Diane (2009). Noun Incorporation: Essentials and Extensions, *Language and Linguistics Compass* 3/4: 1076–96.

Matic, Dejan and Daniel Wedgwood (2013). The Meanings of Focus: The Significance of an Interpretation-Based Category in Cross-Linguistic Analysis, *Journal of Linguistics* 49: 127–63.

Matisoff, James A (1973). Tonogenesis in Southeast Asia, in Larry M Hyman (ed.), *Consonant Types and Tone*, Southern California Occasional Papers in Linguistics No 1. Los Angeles: University of California Los Angeles, 71–95.

Matisoff, James A (1975). Rhinoglottophilia: The Mysterious Connection Between Nasality and Glottality, in Charles A Ferguson, Larry M Hyman and John J Ohala (eds.), *Nasálfest: Papers from A Symposium on Nasals and Nasalization*. Universals Language Project. Stanford: Stanford University, 265–87.

Matisoff, James A (2003). Aslian: Mon-Khmer of the Malay Peninsula, *Mon-Khmer Studies* 33: 1–58.

Matsumura, Hirofumi, Hsiao-Chun Hung, Charles Higham, Chi Zhang et al. (2019). Craniometrics Reveal Two Layers of Prehistoric Human Dispersal in Eastern Eurasia, *Scientific Reports* 9: 1451.

Matsumura, Hirofumi, Ken-Ichi Shinoda, Truman Shimanjuntak, Adhi Agus Oktaviana et al. (2018). Cranio-Morphometric and Adna Corroboration of the Austronesian Dispersal Model in Ancient Island Southeast Asia: Support from Gua Harimau, Indonesia, *PLOS One* 13 (6):E0198689.

Matsumura, Takashi and Michiko Matsumura (1991). A Preliminary Grammar Sketch of the Irarutu Language, *Workpapers in Indonesian Languages and Cultures* 10: 75–110.

Mattes, Veronika (2014). *Types of Reduplication: A Case Study of Bikol*. Berlin/Boston: de Gruyter Mouton.

Mattes, Veronika (2017). Iconicity in the Lexicon: The Semantic Categories of Lexical Reduplication, *Studies in Language* 41: 813–42.

Matthes, B F (1858). *Makassaarsche spraakkunst* [Makasar grammar]. Amsterdam: Frederik Muller.

Matthes, B F (1874). *Boegineesch-Hollandsch woordenboek, met Hollandsch-Boeginesche woordenlijst en verklaring van een tot opheldering bijgevoegde ethnographischen Atlas*. [Bugis–Dutch dictionary with Dutch–Bugis appendix and guidelines for the use of an attached ethnographic atlas]. 's-Gravenhage: Martinus Nijhoff.

Matthes, B F (1875). *Boegineesche spraakkunst*. [Bugis grammar]. 's-Gravenhage: Martinus Nijhoff.

Matti, David F (1991). Phonology of Mamasa, in René van den Berg (ed.), *Sulawesi Phonologies*. Ujung Pandang: Summer Institute of Linguistics in Cooperation with the Department of Education and Culture, 53–97.

Matti, David F (1994). Mamasa Pronoun Sets, in René van den Berg (ed.), *Studies in Sulawesi Linguistics, Part III*. Special issue of *NUSA* 36. Jakarta: Badan Penyelenggara Seri NUSA, Universitas Katolik Indonesia Atma Jaya, 65–89.

Maurer, Jean-Luc (2002). The Javanese in New Caledonia: The Terrors of Exile and the Hazards of Integration, *Autrepart* 2: 67–90.

Maurer, Jean-Luc (2010). The Thin Red Line Between Indentured and Bonded Labour: Javanese Workers in New Caledonia in the Early 20th Century, *Asian Journal of Social Science* 38(6): 866–79.

Maurer, Philippe (2011). *The Former Portuguese Creole of Batavia and Tugu (Indonesia)*. London/Colombo: Battlebridge Publications.

May, Stephen (2012). *Language and Minority Rights: Ethnicity, Nationalism and the Politics of Language*. 2nd edition. New York: Routledge.

Mayani, Luh Anik (2013). *A Grammar of Tajio: A Language Spoken in Central Sulawesi*. PhD Dissertation, University of Cologne.

Mazières S, P Oviedo, C Kamel, P Bailly, C Costedoat and J Chiaroni (2018). Genes Flow by the Channels of Culture: The Genetic Imprint of Matrilocality in Ngazidja, Comoros Islands, *European Journal of Human Genetics* 26(8): 1222–6.

Mbete, Aron Meko (1990). *Rekonstruksi protobahasa Bali-Sasak-Sumbawa*. [A reconstruction of Proto-Bali-Sasak-Sumbawa]. PhD Dissertation, Universitas Indonesia, Jakarta.

McCarthy, John (2001). *A Thematic Guide to Optimality Theory*. Cambridge: Cambridge University Press.

McCarthy, John J and Alan S Prince (1994). The Emergence of the Unmarked: Optimality in Prosodic Morphology, in Mercè González (ed.), *Proceedings of the North East Linguistic Society 24*. Amherst: Graduate Linguistics Students Association, 333–79.

McColl, Hugh, Fernando Racimo, Lasse Vinner, Fabrice Demeter et al. (2018). The Prehistoric Peopling of Southeast Asia, *Science* 361(6397): 88–92.

McConvell, William (unpublished a). A Case for Central-Southern Sulawesi. Manuscript.

McConvell, William (unpublished b). Notes on the Membership and Structure of the South Sulawesi Group. Manuscript.

McDonnell, Bradley (2008a). A Conservative Vowel Phoneme Inventory of Sumatra: The Case of Besemah, *Oceanic Linguistics* 47(2): 409–32.

McDonnell, Bradley (2008b). Possessive Constructions in Ende: A Language of Eastern Indonesia, *Studies in Philippine* Languages *and* Cultures: 10-ICAL Austronesian Papers 18: 108–18.

McDonnell, Bradley J (2016a). Acoustic Correlates of Stress in Besemah, in Yanti and Timothy McKinnon (eds.), *Studies in Language Typology and Change*. Special issue of *NUSA* 60: 1–28.

McDonnell, Bradley (2016b). *Symmetrical Voice Constructions in Besemah: A Usage-Based Approach*. PhD Dissertation, University of California, Santa Barbara.

McDonnell, Bradley and Uri Tadmor (2015). Reconstructing Negation and Negative Suppletive Existentials in Malayic. Presentation: 13th International Conference on Austronesian Linguistics, Taipei, May 2015.

McDonnell, Bradley (2018). Besemah negation in typological and historical perspective. Paper presented at Syntax of the World's Languages 8, Paris, France. September 4.

McDonnell, Bradley (2019). Documentation of the multilingual linguistic practices of the Nasal speech community. Collection BJM02 at PARADISEC. DOI: 10.26278/5f46870d43f29

McDowell, Jonathan and Karl Anderbeck (2020). *The Malay Lects of Southern Sumatra*. Honolulu: University of Hawai'i Press.

McFarland, Curtis D (1974). *The Dialects of the Bikol Area*. PhD Dissertation, Yale University.

McFarland, Curtis D (1978). Definite Objects and Subject Selection in Philippine Languages, in Casilda Edrial-Luzares and Austin Hale (eds.), *Studies in Philippine Linguistics, Vol. 2*. Manila: Linguistic Society of the Philippines, 139–82.

McFarland, Curtis D (1980). *A Linguistic Atlas of the Philippines*. Study of Languages and Cultures of Asia and Africa Monograph Series, No. 15. Tokyo: Institute for the Study of Languages and Cultures of Asia and Africa.

McGinn, Richard (1982). *Outline of Rejang Syntax*. Jakarta: Badan Penyelenggara Seri Nusa, Universitas Atma Jaya.

McGinn, Richard (1999). The Position of the Rejang Language of Sumatra in Relation to Malay and the Ablaut Languages of Northwest Borneo, in Elizabeth Zeitoun and Paul Jen-Kuei Li (eds.), *Selected Papers from the Eighth International Conference on Austronesian Linguistics*. Symposium Series of Linguistics, No 1. Taipei: Academia Sinica, 205–26.

McGinn, Richard (2003). Raising of PMP *a in Bukar-Sadong Land Dayak and Rejang, in John Lynch (ed.), *Issues in Austronesian Historical Phonology*. Canberra: Pacific Linguistics, 37–64.

McGinn, Richard (2005). What the Rawas Dialect Reveals About the Linguistic History of Rejang, *Oceanic Linguistics* 44(1): 12–64.

McGregor, Ronald Stuart (1993). *The Oxford Hindī-English Dictionary*. Oxford: Oxford University Press.

McKaughan, Howard P (1958). *The Inflection and Syntax of Maranao Verbs*. Publications of the Institute of National Language. Manila: Bureau of Printing.

McKaughan, Howard P (1959). Semantic Components of Pronoun Systems: Maranao, *Word* 15(1): 101–2.

McKaughan, Howard P (1962). Overt Relation Markers in Maranao, *Language* 38: 47–51.

McKaughan, Howard P (2002a). *Iranun Traditional Narratives*. Kota Kinabalu, Malaysia: Institut Linguistik (Summer Institute of Linguistics).

McKaughan, Howard P (2002b). *Iranun Word List from Traditional Narratives (with Iranun Verb Structure and an English Index)*. Kota Kinabalu, Malaysia: Institut Linguistik (Summer Institute of Linguistics).

McKaughan, Howard P (2002c). *Short Texts from the Iranun of Sabah*. Kota Kinabalu, Malaysia: Institut Linguistik (Summer Institute of Linguistics).

McKaughan, Howard P and Batua A Macaraya (1967). *A Maranao Dictionary*. Honolulu: University of Hawai'i Press.

McKaughan, Howard P and Batua A Macaraya (1996). *A Maranao Dictionary*. Manila: De La Salle University Press.

McKenzie, Robin (1991). Phonology of Aralle-Tabulahan, in René van den Berg (ed.), *Sulawesi Phonologies*. Ujung Pandang: Summer Institute of Linguistics in Cooperation with the Department of Education and Culture, 98–149.

McKenzie, Robin (1997). Downstream to Here: Geographically Determined Spatial Deictics in Aralle-Tabulahan (Sulawesi), in Gunter Senft (ed.), *Referring to Space: Studies in Austronesian and Papuan Languages*. Oxford: Oxford University Press, 221–490.

McKinnon, Timothy (2011). *The Morphophonology and Morphosyntax of Kerinci Word-Shape Alternations*. PhD Dissertation, University of Delaware.

McKinnon, Timothy (2012). A Survey of Phonation Driven Vowel Shifts in Traditional Malay(ic). Presentation: *Sixteenth International Symposium of Malay/Indonesian Linguistics*, Kelaniya, Sri Lanka, 23 June.

McKinnon, Timothy, Gabriella Hermon, Yanti and Peter Cole (2018). From Phonology to Syntax: Insights from Jangkat Malay, in Huba Bartos, Marcel den Dikken, Zoltan Banreti and Tamas Varati, *Boundaries Crossed, at the Interfaces of Morphosyntax, Phonology, Pragmatics and Semantics*. Cham (Switzerland): Springer International, 349–71.

McKinnon, Timothy, Yanti, Peter Cole and Gabriella Hermon (2011). Object agreement and 'pro-drop' in Kerinci Malay, *Language* 87 (4): 715–50.

McKinnon, Timothy, Yanti, Peter Cole and Gabriella Hermon (2015). Infixation and Apophony in Malay: Description and Developmental States, *Linguistik Indonesia* 33: 1–19.

McLellan, James (2014). Strategies for Revitalizing Endangered Borneo Languages: A Comparison Between Negara Brunei Darussalam and Sarawak, Malaysia, *Southeast Asia: A Multidisciplinary Journal* 14: 14–22.

McWhorter, John (2008a). The Diachrony of Malay: What Just Happens? Presentation: Twelfth International Symposium on Malay/Indonesian Linguistics, Leiden.

McWhorter, John H (2008b). Why Does a Language Undress: Strange Cases in Indonesia, in F Karlsson, M Miestamo and K Sinnemäki (eds.), *Language Complexity: Typology, Contact, Change*. Amsterdam: John Benjamins, 167–90.

McWhorter, John H (2019). The Radically Isolating Languages of Flores: A Challenge to Diachronic Theory, *Journal of Historical Linguistics* 9(2): 177–207.

McWhorter, John H (2007). *Language interrupted: signs of non-native acquisition in standard language grammars*. New York: Oxford University Press.

Meacham, William (1984–85). On the Probability of Austronesian Origins in South China, *Asian Perspectives* 26(1): 89–106.

Meacham, William (1995). Austronesian Origins and the Peopling of Taiwan, in Paul Jen-Kuei Li, Cheng-Hwa Tsang, Dah-an Ho, Ying-Kuei Huang and Chiu-Yu Tseng, (eds.), *Austronesian Studies Relating to Taiwan*. Taipei: Institute of History and Philology, Academia Sinica, Taipei, 227–54.

Mead, David (1996). The Evidence for Final Consonants in Proto-Bungku-Tolaki, *Oceanic Linguistics* 35: 180–94.

Mead, David (1998). *Proto-Bungku-Tolaki: Reconstruction of its Phonology and Aspects of its Morphosyntax*. PhD Dissertation, Rice University.

Mead, David (1999). *The Bungku-Tolaki Languages of South-Eastern Sulawesi, Indonesia*. Canberra: Pacific Linguistics.

Mead, David (2001a). A Preliminary Sketch of the Bobongko Language, in Wyn D Laidig (ed.), *Studies in Sulawesi Linguistics, Part VII*. Special issue of *NUSA* 49. Jakarta: Universitas Atma Jaya, Badan Penyelenggara Seri Nusa, 61–94.

Mead, David (2001b). The Numeral Confix *i- -(e)n, *Oceanic Linguistics* 40: 167–76.

Mead, David (2001c). Ihwal konjungsi dalam Bahasa Mori Bawah di Sulawesi Tengah, [About conjunctions in Mori Bawah, Central Sulawesi], in Kaswanti Purwo (ed.), *Pertemuan Linguistik Lembaga Bahasa Atma Jaya (PELBBA)* 14: Tipologi bahasa pragmatic pengajaran bahasa. Yogyakarta: Kanisius, 1–32.

Mead, David (2003a). Evidence for a Celebic Supergroup, in John Lynch (ed.), *Issues in Austronesian Historical Phonology*. Canberra: Pacific Linguistics, 115–41.

Mead, David (2003b). The Saluan-Banggai Microgroup of Eastern Sulawesi, in John Lynch (ed.), *Issues in Austronesian Historical Phonology*. Canberra: Pacific Linguistics, 65–86.

Mead, David (2005). Mori Bawah, in Alexander Adelaar and Nikolaus P Himmelmann (eds.), *The Austronesian Languages of Asia and Madagascar*. London: Routledge, 683–708.

Mead, David (2008). When to Use a Genitive Pronoun in Mori Bawah (Sulawesi, Indonesia), *Studies in Philippine Languages and Cultures* 17: 137–78.

Mead, David (2013). *Wotu Grammar Notes*. Sulawesi Language Alliance. URL: http://sulang.org

Mead, David (2014). *How Do You Slice the Pie? Ways of Looking at the Kaili Language Area of Central Sulawesi, Indonesia*. Sulawesi Language Alliance. URL: http://sulang.org

Mead, David (2017). *Kaisabu Word List and Notes*. Sulawesi Language Alliance. URL: http://sulang.org

Mead, David (nd a). The Bobongko Voice Inflection System as Flowchart. Unpublished manuscript.

Mead, David (nd b). The fate of Proto Malayo-Polynesian *d, *z, *j, *r and *l in Proto Minahasan and the Minahasan languages. Unpublished manuscript.

Mead, David and Edy Pasanda (2015). *An Initial Appreciation of the Dialect Situation in Saluan and Batui (Eastern Sulawesi, Indonesia)*. Dallas: Summer Institute of Linguistics International.

Mead, David and Joanna Smith (2015). The Voice Systems of Wotu, Barang-Barang and Wolio: Synchronic and Diachronic Perspectives, in Malcolm D Ross and I Wayan Arka (eds.), *Language Change in Austronesian Languages: Papers from 12-ICAL, Volume 3*. Canberra: Asia-Pacific Linguistics, 51–94.

Mead, David and Myung-Young Lee (2007). *Mapping Indonesian Bajau Communities in Sulawesi*. Dallas: Summer Institute of Linguistics International.

Mead, David and Scott Youngman (2008). Verb Serialization in Tolaki, in Gunter Senft and Miriam van Staden (eds.), *Serial Verb Constructions in Austronesian and Papuan Languages*. Canberra: Pacific Linguistics, 113–39.

Merrifield, Scott and Martinus Salea (1996). *North Sulawesi Language Survey*. Dallas: Summer Institute of Linguistics.

Metcalf, Peter (1974). The Baram District: A Survey of Kenyah, Kayan, and Penan Peoples, in Jérôme Rousseau (ed.), *The Peoples of Central Borneo*, Sarawak Museum Journal Special Issue 22 (New Series 43). Kuching: Sarawak Museum, 29–42.

Metslang, Helle, Külli Habicht and Karl Pajusalu (2017). Where Do Polar Question Markers Come from? *STUF - Language Typology and Universals* 70(3): 489–521.

Mettler, Heidi and Mettler, Anton (1990). Yamdena Phonology, *Workpapers in Indonesian Languages and Cultures* 8: 29–79.

Middelkoop, Pieter (1950). Proeve van een Timorese grammatica, [Timorese Grammar]. *Bijdragen tot Taal-, Land- en Volkenkunde* 106: 375–517.

Miestamo, Matti (2005). *Standard Negation. The Negation of Declarative Verbal Main Clauses in A Typological Perspective.* Berlin: Mouton de Gruyter.

Miestamo, Matti, Dik Bakker and Antti Arppe (2016). Sampling for Variety, *Linguistic Typology* 20: 233–96.

Milke, Wilhelm (1958). Ozeanische Verwandtschaftsnamen, *Zeitschrift für Ethnologie* 83: 226–9.

Miller, Carolyn (1993). Kadazan-Dusun Phonology Revisited, in Michael E Boutin and Inka Pekkanen (eds.), *Phonological Descriptions of Sabah Languages.* Kota Kinabalu: Sabah Museum, 1–14.

Miller, Helen and Jeanne Miller (1991). *Mamanwa Texts.* Manila: Studies in Philippine Linguistics Supplementary series, Summer Institute of Linguistics.

Miller, Jeanne (1964). The Role of Verb Stems in the Mamanwa Kernel Verbal Clauses, *Oceanic Linguistics* 3: 87–100.

Miller, Jeanne (1973). Semantic Structure of Mamanwa Verbs, *Linguistics: An International Review* 110: 74–81.

Miller, Jeanne and Helen Miller (1969). Nonverbal Clauses in Mamanwa, in Jeanne Miller and Helen Miller (eds.), *Papers in Philippine Linguistics No. 2.* Canberra: Pacific Linguistics, 1–9.

Miller, Jeanne and Helen Miller (1976). *Mamanwa Grammar.* Huntington Beach, California: Summer Institute of Linguistics.

Miller, Mark T (2007). *A Grammar of West Coast Bajau (Malaysia).* PhD Dissertation, University of Texas at Arlington.

Miller, Mark T (2014). A Comparative Look at the Major Voice Oppositions in Sama-Bajaw Languages and Indonesian/ Malay, in I Wayan Arka and Ni Luh Ketut Mas Indrawati (eds.), *Papers from 12-ICAL, Vol. 2: Argument Realisations and Related Constructions in Austronesian Languages.* Canberra: Asia-Pacific Linguistics, 303–12.

Mills, Roger F (1975a). *Proto South Sulawesi and Proto Austronesian Phonology.* PhD Dissertation, University of Michigan, Ann Arbor.

Mills, Roger F (1975b). The Reconstruction of Proto-South-Sulawesi, *Archipel* 10: 205–24.

Mills, Roger F (1981). Additional Addenda, in Robert Blust (ed.), *Historical Linguistics in Indonesia, Part I.* Special issue of *NUSA* 10. Jakarta: Badan Penyelenggara Seri Nusa, Universitas Atma Jaya, 59–82.

Mills, Roger F (1991). Tanimbar-Kei: An Eastern Austronesian Subgroup, in Robert Blust (ed.), *Currents in Pacific Linguistics: Papers on Austronesian Languages and Ethnolinguistics in Honour of George W Grace.* Canberra: Pacific Linguistics, 241–63.

Milroy, James and Lesley Milroy (1985). Linguistic Change, Social Network and Speaker Innovation, *Journal of Linguistics* 21: 339–84.

Ministry of Education (1972). *Adơi Pơsram Pơnuaĭ Chru: Adŭ Mơgru Chơmrờp* [Study Chru words: a primer], Vol. 3. Saigon: Ministry of Education.

Mintz, Malcolm W (2004). *Bikol Dictionary: Diksionáriong Bíkol. Volume 2 Bikol-English.* Perth: Indonesian/Malay Texts and Resources.

Mintz, Malcolm W and Jose del Rosario Britanico (1985). *Bikol-English Dictionary.* Quezon City, Philippines: New Day Publishers.

Mirante, Edith T (2014). *The Wind in the Bamboo: A Journey in Search of Asia's Negrito Indigenous People.* Hong Kong: Orchid Press.

Mistica, Meladel, Timothy Baldwin and I Wayan Arka (2011). Word Classes in Indonesian: A Linguistic Reality or a Convenient Fallacy in Natural Language Processing? Presentation: 25th PACLIC (Pacific Asia Conference on Language, Information and Computation), at Singapore, 16–18 December 2011.

Mitchell, Peter (2019). Settling Madagascar: When Did People First Colonize the World's Largest Island? *Journal of Island and Coastal Archaeology*, DOI: 10.1080/15564894.2019.1582567

Mithun, Marianne (1984). The Evolution of Noun Incorporation, *Language* 60(4): 847–95.

Mithun, Marianne (1986). On the Nature of Noun Incorporation, *Language* 62(1): 32–8.

Mithun, Marianne (1994). The Implications of Ergativity for a Philippine Voice System, in Barbara A Fox and Paul J Hopper (eds.), *Voice: Form and Function.* Amsterdam/Philadelphia: John Benjamins, 247–77.

Mithun, Marianne and Basri, Hasan (1986). The Phonology of Selayarese, *Oceanic Linguistics* 25: 210–54.

Miyake, Yoshimi (2011). Reduplication in Javanese, *Asian and African Languages and Linguistics* 6: 45–59.

Mofu, Suriel (2009). *Biak Morphosyntax*, PhD Dissertation, University of Oxford.

Mohd Jan, Jariah (2011). Malay Javanese Migrants in Malaysia: Contesting or Creating Identity? in Dipika Mukherjee and Maya Khemlani David (eds.), *National Language Planning and Language Shifts in Malaysian Minority Communities: Speaking in Many Tongues.* Amsterdam: Amsterdam University Press, 163–72.

Montrul, Silvina (2016). *The Acquisition of Heritage Languages.* Cambridge: Cambridge University Press.

Moravcsik, Edith A (1978). Reduplicative Constructions, in Joseph H Greenberg (ed.), *Universals of Human Language, Volume 3.* Stanford: Stanford University Press, 297–334.

Morgan, J L (1978). Two Types of Conventions in Indirect Speech Acts, in P Cole (ed.), *Syntax and Semantics: Pragmatics.* New York: Academic Press.

Moriguchi, Tsunekazu (1983). A Preliminary Report on Ivatan Dialects, in K Shirahihara, Y Aoyagi and M Koomoto (eds.), *Batan Island and Northern Luzon: Archaeological, Ethnological and Linguistic Survey.* Japan: University of Kumamoto Press, 205–53.

Moro, Francesca R (2010). *A Sketch Grammar of Dampelas, A Language of Central Sulawesi.* MA Thesis, University of Leiden.

Moro, Francesca R (2014). Resultative Constructions in Heritage Ambon Malay in the Netherlands, *Linguistics in the Netherlands* 31(1): 78–92.

Moro, Francesca R (2016). *Dynamics of Ambon Malay: Comparing Ambon and the Netherlands.* PhD Dissertation, Radboud University.

Moro, Francesca R (2017). Aspectual Distinctions in Dutch-Ambon Malay Bilingual Heritage Speakers, *International Journal of Bilingualism* 21(2): 178–93.

Moro, Francesca R (2018). Divergence in Heritage Ambon Malay in the Netherlands: The Role of Social-Psychological Factors, *International Journal of Bilingualism* 22(4): 395–411.

Moro, Francesca R (2019). Loss of Morphology in Alorese (Austronesian): Simplification in Adult Language Contact, *Journal of Language Contact* 12(2): 378–403.

Moro, Francesca R and Marian Klamer (2015). Give-Constructions in Heritage Ambon Malay in the Netherlands, *Journal of Language Contact* 8(2): 263–98.

Morris, Max (1900). *Die Mentawai-Sprache.* Berlin: C Skopnik.

Mörseburg A, L Pagani, F X Ricaut, B Yngvadottir, E Harney, C Castillo, T Hoogervorst, T Antao, P Kusuma, N Brucato, A Cardona, D Pierron, T Letellier, J Wee, S Abdullah, M Metspalu and T Kivisild (2016). Multi-Layered Population Structure in Island Southeast Asians, *European Journal of Human Genetics* 24: 1605–11.

Mortensen, Christian J (2018). Subject and Pivot in Symmetrical Voice: The Case of Lun Bawang, *University of Hawai'i Working Papers in Linguistics* 49(4): 1–9.

Mosel, Ulrike and Even Hovdhaugen (1992). *Samoan Reference Grammar.* Oslo: The Institute for Comparative Research in Human Culture.

Moseley, Christopher (ed.) (2007). *Encyclopedia of the World's Endangered Languages.* London: Routledge.

Mourant A E, A C Kopeé and K Domaniewska-Sobczak (1976). *The Distribution of the Human Blood Groups and Other Polymorphisms.* Oxford: Oxford University Press.

Moussay, Gérard (1971). *Dictionnaire căm - vietnamien - français.* Phanrang: Centre Culturel Căm.

Moussay, Gérard (1981). *La langue minangkabau.* Paris: Association Archipel - L'Harmattan.

Moussay, Gérard (1995). *Dictionnaire minangkabau - indonesien - français.* Paris: L'Harmattan. Two Volumes.

Moussay, Gérard (2006). *Grammaire de la langue cam.* Paris: Les Indes Savantes.

Msaidie S, A Ducourneau, G Boetsch, G Longepied, K Papa, C Allibert, A A Yahaya, J Chiaroni and M J Mitchell (2011). Genetic Diversity on the Comoros Islands Shows Early Seafaring as Major Determinant of Human Biocultural Evolution in the Western Indian Ocean, *European Journal of Human Genetics* 19: 89–94.

Mufwene, Salikoko (2002). Competition and Selection in Language Evolution, *Selection* 3(1): 45–56.

Muhadjir (1981). *Morphology of Jakarta dialect, affixation and reduplication.* Jakarta: Badan Penyelenggara Seri Nusa, Universitas Atma Jaya.

Mulder, Jean and Arthur Schwartz (1981). On the Subject of Advancements in the Philippine Languages, *Studies in Language* 5: 227–68.

Müller-Gotama, Franz (2001). *Sundanese.* Munich: LINCOM.

Mundhenk, Alice Tegenfeldt and Hella Goschnick (1977). Haroi Phonemes, in D D Thomas, E W Lee and N Đ Liêm (eds.), *Papers in Southeast Asian Linguistics, No. 4.* Canberra: Pacific Linguistics, 1–15.

Murdock, George Peter (1959). *Africa: its Peoples and Their Culture History.* New York and Toronto and London: McGraw Hill.

Murdock, George Peter (1964). Genetic Classification of the Austronesian Languages: A Key to Oceanic Culture History, *Ethnology* 3(2): 117–26.

Murdock, George Peter (1968). Patterns of Sibling Terminology, *Ethnology* 7: 1–24.

Musgrave, Simon (1998). A Focus Construction, in Peter Austin (ed.), *Working Papers in Sasak, Vol. 1.* Melbourne: Department of Linguistics and Applied Linguistics, University of Melbourne, 91–104.

Musgrave, Simon (2001). *Non-Subject Arguments in Indonesian.* PhD Dissertation, The University of Melbourne.

Musgrave, Simon (2007). Typology and Geography in Eastern Indonesia, in Timothy Jowan Curnow (ed.), *Selected Papers from the 2007 Conference of the Australian Linguistic Society*, 1–27. URL: http://www.als.asn.au

Musgrave, Simon (2010). Reduced Pronouns and Arguments in Sou Amana Teru, Ambon, in Michael C Ewing and Marian Klamer (eds.), *East Nusantara: Typological and Areal Analyses.* Canberra: Pacific Linguistics, 143–64.

Musgrave, Simon and Michael C Ewing (2006). Language and Religion: A Case Study of Two Ambonese Communities, *International Journal of the Sociology of Language* 179: 179–94.

Muthiah, Sasi Rekha (2007). *A Grammar of Singapore Indian Malay.* MA Thesis, National University of Singapore.

Nababan, P W J (1981). *A Grammar of Toba-Batak.* Canberra: Pacific Linguistics.

Nagatsu K (2013). Persisting Maritime Frontiers and Multi-Layered Networks in Wallacea. Presentation: Asian Core Program Seminar (Japan Society for the Promotion of Science), Kyoto.

Nagaya, Naonori (2007). Information Structure and Constituent Order in Tagalog, *Language and Linguistics* 8(1): 343–72.

Nagaya, Naonori (2011). *The Lamaholot Language of Eastern Indonesia.* PhD Dissertation, Rice University.

Nagaya, Naonori (2013). Voice and Grammatical Relations in Lamaholot of Eastern Indonesia, in Alexander Adelaar (ed.), *Voice Variation in Austronesian Languages of Indonesia.* Special issue of *NUSA* 54, 85–119.

Nagaya, Naonori (2014). Ditransitives and Benefactives in Lamaholot, in I Wayan Arka and Ni Luh Ketut Mas Indrawati (eds.), *Argument Realisations and Related Constructions in Austronesian Languages: Papers from 12-ICAL, Volume 2.* Canberra: Asia-Pacific Linguistics, 227–45.

Nagaya, Naonori (2015). Possession and Nominalization in Lamaholot. Presentation: 13th International Conference on Austronesian Linguistics, July 18–23, Academia Sinica, Taiwan.

Na'im, Akhsan and Hendry Syaputra (2011). *Kewarganegaraan, suku bangsa, agama dan bahasa sehari-hari penduduk Indonesia: hasil Sensus Penduduk 2010.* [Citizenship, Ethnicity, Religion and Daily Language of Indonesians: Results of the Population Census 2010]. Jakarta: Badan Pusat Statistik.

Nakhleh, Luay, Don Ringe and Tandy Warnow (2005). Perfect Phylogenetic Networks: A New Methodology for Reconstructing the Evolutionary History of Natural Languages, *Language* 81: 382–420.

Napsin, Syahrul, Zainal Abidin Naning, Selamet Abdullah, Zulkarnain Mustafa (1981). *Struktur Bahasa Sekak* [Sekak structure]. Jakarta: Pusat Pembinaan dan Pengembangan Bahasa.

Narfafan, Sutriani (2011). Arguni Wordlist. Unpublished wordlist.

Nash, David (1997). Comparative Flora Terminology of the Central Northern Territory Area, in Patrick McConvell and Nicholas Evans (eds.), *Comparative Linguistics and Australian Prehistory*. Oxford: Oxford University Press, 187–206.

Natarina, Ari (2018). *Complementation in Balinese: Typological, Syntactic and Cognitive Perspectives*. PhD Dissertation, University of Iowa.

Naw Say Bay (1995). The Phonology of the Dung Dialect of Moken, in David Bradley (ed.), *Studies in Burmese* Languages, *Vol. 13*. Canberra: Pacific Linguistics, 193–205.

Naylor, Paz Buenaventura (1975). Topic, Focus and Emphasis in the Tagalog Verbal Clause, *Oceanic Linguistics* 14: 12–79.

Naylor, Paz Buenaventura (1978). Toward Focus in Austronesian, in Stephen A Wurm and Lois Carrington (eds.), *Second International Conference on Austronesian Linguistics: Proceedings*. Canberra: Pacific Linguistics, 395–442.

Naylor, Paz Buenaventura (1986a). On the Pragmatics of Focus, in Paul Geraghty, Lois Carrington and Stephen A Wurm (eds.), *FOCAL 1: Papers from the Fourth International Conference on Austronesian Linguistics*, 43–57.

Naylor, Paz Buenaventura (1986b). On the Semantics of Reduplication, in Paul Geraghty, Lois Carrington and Stephen A Wurm (eds.), *FOCAL I: Papers from the Fourth International Conference on Austronesian Linguistics*. Canberra: Pacific Linguistics, 175–85.

Nedjalkov, Vladimir P (ed.) (2007). *Typology of Reciprocal Categories and Constructions*. Amsterdam: John Benjamins.

Needham, Rodney (1962). *Structure and Sentiment: A Test Case in Social Anthropology*. Chicago and London: University of Chicago Press.

Nelson, Greg. C and Scott M Fitzpatrick (2006). Preliminary Investigations of the Chelechol Ra Orrak Cemetery, Republic of Palau: I, Skeletal Biology and Paleopathology, *Anthropological Science* 114: 1–12.

Nettle Daniel (2007). Language and Genes: A New Perspective on the Origins of Human Cultural Diversity, *Proceedings of the National Academy of Sciences USA* 104: 10755–6.

Newell, Leonard E and Francis Bon'og Poligon (1993). *Batad Ifugao Dictionary with Ethnographic Notes*. Manila: Linguistic Society of the Philippines.

Newman, John (1984–1985). Nasal Replacement in Western Austronesian: An Overview, *Philippine Journal of Linguistics* 15–16: 1–17.

Nguyen Kim Dung (2017). The Sa Huynh Culture in Ancient Regional Trade Networks: A Comparative Study of Ornaments, in Philip J Piper, Hirofumi Matsumura and David Bulbeck (eds.), *New Perspectives in Southeast Asian and Pacific Prehistory*. Canberra: Australian National University Press, 311–32.

Nguyễn Thị Minh Tâm (2006). *Topics in Ede Syntax*. MA Thesis, University of Oregon.

Nguyễn Thị Minh Tâm (2013a). Expressive Forms in Bih: A Highland Chamic Language of Vietnam, in J P Williams (ed.), *The Aesthetics of Grammar: Sound and Meaning in the Languages of Mainland Southeast Asia*. Cambridge: Cambridge University Press, 207–15.

Nguyễn Thị Minh Tâm (2013b). *A Grammar of Bih*. PhD Dissertation, University of Oregon.

Nguyễn Văn Huệ (2003). Nguyên Âm Mũi Hóa Trong Tiếng Raglai [Nasalized vowels in Raglai], *Những Vấn Đề Văn Hóa Và Ngôn Ngữ Raglai* [Raglai Cultural and Linguistic Questions]. Hồ Chí Minh City: Nhà Xuất Bản Đại Học Quốc Gia [National University Press], 69–78.

Nguyễn Văn Huệ (2007). The Direction of Monosyllabicity in Raglai, in Mark Alves, Paul Sidwell and David Gil (eds.), *SEALS VIII Papers from the 8th Annual Meeting of the Southeast Asian Linguistics Society 1998*. Canberra: Pacific Linguistics, 121–3.

Nichols, Johanna (1988). On Alienable and Inalienable Possession, in William Shipley (ed.), *in Honor of Mary Haas*. Berlin: Mouton de Gruyter, 475–521.

Nichols, Johanna (1997). Modeling Ancient Populations Structures and Movement in Linguistics, *Annual Review of Anthropology* 26: 359–84.

Nichols, Johanna and Balthasar Bickel (2013a). A Possessive Classification, in Matthew S Dryer and Martin Haspelmath (eds.), *The World Atlas of Language Structures Online*. Leipzig: Max Planck Institute for Evolutionary Anthropology.

Nichols, Johanna and Balthasar Bickel (2013b). Locus of Marking in Possessive Noun Phrases, in Matthew S Dryer and Martin Haspelmath (eds.), *The World Atlas of Language Structures Online*. Leipzig: Max Planck Institute for Evolutionary Anthropology.

Nickell, Thomas L (1985). A Partial Stratificational Analysis of Eastern Cagayan Agta Language, in P Bion Griffin and Agnes Estioko-Griffin (eds.), *The Agta of Northeastern Luzon: Recent Studies*. Cebu City: San Carlos Publications, 119–45.

Niemann, George K (1891). Bijdrage tot de kennis der verhouding van het Tjam tot de talen van Indonesië [On the relation between Cam and the languages of Indonesia], *Bijdragen tot de Taal-, Land- en Volkenkunde van Nederlandsch-Indië* 40: 27–44.

Nirmala Sari (1984). *Banjarese verbal morphology*. MA Thesis, Australian National University.

Nishiyama, Kunio and Herman Kelen (2007). *A Grammar of Lamaholot, Eastern Indonesia: The Morphology and Syntax of the Lewoingu Dialect*. München: LINCOM.

Nivens, Richard (1993). Reduplication in Four Dialects of West Tarangan, *Oceanic Linguistics* 32: 353–88.

Nivens, Richard (nd. a). *Proto-Aru database*. Unpublished Toolbox files.

Nivens, Richard (nd. b). *Toward Reconstructing an Immediate Ancestor of the Languages of Aru*. Unpublished Manuscript.

Noerwidi, Sofwan, Dyah Prastiningtyas, Harry Widianto, Fadhilla A Aziz, Adhyanti Putri, Taufiq Senjaya and Rokhus D Awe (2016). The Grave of the Harimau Cave: A Biocultural Study, in Truman Simanjuntak (ed.), *Gua Harimau Cave and the Long Journey of Oku Civilization*. Yogyakarta: Gadjah Mada University Press, 152–78.

Noerwidi, Sofwan, Harry Widianto and Truman Simanjuntak (2020). The Cultural and Biological Context of the Song Keplek 5 Specimen, East Java: Implications for Living Conditions and Human-Environment Interactions During the Later Holocene, in Helen Lewis (ed.), *EurASEAA14 Volume II: Material Culture and Heritage (Papers from the Fourteenth International Conference of the European Association of Southeast Asian Archaeologists)*. Summertown: Archaeopress Publishing Ltd, 133–43.

Nolasco, Ricardo Ma (2003). *Ang Pagkaergatibo at Pagkatransitibo Ng Mga Wikang Pilipino: Isang Pagsusuri Sa Sistemang Bose* [Ergativity and transitivity in the Philippine languages: An investigation of the voice system]. PhD Dissertation, University of the Philippines, Diliman.

Nomoto, Hiroki and Kartini Abd. Wahab (2014). Person Restriction on Passive Agents in Malay: Information Structure and Syntax, in Siaw-Fong Chung and Hiroki Nomoto (eds.), *Current Trends in Malay Linguistics*. Special issue of *NUSA* 57: 31–50.

Noor Azam Haji-Othman (2005). *Changes in the Linguistic Diversity of Negara Brunei Darussalam*. PhD Dissertation, University of Leicester.

Noor Azam Haji-Othman and Siti Ajeerah Najib (2016). The State of Indigenous Languages in Brunei, in Noor Azam Haji-Othman, James McLellan and David Deterding (eds.), *The Use and Status of Language in Brunei Darussalam: A Kingdom of Unexpected Linguistic Diversity*. Singapore: Springer, 17–28.

Noorduyn, J (1963). Mededelingen uit de verslagen van Dr S J Esser, taalambtenaar voor Celebes 1928–1944 [Report statements from Dr Samuel J Esser, official Sulawesi language administrator], *Bijdragen tot de Taal-, Land- en Volkenkunde* 119: 329–70.

Noorduyn, J (1982). Sound Changes in the Gorontalo Language, in Amran Halim, Lois Carrington and Stephen A Wurm (eds.), *Papers from the Third International Conference on Austronesian Linguistics, Vol. 2: Tracking the Travellers*. Canberrra: Pacific Linguistics, 241–61.

Noorduyn, J (1990). Consonant Gemination in Bugis, *Bijdragen tot de Taal-, Land- en Volkenkunde* 146: 470–3.

Noorduyn, J (1991a). *A Critical Survey of Studies on the Languages of Sulawesi*. Leiden: Koninklijk Instituut voor Taal-, Land- en Volkenkunde Press.

Noorduyn, J (1991b). The Languages of Sulawesi, in Hein Steinhauer (ed.), *Papers in Austronesian Linguistics, No. 1*. Canberra: Pacific Linguistics, 137–50.

Nordhoff, Sebastian (2009). *A Grammar of Upcountry Sri Lanka Malay*. PhD Dissertation, University of Amsterdam.

Noresah, Hajah Bt. Baharom (ed.) (2005). *Kamus Dewan, Edisi Keempat* [Official (government-sponsored Malay dictionary, 4th edition]. Kuala Lumpur: Dewan Bahasa dan Pustaka.

Normile, Dennis (2019). Update: Explorers Successfully Voyage to Japan in Primitive Boat in Bid to Unlock an Ancient Mystery. URL: https://www.sciencemag.org/news/2019/07/explorers-voyage-japan-primitive-boat-hopes-unlocking-ancient-mystery

Norwood, Clodagh (2002). Voice and Valency Alternations in Karo Batak, in Fay Wouk and Malcolm Ross (eds.), *The History and Typology of Western Austronesian Voice Systems*. Canberra: Pacific Linguistics, 181–208.

Nothofer, Bernd (1975). *The Reconstruction of Proto-Malayo-Javanic*. The Hague: Martinus Nijhoff.

Nothofer, Bernd (1980). *Dialektgeographischen Untersuchungen in West-Java und im westlichen Zentral-Java*. Wiesbaden: Otto Harrassowitz.

Nothofer, Bernd (1985). The Subgrouping of the Languages of the Javo-Sumatra Hesion: A Reconsideration, *Bijdragen tot de Taal-, Land- en Volkenkunde* 141(2/3): 288–302

Nothofer, Bernd (1986). The Barrier Island Languages in the Austronesian Language Family, in Paul Geraghty, Lois Carrington and Stephen A Wurm (eds.), *FOCAL II: Papers from the Fourth International Conference on Austronesian Linguistics*. Canberra: Pacific Linguistics, 87–109.

Nothofer, Bernd (1988). A Discussion of Two Austronesian Subgroups: Proto-Malay and Proto-Malayic, in Mohd T Ahmad and Z M Zain (eds.), *Rekonstruksi dan Cabang-Cabang Bahasa Melayu Induk* [Reconstruction and branches of Proto-Malay(ic)]. Kuala Lumpur: Dewan Bahasa dan Pustaka, 34–58.

Nothofer, Bernd (1991). Current Interpretations of Western Malayo-Polynesian Linguistic Prehistory, *Bulletin of the Indo-Pacific Prehistory Association* 11: 388–97.

Nothofer, Bernd (1994a). Migrasi Orang Melayu Purba: Kajian Awal [Proto-Malay migrations: a preliminary investigation], *Sari* 14: 33–52.

Nothofer, Bernd (1994b). The Relationship of the Languages of the Barrier Islands and the Sulawesi Philippine Languages, in Tom Dutton and Darrell T Tryon (eds.), *Contact-Induced Language Change in the Austronesian-Speaking Area*. Berlin: Mouton-De Gruyter, 1–41.

Nothofer, Bernd (1995). Dialek Melayu di Kalimantan dan di Bangka: misanan atau mindoan? [Malay dialects in Bangka and in Kalimantan: a first- or second-order relationship?] in S Dardjowidjojo (ed.), *Pertemuan Linguistik Pusat Kajian Bahasa dan Budaya Atma Jaya Kedelapan (PELLBA 8)*. Jakarta: Atma Jaya University Press, 53–84.

Nothofer, Bernd (1996). Borrowing from Javanese in Brunei Malay, in Bernd Nothofer (ed.), *Reconstruction, Classification, Description: Festschrift in Honor of Isidore Dyen*. Hamburg: Abera, 73–84.

Nothofer, Bernd (1997a). A Preliminary Classification of the Malayic Variants Between Sungai Semandang and Sungai Pawan/Sungai Keṛiau (Gerai, Tanjung Beringin, Randau Jeka). Presentation: Eighth International Conference on Austronesian Linguistics (8-ICAL), Taipei, 28 December.

Nothofer, Bernd (1997b). *Dialek Melayu Bangka* [Bangka Malay]. Bangi: Penerbit Universiti Kebangsaan Malaysia.

Nothofer, Bernd (2000). A Preliminary Analysis of the History of Sasak Language Levels. Peter K Austin (ed.), *Working Papers in Sasak*, Vol.2. Melbourne: University of Melbourne, 57–84.

Ntelitheos, Dimitrios (2006). *The Morphosyntax of Nominalizations: A Case Study*. PhD Dissertation, University of California Los Angeles.

Nuger, Justin (2008). Variations on the Palauan Theme. Unpublished Manuscript., University of California Santa Cruz.

Nuger, Justin (2010). *Architecture of the Palauan Verbal Complex*. PhD Dissertation, University of California Santa Cruz.

Nuger, Justin (2016). *Building Predicates. The View from Palauan.* Springer E-Book, DOI: 10.1007/978-3-319-28682-2

Nuraini Chandra (2008). *Langue et production de récits d'une communauté bajau des Îles Kangean (Indonésie)*. PhD Dissertation, Université de La Rochelle.

Nurani, Luisa Marliana (2015). *Changing Language Loyalty and Identity: An Ethnographic Inquiry into the Societal Transformation of the Javanese People*. PhD Dissertation, Arizona State University.

Nurhayani, Ika (2011). *A Unified Account of the Syntax of Valence in Javanese*. PhD Dissertation, Cornell University.

Nurhayani, Ika and Abigail C Cohn (2016). Phonological Strategies for Intensifying Adjectives in Javanese, *NUSA* 61: 19–47.

Nurse, Derek (1988). Review of Pierre Simon (1988). *Ny fiteny fahizany. Reconstitution et périodization du malgache ancien jusqu'au XVe siècle. Études Océan Indien* 10: 141–6.

Nurse, Derek and Hinnebusch, Thomas J. (1993). *Swahili and Sabaki. A Linguistic History*. Berkeley: University of California Publications in Linguistics.

Nyipa, Hang (1956). Migrations of the Kayan People, *Sarawak Museum Journal* 7: 82–8.

O'Connell J F, J Allen, M A J Williams, N A Williams, C S M Turney, N A Spooner, J Kamminga, G Brown and A Cooper (2018). When Did Homo Sapiens First Reach Southeast Asia and Sahul?, *Proceedings of the National Academy of Sciences USA* 115: 8482–90.

O'Connor, Sue (2015). Rethinking the Neolithic in Island Southeast Asia, with Particular Reference to the Archaeology of Timor-Leste and Sulawesi, *Archipel* 90: 15–47.

Odé, Cecilia (1994). On the Perception of Prominence in Indonesian, in Cecilia Odé and V J van Heuven (eds.), *Experimental Studies of Indonesian Prosody* (Semaian 9). Leiden: Vakgroep Talen en Culturen van Zuidoost-Azië en Oceanië, Leiden University, 27–107.

Oetomo, Dédé (1987). *The Chinese of Pasuruan: Their Language and Identity*. Canberra: Pacific Linguistics.

Ogawa, Hidefumi (2005). Typological Chronology of Pottery Assemblages from the Lal-Lo Shell Middens in Northern Luzon, Philippines, *Journal of Southeast Asian Archaeology* 25: 1–30.

Ogloblin, Alexander K (1986). *Madurskij jazyk i Iingvisticeska ya tipologija* [The Madurese language and linguistic typology]. Leningrad: Leningrad University Press.

Ogloblin, Alexander K (2005). Javanese, in Alexander Adelaar and Nikolaus P Himmelmann (eds.), *The Austronesian Languages of Asia and Madagascar*. London: Routledge, 590–624.

Ohala, John J (1983). The Origin of Sound Patterns in Vocal Tract Constraints, in P F MacNeilage (ed.), *The Production of Speech*. New York: Springer-Verlag, 189–216.

Ohala, John J (2011). Accommodation to the Aerodynamic Voicing Constraint and its Phonological Relevance. Presentation: International Congress of Phonetic Sciences, (ICPHS) XVII, Hong Kong 17–21 August, 2011.

Ohala, John J (2018). The Aerodynamic Voicing Constraint and its Phonological Implications, in Eugene Buckley, Thera Crane and Jeff Good (eds.), *Revealing Structure: Papers in Honor of Larry M Hyman*. CSLI Publications, University of Chicago Press.

Oliveira, Sandra, Kathrin Nägele, Irina Pugach, Alexander Hübner et al. (2020). Austronesian-Papuan Contact in North Moluccas and Central Sulawesi. Presentation: Conference of the Society for Molecular Biology and Evolution 2020.

Olson, Kenneth S, Jeff Mielke, Josephine Sanicas-Daguman and Hugh J Patterson III (2010). The Phonetic Status of the (Inter) dental Approximant, *Journal of the International Phonetic Association* 40(2): 199–215.

Olsson, Bruno (2013). *Iamitives: Perfects in Southeast Asia and Beyond*. MA Thesis, Stockholm University.

O'Neill, Timothy (2015). *The Phonology of Betsimisaraka Malagasy*. PhD Dissertation, University of Delaware.

Oostindie, Gert (2012). Postcolonial Migrants in the Netherlands, in Ulbe Bosma, Jan Lucassen, Gert Oostindie (eds.), *Postcolonial Migrants and Identity Politics: Europe, Russia, Japan and the United States in Comparison*. New York: Berghahn Books, 95–126.

Otanes, Fe T (1966). *A Contrastive Analysis of English and Tagalog Verb Complementation*. PhD Dissertation, University of California Los Angeles.

Owens, Melanie (2000). *Agreement in Bimanese*. MA Thesis, University of Canterbury.

Paauw, Scott H (2004). *A Historical Analysis of the Lexical Sources of Sri Lanka Malay*. MA Thesis, York University, Toronto.

Paauw, Scott H (2007). The Malay Contact Varieties of East Nusatenggara. Presentation: Fifth East Nusantara Conference (ENUS V), Kupang, 1 August.

Paauw, Scott H (2008). *The Malay Contact Varieties of Eastern Indonesia: A Typological Comparison*. PhD Dissertation. The State University of New York.

Pagani L, D J Lawson, E Jagoda, A Mörseburg, A Eriksson, M Mitt, F Clemente, G Hudjashov, M Degiorgio, L Saag, J D Wall, A Cardona, et al. (2016). Genome Analyses Inform on Migration Events During the Peopling of Eurasia, *Nature* 538: 238–42.

Pagel, Steve (2018). The Opposite of an Anti-Creole? Why Modern Chamorro is Not a New Language, in Ralph Ludwig, Steve Pagel and Peter Mühlhäusler (eds.), *Linguistic Ecology and Language Contact*. Cambridge: Cambridge University Press, 264–94.

Pakir, Anne Geok-in Sim (1986). *A Linguistic Investigation of Baba Malay*. PhD Dissertation, University of Hawai'i.

Pallesen, A Kemp (1979). The Pepet in Sama-Bajau, in Nguyen Dang Liem (ed.), *South East Asian Linguistic Studies, Vol. 3*. Canberra: Pacific Linguistics, 115–42.

Pallesen, A Kemp (1985). *Culture Contact and Linguistic Convergence*. Manila: Linguistic Society of the Philippines.

Palmer, Bill (2015). Topography in Language: Absolute Frame of Reference and the Topographic Correspondence Hypothesis, in Rik De Busser and Randy J LaPolla (eds.), *Language Structure and Environment: Social, Cultural, and Natural Factors*. Amsterdam: John Benjamins, 179–226.

Palmer, Bill and Dunstan Brown (2007). Heads in Oceanic Indirect Possession, *Oceanic Linguistics* 46: 199–209.

Palmer, Frank R (2001). *Mood and Modality*. New York: Cambridge University Press.

Pampus, Karl-Heinz (1989). Zur dialektgeographischen Gliederung des Mentawai-Archipels, in Wilfried Wagner (ed.), *Mentawai; Identität im Wandel auf indonesischen Ausseninseln*. Bremen: Bersee-Museum, 61–101.

Pancorbo, Luis (1989). *Los viajes del Girasol*. Madrid: Mondadori, 23–35.

Pang Keng-Fong (1998). On the Ethnonym Utsat, in D Thomas (ed.), *Papers in Southeast Asian Linguistics No.15: Further Chamic Studies*. Canberra: Pacific Linguistics, 55–60.

Pangilinan, Michael Raymon M (2006). Kapampángan Or Capampáñgan: Settling the Dispute on the Kapampángan Romanized Orthography. Presentation: 10th International Conference on Austronesian Linguistics, 17–20 January 2006. Puerto Princesa City, Philippines.

Pangilinan, Michael Raymon M (2009). Kapampangan Lexical Borrowing from Tagalog: Endangerment Rather Than Enrichment. Presentation: 11th International Conference on Austronesian Linguistics, 22–26 June 2009, Aussois, France.

Parkin, Harry (1978). *Batak Fruit of Hindu Thought*. Madras: Christian Literature Society.

Parkvall, Mikael and Bart Jacobs (2018). The Genesis of Chavacano Revisited and Solved, *Lingua* 215: 53–77.

Pastika, I Wayan (1999). *Voice Selection in Balinese Narrative Discourse*. PhD Dissertation, Australian National University.

Pateda, Mansoer (1977). *Kamus Bahasa Gorontalo - Indonesia* [Gorontalo–Indonesian dictionary]. Jakarta: Pusat Pembinaan dan Pengembangan Bahasa.

Pateda, Mansoer (1986). *Morfofonologi Bahasa Gorontalo* [Morphophonology of Gorontalo]. PhD Dissertation, Universitas Hasanuddin.

Pattiiha, Magda (2000). *Atur Bahasa = Taal in Orde* [Language in order]. Utrecht: Pusat Edukasi Maluku/Steunpunt Edukatie Molukkers.

Pätzold, Klaus (1968). *Die Palau-Sprache und ihre Stellung zu anderen indonesischen Sprachen*. Berlin: Dietrich Reimer.

Paul, Ileana (1999). On Passive in Malagasy, in *Proceedings of Austronesian Formal Linguistics Association VI*. Special issue of *Toronto Working Papers in Linguistics* 16(2): 265–78.

Paul, Ileana (2000a). *Malagasy Clause Structure*. French Studies Publications, Paper 81. URL: http://ir.lib.uwo.ca/frenchpub/81

Paul, Ileana (2000b). Instrumental Advancement without Instruments and without Advancement, in *Proceedings of Canadian Linguistics Association*. Ottawa: Cahiers Linguistiques d'Ottawa, 257–68.

Paul, Ileana (2001). Concealed Pseudo-Clefts, *Lingua* 111: 707–27.

Paul, Ileana (2009). On the Presence Versus Absence of Determiners in Malagasy, in Jila Ghomeshi, Ileana Paul and Martina Wiltschko (eds.), *Determiners: Universals and Variation*. Amsterdam: John Benjamins, 215–42.

Paul, Ileana (2015). Introduction: Dialectal Microvariation in Madagascar, *Western Papers in Linguistics/Cahiers Linguistiques de Western* 1(1): 1–6.

Pawley, Andrew (1973). Some Problems in Proto-Oceanic Grammar, *Oceanic Linguistics* 12/1–2: 103–88.

Pawley, Andrew (2005). The Meaning(s) of Proto Oceanic *panua, in Claudia Gross, Harriet D Lyons and Dorothy Counts (eds.), *A Polymath Anthropologist: Essays in Honour of Ann Chowning*. Auckland: Department of Anthropology, University of Auckland, 211–23.

Pawley, Andrew and Lawrence Reid (1979). The Evolution of Transitive Constructions in Austronesian, in Paz Naylor (ed.), *Austronesian Studies: Papers from the Second Eastern Conference on Austronesian Languages*. Michigan Papers on South and Southeast Asia, No. 15. Ann Arbor: University of Michigan, 103–30.

Pawley, Andrew and Malcolm D Ross (1995). The Prehistory of Oceanic Languages: A Current View, in Peter Bellwood, James J Fox and Darrell T Tryon (eds.), *The Austronesians: Historical and Comparative Perspectives*. Canberra: Australian National University Press, 39–74.

Pawley, Andrew and Medina Pawley (1994). Early Austronesian Terms for Canoe Parts and Seafaring, in A K Pawley and M D Ross (eds.), *Austronesian Terminologies: Continuity and Change*. Canberra: Australian National University Press, 329–61.

Pawley, Andrew and Timoci Sayaba (1990). Possessive-Marking in Wayan, A Western Fijian Language: Noun Class or Relational System? in Jeremy Davidson (ed.), *Pacific Island Languages: Essays in Honour of G B Milner*. London: School of Oriental and African Studies, and Honolulu: University of Hawai'i Press, 147–71.

Pawley, Meesun and Haekyung Kim (2017). *Jarai Grammar: A Grammatical Analysis of Jarai Spoken in Cambodia*. Unpublished Manuscript.

Payne, Thomas (1982). Role and Reference Related Subject Properties and Ergativity in Yupik Eskimo and Tagalog, *Studies in Language* 6(1): 75–106.

Payne, Thomas (1994). The Pragmatics of Voice in a Philippine Language: Actor-Focus and Goal-Focus in Cebuano Narrative, in Tom Givón (ed.), *Voice and Inversion*. Amsterdam/Philadelphia: John Benjamins, 317–64.

Payne, Thomas (1997). *Describing Morphosyntax: A Guide for Field Linguists*. Cambridge: Cambridge University Press.

Payne, Thomas E and Thomas Laskowske (1997). Voice in Seko Padang, in Joan Bybee, John Haiman and Sandra A Thompson (eds.), *Essays on Language Function and Language Type: Dedicated to T Givón*. Amsterdam: John Benjamins, 423–36.

Pearson, Joel Matthew (1998). Event Structure and the Syntax of Themes and Instruments: The Case of the Malagasy Translative Voice (*a-* Passive). Presentation: Fifth Annual Conference of the Austronesian Formal Linguistics Association, University of Hawai'i.

Pearson, Joel Matthew (2001). *The Clause Structure of Malagasy: A Minimalist Approach*. Los Angeles: University of California Los Angeles Department of Linguistics.

Pearson, Joel Matthew (2005). The Malagasy Subject/Topic as an A'-Element, *Natural Language and Linguistic Theory* 23(2): 381–457.

Pearson, Joel Matthew (2007). Predicate Fronting and Constituent Order in Malagasy, Unpublished Manuscript, Reed College.

Pearson, Joel Matthew (2008). Tense Marked Obliques in Malagasy, in S McQuay (ed.), *Studies in Philippine Languages and Cultures, Vol 18: 10-ICAL Austronesian Papers*. Quezon City: Summer Institute of Linguistics Philippines, 142–58.

Pearson, Joel Matthew (2009). Another Look at NO: Pseudo-Clefts and Temporal Clauses in Malagasy, in Sandra Chung, Dan Finer, Ileana Paul and Eric Potsdam (eds.), *Proceedings of the Sixteenth Meeting of the Austronesian Formal Linguistics Association (AFLA)*. University of California Santa Cruz, 165–79.

Pearson, Joel Matthew (2012). Aspect and Voice Selection in Malagasy: Initial Observations, University of California Los Angeles *Working Papers in Linguistics* 17: 337–47.

Pedersen, Holger (1962) [1931]. *The Discovery of Language: Linguistic Science in the 19th Century*. Bloomington and London: Indiana University Press [Original Danish Title: *Sprogvidenskaben i det nittende aarhundrede: Metoder og resultater*. Copenhagen].

Pejros, I (1994). Some Problems of Austronesian Accent and *t ~ *C (Notes of an Outsider), *Oceanic Linguistics* 33: 105–27.

Pekkanen, Inka (1993). Tatana Phonemics, in Michael E Boutin and Inka Pekkanen (eds.), *Phonological Descriptions of Sabah Languages*, Kota Kinabalu: Sabah Museum, 15–30.

Pellett, Marcian and Alexander Spoehr (1961). Marianas Archaeology: Report on an Excavation on Tinian, *Journal of the Polynesia Society* 70: 321–5.

Peng, Anne Elise (2012). *Aspects of the Syntax of Indonesian Teochew*. PhD Dissertation, University of Delaware, Newark.

Penn, David (2006). *Introducing Dadu'a*. Honours Thesis, University of New England, Australia.

Pennoyer, F Douglas (1980). Buhid and Tawbuid: A New Subgrouping Mindoro, Philippines, in Paz B Naylor, ed., *Austronesian Studies: Papers from the Second Eastern Conference on Austronesian Languages*. Michigan Papers on South and Southeast Asia. Ann Arbor: University of Michigan Press.

Pennoyer, F Douglas (1986–1987). Inati: The Hidden Negrito Language of Panay, Philippines, *Philippine Journal of Linguistics* 17.2–18.1: 1–36.

Penny, David, Bennet J McComish, Michael A Charleston and David M Hendy (2001). Mathematical Elegance with Biochemical Realism: The Covarion Model of Molecular Evolution, *Journal of Molecular Evolution* 53: 711–23.

Pepinsky, Thomas B, Maya Ravindranath Abtihian and Abigail C Cohn (2020). Urbanization, Ethnic Diversity, and Language Shift in Indonesia. Unpublished Manuscript. DOI: 10.2139/ssrn.3529422

Percival, W K (1981). *A Grammar of the Urbanised Toba-Batak of Medan*. Canberra: Pacific Linguistics.

Persons, Gary C (1979). Cohesion by Means of Participant Identification in Bolinao Narrative Discourse, *Studies in Philippine Linguistics* 3(1): 24–57.

Perwitasari, Arum, Marian Klamer, Jurriaan Witteman, and Niels O. Schiller. 2017. Quality of Javanese and Sundanese vowels, *Journal of the Southeast Asian Linguistics Society* 10.2: 1–9.

Petersen, Jennifer (2009). Word-Internal Code-Switching Constraints in a Bilingual Child's Grammar, *Linguistics* 26: 479–94.

Peterson, David A (2007). *Applicative Constructions*. Oxford: Oxford University Press.

Phạm Thị Thu Hà and Marc Brunelle (2014). Ngữ Điệu Và Các Tiểu Từ Cuối Câu Trong Tiếng Cham Phan Rang [Intonation and Sentence-Final Particles in Phan Rang Cham], *Ngôn Ngữ* [Language] 6, 57–69.

Phillips, Timothy C (2005). A survey of nasal preplosion in Aslian languages. Paper: International Conference of Indigenous People, 4-5 July 2005.

Phú Văn Hẳn, Jerold Edmondson and Kenneth Gregerson (1992). Eastern Cham as a Tone Language, *Mon Khmer Studies* 20: 31–43.

Piamenta, Moshe (1990). *Dictionary of Post-Classical Yemeni Arabic*. Leiden: Brill.

Pierron D, H Razafindrazaka, L Pagani, F -X Ricaut, T Antao, M Capredon, C Sambo, C Radimilahy, J -A Rakotoarisoa, R M Blench, T Letellier and T Kivisild (2014). Genome-Wide Evidence of Austronesian–Bantu Admixture and Cultural Reversion in a Hunter-Gatherer Group of Madagascar, *Proceedings of the National Academy of Sciences USA* 111: 936–41.

Pierron D, M Heiske, H Razafindrazaka, I Rakoto, N Rabetokotany, B Ravololomanga, L M Rakotozafy, M M Rakotomalala, M Razafiarivony, B Rasoarifetra, et al. (2017). Genomic Landscape of Human Diversity Across Madagascar, *Proceedings of the National Academy of Sciences USA* 114: E6498–E6506.

Pigafetta, Antonio (1525). *Navigation et Descouvrement de la Inde Superieure et Isles de Malucque ou Naissent les Cloux de Girofle Faicte par Anthoine Pigaphete, Vincentin, Chevallier de Rhodes, Commenceant en l'an Mil Vcc et Xix*. URL: https://brbl-dl.library.yale.edu/vufind/record/3438401

Piper, Philip, Hsiao-Chun Hung, Fredeliza Campos, Peter Bellwood and Rey Santiago (2009). A 4000 Year-Old Introduction of Domestic Pigs into the Philippine Archipelago: Implications for Understanding Routes of Human Migration Through Island Southeast Asia and Wallacea, *Antiquity* 83: 687–95.

Pittayaporn, Pittayaporn (2005). Moken as a Mainland Southeast Asian Language, in Anthony Grant and Paul Sidwell (eds.), *Chamic and Beyond: Studies in Mainland Austronesian Languages*. Canberra: Pacific Linguistics, 189–209.

Pittman, Richard (1966). *Tagalog -um- and mag-, an Interim Report*. Canberra: Linguistic Circle of Canberra Publications, Australian National University.

Platts, John Thompson (1884). *A Dictionary of Urdu, Classical Hindi, and English*. London: W H Allen.

Plutniak, Sébastien, Adhi Agus Oktaviana, Bambang Sugiyanto, Jean-Michel Chazine, François-Xavier Ricaut (2014). New Ceramic Data from East Kalimantan: The Cord-Marked and Red-Slipped Sherds of Liang Abus Layer 2 and Kalimantan's Pottery Chronology, *Journal of Pacific Archaeology* 5(1): 90–9.

Po Dharma (1987). *Le Panduranga (Campa) 1802-1835*. Paris: École Française d'Extrême-Orient.

Po Dharma (1991). Le déclin du Campā entre le XVIe et le XIXe Siècle, in *Le Campā et le monde malais*. Paris: Publications du Centre d'Histoire et Civilisations de la Péninsule Indochinoise, 47–64.

Poedjosoedarmo, Soepomo (1968). Javanese Speech Levels, *Indonesia* 6: 54–87.

Poirot, Gérard (1998). *Dictionnaire vezo-français suivi d'un index français-vezo*. Shopmybook [www.unibook.com].

Poisson, H and G Barbier (1952). *Le cinquantenaire de l'Académie Malgache*. Antananarivo: Imprimerie Officielle.

Polinsky, Maria (2017). Antipassive, in Jessica Coon, Diane Massam and Lisa Demena Travis (eds.), *The Oxford Handbook of Ergativity*. Oxford: Oxford University Press, 308–31.

Polinsky, Maria and Eric Potsdam (nd). *Austronesian Syntax*. Unpublished Manuscript.

Porter, Doris (1977). *A Tboli Grammar*. Manila: Linguistic Society of the Philippines.

Post, Ursula and Mary Jane Gardner (1992). *Binukid Dictionary*. Manila: Linguistic Society of the Philippines and Summer Institute of Linguistics.

Posth C, K Nägele, H Colleran, F Valentin, S Bedford, K W Kami, R Shing, H Buckley, Kinaston, M Walworth, G R Clark, C Reepmeyer, J Flexner, T Maric, J Mose, J Gresky, L Kiko, K J Robson, K Auckland, S J Oppenheimer, A V S Hill, A J Mentzer, J Zech, F Petchey, P Robert, C Jeong, R D Gray, J Krause and A Powell (2018). Language Continuity Despite Population Replacement in Remote Oceania, *Nature Ecology and Evolution* 2(4): 731–40.

Pototanon, Ruchie Mark D and Michael Wilson I Rosero (2012). An Acoustic and Articulatory Characterization of Capiznon Segmental Sounds. Unpublished Manuscript. URL: https://www.academia.edu/3571207/an_acoustic_and_articulatory_investigation_of_capiznon_segmental_sounds

Potsdam, Eric (2006a). More Concealed Pseudoclefts in Malagasy and the Clausal Typing Hypothesis, *Lingua* 116(12): 2154–82.

Potsdam, Eric (2006b). The Cleft Structure of Malagasy Wh-Questions, in Hans-Martin Gärtner, Paul S Law and Joachim Sabel (eds.), *Clause Structure and Adjuncts in Austronesian Languages*. Berlin: Mouton de Gruyter, 195–232.

Potsdam, Eric and Maria Polinsky (2014). Information Questions in Malagasy Dialects: Official Malagasy and Antakarana, *Western Papers in Linguistics/ Cahiers linguistiques de Western* (Ontario): Volume 1, Issue 1, Article 6.

Power, Robert C Power, Tom Güldemann, Alison Crowther, Nicole Boivin (2019). Asian Crop Dispersal in Africa and Late Holocene Human Adaptation to Tropical Environments, *Journal of World Prehistory* 32: 353–92.

Prentice, David J (1971). *The Murut Languages of Sabah*. Canberra: Pacific Linguistics.

Prentice, David J (1981). *A Timugon Murut-English Dictionary*. Canberra: Pacific Linguistics.

Prentice, David J (1987). Malay (Indonesian and Malaysian), in Bernard Comrie (ed.), *The World's major languages*. London: Routledge, 913–35.

Prentice, David J and A Hakim Usman (1978). Kerinci Sound-Changes and Phonotactics, in Stephen A Wurm and Lois Carrington (eds.), *Second International Conference on Austronesian Linguistics, Fascicle I, Western Austronesian*. Canberra: Pacific Linguistics, 121–63.

Prinst, Darwin (2002). *Kamus Karo-Indonesia* [Karo-Batak – Indonesian dictionary]. Medan: Penerbit Bina Media.

Pugach, I, F Delfin, E Gunnarsdottir, M Kayser and M Stoneking (2013). Genomewide Data Substantiate Holocene Gene Flow from India to Australia. *Proceedings of the National Academy of Sciences USA* 110: 1803e1808.

Pugach, Irina, Alexander Hübner, Hsiao-chun Hung, Matthias Meyer, Mike T. Carson and Mark Stoneking (2021). Ancient DNA from Guam and the peopling of the Pacific, *Proceedings of the National Academy of Sciences of the United States of America* 118 (1) e2022112118.

Pulleyblank, Douglas (2009). Patterns of Reduplication in Yoruba, in Kristin Hanson and Sharon Inkelas (eds.), *The Nature of the Word: Studies in Honor of Paul Kiparsky*. Cambridge, MA: Massachusetts Institute of Technology Press, 311–57.

Purwa, I Made, I Wayan Sudiartha, I Ketut Mandala Putra and Mgt. Widaningsih (1994). *Struktur Bahasa Idate* [Idate Structure] Jakarta: Pusat Pembinaan dan Pengembangan Bahasa.

Puspawati and Iman Laili (2013). Malayic Dialects of Northern Sumatra Barat and Southern Sumatra Utara. Presentation: 17th International Symposium on Malay/Indonesian Linguistics, Padang, Indonesia, June 7th 2013.

Putra, Kristian Adi (2018). *Youth, Technology and Indigenous Language Revitalization in Indonesia*. PhD Dissertation, University of Arizona.

Quakenbush, J Stephen (1989). *Language Use and Proficiency in a Multilingual Setting: A Sociolinguistic Survey of Agutaynen Speakers in Palawan, Philippines*. Manila: Linguistic Society of the Philippines. URL: http://www.sil.org/asia/philippines/plb_download.html

Quakenbush, J Stephen (1992). Word Order and Discourse Type: An Austronesian Example, in Doris L Payne (ed.), *Pragmatics of Word Order Flexibility*. Amsterdam: John Benjamins, 279–303.

Quakenbush, J Stephen (2003). Philippine Linguistics from an SIL (Summer Institute of Linguistics) Perspective: Trends and Prospects, *Philippine Journal of Linguistics* 34: 1–27.

Quakenbush, J Stephen and Gary F Simons (2015). Looking at Austronesian Language Vitality Through EGIDS and the Sustainable Use Model, in I Wayan Arka, Ni Luh Nyoman Seri Malini and Ida Ayu Made Puspani (eds.), *Language Documentation and Cultural Practices in the Austronesian World: Papers from 12-ICAL, Volume 4*. Canberra: Asia-Pacific Linguistics, 1–17.

Quakenbush, J Stephen, Gail R Hendrickson and Josenita L Edep (2010). *A Brief Overview of Agutaynen Grammar*. Manila: Summer Institute of Linguistics Publishing. www.sil.org/asia/philippines/plb_download.html

Quick, Phil (2003). *A Grammar of the Pendau Language*. PhD Dissertation, Australian National University.

Quick, Phil (2007). *A Grammar of the Pendau Language of Central Sulawesi, Indonesia*. Canberra: Pacific Linguistics.

Quilis, Antonio (1976). *Hispanismos en cebuano: contribucion al estudio de la lengua española en Filipinas* [Hispanisms in Cebuano: a contribution to the study of Spanish in the Philippines]. Madrid: Ediciones Alcala.

Rackowski, Andrea (2002). *The Structure of Tagalog: Specificity, Voice, and the Distribution of Arguments*. PhD Dissertation, Massachusetts Institute of Technology.

Rackowski, Andrea and Norvin Richards (2005). Phase Edge and Extraction: A Tagalog Case Study, *Linguistic Inquiry* 36: 565–99.

Rafael, Vincente L (1988). *Contracting Colonialism: Translation and Christian Conversion in Tagalog Society Under Early Spanish Rule*. Ithaca and London: Cornell University Press.

Rahajarizafy, A (1960). *Essai de grammaire malgache*. Antanimena, Tananarive: Imprimerie Catholique.

Raharinjanahary, Solo (2004). Langue, dialectes et ethnies à Madagascar, in Solofo Randrianja (ed.), *Madagascar: Ethnies et ethnicité*. Dakar, Senegal: Conseil pour le Développement de la Recherche en Sciences Sociales en Afrique, 137–202.

Rahman, Rudolf and Marcelino N Maceda (1955). Notes on the Negritos of Northern Negros, *Anthropos* 50: 811–37.

Rahyono, F X (2007). Intonation of the Yogyakarta palace language, in Vincent J. van Heuven and Ellen van Zanten (eds.), *Prosody in Indonesian Languages*. Utrecht: LOT Netherlands Graduate School of Linguistics, 177–89.

Rajaona, Siméon (1972). *Structure du malgache - étude des formes prédicatives*. Fianarantsoa: Ambozontany.

Rajaonarimanana, Narivelo (1995). *Grammaire moderne de la langue malgache*. Paris: L'Asiathèque.

Rajaonarimanana, Narivelo (2009). Malagasy, in Kees Versteegh (ed.), *Encyclopedia of Arabic Language and Linguistics. Volume IV: Q-Z*. Leiden and Boston: Brill, 125–8.

Rajaonarimanana, Narivelo and Sarah Fee (1996). *Dictionnaire malgache dialectal - français dialecte tandroy*. Paris: Langues et Mondes/L'Asiathèque.

Rakotofiringa, Hippolyte (1982). *Étude de phonétique experimentale. L'accent et les unités phoniques élémentaires de base en malgache-merina*. PhD Dissertation, Université de Strasbourg II.

Ramos, Teresita (1971). *Tagalog Structures*. PALI Language Texts: Philippines. Honolulu: University of Hawai'i Press.

Randriamasimanana, Charles (2006). Simple Sentences in Malagasy, in Henry Y Chang, Lillian M Huang and Dah-an Ho (eds.), *Streams Converging into an Ocean*. Taipei: Institute of Linguistics, Academia Sinica, 71–96.

Ras, Johannes J (1968). *Hikajat Banjar: A Study in Malay Historiography*. The Hague: Martinus Nijhoff.

Ras, Johannes J (1970). Lange consonanten in enige Indonesische talen (II) [Long consonants in some Indonesian languages Part II], *Bijdragen tot de Taal-, Land- en Volkenkunde* 126: 429–41.

Ras, Johannes J (1985). *Inleiding tot het moderne Javaans* [Introduction to Modern Javanese] (1st edition 1977). Dordrecht: Foris.

Rasoloson, Janie and Carl Rubino (2005). Malagasy, in Alexander Adelaar and Nikolaus P Himmelmann (eds.), *The Austronesian Languages of Asia and Madagascar*. London/New York: Routledge, 456–88.

Rassool, Asmara Romola (2014). *The Sri Lanka Malays: Dominated from the Outside, Dominated from the Inside - Issues of Power, Privilege, and Identity in the Formulation of the Endangerment of the Sri Lanka Malay Language and its Language Revitalisation Initiatives*. PhD Dissertation, University of Melbourne.

Rau D Victoria and Hui-Huan Ann Chang (2015). Yami, in Nicola Grandi and Lívia Körtvélyessy (eds.), *Edinburgh Handbook of Evaluative Morphology*. Edinburgh: Edinburgh University Press, 389–99.

Rau, D Victoria and Maa-Neu Dong (2006). *Yami Texts with Reference Grammar and Dictionary*. Taipei: Academia Sinica.

Ray, Erwin R (1981). *The Material Culture of Prehistoric Tarague Beach, Guam*. MA Thesis, Department of Anthropology, Arizona State University.

Ray, Sidney H (1913). The Languages of Borneo, *The Sarawak Museum Journal* 1(4): 1–196.

Razafindrazaka H, F -X Ricaut, M P Cox, M Mormina, J-M Dugoujon, L P Randriamarolaza, E Guitard, L Tonasso, B Ludes and E Crubézy (2010). Complete Mitochondrial DNA Sequences Provide New Insights into the Polynesian Motif and the Peopling of Madagascar, *European Journal of Human Genetics* 18: 575–81.

Redouane, Rabia (2005). Linguistic Constraints on Codeswitching and Codemixing of Bilingual Moroccan Arabic-French Speakers in Canada, in James Cohen, Kara T McAlister, Kellie Rolstad and Jeff MacSwan (eds.), *ISB4: Proceedings of the 4th International Symposium on Bilingualism*. Somerville: Cascadilla Press, 1921–33.

Reesink, Ger P (1998). The Bird's Head as Sprachbund, in Jelle Miedema, Cecilia Odé and Rien A C Dam (eds.), *Perspectives on the Bird's Head of Irian Jaya, Indonesia: Proceedings of the Conference, Leiden, 13-17 October 1997*. Amsterdam: Rodopi, 603–42.

Reesink, Ger P (1999). *A Grammar of Hatam: Bird's Head Peninsula, Irian Jaya, Indonesia*. Canberra: Pacific Linguistics.

Reesink, Ger P (2002a). Mansim, a Lost Language of the Bird's Head, in G P Reesink (eds.), *Languages of the Eastern Bird's Head*. Canberra: Pacific Linguistics, 277–340.

Reesink, Ger P (2002b). Clause-Final Negation: Structure and Interpretation, *Functions of Language* 9(2): 239–68.

Reich D, N Patterson, M Kircher, F Delfin, R Nandinenim, I Pugach, A M Ko, Y C Ko, T A Jinam, M E Phipps, N Saitou, A Wollstein, M Kayser, S Pääbo and M Stoneking (2011). Denisova Admixture and the First Modern Human Dispersals into Southeast Asia and Oceania, *American Journal of Human Genetics* 89: 516–28.

Reid, Lawrence A (1963). The Phonology of Central Bontoc, *Journal of the Polynesian Society* 72: 21–6.

Reid, Lawrence A (1973). Diachronic Typology of Philippine Vowel Systems, in Thomas A Sebeok (ed.), *Current Trends in Linguistics 11: Diachronic, Areal, and Typological Linguistics*. The Hague and Paris: Mouton and Co., 485–506.

Reid, Lawrence A (1974). The Central Cordilleran Subgroup of Philippine Languages, *Oceanic Linguistics* 13: 511–560.

Reid, Lawrence A (1976). *Bontok-English Dictionary*. Canberra: Pacific Linguistics.

Reid, Lawrence A (1979). Towards A Reconstruction of the Pronominal Systems of Proto-Cordilleran, Philippines, in Nguyen Dang Liem(ed.), *South-East Asian Linguistic Studies* 3. Canberra: Pacific Linguistics, 259–75.

Reid, Lawrence A (1982). The Demise of Proto-Philippines, in Amram Halim, Lois Carrington and Stephen A Wurm (eds.), *Papers from the Third International Conference on Austronesian Linguistics*. Canberra: Pacific Linguistics, 201–16.

Reid, Lawrence A (1987). The Early Switch Hypothesis: Linguistic Evidence for Contact Between Negritos and Austronesians, *Man and Culture in Oceania* 3 (Special Issue): 41–59.

Reid, Lawrence A (1989). Arta, Another Philippine Negrito Language, *Oceanic Linguistics* 28: 47–74.

Reid, Lawrence A (1991). The Alta Languages of the Philippines, in Ray Harlow, ed., *Papers from the Fifth International Conference on Austronesian Linguistics, Western Austronesian and Contact Languages*, 265–97. Auckland: Linguistic Society of New Zealand.

Reid, Lawrence A (1992). On the Development of the Aspect System in Some Philippine Languages, *Oceanic Linguistics* 31(1): 65–91.

Reid, Lawrence A (1994a). Possible Non-Austronesian Lexical Elements in Philippine Negrito Languages, *Oceanic Linguistics* 33: 37–72.

Reid, Lawrence A (1994b). Morphological Evidence for Austric, *Oceanic Linguistics* 33(2): 323–44.

Reid, Lawrence A (1994c). Unravelling the Linguistic Histories of Philippine Negritos, in Tom E Dutton and Darrell T Tryon (eds.), *Language Contact and Change in the Austronesian World*. Berlin: Mouton de Gruyter, 443–75.

Reid, Lawrence A (2002a). Determiners, Nouns or What? Problems in the Analysis of Some Commonly Occurring Forms in Philippine Languages, *Oceanic Linguistics* 41(2): 295–309.

Reid, Lawrence A (2002b). Morphosyntactic Evidence for the Position of Chamorro in the Austronesian Language Family, in Robert S Bauer (ed.), *Collected Papers on Southeast Asian and Pacific Languages*. Canberra: Pacific Linguistics, 63–94.

Reid, Lawrence A (2005). A Cross-Generational View of Contact-Related Phenomena in A Philippine Language: Phonology, in Danilo T Dayag and J Stephen Quakenbush (eds.), *Sociolinguistics and Language Education in the Philippines and Beyond: Festschrift in Honor of Maria Lourdes S Bautista*. Manila: Linguistic Society of the Philippines and the Summer Institute of Linguistics, 383–99.

Reid, Lawrence A (2006a). On the Origin of the Philippine Vowel Grades, *Oceanic Linguistics* 45: 457–73.

Reid, Lawrence A (2006b). On Reconstructing the Morphosyntax of Proto-Northern Luzon, *Philippine Journal of Linguistics* 37(2): 1–66.

Reid, Lawrence A (2006c). Human Noun Pluralization in Northern Luzon Languages, in Henry Y Chang, Lillian M Huang and Dahan Ho (eds.), *Streams Converging into an Ocean: Festschrift in Honor of Professor Paul Jen-Kuei Li on His 70th Birthday*. Language and Linguistics Monograph Series Number W-5. Taipei: Institute of Linguistics, Academia Sinica, 49–69.

Reid, Lawrence A (2007). Another Look at the Marking of Plural Personal Noun Constructions in Austronesian Languages, *Oceanic Linguistics* 46(1): 232–52.

Reid, Lawrence A (2009a). Introduction, in Lawrence A Reid and Ritsuko Kikusawa, *Talking Dictionary of Khinina-Ang Bontok: The Language Spoken in Guina-Ang, Bontoc, Mountain Province, the Philippines*. Osaka: National Museum of Ethnography. URL: https://htq.minpaku.ac.jp/databases/bontok/about introduction.jsp

Reid, Lawrence A (2009b). The Reconstruction of a Dual Pronoun to Proto Malayo-Polynesian, in Bethwyn Evans (ed.), *Discovering History Through Language: Papers in Honour of Malcolm Ross*. Canberra: Pacific Linguistics, 461–77.

Reid, Lawrence A (2009c). On the Diachronic Development of $C_1V_1$- Reduplication in Some Austronesian Languages, *Morphology* 19: 239–61.

Reid, Lawrence A (2009d). Who Are the Indigenous? Origins and Transformations, *Cordillera Review: Journal of Philippine Culture and Society* 1: 3–25.

Reid, Lawrence A (2013). Who Are the Philippine Negritos? Evidence from Language, *Human Biology* 85 (1): 329–58.

Reid, Lawrence A (2016). Accounting for Variability in Malayo-Polynesian Pronouns, *Journal of Historical Linguistics* 6(2): 130–64.

Reid, Lawrence A (2017). Re-Evaluating the Position of Iraya Among Philippine Languages, in Hsiu-Chuan Liao (ed.), *Issues in Austronesian Historical Linguistics*. Journal of the Southeast Asian Linguistics Society Special Publication No. 1, 23–47.

Reid, Lawrence A (2019). Reassessing the Position of Isinay in the Central Cordilleran Family, in Aldrin Lee and Vincent C R Santiago (eds.), *The Archive Special Publication No.16*. Manila: University of the Philippines Diliman, 1–32.

Reid, Lawrence A (2020). Response to Blust 'The Resurrection of Proto-Philippines', *Oceanic Linguistics* 59: 374–93.

Reid, Lawrence A (ed.) (1971). *Philippine Minor Languages: Word Lists and Phonologies*. Honolulu: University of Hawai'i Press.

Reid, Lawrence A and Analyn V Salvador-Amores (2016). *Guide to Isinay Orthography*. Baguio: Cordillera Studies Center, University of the Philippines Baguio.

Reid, Lawrence A and Hsiu-Chuan Liao (2004). A Brief Syntactic Typology of Philippine Languages, *Language and Linguistics* 5(2): 433–90.

Reijffert, Fr. A (1956). *Vocabulary of English and Sarawak Land Dyak (Singhi Tribe)*. Kuching: Sarawak Government Printing Office.

Reinecke, Andreas, Chieu Nguyen and Thi My Dung Lam (2002). *Neue Entdeckungen der Sa-Huynh-Kultur*. Köln: Linden-Soft Press.

Remijsen, Bert (2001a). *Word-Prosodic Systems of Raja Ampat Languages*. PhD Dissertation, Leiden University.

Remijsen, Bert (2001b). Dialectal Variation in the Lexical Tone System of Ma'ya, *Language and Speech* 44(4): 473–99.

Remijsen, Bert (2002). Lexically Contrastive Stress Accent and Lexical Tone in Ma'ya, in Carlos Gussenhoven and Natasha Warner (eds.), *Laboratory Phonology VII*. Berlin: Mouton de Gruyter, 585–614.

Remijsen, Bert (2007). Lexical Tone in Magey Matbat, in Vincent J van Heuven and Ellen van Zanten (eds.), *Prosody in Indonesian Languages*. Utrecht: LOT Netherlands Graduate School of Linguistics, 9–34.

Remijsen, Bert (2010). Nouns and Verbs in Magey Matbat, in Marian Klamer and Michael C Ewing (eds.), *Typological and Areal Analyses: Contributions from East Nusantara*. Canberra: Pacific Linguistics, 285–316.

Remijsen, Bert (2015). *Matbat_Magey dialect_2003_Lexicography*. URL: https://datashare.is.ed.ac.uk/handle/10283/796

Rensch, Calvin R (2012). *Melanau and the Languages of Central Sarawak*. Dallas: Summer Institute of Linguistics International.

Rensch, Carolyn M (2006). Nasality in Bidayuh Phonology, in Calvin R Rensch, Carolyn M Rensch, Jonas Noeb and Robert Sulis Ridu (eds.), *The Bidayuh Language: Yesterday, Today and Tomorrow*. Kuching: Dayak Bidayuh National Association, 31–132.

Rensch, Calvin R Carolyn M. Rensch, Jonas Noeb and Robert Sulis Ridu (2012). *The Bidayuh Language: Yesterday, Today and Tomorrow*. 2nd edition. Kuching: Dayak Bidayuh National Association.

Revel-MacDonald, Nicole (1979). *Le palawan (Philippines)*. Paris: Centre National de la Recherche Scientifique.

Revel-MacDonald, Nicole (1982). Synchronical Description at the Phonetic and Syllabic Level of Modang (Kalimantan Timur) in Contrast to Kenyah, Kayan, and Palawan (Philippines), in Paul Geraghty, Lois Carrington, Stephen A Wurm (eds.), *FOCAL I: Papers from the Fourth International Conference on Austronesian Linguistics 2.* Canberra: Pacific Linguistics, 321–31.

Reynolds, Christopher (2003). *A Maldivian Dictionary.* London/New York: Routledge Curzon.

Richards, Anthony (1981). An *Iban-English Dictionary.* Oxford: Clarendon Press.

Richards, Norvin (2000). Another Look at Tagalog Subjects, in Ileana Paul, Vivianne Phillips and Lisa Travis (eds.), *Formal Issues in Austronesian Linguistics.* Studies in Natural Language and Linguistic Theory, Vol. 49. Dordrecht: Kluwer, 105–16.

Richards, Norvin (2001). *Movement in Language: Interactions and Architectures.* Oxford: Oxford University Press.

Richards, Norvin (2009a). The Tagalog Copula, in Sandra Chung, Daniel Finer, Ileana Paul and Eric Potsdam, eds., *Proceedings of AFLA 16.* London (Ontario): Western Ontario University, 181–95.

Richards, Norvin (2009b). Nouns, Verbs, and Hidden Structure in Tagalog, *Theoretical Linguistics* 35: 139–52.

Richards, Norvin (2010). *Uttering Trees.* Cambridge, MA: Massachusetts Institute of Technology Press.

Richardson, James (1885). *A New Malagasy-English Dictionary.* Antananarivo: The London Missionary Society.

Riedel, J G F (1881). Twee volksverhalen in het dialekt der Orang Lawoet of Orang Sekah van Belitoeng, [Two folktales in the Orang Lawut and Orang Sekah dialects on Belitung Island], *Tijdschrift voor Indische Taal-, Land- en Volkenkunde* 26: 264–73.

Riehl, Anastasia Kay (2008). *The Phonology and Phonetics of Nasal Obstruent Sequences.* PhD Dissertation, Cornell University.

Riesberg, Sonja (2014). *Symmetrical Voice and Linking in Western Austronesian Languages.* Boston/Berlin: de Gruyter Mouton.

Riesberg, Sonja, Janina Kalbertodt, Stefan Baumann and Nikolaus P Himmelmann (2020). Using Rapid Prosody Transcription to Probe Little-Known Prosodic Systems: The Case of Papuan Malay, *Laboratory Phonology* 11(1): 1–35.

Riesberg, Sonja, Kurt Malcher and Nikolaus P Himmelmann (2019). How Universal Is Agent-First? Evidence from Symmetrical Voice Languages, *Language* 95: 523–61.

Riesberg, Sonja, Kurt Malcher and Nikolaus P Himmelmann (2021). The many ways of transitivization in Totoli, in Silvia Luraghi and Elisa Roma (eds.), *Valency over time. Diachronic perspectives on valency patterns and valency orientation.* Berlin: De Gruyter Mouton, 235–264

Riester, Arndt and Asako Shiohara (2018). Information Structure in Sumbawa: A QUD Analysis, in Sonja Riesberg, Asako Shiohara and Atsuko Utsumi (eds.), *Perspectives on Information Structure in Austronesian.* Berlin: Language Science Press, 263–86.

Ringe, Don, Tandy Warnow and Ann Taylor (2002). Indo-European and Computational Cladistics, *Transactions of the Philological Society* 100: 59–129.

Rizki, Syukri (2020). Nurturing Jawi Through Education: Mirroring Jawi Education in Aceh and Malaysia, *The Indonesian Journal of Southeast Asian Studies* 3(2): 217–30.

Robins, Robert (1953). The Phonology of Nasalized Verbal Forms in Sundanese, *Bulletin of the School of Oriental and African Studies* 15: 138–45.

Robins, Robert (1957). Vowel Nasality in Sundanese, in J R Firth (ed.), *Studies in Linguistics Analysis* (Special Volume of the Philological Society). Oxford: Basil Blackwell, 87–103.

Robins, Robert (1968). Basic Sentence Structures in Sundanese, *Lingua* 8: 337–69.

Robinson, Laura C (2006). Dupaningan Agta Recordings, in PARADISEC (Pacific and Regional Archive for Digital Sources in Endangered Cultures). DOI: 10.4225/72/56e825bcc1874

Robinson, Laura C (2008). *Dupaningan Agta: Grammar, Vocabulary, and Texts.* PhD Dissertation, University of Hawai'i.

Robinson, Laura C (2010). Informed Consent Among Analog People in A Digital World, *Language and Communication* 30: 186–91.

Robinson, Laura C (2011). *Dupaningan Agta: Grammar, Vocabulary, and Text.* Canberra: Pacific Linguistics.

Robinson, Laura C and Jason William Lobel (2013). The Northeastern Luzon Subgroup of Philippine Languages, *Oceanic Linguistics* 52(1): 125–68.

Robson, Stuart (2002). *Javanese Grammar for Students*, 2nd edition. Glen Waverley: Monash Papers on Southeast Asia.

Robson, Stuart (2015). *The Old Javanese Rāmāyaṇa: A New English Translation with an Introduction and Notes.* Tokyo: Research Institute for Languages and Cultures of Asia and Africa.

Robson, Stuart and Singgih Wibisono (2002). *Javanese English Dictionary.* Singapore: Periplus.

Rodríguez-Ponga, Rafael (1995). *El elemento español en la lengua chamorra (Islas Marianas)* [The Spanish element in Chamorro]. PhD Dissertation, Universidad Complutense de Madrid, Facultad de Filología.

Rodríguez-Ponga, Rafael (2001). Los numerales hispano-chamorras [Chamorro numerals of Spanish origin], in Thomas Stolz and Klaus Zimmermann (eds.), *Lo propio y lo ajeno en las lenguas amerindias y austronésicas.* Frankfurt am Main: Vervuert.

Rødvand, Linn Iren Sjånes (2023). Possession in Patani, *STUF - Language Typology and Universals* 76(3): 331–368.

Roettger, Timo and Matthew Gordon (2017). Methodological Issues in the Study of Word Stress Correlates, *Linguistics Vanguard* 3(1): 1–11.

Roosman, Lilie (2006). *Phonetic Experiments on the Word and Sentence Prosody of Betawi Malay and Toba Batak.* PhD Dissertation, Leiden University.

Roosman, Lilie (2007). Melodic Structure in Toba Batak and Betawi Malay Word Prosody, in Vincent J Heuven and Ellen van Zanten (eds.), *Prosody in Indonesian Languages.* Utrecht: LOT Netherlands Graduate School of Linguistics, 89–115.

Rosidi, Ajip (1984). *Manusia Sunda: Sebuah esai tentang tokoh-tokoh sastra dan sejarah* [The Sundanese: an essay about literary and historical figures]. Jakarta: Inti Idayu.

Rosnes, Ellen Vea (2019). *The Norwegian Missions Literacy Work in Colonial and Independent Madagascar*. New York: Routledge.

Ross, Malcolm D (1988). *Proto Oceanic and the Austronesian Languages of Western Melanesia*. Canberra: Pacific Linguistics.

Ross, Malcolm D (1992). The Sound of Proto-Austronesian: An Outsider's View of the Formosan Evidence, *Oceanic Linguistics* 31: 23–64.

Ross, Malcolm D (1995a). Some Current Issues in Austronesian Linguistics, in Darrell T Tryon (ed.), *Comparative Austronesian Dictionary: An Introduction to Austronesian Studies, Volume 1*. Berlin/New York: Mouton de Gruyter, 45–120.

Ross, Malcolm D (1995b). Reconstructing Proto Austronesian Verbal Morphology: Evidence from Taiwan in Paul Jen-Kuei Li, Dah-an Ho, Ying-Kuei Huang, Cheng-Hwa Tsang and Chiu-Yu Tseng (eds.), *Austronesian Studies Relating to Taiwan*. Taipei: Institute of History and Philology, Academia Sinica, 727–91.

Ross, Malcolm D (1996). Contact-Induced Change and the Comparative Method: Cases from Papua New Guinea, in Mark Durie and Malcolm Ross (eds.), *The Comparative Method Reviewed: Regularity and Irregularity in Language Change*. Oxford/New York: Oxford University Press, 180–217.

Ross, Malcolm D (1997). Social Networks and Kinds of Speech-Community Event, in Roger M Blench and Matthew Spriggs (eds.), *Archaeology and Language, 1: Theoretical and Methodological Orientations*. London: Routledge, 209–61.

Ross, Malcolm (1998). Possessive-like Attribute Constructions in the Oceanic Languages of Northwest Melanesia, *Oceanic Linguistics* 37(2): 234–76.

Ross, Malcolm D (2001). Contact-Induced Change in Oceanic Languages in North-West Melanesia, in Alexandra Y Aikhenvald and R M W Dixon (eds.), *Areal Diffusion and Genetic Inheritance*. Oxford: Oxford University Press, 134–66.

Ross, Malcolm D (2002a). Final Words: Research Themes in the History and Typology of Western Austronesian Languages, in Fay Wouk and Malcolm Ross (eds.), *The History and Typology of Western Austronesian Voice Systems*. Canberra: Pacific Linguistics, 451–74.

Ross, Malcolm D (2002b). The History and Transitivity of Western Austronesian Voice and Voice Marking, in Fay Wouk and Malcolm Ross (eds.), *The History and Typology of Western Austronesian Voice Systems*. Canberra: Pacific Linguistics, 17–62.

Ross, Malcolm D (2004). Notes on the Prehistory and Internal Subgrouping of Malayic, in John Bowden and Nikolaus P Himmelmann (eds.), *Papers in Austronesian Subgrouping and Dialectology*. Canberra: Pacific Linguistics, 97–109.

Ross, Malcolm D (2005). The Batanic Languages in Relation to the Early History of the Malayo-Polynesian Subgroup of Austronesian, *Journal of Austronesian Studies* 1(2): 1–24.

Ross, Malcolm D (2006). Reconstructing the Case-Marking and Personal Pronoun Systems of Proto Austronesian, in Yung-Li Chang, Lillian M Huang and Dah-an Ho (eds.), *Streams Converging into an Ocean: Festschrift in Honor of Professor Paul Jen-Kuei Li on His 70th Birthday*. Taipei: Institute of Linguistics, Academia Sinica, 521–63.

Ross, Malcolm D (2007). Calquing and Metatypy, *Journal of Language Contact: Thema* 1: 116–43.

Ross, Malcolm D (2009). Proto Austronesian Verbal Morphology: A Reappraisal, in Alexander Adelaar and Andrew K Pawley (eds.), *Austronesian Historical Linguistics and Culture History: A Festschrift for Robert Blust*. Canberra: Pacific Linguistics, 295–326.

Ross, Malcolm D (2014). Reconstructing the History of Languages in Northwest New Britain: Inheritance and Contact, *Journal of Historical Linguistics* 4: 84–132.

Ross, Malcolm D (2017). Languages of the New Guinea Region, in Raymond Hickey (ed.), *The Cambridge Handbook of Areal Linguistics*. Cambridge: Cambridge University Press, 758–820.

Ross, Malcolm D and Mark Durie (1996). Introduction, in Mark Durie and Malcolm D Ross (eds.), *The Comparative Method Reviewed: Irregularity and Regularity in Linguistic Change*. New York: Oxford University Press, 3–38.

Ross, Malcolm and Stacy Fang-Ching Teng (2005). Formosan Languages and Linguistic Typology, *Language and Linguistics* 6: 739–81.

Ross, Malcolm D, Andrew Pawley and Meredith Osmond (2016). *The Lexicon of Proto Oceanic: The Culture and Environment of Ancestral Oceanic Society. Volume 5: People: Body and Mind*. Canberra: Asia-Pacific Linguistics.

Ross, Melody Ann (2017). *Attitudes Toward Tetun Dili: A Language of East Timor*. PhD Dissertation, University of Hawai'i.

Rossel, Gerda (1998). *Taxonomic-Linguistic Study of Plantain in Africa*. Leiden: Research School CNWS.

Rousseau, Jérôme 1974. A Vocabulary of Baluy Kayan, in Jérôme Rousseau (ed.), *The Peoples of Central Borneo. The Peoples of Central Borneo*. (Special Issue of the Sarawak Museum Journal, 22(43)). Kuching (Malaysia): Sarawak Museum, 93–152.

Rubay G S, Adjin Widen, Pagoe Bangel, C Dj. Bandrang, Apria Dansen, C Yus Ngabut (1997). *Kamus Bahasa Maanyan* [Dictionary of the Maanyan language] Edisi II. Palangkaraya: Proyek Pembinaan Perpustakaan Umum Dati II.

Rubino, Carl R Galvez (1997). *A Reference Grammar of Ilocano*. PhD Dissertation, University of California Santa Barbara.

Rubino, Carl R Galvez (2000). *Ilocano Dictionary and Grammar*. Honolulu: University of Hawai'i Press.

Rubino, Carl R Galvez (2001). Iconic Morphology and Word Formation in Ilokano, in F K Erhard Voeltz and Christa Kilian-Hatz (eds.), *Ideophones*. Amsterdam/Philadelphia: John Benjamins, 303–20.

Rubino, Carl R Galvez (2005b). Utudnon, an Undescribed Language of Leyte, in Hsiu-Chuan Liao and Carl R Galvez Rubino (eds.), *Current Issues in Philippine Linguistics and Anthropology: Parangal Kay Lawrence A Reid*. Manila: Linguistic Society of the Philippines and Summer Institute of Linguistics Philippines, 306–37.

Rubino, Carl R Galvez (2006). *Intensive Tausug: A Pedagogical Grammar of the Language of Jolo*. Springfield: Dunwoody Press.

Rubino, Carl R Galvez (2013). Reduplication, in Matthew S Dryer and Martin Haspelmath (eds.), *The World Atlas of Language*

*Structures Online*. Leipzig: Max Planck Institute for Evolutionary Anthropology. URL: https://wals.info/chapter/27

Rubino, Carl Ralph Galvez (2005a). Reduplication: Form, Function and Distribution, in Bernhard Hurch (ed.), *Studies on Reduplication*. Berlin: Mouton de Gruyter, 11–29.

Rubrico, Jessie Grace U (2012). Indigenization of Filipino: The Case of the Davao City Variety. Kuala Lumpur: University of Malaya, Faculty of Education (manuscript).

Ruffolo, Roberta (2004). *Topics in the Morpho-Syntax of Ibaloy, Northern Philippines*. PhD Dissertation, Australian National University.

Ruud, Joergen (1955). Étude grammaticale du dialecte betsimisaraka du sud, *Bulletin de l'Academie Malgache* 33: 33–55.

Sabbagh, Joseph (2009). Existential Sentences in Tagalog, *Natural Language and Linguistic Theory* 27: 675–719.

Sabel, Joachim (2002). Wh-Questions and Extraction Asymmetries in Malagasy, in Andrea Rackowski and Norvin Richards (eds.), *Massachusetts Institute of Technology Working Papers in Linguistics 44: The Proceedings of the Eighth Austronesian Formal Linguistics Association*. Cambridge, MA: Massachusetts Institute of Technology Working Papers in Linguistics, 309–23.

Sacleux, Ch (1939). *Dictionnaire swahili-français*. Paris: Institut d'Ethnologie, Musée de l'Homme.

Sadock, Jerrold M (1986). Some Notes on Noun Incorporation, *Language* 62(1): 19–31.

Safford, William Edwin (1903). The Chamorro Language of Guam-II, *American Anthropologist*, 5(3): 508–29.

Safford, William Edwin (1904a). The Chamorro Language of Guam-III, *American Anthropologist* 6(1): 95–117.

Safford, William Edwin (1904b). The Chamorro Language of Guam-IV, *American Anthropologist* 6(4): 501–34.

Safiah Karim, Nik, Farid M Onn and Hashim Hj Musa (1987). *Tatabahasa Dewan* [Standard Malay grammar sponsored by the Malaysian Bureau for Language and Literature]. Kuala Lumpur: Dewan Bahasa dan Pustaka.

Saldin, B D K (in collaboration with Lisa Lim) (2007). *A Concise Sri Lankan Malay Dictionary: Kamus Ringkas Bahasa Melayu Sri Lanka*. Amsterdam: The Sri Lanka Malay Documentation Project.

Saleh, Rattiya (1986). *The Malay Dialect of Southern Thailand*. Songkhla: Education Service Project, Srinakharinvirot University.

Salmon, Claudine (2019). Contact Languages on the South China Sea and Beyond (15th–18th Centuries), *Asian Culture* 43: 1–24.

Salzner, Richard (1960). *Sprachenatlas des indopazifischen Raumes*. Wiesbaden: Harrassowitz.

Samely, Ursula (1991). *Kedang (Eastern Indonesia): Some Aspects of its Grammar*. Hamburg: Helmut Buske.

Sande, J S (1997). *Tata Bahasa Toraja* [Toraja grammar]. Jakarta: Pusat Pembinaan dan Pengembangan Bahasa.

Sandin, Benedict (1980). *The Living Legends: Borneans Telling Their Tales*. Kuala Lumpur: Dewan Bahasa dan Pustaka.

Sandin, Benedict (1994). *Sources of Iban Traditional History*. Kuching: Sarawak Museum.

Sankararaman S, S Mallick, M Dannemann, K Prüfer, J Kelso, S Pääbo, N Patterson and D Reic (2014). The genomic landscape of Neanderthal ancestry in present-day humans, *Nature* 507(7492): 354–7.

Santa Maria, Luigi (1967). *I Prestiti Portoghesi Nel Malese-Indonesiano* [Portuguese loanwords in Malay/ Indonesian]. Naples: Istituto Orientale.

Santiago, Paul Julian (2010). *The Phonetic Structures of Kalanguya*. MA Thesis, University of the Philippines.

Santos, Pilar C (1975). *Sinauna Tagalog: A Genetic Study Examining its Relationship with Other Philippine Languages*. MA Thesis, Ateneo de Manila University.

Santoso, Dewi Mulyani, Tandang and Diana Sofyan (1991). *Struktur Bahasa Dayak Ngaju*. Pusat Pembinaan dan Pengembangan Bahasa, Departemen Pendidikan dan Kebudayaan.

Sapir, Edward (1916). *Time Perspective in Aboriginal American Culture: A Study in Method*. Canada, Department of Mines, Geological Survey, Memoir 90 Anthropological Series No. 13. Ottawa: Government Printing Bureau. Reprinted in David G Mandelbaum (ed.), (1968). *Selected Writings of Edward Sapir in Language, Culture and Personality*. Berkeley and Los Angeles: University of California Press, 387–462.

Sapir, Edward (1921). *Language: An Introduction to the Study of Speech*. New York: Harcourt, Brace and World, Inc.

Sasse, Hans-Jürgen (1993). Syntactic Categories and Subcategories, in Joachim Jacobs, Arnim von Stechow, Wolfgang Sternefeld and Theo Vennemann (eds.), *Syntax: Ein internationales Handbuch zeitgenössischer Forschung*. Berlin: Walter de Gruyter, 646–86.

Saussure, Ferdinand de (1879). *Mémoire sur le système primitif des voyelles dans les langues*. Leipsick: B. G. Teubner.

Saussure, Ferdinand de (1959)[1915]. *Course in General Linguistics*. New York: McGraw-Hill.

Savage, Dale T (1986). A Reconstruction of Proto-Southern Mindanaon, *Studies in Philippine Linguistics* 6: 181–223.

Sawaki, Yusuf (2016). *A Grammar of Wooi: An Austronesian Language of Yapen Island, Western New Guinea*. PhD Dissertation, Australian National University.

Sawaki, Yusuf and I Wayan Arka (2018). Reflections on Linguistic Fieldwork and Language Documentation in Eastern Indonesia, in Bradley McDonnell, Andrea L Berez-Kroeker and Gary Holton (eds.), *Reflections on Language Documentation 20 Years After Himmelmann 1998*. Honolulu: University of Hawai'i Press, 256–66.

Scebold, Robert (2003). *A Grammar of Central Tagbanwa: A Philippine Language on the Brink of Extinction: Sociolinguistics, Grammar and Lexicon*. Manila: Linguistic Society of the Philippines Publications.

Schachter, Paul (1973). Constraints on Clitic Order in Tagalog, in Andrew B Gonzalez, F S C (ed.), *Parangay Kay Cecilio Lopez: Essays in Honor of Cecilio Lopez on His Seventy-Fifth Birthday*. Quezon City: Linguistic Society of the Philippines, 214–31.

Schachter, Paul (1976). The Subject in Philippine Languages: Actor, Topic, Actor-Topic, Or None of the Above, in Charles Li (ed.), *Subject and Topic*. New York: Academic Press, 491–518.

Schachter, Paul (1977). Reference-Related and Role-Related Properties of Subjects, in Peter Cole and Jerrold M Sadock (eds.), *Syntax and Semantics Vol. 8: Grammatical Relations*. New York: Academic Press, 279–306.

Schachter, Paul (1984). Semantic-Role-Based Syntax in Toba Batak, in Paul Schachter (ed.), *Studies in the Structure of Toba Batak*. Los Angeles: University of California Los Angeles, Department of Linguistics, 122–49.

Schachter, Paul (1985a). Lexical Functional Grammar as a Model of Linguistic Competence, *Linguistics and Philosophy* 8(4): 449–503.

Schachter, Paul (1985b). Part-of-Speech Systems, in Timothy Shopen (ed.), *Language Typology and Syntactic Description I: Clause Structure*. Cambridge: Cambridge University Press, 3–61.

Schachter, Paul (1987). Tagalog, in Bernard Comrie (ed.), *The World's Major Languages*. London, Routledge, 936–58.

Schachter, Paul (1996). *The Subject in Tagalog: Still None of the Above*. UCLA Occasional Papers in Linguistics, 15. Los Angeles: UCLA, Department of Linguistics.

Schachter, Paul and Fay Otanes (1972). *Tagalog Reference Grammar*. Berkeley: University of California Press.

Schadeberg, Thillo C (2003). Derivation, in D Nurse and G Philippson (eds.), *The Bantu Languages*. London: Routledge, 71–89.

Schadeberg, Thillo C (2009). Loanwords in Swahili, (Martin Haspelmath and Uri Tadmor Eds): *Loanwords in the World's Languages: A Comparative Handbook of Lexical Borrowing*. Berlin: Mouton de Gruyter, 717–46.

Schalley, Ewa (2008). *Imperatives: A Typological Approach*. PhD Dissertation, University of Antwerp.

Schapper, Antoinette (2009). Possession in Kemak. Presentation: 11th International Conference on Austronesian Linguistics, June 21–25. Aussois, France.

Schapper, Antoinette (2010a). *Bunaq: A Papuan Language of Central Timor*. PhD Dissertation, Australian National University.

Schapper, Antoinette (2010b). Neuter Gender in Eastern Indonesia, *Oceanic Linguistics* 49(2): 407–35.

Schapper, Antoinette (2011a). Iconicity of Sequence in the Coding of Source and Goal in two Papuan Languages, *Linguistics in the Netherlands* 2011: 101–13.

Schapper, Antoinette (2011b). Phalanger Facts: Notes on Blust's Marsupial Reconstructions, *Oceanic Linguistics* 50: 258–72.

Schapper, Antoinette (2015a). Wallacea, a Linguistic Area, *Archipel* 90: 99–151.

Schapper, Antoinette (2015b). Gender in the Languages of Aru, *Wacana, Journal of the Humanities of Indonesia* 16(1): 1–26.

Schapper, Antoinette (2017a). Farming and the Trans-New Guinea Family: A Consideration, in Martine Robbeets and Alexander Savelyev (eds.), *Language Dispersal Beyond Farming*. Amsterdam: John Benjamins, 155–82.

Schapper, Antoinette (2017b). Introduction to the Papuan Languages of Timor, Alor and Pantar. Volume II, in Antoinette Schapper (ed.), *Papuan Languages of Timor, Alor and Pantar. Sketch Grammars: Volume 2*. Berlin: de Gruyter Mouton, 1–54.

Schapper, Antoinette (2017c). Merging Meanings in Melanesia. Presentation: 9th International Austronesian and Papuan Languages and Linguistics Conference, Paris, 21–23 June 2017.

Schapper, Antoinette (2017d). Negation in Waima'a. Handout from presentation at the University of Cologne. DOI: 10.5281/zenodo.4733336

Schapper, Antoinette (2019). The Ethno-Linguistic Relationship Between Smelling and Kissing: A Southeast Asian Case Study, *Oceanic Linguistics* 58(1): 92–109.

Schapper, Antoinette (2020a). The Origins of Isolating Word Structure in Eastern Timor, in David Gil and Antoinette Schapper (eds.), *Austronesian Undressed: How and Why Languages Become Isolating*. Amsterdam: John Benjamins, 391–446.

Schapper, Antoinette (2020b). Linguistic Melanesia, in Yaron Matras and Evangelia Adamou (eds.), *Routledge Handbook of Language Contact*. London: Routledge, 480–502.

Schapper, Antoinette (2023). From Possessive to Relative Clause Marker: A Grammaticalization Pathway in the Timor-Alor-Pantar Languages, *STUF - Language Typology and Universals* 76(3): 369–401.

Schapper, Antoinette and Emilie Wellfelt (2018). Reconstructing Contact Between Alor and Timor. Evidence from Language and Beyond, in Antoinette Schapper (ed.), *Language Contact and Substrate in the Languages of Wallacea, Part 2*. Special issue of *NUSA* 64: 95–116.

Schapper, Antoinette and Emily Gasser (2023). Adnominal Possession in the Languages of Wallacea: A Survey, *STUF - Language Typology and Universals*, 76(3): 273–329.

Schapper, Antoinette and Harald Hammarström (2013). Innovative Numerals in Malayo-Polynesian Languages Outside of Oceania, *Oceanic Linguistics* 52(2): 423–56.

Schapper, Antoinette and Juliette Huber (2019). The Austronesian-Papuan Contact History of Eastern Timor: What Lexical Borrowing Can Tell Us? Presentation: 11th International Austronesian and Papuan Languages and Linguistics Conference, Leiden, 13–15 June 2019.

Schapper, Antoinette and Juliette Huber. (2023). Papuan borrowings in the Kawaimina languages, in Marian Klamer and Francesca Moro (eds.), *Traces of contact in the lexicon*. Leiden: Brill, 180–209.

Schapper, Antoinette and William McConvell. (2024). Database of Adnominal Possessive Constructions in the Malayo-Polynesian Languages of Southeast Asia. Version 3 DOI: 10.5281/zenodo.12736998.

Schapper, Antoinette and Erik Zobel. (Forthcoming). The classification of Irarutu and Koiwai: A new proposal. *Oceanic Linguistics*.

Scheerer, Otto and Carlos Everett Conant (1908). *The Batan Dialect as a Member of the Philippine Group of Languages*. Manila: Bureau of Printing (Ethnological Survey Publications Vol. 5 Part 1), 1–131.

Schlegel, Gustav (1891). Chinese Loanwords in the Malay Language, *T'oung Pao* 1(5): 391–405.

Schleicher, August (1861). *Compendium der vergleichenden Grammatik der indogermanischen Sprachen, 1: Kurzer Abriss der Lautlehre der indogermanischen Ursprache, Des Altindischen (Sanskrit), Alteranischen (Baktrischen), Altitalischen (Lateinischen, Umbrischen, Oskischen), Altkeltischen (Altirischen), Altslawischen (Altbulgarischen), Litauischen Und Altdeutschen (Gotischen)*. Weimar: Hermann Böhlau.

Schmidt, Christopher K (2014). *Morphosyntax of Wangka, A Dialect of Rembong-Riung*. PhD Dissertation, Rice University.

Schmidt, Wilhelm (1905). Grundzüge einer Lautlehre der Mon-Khmer-Sprachen, *Denkschrift der Akademie der Wissenschaften, Wien, Philologisch-Historische Klasse* 51: 1–233.

Schwaiger, Thomas (2015). Reduplication, in Peter O Müller, Ingeborg Ohnheiser, Susan Olsen and Franz Rainer (eds.), *Word-Formation: An International Handbook of the Languages of Europe*, Volume 1. Berlin: de Gruyter Mouton, 467–84.

Schwaiger, Thomas (2017). *The Structure of Reduplicants: A Typological Investigation of Iconicity and Preferred Form in Reduplication.* PhD Dissertation, University of Graz.

Schwarz, Johannes Albert Traugott (1907). *Tontemboansche teksten.* 3 Volumes. Leiden: Brill.

Schwarz, Johannes Albert Traugott (1908). *Tontemboansch-Nederlandsch woordenboek, met Nederlandsch-Tontemboansch register* [Tontemboan – Dutch dictionary with Dutch – Tontemboan index]. Leiden: Brill.

Scontras, Gregory, Zuzanna Fuchs and Maria Polinsky (2015). Heritage Language and Linguistic Theory, *Frontiers in Psychology* 6: 1545.

Scott, Charles Payson Gurley (1897). The Malayan Words in English, *Journal of the American Oriental Society* 18: 49–124.

Scott, N C (1956). *A Dictionary of Sea Dayak.* London: School of Oriental and African Studies, University of London.

Scott, William H (1984). *Prehispanic Source Materials for the Study of Philippine History* (Revised Edition). Quezon City: Day Publishers.

Scott, William H (1992). *Looking for the Prehispanic Filipino.* Quezon City: New Day Publishers.

Sedeng, I Nyoman (2007). *Morfosintaksis Bahasa Bali dialek Sembiran: Analisis tatabahasa Peran* [The morphosyntax of the Sembiran dialect of Balinese: a Role and Reference Grammar analysis]. Denpasar: Udayana University Press.

Sedghifar A, Y Brandvain, P Ralph and G Coop (2015). The Spatial Mixing of Genomes in Secondary Contact Zones, *Genetics* 201: 243–61.

Segalowitz, Norman and Rosita Galang (1978). Agent-Patient Word Order Preference in the Acquisition of Tagalog, *Journal of Child Language* 5: 47–64.

Seidlitz, E (2005a). *A Study of Jakun Malay: Some Aspects of its Phonology.* MA Thesis, Universiti Kebangsaan Malaysia.

Seidlitz, E (2005b). Duano Fieldnotes. Unpublished Manuscript.

Seidlitz, Eric (2007). Duano: A First Look at its Phonology, in Chong Shin, Karim Harun and Yabit Alas (eds.), *Reflections in Southeast Asian Seas: Essays in honour of Professor James T. Collins*, vol. 2. Pontianak: STAIN Pontianak Press, 23–49.

Sellato, Bernard (1980). The Upper Mahakam Area, *Borneo Research Bulletin* 12(2): 40–6.

Sellato, Bernard (1981). The Three-Gender Personal Pronouns in Some Languages of Central Borneo, *Borneo Research Bulletin* 13: 48–9.

Sellato, Bernard (1986). *Les nomads forestiers de Bornéo et la sédentarisation; essai d'histoire économique et sociale.* PhD Dissertation, EHESS, Paris.

Sellato, Bernard (1988). The Nomads of Borneo: Hoffman and Devolution, *Borneo Research Bulletin* 20(1): 106–20.

Sellato, Bernard (1994). *Nomads of the Bornean Rainforest: The Economics, Politics, and Ideology of Settling Down.* (Translation of Sellato 1986). Honolulu: University of Hawai'i Press.

Sellato, Bernard (2001). *Forest, Resources and People in Bulungan. Elements for a History of Settlement, Trade, and Social Dynamics in Borneo, 1880–2000.* Bogor: Center for International Forestry Research.

Sellato, Bernard and Antonia Soriente (2015). The Languages and Peoples of the Müller Mountains: A Contribution to the Study of the Origins of Borneo's Nomads and their Languages, *Wacana* 16(2): 339–54.

Sells, Peter (2000). Raising and the Order of Clausal Constituents in the Philippine Languages, in Ileana Paul, Vivianne Phillips and Lisa Travis (eds.), *Formal Issues in Austronesian Linguistics.* Dordrecht: Springer/Kluwer Academic Press, 117–43.

Sells, Peter (2006). Optimality-Theoretic Lexical-Functional Grammar, in E Keith Brown and Anne Anderson (ed.), *Encyclopedia of Language and Linguistics.* Amsterdam: Elsevier, 60–8.

Semiun, Agustinus (1993). *The Basic Grammar of Manggarai: Kempo Subdialect.* MA Thesis, La Trobe University.

Senft, Gunter (2004a). *Deixis and Demonstratives in Oceanic Languages.* Canberra: Pacific Linguistics.

Senft, Gunter (2004b). What Do We Really Know about Serial Verb Constructions in Austronesian and Papuan Languages?, in Isabelle Bril and Françoise Ozanne-Rivierre (eds.), *Complex Predicates in Oceanic Languages: Studies in the Dynamics of Binding and Boundness.* Berlin/New York: Mouton de Gruyter, 49–64.

Sercombe, Peter (1996). Ethno-Linguistic Change Among the Penan of Brunei: Some Initial Observations, *Bijdragen tot de Taal-, Land- en Volkenkunde* 152(2): 257–74.

Sercombe, Peter (2020). Identity and Eastern Penan in Borneo, *Journal of Modern Languages* 30(1): 77–100.

Serruys, Henry (1968). Ho-po, ho-pao "pouch" = Turkic qap, xap, *Oriens Extremus* 15(2): 135–48.

Serva, Maurizio and Michele Pasquini (2021). Malagasy Dialects in Mayotte, *Europhysics Letters* 133/6: 133 68003.

Servick, Kelly (2019). Paddlers to Replicate Ancient Voyage, *Science* 365: 1011.

Setiawan, Slamet (2012). *Children's Language in a Bilingual Community in East Java.* PhD Dissertation, University of Western Australia.

Sharma, Mukunda Madhava (1985). *Unsur-unsur Bahasa Sanskerta dalam Bahasa Indonesia* [Sanskrit elements in Indonesian]. Denpasar: Wyasa Sanggaraha.

Shetler, Joanne (1976). *Notes on Balangao Grammar.* Language Data, Asian-Pacific Series #9. Huntington Beach, California: Summer Institute of Linguistics.

Shibatani, Masayoshi (1985). Passives and Related Constructions: A Prototype Analysis, *Language* 61(4): 821–48.

Shibatani, Masayoshi (1988). Introduction, in Masayoshi Shibatani (ed.), *Passive and Voice.* Amsterdam/Philadelphia: John Benjamins, 1–8.

Shibatani, Masayoshi (2006). On the Conceptual Framework for Voice Phenomena, *Linguistics* 44(2): 217–69.

Shibatani, Masayoshi (2008). Relativisation in Sasak and Sumbawa, Eastern Indonesia, *Language and Linguistics* No. 9 (4): 865–916.

Shibatani, Masayoshi and Ketut Artawa (2007). The Middle Voice in Balinese.), *SEALS XIII: Papers from the 13th Meeting of the Southeast Asian Linguistics Society*. Canberra: Pacific Linguistics, 241–63.

Shiohara, Asako (2006). *Sunbawa-Go No Bunpō* [A Grammar of Sumbawa]. PhD Dissertation, Tokyo University.

Shiohara, Asako (2013a). Voice in the Sumbawa Besar Dialect of Sumbawa, in Alexander Adelaar (ed.), *Voice Variation in Austronesian Languages of Indonesia*. Special issue of *NUSA* 54: 145–58.

Shiohara, Asako (2013b). Tense, Aspect, Mood and Polarity in the Sumbawa Besar Dialect of Sumbawa, in John Bowden (ed.), *Tense, Aspect, Mood and Evidentiality in Languages of Indonesia*. Special issue of *NUSA* 55: 173–92.

Shiohara, Asako (2014). Numerals in Sumbawa, in Marian Klamer and František Kratochvíl (eds.), *Number and quantity in East Nusantara*. Canberra: Asia-Pacific Linguistics, 15–25.

Shiohara, Asako and I Ketut Artawa (2012). Grammaticalisation of Verbs of Giving, Using and Inviting in Balinese. Presentation: International Conference on Austronesian Linguistics (ICAL12), Udayana University, Denpasar, Indonesia. July 2, 2012.

Shiohara, Asako and Ketut Artawa (2014). The Definite Marker in Balinese, in Linguistic Science Project 2 (ed.), *Proceedings of the Second International Workshop on Information Structure of Austronesian Languages*. Tokyo: Research Institute of Languages and Cultures of Asia and Africa, Tokyo University of Foreign Studies, 141–60.

Shorto, Harry L (1975). Achinese and Mainland Austronesian, *Bulletin of the School of Oriental and African Studies* 38(1): 81–102.

Shorto, Harry L (1976). In Defense of Austric. *Computational Analyses of Asian and African Languages* 6: 95–104.

Shorto, Harry L (2006). *A Mon-Khmer Comparative Dictionary*. Canberra: Pacific Linguistics.

Sidwell, Paul (2005). Acehnese and the Aceh-Chamic Language Family, in Anthony Grant and Paul Sidwell (eds.), *Chamic and Beyond: Studies in Mainland Austronesian Languages*. Canberra: Pacific Linguistics, 211–46.

Sidwell, Paul (2006). Dating the Separation of Acehnese and Chamic by Etymological Analysis of the Aceh-Chamic Lexicon, *Mon-Khmer Studies* 36: 187–206.

Sidwell, Paul (2007). The Mon-Khmer Substrate in Chamic: Chamic, Bahnaric and Katuic Contact, in Ratree Wayland, John Hartmann and Paul Sidwell (eds.), *SEALS XII Papers from the 12th Annual Meeting of the Southeast Asian Linguistics Society (2002)*. Canberra: Pacific Linguistics, 113–28.

Sidwell, Paul (2008). *On the Sources of Loans in the Proto-Chamic Lexicon*, in Wilaiwan Khanittanan and Paul Sidwell (eds.), *SEALS XIV (Volume 1). Papers from the 14th Annual Meeting of the Southeast Asian Linguistics Society (2004)*. Canberra: Pacific Linguistics, 261–7.

Sidwell, Paul and Pascale Jacq (2003). *A Handbook of Comparative Bahnaric: Volume 1, West Bahnaric*. Canberra, Pacific Linguistics.

Siewierska, Anna (2013). Alignment of Verbal Person Marking, in Matthew S Dryer and Martin Haspelmath (eds.), *The World Atlas of Language Structures Online*. Leipzig: Max Planck Institute for Evolutionary Anthropology. URL: https://wals.info/chapter/100

SIL Philippines (2011). Central Subanen Dictionary. URL: https://philippines.sil.org/resources/works_in_progress/syb

Silverstein, Michael (1979). Language Structure and Linguistic Ideology, in Paul R Clyne, William F Hanks and Carol L Hofbauer (eds.), *The Elements: A Parasession on Linguistic Units and Levels*. Chicago: Chicago Linguistic Society, 193–248.

Silverstein, Michael (1985). Language and the Culture of Gender: At the Intersection of Structure, Usage and Ideology, in Elizabeth Mertz and Richard J Parmentier (eds.), *Semiotic Mediation: Sociocultural and Psychological Perspectives*. Orlando (FL): Academic Press, 219–59.

Silzer, Peter J (1983). *Ambai: An Austronesian Language of Irian Jaya, Indonesia*. PhD Dissertation, Australian National University.

Simanjuntak, Truman (2017). The Western Route Migration: A Second Probable Neolithic Diffusion to Indonesia, in Philip Piper, Hirofumi Matsumura and David Bulbeck (eds.), *New Perspectives in Southeast Asian and Pacific Prehistory*. Canberra: Australian National University Press, 201–11.

Simanjuntak, Truman (ed.) (2016). *Gua Harimau Cave and the Long Journey of Oku Civilization*. Yogyakarta: Gadjah Mada University Press.

Simanjuntak, Truman, Adhi Agus Oktaviana and Retno Handini (2016). Updated Views on the Austronesian Studies in Indonesia, in Bagyo Prasetyo, Titi Surti Nastiti and Truman Simanjuntak (eds.), *Austronesian Diaspora: A New Perspective*. Yogyakarta: Gadjah Mada University Press, 207–22.

Simanjuntak, Truman, M J Morwood, Fadhlan S Intan, Irfan Machmud et al. (2008). Minanga Sipakko and the Neolithic of the Karama River, in Truman Simanjuntak (ed.), *Austronesian in Sulawesi*. Depok: Center for Prehistoric and Austronesian Studies, 57–75.

Simon, Pierre (2006). *La langue des ancêtres (Ny fitenindrazana). Une périodisation du malgache de l'origine au xve Siècle*. Paris: L'Harmattan.

Simons, Gary F and Charles D Fennig (eds.) (2017). *Ethnologue: Languages of the World*, Twentieth Edition. Dallas, Texas: Summer Institute of Linguistics International. URL: http://www.ethnologue.com

Simons, Gary F and Charles D Fennig (eds.) (2018). *Ethnologue: Languages of the World*, Twenty-First Edition. Dallas, Texas: Summer Institute of Linguistics International. URL: http://www.ethnologue.com

Singarimbun, Masri (1975). *Kinship, Descent and Alliance Among the Karo Batak*. Berkeley: University of California Press.

Sippola, Eva (2013). Cavite Chabacano structure dataset, in Susanne M Michaelis, Philippe Maurer, Martin Haspelmath and Magnus Huber (eds.), *The Survey of Pidgin and Creole Languages*, Volume II. Oxford: Oxford University Press, 143–55.

Sirk, Ülo Kh (1981). The South Sulawesi Group and Neighboring Languages, *Indonesia Circle* 25: 29–36.

Sirk, Ülo Kh (1983). *The Buginese Language*. Moscow: Nauka.

Sirk, Ülo Kh (1988). Research Needs: The Wotu Language, *Baruga, Sulawesi Research Bulletin* 2: 10–12.

Sirk, Ülo Kh (1989). On the Evidential Basis for the South Sulawesi Language Group, in James N Sneddon (ed.), *Studies in Sulawesi Linguistics, Part I*. Jakarta: Badan Penyelenggara Seri Nusa, Universitas Atma Jaya, 55–82.

Siwuh Binti, Renate (2015). Spatial Reference in Ngaju Dayak. Presentation: 13th International Conference on Austronesian Linguistics, Taipei.

Skeat, Walter W and Charles O Blagden (1906). *Pagan Races of the Malayan Peninsula (2 Vols)*. New York: Macmillan and Co.

Skoglund, Pontus, Cosimo Posth, Kendra Sirak, Matthew Spriggs et al. (2016). Genomic Insights into the Peopling of the Southwest Pacific, *Nature* 538: 510–13.

Slomanson, Peter (2006). Sri Lankan Malay Morphosyntax: Lankan or Malay? in Ana Deumert and Stephanie Durrleman-Tame (eds.), *Structure and Variation in Language Contact*. Amsterdam: John Benjamins, 135–58.

Slomanson, Peter (2011). Dravidian Features in the Sri Lankan Malay Verb, in C Lefebvre (ed.), *Creoles, Their Substrates, and Language Typology*. Amsterdam: John Benjamins, 383–409.

Slomanson, Peter (2012). Known, Inferable, and Discoverable in Sri Lankan Malay Research, in Sebastian Nordhoff (ed.), *Extreme Language Contact: The Case of Sri Lanka Malay*. Leiden/Boston: Brill, 85–119.

Slomanson, Peter (2013). Sri Lankan Malay, in Susanne Maria Michaelis, Philippe Maurer, Martin Haspelmath and Magnus Huber (eds.), *The Survey of Pidgin and Creole Languages, Vol. III: Contact Languages Based on Languages from Africa, Asia, Australia, and the Americas*. Oxford: Oxford University Press, 77–85.

Slomanson, Peter (2016). Pragmatic Accommodation as a Catalyst for the Development of (non-)finiteness, *The Linguistic Review* 33(3): 365–96.

Slomanson, Peter (2018a). Cross-Linguistic Negation Contrasts in Co-Convergent Contact Languages, in Viviane Déprez and Fabiola Henri (eds.), *Negation and Negative Concord: The View from Creoles*. Amsterdam: John Benjamins, 289–311.

Slomanson, Peter (2018b). The Development of Infinitival Complementation with or without Language Contact, in M Kaunisto, M Höglund and P Rickman (eds.), *Changing Structures: Studies in Constructions and Complementation*. Amsterdam: John Benjamins, 97–213.

Slomanson, Peter (2021). Negative irrealis clauses in Malay/Indonesian and Sri Lankan Malay infinitives, *Wacana* 22/1: 1–21.

Slump, F (1924). *Grammatica en woordenlijst van de Seroei-Laut taal*. Manuscript in het Utrechts Archief, Nummer Toegang 2274, Inventarisnummer 1102–1. [Grammar and wordlist of Serui-Laut. Manuscript in the Utrecht Archive, Access No. 2274, Inventary No. 1102–1].

Smith-Hefner, Nancy (2009). Language Shift, Gender, and Ideologies of Modernity in Central Java, Indonesia, *Journal of Linguistic Anthropology* 19(1): 57–77.

Smith, Alexander D (2015a). On the Classification of Kenyah and Kayanic Languages, *Oceanic Linguistics* 53(2): 333–57.

Smith, Alexander D (2015b). Sebop, Penan, and Kenyah Internal Linguistic Classification, *Borneo Research Bulletin* 46(1): 172–93.

Smith, Alexander D (2017a). *The Languages of Borneo: A Comprehensive Classification*. PhD Dissertation, University of Hawai'i.

Smith, Alexander D (2017b). The Western Malayo-Polynesian Problem, *Oceanic Linguistics* 56(2): 435–89.

Smith, Alexander D (2017c). Merap Historical Phonology in the Context of a Central Bornean Linguistic Area, *Oceanic Linguistics* 56(1): 143–80.

Smith, Alexander D (2017d). Reconstructing Proto-Kenyah Pronouns and the Development of a True five Number System, in Hsiu-Chuan Liao (ed.), *Issues in Austronesian Historical Linguistics*. Special issue of *Journal of the Southeast Asian Linguistic Society* 10(3): 48–66.

Smith, Alexander D (2018a). The Barito Linkage Hypothesis with a Note on the Position of Basap, *Journal of the Southeast Asian Linguistics Society* 11(1): 13–34.

Smith, Alexander D (2018b). Proto-Austronesian Schwa: Phonotactic Restrictions and Weight Phenomena Throughout Austronesian. Presentation: 25th Meeting of the Austronesian Formal Linguistics Association, 10–12 May, 2018, Academia Sinica, Taipei.

Smith, Alexander D (2019a). A Second Look at Proto-Land Dayak Vowels, *Oceanic Linguistics* 58(1): 110–42.

Smith, Alexander D (2019b). A Reconstruction of Proto-Segai Modang, *Oceanic Linguistics* 58(2): 353–85.

Smith, Alexander D (2020). Nasalization in Enggano Historical Phonology, *Oceanic Linguistics* 59(1): 347–65.

Smith, Alexander D (submitted). Reconstructing Non-Contrastive Stress in Austronesian and the Role of Schwa in Stress Shift, Gemination, and Vowel Shift. Unpublished Manuscript, University of North Texas.

Smith, James A and Karla J Smith (2017). Indigenous Language Development in East Malaysia, *International Journal of the Sociology of Language* 244: 119–35.

Smith, Joanna Lee Belding (2002). *Causative Constructions in Barang-Barang*. MA Thesis, University of Auckland.

Smith, Kenneth D (1984). The Languages of Sabah: A Tentative Lexicostatistical Classification, in Julie K King and John Wayne King (eds.), *Languages of Sabah: A Survey Report*. Canberra: Pacific Linguistics, 1–49.

Smits, Leo and C L Voorhoeve (1992). *The J C Anceaux Collection of Wordlists of Irian Jaya Languages A: Austronesian Languages (Part I)*. Leiden/Jakarta: DSALCUL/IRIS.

Smolicz, J J (1986). National Language Policy in the Philippines, in Bernard Spolsky (ed.), *Language and Education in Multilingual Settings*. Clevedon: Multilingual Matters, 96–116.

Sneddon, James N (1975). *Tondano Phonology and Grammar*. Canberra: Pacific Linguistics.

Sneddon, James N (1978). *Proto-Minahasan: Phonology, Morphology, and Wordlist*. Canberra: Pacific Linguistics.

Sneddon, James N (1983). Southern Celebes (Sulawesi), in Stephen A Wurm and Shirô Hattori (eds.), *Language Atlas of the Pacific Area, Part 2: Japan Area, Taiwan (Formosa), Philippines, Mainland and Insular South-East Asia*. Canberra: Pacific Linguistics & Australian Academy of the Humanities and the Japan Academy, Map 44.

Sneddon, James N (1984). *Proto-Sangiric and the Sangiric Languages*. Canberra: Pacific Linguistics.

Sneddon, James N (1989). The North Sulawesi Microgroups: In Search of Higher Level Connections, in James N Sneddon (ed.), *Studies in Sulawesi Linguistics, Part I*. Jakarta: Badan Penyelenggara Seri Nusa, Universitas Katolik Indonesia Atma Jaya, 83–107.

Sneddon, James N (1991). The Position of Lolak, in Ray Harlow, ed., *Papers from the Fifth International Conference on Austronesian Linguistics: Western Austronesian and Contact Languages*. Auckland: Linguistic Society of New Zealand and University of Auckland, 299–318.

Sneddon, James N (1993). The Drift Towards Open Final Syllables in Sulawesi Languages, *Oceanic Linguistics* 32: 1–44.

Sneddon, James N (1996). *Indonesian: A Comprehensive Grammar*. London: Routledge.

Sneddon, James N (2003a). Diglossia in Indonesian, *Bijdragen tot de Taal-, Land- en Volkenkunde* 159(4): 519–49.

Sneddon, James N (2003b). *The Indonesian Language: Its History and Role in Modern Society*. Sydney: University of New South Wales Press.

Sneddon, James N (author), Alexander Adelaar, D Novi Djenar and Michael C Ewing (eds.) (2010). *Indonesian. A Comprehensive Grammar*. 2nd revised edition. London: Routledge.

Sneddon, James N and Hunggu Tadjuddin Usup (1986). Shared Sound Changes in the Gorontalic Language Group: Implications for Subgrouping, *Bijdragen tot de Taal-, Land- en Volkenkunde* 142: 407–26.

Snow, E Bryan, Richard Shutler Jr., D E Nelson, J S Vogel and J R Southon (1986). Evidence of Early Rice Cultivation in the Philippines, *Philippine Quarterly of Culture and Society* 14(1): 3–11.

Soares P A, J A Trejaut, T Rito, B Cavadas, C Hill, K K Eng, M Mormina, A Brandão, R M Fraser, T -Y Wang, J -H Loo, C Snell, T -M Ko, A Amorim, M Pala, V Macaulay, D Bulbeck, J F Wilson, L Gusmão, L Pereira, S Oppenheimer, M Lin and M B Richards (2016). Resolving the Ancestry of Austronesian-Speaking Populations, *Human Genetics* 135: 309–26.

Soares P, J A Trejaut, J H Loo, C Hill, M Mormina, C L Lee, Y M Che, G Hudjashov, P Forster, V Macaulay, D Bulbeck, S Oppenheimer, M Lin and M B Richards (2008). Climate Change and Postglacial Human Dispersals in Southeast Asia, *Molecular Biology and Evolution* 25: 1209–18.

Soares P, T Rito, J Trejaut, M Mormina, C Hill, E Tinkler-Hundal, M Braid, DJ Clark, J H Loo, N Thomson, T Denham, M Donohue, V Macaulay, M Lin, S Oppenheimer and M B Richards (2011). Ancient Voyaging and Polynesian Origins, *American Journal of Human Genetics* 88: 239–47.

Soderberg, Craig (2014). Kedayan, *Journal of the International Phonetic Association* 44(2): 201–5.

Soderberg, Craig, Seymour A Ashley and Kenneth S Olson (2012). Tausug (Suluk), *Journal of the International Phonetic Association* 42: 361–4.

Sokal, Robert R and Peter H A Sneath (1963). *Principles of Numerical Taxonomy*, San Francisco: W H Freeman.

Solheim, Wilhelm G II (1957). The Kalanay Pottery Complex in the Philippines, *Artibus Asiae* XX: 279–88.

Solheim, Wilhelm G II (1964). Pottery and the Malayo-Polynesians, *Current Anthropology* 5(5): 360, 376–406.

Solheim, Wilhelm G II (1968). The Batungan Cave Sites, Masbate, Philippines, in Wilhelm. G Solheim II (ed.), *Anthropology at the Eighth Pacific Science Congress of the Pacific Science Association and the Fourth Far-Eastern Prehistory Congress*. Honolulu: Social Science Research Institute, University of Hawai'i, 21–62.

Solheim, Wilhelm G II (1980). Neue Befunde zur späten Prähistorie Südostasiens und ihre Interpretation, *Saeculum* 31: 275–317, 319–344.

Solheim, Wilhelm G II (1984–1985). The Nusantao Hypothesis: The Origin and Spread of Austronesian Speakers, *Asian Perspectives* 26(1): 77–88.

Solheim, Wilhelm G II (2006). *Archaeology and Culture in Southeast Asia: Unraveling the Nusantao*. Quezon City: The University of the Philippines Press.

Solheim, Wilhelm G II, David Bulbeck and Ambika Flavel (2006). *Archaeology and Culture in Southeast Asia: Unraveling the Nusantao*. Diliman, Quezon City: University of Philippines Press.

Sommerlot, Carly (2020). On *the Syntax of West Kalimantan: Asymmetries and A-Movement in Malayic and Land Dayak Languages*. PhD Dissertation, University of Texas at Arlington.

Sommerlot, Carly (2021). Typological perspectives on the nasal prefix. Presentation: 24th meeting of the International Symposium on Malay/Indonesian Linguistics, 20-22 May 2021.

Song, Jae Jung (1997). The History of Micronesian Possessive Classifiers and Benefactive Marking in Oceanic Languages, *Oceanic Linguistics* 36: 29–64.

Sopher, David Edward (1965). *The Sea Nomads: A Study Based on the Literature of the Maritime Boat People of Southeast Asia*. Singapore: Lim Bian Han, Government Printer.

Sopher, David Edward (1977). *The Sea Nomads: A Study of the Maritime Boat People of Southeast Asia*, 2nd edition. Singapore: National Museum.

Soravia, Giulio (1984). *A Sketch of the Gayo Language*. Gruppo Linguistico Catanese No 1. Catania: Facoltà di Lettere e Filosofia, Università di Catania.

Soravia, Giulio (2007). *A Study of the Alas Language*. Bologna: Università di Bologna, Dipartimento di studi linguistici e orientali.

Soriente, Antonia (2003). *A Classification of the Kenyah Languages in East Kalimantan and Sarawak*. PhD Dissertation, Universiti Kebangsaan Malaysia.

Soriente, Antonia (2006). *Mencalèny and Usung Bayung Marang: A Collection of Kenyah Stories in the Òma Lóngh and Lebu Kulit Languages*. Jakarta: Atma Jaya University.

Soriente, Antonia (2008). The Classification of Kenyah Languages: A Preliminary Assessment, in Wilaiwan Khanittana and Paul Sidwell (eds.), *SEALS XIV(2): Papers from the 14th Meeting of the*

*Southeast Asian Linguistics Society (2004)*. Canberra: Pacific Linguistics, 49–62.

Soriente, Antonia (2013). Undergoer Voice in Borneo: Penan, Punan, Kenyah and Kayan Languages, in Alexander Adelaar (ed.), *Voice Variation in Austronesian Languages of Indonesia*. Special issue of *NUSA* 54: 175–203.

Soriente, Antonia (2020). Hunter-Gatherers of Borneo and their Languages, in Tom Güldemann, Patrick McConvell, Richard A Rhodes (eds.), *The Language of Hunter-Gatherers*. Cambridge: Cambridge University Press, 262–308.

Southwell, C Hudson (1990). *Kayan-English Dictionary, with Appendices*. Kuching: Sarawak Literary Society.

Spitzack, John (1988). Kalabuan Clauses, in Charles Peck, (ed.), *Borneo Language Studies 1: Sabah Syntax Papers*. Dallas: Summer Institute of Linguistics, 100–48.

Spitzack, John (1993). Kalabuan Phonemics, in Michael E Boutin and Inka Pekkanen (eds.), *Phonological Descriptions of Sabah Languages*. Kota Kinabalu: Sabah Museum, 81–96.

Spoehr, Alexander (1957). *Marianas Prehistory: Archaeological Survey and Excavations on Saipan, Tinian and Rota*. Chicago: Chicago Natural History Museum.

Spolsky, Bernard (2018). Language Policy in French Colonies and after Independence, *Current Issues in Language Planning* 19(3): 231–315.

Spriggs, Matthew (2007). The Neolithic and Austronesian Expansion within Island Southeast Asia and Into the Pacific, in S Chiu, C Sand (eds.), *from Southeast Asia to the Pacific: Archaeological Perspectives on the Austronesian Expansion and the Lapita Cultural Complex*. Taipei: Academica Sinica, 104–25.

Spriggs, Matthew (2012). Is the Neolithic Spread in Island Southeast Asia Really as Confusing as the Archaeologists (and Some Linguists) Make it Seem?, in M L Tjoa-Bonatz, A Reinecke, D Bonatz (eds.), *Crossing Borders*. Singapore: NUS Press, 109–21.

Staden, Miriam and Ger Reesink (2008). Serial Verb Constructions in a Linguistic Area, in Gunter Senft (ed.), *Serial Verb Constructions in Austronesian and Papuan Languages*. Canberra: Pacific Linguistics, 17–54.

Starosta, Stanley (1995). A Grammatical Subgrouping of Formosan Languages, in Paul Jen-Kuei Li, Cheng-Hwa Tsang, Ying-Kuei Huang, Dah-an Ho and Chiu-Yu Tseng (eds.), *Austronesian Studies Relating to Taiwan*. Taipei: Academia Sinica, 683–726.

Starosta, Stanley and Louise Pagotto (1985). The Grammatical Genealogy of Chamorro, in Ray Harlow and Robin Hooper (eds.), *Papers from the Fifth International Conference on Austronesian Linguistics: Western Austronesian and Contact Languages*. Te Reo Special Publication. Auckland: Linguistic Society of New Zealand, 319–48.

Starosta, Stanley, Andrew Pawley and Lawrence A Reid (1981). The Evolution of Focus in Austronesian, *Proceedings of the Third International Conference on Austronesian Linguistics*, 329–481.

Starosta, Stanley, Andrew Pawley and Lawrence A Reid (1982). The Evolution of Focus in Austronesian, in Amran Halim, Lois Carrington and Stephen A Wurm (eds.), *Papers from the Third International Conference on Austronesian Linguistics, Vol. 2, Tracking the Travellers*. Canberra: Pacific Linguistics, 145–70.

Stassen, Leon (2013). Predicative Possession, in Matthew S Dryer and Martin Haspelmath (eds.), *The World Atlas of Language Structures Online*. Leipzig: Max Planck Institute for Evolutionary Anthropology. URL: http://wals.info/chapter/117

Steingass, Francis Joseph (1892). *A Comprehensive Persian-English Dictionary*. London: Routledge and K Paul.

Steinhauer, Hein (1983). Notes on the Malay of Kupang (Timor), in James T Collins (ed.), *Studies in Malay Dialects, Part II*. Special issue of *NUSA* 17. Jakarta: Badan penyelenggara seri NUSA, Universitas Atma Jaya, 42–64.

Steinhauer, Hein (1985). Number in Biak: Counterevidence to Two Alleged Language Universals, *Bijdragen tot de Taal-, Land-, en Volkenkunde* 141(2): 462–85.

Steinhauer, Hein (1991a). Problems of Gorontaloese Phonology, in Harry A Poeze and Pim Schoorl (eds.), *Excursies in Celebes: Een bundel bijdragen bij het afscheid van J Noorduyn als directeur-secretaris van het Koninklijk Instituut voor Taal-, Land- en Volkenkunde*. Leiden: Koninklijk Instituut voor Taal-, Land- en Volkenkunde, 325–38.

Steinhauer, Hein (1991b). Malay in East Indonesia: The Case of Larantuka (Flores), in Hein Steinhauer (ed.), *Papers in Austronesian Linguistics, No. 1*. Canberra: Pacific Linguistics, 177–95.

Steinhauer, Hein (1993). Notes on Verbs in Dawanese (Timor), in Ger P Reesink (ed.), *Topics in Descriptive Austronesian Linguistics*. Leiden: Vakgroep Talen en Culturen van Zuidoost-Azië en Oceanië, Rijksuniversiteit te Leiden, 131–58.

Steinhauer Hein (1996). Morphemic Metathesis in Dawanese (Timor), in Hein Steinhauer (ed.), *Papers in Austronesian Linguistics No. 3*. Canberra: Pacific Linguistics, 217–32.

Steinhauer, Hein (2002). More (on) Kerinci Sound Changes, in K Alexander Adelaar and Robert Blust (eds.), *Between Worlds: Linguistic Papers in Memory of David John Prentice*. Canberra: Pacific Linguistics, 149–76.

Steinhauer, Hein (2005). Colonial History and Language Policy in Insular Southeast Asia and Madagascar, in Alexander Adelaar and Nikolaus P Himmelmann (eds.), *The Austronesian Languages of Asia and Madagascar*. London/New York: Routledge, 65–86.

Steinhauer, Hein (2008). On the Development of Urak Lawoi' Malay, *Wacana* 10(1): 117–43.

Steinhauer, Hein (2009). The Sounds of Southeast Babar, in Alexander Adelaar and Andrew Pawley (eds.), *Austronesian Historical Linguistics and Culture History: A Festschrift for Robert Blust*. Canberra: Pacific Linguistics, 399–409.

Steinhauer, Hein (2014). Blagar, in Antoinette Schapper (ed.), *Papuan Languages of Timor-Alor-Pantar: Sketch Grammars, Volume I*. Berlin: de Gruyter Mouton, 115–72.

Steinhauer, Hein and A Hakim Usman (1978). Notes on the Morphemics of Kerinci (Sumatra), in Stephen A Wurm and L Carrington (eds.), *Second International Conference on Austronesian Linguistics, Fascicle I, Western Austronesian*. Canberra: Pacific Linguistics, 483–502.

Steinkrüger, Patrick O (2008a). The Puzzling Case of Chabacano: Creolization, Substrate, Mixing and Secondary Contact, *Studies in Philippine Languages and Cultures* 19: 142–57.

Steinkrüger, Patrick O (2008b). Hispanisation Processes in the Philippines, in Thomas Stolz, Dik Bakker and Rosa Salas Palomo (eds.), *Hispanisation: The Impact of Spanish on the Lexicon and Grammar of the Indigenous Languages of Austronesia and the Americas*. Berlin/New York: Mouton de Gruyter, 203–36.

Steinkrüger, Patrick O (2013). Zamboanga Chavacano, in Susanne Maria Michaelis, Philippe Maurer, Martin Haspelmath and Magnus Huber (eds.), *The Survey of Pidgin and Creole Languages. Volume II: Portuguese-based, Spanish-based and French-based languages*. Oxford: Oxford University Press, 156–62.

Steinmayer, Otto (1999). *Jalai Jako' Iban. A basic grammar of the Iban language of Sarawak* Kuching (Sarawak): Klasik Publishing House.

Steller, K G F and W E Aebersold (1959). *Sangirees-Nederlands woordenboek met Nederlands-Sangirees register* [Sangir – Dutch dictionary with Dutch – Sangir index]. The Hague: Martinus Nijhoff.

Steven, Lee Anthony (1991). *The Phonology of Roma, an Austronesian Language of Eastern Indonesia*. MA Thesis, the University of Texas at Arlington.

Stevens, Alan M (1968). *Madurese Phonology and Morphology*. New Haven: American Oriental Series Publisher.

Stevens, Alan M (1969). Case Grammar in Philippine Languages. Presentation: Fifth Meeting of the Linguistic Society of America, San Francisco.

Stevens, Alan M and A Ed Schmidgall-Tellings (2004). *A Comprehensive Indonesian-English Dictionary*. Athens (OH): Ohio University Press.

Stevens, Mary and John Hajek (2004). A Preliminary Investigation of Some Acoustic Characteristics of Ejectives in Waima'a: VOT and Closure Duration, in S Cassidy, F Cox, R Mannell and S Palethorpe (eds.), *Proceedings of the Tenth Australian International Conference on Speech Science and Technology*. Sydney: ASSTA, 277–82.

Stevens, Mary and John Hajek (2008). Positional Effects on the Characterization of Ejectives in Waima'a, in J Fletcher, D Loakes, R Gocke, D Burnham and M Wagner (eds.), *Proceedings of Interspeech 2008 Incorporating SST 2008*. Brisbane: ISCA, 1124–7.

Stoel, Ruben B (2005). *Focus in Manado Malay: Grammar, Particles, and Intonation*. Leiden: CNWS Publications.

Stoel, Ruben B (2006). The Intonation of Banyumas Javanese, in Rüdiger Hoffmann and Hansjörg Mixdorff (eds.), *Proceedings of the Speech Prosody 2006 Conference*, Dresden, May 2006. Dresden: TUD Press, 827–30.

Stoel, Ruben B (2007). The Intonation of Manado Malay, in Vincent J van Heuven and Ellen van Zanten (eds.), *Prosody in Indonesian Languages*. Utrecht: LOT Netherlands Graduate School of Linguistics, 117–50.

Stokhof, W A L (ed.) in co-operation with Lia Saleh Bronckhorst and Alma E Almanar (1983). *Holle Lists: Vocabularies in Languages of Indonesia Volume 7/1. North Sulawesi: Gorontalo Group and Tontoli*. Canberra: Pacific Linguistics.

Stolz, Thomas (2003). Not Quite the Right Mixture: Chamorro and Malti as Candidates for the Status of Mixed Language, in Yaron Matras and Peter Bakker (eds.), *The Mixed Language Debate. Theoretical and Empirical Advances*. Berlin: Mouton de Gruyter, 271–315.

Stolz, Thomas (2019). The Naked Truth About the Chamorro Dual, *Studies in Language*, 43(3): 533–84.

Stolz, Thomas, Cornelia Stroh and Aina Urdze (2011). *Total Reduplication: The Areal Linguistics of a Potential Universal*. Berlin: Akademie Verlag.

Stone, Jessica H, Scott M Fitzpatrick and John Krigbaum (2019). Stable Isotope Analysis of Human Diet at Chelechol Ra Orrak, Palau, *Bioarchaeology International* 3(2): 142–56.

Storck, Kurt and Margaret Storck (2005). *Ayta Mag-Antsi-English Dictionary*. Manila: Summer Institute of Linguistics, Philippines.

Stresemann, Erwin (1918). *Die Paulohisprache: Ein Beitrag zur Kenntnis der amboinischen Sprachengruppe*. The Hague: Martinus Nijhoff.

Stresemann, Erwin (1927). *Die Lauterscheinungen in den ambonischen Sprachen*. Berlin: Dietrich Reimer.

Strømme, Kari K (1994). Person Marking in the Mamuju Language, in René van den Berg (ed.), *Studies in Sulawesi Linguistics, Part III*. Jakarta: Badan Penyelenggara Seri NUSA, Universitas Atma Jaya, 91–113.

Stuijts, Inge-Lise Marie (1993). *Late Pleistocene and Holocene Vegetation of West Java, Indonesia*. Rotterdam: Balkema.

Subiyantoro, Subiyantoro (2014). Survival Strategies of the Javanese Language in New Caledonia, *Humaniora* 26(1): 43–55.

Subiyantoro, Subiyantoro, Marsono Marsono and Wening Udasmoro (2017). Integration of French Lexicons in New Caledonian Javanese, *Humaniora* 29(1): 85–93.

Sudarsono, P D (2002). *Description of the Bakatik Dayak Language*. PhD Dissertation, La Trobe University.

Sudaryanto (1991). Tata bahasa baku Bahasa Jawa [Standard Javanese grammar]. Yogyakarta: Duta Wacana University Press.

Sudaryat, Yayat, Prawirasumantri, H Abud and H Karna Yudibrata (2007). *Tata bahasa Sunda Kiwari* [Contemporary Sundanese grammar]. Bandung: Yrama Widya.

Suhandono (1994). *Grammatical Relations in Javanese*. MA Thesis, Australian National University.

Sullivan, Robert E (1986). *Maguindanaon Dictionary*. Cotabato City (Philippines): Notre Dame University, Institute of Cotabato Cultures.

Summerhayes, Glenn R (2007). The Rise and Transformations of Lapita in the Bismarck Archipelago, in Scarlett Chiu and Christophe Sand (eds.), *From Southeast Asia to the Pacific*. Taipei: Academia Sinica, 129–72.

Summerhayes, Glenn R (2010). Lapita Interaction – an Update, in Masegseg Z Gadu and Hsiu-Man Lin (eds.), *2009 International Symposium on Austronesian Studies*. Taidong: National Museum of Prehistory, 11–40.

Sutlive, Vinson (1978). *The Iban of Sarawak*. Arlington Heights, Illinois: AHM Publishing.

Sutoko, Soegianto, Sri Surani, Agus Sariono and Budi Suyanto (1998). *Geografi Dialek Bahasa Madura* [Madurese dialect geography]. Jakarta: Pusat Pembinaan dan Pengembangan Bahasa.

Svelmoe, Gordon and Thelma Svelmoe (1990). *Mansaka Dictionary*. Dallas: Summer Institute of Linguistics.

Swastham, Pensiri (1982). *A Description of Moklen: A Malayo-Polynesian Language*. MA Thesis, Institute of Language and Culture for Rural Development, Mahidol University, Nakhon Pathom, Thailand.

Syahrul Napsin, Zainal Abidin Naning, Slamet Abdullah, Sjafran Sjamsuddin, Mohammad Arsyad and Tamizi (1980/1981). *Morfologi dan sintaksis Bahasa Rejang* [Rejang morphology and syntax]. Jakarta: Pusat Pembinaan dan Pengembangan Bahasa.

Szabó, Katherine and Sue O'Connor (2004). Migration and Complexity in Holocene Island Southeast Asia, *World Archaeology* 36(4): 621–8.

Tạ Văn Thông (2009). Tiếng Ra Glai Ở Các Địa Phương [The Raglai language at the local level], in V T Tạ (ed.), *Tìm Hiểu Ngôn Ngữ Các Dân Tộc Ở Việt Nam* [Understanding minority languages in Vietnam]. Hà Nội: Nhà Xuất Bản Khoa Học Xã Hội [Social Science Press], 222–45.

Taber, Kathleen B and Mark H. Taber (1995). On Being Partially Pregnant: Transitivity in Luang, in Wyn D. Laidig (ed.), *Descriptive Studies in Languages of Maluku, Part II*. Jakarta: Universitas Katolik Indonesia Atma Jaya, 88–106.

Taber, Kathleen B and Mark H Taber (2015). *Luang Grammar and Phonology Sketch*. Dallas: Summer Institute of Linguistics International.

Taber, Kathleen B and Mark H. Taber (nd). Luang Dictionary. Unpublished Toolbox files.

Taber, Mark (1993). Toward A Better Understanding of the Indigenous Languages of Southwestern Maluku, *Oceanic Linguistics* 32(2): 389–441.

Tadmor, Uri (1995). *Language Contact and Systemic Restructuring: The Malay Dialect of Nonthaburi, Central Thailand*. PhD Dissertation, University of Hawai'i.

Tadmor, Uri (2000). Rekonstruksi aksen kata Bahasa Melayu [the reconstruction of Malay stress], in Yassir Nasanius and Bambang Kaswanti Purwo (eds.), *PELBBA 13, Pertemuan Linguistik (Pusat Kajian) Bahasa dan Budaya Atma Jaya Ketiga Belas*. Jakarta: Pusat Kajian Bahasa dan Budaya, Universitas Katolik (Unika) Atma Jaya, 153–67.

Tadmor, Uri (2002). Language Contact and the Homeland of Malay. Presentation: 6th International Symposium of Malay/Indonesian Linguistics, Bintan Island, Riau, 3 August.

Tadmor, Uri (2004). Dialect Endangerment: The Case of Nonthaburi Malay, *Bijdragen tot de Taal-, Land- en Volkenkunde* 160(4): 511–31.

Tadmor, Uri (2006). Tanah Air Melayu [The Malay homeland]. Kolokium Kajian Linguistik Melayu/Indonesia (Kalingmi): Metodologi dan Perkembangan Mutakhir, Atma Jaya University, 13 February.

Tadmor, Uri (2007). Grammatical Borrowing in Indonesia, in Yaron Matras and Jeanette Sakel (eds.), *Grammatical Borrowing in Cross-Linguistic Perspective*. Berlin/New York: Mouton de Gruyter, 301–28.

Tadmor, Uri (2009). Loanwords in Indonesian, in Martin Haspelmath and Uri Tadmor (eds.), *Loanwords in the World's Languages: A Comparative Handbook*. Berlin: de Gruyter Mouton, 686–716.

Tadmor, Uri (2014). Dialect Endangerment: The Case of Nonthaburi Malay, *Bijdragen tot de Taal-, Land- en Volkenkunde* 160(4): 511–31.

Tadmor, Uri (2015). When Culture Grammaticalizes. The Pronominal System of Onya Darat, in Rik De Busser and Randy J La Polla (eds.), *Language Structure and Environment: Social, Cultural and Natural Factors*. Amsterdam/Philadelphia: John Benjamins, 77–98.

Tadmor, Uri, Martin Haspelmath and B Taylor (2010). Borrowability and the Notion of Basic Vocabulary, *Diachronica* 27(2): 226–46.

Taguchi, Yushin (1989). Lexicostatistic Survey of the Languages Indigenous to West Seram, in Wyn D Laidig (ed.), *Workpapers in Indonesian Languages and Cultures 6*. Ambon: Pattimura University and the Summer Institute of Linguistics, 15–63.

Tahitu, Egbertus (1989). *Melaju Sini. Het Maleis van Molukse jongeren in Nederland* [Melaju Sini. The Malay of Moluccan youth in the Netherlands]. PhD Dissertation, Leiden University.

Tajolosa, Teresita (2010). Predicting the Ethnolinguistic Vitality of an Endangered Philippine Language: The Case of Three Batak Communities in Palawan, in I Wayan Arka, Ni Luh Nyoman Seri Malini, Ida Ayu Made Puspani (eds.), *Language Documentation and Cultural Practices in the Austronesian World: Papers from 12-ICAL, Volume 4*. Canberra: Asia-Pacific Linguistics, 49–75.

Takata, Masahiro and Yuko Takata (1992). Kola Phonology, in Donald A Burquest and Wyn D Laidig (eds.), *Descriptive studies in languages of Maluku*. Special issue of *NUSA* 34. Jakarta: Badan Penyelenggara Seri NUSA, Universitas Atma Jaya, 31–46.

Takata, Yuko (1992). Word Structure and Reduplication in Kola, in Donald A Burquest and Wyn D Laidig (eds.), *Descriptive Studies in Languages of Maluku*. Jakarta: Badan Penyelenggara Seri NUSA, Universitas Katolik Indonesia Atma Jaya, 47–68.

Talavera, Jezia P, Maira Matsushita and Earvin Pelagio (2013). The Sound Systems of Inivadoy and Ilokano: An Acoustic Phonetics Approach. Unpublished Manuscript. Benguet, Philippines.

Tamil (1924–1936). *Tamil Lexicon*. Madras: University of Madras. Six Volumes.

Tanaka, Kazuhiko (1998). Preliminary Report of the Archaeological Excavation of Catugan Shellmidden, Lal-Lo, Cagayan, Philippines, *Bulletin of Chiba Keiai Junior College* 20: 149–78.

Tanaka, Nozomi, William O'Grady, Kamil Deen and Ivan Paul Bondoc (2019). Comprehension and Production of Word Order and Voice in Bilingual Tagalog Speakers. Poster Presentation: Second Language Research Forum, East Lansing, MI, September 21.

Tanangkingsing, Michael (2009). *A Functional Reference Grammar of Cebuano*. PhD Dissertation, National Taiwan University.

Tanudirjo, Daud Aris (2001). *Islands in Between: Prehistory of the Northeastern Indonesian Archipelago*. PhD Dissertation, Australian National University.

Tätte, Kai, Ene Metspalu, Helen Post et al. (2021). The Ami and Yami aborigines of Taiwan and their genetic relationship to

East Asian and Pacific populations, *European Journal of Human Genetics* 29: 1092–1102.

Taylor-Leech, Kerry (2008). Language and Identity in East Timor: The Discourses of Nation Building, *Language Problems and Language Planning* 32(2): 153–80.

Taylor-Leech, Kerry (2009). The Language Situation in Timor-Leste, *Current Issues in Language Planning* 10(1): 1–68.

Taylor-Leech, Kerry (2013). Finding Space for Non-Dominant Languages in Education: Language Policy and Medium of Instruction in Timor-Leste 2000–2012, *Current Issues in Language Planning* 14(1): 109–26.

Taylor-Leech, Kerry (2019). Postcolonial Language-in-Education Policy in Globalised Times, in Andy Kirkpatrick and Anthony J Liddicoat (eds.), *The Routledge International Handbook of Language Education Policy in Asia*. London: Routledge, 298–311.

Taylor, Paul Michael (1983). North Moluccan Malay: Notes on A Substandard Dialect of Indonesian, in James T Collins (ed.), *Studies in Malay Dialects, Part II*. Special issue of *NUSA* 17. Jakarta: Badan Penyelenggara Seri NUSA, Universitas Atma Jaya, 14–27.

Teeuw, Andries (1951). *Atlas Dialek Pulau Lombok* [Dialect atlas of the Island of Lombok]. Jakarta: Biro Reproduksi Djawatan Topografi.

Teeuw, Andries (1958). *Lombok: Een dialect-geographische studie* [Lombok: A dialect geographical study]. Leiden: Martinus Nijhoff.

Teeuw, Andries (1961). *A Critical Survey of Studies on Malay and Bahasa Indonesia*. The Hague: Martinus Nijhoff.

Teixeira J C and A Cooper (2019). Using Hominin Introgression to Trace Modern Human Dispersals, *Proceedings of the National Academy of Sciences USA* 116: 15327–32.

Teljeur, Dirk (1982). Short Wordlists from South Halmahera, Kayoa, Makian, Ternate, Tidore and Bacan, in C L Voorhoeve (ed.), *The Makian Languages and Their Neighbors*. Canberra: Pacific Linguistics, 129–48.

Teljeur, Dirk (1987). Spatial Orientation Among the Giman of South Halmahera, in E K M Masinambow (ed.), *Halmahera dan Raja Ampat sebagai Kesatuan yang Majemuk*. Jakarta: Lembaga Ekonomi dan Kemasyarakatan Nasional, 347–66.

Teo, Kok Seong (2003). *The Peranakan Chinese of Kelantan: A Study of the Culture, Language, and Communication of an Assimilated Group in Malaysia*. London: ASEAN Academic Press.

Teoh Boon Seong and Lim Beng Soon (2003). A Study of Penang Peranakan Hokkien, *Journal of Modern Languages* 15(1): 169–81.

TFS Working Group (2011a). On the Lam. Totem Field Storyboards. Retrieved from http://totemfieldstoryboards.org/stories/on_the_lam/

TFS Working Group (2011b). Sick Girl. Totem Field Storyboards. Retrieved from http://totemfieldstoryboards.org/stories/sick_girl/

Tharp, James A (1974). Notes on the Ilokano Reflexes of Proto-Austronesian *R, *University of Hawai'i Working Papers in Linguistics* 6(6): 47–51.

Tharp, James A and Y-Bham Đuôn-Ya (1980). *A Rhade-English Dictionary with English-Rhade Finderlist*. Canberra: Pacific Linguistics.

Thiel, Barbara (1984–1985). Austronesian Origins and Expansion: The Philippine Archaeological Data, *Asian Perspective* 26: 119–29.

Thiessen, Henry Arnold (1981). *Phonological Reconstruction of Proto-Palawan* (*Anthropological Papers*, No. 10). Manila: National Museum of the Philippines.

Thoir, Nazir, Ketut Reoni and Ketut Karyawan (1986). *Tata bahasa Bahasa Sasak* [Sasak grammar]. Jakarta: Pusat Pembinaan dan Pengembangan Bahasa.

Thomas-Fattier, Dominique (1982). *Le dialecte sakalava du nord-ouest de Madagascar. Phonologie. Grammaire. Lexique*. Paris: Société d'Études Linguistiques et Anthropologiques de France.

Thomas, David D (1992). On Sesquisyllabic Structure, *Mon-Khmer Studies* 21: 207–10.

Thomas, David D (1955). Three Analyses of the Ilocano Pronoun System, *Word* 11: 204–8.

Thomas, David D (1958). Mansaka Sentence and Sub-Sentence Structures, *Philippine Social Sciences and Humanities Review* 23: 339–58.

Thomas, Nicholas, Harriet Guest and Michael Dettelbach (1996). *Observations Made During a Voyage Round the World*. Honolulu: University of Hawai'i Press.

Thomason, Sarah G (1999). Speakers' Choices in Language Change, *Studies in the Linguistic Sciences* 29(2): 19–43.

Thomason, Sarah G (2009). How to Establish Substratum Interference, *Senri Ethnological Studies* 75: 319–28.

Thomason, Sarah G and Terrence Kaufman (1988). *Language Contact, Creolization and Genetic Linguistics*. Berkeley: University of California Press.

Thompson, Sandra A, Robert E Longacre and Shin Ja J Hwang (2007). Adverbial Clauses, in Timothy Shopen (ed.), *Language Typology and Syntactic Description*, Volume II: Complex Constructions. 2nd edition. Cambridge: Cambridge University Press, 237–300.

Thurgood, Ela (2004). Phonation Types in Javanese, *Oceanic Linguistics* 43(2): 277–95.

Thurgood, Graham (1993). Phan Rang Cham and Utsat: Tonogenetic Themes and Variants, in J Edmondson and K Gregerson (eds.), *Tonality in Austronesian Languages*. Honolulu: University of Hawai'i Press, 91–106.

Thurgood, Graham (1999). *From Ancient Cham to Modern Dialects: Two Thousand Years of Language Contact and Change*. Honolulu: University of Hawai'i Press.

Thurgood, Graham (2000). Learnability and Direction of Convergence in Cham: The Effects of Long-Term Contact on Linguistic Structures, in Vida Samiian (ed.), *Proceedings of the Western Conference on Linguistics. WECOL 2000*. Fresno: California State University, 507–27.

Thurgood, Graham (2005). Phan Rang Cham, in Alexander Adelaar and Nikolaus P Himmelmann (eds.), *The Austronesian Languages of Asia and Madagascar*. London: Routledge, 489–512.

Thurgood, Graham (2007). The Historical Place of Acehnese: The Known and the Unknown. Presentation: First International Conference of Aceh and Indian Ocean Studies.

Thurgood, Graham, Ela Thurgood and Li Fengxiang (2014). *A Grammatical Sketch of Hainan Cham: History, Contact, and Phonology*. Berlin/Boston: de Gruyter Mouton.

Thurston, William R (1987). *Processes of Change in the Languages of North-Western New Britain*. Canberra: Pacific Linguistics.

Ting, Pang-Hsin (1980). The Tan-Chou Dialect of Hainan, *Cahiers de Linguistique - Asie Orientale* 8: 5–27.

Ting, Su-Hie and Fung-Ling Tham (2014). Vitality of Kadazandusun Language in Sabah, Malaysia, *Asia-Pacific Studies* 1(1): 44–57.

Ting, Su-Hie and Teck-Yee Ling (2013). Language Use and Sustainability Status of Indigenous Languages in Sarawak, Malaysia, *Journal of Multilingual and Multicultural Development* 34(1): 77–93.

Tismeer, C M J (1913). Eenige gegevens van de Bahasa Kowiai [Some data on Kowiai], *Bijdragen tot de Taal-, Land- en Volkenkunde van Nederlandsch Indië* 67: 111–22.

Tjia, Johnny (1992). Partikel-partikel dalam klausa, kalimat dan wacana Melayu Ambon: catatan pendahuluan [Clause -, sentence - and discourse particles in Ambon Malay: preliminary notes], *Cakalele* 3: 43–61.

Tjia, Johnny (2007). *A Grammar of Mualang: An Ibanic Language of Western Kalimantan, Indonesia*. PhD Dissertation, Leiden University.

Tollefson, James W (2013). *Language Policies in Education: Critical Issues*. New York: Routledge.

Topping, Donald M (1980). *Spoken Chamorro: With Grammatical Notes and Glossary*. Honolulu: University of Hawai'i Press.

Topping, Donald M, with the assistance of Bernadita Dungca (1973). *Chamorro Reference Grammar*. Honolulu: University of Hawai'i Press.

Trask, Robert L (2015). *Trask's Historical Linguistics*. 3rd edition edited by Robert McColl Miller. Abingdon: Routledge.

Travis, Edgar (nd). Unpublished Ambelau wordlist taken 6 October 1986.

Travis, Lisa (1991). Derived Objects, Inner Aspect, and the Structure of VP. Presentation: Proceedings of the North East Linguistic Society (NELS) 22. Amherst, MA: University of Delaware.

Travis, Lisa (2005). States, Abilities, and Accidents, in C Gurski (ed.), *Proceedings of the 2005 Annual Conference of the Canadian Linguistic Association*. Montreal: Canadian Linguistics Association. URL: http://people.linguistics.mcgill.ca/~lisa.travis/papers/StatesAbilitiesAccidentsCLA5.pdf

Travis, Lisa (2010). *Inner Aspect: The Articulation of VP*. Dordrecht: Springer.

Trick, Douglas (2008). Ergative Control of Syntactic Processes in Southern Sinama, *Studies in Philippine Languages and Cultures* 19: 184–201.

Trosdal, Mimi B (1990). *Formal-Functional Cebuano-English Dictionary: With an English-Cebuano Lexicon*. Cebu City: M B Trosdal.

Tryon, Darrell T (ed.) (1995a). *Comparative Austronesian Dictionary: An Introduction to Austronesian Studies* (5 volumes). Berlin/New York: Mouton de Gruyter.

Tryon, Darrell T (1995b). Proto-Austronesian and the Major Austronesian Subgroups, in Peter Bellwood, James J Fox and Darrell T Tryon (eds.), *The Austronesians*. Canberra: Australian National University Press, 19–42.

Tsang, Cheng-Hwa (1992). *Archaeology of the Penghu Islands*. Taipei: Academia Sinica Press.

Tsang, Cheng-Hwa (2005). Recent Discoveries at the Tapenkeng Culture Sites in Taiwan: Implications for the Problem of Austronesian Origins, in Roger Blench, Laurent Sagart and Alicia Sanchez-Mazas (eds.), *The Peopling of East Asia*. London: Routledge Curzon, 63–73.

Tsang, Cheng-Hwa (2012). Once Again on the Austronesian Origin and Dispersal, *Journal of Austronesian Studies* 3(1): 87–119.

Tsang, Cheng-Hwa, Kuang-Ti Li, Tze-Fu Hsu, Yuan-Ching Tsai, Po-Hsuan Fang and Yue-Ie Caroline Hsing (2017). Broomcorn and Foxtail Millet Were Cultivated in Taiwan About 5000 Years Ago, *Botanical Studies* 58: 3.

Tschacher, Torsten (2009). Tamil, in Kees Versteegh (ed.), *Encyclopedia of Arabic Language and Linguistics. Volume IV: Q-Z*. Leiden/Boston: Brill, 433–6.

Tsimilaza, Alphonse (1981). *Phonologie et morphologie du tsimihety*. PhD Dissertation: Université de Nancy II.

Tsuchida, Shigeru (1976). *Reconstruction of Proto-Tsouic Phonology*. Tokyo: Tokyo Gaikokugo Daigaku, Institute for the Study of Languages and Cultures of Asia and Africa.

Tsuchida, Shigeru, Ernesto Constantino, Yukihiro Yamada and Tsunekazu Moriguchi (1989). *Batanic Languages: Lists of Sentences for Grammatical Features*. Tokyo: University of Tokyo.

Tsuchida, Shigeru, Yukihiro Yamada and Tsunekazu Moriguchi (1987). *Lists of Selected Words of Batanic Languages*. Tokyo: Department of Linguistics, University of Tokyo.

Tucker, Richard (1971). Focus Acquisition by Filipino Children, *Philippine Journal of Psychology* 4(1): 21–4.

Tumonggor M K, T M Karafet, B Hallmark, J S Lansing, H Sudoyo, M F Hammer and M P Cox (2013). The Indonesian Archipelago: An Ancient Genetic Highway Linking Asia and the Pacific, *Journal of Human Genetics* 58: 165–73.

Tumonggor M K, T M Karafet, S Downey, J S Lansing, P Norquest, H Sudoyo, M F Hammer and M P Cox (2014). Isolation, Contact and Social Behavior Shaped Genetic Diversity in West Timor, *Journal of Human Genetics* 59: 494–503.

Tupas, Ruanni (2015). Inequalities of Multilingualism: Challenges to Mother Tongue-Based Multilingual Education, *Language and Education* 29(2): 112–24.

Turcotte, Denis (1981). *La politique linguistique en Afrique francophone: une étude comparative de la Côte-d'Ivoire et de Madagascar*. Québec: Les Presses De l'Université Laval.

Turner, Ralph Lilley (1966). *A Comparative Dictionary of the Indo-Aryan Languages*. London: Oxford University Press.

Tweddell, Colin (1958). *The Iraya (Mangyan) Language of Mindoro, Philippines: Phonology and Morphology*. PhD Dissertation, University of Washington.

Uhlenbeck, Eugenius M (1941). *Beknopte Javaansche grammatica* [Concise grammar of Javanese]. Batavia: Volkslectuur.

Uhlenbeck, Eugenius M (1949). *De structuur van het Javaanse morpheem* [Javanese morpheme structure]. Bandoeng: A C Nix. Dordrecht: Reidel.

Uhlenbeck, Eugenius M (1975). Sentence Segment and Word Group: Basic Concepts of Javanese Syntax, in John W M Verhaar (ed.), *Miscellaneous Studies in Indonesian and Languages in Indonesia, Part I*. Special issue of *NUSA* 1. Jakarta: Badan Penyelenggara Seri NUSA, Universitas Atma Jaya, 6–10.

Uhlenbeck, Eugenius M (1978). *Studies in Javanese morphology* [Studies in Javanese morphology]. Koninklijk Instituut voor Taal-, Land- en Volkenkunde Translation Series 19. The Hague: Martinus Nijhoff.

Urban, Matthias (2010). 'Sun' = 'Eye of the Day': A Linguistic Pattern of Southeast Asia and Oceania, *Oceanic Linguistics* 49: 568–79.

Urdze, Aina (ed.) (2018). *Non-Prototypical Reduplication*. Berlin: de Gruyter Mouton.

Usher, Timothy and Antoinette Schapper (2018). The Lexicons of the Papuan Languages of the Onin Peninsula and their Influences, in Antoinette Schapper (ed.), *Contact and substrate in the languages of Wallacea, Part 2*. Special issue of *NUSA* 64: 39–63.

Usher, Timothy and Antoinette Schapper (2022). The Greater West Bomberai Family, *Oceanic Linguistics* 61(1): 469–527.

Usup, Hunggu Tadjuddin (1981a). *Rekonstruksi fonem proto kelompok Bahasa Gorontalo Sebelah Timur: Laporan Penelitian* [Proto-East Gorontalo phoneme reconstruction: a preliminary report]. Jakarta: Pusat Pembinaan dan Pengembangan Bahasa.

Usup, Hunggu Tadjuddin (1981b). Perbandingan vokal penyokong kata-kata pungutan dalam kelompok Bahasa Gorontalo Timur [A comparison of support vowels in loanwords in East Gorontalo languages], *Bahasa dan Sastra* 7: 36–54.

Usup, Hunggu Tadjuddin (1984). *Rekonstruksi fonologi Bahasa Proto-Gorontalo-Mongondow: Laporan Penelitian* [A reconstruction of Proto-Gorontalo-Mongondow phonology: a preliminary report]. Jakarta: Pusat Pembinaan dan Pengembangan Bahasa.

Usup, Hunggu Tadjuddin (1986). *Rekonstruksi Proto-Bahasa Gorontalo-Mongondow* [A reconstruction of Proto-Gorontalo-Mongondow]. PhD Dissertation, Universitas Indonesia, Jakarta.

Uthai, Ruslan (2007). Kepelbagaian dialek Melayu di wilayah Satun [Malay dialect variety in the Satun region], in Chong Shin, Karim Harun and Yabit Alas (eds.), *Reflections in Southeast Asian Seas: Essays in Honour of Professor James T Collins*, Vol. 2. Pontianak: STAIN Pontianak Press, 93–101.

Utsumi, Atsuko (2011). Reduplication in the Bantik Language. *Asian and African Languages and Linguistics* 6: 5–26.

Utsumi, Atsuko (2013a). The System of Tense and Aspect in the Bantik Language, in John Bowden (ed.), *Tense, Aspect, Mood and Evidentiality in Languages of Indonesia*. Special issue of *NUSA* 55: 219–37.

Utsumi, Atsuko (2013b). Talaud Verbs: Paradigm of Basic Verbs, *Tokyo University Linguistic Papers* 33: 319–61.

Utsumi, Atsuko (2014). Deixis and Relative Height Terms in Bantik, in Anthony Jukes (ed.), *Deixis and Spatial Expressions in Languages of Indonesia*. Special issue of *NUSA* 56: 119–38.

Utsumi, Atsuko (2018). The Tonsawang Language's Basic Morphology and Syntactic Features. Presentation: 28th Annual Meeting of the Southeast Asian Linguistics Society, Kaohsiung, Taiwan, May 17–19.

Valeri, Valerio (1980). Notes on the Meaning of Marriage Prestations Among the Huaulu of Seram, in James J. Fox (ed.), *The Flow of Life: Essays on Eastern Indonesia*. Cambridge, MA: Harvard University Press, 178–92.

Valkama, Kari (1993). *Studies in Duri Grammar: Person Marking, Basic Constitutent Order and Grammatical Relations and Voice in Duri*. MA Thesis, University of Helsinki.

Valkama, Kari (1995). Person Marking in Duri, in René van den Berg (ed.), *Studies in Sulawesi Linguistics, Part IV*. Special issue of *NUSA* 37. Jakarta: Badan Penyelenggara Seri NUSA, Universitas Atma Jaya, 47–95.

Valkama, Suzanne (1995). Notes on Duri Transitivity, in René van den Berg (ed.), *Studies in Sulawesi Linguistics, Part IV*. Special issue of *NUSA* 37. Jakarta: Badan Penyelenggara Seri NUSA, Universitas Atma Jaya, 1–45.

Vallée F, Luciani A and Cox M P (2016). Reconstructing Demography and Social Behavior During the Neolithic Expansion from Genomic Diversity Across Island Southeast Asia, *Genetics* 204: 1495–506.

Van Alsenoy, Lauren (2014). *A New Typology of Indefinite Pronouns, with a Focus on Negative Indefinites*. PhD Dissertation, University of Antwerp.

van Baar, Tim (1997). *Phasal Polarity*. Amsterdam: IFOTT.

van Dam, Nikolaos (2010). Arabic Loanwords in Indonesian Revisited, *Bijdragen tot de Taal-, Land- en Volkenkunde* 166 (2/3): 218–43.

van den Berg, René (1989). *A Grammar of the Muna Language*. Dordrecht: Foris.

van den Berg, René (1991a). Muna Dialects and Munic Languages: Towards a Reconstruction, in Ray Harlow (ed.), *VICAL 2: Western Austronesian and Contact Languages: Papers from the Fifth International Conference on Austronesian Linguistics, Auckland, New Zealand*. Auckland: Linguistic Society of New Zealand, 21–51.

van den Berg, René (1991b). Muna Historical Phonology, in James N Sneddon (ed.), *Studies in Sulawesi Linguistics, Part II*. Special issue of *NUSA* 33. Jakarta: Badan Penyelenggara Seri Nusa, Universitas Atma Jaya, 2–28.

van den Berg, René (1991c). Preliminary Notes on the Cia-Cia Language (South Buton), in Harry A Poeze and Pim Schoorl (eds.), *Excursies in Celebes: Een bundel bijdragen bij het afscheid van J Noorduyn als directeur-secretaris van het Koninklijk Instituut voor Taal-, Land- en Volkenkunde*. [Sulawesi excursions: a festschrift in honour of J Noorduyn at his retirement as Head of the Royal Institute of Linguistics and Anthropology]. Leiden: Koninklijk Instituut voor Taal-, Land- en Volkenkunde, 305–24.

van den Berg, René (1996a). The Demise of Focus and the Spread of Conjugated Verbs in Sulawesi, in Hein Steinhauer (ed.), *Papers in Austronesian Linguistics, No. 3*. Canberra: Pacific Linguistics, 89–114.

van den Berg, René (La Ode Sidu) (1996b). *Muna-English Dictionary*. Leiden: Koninklijk Instituut voor Taal-, Land- en Volkenkunde Press.

van den Berg, René (1997). Spatial Deixis in Muna (Sulawesi), in Gunter Senft (ed.), *Referring to Space: Studies in Austronesian and Papuan Languages*. Oxford: Clarendon Press, 197–220.

van den Berg, René (2001). *Proto Muna-Buton Etyma*. Unpublished Manuscript.

van den Berg, René (2003). The Place of Tukang Besi and the Muna-Buton Languages, in John Lynch (ed.), *Issues in Austronesian Historical Phonology*. Canberra: Pacific Linguistics, 87–113.

van den Berg, René (2004a). Notes on the Southern Muna Dialect, in John Bowden and Nikolaus P Himmelmann (eds.), *Papers in Austronesian Subgrouping and Dialectology*. Canberra: Pacific Linguistics, 129–69.

van den Berg, René (2004b). Some Notes on the Origin of Malay *di-*, *Bijdragen tot de Taal-, Land- en Volkenkunde* 160: 532–54.

van den Berg, René (2008). Notes on the Historical Phonology and Classification of Wolio, in Yury A Lander and Alexander K Ogloblin (eds.), *Language and Text in the Austronesian World: Studies in Honour of Ülo Sirk*. München: LINCOM, 89–113.

van den Berg, René (2009). Possession in South Halmahera-West New Guinea: Typology and Reconstruction, in Alexander Adelaar and Andrew Pawley (eds.), *Austronesian Historical Linguistics and Culture History: A Festschrift for Robert Blust*. Canberra: Pacific Linguistics, 327–57.

van den Berg, René (2010). Elusive Articles in Sulawesi: Between Syntax and Prosody, in Niclas Burenhult, Arthur Holmer, Anastasia Karlsson, Håkan Lundström and Jan-Olof Svantesson (eds.), *Language Documentation and Description, Volume 10: Special Issue on Humanities of the Lesser-Known: New Directions in the Description, Documentation and Typology of Endangered Languages and Musics*. London: School of Oriental and African Studies, 208–27.

van den Berg, René (2013). *A Grammar of the Muna Language*. SIL e-books 53. Dallas (TX): Summer Institute of Linguistics International. (A digital reprint of van den Berg 1989).

van den Berg, René (2015). Muna, in Nicola Grandi and Lívia Körtvélyessy (eds.), *Edinburgh Handbook of Evaluative Morphology*. Edinburgh: Edinburgh University Press, 367–74.

van den Berg, René (2020). *The Busoa Language of Southeast Sulawesi: Grammar Sketch, Texts, Vocabulary*. Dallas: Summer Institute of Linguistics International.

van den Berg, René and La Ode Sidu (2000). *Kamus Muna-Indonesia* [Muna-Indonesian dictionary]. Kupang: Artha Wacana Press.

van den Berg, René and Takashi Matsumura (2008). Possession in Irarutu, *Oceanic Linguistics* 47(1): 213–22.

van den Berg, René and Robert L Busenitz (2012). *A Grammar of Balantak, A Language of Eastern Sulawesi*. Dallas: Summer Institute of Linguistics International.

van den Bergh, J D (1953). *Spraakkunst van het Banggais* [Grammar of Banggai]. 's-Gravenhage: Martinus Nijhoff.

van den Heuvel, Wilco (2006). *Biak: Description of an Austronesian Language of Papua*. PhD Dissertation, Vrije Universiteit, Amsterdam.

van der Auwera, Johan (1998). Phasal Adverbials in the Languages of Europe, in Johan van der Auwera and Dónall P Ó Baoill (eds.), *Adverbial Constructions in the Languages of Europe*. Berlin/New York: Mouton de Gruyter, 25–145.

van der Auwera, Johan (2006). Why Languages Prefer Prohibitives, *Journal of Foreign Languages* 1: 1–25.

van der Auwera, Johan (2021). Phasal Polarity – Warnings from Earlier Research, in Raija L Kramer (ed.), *The Expression of Phasal Polarity in African Languages*. Berlin: Mouton, 23–36.

van der Auwera, Johan and Frens Vossen (2015). Negatives Between Chamic and Bahnaric, *Journal of the Southeast Asian Linguistics Society* 8: 24–38.

van der Auwera, Johan and Lauren Van Alsenoy (2016). On the Typology of Negative Concord, *Studies in Language* 40: 473–512.

van der Auwera, Johan and Lauren Van Alsenoy (2018). More Ado About *Nothing*: On the Typology of Negative Indefinites, in Ken Turner and Laurence R Horn (eds.) *Pragmatics, Truth and Underspecification: Towards an Atlas of Meaning*. Leiden: Brill, 107–46.

van der Auwera, Johan and Ludo Lejeune (2013). The Prohibitive, in Matthew S Dryer and Martin Haspelmath (eds.), *The World Atlas of Language Structures Online*. Leipzig: Max Planck Institute for Evolutionary Anthropology. URL: https://wals.info/chapter/71

van der Auwera, Johan and Nnena Tamarind De Lisser (2019). Negative Concord in Jamaican, *Ampersand* 6. DOI: 10.1016/amper.2019.100051

van der Auwera, Johan, Olga Krasnoukhova and Frens Vossen (2021). Intertwining the Negative Cycles, in Arja Hamari and Ljuba Veselinova (eds.) *The Negative Existential Cycle from A Historical-Comparative Perspective*. Berlin: Language Science Press, 557–96.

van der Leeden, A C (1993). *Ma'ya: A Language Study. A: Phonology*. Jakarta: Lembaga Ilmu Pengetahuan Indonesia and Leiden: Leiden University.

van der Leeden, A C (nd). *Ma'ya Dictionary, Morphology, and Syntax*. Unfinished Manuscript.

van der Molen, Willem (2015). An *Introduction to Old Javanese*. Tokyo: Research Institute for Languages and Cultures of Asia and Africa.

van der Sijs, Nicoline (1996). *Leenwoordenboek: De invloed van andere talen op het Nederlands* [Dictionary of loanwords: the influence on Dutch of other languages]. The Hague: Sdu and Antwerpen: Standaard.

van der Sijs, Nicoline (2010). *Nederlandse Woorden Wereldwijd* [Dutch words worldwide]. The Hague: Sdu.

van der Toorn, J L (1891). *Minangkabausch-Maleis-Nederlandsch woordenboek* [Minangkabau – Malay – Dutch dictionary]. The Hague: Martinus Nijhoff.

van der Tuuk, Herman Neubronner (1865). Note on the Relation of the Kawi to the Javanese, *Journal of the Royal Asiatic Society N S* 1: 442–6.

van der Tuuk, Herman Neubronner (1971). *A Grammar of Toba Batak*. The Hague: Martinus Nijhoff. [Original Dutch version 1864–1867].

van der Veen, H (1929). Nota betreffende de grenzen van de Sa'dansche taalgroep en het haar aanverwante taalgebied [A note about the borders between the Sa'dan language group and related linguistic areas]. *Tijdschrift voor Indische Taal-, Land- en Volkenkunde* 69: 58–96.

van der Veen, H (1940). *Tae' (Zuid-Toradjasch)-Nederlandsch Woordenboek* [Tae' (South Toraja) – Dutch dictionary]. The Hague: Martinus Nijhoff.

van Engelenhoven, Aone (1995). Van Proto Malayo-Polynesisch naar Proto Luangisch-Kisarisch [From Proto-Malayo-Polynesian to Proto-Luang-Kisar], in Connie Baak, Mary Bakker and Dick van der Meij (eds.), *Tales from a Concave World, Liber Amicorum Bert Voorhoeve*. Leiden: Leiden University, 246–64.

van Engelenhoven, Aone (2003). The Incipient Obsolescence and Acute Death of Teun, Nila and Serua (Central and Southwest Maluku), in Mark Janse and Sijmen Tol (eds.), *Language Death and Language Maintenance: Theoretical, Practical and Descriptive Approaches*. Amsterdam: John Benjamins, 49–80.

van Engelenhoven, Aone (2004). *Leti, A Language of Southwest Maluku*. Leiden: Koninklijk Instituut voor Taal-, Land- en Volkenkunde Press.

van Engelenhoven, Aone (2006). Ita-Nia Nasaun Oin-Ida, Ita-Nia Dalen Sira Oin-Seluk. Our Nation Is One, Our Languages Are Different: Language Policy in East Timor, in Paulo Castro Seixas and Aone van Engelenhoven (eds.), *Diversidade cultural na construção da nação e do estado em Timor-Leste* [Cultural diversity in nation and state building in Timor-Leste]. Porto: Universidade Fernando Pessoa, 104–32.

van Engelenhoven, Aone (2009). The Position of Makuva Among the Austronesian Languages in East Timor and Southwest Maluku, in Alexander Adelaar and Andrew Pawley (eds.), *Austronesian Historical Linguistics and Culture History: A Festschrift for Robert Blust*. Canberra: Pacific Linguistics, 425–42.

van Engelenhoven, Aone (2010a). Tentatively Locating West-Damar Among the Languages of Southwest Maluku, in Svetlana Chlenova and Artem Fedorchuk (eds.), *Studia Anthropologica: A Festschrift in Honor of Michael Chlenov*. Moscow-Jerusalem: Gesharim, 297–326.

van Engelenhoven, Aone (2010b). The Makuva Enigma: Locating A Hidden Language in East Timor, *Romanian Review of Linguistics* 55(2): 161–81.

van Engelenhoven, Aone and Williams-van Klinken, Catharina (2005). Tetun and Leti, in Adelaar, Alexander and Himmelmann, Nikolaus P. (eds.), *The Austronesian Languages of Asia and Madagascar*. London: Routledge, 735–68.

van Hasselt, Johannes L and Frans Johannes Frederik van Hasselt (1947). *Noemfoorsch woordenboek* [Numfor dictionary]. Amsterdam: J H de Bussy.

van Heekeren, H R (1972). *The Stone Age of Indonesia*. 2nd Edition. The Hague: Martinus Nijhoff.

van Heuven, Vincent J and Ellen van Zanten (eds.) (2007). *Prosody in Austronesian Languages of Indonesia*. Utrecht: LOT Netherlands Graduate School of Linguistics.

van Heuven, Vincent J and Vera Faust (2009). Are Indonesians Sensitive to Contrastive Accentuation Below the Word Level?, *Wacana, Jurnal Ilmu Pengetahuan Budaya* 11(2): 226–40.

van Heuven, Vincent J, Lilie Roosman and Ellen van Zanten (2008). Betawi Malay Word Prosody, *Lingua* 118: 1271–87.

van Klinken, Catherina (1999). *A Grammar of the Fehan Dialect of Tetun*. Canberra: Pacific Linguistics.

van Klinken, Catharina (2000). From Verb to Coordinator in Tetun, *Oceanic Linguistics* 39(2): 350–63.

van Minde, Don (1997). *Malayu Ambong* [Ambon Malay grammar]: *Phonology, Morphology, Syntax*. Leiden: Centrum voor Niet-Westerse Studiën Publications.

Van Olmen, Daniël (2021). On order and prohibition. *Studies in Language* 45(3): 520–56.

Van Olmen, Daniël (2019). (A)Symmetries in Imperative Negation: A Pilot Study of 60 Languages. Presentation: Association for Linguistic Typology 13 Conference, September, Pavia.

van Rheeden, Hadewych (1995). *Het Petjo van Batavia. Ontstaan en structuur van de Taal van de Indo's* [The Petjo language of Batavia: origin and structure of the language of the Indos (Eurasians)]. Amsterdam: Universiteit van Amsterdam, Instituut voor Algemene Taalwetenschap.

van Ronkel, Philippus Samuel (1899). Over invloed der Arabische syntaxis op de Maleische [The influence of Arabic syntax on the syntax of Malay], *Tijdschrift voor Indische Taal-, Land- en Volkenkunde* 41: 498–528.

van Ronkel, Philippus Samuel (1902a). Het Tamil-element in het Maleisch [The Tamil element in Malay], *Tijdschrift voor Indische Taal- Land- en Volkenkunde* 45: 97–119.

van Ronkel, Philippus Samuel (1902b). L'élément hindoûstânî dans la langue malaise, in *Hommage au Congrès des Orientalistes de Hanoi de la part du Bataviaasch Genootschap van Kunsten en Wetenschappen*. Batavia: Albrecht, 1–6.

van Ronkel, Philippus Samuel (1903a). Tamilwoorden in Maleisch gewaad [Tamil words in Malay disguise], *Tijdschrift voor Indische Taal-, Land- en Volkenkunde* 46: 532–57.

van Ronkel, Philippus Samuel (1903b). Arabische meervoudsvormen van Maleische woorden [Arabic plurals based on Malay vocabulary], in *Opstellen geschreven ter eere van Dr. H Kern, hem aangeboden door vrienden en leerlingen op zijn zeventigsten verjaardag*, 883–6 Leiden: E J Brill.

van Ronkel, Philippus Samuel (1947). Levensbericht van S J Esser [Obituary of Samuel J Esser], in *Jaarboek der Koninklijke Nederlandsche Akademie van Wetenschappen 1946–1947*. Amsterdam: Nederlandsche Akademie van Wetenschappen, 159–69.

van Staden, Miriam (2000). *Tidore: A Linguistic Description of a Language of the North Moluccas*. PhD Dissertation, Leiden University.

van Stein Callenfels, Pieter Vincent (1951). Prehistoric Sites on the Karama River: West Toraja-Land, Central Celebes, *University of Manila Journal of East Asiatic Studies* 1(1): 82–93.

Van Valin, Robert D and Randy J LaPolla (1997). *Syntax: Structure, Meaning and Function*. Cambridge: Cambridge University Press.

van Velzen, Paul (1994). Some Remarks on the Classification of Waropen. Presentation: 7th International Conference on Austronesian Linguistics, Leiden, 22–27 August 1994.

van Velzen, Paul (nd). *Een voorstudie van het Waropen* [Preliminary study of Waropen]. MA Thesis, Universiteit Leiden.

van Zanten, Ellen and Rob Goedemans (2007). A Functional Typology of Austronesian and Papuan Stress Systems, in Vincent van Heuven and Ellen van Zanten (eds.), *Prosody in Indonesian Languages*. Utrecht: LOT Netherlands Graduate School of Linguistics, 63–88.

van Zanten, Ellen and Vincent J van Heuven (1994). Word Stress in Indonesian: Fixed or Free?, in Bambang Kaswanti Purwo (ed.), *Studies in Malay Dialects, Part IV*. Special issue of *NUSA* 53. Jakarta: Badan Penyelenggara Seri NUSA, Universitas Atma Jaya, 1–20.

van Zanten, Ellen and Vincent J van Heuven (1998). Word Stress in Indonesian: Its Communicative Relevance, *Bijdragen tot de Taal-, Land- en Volkenkunde* 154: 129–47.

van Zanten, Ellen, Rob Goedemans and Jos Pacilly (2003). The Status of Word Stress in Indonesian, in Jeroen van de Weijer, Vincent J van Heuven and Harry van der Hulst (eds.), *The Phonological Spectrum. Vol. 2: Suprasegmental Structure*. Amsterdam, Philadelphia: John Benjamins, 151–75.

van Zanten, Ellen, Ruben Stoel and Bert Remijsen (2010). Stress Types in Austronesian Languages, in Harry van der Hulst, Rob Goedemans and Ellen van Zanten (eds.), *A Survey of Word Accentual Patterns in the Languages of the World*. Berlin: de Gruyter, 87–112.

Vander Klok, Jozina (2011). Indirect Modification in Javanese: Evidence from attributive Comparatives, *Proceedings of the 45th Annual Meeting of the Chicago Linguistics Society*. University of Chicago, Chicago, Illinois.

Vander Klok, Jozina (2012). *Tense, Aspect, and Modal Markers in Paciran Javanese*. PhD Dissertation, McGill University, Montreal.

Vander Klok, Jozina (2013a). Pure Possibility and Pure Necessity Modals in Paciran Javanese, *Oceanic Linguistics* 52(2): 341–74.

Vander Klok, Jozina (2013b). On the Nature of Adjectival Modification: A Case Study in Javanese, in S Kan, C Moore-Cantwell and R Staubs (eds.), *Proceedings of the 40th Annual Meeting of the Northeast Linguistics Society*, Vol. II. Amherst, MA: Graduate Linguistics Students Association Publications, 227–38.

Vander Klok, Jozina (2015). The Dichotomy of Auxiliaries in Javanese: Evidence from Two Dialects, *Australian Journal of Linguistics* 35(2): 142–67.

Vander Klok, Jozina (2017). Types of Polar Questions in Javanese, *NUSA* 63: 1–44.

Vander Klok, Jozina (2019). The Javanese Language at Risk? Perspectives from an East Java Village, *Language Documentation and Conservation* 13: 281–326.

Vander Klok, Jozina and Lisa Matthewson (2015). Distinguishing *Already* from Perfect Aspect: A Case Study on Javanese wis, *Oceanic Linguistics* 54(1): 172–205.

Vander Klok, Jozina and Vera Hohaus (2020). Weak Necessity without Weak Possibility: The Composition of Modal Strength Distinctions in Javanese, *Semantics and Pragmatics 13 Article 12*. DOI: 10.3765/sp.13.12

Vander Klok, Jozina and Bethwyn Evans. 2022. The evolution of non-syntactic functions of applicatives: *-i* suffixation in Javanese and neighbouring languages, in Sara Pacchiarotti and Fernando Zúñiga (eds.), *Applicative morphology: Neglected syntactic and non-syntactic functions*. Berlin: Mouton de Gruyter, 437–474.

Vanoverbergh, Morice (1937). *Some Undescribed Languages of Luzon*. Nijmegen: Dekker & van de Vegt NV.

Vanoverbergh, Morice (1954). *Songs in Lepanto-Igorot as It Is Spoken at Bauko* (Studia Instituti Anthropos, Vol. 7). Vienna-Modling: St. Gabriel's Mission Press.

Vanoverbergh, Morice (1955). *Iloko Grammar*. Baguio City: Catholic School Press.

Veiga, Nancy Vásques and Mauro A Fernández (2012). *Maskin, Maski, Masque*, in the Spanish and Portuguese Creoles of Asia: Same Particle, Same Provenance?, in Hugo C Cardoso, Alan N Baxter and Mario Pinharanda Nunes (eds.), *Ibero-Asian Creoles: Comparative Perspectives*. Amsterdam/Philadelphia: John Benjamins, 181–203.

Veloso, Alexandre (2016). *A Grammar Sketch of Naueti, A Language of East Timor*. MA Thesis, Leiden University.

Venago, Martin F (1929). *Ang Mga Paring Pilipino Sa Kasaysayan Ng Inang Bayan* [Filipino priests in the history of the Mother land]. Maynila: [SN].

Verdier, Maud (2013). La constitution de l'idéologie linguistique des chatteurs malgachophones dans les cybercafés de Tananarive, *Langage et Société* 143(1): 87–107.

Verdizade, Allahverdi (2019). *Selected Topics in the Phonology and Morphosyntax of Laboya: A Field Study*. MA Thesis, Stockholm University.

Verhaar, John W M (1984a). Affixation in Contemporary Indonesian, in Kaswanti Purwo (ed.), *Towards a Description of Contemporary Indonesian: Part I*. Special issue of *NUSA* 30. Jakarta: Badan Penyelenggara Seri Nusa, Universitas Atma Jaya, 1–26.

Verhaar, John W M (1984b). The Categorial System in Contemporary Indonesian: Verbs, in Kaswanti Purwo (ed.), *Towards a Description of Contemporary Indonesian: Part I*. Special issue of *NUSA* 30. Jakarta: Badan Penyelenggara Seri Nusa, Universitas Atma Jaya, 27–64.

Verheijen, Jilis A J (1986). *The Sama/Bajau Language in the Lesser Sunda Islands*. Canberra: Pacific Linguistics.

Verheijen, Jilis A J and Charles E Grimes (1995). Manggarai, in Darrell T Tryon (ed.), *Comparative Austronesian Dictionary: An Introduction to Austronesian Studies*. Berlin/New York: Mouton de Gruyter, 585–92.

Vermeulen, Hans and Rinus Penninx (eds.) (2000). *Immigrant Integration: The Dutch Case*. Amsterdam: Het Spinhuis.

Verner, Karl (1967)[1875]. An Exception to the First Sound Shift, in Winfred P Lehman, Editor and Translator. *A Reader in Nineteenth-Century Historical Indo-European Linguistics*: 132–63. Bloomington and London: Indiana University Press (Original Title: Eine Ausnahme der ersten Lautverschiebung, *Zeitschrift für Vergleichende Sprachforschung auf dem Gebiete der Indogermanischen Sprachen* 23(2): 97–130.

Versteegh, Kees (2001a). Arabic in Madagascar, *Bulletin of the School of Oriental and African Studies* 64(2): 177–87.

Versteegh, Kees (2001b). Linguistic Contacts Between Arabic and Other Languages, *Arabica* 48(4): 470–508.

Versteegh, Kees (2003). The Arabic Component of the Indonesian Lexicon, in Lilie Suratminto and Munawar Holil (eds.), *Rintisan dalam kajian leksikologi dan leksikografi: laporan sanggar kerja internasional tentang leksikologi, Depok, 16–17 Desember 2002*. Jakarta: Fakultas Ilmu Pengetahuan Budaya Universitas Indonesia and Kuala Lumpur: Dewan Bahasa dan Pustaka, 216–29.

Veselinova, Ljuba (2013). Negative Existentials: A Cross-Linguistic Study, *Italian Journal of Linguistics* 25: 107–45.

Veselinova, Ljuba (2016). The Negative Existential Cycle Viewed Through the Lens of Comparative Data, in Elly van Gelderen (eds.), *Cyclical Change Continued*. Amsterdam: John Benjamins, 139–87.

Veselinova, Ljuba (2020). Iamitives Vs. Nondums (Already Vs. Not-Yet) Plus Other Phasal Markers as Lexico-Grammatical Categories. Paris: Tulquest: Interactive Space for Sharing Linguistic Questionnaires and Elicitation Stimuli. URL: http://tulquest.huma-num.fr/en/node/162

Veselinova, Ljuba and Leif Asplund. (2020). Geo-coded online database of phasal polarity expressions in Malayo-Polynesian languages. URL: https://arcg.is/1jGeiq

Veselinova, Ljuba and Maud Devos (2020). NOT YET Expressions as a Lexico-Grammatical Category in Bantu Languages, in Raija Kramer (ed.), *Phasal Polarity in African Languages*. Berlin: de Gruyter Mouton, 445–96.

Vickery, Michael (2003). Funan Reviewed: Deconstructing the Ancients, *Bulletin de l'École Française d'Extrême-Orient* 90/91: 101–43.

Vickery, Michael (2005). *Champa Revised*. Singapore: University of Singapore, Asia Research Institute Working Papers Series No.37.

Vikør, Lars S (1988). *Perfecting Spelling: Spelling Discussions and Reforms in Indonesia and Malaysia, 1900–1972*. Dordrecht: Foris.

Villa-Rikkers, Yuri (2014). Inflection in Kei. MA Thesis, Leiden University.

Villerius, Sophie (2017). Developments in Surinamese Javanese, in Kofi Yakpo and Pieter Muysken (eds.), *Boundaries and Bridges: Multilingual Ecologies in the Guianas*. Berlin: de Gruyter Mouton, 151–78.

Villerius, Sophie (2019). *Development of Surinamese Javanese: Language Contact and Change in a Multilingual Context*. PhD Dissertation, Radboud University (Published in 2018 by LOT Netherlands Graduate School of Linguistics [Utrecht]).

Villerius, Sophie, Francesca Moro and Marian Klamer (2019). Encoding Transfer Events in Surinamese Javanese, *Journal of Language Contact* 12(3): 784–822.

Voegelin, C F and F M Voegelin (1977). *Classification and Index of the World's Languages*. New York: Elsevier.

Voigt, Herman (1994). *Code-Wisseling, taalverschuiving en taalverandering in het Melaju Sini* [Code-switching, language shift and language change in Melayu Sini]. PhD Dissertation, University of Tilburg.

Voorhoeve, C L (1982). The West Makian Language, North Moluccas, Indonesia: A Fieldwork Report, in C L Voorhoeve (ed.), *The Makian Languages and their Neighbors*. Canberra: Pacific Linguistics, 1–74.

Voorhoeve, C L (1989). The Masked Bird; Linguistic Relations in the Bird's Head Area, in Paul Haenen and Jan Pouwer (eds.), *Peoples on the Move; Current Themes of Anthropological Research in New Guinea*. Nijmegen: Centre for Australian and Oceanic Studies, 78–101.

Voorhoeve, C L (1994a). Comparative Linguistics and the West Papuan Phylum, in E K M Masinambow (ed.), *Maluku and Irian Jaya*. Jakarta: Lembaga Ilmu Pengetahuan Indonesia, 65–90.

Voorhoeve, C L (1994b). Contact-Induced Language Change in the Non-Austronesian Languages in the North Moluccas, Indonesia, in Tom Dutton and Darrell T Tryon (eds.), *Language Contact and Change in the Austronesian World*. Berlin: Mouton de Gruyter, 649–74.

Voorhoeve, P (1955). *Critical Survey of Studies on the Languages of Sumatra*. 's-Gravenhage: Martinus Nijhoff.

Vossen, Frens (2016). *On the Typology of the Jespersen Cycles*. PhD Dissertation, University of Antwerp.

Vossen, Frens and Johan van der Auwera (2014). The Jespersen Cycles Seen from Austronesian, in M B Mosegaard-Hansen and J Visconti (eds.), *The Diachrony of Negation*. Amsterdam: John Benjamins, 47–83.

Vruggink, Hein (in Collaboration with Johan Sarmo) (2001). *Surinaams-Javaans - Nederlands Woordenboek* [Surinamese Javanese–Dutch dictionary]. Leiden: Koninklijk Instituut voor Taal-, Land- en Volkenkunde Press.

Vuillermet, Marine (2018). Grammatical Fear Morphemes in Ese Ejja: Making the Case for A Morphosemantic Apprehensional Domain, *Studies in Language* 42: 256–93.

Vuorinen, Paula (1995). Person Marking in Padoe, in René van den Berg (ed.), *Studies in Sulawesi Linguistics, Part IV*. Jakarta: Badan Penyelenggara Seri Nusa, Universitas Atma Jaya, 97–121.

Walker, Alan Trevor (1980). *Sawu: A Language of Eastern Indonesia*. PhD Dissertation, Australian National University.

Walker, Alan Trevor (1982). *Grammar of Sawu*. Jakarta: Badan Penyelenggara Seri NUSA, Universitas Atma Jaya.

Walker, Alan and R David Zorc (1981). Austronesian Loanwords in Yolngu-Matha of Northeast Arnhem Land, *Aboriginal History* 5(2): 109–34.

Walker, Dale F (1976). *A Grammar of the Lampung Language: The Pesisir Dialect of Way Lima*. Jakarta: Badan Penyelenggara Seri NUSA, Universitas Atma Jaya.

Walker, Roland and Jean Walker (1991). Unpublished Research Notes on Selected Languages and Cultures of Irian Jaya. Vol. 13a: Kowiai. Abepura: Universitas Cenderawasih – Summer Institute of Linguistics (UNCEN-SIL).

Wallace, Alfred Russel (1962)[1869]. *The Malay Archipelago*. New York: Dover.

Wallace, Stephen (1976). *Linguistic and Social Dimensions of Phonological Variation in Jakarta Malay*. PhD Dissertation, Cornell University.

Wallace, Stephen (1983). Pronouns in Contact, in E B Agard (ed.), *Essays in Honor of Charles E Hockett*. Leiden: Brill, 573–89.

Walsh, Martin (2019). Cockatoos and Crocodiles: Searching for Words of Austronesian Origin in Swahili, *Kenya Past and Present* 46: 32–40.

Walsh, Martin (2021). From Dugouts to Double Outriggers: Lexical Insights into the Development of Swahili Nautical Technology, *Wacana* 22(2): 253–94.

Walsh, Martin T (2007). Island Subsistence: Hunting, Trapping and the Translocation of Wildlife in the Western Indian Ocean, *Azania* 42: 83–113.

Walton, Charles (1986). *Sama Verbal Semantics: Classification, Derivation and Inflection*. Manila: Linguistic Society of the Philippines.

Walton, Janice R and Charles Walton (1992). *English-Pangutaran Sama Dictionary*. Manila: Summer Institute of Linguistics.

Wamad Abdullah, Syamsuar Marlian, Sitti Rohana and Bustami Usman (1991). *Struktur Bahasa Jamee* [The structure of Jamee]. Jakarta: Pusat Pembinaan dan Pengembangan Bahasa.

Wang, Peter, Robert Hunt, Jeff McGriff and Richard E Elkins (2006). *The Grammar of Matigsalug Manobo*. Arlington: Summer Institute of Linguistics and University of Texas.

Ward, J V, J S Athens and C Hotton (1998). Holocene Pollen Records from Babeldaob Island, Palau, Western Caroline Islands. Presentation: Annual Meeting of the Society for American Archaeology, Seattle, March 29, 1998.

Warneck, Johannes (1977). *Toba-Batak - Deutsches Wörterbuch*. The Hague: Martinus Nijhoff.

Wassmann, Jürg and Pierre R Dasen (1998). Balinese Spatial Orientation: Some Empirical Evidence of Moderate Linguistic Relativity, *Journal of the Royal Anthropological Institute* 4: 689–711.

Wassmann, Jürg and Pierre R Dasen (2006). How to Orient Yourself in Balinese Space: Combining Ethnographic and Psychological Methods for the Study of Cognitive Processes, in Jürgen Straub, Doris Weidemann, Carlos Kölbl and Barbara Zielke (eds.), *Pursuit of Meaning. Advances in Cultural and Cross-Cultural Psychology*. Bielefeld, Germany: Transcript Verlag, 351–76.

Waterman, Margaret A (1932). *A Study of the Igorot Language as Spoken by the Bontoc Igorots*. Manila: Bureau of Printing.

Wati Kurniawati, Non Martis, Buha Aritonang and Hidayatul Astar (2002). *Kosakata dasar Swadesh di Kabupaten Berau, Kotamadya Samarinda, dan Kotamadya Balikpapan* [Swadesh basic vocabulary in Berau Regency and in the Samarinda and Balikpapan municipalities]. Jakarta: Pusat Bahasa.

Watuseke, F S and W B Watuseke-Politton (1981). Het Minahasa-of Manado-Maleis [Minahasa - or Manado Malay], *Bijdragen tot de Taal-, Land- en Volkenkunde* 137: 324–46.

Wechsler, Stephen and I Wayan Arka (1998). Syntactic Ergativity in Balinese: An Argument Structure Based Theory, *Natural Language and Linguistic Theory* 16(2): 387–441.

Wedhawati, Nurlina, Wiwin Erni Siti, Setiyanto, Edi, Marsono, Sukesti, Restu and Baryadi, I Praptomo (2006). *Tata Bahasa Jawa Mutakhir* [Contemporary Javanese Grammar]. Yogyakarta: Penerbit Kanisius.

Wehl, David (1961). *Modern Malay Usage*. Singapore: Eastern University Press.

Wehr, Hans (1994). *A Dictionary of Modern Written Arabic: Arabic-English*. Urbana, IL: Spoken Language Services.

Welsh, Alistair (2015). Cocos Malay Language Since Integration with Australia, *Shima* 9(1): 53–68.

Westaway K E, J Louys, R D Awe, M J Morwood, G J Price, J X Zhao, M Aubert, R Joannes-Boyau, T M Smith, M M Skinner, T Compton, R M Bailey, G D van den Bergh, J de Vos, A W G Pike, C Stringer, E W Saptomo, Y Rizal, J Zaim, W D Santoso, A Trihascaryo, L Kinsley and B Sulistyanto (2017). An Early Modern Human Presence in Sumatra 73,000–63,000 Years Ago, *Nature* 548: 322–5.

Wheatley, P (1961). *The Golden Khersonese: Studies in the Historical Geography of the Malay Peninsula Before AD 1500*. Kuala Lumpur: University of Malaya Press.

Whisler, Jacqui (1996). A Grammar of Sawai. Unpublished Manuscript, Pattimura University and Summer Institute of Linguistics.

Whisler, Ronald (1992). Phonology of Sawai, in Donald A Burquest and Wyn D Laidig (eds.), *Phonological Studies in Four Languages of Maluku*. Dallas: Summer Institute of Linguistics and the University of Texas at Arlington, 7–32.

Whisler, Ronald and Jacqui Whisler (1995). Sawai, in Darrell T Tryon (ed.), *Comparative Austronesian Dictionary: An Introduction to Austronesian Studies*. Berlin/New York: Mouton de Gruyter, 659–68.

Wijaya, Juliana (2006). Indonesian Heritage Learners Profiles: A Preliminary Study of Indonesian Heritage Language Learners at University of California Los Angeles, *Journal of Southeast Asian Language Teaching* 12(1): 1–14.

Wilbur, Ronnie Bring (1973). *The Phonology of Reduplication*. Bloomington: Indiana University Linguistics Club Publications.

Wilder J A, M P Cox, A M Paquette, R Alford, A W Satyagraha, A Harahap and H Sudoyo (2011). Genetic Continuity Across a Deeply Divergent Linguistic Contact Zone in North Maluku, Indonesia, *BMC Genetics* 12: 100.

Wilken, N P and Johannes Albert Traugott Schwarz (1868). De taal in Bolaäng-Mongondou [The language in Bolaang-Mongondow], *Mededeelingen van wege het Nederlandsche Zendelinggenootschap* 12: 189–247.

Wilkinson, Richard James (1922). *A History of the Peninsular Malays*. Singapore: Kelly and Walsh.

Wilkinson, Richard James (1932). *A Malay-English Dictionary (Romanised)*. Mytilene: Salavopoulos and Kinderlis.

Wilkinson, Richard James (1959). *A Malay-English Dictonary (Romanised)*. London: Macmillan.

Williams-van Klinken, Catharina and John Hajek (2006). Patterns of Address in Dili Tetum, East Timor, *Australian Review of Applied Linguistics* 29(2): 21.1–21.18.

Williams-van Klinken, Catharina and John Hajek (2018). Language Contact and Functional Expansion in Tetun Dili: The Evolution of a New Press Register, *Multilingua* 37(6): 613–47.

Williams-van Klinken, Catharina and John Hajek (2020). Double agent, double cross? Or how a suffix changes nature in an isolating language: *dór* in Tetun Dili, in David Gil and Antoinette Schapper (eds.), *Austronesian Undressed: How and why languages become isolating*. Amsterdam: John Benjamins, 369–89.

Williams-van Klinken, Catharina, John Hajek and Rachel Nordlinger (2002). *Tetun Dili: A Grammar of an East Timorese Language*. Canberra: Pacific Linguistics.

Williams, Jeffrey P and Lap M Siu (2013). The Aesthetics of Jarai Echo Morphology, in J P Williams (ed.), *The Aesthetics of Grammar: Sound and Meaning in the Languages of Mainland Southeast Asia*. Cambridge: Cambridge University Press, 191–206.

Willms, Alfred. 1955. Lautliche und syntaktische Untersuchungen über die Mentawai Sprache, *Afrika und Übersee* 40: 1–24, 49–72.

Wilson, Helen (1972). *The Phonology and Syntax of Palauan Verb Affixes*. PhD Dissertation, University of Hawai'i.

Winstedt, Richard Olaf (1917). Hindustani Loan-Words in Malay, *Journal of the Straits Branch of the Royal Asiatic Society* (1917): 67–8.

Winstedt, Richard Olaf (1927). *Malay Grammar*. Oxford: Oxford University Press.

Wiradnyana, Ketut and Taufikurrahman Setiawan (2011). *Gayo: Merangkai Identitas* [Gayo: building an identity]. Jakarta: Yayasan Pustaka Obor Indonesia.

Wittke, Jonas (2019). *Status Planning and Regional Identity: The Case of Osing in Banyuwangi, Indonesia*. PhD Dissertation, Rice University.

Woensdregt, Jac (1929). Rampi'-sche verhalen, vertaald en van aanteekeningen voorzien [Translated and annotated Rampi' stories], *Tijdschrift voor Indische Taal-, Land- en Volkenkunde* 69: 254–319.

Wolfenden, Elmer P (1961). *A Re-Statement of Tagalog Grammar*. Manila: Summer Institute of Linguistics and the Institute of National Language.

Wolfenden, Elmer P (1971). *Hiligaynon Reference Grammar*. Honolulu: University of Hawai'i Press.

Wolfenden, Elmer P (1975). *A description of Hiligaynon syntax*. Dallas: Summer Institute of Linguistics.

Wolff, John U (1966). *Beginning Cebuano*. New Haven: Yale University Press.

Wolff, John U (1968). The Historical Development of the Samar-Leyte Vowel System, *Samar Leyte Studies* 2: 33–9.

Wolff, John U (1972). *A Dictionary of Cebuano Visayan*. Ithaca, NY: Cornell University. Two Volumes.

Wolff, John U (1973). Verbal Inflection in Proto-Austronesian, in Andrew B Gonzales (ed.), *Parangal Kay Cecilio Lopez: Essays in Honor of Cecilio Lopez on His Seventy-fifth Birthday*. Quezon City: Linguistic Society of the Philippines, 71–91.

Wolff, John U (1976). Malay Borrowings in Tagalog, in O D Cowan and O W Wolters (eds.), *Southeast Asian History and Historiography Essays Presented to D G E Hall*. Ithaca: Cornell University Press, 345–67.

Wolff, John U (1983). The Indonesian Spoken by the Peranakan Chinese of East Java: A Case of Language Mixture, in F Agard (ed.), *Essays in Honor of Charles F Hockett*. Leiden: Brill, 590–601.

Wolff, John U (1988). The PAN Consonant System, in Richard McGinn (ed.), *Studies in Austronesian Linguistics*. Athens, OH: Ohio University, Center for International Studies, 125–47.

Wolff, John U (1991). The Proto Austronesian Phoneme *t and the Grouping of the Austronesian Languages, in Robert Blust (ed.), *Currents in Pacific Linguistics: Papers on Austronesian Languages and Ethnolinguistics in Honour of George W Grace*. Canberra: Pacific Linguistics, 535–49.

Wolff, John U (1993). Proto-Austronesian Stress, in Jerold A Edmondson and Kenneth J Gregerson (eds.), *Tonality in Austronesian Languages*. Honolulu: University of Hawai'i Press, 1–15.

Wolff, John U (1995). The Position of the Austronesian Languages of Taiwan within the Austronesian Group, in Paul Jen-Kuei Li, Cheng-Hwa Tsang, Ying-Kuei Huang, Dah-an Ho and Chiu-Yu Tseng (eds.), *Austronesian Studies Relating to Taiwan* (Symposium Series of the Institute of History and Philology 3). Taipei: Academia Sinica, 521–83.

Wolff, John U (1996). The Development of the Passive Verb with Pronominal Prefix in Western Austronesian Languages, in Bernd Nothofer (ed.), *Reconstruction, Classification, Description—Festschrift in Honor of Isidore Dyen*. Hamburg: Abera, 15–40.

Wolff, John U (1997). Peranakan Chinese Speech and Identity, *Indonesia* 64: 29–44.

Wolff, John U (2001). The Influence of Spanish on Tagalog, in Klaus Zimmermann and Thomas Stolz (eds.), *Lo propio y lo ajeno en las lenguas austronésicas y amerindias: procesos interculturales en el contacto de Lenguas indígenas con el español en el Pacífico e Hispanoamérica*. Frankfurt am Main: Vervuert, 233–52.

Wolff, John U and Ida Wolff (1967). History of the Dialect of the Camotes Islands, Philippines, and the Spread of Cebuano Bisayan, *Oceanic Linguistics* 6: 63–79.

Wolff, John U and Soepomo Poedjosoedarmo (1982). *Communicative Codes in Central Java*. Linguistics Series VIII. Data Paper Number 116. Southeast Asia Program, Department of Asian Studies. Ithaca: Cornell University.

Wolff, John U with Maria Theresa C Centeno and Der-Hwa V Rau (1991). *Pilipino Through Self-Instruction*. Ithaca: Cornell Southeast Asia Program.

Wolfowitz, Clare (1991). *Language Style and Social Space: Stylistic Choice in Suriname Javanese*. Urbana: University of Illinois Press.

Wolfowitz, Clare (2002). Javanese Speech Styles in Suriname, in Eithne Carlin and Jacques Arends (eds.), *Atlas of the Languages of Suriname*. Leiden: Koninklijk Instituut voor Taal-, Land- en Volkenkunde Press, 265–82.

Wong Chun Wai and Audrey Edwards. Back to Bahasa Malaysia, *The Star* (4 June 2007).

Wood, Esther J (2007). *The Semantic Typology of Pluractionality*, University of California, Berkeley PhD Dissertation.

Wood, L (2000). Language Variation in Kotawaringin Barat and its Implications for Community Development: A Survey Report, in Leigh, M (ed.), *Borneo 2000: Language, Management and Tourism. Proceedings of the Sixth Biennial Borneo Research Conferences Borneo 2000*. Kuching: Institute of East Asian Studies, Universiti Sarawak Malaysia, 189–205.

Woollams, Geoff (1996). *A Grammar of Karo Batak, Sumatra*. Canberra: Pacific Linguistics.

Wouden, F A E Van (1968)[1935]. *Types of Social Structure in Eastern Indonesia*. (Translated by Rodney Needham). The Hague: Martinus Nijhoff.

Wouk, Fay (1984). Scalar Transitivity and Trigger Choice in Toba Batak, University of California Los Angeles *Occasional Papers in Linguistics* 5: 195–219.

Wouk, Fay (2002). Voice in the Languages of Nusa Tenggara Barat, in Fay Wouk and Malcolm Ross (eds.), *The History and Typology of Western Austronesian Voice Systems*. Canberra: Pacific Linguistics, 285–310.

Wouk, Fay and Arafiq (2016). The Particle *kai* in Bimanese, *Oceanic Linguistics* 55(2): 319–49.

Wray, Allison and George W Grace (2007). The Consequences of Talking to Strangers: Evolutionary Corollaries of Socio-Cultural Influences on Linguistic Form, *Lingua* 117: 543–78.

Wu, Jiang (2017). *Plural Words in Austronesian Languages: Typology and History*. MA Thesis, Leiden University.

Wu, Jiang. (2023). *Malayic varieties of Kelantan and Terengganu: Description and linguistic history*. Amsterdam: LOT.

Wumbu, Indra B, Amir Kadir, Nooral Baso and Sy Maranua (1986). *Inventarisasi Bahasa Daerah di Propinsi Sulawesi Tengah* [Inventory of regional languages in Central Sulawesi Province]. Jakarta: Pusat Pembinaan dan Pengembangan Bahasa.

Wurm, Stephen A and Shirô Hattori (eds.) (1981-1983). *Language Atlas of the Pacific Area (Parts I and II)*. Canberra: Pacific Linguistics. The Australian Academy of the Humanities in Collaboration with the Japan Academy.

Wurm, Stephen A (1983). Map 41: Northern Part of Borneo, in Stephen A Wurm and Shirô Hattori (eds.), *Language Atlas of the Pacific Area (Part II)*. Canberra: Pacific Linguistics. The Australian Academy of the Humanities in Collaboration with the Japan Academy.

Xu, S, I Pugach, Mark Stoneking, Manfred Kayser, L Jin and the HUGO Pan-Asian SNP Consortium (2012). Genetic Dating Indicates that the Asian-Papuan Admixture through Eastern Indonesia Corresponds to the Austronesian Expansion, *Proceedings of the National Academy of Sciences USA* 109: 4574–9.

Y-Lách and Alice Mundhenk (1976). *Chơlŏi Blăh Săp Hơrŏi: Bài Học Tiếng Hơroi (Tỉnh Phú-Bổn): Haroi Language Lessons*, Tủ Sách Ngôn-Ngữ Dân-Tộc Thiểu-Số Việt-Nam. Manila: Summer Institute of Linguistics.

Yamada, Yukihiro (2002). *Itbayat-English Dictionary*. Kyoto: Nakanishi Printing Co., Ltd.

Yamada, Yukihiro (2014). *A Grammar of the Itbayat Language*. Himeji: Himeji Dokkyo University.

Yamagata, Mariko (2012). Some Thoughts on the Sa Huynh and Related Pottery: Through A Comparison of the Sa Huynh, Kalanay and Hoa Diem, *Showa Women's University Institute of International Culture Bulletin* 17: 261–68.

Yamaguchi, Masao (2003). Remorango no Keito Kenkyu Hoho [A Study Concerning the Genetic Relationship of the Lemolang Language], *Gengo Bunka Gakkai Ronsyu* [Journal of Linguistic and Cultural Studies] 20: 165–182.

Yamashita, Michiko (1992). *Kakilingan Sambal Texts with Grammatical Analysis*. The Archive, Publication Eight. Quezon City, Metro Manila: The Cecilio Lopez Archives of the Philippine Languages and the Philippine Linguistics Circle, University of the Philippines Diliman.

Yang, Doris Hsiao-Fang (2002). *Subgrouping and Reconstruction of Batanic Languages*. MA Thesis, Providence University.

Yang, Melinda A, Xuechun Fan, Bo Sun, Chungyu Chen et al. (2020). Ancient DNA Indicates Human Population Shifts and Admixture in Northern and Southern China, *Science* 369(6501): 282–8.

Yannuar, Nurenzia (2019). *Bòsò Walikan Malangan: Structure and Development of a Javanese Reversed Language*. PhD Dissertation, Leiden University.

Yanti (2010). *A Reference Grammar of Jambi Malay*. PhD Dissertation, University of Delaware.

Yanti and Eric Raimy (2010). Reduplication in Tanjung Raden Malay, in Raphael Mercado, Eric Potsdam and Lisa deMena Travis (eds.), *Austronesian and Theoretical Linguistics*. Amsterdam: John Benjamins, 25–44.

Yanti, Peter Cole and Gabriella Hermon (to appear). *A Grammar of Jambi Malay*. Manuscript.

Yanti, Peter Cole, Timothy Mckinnon and Gabriella Hermon (2019). The Development of Agent-Demoting Passives in Malayic, *Linguistic Discovery* 16(2): 20–46.

Yanti, Timothy Mckinnon, Peter Cole and Gabriella Hermon (2018). The Phonological Basis of Syntactic Change in Kerinci, *Oceanic Linguistics* 57(2): 433–83.

Yap, Fe Aldave (1967). *A Synchronic Analysis of Tagalog Phonemes*. MA Thesis, University of British Columbia.

Yoder, Brendon E (2010). Syntactic Underspecification in Riau Indonesian. *Working Papers of the Summer Institute of Linguistics* 50.

Yoder, Brendon E (2011). *Phonological and Phonetic Aspects of Enggano Vowels*. MA Thesis, University of North Dakota.

Yoder, Brendon E (2014). *Phonological and Phonetic Aspects of Enggano Vowels*. Dallas TX: Summer Institute of Linguistics International.

Yoder, Brendon E (2018). Prenasalization and Trilled Release of Two Consonants in Nias, *Working Papers of the Summer Institute of Linguistics*, Grand Forks ND: University of North Dakota Session 50(1).

Yoshida, Shuji (1980). Folk Orientation in Halmahera with Special Reference to Insular Southeast Asia, in N Ishige (ed.), *The Galela of Halmahera: A Preliminary Survey*. Osaka: Museum of Ethnology, 19–88.

Yue, Anne O (2003). The Chinese Dialects: Grammar, in Graham Thurgood and Randy J LaPolla (eds.), *The Sino-Tibetan Languages*. London: Routledge, 84–125.

Yupho, Nawanit (1986). Consonant Clusters and Stress Rules in Pattani Malay, *Mon-Khmer Studies* 15: 125–38.

Zainul Arifin Aliana, Siti Salamah Arifin, A Malian Erman, Hasbi Yusuf (1979). *Bahasa Serawai* [The Serawai language]. Jakarta: Pusat Pembinaan dan Pengembangan Bahasa.

Zeitoun, Elizabeth and Chen-Huei Wu (2006). An Overview of Reduplication in Formosan Languages, in Henry Yungli Chang, Lillian M Huang and Dah-an Ho (eds.), *Streams Converging into an Ocean: Festschrift in Honor of Professor Paul Jen-Kuei Li on His 70th Birthday*. Taipei: Academia Sinica, 97–142.

Zentz, Lauren R (2015a). The Porous Borders of Language and Nation: English in Indonesia, *Language Problems and Language Planning* 39(1): 50–69.

Zentz, Lauren R (2015b). Love the Local, Use the National, Study the Foreign: Shifting Javanese Language Ecologies in (Post-)Modernity, Post-Coloniality and Globalization, *Journal of Linguistic Anthropology* 24(3): 339–59.

Zhang Yuhong [張裕宏] (2009). *Tâi-Gí Pe̍h-Ōe Sió Sû-Tián;* TJ台語白話小詞典; *Tjs Dictionary of Non-Literary Taiwanese*. Tainan: Asian A-Tsiu International.

Zhang, Chi and Hsiao-Chun Hung (2010). The Emergence of Agriculture in Southern China, *Antiquity* 84(323): 11–25.

Zheng, Yiqing [鄭貽青] (1997). *Huihui Yu Yanjiu* [A Study of Cham] 回辉语研究. Shanghai: Shanghai Far East Publishers.

Zobel, Erik (2002). The Position of Chamorro and Palauan in the Austronesian Family Tree: Evidence from Verb Morphology and Morphosyntax, in Fay Wouk and Malcolm Ross (eds.), *The History and Typology of Western Austronesian Voice Systems*. Canberra: Pacific Linguistics, 405–34.

Zobel, Erik (2005). Buol, in Alexander Adelaar and Nikolaus P Himmelmann (eds.). *The Austronesian Languages of Asia and Madagascar*. Routledge Language Family Series. London: Routledge, 625–48.

Zobel, Erik (2017a). *Notes on the Position of the Tominic Languages in the Celebic Subgroup*. Unpublished Manuscript. URL: https://www.academia.edu/4219408

Zobel, Erik (2017b). *The Seko-Badaic Languages in the Interior Highlands of Sulawesi*. URL: https://ezlinguistics.blogspot.com/p/seko-badaic.html

Zobel, Erik (2020). *The Kaili-Wolio Branch of the Celebic Languages, Oceanic Linguistics* 59(1/2): 297–346.

Zoetmulder, Petrus Josephus (1983). *De taal van het Adiparwa. Een grammaticale studie van het Oudjavaans* [A grammatical study of Old Javanese based on the Adiparwa prose tekst]. Dordrecht: Foris.

Zoetmulder, Petrus Josephus with the Collaboration of Stuart Robson (1982). *Old Javanese-English Dictionary*, 2 Vols. 's-Gravenhage: Martinus Nijhoff.

Zorc, R David (1971a). *A Proto Philippine Finder List*. Typescript, Cornell University.

Zorc, R David (1971b). Palawano Notes. SEALANG Zorc Papers. URL: http://sealang.net/archives/zorc/

Zorc, R David (1972). Current and Proto-Tagalic Stress, *The Philippine Journal of Linguistics*, 3: 43–57.

Zorc, R David (1974a). Towards A Definitive Philippine Wordlist: The Qualitative Use of Vocabulary in Identifying and Classifying Languages, *Oceanic Linguistics* 13(1–2): 409–55.

Zorc, R David (1974b). Internal and External Relationships of the Mangyan Languages of Mindoro, *Oceanic Linguistics* 13(1–2): 561–600.

Zorc, R David (1977). *The Bisayan Dialects of the Philippines: Subgrouping and Reconstruction*. Canberra: Pacific Linguistics.

Zorc, R David (1978). Proto-Philippine Word Accent: Innovation or Proto-Hesperonesian Retention?, in Stephen A Wurm and Lois Carrington (eds.), *Second International Conference on Austronesian Linguistics: Proceedings, Fascicle 1* Canberra: Pacific Linguistics, 67–119.

Zorc, R David (1979). On the Development of Contrastive Word Accent: Pangasinan, a Case in Point, in Nguyen Dang Liem (ed.), *South-East Asian Linguistic Studies* 3. Canberra: Pacific Linguistics, 241–58.

Zorc, R David (1986). The Genetic Relationships of Philippine Languages, in Paul Geraghty, Lois Carrington and Stephen A Wurm (eds.), *FOCAL II: Papers from the Fourth International Conference on Austronesian Linguistics*. Canberra: Pacific Linguistics, 147–73.

Zorc, R David (1987). Austronesian Apicals (*DdzZ) and the Philippine Non-Evidence, in D C Laycock and W Winter (eds.), *A World of Language: Papers Presented to Professor S A Wurm on His 65th Birthday*. Canberra: Pacific Linguistics, 751–61.

Zorc, R David (1993). Overview of Austronesian and Philippine Accent Patterns, in Jerold A Edmondson and Kenneth J Gregerson (eds.), *Tonality in Austronesian Languages*. Honolulu: University of Hawai'i Press, 17–24.

Zorc, R David (2019). Klata/Giangan: A New Philippine Subgroup, *The Archive: Special Publication* 16: 33–51. Diliman University of the Philippines.

Zorc, R David (2020). Reactions to Blust's the Resurrection of Proto-Philippines, *Oceanic Linguistics* 59: 394–425.

Zorc, R David (ongoing). Zorc Data Sheets (ZDS). [A Collection of Over 6,780 Data Sheets Covering Philippine Macro- and Micro-Groups]; URL: (Zorc.Net/Rdzorc/PHILIPPINE-ETYMA/).

Zorc, R. David and April Almarines (2022). Axis Relationships in the Philippines – When Traditional Subgrouping Falls Short. The Archive: Special Publication No. 17: Selected Papers from the 14th Philippine Linguistics Congress. Diliman: University of the Philippines.

Zorc, R David Paul, Rachel M L San Miguel, Annabelle M Sarra and Patricia O Afable (1993). *Tagalog Slang Dictionary*. Manila: De La Salle University Press.

Zúñiga, Fernando and Seppo Kittilä (2019). *Grammatical Voice*. Cambridge: Cambridge University Press.

Zuraidah Mohd Don, Gerry Knowles and Janet Yong (2008). How Words Can Be Misleading: A Study of Syllable Timing and Stress in Malay, *The Linguistics Journal* 3: 66–81.

Zuraw, Kie (2000). *Patterned Exceptions in Phonology*. PhD Dissertation, University of California Los Angeles.

Zwicky, Arnold M (1985). Clitics and Particles, *Language* 61(2): 283–305.

# Languages Index

# Subject Index